PSYCHOPATHOLOGY

An Integrative Approach to Mental Disorders

Ninth Edition

PSYCHOPATHOLOGY

An Integrative Approach to Mental Disorders

David H. Barlow
Boston University

V. Mark Durand
University of South Florida–St. Petersburg

Stefan G. Hofmann
Philipps University of Marburg, Germany, and Boston University

Cengage

Australia • Brazil • Canada • Mexico • Singapore • United Kingdom • United States

Cengage

***Psychopathology: An Integrative Approach to Mental Disorders,* Ninth Edition**
David H. Barlow, V. Mark Durand,
Stefan G. Hofmann

SVP, Higher Education Product Management:
Erin Joyner

VP, Product Management, Learning Experiences:
Thais Alencar

Product Director: Laura Ross

Product Manager: Colin Grover

Product Assistant: Fantasia Mejia

Learning Designer: Kim Beuttler

Content Manager: Sean Campbell

Digital Delivery Quality Partner: Scott Diggins

VP, Product Marketing: Jason Sakos

Senior Director, Product Marketing: Jennifer Fink

Product Marketing Manager: Chris Walz

IP Analyst: Deanna Ettinger

IP Project Manager: Ilakkiya Jayagopi

Production Service: Lumina Datamatics, Inc.

Designer: Sara Greenwood

Cover Image Source: CoffeeAndMilk/Getty Images

Library of Congress Control Number: 2021952949

Student Edition:
ISBN: 978-0-357-65784-3

Loose-leaf Edition:
ISBN: 978-0-357-65785-0

Cengage
200 Pier 4 Boulevard
Boston, MA 02210
USA

Cengage is a leading provider of customized learning solutions with employees residing in nearly 40 different countries and sales in more than 125 countries around the world. Find your local representative at: **www.cengage.com.**

To learn more about Cengage platforms and services, register or access your online learning solution, or purchase materials for your course, visit **www.cengage.com.**

Printed at CLDPC, USA, 08-22

To my mother, Doris Elinor Barlow-Lanigan, for her multidimensional influence across my life span.

D. H. B.

To Wendy and Jonathan, whose patience, understanding, and love provided me the opportunity to complete such an ambitious project.

V. M. D.

To all of those living and coping with psychopathology.

S. G. H.

About the Authors

David H. Barlow is an internationally recognized pioneer and leader in clinical psychology. Currently professor emeritus of psychology and psychiatry at Boston University, Dr. Barlow is founder and director emeritus of the Center for Anxiety and Related Disorders, one of the largest research clinics of its kind in the world. From 1996 to 2004, he directed the clinical psychology programs at Boston University. From 1979 to 1996, he was distinguished professor at the University at Albany–State University of New York. From 1975 to 1979, he was professor of psychiatry and psychology at Brown University, where he also founded the clinical psychology internship program. From 1969 to 1975, he was professor of psychiatry at the University of Mississippi Medical Center, where he founded the psychology residency program.

Growing up in sports-obsessed Boston, he reached what turned out to be the peak of his athletic career at age 12 when his team went to the Little League Baseball World Series. When it became clear that his athletic career was going no further, he hit the books, receiving his B.A. from the University of Notre Dame, his M.A. from Boston College, and his Ph.D. from the University of Vermont.

A fellow of every major psychological association, Dr. Barlow has received many awards in honor of his excellence in scholarship, including the National Institute of Mental Health Merit Award for his long-term contributions to the clinical research effort. He has also received the two highest awards in psychology—the Distinguished Scientist Award from the American Psychological Association, which is given for applications of psychology, and the James McKeen Cattell Fellow Award from the Association for Psychological Science, which honors individuals for a lifetime of significant intellectual achievements in applied psychological research. Other awards include the Distinguished Scientist Award from the Society of Clinical Psychology of the American Psychological Association and a certificate of appreciation from the APA section on the clinical psychology of women for "outstanding commitment to the advancement of women in psychology." He was awarded an honorary doctorate of science from the University of Vermont, an honorary doctorate of humane letters from William James College, as well as the C. Charles Burlingame Award from the Institute of Living in Hartford Connecticut "for his outstanding leadership in research, education, and clinical care." In 2014, he was awarded a presidential citation from the American Psychological Association "for his lifelong dedication and passion for advancing psychology through science, education, training, and practice." In 2018, he received a second presidential citation for his "far-reaching impact on many psychologists of color and shaping the future of the discipline in valuing and supporting the potential of all students."

He also has received career or lifetime contribution awards from the California, Connecticut, and Massachusetts Psychological Associations, as well as the University of Mississippi Medical Center and the Association for Behavioral and Cognitive Therapies. In 2000, he was named honorary visiting professor at the Chinese People's Liberation Army General Hospital and Postgraduate Medical School in Beijing, China, and in 2015, he was named honorary president of the Canadian Psychological Association. In addition, the annual Grand Rounds in Clinical Psychology at Brown University was named in his honor. During the 1997–1998 academic year, he was Fritz Redlich Fellow at the Center for Advanced Study in the Behavioral Sciences in Palo Alto, California. His research has been continually funded by the National Institutes of Health for over 50 years.

Dr. Barlow has edited several journals, including *Clinical Psychology: Science and Practice* and *Behavior Therapy,* has served on the editorial boards of more than 20 different journals, and is currently editor in chief of the "Treatments That Work" series for Oxford University Press. He has published more than 650 scholarly articles and chapters and written or edited more than 90 books and clinical manuals, including *Anxiety and Its Disorders,* second edition (Guilford Press); *Clinical Handbook of Psychological Disorders: A Step-by-Step Treatment Manual,* fifth edition (Guilford Press); *Single-Case Experimental Designs: Strategies for Studying Behavior Change,* third edition (Allyn & Bacon) (with Matthew Nock and Michael Hersen); *The Scientist–Practitioner: Research and Accountability in the Age of Managed Care,* second edition (Allyn & Bacon) (with Steve Hayes and Rosemary Nelson-Gray); *Mastery of Your Anxiety and Panic* (Oxford University Press) (with Michelle Craske); and, more recently, *The Unified Protocol for Transdiagnostic Treatment of Emotional Disorders,* second edition (Oxford University Press) (with the Unified Protocol team at Boston University). The books and manuals have been translated into more than 20 languages, including Arabic, Chinese, Hindi, and Russian. His research has been cited over 130,000 times with a Google scholar h-index of 160.

Dr. Barlow was one of three psychologists on the task force that was responsible for reviewing the work of more than 1,000 mental health professionals who participated in the creation of DSM-IV, and he continued on as an adviser to the DSM-5 task force. He also chaired the APA task force on Psychological Intervention Guidelines, which created a template for the creation of clinical practice guidelines. His current research program focuses on the nature and treatment of anxiety and related emotional disorders.

At leisure, he plays golf, skis, and retreats to his home on Nantucket Island, where he loves to write, walk on the beach, and visit with his island friends.

V. Mark Durand is known worldwide as an authority in the area of autism spectrum disorder. He is a Distinguished University Professor of psychology at the University of South Florida–St. Petersburg, where he was the founding dean of Arts and Sciences and vice chancellor for academic affairs. Dr. Durand is a fellow of the American Psychological Association. He has received more than $4 million in federal funding since the beginning of his career to study the nature, assessment, and treatment of behavior problems in children with disabilities. Before moving to Florida, he served in a variety of leadership positions at the University at Albany, including associate director for clinical training for the doctoral psychology program from 1987 to 1990, chair of the clinical department from 1995 to 1998, and interim dean of Arts and Sciences from 2001 to 2002. There he established the Center for Autism and Related Disabilities at the University at Albany–SUNY. He received his B.A., M.A., and Ph.D.—all in psychology—at the State University of New York–Stony Brook.

Dr. Durand was awarded the University Award for Excellence in Teaching at SUNY–Albany in 1991 and was given the Chancellor's Award for Excellence in Research and Creative Scholarship at the University of South Florida–St. Petersburg in 2007. He was named a 2014 Princeton Lecture Series Fellow and received the 2015 Jacobson Award for Critical Thinking from the American Psychological Association for his body of work in the field of autism spectrum disorder. Dr. Durand was elected to serve as president of the American Psychological Association's Division 33 (Intellectual and Developmental Disabilities / Autism Spectrum Disorders) for 2019.

Dr. Durand is currently a member of the Professional Advisory Board for the Autism Society of America and was on the board of directors of the International Association of Positive Behavioral Support. He was coeditor of the *Journal of Positive Behavior Interventions*, serves on a number of editorial boards, and has more than 145 publications on functional communication training, educational programming, and behavior therapy. His books include *Severe Behavior Problems: A Functional Communication Training Approach* (Guilford Press); *Sleep Better! A Guide to Improving Sleep for Children with Special Needs* (Brookes); *Helping Parents with Challenging Children: Positive Family Intervention* (Oxford University Press) (with Meme Hieneman); the multiple national award-winning *Optimistic Parenting: Hope and Help for You and Your Challenging Child* (Brookes); and most recently *Autism Spectrum Disorder: A Clinical Guide for General Practitioners* (American Psychological Association).

Dr. Durand developed a unique treatment for severe behavior problems that is currently mandated by states across the country and is used worldwide. He also developed an assessment tool that is used internationally and has been translated into more than 15 languages. Most recently, he developed an innovative approach to help families work with their challenging child (Optimistic Parenting), which was validated in a 5-year clinical trial and is being used all over the world. He has been consulted by the departments of education in numerous states and by the U.S. Departments of Justice and Education. His current research program includes the study of prevention models and treatments for such serious problems as self-injurious behavior.

In his leisure time, he enjoys long-distance running and has completed three marathons.

Stefan G. Hofmann is an international expert on psychotherapy for emotional disorders. He is the Alexander von Humboldt Professor of Translational Clinical Psychology at the Philipps University of Marburg and professor of psychology at Boston University. He was born in a little town near Stuttgart in Germany, which may explain his German accent. He studied psychology at the Philipps University of Marburg, Germany, where he received his B.A., M.S., and Ph.D. A brief dissertation fellowship to spend some time at Stanford University turned into a longer research career in the United States. He eventually moved to the United States in 1994 to join Dr. Barlow's team at the University at Albany–State University of New York. He has been a professor at Boston University since 1996 and received an Alexander von Humboldt Professorship for the Philipps University of Marburg, Germany, in 2021. He now lives in Frankfurt, Germany, Boston, and Cape Cod.

Dr. Hofmann has an actively funded research program studying various aspects of emotional disorders with a particular emphasis on anxiety disorders, cognitive behavioral therapy, and neuroscience. More recently, he has been interested in mindfulness approaches, such as yoga and meditation practices, as treatment strategies of emotional disorders. Furthermore, he has been one of the leaders in translational research methods to enhance the efficacy of psychotherapy and to predict treatment outcome using neuroscience methods. He is codeveloper (with Steven Hayes) of process-based therapy.

He has won many prestigious professional awards, including the Aaron T. Beck Award for Significant and Enduring Contributions to the Field of Cognitive Therapy by the Academy of Cognitive Therapy. He is a fellow of the American Psychological Association and the Association for Psychological Science and was president of various national and international professional societies, including the Association for Behavioral and Cognitive Therapies and the International Association for Cognitive Psychotherapy. He was an adviser to the DSM-5 Development Process and a member of the DSM-5 Anxiety Disorder Sub-Work Group. As part of this, he participated in the discussions about the revisions of the DSM-5 criteria for various anxiety disorders, especially social anxiety disorder, panic disorder, and agoraphobia. Dr. Hofmann is a Thomson Reuters' Highly Cited Researcher.

Dr. Hofmann has been the editor in chief of *Cognitive Therapy and Research,* and he has published more than 400 peer-reviewed journal articles and 20 books, including *An Introduction of Modern CBT* (Wiley-Blackwell) and *Emotion in Therapy* (Guilford Press).

At leisure, he enjoys playing with his sons. He likes traveling to immerse himself into new cultures, make new friends, and reconnect with old ones. When time permits, he occasionally gets out his flute.

Brief Contents

Contents

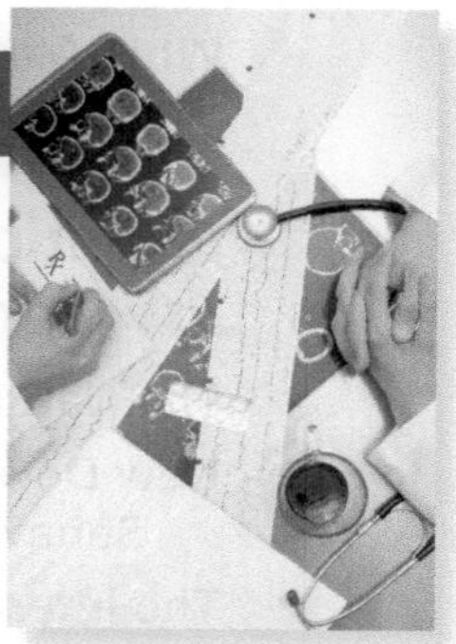

5 Anxiety, Trauma- and Stressor-Related, and Obsessive-Compulsive and Related Disorders 124

6 Somatic Symptom and Related Disorders and Dissociative Disorders 180

7 Mood Disorders and Suicide 210

11 Substance-Related, Addictive, and Impulse-Control Disorders 400

12 Personality Disorders 444

Preface

Science is a constantly evolving field, but every now and then something groundbreaking occurs that alters our way of thinking. For example, evolutionary biologists, who long assumed that the process of evolution was gradual, suddenly had to adjust to evidence that says evolution happens in fits and starts in response to such cataclysmic environmental events as meteor impacts. Similarly, geology has been revolutionized by the discovery of plate tectonics.

Until recently, the science of psychopathology had been compartmentalized, with psychopathologists examining the separate effects of psychological, biological, and social influences. This approach is still reflected in popular media accounts that describe, for example, a newly discovered gene, a biological dysfunction (chemical imbalance), or early childhood experiences as a "cause" of a psychological disorder. This way of thinking still dominates discussions of causality and treatment in some psychology textbooks: "The psychoanalytic views of this disorder are . . . ," "the biological views are . . . ," and, often in a separate chapter, "psychoanalytic treatment approaches for this disorder are . . . ," "cognitive behavioral treatment approaches are . . . ," or "biological treatment approaches are . . ."

In the first edition of this text, we tried to do something very different. We thought the field had advanced to the point that it was ready for an integrative approach in which the intricate interactions of biological, psychological, and social factors are explicated in as clear and convincing a manner as possible. Recent explosive advances in knowledge confirm this approach as the only viable way of understanding psychopathology. To take just two examples, Chapter 2 contains a description of a study demonstrating that stressful life events can lead to depression but that not everyone shows this response. Rather, stress is more likely to cause depression in individuals who already carry a particular gene that influences serotonin at the brain synapses. Similarly, Chapter 9 describes how the pain of social rejection activates the same neural mechanisms in the brain as physical pain. In addition, the entire section on genetics has been rewritten to highlight the new emphasis on gene–environment interaction, along with recent thinking from leading behavioral geneticists that the goal of basing the classification of psychological disorders on the firm foundation of genetics is fundamentally flawed. Descriptions of the emerging field of *epigenetics*, or the influence of the environment on gene expression, is also woven into the chapter, along with new studies on the seeming ability of extreme environments to largely override the effects of genetic contributions. Studies elucidating the mechanisms of epigenetics or specifically how environmental events influence gene expression are described.

These results confirm the integrative approach in this book: Psychopathology cannot be explained by genetic or environmental factors alone but rather arise from their interaction. We now understand that psychological and social factors directly affect neurotransmitter function and even genetic expression. Similarly, we cannot study behavioral, cognitive, or emotional processes without appreciating the contribution of biological and social factors to psychological and psychopathological expression. Instead of compartmentalizing psychopathology, we use a more accessible approach that accurately reflects the current state of our clinical science.

As colleagues, you are aware that we understand some disorders better than others. But we hope you will share our excitement in conveying to students both what we currently know about the causes and treatments of psychopathology and how far we have yet to go in understanding these complex interactions.

Integrative Approach

As noted earlier, the first edition of this book pioneered a new generation of such textbooks, which offer an integrative and multidimensional perspective. (We acknowledge such one-dimensional approaches as biological, psychosocial, and supernatural as historic perspectives on our field.) We include substantial current evidence of the reciprocal influences of biology and behavior and of psychological and social influences on biology. Our examples are designed to hold students' attention. For example, we discuss genetic contributions to divorce, the effects of early social and behavioral experience on later brain function and structure, new information on the relation of social networks to the common cold, and new data on psychosocial treatments for cancer. We note that in the phenomenon of implicit memory and blind sight, which may have parallels in dissociative experiences, psychological science verifies the existence of the unconscious (although it does not much resemble the seething caldron of conflicts envisioned by Freud). We present new evidence confirming the effects of psychological treatments on neurotransmitter flow and brain function. We acknowledge the often neglected area of emotion theory for its rich contributions to psychopathology (such as the effects of anger on cardiovascular disease). We weave scientific findings from the study of emotions together with behavioral, biological, cognitive, and social discoveries to create an integrated tapestry of psychopathology.

Life-Span Developmental Influences

No modern view of psychology can ignore the importance of life-span developmental factors in the manifestation and treatment of psychopathology. Studies highlighting developmental windows for the influence of the environment on gene expression are explained. Accordingly, although we include a chapter on neurodevelopmental disorders (Chapter 14), we consider the importance of development throughout the text. We discuss childhood and geriatric anxiety, for example, in the context of the anxiety, trauma- and stressor-related, and obsessive-compulsive and related disorders chapter (Chapter 5). This system of organization, which is for the most part consistent with DSM-5-TR, helps students appreciate the need to study each disorder from childhood through adulthood and old age. We note findings on developmental considerations in separate sections of each disorder chapter and, as appropriate, discuss how specific developmental factors affect causation and treatment.

Scientist–Practitioner Approach

We go to some lengths to explain why the scientist–practitioner approach to psychopathology is both practical and ideal. Like most of our colleagues, we view this as something more than simple awareness of how scientific findings apply to psychopathology. We show how every clinician contributes to general scientific knowledge through astute and systematic clinical observations, functional analyses of individual case studies, and systematic observations of series of cases in clinical settings. For example, we explain how information on dissociative phenomena provided by early psychoanalytic theorists remains relevant today. We also describe the formal methods used by scientist–practitioners, showing how abstract research designs are actually implemented in research programs.

Clinical Cases of Real People

We have enriched the book with authentic clinical histories to illustrate scientific findings on the causes and treatment of psychopathology. We have run active clinics for years, so 95% of the cases are from our own files, and they provide a fascinating frame of reference for the findings we describe. The beginnings of most chapters include a case description, and most of the discussion of the latest theory and research is related to these very human cases.

Disorders in Detail

We cover the major psychological disorders in 11 chapters (Chapters 5–15), focusing on three broad categories: clinical description, causal factors, and treatment and outcomes. We pay considerable attention to case studies and DSM-5-TR criteria, and we include statistical data, such as prevalence and incidence rates, sex ratio, age of onset, and the general course or pattern for the disorder as a whole. Since several of us were appointed advisers to the DSM-5-TR task force, we are able to include the reasons for changes as well as the changes themselves. Throughout, we explore how biological, psychological, and social dimensions may interact to cause a particular disorder. Finally, by covering treatment and outcomes within the context of specific disorders, we provide a realistic sense of clinical practice.

Treatment

One of the best received innovations in the first eight editions was our strategy of discussing treatments in the same chapter as the disorders themselves instead of in a separate chapter, an approach that is supported by the development of specific psychosocial and pharmacological treatment procedures for specific disorders. We have retained this integrative format and have improved upon it, and we include treatment procedures in the key terms and glossary.

Legal and Ethical Issues

In our closing chapter, we integrate many of the approaches and themes that have been discussed throughout the text. We include case studies of people who have been involved directly with many legal and ethical issues and with the delivery of mental health services. We also provide a historical context for current perspectives so students will understand the effects of social and cultural influences on legal and ethical issues.

Diversity

Issues of culture and gender are integral to the study of psychopathology. Throughout the text, we describe current thinking about which aspects of the disorders are culturally specific and which are universal and about the strong and sometimes puzzling effects of gender roles. For instance, we discuss the current information on such topics as the gender imbalance in depression, the ways panic disorders are expressed differently in various Asian cultures, the ethnic differences in eating disorders, treatment of schizophrenia across cultures, and the diagnostic differences of attention deficit/hyperactivity disorder (ADHD) in boys and girls. We also include a discussion on the influence of social and contextual factors, such as racial/ethnic discrimination, on the prevalence of panic disorder in the different ethnic groups in the United States. Clearly, our field will grow in depth and detail as these subjects and others become standard research topics. For example, why do some disorders overwhelmingly affect females and others appear predominantly in males? And why does this apportionment sometimes change from one culture to another? In answering questions like these, we adhere closely to science, emphasizing that gender and culture are each one dimension among several that constitute psychopathology.

New to This Edition

A Thorough Update

This exciting field moves at a rapid pace, and we take particular pride in how our book reflects the most recent developments. Of course, the most important recent development is the publication of the text revision of DSM-5 (DSM-5 TR). In this revision many of the diagnostic criteria have been updated and there is one brand new disorder described below. All of these revisions have been fully integrated throughout the book. Also, once again, every chapter has been carefully revised to reflect the latest research studies on psychological disorders. Hundreds of new references from 2020 to 2021 (and some still "in press") appear for the first time in this edition, and some of the information they contain stuns the imagination. Nonessential material has been eliminated, some new headings have been added, and DSM-5-TR criteria are included in their entirety as tables in the appropriate disorder chapters.

Several chapters—Chapter 5, Anxiety, Trauma- and Stressor-Related, and Obsessive-Compulsive and Related Disorders; Chapter 7, Mood Disorders and Suicide; Chapter 8, Eating and Sleep–Wake Disorders; Chapter 9, Physical Disorders and Health Psychology; Chapter 11, Substance-Related, Addictive, and Impulse-Control Disorders; Chapter 13, Schizophrenia Spectrum and Other Psychotic Disorders; and Chapter 14, Neurodevelopmental Disorders—have been heavily revised to reflect new research, but all chapters have been significantly updated and freshened.

Chapter 1, Psychopathology in Historical Context, features updated nomenclature to reflect new titles in DSM-5-TR, updated descriptions of research on defense mechanisms, and fuller and deeper descriptions of the historical development of psychodynamic and psychoanalytic approaches. We added a discussion of the definition of the term *mental disorder*, which includes a critique of Jerome Wakefield's influential definition by Richard McNally and examines the historical changes of this term throughout history, including today's struggle with the COVID-19 pandemic. We added a section on causality and discuss the term *etiology* as it relates to psychopathology. Freud's influential psychosexual theory of psychoanalysis is discussed in the context of issues related to LGBTQ2+ and gender identity. His theory was replaced by cognitive behavioral therapy (CBT), which we discuss in more detail.

Chapter 2, An Integrative Approach to Psychopathology, includes an updated discussion of developments in the study of genes and behavior with a focus on gene–environment interaction; new data illustrating the gene–environment correlation model; and new studies illustrating the psychosocial influence on the development of brain structure and function in general and on neurotransmitter systems specifically. We updated, revised, and refreshed sections on behavioral and cognitive science and added discussions of new evidence on the brain-gut connection and of COVID-19 as an example of the importance of social influence on psychopathology. This chapter also includes a major update on genetics, DNA, the definition of a gene based on the DNA structure, coding versus noncoding DNA, transcription of DNA, RNA, the definition of *allele*, the difference between a genotype and phenotype, polymorphism, and the definition of *single nucleotide polymorphism (SNP)*. We also updated the section on epigenetics and added new references, including new research on telomere length and other epigenetic mechanisms. We believe this update is necessary for students to gain a better understanding on the etiology of mental disorders. Finally, we added a discussion on the exploding research field on psychedelics, hallucinogens, and other drugs such as St. John's wort as new pharmacological agents for mental disorders.

Chapter 3, Clinical Assessment and Diagnosis, now presents references to "intellectual disability" instead of "mental retardation" to be consistent with DSM-5-TR and changes within the field; a new discussion about information from the MMPI-2 (noting that it is informative but does not necessarily change how clients are treated and may not improve their outcomes); a description of the organization and structure of DSM-5-TR along with major changes from DSM-IV and DSM-5-TR; a description of methods to coordinate the development of DSM-5 with the ICD-11; a description of likely directions of research as we begin to head toward DSM-6; a discussion and description of the new Rorschach Performance Assessment System (RPAS) that goes beyond U.S. reference values and uses a set of international normative reference values; and a discussion and description of a new version of the MMPI—MMPI-2-Restructured Form (MMPI-2-RF)—that attempts to change the information from the assessment that results in a yes/no outcome about whether a person has a disorder to a continuum of impairment.

In Chapter 4, Research Methods, we note that the study of COVID-19 is a contemporary example of the work of epidemiologists—including identifying the most vulnerable groups (such as people over 65 years of age and those with certain pre-existing conditions). In the discussion of prevalence, we note recent research on binge drinking, including findings that the prevalence of binge drinking (having five or more drinks in a row) among U.S. college students is about 40% and that in states that legalized recreational marijuana use, marijuana use increased but binge drinking decreased.

Chapter 5, Anxiety, Trauma- and Stressor-Related, and Obsessive-Compulsive and Related Disorders, is organized according to the three major groups of disorders: anxiety disorders, trauma- and stressor-related disorders, and obsessive-compulsive and related disorders. Obsessive-compulsive and related disorders include obsessive-compulsive disorder and also body dysmorphic disorder, hoarding disorder, trichotillomania (hair pulling disorder), and excoriation (skin picking disorder). Some of the revisions to Chapter 5 include, most importantly, the addition of an entirely new disorder in the DSM-5-TR, Prolonged Grief Disorder, which appears among the trauma and stressor related disorders. We also added a discussion on the limitations of animal research for studying anxiety disorders in humans, as well as, studies examining biomarkers of anxiety and studies on the inhalation of CO_2-enriched air to induce panic and review new treatments, such as Dr. Barlow's Unified Protocol. We also updated the relationship between anxiety disorders and suicide, and we revised and updated the discussion of benzodiazepine and anxiety disorders in youth to reflect the new black box warning. The section on generalized anxiety disorders (GAD) was revised to reflect the new conceptualization of the role of worry in addition to new clinical trial data supporting the efficacy of cognitive-behavioral therapy (CBT) as compared to other treatments, including yoga. We revised the discussion on the relationship between panic and agoraphobia to reflect the most current view as reflected in the DSM-5-TR, and we updated the prevalence estimates of panic disorder in different age groups. We reviewed and updated the contemporary literature on cultural influences and their associated cultural and social factors, as well as research on internet-supported and smartphone app-delivered treatment options. Finally, we included the newest evidence of the limitations of treatment protocols for posttraumatic stress disorder (PTSD).

The grouping of disorders in Chapter 6, Somatic Symptom and Related Disorders and Dissociative Disorders, reflects a major overarching change, specifically for somatic symptom disorder, illness anxiety disorder (formerly known as hypochondriasis), and psychological factors affecting medical conditions. The chapter discusses the differences between these overlapping disorders and provides a summary of the causes and treatment approaches of these problems. In addition, Chapter 6 now includes a discussion on the perceptual dysregulation model of somatic symptom disorder and an update on the false memory debate related to trauma in individuals with dissociative identity disorder (DID). We now clarify the use of the terms *hypochondriasis* and *hypochondriac* and revised the cultural expression of illness anxiety disorder. The chapter includes an updated review of treatment options for health anxiety, somatic symptom disorder, and other medically unexplained symptoms. We introduce the concept of secondary gain and elaborate on the distinction between organic and functional blindness. We provide more details on the Munchausen syndrome and discuss blind sight and unconscious vision. The chapter now also includes a discussion on the difference between epileptic seizure and functional seizure and the results of a recently published large study examining the clinical correlates of functional seizure. We updated our review on dissociation, derealization, and depersonalization, and we provide a review of the recent data on malingering as it relates to DID. We discuss the contemporary views of these disorders and contrast them with Freudian beliefs on memory as they relate to psychopathology. Finally, we elaborate on the controversies around assessing childhood abuse.

Chapter 7, Mood Disorders and Suicide, provides an updated discussion on the psychopathology and treatment of the DSM-5 mood disorders, including persistent depressive disorder, seasonal affective disorder, disruptive mood dysregulation disorder, bipolar disorder, and suicide. The chapter discusses new data on the genetic and environmental risk factors, such as dysfunctional reward processing, and protective factors, such as optimism. Also included is an update on the pharmacological and psychological treatments, an update on the section on mixed features and predominant polarity, a discussion on paternal peripartum depression, an update on the influence of seasonal change and daylight exposure on depression, and an update on prolonged grief disorder and risk factors for suicide. We also revised and updated the information on the prevalence of mood disorders and added a comparison between bipolar and major depressive disorder in suicidality. We also updated the information on mortality of elderly patients with depression, review elderly depression between different racial and ethnic groups, add updated the information on the genetics of depression and bipolar disorder, discuss the influence of the gut microbiota on depression, expand the influence of social and cultural factors contributing to depression by including racism in this discussion, clarify the relative importance of genetics for depression, add ketamine as a novel treatment strategy for depression, update the section on depression in children and adolescents, update the comparative efficacy of CBT and Interpersonal Psychotherapy update the statistics on suicide, and update and elaborate on suicide contagion by discussing the Werther effect and the competing Papageno effect. We were mindful of the terminology we used, avoiding terms such as "committing suicide" and "successful suicide" and replacing them with more appropriate and generally agreed upon contemporary terminology (such as "to die by suicide" and "fatal versus nonfatal suicide attempts").

Thoroughly rewritten and updated, Chapter 8, Eating and Sleep–Wake Disorders, contains new information on mortality and suicide rates in anorexia nervosa; new epidemiological information on the prevalence of eating disorders in adolescents; new information on the increasing globalization of eating disorders and obesity; updated information on typical patterns of comorbidity accompanying eating disorders; and new and updated research on changes in the incidence of eating disorders among males, racial and ethnic differences on the thin-ideal body image associated with eating disorders, the substantial contribution of emotion dysregulation to etiology and maintenance of anorexia, the role of friendship cliques in the etiology of eating disorders, mothers with eating disorders who also restrict their children's food intake, the contribution of parents and family factors in the etiology of eating disorders, biological and genetic contributions to causes of eating disorders (including the role of ovarian hormones), transdiagnostic treatment applicable to all eating disorders, results from a large multinational trial comparing CBT to psychoanalysis in the treatment of bulimia, the effects of combining Prozac with CBT in the treatment of eating disorders, racial and ethnic differences in people with binge-eating disorder seeking treatment, the phenomenon of night eating syndrome and its role in the development of obesity, and new public health policy developments directed at the obesity epidemic.

Also in Chapter 8, we have realigned coverage of sleep–wake disorders with new information on sleep in women (including risk and protective factors), updated a section on narcolepsy to describe new research on the causes of this disorder, and added new research on the nature and treatment of nightmares. We updated our review of the changes in prevalence rates in eating disorders over time across the world, updated our review of obesity and compare obesity rates internationally and between different age and ethnic groups, updated the clinical description of bulimia, and discuss the role of physical exercise and the individual's distorted sense of self. We also added a discussion on purging disorder, features that distinguish it from binge-eating disorder and bulimia nervosa, predictors of eating disorders, and the relationship between eating disorders, ethnicity, sexual orientation and sexual identity. Finally, we updated the findings on sex difference in body image perception.

In Chapter 9, Physical Disorders and Health Psychology, we updated data on the leading causes of death in the United States; provided new statistics about sexually transmitted diseases, including HIV/AIDS; reviewed psychosocial factors on brain structures and function; summarized the influential Framingham Heart Study and provided new data on the effects of stress on cardiovascular disease, including a discussion on allostatic load; and updated a review into the causes and treatments of chronic pain. We also provided an updated review of psychological and behavioral procedures for preventing injuries; added information on lower back pain, sex differences in pain perception, the effect of cigarette smoking and small airway dysfunction, in particular as it relates to China; and discuss studies on the effect of psychotherapy on cancer survival. Finally, we include a discussion of COVID-19 as an example of the impact of a global pandemic on deaths.

In Chapter 10, Sexual Dysfunctions, Paraphilic Disorders, and Gender Dysphoria, we review sexual practices and preferences based on international surveys, review the biological and genetic contribution of same-sex orientation, added a section on vulvodynia, added an update on the general trend in research on sexual dysfunctions, and updated the section on erectile dysfunction and its treatment with the popular PDE-5 inhibitors (such as Viagra). In general, we were mindful of the preferred terminologies for the various sexual orientations and preferences. As much as possible, we rephrased wordings from the original reports we reviewed about sex differences and differences in sexual orientation to be inclusive and to avoid feelings of discomfort in some of our readers.

A thoroughly revised Chapter 11, Substance-Related, Addictive, and Impulse-Control Disorders, features a new discussion of how the trend to mix caffeinated energy drinks with alcohol may increase the likelihood of later abuse of alcohol; new research on how chronic use of MDMA ("Ecstasy") leads to lasting memory problems; and new research on several factors predicting early alcohol use, including when best friends have started drinking, whether family members are at high risk for alcohol dependence, and the presence of behavior problems in these children.

Chapter 12, Personality Disorders, describes the efforts to begin to address the personality dimensions. The DSM-5 Alternative Model of Personality Disorders (AMPD) was created in a different section of DSM (Section III: Emerging Measures and Models). A similar decision was made for the international version of the DSM—the WHO International Classification of Diseases, 11th version (ICD-11). The DSM-5 and the ICD-11 classifications of personality disorders (PD) are largely commensurate, and, when combined, they delineate six trait domains: negative affectivity, detachment, antagonism/dissociality, disinhibition, anankastia, and psychoticism. More work on the usefulness of these alternatives is necessary to evaluate these alternatives.

Chapter 13, Schizophrenia Spectrum and Other Psychotic Disorders, presents updated information on the economic impact of schizophrenia. The annual cost of schizophrenia in the United States is estimated to exceed $150 billion when factors such as family caregiving, lost wages, and treatment are considered. We updated the prevalence of hallucinations and delusions. Between 60% and 80% of people with schizophrenia experience hallucinations, and approximately 70% experience delusions. We added an interesting study of brief psychotic disorder. Brief psychotic disorder is often precipitated by extremely stressful situations. In one case study in Italy, researchers found an increase in hospitalizations for brief psychotic disorders during the COVID-19 pandemic. Of the six individuals admitted (none of whom had a previous psychiatric disorder), three presented the somatic delusion of being infected with COVID, and all six cases had religious/spiritual delusions and hallucinatory content.

Chapter 14, Neurodevelopmental Disorders, now includes updated prevalence data about attention-deficit/hyperactivity disorder (ADHD) in children. An important analysis of prevalence of ADHD suggests that the disorder is found in about 4% of the U.S. population of children and in 5.2% of the child populations across all regions of the world. We added a new study looking at early detection of ADHD. In this study, much younger children at risk for ADHD were identified as having early signs of ADHD. Infants with an older sibling or parent diagnosed with ADHD were distinguishable from infants with no family history of ADHD as early as 12 months of age based on directly observed and examiner reports of behavior, particularly with respect to hyperactive-impulsive behavior. Parents of infants at familial risk for ADHD also reported significantly more behavior/temperament concerns as early as 12 months of age compared to parents of infants at low risk for ADHD. We expanded the description of savant skills in some persons with autism spectrum disorder (ASD). These special skills typically occur in five areas—music, art, calendar calculating, mathematics, or mechanical/visual-spatial skills—and are usually associated with outstanding memory that is restricted to the area of expertise.

Chapter 15, Neurocognitive Disorders, features a study of the effects of confinement during COVID-19 on the side effects of dementia due to Alzheimer's disease. Perhaps partly because people suffering from neurocognitive disorder are aware that they are deteriorating mentally, emotional changes often occur as well. Common side effects are delusions (irrational beliefs), depression, agitation, aggression, and apathy. One study found that confinement during COVID-19 increased the side effects among some patients. We updated the criteria used to diagnose dementia due to Alzheimer's disease. To make a diagnosis without direct examination of the brain, the course and presence of the following symptoms should be observed—slow, progressive decline, typically in this order: memory, language, visuospatial function (that is, skills needed for movement, depth and distance perception, and spatial navigation), and executive function (that is, a set of mental skills that include working memory, flexible thinking, and self-control).

And Chapter 16, Mental Health Services: Legal and Ethical Issues, presents a brief discussion of a trend to provide individuals needing emergency treatment with court-ordered assisted outpatient treatment (AOT) to avoid commitment in a mental health facility; a new discussion of a major meta-analysis showing that current risk assessment tools are best at identifying persons at low risk of being violent but only marginally successful at accurately detecting who will be violent at a later point; and an updated section on legal rulings on involuntary medication.

Additional Features

In addition to the changes highlighted earlier, *this text* offers other distinct features:

- New, program-specific *learning objectives* at the start of each chapter alert students to what they will achieve. Various instructor resources including the testing program map to these objectives to support assessment. In addition, student learning outcomes mapped to core American Psychological Association goals may be found in the *Instructor Manual*.
- In each disorder chapter, a feature called DSM *Controversies* discusses some of the contentious and thorny decisions made in the process of creating DSM-5. Examples include the creation of new and sometimes controversial disorders appearing for the first time in DSM-5, such as premenstrual dysphoric disorder, binge-eating disorder, and disruptive mood dysregulation disorder. Another example is removing the "grief" exclusion criteria for diagnosing major depressive disorder so that someone can be diagnosed with major depression even if the trigger was the death of a loved one. Finally, changing the title of the paraphilia chapter to "paraphilic disorders" implies that paraphilic sexual arousal patterns such as pedophilia are not disorders in themselves but become disorders only if they cause impairment or harm to others.

DSM-IV, DSM-IV-TR, and DSM-5

Much has been said about the mix of political and scientific considerations that resulted in DSM-5, and naturally we have our own opinions. (DHB had the interesting experience of sitting on the task force for DSM-IV and was an adviser to the DSM-5 task force.) Psychologists are often concerned about "turf issues" in what has become, for better or worse, the nosological standard in our field, and with good reason: In previous DSM editions, scientific findings sometimes gave way to personal opinions. For DSM-IV and DSM-5, however, most professional biases were left at the door while the task force almost endlessly debated the data. This process produced enough new information to fill every psychopathology journal for a year with integrative reviews, reanalysis of existing databases, and new data from field trials. From a scholarly point of view, the process was both stimulating and exhausting. This book contains highlights of various debates that created the nomenclature, as well as recent updates. For example, in addition to the controversies described above, we summarize and update the data and discussion of premenstrual dysphoric disorder, which was designated a new disorder in DSM-5, and mixed anxiety depression, a disorder that did not make it into the final criteria. Students can thus see the process of making diagnoses, as well as the combination of data and inferences that are part of it.

We also discuss the intense continuing debate on categorical and dimensional approaches to classification. We describe some of the compromises the task force made to accommodate data, such as why dimensional approaches to personality disorders did not make it into DSM-5 and why the proposal to do so was rejected at the last minute and included in Section III under "Conditions for Further Study," even though almost everyone agrees that these disorders should not be categorical but rather dimensional.

Prevention

Looking into the future of clinical psychology as a field, it seems our ability to prevent psychological disorders may help the most. Although this has long been a goal of many, we now appear to be at the cusp of a new age in prevention research. Scientists from all over the globe are developing the methodologies and techniques that may at long last provide us with the means to interrupt the debilitating toll of emotional distress caused by the disorders chronicled in this book. We therefore highlight these cutting-edge prevention efforts—such as preventing eating disorders, suicide, and health problems, including HIV and injuries—in appropriate chapters as a means to celebrate these important advancements, as well as to spur on the field to continue this important work.

Retained Features

Visual Summaries

At the end of each disorder chapter is a colorful, two-page visual overview that succinctly summarizes the causes, development, symptoms, and treatment of each disorder covered in the chapter. Our integrative approach is instantly evident in these diagrams, which show the interaction of biological, psychological, and social factors in the etiology and treatment of disorders. The visual summaries will help instructors wrap up discussions, and students will appreciate them as study aids.

Pedagogy

Each chapter contains several Concept Checks that let students verify their comprehension at regular intervals. Answers are listed at the end of each chapter along with a more detailed summary. The key terms are listed in the order they appear in the text and thus form a sort of outline that students can study.

MindTap for Barlow, Durand, and Hofmann's *Psychopathology*

MindTap is a platform that propels students from memorization to proficiency. It also allows instructors to provide engaging content, challenge every learner, and build student confidence. Instructors can customize interactive syllabi to emphasize priority topics and then add material or notes to the ebook as desired. This outcomes-driven application gives you the tools needed to empower students and boost both understanding and performance:

- Guide students: A unique learning path of relevant readings, media, and activities moves students up the learning taxonomy from basic knowledge and comprehension to analysis and application.
- Personalize teaching: A Learning Path built on key student objectives allows you to control what students see and when they see it. Use it as-is, or match to your syllabus exactly: Hide, rearrange, add, and create your own content.
- Promote better outcomes: Empower instructors and motivate students with analytics and reports that provide a snapshot of class progress, time in course, engagement, and completion rates.

In addition to the benefits of the platform, MindTap for Barlow, Durand, and Hofmann's *Psychopathology* includes the following:

- Profiles in Psychopathology guide users through the symptoms, causes, and treatments of individuals who live with mental disorders. Profiles present real-life examples of both celebrities and ordinary people to humanize psychological disorders and tie chapter content to the real world.
- Video polling activities provide real-life video portraits of individuals with psychopathologies in the context of their daily lives. These activities encourage learners to make observations and reflect on what they have observed.
- Concept Clip Videos visually elaborate on specific disorders and psychopathology in a vibrant, engaging manner. Detailed animations teach core concepts with interactive elements, narrated audio, and nongraded concept checks. These videos provide visual examples and delve deeper into chapter content.

- Case studies present real-life examples of people with disorders to humanize psychological disorders and connect learners to authentic cases they may encounter in the field.
- Chapter quizzes are formative assessments that check student comprehension of chapter content.
- Master Training, powered by Cerego, for student personalized learning plans to help them understand and retain key topics and discussions.

Supplements for the Instructor

Additional instructor resources for this product are available online. Instructor assets include an Instructor's Manual, Educator's Guide, PowerPoint® slides, and a test bank powered by Cognero®. Sign up or sign in at www.cengage.com to search for and access this product and its online resources.

Titles of Interest

- DSM-5 *Supplement* by H. Boettcher, J. Q. Wu, D. H. Barlow, and V. M. Durand is a thorough comparison of the changes made in DSM-5 with the previous criteria and language in DSM-IV-TR. It also includes discussion of major controversies resulting from the proposed and realized modifications to the latest diagnostic manual. ISBN: 9781285848181
- *Looking into Abnormal Psychology: Contemporary Readings* by Scott O. Lilienfeld is a fascinating 234-page reader consisting of 40 articles from popular magazines and journals. Each article explores ongoing controversies regarding mental illness and its treatment. ISBN: 0-534-35416-5
- *Casebook in Abnormal Psychology,* fifth edition, by Timothy A. Brown and David H. Barlow, is a comprehensive casebook fully updated to be consistent with DSM-5. *It* reflects the integrative approach, which considers the multiple influences of genetic, biological, familial, and environmental factors in a unified model of causality as well as maintenance and treatment of the disorder. The casebook discusses treatment methods that are the most effective interventions developed for a particular disorder. It also presents three undiagnosed cases in order to give students an appreciation for the complexity of disorders. The cases are strictly teaching/learning exercises, similar to what many instructors use on their examinations. ISBN: 9781305971714

Acknowledgments

Finally, this book in all of its editions would not have begun and certainly would not have been finished without the inspiration and coordination of our senior editors at Cengage, who always keep their eyes on the ball. A special note of thanks to content manager Sean Campbell and his eye for detail and organization. The book is much better for your efforts. We hope to work with you on many subsequent editions.

Numerous colleagues and students provided superb feedback on the previous editions, and to them we express our deepest gratitude. Although not all comments were favorable, all were important. Readers who take the time to communicate their thoughts offer the greatest reward to writers and scholars.

Finally, you share with us the task of communicating knowledge and discoveries in the exciting field of psychopathology, a challenge that none of us takes lightly. In the spirit of collegiality, we would greatly appreciate your comments on the content and style of this book and recommendations for improving it further.

Reviewers

Creating this book has been both stimulating and exhausting, and we could not have done it without the valuable assistance of colleagues who read one or more chapters and provided extraordinarily perceptive critical comments, corrected errors, pointed to relevant information, and, on occasion, offered new insights that helped us achieve a successful, integrative model of each disorder.

We thank the following expert reviewers and survey participants of the ninth edition:

Kanika Bell, *Clark Atlanta University*
Jamie S Bodenlos, *Hobart and William Smith Colleges*
Lawrence Burns, *Grand Valley State University*
Don Evans, *Simpson College*
Susan Frankel, *Lamar Community College*
Tammy Hanna, *Albertus Magnus College*
Sarah Heavin, *University of Puget Sound*
Stephen T. Higgins, *University of Vermont*
Fiyyaz Karim, *University of Minnesota*
Maureen C. Kenny, *Florida International University*
Lissa Lim, *California State University–San Marcos*
Barbara S. McCrady, *University of New Mexico*
Winfried Rief, *Philipps University of Marburg, Germany*
Robert Rotunda, *University of West Florida*
Kyle Stephenson, *Willamette University*
Lynda Szymanski, *St. Catherine University*

We also thank the reviewers of previous editions:

Dale Alden, *Lipscomb University*
Kerm Almos, *Capital University*
Frank Andrasik, *University of Memphis*
Robin Apple, *Stanford University Medical Center*
Barbara Beaver, *University of Wisconsin*
James Becker, *University of Pittsburgh*
Evelyn Behar, *University of Illinois–Chicago*
Dorothy Bianco, *Rhode Island College*
Sarah Bisconer, *College of William & Mary*
Susan Blumenson, *City University of New York, John Jay College of Criminal Justice*
Robert Bornstein, *Adelphi University*
James Calhoun, *University of Georgia*
Montie Campbell, *Oklahoma Baptist University*
Robin Campbell, *Brevard Community College*
Shelley Carson, *Harvard University*
Richard Cavasina, *California University of Pennsylvania*
Antonio Cepeda-Benito, *Texas A&M University*
Kristin Christodulu, *State University of New York–Albany*
Bryan Cochran, *University of Montana*
Julie Cohen, *University of Arizona*

Dean Cruess, *University of Connecticut*
Sarah D'Elia, *George Mason University*
Robert Doan, *University of Central Oklahoma*
Juris Draguns, *Pennsylvania State University*
Melanie Duckworth, *University of Nevada–Reno*
Mitchell Earleywine, *State University of New York–Albany*
Chris Eckhardt, *Purdue University*
Elizabeth Epstein, *Rutgers University*
Donald Evans, *University of Otago*
Ronald G. Evans, *Washburn University*
Janice Farley, *Brooklyn College, CUNY*
Anthony Fazio, *University of Wisconsin–Milwaukee*
Diane Finley, *Prince George's Community College*
Allen Frances, *Duke University*
Louis Franzini, *San Diego State University*
Maximillian Fuhrmann, *California State University–Northridge*
Aubyn Fulton, *Pacific Union College*
Noni Gaylord-Harden, *Loyola University–Chicago*
Trevor Gilbert, *Athabasca University*
David Gleaves, *University of Canterbury*
Frank Goodkin, *Castleton State College*
Irving Gottesman, *University of Minnesota*
Laurence Grimm, *University of Illinois–Chicago*
Mark Grudberg, *Purdue University*
Marjorie Hardy, *Eckerd College*
Keith Harris, *Canyon College*
Christian Hart, *Texas Women's University*
William Hathaway, *Regent University*
Brian Hayden, *Brown University*
Stephen Hinshaw, *University of California, Berkeley*
Alexandra Hye-Young Park, *Humboldt State University*
William Iacono, *University of Minnesota*
Heidi Inderbitzen-Nolan, *University of Nebraska–Lincoln*
Thomas Jackson, *University of Arkansas*
Kristine Jacquin, *Mississippi State University*
James Jordan, *Lorain County Community College*
Boaz Kahana, *Cleveland State University*
Arthur Kaye, *Virginia Commonwealth University*
Christopher Kearney, *University of Nevada–Las Vegas*
Ernest Keen, *Bucknell University*
Elizabeth Klonoff, *San Diego State University*
Ann Kring, *University of California–Berkeley*
Marvin Kumler, *Bowling Green State University*
Thomas Kwapil, *University of North Carolina–Greensboro*
George Ladd, *Rhode Island College*
Michael Lambert, *Brigham Young University*
Travis Langley, *Henderson State University*
Christine Larson, *University of Wisconsin–Milwaukee*
Elizabeth Lavertu, *Burlington County College*
Cynthia Ann Lease, *Salem Veterans Affairs Medical Center, Salem, VA*
Richard Leavy, *Ohio Wesleyan University*
Karen Ledbetter, *Portland State University*
Scott Lilienfeld, *Emory University*
Kristi Lockhart, *Yale University*
Michael Lyons, *Boston University*
Jerald Marshall, *Valencia Community College*
Janet Matthews, *Loyola University–New Orleans*
Dean McKay, *Fordham University*
Mary McNaughton-Cassill, *University of Texas at San Antonio*
Suzanne Meeks, *University of Louisville*
Michelle Merwin, *University of Tennessee–Martin*
Thomas Miller, *Murray State University*
Scott Monroe, *University of Notre Dame*
Greg Neimeyer, *University of Florida*
Sumie Okazaki, *New York University*
John Otey, *South Arkansas University*
Christopher Patrick, *University of Minnesota*
P. B. Poorman, *University of Wisconsin–Whitewater*
Katherine Presnell, *Southern Methodist University*
Lynn Rehm, *University of Houston*
Kim Renk, *University of Central Florida*
Alan Roberts, *Indiana University–Bloomington*
Melanie Rodriguez, *Utah State University*
Carol Rothman, *City University of New York, Herbert H. Lehman College*
Steve Saiz, *State University of New York–Plattsburgh*
Steve Schuetz, *University of Central Oklahoma*
Stefan Schulenberg, *University of Mississippi*
Amanda Sesko, *University of Alaska–Southeast*
Paula K. Shear, *University of Cincinnati*
Jerome Small, *Youngstown State University*
Ari Solomon, *Williams College*
Michael Southam-Gerow, *Virginia Commonwealth University*
John Spores, *Purdue University–North Central*
Brian Stagner, *Texas A&M University*
Irene Staik, *University of Montevallo*
Rebecca Stanard, *State University of West Georgia*
Chris Tate, *Middle Tennessee State University*
Lisa Terre, *University of Missouri–Kansas City*
Gerald Tolchin, *Southern Connecticut State University*
Michael Vasey, *Ohio State University*
Larry Ventis, *College of William & Mary*
Richard Viken, *Indiana University*
Lisa Vogelsang, *University of Minnesota–Duluth*
Philip Watkins, *Eastern Washington University*
Kim Weikel, *Shippensburg University of Pennsylvania*
Amy Wenzel, *University of Pennsylvania*
W. Beryl West, *Middle Tennessee State University*
Michael Wierzbicki, *Marquette University*
Richard Williams, *State University of New York–College at Potsdam*
John Wincze, *Brown University*
Bradley Woldt, *South Dakota State University*
Nancy Worsham, *Gonzaga University*
Ellen Zaleski, *Fordham University*
Raymond Zurawski, *St. Norbert College*

PSYCHOPATHOLOGY

An Integrative Approach to Mental Disorders

1 Psychopathology in Historical Context

Historic Images/Alamy Stock Photo

Learning Objectives

LO1.1 Define psychological disorders according to the three basic criteria of psychopathology.

LO1.2 Describe each of the three basic categories of research in psychopathology.

LO1.3 Compare the three prominent historical approaches to psychopathology in terms of how they explain and treat psychological disorders.

LO1.4 Differentiate Freudian psychoanalysis from the humanistic and behavioral approaches according to their research and therapeutic emphases.

LO1.5 List the main influences on the development of psychopathology according to the integrative approach.

Understanding Psychopathology

Today you may have gotten out of bed, had breakfast, gone to class, studied, and, at the end of the day, enjoyed the company of your friends before dropping off to sleep. For some people going through this routine, it might not occur to them that many physically capable people are not able to do some or any of these activities. What they have in common is a **psychological disorder**, a psychological dysfunction within an individual associated with distress or impairment in functioning and a response that is not typical or culturally expected. Before examining exactly what this means, let's look at one individual's situation.

Janelle... The Girl Who Fainted at the Sight of Blood

Janelle, a 16-year-old, was referred to our anxiety disorders clinic after increasing episodes of fainting. About 2 years earlier, in Janelle's first biology class, the teacher had shown a movie of a frog dissection to illustrate various points about anatomy.

This was a particularly graphic film, with vivid images of blood, tissue, and muscle. About halfway through, Janelle felt a bit lightheaded and left the room. But the images did not leave her. She continued to be bothered by them and occasionally felt slightly queasy. She began to avoid situations in which she might see blood or injury. She stopped looking at magazines that might have gory pictures. She found it difficult to look at raw meat or even Band-Aids because they brought the feared images to mind. Eventually, anything her friends or parents said that evoked an image of blood or injury caused Janelle to feel lightheaded. It got so bad that if one of her friends exclaimed, "Cut it out!" she felt faint.

Beginning about 6 months before her visit to the clinic, Janelle actually fainted when she unavoidably encountered something bloody. Her family physician could find nothing wrong with her, nor could several other physicians. By the time she was referred to our clinic, she was fainting 5 to 10 times a week, often in class. Clearly, this was problematic for her and disruptive in school; each time Janelle fainted, the other students flocked around her, trying to help, and class was interrupted. Because no one could find anything wrong with her, the principal finally concluded that she was being manipulative and suspended her from school, even though she was an honor student.

Janelle was suffering from what we now call *blood–injection–injury phobia.* Her reaction was quite severe, thereby meeting the criteria for phobia, a psychological disorder characterized by marked and persistent fear of an object or situation. But many people have similar reactions that are not as severe when they receive an injection or see someone who is injured, whether blood is visible or not. For people who react as severely as Janelle, this phobia can be disabling. They may avoid certain careers, such as medicine or nursing, and, if they are so afraid of needles and injections that they avoid them even when they need them, they put their health at risk.

What Is a Psychological Disorder?

Keeping in mind the real-life problems faced by Janelle, let's look more closely at the definition of psychological disorder or problematic **abnormal behavior**: It is a psychological dysfunction within an individual that is associated with distress or impairment in functioning and a response that is not typical or culturally expected (see ■ Figure 1.1). On the surface, these three criteria may seem obvious, but they were not easily arrived at and it is worth a moment to explore what they mean. You will learn importantly that no one criterion has yet been developed that fully defines a psychological disorder.

Psychological Dysfunction *Psychological dysfunction* refers to a breakdown in cognitive, emotional, or behavioral functioning. For example, if you are out on a date, it should be fun. But if you

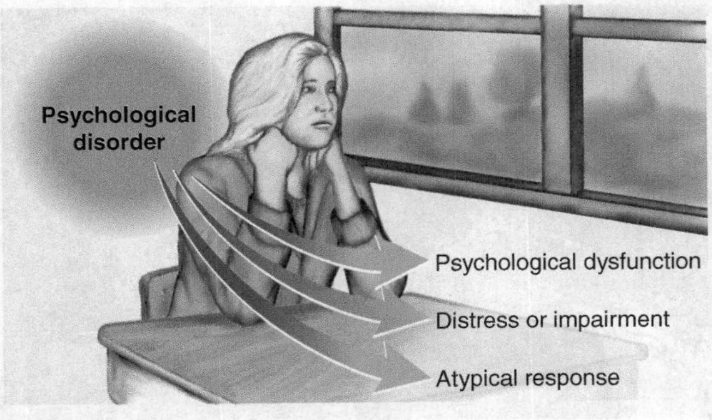

Figure 1.1
The criteria defining a psychological disorder.

experience severe fear all evening and just want to go home, even though there is nothing to be afraid of, and the severe fear happens on every date, your emotions are not functioning properly. However, if all your friends agree that the person who asked you out is unpredictable and dangerous in some way, then it would not be dysfunctional for you to be fearful and avoid the date.

A dysfunction was present for Janelle: She fainted at the sight of blood. But many people experience a mild version of this reaction (feeling queasy at the sight of blood) without meeting the criteria for the disorder, so knowing where to draw the line between normal and abnormal dysfunction is often difficult. For this reason, some of these problems are often considered to be on a continuum or a dimension rather than to be categories that are either present or absent (McNally, 2011; Stein, Phillips, Bolton, Fulford, Sadler, & Kendler, 2010; Widiger & Crego, 2013). This, too, is a reason that just having a dysfunction is not enough to meet the criteria for a psychological disorder.

Distress or Impairment That the behavior must be associated with distress to be classified as a disorder adds an important component and seems clear: The criterion is satisfied if the individual is extremely upset. We can certainly say that Janelle was distressed and even suffered with her **phobia**. But remember, by itself this criterion does not define problematic abnormal behavior. It is often quite normal to be distressed—for example, when someone close to you dies. The human condition is such that suffering and distress are very much part of life. This is not likely to change. Furthermore, for some disorders, by definition, suffering and distress are absent. Consider the person who feels extremely elated and may act impulsively as part of a manic episode. As you will see in Chapter 7, one of the major difficulties with this problem is that some people enjoy the manic state so much they are reluctant to begin treatment or stay long in treatment. Thus, defining psychological disorder by distress alone doesn't work, although the concept of distress contributes to a good definition.

MediaNews Group/Boston Herald via Getty Images

Distress and suffering are a natural part of life and do not in themselves constitute a psychological disorder.

The concept of *impairment* is useful, although not entirely satisfactory. For example, many people consider themselves shy or lazy. This doesn't mean that they're abnormal. But if you are so shy that you find it impossible to date or even interact with people and you make every attempt to avoid interactions even though you would like to have friends, then your social functioning is impaired.

Janelle was clearly impaired by her phobia, but many people with similar, less severe reactions are not impaired. This difference again illustrates the important point that most psychological disorders are simply extreme expressions of otherwise normal emotions, behaviors, and cognitive processes.

Atypical or Not Culturally Expected Finally, the criterion that the response be *atypical* or *not culturally expected* is important but also insufficient to determine if a disorder is present by itself. At times, something is considered abnormal because it occurs infrequently; it deviates from the average. The greater the deviation, the more abnormal it is. You might say that someone is abnormally short or abnormally tall, meaning that the person's height deviates substantially from average, but this obviously isn't a definition of disorder. Many people are far from the average in their behavior, but few would be considered disordered. We might call them *talented* or *eccentric*. Many artists, movie stars, and athletes fall in this category. For example, it's not normal to wear a dress made entirely out of meat, but when Lady Gaga wore this to an awards show, it only enhanced her celebrity. The late novelist J. D. Salinger, who wrote *The Catcher in the Rye*, retreated to a small town in New Hampshire and refused to see any outsiders for years, but he continued to write. In most cases, the more productive you are in the eyes of society, the more eccentricities society will tolerate. Therefore, "deviating from the average" doesn't work well as a definition for problematic abnormal behavior.

Another view is that your behavior is disordered if you are violating social norms, even if a number of people are sympathetic to your point of view. This definition is useful in considering important cultural differences in psychological disorders. For example, to enter a trance state and believe you are possessed reflects a psychological disorder in most Western cultures but not in many other societies, where the behavior is accepted and expected (see Chapter 6). (A cultural perspective is an important point of reference throughout this book.)

A social standard of *normal* has been misused, however. Consider, for example, the practice of committing political dissidents to mental institutions because they protest the policies of their government. Although such dissident behavior clearly violated social norms, it should not alone be cause for commitment.

Steve Granitz/Getty Images

We accept extreme behaviors by entertainers, such as Lady Gaga, that would not be tolerated in other members of our society.

Jerome Wakefield (1999, 2009), in a thoughtful analysis of the matter, uses the shorthand definition of *harmful dysfunction*. However, this definition assumes that we know what the evolutionary function of a behavior is, which is often not the case (McNally, 2001). Another possibility is to determine whether the behavior is out of the individual's control (something the person doesn't want to do) (Widiger & Crego, 2013; Widiger & Sankis, 2000). Variants of these approaches are most often used in current diagnostic practice, as outlined in the fifth edition of the *Diagnostic and Statistical Manual* (American Psychiatric Association, 2013), which contains the current listing of criteria for psychological disorders (Stein et al., 2010). These approaches guide our thinking in this book.

An Accepted Definition In conclusion, it is difficult to define what constitutes a psychological disorder (Lilienfeld & Marino, 1995, 1999)—and the debate continues (Blashfield, Keeley, Flanagan, & Miles, 2014; McNally, 2011; Spitzer, 1999; Stein et al., 2010; Wakefield, 2003, 2009; Zachar & Kendler, 2014). The most widely accepted definition used in the *Diagnostic and Statistical Manual of Mental Disorders, fifth edition* (DSM-5) (American Psychiatric Association, 2013) describes behavioral, psychological, or biological dysfunctions that are unexpected in their cultural context and associated with present distress and impairment in functioning, or increased risk of suffering, death, pain, or impairment. This definition can be useful across cultures and subcultures if we pay careful attention to what is functional or dysfunctional (or out of control) in a given society. But, again, it is never easy to decide what represents a dysfunction, and some scholars have argued persuasively that the health professions will never be able to satisfactorily define *disease* or *disorder* (see, for example, Lilienfeld & Marino, 1995, 1999; McNally, 2011; Stein et al., 2010; Zachar & Kendler, 2014). The best we may be able to do is to consider how the apparent disease or disorder matches a "typical" profile of a disorder—for example, major depression or schizophrenia—when most or all symptoms that experts would agree are part of the disorder are present. We call this typical profile a *prototype*, and as described in Chapter 3, the diagnostic criteria from DSM-5 found throughout this book are all prototypes. This means that patients may have only some features or symptoms of the disorder (a minimum number) and still meet criteria for the disorder because their set of symptoms is close to the prototype. But one of the differences between DSM-5 and its predecessor, DSM-IV, is the addition of dimensional estimates of the severity of specific disorders in DSM-5 (American Psychiatric Association, 2013; Helzer, Wittchen, Krueger, & Kraemer, 2008; Regier, Narrow, Kuhl, & Kupfer, 2009). Thus, for the anxiety disorders, for example, the intensity and frequency of anxiety within a given disorder such as panic disorder is rated on a 0 to 4 scale, where a rating of 1 would indicate mild or occasional symptoms and a rating of 4 would indicate continual and severe symptoms (Beesdo-Baum, et al., 2012; LeBeau, Bogels, Moller, & Craske, 2015; LeBeau et al., 2012). These concepts are described more fully in Chapter 3, where the diagnosis of psychological disorders is discussed.

For a final challenge, take the problem of defining a psychological disorder a step further and consider this: What if Janelle passed out so often that after a while neither her classmates nor her teachers even noticed because she regained consciousness quickly? Furthermore, what if Janelle continued to get good grades? Would frequent fainting at the mere thought of blood be a disorder? Would it be impairing? Dysfunctional? Distressing? What do you think?

Giulio Ercolani/Alamy Stock Photo

Some religious behaviors may seem unusual to us but are culturally or individually appropriate.

The Science of Psychopathology

Psychopathology is the scientific study of psychological disorders. Within this field are specially trained professionals, including clinical and counseling psychologists, psychiatrists, psychiatric social workers, and psychiatric nurses, as well as marriage and family therapists and mental health counselors. *Clinical psychologists* and *counseling psychologists* receive the Ph.D., doctor of philosophy, degree (or sometimes an Ed.D., doctor of education, or Psy.D., doctor of psychology) and follow a course of graduate-level study lasting approximately 5 years, which prepares them to conduct research into the causes and treatment of psychological disorders and to diagnose, assess, and treat these disorders. Although there is a great deal of overlap, counseling psychologists tend to study and treat adjustment and vocational issues encountered by relatively healthy individuals, and clinical psychologists usually concentrate on more severe psychological disorders. Also, programs in professional schools of psychology, where the degree is often a Psy.D., focus on clinical training and deemphasize or eliminate research training. In contrast, Ph.D. programs in universities integrate clinical and research training. Psychologists with other specialty training, such as experimental and social psychologists, concentrate on investigating the basic determinants of behavior but do not assess or treat psychological disorders.

Psychiatrists first earn an M.D. degree in medical school and then specialize in psychiatry during residency training that lasts 3 to 4 years. Psychiatrists also investigate the nature and causes of psychological disorders, often from a biological point of view; make diagnoses; and offer treatments. Many psychiatrists emphasize drugs or other biological treatments, although most use psychosocial treatments as well.

Psychiatric social workers typically earn a master's degree in social work as they develop expertise in collecting information relevant to the social and family situation of the individual with a psychological disorder. Social workers also treat disorders, often concentrating on family problems associated with them. *Psychiatric nurses* have advanced degrees, such as a master's or even a Ph.D., and specialize in the care and treatment of patients with psychological disorders, usually in hospitals as part of a treatment team.

Finally, *marriage and family therapists* and *mental health counselors* typically spend 1 to 2 years earning a master's degree and are employed to provide clinical services by hospitals or clinics, usually under the supervision of a doctoral-level clinician.

The Scientist-Practitioner The most important development in the recent history of psychopathology is the adoption of scientific methods to learn more about the nature of psychological disorders, their causes, and their treatment. Many mental health professionals take a scientific approach to their clinical work and therefore are called **scientist-practitioners** (Barlow, Hayes, & Nelson, 1984; Hayes, Barlow, & Nelson-Gray, 1999). Mental health practitioners may function as scientist-practitioners in one or more of three ways (see ■ Figure 1.2). First, they may keep up with the latest scientific developments in their field and therefore use the most current diagnostic and treatment procedures. In this sense, they are consumers of the science of psychopathology to the advantage of their patients. Second, scientist-practitioners evaluate their own assessments or treatment procedures to see whether they work. They are accountable not only to their patients but also to the government agencies and insurance companies that pay for the treatments, so they must demonstrate clearly whether their treatments are effective or not. Third, scientist-practitioners might conduct research, often in clinics or hospitals, that produces new information about disorders or their treatment, thus becoming immune to the fads that plague our field, often at the expense of patients and their families. For example, new "miracle cures" for psychological disorders that are reported several times a year in popular media would not be used by a scientist-practitioner if there were no sound scientific data showing that they work. Such data flow from research that attempts three basic things: to describe psychological disorders, to determine their causes, and to treat them (see ■ Figure 1.3). These three categories compose an organizational structure that recurs throughout this book and that is formally evident in the discussions of specific disorders beginning in Chapter 5. A general overview of them now will give you a clearer perspective on our efforts to understand abnormality.

Clinical Description In hospitals and clinics, we often say that a patient "presents" with a specific problem or set of problems or we discuss the **presenting problem**. *Presents* is a traditional shorthand way of indicating why the person came to the clinic. Describing Janelle's presenting problem is the first step

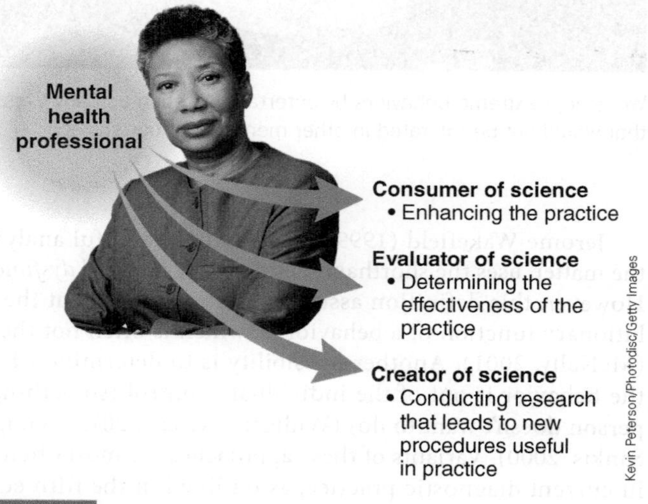

Figure 1.2
Functioning as a scientist-practitioner.

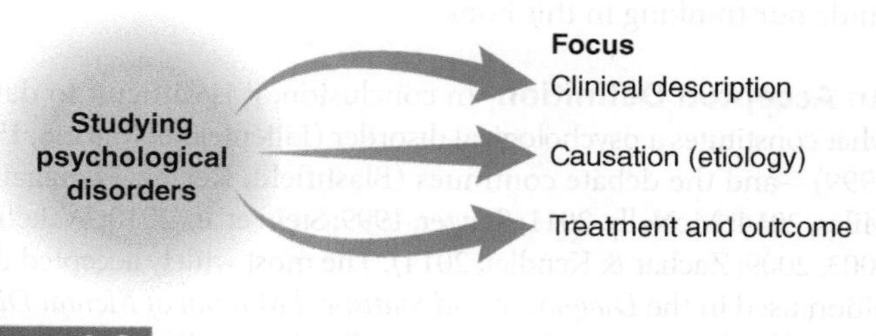

Figure 1.3
Three major categories make up the study and discussion of psychological disorders.

in determining her **clinical description**, which represents the unique combination of behaviors, thoughts, and feelings that make up a specific disorder. The word *clinical* refers both to the types of problems or disorders that you would find in a clinic or hospital and to the activities connected with assessment and treatment. Throughout this text are excerpts from many more individual cases, most of them from our personal files.

One important function of the clinical description is to specify what makes the disorder different from normal behavior or from other disorders. Statistical data may also be relevant.

For example, how many people in the population as a whole have the disorder? This figure is called the **prevalence** of the disorder. Statistics on how many new cases occur during a given period, such as a year, represent the **incidence** of the disorder. You may have become familiar with these terms during the COVID-19 pandemic. Other statistics include the *sex ratio*—that is, what percentage of women and men have the disorder (unfortunately, this traditional term does not consider nonbinary gender identity)—and the typical age of onset, which often differs from one disorder to another.

In addition to having different symptoms, age of onset, and possibly a different sex ratio and prevalence, most disorders follow a somewhat individual pattern, or **course**. For example, some disorders, such as schizophrenia (see Chapter 13), follow a *chronic course*, meaning that they tend to last a long time, sometimes a lifetime. Other disorders, like mood disorders (see Chapter 7), follow an *episodic course*, in that the individual is likely to recover within a few months, only to suffer a recurrence of the disorder at a later time. This pattern may repeat throughout a person's life. Still other disorders may have a *time-limited course*, meaning the disorder will improve without treatment in a relatively short period with little or no risk of recurrence.

Closely related to differences in course of disorders are differences in onset. Some disorders have an *acute onset*, meaning that they begin suddenly; others develop gradually over an extended period, which is sometimes called an *insidious onset*. It is important to know the typical course of a disorder so that we can know what to expect in the future and how best to deal with the problem. This is an important part of the clinical description. For example, if someone is suffering from a mild disorder with acute onset that we know is time limited, we might advise the individual not to bother with expensive treatment because the problem will be over soon enough, like a common cold. If the disorder is likely to last a long time (become chronic), however, the individual might want to seek treatment and take other appropriate steps. The anticipated course of a disorder is called the **prognosis**. So we might say, "the prognosis is good," meaning the individual will probably recover, or "the prognosis is guarded," meaning the probable outcome doesn't look good.

The patient's age may be an important part of the clinical description. A specific psychological disorder occurring in childhood may present differently from the same disorder in adulthood or old age. Children experiencing severe anxiety and panic often assume that they are physically ill because they have difficulty understanding that there is nothing physically wrong. Because their thoughts and feelings are different from those experienced by adults with anxiety and panic, children are often misdiagnosed and treated for a medical disorder.

We call the study of changes in behavior over time *developmental psychology*, and we refer to the study of changes in abnormal behavior as *developmental psychopathology*. When you think of developmental psychology, you probably picture researchers studying the behavior of children. We change throughout our lives, however, and so researchers also study development in adolescents, adults, and older adults. Study of abnormal behavior across the entire age span is referred to as *life-span developmental psychopathology*. The field is relatively new but expanding rapidly.

Causation, Treatment, and Etiology Outcomes **Etiology**, or the study of origins, has to do with why a disorder begins (what causes it) and includes biological, psychological, and social dimensions. The question of causality is deeply philosophical. Just because two events co-occur does not mean that they are in any way causally related: Correlation does not imply causality. Statisticians often use the term *Granger causality* to describe when a series of events temporally predict another series of events. But even if events are related, it is often difficult if not impossible to pinpoint a single cause of something, especially if many factors contribute to it. For example, could we really say that a flap of the wings of a butterfly in the Amazon jungle caused a tornado in Nebraska, even if these events were, in fact, somehow related? As is true for the weather, many factors also "cause" a psychological

Hung Chung Chih /Shutterstock.com

Children experience panic and anxiety differently from adults, so their reactions may be mistaken for symptoms of physical illness.

disorder, and some are more important than others. Because the etiology of psychological disorders is so important to this field, we devote an entire chapter (Chapter 2) to it.

Treatment, also, is often important to the study of psychological disorders. If a new drug or psychosocial treatment is successful in treating a disorder, it may give us some hints about the nature of the disorder and its causes. For example, if a drug with a specific known effect within the nervous system alleviates a certain psychological disorder, we know that something in that part of the nervous system might either be causing the disorder or helping maintain it. Similarly, if a psychological treatment designed to help clients regain a sense of control over their lives is effective with a certain disorder, a diminished sense of control may be an important psychological component of the disorder itself.

As you will see in the next chapter, psychopathology is rarely simple. This is because the *effect* does not necessarily imply the *cause*. To use a common example, you might take an aspirin to relieve a tension headache you developed during a grueling day of taking exams. If you then feel better, that does not mean that the headache was caused by a lack of aspirin. Nevertheless, many people seek treatment for psychological disorders, and treatment can provide interesting hints about the nature of the disorder.

In the past, textbooks emphasized treatment approaches in a general sense, with little attention to the disorder being treated. For example, a mental health professional might be thoroughly trained in a single theoretical approach, such as psychoanalysis or behavior therapy (both described later in the chapter), and then use that approach on every disorder. More recently, as our science has advanced, we have developed specific effective treatments that do not always adhere neatly to one theoretical approach or another but that have grown out of a deeper understanding of the disorder in question. For this reason, there are no separate chapters in this book on such types of treatment approaches as psychodynamic, cognitive behavioral, or humanistic. Rather, the latest and most effective drug and psychosocial treatments (nonmedical treatments that focus on psychological, social, and cultural factors) are described in the context of specific disorders in keeping with our integrative multidimensional perspective.

We now survey many early attempts to describe and treat abnormal behavior and to comprehend its causes, which will give you a better perspective on current approaches. In Chapter 2, we examine exciting contemporary views of causation and treatment. In Chapter 3, we discuss efforts to describe, or classify, abnormal behavior. In Chapter 4, we review research methods—our systematic efforts to discover the truths underlying description, cause, and treatment that allow us to function as scientist-practitioners. In Chapters 5 through 15, we examine specific disorders; our discussion is organized in each case in the now familiar triad of description, cause, and treatment. Finally, in Chapter 16 we examine legal, professional, and ethical issues relevant to psychological disorders and their treatment today. With that overview in mind, let us turn to the past.

Historical Conceptions of Abnormal Behavior

For thousands of years, humans have tried to explain and control problematic behavior. But our efforts always derive from the theories or models of behavior popular at the time. The purpose of these models is to explain why someone is "acting like that." Three major models that have guided us date back to the beginnings of civilization.

Humans have always supposed that agents outside our bodies and environment influence our behavior, thinking, and emotions. These agents—which might be divinities, demons, spirits, or other phenomena such as magnetic fields or the moon or the stars—are the driving forces behind the *supernatural model*. In addition, since the era of ancient Greece, the mind has often been called the *soul* or the *psyche* and considered separate from the body. Although many have thought that the mind can influence the body and, in turn, the body can influence the mind, most philosophers looked for causes of abnormal behavior in one or the other. This split gave rise to two traditions of thought about abnormal behavior, summarized as the *biological model* and the *psychological model*. These three models—the supernatural, the biological, and the psychological—are very old but continue to be used today.

The Supernatural Tradition

For much of our recorded history, deviant behavior has been considered a reflection of the battle between good and evil. When confronted with unexplainable, irrational behavior and by suffering and upheaval, people have perceived evil. In fact, in the great Persian empire from 900 to 600 B.C., all physical and mental disorders were considered the work of the devil (Millon, 2004). Barbara Tuchman, a noted historian, chronicled the second half of the 14th century, a particularly difficult time for humanity, in *A Distant Mirror* (1978). She ably captures the conflicting tides of opinion on the origins and treatment of insanity during that bleak and tumultuous period.

Demons and Witches

One strong current of opinion put the causes and treatment of psychological disorders squarely in the realm of the supernatural. During the last quarter of the 14th century, religious and lay authorities supported these popular superstitions, and society as a whole began to believe more strongly in the existence and power of demons and witches. The Catholic Church had split, and a second center, complete with a pope, emerged in the south of France to compete with Rome. In reaction to this schism, the Roman Church fought back against the evil in the world that it believed must have been behind this heresy.

People increasingly turned to magic and sorcery to solve their problems. During these turbulent times, the bizarre behavior of people afflicted with psychological disorders was seen as the work of the devil and witches. It followed that individuals possessed by evil spirits were probably responsible for any misfortune experienced by people in the local community, which inspired drastic action against the possessed. Treatments included **exorcism**, in which various religious rituals were performed in an effort to rid the victim of evil spirits. Other approaches included shaving the pattern of a cross in the hair of the victim's head and securing sufferers to a wall near the front of a church so that they might benefit from hearing Mass.

Concept Check 1.1

Part A

Write the letter for any or all of the following definitions of abnormality in the blanks: (a) societal norm violation, (b) impairment in functioning, (c) dysfunction, and (d) distress.

1. Miguel recently began feeling sad and lonely. Although still able to function at work and fulfill other responsibilities, he finds himself feeling down much of the time, and he worries about what is happening to him. Which of the definitions of abnormality apply to Miguel's situation? ____________
2. Three weeks ago, Makayla, a 35-year-old business executive, stopped showering, refused to leave her apartment, and started watching television talk shows. Threats of being fired have failed to bring Jane back to reality, and she continues to spend her days staring blankly at the television screen. Which of the definitions seems to describe Jane's behavior? ____________

Part B

Match the following words that are used in clinical descriptions with their corresponding examples: (a) presenting problem, (b) prevalence, (c) incidence, (d) prognosis, (e) course, and (f) etiology.

3. Maria should recover quickly with no intervention necessary. Without treatment, Kofi will deteriorate rapidly. ____________
4. Three new cases of bulimia have been reported in this county during the past month and only one in the next county. ____________
5. Kaliah visited the campus mental health center because of her increasing feelings of guilt and anxiety. ____________
6. Biological, psychological, and social influences all contribute to a variety of disorders. ____________
7. The pattern a disorder follows can be chronic, time-limited, or episodic. ____________
8. How many people in the population as a whole suffer from obsessive-compulsive disorder? ____________

The conviction that sorcery and witches are causes of madness and other evils continued into the 15th century, and evil continued to be blamed for unexplainable behavior, even after the founding of the United States, as evidenced by the Salem, Massachusetts, witch trials in the late 17th century, which resulted in the hanging deaths of 20 innocent people.

Stress and Melancholy

An equally strong opinion, even during this period, reflected the enlightened view that insanity was a natural phenomenon, caused by mental or emotional stress, and that it was curable (Alexander & Selesnick, 1966; Maher & Maher, 1985a). Mental depression and anxiety were recognized as illnesses (Kemp, 1990; Schoeneman, 1977), although symptoms such as despair and lethargy were often identified by the church with the sin of *acedia*, or sloth (Tuchman, 1978). Common treatments were rest, sleep, and a healthy and happy environment. Other treatments included baths, ointments, and various potions. Indeed, during the 14th and 15th centuries, people with insanity, along with those with physical deformities or disabilities, were often moved from house to house in medieval villages as neighbors took turns caring for them. We now know that this medieval practice of keeping people who have psychological disturbances in their own community is beneficial (see Chapter 13). We return to this subject when we discuss biological and psychological models later in this chapter.

In the 14th century, one of the chief advisers to the king of France, a bishop and philosopher named Nicholas Oresme, also suggested that the disease of melancholy (depression) was the

DEA PICTURE LIBRARY/Getty Images

During the Middle Ages, individuals with psychological disorders were sometimes thought to be possessed by evil spirits and exorcisms were attempted through rituals.

source of some bizarre behavior, rather than demons. Oresme pointed out that much of the evidence for the existence of sorcery and witchcraft, particularly among those considered insane, was obtained from people who were tortured and who, quite understandably, confessed to anything.

These conflicting crosscurrents of natural and supernatural explanations for mental disorders are represented more or less strongly in various historical works, depending on the sources consulted by historians. Some assumed that demonic influences were the predominant explanations of abnormal behavior during the Middle Ages (for example, Zilboorg & Henry, 1941); others believed that the supernatural had little or no influence. As in the handling of the severe psychological disorder experienced by late-14th-century King Charles VI of France, both influences were strong, sometimes alternating in the treatment of the same case.

Charles VI... The Mad King

In the summer of 1392, King Charles VI of France was under a great deal of stress, partly because of the division of the Catholic Church. As he rode with his army to the province of Brittany, a nearby aide dropped his lance with a loud clatter, and the king, thinking he was under attack, turned on his own army, killing several prominent knights before being subdued from behind. The army immediately marched back to Paris. The king's lieutenants and advisers concluded that he was mad.

During the following years, at his worst the king hid in a corner of his castle believing he was made of glass or roamed the corridors howling like a wolf. At other times, he couldn't remember who or what he was. He became fearful and enraged whenever he saw his own royal coat of arms and would try to destroy it if it was brought near him.

The people of Paris were devastated by their leader's apparent madness. Some thought it reflected God's anger because the king failed to take up arms to end the schism in the Catholic Church; others thought it was God's warning against taking up arms; and still others thought it was divine punishment for heavy taxes (a conclusion some people might make today). But most thought the king's madness was caused by sorcery, a belief strengthened by a great drought that dried up the ponds and rivers, causing cattle to die of thirst. Merchants claimed their worst losses in 20 years.

Naturally, the king was given the best care available at the time. The most famous healer in the land was a 92-year-old physician whose treatment program included moving the king to one of his residences in the country where the air was thought to be the cleanest in the land. The physician prescribed rest, relaxation, and recreation. After some time, the king seemed to recover. The physician recommended that the king not be burdened with the responsibilities of running the kingdom, claiming that if he had few worries or irritations, his mind would gradually strengthen and further improve.

Unfortunately, the physician died, and the insanity of King Charles VI returned more seriously than before. This time, however, he came under the influence of the conflicting crosscurrent of supernatural causation. "An unkempt evil-eyed charlatan and pseudo-mystic named Arnaut Guilhem was allowed to treat Charles on his claim of possessing a book given by God to Adam by means of which man could overcome all affliction resulting from original sin" (Tuchman, 1978, p. 514). Guilhem insisted that the king's malady was caused by sorcery, but his treatments failed to bring about a cure.

A variety of remedies and rituals of all kinds were tried, but none worked. High-ranking officials and doctors of the university called for the "sorcerers" to be discovered and punished. "On one occasion, two Augustinian friars, after getting no results from magic incantations and a liquid made from powdered pearls, proposed to cut incisions in the King's head. When this was not allowed by the King's council, the friars accused those who opposed their recommendation of sorcery" (Tuchman, 1978, p. 514). Even the king himself, during his lucid moments, came to believe that the source of madness was evil and sorcery. "In the name of Jesus Christ," he cried, weeping in his agony, "if there is any one of you who is an accomplice to this evil I suffer, I beg him to torture me no longer but let me die!" (Tuchman, 1978, p. 515).

Treatments for Possession

With a perceived connection between evil deeds and sin on the one hand and psychological disorders on the other, it is logical to conclude that the sufferer is largely responsible for the disorder, which might well be a punishment for evil deeds. Does this sound familiar? The acquired immune deficiency syndrome (AIDS) epidemic was associated with a similar belief among some people, particularly in the late 1980s and early 1990s. Because the human immunodeficiency virus (HIV) is, in Western societies, still quite prevalent among the gay community, many people believed it was a divine punishment for what they considered immoral behavior. This view became less common as the AIDS virus spread to other segments of the population, yet some people still hold on to this belief.

Possession, however, is not always connected with sin but may be seen as involuntary and the possessed individual as blameless. Furthermore, exorcisms at least have the virtue of being relatively painless. They sometimes work, as do other forms of faith healing, for reasons we explore in subsequent chapters. But what if they did not? In the Middle Ages, if exorcism failed, some authorities thought that steps were necessary to make the body uninhabitable by evil spirits, and many people were subjected to confinement, beatings, and other forms of torture (Kemp, 1990).

Somewhere along the way, a creative "therapist" decided that hanging people over a pit full of poisonous snakes might scare the evil spirits right out of their bodies (to say nothing of terrifying the people themselves). This approach sometimes worked; that is, the most disturbed, oddly behaving individuals would suddenly come to their senses and experience relief from their symptoms, if only temporarily. Naturally, this was reinforcing to the therapist, so snake pits were built in many institutions. Although these torture procedures seemed temporarily effective, these "treatments" are not the kinds of approaches we want to use because there is no good theoretical (or ethical) reason for using them.

Mass Hysteria

Another fascinating phenomenon is characterized by large-scale outbreaks of bizarre behavior. To this day, these episodes puzzle historians and mental health practitioners. During the Middle Ages, they lent support to the notion of possession by the devil. In Europe, whole groups of people were simultaneously compelled to run out in the streets, dance, shout, rave, and jump around in patterns as if they were at a particularly wild party late at night (still called a *rave* today, but with music). This behavior was known by several names, including Saint Vitus's Dance and tarantism. It is most interesting that many people behaved in this strange way at once. In an attempt to explain the inexplicable, several reasons were offered in addition to possession. One reasonable guess was reaction to insect bites. Another possibility was what we now call *mass hysteria* (Veith, 1965). Consider the following example.

Modern Mass Hysteria

One Friday afternoon, an alarm sounded over the public address system of a community hospital, calling all physicians to the emergency room immediately. Arriving from a local school in a fleet of ambulances were 17 students and 4 teachers who reported dizziness, headache, nausea, and stomach pains. Some were vomiting; most were hyperventilating.

All the students and teachers had been in four classrooms, two on each side of the hallway. The incident began when a 14-year-old young woman reported a funny smell that seemed to be coming from a vent. She fell to the floor, crying and complaining that her stomach hurt and her eyes stung. Soon, many of the students and most of the teachers in the four adjoining classrooms, who could see and hear what was happening, experienced similar symptoms. Of 86 susceptible people (82 students and 4 teachers in the four classrooms), 21 patients (17 students and 4 teachers) experienced symptoms severe enough to be evaluated at the hospital. Inspection of the school building by public health authorities revealed no apparent cause for the reactions, and physical examinations by teams of physicians revealed no physical abnormalities. All the patients were sent home and quickly recovered (Rockney & Lemke, 1992).

Mass hysteria may simply demonstrate the phenomenon of *emotion contagion*, in which the experience of an emotion seems to spread to those around us (Hatfield, Cacioppo, & Rapson, 1994; Ntika, Sakellariou, Kefalas, & Stamatpoulou, 2014; Wang, 2006). If someone nearby becomes frightened or sad, chances are that, for the moment, you also will feel fear or sadness. When this kind of experience escalates into full-blown panic, whole communities are affected (Barlow, 2002). People are also suggestible when they are in states of high emotion. Therefore, if one person identifies a "cause" of the problem, others will probably assume that their own reactions have the same source. In popular language, this shared response is sometimes referred to as *mob psychology*. Until recently, it was assumed that victims had to be in contact with each other for the contagion to occur, as were the young women described above in the adjacent classrooms. But lately there are documented cases of emotion contagion occurring across social networks, raising the possibility that episodes of mass hysteria may increase (Bartholomew, Wessely, & Rubin, 2012; Dimon, 2013)

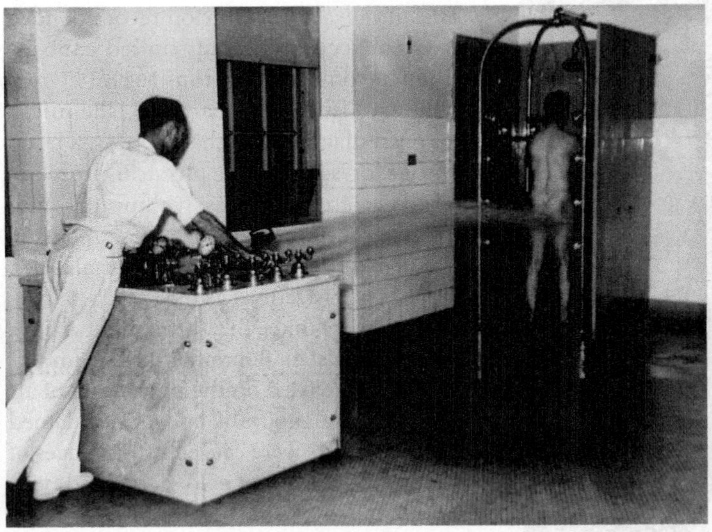

Source: U.S. National Library of Medicine

In hydrotherapy, patients were shocked back to their senses by applications of ice-cold water.

The Moon and the Stars

Paracelsus, a Swiss physician who lived from 1493 to 1541, rejected notions of possession by the devil, suggesting instead that the movements of the moon and stars had profound effects on people's psychological functioning. Echoing similar thinking in ancient Greece, Paracelsus speculated that the gravitational effects of the moon on bodily fluids might be a possible cause of mental disorders (Rotton & Kelly, 1985). This influential theory inspired the word *lunatic*, which is derived from the Latin word *luna*, meaning "moon." You might hear some of your friends explain something crazy they did one night by saying, "It must have been the full moon." The belief that heavenly bodies affect human behavior still exists, although there is no scientific evidence to support it (Raison, Klein, & Steckler, 1999; Rotton & Kelly, 1985). Despite much ridicule, millions of people around the world are convinced that their behavior is influenced by the stages of the moon or the positions of the stars. This belief is most noticeable today in followers of astrology, who hold that their behavior and the major events in their lives can be predicted by their day-to-day relationship to the position of the planets. No serious evidence has ever confirmed such a connection, however.

The Biological Tradition

Physical causes of mental disorders have been sought since early in history. Important to the biological tradition are an ancient Greek physician, Hippocrates; a disease, syphilis; and the early consequences of believing that psychological disorders are biologically caused.

Hippocrates and Galen

The Greek physician Hippocrates (460–377 B.C.) is considered to be the father of modern Western medicine. He and his associates left a body of work called the *Hippocratic Corpus*, written between 450 and 350 B.C. (Maher & Maher, 1985a), in which they suggested that psychological disorders could be treated like any other disease. They did not limit their search for the causes of psychopathology to the general area of "disease" because they believed that psychological disorders might also be caused by brain pathology or head trauma and could be influenced by heredity (genetics). These are remarkably astute deductions for the time, and they have been supported in recent years. Hippocrates considered the brain to be the seat of wisdom, consciousness, intelligence, and emotion. Therefore, disorders involving these functions would logically be located in the brain. Hippocrates also recognized the importance of psychological and interpersonal contributions to psychopathology, such as the sometimes-negative effects of family stress; on some occasions, he removed patients from their families.

The Roman physician Galen (approximately A.D. 129–198) later adopted the ideas of Hippocrates and his associates and developed them further, creating a powerful and influential school of thought within the biological tradition that extended well into the 19th century. One of the more interesting and influential legacies of the Hippocratic-Galenic approach is the *humoral theory* of disorders. Hippocrates assumed that normal brain functioning was related to four bodily fluids or *humors*: blood, black bile, yellow bile, and phlegm. Blood came from the heart, black bile from the spleen, phlegm from the brain, and choler or yellow bile from the liver. Physicians believed that disease resulted from too much or too little of one of the humors; for example, too much black bile was thought to cause melancholia (depression). In fact, the term *melancholer*, which means "black bile," is still used today in its derivative form *melancholy* to refer to aspects of depression. The humoral theory was, perhaps, the first example of associating psychological disorders with a "chemical imbalance," an approach that is widespread today.

The four humors were related to the Greeks' conception of the four basic qualities: heat, dryness, moisture, and cold. Each humor was associated with one of these qualities. Terms derived from the four humors are still sometimes applied to personality traits. For example, *sanguine* (literal meaning "red, like blood") describes someone who is ruddy in complexion, presumably from copious blood flowing through the body, and cheerful and optimistic, although insomnia and delirium were thought to be caused by excessive blood in the brain. *Melancholic* means depressive (depression was thought to be caused by black bile flooding the brain). A *phlegmatic* personality (from the humor phlegm) indicates apathy and sluggishness but can also mean being calm under stress. A *choleric* person (from yellow bile or choler) is hot tempered (Maher & Maher, 1985a).

Excesses of one or more humors were treated by regulating the environment to increase or decrease heat, dryness, moisture, or cold, depending on which humor was out of balance. One reason King Charles VI's physician moved him to the less stressful countryside was to restore the balance in his humors (Kemp, 1990). In addition to rest, good nutrition, and exercise, two treatments were developed. In one, *bleeding* or *bloodletting*, a carefully measured amount of blood was removed from the body, often with leeches. The other was to induce vomiting; indeed, in a well-known treatise on depression published in 1621, *Anatomy of Melancholy*, Robert Burton recommended eating tobacco and a half-boiled cabbage to induce vomiting (Burton, 1621/1977). If Janelle had lived 300 years ago, she might have been diagnosed with an illness, a brain disorder, or some other physical problem, perhaps related to excessive humors, and been given the proper medical treatments of the day: bed rest, bloodletting, a certain diet, and other ministrations as indicated.

In ancient China and throughout Asia, a similar idea existed. But rather than "humors," the Chinese focused on the movement of air or "wind" throughout the body. Unexplained mental disorders were caused by blockages of wind or the presence of cold, dark wind (yin) as opposed to warm, life-sustaining wind (yang). Treatment involved restoring proper flow of wind through various methods, including acupuncture.

Anadolu Agency/Getty Images

Emotions are contagious and can escalate into mass hysteria.

Bloodletting, the extraction of blood from patients, was intended to restore the balance of humors in the body.

Hippocrates also coined the word *hysteria* to describe a concept he learned about from the Egyptians, who had identified what we now call the *somatic symptom disorders*. In these disorders, the physical symptoms appear to be the result of a medical problem for which no physical cause can be found, such as paralysis and some kinds of blindness. Because these disorders occurred primarily in women, the Egyptians (and Hippocrates) mistakenly assumed that they were restricted to women. They also presumed a cause: The empty uterus wandered to various parts of the body in search of conception (the Greek word for "uterus" is *hysteron*). Numerous physical symptoms reflected the location of the wandering uterus. The prescribed cure might be marriage or, occasionally, fumigation of the vagina to lure the uterus back to its natural location (Alexander & Selesnick, 1966). Knowledge of physiology eventually disproved the wandering uterus theory; however, the tendency to stigmatize dramatic women as hysterical continued unabated well into the 1970s, when mental health professionals became sensitive to the prejudicial stereotype the term implied. As you will learn in Chapter 6, somatic symptom disorders (and the traits associated with them) are not limited to any one sex.

The 19th Century

The biological tradition waxed and waned during the centuries after Hippocrates and Galen but was reinvigorated in the 19th century because of two factors: the discovery of the nature and cause of syphilis and strong support from the well-respected American psychiatrist John P. Grey.

Syphilis Behavioral and cognitive symptoms of what we now know as *advanced syphilis*, a sexually transmitted disease caused by a bacterial microorganism entering the brain, include believing that everyone is plotting against you (delusion of persecution) or that you are God (delusion of grandeur), as well as other bizarre behaviors. Although these symptoms are similar to those of *psychosis*—psychological disorders characterized in part by beliefs that are not based in reality (delusions), perceptions that are not based in reality (hallucinations), or both—researchers recognized that a subgroup of apparently psychotic patients deteriorated steadily, becoming paralyzed and dying within 5 years of onset. This course of events contrasted with that of most psychotic patients, who remained fairly stable. In 1825, the condition was designated a disease, *general paresis*, because it had consistent symptoms (presentation) and a consistent course that resulted in death. The relationship between general paresis and syphilis was only gradually established. Louis Pasteur's germ theory of disease, developed in about 1870, facilitated the identification of the specific bacterial microorganism that caused syphilis.

Of equal importance was the discovery of a cure for general paresis. Physicians observed a surprising recovery in patients with general paresis who had contracted malaria, so they deliberately injected other patients with blood from a soldier who was ill with malaria. Many of those who survived this treatment recovered because the high fever "burned out" the syphilis bacteria. Obviously, this type of experiment would not be ethically possible today. Ultimately, clinical investigators discovered that penicillin cures syphilis, but with the malaria cure, "madness" and associated behavioral and cognitive symptoms for the first time were traced directly to a curable infection. Many mental health professionals then assumed that comparable causes and cures might be discovered for all psychological disorders.

John P. Grey The champion of the biological tradition in the United States was the most influential American psychiatrist of the time, John P. Grey (Bockoven, 1963). In 1854, Grey was appointed superintendent of the Utica State Hospital in New York, the largest in the country. He also became editor of the *American Journal of Insanity*, the precursor of the current *American Journal of Psychiatry*, the flagship publication of the American Psychiatric Association (APA). Grey's position was that the causes of insanity were *always* physical. Therefore, the mentally ill patient should be treated as physically ill. The emphasis was again on rest, diet, and proper room temperature and ventilation, approaches used for centuries by previous therapists in the biological tradition. Grey even invented the rotary fan to ventilate his large hospital.

Under Grey's leadership, the conditions in hospitals greatly improved, and they became more humane, livable institutions. But in subsequent years, they also became so large and impersonal that individual attention was not possible.

In fact, leaders in psychiatry at the end of the 19th century were alarmed at the increasing size and impersonality of mental hospitals and recommended that they be downsized. It was almost 100 years before the community mental health movement was successful in reducing the population of mental hospitals with the controversial policy of deinstitutionalization, in which patients were released into their communities. Unfortunately, this practice has as many negative consequences as positive ones, including a large increase in the number of chronically disabled patients experiencing homelessness on the streets of our cities.

In the 19th century, psychological disorders were attributed to mental or emotional stress, so patients were often treated sympathetically in a restful and hygienic environment.

The Development of Biological Treatments

On the positive side, renewed interest in the biological origin of psychological disorders led, ultimately, to greatly increased understanding of biological contributions to psychopathology and to the development of new treatments. In the 1930s, the physical interventions of electric shock and brain surgery were often used. Their effects, and the effects of new drugs, were discovered quite by accident. For example, insulin was occasionally given to stimulate appetite in psychotic patients who were not eating, but it also seemed to calm them down. In 1927, a Viennese physician, Manfred Sakel, began using increasingly higher dosages until, finally, patients convulsed and became temporarily comatose (Sakel, 1958). Some actually recovered their mental health, much to the surprise of everybody, and their recovery was attributed to the convulsions. The procedure became known as *insulin shock therapy*, but it was abandoned because it was too dangerous, often resulting in prolonged coma or even death. Other methods of producing convulsions were needed.

Benjamin Franklin made numerous discoveries during his life with which we are familiar, but most people don't know that he discovered accidentally, and then confirmed experimentally in the 1750s, that a mild and modest electric shock to the head produced a brief convulsion and memory loss (amnesia) but otherwise did little harm. A Dutch physician who was a friend and colleague of Franklin tried it on himself and discovered that the shock also made him "strangely elated" and wondered if it might be a useful treatment for depression (Finger & Zaromb, 2006, p. 245).

Independently in the 1920s, Hungarian psychiatrist Joseph von Meduna observed that schizophrenia was rarely found in individuals with epilepsy (which ultimately did not prove to be true). Some of his followers concluded that induced brain seizures might cure schizophrenia. Following suggestions on the possible benefits of applying electric shock directly to the brain—notably, by two Italian physicians, Ugo Cerletti and Lucio Bini, in 1938—a surgeon in London treated a depressed patient by sending six small shocks directly through his brain, producing convulsions (Hunt, 1980). The patient recovered. Although greatly modified, shock treatment is still with us today. The controversial modern uses of *electroconvulsive therapy* are described in Chapter 7. It is interesting that even now we have little knowledge of how it works.

During the 1950s, the first effective drugs for severe psychotic disorders were developed in a systematic way. Before that time, a number of medicinal substances, including opium (derived from poppies), had been used as sedatives, along with countless herbs and folk remedies (Alexander & Selesnick, 1966). With the discovery of *Rauwolfia serpentine* (later renamed *reserpine*) and another class of drugs called *neuroleptics* (major tranquilizers), for the first time hallucinatory and delusional thought processes could be diminished in some patients; these drugs also controlled agitation and aggressiveness. Other discoveries included *benzodiazepines* (minor tranquilizers), which seemed to reduce anxiety. By the 1970s, the benzodiazepines (known by such brand names as Valium and Librium) were among the most widely prescribed drugs in the world. As drawbacks and side effects of tranquilizers became apparent, along with their limited effectiveness, prescriptions decreased somewhat (we discuss the benzodiazepines in more detail in Chapters 5 and 11).

Throughout the centuries, as Alexander and Selesnick point out, "The general pattern of drug therapy for mental illness has been one of initial enthusiasm followed by disappointment" (1966, p. 287). For example, bromides, a class of sedating drugs, were used at the end of the 19th century and beginning of the 20th century to treat anxiety and other psychological disorders. By the 1920s, they were reported as being effective for many serious psychological and emotional symptoms. By 1928, one of every five prescriptions in the United States was for bromides. When their side effects, including various undesirable physical symptoms, became widely known, and experience began to show that their overall effectiveness was relatively modest, bromides largely disappeared from the scene.

Neuroleptics have also been used less as attention has focused on their many side effects, such as chronic tremors and shaking. However, the positive effects of these drugs on some patients' psychotic symptoms of hallucinations, delusions, and agitation revitalized both the search for biological contributions to psychological disorders and the search for new and more powerful drugs, a search that has paid many dividends, as documented in later chapters.

Consequences of the Biological Tradition

In the late 19th century, Grey and his colleagues ironically reduced or eliminated interest in treating mental patients because they thought that mental disorders were the result of some as-yet-undiscovered brain pathology and were therefore incurable. The only available course of action was to hospitalize these patients. Around the turn of the century, some nurses documented clinical success in treating mental patients but were prevented from treating others for fear of raising hopes of a cure among family members. In place of treatment, interest centered on diagnosis, legal questions concerning the responsibility of patients for their actions during periods of insanity, and the study of brain pathology itself.

The German physician Emil Kraepelin (1856–1926) was the dominant figure during this period and one of the founding fathers of modern psychiatry. He was extremely influential in advocating the major ideas of the biological tradition, but he was little involved in treatment. As a student of Wilhelm Wundt, his lasting contribution was in the area of diagnosis and classification, which we discuss in detail in Chapter 3. Kraepelin (1913) was one of the first to distinguish among various psychological disorders, seeing that each may have a different age of onset and time course, with somewhat different clusters of presenting symptoms, and probably a different cause. Many of his descriptions of schizophrenic disorders are still useful today.

By the end of the 1800s, a scientific approach to psychological disorders and their classification had begun with the search for biological causes. Furthermore, treatment was based on humane principles. There were many drawbacks, however, the most unfortunate being that active intervention and treatment were all but eliminated in some settings, despite the availability of some effective approaches. It is to these that we now turn.

The Psychological Tradition

It is a long leap from evil spirits to brain pathology as the cause of psychological disorders. In the intervening centuries, where was the body of thought that put psychological development, both normal and abnormal, in an interpersonal and social context? In fact, this approach has a long and distinguished tradition. Plato, for example, thought that the two causes of maladaptive behavior were the social and cultural influences in one's life and the learning that took place in that environment. If something was wrong in the environment, such as abusive parents, one's impulses and emotions would overcome reason. The best treatment was to reeducate the individual through rational discussion so that the power of reason would predominate (Maher & Maher, 1985a). This was very much a precursor to modern **psychosocial treatment** approaches to the causation of psychopathology, which focus not only on psychological factors but also on social and cultural ones. Other well-known early philosophers, including Aristotle, also emphasized the influence of social environment and early learning on later psychopathology. These philosophers wrote about the importance of fantasies, dreams, and cognitions and thus anticipated, to some extent, later developments in psychoanalytic thought and cognitive science. They also advocated humane and responsible care for individuals with psychological disturbances.

Concept Check 1.2

For thousands of years, humans have tried to understand and control abnormal behavior. Check your understanding of these historical theories, and match them to the treatments used to "cure" abnormal behavior: (a) bloodletting; induced vomiting; (b) patient placed in socially facilitative environments; and (c) exorcism; burning at the stake.

1. Supernatural causes; evil demons took over the victims' bodies and controlled their behaviors. ______________
2. The humoral theory reflected the belief that normal functioning of the brain required a balance of four bodily fluids or humors. ______________
3. Maladaptive behavior was caused by poor social and cultural influences within the environment. ______________

Moral Therapy

During the first half of the 19th century, a strong psychosocial approach to mental disorders called **moral therapy** became influential. The term *moral* actually referred more to emotional or psychological factors rather than to a code of conduct. Its basic tenets included treating institutionalized patients as normally as possible in a setting that encouraged and reinforced normal social interaction (Bockoven, 1963), thus providing them with many opportunities for appropriate social and interpersonal contact. Relationships were carefully nurtured. Individual attention clearly emphasized positive consequences for appropriate interactions and behavior, and restraint and seclusion were eliminated.

As with the biological tradition, the principles of moral therapy date back to Plato and beyond. For example, the Greek Asclepiad Temples of the 6th century B.C. housed the chronically ill, including those with psychological disorders. Here, patients were well cared for, massaged, and provided with soothing music. Similar enlightened practices were evident in Muslim countries in the Middle East (Millon, 2004). But moral therapy as a system originated with the well-known French psychiatrist Philippe Pinel (1745–1826) and his close associate Jean-Baptiste Pussin (1746–1811), who was the superintendent of the Parisian hospital La Bicêtre (Gerard, 1997; Zilboorg & Henry, 1941).

When Pinel arrived in 1791, Pussin had already instituted remarkable reforms by removing all chains used to restrain patients and instituting humane and positive psychological interventions. Pussin persuaded Pinel to go along with the changes. Much to Pinel's credit, he did, first at La Bicêtre and then at the women's hospital Salpétrière, where he invited Pussin to join him (Gerard, 1997; Maher & Maher, 1985b; Weiner, 1979). Here again, they instituted a humane and socially facilitative atmosphere that produced "miraculous" results.

After William Tuke (1732–1822) followed Pinel's lead in England, Benjamin Rush (1745–1813), often considered the founder of U.S. psychiatry, introduced moral therapy in his early work at Pennsylvania Hospital. It then became the treatment of choice in the leading hospitals. *Asylums* had appeared in the 16th century, but they were more like prisons than hospitals. It was the rise of moral therapy in Europe and the United States that made asylums habitable and even therapeutic.

In 1833, Horace Mann, chair of the board of trustees of the Worcester State Hospital, reported on 32 patients who had been given up as incurable. These patients were treated with moral therapy, cured, and released to their families. Of 100 patients who were viciously assaultive before treatment, no more than 12 continued to be violent a year after beginning treatment. Before treatment, 40 patients had routinely torn off any new clothes provided by attendants; only 8 continued this behavior after a period of treatment. These were remarkable statistics then and would be remarkable even today (Bockoven, 1963).

Asylum Reform and the Decline of Moral Therapy

Unfortunately, after the mid-19th century, humane treatment declined because of a convergence of factors. First, it was widely recognized that moral therapy worked best when the number of patients in an institution was 200 or fewer, allowing for a great deal of individual attention. After the Civil War, enormous waves of immigrants arrived in the United States, yielding their own populations of mentally ill. Patient loads in existing hospitals increased to 1,000 or 2,000, and even more. Because immigrant groups were thought not to deserve the same privileges as "native" Americans (whose ancestors had immigrated perhaps only 50 or 100 years earlier!), they were not given moral treatments even when there were sufficient hospital personnel.

A second reason for the decline of moral therapy has an unlikely source. The great crusader Dorothea Dix (1802–1887) campaigned endlessly for reform in the treatment of insanity. A schoolteacher who had worked in various institutions, she had firsthand knowledge of the deplorable conditions imposed on patients with insanity, and she made it her life's work to inform the American public and their leaders of these abuses. Her work became known as the **mental hygiene movement**.

In addition to improving the standards of care, Dix worked hard to make sure that everyone who needed care received it, including people who experienced homelessness. Through her efforts, humane treatment became more widely available in U.S. institutions. As her career drew to a close, she was rightly acknowledged as a hero of the 19th century.

Unfortunately, an unforeseen consequence of Dix's heroic efforts was a substantial increase in the number of mental patients. This influx led to a rapid transition from moral therapy to custodial

Asylums and Poor Farms in Rural America

In 1822 at an annual town meeting, the town of Nantucket, a small island 30 miles off the coast of Massachusetts, voted to build a permanent town poor farm and asylum (Gavin, 2003). In those days, asylums also cared for low-income and older adults. After the War of 1812, Nantucket had prospered from trade as well as from the beginning of the great whaling era, and its citizens wanted to take care of the less fortunate. Inspired by more modern beliefs at the time about the treatment of insanity, it was decided to place the asylum away from town in an area where residents could work productively in a pleasant and restful rural setting with fresh air, individual attention, and the availability of productive activities. Since misuse of alcohol was considered the principal cause of poverty, moving the asylums as far away from taverns as possible seemed logical and was another reason for locating the asylum in the country. But more important, both alcohol misuse and insanity were considered curable after word reached the island of the very positive results from moral therapy at McLean Asylum near Boston (currently McLean Hospital). Thus, it was arranged for residents of the asylum to engage principally in agricultural labor, producing vegetables, eggs, and dairy products or working outside in the wheat and rye fields or with the livestock. Older adults, or those unable to work outside of the asylum, were provided with productive work in their room, such as weaving. Consistent with the tenets of moral therapy, it was thought that a majority of the inmates might recover under the benefits of this healthy and restorative atmosphere. And the poor farm was well run and profitable for the town!

After building the asylum, town officials appointed a Board of Overseers, responsible leaders of Nantucket who immediately became concerned about the number of people visiting the asylum and poor farm, presumably to gawk at the insane. In a further effort to protect the residents, the town passed an ordinance restricting visits only to those who applied in writing and offered a good reason for visiting. Unfortunately, in the winter of February 1844, the structure burned to the ground. Despite heroic efforts of many townspeople, 10 inmates were killed, and the structure was destroyed.

Eventually, a new asylum was built, but by this time it housed only the sick and elderly who could no longer care for themselves. By that time, the new state asylum for the insane had opened far from the island, and the removal of people suffering from insanity to this large (and impersonal) state institution was seen as desirable. New policies were adopted for cases of poverty (presumably those not suffering from addiction of some kind) that included maintaining the poor in their dwellings and providing them with sufficient (but minimal) materials and resources to see them through. A new town "poor department" was created for this purpose. Thus did moral therapy rise and fall in a small rural town in New England, reflecting the tenor of the time (Gavin, 2003).

Everett Historical/Shutterstock.com

Dorothea Dix (1802–1887) began the mental hygiene movement and spent much of her life campaigning for reform in the treatment of the mentally ill.

care because hospitals were inadequately staffed. Dix reformed our asylums and single-handedly inspired the construction of numerous new institutions here and abroad. But even her tireless efforts and advocacy could not ensure sufficient staffing to allow the individual attention necessary to moral therapy. A final blow to the practice of moral therapy was the decision, in the middle of the 19th century, that mental illness was caused by brain pathology and, therefore, was incurable.

The psychological tradition lay dormant for a time, only to reemerge in several different schools of thought in the 20th century. The first major approach was **psychoanalysis**, based on Sigmund Freud's (1856–1939) elaborate theory of the structure of the mind and the role of unconscious processes in determining behavior. The second was **behaviorism**, associated with John B. Watson, Ivan Pavlov, and B. F. Skinner, which focuses on how learning and adaptation affect the development of psychopathology.

Psychoanalytic Theory

Have you ever felt as if someone cast a spell on you? Have you ever been mesmerized by looking deep and long into someone's eyes or at some spectacular firework? If so, you have something in common with the patients of Franz Anton Mesmer (1734–1815) and with millions of people since his time who have been hypnotized. Mesmer suggested to his patients that their problem was caused by an undetectable fluid found in all living organisms called "animal magnetism," which could become blocked.

Mesmer had his patients sit in a dark room around a large vat of chemicals with rods extending from it and touching them. Dressed in flowing robes, he might then identify and tap various areas of their bodies where their animal magnetism was blocked while suggesting strongly that they were being cured. Because of his rather unusual techniques, Mesmer was considered an oddity and maybe a charlatan, strongly opposed by the medical establishment (Winter, 1998). In fact, none less than Benjamin Franklin put animal magnetism to the test by conducting a brilliant experiment in which patients received either magnetized water or nonmagnetized water with strong suggestions that they would get better. Neither the patient nor the therapist knew which water was which, making it a double-blind experiment (see Chapter 4). When both groups got better, Franklin concluded that animal magnetism, or mesmerism, was nothing more than strong suggestion (Gould, 1991; McNally, 1999). Nevertheless, Mesmer is widely regarded as the father of hypnosis, a state in which extremely suggestible subjects sometimes appear to be in a trance.

Many distinguished scientists and physicians were interested in Mesmer's powerful methods of suggestion. One of the best known, Jean-Martin Charcot (1825–1893), was head of the Salpêtrière Hospital in Paris, where Philippe Pinel had introduced psychological treatments several generations earlier. A distinguished neurologist, Charcot demonstrated that some techniques of mesmerism were effective with a number of psychological disorders, and he did much to legitimize the fledgling practice of hypnosis. Significantly, in 1885 a young man named Sigmund Freud came from Vienna to study with Charcot.

After returning from France, Freud teamed up with Josef Breuer (1842–1925), who had experimented with a somewhat different hypnotic procedure. While his patients were in the highly suggestible state of hypnosis, Breuer asked them to describe their problems, conflicts, and fears in as much detail as they could. Breuer observed two extremely important phenomena during this process. First, patients often became extremely emotional as they talked and felt quite relieved and improved after emerging from the hypnotic state. Second, seldom would they have gained an understanding of the relationship between their emotional problems and their psychological disorder. In fact, it was difficult or impossible for them to recall some details they had described under hypnosis. In other words, the material seemed to be beyond the awareness of the patient. With this observation, Breuer and Freud believed that they had "discovered" the **unconscious** mind and its apparent influence on the production of psychological disorders. This is one of the most important developments in the history of psychopathology and, indeed, of psychology as a whole. However, as we discuss later, many of Freud's beliefs turned out to be incorrect.

A close second was their discovery that it is therapeutic to recall and relive emotional trauma that has been made unconscious and to release the accompanying tension. This release of emotional material became known as **catharsis**. A fuller understanding of the relationship between current emotions and earlier events is referred to as *insight.* As you shall learn throughout this book, particularly in Chapters 5 and 6 on anxiety and somatic symptom disorders,

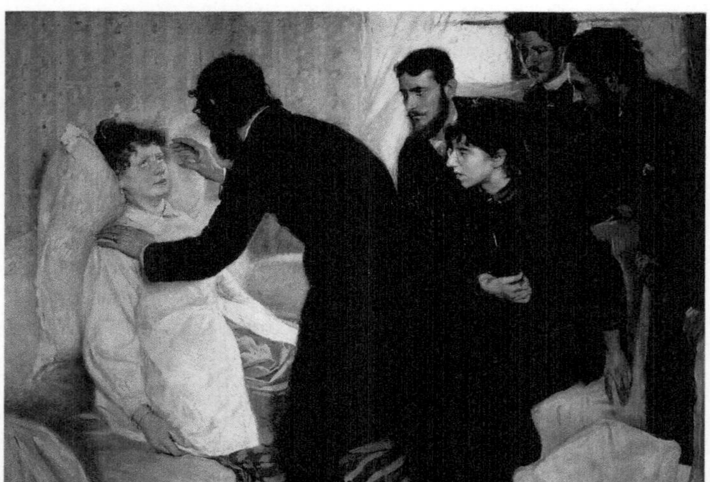

Erich Lessing/Art Resource, NY

Franz Anton Mesmer (1734–1815) and other early therapists often used hypnosis and/or strong suggestions to cure their patients.

the existence of "unconscious" memories and feelings and the importance of processing emotion-filled information have been verified and reaffirmed.

Freud and Breuer's ideas were based on case observations, some of which were made in a surprisingly systematic way for those times. An excellent example is Breuer's classic description of his treatment of "hysterical" symptoms in Anna O. in 1895 (Breuer & Freud, 1895/1957). Anna O. was a bright young woman who was perfectly healthy until she reached 21 years of age. Shortly before her problems began, her father developed a serious chronic illness that led to his death. Throughout his illness, Anna O. had cared for him; she felt it necessary to spend endless hours at his bedside. Five months after her father became ill, Anna noticed that during the day her vision blurred and that from time to time she had difficulty moving her right arm and both legs. Soon, additional symptoms appeared. She began to experience some difficulty speaking, and her behavior became unpredictable. Shortly thereafter, she consulted Breuer.

Bettmann/Getty Images

Jean Charcot (1825–1893) studied hypnosis and influenced Sigmund Freud to consider psychosocial approaches to psychological disorders.

Mary Evans Picture Library/Alamy Stock Photo

Josef Breuer (1842–1925) worked on the celebrated case of Anna O. and, with Sigmund Freud, developed the theory of psychoanalysis.

In a series of treatment sessions, Breuer dealt with one symptom at a time through hypnosis and subsequent "talking through," tracing each symptom to its hypothetical causation in circumstances surrounding the death of Anna's father. One at a time, her "hysterical" ailments disappeared, but only after treatment was administered for each respective behavior. This process of treating one behavior at a time fulfills a basic requirement for drawing scientific conclusions about the effects of treatment in an individual case study, as you will learn in Chapter 4. We return to the fascinating case of Anna O. in Chapter 6.

Freud took these basic observations and expanded them into the **psychoanalytic model**, the most comprehensive theory yet constructed on the development and structure of our personalities. He also speculated on where this development could go wrong and produce psychological disorders. Although many of Freud's views changed over time, the basic principles of mental functioning that he originally proposed remained constant through his writings and are still applied by psychoanalysts today.

Although most of it turned out to be incorrect or remains unproven, psychoanalytic theory has had a strong influence, and it is still important to be familiar with its basic ideas; what follows is a brief outline of the theory. We focus on its three major facets: (1) the structure of the mind and the distinct functions of personality that sometimes clash with one another; (2) the defense mechanisms with which the mind defends itself from these clashes, or conflicts; and (3) the stages of early psychosexual development that provide grist for the mill of our inner conflicts.

The Structure of the Mind The mind, according to Freud, has three major parts or functions: the id, the ego, and the superego (see ■ Figure 1.4). These terms, like many from psychoanalysis, have found their way into our common vocabulary, but although you may have heard them, you may not be aware of their meaning. The **id** is the source of our strong sexual and aggressive feelings or energies. It is, basically, the animal within people; if totally unchecked, it could make someone a rapist or a killer. The energy or drive within the id is the *libido.* Even today, some people explain low sex drive as an absence of libido. A less important source of energy, not as well conceptualized by Freud, is the death instinct, or *thanatos*. These two basic drives, toward life and fulfillment on the one hand and death and destruction on the other, are continually in opposition.

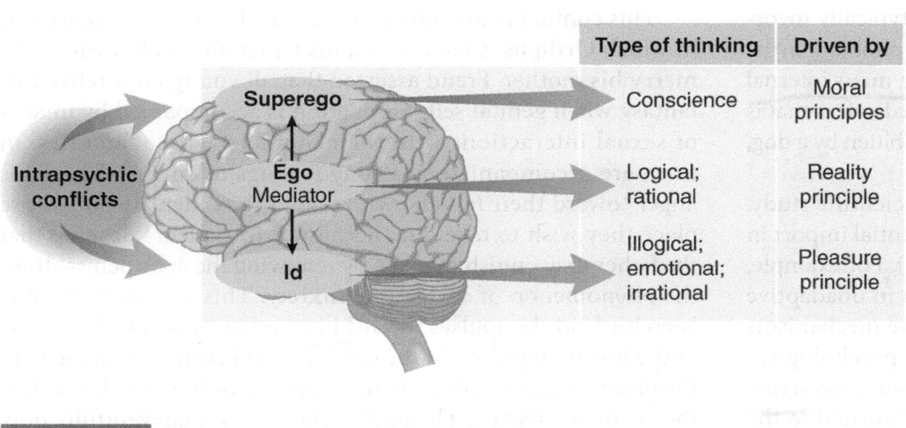

Figure 1.4

Freud's structure of the mind.

The id operates according to the *pleasure principle*, with an overriding goal of maximizing pleasure and eliminating any associated tension or conflicts. The goal of pleasure, which is particularly prominent in childhood, often conflicts with social rules and regulations, as you shall see later. The id has its own characteristic way of processing information; referred to as the *primary process*, this type of thinking is emotional, irrational, illogical, filled with fantasies, and preoccupied with sex, aggression, selfishness, and envy.

Fortunately for all of us, in Freud's view, the id's selfish and sometimes dangerous drives do not go unchecked. In fact, only a few months into life, we know we must adapt our basic demands to the real world. In other words, we must find ways to meet our basic needs without offending everyone around us. Put yet another way, we must act realistically. The part of our mind that ensures that we act realistically is called the **ego**, and it operates according to the *reality principle* instead of the pleasure principle. The cognitive operations or thinking styles of the ego are characterized by logic and reason and are referred to as the *secondary process*, as opposed to the illogical and irrational primary process of the id.

Mary Evans Picture Library/Alamy Stock Photo

Bertha Pappenheim (1859–1936), famous as Anna O., was described as "hysterical" by Breuer.

The third important structure within the mind, the **superego**, or what we might call *conscience*, represents the *moral principles* instilled in us by our parents and our culture. It is the voice within us that nags at us when we know we're doing something wrong. Because the purpose of the superego is to counteract the potentially dangerous aggressive and sexual drives of the id, the basis for conflict is readily apparent.

The role of the ego is to mediate conflict between the id and the superego, juggling their demands with the realities of the world. The ego is often referred to as the executive or manager of our minds. If it mediates successfully, we can go on to the higher intellectual and creative pursuits of life. If it is unsuccessful and the id or superego becomes too strong, conflict will overtake us, and psychological disorders will develop. Because these conflicts are all within the mind, they are referred to as **intrapsychic conflicts**. Now think back to the case of Anna O., in which Breuer observed that patients cannot always remember important but unpleasant emotional events. From these and other observations, Freud conceptualized the mental structures described in this section to explain unconscious processes. He believed that the id and the superego are almost entirely unconscious. We are fully aware only of the secondary processes of the ego, which is a relatively small part of the mind.

Defense Mechanisms The ego fights a continual battle to stay on top of the warring id and superego. Occasionally, their conflicts produce anxiety that threatens to overwhelm the ego. The anxiety is a signal that alerts the ego to marshal **defense mechanisms**, unconscious protective processes that keep primitive emotions associated with conflicts in check so that the ego can continue its coordinating function. Although Freud first conceptualized defense mechanisms, it was his daughter, Anna Freud, who developed the ideas more fully.

We all use defense mechanisms at times: They are sometimes adaptive and at other times maladaptive. For example, have you ever done poorly on a test because the professor was unfair in the grading? And then you go to a store and you start an argument with a store clerk because you can't find an item? This is an example of the defense mechanism of *displacement*. The ego adaptively decides that expressing primitive anger at your professor might not be in your best interest. Because that store clerk doesn't have the authority to affect you in an adverse way, your anger is displaced to them. Some people may redirect energy from conflict or underlying anxiety into a more constructive outlet such as work, where they may be more efficient because of the redirection. This process is called *sublimation*.

More severe internal conflicts that produce a lot of anxiety or other emotions can trigger self-defeating defensive processes or symptoms. Phobic and obsessive symptoms are especially common self-defeating defensive reactions that, according to Freud, reflect an inadequate attempt to deal with an

AP Images

Sigmund Freud (1856–1939) is considered the founder of psychoanalysis.

internally dangerous situation. Phobic symptoms typically incorporate elements of the danger. For example, a dog phobia may be connected to an infantile fear of castration; that is, a man's internal conflict involves a fear of being attacked and castrated, a fear that is consciously expressed as a fear of being attacked and bitten by a dog, even if he knows the dog is harmless.

Defense mechanisms have been subjected to scientific study, and there is some evidence that they may be of potential import in the study of psychopathology (Vaillant, 1992; 2012). For example, Perry and Bond (2012, 2014) noted that reduction in unadaptive defense mechanisms, and strengthening of adaptive mechanisms such as humor and sublimation, correlated with psychological health. Thus, the concept of defense mechanisms—*coping styles*, in contemporary terminology—continues to be important to the study of psychopathology.

Examples of defense mechanisms are listed below (APA, 2000a):

Denial: Refuses to acknowledge some aspect of objective reality or subjective experience that is apparent to others

Displacement: Transfers a feeling about or a response to an object that causes discomfort onto another, usually less threatening, object or person

Projection: Falsely attributes own unacceptable feelings, impulses, or thoughts to another individual or object

Rationalization: Conceals the true motivations for actions, thoughts, or feelings through elaborate reassuring or self-serving but incorrect explanations

Reaction formation: Substitutes behavior, thoughts, or feelings that are the direct opposite of unacceptable ones

Repression: Blocks disturbing wishes, thoughts, or experiences from conscious awareness

Sublimation: Directs potentially maladaptive feelings or impulses into socially acceptable behavior

Psychosexual Stages of Development Freud also theorized that during infancy and early childhood we pass through a number of **psychosexual stages of development** that have a profound and lasting impact. This makes Freud one of the first to take a developmental perspective on the study of abnormal behavior, which we look at in detail throughout this book. The stages—oral, anal, phallic, latency, and genital—represent distinctive patterns of gratifying our basic needs and satisfying our drive for physical pleasure. For example, the oral stage, typically extending for approximately 2 years from birth, is characterized by a central focus on the need for food. In the act of sucking, necessary for feeding, the lips, tongue, and mouth become the focus of libidinal drives and, therefore, the principal source of pleasure. Freud hypothesized that if we did not receive appropriate gratification during a specific stage or if a specific stage left a particularly strong impression (which he termed *fixation*), an individual's personality would reflect the stage throughout adult life. For example, fixation at the oral stage might result in excessive thumb sucking and emphasis on oral stimulation through eating, chewing pencils, or biting fingernails. Adult personality characteristics theoretically associated with oral fixation include dependency and passivity or, in reaction to these tendencies, rebelliousness and cynicism.

One of the more controversial and frequently mentioned psychosexual conflicts occurs during the phallic stage (from age 3 to age 5 or 6), which is characterized by early genital self-stimulation. This conflict is the subject of the Greek tragedy *Oedipus Rex*, in which Oedipus is fated to kill his father and, unknowingly, to marry his mother. Freud asserted that all young boys relive this fantasy when genital self-stimulation is accompanied by images of sexual interactions with their mothers. These fantasies, in turn, are accompanied by strong feelings of envy and perhaps anger toward their fathers, with whom they identify but whose place they wish to take. Furthermore, strong fears develop that the father may punish that lust by removing the son's penis—thus, the phenomenon of **castration anxiety**. This fear helps the boy keep his lustful impulses toward his mother in check. The battle of the lustful impulses on the one hand and castration anxiety on the other creates a conflict that is internal, or intrapsychic, called the *Oedipus complex*. The phallic stage passes uneventfully only if several things happen. First, the child must resolve his ambivalent relationship with his parents and reconcile the simultaneous anger and love he has for his father. If this happens, he may go on to channel his libidinal impulses into heterosexual relationships while retaining harmless affection for his mother.

The counterpart conflict in girls, called the *Electra complex*, is even more controversial. Freud viewed the young girl as wanting to replace her mother and possess her father. Central to this possession is the girl's desire for a penis, so as to be more like her father and brothers—hence the term *penis envy*. According to Freud, the conflict is successfully resolved when females develop healthy heterosexual relationships and look forward to having a baby, which he viewed as a healthy substitute for having a penis. Freudian beliefs about LBGTQ and other forms of sexuality and gender identity are even more speculative. Needless to say, these views are seen as sexist and demeaning. It is important to remember that these views are not based on facts; no systematic research exists to support them.

In Freud's view, all nonpsychotic psychological disorders resulted from underlying unconscious conflicts, the anxiety that resulted from those conflicts, and the implementation of ego defense mechanisms. Freud called such disorders **neuroses**, or *neurotic disorders*, from an old term referring to disorders of the nervous system.

Imagno/Hulton Archive/Getty Images

Anna Freud (1895–1982), here with her father, contributed the concept of defense mechanisms to the field of psychoanalysis.

Later Developments in Psychoanalytic Thought Freud's original psychoanalytic theories have been greatly modified and developed in a number of different directions, mostly by his students or followers. Some theorists simply took one component of psychoanalytic theory and developed it more fully. Others broke with Freud and went in entirely new directions.

Anna Freud (1895–1982), Freud's daughter, concentrated on the way in which the defensive reactions of the ego determine our behavior. In so doing, she was the first proponent of the modern field of **ego psychology**. Her book *Ego and the Mechanisms of Defense* (1946) is still influential. According to Anna Freud, the individual slowly accumulates adaptational capacities, skill in reality testing, and defenses. Abnormal behavior develops when the ego is deficient in regulating such functions as delaying and controlling impulses or in marshaling appropriate normal defenses to strong internal conflicts. In another somewhat later modification of Freud's theories, Heinz Kohut (1913–1981) focused on a theory of the formation of self-concept and the crucial attributes of the self that allow an individual to progress toward health, or conversely, to develop **neurosis**. This psychoanalytic approach became known as **self-psychology** (Kohut, 1977).

A related area that is quite popular today is referred to as **object relations**. Object relations is the study of how children incorporate the images, the memories, and sometimes the values of a person who was important to them and to whom they were (or are) emotionally attached. *Object* in this sense refers to these important people, and the process of incorporation is called *introjection*. Introjected objects can become an integrated part of the ego or may assume conflicting roles in determining the identity, or self. For example, your parents or guardians may have conflicting views on relationships or careers, which, in turn, may be different from your own point of view. To the extent that these varying positions have been incorporated, the potential for conflict arises. One day you may feel one way about your career direction, and the next day you may feel quite differently. According to object relations theory, you tend to see the world through the eyes of the person incorporated into your self. Object relations theorists focus on how these disparate images come together to make up a person's identity and on the conflicts that may emerge.

Carl Jung (1875–1961) and Alfred Adler (1870–1937) were students of Freud who came to reject his ideas and form their own schools of thought. Jung, rejecting many of the sexual aspects of Freud's theory, introduced the concept of the **collective unconscious**, which is a wisdom accumulated by society and culture that is stored deep in individual memories and passed down from generation to generation. Jung also suggested that spiritual and religious drives are as much a part of human nature as are sexual drives; this emphasis and the idea of the **collective unconscious** continue to draw the attention of mystics. Jung emphasized the importance of enduring personality traits such as introversion (the tendency to be shy and withdrawn) and extroversion (the tendency to be friendly and outgoing).

Adler focused on feelings of inferiority and the striving for superiority; he created the term *inferiority complex*. Unlike Freud, both Jung and Adler also believed that the basic quality of human nature is positive and that there is a strong drive toward self-actualization (realizing one's full potential). Jung and Adler believed that by removing barriers to both internal and external growth the individual would improve and flourish.

Others took psychoanalytical theorizing in different directions, emphasizing development over the life span and the influence of culture and society on personality. Karen Horney (1885–1952) and Erich Fromm (1900–1980) are associated with these ideas, but the best-known theorist is Erik Erikson (1902–1994). Erikson's greatest contribution was his theory of development across the life span, in which he described in some detail the crises and conflicts that accompany eight specific stages. For example, in the last of these stages, the *mature age*, beginning about age 65, individuals review their lives and attempt to make sense of them, experiencing both satisfaction at having completed some lifelong goals and despair at having failed at others. Scientific developments have borne out the wisdom of considering psychopathology from a developmental point of view.

Psychoanalytic Psychotherapy Many techniques of psychoanalytic psychotherapy, or psychoanalysis, are designed to reveal the nature of unconscious mental processes and conflicts through catharsis and insight. Freud developed techniques of **free association**, in which patients are instructed to say whatever comes to mind without the usual socially required censoring. Free association is intended to reveal emotionally charged material that may be repressed because it is too painful or threatening to bring into consciousness. Freud's patients lay on a couch, and he sat behind them so that they would not be distracted. This is how the couch became the symbol of psychotherapy. Other techniques include **dream analysis** (still quite popular today), in which the therapist interprets the content of dreams, supposedly reflecting the primary-process thinking of the id, and systematically relates the dreams to symbolic aspects of unconscious conflicts. This procedure is often difficult because the patient may resist the efforts of the therapist to uncover repressed and sensitive conflicts and may deny the interpretations. The goal of this stage of therapy is to help the patient gain insight into the nature of the conflicts.

The relationship between the therapist, called the **psychoanalyst**, and the patient is important. In the context of this relationship as it evolves, the therapist may discover the nature of the patient's intrapsychic conflict. This is because, in a phenomenon called **transference**, patients come to relate to the therapist much as they did to important figures in their childhood, particularly their parents. Patients who resent the therapist but can verbalize no good reason for it may be reenacting childhood resentment toward a parent. More often, the patient will fall deeply in love with the therapist, which reflects strong positive feelings that existed earlier for a parent. In the phenomenon of *countertransference*, therapists project some of their own personal issues and feelings, usually positive, onto the patient. Therapists are trained to deal with their own feelings as well as those of their patients, whatever the mode of therapy, and it is strictly against all ethical canons of the mental health professions to accept overtures from patients that might lead to relationships outside therapy.

Classical psychoanalysis requires therapy four to five times a week for 2 to 5 years to analyze unconscious conflicts, resolve them, and restructure the personality to put the ego back in charge. Reduction of symptoms (psychological disorders) is relatively inconsequential because they are only expressions of underlying intrapsychic conflicts that arise from psychosexual developmental stages. Thus, eliminating a phobia or depressive episode would be of little use unless the underlying conflict was dealt with adequately, because another set of symptoms would almost certainly emerge (*symptom substitution*). Because of the high cost of classical psychoanalysis and the lack of evidence that it is effective in alleviating psychological disorders, this approach is seldom used today.

Psychoanalysis is still practiced, particularly in some large cities, but many psychotherapists employ a loosely related set of approaches referred to as **psychodynamic psychotherapy**. Although conflicts and unconscious processes are still emphasized and efforts are made to identify trauma and active defense mechanisms, therapists use an eclectic mixture of tactics, with a social and interpersonal focus. Seven tactics that characterize psychodynamic psychotherapy include (1) a focus on affect and the expression of patients' emotions; (2) an exploration of patients' attempts to avoid topics or engage in activities that hinder the progress of therapy; (3) the identification of patterns in patients' actions, thoughts, feelings, experiences, and relationships; (4) an emphasis on past experiences; (5) a focus on patients' interpersonal experiences; (6) an emphasis on the therapeutic relationship; and (7) an exploration of patients' wishes, dreams, or fantasies (Blagys & Hilsenroth, 2000). Two additional features characterize psychodynamic psychotherapy. First, it is significantly briefer than classical psychoanalysis. Second, psychodynamic therapists deemphasize the goal of personality reconstruction, focusing instead on relieving the suffering associated with psychological disorders.

Comments Pure psychoanalysis is of historical interest more than current interest, and classical psychoanalysis as a treatment has been diminishing in popularity for years. In 1980, the term *neurosis*, which specifically implied a psychoanalytic view of the causes of psychological disorders, was dropped from the DSM, the official diagnostic system of the APA.

A major criticism of psychoanalysis is that it is basically unscientific, relying on reports by the patient of events that happened years ago. These events have been filtered through the experience of the observer and then interpreted by the psychoanalyst in ways that certainly could be questioned and might differ from one analyst to the next. Finally, there has been no careful measurement of any of these psychological phenomena and no obvious way to prove or disprove the basic hypotheses of psychoanalysis. This is important because measurement and the ability to prove or disprove a theory are the foundations of the scientific approach.

Nevertheless, psychoanalytic concepts and observations have been valuable to the study of psychopathology and psychodynamic psychotherapy and also to the history of ideas in Western civilization. Careful scientific studies of psychopathology have supported the observation of unconscious mental processes, the notion that basic emotional responses are often triggered by hidden or symbolic cues, and the understanding that memories of events in our lives can be repressed and otherwise avoided in a variety of ingenious ways. The relationship of the therapist and the patient, called the *therapeutic alliance*, is an important area of study across most therapeutic strategies. These concepts, along with the importance of various coping styles or defense mechanisms, appear repeatedly throughout this book.

Many of these psychodynamic ideas had been in development for more than a century, culminating in Freud's influential writings (for example, Lehrer, 1995), and they stood in stark contrast to witch trials and ideas of incurable brain pathology. In early years, the source of good and evil and of urges and prohibitions was conceived as external and spiritual, usually in the guise of demons confronting the forces of good. From the psychoanalytic point of view, we ourselves became the battleground for these forces, and we are inexorably caught up in the battle, sometimes for better and sometimes for worse.

Humanistic Theory

You have already learned that Jung and Adler broke sharply with Freud. Their fundamental disagreement concerned the very nature of humanity. Freud portrayed life as a battleground where we are continually in danger of being overwhelmed by our darkest forces. Jung and Adler, by contrast, emphasized the positive, optimistic side of human nature. Jung talked about setting goals, looking toward the future, and realizing one's fullest potential. Adler believed that human nature reaches its fullest potential when we contribute to the welfare of other individuals and to society as a whole. He believed that we all strive to reach superior levels of intellectual and moral development. Nevertheless, both Jung and Adler retained many of the principles of psychodynamic thought. Their general philosophies were adopted in the middle of the century by personality theorists and became known as *humanistic psychology*.

Self-actualizing was the watchword for this movement. The underlying assumption is that all of us could reach our highest potential, in all areas of functioning, if only we had the freedom to grow. Inevitably, a variety of conditions may block our actualization. Because every person is basically good and whole, most blocks originate outside the individual. Difficult living conditions or stressful life or interpersonal experiences may move you away from your true self.

Abraham Maslow (1908–1970) was most systematic in describing the structure of personality. He postulated a *hierarchy of needs*, beginning with our most basic physical needs for food and sex and ranging upward to our needs for self-actualization, love, and self-esteem. Social needs such as friendship fall somewhere between. Maslow hypothesized that we cannot progress up the hierarchy until we have satisfied the needs at lower levels.

Carl Rogers (1902–1987) is, from the point of view of therapy, the most influential humanist. Rogers (1961) originated client-centered therapy, later known as **person-centered therapy**. In this approach, the therapist takes a passive role, making as few interpretations as possible. The point is to give the individual a chance to develop during the course of therapy, unfettered by threats to the self. Humanist theorists have great faith in the ability of human relations to foster this growth. **Unconditional positive regard**, the complete and almost unqualified acceptance of most of the client's feelings and actions, is critical to the humanistic approach. *Empathy* is the sympathetic understanding of the individual's particular view of the world. The hoped-for result of person-centered therapy is that clients will be more straightforward and honest with themselves and will access their innate tendencies toward growth.

Like psychoanalysis, the humanistic approach has had a substantial effect on theories of interpersonal relationships. For example, the human potential movements so popular in the 1960s and 1970s were a direct result of humanistic theorizing. This approach also emphasized the importance of the therapeutic relationship in a way quite different from Freud's approach. Rather than seeing the relationship as a means to an end (transference), humanistic therapists believed that relationships, including the therapeutic relationship, were the single most positive influence in facilitating human growth. In fact, Rogers made substantial contributions to the scientific study of therapist–client relationships.

Nevertheless, the humanistic model contributed relatively little new information to the field of psychopathology. One reason for this is that its proponents, with some exceptions, had little interest in doing research that would discover or create new knowledge. Rather, they stressed the unique, nonquantifiable experiences of the individual, emphasizing that people are more different than alike. As Maslow noted, the humanistic model found its greatest application among individuals without psychological disorders. The application of person-centered therapy to more severe psychological disorders has decreased substantially over the decades, although certain variations have arisen periodically in some areas of psychopathology.

The Cognitive-Behavioral Model

As psychoanalysis swept the world at the beginning of the 20th century, events in Russia and the United States would eventually provide an alternative psychological model. The **cognitive-behavioral model** combines insights from the *behavioral model*, the *cognitive model*, and the *social learning model*. These models revolutionized the field because they brought the systematic development of a more scientific approach to psychological aspects of psychopathology.

Pavlov and Classical Conditioning In his classic study examining why dogs salivate before the presentation of food, physiologist Ivan Petrovich Pavlov (1849–1936) of St. Petersburg, Russia, initiated the study of **classical conditioning**, a type of learning in which a neutral stimulus is paired with a response until it elicits that response. The word *conditioning* (or *conditioned response*) resulted from an accident in translation from the original Russian. Pavlov was really talking about a response that occurred only on the condition of the presence of a particular event or situation (stimulus)—in this case, the footsteps of the laboratory assistant at feeding time. Thus, "conditional response" would have been more accurate. Conditioning is one way in which we acquire new information, particularly information that is somewhat emotional in nature. This process is not as simple as it first seems, and we continue to uncover many more facts about its complexity (Bouton, 2005; Craske, Hermans, & Vansteenwegen, 2006; Lissek et al., 2014; Prenoveau, Craske, Liao, & Ornitz, 2013; Rescorla, 1988). But it can be quite automatic. Let's consider a powerful contemporary example.

Psychologists working in oncology units have studied a phenomenon well known to many cancer patients, their nurses and physicians, and their families. Chemotherapy, a common treatment for some forms of cancer, has side effects including severe nausea and vomiting. But these patients often experience severe nausea and, occasionally, vomiting when they merely see the medical personnel who administered the chemotherapy or any equipment associated with the treatment, even on days when their treatment is not delivered (Kamen et al., 2014; Morrow & Dobkin, 1988; Roscoe, Morrow, Aapro, Molassiotis, & Olver, 2011). For some patients, this reaction becomes associated with a variety of stimuli that evoke people or things present during chemotherapy—anybody in a nurse's uniform or even the sight of the hospital. The strength of the response to similar objects or people is usually a function of how similar these objects or people are. This phenomenon is called *stimulus generalization* because the response generalizes to similar stimuli. In any case, this particular reaction is distressing and uncomfortable, particularly if it is associated with a variety of objects or situations. Psychologists have had to develop specific treatments to overcome this response (Mustian et al., 2011).

Whether the stimulus is food, as in Pavlov's laboratory, or chemotherapy, the classical conditioning process begins with a stimulus that would elicit a response in almost anyone and requires no learning; no conditions must be present for the response to occur. For these reasons, the food or chemotherapy is called the *unconditioned stimulus (UCS)*. The natural or unlearned response to this stimulus—in these cases, salivation or nausea—is called the *unconditioned response (UCR)*. Now the learning comes in. As we have already seen, any person or object associated with the UCS (food or chemotherapy) acquires the power to elicit the same response, but now the response, because it was elicited by the conditional or *conditioned stimulus (CS)*, is termed a *conditioned response (CR)*. Thus, the nurse associated with the chemotherapy becomes a CS. The nauseous sensation (upon seeing the nurse), which is almost the same as that experienced during chemotherapy, becomes the CR.

With unconditioned stimuli as powerful as chemotherapy, a CR can be learned in one trial. Most learning of this type, however, requires repeated pairing of the UCS (for example, chemotherapy) and the CS (for instance, nurses' uniforms or hospital equipment). When Pavlov began to investigate this phenomenon, he substituted a metronome for the footsteps of his laboratory assistants so that he could quantify the stimulus more accurately and, therefore, study the approach more precisely. What he also learned is that presentation of the CS (for example, the metronome) *without* the food for a long enough period would eventually eliminate the CR to the food. In other words, the dog learned that the metronome no longer meant that a meal might be on the way. This process was called **extinction**.

Ivan Pavlov (1849–1936) identified the process of classical conditioning, which is important to many emotional disorders.

Because Pavlov was a physiologist (he won the Nobel Prize in physiology in 1904 for his studies on the digestive system), it was natural for him to study these processes in a laboratory and to be quite scientific about it. This required precision in measuring and observing relationships and in ruling out alternative explanations. Although this scientific approach is common in biology, it was uncommon in psychology at that time. For example, early psychoanalysts did not believe that the scientific method was appropriate to measure and test the effects of unconscious conflicts precisely. Therefore, they relied on examinations of their own inner processes. Even early experimental psychologists such as Edward Titchener (1867–1927) emphasized the study of **introspection**. Subjects simply reported on their inner thoughts and feelings after experiencing certain stimuli, but the results of this "armchair" psychology were inconsistent and discouraging to many experimental psychologists.

Watson and the Rise of Behaviorism An early American psychologist, John B. Watson (1878–1958), is considered the founder of behaviorism. Strongly influenced by the work of Pavlov, Watson decided that to base psychology on introspection was to head in the wrong direction, that psychology could be made as scientific as physiology, and that psychology needs introspection or other nonquantifiable methods no more than chemistry and physics do (Watson, 1913). This point of view is reflected in a famous quotation from a seminal article published by Watson in 1913: "Psychology, as the behaviorist views it, is a purely objective experimental branch of natural science. Its theoretical goal is the prediction and control of behavior. Introspection forms no essential part of its methods" (p. 158).

Most of Watson's time was spent developing behavioral psychology as a radical empirical science, but he did dabble briefly in the study of psychopathology. In 1920, he and a student, Rosalie Rayner, presented an 11-month-old boy named Albert with a harmless fluffy white rat to play with. Albert was not afraid of the small animal and enjoyed playing with it. Every time Albert reached for the rat, however, the experimenters made a loud noise behind him. After only five trials, Albert showed the first signs of fear if the white rat came near. The experimenters then determined that Albert displayed mild fear of any white furry object, even a Santa Claus mask with a white fuzzy beard. You may not think that this is surprising, but keep in mind that this was one of the first examples ever recorded in a laboratory of producing fear of an object not previously feared. This experiment would be considered unethical by today's standards, and it turns out Albert may have also had some neurological impairment that could have contributed to developing fear (Fridlund, Beck, Goldie, & Irons, 2012), but the study remains a classic one.

Mary Cover Jones (1896–1987) was one of the first psychologists to use behavioral techniques to free a patient from phobia.

Another student of Watson's, Mary Cover Jones (1896–1987), thought that if fear could be learned or classically conditioned in this way, perhaps it could also be unlearned or extinguished. She worked with a boy named Peter, who at 2 years, 10 months, old was already quite afraid of furry objects. Jones decided to bring a white rabbit into the room where Peter was playing for a short time each day. She also arranged for other children, whom she knew did not fear rabbits, to be in the same room. She noted that Peter's fear gradually diminished. Each time it diminished, she brought the rabbit closer. Eventually Peter was touching and even playing with the rabbit (Jones, 1924a, 1924b), and years later the fear had not returned.

The Beginnings of Behavior Therapy The implications of Jones's research were largely ignored for two decades, given the fervor associated with more psychoanalytic conceptions of the development of fear. But in the late 1940s and early 1950s, Joseph Wolpe (1915–1997), a pioneering psychiatrist from South Africa, became dissatisfied with prevailing psychoanalytic interpretations of psychopathology and began looking for something else. He turned to the work of Pavlov and became familiar with the wider field of behavioral psychology. He developed a variety of behavioral procedures for treating his patients, many of whom suffered from phobias. His best-known technique was termed **systematic desensitization**. In principle, it was similar to the treatment of little Peter: Individuals were gradually introduced to the objects or situations they feared so that their fear could decline; that is, they could test reality and see that nothing bad happened in the presence of the phobic object or scene. Wolpe added another element by having his patients do something that was incompatible with fear while they were in the presence of the dreaded object or situation. Because he could not always reproduce the phobic object in his office, Wolpe had his patients carefully and systematically *imagine* the phobic scene, and the response he chose was relaxation because it was convenient. For example, Wolpe treated a young man with a phobia of dogs by training him first to relax deeply and then imagine he was looking at a dog across the park. Gradually, he could imagine the dog across the park and remain relaxed, experiencing little or no fear. Wolpe then had him imagine that he was closer to the dog. Eventually, the young man imagined that he was touching the dog while maintaining a relaxed, almost trancelike state.

Wolpe reported great success with systematic desensitization, one of the first wide-scale applications of the new science of behaviorism to psychopathology. Wolpe, working with fellow pioneers Hans-Jürgen Eysenck and Stanley Rachman in London, called this approach **behavior therapy**. Although Wolpe's procedures are seldom used today, they paved the way for modern-day fear and anxiety reduction procedures in which severe phobias can be eliminated in as little as 1 day (see Chapter 5).

B. F. Skinner and Operant Conditioning Sigmund Freud's influence extended far beyond psychopathology into many aspects of our cultural and intellectual history. Only one other behavioral scientist has made a similar impact: Burrhus Frederic (B. F.) Skinner (1904–1990). In 1938 he published *The Behavior of Organisms*, in which he laid out, in a comprehensive manner, the principles of *operant conditioning*, a type of learning in which behavior changes as a function of what follows the behavior.

Skinner observed early on that a large part of our behavior is not automatically elicited by a UCS and that we must account for this. In the ensuing years, Skinner did not confine his ideas to the laboratories of experimental psychology. He ranged far and wide in his writings, describing, for example, the potential applications of a science of behavior to our culture. Some best-known examples of his ideas are in the novel *Walden Two* (Skinner, 1948), in which he depicts a fictional society run on the principles of operant conditioning. In another well-known work, *Beyond Freedom and Dignity* (1971), Skinner lays out a broader statement of problems facing our culture and suggests solutions based on his own view of a science of behavior.

Skinner was strongly influenced by Watson's conviction that a science of human behavior must be based on observable events and relationships among those events. The work of psychologist Edward L. Thorndike (1874–1949) also influenced Skinner. Thorndike is best known for the *law of effect*, which states that behavior is either strengthened (likely to be repeated more frequently) or weakened (likely to occur less frequently) depending on the consequences of that behavior. Skinner took the simple notions that Thorndike had tested in the animal laboratories, using food as a reinforcer, and developed them in a variety of complex ways to apply to much of our behavior. For example, if a 5-year-old child starts shouting at the top of their lungs in a restaurant, much to the annoyance of the people around them, it is unlikely that their behavior was automatically elicited by a UCS. Also, they will be less likely to do it in the future if their parents scold them, take them out to the car to sit for a bit, or consistently reinforce more appropriate behavior. Then again, if the parents think their behavior is cute and laugh, chances are they will do it again.

Skinner coined the term *operant conditioning* because behavior operates on the environment and changes it in some way. For example, the child's behavior affects their parents' behavior and probably the behavior of other customers. Therefore, the child changes their environment. Most things that we do socially provide the context for other people to respond to us in one way or another, thereby providing consequences for our behavior. The same is true of our physical environment, although the consequences may be long term (polluting the air eventually will poison us). Skinner preferred the term **reinforcement** to "reward" because it connotes the effect on the behavior. Skinner once said that he found himself a bit embarrassed to be talking continually about reinforcement, much as Marxists used to see class struggle everywhere. But he pointed out that all of our behavior is governed to some degree by reinforcement, which can be arranged in an endless variety of ways, in *schedules of reinforcement*. Skinner wrote a whole book on different schedules of reinforcement (Ferster & Skinner, 1957). He also believed that using punishment as a consequence is relatively ineffective in the long run and that the primary way to develop new behavior is to positively reinforce desired behavior. Much like Watson, Skinner did not see the need to go beyond the observable and quantifiable to establish a satisfactory science of behavior. He did not deny the influence of biology or the existence of subjective states of emotion or cognition; he simply explained these phenomena as relatively inconsequential side effects of a particular history of reinforcement.

Bettmann/Getty Images

B. F. Skinner (1904–1990) studied operant conditioning, a form of learning that is central to psychopathology.

The subjects of Skinner's research were usually animals, mostly pigeons and rats. Using his new principles, Skinner and his disciples taught the animals a variety of tricks, including dancing, playing Ping-Pong, and playing a toy piano. To do this he used a procedure called **shaping**, a process of reinforcing successive approximations to a final behavior or set of behaviors. For example, if you want a pigeon to play Ping-Pong, first you provide it with a pellet of food every time it moves its head slightly toward a Ping-Pong ball tossed in its direction. Gradually, you require the pigeon to move its head ever closer to the Ping-Pong ball until it touches it. Finally, receiving the food pellet is contingent on the pigeon hitting the ball back with its head.

Pavlov, Watson, and Skinner contributed significantly to behavior therapy (see, for example, Wolpe, 1958), in which scientific principles of psychology are applied to clinical problems. Their ideas have substantially contributed to current psychological treatments and so are referred to repeatedly in this book.

Comments The behavioral model has contributed greatly to the understanding and treatment of psychopathology, as is apparent in the chapters that follow. Nevertheless, this model is incomplete and inadequate to account for what we now know about psychopathology. In the past, there was little or no room for biology in behaviorism because disorders were considered, for the most part, environmentally determined reactions. The model also fails to account for development of psychopathology across the life span. Recent advances in our knowledge of how information is processed, both consciously and subconsciously, have added a layer of complexity. Integrating all these dimensions requires a new model of psychopathology.

The Present: The Scientific Method and an Integrative Approach

As William Shakespeare wrote, "What's past is prologue." We have just reviewed three traditions or ways of thinking about causes of psychopathology: the supernatural, the biological, and the psychological (further subdivided into two major historical components—psychoanalytic and behavioral).

Supernatural explanations of psychopathology are still with us. Superstitions prevail, including beliefs in the effects of the moon and the stars on our behavior. This tradition has little influence on scientists and other professionals, however. Biological, psychoanalytic, and behavioral models, by contrast, continue to further our knowledge of psychopathology, as you will learn in the next chapter.

Each tradition has failed in important ways. First, scientific methods were not often applied to the theories and treatments within a tradition, mostly because methods that would have produced the evidence necessary to confirm or disprove the theories and treatments had not been developed. Lacking such evidence, many people accepted various fads and superstitions that ultimately proved to be untrue or useless. New fads often superseded truly useful theories and treatment procedures. King Charles VI was subjected to a variety of procedures, some of which have since been proved useful and others that were mere fads or even harmful. How we use scientific methods to confirm or disconfirm findings in psychopathology is described in Chapter 4. Second, health professionals tend to look at psychological disorders narrowly, from their own point of view alone. Grey assumed that psychological disorders were the result of brain disease and that other factors had no influence. Watson assumed that all behaviors, including disordered behavior, were the result of psychological and social influences and that the contribution of biological factors was inconsequential.

In the 1990s, two developments came together as never before to shed light on the nature of psychopathology: (1) the increasing sophistication of scientific tools and methodology and (2) the realization that no one influence—biological, behavioral, cognitive, emotional, or social—ever occurs in isolation. Literally, every time we think, feel, or do something, the brain and the rest of the body are hard at work. Perhaps not as obvious, however, is that our thoughts, feelings, and actions inevitably influence the function and even the structure of the brain, sometimes permanently. In other words, our behavior, both normal and abnormal, is the product of a continual interaction of psychological, biological, and social influences.

The view that psychopathology is multiply determined had its early adherents. Perhaps the most notable was Adolf Meyer (1866–1950), often considered the dean of American psychiatry. Whereas most professionals during the first half of the century held narrow views of the cause of psychopathology, Meyer steadfastly emphasized the equal contributions of biological, psychological, and sociocultural determinism. Although Meyer's ideas had some proponents, it took 100 years before the wisdom of his advice was fully recognized in the field.

By 2000, a veritable explosion of knowledge about psychopathology was occurring. The young fields of cognitive science and neuroscience began to grow exponentially as we learned more about the brain and about how we process, remember, and use information. At the same time, startling new findings from behavioral science revealed the importance of early experience in determining later development. It was clear that a new model was needed that would consider biological, psychological, and social influences on behavior. This approach to psychopathology would combine findings from all areas with our rapidly growing understanding of how we experience life during different developmental periods, from infancy to old age.

Concept Check 1.3

Match the treatment with the corresponding psychological theory of behavior: (a) behavioral model, (b) moral therapy, (c) psychoanalytic theory, and (d) humanistic theory.

1. Treating institutionalized patients as normally as possible and encouraging social interaction and relationship development. ____________
2. Hypnosis, psychoanalysis-like free association and dream analysis, and balance of the id, ego, and superego. ____________
3. Person-centered therapy with unconditional positive regard. ____________
4. Classical conditioning, systematic desensitization, and operant conditioning. ____________

This development is in line with the Strategic Plan for Research of the National Institute of Mental Health (NIMH), the main funding agency for research on mental health (NIMH, 2020). This plan specifically states four goals: (1) to define the brain mechanisms underlying complex behaviors, (2) to examine mental illness trajectories across the lifespan, (3) to strive for prevention and cures, and (4) to strengthen the public health impact of research. It still includes but less strongly emphasizes the earlier so-called Research Domain Criteria (RDoC) framework. The goal of this previous NIMH initiative was to offer an alternative to the DSM by utilizing brain circuits and basic biology processes to describe and understand mental disorders. This approach did not turn out to be practically feasible.

In the remainder of this book, we explore the reciprocal influences among neuroscience, cognitive science, behavior science, and developmental science and demonstrate that the only currently valid model of psychopathology is multidimensional and integrative.

Summary

Understanding Psychopathology

- A psychological disorder is (1) a psychological dysfunction within an individual that is (2) associated with distress or impairment in functioning and (3) a response that is not typical or culturally expected. All three basic criteria must be met; no one criterion alone has yet been identified that defines the essence of abnormality.
- The field of psychopathology is concerned with the scientific study of psychological disorders. Trained mental health professionals range from clinical and counseling psychologists to psychiatrists and psychiatric social workers and nurses. Each profession requires a specific type of training.
- Using scientific methods, mental health professionals can function as scientist-practitioners. They not only keep up with the latest findings but also use scientific data to evaluate their own work, and they often conduct research within their clinics or hospitals.

- Research about psychological disorders falls into three basic categories: description, causation, and treatment and outcomes.

The Supernatural, Biological, and Psychological Traditions

- Historically, there have been three prominent approaches to abnormal behavior. In the supernatural tradition, abnormal behavior is attributed to agents outside our bodies or social environment, such as demons, spirits, or the influence of the moon and stars. Although still alive, this tradition has been largely replaced by biological and psychological perspectives. In the biological tradition, disorders are attributed to disease or biochemical imbalances; in the psychological tradition, abnormal behavior is attributed to faulty psychological development and to social context.
- Each tradition has its own way of treating individuals who experience psychological disorders. Supernatural treatments include exorcism to rid the body of the supernatural spirits. Biological treatments typically emphasize physical care and the search for medical cures, especially drugs. Psychological approaches use psychosocial treatments, beginning with moral therapy and including modern psychotherapy.
- Sigmund Freud, the founder of psychoanalytic therapy, offered an elaborate conception of the unconscious mind, much of which is still conjecture. In therapy, Freud focused on tapping into the mysteries of the unconscious through such techniques as catharsis, free association, and dream analysis. Although Freud's followers veered from his path in many ways and although many of his views turned out to be incorrect or remain untested, Freud's influence can still be felt today.
- One outgrowth of Freudian therapy is humanistic psychology, which focuses more on human potential and self-actualizing than on psychological disorders. Therapy that has evolved from this approach is known as person-centered therapy; the therapist shows almost unconditional positive regard for the client's feelings and thoughts.
- The behavioral model moved psychology into the realm of science. Both research and therapy focus on things that are measurable, including such techniques as systematic desensitization, reinforcement, and shaping.

The Present: The Scientific Method and an Integrative Approach

- With the increasing sophistication of our scientific tools, and new knowledge from cognitive science, behavioral science, and neuroscience, we now realize that no contribution to psychological disorders ever occurs in isolation. Our behavior, both normal and abnormal, is a product of a continual interaction of psychological, biological, and social influences.

Key Terms

psychological disorder, 3
abnormal behavior, 3
phobia, 4
psychopathology, 6
scientist-practitioner, 6
presenting problem, 6
clinical description, 7
prevalence, 7
incidence, 7
course, 7
prognosis, 7
etiology, 7
exorcism, 8
psychosocial treatment, 15
moral therapy, 15
mental hygiene movement, 16
psychoanalysis, 17
behaviorism, 17
unconscious, 17
catharsis, 17
psychoanalytic model, 18
id, 18
ego, 19
superego, 19
intrapsychic conflicts, 19
defense mechanisms, 19
psychosexual stages of development, 20
castration anxiety, 20
neurosis (plural neuroses), 21
ego psychology, 21
self-psychology, 21
object relations, 21
collective unconscious, 21
free association, 21
dream analysis, 21
psychoanalyst, 21
transference, 21
psychodynamic psychotherapy, 22
self-actualizing, 22
person-centered therapy, 22
unconditional positive regard, 22
cognitive-behavioral model, 23
classical conditioning, 23
extinction, 23
introspection, 24
systematic desensitization, 24
behavior therapy, 24
reinforcement, 25
shaping, 25

Answers to Concept Checks

1.1

Part A

1. d; **2.** b, c

Part B

3. d; **4.** c; **5.** a; **6.** f; **7.** e; **8.** b

1.2

1. c; **2.** a; **3.** b

1.3

1. b; **2.** c; **3.** d; **4.** a

Timeline of Significant Events

400 B.C.–1875

The Image Works

National Library of Medicine

400 B.C.: Hippocrates suggests that psychological disorders have both biological and psychological causes.

1300s: Superstition runs rampant, and mental disorders are blamed on demons and witches; exorcisms are performed to rid victims of evil spirits.

1400–1800: Bloodletting and leeches are used to rid the body of unhealthy fluids and restore chemical balance.

1793: Philippe Pinel introduces moral therapy and makes French mental institutions more humane.

400 B.C. | **1300s** | **1500s** | **1825–1875**

200 C.E.: Galen suggests that normal and abnormal behaviors are related to four bodily fluids, or humors.

1400s: Enlightened view that insanity is caused by mental or emotional stress gains momentum, and depression and anxiety are again regarded by some as disorders.

1500s: Paracelsus suggests that the moon and the stars, not possession by the devil, affect people's psychological functioning.

1825–1875: Syphilis is differentiated from other types of psychosis in that it is caused by a specific bacterium; ultimately, penicillin is found to cure syphilis.

1930–1968

1930: Insulin shock therapy, electric shock treatments, and brain surgery begin to be used to treat psychopathology.

1943: The Minnesota Multiphasic Personality Inventory is published.

1950: The first effective drugs for severe psychotic disorders are developed. Humanistic psychology (based on ideas of Carl Jung, Alfred Adler, and Carl Rogers) gains some acceptance.

1958: Joseph Wolpe effectively treats patients with phobias using systematic desensitization based on principles of behavioral science.

1930 | **1943** | **1950** | **1968**

1938: B. F. Skinner publishes *The Behavior of Organisms,* which describes the principles of operant conditioning.

1946: Anna Freud publishes *Ego and the Mechanisms of Defense.*

1952: The first edition of the *Diagnostic and Statistical Manual* (DSM-I) is published.

1968: DSM-II is published.

Bettmann/Getty Images

Imagno/Hulton Archive /Getty Images

1848–1920

© Everett Historical/Shutterstock.com

1848: Dorothea Dix successfully campaigns for more humane treatment in U.S. mental institutions.

1870: Louis Pasteur develops his germ theory of disease, which helps identify the bacterium that causes syphilis.

AP Images

1900: Sigmund Freud publishes *The Interpretation of Dreams.*

Granger Historical Picture Archive/Alamy Stock Photo

1913: Emil Kraepelin classifies various psychological disorders from a biological point of view and publishes work on diagnosis.

1848 **1870** **1900** **1920**

1854: John P. Grey, head of New York's Utica Hospital, believes that insanity is the result of physical causes, thus de-emphasizing psychological treatments.

1895: Josef Breuer treats the "hysterical" Anna O., leading to Freud's development of psychoanalytic theory.

Mary Evans Picture Library/Alamy Stock Photo

1904: Ivan Pavlov receives the Nobel Prize for his work on the physiology of digestion, which leads him to identify conditioned reflexes in dogs.

Hulton Archive/Getty Images

1920: John B. Watson experiments with conditioned fear in Little Albert, using a white rat.

1980–2021

1980: DSM-III is published.

1990s: Increasingly sophisticated research methods are developed; no one influence—biological or environmental—is found to cause psychological disorders in isolation from the other.

2000: DSM-IV-TR is published.

1980 **1990s** **2000** **2010**

1987: DSM-III-R is published.

1994: DSM-IV is published.

2013: DSM-5 is published.

2021: DSM-5 TR is published.

2 An Integrative Approach to Psychopathology

Photographee.eu/Shutterstock.com

Learning Objectives

LO2.1 List the relevant dimensions that may cause psychological disorders according to the multidimensional integrative approach.

LO2.2 Distinguish the diathesis–stress model, reciprocal gene–environment model, and epigenetics from each other according to how they explain the development of psychopathology.

LO2.3 State the function of each of the five neurotransmitters that may play a key role in the development of psychological disorders.

LO2.4 Compare the effects of behavioral and cognitive influences on psychopathology, including learned helplessness, modeling, prepared learning, and implicit memory.

LO2.5 Define *mood* in terms of its relationship to emotions and psychological disorders.

LO2.6 Explain the influence of social, cultural, and interpersonal factors on how psychopathology manifests in individuals.

LO2.7 Provide an example of equifinality in the context of psychopathology.

Remember Janelle from Chapter 1? We knew she suffered from blood–injection–injury phobia, but we did not know why. Here, we address the issue of causation. This chapter examines the specific components of a **multidimensional integrative approach** to psychopathology (see ■ Figure 2.1). Biological dimensions include causal factors from the fields of genetics and neuroscience. Psychological dimensions include causal factors from behavioral and cognitive processes, including learned helplessness, social learning, prepared learning, and even unconscious processes (in a different guise than in the days of Sigmund Freud). Emotional influences contribute in a variety of ways to psychopathology, as do social and interpersonal influences. Finally, developmental influences figure in any discussion of causes of psychological disorders. You will become familiar with these areas as they relate to psychopathology and learn about some of the latest developments relevant to psychological disorders. But keep in mind what we confirmed in the previous chapter: No influence operates in isolation. Each dimension—biological or psychological—is strongly influenced by the others and by development, and they weave together in various complex and intricate ways to create a psychological disorder.

Here, we explain briefly why we have adopted a multidimensional integrative model of psychopathology. Then we preview various causal influences and interactions, using Janelle's case as background. After that, we look more deeply at specific causal influences in psychopathology, examining both the latest research and integrative ways of viewing what we know.

One-Dimensional versus Multidimensional Models

A linear or one-dimensional model attempts to trace the origins of behavior to a single cause. For example, a linear causal model might hold that schizophrenia or a phobia is caused by having a chemical imbalance or by growing up surrounded by overwhelming conflicts among family members. In psychology and psychopathology, we still encounter this type of thinking occasionally, but most scientists and clinicians believe that psychopathology results from multiple influences. A system, or feedback loop, may have independent inputs at many different points, but as each input becomes part of the whole, it can no longer be considered independent. This perspective on causality is *systemic*, which derives from the word *system*; it implies that any particular influence contributing to psychopathology cannot be considered out of context. Context, in this case, is the biology and behavior of the individual, as well as the cognitive, emotional, social, and cultural environment, because any one component of the system inevitably affects the other components, forming a complex network. This is a multidimensional model.

What Caused Janelle's Phobia?

From a multidimensional perspective, let's look at what might have caused Janelle's phobia (see Figure 2.1).

Behavioral Influences

The cause of Janelle's phobia might at first seem obvious. She saw a movie with graphic scenes of blood and injury and had a bad reaction to it. Her reaction, an unconditioned response, became associated with situations similar to the scenes in the movie, depending on how similar they were. But Janelle's reaction reached such an extreme that even hearing someone say "Cut it out!" evoked queasiness. Is Janelle's phobia a straightforward case of classical conditioning? It might seem so, but one puzzling question arises: Why didn't the other kids in Janelle's class develop the same phobia? As far as Janelle knew, nobody else even felt queasy.

Biological Influences

We now know that more is involved in blood–injection–injury phobia than a simple conditioning experience, although conditioning and stimulus generalization contribute. We have learned a lot about this phobia (Antony & Barlow, 2002; Ritz, Meuret, & Ayala, 2010; van Overveld, de Jong, & Peters, 2011). Physiologically, Janelle experienced a *vasovagal syncope*, which is a common cause of fainting. *Syncope* means "sinking feeling" or "swoon" caused by low blood pressure in the head. When she saw the film, she became mildly distressed, as many people would, and her heart rate and blood pressure increased accordingly, which she probably did not notice. Then her body took over, immediately overcompensating by decreasing her vascular resistance, lowering her heart rate, and, eventually, lowering her blood pressure too much. The amount of blood reaching her brain diminished until she lost consciousness.

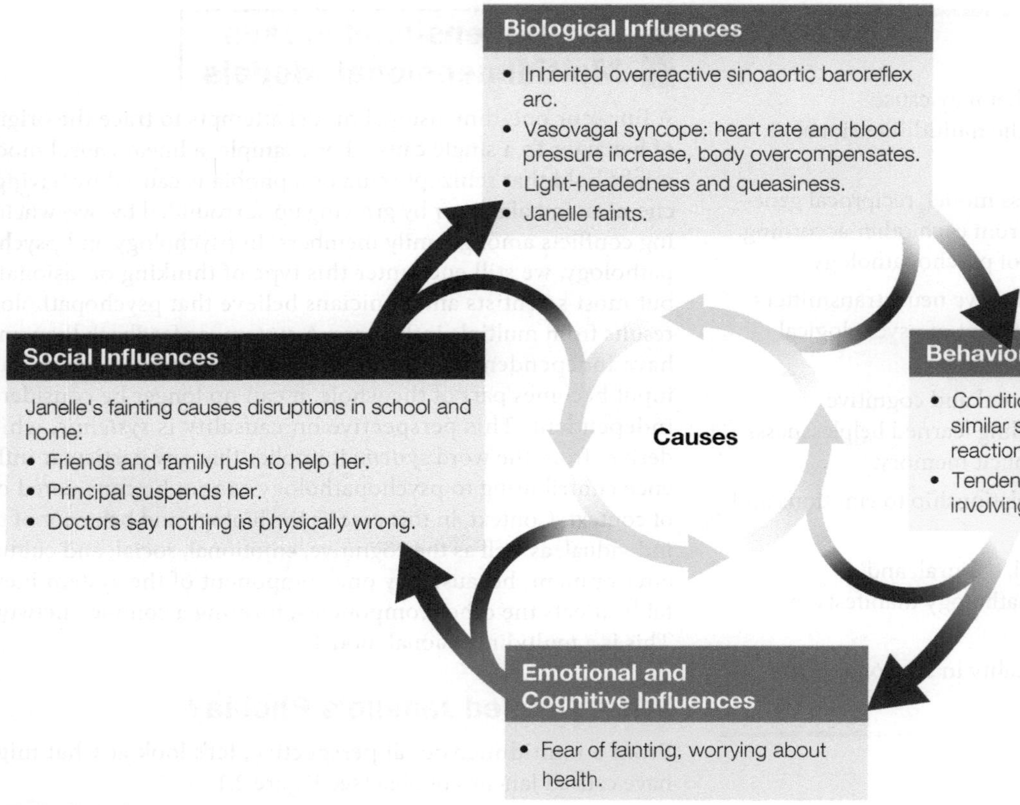

Figure 2.1

Janelle's case.

A possible cause of the vasovagal syncope is an overreaction of a mechanism called the *sinoaortic baroreflex arc*, which compensates for sudden increases in blood pressure by lowering it. The tendency to overcompensate seems to be inherited, a trait that may account for the high rate of blood–injection–injury phobia in families. Do you ever feel queasy at the sight of blood? If so, chances are your mother, your father, or someone else in your immediate family has the same reaction. In one study, 61% of the family members of individuals with this phobia had a similar condition, although somewhat milder in most cases (Öst, 1992). You might think, then, that we have discovered the cause of blood–injury–injection phobia and that all we need to do is develop a pill to regulate the baroreflex. But many people with rather severe syncope reaction tendencies do *not* develop phobias. They cope with their reaction in various ways, including tensing their muscles whenever they are confronted with blood. Tensing the muscles quickly raises blood pressure and prevents the fainting response. Furthermore, some people with little or no syncope reaction develop the phobia anyway (Öst, 1992). Therefore, the cause of blood–injection–injury phobia is more complicated than it seems. If we said that the phobia is caused by a biological dysfunction (an overactive vasovagal reaction probably because of a particularly sensitive baroreflex mechanism) or a traumatic experience (seeing a gruesome film) and subsequent conditioning, we would be partly right on both counts, but in adopting a one-dimensional causal model we would miss the most important point: To cause blood–injection–injury phobia, a complex *interaction* must occur between emotional, cognitive, social, biological, and behavioral factors. Inheriting a strong syncope reaction definitely puts a person at risk for developing this phobia, but other influences are at work as well.

Emotional Influences

Janelle's case is a good example of biology influencing behavior. But behavior, thoughts, and feelings can also influence biology, sometimes dramatically. What role did Janelle's fear and anxiety play in the development of her phobia, and where did they come from? Emotions can affect physiological responses such as blood pressure, heart rate, and respiration, particularly if we know rationally there is nothing to fear, as Janelle did. In her case, rapid increases in heart rate caused by her emotions may have triggered a stronger and more intense baroreflex. Emotions also changed the way she thought about situations involving blood and injury and motivated her to behave in ways she didn't want to, avoiding all situations connected with blood and injury, even if it was important not to avoid them. As we see throughout this book, emotions play a substantial role in the development of many disorders.

Social Influences

Most people are social by nature and tend to live in groups such as families and gather in cities. The COVID-19 pandemic was

People who experience the same traumatic event will have different long-term reactions.

possible because many of us are closely connected socially, which also made social isolation during this time difficult. These social influences are always present and have direct contributions to biology and behavior. Janelle's friends and family rushed to her aid when she fainted. Did their support help or hurt? Her principal rejected her and dismissed her problem. What effect did this behavior have on her phobia? Rejection, particularly by authority figures, can make psychological disorders worse than they otherwise would be. Then again, being supportive only when somebody is experiencing symptoms is not always helpful because the strong effects of social attention may actually increase the frequency and intensity of the reaction.

Developmental Influences

One more influence affects us all—the passage of time. As time passes, many things about ourselves and our environments change in important ways, causing us to react differently at different ages. Thus, at certain times we may enter a *developmental critical period* when we are more or less reactive to a given situation or influence than at other times. To go back to Janelle, it is possible she was previously exposed to other situations involving blood. Important questions to ask are these: Why did this problem develop when she was 16 years old and not before? Is it possible that her susceptibility to having a vasovagal reaction was highest in her teenage years? It may be that the timing of her physiological reaction, along with viewing the disturbing biology film, provided just the right (but unfortunate) combination to initiate her severe phobic response.

Outcome and Comments

Fortunately for Janelle, she responded well to brief but intensive treatment at one of our clinics, and she was back in school within 7 days. Janelle was gradually exposed, with her full cooperation, to words, images, and situations describing or depicting blood and injury, while a sudden drop in blood pressure was prevented. We began with something mild, such as the phrase "Cut it out!" By the end of the week Janelle was witnessing surgical procedures at the local hospital.

Janelle required close therapeutic supervision during this program. At one point, while driving home with her parents from an evening session, she had the bad luck to pass a car crash, and she saw a bleeding accident victim. That night, she dreamed about bloody accident victims coming through the walls of her bedroom. This experience made her call the clinic and request emergency intervention to reduce her distress, but it did not slow her progress. (Programs for treating phobias and related anxiety disorders are described more fully in Chapter 5. It is the issue of etiology or causation that concerns us here.)

Finding the causes of abnormal behavior is a complex and fascinating process. Focusing on biological or behavioral factors would not have given us a full picture of the causes of Janelle's disorder; we had to consider a variety of other influences and the ways they might interact. A discussion in more depth follows, examining the research underlying the many biological, psychological, and social influences that must be considered as causes of any psychological disorder.

Concept Check 2.1

Theorists have abandoned the notion that any one factor can explain abnormal behavior; they favor an integrative model. Match each of the following scenarios to its most likely influence or influences: (a) behavioral, (b) biological, (c) emotional, (d) social, and (e) developmental.

1. The fact that some phobias are more common than others (such as fear of heights and snakes) and may have contributed to the survival of the species in the past suggests that phobias may be genetically prewired. This is evidence for which influence? ____________
2. Miray's husband, Jinx, was an unemployed jerk who spent his life chasing women other than his wife. Miray, happily divorced for years, cannot understand why the smell of Jinx's brand of aftershave causes her to become nauseated. Which influence best explains her response? ____________
3. Ichiro, age 16, finds it more difficult than his 7-year-old sister to adjust to his parents' recent separation. This may be explained by what influences? ____________
4. A traumatic ride on a Ferris wheel at a young age was most likely to have been the initial cause of Isabella's fear of heights. Her strong emotional reaction to heights is likely to maintain or even increase her fear. The initial development of the phobia is likely a result of ____________ influences; however, ____________ influences are likely perpetuating the phobia.

Genetic Contributions to Psychopathology

What causes you to look like one or both of your parents or, perhaps, your grandparents? Obviously, the genes you inherit are from your parents and from your ancestors before them. **Genes** are long molecules of deoxyribonucleic acid (DNA) at various locations on chromosomes, within the cell nucleus. Ever since Gregor Mendel's pioneering work in the 19th century, we have known that some physical characteristics are influenced by our genetic endowment. But other factors in the environment also influence our physical appearance. To some extent, our weight and even our height are affected by nutritional, social, and cultural factors. Consequently, our genes seldom determine our physical development in any absolute way. They do provide some boundaries to our development. Exactly where we go within these boundaries depends on environmental influences.

Although this is true for most of our characteristics, it is not true for all of them. For example, Huntington's disease has been traced to a genetic defect that causes deterioration in a specific area of the brain, the basal ganglia. It is a degenerative brain disease that appears in early to middle age, usually the early 40s, and causes broad changes in personality, cognitive functioning, and, particularly, motor behavior, including involuntary shaking or jerkiness throughout the body. We have not yet discovered a way to environmentally influence the course of Huntington's disease. Another example of genetic influence is a disorder known as phenylketonuria (PKU), which can result in intellectual disability. This disorder, present at birth, is caused by the inability of the body to metabolize (break down) phenylalanine, a chemical compound found in many foods. Like Huntington's disease, PKU is caused by a defect in a single gene, with little contribution from other genes or the environmental background. PKU is inherited when both parents are carriers of the gene and pass it on to the child. Fortunately, researchers have discovered a way to correct this disorder: We can change the way the environment interacts with and affects the genetic expression of this disorder. Specifically, by detecting PKU early enough (which is now routinely done), we can simply restrict the amount of phenylalanine in the baby's diet until the child develops to the point where a normal diet does not harm the brain, usually 6 or 7 years of age. Disorders such as PKU and Huntington's disease, in which cognitive impairment of various kinds is the prominent characteristic, are covered in more detail in Chapters 14 and 15.

Except for identical twins, every person has a unique set of genes unlike those of anyone else in the world. Because there is plenty of room for the environment to influence our development within the constraints set by our genes, there are many reasons for the development of individual differences.

What about our behavior and traits, our likes and dislikes? Do genes influence personality and, by extension, abnormal behavior? This question of nature (genes) versus nurture (upbringing and other environmental influences) is age-old in psychology, and the answers beginning to emerge are fascinating. Before discussing them, let's review briefly what we know about genes and about environmental factors.

The Nature of Genes

Broadly speaking, a gene is the unit of heredity that is passed on from the parent to the offspring. The DNA contains the complete set of genetic instructions (the *genome*). We have known for a long time that each normal human cell has 46 chromosomes arranged in 23 pairs. One chromosome in each pair comes from the father, and one comes from the mother. We can see these chromosomes through a microscope, and we can sometimes tell when one is faulty and predict what problems it will cause.

The first 22 pairs of chromosomes (called *autosomes*) provide programs or directions for the development of the body and brain, and the last pair, called the *sex chromosomes*, also determines an individual's sex. In females, both chromosomes in the 23rd pair are called *X chromosomes*. In males, the mother contributes an X chromosome, but the father contributes a *Y chromosome*. This one difference is responsible for the variance in biological sex. Abnormalities in the sex chromosomal pair can cause ambiguous sexual characteristics (see Chapter 10).

The chromosomes contain DNA, which includes the genetic blueprint. The DNA molecule has a certain structure. It is a double helix, resembling a twisted ladder or spiral staircase. The steps of the ladder are the four *nucleotides* with their nucleobases, adenine, cytosine, guanine, or thymine. These bases form pairs: Adenine forms a pair with thymine, and cytosine forms a pair with guanine. The DNA sequence that defines a gene is called *coding DNA*. For a gene to be *expressed*, the DNA code is first copied (or *transcribed*) into a strand of *ribonucleic acid* (*RNA*). We will revisit this transcription process later again when we discuss epigenetics. On the level of the DNA, therefore, a gene may be defined as a sequence of nucleotides on the DNA that codes for a specific protein or piece of RNA.

The specific location on a chromosome that codes for a gene is the *genetic locus*. Because we have pairs of chromosomes, we always have two alternative forms of a gene at each genetic locus inherited from each parent (except for genes on the Y chromosome). In the population, the same gene can of course have many different additional forms (or variants) because people can differ in the DNA sequence coding for a particular gene. Alternative (or variant) forms of genes are called *alleles*.

The outward appearance of the person (or any organism) is called the person's *phenotype*. Each pair of alleles represents the *genotype* of a specific gene. The different forms of alleles are called *polymorphism* (*poly* stands for many and *morphism* for form). One type of polymorphism is caused by differences in one single nucleotide in the sequence of the coding DNA. In fact, the most common polymorphism in the human genome is the *single nucleotide polymorphism* (SNP, which is pronounced *snip*). This occurs when one nucleotide replaces another. For example, the nucleotide thymine (T) might replace the nucleotide cyctosine (C) in a particular stretch of the DNA (such as GCATCG versus GCACCG).

SNPs are quite common and occur in the coding and noncoding DNA. Most SNPs have no effect on health whatsoever. But other times, these genetic variations can act as biological markers, helping scientists locate genes that are associated with diseases. When SNPs occur within a gene or in a regulatory region near a gene, they may play a more direct role in disease by affecting the gene's function. SNPs may help predict an individual's response to certain drugs, susceptibility to environmental factors such as toxins, and risk of developing particular diseases. We discuss some of them later.

There is a lot more noncoding DNA than there are genes on chromosomes. On the X chromosome, for example, there are approximately 160 million base pairs but only about 800 protein-coding genes, and only some of them are expressed, with lots of variation between individuals. In addition, people differ in whether they have dominant or recessive alleles for certain traits. A *dominant allele* is one of a pair of genes that strongly influences a particular trait, and we need only one of them to determine. A *recessive allele*, by contrast, must be paired with another (recessive) allele to determine a trait. Otherwise, it won't have any effect. Color-blindness is an example of a recessive allele on the X chromosome, and sickle cell disease is an example of a recessive autosomal allele. Dominance occurs when one member of a gene pair is consistently expressed over the other. When we have a dominant allele, using Mendelian laws of genetics we can predict fairly accurately how many offspring will develop a certain trait, characteristic, or disorder, depending on whether one or both parents carry that dominant gene. However, Mendelian inheritance in humans is rare.

Much of our development and most of our behavior, our personality, and even our intelligence are *polygenic*—that is, influenced by many genes, each contributing only a tiny effect, all of which, in turn, may be influenced by the environment. The same is true for psychiatric disorders (Geschwind & Flint 2015). And because the human *genome*—an individual's complete set of genes—consists of more than 20,000 genes (Lander et al., 2001; U.S. Department of Energy Office of Science, 2009), polygenic interactions can be quite complex. For this reason, most geneticists now use sophisticated procedures such as quantitative genetics and molecular genetics that allow them to look for patterns of influence across many genes (Kendler, 2011, 2013; Kendler, Jaffee, & Roemer, 2011; Plomin & Davis, 2009; Rutter, Moffitt, & Caspi, 2006). *Quantitative genetics* examines the contribution of genes that code for dimensional, rather than discrete, traits (phenotypes). *Molecular genetics* focuses on examining the actual structure of genes with increasingly advanced technologies such as *DNA microarrays*; these technologies allow scientists to analyze thousands of genes at once and identify broad networks of genes that may be contributing to a particular trait (Kendler, 2011; Plomin & Davis, 2009). Such studies have indicated that hundreds of genes can contribute to the heritability of a single trait (Hariri et al., 2002; Plomin et al., 1995; Rutter et al., 2006).

What is interesting is that environmental factors, in the form of social and cultural influences, can also contribute to gene expression (Cole, 2011). To take one example, in studies with rat pups, researchers have found that the absence of normal maternal behavior of "licking and grooming" prevents the genetic expression of a glucocorticoid receptor that modulates stress hormones. This means rats with inadequate maternal care have greater sensitivity to stress (Meaney & Szyf, 2005). There is evidence that a similar model may be relevant in humans (Dickens, Turkheimer, & Beam, 2011; Hyman, 2009). We present more examples later in

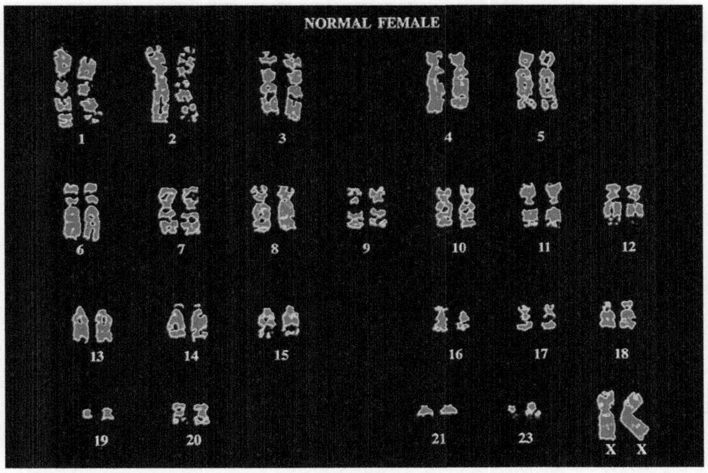

Bio-Photo Associates/Science Source

A normal female has 23 pairs of chromosomes.

the chapter when we discuss the interaction of genes and the environment. The study of gene expression and gene–environment interaction is the current frontier in the study of genetics (Kendler et al., 2011; Plomin & Davis, 2009; Rutter, 2006; Rutter et al., 2006; Thapar & McGuffin, 2009). In Chapter 4, we look at the actual methods that scientists use to study the influence of genes. Here, our interest is in what they are finding.

New Developments in the Study of Genes and Behavior

Scientists have now identified, in a preliminary way, the genetic contribution to psychological disorders and related behavioral patterns. The best estimates attribute about half of our enduring personality traits and cognitive abilities to genetic influence (Rutter, 2006). For example, McClearn and colleagues (1997) compared 110 Swedish identical twin pairs, at least 80 years old, with 130 same-sex fraternal twin pairs of a similar age and found heritability estimates for specific cognitive abilities, such as memory or ability to perceive spatial relations, ranged from 32% to 62%. This work built on earlier important twin studies, with different age groups showing similar results (for example, Bouchard, Lykken, McGue, Segal, & Tellegen, 1990). Furthermore, a study of more than 1,200 twins spanning 35 years confirmed that during adulthood (from early adulthood to late middle age) genetic factors determined stability in cognitive abilities, whereas environmental factors were responsible for any changes (Lyons et al., 2009). In other studies, the same heritability calculation for personality traits such as shyness or activity levels ranges between 30% and 50% (Bouchard et al., 1990; Kendler, 2001; Loehlin, 1992; Rutter, 2006; Saudino et al., 2018).

It has also become clear that adverse life events such as a "chaotic" childhood can overwhelm the influence of genes (Turkheimer, Haley, Waldron, D'Onofrio, & Gottesman, 2003). For example, one member of a set of twins in the Lyons and colleagues (2009) study showed marked variability or change in cognitive abilities if the environment of one of the twins changed dramatically from the other twin's because of some stressful event such as death of a loved one.

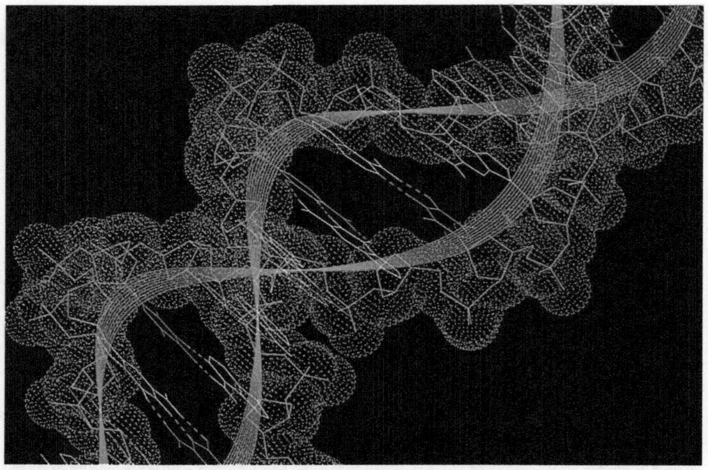

A DNA molecule, which contains genes, resembles a double spiral, or helix.

For psychological disorders, the evidence indicates that genetic factors make some contribution to all disorders but account for less than half of the explanation. This means that if one of a pair of identical twins has schizophrenia, there is a less-than-50% likelihood that the other twin will also have schizophrenia (Gottesman & Erlenmeyer-Kimling, 2001). Similar or lower rates exist for other psychological disorders (Kendler & Prescott, 2006; Rutter, 2006).

Behavioral geneticists have reached general conclusions in the past several years on the role of genes and psychological disorders relevant to this chapter's discussion of integrative approaches to psychopathology. First, specific genes or small groups of genes may ultimately be found to be associated with certain psychological disorders, as suggested in several important studies described later. But as discussed earlier, much of the current evidence suggests that contributions to psychological disorders come from

Genetic contributions to behavior are evident in twins who were raised apart. When these brothers were finally reunited, they were both firefighters, and they discovered many other shared characteristics and interests.

many genes, each having a relatively small effect (Flint, 2009; Rutter, 2006). It is extremely important that we recognize this probability and continue to make every attempt to track the group of genes implicated in various disorders. Advances in gene mapping, molecular genetics, and linkage studies help with this difficult research (for example, Gershon Kelsoe, Kendler, & Watson, 2001; Hettema, Prescott, Myers, Neale, & Kendler, 2005). In linkage studies, scientists study individuals who have the same disorder, such as bipolar disorder, and share other features associated with a known gene location. Scientists can then "link" known gene locations with the possible location of another gene contributing to the disorder (Flint, 2009; see Chapter 4).

Second, as noted earlier, it has become increasingly clear that genetic contributions cannot be studied in the absence of interactions with events in the environment that trigger genetic vulnerability or "turn on" specific genes (Kendler et al., 2011; Rutter, 2010). It is to this fascinating topic that we now turn.

The Interaction of Genes and the Environment

In 1983, the distinguished neuroscientist and Nobel Prize winner Eric Kandel speculated that the process of learning affects more than behavior. He suggested that the very genetic structure of cells may change as a result of learning if genes that were inactive or dormant interact with the environment in such a way that they become active. In other words, the environment may occasionally turn on certain genes. This type of mechanism may lead to changes in the number of receptors at the end of a neuron, which, in turn, would affect biochemical functioning in the brain.

Although Kandel was not the first to propose this idea, he provided convincing evidence to support it. Most people assume that the brain, like other parts of the body, may well be influenced by environmental changes during development. But we also assume that once maturity is reached, the structure and function of our internal organs and most of our physiology are set or, in the case of the brain, hard-wired. The competing idea is that the brain and its functions are plastic, subject to continual change in response to the environment, even at the level of genetic structure. Now there is additional strong evidence supporting that view (Dick, 2011; Kendler et al., 2011; Landis & Insel, 2008; Robinson, Fernald, & Clayton, 2008).

With these new findings in mind, we can now explore gene–environment interactions as they relate to psychopathology. Two models have received the most attention: the diathesis–stress model and the reciprocal gene–environment model (or gene–environment correlations).

The Diathesis–Stress Model

For years, scientists have assumed a specific method of interaction between genes and environment. According to this **diathesis–stress model**, individuals inherit tendencies to express certain traits or behaviors, which may then be activated under conditions of stress (see ■ Figure 2.2). Each inherited tendency is a *diathesis*, which means, literally, a condition that makes someone susceptible to developing a disorder. When the right kind of life event, such as a certain type of stressor, comes along, the disorder

STAN HONDA/Getty Images

Eric Kandel won the Nobel Prize in Medicine for learning on biological functioning among other accomplishments.

develops. For example, according to the diathesis–stress model, Janelle inherited a *tendency* to faint at the sight of blood. This tendency is the diathesis, or **vulnerability**. It would not become prominent until certain environmental events occurred. For Janelle, this event was the sight of an animal being dissected when she was in a situation in which escape, or at least closing her eyes, was not acceptable. The stress of seeing the dissection under these conditions activated her genetic tendency to faint. Together, these factors led to her developing a disorder. If she had not taken biology, she might have gone through life without ever knowing she had this tendency, at least to such an extreme, although she might have felt queasy about minor cuts and bruises. You can see that the diathesis is genetically based and the stress is environmental but that they must interact to produce a disorder.

We might also take the case of someone who inherits a vulnerability to alcohol use disorder, which would make that person substantially different from a close friend who does not have the same tendency. During college, both engage in extended drinking bouts, but only the individual with the so-called addictive genes begins the long downward spiral into alcohol use disorder. The friend doesn't. Having a particular vulnerability doesn't mean someone will necessarily develop the associated disorder. The smaller the vulnerability, the greater the life stress required to produce the disorder; conversely, with greater vulnerability, less life stress is required. This model of gene–environment interactions has been popular, although, in view of the relationship of the environment to the structure and function of the brain, it is greatly oversimplified.

This relationship was demonstrated in an elegant way in a landmark study by Caspi and colleagues (2003). These investigators studied a group of 847 individuals in New Zealand who had undergone a variety of assessments for more than two decades, starting at the age of 3. They also noted whether the participants, at age 26, had been depressed during the past year. Overall, 17% of the study participants reported that they had experienced a major depressive episode during the prior year, and 3% reported that they felt suicidal. But the crucial part of the study is that the investigators also identified the genetic makeup of the individuals and, in particular, a gene that produces a substance called a *chemical transporter* that affects the transmission of serotonin in the brain, called the *5-HTT gene*. Serotonin, one of the neurotransmitters we talk about later in the chapter, is particularly implicated in depression and related disorders. But the gene that Caspi and colleagues were studying comes in two common versions, or *alleles*: the long allele and the short allele. There was reason to believe, from prior work with animals, that individuals with at least two copies of the long allele (LL) were able to cope better with stress than individuals with two copies of the short allele (SS). Because the investigators have been recording stressful life events in these individuals most of their lives, they were able to test this relationship. In people with two S alleles, the risk for having a major depressive episode doubled if they had at least four stressful life events, compared with participants experiencing four stressful events who had two L alleles. But the interesting finding occurs when we look at the childhood experience of these individuals. In people with the SS alleles, severe and stressful maltreatment during childhood more than doubled their risks of depression in adulthood compared with those individuals carrying the SS alleles who were not maltreated or abused (63% versus 30%). For individuals carrying the LL alleles, on the other hand, stressful childhood experiences did not affect the incidence of depression in adulthood; 30% of this group became depressed

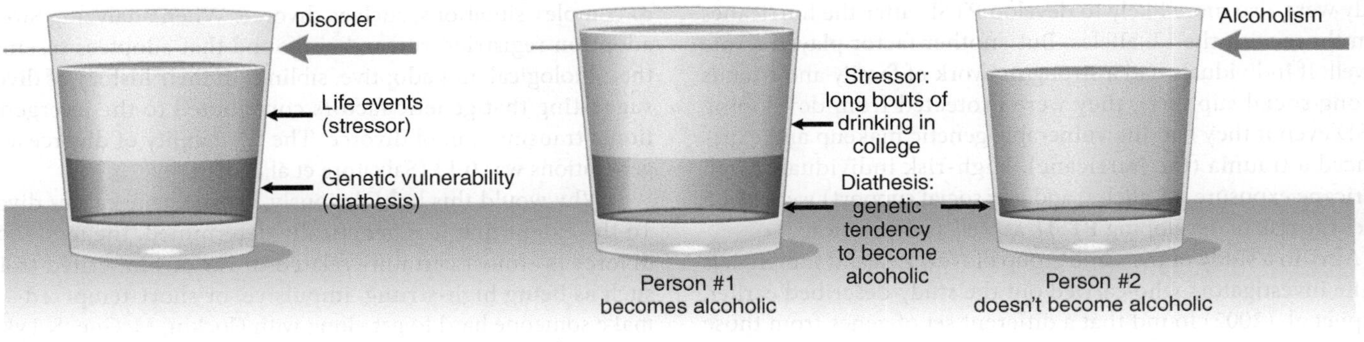

Figure 2.2

In the diathesis–stress model, the greater the underlying vulnerability, the less stress is needed to trigger a disorder.

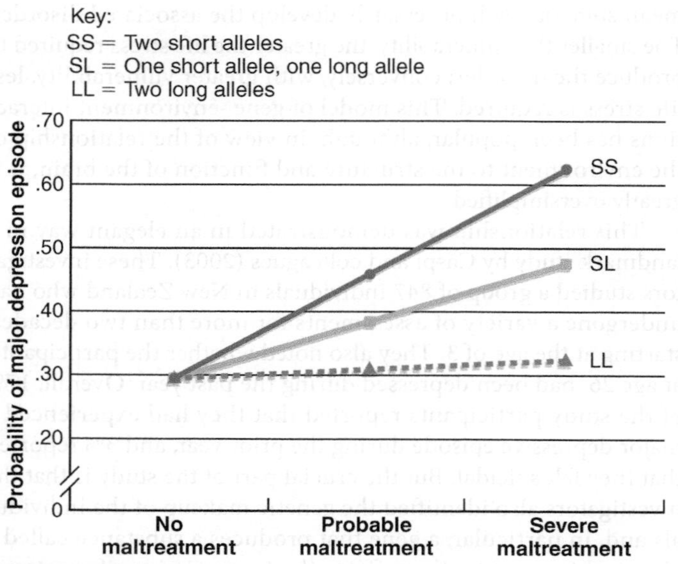

Figure 2.3

Interaction of genes and early environment in producing adult major depression. Reprinted, with permission, from A. Caspi, K. Sugden, T. E. Moffitt, A. Taylor, I. W. Craig, H. Harrington, et al., 2003, Influence of life stress on depression: Moderation by a polymorphism in the 5-HTT gene, *Science, 301*, 386–389. © 2003 AAAS.

whether they had experienced stressful childhoods or not. (This relationship is shown in ■ Figure 2.3.) Therefore, unlike the SS group, depression in the LL allele group seems related to stress in their recent past rather than childhood experiences. This study was very important in demonstrating clearly that neither genes nor life experiences (environmental events) can solely explain the onset of a disorder such as depression. It takes a complex interaction of the two factors.

Other studies have replicated or supported these findings (Binder, 2008; Karg, Burmeister, Shedden, & Sen, 2011; Kilpatrick et al., 2007; Mercer et al., 2012; Rutter et al., 2006). For example, in the Kilpatrick et al. (2007) study on the development of post-traumatic stress disorder (PTSD), 589 adults who experienced the Florida hurricanes of 2004 were interviewed, and their DNA was collected. Individuals with the same genetic makeup (SS) that signaled vulnerability in the Caspi and colleagues (2003) study were also more likely to develop PTSD after the hurricanes than those with the LL alleles. But another factor played a role as well. If individuals had a strong network of family and friends (strong social support), they were protected from developing PTSD even if they had the vulnerable genetic makeup and experienced a trauma (the hurricane). High-risk individuals (high hurricane exposure, SS alleles, and low social support) were at 4.5 times the risk of developing PTSD, as well as depression.

Also, in a study of the same group of New Zealand individuals by the investigators who carried out the study described earlier, Caspi et al. (2002) found that a different set of genes from those associated with depression seems to contribute to violent and antisocial behavior in adults. But again, this genetic predisposition occurs only if the individuals were maltreated as children. That is, some children who were maltreated turned out to be violent and antisocial as adults, but they were four times more likely to do their share of rape, robbery, and assault if they had a certain genetic makeup than were those who didn't have the genetic makeup. Subsequent research suggests that it is not just any one genetic variation that makes people susceptible to stress or other environmental influences (Goldman, Glei, Lin, & Weinstein, 2010; Risch et al., 2009). A large network of genes, not only single genes, plays a role in the development of depression and other disorders. These and subsequent studies, however, do provide powerful, if preliminary, support for the gene–environment interaction model that had only indirect support until this time (Uher, 2011).

The Gene–Environment Correlation Model

With additional study, psychologists have found the web of interrelationships between genes and environment to be even more complex. Some evidence now indicates that genetic endowment may *increase the probability* that an individual will experience stressful life events (see Kendler, 2006, 2011; Rutter, 2006, 2010; Saudino, Pedersen, Lichtenstein, McClearn, & Plomin, 1997; Thapar & McGuffin, 2009). For example, people with a genetic vulnerability to develop a certain disorder, such as blood–injury–injection phobia, may also have a personality trait—let's say impulsiveness—that makes them more likely to be involved in minor accidents that would result in their seeing blood. In other words, they may be accident prone because they are continually rushing to complete things or to get to places without regard for their physical safety. These people, then, might have a genetically determined tendency to create the very environmental risk factors that trigger a genetic vulnerability to blood–injury–injection phobia.

This is the **gene–environment correlation model** or reciprocal gene–environment model (Jaffee, 2011; Kendler, 2011; Thapar & McGuffin, 2009) (see ■ Figure 2.4). Some evidence indicates that it applies to the development of depression because some people may tend to seek out difficult relationships or other circumstances that lead to depression (Eley, 2011). This did not seem to be the case in the New Zealand study described earlier (Caspi et al., 2003), however, because stressful episodes during adulthood occurred with about the same frequency in the SS and the LL groups. Gene–environment correlation even applies to complex situations, such as divorce. When analyzing Swedish adoption registries, researchers found that adoptees resembled their biological, not adoptive, siblings in their history of divorce, suggesting that genetic factors contributed to the intergenerational transmission of divorce. The heritability of divorce across generations was 0.13 (Salvatore et al., 2018).

Why would this be? Obviously, no one gene causes divorce. To the extent that it is genetically determined, the tendency to divorce is almost certainly related to various inherited traits—such as being high-strung, impulsive, or short-tempered—that make someone hard to get along with (Jockin, McGue, & Lykken, 1996). Another possibility is that an inherited trait makes it more likely you will choose an incompatible spouse. To take a simple example, people who are passive and unassertive may well choose a strong, dominant mate who turns out to be difficult to live with.

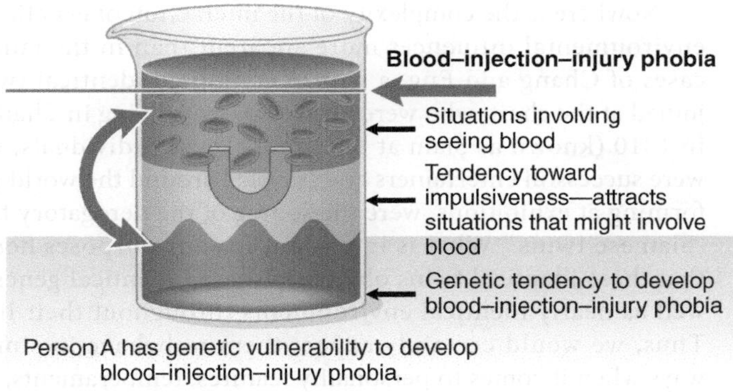

Figure 2.4

Reciprocal Gene–Environment Model.

They get divorced but then find themselves attracted to another individual with the same personality traits, who is also difficult to live with. Some people would simply attribute this kind of pattern to poor judgment. Nevertheless, there's no doubt that social, interpersonal, psychological, and environmental factors play major roles in whether we stay married, and it's quite possible that our genes contribute to how we create our own environment.

Epigenetics and the Nongenomic "Inheritance" of Behavior

To make things more complicated, it has become apparent that the environment also influences biology in a fundamental way. Research on telomeres illustrates this effect. *Telomeres* are certain structures that cap the ends of chromosomes to protect the chromosome from deteriorating or getting entangled with neighboring chromosomes. Telomere length appears to be positively correlated with lifespan and might be a marker for ageing (Chakravarti, LaBella, & DePinho, 2021). Interestingly, exposure to adverse stressors has been associated with shortening of telomere length, as suggested by the results of a Swedish twin and adoption study of aging. This study showed that over a period of 25 years, when adjusting for genetic differences, more life stressors within an individual was related to decreased telomere length over time, suggesting a causal relationship between life stress and accelerated telomere length shortening (Gerritsen et al., 2020).

But the environmental effect of biology is not restricted to telomere length. The environment can also have other effects on the DNA in more lasting and complex ways, as shown in some rodent studies (Cameron et al., 2005; Francis, Diorio, Liu, & Meaney, 1999; Weaver et al., 2004). The investigators examined stress reactivity and the ways it is passed through generations, using a powerful experimental procedure called *cross-fostering*, in which a rat pup born to one mother is assigned to another mother for rearing. They first demonstrated, as had many other investigators, that maternal behavior affected how the young rats tolerated stress. If the mothers were calm and supportive, their rat pups were less fearful and better able to tolerate stress. But we don't know if this effect results from genetic influences or from being raised by calm mothers. This is where cross-fostering comes in. Francis et al. (1999) took some newly born rat pups of fearful and easily stressed mothers and placed them for rearing with calm mothers. Other young rats remained with their easily stressed mothers. With this interesting scientific twist, Francis et al. (1999) demonstrated that calm and supportive behavior by the mothers could be passed down through generations of rats *independent of genetic influences* because rats born to easily stressed mothers but reared by calm mothers grew up more calm and supportive. The authors concluded,

> These findings suggest that individual differences in the expression of genes in brain regions that regulate stress reactivity can be transmitted from one generation to the next through behavior. . . . The results . . . suggest that the mechanism for this pattern of inheritance involves differences in maternal care. (p. 1158)

In subsequent studies from this group (Cameron et al., 2005), the investigators demonstrated that the maternal behavior had lastingly altered the endocrine response to stress by affecting gene expression. But this effect occurred only if the rat mother was calm and nurturing during the rat pups' first week of life. After that, it didn't matter. This highlights the importance of early experience on behavior.

Other scientists have reported similar results (Anisman, Zaharia, Meaney, & Merali, 1998; Harper, 2005). For example, Suomi (1999), working with rhesus monkeys and using the cross-fostering strategies just described, showed that if genetically reactive and emotional young monkeys are reared by calm mothers for the first 6 months of their lives, the animals behaved in later life as if they were nonemotional and not reactive to stress at birth. In other words, the environmental effects of early parenting seem to override any genetic contribution to be anxious, emotional, or reactive to stress. Suomi (1999) also demonstrated that these emotionally reactive monkeys raised by "calm, supportive" parents were also calm and supportive when raising their own children, thereby influencing and even reversing the genetic contribution to the expression of personality traits or temperaments.

Strong effects of the environment have also been observed in humans. For example, Tienari et al. (1994) found that children whose parents had schizophrenia and who were adopted away as babies demonstrated a tendency to develop psychiatric disorders (including schizophrenia) themselves only if they were adopted into dysfunctional families. Those children adopted into functional families with high-quality parenting did not develop the disorders. Thus, it is probably too simplistic to say the genetic contribution to a personality trait or to a psychological disorder is approximately 50%. We can talk of a heritable (genetic) contribution only in the context of the individual's past and present environment (Dickens et al., 2011).

In support of this conclusion, Suomi (2000) demonstrated that for young monkeys with a specific genetic pattern associated with a highly reactive temperament (emotional or susceptible to the effects of stress), early maternal deprivation (disruptions in mothering) will have a powerful effect on their neuroendocrine functioning and their later behavioral and emotional reactions. For animals not carrying this genetic characteristic, however, maternal deprivation will have little effect, just as was found in the New Zealand study in humans by Caspi et al. (2003), and it is likely this effect will be carried down through the generations. But as noted above in the example of genetic influences on cognitive abilities (Turkheimer et al., 2003), extremely chaotic early environments can override genetic factors and alter neuroendocrine function to increase the likelihood of later behavioral and emotional disorders (Dickens et al., 2011; Ouellet-Morin et al., 2008).

How does this work? Although the environment cannot change our DNA sequence, it can have an influence on the DNA by changing the gene expression. This phenomenon is referred to as **epigenetics** (the prefix *epi* means "above" or "over" the gene). These changes in the epigenome can then be passed down to future generations. Not surprisingly, this is an expanding area of research (Arai, Li, Hartley, & Feig, 2009; Champagne, 2018; Crabbe, Wahlsten, & Dudek, 1999; Meany, 2010; Mill, 2011; Schiele, Gottschalk, & Domschke, 2020). The biological process underlying epigenetics on the DNA level is complex and not yet fully understood. For a gene to be expressed, the DNA needs to be transcribed, and this transcription starts in a particular region, the so-called promoter region. Environmental factors influence this region. The most common epigenetic DNA modification is by methylation (addition of a CH_3 group) and hydroxymethylation (addition of a CH_2OH group) of the carbon atoms of the cytosine bases of cytosine-guanine pairs (one of the DNA base pairs) in the promoter region. Methylation leads to the silencing of transcription of the gene, whereas reduced methylation (that is, hypomethylation) of this region increases the transcription rate. Thus, in epigenetics the genomic sequence itself isn't changed, but the expression of the genes is altered through methylation or hypomethylation in the promoter region of genes. These new conceptualizations of the role of genetic contributions as only constraining environmental influences have implications for preventing unwanted personality traits or temperaments and even psychological disorders. Although current research suggests that environmental influences, such as peer groups and schools, affect this genetic expression, the strongest evidence exists for the effects of early parenting influences and other early experiences (Cameron et al., 2005; Mill, 2011; Ouellet-Morin et al., 2008).

Nowhere is the complexity of the interaction of genetic and environmental influences more apparent than in the famous cases of Chang and Eng, a pair of conjoined identical twins, joined at the chest, who were born to parents living in Thailand in 1810 (known as Siam at the time). These individuals, who were successful entertainers and traveled around the world performing at exhibitions, were the source of the derogatory term "Siamese twins." What is important for our purposes here is that these identical twins obviously shared identical genes, as well as nearly identical environments throughout their lives. Thus, we would certainly expect them to behave in similar ways when it comes to personality features, temperaments, and psychological disorders. But everybody who knew these twins noted that they had distinct personalities. Chang was prone to moodiness and depression, and he finally started drinking heavily. Eng, on the other hand, was more cheerful, quiet, and thoughtful (Moore, 2001).

In summary, a complex interaction between genes and the environment plays an important role in every psychological disorder (Kendler et al., 2011; Rutter, 2006, 2010; Turkheimer, 1998). Our genetic endowment does contribute to our behavior, our emotions, and our cognitive processes and constrains the influence of environmental factors, such as upbringing, on our later behavior, as is evident in the New Zealand study (Caspi et al., 2003) and its later replications. Environmental events, in turn, can determine whether some genes are activated or not (Kendler, 2011; Schienle et al., 2020). Thus, neither nature (genes) nor nurture (environmental events) alone, but rather a complex interaction of the two, influences the development of our behavior and personalities.

Concept Check 2.2

Determine whether these statements relating to the genetic contributions of psychopathology are true (T) or false (F).

1. ____________ The first 20 pairs of chromosomes program the development of the body and brain.
2. ____________ No individual genes have been identified that cause any major psychological disorders.
3. ____________ According to the diathesis–stress model, people inherit a vulnerability to express certain traits or behaviors that may be activated under certain stress conditions.
4. ____________ The idea that individuals may have a genetic endowment to increase the probability that they will experience stressful life events and therefore trigger a vulnerability is in accordance with the diathesis–stress model.
5. ____________ Environmental events alone influence the development of our behavior and personalities.

Neuroscience and Its Contributions to Psychopathology

Knowing how the nervous system and, especially, how the brain works is central to any understanding of our behavior, emotions, and cognitive processes. This is the focus of **neuroscience**. To comprehend the newest research in this field, we first need an overview of how the brain and the nervous system function. The human nervous system includes the *central nervous system*, consisting of the brain and the spinal cord, and the *peripheral nervous system*, consisting of the somatic nervous system and the autonomic nervous system (see ■ Figure 2.5).

The Central Nervous System

The central nervous system processes all information received from our sense organs and reacts as necessary. It sorts out what is relevant (such as a certain taste or a new sound) from what isn't (such as a familiar view or ticking clock); checks the memory banks to determine why the information is relevant; and implements the right reaction, whether it is to answer a simple question or to play a Mozart sonata. This is a lot of exceedingly complex work. The spinal cord is part of the central nervous system, but its primary function is to facilitate the sending of messages to and from the brain, which is the other major component of the central nervous system (CNS) and the most complex organ in the body.

Figure 2.5

Divisions of the nervous system. Reprinted from J. W. Kalat, 2009, *Biological psychology*, 10th ed. © 2009 Wadsworth.

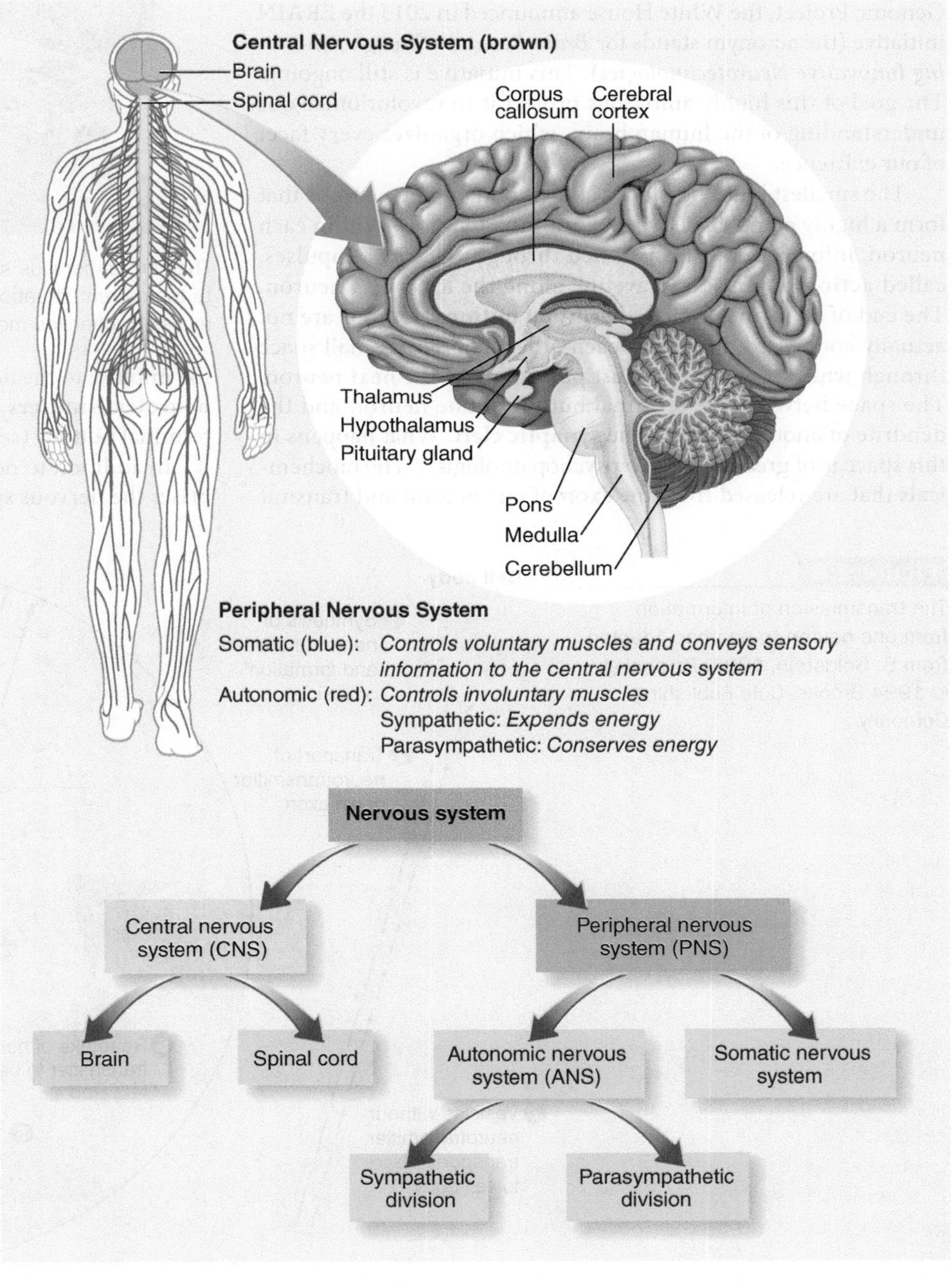

The brain contains **neurons** to control our thoughts and actions. Neurons transmit information throughout the nervous system.

It is important to understand what a neuron is and how it works. The typical neuron contains a central cell body with two kinds of branches. One kind of branch is called a *dendrite*. Dendrites have numerous *receptors* that receive messages in the form of chemical impulses from other nerve cells, which are converted into electrical impulses. The other kind of branch, called an *axon*, transmits these impulses to other neurons. Any one nerve cell may have multiple connections to other neurons. These connections are called *synapses*. The brain has billions of nerve cells, more than 100 billion by some estimates, and trillions of synapses, so you can see how complicated the system becomes—far more complicated than the most powerful computer that has ever been built (or will be for some time). Inspired by the Human Genome Project, the White House announced in 2013 the BRAIN initiative (the acronym stands for *Brain Research through Advancing Innovative Neurotechnologies*). This initiative is still ongoing. The goal of this highly ambitious project is to revolutionize our understanding of the human brain, which organizes every facet of our existence.

The smallest building blocks of the brain are the neurons that form a highly complex network of information flow. Within each neuron, information is transmitted through electrical impulses, called **action potentials**, traveling along the axon of a neuron. The end of an axon is called a **terminal button**. Neurons are not actually connected directly to each other. There is a small space through which the impulse must pass to get to the next neuron. The space between the terminal button of one neuron and the dendrite of another is called the **synaptic cleft**. What happens in this space is of great interest to psychopathologists. The biochemicals that are released from the axon of one neuron and transmit

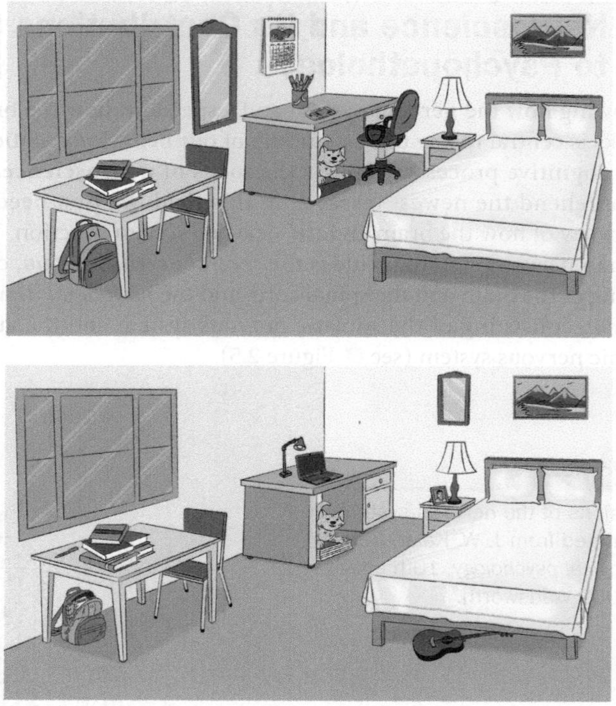

The central nervous system screens out information that is irrelevant to the current situation. From moment to moment, we notice what moves or changes more than what remains the same.

the impulse to the dendrite receptors of another neuron are called **neurotransmitters**, which are chemicals stored in vesicles in the terminal buttons (see ■ Figures 2.6 and 2.12).

In addition to neurons, there is another type of cell that comprises the nervous system—*glia* (or glial) cells. Even though these

Figure 2.6

The transmission of information from one neuron to another. Adapted from B. Goldstein, 1994, *Psychology*. © 1994 Brooks/Cole Publishing Company.

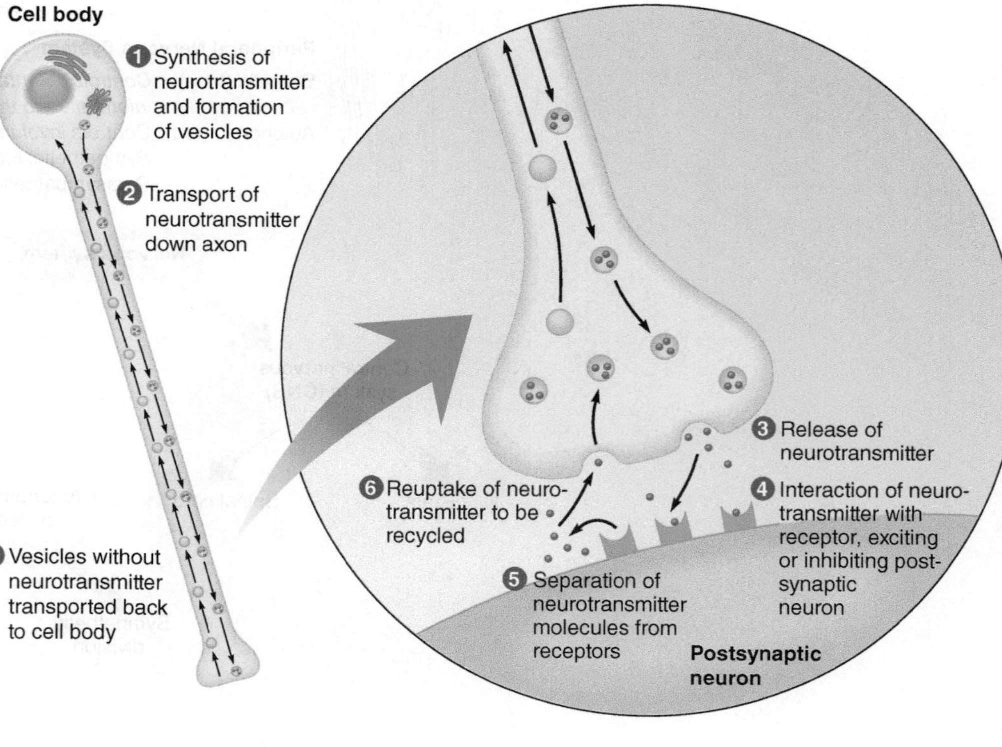

cells outnumber neurons by a ratio of about 10 to 1, for many years they were little studied because scientists believed that they were passive cells that merely served to connect and insulate neurons (Koob, 2009). More recently, scientists have discovered that glia actually play active roles in neural activity (Eroglu & Barres, 2010). It is now known that there are different types of glia cells with several specific functions, some of which serve to modulate neurotransmitter activity (Allen & Barres, 2009; Perea & Araque, 2007). Better understanding the role of glia cells in neurotransmitter processes is an important new area of research. To date, however, the most advanced neuroscience research in psychopathology focuses on neurons.

Major neurotransmitters relevant to psychopathology include *norepinephrine* (also known as noradrenaline), *serotonin, dopamine, gamma-aminobutyric acid (GABA),* and *glutamate* (which is the most common neurotransmitter). You will see these terms many times in this book. Some neurotransmitters are primarily **excitatory** (such as glutamate) because they increase the likelihood that the connecting neuron will fire, whereas other neurotransmitters are primarily **inhibitory** (such as GABA) because they decrease the likelihood that the connecting neuron will fire. Neurons can receive input from both excitatory and inhibitory neurotransmitters. Excesses or insufficiencies in some neurotransmitters are associated with different groups of psychological disorders. For example, reduced levels of GABA were initially thought to be associated with excessive anxiety (Costa, 1985). Early research (Snyder, 1976, 1981) linked increases in dopamine activity to schizophrenia. Other early research found correlations between depression and high levels of norepinephrine (Schildkraut, 1965) and, possibly, low levels of serotonin (Siever, Davis, & Gorman, 1991). However, more recent research, described later in this chapter, indicates that these early interpretations were too simplistic. In view of their importance, we return to the subject of neurotransmitters shortly.

The Structure of the Brain

Having an overview of the brain is useful because many structures described here are later mentioned in the context of specific disorders. One way to view the brain (see ■ Figure 2.7) is to see it in two parts—the *brain stem* and the *forebrain*. The brain stem is the lower and more ancient part of the brain. Found in most animals, this structure handles most of the essential automatic functions, such as breathing, sleeping, and moving around in a coordinated way. The forebrain is more advanced and evolved more recently.

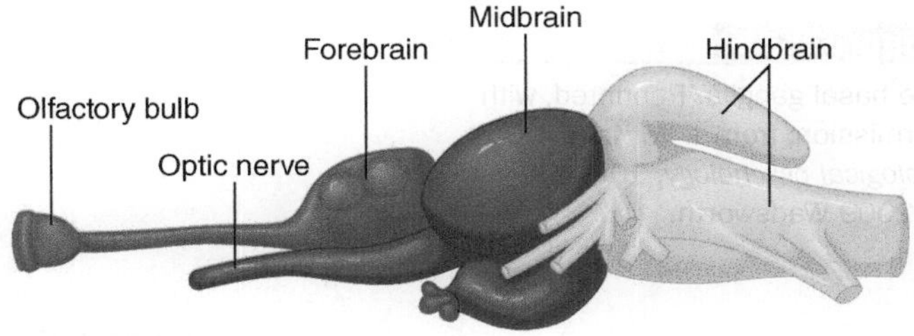

Figure 2.7A

Three divisions of the brain. Reprinted, with permission, from J. W. Kalat, 2009, *Biological psychology*, 10th ed. © 2009 Wadsworth.

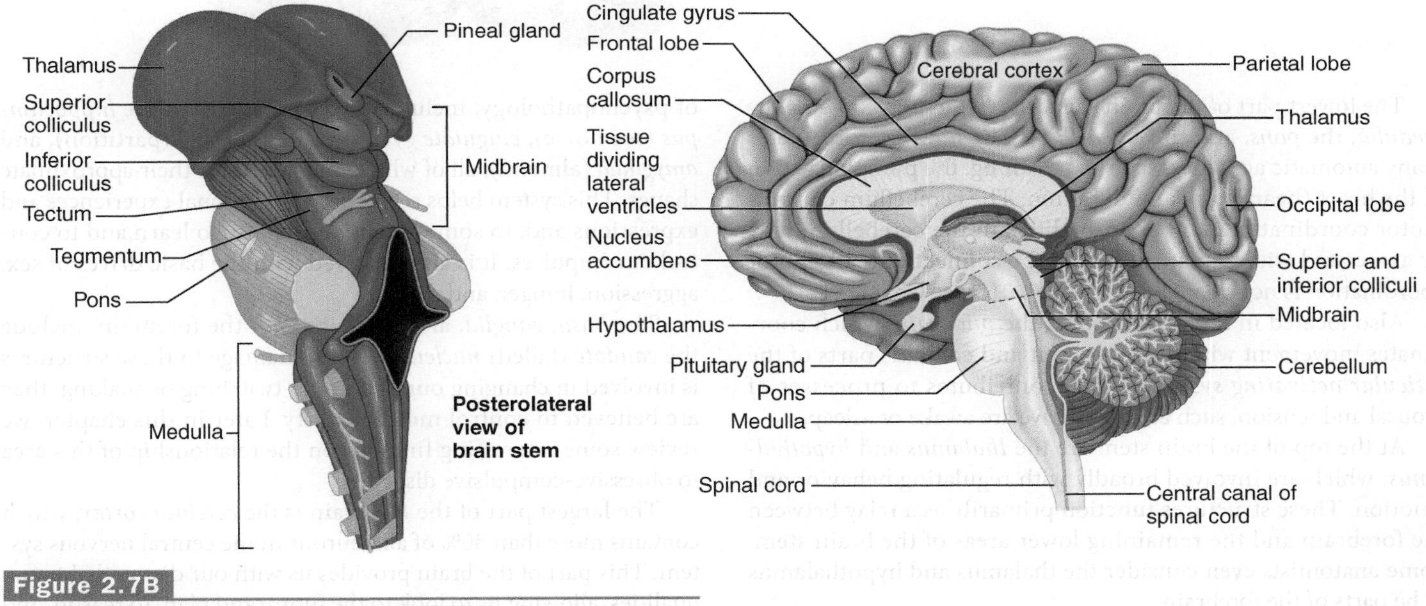

Figure 2.7B

Major structures of the brain. Reprinted, with permission, from J. W. Kalat, 2009, *Biological psychology*, 10th ed. © 2009 Wadsworth.

Figure 2.7C

The limbic system. Reprinted, with permission, from J. W. Kalat, 2009, *Biological psychology*, 10th ed. © 2009 Wadsworth.

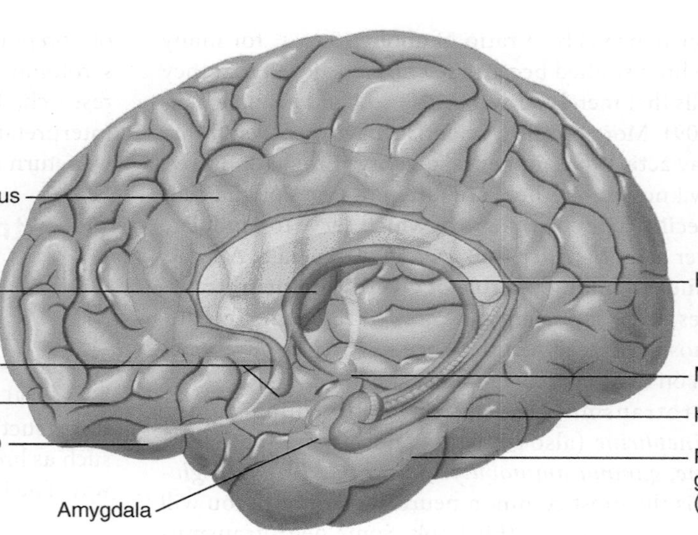

Figure 2.7D

The basal ganglia. Reprinted, with permission, from J. W. Kalat, 2009, *Biological psychology*, 10th ed. © 2009 Wadsworth.

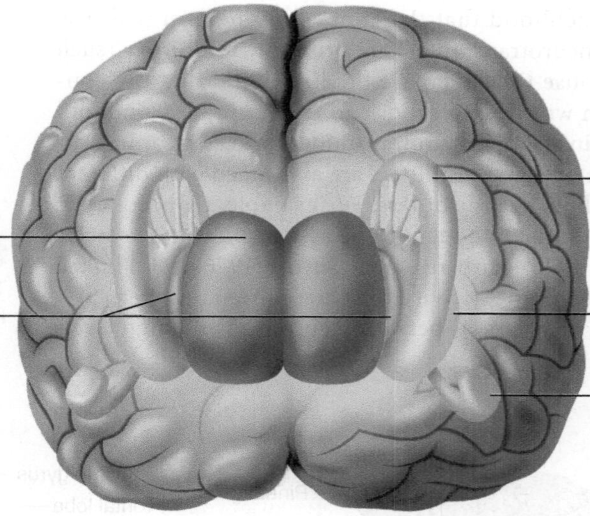

The lowest part of the brain stem, the *hindbrain*, contains the *medulla*, the *pons*, and the *cerebellum*. The hindbrain regulates many automatic activities, such as breathing, the pumping action of the heart (heartbeat), and digestion. The cerebellum controls motor coordination, and abnormalities in the cerebellum may be associated with autism, although the connection with motor coordination is not clear (Fatemi et al., 2012; see Chapter 14).

Also located in the brain stem is the *midbrain*, which coordinates movement with sensory input and contains parts of the *reticular activating system*, which contributes to processes of arousal and tension, such as whether we are awake or asleep.

At the top of the brain stem are the *thalamus* and *hypothalamus*, which are involved broadly with regulating behavior and emotion. These structures function primarily as a relay between the forebrain and the remaining lower areas of the brain stem. Some anatomists even consider the thalamus and hypothalamus to be parts of the forebrain.

At the base of the forebrain, just above the thalamus and hypothalamus, is the *limbic system*. *Limbic* means border, so named because it is located around the edge of the center of the brain. The limbic system, which figures prominently in much of psychopathology, includes such structures as the *hippocampus* (sea horse), *cingulate gyrus* (girdle), *septum* (partition), and *amygdala* (almond), all of which are named for their approximate shapes. This system helps regulate our emotional experiences and expressions and, to some extent, our ability to learn and to control our impulses. It is also involved with the basic drives of sex, aggression, hunger, and thirst.

The *basal ganglia*, also at the base of the forebrain, include the *caudate* (tailed) *nucleus*. Because damage to these structures is involved in changing our posture or twitching or shaking, they are believed to control motor activity. Later in this chapter, we review some interesting findings on the relationship of this area to obsessive-compulsive disorder.

The largest part of the forebrain is the *cerebral cortex*, which contains more than 80% of all neurons in the central nervous system. This part of the brain provides us with our distinctly human qualities, allowing us to look to the future and plan, to reason, and to create. The cerebral cortex is divided into two hemispheres. Although the hemispheres look alike structurally and operate relatively independently (both are capable of perceiving, thinking, and remembering), research indicates that each has different

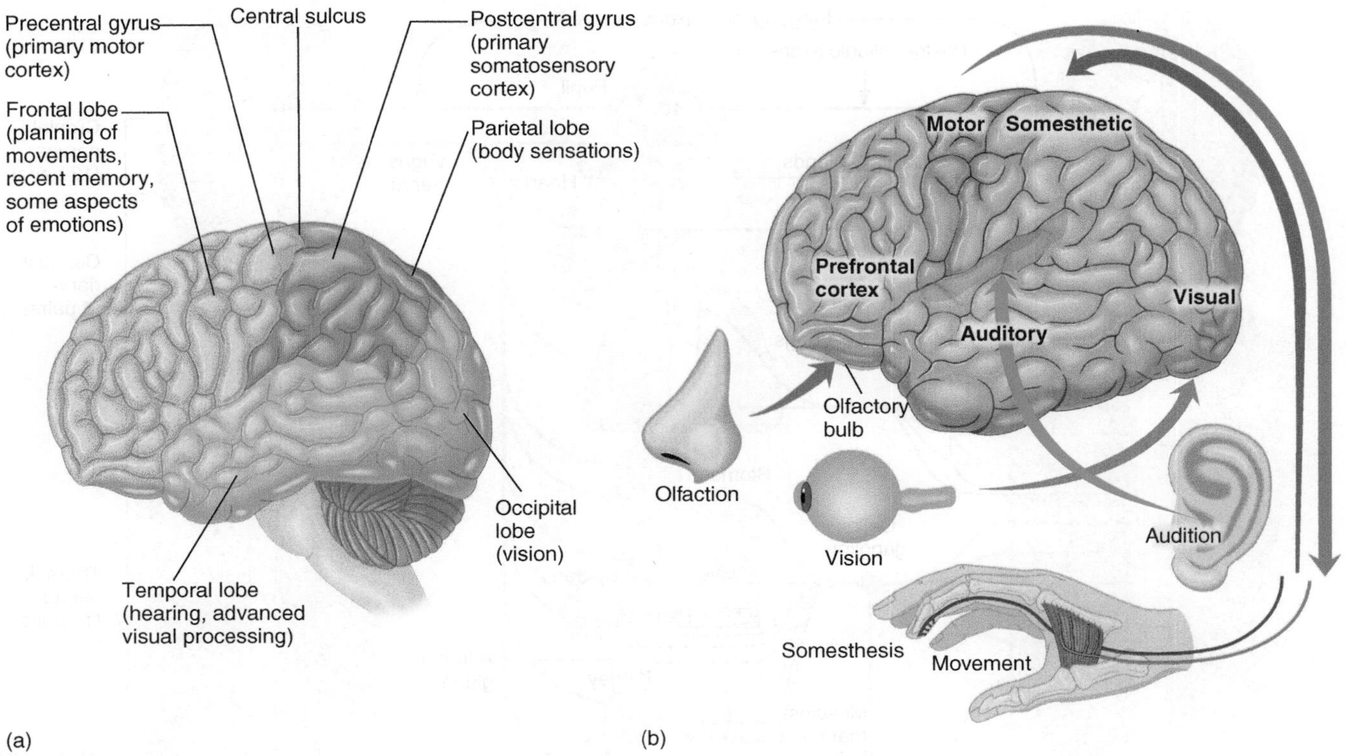

Figure 2.8

Some major subdivisions of the human cerebral cortex and a few of their primary functions. Reprinted, with permission, from J. W. Kalat, 2009, *Biological psychology*, 10th ed. © 2009 Wadsworth.

specialties. The left hemisphere seems to be chiefly responsible for verbal and other cognitive processes. The right hemisphere seems to be better at perceiving the world around us and creating images. The hemispheres may play differential roles in specific psychological disorders. Each hemisphere consists of four separate areas, or *lobes*: temporal, parietal, occipital, and frontal (see ■ Figure 2.8). Each is associated with different processes. Of the first three areas, the *temporal lobe* is associated with recognizing various sights and sounds and with long-term memory storage, the *parietal* lobe is associated with recognizing various sensations of touch and monitoring body positioning, and the *occipital lobe* is associated with integrating and making sense of various visual inputs. These three lobes, located toward the back (posterior) of the brain, work together to process sight, touch, hearing, and other signals from our senses.

The *frontal lobe* is the most interesting from the point of view of psychopathology. The front (or anterior) of the frontal lobe is called the *prefrontal cortex*, and this is the area responsible for higher cognitive functions such as thinking and reasoning, planning for the future, and long-term memory. This area of the brain synthesizes all information received from other parts of the brain and decides how to respond. It is what enables us to relate to the world around us and the people in it. When studying areas of the brain for clues to psychopathology, most researchers focus on the frontal lobe of the cerebral cortex, as well as on the limbic system, the hippocampus, and the basal ganglia.

The Peripheral Nervous System

The peripheral nervous system coordinates with the brain stem to make sure the body is working properly. Its two major components are the *somatic nervous system* and the *autonomic nervous system*. The somatic nervous system controls the muscles, so damage in this area might make it difficult for us to engage in any voluntary movement, including talking. The autonomic nervous system includes the *sympathetic nervous system* and *parasympathetic nervous system*. The primary duties of the autonomic nervous system are to regulate the cardiovascular system (for example, the heart and blood vessels) and the endocrine system (for example, the pituitary, adrenal, thyroid, and gonadal glands) and to perform various other functions, including aiding digestion and regulating body temperature (see ■ Figure 2.9).

The *endocrine system* works a bit differently from other systems in the body. Each endocrine gland produces its own chemical messenger, called a **hormone**, and releases it directly into the bloodstream. The adrenal glands produce *epinephrine* (also called *adrenaline*) in response to stress, as well as salt-regulating hormones; the thyroid gland produces *thyroxine*, which facilitates energy metabolism and growth; the pituitary is a master gland that produces a variety of regulatory hormones; and the gonadal glands produce sex hormones such as estrogen and testosterone. The endocrine system is closely related to the immune system; it is also implicated in a variety of disorders. In addition

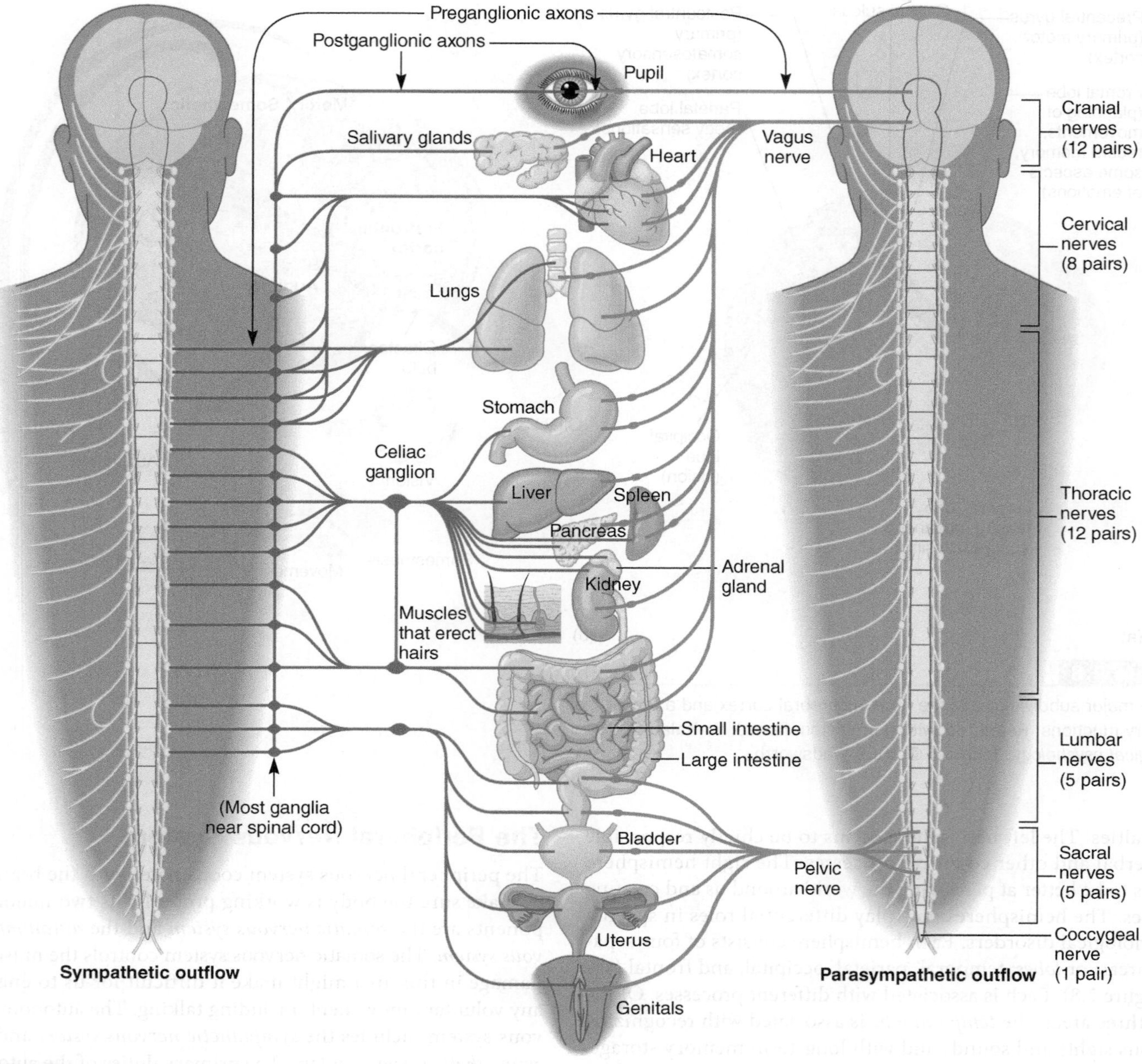

Figure 2.9

The sympathetic nervous system (red lines) and parasympathetic nervous system (blue lines). Reprinted, with permission, from J. W. Kalat, 2009, *Biological psychology*, 10th ed. © 2009 Wadsworth.

to contributing to stress-related physical disorders discussed in Chapter 9, endocrine regulation may play a role in depression, anxiety, schizophrenia, and other disorders (McEwen, 2013). This interdisciplinary area of research is termed *psychoneuroendocrinology* and is a growing subfield.

Sympathetic and parasympathetic divisions of the autonomic nervous system operate in a complementary fashion. The sympathetic nervous system is primarily responsible for mobilizing the body during times of stress or danger by rapidly activating the organs and glands under its control. When the sympathetic division goes on alert, three things happen. The heart beats faster, thereby increasing the flow of blood to the muscles; respiration increases, allowing more oxygen to get into the blood and brain; and the adrenal glands are stimulated. All three changes help mobilize us for action. When you read in the newspaper that a woman lifted a heavy object to free a trapped child, you can be sure her sympathetic nervous system was working overtime. This system mediates a substantial part of our "emergency" or "alarm" reaction, discussed later in this chapter and in Chapter 5.

One of the functions of the parasympathetic system is to balance the sympathetic system. In other words, because we could not operate in a state of hyperarousal and preparedness forever, the parasympathetic nervous system takes over after the sympathetic nervous system has been active for a while, normalizing our arousal and facilitating the storage of energy by helping the digestive process.

One brain connection implicated in some psychological disorders involves the hypothalamus and the endocrine system. The hypothalamus connects to the adjacent pituitary gland, which is the master or coordinator of the endocrine system. The pituitary gland, in turn, may stimulate the cortical part of the adrenal glands on top of the kidneys. As we noted previously, surges of epinephrine tend to energize us, arouse us, and get our bodies ready for threat or challenge. When athletes say their adrenaline was really flowing, they mean they were highly aroused and up for the competition. The cortical part of the adrenal glands also produces the stress hormone cortisol. This system is called the *hypothalamic–pituitary–adrenocortical axis*, or *HPA axis* (see ■ Figure 2.10); it has been implicated in several psychological disorders and is mentioned in Chapters 5, 7, and 9. There is good evidence showing that a dysregulation of the HPA axis and other endocrine systems are linked to depression (Dwyer et al., 2020).

This brief overview should give you a general sense of the structure and function of the brain and nervous system. New procedures for studying brain structure and function that involve imaging the working brain are discussed in Chapter 3. Here, we focus on what these studies reveal about the nature of psychopathology.

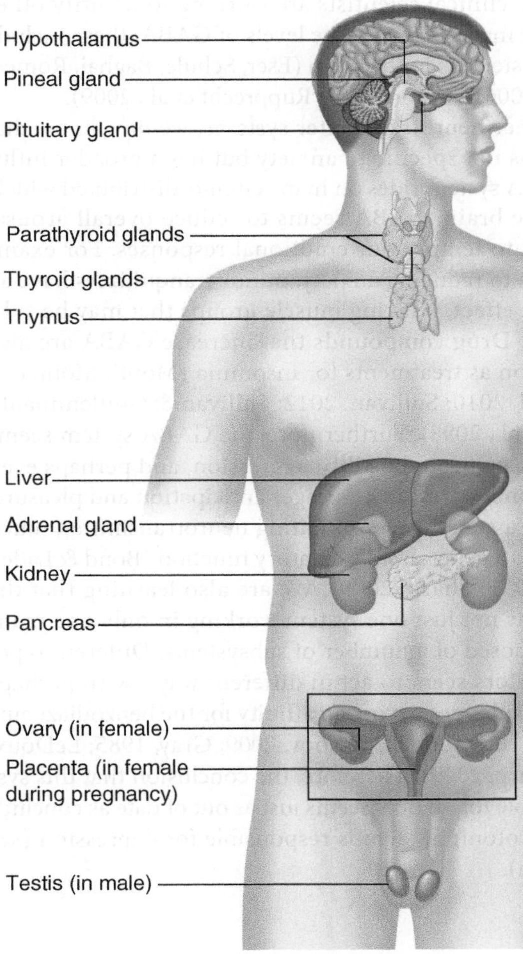

Figure 2.10

Location of some major endocrine glands. Reprinted, with permission, from J. W. Kalat, 2009, *Biological psychology*, 10th ed. © 2009 Wadsworth.

Neurotransmitters

The biochemical neurotransmitters in the brain and nervous system that carry messages from one neuron to another continue to receive intense attention from psychopathologists (Bloom & Kupfer, 1995; LeDoux, 2002; Iverson, 2006; Iverson & Iverson, 2007; Nestler, Hyman, & Malenka, 2008). One good example is the role of the neurotransmitter serotonin in some studies of gene–environment interactions described earlier (for example, Karg et al., 2011). Neurons that are sensitive to one type of neurotransmitter cluster together and form paths from one part of the brain to the other.

These paths may overlap with the paths of other neurotransmitters, but, as often as not, they end up going their separate ways (Bloom, Nelson, & Lazerson, 2001; Dean, Kelsey, Heller, & Ciaranello, 1993). There are thousands, perhaps tens of thousands, of these **brain circuits**, and we are just beginning to discover and map them (Arenkiel & Ehlers, 2009). Neuroscientists have identified several neural pathways that seem to play roles in various psychological disorders (Fineberg et al., 2010; LeDoux, 2002, 2015; Stahl, 2008; Tau & Peterson, 2010).

New neurotransmitters are frequently discovered, and existing neurotransmitter systems must be subdivided into separate classifications. Estimates suggest that more than 100 different neurotransmitters, each with multiple receptors, are functioning in various parts of the nervous system (Borodinsky et al., 2004; Kalat, 2013; Sharp, 2009). Also, scientists are increasingly discovering additional biochemicals and gases that have certain neurotransmitter properties. Because this dynamic field of research is in a state of considerable flux, the neuroscience of psychopathology is an exciting area of study that may lead to new drug treatments among other advances. You may still read reports that certain psychological disorders are "caused" by biochemical imbalances, excesses, or deficiencies in certain neurotransmitter systems. For example, abnormal activity of the neurotransmitter serotonin is often described as causing depression, and abnormalities in the neurotransmitter dopamine have been implicated in schizophrenia. Increasing evidence indicates that this is an enormous oversimplification, however. We are now learning that the effects of neurotransmitter activity are less specific. They often seem to be related to the way we process information (Harmer et al., 2009; Kandel, Schwartz, & Jessell, 2000; LeDoux, 2002; Sullivan & LeDoux, 2004). Changes in neurotransmitter activity may make people more or less likely to exhibit certain kinds of behavior in certain situations without causing the behavior directly. In addition, broad-based disturbances in our functioning are almost always associated with interactions of the various neurotransmitters rather than with alterations in the activity of any one system (Fineberg et al., 2010; LeDoux, 2002; Stahl, 2008; Xing, Zhang, Russell, & Post, 2006).

Research on neurotransmitter function focuses primarily on what happens when activity levels change. We can study this in several ways. We can introduce substances called **agonists** that effectively *increase* the activity of a neurotransmitter by mimicking its effects; substances called **antagonists** that *decrease*, or block, a neurotransmitter; or substances called **inverse agonists** that produce effects *opposite* to those produced by the neurotransmitter. By systematically manipulating the production of a neurotransmitter in different parts of the brain, scientists are able to learn more about its effects. Most drugs could be classified as either agonistic or antagonistic, although they may achieve these results in a variety of ways. That is, these drug therapies work by either increasing or decreasing the flow of specific neurotransmitters. Some drugs directly inhibit, or block, the production of a neurotransmitter. Other drugs increase the production of competing biochemical substances that may deactivate the neurotransmitter. Yet other drugs do not affect neurotransmitters directly but prevent the chemical from reaching the next neuron by closing down, or occupying, the receptors in that neuron.

After a neurotransmitter is released, it is quickly broken down and brought back from the synaptic cleft into the same neuron that released it. This process is called **reuptake**. Normally, the action of a neurotransmitter is fairly brief to ensure that the nervous system can quickly adjust to environmental changes and situational demands. Sometimes, psychological problems are associated with too much of a particular neurotransmitter in the synaptic gap, sometimes with too little. Some drugs work by blocking the reuptake process, thereby causing continued stimulation along the brain circuit; other drugs work by stimulating or blocking the release of a neurotransmitter into the synaptic gap or by blocking the receptor of a neurotransmitter.

Here we focus on several classic neurotransmitters most relevant to psychopathology. Two types of neurotransmitters, *monoamines* and *amino acids*, have been most studied in regard to psychopathology. These are considered the "classic" neurotransmitters because they are synthesized in the nerve. Neurotransmitters in the monoamine class include norepinephrine (also known as *noradrenaline*), serotonin, and dopamine. Amino-acid neurotransmitters include gamma-aminobutyric acid (GABA) and glutamate.

Glutamate and GABA

Two major neurotransmitters affect much of what we do. Each of these substances is in the amino acid category of neurotransmitters. The first, **glutamate**, is an excitatory transmitter that "turns on" many different neurons, leading to action. A second type of amino acid transmitter is **gamma-aminobutyric acid**, or **GABA** for short, which is an inhibitory neurotransmitter. Thus, the job of GABA is to inhibit (or regulate) the transmission of information and action potentials. Because these two neurotransmitters work in concert to balance functioning in the brain, they have been referred to as the "chemical brothers" (LeDoux, 2002). Glutamate and GABA operate relatively independently at a molecular level, but the relative balance of each in a cell will determine whether the neuron is activated (fires) or not.

Another characteristic of these "chemical brothers" is that they are fast acting, as they would have to be for the brain to keep up with the many influences from the environment that require action or restraint. As is true for every neurotransmitter, over- or underactivity can cause some serious problems. We return to some exciting new findings involving glutamate-specific receptors when we discuss new treatments for anxiety disorders in Chapter 5.

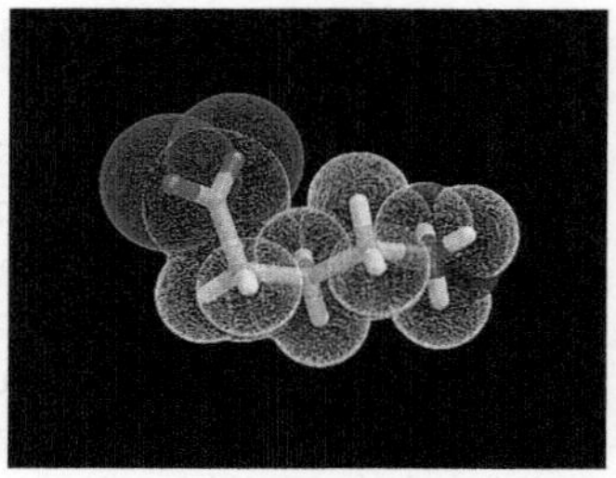
University of California/Lewis Baster, Jr. M.D.

Computer-generated model of GABA.

As noted earlier, GABA often reduces postsynaptic activity, which, in turn, inhibits a variety of behaviors and emotions. GABA was discovered before glutamate and has been studied for a longer period; its best-known effect is to reduce anxiety (Charney & Drevets, 2002; Davis, 2002; Griebel & Holmes, 2013; Sullivan & LeDoux, 2004). Scientists have discovered that a particular class of drugs, the *benzodiazepines*, or minor tranquilizers, makes it easier for GABA molecules to attach themselves to the receptors of specialized neurons. Thus, the higher the level of benzodiazepine, the more GABA becomes attached to neuron receptors, and the calmer we become (to a point). Because benzodiazepines have certain addictive properties, clinical scientists are working to identify other substances that may also modulate levels of GABA; these include certain natural steroids in the brain (Eser, Schule, Baghai, Romeo, & Rupprecht, 2006; Gordon, 2002; Rupprecht et al., 2009).

As with other neurotransmitter systems, we now know that GABA's effect is not specific to anxiety but has a broader influence. The GABA system rides on many circuits distributed widely throughout the brain. GABA seems to reduce overall arousal somewhat and to temper our emotional responses. For example, in addition to reducing anxiety, minor tranquilizers have an anticonvulsant effect, relaxing muscle groups that may be subject to spasms. Drug compounds that increase GABA are also under evaluation as treatments for insomnia (Monti, Möhler, & Pandi-Perumal, 2010; Sullivan, 2012; Sullivan & Guilleminault, 2009; Walsh et al., 2008). Furthermore, the GABA system seems to reduce levels of anger, hostility, aggression, and perhaps even positive emotional states such as eager anticipation and pleasure, making GABA a generalized inhibiting neurotransmitter, much as glutamate has a generalized excitatory function (Bond & Lader, 1979; Lader, 1975; Sharp, 2009). We are also learning that the GABA system is not just one system working in only one manner but is composed of a number of subsystems. Different types of GABA receptors seem to act in different ways, with perhaps only one of the subtypes having an affinity for the benzodiazepine component (D'Hulst, Atack, & Kooy, 2009; Gray, 1985; LeDoux, 2002, 2015; Sharp, 2009). Therefore, the conclusion that this system is responsible for anxiety seems just as out of date as concluding that the serotonin system is responsible for depression (see the next section).

Serotonin

The technical name for **serotonin** is 5-hydroxytryptamine (5HT). It is in the monoamine category of neurotransmitters, along with norepinephrine and dopamine, discussed next. Approximately six major circuits of serotonin spread from the midbrain, looping

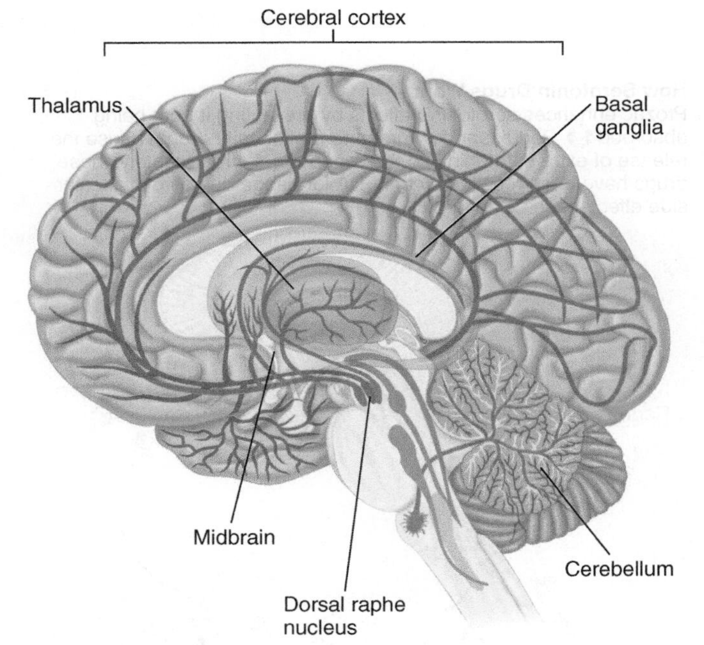

Figure 2.11

Major serotonin pathways in the brain.

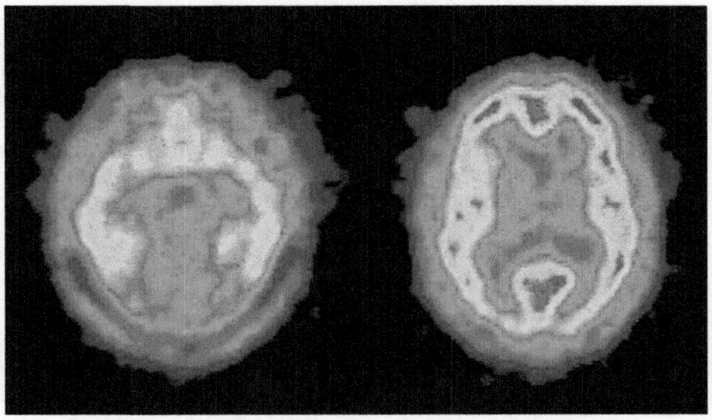

J. James Frost, M.D., Ph.D./Johns Hopkins University School of Medicine

A positron emission tomography scan shows the distribution of serotonergic neurons.

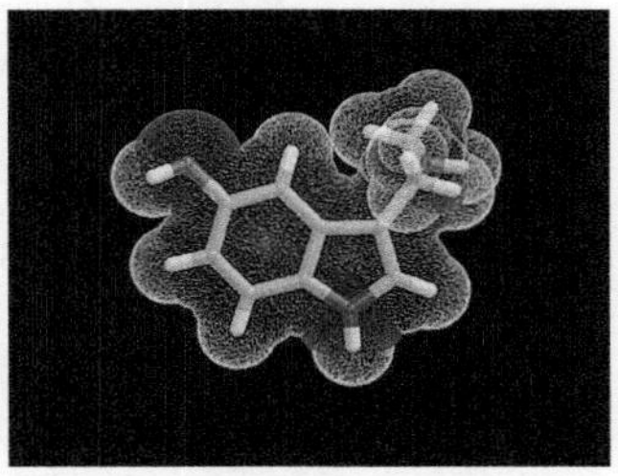

University of California/Lewis Baster, Jr. M.D.

Computer-generated model of serotonin.

around its various parts (Azmitia, 1978) (see ■ Figure 2.11). Because of the widespread nature of these circuits, many of them ending up in the cortex, serotonin is believed to influence a great deal of our behavior, particularly the way we process information (Harmer, 2008; Merens, Willem Van der Does, & Spinhoven, 2007; Spoont, 1992). It was genetically influenced dysregulation in this system that contributed to depression in the New Zealand study described earlier (Caspi et al., 2003).

The serotonin system regulates our behavior, moods, and thought processes. Extremely low activity levels of serotonin are associated with less inhibition and with instability, impulsivity, and the tendency to overreact to situations. Low serotonin activity has been associated with aggression, suicide, impulsive overeating, and excessive sexual behavior (Berman, McCloskey, Fanning, Schumacher, & Coccaro, 2009). These behaviors do not *necessarily* happen if serotonin activity is low, however. Other currents in the brain, or other psychological or social influences, may well compensate for low serotonin activity. Therefore, low serotonin activity may make us more vulnerable to certain problematic behavior without directly causing it (as mentioned earlier). To add to the complexity, serotonin has slightly different effects depending on the type or subtype of receptors involved. There are approximately 15 different receptors in the serotonin system (Olivier, 2015).

Several classes of drugs primarily affect the serotonin system, including the tricyclic antidepressants such as imipramine (known by its brand name, Tofranil). However, the class of drugs called *selective-serotonin reuptake inhibitors (SSRIs)*, including fluoxetine (Prozac) (see ■ Figure 2.12), affects serotonin more directly than other drugs, including the tricyclic antidepressants. SSRIs are used to treat a number of psychological disorders, particularly anxiety, mood, and eating disorders. The herbal medication St. John's wort, available in many drugstores, affects serotonin levels, and so do many psychedelics and hallucinogens, such as *LSD* (lysergic acid diethylamide), *mescaline*, magic mushrooms (*psilocybin*), and *ecstasy* (3,4-methylenedioxy-methamphetamine or MDMA). However, many other neurotransmitters are also involved in the effects of these drugs. For example, *ketamine* (*special-K*) primarily influences glutamate. These substances cause unusual emotional and cognitive experiences in all people by acting on these neurotransmitters in the brain. These substances also appear to reduce symptoms of severe depression, anxiety, and PTSD (Nutt & Carhart-Harris, 2020; Yaden & Yaden, 2020). However, little is known about the efficacy of these drugs, and the underlying mechanism remains unclear. Due to strict laws to stop illegal drugs that began during the Vietnam War era (known as the *War on Drugs*), research on these substances came to a standstill. These laws have been changing and the potential therapeutic value of these drugs have recently become the focus of much scientific interest (Breeksema et al., 2020).

Norepinephrine

A third neurotransmitter system in the monoamine class important to psychopathology is **norepinephrine** (also known as **noradrenaline**) (see ■ Figure 2.13). We have already seen that norepinephrine, like epinephrine (referred to as a catecholamine), is part of the endocrine system.

Norepinephrine seems to stimulate at least two groups (and probably several more) of receptors called *alpha-adrenergic* and *beta-adrenergic receptors.* Someone in your family may be taking a widely used class of drugs called *beta-blockers*, particularly if that person has hypertension or difficulties with regulating heart rate. As the name indicates, these drugs block the beta-receptors so that their response to a surge of norepinephrine is reduced, which keeps blood pressure and heart rate down. In the central

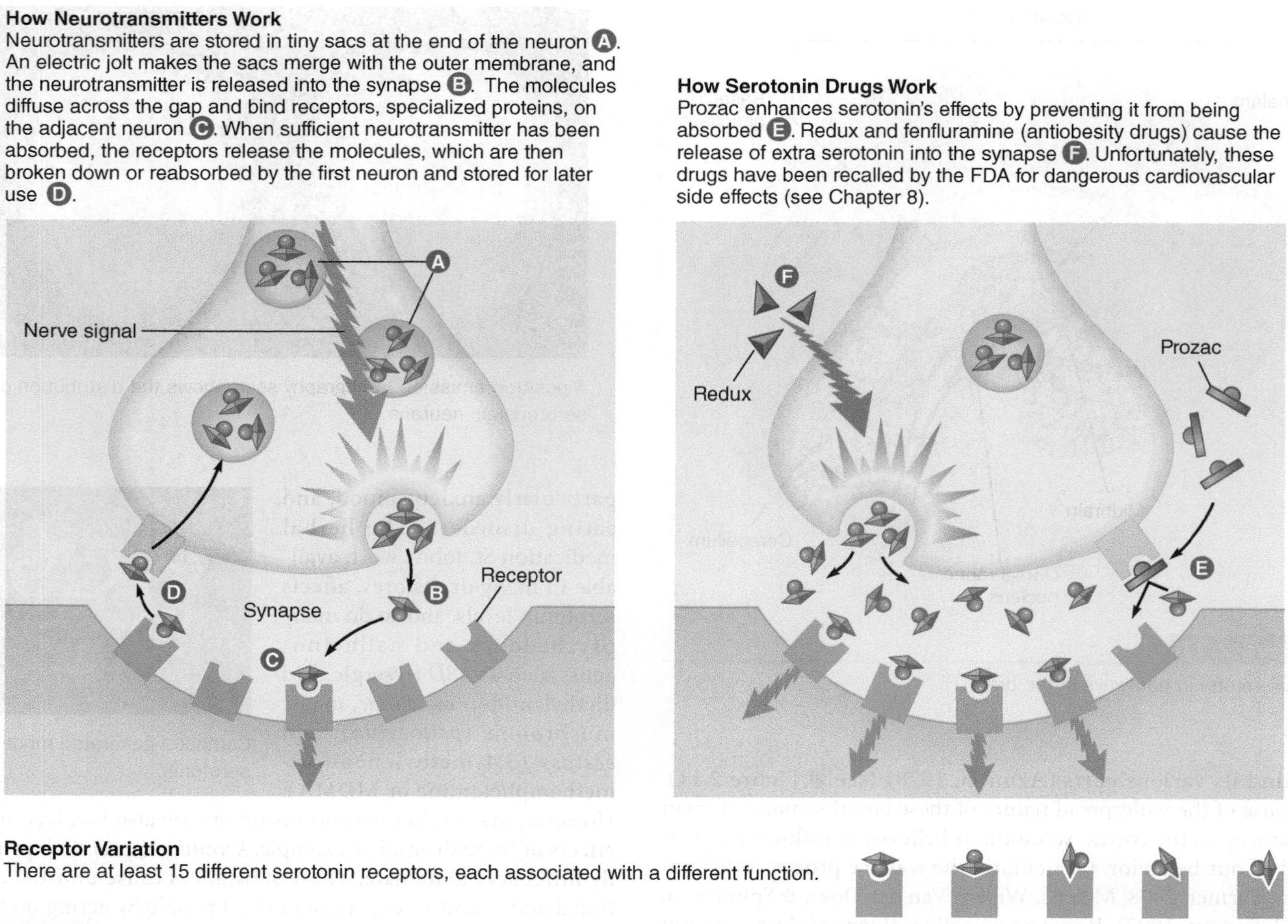

Figure 2.12

Manipulating serotonin in the brain.

nervous system, a number of norepinephrine circuits have been identified. One major circuit begins in the hindbrain, an area that controls basic bodily functions such as respiration. Another circuit appears to influence the emergency reactions or alarm responses (Charney & Drevets, 2002; Gray & McNaughton, 1996; Sullivan & LeDoux, 2004) that occur when we suddenly find ourselves in a dangerous situation, suggesting that norepinephrine may bear some relationship to states of panic (Charney et al., 1990; Gray & McNaughton, 1996). More likely, however, is that this system, with all its varying circuits coursing through the brain, acts in a more general way to regulate or modulate certain behavioral tendencies and is not directly involved in specific patterns of behavior or in psychological disorders.

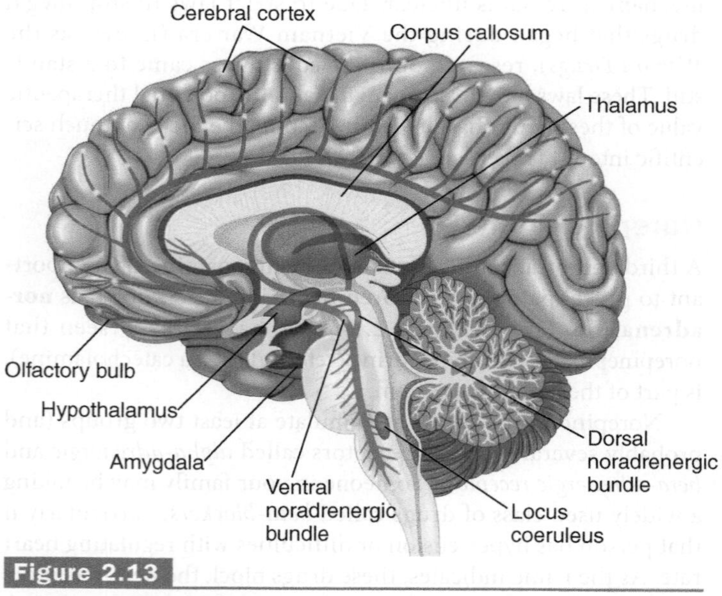

Figure 2.13

Major norepinephrine pathways in the human brain. Adapted from J. W. Kalat, 2009, *Biological psychology*, 10th ed. © 2009 Wadsworth.

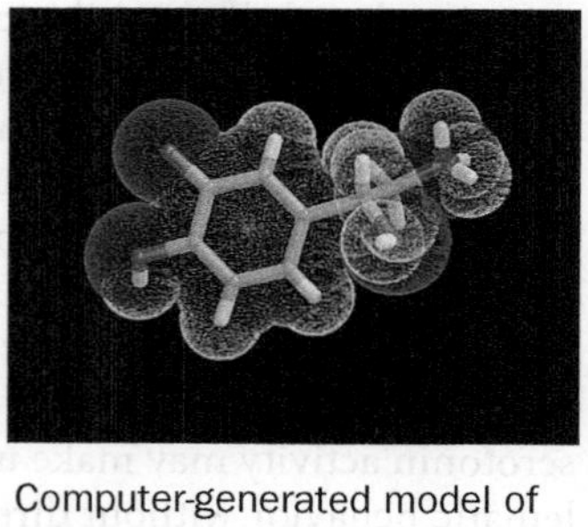

University of California/Lewis Baxter, Jr., M.D.

Computer-generated model of norepinephrine.

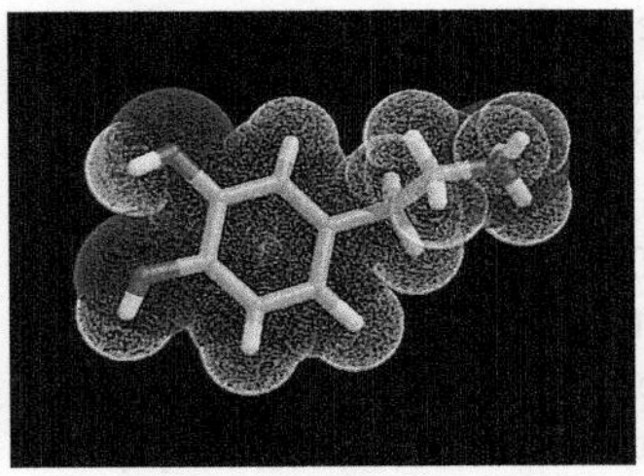

University of California/Lewis Baxter, Jr., M.D.

Computer-generated model of dopamine.

Dopamine

Finally, **dopamine** is another major neurotransmitter that is in the monoamine class and that is also termed a catecholamine because of the similarity of its chemical structure to epinephrine and norepinephrine. Dopamine has been implicated in the pathophysiology of schizophrenia (see ■ Figure 2.14) and disorders of addiction (Le Foll, Gallo, Le Strat, Lu, & Gorwood, 2009). Some research also indicates it may play a significant role in depression (Dunlop & Nemeroff, 2007) and attention deficit hyperactivity disorder (Volkow et al., 2009). Remember the wonder drug reserpine mentioned in Chapter 1 that reduced psychotic behaviors associated with schizophrenia? This drug and more modern antipsychotic treatments affect a number of neurotransmitter systems, but their greatest impact may be that they block specific dopamine receptors, thus lowering dopamine activity (see, for example, Snyder, Burt, & Creese, 1976). Thus, it was long thought possible that in schizophrenia dopamine circuits may be too active. The development of second-generation antipsychotic drugs such as clozapine, which has only weak effects on certain dopamine receptors, suggests this idea may need revising. We explore the dopamine hypothesis in some detail in Chapter 13.

In its various circuits throughout specific regions of the brain, dopamine also seems to have a more general effect, best described as a switch that turns on various brain circuits possibly associated with certain types of behavior. Once the switch is turned on, other neurotransmitters may then inhibit or facilitate emotions or behavior (Armbruster et al., 2009; Oades, 1985; Spoont, 1992; Stahl, 2008). Dopamine circuits merge and cross with serotonin circuits at many points and therefore influence many of the same behaviors. For example, dopamine activity is associated with exploratory, outgoing, pleasure-seeking behaviors (Elovainio, Kivimaki, Viikari, Ekelund, & Keltikangas-Jarvinen, 2005), and serotonin is associated with inhibition and constraint; thus, in a sense they balance each other (Depue, Luciana, Arbisi, Collins, & Leon, 1994).

Again, we see that the effects of a neurotransmitter—in this case, dopamine—are more complex than we originally thought. Researchers have thus far discovered at least five different receptor sites that are selectively sensitive to dopamine (Beaulieu & Gainetdinov, 2011). One of a class of drugs that affects the dopamine circuits specifically is L-dopa, which is a dopamine agonist (increases levels of dopamine). One of the systems that dopamine switches on is the locomotor system, which regulates ability to move in a coordinated way and, once turned on, is influenced by serotonin activity. Because of these connections, deficiencies in dopamine have been associated with disorders such as Parkinson's disease, in which a marked deterioration in motor behavior includes tremors, rigidity of muscles, and difficulty with judgment. L-dopa has been successful in reducing some of these motor disabilities.

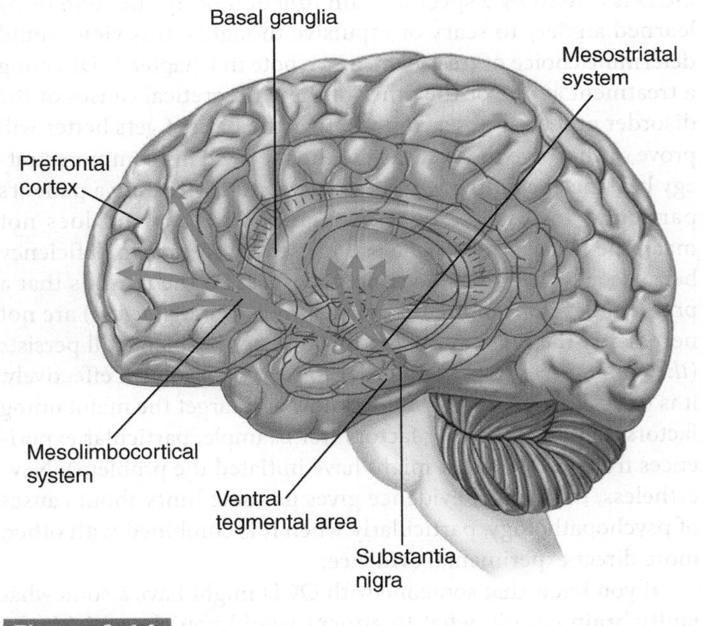

Figure 2.14

Two major dopamine pathways. The mesolimbic system is apparently implicated in schizophrenia; the path to the basal ganglia contributes to problems in the locomotor system, such as tardive dyskinesia, which sometimes results from use of neuroleptic drugs. Adapted from J. W. Kalat, 2009, *Biological psychology*, 10th ed. © 2009 Wadsworth.

Implications for Psychopathology

Psychological disorders typically mix emotional, behavioral, and cognitive symptoms, so identifiable lesions (or damage) localized in specific structures of the brain do not, for the most part, cause the disorders. Even widespread damage most often results in motor or sensory deficits, which are usually the province of the medical specialty of neurology; neurologists often work with neuropsychologists to identify specific lesions. But psychopathologists have been focusing lately on the more general role of brain function in the development of personality, with the goal of considering how different types of biologically driven personalities might be more vulnerable to developing certain types of psychological disorders. For example, genetic contributions might lead to patterns of neurotransmitter activity that influence personality. Thus, some impulsive risk takers may have low serotonergic activity and high dopaminergic activity.

Procedures for studying images of the functioning brain have been applied to a number of disorders, including *obsessive-compulsive disorder (OCD)*. Individuals with this severe anxiety-based disorder (described in Chapter 5) suffer from intrusive, frightening thoughts—for example, some patients may fear that they might have become contaminated with deadly germs and will poison their loved ones if they touch them. To prevent this drastic consequence, they engage in compulsive rituals such as frequent washing to try to scrub off the imagined poison. A number of investigators have found intriguing differences between the brains of patients with OCD and the brains of other people. Although the sizes and structures of the brains are the same, patients with OCD have increased activity in the part of the frontal lobe of the cerebral cortex called the *orbital surface* (Chamberlain et al., 2008; Harrison et al., 2013). Increased activity is also present in the cingulate gyrus and, to a lesser extent, in the caudate nucleus, a circuit that extends from the orbital section of the frontal area of the cortex to parts of the thalamus. Activity in these areas seems to be correlated; that is, if one area is active, the other areas are also. These areas contain several pathways of neurotransmitters, and one of the most concentrated is serotonin.

Remember that one of the roles of serotonin seems to be to moderate our reactions. Eating behavior, sexual behavior, and aggression are under better control with adequate levels of serotonin. Research, mostly on animals, demonstrates that lesions (damage) that interrupt serotonin circuits seem to impair the ability to ignore irrelevant external cues, making the organism overactive. Thus, if we were to experience damage or interruption in this brain circuit, we might find ourselves acting on every thought or impulse that enters our heads.

Thomas Insel (1992) described a case originally reported by Eslinger and Damasio (1985) of a man who had been successful as an accountant, husband, and father of two before undergoing surgery for a brain tumor. He made a good recovery from surgery and seemed to be fine, but in the following year his business failed, and he separated from his family. Although his scores on IQ tests were as high as ever and all his mental functions were intact, he was unable to keep a job or even be on time for an appointment. What was causing all these problems? He was engaging in lengthy and uncontrollable compulsive rituals. Most of his days were consumed with washing, dressing, and rearranging things in the single room where he lived. In other words, he had classic obsessive-compulsive symptoms. The area of his brain damaged by removal of the tumor was a small area of his orbital frontal cortex.

This information seems to support a biological cause for psychopathology—in this case, OCD. You might think there is no need to consider social or psychological influences here. But Insel and other neuroscientists interpret these findings cautiously. First, this finding was based on only one individual. Other individuals with the *same* lesion might react differently. Also, brain-imaging studies are often inconsistent with one another on many important details. Sometimes pinpointing the increased or decreased activity is difficult because brains differ in their structure, just as bodies and faces do. Also, the orbital frontal cortex is implicated in other anxiety disorders and maybe other emotional disorders (Gansler et al., 2009; Goodwin, 2009; Sullivan & LeDoux, 2004), so the damage in this area of the brain may just increase negative affect more generally rather than OCD specifically. It is also possible that activity in this area may simply be a result of the repetitive thinking and ritualistic behavior that characterizes OCD, rather than a cause. To take a simple analogy, if you were late for class and began running, massive changes would occur throughout your body and brain. If someone who did not know that you had just sprinted to class then examined you with brain scans, your brain functions would look different from those of the brain of a person who had walked to class. If you were doing well in the class, the scientist might conclude, wrongly, that your unusual brain function "caused" your intelligence. It is also important to note that today, neuroscientists focus much more on the connectivity between certain brain areas (the brain circuitry) than the activity of any particular brain region that might be associated with a specific mental disorder (for example, Whitfield-Gabrieli et al., 2016).

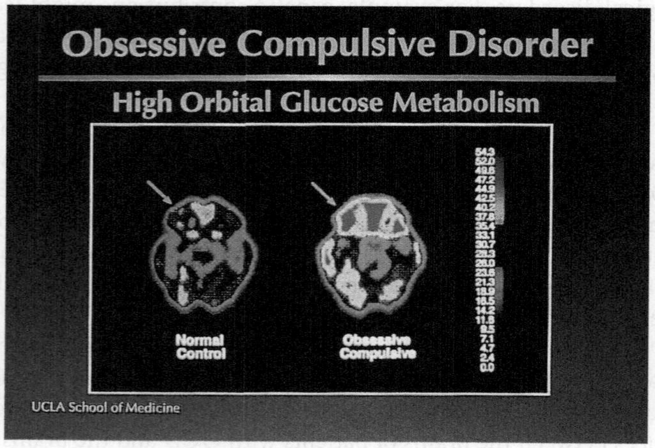

University of California/Lewis Baxter, Jr., M.D.

Brain function is altered in people with OCD, but it normalizes after effective psychosocial treatment.

Psychosocial Influences on Brain Structure and Function

At the same time that psychopathologists are exploring the causes of psychopathology, whether in the brain or in the environment, people are suffering and require the best treatments we have.

Sometimes the effects of treatment tell us something about the nature of psychopathology. For example, if a clinician thinks OCD is caused by a specific brain function or dysfunction or by learned anxiety to scary or repulsive thoughts, this view would determine choice of treatment, as we note in Chapter 1. Directing a treatment at one or the other of these theoretical causes of the disorder and then observing whether the patient gets better will prove or disprove the accuracy of the theory. This common strategy has one overriding weakness. Successfully treating a patient's particular feverish state or toothache with aspirin does not mean the fever or toothache was caused by an aspirin deficiency because an effect does not imply a cause. So the reasons that a problem develops in the first place (*the initiating factors*) are not necessarily the same as the reasons that her problem still persists (*the maintaining factors*). In order to treat the problem effectively, it is typically more important to know and target the maintaining factors than the initiating factors (for example, particular experiences from the past that might have initiated the problem). Nevertheless, this line of evidence gives us some hints about causes of psychopathology, particularly when it is combined with other, more direct experimental evidence.

If you knew that someone with OCD might have a somewhat faulty brain circuit, what treatment would you choose? Maybe you would recommend brain surgery, or neurosurgery. Neurosurgery to correct severe psychopathology (sometimes called *psychosurgery*) is an option still chosen today on occasion, particularly in the case of OCD when the suffering is severe and other treatments have failed (Aouizerate et al., 2006; Bear, Fitzgerald,

Rosenfeld, & Bittar, 2010; Denys et al., 2010; Greenberg, Rauch, & Haber, 2010; see also Chapter 5). For the accountant described previously, the removal of his brain tumor seems to have inadvertently eliminated an inhibitory part of the brain circuit implicated in OCD. Precise surgical lesions might dampen the runaway activity that seems to occur in or near this particular area of the brain triggering the OCD symptoms. This result would probably be welcome if all other treatments have failed, although psychosurgery is used seldom and has not been studied systematically.

Nobody wants to do surgery if less intrusive treatments are available. To use the analogy of a television set that has developed the "disorder" of going fuzzy, if you had to rearrange and reconnect wires on the circuit board every time the disorder occurred, the correction would be a major undertaking. Alternatively, if you could simply push some buttons on the remote and eliminate the fuzziness, the correction would be simpler and less risky. The development of drugs affecting neurotransmitter activity has given us one of those buttons. We now have drugs that, although not a cure or even an effective treatment in all cases, do seem to be beneficial in treating OCD. As you might suspect, most of them act by increasing serotonin activity in one way or another.

But is it possible to get at this brain circuit without either surgery or drugs? Could psychological treatment be powerful enough to affect the circuit directly? The answer seems to be yes. To take one of the first examples, Lewis R. Baxter and his colleagues used brain imaging on patients who had not been treated and then took an additional, important scientific step (Baxter et al., 1992). They treated the patients with a cognitive-behavioral therapy known to be effective in OCD called *exposure and response prevention* (described more fully in Chapter 5) and then repeated the brain imaging. In a remarkable finding, widely noted in the world of psychopathology, Baxter and his colleagues discovered that the brain circuit had been changed (normalized) by a psychological intervention. The same team of investigators then replicated the experiment with a different group of patients and found the same changes in brain function (Schwartz, Stoessel, Baxter, Martin, & Phelps, 1996). In other examples, investigating teams noted changes in brain function after successful psychological treatment for depression, PTSD, obsessive-compulsive disorder, panic disorder, social anxiety disorder, specific phobias, and schizophrenia (Barsaglini, Sartori, Benetti, Pettersson-Yeo, & Mechelli, 2014). A review of the evidence suggests that, depending on the disorder, psychotherapy results in either a normalization of abnormal patterns of activity, the recruitment of additional areas, which did not show altered activation prior to treatment, or both. One study showed that as little as two hours of intense exposure-based therapy for specific phobia changed brain function dramatically, and these effects persisted six months later (Hauner, Mineka, Voss, & Paller, 2012).

The study of placebo effects offers another window on psychological factors directly affecting brain function. Remember that it is common for inactive placebo medications, which are just sugar pills, or other "sham" (inactive) treatments to result in behavioral and emotional changes in patients, presumably as a result of psychological factors such as increasing hope and expectations or conditioning effects (discussed later in the chapter) (Brody & Miller, 2011). Several studies have examined the conditions under which placebos are active. For example, one study administered medications for either pain or anxiety after surgery by means of an infusion pump that was either in plain view of the patients or was hidden behind a screen (Colloca, Lopiano, Lanotte, & Benedetti, 2004). Even though the same dosage of medicine was administered, the effect was consistently greater when patients knew they were receiving the drug because they could see the pump working compared with when the pump was hidden behind a screen. No placebos were actually given in this study, but the difference in effects between knowing and not knowing whether the drug was given was considered a good estimate of the placebo effect. In another study, patients with irritable bowel syndrome (see Chapter 9) received a sham treatment (acupuncture) that was not designed to be effective. The treatment was administered either impersonally or in the context of a warm therapeutic interpersonal relationship. The impersonal administration produced better results than no treatment, (even though there was no active ingredient in the treatment), but the addition of a strong relationship added substantially to the therapeutic benefit (Kaptchuk et al., 2008). But how and why do placebos work?

In an intriguing study, Leuchter, Cook, Witte, Morgan, and Abrams (2002) treated patients with major depressive disorder with either antidepressant medications or placebo medications. Measures of brain function showed that both antidepressant medications and placebos changed brain function but in somewhat different parts of the brain, suggesting different mechanisms of action for these two interventions, at least in the treatment of depression. Placebos alone are not usually as effective as active medication, but every time clinicians prescribe pills, they are also treating the patient psychologically by inducing positive expectation for change, and this intervention changes brain function. Petrovic, Kalso, Petersson, and Ingvar (2002), in an important study, also examined how placebo pills (in other words, psychological factors) can change brain function in the context of treating pain. Normal participants were administered (with their consent) a harmless but painful condition in which their left hand was subjected to intense heat. These participants were informed that two potent analgesics (pain-reducing medications) would be used in the experiment. In fact, one of these drugs was an opioid, and the other was a placebo. Opioid-based drugs are used routinely in medical settings to relieve severe pain. Each participant experienced the painful stimulus under three conditions: (1) under the influence of an opioid drug, (2) under the influence of a placebo pill that the patient assumed was an opioid-based drug, and (3) with no drug (pain only). All participants experienced each condition multiple times, while brain-imaging procedures monitored their brain functioning (see Chapter 3) during administration of the painful stimulus. Whereas both the placebo drug and the opiate drug reduced pain to less than the level with no drug, the surprising results indicated that, unlike the study on depression above, both treatments activated overlapping (although not identical) regions in the brain, primarily within the anterior cingulate cortex and the brain stem. These areas were not activated during the pain-only condition.

Thus, it appears that the anterior cingulate cortex is at least in part responsible for control of the pain response in the brain stem and that cognitive expectations of pain relief created by the placebo condition may cause these brain circuits to be turned on. It would seem that psychological factors are another button on the remote with which we can directly change brain circuits. In a follow-up study, the authors compared the mechanisms of the effect of opioids versus placebo on the brain in more detail and found that the opioid-rich areas of the anterior cingulate cortex were more extensively activated during opioid as compared with placebo analgesia, whereas placebo analgesia was more dependent on a neocortical top-down influence (Petrovic et al., 2010). In general, the literature suggests that multiple brain systems and neurochemical modulators, including opioids and dopamine, seem to be involved in the placebo effect on pain perception (Wager & Atlas, 2015).

A final intriguing area of research is exploring the specific ways in which drug or active psychological treatments work (as opposed to placebos) in terms of changes in brain function. Are the changes in brain function similar or different as a function of drug or psychological treatment? Kennedy et al. (2007) treated individuals with major depressive disorder with either a psychological treatment, cognitive-behavioral therapy (CBT), or the antidepressant drug venlafaxine. Although some brain changes were similar among the three treatment groups, complex differences were also noted, primarily in the way in which CBT facilitated changes in thinking patterns in the cortex that, in turn, affected the emotional brain. Sometimes this is called a "top down" change because it originates in the cortex and works its way down into the lower brain. Drugs, on the other hand, often seem to work more in a "bottom up" manner, reaching higher areas of the cortex (where thinking occurs) last. Because we know that some people respond better to psychological treatments and others respond better to drugs, this research provides hope that we will one day be able to choose the best treatments or better combine treatments based on an analysis of the individual's brain function. Our team has been able to use brain imaging as a tool to predict psychotherapy response (Doehrmann et al., 2013; Whitfield-Gabrieli et al., 2016). The results showed that greater activation in certain brain areas involved in emotion processing and greater connectivity between higher cortical areas with the amygdala predict better outcome after CBT for social anxiety disorder. In the next step, this method could be used to predict whether a particular patient will respond better to pharmacotherapy or psychotherapy. For example, if researchers find that greater (or weaker) connectivity between the amygdala and prefrontal brain areas predict better treatment response to CBT but worse response to drug therapy, this information could then be used to match patients to the most promising treatment option for this particular patient. This is an example for *precision medicine* (that is, tailoring the treatment to the individual patient in order to optimize therapy outcome).

Interactions of Psychosocial Factors and Neurotransmitter Systems

Several experiments illustrate the interaction of psychosocial factors and brain function on neurotransmitter activity, with implications for the development of disorders. Some even indicate that psychosocial factors directly affect levels of neurotransmitters. In one classic experiment, Insel, Scanlan, Champoux, and Suomi (1988) raised two groups of rhesus monkeys identically except for their ability to control things in their cages. One group had free access to toys and food treats, but the second group got these toys and treats only when the first group did. In other words, members of the second group had the same number of toys and treats but could not choose when they got them. In any case, the monkeys in the first group grew up with a sense of control over things in their lives and those in the second group didn't.

Later in their lives, all these monkeys were administered a benzodiazepine inverse agonist, a neurochemical that has the *opposite* effect of the neurotransmitter GABA; the effect is an extreme burst of anxiety. (The few times this neurochemical has been administered to people—usually scientists administering it to one another—the recipients have reported the experience, which lasts only a short time, to be one of the most horrible sensations they had ever endured.) When this substance was injected into the monkeys, the results were interesting. The monkeys that had been raised with little control over their environment ran to a corner of their cage where they crouched and displayed signs of severe anxiety and panic. But the monkeys that had a sense of control behaved quite differently. They did not seem anxious. Rather, they seemed angry and aggressive, even attacking other monkeys near them. Thus, the same level of a neurochemical substance, acting as a neurotransmitter, had different effects, depending on the psychological and environmental histories of the monkeys.

The Insel and colleagues (Insel, Scanlan, Champoux, & Suomi, 1988) experiment is an early example of a significant interaction between neurotransmitters and psychosocial factors. Other experiments suggest that psychosocial influences directly affect the functioning and perhaps even the structure

Thomas Insel/1986 study/National Institute of Mental Health

Rhesus monkeys injected with a specific neurotransmitter react with anger or fear, depending on their early psychological experiences.

of the central nervous system. Scientists have observed that psychosocial factors routinely change the activity levels of many of our neurotransmitter systems (Barik et al., 2013; Cacioppo et al., 2007; Marinelli & McCutcheon, 2014; Sandi & Haller, 2015).

In another remarkable example of the complex interaction among psychosocial factors, brain structure, and brain function as reflected in neurotransmitter activity, Yeh, Fricke, and Edwards (1996) studied two male crayfish battling to establish dominance in their social group. When one of the crayfish won the battle and established dominance, the scientists found that serotonin made a specific set of neurons more likely to fire. In the animal that lost the battle, serotonin made the same neurons less likely to fire. Thus, unlike the Insel et al. (1988) experiment, where monkeys were injected with a neurotransmitter, Yeh and colleagues (1996) discovered that naturally occurring neurotransmitters have different effects depending on the previous psychosocial experience of the organism. Furthermore, this experience directly affects the structure of neurons at the synapse by altering the sensitivity of serotonin receptors. The researchers also discovered that the effects of serotonin are reversible if the losers again become dominant. Similarly, Suomi (2000) demonstrated in primates that early stressful experiences produced deficits in serotonin (as well as other neuroendocrine changes) in genetically susceptible individuals, deficits that did not occur in the absence of early stress.

In another example, Berton and colleagues (2006) discovered, much to their surprise, that putting into a cage big mice that then proceeded to "bully" a smaller mouse produced changes in the mesolimbic dopamine system of the smaller mouse. These changes were associated with the smaller mouse wanting no part of other mice under any circumstances. The small mouse chose to become a recluse. Interestingly, the mesolimbic system is ordinarily associated with reward and even addiction. But in this case, certain chemicals that produce new learning and other positive changes in other parts of the brain, specifically brain development neurotrophic factor (BDNF; a protein that is involved in learning by stimulating growth of new neurons), were turned on in the mesolimbic dopamine system by a psychological experience—bullying—such that the mesolimbic dopamine system had different effects on the mouse than it usually does because of the mouse's unique experience. That is, the "bullying" experience produced BDNF, which changed the usual functioning of the mesolimbic dopamine system from facilitating reinforcement and even addiction to facilitating avoidance and isolation. More recent research implicates glucocorticoid receptors located on dopaminergic neurons specifically in facilitating and maintaining this social aversion (Barik et al., 2013).

Psychosocial Effects on the Development of Brain Structure and Function

It also seems that the structure of neurons themselves, including the number of receptors on a cell, can be changed by learning and experience during development (Clemenson, Deng, & Gage, 2015; Kandel, Dudai, & Mayford, 2014) and that these effects on the central nervous system continue throughout our lives (Cameron et al., 2005; Spinelli et al., 2009; Suárez et al., 2009). We are now beginning to learn how this happens (Clemenson et al., 2015; Kolb, Gibb, & Robinson, 2003; Kolb & Whishaw, 1998; Miller, 2011). For example, William Greenough and his associates, in a series of classic experiments (Greenough, Withers, & Wallace, 1990), studied the cerebellum, which coordinates and controls motor behavior. They discovered that the nervous systems of rats raised in a rich environment requiring a lot of learning and motor behavior develop differently from the nervous systems in rats that were couch potatoes. The active rats had many more connections between nerve cells in the cerebellum and grew many more dendrites. In a follow-up study, Wallace, Kilman, Withers, and Greenough (1992) reported that these structural changes in the brain began in as little as 4 days in rats, suggesting enormous plasticity in brain structure as a result of experience. Similarly, stress during early development can lead to substantial changes in the functioning of the HPA axis (described earlier in this chapter) that, in turn, make primates more or less susceptible to stress later in life (Barlow, 2002; Coplan et al., 1998; Gillespie & Nemeroff, 2007; Spinelli et al., 2009; Suomi, 1999). It may be something similar to this mechanism that was responsible for the effects of early stress on the later development of depression in genetically susceptible individuals in the New Zealand study described earlier (Caspi et al., 2003). More recent experiments with monkeys indicate that housing monkeys in larger groups increases the amount of gray matter in several parts of the brain involved in social cognition. This turns out to be very important since social cognition, including such skills as being able to interpret facial expressions and gestures and successfully predicting what others might be likely to do, makes one more successful socially and, in monkeys, increases one's social ranking (Sallet et al., 2011). Even more intriguing, some studies have suggested increased gray matter density in several temporal lobe regions of the brain in people who have larger Facebook networks. Of course, these findings are only correlational at present (Kanai, Bahrami, Roylance, & Rees, 2012).

So we can conclude that early psychological experience affects the development of the nervous system and thus determines vulnerability to psychological disorders later in life. It seems that the very structure of the nervous system is constantly changing as

William Greenough/University of Illinois

William Greenough and his associates raised rats in a complex environment that required significant learning and motor behavior, which affected the structure of the rats' brains. This supports the role of psychological factors in biological development.

a result of learning and experience, even into old age, and that some of these changes become permanent (Barlow, Ellard, Sauer Zavala, Bullis, & Carl, 2014; Kolb, Gibb, & Gorny, 2003). This plasticity of the central nervous system helps us adapt more readily to our environment. These findings will be important when we discuss the causes of anxiety disorders and mood disorders in Chapters 5 and 7.

The Brain–Gut Connection

Research on neurotransmitters expanded our views of the biology of behavioral and mental disorders. Although the brain has remained central, the path of science has led researchers to another surprising part of the human body: the gut. Our intestines are populated by thousands of microbes, such as fungi, viruses, and bacteria. The entirety of these microorganisms is called the **microbiota**. The combined genome of these organisms (the *microbiome*) adds up to about 20 million genes. This is a lot more than the modest 20,000 genes of our cell's DNA. Some gut bacteria seem to be important for physical and mental health. In other words, our emotional well-being is influenced by our gut though this **brain–gut connection**. The influence of the microbiome of the gut on psychological well-being is sometimes referred to as the *psychobiome*. There has been a lot of circumstantial evidence: For example, many people with irritable bowel syndrome and those frequently taking antibiotics (leading to an imbalance of gut bacteria) often experience depression; autism spectrum disorder is often associated with digestive problems, and constipation is a common problem among people with Parkinson's disease (Cryan & Dinan, 2012).

The exact mechanism through which the gut influences our mental health is not yet fully understood. Bacteria in the gut secrete messenger molecules that travel though the blood to the brain. Other bacteria stimulate the vagus nerve, the largest cerebral nerve that runs from the base of the brain to the abdomen. Healthy gut bacteria are essential for the immune system, and it is possible that the wrong combination of gut bacteria can produce inflammation, which in turn could play a key role in many psychiatric and neurological disorders.

Many of the neurotransmitters discussed earlier are closely linked to some gut bacteria. Microbiota influence some cells in the lining of the gut that then release neurotransmitters, which travel to the brain. This is consistent with recent data that suggest that the gut microbiome mediates and coordinates the effects of genetics on emotional health (Jin et al., 2021). People with depression show deficits in some bacterial species involved in dopamine production (Valles-Colomer et al., 2019), and gut bacteria producing GABA in the rat's digestive tract increases GABA levels in the brain and reduces depression-like behaviors in those animals (Strandwitz, 2018). Moreover, people with relatively fewer of these GABA-producing bacteria have a stronger pattern of hyperactivity in the prefrontal cortex, which is associated with depression (Strandwitz et al., 2019). Serotonin, which is commonly found in the digestive system, is likely also an important gut-brain link. This complex interplay between the gut, neurotransmitters, genetics, and the brain has considerable implications for future treatments and drug developments (Cryan & Dinan, 2012; Pascale et al., 2020).

Comments

The specific brain circuits involved in psychological disorders are complex systems identified by pathways of neurotransmitters traversing the brain. The existence of these circuits suggests that the structure and function of the nervous system play major roles in psychopathology. But other research suggests the circuits are strongly influenced—perhaps even created—by psychological and social factors. Furthermore, both biological interventions, such as drugs, and psychological interventions or experience seem capable of altering the circuits. Therefore, we cannot consider the nature and cause of psychological disorders without examining both biological and psychological factors. We now turn to an examination of psychological factors.

Concept Check 2.3

Check your understanding of the brain structures and neurotransmitters. Match each with its description below: (a) frontal lobe, (b) brain stem, (c) GABA, (d) midbrain, (e) serotonin, (f) dopamine, (g) norepinephrine, and (h) cerebral cortex.

1. Movement, breathing, and sleeping depend on the ancient part of the brain, which is present in most animals. ____________
2. Which neurotransmitter binds to neuron receptor sites, inhibiting postsynaptic activity and reducing overall arousal? ____________
3. Which neurotransmitter is a switch that turns on various brain circuits? ____________
4. Which neurotransmitter seems to be involved in our emergency reactions or alarm responses? ____________
5. This area contains part of the reticular activating system and coordinates movement with sensory output. ____________
6. Which neurotransmitter is believed to influence the way we process information, as well as to moderate or inhibit our behavior? ____________
7. More than 80% of the neurons in the human central nervous system are contained in this part of the brain, which gives us distinct qualities. ____________
8. This area is responsible for most of our memory, thinking, and reasoning capabilities and makes us social animals. ____________

Behavioral and Cognitive Science

Enormous progress has been made in understanding behavioral and cognitive influences in psychopathology. Some new information has come from the rapidly growing field of **cognitive science**, which is concerned with how we acquire and process information and how we store and ultimately retrieve it (one of the processes involved in memory). Scientists have also discovered that we are not necessarily aware of a great deal of what goes on inside our heads. Because, technically, these cognitive processes are unconscious, some findings recall the unconscious mental processes that are so much a part of Sigmund Freud's theory of psychoanalysis (although they do not look much like the ones he envisioned). A brief account of current thinking on what is happening during the process of classical conditioning will start us on our way.

Conditioning and Cognitive Processes

During the 1960s and 1970s, behavioral scientists in animal laboratories began to uncover the complexity of the basic processes of classical conditioning (Bouton, 2005; Bouton, Mineka, & Barlow, 2001; Eelen & Vervliet, 2006; Meyers & Davis, 2002; Mineka & Zinbarg, 1996, 1998). Robert Rescorla (1988) concluded that simply pairing two events closely in time (such as the meat powder and the metronome in Ivan Pavlov's laboratories) is not what's important in this type of learning; at the least, it is a simple summary. Rather, a variety of judgments and cognitive processes combine to determine the final outcome of this learning, even in lower animals such as rats.

To take just one simple example, Pavlov would have predicted that if the meat powder and the metronome were paired, say, 50 times, then a certain amount of learning would take place. But Rescorla and others discovered that if one animal never saw the meat powder except for the 50 trials following the metronome sound, whereas the meat powder was brought to a second animal many times *between* the 50 times it was paired with the metronome, the two animals would learn different things; that is, even though the metronome and the meat powder were paired 50 times for each animal, the metronome was less meaningful to the second animal (see ■ Figure 2.15). Put another way, the first animal learned that the sound of the metronome meant meat powder came next; the second animal learned that the meat sometimes came after the sound and sometimes without the sound. That two different conditions produce two different learning outcomes is a commonsense notion, but it demonstrates, along with many far more complex scientific findings, that basic classical (and operant) conditioning paradigms facilitate the learning of the relationship among events in the environment.

This type of learning enables us to develop working ideas about the world that allow us to make appropriate judgments. We

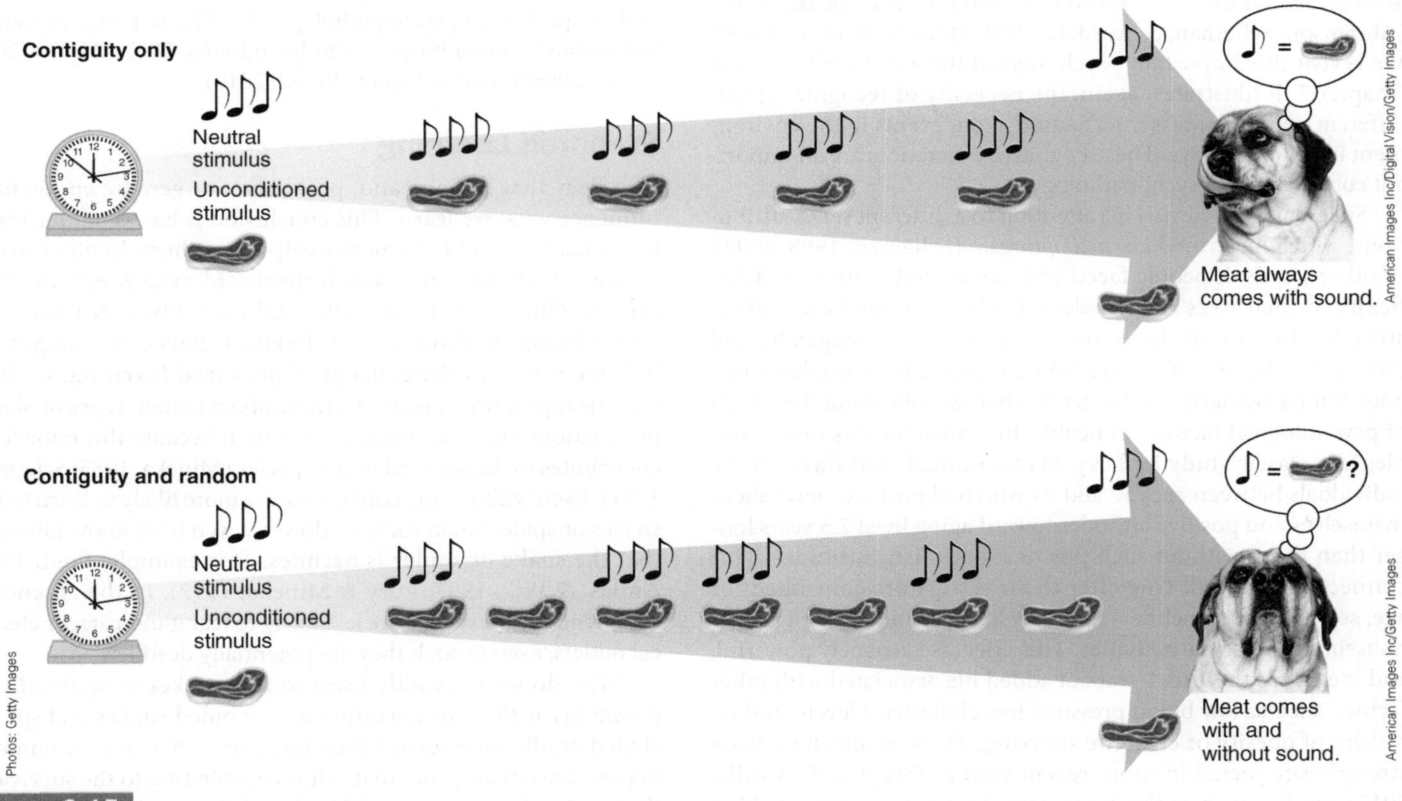

Figure 2.15

Robert Rescorla's experiment that showed contiguity—pairing a neutral stimulus and an unconditioned stimulus—does not result in the same kind of conditioning. The dog in the contiguity-only group (top panel) experiences the usual conditioning procedure: Pairing a tone and meat causes the tone to take on properties of the meat. For the dog in the contiguity-and-random group, the meat appeared away from the tones, as well as with it, making the tone less meaningful.

can then respond in a way that will benefit, or at least not hurt, us. In other words, complex cognitive processing of information, as well as emotional processing, is involved when conditioning occurs, even in animals.

Learned Helplessness

Along similar lines, Martin Seligman and his colleague Steven Maier, also working with animals, described the phenomenon of **learned helplessness**, which occurs when rats or other animals encounter conditions over which they have no control (Maier & Seligman, 1976). If rats are confronted with a situation in which they receive occasional foot shocks, they can function well if they learn they can cope with these shocks by doing something to avoid them (say, pressing a lever). But if the animals learn their behavior has no effect on their environment—sometimes they get shocked and sometimes they don't, no matter what they do—they become "helpless." In other words, they give up attempting to cope and seem to develop the animal equivalent of depression.

Seligman drew some important conclusions from these observations. He theorized that the same phenomenon may happen with people who are faced with uncontrollable stress in their lives. Subsequent work revealed this to be true under one important condition: People become depressed if they "decide" or "think" they can do little about the stress in their lives, even if it seems to others that there is something they could do. People make an *attribution* that they have no control, and they become depressed (Abramson, Seligman, & Teasdale, 1978; Miller & Norman, 1979). We revisit this important psychological theory of depression in Chapter 7. It illustrates, again, the necessity of recognizing that different people process information about events in the environment in different ways. These cognitive differences are an important component of psychopathology.

Seligman later turned his attention to a different set of attributions, which he termed *learned optimism* (Seligman, 1998, 2002). In other words, if people faced with considerable stress and difficulty in their lives nevertheless display an optimistic, upbeat attitude, they are likely to function better psychologically and physically. We return to this theme repeatedly throughout this book but particularly in Chapter 9, when we talk about the effects of psychological factors on health. But consider this one example: In a classic study by Levy, Slade, Kunkel, and Kasl (2002), individuals between ages 50 and 94 who had positive views about themselves and positive attitudes toward aging lived 7.5 years longer than those without such positive, optimistic attitudes. This connection was still true after the investigators controlled for age, sex, income, loneliness, and physical capability to engage in household and social activities. This effect is extremely powerful, and it exceeds the 1 to 4 years of added life associated with other factors, such as low blood pressure, low cholesterol levels, and no history of obesity or cigarette smoking. These results have been strongly supported in more recent studies (Steptoe & Wardle, 2012). Studies such as this have created interest in a new field of study called *positive psychology*, in which investigators explore factors that account for positive attitudes and happiness (Diener, 2000; Lyubomirsky, 2001). We return to these themes in the chapters describing specific disorders.

Social Learning

Another influential psychologist, Albert Bandura (1973, 1986), observed that organisms do not have to experience certain events in their environment to learn effectively. Rather, they can learn just as much by observing what happens to someone else in a given situation. This fairly obvious discovery came to be known as **modeling** (or **observational learning**). What is important is that, even in animals, this type of learning requires a symbolic integration of the experiences of others with judgments of what might happen to oneself. In other words, even an animal that is not intelligent by human standards, such as a monkey, must make a decision about the conditions under which its own experiences would be similar to those of the animal it is observing. Bandura expanded his observations into a network of ideas in which behavior, cognitive factors, and environmental influences converged to produce the complexity of behavior that confronts us. He also specified in some detail the importance of the social context of our learning; that is, much of what we learn depends on our interactions with other people around us. These ideas have been integrated with new findings on the genetic and biological bases of social behavior in a new field of study called social neuroscience (Cacioppo et al., 2007).

The basic idea in all Bandura's work is that a careful analysis of cognitive processes may well produce the most accurate scientific predictions of behavior. Concepts of probability learning, information processing, and attention have become increasingly important in psychopathology (Bar-Haim, Lamy, Pergamin, Bakermans-Kranenburg, & Van Ijzendoorn, 2007; Barlow, 2002; Davey, 2006; Lovibond, 2006; Yiend, 2010).

Prepared Learning

It is clear that biology and, probably, our genetic endowment influence what we learn. This conclusion is based on our learning to fear some objects more easily than others. In other words, we learn fears and phobias selectively (Mineka & Sutton, 2006; Morris, Öhman, & Dolan, 1998; Öhman, Flykt, & Lundqvist, 2000; Öhman & Mineka, 2001; Rakison, 2009). Why might this be? According to the concept of **prepared learning**, we have become highly prepared for learning about certain types of objects or situations over the course of evolution because this knowledge contributes to the survival of the species (Mineka, 1985; Seligman, 1971). Even without any contact, we are more likely to learn to fear snakes or spiders than rocks or flowers, even if we know rationally that the snake or spider is harmless (for example, Fredrikson, Annas, & Wik, 1997; Pury & Mineka, 1997). In the absence of experience, however, we are less likely to fear guns, cars, or electrical outlets, even though they are potentially deadlier.

Why do we so readily learn to fear snakes or spiders? One possibility is that our ancestors who avoided snakes and spiders eluded deadly varieties and therefore survived in greater numbers to pass down their genes to us, thus contributing to the survival of the species. In fact, research has found that a sex difference may exist for this type of learning: Women and girls are particularly sensitive to this learning and, unlike men and boys, demonstrate it as early as 11 months of age (Rakison, 2009). Thus, "prepared learning" may account for the greater incidence of snake and spider phobias in adult women (see Chapter 5). This is just a theory, but at present it seems a likely explanation. According to the theory, it would have been more important for women, in their roles as foragers and gatherers, to develop a tendency to avoid snakes and spiders than males, in their primary roles as risk-taking hunters (Rakison, 2009).

In any case, something within us recognizes the connection between a certain signal and a threatening event. If you've ever gotten sick after having eaten something that was way passed its expiration date, chances are you won't make the same mistake again. This quick, or "one-trial," learning also occurs in animals that eat something that tastes bad, causes nausea, or may contain poison. It is easy to see that survival is associated with quickly learning to avoid poisonous food. If animals are shocked instead of poisoned when eating certain foods, however, they do not learn this association nearly as quickly, probably because in nature shock is not a consequence of eating, whereas food is more closely associated with getting poisoned. Perhaps these selective associations are also facilitated by our genes and depend on the context and the nature of the associated stimuli (Barlow, 2002; Cook, Hodes, & Lang, 1986; Garcia, McGowan, & Green, 1972; Mallan, Lipp & Cochrane, 2013).

Cognitive Science and the Unconscious

Advances in cognitive science have revolutionized our conceptions of the unconscious. We are not aware of much of what goes on inside our heads, but our unconscious is not necessarily the seething caldron of primitive emotional conflicts envisioned by Freud. Rather, we simply seem able to process and store information and to act on it without having the slightest awareness of what the information is or why we are acting on it (Bargh & Chartrand, 1999; Uleman, Saribay, & Gonzalez, 2008). Is this surprising? Consider briefly these two examples.

Lawrence Weiskrantz in a classic study (1992) describes a phenomenon called *blind sight* or *unconscious vision.* He relates the case of a young man who, for medical reasons, had a small section of his visual cortex (the center for the control of vision in the brain) surgically removed. Although the operation was considered a success, the young man became blind in both eyes. Later, during routine tests, a physician raised his hand to the left of the patient who, much to the shock of his doctors, reached out and touched it. Subsequently, scientists determined that he could not only reach accurately for objects but could also distinguish among objects and perform most of the functions usually associated with sight. Yet when asked about his abilities, he would say, "I couldn't see anything, not a darn thing," and that all he was doing was guessing.

The phenomenon in this case is associated with real brain damage. More interesting, from the point of view of psychopathology, is that the same thing seems to occur in healthy individuals who have been hypnotized (Hilgard, 1992; Kihlstrom, 1992); that is, normal individuals, provided with hypnotic suggestions that they are blind, are able to function visually but have no awareness or memory of their visual abilities. This condition, which illustrates a process of *dissociation* between behavior and consciousness, is the basis of the dissociative disorders discussed in Chapter 6.

A second example, more relevant to psychopathology, is called **implicit memory** (Bowers & Marsolek, 2003; Kandel et al., 2014; McNally, 1999; Schacter, Chiu, & Ochsner, 1993). Implicit memory is apparent when someone clearly acts on the basis of things that have happened in the past but can't remember the events. (A conscious memory for events is called *explicit memory.*) But implicit memory can be selective for only certain events or circumstances. Clinically, we have already seen in Chapter 1 an example of implicit memory at work in the story of Anna O., the classic case first described by Breuer and Freud (1895/1957) to demonstrate the existence of the unconscious. It was only after therapy that Anna O. remembered events surrounding her father's death and the connection of these events to her paralysis. Thus, Anna O.'s behavior (occasional paralysis) was evidently connected to implicit memories of her father's death. Many scientists have concluded that Freud's speculations on the nature and structure of the unconscious went beyond the evidence, but the existence of unconscious processes has since been demonstrated, and we must take them into account as we study psychopathology.

What methods do we have for studying the unconscious? The *black box* refers to unobservable feelings and cognitions inferred from an individual's self-report or behaviors. In recent decades, psychologists and neuroscientists, confident in an established science of behavior, have returned to the black box with new methods, attempting to reveal the unobservable. Several methods for studying the unobservable unconscious have been made possible by advances in technology. One of them is the Stroop color-naming paradigm.

In the Stroop paradigm, participants are shown a variety of words, each printed in a different color. They are shown these words quickly and asked to name the colors in which they are printed while ignoring their meaning (for example, they are asked to say "blue" if they see the word *red* printed in a blue color). Color naming is delayed when the meaning of the word attracts the participant's attention, despite efforts to concentrate on the color; that is, the meaning of the word interferes with the participant's ability to process color information. For example, experimenters have determined that people with certain psychological disorders, like Janelle, are much slower at naming the colors of words associated with their problem (for example, *blood, injury,* and *dissect*) than the colors of words that have no relation to the disorder. Thus, psychologists can now uncover particular patterns of emotional significance, even if the participant cannot verbalize them or is not even aware of them.

Cognitive neuroscientists using brain imaging methods (functional magnetic resonance imaging [fMRI]) have noticed differences in the processing of neural activity in the brain depending on whether the person is aware of the information or not (Uehara et al., 2013; see Chapter 4). Generally, the greater the duration, intensity, and coherence of the neural representation of a piece of information in the brain, the more likely that the person will be aware or conscious of the information (Kandel et al., 2014; Schurger, Pereira, Treisman, & Cohen, 2010; Schwarzkopf & Rees, 2010; Wimmer & Shohamy, 2012). But so far, this work has been carried out only in experiments with normal individuals. It remains to be seen if the unconscious experience of people with psychological disorders will look similar during brain imaging.

1. RED	6. GREEN	11. BLUE
2. PURPLE	7. PURPLE	12. PURPLE
3. GREEN	8. BROWN	13. BROWN
4. BLUE	9. BLUE	14. RED
5. BROWN	10. RED	15. GREEN

The Stroop paradigm. Have someone keep time as you name the colors of the words but not the words themselves and again while you name the words and colors together.

These developments in our understanding of the nature of psychopathology will come up repeatedly as we discuss specific disorders. Again, note that these findings support Freud's theories about the unconscious, up to a point. But no assumptions are made about an elaborate structure existing within the mind that is continually in conflict (Freud's id, ego, and superego); and at present, there is no evidence to support the existence of an unconscious with such a complex structure and array of functions.

Emotions

Emotions play an enormous role in our day-to-day lives and can contribute in major ways to the development of psychopathology (Barrett, 2012; Gross, 2015; Kring & Sloan, 2010; Rottenberg & Johnson, 2007). Consider the emotion of fear. Have you ever found yourself in a really dangerous situation? Have you ever been swimming in the ocean and realized you were out too far or caught in a current? Have you ever almost fallen from a height, such as a ladder or a roof? In any of these instances, you would have felt an incredible surge of arousal. As the first great emotion theorist, Charles Darwin (1872), pointed out more than 150 years ago, this kind of reaction seems to be programmed in all animals, including humans, which suggests that it serves a useful evolutionary function. The alarm reaction that activates during potentially life-threatening emergencies is called the **flight or fight response**. If you are caught in ocean currents, your almost instinctual tendency is to struggle toward shore. You might realize rationally that you're best off just floating until the current runs its course and then, more calmly, swimming in later. Yet somewhere, deep within, ancient instincts for survival won't let you relax, even though struggling against the ocean will only wear you out and increase your chance of drowning. Still, this kind of reaction might momentarily give you the strength to lift a car off your trapped brother or fight off an attacker. The whole purpose of the physical rush of adrenaline that we feel in extreme danger is to mobilize us to escape the danger (flight) or to fend it off (fight).

Charles Darwin, *Evolution of the Species*, 1896

Charles Darwin (1809–1882) drew this cat frightened by a dog to show the flight or fight reaction.

The Physiology and Purpose of Fear

How do physical reactions prepare us to respond this way? The great physiologist Walter Cannon (1929) speculated on the reasons. Fear activates your cardiovascular system. Your blood vessels constrict, thereby raising arterial pressure and decreasing the blood flow to your extremities (fingers and toes). Excess blood is redirected to the skeletal muscles, where it is available to the vital organs that may be needed in an emergency. As a result, some people "tremble with fear" or have their hair stand on end, which is a result of shivering and piloerection (in which body hairs stand erect), reactions that conserve heat when your blood vessels are constricted.

These defensive adjustments can also produce the hot-and-cold spells that often occur during extreme fear. Breathing becomes faster and, usually, deeper to provide necessary oxygen to rapidly circulating blood. Increased blood circulation carries oxygen to the brain, stimulating cognitive processes and sensory functions, which make you more alert and able to think more quickly during emergencies. An increased amount of glucose (sugar) is released from the liver into the bloodstream, further energizing various crucial muscles and organs, including the brain. Pupils dilate, presumably to allow a better view of the situation. Hearing becomes more acute, and digestive activity is suspended, resulting in a reduced flow of saliva (the "dry mouth" of fear). In the short term, voiding the body of all waste material and eliminating digestive processes further prepare the organism for concentrated action and activity, so there is often pressure to urinate and defecate and, occasionally, to vomit.

It is easy to see why the flight or fight reaction is fundamentally important. Millennia ago, when our ancestors lived in unstable circumstances, those with strong emergency reactions were more likely to live through attacks and other dangers than those with weak emergency responses, and the survivors passed their genes down to us.

Emotional Phenomena

The **emotion** of fear is a subjective feeling of terror, a strong motivation for behavior (escaping or fighting), and a complex physiological or arousal response. To define "emotion" is difficult, but most theorists agree that it is linked to an *action tendency* (Barlow, 2002; Barlow et al. 2014; Lang, 1985, 1995; Lang, Bradley,

& Cuthbert, 1998); that is, a tendency to behave in a certain way (for example, escape), elicited by an external event (a threat) and a feeling state (terror) and accompanied by a (possibly) characteristic physiological response (Barrett, 2012; Fairholme, Boisseau, Ellard, Ehrenreich, & Barlow, 2010; Gross, 2015; Izard, 1992; Lazarus, 1991, 1995). Any emotional experience is associated with approach and avoidance tendencies. One purpose of a feeling state is to motivate us to carry out a behavior: If we escape, our terror, which is unpleasant, will be decreased, so decreasing unpleasant feelings motivates us to escape (Campbell-Sills, Ellard, & Barlow, 2015; Gross, 2015; Hofmann, 2016; Hofmann & Doan, 2018; Öhman, 1996). As Öhman (1996; Öhman, Flykt, & Lundquist, 2000) points out, the principal function of emotions can be understood as a clever means, guided by evolution, to get us to do what we have to do to pass on our genes successfully to coming generations. How do you think this works with anger or with love? What is the feeling state? What is the behavior?

Emotions are usually short-lived, temporary states lasting from several minutes to several hours, occurring in response to an external event. **Mood** is a more persistent period of affect or emotionality. Thus, in Chapter 7, we describe enduring or recurring states of depression or excitement (mania) as *mood disorders.* But *anxiety disorders*, described in Chapter 5, are characterized by enduring or chronic anxiety and, therefore, could also be called *mood disorders.* Alternatively, both anxiety disorders and mood disorders could be called *emotional disorders*, a term not formally used in psychopathology. This is only one example of the occasional inconsistencies in the terminology of abnormal psychology. A related term you will see occasionally, particularly in Chapters 3 and 13, is **affect**, which often refers to the valence dimension (that is, pleasant or positive versus unpleasant or negative) of an emotion. For example, positive affect is experienced during joy, whereas negative affect is experienced during anger and fear. Together with arousal dimension (that is, activated or high arousal versus deactivated or low arousal), any emotional experience can be assigned as a point on this two-dimensional system. This two-dimensional system is known as the **circumplex model** of emotions (for example, Colibazzi et al., 2010). A third dimension (time) could be added to specify whether the emotional experience is short or long-lasting (for example, surprise versus joy). Affect can also refer to the momentary emotional tone that accompanies what we say or do. For example, if you just got an A+ on your test but you look sad, your friends might think your reaction strange because your affect is not appropriate to the event. Finally, the term *affective style* is sometimes used to summarize commonalities among emotional states characteristic of an individual. Thus, someone who tends to be fearful, anxious, and depressed has a negative affective style, whereas sometimes with a positive affective style would subsume, or include, tendencies to be generally pleasant, joyful, excited, and so on.

The Components of Emotion

Emotion scientists now agree that emotion is composed of three related components—*behavior*, *physiology*, and *cognition*—but most emotion scientists tend to concentrate on one component or another (see ■ Figure 2.16). Emotion scientists who concentrate

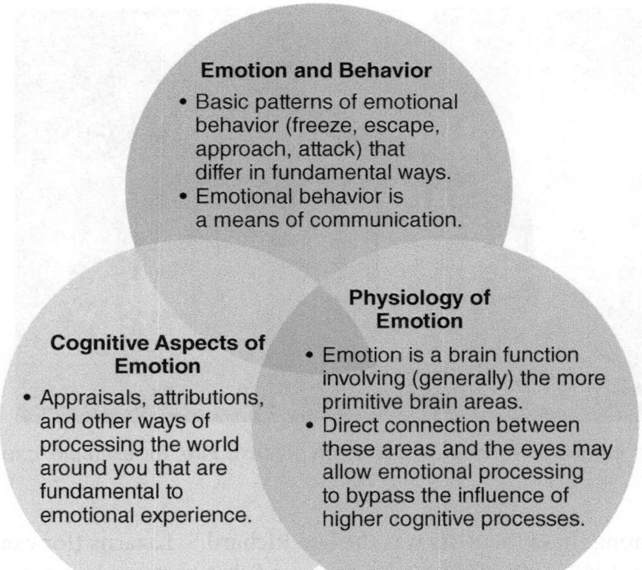

Figure 2.16
Emotion has three important and overlapping components: behavior, cognition, and physiology.

on behavior think that basic patterns of emotion differ from one another in fundamental ways; for example, anger may differ from sadness not only in how it feels but also behaviorally and physiologically. These scientists also emphasize that emotion is a way of communicating between one member of the species and another. One function of fear is to motivate immediate and decisive action, such as running away. But if you look scared, your facial expression will quickly communicate the possibility of danger to your friends, who may not have been aware that a threat is imminent. Your facial communication increases their chance for survival because they can now respond more quickly to the threat when it occurs. This may be one reason emotions are contagious, as we observe in Chapter 1 when discussing mass hysteria (Hatfield, Cacioppo, & Rapson, 1994; Wang, 2006).

Other scientists have concentrated on the physiology of emotions, most notably Cannon (1929). In some pioneering work, he viewed emotion as primarily a brain function. Research in this tradition suggests that areas of the brain associated with emotional expression are generally more ancient and primitive than areas associated with higher cognitive processes, such as reasoning.

Other research demonstrates direct neurobiological connections between emotional centers of the brain and parts of the eye (the retina) or the ear that allow emotional activation without the influence of higher cognitive processes (LeDoux, 1996, 2002; Öhman, Flykt, & Lundqvist, 2000; Zajonc, 1984, 1998). In other words, you may experience various emotions quickly and directly without necessarily thinking about them or being aware of why you feel the way you do.

Finally, a number of prominent emotion scientists concentrate on studying the cognitive aspects of emotion. Notable

Our emotional reaction depends on context. Fire, for example, can be threatening or comforting.

among these theorists was the late Richard S. Lazarus (for example, 1968, 1991, 1995), who proposed that changes in a person's environment are appraised in terms of their potential impact on that person. The type of appraisal you make determines the emotion you experience. For example, if someone sees a person holding a gun in a dark alley, they will probably appraise the situation as dangerous and experience fear. But they would likely make a different appraisal if they saw a tour guide displaying an antique gun in a museum. Lazarus would suggest that thinking and feeling cannot be separated, but other cognitive scientists are concluding otherwise by suggesting that, although cognitive and emotional systems interact and overlap, they are fundamentally separate (Teasdale, 1993). All components of emotion—behavior, physiology, and cognition—are important, and theorists are adopting more integrative approaches by studying their interaction (Barrett, 2009, 2012; Gendron & Barrett, 2009; Gross, 2015; Hofmann, 2016; Hofmann & Doan, 2018).

Anger and Your Heart

When we discussed Janelle's blood phobia, we observed that behavior and emotion may strongly influence biology. Scientists have made important discoveries about the familiar emotion of anger. We have known for years that negatively valenced emotions such as hostility and anger increase a person's risk of developing heart disease (Chesney, 1986; MacDougall, Dembroski, Dimsdale, & Hackett, 1985). Sustained hostility with angry outbursts and repeatedly and continually suppressing anger contributes more strongly to death from heart disease than other well-known risk factors, including smoking, high blood pressure, and high cholesterol levels (Harburg, Kaciroti, Gleiberman, Julius, & Schork, 2008; Williams, Haney, Lee, Kong, & Blumenthal, 1980).

Why is this, exactly? In a classic study, Ironson and colleagues (1992) asked a number of people with heart disease to recall something that made them angry in the past. Sometimes these events had occurred many years earlier. In one case, an individual who had spent time in a Japanese prisoner-of-war camp during World War II became angry every time he thought about it, especially when he thought about reparations paid by the U.S. government to Japanese Americans who had been held in internment camps during the war. Ironson and associates compared the experience of anger with stressful events that increased heart rate but were not associated with anger. For example, some participants imagined making a speech to defend themselves against a charge of shoplifting. Others tried to figure out difficult problems in arithmetic within a time limit. Heart rates during these angry situations and stressful ones were then compared with heart rates that increased as a result of exercise (riding a stationary bicycle). The investigators found that the ability of the heart to pump blood efficiently through the body dropped significantly during anger but not during stress or exercise. In fact, remembering being angry was sufficient to cause the anger effect. If participants were really angry, their heart-pumping efficiency dropped even more, putting them at risk for dangerous disturbances in heart rhythm (arrhythmias).

This study was the first to prove that anger affects the heart through decreased pumping efficiency, at least in people who already have heart disease. This was confirmed in a large high-risk study examining 13,171 participants (Kucharska-Newton et al., 2014). The incidence of heart failure was greater among those with high, as compared to those with low or moderate trait anger, and men had a higher risk for heart failure than women.

Suarez and colleagues (2002) demonstrated how anger may cause this effect. Inflammation produced by an overactive immune system in particularly hostile individuals may contribute to clogged arteries (and decreased heart-pumping efficiency).

Interestingly, it seems that adopting a forgiving attitude can neutralize the toxic effects of anger on cardiovascular activity. In the words of the Buddhist leader, the Dalai Lama: "Harboring anger is like swallowing poison and expecting the other person to die." The antidote to anger is forgiveness, compassion, and kindness. These insights are supported by scientific data. For example, Larsen et al. (2012) had participants think about a previous offense from either an angry perspective or a forgiving perspective or while they were distracted by focusing on a neutral topic. All of them were then distracted by focusing on the neutral topic for five minutes, after which they could freely ruminate on the offense. As expected, thinking about the offense from an angry perspective had negative effects on cardiovascular measures (increased blood pressure and heart rate, etc.) compared with the distraction condition, but taking a forgiving attitude not only greatly reduced this cardiovascular reactivity to a level present in the distraction condition, but these effects were still present during the follow-up free rumination period, even compared to the distraction condition as that group began ruminating on the offense causing increases in their reactivity.

Taken together, these results provide strong support for the effects of anger on the heart, but shall we conclude that too much anger causes heart attacks? This would be another example of one-dimensional causal modeling. Increasing evidence, including the studies just mentioned, suggests that anger and hostility contribute to heart disease, but so do many other factors, including a genetically determined biological vulnerability. We discuss cardiovascular disease in Chapter 9.

Emotions and Psychopathology

We now know that suppressing almost any kind of emotional response, such as anger or fear, increases sympathetic nervous system activity, which may contribute to psychopathology (Barlow, Sauer-Zavala, Carl, Bullis, & Ellard, 2014; Campbell-Sills et al., 2015; Fairholme, Boisseau, Ellard, Ehrenreich, & Barlow, 2010). Other emotions seem to have a more direct effect. In Chapter 5, we study the phenomenon of *panic* and its relationship to anxiety disorders. One interesting possibility is that a panic attack is simply the normal emotion of fear occurring at the wrong time, when there is nothing to be afraid of (Barlow, 2002). Some patients with mood disorders become overly excited and joyful. They think they have the world on a string and they can do anything they want and spend as much money as they want because everything will turn out all right. Every little event is the most wonderful and exciting experience they have ever had. These individuals are suffering from *mania*, which is part of a serious mood disorder called *bipolar disorder*, discussed in Chapter 7. People who suffer from mania usually alternate periods of excitement with periods of extreme sadness and distress, when they feel that all is lost and the world is a gloomy and hopeless place. During extreme sadness or distress, people are unable to experience any pleasure in life and often find it difficult even to get out of bed and move around. If hopelessness becomes acute, they are at risk for suicide. This emotional state is *depression*, a defining feature of many mood disorders.

Thus, basic emotions of fear, anger, sadness or distress, and excitement may contribute to many psychological disorders and may even define them. Emotions and mood also affect our cognitive processes: If your mood is positive, then your associations, interpretations, and impressions also tend to be positive (Diener, Oishi, & Lucas, 2003). A person's first impressions of people they meet and even a person's memories of past events are colored to a great extent by their current mood. If a person is consistently negative or depressed, then their memories of past events are likely to be unpleasant. The pessimist or depressed person sees the bottle filled halfway as half empty. In contrast, the cheerful optimist is said to see the bottle as half full. This is a rich area of investigation for cognitive and emotion scientists (Eysenck, 1992; Rottenberg & Johnson, 2007; Teasdale, 1993), particularly those interested in the close interconnection of cognitive and emotional processes. Leading psychopathologists are beginning to outline the nature of emotion disruption (or dysregulation) and to understand how these disruptions interfere with thinking and behavior in various psychological disorders (Barlow, Allen, & Choate, 2004; Campbell-Sills et al., 2015; Gross, 2015; Hofmann, Sawyer, Fang, & Asnaani, 2012; Kring & Sloan, 2010).

Concept Check 2.4

Check your understanding of behavioral and cognitive influences by identifying the descriptions. Choose your answers from (a) learned helplessness, (b) modeling, (c) prepared learning, and (d) implicit memory.

1. Dalia noticed that every time Tyrone behaved well at lunch, the teacher praised him. Dalia decided to behave better to receive praise herself. ____________
2. Tyler stopped trying to please his father because he never knows whether his father will be proud or outraged. ____________
3. Piper fell into a lake as a baby and almost drowned. Even though Piper has no recollection of the event, they hate to be around large bodies of water. ____________
4. Juanita was scared to death of the tarantula, even though she knew it wasn't likely to hurt her. ____________

Cultural, Social, and Interpersonal Factors

Given the jumble of neurobiological and psychological variables impinging on our lives, is there any room for the influence of social, interpersonal, and cultural factors? Studies are beginning to demonstrate the substantial power and depth of such influences. Researchers have now established that cultural and social influences can kill you. Consider the following example.

Voodoo, the Evil Eye, and Other Fears

Fear and phobias are universal, occurring across all cultures. But *what* we fear is to some extent influenced by our social environment. In many cultures around the world, individuals may suffer from culturally shaped *fright disorders*, which are characterized by exaggerated startle responses and other observable fear and anxiety reactions. One example is the Latin American *susto*, which describes various anxiety-based symptoms, including insomnia, irritability, phobias, and the marked somatic

THONY BELIZAIRE/AFP/Getty Images

A "possessed" person receives treatment in a voodoo ritual.

symptoms of sweating and increased heart rate (tachycardia). But *susto* has only one cause: The individual believes that he or she has become the object of black magic, or witchcraft, and is suddenly badly frightened. In some cultures, the sinister influence is called the *evil eye* (Good & Kleinman, 1985; Tan, 1980), and the resulting fright disorder can be fatal. Cannon (1942), examining the Haitian phenomenon of voodoo death, suggested that the sentence of death by a medicine man may create an intolerable autonomic arousal in the participant, who has little ability to cope because there is no social support. That is, friends and family ignore the individual after a brief period of grieving because they assume death has already occurred. Ultimately, the condition leads to damage to internal organs and death. Thus, from all accounts, an individual who is from a physical and psychological point of view functioning in a perfectly healthy and adaptive way suddenly dies because of marked changes in the social environment.

In another example of how social and cultural framing shapes what people fear, Israeli and Bedouin researchers studied the fears of hundreds of Jewish and Bedouin children living in the same region of Israel (Elbedour, Shulman, & Kedem, 1997). Although they all feared potentially life-threatening events, the study showed that the Israeli children, who lived in a society emphasizing individuality and autonomy, had fewer fears than Bedouin children, who grew up in a strongly paternalistic society in which the group and family were central and who were taught to be cautious about the rest of the world. Bedouin and Jewish children have different fears, and the Bedouin children have more of them, many centering on the possible disintegration of the family. Thus, cultural factors influence the form and content of psychopathology and may differ even among cultures side by side in the same country.

Gender

Gender roles have a strong and sometimes puzzling effect on psychopathology (Kistner, 2009; Maeng & Milad, 2015; Rutter, Caspi, & Moffitt, 2006). Everyone experiences anxiety and fear, and phobias are found all over the world. But phobias have a peculiar characteristic: The likelihood of your having a particular phobia is powerfully influenced by your gender. For example, someone who complains of an insect or small-animal phobia severe enough to prohibit field trips or visits to friends in the country is almost certain to be female, as are 90% of the people with this phobia (possible reasons for this were mentioned on pp. 60–61). But a social phobia strong enough to keep someone from attending parties or meetings affects men and women more or less equally, though perhaps for different reasons.

We think some of these differences have to do with cultural expectations of men and women, or the culture-specific *gender roles*. For example, an equal number of men and women may have an experience that could lead to an insect or small-animal phobia, such as being bitten by one, but in our society it isn't always acceptable for a man to show or even admit fear. So a man is more likely to hide or endure the fear until he gets over it. It is more acceptable for women to acknowledge fearfulness, so a phobia develops. It is also more acceptable for a man to be shy than to show fear, so he is more likely to admit social discomfort.

To avoid or lessen a panic attack, an extreme experience of fear, some males drink alcohol instead of admitting they're afraid (see Chapter 5). In many cases, this attempt to cope may lead to alcoholism, a disorder that affects many more men than women (see Chapter 11). One reason for this gender imbalance is that men are more likely than women to self-medicate their fear and panic with alcohol and in so doing start down the slippery slope to addiction.

It even seems that men and women may respond differently to the same standardized psychological treatment (Felmingham & Bryant, 2012). After exposure therapy for posttraumatic stress disorder (see Chapter 5), both groups benefited, but women maintained their gains significantly better during a follow-up period. The authors suggest that the well-established ability of women to recall emotional memories somewhat better than men may facilitate emotional processing and long-term treatment gains.

Bulimia nervosa, the severe eating disorder, occurs almost entirely in young women. Why? As you will see in Chapter 8, a cultural emphasis on female thinness plagues our society and, increasingly, societies around the world. The pressures for men to be thin are less apparent, and of the few men who develop bulimia, a substantial percentage are gay; for these individuals, cultural imperatives to be thin are present in many specific instances (Rothblum, 2002). In fact, the proportion of gay and bisexual men with symptoms related to disordered eating was 10 times higher than among heterosexual men (10% versus 1%; Strong et al., 2000).

Finally, in an exciting finding, Taylor (2002, 2006; Taylor et al., 2000) described a unique way in which females in many different species respond to stress in their lives. This unique

Jewish children, whose culture emphasizes individuality and autonomy, have been found to be less fearful of outsiders than Bedouin children in the same community, whose culture emphasizes the group and the family.

response to stress is called "tend and befriend" and refers to protecting themselves and their young through nurturing behavior (tend) and forming alliances with larger social groups, particularly other females (befriend). Taylor et al. (2000) supposed that this response fits better with the way females respond to stress because it builds on the brain's attachment–caregiving system and leads to nurturing and affiliative behavior. Furthermore, the response is characterized by identifiable neurobiological processes in the brain that are gender specific.

Our gender doesn't cause psychopathology. But because gender role is a social and cultural factor that influences the form and content of a disorder, we attend closely to it in the chapters that follow.

Social Effects on Health and Behavior

Many studies have demonstrated that the greater the number and frequency of social relationships and contacts, the longer you are likely to live (Miller, 2011). Conversely, the lower one scores on a social index that measures the richness of one's social life, the shorter one's life expectancy. Studies documenting this finding have been reported in the United States (Berkman & Syme, 1979; House, Robbins, & Metzner, 1982; Schoenbach, Kaplan, Fredman, & Kleinbaum, 1986), as well as in Sweden and Finland. They take into account existing physical health and other risk factors for dying young, such as high blood pressure, high cholesterol levels, and smoking habits, and they still produce the same result. Studies also show that social relationships seem to protect individuals against many physical and psychological disorders, such as high blood pressure, depression, alcohol use disorder, arthritis, the progression to AIDS, and bearing low birth weight babies (Cobb, 1976; House, Landis, & Umberson, 1988; Leserman et al., 2000; Thurston & Kubzanksy, 2009). Conversely, the risk of depression for people who live alone is approximately 80% higher than for people who live with others, based on a count of new prescriptions for anti-depressant medication (Pulkki-Raback et al., 2012). Also, social isolation increases the risk of death about as much as smoking cigarettes and more than physical inactivity or obesity (Holt-Lunstad, Smith, & Layton, 2010). Interestingly, it is not just the absolute number of social contacts that is important. It is the actual perception of loneliness. Thus, some people can live alone with few ill effects. Others might feel lonely despite frequent social contacts (Cacioppo, Grippo, London, Goossensm, & Cacioppo, 2015; Cacioppo & William, 2008).

Even whether or not we come down with a cold is strongly influenced by the quality and extent of our social network. Cohen, Doyle, Skoner, Rabin, and Gwaltney (1997) used nasal drops to expose 276 healthy volunteers to one of two different rhinoviruses (cold viruses); then they quarantined the participants for a week. The researchers measured the extent of participation in 12 types of social relationships (for example, spouse, parent, friend, and colleague), as well as other factors, such as smoking and poor sleep quality, that are likely to increase susceptibility to colds. The surprising results were that the greater the extent of social ties, the smaller the chance of catching a cold, even after all other factors were taken into consideration (controlled for). Those with the fewest social ties were more than four times more likely to catch a cold than those with the greatest number of ties. This effect also extends to pets! Compared with people who do not have pets, people with pets evidenced lower resting heart rate and blood pressure and responded with smaller increases in these variables during laboratory stressors (Allen, Bloscovitch, & Mendes, 2002). What could account for this? Again, social and interpersonal factors seem to influence psychological and neurobiological variables such as the immune system—sometimes to a substantial degree (Cacioppo & William, 2008). Thus, we cannot study psychological and biological aspects of psychological disorders (or physical disorders, for that matter) without taking into account the social and cultural context of the disorder.

That a multidimensional point of view is necessary is shown time and again. Consider a classic experiment with primates that illustrates the dangers of ignoring social context. Monkeys were injected with amphetamine, a central nervous system

Yellow Dog Productions/Digital Vision/Getty Images

A long and productive life usually includes strong social relationships and interpersonal relations.

stimulant (Haber & Barchas, 1983). Surprisingly, the drug had no reliable effect on the average behavior of the monkeys as a group. When the investigators divided the monkeys according to whether they were socially dominant or submissive in their group, however, dramatic effects appeared. Amphetamine increased dominant behaviors in primates that were high in the social hierarchy and submissive behaviors in those that were low in the hierarchy. Thus, the effects of a biological factor (the drug) on psychological characteristics (the behavior) were uninterpretable unless the social context of the experiment was considered.

Returning to human studies, how do social relationships have such a profound impact on our physical and psychological characteristics? We don't know for sure, but there are some intriguing hints (Cacioppo & William, 2008; Cacioppo et al., 2007). Some people think interpersonal relationships give meaning to life and that people who have something to live for can overcome physical deficiencies and even delay death. For example, an older person may far outlive their expected time in order to witness a significant family event, such as a grandchild's graduation from college. Once the event has passed, the person dies. Another common observation is that if one spouse in a long-standing marital relationship dies, particularly an older wife, the other often dies soon after, regardless of health status. It is also possible that social relationships facilitate health-promoting behaviors, such as restraint in the use of alcohol and drugs, getting proper sleep, and seeking appropriate health care (House, Landis, & Umberson, 1988; Leserman et al., 2000).

Sometimes social upheaval is an opportunity for studying the impact of social networks on individual functioning. Several decades ago when Israeli settlements in the Sinai Peninsula were dismantled and the Israeli residents were evacuated as part of peace negotiations with Egypt, Steinglass, Weisstub, and Kaplan De-Nour (1988) studied residents of an Israeli community threatened with dissolution. They found that believing oneself embedded firmly in a social context was just as important as having a social network. Poor long-term adjustment was best predicted in those who *perceived* that their social network was disintegrating, regardless of whether it actually was or not.

In another example, whether one lives in a city or the country may be associated with one's chances of developing schizophrenia, a severe disorder. In a study from Sweden, Lewis, David, Andreasson, and Allsbeck (1992) found that the incidence of schizophrenia was 38% greater in men who had been raised in cities than in those raised in rural areas. We have known for a long time that more schizophrenia exists in the city than in the country, but researchers thought people with schizophrenia who drifted to cities *after* developing schizophrenia or other endemic urban factors, such as drug use or unstable family relationships, might account for the disparity. But Lewis and associates carefully controlled for such factors, and it now seems something about cities beyond those influences may contribute to the development of schizophrenia (Boydell & Allardyce, 2011; Pedersen & Mortensen, 2006; Vassos, Pederson, Murray, Collier, & Lewis, 2012). A meta-analysis by Vassos et al. (2012) estimated that the risk for schizophrenia in the most urban environment is 2.37 times higher than in the most rural environment.

We do not yet know what it is. This finding, if it is replicated and shown to be true, may be important in view of the mass migration of individuals to overcrowded urban areas, particularly in less developed countries.

In summary, we cannot study psychopathology independently of social and interpersonal influences, and we still have much to

Neil Cooper/Alamy Stock Photo

In developing countries, personal upheaval because of political strife affects mental health.

learn. Many major psychological disorders, such as schizophrenia and major depressive disorder, seem to occur in all cultures, but they may look different from one culture to another because individual symptoms are strongly influenced by social and interpersonal context (Cheung, 2012; Cheung, van de Vijver, & Leong, 2011). For example, as you will see in Chapter 7, depression in Western culture is reflected in feelings of guilt and inadequacy and in developing countries with physical distress such as fatigue or illness.

Social and Interpersonal Influences on the Elderly

Finally, the effect of social and interpersonal factors on the expression of physical and psychological disorders may differ with age (Charles & Carstensen, 2010; Holland & Gallagher-Thompson, 2011). Grant, Patterson, and Yager (1988) studied 118 men and women 65 years or older who lived independently. Those with fewer meaningful contacts and less social support from relatives had consistently higher levels of depression and more reports of unsatisfactory quality of life. If these individuals became physically ill, however, they had more substantial support from their families than those who were not physically ill. This finding raises the unfortunate idea that it may be advantageous for older people to become physically ill because illness allows them to reestablish the social support that makes life worth living. If further research confirms this finding, we will know for fact what seems to make intuitive sense: involvement with their families before they become ill might help older adults maintain their physical health (and significantly reduce health-care costs).

The study of older adults is growing at a rapid pace. In 2010, an estimated 40 million people in the United States (13% of the population) were 65 and older, and by 2030 this number is expected to reach 71.5 million (20% of the population) (Federal Interagency Forum on Aging-Related Statistics, 2012). With this growth will come a corresponding increase in the number of older adults with mental health problems, many of whom will not receive appropriate care (Holland & Gallagher-Thompson, 2011). As you can see, understanding and treating the disorders experienced by older adults is necessary and important.

Social Stigma

Other factors make the consideration of social and cultural issues imperative to the study of psychopathology. Psychological disorders continue to carry a substantial stigma in our society (Hinshaw & Stier, 2008). To be anxious or depressed is to be weak and cowardly. To be schizophrenic is to be unpredictable and crazy. For physical injuries in times of war, we award medals. For psychological injuries, the unfortunate soldiers earn scorn and derision, as anyone knows who has seen the classic movie *Born on the Fourth of July* depicting the Vietnam War era; the 2010 Academy Award–winning *The Hurt Locker*; or the 2014 Academy Award–winning *American Sniper* portraying events in postinvasion Iraq and Afghanistan. Often a patient with psychological disorders does not seek health insurance reimbursement for fear a coworker might learn about the problem. With far less social support than for physical illness, there is less chance of full recovery and a greater risk of suicide, as we are seeing in the United States in veterans returning from Iraq and Afghanistan. We discuss some consequences of social attitudes toward psychological disorders in Chapters 3 and 16.

Global Incidence of Psychological Disorders

Important surveys from the World Health Organization (WHO) reveal that mental disorders account for 13% of the global burden of disease (WHO, 2015). Behavioral and mental health problems in developing countries are exacerbated by political strife, technological change, and massive movements from rural to urban areas. Ten to twenty percent of all primary medical services in poor countries are sought by patients with psychological disorders, principally anxiety and mood disorders (including suicide attempts), as well as alcohol use disorder, drug misuse, and childhood developmental disorders (WHO, 2015). Treatments for disorders such as depression and addictive behaviors that are successful in the United States can't be administered in countries where mental health care is limited. In Cambodia, during and after the bloody reign of the Khmer Rouge, all mental health professionals either died or disappeared. As of 2006, only 26 psychiatrists were available to see 12 million people. In sub-Saharan Africa, it's even worse, with only one psychiatrist per 2 million people (WHO, 2011). In the United States, approximately 200,000 mental health professionals serve almost 300 million people, yet only 1 in 3 persons with a psychological disorder in the United States has ever received treatment of any kind (Institute of Medicine, 2001). And despite the wonderful efforts of the Bill and Melinda Gates Foundation, there's no mention of mental health among the goals of the foundation's "Grand Challenges in Global Health" initiative. Mental disorders—and especially the most common ones, such as anxiety disorders and depression—not only impose great suffering to the affected individuals, but they also lead to high economic cost to society by being undertreated (Laird & Clark, 2014). These shocking statistics suggest that in addition to their role in causation, social and cultural factors substantially maintain disorders because most societies have not yet developed the social context for alleviating and ultimately preventing them. Changing societal attitudes is just one of the challenges facing us as the century unfolds.

Life-Span Development

Life-span developmental psychopathologists point out that we tend to look at psychological disorders from a snapshot perspective: We focus on a particular point in a person's life and assume it represents the whole person. The inadequacy of this way of looking at people should be clear. Think back on your own life over the past few years. The person you were, say,

3 years ago, is different from the person you are now, and the person you will be 3 years from now will have changed in important ways, even though we tend to have a cognitive bias called "the end of history" illusion that makes us think that we will change very little in the years to come (Quoidbach, Gilbert, & Wilson, 2013). To understand psychopathology, we must appreciate how experiences during different periods of development may influence our vulnerability to other types of stress or to differing psychological disorders (Charles & Carstensen, 2010; Rutter, 2002).

Important developmental changes occur at all points in life. For example, adulthood, far from being a relatively stable period, is highly dynamic, with important changes occurring into old age. Erik Erikson (1982) suggested that we go through eight major crises during our lives, each determined by our biological maturation and the social demands made at particular times. Unlike Freud, who envisioned no developmental stages beyond adolescence, Erikson believed that we grow and change beyond the age of 65. During older adulthood, for example, we look back and view our lives either as rewarding or as disappointing.

Although aspects of Erikson's theory of psychosocial development have been criticized as being too vague and not supported by research (Shaffer, 1993), it illustrates the comprehensive approach to human development advocated by life-span developmentalists. Basic research is beginning to confirm the importance of this approach. In one experiment, Kolb, Gibb, and Gorny (2003) placed animals in complex environments as juveniles, as adults, or in old age when cognitive abilities were beginning to decline (senescence). They found that the environment had different effects on the brains of these animals depending on their developmental stage. Basically, the complex and challenging environments increased the size and complexity of neurons in the motor and sensory cortical regions in the adult and aged animals; however, unlike the older groups, in young animals the complex and challenging environments decreased the size and complexity of neurons in the spine. Nevertheless, this decrease was associated with enhanced motor and cognitive skills when the animals became adults, indicating that stimulating environments can affect brain function in a positive way at any age. For example, it has been shown that the disease progression of disorders that typically begin in adulthood or old age, such as Huntington's disease, Alzheimer's disease, and Parkinson's, and even genetic disorders, such as fragile X and Down syndrome, can be delayed or slowed down through enriched environments (Nithianantharajah & Hannan, 2006). Even prenatal experience seems to affect brain structure because the offspring of an animal housed in a rich and complex environment during the term of her pregnancy has the advantage of more complex cortical brain circuits after birth (Kolb, Gibb, & Robinson, 2003). You may remember the study by Cameron et al. (2005) discussed earlier in the chapter, in which mother rats' behavior in the first week of their pups' lives, but not thereafter, strongly influenced the ability of the pups to handle stress throughout their lives.

Thus, we can infer that the influence of developmental stage and prior experience has a substantial impact on the development and presentation of psychological disorders, an inference that is receiving confirmation from sophisticated life-span developmental psychologists such as Laura Carstensen (Carstensen, Charles, Isaacowitz, & Kennedy, 2003; Carstensen et al., 2011; Charles & Carstensen, 2010; Isaacowitz, Smith, & Carstensen, 2003). For example, in depressive (mood) disorders, children and adolescents do not receive the same benefit from antidepressant drugs as do adults (Hazell, O'Connell, Heathcote, Robertson, & Henry, 1995; Santosh, 2009), and for many of them these drugs pose risks that are not present in adults (Santosh, 2009). Also, the gender distribution in depression is approximately equal until puberty, when it becomes more common in girls (Compas et al., 1997; Hankin, Wetter, & Cheely, 2007).

The Principle of Equifinality

Like a fever, a particular behavior or disorder may have a number of causes. The principle of **equifinality** is used in developmental psychopathology to indicate that we must consider a number of paths to a given outcome (Cicchetti, 1991). There are many examples of this principle. A delusional syndrome may be an aspect of schizophrenia, but it can also arise from amphetamine abuse. Delirium, which involves difficulty focusing attention, often occurs in older adults after surgery, but it can also result from thiamine deficiency or renal (kidney) disease. Autism can sometimes occur in children whose mothers are exposed to rubella during pregnancy, but it can also occur in children whose mothers experience difficulties during labor.

Different paths can also result from the interaction of psychological and biological factors during various stages of development. How someone copes with impairment resulting from physical causes may have a profound effect on that person's overall functioning. For example, people with documented brain damage of approximately equal severity may have different levels of disorder. Those with healthy systems of social support, consisting of family and friends, as well as highly adaptive personality characteristics, such as confidence in their abilities to overcome challenges, may experience only mild behavioral and cognitive disturbance despite physical (organic) pathology. Those without comparable support and personality may be incapacitated. This may be clearer if you think of people you know with physical disabilities. One person paralyzed from the waist down by accident or disease nevertheless becomes a superb athlete, whereas another person with the same experience feels depressed and hopeless and withdraws from life. Even the content of delusions and hallucinations that may accompany a disorder, and the degree to which they are frightening or difficult to cope with, is partly determined by psychological and social factors.

Researchers are exploring not only what makes people experience particular disorders but also what protects others from having the same difficulties. If you were interested in why someone would be depressed, for example, you would first look at people who display depression. But you could also study people in similar situations and from similar backgrounds who are not depressed. An excellent example of this approach is research on "resilient" children, which suggests that social factors may protect some children from being hurt by stressful experiences, such as one or both parents suffering a psychiatric disturbance (Becvar, 2013; Cooper, Feder, Southwick & Charney, 2007; Garmezy & Rutter, 1983; Goldstein, & Brooks, 2013). The presence of a caring adult friend or relative can offset the negative stresses of this environment, as can the child's own ability to understand and cope with unpleasant situations. More recently, scientists are discovering strong biological differences in responsiveness to trauma and stress as a result of protective factors such as social support, or having a strong purpose or meaning of life (Alim et al., 2008; Charney, 2004; Ozbay et al., 2007). Perhaps if we better understand why some people do not encounter the same problems as others in similar circumstances, we can better understand particular disorders, assist those who suffer from them, and even prevent some cases from occurring.

Conclusions

We have examined modern approaches to psychopathology, and we have found the field to be complex indeed. In this brief overview (even though it may not seem brief), we have seen that contributions from (1) psychoanalytic theory, (2) behavioral and cognitive science, (3) emotional influences, (4) social and cultural influences, (5) genetics, (6) neuroscience, and (7) life-span developmental factors all must be considered when we think about psychopathology. Even though our knowledge is incomplete, you can see why we could never resume the one-dimensional thinking typical of the various historical traditions described in Chapter 1.

And yet books about psychological disorders and news reports in the popular press often describe the causes of these disorders in one-dimensional terms without considering other influences. For example, how many times have you heard that a psychological disorder such as depression or perhaps schizophrenia is caused by a "chemical imbalance" without considering other possible causes? When you read that a disorder is *caused* by a chemical imbalance, it sounds like nothing else really matters and all you have to do is correct the imbalance in neurotransmitter activity to "cure" the problem.

Based on the research we review when we talk about specific psychological disorders, there is no question that psychological disorders are associated with altered neurotransmitter activity and other aspects of brain function (a chemical imbalance). But you have learned in this chapter that a chemical imbalance could, in turn, be caused by psychological or social factors such as stress, strong emotional reactions, difficult family interactions, changes caused by aging, or, most likely, some interaction of all these factors. Therefore, it is inaccurate and misleading to say that a psychological disorder is "caused" by a chemical imbalance, even though chemical imbalances almost certainly exist.

Similarly, how many times have you heard that alcohol use disorder or other addictive behaviors were caused by "lack of willpower," implying that if these individuals simply developed the right attitude, they could overcome their addiction? There is no question that people with severe addictions may well have motivational problems and faulty cognitive processes as indicated by rationalizing their behavior, or other faulty appraisals, or by attributing their problems to stress in their lives. They may also misperceive the effects that alcohol has on them, and these cognitions and attitudes all contribute to developing addictions. But considering only cognitive processes without considering other factors, such as genes and brain physiology, as causes of addictions would be as incorrect as saying that depression is caused by a chemical imbalance. Interpersonal, social, and cultural factors also contribute strongly to the development of addictive behaviors. To say, then, that addictive behaviors such as alcohol use disorder are caused by lack of willpower or certain faulty ways of thinking is also highly simplistic and just plain wrong.

If you learn one thing from this book, it should be that psychological disorders do not have just one cause. They have many causes—these causes all interact with one another—and we must understand this interaction to appreciate fully the origins of psychological disorders. To do this requires a multidimensional integrative approach. In chapters covering specific psychological disorders, we return to cases like Janelle's and consider them from this multidimensional integrative perspective. But first we must explore the processes of assessment and diagnosis used to measure and classify psychopathology.

Concept Check 2.5

Fill in the blanks to complete these statements relating to the cultural, social, and developmental factors influencing psychopathology.

1. What we ____________ is strongly influenced by our social environments.
2. The likelihood of your having a particular phobia is powerfully influenced by your ____________.
3. A large number of studies have demonstrated that the greater the number and frequency of ____________ relationships and ____________, the longer you are likely to live.
4. The effect of social and interpersonal factors on the expression of physical and psychological disorders may differ with ____________.
5. The principle of ____________ is used in developmental psychopathology to indicate that we must consider a number of paths to a given outcome.

Summary

One-Dimensional versus Multidimensional Models

- The causes of abnormal behavior are complex and fascinating. Psychological disorders are caused by a complex interplay of nature (biology) and nurture (psychosocial factors).
- To identify the causes of a psychological disorder in a given person, we must consider the interaction of all relevant dimensions: genetic contributions, the role of the nervous system, behavioral and cognitive processes, emotional influences, social and interpersonal influences, and developmental factors. Thus, we have arrived at a multidimensional integrative approach to the causes of psychological disorders.

Genetic Contributions to Psychopathology

- The genetic influence on much of our development and most of our behavior, personality, and even IQ score is polygenic—that is, influenced by many genes. This is assumed to be the case in abnormal behavior as well, although research is beginning to identify specific small groups of genes that relate to some major psychological disorders.
- In studying causal relationships in psychopathology, researchers look at the interactions of genetic and environmental effects. In the diathesis–stress model, individuals are assumed to inherit certain vulnerabilities that make them susceptible to a disorder when the right kind of stressor comes along. In the gene–environment correlation or reciprocal gene–environment model, the individual's genetic vulnerability toward a certain disorder may make it more likely that the person will experience the stressor that, in turn, triggers the genetic vulnerability and thus the disorder. In epigenetics, the immediate effects of the environment (such as early stressful experiences) influence cells that turn certain genes on or off. This effect may be passed down through several generations.

Neuroscience and Its Contributions to Psychopathology

- Brain science and the field of neuroscience promise much as we try to unravel the mysteries of psychopathology. Within the nervous system, levels of neurotransmitter and neuroendocrine activity interact in complex ways to modulate and regulate emotions and behavior and contribute to psychological disorders.
- Critical to our understanding of psychopathology are the neurotransmitter currents called brain circuits. Of the neurotransmitters that may play a key role, we investigated five: serotonin, gamma-aminobutyric acid (GABA), glutamate, norepinephrine, and dopamine.

Behavioral and Cognitive Science

- The relatively new field of cognitive science provides a valuable perspective on how behavioral and cognitive influences affect the learning and adaptation each of us experience throughout life. Clearly, such influences not only contribute to psychological disorders but also may directly modify brain functioning, brain structure, and even genetic expression. We examined some research in this field by looking at learned helplessness, modeling, prepared learning, and implicit memory.

Emotions

- Emotions have a direct and dramatic impact on our functioning and play a central role in many mental disorders. Mood, a persistent period of emotionality, is often evident in psychological disorders.

Cultural, Social, and Interpersonal Factors

- Social and interpersonal influences profoundly affect both psychological disorders and biology.

Life-Span Development

- In considering a multidimensional integrative approach to psychopathology, it is important to remember the principle of equifinality, which reminds us that we must consider the various paths to a particular outcome, not just the result.

Key Terms

multidimensional integrative approach, 31
genes, 34
diathesis–stress model, 36
vulnerability, 37
gene–environment correlation model, 38
epigenetics, 40
neuroscience, 41
neuron, 42
action potentials, 42
terminal button, 42
synaptic cleft, 42
neurotransmitters, 42
excitatory, 43
inhibitory, 43
hormone, 45
brain circuits, 47
agonist, 47
antagonist, 48
inverse agonist, 48
reuptake, 48
glutamate, 48
gamma-aminobutyric acid (GABA), 48
serotonin, 48
norepinephrine (also noradrenaline), 49
dopamine, 51
microbiota, 56
brain–gut connection, 56
cognitive science, 57
learned helplessness, 58
modeling (also observational learning), 58
prepared learning, 58
implicit memory, 59
flight or fight response, 60
emotion, 60
mood, 61
affect, 61
circumplex model, 61
equifinality, 68

Answers to Concept Checks

2.1

1. b; **2.** a (best answer) or c; **3.** e; **4.** a (initial), c (maintenance)

2.2

1. F (first 22 pairs); **2.** T; **3.** T; **4.** F (reciprocal gene–environment model); **5.** F (complex interaction of both nature and nurture)

2.3

1. b; **2.** c; **3.** f; **4.** g; **5.** d; **6.** e; 7. h; **8.** a

2.4

1. b; **2.** a; **3.** d; **4.** c

2.5

1. fear; **2.** gender; **3.** social, contacts; **4.** age; **5.** equifinality

3 Clinical Assessment and Diagnosis

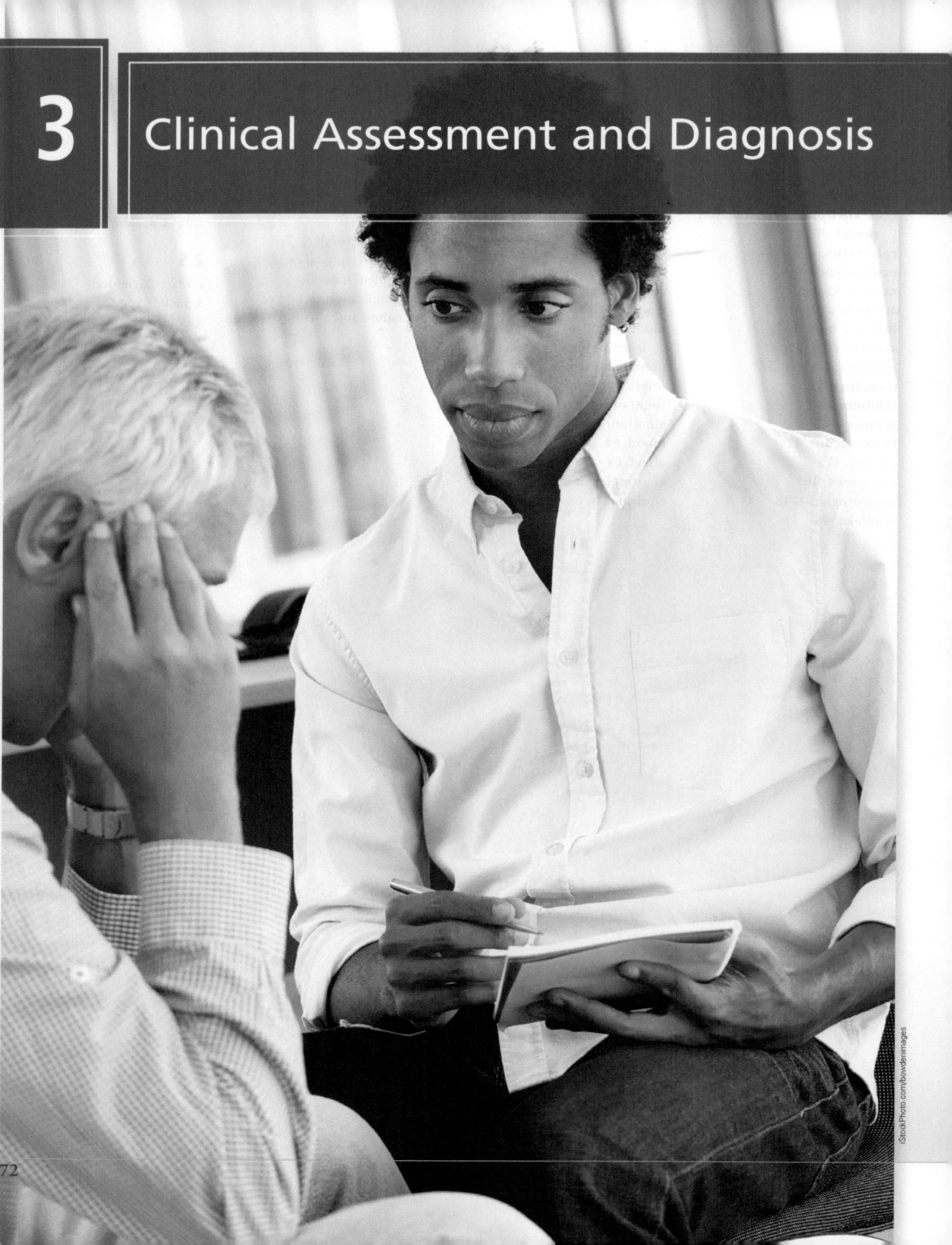

iStockPhoto.com/bowdenimages

Learning Objectives

LO3.1 Define *clinical assessment* in terms of the goals of assessment and key components of high-quality assessments.

LO3.2 Discuss how projective tests, personality inventories, and intelligence testing are used to determine a person's mental functioning.

LO3.3 Explain the benefits of administering neuropsychological testing, neuroimaging, and psychophysiological assessment to individuals with psychological disorders.

LO3.4 Describe the strengths and weaknesses of categorical, dimensional, and prototypical approaches to classifying mental disorders.

Assessing Psychological Disorders

The processes of clinical assessment and diagnosis are central to the study of psychopathology and, ultimately, to the treatment of psychological disorders. **Clinical assessment** is the systematic evaluation and measurement of psychological, biological, and social factors in an individual presenting with a possible psychological disorder. **Diagnosis** is the process of determining whether the particular problem afflicting the individual meets all criteria for a psychological disorder, as set forth in the fifth edition of the *Diagnostic and Statistical Manual of Mental Disorders,* or DSM-5 (American Psychiatric Association, 2013). In this chapter, after demonstrating assessment and diagnosis within the context of an actual case, we examine the development of the DSM into a widely used classification system for abnormal behavior. Then we review the many assessment techniques available to the clinician. Finally, we turn to diagnostic issues and the related challenges of classification.

Frank... Young, Serious, and Anxious

Frank was referred to one of our clinics for evaluation and possible treatment of severe distress and anxiety centering on his marriage. He arrived neatly dressed in his work clothes (he was a mechanic). He reported that he was 24 years old and that this was the first time he had ever seen a mental health professional. He wasn't sure that he needed (or wanted) to be there, but he felt he was beginning to "come apart" because of his marital difficulties. He figured that it certainly wouldn't hurt to come once to see whether we could help. What follows is a transcript of parts of this first interview.

THERAPIST: What sorts of problems have been troubling you during the past month?

FRANK: I'm beginning to have a lot of marital problems. I was married about 9 months ago, but I've been really tense around the house, and we've been having a lot of arguments.

THERAPIST: Is this something recent?

FRANK: Well, it wasn't too bad at first, but it's been worse lately. I've also been really uptight in my job, and I haven't been getting my work done.

Note that we always begin by asking the patient to describe for us, in a relatively open-ended way, the major difficulties that brought them to the office. When dealing with adults or children old enough (or verbal enough) to tell us their story, this strategy tends to break the ice. It also allows us to relate details of the patient's life revealed later in the interview to the central problems as seen through the patient's eyes.

After Frank described this major problem in some detail, we asked him about his marriage, his job, and other current life circumstances. Frank reported that he had worked steadily in an auto body repair shop for the past 4 years and that, 9 months previously, he had married a 17-year-old woman. After getting a better picture of his current situation, we returned to his feelings of distress and anxiety.

THERAPIST: When you feel uptight at work, is it the same kind of feeling you have at home?

FRANK: Pretty much; I just can't seem to concentrate, and lots of times I lose track of what my wife's saying to me, which makes her mad, and then we'll have a big fight.

THERAPIST: Are you thinking about something when you lose your concentration, such as your work or maybe other things?

FRANK: Oh, I don't know; I guess I just worry a lot.

THERAPIST: What do you find yourself worrying about most of the time?

FRANK: Well, I worry about getting fired and then not being able to support my family. A lot of the time I feel like I'm going to catch something—you know, get sick and not be able to work. Basically, I guess I'm afraid of getting sick and then failing at my job and in my marriage, and having my parents and her parents both telling me what an ass I was for getting married in the first place.

During the first 10 minutes or so of the interview, Frank seemed to be quite tense and anxious and would often look down at the floor while he talked, glancing up only occasionally to make eye contact. Sometimes his right leg would twitch a bit. Although it was not easy to see at first because he was looking down, Frank was also closing his eyes tightly for a period of 2 to 3 seconds. It was during these periods when his eyes were closed that his right leg would twitch.

The interview proceeded for the next half hour, exploring marital and job issues. It became increasingly clear that Frank was feeling inadequate and anxious about handling situations in his life. By this time, he was talking freely and looking up a little more at the therapist, but he was continuing to close his eyes and twitch his right leg slightly.

THERAPIST: Are you aware that once in a while you're closing your eyes while you're telling me this?

FRANK: I'm not aware all the time, but I know I do it.

THERAPIST: Do you know how long you've been doing that?

FRANK: Oh, I don't know, maybe a year or two.

THERAPIST: Are you thinking about anything when you close your eyes?

FRANK: Well, actually I'm trying not to think about something.

THERAPIST: What do you mean?

FRANK: Well, I have these really frightening and stupid thoughts, and … it's hard to even talk about it.

THERAPIST: The thoughts are frightening?

FRANK: Yes, I keep thinking I'm going to take a fit, and I'm just trying to get that out of my mind.

THERAPIST: Could you tell me more about this fit?

FRANK: Well, you know, it's those terrible things where people fall down and they froth at the mouth, and their tongues come out, and they shake all over. You know, seizures. I think they call it epilepsy.

THERAPIST: And you're trying to get these thoughts out of your mind?

Frank: Oh, I do everything possible to get those thoughts out of my mind as quickly as I can.

THERAPIST: I've noticed you moving your leg when you close your eyes. Is that part of it?

FRANK: Yes, I've noticed if I really jerk my leg and pray real hard for a little while, the thought will go away.

Excerpt from R. O. Nelson & D. H. Barlow, 1981, Behavioral assessment: Basic strategies and initial procedures, in D. H. Barlow (Ed.), *Behavioral assessment of adult disorders*, Guilford Press. •

What's wrong with Frank? The first interview reveals an insecure young man experiencing substantial stress as he questions whether he is capable of handling marriage and a job. He reports that he loves his wife very much and wants the marriage to work and he is attempting to be as conscientious as possible on his job, a job from which he derives a lot of satisfaction and enjoyment. Also, for some reason, he is having troubling thoughts about seizures. Now let's consider one more case for purposes of illustration.

Brian... Suspicious Ideas

Brian was 20 years old and had recently been discharged from a tour of duty in the army. He was referred by a psychiatrist in another state for evaluation of sexual problems. What follows is a greatly abbreviated transcript.

THERAPIST: What seems to be the problem?

BRIAN: I'm a homosexual.

THERAPIST: You're a homosexual?

BRIAN: Yes, and I want to be straight. Who wants to be queer?

THERAPIST: Do you have any homosexual friends or lovers?

BRIAN: No, I wouldn't get near them.

THERAPIST: How often do you engage in homosexual behavior?

BRIAN: Well, I haven't as of yet, but it's no secret that I'm homosexual, and it's just a matter of time before it happens, I suppose.

THERAPIST: Do you have somebody specifically in mind? Are you attracted to somebody?

BRIAN: No, but others are attracted to me. I can tell by the way they look at me.

THERAPIST: The way they look at you?

BRIAN: Yes, the look in their eyes.

THERAPIST: Has anyone ever actually approached you or said anything to you about being homosexual?

BRIAN: No, not to me; they wouldn't dare. But I know they talk about me behind my back.

THERAPIST: How do you know that?

BRIAN: Well, sometimes the guys will be talking in the next room, and the only thing they could be talking about is that I'm queer. (Nelson & Barlow, 1981, p. 20) •

So where do we go from here? Where do you think Brian got these ideas? And how do we determine whether Frank has a psychological disorder or is simply one of many young men suffering the normal stresses and strains of a new marriage who, perhaps, could benefit from some marital counseling? The purpose of this chapter is to illustrate how mental health clinicians address these types of questions in a systematic way, assessing patients to study the basic nature of psychopathology, as well as to make diagnoses and plan treatment.

Key Concepts in Assessment

The process of clinical assessment in psychopathology has been likened to a funnel (Antony & Barlow, 2010; Hunsley & Mash, 2011; Urbina, 2014). The clinician begins by collecting a lot of information across a broad range of the individual's functioning to determine where the source of the problem may lie. After getting a preliminary sense of the overall functioning of the person, the clinician narrows the focus by ruling out problems in some areas and concentrating on areas that seem most relevant.

To understand the different ways clinicians assess psychological problems, we need to understand three basic concepts that help determine the value of our assessments: reliability, validity, and standardization (Ayearst & Bagby, 2010)

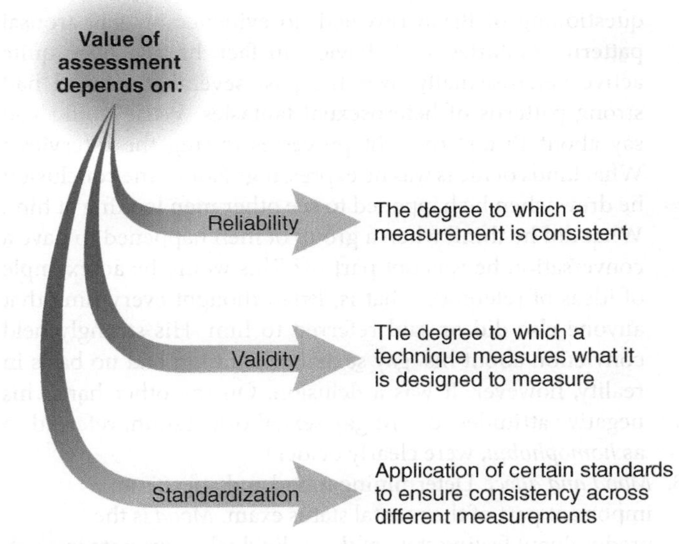

Figure 3.1

Concepts that determine the value of clinical assessments.

(see ■ Figure 3.1). Assessment techniques are subject to a number of strict requirements, not the least of which is some evidence (research) that they actually do what they are designed to do. One of the more important requirements of these assessments is that they be reliable. **Reliability** is the degree to which a measurement is consistent. Imagine how irritated you would be if you had stomach pain and you went to four competent physicians and got four different diagnoses and four different treatments. The diagnoses would be said to be unreliable because two or more "raters" (the physicians) did not agree on the conclusion. We expect, in general, that presenting the same symptoms to different physicians will result in similar diagnoses. One way psychologists improve their reliability is by carefully designing their assessment devices and then conducting research on them to ensure that two or more raters will get the same answers (called *interrater reliability*). They also determine whether these assessment techniques are stable across time. In other words, if you go to a clinician on Tuesday and are told you have an IQ of 110, you should expect a similar result if you take the same test again on Thursday. This is known as *test–retest reliability.* We will return to the concept of reliability when we talk about diagnoses and classification.

Validity is whether something measures what it is designed to measure—in this case, whether a technique assesses what it is supposed to. Comparing the results of an assessment measure under consideration with the results of others that are better known allows you to begin to determine the validity of the first measure. This comparison is called *concurrent* or *descriptive validity.* For example, if the results from a standard, long IQ test were essentially the same as the results from a new, brief version, you could conclude that the brief version had concurrent validity. *Predictive validity* is how well your assessment tells you what will happen in the future. For example, does it predict who will succeed in school and who will not (which is one of the goals of an IQ test)?

During their first meeting, the mental health professional focuses on the problem that brought the person to treatment.

Standardization is the process by which a certain set of standards or norms is determined for a technique to make its use consistent across different measurements. The standards might apply to the procedures of testing, scoring, and evaluating data. For example, the assessment might be given to large numbers of people who differ on important factors such as age, race, gender, socioeconomic status, and diagnosis. Their scores would be pooled with other individuals like them and then be used as a standard, or norm, for comparison purposes. For example, if you are an African American person, 19 years old, and from a middle-class background, your score on a psychological test should be compared with the scores of others like you and not to the scores of different people, such people of Asian descent in their 60s from working-class backgrounds. Reliability, validity, and standardization are important to all forms of psychological assessment.

Clinical assessment consists of a number of strategies and procedures that help clinicians acquire the information they need to understand their patients and assist them. These procedures include a clinical interview and, within the context of the interview, a mental status exam that can be administered either formally or informally; often a thorough physical examination; a behavioral observation and assessment; and psychological tests (if needed).

The Clinical Interview

Psychologists, psychiatrists, and other mental health professionals use the clinical interview, the core of most clinical work. The interview gathers information on current and past behavior, attitudes, and emotions, as well as a detailed history of the individual's life in general and of the presenting problem. Clinicians determine when the specific problem started and identify other events (for example, life stress, trauma, or physical illness) that might have occurred about the same time. In addition, most clinicians gather at least some information on the patient's current and past interpersonal and social history, including family makeup (for example, marital status, number of children, or college student currently living with parents), and on the individual's upbringing. Information on sexual development, religious attitudes (current and past), relevant cultural concerns (such as stress induced by discrimination), and educational history are routinely collected. To organize information obtained during an interview, many clinicians use a mental status exam.

The Mental Status Exam

In essence, the **mental status exam** involves the systematic observation of an individual's behavior. This type of observation occurs when any one person interacts with another. All of us, clinicians and nonclinicians alike, perform daily pseudo–mental status exams. The trick for clinicians is to organize their observations of other people in a way that gives them sufficient information to determine whether a psychological disorder might be present (Nelson & Barlow, 1981). Mental status exams can be structured and detailed (Wiger & Mooney, 2015; Wing, Cooper, & Sartorius, 1974), but mostly they are performed relatively quickly by experienced clinicians in the course of interviewing or observing a patient. The exam covers five categories:

1. *Appearance and behavior.* The clinician notes any overt physical behaviors, such as Frank's leg twitch, as well as the individual's dress, general appearance, posture, and facial expression. For example, slow and effortful motor behavior, sometimes referred to as *psychomotor retardation,* may indicate severe depression.
2. *Thought processes.* When clinicians listen to a patient talk, they're getting a good idea of that person's thought processes. They might look for several things here. For example, what is the rate or flow of speech? Does the person talk quickly or slowly? What about continuity of speech? In other words, does the patient make sense when talking, or are ideas presented with no apparent connection? In some patients with schizophrenia, a disorganized speech pattern, referred to as *loose association* or *derailment,* is quite noticeable. Clinicians sometimes ask specific questions. If the patient shows difficulty with continuity or rate of speech, a clinician might ask, "Can you think clearly, or is there some problem putting your thoughts together? Do your thoughts tend to be mixed up or come slowly?"

   In addition to rate or flow and continuity of speech, what about the content? Is there any evidence of *delusions* (distorted views of reality)? Typical delusions would be *delusions of persecution,* in which someone thinks people are after him and out to get him all the time, or *delusions of grandeur,* in which an individual thinks she is all-powerful in some way. The individual might also have *ideas of reference,* in which everything everyone else does somehow relates back to the individual. The most common example would be thinking that a conversation between two strangers on the other side of the room must be about you. *Hallucinations* are things a person sees or hears when those things really aren't there. For example, the clinician might say, "Let me ask you a couple of routine questions that we ask everybody. Do you ever see things or maybe hear things when you know there is nothing there?"

   Now think back to the case of Brian. Extensive questioning of Brian revealed no evidence of gay arousal patterns, fantasies, or behavior. In fact, he had been quite active heterosexually over the past several years and had strong patterns of heterosexual fantasies. What would you say about Brian's thought processes during the interview? What kinds of ideas was he expressing? Notice the conclusion he drew when he happened to see other men looking at him. What did he think when a group of men happened to have a conversation he was not part of? This would be an example of ideas of reference. That is, Brian thought everything that anyone else did or said referred to him. His strongly held conviction about his gay sexual orientation had no basis in reality, however. It was a delusion. On the other hand, his negative attitudes toward gay sexual orientation, referred to as *homophobia,* were clearly evident.
3. *Mood and affect.* Determining mood and affect is an important part of the mental status exam. *Mood* is the predominant feeling state of the individual, as we note in Chapter 2. Does the person appear to be down in the dumps or continually elated? Does the individual talk in a depressed or hopeless fashion? How pervasive is this mood? Are there times when the depression seems to go away? *Affect,* by contrast, refers to the feeling state that accompanies what we say at a given point. Usually our affect is "appropriate"; that is, we laugh when we say something funny or look sad when we talk about something sad. If a friend just told you his mother died and is laughing about it, or if your friend has just won the lottery and she is crying, you would think it strange, to say the least. A mental health clinician would note that your friend's affect is "inappropriate." Then again, you might observe your friend talking about a range of happy and sad things with no affect whatsoever. In this case, a mental health clinician would say the affect is "blunted" or "flat."
4. *Intellectual functioning.* Clinicians make a rough estimate of others' intellectual functioning just by talking to them. Do they seem to have a reasonable vocabulary? Can they talk in abstractions and metaphors (as most of us do much of the time)? How is the person's memory? Clinicians usually make a rough estimate of intelligence that is noticeable only if it deviates from normal, such as concluding the person is above or below average intelligence.
5. *Sensorium.* The term *sensorium* refers to our general awareness of our surroundings. Does an individual know what the date is, what time it is, where they are, who they are, and who you are? Most of us are fully aware of these facts. People with permanent brain damage or dysfunction—or temporary brain damage or dysfunction, often because of drugs or other toxic states—may not know the answer to these questions. If the patient knows who they are and who the clinician is and has a good idea of the time and place, the clinician would say that the patient's sensorium is "clear" and is "oriented times three" (to person, place, and time).

What can we conclude from these informal behavioral observations? Basically, they allow the clinician to make a preliminary determination of which areas of the patient's behavior and condition should be assessed in more detail and perhaps more formally. If psychological disorders remain a possibility, the clinician may begin to hypothesize which disorders might be present. This process, in turn, provides more focus for the assessment and diagnostic activities to come.

Returning to our case, what have we learned from this mental status exam (see ■ Figure 3.2)? Observing Frank's persistent motor behavior in the form of a twitch led to the discovery of a connection (functional relationship) with his troublesome thoughts regarding seizures. Beyond this, his appearance was appropriate, and the flow and content of his speech was reasonable; his intelligence was well within normal limits, and he was oriented times three. He did display an anxious mood; however, his affect was appropriate to what he was saying. These observations suggested that we direct the remainder of the clinical interview and additional assessment and diagnostic activities to identify the possible existence of a disorder characterized by intrusive, unwanted thoughts and the attempt to resist them—in other words, *obsessive-compulsive disorder (OCD)*. Later we describe some specific assessment strategies, from among many choices, that we would use with Frank.

Patients usually have a good idea of their major concerns in a general sense ("I'm depressed" or "I'm phobic"). Occasionally, the problem reported by the patient may not, after assessment, be the major issue in the eyes of the mental health clinician. The case of Frank illustrates this point well: He complained of distress relating to marital problems, but the clinician decided, on the basis of the initial interview, that the principal difficulties lay elsewhere. Frank wasn't attempting to hide anything from the clinician. Frank just didn't think his intrusive thoughts were the major problem; in addition, talking about them was difficult for him because they were quite frightening.

This example illustrates the importance of conducting the clinical interview in a way that elicits the patient's trust and empathy. Psychologists and other mental health professionals are trained extensively in methods that put patients at ease and facilitate communication, including nonthreatening ways of seeking information and appropriate listening skills. Information provided by patients to psychologists and psychiatrists is protected by laws of "privileged communication" or confidentiality in most states; that is, even if authorities want the information the therapist has received from the patient, they cannot have access to it without the expressed consent of the patient. The only exception to this rule occurs when the clinician judges that, because of the patient's condition, some harm or danger to either the patient or someone else is imminent. At the outset of the initial interview, the therapist should inform the patient of the confidential nature of their conversation and the (quite rare) conditions under which that confidence would not hold.

Despite these assurances of confidentiality and the clinician's interview skills, patients sometimes find it difficult to volunteer sensitive information. In our own files is the case of a man in his early 20s who came to therapy once a week for 5 months. He wanted help with what he viewed as deficient interpersonal skills and anxieties that were impeding his ability to relate to other people. Only after 5 months, and quite by chance during a particularly emotional session, did he reveal his secret. He was strongly sexually attracted to small boys and confessed that he found their feet and associated objects such as socks and shoes to be nearly irresistible. Although he had never actually approached any young boys, he had hidden in his home a large collection of small socks and shoes. Confidentiality had been assured, and the therapist was there to help, so there was no rational reason not to tell the therapist. Nevertheless, the patient found it almost impossible

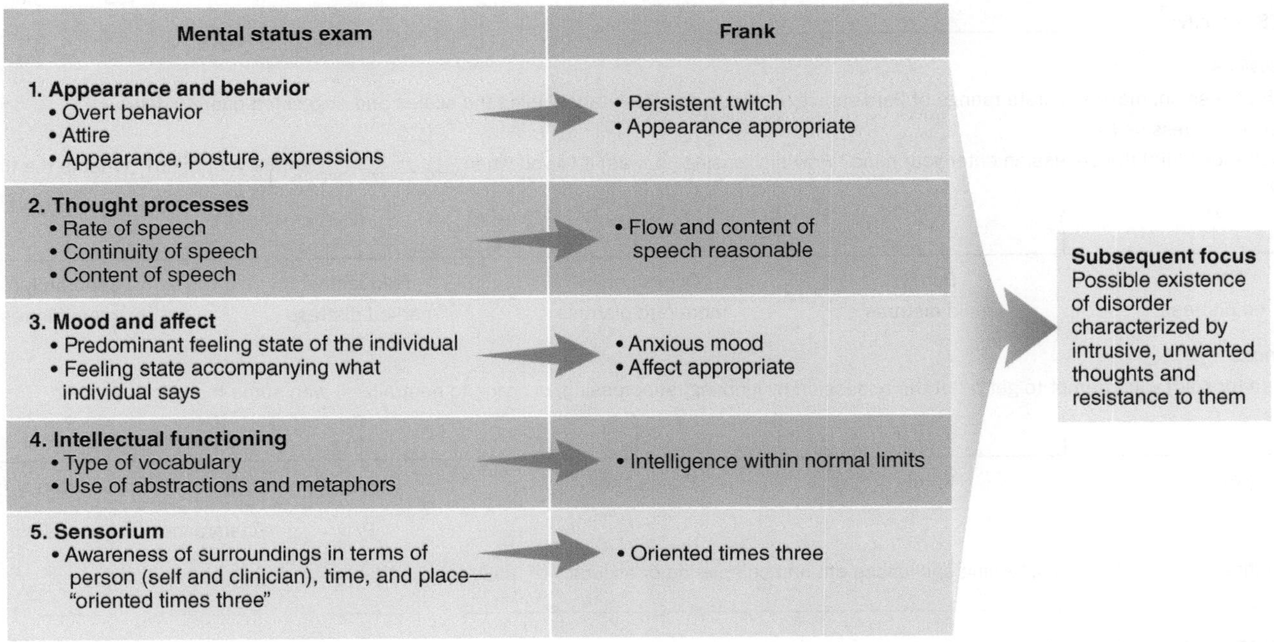

Figure 3.2

Components of the mental status exam.

to volunteer this information. There may well have been signs during the 5 months of treatment that the patient's problems involved issues other than those he had communicated, but if there were, the therapist missed them.

Semistructured Clinical Interviews

Until relatively recently, most clinicians, after training, developed their own methods of collecting necessary information from patients. Different patients seeing different psychologists or other mental health professionals might encounter markedly different types and styles of interviews. Unstructured interviews follow no systematic format. *Semistructured interviews* are made up of questions that have been carefully phrased and tested to elicit useful information in a consistent manner so that clinicians can be sure they have inquired about the most important aspects of particular disorders (Galletta, 2013; Summerfeldt, Kloosterman, & Antony, 2010). Clinicians may also depart from set questions to follow up on specific issues—thus the label "semistructured." Because the wording and sequencing of questions has been carefully worked out over a number of years, the clinician can feel confident that a semistructured interview will accomplish its purpose. The disadvantage is that it robs the interview of some of the spontaneous quality of two people talking about a problem. Also, if applied too rigidly, a semistructured interview may inhibit the patient from volunteering useful information that is not directly relevant to the questions being asked. Because of these few drawbacks associated with semistructured interviews, fully structured interviews administered wholly by a computer have not caught on, although they are used in some settings.

An increasing number of mental health professionals, however, do routinely use semistructured interviews. Some are quite specialized. For example, Frank's clinician, in probing further into a possible obsessive-compulsive disorder, might use the *Anxiety and Related Disorders Interview Schedule for* DSM-5 *(ADIS-5)* (Brown & Barlow, 2014). According to this interview schedule, shown in Table 3.1, the clinician first asks if the patient is bothered by thoughts, images, or impulses (obsessions) or feels driven to experience some behavior or thought repeatedly (compulsions). Based on a 9-point rating scale that ranges from "never" to "constantly," the clinician then asks the patient to rate each obsession on two measures: persistence–distress (how often it occurs and how much distress it causes) and resistance (types of attempts the patient makes to get rid of the obsession). For compulsions, the patient provides a rating of their frequency.

Table 3.1 Sample Questions for Assessing Obsessive-Compulsive Disorder

1. *Initial inquiry*

Currently, are you bothered by thoughts, images, or impulses that keep recurring to you and seem inappropriate or nonsensical but that you can't stop from coming into your mind? yes ____ no ____

If YES, specify: ________________

Currently, do you feel driven to repeat some behavior or to repeat something in your mind over and over again to try to feel less uncomfortable? yes ____ no ____

If YES, specify: ________________

2. *Obsessions:*

For each obsession, make separate ratings of Persistence/Distress and Resistance using the scales and suggested queries below.

Persistence/Distress (P/D):

How often [does/did] the obsession enter your mind? How distressing [is/was] it to you when ________ enters your mind? (What is the time frame?)

0	1	2	3	4	5	6	7	8
Never/ no distress		Rarely/ mild distress		Occasionally/ moderate distress		Frequently/ marked distress		Constantly/ extreme distress

Resistance:

How often [do/did] you attempt to get rid of the obsession by ignoring, suppressing, or trying to neutralize it with some thought or action?

0	1	2	3	4	5	6	7	8
Never		Rarely		Occasionally		Frequently		Constantly

	P/D	Resistance	Comments
1. Doubting (for example, locks, turning appliances off, and completion or accuracy of tasks) ________________	____	____	____
2. Contamination (for example, contracting germs from doorknobs, toilets, or money, etc.) ________________	____	____	____

Table 3.1 **Sample Questions for Assessing Obsessive-Compulsive Disorder *(continued)***

3. Nonsensical urges (for example, shouting or undressing in public)

4. Aggressive urges (for example, hurting oneself or others, destroying objects)

5. Unwanted sexual thoughts/images (for example, distressing obscene thoughts or images)

6. Unwanted religious/Satanic thoughts/images (for example, blasphemous thoughts or impulses)

7. Accidental harm to others (for example, hurting someone unknowingly by poisoning, hitting with a car, etc.)

8. Horrific images (for example, mutilated bodies)

9. Nonsensical thoughts or images (for example, numbers, letters, or songs)

10. Other

11. Other

3. Compulsions:

For each compulsion, make ratings of frequency using the scale and suggested queries below.

Frequency:

How often (are/were) you driven to perform such an action? (What is the time frame?)

0	1	2	3	4	5	6	7	8
Never		Rarely		Occasionally		Frequently		Constantly

Current compulsion

Frequency   Comments

1. Checking (for example, locks, appliances, driving routes, important papers, wastebaskets)

2. Washing (for example, self, household objects)

3. Counting (for example, certain letters or numbers, objects in the environment)

4. Internal repetition (for example, phrases, words, prayers)

5. Adhering to rules or behavioral sequences (for example, ordering/symmetry, ritualistic acts, or adhering to a specific daily routine)

6. Other

7. Other

Source: Adapted and reprinted, with permission, from T. A. Brown & D. H. Barlow, 2013, *Anxiety and Related Disorders Interview Schedule for DSM-5* (ADIS.5), Oxford University Press.

Physical Examination

Many patients with problems first go to a family physician and are given a physical. If the patient presenting with psychological problems has not had a physical exam in the past year, a clinician might recommend one, with particular attention to the medical conditions sometimes associated with the specific psychological problem. Many problems presenting as disorders of behavior, cognition, or mood may, on careful physical examination, have a clear relationship to a temporary toxic state. This toxic state could be caused by a lack of certain nutrients , the wrong amount or type of medicine, or onset of a medical condition. For example, thyroid difficulties, particularly hyperthyroidism (overactive thyroid gland), may produce symptoms that mimic certain anxiety disorders, such as generalized anxiety disorder. Hypothyroidism (underactive thyroid gland) might produce symptoms consistent with depression. Certain psychotic symptoms, including delusions or hallucinations, might be associated with the development of a brain tumor. Withdrawal from cocaine often produces panic attacks, but many patients presenting with panic attacks are reluctant to volunteer information about their addiction, which may lead to an inappropriate diagnosis and improper treatment.

Usually, psychologists and other mental health professionals are well aware of the medical conditions and drug use and misuse that may contribute to the kinds of problems described by the patient. If a current medical condition or substance abuse situation exists, the clinician must ascertain whether it is merely coexisting or is causal, usually by looking at the onset of the problem. If a patient has suffered from severe bouts of depression for the past 5 years but within the past year has also developed hypothyroid problems or begun taking a sedative drug, then the clinician would not conclude the depression was caused by the medical or drug condition. On the other hand, if the depression developed simultaneously with the initiation of sedative drugs and diminished considerably when the drugs were discontinued, the clinician would be likely to conclude the depression was part of a substance-induced mood disorder.

Behavioral Assessment

The mental status exam is one way to begin to sample how people think, feel, and behave and how these actions might contribute to or explain their problems (Black & Andreasen, 2021a). **Behavioral assessment** takes this process one step further by using direct observation to formally assess an individual's thoughts, feelings, and behavior in specific situations or contexts. Behavioral assessment may be more appropriate than an interview in terms of assessing individuals who are not old enough or skilled enough to report their problems and experiences. Clinical interviews sometimes provide limited assessment information. For instance, young children or individuals who are not verbal because of the nature of their disorder or because of cognitive deficits or impairments are not good candidates for clinical interviews. As we already mentioned, sometimes people withhold information deliberately because it is embarrassing or unintentionally because they aren't aware it is important. In addition to talking with a patient in an office about a problem, some clinicians go to the person's home or workplace or even into the local community to observe the person and the reported problems directly. Others set up role-play simulations in a clinical setting to see how people might behave in similar situations in their daily lives. These techniques are all types of behavioral assessment (Chafouleas, Johnson, Riley-Tillman, & Iovino, 2021).

In behavioral assessment, target behaviors are identified and observed with the goal of determining the factors that seem to influence them. It may seem easy to identify what is bothering a particular person (that is, the target behavior), but even this aspect of assessment can be challenging. For example, when the mother of a 7-year-old child with a severe conduct disorder came to one of our clinics for assistance, she told the clinician, after much prodding, that her son "didn't listen to her" and sometimes had an "attitude." The boy's schoolteacher, however, painted a different picture. She spoke candidly of his verbal violence—of his threats toward other children and to herself, threats she took seriously. To get a clearer picture of the situation at home, the clinician visited one afternoon. Approximately 15 minutes after the visit began, the boy got up from the kitchen table without removing the drinking glass he was using. When his mother quite meekly asked him to put the glass in the sink, he picked it up and threw it across the room, sending broken glass throughout the kitchen. He giggled and went into his room to watch television. "See," she said. "He doesn't listen to me!"

Obviously, this mother's description of her son's behavior at home did not portray what he was really like. It also did not accurately describe her response to his violent outbursts. Without the home visit, the clinician's assessment of the problem and recommendations for treatment would have been different. Clearly, this was more than simple disobedience. We developed strategies to teach the mother how to make requests of her son and how to follow up if he was violent.

Getting back to Frank and his anxiety about his marriage: How do we know he is telling the "truth" about his relationship with his wife? Is what he is not telling us important? What would we find if we observed Frank and his wife interacting in their home, or if they had a typical conversation in front of us in a clinical setting? Most clinicians assume that a complete picture of a person's problems requires direct observation in naturalistic environments. But going into a person's home, workplace, or school isn't always possible or practical, so clinicians sometimes arrange *analogue,* or similar, settings (for example, Choi, Kim, Comstock, & Havlik, 2020; Overstreet, Pomerantz, Segrist, & Ro, in press). For example, one of us studies children with autism spectrum disorder (a disorder characterized by social withdrawal and communication problems; see Chapter 14). The reasons for self-hitting (called *self-injurious*) behavior in this disorder are discovered by placing the children in simulated situations, such as sitting alone at home, playing with a sibling, or being asked to complete a difficult task (Durand, Hieneman, Clarke, Wang, & Rinaldi, 2013). Observing how the children behave in these different situations helps us determine why they hit themselves so that we can design a successful treatment to eliminate the behavior. Other researchers are using hypnosis to produce analogue assessments (conditions that mimic real-life clinical symptoms or situations) by inducing symptoms of psychopathology to study these characteristics in a more controlled way (Cioffi et al., 2020). In one example, researchers studied perceptual distortions and delusional thinking (a symptom of schizophrenia we discuss in Chapter 13) in healthy volunteers by giving them the hallucinogenic anesthetic ketamine, all the while conducting brain scans to see how their brain reacted (Stone et al., 2015). As you can see, researchers are using a variety of new creative techniques to study psychological disorders.

Some areas of psychopathology are difficult to study without resorting to analogue models. For instance, one study examined the tendency of some men to sexually harass women (Bosson et al., 2015). Men in the study had the opportunity to send film clips—some with potentially offensive sexual content and others without—to a fake female partner online who claimed to dislike sexual content in films. Choosing to send the explicit film clips corresponded with the men's history of sexual assault over the past year. This type of assessment allowed the researchers to study aspects of sexual harassment without having to subject others to negative behaviors. These types of observations are useful when developing screenings and treatments.

The ABCs of Observation

Observational assessment is usually focused on the here and now. Therefore, the clinician's attention is usually directed to the immediate behavior, its antecedents (what happened just before the behavior), and its consequences (what happened afterward) (Chafouleas et al., 2021). To use the example of the violent boy, an observer would note that the sequence of events was (1) his mother asking him to put his glass in the sink (antecedent), (2) the boy throwing the glass (behavior), and (3) his mother's lack of response (consequence). This antecedent–behavior–consequence sequence (the ABCs) might suggest that the boy was being reinforced for his violent outburst by not having to clean up his mess. And because there was no negative consequence for his behavior (his mother didn't scold or reprimand him), he will probably act violently the next time he doesn't want to do something (see ■ Figure 3.3).

This is an example of a relatively *informal observation*. A problem with this type of observation is that it relies on the observer's recollection, as well as interpretation, of the events.

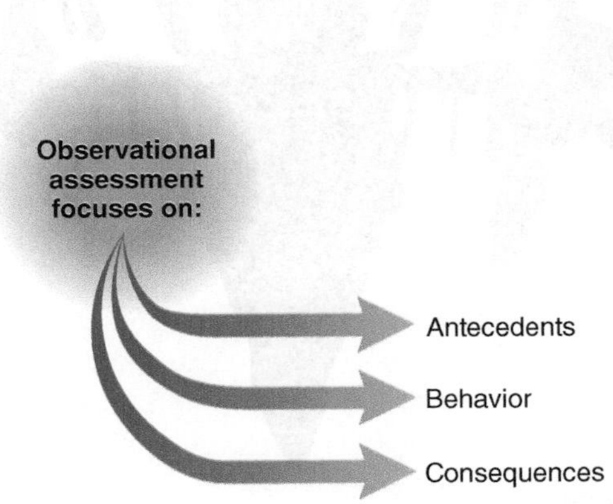

Figure 3.3

The ABCs of observation.

Formal observation involves identifying specific behaviors that are observable and measurable (called an *operational definition*). For example, it would be difficult for two people to agree on what "having an attitude" looks like. An operational definition, however, clarifies this behavior by specifying that this is "any time the boy does not comply with his mother's reasonable requests." Once the target behavior is selected and defined, an observer writes down each time it occurs, along with what happened just before (antecedent) and just after (consequence). The goal of collecting this information is to see whether there are any obvious patterns of behavior and then to design a treatment based on these patterns.

Self-Monitoring

People can also observe their own behavior to find patterns, a technique known as **self-monitoring** or self-observation (Chafouleas et al., 2021). People trying to quit smoking may write down the number of cigarettes they smoke and the times when and places where they smoke. This observation can tell them exactly how big their problem is (for example, they smoke two packs a day) and what situations lead them to smoke more (for example, talking on the phone). The use of smartphones is becoming common in these types of assessments (Melbye, Kessing, Bardram, & Faurholt-Jepsen, 2020). The goal here is to help clients monitor their behavior more conveniently. When behaviors occur only in private (such as purging by people with bulimia nervosa), self-monitoring is essential. Because the people with the problem are in the best position to observe their own behavior throughout the day, clinicians often ask patients to self-monitor their behavior to get more detailed information.

A more formal and structured way to observe behavior is through checklists and *behavior rating scales,* which are used as assessment tools before treatment and then periodically during treatment to assess changes in the person's behavior (Maust et al., 2012). Of the many such instruments for assessing a variety of behaviors, the *Brief Psychiatric Rating Scale* (Clarkin, Howieson, & McClough, 2008), assesses 18 general areas of concern. Each symptom is rated on a 7-point scale from 0 (not present) to 6 (extremely severe). The rating scale screens for moderate to severe psychotic disorders and includes such items as somatic concern (preoccupation with physical health, fear of physical illness, hypochondriasis), guilt feelings (self-blame, shame, remorse for past behavior), and grandiosity (exaggerated self-opinion, arrogance, conviction of unusual power or abilities) (American Psychiatric Association, 2006).

A phenomenon known as *reactivity* can distort any observational data. Any time you observe how people behave, the mere fact of your presence may cause them to change their behavior (Haynes et al., 2011). To test reactivity, you can tell a friend you are going to record every time she says the word *like.* Just before you reveal your intent, however, count the times your friend uses this word in a 5-minute period. You will probably find that your friend uses the word less often when you are recording it. Your friend will react to the observation by changing the behavior. The same phenomenon occurs if you observe your own behavior, or self-monitor. When people self-monitor, behaviors they want to increase (such as talking more in class) tend to increase, and behaviors they want to decrease (such as smoking) tend to decrease (Hufstedler & Varghese, 2020). Clinicians sometimes depend on the reactivity of self-monitoring to increase the effectiveness of their treatments.

Psychological Testing

We are confronted with so-called psychological tests in the popular press almost every week: "12 Questions to Test Your Relationship," "Every Guy's Private Marriage Checklist," "Are You a Type 'Z' Personality?" Although we may not want to admit it, many of us have probably purchased a magazine at some point to take one of these tests. Many are no more than entertainment, designed to make you think about the topic (and to make you buy the magazine). They are typically made up for the purposes of the article and include questions that, on the surface, seem to make sense. We are interested in these tests because we want to understand better why we and our friends behave the way we do. In reality, they usually tell us little.

In contrast, the tests used to assess psychological disorders must meet the strict standards we have noted. They must be reliable so that two or more people administering the same test to the same person will come to the same conclusion about the problem, and they must be valid so that they measure what they say they are measuring (Chafouleas et al., 2021).

Psychological tests include specific tools to determine cognitive, emotional, or behavioral responses that might be associated with a specific disorder and more general tools that assess long-standing personality features, such as a tendency to be suspicious. For example, intelligence testing is designed to determine the structure and patterns of cognition. Neuropsychological testing determines the possible contribution of brain damage or cognitive dysfunction to the patient's condition. Neuroimaging uses sophisticated technology to assess brain structure and function.

Projective Testing

We saw in Chapter 1 how Sigmund Freud brought to our attention the presence and influence of unconscious processes in psychological disorders. At this point we should ask, "If people aren't aware of these thoughts and feelings, how do we assess them?" To address this intriguing problem, psychoanalytic workers developed several assessment measures known as **projective tests** (Searight, 2020). They include a variety of methods in which ambiguous stimuli, such as pictures of people or things, are presented to people who are asked to describe what they see. The theory here is that people project their own personality and unconscious fears onto other people and things—in this case, the ambiguous stimuli—and, without realizing it, reveal their unconscious thoughts to the therapist.

Because these tests are based in psychoanalytic theory, they have been, and remain, controversial. Even so, the use of projective tests is quite common, with a majority of clinicians administering them at least occasionally and many doctoral programs providing training in their use (Butcher, 2009). Three of the more widely used are the Rorschach inkblot test, the Thematic Apperception Test, and the sentence-completion method.

More than 80 years ago, a Swiss psychiatrist named Hermann Rorschach developed a series of inkblots, initially to study perceptual processes and then to diagnose psychological disorders. The *Rorschach inkblot test* is one of the early projective tests. In its current form, the test includes 10 inkblot pictures that serve as the ambiguous stimuli (see ■Figure 3.4). The examiner presents the inkblots one by one to the person being assessed, who responds by telling what they see.

Although Rorschach advocated a scientific approach to studying the answers to the test (Rorschach, 1951), he died at the age of 38, before he had fully developed his method of systematic interpretation. Unfortunately, much of the early use of the Rorschach is extremely controversial because of the lack of data on reliability or validity, among other things. Until relatively recently, therapists administered the test in any way they saw fit, although one of the most important tenets of assessment is that the same test be given in the same way each time—that is, according to standardized procedures. If you encourage someone to give more detailed answers during one testing session but not during a second session, for example, you may get different responses as the result of your administering the test differently on the two occasions—not because of problems with the test or administration by another person (interrater reliability).

To respond to the concerns about reliability and validity, John Exner developed a standardized version of the Rorschach inkblot test, called the *Comprehensive System* (Exner, 2003). Exner's system of administering and scoring the Rorschach specifies

Figure 3.4

This inkblot resembles the ambiguous figures presented in the Rorschach test.

how the cards should be presented, what the examiner should say, and how the responses should be recorded (Mihura, Meyer, Dumitrascu, & Bombel, 2012). Varying these steps can lead to varying responses by the patient. Another system—the Rorschach Performance Assessment System—uses a set of international normative reference values (Meyer & Eblin, 2012). Despite the attempts to bring standardization to the use of the Rorschach test, its use remains controversial. Critics of the Rorschach question whether research on the Comprehensive System supports its use as a valid assessment technique for people with psychological disorders (Smith, Gacono, Fontan, Cunliffe, & Andronikof, 2020).

The *Thematic Apperception Test (TAT)* is perhaps the best-known projective test after the Rorschach. It was developed in 1935 by Christiana Morgan and Henry Murray at the Harvard Psychological Clinic (Nissley & DeFreese, 2020). The TAT consists of a series of 31 cards—30 with pictures on them and 1 blank card—although only 20 cards are typically used during each administration. Unlike the Rorschach, which involves asking for a fairly straightforward description of what the test taker sees, the instructions for the TAT ask the person to tell a dramatic story about the picture. The tester presents the pictures and tells the patient, "This is a test of imagination, one form of intelligence." The person being assessed can "let your imagination have its way, as in a myth, fairy story, or allegory" (Stein, 1978, p. 186). Again, like the Rorschach, the TAT is based on the notion that people will reveal their unconscious mental processes in their stories about the pictures (Nissley & DeFreese, 2020).

Several variations of the TAT have been developed for different groups, including a Children's Apperception Test (CAT) and a Senior Apperception Test (SAT). In addition, modifications of the test have evolved for use with a variety of racial and ethnic groups, including African Americans, Native Americans, and people from India, South Africa, and the South Pacific Micronesian culture (Aronow, Weiss & Reznikoff, 2013; Bellak, 1975; Dana, 1996). These modifications have included changes not only in the appearance of people in the pictures but also in the situations depicted. Like the Comprehensive System used with the Rorschach, researchers have developed formal scoring systems for TAT stories, including the Social Cognition and Object Relations Scale (Stein, Hilsenroth, Slavin-Mulford & Pinkser, 2011; Westen, 1991).

Unfortunately, the TAT and its variants continue to be used inconsistently. How the stories people tell about these pictures are interpreted depends on the examiner's frame of reference, as well as what the patient may say. It is not surprising, therefore, that questions remain about its use in psychopathology (Nissley & DeFreese, 2020).

Despite the popularity and increasing standardization of these tests, most clinicians who use projective tests have their own methods of administration and interpretation. When used as icebreakers for getting people to open up and talk about how they feel about things going on in their lives, the ambiguous stimuli in these tests can be valuable tools. Their relative lack of reliability and validity, however, makes them less useful as diagnostic tests. Concern over the inappropriate use of projective tests should remind you of the importance of the scientist–practitioner approach. Clinicians are not only responsible for knowing how to administer tests but also need to be aware of research that suggests the tests have limited usefulness as a means of diagnosing psychopathology.

Personality Inventories

The questions in psychological tests published in mainstream magazines typically make sense when you read them. This is called having *face validity:* The wording of the questions seems to fit the type of information desired. But is this necessary? A famous psychologist, the late Paul Meehl, presented his position on this issue more than 60 years ago and subsequently influenced a whole field of study on **personality inventories** (self-report questionnaires that assess personal traits) (Meehl, 1945). Put simply, Meehl pointed out that what is necessary from these types of tests is not whether the questions necessarily make sense on the surface but, rather, what the answers to these questions predict. If we find that people who have schizophrenia tend to respond "true" to "I have never been in love with anyone," then it does not matter whether we have a theory of love and schizophrenia. What matters is if people with certain disorders tend, as a group, to answer certain questions in a certain way, this pattern may predict who else has this disorder. The content of the questions becomes irrelevant; again, the importance lies in what the answers predict.

Although many personality inventories are available, we look at the most widely used personality inventory in the United States, the *Minnesota Multiphasic Personality Inventory (MMPI)*. The MMPI was developed in the late 1930s and early 1940s and first published in 1943 (Hathaway & McKinley, 1943). In stark contrast to projective tests, which rely heavily on theory for an interpretation, the MMPI and similar inventories are based on an *empirical* approach—that is, the collection and evaluation of data. The administration of the MMPI is straightforward. The individual being assessed reads statements and answers either "true" or "false." Following are some statements from the MMPI:

- Cry readily
- Often happy for no reason
- Am being followed
- Fearful of things or people that can't hurt me

There is little room for interpretation of MMPI responses, unlike responses to projective tests such as the Rorschach and the TAT. A problem with administering the MMPI, however, is the time and tedium of responding to the 550 items on the original version and now the 567 items on the MMPI-2 (published in 1989). A version of the MMPI that is appropriate for adolescents is also available—MMPI-A (published in 1992)—and other versions are being adapted for people in different cultures (Okazaki, Okazaki, & Sue, 2009). Individual responses on the MMPI are not examined; instead, the pattern of responses is reviewed to see whether it resembles patterns from groups of people who have specific disorders (for example, a pattern similar to a group with schizophrenia). Each group is represented on separate standard scales (Nichols, 2011) (see Table 3.2). A version of the MMPI (MMPI-2-Restructured Form; MMPI-2-RF) attempts to change the information from the assessment from a yes/no outcome about whether a person has a disorder to a continuum of impairment (McCord, 2018). More research is needed on this assessment to determine its value in serving people with psychopathology.

Table 3.2 Scales of the MMPI-2

Validity Scales	Characteristics of High Scorers
Cannot say (reported as a raw score) (?CNS)	Reading difficulties, guardedness, confusion and distractibility, depression, rebellion, or obsessiveness
Variable response inconsistency (VRIN)	Responding to questions in a manner inconsistent with psychological disorder
True response inconsistency (TRIN)	Answering questions all true or all false
Infrequency (F)	Exhibit randomness of responses or psychotic psychopathology
Back F (F_b)	Changing the way the questions are answered at the end of the test
Infrequency–psychopathology (F_r)	Claiming more psychiatric symptoms than expected
Symptom validity (FBS)	Trying to appear to have more disabilities but not psychotic
Lie (L)	Dishonest, deceptive, and/or defended
Correction (K)	Person is very guarded and defensive
Superlative self-presentation (S)	Believes in human goodness and denies personal flaws
Clinical Scales	**Characteristics of High Scorers**
Hypochondriasis	Somatizers, possible medical problems
Depression	Dysphoric, possibly suicidal
Hysteria	Highly reactive to stress, anxious, and sad at times
Psychopathic deviate	Antisocial, dishonest, possible drug abusers
Masculinity–femininity	Exhibit lack of stereotypical masculine interests, aesthetic and artistic
Paranoia	Exhibit disturbed thinking, ideas of persecution, possibly psychotic
Psychasthenia	Exhibit psychological turmoil and discomfort, extreme anxiety
Schizophrenia	Confused, disorganized, possible hallucinations
Mania	Manic, emotionally labile, unrealistic self-appraisal
Social introversion	Very insecure and uncomfortable in social situations, timid

Source: Excerpted from the MMPI® -2 (Minnesota Multiphasic Personality Inventory® -2) Manual for Administration, Scoring, and Interpretation, revised edition.

Fortunately, clinicians can have these responses scored by computer. The program also includes an interpretation of the results, thereby reducing problems of reliability. One concern that arose early in the development of the MMPI was the potential of some people to answer in ways that would downplay their problems. Skilled individuals would ascertain the intent of statements such as "Worry about saying things that hurt people's feelings" and fake the answers. To assess this possibility, the MMPI includes additional scales that determine the validity of each administration. For example, on the Lie scale, a statement such as "Have hurt someone when angry," when answered "false" might be an indication that the person may be falsifying answers to look good. The other scales are the Infrequency scale, which measures false claims about psychological problems or determines whether the person is answering randomly, and the Subtle Defensiveness scale, which assesses whether the person sees herself in unrealistically positive ways (Nichols, 2011).

■Figure 3.5 is an MMPI *profile* or summary of scores from an individual being clinically assessed. Before we tell you why this 27-year-old man (we'll call him James S.) was being evaluated, let's see what his MMPI profile tells us about him (note that these scores were obtained on the original version of the MMPI). The first three data points represent scores on the validity scales. The high scores on these scales were interpreted to mean that James S. made a naive attempt to look good for the evaluator and may have been trying to fake an appearance of having no problems. Another important part of his profile is the very high score on the psychopathic deviation scale, which measures the tendency to behave in antisocial ways. The interpretation of this score from the assessing clinician is that James S. is "aggressive, unreliable, irresponsible; unable to learn from experience; may initially make a good impression but then psychopathic features will surface in longer interactions or under stress."

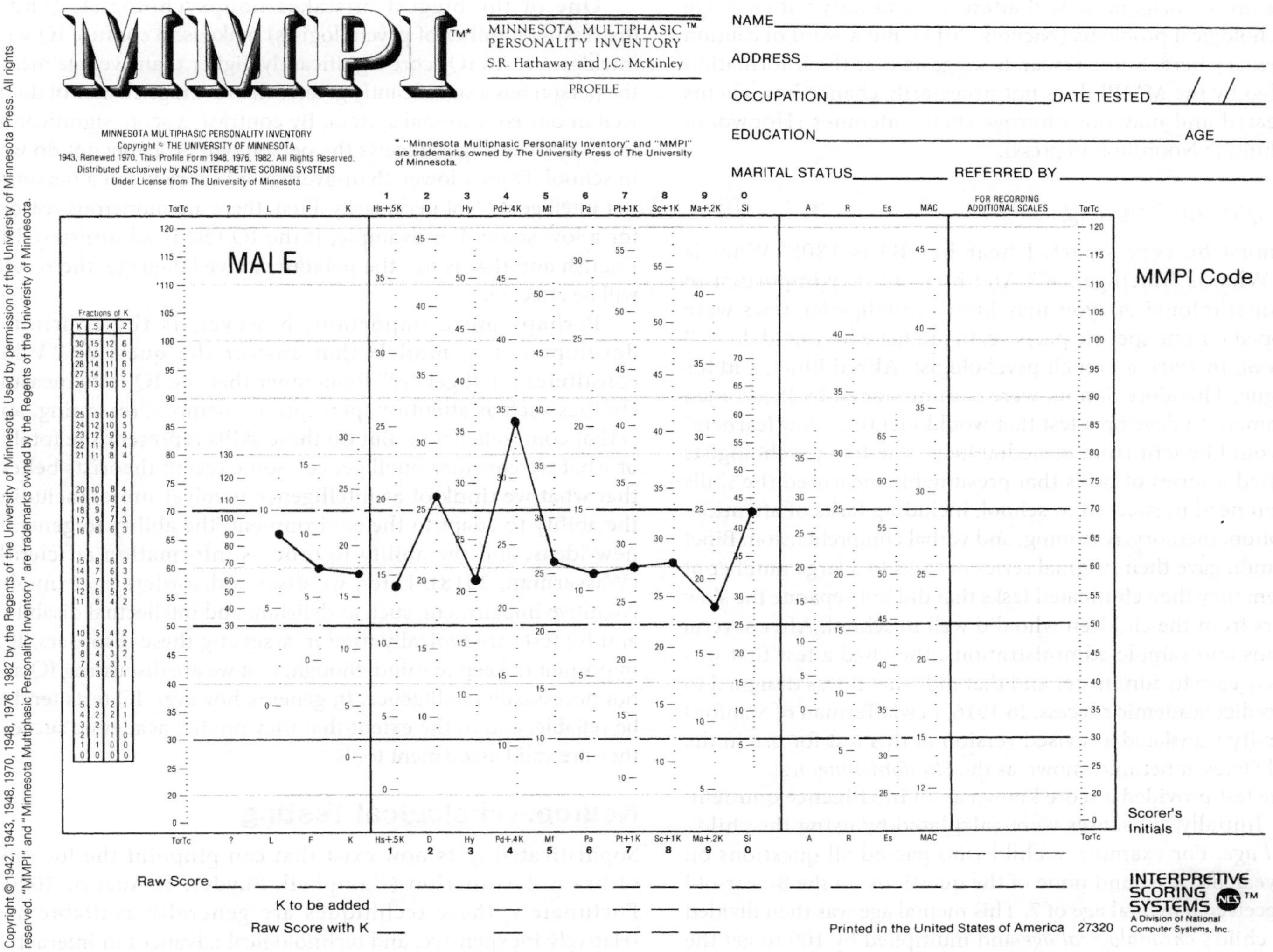

Figure 3.5

Minnesota Multiphasic Personality Inventory Profile Form.

Why was James S. being evaluated? He was a young man with a criminal record that began in his childhood. He was evaluated as part of his trial for kidnapping, raping, and murdering a middle-aged woman. Throughout his trial, he made up a number of contradictory stories to make himself look innocent (remember his high scores on the validity scales), including blaming his brother. There was overwhelming evidence of his guilt, however, and he was sentenced to life in prison. His answers on the MMPI resembled those of others who act in violent and antisocial ways.

The MMPI is one of the most extensively researched assessment instruments in psychology (Cox, Weed, & Butcher, 2009; Friedman, Bonlinskey, Levak & Nichols, 2014). The original standardization sample—the people who first responded to the statements and set the standard for answers—included many people from Minnesota who had no psychological disorders and several groups of people who had particular disorders. The more recent versions of this test, including the MMPI-2-Revised Form (Ben-Porath & Tellegen, 2008), eliminate problems with the original version that partly resulting from the original selective sample of people and partly resulting from the wording of questions (Ranson, Nichols, Rouse, & Harrington, 2009). For example, some questions were sexist. One item on the original version asks the respondent to say whether she has ever been sorry she is a girl (Worell & Remer, 1992). Another item reads, "Any man who is willing to work hard has a good chance of succeeding" (Hathaway & McKinley, 1943). Other items were criticized as insensitive to cultural diversity. Items dealing with religion, for example, referred almost exclusively to Christianity (Butcher, Graham, Williams, & Ben-Porath, 1990). The MMPI-2 has also been standardized with a sample that reflects the 1980 U.S. Census figures, including African Americans and Native Americans for the first time. In addition, new items have been added that deal with contemporary issues such as type A personality, low self-esteem, and family problems.

Reliability of the MMPI is excellent when it is interpreted according to standardized procedures, and thousands of studies on the original MMPI attest to its validity with a range of psychological problems (Nichols, 2011). But a word of caution is necessary here. Some research suggests that the information provided by the MMPI does not necessarily change how clients are treated and may not improve their outcomes (Hopwood, Kamphuis, & Noordhof, in press).

Intelligence Testing

"She must be very smart. I hear her IQ is 180!" What is "IQ"? What is "intelligence"? And how are they important in psychopathology? As you may know, intelligence tests were developed for one specific purpose: to predict who would do well in school. In 1904, a French psychologist, Alfred Binet, and his colleague, Théodore Simon, were commissioned by the French government to develop a test that would identify "slow learners" who would benefit from remedial help. The two psychologists identified a series of tasks that presumably measured the skills children need to succeed in school, including tasks of attention, perception, memory, reasoning, and verbal comprehension. Binet and Simon gave their original series of tasks to a large number of children; they then eliminated tasks that did not separate the slow learners from the children who did well in school. After several revisions and sample administrations, they had a test that was relatively easy to administer and that did what it was designed to do—predict academic success. In 1916, Lewis Terman of Stanford University translated a revised version of this test for use in the United States; it became known as the *Stanford-Binet test.*

The test provided a score known as an **intelligence quotient**, or **IQ**. Initially, IQ scores were calculated by using the child's *mental age*. For example, a child who passed all questions on the 7-year-old level and none of the questions on the 8-year-old level received a mental age of 7. This mental age was then divided by the child's *chronological age* and multiplied by 100 to get the IQ score. There were problems, however, with using this type of formula for calculating an IQ score. For example, a 4-year-old needed to score only 1 year above their chronological age to be given an IQ score of 125, although an 8-year-old had to score 2 years above their chronological age to be given the same score. Current tests use what is called a *deviation IQ*. A person's score is compared only with scores of others of the same age. The IQ score, then, is an estimate of how much a child's performance in school will deviate from the average performance of others of the same age (Fletcher & Hattie, 2011).

In addition to the revised version of the Stanford-Binet (*Stanford-Binet 5*) (Roid, 2003), there is another widely used set of intelligence tests, developed by psychologist David Wechsler. The Wechsler tests include versions for adults (*Wechsler Adult Intelligence Scale,* fourth edition, or *WAIS-IV*), children (*Wechsler Intelligence Scale for Children,* fifth edition, or *WISC-V*), and young children (*Wechsler Preschool and Primary Scale of Intelligence,* fourth edition, or *WPPSI-IV*). All these tests contain *verbal scales* (which measure vocabulary, knowledge of facts, short-term memory, and verbal reasoning skills) and *performance scales* (which assess psychomotor abilities, nonverbal reasoning, and ability to learn new relationships) (Valentine, Block, Eversole, Boxley, & Dawson, 2020).

One of the biggest mistakes nonpsychologists (and a distressing number of psychologists) make is to confuse IQ with intelligence. An IQ score significantly higher than average means the person has a significantly greater than average chance of doing well in our educational system. By contrast, a score significantly lower than average suggests the person will probably not do well in school. Does a lower-than-average IQ score mean a person is not intelligent? Not necessarily. First, there are numerous reasons for a low score. For example, if the IQ test is administered in English and that is not the person's native language, the results will be affected.

Perhaps more important, however, is the continued development of models that answer the question "What constitutes intelligence?" Remember that the IQ tests measure abilities such as attention, perception, memory, reasoning, and verbal comprehension. But do these skills represent the totality of what we consider intelligence? Some recent theorists believe that what we think of as intelligence involves more, including the ability to adapt to the environment, the ability to generate new ideas, and the ability to process information efficiently (Wasserman, 2018). Later, we discuss disorders that involve cognitive impairment, such as delirium and intellectual disability, and IQ tests are typically used in assessing these disorders. It is important to keep in mind, though, that we are discussing IQ and not necessarily intelligence. In general, however, IQ tests tend to be reliable, and to the extent that they predict academic success, they are valid assessment tools.

Neuropsychological Testing

Sophisticated tests now exist that can pinpoint the location of brain dysfunction (Campbell, Snyder, & Austin, 2020). Fortunately, these techniques are generally available and relatively inexpensive, and technological advances in interactive teleconferencing have led to efforts to conduct such assessments for people in remote areas (Lezak, Howieson, Bigler, & Tranel, 2012). **Neuropsychological tests** measure abilities in areas such as receptive and expressive language, attention and concentration, memory, motor skills, perceptual abilities, and learning and abstraction in such a way that the clinician can make educated

Olimpik/Shutterstock.com

This child is concentrating on a standard psychological assessment test.

guesses about the person's performance and the possible existence of brain impairment. In other words, this method of testing assesses brain dysfunction by observing the effects of the dysfunction on the person's ability to perform certain tasks. Although you do not see damage, you can see its effects.

A simple neuropsychological test often used with children is the *Bender Visual–Motor Gestalt Test* (Brannigan & Decker, 2006). A child is given a series of cards on which are drawn various lines and shapes. The task is for the child to copy what is drawn on the card. The errors on the test are compared with test results of other children of the same age; if the number of errors exceeds a certain figure, then brain dysfunction is suspected. This test is less sophisticated than other neuropsychological tests because the nature or location of the problem cannot be determined with this test. The Bender Visual–Motor Gestalt Test can be useful for psychologists, however, because it provides a simple screening instrument that is easy to administer and can detect possible problems. Two of the most popular advanced tests of organic (brain) damage that allow more precise determinations of the location of the problem are the *Luria-Nebraska Neuropsychological Battery* (Golden, Hammeke, & Purisch, 1980) and the *Halstead-Reitan Neuropsychological Battery* (Reitan & Davison, 1974). These offer an elaborate battery of tests to assess a variety of skills in adolescents and adults. For example, the Halstead-Reitan Neuropsychological Battery includes the *Rhythm Test* (which asks the person to compare rhythmic beats, thus testing sound recognition, attention, and concentration), the *Strength of Grip Test* (which compares the grips of the right and left hands), and the *Tactile Performance Test* (which requires the test taker to place wooden blocks in a form board while blindfolded, thus testing learning and memory skills) (McCaffrey, Lynch, & Westervelt, 2011).

Research on the validity of neuropsychological tests suggests they may be useful for detecting organic damage. One study found that the Halstead-Reitan and the Luria-Nebraska test batteries were equivalent in their abilities to detect damage and were about 80% correct (Goldstein & Shelly, 1984). These types of studies, however, raise the issue of **false positives** and **false negatives**. For any assessment strategy, there will be times when the test shows a problem when none exists (false positive) and times when no problem is found even though some difficulty is present (false negative). The possibility of false results is particularly troublesome for tests of brain dysfunction; a clinician who fails to find damage that exists might miss an important medical problem that needs to be treated. Fortunately, neuropsychological tests are used primarily as screening devices and are routinely paired with other assessments to improve the likelihood that real problems will be found. They do well with regard to measures of reliability and validity. On the downside, some of these tests can require hours to administer, score, and interpret and are therefore not used unless specific disorders (for example, neurodevelopmental or learning disorders) are suspected.

Neuroimaging: Pictures of the Brain

For more than a century, we have known that many things we do, think, and remember are partially controlled by specific areas of the brain. In recent years we have developed the ability to look inside the nervous system and take increasingly accurate pictures of the structure and function of the brain, using a technique called **neuroimaging** (Black & Andreasen, 2021b). Neuroimaging can be divided into two categories. One category includes procedures that examine any damage. The other category includes procedures that examine the actual functioning of the brain by mapping blood flow and other metabolic activity.

Images of Brain Structure

The first neuroimaging technique, developed in the early 1970s, uses multiple X-ray exposures of the brain from different angles; that is, X-rays are passed directly through the head. As with any X-ray, these are partially blocked or attenuated more by bone and less by brain tissue. The degree of blockage is picked up by detectors in the opposite side of the head. A computer then reconstructs pictures of various slices of the brain. This procedure, which takes about 15 minutes, is called a *computerized axial tomography (CAT) scan* or *CT scan*. It is relatively noninvasive and has proved useful in identifying and locating abnormalities in the structure or shape of the brain. CT scans are particularly useful in locating brain tumors, injuries, and other structural and anatomical abnormalities. One difficulty, however, is that these scans, like all X-rays, involve repeated x-radiation, which poses some risk of cell damage (Black & Andreasen, 2021b).

Several more recently developed procedures give greater resolution (specificity and accuracy) than a CT scan without the inherent risks of X-ray tests. A now commonly used scanning technique is called nuclear *magnetic resonance imaging (MRI)*. The patient's head is placed in a high-strength magnetic field through which radio frequency signals are transmitted. These signals "excite" the brain tissue, altering the protons in the hydrogen atoms. The alteration is measured, along with the time it takes the protons to "relax" or return to normal. Where there are lesions or damage, the signal is lighter or darker (Filippi, 2015). Technology now exists that allows the computer to view the brain in layers, which enables precise examination of the structure. Although an MRI is more expensive than a CT scan and originally took as long as

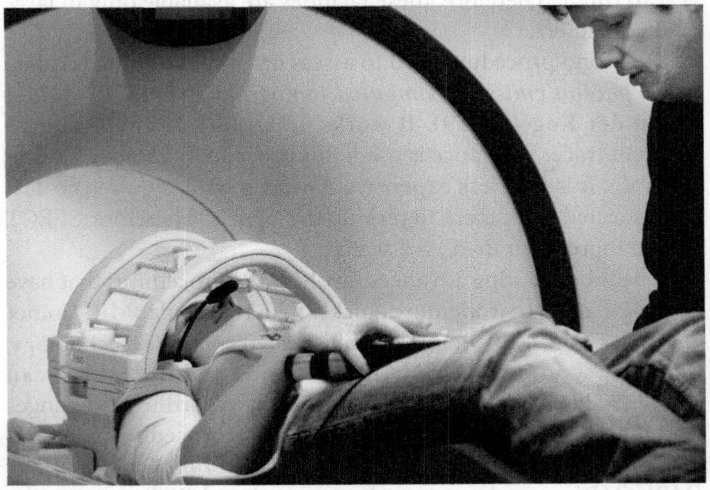

Koen Verheijden/Hollandse Hoogte/Redux

The patient is being positioned for an MRI scan.

45 minutes, this is changing as technology improves. Newer versions of MRI procedures take as little as 10 minutes; the time and cost are decreasing yearly. Another disadvantage of MRI at present is that someone undergoing the procedure is totally enclosed inside a narrow tube with a magnetic coil surrounding the head. People who are somewhat claustrophobic often cannot tolerate an MRI.

Although neuroimaging procedures are useful for identifying damage to the brain, only recently have they been used to determine structural or anatomical abnormalities that might be associated with various psychological disorders. We review some tantalizing studies in subsequent chapters on specific disorders.

Images of Brain Functioning

Several widely used procedures are capable of measuring the actual functioning of the brain, as opposed to its structure (Joiner & van der Kogel, 2019). The first is called *positron emission tomography (PET) scan*. Subjects undergoing a PET scan are injected with a tracer substance attached to radioactive isotopes, or groups of atoms that react distinctively. This substance interacts with blood, oxygen, or glucose. When parts of the brain become active, blood, oxygen, or glucose rushes to these areas of the brain, creating "hot spots" picked up by detectors that identify the location of the isotopes. Thus, we can learn what parts of the brain are working and what parts are not. To obtain clear images, the individual undergoing the procedure must remain motionless for 40 seconds or more. These images can be superimposed on MRI images to show the precise location of the active areas. The PET scans are also useful in supplementing MRI and CT scans when localizing the sites of trauma resulting from head injury or stroke, as well as when localizing brain tumors. More important, PET scans are used increasingly to look at varying patterns of metabolism that might be associated with different disorders. Recent PET scans have demonstrated that many patients with early Alzheimer's-type dementia show reduced glucose metabolism in the parietal lobes. Other intriguing findings have been reported for obsessive-compulsive disorder and bipolar disorder (see Chapters 5 and 7). PET scanning is expensive: The cost is about $6 million to set up a PET facility and $500,000 a year to run it. Therefore, these facilities are available only in large medical centers.

A second procedure used to assess brain functioning is called *single photon emission computed tomography (SPECT)* (Joiner & van der Kogel, 2019). It works much like PET, although a different tracer substance is used; this procedure is somewhat less accurate. It is also less expensive, however, and requires far less sophisticated equipment to pick up the signals. Therefore, SPECT is used more often than PET scans.

The most exciting advances involve MRI procedures that have been developed to work more quickly than the regular MRI (Joiner & van der Kogel, 2019). Using sophisticated computer technology, these procedures take only milliseconds and, therefore, can actually take pictures of the brain at work, recording its changes from one second to the next. Because these procedures measure the functioning of the brain, they are called *functional MRI,* or *fMRI.* fMRI procedures have largely replaced PET scans in the leading brain-imaging centers because they allow researchers to

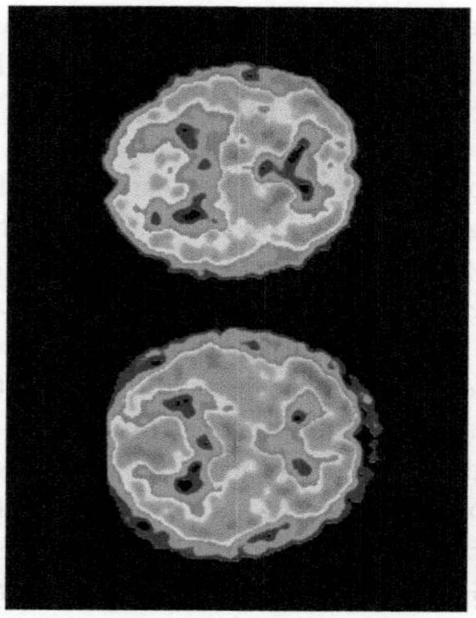

PET scans display areas of high and low neurological activity, as in these scans of a brain affected by HIV.

see the immediate response of the brain to a brief event, such as seeing a new face. BOLD-fMRI (blood-oxygen-level-dependent fMRI) is currently the most common fMRI technique used to study psychological disorders (Joiner & van der Kogel, 2019).

Some of the latest research in neuroimaging seeks to view the brain all the way down to the level of the synapse. These new technologies can detect activity at the receptors for neurochemicals such as dopamine and serotonin, therefore allowing researchers not just to look at action in general areas but also to differentiate activities at different and specific receptor sites. These technologies use radiolabeled neuroreceptor ligands (radioactive chemicals designed to congregate at specific receptor sites) in SPECT and PET imaging to study the distribution and density of neuroreceptors (Filippi, 2015). This up-and-coming technology may prove to be a more accurate way of learning how the brain works.

Brain imagery procedures hold enormous potential for illuminating the contribution of neurobiological factors to psychological disorders. For example, in Chapter 5 you will learn what fMRI procedures reveal about brain functioning in individuals such as Frank, who has obsessive-compulsive disorder. These technological advances will enable researchers to gain more precise insights into the architecture and function of the living brain than ever before. Akin to the *Human Genome Project*, which led to the decoding of the human DNA, the National Institutes of Health has initiated the NIH *Human Connectome Project* (National Institutes of Health, n.d.). The purpose of this project is to collect a large amount of brain imaging data to identify abnormal brain circuits in patients with various mental illnesses (Hubbard et al., 2020). Some of us are part of this initiative, as well as an international project called the *ENIGMA (Enhancing NeuroImaging Genetics through Meta Analysis) Consortium*, a global alliance of over 1,400 scientists across 43 countries studying the human brain in health and disease (Thomson et al., 2020).

Psychophysiological Assessment

Yet another method for assessing brain structure and function specifically and nervous system activity generally is called

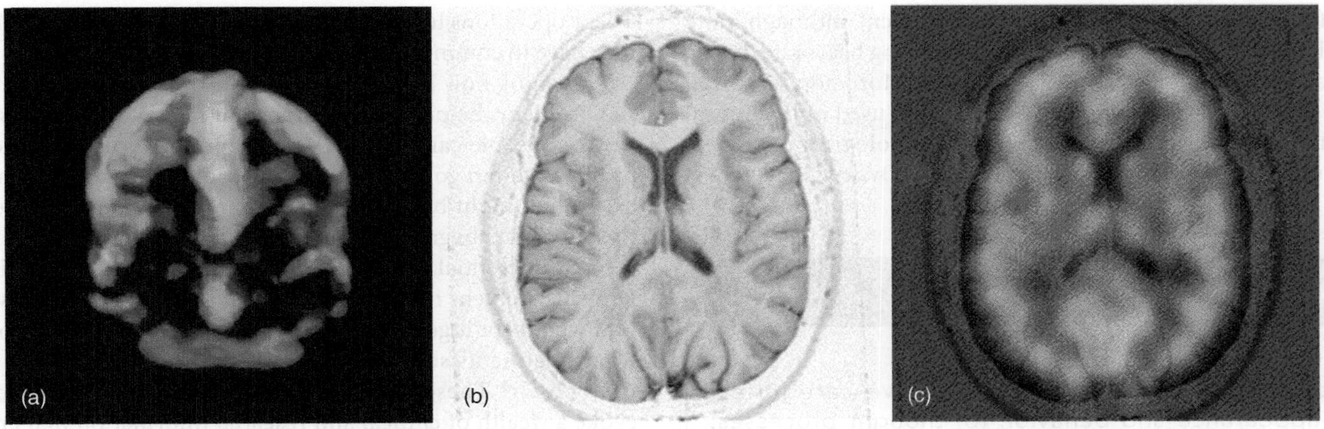

Carl Friston of Stichman Medical Equipment, Medford, MA

A horizontal brain section (a) in a SPECT image clearly reveals parietal lobe damage in a person with schizophrenia. Images (b) and (c) are MRI photographs. SPECT images show metabolic activity and thus indicate the relationship between the person's brain and the person's behavior. The higher-resolution MRI images show tissue variations.

psychophysiological assessment. As the term implies, *psychophysiology* refers to measurable changes in the nervous system that reflect emotional or psychological events. The measurements may be taken either directly from the brain or peripherally from other parts of the body.

Frank feared that he might have seizures. If we had any reason to suspect he might have periods of memory loss or exhibit bizarre, trancelike behavior, if only for a short period, it would be important for him to have an **electroencephalogram (EEG)**. Measuring electrical activity in the head related to the firing of a specific group of neurons reveals brain wave activity; brain waves come from the low-voltage electrical current that runs through the neurons. A person's brain waves can be assessed in both waking and sleeping states. In an EEG, electrodes are placed directly on various places on the scalp to record the different low-voltage currents.

We have learned much about EEG patterns in the past decades (Kim, Schulz, Wilde, & Yudofsky, 2008). Usually, we measure ongoing electrical activity in the brain. When brief periods of WWEEG patterns are recorded in response to specific events, such as hearing a psychologically meaningful stimulus, the response is called an *event-related potential (ERP)* or *evoked potential.* We have learned that EEG patterns are often affected by psychological or emotional factors and can be an index of these reactions or a psychophysiological measure. In a normal, healthy, relaxed adult, waking activities are characterized by a regular pattern of changes in voltage termed *alpha waves.*

Many types of stress-reduction treatments attempt to *increase* the frequency of the alpha waves, often by relaxing the patients in some way. The alpha wave pattern is associated with relaxation and calmness. During sleep, we pass through several stages of brain activity, at least partially identified by EEG patterns. During the deepest, most relaxed stage, typically occurring 1 to 2 hours after a person falls asleep, EEG recordings show a pattern of *delta waves.* These brain waves are slower and more irregular than the alpha waves, which is normal for this stage of sleep. You will see in Chapter 5 that panic attacks occurring while a person is sound asleep come almost exclusively during the delta wave stage. If frequent delta wave activity occurred during the waking state, it might indicate dysfunction of localized areas of the brain.

Psychophysiological assessment of other bodily responses may also play a role in assessment. These responses include heart rate, respiration, and *electrodermal responding,* formerly referred to as *galvanic skin response (GSR),* which is a measure of sweat gland activity controlled by the peripheral nervous system. Remember from Chapter 2 that the peripheral nervous system and, in particular, the sympathetic division of the autonomic nervous system are responsive to stress and emotional arousal.

Assessing psychophysiological response to emotional stimuli is important in many disorders, one being posttraumatic stress disorder. Stimuli such as sights and sounds associated with the trauma evoke strong psychophysiological responses, even if the patient is not fully aware that this is happening.

Psychophysiological assessment is also used with many sexual dysfunctions and disorders. For example, sexual arousal can be assessed through direct measurement of penile circumference or vaginal blood flow in response to erotic stimuli, usually movies or slides (see Chapter 10). Sometimes the individual might be unaware of specific patterns of sexual arousal.

Physiological measures are also important in the assessment and treatment of conditions such as headaches and hypertension (Hazlett-Stevens & Bernstein, 2012); they form the basis for the treatment we call *biofeedback.* In biofeedback, as we explain in Chapter 9, levels of physiological responding, such as blood pressure readings, are fed back to the patient (provided on a continuous basis) by meters or gauges so that the patient can try to regulate these responses.

Nevertheless, physiological assessment is not without its limitations because it requires a great deal of skill and some technical expertise. Even when administered properly, the measures sometimes produce inconsistent results because of procedural or technical difficulties or the nature of the response itself. Therefore, only clinicians specializing in certain disorders in which these measures are particularly important are likely to make extensive use of psychophysiological recording equipment, although more straightforward applications, such as monitoring heart rate during relaxation exercises, are more common. More sophisticated psychophysiological assessment is most often used in theoretical investigations of the nature of certain psychological disorders, particularly emotional disorders (Barlow, 2002; Ovsiew, 2005).

Concept Check 3.1

Part A

The mental status exam includes five categories: (a) appearance and behavior, (b) thought processes, (c) mood and affect, (d) intellectual functioning, and (e) sensorium. Identify which part of the mental status exam is being performed in the following situations.

1. Dr. Swan listened carefully to Zara's speech pattern, noting its speed, content, and continuity. He noticed no loose association but did hear indications of delusional thoughts and visual hallucinations. ________
2. Eli arrived at the clinic accompanied by police, who had found him dressed only in shorts although the temperature was 23°F. He was reported to the police by someone who saw him walking slowly down the street, making strange faces, and talking to himself. ________
3. When Fatma was brought to Dr. García 's office, she asked if she knew the date and time, her identity, and where she was. ________
4. Dr. Jones viewed as inappropriate Tim's laughter after discussing his near-fatal incident and noted that Tim appeared to be elated. ________
5. Holly's vocabulary and memory seemed adequate, leading Dr. Zhong to estimate that she was of average intelligence. ________

Part B

Check your understanding of reliability and validity by marking each test R (reliable) or NR (not reliable) and V (valid) or NV (not valid).

1. ___, ___ EEG to show electrical activity in the brain of someone who has seizures
2. ___, ___ Rorschach inkblots
3. ___, ___ Structured interviews with definite answers
4. ___, ___ Sentence completion

Diagnosing Psychological Disorders

Thus far, we have looked at Frank's functioning on an individual basis; that is, we have closely observed his behavior, cognitive processes, and mood, and we have conducted semistructured interviewing, behavioral assessment, and psychological tests. These operations tell us what is unique about Frank, not what he may have in common with other individuals.

Learning how Frank may resemble other people in terms of the problems he presents is important for several reasons. If in the past people came in with similar problems or psychological profiles, we can go back and find a lot of information from their cases that might be applicable to Frank's case. We can see how the problems began for those other individuals, what factors seemed influential, and how long the problem or disorder lasted. Did the problem in the other cases just go away on its own? If not, what kept it going? Did it need treatment? Most important, what treatments seemed to relieve the problem for those other individuals? These general questions are useful because they evoke a wealth of clinical and research information that enables the investigator to make certain inferences about what will happen next and what treatments may work. In other words, the clinician can form general conclusions and establish a *prognosis,* a term discussed in Chapter 1 that refers to the likely future course of a disorder under certain conditions.

Both strategies are essential in the study and treatment of psychopathology. If we want to determine what is unique about an individual's personality, cultural background, or circumstances, we use what is known as an **idiographic strategy** (Barlow & Nock, 2009). This information lets us tailor our treatment to the person. But to take advantage of the information already accumulated on a particular problem or disorder, we must be able to determine a general class of problems to which the presenting problem belongs. This is known as a **nomothetic strategy**. In other words, we are attempting to name or classify the problem. When we identify a specific psychological disorder, such as a mood disorder, in the clinical setting, we are making a diagnosis. We can also identify a general class or grouping of problems by determining a particular personality profile on a psychological test such as the MMPI. For example, when it was noted earlier in the section on the MMPI that James S. scored high on the psychopathic deviation scale, we concluded that he shared personality features of aggressiveness and irresponsibility with others who have elevated scores on that scale. Before proceeding, let's define some additional terms more precisely.

Because classification is such an integral part of science and, indeed, of our human experience, we describe its various aspects individually (Blashfield, Keeley, Flanagan, & Miles, 2014; Millon, 1991; Widiger & Crego, 2013). The term **classification** itself is broad, referring simply to any effort to construct groups or categories and to assign objects or people to these categories on the basis of their shared attributes or relations—a nomothetic strategy. If the classification is in a scientific context, it is most often called **taxonomy**, which is the classification of entities for scientific purposes, such as insects, rocks, or—if the subject is psychology—behaviors. If you apply a taxonomic system to psychological or medical phenomena or other clinical areas, you use the word **nosology**. All diagnostic systems used in health-care settings, such as those for infectious diseases, are nosological systems. The term **nomenclature** describes the names or labels of the disorders that make up the nosology (for example, anxiety or mood disorders). Most mental health professionals in North America use the classification system contained in the DSM-5

(American Psychiatric Association, 2013). This is the official system in the United States, and it is used widely throughout the world along with the closely related *International Classification of Diseases*, 10th edition (*ICD-10*) (World Health Organization, 1992), discussed below. A clinician refers to the DSM-5 to identify a specific psychological disorder in the process of making a diagnosis.

During the past several years, there have been enormous changes in how psychopathology is classified. Because these developments affect so much of what clinicians do, we examine carefully the processes of classification and diagnosis as they are used in psychopathology. We look first at different approaches, examine the concepts of reliability and validity as they pertain to diagnosis, and then discuss our current system of classification, the DSM-5.

Classification Issues

Classification is at the heart of any science, and much of what we have said about it is common sense. If we could not order and label objects or experiences, scientists could not communicate with one another, and our knowledge would not advance. Everyone would have to develop a personal system that would mean nothing to anyone else. In your biology or geology courses, when you study insects or rocks, classification is fundamental. Knowing how one species of insects differs from another allows us to study its functioning and origins. When we are dealing with human behavior or human behavioral disorders, however, the subject of classification becomes controversial. Some people have questioned whether it is proper or ethical to classify human behavior. Even among those who recognize the necessity of classification, major controversies have arisen in several areas. Within psychopathology, for example, definitions of "normal" and "abnormal" are questioned, as is the assumption that a behavior or cognition is part of one disorder and not another. Some would prefer to talk about behavior and feelings on a continuum from happy to sad or fearful to nonfearful rather than to create such categories as mania, depression, and phobia. For better or worse, classifying behavior and people is something we all do. Few of us talk about our own emotions or those of our friends by using a number on a scale (where 0 is totally unhappy and 100 is totally happy), although this approach might be more accurate. ("How do you feel about that?" "About 65.") Rather, we talk about being happy, sad, angry, depressed, fearful, and so on.

Categorical and Dimensional Approaches

To avoid reinventing the wheel every time we see a new set of problem behaviors and to seek general principles of psychopathology, in what different ways can we classify human behavior? We have already alluded to two possibilities. We can have distinct categories of disorders that have little or nothing in common with one another; for example, either you hear voices talking to you from the refrigerator (auditory hallucination) and have other symptoms of schizophrenia, or you don't. Alternatively, we can quantify the various attributes of a psychological disorder along several dimensions, coming up with a composite score. An MMPI profile is a good example; another is "dimensionalizing" a disorder—for example, depression, on a continuum of severity from feeling mildly depressed in the morning (something most of us experience once in a while) to feeling so deeply depressed and hopeless that suicide seems the only solution. Which system is better? Each has its strengths and its faults (Blashfield et al., 2014; Brown & Barlow, 2005; Helzer et al., 2008; LeBeau, Bogels, Moller, & Craske, 2015; Widiger, 2013). Let's look at both.

Emil Kraepelin (1856–1926) was one of the first psychiatrists to classify psychological disorders from a biological point of view.

The **classical (or pure) categorical approach** to classification originates in the work of the German physician Emil Kraepelin (1856–1926) and the biological tradition in the study of psychopathology. Here we assume that every diagnosis has a clear underlying pathophysiological cause, such as a bacterial infection or a malfunctioning endocrine system, and that each disorder is unique. When diagnoses are thought of in this way, the causes could be psychological or cultural instead of pathophysiological, but there is still only one set of causative factors per disorder, which does not overlap with those of other disorders. Because each disorder is fundamentally different from every other, we need only one set of defining criteria, which everybody in the category has to meet. If the criteria for a major depressive episode are (1) the presence of depressed mood, (2) significant weight loss or gain when not dieting, (3) diminished ability to think or concentrate, and seven additional specific symptoms, then, to be diagnosed with depression, an individual would have to meet all of the criteria. In that case, according to the classical categorical approach, the clinician would know the cause of the disorder.

Classical categorical approaches are quite useful in medicine. It is extremely important for a physician to make accurate diagnoses. If a patient has a fever accompanied by stomach pain, the doctor must determine quickly whether the cause is a stomach flu or an infected appendix or something else. This is not always easy, but physicians are trained to examine the signs and symptoms closely, and they usually reach the correct conclusion. To understand the cause of symptoms (infected appendix) is to know what treatment will be effective (surgery). But if someone is depressed or anxious, is there a similar type of underlying cause? As you saw in Chapter 2, probably not. Most psychopathologists believe psychological and social factors interact with biological factors to produce a disorder. Therefore, despite the beliefs of Kraepelin and other early biological investigators, the classical categorical approach is clearly inappropriate to the complexity of psychological disorders (Helzer et al., 2008; Lillienfeld, 2014; Regier, Narrow, Kuhl, & Kupfer, 2009; Widiger & Edmundson, 2011).

A second strategy is a **dimensional approach**, in which we note the variety of cognitions, moods, and behaviors with which the patient presents and quantify them on a scale. For example,

Despite their wide physical variation, all dogs belong to the same class of animals.

on a scale of 1 to 10, a patient might be rated as severely anxious (10), moderately depressed (5), and mildly manic (2) to create a profile of emotional functioning (10, 5, 2). Although dimensional approaches have been applied to psychopathology in the past—particularly to personality disorders (Blashfield et al., 2014; Helzer et al., 2008; Krueger, Hopwood, Wright, & Markon, 2014; Widiger & Samuel, 2005)—they have been relatively unsatisfactory (Brown & Barlow, 2009; Frances, 2009; Regier et al., 2009; Widiger & Edmundson, 2011). Most theorists have not been able to agree on how many dimensions are required: Some say one dimension is enough; others have identified as many as 33 (Millon, 1991, 2004).

A third strategy for organizing and classifying behavioral disorders has found increasing support in recent years as an alternative to classical categorical or dimensional approaches. It is a categorical approach but with the twist that it basically combines some features of each of the former approaches. Called a **prototypical approach**, this alternative identifies certain essential characteristics of an entity so that you (and others) can classify it, but it also allows certain nonessential variations that do not necessarily change the classification. For example, if someone were to ask you to describe a dog, you could easily give a general description (the essential, categorical characteristics), but you might not exactly describe a specific dog. Dogs come in different colors, sizes, and even breeds (the nonessential, dimensional variations), but they all share certain doggish characteristics that allow you to classify them separately from cats. Thus, requiring a certain number of prototypical criteria and only some of an additional number of criteria is adequate. This system is not perfect because there is a greater blurring at the boundaries of categories, and some symptoms apply to more than one disorder. For this reason, these categories are often called "fuzzy." It has the advantage, however, of fitting better with the current state of our knowledge of psychopathology than a categorical approach, and it is relatively user-friendly.

When a prototypical approach is used in classifying a psychological disorder, many possible features or properties of the disorder are listed, and any candidate must meet enough of them to fall into that category. Consider the DSM-5-TR criteria defining a major depressive episode.

As you can see, the criteria include many nonessential symptoms, but if you have either depressed mood or marked loss of interest or pleasure in most activities and at least four of the remaining eight symptoms, you come close enough to the prototype to meet the criteria for a major depressive episode. One person might have depressed mood, significant weight loss, insomnia, psychomotor agitation, and loss of energy, whereas another person who also meets the criteria for major depressive episode might have markedly diminished interest or pleasure in activities, fatigue, feelings of worthlessness, difficulty thinking or concentrating, and ideas of committing suicide. Although both have the requisite five symptoms that bring them close to the prototype, they look different because they share only one symptom.

DSM 5 **Table 3.1**
Criteria for a Major Depressive Episode

A. Five (or more) of the following symptoms have been present during the same 2-week period and represent a change from previous functioning; at least one of the symptoms is either (a) depressed mood or (b) loss of interest or pleasure.

Note: Do not include symptoms that are clearly attributable to another medical condition.

1. Depressed mood most of the day, nearly every day, as indicated by either subjective report (e.g. feels sad, empty, hopeless) or observation made by others (e.g. appears tearful). (*Note:* In children and adolescents, can be irritable mood.)
2. Markedly diminished interest or pleasure in all, or almost all, activities most of the day, nearly every day (as indicated by either subjective account or observation).
3. Significant weight loss when not dieting or weight gain (e.g., a change of more than 5% of body weight in a month), or decrease or increase in appetite nearly every day. (*Note:* In children, consider failure to make expected weight gain.)
4. Insomnia or hypersomnia nearly every day.
5. Psychomotor agitation or retardation nearly every day (observable by others, not merely subjective feelings of restlessness or being slowed down).
6. Fatigue or loss of energy nearly every day.
7. Feelings of worthlessness or excessive or inappropriate guilt (which may be delusional) nearly every day (not merely self-reproach or guilt about being sick).
8. Diminished ability to think or concentrate ,or indecisiveness, nearly every day (either by subjective account or as observed by others).
9. Recurrent thoughts of death (not just fear of dying), recurrent suicidal ideation without a specific plan, or a suicide attempt or a specific plan for committing suicide.

B. The symptoms cause clinically significant distress or impairment in social, occupational, or other important areas of functioning.

C. The episode is not attributable to the physiological effects of a substance or another medical condition.

From American Psychiatric Association, 2022, *Diagnostic and statistical manual of mental disorders* (5th ed., Text Revision).

Reliability

Any system of classification should describe specific subgroups of symptoms that are clearly evident and can be readily identified by experienced clinicians. If two clinicians interview the patient at separate times on the same day (and assuming the patient's condition does not change during the day), the two clinicians should see, and perhaps measure, the same set of behaviors and emotions. The psychological disorder can thus be identified reliably (Chmielewski, Clark, Bagby, & Watson, 2015; Kraemer, 2014). If the disorder is not readily apparent to both clinicians, the resulting diagnoses might represent bias. For example, someone's clothes might provoke some comment. One of your friends might later say, "She looked kind of sloppy tonight." Another might comment, "No, she's just got swag." Perhaps a third friend would say, "Actually, I thought she was dressed kind of neatly." You might wonder if they had all seen the same person. In any case, there would be no reliability to their observations. Getting your friends to agree about someone's appearance would require a careful set of definitions that they all accept.

As we noted before, unreliable classification systems are subject to bias by clinicians making diagnoses. One of the most unreliable categories in current classification is the area of personality disorders—chronic, trait-like sets of inappropriate behaviors and emotional reactions that characterize a person's way of interacting with the world. Although bias among clinicians is always a potential problem, the more reliable the nosology, or system of classification, the less likely bias is to creep in during diagnosis. The lack of agreement among clinicians when diagnosing personality disorders indicates that more reliable criteria are needed and may be on the way for future revisions described below (Krueger et al., 2014) (see Chapter 12).

Validity

In addition to being reliable, a system of nosology must be valid. Earlier we described *validity* as whether something measures what it is designed to measure. There are several types of diagnostic validity. For one, the system should have *construct validity.* This means the signs and symptoms chosen as criteria for the diagnostic category are consistently associated or "go together" and the things they identify differ from other categories. Someone meeting the criteria for depression should be discriminable from someone meeting the criteria for social phobia. This discriminability might be evident not only in presenting symptoms but also in the course of the disorder and possibly in the choice of treatment. It may also predict **familial aggregation**, the extent to which the disorder would be found among the patient's relatives (Kupfer, First, & Regier, 2002; Lillienfeld, 2014).

In addition, a valid diagnosis tells the clinician what is likely to happen with the prototypical patient; it may predict the course of the disorder and the likely effect of one treatment or another. This type of validity is referred to often as *predictive validity* and sometimes as *criterion validity,* when the outcome is the criterion by which we judge the usefulness of the diagnostic category (for example, Klaus et al., 2015). Finally, there is *content validity,* which simply means that if you create criteria for a diagnosis of, say, social phobia, it should reflect the way most experts in the field think of social phobia, as opposed to, say, depression. In other words, you need to get the label right.

Diagnosis before 1980

The classification of psychopathology, as the old adage goes, has a long past but a recent history (Blashfield et al., 2014). Observations of depressed, phobic, or psychotic symptoms stretch back to the earliest recorded observations of human behavior. Many of these observations were so detailed and complete that we could make a diagnosis today of the individuals they described. Nevertheless, only recently have we attempted the difficult task of creating a formal nosology that would be useful for scientists and clinicians around the world. As late as 1959, there were at least nine systems of varying usefulness for classifying psychological disorders worldwide, but only three of the nine systems listed "phobic disorder" as a separate category (Marks, 1969). One reason for this confusion is that creating a useful nosology is easier said than done.

Early efforts to classify psychopathology arose out of the biological tradition, particularly the work of Kraepelin, as described in Chapter 1 and mentioned earlier in this chapter. Kraepelin first identified what we now know as the disorder of schizophrenia. His term for the disorder at the time was *dementia praecox* (Kraepelin, 1919). Dementia praecox refers to deterioration of the brain that sometimes occurs with advancing age (dementia) and develops earlier than it is supposed to, or "prematurely" (praecox). This label (later changed to *schizophrenia*) reflected Kraepelin's belief that brain pathology is the cause of this particular disorder. Kraepelin's landmark 1913 book (*Psychiatry: A Textbook for Students and Physicians*) describes not only dementia praecox but also bipolar disorder, then called *manic depressive psychosis.* Kraepelin also described a variety of organic brain syndromes. Other well-known figures in their time, such as French psychiatrist Philippe Pinel, characterized psychological disorders, including depression (melancholia), as separate entities, but Kraepelin's theorizing that psychological disorders are basically biological disturbances had the greatest impact on the development of our nosology and led to an early emphasis on classical categorical strategies.

It was not until 1948 that the World Health Organization (WHO) added a section classifying mental disorders to the sixth edition of the *International Classification of Diseases and Related Health Problems (ICD).* This early system did not have much influence, however. Nor did the first *Diagnostic and Statistical Manual* (DSM-I), published in 1952 by the American Psychiatric Association. Only in the late 1960s did systems of nosology begin to have some real influence on mental health professionals. In 1968, the American Psychiatric Association published a second edition of its *Diagnostic and Statistical Manual* (DSM-II), and in 1969, WHO published the eighth edition of the *ICD,* which was all but identical to DSM-II, since leaders in mental health began to realize the importance of at least trying to develop a uniform system of classification. Nevertheless, these systems lacked precision, often relying heavily on unproven theories of etiology not widely accepted by all mental health professionals. To make matters worse, the systems had little reliability. Two mental health practitioners looking at the same patient often came to different conclusions based on the nosology at that time. Even as late as the 1970s, many countries, such as France and Russia, had their own systems of nosology. In these countries, the same disorders would be labeled and interpreted differently.

DSM-III and DSM-III-R

The year 1980 brought a landmark in the history of nosology: the third edition of the *Diagnostic and Statistical Manual* (DSM-III) (American Psychiatric Association, 1980). Under the leadership of Robert Spitzer, DSM-III departed radically from its predecessors. Two changes stood out. First, DSM-III attempted to take an atheoretical approach to diagnosis, relying on precise descriptions of the disorders as they presented to clinicians rather than on psychoanalytic or biological theories of etiology. With this focus, DSM-III became a tool for clinicians with a variety of points of view. For example, rather than classifying phobia under the broad category "neurosis," defined by intrapsychic conflicts and defense mechanisms, it was assigned its own category within a new broader group, "anxiety disorders."

The second major change in DSM-III was that the specificity and detail with which the criteria for identifying a disorder were listed made it possible to study their reliability and validity. Although not all categories in DSM-III (and its 1987 revision, DSM-III-R) achieved perfect or even good reliability and validity, this system was a vast improvement over what was available before. Despite numerous shortcomings, such as low reliability in identifying some disorders and arbitrary decisions on criteria for many disorders, DSM-III and DSM-III-R had a substantial impact.

DSM-IV and DSM-IV-TR

By the late 1980s, clinicians and researchers realized once again the importance of a consistent, worldwide system of nosology. The 10th edition of the *International Classification of Diseases (ICD-10)* (World Health Organization, 1992) was published in 1992, and the United States is required by treaty obligations to use the *ICD-10* codes in all matters related to health. To make the *ICD-10* and DSM as compatible as possible, work proceeded more or less simultaneously on both the *ICD-10* and the fourth edition of the DSM (DSM-IV), published in 1994. The DSM-IV task force decided to rely as little as possible on a consensus of experts. Any changes in the diagnostic system were to be based on sound scientific data. Various committees attempted to review the voluminous literature in all areas pertaining to the diagnostic system (Widiger et al., 1996; Widiger, et al., 1998) and to identify large sets of data that might have been collected for other reasons but that, with reanalysis, would be useful to DSM-IV. Finally, 12 independent studies or field trials examined the reliability and validity of alternative sets of definitions or criteria and, in some cases, the possibility of creating a new diagnosis. (See Widiger et al., 1998; Zinbarg et al., 1994, 1998, for examples.)

David Kupfer was the chair of the task force for the 5th edition of the *Diagnostic and Statistical Manual of Mental Disorders* (DSM), which was published in 2013.

Perhaps the most substantial change in DSM-IV was that the distinction between organically based disorders and psychologically based disorders that was present in previous editions was eliminated. As you saw in Chapter 2, we now know that even disorders associated with known brain pathology are substantially affected by psychological and social influences. Similarly, disorders previously described as psychological in origin certainly have biological components and, most likely, identifiable brain circuits.

In 2000, a committee updated the text that describes the research literature accompanying the DSM-IV diagnostic category and made minor changes to some of the criteria themselves to improve consistency (American Psychiatric Association, 2000a; First & Pincus, 2002). This text revision (DSM-IV-TR) helped clarify many issues related to the diagnosis of psychological disorders.

DSM-5 and DSM-5-TR

In the almost 20 years since the publication of DSM-IV, our knowledge had advanced considerably, and, after over 10 years of concerted effort, DSM-5 was published in the spring of 2013. This massive undertaking was also carried out in collaboration with international leaders working simultaneously on *ICD-11* (published in 2019) such that each "workgroup" responsible for a set of disorders (for example, anxiety disorders) had an international expert deeply involved in the work of the committee. The general consensus is that DSM-5 (note the switch from Roman to Arabic numbering) is largely unchanged from DSM-IV, although some new disorders are introduced and other disorders have been reclassified. Also, there have been some organizational and structural changes in the diagnostic manual itself. For example, the manual is divided into three main sections. The first section introduces the manual and describes how best to use it. The second section presents the disorders themselves, and the third section includes descriptions of disorders or conditions that need further research before they can qualify as official diagnoses.

The use of dimensional axes for rating severity, intensity, frequency, or duration of specific disorders in a relatively uniform manner across all disorders is also a feature of DSM-5 (LeBeau et al., 2015). For example, for posttraumatic stress disorder (PTSD), LeBeau et al. (2014) developed the National Stressful Events Survey PTSD Short Scale (NSESSS2PTSD), which is a nine-item self-report scale developed based on data from a national study of U.S. adults (Kilpatrick, Resnick, & Friedman, 2010). This scale was reviewed and approved by the DSM-5 workgroup to assess the severity of PTSD symptoms over the past seven days (American Psychiatric Association, 2013) and is described in more detail in Chapter 5.

In addition to dimensional assessments of severity or intensity for individual disorders, the DSM-5 introduces cross-cutting dimensional symptom measures. These assessments are not specific to any particular disorder but rather evaluate in a global sense important symptoms that are often present across disorders in almost all patients. Examples include anxiety, depression, and problems with sleep (Narrow et al., 2013). The idea would be to monitor the symptoms, if present, across the course of treatment for the presenting disorder.

Thus, one might diagnose bipolar disorder and provide a dimensional rating of the degree of anxiety also present because a greater degree of anxiety seems to predict a poorer response to treatment and thus may require additional treatment (Deckersbach et al., 2014; Howland et al., 2009). The suggested questions in DSM-5 are: "During the past two weeks, how much (or how often) have you been bothered by (1) feeling nervous, anxious, frightened, worried, or on edge, (2) feeling panic or being frightened, or (3) avoiding situations that make you anxious?" (American Psychiatric Association, 2013, p. 738) The DSM-5 rating would be a 0 to 4 scale, where 0 is no anxiety and 4 is very severe anxiety.

Notice that this does not represent a change to the categories of disorders themselves. Rather, these dimensions are added on to the categorical diagnoses in order to provide clinicians with additional information for assessment, treatment planning, and treatment monitoring. Similar to the text revision of the DSM-IV, the DSM-5 has been updating the text that describes the research literature accompanying the diagnostic category, resulting in the most current nosological system, the DSM-5-TR. This text revision was published in 2022 and includes one new disorder, prolonged grief disorder, presented in Chapter 5.

DSM-5 and Frank

In Frank's case, initial observations indicated an obsessive-compulsive disorder diagnosis. He might also, however, have long-standing personality traits that lead him systematically to avoid social contact. If so, there might also be a diagnosis of schizoid personality disorder. Job and marital difficulties might be indicated where clinicians note psychosocial or environmental problems that are not part of the disorder but might make it worse or affect treatment planning. Similarly, overall severity and impairment would be rated in a dimensional fashion periodically, as described above for PTSD, to monitor response to treatment using a DSM-5 scale devised for that purpose (LeBeau et al., 2013).

It is important to emphasize that impairment is a crucial determination in making any diagnosis. For example, if someone, such as Frank, has all of the symptoms of obsessive-compulsive disorder but finds them only mildly annoying because the intrusive thoughts are not severe and don't occur that often, that person would not meet criteria for a psychological disorder. It is essential that the various behaviors and cognitions comprising the diagnosis interfere with functioning in some substantial manner. Thus, the criteria for disorders include the provision that the disorder must cause clinically significant distress or impairment in social, occupational, or other important areas of functioning. Individuals who have all the symptoms as noted earlier but do not cross this "threshold" of impairment could not be diagnosed with a disorder. As noted above, one change in DSM-5 is to make this judgment of severity and impairment more systematic by using a dimensional scale. In one of our own clinics, we have been doing something similar to this for many years (Brown & Barlow, 2014). That is, in addition to rating overall impairment, impairment specifically associated with the disorder (if present) is also rated. We have used a scale of 0 to 8, where 0 is no impairment and 8 is severely disturbing or disabling (usually housebound and barely functional). The disorder must be rated at least a 4 in severity (definitely disturbing or disabling) to meet criteria for a psychological disorder. Many times, disorders such as obsessive-compulsive disorder would be rated a 2 or 3, meaning that all of the symptoms are there but in too mild a form to impair functioning; in this case, the disorder would be termed *subthreshold*. Using Frank as an example again, the severity of his obsessive-compulsive disorder would be rated 5.

Bob Thomas/The Image Bank/Getty Images

The DSM-5 diagnostic guidelines take cultural considerations into account.

Social and Cultural Considerations in DSM-5

By emphasizing levels of stress in the environment, DSM-III and DSM-IV facilitated a more complete picture of the individual. Furthermore, DSM-IV corrected a previous omission by including a plan for integrating important social and cultural influences on diagnosis, a feature that remains in DSM-5. *Culture* refers to the values, knowledge, and practices that individuals derive from membership in different ethnic groups, religious groups, or other social groups, as well as how membership in these groups may affect the individual's perspective on their experience with psychological disorders (American Psychiatric Association, 2013). The plan, referred to as *cultural formulation*, allows the disorder to be described from the perspective of the patient's personal experience and in terms of their primary social and cultural group, such as Hispanic or Chinese. Answering suggested culture-related questions from the DSM-5 *Cultural Formulation Interview* (American Psychiatric Association, 2013) will help accomplish these goals:

1. Some examples include: What is the primary cultural reference group of the patient? For recent immigrants to the country, as well as other ethnic minorities, how involved are they with their "new" culture versus their own culture? Have they mastered the language of their new country (for example, English in the United States), or is language a continuing problem?
2. Does the patient use terms and descriptions from their country of origin to describe the disorder? For example, *ataques de nervios* in the Hispanic subculture is a type of anxiety disorder close to panic disorder. Does the patient accept Western models of disease or disorder for which treatment is available in health-care systems, or does the patient also have an alternative health-care system in another culture (for example, traditional herbal doctors in Chinese subcultures)?

3. What does it mean to be "disabled?" Which kinds of "disabilities" are acceptable in a given culture, and which are not? For example, is it acceptable to be physically ill but not to be anxious or depressed? What are the typical family, social, and religious supports in the culture? Are they available to the patient? Does the clinician understand the first language of the patient, as well as the cultural significance of the disorder?

These cultural considerations must not be overlooked in making diagnoses and planning treatment, and they are assumed throughout this book. But, as yet, there is no research supporting the use of these cultural formulation guidelines (Aggarwal, Nicasio, DeSilva, Boiler, & Lewis-Fernandez, 2013). The consensus is that we have a lot more work to do in this area to make our nosology truly culturally sensitive.

Criticisms of DSM-5

It is clear that DSM-5 (and the closely related *ICD-11* mental disorder section) are the most advanced, scientifically based systems of nosology ever developed. Nevertheless, any nosological system should be considered a work in progress (Brown & Barlow, 2005; Frances & Widiger, 2012; Millon, 2004; Regier et al., 2009; Smith & Oltmanns, 2009), and DSM-5 has attempted to put operations in place allowing for interim revisions to categories as new information becomes available (American Psychiatric Association, 2013). As is evident with the publication of DSM-5 TR (American Psychiatric Association, 2022).

For the time being, we still have "fuzzy" categories that blur at the edges, making diagnostic decisions difficult at times. As a consequence, individuals are often diagnosed with more than

Anton Vengo/SuperStock

The kinds of disabilities accepted in a given culture are socially determined.

one psychological disorder at the same time, which is called **comorbidity**. How can we conclude anything definite about the course of a disorder, the response to treatment, or the likelihood of associated problems if we are dealing with combinations of disorders (L. Allen et al., 2010; Brown & Barlow, 2009; Krueger et al., 2014)? Is there a way to identify essential features of comorbid disorders and, perhaps, rate them dimensionally (Brown & Barlow, 2009; Rosellini, Boettcher, Brown, & Barlow, 2015)? Resolution of these tough problems simply awaits the long, slow process of science.

Criticisms center on two other aspects of DSM-5 and the *ICD-11*. First, the systems strongly emphasize reliability, sometimes at the expense of validity. This is understandable because reliability is difficult to achieve unless you are willing to sacrifice validity. If the sole criterion for establishing depression were to hear the patient say at some point during an interview, "I feel depressed," the clinician could theoretically achieve perfect reliability. But this achievement would be at the expense of validity because many people with differing psychological disorders (or none) occasionally say they are depressed. Thus, clinicians could agree that the statement occurred, but it would be of little use (Meehl, 1989). Second, methods of constructing a nosology of mental disorders have a way of perpetuating definitions handed down to us from past decades, even if they might be fundamentally flawed (Hayes & Hofmann, 2020; Lilienfield, 2014).

In addition to the daunting complexity of categorizing psychopathology, systems are subject to misuse, some of which can be dangerous and harmful. Diagnostic categories are just a convenient format for organizing observations that help professionals communicate, study, and plan. But if we reify a category, we literally make it a "thing," assuming it has a meaning that, in reality, does not exist. Categories may change occasionally with new knowledge, so none can be written in stone. If a case falls on the fuzzy borders between diagnostic categories, we should not expend all our energy attempting to force it into one category or another. It is a mistaken assumption that everything has to fit neatly somewhere.

A Caution about Labeling and Stigma

A related problem that occurs any time we categorize people is **labeling**. You may remember Kermit the Frog from *Sesame Street* sharing with us that "It's not easy being green." Something in human nature causes us to use a label, even one as superficial as skin color, to characterize the totality of an individual ("He's green, so he's different from me"). We see the same phenomenon among psychological disorders ("He's a schizo"). Furthermore, if the disorder is associated with an impairment in cognitive or behavioral functioning, the label itself has negative connotations and contributes to *stigma*, which is a combination of stereotypic negative beliefs, prejudices, and attitudes resulting in reduced life opportunities for the devalued group in question, such as individuals with mental disorders (Hinshaw & Stier, 2008; Martinez, Piff, Mendoza-Denton, & Hinshaw, 2011; Parcesepe & Cabassa, 2013).

There have been many attempts over the years to categorize intellectual disability. Most of the categories were based on the severity of the impairment or highest level of developmental ability that the individual could reach. But we have had to change the labels for these categories of cognitive impairment periodically as the stigma associated with them builds up. One early categorization described levels of severity as *moron* (least severe), *imbecile*, and *idiot* (most severe). When these terms were introduced, they were rather neutral, simply describing the severity of a person's cognitive and developmental impairment. But as they began to be used in common language, they picked up negative connotations and were used as insults. As these terms gradually became pejorative, it was necessary to eliminate them as categories and come up with a new set of classifying labels that were less derogatory. In DSM-5, the term "mental retardation" has been dropped in favor of the more accurate term "intellectual disability," which is further described as mild, moderate, severe, or profound (American Psychiatric Association, 2013). This is consistent with recent changes by other organizations (see Chapter 14).

In any case, once labeled, individuals with a disorder may identify with the negative connotations associated with the label (Hinshaw & Stier, 2008). This affects their self-esteem, although Ruscio (2004) indicates that the negative meanings associated with labeling are not a necessary consequence of making a diagnosis if it is relayed in a compassionate manner. Nevertheless, if you think of your own reactions to mental illness, you will probably recognize the tendency to generalize inappropriately from the label. In fact, for a variety of reasons Hinshaw and Stier (2008) note that stigmatization of individuals with mental disorders is increasing rather than decreasing. We have to remember that terms in psychopathology do not describe people but identify patterns of behavior that may or may not occur in certain circumstances. Thus, whether the disorder is medical or psychological, we must resist the temptation to identify the person with the disorder: Note the different implications of "John is a diabetic" and "John is a person who has diabetes."

Would we label this man? The late Stephen Hawking, was one of the world's leading physicists and was severely disabled by amyotrophic lateral sclerosis, a rare progressive degenerative disease of the spinal cord. Because he could not activate his voice box or move his lips, Hawking typed his words into an electronic voice synthesizer that "spoke" for him. He used his thumbprint to autograph his books. "I have been lucky," he once said. "I don't have anything to be angry about."

Creating and Abandoning Diagnoses

The DSM and *ICD* are essentially products of data-informed consensus meetings. As members of the DSM-IV, DSM-5, and DSM-5-TR development process, we have gained some insights into the complexity of the problems surrounding psychiatric diagnoses. As discussed in Chapter 1, disorders are always influenced by societal factors. For example, *homosexuality* used to be considered a psychiatric disease. It was removed from the DSM only in 1973 and does not appear in DSM III. To put this in context, Harvey Milk, a prominent figure in the gay rights movement, became the first openly gay city commissioner of San Francisco in 1976, and in 1977, he was instrumental in passing the city's first civil rights ordinance that outlawed discrimination based on sexual orientation. Today, the LBGTQ2+ movement as a whole has become very vocal. Although no sexual identity is considered a psychiatric disorder anymore, the DSM-5 does include the diagnosis *gender dysphoria* for transgender people who experience psychological distress that results from an incongruence between the sex that society assigned them at birth and their own gender identity. This incongruence is a result of societal pressure, and, as society changes, the pressure on the single individual will likely change, which might also impact this DSM diagnosis.

Another example of disorders being influenced by societal factors is the controversial diagnosis of *pediatric bipolar disorder*. Because this diagnosis might encourage some psychiatrists to prescribe medication that could prove dangerous to the child's heath, the DSM-5 created the new childhood diagnosis, *disruptive mood regulation disorder*, for children and adolescents who experience ongoing irritability, anger, and frequent, intense temper outbursts. Many of these children would have been previously diagnosed with pediatric bipolar disorder despite not experiencing other bipolar symptoms. Thus, many considerations factor into the decision to retain, eliminate, or create a new diagnosis.

Other examples are Prolonged grief disorder and premenstrual dysphoric disorder. In both cases, some critics wondered whether the DSM went too far by pathologizing normal human experiences—grieving the loss of a loved one and experiencing mood disturbance before the menstrual period in women. Premenstrual dysphoric disorder is an interesting case because it brings to light many of the controversial issues surrounding a diagnosis, including bias and stigmatization. Evaluation of this extremely controversial category began well before the publication of DSM-III-R in 1987. Clinicians had identified a small group of women who presented with severe and sometimes incapacitating emotional reactions associated with the late luteal phase of their menstrual period (Rivera-Tovar, Pilkonis, & Frank, 1992). Subsequently, proposals were made to consider inclusion of this disorder in the DSM-III-R. In view of the suffering and impairment associated with the condition, the proponents argued, people who menstruate deserved the attention, care, and financial support that inclusion in a diagnostic category would provide. In addition, the creation of this category would promote a substantial increase in research into the nature and treatment of the problem.

Nevertheless, arguments against the category were marshaled along several fronts. First, opponents noted that relatively little scientific information existed in either the clinical or the research literature on this topic. The available information was insufficient to warrant the creation of a new diagnostic category. More important were substantial objections that what could be a normal endocrinological stage experienced by all or most people who menstruate would be stigmatized as a psychiatric disorder. The seeming similarities with the once widely accepted category of "hysteria" described in Chapter 1 were also noted. (Remember that this so-called disorder was diagnosed exclusively in women, was characterized by a variety of incapacitating physical complaints without a medical basis, and was thought to be caused by the wandering of the uterus.) Questions were raised about whether the disorder would best be described as endocrinological or gynecological rather than mental. Because premenstrual dysphoric disorder occurs only in people who menstruate, should a comparable disorder—for example, aggressiveness related to excessive testosterone—be included?

The DSM-III-R task force decided to place this disorder in the appendix with the hope of promoting further study. The task force also wanted to clearly differentiate this syndrome from premenstrual syndrome (PMS), which has less severe and specific premenstrual symptomatology. One way of accomplishing this was by naming the condition *late luteal phase dysphoric disorder (LLPDD).*

After the publication of DSM-III-R, LLPDD attracted a great deal of research attention. By 1991, some observers estimated that one research article per month on LLPDD was published (Gold et al., 1996). A variety of scientific findings began to accrue that supported the inclusion of this disorder in DSM-IV. For example, although the rather vague and less severe symptoms of PMS occur in 20% to 40% of women (Severino & Moline, 1989), only a small proportion of them—about 4.6%—suffer from the more severe and incapacitating symptoms associated with LLPDD (Rivera-Tovar & Frank, 1990). In addition, a substantial number of women with no other psychological disorder meet the criteria for LLPDD. Among other findings supporting the inclusion of this disorder in DSM-IV were abnormalities in several biological systems associated with clinically significant premenstrual dysphoria (Gold et al., 1996) and the revelation that several types of treatment showed some promise of being effective against LLPDD (for example, see Stone, Pearlstein, & Brown, 1991). Hurt and colleagues, in a reanalysis of data from 670 women, recommended a set of criteria for this disorder that were not very different from those proposed in DSM-III-R (Hurt et al., 1992).

Nevertheless, arguments continued against including this disorder in the diagnostic system. Most of them cite the issue of stigmatization, warning that recognition might confirm the cultural belief that menstruation and resulting disability make those people unfit for positions of responsibility. (There have been several cases in which accusations of the less severe condition of PMS have been used against a mother in an attempt to win child custody for the father; see Gold et al., 1996.) Those arguing against the disorder also point out that some symptoms are associated with anger, which would not be viewed as inappropriate in a man.

Interestingly, many people with this disorder are quite comfortable with the label. In contrast, some women presenting with other psychological disorders, such as depression, refuse to accept the suggestion that they have a "psychiatric problem," insisting it is really PMS (Rapkin, Chang, & Reading, 1989). Early in 1994, the DSM-IV task force decided to retain the disorder in the appendix as needing further study. Among other problems, the committee wanted to see more data on the prevalence of this condition using the new criteria and to examine more carefully the data on the relation of this problem to existing mood disorders. Several additional research findings indicated that the name *late luteal phase dysphoric disorder* was not entirely accurate because the symptoms may not be exclusively related to the endocrine state of the late luteal phase. Therefore, the name was changed to *premenstrual dysphoric disorder (PMDD).*

Since 1994, research has continued and even accelerated on the nature and treatment of PMDD, with thousands of papers published on this general topic (Bloch, Schmidt, & Rubinow, 2014; Epperson, et al., 2012; O'Brien et al., 2011; Hartlage, Freels, Gotman, & Yonkers, 2012; Pearlstein, 2010; Zachar & Kendler, 2014). Epidemiological studies from around the world supported the existence of disabling premenstrual symptoms in about 2% to 5% of women, with another 14% to 18% experiencing moderate symptoms (Cunningham, Yonkers, O'Brien, & Eriksson, 2009; Epperson et al., 2012; Gold, 1997; Ko, Lee, Chang, & Huang, 1996; Pearlstein & Steiner, 2008). The American College of Obstetricians and Gynecology has also published systematic clinical practice guidelines recommending specific treatments (American College of Obstetricians and Gynecologists, 2002), and new information on effective treatment is published frequently (Epperson et al., 2012; Freeman, Rickels, Sammel, Lin, & Sondheimer, 2009; Jang, Kim, & Choi, 2014; Yonkers, 2015). One of the difficulties encountered has been distinguishing PMDD from premenstrual exacerbations of other disorders, such as binge eating disorder or mood disorders (Pearlstein, Yonkers, Fayyad, & Gillespie, 2005). Hartlage et al. (2012) proposed a method that carefully considers the nature and timing of the symptoms to make a valid distinction between PMDD and premenstrual exacerbations of other disorders. For example, the symptoms of PMDD must be absent or present only mildly postmenstrually. Also, to distinguish from a mood disorder, at least some symptoms must be different from those associated with a mood disorder, such as certain physical symptoms or anxiety. The accumulating evidence thus far seems to suggest that PMDD is best considered a disorder of mood rather than, for example, an endocrine disorder and that it should continue to be considered a mental disorder (Cunningham et al., 2009; Gold, 1999). Support for

PMDD is now sufficient enough that it was included as a distinct psychological disorder in DSM-5 in the mood disorders chapter (see Chapter 7).

Beyond DSM-5: Dimensions and Spectra

The process of changing the criteria for existing diagnoses and creating new ones will continue as our science advances. New findings on brain circuits, cognitive processes, and cultural factors that affect our behavior could date diagnostic criteria relatively quickly.

As mentioned above, although some new disorders have been added and others relocated from one section to another, overall the DSM-5 has not changed substantially from DSM-IV. Nevertheless, it has been clear to most professionals involved in this process that an exclusive reliance on discrete diagnostic categories has not achieved its objective in achieving a satisfactory system of nosology (Blashfield et al., 2014; Frances & Widiger, 2012; Hayes & Hofmann, 2020; Krueger, Watson, & Barlow, 2005; Lilienfeld, 2014). In addition to problems noted earlier with comorbidity and the fuzzy boundary between diagnostic categories, little evidence has emerged validating these categories, such as discovering specific underlying causes associated with each category (Regier et al., 2009). In fact, not one biological marker, such as a laboratory test, that would clearly distinguish one disorder from another has been discovered (Frances, 2009; Widiger & Crego 2013; Widiger & Samuel, 2005). It is also clear that the current categories lack treatment specificity. That is, certain treatments such as cognitive behavioral therapies or specific antidepressant drugs are effective for a large number of diagnostic categories that are not supposed to be all that similar. Therefore, although some progress has been made, many are beginning to assume that the limitations of the current diagnostic system are substantial enough that continued research on these diagnostic categories may never be successful in uncovering their underlying causes or helping us develop new treatments.

It may be time for a new approach. But it is also clear at this point that research is not sufficiently advanced to attempt a wholesale switch to a dimensional or spectrum approach, so the categories in DSM-5-TR for the most part look very much like the categories in DSM-IV with some updated language and increased precision and clarity. But sparked by research and conceptual advances during the process of creating DSM-5, more conceptually substantial and consistent dimensional approaches are in development and may be ready for the sixth edition of the DSM.

For example, most investigators in the area of personality disorders, in studying both clinical samples of patients with personality disorders and community samples, have concluded that personality disorders are not qualitatively distinct from the personalities of normal-functioning individuals in community samples (Krueger et al., 2014; Trull, Carpenter, & Widiger, 2013). Instead, personality disorders simply represent maladaptive and perhaps extreme variants of common personality traits (Widiger & Edmundson, 2011; Widiger, Livesley & Clark, 2009). Even the genetic structure of personality is not consistent with discrete categorical personality disorders. That is, personality dispositions more broadly defined, such as being shy and inhibited or outgoing, have a stronger genetic influence (higher genetic loading) than personality disorders as currently defined (First et al., 2002; Livesley & Jang, 2008; Livesley, Jang, & Vernon, 1998; Rutter, Moffitt, & Caspi, 2006; Widiger et al., 2009). For the anxiety and mood disorders, Brown & Barlow (2009) have proposed a new dimensional system of classification based on previous research (Brown, Chorpita, & Barlow, 1998) demonstrating that anxiety and depression have more in common than previously thought and may best be represented as points on a continuum of negative affect or a spectrum of emotional disorders (see Barlow, 2002; Brown & Barlow, 2005, 2009; Rosellini et al., 2015). Even for severe disorders with seemingly stronger genetic influences, such as schizophrenia, it appears that dimensional classification strategies or spectrum approaches might prove superior (Ahmed et al., 2013; Charney et al., 2002; Harvey & Bowie, 2013; Widiger & Edmundson, 2011).

At the same time, exciting new developments from the area of neuroscience relating to brain structure and function will provide enormously important information on the nature of psychological disorders. This information could then be integrated with more psychological, social, and cultural information into a diagnostic system. But even neuroscientists are abandoning the notion that groups of genes or brain circuits will be found that are specifically associated with DSM-5 diagnostic categories, as noted in Chapter 2. Rather, it is now assumed that neurobiological processes will be discovered that are associated with specific cognitive, emotional, and behavioral patterns or traits (for example, behavioral inhibition) that do not necessarily correspond closely with current diagnostic categories.

With this in mind, we can turn our attention to the current state of our knowledge about a variety of major psychological disorders. But first we review the all-important area of research methods and strategies used to establish new knowledge of psychopathology.

Concept Check 3.2

Identify each of the following statements related to diagnosing psychological disorders as either true (T) or false (F).

1. __________ The classical categorical approach to classification assumes there is only one set of causative factors per disorder with no overlap between disorders, and the prototypical approach uses essential, defining features, as well as a range of other characteristics.
2. __________ As in earlier versions, DSM-5 retains a distinction between organically and psychologically based disorders.
3. __________ The DSM-5 eradicated the problem of comorbidity, the identification of two or more disorders in an individual at one time, which was previously caused by imprecise categories.
4. __________ If two or more clinicians agree on a patient's classification, the assessments are said to be valid.
5. __________ A danger in psychological classification is that a diagnostic label might be used to characterize personally the total individual.

Summary

Assessing Psychological Disorders

- Clinical assessment is the systematic evaluation and measurement of psychological, biological, and social factors in an individual with a possible psychological disorder; diagnosis is the process of determining that those factors meet all criteria for a specific psychological disorder.
- Reliability, validity, and standardization are important components in determining the value of a psychological assessment.
- To assess various aspects of psychological disorders, clinicians may first interview and take an informal mental status exam of the patient. More systematic observations of behavior are called *behavioral assessment.*
- A variety of psychological tests can be used during assessment, including projective tests, in which the patient responds to ambiguous stimuli by projecting unconscious thoughts; personality inventories, in which the patient takes a self-report questionnaire designed to assess personal traits; and intelligence testing, which provides a score known as an intelligence quotient (IQ).
- Biological aspects of psychological disorders may be assessed through neuropsychological testing designed to identify possible areas of brain dysfunction. Neuroimaging can be used more directly to identify brain structure and function. Finally, psychophysiological assessment refers to measurable changes in the nervous system, reflecting emotional or psychological events that might be relevant to a psychological disorder.

Diagnosing Psychological Disorders

- The term *classification* refers to any effort to construct groups or categories and to assign objects or people to the categories on the basis of their shared attributes or relations. Methods of classification include classical categorical, dimensional, and prototypical approaches. Our current system of classification, the *Diagnostic and Statistical Manual,* fifth edition (DSM-5), is based on a prototypical approach in which certain essential characteristics are identified but certain "nonessential" variations do not necessarily change the classification. The DSM-5 categories are based on empirical findings to identify the criteria for each diagnosis. Although this system is the best to date in terms of scientific underpinnings, it is far from perfect, and research continues on the most useful way to classify psychological disorders.

Key Terms

clinical assessment, 73
diagnosis, 73
reliability, 75
validity, 75
standardization, 75
mental status exam, 76
behavioral assessment, 80
self-monitoring, 81
projective tests, 82
personality inventories, 83
intelligence quotient (IQ), 86
neuropsychological test, 86
false positive, 87
false negative, 87
neuroimaging, 87
psychophysiological assessment, 89
electroencephalogram (EEG), 89
idiographic strategy, 90
nomothetic strategy, 90
classification, 90
taxonomy, 90
nosology, 90
nomenclature, 90
classical (or pure) categorical approach, 91
dimensional approach, 91
prototypical approach, 92
familial aggregation, 93
comorbidity, 96
labeling, 96

Answers to Concept Checks

3.1

Part A

1. b; 2. a; 3. e; 4. c; 5. d

Part B

6. R, V; 7. NR, NV; 8. R, V; 9. NR, NV

3.2

1. T; 2. F; 3. F (still a problem); 4. F (reliable); 5. T

4 Research Methods

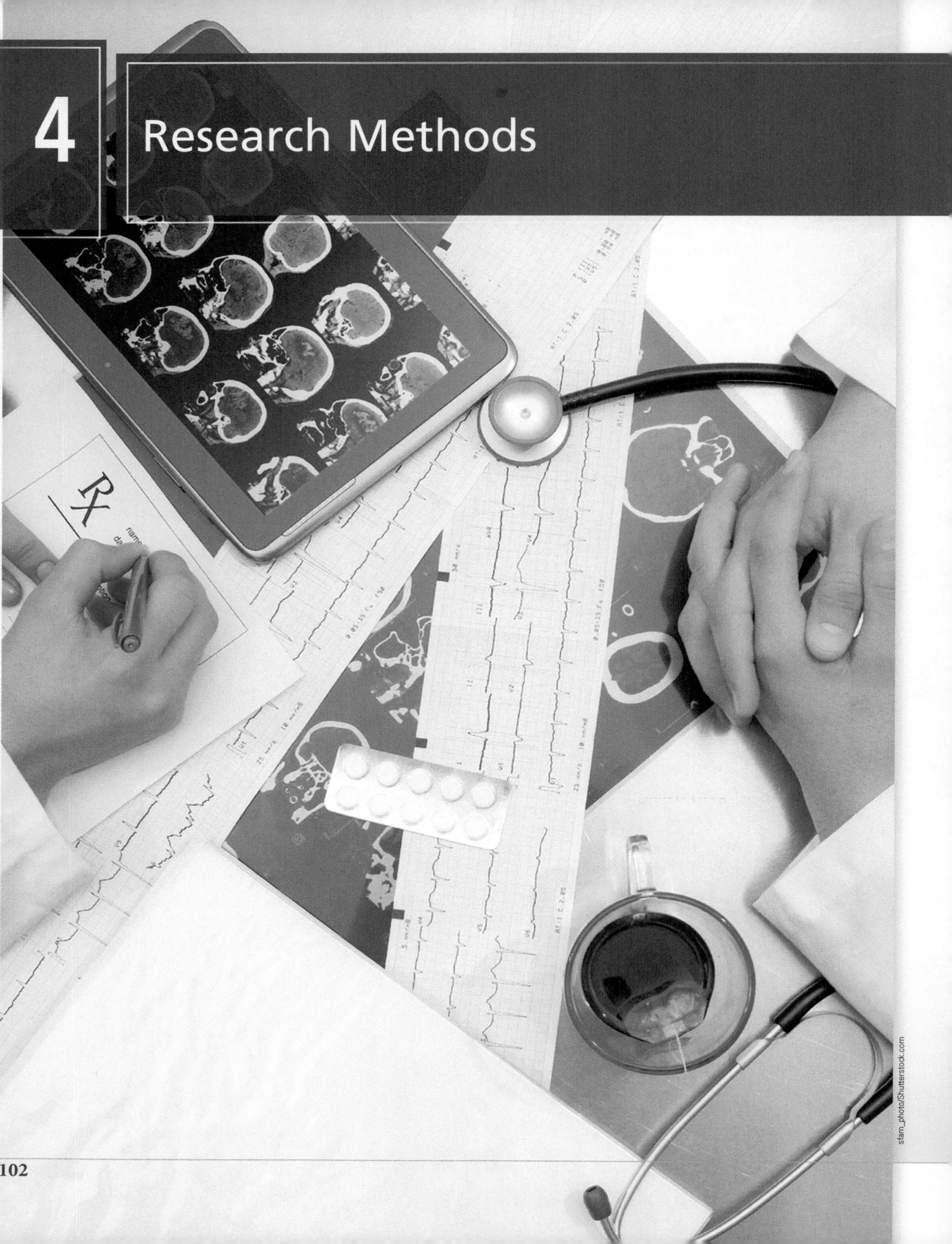

sfam_photo/Shutterstock.com

Learning Objectives

LO4.1 Describe the goals of research as they relate to psychopathology.

LO4.2 Compare the uses of case studies, correlational research, and experimental research as research methods used by psychologists to understand mental disorders.

LO4.3 Distinguish between cross-sectional and longitudinal research designs as research strategies that examine psychopathology across time.

LO4.4 List the ways in which ethical considerations are identified and addressed in modern psychological research.

Examining Psychopathology

Behavioral scientists explore human behavior in the same way other scientists study volcanic activity or the impact of cell phone use on brain cells: They use the scientific method. As you have already learned, psychopathology is a challenging subject because of the interaction of biological and psychological dimensions. Rarely are there any simple answers to such questions as "Why do some people have hallucinations?" or "How do you treat someone who wants to take their own life?"

In addition to the obvious complexity of human nature, another factor that makes an objective study of psychopathology difficult is the inaccessibility of many important aspects of this phenomenon. We cannot get inside the minds of people except indirectly. Fortunately, some creative individuals have accepted this challenge and developed many ingenious methods to studying scientifically what behaviors constitute problems, why people have behavioral disorders, and how to treat these problems. Many critical questions regarding psychopathology have yet to be answered, and we hope that some of you will be inspired to take them on. Understanding research methods is extremely important for everyone, however. You or someone close to you may need the services of a psychologist, psychiatrist, or other mental health provider. You may have questions such as these:

- Should childhood aggression be cause for concern, or is it just a phase my child will grow out of?
- A TV news program just reported that increased exposure to sunlight alleviates depression. Instead of meeting with a therapist, should I buy a ticket to Hawai'i?
- I read online about the horrors of shock therapy. Should I advise my neighbor not to let her daughter have this treatment?
- My brother has been in therapy for 3 years but does not seem to be any better. Should I tell him to look elsewhere for help?
- My mother is still in her 50s but seems to be forgetting things. Friends tell me this is natural as you grow older. Should I be concerned?

To answer such questions, you need to be a good consumer of research. When you understand the correct ways of obtaining information—that is, research methodology—you will know when you are dealing with fact and not fiction. Knowing the difference between a fad and an established approach to a problem can be the difference between months of suffering and a quick resolution to a disturbing problem.

Important Concepts

As we said from the start, we examine several aspects of psychopathology in this book. First, "What problems cause distress and impair functioning?" Second, "Why do people behave in unusual ways?" Third, "How do we help them behave in more adaptive ways?" The first question is about the nature of the problems people report; we explore research strategies that help us answer this question. The second question considers the causes, or *etiology*, of psychopathology; we explore strategies for discovering why a disorder occurred. Finally, because we want to help people who have disorders, we describe how researchers evaluate treatments. Before we discuss specific strategies, however, we must consider several general ways of evaluating research.

Basic Components of a Research Study

The basic research process is simple. You start with an educated guess, called a **hypothesis**, about what you expect to find. When you decide how you want to test this hypothesis, you formulate a **research design** that includes the aspects you want to measure in the people you are studying (the **dependent variable**) and the influences on these characteristics or behaviors (the **independent variable**). Finally, two forms of validity are specific to research studies: internal validity and external validity. **Internal validity** is the extent to which you can be confident that the independent variable is causing the dependent variable to change. **External validity** refers to how well the results relate to things outside your study—in other words, how well your findings describe similar individuals who were not among the study participants. Although we discuss a variety of research strategies, they all have these basic elements. Table 4.1 shows the essential components of a research study.

Hypothesis

Human beings look for order and purpose. We want to know why the world works as it does and why people behave the way they do. Robert Kegan describes us as "meaning-making" organisms, constantly striving to make sense of what is going on around us (Lefrancois, 1990). In fact, fascinating research from social psychology tells us that we may have a heightened motivation to make sense of the world, especially if we experience situations that seem to threaten our sense of order and meaning (Costin & Vignoles, 2020). And for those people who do not seem to want to know why others behave the way they do, we sometimes conclude this is a psychological disorder (for example, autism spectrum disorder; see Chapter 14).

The familiar search for meaning and order also characterizes the field of psychopathology. Almost by definition, psychopathology defies the regularity and predictability we desire. It is this departure from the norm that makes the study of psychopathology so intriguing. In an attempt to make sense of these

Table 4.1 The Basic Components of a Research Study

Component	Description
Hypothesis	An educated guess or statement to be supported by data.
Research design	The plan for testing the hypothesis. Affected by the question addressed, by the hypothesis, and by practical considerations.
Dependent variable	Some aspect of the phenomenon that is measured and is expected to be changed or influenced by the independent variable.
Independent variable	The aspect manipulated or thought to influence the change in the dependent variable.
Internal validity	The extent to which the results of the study can be attributed to the independent variable.
External validity	The extent to which the results of the study can be generalized or applied outside the immediate study.

phenomena, behavioral scientists construct hypotheses and then test them. Hypotheses are nothing more than educated guesses about the world (ideally informed by reviewing previous research on the subject of interest). You may believe that watching violent television programs will cause children to be more aggressive. You may think that bulimia is influenced by media depictions of supposedly ideal female body types. You may suspect that someone abused as a child is likely to abuse their significant other or child. These concerns are all testable hypotheses.

Once a scientist decides what to study, the next step is to put it in words that are unambiguous and in a form that is testable. Consider a study comparing the relative efficacy of two cognitive behavioral therapy (CBT) programs and treatment as usual (TAU) to assess treatment outcomes on anxiety in children with autism spectrum disorder (ASD; see chapter 14) (Wood et al., 2020). Participants in the TAU arm continued in their usual services and were provided with referrals. No specific treatment recommendations were given. One CBT program was a traditional form of CBT, and the second version included components specifically adapted to children with ASD (for example, facilitating parent engagement). Researchers from four universities followed 214 children (ages 7 to 13) who were initially enrolled. Of those children, 167 were randomized into one of the three groups, 145 completed treatment, and 22 discontinued participation. Those who were not randomized failed to meet eligibility criteria (such as confirmed ASD).

In their study, these researchers posed the following research question: "Will one or both of the CBT programs improve anxiety in these children when compared to treatment as usual (TAU)?" They did not know what they would find until the study was completed, but phrasing the hypothesis in this way made it testable. If, for example, children with a history of anxiety had similar levels of anxiety regardless of the treatment, then other components of treatment (such as adding peer instruction) would be studied. This concept of **testability** (the ability to support the hypothesis) is important for science because it allows us to say that in this case, what treatment modality best improves anxiety in children with ASD. The researchers did find that typical CBT was efficacious for children with ASD and the adapted CBT approach showed additional advantages (such as improvements in social-communication symptoms, and adaptive functioning) (Wood et al., 2020).

When they develop an experimental hypothesis, researchers also specify dependent and independent variables. A dependent variable is what is measured, and it may be influenced directly by the study. Psychologists studying psychopathology typically measure an aspect of the disorder in question, such as overt behaviors, self-reported thoughts and feelings, or biological symptoms. In the study by Wood and colleagues, the main dependent variable (anxiety) was measured using several different types of measures (such as the Pediatric Anxiety Rating Scale). Independent variables are those factors thought to affect the dependent variables and may be directly manipulated by the researchers. The independent variable in the study were the three treatments.

Internal and External Validity

The researchers in the study of CBT on anxiety used responses on an intellectual assessment. Suppose they found that among the people in the study, those who did more poorly with CBT happened to have lower IQ scores than those who did better. In other words, there was a systematic difference in the groups (that is, IQ scores). This would have affected the data in a way that would limit what they could conclude about CBT and anxiety and would change the meaning of their results. This situation, which relates to internal validity, is called a **confound** (or **confounding variable**),

Dynamics Graphics Group/Creatas/Alamy Stock Photo

Studying people as part of a group sometimes masks individual differences.

defined as any factor occurring in a study that makes the results uninterpretable because a variable (in this instance, the type of population being studied) other than the independent variable (treatments) may also affect the dependent variable (scores on anxiety scales). You may point out that many different things can affect a dependent variable like cognitive ability, and you would be right. In the example given here, however, the confounding variable is problematic because it differs systematically among the groups being compared (those who participated in standard CBT, adapted CBT and TAU).

Scientists use many strategies to ensure internal validity in their studies, three of which we discuss here: control groups, randomization, and analogue models. In a **control group**, people are similar to the experimental group in every way except that members of the experimental group are exposed to the independent variable and those in the control group are not. Because researchers cannot prevent people from being exposed to many things around them that could affect the outcomes of the study, they try to compare people who receive the treatment with people who go through similar experiences except for the treatment (control group). For example, scientists studying whether a new type of therapy reduces anxiety might compare people who receive the therapy against people who are similar but who do not receive the therapy. Control groups help rule out alternative explanations for results (such as anxiety reducing simply due to the passage of time), thereby strengthening internal validity.

Randomization is the process of assigning people to different research groups in such a way that each person has an equal chance of being placed in any group. Researchers can, for example, randomly place people in groups in the hope that there will be approximately equal numbers of certain people (for example, people with more severe depression) in all groups. Placing people in groups by flipping a coin or using a random number table helps improve internal validity by eliminating any systematic bias in assignment. If random assignment is not used, people sometimes "put themselves in groups," and this self-selection can affect study results. Perhaps a researcher treating people with depression offers them the choice of being either in the treatment group, which requires coming into the clinic twice a week for 2 months, or in a wait-list control group, which means waiting until some later time to be treated. The most severely depressed individuals may not be motivated to come to frequent treatment sessions and so will choose the wait-list group. If members of the treated group are less depressed after several months, it could be because of the treatment or because group members were less depressed to begin with. Groups assembled randomly avoid these problems.

Analogue models create in the controlled conditions of the laboratory aspects that are comparable (analogous) to the phenomenon under study (remember that we described using analogues in assessment in Chapter 3). For example, bulimia researchers could ask volunteers to binge eat in the laboratory, questioning them before they ate, while they were eating, and after they finished to learn whether eating in this way made them feel more or less anxious, guilty, and so on. If they used volunteers of any age, gender, race, or background, the researchers could rule out influences on the participants' attitudes about eating that they might not be able to dismiss if the group contained only people with bulimia. In this way, such "artificial" studies help improve internal validity.

In a research study, internal and external validity often seem to be in opposition. On the one hand, we want to be able to control as many things as possible to conclude that the independent variable (the aspect of the study we manipulated) was responsible for the changes in the dependent variables (the aspects of the study we expected to change). On the other hand, we want the results to apply to people other than the participants of the study and in other settings; this is **generalizability**, the extent to which results apply to everyone in a certain population (such as people with a particular disorder). If we control all aspects of a study so that only the independent variable changes, the result is not relevant to the real world. For example, if you reduce the influence of gender issues by studying only males, and if you reduce age variables by selecting only people from 25 to 30 years of age, and finally, if you limit your study to those with college degrees so that education level isn't an issue—then what you study (in this case, 25- to 30-year-old male college graduates) may not be relevant to many other populations. Internal and external validity are in this way often inversely related. Researchers constantly try to balance these two concerns, and, as you will learn later in this chapter, the best solution for achieving both internal and external validity may be to conduct several related studies.

Statistical versus Clinical Significance

The introduction of statistics is part of psychology's evolution from a prescientific to a scientific discipline. Statisticians gather, analyze, and interpret data from research. In psychological research, statistical significance typically means that the probability of obtaining the observed effect by chance is small. As an example, consider a study evaluating whether watching a video designed to promote a positive mood affects the amount of food eaten by subjects with eating disorders (Cardi, Esposito, Clarke, Schifano, & Treasure, 2015). The study found that participants with anorexia nervosa consumed 75 milliliters of a fruit smoothie after watching the positive video clip, compared to 38 milliliters consumed on average by subjects with anorexia nervosa after watching a neutral video clip. This difference was statistically significant. However, is it an important difference? The difficulty is in the distinction between **statistical significance** (a mathematical calculation about the difference between groups) and **clinical significance** (whether or not the difference was meaningful for those affected) (Mewton, Hodge, Gates, Visontay, Lees, & Teesson, 2020).

Closer examination of the results leads to concern about the size of the effect. Despite this difference in consumption between the positive-mood and neutral-mood groups, these subjects with anorexia nervosa ate less of the smoothie than a group of subjects without eating disorders (who consumed approximately 199 milliliters of the smoothie on average). Therefore, the difference may not be clinically significant because it did not elevate consumption to "nondisordered" levels.

Fortunately, concern for the clinical significance of results has led researchers to develop statistical methods that address not just that groups are different but also how large these differences are, or **effect size**. Calculating the actual statistical measures involves fairly sophisticated procedures that take into account how much each treated and untreated person in a research study improves or worsens (Durand & Wang, 2011; Fritz, Morris, & Richler, 2012). In other words, instead of just looking at the results of the group as a whole, individual differences are considered as well. Some researchers have used more subjective ways of determining whether truly important change has resulted from treatment. The late behavioral scientist Montrose Wolf (1978) advocated the assessment of what he called *social validity.* This technique involves obtaining input from the person being treated, as well as from significant others, about the importance of the changes that have occurred. In the example here, we might ask the participants and family members if they thought the positive video clip led to lasting changes in eating behavior (such as eating more over the week following the study). If the effect of the treatment is large enough to impress those who are directly involved, the treatment effect is clinically significant. Statistical techniques of measuring effect size and assessing subjective judgments of change will let us better evaluate the results of our treatments.

The "Average" Client

Too often we look at results from studies and make generalizations about the group, ignoring individual differences. Kiesler (1966) labeled the tendency to see all participants as one homogeneous group the **patient uniformity myth**. Comparing groups according to their mean scores ("Group A improved by 50% over Group B") hides important differences in individual reactions to our interventions.

The patient uniformity myth leads researchers to make inaccurate generalizations about disorders and their treatments.

Concept Check 4.1

In each of the statements provided, fill in the blanks with one of the following: hypothesis, dependent variable, independent variable, internal validity, external validity, or confound.

1. In a treatment study, the introduction of the treatment to the participants is referred to as the __________.
2. After the treatment study has been completed, you find that many people in the control group received treatment outside of the study. This is called a __________.
3. A researcher's guess about what a study might find is labeled the __________.
4. Scores on a depression scale improved for a treatment group after therapy. The change in these scores would be referred to as a change in the __________.
5. A relative lack of confounds in a study would indicate good __________, whereas good generalizability of the results would be called good __________.

To continue with our previous example, what if the researchers studying the treatment of eating disorders concluded watching positive video clips was a good approach? And suppose we found that, although some participants improved with treatment, others worsened. Such differences would be averaged out in the analysis of the group as a whole, but for the person who continued to be affected by eating disorder symptoms, it would make little difference that "on the average" people improved. Because people differ in such ways as age, cognitive abilities, gender, and history of treatment, a simple group comparison may be misleading. Practitioners who deal with all types of disorders understand the heterogeneity of their clients and therefore do not know whether treatments that are statistically significant will be effective for a given individual. In our discussions of various disorders, we return to this issue.

Types of Research Methods

Researchers who study human behavior use several forms of research when studying the causes of behavior. We now examine individual case studies, correlational research, experimental research, and single-case experimental studies.

Studying Individual Cases

Consider the following scenario: A psychologist thinks she has discovered a new disorder. She has observed several men who seem to have similar characteristics. All complain of a specific sleep disorder: falling asleep at work. Each man has obvious cognitive impairments that were evident during the initial interviews, and all are similar physically, each with significant hair loss and a pear-shaped physique. Finally, their personality styles are extremely egocentric, or self-centered. Based on these preliminary observations, the psychologist has come up with a tentative name, the Homer Simpson disorder, and she has decided to investigate this condition and possible treatments. However, what is the best way to begin exploring a relatively unknown disorder? One method is to use the **case study method**, investigating intensively one or more individuals who display the behavioral and physical patterns (Yin, 2012).

One way to describe the case study method is by noting what it is not. It does not use the scientific method. Few efforts are made to ensure internal validity, and, typically, many confounding variables are present that can interfere with conclusions. Instead, the case study method relies on a clinician's observations of differences among one person or one group with a disorder, people with other disorders, and people with no psychological disorders. The clinician usually collects as much information as possible to obtain a detailed description of the person. Historically, interviewing the person under study yields a great deal of information on personal and family background, education, health, and work history, as well as the person's opinions about the nature and causes of the problems studied.

Case studies are important in the history of psychology. Sigmund Freud developed psychoanalytic theory and the methods of psychoanalysis based on his observations of dozens of cases. Freud and Josef Breuer's description of Anna O. (see Chapter 1) led to development of the clinical technique known as free association. Sexuality researchers Virginia Johnson and William Masters based their work on many case studies and helped shed light on numerous myths regarding sexual behavior (Masters & Johnson, 1966). Joseph Wolpe, author of the landmark book *Psychotherapy by Reciprocal Inhibition* (1958), based his work with systematic desensitization on more than 200 cases. As our knowledge of psychological disorders has grown, psychological researchers' reliance on the case study method has gradually decreased.

One difficulty with depending heavily on individual cases is that sometimes coincidences occur that are irrelevant to the condition under study. Unfortunately, coincidences in people's lives often lead to mistaken conclusions about what causes certain conditions and what treatments are effective. Because a case study does not have the controls of an experimental study, the results may be unique to a particular person without the researcher realizing it or may derive from a special combination of factors that are not obvious. Complicating our efforts to understand psychopathology is the portrayal of sensational cases in the media. For example, on April 16, 2007, a shooter on the campus of Virginia Tech University took the lives of 32 faculty members and students. Immediately after this horrific mass killing, there was speculation about the shooter, including early bullying, descriptions of him being a "loner," and depictions of notes he wrote against "rich kids," "deceitful charlatans," and "debauchery" (Kellner, 2008). Attempts have been made to discover childhood experiences that could possibly explain this later behavior (Harrison & Frederick, in press). We must be careful, however, about concluding anything from such sensational portrayals, since many people are bullied as children, for example, but do not go on to kill dozens of innocent people.

Researchers in cognitive psychology point out that the public and researchers themselves are often, unfortunately, more highly influenced by dramatic accounts than by scientific evidence (Nisbett & Ross, 1980). Remembering our tendency to ignore this fact, we highlight research findings in this book. To advance our understanding of the nature, causes, and treatment of psychopathology, we must guard against premature and inaccurate conclusions.

Research by Correlation

One of the fundamental questions posed by scientists is whether two variables relate to each other. A statistical relationship between two variables is called a **correlation**. For example, is schizophrenia related to the size of ventricles (spaces) in the brain? Are people with depression more likely to have negative attributions (negative explanations for their own and others' behavior)? Is the frequency of hallucinations higher among older people? The answers depend on determining how one variable (for example, number of hallucinations) is related to another (for example, age). Unlike experimental designs, which involve manipulating or changing conditions, correlational designs are used to study phenomena just as they occur. The result of a correlational study—whether variables occur together—is important to the ongoing search for knowledge about psychopathology.

One of the clichés of science is that correlation does not imply causation. In other words, two things occurring together does not necessarily mean that one caused the other. For example, the occurrence of marital problems in families is correlated with behavior problems in children (Zhang, Palmer, Zhang, & Gewirtz, in press). If you conduct a correlational study in this area, you will find that in families with marital problems, you tend to see children with behavior problems; in families with fewer marital problems, you are likely to find children with fewer behavior problems. The most obvious conclusion is that having marital problems will cause children to misbehave. If only it were as simple as that! The nature of the relationship between marital discord and childhood behavior problems can be explained in a number of ways. It may be that problems in a marriage cause disruptive behavior in the children. Some evidence suggests, however, the opposite may be true as well: The disruptive behavior of children may cause marital problems (Rutter & Giller, 1984). In addition, evidence suggests genetic influences may play a role in conduct disorders and in marital discord (D'Onofrio et al., 2006; Lynch et al., 2006). So parents who are genetically more inclined to argue pass on those genes to children, who then have an increased tendency to misbehave.

This example points out the problems in interpreting the results of a correlational study. We know that variable A (marital problems) is correlated with variable B (child behavior problems). We do not know from these studies whether A causes B (marital problems cause child problems), whether B causes A (child problems cause marital problems), or whether some third variable, C, causes both (genes influence both marital problems and child problems).

The association between marital discord and child problems represents a **positive correlation**. This means that great strength or quantity in one variable (a great deal of marital distress) is associated with great strength or quantity in the other variable (more child disruptive behavior). At the same time, lower strength or quantity in one variable (marital distress) is associated with lower strength or quantity in the other (disruptive behavior). If you have trouble conceptualizing statistical concepts, you can think about this mathematical relationship in the same way you would a social relationship. Two people who are getting along well tend to go places together: "Where I go, you will go!" The correlation (or **correlation coefficient**) is represented as +1.00. The plus sign means there is a positive relationship, and the 1.00 means that it is a "perfect" relationship, in which the people are inseparable. But two people who like each other do not go everywhere together. The strength of their relationship ranges between 0.00 and +1.00 (0.00 means no relationship exists). The higher the number, the stronger the relationship, whether the number is positive or negative (for example, a correlation of +0.80 is "stronger" than a correlation of +0.75). You would expect two strangers, for example, to have a relationship of 0.00 because their behavior is not related; they sometimes end up in the same place together, but this occurs rarely and randomly. Two people who know each other but do not like each other would be represented by a negative sign, with the strongest negative relationship being −1.00, which means "Anywhere you go, I won't be there!"

Using this analogy, marital problems in families and behavior problems in children have a relatively strong positive correlation

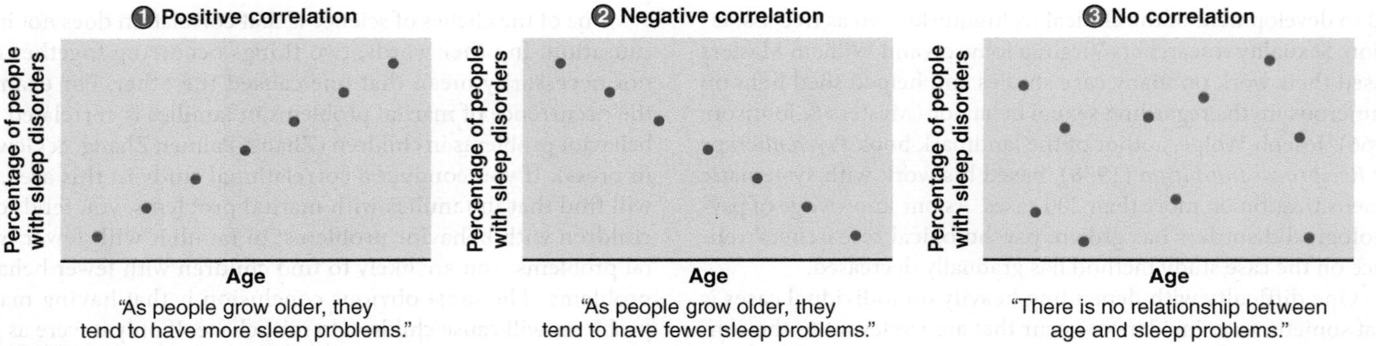

Figure 4.1
These three graphs represent hypothetical correlations between age and sleep problems.

represented by a number around +0.50. They tend to go together. On the other hand, other variables are strangers to each other. Schizophrenia and height are not related, so they do not go together and probably would be represented by a number close to 0.00. If A and B have no correlation, their correlation coefficient would approximate 0.00. Other factors have negative relationships: As one increases, the other decreases. (See ■ Figure 4.1 for an illustration of positive and negative correlations.) We use an example of **negative correlation** in Chapter 2, when we discuss social supports and illness. The more social supports that are present, the less likely it is that a person will become ill. The negative relationship between social supports and illness could be represented by a number such as −0.40. The next time someone wants to break up with you, ask if the goal is to weaken the strength of your positive relationship to something like +0.25 (friends), to become complete strangers at 0.00, or to have an intense negative relationship approximating −1.00 (enemies).

A correlation allows us to see whether a relationship exists between two variables but not to draw conclusions about whether either variable causes the effects. This is a problem of **directionality**. In this case, it means that we do not know whether A causes B, B causes A, or a third variable, C, causes A and B. Therefore, even an extremely strong relationship between two variables (+0.90) shows nothing about the direction of causality.

Epidemiological Research

Scientists often think of themselves as detectives, searching for the truth by studying clues. One type of correlational research that is much like the efforts of detectives is called **epidemiology**, the study of the incidence, distribution, and consequences of a particular problem or set of problems in one or more populations. Epidemiologists expect that by tracking a disorder among many people they will find important clues as to why the disorder exists. The study of COVID-19 is a contemporary example of the work of epidemiologists—including identifying the most vulnerable groups (including people over 65 years of age and those with certain preexisting conditions) (Lipsitch, Swerdlow, & Finelli, 2020). One strategy involves determining *prevalence*, the number of people with a disorder at any one time. For example, the prevalence of binge drinking (having five or more drinks in a row) among U.S. college students is about 40% (Substance Abuse and Mental Health Services Administration, 2014). One study found that in states that legalized recreational marijuana use, marijuana use increased but binge drinking decreased (Alley, Kerr, & Bae, 2020). A related strategy is to determine the *incidence* of a disorder, the estimated number of new cases during a specific period. For example, incidence of binge drinking among college students has lowered slightly from 1980 until the present (Substance Abuse and Mental Health Services Administration, 2014), suggesting that despite efforts to reduce such heavy drinking, it continues to be a problem. Epidemiologists study the incidence and prevalence of disorders among different groups of people. For instance, data from epidemiological research indicate that the prevalence of alcohol abuse among Black Americans is lower than that among White Americans (Substance Abuse and Mental Health Services Administration, 2012).

Although the primary goal of epidemiology is to determine the extent of medical problems, it is also useful in the study of psychopathology. In the early 1900s, a number of Americans displayed symptoms of a strange mental disorder. Its symptoms were similar to those of organic psychosis, which is often caused by mind-altering drugs or great quantities of alcohol. Many patients appeared to be catatonic (immobile for long periods) or exhibited symptoms similar to those of paranoid schizophrenia. Victims were likely to be low-income Black individuals, which led to speculation about racial and class inferiority. Using the methods of epidemiological research, however, researcher Joseph Goldberger found correlations between the disorder and diet, and he identified the cause of the disorder as a deficiency of the B vitamin niacin among people with poor diets. The symptoms were successfully eliminated by niacin therapy and improved diets among low-income populations. A long-term, widespread benefit of Goldberger's findings was the introduction of vitamin-enriched bread in the 1940s (Colp, 2009).

Researchers have used epidemiological techniques to study the effects of stress on psychological disorders. On the morning of September 11, 2001, approximately 3,000 people died from three separate terrorist attacks in lower Manhattan, at the Pentagon, and in Pennsylvania. DeLisi and colleagues (DeLisi et al., 2003) interviewed 1,009 men and women throughout Manhattan to

Monkey Business Images/Shutterstock.com

The more social supports people have, the less likely it is that they will become ill.

assess their long-term emotional reactions to the attacks, especially given their proximity to the destroyed World Trade Center towers. These researchers found that individuals who had the most negative reactions to this traumatic event were those who had preexisting psychological disorders, those who had the greatest exposure to the attack (for example, being evacuated from the World Trade Center), and women. The most common negative reactions included anxiety and painful memories. This is a correlational study because the investigators did not manipulate the independent variable. (The attack was not part of an experiment.)

If you have followed the work on the AIDS virus, you have seen how epidemiologists study a problem. By tracking the incidence of this disease among several populations (gay men, intravenous drug users, and significant others and children of infected individuals) in the early days of the AIDS epidemic (1980s), researchers obtained important information about how the virus is passed from person to person. They inferred from the types of behaviors engaged in by members of these groups that the virus is probably spread by the transfer of bodily fluids through unprotected sex or by nonsterile hypodermic needles. Like other types of correlational research, epidemiological research can't tell us conclusively what causes a particular phenomenon. Knowledge about the prevalence and course of psychological disorders is extremely valuable to our understanding, however, because it points researchers in the right direction.

Research by Experiment

An **experiment** involves the manipulation of an independent variable and the observation of its effects. We manipulate the independent variable to answer the question of causality. If we observe a correlation between social supports and psychological disorders, we cannot conclude which of these factors influenced the other. We can, however, change the extent of social supports and see whether there is an accompanying change in the prevalence of psychological disorders—in other words, do an experiment.

What will this experiment tell us about the relationship between these two variables? If we increase social supports and find no change in the frequency of psychological disorders, it may mean that lack of such supports does not cause psychological problems. On the other hand, if we find that psychological disorders diminish with increased social support, we can be more confident that nonsupport does contribute to psychological disorders. However, because we are never 100% confident that our experiments are internally valid—that no other explanations are possible—we must be cautious about interpreting our results. In the following section, we describe different ways in which researchers conduct experiments and consider how each one brings us closer to understanding psychopathology.

Group Experimental Designs

With correlational designs, researchers observe groups to see how different variables are associated. In group experimental designs, researchers are more active. They actually change an independent variable to see how the behavior of the people in the group is affected. Suppose researchers design an intervention to help reduce insomnia in older adults, who are particularly affected by the condition (Karlin, Trockel, Spira, Taylor, & Manber, 2015). They treat a number of individuals and follow them for 10 years to learn whether their sleep patterns improve. The treatment is the independent variable; that is, it would not have occurred naturally. They then assess the treated group to learn whether their behavior changed as a function of what the researchers did. Introducing or withdrawing a variable in a way that would not have occurred naturally is called *manipulating a variable.*

Unfortunately, a decade later the researchers find that the older adults treated for sleep problems still, as a group, sleep less than 8 hours per night. Is the treatment a failure? Maybe not. The question that cannot be answered in this study is what would have happened to group members if they had not been treated. Perhaps their sleep patterns would have been worse. Fortunately, researchers have devised ingenious methods to help sort out these complicated questions.

A special type of group experimental design is used more and more frequently in the treatment of psychological disorders and is referred to as a *clinical trial* (Durand & Wang, 2011; Pocock, 2013). A clinical trial is an experiment used to determine the effectiveness and safety of a treatment or treatments. The term *clinical trial* implies a level of formality with regard to how it is conducted. As a result, a clinical trial is not a design by itself but rather a method of evaluation that follows a number of generally accepted rules. For example, these rules cover how you should select the research participants, how many individuals should be included in the study, how they should be assigned to groups, and how the data should be analyzed—and this represents only a partial list. Also, treatments are usually applied using formal protocols to ensure that everyone is treated the same.

The terms used to describe these experiments can be confusing. *Clinical trials* is the overarching term used to describe the general category of studies that follow the standards described previously. Within the clinical trial category are *randomized clinical trials,* which are experiments that employ randomization of participants into each experimental group. Another subset of clinical trials is *controlled clinical trials,* which are used to describe experiments that rely on control conditions to be used for comparison purposes. Finally, the preferred method of conducting a clinical trial, which uses both randomization and one or more control conditions, is referred to as a *randomized controlled trial*. We next describe the nature of control groups and randomization and discuss their importance in treatment outcome research.

Control Groups

One answer to the what-if dilemma is to use a control group—people who are similar to the experimental group in every way except they are not exposed to the independent variable. In the previous study looking at sleep in older adults, suppose another group who didn't receive treatment was selected. Further, suppose that the researchers also follow this group of people, assess them 10 years later, and look at their sleep patterns over this period of time. They probably observe that, without intervention, people tend to sleep fewer hours as they age—a finding that cuts across multiple cultures (Lee et al., 2020; Nutakor, Dai, Gavu, & Antwi, 2020; Scarlett, Nolan, Kenny, & O'Connell, 2020). Members of the control group might sleep significantly less than people in the treated group, who might themselves sleep somewhat less than they did 10 years earlier. Using a control group allows the researchers to see that their treatment did help the treated participants keep their sleep time from decreasing further.

Ideally, a control group is nearly identical to the treatment group in such factors as age, gender, socioeconomic backgrounds, and the problems they are reporting. Furthermore, a researcher would do the same assessments before and after the independent variable manipulation (for example, a treatment) to people in both groups. Any later differences between the groups after the change would, therefore, be attributable only to what was changed.

People in a treatment group often expect to get better. When behavior changes as a result of a person's expectation of change rather than as a result of any manipulation by an experimenter, the phenomenon is known as a **placebo effect** (from the Latin word *placebo*, which means "I shall please"). Conversely, people in the control group may be disappointed that they are not receiving treatment (this often called *nocebo effect*, from the Latin word *nocebo*, meaning "to harm") (Geers & Caplandies, 2021). Depending on the type of disorder they experience (for example, depression), disappointment may make them worse. This phenomenon would also make the treatment group look better by comparison.

One way that researchers address the expectation concern is through **placebo control groups**. The word *placebo* typically refers to inactive medications such as sugar pills. The placebo is given to members of the control group to make them believe they are getting treatment (Geers & Caplandies, 2021). A placebo control in a medication study can be carried out with relative ease because people in the untreated group receive something that looks like the medication administered to the treatment group. In psychological treatments, however, it is not always easy to devise something that people believe may help them but does not include the component the researcher believes is effective. Clients in these types of control groups are often given part of the actual therapy—for example, the same homework as the treated group—but not the portions the researchers believe are responsible for improvements.

Note that you can look at the placebo effect as one portion of any treatment (Geers & Caplandies, 2021). If someone you provide with a treatment improves, you would have to attribute the improvement to a combination of your treatment and the client's expectation of improving (placebo effect). Therapists want their clients to expect improvement; this helps strengthen the treatment. When researchers conduct an experiment to determine what portion of a particular treatment is responsible for the observed changes, however, the placebo effect is a confound that can dilute the validity of the research. Thus, researchers use a placebo control group to help distinguish the results of positive expectations from the results of actual treatment.

The **double-blind control** is a variant of the placebo control group procedure. As the name suggests, not only are the participants in the study "blind," or unaware of what group they are in or what treatment they are given (single blind), but so are the researchers or therapists providing treatment (double blind). This type of control eliminates the possibility that an investigator might bias the outcome. For example, a researcher comparing two treatments who expected one to be more effective than the other might "try harder" if the "preferred" treatment wasn't working as well as expected. On the other hand, if the treatment that wasn't expected to work seemed to be failing, the researcher might not push as hard to see it succeed. This reaction might not be deliberate, but it does happen. This phenomenon is referred to as an *allegiance effect* (Dragioti, Dimoliatis, Fountoulakis, & Evangelou, 2015). If, however, both the participants and the researchers or therapists are "blind" there is less chance that bias will affect the results.

A double-blind placebo control does not work perfectly in all cases. If medication is part of the treatment, participants and researchers may be able to tell whether they have received it by the presence or absence of physical reactions (side effects). Even with purely psychological interventions, participants often know whether they are receiving a powerful treatment, and they may alter their expectations for improvement accordingly.

Comparative Treatment Research

As an alternative to using no-treatment control groups to help evaluate results, some researchers compare different treatments. In this design, the researcher gives different treatments to two or more comparable groups of people with a particular disorder and can then assess how or whether each treatment helped the people who received it. This is called **comparative treatment research**. In the sleep study we discussed, two groups of older adults could be selected, with one group given medication for insomnia, the other given a cognitive-behavioral intervention, and the results compared.

The process and outcome of treatment are two important issues to be considered when different approaches are studied. *Process research* focuses on the mechanisms responsible for behavior change, or "Why does it work?" In an old joke, someone goes to a physician for a new miracle cold cure. The physician

Dave & Les Jacobs/Blend Images/Jupiter Images

Tetra Images/Alamy Stock Photo

In comparative treatment research, different treatments are administered to comparable groups of people.

prescribes the new drug and tells the patient the cold will be gone in 7 to 10 days. As most of us know, colds typically improve in 7 to 10 days without so-called miracle drugs. The new drug probably does nothing to further the improvement of the patient's cold. The process aspect of testing medical interventions involves evaluating biological mechanisms responsible for change. Does the medication cause lower serotonin levels, for example, and does this account for the changes we observe? Similarly, in looking at psychological interventions, we determine what is "causing" the observed changes. This is important for several reasons. First, if we understand what the "active ingredients" of our treatment are, we can often eliminate aspects that are not important, thereby saving clients' time and money. For an example, one study of treatments for anxiety in youth found that the introduction of relaxation training did not speed up an individual's progress in treatment, whereas the introduction of treatment elements that focused on thoughts or behaviors did. These results allow clinicians to focus their treatment on only those aspects most likely to improve anxiety (for example, cognitive restructuring and exposures; Peris et al., 2015). In addition, knowing what is important about our interventions can help us create more powerful, newer versions that may be more effective.

Outcome research focuses on the positive, negative, or both results of the treatment. In other words, does it work? Remember, *treatment process* involves finding out why or how your treatment works. In contrast, *treatment outcome* involves finding out what changes occur after treatment.

Single-Case Experimental Designs

B. F. Skinner's innovations in scientific methodology were among his most important contributions to psychopathology. Skinner formalized the concept of **single-case experimental designs**. This method involves the systematic study of individuals under a variety of experimental conditions. Skinner thought it was much better to know a lot about the behavior of one individual than to make only a few observations of a large group for the sake of presenting the "average" response. Psychopathology is concerned with the distress of specific people, and this methodology has greatly helped us understand the factors involved in individual psychopathology (Wendt & Rindskopf, 2020). Many applications throughout this book reflect Skinnerian methods.

Single-case experimental designs differ from case studies in their use of various strategies to improve internal validity, thereby reducing the number of confounding variables. As you will see, these strategies have strengths and weaknesses in comparison with traditional group designs. Although we use examples from treatment research to illustrate the single-case experimental designs, they, like other research strategies, can help explain why people engage in psychopathology, as well as how to treat them.

Repeated Measurements

One of the more important strategies used in single-case experimental design is **repeated measurement**, in which a behavior is measured several times instead of only once before

Figure 4.2

The top graph seems to show Wendy's anxiety dropping significantly after treatment (measuring level). When you look at repeated measures before and after treatment, however, the middle graph reveals little change because her anxiety fluctuated a great deal (measuring variability). A different scenario is illustrated in the bottom graph (measuring trend), where her anxiety also varied. In general, there was a downward movement (improved anxiety) even before treatment, suggesting that she might have improved without help. Examining variability and trend can provide more information about the true nature of the change.

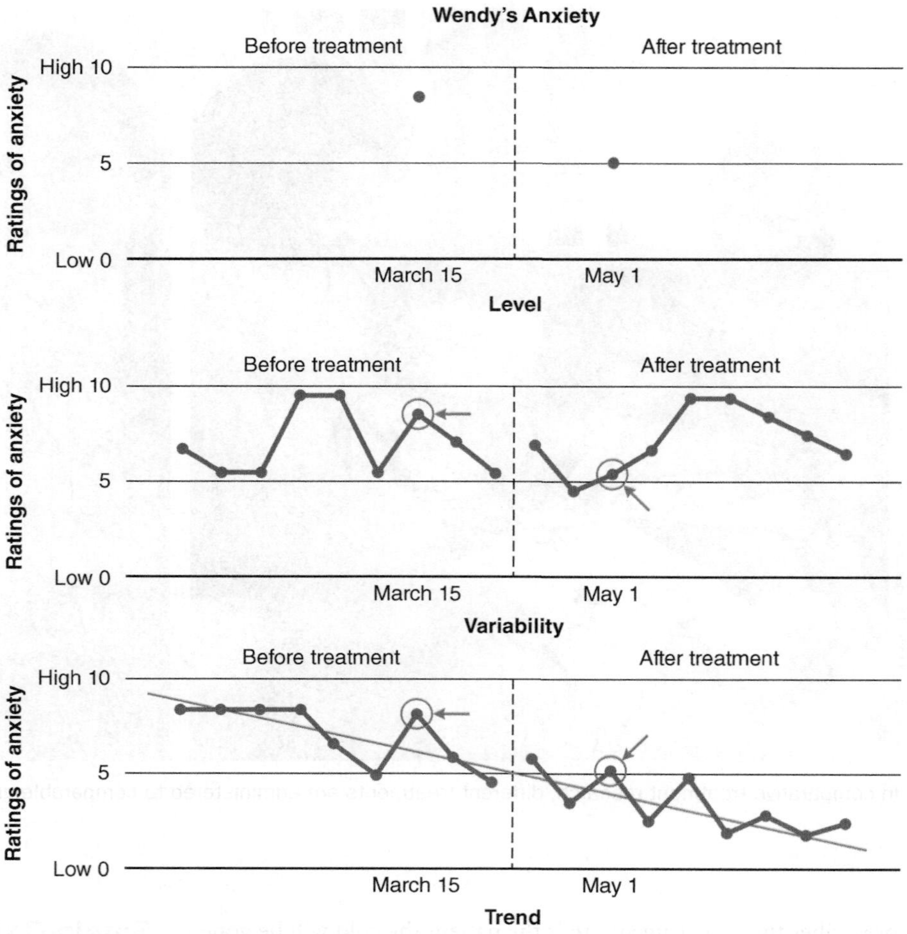

you change the independent variable and once afterward. The researcher takes the same measurements repeatedly to learn how variable the behavior is (how much does it change from day to day?) and whether it shows any obvious trends (is it getting better or worse?). Suppose a young woman, Wendy, comes into the office complaining about feelings of anxiety. When asked to rate the level of her anxiety, she gives it a 9 (10 is the worst). After several weeks of treatment, Wendy rates her anxiety at 6. Can we say that the treatment reduced her anxiety? Not necessarily.

Suppose we had measured Wendy's anxiety each day during the weeks before her visit to the office (repeated measurement) and observed that it differed greatly. On particularly good days, she rated her anxiety from 5 to 7. On bad days, it was between 8 and 10. Suppose further that, even after treatment, her daily ratings continued to range from 5 to 10. The rating of 9 before treatment and 6 after treatment may only have been part of the daily variations she experienced normally. Wendy could just as easily have had a good day and reported a 6 before treatment and then had a bad day and reported a 9 after treatment, which would imply that the treatment made her worse!

Repeated measurement is part of each single-subject experimental design. It helps identify how a person is doing before and after intervention and whether the treatment accounted for any changes. ■ Figure 4.2 summarizes Wendy's anxiety and the added information obtained by repeated measurements. The top graph shows Wendy's original before-and-after ratings of her anxiety. The middle graph shows that with daily ratings her reports are variable and that just by chance the previous measurement was probably misleading. She had good and bad days both before and after treatment and does not seem to have changed much.

The bottom graph shows a different possibility: Wendy's anxiety was on its way down before the treatment, which would also have been obscured with just before-and-after measurements. Maybe she was getting better on her own, and the treatment didn't have much effect. Although the middle graph shows how the **variability** from day to day could be important in an interpretation of the effect of treatment, the bottom graph shows how the **trend** itself can also be important in determining the cause of any change. The three graphs illustrate important parts of repeated measurements: (1) the **level** or degree of behavior change with different interventions (top), (2) the variability or degree of change over time (middle), and (3) the trend or direction of change (bottom). Again, before-and-after scores alone do not necessarily show what is responsible for behavioral changes.

Withdrawal Designs

One of the more common strategies used in single-subject research is a **withdrawal design**, in which a researcher tries to determine whether the independent variable is responsible for changes in behavior (Wendt & Rindskopf, 2020). The effect of Wendy's treatment could be tested by stopping it for some time to see whether her anxiety increased. A simple withdrawal design has three parts. First, a person's condition is evaluated before treatment, to establish a **baseline**. Then comes the change in the independent variable—in Wendy's case, the beginning of treatment. Last, treatment is withdrawn ("return to baseline"), and the researcher assesses whether Wendy's anxiety level changes again as a function of this last step. If with the treatment her anxiety lessens in comparison to baseline and then worsens after treatment is withdrawn, the researcher can conclude the treatment has reduced Wendy's anxiety.

How is this design different from a case study? An important difference is that the change in treatment is designed specifically to show whether treatment caused the changes in behavior. Although case studies often involve treatment, they do not include any effort to learn whether the person would have improved without the treatment. A withdrawal design gives researchers a better sense of whether or not the treatment itself caused behavior change.

Despite their advantages, withdrawal designs are not always appropriate. The researcher is required to remove what might be an effective treatment, a decision that is sometimes difficult to justify for ethical reasons. In Wendy's case, a researcher would have to decide there was a sufficient reason to risk making her anxious again. A withdrawal design is also unsuitable when the treatment cannot be removed. Suppose Wendy's treatment involved visualizing herself on a beach on a tropical island. It would be difficult—if not impossible—to stop her from imagining something. Similarly, some treatments involve teaching people skills, which might be impossible to unlearn. If Wendy learned how to be less anxious in social situations, how could she revert to being socially apprehensive?

Several counterarguments support the use of withdrawal designs (Barlow et al., 2009). Treatment is routinely withdrawn when medications are involved. *Drug holidays* are periods when the medication is withdrawn so that clinicians can determine whether it is responsible for the treatment effects. Any medication can have negative side effects, and unnecessary medication should be avoided. Sometimes treatment withdrawal happens naturally. Withdrawal does not have to be prolonged; a brief withdrawal may still clarify the role of the treatment.

Multiple Baseline

Another single-case experimental design strategy used often that does not have some of the drawbacks of a withdrawal design is the **multiple baseline (Wendt & Rindskopf, 2020).** Rather than stopping the intervention to see whether it is effective, the researcher starts treatment at different times across settings (home versus school), behaviors (yelling at spouse/partner or boss), or people. As an example of treatment across settings, suppose that after waiting for a while and taking repeated measures of Wendy's anxiety both at home and at her office (the baseline), the clinician treats her first at home. When the treatment begins to be effective, intervention could begin at work. If she improves only at home after beginning treatment but improves at work after treatment is used there also, we could conclude the treatment was effective. This is an example of using a multiple baseline across settings. Does internal validity improve with a multiple baseline? Yes. Any time other explanations for results can be ruled out, internal validity is improved. Wendy's anxiety improved only in the settings where it was treated, which rules out competing explanations for her anxiety reduction. If she had won the lottery at the same time treatment started and her anxiety decreased in all situations, however, we couldn't conclude her condition was affected by treatment.

Suppose a researcher wanted to assess the effectiveness of a treatment for a child's problem behaviors. Treatment could focus first on the child's crying then on a second problem, such as fighting with siblings. If the treatment was first effective only in reducing crying and effective for reducing fighting only after the second intervention, the researcher could conclude that the treatment, not something else, accounted for the improvements. This is a multiple baseline conducted across behaviors.

Single-case experimental designs are sometimes criticized because they tend to involve only a small number of cases, leaving their external validity in doubt. In other words, we cannot say the results we saw with a few people would be the same for everyone. However, although they are called *single-case* designs, researchers can and often do use them with several people at once, in part to address the issue of external validity. One of us studied the effectiveness of a treatment for the severe behavior problems of children with autism spectrum disorder (Durand, 1999) (see ■ Figure 4.3). We taught the children to communicate instead of misbehave, using a procedure known as *functional communication training* (we discuss this in more detail in Chapter 14). Using a multiple baseline, we introduced this treatment to a group of five children. Our dependent variables were the incidence of the children's behavior problems and their newly acquired communication skills. As Figure 4.3 shows, only when we began treatment did each child's behavior problems improve and communication begin. This multiple baseline design let us rule out coincidence or some other change in the children's lives as explanations for the improvements.

Among the advantages of the multiple baseline design in evaluating treatments is that it does not require withdrawal of treatment and, as you have seen, withdrawing treatment is sometimes difficult or impossible. Furthermore, the multiple baseline typically resembles the way treatment would naturally be implemented. A clinician cannot help a client with numerous problems simultaneously but can take repeated measures of the relevant behaviors and observe when they change. A clinician who sees predictable and orderly changes related to where and when the treatment is used can conclude the treatment is causing the change.

Figure 4.3

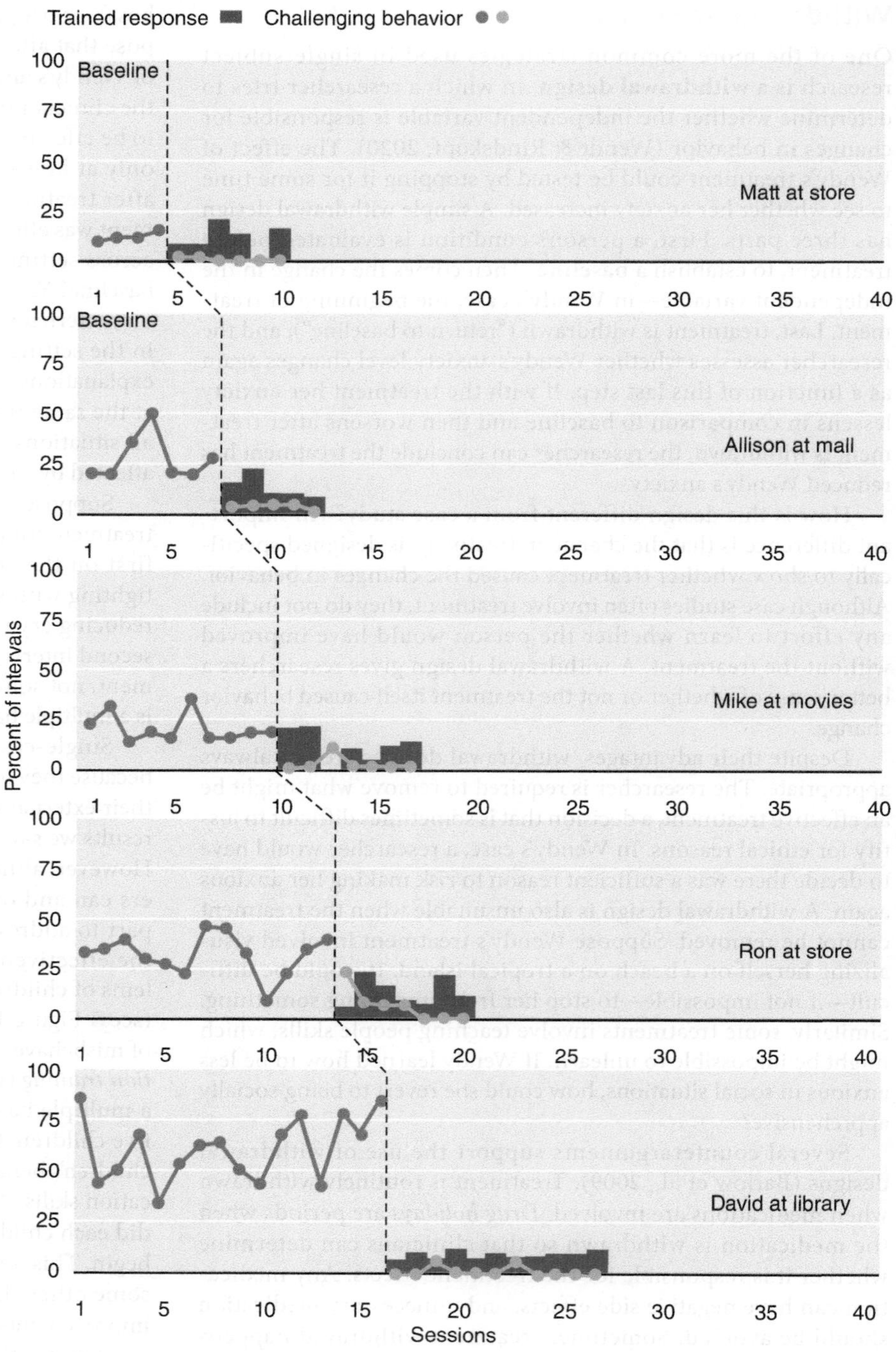

This figure shows how a multiple baseline design was used to illustrate that the treatment—functional communication training—was responsible for improvements in the children's behaviors. The circles represent how often each child exhibited behavior problems (called challenging behavior), and the blue-shaded areas show how often they communicated without help from the teacher (referred to as unprompted communication). From V. M. Durand, 1999, Functional communication training using assistive devices: Recruiting natural communities of reinforcement, *Journal of Applied Behavior Analysis*, 32(3), 247–267. Reprinted by permission of the Society for the Experimental Analysis of Human Behavior.

Genetics and Behavior across Time and Cultures

Examining the origin and strategies for treating an individual's behavior problem or disorder requires several factors to be considered so that multiple possible influences are taken into account. The factors include determining any inherited influences, the ways behavior will change or remain the same over time, and the effects of culture. We discuss these issues, as well as research replication and ethics, as key elements in the research process.

Studying Genetics

We tend to think of genetics in terms of what we inherit from our parents: "He's got his mother's eyes." "She's thin, just like her dad." "She's stubborn, like her mother." This simple view of how we become the people we are suggests that how we look, think, feel, and behave is predetermined. Yet as you saw in Chapter 2, we now know that the interaction between our genetic makeup and our experiences is what determines how we will develop. The goal of behavioral geneticists (people who study the genetics of behavior)

Concept Check 4.2

Check your understanding of research methods by indicating which would be most appropriate in each of the following situations. Choose from (a) case study, (b) correlation, (c) randomized clinical trials, (d) epidemiology, (e) experiment, and (f) single-case experimental design.

1. A researcher changes the level of noise several times to see how it affects concentration in a group of people. ________
2. A group of researchers uses chance assignment to include participants in one of two treatment groups and uses published protocols to make sure treatment is applied uniformly. ________
3. A researcher wants to investigate the hypothesis that as children go through adolescence they listen to louder music. ________
4. A researcher is interested in studying a woman who had no contact with civilization and created her own language. ________
5. A researcher wants to know how different kinds of music will affect a 5-year-old who has never spoken. ________

is to tease out the role of genetics in these interactions (Cai, Choi, & Fried, 2020; Shohat, Amelan, & Shifman, 2020).

Genetic researchers examine **phenotypes**, the observable characteristics or behavior of the individual, and **genotypes**, the unique genetic makeup of individual people. For example, a person with Down syndrome typically has some level of intellectual disability and a variety of other physical characteristics, such as slanted eyes and a thick tongue. These characteristics are the phenotype. The genotype is the extra 21st chromosome that causes Down syndrome.

Our knowledge of the phenotypes of different psychological disorders exceeds our knowledge of the genotypes, but that may soon change. Ever since the discovery of the double helix in 1953 by James Watson and Francis Crick, scientists have known we have to map the structure and location of every gene on all 46 chromosomes if we are to fully understand our genetic endowment. Beginning in 1990, scientists around the world, in a coordinated effort, began the **human genome project** (*genome* means "all the genes of an organism"). Using the latest advances in molecular biology, scientists working on this project completed a rough draft of the mapping of the approximately 25,000 human genes. This work identified hundreds of genes that contribute to inherited diseases. These exciting findings represent truly astounding progress in deciphering the nature of genetic endowment and its role in psychological disorders.

With the rapid advance of science, a third concept is now the focus of intense study—**endophenotypes**. Endophenotypes are the genetic mechanisms that ultimately contribute to the underlying problems causing the symptoms and difficulties experienced by people with psychological disorders (Sanchez-Roige & Palmer, 2020). In the case of schizophrenia (a disorder we discuss in Chapter 13), for example, researchers are not looking for a "schizophrenia gene" (genotype); instead, they are searching for the gene or genes responsible for the working memory problems characteristic of people with this disorder (endophenotype), as well as the genes responsible for other problems experienced by people with this disorder.

What follows is a brief review of the research strategies that scientists use as they study the interaction between environment and genetics in psychological disorders. These complex approaches can be summarized into four categories: basic genetic epidemiology, advanced genetic epidemiology, gene finding, and molecular genetics (Kendler, 2005) (see Table 4.2). The table shows that these categories form a progression that starts by finding whether a disorder has a genetic component (basic genetic epidemiology). Once this is established, researchers explore the nature of the genetic influences by seeing how genetics affect aspects of the disorder (advanced genetic epidemiology). Going deeper still, scientists use sophisticated statistical methods (linkage and association studies), which we describe next, to find out just where the gene or genes are located in the genome (gene

Table 4.2 The Basic Approaches Used to Assess Gene–Environment Influences in Psychological Disorders

Approach	Method	Question
Basic genetic epidemiology	Statistical analysis of family, twin, and adoption studies	Is the disorder inherited (heritability), and if so, how much of the disorder is attributable to genetics?
Advanced genetic epidemiology	Statistical analysis of family, twin, and adoption studies	If the disorder is found to be inherited, what factors influence the disorder (for example, is the change something that occurs early in development, is it different between males and females, and do the genetic influences affect environmental risk factors)?
Gene finding	Statistical analysis of specific families or individuals (linkage and/or association studies)	Where is the gene (or genes) that influences the disorder?
Molecular genetics	Biological analysis of individual DNA samples	What biological processes do the genes affect to produce the symptoms of the disorder?

Source: Adapted from K. S. Kendler, 2005, Psychiatric genetics: A methodological critique, in N. C. Andreasen (Ed.), *Research advances in genetics and genomics: Implications for psychiatry* (Table I, p. 6), American Psychiatric Publishing.

finding). Finally, switching to biological strategies, scientists are just at the genesis of examining what these genes do and how they interact with the environment to create the symptoms associated with psychological disorders (molecular genetics).

The specific research techniques used in the study of genetics—family studies, adoption studies, twin studies, genetic linkage analysis, and association studies—are described next.

Family Studies

In **family studies**, scientists simply examine a behavioral pattern or emotional trait in the context of the family. The family member with the trait singled out for study is called the **proband**. If there is a genetic influence, presumably the trait should occur more often in first-degree relatives (parents, siblings, or offspring) than in second-degree or more distant relatives. The presence of the trait in distant relatives, in turn, should be somewhat greater than in the population as a whole. In Chapter 1, you met Janelle, the adolescent with blood–injury–injection phobia who fainted at the sight of blood. The tendency of a trait to run in families, or familial aggregation, is as high as 60% for this disorder; that is, 60% of the first-degree relatives of someone with blood–injury–injection phobia have the same reaction to at least some degree. This is one of the highest rates of familial aggregation for any psychological disorder we have studied.

The problem with family studies is that family members tend to live together and there might be something in their shared environment that causes the high familial aggregation. For example, Mom might have developed a bad reaction to blood as a young girl after witnessing a serious accident. Every time she sees blood, she has a strong emotional response. Because emotions are contagious, the young children watching Mom probably react similarly. In adulthood, they pass it on, in turn, to their own children.

Adoption Studies

How do we separate environmental from genetic influences in families? One way is through **adoption studies**. Scientists identify adoptees who have a particular behavioral pattern or psychological disorder and attempt to locate first-degree relatives who were raised in different family settings. Suppose a young man has a disorder and scientists discover his brother was adopted as a baby and brought up in a different home. The researchers would then examine the brother to see whether he also displays signs of the disorder. If they can identify enough sibling pairs (and they usually do after a lot of hard work), they can assess whether siblings brought up in different families display the disorder to the same extent as the original participant. If the siblings raised with different families have the disorder more often than would be expected by chance, the researchers can infer that genetic endowment is a contributor.

Twin Studies

Nature presents an elegant experiment that gives behavioral geneticists their closest possible look at the role of genes in development: identical (monozygotic) twins (Atkinson & Vernon, 2020). These twins not only look a lot alike but also have identical genes. Some changes do occur in chemical markers (called epigenetic markers) in the womb, which explains the subtle differences even in identical twins (Schiele, Gottschalk, & Domschke, 2020). Fraternal (dizygotic) twins, on the other hand, come from different eggs and have only about 50% of their genes in common, as do all first-degree relatives. In **twin studies**, the obvious scientific question is whether identical twins share the same trait—say, fainting at the sight of blood—more often than fraternal twins. Determining whether a trait is shared is easy with some physical traits, such as height. As Plomin (1990) points out, correlations in height are 0.45 for both first-degree relatives and fraternal twins and 0.90 for identical twins. These findings show that heritability of height is about 90%, so approximately 10% of the variance is the result of environmental factors. But the case of conjoined identical twins with different personalities (whom we mention in Chapter 2) reminds us that the 90% estimate is the *average* contribution. An identical twin who was severely physically abused or selectively deprived of proper foods might be substantially different in height from the other twin.

Michael Lyons and his colleagues (1995) conducted a study of antisocial behavior among members of the Vietnam Era Twin Registry. The individuals in the study were about 8,000 twin men who served in the military from 1965 to 1975. The investigators found that among identical twins there was a greater degree of resemblance for antisocial traits than among fraternal twins. The difference was greater for adult antisocial behavior—that is, identical twins' behavior was more similar than fraternal twins' behavior in adulthood—than for juvenile antisocial behavior (meaning that nonadult identical and fraternal twin pairs were more similar in childhood than in adulthood). The researchers concluded that the family environment is a stronger influence than genetic factors on juvenile antisocial traits and that antisocial behavior in adulthood is more strongly influenced by genetic factors. In other words, after the individual grew up and left the family of origin, early environmental influences mattered less and less. This way of studying genetics is not perfect. You can assume identical twins have the same genetic makeup and fraternal twins do not. A complicating concern, however, is whether identical twins have the same experiences or environment as fraternal twins. Some identical twins are dressed alike and are even given similar names. Yet the twins themselves influence each other's behavior, and in some cases, identical twins may affect each other more than fraternal twins (Johnson, Turkheimer, Gottesman, & Bouchard, 2009).

One way to address this problem is by combining the adoption study and twin study methods. If you can find identical twins, one or both of whom were adopted as an infant, you can estimate the relative roles of genes and the environment (nature versus nurture) in the development of behavioral patterns.

Genetic Linkage Analysis and Association Studies

The results of a series of family, twin, and adoption studies may suggest that a particular disorder has a genetic component, but they cannot provide the location of the implicated gene or genes. To locate a defective gene, there are two general strategies: genetic linkage analysis and association studies (Avinun, 2020).

The basic principle of **genetic linkage analysis** is simple. When a family disorder is studied, other inherited characteristics are assessed at the same time. These other characteristics—called

iStockPhoto.com/gisele

Family members often resemble each other in physical appearance, but their shared genetics can influence many other aspects of their lives.

genetic markers—are selected because we know their exact location. If a match or link is discovered between the inheritance of the disorder and the inheritance of a genetic marker, the genes for the disorder and the genetic marker are probably close together on the same chromosome. For example, bipolar disorder (manic depression) was studied in a large Amish family (Egeland et al., 1987). Researchers found that two markers on chromosome 11—genes for insulin and a known cancer gene—were linked to the presence of mood disorder in this family, suggesting that a gene for bipolar disorder might be on chromosome 11. Unfortunately, although this is a genetic linkage study, it also illustrates the danger of drawing premature conclusions from research. This linkage study and a second study that purported to find a linkage between bipolar disorder and the X chromosome (Baron et al., 1987) have yet to be replicated; that is, different researchers have not been able to show similar linkages in other families (Merikangas & Risch, 2014).

The inability to replicate findings in these studies is quite common (Flanagan, 2015). This type of failure casts doubt on conclusions that only one gene is responsible for such complex disorders. Be mindful of such limitations the next time you read in a newspaper or hear on television that a gene has been identified as causing some disorder.

The second strategy for locating specific genes, **association studies**, also uses genetic markers. Whereas linkage studies compare markers in a large group of people with a particular disorder, association studies compare such people to people without the disorder. If certain markers occur significantly more often in the people with the disorder, it is assumed the markers are close to the genes involved with the disorder. This type of comparison makes association studies better able to identify genes that may only be weakly associated with a disorder. Both strategies for locating specific genes shed new light on the origins of specific disorders and may inspire new approaches to treatment (Avinun, 2020).

Studying Behavior over Time

Sometimes we want to ask, "How will a disorder or behavior pattern change (or remain the same) over time?" This question is important for several reasons. First, the answer helps us decide whether to treat a particular person. For example, should we begin an expensive and time-consuming program for a young adult who is depressed over the loss of a grandparent? You might not if you knew that with normal social supports the depression is likely to diminish over the next few months without treatment. On the other hand, if you have reason to believe a problem is not likely to go away on its own, you might decide to begin treatment. For example, as you will read later, aggression among young children does not usually go away naturally and should be dealt with as early as possible.

It is also important to understand the developmental changes in psychopathology because sometimes these can provide insight into how problems are created and how they become more serious. For example, you will see that some researchers identify newborns who are at risk for autism spectrum disorder (ASD) because they are siblings of a child with ASD (see Chapter 14 for a discussion of ASD) and then follow them through infancy until some develop the disorder themselves. This type of study is showing us that the pattern of the onset of this disorder is actually much different than parents report after the fact (they tend to remember drastic changes in the child's behavior when, in fact, the changes occur gradually) (Zwaigenbaum, Bryson, & Garon, 2013). Prospective studies (which record changes over time as they occur) sometimes reveal dramatic differences in the development of psychological disorders or their treatment compared with the information discovered through retrospective studies (which ask people to remember what happened in the past).

Prevention Research

An additional reason for studying clinical problems over time is that we may be able to design interventions and services to prevent these problems. For example, a large number of researchers are looking at factors that may slow or prevent the onset of dementia among older adults (for example, childhood education, exercise, maintaining social engagement, reducing smoking, management of hearing loss, depression, diabetes, and obesity across the life course are key protective factors) (Anstey et al., 2020). Clearly, preventing mental health difficulties would save countless families significant emotional distress, and the financial savings could be substantial. Prevention research has expanded over the years to include a broad range of approaches. These different methods can be viewed in four broad categories: positive development strategies (health promotion), universal prevention strategies, selective prevention strategies, and indicated prevention strategies (Kalra et al., 2012).

Health promotion or *positive development strategies* involve efforts to blanket entire populations of people—even those who may not be at risk—to prevent later problems and promote protective behaviors. The intervention is not designed to fix existing problems but, instead, focuses on skill building, for example, to keep problems from developing. For example, the Seattle Social Development Program targets young children in public elementary schools in the Seattle school system that are in high-crime areas, providing intervention with teachers and parents to engage the children in learning and positive behaviors. Although this approach does not target one particular problem (for example, drug use), long-term follow-up of these children suggests multiple positive effects in achievement, reductions in delinquency, and lower odds of contracting a sexually transmitted illness by age 30 (Bailey, 2009; Hill et al., 2014; Lonczak, Abbott, Hawkins, Kosterman, & Catalano, 2002).

Universal prevention strategies focus on entire populations and target certain specific risk factors (for example, behavior problems in classrooms in low-income communities) without focusing on specific individuals. The third approach to prevention intervention—*selective prevention*—specifically targets whole groups at risk (for example, children who have parents who have died) and designs specific interventions aimed at helping them avoid future problems. Finally, *indicated prevention* is a strategy for those individuals who are beginning to show signs of problems (for example, depressive symptoms) but do not yet have a psychological disorder.

To evaluate the effectiveness of each of these approaches, the research strategies used in prevention research for examining psychopathology across time combine individual and group research methods, including both correlational and experimental designs. We look next at two of the most often used: cross-sectional and longitudinal designs.

Cross-Sectional Designs A variation of correlation research is to compare different people at different ages. For a **cross-sectional design**, researchers take a cross section of a population across the different age groups and compare them on some characteristic (Domínguez-Salas, Gómez-Salgado, Andrés-Villas, Díaz-Milanés, Romero-Martín, & Ruiz-Frutos, 2020; Qian, Wu, Wu, Hou, Liang, Cowling, & Yu, 2020). For example, if they were trying to understand the development of alcohol use disorder and dependence, they could take groups of adolescents at 12, 15, and 17 years of age and assess their beliefs about alcohol use. In an early comparison, Brown and Finn (1982) made some interesting discoveries. They found that 36% of the 12-year-olds thought the primary purpose of drinking was to get drunk. This percentage increased to 64% with 15-year-olds, but dropped again to 42% for the 17-year-old students. The researchers also found that 28% of the 12-year-olds reported drinking with their friends at least sometimes, a rate that increased to 80% for the 15-year-olds and to 88% for the 17-year-olds. Brown and Finn used this information to develop the hypothesis that the reason for excessive drinking among teens is a deliberate attempt to get drunk rather than a mistake in judgment once they are under the influence of alcohol. In other words, teenagers do not, as a group, appear to drink too much because once they have had a drink or two they show poor judgment and drink excessively. Instead, their attitudes before drinking seem to influence how much they drink later.

In cross-sectional designs, the participants in each age group are called **cohorts**; Brown and Finn studied three cohorts: 12-year-olds, 15-year-olds, and 17-year-olds. The members of each cohort are the same age at the same time and thus have all been exposed to similar experiences. Members of one cohort differ from members of other cohorts in age and in their exposure to cultural and historical experiences. You would expect a group of 12-year-olds in the 1980s to have received a great deal of education about drug and alcohol use (such as the "Just Say No" program), whereas the 17-year-olds may not have. Differences among cohorts in their opinions about alcohol use may be related to their respective cognitive and emotional development at these different ages and to their dissimilar experiences. This **cohort effect**, the confounding of age and experience, is a limitation of the cross-sectional design.

Researchers prefer cross-sectional designs to study changes over time partly because they are easier to use than longitudinal designs (discussed next). In addition, some phenomena are less likely to be influenced by different cultural and historical experiences and therefore less susceptible to cohort effects. For example, the prevalence of Alzheimer's disease among people at ages 60 and 70—assumed to be strongly influenced by biology—is not likely to be greatly affected by different experiences among the study participants.

One question not answered by cross-sectional designs is how problems develop in individuals. For example, do children who refuse to go to school grow up to have anxiety disorders? Researchers cannot answer this question simply by comparing adults with anxiety problems and children who refuse to go to school. They could ask the adults whether they were anxious about school when they were children, but this **retrospective information** (looking back) is usually less than accurate. To get a better picture of how individuals develop over the years, researchers use longitudinal designs.

Longitudinal Designs Rather than looking at different groups of people of differing ages, researchers may follow one group over time and assess change in its members directly. The advantages of **longitudinal designs** are that they do not suffer from cohort effect problems and they allow the researchers to assess individual change. (■ Figure 4.4 illustrates both longitudinal and cross-sectional designs.) In one such study, researchers followed a large number of patients (3,440) over 17 years to assess how consuming dairy products was associated with changes in their weight. Every three years, participants completed a physical exam and filled out a food frequency assessment to determine how much dairy they consumed in the past year. The results of this study suggested that participants who consumed three or more servings of dairy per day gained less weight over the year than those who did not (Wang et al., 2014). This study lends support to advocates of healthy dairy consumption and shows the value of longitudinal designs when assessing health outcomes over time.

Imagine conducting a major longitudinal study. Not only must the researcher persevere over months and years, but so must the people who participate in the study. They must remain willing to continue in the project, and the researcher must hope they will not move away or, worse, die. Longitudinal research is costly and

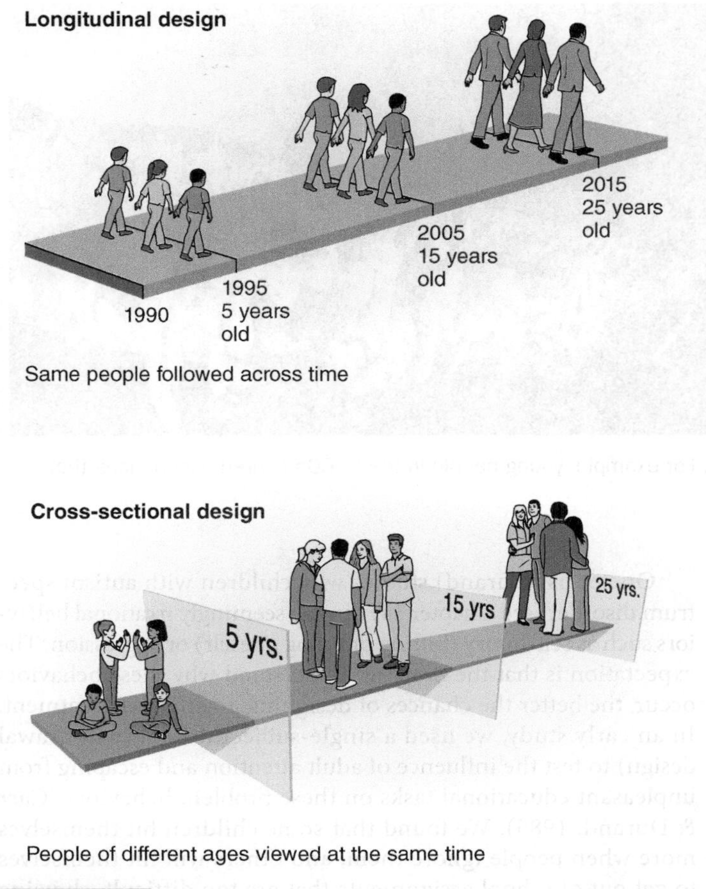

Figure 4.4

Two types of research designs: longitudinal and cross-sectional.

time consuming; it is also possible that the research question will have become irrelevant by the time the study is complete. Finally, longitudinal designs can suffer from a phenomenon similar to the cohort effect on cross-sectional designs. The **cross-generational effect** involves trying to generalize the findings to groups whose experiences are different from those of the study participants. For example, the drug-use histories of people who were young adults in the 1960s and early 1970s are vastly different from those of people born in the 1990s.

Sometimes psychopathologists combine longitudinal and cross-sectional designs in a strategy called **sequential design**, which involves repeated study of different cohorts over time. As an example, we look at work by Laurie Chassin and her colleagues, who study children's beliefs about cigarette smoking (Chassin, Presson, Rose, & Sherman, 2001). These researchers have followed 10 cohorts of middle- and high-school-age children (cross-sectional design) since the early 1980s (longitudinal design). Through questionnaires, they have tracked how these children (and later, adults) viewed the health risks associated with smoking from their youth into their mid-30s. For example, the researchers would ask participants whether they believed in the following statement: "A person who eats right and exercises regularly can smoke without harming his/her health." The results suggest that as middle schoolers (ages 11 to 14) the children viewed smoking as less risky to them personally and believed that there were positive psychological benefits (for example, making them appear more mature). These beliefs changed as the children went into high school and entered adulthood, but they point to the importance of targeting smoking prevention programs during the middle-school period (Macy, Chassin, & Presson, 2012).

Studying Behavior across Cultures

Just as we can become narrowly focused when we study people only at a certain age, we can also miss important aspects by studying people from only one culture. Studying the differences in behavior of people from different cultures can tell us a great deal about the origins and possible treatments of psychopathology. Unfortunately, most research literature originates in Western cultures, producing an ethnocentric view of psychopathology that can limit our understanding of disorders in general and can restrict the way we approach treatment (Teodoro & Afonso, 2020). Researchers in Malaysia—where psychological disorders are commonly believed to have supernatural origins—have described a disorder they call *sakit gila*, which has some features of schizophrenia but differs in important ways (Csordas, 2015). Could we learn more about schizophrenia (and *sakit gila*) by comparing the disorders themselves and the cultures in which they are found? Increasing awareness of the limited cultural scope of our research is creating a corresponding increase in cross-cultural research on psychopathology (Teodoro & Afonso, 2020).

The designs we have described are adapted for studying psychopathology across cultures. Some researchers view the effects of different cultures as though they were different treatments (Teodoro & Afonso, 2020). In other words, the independent variable is the effect of different cultures on behavior, rather than, say, the effect of cognitive therapy versus simple exposure for the treatment of fears. The difference between looking at culture as a "treatment" and our typical design, however, is important. In cross-cultural research, we cannot randomly assign infants to different cultures and observe how they develop. People from varying cultures can differ in any number of important ways—their genetic backgrounds, for one—that could explain variations in their behavior for reasons other than culture.

The characteristics of different cultures can also complicate research efforts. Symptoms, or descriptions of symptoms, can be dissimilar in different societies (Paniagua & Yamada, 2013). Nigerians who are depressed complain of heaviness or heat in the head, crawling sensations in the head or legs, burning sensations in the body, and a feeling that the belly is bloated with water (Ebigno, 1982; James, Jenkins, & Lawani, 2012). In contrast, people in the United States report feeling worthless, being unable to start or finish anything, losing interest in usual activities, and thinking of suicide. Natives of China, on the other hand, are less likely to report feeling depressed or losing interest in favorite things but may have thoughts of suicide or worthlessness (Yu, Tam, Wong, Lam, & Stewart, 2012). These few examples illustrate that applying a standard definition of depression across different cultures will result in vastly different outcomes (Markova, Sandal, & Guribye, 2020).

An additional complicating factor is varying tolerances, or thresholds, for psychopathology. If people in different cultures see

Owen Franken - Corbis/Corbis Historical/Getty Images

Christian Bertrand/Shutterstock.com

Longitudinal studies can be complicated by the cross-generational effect. For example, young people in the 1960s shared experiences that were different from those of young people today.

the same behaviors differently, researchers will have trouble comparing incidence and prevalence rates. For example, traditional Chinese customs include talking to deceased relatives and local deities—behaviors, which might be characteristic of schizophrenia in other cultures (Fuji, Tsushima, Murakami-Brundage, & Kamath, 2014). Understanding cultural attitudes and customs is essential to such research (Paniagua & Yamada, 2013).

Finally, treatment research is also complicated by cross-cultural differences. Cultures develop treatment models that reflect their own values. In Japan, psychiatric hospitalization is organized in terms of a family model, with caregivers assuming parental roles. A family model was common in psychiatric institutions in 19th-century North America until it was replaced with the medical model common today (Colp, 2009). In Saudi Arabia, women are veiled when outside the home, which prevents them from uncovering their faces in the presence of therapists; custom thus complicates efforts to establish a trusting and intimate therapeutic client–therapist relationship and may also prevent the therapist from gathering information about a patient's affective state from her facial expression (Ali, Liu, & Humedian, 2004; Dubovsky, 1983; Mistry, Bhugra, Chaleby, Khan, & Sauer, 2009). Because in the Islamic perspective medicine and religion are inseparable, medical and religious treatments are combined (Tober & Budiani, 2014). As you can see, something as basic as comparing treatment outcomes is highly complex in a cross-cultural context.

Power of a Program of Research

When we examine different research strategies independently, as we have done here, we often have the impression that some approaches are better than others. It is important to understand that this is not true. Depending on the type of question you are asking and the practical limitations inherent in the inquiry, any of the research techniques would be appropriate. Significant issues often are resolved not by one perfectly designed study but rather by a series of studies that examine different aspects of the problem—in a program of research. The research of one of this book's authors will be used to illustrate how complex research questions are answered with a variety of different research designs.

One of us (Durand) studies why children with autism spectrum disorder (see Chapter 14) display seemingly irrational behaviors such as self-injury (hitting or biting oneself) or aggression. The expectation is that the more we understand why these behaviors occur, the better the chances of designing an effective treatment. In an early study, we used a single-subject design (withdrawal design) to test the influence of adult attention and escaping from unpleasant educational tasks on these problem behaviors (Carr & Durand, 1985). We found that some children hit themselves more when people ignore them, and others will hit themselves to get out of school assignments that are too difficult, showing that these disturbing behaviors can be understood by looking at them as primitive forms of communication (for example, "Please come here" or "This is too hard"). This led us to consider what would happen if we taught these children to communicate with us more appropriately (Durand, 1990). The next series of studies again used single-subject designs and demonstrated that teaching more acceptable ways of getting attention or help from others did significantly reduce these challenging behaviors (e.g, Durand & Carr, 1992). Several decades of research on this treatment (called functional communication training) demonstrates its value in significantly improving the lives of people with these once severe behavior problems by reducing the severity of the misbehavior through improving communication skills (Durand, 2012).

One of the questions that faces researchers in this area is why some children develop more severe forms of these behavior problems, while others do not. To begin to answer this question, we conducted a 3-year prospective longitudinal study on more than 100 children with autism spectrum disorder to see what factors might cause more problems (Durand, 2001). We studied the children at age 3 and later at age 6 to determine what about the child or the family led to more severe problems. We found the following two factors to be the most important indicators of severe behavior problems in the children: (1) The parents were pessimistic about their ability to help their child, or (2) the parents were doubtful about their child's ability to change. These parents would "give up" and allow their child to dictate many of the routines around the house (for example, eating dinner in the living room

Janine Wiedel Photolibrary / Alamy Stock Photo

The same behavior—in this case a woman baring her legs and having her head uncovered in public—would be acceptable in some cultures but not in others.

or not going out to the movies because it would cause tantrums) (Durand, 2001).

This important finding then led to the next question: Could we make pessimistic parents more optimistic, and would this help prevent their children from developing more severe behavior problems? To answer this question, we next relied on a randomized clinical trial to see if adding a cognitive behavior intervention (described in more detail in the later chapters on the individual disorders) would help make pessimistic parents more optimistic. We wanted to teach these parents to examine their own pessimistic thoughts ("I have no control of my child" or "My child won't improve because of his/her disorder") and replace them with more hopeful views of their world ("I can help my child" or "My child can improve his/her behavior"). We hypothesized that this cognitive intervention would help them carry out the parenting strategies we offer them (including functional communication training) and in turn improve the outcomes of our behavioral interventions. We randomly assigned groups of pessimistic parents who also had a child with very severe behavior problems to either a group that taught them how to work with their child or a group that used the same techniques but also helped them explore their pessimistic thinking and helped them view themselves and their child in a better light. The treatments were applied very formally, using written protocols to make sure that each group received the treatment as designed (Durand & Hieneman, 2008). What we found was that addition of the cognitive behavioral intervention had the expected effect—improving optimism and also improving child outcomes (Durand, Hieneman, Clarke, Wang, & Rinaldi, 2013). This finding led to articulating a new process that pessimistic parents use with their challenging children called the "concession process" (Durand, in press).

As this example indicates, research is conducted in stages, and a complete picture of any disorder and its treatment can be seen only after looking at it from many perspectives. An integrated program of research can help researchers explore various aspects of psychopathology.

Replication

The motto of the state of Missouri is "Show Me." The motto of science could be "Show Me Again." Scientists, in general, and behavioral scientists, in particular, are never really convinced something is "true." People are skeptical when it comes to claims about causes or treatment outcomes. Replicating findings is what makes researchers confident that what they are observing is not a coincidence. We noted when we described the case study method that if we look at a disorder in only one person, no matter how carefully we describe and document what we observe, we cannot draw strong conclusions.

The strength of a research program is in its ability to replicate findings in different ways to build confidence in the results. If you look back at the research strategies we have described, you will find that replication is one of the most important aspects of each. The more times researchers repeat a process (and the behavior they are studying changes as expected), the surer they are about what caused the changes.

Research Ethics

An important final issue involves the ethics of doing research on psychopathology. For example, the appropriateness of a clinician's delaying treatment to people who need it, just to satisfy the requirements of an experimental design, is often questioned. One single-case experimental design, the withdrawal design, can involve removing treatment for some time. Treatment is also withheld when placebo control groups are used in group experimental designs. Researchers continue to discuss and caution others about just when it is appropriate to use placebo-controlled trials (Boot, Simons, Stohart, & Stutts, 2013). The fundamental question is this: When does a scientist's interest in preserving the internal validity of a study outweigh a client's right to treatment?

One answer to this question involves **informed consent**—a research participant's formal agreement to cooperate in a study following full disclosure of the nature of the research and the participant's role in it (Rost, Nast, Elger, & Shaw, 2020). The concept of informed consent is derived from the war trials after World War II. Revelations that the Nazis had forced prisoners into so-called medical experiments helped establish the informed consent guidelines that are still used today. In studies using some form of treatment delay or withdrawal, the participant is told why it will occur and the risks and benefits, and permission to proceed is then obtained. In placebo control studies, participants are told they may not receive an active treatment (all participants are blind to or unaware of which group they are placed in), but they are usually given the option of receiving treatment after the study ends.

True informed consent is at times elusive. The basic components are competence, voluntarism, full information, and comprehension on the part of the participant (Snyder, 2012). In other words, research participants must be capable of consenting to participation in the research, they must volunteer or not be coerced into participating, they must have all the information they need to make the decision, and they must understand what their participation will involve. In some circumstances, all these conditions are difficult to attain. Children, for example, often do not fully appreciate what will occur during research. Similarly, individuals with cognitive impairments such as intellectual disability or schizophrenia may not understand their role or their rights as participants. In institutional settings, participants should not feel coerced into taking part in research. And individuals from different cultures can have different perspectives about what is important in informed consent (Lakes et al., 2012).

Certain general protections help ensure that these concerns are properly addressed. First, research in university and medical settings must be approved by an institutional review board (IRB) (Lynch & Rosenfeld, 2020). These committees are made up of university faculty and nonacademic people from the community, and their purpose is to see that the rights of research participants are protected. The committee structure allows people other than the researcher to look at the research procedures to determine whether sufficient care is being taken to protect the welfare and dignity of the participants.

To safeguard those who participate in psychological research and to clarify the responsibilities of researchers, the American Psychological Association has published *Ethical Principles of Psychologists and Code of Conduct*, which includes general guidelines for conducting research (American Psychological Association, 2016). People in research experiments must be protected from both physical and psychological harm. In addition to the issue of informed consent, these principles stress the investigators' responsibility for the research participants' welfare because the researcher must ensure that the welfare of the research participants is given priority over any other consideration, including experimental design.

Psychological harm is difficult to define, but its definition remains the responsibility of the investigators. Researchers must hold in confidence all information obtained from participants, who have the right to concealment of their identity on all data, either written or informal. Whenever deception is considered essential to research, the investigator must satisfy a committee of peers that this judgment is correct. If deception or concealment is used, participants must be debriefed—that is, told in language they can understand what the true purpose of the study is and why it was necessary to deceive them.

The Society for Research in Child Development (2007) has endorsed ethical guidelines for research that address some issues unique to research on children. For example, these guidelines not only call for confidentiality, protection from harm, and debriefing but also require informed consent from children's caregivers and from the children themselves if they are age 7 or older. These guidelines specify that the research must be explained to children in language they can understand so that they can decide whether they wish to participate. Many other ethical issues extend beyond protection of the participants, including how researchers deal with errors in their research, fraud in science, and the proper way to give credit to others. Doing a study involves more than selecting the appropriate design. Researchers must be aware of numerous concerns that involve the rights of the people in the experiment, as well as their own conduct.

A final and important development in the field that will help to "keep the face" on psychological disorders is the involvement of consumers in important aspects of this research—referred to as participatory action research (Chevalier & Buckles, 2013). The concern over not only how people are treated in research studies but also how the information is interpreted and used has resulted in many government agencies providing guidance on how the people who are the targets of the research (for example, those with schizophrenia, depression, or anxiety disorders) should be involved in the process. The hope is that if people who experience these disorders are partners in designing, running, and interpreting this research, the relevance of the research, as well as the treatment of the participants in these studies, will be markedly improved.

Concept Check 4.3

Part A

The following are some advantages and limitations of methods used in research across time. Sort them out by marking CS for cross-sectional designs and L for longitudinal designs.

Benefits:

1. ________ Shows individual development

2. ________ Easier

3. ________ No cohort effects

Limitations:

4. ________ Cohort effects

5. ________ Cross-generational effect

6. ________ No individual development data

Part B

Indicate whether the following statements are true (T) or false (F).

7. ________ After participants are told the nature of the experiment and their role in it, they must be allowed to refuse or agree to sign an informed consent form.

8. ________ If the participant is in the control group or taking a placebo, informed consent is not needed.

9. ________ Research in universities or medical settings must be approved by the institution's review board regarding whether the participants lack the cognitive skills to protect themselves from harm.

10. ________ Participants have a right to concealment of their identity on all data collected and reported.

11. ________ When deception is essential to the research, participants do not have to be debriefed regarding the true pose of the study.

Summary

Examining Psychopathology

- Research involves establishing a hypothesis that is then tested. In psychopathology, research focuses on hypotheses meant to explain the nature, the causes, or the treatment of a disorder.

Types of Research Methods

- The individual case study is used to study one or more individuals in depth. Although case studies have an important role in the theoretical development of psychology, they are not subject to experimental control and must necessarily be suspect in terms of both internal and external validity.
- Research by correlation can tell us whether a relationship exists between two variables, but it does not tell us if that relationship is a causal one. Epidemiological research is a type of correlational research that reveals the incidence, distribution, and consequences of a particular problem in one or more populations.
- Research by experiment can follow one of two designs: group or single case. In both designs, a variable (or variables) is manipulated, and the effects are observed to determine the nature of a causal relationship.

Genetics and Behavior across Time and Cultures

- Genetic research focuses on the role of genetics in behavior. These research strategies include family studies, adoption studies, twin studies, genetic linkage analyses, and association studies.
- Research strategies that examine psychopathology across time include cross-sectional and longitudinal designs. Both focus on differences in behavior or attitudes at different ages, but the former does so by looking at different individuals at different ages, and the latter looks at the same individuals at different ages.
- Prevention research can be viewed in four broad categories: health promotion or positive development strategies, universal prevention strategies, selective prevention strategies, and indicated prevention strategies.
- The clinical picture, causal factors, and treatment process and outcome can all be influenced by cultural factors.
- The more the findings of a research program are replicated, the more they gain in credibility.
- Ethics are important to the research process, and ethical guidelines are spelled out by many professional organizations in an effort to ensure the well-being of research participants.
- Ethical concerns are being addressed through informed consent and through the inclusion of consumers in research design, implementation, and interpretation.

Key Terms

hypothesis, 103
research design, 103
dependent variable, 103
independent variable, 103
internal validity, 103
external validity, 103
testability, 104
confound, 104
confounding variable, 104
control group, 105
randomization, 105
analogue models, 105
generalizability, 105
statistical significance, 105
clinical significance, 105
effect size, 106
patient uniformity myth, 106
case study method, 106
correlation, 107
positive correlation, 107
correlation coefficient, 107
negative correlation, 108
directionality, 108
epidemiology, 108
experiment, 109
placebo effect, 110
placebo control groups, 110
double-blind control, 110
comparative treatment research, 110
single-case experimental designs, 111
repeated measurement, 111
variability, 112
trend, 112
level, 112
withdrawal design, 113
baseline, 113
multiple baseline, 113
phenotypes, 115
genotypes, 115
human genome project, 115
endophenotypes, 115
family studies, 116
proband, 116
adoption studies, 116
twin studies, 116
genetic linkage analysis, 116
genetic markers, 117
association studies, 117
cross-sectional design, 118
cohorts, 118
cohort effect, 118
retrospective information, 118
longitudinal designs, 118
cross-generational effect, 119
sequential design, 119
informed consent, 121

Answers to Concept Checks

4.1

1. independent variable; **2.** confound; **3.** hypothesis; **4.** dependent variable; **5.** internal validity, external validity

4.2

1. e; **2.** c; **3.** b; **4.** a; **5.** f

4.3

Part A

1. L; **2.** CS; **3.** L; **4.** CS; **5.** L; **6.** CS

Part B

7. T; **8.** F; **9.** T; **10.** T; **11.** F

5 Anxiety, Trauma- and Stressor-Related, and Obsessive-Compulsive and Related Disorders

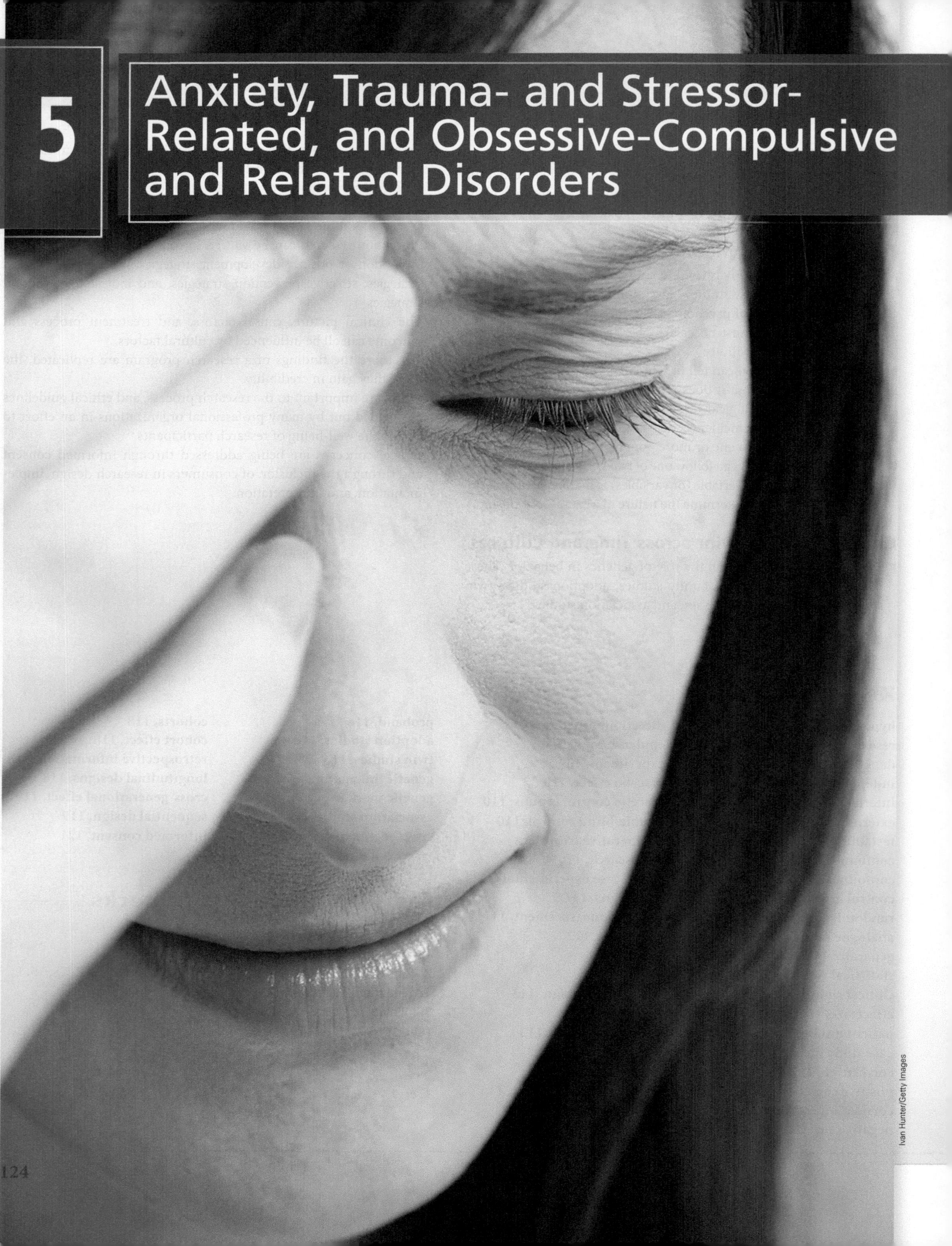

Ivan Hunter/Getty Images

Learning Objectives

LO5.1 Explain how anxiety is related to fear and panic.

LO5.2 Discuss the biological, psychological, and social contributors that produce anxiety and related disorders.

LO5.3 Explain the different types of anxiety disorders according to their symptoms as listed in the DSM-5.

LO5.4 Identify the causal similarities in the development of specific phobias and social anxiety disorder.

LO5.5 Describe the factors involved in the development of posttraumatic stress disorder among trauma victims.

LO5.6 Compare the different forms of treatment for obsessive compulsive disorder according to their overall effectiveness.

LO5.7 Draw connections between obsessive-compulsive disorder and the different types of obsessive-compulsive and related disorders according to their symptoms and causes.

The Complexity of Anxiety Disorders

Anxiety is complex and mysterious, as Sigmund Freud realized many years ago. In some ways, the more we learn about it, the more baffling it seems. "Anxiety" is a specific type of disorder, but it is more than that. It is an emotion implicated so heavily across the full range of psychopathology that our discussion explores its general nature, both biological and psychological. Next, we consider fear, a somewhat different but clearly related emotion. Related to fear is a panic attack, which we propose is fear that occurs when there is nothing to be afraid of and, therefore, at an inappropriate time. With these important ideas clearly in mind, we focus on specific anxiety and related disorders.

Anxiety, Fear, and Panic: Some Definitions

Have you ever experienced anxiety? A silly question, you might say, because most of us feel some anxiety almost every day of our lives. Did you have a test in school today for which you weren't "perfectly" prepared? Did you have a date last weekend with somebody new? And how about that job interview coming up? Even thinking about that might make you nervous. But have you ever stopped to think about the nature of anxiety? What is it? What causes it?

Anxiety is a future-oriented negative mood state characterized by bodily symptoms of physical tension and by apprehension about the future (American Psychiatric Association, 2013; Barlow, 2002). In humans, it can be a subjective sense of unease, a set of behaviors (looking worried and anxious or fidgeting), or a physiological response originating in the brain and reflected in elevated heart rate and muscle tension. For ethical reasons, much of the research on anxiety has been done with animals.

For example, we might teach laboratory rats that a light signals an impending shock. When the light comes on, the animal may fidget, tremble, and perhaps cower in a corner. Can we conclude that the rat is feeling fear or anxiety? Sure, the rat *appears* to be anxious. But does this also mean that the rat *feels* anxious? How do we know that the rat's experience is the same as that of a human? What about the mosquito that you are trying to catch and the bacterium that is detecting toxin in the water? Do they feel the same emotion? Do all species experience the same in moments of threat?

Before you jump to an answer, first consider this: One of the defining differences between humans and other species is self-consciousness and self-awareness. There might be some evidence of self-consciousness in some primates, as well, but no gorilla has ever written a philosophical treatise about the meaning of life. Associated with our human cognitive skills is the ability to use language to communicate and describe our inner experience, our emotions. If an emotional experience in humans, including fear and anxiety, involves consciousness and self-awareness, then how can we know what animals are feeling? The unsatisfying answer is: We don't really know! Children may conclude: "Of course, the rat feels anxious because that's how I would feel if I was a rat." This argumentation is anthropomorphism (that is, the attributing of human characteristics or behaviors to an animal or object), and it limits what we can say about human emotions when studying animals (Brown & LeDoux, 2020; LeDoux & Brown, 2017; LeDoux & Hofmann, 2018). Thus, anxiety remains a mystery, and we are only beginning our journey of discovery. Anxiety is also closely related to depression (Barlow, 2000, 2002; Brown & Barlow, 2005, 2009; Kaiser, Herzog, Voderholzer, & Brakemeier, 2021; Penninx, Pine, Holmes, & Reif, 2021), so much of what we say here is relevant to Chapter 7.

Anxiety is not pleasant, so why do we seem programmed to experience it almost every time we do something important? Surprisingly, anxiety is good for us, at least in moderate amounts. Psychologists have known for over a century that we perform better when we are a little anxious (Yerkes & Dodson, 1908). You would not have done so well on that test the other day if you had had no anxiety. You were a little more charming and lively on that date last weekend because you were a little anxious. And you will be better prepared for that upcoming job interview if you are anxious. In short, social, physical, and intellectual performances are driven and enhanced by anxiety. Without it, few of us would get much done. Howard Liddell (1949) first proposed this idea when he called anxiety the "shadow of intelligence." He thought the human ability to plan in some detail for the future was connected to that gnawing feeling that things could go wrong and we had better be prepared for them. This is why anxiety is a future-oriented mood state. If you were to put it into words, you might say, "Something might go wrong, and I'm not sure I can deal with it, but I've got to be ready to try. Maybe I'd better study a little harder (or check the mirror one more time before my date or do a little more research on that company before the interview)."

But what happens when you have too much anxiety? You might actually fail the exam because you can't concentrate on the questions. All you can think about when you're too anxious is how terrible it will be if you fail. You might blow the interview for the same reason. On that date with a new person, you might spend the evening perspiring profusely, with a sick feeling in your stomach, unable to think of even one reasonably interesting thing to say. Too much of a good thing can be harmful, and few sensations are more harmful than severe anxiety that is out of control.

What makes the situation worse is that severe anxiety usually doesn't go away—that is, even if we "know" there is nothing to be afraid of, we remain anxious. One example of this kind of irrationality involves John Madden, the retired sports announcer and former professional football coach, who suffers from claustrophobia. He has written about his anxiety and used it as a source of humor in several television commercials. Madden, who during his career had to announce a game in New York one Sunday and in San Francisco the next, cannot travel by air because of his claustrophobia. For a long time, he took trains around the country; later, he used a well-equipped private bus. Madden and countless other individuals who experience anxiety-based disorders are well aware that there is little to fear in the situations they find stressful. Madden must have realized long ago that flying is in fact the safest way to travel and that it was in his best interest to fly to save time and help maintain his lucrative career. And yet he could not abandon his anxiety-driven behavior.

All the disorders discussed in this chapter are characterized by excessive anxiety, which takes many forms. In Chapter 2, you saw that **fear** is an immediate alarm reaction to danger. Like anxiety, fear can be good for us. It protects us by activating a massive response from the autonomic nervous system (increased heart rate and blood pressure, for example), which, along with our subjective sense of terror, motivates us to escape (flee) or, possibly, to attack (fight). As such, this emergency reaction is often called the flight or fight response.

There is much evidence that fear and anxiety reactions differ psychologically and physiologically (Barlow, 2002; Bouton, 2005; Li et al., 2021; Molosh et al., 2020; Zych & Gogolla, 2021). As noted earlier, anxiety is a future-oriented mood state, characterized by apprehension because we cannot predict or control upcoming events. Fear, on the other hand, is an immediate emotional reaction to current danger characterized by strong escapist action tendencies and, often, a surge in the sympathetic branch of the autonomic nervous system (Barlow, Brown, & Craske, 1994; Craske et al., 2010).

What happens if you experience the alarm response of fear when there is nothing to be afraid of—that is, if you have a false alarm? Consider the case of Ashlyn, who appeared at one of our clinics.

Ashlyn... Attacked by Panic

I was 25 when I had my first attack. It was a few weeks after I'd come home from the hospital. I had had my appendix out. The surgery had gone well, and I wasn't in any danger, which is why I don't understand what happened. But one night I went to sleep and I woke up a few hours later—I'm not sure how long—but I woke up with this vague feeling of apprehension. Mostly I remember how my heart started pounding. And my chest hurt; it felt like I was dying—that I was having a heart attack. And I felt kind of queer, as if I were detached from the experience. It seemed like my bedroom was covered with a haze. I ran to my sister's room, but I felt like I was a puppet or a robot who was under the control of somebody else while I was running. I think I scared her almost as much as I was frightened myself. She called an ambulance (Barlow, 2002). •

This sudden overwhelming reaction came to be known as **panic**, after the Greek god Pan, who terrified travelers with bloodcurdling screams. In psychopathology, a **panic attack** is defined as an abrupt experience of intense fear or acute discomfort, accompanied by physical symptoms that usually include heart palpitations, chest pain, shortness of breath, and, possibly, dizziness.

Two basic types of panic attacks are described in DSM-5: expected and unexpected. If you know you are afraid of high places or of driving over long bridges, you might have a panic attack in these situations but not anywhere else; this is an *expected (cued) panic attack.* By contrast, you might experience *unexpected (uncued) panic attacks* if you don't have a clue when or where the next attack will occur. We mention these types of attacks because they play a role in several anxiety disorders. Unexpected attacks are important in panic disorder. Expected attacks are more common in specific phobias or social anxiety disorder (see ■ Figure 5.1).

Remember that fear is an intense emotional alarm accompanied by a surge of energy in the autonomic nervous system that motivates us to flee from danger. Does Ashlyn's panic attack sound as if it could be the emotion of fear? A variety of evidence suggests it is (Barlow, 2002; Bouton, 2005; Craske & Barlow, 2014), including similarities in reports of the experience of fear and panic, similar behavioral tendencies to escape, and similar underlying neurobiological processes. The experience of panic attacks is an important severity marker and predictor of persistence of any anxiety disorder across the lifespan (Hovenkamp-Hermelink et al., 2021).

Physiological recordings of people with panic disorder can reveal unexpected results (see, for example, Alpers, 2009; Hofmann & Barlow, 1996; Meuret et al., 2011; Tunnell et al., 2021). The physiological surge during a panic attack recorded in one patient is shown in ■ Figure 5.2. Notice the sudden dramatic increase in heart rate from minute 11 through minute 13, accompanied by increases in muscle tension (frontalis EMG) and finger temperature. This massive autonomic surge peaked and subsided within 3 minutes. The panic attack in the laboratory appeared to have occurred unexpectedly from the patient's point of view and from ours. As the figure shows, fear and panic are experienced suddenly, which is necessary to mobilize us for instantaneous reaction to impending danger.

Causes of Anxiety and Related Disorders

You learned in Chapters 1 and 2 that excessive emotional reactions have no simple one-dimensional cause but come from

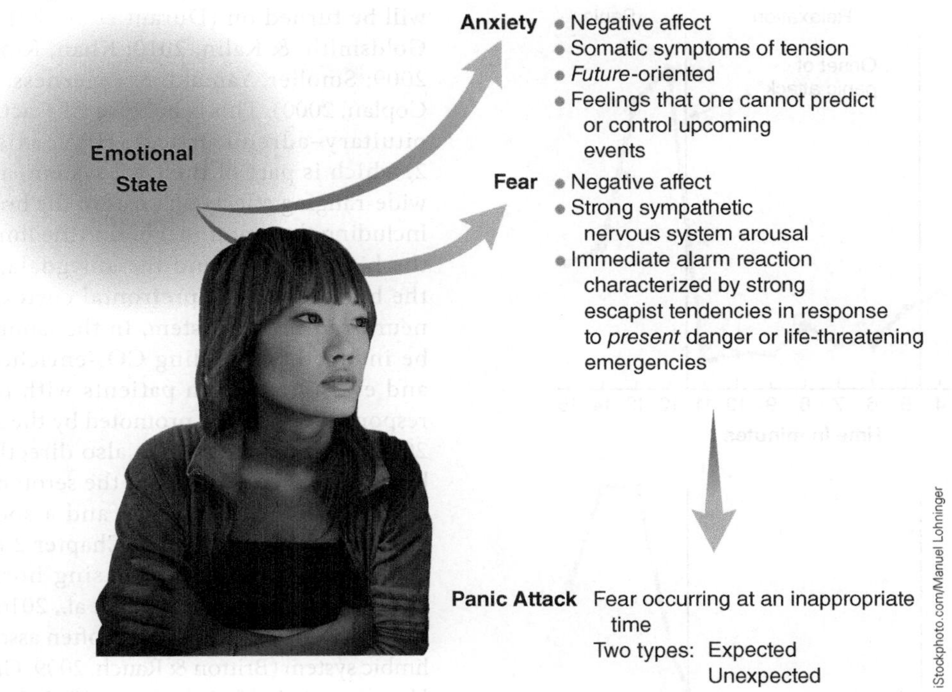

Figure 5.1

The relationships among anxiety, fear, and panic attack.

DSM 5 Table 5.1

Diagnostic Criteria for Panic Attack

An abrupt surge of intense fear or intense discomfort that reaches a peak within minutes, and during which time four (or more) of the following symptoms occur. [*Note:* The abrupt surge can occur from a calm state or an anxious state.]:

1. Palpitations, pounding heart, or accelerated heart rate
2. Sweating
3. Trembling or shaking
4. Sensations of shortness of breath or smothering
5. Feelings of choking
6. Chest pain or discomfort
7. Nausea or abdominal distress
8. Feeling dizzy, unsteady, light-headed, or faint
9. Chills or heat sensations
10. Paresthesias (numbness or tingling sensations)
11. Derealization (feelings of unreality) or depersonalization (being detached from oneself)
12. Fear of losing control or "going crazy"
13. Fear of dying

[*Note:* Culture-specific symptoms (e.g., tinnitus, neck soreness, headache, uncontrollable screaming or crying) may be seen. Such symptoms should not count as one of the four required symptoms.]

American Psychiatric Association. (2022). *Diagnostic and statistical manual of mental disorders* (5th ed., Text Revision).

multiple sources. Next, we explore the biological, psychological, and social contributors and the ways they interact to produce anxiety and related disorders.

Biological Contributions Increasing evidence shows that we inherit a tendency to be tense, uptight, and anxious (Barlow et al., 2014; Clark, 2005; Eysenck, 1967; Gray & McNaughton, 2003). The tendency to panic also seems to run in families and probably has a genetic component that differs somewhat from genetic contributions to anxiety (Ask et al., 2021; Barlow, 2002; Craske & Barlow, 2014; Kendler, 2001). As with almost all emotional traits and psychological disorders, no single gene seems to cause anxiety or panic or any other psychiatric disorder (Ask et al., 2021). Instead, contributions from collections of genes in several areas on chromosomes make us vulnerable when the right psychological and social factors are in place. Furthermore, a genetic vulnerability does not cause anxiety and/or panic directly. That is, stress or other factors in the environment can "turn on" or "turn off" certain genes, as we review in Chapter 2 (Ask et al., 2021; Schiele, Gottschalk, & Domschke, 2020).

Anxiety is also associated with specific brain circuits (Domschke & Dannlowski, 2010; Hermans, Henckens, Joels, & Fernandez, 2014; Tovote et al., 2015) and neurotransmitter systems (Durant, Christmas, & Nutt, 2010). For example, depleted levels of gamma-aminobutyric acid (GABA), part of the GABA–benzodiazepine system, are associated with increased anxiety, although the relationship is not quite so direct. The noradrenergic

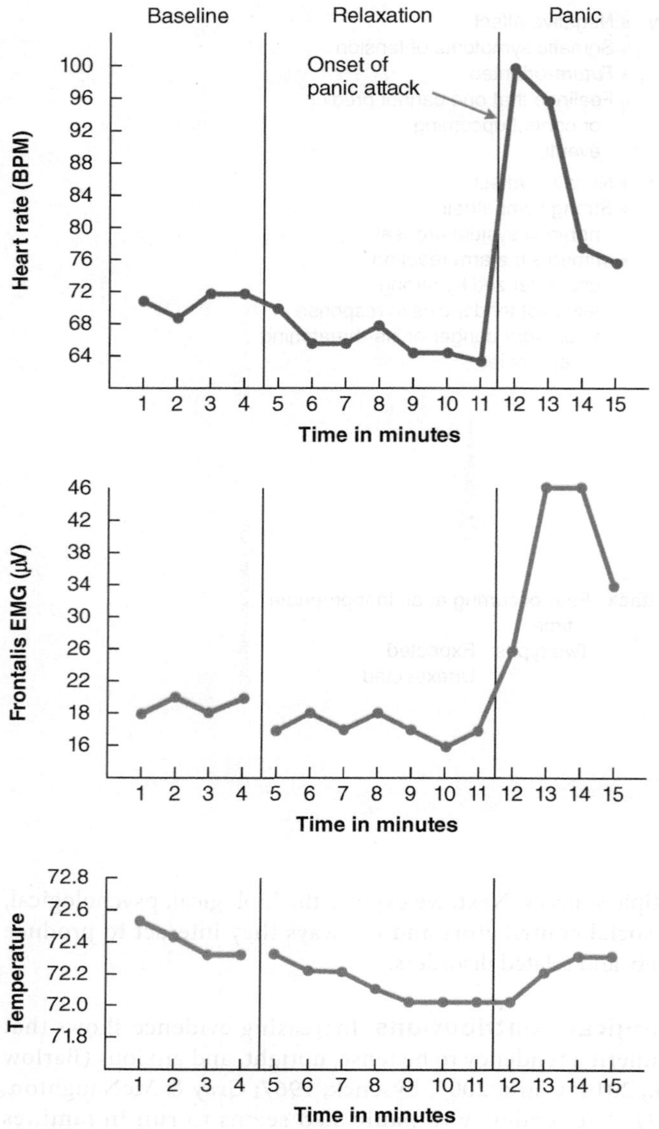

Figure 5.2

Physiological measurements during a panic attack. BPM, beats per minute; EMG, electromyography. (Reprinted, with permission, from A. S. Cohen, D. H. Barlow, & E. B. Blanchard, 1985, Psychophysiology of relaxation-associated panic attacks, *Journal of Abnormal Psychology, 94*, 98. © 1985 by the American Psychological Association.)

system has also been implicated in anxiety (Hermans et al., 2011), and evidence from basic animal studies, as well as studies of normal anxiety in humans, suggests the serotonergic neurotransmitter system is also involved (Canli & Lesch, 2007).

But increasing attention in the past several years is focusing on the role of the corticotropin-releasing factor (CRF) system as central to the expression of anxiety (and depression) and the groups of genes that increase the likelihood that this system will be turned on (Durant et al., 2010; Essex, Klein, Slattery, Goldsmith, & Kalin, 2010; Khan, King, Abelson, & Liberzon, 2009; Smoller, Yamaki, & Fagerness, 2005; Sullivan, Kent, & Coplan, 2000). This is because CRF activates the hypothalamic–pituitary–adrenocortical (HPA) axis, described in Chapter 2, which is part of the CRF system, and this CRF system has wide-ranging effects on areas of the brain implicated in anxiety, including the emotional brain (the limbic system), particularly the hippocampus and the amygdala; the locus coeruleus in the brain stem; the prefrontal cortex; and the dopaminergic neurotransmitter system. In the laboratory, panic attacks can be induced by inhaling CO_2-enriched air in healthy people and even more so in patients with panic disorder, and this response seems to be promoted by the amygdala (Taugher et al., 2020). The CRF system is also directly related to the GABA–benzodiazepine system and the serotonergic and noradrenergic neurotransmitter systems, and a specific single-nucleotide polymorphism (SNP) (see Chapter 2 for more details) coding for the corticotropin-releasing hormone receptor was an important risk allele (Weber et al., 2016).

The area of the brain most often associated with anxiety is the limbic system (Britton & Rauch, 2009; Gray & McNaughton, 2003; Hermans et al., 2011; LeDoux, 2002, 2015; Raber et al., 2019; see Figure 2.7c), which acts as a mediator between the brain stem and the cortex. The more primitive brain stem monitors and senses changes in bodily functions and relays these potential danger signals to higher cortical processes through the limbic system. The late Jeffrey Gray, a prominent British neuropsychologist, identified a brain circuit in the limbic system of animals that seems heavily involved in anxiety (Gray & McNaughton, 2003) and may be relevant to humans. This circuit leads from the septal and hippocampal area in the limbic system to the frontal cortex. (The septal–hippocampal system is activated by CRF and serotonergic- and noradrenergic-mediated pathways originating in the brain stem.) The system that Gray calls the **behavioral inhibition system (BIS)** is activated by signals from the brain stem of unexpected events, such as major changes in body functioning that might signal danger. Danger signals in response to something we see that might be threatening descend from the cortex to the septal–hippocampal system. The BIS also receives a big boost from the amygdala (LeDoux, 1996, 2002, 2015). When the BIS is activated by signals that arise from the brain stem or descend from the cortex, our tendency is to freeze, experience anxiety, and apprehensively evaluate the situation to confirm that danger is present.

The BIS circuit is distinct from the circuit involved in panic. Gray and McNaughton (2003) and Graeff (2004) identified what Gray and others call the **fight/flight system (FFS)**. This circuit originates in the brain stem and travels through several midbrain structures, including the amygdala, the ventromedial nucleus of the hypothalamus, and the central gray matter. When stimulated in animals, this circuit produces an immediate alarm-and-escape response that looks very much like panic in humans (Gray & McNaughton, 2003). The FFS is activated partly by deficiencies in serotonin, suggest Gray and McNaughton (2003) and Graeff (2004).

As is true for other anxiety disorders (such as social anxiety disorder, which we discuss later), activation of a network that involves the prefrontal cortex and the amygdala while performing certain tasks can predict response to Cognitive Behavioral Therapy (CBT) (Hahn et al., 2015). It is likely that factors in your environment can change the sensitivity of these brain circuits, making you more or less susceptible to developing anxiety and its disorders, a finding that has been demonstrated in several laboratories (Francis, Diorio, Plotsky, & Meaney, 2002; Stein, Schork, & Gelernter, 2007). For example, one important study suggested that cigarette smoking as a teenager is associated with greatly increased risk for developing anxiety disorders as an adult, particularly panic disorder and generalized anxiety disorder (Johnson et al., 2000). Nearly 700 adolescents of a community-based sample from upstate New York were followed into adulthood. Teens who smoked 20 or more cigarettes daily were 15 times more likely to develop panic disorder and 5 times more likely to develop generalized anxiety disorder than teens who smoked less or didn't smoke.

Smoking and anxiety disorders show a complex interaction (Leventhal & Zvolensky, 2015). The current thinking about the link between smoking and anxiety is that anxiety sensitivity (the general tendency to fear bodily sensations, which we briefly discuss later), distress tolerance (the amount of distress a person can tolerate), and anhedonia (the inability to feel pleasure) all contribute to smoking. This and other problems, such as acculturative stress (Zvolensky et al., 2020), are the reasons that many people with anxiety find it difficult to quit smoking. Brain-imaging procedures are yielding more information about the neurobiology of anxiety and panic (Britton et al., 2013; Shin & Liberzon, 2010). For example, there is now general agreement that in people with anxiety disorders, the limbic system, including the amygdala, is overly responsive to stimulation or new information (abnormal bottom-up processing); at the same time, controlling functions of the cortex that would down-regulate the hyperexcitable amygdala are deficient (abnormal top-down processing). Despite these biological abnormalities, psychological treatments, in particular CBT, can effectively treat these disorders across the age range (Carpenter et al., 2018; Hofmann, Asnaani, Vonk, Sawyer, & Fang, 2012; Kendall & Peterman, 2015).

Psychological Contributions In Chapter 2, we review some theories on the nature of psychological causes of anxiety. Remember that Freud thought anxiety was a psychic reaction to danger surrounding the reactivation of an infantile fearful situation. Behavioral theorists thought anxiety was the product of early classical conditioning, modeling, or other forms of learning (Bandura, 1986). But new and accumulating evidence supports an integrated model of anxiety involving a variety of psychological factors (see, for example, Barlow, 2002; Barlow, Ellard, et al., 2014; Hofmann & Hay, 2018). In childhood, we may acquire an awareness that events are not always in our control (Chorpita & Barlow, 1998; Gallagher, Bentley, & Barlow, 2014). The continuum of this perception may range from total confidence in our control of all aspects of our lives to deep uncertainty about ourselves and our ability to deal with upcoming events. If you are anxious about schoolwork, for example, you may worry you will do poorly on the next exam, even though all your grades have been A's and B's. A general "sense of uncontrollability" may develop early as a function of upbringing and other disruptive or traumatic environmental factors.

The actions of parents in early childhood seem to do a lot to foster this sense of control or uncontrollability (Barlow, Ellard, et al., 2014; Bowlby, 1980; Chorpita & Barlow, 1998; Racine et al., 2021). Generally, it seems that parents who interact in a positive and predictable way with their children by responding to their needs, particularly when the child communicates needs for attention, food, relief from pain, and so on, perform an important function. These parents teach their children that they have control over their environment and their responses have an effect on their parents and their environment. In addition, parents who provide a "secure home base" but allow their children to explore their world and develop the necessary skills to cope with unexpected occurrences enable their children to develop a healthy sense of control (Chorpita & Barlow, 1998). In contrast, parents who are overprotective and overintrusive and who "clear the way" for their children, never letting them experience any adversity, create a situation in which children never learn how to cope with adversity when it comes along. Therefore, these children don't learn that they can control their environment. A variety of evidence has accumulated supporting these ideas (Barlow, 2002; Chorpita & Barlow, 1998; Dan, Sagi-Schwartz, Bar-haim, & Eshel, 2011; Fulton, Kiel, Tull, & Gratz, 2014; Gallagher et al., 2014; Racine et al., 2021; White, Brown, Somers, & Barlow, 2006). A sense of control (or lack of it) that develops from these early experiences is the psychological factor that makes us more or less vulnerable to anxiety in later life.

Another feature among patients with panic is the general tendency to respond fearfully to anxiety symptoms. This is known as *anxiety sensitivity*, which appears to be an important personality trait that determines who will and who will not experience problems with anxiety under certain stressful conditions (Reiss, 1991).

Most psychological accounts of panic (as opposed to anxiety) invoke conditioning and cognitive explanations that are difficult to separate (Bouton, Mineka, & Barlow, 2001). Thus, a strong fear response initially occurs during extreme stress or perhaps as a result of a dangerous situation in the environment (a true alarm). This emotional response then becomes associated with a variety of external and internal cues. In other words, these cues, or conditioned stimuli, provoke the fear response and an assumption of danger, even if the danger is not actually present (Bouton, 2005; Bouton et al., 2001; Mineka & Zinbarg, 2006; Razran, 1961), so it is really a learned or false alarm. This is the conditioning process described in Chapter 2. External cues are places or situations similar to the one where the initial panic attack occurred. Internal cues are increases in heart rate or respiration that were associated with the initial panic attack, even if they are merely the result of exercise or other routine activities. Thus, when your heart is beating fast, you are more likely to think of and, perhaps, experience a panic attack than when it is beating normally. Furthermore, you may not be aware of the cues or triggers of severe fear; that is, they are unconscious as demonstrated in patients with panic disorder (Meuret et al., 2011). This is most likely, as demonstrated in experimental work with animals, because these cues or triggers may travel from the eyes directly to the amygdala in the emotional brain without going through the cortex, the source of awareness (Bouton et al., 2001; LeDoux, 2002, 2015; LeDoux & Brown, 2017; LeDoux & Hofmann, 2018).

Social Contributions Stressful life events trigger our biological and psychological vulnerabilities to anxiety. Most are social and interpersonal in nature—marriage, divorce, difficulties at work, death of a loved one, pressures to excel in school, and so on. Some might be physical, such as an injury or illness.

The same stressors can trigger physical reactions, such as headaches or hypertension, and emotional reactions, such as panic attacks (Barlow, 2002). The particular way we react to stress seems to run in families. If you get headaches when under stress, chances are other people in your family also get headaches. If you have panic attacks, other members of your family probably do also. This finding suggests a possible genetic contribution, at least to initial panic attacks.

An Integrated Model Putting the factors together in an integrated way, we have described a theory of the development of anxiety called the *triple vulnerability theory* (Barlow, 2000, 2002; Barlow, Ellard, et al., 2014; Brown & Naragon-Gainey, 2013). The first vulnerability (or diathesis) is a *generalized biological vulnerability.* We can see that a tendency to be uptight or high-strung might be inherited. But a generalized biological vulnerability to develop anxiety is not sufficient to produce anxiety itself. The second vulnerability is a *generalized psychological vulnerability.* That is, you might also grow up believing the world is dangerous and out of control, and you might not be able to cope when things go wrong based on your early experiences. If this perception is strong, you have a generalized psychological vulnerability to anxiety. The third vulnerability is a *specific psychological vulnerability* in which you learn from early experience, such as being taught by your parents, that some situations or objects are fraught with danger (even if they really aren't). For example, if one of your parents is afraid of dogs or expresses anxiety about being evaluated negatively by others, you may well develop a fear of dogs or of social evaluation. These triple vulnerabilities are presented in ■ Figure 5.3 and revisited when we describe each anxiety and related disorder. If you are under a lot of pressure, particularly from interpersonal stressors, a given stressor could activate your biological tendencies to be anxious and your psychological tendencies to feel you might not be able to deal with the situation and control the stress. Once this cycle starts, it tends to feed on itself, so it might not stop even when the particular life stressor has long since passed. Anxiety can be general, evoked by many aspects of your life. But it is usually focused on one area, such as social evaluations or grades (Barlow, 2002).

As noted above, panic is also a characteristic response to stress that runs in families and may have a genetic component that is separate from anxiety. Furthermore, anxiety and panic are closely related (Barlow, 2002; Barlow, Ellard, et al., 2014; Suárez et al., 2009): anxiety increases the likelihood of panic. This relationship makes sense from an evolutionary point of view because sensing a possible future threat or danger (anxiety) should prepare us to react instantaneously with an alarm response if the danger becomes imminent (Bouton, 2005). Anxiety and panic need not occur together, but it makes sense that they often do.

Comorbidity of Anxiety and Related Disorders

Before describing the specific disorders, it is important to note that the disorders often co-occur. As we describe in Chapter 3, the co-occurrence of two or more disorders in a single individual is referred to as *comorbidity.* The high rates of comorbidity among anxiety and related disorders (and depression) emphasize how all of these disorders share the common features of anxiety and panic described here. They also share the same vulnerabilities—biological and psychological—to develop anxiety and panic. The various disorders differ only in what triggers the anxiety and, perhaps, the patterning of panic attacks.

This logic laid the foundation for developing a single treatment that targets common features of a variety of anxiety disorders including those that co-occur (Barlow et al., 2020). Another similar argument formulated in *process-based therapy* is that for therapy to

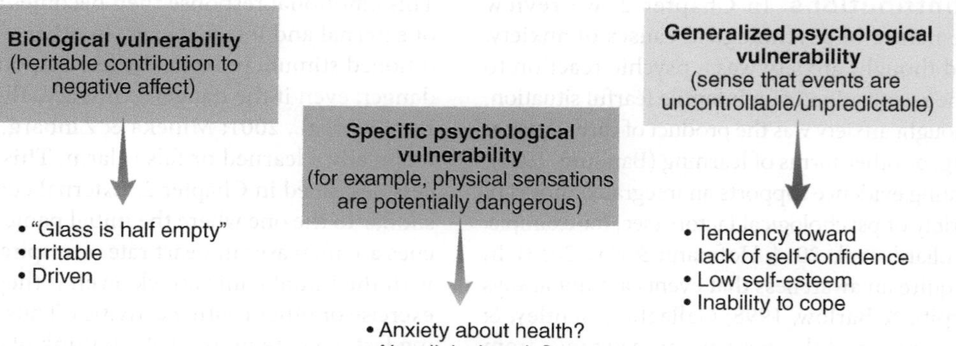

Figure 5.3

The three vulnerabilities that contribute to the development of anxiety disorders. If individuals possess all three, the odds are greatly increased that they will develop an anxiety disorder after experiencing a stressful situation. From D. H. Barlow, 2002, *Anxiety and its disorders: The nature and treatment of anxiety and panic* (2nd ed.), Guilford Press.

be effective, it needs to target the underlying processes of change rather than the DSM-defined psychiatric syndromes (Hofmann & Hayes, 2019). A major clinical trial by one of us (Barlow et al., 2017) examined whether a unified protocol (UP)—a transdiagnostic treatment applicable to all anxiety and related disorders—was at least as efficacious as established treatments for individual anxiety disorders such as panic disorder (single-disorder protocols or SDPs) for treating patients diagnosed with a variety of anxiety disorders. This study recruited 223 patients: 88 were randomized to receive the UP, 91 to receive an SDP, and 44 to the waitlist control condition. Patients received up to 16 sessions of the UP or an SDP for 16 to 21 weeks. The results showed that patients were more likely to complete treatment with the UP than with SDPs and that SDPs were superior to the waitlist control condition immediately after the intervention. Most important, the results also showed that the UP and the SDPs were similarly efficacious at posttreatment and follow-up. This study is important because a unified treatment protocol facilitates dissemination of evidence-based psychological treatments since clinicians have to master the administration of only one protocol rather than six to eight individual treatments.

Although rates of comorbidity are high, they vary somewhat from disorder to disorder (Allen et al., 2010; Bruce et al., 2005; Tsao, Mystkowski, Zucker, & Craske, 2002). A large-scale study completed at one of our centers examined the comorbidity of DSM-IV anxiety and mood disorders (Brown & Barlow, 2005; Brown, Campbell, Lehman, Grisham, & Mancill, 2001). Data were collected from 1,127 patients carefully diagnosed using a semistructured interview in our center. If we examine just rates of comorbidity at the time of assessment, the results indicate that 55% of the patients who received a principal diagnosis of an anxiety or depressive disorder had at least one additional anxiety or depressive disorder at the time of the assessment. If we consider whether patients met criteria for an additional diagnosis at any time in their lives rather than just at the time of the assessment, the rate increases to 76%.

By far the most common additional diagnosis for all anxiety disorders was major depression, which occurred in 50% of the cases over the course of the patient's life, probably due to the shared vulnerabilities between depression and anxiety disorders in addition to the disorder-specific vulnerability. Consistent with this notion are the results by Blanco and colleagues (Blanco, Rubio, Wall, Wang, Jiu, & Kendler, 2014), who reported that the risks for anxiety disorders and depression are mediated partially by a latent variable underlying both disorders (such as low self-esteem and childhood sexual abuse) and partially by disorder-specific effects (such as a family history of depression as a risk factor for depression in the children). This becomes important when we discuss the relationship of anxiety and depression later in this chapter. Also important is the finding that additional diagnoses of depression or alcohol use disorder or drug use or misuse makes it less likely that you will recover from an anxiety disorder and more likely that you will relapse if you do recover (Bruce et al., 2005; Ciraulo et al., 2013; Huppert, 2009).

Comorbidity with Physical Disorders

Anxiety disorders also co-occur with several physical conditions (Foldes-Busque et al., 2021; Kariuki-Nyuthe & Stein, 2015). An important study indicated that the presence of any anxiety disorder was uniquely and significantly associated with thyroid disease, respiratory disease, gastrointestinal disease, arthritis, migraine headaches, and allergic conditions (Sareen et al., 2006). Thus, people with these physical conditions are likely to have an anxiety disorder but are not any more likely to have another psychological disorder. Furthermore, the anxiety disorder most often begins before the physical disorder, suggesting (but not proving) that something about having an anxiety disorder might cause or contribute to the cause of the physical disorder. Finally, if someone has both an anxiety disorder and one of the physical disorders mentioned earlier, that person will suffer, as studies have shown, from greater disability and a poorer quality of life from both the physical problem and the anxiety problem than if that individual had just the physical disorder alone (Belik, Sareen, & Stein, 2009; Comer et al., 2011; Sareen et al., 2006). Other studies have also found the same relationship between anxiety disorders, particularly panic disorders, and cardiovascular (heart) disease (see, for example, Gomez-Caminero, Blumentals, Russo, Brown, & Castilla-Puentes, 2005). Also, the DSM-5 now makes it explicit that panic attacks often co-occur with certain medical conditions, particularly cardio, respiratory, gastrointestinal, and vestibular (inner ear) disorders, even though the majority of these patients would not meet criteria for panic disorder (Kessler et al., 2006).

Image Point Fr/Shutterstock.com

People with certain physical conditions, like asthma, are often at higher risk for anxiety disorders.

Suicide

Earlier studies have found that 20% of patients with panic disorder had attempted suicide and that the risk of someone with panic disorder attempting suicide was comparable to that for individuals with major depression (Johnson, Weissman, & Klerman, 1990; Weissman, Klerman, Markowitz, & Ouellette, 1989).

Concept Check 5.1

Complete the following statements about anxiety and its causes with the following terms: (a) comorbidity, (b) panic attack, (c) expected, (d) neurotransmitter, (e) brain circuits, and (f) stressful.

1. A ____________ is an abrupt experience of intense fear or acute discomfort accompanied by physical symptoms, such as chest pain and shortness of breath.
2. An ____________ panic attack often occurs in certain situations but not anywhere else.
3. Anxiety is associated with specific ____________ (for example, behavioral inhibition system or fight/flight system) and ____________ systems (for example, noradrenergic).
4. The rates of ____________ among anxiety and related disorders are high because they share the common features of anxiety and panic.
5. ____________ life events can trigger biological and psychological vulnerabilities to anxiety.

These investigators also found that having any anxiety or related disorder, not just panic disorder, uniquely increases the chances of having thoughts about suicide (suicidal ideation) or making suicidal attempts (Sareen et al., 2006). However, the relationship is strongest with panic disorder and posttraumatic stress disorder (Nepon, Belik, Bolton, & Sareen 2010; Sareen, 2011), even after accounting for mood disorders and substance use disorders (Chartrand, Sareen, Toews, & Bolton, 2012; Thibodeau, Welch, Sareen, & Asmundson, 2013). People with generalized anxiety disorder and social anxiety disorder who engaged in deliberate self-harm were also likely to engage in this behavior multiple times, and at least one of those times was a suicide attempt.

Clearly, many questions about the relationship between suicide and mood and anxiety disorders remain unanswered. We now turn to descriptions of the individual anxiety and related disorders. But keep in mind that approximately 50% of individuals with these disorders may present with one or more additional anxiety or depressive disorders and, perhaps, some other disorders, particularly substance abuse disorders, as described later. For this reason, we also consider new ideas for classifying and treating anxiety disorders that move beyond just looking at single disorders.

Anxiety Disorders

Disorders traditionally grouped together as anxiety disorders include generalized anxiety disorder, panic disorder and agoraphobia, specific phobia, and social anxiety disorder, as well as two new disorders, separation anxiety disorder and selective mutism. These specific anxiety disorders are complicated by panic attacks or other features that are the focus of the anxiety. But in generalized anxiety disorder, the focus is generalized to the events of everyday life. Therefore, we consider generalized anxiety disorder first.

Generalized Anxiety Disorder

Most of us worry to some extent. As we have said, worry can be useful. It helps us plan for the future, make sure that we're prepared for that test, or double-check that we've thought of everything before we head home for the holidays. But what if you worry indiscriminately about everything? Furthermore, what if worrying is unproductive? What if no matter how much you worry, you can't seem to decide what to do about an upcoming problem or situation? And what if you can't stop worrying, even if you know it is doing you no good and probably making everyone else around you miserable? These features characterize **generalized anxiety disorder (GAD)**. Consider the case of Tanisha.

Tanisha... Ruled by Worry

Tanisha was a 20-year-old college student with an engaging personality but not many friends. She came to the clinic complaining of excessive anxiety and general difficulties in controlling her life. Everything was a catastrophe for Tanisha. Although she carried a 3.7 grade point average, she was convinced she would flunk every test she took. As a result, she repeatedly threatened to drop courses after only several weeks of classes because she feared that she would not understand the material.

Tanisha worried until she dropped out of the first college she attended after 1 month. She felt depressed for a while and then decided to take a couple of courses at a local junior college, believing she could handle the work there better. After achieving straight A's at the junior college for 2 years, she enrolled once again in a 4-year college as a junior. After a short time, she began calling the clinic in a state of extreme agitation, saying she had to drop this or that course because she couldn't handle it. With great difficulty, her therapist and parents persuaded her to stay in the courses and to seek further help. In any course Tanisha completed, her grade was between an A and a B-minus, but she still worried about every test and every paper, afraid she would fall apart and be unable to understand and complete the work.

Tanisha did not worry only about school. She was also concerned about relationships with her friends. Whenever she was with her new boyfriend, she feared making a fool of herself and losing his interest. She reported that each date went extremely well, but she knew the next one would probably be a disaster. As the relationship progressed and some sexual contact seemed natural, Tanisha was worried sick that her inexperience would make her boyfriend consider her naive and stupid. Nevertheless, she reported enjoying the early sexual contact and admitted that he seemed to enjoy it also, but she was convinced that the next time a catastrophe would happen.

Tanisha was also concerned about her health. She had minor hypertension, probably because she was somewhat overweight. She was also very worried about eating the wrong types or amounts of food. She became reluctant to have her blood pressure checked for fear it would be high or to weigh herself for fear she was not losing weight. She severely restricted her eating and as a result had an occasional episode of binge eating, although not often enough to warrant concern.

Although Tanisha had an occasional panic attack, this was not a major issue to her. As soon as the panic subsided, she focused on the next possible catastrophe. In addition to high blood pressure, Tanisha had tension headaches and a "nervous stomach," with a lot of gas, occasional diarrhea, and some abdominal pain. Tanisha's life was a series of impending catastrophes. Her mother reported that she dreaded a phone call from Tanisha, let alone a visit, because she knew she would have to see her daughter through a crisis. For the same reason, Tanisha had few friends. •

Clinical Description

Tanisha was diagnosed with GAD, which is, in many ways, the basic syndrome that characterizes every anxiety and related disorder considered in this chapter (Brown, Barlow, & Liebowitz, 1994). The DSM-5 criteria specify that at least 6 months of excessive anxiety and worry (apprehensive expectation) must be ongoing more days than not. Furthermore, it must be difficult to turn off or control the worry process. This is what distinguishes pathological worrying from the kind we all experience occasionally as we prepare for an upcoming event or challenge. Most of us worry for a time but can set the problem aside and go on to another task. Even if the upcoming challenge is a big one, as soon as it is over, the worrying stops. For Tanisha, it never stopped. She turned to the next crisis as soon as the current one was over.

The physical symptoms associated with generalized anxiety and GAD differ somewhat from those associated with panic attacks and panic disorder (covered next). Whereas panic is associated with autonomic arousal, presumably as a result of a sympathetic nervous system surge (for instance, increased heart rate, palpitations, perspiration, and trembling), GAD is characterized by muscle tension, mental agitation, susceptibility to fatigue (probably the result of chronic excessive muscle tension), some irritability, and difficulty sleeping (Campbell-Sills & Brown, 2010). Focusing one's attention is difficult, as the mind quickly switches from crisis to crisis. For children, only one physical symptom is required for a diagnosis of GAD, and research validates this strategy (Tracey, Chorpita, Douban, & Barlow, 1997). People with GAD mostly worry about minor, everyday life events, a characteristic that distinguishes GAD from other anxiety disorders. When asked, "Do you worry excessively about minor things?," 100% of individuals with GAD respond "yes," compared with approximately 50% of individuals whose anxiety disorder falls within other categories (Barlow, 2002). Major events quickly become the focus of anxiety and worry, too. Adults typically focus on possible misfortune to their children, family health, job responsibilities, and more minor things such as household chores or being on time for appointments. Children with GAD most often worry about competence in academic, athletic, or social performance, as well as family issues (Albano & Hack, 2004; Furr, Tiwari, Suveg, & Kendall, 2009; Weems, Silverman, & La Greca, 2000). Older adults tend to focus, understandably, on health (Beck & Averill, 2004; Person & Borkovec, 1995; Wetherell et al., 2010); they also have difficulty sleeping, which seems to make the anxiety worse (Beck & Stanley, 1997; Brenes, Miller, Stanley, Williamson, Knudson, & McCall, 2009).

Statistics

Approximately 3.1% of the U.S. population meets criteria for GAD during a given 1-year period (Kessler, Chiu, Demler, & Walters, 2005), and 5.7% at some point during their lifetime (Kessler, Berglund, Demler, Jin, Merikangas, & Walters, 2005). For adolescents only (ages 13–17), the 1-year prevalence is somewhat lower at 1.1% (Kessler et al., 2012). This is still quite a large number, making GAD one of the most common anxiety

DSM 5 Table 5.2

Diagnostic Criteria for Generalized Anxiety Disorder

A. Excessive anxiety and worry (apprehensive expectation), occurring more days than not for at least 6 months about a number of events or activities (such as work or school performance).

B. The individual finds it difficult to control the worry.

C. The anxiety and worry are associated with at least three (or more) of the following six symptoms (with at least some symptoms present for more days than not for the past 6 months) [*Note:* Only one item is required in children]:

1. Restlessness or feeling keyed up or on edge
2. Being easily fatigued
3. Difficulty concentrating or mind going blank
4. Irritability
5. Muscle tension
6. Sleep disturbance (difficulty falling or staying asleep or restless, unsatisfying sleep)

D. The anxiety, worry or physical symptoms cause clinically significant distress or impairment in social, occupational, or other important areas of functioning.

E. The disturbance is not attributable to the physiological effects of a substance (e.g., a drug of abuse, a medication) or another medical condition (e.g., hyperthyroidism).

F. The disturbance is not better explained by another mental disorder (e.g., anxiety or worry about having panic attacks in panic disorder, negative evaluation in social anxiety disorder).

American Psychiatric Association. (2022). *Diagnostic and statistical manual of mental disorders* (5th ed., Text Revision).

disorders. Similar rates are reported from around the world—for example, from rural South Africa (Bhagwanjee, Parekh, Paruk, Petersen, & Subedar, 1998). Relatively few people with GAD come for treatment, however, compared with patients with panic disorder. Anxiety clinics like ours report that only approximately 10% of their patients meet criteria for GAD compared with 30% to 50% for panic disorder. This may be because most patients with GAD seek help from their primary care doctors, where they are found in large numbers (Roy-Byrne & Katon, 2000; Wittchen, 2002).

About twice as many individuals with GAD are female than male in epidemiological studies (where individuals with GAD are identified from population surveys), which include people who do not necessarily seek treatment (Grant et al., 2005). But this sex ratio may be specific to developed countries. In the South African study mentioned here, GAD was more common in males. In the United States, the prevalence of the disorder is significantly lower among Asian Americans, Hispanic, and Black adults compared to White adults (Grant et al., 2005).

Some people with GAD report onset in early adulthood, usually in response to a life stressor. Nevertheless, most studies find that GAD is associated with an earlier and more gradual onset than most other anxiety disorders (Barlow, 2002; Brown et al., 1994; Beesdo, Pine, Lieb, & Wittchen, 2010; Sanderson & Barlow, 1990). The median age of onset based on interviews is 31 (Kessler, Berglund, Demler, Jin, Merikangas, & Walters, 2005), but like Tanisha, many people have felt anxious and tense all their lives. Once it develops, GAD is chronic. One study found only an 8% probability of becoming symptom free after 2 years of follow-up (Yonkers et al., 1996). Bruce and colleagues (2005) reported that 12 years after the beginning of an episode of GAD, there was only a 58% chance of recovering. But 45% of those individuals who recovered were likely to relapse later. This suggests that GAD, like most anxiety disorders, follows a chronic course, characterized by waxing and waning of symptoms.

GAD is quite prevalent among older adults in the United States. In the large national comorbidity study and its replication, GAD was found to be most common in the group over 45 years of age and least common in the youngest group, ages 15 to 24 (Byers, Yaffe, Covinsky, Friedman, & Bruce, 2010; Wittchen, Zhao, Kessler, & Eaton, 1994); reported prevalence rates of GAD in older adults were as high as 10%. We also know that the use of minor tranquilizers for older adults is high, and the percentage increases with age (Olfson, King, & Schoenbaum, 2015). It is not entirely clear why drugs are prescribed with such frequency for older adults. One possibility is that the drugs may not be entirely intended for anxiety. Prescribed drugs may be primarily for sleeping problems or other secondary effects of medical illnesses. In any case, benzodiazepines (minor tranquilizers) interfere with cognitive function and put older adults at greater risk for injuries such as falling down and breaking bones, particularly their hips (Barlow, 2002).

Although less common, benzodiazepine use is also a problem in younger people: A large survey of approximately 29,600 high school students showed that 3.9% of U.S. 10th- and 12th-grade students reported nonmedical benzodiazepine use (Johnston et al., 2019). This is concerning because benzodiazepines use in this vulnerable population can easily lead to substance use disorders that may persist through early and late adulthood. For this and other reasons, the U.S. Food and Drug Administration (FDA) is now warning consumers about the serious risks of misuse, addiction, physical dependence, and withdrawal reactions when taking this medication. But as is true for all medications, doctors always need to carefully weigh the benefits and potential harm of benzodiazepines and develop a treatment plan that is safe and effective for the individual patient (Hirschtritt, Olfson, & Kroenke, 2021).

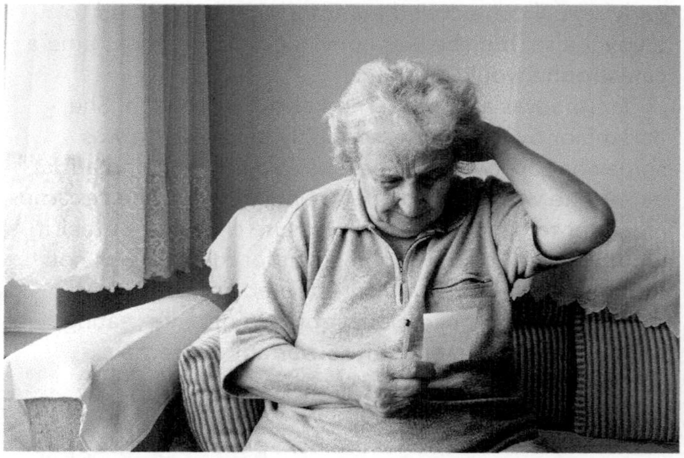

Approximately 1 in 10 older adults suffers from generalized anxiety disorder.

Causes

What causes GAD? We have learned a great deal in the past several years. As with most anxiety disorders, there seems to be a generalized biological vulnerability. This is reflected in studies examining a genetic contribution to GAD, although Kendler and colleagues (1995; Hettema, Prescott, Myers, Neale, & Kendler, 2005; Hettema, Neale, & Kendler, 2001) confirmed that what seems to be inherited is the tendency to become anxious rather than GAD itself. In support of this finding, heritability has been found for a particular trait, called *anxiety sensitivity*, which is the tendency to become distressed in response to arousal-related sensations, arising from beliefs that these anxiety-related sensations have harmful consequences (Davies et al., 2015).

For a long time, GAD has posed a real puzzle to investigators. Although the definition of the disorder is relatively new, originating in 1980 with DSM-III, clinicians and psychopathologists were working with people with generalized anxiety long before diagnostic systems were developed. For years, clinicians thought that people who were generally anxious had simply not focused their anxiety on anything specific. Thus, such anxiety was described as "free floating." But now scientists have looked more closely and have discovered some interesting distinctions from other anxiety disorders.

The first hints of difference were found in the physiological responsivity of individuals with GAD. It is surprising that individuals with GAD do not respond as strongly to stressors as individuals with anxiety disorders in which panic is more prominent. Several studies have found that individuals with GAD show *less responsiveness* on most physiological measures—such as heart rate, blood pressure, skin conductance, and respiration rate (Borkovec & Hu, 1990; Roemer & Orsillo, 2013)—than do individuals with other anxiety disorders. Moreover, GAD patients often show a comparatively low *cardiac vagal tone* (the vagus nerve is the largest parasympathetic nerve innervating the heart and decreasing its activity), leading to *autonomic inflexibility* because the heart is less responsive to certain tasks (Hofmann et al., 2005). Therefore, people with GAD have been called *autonomic restrictors* (Barlow, Chorpita, & Turovsky, 1996; Thayer, Friedman, & Borkovec, 1996).

When individuals with GAD are compared with nonanxious participants, the one physiological measure that consistently distinguishes the anxious group is muscle tension: people with GAD are chronically tense (Andrews et al., 2010; Marten et al., 1993). To understand this phenomenon of chronic muscle tension, we may have to know what's going on in the minds of people with GAD. With new methods from cognitive science, we are beginning to uncover the sometimes unconscious mental processes ongoing in GAD (Teachman, Joormann, Steinman, & Gotlib, 2012).

The evidence indicates that individuals with GAD are highly sensitive to threat in general, particularly to a threat that has personal relevance. That is, they allocate their attention more readily to sources of threat than do people who are not anxious (Aikins & Craske, 2001; Bradley, Mogg, White, Groom, & de Bono, 1999; Roemer & Orsillo, 2013). This high sensitivity may have arisen in early stressful experiences where they learned that the world is dangerous and out of control and they might not be able to cope (generalized psychological vulnerability). Furthermore, this acute awareness of potential threat, particularly if it is personal, seems to be entirely automatic or unconscious. Using the Stroop color-naming task described in Chapter 2, MacLeod and Mathews (1991) presented threatening words on a screen for only 20 milliseconds and still found that individuals with GAD were slower to name the colors of the words than were nonanxious individuals. Remember that in this task, words in colored letters are presented briefly and participants are asked to name the *color* rather than the word. The fact that the colors of threatening words were named more slowly suggests the *words* were more relevant to people with GAD, which interfered with their naming the color—even though the words were not present long enough for the individuals to be conscious of them. Investigators using other paradigms and in different anxiety populations have come to similar conclusions (Bar-Haim, Larry, Pergamin, Bakermans-Kranenburg, Van Ijzendoorn, 2007; Sheppes, Luria, Fukuda, & Gross, 2013).

How do mental processes link up with the tendency of individuals with GAD to be autonomic restrictors? Tom Borkovec and his colleagues noticed that although the peripheral autonomic arousal of individuals with GAD is restricted, they showed intense cognitive processing in the frontal lobes as indicated by EEG activity, particularly in the left hemisphere. This finding would suggest frantic, intense thought processes or worry without accompanying images (which would be reflected by activity in the right hemisphere of the brain rather than the left) (Borkovec, Alcaine, & Behar, 2004). Thus, worry may cause these individuals to be autonomic restrictors (Borkovec, Shadick, & Hopkins, 1991; Hofmann et al., 2005; Roemer & Orsillo, 2013). People with GAD are thinking so hard about upcoming problems that they don't have the attentional capacity left for the all-important process of creating images of the potential threat, images that would elicit more substantial negative affect and autonomic activity. In other words, they *avoid* images associated with the threat (Borkovec et al., 2004; Fisher & Wells, 2009). In therapy, the patient with GAD is taught to "process" the images and negative affect associated with anxiety and to refrain from worrying as a way to cope with their anxiety (Craske & Barlow, 2006; Hofmann, 2020; Zinbarg, Craske, & Barlow, 2006).

Many people with GAD also inherit a tendency to be tense (generalized biological vulnerability), and they develop a sense early on that important events in their lives may be uncontrollable and potentially dangerous (generalized psychological vulnerability), especially under stress. In addition, they use worry as a way to deal with this uncontrollability, and there is a possible rational reason for that. Let's assume that you didn't study as much as you should have for your midterm exam (which of course would never happen). If you expected a B, you would feel pleasantly surprised if you got an A but disappointed with a C. One way to avoid feeling disappointed is to adjust your expectations: If you expect that the outcome will be worse than it probably will turn out to be, then you won't be disappointed! Worrying is an "effective" strategy to do just that. The drawback is that if you constantly expect the worst, you will also feel miserable most of time. It appears that this is what many people with GAD do: They prefer to experience a sustained state of distress as a way to be emotionally prepared for the worst possible outcome to various events. As a result, worry evokes and sustains a chronic level of negative affect but prevents a sharp increase in negative emotion (Newman et al., 2013). This is consistent with our view of anxiety as a future-oriented mood state focused on potential danger or threat, as opposed to an emergency or alarm reaction to actual present danger. A model of the development of GAD is presented in ■ Figure 5.4.

Treatment

GAD is quite common, and available treatments, both drug and psychological, are reasonably effective. Benzodiazepines are most often prescribed for generalized anxiety, and the evidence indicates that they give some relief, at least in the short term. Few studies have looked at the effects of these drugs for a period longer than 8 weeks (Mathew & Hoffman, 2009). But the therapeutic effect is relatively modest.

Furthermore, benzodiazepines carry some risks. First, they seem to impair both cognitive and motor functioning (see, for example, Hindmarch, 1990; van Laar, Volkerts, & Verbaten, 2001). Specifically, people don't seem to be as alert on the job or at school when they are taking benzodiazepines. The drugs may impair driving, and in older adults they seem to be associated with falls, resulting in hip fractures (Ray, Gurwitz, Decker, & Kennedy, 1992; Wang, Bohn, Glynn, Mogun, & Avorn, 2001). More important, benzodiazepines seem to produce both psychological and physical dependence, making it difficult for people to stop

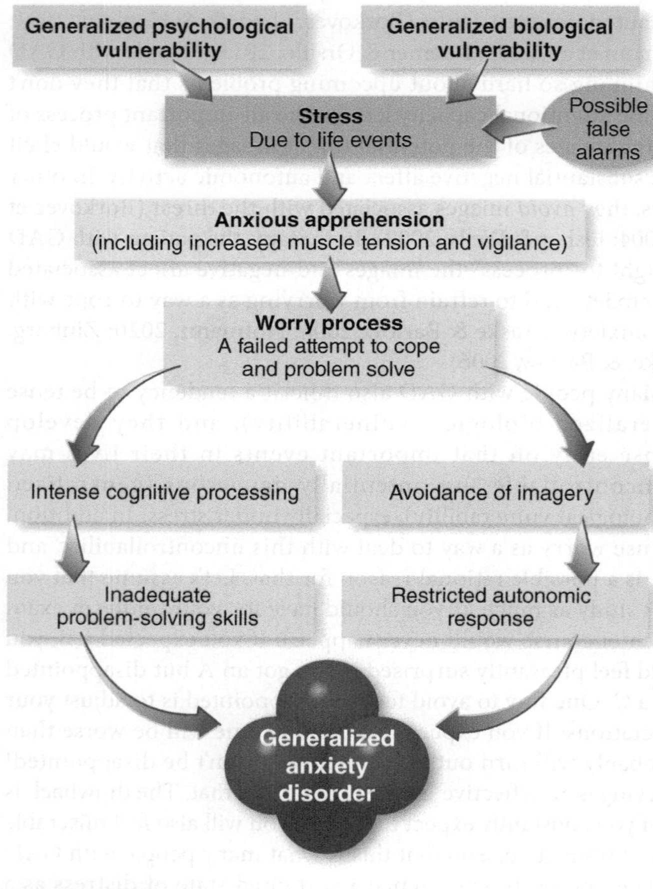

Figure 5.4

An integrative model of GAD.

taking them (Mathew & Hoffman, 2009; Noyes, Garvey, Cook, & Suelzer, 1991; Rickels, Schweizer, Case, & Greenblatt, 1990).

There is reasonably wide agreement that the optimal use of benzodiazepines is for the short-term relief of anxiety associated with a temporary crisis or stressful event, such as a family problem (Craske & Barlow, 2006). Under these circumstances, a physician may prescribe a benzodiazepine until the crisis is resolved but for no more than a week or two. There is stronger evidence for the usefulness of antidepressants in the treatment of GAD, such as paroxetine (also called Paxil) (Rickels, Rynn, Ivengar, & Duff, 2006) and venlafaxine (also called Effexor) (Schatzberg, 2000). These drugs may prove to be a better choice (Brawman-Mintzer, 2001; Mathew & Hoffman, 2009).

In the short term, psychological treatments seem to confer about the same benefit as drugs in the treatment of GAD, but psychological treatments are more effective in the long term (Barlow, Allen, & Basden, 2007; Newman et al., 2011; Roemer & Orsillo, 2013). Reports of innovations in brief psychological treatments are encouraging. Because we now know that individuals with GAD seem to avoid "feelings" of anxiety and the negative affect associated with threatening images, clinicians have designed treatments to help patients with GAD process the threatening information on an emotional level, using images, so that they will experience (rather than avoid feeling) the emotion associated with the images. These treatments have other components, such as teaching patients how to relax deeply to combat tension. Borkovec and his colleagues found such a treatment to be significantly better than a placebo psychological treatment, not only at posttreatment but also at a 1-year follow-up (Borkovec & Costello, 1993).

In the early 1990s, we developed a cognitive-behavioral treatment (CBT) for GAD in which patients evoke the worry process during therapy sessions and confront threatening images and thoughts head-on. The patient learns to use cognitive skills and other coping techniques to counteract and control the worry process (Craske & Barlow, 2006; Hofmann, 2020; Wetherell, Gatz, & Craske, 2003). In a major study, one of these CBT treatment protocols (Hofmann, 2020) was compared to yoga and stress education. The results showed that both CBT and yoga were more effective than stress education, but CBT showed the more robust improvements that were maintained over at 6 months with treatment response rate of around 75% (Simon et al., 2021). Another study showed that a brief adaptation of another one of these treatments (Craske & Barlow, 2006) was also used successfully to decrease anxiety and improve quality of life in a primary care office (family doctors and nurses) where GAD is frequently diagnosed (Rollman et al., 2005). Cuijpers and colleagues (Cuijpers et al., 2014) reviewed 41 studies with 2,132 patients meeting criteria for GAD and found large treatment effects of psychotherapy, which primarily consisted of CBT, as compared to control conditions, which were primarily waitlist groups. This treatment can also be effectively delivered via the internet (Eilert et al., 2021).

Despite this success, it is clear we need more powerful treatments, both drug and psychological, for this chronic, treatment-resistant condition. Meditational and mindfulness-based approaches, which help teach the patient to be more tolerant of these feelings, can be important modules to enhance more traditional treatments (Hayes-Skelton, Roemer, & Orsillo, 2013; Hofmann, Sawyer, Witt, & Oh, 2010; Khoury et al., 2013; Orsillo & Roemer, 2011; Roemer et al., 2002).

There is particularly encouraging evidence that psychological treatments are effective with children who suffer from generalized anxiety (Albano & Hack, 2004; Furr et al., 2009; Perrin, Bevan, Payne, & Bolton, 2019). In a major clinical trial with 488 children ages 7 to 17 years, CBT and the antidepressant drug sertraline (Zoloft) were equally effective immediately following treatment compared with taking placebo pills for children with GAD and other related disorders, but the combination of CBT and sertraline was even better, with 80% showing substantial improvement versus 24% on placebo (Walkup et al., 2008). Follow-up analyses showed that more severe and impairing anxiety, greater caregiver strain, and a principal diagnosis of social anxiety disorder were associated with less favorable outcomes (Compton al., 2014). Also, mindfulness-based therapies for GAD are now being adapted and tested with youth with some indications of success (Semple & Burke, 2012). Similarly, progress is also being made in adapting psychological treatments for older adults, as important studies show (Beck & Stanley, 1997; Stanley et al., 2003; Wetherell, Lenze, & Stanley, 2005). One large clinical trial demonstrated very clearly the efficiency of this treatment for adults over 60 compared to the usual care they received (Stanley et al., 2009).

Other promising new strategies are to help educate patients in increasing their tolerance to uncertainty about the future (Dugas, Schwartz, & Francis, 2012) and changing their beliefs about worrying (Wells, Welford, King, Papageorgiou, Wisely, & Mendel, 2010) because patients often feel a strong need to control the future and hold maladaptive beliefs about worrying, which has been referred to as *metacognitions*—cognitions (beliefs) about cognitions (worrying).

After trying a number of different drugs, Tanisha, the college student diagnosed with GAD, was treated with the CBT approach developed at our clinic and found herself more able to cope with life. She completed college and graduate school, married, and is successful in her career as a counselor in a nursing home. But even now, Tanisha finds it difficult to relax and stop worrying. She continues to experience mild to moderate anxiety, particularly when under stress, and she occasionally takes minor tranquilizers to support her psychological coping skills.

Concept Check 5.2

True (T) or false (F)?

1. ____________ GAD is characterized by muscle tension, mental agitation, irritability, sleeping difficulties, and susceptibility to fatigue.
2. ____________ Most studies show that in the majority of cases of GAD, onset is early in adulthood as an immediate response to a life stressor.
3. ____________ GAD is prevalent in older adults and in females in our society.
4. ____________ GAD has no genetic basis.
5. ____________ Cognitive-behavioral treatment and other psychological treatments for GAD are probably better than drug therapies in the long run.

Panic Disorder and Agoraphobia

People with **panic disorder (PD)** experience severe, unexpected panic attacks; they may think they're dying or otherwise losing control. In many but not all cases, PD is accompanied by a closely related disorder called **agoraphobia**, which is fear and avoidance of situations in which a person feels unsafe or unable to escape to get home or to a hospital in the event of a developing panic, panic-like symptoms, or other physical symptoms, such as loss of bladder control. People develop agoraphobia because they never know when these symptoms might occur. In severe cases, people with agoraphobia are unable to leave the house, sometimes for years on end, as in the example of Mrs. M.

Mrs. M... Self-Imprisoned

Mrs. M. was 67 years old and lived in a second-floor walk-up apartment in a lower-middle-class section of the city. Her adult daughter, one of her few remaining contacts with the world, had requested an evaluation with Mrs. M.'s consent. I rang the bell and entered a narrow hallway. Mrs. M. was nowhere in sight. Knowing that she lived on the second floor, I walked up the stairs and knocked on the door at the top. When I heard Mrs. M. ask me to come in, I opened the door. She was sitting in her living room, and I could quickly see the layout of the rest of the apartment. The living room was in the front; the kitchen was in the back, adjoining a porch. To the right of the stairs was the one bedroom, with a bathroom opening from it.

Mrs. M. was glad to see me and seemed very friendly, offering me coffee and homemade cookies. I was the first person she had seen in 3 weeks. Mrs. M. had not left that apartment in 20 years, and she had suffered from panic disorder and agoraphobia for more than 30 years.

As she told her story, Mrs. M. conveyed vivid images of a wasted life. And yet she continued to struggle in the face of adversity and to make the best she could of her limited existence. Even areas in her apartment signaled the potential for terrifying panic attacks. She had not answered the door herself for the past 15 years because she was afraid to look into the hallway. She could enter her kitchen and go into the areas containing the stove and refrigerator, but for the past 10 years she had not been to the part of the room that overlooked the backyard or out onto the back porch. Thus, her life for the past decade had been confined to her bedroom, her living room, and the front half of her kitchen. She relied on her adult daughter to bring groceries and visit once a week. Her only other visitor was the parish priest, who came to deliver communion every 2 to 3 weeks when he could. Her only other contact with the outside world was through the television and the radio. Her husband, who had alcohol use problems and had abused Mrs. M., had died 10 years earlier of alcohol-related causes. Early in her stressful marriage, she had her first terrifying panic attack and had gradually withdrawn from the world. As long as she stayed in her apartment, she was relatively free of panic. Therefore, and because in her mind there were few reasons left near the end of her life to venture out, she declined treatment. •

Clinical Description

In DSM-IV, panic disorder and agoraphobia were integrated into one disorder called panic disorder with agoraphobia, but investigators discovered that many people experienced panic disorder without developing agoraphobia and some people develop agoraphobia in the absence of panic disorder (Wittchen, Gloster, Beesdo-Baum, Fava, & Craske, 2010). As a result, the DSM-5 lists panic disorder and agoraphobia as two separate diagnoses. Often, however, they go together, so we discuss both disorders in this section.

At the beginning of the chapter, we talked about the related phenomena of anxiety and panic. In PD, anxiety and panic are combined in an intricate relationship that can become as difficult as it was for Mrs. M. Many people who have panic attacks do not necessarily develop panic disorder. To meet criteria for panic disorder, a person must experience an unexpected panic attack *and* develop substantial anxiety over the possibility of having another attack or about the implications of the attack or its consequences. In other words, the person must think that each attack is a sign of impending death or incapacitation. A few individuals do not report concern about another attack but still change their behavior in a way that indicates the distress the attacks cause them. They may avoid going to certain places or neglect their duties around the house for fear an attack might occur if they are too active.

The term *agoraphobia* was coined in 1871 by Karl Westphal, a German physician, and, in the original Greek, refers to fear of the marketplace. This is an appropriate term because the agora *was* the Greek marketplace—a busy, bustling area. One of the most stressful places for individuals with agoraphobia today is the shopping mall, the modern-day agora.

We know that anxiety is diminished for individuals with agoraphobia if they think a location or person is "safe," even if there is nothing effective the person could do if something bad did happen to the patient. For these reasons, when they do venture outside their homes, people with agoraphobia always plan for rapid escape (for example, by sitting near the door). A list of typical situations commonly avoided by someone with agoraphobia is found in Table 5.1.

Although agoraphobia can also exist independent of panic disorder (Wittchen et al., 2010), some people avoid agoraphobic situations as a way to cope with their panic or panic-like symptoms. Other methods of coping with panic attacks include using (and sometimes abusing) drugs and/or alcohol. Some individuals do not avoid agoraphobic situations but endure them with "intense dread." For example, people who must go to work each day or, perhaps, travel as part of the job will suffer high levels of anxiety and panic simply to achieve their goals. Thus, DSM-5 notes that agoraphobia may be characterized either by avoiding the situations or by enduring them with intense fear and anxiety. As noted above, epidemiological surveys have identified a group of people who seem to have agoraphobia without ever having a panic attack or any fearful spells whatsoever. In fact, approximately 50% of individuals with agoraphobia identified in population surveys fit this description, although it is relatively rare to see these cases in the clinic (Wittchen et al., 2010). These individuals may have other distressing unpredictable experiences such as dizzy spells, possible loss of bladder or bowel control such that they can never be far from a bathroom, or fear of falling (particularly for older adults), any of which might be embarrassing or may even become dangerous if away from a safe place or without the presence of a safe person. Most patients with panic disorder and agoraphobic avoidance also display another cluster of avoidant behaviors that we call *interoceptive avoidance*, or avoidance of internal physical sensations (Brown, White, & Barlow, 2005; Craske & Barlow, 2014; Mesri et al., 2020; Shear et al., 1997). These behaviors involve removing oneself from situations or activities that might produce the physiological arousal that somehow resembles the beginnings of a panic attack. Some patients might avoid exercise because it produces increased cardiovascular activity or faster respiration, which reminds them of panic attacks and makes them think one might be beginning. Other patients might avoid sauna baths or any rooms in which they might perspire. Psychopathologists are beginning to recognize that this cluster of avoidance behaviors is every bit as important as more classical agoraphobic avoidance. A list of situations or activities typically avoided within the interoceptive cluster is found in Table 5.2.

Table 5.1 Typical Situations Avoided by People with Agoraphobia

Shopping malls	Being far from home
Cars (as driver or passenger)	Staying at home alone
Buses	Waiting in line
Trains	Supermarkets
Subways	Stores
Wide streets	Crowds
Tunnels	Planes
Restaurants	Elevators
Theaters	Escalators

Source: Adapted, with permission, from D. H. Barlow & M. G. Craske, 2007, *Mastery of your anxiety and panic* (4th ed.), Oxford University Press, p. 5.

Statistics

PD is fairly common. Approximately 2.7% of the US population meet criteria for PD during a given 1-year period (Kessler, Chiu, et al., 2005; Kessler, Chiu, Jin, et al., 2006) and 4.7% met them at some point during their lives, two-thirds of them women (Eaton,

Table 5.2 Interoceptive Daily Activities Typically Avoided by People with Agoraphobia

Running up flights of stairs	Getting involved in "heated" debates
Walking outside in intense heat	
Having showers with the doors and windows closed	Hot, stuffy rooms Hot, stuffy cars
Hot, stuffy stores or shopping malls	Having a sauna Hiking
Walking outside in very cold weather	Sports
Aerobics	Drinking coffee or any caffeinated beverages
Lifting heavy objects	Sexual relations
Dancing	Watching horror movies
Eating chocolate	Eating heavy meals
Standing quickly from a sitting position	Getting angry
Watching exciting movies or sports events	

Source: Adapted, with permission, from D. H. Barlow & M. G. Craske, 2007, *Mastery of your anxiety and panic* (4th ed.), Oxford University Press, p. 11.

Kessler, Wittchen, & Magee, 1994; Kessler, Berglund, Demler, Jin, Merikangas, & Walters, 2005). Some develop agoraphobia without ever having a full-blown panic attack, which was the reason the DSM-5 considered PD and agoraphobia as two separate diagnoses (Wittchen et al., 2010).

Onset of panic disorder usually occurs in early adult life—from midteens through about 40 years of age. The median age of onset is between 20 and 24 (Kessler et al., 2005). Prepubescent children have been known to experience unexpected panic attacks and occasionally panic disorder (Kessler et al., 2012). Most initial unexpected panic attacks begin at or after puberty. Furthermore, many prepubertal children who are seen by general medical practitioners have symptoms of hyperventilation that may well be panic attacks. These children do not report fear of dying or losing control, however, perhaps because they are not at a stage of their cognitive development where they can make these attributions (Nelles & Barlow, 1988).

Important work on anxiety for older adults suggests that health and vitality are the primary focus of anxiety for the older adult population (Mohlman et al., 2012; Wolitzky-Taylor, Castriotta, Lenze, Stanley, & Craske, 2010). The prevalence rates of PD in different age groups are very similar, and the tendency for women to experience a greater prevalence remains present in older adults (Grenier et al., 2019).

Similarly, most (75% or more) of those who suffer from agoraphobia are women (Barlow, 2002; Myers et al., 1984; Thorpe & Burns, 1983). For a long time, we didn't know why, but now it seems the explanation is cultural (Arrindell et al., 2003a; Wolitzky-Taylor et al., 2010). It is more accepted for women to report fear and to avoid numerous situations. Men, however, are expected to be stronger and braver, to "tough it out." The higher the severity of agoraphobic avoidance, the greater the proportion of women. For example, in our clinic, out of a group of patients suffering from panic disorder with mild agoraphobia, 72% were women. If the agoraphobia was moderate, however, the percentage was 81%. Similarly, if agoraphobia was severe, the percentage was 89%.

What happens to men who have severe unexpected panic attacks? Is cultural disapproval of fear in men so strong that most of them simply endure panic? The answer seems to be no. A large proportion of males with unexpected panic attacks cope in a culturally acceptable way: They consume large amounts of alcohol. This can establish a close link between substance use and anxiety (Anker & Kushner, 2019; Grant, Stinson, et al., 2004).

The problem is that some people become dependent on alcohol, and many begin the long downward spiral into serious addiction. Thus, men may end up with an even more severe problem. Because these men are so impaired by alcohol abuse, clinicians may not realize they also have panic disorder and agoraphobia. Furthermore, even if they are successfully treated for their addiction, the anxiety disorder will require treatment (McHugh, 2015).

Cultural Influences Panic disorder exists worldwide, although its expression may vary from place to place. Prevalence rates for panic disorder show some degree of cross-cultural variability, with Asian and African countries usually showing the lowest rates. These findings mirror cross-ethnic comparisons within the United States, with Asian Americans showing the lowest, and White Americans showing the highest prevalence rates (Asnaani, Gutner, Hinton, & Hofmann, 2009; Hofmann & Hinton, 2014; Lewis-Fernandez et al., 2010). But a number of contextual and social factors need to be considered when interpreting this pattern of findings. Among Asian Americans, Hispanic Americans, and Blacks in the United States, panic disorder is associated with reports of racial/ethnic discrimination, even after accounting for the effect of demographic factors (Chou et al. 2012). Also, across different racial and ethnic minority groups, better mental health was associated with male gender, higher income, marriage, and higher education (Lo & Cheng, 2018). The exact reasons for these findings are not well understood and they need to be investigated further.

Courtesy of Michelle Craske

Michelle Craske demonstrated that agoraphobic avoidance is simply one way of coping with panic. She and Ron Rapee, working with David H. Barlow, also developed an effective psychological treatment for panic disorder.

In addition to differences in prevalence rates and chronicity, cross-cultural studies have also identified interesting differences in the expression of the anxiety. In Chapter 2, we described a fright disorder in Latin America that is called *susto*, a disorder that is characterized by sweating, increased heart rate, and insomnia but not by reports of anxiety or fear, even though a severe fright is the cause. An anxiety-related, culturally defined syndrome prominent among Hispanic Americans, particularly those from the Caribbean, is called *ataques de nervios* (Hinton, Chong, Pollack, Barlow, & McNally, 2008; Hinton, Lewis-Fernández, & Pollack, 2009). The symptoms of an *ataque* seem quite similar to those of a panic attack, although such manifestations as shouting uncontrollably or bursting into tears may be associated more often with *ataque* than with panic.

Finally, Devon Hinton, a psychiatrist/anthropologist, and his colleagues have described an interesting manifestation of panic disorder among Khmer (Cambodian) and Vietnamese refugees in the United States. Both of these groups have a high rate of panic disorder. But a substantial number of these panic attacks are associated with orthostatic dizziness (dizziness from standing up quickly) and "sore neck." What Hinton's group discovered is that the Khmer concept of *kyol goeu* or "wind overload" (too much wind or gas in the body, which may cause blood vessels to burst) becomes the focus of catastrophic thinking during panic attacks (Hinton, Hofmann, Pitman, Pollack, & Barlow, 2008; Hinton, Pollack, Pich, Fama, & Barlow, 2005; Hinton et al., 2019).

DSM 5 Table 5.3 Diagnostic Criteria for Panic Disorder

A. Recurrent unexpected panic attacks.

B. At least one of the attacks has been followed by 1 month (or more) of one or both of the following: (a) Persistent concern or worry about additional panic attacks or their consequences (e.g., losing control, having a heart attack, "going crazy"), or (b) A significant maladaptive change in behavior related to the attacks (e.g., behaviors designed to avoid having panic attacks, such as avoidance of exercise or unfamiliar situations).

C. The disturbance is not attributable to the physiological effects of a substance (e.g., a drug of abuse, a medication) or another medical condition (e.g., hyperthyroidism, cardiopulmonary disorders).

D. The disturbance is not better explained by another mental disorder (e.g., the panic attacks do not occur only in response to feared social situations, as in social anxiety disorder).

American Psychiatric Association. (2022). *Diagnostic and statistical manual of mental disorders* (5th ed., Text Revision).

DSM 5 Table 5.4 Diagnostic Criteria for Agoraphobia

A. Marked fear or anxiety about two (or more) of the following five situations:
   1. Using public transportation (e.g., automobiles, buses, trains, ships, planes).
   2. Being in open spaces
   3. Being in enclosed places (e.g. shops, theaters, cinemas)
   4. Standing in line or being in a crowd
   5. Being outside the home alone.

B. The individual fears or avoids these situations due to thoughts that escape might be difficult or help might not be available in the event of developing panic-like symptoms or other incapacitating or embarrassing symptoms (e.g., fear of falling in the elderly; fear of incontinence).

C. The agoraphobic situations almost always provoke fear or anxiety.

D. The agoraphobic situations are actively avoided, require the presence of a companion, or are endured with intense fear or anxiety.

E. The fear or anxiety is out of proportion to the actual danger posed by the agoraphobic situations, and to the sociocultural context.

F. The fear, anxiety, or avoidance is persistent, typically lasting for 6 months or more.

G. The fear, anxiety, or avoidance causes clinically significant distress or impairment in social, occupational, or other important areas of functioning.

H. If another medical condition (e.g., inflammatory bowel disease, Parkinson's disease) is present, the fear, anxiety or avoidance is clearly excessive.

I. The fear, anxiety or, avoidance is not better explained by the symptoms of another mental disorder—for example, the symptoms are not confined to specific phobia, situational type; do not involve only social situations (as in social anxiety disorder) and are not related exclusively to obsessions (as in obsessive-compulsive disorder), perceived defects or flaws in physical appearance (as in body dysmorphic disorder), reminders of traumatic events (as in posttraumatic stress disorder), or fear of separation (as in separation anxiety disorder).

American Psychiatric Association. (2022). *Diagnostic and statistical manual of mental disorders* (5th ed., Text Revision).

Nocturnal Panic Think back to the case of Ashlyn, whose panic attack was described earlier. Is there anything unusual about her report? She was sound asleep when it happened. Approximately 60% of the people with panic disorder have experienced such nocturnal attacks (Craske & Rowe, 1997; Uhde, 1994). In fact, panic attacks occur more often between 1:30 A.M. and 3:30 A.M. than any other time. In some cases, people are afraid to go to sleep at night. What's happening to them? Are they having nightmares? Research indicates they are not. Nocturnal attacks are studied in a sleep laboratory. Patients spend a few nights sleeping while attached to an electroencephalograph machine that monitors their brain waves (see Chapter 3). We all go through various stages of sleep that are reflected by different patterns on the electroencephalogram. (Stages of sleep are discussed fully in Chapter 8.) We have learned that nocturnal panic attacks occur during delta wave or slow-wave sleep, which typically occurs several hours after we fall asleep and is the deepest stage of sleep. People with panic disorder often begin to panic when they start sinking into delta sleep, and then they awaken amid an attack. Because there is no obvious reason for them to be anxious or panicky when they are sound asleep, most of these individuals think they are dying (Craske & Barlow, 1988; Craske & Barlow, 2014).

What causes nocturnal panic? Currently, our best information is that the change in stages of sleep to slow-wave sleep produces physical sensations of "letting go" that are frightening to an individual with panic disorder (Craske, Lang, Mystkowski, Zucker, & Bystritsky, 2002; Smith & Capron, 2020). This process is described more fully later when we discuss causes of panic disorder. Several other events also occur during sleep that resemble nocturnal panic and are mistakenly thought by some to be the cause of nocturnal panic. Initially, these events were thought to be nightmares, but nightmares and other dreamlike activity occur only during a stage of sleep characterized by rapid eye movement (REM) sleep, which typically occurs much later in the sleep cycle. Therefore, people are not dreaming when they have nocturnal panics, a conclusion consistent with patient reports. Some therapists are not aware of the stage of sleep associated with nocturnal panic attacks and so assume that patients are "repressing" their dream material, perhaps because it might relate to an early trauma too painful to be admitted to consciousness. As we've seen, this is virtually impossible because nocturnal panic attacks do not occur during REM sleep, so there is no well-developed dream or nightmare activity going on when they happen. Thus, it is not possible for these patients to be dreaming anything.

Some therapists assume that patients with nocturnal panic might have a breathing disorder called *sleep apnea*, an interruption of breathing during sleep that may feel like suffocation. This condition is often found in people who are substantially overweight. But sleep apnea has a cycle of awakening and falling back to sleep that is not characteristic of nocturnal panics.

A related phenomenon occurring in children is called *sleep terrors*, which we describe in more detail in Chapter 8 (Durand, 2006). Often children awaken imagining that something is chasing them around the room. It is common for them to scream and get out of bed as if something were after them. However, they do not wake up and have no memory of the event in the morning. In contrast, individuals experiencing nocturnal panic attacks do wake up and later remember the event clearly. Sleep terrors also tend to occur at a later stage of sleep (stage 4 sleep), a stage associated with sleepwalking.

Finally, there is a fascinating condition called *isolated sleep paralysis* that seems culturally determined. Have you ever heard the expression "the witch is riding you"? It is a common expression used among African Americans to describe this condition (Bell, Dixie-Bell, & Thompson, 1986; Neal-Barnett & Smith, 1997; Ramsawh, Raffa, White, & Barlow, 2008). Isolated sleep paralysis occurs during the transitional state between sleep and waking, when a person is either falling asleep or waking up, but mostly when waking up (Sharpless & Klikova, 2019). During this period, the individual is unable to move and experiences a surge of terror that resembles a panic attack; occasionally, there are also vivid hallucinations. One possible explanation is that REM sleep is spilling over into the waking cycle. This seems likely because one feature of REM sleep is lack of bodily movement. Another is vivid dreams, which could account for the experience of hallucination.

Rates of sleep paralysis vary a lot by ethnic groups and samples. Sharpless and Barber (2011) showed that rates of sleep paralysis is highest among African American samples in the general population (40.2%) and psychiatric samples (44.3%) and also among Asian American student samples (39.9%). In contrast, the rate in the general population across all groups is 7.6%. Ramsawh and colleagues (2008) also reported that African Americans with isolated sleep paralysis had a history of trauma and more frequent diagnoses of panic disorder and posttraumatic stress disorder than African Americans without isolated sleep paralysis. Even more interesting is that the disorder does not seem to occur in Black Nigerians. The prevalence in Black Nigerian populations is about the same as it is in White American populations. The reasons for this distribution are not clear, although all factors may point to a cultural explanation.

Causes

It is not possible to understand panic disorder without referring to the triad of contributing factors mentioned throughout this book: biological, psychological, and social. Strong evidence indicates that agoraphobia often develops after a person has unexpected panic attacks (or panic-like sensations), but whether agoraphobia develops and how severe it becomes seem to be socially and culturally determined, as we noted earlier. Panic attacks and panic disorder, however, seem to be related most strongly to biological and psychological factors and their interaction.

At the beginning of the chapter, we discussed the triple vulnerability model of how biological, psychological, and social factors may contribute to the development and maintenance of anxiety and to an initial unexpected panic attack (Bouton et al., 2001; Suárez et al., 2009; White & Barlow, 2002) (see ■ Figure 5.3). As noted earlier, we all inherit—some more than others—a vulnerability to stress, which is a tendency to be generally neurobiologically overreactive to the events of daily life (generalized biological vulnerability). But some people are also more likely than others to have an emergency alarm reaction (unexpected panic attack) when confronted with stress-producing events. These may include stress on the job or at school, the death of a loved one, divorce, and even positive events that are nevertheless stressful, such as graduating from school and starting a new career, getting married, or changing jobs. (Remember that other people might be more likely to have headaches or high blood pressure in response to the same kinds of stress.) Particular situations quickly become associated in an individual's mind with external and internal cues that were present during the panic attack (Bouton et al., 2001). The next time the person's heart rate increases during exercise, they might assume they are having a panic attack (conditioning). A regular amount of exercise is an example of an internal cue or a conditioned stimulus for a panic attack. Being in a movie theater when panic first occurred would be an external cue that might become a conditioned stimulus for future panics. Because these cues become associated with a number of different internal and external stimuli through a learning process, we call them *learned alarms*.

But none of this would make much difference without the next step. Why would some people think something terrible is going to happen when they have an attack but others wouldn't? In one study, young women at risk for developing anxiety disorders were followed prospectively for several years. Those women who had a history of various physical disorders and were anxious about their health tended to develop panic disorder rather than another anxiety disorder such as social anxiety disorder (Rudaz, Craske, Becker, Ledermann, & Margraf, 2010). Thus, these women may have learned in childhood that unexpected bodily sensations may be dangerous—whereas other people experiencing panic attacks do not. This tendency to believe that unexpected bodily sensations are dangerous reflects a specific psychological vulnerability to develop panic and related disorders. The causal sequence for the development of panic disorder is depicted in ■ Figure 5.5.

Approximately 8% to 12% of the U.S. population has an occasional unexpected panic attack, often during a period of intense stress over the previous year (Kessler, Chiu, et al., 2006; Mattis & Ollendick, 2002; Norton, Harrison, Hauch, & Rhodes, 1985; Suárez et al., 2009; Telch, Lucas, & Nelson, 1989). Most of these people do not develop anxiety (Telch et al., 1989). Only approximately 5% go on to develop anxiety over future panic attacks and thereby meet the DSM criteria for panic disorder, and these individuals are the ones who are susceptible to developing anxiety over the possibility of having another panic attack (a generalized psychological vulnerability). What happens to those individuals who don't develop anxiety? They seem to attribute the attack to events of the moment—such as an argument with a friend, something they ate, or a bad day—and go on with their lives, perhaps experiencing an occasional panic attack when they are under stress again. This was illustrated by the experiences of professional golfer Charlie Beljan, known to his friends as a fun-loving and free-spirited guy. But in late 2012, on his way to winning his first Professional Golfers Association (PGA) tournament, he experienced a panic attack that he thought was a heart attack. Determined to finish and with

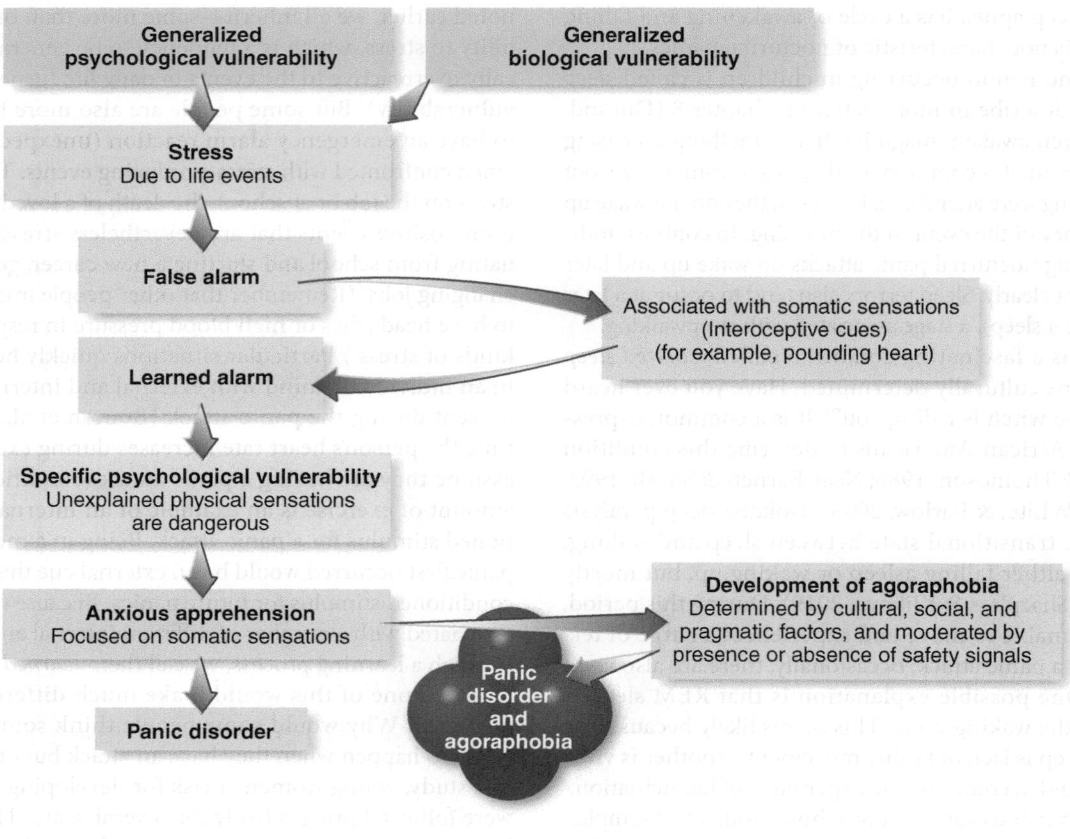

Figure 5.5

A model of the causes of panic disorder with or without agoraphobia. Reprinted, with permission, from K. S. White & D. H. Barlow, 2002, Panic disorder and agoraphobia, in D. H. Barlow, *Anxiety and its disorders: The nature and treatment of anxiety and panic* (2nd ed.), Guilford Press. © 2002 by Guilford Press.

paramedics following him in a golf cart, Beljan would stagger from shot to shot, sometimes having to sit down on the fairway. Nevertheless, he had his best round of the year and, after finishing, took an ambulance to the hospital where he was diagnosed as having a panic attack (Crouse, 2013). Reacting to the news, Bubba Watson, the Masters champion in 2012, reported that panic attacks had put him in the hospital at least three times in his career.

The influential cognitive theories of David Clark (1986, 1996) explicate in more detail some cognitive processes that may be ongoing in panic disorder. Clark emphasizes the specific psychological vulnerability of people with this disorder to interpret normal physical sensations in a catastrophic way. In other words, although we all typically experience rapid heartbeat after exercise, if you have a psychological or cognitive vulnerability, you might interpret the response as dangerous and feel a surge of anxiety. This anxiety, in turn, produces more physical sensations because of the action of the sympathetic nervous system; you perceive these additional sensations as even more dangerous, and a vicious cycle begins that results in a panic attack. Thus, Clark emphasizes the cognitive process as most important in panic disorder.

One hypothesis that panic disorder and agoraphobia evolve from psychodynamic causes suggested that early object loss and/or separation anxiety might predispose someone to develop the condition as an adult. Separation anxiety is what a child might feel at the threat of separation or on actual separation from an important caregiver, such as a parent. Dependent personality tendencies often characterize a person with agoraphobia. These characteristics were hypothesized as a possible reaction to early separation. Nevertheless, despite some intriguing suggestions, little evidence indicates that patients who have panic disorder or agoraphobia experienced separation anxiety during childhood more often than individuals with other psychological disorders or, for that matter, people without this problem (Barlow, 2002; Thyer, 1993). It is still possible, however, that the trauma of early separation might predispose someone to psychological disorders in general. (Separation anxiety disorder is discussed below.)

Treatment

As we note in Chapter 1, research on the effectiveness of new treatments is important to psychopathology. Responses to certain specific treatments, whether drug or psychological, may indicate the causes of the disorder. We now discuss the benefits and some drawbacks of medication, psychological interventions, and a combination of these two treatments.

Medication A large number of drugs affecting the noradrenergic, serotonergic, or GABA–benzodiazepine neurotransmitter systems, or some combination, seem effective in treating panic disorder, including high-potency benzodiazepines, the newer selective-serotonin reuptake inhibitors (SSRIs) such as Prozac and Paxil, and the closely related serotonin-norepinephrine reuptake inhibitors (SNRIs), such as venlafaxine (Barlow, 2002; Caldirola et al., 2018; Ciraulo et al., 2013; Pollack, 2005; Pollack & Simon, 2009).

There are advantages and disadvantages to each class of drugs. SSRIs are currently the indicated drug for panic disorder based on all available evidence, although sexual dysfunction seems to occur in 75% or more of people taking these medications (Lecrubier, Bakker, Dunbar, & the Collaborative Paroxetine Panic Study Investigators, 1997; Lecrubier, Judge, & the Collaborative Paroxetine Panic Study Investigators, 1997). On the other hand, high-potency benzodiazepines such as alprazolam (Xanax), commonly used for panic disorder, work quickly but are hard to stop taking because of psychological and physical dependence and addiction. Therefore, they are not recommended as strongly as the SSRIs. Nevertheless, benzodiazepines remain the most widely used class of drugs in practice (Blanco et al., 2004) and their use continues to increase (Comer, Mojtabai, & Olfson, 2011). Also, all benzodiazepines adversely affect cognitive and motor functions to some degree. Therefore, people taking them in high doses often find their ability to focus (while driving a car or trying to study) somewhat reduced.

Approximately 60% of patients with panic disorder are free of panic as long as they stay on an effective drug (Lecrubier, Bakker, et al., 1997; Pollack & Simon, 2009), but 20% or more stop taking the drug before treatment is done (Otto, Behar, Smits, & Hofmann, 2009), and relapse rates are high (approximately 50%) once the medication is stopped (Hollon et al., 2005). The relapse rate is closer to 90% for those who stop taking benzodiazepines (see, for example, Fyer et al., 1987).

Psychological Intervention Psychological treatments have proved quite effective for panic disorder. Originally, such treatments concentrated on reducing agoraphobic avoidance, using strategies based on exposure to feared situations. The strategy of exposure-based treatments is to arrange conditions in which the patient can gradually face the feared situations and learn there is nothing to fear. Most patients with phobias are well aware of this rationally, but they must be convinced on an emotional level as well by "reality testing" the situation and confirming that nothing dangerous happens. Sometimes the therapist accompanies the patients on their exposure exercises. At other times, the therapist simply helps patients structure their own exercises and provides them with a variety of psychological coping mechanisms to help them complete the exercises, which are typically arranged from least to most difficult. A sample of these is listed in Table 5.3.

Gradual exposure exercises, sometimes combined with anxiety-reducing coping mechanisms such as relaxation or breathing retraining, have proved effective in helping patients overcome agoraphobic behavior whether associated with panic disorder or not (Craske & Barlow, 2014). As many as 70% of patients undergoing these treatments substantially improve as their anxiety and panic are reduced and their agoraphobic avoidance is greatly diminished. Few are cured, however, and many still experience some anxiety and panic attacks, although at a less severe level.

Table 5.3 Situation-Exposure Tasks (From Least to Most Difficult)

Shopping in a crowded supermarket for 30 minutes alone
Walking five blocks away from home alone
Driving on a busy highway for 5 miles with spouse and alone
Eating in a restaurant, seated in the middle
Watching a movie while seated in the middle of the row

Source: Adapted, with permission, from D. H. Barlow & M. G. Craske, 2007, *Mastery of your anxiety and panic* (4th ed.), Oxford University Press, p. 133.

Effective psychological treatments have been developed that treat panic disorder directly even in the absence of agoraphobia (Barlow & Craske, 2007; Clark et al., 1994; Craske & Barlow, 2014). **Panic control treatment (PCT)** developed at one of our clinics concentrates on exposing patients with panic disorder to the cluster of interoceptive (physical) sensations that remind them of their panic attacks. The therapist attempts to create "mini" panic attacks in the office by having the patients exercise to elevate their heart rates or perhaps by spinning them in a chair to make them dizzy. A variety of exercises have been developed for this purpose. Patients also receive cognitive therapy. Basic attitudes and perceptions concerning the dangerousness of the feared but objectively harmless situations are identified and modified. As discussed earlier, many of these attitudes and perceptions are beyond the patient's awareness. Uncovering these unconscious cognitive processes requires a great deal of therapeutic skill. Sometimes, in addition to exposure to interoceptive sensations and cognitive therapy, patients are taught relaxation or breathing retraining to help them reduce anxiety and excess arousal, but we are using these strategies less often because we find they are not necessary.

These psychological procedures are highly effective for panic disorder. Follow-up studies of patients who receive PCT indicate that most of them remain better after at least 2 years (Craske & Barlow, 2014; Craske, Brown, & Barlow, 1991). Remaining agoraphobic behavior can then be treated with more standard exposure exercises.

Nevertheless, some people relapse over time, so our multisite collaborative team began investigating long-term strategies in the treatment of panic disorder including the usefulness of providing booster sessions after therapy is complete to prevent relapse. In the initial phase, 256 patients with panic disorder with all levels of agoraphobia completed 3 months of initial treatment with cognitive-behavioral therapy (Aaronson et al., 2008). Those patients who responded very well to treatment were then randomized to 9 months of monthly booster sessions ($n = 79$) or no booster sessions ($n = 78$), and then followed for additional 12 months without treatment (White et al., 2013). Booster sessions produced significantly lower relapse rates (5.2%) and reduced work and social impairment compared with the assessment-only condition without booster sessions (18.4%) at a 21-month follow-up (see ■ Figure 5.6). Thus, booster sessions aimed at reinforcing acute treatment gains to prevent relapse and offset disorder recurrence improved long-term outcome for panic disorder and agoraphobia, even in those patients who responded well to treatment

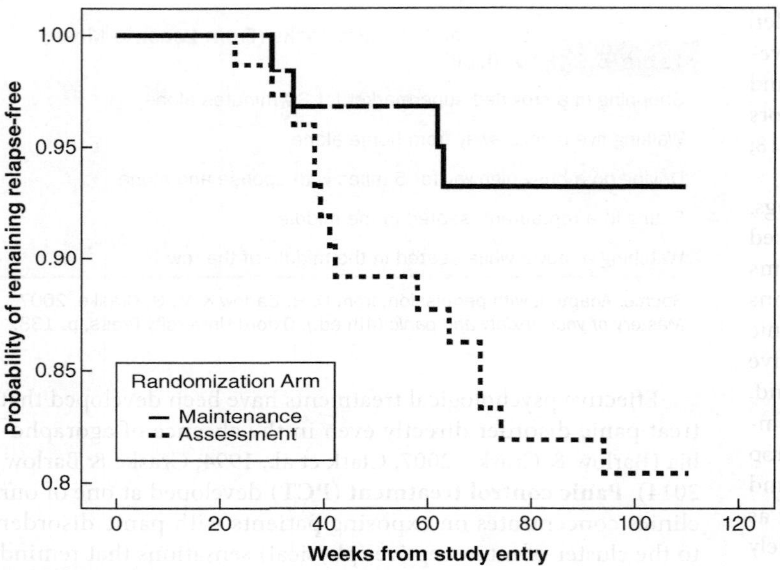

Figure 5.6

Relapse rates in patients with panic disorder who received booster sessions after treatment, compared to those without booster sessions.

initially. Similar treatments have also been successfully used in children (Albon & Schneider, 2007) and older adults (Hendriks, Kampman, Keijers, Hoogduin, & Voshaar, 2014).

Although these treatments are quite effective, they are not available to many individuals who suffer from panic disorder because administering them requires therapists to have advanced training (Barlow, Levitt, & Bufka, 1999; McHugh & Barlow, 2010). Because of this, investigators are evaluating new and creative ways using modern technology to get these programs out to the people who need them. Promising results are reported when CBT is delivered via the internet (Stech et al., 2020) or smart phone apps (Linardon et al., 2019).

Combined Psychological and Drug Treatments Partly because primary care physicians are usually the first clinicians to treat those suffering from panic disorder and psychological treatments are not available in those settings, when patients do get referred for psychological treatment, they are often already taking medications. So important questions are as follows: How do these treatments compare with each other? And do they work together? One major study sponsored by the National Institute of Mental Health looked at the separate and combined effects of psychological and drug treatments (Barlow, Gorman, Shear, & Woods, 2000). In this double-blind study, patients were randomized into five treatment conditions: psychological treatment alone (CBT); drug treatment alone (imipramine—IMI, a tricyclic antidepressant—was used because this study was begun before the SSRIs were available); a combined treatment condition (IMI 1 CBT); and two "control" conditions—one using placebo alone (PBO) and one using PBO 1 CBT (to determine the extent to which any advantage for combined treatment was caused by placebo contribution).

The data indicate that all treatment groups responded significantly better than the placebo group, but approximately the same number of patients responded to both drug and psychological treatments. Combined treatment was no better than individual treatments.

After 6 additional months of maintenance treatment (9 months after treatment was initiated), during which patients were seen once per month, the results looked much as they did after initial treatment, except there was a slight advantage for combined treatment at this point and the number of people responding to placebo had diminished. ■ Figure 5.7 shows the last set of results—6 months after treatment was discontinued (15 months after it was initiated). At this point, patients on medication, whether combined with CBT or not, had deteriorated somewhat, and those receiving CBT without the drug had retained most of their gains. For example, 14 of 29 patients (48% of those who began the 6-month follow-up phase) who were taking the drug combined with CBT (IMI 1 CBT) relapsed, with those who dropped out during this period counted as failures (intent to follow). Of those patients who completed the follow-up phase, 40%, or 10 of 25, relapsed. Notice the much lower relapse figure for the conditions containing CBT. Thus, treatments containing CBT without the drug tended to be more effective at this point, because they had more enduring effects.

Most studies show that drugs, particularly benzodiazepines, may interfere with the effects of psychological treatments (Craske & Barlow, 2014). Furthermore, benzodiazepines taken over a long period are associated with cognitive impairment (Deckersbach, Moshier, Tuschen-Caffier, & Otto, 2011). Because of this, our

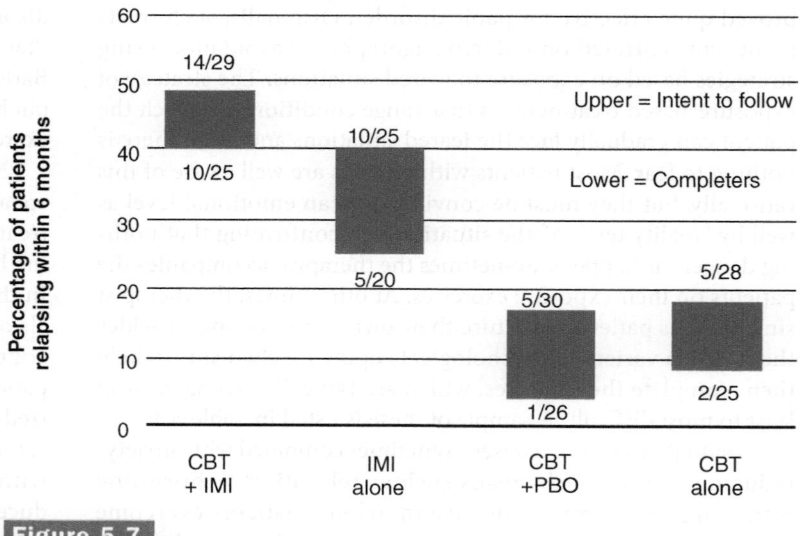

Figure 5.7

Posttreatment relapse rates in patients with panic disorder. Adapted from D. H. Barlow, J. M. Gorman, K. M. Shear, & S. W. Woods, 2000, Cognitive-behavioral therapy, imipramine, or their combination for panic disorder: A randomized controlled trial, *Journal of the American Medical Association, 283*(19), 2529–2536.

multisite collaborative team asked whether a sequential strategy in which one treatment was delayed until later and given only to those patients who didn't do as well as hoped would work better than giving both treatments at the same time. In this study, which was the second part of our long-term strategies research described above (Payne et al., 2016), studied 58 of the original 256 patients treated with CBT who did not respond adequately to the initial treatment and randomized these patients to a study where they either received continued CBT or the SSRI drug paroxetine. Paroxetine was administered for up to 12 months, whereas the CBT was delivered for 3 months. At the end of the 3-month period, patients receiving paroxetine responded better than those receiving continued CBT, but these differences had disappeared by the 1-year follow-up. Specifically, 53% of the inadequate responders receiving paroxetine became responders compared with 33% receiving continued CBT, but at 12 months the results were 56% and 53% respectively. So clinicians must judge if the more rapid response among some patients is worth trying drug treatment given that subsequent improvement will be about the same at a later date. For some patients, the more rapid response will be very important. Others may be less enthusiastic about taking a drug and enduring the potential side effects, knowing that they are likely to improve over time without the drug.

What about those patients already taking drugs? In the primary care setting, adding CBT to the treatment of patients already on medications resulted in significant further improvement compared with those patients on medication who did not have CBT added according to Craske and colleagues (2005). Both of the above studies indicate that a "stepped care" approach in which the clinician begins with one treatment and then adds another if needed may be more effective compared to combining treatments from the beginning.

General conclusions from these studies suggest no advantage to combining drugs and CBT initially for panic disorder and agoraphobia. Furthermore, the psychological treatments seemed to perform better in the long run (6 months after treatment had stopped). This suggests that psychological treatment should be offered initially, followed by drug treatment for those patients who do not respond adequately or for whom psychological treatment is not available.

Concept Check 5.3

True (T) or false (F)?

1. ____________ Panic disorder is a disorder in which an individual experiences anxiety and panic triggered by being in an "unsafe" situation.
2. ____________ About 40% of the population meets the criteria for panic disorder at some point in life.
3. ____________ Some individuals with panic disorder are suicidal, have nocturnal panic, and/or are agoraphobic.
4. ____________ Psychological treatments like PCT or CBT are highly effective for treating panic disorder.

Specific Phobia

Remember Janelle in Chapter 1? When she saw a film of the frog being dissected, Janelle began feeling queasy. Eventually she reached the point of fainting if someone simply said, "Cut it out." Earlier in this chapter, you read about John Madden's difficulties with flying. John Madden and Janelle have in common what we call a specific phobia.

Clinical Description

A **specific phobia** is an irrational fear of a specific object or situation that markedly interferes with an individual's ability to function. In earlier versions of the DSM, this category was called "simple" phobia to distinguish it from the more complex agoraphobia condition, but we now recognize there is nothing simple about it. Many of you might be afraid of something that is not dangerous, such as going to the dentist, or have a greatly exaggerated fear of something that is only slightly dangerous, such as driving a car or flying. Surveys indicate that specific fears of a variety of objects or situations occur in a majority of the U.S. population (Myers et al., 1984). But the very commonness of fears, even severe fears, often causes people to trivialize the more serious psychological disorder known as a specific phobia. These phobias can cause severe impairment, as we saw with Janelle. Table 5.4 lists some other examples of particularly impairing phobias seen at our clinics (Antony & Barlow, 2002).

For people such as John Madden, on the other hand, phobias are a nuisance—sometimes an extremely inconvenient nuisance—but people can adapt to life with a phobia by simply working around it somehow. In upstate New York and New England, some people are afraid to drive in the snow. We have had people come to our clinics who have been so severely phobic that during the winter they were ready to uproot, change their jobs and their lives, and move south. That is one way of dealing with a phobia. We discuss some other ways at the end of this chapter.

The major characteristic held in common by Janelle and Madden is the DSM-5 criterion of marked fear and anxiety about a specific object or situation. Both also recognized that their fear and anxiety were out of proportion to any actual danger. Finally, both went to considerable lengths to avoid situations in which their phobic response might occur.

There the similarities end. There are as many phobias as there are objects and situations. The variety of Greek and Latin names contrived to describe phobias stuns the imagination. Table 5.4 gives only the phobias beginning with the letter A from a long list compiled by Jack D. Maser from medical dictionaries and other diverse sources (Maser, 1985). This sort of list has little or no value for people studying psychopathology, but it does show the extent of the named phobias.

Before the publication of DSM-IV in 1994, no meaningful classification of specific phobias existed. We have now learned, however, that the cases of Janelle and Madden represent types of specific phobia that differ in major ways. Four major subtypes of specific phobia have been identified: blood–injection–injury type, situational type (such as planes, elevators, or enclosed places), natural environment type (for example, heights, storms, and water), and animal type. A fifth category, "other," includes

Table 5.4 Phobias Beginning with "A"

Term	Fear of:
Acarophobia	Insects, mites
Achluophobia	Darkness, night
Acousticophobia	Sounds
Acrophobia	Heights
Aerophobia	Air currents, drafts, wind
Agoraphobia	Open spaces
Agyiophobia	Crossing the street
Aichmophobia	Sharp, pointed objects; knives; being touched by a finger
Ailurophobia	Cats
Algophobia	Pain
Amathophobia	Dust
Amychophobia	Laceration; being clawed, scratched
Androphobia	Men (and sex with men)
Anemophobia	Air currents, wind, drafts
Anginophobia	Angina pectoris (brief attacks of chest pain)
Anthropophobia	Human society
Antlophobia	Floods
Apeirophobia	Infinity
Aphephobia	Physical contact, being touched
Apiphobia	Bees, bee stings
Astraphobia	Thunderstorms, lightning
Ataxiophobia	Disorder
Atephobia	Ruin
Auroraphobia	Northern lights
Autophobia	Being alone, solitude, oneself, being egotistical

Source: Reprinted, with permission, from J. D. Maser, 1985, List of phobias, in A. H. Tuma & J. D. Maser (Eds.), *Anxiety and the anxiety disorders*, Erlbaum, p. 805. © 1985 Lawrence Erlbaum Associates.

phobias that do not fit any of the four major subtypes (for example, situations that may lead to choking, vomiting, or contracting an illness or, in children, avoidance of loud sounds or costumed characters). Although this subtyping strategy is useful, we also know that most people who have a phobia tend to have multiple phobias of several types (Hofmann, Lehman, & Barlow, 1997; LeBeau et al., 2010).

Blood–Injection–Injury Phobia How do phobia subtypes differ from each other? We have already seen one major difference in the case of Janelle. Rather than the usual surge of activity in the sympathetic nervous system and increased heart rate and blood pressure, Janelle experienced a marked drop in heart rate and blood pressure and fainted as a consequence. Many people who suffer from phobias and experience panic attacks in their feared situations report that they feel like they are going to faint, but they never do because their heart rate and blood pressure are actually increasing. Therefore, those with **blood–injection–injury phobias** almost always differ in their physiological reaction from people with other types of phobia (Barlow & Liebowitz, 1995; Hofmann, Alpers, & Pauli, 2009; Öst, 1992). We also noted in Chapter 2 that blood–injection–injury phobia runs in families more strongly than any phobic disorder we know. This is probably because people with this phobia inherit a strong vasovagal response to blood, injury, or the possibility of an injection, all of which cause a drop in blood pressure and a tendency to faint. The phobia develops over the possibility of having this response. The average age of onset for this phobia is approximately 9 years (LeBeau et al., 2010).

DSM 5 **Table 5.5**
Diagnostic Criteria for Specific Phobia

A. Marked fear or anxiety about a specific object or situation (e.g., flying, heights, animals, receiving an injection, seeing blood). [*Note:* In children, the fear may be expressed by crying, tantrums, freezing, or clinging.]

B. The phobic object or situation almost always provokes immediate fear or anxiety.

C. The phobic object or situation is actively avoided or endured with intense fear or anxiety.

D. The fear or anxiety is out of proportion to the actual danger posed by the specific object or situation and to the sociocultural context.

E. The fear, anxiety, or avoidance is persistent, typically lasting for 6 months or more.

F. The fear, anxiety or avoidance causes clinically significant distress or impairment in social, occupational or other important areas of functioning.

G. The disturbance is not better explained by the symptoms of another mental disorder, including fear, anxiety and avoidance of situations associated with panic-like symptoms or other incapacitating symptoms (as in agoraphobia); objects or situations related to obsessions (as in obsessive-compulsive disorder); reminders of traumatic events (as in posttraumatic stress disorder); separation from home or attachment figures (as in separation anxiety disorder); or social situations (as in social anxiety disorder).

Specify type:

1. **Animal** (e.g., spiders, insects, dogs)
2. **Natural environment** (e.g., heights, storms, and water)
3. **Blood–injection–injury** (e.g., needles, invasive medical procedures)
4. **Situational** (e.g., planes, elevators, or enclosed places)
5. **Other** (e.g., situations that may lead to choking or vomiting; in children, e.g., loud sounds or costumed characters)

American Psychiatric Association. (2022). *Diagnostic and statistical manual of mental disorders* (5th ed., Text Revision).

Situational Phobia Phobias characterized by fear of public transportation or enclosed places are called **situational phobias**. Claustrophobia, a fear of small enclosed places, is situational, as is a phobia of flying. Psychopathologists first thought that situational phobia was similar to panic disorder and agoraphobia.

Situational phobia, as well as panic disorder and agoraphobia, tends to emerge from midteens to mid-20s (Craske et al., 2006; LeBeau et al., 2010). The extent to which PD, agoraphobia, and situational phobias run in families is also similar (Curtis, Hill, & Lewis, 1990; Curtis, Himle, Lewis, & Lee, 1989; Fyer et al., 1990), with approximately 30% of first-degree relations having the same or a similar phobia. But some analyses do not support the similarity as anything more than superficial (Antony, Brown, & Barlow, 1997a, 1997b). The main difference between situational phobia and panic disorder is that people with situational phobia never experience panic attacks outside the context of their phobic object or situation. Therefore, they can relax when they don't have to confront their phobic situation. People with panic disorder, in contrast, might experience unexpected, uncued panic attacks at any time.

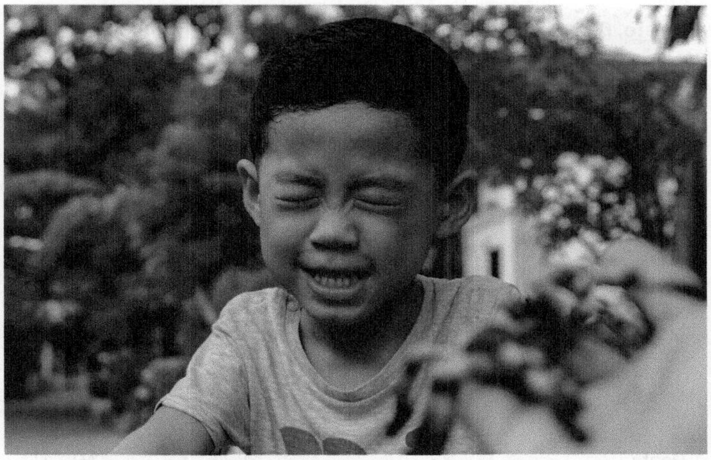
Krisda Ponchaipulltawee/Shutterstock.com
Many specific phobias begin in childhood, including fears of animals.

Natural Environment Phobia Sometimes very young people develop fears of situations or events occurring in nature. These fears are called **natural environment phobias**. The major examples are heights, storms, and water. These fears also seem to cluster together (Antony & Barlow, 2002; Hofmann et al., 1997): If you fear one situation or event, such as deep water, you are likely to fear another, such as storms. Many of these situations have some danger associated with them, and, therefore, mild to moderate fear can be adaptive. For example, we should be careful in a high place or in deep water. It is entirely possible that we are somewhat prepared to be afraid of these situations. As is discussed in Chapter 2, something in our genes makes us sensitive to these situations if any sign of danger is present. In any case, these phobias have a peak age of onset of about 7 years. They are not phobias if they are only passing fears. They have to be persistent (lasting at least 6 months) and to interfere substantially with the person's functioning, leading to avoidance of boat trips or summer vacations in the mountains where there might be a storm.

Animal Phobia Fears of animals and insects are called **animal phobias**. Again, these fears are common but become phobic only if severe interference with functioning occurs. For example, we have seen cases in our clinic in which people with snake or mice phobias are unable to read magazines for fear of unexpectedly coming across a picture of one of these animals. There are many places that these people are unable to go, even if they want to very much, such as to the country to visit someone. The fear experienced by people with animal phobias is different from mild revulsion. The age of onset for these phobias, like that of natural environment phobias, peaks around 7 years (Antony et al., 1997a; LeBeau et al., 2010).

Statistics

Specific fears occur in a majority of people. The ones most commonly found in the population at large, categorized by Agras, Sylvester, and Oliveau (1969), are presented in Table 5.5. Not surprisingly, fears of snakes and heights rank near the top. Notice also that the sex ratio among common fears is overwhelmingly female with a couple of exceptions. Among these exceptions is fear of heights, for which the sex ratio is approximately equal. Few people who report specific fears qualify as having a phobia, but for approximately 12.5% of the population, their fears become severe enough to earn the label "phobia." During a given 1-year period the prevalence is 8.7% overall (Kessler, Berglund, Demler, et al., 2005), but 15.8% in adolescents (Kessler, Petukhova, et al., 2012). This is a high percentage, making specific phobia one of the most common psychological disorders in the United States and around the world (Arrindell et al., 2003b). As with common fears, the sex ratio for specific phobias is, at 4:1, overwhelmingly female; this is also consistent around the world (Craske et al., 2006; LeBeau et al., 2010).

Even though phobias may interfere with an individual's functioning, only the most severe cases come for treatment because more mildly affected people tend to work around their phobias. For example, people with a fear of heights arrange their lives so they never have to be in a tall building or other high place. The median age of onset for specific phobia is 7 years of age, the youngest of any anxiety disorder except separation anxiety disorder (see below) (Kessler, Berglund, Demler, et al., 2005). Once a phobia develops, it tends to last a lifetime (run a chronic course) (see, for example, Antony et al., 1997a; Barlow, 2002; Kessler, Berglund, Demler, et al., 2005); thus, the issue of treatment, described shortly, becomes important.

Although most anxiety disorders look much the same in adults and in children, clinicians must be aware of the types of normal fears and anxieties experienced throughout childhood so that they can distinguish them from specific phobias (Albano et al., 1996; Silverman & Rabian, 1993). Infants, for example, show marked fear of loud noises and strangers. At 1 to 2 years of age, children quite normally are anxious about separating from parents, and fears of animals and the dark also develop and may persist into the fourth or fifth year of life. Fear of various monsters and other imaginary creatures may begin about age 3 and last for several years. At age 10, children may fear evaluation by others and feel anxiety over their physical appearance. Generally,

Table 5.5 Prevalence of Intense Fears and Phobias

Intense Fear	Prevalence per 1,000 Population	Sex Distribution	SE by Sex
Snakes	253	M: 118 F: 376	M: 34 F: 48
Heights	120	M: 109 F: 128	M: 33 F: 36
Flying	109	M: 70 F: 144	M: 26 F: 38
Enclosures	50	M: 32 F: 63	M: 18 F: 25
Illness	33	M: 31 F: 35	M: 18 F: 19
Death	33	M: 46 F: 21	M: 21 F: 15
Injury	23	M: 24 F: 22	M: 15 F: 15
Storms	31	M: 9 F: 48	M: 9 F: 22
Dentists	24	M: 22 F: 26	M: 15 F: 16
Journeys alone	16	M: 0 F: 31	M: 0 F: 18
Being alone	10	M: 5 F: 13	M: 7 F: 11

SE, standard error.

Source: Adapted, with permission, from W. S. Agras, D. Sylvester, & D. Oliveau, 1969, The epidemiology of common fears and phobias, *Comprehensive Psychiatry, 10,* 151–156. © 1969 Elsevier.

reports of fear decline with age, although performance-related fears of such activities as taking a test or talking in front of a large group may increase with age. Specific phobias seem to decline with old age (Ayers et al., 2009; Blazer, George, & Hughes, 1991; Sheikh, 1992).

The prevalence of specific phobias varies from one culture to another (Hinton & Good, 2009). Hispanics are two times more likely to report specific phobias than White non-Hispanic Americans (Magee, Eaton, Wittchen, McGonagle, & Kessler, 1996), for reasons not entirely clear. A variant of phobia in Chinese cultures is called *pa-leng,* sometimes *frigophobia* or "fear of the cold." *Pa-leng* can be understood only in the context of traditional ideas—in this case, the Chinese concepts of *yin* and *yang* (Tan, 1980). Chinese medicine holds that there must be a balance of yin and yang forces in the body for health to be maintained. Yin represents the cold, dark, windy, energy-sapping aspects of life; yang refers to the warm, bright, energy-producing aspects of life. Individuals with *pa-leng* have a morbid fear of the cold. They ruminate over loss of body heat and may wear several layers of clothing even on a hot day. They may complain of belching and flatulence (passing gas), which indicate the presence of wind and therefore of too much yin in the body. As discussed earlier, these ideas also play a role in phobia and anxiety disorders in other Asian cultures (Hinton, Park, Hsia, Hofmann, & Pollack, 2009; Hinton, Pich, Chhean, Pollack, & Barlow, 2004).

Causes

For a long time, we thought that most specific phobias began with a traumatic event. For example, if you were bitten by a dog, you would develop a phobia of dogs. We now know this is not necessarily the case (Barlow, 2002; Craske et al., 2006). This is not to say that traumatic conditioning experiences do not result in subsequent phobic behavior. Almost every person with a choking phobia has had some kind of a choking experience. An individual with claustrophobia who came to our clinic reported being trapped in an elevator for an extraordinarily long period. These are examples of phobias acquired by *direct experience,* where real danger or pain results in an alarm response (a true alarm). This is one way of developing a phobia, and there are at least three others: *experiencing* a false alarm (panic attack) in a specific situation, *observing* someone else experiencing severe fear (vicarious experience), or, under the right conditions, *being told* about danger.

Remember our earlier discussion of unexpected panic attacks? Studies show that many people with specific phobias do not necessarily experience a true alarm resulting from real danger at the onset of their phobia. Many initially have an unexpected panic attack in a specific situation, perhaps related to current life stress. A specific phobia of that situation may then develop.

This was evident in a study with driving phobia (Ehlers, Hofmann, Herda, & Roth, 1994). Although only a minority (14%) met criteria for panic disorder, the majority (81%) of people with excessive fear of driving an automobile reported having had panic attacks. When asked about the primary reason for their phobia, only 15% attributed it to an accident, whereas 53% attributed it to the possibility of having panic attacks. These people were also more concerned about anxiety symptoms while driving than phobics who gave other, nonaccident-related reasons for their driving phobia.

We also learn fears vicariously. Seeing someone else have a traumatic experience or endure intense fear may be enough to instill a phobia in the watcher. Remember, we noted earlier that emotions are contagious. If someone you are with is either happy or fearful, you will probably feel a tinge of happiness or fear also. This has been illustrated in a study with 8- to 11-year-old children who watched a short, 1980s animated film clip of a person trying to score in basketball as part of a try out for a basketball team while being evaluated by judges (Askew, Hagel, & Morgan, 2015). In one of the films, the outcome was neutral; the animated person threw the ball into the basket with positive thoughts appearing in a thought cloud and a neutral expression as if it was a routine practice. In the other film clip, the person missed the basket, slipped, and fell while negative thoughts appeared in a thought cloud. After watching these clips, the children filled out a questionnaire asking them how fearful they thought they would feel in similar performance situations. Results showed that, compared to children who watched the neutral film clip, those who watched the negative film clip with the negative outcome expected that they would feel more fearful and also showed a greater attention bias toward social threat, which was measured with an emotion

A child with separation anxiety disorder persistently worries that parting with an important person drastically endangers either the loved one or the child.

Chinese medicine is based on the concept that *yin* (dark, cold, enervating forces) and *yang* (bright, warm, energizing forces) must harmonize in the body. In this traditional representation of the yin–yang balance, note that each aspect contains something of the other.

Stroop task in which children were asked to name the color of threating words, such as "audience" or "criticize" (rather than naming the word). This suggests that fear can be acquired through vicarious learning even after watching a brief film clip. Sometimes just being warned repeatedly about a potential danger is sufficient for someone to develop a phobia (Muris & Field, 2010). We call this mode of developing a phobia *information transmission.*

Terrifying experiences alone do not create phobias. As we have said, a true phobia also requires anxiety over the possibility of another extremely traumatic event or false alarm, and we are likely to avoid situations in which that terrible thing might occur. If we don't develop anxiety, our reaction would presumably be in the category of normal fears experienced by more than half the population. Normal fear can cause mild distress, but it is usually ignored and forgotten. This point is best illustrated by Peter DiNardo and his colleagues (1988), who studied a group of dog phobics, as well as a matched group who did not have the phobia. Only about 50% of the dog phobics had had a frightening encounter with a dog, usually involving a bite. In the other group of individuals who did not have dog phobia, however, about 50% had also had a frightening encounter with a dog. Why hadn't they become phobics as well? They had not developed anxiety about another encounter with a dog, unlike the people who did become phobic (reflecting a generalized psychological vulnerability). A diagram of the etiology of specific phobia is presented in ■ Figure 5.8.

In summary, several things have to occur for a person to develop a phobia. First, a traumatic conditioning experience often plays a role (even hearing about a frightening event is sufficient for some individuals). Second, fear is more likely to develop if we are "prepared"; that is, we seem to carry an inherited tendency to fear situations that have always been dangerous to the human race, such as being threatened by wild animals or trapped in small places (see Chapter 2).

Third, we also have to be susceptible to developing anxiety about the possibility that the event will happen again. We have discussed the biological and psychological reasons for anxiety and have seen that at least one phobia, blood–injection–injury phobia, is highly heritable (Ayala, Meuret, & Ritz, 2009; Page & Martin, 1998; Öst, 1989). Patients with blood phobia probably also inherit a strong vasovagal response that makes them susceptible to fainting. This alone would not be sufficient to ensure their becoming phobic, but it combines with anxiety to produce strong vulnerability.

Fyer and colleagues (1990) demonstrated that approximately 31% of the first-degree relatives of people with specific phobias also had a phobia, compared with 11% of the first-degree relatives of "normal" controls. In a collaborative study between Fyer's clinic and our center, we replicated these results, finding a 28% prevalence in the first-degree relatives of patients with phobia compared with 10% in relatives of controls. More interesting, it seems that each subtype of phobia was more likely to be present in relatives. Kendler, Karkowski, and Prescott (1999a) and Page and Martin (1998) found relatively high estimates for heritability of individual specific phobias. We do not know for sure whether the tendency for phobias to run in families is caused by genes or by modeling, but the findings are at least suggestive of a unique genetic contribution to specific phobia (Antony & Barlow, 2002; Hettema et al., 2005; Smoller et al., 2005).

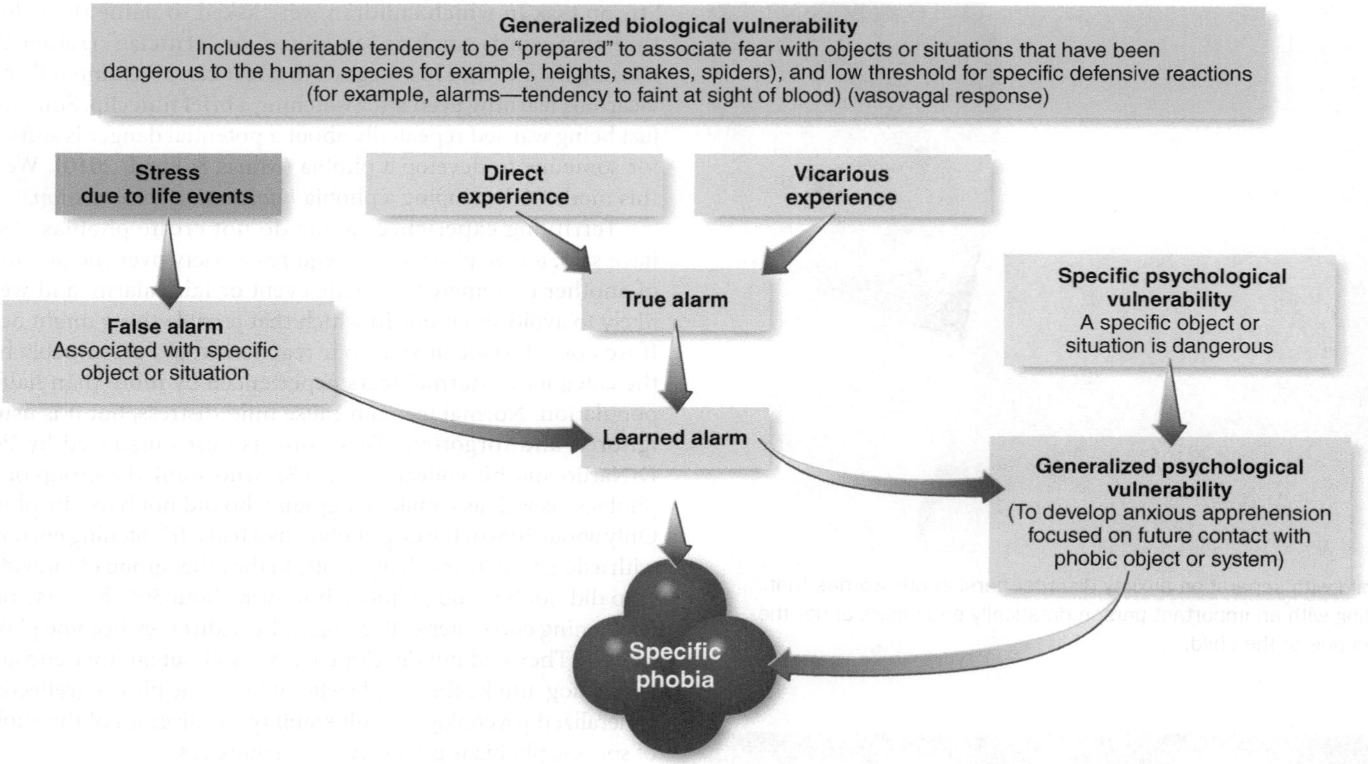

Figure 5.8

A model of the various ways a specific phobia may develop. From D. H. Barlow, 2002, *Anxiety and its disorders: The nature and treatment of anxiety and panic* (2nd ed.), Guilford Press.

Finally, social and cultural factors are strong determinants of who develops and reports a specific phobia. In most societies, it is almost unacceptable for males to express fears and phobias. Thus, the overwhelming majority of reported specific phobias occur in women (Arrindell et al., 2003b; LeBeau et al., 2010). What happens to men? Possibly they work hard to overcome their fears by repeatedly exposing themselves to their feared situations. A more likely possibility is that they simply endure their fears without telling anyone about them and without seeking treatment (Antony & Barlow, 2002). Pierce and Kirkpatrick (1992) asked male and female college students to report their fears on two occasions before watching a videotape of something frightening. Before the second evaluation, subjects were told their heart rate would be monitored to assess the "truthfulness" of their report. Reports from women were the same on both occasions, but men reported substantially more fear when it was important to be truthful. Ginsburg and Silverman (2000) observed that level of reported fear in children with anxiety disorders was a function of gender role but not of biological sex. That is, a more masculine girl would report less fear than a more feminine girl, illustrating the contribution of culture to the development of fear and phobia.

Treatment

Although the development of phobias is relatively complex, the treatment is fairly straightforward. Almost everyone agrees that specific phobias require structured and consistent exposure-based exercises (Barlow, Moscovitch, & Micco, 2004; Craske et al., 2006). Nevertheless, most patients who expose themselves gradually to what they fear must be under therapeutic supervision. Individuals who attempt to carry out the exercises alone often attempt to do too much too soon and end up escaping the situation, which may strengthen the phobia. In addition, if they fear having another unexpected panic attack in this situation, it is helpful to direct therapy at panic attacks in the manner described for panic disorder (Antony, Craske, & Barlow, 2006; Craske et al., 2006). For separation anxiety, parents are often included to help structure the exercises and also to address parental reaction to childhood anxiety (Choate, Pincus, Eyberg, & Barlow, 2005). An intensive 1-week program for girls ages 8 to 11 developed at one of our clinics in which the girls end up having a sleepover at the clinic has proved highly successful (Pincus, Santucci, Ehrenreich, & Eyberg, 2008; Santucci, Ehrenreich, Trosper, Bennett, & Pincus, 2009). Finally, in cases of blood–injection–injury phobia, where fainting is a real possibility, graduated exposure-based exercises must be done in specific ways. Individuals must tense various muscle groups during exposure exercises to keep their blood pressure sufficiently high to complete the practice (Ayala, Meuret, & Ritz, 2009; Öst & Sterner, 1987). New developments make it possible to treat many specific phobias, including blood phobia, in a single session taking anywhere from approximately 2 to 6 hours (see, for example, Antony et al., 2006; Craske et al., 2006; Hauner, Mineka, Voss, & Paller, 2012; Oar, Farrell, Waters, Conlon, & Ollendick,

2015; Öst, Svensson, Hellström, & Lindwall, 2001). Basically, the therapist spends most of the session with the individual, working through exposure exercises with the phobia object or situation. The patient then practices approaching the phobic situation at home, checking in occasionally with the therapist. In these cases, not only does the phobia disappear, but in blood phobia the tendency to experience the vasovagal response at the sight of blood also lessens considerably. It is also now clear based on brain-imaging work that these treatments change brain functioning in an enduring way by modifying neural circuitry in such areas as the amygdala, insula, and cingulate cortex (Hauner et al., 2012). After treatment, responsiveness is diminished in this fear-sensitive network but increased in prefrontal cortical areas, suggesting that more rational appraisals were inhibiting emotional appraisals of danger. Thus, these treatments "rewire" the brain (Paquette et al., 2003).

Separation Anxiety Disorder All anxiety and related disorders described in this chapter may occur during childhood (Rapee, Schniering, & Hudson, 2009), but there is one disorder that is identified more closely with children. **Separation anxiety disorder** is characterized by children's unrealistic and persistent worry that something will happen to their parents or other important people in their life or that something will happen to the children themselves that will separate them from their parents (for example, they will be lost, kidnapped, killed, or hurt in an accident). Children often refuse to go to school or even to leave home, not because they are afraid of school but because they are afraid of separating from loved ones. These fears can result in refusing to sleep alone and may be characterized by nightmares involving possible separation and by physical symptoms, distress, and anxiety (Barlow, Pincus, Heinrichs, & Choate, 2003).

All young children experience separation anxiety to some extent; this fear usually decreases as they grow older. Therefore, a clinician must judge whether the separation anxiety is greater than would be expected at that particular age (Allen, Lavallee, Herren, Ruhe, & Schneider, 2010; Barlow et al., 2003). It is also important to differentiate separation anxiety from school phobia. In school phobia, the fear is clearly focused on something specific to the school situation; the child can leave the parents or other attachment figures to go somewhere other than school. In separation anxiety, the act of separating from the parent or attachment figure provokes anxiety and fear; 4.1% of children have separation anxiety at a severe enough level to meet criteria for a disorder (Shear, Jin, Ruscio, Walters, & Kessler, 2006).

Several years ago, it was discovered that separation anxiety, if untreated, can extend into adulthood in approximately 35% of cases (Shear et al., 2006). Furthermore, evidence suggests that we have overlooked this disorder in adults and that it occurs in approximately 6.6% of the adult population over the course of a lifetime (Shear et al., 2006). In some cases, the onset is in adulthood rather than carrying over from childhood. The focus of anxiety in adults is the same: that harm may befall loved ones during separation (Manicavasagar et al., 2010; Silove, Marnane, Wagner, Manicavasagar, & Rees, 2010). With the recognition that separation anxiety disorder occurs across the life span and is characterized by a unique presentation, a decision was made to elevate this disorder to a full status as a diagnostic category in DSM-5. As with any new disorder, the expectation is that this problem will receive greater attention from a research point of view and that individuals in all age ranges with this problem will find it easier to get the help they need.

In treating separation anxiety in children, parents are often included to help structure the exercises and also to address parental reaction to childhood anxiety (Choate, Pincus, Eyberg, & Barlow, 2005; Pincus, Santucci, Ehrenreich, & Eyberg, 2008). Researchers have explored the use of real-time coaching of parents using a small microphone in parents' ear to allow therapists to actively instruct parents in how to best respond when their child resists separation (Puliafico, Comer, & Pincus, 2012; Sacks, Comer, Pincus, Comacho, & Hunter, 2013). Innovative formats for treatment have also proven highly successful, including, as noted above, an intensive 1-week program for girls with separation anxiety disorder aged 8 to 11 in which the girls end up having a sleepover at the clinic on the final day of treatment (Santucci et al., 2009).

Social Anxiety Disorder (Social Phobia)

Are you shy? If so, you have something in common with 20% to 50% of college students, depending on which survey you read. A much smaller number of people, who suffer severely around others, have **social anxiety disorder (SAD)**, formerly known as **social phobia**. Consider the case of Darnell, a 13-year-old boy.

Darnell... Too Shy

Darnell was the model boy at home. He did his homework, stayed out of trouble, obeyed his parents, and was generally so quiet and reserved he didn't attract much attention. When he got to junior high school, however, something his parents had noticed earlier became painfully evident. Darnell had no friends. He was unwilling to attend social or sporting activities connected with school, even though most of the other kids in his class went to these events. When his parents decided to check with the guidance counselor, they found that she had been about to call them. She reported that Darnell did not socialize or speak up in class and was sick to his stomach all day if he knew he was going to be called on. His teachers had difficulty getting anything more than a yes or no answer from him. More troublesome was that he had been found hiding in a stall in the boy's restroom during lunch, which he said he had been doing for several months instead of eating. After Darnell was referred to our clinic, we diagnosed a severe case of social anxiety disorder—an irrational and extreme fear of social situations. Darnell's phobia took the form of extreme shyness. He was afraid of being embarrassed or humiliated in the presence of almost everyone except his parents. •

Clinical Description

SAD is more than exaggerated shyness (Bögels et al., 2010; Hofmann, Alpers, & Pauli, 2009; Morrison, & Heimberg, 2013; Poole, van Lieshoute, & Schmidt, 2017). The cases described in the box about Steve Sax and Chuck Knoblauch are typical of many that appear occasionally in the press over the years.

Steve and Chuck... Star Players?

In the second inning of a Major League Baseball All-Star Game, Los Angeles Dodger second baseman Steve Sax fielded an easy grounder, straightened up for the lob to first, and bounced the ball past first baseman Al Oliver, who was less than 40 feet away. It was a startling error even in an All-Star Game studded with bush-league mishaps. But hard-core baseball fans knew it was one more manifestation of a leading mystery of the 1983 season: Sax, age 23, the National League Rookie of the Year the previous season, could not seem to make routine throws to first base. (Of his first 27 errors that season, 22 were bad throws.)

Chuck Knoblauch won a Golden Glove Award at second base in 1997 but led the league in errors in 1999 with 26, most of them throwing errors. Announcers and reporters observed that his throws would be hard and on target to first base if he made a difficult play and had to quickly turn and throw the ball "without thinking about it." But if he fielded a routine ground ball and had time to think about the accuracy of his throw, he would throw awkwardly and slowly—and often off target. The announcers and reporters concluded that because his arm seemed fine on the difficult plays, his problem must be "mental." For the 2001 season, he was moved to left field to avoid having to make that throw and by 2003 was out of baseball. •

NFL player Ricky Williams also interrupted his career partly because of severe social anxiety.

Whereas Chuck Knoblauch continued to struggle, Steve Sax and Ricky Williams overcame their problems. Many other athletes are not so fortunate. This problem is not limited to athletes but is also experienced by well-known lecturers and performers. Actress Scarlett Johansson avoided doing Broadway for many years due to intolerable performance anxiety, in this case also called "stage fright." The inability of a skilled athlete to throw a baseball to first base or a seasoned performer to appear on stage certainly does not match the concept of "shyness" with which we are all familiar. Many of these performers may well be among our more gregarious citizens. And what if when you're with other people, you continually worry about a physical reaction you have that is very noticeable to others but difficult to control? For example, what if you blush to the extent that you're so embarrassed that you can't socialize? Or if your palms sweat so much that you're reluctant to shake hands?

What holds these seemingly different conditions together within the category of social anxiety disorder? Darnell, Knoblauch, Sax, Williams, and Johansson (and anyone who worries about blushing or sweating excessively) all experienced marked fear or anxiety focused on one or more social or performance situations. In Darnell's case, these situations were any in which he might have to interact with people. For Knoblauch and Johansson, they were specific to performing some special behavior in public. Individuals with just performance anxiety, which is a subtype of SAD, usually have no difficulty with social interaction, but when they must do something specific in front of people, anxiety takes over, and they focus on the possibility that they will embarrass themselves. The most common type of performance anxiety, to which most people can relate, is public speaking. Other situations that commonly provoke performance anxiety are eating in a restaurant or signing a paper or check in front of a person or people who are watching. Anxiety-provoking physical reactions include blushing, sweating, trembling, or, for males, urinating in a public restroom ("bashful bladder" or paruresis). Males with this problem must wait until a stall is available, a difficult task at times. What these examples have in common is that the individual is very anxious only while others are present, maybe watching, and, to some extent, evaluating their behavior. This is truly social anxiety disorder because the people have no difficulty eating, writing, or urinating in private. Only when others are watching does the behavior deteriorate.

Statistics

As many as 12.1% of the general population suffer from SAD at some point in their lives (Kessler, Berglund, Demler, et al., 2005). In a given 1-year period, the prevalence is 6.8% (Kessler, Chiu, et al., 2005) and 8.2% in adolescents (Kessler et al., 2012). This makes SAD second only to specific phobia as the most prevalent anxiety disorder, afflicting more than 35 million people in the United States alone, based on current population estimates. Many more people are shy but not severely enough to meet criteria for social anxiety disorder. Unlike other anxiety disorders for which females predominate (Hofmann, Alpers, & Pauli, 2009; Magee et al., 1996; Mclean, Asnaani, Litz, & Hofmann, 2011), the sex ratio for SAD is nearly 50:50 (Hofmann & Barlow, 2002; Marks, 1985; McLean et al., 2011). Overall, 45.6% of people suffering from SAD sought professional help in a recent 12-month period (Wang et al., 2005). SAD usually begins during adolescence, with a peak age of onset around 13 years (Kessler, Berglund, Demler, et al., 2005). SAD also tends to be more prevalent in people who are young (18–29 years), undereducated, single, and of low socioeconomic class. Prevalence is less than half as prevalent among individuals over 60 (6.6%) as it is among individuals 18 to 29 (13.6%) (Kessler, Berglund, Demler, et al., 2005).

Considering their difficulty meeting people, it is not surprising that a greater percentage of individuals with SAD are single than in the population at large. In the United States, White Americans are typically more likely to be diagnosed with social anxiety disorder (as well as generalized anxiety disorder and panic disorder) than African Americans, Hispanic Americans, and Asian Americans (Asnaani, Richey, Dimaite, Hinton, &

DSM 5 Table 5.6 Diagnostic Criteria for Social Anxiety Disorder

A. Marked fear or anxiety about one or more social situations in which the individual is exposed to possible scrutiny by others. Examples include social interactions (e.g., having a conversation; meeting unfamiliar people), being observed (e.g., eating or drinking), and performing in front of others (e.g., giving a speech). [*Note:* In children, the anxiety must occur in peer settings and not just in interactions with adults.]

B. The individual fears that he or she will act in a way or show anxiety symptoms that will be negatively evaluated (i.e., will be humiliating or embarrassing; will lead to rejection or offend others).

C. The social situations almost always provoke fear or anxiety. [Note: In children, the fear or anxiety may be expressed by crying, tantrums, freezing, clinging, shrinking, or failing to speak in social situations.]

D. The social situations are avoided or endured with intense fear or anxiety.

E. The fear or anxiety is out of proportion to the actual threat posed by the social situation and to the sociocultural context.

F. The fear, anxiety, or avoidance is persistent, typically lasting for 6 months or more.

G. The fear, anxiety, or avoidance causes clinically significant distress or impairment in social, occupational or other important areas of functioning.

H. The fear, anxiety or avoidance is not attributable to the effects of a substance (e.g., a drug of abuse, a medication) or another medical condition.

I. The fear, anxiety, or avoidance is not better explained by the symptoms of another mental disorder, such as panic disorder, body dysmorphic disorder, or autism spectrum disorder.

J. If another medical condition (e.g., Parkinson's disease, obesity, disfigurement from burns or injury) is present, the fear, anxiety, or avoidance is clearly unrelated or is excessive.

Specify if:

Performance only: If the fear is restricted to speaking or performing in public.

American Psychiatric Association. (2022). *Diagnostic and statistical manual of mental disorders* (5th ed., Text Revision).

Hofmann, 2010). Cross-national data suggest that Asian cultures show the lowest rates of SAD, whereas Russian and U.S. samples show the highest rates (Hofmann, Asnaani, & Hinton, 2010). In Japan, the clinical presentation of anxiety disorders is best summarized under the label *shinkeishitsu*. One of the most common subcategories is referred to as *taijin kyofusho*, which resembles SAD in some of its forms (Hofmann, Asnaani, & Hinton, 2010; Kleinknecht, Dinnel, Kleinknecht, Hiruma, & Harada, 1997). Japanese people with this form of SAD strongly fear that some aspect of their personal presentation (blushing, stuttering, body odor, and so on) will appear reprehensible, causing other people to feel embarrassed. Thus, the focus of anxiety in this disorder is on offending or embarrassing others rather than embarrassing oneself, as in SAD, although these two disorders overlap considerably (Dinnel, Kleinknecht, & Tanaka-Matsumi, 2002). Japanese males with this disorder outnumber females by a 3:2 ratio (Takahasi, 1989). This syndrome is found in many cultures around the world, but predominantly in Asian cultures (Vriends, Pfatz, Novianti, & Hadiyono, 2013). Nevertheless, one manifestation of this set of symptoms called "olfactory reference syndrome" has even been reported in North America (Feusner, Phillips, & Stein, 2010). The key feature once again is preoccupation with a belief that one is embarrassing oneself and offending others with a foul body odor. As such, it seems to resemble obsessive-compulsive disorder (discussed below) more than SAD and seems to respond to psychological treatments used to treat obsessive-compulsive disorder (Martin-Pichora & Antony, 2011).

Causes

We have noted that we seem to be prepared by evolution to fear certain wild animals and dangerous situations in the natural environment. Similarly, it seems we are also prepared to fear angry, critical, or rejecting people (Blair et al., 2008; Mineka & Zinbarg, 2006; Mogg, Philippot, & Bradley, 2004). In a series of studies, Öhman and colleagues (see, for example, Dimberg & Öhman, 1983; Öhman & Dimberg, 1978) noted that we learn more quickly to fear angry expressions than other facial expressions, and this fear diminishes more slowly than other types of learning. Lundh and Öst (1996) demonstrated that people with SAD who saw a number of pictures of faces were likely to remember critical expressions; Mogg and colleagues (2004) showed that socially anxious individuals more quickly recognized angry faces than non-anxious individuals whereas non-anxious individuals remembered the accepting expressions (Navarrete et al., 2009). Other studies show that individuals with SAD react to angry faces with greater activation of the amygdala and less cortical control or regulation than "normals" (Goldin, Manber, Hakimi, Canli, & Gross, 2009; Stein, Goldin, Sareen, Zorrilla, & Brown, 2002). Fox and Damjanovic (2006) demonstrated that the eye region specifically is the threatening area of the face.

Why should we inherit a tendency to fear angry faces? Our ancestors probably avoided hostile, angry, domineering people who might attack or kill them. In all species, dominant, aggressive individuals, high in the social hierarchy, tend to be avoided. Possibly, individuals who avoided people with angry faces were more likely to survive and pass their genes down to us. Of course, this is just a theory.

Jerome Kagan (see, for example, Kagan, 2014a, 2014b) has demonstrated that some infants are born with a temperamental profile or trait of inhibition or shyness that is evident as early as 4 months of age. Four-month-old infants with this trait become more agitated and cry more frequently when presented with toys or other age-appropriate stimuli than infants without the trait. There is now evidence that individuals with excessive behavioral inhibition are at increased risk for developing phobic behavior (Essex et al., 2010; Hirschfeld et al., 1992).

A model of the etiology of SAD would look somewhat like models of panic disorder and specific phobia. Three pathways

Jim Spellman/WireImage/Getty Images

Jerome Kagan discovered that shyness is evident as early as 4 months of age and is probably inherited.

to SAD are possible, as depicted in ■ Figure 5.9. First, someone could inherit a generalized biological vulnerability to develop anxiety, a biological tendency to be socially inhibited, or both. The existence of a generalized psychological vulnerability—such as the belief that events, particularly stressful events, are potentially uncontrollable—would increase an individual's vulnerability. When under stress, a person could have anxiety and self-focused attention increase to the point of disrupting performance, even in the absence of a false alarm (panic attack). Second, when under stress, someone might have an unexpected panic attack in a social situation that would become associated (conditioned) to social cues. The individual would then become anxious about having additional panic attacks in the same or similar social situations. Third, someone might experience a real social trauma resulting in a true alarm. Anxiety would then develop (be conditioned) in the same or similar social situations. Traumatic social experiences may also extend back to difficult periods in childhood. Early adolescence—usually ages 12 through 15—is when children may be brutally taunted by peers who are attempting to assert their own dominance. This experience may produce anxiety and panic that are reproduced in future social situations. For example, McCabe, Antony, Summerfeldt, Liss, and Swinson (2003) noted that 92% of adults with social anxiety disorder in their sample experienced severe teasing and bullying in childhood, compared with only 35% to 50% among people with other anxiety disorders.

But one more factor must fall into place to make it an SAD disorder. The individual with the vulnerabilities and experiences just described must also have learned growing up that social evaluation in particular can be dangerous, creating a specific

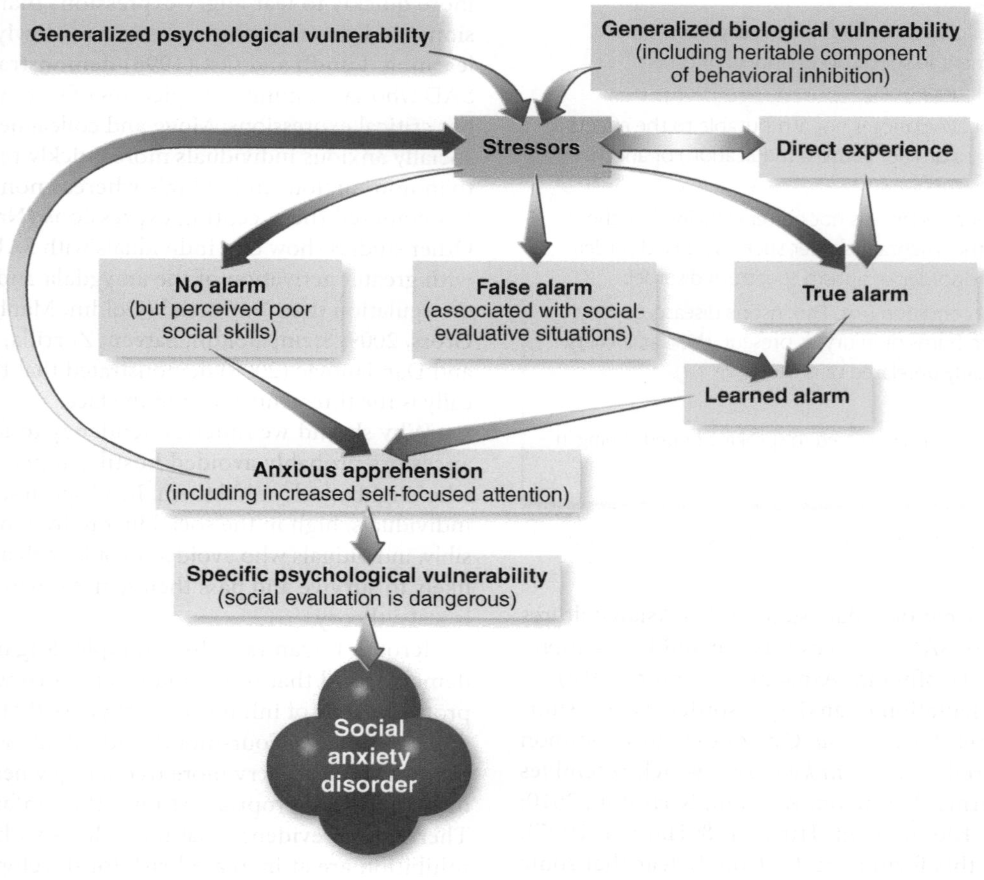

Figure 5.9

A model of the various ways a social anxiety disorder may develop. From D. H. Barlow, 2002, *Anxiety and its disorders: The nature and treatment of anxiety and panic* (2nd ed.), Guilford Press.

psychological vulnerability to develop social anxiety. Evidence indicates that some people with SAD are predisposed to focus their anxiety on events involving social evaluation. Some investigators (Bruch & Heimberg, 1994; Rapee & Melville, 1997) suggest that the parents of patients with social anxiety disorder are significantly more socially fearful and concerned with the opinions of others than are the parents of patients with panic disorder and that they pass this concern on to their children (Lieb et al., 2000). Fyer, Mannuzza, Chapman, Liebowitz, and Klein (1993) reported that the relatives of people with SAD had a significantly greater risk of developing it than the relatives of individuals without SAD (16% versus 5%)—thus, the specific psychological vulnerability depicted in ■ Figure 5.9. As you can see, a combination of biological and psychological events seems to lead to the development of SAD.

Treatment

Effective treatments have been developed for SAD (Barlow & Lehman, 1996; Heimberg & Magee, 2014; Hofmann, 2007b; Hofmann & Otto, 2008; Hofmann & Smits, 2008). Clark and colleagues (2006) evaluated a cognitive therapy program that emphasized real-life experiences during therapy to disprove automatic perceptions of danger. This program substantially benefited 84% of individuals receiving treatment, and these results were maintained at a 1-year follow-up. This outcome is the best yet for this difficult condition and significantly better than previous approaches to which it has been compared. Subsequent studies indicated that this treatment was clearly superior to a second very credible treatment, interpersonal psychotherapy (IPT) both immediately after treatment and at a 1-year follow-up, even when delivered in a center specializing in treatment with IPT (Stangier, Schramm, Heidenreich, Berger, & Clark, 2011).

A similar approach was developed at our center (Hofmann, 2007b; Hofmann & Otto, 2008). This treatment specifically targets the different factors that are maintaining the disorder. One important reason SAD is maintained in the presence of repeated exposure to social cues is that individuals with SAD engage in a variety of avoidance and safety behaviors to reduce the risk of rejection and, more generally, prevent patients from critically evaluating their catastrophic beliefs about how embarrassed and foolish they will look if they attempt to interact with somebody. Social mishap exposures directly target the patients' beliefs by confronting them with the actual consequences of such mishaps, such as what would happen if you spilled something all over yourself while you were talking to somebody for the first time (Hofmann & Otto, 2008). As a group intervention, this treatment was associated with an 82% completion rate and a 73% response rate, which was maintained at 6-month follow-up (Hofmann et al., 2013). Brain imaging studies showed that brain measures before treatment can strongly predict the extent to which CBT reduces symptoms in patients with social anxiety disorder (Doehrmann et al., 2013; Whitfield-Gabrieli et al., 2016) and that CBT leads to changes in brain activity associated with emotional processing (Goldin et al., 2013; Klumpp, Fitzgerald, & Phan, 2013; Månsson et al., 2013).

We have adapted these protocols for use with adolescents, directly involving parents in the group treatment process. Results of numerous studies suggest that severely socially anxious adolescents can attain relatively normal functioning in school and other social settings after receiving cognitive-behavioral treatment (Albano & Barlow, 1996; Garcia-Lopez et al., 2006; Masia-Warner et al., 2005; Scharfstein, Beidel, Finnell, Distler, & Carter, 2011). Several clinical trials have now compared individual and family-based treatment approaches for youth with social anxiety. While both treatment approaches appear to be equally efficacious (Barmish & Kendall 2005), family-based treatment appears to outperform individual treatment when the child's parents also have an anxiety disorder (Kendall, Hudson, Gosch, Flannery-Schroeder, & Suveg, 2008). A long-term follow up study indicates that youth who receive a parent component as part of anxiety treatment are significantly more likely to be diagnosis-free 3 years following treatment (Cobham, Dadds, Spence, & McDermott, 2010), and a family-based intervention can even prevent the onset of anxiety disorders in the children of anxious parents (Ginsburg, Drake, Tein, Teetsel, & Riddle, 2015). Once the child develops an anxiety disorder, early treatment with CBT can be successful to treat the symptoms or prevent future problems with anxiety (Benjamin, Harrison, Settipani, Brodman, & Kendall, 2013; Ginsburg et al., 2014), with a slight advantage of family-based CBT over child-based CBT (Schneider et al., 2013).

Effective drug treatments have been discovered as well (Van Ameringen, Mancini, Patterson, & Simpson, 2009). For a time, clinicians assumed that beta-blockers (drugs that lower heart rate and blood pressure, such as Inderal) would work, particularly for performance anxiety, but the evidence did not seem to support that contention (Liebowitz et al., 1992; Turner, Beidel, & Jacob, 1994). Since 1999, the SSRIs Paxil, Zoloft, and Effexor have received approval from the Food and Drug Administration for treatment of SAD based on studies showing effectiveness compared with placebo (see, for example, Stein et al., 1998).

Several major studies have compared psychological and drug treatments. One impressive study compared Clark's cognitive therapy described earlier with the SSRI drug Prozac, along with instructions to the patients with SAD to attempt to engage in more social situations (self-exposure). A third group received placebo plus instructions to attempt to engage in more social activities. Assessments were conducted before the 16-week treatment, at the midpoint of treatment, posttreatment, and then after 3 months of booster sessions. Finally, researchers followed up with patients in the two treatment groups 12 months later (Clark et al., 2003). Results are presented in ■ Figure 5.10. Both treatments did well, but the psychological treatment was substantially better at all times, with most patients cured or nearly cured with few remaining symptoms. Also, gains made during CT were maintained when assessed after 5 years (Mörtberg, Clark, & Bejerot, 2011).

The evidence is mixed on the usefulness of combining SSRIs or related drugs with psychological treatments. Davidson, Foa, and Huppert (2004) found that a cognitive-behavioral treatment and an SSRI were comparable in efficacy but that the combination was no better than the two individual treatments.

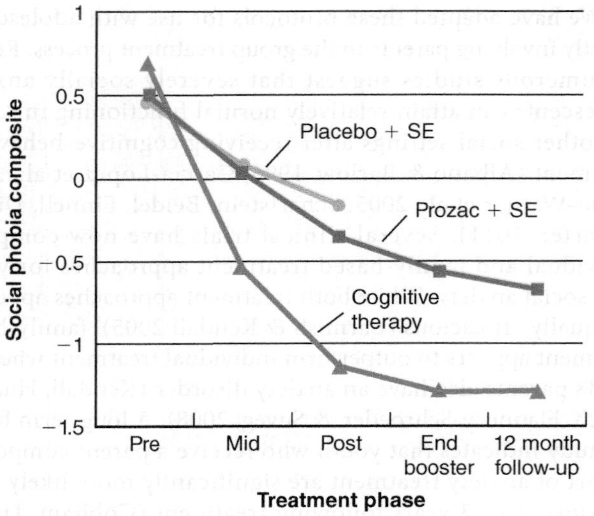

Figure 5.10

Results from a comparison of Prozac and instructions to attempt more social interactions or "self-exposure" (Prozac 1 SE), placebo and the same instruction (placebo 1 SE), and cognitive therapy (CT) in the treatment of patients with generalized social phobia. Reprinted, with permission, from D. M. Clark, A. Ehlers, F. McManus, A. Hackmann, M. Fennell, H. Campbell, T. Flower, C. Davenport, & B. Louis, 2003, Cognitive therapy versus fluoxetine in generalized social phobia: A randomized placebo-controlled trial, *Journal of Consulting and Clinical Psychology, 71,* 1058–1067. © 2003 American Psychological Association.

Several exciting studies suggest that adding the drug D-cycloserine (DCS) to cognitive-behavioral treatments can enhance exposure therapy (Chasson et al., 2010; Wilhelm et al., 2008). Neuroscientists working with rats in the laboratory, such as Michael Davis at Emory University, learned that DCS made extinction work faster and last longer (Walker, Ressler, Lu, & Davis, 2002). Further research indicated that this drug works in the amygdala, a structure in the brain involved in the learning and unlearning of fear and anxiety. Unlike SSRIs, this drug is known to facilitate extinction of anxiety by modifying neurotransmitter flow in the glutamate system as described in Chapter 2 (Hofmann, 2007a). SSRIs and other antidepressants might even interact with DCS to block its facilitating effect on exposure therapy (Andersson et al., 2015).

When used with individuals with SAD (or other anxiety disorders), DCS is given approximately an hour before the extinction or exposure trial, and the individual does not take the drug on an ongoing basis. For example, our research group (Otto et al., 2010) administered cognitive-behavioral intervention to patients with panic disorder either with or without the drug. (That is, one group got the drug, the other group got a placebo, and neither the patients nor the therapists knew which group was getting the drug and which was not, making it a double-blind experiment.) The people who got the drug improved significantly more during treatment than those who didn't get the drug. This is noteworthy because the feared cues for people with panic disorder are physical sensations, and the drug DCS helped extinguish anxiety triggered by sensations such as increased heart rate or respiration. We found a similar result with social anxiety disorder (Hofmann et al., 2006, 2013; Smits et al., 2020). We observed that DCS was associated with a 24% to 33% faster rate of improvement in symptom severity and remission rates relative to placebo during a full course, 12-week CBT intervention (Hofmann et al., 2013). At posttreatment, DCS did not improve the response and remission rates of the CBT intervention as compared with placebo, however (Hofmann et al., 2013). These findings are consistent with other studies suggesting that DCS primarily initiates the treatment effect sooner but does not augment a full course of CBT (Hofmann, Sawyer, & Asnaani, 2012). These research studies pave the way toward enhancing and accelerating the response to psychotherapy for anxiety disorders.

Selective Mutism Now grouped with the anxiety disorders in DSM-5, selective mutism (SM) is a rare childhood disorder characterized by a lack of speech in one or more settings in which speaking is socially expected. As such, it seems clearly driven by social anxiety, since the behavior does not occur due to a lack of knowledge of speech or any physical difficulties, nor is it due to another disorder in which speaking is rare or can be impaired such as autism spectrum disorder. In fact, speech in selective mutism commonly occurs in some settings, such as home, but not others, such as school, hence the word *selective*. In order to meet diagnostic criteria for SM, the lack of speech must occur for more than one month and cannot be limited to the first month of school. Further evidence that this disorder is strongly related to social anxiety is found in the high rates of comorbidity of SM and anxiety disorders, particularly SAD (Bögels et al., 2010). In fact, in one study, nearly 100% of a series of 50 children with selective mutism also met criteria for SAD (Dummit et al., 1997). Another study found substantially more social anxiety in children with SM than a matched control group without SM (Buzzella, Ehrenreich-May, & Pincus, 2011). Estimates of the prevalence of SM average about 0.5% of children with girls more affected than boys (Kumpulainen, 2002; Viana, Beidal, & Rabian, 2009).

Why does lack of speech in certain situations emerge as the specific symptom in selective mutism instead of other socially anxious behaviors? It is not entirely clear yet, but there is some evidence that well-meaning parents enable this behavior by being more readily able to intervene and "do their talking for them" (Buzzella et al., 2011).

Treatment employs many of the same cognitive-behavioral principles used successfully to treat social anxiety in children but with a greater emphasis on speech (Carpenter, Puliafico, Kurtz, Pincus, & Comer, 2014). For example, in one of our clinics, we run a specialized program called the Boston University Brave Buddies Camp. This is a week-long intensive group treatment program for children ages 4 to 8 who have been diagnosed with selective mutism or have difficulty speaking in social or school situations with familiar and/or unfamiliar peers and adults. The BU Brave Buddies Camp provides guided opportunities for children to interact with a number of new children and adults, participate in classroom-like activities (such as morning meeting, circle time, show and tell, and group creative projects), engage in field trips (for example, to the library and the park), and play socializing games that promote verbal participation ("brave talking") and spontaneous speaking. This approach utilizes behavioral interventions such as modeling, stimulus fading, and shaping that allow for gradual exposure to the speaking situation. These techniques are combined with a behavioral reward system for participation in treatment (Furr et al., 2012; Sacks, Comer, Furr, Pincus, & Kurtz, 2011). Results from this program have been very encouraging: 80% of 15 children who participated in this camp successfully initiating speech and maintaining speech productivity at a 2-year follow-up. Unfortunately, these highly specialized programs are not readily available at the present time.

Concept Check 5.4

Identify the following phobias: (a) blood–injection–injury, (b) acrophobia, (c) animal, (d) social, (e) natural environment, and (f) other. The same phobia may apply to more than one statement.

1. Mark had no friends at school and hid in the boys' bathroom during both lunch and recess. ____________
2. Omar fears and strenuously avoids storms. Not surprisingly, on his first oceangoing cruise, he found that deep water terrified him, too. ____________
3. Rita was comfortable at the zoo until the old terror gripped her at the insect display. ____________
4. Armando would love to eat fish with his fishing buddies, but he experiences an inordinate fear of choking on a bone. ____________
5. Khalid had to give up his dream of becoming a surgeon because he faints at the sight of blood. ____________
6. Kacey turned down several lucrative job offers that involved public speaking and took a low-paying desk job instead. ____________
7. Farrah can't visit her rural friends because of her fear of snakes. ____________

Trauma and Stressor-Related Disorders

DSM-5 consolidates a group of formerly disparate disorders that all develop after a relatively stressful life event, often an extremely stressful or traumatic life event. This set of disorders—trauma and stressor-related disorders—include attachment disorders in childhood following inadequate or abusive child-rearing practices, adjustment disorders characterized by persistent anxiety and depression following a stressful life event, and reactions to trauma such as posttraumatic stress disorder and acute stress disorder. Investigators working in this area concluded that these disorders did not fit as neatly with other classes of disorders, such as the anxiety disorders as previously assumed. This is because trauma and stressor-related disorders all share a proximal instigating stressful event followed by intense emotional responses. Also, a wider range of emotions—such as rage, horror, guilt, and shame, in addition to fear and anxiety—may be implicated in the onset, particularly for posttraumatic stress disorder (Friedman et al., 2011; Keane, Marx, Sloan, & DePrince, 2011; Miller, Wolf, & Keane, 2014). We begin with a description of posttraumatic stress disorder.

Posttraumatic Stress Disorder (PTSD)

Traumatic events can have severe and long-lasting emotional consequences. For many Americans, perhaps the most notorious traumatic events of the 21st century so far have been the wars in Iraq and Afghanistan, the terrorist attacks on September 11, 2001, hurricanes, or the COVID pandemic. Still, emotional disorders also occur after physical assault (particularly rape), car accidents, natural catastrophes, or the sudden death of a loved one. **Posttraumatic stress disorder (PTSD)** is the best known of these disorders.

Clinical Description

DSM-5 describes the setting event for PTSD as exposure to a traumatic event during which an individual experiences or witnesses death or threatened death, actual or threatened serious injury, or actual or threatened sexual violation. Learning that the traumatic event occurred to a close family member or friend or enduring repeated exposure to details of a traumatic event (as in first responders to a terrorist attack dealing with human remains) are also setting events. Afterward, victims reexperience the event through memories and nightmares. When memories occur suddenly, accompanied by strong emotion, and the victims find themselves reliving the event, they are having a *flashback*. Victims most often avoid anything that reminds them of the trauma. They often display a characteristic restriction or numbing of emotional responsiveness, which may be disruptive to interpersonal relationships. They are sometimes unable to remember certain aspects of the event. It is possible that victims unconsciously attempt to avoid the experience of emotion itself, like people with panic disorder, because intense emotions could bring back memories of the trauma. Finally, victims typically are chronically overaroused, easily startled, and quick to anger. New to DSM-5 is the addition of "reckless or self-destructive behavior" under the PTSD E criteria as one sign of increased arousal and reactivity. Also new to DSM-5 is the addition of a "dissociative" subtype describing victims who do not necessarily react with the reexperiencing or hyperarousal, characteristic of PTSD. Rather, individuals with PTSD who experience dissociation have less arousal than normal along with (dissociative) feelings of unreality (Atchley & Bedford, 2021; Canan & North, 2019; Wolf, Lunney, et al., 2012; Wolf, Miller, et al., 2012). Victims with PTSD seem to respond somewhat differently to treatment if they meet criteria for a dissociative subtype (Lanius, Brand, Vermetten, Frewen, & Spiegel, 2012).

PTSD was first named in 1980 in DSM-III (American Psychiatric Association, 1980), but it has a long history. In 1666, the

British diarist Samuel Pepys witnessed the Great Fire of London, which caused substantial loss of life and property and threw the city into chaos for a time. He captured the events in an account that is still read today. But Pepys did not escape the effects of the horrific event. Six months later, he wrote, "It is strange to think how to this very day I cannot sleep a night without great terrors of fire; and this very night could not sleep to almost 2 in the morning through thoughts of fire" (Daly, 1983, p. 66). The DSM-5 criteria show that difficulty sleeping and recurring intrusive dreams of the event are prominent features of PTSD. Pepys described his guilt at saving himself and his property while others died. He also experienced a sense of detachment and a numbing of his emotions concerning the fire, common experiences in PTSD (Keane & Miller, 2012).

Since many individuals experience strong reactions to stressful events that typically disappear within a month, the diagnosis of PTSD cannot be made until at least 1 month after the occurrence of the traumatic event. In *PTSD with delayed onset*, individuals show few or no symptoms immediately or for months after a trauma, but at least 6 months later and perhaps years afterward, they develop full-blown PTSD (O'Donnell et al., 2013). A 10-year follow-up study of military service members deployed to Afghanistan showed that the prevalence of PTSD at 10 years after deployment was 8% across all 1,007 service members. Over this 10-year period, the majority of all participants (85%) showed a low and stable trajectory of symptoms (that is, they were resilient). A smaller group (7%) showed increasing symptoms reaching the level of PTSD between 2 and 5 years postdeployment (they had a delayed onset). Others (6%) showed their first elevated symptoms predeployment and shortly after deployment but had gradual recovery after 6 months postdeployment. Another small group (2%) first showed increasing symptoms and then recovery after 5 years postdeployment (van der Wal, Vermetten, & Elbert, 2020). Why people show these different trajectories is not well understood.

As we noted, PTSD cannot be diagnosed until a month after the trauma. In DSM-IV a disorder called **acute stress disorder** was introduced. This is similar to PTSD, occurring within the first month after the trauma, but the different name emphasizes the severe reaction that some people have immediately (Cardeña & Carlson, 2011). Approximately 50% of individuals with acute stress disorder went on to develop PTSD (Bryant, 2010; Bryant, Friedman, Spiegel, Ursano, & Strain, 2011). But these surveys also indicated that as many as 52% of a sample of trauma survivors who went on to develop PTSD did not meet criteria for acute stress disorder in the month following the trauma (Bryant et al., 2011). Acute stress disorder was included in DSM-IV because many people with severe early reactions to trauma could not otherwise be diagnosed and, therefore, could not receive insurance coverage for immediate treatment. The surveys described above confirm that people with early severe reactions to traumatic stress are severely impacted and can benefit from treatment. But these early reactions are not particularly good predictors of who will go on to develop PTSD.

Statistics

Determining the prevalence rates for PTSD seems relatively straightforward: Simply observe victims of a trauma, and view how many are suffering from PTSD. But a number of studies have demonstrated the remarkably low prevalence of PTSD in populations of trauma victims. Rachman, in a classic study, reported on the British citizenry who endured numerous life-threatening air raids during World War II. He concluded that "a great majority of people endured the air raids extraordinarily well, contrary to the universal expectation of mass panic. Exposure to repeated bombings did not produce a significant increase in psychiatric disorders. Although short-lived fear reactions were common, surprisingly few persistent phobic reactions emerged" (Rachman, 1991, p. 162). Similar results have been observed from classic studies following disastrous fires, earthquakes, and floods (for example, Green, Grace, Lindy, Titchener, & Lindy, 1983).

Phillip Saigh (1984) made some interesting observations when he was teaching at the American University in Beirut, Lebanon, just before and during the Israeli invasion in the early 1980s. Saigh had been collecting questionnaires measuring anxiety among university students just before the invasion. When the invasion began, half these students escaped to the surrounding mountains and were safe. The other half endured intense shelling and bombing for a period. Saigh continued administering the questionnaires and found a surprising result. There were no significant long-term differences between the group in the mountains and the group in the city, although a few students in the city who were closely exposed to danger and death did develop emotional reactions that progressed into PTSD. In contrast, some studies have found a high incidence of PTSD after trauma. Large studies are now available on the prevalence of PTSD in veterans of the wars in Iraq and Afghanistan. Based on experiences during the Vietnam War, military mental health officials were very concerned that rates of PTSD might be as high as 30% or more (McNally, 2012b). A survey of women who were active-duty military personnel during the Vietnam War suggested that the lifetime prevalence rate of PTSD among the 4,219 women who responded to the survey was 20.1% (Magruder et al., 2015). In contrast, the results of other investigations are less dire than expected. Based on a study of more than 47,000 members of the armed forces, "only" 4.3% of personnel developed PTSD. For those experiencing combat, exposure rates increased to 7.6% versus 1.4% among those not experiencing combat (Smith et al., 2008). Given the large number of personnel deployed over the past decade, this still amounts to an enormous number of soldiers suffering from PTSD. In the population as a whole, surveys indicate that 6.8% have experienced PTSD at some point in their life (Kessler, Berglund, Demler, et al., 2005) and 3.5% during the past year (Kessler, Chiu, et al., 2005). For adolescents, the corresponding figure is 3.9% (Kessler et al., 2012). Breslau (2012) reports, based on large population surveys, the likelihood of developing PTSD after a specific trauma. Results are presented in Table 5.6. As one can see, the highest rates are associated with experiences of rape; being held captive, tortured, or kidnapped; or being badly assaulted. The rates of PTSD after these experiences, which Breslau collects under the heading of "assaultive violence," are far higher than other categories. Even more tragic are rates of PTSD in women who have experienced repeated sexual assaults. Compared with those for nonvictims, the rates of PTSD are 2.4 to 3.5 times higher for women experiencing a single sexual assault or rape and 4.3 to 8.2 times higher for those who have been re-victimized (Walsh et al., 2012).

Table 5.6 Posttraumatic Stress Disorder (PTSD) Risk Associated with Specific Traumas*

Conditional Risk of PTSD across	Specific Traumas, % PTSD (SE)
Assaultive violence	**20.9 (3.4)**
Military combat	0 (0.0)**
Rape	49.0 (12.2)
Held captive/tortured/kidnapped	53.8 (23.4)
Shot/stabbed	15.4 (13.7)
Sexual assault other than rape	23.7 (10.8)
Mugged/threatened with weapon	8.0 (3.7)
Badly beaten up	31.9 (8.6)
Other injury or shock	6.1 (1.4)
Serious car crash	2.3 (1.3)
Other serious accident	16.8 (6.2)
Natural disaster	3.8 (3.0)
Life-threatening illness	1.1 (0.9)
Child's life-threatening illness	10.4 (9.8)
Witnessed killing/serious injury	7.3 (2.5)
Discovering dead body	0.2 (0.2)
Learning about others	2.2 (0.7)
Close relative raped	3.6 (1.7)
Close relative attacked	4.6 (2.9)
Close relative car crash	0.9 (0.5)
Close relative other accident	0.4 (0.4)
Sudden unexpected death	14.3 (2.6)
Any trauma	9.2 (1.0)

*Labels of traumas are abbreviated

**The risk is 0 because none of these civilian cases were subjected to combat.

What accounts for the discrepancies between the low rate of PTSD in citizens who endured bombing and shelling in London and Beirut and the relatively high rate in victims of assaultive violence? Investigators have now concluded that during air raids, many people may not have directly experienced the horrors of dying, death, and direct attack. Close exposure to the trauma seems to be necessary to developing this disorder (Friedman, 2009; Keane & Barlow, 2002). But this is also evident among Vietnam veterans, among whom 18.7% developed PTSD, with prevalence rates directly related to amount of combat exposure (Dohrenwend, Turner, & Turse, 2006). Surveys of 76 victims of Hurricane Katrina in 2005 also report a doubling of severe mental illness based on extent of direct exposure to danger (Kessler, Galea, Jones, & Parker, 2006). The connection between proximity to the traumatic event and the development of PTSD was starkly evident following the tragedy of 9/11. Galea and colleagues (2002) contacted a representative sample of adults living south of 110th Street in Manhattan and found that 7.5% reported symptoms consistent with a diagnosis of acute stress disorder or PTSD. But among respondents who lived close to the World Trade Center (south of Canal Street), the prevalence of the disorder was 20%. Again, those who experienced the disaster most personally and directly seemed to be the ones most affected.

In addition, tens of thousands of public school children in New York City who lived close to the disaster experienced chronic nightmares, fear of public places, and other symptoms of PTSD. After the attack, a large study conducted with the help of federal agencies estimated that 75,000 schoolchildren in New York City in grades 4 through 12, or 10.5% of children in those grades, suffered PTSD after September 11 (Goodnough, 2002). In addition, 155 suffered from agoraphobia, or a fear of leaving a safe place such as home. Many of these children feared riding public transportation. Two-thirds of the children sampled lived near the World Trade Center or in other neighborhoods directly affected by the tragedy, such as Staten Island, home to many who were killed, or Brooklyn, where smoke drifted over neighborhoods for days. We also know that once it appears, PTSD tends to last (that is, it runs a chronic course) (Breslau, 2012; Perkonigg et al., 2005). Since a diagnosis of PTSD predicts suicidal attempts independently of any other problem, such as alcohol use problems, every case should be taken very seriously (Wilcox, Storr, & Breslau, 2009).

But is this the whole story? It seems not. Some people experience the most horrifying traumas imaginable and emerge psychologically healthy. For others, even relatively mild stressful events are sufficient to produce a full-blown disorder. Moreover, PTSD symptoms change over time, more for some people than for others, which may be due to individual differences in resiliency, coping skills, levels of trauma exposure, early adversities, ongoing stress, and even the presence of mild traumatic brain injuries (Berntsen et al., 2012; Bonnano, 2004; Bryant, O'Donnell, Creamer, McFarlane, & Silove, 2013; Marmar et al., 2015; Nash, Boasso, Steenkamp, Larson, Lubin, & Litz, 2014). To better understand why trauma influences some people more than others, we must consider the etiology of PTSD.

Causes

PTSD is the one disorder for which we know the cause at least in terms of the precipitating event: Someone personally experiences a trauma and develops a disorder. Whether or not a person develops PTSD, however, is a surprisingly complex issue involving biological, psychological, and social factors. We know that intensity of exposure

Andy Nelson/The Christian Science Monitor/Getty Images

Exposure to a traumatic event may create profound fear and helplessness. People who have PTSD may reexperience such feelings in flashbacks, involuntarily reliving the horrifying event.

DSM 5 **Table 5.7**

Diagnostic Criteria for Posttraumatic Stress Disorder

[Note: The following criteria apply to adults, adolescents, and children older than 6 years.]

A. Exposure to actual or threatened death, serious injury, or sexual violence in one (or more) of the following ways:

1. Directly experiencing the traumatic event(s).
2. Witnessing, in person, the event(s) as they occurred to others.
3. Learning that the event(s) occurred to a close relative or close friend. In cases of actual or threatened death of a family member or friend, the event(s) must have been violent or accidental.
4. Experiencing repeated or extreme exposure to aversive details of the traumatic event(s) (e.g., first responders collecting human remains; police officers repeatedly exposed to details of child abuse).

[Note: Criterion A4 does not apply to exposure through electronic media, television, movies, or pictures, unless this exposure is work related.]

B. Presence of one (or more) of the following intrusion symptoms associated with the traumatic event(s), beginning after the traumatic event(s) occurred:

1. Recurrent, involuntary and intrusive distressing memories of the traumatic event(s). [Note: In children older than 6 years, repetitive play may occur in which themes or aspects of the traumatic event(s) are expressed.]
2. Recurrent distressing dreams in which the content and/or affect of the dream are related to the traumatic event(s). [Note: In children, there may be frightening dreams without recognizable content.]
3. Dissociative reactions (e.g., flashbacks) in which the individual feels or acts as if the traumatic event(s) were recurring. (Such reactions may occur on a continuum, with the most extreme expression being a complete loss of awareness of present surroundings.) [Note: In young children, trauma-specific reenactment may occur in play.]
4. Intense or prolonged psychological distress at exposure to internal or external cues that symbolize or resemble an aspect of the traumatic event(s).
5. Marked physiological reactions to internal or external cues that symbolize or resemble an aspect of the traumatic event(s).

C. Persistent avoidance of stimuli associated with the traumatic event(s), beginning after the traumatic event(s) occurred, as evidenced by one or both of the following:

1. Avoidance of or efforts to avoid distressing memories, thoughts, or feelings, about or closely associated with the traumatic event(s).
2. Avoidance of or efforts to avoid external reminders (people, places, conversations, activities, objects, situations) that arouse distressing memories, thoughts, or feelings about or closely associated with the traumatic event(s).

D. Negative alterations in cognitions and mood associated with the traumatic event(s), beginning or worsening after the traumatic event(s) occurred, as evidenced by two (or more) of the following:

1. Inability to remember an important aspect of the traumatic event(s) (typically due to dissociative amnesia and not to other factors such as head injury, alcohol, or drugs).
2. Persistent and exaggerated negative beliefs or expectations about oneself, others, or the world (e.g., "I am bad," "No one can be trusted," "The world is completely dangerous," "My whole nervous system is permanently ruined").
3. Persistent distorted cognitions about the cause or consequences of the traumatic event(s) that lead the individual to blame himself/herself or others.
4. Persistent negative emotional state (e.g., fear, horror, anger, guilt, or shame).
5. Markedly diminished interest or participation in significant activities.
6. Feelings of detachment or estrangement from others.
7. Persistent inability to experience positive emotions (e.g., inability to experience happiness, satisfaction, or loving feelings).

E. Marked alterations in arousal and reactivity associated with the traumatic event(s), beginning or worsening after the traumatic event(s) occurred, as evidenced by two (or more) of the following:

1. Irritable behavior and angry outbursts (with little or no provocation) typically expressed as verbal or physical aggression toward people or objects.
2. Reckless or self-destructive behavior.
3. Hypervigilance.
4. Exaggerated startle response.
5. Problems with concentration
6. Sleep disturbance (e.g., difficulty falling or staying asleep or restless sleep).

F. Duration of the disturbance (Criteria B, C, D, and E) is more than 1 month.

G. The disturbance causes clinically significant distress or impairment in social, occupational, or other important areas of functioning.

H. The disturbance is not attributable to the physiological effects of a substance (e.g., medication, alcohol) or another medical condition.

Specify whether:

With dissociative symptoms: The individual's symptoms meet the criteria for posttraumatic stress disorder, and in addition, in response to the stressor, the individual experiences persistent or recurrent symptoms of either of the following:

1. Depersonalization: Persistent or recurrent experiences of feeling detached from, and as if one were an outside observer of, one's mental processes or body (e.g. feeling as though one were in a dream; feeling a sense of unreality of self or body or of time moving slowly).
2. Derealization: Persistent or recurrent experiences of unreality of surroundings (e.g., the world around the individual is experienced as unreal, dreamlike, distant, or distorted).

[Note: To use this subtype, the dissociative symptoms must not be attributable to the physiological effects of a substance (e.g. blackouts, behavior during alcohol intoxication) or another medication condition (e.g., complex partial seizures).]

Specify whether:

With delayed expression: If the full diagnostic criteria are not met until at least 6 months after the event (although the onset and expression of some symptoms may be immediate).

American Psychiatric Association. (2022). *Diagnostic and statistical manual of mental disorders* (5th ed., Text Revision).

to assaultive violence contributes to the etiology of PTSD (Dohrenwend, Yager, Wall, & Adams, 2012; Friedman, 2009) but does not account for all of it. To take a particularly dramatic example, approximately 67% of prisoners of war in Vietnam developed PTSD (Foy, Resnick, Sipprelle, & Carroll, 1987). This means that 33% of the prisoners who endured long-term deprivation and torture *did not* develop the disorder; perhaps the best known among the group is Senator John McCain. Similarly, children experiencing severe burns are likely to develop PTSD in proportion to the severity of the burns and the pain associated with them (Saxe et al., 2005). At lower levels of trauma, some people develop PTSD, but most do not. What accounts for these differences?

As with other disorders, we bring our own generalized biological and psychological vulnerabilities with us. The greater the vulnerability, the more likely we are to develop PTSD. If certain characteristics run in your family, you have a much greater chance of developing the disorder. A family history of anxiety suggests a generalized biological vulnerability for PTSD. True and colleagues (1993) reported that, given the same amount of combat exposure and one twin with PTSD, a monozygotic (identical) twin was more likely to develop PTSD than a dizygotic (fraternal) twin. The correlation of symptoms in identical twins was between 0.28 and 0.41, whereas for fraternal twins it was between 0.11 and 0.24, which suggests some genetic influence in the development of PTSD. Nevertheless, as with other disorders, there is little or no evidence that genes directly cause PTSD (Norrholm & Ressler, 2009). Rather, the stress–diathesis model described in Chapter 2 comes into play again since genetic factors predispose individuals to be easily stressed and anxious, which then may make it more likely that a traumatic experience will result in PTSD (Uddin, Amstadter, Nugent, & Koenen, 2012). This was demonstrated in a study of female undergraduates who witnessed a tragic shooting on the campus of Northern Illinois University in 2008. While all experienced the same traumatic experience, specific characteristics of what is referred to as the serotonin transporter gene involving two short alleles (SS) described as increasing the probability of becoming depressed in Chapter 2 (Caspi et al., 2003) also increased the probability of experiencing symptoms of acute stress after the shooting, even though other factors such as amount of exposure to the shooting were equalized (Mercer et al., 2012). Wang and colleagues (2011) identified the same genetic risk factors in combat veterans.

Breslau, Davis, and Andreski (1995; Breslau, 2012) demonstrated among a random sample of 1,200 individuals that characteristics such as a tendency to be anxious, as well as factors such as minimal education, predict exposure to traumatic events in the first place and therefore an increased risk for PTSD. Breslau, Lucia, and Alvarado (2006) elaborated on this finding by showing that 6-year-old children with externalizing (acting out) problems were more likely to encounter trauma (such as assaults), probably because of their acting out, and later develop PTSD. Higher intelligence predicted decreased exposure to these types of traumatic events. That is, personality and other characteristics, some of them at least partially heritable, may predispose people to the experience of trauma by making it likely that they will be in (risky) situations where trauma is likely to occur (Norrholm & Ressler, 2009). This is reminiscent of the studies on reciprocal gene–environment interactions we describe in Chapter 2, in which existing vulnerabilities, some of them heritable, may help determine the kind of environment in which someone lives and, therefore, the type of psychological disorder that person may develop.

Also, there seems to be a generalized psychological vulnerability described in the context of other disorders based on early experiences with unpredictable or uncontrollable events. Family instability is one factor that may instill a sense that the world is an uncontrollable, potentially dangerous place (Chorpita & Barlow, 1998; Suárez et al., 2009), so it is not surprising that individuals from unstable families are at increased risk for developing PTSD if they experience trauma. Family instability was found to be a prewar risk factor for the development of PTSD in a study of more than 1,600 male and female Vietnam veterans (King et al., 1996, 2012).

In addition, there are certain biological individual characteristics (biomarkers) that appear to increase the likelihood for developing PTSD. In one study, Telch and colleagues (Telch, Rosenfield, Lee, & Pai, 2012) asked 158 soldiers before their deployment to Iraq to inhale air that was enriched with 35% carbon dioxide. Inhaling such gas mixture typically leads to strong physiological symptoms (shortness of breath, tingling, sweating, etc.) and anxiety in some people. Telch and colleagues found that those who reported more emotional reactivity to the gas mixture also experienced the war zone as much more stressful after they came back from Iraq. These soldiers were also at greater risk for developing PTSD symptoms and other anxiety and stress symptoms later on. This example illustrates how certain vulnerabilities can lead to a disorder when the person is exposed to stressors.

Finally, social factors play a major role in the development of PTSD (Ruzek, 2012; King et al., 2012). The results from a number of studies are consistent in showing that, if you have a strong and supportive group of people around you, it is much less likely you will develop PTSD after a trauma (Friedman, 2009). These factors seem to be true for many cultures, as a study comparing American and Russian adolescents demonstrated (Ruchkin et al., 2005). In a particularly interesting study, Vernberg, La Greca, Silverman, and Prinstein (1996) studied 568 elementary school children 3 months after Hurricane Andrew hit the coast of south Florida. More than 55% of these children reported moderate to severe levels of PTSD symptoms, a typical result for this type of disaster (La Greca & Prinstein, 2002). When the authors examined factors contributing to who developed PTSD symptoms and who didn't, social support from parents, close friends, classmates, and teachers was an important protective factor. Similarly, positive coping strategies involving active problem solving seemed to be protective, whereas becoming angry and placing blame on others were associated with higher levels of PTSD. The broader and deeper the network of social support, the less the chance of developing PTSD. Longer-term follow-up of children at 9 and 21 months after hurricane Charley hit Florida in 2004 confirmed that strong social support systems reduced the persistence of posttraumatic stress symptoms over time (La Greca, Silverman, Lai, & Jaccard, 2010).

Why is this? As you saw in Chapter 2, we are all social animals, and something about having a loving, caring group of people around us directly affects our biological and psychological responses to stress. A number of studies show that support from loved ones reduces cortisol secretion and hypothalamic–pituitary–adrenocortical (HPA) axis activity in children during stress (see, for example, Tarullo & Gunnar, 2006). It is likely that one reason for the high prevalence of PTSD in Vietnam veterans compared with veterans from Iraq and Afghanistan was the tragic absence of social support when those veterans returned from Vietnam.

It seems clear that PTSD involves a number of neurobiological systems, particularly elevated or restricted corticotropin-releasing factor (CRF), which indicates heightened activity in the HPA axis, as described earlier in this chapter and in Chapter 2 (Amat et al., 2005; Gunnar & Fisher, 2006; Shin et al., 2004; Shin et al., 2009; Yehuda, Pratchett, & Pelcovitz, 2012). Chronic arousal associated with HPA axis and some other symptoms of PTSD may be directly related to changes in brain function and structure (Bremner, 1999; McEwen & Magarinos, 2004) that in turn influence treatment response (Rauch et al., 2014). For example, evidence of damage to the hippocampus has appeared in groups of patients with war-related PTSD (Gurvits et al., 1996; Wang et al., 2010), adult survivors of childhood sexual abuse (Bremner et al., 1995), and firefighters exposed to extreme trauma (Shin et al., 2004). The hippocampus is a part of the brain that plays an important role in regulating the HPA axis and in learning and memory. Thus, if there is damage to the hippocampus, we might expect persistent and chronic arousal as well as some disruptions in learning and memory. These memory deficits are evident in veterans of the Gulf War (Vasterling, Brailey, Constans, & Sotker, 1998) and Holocaust survivors with PTSD, as compared with Holocaust survivors without PTSD or healthy Jewish adults (Golier et al., 2002). Fortunately, some evidence indicates this damage to the hippocampus may be reversible. For example, Starkman and colleagues (1999) reported results from patients who had some damage to their hippocampus because of Cushing's disease, which causes chronic activation of the HPA axis and increased flow of cortisol. They found increases of up to 10% in hippocampal volume following successful treatment for this disease. Further studies will confirm if the changes as a result of trauma can be reversed by treatment.

Earlier we described a panic attack as an adaptive fear response occurring at an inappropriate time. We have speculated that the "alarm reaction" that is a panic attack is similar in both panic disorder and PTSD but that in panic disorder the alarm is false. In PTSD, the initial alarm is true in that real danger is present (Jones & Barlow, 1990; Keane & Barlow, 2002). If the alarm is severe enough, we may develop a conditioned or learned alarm reaction to stimuli that remind us of the trauma (Lissek & Grillon, 2012). We may also develop anxiety about the possibility of additional uncontrollable emotional experiences (such as flashbacks, which are common in PTSD). Whether or not we develop anxiety partly depends on our vulnerabilities. This model of the etiology of PTSD is presented in ■ Figure 5.11.

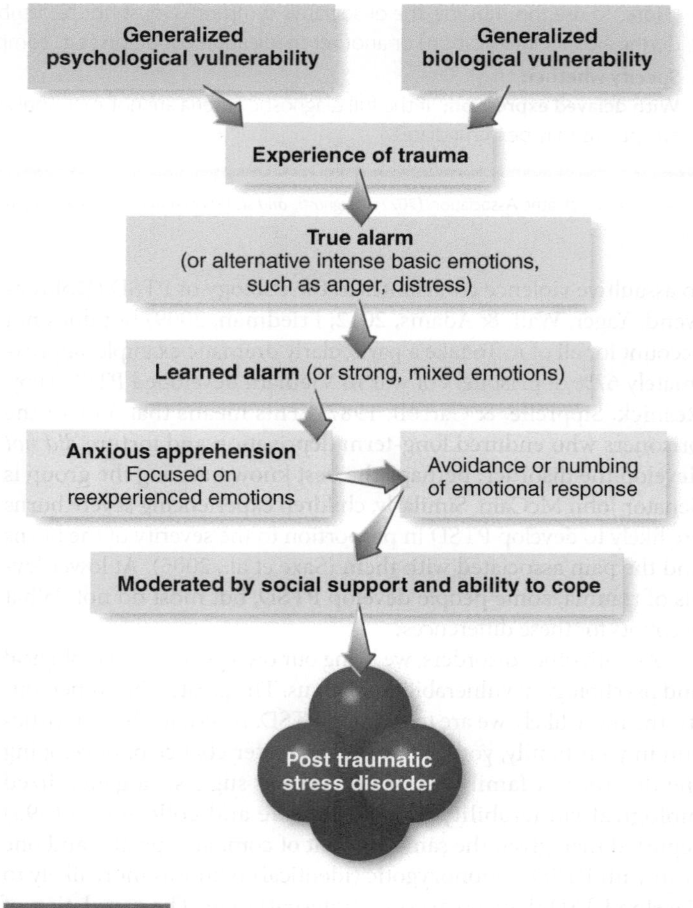

Figure 5.11

A model of the causes of PTSD. Reprinted, with permission, from D. H. Barlow, 2002, *Anxiety and its disorders: The nature and treatment of anxiety and panic* (2nd ed.), Guilford Press. © 2002 Guilford Press.

Treatment

From the psychological point of view, most clinicians agree that individuals with PTSD should face the original trauma, process the intense emotions, and develop effective coping procedures in order to overcome the debilitating effects of the disorder (Beck & Sloan, 2012; Monson, Resick, & Rizvi, 2014; Najavits, 2007). In psychoanalytic therapy, reliving emotional trauma to relieve emotional suffering is called *catharsis*. The challenge is in arranging the reexposure so that it will be therapeutic rather than traumatic. Unlike the object of a specific phobia, a traumatic event is difficult to recreate, and few therapists want to try. Therefore, *imaginal exposure*, in which the content of the trauma and the emotions associated with it are worked through systematically, has been used for decades under a variety of names.

At present, the most common strategy to achieve this purpose with adolescents or adults is to work with the victim to develop a narrative of the traumatic experience and to expose the patients for an extended period of time to the image (*prolonged exposure therapy*) that is then reviewed extensively in treatment (Eftekhari et al., 2013; Foa, Gillihan, & Bryant, 2013; Foa, McLean, Capaldi, & Rosenfield, 2013). One recent review has introduced some caution on generally positive outcomes of psychotherapy for veterans (Steenkamp, Litz, & Marmar, 2020). The effects of the exposure practices may be strengthened by strategically timing the exposure treatment with sleep. Patients in the study were asked to take a nap soon after an exposure because extinction learning appears to take place during slow wave sleep and also because sleep quality reduces anxiety (Pace-Schott, Germain, & Milad, 2015).

Cognitive therapy to correct negative assumptions about the trauma—such as blaming oneself in some way, feeling guilty, or both—is another part of treatment (Ehlers et al., 2014; Monson et al., 2014; Najavits, 2007).

Another complication is that trauma victims often repress the emotional side of their memories of the event and sometimes, it seems, the memory itself. This happens automatically and unconsciously. Occasionally, with treatment, the memories flood back and the patient relives the episode. Although this may be frightening to both patient and therapist, it can be therapeutic if handled appropriately. Evidence is now accumulating that early, structured interventions delivered as soon after the trauma as possible to those who require help are useful in preventing the development of PTSD (Bryant, Moulds, & Nixon, 2003; Ehlers et al., 2003; Kearns, Ressler, Zatzick, & Rothbaum, 2012), and these preventive psychological approaches seem more effective than medications (Shalev et al., 2012). For example, in the study by Ehlers and colleagues (2003) of patients who had experienced a car accident and were clearly at risk for developing PTSD, only 11% developed PTSD after 12 sessions of cognitive therapy, compared with 61% of those receiving a detailed self-help booklet or 55% of those who were just assessed repeatedly over time but had no intervention. All patients who needed it were then treated with cognitive therapy. On the other hand, there is evidence that subjecting trauma victims to a single debriefing session, in which they are forced to express their feelings as to whether they are distressed or not, can be harmful (Ehlers & Clark, 2003).

We now have evidence that the strategies described above produce lasting changes. one hundred forty-four female rape survivors who were treated with evidence-based psychological treatments were reassessed 5 to 10 years after treatment. The substantial decreases in symptoms originally observed were maintained with very little change over this period of time (Resick, Williams, Suvak, Monson, & Gradus, 2012). Another important study evaluated treatment for 40 heterosexual and same-sex couples in which one partner met criteria for PTSD. However, in this study the partner was directly included in treatment in order to address the severe disruptions in intimate relationships that often accompany PTSD and may lead to relapse (Monson et al., 2012). The outcome was significant improvement in PTSD symptoms but also in relationship satisfaction that might contribute substantially to long-term adjustment. Drugs can also be effective for symptoms of PTSD (Dent & Bremner, 2009; Schneier et al., 2012). Some of the drugs, such as SSRIs (such as Prozac and Paxil), that are effective for anxiety disorders in general have been shown to be helpful for PTSD, perhaps because they relieve the severe anxiety and panic attacks so prominent in this disorder. Promising but mixed results have been reported for the use of D-cycloserine (DCS) as an augmentation strategy of CBT for PTSD (de Kleine, Hendriks, Kusters, Broekman, & van Minnen, 2012; Litz et al., 2012; Rothbaum et al., 2014). The study by Litz et al. (2012) suggests that DCS augmentation can lead to even worse outcome than placebo if exposure during CBT was unsuccessful. De Kleine and colleagues (2012) did not find an overall augmentation effect at the end of therapy, but DCS was more beneficial for individuals who had more severe PTSD before therapy and who needed longer treatment. Similarly, Rothbaum and colleagues (2014) showed that for people who are slow responders to CBT, augmentation with DCS may set them on a course for better response by the end of treatment. In general, DCS appears to have a fairly narrow therapeutic window and may not only augment extinction learning but also enhance a process called *fear memory reconsolidation* (referring to the process when fear memory is reactivated and stored back into long-term memory again) (Phelps & Hofmann, 2020). This can make "good" exposures better but also "bad" exposures worse (Hofmann, 2014).

Concept Check 5.5

Match the correct preliminary diagnosis with the cases below: (a) posttraumatic stress disorder, (b) acute stress disorder, and (c) delayed onset posttraumatic stress disorder.

1. Cadence witnessed a horrific tornado level her farm 3 weeks ago. Since then, she's had many flashbacks of the incident, trouble sleeping, and a fear of going outside in storms. ____________
2. Sanjay was involved in a car accident 6 weeks ago in which the driver of the other car was killed. Since then, Sanjay has been unable to get into a car because it brings back the horrible scene he witnessed. Nightmares of the incident haunt him and interfere with his sleep. He is irritable and has lost interest in his work and hobbies. ____________
3. Patricia was raped at the age of 17, 30 years ago. Just recently, she has been having flashbacks of the event, difficulty sleeping, and fear of sexual contact with her husband. ____________

Prolonged Grief Disorder

Many people reading this book have had the tragic experience of losing a loved one such as a grandparent, parent, or sibling. Others will encounter this event eventually and will experience, sometimes intensely, the very natural and human response of acute grief, which involves changes in emotion, thoughts, and behaviors. Our cultures and religions provide rituals, such as funerals, in which friends and loved ones participate in processing the loss and providing comfort to the bereaved.

In most cases, feelings of grief diminish over time, and the loss becomes integrated into our lives. The process of acute and integrated grief and its relationship to depression is discussed more fully in chapter 7. However, for some individuals, the process of adaptation to loss is prolonged and even intensifies with the passage of time instead of diminishing. These individuals may meet criteria for the newest disorder in the DSM: **prolonged grief disorder (PGD)** (see DSM table 5.8). This disorder is estimated to occur in from 9.8% to 11% of all adults experiencing grief (Lundorff, Holmgren, Zachariae, Farver-Vestergaard, & O'Connor, 2017). The experience of grief for these individuals includes intense longing for and preoccupation with the deceased and a range of other symptoms that make it difficult to move on with life even after a year or more has passed (6 months or more for children).

The COVID-19 pandemic has also produced a "grief pandemic" due to the millions of people who have died in an unexpected fashion, which may increase the likelihood of PGD. In addition, many individuals were unable to adequately grieve their losses through funerals and related rituals due to pandemic restrictions.

Intense grief can produce a traumatic reaction, resulting in its classification in this section of the DSM, with other traumatic and stressor related disorders. Furthermore, psychological and biological vulnerabilities increasing the likelihood of intense grief progressing to PGD in some individuals seem to be similar to vulnerabilities for developing other disorders described in this chapter (Barlow, Curreri, & Woodard 2021). Fortunately, new treatments resembling effective treatments for PTSD, but adapted for prolonged grief, have been developed for this condition (Shear, Frank, Houck, & Reynolds, 2005; Shear et al., 2014; Shear et al., 2016).

Several other disorders in addition to PTSD are included in this general category. **Adjustment disorders** describe anxious or depressive reactions to life stress that are generally milder than would be seen in acute stress disorder or PTSD but are nevertheless impairing in terms of interfering with work or school performance, interpersonal relationships, or other areas of living (Friedman et al., 2011; Strain & Friedman, 2011). Sometimes, particularly in adolescence, the life stress may provoke some conduct problems. The stressful events themselves would not be considered traumatic, but it is clear that the individual is nevertheless unable to cope with the demands of the situation and some intervention is typically required. If the symptoms persist for more than 6 months after the removal of the stress or its consequences, the adjustment disorder would be considered "chronic." In the past, adjustment disorder has often been used as a residual diagnostic category for people with significant anxiety or depression associated with an identifiable life stress that does not meet criteria for another anxiety or mood disorder. Partly for this reason, there has been very little research on these reactions. Presumably it describes individuals with the biological and psychological vulnerabilities that are described throughout this chapter and that are associated with trait anxiety that flares up when confronting stressful events, although

DSM 5

Table 5.8

Diagnostic Criteria for Prolonged Grief Disorder

A. The death, at least 12 months ago, of a person who was close to the bereaved individual (for children and adolescents, at least 6 months ago).

B. Since the death, the development of a persistent grief response characterized by one or both of the following symptoms, which have been present most days to a clinically significant degree. In addition, the symptom(s) have occurred nearly every day for at least the last month:

1. Intense yearning/longing for the deceased person
2. Preoccupation with thoughts or memories of the deceased person (in children and adolescents, preoccupation may focus on the circumstances of the death)

C. Since the death, at least 3 of the following symptoms have been present most days to a clinically significant degree. In addition, the symptoms have occurred nearly every day for at least the last month:

1. Identity disruption (e.g., feeling as though part of oneself has died) since the death
2. Marked sense of disbelief about the death
3. Avoidance of reminders that the person is dead (in children and adolescents, may be characterized by efforts to avoid reminders)
4. Intense emotional pain (e.g., anger, bitterness, sorrow) related to the death
5. Difficulty reintegrating into one's relationships and activities after the death (e.g., problems engaging with friends, pursuing interests, or planning for the future)
6. Emotional numbness (absence or marked reduction of emotional experience) as a result of the death
7. Feeling that life is meaningless as a result of the death
8. Intense loneliness as a result of the death

D. The disturbance causes clinically significant distress or impairment in social, occupational, or other important areas of functioning.

E. The duration and severity of the bereavement reaction clearly exceed expected social, cultural, or religious norms for the individual's culture and context.

F. The symptoms are not better explained by major depressive disorder, posttraumatic stress disorder, or another mental disorder or attributable to the physiological effects of a substance (e.g., medication, alcohol) or another medical condition.

American Psychiatric Association. (2022). *Diagnostic and statistical manual of mental disorders* (5th ed., text revision).

not to the extent that it would meet criteria for another more serious disorder.

Attachment disorders refers to disturbed and developmentally inappropriate behaviors in children, emerging before 5 years of age, in which the child is unable or unwilling to form normal attachment relationships with caregiving adults. These seriously maladaptive patterns are due to inadequate or abusive child-rearing practices. In many cases, these inadequate child-rearing practices might be caused by frequent changes in the primary caregiver because of multiple foster care placements or possibly by neglect in the home. In either case, the result is a failure to meet the child's basic emotional needs for affection and comfort or even provide the basic necessities of daily living. As such, these disorders are considered to be pathological reactions to early extreme stress (Kay & Green, 2013). In previous editions of the DSM, two different kinds of presentations were included under the heading "reactive attachment disorder." In DSM-5, two separate disorders are described—the first an emotionally withdrawn inhibited type and the second an indiscriminately social disinhibited type (Zeanah & Gleason 2010; Gleason et al., 2011).

In **reactive attachment disorder**, the child will very seldom seek out a caregiver for protection, support, and nurturance and will seldom respond to offers from caregivers to provide this kind of care. Generally, they would evidence lack of responsiveness, limited positive affect, and additional heightened emotionality, such as fearfulness and intense sadness. In **disinhibited social engagement disorder**, a similar set of child-rearing circumstances—perhaps including early persistent harsh punishment—would result in a pattern of behavior in which the child shows no inhibitions whatsoever to approaching adults. Such a child might engage in inappropriately intimate behavior by showing a willingness to immediately accompany an unfamiliar adult figure somewhere without first checking back with a caregiver. These patterns of behavior were combined into one disorder in DSM-IV but have been separated into two different disorders in the DSM-5, partly because of the markedly different presentations of inadequate detachment behavior (Gleason et al., 2011).

Obsessive-Compulsive and Related Disorders

Another new class of disorders in DSM-5 brings together several disorders that share a number of characteristics, such as driven repetitive behaviors and some other symptoms, and a similar course and treatment response (Abramowitz & Jacoby, 2015). Previously, these disorders had been scattered in other areas of DSM-IV. In addition to obsessive-compulsive disorder, which was classified as an anxiety disorder until DSM-5, this grouping now includes a separate diagnostic category for hoarding disorder, body dysmorphic disorder previously located with the somatoform disorders, and trichotillomania previously grouped with the impulse control disorders. Also, another new disorder in this group is excoriation (skin picking) disorder. We begin with the most prominent disorder in this group, obsessive-compulsive disorder.

Obsessive-Compulsive Disorder

Among the persons suffering from anxiety and related disorders, a client who needs hospitalization is likely to have **obsessive-compulsive disorder (OCD)**. A client who has been referred for psychosurgery (neurosurgery for a psychological disorder) because every psychological and pharmacological treatment has failed and whose suffering is unbearable probably has OCD. OCD is the devastating culmination of the anxiety disorders. It is not uncommon for someone with OCD to experience severe generalized anxiety, recurrent panic attacks, debilitating avoidance, and major depression, all occurring simultaneously with obsessive-compulsive symptoms. With OCD, establishing even a foothold of control and predictability over the dangerous events in life seems so utterly hopeless that victims resort to magic and rituals

Clinical Description

In other anxiety disorders, the danger is usually in an external object or situation or at least in the memory of one. In OCD, the dangerous event is a thought, an image, or an impulse that the client attempts to avoid as completely as someone with a snake phobia avoids snakes (Clark & O'Connor, 2005). For example, has anyone ever told you not to think of pink elephants? If you really concentrate on not thinking of pink elephants, using every mental means possible, you will realize how difficult it is to suppress a suggested thought or image. Individuals with OCD fight this battle all day, every day, sometimes for most of their lives. In Chapter 3, we discuss the case of Frank, who experienced involuntary thoughts of epilepsy or seizures and prayed or shook his leg to try to distract himself. **Obsessions** are intrusive and mostly nonsensical thoughts, images, or urges that the individual tries to resist or eliminate. **Compulsions** are the thoughts or actions used to suppress the obsessions and provide relief. Frank had both obsessions and compulsions, but his disorder was mild compared with the case of Brandon.

Brandon... Bound by Ritual

Brandon, a 19-year-old college freshman majoring in philosophy, withdrew from school because of incapacitating ritualistic behavior. He abandoned personal hygiene because the compulsive rituals that he had to carry out during washing or cleaning were so time consuming that he could do nothing else. Almost continual showering gave way to no showering. He stopped cutting and washing his hair and beard, brushing his teeth, and changing his clothes. He left his room infrequently and, to avoid rituals associated with the toilet, defecated on paper towels, urinated in paper cups, and stored the waste in the closet. He ate only late at night when his family was asleep. To be able to eat, he had to exhale completely, making a lot of hissing noises, coughs, and hacks, and then fill his mouth with as much food as he could while no air was in his lungs. He would eat only a mixture of peanut butter, sugar, cocoa, milk, and mayonnaise. All other foods he considered contaminants. When he walked, he took small steps on his toes while continually looking back, checking and rechecking. Occasionally, he ran quickly in place. He withdrew his left arm completely from his shirt sleeve and used it as a sling as an amputee would for his arm.

Like everyone with OCD, Brandon experienced intrusive and persistent thoughts and impulses; in his case, they were about sex, aggression, and religion. His various behaviors were efforts to suppress sexual and aggressive thoughts or to ward off the disastrous consequences he thought would ensue if he did not perform his rituals. Brandon performed most of the repetitive behaviors and mental acts mentioned in the DSM-5 criteria. Compulsions can be either behavioral (hand-washing or checking) or mental (thinking about certain words in a specific order, counting, praying, and so on) (Foa et al., 1996; Purdon, 2009; Steketee & Barlow, 2002). The important thing is that they are believed to reduce stress or prevent a dreaded event. Compulsions are often "magical" in that they may bear no logical relation to the obsession. •

DSM 5 **Table 5.9**

Diagnostic Criteria for Obsessive-Compulsive Disorder

A. Presence of obsessions, compulsions or both:

Obsessions are defined by (1) and (2):

1. Recurrent and persistent thoughts, urges, or images that are experienced, at some time during the disturbance, as intrusive and unwanted, and that in most individuals cause marked anxiety or distress.
2. The individual attempts to ignore or suppress such thoughts, urges, or images, or to neutralize them with some other thought or action (i.e., by performing a compulsion).

Compulsions are defined by (1) and (2):

1. Repetitive behaviors (e.g., hand washing, ordering, checking) or mental acts (e.g., praying, counting, repeating words silently) that the individual feels driven to perform in response to an obsession, or according to rules that must be applied rigidly.
2. The behaviors or mental acts are aimed at preventing or reducing distress or preventing some dreaded event or situation; however, these behaviors or mental acts are not connected in a realistic way with what they are designed to neutralize or prevent, or are clearly excessive.

B. The obsessions or compulsions are time-consuming (e.g., take more than 1 hour per day) or cause clinically significant distress or impairment in social, occupational or other important areas of functioning.

C. The obsessive-compulsive symptoms are not attributable to the physiological effects of a substance (e.g., a drug of abuse, a medication) or another medical condition.

D. The disturbance is not better explained by the symptoms of another mental disorder (e.g., excessive worries, as in generalized anxiety disorder; preoccupation with appearance, as in body dysmorphic disorder).

Specify if:

With good or fair insight: The individual recognizes that obsessive-compulsive disorder beliefs are definitely or probably not true or that they may or may not be true.

With poor insight: The individual thinks obsessive-compulsive disorder beliefs are probably true.

With absent insight/delusional: The individual is completely convinced that obsessive-compulsive disorder beliefs are true.

Specify if:

Tic-related: The individual has a current or past history of a tic disorder.

American Psychiatric Association. (2022). *Diagnostic and statistical manual of mental disorders* (5th ed., text revision).

Types of Obsessions and Compulsions Based on statistically associated groupings, there are four major types of obsessions (Bloch, Landeros-Weisenberger, Rosario, Pittenger, & Leckman, 2008; Mathews, 2009), and each is associated with a pattern of compulsive behavior (see DSM Table 5.9 and Table 5.7). Symmetry obsessions account for most obsessions (26.7%), followed by "forbidden thoughts or actions" (21%), cleaning and contamination (15.9%), and hoarding (15.4%) (Bloch et al., 2008). Symmetry refers to keeping things in perfect order or doing something in a specific way. As a child, were you careful not to step on cracks in the sidewalk? You and your friends might have kept this up for a few minutes before tiring of it. But what if you had to spend your whole life avoiding cracks, on foot or in a car, to prevent something bad from happening? You wouldn't have much fun. People with aggressive (forbidden) obsessive impulses may feel they are about to yell out a swear word in church. One patient of ours was afraid to ride the bus for fear that if a man sat down beside her, she would grab his crotch! In reality, this would be the last thing she would do, but the aggressive urge was so horrifying that she made every attempt possible to suppress it and to avoid riding the bus or similar situations where the impulse might occur.

Certain kinds of obsessions are strongly associated with certain kinds of rituals (Bloch et al., 2008; Calamari et al., 2004; Leckman et al., 1997). For example, forbidden thoughts or actions, as indicated in Table 5.7, seem to lead to checking rituals. Checking rituals serve to prevent an imagined disaster or catastrophe. Many are logical, such as repeatedly checking the stove to see whether you turned it off, but severe cases can be illogical. For example, Brandon thought that if he did not eat in a certain way, he might become possessed. If he didn't take small steps and look back, some disaster might happen to his family. A mental act, such as counting, can also be a compulsion. Obsessions with symmetry lead to ordering and arranging or repeating rituals; obsessions with contamination lead to washing rituals that may restore a

Table 5.7 Types of Obsessions and Associated Compulsions

Symptom Subtype	Obsession	Compulsion
Symmetry/exactness/"just right"	Needing things to be symmetrical/aligned just so Urges to do things over and over until they feel "just right"	Putting things in a certain order Repeating rituals
Forbidden thoughts or actions (aggressive/sexual/religious)	Fears, urges to harm self or others Fears of offending God	Checking Avoidance Repeated requests for reassurance
Cleaning/contamination	Germs Fears of germs or contaminants	Repetitive or excessive washing Using gloves, masks to do daily tasks
Hoarding	Fears of throwing anything away	Collecting/saving objects with little or no actual or sentimental value such as food wrappings

Source: Adapted from Mathews (2009) and Bloch et al. (2008).

sense of safety and control (Rachman, 2006). Like Brandon, many patients have several kinds of obsessions and compulsions.

On rare occasions, patients, particularly children, will present with compulsions but few or no identifiable obsessions. We saw an 8-year-old child who felt compelled to undress, put on his pajamas, and turn down the covers in a time-consuming fashion each night; he always repeated the ritual three times. He could give no particular reason for his behavior; he simply had to do it.

Tic Disorder and OCD It is also common for tic disorder, characterized by involuntary movement (sudden jerking of limbs, for example), to co-occur in patients with OCD (particularly children) or in their families (Browne et al., 2015; Grados et al., 2001; Leckman et al., 2010; Mataix-Cols et al., 2013). More complex tics with involuntary vocalizations are referred to as Tourette's disorder (Leckman et al., 2010; see Chapter 14). In some cases, these movements are not tics but may be compulsions, as they were in the case of Frank in Chapter 3 who kept jerking his leg if thoughts of seizures entered his head. Approximately 10% to 40% of children and adolescents with OCD also have had tic disorder at some point (Leckman et al., 2010). The obsessions in tic-related OCD are almost always related to symmetry. CBT has been found to be quite effective for treating tic disorders (McGuire et al., 2015).

Observations among one small group of children presenting with OCD and tics suggest that these problems occurred after a bout of strep throat. This syndrome has been referred to as pediatric autoimmune disorder associated with streptococcus infection (PANDAS) (Leckman et al., 2010; Radomsky & Taylor, 2005). Presentation of OCD in these cases differs somewhat from OCD without a history of PANDAS in several ways. The PANDAS group is more likely to be male, experience dramatic onset of symptoms often associated with fever or sore throat, have full remissions between episodes, show remission of symptoms during antibiotic therapy, have evidence of past streptococcal infections, and present with noticeable clumsiness (Murphy, Storch, Lewin, Edge, & Goodman, 2012). This syndrome has been revised and broadened under the umbrella term pediatric autoimmune neuropsychiatric syndrome (PANS) (Swedo, Leckman, & Rose, 2012). The prevalence of this condition has yet to be determined.

Statistics

Estimates of the lifetime prevalence of OCD range from 1.6% to 2.3% (Calamari, Chik, Pontarelli, & DeJong, 2012; Kessler, Berglund, Demler, et al., 2005), and in a given 1-year period the prevalence is 1% (Calamari et al., 2012; Kessler, Chiu, et al., 2005). Not all cases meeting criteria for OCD are as severe as Brandon's. Obsessions and compulsions can be arranged along a continuum, like most clinical features of anxiety disorders. Intrusive and distressing thoughts are common in nonclinical ("normal") individuals (Boyer & Liénard, 2008; Clark & Rhyno, 2005; Fullana et al., 2009). Spinella (2005) found that 13% of a "normal" community sample of people had moderate levels of obsessions or compulsions that were not severe enough to meet diagnostic criteria for OCD.

It would also be unusual *not* to have an occasional intrusive or strange thought. Many people have bizarre, sexual, or aggressive thoughts, particularly if they are bored—for example, when sitting in class. Steketee and Barlow (2002) collected examples of thoughts from ordinary people who do not have OCD. Some of these thoughts are listed in Table 5.8.

Have you had any of these thoughts? Most people do, but they are passing worries. Certain individuals, however, are horrified by such thoughts, considering them signs of an alien, intrusive, evil force. Unlike other anxiety and related disorders, OCD has a ratio of female to male that is nearly 1:1. Although there is some evidence in children that there are more males than females (Hanna, 1995), this seems to be because boys tend to develop OCD earlier. By midadolescence, the sex ratio is approximately equal (Albano et al., 1996). Age of onset ranges from childhood through the 30s, with a median age of onset of 19 (Kessler, Berglund, Demler, et al., 2005). The age of onset peaks earlier in males (13 to 15) than in females (20 to 24) (Rasmussen & Eisen, 1990). Once OCD develops, it tends to become chronic (Calamari et al., 2012; Steketee & Barlow, 2002).

In Arabic countries, OCD is easily recognizable, although as always cultural beliefs and concerns influence the content of the obsessions and the nature of the compulsions. In Saudi Arabia and Egypt, obsessions are primarily related to religious practices, specifically the Muslim emphasis on cleanliness. Contamination themes are also highly prevalent in India. Nevertheless, OCD looks remarkably similar across cultures. Studies from Egypt, England, Hong Kong, India, Japan, and Norway found essentially similar types and proportions of obsessions and compulsions, as did studies from Canada, Finland, Taiwan, Africa, Puerto Rico, Korea, and New Zealand (Horwath & Weissman, 2000; Weissman et al., 1994).

Table 5.8 Obsessions and Intrusive Thoughts Reported by Nonclinical Samples*

Harming
Impulse to jump out of high window
Idea of jumping in front of a car
Impulse to push someone in front of train
Wishing a person would die
While holding a baby, having a sudden urge to kick it
Thoughts of dropping a baby
The thought that if I forget to say goodbye to someone, they might die
Thought that thinking about horrible things happening to a child will cause it
Contamination or Disease
Thought of catching a disease from public pools or other public places
Thoughts I may have caught a disease from touching toilet seat
Idea that dirt is always on my hand
Inappropriate or Unacceptable Behavior
Idea of swearing or yelling at my boss
Thought of doing something embarrassing in public, like forgetting to wear a top
Hoping someone doesn't succeed
Thought of blurting out something in church
Thought of "unnatural" sexual acts
Doubts about Safety, Memory, and So On
Thought that I haven't locked the house up properly
Idea of leaving my curling iron on the carpet and forgetting to pull out the plug
Thought that I've left the heater and stove on
Idea that I've left the car unlocked when I know I've locked it
Idea that objects are not arranged perfectly

*Examples were obtained from Rachman and de Silva (1978) and from unpublished research by Dana Thordarson, Ph.D., and Michael Kyrios, Ph.D. (personal communications, 2000).

Source: Reprinted, with permission, from G. Steketee & D. H. Barlow, 2002, Obsessive-compulsive disorder, in D. H. Barlow, *Anxiety and its disorders: The nature and treatment of anxiety and panic* (2nd ed.), Guilford Press, p. 529. © 2002 Guilford Press.

Causes

Many of us sometimes have intrusive, even horrific, thoughts and occasionally engage in ritualistic behavior, especially when we are under stress (Parkinson & Rachman, 1981a, 1981b). But few of us develop OCD. Again, as with panic disorder and PTSD, someone must develop anxiety focused on the possibility of having additional intrusive thoughts.

The repetitive, intrusive, unacceptable thoughts of OCD may well be regulated by the hypothetical brain circuits described in Chapter 2. The tendency to develop anxiety over having additional compulsive thoughts, however, may have the same generalized biological and psychological precursors as anxiety in general (Barlow et al., 2014; Suárez et al., 2009).

Why would people with OCD focus their anxiety on the occasional intrusive thought rather than on the possibility of a panic attack or some other external situation? One hypothesis is that early experiences taught them that some thoughts are dangerous and unacceptable because the terrible things they are thinking might happen and they would be responsible. These early experiences would result in a specific psychological vulnerability to develop OCD. When clients with OCD equate thoughts with the specific actions or activity represented by the thoughts, this is called *thought–action fusion.* Thought–action fusion may, in turn, be caused by attitudes of excessive responsibility and resulting guilt developed during childhood, when even a bad thought is associated with malevolent intent (Clark & O'Connor, 2005; Steketee & Barlow, 2002; Taylor, Abramowitz, McKay, & Cuttler, 2012). They may learn this through the same process of misinformation that convinced the person with snake phobia that snakes were dangerous and could be everywhere. One patient believed thinking about abortion was the moral equivalent of having an abortion. Brandon finally admitted to having strong same-sex impulses that were unacceptable to him and to his minister father, and he believed the impulses were as sinful as actual acts. Many people with OCD who believe in the tenets of fundamentalist religions—whether Christian, Jewish, or Islamic—present with similar attitudes of inflated responsibility and thought–action fusion. Several studies showed that the strength of religious belief, but not the type of belief, was associated with thought–action fusion and severity of OCD (Rassin & Koster, 2003; Steketee, Quay, & White, 1991). Most people with fundamental religious beliefs do not develop OCD. But what if the most frightening thing in your life was not a snake or speaking in public but a terrible thought that happened to pop into your head? You can't avoid it as you would a snake, so you resist this thought by attempting to suppress it or "neutralize" it using mental or behavioral strategies, such as distraction, praying, or checking. These strategies become compulsions, but they are ineffective in the long term because these strategies backfire and actually increase the frequency of the thought (Franklin & Foa, 2014; Wegner, 1989).

Again, generalized biological and psychological vulnerabilities must be present for this disorder to develop. Believing some thoughts are unacceptable and therefore must be suppressed (a specific psychological vulnerability) may put people at greater risk of OCD (Parkinson & Rachman, 1981b; Salkovskis & Campbell, 1994). A model of the etiology of OCD that is somewhat similar to other models of anxiety disorders is presented in ■ Figure 5.12.

Treatment

The effects of drugs on OCD have been evaluated extensively (Dougherty, Rauch, & Jenike, 2012; Stewart, Jenike, & Jenike, 2009). The most effective seem to be those that specifically inhibit the reuptake of serotonin, such as clomipramine or the SSRIs, which benefit up to 60% of patients with OCD, with no particular advantage to one drug over another. Relapse often occurs when the drug is discontinued, however (Dougherty et al., 2012; Lydiard, Brawman-Mintzer, & Ballenger, 1996).

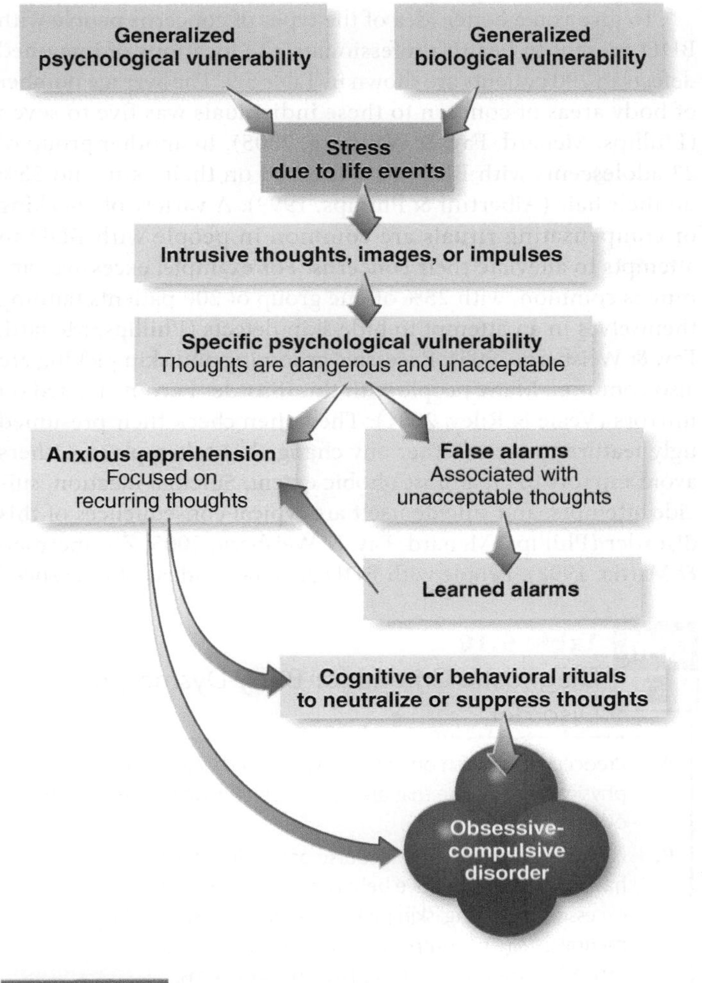

Figure 5.12

A model of the causes of obsessive-compulsive disorder. Reprinted, with permission, from G. Steketee & D. H. Barlow, 2002, Obsessive-compulsive disorder, in *Anxiety and its disorders: The nature and treatment of anxiety and panic* (2nd ed.), Guilford Press, p. 536. © 2002 Guilford Press.

Highly structured psychological treatments work somewhat better than drugs, but they are not readily available. The most effective approach is called *exposure and ritual prevention (ERP)*, a process whereby the rituals are actively prevented and the patient is systematically and gradually exposed to the feared thoughts or situations (Abramowitz, Taylor, & McKay, 2012; Franklin & Foa, 2014). Brandon, for example, would be systematically exposed to harmless objects or situations that he thought were contaminated, including certain foods and household chemicals, and his washing and checking rituals would be prevented. Usually, this can be done by working closely with patients to see that they do not wash or check. In severe cases, patients may be hospitalized, and the faucets removed from the bathroom sink for a period to discourage repeated washing. However the rituals are prevented, the procedures seem to facilitate "reality testing" because the client soon learns, at an emotional level, that no harm will result whether he carries out the rituals or not. Innovative strategies to evidence-based psychological treatments for OCD have examined the efficacy of cognitive treatments with a focus on the overestimation of threat, the importance and control of intrusive thoughts, the sense of inflated responsibility present in patients with OCD who think they alone may be responsible for preventing a catastrophe, as well as the need for perfectionism and certainty present in these patients (Whittal & Robichaud, 2012). Initial results indicate that these strategies are effective, perhaps as effective as ERP.

Studies have evaluated the combined effects of medication and psychological treatments (Romanelli, Wu, Gamba, Mojtabai, & Segal, 2014; Simpson et al., 2013; Tolin, 2011). In one large study (Foa et al., 2005), ERP was compared with the drug clomipramine, as well as with a combined condition. ERP, with or without the drug, produced superior results to the drug alone, with 86% responding to ERP alone versus 48% to the drug alone. Combining the treatments did not produce any additional advantage. Also, relapse rates were high from the medication-only group when the drug was withdrawn. Furthermore, medication such as SSRIs appear to be effective only in a subgroup of patients, possibly because these drugs primarily dampen the symptoms but do not correct the dysregulated neural circuits (Ressler & Rothbaum, 2013). Therefore, adding ERP to people who continue to have OCD symptoms after starting an SSRI can be more beneficial than adding another medication (Simpson et al., 2013).

Psychosurgery is one of the more radical treatments for OCD. "Psychosurgery" is a misnomer that refers to neurosurgery for a psychological disorder. Jenike and colleagues (1991) reviewed the records of 33 patients with OCD, most of them extremely severe cases who did not respond to either drug or psychological treatment. After a specific surgical procedure to lesion the cingulate bundle (cingulotomy), approximately 30% benefited substantially. Similarly, Rück et al. (2008) performed a related surgery (capsulotomy) on 25 patients who had not responded to 5 years of previous treatment; 35% (9 patients) benefited substantially, but 6 of those 9 patients exhibited serious adverse side effects of the surgery. These results seem typical from the surgical procedures (Greenberg, Rauch, & Haber, 2010) and are similar to results from a procedure called deep-brain stimulation in which electrodes are placed through small holes drilled in the skull and are connected to a pacemaker-like device in the brain. The advantage of deep-brain stimulation over more traditional surgery is that it is reversible (McLaughlin & Greenberg, 2012). Considering that these patients did not respond well to other treatments, surgery deserves consideration as a last resort.

Body Dysmorphic Disorder

Did you ever wish you could change part of your appearance? Maybe the size of your nose or the way your ears stick out? Some people are preoccupied with one or more perceived defects or flaws in physical appearance even though they are not really observable to others. This curious affliction is called **body dysmorphic disorder (BDD)**, and at its center is a preoccupation with some imagined defect in appearance by someone who actually looks unremarkable (Fang & Wilhelm, 2015). The disorder has been referred to as "imagined ugliness" (Phillips, 1991). Consider the case of Isaac.

Isaac... Ashamed to Be Seen

In his mid-20s, Isaac was diagnosed with suspected social anxiety disorder, and he was referred to our clinic by another professional. Isaac had just finished rabbinical school and had been offered a position at a synagogue in a nearby city. He found himself unable to accept, however, because of marked social difficulties. Lately, he had given up leaving his small apartment for fear of running into people he knew and being forced to stop and interact with them.

Isaac was a good-looking young man of about average height, with dark hair and eyes. Although he was somewhat depressed, a mental status exam and a brief interview focusing on current functioning and past history did not reveal any remarkable problems. There was no sign of a psychotic process (he was not out of touch with reality). We then focused on Isaac's social difficulties. We expected the usual kinds of anxiety about interacting with people or "doing something" (performing) in front of them. But this was not Isaac's concern. Rather, he was convinced that everyone, even his good friends, was staring at a part of his body that he found grotesque. He reported that strangers would never mention his deformity and his friends felt too sorry for him to mention it. Isaac thought his head was square! Like the Beast in *Beauty and the Beast* who could not imagine people reacting to him with anything less than revulsion, Isaac could not imagine people getting past his square head. To hide his condition as well as he could, Isaac wore soft floppy hats and was most comfortable in winter, when he could all but completely cover his head with a large stocking cap. To us, Isaac looked unremarkable. •

For many years, BDD was considered a somatoform disorder because its central feature is a psychological preoccupation with somatic (physical) issues. But increasing evidence indicated it was more closely related to OCD, accounting for its relocation to the obsessive-compulsive and related disorders section in DSM-5. For example, OCD often co-occurs with BDD and is found among family members of BDD patients (Chosak et al., 2008; Gustad & Phillips, 2003; Phillips et al., 2010; Phillips & Stout, 2006; Tynes, White, & Steketee, 1990; Zimmerman & Mattia, 1998). There are other similarities. People with BDD report of persistent, intrusive, and horrible thoughts about their appearance, and they engage in such compulsive behaviors as repeatedly looking in mirrors to check their physical features. BDD and OCD also have approximately the same age of onset and run the same course. One brain-imaging study demonstrated similar abnormal brain functioning between patients with BDD and patients with OCD (Rauch et al., 2003).

To give you a better idea of the types of concerns people with BDD present to health professionals, the locations of imagined defects in 200 patients are shown in Table 5.9. The average number of body areas of concern to these individuals was five to seven (Phillips, Menard, Fay, & Weisberg, 2005). In another group of 23 adolescents with BDD, 61% focused on their skin, and 55% on their hair (Albertini & Phillips, 1999). A variety of checking or compensating rituals are common in people with BDD in attempts to alleviate their concerns. For example, excessive tanning is common, with 25% of one group of 200 patients tanning themselves in an attempt to hide skin defects (Phillips, Menard, Fay, & Weisberg, 2005). Excessive grooming and skin picking are also common. Many people with this disorder become fixated on mirrors (Veale & Riley, 2001). They often check their presumed ugly feature to see whether any change has taken place. Others avoid mirrors to an almost phobic extent. Suicidal ideation, suicide attempts, and suicide itself are typical consequences of this disorder (Phillips, Menard, Fay, & Weisberg, 2005; Zimmerman & Mattia, 1998). People with BDD also have "ideas of reference,"

DSM 5 **Table 5.10**
Diagnostic Criteria for Body Dysmorphic Disorder

A. Preoccupation with one or more perceived defects or flaws in physical appearance that are not observable or appear slight to others.

B. At some point during the course of the disorder, the individual has performed repetitive behaviors (e.g., mirror checking, excessive grooming, skin picking, reassurance seeking) or mental acts (e.g., comparing his or her appearance with that of others) in response to the appearance concerns.

C. The preoccupation causes clinically significant distress or impairment in social, occupational, or other important areas of functioning.

D. The appearance preoccupation is not better explained by concerns with body fat or weight in an individual whose symptoms meet diagnostic criteria for an eating disorder.

Specify if:

With muscle dysmorphia: The individual is preoccupied with the idea that his or her body build is too small or insufficiently muscular. This specifier is used even if the individual is preoccupied with other body areas, which is often the case.

Specify if:

Indicate degree of insight regarding body dysmorphic beliefs (e.g., "I look ugly" or "I look deformed").

With good or fair insight: The individual recognizes that the body dysmorphic disorder beliefs are definitely or probably not true or that they may or may not be true.

With poor insight: The individual thinks that the body dysmorphic disorder beliefs are probably true.

With absent insight/delusional beliefs: the individual is completely convinced that the body dysmorphic disorder beliefs are true.

American Psychiatric Association. (2022). *Diagnostic and statistical manual of mental disorders* (5th ed., Text Revision).

Table 5.9 Location of Imagined Defects on 200 Patients with Body Dysmorphic Disorder*

Location	%	Location	%
Skin	80	Overall appearance of face	19
Hair	58	Small body build	18
Nose	39	Legs	18
Stomach	32	Face size or shape	16
Teeth	30	Chin	15
Weight	29	Lips	14.5
Breasts	26	Arms or wrists	14
Buttocks	22	Hips	13
Eyes	22	Cheeks	11
Thighs	20	Ears	11
Eyebrows	20		

Source: Adapted from K. A. Phillips, B. A. Menard, C. Fay, & R. Weisberg, 2005, Demographic characteristics, phenomenology, comorbidity, and family history in 200 individuals with body dysmorphic disorder, *Psychosomatics*, *46*(4), 317–325. © 2005 The Academy of Psychosomatic Medicine.

which means they think everything that goes on in their world somehow is related to them—in this case, to their imagined defect. This disorder can cause considerable disruption in the patient's life. Many patients with severe cases become housebound for fear of showing themselves to other people.

If this disorder seems strange to you, you are not alone. For decades, this condition, previously known as *dysmorphophobia* (literally, fear of ugliness), was thought to represent a psychotic delusional state because the affected individuals were unable to realize, even for a fleeting moment, that their ideas were irrational.

For example, in 200 cases examined by Phillips, Menard, Fay, and Weisberg (2005) and in 50 cases reported by Veale, Boocock, and colleagues (1996), between 33% and 50% of participants were convinced their imagined bodily defect was real and a reasonable source of concern. Even though this lack of insight is also present in approximately 10% of patients with OCD, it is much higher in BDD based on direct comparisons of individuals with these two disorders (Phillips et al., 2012). Is this delusional? Phillips, Menard, Pagano, Fay, and Stout (2006) looked closely at differences that may exist between delusional and nondelusional types and found nothing significant, beyond the fact that the delusional type was more severe and found in less educated patients. Other studies have supported this lack of meaningful differences between these two groups (Mancuso, Knoesen, & Castle, 2010; Phillips et al., 2010). It is also the case that these two groups both respond equally well to treatments for BDD and that the "delusional" group does not respond to drug treatments for psychotic disorders (Phillips et al., 2010). Thus, in DSM-5, patients receive a BDD diagnosis, whether they are "delusional" or not.

The prevalence of BDD is hard to estimate because by its very nature it tends to be kept secret. The best estimates, however, are that it is far more common than we had previously thought. Without some sort of treatment, it tends to run a lifelong course (Phillips, 1991; Veale, Boocock, et al., 1996). One of the patients with BDD reported by Phillips and colleagues (Phillips, McElroy, Keck, Pope, & Hudson, 1993) had suffered from her condition for 71 years, since the age of 9. If you think a college friend seems to have at least a mild version of BDD, you're probably correct. Studies suggest that as many as 70% of college students report at least some dissatisfaction with their bodies, with 4% to 28% of these appearing to meet all the criteria for the disorder (Fitts, Gibson, Redding, & Deiter, 1989; Phillips, 2005). This study was done by questionnaire, however, and may well have reflected the large percentage of students who are concerned simply with weight. Another study investigated the prevalence of BDD, specifically in an ethnically diverse sample of 566 adolescents between the ages of 14 and 19. The overall prevalence of BDD in this group was 2.2%, with adolescent girls more dissatisfied with their bodies than boys and African Americans of both genders more satisfied with their bodies than African Americans, European Americans, Asian Americans, and Hispanics (Mayville, Katz, Gipson, & Cabral, 1999; Roberts, Cash, Feingold, & Johnson, 2006). Overall, about 1% to 2% of individuals in community samples and from 2% to 13% of student samples meet criteria for BDD (Koran, Abujaoude, Large, & Serpe, 2008; Phillips, Menard, Fay, & Weisberg, 2005; Woolfolk & Allen, 2011). A somewhat higher proportion of individuals with BDD are interested in art or design compared with individuals without BDD, reflecting, perhaps, a strong interest in aesthetics or appearance (Veale, Ennis, & Lambrou, 2002).

In mental health clinics, the disorder is also uncommon because most people with BDD seek other types of health professionals, such as plastic surgeons and dermatologists. BDD is seen equally in men and women. In the larger series of 200 individuals reported by Phillips, Menard, Fay, and Weisberg (2005), 68.5% were female, but 62% of a large number of individuals with BDD in Japan were males. Generally, there are more similarities than differences between men and women with BDD, but some differences have been noted (Phillips, Menard, & Fay, 2006). Men tend to focus on body build, genitals, and thinning hair and tend to have more severe BDD. A focus on muscle defects and body building is nearly unique to men with the disorder (Pope et al., 2005). Women focus on more varied body areas and are more likely to also have an eating disorder.

Age of onset ranges from early adolescence through the 20s, peaking at age 16 and 17 (Phillips, Menard, Fay, & Weisberg, 2005; Veale, Boocock, et al., 1996; Zimmerman & Mattia, 1998). Individuals are somewhat reluctant to seek treatment. In many cases, a relative will force the issue, demanding the individual get help; this insistence may reflect the disruptiveness of the disorder for family members. Severity is also reflected in the high percentage (24%) of past suicide attempts among the 50 cases described by Veale, Boocock, and colleagues (1996); 27.5% of the 200 cases described by Phillips, Menard, Fay, and Weisberg (2005); and 21% of a group of 33 adolescents (Albertini & Phillips, 1999).

One study of 62 consecutive outpatients with BDD found that the degree of psychological stress, quality of life, and impairment were generally worse than comparable indices in patients with depression, diabetes, or a recent myocardial infarction (heart attack) on several questionnaire measures (Phillips, Dufresne, Wilkel, & Vittorio, 2000). Similar results were reported on a larger sample of 176 patients (Phillips, Menard, Fay, & Pagano, 2005). Thus, BDD is among the more serious of psychological disorders, and depression and substance misuse are common consequences of BDD (Gustad & Phillips, 2003; Phillips et al., 2010). As one might suspect, few people with this disorder get married. Further reflecting the intense suffering that accompanies this disorder, Veale (2000) collected information on 25 patients with BDD who had sought cosmetic surgery in the past. Of these, 9 patients who could not afford surgery or were turned down for other reasons had attempted by their own hand to alter their appearance dramatically, often with severe results. One example was a man preoccupied by his skin, who believed it was too "loose." He used a staple gun on both sides of his face to try to keep his skin taut. The staples fell out after 10 minutes, and he narrowly missed damaging his facial nerve. In a second example, a woman was preoccupied by her skin and the shape of her face. She filed down her teeth to alter the appearance of her jawline. Yet another woman, who was preoccupied by what she perceived as the ugliness of multiple areas of her body and desired liposuction but could not afford it, used a knife to cut her thighs and attempted to squeeze out the fat. BDD is also stubbornly chronic. In a prospective study of 183 patients, only 21% were somewhat improved over the course of a year, and 15% of that group relapsed during that year (Phillips, Pagano, Menard, & Stout, 2006).

Individuals with BDD react to what they think is a horrible or grotesque feature. Thus, the psychopathology lies in their reacting to a "deformity" that others cannot perceive. Social and cultural determinants of beauty and body image largely define what is "deformed." (Nowhere is this more evident than in the greatly varying cultural standards for body weight and shape, factors that play a major role in eating disorders, as is shown in Chapter 8.)

What can we learn about BDD from such practices of mutilation around the world? The behavior of individuals with BDD seems remarkably strange because they go *against* current cultural practices that put less emphasis on altering facial features. In other words, people who conform to the expectations of their culture do not have a disorder (as noted in Chapter 1). Nevertheless, aesthetic plastic surgery, particularly for the nose and lips, is still widely accepted and, because it is most often undertaken by the wealthy, carries an aura of elevated status. In this light, BDD may not be so strange. As with most psychopathology, its characteristic attitudes and behavior may simply be an exaggeration of normal culturally sanctioned behavior.

We know little about the etiology of BDD specifically. There is almost no information on whether it runs in families, so we can't investigate a specific genetic contribution. Similarly, there is no meaningful information on biological or psychological predisposing factors or vulnerabilities. Psychoanalytic speculations are numerous, but most center on the defensive mechanism of displacement—that is, an underlying unconscious conflict would be too anxiety provoking to admit into consciousness, so the person displaces it onto a body part.

What little evidence we do have on etiology comes from the pattern of comorbidity of BDD with OCD described earlier. The marked similarities to OCD suggest, perhaps, somewhat similar patterns of etiology. Approximately 15% of a series of 100 patients with eating disorders suffered from comorbid BDD, with their body dysmorphic concerns unrelated to weight and shape (Kollei, Schieber, de Zwaan, Svitak, & Martin, 2013).

Perhaps more significantly, there are only two treatments for BDD with any evidence of effectiveness, and these treatments are the same found effective in OCD. First, drugs that block the reuptake of serotonin, such as clomipramine (Anafranil) and fluvoxamine (Luvox), provide relief to at least some people (Hadley, Kim, Priday, & Hollander, 2006). One controlled study of the effects of drugs on BDD demonstrated that clomipramine was significantly more effective than desipramine (a drug that does not specifically block reuptake of serotonin) for the treatment of BDD, even BDD of the delusional type (Hollander et al., 1999). A second controlled study reported similar findings for fluoxetine (Prozac), with 53% showing a good response compared with 18% on placebo after 3 months (Phillips, Albertini, & Rasmussen, 2002). Intriguingly, these are the same drugs that have the strongest effect in OCD.

The second treatment—exposure and response prevention, which is the type of cognitive-behavioral therapy effective with OCD—has also been successful with BDD (McKay et al., 1997; Rosen, Reiter, & Orosan, 1995; Veale, Gournay, et al., 1996; Wilhelm, Otto, Lohr, & Deckersbach, 1999). In the Rosen and colleagues (1995) study, 82% of patients treated with this approach responded, although these patients may have been somewhat less severely affected by the disorder than in other studies (Wilhelm et al., 1999; Williams, Hadjistavropoulos, & Sharpe, 2006). Furthermore, patients with BDD and OCD have similar rates of response to these treatments (Saxena et al., 2001; Williams et al., 2006). As with OCD, cognitive-behavioral therapy tends to produce better and longer lasting outcomes compared to medication alone (Buhlmann, Reese, Renaud, & Wilhelm, 2008). But CBT is not as readily available as drugs.

Another interesting lead on causes of BDD comes from cross-cultural explorations of similar disorders. You may remember reading about the Japanese variant of social anxiety disorder, *taijin kyofusho*, in the section on Social Anxiety Disorder (Social Phobia) earlier in this chapter. Individuals with this disorder may believe they have horrendous bad breath or body odor and thus avoid social interaction. But people with *taijin kyofusho* also have all the other characteristics of social anxiety disorder. Patients who would be diagnosed with BDD in our culture might simply be considered to have severe social anxiety in Japan and Korea. Possibly, then, social anxiety is fundamentally related to BDD, a connection that would give us further hints on the nature of the disorder. Indeed, a study of BDD in Western countries indicates that concerns relating to perceived negative evaluation of their appearance by others is every bit as important as self-evaluation of the imagined defects in appearance (Anson, Veale, & de Silva, 2012). Studies of comorbidity indicate that social anxiety

Thierry Falise/LightRocket/Getty Images

In various cultures, a child's head or face is manipulated to produce desirable features, as in the addition of rings to lengthen the necks of these Burmese girls.

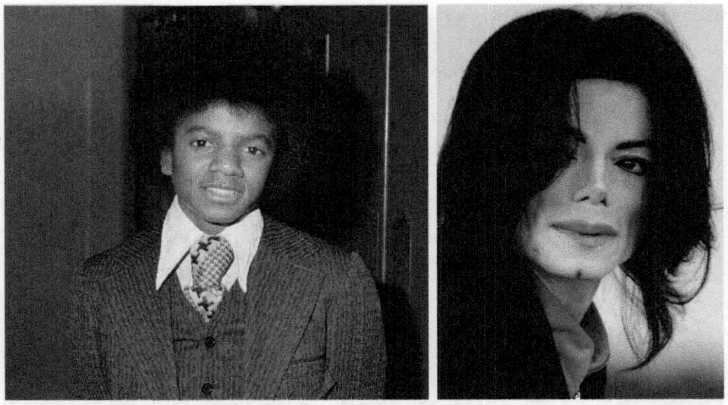

Fotos International/Hulton Archive/Getty Images

Mark Mainz/Getty Images

Michael Jackson as a child and as an adult. Many people alter their features through surgery. However, people with body dysmorphic disorder are seldom satisfied with the results.

disorder, along with OCD, is also commonly found in people with BDD (Fang & Hofmann, 2010; Phillips & Stout, 2006).

Plastic Surgery and Other Medical Treatments

Patients with BDD believe they are physically deformed in some way and go to medical doctors to attempt to correct their deficits (Woolfolk & Allen, 2011). Phillips, Grant, Siniscalchi, and Albertini (2001) studied the treatments sought by 289 patients with BDD, including 39 children or adolescents, and found that fully 76.4% had sought this type of treatment and 66% were receiving it. Dermatology (skin) treatment was the most often received (45.2%), followed by plastic surgery (23.2%). Looking at it another way, in one study of 268 patients seeking care from a dermatologist, 11.9% met criteria for BDD (Phillips et al., 2000).

Because the concerns of people with BDD involve mostly the face or head, it is not surprising that the disorder is big business for the plastic surgery profession—but it is bad business. These patients do not benefit from surgery and may return for additional surgery or, on occasion, file malpractice lawsuits. Investigators estimate that as many as 8% to 25% of all patients who request plastic surgery may have BDD (Barnard, 2000; Crerand et al., 2004). The most common procedures are rhinoplasties (nose jobs), facelifts, eyebrow elevations, liposuction, breast augmentation, and surgery to alter the jawline. Between 2000 and 2012, according to the American Society of Plastic Surgeons (2012), the total number of cosmetic procedures increased 98%. The problem is that surgery on the proportion of these people with BDD seldom produces the desired results. These individuals return for additional surgery on the same defect or concentrate on some new defect. Phillips, Menard, Fay, and Pagano (2005) report that 81% of 50 individuals seeking surgery or similar medical consults were dissatisfied with the result. In 88% of a large group of people with BDD seeking medical rather than psychological treatment, the severity of the disorder and accompanying distress either did not change or *increased* after surgery. Similar discouraging or negative results are evident from other forms of medical treatment, such as skin treatments (Phillips et al., 2001). It is important that plastic surgeons screen out these patients; many do so by collaborating with medically trained psychologists (Pruzinsky, 1988).

Other Obsessive-Compulsive and Related Disorders

Hoarding Disorder

Several years ago, a group of patients came to the attention of specialty clinics because they compulsively hoard things, fearing that if they throw something away, even a 10-year-old newspaper, they then might urgently need it. At first, the specialty clinics assumed that this was just an unusual variant of OCD, but it soon became apparent that it was a major problem in itself, as is obvious to anyone who has seen the spate of television programs showing individuals with this disorder in their almost unlivable homes. Estimates of prevalence range between 2% and 5% of the population, which is twice as high as the prevalence of OCD, with nearly equal numbers of men and women, and is found worldwide (Frost, Steketee, & Tolin, 2012). The three major characteristics of this problem are excessive acquisition of things, difficulty discarding anything, and living with excessive clutter under conditions best characterized as gross disorganization (Frost & Rasmussen, 2012; Grisham & Barlow, 2005; Steketee & Frost, 2007a, 2007b). Maladaptive cognitions and dysfunctional attachments to people and possessions jointly seem to underlie saving behaviors characteristic of this disorder (Mathes et al., 2020). It is not uncommon for some patients' houses and yards to come to the attention of public health authorities (Tolin, 2011). One patient's house and yard was condemned, because junk was piled so high it was both unsightly and a fire hazard. Among her hoard was a 20-year collection of used sanitary napkins. Although only a tiny percentage of fires in residences occur in the homes of individuals who hoard, these fires account for 24% of all fire-related fatalities (Frost et al., 2012).

Basically, these individuals usually begin acquiring things during their teenage years and often experience great pleasure,

WR Publishing/Alamy Stock Photo

People with obsessive-compulsive hoarding are so afraid they may throw something important away that clutter piles up in their homes.

even euphoria, from shopping or otherwise collecting various items. Shopping or collecting things may be a response to feeling down or depressed and is sometimes called, facetiously, "retail therapy." But unlike most people who like to shop or collect, these individuals then experience strong anxiety and distress about throwing anything away because everything has either some potential use or sentimental value in their minds or becomes an extension of their own identity. Their homes or apartments may become almost impossible to live in. Most of these individuals don't consider that they have a problem until family members or authorities insist that they seek help. As with OCD, the extent of insight that the patients have about the problematic status of their hoarding problem is specified when making the diagnosis. The average age when these people come for treatment is approximately 50, after many years of hoarding (Grisham, Frost, Steketee, Kim, & Hood, 2006; Grisham, Norberg, & Certoma, 2012). Often they live alone (Frost & Rasmussen, 2012; Mataix-Cols et al., 2010). Careful analysis of what we know about hoarding suggests it has similarities and differences with both OCD and impulse control disorders. Therefore, it is best considered a separate disorder and now appears as such in the DSM-5.

For example, OCD tends to wax and wane, whereas hoarding behavior can begin early in life and get worse with each passing decade (Ayers, Saxena, Golshan, & Wetherell, 2010). The cognitive and emotional characteristics associated with hoarding alluded to above include extraordinarily strong emotional attachment to possessions, an exaggerated desire for control over possessions, and marked deficits in deciding when a possession is worth keeping or not (all possessions are believed to be equally valuable). One study examined the neural mechanisms of decision-making about whether to keep or discard possessions among individuals with hoarding disorder compared with individuals with OCD without hoarding. The study found specific differences in areas of the brain related to problems identifying the emotional significance of an object and generating the appropriate emotional response (Tolin et al., 2012).

People who hoard animals comprise a separate group that is now being investigated more closely. Occasionally, articles appear in newspapers describing homes occupied by one owner, usually a middle-aged or elderly woman, and 30 or more animals, often cats. Occasionally some of the cats will be dead, either lying on the floor out in the open or stored in the freezer. In addition to owning an unusually large number of animals, animal hoarders are characterized by the inability to care for the animals or provide suitable living quarters, which results in threats to health and safety due to unsanitary conditions associated with accumulated animal waste (Frost, Patronek, & Rosenfield, 2011). One study compared individuals who met criteria for animal hoarding with a small group of nonhoarding controls who owned large number of animals (Steketee et al., 2011). Individuals in both groups were mostly middle-aged White women. While both groups expressed strong caretaking roles and a particularly intense love and attachment to animals, the hoarding group was characterized by attribution of human characteristics to their animals, the presence of more dysfunctional current relationships (with other people), and significantly greater mental health concerns. Much like other individuals with hoarding, animal hoarders typically have little or no realization that they have a problem, despite often living in unsanitary conditions with dead and sick animals.

CBT is a promising treatment for hoarding disorder (Tolin, Frost, Steketee, & Muroff, 2015). These treatments developed at our clinic teach people to assign different values to objects and to reduce anxiety about throwing away items that are somewhat less valued (Grisham et al., 2012; Steketee & Frost, 2007a). Preliminary results are promising, but results are more modest than those achieved with OCD. Also, more information on long-term effects of these treatments is needed. Little or nothing is known about effective interventions for individuals who hoard animals.

Trichotillomania (Hair Pulling Disorder) and Excoriation (Skin Picking Disorder)

The urge to pull out one's own hair from anywhere on the body, including the scalp, eyebrows, and arms, is referred to as **trichotillomania**. This behavior results in noticeable hair loss, distress, and significant social impairments. This disorder can often have severe social consequences, and, as a result, those affected can go to great lengths to conceal their behavior (Grant, Stein, Woods, & Keuthen, 2012; Lochner et al., 2012). Compulsive hair pulling is more common than once believed and is observed in between 1% and 5% of college students, with females reporting the problem more than males (Scott, Hilty, & Brook, 2003). There may be some genetic influence on trichotillomania, with one study finding a unique genetic mutation in a small number of people (Zuchner et al., 2006).

Excoriation (skin picking disorder) is characterized, as the label implies, by repetitive and compulsive picking of the skin, leading to tissue damage (Grant et al., 2012). Many people pick their skin on occasion without any serious damage to their skin or any distress or impairment, but for somewhere between 1% and 5% of the population, noticeable damage to skin occurs, sometimes requiring medical attention. There can be significant embarrassment, distress, and impairment in terms of social and work functioning. In one case, a young woman spent 2 to 3 hours a day picking her skin, resulting in numerous scabs, scars, and open wounds on her face. As a result, she would often be late for work or unable to work if the open wounds were too bad. She had not socialized with friends for over a year (Grant et al., 2012). Excoriation is also largely a disorder observed in women.

Prior to DSM-5, both disorders were classified under impulse control disorders, but it has been established that these disorders often co-occur with obsessive-compulsive disorder and body dysmorphic disorder, as well as with each other (Grant et al., 2012; Odlaug & Grant, 2012). For this reason, all of these disorders, which share repetitive and compulsive behaviors, are now grouped together under obsessive-compulsive and related disorders in DSM-5. Nevertheless, significant differences exist. For example, individuals with BDD may pick at their skin occasionally to improve their appearance, which is not the case for individuals with skin picking disorder.

It is generally assumed that the repetitive behaviors of hair pulling and skin picking function to relieve stress or tension. While this seems to be the case for many patients, a substantial number of individuals do not engage in this behavior to relieve tension and do not evidence tension relief. For this reason, diagnostic criteria referring to tension relief, present in DSM-IV, have been removed in DSM-5 (Nock, Cha, & Dour, 2011).

Psychological treatments, particularly an approach called "habit reversal training," has the most evidence for success with these two disorders. In this treatment, patients are carefully taught to be more aware of their repetitive behavior, particularly as it is just about to begin, and to then substitute a different behavior, such as chewing gum, applying a soothing lotion to the skin, or some other reasonably pleasurable but harmless behavior. Results may be evident in as little as four sessions, but the procedure requires teamwork between the patient and therapist and close monitoring of the behavior throughout the day (Nock et al., 2011). Drug treatments, mostly serotonin-specific reuptake inhibitors, hold some promise, particularly for trichotillomania (Chamberlain, Menzies, Sahakian, & Fineberg, 2007), but the results have been mixed with excoriation (Grant et al., 2012).

Concept Check 5.6

Fill in the blanks to form facts about OCD.

1. ____________ are intrusive and nonsensical thoughts, images, or urges an individual tries to eliminate or suppress.
2. The practices of washing, counting, and checking to suppress obsessions and provide relief are called ____________.
3. The lifetime prevalence of OCD is approximately ____________, or even lower.
4. ____________ is a radical treatment for OCD involving a surgical lesion to the cingulate bundle.

Summary

The Complexity of Anxiety Disorders

- Anxiety is a future-oriented state characterized by negative affect in which a person focuses on the possibility of uncontrollable danger or misfortune. In contrast, fear is a present-oriented state characterized by strong escapist tendencies and a surge in the sympathetic branch of the autonomic nervous system in response to current danger.
- A panic attack represents the alarm response of real fear, but there is no actual danger.
- Panic attacks may be (1) unexpected (without warning) or (2) expected (always occurring in a specific situation). Panic and anxiety combine to create different anxiety and related disorders. Several disorders are grouped under the heading anxiety disorders.

Generalized Anxiety Disorder

- In generalized anxiety disorder (GAD), anxiety focuses on minor, everyday events and not on one major worry or concern.
- Both genetic and psychological vulnerabilities seem to contribute to the development of GAD.
- Although drug and psychological treatments may be effective in the short term, drug treatments are no more effective in the long term than placebo treatments. Successful treatment may help individuals with GAD focus on what is really threatening to them in their lives.

Panic Disorder and Agoraphobia

- In panic disorder, which may or may not be accompanied by agoraphobia (a fear and avoidance of situations considered to be "unsafe"), anxiety is focused on the next panic attack. For some people, agoraphobia develops in the absence of panic attacks or panic-like symptoms.

- We all have some genetic vulnerability to stress, and many of us have had a neurobiological overreaction to some stressful event—that is, a panic attack. Individuals who develop panic disorder and then develop anxiety over the possibility of having another panic attack.
- Both drug and psychological treatments have proved successful in the treatment of panic disorder. One psychological method, panic control treatment, concentrates on exposing patients to clusters of sensations that remind them of their panic attacks. For agoraphobia, therapeutically supervised exposure to feared situations is most effective.

Specific Phobia

- In phobic disorders, the individual avoids situations that produce severe anxiety, panic, or both. In specific phobia, the fear is focused on a particular object or situation.
- Phobias can be acquired by experiencing some traumatic event; they can also be learned vicariously or even be taught.
- Treatment of phobias is rather straightforward, with a focus on structured and consistent exposure-based exercises.

Social Anxiety Disorder (Social Phobia)

- Social anxiety disorder is a fear of being around others, particularly in situations that call for some kind of "performance" in front of other people.
- Although the causes of social anxiety disorder are similar to those of specific phobias, treatment has a different focus that includes rehearsing or role-playing socially phobic situations. In addition, drug treatments have been effective.
- Several disorders are also grouped under the heading trauma- and stressor-related disorders.

Posttraumatic Stress Disorder

- Posttraumatic stress disorder (PTSD) focuses on avoiding thoughts or images of past traumatic experiences.
- The precipitating cause of PTSD is obvious—a traumatic experience. But mere exposure to trauma is not enough. The intensity of the experience seems to be a factor in whether an individual develops PTSD; biological vulnerabilities, as well as social and cultural factors, appear to play a role as well.
- Treatment involves reexposing the victim to the trauma and reestablishing a sense of safety to overcome the debilitating effects of PTSD.

Prolonged Grief Disorder

- Persistent grief after loss of a loved one lasting a year or more (six months or more in children) accompanied by intense preoccupation and longing for the deceased and an inability to move on with one's life.
- Individuals prone to anxiety or depression generally may experience prolonged and impairing complications, particularly after an unexpected loss.
- Effective treatments are similar to those for PTSD but are adapted to the individual circumstances characterizing the loss.

Adjustment Disorders

- Adjustment disorder is the development of anxiety or depression in response to stressful, but not traumatic, life events.
- Individuals prone to anxiety or depression generally may experience increases during stressful life events.

Attachment Disorders

- Children experiencing inadequate, abusive, or absent caregiving in early childhood fail to develop normal attachment relationships with caregivers, resulting in two different disorders.
- Reactive attachment disorder describes children who are inhibited and emotionally withdrawn and unable to form attachment with caregivers.
- Disinhibited social engagement disorder describes children who inappropriately approach all strangers, behaving as if they had always had strong loving relationships with them.
- Several disorders are grouped under the heading obsessive-compulsive and related disorders.

Obsessive-Compulsive Disorder

- Obsessive-compulsive disorder (OCD) focuses on avoiding frightening or repulsive intrusive thoughts (obsessions) or neutralizing these thoughts through the use of ritualistic behavior (compulsions).
- As with all anxiety disorders, biological and psychological vulnerabilities seem to be involved in the development of OCD.
- Drug treatment seems to be only modestly successful in treating OCD. The most effective treatment approach is a psychological treatment called exposure and ritual prevention (ERP).

Body Dysmorphic Disorder

- In body dysmorphic disorder (BDD), a person who looks normal is obsessively preoccupied with some imagined defect in appearance (imagined ugliness). These patients typically have more insight into their problem and may seek out plastic surgery as a remedy. Psychological treatment approaches are also similar to those for OCD and are approximately equally successful.

Hoarding Disorder

- Hoarding disorder is characterized by excessive acquisition of things, difficulty discarding anything, and living with excessive clutter under conditions best characterized as gross disorganization.
- Treatment approaches are similar to those for OCD but are less successful.

Trichotillomania (Hair Pulling Disorder) and Excoriation (Skin Picking Disorder)

- Repetitive and compulsive hair pulling resulting in significant noticeable loss of hair or repetitive and compulsive picking of the skin leading to tissue damage characterize trichotillomania and excoriation disorders respectively.

Key Terms

anxiety, 125
fear, 126
panic, 126
panic attack, 126
behavioral inhibition system (BIS), 128
fight/flight system (FFS), 128
generalized anxiety disorder (GAD), 132
panic disorder (PD), 137
agoraphobia, 137
panic control treatment (PCT), 143
specific phobia, 145
blood–injection–injury phobia, 146
situational phobia, 146
natural environment phobia, 147
animal phobia, 147
separation anxiety disorder, 151
social anxiety disorder (SAD), 151
social phobia, 151
posttraumatic stress disorder (PTSD), 157
acute stress disorder, 158
prolonged grief disorder (PGD), 164
adjustment disorders, 164
attachment disorders, 165
reactive attachment disorder, 165
disinhibited social engagement disorder, 165
obsessive-compulsive disorder (OCD), 165
obsessions, 165
compulsions, 165
body dysmorphic disorder (BDD), 169
trichotillomania, 174
excoriation, 175

Answers to Concept Checks

5.1
1. b; **2.** c; **3.** e, d; **4.** a; **5.** f

5.2
1. T; **2.** F (more gradual); **3.** T; **4.** F; **5.** T

5.3
1. F (panic attacks occur unexpectedly in panic disorder, even in "safe" situations); **2.** F (3.5%); **3.** T; **4.** T

5.4
1. d; **2.** e; **3.** c; **4.** f; **5.** a; **6.** d; **7.** c

5.5
1. b; **2.** a; **3.** c

5.6
1. obsessions; **2.** compulsions; **3.** 1.6%; **4.** psychosurgery

Exploring Anxiety, Trauma- and Stressor-Related,

People with anxiety disorders:

- Feel overwhelming tension, apprehension, or fear when there is no actual danger
- May take extreme action to avoid the source of their anxiety

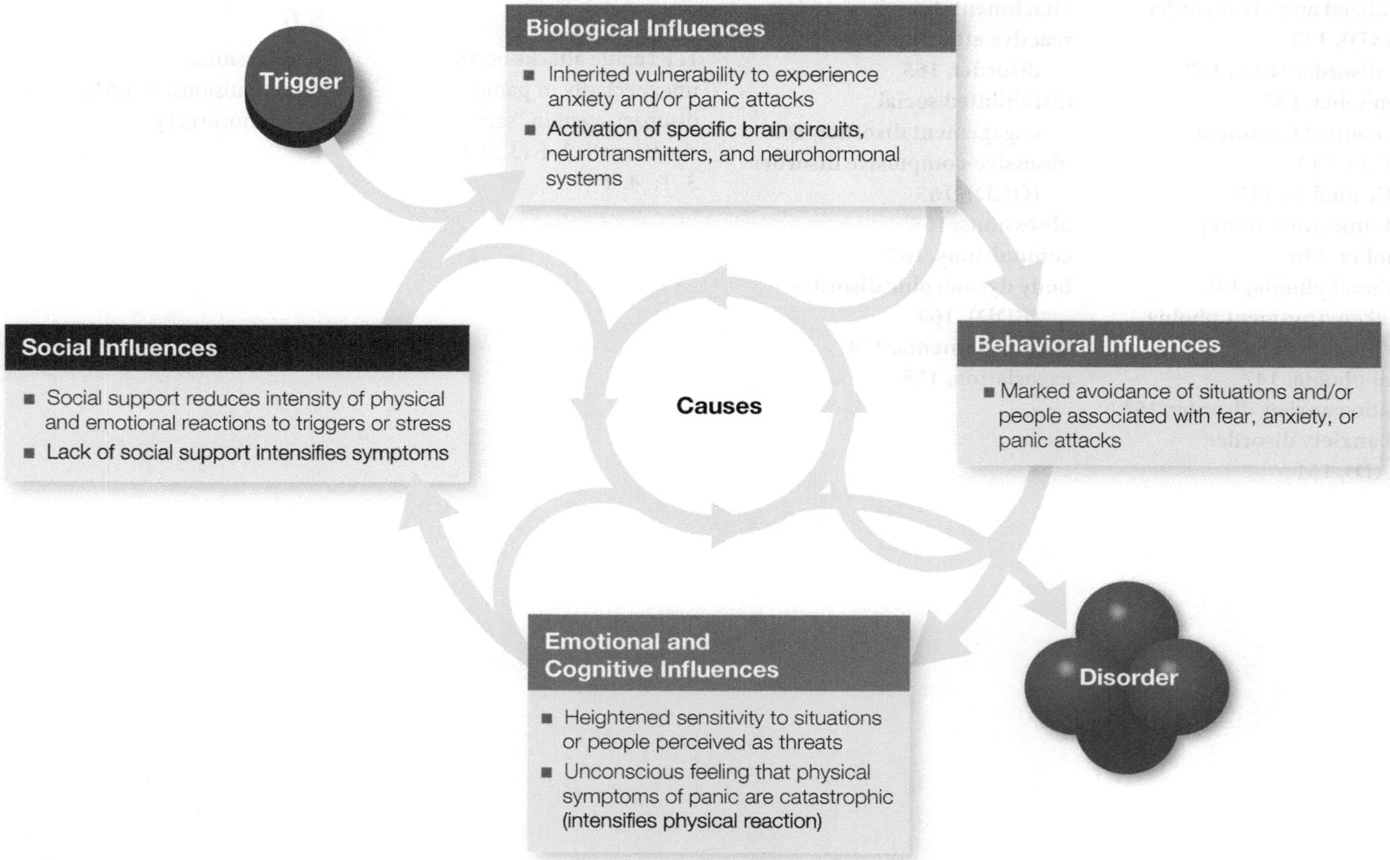

TREATMENT FOR ANXIETY DISORDERS

Cognitive-Behavioral Therapy

- Systematic exposure to anxiety-provoking situations or thoughts
- Learning to substitute positive behaviors and thoughts for negative ones
- Learning new coping skills: relaxation exercises, controlled breathing, etc.

Drug Treatment

- Reduces the symptoms of anxiety disorders by influencing brain chemistry
  —antidepressants (Tofranil, Paxil, Effexor)
  —benzodiazepines (Xanax, Klonopin)

Other Treatments

- Managing stress through a healthy lifestyle: rest, exercise, nutrition, social support, and moderate alcohol or other drug intake

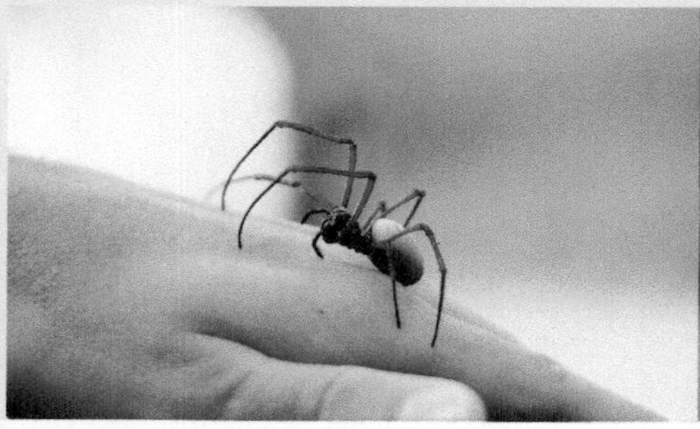
Elena Nasledova/Shutterstock.com

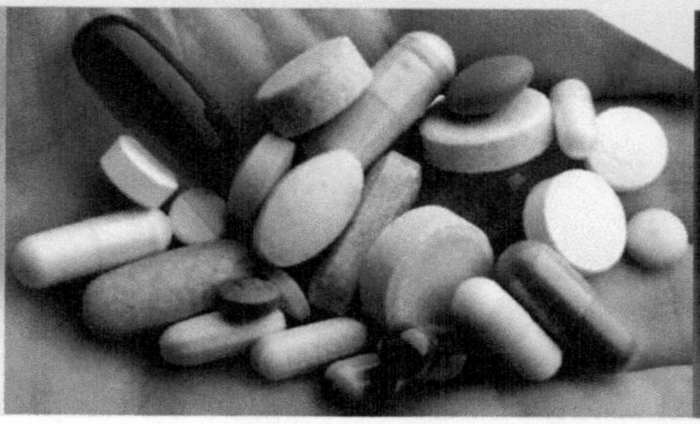
PhotoDisc/Getty Images

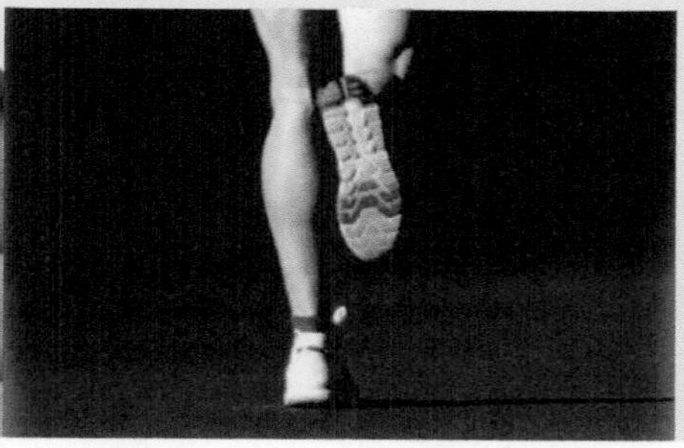
PhotoDisc/Getty Images

and Obsessive-Compulsive and Related Disorders

TYPES OF DISORDERS

Panic

People with panic disorders have had one or more panic attacks and are anxious and fearful about having future attacks.

PhotoDisc/Getty Images

What is a panic attack?

A person having a panic attack feels:

- Apprehension leading to intense fear
- Sensation of "going crazy" or of losing control
- Physical signs of distress: racing heartbeat, rapid breathing, dizziness, nausea, or sensation of heart attack or imminent death

When/why do panic attacks occur?

Panic attacks can be:

- Expected: Always occurring in a specific situation
- Unexpected: Occurring without warning

Phobias

People with phobias avoid situations that produce severe anxiety and/or panic. There are three main types:

PhotoDisc/Getty Images

Agoraphobia

- Fear and avoidance of situations, people, or places where it would be unsafe to have a panic attack: malls, grocery stores, buses, planes, tunnels, etc.
- In the extreme, inability to leave the house or even a specific room
- Begins after a panic attack but can continue for years even if no other attacks occur

Specific Phobia

- Fear of specific object or situation that triggers attack: heights, closed spaces, insects, snakes, or flying
- Develops from personal or vicarious experience of traumatic event with the triggering object or situation or from misinformation

Social Anxiety Disorder (social phobia)

- Fear of being called for some kind of "performance" that may be judged: speaking in public, using a public restroom (for males), or generally interacting with people

Other Types

Eyewire/Getty Images

Generalized Anxiety

- Uncontrollable unproductive worrying about everyday events
- Feeling impending catastrophe even after successes
- Inability to stop the worry–anxiety cycle: for example, Tanisha's fear of failure about school relationships and health even though everything seemed fine
- Physical symptoms of muscle tension

Posttraumatic Stress

- Fear of reexperiencing a traumatic event: rape, war, life-threatening situation, etc.
- Nightmares or flashbacks (of the traumatic event)
- Avoidance of the intense feelings of the event through emotional numbing

Obsessive-Compulsive

- Fear of unwanted and intrusive thoughts (obsessions)
- Repeated ritualistic actions or thoughts (compulsions) designed to neutralize the unwanted thoughts: for example, Brandon's attempts to suppress "dangerous" thoughts about sex, aggression, and religion with compulsive washing and cleaning rituals

6 Somatic Symptom and Related Disorders and Dissociative Disorders

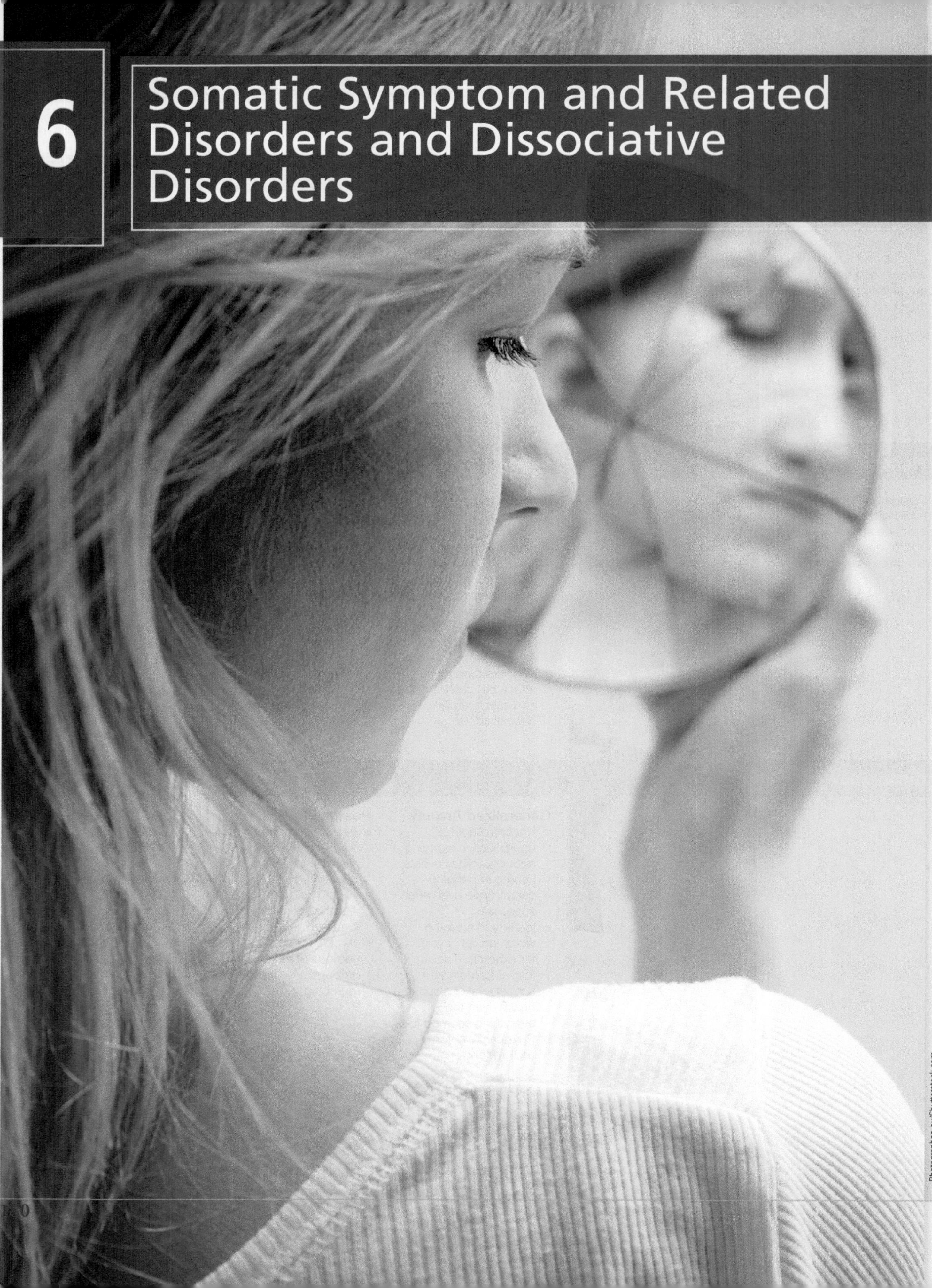

Photographee.eu/Shutterstock.com

Learning Objectives

LO6.1 Describe the main features of somatic symptom and related disorders.

LO6.2 Distinguish between somatic symptom disorder and illness anxiety disorder in terms of symptoms according to the DSM-5.

LO6.3 Differentiate the symptoms of depersonalization-derealization disorder and dissociative amnesia from those of dissociative identity disorder.

LO6.4 Discuss how treatment for trauma addresses the symptoms of dissociative disorders.

Heave you ever had a medical illness? What was your emotional response to it? Were you stressed, depressed, or anxious? Did you spend a lot of time researching the illness on the internet and worrying about it? As the illness subsided or as you learned some ways to cope with it, your negative feelings around the illness and the symptoms probably became less distressing. But imagine what it would be like if these physical symptoms kept bothering you a lot. For some people, these symptoms consume their lives, and their thoughts, feelings, and behaviors related to somatic symptoms are disproportionate, whether or not they are related to a medically diagnosed illness. This is the defining feature of the DSM-5 group of somatic symptom and related disorders. People affected by this problem show a disproportionate response lasting at least 6 months. They sometimes exaggerate the possible cause or consequences of fairly minor somatic symptoms, become very anxious and constantly scan for information about an illness, or avoid situations and behaviors they believe are related to illness. In some cases, the medical cause of the presenting physical symptoms is known, but the emotional distress or level of impairment in response to this symptom is clearly excessive and may even make the condition worse (Kube, Rosenkrantz, Rief, & Barsky, 2020).

Have you ever felt "detached" from yourself or your surroundings? ("This isn't really me," or "That doesn't really look like my hand," or "There's something unreal about this place.") During these experiences, some people feel as if they are dreaming. These mild sensations that most people experience occasionally are slight alterations, or detachments, in consciousness or identity called *dissociation* or *dissociative experiences*, but they are perfectly normal. For a few people, these experiences are so intense and extreme that they lose their identity entirely and assume a new one, or they lose their memory or sense of reality and are unable to function. We discuss several types of **dissociative disorders** in the second half of this chapter.

Somatic symptom and related disorders and dissociative disorders are strongly linked historically, and evidence indicates they share common features (Cernis, Evans, Ehlers, & Freeman, 2020; Lynn et al., 2019). They used to be categorized under one general heading, "hysterical neurosis." You may remember (from Chapter 1) that the term *hysteria*—which dates back to the Greek physician Hippocrates and the Egyptians before him—suggests that the cause of these disorders, which were thought to occur primarily in women, can be traced to a "wandering uterus." But the term *hysterical* came to refer more generally to physical symptoms without known organic cause or to dramatic or "histrionic" behavior thought to be characteristic of women. Sigmund Freud (1894–1962) suggested that in a condition called *conversion hysteria,* unexplained physical symptoms indicated the conversion of unconscious emotional conflicts into a more acceptable form. The historical term *conversion* remains with us (without the theoretical implications); however, the prejudicial and stigmatizing term *hysterical* is no longer used.

The term *neurosis,* as defined in psychoanalytic theory, suggested a specific cause for certain disorders. Specifically, neurotic disorders resulted from underlying unconscious conflicts, anxiety that resulted from those conflicts, and the implementation of ego defense mechanisms. *Neurosis* was eliminated from the diagnostic system in 1980 because it was too vague, applying to almost all nonpsychotic disorders, and because it implied a specific but unproven cause for these disorders.

Somatic symptom disorders and dissociative disorders are not well understood, but they have intrigued psychopathologists and the public for centuries. A fuller understanding provides a rich perspective on the extent to which normal, everyday traits found in all of us can evolve into distorted, strange, and incapacitating disorders.

Somatic Symptom and Related Disorders

DSM-5 lists five basic somatic symptom and related disorders: somatic symptom disorder, illness anxiety disorder, psychological factors affecting medical condition, conversion disorder, and factitious disorder. In each, individuals are pathologically concerned with the functioning of their bodies.

Somatic Symptom Disorder

In 1859, Pierre Briquet, a French physician, described patients who came to see him with seemingly endless lists of somatic complaints for which he could find no medical basis (American Psychiatric Association, 1980). Despite his negative findings, patients returned shortly with either the same complaints or new lists containing slight variations. For many years, this disorder was called *Briquet's syndrome,* but now would be considered **somatic symptom disorder**. Consider the case of Jada.

Jada met the DSM-5 diagnostic criteria for somatic symptom disorder. She was severely impaired and had suffered in the past from symptoms of paralysis (which we refer to as a conversion symptom. People with somatic symptom disorder do not always feel the urgency to take action, but they may often feel weak and ill or avoid exercising, thinking it will make them worse (Henningsen et al., 2018). All of us make likelihood assumptions about having or getting some form of illness if we feel experience certain symptoms in our body. People with somatic symptom disorder make consistent prediction errors about this relationship with major consequences (van den Bergh et al., 2017).

Jada... Full-Time Patient

Jada, an intelligent woman in her 30s, came to our clinic looking distressed and pained. As she sat down, she noted that coming into the office was difficult for her because she had trouble breathing and considerable swelling in the joints of her legs and arms. She was also in some pain from chronic urinary tract infections and might have to leave at any moment to go to the restroom, but she was extremely happy she had kept the appointment. At least she was seeing someone who could help alleviate her considerable suffering. She said she knew we would have to go through a detailed initial interview, but she had something that might save time. At this point, she pulled out several sheets of paper and handed them over. One section, some five pages long, described her contacts with the health-care system for *major difficulties only*. Times, dates, potential diagnoses, and days hospitalized were noted. The second section, one-and-a-half single-spaced pages, consisted of a list of all medications she had taken for various complaints.

Jada felt she had any one of a number of chronic infections that nobody could properly diagnose. She had begun to have these problems in her teenage years. She often discussed her symptoms and fears with doctors and clergy. Drawn to hospitals and medical clinics, she had entered nursing school after high school. During hospital training, however, she noticed her physical condition deteriorating rapidly: She seemed to pick up the diseases she was learning about. A series of stressful emotional events resulted in her leaving nursing school.

After developing unexplained paralysis in her legs, Jada was admitted to a psychiatric hospital, and after a year she regained her ability to walk. On discharge, she obtained disability status, which freed her from having to work full time, and she volunteered at the local hospital. With her chronic but fluctuating incapacitation, on some days she could go in, and on some days she could not. She was currently seeing a family practitioner and six specialists, who monitored various aspects of her physical condition. She was also seeing two ministers for pastoral counseling.

Jada's entire life revolved around her symptoms. She once told her therapist that her symptoms were her identity: Without them, she would not know who she was. By this, she meant that she would not know how to relate to people except in the context of discussing her symptoms much as other people might talk about their day at the office or their kids' accomplishments at school. Her few friends who were not health-care professionals had the patience to relate to her sympathetically, through the veil of her symptoms, and she thought of them as friends because they "understood" her suffering. Jada's case is an extreme example of adopting the "sick role" described earlier.

Another example of a somatic symptom disorder can be severe pain in which psychological factors play a major role in maintaining or exacerbating the pain whether there is a clear physical reason for the pain or not. Consider the case of the medical student.

The Medical Student... Temporary Pain

During her first clinical rotation, a 25-year-old third-year medical student in excellent health was seen at her student health service for intermittent abdominal pain of several weeks' duration. The student claimed no past history of similar pain. Physical examination revealed no physical problems, but she told the physician that she had recently separated from her husband. The student was referred to the health service psychiatrist. No other psychiatric problems were found. She was taught relaxation techniques and given supportive therapy to help her cope with her current stressful situation. The student's pain subsequently disappeared, and she successfully completed medical school.

Once again, the important factor in this condition is not that the physical symptom, in this case pain, has or does not have a clear medical cause or not, but rather that psychological or behavioral factors, particularly anxiety and distress, are compounding the severity and impairment associated with the physical symptoms. The new emphasis in DSM-5 on the psychological symptoms in these disorders highlights the psychological experiences of anxiety and distress focused on the somatic symptoms as the most important target for treatment (Tomenson et al., 2012; Voigt et al., 2012). But an important feature of these physical symptoms, such as pain, is that it is real and it hurts whether there are clear physical reasons for pain or not (Dersh, Polatin, & Gatchel, 2002; Asmundson & Carleton, 2009).

Illness Anxiety Disorder

Illness anxiety disorder was formerly known as *hypochondriasis*. Although the terms *hypochondriasis* and *hypochondriac* are still widely used among the public, they are no longer part of the DSM-5. Still, we will use *hypochondriasis* when we describe studies that examined this DSM-IV category. In illness anxiety disorder as we know it today, physical symptoms are either not experienced at the present time or are very mild, but severe anxiety is focused on the possibility of having or developing a serious disease. If one or more physical symptoms are relatively severe and are associated with anxiety and distress, the diagnosis would be somatic symptom disorder. Using DSM-5 criteria, only about 20% of patients who used to meet the diagnostic criteria for DSM-IV hypochondriasis now meet criteria for illness anxiety disorder, in part because they do not complain about having any somatic symptoms at all despite experiencing serious anxiety about contracting an illness (Rief & Martin, 2014). This justified the creation of the illness anxiety disorder category to cover that 20% segment who does not report symptoms. Once again, in illness anxiety disorder the concern is primarily with the idea of being sick instead of the physical symptom itself (Scarella, Boland, & Barsky, 2019; Lebel et al., 2020). And the threat seems so real that reassurance from physicians does not seem to help. Consider the case of Leinani.

DSM 5 Table 6.1 Diagnostic Criteria for Somatic Symptom Disorder

A. One or more somatic symptoms that are distressing or result in significant disruption of daily life.

B. Excessive thoughts, feelings, or behaviors related to the somatic symptoms or associated health concerns as manifested by at least one of the following:

1. Disproportionate and persistent thoughts about the seriousness of one's symptoms.
2. Persistently high level of anxiety about health or symptoms.
3. Excessive time and energy devoted to these symptoms or health concerns.

C. Although any one symptom may not be continuously present, the state of being symptomatic is persistent (typically more than 6 months).

Specify if:

With predominant pain (previously pain disorder): This specifier is for individuals whose somatic complaints predominantly involve pain.

Specify if:

Persistent: A persistent course is characterized by severe symptoms, marked impairment, and long duration (more than 6 months).

Specify current severity:

Mild: Only one of the symptoms in Criterion B is fulfilled.

Moderate: Two or more of the symptoms specified in Criterion B is fulfilled.

Severe: Two or more of the symptoms specified in Criterion B are fulfilled, plus there are multiple somatic complaints (or one very severe somatic symptom).

American Psychiatric Association. (2022). *Diagnostic and statistical manual of mental disorders* (5th ed., Text Revision).

Clinical Description

Do you notice any differences between Jada, who presented with somatic symptom disorder, and Leinani, who presented with illness anxiety disorder? There is certainly a lot of overlap (Creed & Barsky, 2004; Leibbrand, Hiller, & Fichter, 2000), but Leinani was somewhat less concerned with any specific physical symptom and more worried about the idea that she was either ill or developing an illness. Leinani's problems are fairly typical of illness anxiety disorder.

Research indicates that illness anxiety disorder and somatic symptom disorder share many features with the anxiety and mood disorders, particularly panic disorder (Craske et al., 1996; Creed & Barsky, 2004), including similar age of onset, personality characteristics, and patterns of familial aggregation (running in families). Indeed, anxiety and mood disorders are often comorbid with somatic symptom disorders; that is, if individuals with somatic symptom disorders have additional diagnoses, these most likely are anxiety or mood disorders (Creed & Barsky, 2004; Rief, Hiller, & Margraf, 1998; Simon, Gureje, & Fullerton, 2001; Wollburg, Voigt, Braukhaus, Herzog, & Lowe, 2013).

Leinani... Invisibly Ill

Leinani was married at 21 and looked forward to a new life. As one of many children in a lower-middle-class household, she felt weak and somewhat neglected and suffered from low self-esteem. An older stepbrother berated and belittled her when he was drunk. Her mother and stepfather refused to listen to her or believe her complaints. But she believed that marriage would solve everything; she was finally someone special. Unfortunately, it didn't work out that way. She soon discovered her husband was continuing an affair with an old girlfriend.

Three years after her wedding, Leinani came to our clinic complaining of anxiety and stress. She was working part-time as a waitress and found her job extremely stressful. Although to the best of her knowledge her husband had stopped seeing his former girlfriend, she had trouble getting the affair out of her mind.

Although Leinani complained initially of anxiety and stress, it soon became clear that her major concerns were about her health. Any time she experienced minor physical symptoms such as breathlessness or a headache, she was afraid she had a serious illness. A headache indicated a brain tumor. Breathlessness was an impending heart attack. Other sensations were quickly elaborated into the possibility of AIDS or cancer. Leinani was afraid to go to sleep at night for fear that she would stop breathing. She avoided exercise, drinking, and even laughing because the resulting sensations upset her. Public restrooms and, on occasion, public telephones were feared as sources of infection.

The major trigger of uncontrollable anxiety and fear was the news in the newspaper and on television. Each time an article or show appeared on the "disease of the month," Leinani found herself irresistibly drawn into it, intently noting symptoms that were part of the disease. For days afterward, she was vigilant, looking for the symptoms in herself and others and often noticing some physical sensations that she would interpret as the beginnings of the disease. She even watched her dog closely to see whether he was coming down with the dreaded disease. Only with great effort could she dismiss these thoughts after several days. Real illness in a friend or relative would incapacitate her for days at a time.

Leinani's fears developed during the first year of her marriage, around the time she learned of her husband's affair. At first, she spent a great deal of time and more money than they could afford going to doctors. Over the years, she heard the same thing during each visit: "There's nothing wrong with you; you're perfectly healthy." Finally, she stopped going, as she became convinced her concerns were excessive, but her fears did not go away and she was chronically miserable.

As noted above, illness anxiety disorder is characterized by anxiety or fear that one has a serious disease. Therefore, the essential problem is anxiety, but its expression is different from that of the other anxiety disorders. In illness anxiety disorder, the individual is preoccupied with bodily symptoms, misinterpreting them as indicative of illness or disease. Almost any physical sensation may become the basis for concern. Some may focus on normal bodily functions such as heart rate or perspiration, others on minor physical abnormalities such as a cough. Some individuals complain of vague symptoms, such as aches or fatigue. Because a key feature of this disorder is preoccupation with physical symptoms, individuals with these disorders almost always go initially to family physicians. They come to the attention of mental health professionals only after family physicians have ruled out realistic medical conditions as a cause of the patient's symptoms.

Another important feature of this disorder is that reassurances from numerous doctors that all is well and the individual is healthy have, at best, only a short-term effect. It isn't long before patients like Leinani or Jada are back in the office of another doctor on the assumption that the previous doctors have missed something. This is because many of these individuals mistakenly believe they have a disease, a difficult-to-shake belief sometimes referred to as "disease conviction" (Haenen, de Jong, Schmidt, Stevens, & Visser, 2000). Therefore, along with anxiety focused on the possibility of disease or illness, disease conviction is a core feature of the disorder (Fergus & Valentiner, 2010; Woolfolk & Allen, 2011).

DSM 5 **Table 6.2**

Diagnostic Criteria for Illness Anxiety Disorder

A. Preoccupation having or acquiring a serious illness.

B. Somatic symptoms are not present or, if present, are only mild in intensity. If another medical condition is present or there is a high risk for developing a medical condition (e.g., strong family history is present), the preoccupation is clearly excessive or disproportionate.

C. There is a high level of anxiety about health, and the individual is easily alarmed about personal health status.

D. The individual performs excessive health-related behaviors (e.g., repeatedly checks his or her body for signs of illness) or exhibits maladaptive avoidance (e.g., avoids doctor appointments and hospitals).

E. Illness preoccupation has been present for at least 6 months, but the specific illness that is feared may change over that period of time.

F. The illness-related preoccupation is not better explained by another mental disorde, panic disorder, generalized anxiety disorder, body dysmorphic disorder, obsessive-compulsive disorder, or delucisional disorder, somatic type..

Specify whether:

Care-seeking type: Medical care, including physician visits or undergoing tests and procedures, is frequently used.

Care-avoidant type: Medical care is rarely used

American Psychiatric Association. (2022). *Diagnostic and statistical manual of mental disorders* (5th ed., Text Revision).

If you have just read Chapter 5, you may think that patients with panic disorder resemble patients with both disorders, particularly patients with illness anxiety disorder. Patients with panic disorder also misinterpret physical symptoms as the beginning of the next panic attack, which they believe may kill them. Craske and colleagues (1996) and Hiller, Leibbrand, Rief, and Fichter (2005) suggested several differences between panic disorder and the somatic symptom disorders. Although all disorders include characteristic concern with physical symptoms, patients with panic disorder typically fear immediate symptom-related catastrophes that may occur during the few minutes they are having a panic attack, and these concerns lessen between attacks. Individuals with somatic symptom disorders, on the other hand, focus on a long-term process of illness and disease (for example, cancer or AIDS). Patients with these disorders also continue to seek the opinions of additional doctors in an attempt to rule out (or perhaps confirm) disease and are more likely to demand unnecessary medical treatments. Despite numerous assurances that they are healthy, they remain unconvinced and unreassured. In contrast, panic patients continue to believe their panic attacks might kill them, but most learn rather quickly to stop going to doctors and emergency rooms, where they are told repeatedly that nothing is physically wrong with them. Finally, the anxieties of individuals with panic disorder tend to focus on the specific set of 10 or 15 sympathetic nervous system symptoms associated with a panic attack. Concerns range much wider in somatic symptom disorders. Nevertheless, there are probably more similarities than differences between the symptoms of these disorders.

Statistics

We can only estimate prevalence of somatic symptom disorders in the general population, mostly from studies of similar DSM-IV disorders that were defined a bit differently than the current DSM-5 disorders. For example, the prevalence of DSM-IV hypochondriasis, which would encompass illness anxiety disorder and part of somatic symptom disorder, has been estimated to be from 1% to 5% (American Psychiatric Association, 2000). In primary care settings, the median prevalence rate for hypochondriasis is

SPL/Science Source

In illness anxiety disorder, normal experiences and sensations are often transformed into life-threatening illnesses.

6.7% but as high as 16.6% for distressing somatic symptoms, which should closely approximate the prevalence of somatic symptom disorder and illness anxiety disorder combined in these settings (Creed & Barsky, 2004). Severe illness anxiety has a late age of onset, possibly because more physical health problems occur with aging (El-Gabalawy, Mackenzie, Thibodeau, Asmundson, & Sareen, 2013).

Jada's disorder developed during adolescence. A number of studies have demonstrated that individuals with what would now be somatic symptom disorder tend to be women, unmarried, and from lower socioeconomic groups (see, for example, Creed & Barsky, 2004; Lieb et al., 2002). In addition to a variety of somatic complaints, individuals may have psychological complaints, usually anxiety or mood disorders (Simms, Prisciandaro, Krueger, & Goldberg, 2012; Rief et al., 1998). Patients with these disorders who happened to be in psychiatric clinics reported seemingly endless psychological complaints, including psychotic symptoms, in addition to their physical complaints (Lenze, Miller, Munir, Pornoppadol, & North, 1999). Suicidal attempts that appear to be calls for help rather than true death efforts are frequent (Chioqueta & Stiles, 2004). Individuals with somatic symptom disorders overuse and misuse the health-care system, with medical bills as much as 9 times more than the average patient (Barsky, Orav, & Bates, 2005; Woolfolk & Allen, 2011). In one study, 19% of people with this disorder were on disability (Allen, Woolfolk, Escobar, Gara, & Hamer, 2006). Although symptoms may come and go, somatic symptom disorders and the accompanying sick role behavior are chronic, often continuing into old age.

As with anxiety disorders, culture-specific syndromes seem to fit comfortably with somatic symptom disorders (Kirmayer & Sartorius, 2007). Among these is the disorder of *koro,* in which there is the belief, accompanied by severe anxiety and sometimes panic, that the genitals are retracting into the abdomen. Most individuals with this disorder are Chinese males, although it is also reported in females; there are few reports of the disorder in Western cultures.

Another culture-specific disorder, prevalent in India, is an anxious concern about losing semen, something that obviously occurs during sexual activity. The disorder, called *dhat,* is associated with a vague mix of physical symptoms, including dizziness, weakness, and fatigue. These low-grade depressive or anxious symptoms are simply attributed to a physical factor, semen loss (Ranjith & Mohan, 2004). Other specific culture-bound somatic symptoms associated with emotional factors would include hot sensations in the head or a sensation of something crawling in the head, specific to African patients (Ebigno, 1986), and a sensation of burning in the hands and feet in Pakistani or Indian patients (Kirmayer & Weiss, 1993).

For a long time, researchers thought that expressing psychological distress as somatic complaints was particularly common in non-Western countries. But on closer inspection this does not seem to be the case, and the impression may have resulted from the ways in which early studies were conducted (see, for example, Cheung, 1995). Thus, "somatizing" psychological distress is fairly common and fairly uniform throughout the world (Gureje, 2004). It is particularly important to examine for medical causes of somatic complaints in developing countries, where parasitic and other infectious diseases and physical conditions associated with poor nutrition are common and not always easy to diagnose. Table 6.1 presents data from a large World Health Organization study on individuals presenting to primary care settings with medically unexplained physical symptoms (no longer a required criterion in DSM-5) that either would or would not be sufficient to meet criteria for somatic symptom disorders. Notice that the rates are relatively uniform around the world, as is the sex ratio (Gureje, Simon, Ustun, & Goldberg, 1997; Husain & Chalder, 2021). When the problem is severe enough to meet criteria for disorder, the sex ratio is approximately 2:1 female to male.

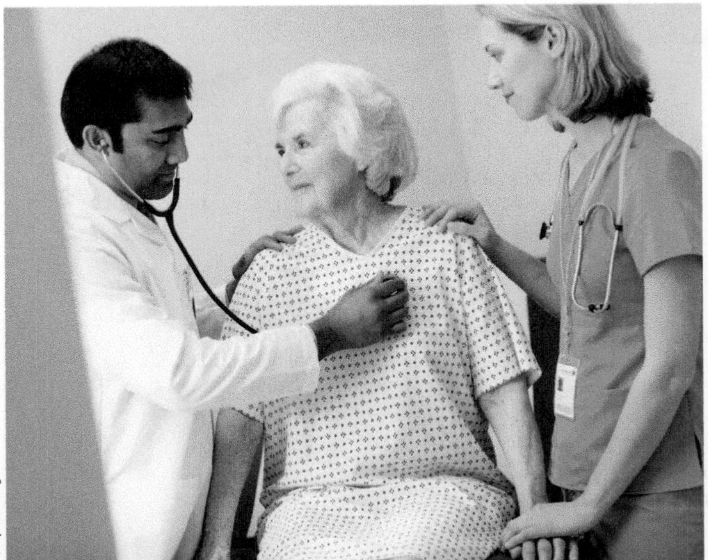

Fuse/Jupiter Images

In somatic symptom disorder, primary relationships are often with medical caregivers; one's symptoms are one's identity.

Causes

Investigators with otherwise differing points of view agree on psychopathological processes ongoing in somatic symptom disorders. Faulty interpretation of physical signs and sensations as evidence of physical illness is central, so almost everyone agrees that these disorders are basically disorders of cognition or perception with strong emotional contributions (Lebel et al., 2020; Taylor & Asmundson, 2004, 2009; Witthöft & Hiller, 2010).

Individuals with somatic symptom disorders experience physical sensations common to many people, but they quickly focus their attention on these sensations. Remember that the very act of focusing on oneself increases arousal and makes the physical sensations seem more intense than they are (see Chapter 5). If people also tend to misinterpret these as symptoms of illness, your anxiety will increase further. Increased anxiety produces additional physical symptoms, which creates a vicious cycle (see ■ Figure 6.1, which was developed to apply to DSM-IV hypochondriasis but, in fact, applies to DSM-5 somatic symptom disorder and illness anxiety disorder) (Lebel et al., 2020; Salkovskis, Warwick, & Deale, 2003; Warwick & Salkovskis, 1990; Witthöft & Hiller, 2010).

Table 6.1 Frequency of Two Forms of Somatization in a Cross-Cultural Study (n = 5,438)*

	ICD-10 Somatization Disorder (%)			Somatic Symptom Index (%)		
Center	Men	Women	Overall Prevalence	Men	Women	Overall Prevalence
Ankara, Turkey	1.3	2.2	1.9	22.3	26.7	25.2
Athens, Greece	0.4	1.8	1.3	7.7	13.5	11.5
Bangalore, India	1.3	2.4	1.8	19.1	20.0	19.6
Berlin, Germany	0.3	2.0	1.3	24.9	25.9	25.5
Groningen, the Netherlands	0.8	4.1	2.8	14.7	19.9	17.8
Ibadan, Nigeria	0.5	0.3	0.4	14.4	5.0	7.6
Mainz, Germany	1.0	4.4	3.0	24.9	17.3	20.6
Manchester, United Kingdom	0	0.5	0.4	21.4	20.0	20.5
Nagasaki, Japan	0	0.2	0.1	13.3	7.9	10.5
Paris, France	0.6	3.1	1.7	18.6	28.2	23.1
Rio de Janeiro, Brazil	1.5	11.2	8.5	35.6	30.6	32.0
Santiago, Chile	33.8	11.2	17.7	45.7	33.3	36.8
Seattle, Washington, United States	0.7	2.2	1.7	10.0	9.8	9.8
Shanghai, China	0.3	2.2	1.5	17.5	18.7	18.3
Verona, Italy	0	0.2	0.1	9.7	8.5	8.9
Total	1.9	3.3	2.8	19.8	19.7	19.7

Note: Criteria from *The International Classification of Diseases* (10th ed.) were used in this study.

*Weighted to the first-stage (intake) sample.

Source: Adapted from O. Gureje, G. E. Simon, T. B. Ustun, & D. P. Goldberg, 1997, Somatization in cross-cultural perspective: A World Health Organization study in primary care, *American Journal of Psychiatry, 154,* 989–995.

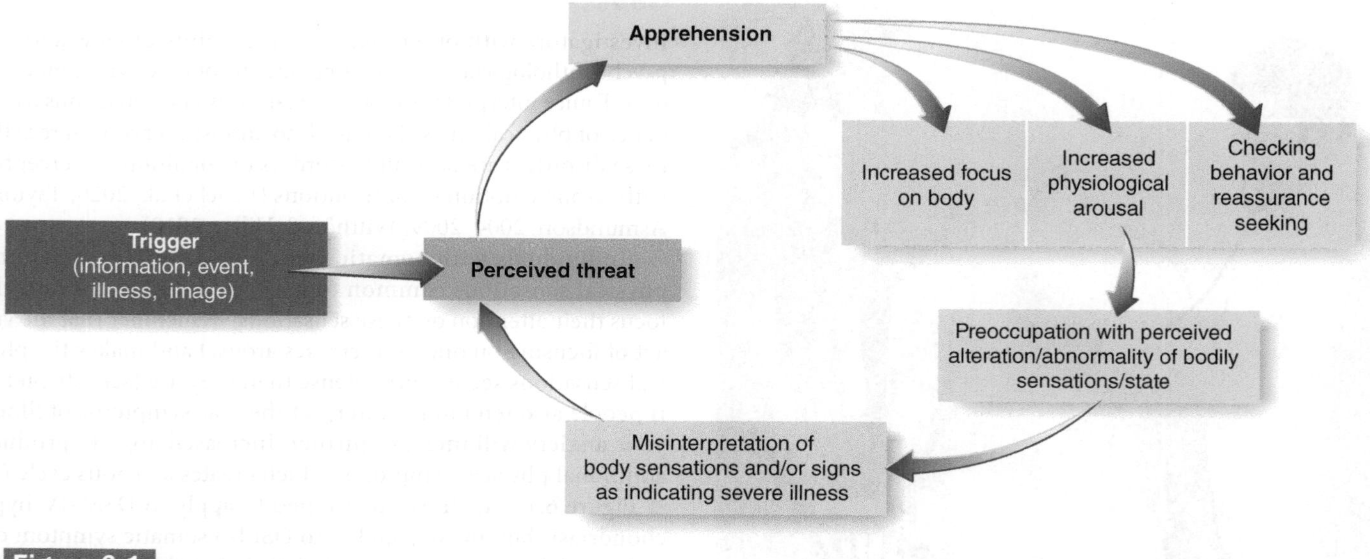

Figure 6.1

Integrative model of causes of hypochondriasis. Based on H. M. Warwick & P. M. Salkovskis, 1990, Hypochondriasis. *Behavior Research Therapy, 28,* 105–117.

Using procedures from cognitive science such as the Stroop test (see Chapter 2), a number of investigators (Hitchcock & Mathews, 1992; Pauli & Alpers, 2002) have confirmed that participants with these disorders show enhanced perceptual sensitivity to illness cues. They also tend to interpret ambiguous stimuli as threatening (Haenen et al., 2000). Thus, they quickly become aware (and frightened) of any sign of possible illness or disease. A minor headache, for example, might be interpreted as a sure sign of a brain tumor. Smeets, de Jong, and Mayer (2000) demonstrated that individuals with these disorders, compared with "normals," take a "better safe than sorry" approach to dealing with even minor physical symptoms by getting them checked out as soon as possible. More fundamentally, they have a restrictive concept of health as being completely symptom-free (Kube et al., 2020; Rief et al., 1998) and show consistent cognitive errors about the meaning and consequences of these somatic symptoms (van den Bergh et al., 2017).

What causes individuals to develop this pattern of somatic sensitivity and distorted beliefs? Although it is not certain, the cause is unlikely to be found in isolated biological or psychological factors. For some patients, the fundamental causes of these disorders are similar to those implicated in the anxiety disorders (Barlow, 2002; Barlow et al., 2014). For example, evidence shows that somatic symptom disorders run in families (Bell, 1994; Guze, Cloninger, Martin, & Clayton, 1986; Katon, 1993) and that there is a modest genetic contribution (Taylor, Thordarson, Jang, & Asmundson, 2006). But this contribution may be nonspecific, such as a tendency to overrespond to stress, and thus may be indistinguishable from the nonspecific genetic contribution to anxiety disorders. Hyperresponsivity might combine with a tendency to view negative life events as unpredictable and uncontrollable and, therefore, to be guarded against at all times (Barlow et al., 2014; Noyes et al., 2004). As we noted in Chapter 5, these factors would constitute biological and psychological vulnerabilities to anxiety.

Why does this anxiety focus on physical sensations and illness? We know that children with these concerns often report the same kinds of symptoms that other family members may have reported at one time (Kirmayer, Looper, & Taillefer, 2003). It is therefore quite possible, as in panic disorder, that some individuals who develop somatic symptom disorder or illness anxiety disorder have *learned* from family members to focus their anxiety on specific physical conditions and illness.

Three other factors may contribute to this etiological process. First, these disorders seem to develop in the context of a stressful life event, as do many disorders, including anxiety disorders. Such events often involve death or illness (Noyes et al., 2004; Sandin, Chorot, Santed, & Valiente, 2004). (Leinani's traumatic first year of marriage seemed to coincide with the beginning of her disorder.) Second, people who develop these disorders tend to have had a disproportionate incidence of disease in their family when they were children. Thus, even if they did not develop somatic symptom disorders until adulthood, they carry strong memories of illness that could easily become the focus of anxiety. Third, an important social and interpersonal influence may be involved (Barlow et al., 2014; Noyes et al., 2003). Some people who come from families where illness is a major issue seem to have learned that an ill person often gets a lot of attention. The "benefits" of being sick might contribute to the development of the disorder in some people. A "sick person" who receives increased attention for being ill and is able to avoid work or other responsibilities is described as adopting a "sick role." The positive consequences of a sick role is sometimes referred to as *secondary gain*. We will come to this point later again.

Treatment

It used to be common clinical practice to uncover unconscious conflicts through psychodynamic psychotherapy. However, the results on the effectiveness of this kind of treatment have seldom been reported.

Scientifically controlled studies have shown some support for cognitive behavioral treatments for health anxiety (for example, Axelsson & Hedman-Lagerloef, 2019; Bouman, 2014; Taylor & Asmundon, 2009), somatic symptom disorder (for example, Kleinstäuber, Witthöft, & Hiller, 2011; Sharma, & Manjula, 2013; Witthoft & Hiller 2010; Woolfolk & Allen, 2011), and other medically unexplained symptoms (Husain & Clader, 2021; Kleinstäuber et al., 2019). These treatments typically target dysfunctional stress coping, attentional processes, cognitions, and behaviors related to somatic symptoms. Mental health professionals may well be able to offer reassurance in a more effective and sensitive manner, devote sufficient time to all concerns the patient may have, and attend to the "meaning" of the symptoms (for example, their relation to the patient's life stress). Fava, Grandi, Rafanelli, Fabbri, and Cazzaro (2000) tested this idea by assigning 20 patients who met diagnostic criteria for DSM-IV hypochondriasis to two groups. One received "explanatory therapy" in which the clinician went over the source and origins of their symptoms in some detail. These patients were assessed immediately after the therapy and again at a 6-month follow-up. The other group was a wait-list control group that did not receive the explanatory therapy until after 6 months of waiting. All patients received usual medical care from their physicians. In both groups, taking the time to explain in some detail the nature of the patient's disorder in an educational framework was associated with a significant reduction in fears and beliefs about somatic symptoms and a decrease in health-care usage, and these gains were maintained at the follow-up. For the wait-list group, treatment gains did not occur until the patients received explanatory therapy, suggesting this treatment is effective. This is a small study and follow-ups occurred for only 6 months, but the results are promising (although explanatory therapy most likely benefits only those with more mild forms of the disorders) (Taylor, Asmundson, & Coons, 2005). Participation in support groups may also give these people the reassurance they need.

Evaluations of more robust treatments are now available (Axelsson & Hedman-Lagerloef, 2019; Barsky & Allen, 2005; Bouman, 2014; Kleinstäuber et al., 2019). For example, Barsky and Ahern (2005) randomized 187 patients with DSM-IV hypochondriasis to receive either six sessions of cognitive-behavioral treatment (CBT) from trained therapists or treatment as usual from primary care physicians. CBT focused on identifying and challenging illness-related misinterpretations of physical sensations and on showing patients how to create "symptoms" by

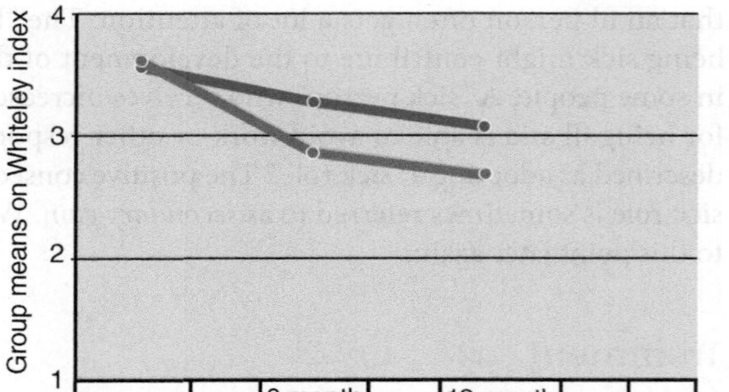

	Baseline	6 month followup	12 month followup
• Treatment group mean	3.58	2.82	2.65
• Control group mean	3.51	3.21	3.02

Figure 6.2

Reduction in symptoms of hypochondriasis after six sessions of CBT or medical care as usual. Adapted from A. J. Barsky & D. K. Ahern, 2005, Cognitive behavior therapy for hypochondriasis: A randomized controlled trial, *JAMA, 291*, 1464–1470.

focusing attention on certain body areas. Bringing on their own symptoms persuaded many patients that such events were under their control. Patients were also coached to seek less reassurance regarding their concerns. Results can be seen in ■ Figure 6.2 as scores on the Whiteley Index of hypochondriacal symptoms. CBT was more effective after treatment and at each follow-up point for both symptoms of hypochondriasis and overall changes in functioning and quality of life. But results were still "modest," and many eligible patients refused to enter treatment because they were convinced their problems were medical rather than psychological.

In another strong study, Allen et al. (2006) found that 40% of patients with more severe somatic symptom disorder treated with CBT (versus 7% of a group receiving standard medical care) evidenced clinical improvement and these gains lasted at least a year. Escobar et al. (2007) reported similar results. Interestingly, cognitive interventions do not seem to be necessary for treating hypochondriasis (Weck, Neng, Richtberg, Jakob, & Stangier, 2015). This study randomly assigned patients with hypochondriasis to receive cognitive therapy alone, exposure therapy without explicit cognitive interventions, or a wait-list control group. Compared to the control group, both treatments resulted in large-sized effects for improving symptoms of hypochondriasis. Although the study found a significant reduction in depressive symptoms and bodily complaints for both treatments in comparison with the wait-list, anxiety symptoms were significantly reduced only by the exposure treatment. The exposure procedures consisted of repeatedly confronting the patient to stimuli that are relevant for health anxieties (such as documentaries about diseases) without using any avoidance and safety behaviors (such as reassurance by doctors or checking the abdomen for cancer). A few other reports suggest that drugs may help some people with somatic symptom disorders (Fallon et al., 2003; Kjernisted, Enns, & Lander, 2002; Kroenke, 2007; Taylor et al., 2005). Not surprisingly, these same types of drugs (antidepressants) are useful for anxiety and depression. In one study, CBT and the drug paroxetine (Paxil), a selective-serotonin reuptake inhibitor (SSRI), were both effective, but only CBT was significantly different from a placebo condition. Specifically, 45% in the CBT group, 30% in the Paxil group, and 14% in the placebo group responded to treatment among all patients who entered the study (Greeven et al., 2007).

In our clinic, we concentrate on initially providing reassurance, reducing stress, and, in particular, reducing the frequency of help-seeking behaviors. One of the most common patterns is the person's tendency to visit numerous medical specialists to address the symptom of the week. There is an extensive medical and physical workup with every visit to a new physician (or to one who has not been seen for a while), at an extraordinary cost to the health-care system (Barsky et al., 2005; Witthöft & Hiller, 2010). In treatment, to limit these visits, a gatekeeper physician is assigned to each patient to screen all physical complaints. Subsequent visits to specialists must be specifically authorized by this gatekeeper. In the context of a positive therapeutic relationship, most patients are amenable to this arrangement.

Additional therapeutic attention is directed at reducing the supportive consequences of relating to significant others on the basis of physical symptoms alone. More appropriate methods of interacting with others are encouraged, along with additional procedures to promote healthy social and personal adjustment without relying on being "sick." In this context, CBT may then be the most helpful (Allen et al., 2006; Mai, 2004; Woolfolk & Allen, 2011). Because Jada, like many patients with this disorder, was receiving disability payments from the state, additional goals involved encouraging at least part-time employment, with the ultimate goal of discontinuing disability.

Now family doctors are being trained in how better to manage these patients using some of these principles (Garcia-Campayo, Claraco, Sanz-Carrillo, Arevalo, & Monton, 2002), but results are mixed (Woolfolk & Allen, 2011).

Psychological Factors Affecting Medical Condition

A related somatic symptom disorder is called **psychological factors affecting medical condition**. The essential feature of this disorder is the presence of a diagnosed medical condition (such as asthma, diabetes, or severe pain) clearly caused by a known medical condition (such as cancer) that is adversely affected (increased in frequency or severity) by one or more psychological or behavioral factors. These behavioral or psychological factors would have a direct influence on the course or perhaps the treatment of the medical condition. One example would be anxiety severe enough to clearly worsen an asthmatic condition. Another example would be a patient with diabetes who is in denial about the need to regularly check insulin levels and intervene when necessary. In this case, the pattern would have to be consistent in the neglect of appropriate monitoring and intervention, but the neglect is clearly a behavioral or psychological factor that is adversely affecting the medical condition. This diagnosis would need to be distinguished from the development of stress or anxiety in response to having a severe medical condition that would more appropriately be diagnosed as an adjustment disorder (see Chapter 5). In Chapter 9, we discuss health psychology and the contribution of psychological factors to physical disorders including cardiovascular disease, cancer, AIDS, and chronic pain.

Conversion Disorder (Functional Neurological Symptom Disorder)

The term *conversion* has been used off and on since the Middle Ages (Mace, 1992) but was popularized by Freud, who believed the anxiety resulting from unconscious conflicts somehow was "converted" into physical symptoms to find expression. This allowed the individual to discharge some anxiety without actually experiencing it. As in phobic disorders, the anxiety resulting from unconscious conflicts might be "displaced" onto another object. In DSM-5, *functional neurological symptom disorder* is a subtitle to *conversion disorder* because the term is more often used by neurologists who see the majority of patients receiving a conversion disorder diagnosis and because the term is more acceptable to patients. *Functional* refers to a symptom without an organic cause (Stone, LaFrance, Levenson, & Sharpe, 2010). It is likely that the old term *conversion* will be dropped in future editions of the DSM because of its problematic psychoanalytic explanation.

Clinical Description

Conversion disorders generally have to do with physical malfunctioning, such as paralysis, blindness, or difficulty speaking (aphonia), without any physical or organic pathology to account for the malfunction. Most conversion symptoms suggest that some kind of neurological disease is affecting sensory–motor systems, although conversion symptoms can mimic the full range of physical malfunctioning (Demartini et al., 2021).

Conversion disorders provide some of the most intriguing, sometimes astounding, examples of psychopathology. What could possibly account for somebody going blind when all visual processes are normal or experiencing paralysis of the arms or legs when there is no neurological damage? Consider the case of Eloise.

Eloise... Unlearning Walking

Eloise sat on a chair with her legs under her, refusing to put her feet on the floor. Her mother sat close by, ready to assist her if she needed to move or get up. Her mother had made the appointment and, with the help of a friend, had all but carried Eloise into the office. Eloise was a 20-year-old of borderline intellectual functioning who was friendly and personable during the initial interview and who readily answered all questions with a big smile. She obviously enjoyed the social interaction.

Eloise's difficulty walking developed over 5 years. Her right leg had given way and she began falling. Gradually, the condition worsened to the point that 6 months before her admission to the hospital Eloise could move around only by crawling on the floor.

Physical examinations revealed no physical problems. Eloise presented with a classic case of conversion disorder. Although she was not paralyzed, her specific symptoms included weakness in her legs and difficulty keeping her balance, with the result that she fell often. This particular type of conversion symptom is called *astasia-abasia*. Eloise lived with her mother, who ran a gift shop in the front of her house in a small rural town. Eloise had been schooled through special education programs until she was about 15; after this, no further programs were available. When Eloise began staying home, her walking began to deteriorate.

In addition to blindness, paralysis, and aphonia, conversion symptoms may include total mutism and the loss of the sense of touch. Some people have seizures, which may be psychological in origin because no significant electroencephalogram (EEG) changes can be documented. These "seizures" are usually called psychogenic nonepileptic seizures. Another relatively common symptom is *globus hystericus,* the sensation of a lump in the throat that makes it difficult to swallow, eat, or sometimes talk (Finkenbine & Miele, 2004).

Distinguishing among conversion reactions, medically explained symptoms, and outright **malingering** (faking) is sometimes difficult. Several factors can help, but one symptom, widely regarded as a diagnostic sign, has proved not to be useful.

It was long thought that patients with conversion reactions had the same quality of indifference to the symptoms thought to be present in some people with severe somatic symptom disorder. This attitude, referred to as *la belle indifférence,* was considered a hallmark of conversion reactions, but this turns out not to be the case. Stone, Smyth, Carson, Warlow, and Sharpe (2006) found a blasé attitude toward illness is sometimes displayed by people with actual physical disorders, and some people with conversion symptoms do become quite distressed. Specifically, only 21% of 356 patients with conversion symptoms displayed *la belle indifférence* compared with 29% of 157 patients with organic disease.

Other factors may be more helpful in making this distinction. Psychosocial stressors are important risk factors for developing conversion disorder, especially in people who have problems-regulating and processing their emotions (Pick et al., 2019). For example, in one survey, 324 out of 869 patients (37%) reported prior physical injury (Stone, Carson, Aditya, et al., 2009). But the occurrence of some identifiable stressor has not been a reliable sign of conversion disorder, since many other disorders are associated with stressful events and stressful events often occur in the lives of people without any disorders. For this reason, the diagnostic criterion that conversion disorder is associated with preceding stress does not appear in DSM-5. Although people with conversion symptoms can usually function normally, they seem truly unaware either of this ability or of sensory input. For example, individuals with the conversion symptom of blindness can usually avoid objects in their visual field, but they will tell you they can't see the objects. Functional blindness can be distinguished from organic blindness with certain neurological and visual tests (Bruce & Newman, 2010). For example, people with

DSM 5 **Table 6.3**

Diagnostic Criteria for Conversion Disorder (Functional Neurological Symptom Disorder)

A. One or more symptoms of altered voluntary motor or sensory function.

B. Clinical findings provide evidence of incompatibility between the symptom and recognized neurological or medical conditions.

C. The symptom or deficit is not better explained by another medical or mental disorder.

D. The symptom or deficit causes clinically significant distress or impairment in social, occupational, or other important areas of functioning or warrants medical evaluation.

American Psychiatric Association. (2022). *Diagnostic and statistical manual of mental disorders* (5th ed., Text Revision).

organic blindness can touch their two index finger tips, whereas many functionally blind people are unable to do this.

But conversion disorder can also become quite evident in everyday life situations. For example, individuals with conversion symptoms of paralysis of the legs might suddenly get up and run in an emergency and then be astounded they were able to do this. It is possible that at least some people who experience miraculous cures during religious ceremonies may have been suffering from conversion reactions. These factors may help in distinguishing between conversion and organically based physical disorders, but clinicians sometimes make mistakes, although it is not common with modern diagnostic techniques. For example, Moene and colleagues (2000) carefully reassessed 85 patients diagnosed with conversion disorder and found 10 (11.8%) had developed some evidence of a neurological disorder approximately 2.5 years after the first exam. Stone and colleagues (2005), summarizing a number of studies, estimate the rate of misdiagnosis of conversion disorders that are really physical problems is approximately 4%, having improved considerably from earlier decades. In any case, ruling out medical causes for the symptoms is crucial to making a diagnosis of conversion and, given advances in medical screening procedures, this is the principal diagnostic criterion in DSM-5 (APA, 2013; Stone et al., 2010).

Some conversion symptoms involve movements such as tremors that are perceived as involuntary. But what makes a movement either voluntary or involuntary? In one well-done study, neuroscientists attempted to find out (Voon et al., 2010). These investigators assessed eight patients who presented with motor tremors without any neurological basis (conversion tremors). In a clever experiment, they used functional magnetic resonance imaging (fMRI) to compare brain activity during the conversion tremor but also during a voluntary "mimicked" tremor in which patients were instructed to produce the tremor on purpose. The investigators found that the conversion tremor, as compared with the voluntary tremor, was associated with lower activity in the right inferior parietal cortex. Interestingly, this is an area of the brain that functions to compare internal predictions with actual events. In other words, if an individual wants to move her arm and then she decides to go ahead and move it, this area of the brain determines if the desired action has occurred. Because we think about making a movement before we do it, the brain concludes (correctly in most cases) that we caused the movement to occur. But if this area of the brain is not functioning properly, then the brain might conclude that the movement is involuntary. It is not clear whether this brain activity is a cause or a result of conversion symptoms, but these sophisticated brain-imaging technologies may eventually bring us closer to understanding at least one part of the puzzle of conversion symptoms in some people.

It can also be difficult to distinguish between individuals who are truly experiencing conversion symptoms in a seemingly involuntary way and malingerers who are good at faking symptoms. Once malingerers are exposed, their motivation is clear: Either they are trying to get out of something (such as work or legal difficulties), or they are attempting to gain something (such as a financial settlement). Malingerers are fully aware of what they are doing and are clearly attempting to manipulate others to gain a desired end.

More puzzling is a set of conditions called **factitious disorder**, also known as **Munchausen syndrome**. The condition was named for a German nobleman called Baron von Münchhausen, who was known as the *Lügenbaron* or Baron of Lies for exaggerating his war stories. He is the basis for a fictional character in Rudolf Erich Raspe's *Baron Munchausen's Narrative of His Marvellous Travels and Campaigns in Russia*, published in English in Oxford, England, in 1786, where the character has impossible adventures, such as visiting the moon and sitting on a cannon ball flying through the air. A diagnosis of Munchausen syndrome suggests that the person is faking an illness, just as the original Münchhausen lied about his adventures. The symptoms in factitious disorder are under voluntary control, as with malingering, but there is *no obvious reason* for voluntarily producing the symptoms except, possibly, to assume the sick role and receive increased attention.

Tragically, this disorder may extend to other members of the family. An adult, almost always a mother, may purposely make her child sick, evidently for the attention and pity given to her as the mother of a sick child. When an individual deliberately makes someone else sick, the condition is called *factitious disorder imposed on another.* It was also known previously as *Munchausen syndrome by proxy.* In any case, it is really an atypical form of child abuse (Check, 1998). The offending parent may resort to extreme tactics to create the appearance of illness in the child (Glaser, 2020; Yates & Bass, 2017). For example, one mother stirred her child's urine specimen with a vaginal tampon obtained during menstruation. Another mother mixed feces into her child's vomit (Check, 1998). Because the mother typically establishes a positive relationship with a medical staff, the true nature of the illness is most often unsuspected and the staff members perceive the parent as remarkably caring, cooperative, and involved in providing for her child's well-being. Therefore, the mother is often successful at eluding suspicion. Helpful procedures to assess the possibility of factitious disorder imposed on another include a trial separation of the mother and the child or video surveillance of

DSM 5 **Table 6.4**
Diagnostic Criteria for Factitious Disorders

A. Falsification of physical or psychological signs or symptoms, or induction of injury or disease, associated with identified deception.
B. The individual presents himself or herself to others as ill, impaired, or injured.
C. The deceptive behavior is evident even in the absence of obvious external rewards.
D. The behavior is not better accounted for by another mental disorder, such as delusional disorder system or acute psychosis.

Specify:

Single episode

Recurrent episodes (two or more events of falsification of illness and/or induction of injury).

American Psychiatric Association. (2022). *Diagnostic and statistical manual of mental disorders* (5th ed., Text Revision).

the child while in the hospital. A systematic review of almost 800 cases showed that almost all perpetrators were women and the mother of the victim (Yates & Bass, 2017). These mothers often had a history of maltreatment and a range of other psychiatric problems, including depression, substance use problems, suicidality, self-harm, and personality disorders, especially borderline personality disorder.

Unconscious Mental Processes

Unconscious cognitive processes seem to play a role in much of psychopathology (although not necessarily as Freud envisioned it), but nowhere is this phenomenon more readily and dramatically apparent than when we attempt to distinguish between conversion disorders and related conditions. To take a closer look at the "unconscious" mental process in these conditions, we review briefly the case of Anna O. (see Chapter 2).

As you may remember, when Anna O. was 21 years old, she was nursing her dying father. This was a difficult time for her. She reported that after many days by the sick bed, her mind wandered. Suddenly she found herself imagining (dreaming?) that a black snake was moving across the bed, about to bite her father. She tried to grab the snake, but her right arm had gone to sleep, and she could not move it. Looking at her arm and hand, she imagined that her fingers had turned into little poisonous snakes. Horrified, all she could do was pray, and the only prayer that came to mind was in English (Anna O.'s native language was German). After this, she experienced paralysis in her right arm whenever she remembered this hallucination. The paralysis gradually extended to the right side of her body and, on occasion, to other parts of her body. She also experienced a number of other conversion symptoms such as deafness and, intriguingly, an inability to speak German, although she remained fluent in English. In Josef Breuer's treatment of Anna O., she relived her traumatic experiences in her imagination. Under hypnosis, she was able to recreate the memory of her horrific hallucination. As she recalled and processed the images, her paralysis left her, and she regained her ability to speak German. Breuer called the therapeutic reexperiencing of emotionally traumatic events *catharsis* (purging, or releasing). Catharsis has proved to be an effective intervention with many emotional disorders, as we note in Chapter 5.

Were Anna O.'s symptoms really "unconscious," or did she realize at some level that she could move her arm and the rest of her body if she wanted to and it simply served her purpose not to? This question has long bedeviled psychopathologists. Now information (reviewed in Chapter 2) on unconscious cognitive processes becomes important. We are all capable of receiving and processing information in a number of sensory channels (such as vision and hearing) without being aware of it. Take, for example, blind sight or unconscious vision, which occurs when people respond to visual stimuli without being aware of it (Weiskrantz, 2009). It appears that this is the result of a number of brain networks, some of which are engaged in nonconscious visual processes, and others in conscious behaviors (Celeghin et al., 2019). Studying these patients and understanding their biology and psychology can provide important new insight into the brain and the way it processes information and responds to the environment (Ajina & Bridge, 2017).

Statistics

We have already seen that conversion disorder may occur with other disorders, particularly somatic symptom disorder, as in the case of Jada. Jada's paralysis passed after several months and did not return, although on occasion she would report "feeling as if" it were returning. Comorbid PTSD, sexual abuse, and anxiety and mood disorders are common (Goleva et al., 2020; Pehlivanturk & Unal, 2002; Rowe, 2010; Stone, Carson, Duncan, et al., 2009). The prevalence estimate in neurological settings is particularly high (Rowe, 2010; Stone, Carson, Duncan, et al., 2009). It is estimated that 30% of all patients referred to epilepsy centers have so-called functional or psychogenic nonepileptic seizures (Benbadis & Allen-Hauser, 2000; Schoenberg, Marsh, & Benbadis, 2012). These seizures are quite different from epileptic seizures, such as the classic grand mal seizure. Functional seizures do not show the abnormal brain activity as measured by an EEG observed during an epileptic seizure. People with functional seizures also usually have their eyes closed, are partially responsive, and show thrashing movements of the entire body for several minutes, whereas people with grand mal epileptic seizures usually have their eyes open, lose consciousness, and show stiffening and then convulsing of their muscles during the tonic-clonic phase lasting only for 1 to 3 minutes (Marcolini & Tolchin, 2021).

Like severe somatic symptom disorder, conversion disorders are found primarily in women (Brown & Lewis-Fernandez, 2011; Deveci et al., 2007) and typically develop during adolescence or slightly thereafter. Conversion reactions have also been reported in soldiers exposed to severe combat, mainly during World Wars I and II (Mucha & Reinhardt, 1970; Perez-Sales, 1990). The conversion symptoms often disappear after a time, only to return later in the same or similar form when a new stressor occurs. In one study, 56 patients with psychogenic nonepileptic seizures (16 males and 40 females), who had their disorder for an average of 8 years, were followed for 18 months after initial diagnosis (Ettinger, Devinsky, Weisbrot, Ramakrishna, & Goyal, 1999). Outcome was generally poor for these patients, with only about half of the patients recovering. Even among those patients whose seizures had gotten better, rehospitalizations were common. Approximately 20% of this group had attempted suicide, and this proportion did not differ between those whose seizures had gotten better during the period and those whose seizures had not gotten better. If the patients believed the diagnosis of conversion disorder when it was given to them and otherwise perceived themselves as being in good health and functioning well at work and at home, they had a better chance of recovering from their psychologically based seizures. Fortunately, children and adolescents seem to have a better long-term outlook than adults. In one study from Turkey, fully 85% of 40 children had recovered 4 years after initial diagnoses, with those diagnosed early having the best chance of recovery (Pehlivanturk & Unal, 2002). In view of the consistency with which this disorder occurs in countries around the world, this outcome would probably be true in other countries as well.

In the beginning of the chapter, we note that conversion disorder and dissociative disorders share common features. Several studies provide evidence for this (Brown & Lewis-Fernandez 2011). In one study, 72 patients with conversion disorders were compared with a control group of 96 psychiatric patients with various emotional disorders who were matched for gender and age. Dissociative symptoms, such as feelings of unreality, were significantly more common in the patients with conversion disorder than in the control group, based on responses to a questionnaire (Spitzer, Spelsberg, Grabe, Mundt, & Freyberger, 1999). This finding was basically replicated in another report on 54 patients with conversion disorder compared with 50 matched patients with mood or anxiety disorders (Roelofs, Keijsers, Hoogduin, Naring, & Moene, 2002). In other cultures, some conversion symptoms are common aspects of religious or healing rituals. Seizures, paralysis, and trances are common in some rural fundamentalist religious groups in the United States (Griffith, English, & Mayfield, 1980), and they are often seen as evidence of contact with God. Individuals who exhibit such symptoms are thus held in high esteem by their peers. These symptoms do not meet criteria for a "disorder" unless they persist and interfere with an individual's functioning.

Causes

Freud described four basic processes in the development of conversion disorder. First, the individual experiences a traumatic event—in Freud's view, an unacceptable, unconscious conflict. Second, because the conflict and the resulting anxiety are unacceptable, the person represses the conflict, making it unconscious. Third, the anxiety continues to increase and threatens to emerge into consciousness, and the person "converts" it into physical symptoms, thereby relieving the pressure of having to deal directly with the conflict. This reduction of anxiety is considered to be the *primary gain* or reinforcing event that maintains the conversion symptom. Fourth, the individual receives greatly increased attention and sympathy from loved ones and may also be allowed to avoid a difficult situation or task. Freud considered such attention or avoidance to be the *secondary gain*, the secondarily reinforcing set of events.

Freud might have been correct on three counts but not on the fourth, although firm evidence supporting any of these ideas is sparse and Freud's views were far more complex than represented here. Most often, individuals with conversion disorder have experienced a traumatic event that must be escaped at all costs (Brown & Lewis-Fernandez, 2011; Stone, Carson, Aditya, et al., 2009). This might be combat, where death is imminent, or an impossible interpersonal situation. Because simply running away is unacceptable in most cases, the socially acceptable alternative of getting sick is substituted; but getting sick on purpose is also unacceptable, so this motivation is detached from the person's consciousness. Finally, because the escape behavior (the conversion symptoms) is successful to an extent in obliterating the traumatic situation, the behavior continues until the underlying problem is resolved.

This idea has some empirical support as shown in one study (Goleva et al., 2020). This study examined 1,431 patients diagnosed with functional seizures, 2,251 with epilepsy and functional seizures (note that people with epilepsy can also have functional seizures), 4,715 with epilepsy without functional seizures, and 502,200 control patients. More than 70% of patients with functional seizures were women (as compared to 59.6% of controls). Functional seizures were associated with more additional psychiatric disorders compared with the general hospital population and also patients with epilepsy. People with functional seizures were diagnosed with an average of 4.75 additional psychiatric diagnoses, whereas patients with epilepsy only received on average 2.6 additional diagnoses. Patients with functional seizures were especially more likely to have additional PTSD, anxiety, and depression than the other groups. Sexual assault trauma and PTSD were approximately 16 times more frequent in patients with functional seizures compared with the general hospital population. However, given sexual assault trauma exposure, there was no difference between men and women in the rate of functional seizures diagnosis, suggesting that men and women who experience sexual assault trauma are at equivalent risk of developing functional seizures.

Mario Tama/Getty Images

The seizures and trances that may be symptomatic of conversion disorder are also common in some rural fundamentalist religious groups in the United States.

The one step in Freud's progression of events about which some questions remain is the issue of primary gain. The notion of primary gain accounts for the feature of *la belle indifférence* (cited previously), where individuals seem not the least bit distressed about their symptoms. In other words, Freud thought that because symptoms reflected an unconscious attempt to resolve a conflict, the patient would not be upset by them. But there is little empirical evidence to support Freud's claim. In fact, people with conversion disorder frequently show emotional problems, including depression and anxiety (Pick et al., 2019). Also, Stone and colleagues (2006) described earlier on "indifference" to conversion symptoms found no difference in distress over symptoms among patients with conversion disorder compared with patients with organic disease.

Social and cultural influences also contribute to conversion disorder, which, like somatic symptom disorder, tends to occur in less educated, lower socioeconomic groups where knowledge about disease and medical illness is not well developed (Brown & Lewis-Fernandez, 2011; Kirmayer et al., 2003; Woolfolk & Allen, 2011; Löwe & Gerloff, 2018; O'Connell et al., 2020). Furthermore, the incidence of these disorders has decreased over the decades (Kirmayer et al., 2003). The most likely explanation is that increased knowledge of the real causes of physical problems by both patients and loved ones eliminates much of the possibility of secondary gain so important in these disorders.

Finally, many conversion symptoms seem to be part of a larger constellation of psychopathology. Jada had broad-ranging somatic symptom disorder, as well as the severe conversion symptoms, that resulted in her hospitalization. In similar cases, individuals may have a marked biological vulnerability to develop conversion disorder when under stress, with biological processes like those discussed in the context of somatic symptom disorder. Neuroscientists are increasingly finding a strong connectivity between the conversion symptom and parts of the brain regulating emotion, such as the amygdala, using brain-imaging procedures (Bryant & Das, 2012; Rowe, 2010; Voon et al., 2010).

For countless other cases, however, biological contributory factors seem to be less important than the overriding influence of interpersonal factors (the actions of Eloise's mother, for example), as we discuss in the next section. There you will learn that the extent of Eloise's suffering and its successful resolution point primarily to a psychological and social etiology.

Treatment

Although few systematic controlled studies have evaluated the effectiveness of treatment for conversion disorders, we often treat these conditions in our clinics, as do others (see, for example, Campo & Negrini, 2000; Gilmour et al., 2020; Moene, Spinhoven, Hoogduin & van Dyck, 2002), and our methods closely follow our thinking on etiology. Because conversion disorder has much in common with somatic symptom disorder, many of the treatment principles are similar.

A principal strategy in treating conversion disorder is to identify and attend to the traumatic or stressful life event if it is still present (either in real life or in memory). As in the case of Anna O., therapeutic assistance in reexperiencing or "reliving" the event (catharsis) is a reasonable first step.

The therapist must also work hard to reduce any reinforcing or supportive consequences of the conversion symptoms (secondary gain). For example, it was quite clear that Eloise's mother found it convenient if Eloise stayed in one place most of the day while her mother attended to the store in the front of the house. Eloise's immobility was thus strongly reinforced by motherly attention and concern. Any unnecessary mobility was punished. The therapist must collaborate with both the patient and the family to eliminate such self-defeating behaviors.

Many times, removing the secondary gain is easier said than done. Eloise was successfully treated in the clinic. Through intensive daily work with the staff, she was able to walk again. To accomplish this, she had to practice walking every day with considerable support, attention, and praise from the staff. When her mother visited, the staff noticed that she verbalized her pleasure with Eloise's progress but that her facial expressions, or *affect*, conveyed a different message. The mother lived a good distance from the clinic so she could not attend sessions, but she promised to carry out the program at home after Eloise was discharged. But she didn't. A follow-up contact 6 months after Eloise was discharged revealed that she had relapsed and was again spending almost all her time in a room in the back of the house while her mother attended to business out front.

Following similar cognitive-behavioral programs, 65% of a group of 45 patients with mostly motor behavior conversions (for example, difficulty walking) responded well to treatment. Interestingly, hypnosis, which was administered to approximately half the patients, added little or no benefit to the CBT (Moene et al., 2002, 2003).

Dissociative Disorders

At the beginning of the chapter, we said that when individuals feel detached from themselves or their surroundings, almost as if they are dreaming or living in slow motion, they are having dissociative experiences. Morton Prince, the founder of the *Journal of Abnormal Psychology*, noted more than 100 years ago that many people experience something like dissociation occasionally (Prince, 1906–1907). It might be likely to happen after an extremely stressful event, such as an accident (Spiegel, 2010). It also is more likely to happen when you're tired or sleep deprived from staying up all night cramming for an exam (Giesbrecht, Smeets, Leppink, Jelicic, & Merckelbach, 2007). If you have had an experience of dissociation, it may not have bothered you much, perhaps because you knew the cause (Barlow, 2002). On the other hand, it may have been extremely frightening. Transient experiences of dissociation will occur in about half of the general population at some point in their lives, and studies suggest that if a person experiences a traumatic event, between 31% and 66% will have this feeling at that time (Hunter, Sierra, & David, 2004; Keane, Marx, Sloan & DePrince, 2011). Because it's hard to measure dissociation, the connection between trauma and dissociation is controversial (Giesbrecht, Lynn, Lilienfeld, & Merckelbach, 2008; Loewenstein, 2018; Lynn et al., 2019).

Concept Check 6.1

Diagnose the somatic symptom and related disorders described here by choosing one of the following: (a) illness anxiety disorder, (b) somatic symptom disorder, (c) conversion disorder.

1. Candice constantly worries about her health. She has been to numerous doctors for her concerns about cancer and other serious diseases—even though she doesn't report current notable physical symptoms—only to be reassured of her well-being. Candice's anxiousness is exacerbated by each small ailment (for example, mild headaches or stomach pains) that she considers to be indications of a major illness. ____________

2. Deion arrived at Dr. Blake's office with a folder crammed full of medical records, symptom documentation, and lists of prescribed treatments and drugs. Several doctors are monitoring him for his complaints, ranging from marked chest pain to difficulty swallowing. Deion recently lost his job for using too many sick days. ____________

3. Sixteen-year-old Russell suddenly lost the use of his arms with no medical cause. The complete paralysis slowly improved to the point that he could slightly raise them. However, Russell cannot drive, pick up objects, or perform most tasks necessary for day-to-day life. ____________

During an episode of *depersonalization,* your perception alters so that you temporarily lose the sense of your own reality, as if you were in a dream and you were watching yourself. During an episode of **derealization**, your sense of the reality of the external world is lost. Things may seem to change shape or size; people may seem dead or mechanical. These sensations of unreality are characteristic of the dissociative disorders because, in a sense, they are a psychological mechanism whereby one "dissociates" from reality. Depersonalization is often part of a serious set of conditions in which reality, experience, and even identity seem to disintegrate. As we go about our day-to-day lives, we ordinarily have an excellent sense of who we are and a general knowledge of the identity of other people. We are also aware of events around us, of where we are, and of why we are there. Finally, except for occasional small lapses, our memories remain intact so that events leading up to the current moment are clear in our minds.

But what happens if we can't remember why we are in a certain place or even who we are? What happens if we lose our sense that our surroundings are real? Finally, what happens if we not only forget who we are but also begin thinking we are somebody else—somebody who has a different personality, different memories, and even different physical reactions, such as allergies we never had? These are examples of disintegrated experience (Dell & O'Neil, 2009; Spiegel, 2010; Spiegel et al., 2013; van der Hart & Nijenhuis, 2009). In each case, there are alterations in our relationship to the self, to the world, or to memory processes.

Electrophysiological recordings in animals and humans suggest that dissociation happens during a low-frequency rhythm coming from a specific brain region, the retrosplenial cortex (Vesuna et al., 2020). This brain area is associated with a wide range of cognitive functions, including episodic memory, navigation, and imagining future events. This study also points to the intriguing possibility that ketamine, which is a psychedelic drug sometimes used for treating depression and trauma (see Chapter 2), might influence this brain area as well.

Although we have much to learn about these disorders, we briefly describe two of them—depersonalization-derealization disorder and dissociative amnesia—before examining the fascinating condition of dissociative identity disorder. As you will see, the influence of social and cultural factors is strong in dissociative disorders. Even in severe cases, the expression of the pathology does not stray far from socially and culturally sanctioned forms (Giesbrecht et al., 2008; Kihlstrom, 2005a; Lynn et al., 2019).

Depersonalization-Derealization Disorder

When feelings of unreality are so severe and frightening that they dominate an individual's life and prevent normal functioning, clinicians may diagnose the rare **depersonalization-derealization disorder**. Consider the case of Mina.

You may remember from Chapter 5 that during an intense panic attack, many people (approximately 50%) experience feelings of unreality. People undergoing intense stress or experiencing a traumatic event may also experience these symptoms, which characterize the newly defined *acute stress disorder.* Feelings of depersonalization and derealization are part of several disorders (Giesbrecht et al., 2008; Lynn et al., 2019; Spiegel et al., 2011; Spiegel et al., 2013). But when severe depersonalization and derealization are the

Mina... Dancing Away from Herself

Mina, a dance teacher in her late 20s, was accompanied by her husband when she first visited the clinic and complained of "flipping out." When asked what she meant, she said, "It's the most scary thing in the world. It often happens when I'm teaching my modern dance class. I'll be up in front, and I will feel focused on. Then, as I'm demonstrating the steps, I just feel like it's not really me and that I don't really have control of my legs. Sometimes I feel like I'm standing in back of myself just watching. Also I get tunnel vision. It seems like I can only see in a narrow space right in front of me and I just get totally separated from what's going on around me. Then I begin to panic and perspire and shake." It turns out that Mina's problems began after she smoked marijuana for the first time about 10 years before. She had the same feeling then and found it scary, but with the help of friends she got through it. Lately, the feeling recurred more often and more severely, particularly when she was teaching dance class.

DSM 5 **Table 6.5**
Diagnostic Criteria for Depersonalization-Derealization Disorder

A. The presence of persistent or recurrent experiences of depersonalization, derealization, or both:
Depersonalization: Experiences of unreality, detachment, or being an outside observer with respect to one's thoughts, feelings, sensations, body or actions (e.g., perceptual alterations, distorted sense of time, unreal or absent self, emotional and/or physical numbing).
Derealization: Experiences of unreality or detachment with respect to surroundings (e.g., individuals or objects are experienced as unreal, dreamlike, foggy, lifeless, or visually distorted).

B. During the depersonalization or derealization experience, reality testing remains intact.

C. The symptoms cause clinically significant distress or impairment in social, occupational, or other important areas of functioning.

D. The disturbance is not attributable to the physiological effects of a substance (e.g., a drug of abuse, medication) or another medical condition (e.g., seizures).

E. The disturbance is not better explained by another mental disorder, such as schizophrenia, panic disorder, major depressive disorder, acute stress disorder, posttraumatic stress disorder, or another dissociative disorder.

American Psychiatric Association. (2022). *Diagnostic and statistical manual of mental disorders* (5th ed., Text Revision).

primary problem (see Table 6.2 for some examples), the individual meets criteria for depersonalization-derealization disorder (APA, 2013). Surveys suggest that this disorder exists in approximately 0.8% to 2.8% of the population (Johnson, Cohen, Kasen, & Brook, 2006; Spiegel et al., 2011). A meta-analysis with 31,905 college students suggests that as many as 11.4% of students sampled meet criteria for depersonalization-derealization disorder based on questionnaire scores. Although this rate is consistent with the prevalence of experiencing multiple types of trauma during childhood (about 12%), it is a lot higher than what has been reported in population samples using interview data (Kate, Hopwood, & Jamieson, 2020). It is quite difficult to determine a diagnosis based on self-report questionnaire data, which probably explains this discrepancy.

Table 6.2 **Dissociative Experiences Scale Item Scores in 117 Participants with Depersonalization-Derealization Disorder (Arranged in Descending Frequency)**

Abbreviated Description	Mean	SD
Surroundings seem unreal	67.4	29.6
Looking at the world through a fog	60.0	37.3
Body does not belong to one	50.6	34.7
Did not hear part of conversation	43.6	29.3
Finding familiar place strange and unfamiliar	35.3	33.0
Staring off into space; unaware of time	32.7	31.8
Can't remember if just did something or thought it	31.6	28.8
Do usually difficult things with ease/spontaneity	31.2	31.2
Act so differently/feel like two different people	28.7	32.5
Talk out loud to oneself when alone	28.4	32.2
SD: 5 standard deviations		

Adapted from D. Simeon, M. Knutelska, D. Nelson, & O. Guralnik, 2003, Feeling unreal: A depersonalization disorder update of 119 cases, *Journal of Clinical Psychiatry, 185*, 31–36. © Physicians Post Graduate Press, Inc.

Two studies (Guralnik, Giesbrecht, Knutelska, Sirroff, & Simeon, 2007; Guralnik, Schmeidler, & Simeon, 2000) compared patients who had what we now call depersonalization-derealization disorder with matched normal-comparison participants on a comprehensive neuropsychological test battery that assessed cognitive function. Although both groups were of equal intelligence, the participants with depersonalization disorder showed a distinct cognitive profile, reflecting some specific cognitive deficits on measures of attention, processing of information, short-term memory, and spatial reasoning. Basically, these patients were easily distracted and were slow to perceive and process new information. It is not clear how these cognitive and perceptual deficits develop, but they seem to correspond with reports of "tunnel vision" (perceptual distortions) and "mind emptiness" (difficulty absorbing new information) that characterize these patients.

Specific aspects of brain functioning are also associated with depersonalization (see, for example, Sierra & Berrios, 1998; Simeon, 2009; Simeon et al., 2000). Sierra and colleagues (2002) compared skin conductance responding, a psychophysiological measure of emotional responding (see Chapter 3), among 15 patients with depersonalization disorder, 11 patients with anxiety disorders, and 15 control participants without any disorder. Patients with depersonalization disorder showed greatly reduced emotional responding compared with other groups, reflecting a tendency to selectively inhibit emotional expression. Brain-imaging studies now confirm deficits in perception (Simeon, 2009; Simeon et al., 2000) and emotion regulation (Phillips et al., 2001). Other studies note dysregulation in the hypothalamic–pituitary–adrenocortical (HPA) axis among these patients, compared with normal controls (Simeon, Guralnik, Knutelska, Hollander, & Schmeidler, 2001; Spiegel et al., 2013), suggesting, again, deficits in emotional responding. Psychological treatments have not been systematically studied. One evaluation of the drug Prozac did not show any treatment effect compared with placebo (Simeon, Guralnik, Schneider, & Knutelska, 2004).

Dissociative Amnesia

Perhaps the easiest to understand of the severe dissociative disorders is one called **dissociative amnesia**, which includes several patterns. People who are unable to remember anything, including who they are, are said to suffer from **generalized amnesia**. Generalized amnesia may be lifelong or may extend from a period in the more recent past, such as 6 months or a year previously. Consider the case study described here.

Far more common than general amnesia is **localized or selective amnesia**, a failure to recall specific events, usually traumatic, that occur during a specific period. Dissociative

DSM 5 **Table 6.6**
Diagnostic Criteria for Dissociative Amnesia

A. An inability to recall important autobiographical information, usually of a traumatic or stressful nature, that is inconsistent with ordinary forgetting. *Note:* Dissociative amnesia most often consists of localized or selective amnesia for a specific event or events; or generalized amnesia for identity and life history.

B. The symptoms cause clinically significant distress or impairment in social, occupational, or other important areas of functioning.

C. The disturbance is not attributable to the physiological effects of a substance (e.g., alcohol or other drug of abuse, a medication) or a neurological or other medical condition (e.g., partial complex seizures, transient global amnesia, sequelae of a closed head injury/traumatic brain injury, or other neurological condition).

D. The disturbance is not better explained by dissociative identity disorder, posttraumatic stress disorder, acute stress disorder, somatic symptom disorder, or major or mild neurocognitive disorder.

Specify if:

With dissociative fugue: Apparently purposeful travel or bewildered wandering that is associated with amnesia for identity or for other important autobiographical information.

American Psychiatric Association. (2022). *Diagnostic and statistical manual of mental disorders* (5th ed., Text Revision).

The Woman Who Lost Her Memory

Several years ago, a woman in her early 50s brought her daughter to one of our clinics because of the girl's refusal to attend school and other severely disruptive behavior. The father, who refused to come to the session, was quarrelsome, a heavy drinker, and, on occasion, abusive. The girl's brother, now in his mid-20s, lived at home and was a burden on the family. Several times a week a major battle erupted, complete with shouting, pushing, and shoving, as each member of the family blamed others for all their problems. The mother, a strong woman, was clearly the peacemaker responsible for holding the family together. Approximately every 6 months, usually after a family battle, the mother lost her memory, and the family had her admitted to the hospital. After a few days away from the turmoil, the mother regained her memory and went home, only to repeat the cycle in the coming months. Although we did not treat this family (they lived too far away), the situation resolved itself when the children moved away and the stress decreased.

amnesia is common during war (Cardeña & Gleaves, 2003; Spiegel et al., 2013). An interesting case of a woman whose father deserted her when she was young and who then was forced to have an abortion at the age of 14 is described by Sackeim and Devanand (1991). Years later, she came for treatment for frequent headaches. In therapy, she reported early events (for example, the abortion) rather matter-of-factly, but under hypnosis she would relive, with intense emotion, the early abortion and remember that subsequently she was raped by the abortionist. She also had images of her father attending a funeral for her aunt, one of the few times she ever saw him. Upon awakening from the hypnotic state, she had no memory of emotionally reexperiencing these events, and she wondered why she had been crying. In this case, the woman did not have amnesia for the *events themselves* but rather for her intense *emotional reactions to the events.* Absence of the subjective experience of emotion that is often present in depersonalization-derealization disorder and confirmed by brain-imaging studies (Phillips et al., 2001) becomes prominent here. In most cases of dissociative amnesia, the forgetting is selective for traumatic events or memories rather than generalized.

Cognitive disorders such as dementia (discussed in Chapter 15) can also be characterized by severe forgetting or amnesia. But there are several differences between cognitive disorders and dissociative amnesia, as outlined in Table 6.3.

A subtype of dissociative amnesia is referred to as **dissociative fugue** (Ross, 2009) with *fugue* literally meaning "flight" (*fugitive* is from the same root). In these curious cases, memory loss revolves around a specific incident—an unexpected trip (or trips). Mostly, individuals just take off and later find themselves in a new place, unable to remember why or how they got there. Usually, they have left behind an intolerable situation. During these trips, a person sometimes assumes a new identity or at least becomes confused about the old identity. Consider the case of Jeffrey Ingram, a 40-year-old man from Washington state, who found himself unexpectedly in Denver.

Dissociative amnesia seldom appears before adolescence and usually occurs in adulthood. It is rare for dissociative amnesia to appear for the first time after an individual reaches the age of 50 (Sackeim & Devanand, 1991). Once dissociative disorders do appear, however, they may continue well into old age. Estimates of prevalence range anywhere from 1.8% to 7.3%, suggesting that dissociative amnesia is the most prevalent of all the dissociative disorders (Spiegel et al., 2011).

Fugue states usually end rather abruptly, and the individual returns home, recalling most, if not all, of what happened. In this disorder, the disintegrated experience is more than memory loss, involving at least some disintegration of identity, if not the complete adoption of a new one.

An apparently distinct dissociative state not found in Western cultures is called *amok* (as in "running amok"). Most people with this disorder are men. Amok has attracted attention because individuals in this trancelike state often brutally assault and sometimes kill people or animals. If the person is not killed himself, he probably will not remember the episode. Running amok is only one of a number of "running" syndromes in which an individual enters a trancelike state and suddenly, imbued with a mysterious source of energy, runs or flees for a long time. Except for amok, the prevalence of running disorders is somewhat greater in women, as with most dissociative disorders. Among native peoples of the

Table 6.3 Differences between DA and Amnesia in Cognitive Disorders

Differences	DA*	Cognitive Disorders
Due to known medical disorder or physical cause	No	Yes
Onset related to psychological trauma/extreme stress	Yes	No
Exacerbated by stress	Yes	Yes/No; anxiety can worsen memory performance in cognitive disorders
Memory deficits primarily in autobiographical recall	Yes	No, but may have circumscribed retrograde memory loss and/or general impairment in autobiographical recall that worsens with illness progression
Reversible with hypnosis	Yes	No
Improvement with sedative-hypnotics (for example, pharmacologically facilitated interviews)	Yes or no change	No or may make worse
Varying extent and nature of the intrusion of the dissociated mental elements to consciousness	Yes	No
Ability to learn new information is intact. Ability to manipulate facts and neutral information is generally normal (for example, finances, current events, etc.)	Yes	No
Disorientation to personal identity generally only occurs in late phase of illness	No	Yes

*DA, dissociative amnesia.

Jeffrey... A Troubled Trip

An amnesia sufferer who had been searching for his identity for more than a month was back in Washington state with his fiancée on Tuesday, but he still doesn't remember his past life or what happened, his mother said.

Jeffrey Alan Ingram, 40, was diagnosed in Denver with dissociative fugue, a type of amnesia.

He has had similar bouts of amnesia in the past, likely triggered by stress, once disappearing for 9 months. When he went missing this time, on September 6, he had been on his way to Canada to visit a friend who was dying of cancer, said his fiancée, Penny Hansen.

"I think that the stress, the sadness, the grief of facing a best friend dying was enough, and leaving me was enough to send him into an amnesia state," Hansen told KCNC-TV.

When Ingram found himself in Denver on September 10, he didn't know who he was. He said he walked around for about 6 hours asking people for help, then ended up at a hospital, where police spokeswoman Virginia Quinones said Ingram was diagnosed with a type of amnesia known as dissociative fugue.

Searched for his identity. Ingram's identity came to light last weekend after he appeared on several news shows asking the public for help: "If anybody recognizes me, knows who I am, please let somebody know."

"Penny's brother called her right away and told her 'Did you watch this newscast?' and 'I think that's Jeff that they're showing on television,'" said Marilyn Meehan, a spokeswoman for Hansen.

Hansen had filed a missing person report after Ingram failed to show up at her mother's home in Bellingham, Washington, on his way to Canada, but officials searching for him had turned up nothing.

On Monday night, two Denver police detectives accompanied Ingram on a flight to Seattle, where he was reunited with his fiancée.

His mother, Doreen Tompkins of Slave Lake, Alberta, was in tears as she talked about the struggle her son and the family still face.

"It's going to be very difficult again, but you know what, I can do it," she told CTV news of Edmonton, Alberta. "I did it before, I can do it again. I'll do it as many times as I have to just so I can have my son."

Memory never fully regained. Ingram had experienced an episode of amnesia in 1995 when he disappeared during a trip to a grocery store. Nine months later, he was found in a Seattle hospital, according to Thurston County, Washington, officials. His mother said he never fully regained his memory.

Meehan, who works with Hansen at the state Utilities and Transportation Commission, said the couple would not give interviews because they want to concentrate on Ingram's effort to regain his memory.

"They're taking it one step at a time," Meehan said.

"He said that while her face wasn't familiar to him, her heart was familiar to him," she said. "He can't remember his home, but he said their home felt like home to him."

AP Images/John Froschauer

Jeffrey Alan Ingram found himself in Denver not knowing who he was or why he was there after having gone missing a month earlier from Washington state.

Arctic, running disorder is termed *pivloktoq*. Among the Navajo nation, it is called *frenzy witchcraft*. Despite their different culturally determined expression, running disorders seem to resemble dissociative fugue, with the possible exception of amok.

Dissociative disorders differ in important ways across cultures. In many areas of the world, dissociative phenomena may occur as a trance or possession. The usual sorts of dissociative symptoms, such as sudden changes in personality, are attributed to possession by a spirit important in the particular culture. Often this spirit demands and receives gifts or favors from the family and friends of the individual with dissociative disorder. Like other dissociative states, trance or possession seems to be most common in women and is often associated with stress or trauma, which, as in dissociative amnesia and fugue states, is current rather than in the past.

Trance and possession are a common part of some traditional religious and cultural practices and are not considered abnormal in that context. Dissociative trances commonly occur in India, Nigeria (where they are called *vinvusa*), Thailand *(phii pob)*, and other Asian and African countries (Mezzich et al., 1992; Saxena & Prasad, 1989; van Duijil, Cardeña, & de Jong, 2005). In the United States, culturally accepted dissociation commonly occurs during African American prayer meetings (Griffith et al., 1980), Native American rituals (Jilek, 1982), and Puerto Rican spiritist sessions (Comas-Diaz, 1981). Among Bahamians and African Americans from the South, trance syndromes are often referred to colloquially as "falling out." The personality profiles of 58 cases of dissociative trance disorder in Singapore, derived from objective testing, revealed that these individuals tended to be nervous, excitable, and emotionally unstable relative to "normals" in Singapore (Ng, Yap, Su, Lim, & Ong, 2002). Although trance and possession are almost never seen in Western cultures, they are among the most common forms of dissociative states elsewhere. When the state is *undesirable* and considered pathological by members of the culture, particularly if the trance involves a perception of being possessed by an evil spirit or another person (described next), the individual would be diagnosed with an "other specified dissociative disorder (**dissociative trance**)" (APA, 2013).

Dissociative Identity Disorder

People with **dissociative identity disorder (DID)** may adopt as many as 100 new identities, all simultaneously coexisting, although the average number is closer to 15. In some cases, the identities are complete, each with its own behavior, tone of voice, and physical gestures. But in many cases, only a few characteristics are distinct because the identities are only partially independent, so it is not true that there are "multiple" complete personalities. Therefore, the name of the disorder was changed in the last edition of the DSM, DSM-IV, from multiple personality disorder to DID. Consider the case of Jonah, originally reported by Ludwig, Brandsma, Wilbur, Bendfeldt, and Jameson (1972).

Clinical Description

During Jonah's hospitalization, the staff was able to observe his behavior directly, both when he had headaches and during other periods that he did not remember. He claimed other names at these times, acted differently, and generally seemed to be another person entirely. The staff distinguished three separate identities, or **alters**, in addition to Jonah. (*Alters* is the shorthand term for the different identities or personalities in DID.) The first alter was named Sammy. Sammy seemed rational, calm, and in control. The second alter, King Young, seemed to be in charge of all sexual activity and was particularly interested in having as many heterosexual interactions as possible. The third alter was the violent and dangerous Usoffa Abdulla. Characteristically, Jonah knew nothing of the three alters. Sammy was most aware of the

DSM 5 **Table 6.7**

Diagnostic Criteria for Dissociative Identity Disorder

A. Disruption of identity characterized by two or more distinct personality states, which may be described in some cultures as an experience of possession. The disruption in identify involves marked discontinuity in sense of self and sense of agency, accompanied by related alterations in affect, behavior, consciousness, memory, perception, cognition, and/or sensory-motor functioning. These signs and symptoms may be observed by others or reported by the individual.

B. Recurrent gaps in the recall of everyday events, important personal information, and/or traumatic events that are inconsistent with ordinary forgetting.

C. The symptoms cause clinically significant distress or impairment in social, occupational, or other important areas of functioning.

D. The disturbance is not a normal part of a broadly accepted cultural or religious practice. *Note:* In children, the symptoms are not attributable to imaginary playmates or other fantasy play.

E. The symptoms are not attributable to the physiological effects of a substance (e.g., blackouts or chaotic behavior during alcohol intoxication) or another medical condition (e.g., complex partial seizures).

American Psychiatric Association. (2022). *Diagnostic and statistical manual of mental disorders* (5th ed., Text Revision).

Jonah... Bewildering Blackouts

Jonah, 27 years old and Black, suffered from severe headaches that were unbearably painful and lasted for increasingly longer periods. Furthermore, he couldn't remember things that happened while he had a headache, except that sometimes a great deal of time passed. Finally, after a particularly bad night, when he could stand it no longer, he arranged for admission to the local hospital. What prompted Jonah to come to the hospital, however, was that other people told him what he did during his severe headaches. For example, he was told that the night before he had a violent fight with another man and attempted to stab him. He fled the scene and was shot at during a high-speed chase by the police. His wife told him that during a previous headache he chased her and his 3-year-old daughter out of the house, threatening them with a butcher knife. During his headaches, and while he was violent, he called himself "Usoffa Abdulla, son of Omega." Once he attempted to drown a man in a river. The man survived, and Jonah escaped by swimming a quarter of a mile upstream. He woke up the next morning in his own bed, soaking wet, with no memory of the incident.

other personalities. King Young and Usoffa Abdulla knew a little bit about the others but only indirectly.

In the hospital, psychologists determined that Sammy first appeared when Jonah was about age 6, immediately after Jonah saw his mother stab his father. Jonah's mother sometimes dressed him as a girl in private. On one of these occasions, shortly after Sammy emerged, King Young appeared. When Jonah was 9 or 10, he was brutally attacked by a group of white youths. At this point, Usoffa Abdulla emerged, announcing that his sole reason for existence was to protect Jonah.

DSM-5 criteria for DID include amnesia, as in dissociative amnesia. In DID, however, identity has also fragmented. How many personalities live inside one body is relatively unimportant, whether there are 3, 4, or even 100 of them. Again, the defining feature of this disorder is that certain aspects of the person's identity are dissociated (Spiegel et al., 2013).

Characteristics

The person who becomes the patient and asks for treatment is usually a "host" identity. Host personalities usually attempt to hold various fragments of identity together but end up being overwhelmed. The first personality to seek treatment is seldom the original personality of the person. Usually, the host personality develops later (Putnam, 1992). Many patients have at least one impulsive alter who handles sexuality and generates income, sometimes by acting as a sex worker. In other cases, all alters may abstain from sex. Cross-gendered alters are not uncommon. For example, a small agile woman might have a strong powerful male alter who serves as a protector.

The transition from one personality to another is called a *switch.* Usually, the switch is instantaneous (although in movies and on television it is often drawn out for dramatic effect). Physical transformations may occur during switches. Posture, facial expressions, patterns of facial wrinkling, and even physical disabilities may emerge. In one study, changes in handedness occurred in 37% of the cases (Putnam, Guroff, Silberman, Barban, & Post, 1986).

Can DID Be Faked?

Are the fragmented identities "real," or is the person faking them to avoid responsibility or stress? As with conversion disorders, it is difficult to answer this question, for several reasons (Kluft, 1999; Paris, 2019). First, evidence indicates that individuals with DID are suggestible (Bliss, 1984; Giesbrecht et al., 2008; Kihlstrom, 2005a; Paris, 2019). It is possible that alters are created in response to leading questions from therapists, either during psychotherapy or while the person is in a hypnotic state.

Kenneth... The Hillside Strangler

During the late 1970s, Kenneth Bianchi brutally raped and murdered 10 young women in the Los Angeles area and left their bodies naked and in full view on the sides of various hills. Despite overwhelming evidence that Bianchi was the "Hillside Strangler," he continued to assert his innocence, prompting some professionals to think he might have DID. His lawyer brought in a clinical psychologist, who hypnotized him and asked whether there were another part of Ken with whom he could speak. Guess what? Somebody called "Steve" answered and said he had done all the killing. Steve also said that Ken knew nothing about the murders. With this evidence, the lawyer entered a plea of not guilty by reason of insanity.

The prosecution called on the late Martin Orne, a distinguished clinical psychologist and psychiatrist who was one of the world's leading experts on hypnosis and dissociative disorders (Orne, Dinges, & Orne, 1984). Orne used procedures similar to those we described in the context of conversion blindness to determine whether Bianchi was simulating DID or had a true psychological disorder. For example, Orne suggested during an in-depth interview with Bianchi that a true multiple personality disorder included at least three personalities. Bianchi soon produced a third personality. By interviewing Bianchi's friends and relatives, Orne established that there was no independent corroboration of different personalities before Bianchi's arrest. Psychological tests also failed to show significant differences among the personalities; true fragmented identities often score differently on personality tests. Several textbooks on psychopathology were found in Bianchi's room; therefore, he presumably had studied the subject. Orne concluded that Bianchi responded like someone simulating hypnosis, not someone deeply hypnotized. On the basis of Orne's testimony, Bianchi was found guilty and sentenced to life in prison.

Objective assessment of memory, particularly implicit (unconscious) memory, reveals that the memory processes in patients with DID do not differ from "normals" when the methodologies of cognitive science are used (Allen & Movius, 2000; Huntjens et al., 2002; Huntjens, Postma, Peters, Woertman, & van der Hart, 2003). Huntjens and colleagues (2006) showed that patients with DID acted more like simulators concerning other identities, about which they profess no memory (interidentity amnesia), suggesting the possibility of faking. This is in contrast to reports from interviews with patients with DID that suggest that memories are different from one alter to the next. Furthermore, Kong, Allen, and Glisky (2008) found that, much as with normal participants, patients with DID who memorized words as one identity could remember the words just as well after switching to another identity, contrary to their self-report of interidentity amnesia.

These findings on faking and the effect of hypnosis led Spanos (1996) to suggest that the symptoms of DID could mostly be accounted for by therapists who inadvertently suggested the existence of alters to suggestible individuals, a model known as the "sociocognitive model" because the possibility of identity fragments and early trauma is socially reinforced by a therapist (Kihlstrom, 2005a; Lilienfeld et al., 1999). A survey of American psychiatrists showed little consensus on the scientific validity of DID, with only one-third in the sample believing that the diagnosis should have been included without reservation in the DSM (Pope, Oliva, Hudson, Bodkin, & Gruber, 1999). (We return to this point of view when we discuss false memories.) The diagnosis captured the fascination of the public after popular books, movies, and TV series appeared on this topic. Chris Costner Sizemore was the real-life subject of a popular book and movie *The Three Faces of Eve.* Sizemore, who used the pseudonym Evelyn Lancaster in her book, was played by Joanne Woodward, who later received the Academy Award for best actress for her role in the movie. Woodward later also played the psychiatrist who treated another patient with DID in the 1976 TV miniseries *Sybil.* The patient in Sybil was played by Sally Fields, who won an Emmy Award for her role in the film. Although these two cases of DID became very popular, critics soon questioned the patients' reports and accuracy of the diagnosis. On the other hand, in the case of Chris Costner Sizemore, some objective tests suggest that many people with fragmented identities are not consciously and voluntarily simulating (Kluft, 1991, 1999). Condon, Ogston, and Pacoe (1969) examined Sizemore and determined that one of the personalities (Eve Black) showed a transient microstrabismus (difference in joined lateral eye movements) that was not observed in the other personalities. These optical differences have been confirmed by S. D. Miller (1989), who demonstrated that DID patients had 4.5 times the average number of changes in optical functioning in their alter identities than control patients who simulated alter personalities. Miller concludes that optical changes—including measures of visual acuity, manifest refraction, and eye muscle balance—would be difficult to fake. Ludwig and colleagues (1972) found that Jonah's various identities had different physiological responses to emotionally laden words, including electrodermal activity, a measure of otherwise imperceptible sweat gland activity, and EEG brain waves. Using functional magnetic resonance imaging (fMRI) procedures, changes in brain function were observed in one patient while switching from one personality to another. Specifically, this patient showed changes in hippocampal and medial temporal activity after the switch (Tsai, Condie, Wu, & Chang, 1999). A number of subsequent studies confirm that various alters have unique psychophysiological profiles (Cardeña & Gleaves, 2003; Putnam, 1997). Kluft (1999) suggests a number of additional clinical strategies to distinguish malingerers from patients with DID, including the observations that malingerers are usually eager to demonstrate their symptoms and do so in a fluid fashion. Patients with DID, on the other hand, are more likely to attempt to hide symptoms. Some scientists have also developed tests to detect malingering in DID (Brand et al., 2019). Still, DID is a highly controversial diagnosis, especially as it relates to the criminal justice system, because in the United States this diagnosis is sometimes used to support a defense of "not guilty by reason of insanity." This is problematic because the accused often has no other defense than DID (Paris, 2019).

Anna O... Revealed

We return one more time to the famous case that prompted early insights into the unconscious and contributed to the development of psychoanalysis. Earlier we described Anna O.'s conversion symptoms of paralysis in her right arm, anesthesia of her right side, and the loss of the ability to speak her native German (although she retained perfect command of English). As Anna confronted her traumatic memories of watching her father die while she nursed him, she increasingly recovered her physical abilities.

Anna O.'s real name was Bertha Pappenheim, and she was an extraordinary woman. What many people don't realize is that she was never completely cured by Breuer, who finally gave up on her in 1882. During the next decade, she was institutionalized several times with severe recurrences of her conversion symptoms before beginning a slow recovery. She went on to become a pioneering social worker and staunch crusader against the sexual abuse of women (Putnam, 1992). She devoted her life to freeing women who were trapped in prostitution and slavery throughout Europe, Russia, and the Near East. Risking her own life, she entered brothels to liberate women from their captors. She wrote a play, *Women's Rights*, about sadistic men and the ongoing abuse of women. She founded a league of Jewish women in 1904 and a home for unwed mothers in 1907. In recognition of her extraordinary contributions as one of the first militant feminists, a commemorative stamp was later issued in her honor by the West German government (Sulloway, 1979).

Pappenheim's friends remarked that she seemed to lead a "double life." On the one hand, she was a radical feminist and reformer. On the other hand, she belonged to the cultural elite in Vienna at the end of the 19th century. It is clear from Breuer's notes that there were "two Anna O.'s" and that she suffered from DID. One personality was somewhat depressed and anxious but otherwise relatively normal. But in an instant, she would turn dark and foreboding. Breuer was convinced that during these times "Anna" was someone else, someone who hallucinated and was verbally abusive. And it was the second Anna O. who experienced conversion symptoms. The second Anna O. spoke only English or garbled mixtures of four or five languages. The first Anna O. spoke fluent French and Italian, as well as her native German. Characteristically, one personality had no memory of what happened when the other was "out." Almost anything might cause an instant switch in personalities—for example, the sight of an orange, which was Anna O.'s primary source of nourishment when she nursed her dying father. Putnam (1992, p. 36) reports that when Pappenheim died of cancer in 1936, "It is said that she left two wills, each written in a different hand."

Statistics

Jonah had four identities and Anna O. only two, but the average number of alter personalities is reported by clinicians as closer to 15 (Ross, 1997; Sackeim & Devanand, 1991). Of people with DID, the ratio of women to men is as high as 9:1, although these data are based on accumulated case studies rather than survey research (Maldonado, Butler, & Spiegel, 1998). The onset is almost always in childhood, often as young as 4 years of age, although it is usually approximately 7 years after the appearance of symptoms before the disorder is identified (Maldonado et al., 1998; Putnam et al., 1986). Once established, the disorder tends to last a lifetime in the absence of treatment. The form DID takes does not seem to vary substantially over the person's lifespan, although some evidence indicates the frequency of switching decreases with age (Sackeim & Devanand, 1991). Different personalities may emerge in response to new life situations, as was the case with Jonah.

There are not good epidemiological studies on the prevalence of the disorder in the population at large, although investigators now think it is more common than previously estimated (Kluft, 1991; Ross, 1997). For example, semistructured interviews of large numbers of severely disturbed inpatients found prevalence rates of DID of between 3% and 6% in North America (Ross, 1997; Ross, Anderson, Fleisher, & Norton, 1991; Saxe et al., 1993) and approximately 2% in Holland (Friedl & Draijer, 2000). In the best survey to date in a nonclinical (community) setting, a prevalence of 1.5% was found during the previous year (Johnson et al., 2006).

A large percentage of DID patients have simultaneous psychological disorders that may include anxiety, substance use disorder, depression, and personality disorders (Giesbrecht et al., 2008; Johnson et al., 2006; Kluft, 1999; Ross et al., 1990). In one sample of more than 100 patients, more than seven additional diagnoses were noted on the average (Ellason & Ross, 1997). Another study of 42 patients documented a pattern of severe comorbid personality disorders, including severe borderline features (Dell, 1998). In some cases, this high rate of comorbidity may reflect that certain disorders, such as borderline personality disorder, share many features with DID—for example, self-destructive, sometimes suicidal behavior, and emotional instability. Because auditory hallucinations are common, DID is often misdiagnosed as a psychotic disorder (Martinez et al., 2020; Ross, 2020). But the voices in DID are reported by patients as coming from inside their heads, not outside as in psychotic disorders. Because patients with DID are usually aware the voices are hallucinations, they don't report them and try to suppress them. These voices often encourage doing something against the person's will, so some individuals, particularly in other cultures, appear to be possessed by demons (Putnam, 1997). DID seems to occur in a variety of cultures throughout the world, particularly in terms of experiencing possession, which is one manifestation of DID (Boon & Draijer, 1993; Coons, Bowman, Kluft, & Milstein, 1991; Ross, 1997). Coons and colleagues (1991) found reports of DID in 21 different countries.

Causes

It is informative to examine current evidence on causes for all dissociative disorders, as we do later, but our emphasis here is on the etiology of DID. Life circumstances that encourage the development of DID seem quite clear in at least one respect. Almost every patient presenting with this disorder reports to their mental health professional being horribly, often unspeakably, abused as a child.

Imagine you are a child in a situation like this. What can you do? You're too young to run away. You're too young to call the authorities. Although the pain may be unbearable, you have no way of knowing it is unusual or wrong. But you can do one thing. You can escape into a fantasy world; you can be somebody else. If the escape blunts the physical and emotional pain just for a minute or makes the next hour bearable, chances are you'll escape again. Your mind learns there is no limit to the identities that can be created as needed. Fifteen? Twenty-five? A hundred? Such numbers have been recorded in some cases. You do whatever it takes to get through life. Most surveys report a high rate of childhood trauma in cases of DID (Gleaves, 1996; Ross, 1997). Putnam and colleagues (1986) examined 100 cases and found that 97% of the patients had experienced significant trauma, usually sexual or physical abuse. Sixty-eight percent reported incest. Ross and colleagues (1990) reported that, of 97 cases, 95% reported physical or sexual abuse. Some children reported being buried alive. Some were tortured with matches, steam irons, razor blades, or glass. Investigators have corroborated the existence of at least some early sexual abuse in 12 patients with DID, whose backgrounds were extensively investigated by examining early records, interviewing relatives and acquaintances, and so on (Lewis, Yeager, Swica, Pincus, & Lewis, 1997), although Kluft (1996, 1999) notes that some reports by patients are not true but have been confabulated (made up).

Not all the trauma is caused by abuse. Putnam (1992) describes a young girl in a war zone who saw both her parents blown to bits in a minefield. In a heart-wrenching response, she tried to piece the bodies back together, bit by bit.

Such observations have led to wide-ranging agreement that DID is rooted in a natural tendency to escape or "dissociate" from the unremitting negative affect associated with severe abuse (Kluft, 1984, 1991). A lack of social support during or after the abuse also seems implicated. A study of 428 adolescent twins demonstrated that a surprisingly major portion of the cause of dissociative experience could be attributed to a chaotic, nonsupportive family environment. Individual experience and personality factors also contributed to dissociative experiences (Waller & Ross, 1997).

The behavior and emotions that make up dissociative disorders seem related to otherwise normal tendencies present in all of us to some extent. It is quite common for otherwise normal individuals to escape in some way from emotional or physical pain (Butler, Duran, Jasiukaitis, Koopman, & Spiegel, 1996; Spiegel et al., 2013). Noyes and Kletti (1977) surveyed more than 100 survivors of various life-threatening situations and found that most had experienced some type of dissociation, such as feelings of unreality, a blunting of emotional and physical pain, and even separation from their bodies. Dissociative amnesia and fugue states are clearly reactions to severe life stress. But the life stress or trauma is in the present rather than the past, as in the case of the overwrought mother who suffered from dissociative amnesia. Many patients are escaping from legal difficulties or severe stress at home or on the job (Sackeim & Devanand, 1991). But sophisticated statistical analyses indicate that "normal" dissociative reactions differ substantially from the pathological experiences we've described (Waller, Putnam, & Carlson, 1996; Waller & Ross, 1997) and that at least some people do not develop severe pathological dissociative experiences, no matter how extreme the stress. These findings are consistent with our diathesis–stress model in that only with the appropriate vulnerabilities (the diathesis) will someone react to stress with pathological dissociation.

You may have noticed that DID seems similar in its etiology to posttraumatic stress disorder (PTSD). Both conditions feature strong emotional reactions to experiencing a severe trauma (Butler et al., 1996). But remember that not everyone goes on to experience PTSD after severe trauma. Only people who are biologically and psychologically vulnerable to anxiety are at risk for developing PTSD in response to moderate levels of trauma. As the severity of the trauma increases, however, a greater percentage of people develop PTSD as a consequence, some with the dissociative subtype of PTSD (see Chapter 5). Still, some people do not become victims of the disorder even after the most severe traumas, suggesting that individual psychological and biological factors interact with the trauma to produce PTSD.

One perspective suggests that DID is an extreme subtype of PTSD, with a much greater emphasis on the process of dissociation than on symptoms of anxiety, although both are present in each disorder (Butler et al., 1996). Some evidence also shows that the "developmental window" of vulnerability to the abuse that leads to DID closes at approximately 9 years of age (Putnam, 1997). After that, DID is unlikely to develop, although severe PTSD might. If true, this is a particularly good example of the role of development in the etiology of psychopathology.

We also must remember that we know relatively little about DID. Our conclusions are based on retrospective case studies or correlations rather than on the prospective examination of people who may have undergone the severe trauma that seems to lead to DID (Kihlstrom, 2005a; Kihlstrom, Glisky, & Anguilo, 1994). Therefore, it is hard to say what psychological or biological factors might contribute, but there are hints concerning individual differences that might play a role.

Suggestibility

Suggestibility is a personality trait distributed normally across the population, much like weight and height. Some people are more suggestible than others; some are relatively immune to suggestibility; and the majority fall in the midrange.

Did you ever have an imaginary childhood playmate? Many people did, and it is one sign of the ability to lead a rich fantasy life, which can be helpful and adaptive. But it also seems to correlate with being suggestible or easily hypnotized (some people equate the terms *suggestibility* and *hypnotizability*). A hypnotic trance is also similar to dissociation (Butler et al., 1996; Spiegel et al., 2013). People in a trance tend to be focused on one aspect of their world, and they become vulnerable to suggestions by the hypnotist. There is also the phenomenon of self-hypnosis, in which individuals can dissociate from most of the world around them and "suggest" to themselves that, for example, they won't feel pain in one of their hands.

According to the *autohypnotic model,* people who are suggestible may be able to use dissociation as a defense against extreme trauma (Putnam, 1991). As many as 50% of DID patients clearly remember imaginary playmates in childhood (Ross et al., 1990); whether they were created before or after the trauma is not entirely clear. According to this view, when the trauma becomes unbearable, the person's very identity splits into multiple dissociated identities. Children's ability to distinguish clearly between reality and fantasy as they grow older may be what closes the developmental window for developing DID at approximately age 9. People who are less suggestible may develop a severe posttraumatic stress reaction but not a dissociative reaction. Once again, these explanations are all speculative because there are no controlled studies of this phenomenon (Giesbrecht et al., 2008; Kihlstrom, 2005b).

Biological Contributions

As in PTSD, where the evidence is more solid, there is almost certainly a biological vulnerability to DID, but it is difficult to pinpoint. For example, in the large twin study mentioned earlier

BSIP/UIG via Getty Images

A person in a hypnotic trance is suggestible and may become absorbed in a particular experience.

(Waller & Ross, 1997), none of the variance or identifiable causal factors was attributable to heredity: All of it was environmental. As with anxiety disorders, more basic heritable traits, such as tension and responsiveness to stress, may increase vulnerability. On the other hand, much as in PTSD, there is some evidence of smaller hippocampal and amygdala volume in patients with DID compared with "normals" (Vermetten, Schmahl, Lindner, Loewenstein, & Bremner, 2006). Future studies might use this and other information to aid in the diagnosis of DID, such as by identifying patterns of structural brain abnormalities and other biological markers of DID (Reinders et al., 2019; Roydeva & Reinders, 2021)

Interesting observations may provide some hints about brain activity during dissociation. Individuals with certain neurological disorders, particularly seizure disorders, experience many dissociative symptoms (Bob, 2003; Bowman & Coons, 2000; Cardeña, Lewis-Fernandez, Bear, Pakianathan, & Spiegel, 1996). Temporal lobe epileptic seizure especially can be associated with dissociative symptoms (Bob, 2003). Patients with dissociative experiences who have seizure disorders are clearly different from those who do not (Ross, 1997). The seizure patients develop dissociative symptoms in adulthood that are not associated with trauma, in clear contrast to DID patients without seizure disorders. This is an area for future study (Hara et al., 2015).

Head injury and resulting brain damage may induce amnesia or other types of dissociative experience. But these conditions are usually easily diagnosed because they are generalized and irreversible and are associated with an identifiable head trauma (Butler et al., 1996). Finally, strong evidence exists that sleep deprivation produces dissociative symptoms such as marked hallucinatory activity (Giesbrecht et al., 2007; van der Kloet, Giesbrecht, Lynn, Merckelbach, & de Zutter, 2012). In fact, the symptoms of individuals with DID seem to worsen when they feel tired. Simeon and Abugal (2006) report that patients with DID "often liken it to bad jet lag and feel much worse when they travel across time zones" (p. 210).

Real Memories and False

Again, retrospective case studies suggest that individuals presenting with dissociation, and particularly DID, may have experienced severe trauma, such as sexual abuse, early in their lives but that they have dissociated themselves from this experience and "repressed" the memory. But some clinical scientists suggest that many such memories are simply the result of strong suggestions by careless therapists who assume people with this condition have been abused. One of the most controversial issues in the field of abnormal psychology today concerns the extent to which memories of early trauma, particularly sexual abuse, are accurate. This issue is not specific to any one particular mental disorder. Rather, whenever clinical decisions are based on a person's memory, it is important to consider the fact that memories are not always very accurate or even true, even if they *feel* true.

Freud assumed that, similar to a videorecorder, almost everything we experience is permanently stored in our brains as highly preserved and almost complete records of our past, except for some important details that reveal themselves through hypnosis and other strategies, such as dream analysis and free association. Today, we know that this idea of memory is incorrect. Memory is not a state but a process that changes with time and usage, depending on the particular processing stage.

In particular, there are two windows of memory vulnerability when our memories can be changed significantly: First, when we initially store it (or consolidate it), and second, when we restore (or reconsolidate) it after retrieval (Phelps & Hofmann, 2019). As a result, sometimes, we can't remember important things that did happen and other times, we seem to remember things that actually never happened. But this controversy often arises in the context of studying traumatic memories, particularly as identified in DID, so we discuss the research, both pros and cons, bearing on this important topic because the stakes in this controversy are enormous, with considerable opportunity for harm to innocent people on each side of the controversy.

On the one hand, if early sexual abuse did occur but is not remembered because of dissociative amnesia, it is crucially important to reexperience aspects of the trauma under the direction of a skilled therapist to relieve current suffering. Without therapy, the patient is likely to suffer from PTSD or a dissociative disorder indefinitely. It is also important that perpetrators are held accountable for their actions because abuse of this type is a crime and prevention is an important goal.

On the other hand, if memories of early trauma are inadvertently created in response to suggestions by a careless therapist but seem real to the patient, false accusations against loved ones could lead to irreversible family breakup and, perhaps, unjust prison sentences for those falsely accused as perpetrators. Allegedly inaccurate accusations based on false memories have led to substantial lawsuits against therapists, resulting in awards of millions of dollars in damages. As with most issues that reach this level of contention and disagreement, it is clear that the final answer will not involve an all-or-none resolution. There is irrefutable evidence that false memories *can* be created by reasonably well-understood psychological processes (Bernstein & Loftus, 2009; Ceci, 2003; Frenda, Nichols, & Loftus, 2011; Geraerts et al., 2009; Lilienfeld et al., 1999; Loftus & Davis, 2006; McNally, 2003, 2012a; Shaw & Porter, 2015; Toth, Harris, Goodman, & Cicchetti, 2011; Wilson, Mickes, Stolarz-Fantino,

Evrard, & Fantino, 2015). Some authors content that early traumatic experiences can cause selective dissociative amnesia, with substantial implications for psychological functioning (Dahlenberg et al., 2012; Gleaves, Smith, Butler, & Spiegel, 2004; Kluft, 1999; Spiegel et al., 2013). In contrast, others question the assumption that people can encode traumatic experiences without being able to recall them (for example, Lynn et al., 2014).

Evidence supporting the existence of distorted or illusory memories comes from experiments like one by the distinguished cognitive psychologist Elizabeth Loftus and her colleagues (Loftus, 2003; Loftus & Davis, 2006). Loftus, Coan, and Pickrell (1996) successfully convinced a number of individuals that they had been lost for an extended period when they were approximately 5 years old, which was not true. A trusted companion was recruited to "plant" the memory. In one case, a 14-year-old boy was told by his older brother that he had been lost in a nearby shopping mall when he was 5 years old, rescued by an older man, and reunited with his mother and brother. Several days after receiving this suggestion, the boy reported remembering the event and even that he felt frightened when he was lost. As time went by, the boy remembered more and more details of the event, beyond those described in the "plant," including an exact description of the older man. When he was finally told the incident never happened, the boy was surprised, and he continued to describe details of the event as if they were true. Bernstein and Loftus (2009) reviewed a series of experiments demonstrating that, for example, creating a false memory of becoming ill after eating egg salad led to eating less egg salad and reporting a distaste for egg salad up to 4 months later during a test in which the participants didn't know they were being tested for food preferences.

Young children are quite unreliable in reporting accurate details of events (Bruck, Ceci, Francouer, & Renick, 1995), particularly emotional events (Howe, 2007; Howe & Knott, 2015; Toth et al., 2011). In one study (Bruck et al., 1995), 35 3-year-old girls were given a genital exam as part of their routine medical checkup; another 35 girls were not (the control group). Shortly after the exam, with her mother present, each girl was asked to describe where the doctor had touched her. She was then presented with an anatomically correct doll and asked again to point out where the doctor had touched her. The findings indicated that the children were inaccurate in reporting what happened. Approximately 60% of those who were touched in the genital region refused to indicate this, whether the dolls were used or not. On the other hand, of the children in the control group, approximately 60% indicated genital insertions or other intrusive acts by the doctor, even though nothing of the sort had occurred.

In another set of studies (Ceci, 2003), preschool children were asked to think about actual events that they had experienced, such as an accident, and about fictitious events, such as having to go to the hospital to get their fingers removed from a mousetrap. Each week for 10 consecutive weeks, an interviewer asked each child to choose one of the scenes and to "think very hard and tell me if this ever happened to you." The child thus experienced thinking hard and visualizing both real and fictitious scenes over an extended period. After 10 weeks, the children were examined by a new interviewer who had not participated in the experiment.

Ceci and his colleagues conducted several experiments using this paradigm (Ceci, 1995, 2003). In one study, 58% of the preschool children described the fictitious event as if it had happened. Another 25% of the children described the fictitious events as real a majority of the time. Furthermore, the children's narratives were detailed, coherent, and embellished in ways that were not suggested originally. More telling was that in one study, 27% of the children, when told their memory was false, claimed that they really did remember the event.

Clancy and colleagues, in a fascinating experiment, studied the process of false memory creation in a group who reported having recovered memories of traumatic events unlikely to have occurred: abduction by space aliens. Among three groups—those reporting recovered memories of alien abduction, those who believe they were abducted but have no memories of it (repressed memories), and people who have no such beliefs or memories—some interesting differences emerged (Clancy, McNally, Schacter, Lenzenweger, & Pitman, 2002; McNally 2012). Those reporting recovered and repressed memories of abduction also evidenced more false recall and recognition on some cognitive tasks in the laboratory and scored higher on measures of suggestibility and depression than control participants. These studies collectively indicate that memories are malleable and easily distorted, particularly in some individuals with certain personality traits and characteristics such as vivid imaginal capabilities (absorption) and an openness to unusual ideas (McNally, 2012a).

But there is also plenty of evidence that therapists need to be sensitive to signs of trauma that may not be fully remembered in patients presenting with symptoms of dissociative disorder or PTSD. Even if patients are unable to report or remember early trauma, it can sometimes be confirmed through corroborating evidence (Coons, 1994). In one study, Williams (1994) interviewed 129 women with documented histories, such as hospital records, of having been sexually abused as children. Thirty-eight percent did not recall the incidents that had been reported to authorities at least 17 years earlier, even with extensive probing of their abuse histories. This lack of recall was more extensive if the victim had been young and knew the abuser. But Goodman and colleagues (2003) interviewed 175 individuals with documented child sexual abuse histories and found that most participants (81%) remembered and reported the abuse. Older age when the abuse ended and emotional support following initial disclosure of the abuses were associated with higher rates of disclosures.

Prospective measures of abuse are rarely available in clinical practice. Therefore, clinicians (and the judicial system) usually rely on retrospective measures of abuse, using retrospective measures as a shortcut to gather the same information. However, prospective and retrospective reports of childhood abuse show poor agreement as reported in a meta-analysis (Baldwin et al., 2019). This study showed that more than half of individuals with prospective observations of childhood maltreatment did not report it retrospectively, and likewise more than half of individuals retrospectively reporting childhood abuse did not have concordant prospective observations. The agreement between prospective and retrospective measures of childhood abuse was higher in studies that used interviews rather than questionnaires to gather this information. Clearly, childhood abuse can have serious adverse consequences on people's lives. However, many factors should be taken into consideration before we can be reasonably certain that an abuse has happened. Some of these factors include the reporter's motivation, measurement factors, and memory biases. Memory, especially, is highly malleable.

McNally and Geraerts (2009), for example, present evidence suggesting that some people, after many years, simply forget these early experiences and recall them after encountering some reminders outside of therapy. In this group, it's not necessary to invoke the concepts of repression, trauma, or false memory. It is simple forgetting. In summary, among those individuals reporting memories of sexual abuse, some may have experienced it and remembered it all along, some people may have false memories, some may have recovered memories in therapy of "repressed" sexual abuse, and some may have simply forgotten the incident but remember later.

How will this controversy be resolved? Because false memories can be created through strong repeated suggestions by an authority figure, therapists must be fully aware of the conditions under which this is likely to occur, particularly when dealing with young children. This requires extensive knowledge of the workings of memory and other aspects of psychological functioning and illustrates, again, the dangers of dealing with inexperienced or inadequately trained psychotherapists. Elaborate tales of satanic abuse of children under the care of older women in day care centers are most likely cases of memories implanted by aggressive and careless therapists or law enforcement officials (Lilienfeld et al., 1999; Loftus & Davis, 2006; McNally, 2003). In some cases, older caregivers have been sentenced to life in prison.

On the other hand, many people with dissociative disorder and PTSD have suffered documented extreme abuse and trauma, which could then become dissociated from awareness. It may be that future research will find that the severity of dissociative amnesia is directly related to the severity of the trauma in vulnerable individuals with certain specific coping styles (Toth et al., 2011), and this type of severe dissociative reaction is also likely to be proved as qualitatively different from "normal" dissociative experiences we all have occasionally, such as feeling unreal or not here for a moment or two (see, for example, Kluft, 1999; Waller et al., 1996). Advocates on both sides of this issue agree that clinical science must proceed as quickly as possible to specify the processes under which the implantation of false memories is likely and to define the presenting features that indicate a real but dissociated traumatic experience (Frenda et al., 2011; Goodman, Quas, & Ogle, 2010; Kihlstrom, 1997, 2005a; Lilienfeld et al., 1999; Pope, 1996, 1997). Until then, mental health professionals must be extremely careful not to prolong unnecessary suffering among both victims of actual abuse and victims falsely accused as abusers (for example, Lynn et al., 2014).

Treatment

Individuals who experience dissociative amnesia or a fugue state usually get better on their own and remember what they have forgotten. The episodes are so clearly related to current life stress that prevention of future episodes usually involves therapeutic resolution of the distressing situations and increasing the strength of personal coping mechanisms. When necessary, therapy focuses on recalling what happened during the amnesic or fugue states, often with the help of friends or family who know what happened, so that patients can confront the information and integrate it into their conscious experience.

For DID, however, the process is not so easy. With the person's very identity shattered into many elements, reintegrating the personality might seem hopeless. Fortunately, this is not always the case. There are some documented successes of attempts to reintegrate identities through long-term psychotherapy (Brand et al., 2009; Ellason & Ross, 1997; Kluft, 2009). Nevertheless, the prognosis for most people remains guarded. Coons (1986) found that only 5 of 20 patients achieved a full integration of their identities. Ellason and Ross (1997) reported that 12 of 54 (22.2%) patients had achieved integration 2 years after presenting for treatment, which in most cases had been continuous. These results could be attributed to other factors than therapy because no experimental comparison was present (Powell & Howell, 1998).

The strategies that therapists use today in treating DID are based on accumulated clinical wisdom, as well as on procedures that have been successful with PTSD (Gentile, Dillin, & Gillig, 2013; Gold & Seibel, 2009; Keane et al., 2011; Maldonado et al., 1998; see Chapter 5). The fundamental goal is to identify cues or triggers that provoke memories of trauma, dissociation, or both and to neutralize them. More important, the patient must confront and relive the early trauma and gain control over the horrible events, at least as they recur in the patient's mind (Kluft, 2009; Ross, 1997). To instill this sense of control, the therapist must skillfully and slowly help the patient visualize and relive aspects of the trauma until it is simply a terrible memory instead of a current event. Because the memory is unconscious, aspects of the experience are often not known to either the patient or the therapist until they emerge during treatment. Hypnosis is often used to access unconscious memories and bring various alters into awareness. Because the process of dissociation may be similar to the process of hypnosis, the latter may be a particularly efficient way to access traumatic memories (Maldonado et al., 1998). (There is as yet no evidence that hypnosis is a *necessary* part of treatment.) DID seems to run a chronic course and seldom improves spontaneously, which confirms that current treatments, primitive as they are, have some effectiveness.

It is possible that reemerging memories of trauma may trigger further dissociation. The therapist must be on guard against this happening. Trust is important to any therapeutic relationship, but it is essential in the treatment of DID. Occasionally, medication is combined with therapy, but there is little indication that it helps much. What little clinical evidence there is indicates that antidepressant drugs might be appropriate in some cases (Gentile, Dillin, & Gillig, 2013; Kluft, 1996; Putnam & Loewenstein, 1993).

Concept Check 6.2

Diagnose the dissociative disorders described here by choosing one of the following: (a) dissociative fugue, (b) depersonalization-derealization disorder, (c) generalized amnesia, (d) dissociative identity disorder, and (e) localized amnesia.

1. Nylah was found wandering the streets, unable to recall any important personal information. After searching her purse and finding an address, doctors were able to contact her mother. They learned that Nylah had just been in a terrible accident and was the only survivor. Nylah could not remember her mother or any details of the accident. She was distressed. ________

2. Gabriel was brought to a clinic by his mother. She was concerned because at times his behavior was strange. His speech and his way of relating to people and situations would change dramatically, almost as if he were a different person. What bothered her and Gabriel most was that he could not recall anything he did during these periods. ________

3. Jhené complained about feeling out of control. She said she felt sometimes as if she were floating under the ceiling and just watching things happen to her. She also experienced tunnel vision and felt uninvolved in the things that went on in the room around her. This always caused her to panic and perspire. ________

4. Rashadis 64 and recently arrived in town. He does not know where he is from or how he got here. His driver's license proves his name, but he is unconvinced it is his. He is in good health and not taking any medication. ________

5. Rosita cannot remember what happened last weekend. On Monday, she was admitted to a hospital, suffering from cuts, bruises, and contusions. It also appeared that she had been sexually assaulted. ________

DSM Controversies: *Radical Changes in Classification*

As noted in the beginning of this chapter, somatic symptom and related disorders and dissociative disorders are among the oldest recognized mental disorders. And yet we have much to learn about the nature of these disorders, and neither grouping of disorders may comprise a uniform category that reflects shared characteristics for purposes of classification (Mayou et al., 2005). For example, the grouping of somatic symptom disorders was based in the past on the assumption that "somatization" is a common process in which a mental disorder manifests itself in the form of physical symptoms. The specific disorders, then, simply reflect the different ways in which symptoms can be expressed physically. But major questions arose concerning the classification of these disorders (Noyes, Stuart, & Watson, 2008; Voigt et al., 2010; Voigt et al., 2012).

Specifically, and as noted at the beginning of the chapter, the somatic symptom disorders all share presentations of somatic symptoms accompanied by cognitive distortions in the form of misattributions of or excessive preoccupation with symptoms. These cognitive distortions may include excessive anxiety about health or physical symptoms, a tendency to think the worst or "catastrophize" about these symptoms, and very strong beliefs that physical symptoms might be more serious than health-care professionals have recognized. Also, people presenting with these disorders often make health concerns a very central part of their lives; in other words, they adopt the "sick role."

For this reason, DSM-5 has changed very substantially the definitions of these disorders to focus on two major factors: the severity and number of physical symptoms, as well as the severity of anxiety focused on the symptoms and the degree of behavior change as a consequence of the symptoms. In illness anxiety disorder, physical symptoms need not even be present beyond just mild complaints, and the focus is solely on severe anxiety over the prospect that one is ill or will become ill. Preliminary explorations of the validity and utility of this strategy indicate that this new dimensional approach, reflecting both physical and psychological symptom severity, may be very helpful to clinicians in predicting the course of the disorder as well as selecting among possible treatments (Noyes et al., 2008; Voigt et al., 2010; Voigt et al., 2012; Wollburg et al., 2013).

Another advantage of this approach is that there is less burden on physicians to make very tricky determinations on whether the symptoms have physical causes as was the case in DSM-IV. Rather, the combination of chronic physical symptoms accompanied by the psychological factors of misattributing the meaning of the symptoms and excessive concern is sufficient to make the diagnosis. This new category also includes psychological factors affecting medical condition (see Chapter 9) and the factitious disorders because all involve the presentation of physical symptoms and/or concern about medical illness. Needless to say, the very radical nature of change in this major category of disorders is proving to be very controversial, primarily because so little data exist on the validity of these new categories or even the reliability with which they can be diagnosed. But they appear to be an improvement, and clinical investigators are already busy attempting to confirm or disconfirm the utility of this new approach.

Summary

Somatic Symptom and Related Disorders

- Individuals with somatic symptom and related disorders are pathologically concerned with the functioning of their bodies and bring these concerns to the attention of health professionals, who usually find no identifiable medical basis for the physical complaints.
- There are several types of somatic symptom disorders. Somatic symptom disorder is characterized by a focus on one or more physical symptoms accompanied by marked distress focused on the symptom that is disproportionate to the nature or severity of the physical symptoms. This condition may dominate the individual's life and interpersonal relationships. Illness anxiety disorder is a condition in which individuals believe they are seriously ill and become anxious over this possibility, even though they are not experiencing any notable physical symptoms at the time. In conversion disorder, there is physical malfunctioning, such as paralysis, without any apparent physical problems. Distinguishing among conversion reactions, real physical disorders, and outright malingering, or faking, is sometimes difficult. Even more puzzling can be factitious disorder, in which the person's symptoms are feigned and under voluntary control, as with malingering, but for no apparent reason.
- The causes of somatic symptom disorder are not well understood. Patients with this disorder are often preoccupied with physical symptoms that significantly distress or interfere with their lives. In the case of illness anxiety disorder (formerly known as hypochondriasis), the person experiences significant anxiety about having or developing a serious medical disease. The latter diagnosis is similar to an anxiety disorder. Treatment of somatic symptom disorders ranges from basic techniques of reassurance and social support to interventions meant to reduce stress and remove any secondary gain for the behavior. Specifically tailored cognitive-behavioral therapy has proved successful with these conditions.

Dissociative Disorders

- Dissociative disorders are characterized by alterations in perceptions: a sense of detachment from one's own self, from the world, or from memories.
- Dissociative disorders include depersonalization-derealization disorder, in which the individual's sense of personal reality is temporarily lost (depersonalization), as is the reality of the external world (derealization). In dissociative amnesia, the individual may be unable to remember important personal information. In generalized amnesia, the individual is unable to remember anything; more commonly, the individual is unable to recall specific events that occur during a specific period (localized or selective amnesia). In dissociative fugue, a subtype of dissociative amnesia, memory loss is combined with an unexpected trip (or trips). In the extreme, new identities, or alters, may be formed, as in dissociative identity disorder (DID). The causes of dissociative disorders are not well understood but often seem related to the tendency to escape psychologically from stress or memories of traumatic events.
- Treatment of dissociative disorders involves helping the patient reexperience the traumatic events in a controlled therapeutic manner to develop better coping skills. In the case of DID, therapy is often long term. Particularly essential with this disorder is a sense of trust between therapist and patient.

Key Terms

dissociative disorder, 181
somatic symptom disorder, 181
illness anxiety disorder, 182
psychological factors affecting medical condition, 188
conversion disorder, 189
malingering, 189
factitious disorder, 190
Munchausen syndrome, 190
derealization, 194
depersonalization-derealization disorder, 194
dissociative amnesia, 195
generalized amnesia, 195
localized or selective amnesia, 195
dissociative fugue, 196
dissociative trance, 198
dissociative identity disorder (DID), 198
alters, 198

Answers to Concept Checks

6.1

1. a; 2. b; 3. c

6.2

1. c; 2. d; 3. b; 4. a; 5. e

Exploring Somatic Symptom and Dissociative Disorders

These two sets of disorders share some common features and are strongly linked historically as "hysterical neuroses." Both are relatively rare and not yet well understood.

SOMATIC SYMPTOM AND RELATED DISORDERS

Characterized by a pathological concern with physical functioning or appearance

Illness Anxiety Disorder

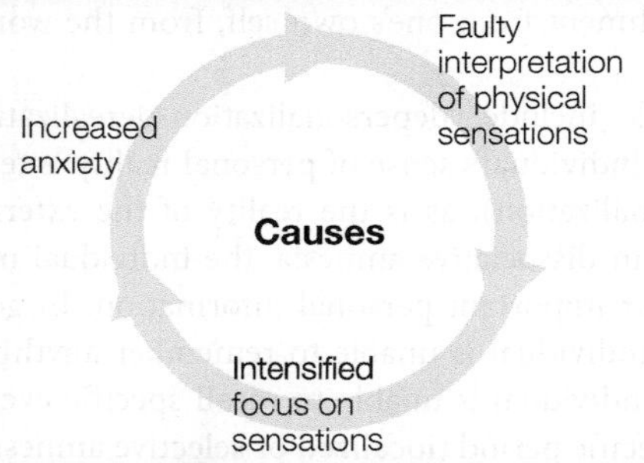

Characteristics

- Severe anxiety over physical problems that are medically undetectable
- Affects women and men equally
- May emerge at any age
- Evident in diverse cultures

Treatment

- Psychotherapy to challenge illness perceptions
- Counseling and/or support groups to provide reassurance

Somatic Symptom Disorder

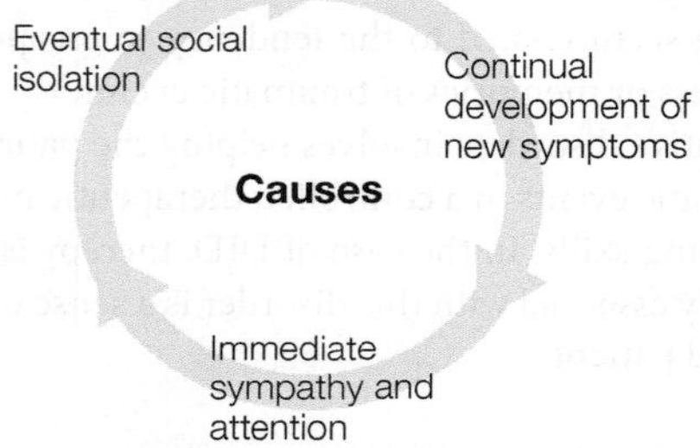

Characteristics

- Reports of multiple physical symptoms without a medical basis
- Runs in families; probably heritable basis
- Rare—most prevalent among unmarried women in low socioeconomic groups
- Onset usually in adolescence; often persists into old age

Treatment

- Hard to treat
- Cognitive-behavioral therapy (CBT) to provide reassurance, reduce stress, and minimize help-seeking behaviors
- Therapy to broaden basis for relating to others

Conversion Disorder

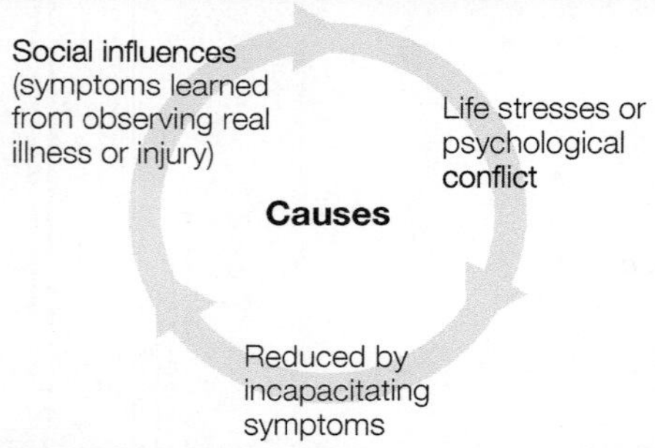

Characteristics

- Severe physical dysfunctioning (for example, paralysis and blindness) without corresponding physical pathology
- Affected people are genuinely unaware that they can function normally
- May coincide with other problems, especially somatic symptom disorder
- Most prevalent in low socioeconomic groups, women, and men under extreme stress (for example, soldiers)

Treatment

- Same as for somatic symptom disorder, with emphasis on resolving life stress or conflict and reducing help-seeking behaviors

DISSOCIATIVE DISORDERS

Characterized by detachment from the self (depersonalization) and objective reality (derealization)

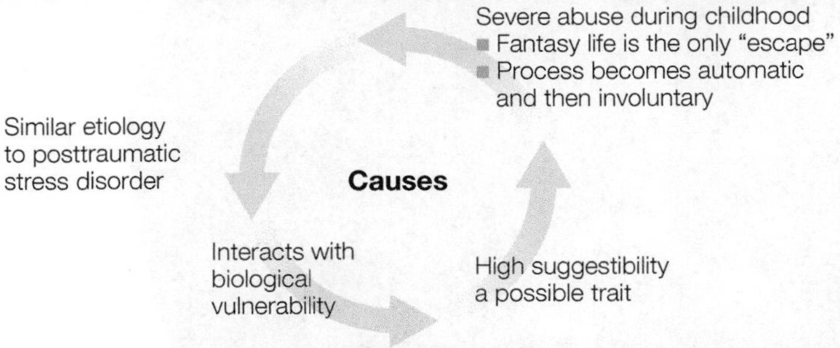

istockphoto.com/track5/Vetta Collection

Controversy

The scientific community is divided over the question of whether multiple identities are a genuine experience or faked. Studies have shown that "false memories" can be created ("implanted") by therapists. Other tests confirm that various alters are physiologically distinct.

Disorder	Characteristics	Treatment
Dissociative Identity Disorder (DID)	■ Affected person adopts new identities, or alters, that coexist simultaneously; the alters may be complete and distinct personalities or only partly independent ■ Average number of alters is 15 ■ Childhood onset; affects more women than men ■ Patients often suffer from other psychological disorders simultaneously ■ Rare outside of Western cultures	■ Long-term psychotherapy may reintegrate separate personalities in 25% of patients ■ Treatment of associated trauma similar to posttraumatic stress disorder; lifelong condition without treatment
Depersonalization-Derealization Disorder	■ Severe and frightening feelings of detachment dominate the person's life ■ Affected person feels like an outside observer of his or her own mental or body processes ■ Causes significant distress or impairment in functioning, especially emotional expression and deficits in perception ■ Some symptoms are similar to those of panic disorder ■ Rare; onset usually in adolescence	■ Psychological treatments similar to those for panic disorder may be helpful ■ Stresses associated with onset of disorder should be addressed ■ Tends to be lifelong
Dissociative Amnesia	■ Generalized: Inability to remember anything, including identity; comparatively rare ■ Localized: Inability to remember specific events (usually traumatic); frequently occurs in war ■ More common than general amnesia ■ Usually adult onset for both types ■ Dissociative Fugue Subtype: Memory loss is accompanied by purposeful travel or bewildered wandering	■ Usually self-correcting when current life stress is resolved ■ If needed, therapy focuses on retrieving lost information
Dissociative Trance	■ Sudden changes in personality accompany a trance or "possession" ■ Causes significant distress and/or impairment in functioning ■ Often associated with stress or trauma ■ Prevalent worldwide, usually in a religious context; rarely seen in Western cultures ■ More common in women than in men	■ Little is known

©Getty Images

7 Mood Disorders and Suicide

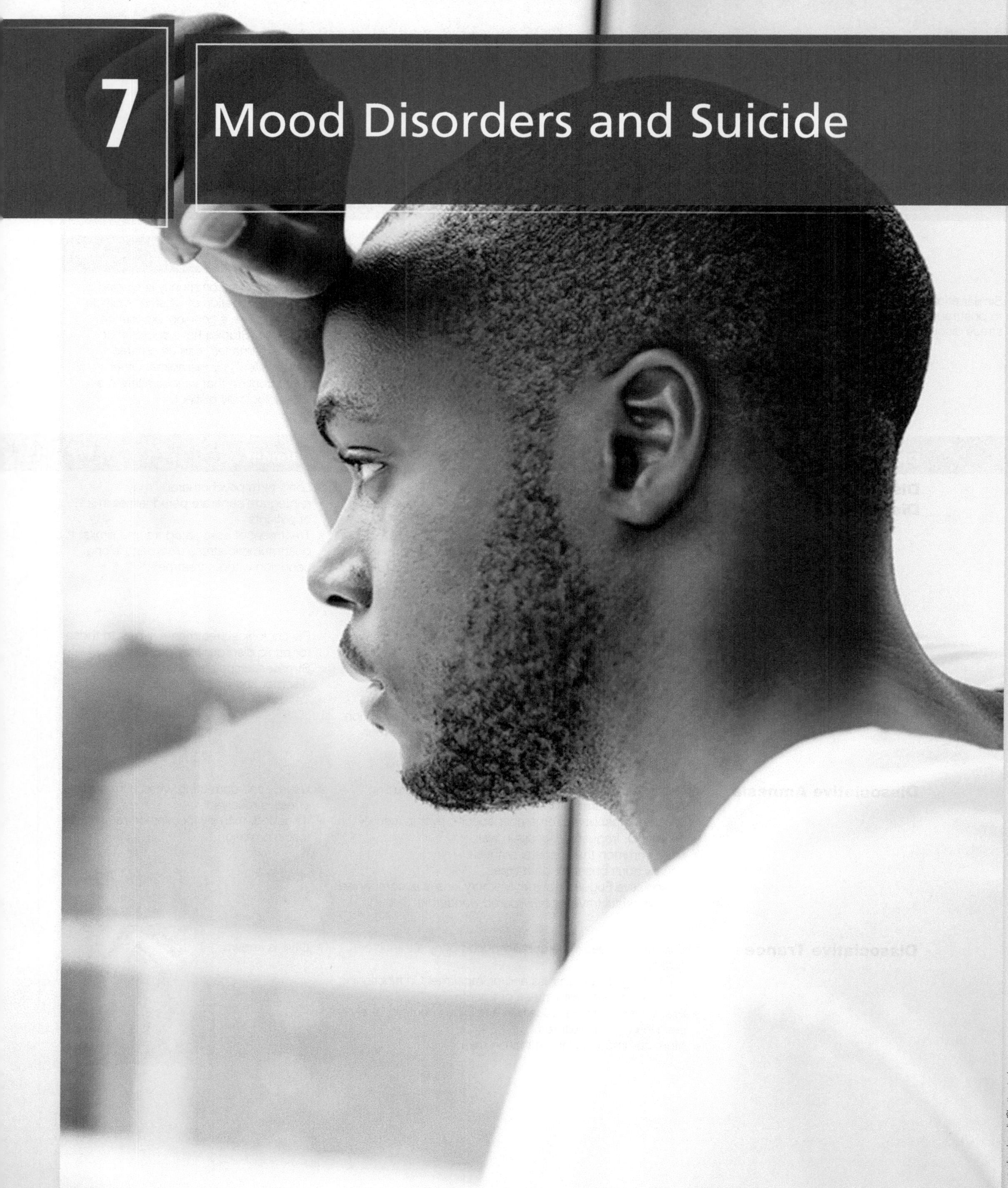

Learning Objectives

LO7.1 Discuss the key features of depression and mania in terms of their symptoms as defined by the DSM-5.

LO7.2 Compare the similarities and differences between unipolar depression and bipolar disorder in terms of their key features as described in the DSM-5.

LO7.3 Explain the challenges of comparing experiences of depression and anxiety across different cultures.

LO7.4 Identify the main factors involved in the development of mood disorders from biological, psychological, and social perspectives.

LO7.5 Differentiate between the leading biological and psychological treatments for mood disorders in terms of their main features and efficacy.

LO7.6 Describe the three indices involved in the progression of suicidal thinking and behavior.

Understanding and Defining Mood Disorders

Think back over the past month of your life. Maybe sometime during the past month you felt kind of down because you received a lower mark than you expected on a test after studying hard, or you broke up with your partner, or worse yet, somebody close to you became sick or died. Think about your feelings during this period. Were you sad? Perhaps you remember crying. Maybe you felt listless, and you couldn't seem to get up the energy to study or go out with your friends. It may be that you feel this way once in a while for no good reason you can think of and your friends think you're moody.

If you are like most people, you know that such a mood will pass. You will be back to your old self in a few days or a week. If you never felt down and always saw only what was good in a situation, it would be more unusual (and would also seem so to your friends) than if you felt depressed once in a while. Feelings of depression (and joy) are universal, which makes it all the more difficult to understand disorders of mood—disorders that can be so incapacitating that violent suicide may seem by far a better option than living. Consider the case of Keisha.

Keisha... Weathering Depression

Keisha was a shy 16-year-old who came to our clinic with her parents. For several years, Keisha had seldom interacted with anybody outside her family because of her considerable social anxiety. Going to school was difficult, and as her social contacts decreased, her days became empty and dull. By the time she was 16, a deep, all-encompassing depression blocked the sun from her life. Here is how she described it later:

> The experience of depression is like falling into a deep, dark hole that you cannot climb out of. You scream as you fall, but it seems like no one hears you. Some days you float upward without even trying; on other days, you wish that you would hit bottom so that you would never fall again. Depression affects the way you interpret events. It influences the way you see yourself and the way you see other people. I remember looking in the mirror and thinking that I was the ugliest creature in the world. Later in life, when some of these ideas would come back, I learned to remind myself that I did not have those thoughts yesterday and chances were that I would not have them tomorrow or the next day. It is a little like waiting for a change in the weather.

But at 16, in the depths of her despair, Keisha had no such perspective. She often cried for hours at the end of the day. She had begun drinking alcohol the year before, with the blessing of her parents, strangely enough, because the pills prescribed by her family doctor did no good. A glass of wine at dinner had a temporary soothing effect on Keisha, and both she and her parents, in their desperation, were willing to try anything that might make her a more functional person. But one glass was not enough. She drank increasingly more often. She began drinking herself to sleep. It was a means of escaping what she felt: "I had very little hope of positive change. I do not think that anyone close to me was hopeful, either. I was angry, cynical, and in a great deal of emotional pain." Keisha's life continued to spiral downward.

For several years, Keisha had thought about suicide as a solution to her unhappiness. At 13, in the presence of her parents, she reported these thoughts to a psychologist. Her parents wept, and the sight of their tears deeply affected Keisha. From that point on, she never expressed her suicidal thoughts again, but they remained with her. By the time she was 16, her preoccupation with her own death had increased:

> I think this was just exhaustion. I was tired of dealing with the anxiety and depression, day in and day out. Soon I found myself trying to sever the few interpersonal connections that I did have, with my closest friends, with my mother, and my oldest brother. I was almost impossible to talk to. I was angry and frustrated all the time. One day I went over the edge. My mother and I had a disagreement about some unimportant little thing. I went to my bedroom where I kept a bottle of whiskey or vodka or whatever I was drinking at the time. I drank as much as I could until I could pinch myself as hard as I could and feel nothing. Then I got out a very sharp knife that I had been saving and slashed my wrist deeply. I did not feel anything but the warmth of the blood running from my wrist.
>
> The blood poured out onto the floor next to the bed that I was lying on. The sudden thought hit me

that I had failed, that this was not enough to cause my death. I got up from the bed and began to laugh. I tried to stop the bleeding with some tissues. I stayed calm and frighteningly pleasant. I walked to the kitchen and called my mother. I cannot imagine how she felt when she saw my shirt and pants covered in blood. She was amazingly calm. She asked to see the cut and said that it was not going to stop bleeding on its own and that I needed to go to the doctor immediately. I remember as the doctor shot novocaine into the cut he remarked that I must have used an anesthetic before cutting myself. I never felt the shot or the stitches.

After that, thoughts of suicide became more frequent and more real. My father asked me to promise that I would never do it again, and I said I would not, but that promise meant nothing to me. I knew it was to ease his pains and fears and not mine, and my preoccupation with death continued.

Think for a moment about your own experiences of feeling depressed. What are the major differentiating factors between your feelings and Keisha's? Clearly, Keisha's depression was outside the boundaries of normal experience because of its intensity and duration. In addition, her severe or "clinical" depression interfered substantially with her ability to function. Finally, a number of associated psychological and physical symptoms accompany clinical depression.

Sometimes, mood disorders lead to tragic consequences. So developing a full understanding is key. In the following sections, we describe how various emotional experiences and symptoms interrelate to produce specific mood disorders. We offer detailed descriptions of different mood disorders and examine the many criteria that define them. We discuss the relationship of anxiety and depression and the causes and treatment of mood disorders. We conclude with a discussion of suicide.

An Overview of Depression and Mania

The disorders described in this chapter used to be categorized under several general labels, such as "depressive disorders," "affective disorders," or even "depressive neuroses." Beginning with the third edition of the *Diagnostic and Statistical Manual* (DSM-III), published by the American Psychiatric Association in 1980, these problems have been grouped under the heading **mood disorders** because they are characterized by gross deviations in mood.

The fundamental experiences of depression and mania contribute, either singly or together, to all the mood disorders. We describe each state and discuss its contributions to the various mood disorders. Then we briefly describe the additional defining criteria, features, or symptoms that define the specific disorders.

The most commonly diagnosed and most severe depression is called a **major depressive episode**. The DSM-5 criteria describe it as an extremely depressed mood state that lasts at least 2 weeks and includes cognitive symptoms (such as feelings of worthlessness and indecisiveness) and disturbed physical functions (such as altered sleeping patterns, significant changes in appetite and weight, or a notable loss of energy) to the point that even the slightest activity or movement requires an overwhelming effort. The episode is typically accompanied by a general loss of interest in things and an inability to experience any pleasure from life, including interactions with family or friends or accomplishments at work or at school. Although all symptoms are important, evidence suggests that the most central indicators of a full major depressive episode are the physical changes (sometimes called *somatic* or *vegetative* symptoms) (Regier et al., 2013; Tang & Thomas, 2020), along with the behavioral and emotional "shutdown," as reflected by low behavioral activation (Dimidjian, Barrera, Martell, Muñoz, & Lewinsohn, 2011). If something good

DSM 5

Table 7.1
Criteria for Major Depressive Episode

A. Five (or more) of the following symptoms have been present during the same 2-week period and represent a change from previous functioning; at least one of the symptoms is either (1) depressed mood or (2) loss of interest or pleasure. *Note:* Do not include symptoms that are clearly due to a general medical condition or mood-incongruent delusions or hallucinations.

1. Depressed mood most of the day, nearly every day, as indicated by either subjective report (e.g., feels sad, empty, hopeless) or observation made by others (e.g., appears tearful). (*Note:* In children and adolescents can be irritable mood.)
2. Markedly diminished interest or pleasure in all, or almost all, activities most of the day, nearly every day (as indicated by either subjective account or observation).
3. Significant weight loss when not dieting or weight gain (e.g., a change of more than 5% of body weight in a month), or decrease or increase in appetite nearly every day. (*Note:* In children, consider failure to make expected weight gains.)
4. Insomnia or hypersomnia nearly every day.
5. Psychomotor agitation or retardation nearly every day (observable by others, not merely subjective feelings of restlessness or being slowed down).
6. Fatigue or loss of energy nearly every day.
7. Feelings of worthlessness or excessive or inappropriate guilt (which may be delusional) nearly every day (not merely self-reproach or guilt about being sick).
8. Diminished ability to think or concentrate, or indecisiveness, nearly every day (either by subjective account or as observed by others).
9. Recurrent thoughts of death (not just fear of dying), recurrent suicidal ideation without a specific plan, or a suicide attempt or a specific plan for suicide.

B. The symptoms cause clinically significant distress or impairment in social, occupational, or other important areas of functioning.

C. The episode is not attibutable to the direct physiological effects of a substance or another medical condition.

American Psychiatric Association. (2022). *Diagnostic and statistical manual of mental disorders* (5th ed., Text Revision).

happens to you, you feel pleasure. But people with depression show *dysfunctional reward processing* (Halahakoon et al., 2020) and *anhedonia* (loss of energy and inability to engage in pleasurable activities or have any "fun"). This is more characteristic of these severe episodes of depression than are, for example, reports of sadness or distress (Cooper, Arulpragasam, & Treadway, 2018; Pizzagalli, 2014). Nor does the tendency to cry, which occurs equally in depressed and nondepressed individuals (mostly women in both cases) reflect severity—or even the presence of a depressive episode (Vingerhoets, Rottenberg, Cevaal, & Nelson, 2007). This anhedonia reflects that these episodes represent a state of low positive affect and not just high negative affect (Brown & Barlow, 2009). The duration of a major depressive episode, if untreated, is approximately 4 to 9 months (Hasin, Goodwin, Stinson, & Grant, 2005; Kessler & Wang, 2009).

The second fundamental state in mood disorders is abnormally exaggerated elation, joy, or euphoria. In **mania**, individuals find extreme pleasure in every activity; some patients compare their daily experience of mania with a continuous sexual orgasm. They become extraordinarily active (hyperactive), require little sleep, and may develop grandiose plans, believing they can accomplish anything they desire. DSM-5 highlights this feature by adding "persistently increased goal-directed activity or energy" to the "A" criteria (see DSM-5 Table 7.2) (American Psychiatric Association, 2013). Speech is typically rapid and may become incoherent, because the individual is attempting to express so many exciting ideas at once; this feature is typically referred to as *flight of ideas*.

DSM-5 criteria for a manic episode require a duration of only 1 week, less if the episode is severe enough to require hospitalization. Hospitalization could occur, for example, if the individual was engaging in a self-destructive buying spree, charging thousands of dollars in the expectation of making a million dollars the next day. Irritability is often part of a manic episode, usually near the end. Paradoxically, being anxious or depressed is also commonly part of mania, as described later. The duration of an untreated manic episode is typically 3 to 4 months (Angst, 2009; Solomon et al., 2010).

DSM-5 also defines a **hypomanic episode**, a less severe version of a manic episode that does not cause marked impairment in social or occupational functioning and need last only 4 days rather than a full week. (*Hypo* means "below"; thus the episode is below the level of a manic episode.) A hypomanic episode is not in itself necessarily problematic, but its presence does contribute to the definition of several mood disorders.

The Structure of Mood Disorders

Individuals who experience either depression or mania are said to suffer from a *unipolar mood disorder* because their mood remains at one "pole" of the usual depression–mania continuum. Mania by itself (unipolar mania) probably does occur (Angst & Grobler, 2015; Baek, Eisner, & Nierenberg, 2014; Tazici, 2014) but seems to be rare because most people with a unipolar mood disorder eventually develop depression. On the other hand, manic episodes alone may be somewhat more frequent in adolescents (Merikangas et al., 2012). Someone who alternates between depression and mania is said to have a bipolar mood disorder traveling from one "pole" of the depression–elation continuum to the other and back again. This label is somewhat misleading, however, because depression and elation may not be at exactly opposite ends of the same mood state; although related, they are often relatively

DSM 5 Table 7.2
Criteria for Manic Episode

A. A distinct period of abnormally and persistently elevated, expansive, or irritable mood and abnormally and persistently increased activity or energy, lasting at least 1 week and present most of the day, nearly every day (or any duration if hospitalization is necessary).

B. During the period of mood disturbance and increased energy or activity, three (or more) of the following symptoms (four if the mood is only irritable) are present to a significant degree and represent a noticeable change from usual behavior:

1. Inflated self-esteem or grandiosity
2. Decreased need for sleep (e.g., feels rested after only 3 hours of sleep)
3. More talkative than usual or pressure to keep talking
4. Flight of ideas or subjective experience that thoughts are racing
5. Distractibility (i.e., attention too easily drawn to unimportant or irrelevant external stimuli), as reported or observed
6. Increase in goal-directed activity (either socially, at work or school, or sexually) or psychomotor agitation (i.e., purposeless non-goal-directed activity)
7. Excessive involvement in activities that have a high potential for painful consequences (e.g., engaging in unrestrained buying sprees, sexual indiscretions, or foolish business investments)

C. The mood disturbance is sufficiently severe to cause marked impairment in social or occupational functioning or to necessitate hospitalization to prevent harm to self or others, or there are psychotic features.

D. The episode is not attributable to the physiological effects of a substance (e.g., a drug of abuse, a medication, other treatment) or to another general medical condition.

Note: A full manic episode that emerges during antidepressant treatment (e.g., medication, electroconvulsive therapy) but persists at a fully syndromal level beyond the physiological effect of that treatment is sufficient evidence of a manic episode and, therefore, a bipolar I diagnosis.

American Psychiatric Association. (2022). *Diagnostic and statistical manual of mental disorders* (5th ed., Text Revision).

independent. An individual can experience manic symptoms but feel somewhat depressed or anxious at the same time or be depressed with a few symptoms of mania. This episode is characterized as having "**mixed features**" (Baldessarini, Vazques, & Tondo, 2020; Na, Kang, & Cho, 2021). Research suggests that manic episodes are characterized by dysphoric (anxious or depressive) features more commonly than was thought, and dysphoria can be severe (Cassidy, Yatham, Berk, & Grof, 2008; Swann et al., 2013). In one study, 30% of 1,090 patients hospitalized for acute mania had mixed episodes (Hantouche et al., 2006). In another carefully constructed study of more than 4,000 patients, as many as two-thirds of patients with bipolar depressed episodes also had manic symptoms, most often racing thoughts (flight of ideas), distractibility, and agitation. These patients were also more severely impaired than those without concurrent depression and manic symptoms (Goldberg et al., 2009; Swann et al., 2013). The rare individual who suffers from manic episodes alone also meets criteria for bipolar mood disorder because experience shows that most of these individuals can be expected to become depressed at a later time. In general, newer models view bipolar disorder as an evolving condition, proceeding through different "at risk" stages with mild symptoms early in the disease progressing to a later chronic disorder (Frank, Nimgaonkar, Philips, & Kupfer, 2015; Kupfer, Frank, & Ritchey, 2015). In DSM-5, the term *mixed features* requires specifying whether a predominantly manic or predominantly depressive episode is present and then noting if enough symptoms of the opposite polarity are present to meet the mixed features criteria. Predominant polarity exists if one polarity occurs during at least two-thirds of the person's lifetime. In one study, out of 356 patients with bipolar disorder, 62 (17.4%) were predominantly depressed, 41 (11.5%) were predominantly manic, and 253 (71.1%) were neither predominantly depressed nor manic (Sentissi et al., 2019).

It is important to determine the course or temporal patterning of the depressive or manic episodes. For example, do they tend to recur? If they do, does the patient recover fully for at least 2 months between episodes (termed *full remission*) or only partially recover retaining some depressive symptoms ("partial remission")? Do the depressive episodes alternate with manic or hypomanic episodes or not? All these patterns for mood disorders are important to note, since they contribute to decisions on which diagnosis is appropriate.

The importance of temporal course (patterns of recurrence and remittance) makes the goals of treating mood disorders somewhat different from those for other psychological disorders. Clinicians want to do everything possible to relieve people like Keisha from their current depressive episode, but an equally important goal is to prevent future episodes—in other words, to help people like Keisha stay well for a longer period. Studies have been conducted that evaluate the effectiveness of treatment in terms of this second goal (Cuijpers, 2015; Fava et al., 2004; Hollon, Stewart, & Strunk, 2006; Otto & Applebaum, 2011; Teasdale et al., 2001).

Depressive Disorders

DSM-5 describes several types of depressive disorders. These disorders differ from one another in the frequency and severity with which depressive symptoms occur and the course of the symptoms (chronic—meaning almost continuous—or nonchronic). In fact, a strong body of evidence indicates that the two most important factors that describe mood disorders are severity and chronicity (Klein, 2010, and see below).

Clinical Descriptions The most easily recognized mood disorder is **major depressive disorder**, defined by the presence of depression and the absence of manic, or hypomanic episodes, before or during the disorder. An occurrence of just one isolated depressive episode in a lifetime is now known to be relatively rare (Angst, 2009; Eaton et al., 2008; Kessler & Wang, 2009). If two or more major depressive episodes occurred and were separated by at least 2 months during which the individual was not depressed, the major depressive disorder is noted as being **recurrent**. Recurrence is important in predicting the future course of the disorder, as well as in choosing appropriate treatments.

From 35% to 85% of people with single-episode occurrences of major depressive disorder later experience a second episode (Angst, 2009; Eaton et al., 2008; Judd, 2000; Souery, et al., 2012),

DSM 5 Table 7.3
Diagnostic Criteria for Major Depressive Disorder

A. At least one major depressive episode (*DSM*-5 Table 7.1, criteria A–C).

B. At least one major depressive episode is not better explained by schizoaffective disorder and is not superimposed on schizophrenia, schizophreniform disorder, delusional disorder, or other specified and unspecified schizophrenia spectrum and other psychotic disorders.

C. There has never been a manic episode or hypomanic episode. *Note:* This exclusion does not apply if all of the manic-like or hypomanic-like episodes are substance-induced or are attributable to the direct physiological effects of another medical condition.

Specify if:

Single episode or recurrent episode
Mild, moderate, severe
With psychotic features
With anxious distress
With mixed features
With melancholic features
With atypical features
With mood-congruent psychotic features
With mood-incongruent psychotic features
With catatonia
With peripartum onset
With seasonal pattern (recurrent episode only)
In partial remission, in full remission

American Psychiatric Association. (2022). *Diagnostic and statistical manual of mental disorders* (5th ed., Text Revision).

based on follow-ups as long as 23 years (Eaton et al., 2008). In the 1st year following an episode, the risk of recurrence is 20%, but it rises as high as 40% in the 2nd year (Boland & Keller, 2009). Unipolar depression is often a chronic condition that waxes and wanes over time but seldom disappears (Judd, 2012). The median lifetime number of major depressive episodes is four to seven; in one large sample, 25% experienced six or more episodes (Angst, 2009; Kessler & Wang, 2009). The median duration of recurrent major depressive episodes is 4 to 5 months (Boland & Keller, 2009; Kessler et al., 2003), somewhat shorter than the average length of the first episode.

On the basis of these criteria, how would you diagnose Keisha? Keisha was severely depressed and had feelings of worthlessness, difficulty concentrating, recurrent thoughts of death, sleep difficulties, and loss of energy. She clearly met the criteria for major depressive disorder, recurrent. Keisha's depressive episodes were quite severe when they occurred, but she tended to cycle in and out of them.

Persistent depressive disorder (dysthymia) shares many of the symptoms of major depressive disorder but differs in its course. There may be fewer symptoms (as few as two; see DSM-5 Table 7.4), but depression remains relatively unchanged over long periods, sometimes 20 or 30 years or more (Angst, 2009; Cristancho, Kocsis, & Thase, 2012; Klein, 2008; Klein, Shankman, & Rose, 2006; Murphy & Byrne, 2012).

Persistent depressive disorder is defined as depressed mood that continues at least 2 years, during which the patient cannot be symptom free for more than 2 months at a time even though they may not experience all of the symptoms of a major depressive episode. It identifies patients who were formerly diagnosed with dysthymic disorder and other depressive disorders (Rhebergen & Graham, 2014). Persistent depressive disorder differs from a major depressive disorder in the number of symptoms required, but mostly it is in the chronicity (Schramm, Klein, Elsaesser, Furukawa, & Domschke, 2020). It is considered more severe, since patients with persistent depression present with higher rates of comorbidity with other mental disorders, are less responsive to treatment, and show a slower rate of improvement over time. Klein and colleagues (2006), in a 10-year prospective follow-up study, suggest that chronicity (versus nonchronicity) is the most important distinction in diagnosing depression independent of whether the symptom presentation meets criteria for a major depressive disorder (as noted above) because these two groups (chronic and nonchronic) seem different, not only in course over time but also in family history and cognitive style. About 20% of patients with a major depressive episode report chronicity of this episode for at least 2 years, thereby meeting criteria for persistent depressive disorder (Klein, 2010).

Also, 22% of people suffering from persistent depression with fewer symptoms (specified as "with pure dysthymic syndrome"; see below) eventually experienced a major depressive episode (Klein et al., 2006). Individuals who have major depressive episodes and persistent depression with fewer symptoms are said to have **double depression**. Typically, a few depressive symptoms develop first, perhaps at an early age, and then one or more major depressive episodes occur later only to revert to the underlying pattern of depression once the major depressive episode has run its course (Boland & Keller, 2009; Klein et al., 2006). Identifying this particular pattern is important because it is associated with even more severe psychopathology and a problematic future course (Boland & Keller, 2009; Rubio, Markowitz, Alegria, Perez-Fuentes, Liu, Lin, & Blanco, 2011; Schramm et al., 2020). For example, Klein et al. (2006) found that the relapse rate of depression among people meeting criteria for DSM-IV dysthymia was 71.4%. Also, double depression is more difficult to treat than either the major depression or the dysthymia alone (May, Shaffer, & Yoon, 2020). Consider the case of Jack.

Jack... A Life Kept Down

Jack was a 49-year-old divorced white man who lived at his mother's home with his 10-year-old son. He complained of chronic depression, saying he finally realized he needed help. Jack reported that he had been a pessimist and a worrier for much of his adult life. He consistently felt kind of down and depressed and did not have much fun. He had difficulty making decisions, was generally pessimistic about the future, and thought little of himself. During the past 20 years, the longest period he could remember in which his mood was "normal" or less depressed lasted only 4 or 5 days.

Despite his difficulties, Jack had finished college and obtained a master's degree in public administration. People told him his future was bright and he would be highly valued in state government. Jack did not think so. He took a job as a low-level clerk in a state agency, thinking he could always work his way up. He never did, remaining at the same desk for 20 years.

Jack's wife, fed up with his continued pessimism, lack of self-confidence, and relative inability to enjoy day-to-day events, became discouraged and divorced him. Jack moved in with his mother so that she could help care for his son and share expenses.

About 5 years before coming to the clinic, Jack had experienced a bout of depression worse than anything he had previously known. His self-esteem went from low to nonexistent. From indecisiveness, he became unable to decide anything. He was exhausted all the time and felt as if lead had filled his arms and legs, making it difficult even to move. He became unable to complete projects or to meet deadlines. Seeing no hope, he began to consider suicide. After tolerating a listless performance for years from someone they had expected to rise through the ranks, Jack's employers finally fired him.

After about 6 months, the major depressive episode resolved and Jack returned to his chronic but milder state of depression. He could get out of bed and accomplish some things, although he still doubted his own abilities. He was unable to obtain another job, however. After several years of waiting for something to turn up, he realized he was unable to solve his own problems and that without help his depression would continue. After a thorough assessment, we determined that Jack suffered from a classic case of double depression.

DSM 5 **Table 7.4**

Diagnostic Criteria for Persistent Depressive Disorder (Dysthymia)

A. Depressed mood for most of the day, for more days than not, as indicated by either subjective account or observation by others, for at least 2 years. *Note:* In children and adolescents, mood can be irritable and duration must be at least 1 year.

B. Presence, while depressed, of two (or more) of the following:

1. Poor appetite or overeating
2. Insomnia or hypersomnia
3. Low energy or fatigue
4. Low self-esteem
5. Poor concentration or difficulty making decisions
6. Feelings of hopelessness

C. During the 2-year period (1 year for children or adolescents) of the disturbance, the individual has never been without the symptoms in criteria A and B for more than 2 months at a time.

D. Criteria for major depressive disorder may be continuously present for 2 years.

E. There has never been a manic episode or a hypomanic episode.

F. The disturbance is not better explained by a persistent schizoaffective disorder, schizophrenia, delusional disorder, or other specified or unspecified schizophrenia spectrum and other psychotic disorder.

G. The symptoms are not attributable to the physiological effects of a substance (e.g., a drug of abuse, a medication) or another medical condition (e.g., hypothyroidism).

H. The symptoms cause clinically significant distress or impairment in social, occupational, or other important areas of functioning.

Specify if:

With anxious distress

With atypical features

Specify if:

In partial remission

In full remission

Specify if:

Early onset: If onset is before age 21 years

Late onset: If onset is at age 21 years or older

Specify if (for most recent 2 years of persistent depressive disorder):

With pure dysthymic syndrome: Full criteria for a major depressive episode have not been met in at least the preceding 2 years.

With persistent major depressive episode: Full criteria for a major depressive episode have been met throughout the preceding 2-year period

With intermittent major depressive episodes, with current episode: Full criteria for a major depressive episode are currently met, but there have been periods of at least 8 weeks in at least the preceding 2 years with symptoms below the threshold for a full major depressive episode

With intermittent major depressive episodes, without current episode: Full criteria for a major depressive episode are not currently met, but there has been one or more major depressive episodes in at least the preceding 2 years.

Specify current severity:

Mild

Moderate

Severe

American Psychiatric Association. (2022). *Diagnostic and statistical manual of mental disorders* (5th ed., Text Revision).

Persistent depressive disorder is further specified depending on whether a major depressive episode is part of the picture or not. Thus, one might meet criteria for the disorder "with pure dysthymic syndrome," meaning one has not met criteria for a major depressive episode in at least the preceding 2 years, "with persistent major depressive episode," indicating the presence of a major depressive episode over at least a 2-year period, or "with intermittent major depressive episodes," which is the double depression that Jack was diagnosed with. In these cases, it is important to note whether the patient is currently in a major depressive episode or not. For both major depressive disorder and persistent depressive disorder, a depiction of the various course configurations of depression can be seen in ■ Figure 7.1.

Additional Defining Criteria for Depressive Disorders

Look again at DSM-5 Table 7.3 on the diagnostic criteria for major depressive disorder, and notice the section at the bottom that asks the clinician to specify the features of the latest depressive

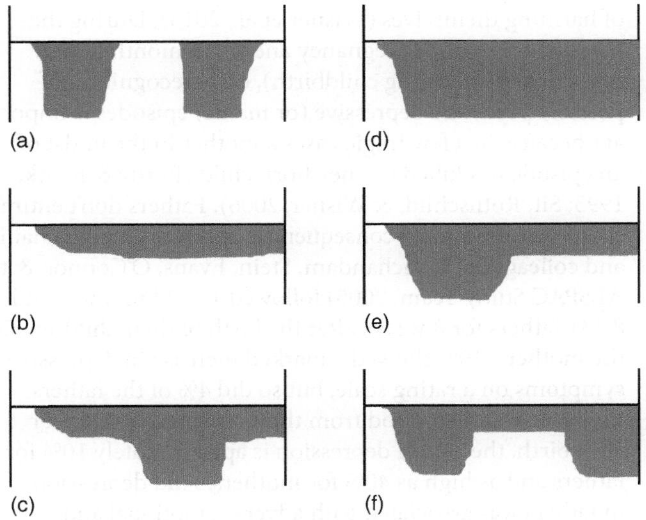

Figure 7.1

Pictorial representation of various course configurations of nonbipolar depression. The horizontal axis represents time, and the vertical axis represents mood, with the horizontal black line representing euthymic, or normal, mood, and the magnitude of downward deflection (the blue area) reflecting severity of depressive symptoms. Panel (a) is nonchronic major depressive disorder (in this case, recurrent, as two depressive episodes are depicted). Panel (b) is persistent depressive disorder with pure dysthymic syndrome. Panel (c) is double depression (major depressive episode occurring within the course of persistent depressive disorder or dysthymia). Panel (d) is chronic major depressive episode. Panel (e) is major depressive episode in partial remission. Panel (f) is recurrent major depression without full interepisode recovery. Based on D. N. Klein, 2010, Chronic depression: Diagnosis and classification, *Current Directions in Psychological Science, 19*(2), 96–100.

episode. These instructions are here because these symptoms, or *specifiers*, may or may not accompany a depressive disorder, but when they do, they are often helpful in determining the most effective treatment or likely course.

In addition to rating severity of the episode as mild, moderate, or severe, clinicians use eight basic specifiers to describe depressive disorders. These are (1) with psychotic features (mood-congruent or mood-incongruent), (2) with anxious distress (mild to severe), (3) with mixed features, (4) with melancholic features, (5) with atypical features, (6) with catatonic features, (7) with peripartum onset, and (8) with seasonal pattern. Some of these specifiers apply only to major depressive disorder. Others apply to both major depressive disorder and persistent depressive disorder. Each is described briefly below.

1. *Psychotic features specifiers.* Some individuals in the midst of a major depressive (or manic) episode may experience psychotic symptoms, specifically **hallucinations** (seeing or hearing things that aren't there) and **delusions** (strongly held but inaccurate beliefs) (Rothschild, 2013). Patients may also have *somatic (physical) delusions*, believing, for example, that their bodies are rotting internally and deteriorating into nothingness. Some may hear voices telling them how evil and sinful they are *(auditory hallucinations)*. Such hallucinations and delusions are called *mood congruent* because they seem directly related to the depression. On rare occasions, depressed individuals might have other types of hallucinations or delusions such as *delusions of grandeur* (believing, for example, they are supernatural or supremely gifted) that do not seem consistent with the depressed mood. This is a *mood-incongruent* hallucination or delusion. Although quite rare, this condition signifies a serious type of depressive episode that may progress to schizophrenia (or may be a symptom of schizophrenia to begin with). Delusions of grandeur accompanying a manic episode are mood congruent. Conditions in which psychotic symptoms accompany depressive episodes are relatively rare, occurring in 5% to 20% of identified cases of depression (Flores & Schatzberg, 2006; Ohayon & Schatzberg, 2002). Psychotic features in general are associated with a poor response to treatment, greater impairment, and fewer weeks with minimal symptoms, compared with nonpsychotic depressed patients over a 10-year period (Busatto, 2013; Flint, Schaffer, Meyers, Rothschild, & Mulsant, 2006).
2. *Anxious distress specifier.* The presence and severity of accompanying anxiety, whether in the form of comorbid anxiety disorders (anxiety symptoms meeting the full criteria for an anxiety disorder) or anxiety symptoms that do not meet all the criteria for disorders (Goldberg & Fawcett, 2012; Murphy & Byrne, 2012). This is perhaps the most important addition to specifiers for mood disorders in DSM-5. For all depressive and bipolar disorders, the presence of anxiety indicates a more severe condition, makes suicidal thoughts and fatal suicide attempts more likely, and predicts a less effective outcome from treatment.
3. *Mixed features specifier.* Predominantly depressive episodes that have several (at least three) symptoms of mania as described above would meet this specifier, which applies to major depressive episodes both within major depressive disorder and persistent depressive disorder.
4. *Melancholic features specifier.* This specifier applies only if the full criteria for a major depressive episode have been met, whether in the context of a persistent depressive disorder or not. Melancholic specifiers include some of the more severe somatic (physical) symptoms, such as early-morning awakenings, weight loss, loss of libido (sex drive), excessive or inappropriate guilt, and anhedonia (diminished interest or pleasure in activities). The concept of "melancholic" does seem to signify a severe type of depressive episode. Whether this type is anything more than a different point on a continuum of severity remains to be seen (Johnson, Cueller, & Miller, 2009; Klein, 2008; Parker, McCraw, et al., 2013; Sun et al., 2012).
5. *Catatonic features specifier.* This specifier can be applied to major depressive episodes whether they occur in the context of a persistent depressive order or not, and even to manic episodes, although it is rare—and rarer still in mania. This serious condition involves an absence of movement (a stuporous state) or **catalepsy**, in which the muscles are waxy and semirigid, so a patient's arms or legs remain in any position in which they are placed. Catatonic symptoms may also involve excessive but random or purposeless movement. Catalepsy was thought to be more commonly associated with schizophrenia, but some studies have suggested it may be more common in depression than in schizophrenia (Huang, Lin, Hung, & Huang, 2013).

This response may be a common "end state" reaction to feelings of imminent doom and is found in many animals about to be attacked by a predator (Moskowitz, 2004).

6. *Atypical features specifier.* This specifier applies to both depressive episodes, whether in the context of persistent depressive disorder or not. While most people with depression sleep less and lose their appetite, individuals with this specifier consistently oversleep and overeat during their depression and therefore gain weight, leading to a higher incidence of diabetes (Glaus et al., 2012; Kessler & Wang, 2009). Although they also have considerable anxiety, they can react with interest or pleasure to some things, unlike most depressed individuals. In addition, depression with atypical features, compared with more typical depression, is associated with a greater percentage of women and an earlier age of onset. The atypical group also has more symptoms, more severe symptoms, more suicide attempts, and higher rates of comorbid disorders including alcohol use disorder (Bech, 2009; Blanco et al., 2012; Glaus et al., 2012; Matza, Revicki, Davidson, & Stewart, 2003).
7. *Peripartum onset specifier. Peri* means "surrounding"—in this case, the period of time just before and just after the birth. This specifier can apply to both major depressive and manic episodes. Between 13% and 19% of all women giving birth (one in eight) meet criteria for a diagnosis of depression, referred to as *peripartum depression*. In one study, 7.2% met criteria for a full major depressive episode (Gavin et al., 2005). Typically, a somewhat higher incidence of depression is found postpartum (after the birth) than during the period of pregnancy itself (Viguera et al., 2011). In another important study, 14% of 10,000 women who gave birth screened positively for depression, and fully 19.3% of those depressed new mothers had serious thoughts of harming themselves (Wisner et al., 2013). During the peripartum period (pregnancy and the 6-month period immediately following childbirth), early recognition of possible psychotic depressive (or manic) episodes is important because in a few tragic cases a mother in the midst of an episode has killed her newborn child (Purdy & Frank, 1993; Sit, Rothschild, & Wisner, 2006). Fathers don't entirely escape the emotional consequences of birth. Ramchandani and colleagues (Ramchandani, Stein, Evans, O'Connor, & the ALSPAC Study Team, 2005) followed 11,833 mothers and 8,431 fathers for 8 weeks after the birth of their children. Of the mothers, 10% showed a marked increase in depressive symptoms on a rating scale, but so did 4% of the fathers. If you extend the period from the 1st trimester to 1 year after birth, the rate of depression is approximately 10% for fathers and as high as 40% for mothers. And depression in fathers was associated with adverse emotional and behavioral outcomes in children 3.5 years later (Paulson & Bazemore, 2010). A review of the literature shows that psychological interventions for paternal peripartum depression has a positive impact on the father and also on the father-child and the marital relationship (Goldstein, Rosen, Howlett, Anderson, & Herman, 2020). In general, guidelines for treating and preventing peripartum depression include cognitive behavioral therapy and interpersonal therapy (Curry et al., 2020).

While his bride awaited him, Abraham Lincoln was suffering from a depressive episode that was so severe he was unable to proceed with the wedding until several days later.

More minor reactions in adjustment to childbirth—called the "baby blues"—typically last a few days and occur in 40% to 80% of women between 1 and 5 days after delivery. During this period, new mothers may be tearful and have some temporary mood swings, but these are normal responses to the stresses of childbirth and disappear quickly; the peripartum onset specifier does not apply to them (Fonseca et al., 2020; O'Hara & McCabe, 2013; Wisner, Moses-Kolko, & Sit, 2010). However, in peripartum depression, most people, including new mothers, have difficulty understanding why they are depressed because they assume this is a joyous time. Many people forget that extreme stress can be brought on by physical exhaustion, new schedules, adjusting to nursing, and other changes that follow the birth. There is also some evidence that women with a history of peripartum depression meeting full criteria for an episode of major depression may be affected differently by the rapid decline in reproductive hormones that occurs after delivery (Wisner, Parry, & Piontek, 2002; Workman, Barha, & Galea, 2012) or may have elevated corticotrophin-releasing hormone (see Chapter 2) in the placenta (Meltzer-Brody et al., 2011; Yim et al., 2009) and that these factors may contribute to peripartum depression. But these findings need replication because all women experience very substantial shifts in hormone levels after delivery, but only a few develop a depressive disorder. Nor is there strong evidence that hormonal levels are significantly different in peripartum depressed and nondepressed women (Workman et al., 2012). A close examination of women with peripartum depression revealed no essential differences between the characteristics of this mood disorder and others (O'Hara & McCabe, 2013; Wisner et al., 2002). Therefore, peripartum depression did not require a separate category in DSM-5 and is simply a specifier for a depressive disorder. (Approaches to treatment for peripartum depression do not differ from those for nonperipartum depression.)

8. *Seasonal pattern specifier.* This temporal specifier applies to recurrent major depressive disorder (and also to bipolar disorders). It accompanies episodes that occur during certain seasons (e.g., winter depression). The most usual pattern is a depressive episode that begins in the late fall and ends with the beginning of spring. (In bipolar disorder, individuals may become depressed during the winter and manic during the summer.) These episodes must have occurred for at least 2 years with no evidence of nonseasonal major depressive episodes occurring during that period of time. This condition is called **seasonal affective disorder (SAD)**.

Although some studies have reported seasonal cycling of manic episodes, the overwhelming majority of seasonal mood disorders involve winter depression, which has been estimated to affect as many as 2.7% of North Americans (Lam et al., 2006; Levitt & Boyle, 2002). But fully 15% to 25% of the population might have some vulnerability to seasonal cycling of mood that does not reach criteria for a disorder (Kessler & Wang, 2009; Sohn & Lam, 2005). Unlike more severe melancholic types of depression, people with winter depressions tend toward excessive sleep (rather than decreased sleep) and increased appetite and weight gain (rather than decreased appetite and weight loss), symptoms shared with atypical depressive episodes. Although SAD seems a bit different from other major depressive episodes, family studies have not yet revealed any significant differences that would suggest winter depressions are a separate type (Lam & Lavitan, 2000).

Emerging evidence suggests that SAD may be related to daily and seasonal changes in the production of melatonin, a hormone secreted by the pineal gland. Because exposure to light suppresses melatonin production, it is produced only at night. Melatonin production also tends to increase in winter, when there is less sunlight. One theory is that increased production of melatonin might trigger depression in vulnerable people (Goodwin & Jamison, 2007; Lee et al., 1998). Wehr and colleagues (2001) have shown that melatonin secretion does increase in winter but only in patients with SAD and not healthy controls. (We return to this topic when we discuss biological contributions to depression.) Another possibility is that circadian rhythms, which occur in approximately 24-hour periods, or cycles, and are thought to have some relationship to mood, are delayed in winter. According to this "phase shift hypothesis," SAD is a result of phase-delayed circadian misalignment, meaning that the patient's circadian rhythm is misaligned with the environmental day–night cycle. Bright light exposure and melatonin at wake time, therefore, can realign the circadian rhythm in some patients (Lewy, Tutek, Havel, & Nikia, 2014; Van Maanen, Meijer, van der Heijden, & Oort, 2016). We come back to these treatment options below.

Cognitive and behavioral factors are also associated with SAD (Rohan, 2009; Rohan, Sigmon, & Dorhofer, 2003). Women with SAD, compared with well-matched nondepressed women, reported more autonomous negative thoughts throughout the year and greater emotional reactivity to light in the laboratory, with low light associated with lower mood. Severity of worrying, or rumination, in the fall predicted symptom severity in the winter.

As you might expect, the prevalence of SAD is higher in extreme northern and southern latitudes because there is less winter sunlight. However, there is a big variation in the degree to which people are affected by seasonal changes and daylight exposure. We discuss some of the reasons, which are also linked to sleep–wake cycles, in Chapter 8.

Some clinicians reasoned that exposure to bright light might slow melatonin production in individuals with SAD (Lewy et al., 2014). In phototherapy, a current treatment, most patients are exposed to 2 hours of bright light (2,500 lux) immediately on awakening. If the light exposure is effective, the patient begins to notice a lifting of mood within 3 to 4 days and a remission of winter depression in 1 to 2 weeks. Patients are also asked to avoid bright lights in the evening (from shopping malls and the like) so as not to interfere with the effects of the morning treatments. But this treatment is not without side effects. Approximately 19% of patients experience headaches, 17% have eyestrain, and 14% just feel "wired" (Levitt et al., 1993). Several controlled studies generally support phototherapy's effectiveness (Eastman, Young, Fogg, Liu, & Meaden, 1998; Golden et al., 2005; Martensson, Petterson, Berglund, & Ekselius, 2015; Reeves et al., 2012; Terman, Terman, & Ross, 1998). In these studies, morning light was compared with evening light, which was predicted to be less effective, or to a placebo. In two of these studies (Eastman et al., 1998; Terman et al., 1998), a clever "negative ion generator" served as a placebo treatment in which patients sat in front of the box for the same amount of time as in the phototherapy and "expected" the treatment would work following instructions from the investigator but did not see the light. The results, presented in Table 7.1, showed a significantly better response for morning light compared with evening light or placebo. Evening light was better than placebo. The mechanism of action of this treatment has not been fully established, but one study indicated that morning light was more effective to evening light because morning light produced phase advances of the melatonin rhythm, suggesting that changes in circadian rhythm are an important factor in treatment (Terman, Terman, Lo, & Cooper, 2001). In any case, it seems clear that light therapy is one important treatment for winter depression for some people (Golden et al., 2005; Lam et al., 2006; Pjrek et al., 2020).

MediaNews Group/Reading Eagle via Getty Images/Getty Images

Light therapy is a promising treatment for seasonal affective disorder, often providing relief from depressive symptoms in just a few days.

Table 7.1 Summary of Remission Rates

	Remission Rate % (Number of Patients)		
	Morning Light	Evening Light	Placebo (Negative-Ion Generator)
Terman et al., 1998			
First treatment	54% (25 of 46)	33% (13 of 39)	11% (2 of 19)
Crossover	60% (28 of 47)	30% (14 of 47)	Not done
Eastman et al., 1998			
First treatment	55% (18 of 33)	28% (9 of 32)	16% (5 of 31)
Lewy et al., 1998			
First treatment	22% (6 of 27)	4% (1 of 24)	Not done
Crossover	27% (14 of 51)	4% (2 of 51)	Not done

Seemingly unique cognitive and behavioral factors are associated with SAD, as noted earlier, which suggests a role for cognitive-behavioral therapy (CBT). In an important study of 177 adults by Rohan and colleagues (2015), each participant received either light therapy or CBT (twice a week in groups for 6 weeks) and were assessed during the following winter and again 2 years following the treatment. Both treatments had a similar effect on depression during the winter after the 1st year. However, during the second winter, the CBT group, as compared to the light therapy group, showed less severe symptoms of depression, had a smaller proportion of people relapse (27.3% vs. 45.6%), and demonstrated a greater proportion of remissions (68.3% vs. 44.5%). These results suggest that CBT has greater durability than light therapy for SAD, replicating and extending an earlier study (Rohan et al., 2007).

Onset and Duration Generally, the risk for developing major depression is fairly low until the early teens, when it begins to rise in a steady (linear) fashion (Rohde, Lewinsohn, Klein, Seeley, & Gau, 2013). A longitudinal study with 2,320 individuals from the Baltimore Longitudinal Study of Aging spanning from age 19 to 95 showed that symptoms of depression followed a U-shaped pattern, such that symptoms of depression were highest in young adults, decreased across middle adulthood, and then increased again in older age, with older people also experiencing an increase in distress associated with these symptoms (Sutin et al., 2013). Another alarming finding is that the incidence of depression and consequent suicide seem to be steadily increasing. Kessler and colleagues (2003) compared four age groups and found that fully 25% of people 18 to 29 years had already experienced major depression, a rate far higher than the rate for older groups when they were that age. Rohde and colleagues (2013) also looked at the incidence of major depressive disorder and four age groups spanning a longer period of time. They found that in children ages 5 to 12, 5% had experienced major depressive disorder. The corresponding figures in adolescence (ages 13 to 17) was 19%; in emerging adulthood (ages 18 to 23), 24%; and in young adulthood (ages 24 to 30), 16%.

As we noted previously, the length of depressive episodes is variable, with some lasting as little as 2 weeks; in more severe cases, an episode might last for several years, with the typical duration of the first episode being 2 to 9 months if untreated (Angst, 2009; Boland & Keller, 2009; Rohde et al., 2013). Although 9 months is a long time to suffer with a severe depressive episode, evidence indicates that, even in the most severe cases, the probability of remission of the episode within 1 year approaches 90% (Kessler & Wang, 2009). In those severe cases in which the episode lasts 5 years or longer, 38% can be expected to eventually recover (Mueller et al., 1996). Occasionally, however, episodes may not entirely clear up, leaving some residual symptoms. In this case, the likelihood of a subsequent episode with another incomplete recovery is much higher (Boland & Keller, 2009; Judd, 2012). Awareness of this increased likelihood is important to treatment planning because treatment should be continued much longer in these cases.

Investigators have found a lower (0.07%) prevalence of persistent mild depressive symptoms in children compared with adults (3% to 6%) (Klein, Schwartz, Rose, & Leader, 2000), but symptoms tend to be stable throughout childhood (Garber, Gallerani, & Frankel, 2009). Kovacs, Akiskal, Gatsonis, and Parrone (1994) found that 76% of a sample of children with persistent mild depressive symptoms later developed major depressive disorder.

Persistent depressive disorder may last 20 to 30 years or more, although studies have reported a median duration of approximately 5 years in adults (Klein et al., 2006) and 4 years in children (Kovacs et al., 1994). Klein and colleagues (2006), in the study mentioned earlier, conducted a 10-year follow-up of 97 adults with DSM-IV dysthymia (now known as persistent depressive disorder, which is characterized by fewer or more mild symptoms of depression) and found that 74% had recovered at some point but 71% of those had relapsed. The whole sample of 97 patients spent approximately 60% of the 10-year follow-up period meeting full criteria for a mood disorder. This compares with 21% of a group of patients with major depressive disorder also followed for 10 years. Even worse, patients with persistent depressive disorder with less severe depressive symptoms (dysthymia) were more likely to attempt suicide than a comparison group with (nonpersistent) episodes of major depressive disorder during a 5-year period. As noted above, it is relatively common for major depressive episodes and dysthymia (now persistent depressive disorder) to co-occur (double depression) (Boland & Keller, 2009; McCullough et al., 2000). Among those who have had persistent depressive disorder, as many as 79% have also had a major depressive episode at some point in their lives.

■ Figure 7.2 presents data on the 10-year course of patients presenting with DSM-IV persistent depressive disorder alone, nonchronic major depressive disorder, or double depression. The group with persistent depressive disorder, on the average, stays depressed. The double depression group (a subset of persistent depressive disorder), starts off more severe, recovers from its major depressive episode, as did Jack, but remains the most severely depressed after 10 years. The nonchronic major depressive disorder group evidences the most recovery (on average).

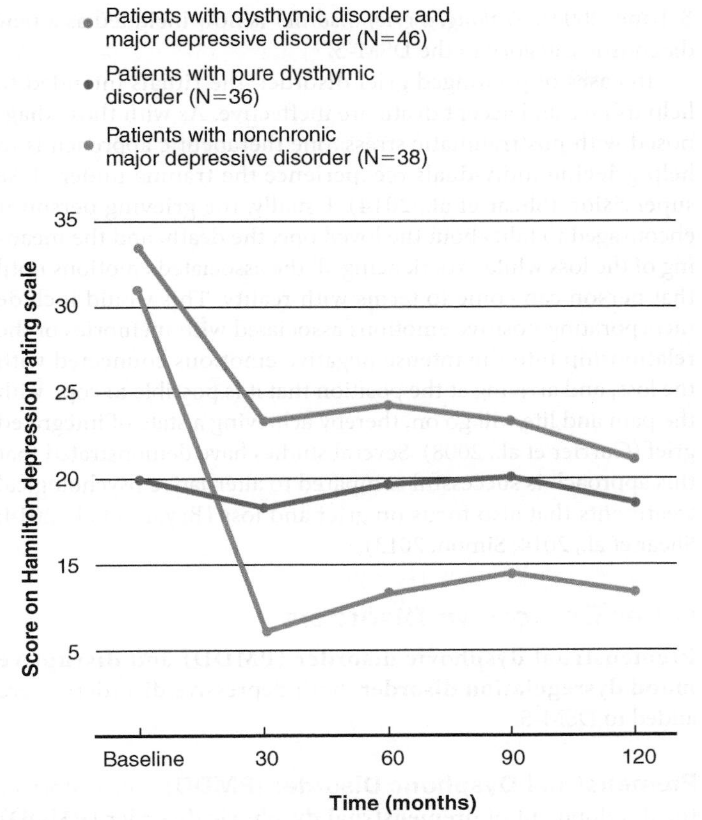

Figure 7.2

Hamilton Depression Rating Scale scores of dysthymic disorder patients with and without concurrent major depressive disorder episode and patients with nonchronic major depressive disorder over a 10-year follow-up period. Based on D. Klein, S. Shankman, & S. Rose, 2006, 10-year prospective follow-up study of the naturalistic course of dysthymic disorder and double depression, *American Journal of Psychiatry, 163*, 872–880. © American Psychiatric Association.

Once again, these results emphasize the overriding importance of considering chronicity or persistence when diagnosing depressive disorders.

From Grief to Depression A new diagnosis of prolonged grief disorder where individuals experience intense grief that lasts a year or more was described in chapter 5. But the natural grieving process called **acute grief** can also be closely related to depression. At the beginning of the chapter, we asked whether you had ever felt down or depressed. Almost everyone has. But if someone you love has died—particularly if the death was unexpected and the person was a member of your immediate family—you may, after your initial reaction to the trauma, have experienced a number of depressive symptoms as well as anxiety, emotional numbness, and denial (Shear, 2012; Shear et al., 2011; Simon, 2012). Sometimes individuals experience very severe symptoms requiring immediate treatment, such as a full major depressive episode, perhaps with psychotic features, suicidal ideation, or severe weight loss and so little energy that the individual cannot function (Maciejewski, Zhang, Block, & Prigerson, 2007). We must confront death and process it emotionally. All religions and cultures have grieving rituals, such as funerals and burial ceremonies, to help us work through our losses with the support and love of our relatives and friends (Bonanno & Kaltman, 2001; Gupta & Bonanno, 2011; Shear, 2012). Usually, the natural grieving process has peaked within the first 6 months, although some people grieve for a year or longer (Currier, Neimeyer, & Berman, 2008; Maciejewski et al., 2007). The acute grief most of us would feel eventually evolves into what is called **integrated grief**, in which the finality of death and its consequences are acknowledged and the individual adjusts to the loss. New, bittersweet, but mostly positive memories of the deceased person that are no longer dominating or interfering with functioning are then incorporated into memory (Shear et al., 2011).

Integrated grief often recurs at significant anniversaries, such as the birthday of the loved one, holidays, and other meaningful occasions, including the anniversary of the death. This is all a very normal and positive reaction. In fact, mental health professionals are concerned when someone does not grieve after a death because grieving is our natural way of confronting and handling loss. When grief lasts beyond typical time, mental health professionals again become concerned (Neimeyer & Currier, 2009). After 6 months to a year or so, the chance of recovering from severe grief without treatment is considerably reduced. At this stage, suicidal thoughts increase substantially and focus mostly on joining the beloved deceased (Stroebe, Stroebe, & Abakoumkin, 2005). The ability to imagine events in the future is generally impaired, since it is difficult to think of a future without the deceased (MacCallum & Bryant, 2011; Robinaugh & McNally, 2013). Individuals also have difficulty regulating their own emotions, which tend to become rigid and inflexible (Gupta & Bonanno, 2011). Many of the psychological and social factors related to mood disorders in general, including a history of past depressive episodes, also predict the development of the new disorder described in chapter 5, prolonged grief disorder, (Nakajima, 2018; Shear et al., 2011), although this reaction can develop without a preexisting depressed state (Bonanno, Westphal, & Mancini, 2011).

In children and young adults, the sudden loss of a parent makes them particularly vulnerable to severe depression beyond the normal time for grieving, suggesting the need for immediate intervention for some (Brent, Melhem, Donohoe, & Walker, 2009;

Queen Victoria remained in such deep mourning for her husband, Prince Albert, that she was unable to perform as monarch for several years after his death. The chart-topping singer Mariah Carey lived in denial and isolation for years until she received treatment for bipolar disorder.

Melhem, Porta, Shamseddeen, Payne, & Brent, 2011). Features of normal (acute) grief, and integrated grief, are listed in Table 7.2 (Nakajima, 2018; Shear et al., 2011). The unique cluster of symptoms described above, combined with other differences, was sufficient to make prolonged grief disorder a separate diagnostic category distinct from depression as described in chapter 5, (Bonanno, 2006; Nakajima, 2018; Shear et al., 2011). For example, the very strong yearning in complicated grief seems to be associated with the activation of the dopamine neurotransmitter system. This is in contrast to major depressive disorder, in which activation is reduced in this system (O'Connor et al., 2008). Also, brain-imaging studies indicate that areas of the brain associated with close relationships and attachment are active in grieving people, in addition to areas of the brain associated with more general emotional responding (Gündel, O'Connor, Littrell, Fort, & Lane, 2003). *Prolonged grief disorder* is now included as a new diagnostic category in the DSM-5.

In cases of prolonged grief disorder, the rituals intended to help us face and accept death are ineffective. As with those diagnosed with posttraumatic stress, one therapeutic approach is to help grieving individuals reexperience the trauma under close supervision (Shear et al., 2014). Usually, the grieving person is encouraged to talk about the loved one, the death, and the meaning of the loss while experiencing all the associated emotions until that person can come to terms with reality. This would include incorporating positive emotions associated with memories of the relationship into the intense negative emotions connected with the loss, and arriving at the position that it is possible to cope with the pain and life will go on, thereby achieving a state of integrated grief (Currier et al., 2008). Several studies have demonstrated that this approach is successful compared to alternative psychological treatments that also focus on grief and loss (Bryant et al., 2014; Shear et al., 2014; Simon, 2013).

Table 7.2 Acute and Integrated Grief.

Common symptoms of acute grief that are within normal limits within the first 6–12 months after:
· Recurrent, strong feelings of yearning, wanting very much to be reunited with the person who died; possibly even a wish to die in order to be with deceased loved one
· Pangs of deep sadness or remorse, episodes of crying or sobbing, typically interspersed with periods of respite and even positive emotions
· Steady stream of thoughts or images of deceased, may be vivid or even entail hallucinatory experiences of seeing or hearing deceased person
· Struggle to accept the reality of the death, wishing to protest against it; there may be some feelings of bitterness or anger about the death
· Somatic distress, for example, uncontrollable sighing, digestive symptoms, loss of appetite, dry mouth, feelings of hollowness, sleep disturbance, fatigue, exhaustion or weakness, restlessness, aimless activity, difficulty initiating or maintaining organized activities, and altered sensorium
· Feeling disconnected from the world or other people, indifferent, not interested, or irritable with others
Symptoms of integrated grief that are within normal limits:
· Sense of having adjusted to the loss
· Interest and sense of purpose, ability to function, and capacity for joy and satisfaction are restored
· Feelings of emotional loneliness may persist
· Feelings of sadness and longing tend to be in the background but still present
· Thoughts and memories of the deceased person accessible and bittersweet but no longer dominate the mind
· Occasional hallucinatory experiences of the deceased may occur
· Surges of grief in response to calendar days or other periodic reminders of the loss may occur

Source: M. K. Shear, N. Simon, M. Wall, S. Zisook, R. Neimeyer, N. Duan, & A. Keshaviah, (2011), Complicated grief and related bereavement issues for DSM-5, *Depression and Anxiety, 28,* 103–117.

Other Depressive Disorders

Premenstrual dysphoric disorder (PMDD) and **disruptive mood dysregulation disorder**, both depressive disorders, were added to DSM-5.

Premenstrual Dysphoric Disorder (PMDD) The history of the development of **premenstrual dysphoric disorder (PMDD)** over the past several decades as a diagnosis is described in some detail in Chapter 3 (see pp. 000–000). Basically, clinicians identified a small group of women, from 2% to 5%, who suffered from severe and sometimes incapacitating emotional reactions during the premenstrual period (Epperson et al., 2012). But strong objections to making this condition an official diagnosis were based on concerns that women who were experiencing a very normal monthly physiological cycle, as part of being female, would now be classified as having a disorder, which would be very stigmatizing. As noted above, the history of this controversy is described in Chapter 3. It has now been clearly established that this small group of women differs in a number of ways from the 20% to 40% of women who experience uncomfortable premenstrual symptoms (PMS) that, nevertheless, are not associated with impairment of functioning. Criteria defining PMDD are presented in DSM-5 Table 7.5. As one can see, a combination of physical symptoms, severe mood swings, and anxiety are associated with incapacitation during this period of time (Hartlage, Freels, Gotman, & Yonkers, 2012). All of the evidence indicates that PMDD is best considered a disorder of mood as opposed to a physical disorder (such as an endocrine disorder), and, as pointed out in Chapter 3, the creation of this diagnostic category should greatly assist the thousands of women suffering from this disorder to receive the treatment they need to relieve their suffering and improve their functioning.

Disruptive Mood Dysregulation Disorder Children and adolescents are being diagnosed with bipolar disorder at greatly increasing rates over the past several years. In fact, from 1995 to 2005, the diagnosis of bipolar disorder in children increased 40-fold overall and has quadrupled in U.S. community hospitals

DSM 5 **Table 7.5**
Diagnostic Criteria for Premenstrual Dysphoric Disorder

A. In the majority of menstrual cycles, at least five symptoms must be present in the final week before the onset of menses, start to *improve* within a few days after the onset of menses, and become absent in the week postmenses.

B. One (or more) of the following symptoms must be present:

1. Marked affective lability (e.g., mood swings; feeling suddenly sad or tearful, or increased sensitivity to rejection).
2. Marked irritability or anger or increased interpersonal conflicts.
3. Marked depressed mood, feelings of hopelessness, or self-deprecating thoughts.
4. Marked anxiety, tension, and/or feelings of being keyed up or on edge.

C. One (or more) of the following symptoms must additionally be present, to reach a total of *five* symptoms when combined with symptoms from Criterion B above:

1. Decreased interest in usual activities (e.g., work, school, friends, hobbies).
2. Subjective difficulty in concentration.
3. Lethargy, easy fatigability, or marked lack of energy.
4. Marked change in appetite; overeating; or specific food cravings.
5. Hypersomnia or insomnia.
6. A sense of being overwhelmed or out of control.
7. Physical symptoms such as breast tenderness or swelling, joint or muscle pain, a sensation of "bloating," or weight gain.

Note: The symptoms in criteria A–C must have been met for most menstrual cycles that occurred in the preceding year.

D. The symptoms cause clinically significant distress or interference with work, school, usual social activities, or relationships with others (e.g., avoidance of social activities; decreased productivity and efficiency at work, school, or home).

E. The disturbance is not merely an exacerbation of the symptoms of another disorder, such as major depressive disorder, panic disorder, persistent depressive disorder, or a personality disorder (although it may co-occur with any of these disorders).

F. Criterion A should be confirmed by prospective daily ratings during at least two symptomatic cycles. (*Note:* The diagnosis may be made provisionally prior to this confirmation.)

G. The symptoms are not attributable to the physiological effects of a substance (e.g., a drug of abuse, a medication) or another medical condition (e.g., hypothyroidism).

American Psychiatric Association. (2022). *Diagnostic and statistical manual of mental disorders* (5th ed., Text Revision).

(up to 40%) (Leibenluft & Rich, 2008; Moreno et al., 2007). Why the increase? Many clinicians are now using much broader diagnostic criteria that would not correspond to current definitions of bipolar I or bipolar II disorder but rather fall under the relatively vague category of bipolar disorder not otherwise specified (NOS) and include children with chronic irritability, anger, aggression, hyperarousal, and frequent temper tantrums that are not limited to an occasional episode (as might be the case if the child were cycling into a manic episode, since irritability sometimes accompanies discrete manic episodes).

But the most important observation is that these children show no evidence of periods of elevated mood (mania), which has been a requirement for a diagnosis of bipolar disorder (Liebenluft, 2011). Additional research demonstrated that these children with chronic and severe irritability and difficulty regulating their emotions resulting in frequent temper tantrums are at increased risk for additional depressive and anxiety disorders rather than manic episodes and that there is no evidence of excessive rates of bipolar disorder in their families, which one would expect if this condition were truly bipolar disorder. It was also recognized that this severe irritability is more common than bipolar disorder but has not been well studied (Brotman et al., 2006). This irritability is associated with substantial suffering in the children themselves, reflecting as it does chronically high rates of negative affect and marked disruption of family life. Though these broader definitions of symptoms do display some similarities with more classic bipolar disorder symptoms (Biederman et al., 2005; Biederman et al., 2000), the danger is that these children are being misdiagnosed when they might better meet criteria for more classic diagnostic categories, such as ADHD or conduct disorder (see Chapter 14). In that case, the very potent drug treatments for bipolar disorder with substantial side effects would pose more risks for these children than they would benefit. But these cases also differ from more typical conduct or ADHD conditions as well, since it is the intense negative affect that seems to be driving the irritability and marked inability to regulate mood. In view of the distinctive features of this condition reviewed above, it seemed very important to better describe these children up to 12 years of age as suffering from a diagnosis termed disruptive mood dysregulation disorder rather than have them continue to be mistakenly diagnosed with bipolar disorder or perhaps conduct disorder (Roy, Lopes, & Klein, 2014). Criteria for this new disorder are presented in DSM-5 Table 7.6. In one case seen at our clinic, a 9-year-old girl we will call Betsy was brought in by her father for evaluation for severe anxiety. The father described a situation in which Betsy, although a very bright child from an upper middle-class family who had done well in school, was continually irritable and increasingly unable to get along at home, engaging in intense arguments, particularly with her mother, at the slightest provocation. Her mood would then deteriorate into a full-blown aggressive temper tantrum and she would run to her room and on occasion begin throwing things. She began refusing to eat meals with the family since bitter arguments would often arise, and it just became easier to allow her to eat in her room. Since nothing else seemed to work to calm her down, her father resorted to something he used to do when she was a baby: take her for a long ride in the family car. After a while, Betsy would begin to relax but during one long ride turned to her father and said, "Daddy, please help me feel better because if I keep feeling like this, I just want to die."

Adults with a history of disruptive mood dysregulation disorder are at increased risk for developing mood and anxiety disorders as well as many other adverse health outcomes (Copeland, Shanahan, Egger, Angold, & Costello, 2014). Therefore, a very important objective for the immediate future will be developing and evaluating treatments for this difficult condition, both psychological and drug. For example, it is very possible that new psychological treatments under development for severe emotional dysregulation in children may be useful with this condition (Ehrenreich, Goldstein, Wright, & Barlow, 2009).

DSM 5 **Table 7.6**

Diagnostic Criteria for Disruptive Mood Dysregulation Disorder

A. Severe recurrent temper outburst manifested verbally (e.g., verbal rages) and/or behaviorally (e.g., physical aggression toward people or property) that are grossly out of proportion in intensity or duration to the situation or provocation.

B. The temper outbursts are inconsistent with developmental level.

C. The temper outbursts occur, on average, three or more times per week.

D. The mood between temper outbursts is persistently irritable or angry most of the day, nearly every day, and is observable by others (e.g., parents, teachers, peers).

E. Criteria A–D have been present for 12 or more months. Throughout that time, the individual has not had a period lasting 3 or more consecutive months without all of the symptoms in criteria A–D.

F. Criteria A and D are present in at least two of three settings (i.e., at home, at school, with peers) and are severe in at least one of these.

G. The diagnosis should not be made for the first time before age 6 years or after age 18 years.

H. By history or observation, the age at onset of criteria A–E is before 10 years.

I. There has never been a distinct period lasting more than 1 day during which the full symptom criteria, except duration, for a manic or hypomanic episode have been met.

Note: Developmentally appropriate mood elevation, such as occurs in the context of a highly positive event or its anticipation, should not be considered as a symptom of mania or hypomania.

J. The behaviors do not occur exclusively during an episode of major depressive disorder and are not better explained by another mental disorder (e.g., autism spectrum disorder, post-traumatic stress disorder, separation anxiety disorder, persistent depressive disorder).

K. The symptoms are not attributable to the physiological effects of a substance or to another medical or neurological condition.

American Psychiatric Association. (2022). *Diagnostic and statistical manual of mental disorders* (5th ed., Text Revision).

Bipolar Disorders

The original term for this group of disorders was *manic-depressive illness*, which was first introduced by Emil Kraepelin (Kendler, 2021). The key identifying feature of bipolar disorders is the tendency of manic episodes to alternate with major depressive episodes in an unending roller-coaster ride from the peaks of elation to the depths of despair (McIntyre et al., 2020). Beyond that, bipolar disorders are parallel in many ways to depressive disorders. For example, a manic episode might occur only once or repeatedly. Consider the case of Aniyah.

Aniyah... Funny, Smart, and Desperate

Aniyah was the wife of a well-known surgeon and the loving mother of three children. The family lived in an old country house on the edge of town with plenty of room for family members and pets. Aniyah was nearly 50. The older children had moved out, and the youngest son, 16-year-old Wyatt, was having substantial academic difficulties in school and seemed anxious. Aniyah brought Wyatt to the clinic to find out why he was having problems.

As they entered the office, I observed that Aniyah was well dressed, neat, vivacious, and personable; she had a bounce to her step. She began talking about her wonderful and successful family before she and Wyatt even reached their seats. Wyatt, by contrast, was quiet and reserved. He seemed resigned and perhaps relieved that he would have to say little during the session. By the time Aniyah sat down, she had mentioned the personal virtues and material achievement of her husband and the brilliance and beauty of one of her older children, and she was proceeding to describe the second child. But before she finished, she noticed a book on anxiety disorders and, having read voraciously on the subject, began a litany of various anxiety-related problems that might be troubling Wyatt.

In the meantime, Wyatt sat in the corner with a small smile on his lips that seemed to be masking considerable distress and uncertainty over what his mother might do next. It became clear as the interview progressed that Wyatt suffered from obsessive-compulsive disorder, which disturbed his concentration both in and out of school. He was failing all his courses.

It also became clear that Aniyah herself was in the midst of a hypomanic episode, evident in her unbridled enthusiasm, grandiose perceptions, "uninterruptable" speech, and report that she needed little sleep these days. She was also easily distracted, as when she quickly switched from describing her children to the book on the table. When asked about her own psychological state, Aniyah readily admitted that she was a "manic depressive" (the old name for bipolar disorder) and that she alternated rather rapidly between feeling on top of the world and feeling depressed; she was taking medication for her condition. I immediately wondered if Wyatt's obsessions had anything to do with his mother's condition.

Wyatt was treated intensively for his obsessions and compulsions but made little progress. He said that life at home was difficult when his mother was depressed. She sometimes went to bed and stayed there for 3 weeks. During this time, she seemed be in a depressive stupor, essentially unable to move for days. It was up to the children to care for themselves and their mother, whom they fed by hand. Because the older children had now left home, much of the burden had fallen on Wyatt. Aniyah's profound depressive episodes would remit after about 3 weeks, and she would immediately enter a hypomanic episode that might last several months or more. During hypomania, Aniyah was mostly funny, entertaining, and a delight to be with—if you could get a word in edgewise. Consultation with her therapist, an expert in the area, revealed that he had prescribed a number of medications but was so far unable to bring her mood swings under control.

Aniyah suffered from **bipolar II disorder**, in which major depressive episodes alternate with hypomanic episodes rather than full manic episodes. As we noted earlier, hypomanic episodes are less severe. Although she was noticeably "up," Aniyah functioned pretty well while in this mood state. The criteria for **bipolar I disorder** are the same, except the individual experiences a full manic episode. As in the criteria set for major depressive disorder, for the manic episodes to be considered separate, there must be a symptom-free period of at least 2 months between them. Otherwise, one episode is seen as a continuation of the last.

The case of Taio illustrates a full manic episode. This individual was first encountered when he was admitted to a hospital.

Taio... The World's Best at Everything

Before Taio reached the ward, you could hear him laughing and carrying on in a deep voice; it sounded as if he was having a wonderful time. As the nurse brought Taio down the hall to introduce him to the staff, he spied the Ping-Pong table. Loudly, he exclaimed, "Ping-Pong! I love Ping-Pong! I have only played twice, but that is what I am going to do while I am here; I am going to become the world's greatest Ping-Pong player! And that table is gorgeous! I am going to start work on that table immediately and make it the finest Ping-Pong table in the world. I am going to sand it down, take it apart, and rebuild it until it gleams and every angle is perfect!" Taio soon went on to something else that absorbed his attention.

The previous week, Taio had emptied his bank account, taken his credit cards and those of his elderly parents with whom he was living, and bought every piece of fancy stereo equipment he could find. He thought that he would set up the best sound studio in the city and make millions of dollars by renting it to people who would come from far and wide. This episode had precipitated his admission to the hospital.

During manic or hypomanic phases, patients often deny they have a problem, which was characteristic of Taio. Even after spending inordinate amounts of money or making foolish business decisions, these individuals, particularly if they are in the midst of a full manic episode, are so wrapped up in their enthusiasm and expansiveness that their behavior seems reasonable to them. The high during a manic state is so pleasurable that people may stop taking their medication during periods of distress or discouragement in an attempt to bring on a manic state again; this is a serious challenge to professionals.

Returning to the case of Aniyah, we continued to treat Aniyah's son Wyatt for several months. We made little progress before the school year ended. Because Wyatt was doing so poorly, the school administrators informed his parents that he would not be accepted back the next year. Wyatt and his parents wisely decided it might be a good idea if he got away from the house and did something different for a while, and he began working and living at a ski and tennis resort. Several months later, his father called to tell us that Wyatt's obsessions and compulsions had completely lifted since he'd been away from home. The father thought Wyatt should continue living at the resort, where he had entered school and was doing better academically. He now agreed with our previous assessment that Wyatt's condition might be related to his relationship with his mother. Several years later, we heard that Aniyah, in a depressive stupor, had killed herself, a tragic outcome in bipolar disorder.

A milder but more chronic version of bipolar disorder is called **cyclothymic disorder** (Akiskal, 2009; Parker, McCraw, & Fletcher, 2012). Cyclothymic disorder is a chronic alternation of mood elevation and depression that does not reach the severity of manic or major depressive episodes. Individuals with cyclothymic disorder tend to be in one mood state or the other for years with relatively few periods of neutral (or euthymic) mood. This pattern must last for at least 2 years (1 year for children and adolescents) to meet criteria for the disorder. Individuals with cyclothymic disorder alternate between the kinds of mild depressive symptoms Jack experienced during his dysthymic states and the sorts of hypomanic episodes Aniyah experienced. In neither case was the behavior severe enough to require hospitalization or immediate intervention. Much of the time, such individuals are just considered moody. However, the chronically fluctuating mood states are, by definition, substantial enough to interfere with functioning. Furthermore, people with cyclothymia should be treated because of their increased risk to develop the more severe bipolar I or bipolar II disorder (Akiskal, 2009; Goodwin & Jamison, 2007; Otto & Applebaum, 2011; Parker et al., 2012).

Additional Defining Criteria for Bipolar Disorders

For depressive disorders, we discussed additional defining criteria that may or may not accompany a mood disorder and noted that it was important to identify these specifiers or symptoms in order to plan the most effective treatment. All of these same specifiers apply to bipolar disorders (see DSM-5 Table 7.5). Specifically, the catatonic features specifier applies mostly to major depressive episodes, though rarely may apply to a manic episode. The psychotic features specifier may apply to manic episodes, during which it is common to have delusions of grandeur. The anxious distress specifier is also present in bipolar disorders, as it is in depressive disorders. New to DSM-5 is the "mixed features" specifier, which, as in depressive disorders, is meant to describe the major depressive or manic episode that has some symptoms from the opposite polarity—for example, a depressive episode with some manic symptoms. The seasonal pattern specifier may also apply to bipolar disorders. In the usual presentation, individuals may become depressed during the winter and manic during the summer. Finally, manic episodes may occur surrounding but mostly after childbirth in the peripartum period.

Just as for depression, it is important to determine if a patient suffering from a manic episode has had episodes of major depression or mania in the past as well as whether the individual has fully recovered between past episodes. Just as it is important to determine if persistent depressive disorder preceded a major depressive episode (double depression), it is also important to determine if cyclothymia preceded the onset of bipolar disorder. This is because the presence of cyclothymia predicts a decreased chance for a full inter-episode recovery (Akiskal, 2009).

Rapid-Cycling Specifier There is one specifier that is unique to bipolar I and II disorders: rapid-cycling specifier. Some people move quickly in and out of depressive or manic episodes. An individual with bipolar disorder who experiences at least four manic or depressive episodes within a year is considered to have a rapid-cycling pattern, which appears to be a severe variety of bipolar disorder that does not respond well to standard treatments (Angst, 2009; Kupka et al., 2005; Schneck et al., 2004; Schneck et al., 2008). Coryell and colleagues (2003) demonstrated a higher probability of suicide attempts and more severe episodes of depression in 89 patients with a rapid-cycling pattern compared with a non-rapid-cycling group. Kupka and colleagues (2005) and Nierenberg and colleagues (2010) also found these patients' symptoms were more severe on a number of measures. Some evidence indicates that alternative drug treatment, such as anticonvulsants and mood stabilizers, rather than antidepressants may be more effective with this group of patients (Kilzieh & Akiskal, 1999).

Approximately 20% to 50% of bipolar patients experience rapid cycling. From 60% to 90% are female, a higher rate than in other variations of bipolar disorder (see, for example, Altshuler et al., 2010; Coryell et al., 2003; Kupka et al., 2005; Schneck et al., 2004), and this finding is consistent across 10 studies (Kilzieh & Akiskal, 1999). In most cases, rapid cycling tends to increase in frequency over time and can reach severe states in which patients cycle between mania and depression without any break. When this direct transition from one mood state to another happens, it is referred to as *rapid switching* or *rapid mood switching* and is a particularly treatment-resistant form of the disorder (MacKinnon, Zandi, Gershon, Nurnberger, & DePaulo, 2003; Maj, Pirozzi, Magliano, & Bartoli, 2002). One precipitant of rapid cycling may be taking antidepressant medication, which is prescribed for some individuals with bipolar disorder, because the frequency of rapid cycling is considerably higher among those taking antidepressants compared with those who are not taking them (Schneck et al., 2008). Fortunately, rapid cycling does not seem to be permanent because only 3% to 5% of patients continue with rapid cycling across a 5-year period (Schneck et al., 2008), with 80% returning to a non-rapid-cycling pattern within 2 years (Coryell et al., 2003). There are also cases of *ultra-rapid* cycle lengths that only last for days to weeks and *ultra-ultra-rapid cycling* in cases where cycle lengths are less than 24 hours (Wilk & Hegerl, 2010). In ultra-ultra-rapid cycling, switches into depression occurred at night, and switches into mania occurred at daytime, suggesting that for patients with mood cycles of 48 hours or less, the switch process is closely linked to circadian aspects.

DSM 5 **Table 7.7**

Diagnostic Criteria for Cyclothymic Disorder

A. For at least 2 years (at least 1 year in children and adolescents) there have been numerous periods with hypomanic symptoms that do not meet criteria for a hypomanic episode and numerous periods with depressive symptoms that do not meet criteria for a major depressive episode.

B. During the above 2-year period (1 year in children and adolescents), Criterion A symptoms have been present for at least half the time and the individual has not been without the symptoms for more than 2 months at a time.

C. Criteria for a major depressive, manic, or hypomanic episode have never been met.

D. The symptoms in Criterion A are not better explained by schizoaffective disorder, schizophrenia, schizophreniform disorder, delusional disorder, or other specified or unspecified schizophrenia spectrum and other psychotic disorder.

E. The symptoms are not attributable to the physiological effects of a substance (e.g., a drug of abuse, a medication) or another medical condition (e.g., hyperthyroidism).

F. The symptoms cause clinically significant distress or impairment in social, occupational, or other important areas of functioning.

Specify if:

With anxious distress

American Psychiatric Association. (2022). *Diagnostic and statistical manual of mental disorders* (5th ed., Text Revision).

Onset and Duration The average age of onset for bipolar I disorder is from 15 to 18 years and for bipolar II disorder from 19 and 22 years, although cases of both can begin in childhood (Angst, 2009; Judd et al., 2003; Merikangas & Pato, 2009). This is somewhat younger than the average age of onset for major depressive disorder, and bipolar disorders begin more acutely; that is, they develop more suddenly (Angst & Sellaro, 2000; Johnson et al., 2009). About one third of the cases of bipolar disorder begin in adolescence, and the onset is often preceded by minor oscillations in mood or mild cyclothymic mood swings (Goodwin & Jamison, 2007; Merikangas et al., 2007). Between 10% and 25% of people with bipolar II disorder will progress to full bipolar I disorder (Birmaher et al., 2009; Coryell et al., 1995).

Though unipolar and bipolar disorder have been thought distinct disorders, Angst and Sellaro (2000), in reviewing some older studies, estimated the rate of depressed individuals later experiencing a full manic episode at closer to 25%. And Cassano and colleagues (2004), along with Akiskal (2006) and Angst and colleagues (2010), found that as many as 67.5% of patients with unipolar depression experienced some manic symptoms. These studies raise questions about the true distinction between unipolar depression and bipolar disorder and suggest they may be on a continuum (called a *spectrum* in psychopathology) (Johnson et al., 2009; Merikangas et al., 2011).

It is relatively rare for someone to develop bipolar disorder after the age of 40. Once it does appear, the course is chronic; that is, mania and depression alternate indefinitely. Therapy usually involves managing the disorder with ongoing drug regimens that prevent recurrence of episodes. As we already briefly discussed, suicide is an all-too-common consequence of bipolar disorder, almost always occurring during depressive episodes, as it did in the case of Aniyah (Angst, 2009; Valtonen et al., 2007). A large Swedish study showed that, on average, people with bipolar disorder died 8 to 9 years earlier of various medical diseases and suicide compared to the general population (Crump, Sundquist, Winkleby, & Sundquist, 2013). However, when patients receive treatment early, the mortality rate was comparable to that of the general population. Bipolar disorder is associated with a high risk of suicide attempts and suicide death, the latter being associated with male sex and having a first-degree relative who died by suicide (Schaffer et al., 2015). Other risk factors include living alone, being divorced, having no children, being White, being either relatively young (< 35 years) or old (> 75 years), and being unemployed (Miller & Black, 2020). The risk of suicide is not limited to Western countries but occurs in countries around the world (Merikangas et al., 2011).

In typical cases, cyclothymia is chronic and lifelong. In about one third to one half of patients, cyclothymic mood swings develop into full-blown bipolar disorder (Kochman et al., 2005; Parker et al., 2012). In one sample of cyclothymic patients, 60% were female, and the age of onset was often during the teenage years or before, with some data suggesting the most common age of onset to be 12 to 14 years (Goodwin & Jamison, 2007). The disorder is often not recognized, and individuals with the disorder are thought to be high-strung, explosive, moody, or hyperactive (Akiskal, 2009; Goodwin & Jamison, 2007). One subtype of cyclothymia is based on the predominance of mild depressive symptoms, one on the predominance of hypomanic symptoms, and another on an equal distribution of both.

Prevalence of Mood Disorders

Approximately 20.6% of the U.S. population has experienced a major depressive disorder over a lifetime (Hasin et al., 2018. For bipolar disorder, the estimates are 2.4% lifetime prevalence and 1.5% during the past year (Merikangas et al., 2011). The similarity of the lifetime and past-year rates for bipolar disorder reflects the fact that this chronic condition has a substantial negative impact on one's life (Carvalho, Firth, & Vieta, 2020). About 6% to 7% of people with bipolar disorder die by suicide, which means that the risk of dying by suicide is 20 to 30 times higher among people with bipolar disorder than in the general population (Plans et al., 2018). Suicidality is also greater in bipolar disorder than in major depressive disorder, as shown in the difference in suicidal ideation (29.2% vs. 17.3%) and attempts (18.8% vs. 4.8%) (Baldessarini, Tondo, Pinna, Nuñez, & Vázquez, 2019).

Studies indicate that women are twice as likely to have mood disorders as men (Kessler, 2006; Kessler & Wang, 2009), but the imbalance in prevalence between males and females is accounted for solely by major depressive disorder and persistent depressive disorder (dysthymia) because bipolar disorders are distributed approximately equally across gender

Concept Check 7.1

Match each description or case by choosing its corresponding disorder: (a) mania, (b) double depression, (c) persistent depressive disorder, (d) major depressive episode, and (e) bipolar I disorder.

1. Last week, as he does about every 3 months, Michael went out with his friends, buying rounds of drinks, socializing until early morning, and feeling on top of the world. Today Michael will not even get out of bed to go to work, see his friends, or even turn on the lights. ____________
2. Feeling certain he would win the lottery, Charles went on an all-night shopping spree, maxing out all his credit cards without a worry. We know he's done this several times, feeling abnormally extreme elation, joy, and euphoria. ____________
3. Ayana has had some mood disorder problems in the past, although some days she's better than others. Many days it seems like she has fallen into a rut. Although she manages to get by, she has trouble making decisions because she doesn't trust herself. ____________
4. For the past few weeks, Imani has been sleeping a lot. She feels worthless, can't get up the energy to leave the house, and has lost a lot of weight. Her problem is the most common and extreme mood disorder. ____________
5. Eusebio is always down and a bit blue, but occasionally he becomes so depressed that nothing pleases him. ____________

(Merikangas & Pato, 2009). Although equally prevalent, there are some sex-based differences in bipolar disorder. As noted above, women are more likely than men to experience rapid cycling but also to be anxious and to be in a depressive phase rather than a manic phase (Altshuler et al., 2010).

The prevalence of major depressive disorder and persistent depressive disorder (dysthymia) is significantly lower among Black people than among White people (Hasin et al., 2005), although, again, no differences appear in bipolar disorders. One study of major depressive disorder in a community sample of Black individuals found a prevalence of 3.1% during the previous year (Brown, Ahmed, Gary, & Milburn, 1995), and another found a prevalence of 4.52% during the previous year (Hasin et al., 2005), compared with 5.53% among Whites. Fair or poor health status was the major predictor of depression in Blacks. Few of these individuals received appropriate treatment, with only 11% coming in contact with a mental health professional (Brown et al., 1995). Native Americans, on the other hand, present with a significantly higher prevalence of depression (Hasin et al., 2005), although difficulties in translating the concept of depression to Native American cultures suggest this finding needs more study (Beals et al., 2005; Kaufmann et al., 2013; see section later in this chapter on culture).

Prevalence in Children, Adolescents, and Older Adults

Estimates on the prevalence of mood disorders in children and adolescents vary widely, although more sophisticated studies are beginning to appear. The general conclusion is that depressive disorders occur less often in prepubertal children than in adults but rise dramatically in adolescence (Brent & Birmaher, 2009; Garber et al., 2009; Kessler et al., 2012; Rohde et al., 2013; Rudolph, 2009). Among children ages 2 to 5, rates of major depression are about 1.5% and a bit lower later in childhood (Garber et al., 2009), but as many as 20% to 50% of children experience some depressive symptoms that are not frequent or severe enough to meet diagnostic criteria, though are nevertheless impairing (Kessler, Avenevoli, & Ries Merikangas, 2001; Rudolph, 2009). Adolescents experience major depressive disorder about as often as adults (Kessler et al., 2012; Rohde et al., 2013; Rudolph, 2009). But this pattern seems to be changing over the years. Weinberger, Gbedemah, Martinez, Nash, Galea, and Goodwin (2018) conducted a cross-sectional study over multiple years with more than 600,000 people living in the United States age 12 and older. The results showed that the prevalence of depression increased overall from 2005 to 2015 and the rate of increase in depression was faster among the younger as compared to the older age groups.

In children, the sex ratio for depressive disorders is approximately 50:50, but this changes dramatically in adolescence. Major depressive disorder in adolescents is largely a female disorder (we further discuss sex differences in depression later in the chapter), as it is in adults, with puberty and greater interpersonal stress in adolescent girls than boys seemingly triggering this sex imbalance (Garber & Carter, 2006; Garber, Clarke et al., 2009; Hamilton, Stange, Abramson, & Alloy, 2015; Nolen-Hoeksema & Hilt, 2009). This sex imbalance is not evident for more mild depression.

DSM 5 **Table 7.8**

Diagnostic Criteria for Bipolar II Disorder

A. Criteria have been met for at least one hypomanic episode *and* at least one major depressive episode. Criteria for a hypomanic episode are identical to those for a manic episode (see DSM-5 Table 7.2), with the following distinctions: (1) Minimum duration is 4 days; (2) although the episode represents a definite change in functioning, it is not severe enough to cause marked social or occupational impairment or hospitalization; (3) there are no psychotic features.

B. There has never been a manic episode.

C. At least one hypomanic episode and at least one major depressive episode are not better explained by schizoaffective disorder and are not superimposed on schizophrenia, schizophreniform disorder, delusional disorder, or other specified or unspecified schizophrenia spectrum and other psychotic disorder.

D. The symptoms of depression or the unpredictability caused by frequent alternation between periods of depression and hypomania causes clinically significant distress or impairment in social, occupational, or other important areas of functioning.

Specify current or most recent episode:

Hypomanic:

Depressed:

If current episode is **hypomanic** (or most recent episode if bipolar II disorder is in partial or full remission):

Note: The specifiers "with rapid cycling" and "with seasonal pattern" describe the pattern of mood episodes.

Specify if:

With anxious distress
With mixed features
With rapid cycling
With peripartum onset.
With seasonal pattern.

If current episode is **depressed** (or most recent episode if bipolar II disorder is in partial or full remission):

Specify if:

With anxious distress
With mixed features
With rapid cycling
With melancholic features
With atypical features
With mood-congruent psychotic features
With mood-incongruent psychotic features
With catatonia
With peripartum onset
With seasonal pattern

Specify severity if full criteria for a mood episode are currently met:

In full remission
In partial remission

Specify severity if full criteria for a major depressive episode are currently met:

Mild

Moderate

Severe

American Psychiatric Association. (2022). *Diagnostic and statistical manual of mental disorders* (5th ed., Text Revision).

Corbis

Among adolescents, severe major depressive disorder occurs mostly in girls.

The overall prevalence of major depressive disorder for individuals over age 65 is about half that of the general population (Blazer & Hybels, 2009; Byers, Yaffe, Covinsky, Friedman, & Bruce, 2010; Fiske, Wetherell, & Gatz, 2009; Hasin et al., 2005; Kessler et al., 2003), perhaps because stressful life events that trigger major depressive episodes decrease with age. But milder symptoms that do not meet criteria for major depressive disorder seem to be more common among older adults (Beekman et al., 2002; Gotlib & Nolan, 2001) and may be associated with illness and infirmity (Delano-Wood & Abeles, 2005; Alexopoulos, 2005). Depression was even associated with excess mortality in the elderly, but only among those living in low- and middle-income countries (Brandao, Fontenelle, da Silva, Menezes, & Pastor-Valero, 2019) and not in those from high-income countries (Jeuring, Comijs, Deeg, Hoogendijk, Beekman, Stek, & Huisman, 2018).

Bipolar disorder seems to occur at about the same rate (1%) in childhood and adolescence as in adults (Brent & Birmaher, 2009; Kessler et al., 2012; Merikangas & Pato, 2009). The rates of diagnosis of bipolar disorder in clinics has increased substantially, however, due to greater interest and a controversial tendency described above to broaden the diagnostic criteria in children to include what will now be subsumed under disruptive mood dysregulation disorder. Considering the chronicity and seriousness of mood disorders (Gotlib & Hammen, 2009), the prevalence in all age groups is high, indeed, demonstrating a substantial impact not only on the affected individuals and their families but also on society.

Life Span Developmental Influences on Mood Disorders

blue jean images/Getty Images

Children of depressed mothers may show depressive behavior at less than a year old.

The prevalence of mood disorders varies with age, and age and development also impact many of the characteristics of mood disorders. We review and highlight these developmental characteristics—first for children and adolescents and then for older adults. You might assume that depression requires some experience with life—that an accumulation of negative events or disappointments might create pessimism, which then leads to depression. Like many reasonable assumptions in psychopathology, this one is not uniformly correct. There is some evidence that even 3-month-old babies can become depressed. Infants of depressed mothers display marked depressive behaviors (sad faces, slow movement, lack of responsiveness) even when interacting with a nondepressed adult (Garber et al., 2009; Guedeney, 2007). Whether this behavior or temperament is caused by a genetic tendency inherited from the mother, the result of early interaction patterns with a depressed mother or primary caregiver, or a combination is not yet clear.

Most investigators agree that mood disorders are fundamentally similar in children and in adults (Brent & Birmaher, 2009; Garber et al., 2009; Weiss & Garber, 2003). Therefore, no "childhood" mood disorders in DSM-5 are specific to a developmental stage, with the exception of disruptive mood dysregulation disorder, which can be diagnosed only up to 12 years of age. This is unlike the anxiety disorders in which a number of conditions occur only early in development. It seems clear, however, that the "look" of depression changes with age. For example, children under 3 years of age might manifest depression by sad facial expressions, irritability, fatigue, fussiness, and tantrums, as well as by problems with eating and sleeping. In the extreme, this could develop into disruptive mood dysregulation disorder. In children between the ages of 9 and 12, many of these features would not occur. Also, for preschool children (6 years old and under), Luby and colleagues (2003) report the necessity of setting aside the strict 2-week duration requirement for major depression because it is normal for mood to fluctuate at this young age. However, once depression develops, it cannot be expected that children simply "grow out of it" (Luby, 2012). For example, a study by Luby and colleagues (2014) found that preschool depression was a significant and robust predictor for later depression at the ages of 6 to 13. Preschool depression was also a risk factor for other problems, such as anxiety disorders and attention deficit/hyperactivity disorder (ADHD) at school age. These results are consistent with an earlier study showing that emotional and behavioral problems in general at age 3 were associated with an almost fivefold greater risk of having an emotional or behavioral disorder at age 6. Conversely, more than 50% of children who met criteria for a disorder at age 6 already had clinically significant problems by age 3 (Bufferd et al., 2012).

As far as mania is concerned, children under the age of 9 seem to present with more irritability and emotional swings as compared with classic manic states, particularly irritability (Fields & Fristad, 2009; Leibenluft & Rich, 2008), but it is also important to recognize that irritability alone is insufficient to diagnose mania because it is associated with many different types of problems in childhood (it is nonspecific to mania). "Emotional swing," or oscillating manic states that are less distinct than in adults, may also be characteristic of children, as are brief or rapid-cycling manic episodes lasting only part of a day (Youngstrom, 2009).

One developmental difference between children and adolescents compared with adults concerns patterns of comorbidity. For example, childhood depression (and mania) is often associated with and sometimes misdiagnosed as ADHD or, more often, conduct disorder in which aggression and even destructive behavior are common (Fields & Fristad, 2009; Garber et al., 2009). Conduct disorder and depression often co-occur in bipolar disorder. But once again, many of these children might now meet criteria for disruptive mood dysregulation disorder, which would better account for this comorbidity. In any case, successful treatment of the underlying depression (or spontaneous recovery) may resolve the associated ADHD or conduct disorder in these patients. Adolescents with bipolar disorder may also become aggressive, impulsive, sexually provocative, and accident prone (Carlson & Klein, 2014; Carlson & Meyer, 2006).

Whatever the presentation, mood disorders in children and adolescents are serious because of their likely consequences (Garber et al., 2009). Fergusson and Woodward (2002), in a large prospective study, identified 13% of a group of 1,265 adolescents who developed major depressive disorder between 14 and 16 years of age. Later, between ages 16 and 21, this group was significantly at risk for occurrence of major depression, anxiety disorders, nicotine dependence, suicide attempts, and drug and alcohol misuse, as well as educational underachievement and early parenting, compared with adolescents who were not depressed. Weissman and colleagues (1999) identified a group of 83 children with an onset of major depressive disorder before puberty and followed them for 10 to 15 years. Generally, there was also a poor adult outcome in this group, with high rates of suicide attempts and social impairment, compared with children without major depressive disorder. These prepubertal children were more likely to develop substance misuse or other disorders as adults than to continue with their depression, unlike adolescents with major depressive disorder. Fergusson, Horwood, Ridder, and Beautrais (2005) found that extent and severity of depressive symptoms as an adolescent predicted extent of depression and suicidal behaviors as an adult. Other studies support the idea that age of onset distinguishes different depressive trajectories (Rice, Riglin, Thapar, Heron, Anney, O'Donovan, & Thapar, 2019; Hofmann, 2020). Clearly, becoming depressed as a child or adolescent is a dangerous, threatening event to be treated immediately or prevented if possible. Fortunately, CBT can effectively prevent the onset of depressive episodes in at-risk youth (Beardslee et al., 2013)

Age-Based Influences on Older Adults Depression in older adults is a serious problem (Blazer, 2003; Wang & Blazer, 2015; Wittchen, 2012), in part because social isolation and loneliness (Blazer, 2020). Some studies estimate that 14% to 42% of nursing home residents may experience major depressive episodes (Djernes, 2006; Fiske et al., 2009). In one large study, depressed elderly patients between 56 and 85 years of age were followed for 6 years; approximately 80% did not remit but continued to be depressed (or cycled in and out of depression) even if their depressive symptoms were not severe enough to meet diagnostic criteria for a disorder (Beekman et al., 2002).

Depression in older adults is strongly associated with race and ethnicity (Vyas et al., 2020), as shown in a large survey of 25,503 depressed older people (50.5% of those were women, 69.9% were non-Hispanic White, 19.6% Black, 3.9% Hispanic, 1.5% Asian, and 5.1% other/unspecified). After adjusting for sociodemographic, lifestyle, and other health confounders, the results showed that people from ethnic underrepresented groups had 1.5-fold to 2-fold higher risk for experiencing anhedonia, sadness, and psychomotor symptoms as compared with non-Hispanic White participants. Black participants were also 61% less likely to report any pharmacological or psychological treatments than non-Hispanic White individuals.

Late-onset depressions are associated with marked sleep difficulties, illness anxiety disorder (anxiety focused on possibly being sick or injured in some way), and agitation (Baldwin, 2009). It can be difficult to diagnose depression in older adults because elderly people who become physically ill or begin to show signs of dementia might become depressed about it, but the signs of depression or mood disorder would be attributed to the illness or dementia and thus missed (see, for example, Blazer & Hybels, 2009; Delano-Wood & Abeles, 2005). As many as 50% of patients with Alzheimer's disease suffer from comorbid depression, which makes life more difficult for their families (Lyketsos & Olin, 2002; Modrego, 2010).

Anxiety disorders accompany depression in from one third to one half of elderly patients, particularly generalized anxiety disorder and panic disorder (Fiske et al., 2009; Lenze et al., 2000), and when they do appear together, patients are more severely depressed. In DSM-5 as described above, clinicians now must specify the presence and severity of anxiety when diagnosing a mood disorder because of the implications for severity and course of the mood disorder, as well as treatment. One third will also suffer from comorbid alcohol abuse (Devanand, 2002). Several studies have shown that entering menopause also increases rates of depression among women who have never previously been depressed (Cohen, Soares, Vitonis, Otto, & Harlow, 2006; Freeman, Sammel, Lin, & Nelson, 2006). This may be because of biological factors, such as hormonal changes, or the experience of distressing physical symptoms or other life events occurring during this period. Depression can also contribute to physical disease and death in the elderly (Blazer, 2020; Blazer & Hybels, 2009). Being depressed doubles the risk of death in elderly patients who have suffered a heart attack or stroke (Schulz, Drayer, & Rollman, 2002; Whooley & Wong, 2013). Wallace and O'Hara (1992), in a longitudinal study, found that elderly citizens became increasingly depressed over a 3-year period. They suggest, with some evidence, that this trend is related to increasing illness and reduced social support. In other words, as we become frailer and more alone, the psychological result is depression, which increases the probability that we will become even frailer and have even less social support (Wittchen, 2012).

Bruce (2002) confirmed that death of a spouse, caregiving burden for an ill spouse, and loss of independence because of medical illness are among the strongest risk factors for depression in this age group. This vicious cycle is deadly because suicide rates are higher in older adults than in any other age group (Conwell, Duberstein, & Caine, 2002), although rates have been decreasing lately (Blazer & Hybels, 2009). In contrast, optimism prevents depression after medical illnesses and promotes longevity. For example, Galatzer-Levy and Bonanno (2014) studied more than 2,000 older adults from 6 years prior to their first heart attack to 4 years after their first heart attack. People were more likely to die if they became depressed after their first heart attack, as compared with people who did not become depressed. However, optimism measured before the heart attack distinguished all people who became depressed from those who did not become depressed after the first heart attack, suggesting that optimism prospectively predicted depression and thereby also mortality following the first heart attack. Approximately half of the sample in this study was male, and the results were similar in both sexes.

The earlier gender imbalance in depression lessens considerably after the age of 65. In early childhood, boys are more likely to be depressed than girls, but an overwhelming surge of depression in adolescent girls produces an imbalance in the sex ratio that is maintained until old age, when just as many women are depressed but increasing numbers of men are also affected (Fiske et al., 2009). From the perspective of the life span, this is the first time since early childhood that the sex ratio for depression is more closely balanced.

Across Cultures

We noted the strong tendency of anxiety to take somatic (physical) forms in some cultures. Instead of talking about fear, panic, or general anxiety, many people describe stomachaches, chest pains or heart distress, and headaches. Much the same tendency exists across cultures for mood disorders (Kim & Lopez, 2014), which is not surprising given the close relationship of anxiety and depression (Kessler and Bromet, 2013). Feelings of weakness or tiredness particularly characterize depression that is accompanied by mental or physical slowing or retardation (Kleinman, 2004; Ryder et al., 2008). Some cultures have their own idioms for depression; for instance, the Hopi, a Native American tribe, say they are "heartbroken" (Manson & Good, 1993), whereas aboriginal men in central Australia who are clearly depressed attribute it to weakness or injury of the spirit (Brown, Scales, et al., 2012).

Although somatic symptoms that characterize mood disorders seem roughly equivalent across cultures, it is difficult to compare subjective feelings. The way people think of depression may be influenced by the cultural view of the individual and the role of the individual in society (Kleinman, 2004; Ryder et al., 2008). For example, in societies that focus on the *individual* instead of the *group*, it is common to hear statements such as, "I feel blue" or "I am depressed." In cultures where the individual is tightly integrated into the larger group, however, someone might say, "Our life has lost its meaning," referring to the group in which the individual resides (Manson & Good, 1993).

In specific locations, prevalence of depression can differ dramatically. A structured interview was used by Kinzie, Leung, Boehnlein, and Matsunaga (1992) to determine the percentage of adult members of a Native American village who met criteria for mood disorders. The lifetime prevalence for any mood disorder was 19.4% in men, 36.7% in women, and 28% overall, approximately four times higher than in the general population. Examined by disorder, almost all the increase is accounted for by greatly elevated rates of major depression. Findings in the same village for substance abuse are similar to the results for major depressive disorder (see Chapter 11). Hasin and colleagues (2005) found a somewhat lower overall percentage of 19.17% in a different village, which was still 1.5 times higher than the percentage found in Whites, a significant difference. Beals and colleagues (2005), on the other hand, reported a considerably lower prevalence in two tribes they studied, perhaps because of differences in interviewing methods or because conditions and culture can differ greatly from tribe to tribe. Still, appalling social and economic conditions on many reservations fulfill all requirements for chronic major life stress, which is so strongly related to the onset of mood disorders, particularly major depressive disorder.

Among Creative Individuals

Early in the history of the United States, Benjamin Rush, one of the signers of the Declaration of Independence and a founder of American psychiatry, observed something curious:

> From a part of the brain preternaturally elevated, but not diseased, the mind sometimes discovers not only unusual strengths and acuteness, but certain talents it never exhibited before. Talents for eloquence, poetry, music and painting, and uncommon ingenuity in several of the mechanical arts, are often evolved in this state of madness." (Rush, 1812, p. 153)

This clinical observation has been made many times for thousands of years and applies not only to creativity but also to leadership. Aristotle pointed out that leading philosophers, poets, politicians, and artists all have tendencies toward "melancholia" (Ludwig, 1995).

Is there truth in the enduring belief that genius is allied to madness? Several researchers, including Kay Redfield Jamison and Nancy Andreasen, have attempted to find out. The results are surprising. Table 7.3 lists a group of famous American poets, many of whom won the Pulitzer Prize. As you can see, all almost certainly had bipolar disorder.

Musician Demi Lovato was diagnosed with bipolar disorder while being treated for other mental health problems.

Many died by suicide. These eight poets are among the 36 born in the 20th century who were represented in *The New Oxford Book of American Verse (the 1976 edition, edited by Richard Ellman)*, a collection reserved for the most distinguished poets in the country. It is certainly striking that about 20% of these 36 poets exhibited bipolar disorder, given the population prevalence of slightly less than 1%. Goodwin and Jamison (2007) think that 20% is probably a conservative estimate because the 28 remaining poets have not been studied in sufficient detail to determine whether they also had bipolar disorder. Andreasen (1987) reported results similar to those shown in Table 7.3 in a study of 30 other creative writers, and Kaufman (2001, 2002) observed that this effect was far more common in women poets, even when compared with other artists or leaders. Why female poets in particular? Kaufman and Baer (2002) wonder whether the independent and sometimes rebellious qualities associated with creativity might be more stressful in a society that puts demands on women to be supportive and affiliative.

Many artists and writers, whether suspected of mood disorders or not, speak of periods of inspiration when thought processes quicken, moods lift, and new associations are generated (Jamison, 1989, 1993). Perhaps something inherent in manic states fosters creativity, and some studies confirm that creativity is specifically associated with manic episodes and not depressive states (Soeiro-de-Souza, Dias, Bio, Post, & Moreno, 2011). On the other hand, it is possible that the genetic vulnerability to mood disorders is independently accompanied by a predisposition to creativity (Richards, Kinney, Lunde, Benet, & Merzel, 1988). In other words, the genetic patterns associated with bipolar disorder may also carry the spark of creativity. Subsequent studies have confirmed heightened creativity in bipolar (but not unipolar) patients on tests of creativity, even when not afflicted by manic or depressive states and functioning normally (referred to as being euthymic) (Santosa et al., 2007; Srivastava et al., 2010; Strong et al., 2007). These ideas need further confirmation, but the study of creativity and leadership, so highly valued in all cultures, may well be enhanced by a deeper understanding of "madness" (Goodwin & Jamison, 2007; Ludwig, 1995).

Causes of Mood Disorders

In Chapter 2, we describe *equifinality* as the same product resulting from possibly different causes. Just as there may be many reasons for a fever, there may also be a number of reasons for depression. For example, a depressive disorder that arises in winter has a different precipitant than a severe depression following a death, even though the episodes might look quite similar. Nevertheless, psychopathologists are identifying biological, psychological, and social factors that seem strongly implicated in the etiology of mood disorders, whatever the precipitating factor. An integrative theory of the etiology of mood disorders considers the interaction of biological, psychological, and social dimensions and notes the strong relationship of anxiety and depression. Before describing these interactions, we review evidence pertaining to each contributing factor.

Concept Check 7.2

Identify each of the following statements related to prevalence of mood disorders as either true (T) or false (F).

1. ____________ Women are approximately twice as likely as men to be diagnosed with a mood disorder.
2. ____________ Depression requires some life experience, indicating that babies and young children cannot experience the disorder.
3. ____________ It's often difficult to diagnose depression in the elderly because its symptoms are similar to those of medical ailments or dementia.
4. ____________ Somatic symptoms characterizing mood disorders are nearly equivalent across cultures.

Table 7.3 Partial Listing of Major 20th-Century American Poets, born between 1895 and 1935, with Documented Histories of Manic-Depressive Illness (Bipolar Disorder)

Poet	Pulitzer Prize in Poetry	Treated for Major Depressive Illness	Treated for Mania	Died by Suicide
Hart Crane (1899–1932)		×	×	×
Theodore Roethke (1908–1963)	×		×	
Delmore Schwartz (1913–1966)		×	×	
John Berryman (1914–1972)	×	×	×	×
Randall Jarrell (1914–1965)		×	×	×
Robert Lowell (1917–1977)	×	×	×	
Anne Sexton (1928–1974)	×	×	×	×
Sylvia Plath* (1932–1963)	×	×		×

*Plath, although not treated for mania, was probably bipolar II.

Source: F. K. Goodwin K. R. & Jamison, 1990, *Manic depressive illness*, Oxford University Press.

Biological Dimensions

Conducting research to determine the genetic contribution to a particular disorder or class of disorders is complex and difficult to do. But several traditional strategies—such as family studies and twin studies—can help us estimate this contribution.

Familial and Genetic Influences In *family studies*, we look at the prevalence of a given disorder in the first-degree relatives of an individual known to have the disorder (the *proband*). We have found that, despite wide variability, the rate in relatives of probands with mood disorders is consistently about two to three times greater than in relatives of controls who don't have mood disorders (Klein, Lewinsohn, Rohde, Seeley, & Durbin, 2002; Lau & Eley, 2010; Levinson, 2009). Increasing severity, recurrence of major depression, and earlier age of onset in the proband is associated with the highest rates of depression in relatives (Kendler, Gatz, Gardner, & Pedersen, 2007; Klein et al., 2002; Weissman et al., 2005).

The best evidence that genes have something to do with mood disorders comes from *twin studies*, in which we examine the frequency with which identical twins (with identical genes) have the disorder, compared with fraternal twins, who share only 50% of their genes (as do all first-degree relatives). If a genetic contribution exists, the disorder should be present in identical twins to a much greater extent than in fraternal twins. A number of twin studies suggest that mood disorders are heritable (see, for example, Hodgson & McGuffin, 2013; Kendler, Neale, Kessler, Heath, & Eaves, 1993; McGuffin et al., 2003).

One strong study is presented in ■ Figure 7.3 (McGuffin et al., 2003). As you can see, an identical twin is two to three times more likely to present with a mood disorder than a fraternal twin if the first twin has a mood disorder (66.7% of identical twins compared with 18.9% of fraternal twins if the first twin has bipolar disorder; 45.6% versus 20.2% if the first twin has unipolar disorder). But notice that if one identical twin has unipolar disorder, the chances of a co-twin having bipolar disorder are slim to none. In a large meta-analysis of twin studies, Sullivan et al. (2000) estimated the heritability of depression to be 37%. Shared environmental factors have little influence, whereas 63% of the variance in depression can be attributed to non-shared environmental factors.

Two reports have appeared suggesting sex differences in genetic vulnerability to depression. Bierut and colleagues (1999) studied 2,662 twin pairs in the Australian twin registry and found the characteristically higher rate of depressive disorders in women. Estimates of heritability in women ranged from 36% to 44%, consistent with other studies. But estimates for men were lower and ranged from 18% to 24%. These results mostly agree with an important study of men in the United States by Lyons and colleagues (1998). The authors conclude that environmental events play a larger role in causing depression in men than in women.

Note from the studies just described that bipolar disorder confers an increased risk of developing some mood disorder, but not necessarily bipolar disorder, in close relatives. This conclusion supports an assumption noted previously that bipolar disorder may simply be a more severe variant of mood disorders rather than a fundamentally different disorder. Then again, of identical twins both having (concordant for) a mood disorder, 80% are also concordant for polarity. In other words, if one identical twin is unipolar, there is an 80% chance the other twin is unipolar as opposed to bipolar. This finding suggests these disorders may be inherited separately and therefore be separate disorders after all (Nurnberger, 2012; Nurnberger & Gershon, 1992).

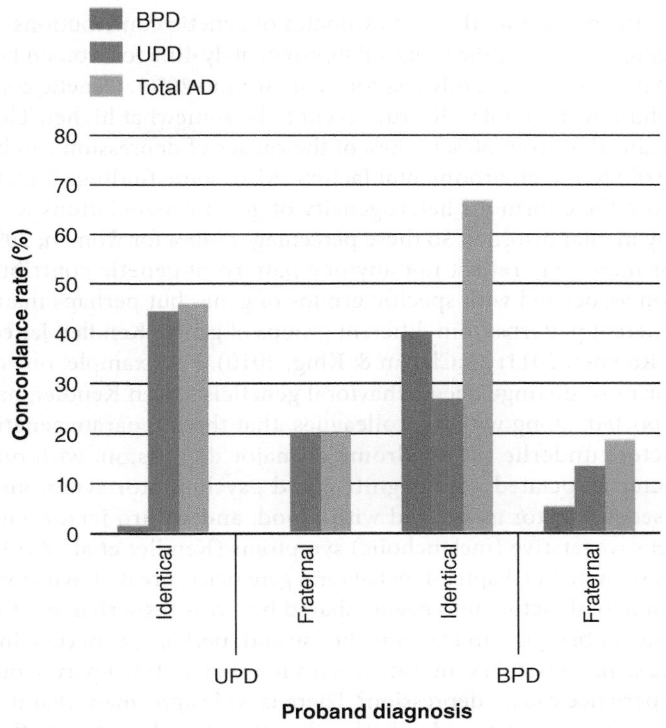

Figure 7.3

Co-occurrence of types of mood disorders in twins for unipolar (UPD) and bipolar (BPD) affective disorder (AD). Adapted from P. McGuffin, F. Rijsdijk, M. Andrew, P. Sham, R. Katz, & A. Cardno, 2003, The heritability of bipolar affective disorder and the genetic relationship to unipolar depression, *Archives of General Psychiatry, 60*, 497–502, © 2003 American Medical Association.

McGuffin and colleagues (2003) conclude that both points are partially correct. Basically, they found that the genetic contributions to depression in both disorders are the same or similar but that the genetics of mania are distinct from depression. Thus, individuals with bipolar disorder are genetically susceptible to depression and independently genetically susceptible to mania. This hypothesis still requires further confirmation.

Although these findings do raise continuing questions about the relative contributions of psychosocial and genetic factors to mood disorders, overwhelming evidence suggests that such disorders are familial and almost certainly reflect an underlying genetic vulnerability, particularly for women. As described in some detail in Chapter 2 (see pp. 00–00), studies are now beginning to identify different patterns of genes that may confer this vulnerability, at least for some types of depression (Bradley et al., 2008; Caspi et al., 2003; Garlow, Boone, Li, Owens, & Nemeroff, 2005; Kendler, Aggen, & Neale, 2013; Levinson, 2009; Nurnberger, 2012). In this complex field, it is likely that many additional patterns of gene combinations will be found to contribute to varieties of depression.

In conclusion, the best estimates of genetic contributions to depression fall in the range of approximately 40% for women but seem to be significantly less for men (around 20%). Genetic contributions to bipolar disorder seem to be somewhat higher. This means that from 60% to 80% of the causes of depression can be attributed to environmental factors. Also, some findings underscore the enormous heterogeneity of genetic associations with any mental disorder. So these percentages (40% for women, 20% for men) may reflect not any one pattern of genetic contribution associated with specific groups of genes but perhaps many different patterns from different groups of genes (Kendler, Jaffee, & Roemer, 2011; McClellan & King, 2010). For example, one of our most distinguished behavioral geneticists, Ken Kendler, has reported, along with his colleagues, that three separate genetic factors underlie the syndrome of major depression, with one factor associated with cognitive and psychomotor symptoms, a second factor associated with mood, and a third factor with neurovegetative (melancholic) symptoms (Kendler et al., 2013). As we note in Chapter 4, behavioral geneticists break down environmental factors into events shared by twins (experiencing the same upbringing in the same house and, perhaps, experiencing the same stressful events) and events not shared. What part of our experience causes depression? There is wide agreement that it is the unique, nonshared events rather than the shared ones that interact with biological vulnerability to cause depression (Lau & Eley, 2010; Plomin, DeFries, McClearn, & Rutter, 1997).

Depression and Anxiety: Same Genes? Although most studies have looked at specific disorders in isolation, a growing trend is to examine the heritability of related groups of disorders. Evidence supports the assumption of a close relationship among depression and anxiety (as well as other emotional disorders). For example, data from family studies indicate that the more signs and symptoms of anxiety and depression there are in a given patient, the greater the rate of anxiety, depression, or both in first-degree relatives and children (Hudson et al., 2003; Leyfer & Brown, 2011). This is consistent with genome-wide association studies pointing to a genetic link between depression and anxiety (Purves et al., 2020), and especially between depression and generalized anxiety disorder (Morneau-Vaillancourt et al., 2020). But many other psychiatric disorders are also genetically linked to depression. For example, a genome-wide association study examined the genetic link of various psychiatric and neurological illnesses from 1,191,588 individuals and showed that mood disorders (major depressive disorder and bipolar disorder) share common genetic risks with schizophrenia, anxiety disorders, and ADHD. In contrast, neurological illnesses (such as epilepsy, Parkinson's disease, and Alzheimer's disease) are more distinct from one another and from the psychiatric disorders (Anttila et al., 2018).

Social and psychological explanations seemed to account for the factors that differentiate anxiety from depression rather than genes. These findings again suggest that, with the possible exception of mania, the biological vulnerability for mood disorders may not be specific to that disorder but may reflect a more general predisposition to anxiety or mood disorders or, more likely, to a basic temperament underlying all emotional disorders, such as neuroticism (Barlow et al., 2013). The specific form of the disorder would be determined by unique psychological, social, or additional biological factors (Kilpatrick et al., 2007; Rutter, 2010; Slavich & Irwin, 2014).

Neurotransmitter Systems Mood disorders have been the subject of more intense neurobiological study than almost any other area of psychopathology, with the possible exception of schizophrenia. In Chapter 2, we observe that we now know that neurotransmitter systems have many subtypes and interact in many complex ways with one another and with neuromodulators (products of the endocrine system). Research implicates low levels of serotonin in the causes of mood disorders, but only in relation to other neurotransmitters, including norepinephrine and dopamine (see, for example, Thase, 2005, 2009). Remember that the apparent primary function of serotonin is to regulate our emotional reactions. For example, we are more impulsive and our moods swing more widely when our levels of serotonin are low. This may be because one of the functions of serotonin is to regulate systems involving norepinephrine and dopamine. According to the "permissive" hypothesis, when serotonin levels are low, other neurotransmitters are "permitted" to range more widely, become dysregulated, and contribute to mood irregularities, including depression. Current thinking is that the balance of the various neurotransmitters and their interaction with systems of self-regulation are more important than the absolute level of any one neurotransmitter (Carver, Johnson, & Joormann, 2009; Whisman, Johnson, & Smolen, 2011; Yatham et al., 2012).

In the context of this delicate balance, there is continued interest in the role of dopamine, particularly in relationship to manic episodes, atypical depression, or depression with psychotic features (Dunlop & Nemeroff, 2007; Garlow & Nemeroff, 2003; Thase, 2009). For example, the dopamine agonist L-dopa seems to produce hypomania in bipolar patients (see, for instance, Van Praag & Korf, 1975), along with other dopamine agonists (Silverstone, 1985). Chronic stress also reduces dopamine levels and produces depressive-like behavior (Thase, 2009). But as with other research in this area, it is quite difficult to pin down any relationships with certainty.

The Endocrine System During the past several years, most attention has shifted away from a focus on neurotransmitters to the endocrine system and the "stress hypothesis" of the etiology of depression (Nemeroff, 2004). This hypothesis focuses on overactivity in the hypothalamic–pituitary–adrenocortical (HPA) axis (discussed later), which produces stress hormones. Again, notice the similarity with the description of the neurobiology of anxiety in Chapter 5 (see, for example, Barlow et al., 2014; Britton & Rauch, 2009; Charney & Drevets, 2002). Investigators became interested in the endocrine system when they noticed that patients with diseases affecting this system sometimes became depressed. For example, hypothyroidism, or Cushing's disease, which affects the adrenal cortex, leads to excessive secretion of cortisol and often to depression (and anxiety).

In Chapter 2 and again in Chapter 5, we discuss the brain circuit called the HPA axis, beginning in the hypothalamus and running through the pituitary gland, which coordinates the endocrine system (see Figure 2.10, p. 00). Investigators have also discovered that neurotransmitter activity in the hypothalamus regulates the release of hormones that affect the HPA axis. These **neurohormones** are an increasingly important focus of study in psychopathology (see, for example, Garlow & Nemeroff, 2003; Hammen & Keenan-Miller, 2013; Nemeroff, 2004; Thase, 2009). There are thousands of neurohormones. Sorting out their relationship to antecedent neurotransmitter systems (as well as determining their independent effects on the central nervous system) is likely to be a complex task indeed. One of the glands influenced by the pituitary is the cortical section of the adrenal gland, which produces the stress hormone cortisol that completes the HPA axis. Cortisol is called a *stress hormone* because it is elevated during stressful life events. (We discuss this system in more detail in Chapter 9.) For now, it is enough to know that cortisol levels are elevated in depressed patients, a finding that makes sense considering the relationship between depression and severe life stress (Barlow et al., 2014; Bradley et al., 2008; Thase, 2009).

This connection led to the development of what was thought to be a biological test for depression, the *dexamethasone suppression test (DST)*. Dexamethasone is a glucocorticoid that suppresses cortisol secretion in normal participants. When this substance was given to patients who were depressed, however, much *less* suppression was noticed than in normal participants, and what did occur didn't last long (Carroll, Martin, & Davies, 1968; Carroll et al., 1980). Approximately 50% of depressed patients show this reduced suppression, particularly if their depression is severe (Rush et al., 1997). The thinking was that in depressed patients, the adrenal cortex secreted enough cortisol to overwhelm the suppressive effects of dexamethasone. This theory was heralded as important because it promised the first biological laboratory test for a psychological disorder. However, later research demonstrated that individuals with other disorders, particularly anxiety disorders, also demonstrate nonsuppression (Feinberg & Carroll, 1984; Goodwin & Jamison, 2007), which eliminated its usefulness as a test to diagnose depression.

Over the past decade, research has taken some exciting turns. Recognizing that stress hormones are elevated in patients with depression (and anxiety), researchers have begun to focus on the consequences of these elevations. Preliminary findings indicate that these hormones can be harmful to neurons in that they decrease a key ingredient that keeps neurons healthy and growing. As is shown in Chapter 5 on anxiety disorders, individuals experiencing heightened levels of stress hormones over a long period undergo some shrinkage of a brain structure called the *hippocampus*. The hippocampus, among other things, is responsible for keeping stress hormones in check and serves important functions in facilitating cognitive processes such as short-term memory. But the new finding, at least in animals, is that long-term overproduction of stress hormones makes the organism unable to develop new neurons (neurogenesis). Thus, some theorists suspect that the connection between high stress hormones and depression is the suppression of neurogenesis in the hippocampus (Glasper, Schoenfeld, & Gould, 2012; Heim, Plotsky, & Nemeroff, 2004; Snyder, Soumier, Brewer, Pickel, & Cameron, 2011; Thase, 2009). Evidence reveals that healthy girls at risk for developing depression because their mothers suffer from recurrent depression have reduced hippocampal volume compared with girls with nondepressed mothers (Chen, Hamilton, & Gotlib, 2010). This finding suggests that low hippocampal volume may precede and perhaps contribute to the onset of depression. Scientists have already observed that successful treatments for depression, including electroconvulsive therapy, seem to produce neurogenesis in the hippocampus, thereby reversing this process (Duman, 2004; Santarelli et al., 2003; Sapolsky, 2004). In fact, it has been demonstrated in animal laboratories that exercise increases neurogenesis, which could possibly be one mechanism of action in successful psychological treatments utilizing exercise, such as behavioral activation described below (Speisman, Kumar, Rani, Foster, & Ormerod, 2013). Despite strong preliminary evidence, this is just a theory that must now undergo the slow process of scientific confirmation.

Another exciting new field of research is the role of the gut microbiota, which are the bacteria and other microorganisms residing in the human intestines (see Chapter 2). Because some of them are directly or indirectly involved in the production and actions of many neurohormones, researchers are now examining their roles in psychiatric conditions, including depression (Evrensel & Tarhan, 2021; Simpson, Diaz-Arteche, Eliby, Schwartz, & Cowan, 2021; Spichak, Bastiaanssen, Berding, Vickova, Clark , Dinan, & Cryan, 2021). This opens up exciting new avenues for research that could show that people's diet might have a role in depression (Marx et al., 2021).

Sleep and Circadian Rhythms We have known for several years that sleep disturbances are a hallmark of most mood disorders (Alloy, Ng, Titone, & Boland, 2017; Carpenter et al., 2021; Fang, Tu, Sheng, & Shao, 2019). Most important, in people who are depressed, there is a significantly shorter period after falling asleep before *rapid eye movement (REM) sleep* begins. As you may remember from your introductory psychology or biology course, there are two major stages of sleep: REM sleep and non-REM sleep. When we first fall asleep, we go through several substages of progressively deeper sleep during which we achieve most of our rest. After about 90 minutes, we begin to experience REM sleep, when the brain arouses, and we begin to dream. Our eyes move rapidly back and forth under our eyelids—hence the name *rapid eye movement* sleep. As the night goes on, we have increasing amounts of REM sleep. (We discuss the process of sleep in more detail in Chapter 8.) In addition to entering REM sleep more quickly, depressed patients experience REM activity that is more intense, and the stages of deepest sleep, called *slow-wave sleep*, don't occur until later, if at all (Jindal et al., 2002; Kupfer, 1995; Thase, 2009). It seems that some sleep characteristics occur only while we are depressed and not at other times (Riemann, Berger, & Voderholzer, 2001; Rush et al., 1986). But other evidence suggests that, at least in more severe cases with recurrent depression, disturbances in sleep continuity, as well as reduction of deep sleep, may be present even when the individual is not depressed (Kupfer, 1995; Thase, 2009). In addition, unusually short and long sleep durations were associated with an increased risk for depression in adults (Zhai, Zhang, & Zhang, 2015).

Sleep pattern disturbances in depressed children are less pronounced than in adults, perhaps because children are very deep sleepers, illustrating once again the importance of developmental stage to psychopathology (Brent & Birmaher, 2009; Garber et al., 2009). But sleep disturbances are even more severe among depressed older adults. In fact, insomnia, frequently experienced by older adults, is a risk factor for both the onset and persistence of depression (Fiske et al., 2009; Perlis et al., 2006; Talbot et al., 2012). In an interesting study, researchers found that treating insomnia directly in those patients who have both insomnia and depression may enhance the effects of treatment for depression (Manber et al., 2008). Sleep disturbances also occur in bipolar patients, where they are particularly severe and are characterized not only by decreased REM latency but also by severe insomnia and hypersomnia (excessive sleep) (Goodwin & Jamison, 2007; Harvey, 2008; Harvey, Talbot, & Gershon, 2009). Talbot and colleagues (2012) studied the relationship between sleep and mood in patients with bipolar disorder who were not currently in a depressed or manic state (interepisode), compared with a group of patients suffering from insomnia. Both the bipolar and insomnia patients had greater sleep disturbance compared with a healthy control group. But the investigators discovered that the relationship between sleep and mood was bidirectional in both groups. That is, negative mood predicted sleep disruptions, and sleep disruptions subsequently resulted in negative mood. Treating the insomnia of bipolar I patients between episodes with CBT has been shown to reduce the risk of relapse and improve sleep, mood, and functioning (Harvey et al., 2015). Thus, it seems that the relationship between sleep and mood may cut across different diagnoses and that treating sleep disruptions directly might positively affect mood not only in insomnia but also in mood disorders

Another interesting finding is that depriving depressed patients of sleep, particularly during the second half of the night, causes temporary improvement in their condition (Giedke & Schwarzler, 2002; Thase, 2009), particularly for patients with bipolar disorder in a depressive state (Harvey, 2008; Johnson et al., 2009), although the depression returns when the patients start sleeping normally again. In any case, because sleep patterns reflect a biological rhythm, there may be a relationship among SAD, sleep disturbances in depressed patients, and a more general disturbance in biological rhythms (Soreca, Frank, & Kupfer, 2009). This would not be surprising if it were true, because most mammals are exquisitely sensitive to day length at the latitudes at which they live, and this "biological clock" controls eating, sleeping, and weight changes. Thus, substantial disruption in circadian rhythm might be particularly problematic for some vulnerable individuals (Moore, 1999; Sohn & Lam, 2005; Soreca et al., 2009).

Finally, abnormal sleep profiles and, specifically, disturbances in REM sleep and poor sleep quality predict a somewhat poorer response to psychological treatment (Buysse et al., 1999; Thase, 2009; Thase, Simons, & Reynolds, 1996), further supporting the potential usefulness of treating disrupted sleep directly.

Additional Studies of Brain Structure and Function

Measuring electrical activity in the brain with an electroencephalogram (EEG) is described in Chapter 3, where we also describe a type of brain wave activity, alpha waves, that indicate calm, positive feelings. In the 1990s, Davidson (1993) and Heller and Nitschke (1997) demonstrated that depressed individuals exhibit greater right-sided anterior activation of their brains, particularly in the prefrontal cortex (and less left-sided activation and, correspondingly, less alpha wave activity) than nondepressed individuals (Davidson, Pizzagalli, Nitschke, & Putnam, 2002). Furthermore, right-sided anterior activation was also found in patients who are no longer depressed (Gotlib, Ranganath, & Rosenfeld, 1998; Tomarken & Keener, 1998), suggesting this brain function might also exist *before* the individual becomes depressed and represent a vulnerability to depression. Follow-up studies showed that adolescent offspring of depressed mothers tend to show this pattern, compared with offspring of nondepressed mothers (Tomarken, Dichter, Garber, & Simien, 2004), also suggesting that this type of brain functioning could become an indicator of a biological vulnerability to depression (Gotlib & Abramson, 1999). In contrast, one study suggests that bipolar spectrum patients (individuals with subthreshold swings in mood) show elevated rather than diminished relative left-frontal EEG activity and that this brain activity predicts the onset of a full bipolar I disorder (Nusslock et al., 2012). In addition to studying the prefrontal cortex and hippocampus, neuroscientists are also studying the anterior cingulate cortex and the amygdala for clues to understanding brain function in depression and finding that some areas are less active, and other areas more active, in people with depression than in normals, confirming the EEG studies mentioned above (Davidson, Pizzagalli, & Nitschke, 2009). These areas of the brain are all interconnected and seem to be associated with increased inhibition as well as deficits in pursuing desired goals, which happen to be characteristics of depression. Scientists hope that further study of these brain circuits will lead to a deeper understanding of what the origins of differences in depressed individuals are, whether these differences precede depression and may contribute to causing depression as some studies suggest, or whether they are simply a consequence of being depressed.

Psychological Dimensions

Thus far we have reviewed genetic and biological factors, including findings from studies of neurotransmitters, the endocrine system, sleep and circadian rhythms, and relative activity in certain areas of the brain associated with depression. But these factors are all inextricably linked to psychological and social dimensions where scientists are also discovering strong associations with depression. We now review some of these findings.

Stressful Life Events Stress and trauma are among the most striking unique contributions to the etiology of all psychological disorders. This is reflected throughout psychopathology and is evident in the wide adoption of the diathesis–stress model of psychopathology presented in Chapter 2 (and referred to throughout this book), which describes possible genetic and psychological vulnerabilities. But in seeking what activates this vulnerability (diathesis), we usually look for a stressful or traumatic life event.

Stress and Depression You would think it would be sufficient to ask people whether anything major had happened in their lives before they developed depression or some other psychological disorder. Most people who develop depression report losing a job, getting divorced, having a child, or graduating from school and starting a career. But as with most issues in the study of psychopathology, the significance of a major event is not easily discovered (Carter & Garber, 2011; Hammen, 2005; Hammen & Keenan-Miller, 2013; Monroe & Reid, 2009; Monroe, Slavich, & Georgiades, 2009), so most investigators have stopped simply asking patients whether something bad (or good) happened and have begun to look at the context of the event, as well as the meaning it has for the individual.

For example, losing a job is stressful for most people, but it is far more difficult for some than others. A few people might even see it as a blessing. If you were laid off as a manager in a large corporation because of a restructuring but your partner is the president of another corporation and makes more than enough money to support the family, it might not be so bad. Furthermore, if you are an aspiring writer or artist who has not had time to pursue your art, becoming unemployed might be the opportunity you have been waiting for, particularly if your partner has been telling you for years to devote yourself to your creative pursuits.

Now consider losing your job if you are a single parent of two young children living from paycheck to paycheck and, on account of a recent doctor's bill, you have to choose between paying the electric bill or buying enough food. The stressful life event is the same, but the context is different and transforms the significance of the event substantially. To complicate the scenario further, think for a minute about how various individuals in this situation might react to losing their job. Some people might well decide they are a total failure and thus become unable to carry on and provide for their children. Others might realize the job loss was not their fault and take advantage of a job training program while scraping by somehow. Thus, both the context of the life event and its meaning are important. This approach to studying life events, was developed by George W. Brown (1989b) and associates in England.

Brown's study of life events is difficult to carry out, and the methodology is still evolving. Psychologists such as Scott Monroe and Constance Hammen (Hammen, 2005; Monroe et al., 2009; Monroe, Rohde, Seeley, & Lewinsohn, 1999; Dohrenwend & Dohrenwend, 1981) have developed new methods. One crucial issue is the bias inherent in remembering events. If you ask people who are currently depressed what happened when they first became depressed more than 5 years ago, you will probably get answers different from those that they would give if they were not currently depressed. Because current moods distort memories, many investigators have concluded that the only useful way to study stressful life events is to follow people *prospectively*, to determine more accurately the precise nature of events and their relation to subsequent psychopathology.

In any case, in summarizing a large amount of research, it is clear that stressful life events are strongly related to the onset of mood disorders (Grant, Compas, Thurm, McMahon, & Gipson, 2004; Hammen, 2005; Kendler & Gardner, 2010; Monroe et al., 2009; Monroe & Reid, 2009). Measuring the context of events and their impact in a random sample of the population, a number of studies have found a marked relationship between severe and, in some cases, traumatic life events and the onset of depression (Brown, 1989a; Brown, Harris, & Hepworth, 1994; Kendler et al., 1999b; Mazure, 1998). Severe events precede all types of depression except, perhaps, for a small group of patients with melancholic or psychotic features who are experiencing subsequent episodes where depression emerges in the absence of life events (Brown et al., 1994). For example, childhood sexual abuse (in addition to a family history of depression and anxiety disorders) is a significant predictor of a first onset of depression in young adults (Klein et al., 2013). In addition, for people with recurrent depression, the clear occurrence of a severe life stress before or early in the latest episode predicts a poorer response to treatment and a longer time before remission (Monroe et al., 2009; Monroe, Kupfer, & Frank, 1992), as well as a greater likelihood of recurrence (Monroe et al., 2009; Monroe, Roberts, Kupfer, & Frank, 1996).

Although the context and meaning are often more important than the exact nature of the event itself, there are some events that are particularly likely to lead to depression. One of them is the breakup of a relationship, which is difficult for both adolescents (Carter & Garber, 2011; Monroe, Rohde, Seeley, & Lewinsohn, 1999) and adults (Kendler, Hettema, Butera, Gardner, & Prescott, 2003). Kendler and colleagues (2003) demonstrated in a twin study that if one twin experienced a loss, such as the death of a loved one, that twin was 10 times more likely to become depressed than the twin who didn't experience the loss. But if one twin is also humiliated by the loss, as when, for example, a partner or spouse leaves the twin for a best friend and the twin still sees them all the time, then that twin would be 20 times more likely to get depressed than a twin with the same genes who didn't experience the event. Scientists have confirmed that humiliation, loss, and social rejection are the most potent stressful life events likely to lead to depression (Monroe et al., 2009).

Clearly, there is a strong relationship between stress and depression, and scientists are discovering that the cause-and-effect connection between the two might go both ways. Remember in Chapter 2 where we note that our genetic endowment might increase the probability that we will experience stressful life events? We refer to this as the *gene–environment correlation model* (Kendler, 2011; Kendler, Jaffee, & Roemer, 2011). One example would be people who tend to seek difficult relationships because of genetically based personality characteristics that then lead to depression. Kendler and colleagues (1999a) report that about one third of the association between stressful life events and depression is not the usual arrangement where stress triggers depression but rather a situation where individuals vulnerable to depression place themselves in high-risk stressful environments, such as difficult relationships or other risky situations where bad outcomes are common. What is important about the reciprocal model is that it can happen both ways in the same individual: Stress triggers depression, and depressed individuals create or seek stressful events. If you ask mothers, they tend to say their depressed adolescents created the problem, but adolescents blame the stressful event itself (Carter, Garber, Cielsa, & Cole, 2006; Eley, 2011). According to the reciprocal model, the truth lies somewhere between these two views. Moreover, the relative importance of the contribution of genetic factors versus environmental effects seems to differ depending on age: Whereas heritability depression (and anxiety) symptoms is high during childhood, the importance of environmental effects increases with age (Nivard et al., 2015).

Stress and Bipolar Disorder The relationship of stressful events to the onset of episodes in bipolar disorder is also strong (Alloy & Abramson, 2010; Goodwin & Jamison, 2007; Johnson, Gruber, & Eisner, 2007; Johnson et al., 2008). Several issues may be particularly relevant to the causes of bipolar disorders, however (Goodwin & Ghaemi, 1998). First, typically negative stressful life events trigger depression, but a somewhat different, more positive, set of stressful life events seems to trigger mania (Alloy et al., 2012; Johnson et al., 2008). Specifically, experience associated with striving to achieve important goals—such as getting accepted into graduate school, obtaining a new job or promotion, getting married, or striving for popularity or financial success —trigger mania in vulnerable individuals (Alloy et al., 2012). Second, stress seems to initially trigger mania and depression, but as the disorder progresses, these episodes seem to develop a life of their own. In other words, once the cycle begins, a psychological or pathophysiological process takes over and ensures the disorder will continue (see, for example, Post, 1992; Post et al., 1989). Third, some precipitants of manic episodes seem related to loss of sleep, as in the postpartum period (Goodwin & Jamison, 2007; Harvey, 2008; Soreca et al., 2009) or as a result of jet lag—that is, disturbed circadian rhythms (Alloy, Nusslock, & Boland, 2015). In most cases of bipolar disorder, nevertheless, stressful life events are substantially indicated not only in provoking relapse but also in preventing recovery (Alloy, Abramson, Urosevic, Bender, & Wagner, 2009; Johnson & Miller, 1997).

Finally, although almost everyone who develops a mood disorder has experienced a significant stressful event, most people who experience such events do not develop mood disorders. Although the data are not yet as precise as we would like, somewhere between 20% and 50% of individuals who experience severe events develop mood disorders. Thus, between 50% and 80% of individuals do *not* develop mood disorders or, presumably, any other psychological disorder. Again, data strongly support the interaction of stressful life events with some kind of vulnerability: genetic, psychological, or, more likely, a combination of the two influences (Barlow, 2002; Haeffel & Hames, 2014; Kendler, Kuhn, Vittum, Prescott, & Riley, 2005; Thase, 2009).

Given a genetic vulnerability (diathesis) and a severe life event (stress), what happens then? Research has isolated a number of psychological and biological processes. To illustrate one, let's return to Keisha. Her stressful life event was attending a new school. Keisha's feeling of loss of control leads to another important psychological factor in depression: learned helplessness.

Learned Helplessness As discussed in Chapter 2, Martin Seligman discovered that dogs and rats have an interesting emotional reaction to events over which they have no control. If rats receive occasional shocks, they can function reasonably well as long as they can cope with the shocks by doing something to avoid them, such as pressing a lever. But if they learn that nothing they do helps them avoid the shocks, they eventually become helpless, give up, and manifest an animal equivalent of depression (Seligman, 1975).

Do humans react the same way? Seligman suggests we seem to, but only under one important condition: People become anxious and depressed when they decide that they have no control over the stress in their lives (Abramson, Seligman, & Teasdale, 1978; Miller & Norman, 1979). These findings evolved into an important model called the **learned helplessness theory of depression**. Often overlooked is Seligman's point that anxiety is the first response to a stressful situation. Depression may follow marked hopelessness about coping with the difficult life events (Barlow, 1988, 2002). The depressive attributional style is (1) *internal*, in that the individual attributes negative events to personal failings ("it is all my fault"); (2) *stable*, in that, even after a particular negative event passes, the attribution that "additional bad things will always be my fault" remains; and (3) *global*, in that the attributions extend across a variety of issues. Research continues on this interesting concept, but you can see how it applies to Keisha. Early in her difficulties with attending school, she began to believe events were out of her control and that she was unable even to begin to cope. More important, in her eyes the bad situation was all her fault: "I blamed myself for my lack of control." A downward spiral into a major depressive episode followed.

But a major question remains: Is learned helplessness a cause of depression or a correlated side effect of becoming depressed? If it were a cause, learned helplessness would have to exist *before* the depressive episode. Results from a classic 5-year longitudinal study of children shed some light on this issue. Nolen-Hoeksema, Girgus, and Seligman (1992) reported that negative attributional

Keisha... No Easy Transitions

I was a serious and sensitive 11-year-old at the edge of puberty and at the edge of an adventure that many teens and preteens embark on—the transition from elementary to junior high school. A new school, new people, new responsibilities, new pressures. Academically, I was a good student up to this point, but I didn't feel good about myself and generally lacked self-confidence.

Keisha began to experience severe anxiety reactions. Then she became quite ill with the flu. After recovering and attempting to return to school, Keisha discovered that her anxieties were worse than ever. More important, she began to feel she was losing control:

> As I look back, I can identify events that precipitated my anxieties and fears, but then everything seemed to happen suddenly and without cause. I was reacting emotionally and physically in a way that I didn't understand. I felt out of control of my emotions and body. Day after day I wished, as a child does, that whatever was happening to me would magically end. I wished that I would awake one day to find that I was the person I was several months before.

style did not predict later symptoms of depression in young children; rather, stressful life events seemed to be the major precipitant of symptoms. As children under stress grew older, however, they tended to develop more negative cognitive styles, which did tend to predict symptoms of depression in reaction to additional negative events. Nolen-Hoeksema and colleagues speculate that meaningful negative events early in childhood may lead to negative attributional styles, making these children more vulnerable to future depressive episodes when stressful events occur. Indeed, most studies support the finding that negative cognitive styles precede and are a risk factor for depression (Alloy & Abramson, 2006; Garber & Carter, 2006; Garber et al., 2009).

This thinking recalls the types of psychological vulnerabilities theorized to contribute to the development of anxiety disorders (Barlow, 1988, 2002; Barlow et al., 2013). That is, in a person who has a nonspecific genetic vulnerability to either anxiety or depression, stressful life events activate a psychological sense that life events are uncontrollable (Barlow, 2002; Chorpita & Barlow, 1998). Evidence suggests that negative attributional styles are not specific to depression but also characterize people with anxiety (Barlow, 2002; Barlow et al., 2013; Hankin & Abramson, 2001). This may indicate that a psychological (cognitive) vulnerability is no more specific for mood disorders than a genetic vulnerability. Both types of vulnerabilities may underlie numerous disorders.

Abramson, Metalsky, and Alloy (1989) revised the learned helplessness theory to deemphasize the influence of negative attributions and highlight the development of a sense of hopelessness as a crucial cause of many forms of depression. Attributions are important only to the extent that they contribute to a sense of hopelessness. This fits well with the current thinking on crucial differences between anxiety and depression. Both anxious and depressed individuals feel helpless and believe they lack control, but only in depression do they give up and become hopeless about ever regaining control (Alloy & Abramson, 2006; Barlow, 1991, 2002; Chorpita & Barlow, 1998).

Negative Cognitive Styles In 1967, Aaron T. Beck (1967, 1976) suggested that depression may result from a tendency to interpret everyday events in a negative way. According to Beck, people with depression make the worst of everything; for them, the smallest setbacks are major catastrophes. In his extensive clinical work, Beck observed that all of his depressed patients thought this way, and he began classifying the types of "cognitive errors" that characterized this style. From the long list he compiled, two representative examples are *arbitrary inference* and *overgeneralization*. Arbitrary inference is evident when a depressed individual emphasizes the negative rather than the positive aspects of a situation. A high school teacher may assume they are a terrible instructor because two students in their class fell asleep. They fail to consider other reasons the students might be sleeping (up all night partying, perhaps) and "infers" that their teaching style is at fault. As an example of overgeneralization, when your professor makes one critical remark on your paper, you then assume you will fail the class despite a long string of positive comments and good grades on other papers. You are overgeneralizing from one small remark. According to Beck, people who are depressed think like this all the time. They make cognitive errors in thinking negatively about themselves, their immediate world, and their future, three areas that together are called the **depressive cognitive triad** (see ■ Figure 7.4).

In addition, Beck theorized, after a series of negative events in childhood, individuals may develop a deep-seated *negative schema*, an enduring negative cognitive belief system about some aspect of life (Alloy et al., 2012; Beck, Epstein, & Harrison, 1983; Gotlib & Krasnoperova, 1998; Young, Rygh, Weinberger, & Beck, 2014). In a self-blame schema, individuals feel personally responsible for every

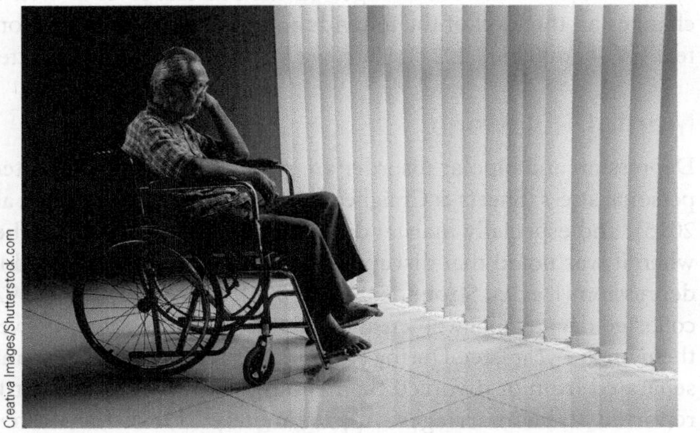

According to the learned helplessness theory of depression, people become depressed when they believe they have no control over the stress in their lives.

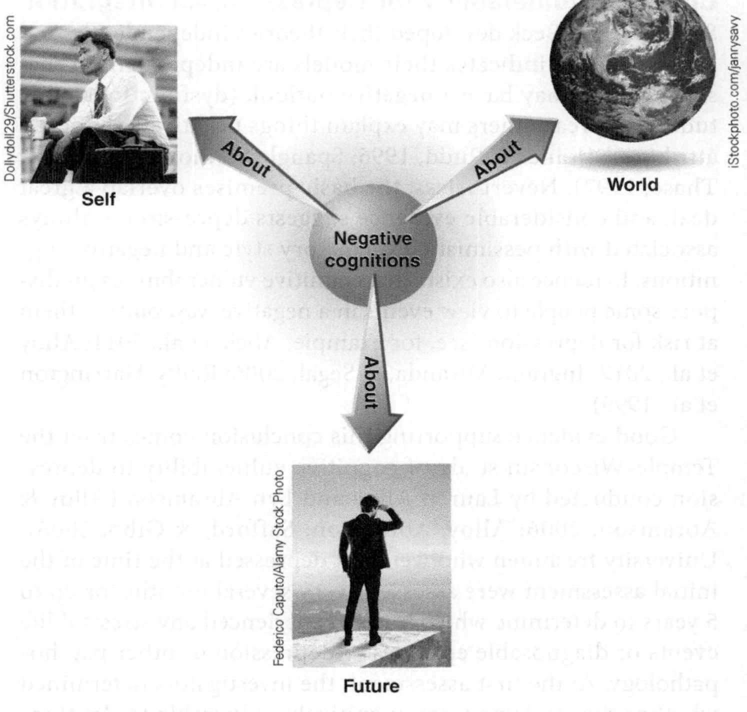

Figure 7.4

Beck's cognitive triad for depression.

bad thing that happens. With a negative self-evaluation schema, they believe they can never do anything correctly. In Beck's view, these cognitive errors and schemas are automatic—that is, not necessarily conscious. Indeed, an individual might not even be aware of thinking negatively and illogically. Thus, minor negative events can lead to a major depressive episode.

A variety of evidence supports a cognitive theory of emotional disorders in general and depression in particular (Gotlib, Joormann, & Foland-Ross, 2014; Hammen & Keenan-Miller, 2013; Ingram, Miranda, & Segal, 2006; Mazure, Bruce, Maciejewski, & Jacobs, 2000). The thinking of depressed individuals is consistently more negative than that of nondepressed individuals (Gotlib & Abramson, 1999; Gotlib et al., 2014) in each dimension of the cognitive triad—the self, the world, and the future (see, for example, Garber & Carter, 2006). Depressive cognitions seem to emerge from distorted and probably automatic methods of processing information. People prone to depression are more likely to recall negative events when they are depressed than when they are not depressed or than are nondepressed individuals (Gotlib et al., 2014).

The implications of this theory are important. By recognizing cognitive errors and the underlying schemas, we can correct them and alleviate depression and related emotional disorders. In developing ways to do this, Beck became the father of cognitive therapy, one of the most important developments in psychotherapy in the past 50 years (see pp. 000–000). Individuals with bipolar disorder also exhibit negative cognitive styles, but with a twist. Cognitive styles in these individuals are characterized by ambitious striving for goals, perfectionism, and self-criticism in addition to the more usual depressive cognitive styles (Alloy & Abramson, 2010; Johnson et al., 2008).

Cognitive Vulnerability for Depression: An Integration

Seligman and Beck developed their theories independently, and good evidence indicates their models are independent in that some people may have a negative outlook (dysfunctional attitudes), whereas others may explain things negatively (hopeless attributes) (Joiner & Rudd, 1996; Spangler, Simons, Monroe, & Thase, 1997). Nevertheless, the basic premises overlap a great deal, and considerable evidence suggests depression is always associated with pessimistic explanatory style and negative cognitions. Evidence also exists that cognitive vulnerabilities predispose some people to view events in a negative way, putting them at risk for depression (see, for example, Abela et al., 2011; Alloy et al., 2012; Ingram, Miranda, & Segal, 2006; Reilly-Harrington et al., 1999).

Good evidence supporting this conclusion comes from the Temple-Wisconsin study of cognitive vulnerability to depression conducted by Lauren Alloy and Lyn Abramson (Alloy & Abramson, 2006; Alloy, Abramson, Safford, & Gibb, 2006). University freshmen who were not depressed at the time of the initial assessment were assessed every several months for up to 5 years to determine whether they experienced any stressful life events or diagnosable episodes of depression or other psychopathology. At the first assessment, the investigators determined whether the students were cognitively vulnerable to developing depression or not on the basis of their scores on questionnaires that measure dysfunctional attitudes and hopelessness attributions. Results indicated students at high risk because of dysfunctional attitudes reported higher rates of depression in the past compared with the low-risk group.

But the really important results come from the prospective portion of the study. Negative cognitive styles do indicate a vulnerability to later depression. Even if participants had never suffered from depression before in their lives, high-risk participants (who scored high on the measures of cognitive vulnerability) were 6 to 12 times more likely than low-risk participants to experience a major depressive episode. In addition, 16% of the high-risk participants versus only 2.7% of the low-risk participants experienced major depressive episodes, and 46% versus 14% experienced minor depressive symptoms (Alloy & Abramson, 2006). In another important study, Abela and Skitch (2007) demonstrated that children at high risk for depression because of a depressed mother showed depressive cognitive styles when under minor stress, unlike children not at risk. Finally, a somewhat frightening recent finding suggests that this cognitive vulnerability to depression can be contagious (Haeffel & Hames, 2014). In this study, college students who happened to live with roommates with high levels of vulnerability began to develop a similar cognitive style over time and also evidenced increases in depressive symptoms. All of these data suggest that cognitive vulnerabilities to developing depression do exist and, when combined with biological vulnerabilities, create a slippery path to depression.

Social and Cultural Dimensions

A number of social and cultural factors contribute to the onset or maintenance of depression. Among these, marital relationships, gender, racial discrimination, and social support are most prominent. None of these issues is unique to depression; all of them influence virtually all aspects of health to some degree in many, if not all, cultures and nations (Stein, Bass, & Hofmann, 2019). In the United States, for example, there is convincing evidence linking various domains of racism (structural racism, cultural racism, and individual-level discrimination) to physical and emotional health, including, but not limited to, depression (Williams, Lawrence, & Davis, 2021). Effective interventions for racism and other dimensions affecting health will require both systemic and structural changes on the societal level as well as changes on the level of the individual person within a given context (Williams et al., 2021). Here, we focus primarily on the latter.

Marital Relations

Depression and bipolar disorder are strongly influenced by interpersonal stress (Sheets & Craighead, 2014; Vrshek-Schallhorn et al., 2015), and especially marital dissatisfaction, as suggested earlier when it was noted that disruptions in relationships often lead to depression (Davila, Stroud, & Starr, 2009). Bruce and Kim (1992) collected data on 695 women and 530 men and then reinterviewed them up to 1 year later. During this period, a number of participants separated from or divorced their spouses, although the majority reported stable marriages. Approximately 21% of the women who reported a marital split during the study experienced severe depression, a rate three times higher than that for women who remained married. Nearly 17% of the men who reported a marital split developed severe depression, a rate *nine times* higher than that for men who remained married. When the researchers considered only those participants with no history of severe depression, 14% of the men who separated or divorced during the period experienced severe depression, as did approximately 5% of the women.

To further examine the nature of sex differences in the etiologic pathways to major depression, Kendler and Gardner (2014) examined 1,057 opposite-sex dizygotic twin pairs and compared men and women in various risk factors for depression, including marital relations. Such a cot-win control design matches sisters and brothers on genetic and familial–environmental background. Overall, personality and failures in interpersonal relationships played a stronger etiologic role in major depression for women than for men. For example, divorce, social support, marital satisfaction, parental warmth, and neuroticism had a greater impact in women, whereas childhood sexual abuse, conduct disorder, drug abuse, prior history of major depression, and stressful life events (related to financial, occupational, and legal issues) had a greater impact on men.

Another finding with considerable support is that depression including bipolar disorder, particularly if it continues, may lead to substantial deterioration in marital relationships (Beach, Jones, & Franklin, 2009; Beach, Sandeen, & O'Leary, 1990; Davila et al., 2009; Uebelacker & Whisman, 2006). It is not hard to figure out why. Being around someone who is continually negative, ill tempered, and pessimistic becomes tiring after a while. Because emotions are contagious, the spouse probably begins to feel bad also. These kinds of interactions precipitate arguments or, worse, make the nondepressed spouse want to leave (Joiner & Timmons, 2009; Whisman, Weinstock, & Tolejko, 2006).

But conflict within a marriage seems to have different effects on men and women. Depression seems to cause men to withdraw or otherwise disrupt the relationship. For women, on the other hand, problems in the relationship most often cause depression. Thus, for both men and women, depression and problems in marital relations are associated, but the causal direction is different (Fincham, Beach, Harold, & Osborne, 1997; Goldfarb & Trudel, 2019; Spangler, Simons, Monroe, and Thase, 1996). Given these factors, Beach, Jones, & Franklin (2009) suggest that therapists treat disturbed marital relationships at the same time as the mood disorder to ensure the highest level of success for the patient and the best chance of preventing future relapses. Individuals with bipolar disorder are less likely to be married at all and more likely to get divorced if they do marry, although those who stay married have a somewhat better prognosis perhaps because their spouses are helpful in regulating their treatments and keeping them on medications (Davila et al., 2009).

Mood Disorders in Women Data on the prevalence of mood disorders indicate dramatic gender imbalances. Although bipolar disorder is evenly divided between men and women, almost 70% of the individuals with major depressive disorder and persistent depressive disorder (dysthymia) are women (Hankin & Abramson, 2001; Kessler, 2006; Kessler & Bromet, 2013). What is particularly striking is that this gender imbalance is constant around the world, even though overall rates of disorder may vary from country to country (Kessler & Bromet, 2013; Seedat et al., 2009; Weissman & Olfson, 1995; see ■ Figure 7.5). Often overlooked is the similar ratio for most anxiety disorders, particularly panic disorder and generalized anxiety disorder. Women represent an even greater proportion of specific phobias, as we note in Chapter 2. What could account for this?

It may be that gender differences in the development of emotional disorders are strongly influenced by perceptions of uncontrollability (Barlow, 1988; Barlow et al., 2014). If you feel a sense of mastery over your life and the difficult events we all encounter, you might experience occasional stress, but you will not feel the helplessness central to anxiety and mood disorders. The source of these differences is cultural, in the sex roles assigned to men and women in our society. Males are strongly encouraged to be independent, masterful, and assertive; females, by contrast, are expected to be more passive, be sensitive to other people, and perhaps rely on others more than males do (needs for affiliation) (Cyranowski, Frank, Young, & Shear, 2000; Hankin & Abramson, 2001). Although these stereotypes are changing, they still describe current sex roles to a large extent in many cultures. But this culturally induced dependence and passivity may well put women at heightened

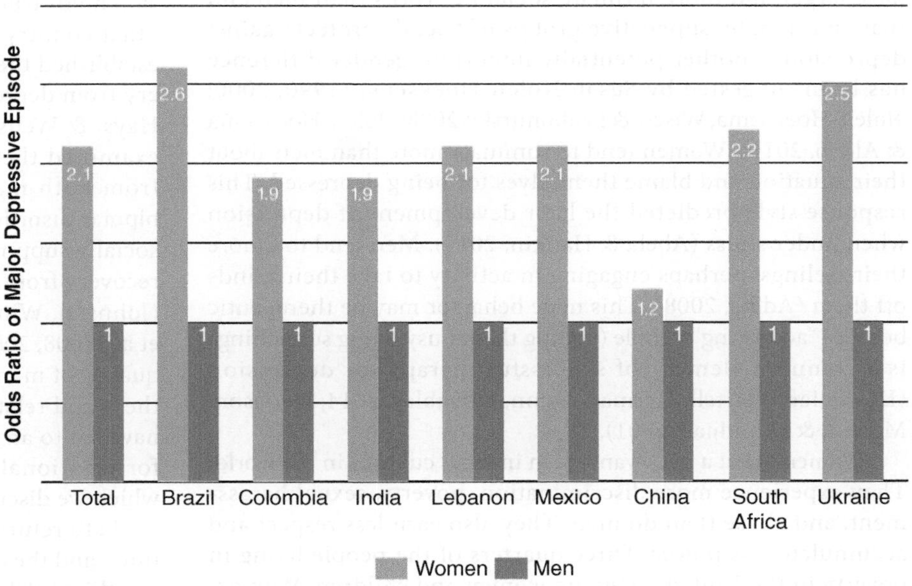

Figure 7.5

The gender disparity in depression diagnoses worldwide, expressed as odds ratios. These odds ratios express the comparative likelihood of women experiencing a major depressive episode in the past year, relative to men. In Brazil, for example, women are 2.6 times more likely than men to report having had a major depressive episode in the last year. Adapted from Bromet et al., 2011, p. 11.

risk for emotional disorders by increasing their feelings of uncontrollability and helplessness. Evidence has accumulated that parenting styles encouraging stereotypic gender roles are implicated in the development of early psychological vulnerability to later depression or anxiety (Chorpita & Barlow, 1998; Barlow et al., 2013; Suárez et al., 2009)—specifically, a smothering, overprotective style that prevents the child from developing initiative. Also interesting is the "sudden surge" in depression among girls mentioned earlier that occurs during puberty. Many thought this might be biologically based. Kessler (2006) notes, however, that low self-esteem emerges quickly in girls in seventh grade if the school system has a grade 7 to grade 9 middle school, but low self-esteem among girls does not emerge until ninth grade when the school has a kindergarten through grade 8 primary school and a 4-year high school (Simmons & Blyth, 1987). These results suggest that the younger girls just entering a new school, whether it is seventh, ninth, or some other grade, find it stressful. Also, girls who mature early physically have more distress and depression than girls who don't (Ge, Conger, & Elder, 1996).

Women tend to place greater value on intimate relationships than men, which can be protective if social networks are strong, but it may also put them at risk. Disruptions in such relationships, combined with an inability to cope with the disruptions, seem to be more damaging to women than to men (Kendler & Gardner, 2014; Nolen-Hoeksema & Hilt, 2009). Cyranowski and associates (2000) note that the tendency for adolescent girls to express aggression by rejecting other girls, combined with a greater sensitivity to rejection, may precipitate more depressive episodes in these adolescent girls compared with boys. Kendler, Myers, and Prescott (2005) also observed that women tend to have larger and more intimate social networks than men and that emotionally supportive groups of friends protect against depression. Another potentially important gender difference has been suggested by Susan Nolen-Hoeksema (1990, 2000; Nolen-Hoeksema, Wisco, & Lyubomirsky, 2008; Nolen-Hoeksema & Aldao, 2011). Women tend to ruminate more than men about their situation and blame themselves for being depressed. This response style predicted the later development of depression when under stress (Abela & Hankin, 2011). Men tend to ignore their feelings, perhaps engaging in activity to take their minds off them (Addis, 2008). This male behavior may be therapeutic because "activating" people (getting them busy doing something) is a common element of successful therapy for depression (Dimidjian, Martell, Herman-Dunn, & Hubley, 2014; Jacobson, Martell, & Dimidjian, 2001).

Women are at a disadvantage in in most cultures in the world: They experience more discrimination, poverty, sexual harassment, and abuse than do men. They also earn less respect and accumulate less power. Three quarters of the people living in poverty in the United States are women and children. Women, particularly single mothers, have a difficult time entering the workplace. It is interesting that married women employed full time outside the home report levels of depression no greater than those of employed married men. Single, divorced, and widowed women experience significantly more depression than men in the same categories (Davila et al., 2009). This does not necessarily mean that anyone should get a job to avoid becoming depressed. Indeed, for a man or woman, feeling mastery, control, and value in a strongly socially supported role of homemaker and parent should be associated with low rates of depression.

Finally, other disorders may reflect gender role stereotypes but in the opposite direction. Disorders associated with aggressiveness, overactivity, and substance abuse occur far more often in men than in women (Barlow, 1988, 2002). Identifying the reasons for gender imbalances across the full range of psychopathological disorders may prove important in discovering causes of disorders.

Social Support In Chapter 2, we examine the powerful effect of social influences on our psychological and biological functioning. We cite several examples of how social influences seem to contribute to early death, such as the evil eye or lack of social support in old age. It is not surprising, then, that social factors influence whether we become depressed (Beach et al., 2009). To take one example, the risk of depression for people who live alone is almost 80% higher than for people who live with others (Pulkki-Råback et al., 2012). In an early landmark study, Brown and Harris (1978) first suggested the important role of social support in the onset of depression. In a study of a large number of women who had experienced a serious life stress, they discovered that only 10% of the women who had a friend in whom they could confide became depressed, compared with 37% of the women who did not have a close supportive relationship. Later prospective studies have also confirmed the importance of social support (or lack of it) in predicting the onset of depressive symptoms at a later time (see, for instance, Joiner, 1997; Kendler, Kuhn et al., 2005; Monroe, Anderson, & Harkness, 2019). The importance of social support in preventing depression holds true in China (Wang, Wang, & Shen, 2006) and every other country in which it has been studied. Other studies have established the importance of social support in speeding recovery from depressive episodes (Keitner et al., 1995; Sherbourne, Hays, & Wells, 1995). In an interesting twist, several studies examined the effects of social support in speeding recovery from both manic and depressive episodes in patients with bipolar disorder, and they came up with a surprising finding. A socially supportive network of friends and family helped speed recovery from depressive episodes but not from manic episodes (Johnson, Winett, Meyer, Greenhouse, & Miller, 1999; Johnson et al., 2008, 2009). This finding highlights the uniquely different quality of manic episodes (McGuffin et al., 2003). In any case, these and related findings on the importance of social support have led to an exciting new psychological therapeutic approach for emotional disorders called interpersonal psychotherapy, which we discuss later in this chapter.

Let's return again to Keisha. In reflecting on her turbulent times and the days when death seemed more rewarding than life, one thing sticks out clearly in her mind:

> My parents are the true heroes of these early years. I will always admire their strength, their love, and their commitment. My father is a high school graduate, and my mother has an eighth-grade education. They dealt with complicated legal, medical, and psychological issues. They

Self-blame and rumination may contribute to the higher rates of mood disorders among women compared with men.

> had little support from friends or professionals, yet they continued to do what they believed best. In my eyes, there is no greater demonstration of courage and love.

Keisha's parents did not have the social support that might have helped them through these difficult years, but they gave it to Keisha. We return to her case later.

An Integrative Theory

How do we put all this together? Basically, depression and anxiety may often share a common, genetically determined biological vulnerability (Barlow, 2002) that can be described as an overactive neurobiological response to stressful life events. One genetic pattern implicated in this vulnerability is in the serotonin transporter gene-linked polymorphic region described earlier. Again, this vulnerability is simply a general tendency to develop depression (or anxiety) rather than a specific vulnerability for depression or anxiety itself. To understand the causes of depression, we must look at psychological vulnerabilities as well as life experiences that interact with genetic vulnerabilities.

People who develop mood disorders also possess a psychological vulnerability experienced as feelings of inadequacy for coping with the difficulties confronting them as well as depressive cognitive styles. As with anxiety, we may develop this sense of control in childhood (Barlow, 2002; Chorpita & Barlow, 1998). It may range on a continuum from total confidence to a complete inability to cope. When vulnerabilities are triggered, the pessimistic "giving up" process seems crucial to the development of depression (Alloy et al., 2000; Alloy & Abramson, 2006).

These psychological processes of inadequate coping and depressive cognitive style in combination with certain genetic patterns mentioned above comprise the temperament of neuroticism or negative affect (Barlow et al., 2014). You will remember from Chapter 5 that neuroticism is associated with biochemical markers of stress and depression (see, for example, Nemeroff, 2004; Thase, 2009), as well as differential levels of arousal in different hemispheres in the brain (hemispheric lateral asymmetry and activation of specific brain circuits (Barlow et al., 2013; Davidson et al., 2009; Liotti, Mayberg, McGinnis, Brannan, & Jerabek, 2002). Some research illustrates the strong associations between the genetic and generalized psychological vulnerabilities (for example, Whisman, Johnson, & Smolen, 2011). There is also good evidence that stressful life events trigger the onset of depression in most cases in these vulnerable individuals, particularly initial episodes (Jenness, Hankin, Abela, Young, & Smollen, 2011). How do these factors interact? Current thinking is that stressful life events in vulnerable individuals activate stress hormones, which, in turn, have wide-ranging effects on neurotransmitter systems, particularly those involving serotonin, norepinephrine, and the corticotropin-releasing factor system. Booij and Van der Does (2007) have illustrated how neurotransmitter function and negative cognitive styles interact. They collaborated with 39 patients who had suffered an episode of major depression but had recovered. These patients participated in two biological test or "challenge" procedures called acute tryptophan depletion (ATD) that had the effect of temporarily lowering levels of serotonin. This is accomplished fairly easily by altering diet for 1 day by restricting intake of tryptophan (a precursor to serotonergic functioning) and increasing a mixture of essential amino acids. Participants in the experiment, of course, were fully informed of these effects and collaborated willingly.

What Booij and Van der Does (2007) found was that this biological challenge was, as usual, effective in temporarily inducing a variety of depressive symptoms in some of these individuals but that these symptoms were more pronounced in those who also had evidence of the cognitive vulnerability marker. That is, cognitive vulnerability assessed before the biological challenge clearly predicted a depressive response. It is interesting that a challenge with ATD causes no significant changes in mood in healthy samples; rather, it is limited to those individuals who are vulnerable to depression.

What we have so far is a possible mechanism for the diathesis–stress model. Finally, it seems clear that factors such as interpersonal relationships (Tsai, Lucas, & Kawachi, 2015) or cognitive style (Gotlib et al., 2014) may protect us from the effects of stress and therefore from developing mood disorders. Alternatively, these factors may at least determine whether we quickly recover from these disorders or not. But remember that bipolar disorder, and particularly activation of manic episodes, seems to have a somewhat different genetic basis, as well as a different response to social support. Scientists are beginning to theorize that individuals with bipolar disorder, in addition to factors outlined so far, are also highly sensitive to the experience of life events connected with striving to reach important goals, perhaps because of an overactive brain circuit called the behavioral approach system (BAS) (Alloy & Abramson, 2010; Gruber, Johnson, Oveis, & Keltner, 2008). In these cases, stressful life events that are more positive but still stressful, such as starting a new job or pulling all-nighters to finish an important term paper, might precipitate a manic episode in vulnerable individuals instead of a depressive episode. Individuals with bipolar disorder are also highly sensitive to disruptions in circadian rhythm. So individuals with bipolar disorder might possess brain circuits that predispose them to both depression and mania. Research of this hypothesis is just commencing.

In summary, biological, psychological, and social factors all influence the development of mood disorders, as depicted in ■Figure 7.6. This model does not fully account for the varied presentation of mood disorders—seasonal, bipolar, and so on—although mania in bipolar disorder seems to be associated with unique genetic contributions and is triggered by relatively unique life events as noted above. But why would someone with an underlying genetic vulnerability who experiences a stressful life event develop a mood disorder rather than an anxiety or somatic symptom disorder? As with the anxiety disorders and other stress disorders, specific psychosocial circumstances, such as early learning experiences, may interact with specific genetic vulnerabilities and personality characteristics to produce the rich variety of emotional disorders.

Treatment of Mood Disorders

Researchers have learned a great deal about the neurobiology of mood disorders during the past several years. Findings on the complex interplay of neurochemicals are beginning to shed light on the nature of mood disorders. As we have noted, the principal effect of medications is to alter levels of these neurotransmitters and other related neurochemicals. Other biological treatments, such as electroconvulsive therapy, dramatically affect brain chemistry. A more interesting development, however, alluded to throughout this book, is that powerful psychological treatments also alter brain chemistry. The rate of outpatient treatment of depression increased substantially in the United States in the 20 years from 1987 to 2007. But almost all of this increase was due

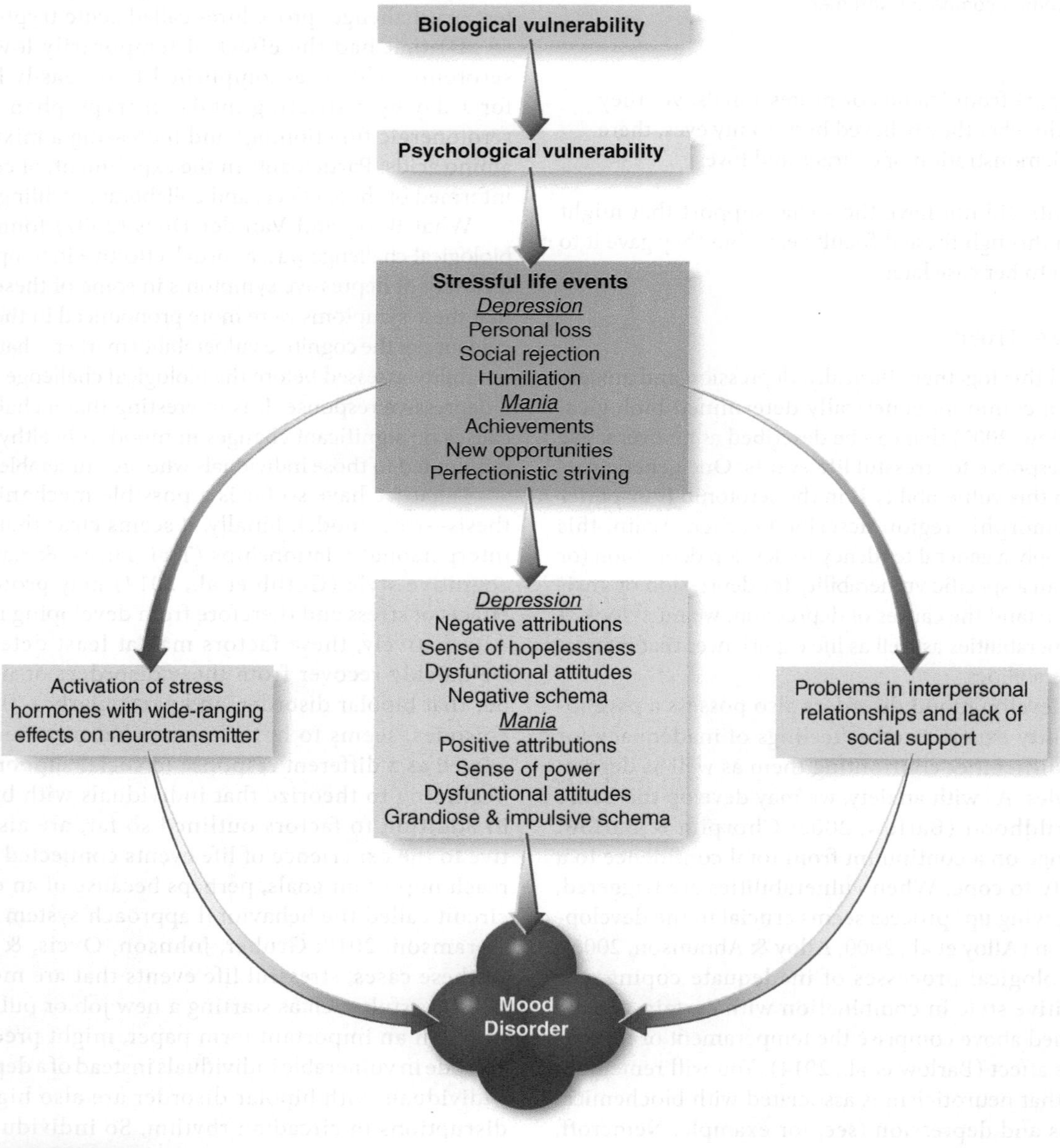

Figure 7.6
An integrative model of mood disorders.

Concept Check 7.3

Answer these questions about the various causes of mood disorders.

1. List five biological sources that can contribute to mood disorders. ____________ ____________ ____________ ____________ ____________
2. What psychological factors can have an impact on mood disorders? ____________ ____________ ____________ ____________
3. Name several social and cultural dimensions that contribute to mood disorders. ____________ ____________ ____________

to treatment with antidepressant drugs (approximately 75% of all patients treated). The percentage receiving psychotherapy during this period actually declined somewhat (Marcus & Olfson, 2010). Despite these advances, most cases of depression go untreated because neither health-care professionals nor patients recognize and correctly identify or diagnose depression. Similarly, many professionals and patients are unaware of the existence of effective and successful treatments (Delano-Wood & Abeles, 2005; Hirschfeld et al., 1997). Therefore, it is important to learn about treatments for depression.

Medications

A number of medications are effective treatments for depression. New information often becomes available on new medications or the latest estimates of effectiveness of older medications.

Antidepressants Four basic types of antidepressant medications are used to treat depressive disorders: selective-serotonin reuptake inhibitors (SSRIs), mixed reuptake inhibitors, tricyclic antidepressants, and monoamine oxidase (MAO) inhibitors. It is important to note at the outset that there are few, if any, differences in effectiveness among the different antidepressants; approximately 50% of patients receive some benefit, with about half of the 50% coming very close to normal functioning (remission). If dropouts are excluded and only those who complete treatment are counted, the percentage of patients receiving at least some benefit increases to between 60% and 70% (American Psychiatric Association, 2010), but one thoroughgoing meta-analysis indicated that antidepressants were relatively ineffective for mild to moderate depression compared with placebo. Only in severely depressed patients is there a clear advantage for taking an antidepressant compared with placebo (Fournier et al., 2010).

The class of drugs currently considered the first choice in drug treatment for depression seems to have a specific effect on the serotonin neurotransmitter system (although such drugs affect other systems to some extent). These *selective-serotonin reuptake inhibitors (SSRIs)* specifically block the presynaptic reuptake of serotonin. This temporarily increases levels of serotonin at the receptor site, but again the precise long-term mechanism of action is unknown, although levels of serotonin are eventually increased (Gitlin, 2009; Thase & Denko, 2008). Perhaps the best-known drug in this class is *fluoxetine* (Prozac). Like many other medications, Prozac was initially hailed as a breakthrough drug; it even made the cover of *Newsweek* (Cowley & Springen, 1990). Then reports began to appear that it might lead to suicidal preoccupation, paranoid reactions, and, occasionally, violence (see, for example, Mandalos & Szarek, 1990; Teicher, Glod, & Cole, 1990). Prozac went from being a wonder drug in the eyes of the press to a potential menace to modern society. Neither conclusion was true. Findings indicated that the risks of suicide with this drug for the general population were no greater than with any other antidepressant (Fava & Rosenbaum, 1991), and the effectiveness is about the same as that of other antidepressants, including the tricyclics.

Several years ago, concerns about suicidal risks (increased thoughts, and so on) surfaced again, particularly among adolescents, and this time it looks like the concerns are justified, at least for adolescents (Baldessarini, Pompili, & Tondo, 2006; Berman, 2009; Olfson, Marcus, & Schaffer, 2006). These findings have led to warnings from the Food and Drug Administration (FDA) and other regulatory agencies around the world about these drugs. On the other hand, Gibbons, Hur, Bhaumik, and Mann (2006) found that actual suicide rates were lower in sections of the United States where prescriptions for SSRIs were higher. In addition, the SSRIs were also associated with a small but statistically significant *decrease* in actual suicides among adolescents compared with depressed adolescents not taking these drugs, based on a large community survey (Olfson, Shaffer, Marcus, & Greenberg, 2003). These findings are *correlational*, meaning we can't conclude that increased prescriptions for SSRIs caused lower suicide rates. Research will continue on this important question. One possible conclusion is that SSRIs cause increased thoughts about suicide in the first few weeks in some adolescents but, once they start working after a month or more, may prevent the depression from leading to suicide (Berman, 2009; Simon, 2006). Prozac and other SSRIs have their own set of side effects, the most prominent of which are physical agitation, sexual dysfunction, low sexual desire (which is prevalent, occurring in 50% to 75% of cases), insomnia, and gastrointestinal upset. But these side effects, on the whole, seem to bother most patients less than the side effects associated with tricyclic antidepressants, with the possible exception of the sexual dysfunction.

Another class of antidepressants (sometimes termed *mixed reuptake inhibitors*) seem to have somewhat different mechanisms of neurobiological action. The best known, venlafaxine (Effexor), is related to tricyclic antidepressants but acts in a slightly different

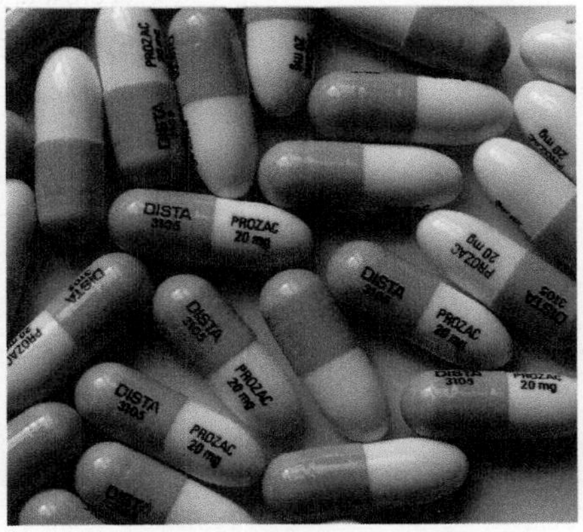

SCOTT CAMAZINE/Getty Images

Of the synthetic drugs for depression, fluoxetine (Prozac) is the most widely used.

manner, blocking reuptake of norepinephrine as well as serotonin. Some side effects associated with the SSRIs are reduced with venlafaxine, as is the risk of damage to the cardiovascular system. Other typical side effects remain, including nausea and sexual dysfunction. Table 7.4 shows the commonly prescribed antidepressants.

Monomine oxidase (MAO) inhibitors work differently. As their name suggests, they block the enzyme MAO that breaks down such neurotransmitters as norepinephrine and serotonin. The result is roughly equivalent to the effect of the tricyclics. Because they are not broken down, the neurotransmitters pool in the synapse, leading to a down-regulation. The MAO inhibitors seem to be as effective as the tricyclics (American Psychiatric Association, 2010), with somewhat fewer side effects. Some evidence suggests they are relatively more effective for depression with atypical features (American Psychiatric Association, 2010; Thase & Kupfer, 1996). But MAO inhibitors are used far less often because of two potentially serious consequences: Eating and drinking foods and beverages containing tyramine—such as cheese, red wine, or beer—can lead to severe hypertensive episodes and, occasionally, death. In addition, many other drugs that people take daily, such as cold medications, are dangerous and even fatal in interaction with an MAO inhibitor. Therefore, MAO inhibitors are usually prescribed only when other antidepressants are not effective.

Tricyclic antidepressants were the most widely used treatments for depression before the introduction of SSRIs but are now used less commonly (Gitlin, 2009; Thase & Denko, 2008). The best-known variants are probably imipramine (Tofranil) and amitriptyline (Elavil). It is not yet clear how these drugs work, but initially, at least, they block the reuptake of certain neurotransmitters, allowing them to pool in the synapse and, as the theory goes, desensitize or down-regulate the transmission of that particular neurotransmitter (so less of the neurochemical is transmitted). Tricyclic antidepressants seem to have their greatest effect by down-regulating norepinephrine, although other neurotransmitter systems, particularly serotonin, are also affected. This process then has a complex effect on both presynaptic and postsynaptic regulation of neurotransmitter activity, eventually restoring appropriate balance. Side effects include blurred vision, dry mouth, constipation, difficulty urinating, drowsiness, weight gain (at least 13 pounds on average), and sometimes sexual dysfunction. Therefore, as many as 40% of these patients may stop taking the drug, thinking the cure is worse than the disease. Nevertheless, with careful management, many side effects disappear over time. Another issue clinicians must consider is that tricyclics are *lethal* if taken in excessive doses; therefore, they must be prescribed with great caution to patients with suicidal tendencies.

Finally, there was a great deal of interest several years ago in the antidepressant properties of the natural herb St. John's wort (hypericum). St. John's wort is popular in Europe, and a number of preliminary studies demonstrated it was better than placebo and worked about as well as low doses of other antidepressants (American Psychiatric Association, 2010). St. John's wort produces few side effects and is relatively easy to produce. It is available at many drugstores and nutritional supplement stores, but there is no guarantee that any given brand of St. John's wort contains the appropriate ingredients. Some preliminary evidence suggests the herb also somehow alters serotonin function. But the National Institutes of Health in the United States completed a major study examining its effectiveness (Hypericum Depression Trial Study Group, 2002), and surprisingly, this large study found no benefits from St. John's wort compared with placebo.

Because the SSRIs and other drugs relieve symptoms of depression to some extent in about 50% of all patients treated

Table 7.4 Most Commonly Prescribed Antidepressants: Classes, Drug Names, Dosages, and Side Effects

Class	Generic Name	Brand Name	Usual Dose (mg/day)	Prominent Side Effects
Selective Serotonin Reuptake Inhibitors (SSRIs)	Citalopram Escitalopram Fluoxetine Fluvoxamine Paroxetine Sertraline	Celexa Lexapro Prozac Luvox Paxil Zoloft	20–60 10–20 20–60 100–300 20–50 50–100	Nausea, diarrhea, insomnia, sexual dysfunction, agitation/restlessness, and daytime sedation
Mixed Reuptake Inhibitors	Bupropion	Wellbutrin	300–450	Nausea, vomiting, insomnia, headaches, seizures
	Venlafaxine	Effexor	7–225	Nausea, diarrhea, nervousness, increased sweating, dry mouth, muscle jerks, and sexual dysfunction
	Duloxetine	Celexa	60–80	Nausea, diarrhea, vomiting, nervousness, increased sweating, dry mouth, headaches, insomnia, daytime drowsiness, sexual dysfunction, tremor, and elevated liver enzymes

Adapted from M. E. Thase & T. Denko, 2008, Pharmacotherapy of mood disorders, *Annual Review of Clinical Psychology, 4*, 53–91.

but eliminate depression or come close to it in only 25% to 30% of all patients treated (termed *remission*) (Trivedi et al., 2006), the question remains: What do clinicians do when depression does not respond adequately to drug treatment, often called *treatment-resistant depression*? A large study called the Sequenced Treatment Alternatives to Relieve Depression (STAR*D) examined whether it is useful to offer those individuals who did not achieve remission the alternatives of either adding a second drug or switching to a second drug. Among those who were willing, approximately 20% (for switching) to approximately 30% (for adding a second drug) achieved remission. When repeating this with a third drug among those who had failed to achieve remission with the first two drugs, the results weren't as good (between 10% and 20% achieved remission) (Insel, 2006; Menza, 2006; Rush, 2007), and very few clinicians would go to a third drug in the same class after failing on the first two (Gitlin, 2009). The conclusion is that it's worth being persistent, as long as individuals with depression are still willing to try a second drug, because some people who don't improve with the first drug could improve with a different drug. Later, we report on combining psychological treatments with drugs. In summary, all antidepressant medications work about the same in large clinical trials, but sometimes a patient will not do well on one drug but respond better to another.

Current studies indicate that drug treatments effective with adults are not necessarily effective with children (American Psychiatric Association, 2010; Geller et al., 1992; Kaslow, Davis, & Smith, 2009; Ryan, 1992). Sudden deaths of children under 14 who were taking tricyclic antidepressants have been reported, particularly during exercise, as in routine school athletic competition (Tingelstad, 1991). Cardiac side effects have been implicated in these deaths. But evidence indicates that, unlike tricyclic antidepressants, at least one of the SSRIs, fluoxetine (Prozac), is safe and has some evidence for efficacy with adolescents both initially (Kaslow et al., 2009; Treatment for Adolescents with Depression Study [TADS] Team, 2004) and at follow-up (TADS Team, 2009), particularly if combined with cognitive behavioral therapy (CBT) (March & Vitiello, 2009). Traditional antidepressant drug treatments are usually effective with the elderly, but administering them takes considerable skill because older people may suffer from a variety of side effects not experienced by younger adults, including memory impairment and physical agitation (Blazer & Hybels, 2009; Delano-Wood & Abeles, 2005; Fiske et al., 2009). Use of a depression care manager to deliver care to depressed elderly patients right in the office of their primary medical care doctor including encouraging compliance with drug taking, monitoring side effects unique to older adults, and delivering a bit of psychotherapy was more effective than usual care (Alexopoulos et al., 2005; Unutzer et al., 2002).

Clinicians and researchers have concluded that recovery from depression, although important, may not be the most important therapeutic outcome (Frank et al., 1990; Thase, 2009). Most people eventually recover from a major depressive episode, some rather quickly. A more important goal is often to delay the next depressive episode or even prevent it entirely (National Institute of Mental Health, 2003; Thase, 2009; Thase & Kupfer, 1996). This is particularly important for patients who retain some symptoms of depression or have a past history of chronic depression or multiple depressive episodes (Forand & DeRubeis, 2013; Hammen & Keenan-Miller, 2013). Because all these factors put people at risk for relapse, it is recommended that drug treatment go well beyond the termination of a depressive episode, continuing perhaps 6 to 12 months after the episode is over, or even longer (American Psychiatric Association, 2010; Insel, 2006). The drug is then gradually withdrawn over weeks or months. (We return later to strategies for maintaining therapeutic benefits.) Long-term administration of antidepressants has not been studied extensively, and there is even some evidence that long-term treatment lasting several years may worsen the course of depression (Fava, 2003).

Antidepressant medications have relieved severe depression and undoubtedly prevented suicide in tens of thousands of patients around the world, particularly in cases of more severe depression. Although these medications are readily available, many people refuse or are not eligible to take them. Some are wary of long-term side effects. Women of childbearing age must protect themselves against the possibility of conceiving while taking antidepressants because of possible damage to the fetus. In one study of all births over a 10-year period in the country of Denmark, infants of mothers who were taking SSRIs during pregnancy, but not other antidepressants, had an almost twofold increased risk of having a low Apgar score (a measure of infant health immediately after birth that predicts IQ scores, performance in school, as well as neurological disability including cerebral palsy, epilepsy, and cognitive impairment lasting for many years after birth) (Jensen et al., 2013). On the other hand, a large population-based prospective study in the United States showed that depressed mothers who were taking SSRIs during pregnancy had a *lower* risk for birth complications (such as preterm birth or cesarean delivery) than those who did not take SSRIs, suggesting that SSRIs may also have a protective effect on the process of giving birth (Malm et al., 2015). The current recommendation is to individualize clinical decision making.

As we noted in Chapter 2, some psychedelics (in particular *ketamine* and a metabolite, *S-ketamine*) are promising as a stand-alone treatment or in conjunction with psychotherapy (for example, Zanos et al., 2018). Although research on ketamine and other psychedelics has been limited and restricted since the passage of the Controlled Substances Act in 1970, this is now changing since earlier well-controlled clinical trials by investigators from the National Institute of Mental Health showed some remarkably positive results (Zarate et al., 2006).

Lithium Another type of antidepressant drug, *lithium carbonate*, is a common salt widely available in the natural environment (Alda, 2015). It is found in our drinking water in amounts too small to have any effect. The side effects of therapeutic doses of lithium are potentially more serious, however, than the side effects of other antidepressants. Dosage has to be carefully regulated to prevent toxicity (poisoning) and lowered thyroid functioning, which might intensify the lack of energy associated with depression. Substantial weight gain is also common. Lithium, however, has one major advantage that distinguishes it from other antidepressants: It is also often effective in preventing and treating manic episodes. Therefore, it is most often referred to as a **mood-stabilizing drug**. Antidepressants can induce manic episodes, even in individuals without preexisting bipolar disorder (Goodwin & Ghaemi, 1998; Goodwin & Jamison, 2007), and lithium remains the gold standard for treatment of bipolar disorder, although the mechanism of action remains only partially understood (Alda, 2015; Nivoli, Murru, & Vieta, 2010). Other pharmacological treatments for acute bipolar depression include antidepressants, anticonvulsants, and antipsychotics (Vazques, Holtzman, Tondo, & Baldessarini, 2015).

Results indicate that 50% of bipolar patients respond well to lithium initially, meaning at least a 50% reduction in manic symptoms (Goodwin & Jamison, 2007). Thus, although effective, lithium provides many people with inadequate therapeutic benefit. Patients who don't respond to lithium can take other drugs with antimanic properties, including anticonvulsants such as carbamazepine and valproate (Divalproex), as well as calcium channel blockers such as verapamil (Keck & McElroy, 2002; Sachs & Rush, 2003; Thase & Denko, 2008). Valproate has now overtaken lithium as the most commonly prescribed mood stabilizer for bipolar disorder (Thase & Denko, 2008) and is equally effective, even for patients with rapid-cycling symptoms (Calabrese et al., 2005). But newer studies show that these drugs have one distinct disadvantage: They are less effective than lithium in preventing suicide (Thase & Denko, 2008; Tondo, Jamison, & Baldessarini, 1997). Goodwin and colleagues (2003) reviewed records of more than 20,000 patients taking either lithium or valproate and found the rate of fatal suicide attempts was 2.7 times higher in people taking valproate than in people taking lithium. Thus, lithium remains the preferred drug for bipolar disorder although other mood stabilizing drugs are often combined with therapeutic doses of lithium (Dunlop, Rakofsky, & Rapaport, 2013; Goodwin & Jamison, 2007; Nierenberg et al., 2013). This finding on the importance of mood-stabilizing drugs was confirmed in a large trial demonstrating no advantage to adding a traditional antidepressant drug such as an SSRI to a mood stabilizer such as lithium (Sachs et al., 2007).

For those patients who do respond to lithium, studies following patients for up to 5 years report that approximately 70% relapse, even if they continue to take the lithium (Frank et al., 1999; Hammen & Keenan-Miller, 2013). Nevertheless, for almost anyone with recurrent manic episodes, maintenance on lithium or a related drug is recommended to prevent relapse (Yatham et al., 2006). Another problem with drug treatment of bipolar disorder is that people usually like the euphoric or high feeling that mania produces, and they often stop taking lithium to maintain or regain the state; that is, they do not comply with the medication regimen. Because the evidence now clearly indicates that individuals who stop their medication are at considerable risk for relapse, other treatment methods, usually psychological in nature, are used to increase compliance.

Courtesy of Nubar Alexanian

Kay Redfield Jamison, an internationally respected authority on bipolar disorder, has suffered from the disease since adolescence.

Electroconvulsive Therapy and Transcranial Magnetic Stimulation

When someone does not respond to medication (or in an extremely severe case), clinicians may consider a more dramatic treatment, **electroconvulsive therapy (ECT)**, the most controversial treatment for psychological disorders after psychosurgery. In Chapter 1, we describe how ECT was used in the early 20th century. Despite many unfortunate abuses along the way, ECT is considerably changed today. It is now a safe and reasonably effective treatment for those cases of severe depression that do not improve with other treatments (American Psychiatric Association, 2010; Gitlin, 2009; Kellner et al., 2012; National Institute of Mental Health, 2003).

In current administrations, patients are anesthetized to reduce discomfort and given muscle-relaxing drugs to prevent bone breakage from convulsions during seizures. Electric shock is administered directly through the brain for less than a second, producing a seizure and a series of brief convulsions that usually lasts for several minutes. In current practice, treatments are administered once every other day for a total of 6 to 10 treatments (fewer if the patient's mood returns to normal). Side effects are generally limited to short-term memory loss and confusion that disappear after a week or 2, although some patients may have long-term memory problems. For severely depressed inpatients with psychotic features, controlled studies indicate that approximately 50% of those *not responding* to medication will benefit. Continued treatment with medication or psychotherapy is then necessary because the relapse rate approaches 60% or higher (American Psychiatric Association, 2010a; Gitlin, 2009). For example, Sackeim and colleagues (2001) treated 84 patients with ECT and then randomly assigned them to follow-up placebo or one of several antidepressant drug treatments. All patients assigned to placebo relapsed within 6 months, compared with 40% to 60% on medication. Thus, follow-up treatment with antidepressant drugs or psychological treatments is necessary, but relapse is still high. Nevertheless, it may not be in the best interest of psychotically depressed and acutely suicidal inpatients to wait 3 to 6 weeks to determine whether a drug or psychological treatment is working; in these cases, immediate ECT may be appropriate.

We do not really know why ECT works. Repeated seizures induce massive functional and perhaps structural changes in the brain, which seems to be therapeutic. There is some evidence that ECT increases levels of serotonin, blocks stress hormones, and promotes neurogenesis in the hippocampus. Because of the controversial nature of this treatment, its use declined considerably during the 1970s and 1980s (American Psychiatric Association, 2001; De Raedt, Vanderhasselt, & Baeken, 2015).

Another method for altering electrical activity in the brain by setting up a strong magnetic field has been introduced. This procedure is called *transcranial magnetic stimulation (TMS)*, and it works by placing a magnetic coil over the individual's head to generate a precisely localized electromagnetic pulse. Anesthesia is not required, and side effects are usually limited to headaches. Initial reports, as with most new procedures, showed promise in treating depression (George, Taylor, & Short, 2013), and some observations and reviews have confirmed that TMS can be effective (De Raedt et al., 2015; Mantovani et al., 2012; Schutter, 2009). But results from several important clinical trials with severe or treatment-resistant psychotic depression reported ECT to be clearly more effective than TMS (Eranti et al., 2007). It may be that TMS is more comparable to antidepressant medication than to ECT, and one study reported a slight advantage for combining TMS and medication compared to using either treatment alone (Brunoni et al., 2013; Gitlin, 2009).

Several other nondrug approaches for treatment-resistant depression are in development. Vagus nerve stimulation involves implanting a pacemaker-like device that generates pulses to the vagus nerve in the neck, which, in turn, is thought to influence neurotransmitter production in the brain stem and limbic system (Gitlin, 2009; Marangell et al., 2002). Sufficient evidence has accumulated so that the FDA has approved this procedure, but results are generally weak and it has been little-used. Deep brain stimulation has been used with a few severely depressed patients. In this procedure, electrodes are surgically implanted in the limbic system (the emotional brain). These electrodes are also connected to a pacemaker-like device (Mayberg et al., 2005). Initial results show some promise in treatment-resistant patients, but time will tell if this is a useful treatment (Kennedy et al., 2011; Lozano et al., 2012).

Psychological Treatments for Depression

Of the effective psychological treatments now available for depressive disorders, two major approaches have the most evidence supporting their efficacy. The first is a cognitive-behavioral approach. Aaron T. Beck, the founder of cognitive therapy, is most closely associated with this approach. The second approach, interpersonal psychotherapy, was developed by Myrna Weissman and Gerald Klerman.

Cognitive-Behavioral Therapy Beck's **cognitive therapy** grew directly out of his observations of the role of deep-seated negative thinking in generating depression (Beck, 1967, 1976; Young et al., 2014). Clients are taught to examine carefully their thought processes while they are depressed and to recognize "depressive" errors in thinking. This task is not always easy because many thoughts are automatic and beyond clients' awareness. Clients are taught that errors in thinking can directly cause depression. Treatment involves correcting cognitive errors and substituting less depressing and (perhaps) more realistic thoughts and appraisals. Later in therapy, underlying negative cognitive schemas (characteristic ways of viewing the world) that trigger specific cognitive errors are targeted, not only in the clinic but also as part of the client's day-to-day life. The therapist purposefully takes a Socratic approach (teaching by asking questions—see the dialogue below),

Beck and Irene... A Dialogue

Because an intake interview had already been completed by another therapist, Beck did not spend time reviewing Irene's symptoms in detail or taking a history. Irene began by describing her "sad states." Beck almost immediately started to elicit her automatic thoughts during these periods.

Therapist: What kind of thoughts go through your mind when you've had these sad feelings this past week?

Patient: Well, ... I guess I'm thinking, "What's the point of all this?" My life is over. It's just not the same. ... I have thoughts like, "What am I going to do?" ... Sometimes I feel mad at him—you know, my husband. How could he leave me? Isn't that terrible of me? What's wrong with me? How can I be mad at him? He didn't want to die a horrible death. ... I should have done more. I should have made him go to the doctor when he first started getting headaches. ... Oh, what's the use? . . .

T: It sounds like you are feeling quite bad right now. Is that right?

P: Yes.

T: Keep telling me what's going through your mind right now.

P: I can't change anything. ... It's over. ... I don't know. ... It all seems so bleak and hopeless. ... What do I have to look forward to? ... Sickness and then death. ...

T: So one of the thoughts is that you can't change things and that it's not going to get any better?

P: Yes.

T: And sometimes you believe that completely?

P: Yeah, I believe it, sometimes.

T: Right now, do you believe it?

P: I believe it—yes.

T: Right now, you believe that you can't change things and it's not going to get better?

P: Well, there is a glimmer of hope but it's mostly. ...

T: Is there anything in your life that you kind of look forward to in terms of your own life from here on?

P: Well, what I look forward to—I enjoy seeing my kids, but they are so busy right now. My son is a lawyer, and my daughter is in medical school. ... So they are very busy. ... They don't have time to spend with me.

making it clear that therapist and client are working as a team to uncover faulty thinking patterns and the underlying schemas from which they are generated. Therapists must be skillful and highly trained. Following is an example of an actual interaction between Beck and a depressed client named Irene.

By inquiring about Irene's automatic thoughts, the therapist began to understand her perspective—that she would go on forever, mostly alone. This illustrates the hopelessness about the future that is characteristic of most depressed patients. A second advantage to this line of inquiry is that the therapist introduced Irene to the idea of looking at her own thoughts, which is central to cognitive therapy (Young et al., 2014).

Related cognitive-behavioral approaches to depression include the Cognitive-Behavioral Analysis System of Psychotherapy (CBASP) (McCullough, 2000, 2014), which integrates cognitive, behavioral, and interpersonal strategies and focuses on problem-solving skills, particularly in the context of important relationships. This treatment was designed for individuals with persistent (chronic) depression and has been tested in a large clinical trial (see below). Finally, mindfulness-based therapy has been found to be effective for treating depression (Hofmann, Sawyer, Witt, & Oh, 2010; Khoury et al., 2013) and preventing future depressive relapse and recurrence (Kuyken et al., 2015). These techniques have also been combined with cognitive therapy in mindfulness-based cognitive therapy (MBCT) (Barnhofer et al., 2015; Michalak, Schultze, Heidenreich, & Schramm, 2015; Williams, Teasdale, Segal, & Kabat-Zinn, 2007; Segal, Williams, & Teasdale, 2002). MBCT has been evaluated and found effective for the most part in the context of preventing relapse or recurrence in patients who are in remission from their depressive episode. This approach seems particularly effective for individuals with more severe disorders, as indicated by a history of three or more prior depressive episodes (Segal et al., 2002; Segal et al., 2010).

The late Neil Jacobson and colleagues have shown that increased activities alone can improve self-concept and lift depression (Dimidjian et al., 2014; Jacobson et al., 1996). This more behavioral treatment has been reformulated because initial evaluation suggests it is as effective as or more effective than cognitive approaches (Hollon, 2011; Jacobson, Martell, & Dimidjian, 2001). The new focus of this approach is on preventing avoidance of social and environmental cues that produce negative affect or depression and result in avoidance and inactivity. Rather, the individual is helped to face the cues or triggers and work through them and the depression they produce, with the therapist, by developing better coping skills. Similarly, programmed exercise over the course of weeks or months is surprisingly effective in treating depression (Mead et al., 2009; Stathopoulou, Powers, Berry, Smits, & Otto, 2006). Babyak and colleagues (2000) demonstrated that programmed aerobic exercise three times a week was as effective as treatment with antidepressive medication (Zoloft) or the combination of exercise and Zoloft after 4 months. More important, exercise was *better* at preventing relapse in the 6 months following treatment compared with the drug or combination treatment, particularly if the patients continued exercising. It was noted above that there is some new evidence that exercise increases neurogenesis in the hippocampus, which is known to be associated with resilience to depression. This general approach of focusing on fitness activities is also consistent with findings about the most powerful methods to change dysregulated emotions (Barlow, Allen, & Choate, 2004; Campbell-Sills, Ellard, & Barlow, 2015), and we are likely to see more research on this approach in the near future.

Interpersonal Psychotherapy We have seen that major disruptions in our interpersonal relationships are an important category of stresses that can trigger mood disorders (Joiner & Timmons, 2009; Kendler et al., 2003). In addition, people with few, if any, important social relationships seem at risk for developing and sustaining mood disorders (Beach et al., 2009). **Interpersonal psychotherapy (IPT)** (Bleiberg & Markowitz, 2014; Klerman, Weissman, Rounsaville, & Chevron, 1984; Weissman, 1995) focuses on resolving problems in existing relationships and learning to form important new interpersonal relationships.

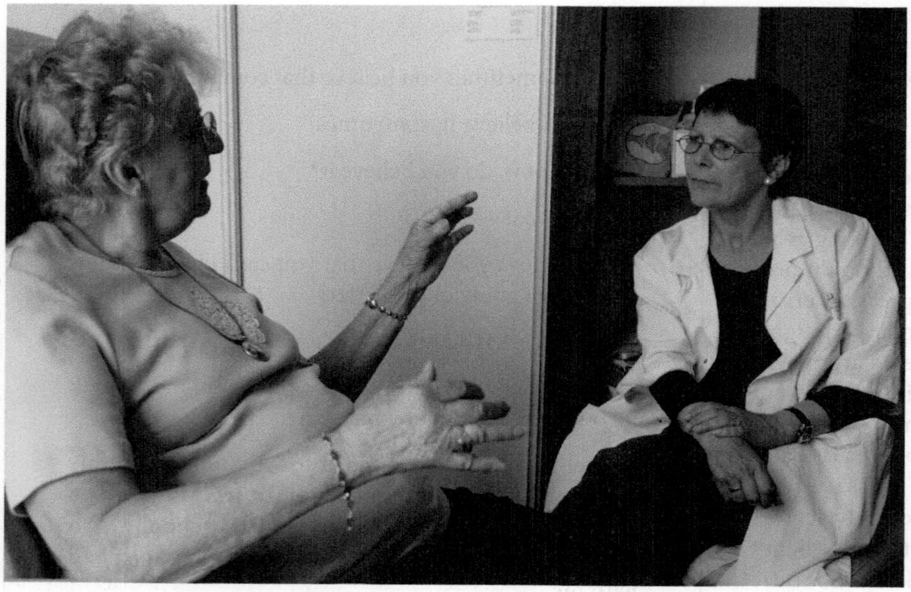

BSIP/Contributor/Universal Images Group/Getty Images

In interpersonal psychotherapy, the therapist and patient identify strategies for mitigating social conflict and forming new relationships.

Like cognitive-behavioral approaches, IPT is highly structured and seldom takes longer than 15 to 20 sessions, usually scheduled once a week (Cuijpers et al., 2011). After identifying life stressors that seem to precipitate the depression, the therapist and patient work collaboratively on the patient's current interpersonal problems. Typically, these include one or more of four interpersonal issues: *dealing with interpersonal role disputes*, such as marital conflict; *adjusting to the loss of a relationship*, such as grief over the death of a loved one; *acquiring new relationships*, such as getting married or establishing professional relationships; and *identifying and correcting deficits in social skills* that prevent the person from initiating or maintaining important relationships.

To take a common example, the therapist's first job is to identify and define an interpersonal dispute (Bleiberg & Markowitz, 2014; Weissman, 1995). Perhaps a patient has a spouse who expects to be supported but has to take an outside job to help pay bills. The patient might expect their spouse to share equally in generating income. If this dispute seems to be associated with the onset of depressive symptoms and to result in a continuing series of arguments and disagreements without resolution, it would become the focus for IPT.

After helping identify the dispute, the next step is to bring it to a resolution. First, the therapist helps the patient determine the stage of the dispute.

1. *Negotiation stage.* Both partners are aware it is a dispute, and they are trying to renegotiate it.
2. *Impasse stage.* The dispute smolders beneath the surface and results in low-level resentment, but no attempts are made to resolve it.
3. *Resolution stage.* The partners are taking some action, such as divorce, separation, or recommitting to the marriage.

The therapist works with the patient to define the dispute clearly for both parties and develop specific strategies for resolving it. Along similar lines, Daniel O'Leary, Steve Beach, and their colleagues, as well as Neil Jacobson and his colleagues, have demonstrated that marital therapy is applicable to the large numbers of depressed patients they see, particularly women, who are in the midst of dysfunctional marriages (as is the case for as many as 50% of all depressed patients) (Beach & O'Leary, 1992; Beach et al., 2009; Jacobson, Fruzzetti, Dobson, Whisman, & Hops, 1993).

Studies comparing the results of cognitive therapy and IPT with those of antidepressant drugs and other control conditions have found that psychological approaches and medication are equally effective immediately following treatment, and all treatments are more effective than placebo conditions, brief psychodynamic treatments, or other appropriate control conditions for both major depressive disorder and persistent depressive disorder (Hollon, 2011; Hollon & Dimidjian, 2009; Miller, Norman, & Keitner, 1989; Paykel & Scott, 2009; Schulberg et al., 1996). Depending on how "success" is defined, approximately 50% or more of people benefit from treatment to a significant extent, compared with approximately 30% in placebo or control conditions (Craighead, Hart, Craighead, & Ilardi, 2002; Hollon, 2011; Hollon & Dimidjian, 2009).

Similar results have been reported in depressed children and adolescents (Kaslow et al., 2009). In one notable clinical trial, Brent and colleagues (2008) demonstrated that, in more than 300 severely depressed adolescents who had failed to respond to an SSRI antidepressant, CBT was significantly more effective than switching to another antidepressant. Kennard and colleagues (2009) showed that this was particularly true if the adolescents received at least nine sessions of the CBT.

Furthermore, studies have not found differences in treatment effectiveness based on severity of depression (Fournier et al., 2010; Hollon, Stewart, & Strunk, 2006; McLean & Taylor, 1992; Stangier et al., 2013). For example, DeRubeis, Gelfand, Tang, and Simons (1999) evaluated the effects of cognitive therapy versus medication in severely depressed patients only, across four studies, and found no advantage for one treatment or the other. Similarly, another quantitative review showed that baseline depression severity did not predict the efficacy of CBT and antidepressant medications (Weitz et al., 2015). However, adding CBT to antidepressant medications only enhanced treatment efficacy in patients with severe and nonchronic depression (Hollon et al., 2014). These findings can help clinicians personalize the treatment to the individual patient (Maj et al., 2020)

O'Hara, Stuart, Gorman, and Wenzel (2000) reported positive effects for IPT in a group of women with postpartum depression, demonstrating that this approach is a worthwhile strategy in patients with postpartum depression who are reluctant to go on medication because, for example, they are breastfeeding. In an important related study, Spinelli and Endicott (2003) compared IPT with an alternative psychological approach in 50 depressed pregnant women unable to take drugs because of potential harm to the fetus. Fully 60% of these women recovered, leading the authors to recommend that IPT should be the first choice for pregnant depressed women, although it is likely that CBT would produce similar results. IPT has also been successfully administered to depressed adolescents by school-based clinicians trained to deliver IPT right in the school setting (Mufson et al., 2004). This practical approach shows good promise of reaching a larger number of depressed adolescents. In general, these studies paint a complex picture, suggesting that depression identifies a heterogeneous group of patients. In the near future, we might be able to maximize treatment outcome by assigning a patient to the most suitable treatment, depending on the person's individual characteristics, in line with the general move toward precision medicine.

Prevention In view of the seriousness of mood disorders in children and adolescents, work has begun on preventing these disorders in these age groups (Horowitz & Garber, 2006; Muñoz, Cuijpers, Smit, Barrera, & Leykin, 2010; Muñoz, Beardslee, & Leykin, 2012). The Institute of Medicine (IOM) delineated three types of programs: *universal* programs, which are applied to everyone; *selected* interventions, which target individuals at risk for depression because of factors such as divorce, a family history of alcohol use disorder, and so on; and *indicated* interventions, in which the individual is already showing mild symptoms of depression (Muñoz et al., 2009). As an example of selected interventions, Gillham and colleagues (2012) taught cognitive and social problem-solving techniques to more than 400 middle school children ages 10 to 15 who were at risk for depression because of negative thinking styles. Compared with children in a matched no-treatment control group, the prevention group reported fewer depressive symptoms during follow up. Seligman, Schulman, DeRubeis, and Hollon (1999) conducted a similar course for university students who were also at risk for depression based on a pessimistic cognitive style. After 3 years, students taking the eight-session program experienced less anxiety and depression than a control group receiving the assessments only. This suggests that it might be possible to "psychologically immunize" at-risk children and adolescents against depression by teaching appropriate cognitive and social skills before they enter puberty.

Results from a major clinical trial that combined "selected" and "indicated" approaches have been reported targeting adolescents at risk for depression (Garber et al., 2009). In the trial, 316 adolescent offspring of parents with current or prior depressive disorders were randomized to a CBT prevention program or to usual care. To be included, adolescents had to have either a past history of depression, current depressive symptoms that would not be severe enough to meet criteria for a disorder, or both. The adolescents in the CBT prevention group received eight weekly group sessions as well as six monthly continuation sessions. The usual care group included a fairly active use of mental health or other health-care services that, however, did not include any of the procedures used in the CBT group. The results, shown in ■ Figure 7.7, indicate that the CBT prevention program was significantly more effective than usual care in preventing future episodes of depression, but only for those adolescents whose parents were not currently in a depressive episode themselves. If the parents were in a depressive episode while the adolescents were receiving care, the adolescents became somewhat less depressed based on their own report but did not have significantly fewer depressive episodes during the follow-up period. These results are important because they show not only that preventive programs are potentially powerful but also that living with a depressed parent lessens the power of preventive programs to some degree (Hammen, 2009). The results also suggest that to prevent future depressive episodes, it is necessary to treat depression in the whole family in a coordinated manner.

Another study also demonstrated that meeting in an integrated fashion with families that included parents who had a history of depression and included their 9- to 15-year-old children (who were at risk because of their parents' depression) was successful in preventing depression in these families during a follow-up period (Compas et al., 2009). Additional studies have indicated that preventing depression is possible in older adults in primary care settings (van't Veer-Tazelaar et al., 2009) and also in poststroke patients, a particularly high-risk group (Reynolds, 2009; Robinson et al., 2008). It appears that CBT, delivered during the acute phase, has an enduring effect that protects some patients against relapse and others from recurrence following treatment termination. Furthermore, continuation CBT seems to reduce the risk for relapse, and maintenance CBT appears to reduce the risk for recurrence (Bockting, Hollon, Jarrett, Kuyken, & Dobson, 2015). However, more prevention studies are needed. In view of the enormous burden depression places on society, a consensus has developed that preventing depression is a global priority in public health (Cuijpers, Beekman, & Reynolds, 2012).

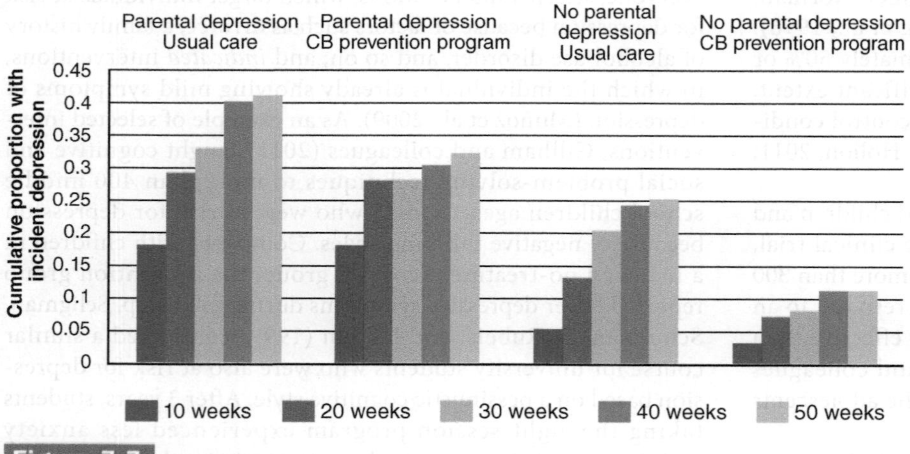

Figure 7.7

Risk of incident depression by intervention condition and baseline parental depression. Adapted from J. Garber, G. N. Clarke, V. R. Weersing, W. R. Beardslee, D. A. Brent, T. R. G. Gladstone, & S. Iyengar, 2009, Prevention of depression in at-risk adolescents: A randomized controlled trial, *Journal of the American Medical Association, 301*, 2215–2224.

Combined Treatments for Depression

One important question is whether combining psychosocial treatments with medication is more effective than either treatment alone in treating depression or preventing relapse. In a large study reported by Keller and colleagues (2000) on the treatment of persistent (chronic) major depression, 681 patients at 12 clinics around the country were assigned to receive antidepressant medication (nefazodone), a CBT constructed specifically for chronically depressed patients (CBASP, discussed earlier) (McCullough, 2014), or the combination of two treatments. Researchers found that 48% of patients receiving each of the individual treatments went into remission or responded in a clinically satisfactory way, compared with 73% of the patients receiving combined treatment. Because this study was conducted with only a subset of depressed patients, those with persistent depression, the findings would need to be replicated before researchers could say combined treatment was useful for depression in general. In addition, because the study did not include a fifth condition in which the CBT was combined with placebo, we cannot rule out that the enhanced effectiveness of the combined treatment was the result of placebo factors. Nevertheless, the consensus is that combined treatment does provide some advantage. The same seems to be true for treating depression in children and adolescents. A meta-analytic review of 71 trials (9,510 participants) comparing various forms of pharmacotherapy and psychotherapy for depression in children and adolescents showed that no pharmacotherapy alone was more effective than psychotherapy alone and fluoxetine plus CBT was more effective than CBT alone (Zhou et al., 2020).

Notice how this conclusion differs from the conclusion in Chapter 5 on anxiety disorders, where no advantage of combining treatments was apparent. But combining two treatments is also expensive, so many experts think that it makes more sense to use a sequential strategy, in which you start with one treatment (maybe the one the patient prefers or the one that's most convenient) and then switch to the other only if the first choice is not entirely satisfactory (see, for example, Lynch et al., 2011; Payne et al., 2016; Schatzberg et al., 2005).

Preventing Relapse of Depression

Drugs and CBT seem to operate in different ways, but it remains uncertain which is more effective. It might just be that the most effective treatment depends on the particular individual, but we know little about these patient characteristics that could be used to personalize therapies (Maj et al., 2020). Until we develop such methods, studies continue to compare groups of individuals who share the same diagnosis. Moreover, it is possible that medication, when it works, does so more quickly than psychological treatments for the most part, which in turn have the advantage of increasing the patient's long-range social functioning (particularly in the case of IPT) and protecting against relapse or recurrence (particularly CBT). Combining treatments, therefore, might take advantage of the drugs' rapid action and the psychosocial protection against recurrence or relapse, thereby allowing eventual discontinuation of the medications.

Given the high rate of recurrence in depression, it is not surprising that more than 50% of patients on antidepressant medication relapse if their medication is stopped within 4 months after their last depressive episode (Thase, 1990). Therefore, one important question has to do with **maintenance treatment** to prevent relapse or recurrence over the long term. In a number of studies, cognitive therapy reduced rates of subsequent relapse in depressed patients by more than 50% over groups treated with antidepressant medication (see, for example, Hollon et al., 2005, 2006; Teasdale et al., 2000). A study by Jarrett and colleagues (Jarrett, Minhajuddin, Gershenfeld, Friedman, & Thase, 2013) compared CBT, an SSRI (fluoxetine) and a pill placebo as a relapse prevention strategy for people with recurrent major depressive disorder. The study first treated everybody with CBT and then randomized people to receive either continued CBT, or the SSRI, or the placebo for 8 months. Then treatment was stopped, and patients were followed up for 2 years to examine relapse rates. The study showed that, overall, both CBT and the SSRI prevented relapse equally well and more so than the placebo. Relapse rates after having received CBT and fluoxetine did not differ.

In another study, patients were treated with either antidepressant medication or cognitive therapy compared with placebo (see DeRubeis et al., 2005), and then the study began (Hollon et al., 2005; Hollon, Stewart, & Strunk, 2006). All patients who had responded well to treatment were followed for 2 years. During the 1st year, one group of patients who were originally treated with antidepressant medication continued on the medication but then stopped for the 2nd year. Also included in this figure is a subgroup of patients from the antidepressant medication group who took their medication exactly as prescribed and, therefore, should have received maximum benefit from the drugs (perfect adherence). A second group of patients originally receiving cognitive therapy were given up to three additional (booster) sessions during that 1st year but none after that. A third group was also originally treated with antidepressant medication but then switched to placebo. Outcomes during the 2 years are presented in ■ Figure 7.8. During the 1st year, patients who were withdrawn from medication and placed onto pill placebo were considerably more likely to relapse over the ensuing 12-month interval than were patients continued on medication (23.8% did not relapse on placebo versus 52.8% on medication). In comparison, 69.2% of patients with a history of cognitive therapy did not relapse. At this point, there was no statistically significant difference in relapse rates among patients who had received cognitive therapy versus those who continued on antidepressant medication. This suggests that prior cognitive therapy has an enduring effect that is at least as large in magnitude as keeping the patients on medications. In the 2nd year, when all treatments had stopped, patients who had received medications were more likely to experience a recurrence than patients who had originally received cognitive therapy. Thus, the adjusted recurrence rates were 17.5% for prior cognitive therapy versus 56.3% for prior continuation of antidepressant medication. Stangier and colleagues (2013) compared the effects of CBT with psychoeducation (a control condition) as a maintenance intervention for recurrent depression and found that CBT was more effective than the control treatment only in patients with five or more previous depressive episodes. These studies would seem to confirm that psychological treatments for depression are most notable for their enduring ability to prevent relapse or recurrence, especially for the more chronic or severe cases.

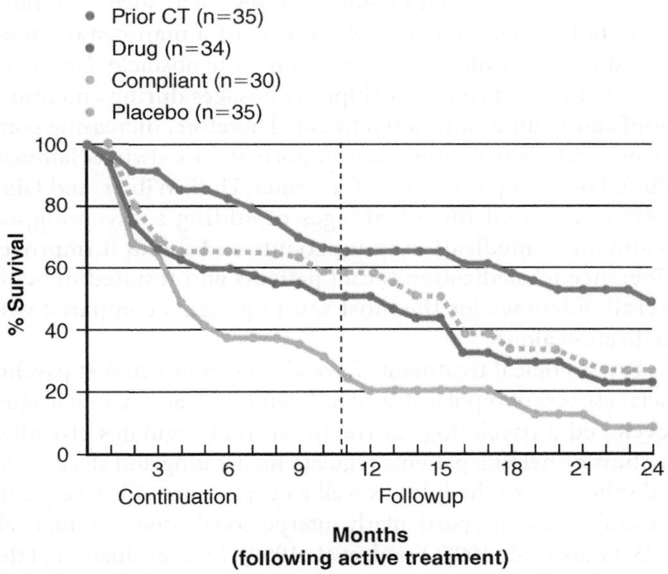

Figure 7.8

Cumulative proportion of depressed treatment responders who survived without relapse during continuation (first 12 months), and cumulative proportion of recovered patients who survived without recurrence during the subsequent follow-up (months 13–24). Prior cognitive therapy (CT) allowed only three booster sessions following acute response (first 12 months) and no sessions following recovery (months 13–24). Continuation antidepressant medication patients (drug condition) continued on active medications following acute responses (first 12 months) then withdrew from all pills following recovery (months 13–24); compliant refers to a subset of drug condition who took the medication exactly as prescribed and should have received maximum benefit during the continuation phase. Placebo patients withdrew from active medications onto pill placebo following acute responses (first 12 months) then withdrew from all pills following recovery (months 13–24). Adapted, with permission, from S. Hollon, M. Stewart, & D. Strunk, 2006, Enduring effects for cognitive behavior therapy in the treatment of depression and anxiety, *Annual Review of Psychology, 57,* 285–315. © 2006 American Medical Association.

Early intervention of high-risk children and adolescents is a particularly important area of future research, as shown in studies comparing CBT with usual care for preventing depression in high-risk adolescents (Beardslee et al., 2013; Brent et al., 2015). Subjects received eight weekly sessions followed by six monthly continuation sessions. The results showed that CBT was more effective than usual care (consisting of family-initiated mental health treatment) at preventing the onset of depression within 3 years (Beardslee et al., 2013) and 6 years (Brent et al., 2015) following the treatment. These are important and encouraging results.

Psychological Treatments for Bipolar Disorder

Although medication, particularly lithium, seems a necessary treatment for bipolar disorder, most clinicians emphasize the need for psychological interventions to manage interpersonal and practical problems (for example, marital and job difficulties that result from the disorder) (Otto & Applebaum, 2011). The principal objective of psychological intervention is often to increase compliance with medication regimens such as lithium. We noted before that the "pleasures" of a manic state make refusal to take lithium a major therapeutic obstacle. Giving up drugs between episodes or skipping dosages during an episode significantly undermines treatment. Therefore, increasing compliance with drug treatments is important (Goodwin & Jamison, 2007). For example, Clarkin, Carpenter, Hull, Wilner, and Glick (1998) evaluated the advantages of adding a psychological treatment to medication in inpatients and found it improved adherence to medication for all patients and resulted in better overall outcomes for the most severe patients compared with medication alone.

Psychological treatments have also been directed at psychosocial aspects of bipolar disorder. Ellen Frank and her colleagues developed a psychological treatment that regulates circadian rhythms by helping patients regulate their eating and sleep cycles and other daily schedules as well as cope more effectively with stressful life events, particularly interpersonal issues (Frank et al., 2005; Frank et al., 1997; Frank et al., 1999). In an evaluation of this approach, called *interpersonal and social rhythm therapy (IPSRT)*, patients receiving IPSRT survived longer without a new manic or depressive episode compared with patients undergoing standard, intensive clinical management. Initial results with adolescents are also promising (Hlastala, Kotler, McClellan, & McCauley, 2010).

Courtesy Dr. Ellen Frank

Ellen Frank and colleagues have developed important new treatments to prevent recurrences of mood disorders.

David Miklowitz and his colleagues found that family tension is associated with relapse in bipolar disorder. Preliminary studies indicate that treatments directed at helping families understand symptoms and develop new coping skills and communication styles do change communication styles (Simoneau, Miklowitz, Richards, Saleem, & George, 1999) and prevent relapse (Miklowitz, 2014). Miklowitz, George, Richards, Simoneau, and Suddath (2003) demonstrated that their family-focused treatment combined with medication results in significantly less relapse 1 year following initiation of treatment than occurs in patients receiving crisis management and medication over the same period (see ■ Figure 7.9). Specifically, only 35% of patients receiving family therapy plus medication relapsed versus 54% in the comparison group. Similarly, family therapy patients averaged over a year and a half (73.5 weeks) before relapsing, significantly longer than the comparison group.

Rea, Tompson, and Miklowitz (2003) compared this approach to an individualized psychotherapy in which patients received the same number of sessions over the same period and continued to find an advantage for the family therapy after 2 years. Reilly-Harrington and colleagues (2007) found some evidence that CBT is effective for bipolar patients with the rapid-cycling feature. In view of the relative ineffectiveness of antidepressant medication for the depressive stage of bipolar disorder reviewed above, Miklowitz and colleagues (2007) reported an important study showing that up to 30 sessions of an intensive psychological treatment was significantly more effective than usual and customary best treatment in promoting recovery from bipolar depression and remaining well. One trial compared the effects of a 4-month family-focused therapy and an educational control condition on preventing on the 1-year course of mood symptoms in youths who are at high risk for developing bipolar disorder based on their family history and environment (Miklowitz et al., 2013). The study showed that participants who received the family-focused therapy had a more rapid recovery from their initial mood symptoms and were more often in remission over the 1 year following treatment than those in the education control condition. The specificity of this effect on bipolar depression, which is the most common stage of bipolar disorder, combined with the lack of effectiveness of antidepressants, suggest that these procedures will provide an important contribution to the comprehensive treatment of bipolar disorder. A meta-analytic review of 39 randomized clinical trials with 3,863 participants (60.8% were female) showed that various forms of psychotherapy used as adjuncts to pharmacotherapy were associated with lower recurrence rates than control treatments. The strongest evidence was found for CBT and less so for family and interpersonal therapy (Miklowitz et al., 2021). Otto and colleagues (2008a, 2008b) have synthesized some of these evidence-based psychological treatment procedures for bipolar disorder into a treatment protocol.

Let us now return to Keisha, who, you will remember, had made a serious suicide attempt amid a major depressive episode.

Suicide

Most days we are confronted with news about the war on cancer or the frantic race to find a cure for AIDS. We also hear never-ending admonitions to improve our diet and to exercise more to prevent heart disease. But another cause of death ranks right up there with the most frightening and dangerous medical conditions. This is the seemingly inexplicable decision to kill themselves made by approximately 40,000 people a year in the United States alone.

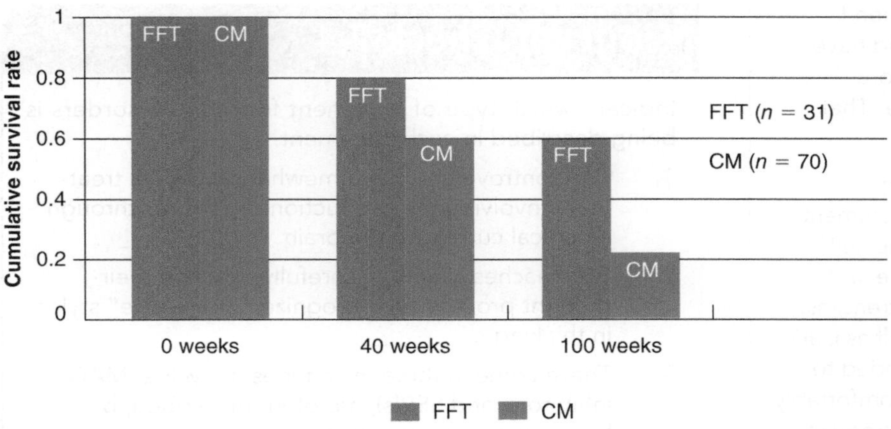

Figure 7.9

Survival curves for bipolar patients assigned to family-focused treatment (FFT) and medication or crisis management (CM) and medication (intent-to-treat analysis, $n = 101$). Comparison of the curves revealed that patients undergoing FFT had longer survival intervals without experiencing disease relapse than patients undergoing CM (Wilcoxon $X^2_1 = 8.71$, $P = 0.003$). Based on D. J. Miklowitz, E. L. George, J. A. Richards, T. L. Simoneau, & R. L. Suddath, 2003, A randomized study of family-focused psychoeducation and pharmacotherapy in the outpatient management of bipolar disorder, *Archives of General Psychiatry, 60*, 904–912.

Statistics

Consider a group of 1,000 people, randomly selected from the world's population. Each year, four of these people will die by suicide, seven will make plans to kill themselves, and 20 will seriously consider suicide (Borges et al., 2010). Suicide accounts for 1.5% of all deaths in the world and is the foremost cause of death worldwide among people 15 to 24 years of age (Fazel & Runeson, 2020)

In the United States, suicide is officially the 10th leading cause of death (Fazel & Runeson, 2020), and most epidemiologists agree that the actual number of suicides may be two to three times higher than what is reported. Many of these unreported suicides occur when people deliberately drive into a bridge or off a cliff (Blumenthal, 1990), and in the past, it was not uncommon to attribute deaths by suicide to medical causes out of respect for the deceased (Marcus, 2010). Around the world, suicide causes more deaths per year than homicide or HIV/AIDS (Nock, Borges, Bromet, Cha, et al., 2008).

Suicide is overwhelmingly a phenomenon among White populations. Most other ethnic groups, including Black and Latinx individuals, seldom resort to this desperate alternative. As you might expect from the incidence of depression in Native Americans, however, their suicide rate is extremely high, far outstripping the rates in other ethnic groups (Centers for Disease Control and Prevention [CDC], 2015); although there is great variability across tribes—among the Apache, the rates are nearly four times the national average (Mullany et al., 2009). Even more alarming is the dramatic increase in death by suicide beginning in adolescence. In 2012 in the United States, the number of deaths by suicide per 100,000 people was from 1.73 in the 10 to 14 age group and increased to 14.26 in the 20 to 24 age group (CDC, 2015). Firearms account for almost half of all suicides in this age group (CDC, 2015). Sadly, adolescents who are at risk for suicide have just as easy access to firearms (1 in 3 adolescents live in a home with a firearm) as those who are not at risk (Simonetti et al., 2015). Prevalence rates for suicide in adolescents differ greatly depending on ethnic group. This fact underscores the importance of attending to cultural considerations in the prevention and treatment of adolescent suicide (Goldston et al., 2008).

There is also a dramatic increase in suicide rates among the elderly compared with rates for younger age groups. This rise has been connected to the growing incidence of medical illness in our oldest citizens and to their increasing loss of social support (Conwell, Duberstein, & Caine, 2002) and resulting depression (Fiske et al., 2009; Boen, Dalgard, & Bjertness, 2012). Age-related neurological (Erlangsen et al., 2020) and neurodegenerative illnesses, such as Parkinson's disease (Chen et al., 2021), increase the risk for suicide. As we have noted, a strong relationship exists between illness or infirmity and hopelessness or depression.

Keisha... The Thinner, the Better

Like the overwhelming majority of people with serious psychological disorders, Keisha had never received an adequate course of treatment, although she was evaluated occasionally by various mental health professionals. She lived in a rural area where competent professional help was not readily available. Her life ebbed and flowed with her struggle to subdue anxiety and depression. When she could manage her emotions sufficiently, she took an occasional course in the high school independent study program.

Keisha discovered that she was fascinated by learning. She enrolled in a local community college at the age of 19 and did extremely well, even though she had not progressed beyond her freshman year in high school. At the college, she earned a high school equivalency degree. She went to work in a local factory. But she continued to drink heavily and to take Valium. Occasionally, anxiety and depression would return and disrupt her life.

Finally, Keisha left home, attended college full time, and fell in love. But the romance was one-sided, and she was rejected:

> One night after a phone conversation with him, I nearly drank myself to death. I lived in a single room alone in the dorm. I drank as much vodka as quickly as I could. I fell asleep. When I awoke, I was covered in vomit and couldn't recall falling asleep or being

sick. I was drunk for much of the next day. When I awoke the following morning, I realized I could have killed myself by choking on my own vomit. More important, I wasn't sure if I fully wanted to die. That was the last of my drinking.

Keisha decided to make some changes. Taking advantage of what she had learned in the little treatment she had received, she began looking at life and herself differently. Instead of dwelling on how inadequate and evil she was, she began to pay attention to her strengths. "But I now realized that I needed to accept myself as i, and work with any stumbling blocks that I faced. I needed to get myself through the world as happily and as comfortably as I could. I had a right to that." Other lessons learned in treatment now became valuable, and Keisha became more aware of her mood swings:

I learned to objectify periods of depression as [simply] periods of "feeling." They are a part of who I am but not the whole. I recognize when I feel that way, and I check my perceptions with someone that I trust when I feel uncertain of them. I try to hold on to the belief that these periods are only temporary.

Keisha developed other strategies for coping successfully with life:

I try to stay focused on my goals and what is important to me. I have learned that if one strategy to achieve some goal doesn't work, there are other strategies that probably will. My endurance is one of my blessings. Patience, dedication, and discipline are also important. None of the changes that I have been through occurred instantly or automatically. Most of what I have achieved has required time, effort, and persistence.

Keisha dreamed that if she worked hard enough, she could help other people who had problems similar to her own. Keisha pursued that dream and earned her Ph.D. in psychology.

Concept Check 7.4

Indicate which type of treatment for mood disorders is being described in each statement.

1. The controversial but somewhat successful treatment involving the production of seizures through electrical current to the brain. ___________
2. This teaches clients to carefully examine their thought process and recognize "depressive" styles in thinking. ___________
3. These come in three main types (tricyclics, MAO inhibitors, and SSRIs), are often prescribed, but have numerous side effects. ___________
4. This antidepressant must be carefully regulated to avoid illness but has the advantage of affecting manic episodes. ___________
5. This therapy focuses on resolving problems in existing relationships and learning to form new interpersonal relationships. ___________
6. This is an effort to prevent relapse or recurrence over the long run. ___________

Suicide is not attempted only by adolescents and adults. Several reports exist of children 2 to 5 years of age who had attempted suicide at least once, many injuring themselves severely (Rosenthal & Rosenthal, 1984; Tishler, Reiss, & Rhodes, 2007), and suicide is the fifth leading cause of death from ages 5 to 14 (Minino et al., 2002).

Regardless of age, in every country around the world except China, males are four times more likely to *die by* suicide than females (Nock et al., 2011; World Health Organization, 2010). This startling fact seems to be related partly to gender differences in the types of suicide *attempts*. Males generally choose far more violent methods, such as guns and hanging; females tend to rely on less violent options, such as drug overdose (Callanan & Davis, 2012; Nock et al., 2011). More men die by suicide during old age and more women during middle age, partly because most attempts by older women are nonfatal (Berman, 2009; Kuo, Gallo, & Tien, 2001).

Uniquely in China, more women die by suicide than men, particularly in rural settings (Nock, Borges, Bromet, Cha, et al., 2008; Phillips, Li, & Zhang, 2002; Sun, 2011; Wu, 2009). What accounts for this culturally determined reversal? Chinese scientists agree that China's suicide rates, probably the highest in the world, are the result of an absence of stigma. Suicide, particularly among women, is often portrayed in classical Chinese literature as a reasonable solution to problems. A rural Chinese woman's family is her entire world, and suicide is an honorable solution if the family collapses. Furthermore, highly toxic farm pesticides are readily available, and it is possible that many women who did not necessarily intend to kill themselves die after accidentally swallowing poison.

In addition to fatal suicide attempts, three other important indices of suicidal behavior are **suicidal ideation** (thinking seriously about suicide), **suicidal plans** (the formulation of a specific method for killing oneself), and nonfatal **suicidal attempts** (the person survives) (Kessler et al., 2005; Nock et al., 2011). Also, Nock and Kessler (2006) distinguish "attempters" (self-injurers with the intent to die) from "gesturers" (self-injurers who intend not to die but to influence or manipulate somebody or communicate a cry for help). In a carefully done cross-national study using consistent definitions, the prevalence of suicide ideation has been estimated at 9.2%; 3.1% reported a suicide plan, and 2.7% attempted suicide during their lifetime (Nock, Borges, Bromet, Alonso, et al., 2008). Although males *die by* suicide more often than females in most of the world, females *attempt* suicide at least three times as often (Berman & Jobes, 1991; Kuo et al., 2001). And the overall rate of nonlethal suicidal thoughts, plans, and (nonfatal) attempts is 40% to 60% higher in women than in men (Nock et al., 2011). This high incidence may reflect that more women than men are depressed and that depression is strongly related to suicide attempts (Berman, 2009). It is also interesting that despite the much higher rate of fatal suicide attempts among Whites, there are no significant ethnic or racial differences in rates of suicide ideation, plans, or attempts (Kessler et al., 2005). Among adolescents, the ratio of *thoughts* about suicide to *attempts* is also between 3:1 and 6:1. In other words, between 16% and 30% of adolescents who think about killing themselves actually attempt it (Kovacs, Goldston, & Gatsonis, 1993; Nock, Borges, Bromet, Cha, et al., 2008). "Thoughts" in this context does not refer to a fleeting philosophical type of consideration but rather to a serious contemplation of the act. The first step down the dangerous road to suicide is thinking about it.

In a study of college students (among whom suicide is the second leading cause of death), approximately 12% had serious thoughts about suicide during the past 12 months (Wilcox et al., 2010). Only a minority of these college students with thoughts of suicide (perhaps around 10%) attempt to kill themselves, and only a few succeed (Schwartz, 2011). Nevertheless, given the enormity of the problem, suicidal thoughts are taken seriously by mental health professionals.

Causes

In the spring of 2003, Bernard Loiseau, one of the all-time great French chefs, learned that an important French restaurant guide, *Gault Millau*, was reducing the rating on one of his restaurants. This was the first time in his career that any of his restaurants had a rating reduced. Later that week, he killed himself. Although police quickly ruled his death a suicide, most people in France did not consider it a suicide. Along with his fellow chefs, they accused the guidebook of murder! They claimed that he had been deeply affected by the ratings demotion, as well as speculation in the press that he might lose one of his three Michelin stars (Michelin publishes the most famous French restaurant guide). This series of events caused a sensation throughout France and, indeed, throughout the culinary world. But did *Gault Millau* kill Loiseau? Let's examine the causes of suicide.

Past Conceptions The great sociologist Emile Durkheim (1951) defined a number of suicide types, based on the social or cultural conditions in which they occurred. One type is "formalized" suicides that were approved of, such as the ancient custom in Japan of *hara-kiri* (lit. stomach-cut), in which individuals slit open their stomach and another person beheaded them. The purpose of *hara-kiri*, or *seppuku*, was to preserve one's honor. Durkheim referred to this as *altruistic suicide*. Durkheim also recognized the loss of social supports as an important provocation for suicide; he called this *egoistic suicide*. (Older adults who kill themselves after losing touch with their friends or family fit into this category.) Magne-Ingvar, Ojehagen, and Traskman-Bendz (1992) found that only 13% of 75 individuals who had seriously attempted suicide had an adequate social network of friends and relationships. Similarly, another study found that suicide attempters perceived themselves to have lower social support than did nonattempters (Riihimaki, Vuorilehto, Melartin, Haukka, & Isometsa, 2013). *Anomic suicides* are the result of marked disruptions, such as the sudden loss of a high-prestige job. (*Anomie* is feeling lost and confused.) Finally, *fatalistic suicides* result from a loss of control over one's own destiny. The mass suicide of 39 Heaven's Gate cult members in 1997 is an example of this type because the lives of those people were largely in the hands of Marshall Applewhite, a supreme and charismatic leader. Durkheim's work was important in alerting us to the social contribution to suicide. Sigmund Freud (1917/1957) believed that suicide (and depression, to some extent) indicated unconscious hostility directed inward to the self rather than outward to the person or situation causing the anger. Indeed, suicide victims often seem to be psychologically "punishing" others who may have rejected them or caused some other personal hurt. Current thinking considers social and psychological factors but also highlights the potential importance of biological contributions.

Risk Factors

Edward Shneidman pioneered the study of risk factors for suicide (Shneidman, 1989; Shneidman, Farberow, & Litman, 1970). Among the methods he and others have used to study those conditions and events that make a person vulnerable is **psychological autopsy**. The psychological profile of the person who died by suicide is reconstructed through extensive interviews with friends and family members who are likely to know what the individual was thinking and doing in the period before death. This and other methods have allowed researchers to identify a number of risk factors for suicide.

Family History If a family member died by suicide, there is an increased risk that someone else in the family will also (Brent et al., 2015; Mann et al., 2005; Nock et al., 2011). In fact, among depressed patients, the strongest predictor of suicidal behavior was having a family history of suicide (Hantouche et al., 2010). Brent and colleagues (2002) noted that offspring of family members who had attempted suicide had six times the risk of suicide attempts compared with offspring of nonattempters. If a sibling was also a suicide attempter, the risk increased even more (Brent et al., 2003). This may not be surprising because many people who kill themselves are depressed or have some related mental disorder, and these disorders run in families (Nock et al., 2011). Nevertheless, the question remains: Are people who kill themselves simply adopting a familiar solution that they've witnessed in family members, or does an inherited trait, such as impulsivity, account for increased suicidal behavior in families? It seems both factors may contribute. If individuals have an early onset of their mood disorder, as well as aggressive or impulsive traits, then their families are at a greater risk for suicidal behavior (Mann et al., 2005). The possibility that something is inherited is also supported by several adoption studies. One found an increased rate of suicide in the biological relatives of adopted individuals who had died by suicide compared with a control group of adoptees who had not died by suicide (Nock et al., 2011). Also, reviewing studies of adopted children and their biological and adopted families, Brent and Mann (2005) found that adopted individuals' suicidal behavior was predicted only by suicidal behavior in their biological relatives. This suggests some biological (genetic) contribution to suicide, even if it is relatively small, although it may not be independent of genetic contribution to depression or associated disorders.

Neurobiology A variety of evidence suggests that low levels of serotonin may be associated with suicide and with violent suicide attempts (Pompili et al., 2010; Asberg, Nordstrom, & Traskman-Bendz, 1986; Cremniter et al., 1999; Winchel, Stanley, & Stanley, 1990). As we have noted, extremely low levels of serotonin are associated with impulsivity, instability, and the tendency to overreact to situations. It is possible then that low levels of serotonin may contribute to creating a vulnerability to act impulsively. This may include killing oneself, which is sometimes an impulsive act. The studies by Brent and colleagues (2002) and Mann and colleagues (2005) suggest that transmission of vulnerabilities for a mood disorder, including the trait of impulsivity, may mediate family transmission of suicide attempts.

Existing Psychological Disorders and Other Psychological Risk Factors

More than 80% of people who kill themselves suffer from a psychological disorder, usually mood, substance use, or impulse control disorders (Berman, 2009; Brent & Kolko, 1990; Conwell et al., 1996; Joe, Baser, Breeden, Neighbors, & Jackson, 2006; Nock, Hwang, Sampson, & Kessler, 2009). Suicide is often associated with mood disorders, and for good reason. As many as 60% of suicides (75% of adolescent suicides) are associated with an existing mood disorder (Berman, 2009; Brent & Kolko, 1990; Oquendo et al., 2004). But many people with mood disorders do not attempt suicide, and, conversely, many people who attempt suicide do not have mood disorders. Therefore, depression and suicide, although strongly related, are still independent. Looking more closely at the relationship of mood disorder and suicide, some investigators have isolated hopelessness, a specific component of depression, as strongly predicting suicide (Beck, 1986; Goldston, Reboussin, & Daniel, 2006). But hopelessness also predicts suicide among individuals whose primary mental health problem is not depression (David Klonsky et al., 2012; Simpson, Tate, Whiting, & Cotter, 2011), a finding that also holds true in China (Cheung, Law, Chan, Liu, & Yip, 2006). An important theoretical account of suicide termed the *interpersonal theory of suicide* cites a perception of oneself as a burden on others and a diminished sense of belonging as powerful predictors of hopelessness and subsequently suicide (van Orden et al., 2010).

Tinseltown/Shutterstock.com

Men often choose violent methods of suicide. Actor Robin Williams, shown here, hanged himself. Singer Kurt Cobain shot himself.

Alcohol use and abuse are associated with approximately 25% to 50% of suicides and are particularly evident in suicide among college students (Lamis, Malone, Langhinrichsen-Rohling, & Ellis, 2010) and adolescents (Pompili et al., 2012; Berman, 2009; Conwell et al., 1996; Hawton, Houston, Haw, Townsend, & Harriss, 2003). In fact, Brent and colleagues (1988) found that about one third of adolescents who died by suicide were intoxicated when they died and that many more might have been under the influence of drugs. Combinations of disorders, such as substance abuse and mood disorders in adults or mood disorders and conduct disorder in children and adolescents, seem to create a stronger vulnerability than any one disorder alone (Conwell et al., 1996; Nock, Hwang, et al., 2010; Woods et al., 1997). For example, Nock, Hwang, and colleagues (2010) noticed that depression alone did not predict suicidal ideation or attempts but depression combined with impulse control problems and anxiety/agitation did. Woods and colleagues (1997) also found that substance abuse with other risk-taking behaviors—such as getting into fights, carrying a gun, or smoking—were predictive of teenage suicide, possibly reflecting impulsivity in these troubled adolescents. A closely related trait termed *sensation-seeking* predicts teenage suicidal behavior as well, above and beyond its relationship with depression and substance use (Ortin, Lake, Kleinman, & Gould, 2012). Past suicide attempts are another strong risk factor and must be taken seriously (Berman, 2009). Cooper and colleagues (2005) followed almost 8,000 individuals who were treated in the emergency room for deliberate self-harm for up to 4 years. Sixty of these people later killed themselves, which equates to 30 times the rate for the general population.

A disorder characterized more by impulsivity than depression is borderline personality disorder (see Chapter 12). Individuals with this disorder, known for making manipulative and impulsive suicidal gestures without necessarily wanting to destroy themselves, sometimes kill themselves by mistake in as many as 10% of the cases. The combination of borderline personality disorder and depression is particularly deadly (Perugi et al., 2013; Soloff, Lynch, Kelly, Malone, & Mann, 2000).

The association of suicide with severe psychological disorders, especially depression, belies the myth that it is a response to disappointment in people who are otherwise healthy.

Stressful Life Events

Perhaps the most important risk factor for suicide is a severe, stressful event experienced as shameful or humiliating, such as a failure (real or imagined) in school or at work, an unexpected arrest, or a rejection by a loved one (Blumenthal, 1990; Conwell et al., 2002; Joiner & Rudd, 2000). Physical and sexual abuse are also important sources of stress (Wagner, 1997). Evidence confirms that the stress and disruption caused by natural disasters increase the likelihood of suicide (Stratta et al., 2012; Krug et al., 1998), particularly in the case of extreme catastrophes like massive earthquakes (Matsubayashi, Sawada, & Ueda, 2012). Based on data from 337 countries experiencing natural disasters in the

1980s, Krug and colleagues (1998) concluded that the rates of suicide increased 13.8% in the 4 years after severe floods, 31% in the 2 years after hurricanes, and 62.9% in the 1st year after an earthquake. Given preexisting vulnerabilities—including psychological disorders, traits of impulsiveness, and lack of social support—a stressful event can often put a person over the edge. An integrated model of the causes of suicidal behavior is presented in ■ Figure 7.10.

Is Suicide Contagious?

The year 1774 marked the publication of *The Sorrows of Young Werther* by Johann Wolfgang von Goethe, one of the most influential books in German literature. The book tells the story of young Werther, who falls madly in love with a woman who is unable to requite his love. In the story, Werther ends up dying by shooting himself to escape the emotional pain caused by his unrequited love. After publication of this book, suicide rates in Germany increased. Men sometimes dressed in the same clothing as Werther and killed themselves with the kind of pistol that is described in the book. Sometimes the book was found at the scene of suicides. Suicides as imitations of other suicides have since been named the *Werther effect*. Research has confirmed that certain media content is associated with an increase in suicide rates (Sisask & Varnik, 2012). However, other media content can be associated with a decrease in suicide. This is sometimes referred as the *Papageno effect* (Thorson & Öberg, 2003), based on a character from Mozart's opera *The Magic Flute*. In the opera, Papageno contemplates suicide but chooses a different option after other characters suggest more adaptive ways to resolve his problems (Niederkrotenthaler et al., 2010). Thus, it appears that repetitive reporting of the same suicide, romanticizing suicide, and reporting suicide myths can, in fact, lead to an increase in suicide rates, whereas presenting adaptive coping strategies in response to suicidal ideation but without suicidal behavior can decrease suicide rates.

Why would anyone want to copy a suicide? First, suicides are often romanticized in the media: An attractive young person under unbearable pressure dies by suicide and becomes a martyr to friends and peers by getting even with the (adult) world for creating such a difficult situation. Also, media accounts often describe in detail the methods used in the suicide, thereby providing a guide to potential victims. Little is reported about the paralysis, brain damage, and other tragic consequences of the nonfatal suicide attempts or about how suicide is almost always associated with a severe psychological disorder. More important, even less is said about the futility of this method of solving problems (Gould, 1990, 2001; O'Carroll, 1990). To prevent these tragedies, mental health professionals must intervene immediately in schools and other locations with people who might be depressed or otherwise vulnerable to the contagion of suicide (Boyce, 2011). But it isn't clear that suicide is "contagious" in the infectious disease sense. Rather, the stress of a friend's suicide or some other major stress may affect several individuals who are vulnerable because of existing psychological disorders (Joiner, 1999; Blasco-Fontecilla, 2012).

Treatment

Despite the identification of important risk factors, predicting suicide is still an uncertain art. Individuals with few precipitating factors unexpectedly kill themselves, and many who live with seemingly insurmountable stress and illness and have little social support or guidance somehow survive and overcome their difficulties.

Chris Hondros/Getty Images

Cognitive behavioral group therapy has been shown to decrease suicidal behavior in individuals who have previously attempted suicide.

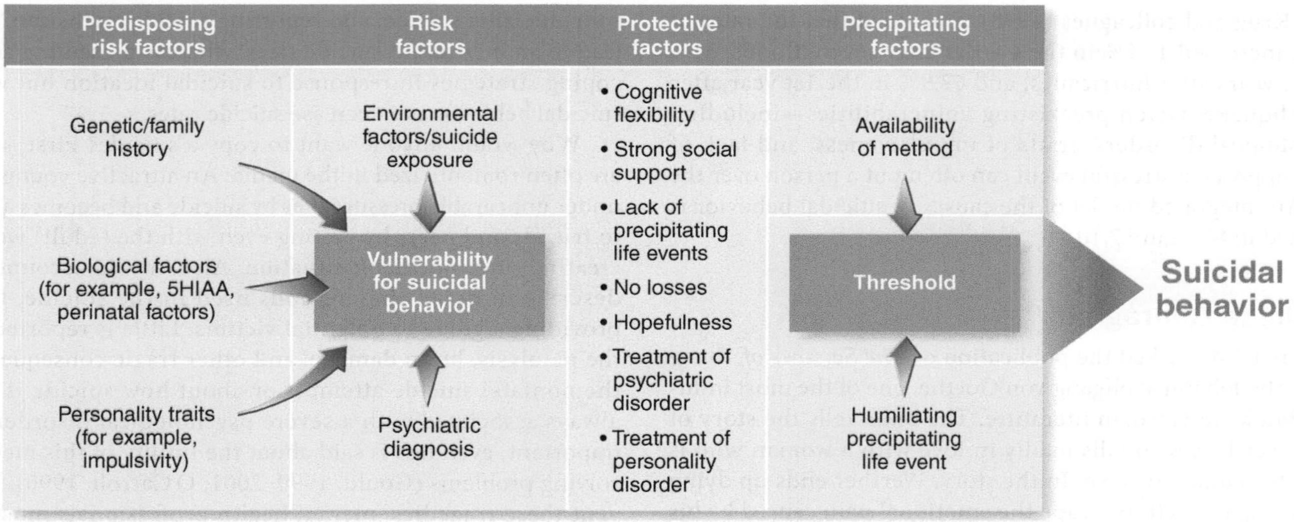

Figure 7.10

Threshold model for suicidal behavior. 5HIAA 5 5-hydroxyindoleacetic acid. Based on S. J. Blumenthal & D. J. Kupfer, 1988, Clinical assessment and treatment of youth suicide, *Journal of Youth and Adolescence, 17,* 1–24.

Mental health professionals are thoroughly trained in assessing for possible suicidal ideation (Fowler, 2012; Joiner et al., 2007). Others might be reluctant to ask leading questions for fear of putting the idea in someone's head. We know, however, it is far more important to check for these "secrets" than to do nothing because the risk of inspiring suicidal thoughts is small to nonexistent and the risk of leaving them undiscovered is enormous (Berman, 2009). Gould and colleagues (2005) found that more than 1,000 high school students who were asked about suicidal thoughts or behaviors during a screening program showed no risk of increased suicidal thoughts compared with a second group of 1,000 students who had the screening program without the questions about suicide. Therefore, if there is any indication that someone is suicidal, the mental health professional will inquire, "Has there been any time recently when you've thought that life wasn't worth living or had some thoughts about hurting yourself or possibly killing yourself?"

One difficulty with this approach is that sometimes these thoughts are implicit or out of awareness. Now Cha, Najmi, Park, Finn, and Nock (2010) have developed measures of implicit (unconscious) cognition, adapted from cognitive psychology, to assess implicit suicidal ideation. In this assessment using the Stroop test described in Chapter 2, people who demonstrated an implicit association between the words *death/suicide* and *self,* even if they weren't aware of it, were six times more likely to make a suicide attempt in the next 6 months than those without this specific association; thus, this assessment is a better predictor of suicide attempts than both patients' own predictions and clinicians' predictions (Nock, Park, et al., 2010). These results appear in ■ Figure 7.11. This procedure holds considerable promise for improving screening for people at risk.

The mental health professional will also check for possible recent humiliations and determine whether any of the factors are present that might indicate a high probability of suicide. For example, does a person who is thinking of suicide have a detailed plan or just a vague fantasy? If a plan is discovered that includes a specific time, place, and method, the risk is high. Does the detailed plan include putting all personal affairs in order, giving away possessions, and other final acts? If so, the risk is higher still. What specific method is the person considering? Generally, the more lethal and violent the method (guns, hanging, poison, and so on), the greater the risk it will be used. Does the person understand what might actually happen? Many people do not understand the effects of the pills on which they might overdose. Finally, has the person taken any precautions against being discovered? If so, the risk is extreme (American Psychiatric Association, 2003). In summary, the clinician must assess for (1) suicidal desire (ideation, hopelessness, burdensomeness, feeling trapped); (2) suicidal capability (past attempts, high anxiety and/or rage, available means); and (3) suicidal intent (available plan, expressed intent to die, preparatory behavior) (Joiner et al., 2007). If all three conditions are present, immediate action is required.

If a risk is present, clinicians attempt to get the individual to agree to or perhaps even sign a "no-suicide" contract. Usually, this includes a promise not to do anything remotely connected with suicide without contacting the mental health professional first. Although signing a contract will not prevent a suicide attempt in someone who is determined, if the person at risk refuses a contract (or the clinician has serious doubts about the patient's sincerity) and the suicidal risk is judged to be high, immediate hospitalization is indicated, even against the will of the patient. Whether the person is hospitalized or not, treatment aimed at resolving underlying life stressors and treating existing psychological disorders should be initiated immediately.

In view of the public health consequences of suicide, a number of programs have been implemented to reduce the rates of suicide. Most research indicates that such curriculum-based programs targeting the general population (universal programs) in schools or organizations on how to handle life stress or increase social support are not effective

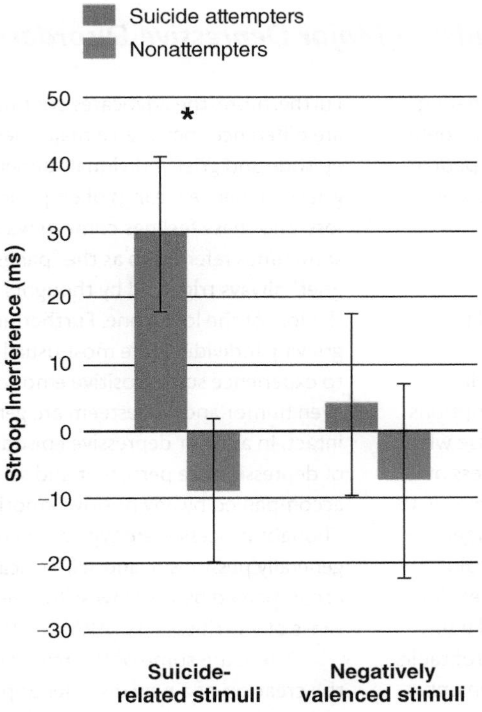

Figure 7.11

Attentional biases toward suicide-related stimuli in suicide attempters versus nonattempters. Among adults presenting to a psychiatric emergency department ($n = 124$), those presenting following a suicide attempt displayed greater attentional bias to suicide-related words (as indicated by more interference and slower reaction times on the Stroop test) than those who did not attempt suicide. Adapted from C. B. Cha, S. Najmi, J. M. Park, C. T. Finn, & M. K. Nock, 2010, Attentional bias toward suicide-related stimuli predicts suicidal behavior, *Journal of Abnormal Psychology, 119*, 616–622.

(Berman, 2009; Garfield & Zigler, 1993). More helpful are programs targeted to at-risk individuals, including adolescents in schools where a student has died by suicide. The Institute of Medicine (2002) recommends making services available immediately to friends and relatives of the deceased. An important step is limiting access to lethal weapons for anyone at risk for suicide. This may be one of the most powerful parts of a suicide prevention program (Mann and colleagues, 2005). Telephone hotlines and other crisis intervention services also seem to be useful. Nevertheless, as Garfield and Zigler (1993) point out, hotline volunteers must be backed up by competent mental health professionals who can identify potentially serious risks. One large health maintenance organization carefully screened all of its approximately 200,000 members who came in for services for suicide risk and then intervened if any risk was noted. Suicides were greatly reduced in this very promising program (Hampton, 2010).

Specific treatments for people at risk have also been developed. Suicide prevention programs for the elderly, for example, tend to focus on decreasing risk factors (for example, treating depression) rather than shoring up protective factors like familial support, and could be improved by greater involvement of individuals' social networks (Lapierre et al., 2011). Other interventions target specific mental health problems associated with suicide. For instance, Marsha Linehan and colleagues developed a noteworthy treatment for borderline personality disorder that addresses impulsive suicidal behavior associated with this condition (see Chapter 12).

Empirical research indicates that cognitive-behavioral interventions can be efficacious in decreasing suicide risk. For example, David Rudd and colleagues developed a brief psychological treatment targeting young adults who were at risk for suicide because of the presence of suicidal ideation accompanied by previous suicidal attempts, mood or substance use disorders, or both (Rudd et al., 1996). Patients were assessed up to 2 years following treatment, and results indicated reductions in suicidal ideation and behavior, as well as marked improvement in problem-solving ability. This program was expanded into a psychological treatment for suicidal behavior with empirical support for its efficacy (Rudd, Joiner, & Rajab, 2001). Attending as few as 10 sessions of cognitive therapy for recent suicide attempters cuts the risk of additional attempts by 50% over the next 18 months (Brown et al., 2005). Specifically, 24% of those in the cognitive therapy group made a repeat attempt compared with 42% in the care-as-usual group. Because cognitive therapy is relatively widely available, this is an important development in suicide prevention (Joiner, 2014).

With the increased rate of suicide, particularly in adolescents, the tragic and paradoxical act is receiving increased scrutiny from public health authorities. The quest will go on to determine more effective and efficient ways of preventing one of the most serious consequences of any psychological disorder, the taking of one's own life.

Concept Check 7.5

Match each of the following summaries with the correct suicide type, choosing from (a) altruistic, (b) egoistic, (c) anomic, and (d) fatalistic.

1. Jordan's wife left him and took the children. He is a well-known television personality, but because of a conflict with the new station owners, he was recently fired. If Jordan kills himself, his suicide would be considered __________.
2. James killed himself while a prisoner of war in Vietnam. __________
3. Sheiba lives in a remote village in Africa. She was recently caught in an adulterous affair with a man in a nearby village. Her husband wants to kill her but won't have to because of a tribal custom that requires her to kill herself. She leaps from the nearby "sinful woman's cliff." __________
4. Mabel lived in a nursing home for many years. At first, her family and friends visited her often; now they come only at Christmas. Her two closest friends in the nursing home died recently. She has no hobbies or other interests. Mabel's suicide would be identified as what type? __________

DSM Controversies: *When Should Normal Grief Be Considered Major Depressive Disorder?*

Prior to DSM-5, if you met criteria for a major depressive episode in the 2 months following the loss, you would not receive a diagnosis of major depressive disorder, even if you otherwise met criteria for it (unless you had very severe symptoms such as strong suicidal ideation or psychotic features). This was called the "bereavement exclusion." This exclusion was dropped in DSM-5 for several reasons (Zisook et al., 2012). For example, it was noted that major depressive episodes often are triggered by stressful events other than loss of a loved one in vulnerable individuals and that, if all of the criteria are otherwise met for a major depressive episode, there seemed no reason to exclude people simply because the precipitating event was the death of a loved one. Furthermore, data from a number of sources suggested that there are no differences between depressive episodes triggered by loss or not triggered by loss and that the biological, psychological, and social factors that make one vulnerable to developing major depression are the same whether the trigger is loss of a loved one or not (Shear et al., 2011; Zisook et al., 2012). Finally, the data indicated that eliminating the 2-month bereavement exclusion would not greatly increase the numbers of people requiring treatment for major depression (Gilman et al., 2012; Zisook et al., 2012).

Nevertheless, this change was controversial, since some concluded that DSM-5 would be making the natural grieving process a disorder resulting in, among other things, frequent prescriptions of antidepressant medication to those who might be undergoing a normal process of grieving (Fox & Jones, 2013; Nakajiama, 2018; Maj, 2008). This is one part of the larger criticism levied at DSM-5 that the major purpose of DSM is to increase business for mental health professionals and make sure that large drug companies remain profitable. Advocates for dropping the bereavement exclusion point out that the diagnosis of major depressive disorder or posttraumatic stress disorder in response to other major life stressors is not controversial and that the development of major depressive disorder in some people in response to the loss of a loved one shouldn't be controversial, either. Furthermore, the advocates continue, there are differences between a major depressive episode and grief. Individuals undergoing grief experience feelings of emptiness and loss, and these feelings come in waves sometimes referred to as the "pangs of grief," always triggered by thoughts of the loss of the loved one. Furthermore, grieving individuals are most usually able to experience some positive emotions, and even humor and self-esteem are generally intact. In a major depressive episode, feelings of depression are persistent and seldom accompanied by any positive emotions. Thought processes are typically very generally pessimistic and self-critical and are accompanied by very low self-esteem and a sense of worthlessness (APA, 2013).

These are some of the reasons for the creation of a new disorder appearing in DSM-5-TR, prolonged grief disorder described in chapter 5, while continuing to acknowledge that in some cases, a significant loss could lead to a major depressive episode.

Summary

Understanding and Defining Mood Disorders

- Mood disorders are among the most common psychological disorders, and the risk of developing them is increasing worldwide, particularly in younger people.
- Two fundamental experiences can contribute either singly or in combination to all specific mood disorders: a major depressive episode and mania. A less severe episode of mania that does not cause impairment in social or occupational functioning is known as a hypomanic episode. An episode of mania coupled with anxiety or depression is known as a mixed episode or mixed state.
- An individual who suffers only from episodes of depression is said to have a unipolar disorder. An individual who alternates between depression and mania has a bipolar disorder.
- Major depressive disorder may be a single episode or recurrent, but it is always time-limited. In another form of depression, persistent depressive disorder (dysthymia), the symptoms are often somewhat milder but remain relatively unchanged over long periods. In some cases, fewer symptoms are observed than in a major depressive episode, but they persist for at least 2 years (persistent depressive disorder) (dysthymia). In other cases, a major depressive episode will last at least 2 years (chronic major depressive episode). In cases of double depression, a form of persistent depressive disorder, an individual experiences both major depressive episodes and persistent depressive disorder (dysthymia).
- The key identifying feature of bipolar disorders is an alternation of manic episodes and major depressive episodes. Cyclothymic disorder is a milder but more chronic version of bipolar disorder.
- Patterns of additional features that sometimes accompany mood disorders, called *specifiers*, may predict the course or patient response to treatment, as does the temporal patterning or course of mood disorders. One pattern, seasonal affective disorder, most often occurs in winter.

Prevalence of Mood Disorders

- Mood disorders in children are fundamentally similar to mood disorders in adults.
- Symptoms of depression are increasing dramatically in our elderly population.

- The experience of anxiety across cultures varies, and it can be difficult to make comparisons—especially, for example, when we attempt to compare subjective feelings of depression.

Causes of Mood Disorders

- The causes of mood disorders lie in a complex interaction of biological, psychological, and social factors. From a biological perspective, researchers are particularly interested in the stress hypothesis and the role of neurohormones. Psychological theories of depression focus on learned helplessness and the depressive cognitive schemas, as well as interpersonal disruptions.

Treatment of Mood Disorders

- A variety of treatments, both biological and psychological, have proved effective for the mood disorders, at least in the short term. For those individuals who do not respond to antidepressant drugs or psychosocial treatments, a more dramatic physical treatment, electroconvulsive therapy, is sometimes used. Two psychological treatments—cognitive therapy and interpersonal psychotherapy—seem effective in treating depressive disorders.
- Relapse and recurrence of mood disorders are common in the long term, and treatment efforts must focus on maintenance treatment—that is, on preventing relapse or recurrence.

Suicide

- Suicide is often associated with mood disorders but can occur in their absence or in the presence of other disorders. It is the 10th leading cause of death among all people in the United States, but among adolescents, it is the 3rd leading cause of death.
- In understanding suicidal behavior, three indices are important: suicidal ideation (serious thoughts about suicide), suicidal plans (a detailed method for killing oneself), and suicidal attempts (that are nonfatal). Important, too, in learning about risk factors for suicides is the psychological autopsy, in which the psychological profile of an individual who has died by suicide is reconstructed and examined for clues.

Key Terms

mood disorders, 212
major depressive episode, 212
mania, 213
hypomanic episode, 213
mixed features, 214
major depressive disorder, 214
recurrent, 214
persistent depressive disorder (dysthymia), 215
double depression, 215
hallucinations, 217
delusion, 217
catalepsy, 217
seasonal affective disorder (SAD), 219
integrated grief, 221
acute grief, 221
premenstrual dysphoric disorder, 222
disruptive mood dysregulation disorder, 222
bipolar II disorder, 225
bipolar I disorder, 225
cyclothymic disorder, 225
neurohormones, 235
learned helplessness theory of depression, 238
depressive cognitive triad, 239
mood-stabilizing drug, 248
electroconvulsive therapy (ECT), 248
cognitive therapy, 249
interpersonal psychotherapy (IPT), 250
maintenance treatment, 253
suicidal ideation, 256
suicidal plans, 256
suicidal attempts, 256
psychological autopsy, 257

Answers to Concept Checks

7.1

1. e; 2. a; 3. c; 4. d; 5. b

7.2

1. T; 2. F (it does not require life experience); 3. T; 4. T

7.3

1. genetics, neurotransmitter system abnormalities, endocrine system, circadian or sleep rhythms, neurohormones;
2. stressful life events, learned helplessness, depressive cognitive triad, a sense of uncontrollability;
3. marital dissatisfaction, gender, few social supports

7.4

1. electroconvulsive therapy; 2. cognitive therapy; 3. antidepressants; 4. lithium; 5. interpersonal psychotherapy; 6. maintenance treatment

7.5

1. c; 2. d; 3. a; 4. b

Exploring Mood Disorders

People with mood disorders experience one or both of the following:

- **Mania:** A frantic "high" with extreme overconfidence and energy, often leading to reckless behavior
- **Depression:** A devastating "low" with extreme lack of energy, interest, confidence, and enjoyment of life

Trigger

- Negative or positive life changes (death of a loved one, promotion, etc.)
- Physical illness

PhotoDisc/Getty Images

Social Influences

- Women and underrepresented—social inequality and oppression and a diminished sense of control
- Social support can reduce symptoms
- Lack of social support can aggravate symptoms

Biological Influences

- Inherited vulnerability
- Altered neurotransmitters and neurohormonal systems
- Sleep deprivation
- Circadian rhythm disturbances

Causes

Behavioral Influences

Depression

- General slowing down
- Neglect of responsibilities and appearance
- Irritability; complaints about matters that used to be taken in stride

Mania

- Hyperactivity
- Reckless or otherwise unusual behavior

PhotoDisc/Getty Images

Disorder

Emotional and Cognitive Influences

Depression

- Emotional flatness or emptiness
- Inability to feel pleasure
- Poor memory
- Inability to concentrate
- Hopelessness and/or learned helplessness
- Loss of sexual desire
- Loss of warm feelings for family and friends
- Exaggerated self-blame or guilt
- Overgeneralization
- Loss of self-esteem
- Suicidal thoughts or actions

Mania

- Exaggerated feelings of euphoria and excitement

PhotoDisc/Getty Images

TYPES OF MOOD DISORDERS

Depressive

PhotoDisc/Getty Images

Major Depressive Disorder
Symptoms of major depressive disorder:
- begin suddenly, often triggered by a crisis, change, or loss
- are extremely severe, interfering with normal functioning
- can be long term, lasting months or years if untreated

Some people have only one episode, but the pattern usually involves repeated episodes or lasting symptoms.

Persistent Depressive Disorder (Dysthymia)
Long-term unchanging symptoms of mild depression, sometimes lasting 20 to 30 years if untreated. Daily functioning not as severely affected, but over time impairment is cumulative.

Double Depression
Alternating periods of major depression and dysthymia

Bipolar

People who have a bipolar disorder live on an unending emotional roller coaster.

Types of Bipolar Disorders
- **Bipolar I:** major depression and full mania
- **Bipolar II:** major depression and mild mania
- **Cyclothymia:** mild depression with mild mania, chronic and long term

During the **Depressive Phase**, the person may:
- lose all interest in pleasurable activities and friends
- feel worthless, helpless, and hopeless
- have trouble concentrating
- lose or gain weight without trying
- have trouble sleeping or sleep more than usual
- feel tired all the time
- feel physical aches and pains that have no medical cause
- think about death or attempt suicide

During the **Manic Phase**, the person may:
- feel extreme pleasure and joy from every activity
- be extraordinarily active, planning excessive daily activities
- sleep little without getting tired
- develop grandiose plans leading to reckless behavior: unrestrained buying sprees, sexual indiscretions, foolish business investments, and so on.
- have "racing thoughts" and talk on and on
- be easily irritated and distracted

TREATMENT OF MOOD DISORDERS

Treatment for mood disorders is most effective and easiest when it's started early. Most people are treated with a combination of these methods.

Treatment

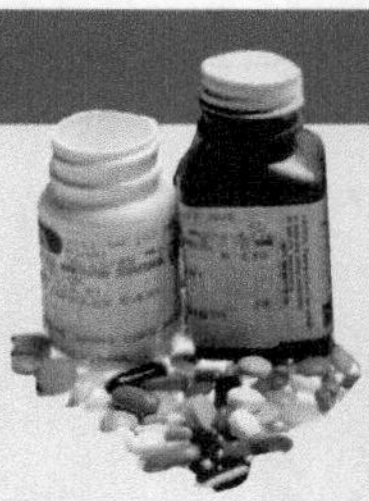

PhotoDisc/Getty Images

Medication
Antidepressants can help to control symptoms and restore neurotransmitter functioning.
Common types of antidepressants:
- Tricyclics (Tofranil, Elavil)
- Monamine oxidase inhibitors (MAO inhibitors): (Nardil, Parnate); MAO inhibitors can have severe side effects, especially when combined with certain foods or over-the-counter medications
- Selective-serotonin reuptake inhibitors or SSRIs (Prozac, Zoloft) are newer and cause fewer side effects than tricyclics or MAO inhibitors
- Lithium is the preferred drug for bipolar disorder; side effects can be serious; and dosage must be carefully regulated

Cognitive-Behavioral Therapy
Helps depressed people:
- learn to replace negative depressive thoughts and attributions with more positive ones
- develop more effective coping behaviors and skills

Interpersonal Psychotherapy
Helps depressed people:
- focus on the social and interpersonal triggers for their depression (such as the loss of a loved one)
- develop skills to resolve interpersonal conflicts and build new relationships

Electroconvulsive Therapy (ECT)
- For severe depression, ECT is used when other treatments have been ineffective. It usually has temporary side effects, such as memory loss and lethargy. In some patients, certain intellectual and/or memory functions may be permanently lost.

Light Therapy
- For seasonal affective disorder

PhotoDisc/Getty Images

8 Eating and Sleep–Wake Disorders

Justin Pumfrey/The Image Bank/Getty Images

Learning Objectives

LO8.1 Differentiate bulimia nervosa, binge-eating disorder, and anorexia nervosa in terms of their key features as outlined in the DSM-5.

LO8.2 List the reasons that the development of an eating disorder is a particular risk for young women in developed countries.

LO8.3 Draw connections between the biological, psychological, and social causes of eating disorders and the symptoms of eating disorders.

LO8.4 Compare the effectiveness of psychological treatments for eating disorders versus medical treatments for eating disorders.

LO8.5 Explain how obesity as a medical condition differs from eating disorders.

LO8.6 Discuss how to test an individual for the presence of dyssomnias in terms of formal medical assessment.

LO8.7 Describe the different types of parasomnias in terms of their symptoms and treatment.

We now begin a series of three chapters on the interaction of psychological and social factors in relation to physical functioning. Many people take their bodies for granted. People wake up in the morning assuming they will be alert enough to handle their required daily activities; they eat two or three meals a day and perhaps a number of snacks; they may engage in some vigorous exercise and, on some days, in sexual activity. They don't focus on their functioning to any great degree unless it is disrupted by illness or disease. Yet psychological and social factors can significantly disrupt these "activities of survival."

In this chapter, we talk about psychological disruptions of two of our relatively automatic behaviors, eating and sleeping, which substantially affect the rest of our behavior. In Chapter 9, we discuss the psychological factors involved in physical malfunctioning: specifically, illness and disease. Finally, in Chapter 10, we discuss disordered sexual behavior.

Major Types of Eating Disorders

Although some disorders we discuss in this chapter can be deadly, many people do not understand the differences or prevalence of eating disorders. They began to increase during the 1950s or early 1960s and have spread insidiously over the ensuing decades. In **bulimia nervosa**, out-of-control eating episodes, or **binges**, are followed by self-induced vomiting, excessive use of laxatives, or other attempts to purge (get rid of) the food. In **anorexia nervosa**, the person eats only minimal amounts of food or exercises vigorously to offset food intake so body weight sometimes drops dangerously. In **binge-eating disorder**, individuals may binge repeatedly and find it distressing, but they do not attempt to purge the food. The chief characteristic of these and related disorders is an overwhelming, all-encompassing drive to be thin. Another type of eating disorder is **avoidant/restrictive food intake disorder (ARFID)**. People with this problem limit their food intake not because they are concerned about weight or body shape but because they are simply not interested in eating or food or because they avoid certain sensory characteristics or consequences of food or eating. This can lead to impaired growth in children and to significant weight loss in adults.

Eating disorders were included for the first time as a separate group of disorders in the DSM-IV. Of the people with anorexia nervosa who are followed over a sufficient period, up to 20% die as a result of their disorder, with slightly more than 5% dying within 10 years (see, for example, Franko et al., 2013; Millar et al., 2005; Papadopoulos, Ekbom, Brandt, & Ekselius, 2009). In fact, anorexia nervosa has the highest mortality rate of any psychological disorder reviewed in this book, including mood disorders (Keshaviah et al., 2014; Papadopoulos et al., 2009). Women with anorexia nervosa were 18 times more likely to die by suicide than 15- to 34-year-old females in the general population (Keshaviah et al., 2014).

Are eating disorders on the rise? To answer this question, one literature review examined 94 studies published between 2000 and 2018 (Galmiche, Déchelotte, Lambert, & Tavolacci, 2019). The results showed that eating disorders are highly prevalent worldwide, especially in women. The point prevalence rates increased from 3.5% during the years 2000 to 2006 to 7.8% during the years 2013 to 2018. On average, these rates were higher in the United States (4.6%) than in Europe (2.2%) or Asia (3.5%). But not all investigators agree that eating disorders are on the rise (for example, Geddes, Andreasen, Goodwin, & Halmi, 2020). Still, the difference in the prevalence rates of eating disorders between different regions in the world gives us some clues about the sociocultural factors that contribute to these problems. Until recently, eating disorders, particularly bulimia, were not a major problem in developing countries, where access to sufficient food is so often a daily struggle. Thus, it appears that the challenges associated with industrialization and urbanization are at least partly responsible for the increase in eating disorders in many countries, including China, Singapore, South Korea, Egypt, Pakistan, United Arab Emirates, Oman, Lebanon, Kuwait, Iran, and Jordan (Pike, Hoek, & Dunne, 2014). **Obesity** is not considered an official disorder in DSM-5, but we discuss it in this chapter because it is thought to be one of the most dangerous epidemics confronting public health authorities around the world today. Definitions of underweight, overweight, and obesity will be discussed further later, but they are based in part on *body mass index (BMI)*, which is highly correlated with body fat. To determine your own BMI, refer to Table 8.1, which is applicable to both men and women. Keep in mind that the table may be off for some people, such as a muscular football player who may look overweight on the charts or a person with normal weight who is out of shape and has a lot of fat. But this table is useful for most people and is in use around the world. In this chapter, we focus on serious undernourishment (BMI less than 18.5), as well as obesity (BMI 30 or greater). People with a BMI of 40 or greater are considered severe (or morbidly) obese.

Table 8.1 Body Mass Index (BMI) Table

Height in Feet and Inches	Weight in Pounds													
	120	130	140	150	160	170	180	190	200	210	220	230	240	250
4′6″	29	31	34	36	39	41	43	46	48	51	53	56	58	60
4′8″	27	29	31	34	36	38	40	43	45	47	49	52	54	56
4′10″	25	27	2	31	34	36	38	40	42	44	46	48	50	52
5′0″	23	25	27	29	31	33	35	37	39	41	43	45	47	49
5′2″	22	24	26	27	29	31	33	35	37	38	40	42	44	46
5′4″	21	22	24	26	28	29	31	33	34	36	38	40	41	43
5′6″	19	21	23	24	26	27	29	31	32	34	36	37	39	40
5′8″	18	20	21	23	24	26	27	29	30	32	34	35	37	38
5′10″	17	19	20	22	23	24	26	27	29	30	32	33	35	36
6′0″	16	18	19	20	22	23	24	26	27	28	30	31	33	34
6′2″	15	17	18	19	21	22	23	24	26	27	28	30	31	32
6′4″	15	16	17	18	20	21	22	23	24	26	27	28	29	30
6′6″	14	15	16	17	19	20	21	22	23	24	25	27	28	29
6′8″	13	14	15	17	18	19	20	21	22	23	24	25	26	28
	Underweight				Healthy weight		Overweight					Obese		

Obesity is rampant in most Western countries and especially in the United States. A review of 18 countries across five continents showed that the prevalence of morbidly obese people ranged from 1.3% (Spain) to 7.7% (USA) for all adults and between 0.7% (Serbia) to 5.6% (USA) for men, and 1.8% (Poland) to 9.7% (USA) for women (Williamson, Nimegeer, & Lean, 2020).

If these trends continue, severe obesity will surpass 6% in men and 9% in women by 2025 globally, whereas underweight remains prevalent in the world's low-income regions (DiCesare et al., 2016). For the most obese nation—the United States—it is projected that by 2030, 1 in 2 adults (48.9%) will have obesity and almost 1 in 4 adults (24.2%) will be morbidly obese by 2030. In 25 of the 50 U.S. states, this prevalence will be higher than 25% (Ward et al., 2019). Similarly disturbing trends can be seen in adolescents, and especially Black or Hispanic boys (Neurmark-Szteiner et al., 2012).

Obesity is a significant health problem because the more overweight someone is at a given height, the greater the risks to health (Convit, 2012). These risks are widespread and involve greatly increased prevalence of cardiovascular disease, diabetes, hypertension, stroke, gallbladder disease, respiratory disease, muscular skeletal problems, and hormone-related cancers (Convit, 2012; Flegal, Graubard, Williamson, & Gail, 2005; Henderson & Brownell, 2004). These risks may be even greater than previously thought (Stokes & Preston, 2015), especially when obesity is comorbid with diabetes (which it often is), a condition so common and concerning that it has become known as *diabesity* (Ng, Delgado, Borlaug, & Bax, 2021). Obesity is included in this chapter because eating is often used as a maladaptive emotion regulation strategy, while also being associated with great emotion distress and significant physical and other mental health problems. It is often produced by the consumption of a greater number of calories than are expended in energy. The behavior that produces this distorted energy equation contradicts a common assumption—namely, that most people with obesity do not necessarily eat more or exercise less than their lean counterparts. They often do, especially those people who are morbidly obese. Although the tendency to overeat and exercise too little unquestionably has a genetic component, as described later, the excessive eating and emotional factors associated with overeating at the core of the problem are the reason that morbid obesity could be considered a disorder of eating.

We begin by examining bulimia nervosa, anorexia nervosa, and a closely related disorder, binge-eating disorder, where individuals binge on food as they do in bulimia nervosa, but they don't compensate for the binging by purging. We then briefly review obesity.

Bulimia Nervosa

Many people are familiar with bulimia nervosa from their own experiences or someone close to them. It is one of the most common psychological disorders on college campuses. Consider the case of Phoebe.

Phoebe . . . Apparently Perfect

Phoebe was a classic all-American girl: popular, attractive, intelligent, and talented. By the time she was a senior in high school, she had accomplished a great deal. She was a class officer throughout high school, homecoming princess her sophomore year, and junior prom queen. She dated the captain of the football team. Phoebe had many talents, among them a beautiful singing voice and marked ability in ballet. Each year at Christmastime, her ballet company performed *The Nutcracker Suite*, and Phoebe attracted much attention with her poised performance in a lead role. She played on several school athletic teams. Phoebe maintained an A-minus average, was considered a model student, and was headed for a top-ranked university.

But Phoebe had a secret: She was haunted by her belief that she was fat and ugly. Every single bite of food that she put in her mouth was, in her mind, another step down the inexorable path that led to the end of her success and popularity. Phoebe had been concerned about her weight since she was 11. Ever the perfectionist, she began regulating her eating in junior high school. She would skip breakfast (over the protestations of her mother), eat a small bowl of pretzels at noon, and allow herself one half of whatever she was served for dinner.

This behavior continued into high school, but as Phoebe struggled to restrict her eating, occasionally she would binge on junk food. Sometimes she stuck her fingers down her throat after a binge (she even tried a toothbrush once), but this tactic was unsuccessful. During her sophomore year in high school, Phoebe reached her full adult height of 5 feet 2 inches and weighed 110 pounds; she continued to fluctuate between 105 and 110 pounds throughout high school. By the time she was a senior, Phoebe was obsessed with what she would eat and when. She used every bit of her willpower attempting to restrict her eating, but occasionally she failed. One day during the fall of her senior year, she came home after school and, alone in front of the television, she ate two big boxes of candy. Depressed, guilty, and desperate, she went to the bathroom and stuck her fingers farther down her throat than she had ever before dared. She vomited. And she kept vomiting. Although so physically exhausted that she had to lie down for half an hour, Phoebe had never in her life felt such an overwhelming sense of relief from the anxiety, guilt, and tension that always accompanied her binges. She realized that she had gotten to eat all that candy and now her stomach was empty. It was the perfect solution to her problems.

Phoebe learned quickly what foods she could easily vomit. And she always drank lots of water. She began to restrict her eating even more, and her bingeing increased.

This routine went on for about 6 months, until April of her senior year in high school. By this time, Phoebe had lost much of her energy, and her schoolwork was deteriorating. Her teachers noticed this and saw that she looked bad. She was continually tired, her skin was broken out, and her face puffed up, particularly around her mouth. Her teachers and mother suspected that she might have an eating problem. When they confronted her, she was relieved her problem was finally out in the open, and stopped binging for a while, but mortally afraid of gaining weight and losing her popularity, Phoebe resumed her pattern, but she was now much better at hiding it. For 6 months, Phoebe binged and purged approximately 15 times a week.

When Phoebe went away to college that fall, things became more difficult. Now she had a roommate to contend with, and she was more determined than ever to keep her problem a secret. Although the student health service offered workshops and seminars on eating disorders for the freshman women, Phoebe knew that she could not break her cycle without the risk of gaining weight. To avoid the communal bathroom, she went to a deserted place behind a nearby building to vomit.

She kept her secret until the beginning of her sophomore year, when her world fell apart. One night, after drinking beer and eating fried chicken at a party she attempted to cope with her guilt anxiety and tension in the usual manner, but when she tried to vomit, her gag reflex seemed to be gone. Breaking into tears, she called her boyfriend and told him she was ready to kill herself. Her loud sobbing and crying attracted the attention of her friends in her dormitory, who attempted to comfort her. She confessed her problem to them. She also called her parents. At this point, Phoebe realized that her life was out of control and that she needed professional help.

Clinical Description

The hallmark of bulimia nervosa is eating a larger amount of food—typically, more junk food than fruits and vegetables—than most people would eat under similar circumstances (Fairburn & Cooper, 2014; Treasure, Duarte, & Schmidt, 2020). Patients with bulimia readily identify with this description, even though the actual caloric intake for binges varies significantly from person to person (Franko, Wonderlich, Little, & Herzog, 2004). Just as important as the *amount* of food eaten is that the eating is experienced as *out of control* (Leslie, Lambert, & Treasure, 2019), a criterion that is an integral part of the definition of binge eating. Both criteria characterized Phoebe.

Another important criterion is that the individual attempts to *compensate* for the binge eating and potential weight gain, almost always by **purging techniques**. Techniques include self-induced vomiting immediately after eating, as in the case of Phoebe, and using laxatives (drugs that relieve constipation) and diuretics (drugs that result in loss of fluids through greatly increased frequency of urination). Some people use both methods; others attempt to compensate in other ways. Some exercise excessively (although rigorous exercising is more usually a characteristic of anorexia nervosa (Cook et al., 2016; Di Lodovico, Hatteea, Couton, Duriez, Treasure, & Gorwood, 2021). Others fast for long periods between binges. Bulimia nervosa was subtyped in DSM-IV-TR into *purging type* (for example, vomiting, laxatives, or diuretics) or *nonpurging type* (for example, exercise and/or fasting). But the nonpurging type has turned out to be quite rare, accounting for only 6% to 8% of patients with bulimia (Hay & Fairburn, 1998; Striegel-Moore et al., 2001). Furthermore, these studies found little evidence of any differences between purging and nonpurging types of bulimia, nor were any differences evident in severity of psychopathology, frequency of binge episodes, or prevalence of major depression and panic disorder (van Hoeken, Veling, Sinke, Mitchell, & Hoek, 2009). As a result, this distinction was dropped in DSM-5.

Purging is not a particularly efficient method of reducing caloric intake (Fairburn, 2013). Vomiting reduces approximately 50% of the calories just consumed—less if it is delayed at all (Kaye, Weltzin, Hsu, McConaha, & Bolton, 1993); laxatives and related procedures have little effect, acting, as they do, so long after the binge (Fairburn, 2013).

One of the more important additions to the DSM-IV criteria in 1994 was the specification of a psychological characteristic clearly present in Phoebe. Despite her accomplishments and success, she felt her continuing popularity and self-esteem would largely be determined by the weight and shape of her body. This is consistent with research suggesting that people with eating disorders have a distorted sense of self (Bardone-Cone, Thompson, & Miller, 2020; Mason et al., 2016; Lantz Lesser et al., 2021). A number of studies confirm that the major features of the disorder (bingeing, purging, overconcern with body shape, and so on) "cluster together" in someone with this problem, which strongly supports the validity of the diagnostic category (Bulik, Sullivan, & Kendler, 2000; Fairburn & Cooper, 2014; Fairburn, Stice, et al., 2003; Franko et al., 2004).

DSM 5 Table 8.1

Diagnostic Criteria for Bulimia Nervosa

A. Recurrent episodes of binge eating. An episode of binge eating is characterized by both of the following:

1. Eating, in a discrete period of time (e.g., within any 2-hour period), an amount of food that is definitely larger than most people would eat during a similar period of time under similar circumstances.
2. A sense of lack of control over eating during the episode (e.g., a feeling that one cannot stop eating or control what or how much one is eating).

B. Recurrent inappropriate compensatory behaviors in order to prevent weight gain, such as self-induced vomiting; misuse of laxatives, diuretics, or other medications; fasting; or excessive exercise.

C. The binge eating and inappropriate compensatory behaviors both occur, on average, at least once a week for 3 months.

D. Self-evaluation is unduly influenced by body shape and weight.

E. The disturbance does not occur exclusively during episodes of anorexia nervosa.

American Psychiatric Association. (2022). *Diagnostic and statistical manual of mental disorders* (5th ed., Text Revision).

Medical Consequences

Chronic bulimia with purging has a number of medical consequences (Mehler, 2017). One is salivary gland enlargement caused by repeated vomiting, which gives the face a chubby appearance. This was noticeable with Phoebe. Repeated vomiting also may erode the dental enamel on the inner surface of the front teeth as well as tear the esophagus. More important, continued vomiting may upset the chemical balance of bodily fluids, including sodium and potassium levels. This condition, called an *electrolyte imbalance*, can result in serious medical complications if unattended, including cardiac arrhythmia (disrupted heartbeat), seizures, and renal (kidney) failure, all of which can be fatal. Surprisingly, young women with bulimia also develop more body fat than age- and weight-matched healthy controls (Ludescher et al., 2009), the very effect they are trying to avoid! Normalization of eating habits will quickly reverse the imbalance. Intestinal problems resulting from laxative abuse are also potentially serious; they can include severe constipation or permanent colon damage. Finally, some individuals with bulimia have marked calluses on their fingers or the backs of their hands caused by the friction of contact with the teeth and throat when repeatedly sticking their fingers down their throat to stimulate the gag reflex.

Associated Psychological Disorders

An individual with bulimia usually presents with additional psychological disorders, particularly anxiety and mood disorders (Steiger et al., 2013; Swanson, Crow, Le Grange, Swendsen, & Merikangas, 2011; Sysko & Wilson, 2011; Treasure, Duarte, & Schmidt, 2020). Results from a definitive national survey on the prevalence of eating disorders and associated psychological disorders found that 80.6% of individuals with bulimia had an anxiety disorder at some point during their lives (Hudson et al., 2007), and 66% of adolescents with bulimia presented with a co-occurring anxiety disorder when interviewed (Swanson et al., 2011). But patients with anxiety disorders, on the other hand, do not necessarily have elevated rates of eating disorders (Schwalberg, Barlow, Alger, & Howard, 1992). Mood disorders, particularly depression, also commonly co-occur with bulimia, with about 20% of bulimic patients meeting criteria for a mood disorder when interviewed, and between 50% and 70% meeting criteria at some point during the course of their disorder (Hudson et al., 2007; Swanson et al., 2011).

For a number of years, one prominent theory suggested that eating disorders are simply a way of expressing depression. But most evidence indicates that depression *follows* bulimia and may be a reaction to it (Brownell & Fairburn, 1995; Steiger et al.,

Lady Gaga Talks Eating Disorders
Singer Reveals She Was Bulimic in High School

Lady Gaga battled bulimia during her teen years. In February 2012, she discussed her past eating disorders in an interview with Maria Shriver.

How and why did she have eating disorders? Gaga admitted, "I used to throw up all the time in high school. So I'm not that confident. I wanted to be a skinny little ballerina, but I was a voluptuous little Italian girl whose dad had meatballs on the table every night. I used to come home and say, 'Dad, why do you always give us this food? I need to be thin.' And he'd say, 'Eat your spaghetti.'"

What was her advice to those who have their own weight and body issues? Thoughtfully, she said, "It's really hard, but . . . you've got to talk to somebody about it. It made my voice bad, so I had to stop. The acid on your vocal cords . . . it's very bad."

Lady Gaga is famous, successful, talented, and idolized by many. But her struggle with weight, body issues, and confidence continues:

Karwai Tang/Getty Images

"Weight is still a struggle. Every video I'm in, every magazine cover, they stretch you —they make you perfect," she confessed. "It's not real life. I'm gonna say this about girls: The dieting has got to stop. Everyone just knock it off. Because at the end of the day, it's affecting kids your age—and it's making girls sick."

Interestingly, in 2010 Gaga told *New York* magazine, "Pop stars should not eat." The magazine dutifully mentioned that Gaga "looked flush from a strict diet of starvation."

Source: Adapted from http://www.huffingtonpost.com/2012/02/09/lady-gaga-reveals-she-was-bulimic-in-highschool_n_1266646.html

2013). Finally, substance abuse commonly accompanies bulimia nervosa. For example, Hudson and colleagues (2007) reported that 36.8% of individuals with bulimia and 27% of individuals with anorexia also had substance use disorders when interviewed, with even higher lifetime rates of substance use disorder. Wade, Bulik, Prescott, and Kendler (2004), in a twin study, found that shared risk factors of novelty seeking and emotional instability accounted for the high rates of comorbidity between bulimia and anxiety and substance use disorder, although these factors differed somewhat between men and women. In summary, bulimia seems strongly related to anxiety disorders and somewhat less so to mood and substance use disorders. Underlying traits of emotional instability and novelty seeking in these individuals may account for these patterns of comorbidity.

Anorexia Nervosa

Like Phoebe, the overwhelming majority of individuals with bulimia are within 10% of their normal weight (Fairburn & Cooper, 2014; Hsu, 1990). In contrast, individuals with anorexia nervosa (which literally means a "nervous loss of appetite"—an incorrect definition because appetite often remains healthy) differ in one important way from individuals with bulimia. People with anorexia are so successful at losing weight that they put their lives in considerable danger. Both anorexia and bulimia are characterized by a morbid fear of gaining weight and losing control over their eating. The major difference seems to be whether the individual is successful at losing weight. People with anorexia are proud of both their diets and their extraordinary control. People with bulimia are ashamed of both their eating issues and their lack of control (Blythin et al., 2020; Brownell & Fairburn, 1995). Consider the case of Zahra.

Zahra... The Thinner, the Better

Zahra was 17 years old when she first came for help. If you looked hard enough past her sunken eyes and pasty skin, you could see that she had once been attractive. But at present, she looked emaciated and unwell. Eighteen months earlier she had been overweight, weighing 140 pounds at 5 feet 1 inch. Her mother, a well-meaning but overbearing and demanding woman, criticized Julie Zahra incessantly about her appearance. Her friends were kinder but no less relentless. Zahra, who had never had a date, was told by a friend she was cute and would have no trouble getting dates if she lost some weight. So she did! After many previous unsuccessful attempts, she was determined to succeed this time.

After several weeks on a strict diet, Zahra noticed she was losing weight. She felt a control and mastery that she had never known before. It wasn't long before she received positive comments, not only from her friends but also from her mother. Zahra began to feel good about herself. The difficulty was that she was losing weight too fast. She stopped menstruating. But now nothing could stop her from dieting. By the time she reached our clinic, she weighed 75 pounds but she thought she looked fine and, perhaps, could even stand to lose a bit more weight. Her parents had just begun to worry about her. Zahra did not initially seek treatment for her eating behavior. Rather, she had developed a numbness in her left lower leg and a left foot drop —an inability to lift up the front part of the foot—that a neurologist determined was caused by peritoneal nerve paralysis believed to be related to inadequate nutrition. The neurologist referred her to our clinic.

Like most people with anorexia, Zahra said she probably should put on a little weight, but she didn't mean it. She thought she looked fine, but she had "lost all taste for food," a report that may not have been true because most people with anorexia crave food at least some of the time but control their cravings. Nevertheless, she was participating in most of her usual activities and continued to do extremely well in school and in her extracurricular pursuits. Her parents were happy to buy her most of the workout videotapes available, and she began doing one every day and then two. When her parents suggested she was exercising enough, perhaps too much, she worked out when no one was around. After every meal, she exercised with a workout tape until, in her mind, she burned up all the calories she had just taken in.

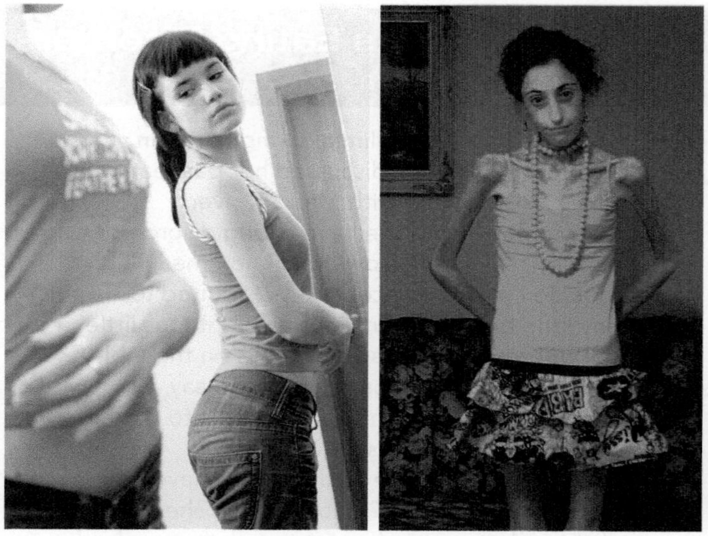

Banos/Alamy Stock Photo

Fairfax Media/Getty Images

These women are at different stages of anorexia.

The tragic consequences of anorexia among young celebrities and within the modeling world have been well publicized in the media. In November 2010, 28-year-old French model and actress Isabelle Caro died, weighing 93 pounds. At 5 feet 5 inches, she had a BMI of 15.47 (16 is considered starvation). Around 2006, first Spain, then Italy, Brazil, and India, instituted bans on models with BMIs less than 18 from their top fashion shows (30% of models in Spain were turned away). In 2015, France instituted a similar ban. It is not clear yet whether the bans have impacted popular perception of ideal body size in these countries.

Clinical Description

Anorexia nervosa is less common than bulimia, but there is a great deal of overlap. For example, many individuals with bulimia have a history of anorexia; that is, they once used fasting to reduce their body weight below desirable levels (Fairburn & Cooper, 2014; Fairburn, Welch, et al., 1997).

David Gray/Reuters/Landov/Getty Images

Before her death at age 28, French model Isabelle Caro contributed to advertisements warning against the dangers of anorexia nervosa.

Although decreased body weight is the most notable feature of anorexia nervosa, it is not the core of the disorder. Many people lose weight because of a medical condition, but people with anorexia have an intense fear of obesity and relentlessly pursue thinness (Fairburn & Cooper, 2014; Hsu, 1990; Russell, 2009). As with Zahra, the disorder most commonly begins in an adolescent who is overweight or who perceives herself to be. She then starts a diet that escalates into an obsessive preoccupation with being thin. As we noted, severe, almost punishing exercise is common (Davis et al., 1997; Russell, 2009), as with Zahra. Dramatic weight loss is achieved through severe caloric restriction or by combining caloric restriction and purging.

DSM-5 specifies two subtypes of anorexia nervosa. In the *restricting type*, individuals diet to limit calorie intake; in the *binge-eating–purging type*, they rely on purging. Unlike individuals with bulimia, binge-eating–purging anorexics binge on relatively small amounts of food and purge more consistently, in some cases each time they eat. Approximately half the individuals who meet criteria for anorexia engage in binge eating and purging (Fairburn & Cooper, 2014). Prospective data collected over 8 years on 136 individuals with anorexia reveal few differences between these two subtypes on severity of symptoms or personality (Eddy et al., 2002). At that time, fully 62% of the restricting subtype had begun bingeing or purging. Another study showed few differences between these subtypes and comorbidity with anxiety disorders (Kaye et al., 2014). Thus, subtyping may not be useful in predicting the future course of the disorder but rather may reflect a certain phase or stage of anorexia (Eddy et al., 2008). For this reason, DSM-5 criteria specify that subtyping refer only to the past 3 months (Peat, Mitchell, Hoek, & Wonderlich, 2009).

Individuals with anorexia are never satisfied with their weight loss. Staying the same weight from one day to the next or gaining any weight is likely to cause intense panic, anxiety, and depression. Only continued weight loss every day for weeks on end is satisfactory. Although DSM-5 criteria specify only "significantly low" body weight 15% below that expected, one study suggests that BMI averages close to 15.8 by the time treatment is sought (Berner, Shaw, Witt, & Lowe, 2013). Another key criterion of anorexia is a marked disturbance in body image. When Zahra looked at herself in the mirror, she saw something different from what others saw. They saw an emaciated, sickly, frail girl in the

DSM 5 **Table 8.2**
Diagnostic Criteria for Anorexia Nervosa

A. Restriction of energy intake relative to requirements, leading to a significantly low body weight in the context of age, sex, developmental trajectory, and physical health. *Significantly low weight* is defined as a weight that is less than minimally normal or, for children and adolescents, less than that minimally expected.

B. Intense fear of gaining weight or of becoming fat, or persistent behavior that interferes with weight gain, even though at a significantly low weight.

C. Disturbance in the way in which one's body weight or shape is experienced, undue influence of body weight or shape on self-evaluation, or persistent lack of recognition of the seriousness of the current low body weight.

Specify whether:

Restricting type: During the past 3 months, the individual has not engaged in recurrent episodes of binge eating or purging behavior (i.e., self-induced vomiting or the misuse of laxatives, diuretics, or enemas). This subtype describes presentations in which weight loss is accomplished primarily through dieting, fasting, and/or excessive exercise.

Binge-eating/purging type: During the past 3 months, the individual has engaged in recurrent episodes of binge eating or purging behavior (i.e., self-induced vomiting or the misuse of laxatives, diuretics, or enemas).

American Psychiatric Association. (2022). *Diagnostic and statistical manual of mental disorders* (5th ed., Text Revision).

throes of semistarvation. Zahra saw a girl who still needed to lose at least a few pounds from some parts of her body. For Zahra, her face and buttocks were the problems. Other people might focus on other parts, such as the arms or legs or stomach.

After seeing numerous doctors, people like Zahra become good at mouthing what others expect to hear. They may agree they are underweight and need to gain a few pounds—but they do not really believe it themselves. When questioned further, they will tell you the girl in the mirror is fat. Therefore, individuals with anorexia seldom seek treatment on their own. Usually, pressure from somebody in the family leads to the initial visit (Agras, 1987; Fairburn & Cooper, 2014), as in Zahra's case. Perhaps as a demonstration of absolute control over their eating, some individuals with anorexia show increased interest in cooking and food. Some have become expert chefs, preparing all food for the family. Others hoard food in their rooms, looking at it occasionally.

Medical Consequences

One common medical complication of anorexia nervosa is cessation of menstruation (amenorrhea), which also occurs relatively often in bulimia (Crow, Thuras, Keel, & Mitchell, 2002). This feature can be an objective physical index of the degree of food restriction but is inconsistent because it does not occur in all cases (Franko et al., 2004). Because of this inconsistency, amenorrhea was dropped as a diagnostic criterion in DSM-5 (Attia & Roberto, 2009; Fairburn & Cooper, 2014). Other medical signs and symptoms of anorexia include dry skin, brittle hair or nails, and sensitivity to or intolerance of cold temperatures. Also, it is relatively common to see *lanugo*, downy hair on the limbs and cheeks. Cardiovascular problems, such as chronically low blood pressure and heart rate, can also result. If vomiting is part of the anorexia, electrolyte imbalance and resulting cardiac and kidney problems can result, as in bulimia (Mehler et al., 2017).

Associated Psychological Disorders

As with bulimia nervosa, anxiety disorders and mood disorders are often present in individuals with anorexia (Agras, 2001; Russell, 2009; Sysko & Wilson, 2011), with rates of depression occurring at some point during their lives in as many as 71% of cases (Godart et al., 2007). One anxiety disorder that seems to co-occur often with anorexia is obsessive-compulsive disorder (OCD) (see Chapter 5; Cederlöf et al., 2015; Keel et al., 2004; Kaye et al., 2014). In anorexia, unpleasant thoughts are focused on gaining weight, and individuals engage in a variety of behaviors, some of them ritualistic, to rid themselves of such thoughts. A large genetic study pointed to some shared genetic risk markers, together with some other disorders, such as bipolar disorder (Yilman et al. 2020). Substance abuse is also common in individuals with anorexia nervosa (Keel et al., 2003; Root et al., 2010; Swanson et al., 2011) and, in conjunction with anorexia, is a strong predictor of mortality, particularly by suicide.

Binge-Eating Disorder

Beginning in the 1990s, research focused on a group of individuals who experience marked distress because of binge eating but do *not* engage in extreme compensatory behaviors and therefore cannot be diagnosed with bulimia (Castonguay, Eldredge, & Agras, 1995; Fairburn et al., 1998). These individuals have binge-eating disorder (BED). After classification in DSM-IV as a disorder needing further study, BED is now included as a full-fledged disorder in DSM-5 (Wonderlich, Gordon, Mitchell, Crosby, & Engel, 2009). Evidence that supports its elevation to disorder status includes somewhat different patterns of heritability compared with other eating disorders (Bulik et al., 2000; Thornton, Mazzeo, & Bulik, 2010), as well as a greater likelihood of occurring in males and a later age of onset. There is also a greater likelihood of remission and a better response to treatment in BED compared with other eating disorders (Striegel-Moore & Franko, 2008; Wonderlich et al., 2009). Individuals who meet preliminary criteria for BED are often found in weight-control programs. For example, Brody, Walsh, and Devlin (1994) studied mildly obese participants in a weight-control program and identified 18.8% who met criteria for BED. In other programs, with participants ranging in degree of obesity, close to 30% met criteria (see, for example, Spitzer et al., 1993). But Hudson and colleagues (2006) concluded that BED is a disorder caused by a separate set of factors from obesity without BED and is associated with more severe obesity. The general consensus is that about 20% of obese individuals in weight-loss programs engage in binge eating, with the number rising to approximately 50% among candidates for bariatric surgery (surgery to correct severe or morbid obesity).

Fairburn, Cooper, Doll, Norman, and O'Connor (2000) identified 48 individuals with BED and were able to prospectively follow 40 of them for 5 years. The prognosis was relatively good for this group, with only 18% retaining the full diagnostic criteria for BED at a 5-year follow-up. The percentage of this group that was obese, however, increased from 21% to 39% at the 5-year mark, and crossing over to bulimia is very common among individuals with BED (Allen, Byrne, Oddy, & Crosby, 2013; Stice, Marti, & Rohde, 2013).

About half of individuals with BED try dieting before bingeing, and half start with bingeing and then attempt to diet (Abbott et al., 1998); those who begin bingeing first become more severely affected by BED and are more likely to have additional disorders (Brewerton, Rance, Dansky, O'Neil, & Kilpatrick, 2014; Spurrell, Wilfley, Tanofsky, & Brownell, 1997). It's also increasingly clear that individuals with BED have some of the same concerns about shape and weight as people with anorexia and bulimia, which distinguishes them from individuals who are obese without BED (Fairburn & Cooper, 2014; Goldschmidt et al., 2010; Grilo, Masheb, & White, 2010; Steiger et al., 2013). It also seems that approximately 33% of those with BED binge to alleviate "bad moods" or negative affect (see, for example, Grilo, Masheb, & Wilson, 2001; Steiger et al., 2013; Stice, Akutagawa, Gaggar, & Agras, 2000). These individuals are more psychologically disturbed than the 67% who do not use bingeing to regulate mood (Grilo et al., 2001).

Some individuals may engage in purging behavior to influence their weight or shape by self-induced vomiting, using laxatives, diuretics, or other medications, but they do not show binge eating as in BED or behaviors typical for other eating disorders. These individuals might meet criteria for another DSM-5 eating disorder, **purging disorder** (Keel, 2019)

To examine predictors of eating problems, young women with body dissatisfaction (n = 1,272) were followed up over a 3-year period (Stice, Gau, Rohde, & Shaw, 2017). The results showed that negative affect and functional impairment predicted all DSM-5 eating disorders and that the internalization of the thin-ideal, body dissatisfaction, dieting, overeating, and mental health care predicted bulimia nervosa, binge-eating disorder, and purging disorder. Low BMI and dieting specifically predicted anorexia nervosa.

DSM 5 **Table 8.3**

Diagnostic Criteria for Binge-Eating Disorder

A. Recurrent episodes of binge eating. An episode of binge eating is characterized by both of the following:

1. Eating, in a discrete period of time (e.g., within any 2-hour period), an amount of food that is definitely larger than what most people would eat in a similar period of time under similar circumstances.
2. A sense of lack of control over eating during the episode (e.g., a feeling that one cannot stop eating or control what or how much one is eating).

B. The binge-eating episodes are associated with three (or more) of the following:

1. Eating much more rapidly than normal.
2. Eating until feeling uncomfortably full.
3. Eating large amounts of food when not feeling physically hungry.
4. Eating alone because of feeling embarrassed by how much one is eating.
5. Feeling disgusted with oneself, depressed, or very guilty afterward.

C. Marked distress regarding binge eating is present.

D. The binge eating occurs, on average, at least once a week for 3 months.

E. The binge eating is not associated with the recurrent use of inappropriate compensatory behavior as in bulimia nervosa and does not occur exclusively during the course of bulimia nervosa or anorexia nervosa.

American Psychiatric Association. (2022). *Diagnostic and statistical manual of mental disorders* (5th ed., Text Revision).

Statistics

Clear cases of bulimia have been described for thousands of years (Parry-Jones & Parry-Jones, 2002), but bulimia nervosa was recognized as a distinct psychological disorder only in the 1970s (Boskind-Lodahl, 1976; Russell, 1979). Therefore, information on prevalence has been acquired relatively recently.

Among those who present for treatment, the overwhelming majority (90% to 95%) of individuals with bulimia are women. Males with bulimia have a slightly later age of onset, and a large minority are predominantly gay males, bisexual, and transgender (Matthews-Ewald, 2014; Nagata, Ganson, & Austin, 2020; Rothblum, 2002). For example, in their review, Nagata et al. (2020) found that the lifetime prevalence rates of anorexia nervosa, bulimia nervosa, and binge-eating disorder are higher in sexual minority groups as compared to the sexual majority group and that body dissatisfaction seems to be a particular stressor experienced by transgender people.

Male athletes in sports that require weight regulation—such as wrestling, baseball, and cycling—are another large group of males with eating disorders (Nagata, Gansen, & Murray, 2021; Ricciardelli & McCabe, 2004). During 1998, stories were widely published about the deaths of three wrestlers from complications of eating disorders. In fact, the incidence among males is increasing (Dominé, Berchtold, Akré, Michaud, & Suris, 2009), with one study showing 0.8% of a large group of males having at least some of the symptoms of bulimia and another 2.9% having at least some of the symptoms of BED (Field et al., 2014). The gender imbalance in bulimia was not always present. Historians of psychopathology note that for hundreds of years, the vast majority of (unsystematically) recorded cases were male (Parry-Jones & Parry-Jones, 1994, 2002). Because women with bulimia are more common today, most of our examples are women.

Among women, adolescent girls are most at risk. A prospective 8-year survey of 496 adolescent girls reported that more than 13% experienced some form of eating disorder by the time they were 20 (Stice, Marti, Shaw, & Jaconis, 2009; Stice et al., 2013). In another elegant prospective study, eating-related problems of 1,498 freshmen women at a large university were studied over the 4-year college experience. Only 28% to 34% had no eating-related concerns. But 29% to 34% consistently attempted to limit their food intake because of weight/shape concerns; 14% to 18% engaged in overeating and binge eating; another 14% to 17% combined attempts to limit intake with binge eating; and 6% to 7% had pervasive bulimic-like concerns. And these tendencies were stable for the most part throughout their 4 years of college (Cain, Epler, Steinley, & Sher, 2010).

A somewhat different view of the prevalence of bulimia comes from studies of the population rather than of specific groups of adolescents, with the most definitive study appearing in 2007 (Hudson et al., 2007). These results from the National Comorbidity Survey reflect lifetime and 12-month prevalence, not only for the three major eating disorders described here but also for "subthreshold" BED, where binge eating occurred at a high-enough frequency but some additional criteria, such as "marked distress" regarding the binge eating, were not met. Therefore, the disorder did not meet the diagnostic "threshold" for BED. Although the study was conducted prior to the publication of DSM-5, the 3-month duration required for BED (or subthreshold BED), found in DSM-5, rather than the 6 months required in DSM-IV-TR, was used. Finally, if binge eating occurred at least twice a week for 3 months—even if it was just a symptom of the four other disorders in Table 8.2 rather than a separate condition—the case was listed under "Any binge eating." This latter category provides an overall picture of the prevalence of binge eating.

These data are all presented in Table 8.2. As you can see, lifetime prevalence was consistently two to three times greater for women, with the exception of subthreshold BED. This sex ratio reflects a somewhat higher proportion of men than found in other samples, but it agrees with data from the study mentioned above by Field and colleagues (2014), showing that some binge-eating symptoms are relatively common in males. No 12-month cases of anorexia were found in this sample, but a large study in Finland based on a telephone survey found a higher lifetime prevalence of anorexia of 2.2%, and half those cases had not been detected in the health-care system (Keski-Rahkonen et al., 2007). So it is possible that the prevalence of anorexia is underrepresented in some surveys. In the adolescent supplement to the National Comorbidity Survey that reports results just for adolescents from ages 13 to 18, lifetime prevalence rates were 0.3% for anorexia (compared with 0.6% for the full age range in Table 8.2), 0.9 % for bulimia (compared with 1.0 % in Table 8.2), and 1.6% for BED (compared with 2.8 % in Table 8.2) (Swanson et al., 2011). This suggests that many cases of anorexia and BED, but not bulimia, begin after age 18.

Table 8.2 Lifetime and 12-Month Prevalence Estimates of DSM-IV-TR Eating Disorders and Related Problems

	Male	Female	Total
	%	%	%
I. Lifetime prevalence			
Anorexia nervosa	0.3	0.9	0.6
Bulimia nervosa	0.5	1.5	1.0
Binge-eating disorder	2.0	3.5	2.8
Subthreshold binge-eating disorder	1.9	0.6	1.2
Any binge eating	4.0	4.9	4.5
II. 12-month prevalence*			
Bulimia nervosa	0.1	0.5	0.3
Binge-eating disorder	0.8	1.6	1.2
Subthreshold binge-eating disorder	0.8	0.4	0.6
Any binge eating	1.7	2.5	2.1
(n) Number of participants	(1,220)	(1,760)	(2,980)

*None of the respondents met criteria for 12-month anorexia nervosa.

Source: From Hudson et al., 2007, The prevalence and correlates of eating disorders in the national comorbidity survey replication, *Biological Psychiatry, 61*, 348–358. © Society for Biological Psychiatry.

The median age of onset for all eating-related disorders occurred in a narrow range of 18 to 21 years (Hudson et al., 2007; Stice et al., 2013). For anorexia, this age of onset was fairly consistent, with younger cases tending to begin at age 15, but it was more common for cases of bulimia to begin as early as age 10, as it did for Phoebe.

Once bulimia develops, it tends to be chronic if untreated (Fairburn, Stice, et al., 2003; Hudson et al., 2007). In an important study of the course of bulimia, referred to earlier, Fairburn and colleagues (2000) identified a group of 102 females with bulimia nervosa and followed 92 of them prospectively for 5 years. About a third improved to the point where they no longer met diagnostic criteria each year, but another third who had improved previously relapsed. Between 50% and 67% exhibited serious eating disorder symptoms at the end of each year of the 5-year study, indicating this disorder has a relatively poor prognosis. In a follow-up study, Fairburn, Stice, and colleagues (2003) reported that the strongest predictors of persistent bulimia were a history of childhood obesity and a continuing overemphasis on the importance of being thin. In addition, individuals tend to retain their bulimic symptoms instead of shifting to symptoms of other eating disorders (Eddy et al., 2008; Keel et al., 2000).

Similarly, once anorexia develops, its course seems chronic—although not so chronic as bulimia, based on data from Hudson and colleagues (2007), particularly if it is caught early and treated. But individuals with anorexia tend to maintain a low BMI over a long period, along with distorted perceptions of shape and weight, indicating that even if they no longer meet criteria for anorexia, they continue to restrict their eating (Fairburn & Cooper, 2014). Perhaps for this reason, anorexia is thought to be more resistant to treatment than bulimia, based on clinical studies (Vitiello & Lederhendler, 2000). In one 7-year study following individuals who had received treatment, 33% of those with anorexia versus 66% of those with bulimia reached full remission at some point during the follow-up (Eddy et al., 2008).

Cross-Cultural Considerations

We have already discussed the highly culturally specific nature of anorexia and bulimia. A review of the literature shows that White individuals report more eating disturbance than non-Whites, especially among college samples (Wildes, Emery, & Simons, 2001). A particularly striking finding is that these disorders develop in immigrants who have recently moved to Western countries

(Anderson-Fye, 2009). One of the more interesting classic studies is Nasser's survey of 50 Egyptian women in London universities and 60 Egyptian women in Cairo universities (Nasser, 1988). There were no instances of eating disorders in Cairo, but 12% of the Egyptian women in England had developed eating disorders. Mumford, Whitehouse, and Platts (1991) found comparable results with Asian women living in the United States.

Later, we discuss the increase in obesity among recent immigrant groups to the United States that also seems to illustrate cultural contributions to eating problems (Goel, McCarthy, Phillips, & Wee, 2004). The prevalence of eating disorders varies somewhat among most North American people of color, including African Americans, Hispanics, Native Americans, and Asians. Earlier surveys revealed that African American adolescent girls have less body dissatisfaction, fewer weight concerns, and a more positive self-image and perceive themselves to be thinner than they are, compared with the attitudes of White adolescent girls (Celio, Zabinski, & Wilfley, 2002). Another study (Hoek et al., 2005) on the small relatively isolated Caribbean island of Curaçao in the Netherlands Antilles, where the population is only approximately 150,000, found that the incidence of anorexia from 1995 to 1998 was zero among the majority Black population but approached levels observed in the Netherlands and United States for the minority White and multiracial population.

Several years ago, Striegel-Moore and colleagues (2003) surveyed 985 White women and 1,061 Black women who had participated in a 10-year government study on growth and health and who were now 21 years old on average. The number in each group who developed anorexia, bulimia, or BED during that 10-year period is presented in ■ Figure 8.1. Major risk factors for eating

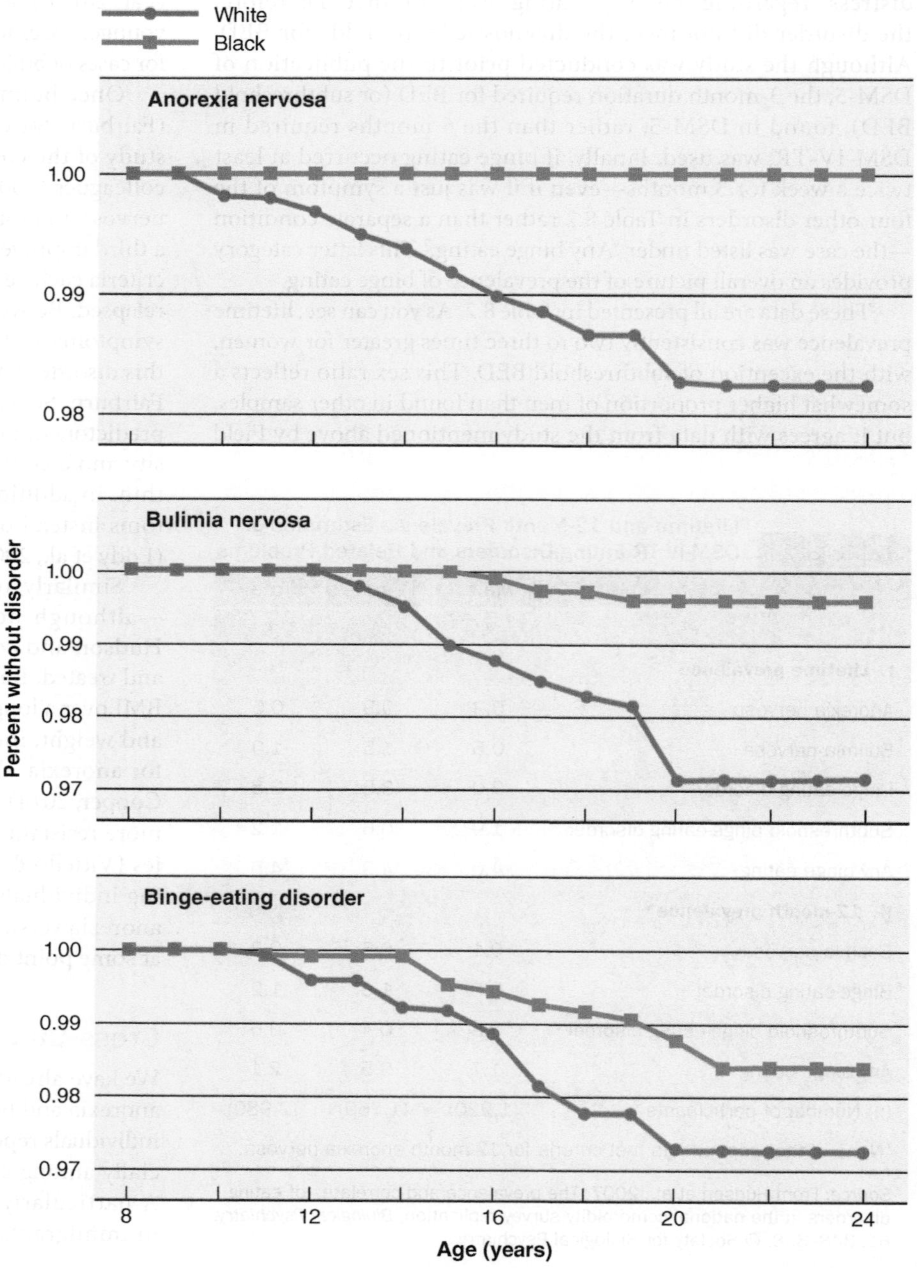

Figure 8.1

Time to onset over 10 years of anorexia nervosa, bulimia nervosa, and BED for 2,046 white and black women, age 19–24 years, who ever met the DSM-IV criteria for each eating disorder. Reprinted, with permission, from R. H. Striegel-Moore, F. A. Dohm, H. C. Kraemer, C. B. Taylor, S. Daniels, P. B. Crawford, & G. B. Schreiber, 2003, Eating disorders in white and black women, *American Journal of Psychiatry, 160*(7), 1329. © 2003 American Psychiatric Press.

disorders in all groups included being overweight, higher social class, and acculturation to the majority (Crago et al., 1997; Grabe & Hyde, 2006; Wilfley & Rodin, 1995). Chao et al. (2008) observe that compared to White women, African American women feel less pressure to lose weight and are more satisfied and comfortable with their bodies, which may contribute to the somewhat lower incidence of eating disorders in African American women. But some of these ethnic differences may be changing. Marques and colleagues (2011) found that the prevalence of eating disorders is now more similar among non-Hispanic Whites, African American, Asian American, and Hispanic females. Eating disorders are generally more common among Native Americans than other ethnic groups (Crago, Shisslak, & Estes, 1997). Body dissatisfaction and desire for thinness is commonly reported by women in high-SES settings across world regions (Swami et al, 2020).

In conclusion, anorexia and bulimia are relatively homogeneous, and both—particularly bulimia—were overwhelmingly associated with Western cultures until recently. In addition, the frequency and pattern of occurrence among minority Western cultures differed somewhat in the past, but those differences seem to be diminishing (Marques et al., 2011; Pike, Hoek, & Dunne, 2014).

Developmental Considerations

Because the overwhelming majority of cases begin in adolescence, it is clear that anorexia and bulimia are strongly related to development (Smith, Simmons, Flory, Annus, & Hill, 2007; Steiger et al., 2013). As pointed out in classic studies by Striegel-Moore, Silberstein, and Rodin (1986) and Attie and Brooks-Gunn (1995), differential patterns of physical development in girls and boys interact with cultural influences to create eating disorders. After puberty, girls gain weight primarily in fat tissue, whereas boys develop muscle and lean tissue. As the ideal look in Western countries is tall and muscular for men and thin and prepubertal for women, physical development brings boys closer to the ideal and takes girls further away.

Eating disorders, particularly anorexia nervosa, occasionally occur in children under the age of 11 (Walsh, 2010). In those rare cases of young children developing anorexia, they are likely to restrict fluid intake, as well as food intake, perhaps not understanding the difference (Gislason, 1988; Walsh, 2010). This is particularly dangerous. Concerns about weight are somewhat less common in young children. Nevertheless, negative attitude toward being overweight emerges as early as 3 years of age, and more than half of girls age 6 to 8 would like to be thinner (Striegel-Moore & Franko, 2002). By 9 years of age, 20% of girls reported trying to lose weight, and by 14, 40% were trying to lose weight (Field et al., 1999). Another study that followed girls and boys for 10 years starting around age 12

Concept Check 8.1

Check your understanding of eating disorders by identifying the proper disorder in the following scenarios: (a) bulimia nervosa, (b) anorexia nervosa, and (c) binge-eating disorder.

1. Manny has been having episodes lately when he eats prodigious amounts of food. He's been putting on a lot of weight because of it. ____________
2. I noticed Elena eating a whole pie, a cake, and two bags of potato chips the other day when she didn't know I was there. She ran to the bathroom when she was finished and it sounded like she was vomiting. This disorder can lead to an electrolyte imbalance, resulting in serious medical problems. ____________
3. Joo-Yeon eats large quantities of food in a short time. She then takes laxatives and exercises for long periods to prevent weight gain. She has been doing this almost daily for several months and feels she will become worthless and ugly if she gains even an ounce. ____________
4. Kirsten has lost several pounds and now weighs less than 90 pounds. She eats only a small portion of the food her father serves her and fears that intake above her current 500 calories daily will make her fat. Since losing the weight, Kirsten has stopped having periods. She sees a fat person in the mirror. ____________

Olesia Bilkei/Shutterstock.com

Anorexia seldom occurs among North American Black women.

found that about 55% of the girls at age 12 were dieting, and about 59% were dieting at age 22. Further, they found that extreme weight control behaviors increased over time in this group with a particular increase between adolescence and young adulthood (Neumark-Sztainer, Wall, Larson, Eisenberg, & Loth, 2011).

Both bulimia and anorexia can occur in later years, particularly after the age of 55. Hsu and Zimmer (1988) reported that most of these individuals had had an eating disorder for decades with little change in their behavior. In a few cases, however, onset did not occur until later years, and it is not yet clear what factors were involved. Generally, concerns about body image decrease with age (Peat, Peyeri, & Muehlenkamp, 2008; Tiggemann & Lynch, 2001; Whitbourne & Skultety, 2002).

Causes of Eating Disorders

As with all disorders discussed in this book, biological, psychological, and social factors contribute to the development of these serious eating disorders. The evidence is increasingly clear, however, that the most dramatic factors are social and cultural.

Social Dimensions

Remember that anorexia and particularly bulimia are the most culturally specific psychological disorders yet identified. What drives so many young people into a punishing and life-threatening routine of semistarvation or purging? For many young women, being seen as thin is more important than being healthy. For young women in competitive environments, self-worth, happiness, and success are largely determined by body measurements and percentage of body fat, factors that have little or no correlation with personal happiness and success in the long run. The cultural imperative for thinness directly results in dieting, the first dangerous step down the slippery slope to anorexia and bulimia.

Levine and Smolak (1996) referred to "the glorification of slenderness" in magazines and on television, where most females are thinner than the average American woman. Because overweight men are two to five times more common as television characters than overweight women, the message from the media to be thin is clearly aimed at women, and the message continues to get through loud and clear. Grabe, Ward, and Hyde (2008), reviewing 77 studies, demonstrated a strong relationship between exposure to media images depicting the thin-ideal body and body image concerns in women. An analysis of prime-time situation comedies revealed that 12% of female characters were dieting and many were making disparaging comments about their body image (Tiggemann, 2002). An analysis of images of women in *Ebony* magazine, which has wide African American readership, generally does not show this thin-ideal body image, seemingly reflecting the somewhat lower prevalence of body image disturbances in African American women (Thompson-Brenner, Boisseau, & St. Paul, 2011). Finally, Thompson and Stice (2001) found that risk for developing eating disorders was directly related to the extent to which women internalize or "buy in" to media messages and images glorifying thinness, a finding also confirmed by Cafri, Yamamiya, Brannick, and Thompson (2005), as well as Keel and Forney (2013).

The problem with today's standards is that they are increasingly difficult to achieve because the size and weight of the average woman has increased over the years with improved nutrition; there is also a general increase in size throughout history (Brownell, 1991; Brownell & Rodin, 1994). Whatever the cause, the collision between our culture and our physiology (Brownell, 1991; Fairburn & Brownell, 2002) has had some negative effects, one of which is that women became dissatisfied with their bodies.

In a classic case study, Fallon and Rozin (1985), studying male and female undergraduates, found that men rated their current size, their ideal size, and the size they figured would be most attractive to the opposite sex as approximately equal. Indeed, they rated their ideal body weight as *heavier* than the weight females thought most attractive in men (see ■ Figure 8.2). Women, however, rated their current figures as much heavier than what they judged the most attractive, which in turn, was rated as heavier than what they thought was ideal. This is a well-replicated finding (Novella, Gosselin, & Danowski, 2015). This conflict between reality and fashion seems most closely related to the current epidemic of eating disorders.

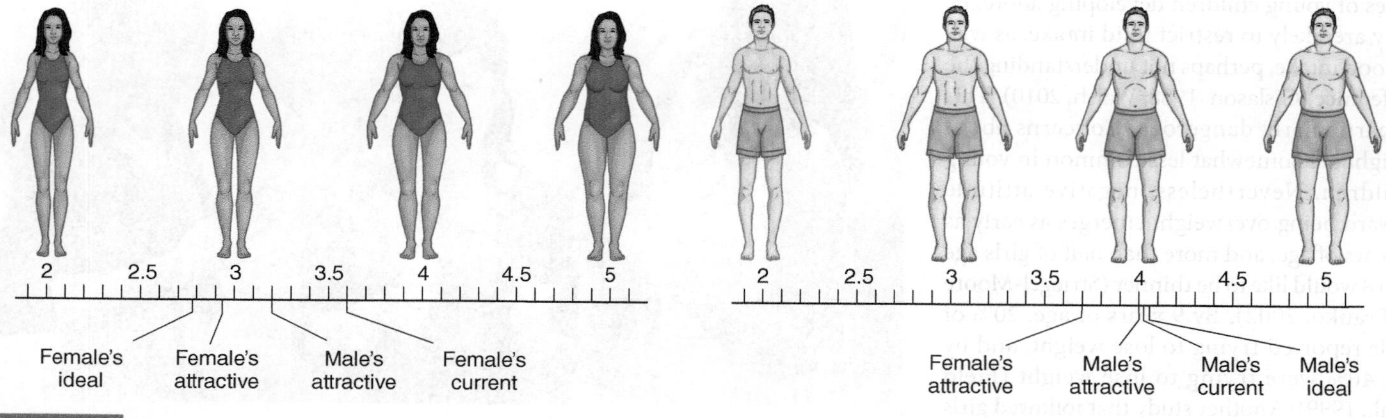

Figure 8.2
Male and female ratings of body size. Based on Fallon & Rozin (1985).

Other researchers have presented interesting data that support Fallon and Rozin's findings that men have different body image perceptions than women. Several studies confirmed that men generally desire to be heavier and more muscular than they are, (Grogan, 2016; Field et al., 2014; Neumark-Sztainer & Eisenberg, 2014). For example, when presented with thin to muscular images, college-age men tend to overestimate the degree of musculature women find attractive, and they tend to choose an ideal image that is more muscular than they currently are (Grossbard, Neighbors, & Larimer, 2011). Pope and colleagues, (2000) measured the height, weight, and body fat of college-age men in three countries —Austria, France, and the United States. They asked the men to choose the body image that they felt represented (1) their own body, (2) the body they ideally would like to have, (3) the body of an average man of their age, and (4) the male body they believed was preferred by women. In all three countries, men chose an ideal body weight that was approximately 28 pounds more muscular than their current one. They also estimated that women would prefer a male body about 30 pounds more muscular than their current one. In contradiction to this impression in men, Pope and colleagues (2000) demonstrated, in a pilot study, that most women preferred an ordinary male body without the added muscle. Men who abuse anabolic–androgenic steroids to increase muscle mass and "bulk up" possess these distorted attitudes toward muscles, weight, and the "ideal man" to a greater degree than men who don't use steroids (Kanayama, Barry, & Pope, 2006), and utilizing these unhealthy substances can lead to other serious problems such as binge drinking or other drug addictions (Field et al., 2014; Neumark-Sztainer & Eisenberg, 2014).

We have some specific information on how these attitudes are socially transmitted in adolescent girls. In an early study, Paxton, Schutz, Wertheim, and Muir (1999) explored the influence of close friendship groups on attitudes concerning body image, dietary restraint, and extreme weight-loss behaviors. In a clever experiment, the authors identified 79 different friendship cliques in a group of 523 adolescent girls. They found that these friendship cliques tended to share the same attitudes toward body image, dietary restraint, and the importance of attempts to lose weight. They assumed from the study that these friendship cliques are significantly associated with individual body image concerns and eating behaviors. In other words, if your friends tend to use extreme dieting or other weight-loss techniques, there is a greater chance that you will, too (Hutchinson & Rapee, 2007). While young girls do tend to share body image concerns, these friendship cliques do not necessarily cause these attitudes or the disordered eating that follows. Rather, adolescent girls simply tend to choose friends who already share these attitudes (Rayner, Schniering, Rapee, Taylor, & Hutchinson, 2012). Nevertheless, any attempts to treat eating disorders must take into account the influence of the social network in maintaining these attitudes.

Courtesy of Kelly Brownell

Kelly Brownell documented the collision between culture and physiology that results in overwhelming pressure to be thinner.

The dangerous obsession with body weight can have tragic consequences. In one early study, toddlers with affluent parents appeared at hospitals with "failure to thrive" syndrome, in which growth and development are severely stunted because of inadequate nutrition. In each case, the parents had put their young, healthy, but somewhat chubby toddlers on diets in the hope of preventing obesity at a later date (Pugliese, Weyman-Daun, Moses, & Lifshitz, 1987). Mothers who have anorexia restrict food intake in not only themselves but also their children, sometimes to the detriment of their children's health (Russell, 2009).

Most people who diet don't develop eating disorders, but Patton, Johnson-Sabine, Wood, Mann, and Wakeling (1990) determined in a prospective study that adolescent girls who dieted were eight times more likely to develop an eating disorder 1 year later than those who weren't dieting. And Telch and Agras (1993) noted marked increases in bingeing during and after rigorous dieting in 201 obese women.

Stice and colleagues (1999) demonstrated that one of the reasons attempts to lose weight may lead to eating disorders is that weight-reduction efforts in adolescent girls are more likely to result in weight *gain* than weight loss! To establish this finding, 692 girls, initially the same weight, were followed for 4 years. Girls who attempted dieting faced more than 300% greater risk of obesity than those who did not diet. Results are presented in ■ Figure 8.3.

Why does dieting cause weight gain? Cottone and colleagues (2009) began feeding rats junk food, which the rats came to love, instead of a boring diet of pellets. They then withdrew the junk food but not the pellets. Based on observations of brain function compared with rats who never had junk food, it was clear that these rats became extremely stressed and anxious. Furthermore, the "junk food" rats began eating more of the pellets than the control group;

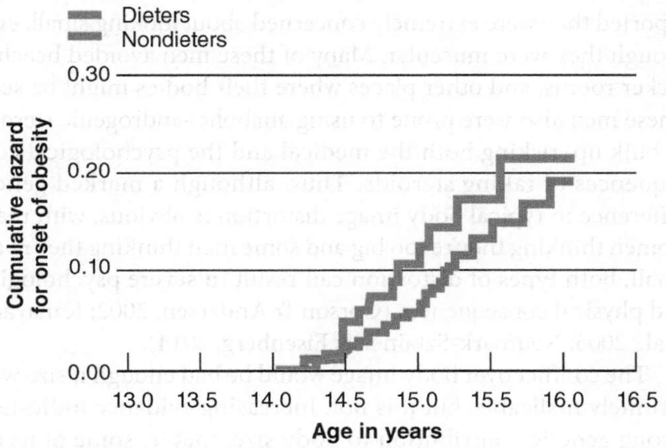

Figure 8.3

The onset of obesity over 4 years for self-labeled dieters versus self-labeled nondieters. From E. Stice, R. P. Cameron, J. D. Killen, C. Hayward, & C. B. Taylor, 1999, Naturalistic weight-reduction efforts prospectively predict growth in relative weight and onset of obesity among female adolescents, *Journal of Consulting and Clinical Psychology, 67*, 967–974.

Peter Willi /Superstock

MICHAEL BUSH/UP/Landow/Shutterstock.com

Changing concepts of ideal weight are evident in a 17th-century painting by Peter Paul Rubens and in a photograph of a current fashion model.

which then seemed to relieve the stress. Thus, repeated cycles of "dieting" seems to produce stress-related withdrawal symptoms in the brain, much like other addictive substances, resulting in more eating than would have occurred without dieting.

Fairburn, Cooper, Doll, and Davies (2005) examined a group of 2,992 young women who were dieting and identified 104 who developed an eating disorder over the next 2 years. Among all of these dieters, several risk factors were identified. Those most at risk for developing an eating disorder were already binge eating and purging, were eating in secret, expressed a desire to have an empty stomach, were preoccupied with food, and were afraid of losing control over eating.

Distortions of body image in some males can also have tragic consequences. Olivardia, Pope, and Hudson (2000) have described a syndrome in men, particularly male weight lifters, that they initially termed *reverse anorexia nervosa*. Men with this syndrome reported they were extremely concerned about looking small, even though they were muscular. Many of these men avoided beaches, locker rooms, and other places where their bodies might be seen. These men also were prone to using anabolic–androgenic steroids to bulk up, risking both the medical and the psychological consequences of taking steroids. Thus, although a marked gender difference in typical body image distortion is obvious, with many women thinking they're too big and some men thinking they're too small, both types of distortion can result in severe psychological and physical consequences (Corson & Andersen, 2002; Kanayama et al., 2006; Neumark-Sztainer & Eisenberg, 2014).

The conflict over body image would be bad enough if size were infinitely malleable, but it is not. Increasing evidence indicates a strong genetic contribution to body size; that is, some of us are born to be heavier than others, and we are all shaped differently. Although most of us can be physically fit, few can achieve the levels of fitness and shape so highly valued today. Biologically, it is nearly impossible (Brownell, 1991; Brownell & Fairburn, 2002). Nevertheless, many young people in our society fight biology to the point of starvation. In adolescence, cultural standards are often experienced as peer pressure and are more influential than reason and fact. The high number of men who are gay among the relatively small numbers of men with eating disorders has also been attributed to pressures among gay men to be physically trim (Carlat et al., 1997; Feldman & Meyer, 2007; Hadland, Austin, Goodenow, & Calzo, 2014). Conversely, pressure to appear more fit and muscular is also apparent for a substantial proportion of men (Neumark-Sztainer & Eisenberg, 2014; Pope et al., 2000).

Dietary Restraint

During World War II, in what has become a classic study, Keys and colleagues (Keys, Brozek, Henschel, Michelson, & Taylor, 1950) conducted a semistarvation experiment involving 36 conscientious objectors who volunteered for the study as an alternative to military service. For 6 months, these healthy men were given about half their former full intake of food. This period was followed by a 3-month rehabilitation phase, during which food was gradually increased. During the diet, the participants lost an average of 25% of their body weight. The results were carefully documented, particularly the psychological effects.

The investigators found that the participants became preoccupied with food and eating. Conversations, reading, and daydreams revolved around food. Many began to collect recipes and to hoard food-related items.

If cultural pressures to be thin are as important as they seem to be in triggering eating disorders, then such disorders would be expected to occur where these pressures are particularly severe, which is just what happens to ballet dancers, who are under extraordinary pressures to be thin. Garner, Garfinkel, Rockert, and Olmsted (1987) followed a group of 11- to 14-year-old female students in ballet school. The conservative estimate was that at least 25% of these girls developed eating disorders during the 2 years of the study. Similar results are apparent among athletes, particularly females, such as gymnasts. What goes on in ballet classes that has such a devastating effect on girls?

Consider the case of Phoebe again.

Phoebe... Dancing to Destruction

Phoebe remembered clearly that during her early years in ballet the older girls talked incessantly about their weight. Phoebe performed well and looked forward to the rare compliment. The ballet mistress seemed to comment more on weight than on dance technique, often remarking, "You'd dance better if you lost weight." If one little girl lost a few pounds through heroic dieting, the instructor always pointed it out: "You've done well working on your weight; the rest of you had better follow this example." One day, without warning, the instructor said to Phoebe, "You need to lose 5 pounds before the next class." At that time, Phoebe was 5 feet 2 inches and weighed 98 pounds. The next class was in 2 days. After one of these admonitions and several days of restrictive eating, Phoebe experienced her first uncontrollable binge.

Early in high school, Phoebe gave up the rigors of ballet to pursue a variety of other interests. She did not forget the glory of her starring roles as a young dancer or how to perform the steps. She still danced occasionally by herself and retained the grace that serious dancers effortlessly display. But in college, as she stuck her head in the toilet bowl, vomiting her guts out for perhaps the third time that day, she realized there was one lesson she had learned in ballet class more deeply and thoroughly than any other—the life-or-death importance of being thin at all costs.

Thus, dieting is one factor that can contribute to eating disorders (Polivy & Herman, 2002) and, along with dissatisfaction with one's body, is a primary risk factor for later eating disorders (Stice, Ng, & Shaw, 2010).

Family Influences

In the past, much has been made of the possible significance of family interaction patterns in cases of eating disorders. A number of clinicians and investigators in decades past (see, for example, Attie & Brooks-Gunn, 1995; Bruch, 1985; Humphrey, 1989; Minuchin, Rosman, & Baker, 1978) observed that the "typical" family of someone with anorexia is successful, hard-driving, concerned about external appearances, and eager to maintain harmony. To accomplish these goals, family members often deny or -ignore conflicts or negative feelings and tend to attribute their problems to other people at the expense of frank communication among themselves (Fairburn, Shafran, & Cooper, 1999; Hsu, 1990).

Pike and Rodin (1991) confirmed some differences in interactions within the families of girls with disordered eating in comparison with control families. Basically, mothers of girls with disordered eating seemed to act as "society's messengers" in wanting their daughters to be thin, at least initially (Steinberg & Phares, 2001). They were likely to be dieting themselves and, generally, were more perfectionistic than comparison mothers in that they were less satisfied with their families and family cohesion (Fairburn, Cooper, et al., 1999; Fairburn, Welch, et al., 1997). But the contributions of parents or family factors are not the primary causes for eating disorders (Steiger et al., 2013; Russell, 2009). Reflecting this development, the Academy for Eating Disorders (le Grange, Lock, Loeb, & Nicholls, 2010) concluded: "It is the position of the Academy for Eating Disorders (AED) that whereas family factors can play a role in the genesis and maintenance of eating disorders, current knowledge refutes the idea that they are either the exclusive or even the primary mechanisms that underlie risk" (p. 1).

Whatever the preexisting relationships, after the onset of an eating disorder, particularly anorexia, family relationships can deteriorate quickly. Nothing is more frustrating for parents than watching their child starve themselves at a dinner table where food is plentiful. Educated and knowledgeable parents, including psychologists and psychiatrists with full understanding of the disorder, have reported resorting to physical violence (for example, hitting or slapping) in moments of extreme frustration, in a vain attempt to get their children to put some food, however little, in their mouths. The parents' guilt and anguish was considerable, and this kind of behavior is associated with poorer outcomes of the eating disorder (Ducios, Vibert, Mattar, & Godart, 2012).

Biological Dimensions

Like most psychological disorders, eating disorders run in families and thus seem to have a genetic component (Trace, Baker, Penas-Lledo, & Bulik, 2013). Studies suggest that relatives of patients with eating disorders are four to five times more likely than the general population to develop eating disorders themselves, with the risks for female relatives of patients with anorexia higher (see, for example, Strober, Freeman, Lampert, Diamond, & Kaye, 2000). In important twin studies of bulimia by Kendler and colleagues (1991) and of anorexia by Walters and Kendler (1995), researchers used structured interviews to ascertain the prevalence of the disorders among 2,163 female twins. In 23% of identical twin pairs, both twins had bulimia, as compared with 9% of fraternal twins. Because no adoption studies have yet been reported, strong sociocultural influences cannot be ruled out, and other studies have produced inconsistent results (Fairburn, Cowen, & Harrison, 1999). For anorexia, numbers were too small for precise estimates, but the disorder in one twin did seem to confer a significant risk for both anorexia and bulimia in the co-twin. Bulik and colleagues (2006), in a large twin study, estimated heritability at 0.56. Thus, the consensus is that genetic makeup is about half of the equation among causes of anorexia and bulimia (Trace et al., 2013).

Again, there is no clear agreement on just *what* is inherited (Steiger et al., 2013; Trace et al., 2013). Hsu (1990) and Steiger and colleagues (2013) speculate that nonspecific personality traits such as emotional instability and, perhaps, poor impulse control might be inherited. In other words, a person might inherit a tendency to be emotionally responsive to stressful life events and, as one consequence, might eat impulsively in an attempt to relieve stress and anxiety (Kaye, 2008; Pearson, Wonderlich, & Smith, 2015; Strober, 2002). Klump and colleagues (2001) mention perfectionist traits, along with negative affect. This biological vulnerability might then interact with social and psychological factors to produce an eating disorder. Wade and colleagues (2008) found support for this idea in a study of 1,002 same-sex twins in which anorexia was associated with, and maybe a reflection of, a trait of perfectionism and a need for order that runs in families.

Biological processes are quite active in the regulation of eating and thus of eating disorders, and substantial evidence points to the hypothalamus as playing an important role. Investigators have studied the hypothalamus and the major neurotransmitter systems—including norepinephrine, dopamine, and, particularly,

Courtesy of Tim Walsh

Tim Walsh has made significant scientific contributions to our understanding of eating disorders.

Dr. Kelly Klump and her colleagues have conducted research highlighting the importance of ovarian hormones in predicting disordered eating, particularly binge-eating episodes.

serotonin—that pass through it to determine whether something is malfunctioning when eating disorders occur (Kaye, 2008; Vitiello & Lederhendler, 2000). Low levels of serotonergic activity, the system most often associated with eating disorders (Russell, 2009; Steiger, Bruce, & Groleau, 2011), are associated with impulsivity generally and binge eating specifically (see Chapter 2). Thus, most drugs under study as treatments for eating disorders target the serotonin system (see, for example, Grilo, Crosby, Wilson, & Masheb, 2012; Kaye, 2008).

Biological investigators are also interested in the influence of hormones on eating behavior, particularly binge eating, which is an important component of bulimia. In an impressive program of research, Kelly Klump and colleagues found strong associations between ovarian hormones and dysregulated or impulsive eating in women prone to binge-eating episodes (Klump et al., 2014). Furthermore, emotional eating behavior (eating to relieve stress or anxiety) and binge-eating frequencies peaked in the postovulatory phases of the menstrual cycle for all women whether they binged or not during other phases of their cycle. High levels of hormones at least partially accounted for these peaks. In an interesting bit of theorizing, Klump and her colleagues, noting the strong association between the onset of bulimia and puberty, speculate that the onset of puberty and associated hormonal changes may "turn on" certain hormone responsive risk genes in women prone to binge eating to begin with because they possess these genetic patterns. If true, this would be another example of the kind of gene–environment interactions discussed in Chapter 2.

If investigators do find a strong association between neurobiological functions and eating disorders, the question of cause or effect remains. At present, the consensus is that some neurobiological abnormalities do exist in people with eating disorders (for example, Marsh et al., 2011; Mainz, Schulte-Rüther, Fink, Herpertz-Dahlmann, & Konrad, 2012) but that they may be a *result* of semistarvation or a binge–purge cycle rather than a cause, although they may well contribute to the *maintenance* of the disorder once it is established. Bodell and Keel (2015) uncovered an interesting example of this type of finding while studying the biological effects of attempts to lose weight (weight suppression), a known risk factor for binge eating and bulimia. They hypothesized that reduced levels of leptin, a hormone acting in the hypothalamus to produce feelings of fullness (and therefore keep people from overeating) might be associated with excessive efforts to keep weight down and therefore lead to increases in the reinforcing value of food and possibly binge eating. Contrary to their hypotheses, they found that patients with bulimia compared to control participants did not differ on leptin levels, which were therefore not significantly associated with the reinforcing value of food. So while it's clear that weight suppression efforts increase the reinforcing value of food and binge eating, at a biological level it is not yet clear why.

Psychological Dimensions

Clinical observations over the years have indicated that many young women with eating disorders have a diminished sense of personal control and confidence in their own abilities and talents (Bruch, 1973, 1985; Striegel-Moore, Silberstein, & Rodin, 1993; Walters & Kendler, 1995). This may manifest as strikingly low self-esteem (Fairburn, Cooper, & Shafran, 2003). They also display more perfectionistic attitudes, perhaps learned or inherited from their families, which may reflect attempts to exert control over important events in their lives (Boone, Soenens, Vansteenkiste, & Braet, 2012; Bulik et al., 2014; Fairburn, Halmi et al., 2012; Joiner et al., 1997; Martinez & Craighead, 2015; Welch, et al., 1997). Shafran, Lee, Payne, and Fairburn (2006) artificially raised perfectionistic standards in otherwise normal women by instructing them to pursue the highest possible standards in everything they did for the next 24 hours. These instructions caused them to eat fewer high-calorie foods, to restrict their eating, and to have more regret after eating than women told to just do the minimum for 24 hours. This occurred even though eating was not specifically mentioned as part of pursuing the "highest standards." Perfectionism alone, however, is only weakly associated with the development of an eating disorder because individuals must consider themselves overweight and manifest low self-esteem before the trait of perfectionism makes a contribution (Vohs, Bardone, Joiner, Abramson, & Heatherton, 1999). But when perfectionism is directed to distorted perception of body image, a powerful engine to drive eating disorder behavior is in place (Lilenfeld, Wonderlich, Riso, Crosby, & Mitchell, 2006; Shafran, Cooper, & Fairburn, 2002).

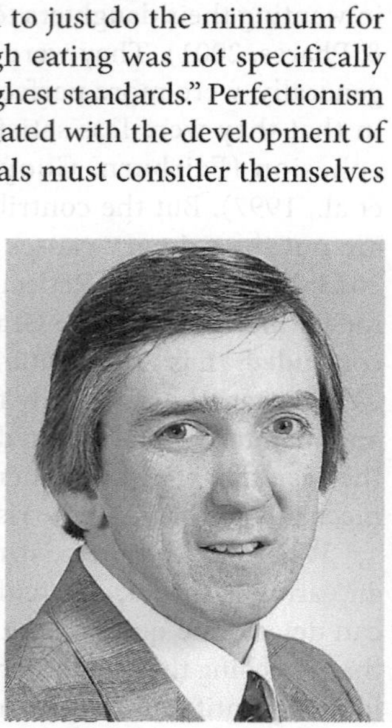

Christopher Fairburn developed an effective psychosocial treatment for bulimia nervosa.

Women with eating disorders are intensely preoccupied with how they appear to others (Fairburn, Stice, et al., 2003; Smith et al., 2007). They also perceive themselves as frauds, considering false any impressions they make of being adequate, self-sufficient, or worthwhile. In this sense, they feel like impostors in their social groups and experience heightened levels of social anxiety (Bardone-Cone et al., 2010; Clance & Imes, 1978; Smolak & Levine, 1996), which may explain why they choose social groups with similar attitudes toward eating and body shape (Rayner et al., 2012). Striegel-Moore and colleagues (1993) suggest these social self-deficits are likely to increase as a consequence of the eating disorder, further isolating the woman from the larger social world.

Specific distortions in perception of body shape change often, depending on day-to-day experience. McKenzie, Williamson, and Cubic (1993) found that women with bulimia judged that their bodies were larger after they ate a candy bar and soft drink, whereas the judgments of women in control groups were unaffected by snacks. Thus, rather minor events related to eating may activate fear of gaining weight, further distortions in body image, and corrective schemes such as purging.

Another important observation is that at least a subgroup of these patients has difficulty tolerating any negative emotion (mood intolerance) and may binge or engage in other behaviors, such as self-induced vomiting or intense exercise, in an attempt to regulate their mood (reduce their anxiety or distress by doing something they think will help them avoid being fat) (Haynos & Fruzzetti, 2011; Paul, Schroeter, Dahme, & Nutzinger, 2002). This seemed to be true for Phoebe. For example, Mauler, Hamm, Weike, and Tuschen-Caffier (2006) investigated reaction to food cues in women with bulimia and a comparison group without disordered eating who had been food deprived. They discovered that women with bulimia, when hungry, had more intense negative emotional reactions (distress, anxiety, and depression) when viewing pictures of food and subsequently ate more at a buffet, presumably to decrease their anxiety and distress and make themselves feel better, even though this overeating would cause problems in the long run. These individuals, understandably, then evidenced even more intense negative affect after overeating and seemed threatened by food cues, which could lead to the extreme food restriction or intense exercise noted above. Fairburn and Cooper (2014) also noted the importance in treatment of countering the tendency to overly restrict food intake and the associated negative attitudes about body image that lead to bingeing and purging. What all of these studies have in common is the role of intense emotions triggered by food cues and fear of becoming fat and faulty attempts to regulate these emotions as factors driving eating disorders.

An Integrative Model

Although the three major eating disorders are identifiable by their unique characteristics and the specific diagnoses have some validity, it is becoming increasingly clear that all eating disorders have much in common in terms of causal factors. It may be more useful to lump the eating disorders into one diagnostic category, simply noting which specific features occur, such as dietary restraint, bingeing, or purging. Christopher Fairburn and colleagues have attempted to develop this approach (see, for example, Fairburn et al., 2007; Fairburn & Cooper, 2014). Thus, we have integrated a discussion of the causes of eating disorders.

In putting together what we know about eating disorders, it is important to remember, again, that no one factor seems sufficient to cause them (see ■ Figure 8.4). Individuals with eating disorders may have some of the same biological vulnerabilities (such as being highly responsive to stressful life events) as individuals with anxiety disorders (Kendler et al., 1995; Klump et al., 2014; Rojo, Conesa, Bermudez, & Livianos, 2006). Anxiety and mood disorders are also common in the families of individuals with eating disorders (Steiger et al., 2013), and negative emotions, along with "mood intolerance," seem to trigger binge eating in many patients. In addition, as you will see, drug and psychological treatments with proven effectiveness for anxiety disorders are also the treatments of choice for eating disorders. Indeed, we could conceptualize eating disorders as anxiety disorders focused exclusively on a fear of becoming overweight.

In any case, it is clear that social and cultural pressures to be thin motivate significant restriction of eating, usually through severe dieting. Remember, however, that many people, including adolescent women, go on strict diets, but only a small minority develops eating disorders, so dieting alone does not account for the disorders. It is also important to note that the social interactions in high-achieving families play at least some role. An emphasis in these families on looks, achievement, and perfectionistic tendencies may help establish strong attitudes about the overriding importance of physical appearance to popularity and success, attitudes reinforced in peer groups. These attitudes result in an exaggerated focus on body shape and weight. Finally, there is the question of why a small minority of individuals with eating disorders can control their intake through dietary restraint, resulting in alarming weight loss (anorexia), whereas the majority are unsuccessful at losing weight and compensate in a cycle of bingeing and purging (bulimia) (Eddy et al., 2002; Eddy et al., 2008). These differences, at least initially, may be determined by biology or physiology, such as a genetically determined disposition to be somewhat thinner initially. Then again, perhaps preexisting personality characteristics, such as a tendency to be overcontrolling, are important determinants of which disorder an individual develops. In any case, most individuals with anorexia do go on to bingeing and purging at some point.

Treatment of Eating Disorders

There is good support for the efficacy of psychological and medical treatments for the different eating disorders (Atwood & Friedman, 2020; Hilbert et al. 2019; Hilbert et al., 2020; Slade et al., 2018; Svaldi et al., 2019).

Drug Treatments

At present, drug treatments have not been found to be effective in the treatment of anorexia nervosa (see, for example, Crow, Mitchell, Roerig, & Steffen, 2009; Wilson & Fairburn, 2007). For example, one definitive study reported that fluoxetine (Prozac) had no benefit in preventing relapse in patients with anorexia after weight has been restored (Walsh et al., 2006).

On the other hand, there is some evidence that drugs may be useful for some people with bulimia, particularly during the

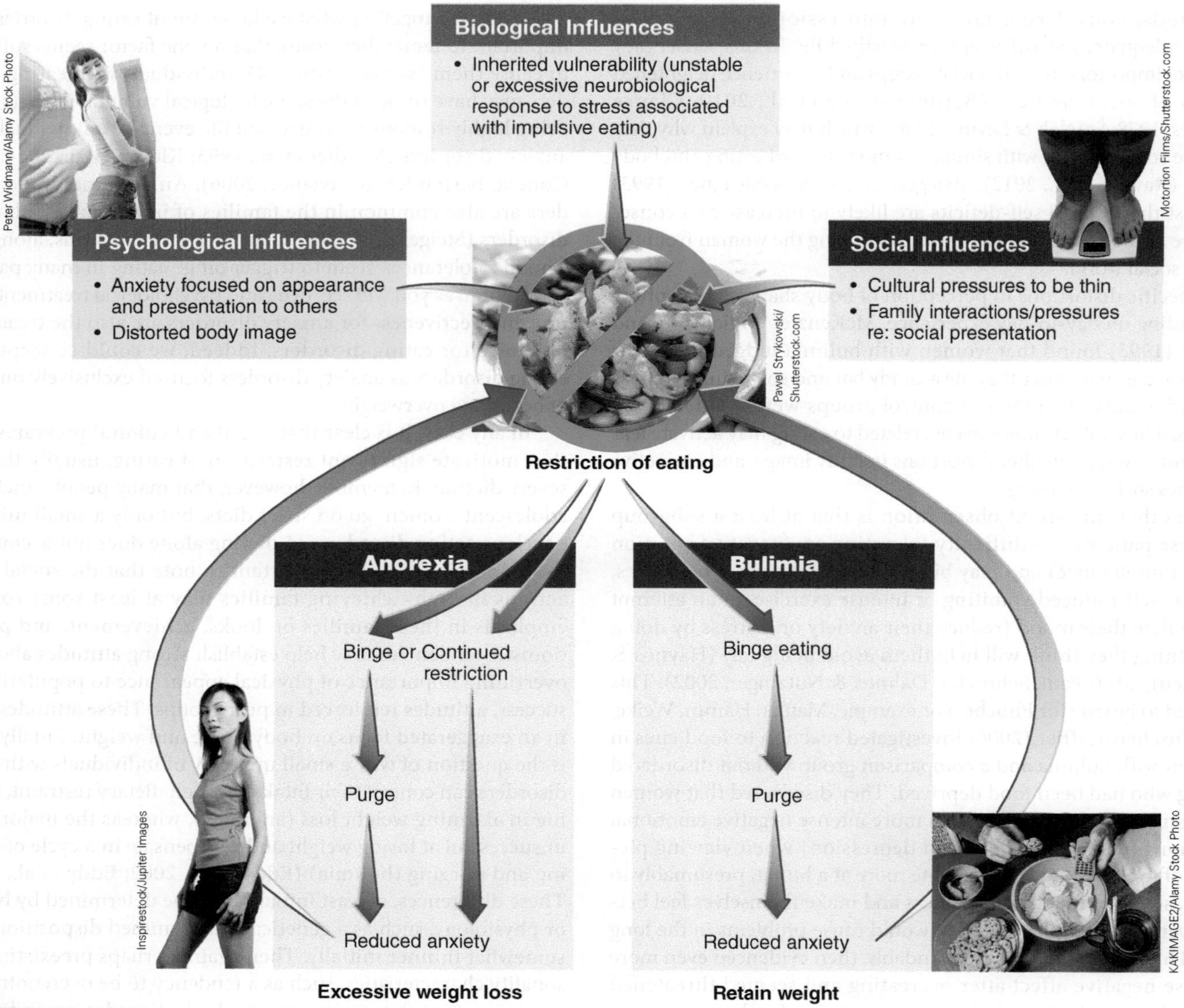

Figure 8.4

An integrative causal model of eating disorders.

bingeing and purging cycle. The drugs generally considered the most effective for bulimia are the same antidepressant medications proven effective for mood disorders and anxiety disorders (Broft, Berner, & Walsh, 2010; Shapiro et al., 2007; Wilson & Fairburn, 2007). The Food and Drug Administration (FDA) in 1996 approved Prozac as effective for eating disorders. Effectiveness is usually measured by reductions in the frequency of binge eating, as well as by the percentage of patients who stop binge eating and purging altogether, at least for a while. In two studies, one utilizing several tricyclic antidepressant drugs and the other utilizing Prozac, researchers found the average *reduction* in binge eating and purging was, respectively, 47% and 65% (Walsh, 1991; Walsh, Hadigan, Devlin, Gladis, & Roose, 1991). In particular, selective serotonin reuptake inhibitors can be helpful in the treatment of bulimia (Tortorella, Fabrazzo, Monteleone, Steardo, & Monteleone, 2014). However, although antidepressants are more effective than placebo in the short term and may enhance the effects of psychological treatment somewhat (Whittal, Agras, & Gould, 1999; Wilson et al., 1999), the available evidence suggests that antidepressant drugs alone do not have substantial long-lasting effects on bulimia nervosa, and current expert opinions suggest that medications are likely most useful in conjunction with psychological treatments (Reas & Grilo, 2014; Walsh, 1995; Wilson & Fairburn, 2007).

Psychological Treatments

Until the 1980s, psychological treatments for people with eating disorders were directed at the patient's low self-esteem and difficulties in developing an individual identity. Disordered patterns of family interaction and communication were also targeted for treatment. These treatments alone, however, did not have the effectiveness that clinicians hoped they might (see, for example, Minuchin et al., 1978; Russell, Szmukler, Dare, & Eisler, 1987).

Short-term cognitive-behavioral treatments target problem eating behavior and associated attitudes about the overriding importance and significance of body weight and shape, and these strategies became the treatment of choice for bulimia (Fairburn & Cooper, 2014; Sysko & Wilson, 2011).

This approach has been updated and improved in two major ways based on more than a decade of experience. First, a variety of new procedures intended to improve outcome have been added. Second, noting the common concern with body shape and weight at the core of all eating disorders, the treatment has become "transdiagnostic" in that it is applicable with minor alterations to all eating disorders. This is an important development because in DSM-IV, eating disorders, for the most part, were considered to be mutually exclusive. For example, according to DSM-IV guidelines, a person could not meet criteria for both anorexia and bulimia. But investigators working in this area discovered that features of the various eating disorders overlapped considerably (Fairburn, 2008; Keel, Brown, Holland, & Bodell, 2012). Furthermore, a large portion of patients, perhaps as many as 50% or more, who met criteria for a clinically severe eating disorder in DSM-IV did not meet criteria for anorexia or bulimia and were diagnosed with "eating disorder not otherwise specified" (eating disorder NOS) (Fairburn & Bohn, 2005). As described earlier in the chapter, some of these patients would now meet criteria for "binge-eating disorder," which is included as a full-fledged diagnostic category in DSM-5. As noted above, these eating disorders have very similar causal influences, including similar inherited biological vulnerabilities, similar social influences (primarily cultural influences glorifying thinness), and a strong family influence toward perfectionism in all things (Guerdjikova, Mori, Casuto, & McElroy, 2019). Finally, all eating disorders seem to share anxiety focused on one's appearance and presentation to others, as well as distorted body image.

In this treatment protocol, the essential components of cognitive-behavioral therapy (CBT) directed at causal factors common to all eating disorders are targeted in an integrated way. (Individuals with anorexia and a very low weight—BMI of 17.5 or less —who would need inpatient treatment would be excluded until their weight was restored to an adequate level when they could then benefit from the program.) Thus, the principal focus of this protocol is on the distorted evaluation of body shape and weight and on maladaptive attempts to control weight in the form of strict dieting (possibly accompanied by binge eating) and methods to compensate for overeating (such as purging and laxative misuse). Fairburn refers to this treatment as cognitive-behavioral therapy-enhanced (CBT-E) (Fairburn & Cooper, 2014). Nevertheless, since there are some differences in outcomes across the eating disorders, we will review treatment of each separately.

Bulimia Nervosa

In the CBT-E pioneered by Fairburn (2008), the first stage is teaching the patient the physical consequences of binge eating and purging, as well as the ineffectiveness of vomiting and laxative abuse for weight control. The adverse effects of dieting are also described, and patients are scheduled to eat small, manageable amounts of food five or six times per day with no more than a 3-hour interval between any planned meals and snacks, which eliminates the alternating periods of overeating and dietary restriction that are hallmarks of bulimia. In later stages of treatment, CBT-E focuses on altering dysfunctional thoughts and attitudes about body shape, weight, and eating. Coping strategies for resisting the impulse to binge and/or purge are also developed, including arranging activities so that the individual will not spend time alone after eating during the early stages of treatment (Fairburn & Cooper, 2014). Evaluations of the earlier versions of short-term (approximately 3 months) cognitive-behavioral treatments for bulimia have been good, showing superior efficacy to credible alternative psychological treatments not only for bingeing and purging but also for distorted attitudes and accompanying depression. Furthermore, these results seem to last (Pike, Walsh, Vitousek, Wilson, & Bauer, 2003; Thompson-Brenner, Glass, & Westen, 2003), although there were, of course, a number of patients who improved only modestly or did not benefit.

Stewart Agras has made many important contributions to our understanding of eating disorders.

In a widely noted study using the earlier version of treatment, Agras, Walsh, Fairburn, Wilson, and Kraemer (2000) randomly assigned 220 patients meeting diagnostic criteria for bulimia nervosa to 19 sessions of either cognitive-behavioral therapy (CBT) or interpersonal psychotherapy (IPT) focused on improving interpersonal functioning. The investigators found that, for those who completed treatment, CBT was significantly superior to IPT at the end of treatment. The percentage who remitted (no longer met diagnostic criteria for an eating disorder but still had some problems) was 67% in the CBT group versus 40% in the IPT group. After 1 year, however, these differences again were no longer significant, as patients in the IPT group tended to "catch up" to patients in the CBT group. More recent evaluations of CBT-E are very promising, particularly since a wider range of patients with bulimia-like symptoms can be included (for example, Fairburn et al., 2009). Results from a major clinical trial comparing 20 weeks of CBT-E with 2 years of weekly long-term psychoanalytic psychotherapy (PPT) in 70 patients with bulimia revealed that patients in each group were comfortable with their treatment, but at5 months (when the CBT-E treatment concluded), 42% of CBT-E patients were recovered compared to 6% of PPT patients. After 2 years (when the PPT treatment concluded), the comparable figures were 44% and 15% (Poulsen et al., 2014). Thus, CBT-E was more efficient in terms of the number of sessions required and more effective at each time point assessed, with evidence for the durability in improvement among those who responded to CBT-E. Results from a major clinical trial similar to the Agras and colleagues (2000) study described above but comparing the transdiagnostic version of CBT (CBT-E) to interpersonal psychotherapy (IPT) in 130 patients with any form of eating disorder have been reported (Fairburn et al., 2015). Just after treatment, 65.5% of the CBT-E participants met criteria for remission compared to 33.3% of the IPT participants. One year later, the figures were 69.4% for CBT-E compared to 49% for IPT, with IPT catching up somewhat but still significantly less effective. Therefore, at the present time, CBT-E would seem to be the treatment of choice for adults based on these studies.

There is also good evidence that family therapy directed at the painful conflicts present in families with an adolescent who has an eating disorder can be helpful (le Grange, Crosby, Rathouz, & Leventhal, 2007). Integrating family and interpersonal strategies into CBT is a promising new direction (Sysko & Wilson, 2011). Clearly, we need to understand more about how to improve such treatments to deal more successfully with the growing number of patients with eating disorders. One of the problems with the best treatment, CBT, is that access to the treatment is limited because trained therapists are not always available. Guided self-help programs that use CBT principles also seem to be effective, at least for less severe cases (Schmidt et al., 2007; Wagner et al., 2013).

Binge-Eating Disorder

Early studies adapting CBT for bulimia to obese binge eaters were quite successful (Smith, Marcus, & Kaye, 1992). To take one example, Agras, Telch, Arnow, Eldredge, and Marnell (1997) followed 93 obese individuals with BED for 1 year and found that immediately after treatment with CBT, 41% of the participants abstained from bingeing and 72% binged less frequently. After 1 year, binge eating was reduced by 64%, and 33% of the group refrained from bingeing altogether. Those who had stopped binge eating during CBT maintained a weight loss of approximately 9 pounds over this 1-year follow-up period; those who continued to binge gained approximately 8 pounds. Thus, stopping binge eating is critical to sustaining weight loss in obese patients, a finding consistent with other studies of weight-loss procedures (Marcus et al., 1990).

In contrast to results with bulimia, it appears that IPT is every bit as effective as CBT for binge eating. Wilfley and colleagues (2002) treated 162 overweight or obese men and women with BED with either CBT or IPT and found comparable results from each treatment. Fully 60% refrained from bingeing at a 1-year follow-up. But in a study examining the effectiveness of the antidepressant drug Prozac compared with CBT for BED, Prozac was ineffective (compared with placebo), and Prozac did not add anything to CBT when the two treatments were combined (Grilo, Masheb, & Wilson, 2005). The positive results from CBT were reasonably durable at follow-up 1 year later (Grilo et al., 2012). If individuals began to respond rapidly to CBT treatment (by the 4th week), the response was particularly good, in both the short term and long term (Grilo, Masheb, & Wilson, 2006).

Widely available behavioral weight loss programs for obese patients with BED, such as Weight Watchers, have some positive effect on binging, but not nearly so much as CBT (Grilo, Masheb, Wilson, Gueorguieva, & White, 2011). Some racial and ethnic differences are apparent in people with BED seeking treatment (Franko et al., 2012). Black participants tend to have higher BMI, and Hispanic participants have greater concerns with shape and weight than White participants. Thus, it would seem that tailoring treatment to these ethnic groups would be useful. Also, males may respond somewhat differently than females to treatment since one recent study demonstrated that men with lower shape/weight concerns responded well to brief treatments, whereas females with shape/weight concerns at any level of severity and men at more severe levels all required longer treatment (Shingleton, Thompson, Pratt, & Franko, 2015).

Fortunately, it appears that self-help procedures may be useful in the treatment of BED (Carter & Fairburn, 1998; Wilson & Zandberg, 2012). For example, CBT delivered as guided self-help was demonstrated to be more effective than a standard behavioral weight-loss program for BED both after treatment and at a 2-year follow up (Wilson, Wilfley, Agras, & Bryson, 2010), and this same program is effective when delivered out of a doctor's office in a primary care setting (Striegel-Moore et al., 2010). In view of these results, it would seem a self-help approach should probably be the first treatment offered for BED before engaging in more expensive and time-consuming therapist-led treatments. Much as with bulimia, however, more severe cases may need the more intensive treatment delivered by a therapist, particularly cases with multiple (comorbid) disorders in addition to BED, as well as low self-esteem (Wilson et al., 2010). A report following up the Wilson and colleagues (2010) study indicated that rapid response (at least 70% reduction in binge eating by week 4) was a

Phoebe... Taking Control

During her sophomore year in college, Phoebe entered a short-term CBT program similar to the program discussed here. She made good progress during the first several months and worked carefully to eat regularly and gain control over her eating. She also made sure that she was with somebody during her high-risk times and planned alternative activities that would reduce her temptation to purge if she felt she had eaten too much at a restaurant or drunk too much beer at a party. During the first 2 months, Phoebe had three slips, and she and her therapist discussed what led to her temporary relapse. Much to Phoebe's surprise, she did not gain weight on this program, even though she did not have time to increase her exercise. Nevertheless, she still was preoccupied with food, was concerned about her weight and appearance, and had strong urges to vomit if she thought she had overeaten the slightest amount.

During the 9 months following treatment, Phoebe reported that her urges seemed to decrease somewhat, although she had one major slip after eating a big pizza and drinking a lot of beer. She reported that she was thoroughly disgusted with herself for purging and was quite careful to return to her program after this episode. Two years after finishing treatment, Phoebe reported that her urges to vomit had disappeared, a report confirmed by her parents. All that remained of her problem were some bad but increasingly vague and distant memories.

specific positive indicator of greater rates of remission compared to nonrapid responders up to 2 years later in the CBT guided self-help treatment but not in the IPT or the behavioral weight-loss group (Hilbert, Hildebrandt, Agras, Wilfley, and Wilson, 2015). The authors suggest that since IPT was effective for both rapid and nonrapid responders, participants who do not show a rapid response to CBT might be switched over to IPT. Matching treatment to individuals on the basis of their personal characteristics or patterns of responding (personalized medicine) is regarded by many as the next important step for improving success rates of our treatments. It is also important to emphasize again that if an obese person is bingeing, standard weight-loss procedures will be ineffective without treatment directed at bingeing.

Anorexia Nervosa

In anorexia, the most important initial goal is to restore the patient's weight to a point that is at least within the low–normal range (American Psychiatric Association, 2010b). If body weight is below approximately 75% of the average healthy body weight for a given individual or if weight has been lost rapidly and the individual continues to refuse food, inpatient treatment is recommended (Schwartz, Mansbach, Marion, Katzman, & Forman, 2008; Russell, 2009) because severe medical complications, particularly acute cardiac failure, could occur if weight is not restored immediately. If the weight loss has been more gradual and seems to have stabilized, weight restoration can be accomplished on an outpatient basis.

Restoring weight, although often a difficult task, is probably the easiest part of treatment. Clinicians who treat patients in different settings, as reported in a variety of studies, find that at least 85% will be able to gain weight. The gain is often as much as a half-pound to a pound a day until weight is within the normal range. Knowing they cannot leave the hospital until their weight gain is adequate is often sufficient to motivate adolescents with anorexia (Agras, Barlow, Chapin, Abel, & Leitenberg, 1974). Zahra gained about 18 pounds during her 5-week hospital stay. Weight gain is very important, since starvation induces loss of gray matter and hormonal dysregulation in the brain (Mainz et al., 2012), changes that are reversible when normal weight is restored.

Then the more difficult stage begins. As Hsu (1988) and others have demonstrated, initial weight gain is a poor predictor of long-term outcome in anorexia. Without attention to patients' underlying dysfunctional attitudes about body shape and the interpersonal disruptions in their lives, they will almost always relapse. For restricting anorexics, the focus of treatment must shift to their marked anxiety over becoming obese and losing control of eating, as well as to their undue emphasis on thinness as a determinant of self-worth, happiness, and success. In this regard, effective treatments for restricting anorexics are similar to those for patients with bulimia nervosa, particularly in the "transdiagnostic" approach (CBT-E) described earlier (Fairburn & Cooper, 2014). In a well-done earlier study (Pike, Walsh, Vitousek, Wilson, & Bauer, 2003), extended (1-year) outpatient CBT was found to be significantly better than continued nutritional counseling in preventing relapse after weight restoration, with only 22% failing (relapsing or dropping out) with CBT versus 73% failing with nutritional counseling. Carter and colleagues (2009) reported similar findings, and both studies demonstrate the ineffectiveness of nutritional counseling alone. Results from 99 adults with anorexia treated with CBT-E suggest the efficiency of this transdiagnostic treatment (only "suggest" because there was no control or comparison group). In the 64% who completed treatment after 40 sessions, weight increased substantially, and eating disorder features improved markedly; this improvement was stable at a 60-week follow-up (Fairburn et al., 2013). In any case, one recent study underscored dramatically the importance of reducing anxiety and general emotion dysregulation concerning shape/weight in the treatment of individuals with anorexia. Racine and Wildes (2015) followed 191 patients who had received intensive inpatient or day hospital treatment who had recovered sufficiently to be discharged and demonstrated that the presence of continued emotion dysregulation at discharge predicted an increase in anorexia psychopathology over the following year, whereas low emotion dysregulation predicted a decrease in anorexics' symptoms. These results are presented in ■ Figure 8.5.

CBT is not the only treatment option. A comprehensive meta-analysis examined 13 randomized controlled trials for various psychological treatments, including CBT, family-based treatment, psychodynamic-oriented therapies, and treatment as usual. In total, 1,047 patients were included in the analysis (of whom 97.4% were female). Compared with treatment as usual, the specific psychological treatments for adult outpatients with anorexia nervosa were modestly effective for improving clinical symptoms and quality of life. However, none of these therapies outperformed treatment as usual in the primary outcome measures. Although dropout rates were lower for CBT than for psychodynamic-oriented psychotherapies, these results did not clearly favor one treatment over another (Solmi et al., 2021).

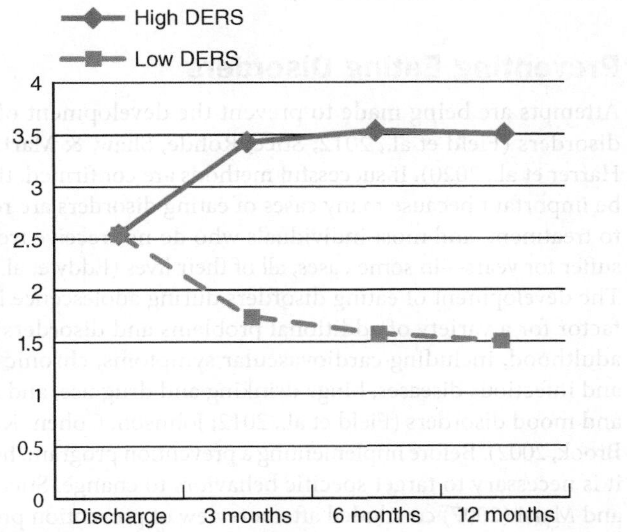

Figure 8.5

Patients with emotion dysregulation (high DERS) show elevated eating disorder symptoms compared to patients with less emotion dysregulation (low DERS) over the year following discharge from a treatment facility. From S. E. Racine & J. E. Wildes, 2015, Dynamic longitudinal relations between emotion regulation difficulties and anorexia nervosa symptoms over the year following intensive treatment, *Journal of Clinical and Consulting Psychology, 83*(4), 785–795.

Although there is not a single treatment of choice, a family-focused approach can often be beneficial for a number of reasons. First, the negative and dysfunctional communication in the family regarding food and eating must be eliminated, and meals must be made more structured and reinforcing. Second, attitudes toward body shape and image distortion are discussed at some length in family sessions. Unless the therapist attends to these attitudes, individuals with anorexia are likely to face a lifetime preoccupation with weight and body shape, struggle to maintain marginal weight and social adjustment, and be subject to repeated hospitalization. Family therapy directed at the goals mentioned above seems effective, particularly with young girls (less than 19 years of age) with a short history of the disorder (Eisler et al., 2000; Lock, le Grange, Agras, & Dare, 2001). Until recently, the long-term results of treatment for anorexia have been more discouraging than for bulimia, with substantially lower rates of full recovery than for bulimia over a 7.5-year period (Eddy et al., 2008; Herzog et al., 1999). But this may be changing. In one clinical trial, 121 adolescents with anorexia received 24 sessions of either family-based treatment (FBT), in which the parents became intimately involved in the treatment program with a focus on facilitating weight gain, or individual psychotherapy. At treatment conclusion, 42% met criteria for remission in the FBT condition and 49% at a 1-year follow up, compared with 23% at both points in time in the individual psychotherapy condition (Lock et al., 2010). A subsequent study demonstrated that FBT was at least as effective and less costly than other forms of family therapy addressing general family processes (Agras et al., 2014). As in some studies of bulimia, a positive early response (gaining at least 5 pounds in the first 4 weeks) predicts a better outcome in the long run (Lock et al., 2015). Promising results have also been reported for e-health treatments of eating disorders (Ahmadiankalati, Steins-Loeber, & Paslakis, 2020).

Preventing Eating Disorders

Attempts are being made to prevent the development of eating disorders (Field et al., 2012; Stice, Rohde, Shaw, & Marti, 2012; Harrer et al., 2020). If successful methods are confirmed, they will be important because many cases of eating disorders are resistant to treatment, and most individuals who do not receive treatment suffer for years—in some cases, all of their lives (Eddy et al., 2008). The development of eating disorders during adolescence is a risk factor for a variety of additional problems and disorders during adulthood, including cardiovascular symptoms, chronic fatigue and infectious diseases, binge drinking and drug use, and anxiety and mood disorders (Field et al., 2012; Johnson, Cohen, Kasen, & Brook, 2002). Before implementing a prevention program, however, it is necessary to target specific behaviors to change. Stice, Shaw, and Marti (2007) concluded after a review of prevention programs that selecting girls age 15 or over and focusing on eliminating an exaggerated focus on body shape or weight and encouraging acceptance of one's body stood the best chance of success in preventing eating disorders. This finding is similar to results from prevention efforts for depression, where a "selective" approach of targeting high-risk individuals was most successful rather than a "universal" approach targeting everyone in a certain age range (Stice & Shaw, 2004). Using this selective approach, a program developed by Stice and colleagues (2012) called "Healthy Weight" was compared with just handing out educational material in 398 college women at risk for developing eating disorders because of weight and shape concerns. During 4 weekly hour-long group sessions with 6,210 participants, the women were educated about food and eating habits (and motivated to alter these habits using motivational enhancement procedures). Eating disorder risk factors and symptoms were substantially reduced in the "Healthy Weight" group compared with the comparison group, particularly for the most severely at-risk women, and the effect was durable at a 6-month follow up.

Could these preventive programs also be delivered via e-health intervention? It seems they can! Winzelberg and colleagues (2000) studied a group of university women who did not have eating disorders at the time of the study but were concerned about their body image and the possibility of being overweight. College women in general are a high-risk group, and sorority women in particular are often the targets of important prevention studies (Becker, Smith, & Ciao, 2005). The investigators developed the "student bodies" program (Winzelberg et al., 1998), a structured, interactive health education program designed to improve body image satisfaction and delivered through the internet. The results indicated this program was markedly successful because participants, compared to controls, reported a significant improvement in body image and a decrease in drive for thinness. Subsequently, these investigators developed innovations to improve compliance with this program to levels of 85% (Celio, Winzelberg, Dev, & Taylor, 2002). The developers have since added an online guided discussion group to accompany the program, with initial results indicating more substantially reduced weight/shape concerns in students at risk for eating disorders who participated in this online discussion group (Kass et al., 2014).

A briefer and more efficient program termed *The Body Project* developed independently from the "Student Bodies Program" has now been adapted as a stand-alone intervention delivered over the internet (eBody Project; Stice, Rohde, Durant, & Shaw, 2012), with no clinician required. Initial results indicate that this program is just as good as the program delivered in groups by a clinician, and it avoids problems with relying on institutions (in this case universities) to sustain these programs after the initial trial (Rohde, Shaw, Butryn., & Stice, 2015), a problem often encountered in disseminating new treatment programs.

In view of the severity and chronicity of eating disorders, preventing these disorders through widespread educational and intervention efforts would be clearly preferable to waiting until the disorders develop.

Concept Check 8.2

Mark the following statements about the causes and treatment of eating disorders as either true (T) or false (F).

1. ____________ Many young women with eating disorders have a diminished sense of personal control and confidence in their own abilities and talents, are perfectionists, and/or are intensely preoccupied with how they appear to others.

2. ____________ Biological limitations, as well as the societal pressure to use diet and exercise to achieve nearly impossible weight goals, contribute to the high numbers of people with anorexia nervosa and bulimia nervosa.
3. ____________ One study showed that males consider a smaller female body size to be more attractive than women do.
4. ____________ Antidepressants help individuals overcome anorexia nervosa but have no effect on bulimia nervosa.
5. ____________ Cognitive-behavioral treatment (CBT) and interpersonal psychotherapy (IPT) are both successful treatments for bulimia nervosa, although CBT is the preferred method.
6. ____________ Attention must be focused on dysfunctional attitudes about body shape in anorexia, or relapse will most likely occur after treatment.

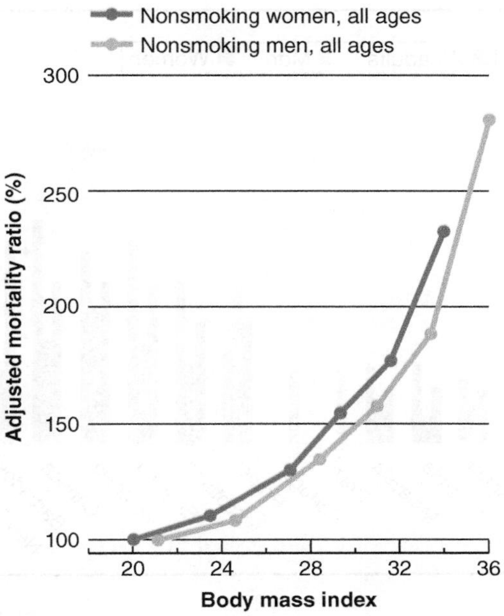

Figure 8.6
Mortality rates in relation to the BMI of nonsmoking men and women (of all ages) who participated in the American Cancer Society study. Reprinted, with permission, from T. B. Vanitallie & E. A. Lew, 1992, Assessment of morbidity and mortality risk in the overweight patient, in T. A. Wadden & T. B. Vanitallie (Eds.), *Treatment of the seriously obese patient* (p. 28) (Guilford Press). © 1992 Guilford Press.

Obesity

As noted at the beginning of the chapter, obesity is not formally considered an eating disorder in the DSM. Rates of anxiety and mood disorders are only somewhat elevated over the normal population among individuals with obesity, and rates of substance abuse are actually somewhat lower (Phelan & Wadden, 2004; Simon et al., 2006). But in the year 2000, the human race reached a historic landmark. For the first time in human evolution, the number of adults with excess weight worldwide surpassed the number of those who were underweight (Caballero, 2007). Indeed, the prevalence of obesity is so high that one might consider it statistically "normal" if it weren't for the serious implications for health, as well as for social and psychological functioning.

Statistics

The prevalence of obesity (BMI 30 or greater) among adults in the United States in 2000 was fully 30.5% of the population, increasing to 30.6% in 2002, 32.2% in 2004, 33.8% in 2008, 35.7% in 2010, and 37.7% in 2013–2014, with no difference in prevalence between men and women (Flegal et al., 2010; Flegal et al., 2012; Flegal, Kruszon-Moran, Carroll, Fryar, & Ogden, 2016; Ogden et al., 2006). This prevalence of obesity represents close to a tripling from 12% of adults in 1991. Medical costs for obesity and overweight are estimated at $147 billion, or 9.1% of U.S. health-care expenditures (Brownell et al., 2009). This condition accounts for significantly higher mortality across the population as a whole (Flegal, Kit, Orpana, & Graubard, 2013). The direct relationship between obesity and mortality (dying prematurely) is shown in ■ Figure 8.6. At a BMI of 30, risk of mortality increases by 30%, and at a BMI of 40 or more, risk of mortality is 100% or more (Manson et al., 1995; Wadden, Brownell, & Foster, 2002). Because 6.3% of the adult population has a BMI over 40 (Flegal et al., 2012), a substantial number of people, perhaps 10 million or more in the United States alone, are in serious danger, and there is evidence to suggest that this may be an underestimate (Stokes & Preston, 2015). In spite of overwhelming evidence pointing to the deleterious effects of obesity, some research is starting to suggest that the distribution of one's fat tissue is more important than BMI when it comes to predicting health outcomes, but more research is needed (Ahima & Lazar, 2013).

For children and adolescents, the numbers are even worse, with the number of overweight youngsters tripling in the past 25 years (Critser, 2003). In the past decade, the obesity rates for children ages 2 to 19 (defined as above the 95th percentile for sex-specific BMI for that age) have increased from 13.9% in 2000 to 17.1% in 2004 (Ogden et al., 2006), but they now may be leveling off with a 16.9% rate in 2008, 2010, and 2011 (Ogden, Carroll, Curtin, Lamb, & Flegal, 2010; Ogden, Carroll, Kit, & Flegal, 2012; 2014; Ogden et al., 2016). Rates may be even dropping a bit in preschoolers (Ogeden et al., 2016; Pan, Blanck, Sherry, Dalenius, & Grummer-Strawn, 2012), indicating, perhaps, that public education campaigns are just beginning to have an effect. If one looks at children and adolescents either overweight (above the 85th percentile in BMI) or obese, the rate is 30.4%. The stigma of obesity has a major impact on quality of life (Gearhardt et al., 2012; Neumark-Sztainer & Haines, 2004). For example, most overweight individuals are subjected to prejudice and discrimination in college, at work, and in housing (Gearhardt et al., 2012). Further, the experience of weight discrimination is associated with increased mortality risk (Sutin, Stephan, & Terracciano, 2015). Ridicule and teasing in children may increase obesity through depression and binge eating (Schwartz & Brownell, 2007).

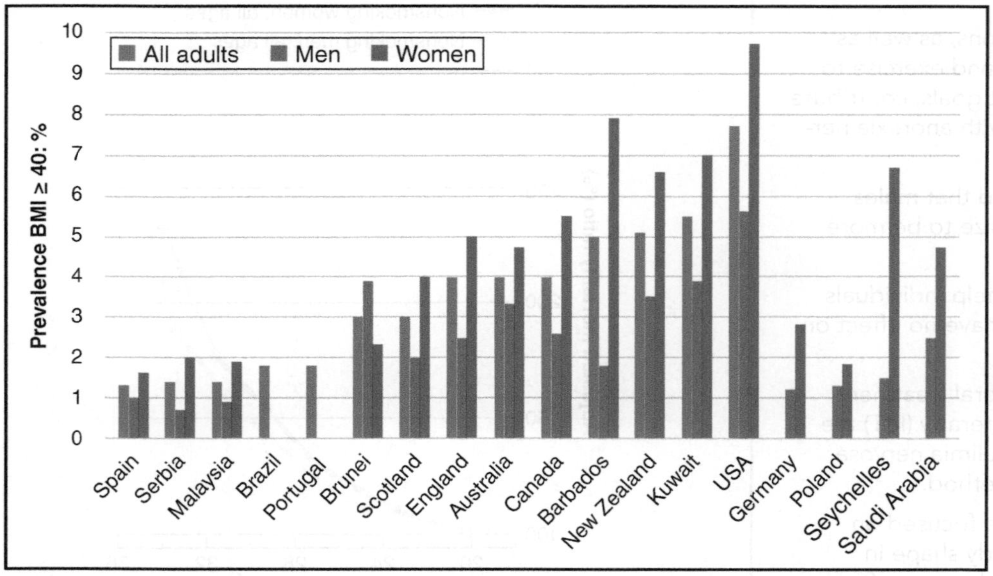

Figure 8.7

Prevalence rates of severe obesity in all adults (A), men (B), and women (C) in different countries. Severe obesity is defined as a body mass index (BMI) of 40 or greater. Adapted from K. Williamson, A. Nimegeer, & M. Lean, 2020, Rising prevalence of BMI ≥40 kg/m2: A high-demand epidemic needing better documentation, *Obesity Reviews, 21*(4), doi: 10.1111/obr.1298

Source: Adapted from Williamson, K., Nimegeer, A., & Lean, M. (2020). Rising prevalence of BMI ≥40 kg/m2: A high-demand epidemic needing better documentation. Obesity Reviews, 21(4) doi:10.1111/obr.1298

Obesity is not limited to North America. Rates of obesity in eastern and southern European nations are as high as 50% (Berghöfer et al., 2008; Bjorntorp, 1997; Ng et al., 2014), and the rate is greatly increasing in industrializing nations. In Japan, although still comparatively low, obesity rates in men have doubled since 1992 and have nearly doubled in young women (Organization for Economic Co-operation and Development, 2012). Although less extreme, increases in obesity are also occurring in China (Henderson & Brownell, 2004), where the proportion of Chinese who are overweight increased from 6% to 8% in a 7-year period (Holden, 2005). Obesity is also the main driver of type 2 diabetes, which has reached epidemic status (Yach, Stuckler, & Brownell, 2006). Additional facts documenting the global epidemic of obesity and its consequences are presented in ■ Figure 8.7 (Brownell & Yach, 2005).

Ethnicity also is a factor in rates of obesity. In the United States, fully 47.8% of African American women and 42% of Hispanic American women are obese, compared with 33.4% of White women (Ogden et al., 2014). Rates among adolescents among underrepresented groups are even more concerning. Table 8.3 shows considerably higher rates of obesity and being overweight among Black and Hispanic adolescents compared with White adolescents.

Disordered Eating Patterns in Cases of Obesity

There are two forms of maladaptive eating patterns in people who are obese. The first is binge eating, and the second is **night eating syndrome** (Lundgren, Allison, & Stunkard, 2012; Vander Wal, 2012). We discussed BED earlier in the chapter, but it is important to note that only a minority of patients with obesity, between 7% and 19%, present with patterns of binge eating. When they do, treatment for binge eating reviewed earlier should be integrated into weight-loss programs.

More interesting is the pattern of night eating syndrome that occurs in between 6% and 16% of obese individuals seeking weight-loss treatment but in as many as 55% of those with extreme obesity seeking bariatric surgery (discussed later) (Colles & Dixon, 2012; Lamberg, 2003; Sarwer, Foster, & Wadden, 2004; Stunkard, Allison, & Lundgren, 2008). Individuals with night eating syndrome consume a third or more of their daily intake after their evening meal and get out of bed at least once during the night to have a high-calorie snack. In the morning, however, they are not hungry and do not usually eat breakfast. These individuals do not binge during their night eating and seldom purge. Occasionally, nonobese individuals will engage in night eating, but the behavior is overwhelmingly associated with being overweight or obese (Gallant, Lundgren, & Drapeau, 2012; Lundgren et al., 2012; Striegel-Moore et al., 2010). Notice the relationship of night eating syndrome with increasing levels of obesity in ■ Figure 8.8 (Colles, Dixon, & O'Brien, 2007). This condition is not the same as the nocturnal eating syndrome described later in the chapter in the section about sleep disorders. In that condition, individuals get up during the night and raid the refrigerator but never wake up. They also may eat uncooked or other dangerous foods while asleep. On the contrary, in night eating syndrome, the individuals are awake as they go about their nightly eating patterns. Night eating syndrome is an important target for treatment in any obesity program to reregulate patterns of eating so that individuals eat more during the day, when their energy expenditure is highest.

Table 8.3 Percentage of U.S. Adolescents Ages 12–19 Who Are Overweight or Obese by Race/Ethnicity

	Hispanic Adolescents	Black Adolescents	Non-Hispanic White Adolescents
BMI for age ≥95th percentile	19.8%	24.8%	14.7%
BMI for age ≥85th percentile	41.9%	45.1%	27.6%

Adapted from C. L. Ogden, M. D. Carroll, B. K. Kit, & K. M. Flegal, 2012, Prevalence of obesity and trends in body mass index among U.S. children and adolescents, 1999–2010, *Journal of American Medical Association, 307*, 483–490.

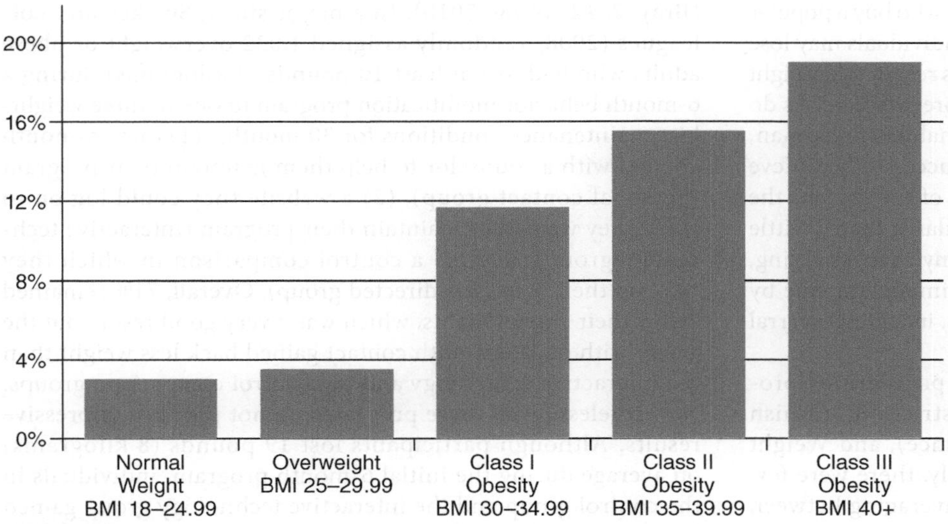

Figure 8.8

Prevalence of night eating syndrome by level of obesity. From S. L. Colles, J. B. Dixon, & P. E. O'Brien, 2007, Night eating syndrome and nocturnal snacking: Association with obesity, binge eating, and psychological distress, *International Journal of Obesity, 31*, 1722–1730.

Causes

Henderson and Brownell (2004) make a point that this obesity epidemic is clearly related to the spread of modernization. In other words, as we advance technologically, we are getting fatter. That is, the promotion of an inactive, sedentary lifestyle and the consumption of a high-fat, energy-dense diet is the largest single contributor to the obesity epidemic (Caballero, 2007; Levine et al., 2005). Kelly Brownell (2003; Brownell et al., 2010) notes that in our modern society, individuals are continually exposed to heavily advertised, inexpensive fatty foods that have low nutritional value. When consumption of these is combined with an increasingly inactive lifestyle, it is not surprising that the prevalence of obesity is increasing (Esparza-Romero et al., 2015; Gearhardt et al., 2012). Brownell has referred to this as the "toxic environment" (Schwartz & Brownell, 2007). He notes that the best example of this phenomenon comes from a classic study of the Pima Indians from Mexico. A portion of this tribe of Indians migrated to Arizona relatively recently. Examining the result of this migration, Ravussin, Valencia, Esparza, Bennett, and Schulz (1994) determined that Arizona Pima women consumed 41% of their total calories in fat on the average and weighed 44 pounds on average more than Pima women who stayed in Mexico, who consumed 23% of their calories from fat. Because this relatively small tribe retains a strong genetic similarity, it is likely that the "toxic environment" in the more modern United States has contributed to the obesity epidemic among the Arizona Pima women. Immigrants to the United States in general more than doubled their prevalence of obesity from 8% to 19% after at least 15 years of living in this country (Goel et al., 2004; Ro, Geronimus, Bound, Griffith, & Gee, 2015).

Not everyone exposed to the modernized environment such as that in the United States becomes obese, and this is where genetics, physiology, and personality come in. On average, genetic contributions may constitute a smaller portion of the cause of obesity than cultural factors, but it helps explain why some people become obese and some don't when exposed to the same environment. For example, genes influence the number of fat cells an individual has, the likelihood of fat storage, saiety, and, most likely, activity levels (Cope, Fernandez, & Allison, 2004; Hetherington & Cecil, 2010; Llewellyn, Trzaskowski, Jaarsveid, & Plomin, 2014). Generally, genes are thought to account for about 30% of the equation in causation of obesity (Bouchard, 2002), but this is misleading because it takes a "toxic" environment to turn on these genes. Physiological processes, particularly hormonal regulation of appetite, play a large role in the initiation and maintenance of eating and vary considerably from individual to individual (Friedman, 2009; Smith & Gibbs, 2002; Yeo & Heisler, 2012). Indeed, individuals with addictive obese eating behavior, which includes less control over eating and feelings of withdrawal if access to food is limited, show similar patterns of reward neurocircuitry in the brain as do individuals with substance use disorders (Gearhardt et al., 2011). Psychological processes of emotional regulation (for example, eating to try to cheer yourself up when you're feeling down), impulse control, attitudes and motivation toward eating, and responsiveness to the consequences of eating are also important (Blundell, 2002; Stice, Presnell, Shaw, & Rohde, 2005). In some lower-income groups, particularly African American communities, unhealthy eating and drinking in readily available fast-food outlets actually does seem to reduce stress, but with damaging physical consequences (Jackson, Knight, & Rafferty, 2010). Many of these attitudes as well as eating habits are strongly influenced by family and close friends. In an important study, Christakis and Fowler (2007) studied the social networks (close friends and neighbors) of more than 12,000 people for more than 30 years. They found that a person's chance of becoming obese increased from 37% to 57% if a spouse, sibling, or even a close friend was obese, but it did not if a neighbor or coworker with whom the person did not socialize was obese. Thus, it seems that obesity spreads through social networks. Although the etiology of obesity is extraordinarily complex, as with most mental health problems, an interaction of biological and psychological factors with a notably strong environmental and cultural contribution provides the most complete account.

Treatment

The treatment of obesity is only moderately successful at the individual level (Bray, 2012; Ludwig, 2012), with somewhat greater long-term evidence for effectiveness in children compared to adults (Sarwer et al., 2004; Waters et al., 2011). Treatment is usually organized in a series of steps from least intrusive to most intrusive depending on the extent of obesity. The first step is usually a self-directed weight-loss program in individuals who buy a popular diet book. The most usual result is that some individuals may lose some weight in the short term but almost always regain that weight (Mann, Tomiyama, & Ward, 2015). Furthermore, these books do little to change lifelong eating and exercise habits (Freedman, King, & Kennedy, 2001) and few individuals successfully achieve long-term results on these diets, which is one of the reasons the latest one is always on the best-seller list. Similarly, there is little evidence that physician counseling results in any changes (Wing, 2010). Nevertheless, physicians can play an important role by providing specific treatment recommendations, including referral to professionals (Sarwer et al., 2004).

Several studies have compared the most popular diet programs, such as the Atkins (carbohydrate restriction), Ornish (fat restriction), Zone (macronutrients balance), and Weight Watchers (calorie restriction) diets. Generally, there were few differences among groups, with weight loss averaging between 4 and 7 pounds after 1 year. But only 50% to 65% stuck with the diet (Dansinger, Gleason, Griffith, Secker, & Schaefer, 2005; Gardiner et al., 2007; Johnston et al., 2014). The Atkins diet did seem safe in these studies, contrary to some previous assumptions about carbohydrate restrictions.

The next step is commercial self-help programs such as Weight Watchers and Jenny Craig. Weight Watchers reports that, in 2014, more than 800,000 people attended more than 36,000 meetings weekly around the world (Weight Watchers International, 2014). These programs stand a better chance of achieving some success, at least compared with self-directed programs (Jakicic et al., 2012; Johnston, Rost, Miller-Kovach, Moreno, & Foreyt, 2013; Wing, 2010). In an earlier study (Heshka et al., 2003) among members who successfully lost weight initially and kept their weight off for at least 6 weeks after completing the program, between 19% and 37% weighed within 5 pounds of their goal weight at least 5 years after treatment (Lowe, Miller-Kovach, Frie, & Phelan, 1999; Sarwer et al., 2004). But this means that up to 80% of individuals, even if they are initially successful, are not successful in the long run.

But there is one modification that not only keeps almost everyone in the program but also produces results that are as much as twice is good after 2 years (Rock et al., 2010). What is this modification? The program, including the food, was provided free of charge, thereby providing a strong incentive. Many would question why people should be paid to stay in weight-loss programs. But given the substantial medical costs associated with obesity, particularly in lower-income groups, many public health professionals would judge that these incentives save the health-care system and taxpayers far more money than they cost, particularly since other studies have shown the value of incentives on initial weight loss (John et al., 2011).

The most successful programs are professionally directed behavior modification programs. The combination of restricted calorie intake, increased physical activity, and behavior therapy tends to lead to more weight loss than any of these components on their own (Wadden, Butryn, Hong, & Tsai, 2014). Other research has suggested that behavior modification programs are particularly effective if patients attend group maintenance sessions periodically in the year following initial weight reduction (Bray, 2012; Wing, 2010). In a major study, Svetkey and colleagues (2008) randomly assigned 1,032 overweight or obese adults who had lost at least 10 pounds (4 kilograms) during a 6-month behavior modification program to one of three weight-loss maintenance conditions for 30 months: (1) once-a-month contact with a counselor to help them maintain their program (personal contact group), (2) a website they could log on to when they wanted to maintain their program (interactive technology group), and (3) a control comparison in which they were on their own (self-directed group). Overall, 71% remained below their entry weights, which was a very good result, but the group with once-a-month contact gained back less weight than the interactive technology and the control comparison groups. Nevertheless, even these programs do not produce impressive results. Although participants lost 19 pounds (8 kilograms) on average during the initial 6-month program, individuals in the control group and the interactive technology group gained back approximately 12 pounds (5.2–5.5 kilograms), and those in the once-a-month contact group gained back approximately 9 pounds (4 kilograms) after 2.5 years.

For those individuals who have become more dangerously obese, very low-calorie diets and possibly drugs, combined with behavior modification programs, are recommended (Yanovski & Yanovski, 2014). Patients lose as much as 20% of their weight on very low-calorie diets, which typically consist of 4 to 6 liquid meal replacement products, or "shakes," a day. At the end of 3 or 4 months, they are then placed on a low-calorie balanced diet. As with all weight-loss programs, patients typically regain up to 50% of their lost weight in the year following treatment (Ames, et al., 2014; Wadden & Osei, 2002). But more than half of them are able to maintain a weight loss of at least 5%, which is important in very obese people (Sarwer et al., 2004). Similarly, drug treatments that reduce internal cues signaling hunger may have some effect, particularly if combined with a behavioral approach targeting lifestyle change, but concerns about cardiovascular side effects have plagued these medications (Morrato & Allison, 2012, Yanovski & Yanovski, 2014). Currently, the FDA has only a few approved drugs approved for this purpose, such as lorcaserin (Belviq) and phentermine/topiramate (Osymia). Another drug, sibutramine (Meridia), was removed from the market in 2010 due to adverse cardiovascular side effects (Kuehn, 2010). Finally, the surgical approach to extreme obesity—called **bariatric surgery**—is an increasingly popular approach for individuals with a BMI of at least 40 (Adams et al., 2012; Arteburn & Fisher, 2014; Courcoulas, 2012; Livingston, 2012). This surgery has been performed on several celebrities, such as music producer/*American Idol* judge Randy Jackson, and television personalities Sharon Osbourne and Al Roker. As noted earlier, 6.3% of the population in the United States now falls into this BMI of 40 or above category (Flegal et al., 2012). Up to 220,000 individuals received bariatric surgery in 2009 (American Society for Metabolic & Bariatric Surgery, 2010). Furthermore, it is usually more successful than diets, with patients losing approximately 20% to 30% of their body weight postoperatively and maintaining these results over a number of years (Adams et al., 2012; Buchwald et al., 2004; Courcoulas et al., 2013). Sjöström et al. (2012) studied a large group of more than

2,000 patients receiving surgery and reported an average 23% weight loss after 2 years and 18% after 20 years, compared with essentially no weight loss on average for 2,000 severely obese individuals who did not have the surgery. Bariatric surgery is also associated with lower mortality in obese individuals up to 14 years after the procedure (Arteburn et al., 2015). Surprisingly few studies report long-term outcomes from this procedure, and more research is needed in this area (Ikramuddin & Livingston, 2013; Puzziferri et al., 2014) This surgery is reserved only for the most severely obese individuals for whom the obesity is an imminent health risk because the surgery is permanent. Typically, patients must have one or more obesity-related physical conditions, such as heart disease or diabetes. In the most common surgery, part of the stomach is removed to create a sleeve or tubelike structure (Reames, Finks, Bacal, Carline, & Dimick, 2014). Alternatively, a gastric bypass operation creates a bypass of the stomach, as the name implies, which limits not only food intake but also absorption of calories.

Approximately 15% of patients who have bariatric surgery fail to lose significant weight, or they regain lost weight after surgery (Latfi, Kellum, DeMaria, & Sugarman, 2002; Livhits et al., 2012). A small percentage of individuals, from 0.1% to 0.5%, do not survive the operation, and an additional 15% to 20% experience severe complications requiring rehospitalization and additional surgery within the first year after surgery and in each of the next 2 years after that (Birkmeyer et al., 2013; O'Brien et al., 2010; Zingmond, McGory, & Ko, 2005). The mortality rate may increase to as much as 2% in hospitals where the surgery is done less often (usually fewer than 100 operations for a given surgeon), but the 30-day mortality rate averages about 1% and nearly 6% after 5 years (Omalu et al., 2007). There is some evidence that these rates are not different from severely obese individuals who do not have the surgery at the 5-year point (Livingston, 2007). Furthermore, if the surgery is successful, risk of death from obesity-related diseases such as diabetes is reduced substantially, as much as 90% in some studies (Adams et al., 2007). Although some data from the very large Sjöström et al. (2012) study mentioned above also indicates that reductions in mortality, at least from cardiovascular events, are significant but relatively small, more puzzling is the finding that reduction in cardiovascular events was not related simply to the weight loss itself, which implies that some other life change may be responsible. This suggests that this surgery should not become routine until we know more about it (Livingston, 2012; Wolfe & Belle, 2014). In any case, surgeons typically require patients to exhaust all other treatment options and to undergo a thorough psychological assessment to ascertain whether they can adapt to the radically changed eating patterns required postsurgery (Kral, 2002; Livingston, 2010; Sarwer et al., 2004). New psychological programs have been designed specifically to prepare patients for this surgery and help them adapt following surgery (Apple, Lock, & Peebles, 2006). With these new programs, surgery may be the best bet for severely obese individuals, but only a small proportion of those eligible are getting the surgery because of its controversial nature (Livingston, 2007; Santry, Gillen, & Lauderdale, 2005). This may change in the coming years as the surgical procedures become more sophisticated and we learn more about the precise nature of the benefits of surgery. But we are also learning more about diet and exercise programs and, contrary to earlier assumptions, find that well-designed programs will benefit even severely obese individuals (Goodpaster et al., 2010; Ryan & Kushner, 2010).

Gary Gershoff/WireImages/Getty Images
Robin Marchant/Getty Images

Celebrities Star Jones and Al Roker had weight loss surgery to address their morbid obesity.

Turning to public health policy approaches, many states are removing soft drink machines and other sources of unhealthy snack foods from public schools. New York City attempted to ban the sale of sweetened soda in sizes over 16 oz altogether in 2012, but after big beverage companies and others objected, this proposed regulation was struck down by the New York Court of Appeals (Grynbaum, 2014). Nine states have also requested permission from the federal government to eliminate the option of buying sugar-sweetened beverages with food stamps, a proposal that is supported by the American Medical Association (Brownell & Ludwig, 2011).

Food taxes have also been discussed as a way to raise revenue that could be used in the fight against the obesity epidemic to promote education and policy changes on food consumption. Could the government make it more attractive to eat healthy foods and less attractive to eat unhealthy foods by making the former less expensive and the latter more expensive? The Rudd Center for Food Policy and Obesity at Yale is studying the issue intensely. By 2009, 40 states had put into place some taxes on snack foods or soft drinks (Brownell & Frieden, 2009). The thinking is that taxes would have to be increased considerably to provide a substantial disincentive. Several years ago, a prestigious group of scientists proposed in the *New England Journal of Medicine* that an excise tax of 1 cent per ounce be placed on beverages that have any added caloric sweetener. This would raise the cost of a 20-ounce soft drink by approximately 20%. Any substantial tax, with its implications of government control of our behavior, would be controversial and roundly criticized by many. But counterarguments point out the obligation of the government to create policy that supports the individual efforts of all people to be healthy (Brownell et al., 2010).

Can We Prevent Obesity?

Society is increasingly turning its attention to ways in which we might prevent continuation of the obesity epidemic. The greatest benefits may come from strategies that focus on prevention by altering factors in the "toxic environment" that strongly encourage the intake of unhealthy foods and a sedentary lifestyle (Brownell, 2002; Gearhardt et al., 2012).

For example, ■ Figure 8.9 shows the relative price over the past 30 years of sugar and sweets versus healthy fresh food. Several years ago, Kelly Brownell, now professor and dean of the School of Public Policy at Duke University, proposed in the *New York Times* that we should consider taxing high-calorie, high-fat, or high-sugar foods as a means of addressing the obesity epidemic. This proposal sparked a firestorm of controversy and came to be known as the "Twinkie tax." Although adding such a tax may not be enough, it is probably needed in a multicomponent strategy to curb the obesity epidemic (Bes-Rastrollo, Sayon-Orea, Ruiz-Canela, & Martinez-Gonzalez, 2016). Taxation is a powerful and commonly used tactic by governments around the world to set policy and shape the behavior of its citizens (Brownell & Frieden, 2009). A rapid increase in taxes on cigarettes has the goal of reducing smoking in our citizens and improving health. Increasing taxes on fossil fuels, including gasoline, is conceived by many as one tool for promoting conservation and diminishing the release of harmful chemicals into our environment that contribute to global warming. Substantial tax breaks on alternative sources of energy such as wind power and solar energy are another government tool for promoting these sources.

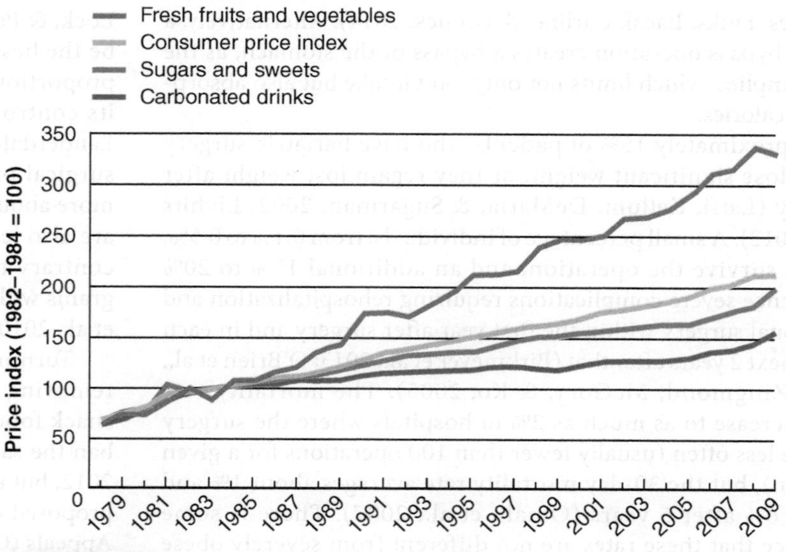

Figure 8.9

Price changes for fruits and vegetables versus sugar and sweets and carbonated drinks, 1978–2009. From K. D. Brownell & T. R. Frieden, 2009, Ounces of prevention: The public policy case for taxes on sugared beverages, *New England Journal of Medicine, 360*, 1805–1808.

These debates are now raging around the country and around the world. What would you do? Would you propose that governments intervene economically to change the nutrition of our citizens? Or would you rely solely on education and other means of persuasion? Governments will have to make these choices because it seems clear that the obesity epidemic is one of the greatest threats to health in recent history.

Another public health approach is choice architecture—that is, designing different ways in which choices can be presented to consumers. One line of research has explored the effects of labeling foods with traffic light colors (i.e., red, yellow, or green) based on their nutritional value. In two studies (Thorndike, Riis, Sonnenberg, & Levy, 2014; Thorndike, Sonnenberg, Riis, Barraclough, & Levy, 2012) researchers found that labeling food in this manner led to decreases in purchases of red (i.e., unhealthy) foods and increases in purchases of green (i.e., healthy foods). While promising, more research is needed in this area.

In contrast to adults, the treatment of obesity in children and adolescents has achieved somewhat better outcomes both the short term and long term (Cooperberg & Faith, 2004; Epstein, Myers, Raynor, & Saelens, 1998; Oude Luttikhuis et al., 2011), particularly for children. A number of studies report that behavior modification programs, especially those that include parents, may produce a 20% reduction in overweight children or adolescents, a change maintained for at least several years after the end of the study. Again, these behavior modification programs include a number of strategies to change dietary habits, particularly decreasing high-calorie, high-fat snacks. These programs also target reduction of sedentary habits in children and adolescents, such as viewing television, playing video games, and sitting in front of a computer. These programs may be more successful than with adults because parents are typically fully engaged in the program in a constructive way and provide constant and continuing support (Altman & Wilfey, 2015; Ludwig, 2012). This is

Concept Check 8.3

Mark the following statements about obesity as either true (T) or false (F).

1. ____________ Obesity is the single most expensive health problem in the United States, surpassing both smoking and alcohol dependency.
2. ____________ Individuals with night eating syndrome consume at least half their daily intake after their evening meal.
3. ____________ Fatty foods and technology are not to blame for the obesity epidemic in the United States.
4. ____________ Professionally directed behavior modification programs represent the most successful treatment for obesity.

important because many parents who are not part of structured program have a tendency to continually pressure their overweight children not to eat, which has the opposite effect of causing them to eat more (Agras et al., 2012). Also, dietary habits in children are less engrained than in adults. In addition, children are generally more physically active if provided with appropriate activities (Cooperberg & Faith, 2004). In addition, programs that directly involve children and their parents seem to have a better chance of working to some extent if they are brief, intensive, and focused on just eating and exercise, as opposed to focused on general health issues (Stice, Shaw, & Marti, 2006). For the most severely obese adolescents with a BMI greater than 35, a less intrusive and safer bariatric surgical procedure than the one typically done on adults is now being evaluated, and initial results suggest short-term reduction in weight, but the long-term effects remain to be seen (Black, White, Viner, & Simmons, 2013; O'Brien et al., 2010).

Most of us recognize that eating is essential to our survival. Equally important is sleep, a still relatively mysterious process crucial to everyday functioning and strongly implicated in many psychological disorders. We turn our attention to this additional survival activity in an effort to understand better how and why we can be harmed by sleep disturbances.

Sleep–Wake Disorders: The Major Dyssomnias

We spend about one third of our lives asleep. That means most of us sleep nearly 3,000 hours per *year*. For many, sleep is energizing, both mentally and physically. Unfortunately, most people do not get enough sleep, and 28% of people in the United States report feeling excessively sleepy during the day (Ohayon, Dauvilliers, & Reynolds, 2012). Most of us know what it is like to have a bad night's sleep. The next day we are a little groggy, and as the day wears on, we may become irritable. Research tells us that even minor sleep deprivation over only 24 hours impedes our ability to think clearly (Hudson, Van Dongen, & Honn, 2020). Now imagine, if you can, that it has been years since you've had a good night's sleep. Your relationships suffer, it is difficult to do your schoolwork, and your efficiency and productivity at work are diminished. Lack of sleep also affects you physically. People who do not get enough sleep are more susceptible to illnesses such as the common cold, perhaps because immune system functioning is reduced with the loss of even a few hours of sleep (Ruiz et al., 2012). It has also been suggested that sleep deprivation may have made people more susceptible to viruses such as COVID-19 (Silva et al., 2020).

Here you might ask yourself how sleep–wake disorders fit into a textbook on abnormal psychology. Different variations of disturbed sleep clearly have physiological bases and therefore could be considered purely medical concerns. Like other physical disorders, however, sleep problems interact in important ways with psychological factors (During, 2021a).

An Overview of Sleep–Wake Disorders

The study of sleep has long influenced concepts of psychopathology. Moral treatment, used in the 19th century for people with severe mental illness, included encouraging patients to get adequate amounts of sleep as part of therapy (Charland, 2008). Sigmund Freud greatly emphasized dreams and discussed them with patients as a way of better understanding their emotional lives (Ursano, Sonnenberg, & Lazar, 2008). Researchers who prevented people from sleeping for prolonged periods found that chronic sleep deprivation often had profound effects. An early study in this area looked at the effects of keeping 350 volunteers awake for 112 hours (Tyler, 1955). Seven volunteers engaged in bizarre behavior that seemed psychotic. Subsequent research suggested that it was interfering with the sleep of people with preexisting psychological problems that can create these disturbing results (Brauchi & West, 1959). A number of the disorders covered in this book are often associated with sleep complaints, including autism spectrum disorder, schizophrenia, major depression, bipolar disorder, anxiety-related disorders (During, 2021a), and seasonal affective disorder. You may think at first that a sleep problem is the result of a psychological disorder. For example, how often have you been anxious about a future event (an upcoming exam, perhaps) and not been able to fall asleep? The relationship between sleep disturbances and mental health is more complex, however (Pires, Tufik, & Andersen, 2015; McEwen & Karatsoreos, 2015). Sleep problems may cause the difficulties people experience in everyday life (for example, Almklov, Drummond, Orff, & Alhassoon, 2015; Kreutzmann, Havekes, Abel, & Meerlo, 2015; McKenna & Eyler, 2012; Talbot et al., 2012; van der Kloet, Giesbrecht, Lynn, Merckelbach, & de Zutter, 2012), or they may result from some disturbance common to a psychological disorder. For example, the disordered behavior of persons with borderline personality disorder (see Chapter 12) may be attributed to the genes associated with circadian rhythms (circadian CLOCK genes) (Vanek et al., 2021).

In Chapter 5, we explain how a brain circuit in the limbic system might be involved with anxiety. We know that this region of the brain is also involved with our dream sleep, which is called **rapid eye movement (REM) sleep** (Marques et al., in press). This mutual neurobiological connection suggests that anxiety and sleep may be interrelated in important ways, although the exact nature of the relationship is still unknown. Insufficient sleep, for example, can stimulate overeating and may contribute to the epidemic of obesity (Hanlon & Knutson, 2014). Similarly, REM sleep seems related to depression, as noted in Chapter 7 (Vanek et al., 2021). Sleep abnormalities are preceding signs of serious clinical depression, which may suggest that sleep problems can help predict who is at risk for later mood disorders (Murphy & Peterson, 2015). In an intriguing study, researchers found that CBT improved symptoms among a group of depressed men and normalized REM sleep patterns (Nofzinger et al., 1994). Furthermore, sleep deprivation has temporary antidepressant effects on some people, although in people who are not already depressed, sleep deprivation may bring on a depressed mood (Voderhozer et al., 2014). We do not fully understand how psychological disorders are related to sleep, yet accumulating research points to the importance of understanding sleep if we are to complete the broader picture of psychopathology.

People differ greatly in their preferred timing of their sleep and activity schedules, and this seems to have an effect on their health. Some like to stay up late and sleep late, whereas others like to get up early and are very active in the morning. Are you an evening person or a morning person? The answer to this question defines your **chronotype** (Roenneberg, Pilz, Zerbini, & Winnebeck, 2019). Your chronotype (i.e., whether you are a morning or evening type) is regulated by both your circadian clock and genetic variations in the clock genes and the environment (Merikanto, Kantojärvi, Partonen, Pesonen, & Paunio, 2021). Social influences, such as school and work schedules, can easily interfere with your sleep preferences. Is your sleep–wake rhythm very different during the weekend when you can go to bed and sleep as long as you want? If you are an evening person based on your chronotype, then you might go to bed late and also get up 2 hours later on Saturday and Sunday than during a weekday.

Switching your schedule because of social factors is similar to changing time zones when you travel, which is why it is called **social jetlag** (Roenneberg et al., 2019; Wittmann, Dinich, Merrow, & Roenneberg, 2006). When you cross time zones during your travel, the sun rises and sets at a different time, and your body slowly gets used to it to match the new rhythm. But during social jetlag, your body can't adjust because this disruption is often repeated. As is true for travel jet lag (and shift workers), social jet lag can take a toll on people's health and performance. It is associated with sleep problems and many other health issues, such as obesity (Roenneberg et al., 2019). For example, one study examined 804 adolescents (418 girls and 386 boys) with a mean age of 13.2. For girls, social jet lag and evening chronotype was associated with greater waist circumference and body mass. These associations persisted even after adjustment for sleep duration and other lifestyle behaviors. By contrast, boys did not show these associations between weight measures, social jetlag, and evening chronotypes (Cespedes Feliciano et al. 2020). Even academic performance is affected when school times are not aligned with student's chronotypes (Goldin, Sigman, Braier, Golombek, & Leone, 2020).

Sleep–wake disorders are divided into two major categories: **dyssomnias** and **parasomnias** (see Table 8.4). Dyssomnias involve difficulties in getting enough sleep, problems with sleeping when you want to (not being able to fall asleep until 2 a.m. when you have a 9 a.m. class), and complaints about the quality of sleep, such as not feeling refreshed even though you have slept the whole night. Parasomnias are characterized by abnormal behavioral or physiological events that occur during sleep, such as nightmares and sleepwalking.

A number of assessments for sleep problems including questionnaires and taking a history of sleep problems. However, the clearest and most comprehensive picture of your sleep habits can be determined only by a **polysomnographic (PSG) evaluation** (Neubauer, 2021). The patient spends one or more nights sleeping in a sleep laboratory and being monitored on a number of measures, including respiration and oxygen desaturation (a measure of airflow); leg movements; brain wave activity, measured by an *electroencephalogram*; eye movements, measured by an *electrooculogram*; muscle movements, measured by an *electromyogram*; and heart activity, measured by an *electrocardiogram*. Daytime behavior and typical sleep patterns are also noted—for example, whether the person uses drugs or alcohol, is anxious about work or interpersonal problems, takes afternoon naps, or has a psychological disorder (Neubauer, 2021). Collecting all these data can be both time consuming and costly, but it is important to ensure an accurate diagnosis and treatment plan. One alternative to the comprehensive assessment of sleep is to use a wristwatch-size device called an **actigraph** (Maness & Trotti, 2021). This instrument records the number of arm movements,

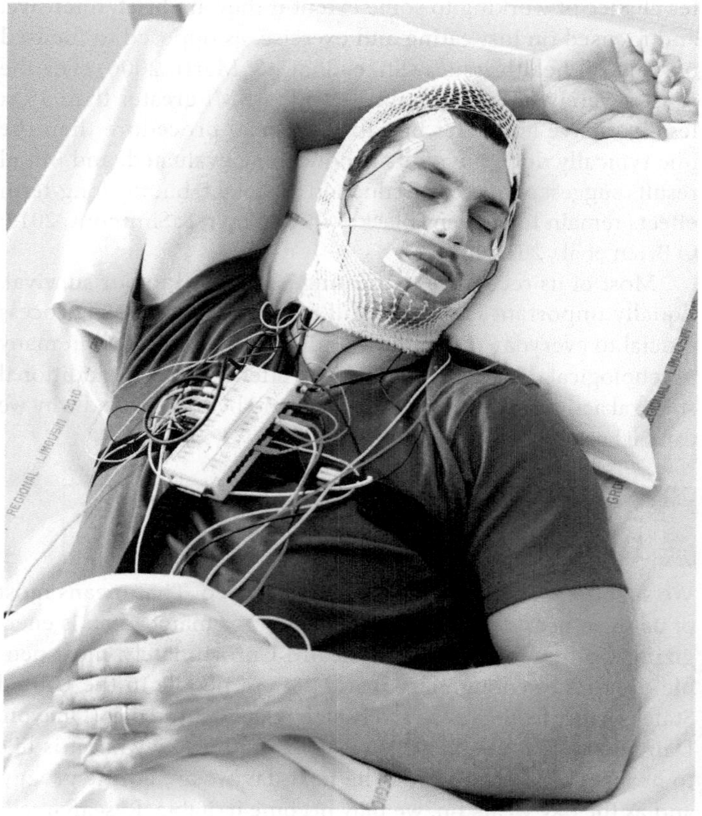

Burger/Phanie/Science Source

This participant is undergoing a polysomnograph, an overnight electronic evaluation of sleep patterns.

Table 8.4 Summary of DSM-5 Sleep–Wake Disorders

Sleep Disorder	Description
DYSSOMNIAS	(Problems in the amount, timing, or quality of sleep)
Insomnia disorder	Difficulty falling asleep at bedtime, problems staying asleep throughout the night, or sleep that does not result in the person feeling rested even after normal amounts of sleep.
Hypersomnolence disorders	Excessive sleepiness that is displayed as either sleeping longer than is typical or frequent falling asleep during the day.
Narcolepsy	Episodes of irresistible attacks of refreshing sleep occurring daily, accompanied by episodes of brief loss of muscle tone (cataplexy).
Breathing-related sleep disorders (obstructive sleep apnea hypopnea syndrome, central sleep apnea, and sleep-related hypoventilation)	A variety of breathing disorders that occur during sleep and that lead to excessive sleepiness or insomnia.
Circadian rhythm sleep–wake disorder	A discrepancy between the sleep–wake schedule required by a person to be rested and the requirements of the person's environment (for example, work schedules) that leads to excessive sleepiness or insomnia.
PARASOMNIAS	
Disorder of arousal	Motor movements and behaviors that occur during NREM sleep including incomplete awakening (confusional arousals), sleep walking, or sleep terrors (abrupt awakening from sleep that begins with a panicky scream).
Nightmare disorder	Frequently being awakened by extended and extremely frightening dreams that cause significant distress and impaired functioning.
Rapid eye movement sleep behavior disorder	Episodes of arousal during REM sleep that result in behaviors that can cause harm to the individual or others.
Restless legs syndrome	Irresistible urges to move the legs as a result of unpleasant sensations (sometimes labeled "creeping," "tugging," or "pulling" in the limbs) (otherwise referred to as Willis-Ekbom disease).
Substance-induced sleep disorder	Severe sleep disturbance that is the result of substance intoxication or withdrawal.

Source: Adapted from American Psychiatric Association, 2022, *Diagnostic and statistical manual of mental disorders* (5th ed., Text Revision).

and the data can be downloaded to a computer to determine the length and quality of sleep. Several studies have now tested the usefulness of this type of device in measuring the sleep of astronauts during space travel, and they find it can reliably detect when they fall asleep, when they wake up, and how restful their in-space sleep is (for example, Barger et al., 2014). The use of apps available through smartphones and separate wristband devices can also provide some of this information (de Zambotti, Claudatos, Inkelis, Colrain, & Baker, 2015). In addition, clinicians and researchers find it helpful to know the average number of hours the individual sleeps each day, taking into account **sleep efficiency (SE)**, the percentage of time actually spent asleep, not just lying in bed trying to sleep. SE is calculated by dividing the amount of time sleeping by the amount of time in bed. A SE of 100% would mean you fall asleep as soon as your head hits the pillow and do not wake up during the night. In contrast, a SE of 50% would mean half your time in bed is spent trying to fall asleep—that is, you are awake half the time. Such measurements help the clinician determine objectively how well you sleep.

One way to determine whether a person has a problem with sleep is to observe his daytime sequelae, or behavior while awake. For example, if it takes you 90 minutes to fall asleep at night but this does not bother you and you feel rested during the day, then you do not have a problem. A friend who also takes 90 minutes to fall asleep but finds this delay anxiety-provoking and is fatigued the next day might be considered to have a sleep problem. It is, to some degree, a subjective decision, partly depending on how the person perceives the situation and reacts to it.

Insomnia Disorder

Insomnia is one of the most common sleep–wake disorders (Neubauer, 2021). You may picture someone with insomnia as being awake all the time. It is not possible to go completely without sleep, however. For example, after being awake for one or two nights, a person begins having **microsleeps** that last approximately 15 seconds or shorter (Skorucak et al., 2020). In the rare occurrences of fatal familial insomnia (a degenerative brain disorder), total lack of sleep eventually leads to death (Baldelli, Calandra-Buonaura, Provini, & Cortelli, in press). Despite the common use of the term *insomnia* to mean "not sleeping," it actually applies to a number of complaints. People

DSM 5 **Table 8.4**

Diagnostic Criteria for Insomnia Disorder

A. A predominant complaint of dissatisfaction with sleep quantity or quality, associated with (one or more) of the following symptoms:

1. Difficulty initiating sleep. (In children, this may manifest as difficulty initiating sleep without caregiver intervention.)
2. Difficulty maintaining sleep, characterized by frequent awakenings or problems returning to sleep after awakenings. (In children, this may manifest as difficulty returning to sleep without caregiver intervention.)
3. Early-morning awakening with inability to return to sleep.

B. The sleep disturbance causes clinically significant distress in social, occupational, educational, academic, behavioral, or other important areas of functioning.

C. The sleep difficulty occurs at least 3 nights per week.

D. The sleep difficulty is present for at least 3 months.

E. The sleep difficulty occurs despite adequate opportunity for sleep.

F. The insomnia is not better explained by and does not occur exclusively during the course of another sleep–wake disorder (e.g., narcolepsy, a breathing-related sleep disorder, a circadian rhythm sleep–wake disorder, a parasomnia).

G. The insomnia is not attributable to the physiological effects of a substance (e.g., a drug of abuse, a medication).

H. Coexisting mental disorders and medical conditions do not adequately explain the predominant complaint of insomnia.

Specify if:

Episodic: Symptoms last at least 1 month but less than 3 months

Persistent: Symptoms last 3 months or longer

Recurrent: Two (or more) episodes within the space of 1 year

American Psychiatric Association. (2022). *Diagnostic and statistical manual of mental disorders* (5th ed., Text Revision).

are considered to have insomnia if they have trouble falling asleep at night (difficulty initiating sleep), if they wake up frequently or too early and can't go back to sleep (difficulty maintaining sleep), or even if they sleep a reasonable number of hours but are still not rested the next day (nonrestorative sleep). Consider the case of Indira.

Indira... School on Her Mind

Indira was a 23-year-old law student with a history of sleep problems. She reported that she never really slept well, both having trouble falling asleep at night and usually awakening again in the early morning. She had been using the nighttime cold medication Nyquil several times per week over the past few years to help her fall asleep. Unfortunately, since she started law school last year, her sleep problems had grown even worse. She would lie in bed awake until the early morning hours thinking about school, getting only 3 to 4 hours of sleep on a typical night. In the morning, she had a great deal of difficulty getting out of bed and was frequently late for her early morning class.

Indira's sleep problems and their interference with her schoolwork were causing her to experience increasingly severe depression. In addition, she recently reported having a severe anxiety attack that woke her in the middle of the night. All of these difficulties caused her to be increasingly isolated from family and friends, who finally convinced her to seek help.

We return to Indira later in this chapter.

Clinical Description

Indira's symptoms meet the DSM-5-TR criteria for **insomnia disorder** because her sleep problems were not related to other medical or psychiatric problems (also referred to as **primary insomnia**). Looking at sleep-wake disorders as primary recalls the overlap of sleep problems with psychological disorders such as anxiety and depression. Because not sleeping makes you anxious and anxiety further interrupts your sleep—which makes you more anxious, and so on—it is uncommon to find a person with a simple sleep–wake disorder and no related problems.

Indira's is a typical case of insomnia disorder. She had trouble both initiating and maintaining sleep. Other people sleep all night but still feel as if they have been awake for hours. Although most people can carry out necessary day-to-day activities, their inability to concentrate can have serious consequences, such as debilitating accidents when they attempt to drive long distances (like bus drivers) or handle dangerous material (like electricians). Students with insomnia like Indira's may do poorly in school because of difficulty concentrating.

Statistics

Approximately one third of the population reports some symptoms of insomnia during any given year (Chung et al., 2015). The prevalence of insomnia in the general population across 66 sites and 57,298 participants of different economic levels and sociocultural values among 13 countries around the world found that it ranged from 2.3% to 25.5% (Eva et al., 2021). For many of these individuals, sleep difficulties are a lifetime affliction (Lind, Aggen, Kirkpatrick, Kendler, & Amstadter, 2015). Approximately 15% of older adults report excessive daytime sleepiness (Berkley, Carter, Yoder, Acton, & Holahan, 2020), with older Black men reporting the most problems, and this contributes to increased risk for falling (Green, Ndao-Brumblay, & Hart-Johnson, 2009; Hayley et al., 2015).

A number of psychological disorders are associated with insomnia. Total sleep time often decreases with depression, substance use disorders, anxiety disorders, and neurocognitive disorder due to Alzheimer's disease. The interrelationship between alcohol use and sleep disorders can be particularly troubling. Alcohol is often used to initiate sleep (Morin et al., 2012). In small amounts, it helps make people drowsy, but it also interrupts ongoing sleep. Interrupted sleep causes anxiety, which often leads to repeated alcohol use and an obviously vicious cycle.

Women report insomnia twice as often as men. Women more often report problems initiating sleep, which may be related to hormonal differences or to differential reporting of sleep problems, with women generally more negatively affected by poor sleep than men (Jaussent et al., 2011). There may be some protective factors that can improve sleep in women, including moderate alcohol and caffeine use and following a Mediterranean diet (for example, a high intake of vegetables, legumes, and fruits and unsaturated fatty acids mostly in the form of olive oil) (Jaussent et al., 2011). Just as people's needs concerning normal sleep change over time, complaints of insomnia differ in frequency among people of different ages. Children who have difficulty falling asleep usually throw a tantrum at bedtime or do not want to go to bed. Many children cry when they wake in the middle of the night. Approximately 30% young children experiences insomnia (Bruni et al., 2020). Growing evidence points to both biological and cultural explanations for poor sleep among adolescents. As children move into adolescence, their biologically determined sleep schedules shift toward a later bedtime (Skeldon, Dirks, & Dijk, 2015). At least in the United States, however, children are still expected to rise early for school, causing chronic sleep deprivation. This problem is not observed among all adolescents, with ethnocultural differences reported among youth from different backgrounds. One study, for example, found that Chinese American youth reported the fewest problems with insomnia, and Mexican American adolescents reported the most difficulty sleeping (Roberts, Roberts, & Chen, 2000). The percentage of individuals who complain of sleep problems increases as they become older adults. A national sleep poll revealed that among adults from 55 to 64 years of age, 26% complain of sleep problems, but this decreases to about 21% for those from 65 to 84 years (National Sleep Foundation, 2009). This higher rate in reports of sleeping problems among older people makes sense when you remember that the number of hours we sleep decreases as we age. It is not uncommon for someone over 65 to sleep fewer than 6 hours and wake up several times each night.

Causes

Insomnia accompanies many medical and psychological disorders, including pain and physical discomfort, physical inactivity during the day, and respiratory problems. Sometimes insomnia is related to problems with the biological clock and its control of temperature. Some people who can't fall asleep at night may have a delayed temperature rhythm: Their body temperature doesn't drop, and they don't become drowsy until later at night. As a group, people with insomnia seem to have higher body temperatures than good sleepers, and their body temperatures seem to vary less; this lack of fluctuation may interfere with sleep (Vargas et al., 2020).

Among the other factors that can interfere with sleeping are drug use and a variety of environmental influences such as changes in light, noise, or temperature. People admitted to hospitals often have difficulty sleeping because the noises and routines differ from those at home. Other sleep disorders, such as *sleep apnea* (a disorder that involves obstructed nighttime breathing) (Singh, 2021) or *periodic limb movement disorder* (excessive jerky leg movements) (Buchfuhrer & Buchfuhrer, 2021), can cause interrupted sleep and may seem similar to insomnia.

Finally, various psychological stresses can also disrupt your sleep. For example, one study looked at how medical and dental school students were affected by a particularly stressful event —in this case, participating in cadaver dissection (Snelling, Sahai, & Ellis, 2003). Among the effects reported by the students was a decrease in their ability to sleep.

People with insomnia may have unrealistic expectations about how much sleep they need ("I need a full 8 hours") and about how disruptive disturbed sleep will be ("I won't be able to think or do my job if I sleep for only 5 hours") (Neubauer, 2021). The actual amount of sleep each person needs varies and is assessed by how it affects you during the day. It is important to recognize the role of cognition in insomnia; our thoughts alone may disrupt our sleep.

Is poor sleeping a learned behavior? It is generally accepted that people suffering from sleep problems associate the bedroom and bed with the frustration and anxiety that go with insomnia. Eventually, the arrival of bedtime itself may cause anxiety (Morin & Benca, 2012). Interactions associated with sleep may contribute to children's sleep problems. For example, one study found that a parent's depression and negative thoughts about child sleep negatively influenced infant night waking (Teti & Crosby, 2012). Researchers think that some children learn to fall asleep only with a parent present; if they wake up at night, they are frightened at finding themselves alone, and their sleep is disrupted. Despite widespread acceptance of the role of learning in insomnia, relatively little research has been done on this phenomenon, perhaps partly because this type of research would involve going into homes and bedrooms at an especially private time.

Cross-cultural sleep research has focused primarily on children. In the predominant culture in the United States, infants are expected to sleep on their own, in a separate bed, and, if possible, in a separate room (see Table 8.5). In other cultures as diverse as rural Guatemala and Korea and urban Japan, however, the child spends the first few years of life in the same room and sometimes the same bed as the mother (Burnham & Gaylor, 2011). In many cultures, mothers report that they do not ignore the cries of their children (Giannotti & Cortesi, 2009), in stark contrast to the United States, where many pediatricians recommend that parents ignore the cries of their infants over a certain age at night (Moore, 2012). One conclusion from this research is that sleep can be affected by cultural norms. Unmet demands can result in stress that negatively affects the ultimate sleep outcome for children (Durand, 2008, 2014).

An Integrative Model

An integrative view of sleep disorders includes several assumptions. The first is that, at some level, both biological and psychological factors are present in most cases. A second assumption is that these multiple factors are reciprocally related. This can be seen in the study we noted earlier, where a parent's depression and negative thoughts about child sleep negatively influenced infant night waking (Teti & Crosby, 2012). In other words, personality characteristics, sleep difficulties, and parental reaction interact in a reciprocal manner to produce and maintain sleep problems.

Table 8.5 Cross-Cultural Differences in Child Sleep

When Children Sleep	
United States	Non-White children will often go to bed later, get up later, and sleep less than White children.
Italy	Italian children have a shorter nightly sleep duration—going to bed later and waking up earlier—than children in the United States.
Japan	Japanese children sleep less, sometimes napping after dinner but waking up to study late into the night.
Netherlands	Dutch infants sleep longer, going to bed earlier.
Bali	Balinese children may participate in occasional spiritual observances throughout the night and sleep on and off.
China	Chinese children's sleep changes seasonally, presumably to coincide with family work patterns.
Bedtime Routines	
Guatemala (Mayan), Spain, Greece, and Italy	In these countries, there is no bedtime routine, and children are often allowed to fall asleep during family activities and then be put to bed.
Bali	Balinese infants are held all day long and sleep as needed.
Where Children Sleep	
Italy	It is common for Italian children to sleep in the same room as the parents.
Japan	Japanese children often sleep in the same bed as parents.

Adapted from V. M. Durand, 2008, *When children don't sleep well: Interventions for pediatric sleep disorders. A therapist guide* (Oxford University Press); O. G. Jenni & B. B. O'Connor, 2005, Children's sleep: An interplay between culture and biology, *Pediatrics, 115*(1), 204–216.

People may be biologically vulnerable to disturbed sleep. This vulnerability differs from person to person and can range from mild to more severe disturbances. For example, a person may be a light sleeper (easily aroused at night) or have a family history of insomnia, narcolepsy, or obstructed breathing. All these factors can lead to eventual sleeping problems. Such influences have been referred to as *predisposing conditions* (Spielman & Glovinsky, 1991); they may not, by themselves, always cause problems, but they may combine with other factors to interfere with sleep (see ■ Figure 8.10).

Biological vulnerability may, in turn, interact with *sleep stress* (Durand, 2008), which includes a number of events that can negatively affect sleep. For example, poor bedtime habits (such as having too much alcohol or caffeine) can interfere with falling asleep (Morin et al., 2012). Note that biological vulnerability and sleep stress influence each other (as shown in ■ Figure 8.10). Although we may intuitively assume that biological factors come first, extrinsic influences such as poor sleep hygiene (the daily activities that affect how we sleep) can affect the physiological activity of sleep. One of the most striking examples of this phenomenon is jet lag, in which people's sleep patterns are disrupted, sometimes seriously, when they fly across several time zones. Whether disturbances continue or become more severe may depend on how they are managed. For example, many people react to disrupted sleep by taking over-the-counter sleeping pills. Unfortunately, most people are not aware that **rebound insomnia**—where sleep problems reappear, sometimes worse—may occur when the medication is withdrawn. This rebound leads people to

iStock.com/RonTech2000

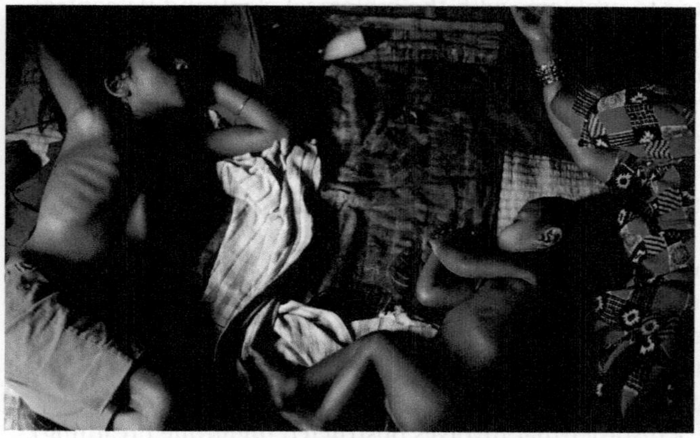

Ridofranz/Getty Images

In the United States, children usually sleep alone (left). In many cultures, all family members share the same bed (right).

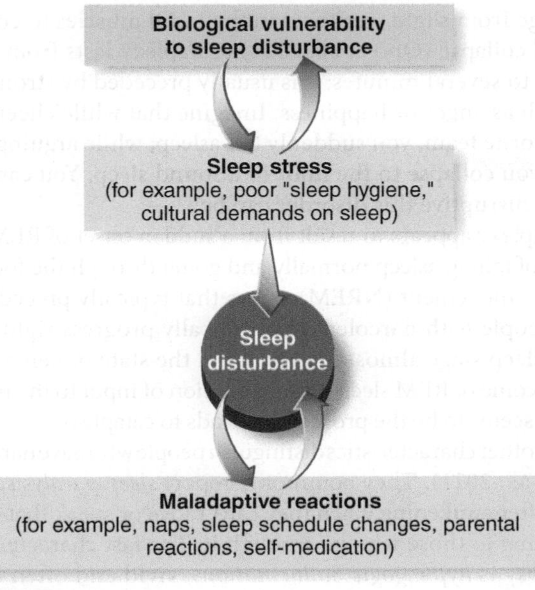

Figure 8.10

An integrative, multidimensional model of sleep disturbance.

think they still have a sleep problem, readminister the medicine, and go through the cycle repeatedly. In other words, taking sleep aids can perpetuate sleep problems.

Other ways of reacting to poor sleep can also prolong problems. It seems reasonable that a person who hasn't had enough sleep can make up for this loss by napping during the day. Unfortunately, naps that alleviate fatigue during the day can also disrupt sleep that night. Anxiety can also extend the problem. Lying in bed worrying about school, family problems, or even about not being able to sleep will interfere with sleep (O'Kearney & Pech, 2014). The behavior of parents can also help maintain these problems in children. Children who receive a great deal of positive attention at night when they wake up may wake up during the night more often (Durand, 2014). Such maladaptive reactions, when combined with a biological predisposition to sleep problems and sleep stress, may account for continuing problems.

Hypersomnolence Disorders

Insomnia disorder involves not getting enough sleep (the prefix *in* means "lacking" or "without"), and **hypersomnolence disorders** involve sleeping too much (*hyper* means "in great amount" or "abnormal excess") (Maness & Trotti, 2021). Many people who sleep all night find themselves falling asleep several times the next day. Consider the case of Hoa.

The DSM-5-TR diagnostic criteria for hypersomnolence include not only the excessive sleepiness that Hoa describes but also the subjective impression of this problem (American Psychiatric Association, 2022). Remember that whether insomnia disorder is a problem depends on how it affects each person. Hoa found her disorder disruptive because it interfered with driving and paying attention in class. Hypersomnolence caused her to be less successful academically and upset her personally, both of which are defining features of this disorder. She slept approximately 8 hours each night, so her daytime sleepiness could not be attributed to insufficient sleep.

Several factors that can cause excessive sleepiness would not be considered hypersomnolence. For example, people with insomnia disorder (who get inadequate amounts of sleep) often report being tired during the day. In contrast, people with hypersomnolence sleep through the night (sometimes longer than is typical) but still complain of being excessively tired throughout the day (Maness & Trotti, 2021). Another sleep problem that can cause a similar excessive sleepiness is a breathing-related sleep disorder called **sleep apnea** (Gu & Sullivan, 2021; Wu & Guilleminault, 2021). People with this problem have difficulty breathing at night. They often snore loudly, pause between breaths, and wake in the morning with a dry mouth and headache. In identifying hypersomnolence, the clinician needs to rule out insomnia, sleep apnea, or other reasons for sleepiness during the day (American Psychiatric Association, 2022).

We are just beginning to understand the nature of hypersomnolence, so relatively little research has been done on its causes (Maness & Trotti, 2021). Genetic influences seem to be involved in a portion of cases, with individuals having an increased

Hoa... Sleeping in Public

Hoa, a college student, came to my office to discuss her progress in class. We talked about several questions that she got wrong on the last exam, and as she was about to leave, she said that she never fell asleep during my class. This seemed like faint praise, but I thanked her for the feedback. "No," she said, "you don't understand. I usually fall asleep in *all* of my classes, but not in yours." Again, I didn't quite understand what she was trying to tell me and joked that she must pick her professors more carefully. She laughed. "That's probably true. But I also have this problem with sleeping too much."

As we talked more seriously, Hoa told me that excessive sleeping had been a problem since her teenage years. In situations that were monotonous or boring or when she couldn't be active, she fell asleep. This could happen several times a day, depending on what she was doing. Recently, large lecture classes had become a problem unless the lecturer was particularly interesting or animated. Watching television and driving long distances were also problematic.

Hoa reported that her father had a similar problem. He had recently been diagnosed with narcolepsy (which we discuss next) and was now getting help at a clinic. Both she and her brother had been diagnosed with hypersomnolence disorder. Hoa had been prescribed Ritalin (a stimulant medication) about 4 years ago and said that it was only somewhat effective in keeping her awake during the day. She said the drug helped reduce the sleep attacks but did not eliminate them altogether.

DSM 5 **Table 8.5**
Diagnostic Criteria for Hypersomnolence Disorder

A. Self-reported excessive sleepiness (hypersomnolence) despite a main sleep period lasting at least 7 hours, with at least one of the following symptoms:

1. Recurrent periods of sleep or lapses into sleep within the same day.

2. A prolonged main sleep episode of more than 9 hours per day that is nonrestorative (i.e., unrefreshing).

3. Difficulty being fully awake after abrupt awakening.

B. The hypersomnolence occurs at least three times per week, for at least 3 months.

C. The hypersomnolence is accompanied by significant distress or impairment in cognitive, social, occupational, or other important areas of functioning.

D. The hypersomnolence is not better explained by and does not occur exclusively during the course of another sleep disorder (e.g., narcolepsy, breathing-related sleep disorder, circadian rhythm sleep–wake disorder, or a parasomnia).

E. The hypersomnolence is not attributable to the physiological effects of a substance (e.g., a drug of abuse, a medication).

F. Coexisting mental and medical disorders do not adequately explain the predominant complaint of hypersomnolence.

Specify if:

Acute: Duration of less than 1 month

Subacute: Duration of 1–3 months

Persistent: Duration of more than 3 months

Specify current severity:

Specify severity based on degree of difficulty maintaining daytime alertness as manifested by the occurrence of multiple attacks of irresistible sleepiness within any given day occurring, for example, while sedentary, driving, visiting with friends, or working.

Mild: Difficulty maintaining daytime alertness 1–2 days/week

Moderate: Difficulty maintaining daytime alertness 3–4 days/week

Severe: Difficulty maintaining daytime alertness 5–7 days/week

American Psychiatric Association. (2022). *Diagnostic and statistical manual of mental disorders* (5th ed., Text Revision).

likelihood of having certain genetic factors (HLA-Cw2 and HLA-DR11) (Buysse et al., 2008). A significant subgroup of people diagnosed with hypersomnolence disorder previously were exposed to a viral infection such as mononucleosis, hepatitis, and viral pneumonia, which suggests there may be more than one cause (Hirshkowitz, Seplowitz, & Sharafkhaneh, 2009).

Narcolepsy

Hoa described her father as having **narcolepsy**, a different form of the sleeping problem she and her brother shared (Ono, Matsumura, & Nishino, 2021). In addition to daytime sleepiness, some people with narcolepsy experience *cataplexy*, a sudden loss of muscle tone. Cataplexy occurs while the person is awake and can range from slight weakness in the facial muscles to complete physical collapse (Ono et al., 2021). Cataplexy lasts from several seconds to several minutes; it is usually preceded by strong emotion such as anger or happiness. Imagine that while cheering for your favorite team, you suddenly fall asleep; while arguing with a friend, you collapse to the floor in a sound sleep. You can imagine how disruptive this disorder can be!

Cataplexy appears to result from a sudden onset of REM sleep. Instead of falling asleep normally and going through the four nonrapid eye movement (NREM) stages that typically precede REM sleep, people with narcolepsy periodically progress right to this dream-sleep stage almost directly from the state of being awake. One outcome of REM sleep is the inhibition of input to the muscles, and this seems to be the process that leads to cataplexy.

Two other characteristics distinguish people who have narcolepsy (Ono et al., 2021). They commonly report *sleep paralysis*, a brief period after awakening when they can't move or speak that is often frightening to those who go through it. The last characteristic of narcolepsy is *hypnagogic hallucinations*, vivid and often terrifying experiences that begin at the start of sleep and are said to be unbelievably realistic because they include not only visual aspects but also touch, hearing, and even the sensation of body movement (Cohen & Avidan, 2021). Examples of hypnagogic hallucinations—which, like sleep paralysis, can be quite terrifying—include the vivid illusion of being caught in a fire or flying through the air. Narcolepsy is relatively rare, occurring in 0.03% to 0.16% of the population, with the numbers slightly higher among males (Ono et al., 2021). Although some cases have been reported in young children, the problems associated with narcolepsy usually are first seen during the teenage years. Excessive sleepiness usually occurs first, with cataplexy appearing either at the same time or with a delay of up to 30 years. Fortunately, the cataplexy, hypnagogic hallucinations, and sleep paralysis often decrease in frequency over time, although sleepiness during the day does not seem to diminish with age.

Sleep paralysis and hypnagogic hallucinations may serve a role in explaining a phenomenon—unidentified flying object (UFO) or alien abduction experiences (Sharpless & Doghramji, 2015). Each year, numerous people report sighting UFOs, and some even tell

Monkey Business Images/Shutterstock.com

Excessive sleepiness can be disruptive.

DSM 5 **Table 8.6**
Diagnostic Criteria for Narcolepsy

A. Recurrent periods of irrepressible need to sleep, lapsing into sleep, or napping occurring within the same day. These must have been occurring at least three times per week over the past 3 months.

B. The presence of at least one of the following:

1. Episodes of cataplexy defined as either (a) or (b), occurring at least a few times per month:
   (a) In individuals with long-standing disease, brief (seconds to minutes) episodes of sudden bilateral loss of muscle tone with maintained consciousness, precipitated by laughter or joking.
   (b) In children or in individuals within 6 months of onset, spontaneous grimaces or jaw-opening episodes with tongue thrusting or a global hypotonia, without any obvious emotional triggers.
2. Hypocretin deficiency, as measured using cerebrospinal fluid (CSF) hypocretin-1 immunoreactivity values (less than or equal to one third of values obtained in healthy subjects tested using the same assay or less than or equal to 110 pg/mL). Low CSF levels of hypocretin-1 must not be observed in the context of acute brain injury, inflammation or infection.
3. Nocturnal sleep polysomnography showing rapid eye movement (REM) sleep latency less than or equal to 15 minutes, or a multiple sleep latency test showing a mean sleep latency less than or equal to 8 minutes and two or more sleep onset REM periods.

Specify current severity:

Mild: Need for naps only once or twice per day. Sleep disturbance, if present, is mild. Cataplexy, when present, is infrequent (occurring less than once per week).

Moderate: Need for multiple naps daily. Sleep may be moderately disturbed. Cataplexy, when present, occurs daily or every few days.

Severe: Nearly constant sleepiness and, often, highly disturbed nocturnal sleep (which may include excessive body movement and vivid dreams). Cataplexy, when present, is drug-resistant, with multiple attacks daily.

American Psychiatric Association. (2022). *Diagnostic and statistical manual of mental disorders* (5th ed., Text Revision).

of visiting with inhabitants of other planets. A group of scientists examined people who had had such experiences, separating them into those who had nonintense experiences (seeing only lights and shapes in the sky) and those with intense experiences (seeing and communicating with aliens) (Spanos, Cross, Dickson, & DuBreuil, 1993). They found that a majority of the reported UFO incidents occurred at night and that 60% of the intense UFO stories were associated with sleep episodes. Specifically, the reports of these intense accounts were often described in ways that resembled accounts of people experiencing a frightening episode of sleep paralysis and hypnagogic hallucination, as illustrated by the following account (Spanos et al., 1993):

> I was lying in bed facing the wall, and suddenly my heart started to race. I could feel the presence of three entities standing beside me. I was unable to move my body but could move my eyes. One of the entities, a male, was laughing at me, not verbally but with his mind. He made me feel stupid. He told me telepathically, "Don't you know by now that you can't do anything unless we let you?" (p. 627)

The realistic and frightening stories of people who have had UFO sightings may not be the products of an active imagination or the results of a hoax, but at least in some cases they may be a disturbance of sleep. Sleep paralysis and hypnagogic hallucinations do occur in a portion of people without narcolepsy, a phenomenon that may help explain why not everyone with these "otherworldly" experiences has narcolepsy. Sleep paralysis commonly co-occurs with anxiety disorders, in which case the condition is termed *isolated sleep paralysis* (Cohen & Avidan, 2021).

Specific genetic models of narcolepsy are now being developed (Ono et al., 2021). Previous research with Doberman pinschers and Labrador retrievers, which also inherit this disorder, suggests that narcolepsy is associated with a cluster of genes on chromosome 6, and it may be an autosomal recessive trait. It appears that there is a significant loss of a certain type of nerve cell (hypocretin neurons) in those with narcolepsy. These neurons create peptides that appear to play an important role in wakefulness, although why these individuals lack just these specific neurons is not yet understood (Ono et al., 2021).

Breathing-Related Sleep Disorders

For some people, sleepiness during the day or disrupted sleep at night has a physical origin—namely, problems with breathing while asleep. In DSM-5-TR, these problems are diagnosed as **breathing-related sleep disorders**. People whose breathing is interrupted during their sleep often experience numerous brief arousals throughout the night and do not feel rested even after 8 or 9 hours asleep (Mindell & Owens, 2015). For all of us, the muscles in the upper airway relax during sleep, constricting the passageway somewhat and making breathing a little more difficult. For some, unfortunately, breathing is constricted a great deal and may be labored *(hypoventilation)* or, in the extreme, there may be short periods (10 to 30 seconds) when they stop breathing altogether, called *sleep apnea*. Often the affected person is only minimally aware of breathing difficulties and doesn't attribute the sleep problems to the breathing. A bed partner usually notices loud snoring (which is one sign of this problem), however, or will

DSM 5 Table 8.7

Diagnostic Criteria for Obstructive Sleep Apnea Hypopnea

A. Either (1) or (2):

1. Evidence by polysomnography of at least five obstructive apneas or hypopneas per hour of sleep and either of the following sleep symptoms:
   - **(a)** Nocturnal breathing disturbances: snoring, snorting/gasping, or breathing pauses during sleep.
   - **(b)** Daytime sleepiness, fatigue, or unrefreshing sleep despite sufficient opportunities to sleep that is not better explained by another mental disorder (including a sleep disorder) and is not attributable to another medical condition.
2. Evidence by polysomnography of 15 or more obstructive apneas and/or hypopneas per hour of sleep regardless of accompanying symptoms.

Specify current severity:

Mild: Apnea hypopnea index is less than 15

Moderate: Apnea hypopnea index is 15–30

Severe: Apnea hypopnea index is greater than 30

American Psychiatric Association. (2022). *Diagnostic and statistical manual of mental disorders* (5th ed., Text Revision).

DSM 5 Table 8.8

Diagnostic Criteria for Central Sleep Apnea

A. Evidence by polysomnography of five or more central apneas per hour of sleep.

B. The disorder is not better explained by another current sleep disorder.

Specify current severity:

Severity of central sleep apnea is graded according to the frequency of the breathing disturbances as well as the extent of associated oxygen desaturation and sleep fragmentation that occur as a consequence of repetitive respiratory disturbances.

American Psychiatric Association. (2022). *Diagnostic and statistical manual of mental disorders* (5th ed., Text Revision).

DSM 5 Table 8.9

Diagnostic Criteria for Sleep-Related Hypoventilation

A. Polysomnography demonstrates episodes of decreased respiration associated with elevated CO_2 levels. (*Note:* In the absence of objective measurement of CO_2, persistent low levels of hemoglobin oxygen saturation unassociated with apneic/hypopneic events may indicate hypoventilation.)

B. The disorder is not better explained by another current sleep disorder.

Specify current severity:

Severity is graded according to the degree of hypoxemia and hypercarbia present during sleep and evidence of end organ impairment due to these abnormalities (e.g., right-sided heart failure). The presence of blood gas abnormalities during wakefulness is an indicator of greater severity.

American Psychiatric Association. (2022). *Diagnostic and statistical manual of mental disorders* (5th ed., Text Revision).

have noticed frightening episodes of interrupted breathing. Other signs that a person has breathing difficulties are heavy sweating during the night, morning headaches, and episodes of falling asleep during the day *(sleep attacks)* with no resulting feeling of being rested (Overeem & Reading, 2010).

There are three types of apnea, each with different causes, daytime complaints, and treatment: obstructive, central, and mixed sleep apnea. *Obstructive sleep apnea hypopnea syndrome* occurs when airflow stops despite continued activity by the respiratory system (Wu & Guilleminault, 2021). In some people, the airway is too narrow; in others, some abnormality or damage interferes with the ongoing effort to breathe. Everyone in a group of people with obstructive sleep apnea hypopnea syndrome reported snoring at night (Goel, Talwar, & Jain, 2015). Obesity is sometimes associated with this problem, as is increasing age. Some work now suggests that the use of MDMA (ecstasy) can lead to obstructive apnea hypopnea syndrome even in young and otherwise healthy adults (McCann, Sgambati, Schwartz, & Ricaurte, 2009). Obstructive sleep apnea is most common in males. The prevalence rates have increased over time, with estimates that 33.9% of men and 17.4% of women meet criteria for mild sleep apnea. The increase has been attributed to the increase in obesity among adults, which can increase the risk for apnea (Wu & Guilleminault, 2021).

The second type of apnea, *central sleep apnea*, involves the complete cessation of respiratory activity for brief periods and is often associated with certain central nervous system disorders, such as cerebral vascular disease, head trauma, and degenerative disorders (Wu & Guilleminault, 2021). Unlike people with obstructive sleep apnea hypopnea syndrome, those with central sleep apnea wake up frequently during the night, but they tend not to report excessive daytime sleepiness and often are not aware of having a serious breathing problem. Because of the lack of daytime symptoms, people tend not to seek treatment, so we know relatively little about this disorder's prevalence or course. The third breathing disorder, *sleep-related hypoventilation*, is a decrease in airflow without a complete pause in breathing. This tends to cause an increase in carbon dioxide (CO_2) levels because insufficient air is exchanged with the environment. All these breathing difficulties interrupt sleep and result in symptoms similar to those of insomnia.

Circadian Rhythm Sleep Disorder

"Spring ahead; fall back": People in most of the United States use this mnemonic device to remind themselves to turn the clocks ahead 1 hour in the spring and back again 1 hour in the fall. Most of us consider the shift to daylight saving time a minor inconvenience and are thus surprised to see how disruptive this time change can be (see the previous discussion of chronotypes). For at least a day or two, we may be sleepy during the day and have difficulty falling asleep at night, almost as if we had jet lag. The reason for this disruption is not just that we gain or lose 1 hour of sleep; our bodies adjust to this fairly easily. The difficulty has to do with how our biological clocks adjust to this change in time. Convention says to go to sleep at this new time while our brains are saying something different. If the struggle continues for any length of time, you may have what is called a **circadian rhythm sleep disorder** (Blum & Zeitzer, 2021). This disorder is characterized by disturbed sleep (either insomnia or excessive sleepiness during the day) brought on by the brain's inability to synchronize its sleep patterns with the current patterns of day and night.

In the 1960s, German and French scientists identified several bodily rhythms that seem to persist without cues from the environment and that are self-regulated (Aschoff & Wever, 1962; Siffre, 1964). Because these rhythms don't exactly match our 24-hour day, they are called circadian (from *circa* meaning "about" and *dian* meaning "day"). If our circadian rhythms don't match the 24-hour day, why isn't our sleep completely disrupted over time?

Fortunately, our brains have a mechanism that keeps us in sync with the outside world. Our biological clock is in the *suprachiasmatic nucleus* in the hypothalamus. Connected to the suprachiasmatic nucleus is a pathway that comes from our eyes. The light we see in the morning and the decreasing light at night signal the brain to reset the biological clock each day. Unfortunately, some people have trouble sleeping when they want to because of problems with their circadian rhythms. The causes may be outside the person (for example, crossing several time zones in a short amount of time) or internal.

Not being synchronized with the normal wake and sleep cycles causes people's sleep to be interrupted when they do try to sleep during the day. There are several types of circadian rhythm sleep disorders. *Jet lag type* is, as its name implies, caused by rapidly crossing multiple time zones (Blum & Zeitzer, 2021). People with jet lag usually report difficulty going to sleep at the proper time and feeling fatigued during the day. Traveling more than two time zones westward usually affects people the most. Traveling eastward and/or less than three time zones are usually tolerated better (Kolla, Auger, & Morgenthaler, 2012). Research with mice suggests that the effects of jet lag can be quite serious—at least among older adults. When older mice were exposed to repeated artificial jet lag, a significant number of them lived shorter lives (Davidson et al., 2006), and artificial jet lag has also been shown to increase cancer risk in mice (van Dycke et al., 2015). *Shift work type* sleep problems are associated with work schedules (Abbott et al., 2012). Many people—such as hospital employees, police, or emergency personnel—work at night or must work irregular hours; as a result, they may have problems sleeping or experience excessive sleepiness during waking hours. Unfortunately, the problems of working (and thus staying awake) at unusual times can go beyond sleep and may contribute to cardiovascular disease, ulcers, and breast cancer in women (Truong et al., 2014). Working rotating shifts is consistently predictive of poor sleep (Linton et al., 2015).

DSM 5 **Table 8.10**
Diagnostic Criteria for Circadian Rhythm Sleep–Wake Disorders

A. A persistent or recurrent pattern of sleep disruption that is primarily due to an alteration of the circadian system or to a misalignment between the endogenous circadian rhythm and the sleep–wake schedule required by an individual's physical environment or social or professional schedule.

B. The sleep disruption leads to excessive sleepiness or insomnia, or both.

C. The sleep disturbance causes clinically significant distress or impairment in social, occupational, and other important areas of functioning.

Specify if:

Episodic: Symptoms last at least 1 month but less than 3 months

Persistent: Symptoms last 3 months or longer

Recurrent: Two or more episodes occur within the space of 1 year

American Psychiatric Association. (2022). *Diagnostic and statistical manual of mental disorders* (5th ed., Text Revision).

In contrast with jet lag and shift work sleep-related problems, which have external causes such as long-distance travel and job selection, several circadian rhythm sleep disorders seem to arise from within the person experiencing the problems. Extreme night owls, people who stay up late and sleep late, may have a problem known as *delayed sleep phase type*, where sleep is delayed or there is a later than normal bedtime. At the other extreme, people with an *advanced sleep phase type* of circadian rhythm disorder are "early to bed and early to rise." Here, sleep is advanced or earlier than normal bedtime. Finally, two other types, *irregular sleep–wake type* (people who experience highly varied sleep cycles) and *non-24-hour sleep–wake type* (for example, sleeping on a 25- or 26-hour cycle with later and later bedtimes ultimately going throughout the day), illustrate the diversity of circadian rhythm sleep–wake problems some people experience.

Research on why our sleep rhythms are disrupted is advancing at a great pace, and we are beginning to understand the circadian rhythm process. Scientists believe the hormone *melatonin* contributes to the setting of our biological clocks that tell us when to sleep. This hormone is produced by the pineal gland in the center of the brain. Melatonin (don't confuse this with *melanin*, the chemical that determines skin color) has been nicknamed the "Dracula hormone" because its production is stimulated by darkness and ceases in daylight. When our eyes see that it is nighttime, this information is passed on to the pineal gland, which, in turn, begins producing melatonin. Researchers believe that both light and melatonin help set the biological clock (Blum & Zeitzer, 2021) (see ■ Figure 8.11).

Concept Check 8.4

Match the following descriptions of sleeping problems with the correct term: (a) cataplexy, (b) hypersomnolence disorder, (c) insomnia disorder, (d) sleep apnea, (e) sleep paralysis, (f) narcolepsy, (g) circadian rhythm sleep disorder, and (h) breathing-related sleep disorder.

1. Timothy wakes up frequently every night because he feels he is about to hyperventilate. He can't seem to get enough air, and many times his wife will wake him to tell him to quit snoring. He is suffering from a(n) ________________.
2. Sonia has problems staying awake throughout the day. Even while talking on the phone or riding the bus, she unexpectedly loses muscle tone and falls asleep for a while. This is due to ________________.
3. Jaime sometimes awakens and cannot move or speak. This is a particularly frightening experience known as ________________.
4. Brett has started a new job that requires him to change shifts monthly. He sometimes has day shifts and at other times has night shifts. Since then he has had considerable trouble sleeping.
5. Rama is extremely overweight. His wife suspects he may be suffering from ________________ because he snores every night and often wakes up exhausted as though he never slept.
6. Melinda sleeps all night and still finds herself falling asleep throughout the next day. This happens even when she goes to bed early and gets up as late as possible. ________________

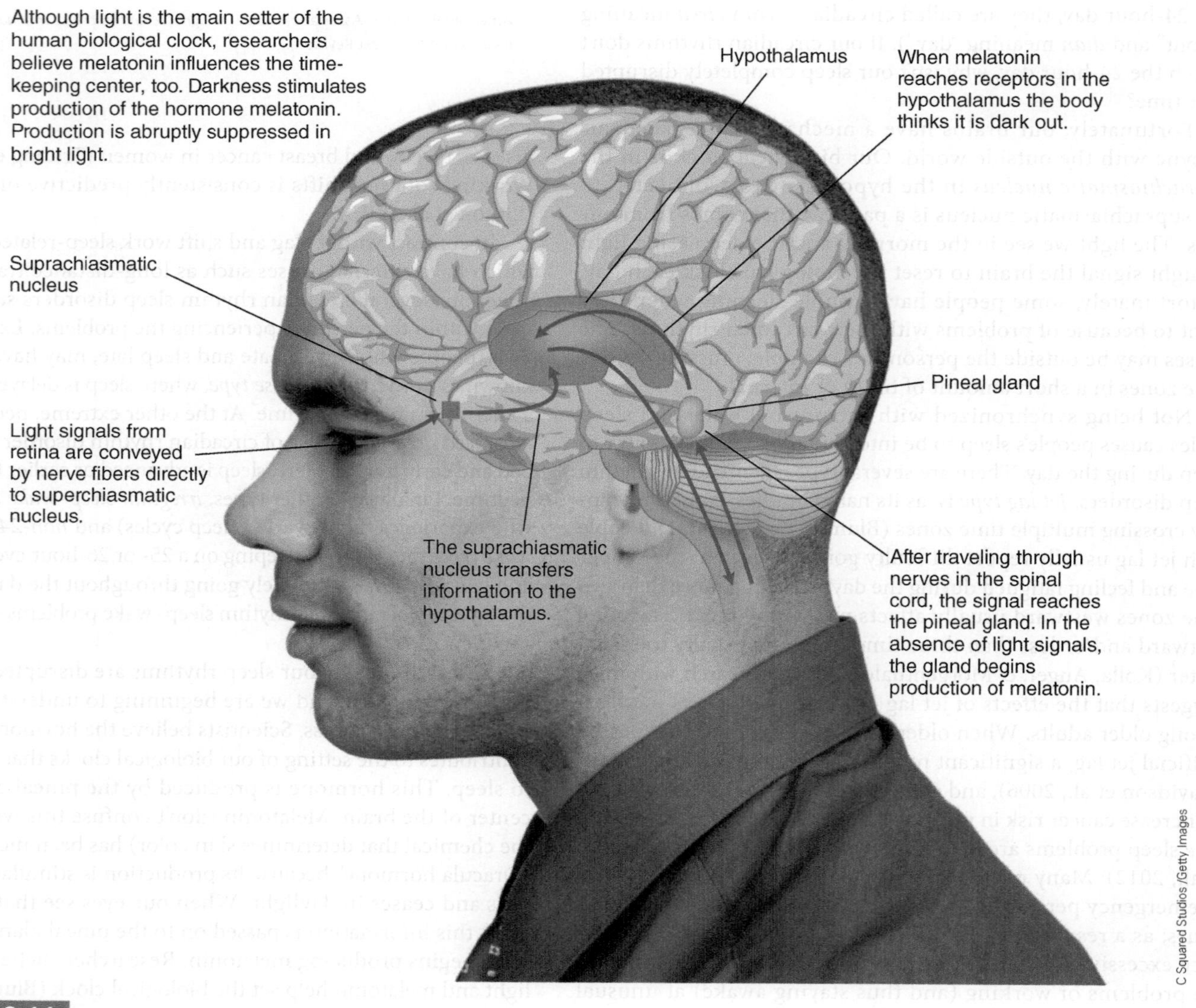

Figure 8.11

Understanding the hormone of darkness. Based on *New York Times*, 1992, November 3.

Treatment of Sleep Disorders

When we cannot fall asleep or when we awaken frequently or when sleep does not restore our energy and vitality, we need help. A number of biological and psychological interventions have been designed and evaluated to help people regain the benefits of normal sleep.

Medical Treatments

Perhaps the most common treatments for insomnia are medical. People who complain of insomnia to a medical professional are likely prescribed one of several benzodiazepine or related medications (see Table 8.6), which include short-acting drugs such as triazolam (Halcion), zaleplon (Sonata), and zolpidem (Ambien) and long-acting drugs such as flurazepam (Dalmane). Short-acting drugs (those that cause only brief drowsiness) are preferred, because the long-acting drugs sometimes do not stop working by morning and people report more daytime sleepiness. The long-acting medications are sometimes preferred when negative effects such as daytime anxiety are observed in people taking the short-acting drugs (Neubauer, 2009). Newer medications, such as those that work directly with the melatonin system (for example, ramelteon [Rozerem]), are also being developed to help people fall and stay asleep. People over the age of 65 are most likely to use medication to help them sleep, although people of all ages, including young children (Durand, 2008), have been prescribed medications for insomnia.

There are several drawbacks to medical treatments for insomnia (During, 2021b). First, benzodiazepine medications can cause excessive sleepiness. Second, people can easily become dependent on them and rather easily misuse them, deliberately or not. Third, these medications are meant for short-term treatment and are not recommended for use longer than 4 weeks. Longer use can cause dependence and rebound insomnia. A concern for some medications (for example, Ambien) is that they may increase the likelihood of sleepwalking-related problems, such as sleep-related eating disorder (Irfan, Schenck, & Howell, 2021). Therefore, although medications may be helpful for sleep problems that will correct themselves in a short period (such as insomnia because of anxiety related to hospitalization), they are not intended for long-term chronic problems.

To help people with hypersomnolence or narcolepsy, physicians usually prescribe a stimulant such as methylphenidate (Ritalin, the medication Hoa was taking) or modafinil (Nevsimalova, 2009). Cataplexy, or loss of muscle tone, can be treated with antidepressant medication, not because people with narcolepsy are depressed but because antidepressants suppress REM (or dream) sleep. Also, sodium oxybate is recommended to treat cataplexy (Bogan, Roth, Schwartz, & Miloslavsky, 2014).

Treatment of breathing-related sleep disorders focuses on helping the person breathe better during sleep. For some, this means recommending weight loss. In some people who are obese, the neck's soft tissue compresses the airways. Unfortunately, as we have seen earlier in this chapter, voluntary weight loss is rarely successful in the long term; as a result, it is not an adequate stand-alone treatment for breathing-related sleep disorders (Anandam, Akinnusi, Kufel, Porhomayon, & El-Solh, 2013).

Table 8.6 Medications for Insomnia

Class	Example*	Elimination Half-Life in Hours**
Immediate-Release Benzodiazepines		
	Estazolam/*ProSom*	10–24
	Flurazepam/*Dalmane*	48–120
	Quazepam/*Doral*	40–70
	Temazepam/*Restoril*	4–20
	Triazolam/*Halcion*	2–4
Immediate-Release Non-Benzodiazepines		
	Eszopiclone/*Lunesta*	6
	Zaleplon/*Sonata*	1
	Zolpidem/*Ambien* Zolpidem/Ambien (SL) Zolpidem/Ambien (XR)	1.5–2.4 2–3 3
Modified-Release Non-Benzodiazepines		
	Zolpidem ER/*Ambien CR*	2.8–2.9
	Selective melatonin receptor agonist	
	Ramelteon/*Rozerem*	1–2.6

ER = extended release; CR = controlled release; SL = sublingual, XR = extended release

*The trade name is in italics.

**Half-life refers to how long it takes to no longer affect the user.

Source: Adapted from E. H. During, 2021, Pharmacological treatment of insomnia, in E. H. During & C. A. Kushida (Eds.), *Clinical sleep medicine: A comprehensive guide for mental health and other medical professionals* (pp. 61–77) (American Psychiatric Association Publishing).

The gold standard for the treatment of obstructive sleep apnea involves the use of a mechanical device—called the continuous positive air pressure (CPAP) machine—that improves breathing (Ishak, Ramsay, Hart, & Steier, 2020). Patients wear a mask that provides slightly pressurized air during sleep, and it helps them breathe more normally throughout the night. Unfortunately, many people have difficulty using the device because of issues of comfort, and some even experience a form of claustrophobia. To assist these individuals, a variety of strategies are tried, including the use of psychological interventions including desensitization for claustrophobia, patient and partner education, and motivational interviewing (a counseling technique used to help patients match their goals with their behaviors) (Olsen, Smith, Oei, & Douglas, 2012). Severe breathing problems may require surgery to help remove blockages in parts of the airways.

An interesting treatment for people with mild apnea was developed by researchers in collaboration with a Swiss didgeridoo instructor. A didgeridoo is a long instrument constructed from tree limbs hollowed out by termites. The instructor observed that people who practiced using this wind instrument had less daytime sleepiness. Evidence points to the effectiveness of several months of daily practice using this instrument in improving the sleep of people with interrupted breathing (Puhan et al., 2006; Sutherland & Cistulli, 2015). Some preliminary evidence points to the positive impact of playing certain types of wind instruments on developing apnea (de Jong, Maroda, Camacho, & Chen, 2020).

Environmental Treatments

Because medication as a primary treatment is not usually recommended for long-term use, other ways of getting people back in step with their sleep rhythms are usually tried (Barwick, 2021). One general principle for treating circadian rhythm disorders is that *phase delays* (moving bedtime later) are easier than *phase advances* (moving bedtime earlier). In other words, it is easier to stay up several hours later than usual than to force yourself to go to sleep several hours earlier. Scheduling shift changes in a clockwise direction (going from day to evening schedule) seems to help workers adjust better. People can best readjust their sleep patterns by going to bed several hours later each night until bedtime is at the desired hour (Sack et al., 2007). A drawback of this approach is that it requires the person to sleep during the day for several days, which is difficult for people with regularly scheduled responsibilities.

Another strategy to help people with sleep problems involves using bright light to trick the brain into readjusting the biological clock. (In Chapter 7, we describe light therapy for seasonal affective disorder.) Research indicates that bright light (also referred to as *phototherapy*) may help people with circadian rhythm problems readjust their sleep patterns (Palermo & Sharkey, 2021). People typically sit in front of a bank of fluorescent lamps that generate light greater than 2,000 lux, an amount significantly different from normal indoor light (250 lux). Several hours of exposure to this bright light have successfully reset the circadian rhythms of many individuals. This type of treatment provides some hope for people with schedule-related sleep problems.

Psychological Treatments

As you can imagine, the limitations of using medication to help people sleep better have led to the development of psychological treatments. Table 8.7 briefly describes some psychological approaches to insomnia. Different treatments help people with different kinds of sleep problems. For example, relaxation treatments reduce the physical tension that seems to prevent some people from falling asleep at night. Some people report that their anxiety about work, relationships, or other situations prevents them from sleeping or wakes them up in the middle of the night. To address this problem, cognitive treatments are used. Cognitive treatment may also focus on worries about sleep itself, such as by helping patients to change their assumptions that they cannot function well on little sleep, which can trigger anxiety that disrupts falling asleep (Barwick, 2021).

Research shows that some psychological treatments for insomnia may be more effective than others. For adult sleep problems, stimulus control may be recommended. People are instructed to use the bedroom only for sleeping and for sex and *not* for work or other anxiety-provoking activities (for example, watching the news on television). Progressive relaxation or sleep hygiene (changing daily habits that may interfere with sleep) alone may not be as effective as stimulus control alone for some people (Means & Edinger, 2006). Because sleep problems are so widespread, there is a growing interest in developing internet-based treatments to determine if certain sufferers can help themselves with appropriate guidance. One study, for example, randomly assigned adults to a control group or an internet-based education group (Ritterband et al., 2009). The internet group received online instruction on the proper use of several of the psychological treatments (such as sleep restriction, stimulus control, sleep hygiene, cognitive restructuring, and relapse prevention). The findings were striking, suggesting that not only could the treatment be delivered over the internet but also that sleep improved in this group even 6 months later. Under certain circumstances, people are able to use *evidence-based instruction* (education on the use of a treatment that has empirical support) to improve a variety of psychological problems.

Table 8.7 Psychological Treatments for Insomnia

Sleep Treatment	Description
Cognitive	This approach focuses on changing the sleepers' unrealistic expectations and beliefs about sleep ("I must have 8 hours of sleep each night"; "If I get less than 8 hours of sleep, it will make me ill"). The therapist attempts to alter beliefs and attitudes about sleeping by providing information on topics such as normal amounts of sleep and a person's ability to compensate for lost sleep.
Guided imagery relaxation	Because some people become anxious when they have difficulty sleeping, this approach uses meditation or imagery to help with relaxation at bedtime or after a night waking.
Graduated extinction	Used for children who have tantrums at bedtime or wake up crying at night, this treatment instructs the parent to check on the child after progressively longer periods until the child falls asleep on his or her own.
Paradoxical intention	This technique involves instructing individuals in the opposite behavior from the desired outcome. Telling poor sleepers to lie in bed and try to stay awake as long as they can is used to try to relieve the performance anxiety surrounding efforts to try to fall asleep.
Progressive relaxation	This technique involves relaxing the muscles of the body in an effort to introduce drowsiness.

Often, psychological treatment of insomnia takes the form of a "package" of different skills known as cognitive-behavioral therapy for insomnia (CBT-I) (Barwick, 2021). Such was the case for Indira, the law student we profile in the beginning of this section, who was helped with her sleep problems using several techniques. She was instructed to limit her time in bed to about 4 hours of sleep time (sleep restriction), about the amount of time she slept each night. The period was lengthened when she began to sleep through the night. Indira was also asked not to do any schoolwork while in bed and to get out of bed if she couldn't fall asleep within 15 minutes (stimulus control). Finally, therapy involved confronting her unrealistic expectations about how much sleep was enough for a person of her age (cognitive therapy). Within about 3 weeks of treatment, Indira was sleeping longer (6 to 7 hours per night as opposed to 4 to 5 hours previously) and had fewer interruptions in her sleep. Also, she felt more refreshed in the morning and had more energy during the day. Indira's results mirror those of studies that find combined treatments to be effective in older adults with insomnia (Savard, Savard, & Morin, 2011). One important study, using a randomized placebo-control design, found that cognitive-behavioral therapy (CBT) may be more successful treating sleep disorders in older adults than a medical (drug) intervention (Siddiqui & D'Ambrosio, 2012). In contrast, a review of insomnia treatments found almost no differences in the effectiveness of drug interventions compared to CBT interventions, except that behavioral interventions more effectively reduced sleep latency (the time it takes to fall asleep) (Smith et al., 2014).

For young children, some cognitive treatments may not be possible. Instead, treatment often includes setting up bedtime routines, such as a bath followed by a parent's reading a story, to help children go to sleep at night. Graduated extinction (described in Table 8.8) has been used with some success for bedtime problems, as well as for waking up at night (Durand, 2014; Hill, 2011).

Preventing Sleep Disorders

Sleep professionals generally agree that a significant portion of the sleep problems people experience daily can be prevented by following a few steps during the day. Referred to as *sleep hygiene*, these changes in lifestyle can be relatively simple to follow and can help avoid problems such as insomnia for some people (Goodman & Scott, 2012). Some sleep hygiene recommendations rely on allowing the brain's normal drive for sleep to take over, replacing the restrictions we place on our activities that interfere with sleep. For example, setting a regular time to go to sleep and awaken each day can help make falling asleep at night easier. Avoiding the use of caffeine and nicotine—which are both stimulants—can also help prevent problems such as nighttime awakening. Table 8.8 illustrates a number of the sleep hygiene steps recommended for preventing sleep problems. Although there is little controlled prospective research on preventing sleep disorders, practicing good sleep hygiene appears to be among the most promising techniques available (Shriane, Ferguson, Jay, & Vincent, 2020).

Table 8.8 Good Sleep Habits

Establish a set bedtime routine.
Develop a regular bedtime and a regular time to awaken.
Eliminate all foods and drinks that contain caffeine 6 hours before bedtime.
Limit any use of alcohol or tobacco.
Try drinking milk before bedtime.
Eat a balanced diet, limiting fat.
Go to bed only when sleepy, and get out of bed if you are unable to fall asleep or back to sleep after 15 minutes.
Do not exercise or participate in vigorous activities in the hours before bedtime.
Do include a weekly program of exercise during the day.
Restrict activities in bed to those that help induce sleep.
Reduce noise and light in the bedroom.
Increase exposure to natural and bright light during the day.
Avoid extreme temperature changes in the bedroom (i.e., too hot or too cold).

Source: Adapted, with permission, from V. M. Durand, 2014, Good sleep habits, in V. M. Durand (Ed.), *Sleep better: A guide to improving sleep for children with special needs* (p. 60) (Paul H. Brookes).

A few studies have investigated the value of educating parents about the sleep of their young children in an effort to prevent later difficulties (Malow et al., 2014). Adachi and colleagues (2009), for example, provided 10 minutes of group guidance and a simple educational booklet to the parents of 4-month-old children. They followed up on these children 3 months later and found that, compared with a randomly selected control group of children, the ones whose parents received education about sleep experienced fewer sleep problems. Because so many children display disruptive sleep problems, this type of preventive effort could significantly improve the lives of many families.

Parasomnias and Their Treatment

Have you ever been told that you walk in your sleep? Talk in your sleep? Have you ever had troublesome nightmares? Do you grind your teeth in your sleep? If you answered yes to one or more of these questions (and it is likely you did), you have experienced sleep problems in the category of parasomnia. Parasomnias are not problems with sleep itself but abnormal events that occur either during sleep or during that twilight time between sleeping and waking (Cohen & Avidan, 2021; Irfan et al., 2021). Some events associated with parasomnia are not unusual if they happen while you are awake (such as walking to the kitchen to look into the refrigerator) but can be distressing if they take place while you are sleeping.

DSM-5-TR identifies a number of different parasomnias (American Psychiatric Association, 2022). As you might have guessed, **nightmares** (or nightmare disorder) occur during REM

A nightmare is distressing for both child and parent.

or dream sleep (Cohen & Avidan, 2021). About 10% to 50% of children and about 9% to 30% of adults experience them regularly (Schredl, 2010). To qualify as a nightmare disorder, according to DSM-5 criteria, these experiences must be so distressful that they impair a person's ability to carry on normal activities (such as making a person too anxious to try to sleep at night). Some researchers distinguish nightmares from bad dreams by whether or not you wake up as a result. Nightmares are defined as disturbing dreams that awaken the sleeper; bad dreams are those that do not awaken the person experiencing them. Based on this definition, college students report an average of 30 bad dreams and 10 nightmares per year (Zadra & Donderi, 2000).

Nightmares are thought to be influenced by genetics (Barclay & Gregory, 2013), trauma, and medication use and are associated with some psychological disorders (such as substance abuse, anxiety, borderline personality disorder, and schizophrenia spectrum disorders) (Augedal et al., 2013). Research on the treatment of nightmares suggests that both psychological intervention (such as cognitive-behavioral therapy) and pharmacological treatment (such as prazosin) can help reduce these unpleasant sleep events (Augedal et al., 2013; Aurora et al., 2010).

Disorder of arousal includes a number of motor movements and behaviors during NREM sleep such as sleepwalking, sleep terrors, and incomplete awakening (Irfan et al., 2021). **Sleep terrors**, which most commonly afflict children, usually begin with a piercing scream. The child is extremely upset, often sweating, and frequently has a rapid heartbeat. On the surface, sleep terrors appear to resemble nightmares—the child cries and appears frightened—but they occur during NREM sleep and therefore are not caused by frightening dreams. During sleep terrors, children cannot be easily awakened and comforted, as they can during a nightmare. Children do not remember sleep terrors, despite their often dramatic effect on the observer (Irfan et al., 2021). As many as one third of 18-month-old children may experience sleep terrors, but this number drops to 13% by age 5 and just 5% by age 13 (Petit et al., 2015). We know relatively little about sleep terrors, although several theories have been proposed—including the possibility of a genetic component because the disorder tends to occur in families (Irfan et al., 2021). Treatment for sleep terrors usually begins with a recommendation to wait and see if they disappear on their own.

One approach to reducing chronic sleep terrors is the use of *scheduled awakenings*. In the first controlled study of its kind, Durand and Mindell (1999) instructed parents of children who were experiencing almost nightly sleep terrors to awaken their child briefly approximately 30 minutes before a typical episode (these usually occur around the same time each evening). This simple technique, which was faded out over several weeks, was successful in almost eliminating these disturbing events.

DSM 5 **Table 8.11**

Diagnostic Criteria for Nonrapid Eye Movement Sleep Arousal Disorders

A. Recurrent episodes of incomplete awakening from sleep usually occurring during the first third of the major sleep episode, accompanied by either one of the following:

1. Sleepwalking: Repeated episodes of rising from bed during sleep and walking about. While sleepwalking, the person has a blank, staring face; is relatively unresponsive to the efforts of others to communicate with him or her; and can be awakened only with great difficulty.
2. Sleep terrors: Recurrent episodes of abrupt terror arousals from sleep, usually beginning with a panicky scream. There is intense fear and signs of autonomic arousal, such as mydriasis, tachycardia, rapid breathing, and sweating, during each episode. There is relative unresponsiveness to efforts of others to comfort the individual during the episodes.

B. No or little (e.g., only a single-visual-scene) dream imagery is recalled.

C. Amnesia for the episodes is present.

D. The episodes cause clinically significant distress or impairment in social, occupational, or other important areas of functioning.

E. The disturbance is not attributable to the physiological effects of a substance (e.g., a drug of abuse, a medication).

F. Coexisting mental and medical disorders do not explain the episodes of sleepwalking or sleep terrors.

American Psychiatric Association. (2022). *Diagnostic and statistical manual of mental disorders* (5th ed., Text Revision).

It might surprise you to learn that **sleepwalking** (also called **somnambulism**) occurs during NREM sleep (Irfan et al., 2021). This means that when people walk in their sleep, they are probably not acting out a dream. This parasomnia typically occurs during the first few hours while a person is in the deep stages of sleep. The DSM-5 criteria for sleepwalking require that the person leave the bed, although less active episodes can involve small motor behaviors, such as sitting up in bed and picking at the blanket or gesturing. Because sleepwalking occurs during the deepest stages of sleep, waking someone during an episode is difficult; if people are wakened, they typically will not remember what has happened. It is not true, however, that waking a sleepwalker is somehow dangerous.

Sleepwalking is primarily a problem during childhood, affecting more than 10% of school-aged children (Petit et al., 2015), but a small proportion of adults are affected. Mostly, the course of sleepwalking is short, and few people over the age of 15 continue to exhibit this parasomnia.

We do not yet clearly understand why some people sleepwalk, although factors such as extreme fatigue, previous sleep deprivation, the use of sedative or hypnotic drugs, and stress have been implicated (Shatkin & Ivanenko, 2009). On occasion, sleepwalking episodes have been associated with violent behavior, including homicide and suicide (Cartwright, 2006). In one case, a man drove to his in-laws' house, succeeded in killing his mother-in-law, and attempted to kill his father-in-law. He was acquitted of the charges of murder, using sleepwalking as his legal defense (Broughton, Billings, & Cartwright, 1994). These cases are still controversial, although there is evidence for the legitimacy of some violent behavior coinciding with sleepwalking episodes. There also seems to be a genetic component to sleepwalking, with a higher incidence observed and within families (Petit et al., 2015).

A related disorder, *nocturnal eating syndrome*, is when individuals rise from their beds and eat while they are still asleep (Yamada, 2015). This problem, which is different than the *night eating syndrome* discussed earlier in the chapter in the eating disorders section, may be more frequent than previously thought; it was found in almost 6% of individuals in one study who were referred because of insomnia complaints (Irfan et al., 2021). Another uncommon parasomnia is *sexsomnia*; acting out sexual behaviors such as masturbation and sexual intercourse with no memory of the event (Irfan et al., 2021). This rare problem can cause relationship problems and, in extreme cases, legal problems when cases occur without consent or with minors (Howell, 2012; Schenck, Arnulf, & Mahowald, 2007).

There is an increasing awareness that sleep is important for both our mental and our physical well-being. Sleep problems are also comorbid with many other disorders and therefore can compound the difficulties of people with significant psychological difficulties (During, 2021a). Researchers are coming closer to understanding the basic nature of sleep and its disorders, and we anticipate significant treatment advances in the years to come.

DSM 5 **Table 8.12**

Diagnostic Criteria for Nightmare Disorder

A. Repeated occurrences of extended, extremely dysphoric, and well-remembered dreams that usually involve efforts to avoid threats to survival, security, or physical integrity and that generally occur during the second half of the major sleep episode.

B. On awakening from the dysphoric dreams, the individual rapidly becomes oriented and alert.

C. The sleep disturbance causes clinically significant distress or impairment in social, occupational, or other important areas of functioning.

D. The nightmare symptoms are not attributable to the physiological effects of a substance (e.g., a drug of abuse, a medication).

E. Coexisting mental and medical disorders do not adequately explain the predominant complaint of dysphoric dreams.

Specify current severity:

Severity can be rated by the frequency with which the nightmares occur:

Mild: Less than one episode per week on average

Moderate: One or more episodes per week but less than nightly

Severe: Episodes nightly

American Psychiatric Association. (2022). *Diagnostic and statistical manual of mental disorders* (5th ed., Text Revision).

DSM 5 **Table 8.13**

Diagnostic Criteria for Rapid Eye Movement Sleep Behavior Disorder

A. Repeated episodes of arousal during sleep associated with vocalization and/or complex motor behaviors.

B. These behaviors arise during rapid eye movement (REM) sleep and therefore usually occur more than 90 minutes after sleep onset, are more frequent during the later portions of the sleep period, and uncommonly occur during daytime naps.

C. Upon awakening from these episodes, the individual is completely awake, alert, and not confused or disoriented.

D. Either of the following:

1. REM sleep without atonia on polysomnographic recording.
2. A history suggestive of REM sleep behavior disorder and an established synucleinopathy diagnosis (e.g., Parkinson's disease, multiple system atrophy).

E. The behaviors cause clinically significant distress or impairment in social, occupational, or other important areas of functioning (which may include injury to self or the bed partner).

F. The disturbance is not attributable to the physiological effects of a substance (e.g., a drug of abuse, a medication) or another medical condition.

G. Coexisting mental and medical disorders do not explain the episodes.

American Psychiatric Association. (2022). *Diagnostic and statistical manual of mental disorders* (5th ed., Text Revision).

Concept Check 8.5

Part A

Diagnose the sleep problems of the cases here using one of the following: (a) nocturnal eating syndrome, (b) sleep terrors, and (c) nightmares.

1. Jaclyn's dad is sometimes awakened by his daughter's screams. He runs to Jaclyn's room to comfort her and is eventually able to calm her down. Jaclyn usually explains that she was being chased by a big, one-eyed, purple monster. The events typically happen after watching scary movies with friends. ____________

2. Sho-jen's parents hear her piercing screams on many nights and rush to comfort her, but she does not respond. During these episodes, her heart rate is elevated, and her pajamas are soaked in sweat. When she gets up the next day, however, she has no memory of the experience. ____________

3. Aiden has made a serious commitment to his diet for more than a month but continues to gain weight. He has no memory of eating but noticed that food is always missing from the refrigerator. ____________

Part B

Fill in the blanks to make the following statements correct about the treatment of sleep disorders.

4. Rin wakes up screaming every night, disregarding her parents' efforts to comfort her. Her heart rate is elevated in these episodes, and her pajamas are soaked in sweat. The next day, she has no memory of the experience. To help reduce these night terrors, Karen's pediatrician used ____________.

5. After Mateo's wife died at the age of 68, he could not sleep. To help him through the hardest first week, Dr. Brown prescribed ____________ for his insomnia.

6. Rajesh's doctor suggested some relatively simple lifestyle changes otherwise known as good ____________ when he expressed concern about developing a sleep disorder.

DSM Controversies: *Binge-Eating Disorder*

Binge-eating disorder is a new diagnosis in DSM-5, but as with most new disorders, some controversy has surrounded its inclusion. Alan J. Frances, the psychiatrist who chaired the task force that created DSM-IV, has criticized binge-eating disorder as he has many of the new disorders introduced into DSM-5. He notes that the history of our system of nosology in mental health has been littered with fad diagnoses that in retrospect have done more harm than good (Frances, 2012). And in his view, binge-eating disorder may be one of those fads. He notes that eating excessively at least 12 times over a period of 3 months (part of the criteria for binge-eating disorder; see DSM-5 Table 8.3) could really be considered just a manifestation of modern-day gluttony caused by the easy availability of great-tasting food (Frances, 2012). How many of us have "overeaten" approximately once a week over the past month? If you continued that for 3 months, you might be eligible for this diagnosis.

But look again at the description of binge-eating disorder. Notice that only a small minority of individuals who are obese and have joined commercial weight control programs to deal with their problem also evidence binge eating. Notice also that the percentage of obese individuals who binge rises considerably in groups who are so severely obese that they would be candidates for bariatric surgery. Also note that these individuals, but not those who are obese without binging, share the same concerns about shape and weight as people with anorexia and bulimia and their binging is often driven by attempts to alleviate bad moods. These factors—along with other factors, such as the tendency of binge eating to run in families, to have a heritable component, and to be responsive to the same types of treatments effective for other eating disorders (something that is not the case for individuals who are obese without bingeing)—were sufficient to convince the eating disorders workgroup and the DSM-5 task force that this condition should be a diagnosis. With this designation, this condition will now achieve greater recognition, and its treatment can be reimbursed by health insurance, thereby increasing the likelihood that individuals suffering from this disorder will receive appropriate care.

Summary

- The prevalence of eating disorders has increased rapidly over the past half century. As a result, they were included for the first time as a separate group of disorders in DSM-IV.

Bulimia Nervosa, Binge-Eating Disorder, and Anorexia Nervosa

- There are three prevalent eating disorders. In bulimia nervosa, dieting results in out-of-control binge-eating episodes that are often followed by purging the food through vomiting or other means. In binge-eating disorder, a pattern of binge eating is not followed by purging. Anorexia nervosa, in which food intake is cut dramatically, results in substantial weight loss and sometimes dangerously low body weight.

Statistics and Course for Eating Disorders

- Bulimia nervosa and anorexia nervosa are largely confined to young women in industrialized countries who are pursuing a thin body shape that is culturally mandated and biologically inappropriate, making it extremely difficult to achieve.
- Without treatment, eating disorders become chronic and can, on occasion, result in death.

Causes of Eating Disorders

- In addition to sociocultural pressures, causal factors include possible biological and genetic vulnerabilities (the disorders tend to run in families), psychological factors (low self-esteem), social anxiety (fears of rejection), and distorted body image (relatively normal-weight individuals view themselves as fat and ugly).

Treatment of Eating Disorders

- Several psychosocial treatments are effective, including cognitive-behavioral approaches combined with family therapy and interpersonal psychotherapy. Drug treatments are less effective at the current time.

Obesity

- Obesity is not a disorder in DSM but is one of the more dangerous epidemics confronting the world today. Cultural norms that encourage eating high-fat foods combine with genetic and other factors to cause obesity, which is difficult to treat. Professionally directed behavior modification programs emphasizing diet and exercise are moderately successful, but prevention effort in the form of changes in government policy on nutrition seem the most promising.

Sleep–Wake Disorders

- Sleep–wake disorders are highly prevalent in the general population and are of two types: dyssomnias (disturbances of sleep) and parasomnias (abnormal events such as nightmares and sleepwalking that occur during sleep).
- Of the dyssomnias, the most common disorder, insomnia disorder, involves the inability to initiate sleep, problems maintaining sleep, or failure to feel refreshed after a full night's sleep. Other dyssomnias include hypersomnolence (excessive sleep), narcolepsy (sudden and irresistible sleep attacks), circadian rhythm sleep disorders (sleepiness or insomnia caused by the body's inability to synchronize its sleep patterns with day and night), and breathing-related sleep disorders (disruptions that have a physical origin, such as sleep apnea, that leads to excessive sleepiness or insomnia).
- The formal assessment of sleep disorders, a polysomnographic evaluation, is typically done by monitoring the heart, muscles, respiration, brain waves, and other functions of a sleeping client in the lab. In addition to such monitoring, it is helpful to determine the individual's sleep efficiency, a percentage based on the time the individual actually sleeps as opposed to time spent in bed trying to sleep.
- Benzodiazepine medications have been helpful for short-term treatment of many of the dyssomnias, but they must be used carefully or they might cause rebound insomnia, a withdrawal experience that can cause worse sleep problems after the medication is stopped. Any long-term treatment of sleep problems should include psychological interventions such as stimulus control and sleep hygiene.
- Parasomnias such as nightmares occur during rapid eye movement (or dream) sleep, and sleep terrors and sleepwalking occur during nonrapid eye movement sleep.

Key Terms

bulimia nervosa, 267
binge, 267
anorexia nervosa, 267
binge-eating disorder (BED), 267
avoidant/restrictive food intake disorder (ARFID), 267
obesity, 267
purging techniques, 269
purging disorder, 274
night eating syndrome, 290
bariatric surgery, 292
rapid eye movement (REM) sleep, 295
chronotype, 296
social jet lag, 296
dyssomnias, 296
parasomnias, 296
polysomnographic (PSG) evaluation, 296
actigraph, 296
sleep efficiency (SE), 297
microsleeps, 297
insomnia disorder, 298
primary insomnia, 298
rebound insomnia, 300
hypersomnolence disorders, 301
sleep apnea, 301
narcolepsy, 302
breathing-related sleep disorders, 303
circadian rhythm sleep disorders, 305
nightmares, 309
disorder of arousal, 310
sleep terrors, 310
sleepwalking (somnambulism), 311

Answers to Concept Checks

8.1

1. c; 2. a; 3. a; 4. b

8.2

1. T; 2. T; 3. F (females find a smaller size more attractive than do men); 4. F (they help with bulimia nervosa, not anorexia); 5. T; 6. T

8.3

1. T; 2. F (it's at least one third or more); 3. F; 4. T

8.4

1. h; 2. f; 3. e; 4. g; 5. d; 6. b

8.5

Part A

1. c; 2. b; 3. a

Part B

4. scheduled awakenings;
5. benzodiazepines;
6. sleep hygiene

Exploring Eating Disorders

Individuals with eating disorders:

- Feel a relentless, all-encompassing drive to be thin
- Are overwhelmingly young females from middle- to upper-class families, who live in socially competitive environments
- Lived only in Western countries until recently

Causes

Psychological Influences
Diminished sense of personal control and self-confidence, causing low self-esteem. Distorted body image.

Social Influences
Cultural and social emphasis on slender ideal, leading to body dissatisfaction and preoccupation with food and eating.

Biological Influences
Possible genetic tendency to poor impulse control, emotional instability, and perfectionistic traits

EATING DISORDERS

Disorder	Characteristics	Treatment
Bulimia Nervosa	■ Out-of-control consumption of excessive amounts of mostly non-nutritious food within a short time ■ Elimination of food through self-induced vomiting and/or abuse of laxatives or diuretics ■ To compensate for binges, some bulimics exercise excessively or fast between binges ■ Vomiting may enlarge salivary glands (causing a chubby face), erode dental enamel, and cause electrolyte imbalance resulting in cardiac failure or kidney problems ■ Weight usually within 10% of normal ■ Age of onset is typically 18 to 21 years of age, although it can be as early as 10	■ Drug treatment, such as antidepressants ■ Short-term cognitive-behavioral therapy (CBT) to address behavior and attitudes on eating and body shape ■ Interpersonal psychotherapy (IPT) to improve interpersonal functioning ■ Tends to be chronic if left untreated
Anorexia Nervosa	■ Intense fear of obesity and persistent pursuit of thinness; perpetual dissatisfaction with weight loss ■ Severe caloric restriction, often with excessive exercise and sometimes with purging, to the point of semi-starvation ■ Severely limiting caloric intake may cause cessation of menstruation, downy hair on limbs and cheeks, dry skin, brittle hair or nails, sensitivity to cold, and danger of acute cardiac or kidney failure ■ Weight at least 15% below normal ■ Average age of onset is between 18 and 21 years of age, with younger cases tending to begin at 15	■ Hospitalization (at 75% below normal weight) ■ Outpatient treatment to restore weight and correct dysfunctional attitudes on eating and body shape ■ Family therapy ■ Tends to be chronic if left untreated; more resistant to treatment than bulimia
Binge Eating	■ Similar to bulimia with out-of-control food binges, but no attempt to purge the food (vomiting, laxatives, diuretics) or compensate for excessive intake ■ Marked physical and emotional stress; some sufferers binge to alleviate bad moods ■ Binge eaters share some concerns about weight and body shape as individuals with anorexia and bulimia ■ Tends to affect more older people than either bulimia or anorexia	■ Short-term CBT to address behavior and attitudes on eating and body shape ■ IPT to improve interpersonal functioning ■ Drug treatments that reduce feelings of hunger ■ Self-help approaches

Photodisc/Getty Images

Exploring Sleep–Wake Disorders

Characterized by extreme disruption in the everyday lives of affected individuals, and are an important factor in many psychological disorders.

SLEEP–WAKE DISORDERS

Diagnosing Sleep–Wake Disorders

A polysomnographic (PSG) evaluation assesses an individual's sleep habits with various electronic tests to measure airflow, brain activity, eye movements, muscle movements, and heart activity. Results are weighed with a measure of sleep efficiency (SE), the percentage of time spent asleep.

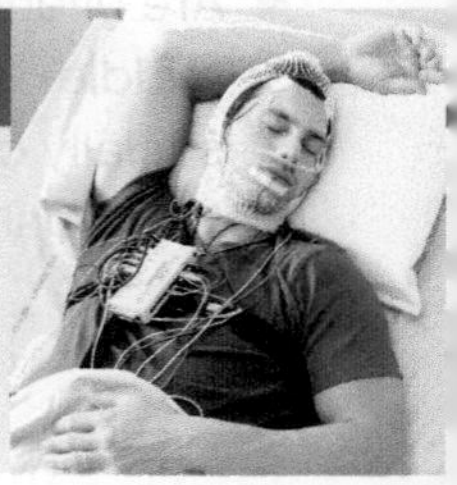

Dyssomnias

Disturbances in the timing, amount, or quality of sleep

Disorder	Characteristics	Causes	Treatment
Insomnia Disorder	■ Characteristics include difficulty initiating sleep, difficulty maintaining sleep, or nonrestorative sleep.	■ Causes include pain, insufficient exercise, drug use, environmental influences, anxiety, respiratory problems, and biological vulnerability.	■ Treatment may be medical (benzodiazepines) or psychologica (anxiety reduction, improved sleep hygiene); combined approach is usually most effective.
Narcolepsy	■ Characteristics include sudden daytime onset of REM sleep combined with cataplexy, a rapid loss of muscle tone that can be quite mild or result in complete collapse. Often accompanied by sleep paralysis and/or hypnagogic hallucinations.	■ Causes are likely to be genetic.	■ Treatment is medical (stimulant drugs).
Hypersomnolence Disorder	■ Characteristics include abnormally excessive sleep and sleepiness, and involuntary daytime sleeping. Classified as a disorder only when it's subjectively perceived as disruptive.	■ Causes may involve genetic link and/or excess serotonin.	■ Treatment is usually medical (stimulant drugs).
Breathing-Related Sleep Disorders	■ Characteristics include disturbed sleep and daytime fatigue resulting from hypoventilation (labored breathing) or sleep apnea (suspended breathing).	■ Causes may include narrow or obstructed airway, obesity, and increasing age.	■ Treatment using continuous positi air pressure (CPAP) machines is th gold standard; weight loss is also often prescribed.
Circadian Rhythm Sleep–Wake Disorders	■ Characteristics include sleepiness or insomnia.	■ Caused by inability to synchronize sleep patterns with current pattern of day and night due to jet lag, shift work, delayed sleep, or advanced sleep (going to bed earlier than normal bedtime).	■ Treatment includes phase delays to adjust bedtime and bright light to readjust biological clock.

Parasomnias

Abnormal behaviors that occur during sleep

Nightmares

Frightening REM dreams that awaken the sleeper. Nightmares qualify as nightmare disorder when they are stressful enough to impair normal functioning. Causes are unknown, but they tend to decrease with age.

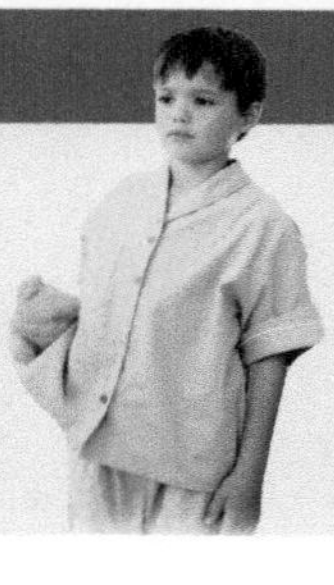

Sleep Terrors

Occur during non-REM (nondreaming) sleep and most commonly afflict children. Sleeping child screams, cries, sweats, sometimes walks, has rapid heartbeat, and cannot easily be awakened or comforted. More common in boys than girls, and possible genetic link since they tend to run in families. May subside with time.

Sleepwalking

Occurs at least once during non-REM sleep in 15% to 30% of children under age 15. Causes may include extreme fatigue, sleep deprivation, sedative or hypnotic drugs, and stress. Adult sleepwalking is usually associated with other psychological disorders. May have a genetic link.

9 Physical Disorders and Health Psychology

© Phil Date/ShutterStock.com

Learning Objectives

LO9.1 Distinguish between behavioral medicine and health psychology as subfields of psychology according to their areas of study.

LO9.2 Explain how psychological and social factors impact the functioning of the immune system via stress.

LO9.3 List psychosocial patterns of lifestyle and behavior that can have an impact on physical health and well-being.

LO9.4 Describe the benefits of comprehensive stress- and pain-reduction programs for treating or preventing physical disorders.

Psychological and Social Factors That Influence Health

At the beginning of the 20th century, the leading causes of death were infectious diseases such as influenza, pneumonia, diphtheria, tuberculosis, typhoid fever, measles, and gastrointestinal infections. Since then, the percentage of yearly total deaths from these diseases has been reduced greatly, showing even a decline from year to year. ■ Figure 9.1 shows the 10 leading causes of death in the United States in 2018 and 2019 (Kochanek, Xu, & Arias, 2020). Unfortunately, the mortality rate in 2020 increased from the previous year by 15.9% due to COVID-19 (SARS-CoV-2). In 2020, the COVID-19 pandemic became the third leading cause of death in the United States, with a particularly devastating impact on people of color (Ahmad et al., 2021). Without the vaccination efforts in 2021 and social distancing strategies early on to control the virus, many more deaths would have been added to the already grim number of fatalities. This has revealed a complex and challenging problem: Some major contributing factors to illness and death are *psychological* and *behavioral* (Ezzati & Riboli, 2012; Marteau, Hollands, & Fletcher, 2012).

In Chapter 2, we described the profound effects of psychological and social factors on brain structure and function. These factors seem to influence neurotransmitter activity, the secretion of neurohormones in the endocrine system, and, at a more fundamental level, gene expression. We have repeatedly looked at the complex interplay of biological, psychological, and social factors in the production and maintenance of psychological disorders. But psychological and social factors are important to a number of additional disorders, including endocrinological disorders such as diabetes, cardiovascular disorders, and disorders of the immune system such as acquired immune deficiency syndrome (AIDS). These and the other disorders discussed in this chapter are clearly *physical disorders.* They have known (or strongly inferred) physical causes and mostly observable physical pathology (for example, genital herpes, damaged heart muscle, malignant tumors, or measurable hypertension). Contrast this with the somatic symptom disorders discussed in Chapter 6: In conversion disorders, for example, clients report physical damage or disease but show no physical pathology.

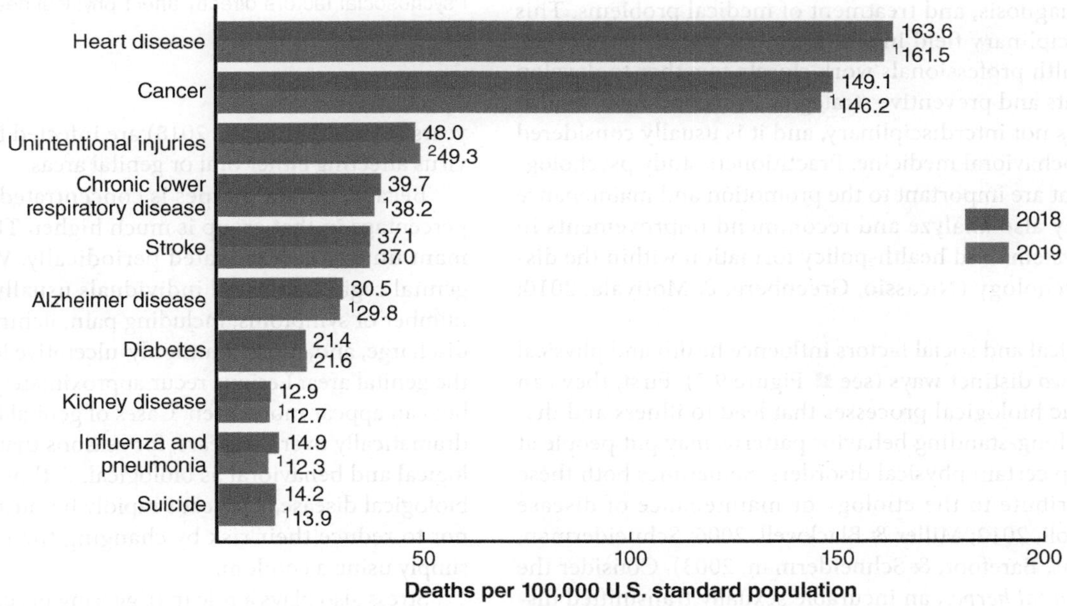

Mortality rates in 2018 and 2019: K. D. Kochanek, J. Q. Xu, & E. Arias, 2020, Mortality in the United States, 2019, NCHS Data Brief, no 395, National Center for Health Statistics, retrieved from https://www.cdc.gov/nchs/products/databriefs/db395.htm

Figure 9.1

Age-adjusted death rates for the 10 leading causes of death in 2019: United States, 2018 and 2019

The study of how psychological and social factors affect physical disorders used to be distinct and somewhat separate from the remainder of psychopathology. Early on, the field was called *psychosomatic medicine* (Alexander, 1950), which meant that *psychological* factors affected *somatic* (physical) function. The label *psychophysiological disorders* was used to communicate a similar idea. Such terms are less often used today because they are misleading. Describing as psychosomatic a disorder with an obvious physical component gave the impression that psychological (mental) disorders of mood and anxiety did not have a strong biological component. As we now know, this assumption is not viable. Biological, psychological, and social factors are implicated to varying degrees in the cause and maintenance of virtually every disorder, both mental and physical.

The contribution of psychosocial factors to the etiology and treatment of physical disorders is widely studied. Some of the discoveries are among the more exciting findings in all of psychology and biology. For example, we describe briefly in Chapter 2 that lowering stress levels and having a rich social network of family and friends are associated with better health, living longer, and less cognitive decline as one ages (Cohen & Janicki-Deverts, 2009). Remember, too, the tragic physical and mental deterioration among older adults who are removed from social networks of family and friends (Hawkley & Cacioppo, 2007).

Health and Health-Related Behavior

Two closely related new fields of health study have developed. In the first, **behavioral medicine** (Feldman & Christensen, 2014), knowledge derived from behavioral science is applied to the prevention, diagnosis, and treatment of medical problems. This is an interdisciplinary field in which psychologists, physicians, and other health professionals work closely together to develop new treatments and preventive strategies. A second field, **health psychology**, is not interdisciplinary, and it is usually considered a subfield of behavioral medicine. Practitioners study psychological factors that are important to the promotion and maintenance of health; they also analyze and recommend improvements in health-care systems and health-policy formation within the discipline of psychology (Nicassio, Greenberg, & Motivala, 2010; Taylor, 2009).

Psychological and social factors influence health and physical problems in *two* distinct ways (see ■ Figure 9.2). First, they can affect the basic biological processes that lead to illness and disease. Second, long-standing behavior patterns may put people at risk to develop certain physical disorders. Sometimes both these avenues contribute to the etiology or maintenance of disease (Ezzati & Riboli, 2012; Miller & Blackwell, 2006; Schneiderman, 2004; Williams, Barefoot, & Schneiderman, 2003). Consider the example of *genital herpes*, an incurable sexually transmitted disease. There's a chance that you or someone you know has genital herpes. The majority of infected people don't know that they have it. This disease is very common, as are other sexually transmitted diseases. About 1 in 5 people in the United States have a sexually transmitted disease (Centers for Disease Control, 2021) and estimates indicate that more than 12.1% of Americans aged 14 to 49 years (McQuillan et al., 2018) are infected by the herpes simplex virus affecting either oral or genital areas.

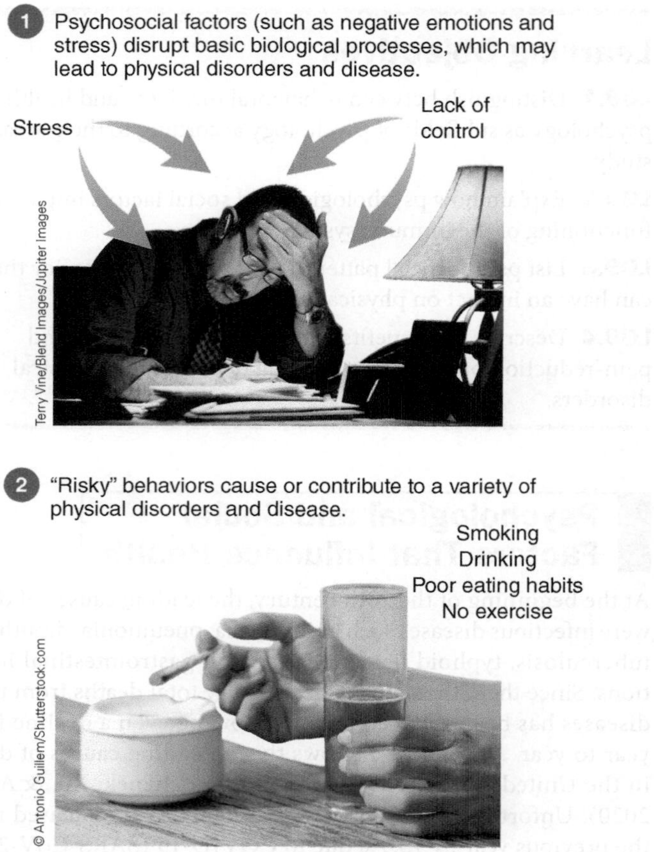

Figure 9.2

Psychosocial factors directly affect physical health in two ways.

Because genital herpes is concentrated in young adults, the percentage in that group is much higher. The virus remains dormant until it is reactivated periodically. When it recurs in the genital region, infected individuals usually experience any of a number of symptoms, including pain, itching, vaginal or urethral discharge, and, most commonly, ulcerative lesions (open sores) in the genital area. Lesions recur approximately four times each year but can appear more often. Cases of genital herpes have increased dramatically over the years, for reasons that are as much psychological and behavioral as biological. Although genital herpes is a biological disease, it spreads rapidly because some people choose not to reduce their risk by changing their behavior, such as by simply using a condom.

Stress also plays a role in triggering herpes recurrences (Chida & Mao, 2009; Coe 2010; Goldmeier, Garvey, & Barton, 2008). Stress-control procedures, particularly stress management, seem to decrease recurrences of genital herpes, as well as the duration of each episode, most likely through the positive effects of such practices on the immune system (Goldmeier, Garvey, & Barton, 2008; Pereira et al., 2003).

Consider also the tragic example of AIDS. AIDS is a disease of the immune system that is directly affected by stress (Kennedy, 2000), so stress may promote the deadly progression of AIDS. This is an example of how psychological factors may directly influence biological processes. We also know that a variety of things we may choose to do put us at risk for AIDS—for example, having unprotected sex or sharing contaminated needles. Because there is no medical cure for AIDS yet, our best weapon is large-scale behavior modification to *prevent acquisition* of the disease (Fauci & Folkers, 2012; Mermin & Fenton, 2012).

Other behavioral patterns contribute to disease. The roots of many of the leading causes of death, such as heart disease, cancer, and diabetes, can be traced to lifestyle factors, principally smoking, diet, and physical activity (Ford et al., 2013).

Smoking is the leading preventable cause of death in the United States and has been estimated to cause nearly half a million of premature deaths every year in the nation and reduces life expectancy by more than a decade (U.S. Department of Health and Human Services, 2014). Other unhealthy behaviors include poor eating habits, lack of exercise, and insufficient injury control (not wearing seat belts, for example). These behaviors are grouped under the label *lifestyle* because they are mostly enduring habits that are an integral part of a person's daily living pattern (Lewis, Statt, & Marcus, 2011; Oldenburg, de Courten, & Frean, 2010). We return to lifestyles in the closing pages of this chapter when we look at efforts to modify them and promote health.

We have much to learn about how psychological factors affect physical disorders and disease. Available evidence suggests that the same kinds of causal factors active in psychological disorders—social, psychological, and biological—play a role in some physical disorders (Mostofsky & Barlow, 2000; Uchino, 2009). But the factor attracting the most attention is *stress,* particularly the neurobiological components of the stress response.

The Nature of Stress

In 1936, a young scientist in Montreal, Canada, named Hans Selye noticed that one group of rats he injected with a certain chemical extract developed ulcers and other physiological problems, including atrophy of immune system tissues. But a control group of rats who received a daily saline (salty water) injection that should not have had any effect developed the *same* physical problems. Selye pursued this unexpected finding and discovered that the daily injections themselves seemed to be the culprit rather than the injected substance. Furthermore, many types of environmental changes produced the same results. Borrowing a term from engineering, he decided the cause of this nonspecific reaction was *stress.* As so often happens in science, an accidental or serendipitous observation led to a new area of study, in this case, *stress physiology* (Selye, 1936).

Courtesy of Hans Selya

Hans Selye suggested in 1936 that stress contributes to certain physical problems.

Selye theorized that the body goes through several stages in response to *sustained stress*. The first phase is a type of *alarm* response to immediate danger or threat. With continuing stress, we seem to pass into a stage of *resistance,* in which we mobilize various coping mechanisms to respond to the stress. Finally, if the stress is too intense or lasts too long, we may enter a stage of *exhaustion,* in which our bodies suffer permanent damage or death (Selye, 1936, 1950). Selye called this sequence the **general adaptation syndrome (GAS)**. Although Selye was not correct in all of the details of his theory, the idea that chronic stress may inflict permanent bodily damage or contribute to disease has been confirmed and elaborated on in later years (Kemeny, 2003; Robles, Glaser, & Kiecolt-Glaser, 2005; Sapolsky, 1990, 2000b).

The word *stress* means many things in modern life. In engineering, stress is the strain on a bridge when a heavy truck drives across it; stress is the *response* of the bridge to the truck's weight. But stress is also a *stimulus.* The truck is a "stressor" for the bridge, just as being fired from a job or facing a difficult final exam is a stimulus or stressor for a person. These varied meanings can create some confusion, but we concentrate on **stress** as the physiological response of the individual to a stressor.

There is a strong, clear association between stress, the brain systems processing threat (such as the amygdala) and other areas (especially the hippocampus), and the neuroendocrine system, releasing cortisol, epinephrine, and norepinephrine into the bloodstream (O'Donovan, Slavich, Epel, & Neylan, 2013). These responses are initially adaptive and mobilize the needed resources to address the threat. But when the threat persists, these same processes can take a toll on the body. This is known as *allostatic load*—the "wear and tear" of stress on the body (McEwen, 2020). Studies have shown that this can negatively affect the brain (such as hippocampus), the cardiovascular system (leading to high blood pressure), and the immune system (leading to increased inflammation), making the body more vulnerable to infection and even cancer (Furman et al., 2019).

The Physiology of Stress

In Chapter 2, we describe the physiological effects of the early stages of stress, noting in particular its activating effect on the sympathetic nervous system, which mobilizes our resources during times of threat or danger by activating internal organs to prepare the body for immediate action, either fight or flight. These changes increase our strength and mental activity. We also note in Chapter 2 that the activity of the endocrine system increases when we are stressed, primarily through activation of the hypothalamic–pituitary–adrenocortical (HPA) axis (see p. 47). Although a variety of neurotransmitters begin flowing in the nervous system, much attention has focused on the endocrine system's neuromodulators or neuropeptides, hormones affecting the nervous system that are secreted by the glands directly into the bloodstream (Chaouloff & Groc, 2010; Owens, Mulchahey, Taylor, Maloney, Dearborn, & Weiss, 2009). These neuromodulating hormones act much like neurotransmitters in carrying the brain's messages to various parts of the body. One of the neurohormones, *corticotropin-releasing factor (CRF),* is secreted by the hypothalamus and stimulates the pituitary gland. Farther down the chain of the HPA axis, the pituitary gland (along with the autonomic nervous system) activates the adrenal gland, which secretes, among other things, the hormone *cortisol.* Because of their close relationship to the stress response, cortisol and other related hormones are known as the *stress hormones.*

Remember that the HPA axis is closely related to the limbic system. The hypothalamus, at the top of the brain stem, is right next to the limbic system, which contains the hippocampus and seems to control our emotional memories. The hippocampus is responsive to cortisol. When stimulated by this hormone during HPA axis activity, the hippocampus helps to *turn off* the stress response, completing a feedback loop between the limbic system and the various parts of the HPA axis (see ■ Figure 9.3).

This loop may be important for a number of reasons. Working with primates, Robert Sapolsky and his colleagues (see, for example, Sapolsky, 2000b, 2007; Sapolsky & Meaney, 1986) showed that increased levels of cortisol in response to chronic stress may kill nerve cells in the hippocampus. If hippocampal activity is thus compromised, excessive cortisol is secreted, and, over time, the ability to turn off the stress response decreases, which leads to further aging of the hippocampus. These findings indicate that chronic stress leading to chronic secretion of cortisol may have long-lasting effects on physical function, including brain damage. Cell death may, in turn, lead to deficient problem-solving abilities among older adults and, ultimately, dementia. This physiological process may also affect susceptibility to infectious disease and recovery from it in other pathophysiological systems. Sapolsky's work is important because we now know that hippocampal cell death associated with chronic stress and anxiety occurs in humans with, for example, posttraumatic stress disorder (see Chapter 5) and depression (see Chapter 7). The long-term effects of this cell death are not yet known.

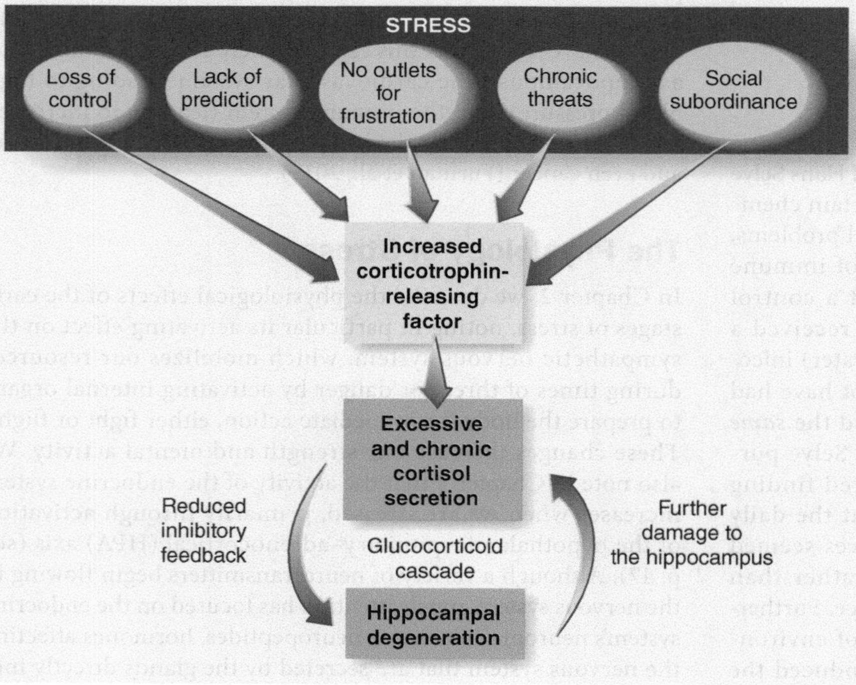

Figure 9.3

Effects of psychological stress on the HPA axis and the hippocampus. Adapted from Sapolsky (1992, 2007) and Sapolsky and Ray (1989).

Contributions to the Stress Response

Stress physiology is profoundly influenced by psychological and social factors (Adler, 2013; Lovallo, 2010; Slavich, 2020; Taylor et al., 2009). This link has been demonstrated by Sapolsky (1990, 2000b, 2007; Gesquiere et al., 2011). He studied baboons living freely in a national reserve in Kenya because their primary sources of stress, like those of humans, are psychological rather than physical. As with many species, baboons arrange themselves in a social hierarchy with dominant members at the top and submissive members at the bottom. And life is tough at the bottom! The lives of subordinate animals are made difficult (Sapolsky calls it "stressful") by continual bullying from the dominant animals, and they have less access to food, preferred resting places, and sexual partners. Particularly interesting are Sapolsky's findings on levels of cortisol in the baboons as a function of their social rank in a dominance hierarchy. Remember from our description of the HPA axis that the secretion of cortisol from the adrenal glands is the final step in a cascade of hormone secretion that originates in the limbic system in the brain during periods of stress. The secretion of cortisol contributes to our arousal and mobilization in the short run, but if produced chronically, it can damage the hippocampus. In addition, muscles atrophy, fertility is affected by declining testosterone, hypertension develops in the cardiovascular system, and the immune response is impaired. Sapolsky discovered that dominant males in the baboon hierarchy ordinarily had *lower* resting levels of cortisol than subordinate males. When an emergency occurred, however, cortisol levels rose more quickly in the dominant males than in the subordinate males.

Sapolsky and his colleagues sought the causes of these differences by working backward up the HPA axis. They found an excess secretion of CRF by the hypothalamus in subordinate animals, combined with a diminished sensitivity of the pituitary gland (which is stimulated by CRF). Therefore, subordinate animals, unlike dominant animals, continually secrete cortisol, probably because their lives are so stressful. In addition, their HPA system is less sensitive to the effects of cortisol and therefore less efficient in turning off the stress response.

Sapolsky also discovered that subordinate males have fewer circulating lymphocytes (white blood cells) than dominant males, a sign of immune system suppression. In addition, subordinate males evidence less circulating high-density lipoprotein cholesterol, which puts them at higher risk for atherosclerosis and coronary heart disease, a subject we discuss later in this chapter.

Baboons at the top of the social hierarchy have a sense of predictability and control that allows them to cope with problems and maintain physical health. Baboons at the bottom of the hierarchy suffer the symptoms of stress because they have little control over access to food, resting places, and mates.

What is it about being on top of the social hierarchy that produces positive effects? Sapolsky concluded that it is primarily the psychological benefits of having *predictability* and *controllability* concerning events in one's life. Parts of his data were gathered during years in which a number of male baboons were at the top of the hierarchy, with no clear "winner." Although these males dominated the rest of the animals in the group, they constantly attacked one another. Under these conditions, they displayed hormonal profiles more like those of subordinate males. Thus, dominance combined with stability produced optimal stress hormone profiles. But the most important factor in regulating stress physiology seems to be a sense of control (Sapolsky & Ray, 1989), a finding strongly confirmed in subsequent research (Kemeny, 2003; Sapolsky, 2007). Control of social situations and the ability to cope with any tension that arises go a long way toward blunting the long-term effects of stress.

Stress, Anxiety, Depression, and Excitement

If you have read the chapters on anxiety, mood, and related psychological disorders, you might conclude, correctly, that stressful life events combined with psychological vulnerabilities such as an inadequate sense of control are a factor in both psychological and physical disorders. Is there any relationship between psychological and physical disorders? There seems to be a strong one. In a classic study, George Vaillant (1979) studied more than 200 Harvard University sophomore men between 1942 and 1944 who were mentally and physically healthy. He followed these men closely for more than 30 years. Those who developed psychological disorders or who were highly stressed became chronically ill or died at a significantly higher rate than men who remained well adjusted and free from psychological disorders, a finding that has been repeatedly confirmed (see, for example, Katon, 2003; Robles et al., 2005; Scott et al., 2016). The study by Scott and colleagues (2016) surveyed more than 47,000 individuals across 17 countries to examine the temporal relationship between 16 different mental disorders (such as mood and anxiety disorders and substance use disorders) and 10 chronic physical conditions (such as arthritis, cancer, chronic pain, and heart disease). The results showed that mental disorders of all kinds were associated with an increased risk for developing chronic physical conditions. This suggests that the same types of stress-related psychological factors that contribute to psychological disorders may contribute to the later development of physical disorders and that stress, anxiety, and depression are closely related. Another study examined deaths, health-care use, and chronic physical disease diagnoses made in public hospitals for all individuals who were born in New Zealand between 1928 and 1978 and who resided in the country at any time during the 30-year observation period (a total of 2,349,897 individuals). The results showed that mental disorders often began and peaked in young adulthood and preceded physical diseases and early mortality, suggesting that improving mental health might also reduce the likelihood for physical diseases and improve people's length and quality of life (Richmond-Raker et al., 2021). A history of psychopathology was also associated with accelerated aging at midlife years before the typical onset of age-related diseases (Wertz et al., 2021). Similar results were reported in a large Danish study, showing that most mental disorders were associated with an increased risk of a subsequent medical condition (Momen et al., 2020).

Can you tell the difference among feelings of stress, anxiety, depression, and excitement? You might say, "No problem," but these four states have a lot in common. Which one you experience may depend on your *sense of control* at the moment or how well you think you can cope with the threat or challenge you are facing (Barlow, 2002; Barlow, Sauer-Zavala, Carl, Bullis, & Ellard, 2014; Suárez, Bennett, Goldstein, & Barlow, 2009). This continuum of feelings from excitement to stress to anxiety to depression is shown in ■ Figure 9.4.

Consider how you feel when you are excited. You might experience a rapid heartbeat, a sudden burst of energy, or a jumpy stomach. But if you're well prepared for the challenge—for example, if you're an athlete up for the game and confident in your abilities or a musician sure you are going to give an outstanding performance—these feelings of *excitement* can be pleasurable and might even enhance your performance.

Sometimes when you face a challenging task, you feel you could handle it if you only had the time or help you need, but because you don't have these resources, you feel pressured. In response, you may work harder to do better and be perfect, even though you think you will be all right in the end. If you are under too much pressure, you may become tense and irritable or develop a headache or an upset stomach. This is what *stress* feels like. If something really is threatening and you believe there is little you can do about it, you may feel *anxiety.* The threatening situation could be anything from facing a physical attack to making a fool of yourself in front of someone. As your body prepares for the challenge, you worry about it incessantly. In some cases, there may not be a difficult situation. Sometimes we are anxious for no reason except that we feel certain aspects of our lives are out of control. Finally, individuals who always perceive life as threatening may lose hope about ever having control and slip into a state of *depression,* no longer trying to cope.

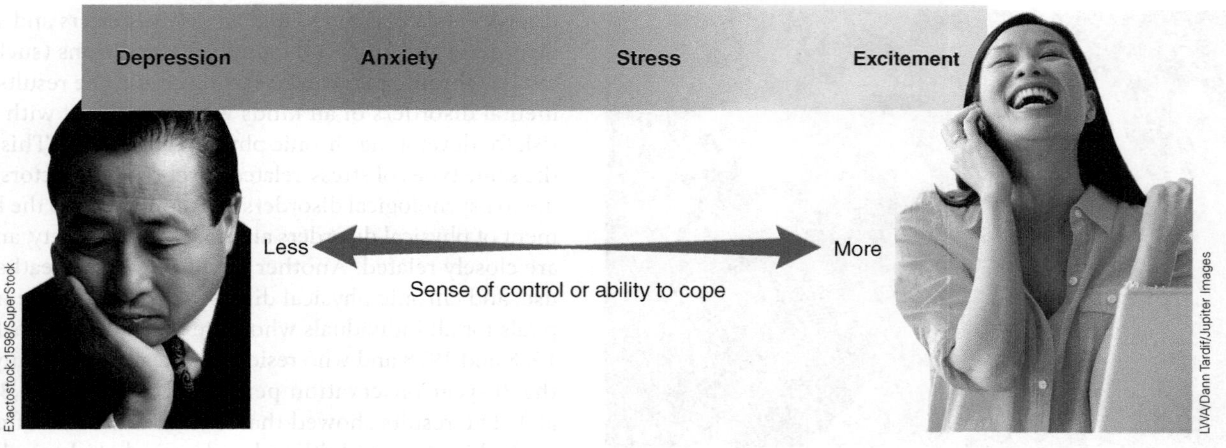

Figure 9.4

Responses to threats and challenges. Our feelings range along a continuum from depression to anxiety to stress to excitement, depending partly on our sense of control and ability to cope. Adapted, with permission, from D. H. Barlow, R. M. Rapee, & S. Perini, 2014, *10 steps to mastering Stress: A lifestyle approach*, Oxford University Press.

To sum up, the underlying physiology of these particular emotional states seems relatively similar in some basic ways. This is why we refer to a similar pattern of sympathetic arousal and activation of specific neurotransmitters and hormones in discussing anxiety, depression, and stress-related physical disorders. On the other hand, there seem to be some differences. Blood pressure may increase when the challenges seem to overwhelm coping resources, resulting in a low sense of control (anxiety, depression), but blood pressure will be unchanged during excitement or marked stress (Blascovich & Tomaka, 1996). Nevertheless, it is psychological factors—specifically a sense of control and confidence that we can cope with stress or challenges, called **self-efficacy** by Bandura (1986)—that differ most markedly among these emotions, leading to different feelings (Taylor et al., 1997).

Stress and the Immune Response

Have you had a cold during the past several months? How did you pick it up? Did you spend the day with someone else who had a cold? Did someone sneeze nearby while you were sitting in class? Exposure to cold viruses is a necessary factor in developing a cold, but, as mentioned briefly in Chapter 2, the level of stress you are experiencing at the time seems to play a major role in whether the exposure results in a cold. Sheldon Cohen and his associates (Cohen, 1996; Cohen, Doyle, & Skoner, 1999) exposed volunteer participants to a specific dosage of a cold virus and followed them closely. They found that the chance a participant would get sick was directly related to how much stress the person had experienced during the past year. Cohen and colleagues (1995) also linked the intensity of stress and negative affect at the time of exposure to the later *severity* of the cold, as measured by mucus production. In an interesting twist, Cohen, Doyle, Turner, Alper, and Skoner (2003) have demonstrated that how sociable you are—that is, the quantity and quality of your social relationships—affects whether you come down with a cold when exposed to the virus, perhaps because socializing with friends relieves stress (Cohen & Janicki-Devarts, 2009). Finally, a positive and optimistic cognitive style protects against developing a cold (Cohen & Pressman, 2006). These are among the first well-controlled studies to demonstrate that stress and related factors increase the risk of infection.

Think back to your last exam. Did you (or your roommate) have a cold? Exam periods are stressors that have been shown to produce increased infections, particularly of the upper respiratory tract (Glaser et al., 1987, 1990). Therefore, if you are susceptible to colds, maybe one way out is to skip final exams! A better solution is to learn how to control your stress before and during exams. Almost certainly, the effect of stress on susceptibility to infections is mediated through the **immune system**, which protects the body from any foreign materials that may enter it, including cold viruses.

Research dating back to the original reports of Selye (1936) demonstrates the detrimental effects of stress on immune system functioning. Humans under stress show clearly increased rates of infectious diseases, including colds, herpes, and mononucleosis (Coe 2010; Taylor, 2009). Direct evidence links a number of stressful situations to lowered immune system functioning, including marital discord or relationship difficulties (Kiecolt-Glaser et al., 2005; Kiecolt-Glaser & Newton, 2001; Uchino, 2009), job loss, and the death of a loved one (Hawkley & Cacioppo, 2007). Furthermore, these stressful events affect the immune system rapidly. Studies in laboratories have demonstrated weakened immune system response within 2 hours of exposure to stress (Glaser & Kiecolt-Glaser, 2005; Weisse, Pato, McAllister, Littman, & Breier, 1990; Zakowski, McAllister, Deal, & Baum, 1992). Cohen and colleagues (1999) infected 55 participants with the influenza A virus. As expected, higher psychological stress was associated with a more severe case of the flu. But Cohen and colleagues (1999; Coe, 2010) also demonstrated that the stress hormones triggered cytokine interleukin-6, an immune system component that produces inflammation of tissues. It seems that this inflammatory response may be one mechanism through which stress breaks down resistance to the infection and injury. There is also evidence to suggest that early-life stress contributes to inflammation in adulthood, which in turn might contribute to cardiovascular disease, type 2 diabetes, and even cancer (Fugundes & Way, 2014; Morey et al., 2015).

We have already noted that psychological disorders seem to make us more susceptible to developing physical disorders (Katon, 2003; Robles et al., 2005; Scott et al., 2016; Vaillant, 1979). In fact, direct evidence indicates that depression lowers immune system functioning (Herbert & Cohen, 1993; Miller & Blackwell, 2006), particularly in older adults (Herbert & Cohen, 1993), whereas optimism and positive affect is associated with a stronger immune system (Segerstrom & Sephton, 2010). It may be that the level of depression—and, more important, the underlying sense of uncontrollability that accompanies most depressions—is the crucial mechanism in lowering immune system functioning, a mechanism present during most negative stressful life events, such as job loss (Miller & Blackwell, 2006; Robles et al., 2005). Depression can also lead to poor self-care and a tendency to engage in riskier behaviors. For humans, like Sapolsky's baboons, the ability to retain a sense of control over events in our lives may be one of the most important psychological contributions to good health.

Most studies concerning stress and the immune system have examined a sudden or acute stressor. But *chronic stress* may be more problematic because the effects, by definition, last longer (Schneiderman, 2004). For example, lowered immune system functioning has been reported for people who care for chronically ill family members, such as Alzheimer's disease patients (Holland & Gallagher-Thompson, 2011; Mills et al., 2004).

To understand how the immune system protects us, we must first understand how it works. We take a brief tour of the immune system next, using ■ Figure 9.5 as a visual guide, and then we examine psychological contributions to the biology of two diseases strongly related to immune system functioning: AIDS and cancer.

How the Immune System Works

The immune system identifies and eliminates foreign materials, called **antigens**, in the body. Antigens can be any of a number of substances, usually bacteria, viruses, or parasites. But the immune system also targets the body's own cells that have become aberrant or damaged in some way, perhaps as part of a malignant tumor. Donated organs are foreign, so the immune system attacks them after surgical transplant; consequently, it is necessary to suppress the immune system temporarily after transplant surgery.

The immune system has two main parts: the humoral and the cellular. Specific types of cells function as agents of both. White blood cells, called *leukocytes,* do most of the work. There are several types of leukocytes. *Macrophages* might be considered one of the body's first lines of defense: They surround identifiable antigens and destroy them. They also signal *lymphocytes,* which consist of two groups, B cells and T cells.

The *B cells* operate within the humoral part of the immune system, releasing molecules that seek antigens in blood and other bodily fluids with the purpose of neutralizing them. The B cells produce highly specific molecules called *immunoglobulins* that act as *antibodies,* which combine with the antigens to neutralize them. After the antigens are neutralized, a subgroup called *memory B cells* are created so that the next time that antigen is encountered, the immune system response will be even faster. This action accounts for the success of inoculations, or vaccinations, you may have received for mumps or measles as a child.

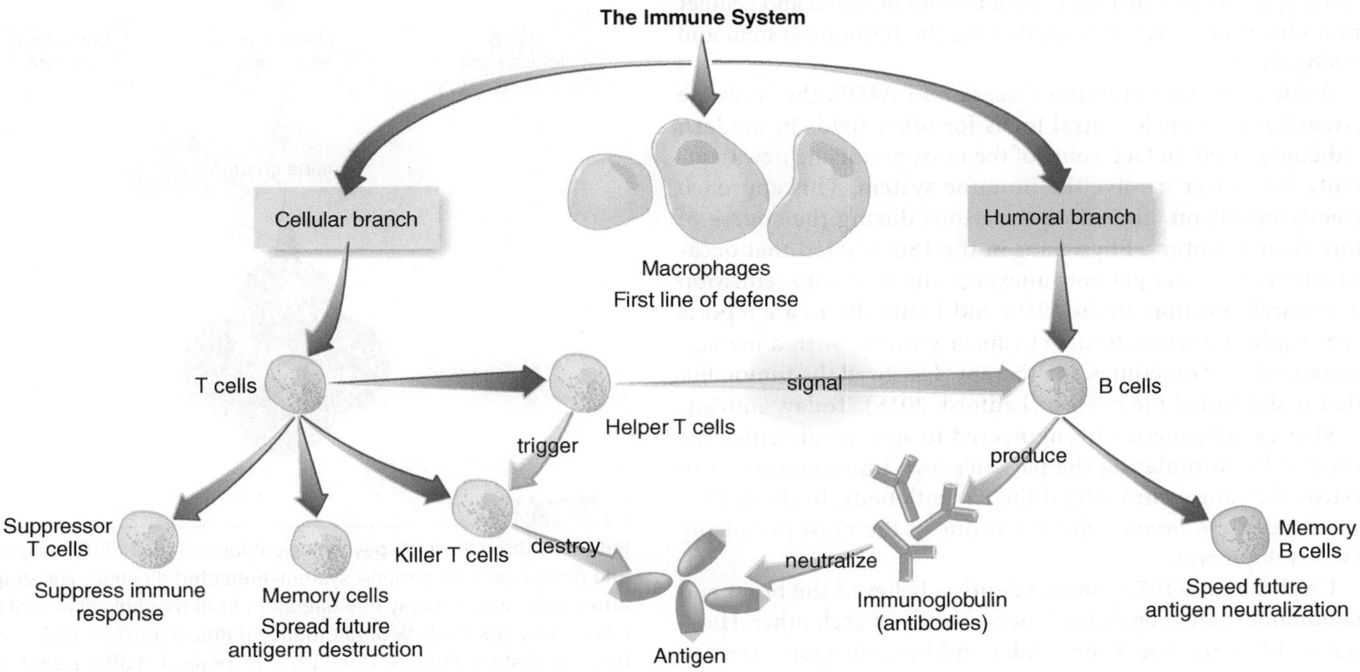

Figure 9.5

An overview of the immune system.

Robert Ader demonstrated that the immune system is responsive to environmental cues.

An inoculation contains small amounts of the targeted organism but not enough to make you sick. Your immune system then "remembers" this antigen and prevents you from coming down with the full disease when you are exposed to it.

Members of the second group of lymphocytes, called *T cells,* operate in the cellular branch of the immune system. These cells don't produce antibodies. Instead, one subgroup, *killer T cells,* directly destroys viruses and cancer cells (Dustin & Long, 2010; Wan, 2010). When the process is complete, *memory T cells* are created to speed future responses to the same antigen. Other subgroups of T cells help regulate the immune system. For example, *T4 cells* are called *helper T cells* because they enhance the immune system response by signaling B cells to produce antibodies and telling other T cells to destroy the antigen. *Suppressor T cells* suppress the production of antibodies by B cells when they are no longer needed.

We should have twice as many T4 (helper) cells as suppressor T cells. With too many T4 cells, the immune system is overreactive and may attack the body's normal cells rather than antigens. When this happens, we have what is called an **autoimmune disease**, such as **rheumatoid arthritis**. With too many suppressor T cells, the body is subject to invasion by a number of antigens. The human immunodeficiency virus (HIV) directly attacks the helper T cells, lymphocytes that are crucial to both humoral and cellular immunity, thereby severely weakening the immune system and causing AIDS.

Aside from autoimmune disease and AIDS, the immune system has become a central focus for other fields in modern medicine as well. In fact, some of the most promising new treatments for cancer involve the immune system. This approach directly builds on clinical observations during the course of more than a century. Physicians in the 1800s noted that occasionally their cancer patients unexpectedly went into remission after a viral infection. In the 1950s and 1960s, these case reports then inspired doctors to inject cancer patients with a menagerie of viruses. Sometimes, the therapy destroyed the tumor, but often it also killed the person (Ledford, 2015). Today, anticancer viruses are genetically engineered to specifically enter the cancer cells, stimulating the patient's own immune system to destroy the cancer throughout the patient's body. In the field of cancer research, *immunotherapy* is one of the most promising new developments.

Until the mid-1970s, most scientists believed the brain and the immune system operated independently of each other. However, in 1974, the late Robert Ader and his colleagues (see, for example, Ader & Cohen, 1975, 1993) made a startling discovery. Working with a classical conditioning paradigm, they gave sugar-flavored water to rats, together with a drug that suppresses the immune system. Ader and Cohen then demonstrated that giving the same rats only the sweet-tasting water produced similar changes in the immune system. In other words, the rats had "learned" (through classical conditioning) to respond to the water by suppressing their immune systems. We now know there are many connections between the nervous system and the immune system. These findings have generated a field of study known as **psychoneuroimmunology**, or **PNI** (Ader & Cohen, 1993; Coe, 2010), which simply means the object of study is *psychological* influences on the *neuro*logical responding implicated in our *immune* response.

Researchers have learned a great deal about pathways through which psychological and social factors may influence immune system functioning. Direct connections among the brain (central nervous system), the HPA axis (hormonal), and the immune system have already been described. Behavioral changes in response to stressful events, such as increased smoking or poor eating habits, may also suppress the immune system (Cohen & Herbert, 1996) (see ■ Figure 9.6). Now scientists have uncovered a chain of molecules that connects stress to the onset of disease by turning on certain genes (Cole et al., 2010). Basically, stress seems to activate certain molecules in cells that activate genes (called a *transcription factor*)—in this case, the GABA-1 transcription factor that activates the interleukin-6 gene. This gene makes a protein that turns on the inflammatory response, which brings infection-fighting cells of the immune system to the area. This is

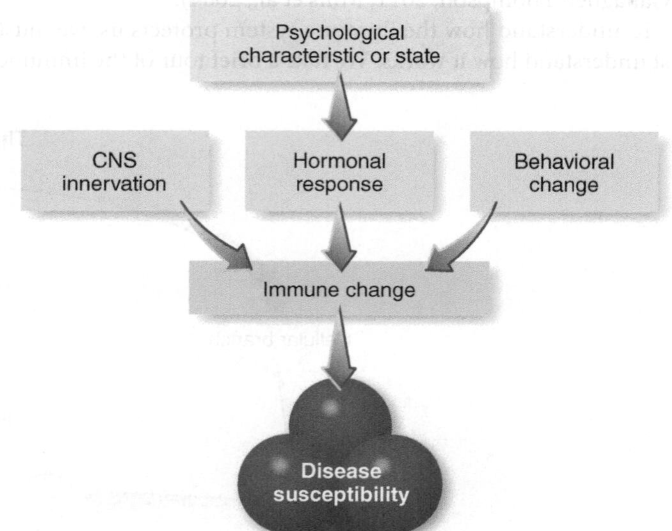

Figure 9.6

Pathways through which psychological factors might influence onset and progression of immune system–mediated disease. For simplicity, arrows are drawn in only one direction, from psychological characteristics to disease. No lack of alternative paths is implied. CNS = central nervous system. From S. Cohen & T. B. Herbert, 1996, Health psychology: Psychological factors and physical disease from the perspective of human psychoneuroimmunology, *Annual Review of Psychology, 47,* 113–142.

Concept Check 9.1

Assess your knowledge of the immune system by matching components of the immune system with their function in the body: (a) macrophages, (b) B cells, (c) immunoglobulins, (d) killer T cells, (e) suppressor T cells, and (f) memory B cells.

1. This subgroup targets viral infections within the cells by directly destroying the antigens. ________
2. A type of leukocyte that surrounds identifiable antigens and destroys them. ________
3. Highly specific molecules that act as antibodies. They combine with antigens to neutralize them. ________
4. Lymphocytes that operate within the humoral part of the system and circulate in the blood and bodily fluids. ________
5. These are created so that when a specific antigen is encountered in the future, the immune response will be faster. ________
6. These T cells stop the production of antibodies by B cells when they are no longer needed. ________

great if you've cut yourself but very damaging if it occurs over a long period of time. It is this chronic inflammatory response that exacerbates cancer, heart disease, and diabetes and shortens life. Other genes, such as the serotonin transporter gene mentioned in Chapter 2, are also implicated in making one vulnerable to certain types of stressors (Way & Taylor, 2010). Many more groups of genes and integrative psychobiological paths implicated in the effects of the stress response will undoubtedly be discovered (Segerstrom & Sephton, 2010).

Psychosocial Effects on Physical Disorders

With an enhanced understanding of the effects of emotional and behavioral factors on the immune system, we can now examine how these factors influence specific physical disorders. We begin with AIDS.

AIDS

The ravages of the AIDS epidemic have made this disease the highest priority of public health systems around the world. The Centers for Disease Control and Prevention estimated that at the end of 2018, 1.2 million people age 13 and older had HIV in the United States (CDC, 2021). Approximately 23% of new infections are transmitted by individuals who are unaware of their infection, and approximately 69% of new infections are transmitted by those who are diagnosed with HIV infection but who are not in medical care (Frieden et al., 2015).

In the hardest-hit regions in southern Africa, between 15% and 28% of the adult population are believed to be HIV positive, comprising two-thirds of cases worldwide, with approximately 18 million children orphaned by the disease (Kates et al., 2012; Klimas, Koneru, & Fletcher, 2008). AIDS is also spreading rapidly to the densely populated regions of India and China (Normile, 2009), and in Latin America, rates are projected to rise from 2 million in 2006 to 3.5 million by 2015 (Cohen, 2006). About a decade after the HIV/AIDS pandemic swept through central Africa, Europe, the Caribbean, and North America, it began to expand rapidly in southern Africa, making it now the highest-priority region for HIV prevention and care (Vermund, Sheldon, & Sidat, 2015). With the exception of Asians, underrepresented groups are disproportionately affected by this deadly disease. In fact, the epidemic is very clearly concentrated in the United States in disenfranchised sexual minorities and communities of color, with effective treatment alternatives few and far between (Pellowski, Kalichman, Matthews, & Adler, 2013). And yet the perceived urgency of this problem in the United States and around the world has decreased considerably over the past decade.

Although intravenous drug use and same-sex activity remain the primary modes of acquiring HIV in the United States, in most of the world (and particularly the underdeveloped world), it is heterosexual activity that brings people in contact with HIV (see Table 9.1). Once a person is infected with HIV, the course of the disease is quite variable. After several months to several years with no symptoms, patients may develop minor health problems such as weight loss, fever, and night sweats—symptoms that make up the condition known as **AIDS-related complex (ARC)**. A diagnosis of AIDS itself is not made until one of several serious diseases appears, such as pneumocystis pneumonia, cancer, dementia, or a wasting syndrome in which the body literally withers away. The median time from initial infection to the development of full-blown AIDS has been estimated to range from 7.3 to 10 years or more (Pantaleo, Graziosi, & Fauci, 1993). Clinical scientists have developed powerful new combinations of drugs referred to as highly active antiretroviral therapy (HAART) that suppress the virus in those infected with HIV, even in advanced cases (Hammer et al., 2006; Thompson et al., 2010). This has been a very positive development that has slowed disease progression and decreased mortality. For example, most people with AIDS die within 1 year of diagnosis without treatment, as is the case in many developing countries (Zwahlen & Egger, 2006). But the proportion of people who receive treatment surviving with AIDS 2 years or longer increased to 85% by 2005, and the death rates from AIDS from 2002 to 2010 declined by at least 50% in the United States, where the drugs are most available (Fauci & Folkers, 2012).

Surveillance data showed that the prevalence of HIV declined from 2009 to 2018 overall, but there were geographic, economic, and racial/ethnic disparities. In the United States, HIV was disproportionately higher among young, racial, or ethnic underrepresented groups living in the South. Although new diagnoses decreased overall, it remained unchanged for Black and increased

Table 9.1 Aids Cases by Mode of Transmission (World, 2009; United States, 2008), Percentage Estimates of Total Cases

Transmission Category	World	United States
Male-to-male sexual contact	5–10%	50%
Injection drug use	10%	17%
Heterosexual contact	59–69%	32%
Other*	16–21%	1%

*Includes hemophilia, blood transfusion, perinatal exposure, transmission within health-care settings, and risk not reported or identified.

Source: Figures for the world adapted from UNAIDS (2009, November), *AIDS Epidemic Update.* Figures for the United States adapted from Centers for Disease Control and Prevention (2010), *Diagnosis of HIV infection and AIDS in the U.S. and dependent areas, 2008*, HIV Surveillance Report, Vol. 20.

for Hispanic or Latino men who have sex with men. Among individuals age 25 to 34 years, HIV also increased (Mayer et al., 2021; Sullivan et al., 2021). Also, HAART is not a cure because the virus is not eliminated but rather lies dormant in reduced numbers; thus, infected patients face a lifetime of taking multiple medications (Buscher & Giordano, 2010; Thompson et al., 2012). Also, the percentage who drop out of HAART because of severe side effects, such as nausea and diarrhea, is high—61% in one study (O'Brien, Clark, Besch, Myers, & Kissinger, 2003; Thompson et al., 2012). For this reason, earlier recommendations were to postpone treatment until those infected are in imminent danger of developing symptomatic disease (Cohen, 2002; Hammer et al., 2006), but in view of the success of this treatment regimen with cases of newly acquired HIV, current recommendations are to start as early as possible after detecting infection and to work closely with patients to increase adherence to the schedule for the medication (Mermin & Fenton, 2012; Thompson et al., 2012). Some studies have even shown that this treatment regimen can prevent acquisition of the virus in high-risk populations (Cohen, 2011; Mermin & Fenton, 2012). Unfortunately, drug-resistant strains of HIV are now being transmitted. It appears that in order to end the HIV/AIDS pandemic, a vaccine will be necessary (Fauci, 2017; Fauci et al., 2019). But until then, psychological strategies are urgently needed to contain the pandemic.

Because AIDS takes at least several years to develop, we are still learning about the factors, including possible psychological factors, that extend survival (Klimas et al., 2008; Taylor, 2009). What we do know is that sexual health interventions are significantly associated with improvements in psychological outcomes, as shown is a meta-analytic review of 29 studies including 11,918 Black adolescents (Evans, 2020). Sexual health interventions led to improvements in sexual abstinence, condom use, and sexual well-being. Psychoeducation is key for preventing this disease. Once a person is infected with the virus, a number of factors influence the course of the disease. Investigators identified a group of people who have been exposed repeatedly to the AIDS virus but have not contracted the disease. A major distinction of these people is that their immune systems, particularly the cellular branch, are robust and strong (Ezzel, 1993), partly due to genetic factors (Kaiser, 2006), but psychological factors also seem to play a role. For example, one study demonstrated that people with the virus who have not progressed to AIDS were characterized by particularly strong confidence in their clinical providers and strong social support from their loved ones, factors that have been linked to stronger immune system functioning (Ruffin, Ironson, Fletcher, Balbin, & Schneiderman, 2012). Therefore, efforts to boost the immune system may contribute to the prevention of AIDS.

Because psychological factors impact immune system functioning, investigators have begun to examine whether these psychological factors influence the progression of HIV. For example, high levels of stress and depression and low levels of social support have been associated with a faster progression to disease (Leserman, 2008; Leserman et al., 2000). One reason for this faster progression is that depression is very strongly associated with decreased adherence to the drug regimen (Gonzalez, Batchelder, Psaros, & Safren, 2011). But an even more intriguing question is whether psychological interventions can slow the progression of the disease, even among those who are symptomatic (Cole, 2008; Gore-Felton & Koopman, 2008). In fact, several important studies suggest that cognitive-behavioral stress-management (CBSM) programs may have positive effects on the immune systems of individuals who are already symptomatic (Antoni et al., 2000; Carrico & Antoni, 2008; Lerner, Kibler, & Zeichner, 2013; Lutgendorf et al., 1997). Specifically, Lutgendorf and colleagues (1997) used an intervention program that significantly decreased depression and anxiety compared with a control group that did not receive the treatment. More important, there was a significant reduction in antibodies to the herpes simplex virus II in the treatment group compared with the control group, which reflects the greater ability of the cellular component of the immune system to control the virus. In a study by Antoni and colleagues (2000), 73 gay or bisexual men already infected with HIV and symptomatic with the disease were assigned to a CBSM program or a control group receiving usual care without the program. As in previous studies, men receiving the stress-management treatment showed significantly lower posttreatment levels of anxiety, anger, and perceived stress than those in the control group, indicating the treatment was effective. More important, as long as a year after the intervention had ended, men who had received the treatment evidenced better immune system functioning as indicated by higher levels of T cells. These findings are presented in ■ Figure 9.7.

Similarly, Goodkin and colleagues (2001) reported that a 10-week psychological treatment significantly buffered against an increase in HIV viral load, which is a powerful and reliable predictor of progression to full-blown AIDS, while a control group had no such result. Antoni and colleagues (2006) took their important line of research a step further. HIV-positive men on HAART drug regimens received 10 weeks of training in how to take their medication properly by taking the exact amount prescribed as closely as possible to the assigned times. Half of this group also received the investigators' CBSM program. Men receiving CBSM actually showed a decrease in viral load 15 months later compared with those with medication training only, who showed no change. This reduction in viral load was primarily the result of decreases in depression, which, in turn, reduced the stress hormone cortisol. Thus, even in progressed, symptomatic HIV disease,

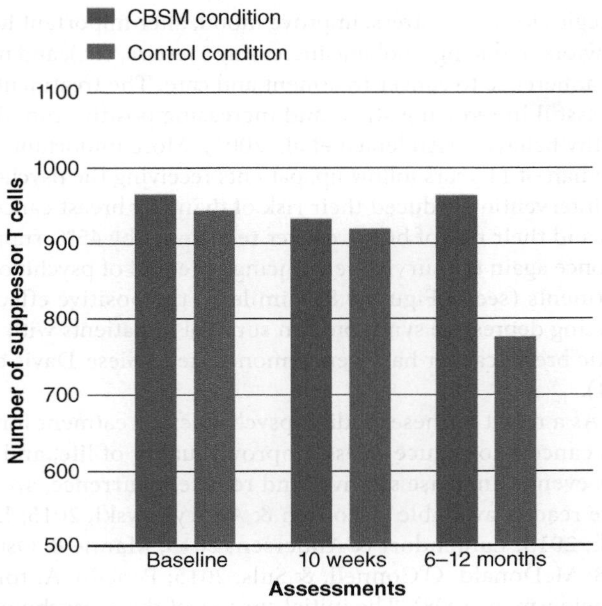

Figure 9.7

Means for T suppressor/cytotoxic cells at preintervention (baseline), postintervention (10 weeks), and follow up (6 to 12 months) in HIV-positive gay men assigned to CBSM (n = 47) versus control (n = 26). Adapted from M. H. Antoni, D. G. Cruess, S. Cruess, S. Lutgendorf, M. Kumar, G. Ironson, N. Klimas, M. A. Fletcher, & N. Schneiderman, 2000, Cognitive-behavioral stress management intervention effects on anxiety, 24-hr urinary norepinephrine output, and T-cytotoxic/suppressor cells over time among symptomatic HIV-infected gay men, *Journal of Consulting and Clinical Psychology, 68*, 31–45.

psychological interventions may not only enhance psychological adjustment but also influence immune system functioning, and this effect may be long lasting.

It is too early to tell whether these results will be strong or persistent enough to translate into increased survival time for AIDS patients, although results from Antoni and colleagues (2000, 2006) suggest they might. A review of randomized controlled trials examining the efficacy of psychological interventions on neuroendocrine hormone regulation and immune status in HIV-positive individuals showed little support for differential efficacy of different interventions (Antoni, 2012; Carrico & Antoni, 2008). However, regardless of the treatment modality, the treatments that are successful in improving psychological adjustment are more likely to have beneficial effects on neuroendocrine regulation and immune status. If stress and related variables *are* clinically significant to immune response, functioning, and disease progression in HIV-infected patients, as suggested by a number of studies (Cole, 2008; Leserman, 2008), then psychosocial interventions to bolster the immune system might increase survival rates and, in the most optimistic scenario, prevent the slow deterioration of the immune system (Carrico & Antoni, 2008; Kennedy, 2000).

Of course, the most effective interventions focus on changing behavior to prevent acquiring HIV in the first place, such as reducing risky behavior and promoting safe sexual practices (Mermin & Fenton, 2012; Temoshok, Wald, Synowski, & Garzino-Demo, 2008), particularly in underrepresented groups such as Latinx and African Americans (Gonzalez, Hendriksen, Collins, Duran, & Safren, 2009).

Beyond that, and in view of the disparities in health care provided to the socially marginalized groups most likely to acquire HIV, robust combined intervention strategies directed at these populations are needed. This would include strategies to make patients more aware of positive HIV status earlier, linking them to treatment earlier, and maximizing adherence to treatment, all goals that rely primarily on behavior change (Grossman, Purcell, Rotheram-Borus, & Veniegas, 2013). Few areas of study in behavioral medicine and health psychology are more urgent. In 2019, Anthony Fauci, director of the National Institute of Allergy and Infectious Diseases, and Robert Redfield, director of the Centers for Disease Control and Prevention, contributed to an article for the *Journal of the American Medical Association* entitled "Ending the HIV Epidemic: A Plan for the United States." The authors make an urgent call for action and suggest ways to end the HIV/AIDS pandemic, noting that "In the United States, more than 700,000 people have died as a result of HIV/AIDS since the disease was first recognized in 1981" (Fauci et al., 2019, p. 844). A few months after the publication of this article, the COVID-19 pandemic spread across the globe, and the death toll quickly rose to 500,000 in the United States within 1 year after the pandemic was recognized (or acknowledged). These statistics are cited not to downplay the danger and significance of HIV/AIDS but to put the COVID-19 pandemic in perspective. Both COVID-19 and HIV/AIDS are dangerous viruses with deadly outcomes. What made COVID-19 so catastrophic was its high transmissibility.

The 1918 H1N1 pandemic (also known as the Spanish flu) was the most severe pandemic of the 20th century, infecting a third of the world's population and killing about 50 million people worldwide. All viruses cause major public health problems, and we need to be prepared for any future deadly and transmissible viruses that may strike without warning. Unless there are effective vaccines and other medications available to treat the symptoms, the most effective way to fight a pandemic is through psychoeducation and other psychological interventions interrupting the virus transmission.

Cancer

Among the more mind-boggling developments in the study of illness and disease is the discovery that the development and course of different varieties of **cancer** are subject to psychosocial influences (Emery, Anderson, & Andersen, 2011; Fagundes et al., 2012; Giese-Davis et al., 2011; Williams & Schneiderman, 2002). This has resulted in a new field of study called **psychoncology** (Antoni & Lutgendorf, 2007; Helgeson, 2005; Lutgendorf, Costanzo, & Siegel, 2007). *Oncology* means the study of cancer.

Psychological interventions have shown to improve the quality of life of people struggling with cancer (Fava, Cosci, & Sonin, 2017; Rehse & Pukrop, 2003). In addition, these treatments might also change the course of the illness. In a widely noted study, David Spiegel, a psychiatrist at Stanford University,

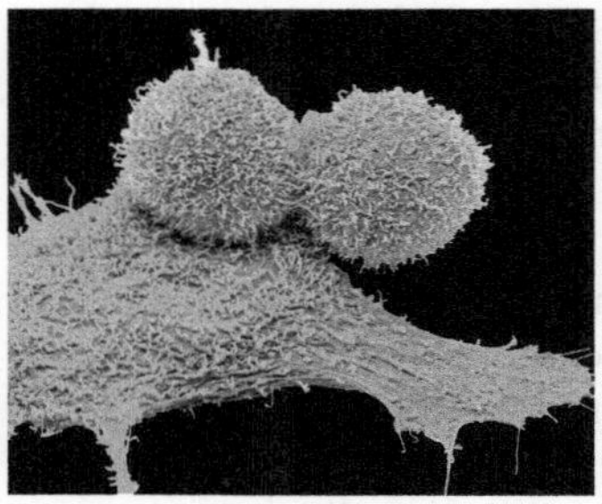

STEVE GSCHMEISSNER/Science Photo Library/Getty Images

Breast cancer cell.

and his colleagues (Spiegel, 2013; Spiegel, Bloom, Kramer, & Gotheil, 1989) studied 86 women with advanced breast cancer that had metastasized to other areas of their bodies and was expected to kill them within 2 years. Clearly, the prognosis was poor indeed. Although Spiegel and his colleagues had little hope of affecting the disease itself, they thought that by treating these people in group psychotherapy at least they could relieve some of their anxiety, depression, and pain. All patients had routine medical care for their cancer. In addition, 50 patients (of the 86) met with their therapist for psychotherapy once a week in small groups. Much to everyone's surprise, including Spiegel's, the therapy group's survival time was significantly longer than that of the control group who did not receive psychotherapy but otherwise benefited from the best care available. The group receiving therapy lived twice as long on average (approximately 3 years) as the controls (approximately 18 months). Four years after the study began, a third of the therapy patients were still alive, and all the patients receiving the best medical care available *without* therapy had died. Subsequently, a careful reanalysis of medical treatment received by each group revealed no differences that could account for the effects of psychological treatment (Kogon, Biswas, Pearl, Carlson, & Spiegel, 1997). These findings do not mean that psychological interventions cured advanced cancer. At 10 years, only three patients in the therapy group still survived.

In another important study, Andersen and colleagues (2008) randomized 227 patients who had been surgically treated for breast cancer to a psychological intervention plus assessment or to an assessment-only condition. The intervention included strategies to reduce stress, improve mood, alter important health behaviors (reducing smoking, increasing exercise, etc.), and maintain adherence to cancer treatment and care. The treatment was successful in reducing stress and increasing positive mood and healthy behavior (Andersen et al., 2007). More important, after a median of 11 years follow up, patients receiving the psychological intervention reduced their risk of dying by breast cancer by 56% and their risk of breast cancer recurrence by 45%, supporting once again the survival-enhancing potential of psychological treatments (see ■ Figure 9.8). Similarly, the positive effects of reducing depressive symptoms on survival in patients with metastatic breast cancer has been demonstrated (Giese-Davis et al., 2011).

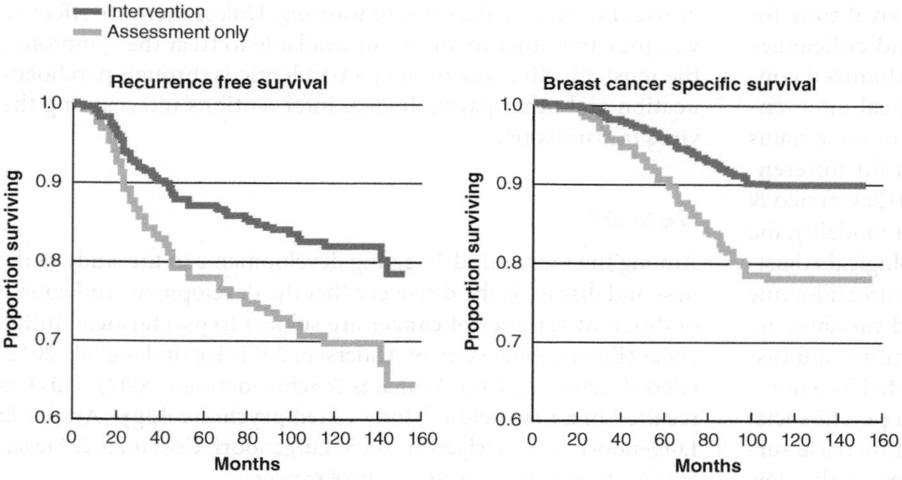

Figure 9.8

Recurrence and survival rates in months following a psychological intervention for breast cancer. From B. L. Andersen et al., 2008, Psychologic intervention improves survival for breast cancer patients, *Cancer, 15,* 3456.

As a result of these studies, psychosocial treatment for various cancers to reduce stress, improve quality of life, and perhaps even to increase survival and reduce recurrence, are now more readily available (Jacobsen & Andrykowski, 2015; Lewis et al., 2015; Lutgendorf & Andersen, 2015; Manne & Ostroff, 2008; McDonald, O'Connell, & Suls, 2015; Penedo, Antoni, & Schneiderman, 2008). The initial success of these psychological treatments on length of survival in at least some studies generated a great deal of interest in exactly how they might work (Antoni et al., 2009; Antoni & Lutgendorf, 2007; Emery et al., 2011; Nemeroff, 2013). Possibilities include better health habits, closer adherence to medical treatment, and improved endocrine functioning and response to stress, all of which may improve immune function (Antoni et al., 2006, 2009; Foley, Baillie, Huxter, Price, & Sinclair, 2010; Emery et al., 2011; Nezu et al., 1999). For example, the experience of a severely stressful life event in the past year, particularly in individuals with troubled early parent–child relationships, predicted greatly decreased immune system reactivity to a basal cell carcinoma tumor (skin cancer) (Fagundes et al., 2012). Also, anything that promotes closer, more supportive relationships in cancer patients is very important because it buffers stress (Hostinar, Sullivan, & Gunnar, 2013) and slows disease progression (Antoni et al., 2006; Foley, Baillie, Huxter, Price, & Sinclair, 2010; Nezu et al., 1999). There is even preliminary evidence that psychological factors may contribute not only to the *course* but also to the *development* of cancer and other diseases (Antoni & Lutgendorf, 2007; Lutgendorf et al., 2007). Perceived lack of control, inadequate coping responses, overwhelmingly stressful life events, or the use of inappropriate coping responses (such as denial) may all contribute to the development of cancer, probably through changes in immune function but also through regulating the activity of cancer-causing viruses, deoxyribonucleic acid (DNA) repair processes, and the expression of genes that control the growth of tumors (Antoni & Dhabhar, 2019; Lutgendorf et al., 2007; Nemeroff, 2013). For example, chronic psychological stress is associated with accelerated cellular aging as indexed by short

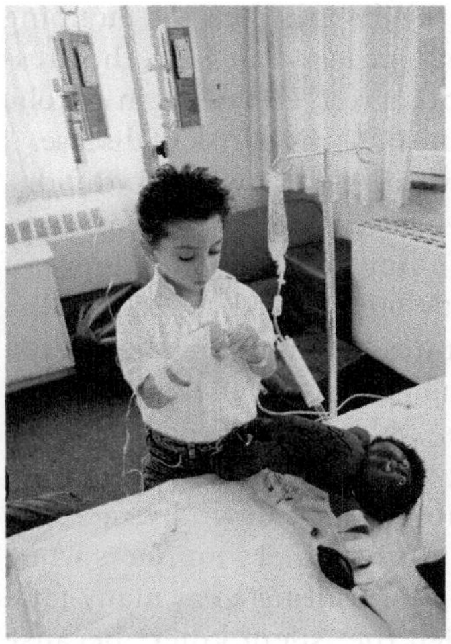

Psychological preparation reduces suffering and facilitates recovery in children who undergo surgery.

telomere length. Telomeres are basically DNA protein complexes located on the ends of chromosomes that protect against damage to the DNA that encodes genetic information. But once again, it is not the absolute level of stress that is responsible for cellular aging but rather negative interpretations and appraisals of the stressful situations (O'Donovan et al., 2012).

Many more studies exist on the effect of psychotherapy on cancer survival, with only some finding a beneficial effect of psychotherapy on survival rate. A meta-analytic review, which was coauthored by David Spiegel (Mirosevic et al., 2019), demonstrated a small to moderate effect of psychotherapy on survival rate overall. This result was consistent with some but not all meta-analytic reviews. A closer look at the data showed an interesting pattern: This effect of psychotherapy on survival rate was stronger in studies that examined more single or unmarried (versus married) patients, when CBT was applied, when patients were still in an early (versus late) stage cancer, and when patients were older (versus younger) than age 50. Thus, it appears that cancer survival can be prolonged with CBT in patients who are unmarried, older, and at an early cancer stage.

But even if psychological treatments cannot reliably influence the course of cancer in most people, they can certainly enhance well-being and quality of life for those affected by this terrible disease, as we discussed earlier. Some people even discover some positive consequences. For example, many patients with breast cancer experience an enhanced sense of purpose, deepening spirituality, closer ties to others, and changes in life priorities (Lechner & Antoni, 2004; Park, Edmondson, Fenster, & Blank, 2008; Yanez et al., 2009). These experiences have been called "benefit finding" and may reflect the types of traits—such as coping skills, a sense of control, and optimism—that underlie resiliency and reduce the harmful effect of stress (Bower, Moskowitz, & Epel, 2009). These traits and skills are among the most important goals of psychological treatment. Antoni and colleagues (2006) targeted these goals in 199 women with nonmetastatic breast cancer using a CBSM program, and they found substantially improved quality of life in the year following treatment.

Psychological factors are also prominent in treatment and recovery from cancer in children (Kazak & Noll, 2015). Many types of cancer require invasive and painful medical procedures; the suffering can be difficult to bear, not only for children but also for parents and health-care providers. Children usually struggle and cry hysterically, so to complete many of the procedures, they must be physically restrained. Not only does their behavior interfere with successful completion, but also the stress and anxiety associated with repeated painful procedures may have their own detrimental effect on the disease process. Psychological procedures designed to reduce pain and stress in these children include breathing exercises, watching films of exactly what happens to take the uncertainty out of the procedure, and rehearsal of the procedure with dolls, all of which make the interventions more tolerable and therefore more successful for young patients (Brewer, Gleditsch, Syblik, Tietjens, & Vacik, 2006; Hubert, Jay, Saltoun, & Hayes, 1988). Pediatric psychologists are making more routine use of these procedures.

Reducing stress in parents who could then provide more supportive care is important because almost all parents develop posttraumatic stress symptoms after hearing that their children have cancer (Kazak, Boeving, Alderfer, Hwang, & Reilly, 2005). Sahler and colleagues (2005) treated mothers of children with newly diagnosed cancer with a cognitive-behavioral problem-solving intervention and compared the results to the usual care available to these mothers. Mothers in the problem-solving group became less negative, less stressed, and better problem solvers, certainly a positive outcome in parents who have to deal with the tragedy of cancer in their own children.

Cardiovascular Problems

The *cardiovascular system* consists of the heart, blood vessels, and complex control mechanisms for regulating their function. Many things can go wrong with this system and lead to **cardiovascular disease**. For example, many individuals, particularly older individuals, suffer **strokes**, also called **cerebral vascular accidents (CVAs)**. Strokes are temporary blockages of blood vessels leading to the brain or a rupture of blood vessels in the brain that result in temporary or permanent brain damage and loss of functioning. People with Raynaud's disease lose circulation to peripheral parts of their bodies such as their fingers and toes, suffering some pain and continual sensations of cold in their hands and feet. The cardiovascular problems receiving the most attention these days are hypertension and coronary heart disease, and we look at both. It has been shown that heightened responsivity to acute mental stress has adverse effects on cardiovascular health (Chida & Steptoe, 2010). But chronic stress and personality factors are also very important. First, let's consider the case of Cameron.

Cameron... The Human Volcano Better

Cameron is a 55-year-old business executive who is married with two teenage children. For most of his adult life, Cameron has smoked about a pack of cigarettes each day. Although he maintains a busy and active schedule, Cameron is mildly obese, partly from regular meals with business partners and colleagues. He has been taking several medications for high blood pressure since age 42. Cameron's doctor has warned him repeatedly to cut down on his smoking and to exercise more often, especially because Cameron's father died of a heart attack. Although Cameron has episodes of chest pain, he continues his busy and stressful lifestyle. It is difficult for Cameron to slow down, as his business has been doing extremely well during the past 10 years.

Moreover, Cameron believes that life is too short and that there is no time to slow down. He sees relatively little of his family and works late most evenings. Even when he's at home, Cameron typically works into the night. It is difficult for him to relax; he feels a constant urgency to get as many things done as possible and prefers to work on several tasks simultaneously. For instance, Cameron often proofreads a document, engages in a phone conversation, and eats lunch all at the same time. He attributes much of the success of his business to his working style. Despite his success, Cameron is not well liked by his peers. His coworkers and employees often find him to be overbearing, easily frustrated, and, at times, even hostile. His subordinates in particular claim he is overly impatient and critical of their performance.

Do you think Cameron has a problem? Most people would recognize that his behaviors and attitudes make his life unpleasant and possibly lethal. Some of these behaviors and attitudes appear to operate directly on the cardiovascular system and may result in hypertension and coronary heart disease. Cameron's personality could be described as a *type A personality*. We will come back to this further below when we discuss coronary heart disease.

Hypertension

Hypertension (high blood pressure) is a major risk factor not only for stroke and heart disease but also for kidney disease. This makes hypertension an extremely serious medical condition. Blood pressure increases when the blood vessels leading to organs and peripheral areas constrict (become narrower), forcing increasing amounts of blood to muscles in central parts of the body. Because so many blood vessels have constricted, the heart muscles must work much harder to force the blood to all parts of the body, which causes the increased pressure. These factors produce wear and tear on the ever-shrinking blood vessels and lead to cardiovascular disease. A small percentage of cases of hypertension can be traced to specific physical abnormalities, such as kidney disease or tumors on the adrenal glands (Chobanian et al., 2003; Papillo & Shapiro, 1990), but the overwhelming majority (close to 90%) have no specific verifiable physical cause and are considered **essential hypertension**. Blood pressure is defined as high by the World Health Organization if it exceeds 160 over 95 (Papillo & Shapiro, 1990), although measures of 140/90 or higher are cause for concern and more usually used to define hypertension (Chobanian et al., 2003; James et al., 2013; Taylor, 2009; Wolf-Maier et al., 2003). The first value is called the *systolic blood pressure,* the pressure when the heart is pumping blood. The second value is the *diastolic blood pressure,* the pressure between beats when the heart is at rest. Elevations in systolic pressure seem to be more worrisome in terms of risk of disease.

According to a comprehensive survey, 27.6% of individuals between the ages of 35 and 64 suffer from hypertension in North America, with a corresponding and shocking figure of 44.2% in six European countries (Wolf-Maier et al., 2003). One survey examined hypertension rates by county in the United States and found a staggering median prevalence of 38% for men and 40% for women (Olives, Myerson, Mokdad, Murray, & Lim, 2013). These data, along with the percentage treating and controlling their hypertension broken down by race, are presented in Table 9.2. These are extraordinary numbers when you consider that hypertension, contributing to as many fatal diseases as it does, has been called the "silent killer" because there are few—if any—symptoms and most people don't know they have it. These numbers are much higher than for any single psychological disorder.

Data showing the relationship of hypertension to risk of death from stroke in each country are presented in ■ Figure 9.9. These data illustrate that hypertension is associated with premature mortality. Even more striking is that African Americans, both men and women, are between 1.5 and two times as likely to develop hypertension as White Americans (CDC, 2011; Egan et al., 2010; Lewis et al., 2006; Yan et al., 2003). Furthermore, among people with hypertension and other cardiovascular concerns, underrepresented groups have poorer management of these conditions compared with White Americans (McWilliams, Meara, Zaslavsky, & Ayanian, 2009).

Prevalence rates of hypertension in Blacks, Whites, and Hispanics are presented in ■ Figure 9.10. More important, African Americans have hypertensive vascular diseases at a rate 5 to 10 times greater than White Americans. Another study confirms that hypertension is a principal disorder of concern within the African American population (Safford et al., 2012). Saab and colleagues (1992) demonstrated in a classic study that during laboratory stress tests, African Americans without high blood pressure show greater vascular responsiveness, including heightened blood pressure. Thus, African Americans in general may be at greater risk to develop hypertension. Other research has suggested that African Americans' risk for hypertension may be augmented by chronic experiences of stereotype threat (that is, situations in which an individual fears that they will confirm negative beliefs about their demographic group), which increase blood pressure both during and after the experience (Blascovich, Spencer, Quinn, & Steele, 2001).

You will not be surprised to learn there are biological, psychological, and social contributions to the development of this potentially deadly condition. It has long been clear that hypertension runs in families and likely is subject to marked genetic influences (for example, Padmanabhan, Caufrield, & Dominiczak, 2015). When stressed in the laboratory, even individuals with *average* blood pressure show greater reactivity in their blood pressure if their parents have high blood pressure than do individuals with average blood pressure whose parents also had average blood

Table 9.2 Prevalence, Treatment, and Control of Hypertension among American Adults, 2001 and 2009

	Prevalence		Treatment		Control	
	2001	2009	2001	2009	2001	2009
Men	32.58	37.56	64.96	73.05	47.25	57.69
	(23.56–47.25)	(26.53–54.43)	(44.74–75.03)	(55.04–82.01)	(32.03–55.49	(43.42–65.86)
White	32.35	37.23	64.17	72.29	49.32	58.63
	(23.75–40.93)	(26.83–46.95)	(41.72–74.75)	(51.04–82.23)	(29.89–58.1)	(39.37–66.31)
Black	45.57	50.84	64.73	72.24	47.07	55.68
	(34.94–54.97)	(38.67–60.92)	(43.41–74.78)	(52.19–81.77)	(29.24–54.96)	(38.12–62.7)
Hispanic	33.65	38.13	58.99	67.41	40.95	50.46
	(25.03–42.10)	(27.72–47.70)	(37.21–70.32)	(45.86–78.67)	(23.37–49.83)	(31.84–58.84)
Other	36.48	41.39	61.7	69.86	45.87	55.1
	(27.27–45.29)	(30.43–51.22)	(39.63–72.52)	(48.56–80.28)	(27.26–54.61)	(36.22–62.95)
Women	36.94	40.08	67.56	74.08	43.83	57.06
	(26.75–52.97)	(28.52–57.88)	(50.87–81.53)	(57.68–86.43)	(30.86–53.48)	(43.04–65.46)
White	35.69	38.85	68.95	75.53	43.2	57.93
	(26.6–42.95)	(28.35–48.01)	(51.62–78.76)	(59.06–84.53)	(29.78–53.46)	(43.98–67.66)
Black	50.6	54.39	80.32	84.8	50.46	63.7
	(39.16–58.89)	(41.85–64.18)	(67.44–86.65)	(73.72–90.13)	(39.55–58.13)	(54.29–69.86)
Hispanic	39.19	42.64	69.11	75.8	45.23	59.53
	(29.58–46.7)	(31.68–51.98)	(51.96–78.82)	(59.76–84.53)	(31.61–55.32)	(45.81–68.76)
Other	42.66	46.03	65.12	71.98	42.16	56.10
	(33.19–50.01)	(35.27–55.16)	(47.55–75.51)	(55.03–81.64)	(28.48–52.52)	(41.77–65.98)

Source: Adapted from C. Olives, R. Myerson, A. H. Mokdad, C. J. Murray, & S. S. Lim, 2013, Prevalence, awareness, treatment, and control of hypertension in United States counties, 200122009, *PLoS One, 8*(4), e60308. *Note: Prevalence* refers to the rates of hypertension in 2009; *Treatment* refers to the rates of treated hypertension; and *Control* lists the rates of hypertension control (systolic BP < 140 mmHg).

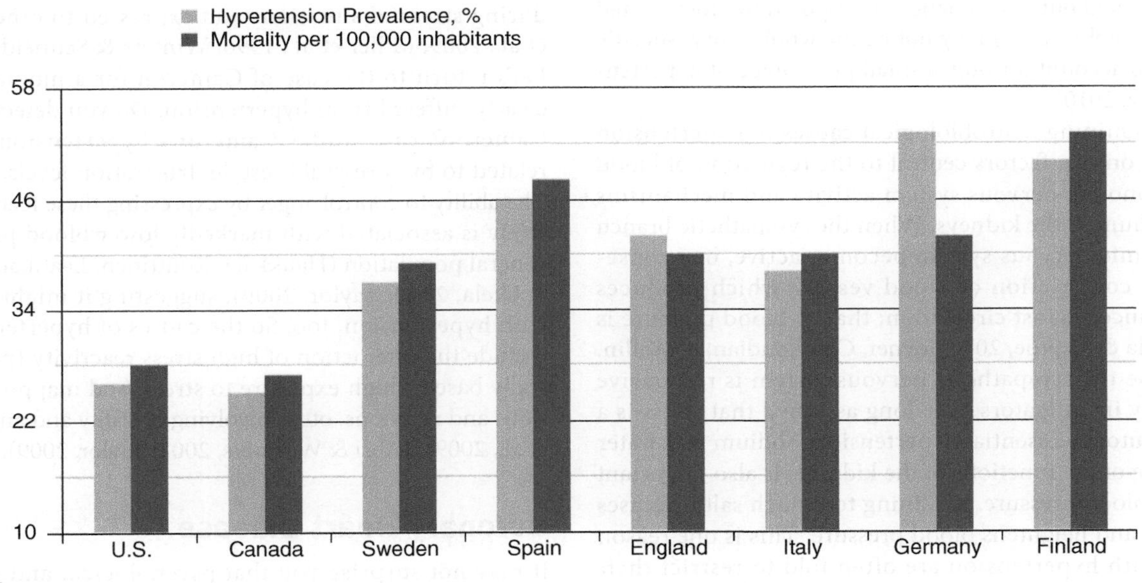

Figure 9.9

Prevalence (per 100,000 inhabitants) of hypertension versus stroke mortality in six European and two North American countries in men and women 35 to 64 years old, age adjusted. Across eight developed countries, higher rates of hypertension were generally associated with higher mortality from stroke. Adapted from K. Wolf-Maier, R. S. Cooper, J. R. Banegas, S. Giampaoli, H. Hense, M. Joffres, M. Kastarinen, N. Poulter, et al., 2003, Hypertension prevalence and blood pressure levels in six European countries, Canada, and the United States, *JAMA: Journal of the American Medical Association, 289,* 2367 (Fig. 4). © 2003 American Medical Association.

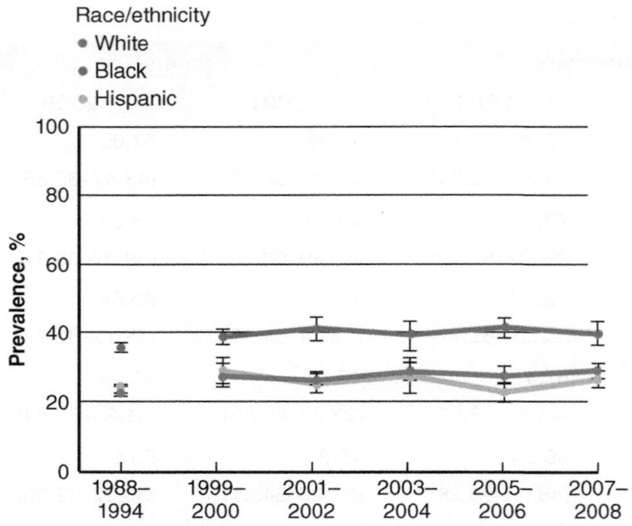

Data are presented as means with 95% confidence intervals (error bars). For all curves, $P \leq .05$ for change over time between 1988–1994 and 2007–2008, except for prevalent hypertension of Hispanic race ($P = .65$), prevalent hypertension in women ($P = .10$), and hypertension awareness in women ($P = .09$).

Figure 9.10

Clinical prevalence of hypertension by race in 2-year blocks for 1988–1994 and 1999–2008. From B. M. Egan et al., 2010, U.S. trends in prevalence, awareness, treatment, and control of hypertension, 1988–2008, *JAMA: Journal of the American Medical Association, 303*, 2048.

pressure (Clark, 2003; Fredrikson & Matthews, 1990). In other words, it doesn't take much to activate an inherited vulnerability to hypertension. The offspring of parents with hypertension are at twice the risk of developing hypertension as children of parents with average blood pressure (Taylor, 2009). Nevertheless, others have pointed out that genetics (as opposed to other related factors, such as upbringing) may not be the whole story; specific gene variations account for only a small percentage of hypertension risk (Kurtz, 2010).

Studies examining neurobiological causes of hypertension have centered on two factors central to the regulation of blood pressure: autonomic nervous system activity and mechanisms regulating sodium in the kidneys. When the sympathetic branch of the autonomic nervous system becomes active, one consequence is the constriction of blood vessels, which produces greater resistance against circulation; that is, blood pressure is elevated (Chida & Steptoe, 2010; Joyner, Charkoudian, & Wallin, 2010). Because the sympathetic nervous system is responsive to stress, many investigators have long assumed that stress is a major contributor to essential hypertension. Sodium and water regulation, one of the functions of the kidneys, is also important in regulating blood pressure. Retaining too much salt increases blood volume and heightens blood pressure. This is one reason that people with hypertension are often told to restrict their intake of salt.

Psychological factors—such as personality, coping style, and, again, level of stress—have been used to explain individual differences in blood pressure (Lehman, Taylor, Kiefe, & Seeman, 2009; Taylor, 2009; Winters & Schneiderman, 2000). In addition, social support emerges as an important contributor to cardiovascular health (Cuffee et al., 2014; Hawkley, Thisted, Masi, & Cacioppo, 2010). Similarly, loneliness, depression, and feelings of uncontrollability are psychological factors that contribute to cardiovascular problems (Wooley & Wong, 2013), whereas happiness and optimism are associated with cardiovascular health (Boehm & Kubzansky, 2012). For example, one study with married couples found that practicing a "warm touch" (frequent affectionate touching) as a way of communicating love and support significantly decreased blood pressure (Holt-Lunstad, Birmingham, & Light, 2008). Similarly, it has been shown that hugging has a stress-buffering effect and can prevent the outbreak of the symptoms of a viral infection and reduce the severity of the symptoms (Cohen et al., 2015).

A long-term study identified two psychological factors, each of which almost doubles the risk of hypertension: hostility, particularly in interpersonal relations, and a sense of time urgency or impatience. To reach this conclusion, more than 5,000 adults (including both Blacks and Whites) were followed for 15 years in the Coronary Artery Risk Development in Young Adults (CARDIA) study (Yan et al., 2003). It is likely that the combination of these two factors creates an even more powerful risk. Also, both anger and hostility have been associated with increases in blood pressure in laboratory and applied settings (Brondolo et al., 2009; Mezick et al., 2010; Miller, Smith, Turner, Guijarro, & Hallet, 1996).

The notion that hostility or repressed hostility predicts hypertension (and other cardiovascular problems) can be traced back to Alexander (1939), who suggested that an inability to express anger could result in hypertension and other cardiovascular problems. What may be more important is not whether anger is suppressed but rather how often anger and hostility are experienced during stressful situations and expressed to others (Brondolo et al., 2009; Miller et al., 1996; Winters & Schneiderman, 2000). Let's return to the case of Cameron for a moment. Cameron clearly suffered from hypertension. Do you detect any anger in Cameron's case study? Cameron's hypertension may well be related to his stressful lifestyle, frustration levels, and hostility. The ability to control anger by expressing these feelings constructively is associated with markedly lower blood pressure in the general population (Haukkala, Konttinen, Laatikainen, Kawachi, & Utela, 2010; Taylor, 2009), suggesting it might help patients with hypertension, too. So the causes of hypertension seem to include the interaction of high stress reactivity (possibly genetically based), high exposure to stress, and inappropriate coping skills and reactions, often involving hostility and anger (Brondolo et al., 2009; al'Absi & Wittmers, 2003; Taylor, 2009).

Coronary Heart Disease

It may not surprise you that psychological and social factors contribute to high blood pressure, but can changes in behavior and attitudes prevent heart attacks? The answers are still not entirely clear, but increasing evidence indicates that psychological and social factors are implicated in coronary heart disease

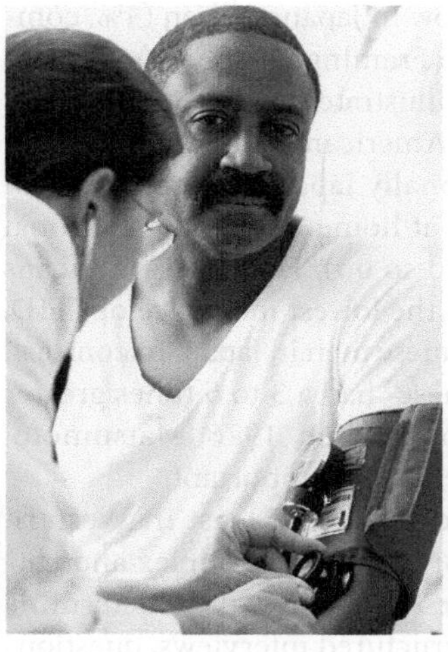

African Americans suffer from hypertension in disproportionately high numbers.

(Clark et al., 2012; Emery et al., 2011; Gulliksson et al., 2011; Kivimaki et al., 2012; Winters & Schneiderman, 2000). Why is this important? Heart disease is the number one cause of death in Western cultures, as already noted.

Coronary heart disease (CHD) is a blockage of the arteries supplying blood to the heart muscle (the *myocardium*). A number of terms describe heart disease. Chest pain resulting from partial obstruction of the arteries is called *angina pectoris* or, usually, just *angina*. *Atherosclerosis* occurs when a fatty substance or plaque builds up inside the arteries and causes an obstruction. *Ischemia* is the name for deficiency of blood to a body part caused by the narrowing of the arteries by too much plaque. And *myocardial infarction*, or *heart attack*, is the death of heart tissue when a specific artery becomes clogged with plaque. Arteries can constrict or become blocked for a variety of reasons other than plaque. For example, a blood clot might lodge in the artery.

It seems clear that we inherit a vulnerability to CHD (and to many other physical disorders) and that other factors such as diet, exercise, and culture make important contributions to our cardiovascular status (Allender, Peto, Scarborough, Boxer, & Rayner, 2007; Cuffee et al., 2014). But what sort of psychological factors contribute to CHD?

A variety of studies suggest strongly that stress, anxiety, and anger, combined with poor coping skills and low social support, are implicated in CHD (Emery et al., 2011; Jiang et al., 2013; Matthews, 2005; Suls & Bunde, 2005; Taylor, 2009). Severe stress, as in learning that a family member suddenly died, can lead on rare occasions to a condition called *myocardial stunning*, which is basically heart failure (Wittstein et al., 2005). Some evidence suggests that heart attacks in response to emotional triggers, though rare, are found with disproportionate frequency among individuals high in negative affectivity and social inhibition to begin with (Compare et al., 2013). Some studies indicate that even healthy men who experience stress are later more likely to experience CHD than low-stress groups (Rosengren, Tibblin, & Wilhelmsen, 1991). For such individuals, stress-reduction procedures may prove to be an important preventive technique. There is a great deal of evidence on the value of stress-reduction procedures in preventing future heart attacks and prolonging life (Emery et al., 2011; Orth-Gomer et al., 2009; Williams & Schneiderman, 2002). In one report summarizing results from 37 studies and using analytic procedures that combine the results from these studies (meta-analysis), the effects of stress-reduction programs on CHD were quite apparent. Specifically, as a group, these studies yielded a 34% reduction in death from heart attacks; a 29% reduction in the recurrence of heart attacks; and a significant positive effect on blood pressure, cholesterol levels, body weight, and other risk factors for CHD (Dusseldorp, van Elderen, Maes, Meulman, & Kraaij, 1999).

Clinical studies confirmed the benefits of CBT focusing on stress reduction and exercise in reducing emotional distress and improving heart function and risk for future attacks in a group of individuals with established heart disease (Blumenthal et al., 2005; Gulliksson et al., 2011). For example, the study by Gulliksson and colleagues (2011) showed that a CBT program focusing on stress management can prevent recurrent heart problems in patients who experienced their first cardiovascular events. This study randomized 362 men and women aged 75 or younger after a coronary heart disease event to receive either 20 sessions of CBT in addition to traditional care, or traditional care alone. During the 94 months follow-up period, patients who received CBT had a 41% lower rate of fatal or nonfatal recurrence of cardiovascular events (such as a stroke or heart attacks) than those who received only traditional care. Similar results were reported in a Swedish study (Orth-Gomer et al., 2013), which randomized 237 women aged 75 or younger with a first cardiovascular event to receive either CBT for stress reduction or usual care. Approximately 7 years after randomization, patients in the CBT group were 3 times more likely to survive than people in the usual care group.

This brings us to an important question: Can we identify, before an attack, people who are under a great deal of stress that might make them susceptible to a first heart attack? The answer seems to be yes, but the answer is more complex than we first thought.

Clinical investigators reported several decades ago that certain groups of people engage in a cluster of behaviors in stressful situations that seem to put them at considerable risk for CHD. These behaviors include excessive competitive drive, a sense of always being pressured for time, impatience, incredible amounts of energy that may show up in accelerated speech and motor activity, and angry outbursts. This set of behaviors, which came to be called the **type A behavior pattern**, was first identified by two cardiologists, Meyer Friedman and Ray Rosenman (1959, 1974). The **type B behavior pattern**, also described by these clinicians, applies to people who basically do not have type A attributes. In other words, the type B individual is more relaxed, less concerned about deadlines, and seldom feels the pressure or, perhaps, the excitement of challenges or overriding ambition.

The concept of the type A personality or behavior pattern is widely accepted in our hard-driving, goal-oriented culture. Indeed, some early studies supported the concept of type A behavior as putting people at risk for CHD (Friedman & Rosenman, 1974; Matthews, 2013), and individual elements of the type A personality, such as anger, continue to emerge as presenting increased cardiovascular risk (Chida & Steptoe, 2009). But the most convincing evidence came from two large prospective studies that followed thousands of patients over a long period to determine the relationship of their behavior to heart disease. The first study was the Western Collaborative Group Study (WCGS). In this project, 3,154 healthy men, aged 39 to 59, were interviewed at the beginning of the study to determine their typical behavioral patterns. They were then followed for 8 years. The basic finding

Pictor International, Ltd./Jupiterimages

Both type A behavior and CHD seem to be culturally determined.

was that the men who displayed a type A behavior pattern at the beginning of the study were at least twice as likely to develop CHD as the men with a type B behavior pattern. When the investigators analyzed the data for the younger men in the study (aged 39 to 49), the results were even more striking, with CHD developing approximately 6 times more often in the type A group than in the type B group (Rosenman et al., 1975).

One important study that has dramatically advanced our understanding of risk factors for cardiovascular disease is the Framingham Heart Study. Funded by the National Heart, Lung, and Blood Institute, this study began in 1948. Initially, researchers recruited 5,209 men and women between the ages of 30 and 62 from the town of Framingham, Massachusetts. Participants underwent extensive physical examinations and lifestyle interviews to study cardiovascular disease development. Participants returned to the study approximately every 2 to 6 years. In 1971, the study enrolled a second generation with 5,124 of the original participants' adult children and their spouses to participate in similar examinations. In 2002, the study finally enrollment a third generation of participants, the grandchildren of the original cohort. In total, the study examined over 14,000 people from 3 generations. The study led to many insights and provided strong evidence that high blood pressure and high blood cholesterol are major risk factors for cardiovascular disease. The study also showed that tobacco use, an unhealthy diet, physical inactivity, obesity, and diabetes increase the risk of cardiovascular disease. All of these seem obvious risk factors (Cooper et al., 2021; Mahmood et al., 2014; Mendis, 2010). But they were novel findings when they were first published and have since become the major focus for global prevention programs to reduce the risk of cardiovascular disease.

Population-based studies in Europe essentially replicated these results (De Backer, Kittel, Kornitzer, & Dramaix, 1983; French-Belgian Collaborative Group, 1982). It is interesting that a large study of Japanese men conducted in Hawai'i did *not* replicate these findings (Cohen & Reed, 1985). The prevalence of type A behavior among Japanese men is much lower than among men in the United States (18.7% versus approximately 50%). Similarly, the prevalence of CHD is equally low in Japanese men (4%, compared with 13% in U.S. men in the Framingham study) (Haynes & Matthews, 1988). In a study that illustrates the effects of culture more dramatically, 3,809 Japanese Americans were classified into groups according to how "traditionally Japanese" they were (in other words, they spoke Japanese at home, retained traditional Japanese values and behaviors, and so on). Japanese Americans who were the "most Japanese" had the lowest incidence of CHD, not significantly different from Japanese men in Japan. In contrast, the group that was the "least Japanese" had a 3 to 5 times greater incidence of CHD levels (Marmot & Syme, 1976; Matsumoto, 1996). Clearly, sociocultural differences are important.

Despite these straightforward results, at least in Western cultures, the type A concept has proved more complex and elusive than scientists had hoped. First, it is difficult to determine whether someone is type A from structured interviews, questionnaires, or other measures of this construct because the measures often do not agree with one another. Many people have *some* characteristics of type A but not all of them, and others present with a mixture of types A and B. The notion that we can divide the world into two types of people—an assumption underlying the early work in this area—has long since been discarded. As a result, subsequent studies did not necessarily support the relationship of type A behavior to CHD (Dembroski & Costa, 1987; Hollis, Connett, Stevens, & Greenlick, 1990).

The Role of Chronic Negative Emotions

At this point, investigators decided that something might be wrong with the type A construct itself (Matthews, 1988; Rodin & Salovey, 1989). A consensus developed that some—but not all—behaviors and emotions representative of the type A personality might be important in the development of CHD. One factor that seems to be responsible for much of the type A–CHD relationship is anger (Chida & Steptoe, 2009; Miller et al., 1996), which will come as no surprise if you read the Ironson study in Chapter 2 and the previous section on hypertension. As you may remember, Ironson and colleagues (1992) compared increased heart rate when they instructed individuals with heart disease to imagine situations or events in their own lives that made them angry with heart rates when they imagined other situations, such as exercise. They found that anger impaired the pumping efficiency of the heart, putting these individuals at risk for dangerous disturbances in heart rhythm (arrhythmias). This study confirms earlier findings relating the frequent experience of anger to later CHD (Houston, Chesney, Black, Cates, & Hecker, 1992; Smith, 1992). Results from an important study strengthen this conclusion. Iribarren and colleagues (2000) evaluated 374 young, healthy adults—both White Americans and African American—over a period of 10 years. Those with high hostility and anger showed evidence of coronary artery calcification, an early sign of CHD.

Is type A irrelevant to the development of heart disease? Most investigators conclude that some components of the type A construct are important determinants of CHD, particularly a chronically high level of negative affect (such as anger) and the time urgency or impatience factor (Matthews, 2005; Thoresen & Powell, 1992; Williams, Barefoot, & Schneiderman, 2003; Winters &

Schneiderman, 2000). Recall again the case of Cameron, who had all the type A behaviors, including time urgency, but also had frequent angry outbursts. But what about people who experience closely related varieties of negative affect on a chronic basis? Look back to Figure 9.4, and notice the close relationship between stress, anxiety, and depression. Some evidence indicates that the physiological components of these emotions and their effects on the cardiovascular system may be identical or at least similar (Suls & Bunde, 2005). We also know that the emotion of anger, so commonly associated with stress, is closely related to the emotion of fear, as evidenced in flight or fight response. Fight is the typical behavioral action tendency associated with anger, and flight or escape is associated with fear. But our bodily alarm response, activated by an immediate danger or threat, is associated with both emotions.

Some investigators, after reviewing the literature, have concluded that anxiety and depression are as important as anger in the development of CHD (Albert, Chae, Rexrode, Manson, & Kawachi, 2005; Barlow, 1988; Frasure-Smith & Lesperance, 2005; Strike & Steptoe, 2005; Suls & Bunde, 2005), even anxious and depressive features noticeable at an early age (Grossardt, Bower, Geda, Colligan, & Rocca, 2009). In a study of 896 people who had heart attacks, Frasure-Smith and colleagues (Frasure-Smith, Lesperance, Juneau, Talajic, & Bourassa, 1999) found that patients who were depressed were 3 times more likely to die in the year following their heart attacks than those who were not depressed, regardless of how severe their initial heart disease was. In a study of 1,017 patients with CHD, Whooley and colleagues (2008) found a 31% higher rate of cardiovascular events such as heart attacks or arrhythmias in patients with depressive symptoms compared with those without depressive symptoms. Severe depression, as in major depressive episodes, is particularly implicated in cardiovascular damage (Agatisa et al., 2005; Emery et al., 2011). In a study of 80,000 women aged 54 to 79, those women with a history of depression had a 29% greater risk of having a stroke than women who were not depressed (Pan et al., 2011). Thus, it may be that the chronic experience of the negative emotions of stress (anger), anxiety (fear), and depression (ongoing) and the neurobiological activation that accompanies these emotions provide the most important psychosocial contributions to CHD, and perhaps to other physical disorders. Indeed, several studies have confirmed that not only depression but also anxiety predicts future arrhythmias, myocardial infarction, and other cardiovascular events in people with CHD (Martens et al., 2010; Shen et al., 2008; Todaro, Shen, Raffa, Tilkemeier, & Niaura, 2007). A large study following nearly 50,000 Swedish men over four decades found that early-onset anxiety was predictive of later coronary heart disease (Janszky, Ahnve, Lundberg, & Hemmingsson, 2010).

Partly because of these findings, some investigators are proposing another personality type, type D, which is characterized by social inhibition and heightened negative emotions. Type D personality has been implicated in CHD in some research (Compare et al., 2013), although not all studies have found an association between D-type behavior and cardiovascular risk (Larson, Barger, & Sydeman, 2013), highlighting a need for further research (Hausteiner, Klupsch, Emeny, Baumert, & Ladwig, 2010).

Investigators are also learning more about the process through which negative emotions contribute to CHD. Once again, the inflammatory processes associated with the stress response (and with all negative emotions) play a major role because inflammation directly contributes to atherosclerosis and heart failure (Matthews et al., 2007; Taylor, 2009). Matthews and colleagues (Gallo & Matthews, 2003; Matthews, 2005, 2013) provide a model of the contribution of psychosocial factors to CHD (see ■ Figure 9.11). Lower socioeconomic status and relatively few resources or low prestige is in the first box. Stressful life events are in the second. Coping skills and social support contribute to a reserve capacity that may buffer the effects of stress, as represented in the third box. Both negative emotions and negative cognitive styles then constitute a major risk factor. Positive emotions and an optimistic style, on the other hand, reduce the risk of CHD (Davidson, Mostofsky, & Whang, 2010; Giltay, Geleijnse, Zitman, Hoekstra, & Schouten, 2004) and may turn out to be just as important as negative emotions in their effects on CHD. Both negative and positive emotions are in the fourth box. This model summarizes nicely what we know about the influence of psychosocial factors on CHD.

Some people with chronic pain or disability can cope extremely well and become high achievers.

Chronic Pain

Pain is not in itself a disorder, yet for most of us it is the fundamental signal of injury, illness, or disease. The importance of pain in our lives cannot be underestimated. Without low levels of pain providing feedback on the functioning of the body and its various systems, we would incur substantially more injuries. For example, you might lie out in the hot sun a lot longer and be badly burned. In many other cases, however, the pain does not seem to serve any adaptive function. Instead, the pain itself is the problem. For example, low back pain is very common, but only for a minority of people is the cause (such as a vertebral fracture) understood.

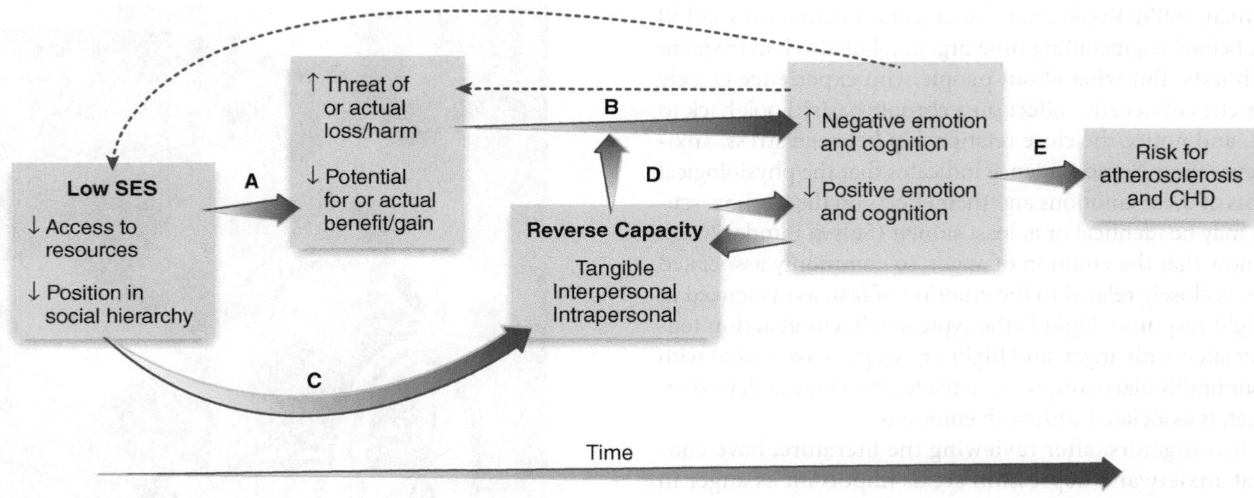

Figure 9.11

The reserve capacity model for associations among environments of low socioeconomic status (SES), stressful experiences, psychosocial resources, and emotions and cognitions, which represent pathways to increased risk for CHD. *Note:* Arrow A depicts the direct influence of SES on exposure to stressful experiences. Arrow B indicates the direct impact of stress experiences on emotion and cognition. Arrow C shows that SES conditions and shapes the bank of resources (that is, the reserve capacity) available to manage stress. Arrow D shows that reserve capacity represents a potential moderator of the association between stress and emotional-cognitive factors. Arrow E indicates the direct effects of emotional-cognitive factors on intermediate pathways and risk for atherosclerosis and CHD. The dashed lines note the possible reverse influences. Adapted from L.B. Gallo & K. A. Matthews, 2003, Understanding the association between socioeconomic status and physical health: Do negative emotions play a role?, *Psychological Bulletin, 129,* 34 (Fig. 1). © 2003 American Psychological Association. Reprinted, with permission, from K. A. Matthews, 2005, Psychological perspectives on the development of coronary heart disease, *American Psychologist, 60*(8), 791 (Fig. 2). © 2005 American Psychological Association.

People at greatest risk for low back pain are those with physically demanding jobs, physical and psychiatric comorbidities, smokers, and obese people. Low back pain has increased by 54% between 1990 and 2015, primarily because of population increase and aging. It has now become the leading cause of disability worldwide (Hartvigsen et al., 2018; Vlaeyen et al., 2018).

In general, there are two kinds of clinical pain: acute and chronic. **Acute pain** typically follows an injury and disappears once the injury heals or is effectively treated, often within a month. **Chronic pain**, by contrast, may begin with an acute episode but *does not decrease* over time, even when the injury has healed or effective treatments have been administered. Typically, chronic pain is in the muscles, joints, or tendons, particularly in the lower back. Vascular pain because of enlarged blood vessels may be chronic, as may headaches; pain caused by the slow degeneration of tissue, as in some terminal diseases; and pain caused by the growth of cancerous tumors that impinge on pain receptors (Otis & Pincus, 2008; Taylor, 2009).

To better understand the experience of pain, clinicians and researchers generally make a clear distinction between the subjective experience termed *pain,* reported by the patient, and the overt manifestations of this experience, termed *pain behaviors.* Pain behaviors include changing the way one sits or walks, continually complaining about pain to others, grimacing, and, most important, avoiding various activities, particularly those involving work or leisure. Finally, an emotional component of pain called *suffering* sometimes accompanies pain and sometimes does not (Fordyce, 1988; Liebeskind, 1991). We first review psychological and social contributions to pain, because they are so important.

Psychological and Social Aspects of Pain

In mild forms, chronic pain can be an annoyance that eventually wears you down and takes the pleasure out of your life. Severe chronic pain may cause you to lose your job, withdraw from your family, give up the fun in your life, and focus your entire awareness on seeking relief. What is interesting for our purposes is that the *severity* of the pain does not seem to predict the *reaction* to it. Some individuals experience intense pain frequently yet continue to work productively, rarely seek medical services, and lead reasonably normal lives; others become invalids. These differences appear to be primarily the result of psychological factors (Dersh et al., 2002; Flor & Turk, 2011; Gatchel, 2005; Gatchel & Turk, 1999). It will come as no surprise that these factors are the same as those implicated in the stress response and other negative emotional states, such as anxiety and depression (Ohayon & Schatzberg, 2003; Otis, Pincus, and Murawski, 2011) (see Chapters 5 and 7). The determining factor seems to be the individual's general sense of control over the situation: whether they can deal with the pain and its consequences in an effective and meaningful way. When a positive sense of control is combined with a generally optimistic outlook about the future, there is substantially less distress and disability (Keefe & France, 1999; Otis & Pincus, 2008; Zautra, Johnson, & Davis, 2005). Positive psychological factors are also associated with active attempts to cope, such as exercise and other regimens, as opposed to suffering passively (Gatchel & Turk, 1999; Otis et al., 2011; Zautra et al., 2005), and successfully treating depression diminishes the experience of chronic pain (Teh, Zaslavsky, Reynolds, & Cleary, 2009).

In one classic example, Philips and Grant (1991) studied 117 patients who suffered from back and neck pain after an injury. Almost all were expected to recover quickly, but fully 40% of them still reported substantial pain at 6 months, thereby qualifying for "chronic pain" status. Of the 60% who reported no pain at the 6-month point, most had been pain free since approximately 1 month after the accident. Furthermore, Philips and Grant reported that the relationship between the experience of pain and the subsequent disability was not as strongly related to the intensity of the pain as other factors, such as personality and socioeconomic differences and whether the person planned to initiate a lawsuit concerning the injury. Preexisting anxiety and personality problems predict who will suffer chronic pain (Flor & Turk, 2011; Taylor, 2009). Generally, a profile of negative emotion such as anxiety and depression, poor coping skills, low social support, and the possibility of being compensated for pain through disability claims predict most types of chronic pain (Dersh et al., 2002; Gatchel et al., 2007; Gatchel & Dersh, 2002). Conversely, developing a greater sense of control and less anxiety focused on the pain results in less severe pain and less impairment (Burns, Glenn, Bruehl, Harden, & Lofland, 2003; Edwards et al., 2009; Otis et al., 2011). Finally, Zautra and colleagues (2005) observed that positive affect in a group of 124 women with severe pain from arthritis or fibromyalgia predicted that they would have less pain in subsequent weeks than would women with lower levels of positive affect.

That the experience of pain can be largely disconnected from disease or injury is perhaps best exemplified by *phantom limb pain.* In this not uncommon condition, people who have lost an arm or leg feel excruciating pain in the limb that is no longer there. Furthermore, they can describe in exquisite detail the exact location of the pain and its type, such as a dull ache or a sharp cutting pain. They are fully aware the limb is amputated, but this does nothing to relieve the pain. Unfortunate victims of the Boston Marathon bombing in April 2013 have reported this experience and have benefited from sharing their feelings among themselves and ways they had discovered to cope with it. These coping methods include looking in a full-length mirror for several minutes each morning so that the brain can register that the limb is no longer there. Evidence suggests that changes in the sensory cortex of the brain may contribute to this phenomenon (Flor et al., 1995; Katz & Gagliese, 1999; Ramachandran, 1993). Generally, someone who thinks pain is disastrous, uncontrollable, or reflective of personal failure experiences more intense pain and greater psychological distress than someone who does not feel this way (Edwards et al., 2009; Gatchel et al., 2007). Thus, treatment programs for chronic pain concentrate on psychological factors.

Social factors also influence how we experience pain (Koban & Wager, 2015). For example, family members who were formerly critical and demanding may become caring and sympathetic (Kerns, Rosenberg, & Otis, 2002; Otis & Pincus, 2008). This phenomenon is referred to as *operant* control of pain behavior

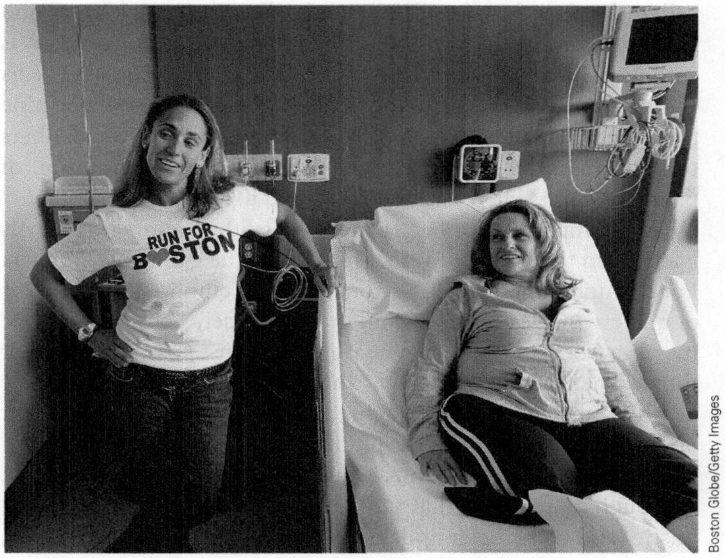

It is not uncommon for people to feel specific pain in limbs that are no longer part of them.

because the behavior clearly seems under the control of social consequences (Flor & Turk, 2011). But these consequences have an uncertain relation to the amount of pain being experienced.

By contrast, a strong network of social support may reduce pain. Jamison and Virts (1990) studied 521 chronic pain patients (with back, abdominal, and chest conditions) and discovered that those who lacked social support from their families reported more pain sites and showed more pain behavior, such as staying in bed. These patients also exhibited more emotional distress *without* rating their pain as any more intense than participants with strong socially supportive families. The participants with strong support returned to work earlier, showed less reliance on medications, and increased their activity levels more quickly than the others. Even having just a photo of a loved one to look at reduces the experience of pain (Master et al., 2009).

Although these results may seem to contradict studies on the operant control of pain, different mechanisms may be at work (Burns et al., 2014). General social support may reduce the stress associated with pain and injury and promote more adaptive coping procedures and control. Specifically reinforcing pain behaviors, however, particularly in the absence of social supports, may powerfully increase such behavior.

Biological Aspects of Pain

No one thinks pain is entirely psychological, just as no one thinks it is entirely physical. As with other disorders, we must consider how psychological and physical factors interact.

Mechanisms of Pain Experience and Pain Control

The *gate control theory of pain* (Melzack & Wall, 1965, 1982) accommodates both psychological and physical factors. According to this theory, nerve impulses from painful stimuli make their way to the spinal column and from there to the brain. An area called the *dorsal horns of the spinal column* acts as a "gate" and may open and transmit sensations of pain if the stimulation is sufficiently intense. Specific nerve fibers referred to as *small fibers* (A-delta and C fibers) and *large fibers* (A-beta fibers) determine the pattern, as well as the intensity, of the stimulation. Small fibers tend to open the gate, thereby increasing the transmission of painful stimuli, whereas large fibers tend to close the gate.

Most important for our purpose is that the brain sends signals back down the spinal cord that may affect the gating mechanism. For example, a person with strong negative emotions such as fear or anxiety may experience pain more intensely because the basic message from the brain is to be vigilant against possible danger or threat. Then again, in a person whose emotions are more positive or who is absorbed in an engaging activity (such as a runner intent on finishing a long race), the brain sends down an inhibitory signal that closes the gate, thus reducing their experience of pain. Although many think that the gate control theory is overly simplistic (and it has been updated periodically; see Melzack, 1999, 2005), research findings continue to support its basic elements, particularly as it describes the complex interaction of psychological and biological factors in the experience of pain (Edwards et al., 2009; Gatchel et al., 2007; Otis & Pincus, 2007).

Endogenous Opioids

The neurochemical means by which the brain inhibits pain is an important discovery (Taylor, 2009). Drugs such as heroin and morphine are manufactured from opioid substances. It now turns out that **endogenous (natural) opioids** exist within the body. Called *endorphins* or *enkephalins,* they act much like neurotransmitters. Because endogenous opioids are distributed widely throughout the body, they may be implicated in a variety of psychopathological symptoms and conditions, including tolerance and dependence, eating disorders, and stress reactions (Bodnar, 2012). They are commonly associated with the "runner's high" that occurs after intense (and sometimes painful) physical activity. The brain uses endorphins to shut down pain, even in the presence of marked tissue damage or injury. Bandura and colleagues (1987) found that people with a greater sense of self-efficacy and control had a higher tolerance for pain than individuals with low self-efficacy and that they increased their production of endogenous opioids when they were confronted with a painful stimulus.

Edwards and colleagues (2009) have articulated the neurobiological processes underlying the effectiveness of psychological coping procedures that successfully alter the experience of pain (see ■ Figure 9.12). Certain procedures, such as reappraising the significance of the pain instead of catastrophizing or thinking the worst about it, activate a variety of brain circuits that modulate or diminish pain experience and allow for more normal functioning. ■ Figure 9.12 schematically illustrates the pain-modulatory pathways. Distraction or reappraisal are associated with activation of prefrontal cortical regions (DLPFC = dorsolateral prefrontal cortex, VLPFC = ventrolateral prefrontal cortex) that modulate activity in cortical regions responsible for the processing of pain-related information, including the insula; primary somatosensory cortex, SI; secondary somatosensory cortex, SII; and thalamus. In addition, brainstem areas such as the periaqueductal gray (PAG) are important sites for opioid-based inhibition of ascending pain-related (nociceptive) neural input. Adaptive cognitive coping appears to have a generally inhibitory effect on cortical pain processing and an excitatory effect on PAG activity, which reduces subsequent ascending pain-related input from the spinal cord. In the figure, modulatory areas are in orange and pain processing areas are in blue. The anterior cingulate cortex (ACC) is involved in both pain processing and pain modulation.

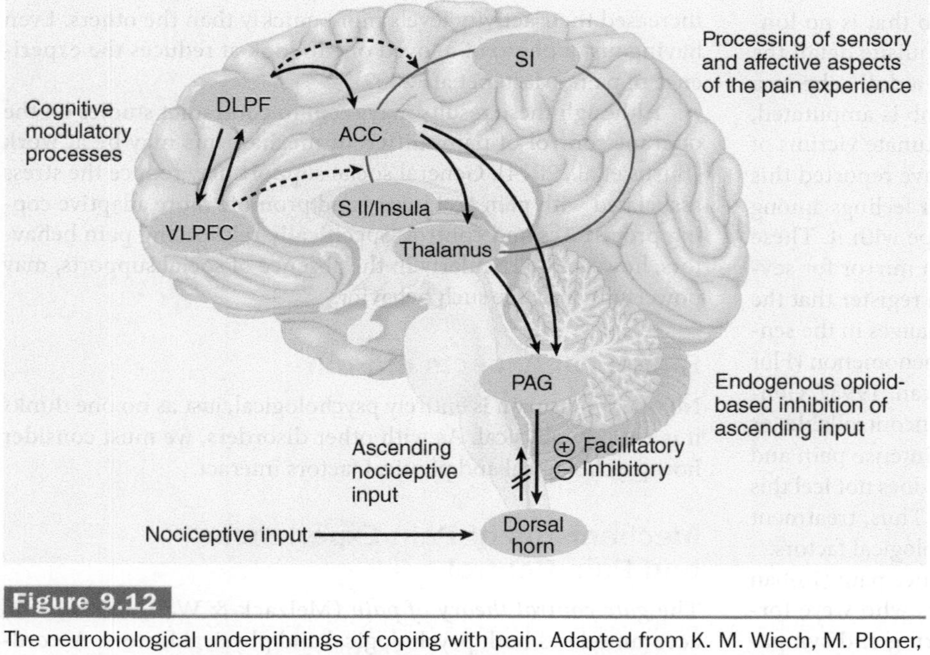

Figure 9.12

The neurobiological underpinnings of coping with pain. Adapted from K. M. Wiech, M. Ploner, & I. Tracey, 2008, Neurocognitive aspects of pain perception, *Trends in Cognitive Sciences, 12,* 306–313.

Gender Differences in Pain

Most animal and human studies have been conducted on males to avoid the complications of hormonal variation. But men and women seem to experience different types of pain as shown in a comprehensive review of the literature (Racine et al., 2012a, 2012b). The authors examined 172 articles published during a 10-year interval (between 1998 and 2008) and examined sex differences in the perception of different laboratory-induced pain stimuli, including thermal, pressure, ischemic (chest), muscle, electrical, chemical, and visceral pain in healthy subjects. The review showed that men and women have comparable thresholds for cold and ischemic pain, but women are more sensitive to pressure pain and thermal (heat, cold) pain than men.

In addition to menstrual cramps and labor pains, women suffer more often than men from migraine headaches, arthritis, carpal tunnel syndrome, and temporomandibular joint (TMJ) pain in the jaw (Lipchik, Holroyd, & Nash, 2002; Smitherman, Burch, Sheikh, & Loder, 2013). Men, on the other hand, have more cardiac pain and backache. Both males and females have endogenous opioid systems, although in males it may be more powerful. But women seem to have additional pain-regulating mechanisms that may be different. The female neurochemistry may be based on an estrogen-dependent neuronal system that may have evolved to cope with the pain associated with reproductive activity (Mogil, Sternberg, Kest, Marek, & Liebeskind, 1993). It is an "extra" pain-regulating pathway in females that, if taken away by removing hormones, has no implications for the remaining pathways, which continue to work. One implication of this finding is that males and females may benefit from different kinds of drugs, different kinds of psychological interventions, or unique combinations of these treatments to best manage and control pain.

The Inseparability of Psychological and Physical Experience of Pain

In this chapter and earlier chapters, we have described the profound influence of psychological factors on brain function and structure, showing how, for example, psychological interventions may affect physical illnesses such as CHD and AIDS. The fascinating study of the placebo response adds another layer to the discussion. To take one example, do "phony" placebo pills really decrease pain, or is it just that individuals think or report that they are feeling less pain? This is one of the major controversies in the study of placebo responses, not only for pain but also for other mental health conditions, such as depression.

With the help of the latest brain-imaging technology, several experiments have demonstrated that when pain is induced in some volunteers (for example, by injecting salt water in their jaws) after they are given a placebo, their brains operate in such a way that they actually feel less pain as opposed to simply thinking they feel less pain or reporting that they feel less pain (Wager, 2005; Zubieta et al., 2005). Specifically, broad areas of the brain are affected, but the most important system that is activated may be the endogenous opioid system (or endorphins), which, among other functions, suppresses pain. Increased endorphin activity across broad areas of the brain was associated with lower ratings of pain intensity, as well as reductions in the sensations of pain and emotional reactions to it. One study examined whether distraction, a procedure well known for reducing pain as when people become totally absorbed in their work or some other task, operates through the same brain circuits as the placebo response (Buhle, Stevens, Friedman, & Wager, 2012). Participants were subjected to thermal pain on their arms while they were either absorbed in a distracting task, received a placebo (a cream that was applied to the participants' skin that, they were told, would reduce pain), or assigned to a control condition in which they were told that a different cream would have no pain reducing effects. Both the placebo and the distraction task separately reduced the experience of pain, but when they were combined, there was an additive effect in that pain was reduced substantially more than it was with either condition alone. This suggests that these procedures operate through somewhat different brain circuits. Thus, the studies show that the placebo effect is certainly not "all in your head." "Phony" pills or other placebo substances really do spur chemical changes in the brain that reduce pain, even if the pill contains only sugar.

But does it also work the other way? Do medical treatments, such as drugs, affect what are clearly psychological processes, and if they do, are drugs affecting different regions in the brain compared with purely psychological interventions to achieve the same end? For example, we know that drugs can relieve anxiety and depression, but the presumption is that these medications are having their effects in different areas of the brain compared with psychological treatments. Several studies have demonstrated that physical pain (such as that caused by physical injury) and social pain (such as hurt feelings caused by social rejection) may rely on some of the same behavioral and neural mechanisms (DeWall et al., 2010; Eisenberger, 2012). In one experiment, participants took a drug commonly used for physical pain, acetaminophen (Tylenol), while another group took a placebo. They then recorded on a form their hurt feelings every day for 3 weeks. Subjects taking the acetaminophen reported substantially fewer hurt feelings than the placebo group. In a second experiment, the investigators found that the acetaminophen reduced neural responses to social rejection in brain regions known to be associated with both social pain as well as physical pain (the dorsal anterior cingulate cortex and the anterior insula). These findings indicate substantial overlap between social and physical pain (Eisenberger, 2012; Wager, 2005). Finally, another fascinating study indicated that stimulating the right ventrolateral prefrontal cortex, an area of the brain implicated in emotion regulation to negative stimulate, reduced pain following social exclusion (Riva, Lauro, DeWall, & Bushman, 2012). All of these findings illustrate again the theme of this book: You cannot easily separate brain function induced biochemically from brain function induced by psychological factors, including expectancies and appraisals. The body and the mind are indeed inseparable, and only a multidimensional integrative approach focusing on the full spectrum of responding will produce a complete understanding of behavior, either normal or pathological.

Chronic Fatigue Syndrome

In the mid-19th century, a rapidly growing number of patients suffered from lack of energy, marked fatigue, a variety of aches and pains, and occasionally low-grade fever. No physical pathology could be discovered, and George Beard (1869) labeled the condition *neurasthenia*, literally "lack of nerve strength" (Abbey & Garfinkel, 1991; Costa e Silva & De Girolamo, 1990). The disease was attributed to the demands of the time, including a preoccupation with material success, a strong emphasis on hard work, and the changing role of women. Neurasthenia disappeared in the early 20th century in Western cultures but continues to remain one of the most common psychological diagnoses in China (Good & Kleinman, 1985; Kleinman, 1986). Now **chronic fatigue syndrome (CFS)** is prevalent throughout the Western world (Brown, Bell, Jason, Christos, & Brown,

Table 9.3 Definition of Chronic Fatigue Syndrome

Inclusion Criteria
Clinically evaluated, medically unexplained fatigue of at least 6 months duration that is:
of new onset (not lifelong)
not resulting from ongoing exertion
not substantially alleviated by rest
a substantial reduction in previous level of activities
The occurrence of four or more of the following symptoms:
Subjective memory impairment
Sore throat
Tender lymph nodes
Muscle pain
Joint pain
Headache
Unrefreshing sleep
Postexertional malaise lasting more than 24 hours

Source: Adapted from K. Fukuda, S. E. Straus, I. Hickie, M. B. Sharpe, J. G. Dobbins, & A. L. Komaroff, 1994, Chronic fatigue syndrome: A comprehensive approach to its diagnosis and management, *Annals of Internal Medicine, 121,* 953–959.

2012; Jason, Fennell, & Taylor, 2003; Prins, van der Meer, & Bleijenberg, 2006). The symptoms of CFS, listed in Table 9.3, were initially attributed to XMRV (xenotropic murine leukemia virus-related virus), a retrovirus with some similarities to HIV and the so-called polytropic murine leukemia virus (pMLV) (Lombardi et al., 2009; Lo et al., 2010). However, after unusually heated scientific debates around a senior scientist who manipulated the data (Dr. Judy Mikovits) and a retraction of original studies (one even published in the prestigious journal *Science*), the evidence now clearly shows that XMRV and pMLV are not related to CFS (Alter et al., 2012).

Jason and colleagues (1999) conducted a sophisticated study of the prevalence of CFS in the community and reported that 0.4% of their sample was determined to have CFS, with higher rates in Latino and African American respondents compared with White Americans. CFS occurs in up to 3% of patients in a primary care clinic, predominantly in women, and usually begins in early adulthood (Afari & Buchwald, 2003), but it can occur in children as young as 7 years (Sankey, Hill, Brown, Quinn, & Fletcher, 2006). A study of 4,591 twins yielded a 2.7% prevalence rate (Furberg et al., 2005), and a prospective study of a larger birth cohort revealed that by age 53, 1.1% reported a diagnosis of CFS (Harvey, Wadsworth, Wessely, & Hotopf, 2008). To get a better idea of prevalence, psychologists will need to do large-scale population studies.

People with CFS suffer considerably and often must give up their careers because the disorder runs a chronic course (Clayton, 2015; Taylor et al., 2003). In a group of 100 patients followed for 18 months, chronic fatigue symptoms did not decrease significantly in fully 79% of cases. Better mental health to begin with—as well as less use of sedating medications and a more "psychological" as opposed to medical attribution for causes—led to better outcomes (Schmaling, Fiedelak, Katon, Bader, & Buchwald, 2003). Results from longer-term follow ups are a bit more encouraging. Of 25 patients diagnosed with CFS 25 years ago, only 5 self-reported that they maintained a diagnosis of CFS, while 20 reported no longer having a diagnosis. But even those 20 patients were significantly more impaired than a control group that had never had the diagnosis (Brown et al., 2012). This was a very small study, so results must be interpreted cautiously. Fortunately, CFS patients do not seem to be at risk for increased mortality (death) through disease or suicide compared with the general population (Smith, Noonan, & Buchwald, 2006).

As Abbey and Garfinkel (1991) and Sharpe (1997) point out, both neurasthenia in the 19th century and CFS in the 20th century through the present have been attributed to an extremely stressful environment, the changing roles of women, and the rapid dissemination of new technology and information. Both disorders are most common in women. It is possible that a virus or a specific immune system dysfunction will someday be found to account for CFS, although, as noted above, the search has been very disappointing so far. Another possibility suggested by Abbey and Garfinkel (1991) is that the condition represents a rather nonspecific response to stress, and Heim and colleagues (2006) found a higher level of adverse early stressful events in people with CFS compared with nonfatigued controls, reminiscent of Sapolsky's monkeys (discussed earlier in the chapter). Furthermore, a large study looking at personality factors that may contribute to CFS found preexisting stress and emotional instability to be important factors (Kato, Sullivan, Evengard, & Pederson, 2006). But it is not clear why certain individuals respond to stress with chronic fatigue instead of some other psychological or physical disorder.

Michael Sharpe (1997) has developed one of the first models of the causes of CFS that accounts for all of its features (see ■ Figure 9.13). Sharpe theorizes that individuals with particularly achievement-oriented lifestyles (driven, perhaps, by a basic sense of inadequacy) undergo a period of extreme stress or acute illness. They misinterpret the lingering symptoms of fatigue, pain, and inability to function at their usual high levels as a continuing disease that is worsened by activity and improved by rest. This results in behavioral avoidance, helplessness, depression, and frustration. They think they should be able to conquer the problem and cope with its symptoms. Chronic inactivity leads to lack of stamina, weakness, and increased feelings of depression and helplessness that in turn result in episodic bursts of long activity followed by further fatigue. Genetic factors probably influence the impact of stress and psychological variables in causing CFS, as is the case with all disorders (Kaiser, 2006). Harvey and colleagues (2008) studied 34 individuals with CFS and found very high levels of exercise prior to the development of CFS and increased long bursts of exercise even after the onset of CFS, perhaps as an attempt to compensate for feelings of fatigue. On the other hand, physical activity that is too vigorous can perpetuate CFS symptoms (Nijs, Paul, & Wallman, 2008). As a result, some patients restrict their physical activity, which can also perpetuate fatigue. A meta-analytic review

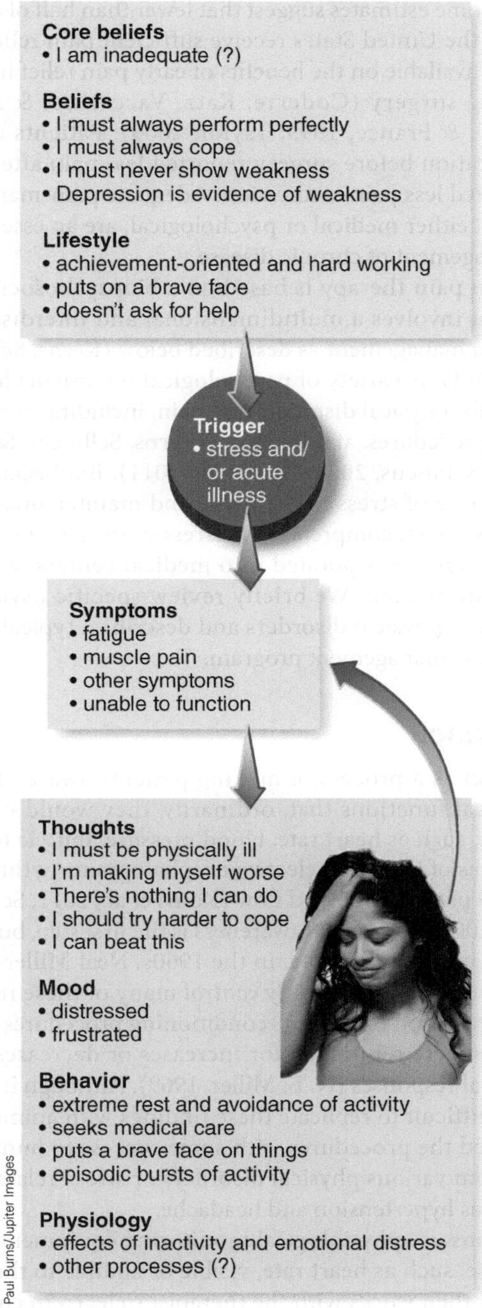

Figure 9.13

A complex-specific model of CFS. Adapted, with permission, from M. Sharpe, 1997, Chronic fatigue syndrome, in D. M. Clark & C. G. Fairburn (Eds.), *Science and practice of cognitive behavior therapy,* Oxford University Press, pp. 381–414. © 1997 Oxford University Press.

suggests that a behavioral intervention that encourages patients to slowly increase and maintain their physical activities (such as aerobic exercise and housework) without leading to exertion has sustained benefits on CFS symptoms (Marques, De Gucht, Gouveia, Leal, & Maes, 2015).

Table 9.4 Patients with Chronic Fatigue Syndrome Who Had Good Outcomes at 6-Month Follow Up*

Study Group	*N*	%
Treatment completers		
Cognitive-behavioral therapy (*n* = 27)	19	70
Relaxation (*n* = 26)	5	19
Completers plus dropouts		
Cognitive-behavioral therapy (*n* = 30)	19	63
Relaxation (*n* = 30)	5	17

*An increase of 50 or more, from pretreatment to 6-month follow up, or an end score of 83 or more on the physical functioning scale of the Medical Outcome Study Short-Form General Health Survey.

Source: Reprinted, with permission, from A. Deale, T. Chalder, I. Marks, & S. Wessely, 1997, Cognitive behavior therapy for chronic fatigue syndrome: A randomized controlled trial, *American Journal of Psychiatry, 154,* 408–414. © 1997 American Psychiatric Association.

Pharmacological treatment has not proved effective for CFS (Afari & Buchwald, 2003; Chalder et al., 2000), but Sharpe has developed a cognitive-behavioral program that includes procedures to increase activity, regulate periods of rest, and direct cognitive therapy at the cognitions specified in ■ Figure 9.13. This treatment also includes relaxation, breathing exercises, and general stress-reduction procedures, interventions we describe in the next section (Sharpe, 1992, 1993, 1997). In an early controlled trial evaluating this approach, 60 patients were assigned to the cognitive-behavioral treatment or to treatment as usual. Seventy-three percent of the patients in the cognitive-behavioral treatment group improved on measures of fatigue, disability, and illness belief, a result far superior to that in the control group (Sharpe et al., 1996).

In a second, more sophisticated, large-scale evaluation of a similar cognitive-behavioral approach to CFS (Deale, Chalder, Marks, & Wessely, 1997), 60 patients with CFS were randomly assigned to cognitive-behavioral therapy or relaxation exercises alone. The results indicated that fatigue diminished and overall functioning improved significantly more in the group that received cognitive-behavioral therapy. As is evident in Table 9.4, 70% of individuals who completed cognitive-behavioral therapy achieved substantial improvement in physical functioning at a 6-month follow up, compared with only 19% of those in the relaxation-only group. A 5-year follow up indicates the gains were largely maintained (Deale, Husain, Chalder, & Wessely, 2001). Subsequent studies confirm the value of this basic approach in adults (Knoop, Prins, Moss-Morris, & Bleijenberg, 2010; Price, Mitchell, Tidy, & Hunot, 2008) and adolescents (Chalder, Deary, Husain, & Walwyn, 2010). Increasing emphasis is now placed on preventing bursts of overexercise (for example, Harvey & Wessely, 2009; Jason et al., 2010). There is some evidence that moderate and graded as opposed to intense exercise can be useful in treatment, but CBT seems clearly indicated when patients have comorbid anxiety and depression (Castell, Kazantzis, & Moss-Morris, 2011; White et al., 2011), since cognitive reappraisal of the meaning of fatigue in one's life and increased self-efficacy seem important (Friedberg & Sohl, 2009).

Concept Check 9.2

Answer the following questions about the psychosocial effects on physical disorders.

1. Which of the following is not considered part of the experience of pain?
   a. The subjective impression of pain as reported by the patient
   b. Pain behaviors or overt manifestations of pain
   c. Cuts, bruises, and other injuries
   d. An emotional component called suffering
2. Some evidence shows that psychological factors may contribute to both the course and the ________ of cancer, AIDS, and other diseases, as well as treatment and recovery.
3. Psychosocial and biological factors contribute to the development of ________, a potentially deadly condition of high blood pressure, and to the development of ________, the blockage of arteries supplying blood to the heart muscle.
4. Psychologists have found that behavior pattern "types" impact physical health. ________ is associated with the development of illness to a greater extent than is ________.
5. No confirmed evidence exists to show that there is a physical cause for the disease of ________, which often causes individuals to give up their careers and suffer considerably.

Psychosocial Treatment of Physical Disorders

Certain experiments suggest that pain not only is bad for you but also may kill you. Several years ago, John Liebeskind and his colleagues (Page, Ben-Eliyahu, Yirmiya, & Liebeskind, 1993) demonstrated that postsurgical pain in rats doubles the rate at which a certain cancer metastasizes (spreads) to the lungs. Rats undergoing abdominal surgery *without* morphine developed twice the number of lung metastases as rats who were given morphine for the same surgery. The rats undergoing surgery with the pain-killing drug had even lower rates of metastases than rats that did not have surgery.

This effect may result from the interaction of pain with the immune system. Pain may reduce the number of natural killer cells in the immune system, perhaps because of the general stress reaction to the pain. Thus, if a rat is in *extreme* pain, the associated stress may further enhance the pain, completing a vicious circle. This finding also seems to apply to humans (Flor & Turk, 2011; Taylor, 2009), so it is important because the consensus is that we are reluctant to use pain-killing medication in chronic diseases such as cancer. Some estimates suggest that fewer than half of all cancer patients in the United States receive sufficient pain relief. Direct evidence is available on the benefits of early pain relief in patients undergoing surgery (Coderre, Katz, Vaccarino, & Melzack, 1993; Keefe & France, 1999; Taylor, 2009). Patients receiving pain medication before surgery reported less pain after surgery and requested less pain medication. Adequate pain-management procedures, either medical or psychological, are an essential part of the management of chronic disease.

Modern pain therapy is based on a biopsychosocial model of pain that involves a multidimensional and interdisciplinary plan of pain management as described below (Kerns, Sellinger, & Goodin, 2011). A variety of psychological treatments have been developed for physical disorders and pain, including biofeedback, relaxation procedures, and hypnosis (Kerns, Sellinger, & Goodin, 2011; Otis & Pincus, 2008; Otis et al., 2011). But because of the overriding role of stress in the cause and maintenance of many physical disorders, comprehensive stress-management programs are increasingly incorporated into medical centers where such disorders are treated. We briefly review specific psychosocial approaches to physical disorders and describe a typical comprehensive stress-management program.

Biofeedback

Biofeedback is a process of making patients aware of specific physiological functions that, ordinarily, they would not notice consciously, such as heart rate, blood pressure, muscle tension in specific areas of the body, electroencephalogram rhythms (brain waves), and patterns of blood flow (Kerns et al., 2011; Schwartz & Andrasik, 2003). Conscious awareness is the first step, but the second step is more remarkable. In the 1960s, Neal Miller reported that rats could *learn to directly control* many of these responses. He used a variation of operant-conditioning procedures in which the animals were reinforced for increases or decreases in their physiological responses (N. E. Miller, 1969). Although it was subsequently difficult to replicate these findings with animals, clinicians applied the procedures with some success to humans who suffered from various physical disorders or stress-related conditions, such as hypertension and headache.

Clinicians use physiological monitoring equipment to make the response, such as heart rate, visible or audible to the patient. The patient then works with the therapist to learn to control the response. A successful response produces some type of signal. For example, if the patient is successful in lowering their blood pressure by a certain amount, the pressure reading will be visible on a gauge, and a tone will sound. It wasn't long before researchers discovered that humans could discriminate changes in autonomic nervous system activity with a high degree of accuracy (Blanchard & Epstein, 1977). The question then became this: Why are people ordinarily so poor at discriminating their internal states? Zillmann (1983) suggested that our abilities have always been highly developed in this regard but that over the millennia we have simply lost our skills through lack of practice. Shapiro (1974) suggests that, in an evolutionary sense, it might have been adaptive to turn our attention from precise monitoring of our internal responses. He proposes that whether humans function as hunter-gatherers or in the home or office, they would be far less efficient if they were continually distracted by a turmoil of internal stimuli. In other words, to focus successfully on the task at hand, we may have found it necessary to ignore our internal functioning and leave it to the more automatic and less aware parts of the brain. Still, internal sensations often take control of our consciousness and make us fully aware of our needs. Consider, for example, the compelling sensations that signal the need to urinate or the insistence of hunger pangs. In any case, it does seem that through precise physiological feedback we can learn to control our responses, although the mechanisms by which we do so are not yet clearly known.

One goal of biofeedback has been to reduce tension in the muscles of the head and scalp, thereby relieving headaches. Pioneers such as Ed Blanchard, Ken Holroyd, and Frank Andrasik found that biofeedback was successful in this area (Holroyd, Andrasik, & Noble, 1980), although no more successful than deep muscle relaxation procedures (Andrasik, 2000; Blanchard & Andrasik, 1982; Holroyd & Penzien, 1986). Because of these results, some have thought that biofeedback might achieve its effects with tension headaches by simply teaching people to relax. However, Holroyd and colleagues (1984) concluded instead that the success of biofeedback, at least for headaches, may depend not on the reduction of tension but on the extent to which the procedures instill a sense of *control* over the pain. (How do you think this relates to the study of stress in baboons described in the beginning of the chapter?) Whatever the mechanism, biofeedback and relaxation are more effective treatments than, for example, placebo medication interventions, and the results of these two treatments are not altogether interchangeable, in that some people benefit more from biofeedback and others benefit from relaxation procedures. Therefore, applying one treatment or the other is a safe strategy (Andrasik, 2000; Kerns et al., 2011). Several reviews have found that 38% to 63% of patients undergoing relaxation or biofeedback achieve significant reductions in headaches compared with approximately 35% who receive placebo medication (Blanchard, 1992; Holroyd & Penzien, 1986). Furthermore, the effects of biofeedback and relaxation seem to be long lasting (Kerns et al., 2011; Andrasik, 2000).

Table 9.5 Suggestions for Tensing Muscles

Large Muscle Groups	Suggestions for Tensing Muscles
Lower arm	Make fist, palm down, and pull wrist toward upper arm.
Upper arm	Tense biceps; with arms by side, pull upper arm toward side without touching. (Try not to tense lower arm while doing this; let lower arm hang loosely.)
Lower leg and foot	Point toes upward to knees.
Thighs	Push feet hard against floor.
Abdomen	Pull in stomach toward back.
Chest and breathing	Take deep breath, and hold it about 10 seconds, then release.
Shoulders and lower neck	Shrug shoulders, bring shoulders up until they almost touch ears.
Back of neck	Put head back, and press against back of chair.
Lips	Press lips together; don't clench teeth or jaw.
Eyes	Close eyes tightly, but don't close too hard (be careful if you have contacts).
Lower forehead	Pull eyebrows down and in (try to get them to meet).
Upper forehead	Raise eyebrows, and wrinkle forehead.

Source: Adapted, with permission, from D. H. Barlow, R. M. Rapee, & S. Perini, 2014, *10 steps to mastering Stress: A lifestyle approach,* Oxford University Press.

Relaxation and Meditation

Various types of relaxation and meditation procedures have also been used, either alone or with other procedures, to treat physical disorder and pain patients (Kerns et al., 2011). In *progressive muscle relaxation,* devised by Edmund Jacobson in 1938, people purposely tense different muscle groups in a sequential fashion (lower arm, upper arm, and so on) (see Table 9.5) followed by relaxing each specific muscle group. In this way they learn to recognize tension in different muscle groups and how to reduce it. A number of meditation-based procedures focus attention either on a specific part of the body or on a single thought or image. This attentional focus is often accompanied by regular, slowed breathing.

Herbert Benson developed a brief procedure he calls the **relaxation response**, in which a person silently repeats a mantra (focusing attention solely on a repeated syllable) to minimize distraction by closing the mind to intruding thoughts. Although Benson suggested focusing on the word *one,* any neutral word or phrase would do. Individuals who meditate for 10 or 20 minutes a day report feeling calmer or more relaxed throughout the day. These brief, simple procedures can be powerful in reducing the flow of certain neurotransmitters and stress hormones, an effect that may be mediated by an increased sense of control and mastery (Benson, 1975, 1984). Benson's ideas are popular and have traditionally been taught in 60% of U.S. medical schools and offered by many major hospitals (Roush, 1997). Relaxation has generally positive effects on headaches, hypertension, and acute and chronic pain, although the results are sometimes relatively modest (Taylor, 2009). In addition, and as we discuss in Chapter 7, mindfulness meditation appears to be effective for a range of problems, including stress and especially anxiety and depression (Goyal et al., 2014; Hofmann, et al., 2010; Khoury et al., 2013; Kuyken et al., 2015) Therefore, relaxation and meditation are almost always part of a comprehensive pain-management program.

Courtesy of Edward Blanchard

Edward Blanchard was a pioneer in the development and testing of biofeedback.

A Comprehensive Stress- and Pain-Reduction Program

In our own stress-management program (Barlow, Rapee, & Parini, 2014), individuals practice a variety of stress-management procedures presented to them in a workbook. First, they learn to monitor their stress closely and to identify the stressful events in their daily lives. (A sample of a daily stress record is in ■ Figure 9.14.) Clients are taught to be specific about recording the times they experience stress, the intensity of the stress, and the possible triggers of the stress. They also note the somatic symptoms and thoughts that occur when they are stressed. All this monitoring becomes important in carrying through with the program, but it can be helpful in itself because it reveals precise patterns and causes of stress and helps clients learn what changes to make to cope better.

Microgen/Shutterstock.com

In biofeedback, the patient learns to control physiological responses that are visible on a screen.

After learning to monitor stress, clients are taught deep muscle relaxation, which first involves tensing various muscles to identify the location of different muscle groups. (Instructions for tensing specific muscle groups are included in Table 9.5.) Clients are then systematically taught to relax the muscle groups beyond the point of inactivity—that is, to actively let go of the muscle so that no tension remains in it. Appraisals and attitudes are an important part of stress, and clients learn how they exaggerate the negative impact of events in their day-to-day lives. In the program, therapist and client use cognitive therapy to develop

Daily Stress Record
(sample)

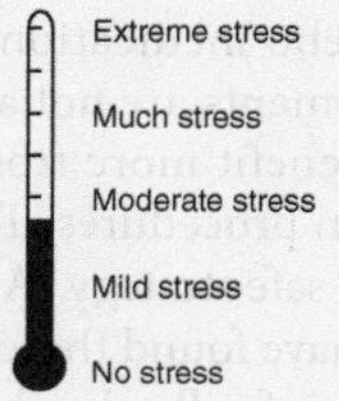

Week of ____________

Date	(1) Starting time	(2) Ending time	(3) Highest stress (0–8)	(4) Triggers	(5) Symptoms	(6) Thoughts
1-5	10:00am	11:00am	7	Sales meeting	Sweating, headache	my figures are bad
1-7	5:15 pm	5:35 pm	6	Traffic jam	Tension, impatience	I'll never get home
1-8	12:30pm	12:32pm	3	Lost keys	Tension	I can't find my keys
1-9	3:30pm	4:30pm	4	Waiting for guests	Sweating, nausea	Are they lost?

Figure 9.14

Methods for monitoring stress. Adapted, with permission, from D. H. Barlow, R. M. Rapee, & S. Perini, 2014, *10 steps to mastering Stress: A lifestyle approach,* Oxford University Press.

Mei Lin... Improving Her Perception

(Mei Lin is a 45-year-old real estate agent.)

Patient: My mother is always calling just when I'm in the middle of doing something important, and it makes me so angry, I find that I get short with her.

Therapist: Let's try and look at what you just said in another way. When you say that she *always* phones in the middle of something, it implies 100% of the time. Is that true? How likely is it really that she will call when you are doing something important?

P: Well, I suppose that when I think back over the last 10 times she's called, most of the times I was just watching TV or reading. There was once when I was making dinner and it burned because she interrupted me. Another time, I was busy with some work I had brought home from the office, and she called. I guess that makes it 20% of the time.

T: OK, great. Now let's go a bit further. So what if she calls at an inconvenient time?

P: Well, I know that one of my first thoughts is that she doesn't think anything I do is important. But before you say anything, I know that is a major overestimation since she obviously doesn't know what I'm doing when she calls. However, I suppose I also think that it's a major interruption and inconvenience to have to stop at that point.

T: Go on. What is the chance that it is a major inconvenience?

P: When I was doing my work, I forgot what I was up to, and it took me 10 minutes to work it out again. I guess that's not so bad; it's only 10 minutes. And when the dinner burned, it was really not too bad, just a little burned. Part of that was my fault anyway because I could have turned the stove down before I went to the phone.

T: So it sounds like quite a small chance that it would be a major inconvenience, even if your mother does interrupt you.

P: True. And I know what you are going to say next. Even if it is a major inconvenience, it's not the end of the world. I have handled plenty of bigger problems than this at work.

more realistic appraisals and attitudes, as exemplified in the case of Mei Lin.

In this program, individuals work hard to identify unrealistic negative thoughts and to develop new appraisals and attitudes almost instantaneously when negative thoughts occur. Such assessment is often the most difficult part of the program. After the session just related, Mei Lin began using what she had learned in cognitive therapy to reappraise stressful situations. Finally, clients in stress-reduction programs develop new coping strategies, such as time-management and assertiveness training. During *time-management training,* patients are taught to prioritize their activities and pay less attention to nonessential demands. During *assertiveness training,* they learn to stand up for themselves in an appropriate way. Clients also learn other procedures for managing everyday problems.

A number of studies have evaluated some version of this comprehensive program. The results suggest that it is generally more effective than individual components alone, such as relaxation or biofeedback, for chronic pain (Keefe et al., 1992; Otis & Pincus, 2008; Turk & Monarch, 2002), CFS (Deale et al., 1997), tension headaches (Lipchik et al., 2002), hypertension (Ward, Swan, & Chesney, 1987), temporomandibular joint (jaw) pain (Turner, Mancl, & Aaron, 2006), and cancer pain (Andersen et al., 2007; Crichton & Morey, 2003). A summary meta-analysis of 22 studies of treatments for chronic lower back pain also found comprehensive psychological treatments effective (Hoffman, Papas, Chatkoff, & Kerns, 2007).

Drugs and Stress-Reduction Programs

We have already noted the enormous nationwide reliance on over-the-counter analgesic medication for pain, particularly headaches. Some evidence suggests that *chronic* reliance on these medications lessens the efficacy of comprehensive programs in the treatment of headache and may make headaches worse because patients experience *increased* headache pain every time the medication wears off or is stopped (rebound headaches) (Capobianco, Swanson, & Dodick, 2001). In a classic study, Michultka, Blanchard, Appelbaum, Jaccard, and Dentinger (1989) matched high analgesic users (people who took a lot of pain pills) to low analgesic users (people who took few or no pain pills) in terms of age, duration of headache activity, and response to comprehensive treatment. Only 29% of high users versus 55% of low users achieved at least a 50% reduction in a measure of frequency and severity of headaches.

Traditional medical advice for people suffering from headache is to avoid the triggers leading to headache. However, it is possible that avoiding triggers is not as effective as learning how to cope with the triggers (Martin & MacLeod, 2009; Martin et al., 2014), which includes general stress-reduction techniques and "planned exposures" to achieve desensitization and to examine whether an alleged trigger does, in fact, precipitate headaches.

Pain medication is an obvious and commonly practiced strategy to avoid pain. Despite its frequent use, it is not overly effective and can lead to overuse and even dependency. Grazzi and colleagues (2002) treated 61 patients with migraine headaches and analgesic overuse by withdrawing the patients from analgesics and then starting them on a more comprehensive but nonaddicting medication regimen, either with biofeedback and relaxation or without these (drugs only). After 3 years, significantly more individuals in the medication-only condition had relapsed by resuming analgesic use and were experiencing more headache pain. Psychological treatment also seems to reduce drug consumption fairly consistently as it did in the study by Grazzi and colleagues (2002), not only for headaches but also for severe hypertension.

Denial as a Means of Coping

We have emphasized the importance of confronting and working through our feelings, particularly after stressful or traumatic events. Beginning with Sigmund Freud, mental health professionals have recognized the importance of reliving or processing intense emotional experiences to put them behind us and to develop better coping responses. For example, individuals undergoing coronary artery bypass surgery who were optimistic recovered more quickly, returned to normal activities more rapidly, and reported a stronger quality of life 6 months after surgery than those who were not optimistic (Scheier et al., 1989). Scheier and colleagues also discovered that optimistic people are less likely to use denial as a means of coping with a severe stressor such as surgery. Bruce Compas and colleagues (2006) studied anxiety and pain complaints in 164 adolescents with recurrent abdominal pain. Adolescents who regularly used denial, avoidance, and wishful thinking had higher levels of anxiety and somatic complaints than those who attempted to cope more directly with the pain. Most mental health professionals work to eliminate denial because it has many negative effects. For example, people who deny the severe pain connected with disease may not notice meaningful variations in their symptoms, and they typically avoid treatment regimens or rehabilitation programs.

But is denial always harmful? The well-known health psychologist Shelley Taylor (2009) points out that most individuals who are functioning well deny the implications of a potentially serious condition, at least initially. A common reaction is to assume that what they have is not serious or will go away quickly. Most people with serious diseases react this way, including those with cancer and CHD. Several groups of investigators (see, for example, Hackett & Cassem, 1973; Meyerowitz, 1983) have found that during that extremely stressful period when a person is first diagnosed, denial may help patients endure the shock more easily. They are then better able to develop coping responses later. The value of denial as a coping mechanism may depend more on timing than on anything else. In the long run, however, all evidence indicates that at some point we must face the situation, process our emotions, and come to terms with what is happening (Compas et al., 2006).

Modifying Behaviors to Promote Health

In the beginning of the chapter, we talk about two distinct ways in which psychological and social factors influence health and physical problems: by directly affecting biological processes and through unhealthy lifestyles. In this section, we consider the effects of an unhealthy lifestyle.

As early as 1991, the director of the National Institutes of Health said, "Our research is teaching us that many common diseases can be prevented and others can be postponed or controlled simply by making possible lifestyle changes" (U.S. Department of Health and Human Services, 1991). Unhealthy eating habits, lack of exercise, and smoking are three of the most common behaviors that put us at risk in the long term for a number of physical disorders (Lewis et al., 2011). Other high-risk behaviors and conditions include unprotected sex, failure to take precautions to avoid injuries, excessive use of alcohol, and excessive exposure to the sun, just to name a few. Many of these behaviors contribute to diseases and physical disorders that are among the leading causes of death, including not only CHD and cancer but also accidents of various kinds (related to consumption of alcohol and the nonuse of safety restraints), cirrhosis of the liver (related to excessive consumption of alcohol), and a variety of respiratory diseases, including influenza and pneumonia (related to smoking and stress) (Lewis et al., 2011). Even now, fully 21% of adults in the United States are regular smokers (CDC, 2007), and smoking is the leading preventable cause of death, accounting for 20% of deaths from all causes and killing approximately 443,000 people each year (CDC, 2008; Ezzati & Roboli, 2012). Considerable work is ongoing to develop effective behavior modification procedures that improve diet, increase adherence to drug and medical treatment programs, and develop optimal exercise programs. Here we review briefly four areas of interest: injury control, the prevention of AIDS, efforts to reduce smoking in China, and a major community intervention known as the Stanford Three Community Study.

Injury Prevention

Accidents (unintentional injuries) are the third leading cause of death among all causes in the United States (see Figure 9.1). Accidents caused by burns, drowning, falls, poisoning, and motor vehicle accidents are the leading cause of death among children in the United States. For adults, accidents are a major cause for lost productivity to the individual and society. The number of years of life lost from injuries is far greater than from the other four leading causes of death: heart disease, cancer, stroke, and respiratory disease (Institute of Medicine, 1999; National Safety Council, 2013). For example, the National Safety Council estimates that when an individual dies in an automobile accident, the average cost to society, including economic costs and loss of quality of life, is a staggering $4.5 million. Even nonfatal automobile injuries carry associated costs of between $50,000 and $225,000 (National Safety Council, 2013). Therefore, the U.S. government has become interested in methods for reducing injury (CDC, 2010; Scheidt, Overpeck, Trifiletti, & Cheng, 2000). Spielberger and Frank (1992) pointed out that psychological variables are crucial in leading to virtually all factors that lead to injury. A good example is the work of the late Lizette Peterson and her colleagues (see, for example, Damashek, Williams, Sher, & Peterson, 2009; Peterson & Roberts, 1992). Peterson was particularly interested in preventing accidents in children. Injuries kill more children than the next six causes of childhood death combined (Scheidt et al., 1995; Taylor, 2009), and nearly half of all cases of poisoning each year occur in children under 6 (CDC, 2006). Yet most people, including parents, don't think too much about prevention, even in their own children, because they usually consider injuries to be fated and, therefore, out of their hands (Peterson & Roberts, 1992). Furthermore, some parents believe that there is value in children experiencing minor injuries as they grow up, which may compromise caregivers' injury prevention efforts (Lewis, DiLillo, & Peterson, 2004).

A variety of programs focusing on behavior change, however, have proved effective for preventing injuries in children. For example, children have been systematically and successfully taught to prevent burns, escape fires, and prevent other serious injuries (Gielen, McDonald, & Shields, 2015; Gielen, Sleet, & DiClemente, 2006; Kendrick et al., 2012; Sleet, Hammond, Jones, Thomas, & Whitt, 2003; Taylor, 2009; Turner et al., 2004). In many of these programs, the participating children maintained the safety skills they

Courtesy of Lizette Peterson

Lizette Peterson developed important behavior-change procedures for preventing injuries in children.

had learned for months after the intervention—as long as assessments were continued, in most cases. Because little evidence indicates that repeated warnings are effective in preventing injuries, programmatic efforts to change behavior are important. Such programs, however, are nonexistent in most communities. Fortunately, parental responses to childhood injury can be improved through cognitive behavioral interventions, leading to more informed care for recovering children (Marsac, Kassam-Adams, Hildenbrand, Kohser, & Winston, 2011).

AIDS Prevention

Earlier we documented the horrifying spread of AIDS, particularly in developing countries. Table 9.1 illustrates modes of transmission of AIDS in the United States and the world as they existed through 2008 and 2009. In developing countries, such as Africa, for instance, AIDS is almost exclusively linked to heterosexual intercourse with an infected partner. There is no vaccine for the disease. *Changing high-risk behavior is the most effective prevention strategy* (Grossman, Purcell, Rotheram-Borus, & Veniegas, 2013; Mermin & Fenton, 2012).

Comprehensive programs are particularly important because testing alone to learn whether one is HIV positive or HIV negative does little to change behavior (see, for example, Grossman et al., 2013). Even educating at-risk individuals is generally ineffective in changing high-risk behavior. One of the most successful behavior-change programs was carried out in San Francisco relatively early in the development of the AIDS epidemic. Table 9.6 shows what

Table 9.6 The San Francisco Model: Coordinated Community-Level Program to Reduce New HIV Infection

Information	
Media: Educate about how HIV is and is not transmitted.	*STI, family planning, and drug abuse treatment centers:* Distribute materials and video models about HIV transmission.
Health-care establishments and providers: Provide educational materials and classes about HIV transmission.	*Community organizations (churches, clubs):* Make guest speakers, materials, and videos available.
Schools: Distribute materials about HIV transmission and prevention.	
Worksites: Distribute materials about HIV transmission and prevention.	*Antibody testing centers:* Distribute materials and instruction about HIV transmission.
Motivation	
Provide examples of different kinds of individuals who have become HIV infected.	Provide examples of coworkers who became infected with HIV.
Ask all patients about risk factors for HIV transmission.	Make detailed assessment of HIV risk.
Advise high-risk patients to be tested for HIV antibodies.	Advise about testing for antibodies to HIV.
Provide models of teens who became infected with HIV.	Provide examples that HIV-infected individuals are similar to club or organization membership.
Skills	
Model how to clean needles and use condoms and spermicides.	Provide classes and models for safe-sex and drug injection skills.
Model skills for safe-sex and needle negotiation.	Instruct and rehearse safe-sex and drug injection skills during medical and counseling encounters.
Provide classes and videos to demonstrate safe-sex skills.	Provide classes and videos for AIDS risk-reduction skills.
Norms	
Publicize the low prevalence of high-risk behaviors.	Publicize student perceptions about desirability of safe-sex.
Publicize the public desirability of safe-sex classes and condom advertisements.	Create a climate of acceptance for HIV-infected people.
Advise patients about prevalent community norms.	Provide classes and videos for AIDS risk-reduction skills.
Create a climate of acceptance for HIV-infected students and teachers.	
Policy and Legislation	
Generate concern and action about policy.	Mobilize clients to request additional treatment slots and facilities.
Advocate policies and laws that will prevent spread of HIV.	Advocate beneficial laws and policies.
Mobilize students and faculty to work to allow sex-education to take place in the schools.	Advocate confidentiality and nondiscrimination.
Install condom machines in public bathrooms.	
Allow HIV-infected people to work.	

STI = sexually transmitted infection

Source: Reprinted, with permission, from T. J. Coates, 1990, Strategies for modifying sexual behavior for primary and secondary prevention of HIV disease, *Journal of Consulting and Clinical Psychology, 58*(1), 57–69.

behaviors were specifically targeted and what methods were used to achieve behavior change in various groups. Before this program was introduced, frequent unprotected sex was reported by 37.4% of one sample of gay men and 33.9% of another sample (Stall, McKusick, Wiley, Coates, & Ostrow, 1986). At a follow-up point in 1988, the incidence had dropped to 1.7% and 4.2%, respectively, in the same two samples (Ekstrand & Coates, 1990). These changes did not occur in comparable groups where a program of this type had not been instituted.

It is crucial that these programs be extended to people of color and women, who often do not consider themselves at risk, probably because most media coverage in the United States has primarily focused on gay white males. In 2003, women accounted for 50% of new AIDS cases (World Health Organization, 2003). Furthermore, the age of highest risk for women is between 15 and 25 years; the peak risk for men is during their late 20s and early 30s. In view of the different circumstances in which women put themselves at risk for HIV infection—for example, sex work in response to economic deprivation—effective behavior-change programs for them must be different from those developed for men (World Health Organization, 2000).

One very strong program focused on inner-city African American adolescent females is called SiHLE (Sistas Informing, Healing, Living, Empowering) (DiClemente et al., 2004, 2008). It is clear that HIV and other sexually transmitted infections are highly prevalent among adolescents, particularly among African American adolescents (Weinstock, Berman, & Cates, 2004). In the SiHLE program, HIV-related interpersonal and social processes that are more characteristic of inner-city African American adolescent females are targeted, such as having older male sex partners who are more demanding, having violent dating partners, being stereotyped by the media, perceiving society as having limited regard for African American teens, and being reluctant to negotiate about safer sex. Unlike many prevention programs that focus only on cognitive decision-making skills, SiHLE also focuses on developing relational skills; building motivation through instilling pride, self-efficacy, perceived value, and importance in the community; and modifying the usual and customary peer influences these teens' experience. The purpose of this intervention is to create an environment that enhances adolescents' likelihood of reducing risky sexual behavior and adopting and sustaining preventative behaviors. Five hundred and twenty-two sexually active African American girls aged 14 to 18 participated, with half randomized to SiHLE and half to a comparison condition. The program consisted of four 1-hour group sessions emphasizing ethnic and gender pride, HIV knowledge, communication, condom-use skills, and healthy relationships. A comparison condition also meeting in groups emphasized exercise and nutrition. Results from this program were very promising (DiClemente et al., 2004, 2008). Girls receiving the SiHLE intervention used condoms more often, had less unprotected sex, had fewer sexual partners, and reduced sexually transmitted infections and unwanted pregnancies at a 1-year follow up than girls in the comparison groups. Some initiatives under way focus on integrating the family as behavioral change agents by working together with counselors to help delay adolescents' first experience with sexual intercourse, limit the number of sexual partners, and support health-promoting behaviors, such as protected sex.

In Africa, where the primary mode of transmission of HIV is heterosexual, a greater focus on the interpersonal and social system of the individual at risk has also begun. One important new initiative is to focus prevention techniques on couples rather than individuals (Grabbe & Bunnell, 2010). This is important, because studies demonstrate that only 22% of adults aged 15 to 49 years know their HIV status in Africa, and condom use within regular partnerships is very low because the assumption is that their partner is "safe" and they are at low risk. Because 55% to 93% of new HIV infections occur within cohabiting relationships, this means that most transmissions occur within couples who are unaware of their HIV status. The successful initiation of couples counseling and testing has occurred in Rwanda, Uganda, and Kenya. Couples counseling for HIV prevention also provides opportunities for delivering and providing more comprehensive maternal and child health services.

Smoking in China

Despite efforts by the government to reduce smoking among its citizens, China has one of the most tobacco-addicted populations in the world. Approximately 320 million people in China are habitual smokers, a number that is greater than the entire population of the United States. About 90% of China's smokers are male. China consumes 33% of all cigarettes in the world, and smoking is projected to kill 100 million Chinese people in the next 50 years (Gu et al., 2009; Lam, Ho, Hedley, Mak, & Peto, 2001; Zhang & Cai, 2003).

Cigarette smoking is a major and modifiable risk factor for many respiratory problems, including small airway dysfunction. Small airways are airways with a luminal diameter of less than 2 mm in the lungs. Initially, obstruction of these airways causes very little change in measurable airway resistance. But when the disease advances, obstruction of the small airways can have severe negative effects on lung function. For example, they can lead to premature airway closure and air trapping. In patients

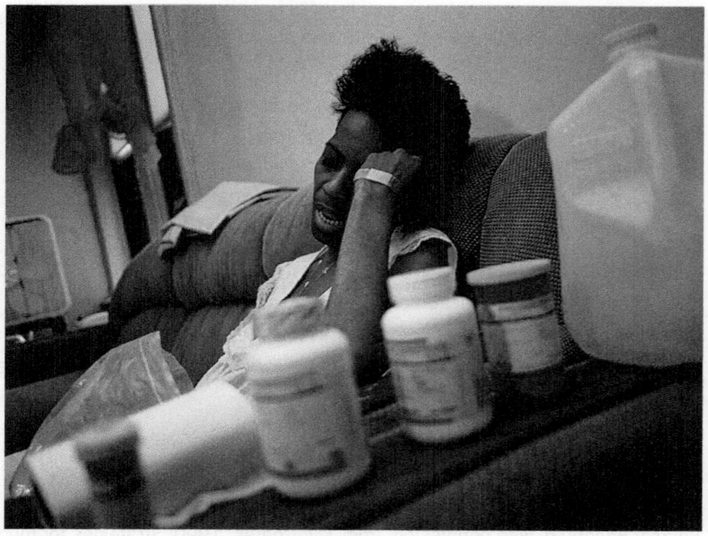
Meryl Levin

Women are increasingly at risk for AIDS.

with chronic obstructive pulmonary disease (COPD), the small airways often show thickening of the airway wall, obstructing the inside airway by mucous and inflammation. The nationally representative China Pulmonary Health Study examined 57,779 adults from 10 provinces and found that the prevalence of small airway dysfunction was 43.5% (Xiao et al., 2020). Xiao and colleagues also found a dose-response association between cigarette smoking and small airway dysfunction among men but not among women.

Unger and colleagues (2001) reported that 47% of Chinese boys in the seventh through ninth grades—but only 16% of girls —had already smoked cigarettes. In one early attempt to reach these individuals, health professionals took advantage of the strong family ties in China and decided to persuade the *children* of smokers to intervene with their fathers. In so doing, they conducted the largest study yet reported of attempted behavior modification to promote health. In 1989, they developed an antismoking campaign in 23 primary schools in Hangzhou, capital of Zhejiang province. Children took home antismoking literature and questionnaires to almost 10,000 fathers. They then wrote letters to their fathers asking them to quit smoking, and they submitted monthly reports on their fathers' smoking habits to the schools. Approximately 9 months later, the results were assessed. Indeed, the children's intervention had some effect. Almost 12% of the fathers in the intervention group had quit smoking for at least 6 months. By contrast, in a control group of another 10,000 males, the quit rate was only 0.2%.

The public health challenge of smoking is evident. Therefore, the Chinese government has become quite involved in smoking prevention efforts. For example, Ma and colleagues (2008) identified several myths that characterize Chinese smokers. These include (1) the identification of smoking as a symbol of personal freedom, (2) a perception that tobacco is important in social and cultural interactions, (3) the perception that the health effects of smoking can be controlled through reasonable and measured use, and (4) the importance of tobacco to the economy. At present, the Chinese government is considering ways to counter these prevailing misconceptions as a prelude to developing more effective preventative programs.

Stanford Three Community Study

One of the best-known and most successful efforts to reduce risk factors for disease in the community is the Stanford Three Community Study (Meyer, Nash, McAlister, Maccoby, & Farquhar, 1980). Although it was conducted several decades ago, it remains a model program. Rather than assemble three groups of people, these investigators studied three entire communities in central California that were reasonably alike in size and type of residents between 1972 and 1975. The target was reduction of risk factors for CHD. The positive behaviors that were introduced focused on smoking, high blood pressure, diet, and weight reduction. In Tracy, the first community, no interventions were conducted, but detailed information was collected from a random sample of adults to assess any increases in their knowledge of risk factors, as well as any changes in risk factors over time. In addition, participants in Tracy received a medical assessment of their cardiovascular factors. The residents of Gilroy and part of Watsonville were subjected to a media blitz on the dangers of behavioral risk factors for CHD, the importance of reducing these factors, and helpful hints for doing so. Most residents of Watsonville, the third community, also had a face-to-face intervention in which behavioral counselors worked with the townspeople judged to be at particularly high risk for CHD. Participants in all three communities were surveyed once a year for a 3-year period following the intervention. Results indicate that the interventions were markedly successful at reducing risk factors for CHD in these communities (see ■ Figure 9.15). Furthermore, for the residents of Watsonville who also received individual counseling, risk factors were substantially lower than for people in Tracy or even for those in Gilroy and people in the part of Watsonville that received only the media blitz, and their knowledge of risk factors was substantially higher.

A similar community-wide study on CHD (Record et al., 2015) was conducted in Franklin County in rural Maine over a period of 40 years (1970 to 2010). Franklin County is a low-income community with fewer than 31,000 inhabitants. Using modest grants and many volunteers, a community-wide program was implemented to reduce hypertension, cholesterol, and smoking and to improve diet and exercise. Compared to other areas of Maine and also compared to the same county 10 years prior to implementing the program, these efforts resulted in fewer hospitalizations and mortality rates over a period of 40 years. These results show that mounting an effort like this is worthwhile to individuals, to the community, and to public health officials because many lives will be saved and disability leave will be decreased to an extent that will more than cover the original cost of the program. Unfortunately, implementation of these types of programs is still not widespread. Perhaps the Affordable Care Act and the expansion of Medicare and Medicaid might bring about a sea change by focusing on preventing rather treating disorders.

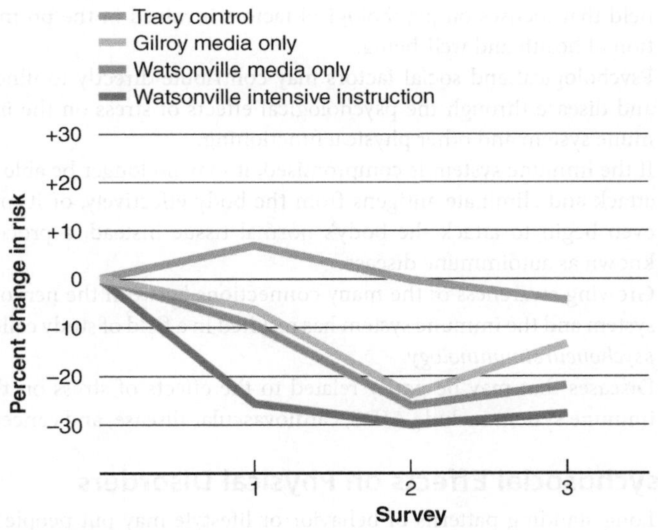

Figure 9.15

Results of the Stanford Three Community Study. Reprinted, with permission, from A. J. Meyer, J. D. Nash, A. L. McAlister, N. Maccoby, & J. W. Farquhar, 1980, Skills training in a cardiovascular health education campaign, *Journal of Consulting and Clinical Psychology, 48*, 129–142. © 1980 American Psychological Association.

Concept Check 9.3

Check your understanding of psychosocial treatment by matching the treatments to the correct scenarios or statements: (a) biofeedback, (b) meditation and relaxation, (c) cognitive coping procedures, (d) denial, (e) modify behaviors to promote health, and (f) Stanford Three Community Study.

1. Gabrielle is often upset by stupid things other people are always doing. Her doctor wants her to realize her exaggeration of these events and suggests ________.
2. Tyrone can't seem to focus on anything at work. He feels too stressed. He needs ________, a way of minimizing intruding thoughts that he can do at work in a short amount of time.
3. Naseem's blood pressure soars when he feels stressed. His doctor showed him how to become aware of his body process to control them better by using ________.
4. At a world conference, leaders met to discuss how to reduce the risk of childhood injuries, AIDS risks, and the number of smoking-related diseases. Professionals suggested programs involving teaching individuals how to ________.
5. Initially, strong ________ can help a patient endure the shock of bad news; however, later it can inhibit or prevent the healing process.
6. The ________ is one of the best-known efforts to reduce community disease risk factors.

Summary

Psychological and Social Factors That Influence Health

- Psychological and social factors play a major role in developing and maintaining a number of physical disorders.
- Two fields of study have emerged as a result of a growing interest in psychological factors contributing to illness. Behavioral medicine involves the application of behavioral science techniques to prevent, diagnose, and treat medical problems. Health psychology is a subfield that focuses on psychological factors involved in the promotion of health and well-being.
- Psychological and social factors may contribute directly to illness and disease through the psychological effects of stress on the immune system and other physical functioning.
- If the immune system is compromised, it may no longer be able to attack and eliminate antigens from the body effectively, or it may even begin to attack the body's normal tissue instead, a process known as autoimmune disease.
- Growing awareness of the many connections between the nervous system and the immune system has resulted in a field of study called *psychoneuroimmunology*.
- Diseases that may be partly related to the effects of stress on the immune system include AIDS, cardiovascular disease, and cancer.

Psychosocial Effects on Physical Disorders

- Long-standing patterns of behavior or lifestyle may put people at risk for developing certain physical disorders. For example, unhealthy sexual practices can lead to AIDS and other sexually transmitted diseases, and unhealthy behavioral patterns—such as poor eating habits, lack of exercise, or type A behavior pattern—may contribute to cardiovascular diseases such as stroke, hypertension, and coronary heart disease.
- Of the 10 leading causes of death in the United States, fully 50% of deaths can be traced to lifestyle behaviors.
- Psychological and social factors also contribute to chronic pain. The brain inhibits pain through naturally occurring endogenous opioids, which may also be implicated in a variety of psychological disorders.
- Chronic fatigue syndrome is a relatively new disorder that is attributed at least partly to stress but may also have an as yet undiscovered viral or immune system dysfunction component.

Psychosocial Treatment of Physical Disorders

- A variety of psychosocial treatments have been developed with the goal of either treating or preventing physical disorders. Among these are biofeedback and the relaxation response.
- Comprehensive stress- and pain-reduction programs include not only relaxation and related techniques but also new methods to encourage effective coping, including stress management, realistic appraisals, and improved attitudes through cognitive therapy.
- Comprehensive programs are generally more effective than individual components delivered singly.
- Other interventions aim to modify such behaviors as unsafe sexual practices, smoking, and unhealthy dietary habits. Such efforts have been made in a variety of areas, including injury control, AIDS prevention, smoking cessation campaigns, and programs to reduce risk factors for diseases such as CHD.

Key Terms

behavioral medicine, 320
health psychology, 320
general adaptation syndrome (GAS), 321
stress, 321
self-efficacy, 324
immune system, 324
antigens, 325
autoimmune disease, 326
rheumatoid arthritis, 326
psychoneuroimmunology (PNI), 326
AIDS-related complex (ARC), 327
cancer, 329
psychoncology, 329
cardiovascular disease, 331
stroke/cerebral vascular accident (CVA), 331
hypertension, 332
essential hypertension, 332
coronary heart disease (CHD), 335
type A behavior pattern, 335
type B behavior pattern, 335
acute pain, 338
chronic pain, 338
endogenous (natural) opioids, 340
chronic fatigue syndrome (CFS), 341
biofeedback, 344
relaxation response, 345

Answers to Concept Checks

9.1

1. d; 2. a; 3. c; 4. b; 5. f; 6. e

9.2

1. c; 2. development; 3. hypertension, coronary heart disease; 4. type A (hard-driving, impatient), type B (relaxed, less concerned); 5. chronic fatigue syndrome

9.3

1. c; 2. b; 3. a; 4. e; 5. d; 6. f

Exploring Physical Disorders and Health Psychology

Psychological and behavioral factors are major contributors to illness and death.

- Behavioral medicine applies behavioral science to medical problems.
- Health psychology focuses on psychological influences on health and improving health care.

PSYCHOLOGICAL AND SOCIAL FACTORS INFLUENCE BIOLOGY

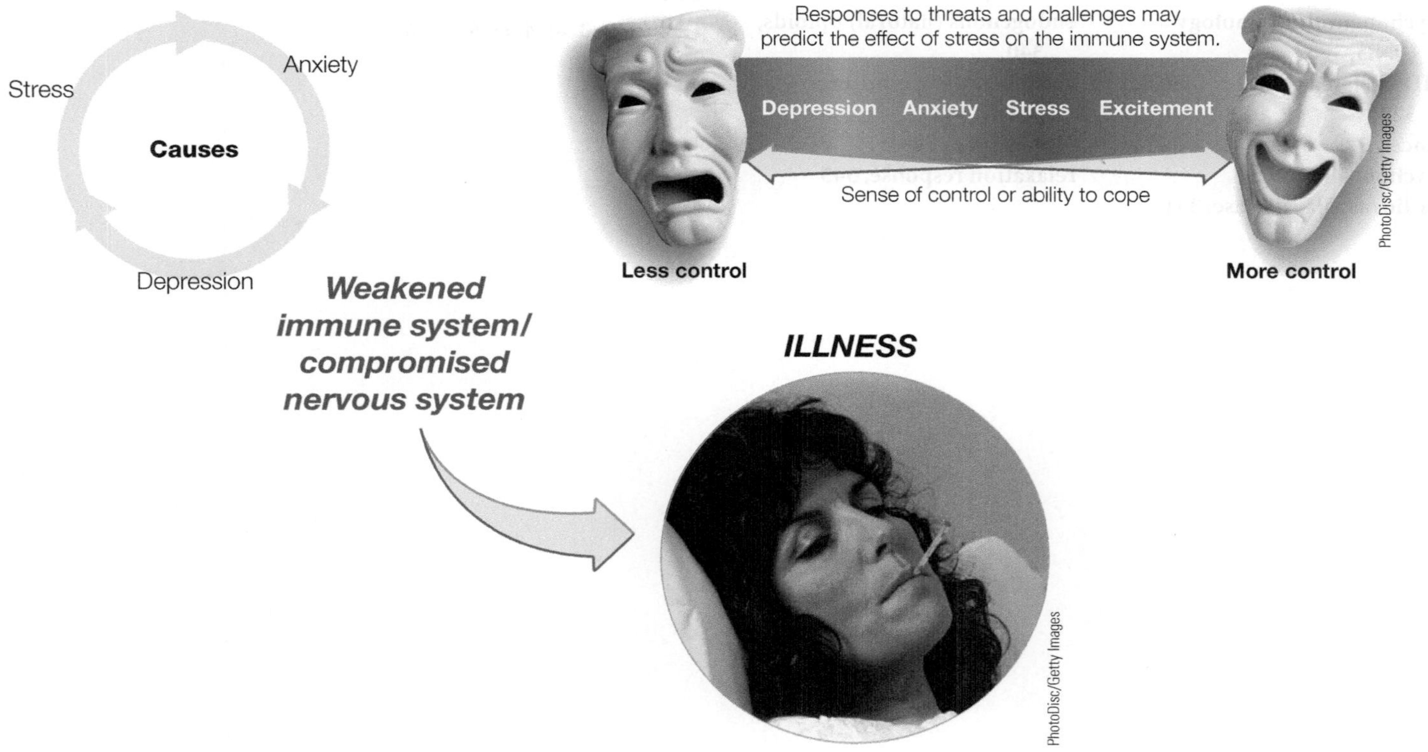

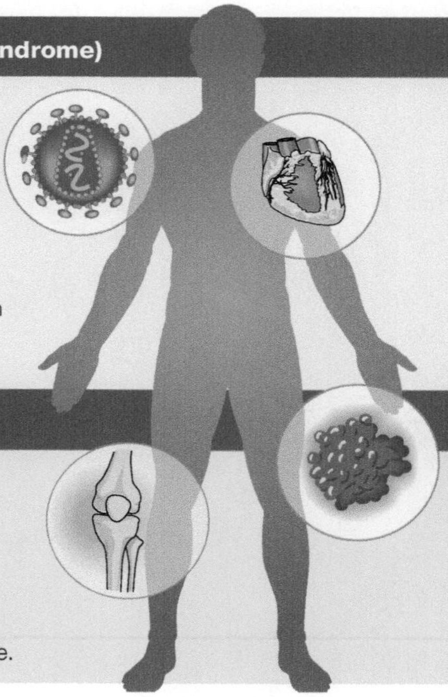

AIDS (Acquired Immune Deficiency Syndrome)

- The human immunodeficiency virus (HIV) attacks the immune system and opportunistic infections develop uncontrollably.
- Psychological treatments focus on strengthening the immune system and gaining a sense of control.
- Although drug therapy may control the virus, there is so far no biological means of prevention and the disease is still always fatal.

Cardiovascular Problems

- The heart and blood vessels can be damaged by
  - *Stroke:* Blockage or rupture of blood vessels in the brain
  - *Hypertension:* Constriction of blood vessels at organs and extremities puts extra pressure on the heart, which eventually weakens
  - *Coronary heart disease:* Blockage of arteries supplying blood to the heart
- Biological, psychological, and social factors contribute to all these conditions and are addressed in treatment.

Chronic Pain

- May begin with an acute episode but does not diminish when injury heals.
- Typically involves joints, muscles, and tendons; may result from enlarged blood vessels, tissue degeneration, or cancerous tumors.
- Psychological and social influences may cause and maintain chronic pain to a significant degree.

Cancer

- Abnormal cell growth produces malignant tumors.
- Psychosocial treatments may prolong life, alleviate symptoms, and reduce depression and pain.
- Different cancers have different rates of recovery and mortality.
- Psychoncology is the study of psychosocial factors involved in the course and treatment of cancer.

PSYCHOSOCIAL TREATMENTS FOR PHYSICAL DISORDERS

The stress reaction associated with pain may reduce the number of natural killer cells in the immune system.

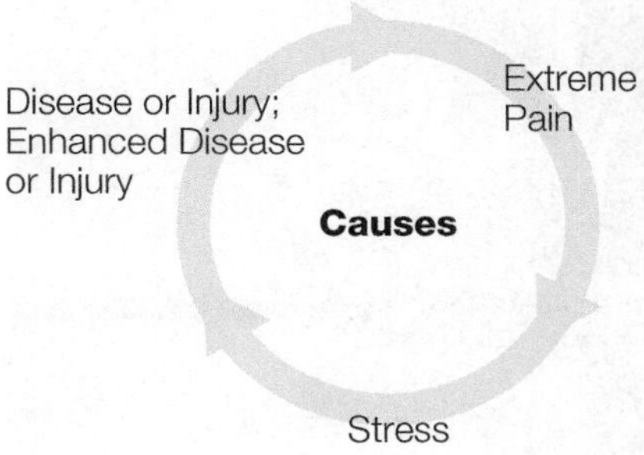

Biofeedback

- Electronic monitors make physiological responses such as heartbeat visible on a computer screen.
- Patient learns to increase or decrease the response, thereby improving functioning (decreasing tension).
  - Developing a sense of control may be therapeutic.

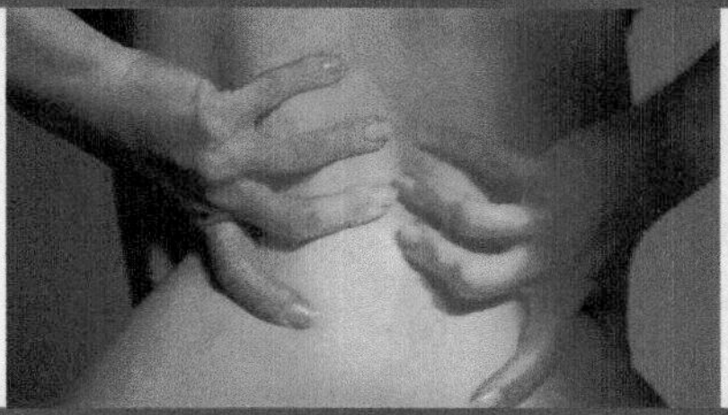
PhotoDisc/Getty Images

Relaxation and Meditation

- ***Progressive muscle relaxation:*** Person learns to locate physical tension and to counteract it by relaxing a specific muscle group.
- ***Meditation:*** Focusing attention on a specific body part or process or on an affirming thought or image; in some forms, focusing on a single silently repeated syllable (mantra) "empties" the mind. Meditation is accompanied by slow, regular breathing.
  - Meditating daily for at least 10 to 20 minutes imparts calm and relaxation by reducing certain neurotransmitters and stress hormones and increasing a sense of control.

PhotoDisc/Getty Images

BEHAVIOR MODIFICATION TO PROMOTE HEALTH

Many injuries and diseases can be prevented or controlled through lifestyle changes involving diet, substance use, exercise, and safety precautions.

Injury Control

- Injuries are the leading cause of death for people age 1 to 45, especially children.
- Most people consider injuries to be out of their control and therefore do not change high-risk behaviors.
- In children, prevention focuses on
  - escaping fires
  - crossing streets
  - using car seats, seat belts, and bicycle helmets
  - first aid

PhotoDisc/Getty Images

AIDS Prevention

- Changing high-risk behavior through individual and community education is the only effective strategy.
  - Eliminate unsafe sexual practices through cognitive-behavioral self-management training and social support networks.
  - Show drug abusers how to clean needles and make safe injections.
- Target minorities and women, groups that do not perceive themselves to be at risk.
  - Media coverage focuses on gay white males.
  - More women are infected through heterosexual interactions than through intravenous drug use.

PhotoDisc/Getty Images

10 Sexual Dysfunctions, Paraphilic Disorders, and Gender Dysphoria

Elke Selzle/Photographer's Choice RF/Getty Images

Learning Objectives

LO10.1 Define sexual dysfunctions according to their key criteria in the DSM-5.

LO10.2 Identify typical sexual behaviors that are not considered disorders by the DSM-5.

LO10.3 Explain how gender dysphoria differs from sexual disorders.

LO10.4 Distinguish between disorders of sexual desire, disorders of sexual arousal, and orgasmic disorders.

LO10.5 List the three components of sexual behavior assessments.

LO10.6 Identify the causes of sexual dysfunction and recommended treatments.

LO10.7 Discuss the root causes and various types of paraphilic disorders, including how they differ from sexual disorders.

LO10.8 Describe the psychological and medical treatment approaches available to individuals with gender dysphoria.

What Is "Normal" Sexuality?

You may have read magazine or online surveys reporting sensational information on sexual practices. According to one, men can reach orgasm 15 or more times a day (in reality, such ability is rare), and women fantasize about being raped. (Women do have idealized fantasies of submission in the context of being desired, but these fantasies are far from imagining an actual rape [Critelli & Bivona, 2008].) Surveys like this fail us on two counts: First, they claim to reveal sexual norms, but they are actually reporting mostly distorted half-truths. Second, the facts they present typically are not based on any scientific methodology that would make them reliable, although they do sell magazines.

What is normal sexual behavior? As you will see, it depends. More to the point, when is sexual behavior that is somewhat different from the norm a disorder? Again, it depends. Current views tend to be quite tolerant of a variety of sexual expressions, even if they are unusual, unless the behavior is associated with a substantial impairment in functioning or involves nonconsenting individuals such as children. Two kinds of sexual behavior meet this definition. Individuals with *sexual dysfunction* find it difficult to function adequately while having sex; for example, they may not become aroused or achieve orgasm. In *paraphilic* disorders, the relatively new term for sexual deviation, sexual arousal occurs primarily in the context of inappropriate objects or individuals. *Philia* refers to a strong attraction or liking, and *para* indicates the attraction is abnormal. Paraphilic arousal patterns tend to be focused rather narrowly, often precluding mutually consenting adult partners, even if desired. In actuality, paraphilic disorders have little to do with sexual dysfunctions except for the fact that they both involve sexual behavior. For this reason, paraphilic disorders now comprise a separate category of disorders in DSM-5. Another condition that has been separated from sexual disorders altogether is *gender dysphoria*. In gender dysphoria, there is incongruence and psychological distress and dissatisfaction with the gender one has been assigned at birth (boy or girl). The disorder is not sexual but rather a disturbance in the person's sense of gender identity. Before describing these three conditions, we return to our initial question ("What is normal sexual behavior?") to gain an important perspective, particularly on sexual dysfunctions and paraphilic disorders. We spend a bit more time on what is "normal" in this chapter compared to other chapters since so many misconceptions exist.

Determining the prevalence of sexual practices accurately requires careful surveys that randomly sample the population. In the United States, one such survey is the *National Survey of Sexual Health and Behavior* by Indiana University Bloomington (https://nationalsexstudy.indiana.edu/), and another is the *National Survey of Family Growth* by the *Centers for Disease Control and Prevention (CDC)* (https://www.cdc.gov/nchs/nsfg/). These surveys are often repeated, and the data are updated frequently on these websites or published elsewhere (Copen, Chandra, & Febo-Vazquez, 2016). Copen and colleagues reported data from 9,175 men and women in the United States ages 18 to 44. The participants were interviewed, which is more reliable than having them fill out a questionnaire, and the responses were analyzed in detail. Virtually all men and women in this study were sexually experienced, with vaginal intercourse being a nearly universal experience. When asked about their sexual orientation, 92.3% of women and 95.1% of men said they were "heterosexual or straight"; 1.3% of women and 1.9% of men reported that they were "homosexual, gay, or lesbian"; 5.5% of women and 2.0% of men reported that they were bisexual; and 0.9% of women and 1.0% of men said that didn't know or chose not to give an answer. Among those who had experienced **heterosexual behavior** (had sex with members of the opposite gender), the vast majority (94.2% of women and 92.0% of men) reported that they have had vaginal intercourse, and 86.2% of women and 87.4% of men had ever had oral sex; whereas only 35.9% of women and 42.3% of men ever had anal sex. More women (17.4%) than men (6.2%) reported experiencing **same-sex sexual behavior** (had sex with members of the same gender) in their lifetime. Feelings of attraction "only to the opposite sex" were more common for men (92.1%) compared with women (81.0%). **Nonbinary** refers to a spectrum of gender identities that are neither female or male. There is a general trend in society to see gender identity as a dimensional rather than a categorical variable.

Sexual behaviors are strongly influenced by social, generational, cultural, regional, religious, and economic factors. A review of surveys between 1996 and 2006 from 59 countries showed a large diversity in sexual behaviors by region and sex (Wellings et al., 2006). Women reported their first intercourse at much younger ages in regions in which early marriage is the norm (for example, in South Asia and in Central, West, and East Africa) and at later ages in Latin America and in some countries of the Middle East and Southeast Asia. Interestingly, for men, their first intercourse was in general not linked to age at marriage. In most African and Asian countries, men started to have sex later than women. The gender differences were most pronounced in less industrialized countries. There was a general shift over the years toward later marriage in most countries, which led to an increase in premarital sex. Monogamy was dominant across the globe. At the same time, having had two or more sexual partners in the past year was more common in men than in women and higher in industrialized than in nonindustrialized countries. Condom use became more common over the years almost everywhere but was less common in developing countries. An international survey of studies from 2000 to 2020 showed that over the years the number of women who were sexually active increased and that they also were more open to modern contraceptives (Slaymaker et al., 2020). This increase correlated with increases in gender equality and with women's time in education.

One study from Britain (Johnson, Wadsworth, Wellings, Bradshaw, & Field, 1992) and one from France (Spira et al., 1992) surveyed sexual behavior and practices among more than 20,000 men and women in each country. The results were surprisingly similar to those reported for U.S. men. More than 70% of the respondents from all age groups in the British and French studies reported no more than one sexual partner during the past year. Women were somewhat more likely than men to have had fewer than two partners. Only 4.1% of French men and 3.6% of British men reported ever having had a male sexual partner, and this figure drops to 1.5% for British men if we consider only the past 5 years. Almost certainly, the percentage of men having exclusively sex with men would be considerably lower. The consistency of these data across three countries suggests strongly that the results represent something close to the norm, at least for Western countries. This has been confirmed in similar surveys (Mosher et al., 2005; Norris, Marcus, & Green, 2015). An update of the British survey (Johnson et al., 2001) indicates a small increase in number of partners over 5 years but also an increase in condom use. Still, more than 53% of males and 62% of females of all ages reported no more than one sexual partner over the past 5 years. Also interesting is that sexual practices and the determinants of sexual satisfaction are now remarkably similar around the world, as recently demonstrated in a large survey of Chinese urban adults (Garcia, Kincannon, Poston, & Walther, 2014).

The generational influence was evident in a nationally representative U.S. sample with 33,380 participants (Twenger, Sherman, & Wells, 2015). This survey found that adults from 2000 to 2012 (versus the 1970s and 1980s) had more sexual partners, were more likely to have had sex with a casual date or pickup or an acquaintance, and were more accepting of most nonmarital sex (premarital sex, teen sex, and same-sex sexual activity but not extramarital sex). The percentage who believed nonmarital sex among adults was "not wrong at all" was 29% in the early 1970s, 42% in the 1980s and 1990s, 49% in the 2000s, and 58% between 2010 and 2012. Separating this by generations, this means that acceptance of nonmarital sex rose steadily between the G.I. generation (born 1901–1924) and Baby Boomers (born 1946–1964), dipped slightly among early Generation Xers (born 1965–1981), and then rose again. Millennials (also known as Generation Y or Generation Me, born 1982–1999) were the most accepting of nonmarital sex. Number of sexual partners increased steadily between the G.I.s and 1960s-born Gen Xers and then dipped among Millennials to return to Boomer levels. The largest changes appeared among White men, with few changes among Black Americans. No large-scale surveys have been done yet of Generation Z (born after 1996) and Generation Alpha (born since 2010).

Another interesting set of data counters the many views we have of sexuality among older adults. Sexual behavior can continue well into old age, even past 80 for some people. Table 10.1 presents the percentage by age group of older individuals in a community sample who were sexually active and continuing to have sexual intercourse (Lindau et al., 2007). Notably, 38.5% of men and 16.7% of women aged 75 to 85 were sexually active. Reasons for the discrepancy between men and women are not clear, although given the earlier mortality of men, many older

Ryuhei Shindo/Fancy/PhotoLibrary/Getty Images

Sexual behavior often continues well into old age.

Table 10.1 Prevalence of Sexual Activity on Older Adults Classified by Age and Sex

	Sexual activity with a partner			
	In previous 12 months		≥2–3 times per month[a]	
Age	Men (%)	Women (%)	Men (%)	Women (%)
57–64	83.7	61.6	67.5	62.6
65–74	67.0	39.5	65.4	65.4
75–85	38.5	16.7	54.2	54.1

[a]Respondents were asked about this activity or behavior if they reported having sex in the previous 12 months.

Source: From S. T. Lindau, L. P. Schumm, E. O. Laumann, W. Levinson, C. A. O'Muircheartaigh, & L. J. Waite, A study of sexuality and health among older adults in the United States, *New England Journal of Medicine*, *357*(8), 762–774. Copyright © 2007 Massachusetts Medical Society. Reprinted with permission from Massachusetts Medical Society.

women lack a suitable partner; it is also possible that some women are married to men in an older age bracket. Many older women also indicated that sex was "not at all important" and generally reported less interest in sex than their male counterparts. Decreases in sexual activity are mostly correlated with decreases in general mobility and various disease processes and consequent medication, which may reduce arousal. Furthermore, the speed and intensity of various vasocongestive responses decrease with age. A large study of older individuals around the world, aged 40 to 80, found men were generally more satisfied with their sexuality than women, particularly in non-Western countries, and that good physical and mental health, as well as a good relationship with a partner, were the best predictors of sexual well-being (Laumann et al., 2006).

Gender Differences

Although both men and women tend toward a monogamous (one partner) pattern of sexual relationships, gender differences in sexual behavior do exist, and some of them are quite dramatic. Petersen and Hyde (2010) reported a sophisticated analysis summarizing results from hundreds of studies examining gender differences in sexual attitudes and behaviors. Their findings will be reviewed in the following paragraphs. One common finding among sexual surveys is a much higher percentage of men than women report that they masturbate (self-stimulate to orgasm) (Oliver & Hyde, 1993; Peplau, 2003; Petersen & Hyde, 2010). When Richters and colleagues (2014) surveyed Australian adults, they also found this discrepancy (72% of men versus only 42% of women reported masturbating in the past year).

Why women masturbate less frequently than men puzzles sex researchers, particularly when other long-standing gender differences in sexual behavior, such as the probability of engaging in premarital intercourse, have virtually disappeared (Clement, 1990; Petersen & Hyde, 2010). One traditional view accounting for differences in masturbatory behavior is that women have been taught to associate sex with romance and emotional intimacy, whereas men are more interested in physical gratification. But the discrepancy continues despite decreases in gender-specific attitudes toward sexuality.

Another continuing gender difference is reflected in the incidence of casual sex, attitudes toward casual premarital sex, and pornography use, with men expressing more permissive attitudes and behaviors than women (for example, England & Bearak, 2014). The most current term for casual sex, particularly among college students, is "hooking up," which refers specifically to a range of physically intimate behaviors outside of a committed relationship (Owen, Rhoades, Stanley, & Fincham, 2010). Studies of "hooking up" demonstrate similar findings to older studies of casual sex, in that it is often precipitated by alcohol, and women are less likely to consider it a positive experience than men (Olmstead, Pasley, & Fincham, 2013; Strokoff, Owen, & Fincham, 2014). For example, Owen & Fincham (2011) found that greater alcohol use leads to greater engagement in "friends with benefits" relationships (a particular type of "hooking up" that involves an ongoing nonromantic relationship), and this was especially true for women. Interestingly, even when women deliberately engage in casual sex, having a greater number of partners is associated with greater worry and vulnerability on the part of the woman, while the opposite was true for men (Furman & Collibee, 2014; Townsend & Wasserman, 2011). It is then not surprising that, despite the high prevalence of hooking up, with 40% of the female students engaging in it during their first year at college in one study, sex within a romantic relationship was still twice as common as "hook-up" sex for young women (Fielder, Carey, & Carey, 2013). However, longitudinal studies show no association between the number of sex partners and later anxiety or depression, although there is an association with increased risk for substance abuse (Ramrakha et al., 2013).

By contrast, results from a large number of studies suggest that *no* gender differences are currently apparent in attitudes about same-sex sexual behaviors (generally acceptable), the experience of sexual satisfaction (important for both), or attitudes toward masturbation (generally accepting). Small to moderate gender differences were evident in attitudes toward premarital intercourse when the couple was engaged or in a committed relationship (with men more approving than women) and in attitudes toward extramarital sex (sex outside of the marital relationship, which men also approved of more than women). As in the British and French studies, the number of sexual partners and the frequency of intercourse were slightly greater for men, and men were slightly younger at age of first sexual intercourse. Examining trends from 1943 to 1999, we find that almost all existing gender differences became smaller over time, especially in regard to attitudes toward premarital sex. Specifically, only 12% of young women approved of premarital sex in 1943, compared with 73% in 1999. The figures for men were 40% in 1943 and 79% in 1999 (Wells & Twenge, 2005). In the late 1990s and after 2000, investigators have noted a *decrease* in number of sexual partners and a tendency to delay sexual intercourse among adolescent boys, perhaps due to a fear of AIDS and other sexually transmitted diseases. Few changes over this time period were noted for adolescent girls (Petersen & Hyde, 2010).

Although they are decreasing, differences still exist between men and women in sexual behavior and attitudes toward sexuality (Peplau, 2003; Petersen & Hyde, 2010). For example, differences seem to exist in patterns of sexual arousal (Chivers, Rieger, Latty, & Bailey, 2004; Samson & Janssen, 2014). On average, men are more specific and narrow in their patterns of arousal. That is, heterosexual men are aroused by female sexual stimuli but not male sexual stimuli. For gay men, it's the opposite. Trans women with gender dysphoria who were assigned male at birth (discussed later) who had gender-affirming surgery retained this specificity (attracted to men but not women). Trans men with gender dysphoria (assigned female at birth), on the other hand, whether they were attracted to the opposite sex or lesbian, experience arousal to both male and female sexual stimuli, demonstrating a broader, more general pattern of arousal. It is important to note, however, that there is a large degree of variation among people in what they find sexually arousing.

In an impressive series of studies, Barbara Andersen and her colleagues have assessed gender differences in basic or core beliefs about sexual aspects of one's self. These core beliefs about sexuality are referred to as "sexual self-schemas." Specifically, in a series of studies (Andersen & Cyranowski, 1994; Andersen, Cyranowski, & Espindle, 1999; Cyranowski, Aarestad, & Andersen, 1999), Andersen and colleagues demonstrated that women tend to report the experience of passionate and romantic feelings as an integral part of their sexuality, as well as an openness to sexual experience. A substantial number of women, however, also hold an embarrassed, conservative, or self-conscious schema that sometimes conflicts with more positive aspects of their sexual attitudes. Men, on the other hand, evidence a strong component of feeling powerful, independent, and aggressive as part of their sexuality, in addition to being passionate, loving, and open to experience. Also, men do not generally possess negative core beliefs reflecting self-consciousness, embarrassment, or feeling behaviorally inhibited. Peplau (2003) summarizes research to date on gender differences in human sexuality as highlighting four themes: (1) men show more sexual desire and arousal than women; (2) women emphasize committed relationships as a context for sex more than men; (3) men's sexual self-concept, unlike women's, is characterized partly by power, independence, and aggression; and (4) women's sexual beliefs are more "plastic" in that they are more easily shaped by cultural, social, and situational factors. For example, women are more likely to change sexual orientation over time (Diamond, 2007; Diamond et al., 2011; Mock & Eibach, 2012) or may be more variable in frequency of sex, alternating periods of high frequency with low frequency if a sexual partner leaves.

In addition to gender differences in sexual behavior, it also seems that there are differences in sexual behavior based on sexual orientation. For example, in one study using U.S. college students (Oswalt & Wyatt, 2013), researchers found that men who identified "unsure" had more partners than those who identified as gay, bisexual, or heterosexual and that heterosexual men had fewer partners than gay men, bisexual men, and men who described themselves as "unsure" about their sexual orientation. On the other hand, women who identified as bisexual had more partners than women who identified with other orientations.

In most industrialized Western societies, sexes have been drawing together in their attitudes and behavior, although some differences in attitudes, core beliefs, and behavior remain. Regardless, the overwhelming majority of individuals engage in heterosexual sexual behavior, such as vaginal intercourse in the context of a relationship with one partner.

Cultural Differences

What is normal in Western countries may not necessarily be normal in other parts of the world (McGoldrick, Loonan, & Wohlsifer, 2007). The Sambia in Papua New Guinea believe semen is an essential substance for growth and development in young boys of the tribe. They also believe semen is *not* produced naturally; that is, the body is incapable of producing it spontaneously. Therefore, all young boys in the tribe, beginning at approximately age 7, become semen recipients by engaging exclusively in oral sex with teenage boys. Only oral sexual practices are permitted; masturbation is forbidden and absent. Early in adolescence, the boys switch roles and become semen providers to younger boys. Heterosexual relations and even contact with the opposite sex are prohibited until the boys become teenagers. Late in adolescence, the boys are expected to marry and begin exclusive heterosexual activity. And they do, with no exceptions (Herdt, 1987; Herdt & Stoller, 1989). By contrast, the Munda of northeast India require adolescents and children to live together. But in this group, both male and female children live in the same setting, and the sexual activity, consisting mostly of petting and mutual masturbation, is all heterosexual in nature (Bancroft, 1989).

John Bancroft was one of the first researchers to describe the interaction of biology and psychology as determinants of sexual behavior.

Even within Western cultures, there are some variations (Herlitz & Forsberg, 2010; Weinberg, Lottes, & Shaver, 1995) (see Table 10.2). In about half of more than 100 societies surveyed worldwide, premarital sexual behavior is culturally accepted and encouraged; in the remaining half, premarital sex is unacceptable and discouraged (Bancroft, 1989; Broude & Greene, 1980). In terms of sex in midlife, both in the context of a marriage and not, there are also different attitudes toward and engagement in sexual behavior, even among Americans. For example, a large survey of multiethnic middle-aged women in the United States found that Chinese and Japanese women were less likely than White women to report sex as very important, while African American women were more likely to do so (Cain et al., 2003). Moreover, of those who had sex in the past 6 months, Hispanic women were less likely to cite "for pleasure" as their reason for doing so compared with other ethnic groups. In a follow-up study, the same women were examined again when they were shortly before or during the early stage of menopause (early perimenopause). African American women reported more often sexual intercourse than

Table 10.2 Group Differences between U.S. and Swedish Female Undergraduates Regarding Premarital Sex

Variable	United States Mean (SD)	Sweden Mean (SD)
Age at first coitus	16.97 (1.83)	16.80 (1.92)
Age of first coital partner	18.77 (2.88)	19.10 (2.96)
Perceived age of social acceptance for *females* to engage in premarital coitus	18.76 (2.57)	15.88 (1.43)
Perceived age of social acceptance for *males* to engage in premarital coitus	16.33 (2.13)	15.58 (1.20)

Source: Reprinted, with permission, from I. M. Schwartz, 1993 Affective reactions of American and Swedish women to their first premarital coitus: A cross-cultural comparison, *Journal of Sex Research, 30*(1), 18–26. © 1993 Society for the Scientific Study of Sex.

White women, and Hispanic women reported again less physical pleasure and arousal. Chinese women reported more pain and less desire and arousal than the White women (Avis et al., 2018). Thus, what is normal sexual behavior in one culture is not necessarily normal in another, even among cultures in the same country, and the range of sexual expression must be considered in diagnosing the presence of a disorder.

The Development of Sexual Orientation

In studying the development of sexual orientation, the emphasis is on the breadth and variety of sexual arousal patterns within otherwise normal and adaptive sexual expression. This was not always the case. Until the 1970s, many forms of sexual expression, including same-sex sexual behaviors, were considered pathological, and individuals received treatment for it, such as "conversion therapy" (an attempt to convert a person's sexual orientation from same-sex sexual to heterosexual). But after "homosexuality" was eliminated as a diagnosis from the DSM, based on scientific studies and motivated by the gay and human rights movement in the 1960s and 1970s, the situation changed considerably in many democratic societies. However, there are still many countries in the world that discriminate against or even punish same-sex sexual orientation.

Many factors influence sexual orientation. Some reports suggest that sexual orientation is mediated by early actions of sex steroids, the direct actions of sex-specific genes, and epigenetic mechanisms (Balthazart, 2020). In two twin studies, same-sex sexual orientation was shared in approximately 50% of identical twins, compared with 16% to 22% of fraternal twins. Approximately the same or a slightly lower percentage of nontwin brothers or sisters were gay (Bailey & Pillard, 1991; Bailey, Pillard, Neale, & Agyei, 1993; Whitnam, Diamond, & Martin, 1993). Other studies on the causes of same-sex sexual behavior reveal that genes account for approximately 34% to 39% of the cause in men and 18% to 19% of the cause in women, with the remainder accounted for by environmental influences (Långström, Rahman, Carlström, & Lichtenstein, 2010). Unfortunately, these and other twin and family studies were relatively small for genetic analyses, limiting the validity of the findings. A large, genome-wide association study (GWAS) on 477,522 individuals revealed five gene loci that were significantly associated with same-sex sexual behavior. Together, these genetic variants accounted for 8% to 25% of variation in same-sex sexual behavior. This means that there is some genetic basis but it is not overly strong. The results further showed that there is no single dimension from heterosexual to same-sex sexual preference (that is, a person can have both same-sex sexual *and* heterosexual orientation) and these variants did not reliably predict an individual's sexual behavior, pointing to the complexity of human sexuality (Ganna et al., 2019).

Interestingly, some of the identified genetic loci are linked to hormone regulation, which is also associated with a higher rate of male pattern balding. Remember from Chapter 2 that environmental influences might include unique biological experiences—for example, differential hormone exposure in utero (before birth). Other reports indicate that same-sex sexual orientation and also gender-atypical behavior during childhood is associated with differential exposure to hormones, particularly androgen levels in utero (Auyeng et al., 2009; Ehrhardt et al., 1985; Gladue, Green, & Hellman, 1984; Hershberger & Segal, 2004) and that the actual structure of the brain might be different in individuals with same-sex sexual as compared with heterosexual arousal patterns (Allen & Gorski, 1992; Byne et al., 2000; LeVay, 1991).

Several findings lend some support to the theory of differential hormone exposure in utero. One is the observation that individuals with same-sex sexual orientation have a 39% greater chance of being non–right-handed (left-handed or mixed-handed) than those with heterosexual orientation (Lalumière, Blanchard, & Zucker, 2000), although these findings were not replicated in a later study (Mustanski, Bailey, & Kaspar, 2002). There is also the finding that gay/bisexual men are significantly shorter and lighter than heterosexual men, though no differences were found for women (Bogart, 2010). Another is the intriguing findings that heterosexual men and masculine lesbians tend to have a longer fourth ("ring") finger than index (second) finger but that heterosexual females and gay males show less of a difference or even have a longer index finger than fourth finger (Brown, Finn, Cooke, & Breedlove, 2002; Hall & Love, 2003), although this finding seems to be influenced by ethnic group membership (Loehlin, McFadden, Medland, & Martin, 2006; McFadden et al., 2005). All of these findings point to biological correlates of sexual orientation.

Do such arguments over biological causes sound familiar? Think back to studies described in Chapter 2 that attempted to link complex behavior to particular genes. In almost every case, these studies could not be replicated, and investigators fell back on a model in which genetic contributions to behavioral traits and psychological disorders come from many genes, each making a relatively small contribution. The large GWAS study described earlier supports this notion (Ganna et al., 2019). We also discussed reciprocal gene–environment interactions in which certain learning experiences and environmental events may affect a person's biology and genetic expression. Most theoretical models outlining these complex interactions for sexual orientation imply that there may be many pathways to the development of sexual orientation and that no one factor—biological or psychological—can predict the outcome (Bancroft, 1994; Brakefield et al., 2014; Byne & Parsons, 1993). One of the more intriguing findings from the twin studies of Bailey and his colleagues is that approximately 50% of the identical twins with exactly the same genetic structure, as well as the same environment (growing up in the same house), *did not* have the same sexual orientation (Bailey & Pillard, 1991). Also intriguing is the finding in a study of 302 gay males that those growing up with older brothers are more likely to be gay, whereas having older sisters, or younger brothers or sisters, is not correlated with later sexual orientation. This study found that each additional older brother increased the odds of being gay by one third. This effect is fairly robust, as shown by a meta-analytic review (Blanchard, 2018). This "fraternal birth order hypothesis" could be due to environmental influences (Blanchard, 2008; Blanchard & Bogaert, 1996, 1998; Cantor, Blanchard, Paterson, & Bogaert, 2002). Other research has implicated the importance of the mother's immunological response to Y-linked proteins (a substance important in male fetal development) as a potential explanation for this finding (Bogaert & Skorska, 2011). Finally, some genetic research has found that epigenetic effects (chemical modifications of the genome without changing the actual DNA sequence) may influence sexual orientation (Balter, 2015). This would be consistent with emerging findings in other areas of development as reviewed in Chapter 2.

It is likely, too, that sexual orientation is malleable or changeable over time, at least for some people (Mock & Eibach, 2012). Lisa Diamond has studied women over time (longitudinal studies) and discovered that interpersonal and situational factors exert a substantial influence on women's patterns of sexual behavior and sexual identities, a finding much less true for men (Diamond, 2007, 2012; Diamond et al., 2011). Among women who initially identified themselves as "heterosexual," lesbian, bisexual, or "unlabeled," after 10 years more than two thirds of women had changed their self-reported sexual orientation a few times. This has been referred to as *sexual fluidity* (Diamond et al., 2020). When women changed their sexual orientation, they typically broadened rather than narrowed their potential range of attractions and relationships.

Why is this true for women but not so much for men? Researchers don't know for certain, but these innovative longitudinal studies have already taught us a lot about the origins of sexual orientation.

In any case, the belief that sexual orientation is determined by a gene may continue to appeal to some segments of the general population. Neither explanation is likely to be proved correct. Almost certainly, biology sets certain limits within which social and psychological factors affect development. Scientists will ultimately pin down biological contributions to the formation of sexual orientation and the environment and experience will be found to powerfully influence how these patterns of potential sexual arousal develop (Diamond, 1995; Diamond et al., 2011; Långström et al., 2010).

An Overview of Sexual Dysfunctions

Before we describe **sexual dysfunction**, it's important to note that the problems that arise in the context of sexual interactions may occur in all relationships regardless of sexual orientation. Inability to become aroused or reach orgasm seems to be as common in all relationships, including gay and lesbian couples, but we discuss them in the context of heterosexual relationships, which are the majority of cases we see in clinics. Of the different stages in the sexual response cycle, three of them—desire, arousal, and orgasm (see ■ Figure 10.1)—are each associated with specific sexual dysfunctions. In addition, pain can become associated with sexual functioning in women, which leads to an additional dysfunction.

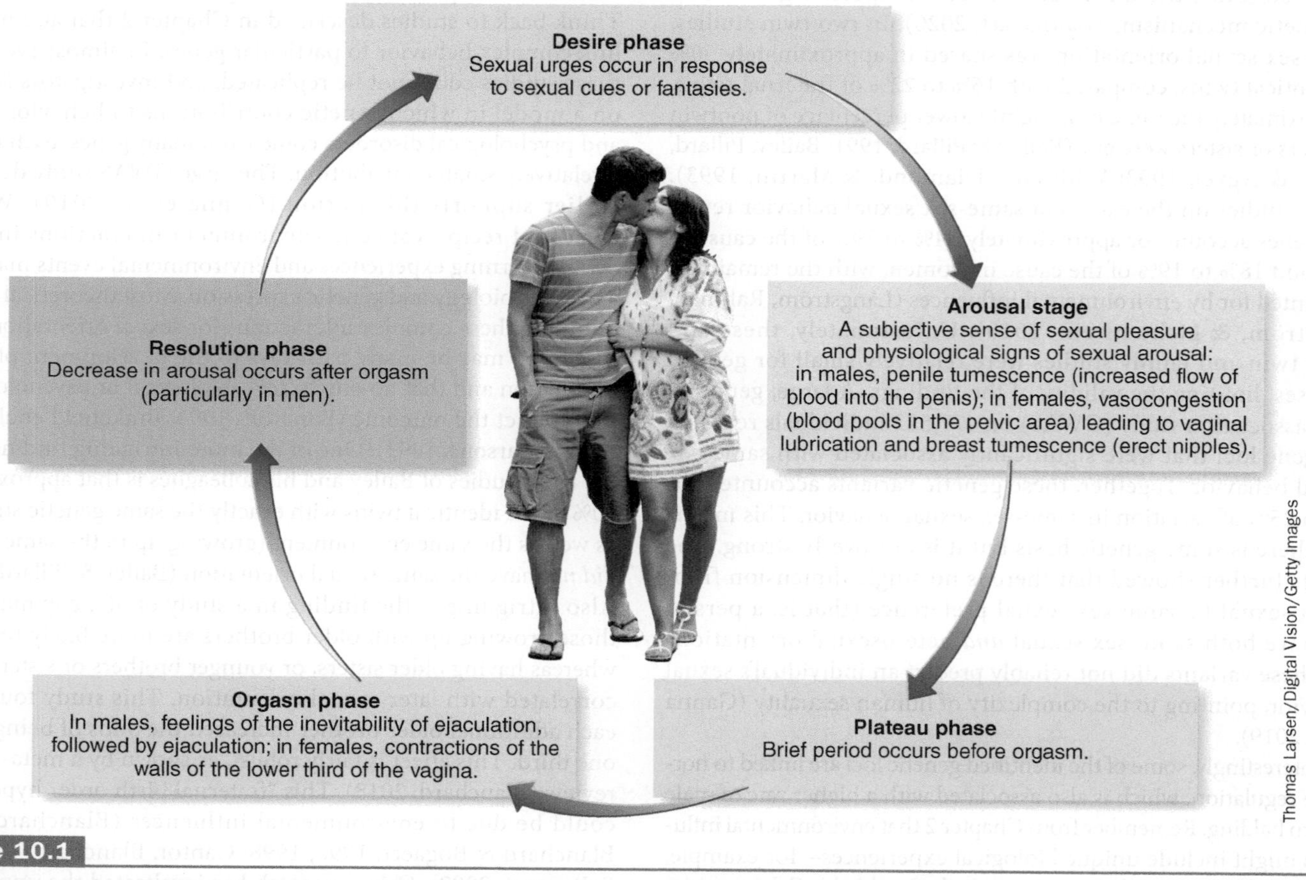

Figure 10.1

The human sexual response cycle. Based on H. S. Kaplan, 1979, *Disorders of sexual desire*, Brunner/Mazel; and W. H. Masters & V. E. Johnson, 1966, *Human sexual response*, Little, Brown.

An overview of the DSM-5 categories of the sexual dysfunctions we examine is provided in Table 10.3. As you can see, both males and females can experience parallel versions of most disorders, which take on specific forms determined by anatomy and other gender-specific characteristics. However, two disorders are sex specific: Premature (early) ejaculation occurs only in males, and genito-pelvic pain/penetration disorder (which includes difficulties with penetration during intercourse due in many cases to painful contractions or spasms of the vagina) appears only in females. Sexual dysfunctions can be either lifelong or acquired. *Lifelong* refers to a chronic condition that is present during a person's entire sexual life; *acquired* refers to a disorder that begins after sexual activity has been relatively normal. In addition, disorders can either be *generalized*, occurring every time the individual attempts sex, or they can be *situational*, occurring with some partners or at certain times but not with other partners or at other times. Before we describe the prevalence of specific sexual dysfunctions, we should note that many couples are in happy and satisfying sexual relations despite experiencing sexual problems, but these dysfunctions do not detract from their overall sexual satisfaction. In one study, only 45% of women experiencing difficulties with orgasm reported the issue as problematic (Fugl-Meyer & Sjogren Fugl-Meyer, 1999). Bancroft, Loftus, and Long (2003) extended this analysis in a survey of close to 1,000 women in the United States involved in a heterosexual relationship for at least 6 months. The interesting results indicate that, although 44.3% met objective criteria for one of the disorders in Table 10.3, only 24.4% of these individuals were distressed about it. Many of these women just did not consider the issue to be a problem. Indeed, the best predictor of sexual distress among these women were deficits in general emotional well-being or emotional relationships with the partner during sexual relations, not lack of lubrication or orgasm. These studies indicate that sexual satisfaction and occasional sexual dysfunction are not mutually exclusive categories (Bradford & Meston, 2011; Graham, 2010). In the context of a healthy relationship, occasional or partial sexual dysfunctions are easily accommodated. But this does raise problems for diagnosing sexual dysfunctions. Should a sexual problem be identified as a diagnosis when dysfunction is clearly present but the person is not distressed about it (Balon, Segraves, & Clayton, 2007; Zucker, 2010)? In DSM-5, the symptoms must clearly cause clinically significant distress in the individual or in the couple.

Sexual Desire Disorders

Three disorders reflect problems with the desire or arousal phase of the sexual response cycle. Two of these disorders are characterized by little or no interest in sex that is causing significant distress in the individual or couple. In men, this disorder is called **male hypoactive sexual desire disorder**, which often leads to infertility in some individuals (Lotti & Maggi, 2018). In females, low sexual interest is almost always accompanied by a diminished ability to become excited or aroused by erotic cues or sexual activity. Thus, deficits in interest or the ability to become aroused in women is combined in a disorder called **female sexual interest/arousal disorder** (Basson, Wierman, van Lankveld, & Brotto, 2010; Brotto, 2010a; Brotto & Luria, 2014). For males, there is a specific disorder of arousal—erectile dysfunction.

Male Hypoactive Sexual Desire Disorder and Female Sexual Interest/Arousal Disorder

Males with and females with sexual interest/arousal disorder have little or no interest in any type of sexual activity. It is difficult to assess low sexual desire, and a great deal of clinical judgment is required (Leiblum, 2010; Segraves & Woodard, 2006; Wincze, 2009; Wincze, Bach, & Barlow, 2008; Wincze & Weisberg, 2015). You might gauge it by frequency of sexual activity—say, less than twice a month for a married couple. Or you might determine whether someone ever thinks about sex or has sexual fantasies. Then there is the person who has sex twice a week but really doesn't want to and thinks about it only because their partner is on their case to live up to their end of the marriage and have sex more often. This individual might have no desire, despite having frequent sex. Consider the cases of Judy and Ira and of Mr. and Mrs. C. The treatment of Mr. and Mrs. C. is discussed later in this chapter.

Table 10.3 Categories of Sexual Dysfunction among Men and Women

	Sexual Dysfunction	
Type of Disorder	**Men**	**Women**
Desire	Male hypoactive sexual desire disorder (little or no desire to have sex)	Female sexual interest/arousal disorder (little or no desire to have sex)
Arousal	Erectile disorder (difficulty attaining or maintaining erections)	Female sexual interest/arousal disorder (little or no desire to have sex)
Orgasm	Delayed ejaculation; premature (early) ejaculation	Female orgasmic disorder
Pain		Genito-pelvic pain/penetration disorder (pain, anxiety, and tension associated with sexual activity; vaginismus, that is, muscle spasms in the vagina that interfere with penetration)

Source: American Psychiatric Association, 2013, *Diagnostic and statistical manual of mental disorders* (5th ed.).

Judy and Ira... A Loving Marriage?

Judy, a married woman in her late 20s, reached a clinic staff member on the phone and reported that she thought her husband, Ira, was having an affair and that she was upset about it. The reason for her assumptions? He had demonstrated no interest in sex during the past 3 years, and they had not had sex for 9 months. Ira was willing to come into the clinic.

When he was interviewed, it became clear that Ira was not having an affair. In fact, he did not masturbate and hardly ever thought about sex. He noted that he loved his wife but that he had not been concerned about the issue until she raised it because he had too many other things to think about and he assumed they would eventually get back to having sex. He now realized that his wife was quite distressed about the situation, particularly because they were thinking about having children.

Although Ira did not have extensive sexual experience, he had engaged in several erotic relationships before his marriage, which Judy knew. During a separate interview, Ira confided that during his premarital affairs he would get a "hard-on" just thinking about his lovers, each of whom was quite promiscuous. His wife, in contrast, was a pillar of the community and otherwise unlike these women, although attractive. Because he did not become aroused by thinking about his wife, he did not initiate sex. •

Mr. and Mrs. C... Getting Started

Mrs. C., a 31-year-old successful businesswoman, was married to a 32-year-old lawyer. They had two children, ages 2 and 5, and had been married 8 years when they entered therapy. The presenting problem was Mrs. C.'s lack of sexual desire. Mr. and Mrs. C. were interviewed separately during the initial assessment, and both professed attraction to and love for their partner. Mrs. C. reported that she could enjoy sex once she got involved and almost always was orgasmic. The problem was her lack of desire to get involved. She avoided her husband's sexual advances and looked on his affection and romanticism with great skepticism and, usually, anger and tears. Mrs. C. was raised in an upper-middle-class family that was supportive and loving. From age 6 to age 12, however, she had been repeatedly pressured into sexual activity by a male cousin who was 5 years her senior. This sexual activity was always initiated by the cousin, always against her will. She did not tell her parents because she felt guilty, as the boy did not use physical force to make her comply. It appeared that romantic advances by Mr. C. triggered memories of abuse by her cousin. •

Problems of sexual interest or desire used to be considered marital rather than sexual difficulties. Since the recognition in the late 1980s of low sexual desire as a distinct disorder, however, increasing numbers of couples present to sex therapy clinics with one of the partners reporting this problem (Kleinplatz, Moser, & Lev, 2012; Leiblum, 2010; Pridal & LoPiccolo, 2000). Best estimates suggest that more than 50% of patients who come to sexuality clinics for help complain of low sexual desire or interest (Leiblum 2010; Pridal & LoPiccolo, 2000). In many clinics, it is the most common presenting complaint of women; men present more often with erectile dysfunction (Hawton, 1995). The U.S. survey confirmed that 22% of women and 5% of men suffer from low sexual interest (hypoactive sexual disorder in man). But in a larger international survey, as many as 43% of women reported this problem (Laumann et al., 2005). For men, the prevalence increases with age; for women, it decreases with age (DeLamater & Sill, 2005; Fileborn et al., 2015; Laumann, Paik, & Rosen, 1999). Schreiner-Engel and Schiavi (1986) noted that patients with this disorder rarely have sexual fantasies, seldom masturbate (35% of the women and 52% of the men never masturbated, and most of the rest in their sample masturbated no more than once a month), and attempt intercourse once a month or less.

Sexual Arousal Disorders

Erectile disorder is a specific disorder of arousal. The problem here is not desire. Many males with erectile dysfunction have

DSM 5 Table 10.1
Criteria for Male Hypoactive Sexual Desire Disorder

A. Persistently or recurrently deficient (or absent) sexual/erotic thoughts or fantasies and desire for sexual activity. The judgment of deficiency is made by the clinician, taking into account factors that affect sexual functioning, such as age and general and sociocultural contexts of the individual's life.

B. The symptoms in Criterion A have persisted for a minimum duration of approximately 6 months.

C. The symptoms in Criterion A cause clinically significant distress in the individual.

D. The sexual dysfunction is not better explained by a nonsexual mental disorder or as a consequence of severe relationship distress or (e.g. partner violence) other significant stressors and is not attributable to the effects of a substance/medication or another medical condition.

Specify whether:

Lifelong: The disturbance has been present since the individual became sexually active.

Acquired: The disturbance began after a period of relatively normal sexual function.

Specify whether:

Generalized: Not limited to certain types of stimulation, situations, or partners.

Situational: Only occurs with certain types of stimulation, situations, or partners.

American Psychiatric Association. (2022). *Diagnostic and statistical manual of mental disorders* (5th ed., Text Revision).

frequent sexual urges and fantasies and a strong desire to have sex. Their problem is in becoming physically aroused: For females who are also likely to have low interest, deficits in arousal are reflected in an inability to achieve or maintain adequate lubrication (Basson, 2007; Rosen, 2007; Wincze, 2009; Wincze et al., 2008; Wincze & Weisberg, 2015). Consider the case of Bill.

The old and somewhat derogatory terms for male erectile disorder and female interest and arousal difficulties are *impotence* and *frigidity*, but these are imprecise labels that do not identify the specific phase of the sexual response in which the problems are localized. A man typically feels more impaired by his problem than a woman does by hers. Inability to achieve and maintain an erection makes intercourse difficult or impossible. Women who are unable to achieve vaginal lubrication, however, may be able to compensate by using a commercial lubricant (Leiblum 2010; Wincze, 2009). In women, arousal and lubrication may decrease at any time but, as in men, such problems tend to accompany aging (Bartlik & Goldberg, 2000; Basson, 2007; DeLamater & Sill, 2005; Rosen, 2000; Shamloul & Ghanem, 2013). In addition, in years past, some women were not as concerned as men about experiencing intense pleasure during sex as long as they could consummate the act; this is generally no longer the case. It is unusual for a man to be completely unable to achieve an erection. More typical is a situation like Bill's, where full erections are possible during masturbation and partial erections occur during attempted intercourse but with insufficient rigidity to allow penetration.

Bill... Long Marriage, New Problem

Bill, a 58-year-old white man, was referred to our clinic by his urologist. He was a retired accountant who had been married for 29 years to his 57-year-old wife, a retired nutritionist. They had no children. For the past several years, Bill had had difficulties obtaining and maintaining an erection. He reported a rather rigid routine he and his wife had developed to deal with the problem. They scheduled sex for Sunday mornings. Bill had to do a number of chores first, however, including letting the dog out, washing the dishes, and shaving. The couple's current behavior consisted of mutual hand stimulation. Bill was "not allowed" to attempt insertion until after his wife had climaxed. Bill's wife was adamant that she was not going to change her sexual behavior and "become a whore," as she put it. This included refusing to try K-Y jelly as a lubricant appropriate to her postmenopausal decrease in lubrication. She described their behavior as "lesbian sex."

Bill and his wife agreed that despite marital problems over the years, they had always maintained a good sexual relationship until the onset of the current problem and that sex had kept them together during their earlier difficulties. Useful information was obtained in separate interviews. Bill masturbated on Saturday night in an attempt to control his erection the following morning; his wife was unaware of this. In addition, he quickly and easily achieved a full erection when viewing erotica in the privacy of the sexuality clinic laboratory (surprising the assessor). Bill's wife privately acknowledged being angry at her husband for an affair that he had had 20 years earlier.

At the final session, three specific recommendations were made: for Bill to cease masturbating the evening before sex, for the couple to use a lubricant, and for them to delay the morning routine until after they had had sexual relations. The couple called back 1 month later to report that their sexual activity was much improved. •

The prevalence of erectile dysfunction is startlingly high and increases with age. Although data from the U.S. survey indicate that 5% of men between 18 and 59 fully meet a stringent set of criteria for erectile dysfunction (Laumann et al., 1999), this figure certainly underestimates the prevalence because erectile dysfunction increases rapidly in men after age 60. Rosen, Wing, Schneider, and Gendrano (2005) reviewed evidence from around the world and found that 60% of men 60 and over suffered from erectile dysfunction. Data from another study (shown in ■Figure 10.2) suggest that at least some impairment is present in approximately 40% of men in their 40s and 70% of men in their 70s (Feldman, Goldstein, Hatzichristou, Krane, & McKunlay, 1994; Kim & Lipshultz, 1997; Rosen, 2007); incidence (new cases) increases dramatically with age, with 46 new cases reported each year for every 1,000 men in their 60s (Johannes et al., 2000). In the past, erectile disorder was the most common problem for which men sought help (Hawton, 1995), but this has changed since the discovery of the phosphodiesterase type 5 inhibitors, such as Viagra (Shamloul & Ghanem, 2013), which we discuss in more detail below.

The prevalence of female interest and arousal disorders is somewhat more difficult to estimate because many women still do not consider absence of arousal to be a problem, let alone a disorder. The U.S. survey reports a prevalence of 14% of females

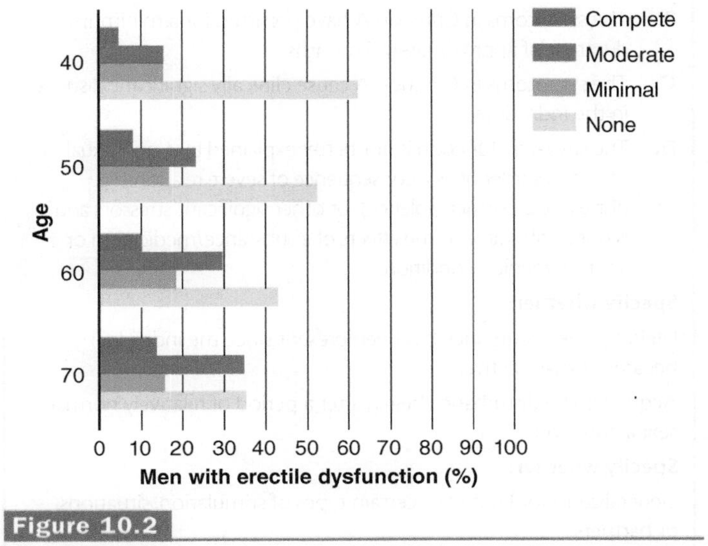

Figure 10.2

Estimated prevalence and severity of erectile dysfunction in a sample of 1,290 men between 40 and 70 years of age. Adapted from H. A. Feldman et al., 1994, Impotence and its medical and psychosocial correlates: Results of the Massachusetts male aging study, *Journal of Urology*, *51*, 54–61.

experiencing an arousal disorder (Laumann et al., 1999). One study (Rosen et al., 2014) reported a prevalence of 7.4%. Because disorders of desire, arousal, and orgasm often overlap, it is difficult to estimate precisely how many women with specific interest and arousal disorders present to sex clinics (Basson, 2007; Wincze & Weisberg, 2015).

Orgasm Disorders

The orgasm phase of the sexual response cycle can also become disrupted in one of several ways. As a result, either the orgasm occurs at an inappropriate time, or it does not occur.

DSM 5 Table 10.2

Criteria for Female Sexual Interest/Arousal Disorder

A. Lack of, or significantly reduced, sexual interest/arousal, as manifested by at least three of the following:

1. Absent/reduced interest in sexual activity.
2. Absent/reduced sexual/erotic thoughts or fantasies.
3. No/reduced initiation of sexual activity, and typically unreceptive to a partner's attempts to initiate.
4. Absent/reduced sexual excitement/pleasure during sexual activity in almost all or all (approximately 75% to 100%) sexual encounters (in identified situational contexts or, if generalized, in all contexts).
5. Absent/reduced sexual interest/arousal in response to any internal or external sexual/erotic cues (e.g., written, verbal, visual).
6. Absent/reduced genital or nongenital sensations during sexual activity in almost all or all (approximately 75% to 100%) sexual encounters (in identified situational contexts or, if generalized, in all contexts).

B. The symptoms in Criterion A have persisted for a minimum duration of approximately 6 months.

C. The symptoms in Criterion A cause clinically significant distress in the individual.

D. The sexual dysfunction is not better explained by a nonsexual mental disorder or as a consequence of severe relationship distress (e.g. partner violence) or other significant stressors and is not attributable to the effects of a substance/medication or another medical condition.

Specify whether:

Lifelong: The disturbance has been present since the individual became sexually active.

Acquired: The disturbance began after a period of relatively normal sexual function.

Specify whether:

Generalized: Not limited to certain types of stimulation, situations, or partners.

Situational: Only occurs with certain types of stimulation, situations, or partners.

American Psychiatric Association. (2022). *Diagnostic and statistical manual of mental disorders* (5th ed., Text Revision).

An inability to achieve an orgasm despite adequate sexual desire and arousal is commonly seen in women and less commonly seen in men. Men who achieve orgasm only with great difficulty or not at all meet criteria for a condition called **delayed ejaculation**. In women, the condition is referred to as **female orgasmic disorder** (Kleinplatz et al., 2013; Wincze, 2009; Wincze & Weisberg, 2015). Consider the case of Greta and Will. We discuss Greta and Will's treatment later.

An inability to reach orgasm is the most common complaint among women who seek therapy for sexual problems. Although the U.S. survey did not estimate the prevalence of female orgasmic disorder specifically, approximately 25% of women report significant difficulty reaching orgasm (Heiman, 2000; Laumann et al., 1999), although estimates vary widely (Graham, 2010). The problem is equally present in different age groups, and unmarried women were 1.5 times more likely than married women to experience orgasm disorder. In diagnosing this problem, it is necessary to determine that the women "never or almost never"

Greta and Will... Loving Disunion

Greta, a teacher, and Will, an engineer, were an attractive couple who came together to the first interview and entered the office clearly showing affection for each other. They had been married for 5 years and were in their late 20s. When asked about the problems that had brought them to the office, Greta quickly reported that she didn't think she had ever had an orgasm—"didn't think" because she wasn't really sure what an orgasm was. She loved Will and occasionally would initiate lovemaking, although with decreased frequency over the past several years.

Will certainly didn't think Greta was reaching orgasm. In any case, he reported, they were clearly going in "different directions" sexually, in that Greta's interest was decreasing. She had progressed from initiating sex occasionally early in their marriage to almost never doing so, except for an occasional spurt every 6 months or so, when she would initiate two or three times in a week. But Greta noted that it was the physical closeness she wanted most during these times rather than sexual pleasure. Further inquiry revealed that she did become sexually aroused occasionally but had never reached orgasm, even during several attempts at masturbation mostly before her marriage. Both Greta and Will reported that the sexual problem was a concern to them because everything else about their marriage was positive.

Greta had been brought up in a strict but loving and supportive Catholic family that more or less ignored sexuality. The parents were always careful not to display their affection in front of Greta, and when her mother caught Greta touching her genital area, she was cautioned rather severely to avoid that kind of activity. •

DSM 5 **Table 10.3**
Criteria for Female Orgasmic Disorder

A. Presence of either of the following symptoms and experienced on almost all or all (approximately 75% to 100%) occasions of sexual activity (in identified situational contexts or, if generalized, in all contexts):
   1. Marked delay in, marked infrequency of, or absence of orgasm.
   2. Markedly reduced intensity of orgasmic sensations.

B. The symptoms in Criterion A have persisted for a minimum duration of approximately 6 months.

C. The symptoms in Criterion A cause clinically significant distress in the individual.

D. The sexual dysfunction is not better explained by a nonsexual mental disorder or as a consequence of severe relationship distress (e.g. partner violence) or other significant stressors and is not attributable to the effects of a substance/medication or another medical condition.

Specify whether:

Lifelong: The disturbance has been present since the individual became sexually active.

Acquired: The disturbance began after a period of relatively normal sexual function.

Specify whether:

Generalized: Not limited to certain types of stimulation, situations, or partners.

Situational: Only occurs with certain types of stimulation, situations, or partners.

Specify:

Never experienced an orgasm under any situation.

American Psychiatric Association. (2022). *Diagnostic and statistical manual of mental disorders* (5th ed., Text Revision).

reach orgasm (Wincze & Weisberg, 2015). This distinction is important because only approximately 20% of all women reliably experience regular orgasms during sexual intercourse (Graham, 2010; Lloyd, 2005). Therefore, approximately 80% do not achieve orgasm with every sexual encounter, unlike most men, who tend to experience orgasm more consistently. Thus, the "never or almost never" inquiry is important, along with establishing the extent of the woman's distress, in diagnosing orgasmic dysfunction.

In the U.S. survey, approximately 8% of men report having delayed ejaculation or none during sexual interactions (Laumann et al., 1999). Men seldom seek treatment for this condition. It is quite possible that in many cases some men reach climax through alternative forms of stimulation and that this condition is accommodated by the couple (Apfelbaum, 2000).

Some men who are unable to ejaculate with their partners can obtain an erection and ejaculate during masturbation. Occasionally men suffer from *retrograde ejaculation*, in which ejaculatory fluids travel backward into the bladder rather than forward. This phenomenon is almost always caused by the effects of certain drugs or a coexisting medical condition and should not be confused with delayed ejaculation.

Gary... Running Scared

Gary, a 31-year-old sales representative, engaged in sexual activity with his wife three or four times a month. He noted that he would have liked to have had sex more often, but his busy schedule kept him working about 80 hours a week. His primary difficulty was an inability to control the timing of his ejaculation. Approximately 70% to 80% of the time, he ejaculated within seconds of penetration. This pattern had been constant since he met his wife approximately 13 years earlier. Previous experience with other women, although limited, was not characterized by premature ejaculation. In an attempt to delay his ejaculation, Gary distracted himself by thinking of nonsexual things (scores of ball games or work-related issues) and sometimes attempted sex soon after a previous attempt because he seemed not to climax as quickly under these circumstances. Gary reported masturbating seldom (three or four times a year at most). When he did masturbate, he usually attempted to reach orgasm quickly, a habit he acquired during his teens to avoid being caught by a family member.

One of his greatest concerns was that he was not pleasing his wife, and under no circumstances did he want her to know that he was seeking treatment. Further inquiry revealed that he made many extravagant purchases at his wife's request, even though it strained their finances, because he wished to please her. He felt that if they had met recently, his wife probably would not even accept a date with him because he had lost much of his hair and she had lost weight and was more attractive than she used to be. •

A far more common male orgasmic disorder is **premature ejaculation**, ejaculation that occurs well before the man and his partner wish it to (Althof, 2006; Polonsky, 2000; Wincze, 2009; Wincze & Weisberg, 2015), defined as approximately 1 minute after penetration in DSM-5. Consider the rather typical case of Gary. Treatment for Gary and his wife is described shortly.

The frequency of premature ejaculation seems to be quite high. In the U.S. survey, 21% of all men met criteria for premature ejaculation, making it the most common male sexual dysfunction (Laumann et al., 1999; Serefoglu & Saitz, 2012). This difficulty is also a presenting complaint in as many as 60% of men who seek treatment for sexual dysfunction (Polonsky, 2000). (But many of these men also present with erectile dysfunction as their major problem.) In one clinic, premature ejaculation was the principal complaint of 16% of men seeking treatment (Hawton, 1995).

Although DSM-5 specifies a duration of less than approximately 1 minute, it is difficult to define "premature." An adequate length of time before ejaculation varies from individual to individual. Patrick and colleagues (2005) found that men who complain of premature ejaculation ejaculated 1.8 minutes after penetration, compared with 7.3 minutes in individuals without this complaint. A perceived

DSM 5 **Table 10.4**
Criteria for Premature Ejaculation

A. A persistent or recurrent pattern of ejaculation occurring during partnered sexual activity within approximately 1 minute following vaginal penetration and before the person wishes it. *Note:* Although the diagnosis of premature (early) ejaculation may be applied to individuals engaged in nonvaginal sexual activities, specific duration criteria have not been established for these activities.
B. The symptom in Criterion A must have been present for at least 6 months and must be experienced on almost all or all (approximately 75% to 100%) occasions of sexual activity (in identified situational contexts or, if generalized, in all contexts).
C. The symptoms in Criterion A cause clinically significant distress in the individual.
D. The sexual dysfunction is not better explained by a nonsexual mental disorder or as a consequence of severe relationship distress or other significant stressors and is not attributable to the effects of a substance/medication or another medical condition.

Specify whether:

Lifelong: The disturbance has been present since the individual became sexually active.

Acquired: The disturbance began after a period of relatively normal sexual function.

Specify whether:

Generalized: Not limited to certain types of stimulation, situations, or partners.

Situational: Only occurs with certain types of stimulation, situations, or partners.

American Psychiatric Association. (2022). *Diagnostic and statistical manual of mental disorders* (5th ed., Text Revision).

lack of control over orgasm, however, may be the more important psychological determinant of premature ejaculation (Wincze et al., 2008). Although occasional early ejaculation is normal, consistent premature ejaculation appears to occur primarily in inexperienced men with less education about sex (Laumann et al., 1999).

Sexual Pain Disorder

Sexual pain disorders are quite common in women. A large survey from the United States showed that 21% of sexually active women of 18 to 29 years of age complained of pain during sexual intercourse during the past 12 months (Laumann et al., 1999). One common experience among women of all ages is **vulvodynia**, which is chronic pain in the area on the outside of a woman's genitals (the vulva) (Bergeron et al., 2020). Women with this problem often describe a sensation of burning, rawness, or stinging. The condition is often associated with tensing and tightening of the pelvic floor muscle during intercourse. Women with this problem sometimes report childhood maltreatment and often show significant anxiety around intercourse and feel depressed because of it. Vulvodynia does not have a clearly identifiable cause (such as an infection or a skin disorder) and is often a chronic condition (but has to last for at least 3 months). As a result, vulvodynia can have a negative impact on a woman's quality of life. A related sexual dysfunction specific to women refers to difficulties with penetration during attempted intercourse or significant pain during intercourse. In the DSM-5, vulvodynia is classified as a **genito-pelvic pain/penetration disorder**.

Another presentation of this disorder is referred to as **vaginismus**, in which the pelvic muscles in the outer third of the vagina undergo involuntary spasms when intercourse is attempted (Binik et al., 2007; Kleinplatz et al., 2013). The spasm reaction of vaginismus may occur during any attempted penetration, including a gynecological exam or insertion of a tampon (Beck, 1993; Bradford & Meston, 2011). Women report sensations of "ripping, burning, or tearing during attempted intercourse" (Beck, 1993, p. 384). Consider the case of Jill.

Although there are no data on the prevalence of vaginismus in community samples, best estimates are that it affects 6% of women (Bradford & Meston, 2011). According to Crowley, Richardson, and Goldmeir (2006), 25% of women who report suffering from some sexual dysfunction experience vaginismus. Because vaginismus and the experience of pain during intercourse overlap quite a bit in women, these conditions have been combined in DSM-5 into genito-pelvic pain/penetration disorder (Binik, 2010; Bradford & Meston, 2011; Payne et al., 2005). Results from the U.S. survey indicate that approximately 7% of women suffer from one or the other type of sexual pain disorder, with higher proportions of younger and less educated women reporting this problem (Laumann et al., 1999). Somewhat higher estimates of 15% of women in North America reporting recurring pain during intercourse have been reported in DSM-5 (APA, 2013).

Jill... Sex and Spasms

Jill was referred to our clinic by another therapist because she had not consummated her marriage of 1 year. At 23 years of age, she was an attractive and loving wife who managed a motel while her husband worked as an accountant. Despite numerous attempts in a variety of positions to engage in intercourse, Jill's severe vaginal spasms prevented penetration of any kind. Jill was also unable to use tampons. With great reluctance, she submitted to gynecological exams at infrequent intervals. Sexual behavior with her husband consisted of mutual masturbation or, occasionally, Jill had him rub his penis against her breasts to the point of ejaculation. She refused to engage in oral sex. Jill, an anxious young woman, came from a family in which sexual matters were seldom discussed and sexual contact between the parents had ceased some years before. Although she enjoyed petting, Jill's general attitude was that intercourse was disgusting. Furthermore, she expressed some fears of becoming pregnant despite taking adequate contraceptive measures. She also thought that she would perform poorly when she did engage in intercourse, therefore embarrassing herself with her new husband. •

Assessing Sexual Behavior

There are three major aspects to the assessment of sexual behavior (Wiegel, Wincze, & Barlow, 2002):

1. *Interviews*, usually supported by numerous questionnaires because patients may provide more information on paper than in a verbal interview
2. A *thorough medical evaluation*, to rule out the variety of medical conditions that can contribute to sexual problems
3. A *psychophysiological assessment*, to directly measure the physiological aspects of sexual arousal

Interviews

All clinicians who conduct interviews for sexual problems should be aware of several useful assumptions (Wiegel et al., 2002; Wincze, 2009). For example, they must demonstrate to the patient through their actions and interviewing style that they are comfortable talking about these issues. Because many patients do not know the various clinical terms professionals use to describe the sexual response cycle and various aspects of sexual behavior, clinicians must always be prepared to use the vernacular (language) of the patient, realizing also that terms vary from person to person.

The following are examples of the questions asked in semistructured interviews in our sexuality clinic:

How would you describe your current interest in sex?
Do you avoid engaging in sexual behavior with a partner?
Do you have sexual fantasies?
How often do you currently masturbate?
How often do you engage in sexual intercourse?
How often do you engage in mutual caressing or cuddling without intercourse?
Have you ever been sexually abused or raped or had a negative experience associated with sex?
Do you have problems attaining an erection? (or) Do you have problems achieving or maintaining vaginal lubrication?
Do you ever have problems reaching orgasm?
Do you ever experience pain associated with sexual activity?

A clinician must be careful to ask these questions in a manner that puts the patient at ease. During an interview lasting approximately 2 hours, the clinician also covers nonsexual relationship issues and physical health and screens for the presence of additional psychological disorders. When possible, the partner is interviewed concurrently.

Patients may volunteer in writing some information they are not ready to talk about, so they are usually given a variety of questionnaires that help reveal sexual activity and attitudes toward sexuality.

Medical Examinations

Human sexuality clinicians routinely inquire about medical conditions that affect sexual functioning. A variety of drugs—including some commonly prescribed for hypertension, anxiety, and depression—often disrupt sexual arousal and functioning. Recent surgery or concurrent medical conditions must be evaluated for their impact on sexual functioning. Often the surgeon or treating physician may not have described possible side effects, or the patient may not have told the physician that a medical procedure or drug has affected sexual functioning. Some males with specific sexual dysfunctions such as erectile disorder have already visited a urologist—a physician specializing in disorders of the genitals, bladder, and associated structures—before coming to a sexuality clinic, and many females already have visited a gynecologist. These specialists may check levels of sexual hormones necessary for adequate sexual functioning and, in the case of males, evaluate vascular functioning necessary for an erectile response.

© Ray Rosen

© Gayle Beck

Ray Rosen (left) and Gayle Beck (right) pioneered research on the psychophysiological measurement of sexual arousal.

Psychophysiological Assessments

Many clinicians assess the ability of individuals to become sexually aroused under a variety of conditions by taking psychophysiological measurements while the patient is either awake or asleep. In men, penile erection is measured directly, using, for example, a *penile strain gauge* developed in our clinic (Barlow, Becker, Leitenberg, & Agras, 1970). As the penis expands, the strain gauge picks up the changes and records them on a polygraph. Note that participants are often not aware of these more objective measures of their arousal; that is, their self-report of how aroused they are differs from the objective measure, and this discrepancy increases or decreases as a function of the type of sexual problem they have. Measuring penile rigidity is also important in cases of erectile dysfunction because large erections with insufficient rigidity will not be adequate for intercourse (Wiegel et al., 2002).

The comparable device for women is a *vaginal photoplethysmograph*, developed by James Geer and his associates (Geer, Morokoff, & Greenwood, 1974; Prause & Janssen, 2006; Rosen & Beck, 1988). This device, which is smaller than a tampon, is inserted by the woman into her vagina. A light source at the tip of the instrument and two light-sensitive photoreceptors on the sides of the instrument measure the amount of light reflected back from the vaginal walls. Because blood flows to the vaginal walls during arousal, the amount of light passing through them decreases with increasing arousal.

Typically in our clinic, individuals undergoing physiological assessment view an erotic videotape for 2 to 5 minutes or, occasionally, listen to an erotic audiotape (see, for example, Bach, Brown, &

John Wincze developed new approaches for treating sexual dysfunction.

Barlow, 1999; Weisburg, Brown, Wincze, & Barlow, 2001). The patient's sexual responsivity during this time is assessed psychophysiologically using the strain gauge or photoplethysmograph just described. Patients also report subjectively on the amount of sexual arousal they experience. This assessment allows the clinician to carefully observe the conditions under which arousal is possible for the patient. For example, many individuals with psychologically based sexual dysfunctions may achieve strong arousal in a laboratory but be unable to become aroused with a partner (Bancroft, 1997; Bradford & Meston, 2011; Sakheim, Barlow, Abrahamson, & Beck, 1987).

Causes and Treatment of Sexual Dysfunction

As with most disorders, biological, psychological, and social factors contribute to the development of sexual dysfunction. And these problems can be treated either psychologically or medically.

Concept Check 10.1

Diagnose the following sexual dysfunctions.

1. After Justin's football team won the championship, his interest in sexual activity diminished. All his thoughts and fantasies centered on football and winning again next season, and his wife was threatening to leave him. Justin is probably displaying (a) male hypoactive sexual desire disorder, (b) vaginismus, (c) penile strain gauge, or (d) male orgasmic disorder.
2. Alyssa has no real desire for sex. She has sex only because she feels that otherwise her wife may leave her. Alyssa suffers from (a) sexual insecurities, (b) hypoactive sexual desire disorder, (c) boredom, or (d) female sexual interest/ arousal disorder.
3. Aadarsh lacks the ability to control ejaculation. The majority of the time he ejaculates within seconds of penetration. He suffers from (a) erectile disorder, (b) stress, (c) premature ejaculation, or (d) both a and b.
4. Yolanda came into the office because she is unable to reach orgasm. She loves her husband but stopped initiating sex. She is most likely suffering from (a) female orgasmic disorder, (b) female sexual interest/arousal arousal disorder, (c) vaginismus, or (d) dislike for her husband.

Causes of Sexual Dysfunction

Individual sexual dysfunctions seldom occur in isolation. Usually, a patient referred to a sexuality clinic complains of a wide assortment of sexual problems, although one may be of most concern (Rosen, 2007; Wincze, 2009). A 45-year-old man referred to our clinic had been free of problems until 10 years earlier, when he was under a great deal of pressure at work and was preparing to take a major career-related licensing examination. He began experiencing erectile dysfunction about 50% of the time, a condition that had progressed to approximately 80% of the time. In addition, he reported that he had no control over ejaculation, often ejaculating before penetration with only a semi-erect penis. Over the past 5 years, he had lost most interest in sex and was coming to treatment only at his wife's insistence. Thus, this man suffered simultaneously from erectile dysfunction, premature ejaculation, and low sexual desire.

Because of the frequency of such combinations, we discuss the causes of various sexual dysfunctions together, reviewing briefly the biological, psychological, and social contributions and specifying causal factors thought to be associated exclusively and specifically with one or another dysfunction.

Biological Contributions

A number of physical and medical conditions contribute to sexual dysfunction (Basson, 2007; Bradford & Meston, 2011; Rosen, 2007; Wincze et al., 2008; Wincze & Weisburg, 2015). Although this is not surprising, most patients and even many health professionals are, unfortunately, unaware of the connection. Neurological diseases and other conditions that affect the nervous system, such as diabetes and kidney disease, may directly interfere with sexual functioning by reducing sensitivity in the genital area, and they are a common cause of erectile dysfunction in males (Rosen, 2007; Wincze, 2009; Wincze & Weisburg, 2015). Feldman and colleagues (1994) reported that 28% of men with diabetes experienced complete erectile failure, and other studies have replicated these high prevalence rates (Phé & Rouprêt, 2012). Vascular disease is a major cause of sexual dysfunction because erections in men and vaginal engorgement in women depend on adequate blood flow. The two relevant vascular problems in men are arterial insufficiency (constricted arteries), which makes it difficult for blood to reach the penis, and venous leakage (blood flows out too quickly for an erection to be maintained; Wincze & Weisburg, 2015).

Chronic illness can also indirectly affect sexual functioning. For example, it is not uncommon for individuals who have had heart attacks to be wary of the physical exercise involved in sexual activity to the point of preoccupation. They often become unable to achieve arousal despite being assured by their physicians that sexual activity is safe for them (Cooper, 1988). Also, coronary artery disease and sexual dysfunction commonly coexist, and it is now recommended that men presenting with erectile dysfunction should be screened for cardiovascular disease (Gandaglia et al., 2014; Jackson, Rosen, Kloner, & Kostis, 2006).

A major physical cause of sexual dysfunction is prescription medication. Drug treatments for high blood pressure, called *antihypertensive medications*, in the class known as beta-blockers (including propranolol) may contribute to sexual dysfunction.

Selective-serotonin reuptake inhibitor (SSRI) antidepressant medications and other antidepressant and antianxiety drugs may also interfere with sexual desire and arousal in both men and women (Balon, 2006; Kleinplatz et al., 2013). A number of these drugs, particularly the psychoactive drugs, may dampen sexual desire and arousal by altering levels of certain subtypes of serotonin in the brain. Sexual dysfunction—specifically low sexual desire and arousal difficulties—is the most widespread side effect of the antidepressant SSRIs, such as Prozac (see Chapter 7), and as many as 80% of individuals who take these medications may experience some degree of sexual dysfunction, although estimates closer to 50% seem more reliable (Balon, 2006; Clayton, Croft, & Handiwala, 2014; Montejo-Gonzalez et al., 1997). Some people are aware that alcohol suppresses sexual arousal, but they may not know that most other drugs of abuse, such as cocaine and heroin, also produce widespread sexual dysfunction in frequent users and misusers, both men and women. Researchers reported that more than 60% of a large number of cocaine users had a sexual dysfunction (Cocores, Miller, Pottash, & Gold, 1988; Macdonald, Waldorf, Reinarman, & Murphy, 1988). In the Cocores group's study, some patients also abused alcohol.

There is also the misconception that alcohol facilitates sexual arousal and behavior. What actually happens is that alcohol at low and moderate levels reduces social inhibitions so that people feel more like having sex (and perhaps are more willing to request it) (Wiegel, Scepkowski & Barlow, 2006). Physically, alcohol is a central nervous system suppressant, and for men to achieve erection and women to achieve lubrication is more difficult when the central nervous system is suppressed (Schiavi, 1990). Chronic alcohol use disorder may cause permanent neurological damage and may virtually eliminate the sexual response cycle. Such misuse may lead to liver and testicular damage, resulting in decreased testosterone levels and related decreases in sexual desire and arousal. This dual effect of alcohol (social disinhibition and physical suppression) has been recognized since the time of Shakespeare: "It provokes the desire, but it takes away the performance" (*Macbeth*, II, iii, 29).

Chronic alcohol use disorder can also cause fertility problems in both men and women (Malatesta & Adams, 2001). Fahrner (1987) examined the prevalence of sexual dysfunction among male alcoholics and found that 75% had erectile dysfunction, low sexual desire, and premature or delayed ejaculation.

Many people report that cocaine or marijuana enhances sexual pleasure. Although little is known about the effects of marijuana across the range of use, it is unlikely that chemical effects increase pleasure. Rather, in those individuals who report some enhancement of sexual pleasure (and many don't), the effect may be psychological in that their attention is focused more completely and fully on sensory stimulation (Buffum, 1982), a factor that seems to be an important part of healthy sexual functioning. If so, imagery and attentional focus can be enhanced with nondrug procedures such as meditation, in which a person practices concentrating on something with as few distractions as possible.

Nicotine is similarly associated with impaired sexual performance. One report from Mannino, Klevens, and Flanders (1994), studying more than 4,000 male army veterans, found that cigarette smoking alone was associated with increased erectile dysfunction after controlling for other factors, such as alcohol and vascular disease (Wincze et al., 2008). Similarly, nicotine used before viewing an erotic film was associated with reduced erectile response to the film for men (Harte & Meston, 2008a). A parallel study also found decreased arousal in women who used nicotine before viewing the film (Harte & Meston, 2008b).

Psychological Contributions

For years, most sex researchers and therapists thought the principal cause of sexual dysfunctions was anxiety (see, for example, Kaplan, 1979; Masters & Johnson, 1970). While evaluating the role of anxiety and sexual functioning in our own laboratory, we discovered it was not that simple. In certain circumstances, anxiety *increases* sexual arousal (Barlow, Sakheim, & Beck, 1983). We designed an experiment in which the same group of young, sexually functional men viewed erotic films under three conditions. Before viewing the film, all participants were exposed to a harmless but somewhat painful electric shock to the forearm. We then attempted to replicate the kinds of performance anxiety that males might experience during a sexual interaction. In the first condition, which served as a control condition, the participants were told to relax and enjoy the film and that there was no chance of shock. In the second condition, participants were told there was a 60% chance they would receive the shock at some time while they were watching the erotic film, no matter what they did (noncontingent shock threat). In the third condition, most closely paralleling the types of performance anxiety that some individuals might experience, the same group of participants were told there was a 60% chance they would receive a shock if they did not achieve the average level of erection achieved by the previous participants (contingent shock threat). No shocks were delivered during the viewing of the erotic films in any of the conditions, although participants believed they might be administered.

The results, presented in ■ Figure 10.3, indicate that the noncontingent shock threat condition *increased* sexual arousal compared with the no-shock threat control condition. In an even more surprising development, however, the contingent shock threat condition (in which participants were told there was a 60% chance they would be shocked if they did not achieve adequate arousal) increased sexual response even more significantly than the no-shock threat control condition. Similar results for women were reported by Hoon, Wincze, and Hoon (1977), Palace (1995), and Palace and Gorzalka (1990), who developed slightly different experimental paradigms, using the vaginal photoplethysmograph (Wiegel, Scepkowski, & Barlow, 2006).

These counterintuitive findings have some parallels outside the laboratory. In one unusual and startling report, Sarrel and Masters (1982) described the ability of men to perform sexually under threat of physical harm. These men, the victims of gang rape by women, reported later that they had been able to achieve erections and repeatedly engage in intercourse despite being constantly threatened with knives and other weapons if they

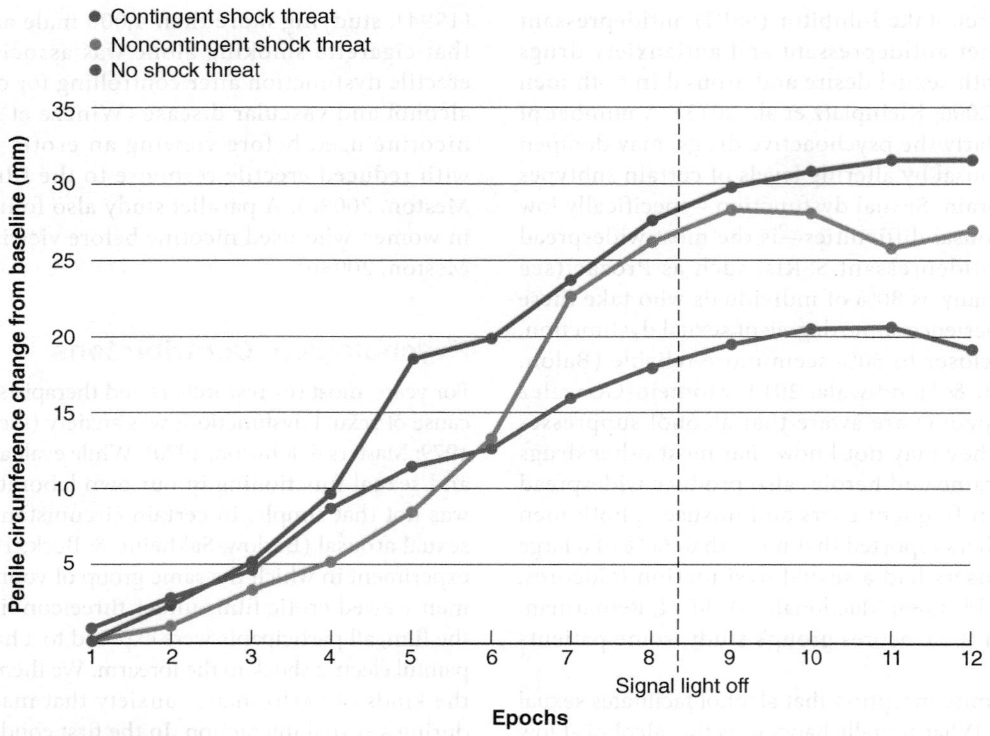

Figure 10.3

Performance anxiety and sexual arousal in males. Shown here are the average changes in male sexual arousal (penile circumference change) during each of three conditions. An epoch is a period of 10 seconds. From D. H. Barlow, D. K. Sakheim, & J. G. Beck, 1983, Anxiety increases sexual arousal, *Journal of Abnormal Psychology, 92*, 49–54.

failed. Certainly they experienced extreme levels of anxiety, yet they reported that their sexual performance was not impaired.

If anxiety does not necessarily decrease sexual arousal and performance, what does? A partial answer is distraction. In one experiment, participants were asked to listen to a narrative through earphones while they watched an erotic film and were told that they would later have to report on the narrative to make sure they were listening. Sexually functional males demonstrated significantly less arousal based on penile strain gauge measurements when they were distracted by the narrative than when they were not distracted (Abrahamson, Barlow, Sakheim, Beck, & Athanasiou, 1985). To anyone who has tried to concentrate on baseball scores or some other nonsexual event to reduce unwanted arousal, this result will come as no surprise. People with erectile dysfunction in whom physical disease processes had been ruled out reacted somewhat differently from functional men to both shock threat and distraction conditions. Anxiety induced by shock threat ("You'll be shocked if you don't get aroused") did seem to reduce sexual arousal in men who were dysfunctional. Remember that the reverse was true for the normally functioning men. In contrast, the kind of neutral distracting conditions present in the experiment by Abrahamson and colleagues (1985) did not reduce arousal in those men who were dysfunctional. This discovery is puzzling.

Two other findings from different experiments are important. One revealed that patients with erectile dysfunction consistently underreport their actual levels of arousal; that is, at the same level of erectile responses (as measured by the penile strain gauge), men who are dysfunctional report far less sexual arousal than do sexually functional men (Sakheim et al., 1987). This result seems to be true for dysfunctional women as well (Meston & Gorzalka, 1995; Morokoff & Heiman, 1980; Wiegel et al., 2006). Another finding showed that inducing positive or negative mood by playing joyful or sad music directly affected sexual arousal, at least in individuals without sexual dysfunctions with sad music decreasing sexual arousal (Mitchell, DiBartolo, Brown, & Barlow, 1998). Although the original studies described above were carried out mostly with men because of the early availability of the strain gauge measure, subsequent studies with women reveal a similar pattern of results (Bradford & Meston, 2006).

How do we interpret this complex series of experiments to account for sexual dysfunction from a psychological perspective? Basically, we have to break the concept of performance anxiety into several components. One component is arousal, another is cognitive processes, and the third is negative affect (Wiegel et al., 2006; Wincze et al., 2008; Wincze & Weisburg, 2015).

When confronted with the possibility of having sexual relations, individuals who are dysfunctional tend to expect the worst and find the situation to be relatively negative and unpleasant (Weisburg et al., 2001; Wincze & Weisburg, 2015). As far as possible, they avoid becoming aware of any sexual cues (and therefore are not aware of how aroused they are physically, thus underreporting their arousal). They also may distract themselves with negative thoughts, such as, "I'm going to make a fool of myself. I'll never be able to get aroused. They will think I'm stupid." We know that as arousal increases, a person's attention focuses more intently and consistently. But the person who is focusing on negative thoughts will find it impossible to become sexually aroused.

People with normal sexual functioning react to a sexual situation positively. They focus their attention on the erotic cues and do not become distracted. When they become aroused, they focus even more strongly on the sexual and erotic cues, allowing themselves to become increasingly sexually aroused. The model presented in ■ Figure 10.4 illustrates both functional and dysfunctional sexual arousal (Barlow, 1986, 2002). These experiments demonstrate that sexual arousal is strongly determined by psychological factors (particularly cognitive and emotional factors) that are powerful enough to determine whether blood flows to the appropriate areas of the body (such as the genitals), confirming again the strong interaction of psychological and biological factors in most of our functioning.

In summary, normally functioning individuals show increased sexual arousal during "performance demand" conditions, experience positive affect, are not distracted by nonsexual stimuli, and have a good idea of how aroused they are. Individuals with sexual problems (such as erectile dysfunction) show decreased arousal during performance demand, experience negative affect, are distracted by nonsexual stimuli, and do not have an accurate sense of how aroused they are. This process seems to apply to most sexual dysfunctions, which, you will remember, tend to occur together, but it is particularly applicable to sexual arousal disorders (Wiegel et al., 2006).

Though little is known about the psychological (or biological) factors associated with premature ejaculation (Althof, 2007; Bradford & Meston, 2011; Malavige & Jayawickrema, 2015; Weiner, 1996),

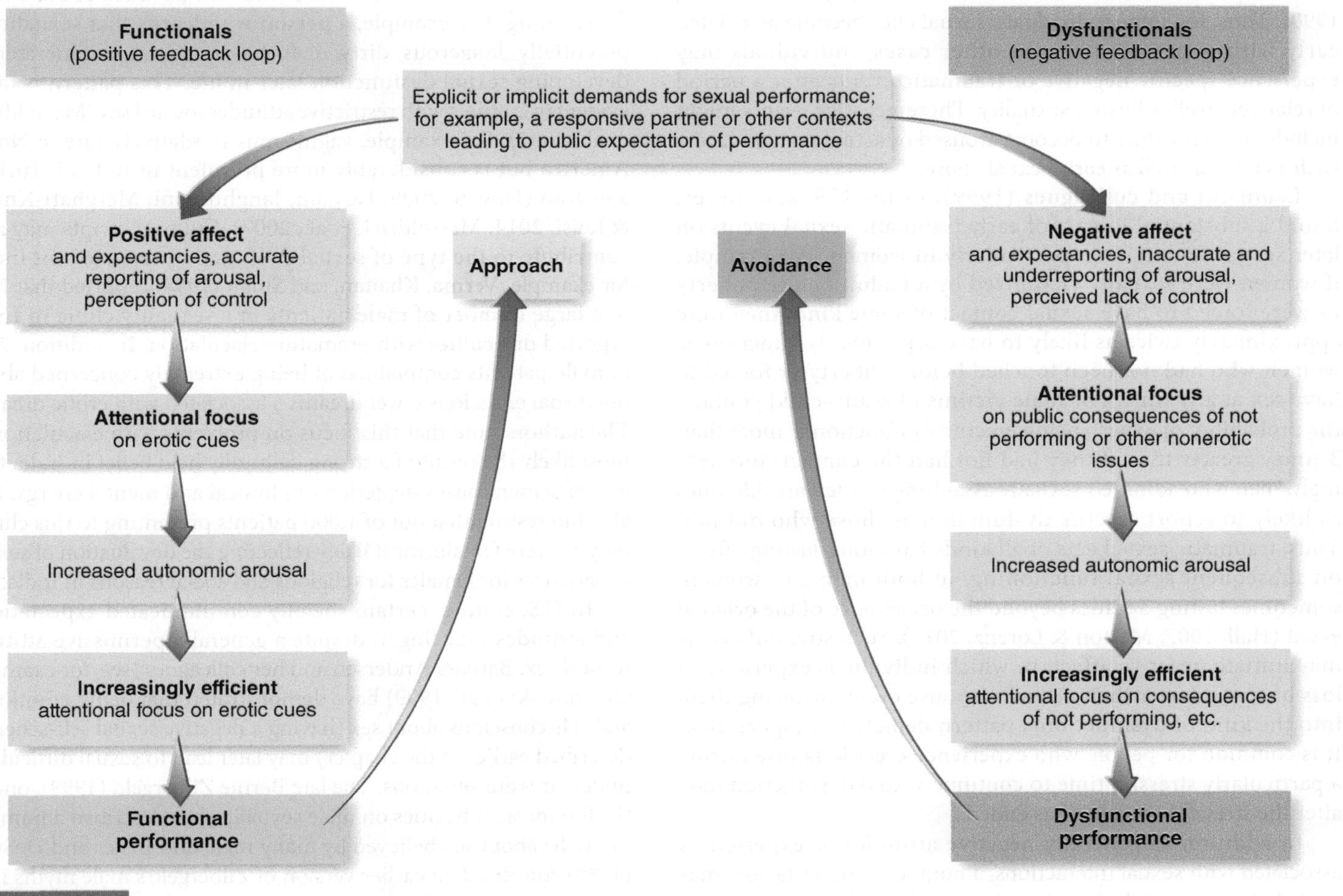

Figure 10.4

A model of functional and dysfunctional sexual arousal. Adapted from D. H. Barlow, 1986, Causes of sexual dysfunction: The role of anxiety and cognitive interference, *Journal of Consulting and Clinical Psychology*, *54*, 140–148.

the condition is most prevalent in young men, and excessive physiological arousal in the sympathetic nervous system may lead to rapid ejaculation. These observations suggest some men may have a naturally lower threshold for ejaculation; that is, they require less stimulation and arousal to ejaculate. Unfortunately, the psychological factor of anxiety also increases sympathetic arousal. Thus, when a man becomes anxiously aroused about ejaculating too quickly, his concern makes the problem worse. We return to the role of anxiety in sexual dysfunctions later.

Social and Cultural Contributions

The model of sexual dysfunction displayed in Figure 10.4 helps explain why some individuals may be dysfunctional *at the present time* but not how they *became* that way. Although it is not known for sure why some people develop problems, many people learn early that sexuality can be negative and somewhat threatening, and the responses they develop reflect this belief. Donn Byrne and his colleagues call this negative cognitive set *erotophobia.* They have demonstrated that erotophobia—presumably learned early in childhood from families, religious authorities, or others—seems to predict sexual difficulties later in life (Byrne & Schulte, 1990). Thus, for some individuals, sexual cues become associated early with negative affect. In other cases, individuals may experience specific negative or traumatic events after a period of relatively well-adjusted sexuality. These negative events might include sudden failure to become aroused or actual sexual trauma such as rape, as well as early sexual abuse.

Laumann and colleagues (1999), in the U.S. sex survey, found a substantial impact of early traumatic sexual events on later sexual functioning, particularly in women. For example, if women were sexually victimized by an adult before puberty or were forced to have sexual contact of some kind, they were approximately twice as likely to have orgasmic dysfunction as women who had not been touched before puberty or forced to have sex at any time. For male victims of adult–child contact, the probability of experiencing erectile dysfunction is more than 3 times greater than if they had not had the contact. Interestingly, men who admitted sexually assaulting women are 3.5 times as likely to report erectile dysfunction as those who did not. Thus, traumatic sexual acts of all kinds have long-lasting effects on subsequent sexual functioning, in both men and women, sometimes lasting decades beyond the occurrence of the original event (Hall, 2007; Meston & Lorenz, 2013). Such stressful events may initiate negative affect, in which individuals experience a loss of control over their sexual response cycle, throwing them into the kind of dysfunctional pattern depicted in Figure 10.4. It is common for people who experience erectile failure during a particularly stressful time to continue sexual dysfunction long after the stressful situation has ended.

In addition to generally negative attitudes or experiences associated with sexual interactions, a number of other factors may contribute to sexual dysfunction. Among these, the most common is a marked deterioration in close interpersonal relationships (Burri, Spector, & Rahman, 2013; Jiann, Su, Yu, Wu, & Huang, 2009; Wincze, Bach, & Barlow, 2008; Wincze & Weisberg, 2015). It is difficult to have a satisfactory sexual relationship in the context of growing dislike for a partner. Occasionally, the partner may no longer seem physically attractive. Finally, it is also important to feel attractive yourself. Koch, Mansfield, Thurau, and Carey (2005) found that the more a woman perceived herself as less attractive than before, the more likely she was to have sexual problems. Kelly, Strassberg, and Kircher (1990) found that anorgasmic women—in addition to displaying more negative attitudes toward masturbation, greater sex guilt, and greater endorsement of sex myths—reported discomfort in telling their partners what sexual activities might increase their arousal or lead to orgasm, such as direct clitoral stimulation. Poor sexual skills might also lead to frequent sexual failure and, ultimately, lack of desire. For example, men with erectile dysfunction report a greatly restricted range of sexual behaviors, compared with men without these problems (Wincze et al., 2008; Wincze & Weisberg, 2015).

Thus, social and cultural factors seem to affect later sexual functioning. John Gagnon has studied this phenomenon and constructed an important concept called *script theory* of sexual functioning, according to which we all operate by following "scripts" that reflect social and cultural expectations and guide our behavior (Gagnon, 1990; Laumann, Gagnon, Michael, & Michaels, 1994; Simon & Gagnon, 1986). Discovering these scripts, both in individuals and across cultures, will tell us much about sexual functioning. For example, a person who learns that sexuality is potentially dangerous, dirty, or forbidden is more vulnerable to developing sexual dysfunction later in life. This pattern is most evident in cultures with restrictive attitudes toward sex (McGoldrick et al., 2007). For example, vaginismus is relatively rare in North America but is considerably more prevalent in Ireland, Turkey, and Iran (Doğan, 2009; Farnam, Janghorbani, Merghati-Khoei, & Raisi, 2014; McGoldrick et al., 2007). Cultural scripts may also contribute to the type of sexual dysfunction reported. In India, for example, Verma, Khaitan, and Singh (1998) reported that 77% of a large number of male patients in a sexuality clinic in India reported difficulties with premature ejaculation. In addition, 71% of male patients complained of being extremely concerned about nocturnal emissions ("wet dreams") associated with erotic dreams. The authors note that this focus on problems with ejaculation is most likely the result of a strong culturally held belief in India that loss of semen causes depletion of physical and mental energy. It is also interesting that out of 1,000 patients presenting to this clinic, only 36 were female, most likely reflecting the devaluation of sexual experiences for females for religious and social reasons in India.

In U.S. culture, certain socially communicated expectations and attitudes may linger, despite a generally permissive attitude toward sex. Barbara Andersen and her colleagues (see, for example, Cyranowski et al., 1999) have demonstrated that being emotional and self-conscious about sex (having a negative sexual self-schema, described earlier in the chapter) may later lead to sexual difficulties under stressful situations. The late Bernie Zilbergeld (1999), one of the foremost authorities on male sexuality, has described a number of myths about sex believed by many men, and Baker and DeSilva (1988) converted an earlier version of Zilbergeld's male myths into a questionnaire and presented it to groups of sexually functional and dysfunctional men. They found that men with dysfunctions showed significantly greater belief in the myths than did men who were sexually functional. We explore such myths further in our discussion of treatment.

Interaction of Psychological and Physical Factors

Having reviewed the various causes, we must now say that seldom is any sexual dysfunction associated exclusively with either psychological or physical factors (Bancroft, 1997; Rosen, 2007; Wiegel et al., 2006; Wincze & Weisburg, 2015). More often, there is a subtle combination of factors. To take a typical example, a young man vulnerable to developing anxiety and holding to a certain number of sexual myths (the social contribution) may experience erectile failure unexpectedly after using drugs or alcohol, as many men do (the biological contribution). He will anticipate the next sexual encounter with anxiety, wondering if the "failure" might happen again. This combination of experience and apprehension activates the psychological sequence depicted in Figure 10.4, regardless of whether he's had a few drinks.

In summary, socially transmitted negative attitudes about sex may interact with a person's relationship difficulties and predispositions to develop performance anxiety and, ultimately, lead to sexual dysfunction. From a psychological point of view, it is not clear why some individuals develop one dysfunction and not another, although it is common for several dysfunctions to occur in the same patient. Possibly, an individual's specific biological predispositions interact with psychological factors to produce a specific sexual dysfunction.

Treatment of Sexual Dysfunction

Over the years, the treatment of sexual dysfunctions has become increasingly medicalized (Kleinplatz, 2018). This trend was greatly driven by the success and marketing of Viagra (which we discuss in more detail later). This powerful "little blue pill" (Pfizer's original Viagra pill was blue and shaped as a diamond) led people to believe that most sexual dysfunctions were primarily due to physical rather than psychological causes. However, even the potent Viagra pill leads to erections only if patients are sexually aroused, which is a psychological process. In fact, psychological factors are essential for understanding and treating all sexual dysfunctions. Some of the treatments targeting these factors are relatively simple. One such simple treatment that is effective for a large number of individuals who experience sexual dysfunction is education. Ignorance of the most basic aspects of the sexual response cycle and intercourse often leads to long-lasting dysfunctions (Bach, Wincze, & Barlow, 2001; Wincze et al., 2008; Wincze & Weisberg, 2015). Consider the case of Carl, who recently came to our sexuality clinic.

Carl... Never Too Late

Carl, a 55-year-old white man, was referred to our clinic by his urologist because he had difficulty maintaining an erection. Although he had never been married, he was involved in an intimate relationship with a 50-year-old woman. This was only his second sexual relationship. He was reluctant to ask his partner to come to the clinic because of his embarrassment in discussing sexual issues. A careful interview revealed that Carl engaged in sex twice a week, but requests by the clinician for a step-by-step description of his sexual activities revealed an unusual pattern: Carl skipped foreplay and immediately proceeded to intercourse. Unfortunately, because his partner was not aroused and lubricated, he was unable to penetrate her. His valiant efforts sometimes resulted in painful abrasions for both of them. Two sessions of extensive sex education, including specific step-by-step instructions for carrying out foreplay, provided Carl with a new outlook on sex. For the first time, he had successful, satisfying intercourse, much to his and his partner's delight. •

In the case of hypoactive sexual desire disorder, a marked difference within a couple often leads to one partner being labeled as having low desire. For example, if one partner is quite happy with sexual relations once a week but the other partner desires sex every day, the latter partner may accuse the former of having low desire, and, unfortunately, the former partner might agree. Facilitating better conditions often resolves these misunderstandings. Fortunately, for people with this and more complex sexual dysfunctions, treatments are now available, both psychosocial and medical. Advances in medical treatments, particularly for erectile dysfunction, have been dramatic in just the past few years. We look first at psychosocial treatments; then we examine the latest medical procedures.

Psychosocial Treatments

Among the many advances in our knowledge of sexual behavior, none was more dramatic than the publication in 1970 by William Masters and Virginia Johnson of *Human Sexual Inadequacy.* The procedures outlined in this book literally revolutionized sex therapy by providing a brief, direct, and reasonably successful therapeutic program for sexual dysfunctions. Underscoring again the common basis of most sexual dysfunctions, a similar approach to therapy is taken with all patients, with slight variations depending on the specific sexual problem (for example, premature ejaculation or orgasmic disorder). This intensive program involves a male and a female therapist to facilitate communication between the dysfunctional partners. (Masters and Johnson were the original male and female therapists.) Therapy is conducted daily over a 2-week period.

The actual program is quite straightforward. In addition to providing basic education about sexual functioning, altering deep-seated myths, and increasing communication, the clinicians' primary goal is to eliminate psychologically based performance anxiety (refer back to Figure 10.4). To accomplish this, Masters and Johnson introduced *sensate focus* and *nondemand pleasuring.* In this exercise, couples are instructed to refrain from intercourse or genital caressing and simply to explore and enjoy each other's body through touching, kissing, hugging, massaging, or similar kinds of behavior. In the first phase, nongenital pleasuring, breasts and genitals are excluded from the exercises. After successfully accomplishing this phase, the couple moves to genital pleasuring but with a ban on orgasm and intercourse and clear instructions to the man that achieving an erection is not the goal.

At this point, arousal should be reestablished, and the couple should be ready to attempt intercourse. So as not to proceed too quickly, this stage is also broken down into parts. For example, a couple might be instructed to attempt the beginnings of penetration; that is, the depth of penetration and the time it lasts are only gradually built up, and both genital and nongenital pleasuring continue. Eventually, full intercourse and thrusting are accomplished. After this 2-week intensive program, recovery was reported by Masters and Johnson for the vast majority of more than 790 sexually dysfunctional patients, with some differences in the rate of recovery depending on the disorder. Close to 100% of individuals with premature ejaculation recovered, whereas the rate for more difficult cases of lifelong generalized erectile dysfunction was closer to 60%.

After these results were published, specialty sexuality clinics based on the pioneering work of Masters and Johnson were established around the country to administer these new treatment techniques. Subsequent research revealed that many of the structural aspects of the program did not seem necessary. For example, one therapist seems to be as effective as two (LoPiccolo, Heiman, Hogan, & Roberts, 1985), and seeing patients once a week seems to be as effective as seeing them every day (Heiman & LoPiccolo, 1983). It has also become clear in the succeeding decades that the results achieved by Masters and Johnson were better than those achieved in clinics around the world using similar procedures. Reasons for this are not entirely clear. One possibility is that patients were highly motivated because they had to take at least 2 weeks off and fly to St. Louis to meet with Masters and Johnson.

Sex therapists have expanded on and modified these procedures over the years to take advantage of recent advances in knowledge (see, for example, Bradford & Meston, 2011; Rosen, 2007; Weiner & Avery-Clark, 2014; Wincze, 2009; Wincze et al., 2008). Results with sex therapy for erectile dysfunction indicate that as many as 60% to 70% of the cases show a positive treatment outcome for at least several years, although results are mixed and there may be some slipping after that (Frühauf, Gerger, Schmidt, Munder, & Barth, 2013; Rosen, 2007; Segraves & Althof, 1998). For better treatment of specific sexual dysfunctions, sex therapists integrate specific procedures into the context of general sex therapy. For example, to treat premature ejaculation, most sex therapists use a procedure developed by Semans (1956), sometimes called the *squeeze* technique, in which the penis is stimulated, usually by the partner, to nearly full erection. At this point, the partner firmly squeezes the penis near the top where the head of the penis joins the shaft, which quickly reduces arousal. These steps are repeated until (for heterosexual partners) eventually the penis is briefly inserted in the vagina without thrusting. If arousal occurs too quickly, the penis is withdrawn, and the squeeze technique is employed again. In this way, the man develops a sense of control over arousal and ejaculation. Reports of success with this approach over the past 20 years suggest that 60% to 90% of men benefit, but the success rates drop to about 25% after 3 years or more of follow up (Althof, 2007; Malavige & Jayawickrema, 2015; Polonsky, 2000). Gary, the 31-year-old sales representative, was treated with this method, and his wife was cooperative during the procedures. Brief marital therapy also persuaded Gary that his insecurity over his perception that his wife no longer found him attractive was unfounded. After treatment, he reduced his work hours somewhat, and the couple's marital and sexual relations improved.

Lifelong female orgasmic disorder may be treated with explicit training in masturbatory procedures (Bradford & Meston, 2011). For example, Greta was still unable to achieve orgasm with manual stimulation by her husband, even after proceeding through the basic steps of sex therapy. At this point, following certain standardized treatment programs for this problem (see, for example, Heiman, 2000; Heiman & LoPiccolo, 1988), Greta and Will purchased a vibrator, and Greta was taught to let go of her inhibitions by talking out loud about how she felt during sexual arousal, even shouting or screaming if she wanted to. In the context of appropriate genital pleasuring and disinhibition exercises, the vibrator brought on Greta's first orgasm. With practice and good communication, the couple eventually learned how to bring on Greta's orgasm without the vibrator. Although Will and Greta were both delighted with her progress, Will was concerned that Greta's screams during orgasm would attract the attention of the neighbors! Summaries of results from a number of studies suggest 70% to 90% of women will benefit from treatment, and these gains are stable and even improve further over time (Fruhauf et al., 2013; Heiman, 2007; Heiman & Meston, 1997; Segraves & Althof, 1998). As we already discussed, vulvodynia is often associated with a tensing and tightening of the pelvic floor muscle, anxiety, and depression. Women with this problem also sometimes report childhood maltreatment. Therefore, treatment of vulvodynia usually involves physical therapy of the pelvic floor to relax the muscles, cognitive-behavioral treatment (CBT), and medical management for pain (Bergeron et al., 2020).

To treat vaginismus and pain related to penetration in genito-pelvic pain/penetration disorder, the woman and, eventually, the partner gradually insert increasingly larger dilators at the woman's pace. After the woman (and then the partner) can insert the largest dilator, in a heterosexual couple, the woman gradually inserts the man's penis. These exercises are carried out in the context of genital and nongenital pleasuring so as to retain arousal. Close attention must be accorded to any increased fear and anxiety that may be associated with the process, which may trigger memories of early sexual abuse that may have contributed to the onset of the

A therapist usually treats a dysfunction in one partner by seeing the couple together.

condition. These procedures are highly successful, with a large majority of women (80% to 100%) overcoming vaginismus in a relatively short period (Binik et al., 2007; Leiblum & Rosen, 2000; ter Kuile et al., 2007; ter Kuile, Melles, de Groot, Tuijnman-Raasveld, & van Lankveld, 2013).

A variety of treatment procedures have also been developed for low sexual desire (see, for example, Pridal & LoPiccolo, 2000; Wincze, 2009; Wincze & Weisberg, 2015). At the heart of these treatments are the standard reeducation and communication phases of traditional sex therapy with, possibly, the addition of masturbatory training and exposure to erotic material. Each case may require individual strategies. Remember Mrs. C., who was sexually abused by her cousin? Therapy involved helping the couple understand the impact of the repeated, unwanted sexual experiences in Mrs. C.'s past and to approach sex so that Mrs. C. was more comfortable with foreplay. She gradually lost the idea that once sex was started she had no control. She and her husband worked on starting and stopping sexual encounters. Cognitive restructuring was used to help Mrs. C. interpret her husband's amorousness in a positive rather than a skeptical light. In general, approximately 50% to 70% of individuals with low sexual desire benefit from sex therapy, at least initially (Basson, 2007; Brotto, 2006).

Medical Treatments

A variety of pharmacological and surgical techniques have been developed in recent years to treat sexual dysfunction, almost all focusing on male erectile disorder. Regardless of the treatments, it is important to combine any medical treatment with a comprehensive educational and sex therapy program to ensure maximum benefit, as recommended by the American Urological Association (Burnett et al., 2018). The drugs sildenafil (for example, Viagra), vardenafil (for example, Lavitra), and tadalafil (for example, Cialis) are some of the most common and most effective drugs for erectile dysfunction (ED). These drugs work by blocking a particular enzyme (phosphodiesterase-5 or PDE5), that promotes the breakdown of a particular phosphate (cyclic GMP) that regulates blood flow in the penis. The first drug of this class, Viagra (sildenafil), was first developed in 1989 by Pfizer as a possible new drug to treat high blood pressure and angina, which is chest pain caused by reduced blood flow to the heart. The first medical trial of Viagra showed disappointing results for treating blood pressure or chest pain but a lot of promise for treating ED. Since then, researchers examined the biochemical pathway involved in the erection process, which helped amplify the effects of sexual stimulation in opening up the blood vessels in the penis. As a result, Viagra became a highly effective and commonly used drug, revolutionizing the treatment of ED (Carson et al., 2002). Viagra is typically taken 1 hour before the planned sexual activity, but sexual stimulation is still necessary for an erection to occur. The effect usually lasts 3 to 4 hours. The side effects are mild, depending on the dose, and can include a stuffy nose, flushing, headache, and stomach pain. Cialis lasts up to 36 hours and can be taken daily at a very small dose, limiting the adverse effects of the drug. Although all PDE5 inhibitors are very effective for treating ED (Briganti et al., 2005), the drug can be dangerous for some people with certain heart conditions and when mixing them with other drugs. Also, response to the drugs vary by individuals. Remember that sexual arousal is necessary for the drug to work. If men are particularly anxious about sex, results are not as good (Rosen et al., 2006). To address this issue, Bach, Barlow, and Wincze (2004) evaluated the addition of CBT to treatment with Viagra. Results were encouraging because couples reported greater satisfaction and increased sexual activity after combined drug therapy and CBT, compared with a period when only the drug was used.

There was also some hope that Viagra would be useful for dysfunction in postmenopausal women, but results were disappointing (Bradford & Meston, 2011; Kaplan et al., 1999). Now interest has centered on a new drug, flibanserin, as a possible treatment for hypoactive sexual desire in women. Indeed, initial research findings suggest that this medication may be effective since there is preliminary evidence for increases in sexual desire and reduced distress associated with hypoactive sexual desire in women (DeRogatis et al., 2012; Katz et al., 2013). These findings are controversial since the data show that the effects of what has been called "pink Viagra" are so modest as to be relatively unnoticeable for many women, leading some to question whether pharmaceutical companies may be misleading the public in order to cash in on a sexual enhancement drug for women given the enormous profits associated with Viagra and similar drugs for men (Brotto, 2015; Laan & Tiefer, 2014; Levine, 2015). This research is still in its infancy.

For some time, testosterone (Schiavi, White, Mandeli, & Levine, 1997) has been used to treat erectile dysfunction. But although it is safe and has relatively few side effects, only negligible effects on erectile dysfunction have been reported (Forti, Corona, Vignozzi, & Maggi, 2012; Mann et al., 1996). Some urologists teach patients to inject vasodilating drugs such as *papaverine* or *prostaglandin* directly into the penis when they want to have sexual intercourse. These drugs dilate the blood vessels, allowing blood to flow to the penis and thereby producing an erection within 15 minutes that can last from 1 to 4 hours (Rosen, 2007; Segraves & Althof, 1998). Because this procedure is a bit painful (although not as much as one might think), a substantial number of men, usually 50% to 60%, stop using it after a short time. In one study, 50 of 100 patients discontinued papaverine for various reasons (Lakin, Montague, Vanderbrug Medendorp, Tesar, & Schover, 1990; Segraves & Althof, 1998). A soft capsule that contains papaverine (called MUSE, for Medical Urethral System for Erections) can be inserted directly into the urethra, but this is somewhat painful, is less effective than injections, and remains awkward and artificial enough to preclude wide acceptance (Delizonna, Wincze, Litz, Brown, & Barlow, 2001). Insertion of *penile prostheses* or implants has been a surgical option for almost 100 years; only recently have they become good enough to approximate normal sexual functioning. One procedure involves implanting a semirigid silicone rod that can be bent by the man into correct position for intercourse and maneuvered out of the way at other times. In a more popular procedure, the man squeezes a small pump that is surgically implanted into the scrotum, forcing fluid into an inflatable cylinder and thus producing an erection. A newer penile prosthetic device is an inflatable rod that contains the pumping device, which is more convenient than having the pump outside the rod. However, surgical implants fall short of restoring presurgical sexual functioning or assuring satisfaction in most patients (Gregoire, 1992; Kim &

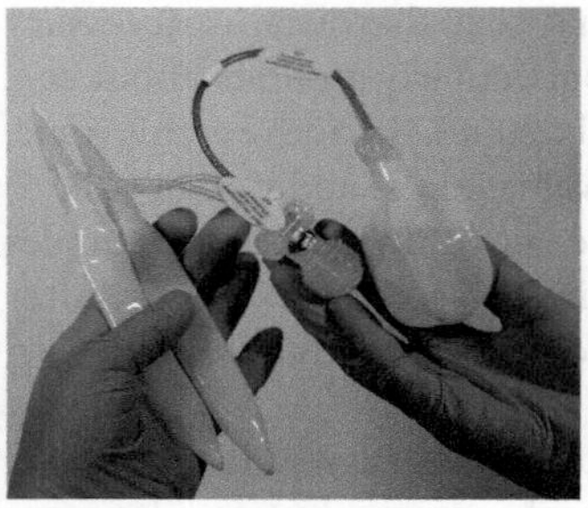
Larry Mulvehill/The Image Works

An inflatable penile implant may be used for people with inadequate sexual functioning.

Lipshultz, 1997); they are now generally used only if other approaches don't work. On the other hand, this procedure has proved useful for men who must have a cancerous prostate removed because this surgery often causes erectile dysfunction, although newer "nerve-sparing" surgeries lessen the effect to some extent (Ramsawh, Morgentaler, Covino, Barlow, & DeWolf, 2005).

Another approach is *vacuum device therapy*, which works by creating a vacuum in a cylinder placed over the penis. The vacuum draws blood into the penis, which is then trapped by a specially designed ring placed around the base of the penis. Although using the vacuum device is rather awkward, between 70% and 100% of users report satisfactory erections, particularly if psychological sex therapy is ineffective (Segraves & Althof, 1998; Witherington, 1988). The procedure is also less intrusive than surgery or injections, but it remains awkward and artificial (Delizonna et al., 2001). However, this therapy has gained traction as a first-line therapy for men who have been treated for prostate cancer (Pahlajani, Raina, Jones, & Zippe, 2012).

Summary

Treatment programs, both psychosocial and medical, offer hope to most people who suffer from sexual dysfunctions. Unfortunately, such programs are not readily available in many locations because few health and mental health professionals are trained to apply them, although the availability of drugs for male erectile dysfunction is widespread. Further, government agencies such as the NIH have been slow to fund research dedicated to understanding sexual dysfunctions and their treatments since any research focused on sex has occasionally proved to be controversial among some members of Congress serving on oversight committees for NIH funding. Psychological treatment of sexual arousal disorders requires further improvement, and treatments for low sexual desire are largely untested. Even with effective PDE5 inhibitors, there is a great need for psychological treatment for sexual dysfunctions.

Unfortunately, most health professionals tend to ignore the issue of sexuality in older adults. Along with the usual emphasis on communication, education, and sensate focus, appropriate lubricants and a discussion of methods to maximize the erectile response should be a part of any sexual counseling for older couples. More important, even with reduced physical capabilities, continued sexual relations, not necessarily including intercourse, should be an enjoyable and important part of an aging couple's relationship. Further research and development in the treatment of sexual dysfunction must address all these issues. Nevertheless, the overwhelming consensus is that a combination of psychological and drug treatment, when indicated, will continue to be the treatment strategy of choice.

Concept Check 10.2

Determine whether the following statements are true (T) or false (F) in regard to the causes and treatments of sexual dysfunctions.

1. ___________ Many physical and medical conditions and their treatments (for example, prescription medications) contribute to sexual dysfunction; however, many doctors are unaware of the connection.
2. ___________ Anxiety always decreases or even eradicates sexual arousal.
3. ___________ Sexual dysfunctions can result from a growing dislike for a partner, traumatic sexual events, or childhood lessons about the negative consequences of sexual behavior.
4. ___________ A simple, effective treatment for many disorders is education.
5. ___________ All sexual dysfunctions are treated with the same psychosocial technique.
6. ___________ Most surgical and pharmacological treatments of recent years have focused on erectile disorder.

Paraphilic Disorders: Clinical Descriptions

Most people's sexual interest is directed to other physically mature adults (or late adolescents), all of whom are capable of freely offering or withholding their consent. But what if someone is sexually attracted to something or somebody other than another adult, such as animals (particularly horses and dogs) (Williams & Weinberg, 2003) or a vacuum cleaner? Or what if your only means of obtaining sexual satisfaction is to commit a brutal murder? Such patterns of sexual arousal and countless others exist in a large number of individuals, causing untold human suffering both for them and, if their behavior involves other people, for their victims. As noted in the beginning of the chapter, these disorders of sexual arousal—if they cause distress or impairment to the individual or cause personal harm or the risk of harm to others—are called **paraphilic disorders**. It is important to note that DSM-5 does not consider a paraphilia a disorder unless it is associated with distress and impairment or harm or the threat of harm to others. Thus, unusual patterns of sexual attraction are not considered to be sufficient to meet criteria for a disorder. This is a controversial change in DSM-5 (see the DSM *Controversies* box on page 395).

Over the years, we have assessed and treated a large number of individuals with paraphilias and paraphilic disorders, ranging from the slightly eccentric and sometimes pitiful cases to some of the most dangerous killer-rapists encountered anywhere. As noted above, there are many harmless aberrations, such as some fetishistic arousal patterns (see next section), which harm no one, are not distressful or impairing, and therefore do not meet criteria for a disorder. We begin

A crowded subway car is a typical setting for frotteuristic activity, in which a person takes advantage of forced physical contact with strangers to become aroused.

by describing briefly the major types of paraphilic disorders, using in all instances cases from our own files. As with sexual dysfunctions, it is unusual for an individual to have just one paraphilic pattern of sexual arousal (Bradford & Meston, 2011; Krueger & Kaplan, 2015; Laws & O'Donohue, 2008; Seto, Kingston, & Bourget, 2014). Many of our patients may present with two, three, or more patterns, although one is usually dominant (Abel, Becker, Cunningham-Rathner, Mittelman, & Rouleau, 1988; American Psychiatric Association, 2013; Brownell, Hayes, & Barlow, 1977). Furthermore, it is not uncommon for individuals with paraphilic disorder to also suffer from comorbid mood, anxiety, and substance abuse disorders (Kafka & Hennen, 2003; Krueger & Kaplan, 2015; Raymond, Coleman, Ohlerking, Christenson, & Miner, 1999). Although paraphilic disorders are not widely prevalent and estimates of their frequency are hard to come by, some disorders, such as transvestic disorder (cross-dressing, discussed later), seem relatively common (Bancroft, 1989; Mason, 1997). You may have been the victim of **frotteuristic disorder** in a large city, typically on a crowded subway or bus. (We mean really crowded, with people packed in like sardines.) In this situation, women have been known to experience more than the usual jostling and pushing from behind. What they discover, much to their horror, is a man with a frotteuristic arousal pattern rubbing against them until he is stimulated to the point of ejaculation. Because the victims cannot escape easily, the frotteuristic act is usually successful (Lussier & Piché, 2008).

Fetishistic Disorder

In **fetishistic disorder**, a person is sexually attracted to nonliving objects. There are almost as many types of fetishes as there are objects, although women's undergarments and shoes are popular (Darcangelo, 2008; Kafka, 2010). Fetishistic arousal is associated with two classes of objects or activities: (1) an inanimate object or (2) a source of specific tactile stimulation, such as rubber, particularly clothing made out of rubber. Shiny black plastic is also used (Bancroft, 1989; Junginger, 1997). Most of the person's sexual fantasies, urges, and desires focus on this object. A third source of attraction (sometimes called *partialism*) is a part of the body, such as the foot, buttocks, or hair.

In one U.S. city for several months, bras hung out on a woman's backyard clothesline disappeared. The women in the neighborhood soon began talking to each other and discovered that bras were missing from every clothesline for blocks around. A police stakeout caught the perpetrator, who turned out to have a strong fetish for brassieres. As another example of fetishistic behavior related to tactile stimulation, it is relatively common for a urologist to be called to the emergency room to remove surgically a long thin object, such as a pencil or the arm of an eyeglass frame, from a man's urethra. Men who insert such objects think that partially blocking the urethra in this way can increase the intensity of ejaculation during masturbation. If the entire object slips into the penis, however, major medical intervention is required.

DSM 5 **Table 10.5**
Criteria for Genito-Pelvic Pain/Penetration Disorder

A. Persistent or recurrent difficulties with one (or more) of the following:
1. Vaginal penetration during intercourse.
2. Marked vulvovaginal or pelvic pain during vaginal intercourse or penetration attempts.
3. Marked fear or anxiety about vulvovaginal or pelvic pain in anticipation of, during, or as a result of vaginal penetration.
4. Marked tensing or tightening of the pelvic floor muscles during attempted vaginal penetration.

B. The symptoms in Criterion A have persisted for a minimum duration of approximately 6 months.

C. The symptoms in Criterion A cause clinically significant distress in the individual.

D. The sexual dysfunction is not better explained by a nonsexual mental disorder or as a consequence of severe relationship distress (e.g., partner violence) or other significant stressors and is not attributable to the effects of a substance/medication or another medical condition.

Specify whether:

Lifelong: The disturbance has been present since the individual became sexually active.

Acquired: The disturbance began after a period of relatively normal sexual function.

American Psychiatric Association. (2022). *Diagnostic and statistical manual of mental disorders* (5th ed., Text Revision).

Voyeuristic and Exhibitionistic Disorders

Voyeuristic disorder is the practice of observing, to become aroused, an unsuspecting individual undressing or naked. **Exhibitionistic disorder**, by contrast, is achieving sexual arousal and gratification by exposing genitals to unsuspecting strangers (Långström, 2010). Consider the case of Robert.

Robert... Outside the Curtains

Robert, a 31-year-old, married, blue-collar worker, reported that he first started "peeping" into windows when he was 14. He rode around the neighborhood on his bike at night, and when he spotted a female through a window, he stopped and stared. During one of these episodes, he felt the first pangs of sexual arousal. Eventually, he began masturbating while watching, thereby exposing his genitals, although out of sight. When he was older, he drove around until he spotted some prepubescent girls. He parked his car near them, unzipped his fly, called them over, and attempted to carry on a nonsexual conversation. Later he was sometimes able to talk a girl into mutual masturbation and *fellatio*, or oral stimulation of the penis. Although he was arrested several times, paradoxically, the threat of arrest increased his arousal (Barlow & Wincze, 1980). •

Remember that anxiety actually increases arousal under some circumstances. Many voyeurs just don't get the same satisfaction from attending readily available strip shows at a local bar. Exhibitionistic disorder is often associated with lower levels of education, but not always. Note again that the thrilling element of risk is an important part of exhibitionistic disorder.

DSM 5 Table 10.6
Criteria for Frotteuristic Disorder

A. Over a period of at least 6 months, recurrent and intense sexual arousal from touching or rubbing against a nonconsenting person, as manifested by fantasies, urges, or behaviors.

B. The person has acted on these sexual urges with a nonconsenting person, or the sexual urges or fantasies cause clinically significant distress or impairment in social, occupational, or other important areas of functioning

American Psychiatric Association. (2022). *Diagnostic and statistical manual of mental disorders* (5th ed., Text Revision).

The Lawyer Who Needed the Bus

Several years ago, a distinguished lawyer reported that he needed help and that his career was on the line. An intelligent, good-looking single man, he noted without bragging that he could have sex with any number of beautiful women in the course of his law practice. The only way he could become aroused, however, was to leave his office, go down to the bus stop, ride around the city until a reasonably attractive young woman got on, expose himself just before the next stop, and then run off the bus, often with people chasing after him. To achieve maximal arousal, the bus could not be full or empty; there had to be just a few people sitting on the bus, and the woman getting on had to be the right age. Sometimes hours would pass before these circumstances lined up correctly. The lawyer observed that if he was not fired for exhibitionism, he would be fired for all the time he was missing from work. On several occasions, he had requested a girlfriend to role-play sitting on a bus in his apartment. Although he exposed himself to her, he could not achieve sexual arousal and gratification because the activity just wasn't exciting. •

Although prevalence is unknown (Murphy & Page, 2008), in a random sample of 2,450 adults in Sweden, 31% reported at least one incident of being sexually aroused by exposing their genitals to a stranger, and 7.7% reported at least one incident of being sexually aroused by spying on others having sex (Långström & Seto, 2006). To meet diagnosis for exhibitionistic disorder, the behavior must occur repeatedly and be compulsive or out of control.

Transvestic Disorder

In **transvestic disorder**, sexual arousal is strongly associated with the act of (or fantasies of) dressing in clothes of the opposite sex, or cross-dressing (Blanchard, 2010; Wheeler, Newring, & Draper, 2008). Consider the case of Mr. M.

Note that Mr. M. was in the Marine Corps before he joined the police force. It is not unusual for men who are strongly inclined to dress in feminine clothes to compensate by associating with so-called macho organizations. Some of our cross-dressing patients have been associated with various paramilitary organizations. Nevertheless, most individuals with this disorder do not seem to display any compensatory behaviors. The same survey in Sweden mentioned earlier found 2.8% of men and 0.4% of women reported at least one episode of transvestistic disorder (Långström & Zucker, 2005). The 3% prevalence rate in males, while a rough estimate, is generally accepted (American Psychiatric Association, 2013).

Mr. M.... Strong Man in a Dress

Mr. M., a 31-year-old married police officer, came to our clinic seeking treatment for uncontrollable urges to dress in women's clothing and appear in public. He had been doing this for 16 years and had been discharged from the Marine Corps for cross-dressing. Since then, he had risked public disclosure on several occasions. Mr. M.'s wife had threatened to divorce him because of the cross-dressing, yet she often purchased women's clothing for him and was "compassionate" while he wore them. •

DSM 5 **Table 10.7**
Criteria for Fetishistic Disorder

A. Over a period of at least 6 months, recurrent and intense sexual arousal from the use of nonliving objects or a highly specific focus on nongenital body part(s), as manifested by fantasies, urges, or behaviors.
B. The fantasies, sexual urges, or behaviors cause clinically significant distress or impairment in social, occupational, or other important areas of functioning.
C. The fetish objects are not limited to articles of clothing used in cross-dressing (as in transvestic disorder) or devices specifically designed for the purpose of tactile genital stimulation (e.g., a vibrator).

American Psychiatric Association. (2022). *Diagnostic and statistical manual of mental disorders* (5th ed., Text Revision).

DSM 5 **Table 10.8**
Criteria for Voyeuristic and Exhibitionistic Disorders

Voyeuristic Disorder

A. Over a period of at least 6 months, recurrent and intense sexual arousal from observing an unsuspecting person who is naked, in the process of disrobing, or engaging in sexual activity, as manifested by fantasies, urges, or behaviors.
B. The person has acted on these sexual urges with a nonconsenting person, or the sexual urges or fantasies cause clinically significant distress or impairment in social, occupational, or other important areas of functioning.
C. The individual experiencing the arousal and/or acting on the urges is at least 18 years of age.

Exhibitionistic Disorder

A. Over a period of at least 6 months, recurrent and intense sexual arousal from the exposure of one's genitals to an unsuspecting person, as manifested by fantasies, urges, or behaviors.
B. The person has acted on these sexual urges with a nonconsenting person, or the sexual urges or fantasies cause clinically significant distress or impairment in social, occupational, or other important areas of functioning.

American Psychiatric Association. (2022). *Diagnostic and statistical manual of mental disorders* (5th ed., Text Revision).

Interestingly, the wives of many men who cross-dress have accepted their husbands' behavior and can be quite supportive if it is a private matter between them. Docter and Prince (1997) reported that 60% of more than 1,000 men with transvestistic disorder were married at the time of the survey. Some people join cross-dressing clubs that meet periodically or subscribe to newsletters devoted to the topic. If sexual arousal is primarily focused on the clothing itself, the diagnostic criteria require a specification "with fetishism." Research suggests that transvestism of this type is indistinguishable from other fetishes in most respects (Freund, Seto, & Kuban, 1996).

Another specifier for transvestism describes a pattern of sexual arousal for a man associated not with clothing itself but rather with thoughts or images of oneself as a woman (for example). This specifier is called "autogynephilia." Consider the case of Ron, who was seen in our clinic.

Ron and Rhonda... Sexual Confusion

Ron was a 47-year-old divorced male with a 6-year-old son who lived with his son's mother. For the past several years, Ron had been living with his girlfriend and his girlfriend's 7-year-old daughter, mother, and sister. He was large and muscular with a short but full beard. His initial complaint was severe social anxiety, which he felt had interfered with his ability to make friends and advance in his job since he sought out positions that required only limited social interaction. He reported that he loved his girlfriend and wanted to get married and was particularly concerned about being the best father he could be for his son. He was assigned to group treatment for social anxiety, but he showed up for the first session much to our surprise dressed in a jean miniskirt, knee-high black leather boots, and a blouse. During the session he expressed considerable confusion about his sexuality, and we decided his needs would be better met in individual treatment.

At that point, he requested to be called Rhonda and began volunteering a previous history of cross-dressing and frequenting gay nightclubs from time to time. He reported that his first marriage had ended after his wife discovered photos of him wearing her wedding dress. Presently, the most sexually arousing scenario for him was the image of himself as a woman, such as imagining himself performing domestic chores or activities such as cooking for a male partner while wearing an apron. But he was clear that it was not the clothes that were arousing so much as the image in his own mind of himself as a woman. He also reported engaging in risky sexual behaviors such as unprotected sex, meeting up with strangers to engage in sexual behaviors in parking lots, texting naked/provocative photos of himself to potential partners, and engaging in sexual acts in public places such as the gym shower, all of which would begin with him dressed in his female clothes and assuming the role of a woman. He had kept this behavior from his girlfriend mostly by hiding his clothes in the trunk of his car or in a back closet at work. In spite of this behavior, he maintained a strong and frequent sexual relationship with his girlfriend and was terrified of contracting AIDS and infecting her. He also couldn't imagine giving up the strong relationship with his son. Treatment focused on eliminating risky sexual behavior and targeting his conflicting feelings around his sexuality. After a course of treatment and occasional follow-up sessions, he reported to be at peace with his sexuality and he had given up his risky infidelities with no reports of slips or relapses. •

This specifier is controversial because the "sexual confusion" experienced by Ron overlaps to some degree with gender dysphoria (described below), and some think this confusion is better captured by the concept of gender dysphoria. Indeed, there is a somewhat greater risk that individuals with this paraphilic disorder will develop gender dysphoria and request transition through gender-affirming surgery (Blanchard, 2010; Lawrence, 2013). But as one can see in the case of Ron/Rhonda, gender dysphoria was not a major component of his presentation, and he did not once consider surgical gender-affirmation. Rather, he was very strongly sexually aroused by thoughts and images of himself as a woman.

Sexual Sadism and Sexual Masochism Disorders

Both **sexual sadism** and **sexual masochism** are associated with either inflicting pain or humiliation (sadism) or suffering pain or humiliation (masochism) (Hucker, 2008; Krueger, 2010a, 2010b; Yates, Hucker, & Kingston, 2008), and becoming sexually aroused is specifically associated with violence and injury in these conditions (Seto, Lalumiere, Harris, & Chivers, 2012). Although Mr. M. was extremely concerned about his cross-dressing, he was also disturbed by another problem. To maximize his sexual pleasure during intercourse with his wife, he had her wear a collar and leash, tied her to the bed, and handcuffed her. He sometimes tied himself with ropes, chains, handcuffs, and wires, all while he was cross-dressed. Mr. M. was concerned he might injure himself seriously. As a member of the police force, he had heard of cases and even investigated one himself in which an individual was found dead, tightly and completely bound in harnesses, handcuffs, and ropes. In many such cases, something goes wrong and the individual accidentally hangs themselves, an event that should be distinguished from the closely related condition called *hypoxiphilia*, which involves self-strangulation to reduce the flow of oxygen to the brain and enhance the sensation of orgasm. It may seem paradoxical that someone has to either inflict or receive pain to become sexually aroused, but these types of cases are not uncommon. On many occasions, the behaviors themselves are quite mild and harmless (Krueger, 2010a, 2010b), but they can become dangerous and costly. It was not unusual that Mr. M. presented with three patterns of deviant arousal—in his case, sexual masochism, sexual sadism, and transvestism.

Sadistic Rape

After murder, rape is the most devastating assault one person can make on another. It is not classified as a paraphilic disorder because most instances of rape are better characterized as an assault by a man (or, rarely, a woman) whose patterns of sexual arousal are not paraphilic. Instead, many rapists meet criteria for antisocial personality disorder (see Chapter 12) and may engage in a variety of antisocial and aggressive acts (Bradford & Meston, 2011; Davison & Janca, 2012; McCabe & Wauchope, 2005; Quinsey, 2010). Many rapes could be described as opportunistic, in that an aggressive or antisocial individual with a marked lack of empathy and disregard for inflicting pain on others (Bernat, Calhoun, & Adams, 1999) spontaneously took advantage of a vulnerable and unsuspecting woman. These unplanned assaults often occur during robberies or other criminal events. Rapes can also be motivated by anger and vindictiveness against specific women and may have been planned in advance (Hucker, 1997; McCabe & Wauchope, 2005; Rebocho & Silva, 2014; Quinsey, 2010).

A number of years ago, we determined in our sexuality clinic that certain rapists do closely fit definitions of paraphilic disorder and could probably better be described as sadists, a finding that has since been confirmed (McCabe & Wauchope, 2005; Quinsey, 2010; Seto et al., 2012). We constructed two audiotapes on which were described (1) mutually enjoyable sexual intercourse and (2) sexual intercourse involving force on the part of the male (rape). Each tape was played twice for selected listeners. The nonrapists became sexually aroused to descriptions of mutually consenting intercourse but not to those involving force. Rapists, however, became aroused by both types of descriptions (Abel, Barlow, Blanchard, & Guild, 1977).

Among the rapists we were evaluating, a subgroup seemed to be particularly aroused when force and acts of cruelty were involved. To assess this reaction more completely, we put together a third audiotape consisting of aggression and assault without any

Marny Malin/Getty Images

Murderer Jeffrey Dahmer obtained sexual gratification from acts of sadism and cannibalism. (In prison, he was killed by fellow inmates.)

DSM 5 Table 10.9
Criteria for Transvestic Disorder

A. Over a period of at least 6 months, recurrent and intense sexual arousal from cross-dressing, as manifested by fantasies, urges, or behaviors.

B. The fantasies, sexual urges, or behaviors cause clinically significant distress or impairment in social, occupational, or other important areas of functioning.

Specify if:

With fetishism

With autogynephilia

American Psychiatric Association. (2022). *Diagnostic and statistical manual of mental disorders* (5th ed., Text Revision).

Pool/Getty Images

In 2002, the Catholic church in the United States was forced to acknowledge a series of cover-ups involving pedophilia by a number of clergy, including one involving defrocked priest Paul Shanley (above).

sexual content. A number of individuals displayed strong sexual arousal to nonsexual aggressive themes, as well as to rape, and little or no arousal to mutually enjoyable intercourse. One of our patients was the most brutal rapist we have ever encountered. By his own report, he had raped more than 100 times. His last victim spent 2 weeks in the hospital recovering from various injuries. He would bite his victim's breasts, burn her with cigarettes, beat her with belts and switches, and pull out her pubic hair while shoving objects in her vagina. Although some evidence indicated he had killed at least three of his victims, it was not sufficient to convict him of murder. Nevertheless, he was convicted of multiple assaults and rapes and was about to begin a life sentence in a closely guarded area of the maximum-security state prison. Realizing his behavior was hopelessly out of control, he was eager to get there. He reported that all his waking hours were spent ruminating uncontrollably on sadistic fantasies. He knew he was going to spend the rest of his life in prison, probably in solitary confinement, but he hoped there was something we could do to relieve him of his obsession. By any definition, this man met criteria for sexual sadism disorder.

Pedophilic Disorder and Incest

Perhaps the most tragic sexual deviance is sexual attraction to children (or young adolescents generally aged 13 years or younger), called **pedophilia** (Blanchard, 2010; Seto, 2009, 2012). People around the world have become more aware of this problem following the well-publicized scandal in the Catholic Church, where priests, many of whom undoubtedly met criteria for pedophilic disorder, abused children repeatedly, only to be transferred to another church and repeat these offences. Individuals with this pattern of arousal may be attracted to male children, female children, or both. In one survey, as many as 12% of men and 17% of women reported being touched inappropriately by adults when they were children (Fagan, Wise, Schmidt, & Berlin, 2002). One study estimated the prevalence of sexual abuse before age 18 to be 10.14% (Pérez-Fuentes et al., 2013). Approximately 90% of abusers are male, and 10% are female (Fagan et al., 2002; Seto, 2009). Much as with adult rape, as many as 40% to 50% of sexual offenders do not have pedophilic arousal patterns and do not meet criteria for pedophilic disorder. Rather, their offenses are associated with brutal antisocial and aggressive opportunistic acts (Blanchard, 2010; Seto, 2009). Child pornography investigations have made much news lately, and individuals convicted of downloading child pornography often defend themselves by pointing out that they were "just looking" and are not pedophiles. But an important study indicates that being charged with a child pornography offense is one of the best diagnostic indications of pedophilic disorder (Seto, Cantor, & Blanchard, 2006).

If the children are the person's relatives, the pedophilia takes the form of **incest**. Although pedophilia and incest have much in common, victims of pedophilic disorder tend to be young children, and victims of incest tend to be girls beginning to mature physically (Rice & Harris, 2002). By using penile strain gauge measures, Marshall, Barbaree, and Christophe (1986) and Marshall (1997) demonstrated that incestuous males are, in general, more aroused by adult women than are males with pedophilic disorder, who tend to focus exclusively on children. Thus, incestuous relations may have more to do with availability and interpersonal issues ongoing in the family than pedophilia, as in the case of Tony.

Tony... More and Less a Father

Tony, a 52-year-old married television repairman, came in depressed. About 10 years earlier, he had begun sexual activity with his 12-year-old daughter. Light kissing and some fondling gradually escalated to heavy petting and, finally, mutual masturbation. When his daughter was 16 years old, his wife discovered the ongoing incestuous relationship. She separated from her husband and eventually divorced him, taking her daughter with her. Soon, Tony remarried. Just before his initial visit to our clinic, Tony visited his daughter, then 22 years old, who was living alone in a different city. They had not seen each other for 5 years. A second visit, shortly after the first, led to a recurrence of the incestuous behavior. At this point, Tony became extremely depressed and told his new wife the whole story. She contacted our clinic with his full cooperation while his daughter sought treatment in her own city. •

We return to the case of Tony later, but several features are worth noting. First, Tony loved his daughter and was bitterly disappointed and depressed over his behavior. Occasionally, a child molester is abusive and aggressive, sometimes killing the victims; in these cases, the disorder is often both sexual sadism and pedophilia. But most child molesters are *not* physically abusive. Rarely is a child physically forced or injured. From the molester's perspective, no harm is done because there is no physical force or threats. Child molesters often rationalize their behavior as "loving" the child or teaching the child useful lessons about sexuality. The child molester almost never considers the psychological damage the victim suffers, yet these interactions often destroy the child's trust and ability to share intimacy. Child molesters rarely gauge their power over the children, who may participate in the molestation without protest yet be frightened and unwilling. Often children feel responsible for the abuse because no outward force or threat was used by the adult, and only after the abused children grow up are they able to understand they were powerless to protect themselves and not responsible for what was done to them.

Paraphilic Disorders in Women

Paraphilic disorders are seldom seen in women and were thought to be absent in women for many years, with the possible exception of sadomasochistic practices. But several reports have appeared describing individual cases or small series of cases (Davis, 2014; Seto, 2009). Now estimates suggest that approximately 5% to 10% of all sexual offenders are women (Cortoni & Gannon, 2011; Logan, 2009; Wiegel, 2008). For example, Federoff, Fishell, and Federoff (1999) have reported 12 cases of women with paraphilic disorders seen in their clinic. Although some women had more than one paraphilic disorder, 5 of the 12 presented with pedophilia, 4 presented with exhibitionism, and 3 presented with sadomasochistic tendencies. Female sexual offenders are often treated similarly to male sexual offenders; however, more attention is needed to understand the differences between these offenders and the best ways to treat them (Cortoni & Gannon, 2016).

To take several examples, one heterosexual woman was convicted of sexually molesting an unrelated 9-year-old boy while she was babysitting. It seems she had touched the boy's penis and asked him to masturbate in front of her while she watched religious programs on television. It is not unusual for individuals

DSM 5 Table 10.10
Criteria for Sexual Sadism Disorder and Sexual Masochism Disorder

Sexual Sadism Disorder

A. Over a period of at least 6 months, recurrent and intense sexual arousal from the psychological or physical suffering of another person, as manifested by fantasies, urges, or behaviors.

B. The person has acted on these sexual urges with a nonconsenting person, or the sexual urges or fantasies cause clinically significant distress or impairment in social, occupational, or other important areas of functioning.

Sexual Masochism Disorder

A. Over a period of at least 6 months, recurrent and intense sexual arousal from the act of being humiliated, beaten, bound, or otherwise made to suffer, as manifested by fantasies, urges, or behaviors.

B. The fantasies, sexual urges, or behaviors cause clinically significant distress or impairment in social, occupational, or other important areas of functioning.

American Psychiatric Association. (2022). *Diagnostic and statistical manual of mental disorders* (5th ed., Text Revision).

DSM 5 Table 10.11
Criteria for Pedophilic Disorder

A. Over a period of at least 6 months, recurrent, intense sexually arousing fantasies, sexual urges, or behaviors involving sexual activity with a prepubescent child or children (generally age 13 years or younger).

B. The person has acted on these sexual urges, or the sexual urges or fantasies cause marked distress or interpersonal difficulty.

C. The individual is at least age 16 years and at least 5 years older than the child or children in Criterion A.

Note: Do not include an individual in late adolescence involved in an ongoing sexual relationship with a 12- or 13-year-old.

Specify type:

Exclusive type (attracted only to children)

Nonexclusive type

Specify if:

Sexually attracted to males

Sexually attracted to females

Sexually attracted to both

Specify if:

Limited to incest

American Psychiatric Association. (2022). *Diagnostic and statistical manual of mental disorders* (5th ed., Text Revision).

DSM 5 Table 10.12
Criteria for Other Specified Paraphilic Disorder

This category applies to presentations in which symptoms characteristic of a paraphilic disorder that cause clinically significant distress or impairment in social, occupational, or other important areas of functioning predominate but do not meet the full criteria for any of the disorders in the paraphilic disorders diagnostic class. Examples include, but are not limited to, telephone scatologia (obscene phone calls), necrophilia (corpses), zoophilia (animals), coprophilia (feces), klismaphilia (enemas), and urophilia (urine).

American Psychiatric Association. (2022). *Diagnostic and statistical manual of mental disorders* (5th ed., Text Revision).

with paraphilic disorders to rationalize their behavior by engaging in some other practices that they consider to be morally correct or uplifting at the same time, a practice sometimes referred to as "moral cleansing." Yet another woman came to treatment because of her "uncontrollable" rituals of undressing in front of her apartment window and masturbating approximately five times a month. In addition, she would, occasionally, drive her truck through the neighborhood, where she would attempt to befriend cats and dogs by offering them food. She would then place honey or other food substances on her genital area so that the animals would lick her. As with most people with paraphilic disorders, the woman was horrified by this activity and was seeking treatment to eliminate it, although she found it highly sexually arousing. Wiegel (2008) reported on more than 175 females who admitted sexually abusing children or adolescents.

Causes of Paraphilic Disorders

Although no substitute for scientific inquiry, case histories often provide hypotheses that can then be tested by controlled scientific observations. Let's return to the cases of Robert and Tony to see if their histories contain any clues.

Robert... Revenge on Repression

Robert, who sought help for exhibitionism, was raised by a stern authoritarian father and a passive mother in a small Texas town. His father often preached the evils of sexual intercourse to his family. Robert learned little about sex from his father except that it was bad, so he suppressed any emerging opposite-sex sexual urges and fantasies and as an adolescent felt uneasy around girls his own age. By accident, he discovered a private source of sexual gratification: staring at attractive and unsuspecting females through the window. This led to his first masturbatory experience.

Robert reported in retrospect that being arrested was not so bad because it disgraced his father, which was his only way of getting back at him. The courts treated him lightly (which is not unusual), and his father was publicly humiliated, forcing the family to move from their small Texas town (Barlow & Wincze, 1980). •

Tony... Trained Too Young

Tony, who sought help because of an incestuous relationship with his daughter, reported an early sexual history that contained a number of interesting events. Although he was brought up in a reasonably loving and outwardly normal Catholic family, he had an uncle who did not fit the family pattern. When he was 9 or 10, Tony was encouraged by his uncle to observe a game of strip poker that the uncle was playing with a neighbor's wife. During this period, he also observed his uncle fondling a waitress at a drive-in restaurant and shortly thereafter was instructed by his uncle to fondle his young female cousin. Thus, he had an early model for mutual fondling and masturbation and obtained some pleasure from interacting in this way with young girls. Although the uncle never touched Tony, his behavior was clearly abusive. When Tony was about 13, he engaged in mutual manipulation with a sister and her girlfriend, which he remembers as pleasurable. Later, when Tony was 18, a brother-in-law took him to a sex worker, and he first experienced sexual intercourse. He remembered this visit as unsatisfactory because, on that and subsequent visits to sex workers, he ejaculated prematurely—a sharp contrast to his early experience with young girls. Other experiences with adult women were also unsatisfactory. When he joined the service and was sent overseas, he sought out underaged girls who were often as young as 12. •

These cases remind us that deviant patterns of sexual arousal often occur in the context of other sexual and social problems. Undesired kinds of arousal may be associated with deficiencies in levels of "desired" arousal with consensual adults; this was certainly true for both Tony and Robert, whose sexual relationships with adults were incomplete. In many cases, an inability to develop adequate social relations with the appropriate people for sexual relationships seems to be associated with a developing of inappropriate sexual outlets (Marshall, 1997). Indeed, integrated theories of the causes of paraphilic disorders all note the presence of disordered relationships during childhood and adolescence with resulting deficits in healthy sexual development (Marshall & Barbaree, 1990; Ward & Beech, 2008). Many people with deficient sexual and social skills do not develop deviant patterns of arousal, however.

Early experience seems to have an effect that may be quite accidental. Tony's early sexual experiences just happened to be of the type he later found sexually arousing. Many individuals with pedophilic disorder also report being abused themselves as children, which turns out to be a strong predictor of later sexual abuse by the victim (Fagan et al., 2002; Nunes, Hermann, Malcom, & Lavoie, 2013). Robert's first erotic experience occurred while he was "peeping." But many of us do not find our early experiences reflected in our sexual patterns.

Another factor may be the nature of the person's early sexual fantasies. For example, Rachman and Hodgson (1968; see also Bancroft, 1989) demonstrated that sexual arousal could become associated with a neutral object—a boot, for example—if the boot was repeatedly presented while the individual was sexually aroused. One of the most powerful engines for developing unwanted arousal may be early sexual fantasies that are repeatedly reinforced through the strong sexual pleasure associated with masturbation (Bradford & Meston, 2011). Before an individual with a pedophilic or sadism disorder ever acts on his behavior, he may fantasize about it thousands of times while masturbating.

Expressed as a clinical or operant-conditioning paradigm, this is another example of a learning process in which a behavior (sexual arousal to a specific object or activity) is repeatedly reinforced through association with a pleasurable consequence (orgasm). This mechanism may explain why paraphilic disorders are almost exclusively male disorders. The basic differences in frequency of masturbation between men and women that exist across cultures may contribute to the differential development of paraphilic disorders. As you have seen, on rare occasions, cases of women with paraphilic disorders do turn up (Cortoni & Gannon, 2011; Federoff et al., 1999; Ford & Cortoni, 2008; Hunter & Mathews, 1997; Logan, 2009), and a comprehensive national study of 175 female child sexual abusers exists (Wiegel, 2008).

However, if early experiences contribute strongly to later sexual arousal patterns, then what about the Sambia males who practice exclusive same-sex sexual behaviors during childhood and early adolescence and yet show exclusively heterosexual behaviors as adults? In such cohesive societies, the social demands or "scripts" for sexual interactions are stronger and more rigid than in our culture and thus may override the effects of early experiences (Baldwin & Baldwin, 1989).

In addition, therapists and sex researchers who work with individuals with paraphilic disorders have observed what seems to be an incredibly strong sex drive. It is not uncommon for some individuals to masturbate three or four times a day. In one case seen in our clinic, a sadistic rapist masturbated approximately every half hour all day long, just as often as it was physiologically possible. We have speculated elsewhere that activity this consuming may be related to the obsessional processes of obsessive-compulsive disorder (Barlow, 2002). In both instances, the very act of trying to suppress unwanted, emotionally charged thoughts and fantasies seems to have the paradoxical effect of *increasing* their frequency and intensity (see Chapter 5). This process is also ongoing in people with eating disorders and addictions, when attempts to restrict strong addictive cravings lead to uncontrollable increases in the undesired behaviors.

Psychopathologists are also becoming interested in the phenomenon of weak inhibitory control across these paraphilic disorders, which may indicate a weak biologically based behavioral inhibition system (BIS) in the brain (Ward & Beech, 2008) that might repress serotonergic functioning. (You may remember from Chapter 5 that the BIS is a brain circuit associated with anxiety and inhibition.)

The model shown in ■ Figure 10.5 incorporates the factors thought to contribute to the development of paraphilic disorders. Nevertheless, all speculations, including the hypotheses we have described, have little scientific support at this time. For example, this model does not include the biological dimension. Excess arousal in paraphilic disorders could be biologically based. Before we can make any steadfast conclusions here, more research is needed.

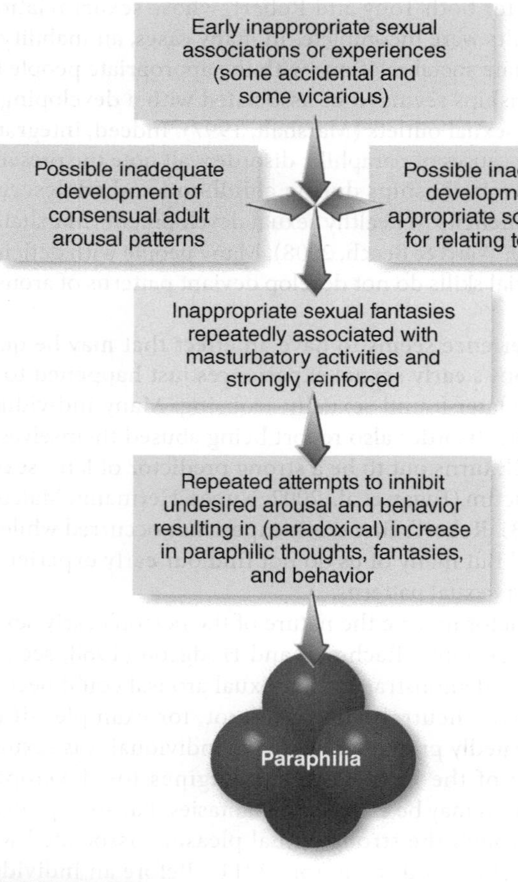

Figure 10.5

A model of the development of paraphilia.

Assessing and Treating Paraphilic Disorders

Researchers have developed sophisticated methods for assessing specific patterns of sexual arousal (Ponseti et al., 2012; Wincze, 2009; Wincze & Weisberg, 2015). This development is important in studying paraphilic disorder because sometimes even the individual presenting with the problem is not fully aware of what caused arousal. An individual once came in to our clinic complaining of uncontrollable arousal to open-toed white sandals worn by women. He noted that he was irresistibly drawn to any woman wearing such sandals and would follow her for miles. These urges occupied much of his summer. Subsequent objective assessment revealed that the sandal itself had no erotic value for this individual; rather, he had a strong sexual attraction to women's feet, particularly moving in a certain way. He had no reason to hide this fact; it was just that he did not realize it himself.

Using the model of paraphilic disorders described previously, we assess each patient not only for the presence of paraphilic arousal but also for levels of desired arousal to adults, for social skills, and for the ability to form relationships. Tony had no problems with social skills: He was 52 years old, reasonably happily married, and generally compatible with his second wife. His major difficulty was his continuing strong, incestuous attraction to his daughter. Nevertheless, he loved his daughter and wished strongly to interact in a normal fatherly way with her.

Psychological Treatment

A number of treatment procedures are available for decreasing unwanted arousal. Most are behavior therapy procedures directed at changing the associations and context from arousing and pleasurable to neutral. One procedure, carried out entirely in the imagination of the patient, called **covert sensitization**, was first described by Joseph Cautela (1967; see also Barlow, 2004). In this treatment, patients associate sexually arousing images in their imagination with some reasons why the behavior is harmful or dangerous. Before treatment, the patient knows about these reasons, but the immediate pleasure and strong reinforcement the sexual activity provides is enough to overcome any thoughts of possible harm or danger that might arise in the future. This process is what happens in much unwanted addictive behavior, where the short-term pleasure outweighs the long-term harm, including bulimia.

In imagination, harmful or dangerous consequences can be associated quite directly with the unwanted behavior and arousal in a powerful and emotionally meaningful way. One of the most powerful negative aspects of Tony's behavior was his embarrassment over the thought of being discovered by his current wife, other family members, or, most important, the family priest. Therefore, he was guided through the fantasy described here.

Tony . . . Imagining the Worst

You are alone with your daughter in your trailer. You realize that you want to caress her breasts. So you put your arm around her, slip your hand inside her blouse, and begin to caress her breasts. Unexpectedly, the door to the trailer opens, and in walks your wife with Father X (the family priest). Your daughter immediately jumps up and runs out the door. Your wife follows her. You are left alone with Father X. He is looking at you as if waiting for an explanation of what he has just seen. Seconds pass, but they seem like hours. You know what Father X must be thinking as he stands there staring at you. You are embarrassed and want to say something, but you can't seem to find the right words. You realize that Father X can no longer respect you as he once did. Father X finally says, "I don't understand this; this is not like you." You both begin to cry. You realize that you may have lost the love and respect of both Father X and your wife, who are important to you. Father X asks, "Do you realize what this has done to your daughter?" You think about this, and you hear your daughter crying; she is hysterical. You want to run, but you can't. You are miserable and disgusted with yourself. You don't know if you will ever regain the love and respect of your wife and Father X. •

Source: Reproduced, with permission of the authors and publisher, from T. L. Harbert, D. H. Barlow, M. Hersen, & J.B. Austin, 1974, Measurement and modification of incestuous behavior: A case study, *Psychological Reports, 34*, 79–86. © 1974 Psychological Reports.

During six or eight sessions, the therapist narrates such scenes dramatically, and the patient is then instructed to imagine them daily until all arousal disappears. The results of Tony's treatment are presented in ■ Figure 10.6. "Card-sort scores" are a measure of how much Tony wanted sexual interactions with his daughter in comparison with his wish for nonsexual fatherly interactions. His incestuous arousal was largely eliminated after 3 to 4 weeks, but the treatment did not affect his desire to interact with his daughter in a healthier manner. These results were confirmed by psychophysiological measurement of his arousal response. A return of some arousal at a 3-month follow-up prompted us to ask Tony if anything unusual was happening in his life. He confessed that his marriage had taken a turn for the worse, and sexual relations with his wife had all but ceased. A period of marital therapy restored the therapeutic gains (see Figure 10.6). Several years later, after his daughter's therapist decided she was ready, she and Tony resumed a nonsexual relationship, which they both wanted.

Two major areas in Tony's life needed treatment: deviant (incestuous) sexual arousal and marital problems. Most individuals with paraphilic arousal patterns need a great deal of attention to family functioning or other interpersonal systems in which they operate (Fagan et al., 2002; Rice & Harris, 2002). In addition, many require intervention to help strengthen appropriate desired patterns of arousal. In **orgasmic reconditioning**, patients are instructed to masturbate to their usual fantasies but to substitute more desirable ones just before ejaculation. With repeated practice, patients should be able to begin the desired fantasy earlier in the masturbatory process and still retain their arousal. This technique, first described by Gerald Davison (1968), has been used with some success in a variety of settings (Brownell et al., 1977; Maletzky, 2002). Finally, as with most strongly pleasurable but undesirable behaviors (including addiction), care must be taken to provide

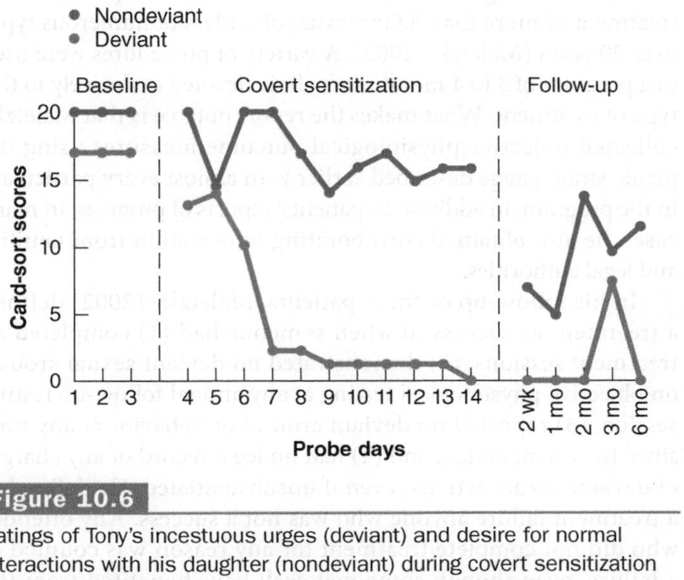

Figure 10.6

Ratings of Tony's incestuous urges (deviant) and desire for normal interactions with his daughter (nondeviant) during covert sensitization treatment. Reproduced, with permission, from T. L. Harbert, D. H. Barlow, M. Hersen, & J. B. Austin, 1974, Measurement and modification of incestuous behavior: A case study, *Psychological Reports*, *34*, 79–86. © 1974 Psychological Reports.

the patient with coping skills to prevent slips or relapses. *Relapse prevention* treatment created for addictions (Laws & O'Donohue, 1997) does just that. Patients are taught to recognize the early signs of temptation and to institute a variety of self-control procedures before their urges become too strong.

Evidence on the effects of psychological treatments for sexual offenders is decidedly mixed at this time. For sexual offenders who have come into contact with the legal system, including those who are incarcerated (obviously a very severe group), the results are modest at best in terms of preventing later occurrences of offending (termed recidivism). Reviews of large numbers of studies with these populations are hampered because of the substantially different methods and procedures in accessing recidivism rates. But several large surveys following up sexual offenders for a period of 4 to 5 years indicate reductions in sexual recidivism (that is, reoffending) among patients who have received psychological treatments of up to 11% to 20% over what would be expected with the usual and customary treatment, with cognitive-behavioral programs proving to be the most effective in reducing recidivism (Hanson et al., 2002; Lösel & Schmucker, 2005). On the other hand, a large study from the state of California with participants who were incarcerated for their sexual offense showed very little effect of any intervention in rates of sexual or violent offending over an 8-year follow-up period after these individuals were released (Marques, Wiederanders, Day, Nelson, & van Ommeren, 2005). New techniques have been incorporated to psychological treatments for sex offenders—including techniques to enhance motivation (motivational interviewing) described in Chapter 11, and a focus on the patient's strengths—with the hope that the addition of these techniques will increase the efficacy of treatment; however, more research is needed (Marshall & Marshall, 2014).

For outpatients, on the other hand, there is at least some evidence for success when treatment is carried out by an experienced professional. For example, Barry Maletzky, a psychiatrist at the University of Oregon Medical School, and his staff reported on the treatment of more than 8,000 sexual offenders of numerous types over 20 years (Maletzky, 2002). A variety of procedures were used in a program of 3 to 4 months in a clinic devoted exclusively to this type of treatment. What makes the report notable is that Maletzky collected objective physiological outcome measures using the penile strain gauge described earlier with almost every participant in the program, in addition to patients' reports of progress. In many cases, he also obtained corroborating information from families and legal authorities.

In his follow-up of these patients, Maletzky (2002) defined a treatment as successful when someone had (1) completed all treatment sessions, (2) demonstrated no deviant sexual arousal on objective physiological testing at any annual follow-up testing session, (3) reported no deviant arousal or behavior at any time since treatment ended, and (4) had no legal record of any charges of deviant sexual activity, even if unsubstantiated. He defined as a treatment failure anyone who was not a success. Any offender who did not complete treatment for any reason was counted as a failure, even though some may well have benefited from the partial treatment and gone on to recover. Using these criteria, from 75% to 95% of individuals, depending on the type of sexual offense (such as pedophilia, rape, or voyeurism), had a successful outcome. Maletzky's results were not derived from a scientifically controlled clinical trial, however.

Men who rape had the lowest success rate among all offenders with a single diagnosis (75%), and individuals with multiple paraphilic disorders had the lowest success rate of any group. Maletzky (2002) also examined factors associated with failure. Among the strongest predictors were a history of unstable social relationships, an unstable employment history, strong denial the problem exists, a history of multiple victims, and a situation in which the offender continues to live with a victim (as might be typical in cases of incest). Many of these problems characterize the presumably more severe incarcerated population mentioned above.

Nevertheless, other groups using similar treatment procedures have achieved comparable success rates (Abel, 1989; Becker, 1990; Fagan et al., 2002). Therapist knowledge and expertise seem to be important in successfully carrying out these treatments to prevent future sexual offenses among patients.

Judith Becker used the procedures described previously in a program for adolescent sexual offenders in an urban setting (see, for example, Becker, 1990; Morenz & Becker, 1995). Results indicate that a relatively low 10% of those who completed treatment had committed further sex crimes. These findings were important both because many adolescent offenders carry the AIDS virus and literally are putting their victims' lives in danger and also because the recidivism rate of sexual offenders without treatment is high (see, for example, Hanson, Steffy, & Gauthier, 1993; Nagayama Hall, 1995), just as it is for all pleasurable but undesirable behavior, including substance abuse. One important study found that intervening with aggressive, victimizing, or highly inappropriate sexual behavior in children age 5 to 12 with a CBT was effective in preventing sexual offending once they reached adolescence and adulthood 10 years later compared to a group receiving play therapy (Carpentier, Silovsky, & Chaffin, 2006). Only 2% of children receiving CBT had future sexual offenses. Preventing adult sexual offending would be an important advance if these results were replicated.

Drug Treatments

The most popular drug used to treat individuals with paraphilic disorders is an antiandrogen called *cyproterone acetate* (Bradford, 1997; Assumpção, Garcia, Garcia, Bradford, & Thibaut, 2014; Seto, 2009). This "chemical castration" drug eliminates sexual desire and fantasy by reducing testosterone levels dramatically, but fantasies and arousal return as soon as the drug is removed. A second drug is *medroxyprogesterone* (Depo-Provera is the injectable form), a hormonal agent that reduces testosterone (Assumpção et al., 2014; Fagan et al., 2002). These drugs may be useful for dangerous sexual offenders who do not respond to alternative treatments or to temporarily suppress sexual arousal in some patients, but they are not always successful. In an earlier report of the Maletzky series (1991), only 8 of approximately 5,000 patients required the drug because they showed no response whatsoever to psychological treatments. Rösler and Witztum (1998) report successful "chemical castration" of 30 men with severe long-standing paraphilic disorders using triptorelin, which inhibits gonadotropin secretion in men. This drug appears to be somewhat more effective than the other drugs mentioned here with fewer side effects, based on this one study. Of course, the drug is effective only if taken regularly, but most individuals, facing prison as the alternative, are highly motivated to comply with treatment. In another study, Maletzky, Tolan, and McFarland (2006) found that among sexual offenders released from prison for whom medication was considered to be possibly useful, a subset who actually received the medication had significantly fewer subsequent sexual offenses than a group who, for a variety of reasons, did not receive the medication.

Summary

Based on evidence from a number of settings, evidence for the psychosocial treatment of paraphilic disorders is mixed, with more success reported in outpatient settings with presumably less severe, more stable patients. But most results are uncontrolled observations from a small number of clinical research centers, and results may not be as good in other clinics and offices. In any case, as with treatment for sexual dysfunctions, psychosocial approaches to paraphilic disorders are not readily available outside of specialized treatment centers. In the meantime, the outlook for most individuals with these disorders is bleak because paraphilic disorders run a chronic course and recurrence is common.

Concept Check 10.3

Check your understanding of sexual paraphilic disorders by matching the scenarios with the correct label: (a) exhibitionistic disorder, (b) voyeuristic disorder, (c) fetishistic disorder, or (d) sexual masochism disorder.

1. Mae enjoys being slapped with leather whips during foreplay. Without such stimulation, she is unable to achieve orgasm during sex. ____________
2. Kai has a collection of women's panties that arouse him. He loves to look at, collect, and wear them. ____________
3. Sam finds arousal in walking up to strangers in the park and showing them his genitals. ____________
4. Peeping Tom loves to look through Susie's bedroom window and watch her undress. He gets extremely excited as she disrobes. He is practicing ____________.
5. What Peeping Tom does not realize is that Susie knows that he is watching. She is aroused by slowly undressing while others are watching, and she fantasizes about what they are thinking. Susie's behavior is called ____________.
6. What Peeping Tom will be shocked to find out is that "Susie" is actually Scott, a man who can become aroused only if he wears feminine clothing. Scott's behavior is ____________.

Gender Dysphoria

How does a person know their gender identity? It's more than your sexual arousal patterns or your anatomy. It's also more than the reactions and experiences of your family and society. The essence of your feelings toward being a man, a woman, gender fluid, or nonbinary or toward having other experiences, including social constructed definitions of masculinity and/or femininity, is a deep-seated personal sense called gender identity. **Gender dysphoria** is present if a person's assigned sex at birth (which is often based on visible genitals) is not consistent with the person's sense of who they really are or with their experienced gender. This condition is associated with clinically significant distress or impairment in social, school, or other important areas of functioning. While gender dysphoria can occur on a continuum (American Psychological Association Task Force of Gender Identity and Gender Variance, 2008; Cohen-Kettenis & Pfäfflin, 2010), at the extreme end of the continuum are individuals who reject their sex assigned at birth altogether and wish to change it. People with this disorder often feel trapped in a body of the wrong sex. Consider the case of Joe.

If the sex assigned at birth is female but the experienced gender (gender identity) is strongly male, the individual is typically referred to as a transgender man or "trans man," and a person assigned male at birth would be a trans woman. If the individual has made the transition to full-time living in their experienced gender (by interacting with people in their daily lives in a consistent manner in their desired gender) and they are

Joe... Trapped in the Wrong Body

Joe was a 17-year-old male and the last of five children. Although his mother had wanted a girl, he became her favorite child. His father worked long hours and had little contact with the boy. For as long as Joe could remember, he had thought of himself as a girl. He began dressing in girls' clothes of his own accord before he was 5 years old and continued cross-dressing into junior high school. He developed interests in cooking, knitting, crocheting, and embroidering, skills he acquired by reading an encyclopedia. His older brother often scorned him for his distaste of such "masculine" activities as hunting.

Joe associated mostly with girls during this period, although he remembered being strongly attached to a boy in the first grade. In his sexual fantasies, which developed around 12 years of age, he pictured himself as a female having intercourse with a male. His extremely effeminate behavior made him the object of scorn and ridicule when he entered high school at age 15. Usually passive and unassertive, he ran away from home and attempted suicide. Unable to continue in high school, he attended secretarial school, where he was the only boy in his class. During his first interview with a therapist, he reported, "I am a woman trapped in a man's body, and I would like to have surgery to become a woman." •

DSM 5 **Table 10.13**
Criteria for Gender Dysphoria

In Children:

A. A marked incongruence between one's experienced/expressed gender and assigned gender, of at least 6 months' duration, as manifested by at least six of the following (one of which must be Criterion A1):

1. A strong desire to be of the other gender or an insistence that one is the other gender (or some alternative gender different from one's assigned gender).
2. In boys (assigned gender), a strong preference for cross-dressing or simulating female attire; or in girls (assigned gender), a strong preference for wearing only typical masculine clothing and a strong resistance to the wearing of typical feminine clothing.
3. A strong preference for cross-gender roles in make-believe play or fantasy play.
4. A strong preference for the toys, games, or activities stereotypically used or engaged in by the other gender.
5. A strong preference for playmates of the other gender.
6. In boys (assigned gender), a strong rejection of typically masculine toys, games, and activities and a strong avoidance of rough-and-tumble play or in girls (assigned gender), a strong rejection of typically feminine toys, games, and activities.
7. A strong dislike of one's sexual anatomy.
8. A strong desire for the primary and/or secondary sex characteristics that match one's experienced gender.

B. The condition is associated with clinically significant distress or impairment in social, school, or other important areas of functioning.

In adolescents and adults:

A. A marked incongruence between one's experienced/expressed gender and assigned gender, of at least 6 months' duration, as manifested by at least two of the following:

1. A marked incongruence between one's experienced/expressed gender and primary and/or secondary sex characteristics (or in young adolescents, the anticipated secondary sex characteristics).
2. A strong desire to be rid of one's primary and/or secondary sex characteristics because of a marked incongruence with one's experienced/expressed gender (or in young adolescents, a desire to prevent the development of the anticipated secondary sex characteristics).
3. A strong desire for the primary and/or secondary sex characteristics of the other gender.
4. A strong desire to be of the other gender (or some alternative gender different from one's assigned gender).
5. A strong desire to be treated as the other gender (or some alternative gender different from one's assigned gender).
6. A strong conviction that one has the typical feelings and reactions of the other gender (or some alternative gender different from one's assigned gender).

B. The condition is associated with clinically significant distress or impairment in social, school, or other important areas of functioning.

American Psychiatric Association. (2022). *Diagnostic and statistical manual of mental disorders* (5th ed., Text Revision).

preparing for or have undergone gender-affirming surgery, then they are referred to as *posttransition*, and this is specified in the diagnostic criteria for gender dysphoria (see DSM-5 Table 10.13). Some also prefer not to be referred to as a specific gender at all, embracing a nonbinary view. Others might identify with multiple genders and embrace a gender fluid view.

Defining Gender Dysphoria

Gender dysphoria must be distinguished from transvestic fetishism, a paraphilic disorder (discussed earlier) in which individuals, usually males, are sexually aroused by wearing articles of clothing associated with gender performances not associated with their assigned sex. There is an occasional preference on the part of the male with transvestite patterns of sexual arousal for the female role, but the primary purpose of cross-dressing is sexual gratification. In the case of gender dysphoria, the primary goal is not sexual gratification but rather the desire to live life openly in a manner consistent with that of the person's gender.

Gender dysphoria can also occur among individuals with disorders of sex development (DSD), formerly known as *intersexuality* or *hermaphroditism*, who are born with ambiguous genitalia associated with documented hormonal or other physical abnormalities. Depending on their particular mix of characteristics, individuals with DSDs are usually "assigned" to a specific sex at birth, sometimes undergoing surgery, as well as hormonal treatments, to alter their sexual anatomy. If gender dysphoria occurs in the context of a DSD, this should be specified when making a diagnosis. But most individuals with gender dysphoria have no demonstrated physical abnormalities. (We return to the issue of DSD later.)

Finally, gender dysphoria must be distinguished from the same-sex sexual arousal patterns of a man who sometimes behaves effeminately or a woman with same-sex sexual arousal patterns and masculine mannerisms. Such an individual does not feel like a woman trapped in a man's body or have any desire to be a woman, or vice versa. Note also, as the DSM-5 criteria do, that gender identity is independent of sexual arousal patterns

(American Psychiatric Association, 2013; Savin-Williams, 2006). For example, a trans woman (assigned male at birth with a strongly experienced female gender identity) may be sexually attracted to females. Similarly, Eli Coleman and his associates (Coleman, Bockting, & Gooren, 1993) reported on nine trans men in which the individuals were sexually attracted to men. Thus, heterosexual women before surgery were gay men after surgery. Chivers and Bailey (2000) compared a group of trans men who were attracted to men (a rare occurrence) with a group of trans men who were attracted to women (the usual pattern) both before and after surgery. They found the groups did not differ in the strength of their gender identity (as males), although the latter group was more sexually assertive and more interested in surgery to create an artificial penis.

Lawrence (2005) studied 232 trans women both before and after surgery and found that the majority (54%) were mostly heterosexual (attracted to women) before the surgery. This changed after surgery slightly for some and dramatically for a few, such that only 25% remained attracted to women after surgery, thus making them lesbians. This latter group may constitute a distinct subset of trans women with a different pattern of development called *autogynephilia*, in which gender dysphoria begins with a strong and specific sexual attraction to a fantasy of oneself (*auto*) as a female (*gyne*). This fantasy then progresses to a more comprehensive all-encompassing experienced gender as a female. Individuals in this subgroup of biological males were not effeminate as boys but became sexually aroused while cross-dressing and to fantasies of themselves as women. Over time, these fantasies progress to *becoming* a woman (Bailey, 2003; Carroll, 2007; Lawrence, 2013). This distinction is controversial, but it is supported by research (Carroll, 2007) (see p. 375).

Gender dysphoria resulting in not identifying with the sex assigned at birth is relatively rare. The estimated prevalence of gender affirmation in people assigned male at birth is between 5 and 14 per 1,000. The estimated prevalence among those assigned female at birth is between 2 and 3 per 1,000 (American Psychiatric Association, 2013, 2015). Therefore, gender affirmation occurs approximately three times more frequently among people assigned male at birth than those assigned female at birth (American Psychological Association, 2008; Judge, O'Donovan, Callaghan, Gaoatswe, & O'Shea, 2014; Sohn & Bosinski, 2007). Many countries now require a series of legal steps to change gender. In Germany, between 2.1 and 2.4 per 100,000 in the population took at least the first legal step of changing their first names in the 1990s; in that country, the male-to-female ratio of people with gender dysphoria is 2.3:1 (Weitze & Osburg, 1996). Since 2006 in New York City, people may choose to alter the sex assigned at birth listed on their birth certificates following surgery.

In some cultures, individuals with a different gender experience are often accorded the status of "shaman" or "seer" and treated as wisdom figures. A shaman is almost always a male adopting a female role (see, for example, Coleman, Colgan, & Gooren, 1992). Stoller (1976) reported on two contemporary feminized Native American men who were not only accepted but also esteemed by their tribes for their expertise in healing rituals. Contrary to the respect accorded these individuals in some cultures, social tolerance for them remains relatively low in Western cultures, although that is changing particularly as individuals such as Caitlyn Jenner and Chaz Bono forthrightly and openly discuss gender dysphoria. Actors such as Laverne Cox, books such as *Becoming Nicole*, and movies such as *The Danish Girl* have also begun to raise awareness about gender dysphoria and encourage more discussion on the topic.

Causes

Research has yet to uncover any specific biological contributions to gender dysphoria or alternative gender experience, for that matter, although it seems likely that a biological predisposition will be discovered. Coolidge, Thede, and Young (2002) estimated that genetics contributed about 62% to creating a vulnerability to experience gender dysphoria in their twin sample and that about 38% of the vulnerability came from nonshared (unique) environmental events. A study from the Netherlands twin registry suggested that 70% of the vulnerability for cross-gender behavior (behaving in a manner consistent with the opposite assigned sex) was genetic as opposed to environmental, but this behavior is not the same as gender identity, which was not measured (as explained later) (van Beijsterveldt, Hudziak, & Boomsma, 2006). Gomez-Gil and colleagues (2010) found a somewhat higher prevalence of gender dysphoria than would be expected by chance in nontwin siblings of a larger group (995) of individuals with gender dysphoria. Segal (2006), on the other hand, found two monozygotic (identical) female twin pairs in which one twin had gender dysphoria and the other did not; no unusual medical or life history factors were identified to account for this difference. Nevertheless, genetic contributions are clearly part of the picture (Heylens et al., 2012).

Featureflash Photo Agency/Shutterstock.com

Theo Wargo/Getty Images

Laverne Cox and Caitlin Jenner are both male-to-female transgender (trans women) who are strong and effective advocates for the transgender community.

Early research suggested that, as with sexual orientation, slightly higher levels of testosterone or estrogen at certain critical periods of development might masculinize a female fetus or feminize a male fetus (see, for example, Keefe, 2002). Variations in hormonal levels could occur naturally or because of medication that a pregnant person is taking. Scientists have studied girls aged 5 to 12 with an intersex condition known as congenital adrenal hyperplasia (CAH). In CAH, the brains of these chromosomal females are flooded with male hormones (androgens), which, among other results, produce mostly masculine external genitalia, although internal organs (ovaries and so on) remain female. Meyer-Bahlburg and colleagues (2004) studied 15 girls with CAH who had been correctly identified as female at birth and raised as girls and looked at their development. Compared with groups of girls and boys without CAH, the CAH girls were masculine in their behavior, but there were no differences in gender identity. Thus, scientists have yet to establish a link between prenatal hormonal influence and later gender identity, although it is still possible that one exists. Structural differences in the area of the brain that controls male sex hormones have also been observed in individuals with male-to-female gender dysphoria (Hannema et al., 2014; Zhou, Hofman, Gooren, & Swaab, 1995), with the result that the brains are comparatively more feminine. But it isn't clear whether this is a cause or an effect.

At least some evidence suggests that gender identity firms up between 18 months and 3 years of age (Ehrhardt & Meyer-Bahlburg, 1981; Money & Ehrhardt, 1972) and is relatively fixed after that. But newer studies suggest that possible preexisting biological factors have already had their impact. One interesting case illustrating this phenomenon was originally reported by Green and Money (1969), who described the sequence of events that occurred in the case of Bruce/Brenda. There do seem to be other case studies of children whose gender was reassigned at birth who adapted successfully (see, for example, Gearhart, 1989), but it certainly seems that biology expressed itself in Bruce's case.

Bruce/Brenda... Gender and Biology

A set of male identical twins was born into a well-adjusted family. Several months later, an unfortunate accident occurred. Although circumcision went routinely for one of the boys, the physician's hand slipped so that the electric current in the device burned off the penis of the second baby. After working through their hostility toward the physician, the parents consulted specialists in children with intersexual problems and were faced with a choice. The specialists pointed out that the easiest solution would be to reassign their son Bruce as a girl, and the parents agreed. At the age of several months, Bruce became "Brenda." The parents purchased a new wardrobe and treated the child in every way possible as a girl. These twins were followed through childhood and, upon reaching puberty, the young girl was given hormonal replacement therapy. After 6 years, the doctors lost track of the case but assumed the child had adjusted well. However, Brenda endured almost intolerable inner turmoil. We know this because two clinical scientists found this individual and reported a long-term follow-up (Diamond & Sigmundson, 1997). Brenda never adjusted to her assigned gender. As a child, she preferred rough-and-tumble play and resisted wearing girls' clothes. In public bathrooms, she often insisted on urinating while standing up, which usually made a mess. By early adolescence, Brenda was pretty sure she was a boy, but her doctors pressed her to act more feminine. When she was 14, she confronted her parents, telling them she was so miserable she was considering suicide. At that point, they told her the true story, and the muddy waters of her mind began to clear. Shortly thereafter, Brenda had additional surgery changing himself back to Bruce, who married and became the father of three adopted children. But the turmoil of his early life never fully resolved. Perhaps because of this, perhaps because his twin brother had recently died, perhaps because he had lost his job and was divorcing, or perhaps because of a combination of these factors, David Reimer (his real name) committed suicide at age 38 in 2004. •

Richard Green, a pioneering researcher in this area, has studied boys who behave in feminine ways and girls who behave in masculine ways, investigating what makes them that way and following what happens to them (Green, 1987). This set of behaviors and attitudes is referred to as **gender nonconformity** (see, for example, Skidmore, Linsenmeier, & Bailey, 2006). Green discovered that when most young boys spontaneously display "feminine" interests and behaviors, they are typically discouraged by most families, and these behaviors usually cease. Boys who consistently display these behaviors are not discouraged, however, and are sometimes encouraged.

Other factors, such as excessive attention and physical contact on the part of the mother, may also play some role, as may a lack of male playmates during the early years of socialization. These are just some factors identified by Green as characteristic of gender-nonconforming boys. Remember that as-yet-undiscovered biological factors may also contribute to the spontaneous display of cross-gender behaviors and interests. For example, one study found that exposure to higher levels of fetal testosterone was associated with more masculine play behavior in both boys and girls during childhood (Auyeng et al., 2009). In following up with these boys, however, Green discovered that few seem to develop the gender incongruence. The most likely outcome is the development of same-sex sexual preferences, but even this particular sexual arousal pattern seems to occur exclusively in only approximately 40% of the gender-nonconforming boys. Another 32% show some degree of *bisexuality,* sexual attraction to both their own and other sexes. Looking at it from the other side, 60% were heterosexual. These results were replicated in subsequent prospective studies of boys (Zucker, 2005). Girls with gender-nonconforming behavior are seldom studied because their behavior attracts much less attention in Western societies. But one study followed 25 girls prospectively, beginning at approximately 9 years of age, whose behavior was extreme enough that they were referred to a gender identity clinic. Most of these girls met criteria for childhood gender dysphoria disorder or came very close to it. At a follow up, when these girls (now women) averaged 25 years of age, only three met criteria for gender dysphoria. Another six reported bisexual/same-sex sexual behavior; eight more would have same-sex sexual fantasies but not behavior. The remaining eight women were heterosexual (Drummond, Bradley, Peterson-Badali, & Zucker, 2008).

This finding of only a very loose relationship between gender-nonconforming behavior and later sexual development is not unique to American culture. For example, similar relationships between early gender-nonconforming behavior and later development exist among the Fa'afafine, a group of males with same-sex sexual orientation in the Pacific Islands country of Samoa (Bartlett & Vasey, 2006). And even in strict Muslim societies where any hint of gender-nonconforming behavior is severely discouraged, gender-nonconforming behavior, gender dysphoria, or both may develop (Doğan & Doğan, 2006). We can safely say that the causes of the development of incongruent experienced gender is still something of a mystery. Societal and cultural norms and expectations certainly play an important role, as shown in the case of Albania's "sworn virgins," also known as *burrneshat* (female-men) (Higgins, 2021). In the traditional male-oriented Albanian culture, women are subservient to men and are sometimes forced into marriage. As a result of family feuds, families sometimes do not have any male members left to lead the family. To solve this problem, some families want their daughters to take on the traditional male roles. As part of this centuries-old tradition, these *burrneshats* make all important family decisions, take the oath of celibacy, and enjoy all privileges that are usually limited to men, such as drinking and smoking. Although some of these women say that they always wanted to be a man, they do not consider themselves as transgender women. In fact, the traditional Albanian culture is strongly opposed to transgender sexuality and homosexuality. Although a traditional *burrneshat* occupies a male role and feels like a man, she does not want to change her sex. In many other cultures, on the other hand, such a mismatch between the biological sex and the desired gender can create psychological distress requiring treatment.

Treatment

Treatment is available for gender dysphoria in specialty clinics around the world, although much controversy surrounds treatment (Carroll, 2007; Meyer-Bahlburg, 2010). For adults requesting full sex transition treatment, guidelines from both the American Psychiatric Association and the American Psychological Association have now been published (American Psychological Association, 2015; Byne et al., 2012). The treatment guidelines published by the American Psychological Association (2015) highlight the diversity of problems facing gender-nonconforming individuals and encourage therapists to take a holistic view of these patients (that is, helping to build resilience, working within existing family structures, and collaborating with other care providers). Recommendations from the American Psychiatric Association guidelines, when addressing adult patients with gender dysphoria more specifically, begin with the least intrusive step of full psychological evaluation and education before proceeding to partially reversible steps such as administration of gonadal hormones to bring about desired secondary sex characteristics. The final nonreversible step is to alter anatomy physically to be consistent with gender identity through **gender-affirming surgery**.

Gender Affirming Surgery

To qualify for gender-affirming surgery at a reputable clinic, individuals must live in the gender they identify as for 1 to 2 years so that they can be sure they want to change sex. They also must be stable psychologically, financially, and socially. In trans women, hormones are administered to promote *gynecomastia* (the growth of breasts) and the development of other secondary sex characteristics. Facial hair is typically removed through electrolysis. If the individual is satisfied with the events of the trial period, the genitals are removed, and a vagina is constructed.

For trans men, an artificial penis is typically constructed through plastic surgery, using sections of skin and muscle from elsewhere in the body, such as the thigh. Breasts are surgically removed. Genital surgery is more difficult and complex in people assigned female at birth. Estimates of satisfaction with surgery indicate predominantly successful adjustment (between 75% and 100% generally satisfied) among those who could be reached for follow-ups, with trans men generally adjusting better than trans women (Blanchard & Steiner, 1992; Bodlund & Kullgren, 1996; Byne et al., 2012; Carroll, 2007; Costantino et al., 2013, Johansson, Sundbom, Höjerback, & Bodlund, 2010). Many people were not available for follow-up, however. Approximately 1% to 7% of individuals who have gender-affirming surgery and were reached for follow-up later regret having the surgery possibly due to insufficient social support (Bancroft, 1989; Byne et al., 2012; Dhejne, Öberg, Aryer, & Landén, 2014; Johansson et al., 2010; Lundstrom, Pauly, & Walinder, 1984). This can result in additional complications because the surgery is often irreversible. Also, as many as 2% attempt suicide after surgery, a rate much higher than the rate for the general population, perhaps again due to insufficient

Reuters/Str Old

After gender reassignment as a baby and subsequently being raised as a girl, David Reimer reclaimed his male gender identity in his teens and lived his life as a man. He spoke out against infant gender reassignment until his death in 2004.

social support. One possible problem may be incorrect diagnosis and assessment. For example, one study of 186 Dutch psychiatrists reporting on 584 patients presenting with gender dysphoria revealed little consensus on diagnostic features or the minimum age at which gender-affirming surgery is safe. Rather, the decision seemed to rest on personal preferences of the psychiatrist (Campo, Nijman, Merckelbach, & Evers, 2003). These assessments are complex and should always be done at highly specialized gender clinics. Predictors of regret, in addition to misdiagnosis, include the presence of comorbid diagnoses (such as alcohol use and psychosis) and poor family support (Byne et al., 2012). Nevertheless, surgery has made life worth living for many people who suffered the effects of existing in what they felt to be the wrong body with rates of satisfaction averaging about 90% (Johansson et al., 2010).

Treatment of Gender Nonconformity in Children

Even more controversial is the treatment of gender-nonconforming children. On the one hand, some segments of society, particularly in more traditionally tolerant areas of the country such as San Francisco and New York, are becoming more open to gender variations in both children and adults. In some schools, children are being allowed and even encouraged to dress and appear in gender-nonconforming ways on the assumption that this gives freer rein to who they "really are" (Brown, 2006). Indeed, one study suggests that gender-nonconforming children who presented themselves according to their gender identity in everyday life exhibit cognitions more consistent with their expressed gender than their assigned sex (Olson, Key, & Eaton, 2015). On the other hand, Skidmore and colleagues (2006) examined whether gender nonconformity was related to psychological distress in a community-based sample of gay men and lesbians. Gender nonconformity was measured by self-reports of childhood gender nonconformity, as well as ratings of current behavior. The researchers found that gender nonconformity was related to psychological distress (depression, anxiety), but only for gay men and not for lesbians. Research suggests that gender nonconformity is associated with lower levels of psychological well-being, but it has not found the same interaction with sexual orientation (Rieger & Savin-Williams, 2012); thus, more research is needed in this area.

Although only a minority of gay men report gender nonconformity as boys, research indicates that many of these gender-nonconforming boys defeminize as they reach adulthood, perhaps because of persistent social pressure from their family and peers. Also, interventions exist to alter gender-nonconforming behavior in young children to avoid the ostracism and scorn these children encounter in most school settings (for example, Rekers, Kilgus, & Rosen, 1990). Other interventions exist to build resilience in children who exhibit gender-nonconforming behavior by strengthening their relationships with peers and caregivers, increasing their sense of self-control, and increasing their sense of belonging within a community or culture (Allan & Ungar, 2014).

Thus, society is faced with a dilemma that requires more research. Should the free expression of gender nonconformity be encouraged knowing that, in most parts of world, gender nonconformity will make for difficult social adaptation, leading to substantial psychological distress for decades to come, particularly since the gender nonconformity is unlikely to persist into adolescence or adulthood? Or will psychological adjustment be more positive if gender nonconformity is allowed and facilitated? If research confirms that adjustment is more positive if individuals find their own place on a gender continuum, then large-scale campaigns to alter social norms may well occur along the lines of the successful campaigns of the past several decades for gay rights, after a consensus developed in the 1970s that "homosexuality" was not a disorder. Research will continue on this important and interesting topic.

Treatment guidelines developed by the American Psychiatric Association and the American Psychological Association for gender nonconformity in youth simply outline the options available (American Psychological Association, 2015; Byne et al., 2012). One option would be to work with the child and caregivers to lessen gender dysphoria and decrease cross-gender behaviors and identification on the assumption that these behaviors are unlikely to persist anyway, the negative consequences of social rejection could be avoided, and avoiding later intrusive surgery would be desirable. A second approach could be described as "watchful waiting" by letting expressed gender unfold naturally. This goal requires strong support from caregivers and the community because of the potential social and interpersonal risks and lack of integration with peer groups. Yet a third approach advocates actively affirming and encouraging cross-gender identification, but critics point out that gender nonconformity usually does not persist and that taking this course would increase the likelihood of persistence. There is very little hard scientific information on which course would be the most beneficial for a given child.

New treatment approaches have been developed in some clinics for children who more clearly identify as transgender. Given the irreversible nature of many treatments for gender dysphoria, treatment for these children needs to be administered with caution. In prepubescent children, first-line treatments include psychoeducation and therapy to help clarify gender identity and navigate the complex social issues associated with cross-gender identification. In individuals closer to puberty, psychotherapy is also recommended. However, a medical intervention that blocks puberty is also available (if, after detailed assessment, it is determined that such treatment would be in the best interest of the patient based on the severity of the discordance between gender identity and their assigned sex at birth as well as family and social considerations). This medication allows the adolescent time to continue exploring gender identity issues without the added of stress of beginning puberty in a gender that is inconsistent with their identify (Tishelman et al., 2014). This treatment remains controversial in many parts of the United States.

Treatment of Disorders of Sex Development (Intersexuality)

Based on the best evidence available, for every 1,000 children born, 17, or 1.7%, may present with a DSD in some form (Fausto-Sterling, 2000a, 2000b). As we noted, surgery and hormonal replacement therapy has been standard treatment for many individuals with DSDs, who may be born with physical characteristics of both sexes, in order to make their sexual anatomy match as closely to their assigned gender as possible. These procedures usually take place soon after birth. But in later years, gender dysphoria may also develop in these individuals, and, if it does, a similar sequence of treatment steps beginning with the least intrusive would be initiated as described above (Byne et al., 2012). Of course, treatment for gender dysphoria in any form has always been controversial and particularly so when a DSD is present. Anne Fausto-Sterling, a biologist from Brown University, proposed early on that even in biologically intersexed individuals gender identity is on a continuum and early surgical intervention may cause more problems than it solves (Fausto-Sterling, 2000a, 2000b, 2015). What Fausto-Sterling (2000b) and others have noted is that individuals in this group are often dissatisfied with surgery, much as Bruce was in the case we described. There have been instances in which doctors, upon observing anatomical sexual ambiguity after birth, treat it as an emergency and immediately perform surgery. Fausto-Sterling suggests that an increasing number of pediatric endocrinologists, urologists, and psychologists are examining the wisdom of early genital surgery that results in an irreversible gender assignment. Instead, health professionals may want to examine closely the precise nature of the DSD and consider surgery only as a last resort and only when they are quite sure the particular condition will lead to a specific psychological gender identity. Otherwise, psychological treatments to help individuals adapt to their particular sexual anatomy or watchful waiting to determine their emerging gender experience might be more appropriate.

Concept Check 10.4

Answer the following questions about normal sexuality and gender dysphoria.

1. Name some gender differences that exist in sexual attitudes and sexual behavior. __________
2. Which sexual preference or preferences are normal, and how are they developed? __________
3. Charlie always felt out of place with boys. At a young age, he preferred to play with girls and insisted that his parents call him "Charlene." He later claimed that he felt like a woman trapped in a man's body. What disorder could Charlie have? __________
4. What could be the cause(s) of Charlie's disorder? __________
5. What treatments could be given to Charlie? __________

DSM Controversies: *Paraphilia or Paraphilic Disorder?*

In DSM-IV, a paraphilia was diagnosed based on the presence of intense and persistent sexual interest as determined by the presence of strong sexual fantasies, sexual urges, or behaviors generally involving nonhuman objects, the suffering or humiliation of oneself or one's partner, or children or other nonconsenting persons. It was also noted that these fantasies, urges, or behaviors cause clinically significant distress or impairment. In DSM-5, an explicit distinction is made between paraphilia, which denotes any intense and persistent sexual interest other than sexual interest and behaviors with phenotypically normal, physically mature, consenting human partners, and paraphilic disorder.

A paraphilic disorder is a paraphilia that causes either distress or impairment to the individual or personal harm or risk of harm to others. Thus, one might have a strong and persistent sexual interest and arousal pattern in young children, but if it is not acted on and does not cause personal distress, it is not by definition a disorder; although abnormal, it is no different than being non-normally tall or short. This change was made to accommodate the high prevalence of "paraphilic" type fantasies that might occasionally occur among people without mental disorders (Ahlers et al., 2011). An example would be a harmless fetish for an article of clothing that is incorporated into sexual activity with a willing partner. Here, the individual would have a paraphilia but not a paraphilic disorder. But what if the paraphilia focused on sex with small children or inflicting grievous harm on other individuals? Advocates of the change would point out that if these fantasies are not acted upon in any way, no harm is done and it is not a disorder and that it does more harm to pathologize this very private behavior than to call it a mental disorder. Critics would point out that anyone with such a strong and persistent pattern of sexual arousal would probably at least watch an occasional video on the internet if it were readily available, and in so doing, harm would occur. This example is yet another point of contention in the fundamental question of what defines a mental disorder, discussed in Chapter 1.

Summary

What Is Normal Sexuality?

- Patterns of all sexual behavior, both same-sex sexual and heterosexual, vary around the world in terms of both behavior and risks. Approximately 20% of individuals who have been surveyed engage in sex with numerous partners, which puts them at risk for sexually transmitted diseases such as AIDS. Some surveys also suggest that as many as 60% of U.S. college females practice unsafe sex by not using condoms.
- Two types of disorders are associated with sexual functioning—sexual dysfunctions and paraphilic disorders. Gender dysphoria is not specifically a sexual disorder but rather a marked incongruence between one's assigned sex and the gender one experiences or identifies with.

An Overview of Sexual Dysfunctions

- Sexual dysfunction includes a variety of disorders in which people find it difficult to function adequately during sexual relations.
- Specific sexual dysfunctions include disorders of sexual desire (hypoactive sexual desire disorder in males and female sexual interest/arousal disorder) in which interest in sexual relations is extremely low or nonexistent, disorders of sexual arousal (erectile disorder and female sexual interest/arousal disorder) in which achieving or maintaining adequate penile erection or sexual excitement and vaginal lubrication is problematic; and orgasmic disorders (female orgasmic disorder and delayed or premature ejaculation in males) in which orgasm occurs too quickly or not at all. The most common disorder in this category is premature ejaculation, which occurs in males; inhibited orgasm is commonly seen in females.
- Sexual pain disorder is known as genito-pelvic pain/penetration disorder in women, in which unbearable pain is associated with sexual relations, and includes vaginismus, in which the pelvic muscles in the outer third of the vagina undergo involuntary spasms when intercourse is attempted.

Assessing Sexual Behavior

- The three components of assessment are interviews, a complete medical evaluation, and psychophysiological assessment.

Causes and Treatment of Sexual Dysfunction

- Sexual dysfunction is associated with socially transmitted negative attitudes about sex, current relationship difficulties, and anxiety focused on sexual activity.
- Psychosocial treatment of sexual dysfunctions is generally successful but not readily available. Various medical approaches have become available, including the drug Viagra and similar drugs. These treatments focus mostly on erectile dysfunction and are effective and satisfying for about one third of patients who try them. Some preliminary evidence exists on a new drug, flibanserin, as a possible treatment for hypoactive sexual desire in women, but more research is needed.

Paraphilic Disorders: Clinical Descriptions

- Paraphilia is sexual attraction to inappropriate people, such as children, or to inappropriate objects, such as articles of clothing. Paraphilia becomes a paraphilic disorder when the sexual attraction causes significant distress or impairment to the individual or causes harm or the risk of harm to others.
- The paraphilic disorders include fetishistic disorder, in which sexual arousal occurs almost exclusively in the context of inappropriate objects or individuals; exhibitionistic disorder, in which sexual gratification is attained by exposing one's genitals to unsuspecting strangers; voyeuristic disorder, in which sexual arousal is derived from observing unsuspecting individuals undressing or naked; transvestic disorder, in which individuals are sexually aroused by wearing clothing of the "opposite" sex; sexual sadism disorder, in which sexual arousal is associated with inflicting pain or humiliation; sexual masochism disorder, in which sexual arousal is associated with experiencing pain or humiliation; and pedophilic disorder, in which there is a strong sexual attraction toward children. Incest is a type of pedophilia in which the victim is related, often a son or daughter.
- The development of paraphilic disorders is associated with deficiencies in consensual adult sexual arousal, deficiencies in consensual adult social skills, deviant sexual fantasies that may develop before or during puberty, and attempts by the individual to suppress thoughts associated with these arousal patterns.

Assessing and Treating Paraphilic Disorders

- Psychosocial treatments of these disorders are only modestly effective at best among individuals who are incarcerated, but somewhat more successful in less severe outpatients.

Gender Dysphoria

- Gender dysphoria is a dissatisfaction with one's assigned sex and the sense that one is a different gender (for example, a woman assigned male at birth). A person develops a sense of gender or gender identity between 18 months and 3 years of age, and it seems that both congruent gender identity and incongruent gender identity have biological roots influenced by learning.
- Treatment for adults with marked gender incongruence (transgender) may include gender-affirming surgery integrated with psychological approaches.

Key Terms

heterosexual behavior, 357
same-sex sexual behavior, 357
nonbinary, 357
sexual dysfunction, 362
male hypoactive sexual desire disorder, 363
female sexual interest/arousal disorder, 363
erectile disorder, 364
delayed ejaculation, 366
female orgasmic disorder, 366
premature ejaculation, 367
vulvodynia, 368
genito-pelvic pain/penetration disorder, 368
vaginismus, 368
paraphilic disorders, 378
frotteuristic disorder, 379
fetishistic disorder, 379
voyeuristic disorder, 379
exhibitionistic disorder, 379
transvestic disorder, 380
sexual sadism, 382
sexual masochism, 382
pedophilia, 383
incest, 383
covert sensitization, 387
orgasmic reconditioning, 387
gender dysphoria, 389
gender nonconformity, 392
gender-affirming surgery, 393

Answers to Concept Checks

10.1

1. a; **2.** d; **3.** c; **4.** a

10.2

1. T; **2.** F (sometimes increases arousal); **3.** T; **4.** T; **5.** F (nondemand pleasuring, squeeze technique, and so on); **6.** T

10.3

1. d; **2.** c; **3.** a; **4.** b; **5.** a; **6.** c

10.4

1. More men masturbate and do it more often; men are more permissive about casual sex; women want more intimacy from sex; and so on.
2. Both same-sex sexual and heterosexual behaviors are normal; genetics appear to play some role in the development of sexual orientation.
3. Gender dysphoria
4. Abnormal hormone levels during development; social or parental influences
5. Gender-affirming surgery; psychosocial treatment to adjust to expressed or desired gender

Exploring Sexual Disorders and Gender Dysphoria

- Sexual behavior is considered normal in our culture unless it is associated with one of three kinds of impaired functioning—gender dysphoria, sexual dysfunction, or paraphilic disorders.
- Sexual orientation probably has a strong biological basis that is influenced by environmental and social factors.

GENDER DYSPHORIA

Present when a person feels trapped in a body that is the "wrong" sex, that does not match his or her innate sense of personal identity. (Gender identity is independent of sexual arousal patterns.) Relatively rare.

Thinkstock/Getty Images

Causes

Biological Influences

- Not yet confirmed, although likely to involve prenatal exposure to hormones
  - Hormonal variations may be natural or result from medication

Psychological Influences

- Gender identity develops between 1 1/2 and 3 years of age
  - "Masculine" behaviors in girls and "feminine" behaviors in boys evoke different responses in different families

Treatment

- Gender affirming surgery: removal of breasts or penis; genital reconstruction
  - Requires rigorous psychological preparation and financial and social stability
- Psychosocial intervention to change gender identity
  - Usually unsuccessful except as temporary relief until surgery

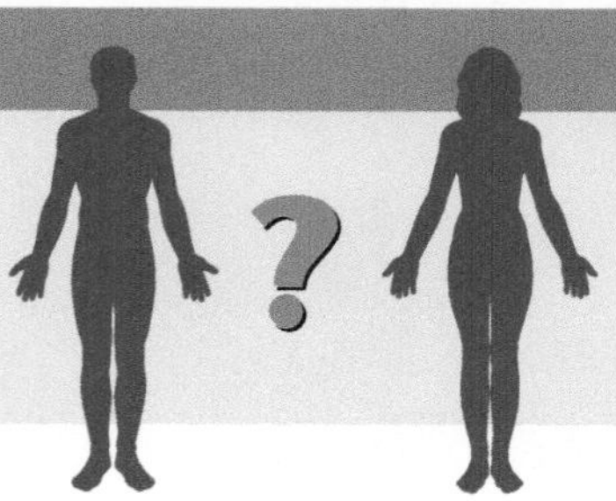

PARAPHILIC DISORDERS

Sexual arousal occurs almost exclusively in the context of inappropriate objects or individuals.

Types

- ***Fetishistic disorder:*** Sexual attraction to nonliving objects
- ***Voyeuristic disorder:*** Sexual arousal achieved by viewing unsuspecting person undressing or naked
- ***Exhibitionistic disorder:*** Sexual gratification from exposing one's genitals to unsuspecting strangers
- ***Transvestic disorder:*** Sexual arousal from wearing opposite-sex clothing (cross-dressing)
- ***Sexual sadism disorder:*** Sexual arousal associated with inflicting pain or humiliation
- ***Sexual masochism disorder:*** Sexual arousal associated with experiencing pain or humiliation
- ***Pedophilic disorder:*** Strong sexual attraction to children
- ***Incest:*** Sexual attraction to family member

Causes

- Preexisting deficiencies
  - In levels of arousal with consensual adults
  - In consensual adult social skills
- Treatment received from adults during childhood
- Early sexual fantasies reinforced by masturbation
- Extremely strong sex drive combined with uncontrollable thought processes

Treatment

- *Covert sensitization:* Repeated mental reviewing of aversive consequences to establish negative associations with behavior
- *Relapse prevention:* Therapeutic preparation for coping with future situations
- *Orgasmic reconditioning:* Pairing appropriate stimuli with masturbation to create positive arousal patterns
- *Medical:* Drugs that reduce testosterone to suppress sexual desire; fantasies and arousal return when drugs are stopped

PhotoDisc/Getty Images

Thinkstock/Getty Images

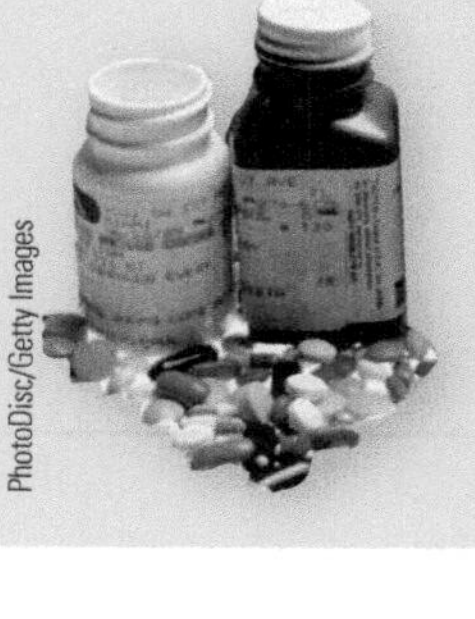

PhotoDisc/Getty Images

SEXUAL DYSFUNCTIONS

Sexual dysfunctions can be

- ***Lifelong:*** Present during entire sexual history
- ***Acquired:*** Interrupts normal sexual pattern
- ***Generalized:*** Present in every encounter
- ***Situational:*** Present only with certain partners or at certain times

The Human Sexual Response Cycle

A dysfunction is an impairment in one of the sexual response stages.

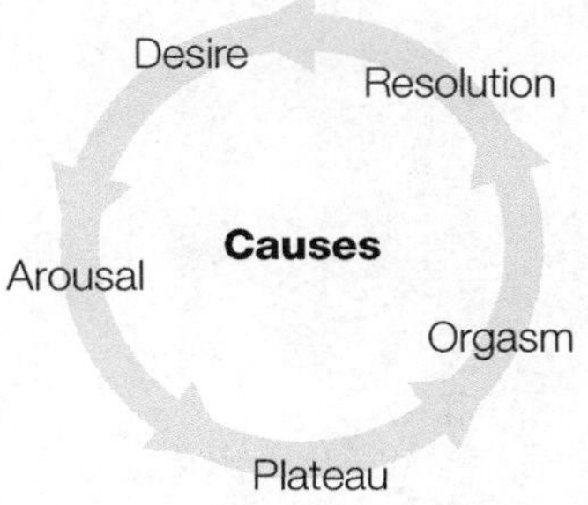

Types of Sexual Dysfunctions

Sexual Desire Disorders

- ***Male hypoactive sexual desire disorder:*** Apparent lack of interest in sexual activity or fantasy

Sexual Arousal Disorders

- ***Erectile disorder:*** Recurring inability to achieve or maintain adequate erection
- ***Female sexual interest/arousal disorder:*** Recurring inability to achieve or maintain adequate lubrication

Orgasm Disorders

- ***Female orgasmic disorder:*** Inability to achieve orgasm despite adequate desire and arousal
- ***Premature ejaculation:*** Ejaculation before it is desired, with minimal stimulation

Sexual Pain Disorders

- ***Genito-pelvic pain/penetration disorder:*** Marked pain, anxiety, and tension associated with intercourse for which there is no medical cause; vaginismus (that is, involuntary muscle spasms in the front of the vagina that prevent or interfere with intercourse); occurs in females

Psychological Contributions

- Distraction
- Underestimates of arousal
- Negative thought processes

Sociocultural Contributions

- Erotophobia, caused by formative experiences of sexual cues as alarming
- Negative experiences, such as rape
- Deterioration of relationship

Causes

Biological Contributions

- Neurological or other nervous system problems
- Vascular disease
- Chronic illness
- Prescription medication
- Drugs of abuse, including alcohol

Psychological and Physical Interactions

- A combination of influences is almost always present
  - Specific biological predisposition *and* psychological factors may produce a particular disorder

Treatment

- *Psychosocial:* Therapeutic program to facilitate communication, improve sexual education, and eliminate anxiety. Both partners participate fully.
- *Medical:* Almost all interventions focus on male erectile disorder, including drugs, prostheses, and surgery. Medical treatment is combined with sexual education and therapy to achieve maximum benefit.

11 Substance-Related, Addictive, and Impulse-Control Disorders

Jan Mika/Shutterstock.com

Learning Objectives

LO11.1 Discuss the differences between substance intoxication and substance withdrawal as a feature of substance use disorders.

LO11.2 List the categories of substances that can contribute to the development of substance use disorders.

LO11.3 Compare biological, psychosocial treatments, and prevention according to their effectiveness at preventing substance use disorder.

LO11.4 Draw connections between the symptoms and brain factors involved in the development of substance use disorders and gambling disorder.

LO11.5 Describe the similarities and differences of impulse-control disorders according to their symptoms as listed in the DSM-5.

Would you be surprised if we told you that a group of psychological disorders costs U.S. citizens hundreds of billions of dollars each year, kills 500,000 Americans annually, and is implicated in street crime, homelessness, and gang violence? Would you be even more surprised to learn that most of us have behaved in ways characteristic of these disorders at some point in our lives? You should not. Smoking cigarettes, drinking alcohol or caffeine, and using illegal drugs are all related to these disorders, and they are responsible for astronomical financial costs and the tragic waste of hundreds of thousands of human lives each year. In this chapter, we explore **substance-related and addictive disorders**, which are associated with the misuse of drugs and other substances people take to alter the way they think, feel, and behave. In addition, the newly added disorder to this category in DSM-5—gambling disorder—will be discussed. These disorders have been with us for centuries and continue to affect how we live, work, and play.

Equally disruptive to the people affected, **impulse-control disorders** represent a number of related problems that involve the inability to resist acting on a drive or temptation. Included in this group are those who cannot resist aggressive impulses or the impulse to steal, for example, or to set fires. Controversy surrounds substance-related, addictive, and impulse-control disorders because society sometimes believes that these problems result simply from a lack of "will." If people wanted to stop drinking, using cocaine, or gambling, well, they would just stop. We first examine those individuals who are being harmed by their use of a variety of chemical substances (substance-related disorders) or their addictive behaviors (gambling disorder) and then turn our attention to the puzzling array of disorders that are under the heading of impulse-control disorders.

Perspectives on Substance-Related and Addictive Disorders

The cost in lives, money, and emotional turmoil has made the issue of excessive drug use a major concern worldwide. Among people in the United States age 12 or older in 2019, 60.1% (or 165.4 million people) used a substance (such as tobacco, alcohol, kratom, or an illicit drug) in the past month (Substance Abuse and Mental Health Services Administration, 2020). Many U.S. presidential administrations have declared various "wars on drugs," but the problem remains. The Roman Catholic Church issued a universal catechism in 1992 that officially declared drug misuse and drunk driving to be sins (Riding, 1992). Yet from the drug-related deaths of rock stars Jimi Hendrix and Janis Joplin in 1970 to contemporary celebrities such as Michael Jackson, Whitney Houston, Prince, and Lil Peep, drug use continues to negatively impact the lives of many. In addition, stories such as these not only are about the rich and famous but also are retold in every corner of society.

As we have just seen, a significant number of people continue to use illicit drugs and misuse prescription drugs regularly. Consider the case of Danny, who has the disturbing but common habit of **alcohol use disorder** and several substance use disorders.

Danny... Comorbid Substance Use Disorders

At the age of 43, Danny was in jail, awaiting trial on vehicular manslaughter charges stemming from a DUI accident that left one woman dead. Danny's story illustrates the lifelong pattern that characterizes the behavior of many people who are affected by substance-related disorders.

Danny grew up in the suburbs in the United States, the youngest of three children. He was well liked in school and an average student. Like many of his friends, he smoked cigarettes in his early teens and drank beer with his friends at night behind his high school. Unlike most of his friends, however, Danny almost always drank until he was obviously drunk. He also experimented with many other drugs, including cocaine, heroin, "speed" (amphetamines), and "downers" (barbiturates).

After high school, Danny attended a local community college for one semester, but he dropped out after failing most of his courses. His dismal performance in school seemed to be related to his missing most classes rather than to an inability to learn and understand the material. He had difficulty getting up for classes after partying most of the night, which he did with increasing frequency. His moods were highly variable, and he was often unpleasant. Danny's family knew he occasionally drank too much, but they didn't know (or didn't want to know) about his other drug use. He had for years forbidden anyone to go into his room after his mother found little packets of white powder (probably cocaine) in his sock drawer. He said he was keeping them for a friend and that he would return them immediately. He was furious that his family might suspect him of using drugs. Money was sometimes missing from the house, and once some stereo equipment "disappeared," but if his family members suspected Danny, they never admitted it.

Danny held a series of low-paying jobs, and when he was working, his family reassured themselves that he was back on track and things would be fine. Unfortunately, he rarely held a job for more than a few months. The money he earned usually turned into drugs, and he was usually fired for his frequent absences from work and performance. Because he continued to live at home, Danny could survive despite frequent periods of unemployment. When he was in his late 20s, Danny seemed to have a personal revelation. He announced that he needed help and planned to check into an alcohol rehabilitation center; he still would not admit to using other drugs. His family's joy and relief were overwhelming, and no one questioned his request for several thousand dollars to help pay for the private program he said he wanted to attend. Danny disappeared for several weeks, presumably because he was in the rehabilitation program. However, a call from the local police station put an end to this fantasy: Danny had been found quite high, living in an abandoned building. As with many of these incidents, we never learned all the details, but it appears that Danny spent his family's money on drugs and had a 3-week binge with some friends. Danny's deceptiveness and financial irresponsibility greatly strained his relationship with his family. He was allowed to continue living at home, but his parents and siblings excluded him from their emotional lives. Following this, Danny seemed to straighten out, and he held a job at a gas station for almost 2 years. He became friendly with the station owner and his son, and he often went hunting with them during the season. Without any obvious warning, however, Danny resumed drinking and using drugs and was arrested for robbing the very place that had kept him employed for many months.

Although he received probation for that offense after promising to attend drug treatment, his pattern continued. Years later, while driving under the influence of multiple substances, he hit another car, and the 28-year-old driver of that car was killed.

Why did Danny's drug use become so problematic when many of his friends' and siblings' use did not? Why did he steal from his family and friends? What ultimately became of him? We return to Danny's frustrating story later when we look at the causes and treatment of substance-related disorders.

Levels of Involvement

Although each drug described in this chapter has unique effects, there are similarities in the ways they are used and the people who misuse them are treated. First, we present some concepts that apply to substance-related disorders in general, noting important terminology and addressing several diagnostic issues.

Can you use drugs without meeting criteria for a disorder? Can you use drugs and not become addicted to them? To answer these important questions, we first need to outline what we mean by *substance use, substance intoxication, substance use disorder,* and *substance dependence/addiction.* The term *substance* refers to chemical compounds that are ingested to alter mood or behavior. **Psychoactive substances** alter mood, behavior, or both. Although one might first think of drugs such as cocaine and heroin, this definition also includes more commonplace legal drugs such as alcohol, the nicotine found in tobacco, and the caffeine in coffee, soft drinks, and chocolate (Black & Andreasen, 2021). As you will see, these so-called safe drugs also affect mood and behavior, they can be addictive, and they account for more health problems and a greater mortality rate than all illegal drugs combined. You could make a good argument for directing the war on drugs to cigarette smoking (nicotine use) because of its addictive properties and negative health consequences.

Substance Use **Substance use** is the ingestion of psychoactive substances in moderate amounts that does not significantly interfere with social, educational, or occupational functioning. Most of you reading this chapter probably use some sort of psychoactive substance occasionally. Drinking a cup of coffee in the morning to wake up or smoking a cigarette and having a drink with a friend to relax are examples of substance use, as is the occasional ingestion of drugs such as cannabis, cocaine, amphetamines, or barbiturates (Black & Andreasen, 2021).

Intoxication Our physiological reaction to ingested substances—drunkenness or getting high—is **substance intoxication**. For a person to become intoxicated, many variables interact, including the type of drug taken, the amount ingested, and the person's individual biological reaction. For many of the substances we discuss here, intoxication is experienced as impaired judgment, mood changes, and lowered motor ability (for example, problems walking or talking) (Black & Andreasen, 2021).

Substance Use Disorders Defining **substance use disorders** by how much of a substance is ingested is problematic. For example, is drinking two glasses of wine in an hour excessive use? Three glasses? Six? Is taking one injection of heroin considered misuse? The fifth edition of the *Diagnostic and Statistical Manual* (DSM-5) (American Psychiatric Association, 2013) defines substance use disorders in terms of how significantly the use interferes with the user's life. If substances disrupt your education, job, or relationships with others and put you in physically dangerous situations (for example, while driving), you would be considered to have a disorder. Some evidence suggests that drug use can predict later job outcomes. In one study, researchers controlled for factors such as educational interests and problem behaviors other than drug use and still found that repeated hard drug use (using one or more of the following: amphetamines, barbiturates, cocaine, crack, crystal meth, heroin or other narcotics, inhalants, LSD and other psychedelics, and PCP) predicted poor job outcomes after college (Arria et al., 2013).

Danny seems to fit this definition of a disorder. His inability to complete a semester of community college was a direct result of drug use. Danny often drove while drunk or under the influence of other drugs, and he had already been arrested twice for driving while intoxicated. Danny's use of multiple substances was so relentless and pervasive that he would probably be diagnosed with severe forms of the disorders.

Intoxication.

Psychiatric Association, 2013), and withdrawal from cannabis includes such symptoms as irritability, nervousness, appetite change, and sleep disturbance (DSM-5). We return to the ways drugs act on our bodies when we examine the causes of excessive misuse and addiction.

Other symptoms that make up a substance use disorder include "drug-seeking behaviors." The repeated use of a drug, a desperate need to ingest more of the substance (stealing money to buy drugs, standing outside in the cold to smoke), and the likelihood that use will resume after a period of abstinence are behaviors that define the extent of substance use disorders. Such behavioral reactions are different from the physiological responses to drugs we described before and are sometimes referred to in terms of psychological dependence. The previous version of the DSM considered substance abuse and **substance dependence** as separate diagnoses. The DSM-5 combines the two into the general definition of substance-related disorders based on research that suggests the two co-occur (American Psychiatric Association, 2013; Dawson, Goldstein, & Grant, 2012; O'Brien, 2011).

Substance use disorder is usually described as addiction. Although we use the term *addiction* routinely when we describe people who seem to be under the control of drugs, there is some disagreement about how to define addiction (Gray & Milin, 2021). In order to meet criteria for a disorder, people must meet criteria for at least two symptoms in the past year that interfered with their life or bothered them a great deal. When a person has four or five symptoms, they are considered to fall in the moderate range. A severe substance use disorder would be someone like Danny that has six or more symptoms (Black & Andreasen, 2021). Symptoms for substance use disorders can include a **physiological dependence** on the drug or drugs, meaning the use of increasingly greater amounts of the drug to experience the same effect (**tolerance**), and a negative physical response when the substance is no longer ingested (**withdrawal**) (Higgins, Sigmon, & Heil, 2014). Tolerance and withdrawal are physiological reactions to the chemicals being ingested. If you're a daily coffee drinker, have you ever experienced a headache when you didn't have your coffee? You were probably going through caffeine withdrawal. In a more extreme example, withdrawal from alcohol can cause *alcohol withdrawal delirium*, in which a person can experience frightening hallucinations and body tremors (a condition described later in this chapter). Withdrawal from many substances can bring on chills, fever, diarrhea, nausea and vomiting, and aches and pains. Not all substances are physiologically addicting, however. For example, you do not go through severe physical withdrawal when you stop taking LSD. Cocaine withdrawal has a pattern that includes anxiety, sleep changes, lack of motivation, and boredom (DSM-5; American

Let's go back to the questions we started with: "Can you use drugs and not misuse them?" and "Can you misuse drugs and not become addicted to them?" The answer to the first question is yes. Some people drink wine or beer regularly without drinking to excess. In addition, contrary to popular belief, some people use drugs such as heroin, cocaine, or crack (a form of cocaine) occasionally (for instance, several times a year) without misusing them (Ray, 2012). What is disturbing is that we do not know ahead of time who might be likely to lose control and misuse these drugs and who is likely to become dependent with even a passing use of a substance.

Substance Use.

Monkey Business Images/Shutterstock.com

substance use disorder.

considered to have a cocaine use disorder in the severe range because of the tolerance he showed for the drug, his use of larger amounts than he intended, his unsuccessful attempts to stop using it, and the activities he gave up to buy it. His pattern of use was more pervasive than simple misuse, and the diagnosis provided a clear picture of his need for help.

Symptoms of other disorders can complicate the substance use disorder picture significantly. For example, do some people take drugs to excess because they are depressed, or does drug use and its consequences (for example, loss of friends or job) create depression? Researchers estimate that almost three quarters of the people in addiction treatment centers have an additional psychiatric disorder, with mood disorders (such as major depression) observed in more than 40% and anxiety disorders and posttraumatic stress disorder seen in more than 25% of the cases (Dawson et al., 2012; Lieb, 2015). The onset of COVID-19 is having a significant negative impact on the mental health of the general population through a range of mechanisms: fear, uncertainty, and anxiety; social distancing/isolation; loneliness; and economic repercussions (Chiappini, Guirguis, John, Corkery, & Schifano, 2020).

Substance use might occur concurrently with other disorders for several reasons. Substance-related disorders and anxiety and mood disorders are highly prevalent in society and may occur together so often just by chance. Drug intoxication and withdrawal can cause symptoms of anxiety, depression, and psychosis. Disorders such as schizophrenia and antisocial personality disorder are highly likely to include a secondary problem of substance use.

Because substance-related disorders can be so complicated, DSM-5 tries to define when a symptom is a result of substance use and when it is not. If symptoms seen in schizophrenia or in extreme states of anxiety appear during intoxication or within 6 weeks after withdrawal from drugs, they are not considered signs of a separate psychiatric disorder. For example, individuals who show signs of severe depression just after they have stopped taking heavy doses of stimulants would not be diagnosed with a major mood disorder. However, individuals who were severely depressed before they used stimulants and those whose symptoms persist more than 6 weeks after they stop might have a separate disorder (Sheperis, Lionetti, & Snook, 2015).

We now turn to the individual substances themselves, their effects on our brains and bodies, and the ways they are used in our society. We have grouped the problematic behaviors into six general categories.

It may seem counterintuitive, but dependence can be present without excessive use. For example, cancer patients who take morphine for pain may become dependent on the drug—build up a tolerance and go through withdrawal if it is stopped—without misusing it (Ho et al., 2020). Later in this chapter, we discuss biological and psychosocial theories of the causes of substance-related disorders and the reasons we have individualized reactions to these substances.

Diagnostic Issues

In early editions of the DSM, alcoholism and drug misuse were not treated as separate disorders. Instead, they were categorized as "sociopathic personality disturbances"—a forerunner of the current *antisocial personality disorder* we discuss in Chapter 12—because substance use was seen as a symptom of other problems. It was considered a sign of moral weakness, and the influence of genetics and biology was hardly acknowledged. A separate category was created for substance use disorders in DSM-III, in 1980, and since then we have acknowledged the complex biological and psychological nature of the problem.

In DSM-5, *substance-related disorders* include 11 symptoms that range from relatively mild (such as substance use results in a failure to fulfill major role obligations) to more severe (for example, occupational or recreational activities are given up or reduced because of substance use). DSM-5 removed the previous symptom that related to substance-related legal problems and added a symptom that indicates the presence of craving or a strong desire to use the substance (Black & Andreasen, 2021). These distinctions help clarify the problem and focus treatment on the appropriate aspect of the disorder. Danny would be

- **Depressants:** These substances result in behavioral sedation and can induce relaxation. They include alcohol (ethyl alcohol) and the sedative and hypnotic drugs in the families of barbiturates (for example, Seconal) and benzodiazepines (for example, Valium and Xanax).
- **Stimulants:** These substances cause us to be more active and alert and can elevate mood. Included in this group are amphetamines, cocaine, nicotine, and caffeine.
- **Opiates:** The major effect of these substances is to produce temporary analgesia (reduce pain) and euphoria. Heroin, kratom, opium, codeine, and morphine are included in this group.
- **Hallucinogens:** These substances alter sensory perception and can produce delusions, paranoia, and hallucinations. Cannabis and LSD are included in this category
- **Other commonly misused substances:** Other substances that are misused but do not fit neatly into one of the categories here include inhalants (for example, airplane glue), anabolic steroids, and other over-the-counter and prescription medications (for example, nitrous oxide). These substances produce a variety of psychoactive effects that are characteristic of the substances described in the previous categories.
- **Gambling disorder:** As with the ingestion of the substances just described, individuals who display gambling disorder are unable to resist the urge to gamble which, in turn, may results in negative personal consequences (such as divorce and loss of employment).

Depressants

Depressants primarily *decrease* central nervous system activity. Their principal effect is to reduce the body's levels of physiological arousal and help people relax. Included in this group are alcohol and the sedative, hypnotic, and anxiolytic drugs, such as those prescribed for insomnia (see Chapter 8). These substances are among those most likely to produce symptoms of physical dependence, tolerance, and withdrawal. We first look at the most commonly used of these substances—**alcohol**—and the **alcohol-related disorders** that can result.

Alcohol-Related Disorders

Danny's substance use began when he drank beer with friends, a rite of passage for many teenagers. Alcohol has been widely used throughout history. For example, scientists have found evidence of wine or beer in pottery jars at the site of a Sumerian trading post in western Iran and the country of Georgia that date back 7,000 years (McGovern, 2007). For hundreds of years, Europeans drank large amounts of beer, wine, and hard liquor. When they came to North America in the early 1600s, they brought their considerable thirst for alcohol with them. In the United States during the early 1800s, consumption of alcohol (mostly whiskey) was more than 7 gallons per year for every person older than 15. This is more than three times the current rate of U.S. alcohol use (Slater & Alpert, 2020).

Alcohol is produced when certain yeasts react with sugar and water and *fermentation* takes place. Historically, we have been creative about fermenting alcohol from just about any fruit or vegetable, partly because many foods contain sugar. Alcoholic drinks have included mead from honey, sake from rice, wine from palm, mescal and pulque from agave and cactus, liquor from maple syrup, liquor from South American jungle fruits, wine from grapes, and beer from grains (Lazare, 1989).

Clinical Description Apparent stimulation is the initial effect of alcohol, although it is a depressant. We generally experience a feeling of well-being, our inhibitions are reduced, and we become more outgoing. This is because the inhibitory centers in the brain are initially depressed—or slowed. With continued drinking, however, alcohol depresses more areas of the brain, which impedes the ability to function properly. Motor coordination is impaired (staggering, slurred speech), reaction time is slowed, we become confused, our ability to make judgments is reduced, and even vision and hearing can be negatively affected, all of which help explain why driving while intoxicated is clearly dangerous.

Effects Alcohol affects many parts of the body (see ■ Figure 11.1). After it is ingested, it passes through the esophagus (1 in Figure 11.1) and into the stomach (2), where small amounts are absorbed. From there, most of it travels to the small intestine (3), where it is easily absorbed into the bloodstream. The circulatory system distributes the alcohol throughout the body, where it contacts every major organ, including the heart (4). Some of the alcohol goes to the lungs, where it vaporizes and is exhaled, a phenomenon that is the basis for the *breathalyzer test* that measures levels of intoxication. As alcohol passes through the liver (5), it is broken down or metabolized into carbon dioxide and water by enzymes (Maher, 1997). ■ Figure 11.2 shows how much time it takes to metabolize one to four drinks, with the dotted line showing when driving becomes impaired (National Institute on Alcohol Abuse and Alcoholism, 1997).

Most substances we describe in this chapter— including cannabis, opiates, and tranquilizers—interact with specific receptors in the brain cells. The effects of alcohol, however, are more complex. Alcohol influences a number of neuroreceptor systems, which makes it difficult to study (Lees, Meredith, Kirkland, Bryant, & Squeglia, 2020). For example, the *gamma-aminobutyric acid (GABA)* system, which we discuss in Chapters 2 and 5, seems to be particularly sensitive to alcohol. GABA, as you will recall, is an inhibitory neurotransmitter. Its major role is to interfere with the firing of the neuron it attaches to. Because the GABA system seems to affect the emotion of anxiety, alcohol's antianxiety properties may result from its interaction with the GABA system. In addition, when GABA attaches to its receptor, chloride ions enter the cell and make it less sensitive to the effects of other neurotransmitters. Alcohol seems to reinforce the movement of these chloride ions; as a result, the neurons have difficulty firing. In other words, although alcohol seems to "loosen our tongues" and makes us more sociable, it makes it difficult for neurons to communicate with one another (Joslyn, Ravindranathan, Brush, Schuckit, & White, 2010). For example, there is some evidence

DSM 5 **Table 11.1**

Diagnostic Criteria for Alcohol Use Disorder

A. A problematic pattern of alcohol use leading to clinically significant impairment or distress, as manifested by at least two of the following, occurring within a 12-month period:

1. Alcohol is often taken in larger amounts or over a longer period than was intended.
2. There is a persistent desire or unsuccessful efforts to cut down or control alcohol use.
3. A great deal of time is spent in activities necessary to obtain alcohol, use alcohol, or recover from its effects.
4. Craving, or a strong desire or urge to use alcohol.
5. Recurrent alcohol use resulting in a failure to fulfill major role obligations at work, school, or home.
6. Continued alcohol use despite having persistent or recurrent social or interpersonal problems caused or exacerbated by the effects of alcohol.
7. Important social, occupational, or recreational activities are given up or reduced because of alcohol use.
8. Recurrent alcohol use in situations in which it is physically hazardous.
9. Alcohol use is continued despite knowledge of having a persistent or recurrent physical or psychological problem that is likely to have been caused or exacerbated by alcohol.
10. Tolerance, as defined by either or both of the following:
    - **(a)** A need for markedly increased amounts of alcohol to achieve intoxication or desired effect.
    - **(b)** A markedly diminished effect with continued use of the same amount of alcohol.
11. Withdrawal, as manifested by either of the following:
    - **(a)** The characteristic withdrawal syndrome for alcohol (refer to criteria A and B of the criteria set for alcohol withdrawal).
    - **(b)** Alcohol (or a closely related substance such as benzodiazepine) is taken to relieve or avoid withdrawal symptoms.

Specify current severity:

Mild: Presence of 2 to 3 symptoms

Moderate: Presence of 4 to 5 symptoms

Severe: Presence of 6 or more symptoms

American Psychiatric Association. (2022). *Diagnostic and statistical manual of mental disorders* (5th ed., Text Revision).

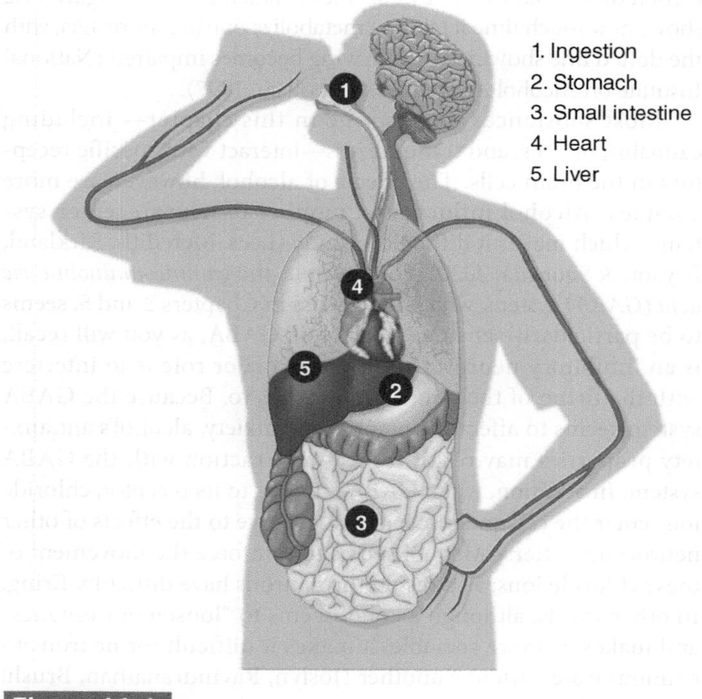

Figure 11.1

The path traveled by alcohol throughout the body (see the text for a complete description).

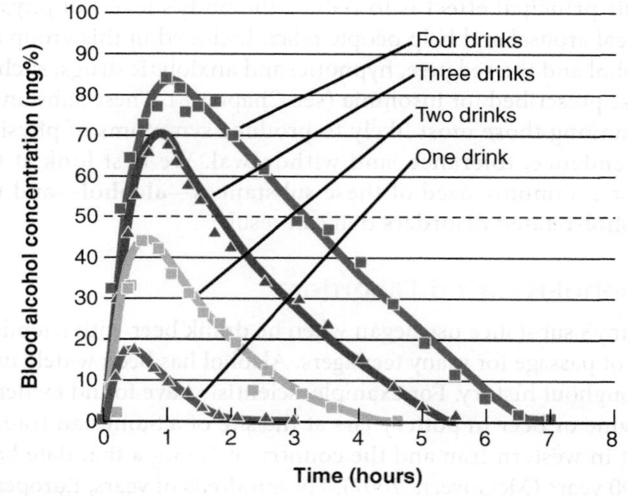

Figure 11.2

Blood alcohol concentration after the rapid consumption of different amounts of alcohol by eight adult, fasting, male subjects. The legal level of intoxication in most states is 100 mg%. The level at which deterioration of driving skills begins is 50 mg%. From National Institute on Alcohol Abuse and Alcoholism, 1997, *Alcohol alert: Alcohol-metabolism*, No. 35, PH 371.

from genetic research (further discussed below) that the genes responsible for communication between neurons may also be responsible for individual differences in response to alcohol.

The *glutamate system* is under study for its role in the effects of alcohol. In contrast to the GABA system, the glutamate system is excitatory, helping neurons fire. It is suspected to involve learning and memory, and it may be the avenue through which alcohol affects our cognitive abilities. Blackouts, the loss of memory for what happens during intoxication, may result from the interaction of alcohol with the glutamate system. The serotonin system also appears to be sensitive to alcohol. This neurotransmitter system affects mood, sleep, and eating behavior and is thought to be responsible for alcohol cravings (Müller, Schumann, Kornhuber, & Kalinichenko, 2020). Because alcohol affects so many neurotransmitter systems, we should not be surprised that it has such widespread and complex effects.

The long-term effects of heavy drinking are often severe. Withdrawal from chronic alcohol use typically includes hand tremors and, within several hours, nausea or vomiting, anxiety, transient hallucinations, agitation, insomnia, and, at its most extreme, **withdrawal delirium** (or **delirium tremens**—the **DTs**), a condition that can produce frightening hallucinations and body tremors. The devastating experience of delirium tremens can be reduced with adequate medical treatment (Muronov, 2020).

Whether alcohol will cause organic damage depends on genetic vulnerability, frequency of use, length of drinking binges, blood alcohol levels attained during the drinking periods, and amount of time given to the body to recover between binges. Consequences of long-term excessive drinking include liver disease, pancreatitis, cardiovascular disorders, and brain damage.

One of the common misperceptions concerning alcohol is that it permanently kills brain cells (neurons). As you will see later, this may not be true. Some evidence for brain damage comes from the experiences of people who are alcohol dependent and experience blackouts, seizures, and hallucinations. Memory and the ability to perform certain tasks may also be impaired. More seriously, two types of organic brain syndromes may result from long-term heavy alcohol use: dementia and **Wernicke-Korsakoff syndrome**. *Dementia,* (or *neurocognitive disorder*), which we discuss more fully in Chapter 15, involves the general loss of intellectual abilities and can be a direct result of neurotoxicity or "poisoning of the brain" by excessive amounts of alcohol (Pagaling et al., 2020). *Wernicke-Korsakoff syndrome* results in confusion, loss of muscle coordination, and unintelligible speech (Isenberg-Grzeda, Kutner, & Nicolson, 2012); it is believed to be caused by a deficiency of thiamine, a vitamin metabolized poorly by heavy drinkers. The dementia caused by this disease does not go away once the brain is damaged. Although it was previously thought that mild to moderate intake of alcohol (especially wine) could actually serve a protective role in cognitive decline as we age, further research shows that this is not the case (Immonen et al., 2020; Topiwala et al., 2017).

The effects of excessive alcohol use extend beyond the health and well-being of the drinker. **Fetal alcohol syndrome (FAS)** is now generally recognized as a combination of problems that can occur in a child whose mother drank while pregnant. These problems include fetal growth retardation, cognitive deficits, behavior problems, and learning difficulties (Kaminen-Ahola, 2020). In addition, children with FAS often have characteristic facial features.

We metabolize alcohol with the help of an enzyme called **alcohol dehydrogenase (ADH)** (Schuckit, 2009b, 2014a). Three different forms of this enzyme have been identified (beta-1, beta-2, and beta-3 ADH). Among children with FAS, beta-3 ADH may be prevalent according to research. Beta-3 ADH is also found most often in African Americans. What these two findings suggest is that, in addition to the drinking habits of the mother, the likelihood a child will have FAS may depend on whether there is a genetic tendency to have certain enzymes. Children from certain racial groups may thus be more susceptible to FAS than are others. If this research is confirmed, we may have a way of identifying parents who might put their unborn children at increased risk for FAS.

Statistics on Use and Misuse Because alcohol consumption is legal in the United States, we know more about it than about most other psychoactive substances we discuss in this chapter (with the possible exception of nicotine and caffeine). Despite a national

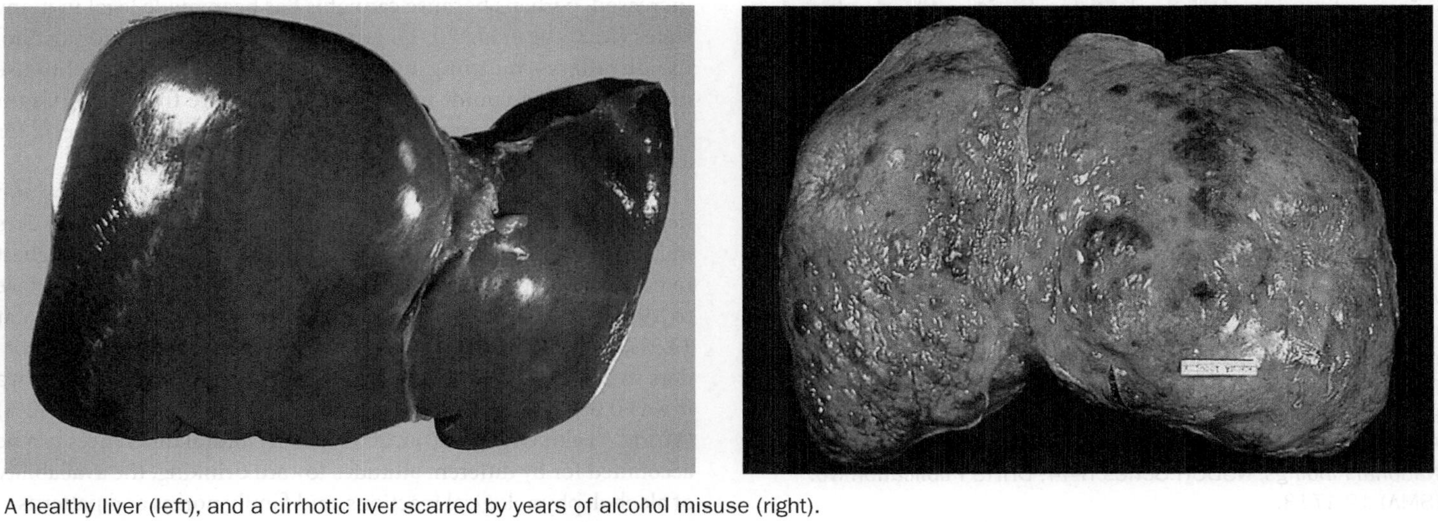

Southern Illinois University/Science Source

Martin M Rotker/Getty Images

A healthy liver (left), and a cirrhotic liver scarred by years of alcohol misuse (right).

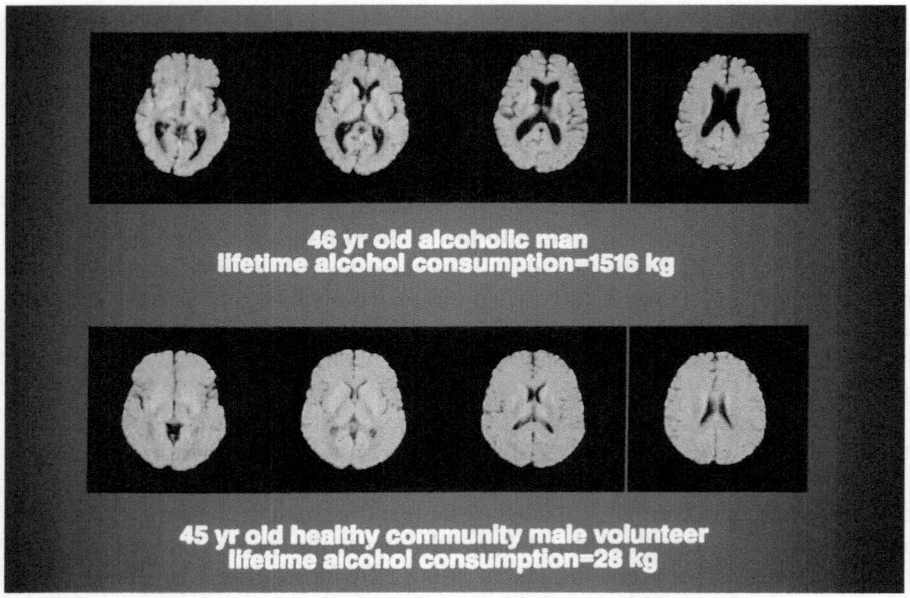

Source: Dr. Adolf Pfefferbaum, Stanford University

The dark areas in the top brain images show the extensive loss of brain tissue caused by heavy alcohol use.

history of heavy alcohol use, most adults in the United States characterize themselves as light drinkers or abstainers. On the other hand, about half of all Americans over the age of 12 report being current drinkers of alcohol, and there are considerable differences among people from different racial and ethnic backgrounds (see ■ Figure 11.3; SAMHSA, 2012). White people report the highest

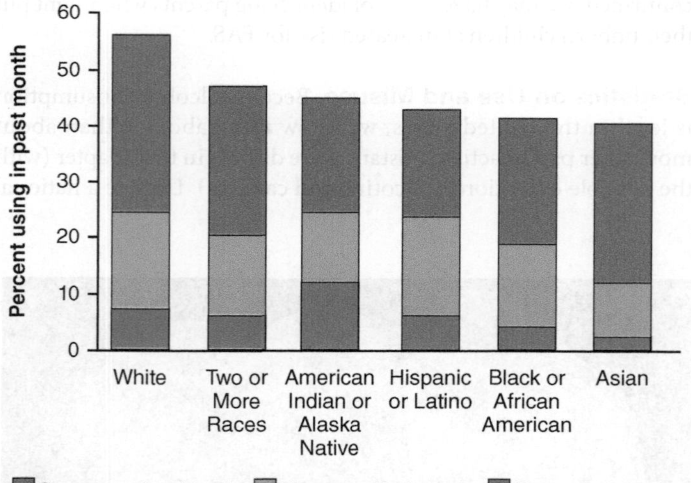

Figure 11.3

Alcohol use across racial groups. Binge drinking is defined as drinking five or more drinks on one occasion at least once per month, and heavy alcohol use is defined as binge drinking for five or more days in a month. From Substance Abuse and Mental Health Services Administration, Office of Applied Studies, 2012, *Results from the 2011 National Survey on Drug Use and Health: National Findings*, NSDUH Series H-44, DHHS Publication No. (SMA) 12-4713.

frequency of drinking (56.8%); drinking is lowest among Asian Americans (40.0%). Unfortunately, despite these differences in drinking among racial groups, Native American /Alaska Native, Latino, and Black persons are more likely than White persons to be booked into jail as opposed to cited and released for drug use (Camplain et al., 2020).

Among the 139.7 million current alcohol users age 12 or older in 2019, 65.8 million people (47.1%) were past month binge drinkers—an alarming statistic (Substance Abuse and Mental Health Services Administration, 2020). Again, there are racial differences, with Asians reporting the lowest level of binge drinking (12.4%), White people (24.0%), and Hispanic or Latino groups (24.1%) reporting the highest. Age seems to also be important given that peak lifetime alcohol use happens around late teens to early adolescence. In surveys across 100 4-year universities and colleges, about 36% of respondents said they had gone on a binge of heavy drinking once in the preceding 2 weeks (Johnston, O'Malley, Bachman, & Schulenberg, 2012). Unfortunately, this binge-drinking trend seems to have increased in college students along with drunk driving and alcohol-related deaths (Whiteside, Bittinger, Kilmer, Lostutter, & Larimer, 2015). Men, however, were more likely to report several binges in the 2-week period (White & Hingson, 2014; Presley & Meilman, 1992). The same survey found that students with a grade point average of A had no more than 3 drinks per week, whereas D and F students averaged 11 alcoholic drinks per week (Presley & Meilman, 1992). Overall, these data point to the popularity and pervasiveness of drinking in our society (Donath et al., 2012).

We know that not everyone who drinks develops an alcohol use disorder. Researchers estimate, however, that among people age 12 or older, the percentage with a past year alcohol use disorder declined from 7.7% (or 18.1 million people) in 2002 to 5.3% (or 14.5 million people) in 2019 (Substance Abuse and Mental Health Services Administration, 2020). Statistics suggest that the prevalence of alcohol use has declined but the use of cannabis has increased, perhaps because cannabis has been made legal in many states (McCabe et al., 2021). Lifetime prevalence rates for alcohol use disorders—meaning a person met criteria for an alcohol use disorder at some point in their life—are more than 29% (Grant et al, 2015). This means one in three people will meet criteria for an alcohol use disorder at some point in their lives.

Outside the United States, rates of alcohol use problems and dependence vary widely. The prevalence of alcohol use disorders in 2004 as measured by the World Health Organization was highest in eastern European countries (for example, in Russia it was close to 19% in 2004), followed by Colombia at 13%, South Korea at 13.5%, and Thailand at 11%. The prevalence for alcohol use disorders in 2004 was lowest in Northern Africa (for example, in Libya it was 0.05%) and the Middle East (in Afghanistan it was 0.2%) (World Health Organization, 2004). Such cultural differences can be accounted for by different attitudes toward drinking, the availability of alcohol, physiological reactions, and family norms and patterns.

Progression Remember that Danny went through periods of heavy alcohol and drug use but also had times when he was relatively sober and did not use drugs. Similarly, many people with an alcohol use disorder fluctuate between drinking heavily, drinking "socially" without negative effects, and being abstinent (not drinking) (McCrady, 2014). It seems that about 20% of people with severe alcohol dependence have a spontaneous remission (they are able to stop drinking on their own) and do not reexperience problems with drinking.

It used to be thought that once problems arose with drinking, they would become steadily worse, following a predictable downward pattern as long as the person kept drinking (Sobell & Sobell, 1993). In other words, like a disease that is not treated properly, unhealthy alcohol use will get progressively worse if left unchecked. First championed by Jellinek more than 50 years ago, this view continues to influence the way people view and treat the disorder (Jellinek, 1946, 1952, 1960). Unfortunately, Jellinek based his model of the progression of alcohol use on a now famous but faulty study (Jellinek, 1946), which we briefly review.

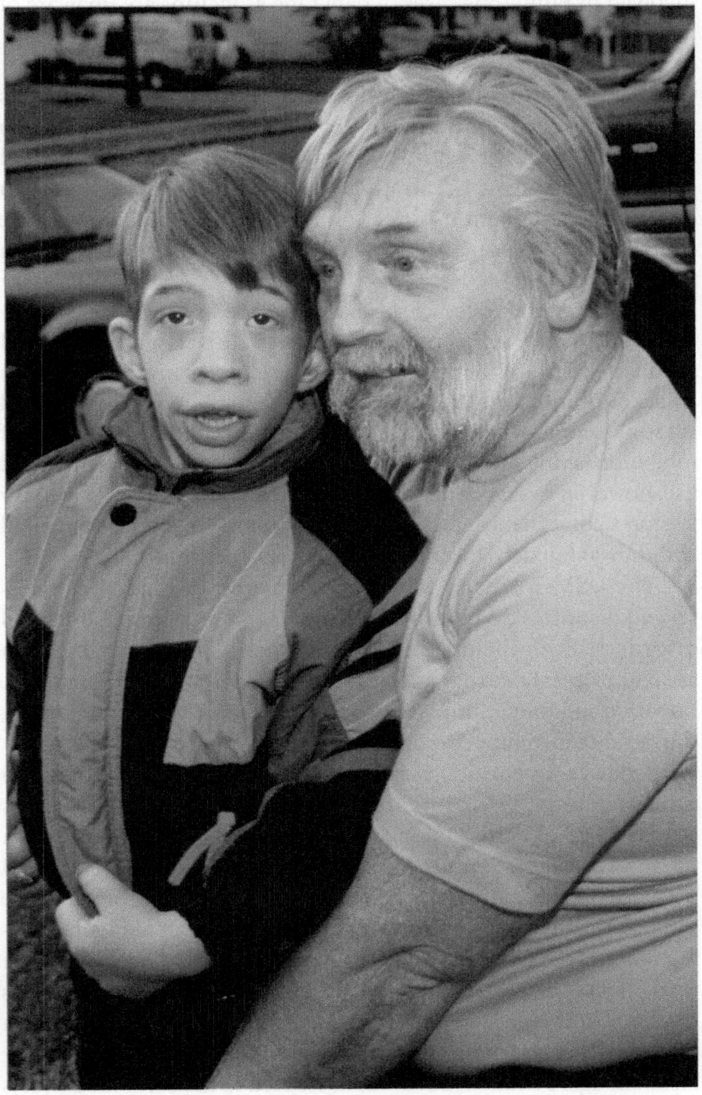

David H. Wells/Getty Images

Physical characteristics of fetal alcohol syndrome (FAS) include skin folds at the corners of the eyes, low nasal bridge, short nose, no groove between nose and upper lip, small head circumference, small eye opening, small midface, and thin upper lip.

In 1945, the newly formed self-help organization Alcoholics Anonymous (AA) sent out some 1,600 surveys to its members asking them to describe symptoms related to drinking, such as feelings of guilt or remorse and rationalizations about their actions, and to note when these reactions first occurred. Only 98 of the almost 1,600 surveys were returned, however. As you know, such a small response could seriously affect data interpretation. A group of 98 may be different from the group as a whole, so they may not represent the typical person with alcohol problems. Also, because the responses were retrospective (participants were recalling past events), their reports may be inaccurate. Despite these and other problems, Jellinek agreed to analyze the data, and he developed a four-stage model for the progression of alcoholism based on this limited information (Jellinek, 1952). According to his model, individuals go through a *prealcoholic stage* (drinking occasionally with few serious consequences), a *prodromal stage* (drinking heavily but with few outward signs of a problem), a *crucial stage* (loss of control, with occasional binges), and a *chronic stage* (the primary daily activities involve getting and drinking alcohol). Attempts by other researchers to confirm this progression of stages have not been successful (Schuckit, Smith, Anthenelli, & Irwin, 1993).

It appears instead that the course of a severe alcohol use disorder may be progressive for most people. For example, early use of alcohol may predict later misuse. A study of more than 1,800 Australian adolescents found four groups—abstaining (n = 352); late-onset moderate drinking (n = 503); early-onset moderate drinking (n = 663); and early-onset heavy drinking (n = 295) (Yuen et al., 2020). They found that early-onset heavy drinking at an early age was predictive of later alcohol-related disorders. Similarly, a study tracking alcohol use onset and later use found that those who started drinking at age 11 or earlier were at higher risk for chronic and severe alcohol use disorders (Guttmannova et al., 2011). A third classic study followed 636 male inpatients in an alcohol rehabilitation center (Schuckit et al., 1993). Among these chronically alcohol-dependent men, a general progression of alcohol-related life problems did emerge, although not in the specific pattern proposed by Jellinek. Three quarters of the men reported moderate consequences of their drinking, such as demotions at work, in their 20s. During their 30s, the men had more serious problems, such as regular blackouts and signs of alcohol withdrawal. By their late 30s and early 40s, these men demonstrated long-term serious consequences of their drinking, which included hallucinations, withdrawal convulsions, and hepatitis or pancreatitis. This study suggests a common pattern among people with chronic alcohol misuse and dependence, one with increasingly severe consequences. This progressive pattern is not inevitable for everyone who misuses alcohol, although we do not yet understand what distinguishes those who are and those who are not susceptible (Krenek & Maisto, 2013).

Research on the mechanism responsible for the differences in early alcohol use suggests that a person's response to the sedative effects of the substance affects later use. In other words, those individuals who tend not to develop the slurred speech, staggering, and other sedative effects of alcohol use are more likely to misuse it in the future (Chung & Martin, 2009; Schuckit, 2014a). This is of particular concern given the trend to mix highly caffeinated energy drinks with alcohol (Nadeem et al., 2020). This combination of drinks can reduce the sedative effect of alcohol, which may increase the likelihood of later excessive use.

Finally, statistics often link alcohol with violent behavior (Boden, Fergusson, & Horwood, 2012; Bye, 2007). Numerous studies have found that many people who commit such violent acts as murder, rape, and assault are intoxicated at the time of the crime (Rossow & Bye, 2012). We hope you are skeptical of this type of correlation. Just because drunkenness and violence overlap does not mean that alcohol will necessarily make you violent. Laboratory studies show that alcohol may increase participants' aggression (Bushman, 1993). Whether a person behaves aggressively outside the laboratory, however, probably involves a number of interrelated factors, such as the quantity and timing of alcohol consumed, the person's history of violence, expectations about drinking, and the individual's experiences while intoxicated. Alcohol does not *cause* aggression, but it may increase a person's likelihood of engaging in impulsive acts, and it may impair the ability to consider the consequences of acting impulsively (Kuypers, Verkes, Van den Brink, Van Amsterdam, & Ramaekers, 2020). Given the right circumstances, such impaired rational thinking may increase a person's risk of behaving aggressively.

Sedative-, Hypnotic-, or Anxiolytic-Related Disorders

The general group of depressants also includes sedative (calming), hypnotic (sleep-inducing), and anxiolytic (anxiety-reducing) drugs (Black & Andreasen, 2021). These drugs include barbiturates and benzodiazepines. **Barbiturates** (which include Amytal, Seconal, and Nembutal) are a family of sedative drugs first synthesized in Germany in 1882 (Cozanitis, 2004). They were prescribed to help people sleep and replaced such drugs as alcohol and opium. Barbiturates were widely prescribed by physicians during the 1930s and 1940s, before their addictive properties were fully understood. By the 1950s, they were among the drugs most misused by adults in the United States (Franklin & Frances, 1999).

dean bertoncelj/Shutterstock.com

Intoxication is often involved in cases of domestic violence.

Benzodiazepines (which today include Valium, Xanax, and Ativan) have been used since the 1960s, primarily to reduce anxiety. These drugs were originally touted as a miracle cure for the anxieties of living in our highly pressured technological society. Although in 1980, the U.S. Food and Drug Administration ruled that they are not appropriate for reducing the tension and anxiety resulting from everyday stresses and strains, an estimated 66 million prescriptions are written for benzodiazepines in the United States each year (He et al., 2020). In general, benzodiazepines are considered much safer than barbiturates, with less risk of excessive use and dependence. Reports on the misuse of Rohypnol, however, show how dangerous even some benzodiazepine drugs can be. Rohypnol (otherwise known as "forget-me-pill," "roofenol," "roofies," "ruffies") gained a following among teenagers in the 1990s because it has the same effect as alcohol without the telltale odor. The drug has been involved in numerous cases of date rape as victims are unaware of being drugged (Sandal, 2020).

Clinical Description At low doses, barbiturates relax the muscles and can produce a mild feeling of well-being. Larger doses can have results similar to those of heavy drinking: slurred speech and problems walking, concentrating, and working. At extremely high doses, the diaphragm muscles can relax so much that they cause death by suffocation. Overdosing on barbiturates is a common means of suicide.

Like the barbiturates, benzodiazepines are used to calm an individual and induce sleep. In addition, drugs in this class are prescribed as muscle relaxants and anticonvulsants (antiseizure medications) (Black & Andreasen, 2021). People who use them for nonmedical reasons report first feeling a pleasant high and a reduction of inhibition, similar to the effects of drinking alcohol. With continued use, however, tolerance and dependence can develop. Users who try to stop taking the drug experience symptoms like those of alcohol withdrawal (anxiety, insomnia, tremors, and delirium).

The DSM-5 criteria for sedative-, hypnotic-, and anxiolytic-related disorders do not differ substantially from those for alcohol disorders. Both include maladaptive behavioral changes, such as inappropriate sexual or aggressive behavior, variable moods, impaired judgment, impaired social or occupational functioning, slurred speech, motor coordination problems, and unsteady gait.

Sedative, hypnotic, and anxiolytic drugs affect the brain by influencing the GABA neurotransmitter system (Jufer-Phipps & Levine, 2020), although by mechanisms slightly different from those involving alcohol. As a result, when people use alcohol with any of these drugs or combine multiple types there can be synergistic effects. In other words, if you drink alcohol after taking a benzodiazepine or barbiturate or combine these drugs, the total effects can reach dangerous levels. One theory about actress Marilyn Monroe's death in 1962 is that she combined alcohol with too many barbiturates and unintentionally killed herself. Actor Heath Ledger's death in 2008 was attributed to the combined effects of oxycodone and a variety of barbiturates and benzodiazepines.

Statistics Barbiturate use has declined and benzodiazepine use has increased since 1960 (Substance Abuse and Mental Health

DSM 5 **Table 11.2**

Diagnostic Criteria for Sedative-, Hypnotic-, or Anxiolytic Use Disorders

A. A problematic pattern of sedative, hypnotic, or anxiolytic use leading to clinically significant impairment or distress, as manifested by at least two of the following, occurring within a 12-month period:

1. Sedatives, hypnotics, or anxiolytics are often taken in larger amounts or over a longer period than was intended.
2. There is a persistent desire or unsuccessful efforts to cut down or control sedative, hypnotic, or anxiolytic use.
3. A great deal of time is spent in activities necessary to obtain the sedative, hypnotic, or anxiolytic; use the sedative, hypnotic, or anxiolytic; or recover from its effects.
4. Craving, or a strong desire to use the sedative, hypnotic, or anxiolytic.
5. Recurrent sedative, hypnotic, or anxiolytic use resulting in a failure to fulfill major role obligations at work, school, or home (e.g., repeated absences from work or poor work performance related to sedative, hypnotic, or anxiolytic use; sedative-, hypnotic-, or anxiolytic-related absences, suspensions, or expulsions from school; neglect of children or household).
6. Continued sedative, hypnotic or anxiolytic use despite having persistent or recurrent social or interpersonal problems caused or exacerbated by the effects of sedatives, hypnotics or anxiolytics (e.g., arguments with a spouse about consequences of intoxication; physical fights).
7. Important social, occupational, or recreational activities are given up or reduced because of sedative, hypnotic or anxiolytic use.
8. Recurrent sedative, hypnotic or anxiolytic use in situations in which it is physically hazardous (e.g., driving in automobile or operating a machine when impaired by sedative, hypnotic, or anxiolytic use).
9. Sedative, hypnotic, or anxiolytic use is continued despite knowledge of having a persistent or recurrent physical or psychological problem that is likely to have been caused or exacerbated by the sedative, hypnotic, or anxiolytic.
10. Tolerance, as defined by either of the following:
    (a) A need for markedly increased amounts of sedative, hypnotic, or anxiolytic to achieve intoxication or desired effect.
    (b) A markedly diminished effect with continued use of the same amount of sedative, hypnotic, or anxiolytic.
    Note: This criterion is not considered to be met for individuals taking sedatives, hypnotics, or anxiolytics under medical supervision.
11. Withdrawal, as manifested by either of the following:
    (a) The characteristic withdrawal syndrome for sedatives, hypnotics, or anxiolytics (refer to Criteria A and B of the criteria set for sedative, hypnotic or anxiolytic withdrawal).
    (b) Sedatives, hypnotics, or anxiolytics (or closely related substance, such as alcohol) are taken to relieve or avoid withdrawal symptoms.
    Note: This criterion is not considered to be met for individuals taking sedatives, hypnotics, or anxiolytics under medical supervision.

Specify current severity:
Mild: Presence of 2 to 3 symptoms
Moderate: Presence of 4 to 5 symptoms
Severe: Presence of 6 or more symptoms

American Psychiatric Association. (2022). *Diagnostic and statistical manual of mental disorders* (5th ed., Text Revision).

Services Administration, 2020). Of those seeking treatment for substance-related problems, less than 1% present problems with benzodiazepines compared with other commonly misused substances. Those who do seek help with their use of these drugs tend to be female, White, and over the age of 35.

Stimulants

Of all the psychoactive drugs used in the United States, the most commonly consumed are stimulants. Included in this group are caffeine (in coffee, chocolate, and many soft drinks), nicotine (in tobacco products such as cigarettes), amphetamines, and cocaine. Many people consume caffeine at the start of their day. In contrast to the depressant drugs, stimulants—as their name suggests—make you more alert and energetic. They have a long history of use. Chinese physicians, for example, prescribed an amphetamine compound called ma-huang *(Ephedra sinica)* for more than 5,000 years for illnesses such as headaches, asthma, and the common cold (Iqbal, Khera, Hanif, Ayub, & Zafar, 2020). We describe several stimulants and their effects on behavior, mood, and cognition.

Stimulant-Related Disorders

Amphetamines At low doses, **amphetamines** can induce feelings of elation and vigor and can reduce fatigue. You feel "up." After a period of elevation, however, you come back down and "crash," feeling depressed or tired. Amphetamines are manufactured in laboratories; they were first synthesized in 1887 and later used as a treatment for asthma and as a nasal decongestant (Carvalho et al., 2012). Because amphetamines also reduce appetite, some people take them to lose weight. Adolph Hitler, partly because of his other physical maladies, became addicted to amphetamines (Judge & Rusyniak, 2009). Long-haul truck drivers, pilots, and some college students trying to "pull all-nighters" use amphetamines to get an extra energy "boost" and stay awake. Amphetamines are prescribed for people with narcolepsy, a sleep disorder characterized by excessive sleepiness

Concept Check 11.1

Part A

Check your understanding of substance use definitions by stating whether the following case summaries describe (a) use, (b) intoxication, or (c) use disorder.

1. Giya started a new job 5 weeks ago and is about to be fired. This is her third job this year. She has been absent from work at least once a week for the past 5 weeks. She was reprimanded in the past after being seen at a local pub in a drunken state during regular office hours although she called in sick. At her previous job, she was fired after she came to work unable to conduct herself appropriately and with alcohol on her breath. When confronted about her problems, Giya went to the nearest bar and drank some more to try to forget about the situation. ____________

2. Brennan scored the winning goal for his high school soccer team, and his friends take him out to celebrate. He doesn't smoke, but he doesn't mind drinking alcohol occasionally. Because Brennan had such a good game, he decides to have a few drinks. Despite his great performance in the game, he is easily irritated, laughing one minute and yelling the next. The more Brennan rambles on about his game-winning goal, the more difficult it is to understand him. ____________

3. Marti is a 24-year-old college student who started drinking heavily when he was 15. Marti drinks a moderate amount every night, unlike his schoolmates who get drunk at weekend parties. In high school, he would become drunk after about four beers; now his tolerance has more than doubled. Marti claims alcohol relieves the pressures of college life. He once attempted to quit drinking, but he had chills, fever, diarrhea, nausea and vomiting, and body aches and pains. ____________

4. Over the past year, Henry picked up a habit of having a cigarette every day after lunch. Instead of sitting in the lounge with his friends, he goes to his favorite spot in the courtyard and has his cigarette. If for some reason he is unable to have his cigarette after lunch, he is not dependent on it and can still function without any detrimental change in his performance at work. ____________

Part B

Match the following disorders with their corresponding effects: (a) substance-related and addictive disorder, (b) dementia, (c) impulse-control disorder, (d) alcohol use disorder, and (e) Wernicke-Korsakoff syndrome.

5. Disorder that deprives a person of the ability to resist acting on a drive or temptation. ____________

6. Disorder in which the effects of the drug impede vision, motor control, reaction time, memory, and hearing. ____________

7. The decline of intellectual abilities through, for example, excess consumption of alcohol. ____________

8. A class of disorders that affects the way people think, feel, and behave. ____________

(discussed in Chapter 8). Some of these drugs (Ritalin, Adderall) are even given to children with attention-deficit/hyperactivity disorder (ADHD) (discussed in Chapter 14). Amphetamines too are being misused for their psychostimulant effects. One large study found that almost two thirds of college students in their fourth year had been offered illegal prescription stimulants and 31% used them—usually to improve studying (Garnier-Dykstra, Caldeira, Vincent, O'Grady, & Arria, 2012).

DSM-5 diagnostic criteria for intoxication in **amphetamine use disorders** include significant behavioral symptoms, such as euphoria or affective blunting (a lack of emotional expression), changes in sociability, interpersonal sensitivity, anxiety, tension, anger, stereotyped behaviors (repetitive motor movements), impaired judgment, and impaired social or occupational functioning. In addition, physiological symptoms occur during or shortly after amphetamine or related substances are ingested and can include heart rate or blood pressure changes, perspiration or chills, nausea or vomiting, weight loss, muscular weakness, respiratory depression, chest pain, seizures, or coma. Severe intoxication or overdose can cause hallucinations, panic, agitation, and paranoid delusions (Black & Andreasen, 2021). Amphetamine tolerance builds quickly, making it doubly dangerous. Withdrawal often results in apathy, prolonged periods of sleep, irritability, and depression.

Periodically, certain "designer drugs" appear in local epidemics. An amphetamine called methylene-dioxymethamphetamine (MDMA), first synthesized in 1912 in Germany, was used as an appetite suppressant (McCann & Ricaurte, 2009). Recreational use of this drug, now commonly called Ecstasy, rose sharply in the late 1980s. After cocaine and methamphetamine, MDMA is the club drug most often bringing people to emergency rooms, and it has passed LSD in frequency of use (SAMHSA, 2011). Its effects are described by users in a variety of ways: Ecstasy makes you "feel happy" and "love everyone and everything"; "music feels better" and "it's more fun to dance"; "You can say what is on your mind without worrying what others will think" (Levy, O'Grady, Wish, & Arria, 2005, p. 1431). Recent years have also seen a rise in a variation of MDMA called "Molly" that has been marketed as a purified powder in capsules instead of the pressed pills of Ecstasy (National Institute of Drug Abuse, 2013). A large international study of wastewater in eight countries found 16 new—previously unidentified—psychoactive substances (Bade et al., 2021).

A purified, crystallized form of amphetamine, called methamphetamine (commonly referred to as "crystal meth" or "ice"), is ingested through smoking. This drug causes marked aggressive tendencies and stays in the system longer than cocaine, making it particularly dangerous. This drug gained and dropped in popularity since it was invented in the 1930s, although its use has now spread wider than before (Maxwell & Brecht, 2011). However enjoyable these various amphetamines may be in the short term, the potential for users to become dependent on them is extremely high, with great risk for long-term difficulties. Some research also shows that repeated use of MDMA can cause lasting memory problems (Wagner, Becker, Koester, Gouzoulis-Mayfrank, & Daumann, 2013).

Amphetamines stimulate the central nervous system by enhancing the activity of norepinephrine and dopamine. Specifically, amphetamines help the release of these neurotransmitters and block their reuptake, thereby making more of them available throughout the system (Black & Andreasen, 2021). Too much amphetamine—and therefore too much dopamine and norepinephrine—can lead to hallucinations and delusions. As we see in Chapter 13, this effect has stimulated theories on the causes of schizophrenia, which can also include hallucinations and delusions.

Cocaine The use and misuse of drugs wax and wane according to societal fashion, moods, and sanctions. Cocaine replaced amphetamines as the stimulant of choice in the 1970s in America (Jaffe, Rawson, & Ling, 2005). Cocaine is derived from the leaves of the coca plant, a flowering bush indigenous to South America. In his essay "On Coca" (1885/1974, p. 60), a young Sigmund Freud wrote of cocaine's magical properties: "I have tested [the] effect of coca, which wards off hunger, sleep, and fatigue and steels one to intellectual effort, some dozen times on myself."

Historically, some communities in Latin America have chewed coca leaves for centuries to get relief from hunger and fatigue (Mendoza-Azpur et al., 2021). Cocaine was introduced into the United States in the late 19th century; it was widely used from then until the 1920s. In 1885, Parke, Davis & Co. manufactured coca and cocaine in 15 forms, including coca-leaf cigarettes and cigars, inhalants, and crystals. For people who could not afford these products, a cheaper way to get cocaine was in Coca-Cola, which up until 1903 contained a small amount (60 mg of cocaine per 8-ounce serving) (Daamen et al., 2012).

DSM 5

Table 11.3
Diagnostic Criteria for Stimulant Use Disorder

A. A pattern of amphetamine-type substance, cocaine, or other stimulant use leading to clinically significant impairment or distress, as manifested by at least two of the following, occurring within a 12-month period:

1. The stimulant is often taken in larger amounts or over a longer period than was intended.
2. There is a persistent desire or unsuccessful efforts to cut down or control stimulant use.
3. A great deal of time is spent in activities necessary to obtain the stimulant, use the stimulant, or recover from its effects.
4. Craving, or a strong desire or urge to use the stimulant.
5. Recurrent stimulant use resulting in a failure to fulfill major role obligations at work, school, or home.
6. Continued stimulant use despite having persistent or recurrent social or interpersonal problems caused or exacerbated by the effects of the stimulant.
7. Important social, occupational, or recreational activities are given up or reduced because of stimulant use.
8. Recurrent stimulant use in situations in which it is physically hazardous.
9. Stimulant use is continued despite knowledge of having a persistent or recurrent physical or psychological problem that is likely to have been caused or exacerbated by the stimulant.
10. Tolerance, as defined by either of the following:
    (a) A need for markedly increased amounts of the stimulant to achieve intoxication or desired effect.
    (b) A markedly diminished effect with continued use of the same amount of the stimulant.
    Note: This criterion is not considered to be met for those taking stimulant medications solely under appropriate medical supervision, such as medications for attention-deficit/hyperactivity disorder or narcolepsy
11. Withdrawal, as manifested by either of the following:
    (a) The characteristic withdrawal syndrome for the stimulant (refer to Criteria A and B of the criteria set for stimulant withdrawal).
    (b) The stimulant (or a closely related substance) is taken to relieve or avoid withdrawal symptoms.
    Note: This criterion is not considered to be met for those taking stimulant medications solely under appropriate medical supervision, such as medications for attention-deficit/hyperactivity disorder or narcolepsy.

Specify current severity:

Mild: Presence of 2 to 3 symptoms

Moderate: Presence of 4 to 5 symptoms

Severe: Presence of 6 or more symptoms

American Psychiatric Association. (2022). *Diagnostic and statistical manual of mental disorders* (5th ed., Text Revision).

Shanti Hesse/Shutterstock.com

For centuries, some people from Latin American countries have chewed coca leaves for relief from hunger and fatigue.

Clinical Description Like amphetamines, in small amounts cocaine increases alertness, produces euphoria, increases blood pressure and pulse, and causes insomnia and loss of appetite. Remember that Danny snorted (inhaled) cocaine when he partied through the night with his friends. He later said the drug made him feel powerful and invincible—the only way he really felt self-confident. The effects of cocaine are short lived; for Danny they lasted less than an hour, and he had to snort repeatedly to keep himself up. During these binges, he often became paranoid, experiencing exaggerated fears that he would be caught or that someone would steal his cocaine. Such paranoia—referred to as *cocaine-induced paranoia*—is common among persons with **cocaine use disorders**, occurring in two thirds or more (Karsinti et al., 2020). Cocaine also makes the heart beat more rapidly and irregularly, and it can have fatal consequences, depending on a person's physical condition and the amount of the drug ingested.

We saw that alcohol can damage the developing fetus. It has also been suspected that the use of cocaine (especially crack) by pregnant women may adversely affect their babies. Babies with prior exposure to crack in the womb appear to be more irritable at birth than average babies and have long bouts of high-pitched crying. They were originally thought to have permanent brain damage, although subsequent research suggests that the effects are less dramatic than first feared (Harp & Bunting, 2020). Some work suggests that many children born to mothers who have used cocaine during pregnancy may have decreased birth weight and decreased head circumference, and are at increased risk for later behavior problems (Richardson, Goldschmidt, & Willford, 2009). Complicating the evaluation of children born to mothers who use cocaine is that their mothers almost always used other substances as well, including alcohol and nicotine. Many of these children are raised in disrupted home environments, which further complicates the picture (Barthelemy et al., 2016). Continuing research should help us better understand the negative effects of cocaine on children.

Statistics Worldwide, almost 5% of adults report using cocaine at some point in their lives, and in the United States, nearly 3% of males and approximately 1.5% of females report using cocaine each year (Cano, Oh, Salas-Wright, & Vaughn, 2020). Those age 18 to 25 are about twice as likely to use cocaine compared with other age groups. In 2018, prevalence of past-year cocaine use did not significantly differ between non-Hispanic Black individuals and non-Hispanic White individuals; however, cocaine-involved overdose deaths were more than twice as high among NH Black individuals as NH White individuals. NH Black individuals accounted for 11.37% of the adults reporting cocaine use, yet were 27.04% of the cocaine-involved overdose deaths. Approximately 17% of cocaine users have also used crack cocaine (a crystallized form of cocaine that is smoked) (Closser, 1992). One estimate is that about 0.1% of people in the United States have tried crack and that an increasing proportion of the users seeking treatment are young, unemployed adults living in urban areas (SAMHSA, 2014).

Cocaine is in the same group of stimulants as amphetamines because it has similar effects on the brain. The "up" seems to come primarily from the effect of cocaine on the dopamine system. Look at ■ Figure 11.4 to see how this action occurs. Cocaine enters the bloodstream and is carried to the brain. There the cocaine molecules block the reuptake of dopamine. As you know, neurotransmitters released at the synapse stimulate the next neuron and then are recycled back to the original neuron. Cocaine seems to bind to places where dopamine neurotransmitters reenter their home neuron, blocking their reuptake. The dopamine that cannot be taken in by the neuron remains in the synapse, causing repeated stimulation of the next neuron. This stimulation of the dopamine neurons in the "pleasure pathway" (the site in the brain that seems to be involved in the experience of pleasure) causes the high associated with cocaine use.

As late as the 1980s, many felt cocaine was a wonder drug that produced feelings of euphoria without being addictive (Weiss & Iannucci, 2009). Such a conservative source as the *Comprehensive Textbook of Psychiatry* in 1980 indicated that "taken no more than two or three times per week, cocaine creates no serious problems" (Grinspoon & Bakalar, 1980). Just imagine—a drug that gives you extra energy, helps you think clearly and more creatively, and lets you accomplish more throughout the day, all without any negative side effects! In our highly competitive and complex technological society, this would be a dream come true. But, as you probably realize, such temporary benefits have a high cost. Cocaine fooled us. Early on, cocaine addiction did not resemble that of many other drugs; typically, people find only that they have a growing inability to resist taking more (Black & Andreasen, 2021). Few negative effects are noted at first; however, with continued use, sleep is disrupted, increased tolerance causes a need for higher doses, paranoia and other negative symptoms set in, and the cocaine user gradually becomes socially isolated. Chronic use may result in premature aging of the brain (Vicario, Pérez-Rivas, de Guevara-Miranda, Santín, & Sampedro-Piquero, 2020).

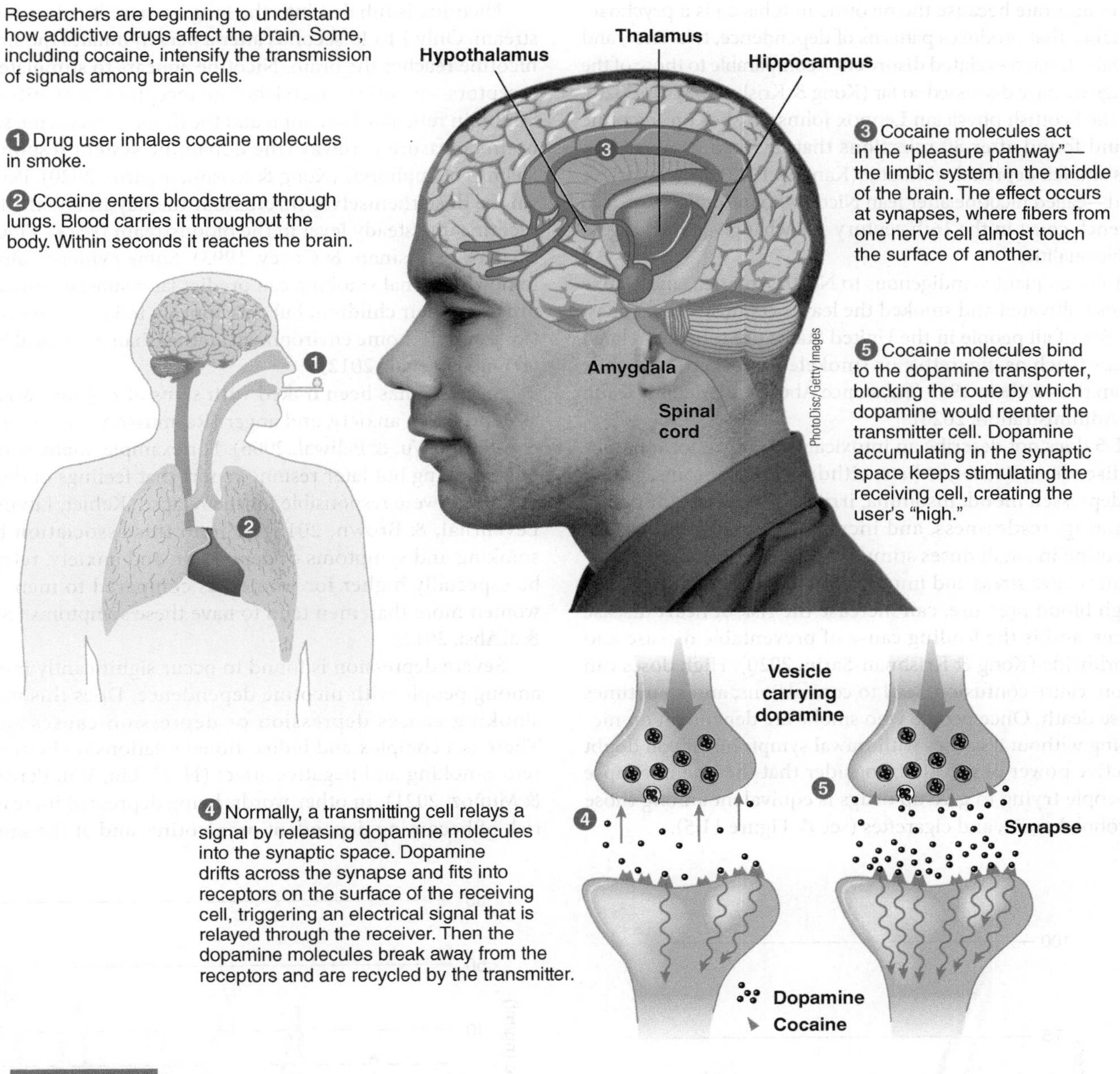

Figure 11.4

Anatomy of a high. Reprinted, with permission, from W. Booth, 1990, The anatomy of a high, *Washington Post* (National Weekly Edition), March 26–April 1, p. 38. © 1990 The Washington Post.

Again, Danny's case illustrates this pattern. He was a social user for a number of years, using cocaine only with friends and only occasionally. Eventually, he had more frequent episodes of excessive use or binges, and he found himself increasingly craving the drug between binges. After the binges, Danny would crash and sleep. Cocaine withdrawal isn't like that of alcohol. Instead of rapid heartbeat, tremors, or nausea, withdrawal from cocaine produces pronounced feelings of apathy and boredom. Think for a minute how dangerous this type of withdrawal is. First, you are bored with everything and find little pleasure from the everyday activities of work or relationships. The one that can "bring you back to life" is cocaine. As you can imagine, a particularly vicious cycle develops: Cocaine is used, withdrawal causes apathy, cocaine misuse develops. The atypical withdrawal pattern misled people into believing that cocaine was not addictive. We now know that cocaine misusers go through patterns of tolerance and withdrawal comparable to those experienced by misusers of other psychoactive drugs (Denomme & Shane, 2020).

Tobacco-Related Disorders

When you think of people who are addicted to substances, what image comes to mind? Do you see dirty and disheveled people huddled on an old mattress in an abandoned building, waiting for the next fix? Do you picture businesspeople huddled outside a city building on a rainy afternoon furtively smoking cigarettes? Both these images are accurate because the nicotine in tobacco is a psychoactive substance that produces patterns of dependence, tolerance, and withdrawal—**tobacco-related disorders**—comparable to those of the other drugs we have discussed so far (Kong & Krishnan-Sarin, 2020). In 1942, the Scottish physician Lennox Johnson "shot up" nicotine extract and found after 80 injections that he liked it more than cigarettes and felt deprived without it (Kanigel, 1988). This colorless, oily liquid—called nicotine after Jean Nicot, who introduced tobacco to the French court in the 16th century—is what gives smoking its pleasurable qualities.

The tobacco plant is indigenous to North America, and Native Americans cultivated and smoked the leaves centuries ago. Today, about 27.5% of all people in the United States use tobacco-related substances (such as cigarettes or smokeless tobacco), which is down from the 42.4% in 1965 (Substance Abuse and Mental Health Services Administration, 2020).

DSM-5 does not describe an intoxication pattern for tobacco-related disorders. Rather, it lists withdrawal symptoms, which include depressed mood, insomnia, irritability, anxiety, difficulty concentrating, restlessness, and increased appetite and weight gain. Nicotine in small doses stimulates the central nervous system; it can relieve stress and improve mood. However, it can also cause high blood pressure, can increase the risk of heart disease and cancer, and is the leading cause of preventable disease and death worldwide (Kong & Krishnan-Sarin, 2020). High doses can blur vision, cause confusion, lead to convulsions, and sometimes even cause death. Once people who smoke are dependent on nicotine, going without it causes withdrawal symptoms. If you doubt the addictive power of nicotine, consider that the rate of relapse among people trying to give up drugs is equivalent among those using alcohol, heroin, and cigarettes (see ■ Figure 11.5).

Nicotine is inhaled into the lungs, where it enters the bloodstream. Only 7 to 19 seconds after a person inhales the smoke, the nicotine reaches the brain. Nicotine appears to stimulate specific receptors—nicotinic acetylcholine receptors (nAChRs)—in the midbrain reticular formation and the limbic system, the site of the brain's pleasure pathway (the dopamine system responsible for feelings of euphoria) (Kong & Krishnan-Sarin, 2020). People who smoke dose themselves throughout the day in an effort to keep nicotine at a steady level in the bloodstream (see ■ Figure 11.6) (Dalack, Glassman, & Covey, 1993). Some evidence also points to how maternal smoking can predict later substance-related disorders in their children, but this appears to be an environmental (for example, home environment) rather than biological influence (D'Onofrio et al., 2012).

Smoking has been linked with signs of negative affect, such as depression, anxiety, and anger (Rasmusson, Anderson, Krishnan-Sarin, Wu, & Paliwal, 2006). For example, many people who quit smoking but later resume report that feelings of depression or anxiety were responsible for the relapse (Kahler, Litvin Bloom, Leventhal, & Brown, 2015). Due to this association between smoking and symptoms of depression and anxiety, relapse may be especially higher for women as compared to men, because women more than men tend to have these symptoms (Nakajima & al'Absi, 2012).

Severe depression is found to occur significantly more often among people with nicotine dependence. Does this mean that smoking causes depression or depression causes smoking? There is a complex and bidirectional relationship between cigarette smoking and negative affect (N. H. Liu, Wu, Pérez-Stable, & Muñoz, 2021). In other words, being depressed increases your risk of becoming dependent on nicotine, and at the same time,

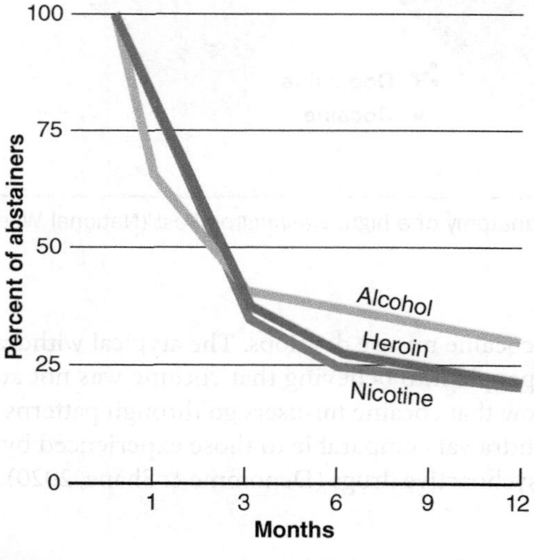

Figure 11.5

Relapse rates for nicotine compared to alcohol and heroin. Individuals trying to give up cigarettes backslide about as often as those who are addicted to alcohol or heroin. Adapted from R. Kanigel, 1988, October–November, Nicotine becomes addictive, *Science Illustrated*, pp. 12–14, 19–21.

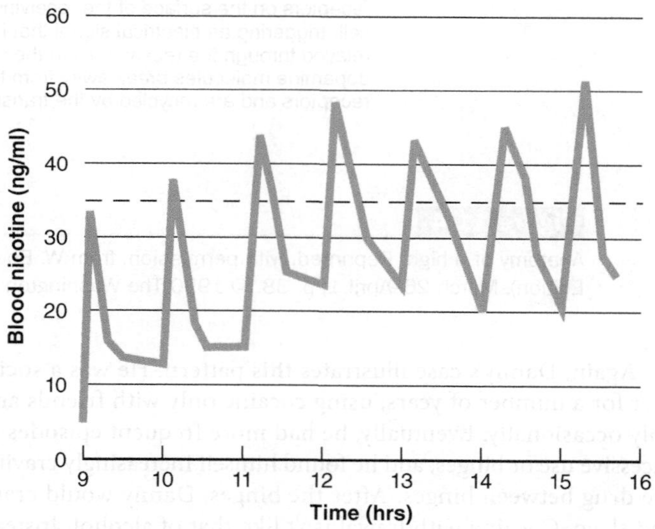

Figure 11.6

Smoking patterns and nicotine levels. This subject smoked one cigarette an hour, illustrating how those who smoke inhale more or less deeply or often, to get the desired blood levels of nicotine—on average 35 nanograms per milliliter. Adapted from R. Kanigel, 1988, October/November, Nicotine becomes addictive, *Science Illustrated*, pp. 12–14, 19–21.

DSM 5 Table 11.4
Diagnostic Criteria for Tobacco Use Disorder

A. A problematic pattern of tobacco use leading to clinically significant impairment or distress, as manifested by at least two of the following, occurring within a 12-month period:
  1. Tobacco is often taken in larger amounts or over a longer period than was intended.
  2. There is a persistent desire or unsuccessful efforts to cut down or control tobacco use.
  3. A great deal of time is spent in activities necessary to obtain or use tobacco.
  4. Craving, or a strong desire or urge to use tobacco.
  5. Recurrent tobacco use resulting in a failure to fulfill major role obligations at work, school, or home (e.g., interference with work).
  6. Continued tobacco use despite having persistent or recurrent social or interpersonal problems caused or exacerbated by the effects of tobacco (e.g., arguments with others about tobacco use).
  7. Important social, occupational, or recreational activities are given up or reduced because of tobacco use.
  8. Recurrent tobacco use in situations in which it is physically hazardous (e.g., smoking in bed).
  9. Tobacco use is continued despite knowledge of having a persistent or recurrent physical or psychological problem that is likely to have been caused or exacerbated by tobacco.
  10. Tolerance, as defined by either of the following:
     (a) A need for markedly increased amounts of tobacco to achieve the desired effect.
     (b) A markedly diminished effect with continued use of the same amount of tobacco.
  11. Withdrawal, as manifested by either of the following:
     (a) The characteristic withdrawal syndrome for tobacco (refer to Criteria A and B of the criteria set for tobacco withdrawal).
     (b) Tobacco (or a closely related substance such as nicotine) is taken to relieve or avoid withdrawal symptoms.

Specify current severity:

Mild: Presence of 2 to 3 symptoms

Moderate: Presence of 4 to 5 symptoms

Severe: Presence of 6 or more symptoms

American Psychiatric Association. (2022). *Diagnostic and statistical manual of mental disorders* (5th ed., Text Revision).

being dependent on nicotine will increase your risk of becoming depressed. Genetic studies suggest that a genetic vulnerability combined with certain life stresses may combine to make people vulnerable to both a nicotine use disorder and depression (for example, Edwards & Kendler, 2012). (We discuss evidence for the genetics of smoking when we cover the causes of substance misuse later in this chapter.)

There was a substantial increase in youth vaping (inhaling nicotine) prevalence beginning in about 2014 (Levy et al., 2019). Analyses show that the decline in past 30-day smoking prevalence accelerated by 2 to 4 times after 2014. Indicators of more established smoking rates, including the proportion of daily smokers among past 30-day smokers, also decreased more rapidly as vaping became more prevalent. In other words, youth in the United States smoked cigarettes less but it was replaced by vaping nicotine (Levy et al., 2019).

Caffeine-Related Disorders

Caffeine is the most common of the psychoactive substances. Estimates indicate that upward of 85% of the U.S. population has at least one caffeinated beverage per day (Black & Andreasen, 2021; Mitchell, Knight, Hockenberry, Teplansky, & Hartman, 2014). Called the "gentle stimulant" because it is thought to be the least harmful of all addictive drugs, caffeine can still lead to problems similar to that of other drugs (such as interfering with social and work obligations) (Meredith, Juliano, Hughes & Griffiths, 2013). This drug is found in tea, coffee, many soda drinks, and cocoa products. High levels of caffeine are added to the "energy drinks" that are widely consumed in the United States today but are banned in some European countries (including France, Denmark, and Norway) due to health concerns mentioned above (Price, Hilchey, Darredeau, Fulton, & Barrett, 2010; Thorlton, Colby & Devine, 2014).

DSM 5 Table 11.5
Diagnostic Criteria for Caffeine Intoxication

A. Recent consumption of caffeine (typically a high dose well in excess of 250 mg).

B. Five (or more) of the following signs or symptoms developing during, or shortly after, caffeine use:
  1. Restlessness.
  2. Nervousness.
  3. Excitement.
  4. Insomnia.
  5. Flushed face.
  6. Diuresis.
  7. Gastrointestinal disturbance.
  8. Muscle twitching.
  9. Rambling flow of thought and speech.
  10. Tachycardia or cardiac arrhythmia.
  11. Periods of inexhaustibility.
  12. Psychomotor agitation.

C. The signs or symptoms in criterion B cause clinically significant distress or impairment in social, occupational, or other important areas of functioning.

D. The signs or symptoms are not attributable to another medical condition and are not better explained by another mental disorder, including intoxication with another substance.

American Psychiatric Association. (2022). *Diagnostic and statistical manual of mental disorders* (5th ed., Text Revision).

Caffeine in small doses can elevate mood and decrease fatigue. In larger doses, it can make one feel jittery and can cause insomnia. Because caffeine takes a relatively long time to leave the body (about 6 hours), sleep can be disturbed if the caffeine is ingested in the hours close to bedtime. This effect is especially pronounced among those already suffering from insomnia (Byrne et al., 2012). As with the other psychoactive drugs, people react variously to caffeine; some are sensitive to it, and others can consume relatively large amounts with little effect. Previously, it was though that moderate use of caffeine (a cup of coffee per day) by pregnant women did not harm the developing fetus (Loomans et al., 2012). Research that is more contemporary suggests that developing fetus may be negatively impacted by any maternal caffeine use (Christensen, Freedman, & Foxe, 2021).

DSM-5 includes **caffeine use disorder**—defined as problematic caffeine use that causes significant impairment and distress—as a condition for further study (American Psychiatric Association, 2013). As with other stimulants, regular caffeine use can result in tolerance and dependence on the drug. Those of you who have experienced headaches, drowsiness, and a generally unpleasant mood when denied your morning coffee have had the withdrawal symptoms characteristic of this drug (Favrod-Coune & Broers, 2021). Caffeine's effect on the brain seems to involve the neuromodulator *adenosine* and, to a lesser extent, the neurotransmitter *dopamine* (Juliano, Ferré, & Griffiths, 2015). Caffeine seems to block adenosine reuptake. Adenosine plays an important role on the release of dopamine and glutamate in the striatum, which may explain the elation and increased energy that come with caffeine use (Jacobson, Gao, Matricon, Eddy, & Carlsson, 2020).

Opioid-Related Disorders

The word *opiate* refers to the natural chemicals in the opium poppy that have a narcotic effect (they relieve pain and induce sleep). In some circumstances, they can cause **opioid-related disorders**. The broader term *opioids* refers to the family of substances that includes natural opiates, synthetic variations (such as heroin, fentanyl, methadone, hydrocodone, and oxycodone), and the comparable substances that occur naturally in the brain (enkephalins, beta-endorphins, and dynorphins) (Arias, Welch, & Kaminer, 2020). References to the use of opium as a medicine date back more than 3,500 years (Strain, Lofwall, & Jaffe, 2009). In *The Wizard of Oz*, the Wicked Witch of the West puts Dorothy, Toto, and the Cowardly Lion to sleep by poisoning poppies in a field that is on the way to Oz, a literary allusion to the opium poppies used to produce morphine, codeine, and heroin.

Just as the poppies lull Dorothy, the Cowardly Lion, and Toto, opiates induce euphoria, drowsiness, and slowed breathing. High doses can lead to death if respiration is completely depressed. Opiates are also analgesics, substances that help relieve pain (Hammond, Hendrickson, & Fishman, 2020). People are sometimes given morphine before and after surgery to calm them and help block pain.

Withdrawal from opioids can be so unpleasant that people may continue to use these drugs despite a sincere desire to stop (Sneyers et al., 2020). Barbiturate and alcohol withdrawal can be even more distressing, however. Even so, people who cease or reduce their opioid intake begin to experience symptoms within 6 to 12 hours. These include excessive yawning, nausea and vomiting, chills, muscle aches, diarrhea, and insomnia—temporarily disrupting work, school, and social relationships. The symptoms can persist for 1 to 3 days, and the withdrawal process is completed in about a week.

In 2018, addiction to heroin was reported in about almost a half million people in the United States, double the number estimated between 2002 and 2013. Over the past quarter century, the United States saw a sharp increase in opioid use disorder (OUD) that disproportionately impacted White individuals in nonurban areas. In contrast, the heroin epidemic of the 1970s disproportionately impacted people of color in urban communities, where prevalence of OUD remains elevated. Despite a decline in opioid-related mortality among White individuals in the United States in 2018, overdose deaths continued to increase among Black individuals in the United States (Warren & Kolodny, 2021).

Illicit use of opioid-containing prescription medicines—the most commonly misused opiate class—declined from 425,000 people in 2015 to 239,000 people in the United States in 2019 (Substance Abuse and Mental Health Services Administration, 2020). This population number in 2019 was lower than the number in 2015, but it was similar to the numbers in 2016 to 2018. One survey found that 12.3% of high school seniors in the United States reported using opioids (such as hydrocodone and oxycodone) for nonmedical reasons (McCabe, West, Teter, & Boyd, 2012). Individuals with opioid use disorder seemed to have been at heightened risk of opioid overdose during the COVID-19 period of social isolation, economic distress, and disrupted treatment services delivery (Slavova, Rock, Bush, Quesinberry, & Walsh, 2020). Research also suggests that individuals who first became addicted to prescription pain medication transitioned to using heroin (Muhuri, Gfroerer & Davies, 2013). People who use opiates face risks beyond addiction and the threat of overdose. Because these drugs are usually injected intravenously, users are at increased risk for other chronic life-threatening illness such as hepatitis C, HIV infection, and AIDS (Compton, Boyle & Wargo, 2015).

The life of someone addicted to an opiate can be bleak. Research suggests that mortality rates in this population range from 6 to 20 times higher than the general population's. And those individuals who do live face much hardship recovering from addiction, with stable abstinence rates as low as 30% and most individuals undergoing many relapses. Even those that discontinue opioids often use alcohol and other drugs in their place to mitigate the withdrawal symptoms (Hser, Evans, Grella, Ling, & Anglin, 2015). Results from a classic 33-year follow-up study of more than 80 opioid users in an English town highlight this pessimistic view (Rathod, Addenbrooke, & Rosenbach, 2005). At the follow up, 22% of opioid users had died—about twice the national rate of about 12% for the general population. More than half the deaths were the result of drug overdose, and several took their own lives. The good news from this study was that of those who survived, 80% were no longer using opioids, and the remaining 20% were being treated with methadone. Persistence opioid use may be related to comorbid mental disorders and sexual or physical abuse. Long-term recovery has been shown to be associated with family and social support, employment, and opioid abstinence of at least five years (Hser et al., 2015).

The high or "rush" experienced by users comes from activation of the body's natural opioid system. In other words, the brain already has its own opioids—called enkephalins and endorphins—that provide narcotic effects (Blum, Baron, McLaughlin, & Gold, 2020). Heroin, opium, morphine, and other opiates activate this system. The discovery of the natural opioid system was a major breakthrough in the field of psychopharmacology: Not only does it allow us to study the effects of addictive drugs on the brain, but it also has led to important discoveries that may help us treat people dependent on these drugs.

Cannabis-Related Disorders

Cannabis (*Cannabis sativa*) (marijuana) was the drug of choice in the 1960s and early 1970s. Prior to its legal acceptance in some U.S. states, it was the most routinely used illegal substance, with 5% to 15% of people in Western countries reporting regular use (Yu, Chen, Chen, & Yan, 2020). Among adolescents age 12 to 17 in the United States, perceived great risk of harm from smoking marijuana weekly declined from 40.6% in 2015 to 34.6% in 2019 (Yu et al., 2020). Marijuana is the name given to the dried parts of the cannabis or hemp plant (its full scientific name is *Cannabis sativa*). Cannabis grows wild throughout the tropical and temperate regions of the world, which accounts for one of its nicknames—"weed."

As demonstrated by the following parable, people who smoke marijuana often experience altered perceptions of the world.

> Three men, so the story goes, arrived one night at the closed gates of a Persian city. One was intoxicated by alcohol, another was under the spell of opium, and the third was steeped in marijuana.
>
> The first blustered: "Let's break the gates down."
>
> "Nay," yawned the opium eater, "let us rest until morning, when we may enter through the wide-flung portals."
>
> "Do as you like," was the announcement of the marijuana addict. "But I shall stroll in through the keyhole!" (Rowell & Rowell, 1939, p. 66)

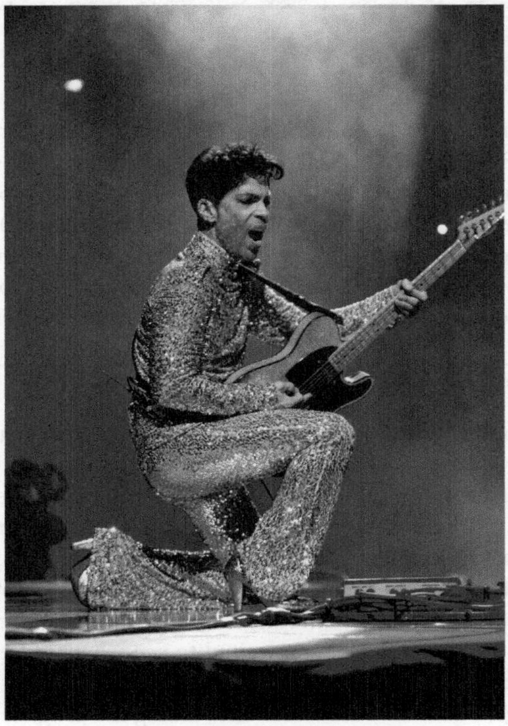
Kevin Mazur/Getty Images

The pop icon Prince died in 2016 at the age of 57 from an accidental overdose of the prescribed opioid, fentanyl.

Reactions to cannabis usually include mood swings. Otherwise typical experiences seem extremely funny, or the person might enter a dreamlike state in which time seems to stand still. Users often report having heightened sensory experiences, seeing vivid colors, or appreciating the subtleties of music (Thurstone & Kaminer, 2020). The feelings of well-being produced by small doses can change to paranoia, hallucinations, and dizziness when larger doses are taken. High school–age marijuana smokers get lower grades and are less likely to graduate, although it is not clear if this is the direct result of cannabis use or concurrent other drug use (Jager, 2012). Research on frequent cannabis users suggests that impairments of memory, concentration, relationships with others, and employment may be negative outcomes of long-term use (possibly leading to **cannabis use disorders**), although some researchers suggest that some psychological problems precede usage—increasing the likelihood that someone will use cannabis (Thurstone & Kaminer, 2020). The introduction of synthetic marijuana (referred to with a number of different names such as "fake weed," "K2," or "Spice" and marketed as "herbal incense") has caused alarm because in many places it can be purchased legally and the reaction to its use can be extremely harmful (for example, hallucinations, seizures, and heart rhythm problems) (Palamar & Barratt, 2016; Wells & Ott, 2011).

The evidence for cannabis tolerance is contradictory. Chronic and heavy users report tolerance, especially to the euphoric high (Ramaekers, Mason, & Theunissen, 2020); they are unable to reach the levels of pleasure they experienced earlier. However, evidence also indicates "reverse tolerance," when regular users experience more pleasure from the drug after repeated use. Chronic users who stop taking the drug report a period of irritability, restlessness, appetite loss, nausea, and difficulty sleeping (Bahji, Stephenson, Tyo, Hawken, & Seitz, 2020).

Controversy surrounds the use of cannabis for medicinal purposes. However, there appears to be an increasing database documenting the successful use of cannabis and its by-products for the symptoms of certain diseases. In Canada and in all but three U.S. states including Washington, D.C., cannabis products are available for medical use, including an herbal cannabis extract (Sativex, delivered in a nasal spray), dronabinol (Marinol), nabilone (Cesamet), and the herbal form of cannabis that is typically smoked (Alharbi, 2020). These cannabis-derived products are prescribed for chemotherapy-induced nausea and vomiting, HIV-associated anorexia, neuropathic pain in multiple sclerosis, and cancer pain. Unfortunately, marijuana smoke may contain as many carcinogens as tobacco smoke, although one long-term study that followed more than 5,000 men and women over 20 years suggested that occasional use does not appear to have a negative effect on lung functioning (Pletcher et al., 2012).

Most people who use cannabis typically inhale the drug by smoking the dried leaves in marijuana cigarettes. Others use preparations such as hashish, which is the dried form of the resin

DSM 5 **Table 11.6**
Diagnostic Criteria for Opioid Use Disorder

A. A problematic pattern of opioid use leading to clinically significant impairment or distress, as manifested by at least two of the following, occurring within a 12-month period:

1. Opioids are often taken in larger amounts or over a longer period than was intended.

2. There is a persistent desire or unsuccessful efforts to cut down or control opioid use.

3. A great deal of time is spent in activities necessary to obtain the opioid, use the opioid, or recover from its effects.

4. Craving, or a strong desire or urge to use opioids.

5. Recurrent opioid use resulting in a failure to fulfill major role obligations at work, school, or home.

6. Continued opioid use despite having persistent or recurrent social or interpersonal problems caused or exacerbated by the effects of opioids.

7. Important social, occupational, or recreational activities are given up or reduced because of opioid use.

8. Recurrent opioid use in situations in which it is physically hazardous.

9. Continued opioid use despite knowledge of having a persistent or recurrent physical or psychological problem that is likely to have been caused or exacerbated by the substance.

10. Tolerance, as defined by either of the following:

(a) A need for markedly increased amounts of opioids to achieve intoxication or desired effect.

(b) A markedly diminished effect with continued use of the same amount of an opioid.

Note: This criterion is not considered to be met for those taking opioids solely under appropriate medical supervision.

11. Withdrawal, as manifested by either of the following:

(a) The characteristic opioid withdrawal syndrome (refer to criteria A and B of the criteria set for opioid withdrawal).

(b) Opioids (or a closely related substance) are taken to relieve or avoid withdrawal symptoms.

Note: This criterion is not considered to be met for those taking opioids solely under appropriate medical supervision.

Specify current severity:

Mild: Presence of 2 to 3 symptoms

Moderate: Presence of 4 to 5 symptoms

Severe: Presence of 6 or more symptoms

American Psychiatric Association. (2022). *Diagnostic and statistical manual of mental disorders* (5th ed., Text Revision).

in the leaves of the female plant. Marijuana contains more than 80 varieties of the chemicals called *cannabinoids,* which are believed to alter mood and behavior. The most common of these chemicals includes the *tetrahydrocannabinols,* otherwise known as *THC.* An exciting finding in the area of cannabis research was that the brain makes its own version of THC, a neurochemical called *anandamide* (after the Sanskrit word *ananda,* which means "bliss") (Sedlak & Kaplin, 2009; Volkow, Baler, Compton, & Weiss, 2014). Subsequent research points to several other naturally occurring brain chemicals, including 2-AG (2-arachidonylglecerol), noladin ether, virodhamine, and N-arachidonoyldopamine (Mechoulam & Parker, 2013; Piomelli, 2003). Scientists continue to explore how this neurochemical affects the brain and behavior (Piomelli, 2014).

Triff/Shutterstock.com

Marijuana.

Hallucinogen-Related Disorders

On a Monday afternoon in April 1943, Albert Hoffmann, a scientist at a large Swiss chemical company, prepared to test a newly synthesized compound. He had been studying derivatives of ergot, a fungus that grows on diseased kernels of grain, and sensed that he had missed something important in the 25th compound of the lysergic acid series. Ingesting what he thought was an infinitesimally small amount of this drug, which he referred to in his notes as LSD-25, he waited to see what subtle changes might come over him as a result. Thirty minutes later, he reported no change, but some 40 minutes after taking the drug, he began to feel dizzy and had a noticeable desire to laugh. Riding his bicycle home, he hallucinated that the buildings he passed were moving and melting. By the time he arrived home, he was terrified he was losing his mind. Hoffmann was experiencing the first recorded "trip" on LSD (Jones, 2009).

LSD (d-lysergic acid diethylamide), sometimes referred to as "acid," is the most common hallucinogenic drug. It is produced synthetically in laboratories, although naturally occurring derivatives of this grain fungus (ergot) have been found historically. In Europe during the Middle Ages, an outbreak of illnesses occurred as a result of people's eating grain that was infected with the fungus. One version of this illness—later called *ergotism*—constricted the flow of blood to the arms or legs and eventually resulted in gangrene and the loss of limbs. Another type of illness resulted in convulsions, delirium, and hallucinations. Years later, scientists connected ergot with the illnesses and began studying versions of this fungus for possible benefits. This is the type of work Hoffmann was engaged in when he discovered LSD's hallucinogenic properties.

LSD largely remained in the laboratory until the 1960s, when it was first produced illegally for recreational use. The Central Intelligence Agency (CIA) tested LSD as a "truth serum" during interrogations, but the agency abandoned its efforts after several serious incidents and no evidence of truth (Lee & Shlain, 1992). The mind-altering effects of the drug suited the social effort to reject established culture and enhanced the search for enlightenment that characterized the mood and behavior of many people during that decade (Parrott, 2012). The late Timothy Leary, at the time a Harvard University research professor, first used LSD in 1961 and immediately began a movement to have every child and adult try the drug and "turn on, tune in, and drop out."

There are a number of other hallucinogens, some occurring naturally in a variety of plants: *psilocybin* (found in certain species of mushrooms), *lysergic acid amide* (found in the seeds of the morning glory plant), *dimethyltryptamine (DMT)* (found in the bark of the Virola tree, which grows in South and Central America), and *mescaline* (found in the peyote cactus plant). Phencyclidine (or PCP) is snorted, smoked, or injected intravenously, and it causes impulsivity and aggressiveness.

The DSM-5 diagnostic criteria for hallucinogen intoxication are similar to those for cannabis: perceptual changes such as the subjective intensification of perceptions, depersonalization, and hallucinations. Physical symptoms include pupillary dilation, rapid heartbeat, sweating, and blurred vision (American Psychiatric Association, 2013). Many users have written about hallucinogens, and they describe a variety of experiences. In one well-designed placebo-controlled study of hallucinogens, researchers at the Johns Hopkins School of Medicine gave volunteers either the hallucinogen psilocybin or a control drug (the ADHD medication Ritalin) and assessed their reactions (Griffiths, Richards, McCann, & Jesse, 2006). Psilocybin ingestion resulted in individualized reactions including perceptual changes (for example, mild visual hallucinations) and mood changes (for example, joy or happiness, anxiety, or fearfulness). Interestingly, the drug increased reports of mystical experiences (for example, deeply felt positive mood), and even 14 months later many rated the experience as having a spiritual significance (Griffiths, Richards, Johnson, McCann, & Jesse, 2008). Additional research explores how these types of drugs work with increased specificity, and this research may also tell us how our brains process experiences such as personal meaning and spirituality (James, Robertshaw, Hoskins, & Sessa, 2020).

Tolerance develops quickly to a number of hallucinogens, including LSD, psilocybin, and mescaline (**hallucinogen use disorders**) (Passie & Halpern, 2015). If taken repeatedly over a period of days, these drugs lose their effectiveness. Sensitivity returns after about a week of abstinence, however. For most hallucinogens, no withdrawal symptoms are reported. Even so, a number of concerns have been expressed about their use. One is the possibility of psychotic reactions. Stories in the popular press

DSM 5 **Table 11.7**
Diagnostic Criteria for Cannabis Use Disorder

A. A problematic pattern of cannabis use leading to clinically significant impairment or distress, as manifested by at least two of the following, occurring within a 12-month period:

1. Cannabis is often taken in larger amounts or over a longer period than was intended.
2. There is a persistent desire or unsuccessful efforts to cut down or control cannabis use.
3. A great deal of time is spent in activities necessary to obtain cannabis, use cannabis, or recover from its effects.
4. Craving, or a strong desire or urge to use cannabis.
5. Recurrent cannabis use resulting in a failure to fulfill major role obligations at work, school, or home.
6. Continued cannabis use despite having persistent or recurrent social or interpersonal problems caused or exacerbated by the effects of cannabis.
7. Important social, occupational, or recreational activities are given up or reduced because of cannabis use.
8. Recurrent cannabis use in situations in which it is physically hazardous.
9. Cannabis use is continued despite knowledge of having a persistent or recurrent physical or psychological problem that is likely to have been caused or exacerbated by cannabis.
10. Tolerance, as defined by either of the following:
    - **(a)** A need for markedly increased amounts of cannabis to achieve intoxication or desired effect.
    - **(b)** A markedly diminished effect with continued use of the same amount of cannabis.
11. Withdrawal, as manifested by either of the following:
    - **(a)** The characteristic withdrawal syndrome for cannabis (refer to criteria A and B of the criteria set for cannabis withdrawal).
    - **(b)** Cannabis (or a closely related substance) is taken to relieve or avoid withdrawal symptoms.

Specify current severity:

Mild: Presence of 2 to 3 symptoms

Moderate: Presence of 4 to 5 symptoms

Severe: Presence of 6 or more symptoms

American Psychiatric Association. (2022). *Diagnostic and statistical manual of mental disorders* (5th ed., Text Revision).

about people who jumped out of windows because they believed they could fly or who stepped into moving traffic with the mistaken idea that they could not be hurt have provided for sensational reading, but little evidence suggests that using hallucinogens produces a greater risk than being drunk or under the influence of any other drug. People do report having "bad trips"; these are the sort of frightening episodes in which clouds turn into threatening monsters or deep feelings of paranoia take over. Usually, someone on a bad trip can be "talked down" by supportive people who provide constant reassurance that the experience is the temporary effect of the drug and it will wear off in a few hours (Parrott, 2012).

Hallucinogens seem to affect the brain in diverse and nonspecific ways, meaning by affecting multiple different receptors at one time in opposing ways. It is thought that this broad impact on brain receptors may lead to consciousness expanding experienced by some (De Gregorio et al., 2021). Most of these drugs bear some resemblance to neurotransmitters; LSD, psilocybin, lysergic acid amide, and DMT are chemically similar to serotonin; mescaline resembles norepinephrine; and a number of other hallucinogens we have not discussed are similar to acetylcholine. Psilocybin, for example, seems to increase serotonin as an agonist at 5HT2A/C and 5HT1A receptors to produce hallucinogenic effects, but the remaining neural activity is less understood, and it seems that psilocybin may also impact dopamine receptors. Recent fMRI studies show activation in "resting state networks" that are typically activated during a resting state or introspection, as well as networks that increase focused attention (Grandjean et al., 2021). Alternation and activation of these two networks typically happens during states like meditation or psychosis. Research in human and animal laboratory studies shows no short-term or long-term toxicity, meaning one's body processes the substances without incurring any harm to organs including the brain. This may be, in part, why some researchers are exploring psilocybin as a "model" for psychosis as well as a substance with possible therapeutic potential (Goldberg, Pace, Nicholas, Raison, & Hutson, 2020).

DSM 5 **Table 11.8**

Diagnostic Criteria for Other Hallucinogen Use Disorder

A. A problematic pattern of hallucinogen (other than phencyclidine) use leading to clinically significant impairment or distress, as manifested by at least two of the following, occurring within a 12-month period:

1. The hallucinogen is often taken in larger amounts or over a longer period than was intended.
2. There is a persistent desire or unsuccessful efforts to cut down or control hallucinogen use.
3. A great deal of time is spent in activities necessary to obtain the hallucinogen, use the hallucinogen, or recover from its effects.
4. Craving, or a strong desire or urge to use the hallucinogen.
5. Recurrent hallucinogen use resulting in a failure to fulfill major role obligations at work, school, or home (e.g., repeated absences from work or poor work performance related to hallucinogen use; hallucinogen-related absences, suspensions, or expulsions from school; neglect of children or household).
6. Continued hallucinogen use despite having persistent or recurrent social or interpersonal problems caused or exacerbated by the effects of the hallucinogen (e.g., arguments with a spouse about consequences of intoxication; physical fights).
7. Important social, occupational, or recreational activities are given up or reduced because of hallucinogen use.
8. Recurrent hallucinogen use in situations in which it is physically hazardous (e.g., driving an automobile or operating a machine when impaired by hallucinogen).
9. Hallucinogen use is continued despite knowledge of having a persistent or recurrent physical or psychological problem that is likely to have been caused or exacerbated by the hallucinogen.
10. Tolerance, as defined by either of the following:
    - **(a)** A need for markedly increased amounts of the hallucinogen to achieve intoxication or desired effect.
    - **(b)** A markedly diminished effect with continued use of the same amount of the hallucinogen.

    Note: Withdrawal symptoms and signs are not established for hallucinogens, and so this criterion does not apply.

Specify current severity:

Mild: Presence of 2 to 3 symptoms

Moderate: Presence of 4 to 5 symptoms

Severe: Presence of 6 or more symptoms

American Psychiatric Association. (2022). *Diagnostic and statistical manual of mental disorders* (5th ed., Text Revision).

Other Commonly Misused Substances

A number of other substances are used by individuals to alter sensory experiences. These drugs do not fit neatly into the classes of substances we just described but are nonetheless of great concern because they can be physically damaging to those who ingest them. We briefly describe inhalants, steroids, and a group of drugs commonly referred to as *designer drugs*.

Inhalants

Inhalants include a variety of substances found in volatile solvents—making them available to breathe into the lungs directly. Some common inhalants that are ingested include spray paint, hair spray, paint thinner, gasoline, amyl nitrate, nitrous oxide ("laughing gas"), nail polish remover, felt-tipped markers, airplane glue, contact cement, dry-cleaning fluid, and spot remover (Ridenour & Howard, 2012). Inhalant use is highest during early adolescence, ages 13 to 14, especially in those in correctional or psychiatric institutions. Additionally, higher rates of inhalant use are found among Native Americans and White persons, as well as those who live in rural or small towns, come from disadvantaged backgrounds, have higher levels of anxiety and depression, and show more impulsive and fearless temperaments (Garland, Howard, Vaughn, & Perron, 2011; Halliburton & Bray, 2016). These drugs are rapidly absorbed into the bloodstream through the lungs when inhaled from containers or on a cloth held up to the mouth and nose.

The high associated with the use of inhalants resembles that of alcohol intoxication and usually includes dizziness, slurred speech, lack of coordination, euphoria, and lethargy (American Psychiatric Association, 2013). Users build up a tolerance to the drugs, and withdrawal—which involves sleep disturbance, tremors, irritability, and nausea—can last from 2 to 5 days. Unfortunately, use can also increase aggressive and antisocial behavior, and long-term use can damage bone marrow, kidneys, liver, lung, nervous system, and the brain (for example, leading to cognitive impairment for the user and for infants in the womb) (Broussard, 2020). If users are startled, this can cause a cardiac event that can lead to death (called "sudden sniffing death") (Broussard, 2020).

Steroids

Anabolic–androgenic steroids (more commonly referred to as steroids, "roids," or "juice") are derived from or are a synthesized form of the hormone testosterone (Sivalokanathan, Małek, & Malhotra, 2021). The legitimate medical uses of these drugs focus on people with asthma, anemia, and breast cancer and males with inadequate sexual development. However, the anabolic action of these drugs (that can produce increased body mass) has resulted in their illicit use by those wishing to try to improve their physical abilities by increasing muscle bulk. Steroids can be taken orally or through injection, and some estimates suggest that approximately 2% to 6% of males will use the drug illegally at some point in their lives (Pope & Kanayama, 2012). Users sometimes administer the drug on a schedule of several weeks or months followed by a break from its use (called "cycling") or combine several types of steroids (called "stacking"). Steroid use differs from other drug use because the substance does not produce a desirable high but instead is used to enhance performance and body size. Dependence on the substance therefore seems to involve the desire to maintain the performance gains obtained rather than a need to reexperience an altered emotional or physical state. Research on the long-term effects of steroid use seems to suggest that mood disturbances are common (for example, depression, anxiety, and panic attacks)

AP Images/CHARLES REX ARBOGAST

The proliferation of new recreational drugs such as Ecstasy inspires ever more vigilance on the part of the legal system.

DSM 5

Table 11.9

Diagnostic Criteria for Inhalant Use Disorder

A. A problematic pattern of use of a hydrocarbon-based inhalant substance leading to clinically significant impairment or distress, as manifested by at least two of the following, occurring within a 12-month period:

1. The inhalant substance is often taken in larger amounts or over a longer period than was intended.
2. There is a persistent desire or unsuccessful efforts to cut down or control use of the inhalant substance.
3. A great deal of time is spent in activities necessary to obtain the inhalant, use it, or recover from its effects.
4. Craving, a strong desire or urge to use the inhalant substance.
5. Recurrent use of the inhalant substance resulting in a failure to fulfill major role obligations at work, school, or home.
6. Continued use of the inhalant substance despite having persistent or recurrent social or interpersonal problems caused or exacerbated by the effects of its use.
7. Important social, occupational, or recreational activities are given up or reduced because of use of the inhalant substance.
8. Recurrent use of the inhalant substance in situations in which it is physically hazardous.
9. Use of the inhalant substance is continued despite knowledge of having a persistent or recurrent physical or psychological problem that is likely to have been caused or exacerbated by the substance.
10. Tolerance, as defined by either of the following:
    - **(a)** A need for markedly increased amounts of inhalant substance to achieve intoxication or desired effect.
    - **(b)** A markedly diminished effect with continued use of the same amount of the inhalant substance.

Specify current severity:

Mild: Presence of 2 to 3 symptoms

Moderate: Presence of 4 to 5 symptoms

Severe: Presence of 6 or more symptoms

American Psychiatric Association. (2022). *Diagnostic and statistical manual of mental disorders* (5th ed., Text Revision).

Concept Check 11.2

Determine whether the following statements about stimulants are true (T) or false (F).

1. ______________ Use of crack cocaine during pregnancy always adversely affects the developing fetus.
2. ______________ Regular use of stimulants can result in tolerance and dependence on the drugs.
3. ______________ Amphetamines have been used as appetite suppressants.
4. ______________ Compared with all other drugs, caffeine can produce the most variable reactions in people.
5. ______________ Amphetamines are naturally occurring drugs that induce feelings of elation and vigor and can reduce fatigue.
6. ______________ An ingredient of the beverage Coca-Cola in the 1800s was cocaine.
7. ______________ Stimulants are produced only in a laboratory.

(Sivalokanathan et al., 2021), and there is a concern that more serious physical consequences may result from regular use.

Designer Drugs

Another class of drugs—dissociative anesthetics—causes drowsiness, pain relief, and the feeling of being out of one's body (Domino & Miller, 2015; Javitt & Zukin, 2009). Sometimes referred to as *designer drugs*, this growing group of drugs was originally developed by pharmaceutical companies to target specific diseases and disorders. Soon some companies began using the developing technology to design "recreational drugs." We have already described one of the more common illicit designer drugs—MDMA, street names of Ecstasy or Molly—in the section on stimulants. This amphetamine is one of a small but feared growing list of related substances that includes 3,4-methelenedioxyethamphetamine (MDEA, or Eve), and 2-(4-bromo-2,5-dimethoxy-phenyl)-ethylamine (BDMPEA, or Nexus) (Wu et al., 2009). Their ability to heighten a person's auditory and visual perceptions and their senses of taste and touch has been incorporated into the activities of those who attend nightclubs, all-night electronic dance music (EDM) parties (raves). A drug related to phencyclidine and associated with the "drug club" scene is ketamine (street names include K, Special K, and Cat Valium), a dissociative anesthetic that produces a sense of detachment, along with a reduced awareness of pain (Lavender, Hirasawa-Fujita, & Domino, 2020). Gamma-hydroxybutyrate (GHB, or liquid Ecstasy) is a central nervous system depressant that was marketed in health food stores in the 1980s as a means of stimulating muscle growth. Users report that, at low doses, it can produce a state of relaxation and increased tendency to verbalize but that at higher doses or with alcohol or other drugs it can result in seizures, severe respiratory depression, and coma. Due to their high toxicity, these drugs taken at high doses may be especially dangerous for the developing teenager brain, which may cause irreversible memory loss and other cognitive problems (Domino & Miller, 2015).

Since 2010, there has been a rise in the use of synthetic cathinones ("bath salts") *3,4-methylenedioxypyrovalerone* (MDPV), synthetic form of a stimulant found in the khat plant from East Africa and Saudi Arabia known for its stimulant effects (Schifano et al., 2020). The effects of synthetic cathiones are much stronger, and though similar to stimulants, they have an excitatory or agitating effect that can include paranoia, delirium, hallucinations, and panic attacks (Schifano et al., 2020). Use of all these drugs can result in tolerance and dependence, and their increasing popularity among adolescents and young adults raises significant public health concerns.

Causes of Substance-Related Disorders

People continue to use psychoactive drugs for their effects on mood, perception, and behavior despite the obvious negative consequences of misuse and dependence. We saw that despite his clear potential as an individual, Danny continued to use drugs to his detriment. Various factors help explain why people like Danny persist in using drugs. Drug misuse and dependence, once thought to be the result of moral weakness, are now understood to be influenced by a combination of biological and psychosocial factors.

Why do some people use psychoactive drugs without abusing or becoming dependent on them? Why do some people stop using these drugs or use them in moderate amounts after being dependent on them and others continue a lifelong pattern of dependence despite their efforts to stop? These questions continue to occupy the time and attention of numerous researchers throughout the world.

Biological Dimensions

In 2007, American model and television personality Anna Nicole Smith died from an apparently accidental overdose of at least nine prescription medications—including methadone, Valium, and the sedative chloral hydrate. The tragedy was compounded by the fact that, just months before, her only son Daniel had died, also from an apparent drug overdose. Did the son inherit a vulnerability to addiction from his mother? Did he pick up Anna Nicole's habits from living with her over the years? Is it just a coincidence that both mother and son were so involved with drugs?

Familial and Genetic Influences As you already have seen throughout this book, many psychological disorders are influenced in important ways by genetics. Mounting evidence indicates that excessive drug use follows this pattern. Researchers conducting twin, family, and adoption and other genetic studies have found that certain people are genetically vulnerable to excessive drug use (Skóra et al., 2020). Twin studies of smoking, for example, indicate a moderate genetic influence (for example, Hardie, Moss, & Lynch, 2006; Seglem, Waaktaar, Ask, & Torgersen, 2015). Most genetic data on substance misuse come from research on alcoholism, which is widely studied because alcohol use is legal and many people are dependent on it. Research in general suggests that genetic risk factors cut across all mood-altering drugs (Kendler et al., 2012).

Gregg DeGuire/Getty Images

Model and TV personality Anna Nicole Smith and her son Daniel both died from drug complications, raising questions about how environment and biology played roles in their drug use.

In a major twin study, the roles of the environment and of genetics were examined in substance use problems. Researchers studied more than 1,000 pairs of male twins and questioned them about their use of cannabis, cocaine, hallucinogens, sedatives, stimulants, and opiates (Kendler, Jacobson, Prescott, & Neale, 2003). The findings—which may have major implications for how we approach treatment and prevention—suggest that there are common genetic influences on the use of all of these drugs. Although it is clear that genetics plays an important role in substance-related disorders, specific genes and their influence on these disorders are still being explored (Ray, 2012; Volkow & Warren, 2015). As the search for the genes influencing substance use disorders, the next obvious question is how these genes function when it comes to addiction—a field of research called *functional genomics* (Knopf, 2020).

Genetic factors may affect how people experience and metabolize certain drugs, which in turn may partly determine who will or will not become regular users (Volkow & Warren, 2015). These relationships can be complex. Research has found that certain genes are associated with a greater likelihood of heroin addiction in Hispanic and African American populations (Nielsen et al., 2008). Other research points out that a pharmacological treatment for alcohol use disorder—naltrexone (an opioid antagonist)—may be most effective with individuals who have a particular genetic variant in their opioid receptors (for example, the OPRM1 gene) (Hartwell et al., 2020). In other words, your genetics may not only influence whether you develop a substance-related disorder but also help predict which treatments may be effective in reducing these problems.

Neurobiological Influences In general, the pleasurable experiences reported by people who use psychoactive substances partly explain why people continue to use them. In behavioral terms, people are positively reinforced for using drugs. However, what mechanism is responsible for such experiences? Studies indicate the brain appears to have a natural "pleasure pathway" that mediates our experience of reward. All psychoactive substances seem to affect this internal reward center in the same way as you experience pleasure from certain foods or from sex (Ray, 2012). In other words, what psychoactive drugs may have in common is their ability to activate this reward center and provide the user with a pleasurable experience, at least for a time.

The pleasure center was discovered more than 65 years ago by James Olds, who studied the effects of electrical stimulation on rat brains (Olds, 1956; Olds & Milner, 1954). If certain areas were stimulated with small amounts of electricity, the rats behaved as if they had received something pleasant, such as food. The exact location of the area in the human brain is still subject to debate. It is believed that the *dopaminergic system* and its *opioid-releasing neurons* known as MOP-r receptors are involved. Opioids have an agonist effect at MOP-r receptors, which are spread throughout the central nervous system and are encoded by mu opioid receptor gene of OPRM1. This means opioids encourage more production of the brains' own opioids. The pleasure center of reward that keeps opioid users using is made up of MOP-r receptors mostly found in ventral and dorsal striatal areas and is highly influenced by the downstream activation of the dopaminergic mesocorticolimbic and nigrostriatal systems (Berridge & Kringelbach, 2015; Borg et al., 2015).

How do different drugs that affect different neurotransmitter systems all converge to activate the pleasure pathway, which is primarily made up of dopamine-sensitive neurons? Researchers are only beginning to sort out the answers to this question, but some surprising findings have emerged in recent years. For example, we know that amphetamines and cocaine act directly on the dopamine system. Other drugs, however, appear to increase the availability of dopamine in more roundabout and intricate ways. For example, the neurons in the brain's ventral tegmental area are kept from continuous firing by GABA neurons. (Remember that the GABA system is an inhibitory neurotransmitter system that blocks other neurons from sending information.) One thing that keeps us from being on an unending high is the presence of these GABA neurons, which act as the "brain police," or superegos of the reward neurotransmitter system. Opiates (opium, morphine, heroin) inhibit GABA, which in turn stops the GABA neurons from inhibiting dopamine, which makes more dopamine available in the brain's pleasure pathway. Drugs that stimulate the reward center directly or indirectly include not only amphetamine, cocaine, and opiates but also nicotine and alcohol (Strain, 2009; Volkow & Warren, 2015).

This complicated picture is far from complete. We now understand that other neurotransmitters in addition to dopamine—including serotonin and norepinephrine—are also involved in the brain's reward system (Khokhar et al., 2010; Volkow & Warren, 2015). The coming years should yield interesting insights into the interaction of drugs and the brain. One aspect that awaits explanation is how drugs not only provide pleasurable experiences (positive reinforcement) but also help remove unpleasant experiences such as pain, feelings of illness, or anxiety (negative reinforcement). Aspirin is a negative reinforcer: We take it not because it makes us feel good but because it stops us from feeling bad. In much the same way, one property of the psychoactive drugs is that they stop people from feeling bad, an effect as powerful as making them feel good.

With several drugs, negative reinforcement is related to the anxiolytic effect, the ability to reduce anxiety (discussed briefly in the section on the sedative, hypnotic, and anxiolytic drugs). Alcohol has an anxiolytic effect. The neurobiology of how these drugs reduce anxiety seems to involve the septal–hippocampal system (Heilig & Spanagel, 2021), which includes a large number of GABA-sensitive neurons. Certain drugs may reduce anxiety by enhancing the activity of GABA in this region, thereby inhibiting the brain's normal reaction (anxiety or fear) to anxiety-producing situations. ■ Figure 11.7 illustrates how a drug such as nicotine has a multifaceted impact on a variety of neurotransmitter systems and in turn their effects on the experience of smoking.

Researchers have identified individual differences in the way people respond to alcohol. Understanding these response differences is important because they may help explain why some people continue to use drugs until they acquire a dependence on them, whereas others stop before this happens. A number of studies compare individuals with and without a family history of alcoholism (Gordis, 2000). They concluded that, compared with the sons of those not addicted to alcohol, the sons of people addicted to alcohol may be more sensitive to alcohol when it is first ingested and then become less sensitive to its effects as the hours pass after drinking. This finding is significant because the euphoric effects of alcohol occur just after drinking but the experience after several hours is often sadness and depression. People who are at risk for developing alcoholism (in this case, the sons of individuals addicted to alcohol) may be better able to appreciate the initial highs of drinking and be less sensitive to the lows that come later, making them ideal candidates for continued drinking. In support of this observation, follow-up research over a 10-year period found that those men who tended to be less sensitive to alcohol also tended to drink more heavily and more often (Schuckit, 1994, 1998).

One line of research involves analyzing the brain wave patterns of people at risk for developing alcoholism. This research is studying the sons of people with alcohol problems because of their own increased likelihood of having alcohol problems. Participants are asked to sit quietly and listen for a particular tone. When they hear the tone, they are to signal the researcher. During this time, their brain waves are monitored and a particular pattern emerges called the *P300 amplitude*. Approximately 300 milliseconds (the origin of the "P300" designation) after the tone is presented, a characteristic spike in brain waves occurs that indicates the brain is processing this information. In general, researchers find this spike is lower among those with a family history of alcoholism (X. Liu et al., 2020).

Is this brain wave difference somehow connected to the reasons people later develop a dependence on alcohol, or is it just a marker or sign that these individuals have in common but is not related to their drinking? One piece of evidence that argues against the P300 differences as a marker for excessive alcohol use is that individuals with a variety of other substance use problems (for example, opioid users) and psychological disorders (for example, schizophrenia and depression) also show lower P300 amplitude than control participants (Singh, Basu, Kohli, & Prabhakar, 2009). Researchers are continuing to try to understand this interesting but puzzling phenomenon (X. Liu et al., 2020).

Psychological Dimensions

We have shown that the substances people use to alter mood and behavior have unique effects. The high from heroin differs substantially from the experience of smoking a cigarette, which in turn differs from the effects of amphetamines or LSD. Nevertheless, it is important to point out the similarities in the way people mentally react to most of these substances.

Positive Reinforcement The feelings that result from using psychoactive substances are pleasurable in some way, and people will continue to take the drugs to recapture the pleasure. Research shows quite clearly that many drugs used and misused by humans also seem to be pleasurable to animals (Young & Herling, 1986). Laboratory animals will work to have their bodies injected with drugs such as cocaine, amphetamines, opiates, sedatives, and alcohol, which demonstrates that even without social and cultural influences these drugs are pleasurable.

Human research also indicates that to some extent all psychoactive drugs provide a pleasurable experience (for example, Heilig & Spanagel, 2021). In addition, the social contexts for drug taking may encourage its use, even when the use alone is not the desired

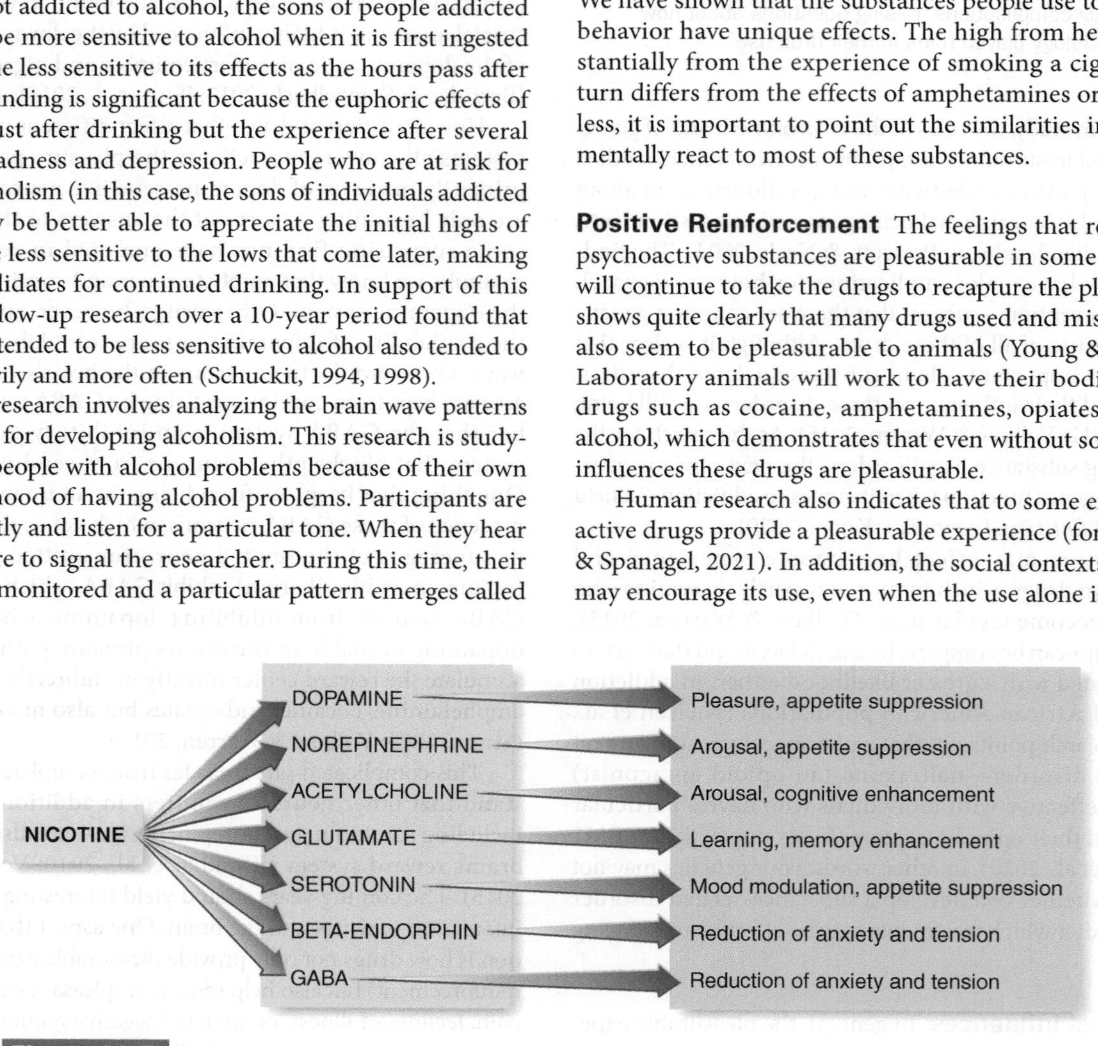

Figure 11.7

Nicotine influences multiple neurotransmitters, causing a number of different mood changes. Figure from N. Benowitz, 2008, Neurobiology of nicotine addiction: Implications for smoking cessation treatment, *American Journal of Medicine 121*(Suppl. 4), S1.

outcome. One study found that among volunteers who preferred not to take Valium, pairing money with pill taking caused participants to switch from a placebo to Valium (Alessi, Roll, Reilly, & Johanson, 2002). Positive reinforcement in the use and the situations surrounding the use of drugs contributes to whether or not people decide to try to continue using drugs.

Negative Reinforcement Most researchers have looked at how drugs help reduce unpleasant feelings through negative reinforcement. Many people are likely to initiate and continue drug use to escape from unpleasantness in their lives. In addition to the initial euphoria, many drugs provide escape from physical pain (opiates), from stress (alcohol), or from panic and anxiety (benzodiazepines). This phenomenon has been explored under a number of different names, including *tension reduction, negative affect,* and *self-medication,* each of which has a somewhat different focus (Heilig & Spanagel, 2021).

One premise is that substance use becomes a way for users to cope with the unpleasant feelings that go along with life circumstances. For example, one study of 1,252 U.S. Army soldiers returning home from Operation Iraqi Freedom found that those who were exposed to violent combat and human trauma and had direct responsibility for taking the life of another person were at increased risk for risk taking and for more frequent and greater alcohol use (Killgore et al., 2008; Stappenbeck, Hellmuth, Simpson, & Jakupcak, 2014). People who experience other types of trauma, such as sexual abuse, are also more likely to misuse alcohol (Evans & Reed, in press). These observations emphasize the important role played by each aspect of misuse and dependence—biological, psychological, social, and cultural—in determining who will and who will not have difficulties with these substances.

In a study that examined substance use among adolescents as a way to reduce stress (Chassin, Pillow, Curran, Molina, & Barrera, 1993), researchers compared a group of adolescents whose parents had an alcohol addiction with a group whose parents did not. The average age of the adolescents was 12.7 years. The researchers found that just having a parent with alcohol dependence was a major factor in predicting who would use alcohol and other drugs. However, they also found that adolescents who reported negative affect—such as feeling lonely, crying a lot, or being tense—were more likely than others to use drugs. The researchers further determined that the adolescents from both groups tended to use drugs as a way to cope with unpleasant feelings. This study and others (see, for example, Pardini, Lochman, & Wells, 2004) suggest that one contributing factor to adolescent drug use is the desire to escape from unpleasantness. It also suggests that to prevent people from using drugs we may need to address influences such as stress and anxiety, a strategy we discuss in our section on treatment.

Many people who use psychoactive substances experience a crash after being high. If people reliably crash, why don't they just stop taking drugs? One explanation is given by Solomon and Corbit in an interesting integration of both the positive and the negative reinforcement processes (Solomon, 1980; Solomon & Corbit, 1974). The *opponent-process theory* holds that an increase in positive feelings will be followed shortly by an increase in negative feelings. Similarly, an increase in negative feelings will be followed by a period of positive feelings (Karin, Raz, & Alon, 2021). Athletes often report feeling depressed after finally attaining a long-sought goal. The opponent-process theory claims that this mechanism is strengthened with use and weakened by disuse. So a person who has been using a drug for some time will need more of it to achieve the same results (tolerance). At the same time, the negative feelings that follow drug use tend to intensify. For many people, this is the point at which the motivation for drug taking shifts from desiring the euphoric high to alleviating the increasingly unpleasant crash. Unfortunately, they come to believe that the best remedy is more of the same drug. People who are hung over after drinking too much alcohol are often advised to have "the hair of the dog that bit you" (that is, have another drink). The sad irony here is that the very drug that can make you feel so bad is also the one thing that can take away your pain. You can see why people can become tyrannized by this insidious cycle.

Researchers have also looked at substance misuse as a way of self-medicating for other problems (Bailey & Baillie, 2012). If people have difficulties with anxiety, for example, they may be attracted to barbiturates or alcohol because of their anxiety-reducing qualities. In one study, researchers were successful in treating a group of people with cocaine addiction who had ADHD with methylphenidate (Ritalin) (Dursteler et al., 2015; Levin, Evans, Brooks, & Garawi, 2007). They had hypothesized that these individuals used cocaine to help focus their attention. Once their ability to concentrate improved with the methylphenidate, the users reduced their use of cocaine. Research is just beginning to outline the complex interplay among stressors, negative feelings, other psychological disorders, and negative reactions to the drugs themselves as causative factors in psychoactive drug use.

Cognitive Dimensions

What people expect to experience when they use drugs influences how they react to them. People who expect to be less inhibited when they drink alcohol will act less inhibited whether they actually drink alcohol or a placebo they think is alcohol (Bailey & Baillie, 2012). This observation about the influence of how we think about drug use has been labeled an *expectancy effect* and has received considerable research attention.

Expectancies develop before people actually use drugs, perhaps as a result of parents' and peers' drug use, advertising, and media figures who model drug use (Le, Zhornitsky, Zhang, & Li, 2020). In an important study, students in Canada in grades 7 to 11 were questioned each year for 3 years about their thoughts about alcohol and marijuana use (Fulton, Krank, & Stewart, 2012; Young, 2013). Included were instructions for them to list three or four things they expected would happen if they used a particular substance. Positive expectancies about the effects of alcohol or marijuana use predicted who was more likely to use and increase their use of these drugs 3 years later. These results suggest that adolescents may begin drinking or using other drugs partly because they believe these substances will have positive effects.

Expectations appear to change as people have more experience with drugs, although their expectations are similar for alcohol, nicotine, cannabis, and cocaine (Simons, Dvorak, & Lau-Barraco, 2009; Young, 2013). Some evidence points to positive expectancies—believing you will feel good if you take a drug—as an indirect influence on drug problems. In other words, what these beliefs may do is increase the likelihood you will take certain drugs, which in turn will increase the likelihood that problems will arise.

Once people stop taking drugs after prolonged or repeated use, powerful urges called "cravings" can interfere with efforts to remain off these drugs (Zhang et al., 2020). DSM-5 includes cravings as one of the criteria for diagnosing a substance-related disorder. If you have ever tried to give up ice cream and then found yourself compelled to have some, you have a limited idea of what it might be like to crave a drug. These urges seem to be triggered by factors such as the availability of the drug, contact with things associated with drug taking (for example, sitting in a bar), specific moods (for example, being depressed), or having a small dose of the drug. For example, one study used a virtual reality apparatus to simulate visual, auditory, and olfactory (an alcohol-dipped tissue) cues (Lee et al., 2009) for alcohol-dependent adults. The participants could choose among kinds of alcoholic beverages (such as beer, whiskey, or wine), snacks, and drinking environments (beer garden, restaurant, and pub). The researchers found significant increases in cravings for alcohol under these conditions (Lee et al., 2009). This type of technology may make it easier for clinicians to assess potential problem areas for clients, which can then be targeted to help keep them from relapsing. Research is under way to determine how cravings may work in the brain and if certain medications can be used to reduce these urges and help supplement treatment (Hollander & Kenny, 2012).

Social Dimensions

Exposure to psychoactive substances is a necessary prerequisite to their use and possible misuse, as previously discussed. You could probably list a number of ways people are exposed to these substances—through friends, through the media, and so on. Research on the consequences of cigarette advertising, for example, suggests the effects of media exposure may be more influential than peer pressure in determining whether teens smoke (Hong & Kim, 2020). In one large study, 820 adolescents (age 14 to 17) were studied to assess what factors influenced the age at which they would have their first drink of alcohol (Kuperman et al., 2013). This study found several factors predicted early alcohol use, including when their best friends started drinking, whether their family was at high risk for alcohol dependence, and whether behavior problems were present in these children.

Research suggests that parents who excessively use addictive substances spend less time monitoring their children than parents without drug problems (Dishion, Patterson, & Reid, 1988) and that this is an important contribution to early adolescent substance use (Kerr, Stattin, & Burk, 2010). When parents do not provide appropriate supervision, their children tend to develop friendships with peers who supported drug use (Van Ryzin, Fosco, & Dishion, 2012). Children influenced by drug use at home may be exposed to peers who use drugs as well. A self-perpetuating pattern seems to be associated with drug use that extends beyond the genetic influences we discussed previously (Hong & Kim, 2020).

How does our society view people who are dependent on drugs? This issue is of tremendous importance because it affects efforts to legislate the sale, manufacture, possession, and use of these substances. It also dictates how drug-dependent individuals are treated. Two views of substance-related disorders characterize contemporary thought: the moral weakness and the disease models of dependence. According to the *moral weakness model of chemical dependence*, drug use is seen as a failure of self-control in the face of temptation; this is a psychosocial perspective. Proponents of this model see drug users as lacking the character or moral fiber to resist the lure of drugs. We saw earlier, for example, that the Catholic Church made drug use an official sin—an indication of its disdain. The *disease model of physiological dependence*, in contrast, assumes that drug use disorders are caused by an underlying physiological cause; this is a biological perspective. Those who ascribe to this model think that just as diabetes or asthma can't be blamed on the afflicted individuals, neither should drug use disorders. AA and similar organizations see drug use disorders as an incurable disease over which the addict has no control (Kelly, Stout, Magill, Tonigan, & Pagano, 2010).

Neither perspective does justice to the complex interrelationship between the psychosocial and biological influences that affect substance disorders. Viewing drug use as moral weakness leads to punishing those afflicted with the disorder, whereas a disease model includes seeking treatment for a medical problem. Messages

Many young children are exposed to drug use.

that the disorder is out of their control can at times be counterproductive. A comprehensive view of substance-related disorders that includes both psychosocial and biological influences is needed for this important societal concern to be addressed adequately.

Cultural Dimensions

Culture is a pervasive factor in the influence of drug use and treatment. For example, the extent to which and how well people adapt to new cultures (*acculturation*) can be either a source of strength or a stress that can impact drug use. Cultural factors such as *machismo* (male dominance in Latin cultures), *marianismo* (female Latin role of motherly nurturance and identifying with the Virgin Mary), spirituality, and *tiu lien* ("loss of face" among some Asian cultures, which can lead to shame for not living up to cultural expectations) are just a few cultural viewpoints that can affect drug use and treatment in either a positive or negative way (Castro & Nieri, 2010; Wang, Nieri, Do, & Llanes, 2020). In addition, when we examine a behavior as it appears in different cultures, it is necessary to reexamine what is considered acceptable (Kohn, Wintrob, & Alarcón, 2009). Each culture has its own preferences for acceptable psychoactive drugs, as well as its own prohibitions for substances it finds unacceptable. Keep in mind that in addition to defining what is or is not acceptable, cultural norms affect the rates of substance use in important ways. For example, research suggests that alcohol may be more available in low-income Mexican towns (that is, more stores or individuals selling alcohol), leading to higher rates of alcoholism in these areas (Parker, McCaffree, & Alaniz, 2013).

On the other hand, in certain cultures, including Korea, people are expected to drink alcohol heavily on certain social occasions (Lee & Chung, 2020). As we have seen before, exposure to these substances, in addition to social pressure for heavy and frequent use, may facilitate their misuse, and this may explain the high alcohol use rates in countries like Korea. This cultural influence provides an interesting natural experiment when exploring gene–environment interactions. People of Asian descent are more likely to have the ALDH2 gene, which produces a severe "flushing" effect (reddening and burning of the face) after drinking alcohol. This flushing effect was thought to be responsible for a relatively low rate of drinking in the population (de Wit & Phillips, 2012). However, between 1979 and 1992—when increased drinking became socially expected—there was an increase in alcohol use (Higuchi et al., 1994). The protective value of having the ALDH2 gene was diminished by the change in cultural norms (Rutter, Moffit, & Caspi, 2006).

Cultural factors not only influence the rates of substance misuse but also determine how it is manifested. Research indicates that alcohol consumption in Poland and Finland is relatively low, yet conflicts related to drinking and arrests for drunkenness in those countries are high compared with those in the Netherlands, which has about the same rate of alcohol consumption (Osterberg, 1986). Our discussion of expectancies may provide some insight into how the same amount of drinking can have different behavioral outcomes. Expectancies about the effects of alcohol use differ across cultures (for example, "Drinking makes me more aggressive" versus "Drinking makes me more withdrawn"); these differing expectancies may partially account for the variations in the consequences of drinking in Poland, Finland, and the Netherlands. Whether substance use is considered a harmful dysfunction often depends on the assumptions of the cultural group.

An Integrative Model

Any explanation of substance use disorders must account for the basic issue raised earlier in this chapter: Why do some people use drugs but not misuse them or become dependent? ■ Figure 11.8 illustrates how the multiple influences we have discussed may interact to account for this process. Access to a drug is a necessary but not a sufficient condition for excessive use or dependence. Exposure has many sources, including the media, parents, peers, and, indirectly, lack of supervision. Whether people use a drug depends also on social and cultural expectations, some encouraging and some discouraging, such as laws against possession or sale of the drug.

W. Perry Conway/Getty Images

James Sturcke/Alamy Stock Photo

In both traditional and contemporary cultures, alcohol is used as part of certain rituals.

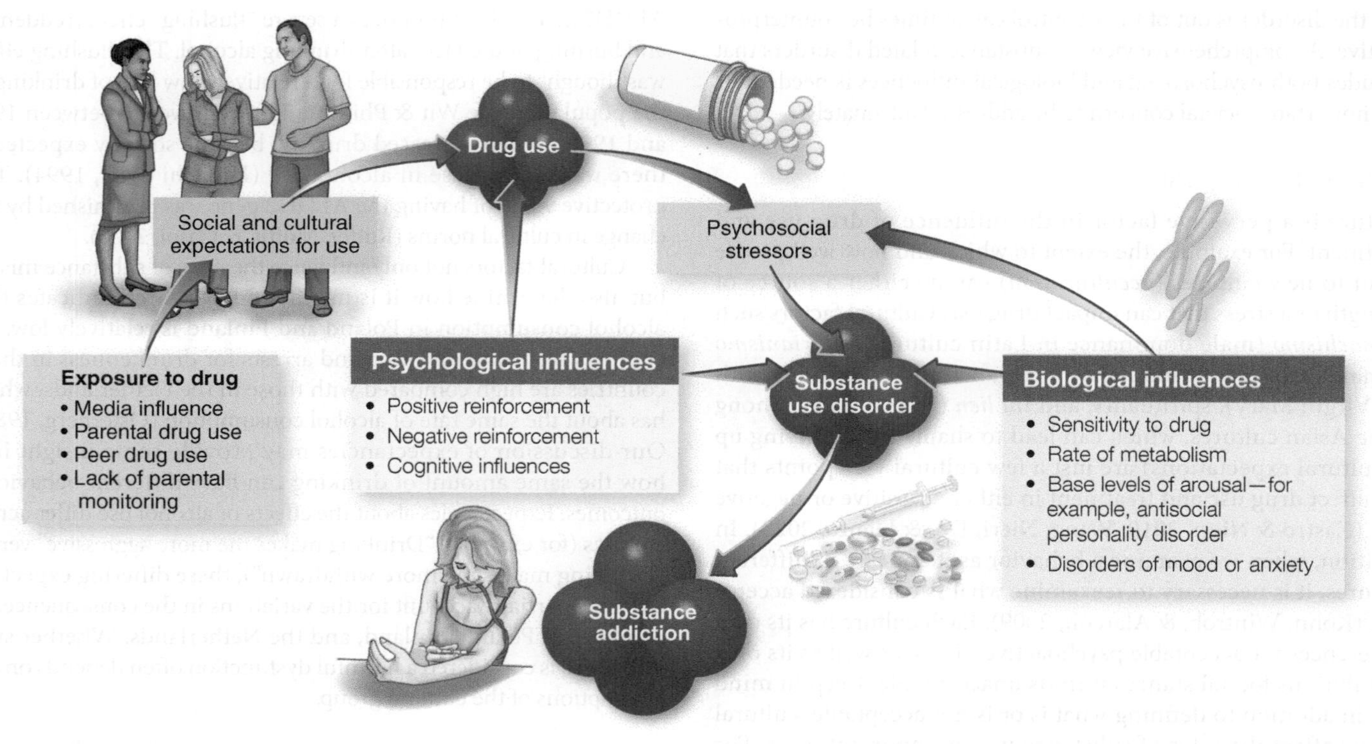

Figure 11.8

An integrative model of substance-related disorders.

The path from drug use to misuse and dependence is more complicated (see Figure 11.8). As major stressors aggravate many disorders we have discussed, so do they increase the risk of excessive use and dependence on psychoactive substances. Genetic influences may be of several types. Some individuals may inherit a greater sensitivity to the effects of certain drugs; others may inherit an ability to metabolize substances more quickly and are thereby able to tolerate higher (and more dangerous) levels (Young-Wolff, Enoch, & Prescott, 2011). Other psychiatric conditions may indirectly put someone at risk for substance misuse. Antisocial personality disorder, characterized by the frequent violation of social norms (see Chapter 12), is thought to include a lowered rate of arousal; this may account for the increased prevalence of substance misuse in this group. People with mood disorders or anxiety disorders may self-medicate by using drugs to relieve the negative symptoms of their disorder, and this may account for the high rates of substance use in this group.

We know also that continued use of certain substances changes the way our brains work through a process called *neuroplasticity* (Umberger & Gaddis, 2020). We tend to think of neuroplasticity—the brain's tendency to reorganize itself by forming new neural connections—when we hear stories of people recovering abilities after some brain damage. This ability to adapt to change is something we hope for when injury occurs to the brain. The other side of this ability shows itself in drug addiction. With the continued use of substances such as alcohol, cocaine, or the other drugs we explore in this chapter, the brain reorganizes itself to adapt. Unfortunately, this change in the brain increases the drive to obtain the drug and decreases the desire for other nondrug experiences—both of which contribute to continued use and relapse (Russo et al., 2010).

It is clear that misuse and dependence cannot be predicted from one factor, whether genetic, neurobiological, psychological, or cultural. For example, some people with the genes common to many with substance use problems do not become misusers. Many people who experience the most crushing stressors, such as abject poverty or bigotry and violence, cope without resorting to drug use. There are different pathways to misuse, and we are only now beginning to identify their basic outlines.

Once a drug has been used repeatedly, biology and cognition conspire to create dependence. Continual use of most drugs causes tolerance, which requires the user to ingest more of the drug to produce the same effect. Conditioning is also a factor. If pleasurable drug experiences are associated with certain settings, a return to such a setting will later cause urges to develop, even if the drugs themselves are not available.

This complex picture still does not convey the intricate lives of people who develop substance-related disorders. Each person has a story and path to misuse and dependence. We have only begun to discover the commonalities of substance disorders; we need to understand a great deal more about how all the factors interact to produce them.

Treatment of Substance-Related Disorders

When we left Danny, he was in jail, awaiting the legal outcome of being arrested for vehicular manslaughter. At this point in his

Concept Check 11.3

Part A

Match the following descriptions with their corresponding substance: (a) opioids, (b) amphetamines, (c) cocaine, (d) hallucinogens, (e) nicotine, and (f) caffeine.

1. This is the most common psychoactive substance because it is legal, elevates mood, and decreases fatigue. It's readily available in many beverages. ____________
2. This substance causes euphoria, appetite loss, and increased alertness. Dependence appears after years of use. Its use during pregnancy has the potential to result in irritable babies. ____________
3. These drugs, including LSD, influence perception, distorting feelings, sights, sounds, and smells. ____________
4. These lead to euphoria, drowsiness, and slowed breathing. These substances are analgesics, relieving pain. Users tend to be secretive, preventing a great deal of research in this area. ____________
5. This substance stimulates the nervous system and relieves stress. DSM-5 describes withdrawal symptoms instead of an intoxication pattern. ____________
6. These create feelings of elation and vigor and reduce fatigue. They are prescribed to people with narcolepsy and ADHD. ____________

Part B

Indicate whether these statements about the causes of substance-related disorders are true (T) or false (F).

7. ____________ Negative reinforcement is involved in the continuance of drug use because drugs often provide escape from pain, stress, panic, and so on.
8. ____________ Research with both animals and humans indicates that substance misuse in general is affected by our genes, although not one particular gene.
9. ____________ The media and parental influences have no effect on adolescent drug use; it is solely a peer pressure factor.
10. ____________ The expectancy effect is illustrated when a person who expects to be less inhibited when drinking alcohol is given a placebo and has no noticeable change in behavior or cognition.
11. ____________ To some extent, all psychoactive drugs provide a pleasurable experience, creating positive reinforcement.

life, Danny needs more than legal help; he needs to free himself from his addiction to alcohol and cocaine. And the first step in his recovery has to come from him. Danny must admit he needs help, that he does indeed have a problem with drugs, and that he needs others to help him overcome his chronic dependence. The personal motivation to work on a drug problem appears to be important but not necessarily essential in the treatment of substance misuse (National Institute on Drug Abuse [NIDA], 2009). Unfortunately, although Danny's arrest seemed to shock him into realizing how serious his problems had become, he was not ready to confront them head-on. He spent many hours researching how the antidepressant medication he was also taking could have caused the deadly accident and did not own up to his drug use as the cause.

Treating people who have substance-related disorders is a difficult task. Perhaps because of the combination of influences that often work together the outlook for those who are dependent on drugs is often not positive. You will see in the case of heroin dependence, for example, that a best-case scenario is often just trading one addiction (heroin) for another (methadone) (Joudrey et al., 2020). And even people who successfully cease taking drugs may feel the urge to resume drug use all their lives.

Treatment for substance-related disorders focuses on multiple areas (Higgins et al., 2014). The National Institute on Drug Abuse recommends 13 principles of effective treatment for illicit drug use based on more than 35 years of research (NIDA, 2009) (see Table 11.1). Sometimes the first step is to help someone through the withdrawal process; typically, the ultimate goal is abstinence. In other situations, the goal is to get a person to maintain a certain level of drug use without escalating its intake, and sometimes it is geared toward preventing exposure to drugs. Because substance misuse arises from so many influences, it should not be surprising that treating people with substance-related disorders is not a simple matter of finding just the right drug or the best way to change thoughts or behavior. Some research suggests that two principles—adequate length of treatment and frequency of testing for drug use—may not be among the strongest aspects of treatment (Pearson et al., 2012).

It is estimated that fewer than 25% of the people who have significant problems with substance use seek treatment for their problems (Gutierrez, Crowe, Mullen, Pignato, & Fan, 2020). This was complicated in early 2020 with the beginning of the COVID-19 pandemic, which increased the use of substances to reduce symptoms such as stress and anxiety (Du et al., 2020). In order to reach out to these individuals, efforts are under way to put in place routine screenings for substance use problems in settings such as doctor's offices, hospital emergency rooms, and college and university health clinics. This community-wide approach is an important part of identifying difficulties and bringing treatment to those in need (Dahlem et al., 2020).

We discuss the treatment of substance-related disorders as a group because treatments have so much in common. For example, many programs that treat people for dependence on a variety of substances also teach skills for coping with life stressors. Some biological treatments focus on how to cancel out the effects of the ingested substances. We discuss the obvious differences among substances as they arise.

Table 11.1 Principles of Effective Treatment

1.	No single treatment is appropriate for all individuals.
2.	Treatment needs to be readily available.
3.	Effective treatment attends to multiple needs of individuals, not just their drug use.
4.	An individual's treatment and services plan must be assessed continually and modified as necessary to ensure that the plan meets the person's changing needs.
5.	Remaining in treatment for an adequate period of time is critical for treatment effectiveness (that is, 3 months or longer).
6.	Counseling (individual and/or group) and other behavioral therapies are critical components of effective treatment for addiction.
7.	Medications are an important element of treatment for many patients, especially when combined with counseling and other behavioral therapies.
8.	Addicted or drug-abusing individuals with coexisting mental disorders should have both disorders treated in an integrated way.
9.	Medical detoxification is only the first stage of addiction treatment and by itself does little to change long-term drug use.
10.	Treatment does not need to be voluntary to be effective.
11.	Possible drug use during treatment must be monitored continuously.
12.	Treatment programs should provide assessment for HIV/AIDS, hepatitis B and C, tuberculosis and other infectious diseases, and counseling to help patients modify or change behaviors that place themselves or others at risk of infection.
13.	Recovery from drug addiction can be a long-term process and frequently requires multiple episodes of treatment.

Source: National Institute on Drug Abuse (NIDA), 2009, *Principles of addiction treatment: A research-based guide* (2nd ed.), NIH Publication No. 09-4180 (National Institute on Drug Abuse).

Table 11.2 Medical Treatments

	Substance Treatment Goal	Treatment Approach
Nicotine	Reduce withdrawal symptoms and cravings.	Nicotine replacement therapy (patch, gum, spray, lozenge, and inhaler)
	Reduce withdrawal symptoms and cravings.	Bupropion (Zyban)
Alcohol	Reduce reinforcing effects of alcohol.	Naltrexone
	Reduce alcohol craving in abstinent individuals.	Acamprosate (Campral)
	Maintain abstinence.	Disulfiram (Antabuse)
Cannabis		No specific medical interventions recommended
Cocaine		No specific medical interventions recommended
Opioids	Maintain abstinence.	Methadone
	Maintain abstinence.	Buprenorphine (Subutex)

Source: From American Psychiatric Association, 2007, Practice guidelines for the treatment of patients with substance use disorders (2nd ed.), *American Journal of Psychiatry, 164* (Suppl.), 1–14.

Biological Treatments

There have been a variety of biologically based approaches designed primarily to change the way substances are experienced. In other words, scientists are trying to find ways to prevent people from experiencing the pleasant highs associated with drug use or to find alternative substances that have some of the positive effects (for example, reducing anxiety) without their addictive properties. Table 11.2 lists the current recommended medical treatments for many of the more intractable substance dependence problems.

Agonist Substitution Increased knowledge about how psychoactive drugs work on the brain has led researchers to explore ways of changing how they are experienced by people who are dependent on them. One method, **agonist substitution**, involves providing the person with a safe drug that has a chemical makeup similar to the addictive drug (therefore the name *agonist*). *Methadone* is an opiate agonist that is often given as a heroin substitute (Black & Andreasen, 2021). Methadone is a synthetic narcotic developed in Germany during World War II when morphine was not available for pain control; it was originally called *adolphine* after Adolph Hitler (Martínez-Fernández, 2002). Although it does not give the quick high of heroin, methadone initially provides the same analgesic (pain reducing) and sedative effects. When users develop a tolerance for methadone, however, it loses its analgesic and sedative qualities. Because heroin and methadone have *cross-tolerance,* meaning they act on the same neurotransmitter receptors, a person addicted to heroin who takes methadone may become addicted to the methadone instead, but this is not always the case (Maremmani et al., 2009). Research suggests that when persons addicted to heroin combine methadone with counseling, many reduce their use of heroin and engage in less criminal activity (Schwartz et al., 2009). A newer agonist—buprenorphine—blocks the effects of opiates and seems to encourage better compliance than would a nonopiate or opiate antagonist (Black & Andreasen, 2021).

Addiction to cigarette smoking is also treated by a substitution process. The drug—**nicotine**—is provided to smokers in the form of gum, patch, inhaler, or nasal spray, which lack the carcinogens included in cigarette smoke; the dose is later tapered off to lessen withdrawal from the drug. In general, these replacement strategies successfully help people stop smoking, although they work best with psychological therapy (Carpenter et al., 2013; Hughes, 2009). People must be taught how to use the gum properly, and a portion of the people who successfully quit smoking become dependent on the gum itself (Etter, 2009). The **nicotine patch** requires less effort and provides a steadier nicotine replacement (Hughes, 2009). The medications used for replacement treatment are varenicline (trade name Chantix) and bupropion (Zyban) (Black & Andreasen, 2021). The latter drug is also commonly prescribed under the trade name Wellbutrin as an antidepressant. These drugs curb the cravings without being an agonist for nicotine (rather than helping smokers trying to quit by making them less depressed). All of these medical treatments have roughly the same effectiveness in helping people quit smoking, although fewer than 10% of the people who try to quit are successful (Barry & Finke, 2020).

Antagonist Treatments We described how many psychoactive drugs produce euphoric effects through their interaction with the neurotransmitter systems in the brain. What would happen if the effects of these drugs were blocked so that the drugs no longer produced the pleasant results? Would people stop using the drugs? **Antagonist drugs** block or counteract the effects of psychoactive drugs, and a variety of drugs that seem to cancel out the effects of opiates have been used with people dependent on a variety of substances. The most often prescribed opiate-antagonist drug, naltrexone, has had only limited success with individuals who are not simultaneously participating in a structured treatment program (Krupitsky & Blokhina, 2010). Some very sophisticated research has found that individuals with a certain genetic makeup may be better responders to naltrexone. Individuals with alcohol use disorder with a more opioid-responsive genotype (OPRM1 G carriers) respond better to naltrexone if they have genotypes indicating normal/less dopamine tone (DAT1 10,10 or COMT val,val), while those with a less responsive opioid-responsive genotype (OPRM1 A homozygotes) respond better to naltrexone if they have genotypes indicating greater dopamine tone (DAT1 9-repeat or COMT met carriers) (Anton et al., 2020). This type of research may lead to more personalized treatment approaches.

When naltrexone is given to a person who is dependent on opiates, it produces immediate withdrawal symptoms, an extremely unpleasant effect. A person must be free from these withdrawal symptoms completely before starting naltrexone, and because it removes the euphoric effects of opiates, the user must be highly motivated to continue treatment. Acamprosate also seems to decrease cravings in people dependent on alcohol, and it works best with highly motivated people who are also participating in psychosocial interventions (Kennedy et al., 2010). The brain mechanisms for the effects of this drug are not well understood, and there may be more people who stop using this drug as compared to those who use naltrexone (Kumar et al., 2020).

Overall, naltrexone or the other drugs being explored are not the panacea that would shut off the response to psychoactive drugs and put an end to dependence. They do appear to help some drug users handle withdrawal symptoms and the cravings that accompany attempts to abstain from drug use; antagonists may therefore be a useful addition to other therapeutic efforts.

Aversive Treatment In addition to looking for ways to block the euphoric effects of psychoactive drugs, clinicians in this area may prescribe drugs that make ingesting the misused substances extremely unpleasant. The expectation is that a person who associates the drug with feelings of illness will avoid using the drug. The most commonly known aversive treatment uses disulfiram (Antabuse) with people who have an alcohol use disorder (Ivanov, 2009). Antabuse prevents the breakdown of acetaldehyde, a by-product of alcohol, and the resulting buildup of acetaldehyde causes feelings of illness. People who drink alcohol after taking Antabuse experience nausea, vomiting, and elevated heart rate and respiration. Ideally, Antabuse is taken each morning before the desire to drink arises. Unfortunately, noncompliance is a major concern, and a person who skips the Antabuse for a few days is able to resume drinking (Ellis & Dronsfield, 2013).

Efforts to make smoking aversive have included the use of silver nitrate in lozenges or gum. This chemical combines with the saliva of a smoker to produce a bad taste in the mouth. Research has not shown it to be particularly effective (Jensen, Schmidt, Pedersen, & Dahl, 1991). Both Antabuse for alcohol misuse and silver nitrate for cigarette smoking have generally been less than successful as treatment strategies on their own, primarily because they require that people be extremely motivated to continue taking them outside the supervision of a mental health professional.

Other Biological Approaches Medication is often prescribed to help people deal with the often disturbing symptoms of withdrawal. Clonidine, developed to treat hypertension, has been given to people withdrawing from opiates. Because withdrawal from certain prescribed medications such as sedative drugs can cause cardiac arrest or seizures, these drugs are gradually tapered off to minimize dangerous reactions. In addition, sedative drugs (benzodiazepines) are often prescribed to help minimize discomfort for people withdrawing from other drugs, such as alcohol (Farrokh, Roels, Owusu, Nelson, & Cook, in press).

Psychosocial Treatments

Most biological treatments for excessive substance use show some promise with people who are trying to treat their drug habit. Not one of these treatments alone is successful for most people, however (Schuckit, 2009b). Most research indicates a need for social support or therapeutic intervention. Because so many people need help to overcome their substance disorder, a number of models and programs have been developed. Unfortunately, in no other area of psychology have unvalidated and untested methods of treatment been so widely accepted. A reminder: A program that has not been subject to the scrutiny of research *may* work, but the sheer number of people receiving services of unknown value is still cause for concern. We next review several therapeutic approaches that *have* been evaluated.

Inpatient Facilities The first specialized facility for people with substance use problems was established in 1935, when the first federal narcotic "farm" was built in Lexington, Kentucky. Now mostly privately run, such facilities are designed to help people get through the initial withdrawal period and to provide supportive therapy so that they can go back to their communities (Morgan, 1981). Inpatient care can be extremely expensive (Bender, 2004). The question arises, then, as to how effective this type of care is compared with outpatient therapy that can cost 90% less. Research suggests there may be no difference between intensive residential setting programs and quality outpatient care in the outcomes for alcoholic patients (Miller & Hester, 1986) or for drug treatment in general (NIDA, 2009). Although some people do improve as inpatients, they may do equally well in outpatient care that is significantly less expensive.

Alcoholics Anonymous and Its Variations Without question, the most popular model for the treatment of substance misuse is a variation of the 12-step program first developed by Alcoholics Anonymous (AA). Established in 1935 by two alcoholic professionals, William "Bill W." Wilson and Robert "Dr. Bob" Holbrook Smith, the foundation of AA is the notion that alcoholism is a disease and alcoholics must acknowledge their addiction to alcohol and its destructive power over them. The addiction is seen as more powerful than any individual; therefore, they must look to a higher power to help them overcome their shortcomings. Central to the design of AA is its independence from the established medical community and the freedom it offers from the stigmatization of alcohol misuse or dependence (Denzin, 1987; Robertson, 1988). An important component is the social support it provides through group meetings.

Since 1935, AA has steadily expanded to include almost 106,000 groups in more than 100 countries (White & Kurtz, 2008). In one survey, 9% of the adult population in the United States reported they had at one time attended an AA meeting (Room & Greenfield, 2006). The 12 steps of AA are the basis of its philosophy (see Table 11.3). In them, you can see the reliance on prayer and a belief in the Christian God.

Many people credit AA and similar organizations, such as Cocaine Anonymous and Narcotics Anonymous, with saving their lives. Despite challenges conducting systematic research on AA because participants attend meetings anonymously and only when they feel the need to, there have been numerous attempts to evaluate the program's effect on people who have a dependence on alcohol (McCrady & Tonigan, 2015). Research finds that those people who regularly participate in AA activities—or other similar supportive approaches—and follow its guidelines carefully are more likely to have positive outcomes, such as reduced drinking and improved psychological health (Kelly, Abry, Ferri, & Humphreys, 2020). Studies suggest that those who are more likely to engage with AA tend to have more severe alcohol use problem and seem to be more committed to abstinence (McCrady & Tonigan, 2015). Thus, AA can be an effective treatment for highly motivated people with alcohol dependence. However, preliminary evidence shows that AA can be helpful for individuals seeking to achieve total abstinence and may be more cost effective than other treatments (Kelly et al., 2020). Researchers are still trying to understand exactly why AA and the 12-step program work, but it seems that social support plays an important role (McCrady & Tonigan, 2015).

Some individuals—including agnostics and atheists, women, and minority groups—have more mixed experiences with AA (McCrady & Tonigan, 2015). Other groups now exist (such as Rational Recovery, Moderation Management, Women for Sobriety, and SMART Recovery) for individuals who benefit from the social support of others but who may not want the abstinence-oriented 12-step program offered by groups modeled after AA (Tucker et al., 2011).

Controlled Use One of the tenets of AA is total abstinence; recovering alcoholics who have just one sip of alcohol are believed to have "slipped" until they again achieve abstinence. Some researchers question this assumption, however, and believe at least a portion of misusers of several substances (notably alcohol and nicotine) may be capable of becoming social users without resuming their problematic use of these drugs.

In the alcoholism treatment field, the notion of teaching people **controlled drinking** is controversial, partly because of a classic study showing partial success in teaching severe misusers to drink in a limited way (Sobell & Sobell, 1978). The participants were 40 male alcoholics in an alcoholism treatment program at a state hospital who were thought to have a good prognosis. The men were assigned either to a program that taught them how to drink in moderation (experimental group) or to a group that was abstinence oriented (control group). The researchers, Mark and Linda Sobell, followed the men for more than 2 years, maintaining contact with 98% of them. During the second year after treatment, those who participated in the controlled drinking group were functioning well 85% of the time, whereas the men in the abstinence group were reported to be doing well only 42% of the time. Although results in the two groups differed significantly, some men in both groups suffered serious relapses and required rehospitalization and some were incarcerated. The results of this study suggest that controlled drinking may be a viable alternative to abstinence for some alcohol misusers, although it clearly isn't a cure.

The controversy over this study began with a paper published in the prestigious journal *Science* (Pendery, Maltzman, & West, 1982). The authors reported they had contacted the men in the Sobell study after 10 years and found that only 1 of the 20 men in the experimental group maintained a pattern of controlled drinking. Although this reevaluation made headlines and was the subject of a segment on the *60 Minutes* television show, it

Table 11.3 The Twelve Steps of Alcoholics Anonymous

1.	We admitted we were powerless over alcohol—that our lives had become unmanageable.
2.	Came to believe that a power greater than ourselves could restore us to sanity.
3.	Made a decision to turn our will and our lives over to the care of God as we understood Him.
4.	Made a searching and fearless moral inventory of ourselves.
5.	Admitted to God, to ourselves, and to another human being the exact nature of our wrongs.
6.	Were entirely ready to have God remove all these defects of character.
7.	Humbly asked Him to remove our shortcomings.
8.	Made a list of all persons we had harmed, and became willing to make amends to them all.
9.	Made direct amends to such people wherever possible, except when to do so would injure them or others.
10.	Continued to take personal inventory and, when we were wrong, promptly admitted it.
11.	Sought through prayer and meditation to improve our conscious contact with God as we understood Him, praying only for knowledge of His will for us and the power to carry that out.
12.	Having had a spiritual awakening as the result of these steps, we tried to carry this message to alcoholics and to practice these principles in all our affairs.

Source: The Twelve Steps are reprinted with permission of Alcoholics Anonymous World Services (AAWS). Permission to reprint the Twelve Steps does not mean that AAWS has reviewed or approved the contents of the publication or that AAWS necessarily agrees with the views expressed herein. AA is a program of recovery from alcoholism only. The use of the Twelve Steps in connection with programs and activities that are patterned after AA but that address other problems or in any other non-AA context does not imply otherwise.

had a number of flaws (Marlatt, Larimer, Baer, & Quigley, 1993). Most serious was the lack of data on the abstinence group over the same 10-year follow-up period. Because no treatment study on substance misuse pretends to help everyone who participates, control groups are added to compare progress. In this case, we need to know how well the controlled drinking group fared compared with the abstinence group.

The controversy over the Sobell study still has a chilling effect on controlled drinking as a treatment of alcohol misuse in the United States. In contrast, controlled drinking is widely accepted as a treatment for alcoholism in the United Kingdom. Despite opposition, research on this approach has been conducted in the ensuing years (Kelly et al., 2020), and the results seem to show that controlled drinking is at least as effective as abstinence but that neither treatment is successful for 70% to 80% of patients over the long term—a rather bleak outlook for people with alcohol dependence problems.

Component Treatment Most comprehensive treatment programs aimed at helping people with substance use disorder have a number of components thought to boost the effectiveness of the "treatment package" (for example, Barbosa-Leiker et al., 2020). We saw in our review of biological treatments that their effectiveness is increased when psychologically based therapy is added. In aversion therapy, which uses a conditioning model, substance use is paired with something extremely unpleasant, such as a brief electric shock or feelings of nausea. For example, people might be offered a drink of alcohol and receive a painful shock when the glass reaches their lips. The goal is to counteract the positive associations with substance use with negative associations. The negative associations can also be made by imagining unpleasant scenes in a technique called *covert sensitization* (Cautela, 1966); people might picture themselves beginning to drink alcohol and be interrupted with visions of becoming violently ill (Suneel & Siddique, 2020).

One component that seems to be a valuable part of therapy for substance use is *contingency management* (Oluwoye et al., 2020). Here, the clinician and the client together select the behaviors that the client needs to change and decide on the reinforcers that will reward reaching certain goals, perhaps money or small retail items like music downloads. In a study of cocaine users, clients received cash vouchers (up to almost $2,000) for having cocaine-negative urine specimens (Higgins et al., 2006). This study found greater abstinence rates among cocaine-dependent users with the contingency management approach and other skills training than among users in a more traditional counseling program that included a 12-step approach to treatment.

Another package of treatments is the *community reinforcement approach* (Archer, Harwood, Stevelink, Rafferty, & Greenberg, 2020). In keeping with the multiple influences that affect substance use, several facets of the drug problem are addressed to help identify and correct aspects of the person's life that might contribute to substance use or interfere with efforts to abstain. First, a spouse, friend, or relative who is not a substance user is recruited to participate in relationship therapy to help the misuser improve relationships with other important people. Second, clients are taught how to identify the antecedents and consequences that influence their drug taking. For example, if they are likely to use cocaine with certain friends, clients are taught to recognize the relationships and encouraged to avoid the associations. Third, clients are given assistance with employment, education, finances, or other social service areas that may help reduce their stress. Fourth, new recreational options help the person replace substance use with new activities. There is now strong empirical support for the effectiveness of this approach with alcohol and cocaine misusers (Higgins et al., 2014).

Obstacles to successful treatment for substance use and dependence include a lack of personal awareness that one has a problem and an unwillingness to change. An increasingly common intervention approach that directly addresses these needs is referred to as *motivational enhancement therapy (MET)* (Archer et al., 2020). MET is based on the work of Miller and Rollnick (2012), who proposed that behavior change in adults is more likely with empathetic and optimistic counseling (the therapist understands the client's perspective and believes that they can change) and a focus on a personal connection with the client's core values (for example, drinking and its consequences interferes with spending more time with family). By reminding the client about what they cherish most, MET intends to improve the individual's belief that any changes made (such as drinking less) will have positive outcomes (such as more family time), and the individual is therefore more likely to make the recommended changes. MET has been used to assist individuals with a variety of substance use problems, and it appears to be a useful component to add to psychological treatment (Archer et al., 2020).

Cognitive-behavioral therapy (CBT) is an effective treatment approach for many psychological disorders (see Chapter 5, for example), and it is also one of the best-designed and -studied approaches for treating substance dependence (Tetrault et al., 2020). This treatment addresses multiple aspects of the disorder, including a person's reactions to cues that lead to substance use (for example, being among certain friends) and thoughts and behaviors to resist use. Another target of CBT addresses the problem of relapse. Marlatt and Gordon's (1985) **relapse prevention** treatment model looks at the learned aspects of dependence and sees relapse as a failure of cognitive and behavioral coping skills (Witkiewitz & Marlatt, 2004). Therapy involves helping people remove any ambivalence about stopping their drug use by examining their beliefs about the positive aspects of the drug ("There's nothing like a cocaine high") and confronting the negative consequences of its use ("I fight with my wife when I'm high"). High-risk situations are identified ("having extra money in my pocket"), and strategies are developed to deal with potentially problematic situations, as well as with the craving that arises from abstinence. Incidents of relapse are dealt with as occurrences from which the person can recover. Instead of looking on these episodes as inevitably leading to more drug use, people in treatment are encouraged to see them as episodes brought on by temporary stress or a situation that can be changed. Research on this technique suggests that it may be particularly effective in treating alcohol problems (McCrady, 2014) as well as a variety of other substance-related disorders (for example, Senn et al., 2020).

Prevention

Adolescents are at high risk for drug addiction due to their higher rates of experimentation with drugs. When done right, education about drugs' risks can lead to decreases in drugs use (such as Ecstasy and tobacco) (Volkow & Warren, 2015). However, over the past few years, the strategies for preventing substance misuse and dependence have shifted from education-based approaches (for example, teaching schoolchildren that drugs can be harmful) to more wide-ranging approaches, including changes in the laws regarding drug possession and use and community-based interventions (Sher et al., 2011). Many states, for example, have implemented education-based programs in schools to try to deter students from using drugs. The widely used Drug Abuse Resistance Education (DARE) program encourages a "no drug use" message through fear of consequences, rewards for commitments not to use drugs, and strategies for refusing offers of drugs. Unfortunately, several extensive evaluations suggest that this type of program may not have its intended effects. Some research shows an overall effect for illicit drug use but not for tobacco or alcohol use (Hodder et al., 2017). Fortunately, more comprehensive programs that involve skills training to avoid or resist social pressures (such as peers) and environmental pressures (such as media portrayals of drug use) can be effective in preventing drug misuse among some. For example, one large-scale longitudinal study used a

Two New Paths to Prevention

We see that the problem with drug misuse is not just use of the drug. A complicating factor in drug misuse includes the brain's desire to continue to use the drug, especially when in the presence of stimuli and situations usually associated with the drug. This "drug seeking" and relapse continue to interfere with successful treatment. Groundbreaking research is now exploring where in the brain these processes occur, which in turn may lead to new approaches to help people remain drug-free (Kalivas, 2005).

Taking this one step further, research with animals suggests the possibility of creating "vaccines" that would use the immune system to fight drugs such as heroin, just as your body attacks infectious bacteria (Anton & Leff, 2006). A vaccine that would take away the pleasurable aspects of smoking is now being tested with humans (Moreno, et al., 2010). What this means is that—theoretically—children could be vaccinated early in their lives and that if they tried a drug, it would not have the pleasurable effects that would encourage repeated use. These "vice vaccines" could hold the answer to one of our most pressing social issues.

On the other end of the intervention spectrum, new and more comprehensive prevention approaches may help many individuals avoid initially trying dangerous drugs. One such approach being used in Montana is called the Montana Meth Project (Generations United, 2006). Initially funded by software billionaire Timothy Siegel, this initiative supports advertising and community action programs to inform youth across the state about the devastating effects of methamphetamine use. The project uses dramatic and sometimes shocking pictures and video ads, and its surveys suggest that the methods were successful in changing attitudes about meth use in many 12- to 17-year-olds. Although no controlled research yet exists, this may be an additional powerful tool for reducing drug dependence.

The Montana Meth Project used photos like these from Faces of Meth, a project of the Multnomah County Sheriff's Office in Portland, Oregon.

community-based intervention strategy to reduce binge drinking and alcohol-related injuries (for example, car crashes and assaults) (Holder et al., 2000). Three communities were mobilized to encourage responsible beverage service (that is, not serving too much alcohol to bar patrons), limit alcohol access to underage drinkers, and increase local enforcement of drinking and driving laws to limit access to alcohol. People's self-reports of drinking too much and drinking and driving were fewer after the intervention, as were alcohol-related car accidents and assaults. These types of comprehensive programs may need to be replicated across communities and extended to more pervasive influences (for example, how drug use is portrayed in the media) to effect significant prevention results (Newton, Conrod, Teesson, & Faggiano, 2012).

It may be that our most powerful preventive strategy involves cultural change. Over the past 50 years or so, we have gone from a "turn on, tune in, drop out," "if it feels good, do it," and "I get high with a little help from my friends" society to one that champions statements like "Just say no to drugs." The social unacceptability of excessive drinking, smoking, and other drug use is probably responsible for this change. The sociocultural disapproval of cigarette smoking, for example, is readily apparent in the following description by a person who used to smoke:

> I began smoking (in Boy Scouts!) at age 11. By the time I was a college freshman, freed from the restrictions of school and home, my smoking had increased to a pack a day. The seminal Surgeon General's Report *Smoking and Health* was issued that year (1964), but I didn't notice. The warnings that began appearing on cigarette packs a couple of years later were also easy to ignore, since I had grown up knowing that smoking was unhealthy. As a graduate student and young professor I often smoked while leading class discussions, as had some of my favorite teachers. That ended in 1980, when an undergraduate student, no doubt empowered by the antismoking movement, asked me to stop because smoke bothered him. A few years later there were hardly any social situations left in which it was acceptable to smoke. Even my home was no longer a refuge, since my children were pestering me to quit. And so I did. Now my status as former smoker puts me in company with fully half of all those who have ever smoked regularly and are alive today. For many of us, the deteriorating social environment for smoking made it easier to quit. (Cook, 1993, p. 1750)

Implementing this sort of intervention is beyond the scope of one research investigator or even a consortium of researchers collaborating across many sites. It requires the cooperation of governmental, educational, and even religious institutions. We may need to rethink our approach to preventing drug use and misuse (Tremblay et al., 2020).

Concept Check 11.4

Determine whether you understand how treatments for substance-related disorders work by matching the examples with the following terms: (a) dependent, (b) cross-tolerant, (c) agonist substitution, (d) antagonist, (e) relapse prevention, (f) controlled drinking, (g) aversion therapy, (h) covert sensitization, (i) contingency management, and (j) anonymous.

1. ______________ is a controversial treatment for alcohol misuse because of a negative but flawed experimental finding but also because it conflicts with the belief in total abstinence.
2. Methadone is used to treat heroin addiction with a method called ______________.
3. ______________ drugs block or counteract the effects of psychoactive drugs and are sometimes effective in treating those addicted to substances.
4. In ______________ the clinician and the client work together to decide which behaviors the client needs to change and which reinforcers will be used as rewards for reaching set goals.
5. It has been difficult to evaluate rigorously the effectiveness of Alcoholics Anonymous, because the participants are ______________.
6. In ______________, substance use is paired with something extremely unpleasant (like alcohol and vomiting with Antabuse).
7. Heroin and methadone are ______________, which means they affect the same neurotransmitter receptors.
8. The ______________ model involves therapy that helps individuals remove ambivalence about stopping their drug use by examining their beliefs about the positive and negative aspects of drug use.
9. By imagining unpleasant scenes, the ______________ technique helps the person associate the negative effects of the drug with drug use.
10. Unfortunately, the heroin user may become permanently ______________ on methadone.

Gambling Disorder

Gambling has a long history—for example, dice have been found in Egyptian tombs that are thousands of years old (Greenberg, 2005). It is growing in popularity in this country, and in many places, it is a legal and acceptable form of entertainment. Perhaps as a result, **gambling disorder** affects an increasing number of people, with a lifetime estimate of approximately 1.9% of adult Americans (Rash & Petry, 2015). Research suggests that among pathological gamblers, 14% have lost at least one job, 19% have declared bankruptcy, 32% have been arrested, and 21% have been incarcerated (Gerstein et al., 1999). The DSM-5 criteria for gambling disorder set forth the associated behaviors that characterize people who have this addictive disorder. These include the same pattern of urges we observe in the other substance-related disorders. Note, too, the parallels with substance dependence, with the need to gamble increasing amounts of money over time and the "withdrawal symptoms" such as restlessness and irritability when attempting to stop. These parallels to substance-related disorders led to the recategorization of gambling disorder as an "Addictive Disorder" in DSM-5 (Rash & Petry, 2015).

There is a growing body of research on the nature and treatment of gambling disorder. For example, work is under way to explore the biological origins of the urge to gamble among pathological gamblers. Research in this area and others (such as genetic research) show strong similarities in the biological origins of gambling disorders and substance use disorders. In one study, brain-imaging technology (echoplanar functional magnetic resonance imaging) was used to observe brain function while gamblers observed videotapes of other people gambling (Potenza et al., 2003). A decreased level of activity was observed in those regions of the brain that are involved in impulse regulation when compared with controls, suggesting an interaction between the environmental cues to gamble and the brain's response (which may be to decrease the ability to resist these cues). Studies have found that the ventromedial prefrontal cortex and orbitofrontal cortex ("the executive parts" of the brain) do not function as normal in those with gambling disorder (Pettorruso et al., in press). Poor impulse control and risky decisions are both processes that involve ventromedial prefrontal cortex, and those individuals with higher problems in these areas also show poorer response to treatment and higher relapse rates (Yau, Yip, & Potenza, 2015).

Treatment of gambling problems is difficult. Those with gambling disorder exhibit a combination of characteristics—including denial of the problem, impulsivity, and continuing optimism ("One big win will cover my losses!")—that interfere with effective treatment. Pathological gamblers often experience cravings similar to people who are substance dependent (Hawker, Merkouris, Youssef, & Dowling, 2021). Treatment is often similar to substance dependence treatment, and there is a parallel Gambler's Anonymous that incorporates the same 12-step program we discussed previously. However, the evidence of effectiveness for Gambler's Anonymous suggests that 70% to 90% drop out of these programs and that the desire to quit must be present before intervention (Ashley & Boehlke, 2012). Cognitive-behavioral interventions help reduce the symptoms of gambling disorder. Brief and full course treatments have both been found to help and both are recommended. Given the higher rates of impulsivity of those with these disorder and thus their high dropout rates from treatment, more research is starting to compare the brief versions to the full course ones (Grant et al., 2015).

In addition to gambling disorder being included under the heading of "Addictive Disorders," DSM-5 includes another potentially addictive behavior—"Internet Gaming Disorder"—as a condition for further study (American Psychiatric Association, 2013). There are indications that some individuals are so preoccupied with online games (sometimes in a social context with other players) that a similar pattern of tolerance and withdrawal develops (Taneli, Guo, & Mushtaq, 2015). The goal of including this potentially new category of addictive behavior is to encourage additional research on its nature and treatment.

DSM 5 **Table 11.10**

Diagnostic Criteria for Gambling Disorder

A. Persistent and recurrent problematic gambling behavior leading to clinically significant impairment of distress, as indicated by the individual exhibiting four (or more) of the following in a 12-month period:

1. Needs to gamble with increasing amounts of money in order to achieve the desired excitement.
2. Is restless or irritable when attempting to cut down or stop gambling.
3. Has made repeated unsuccessful efforts to control, cut back, or stop gambling.
4. Is often preoccupied with gambling (e.g., having persistent thoughts of reliving past gambling experiences, handicapping or planning the next venture, or thinking of ways to get money with which to gamble).
5. Often gambles when feeling distressed (e.g., helpless, guilty, anxious, depressed).
6. After losing money gambling, often returns another day to get even ("chasing" one's losses).
7. Lies to conceal the extent of involvement with gambling.
8. Has jeopardized or lost a significant relationship, job, or educational or career opportunity because of gambling.
9. Relies on others to provide money to relieve desperate financial situations caused by gambling.

B. The gambling behavior is not better explained by a manic episode.

Specify current severity:

Mild: 4 to 5 criteria met

Moderate: 6 to 7 criteria met

Severe: 8 to 9 criteria met

American Psychiatric Association. (2022). *Diagnostic and statistical manual of mental disorders* (5th ed., Text Revision).

Impulse-Control Disorders

A number of the disorders we describe in this book start with an irresistible impulse—usually one that will ultimately be harmful to the person affected. Typically, the person experiences increasing tension leading up to the act and, sometimes, pleasurable anticipation of acting on the impulse. For example, eating disorders and the substance-related disorders in this chapter often commence with temptations or desires that are destructive but difficult to resist. DSM-5 includes three additional impulse-control disorders: intermittent explosive disorder, kleptomania, and pyromania (Muresanu, Stan, & Buzoianu, 2012). In *DMS-IV-TR*, gambling disorder was included as an impulse-control disorder, but as we have seen, it is listed as an addictive disorder in DSM-5.

Finally, trichotillomania (hair pulling disorder) was also moved out of this category and is now included under the obsessive compulsive-related disorders (see Chapter 5).

Intermittent Explosive Disorder

People with **intermittent explosive disorder** have episodes in which they act on aggressive impulses that result in serious assaults or destruction of property (Coccaro, 2020; Dahlem et al., 2020). Although it is unfortunately common among the general population to observe aggressive outbursts, when you rule out the influence of other disorders (for example, antisocial personality disorder, borderline personality disorder, a psychotic disorder, and Alzheimer's disease) or substance use, this disorder is not often diagnosed. In a rare but important large study of more than 9,000 people, researchers found that the lifetime prevalence of this disorder was 7.3% (Kessler et al., 2006).

This diagnosis is controversial and has been debated throughout the development of the DSM. One concern, among others, is that by validating a general category that covers aggressive behavior, it may be used as a legal defense—insanity—for all violent crimes (Coccaro, 2020).

Research is at the beginning stages for intermittent explosive disorder and focuses on the brain regions involved as well as the influence of neurotransmitters such as serotonin and norepinephrine and testosterone levels, along with their interaction with psychosocial influences (stress, disrupted family life, and parenting styles). Recent studies have proposed that there is a disruption of the orbital frontal cortex's role ("the executive parts" of the brain) in inhibiting amygdala activation (the "emotional part" of the brain) combined with changes in the serotonin system in those with this disorder (Yau et al., 2015). These and other influences are being examined to explain the origins of this disorder (Coccaro, 2020). Cognitive-behavioral interventions (for example, helping the person identify and avoid "triggers" for aggressive outbursts) and approaches modeled after drug treatments appear the most effective for these individuals, although few controlled studies yet exist (McCloskey, Noblett, Deffenbacher, Gollan, & Coccaro, 2008).

Kleptomania

The story of wealthy actress Winona Ryder stealing $5,500 worth of merchandise from Saks Fifth Avenue in Beverly Hills, California, in December 2001 was as puzzling as it was titillating. Why risk a multimillion-dollar career over some clothes that she could easily afford? Was hers a case of **kleptomania**—a recurrent failure to resist urges to steal things that are not needed for personal use or their monetary value? This disorder appears to be rare, but it is not well studied, partly because of the stigma associated with identifying oneself as acting out this illegal behavior. Some studies suggest that that disorder may be more common in women than in men and that it typically starts in adolescence (Torales, González, Castaldelli-Maia, & Ventriglio, 2020). One study has reported a lifetime prevalence rate of close to 1% in the United States (Grant, 2003). The patterns described by those with this disorder are strikingly similar: The person begins to feel a sense of tension just before stealing, which is followed by feelings of pleasure or relief while the theft is committed (Zerbo & Deringer, 2015). People with kleptomania score high on assessments of impulsivity, reflecting their inability to judge the immediate gratification of stealing compared with the long-term negative consequences (for example, arrest, embarrassment) (Grant & Kim, 2002). Patients with kleptomania often report having no memory (amnesia) about the act of shoplifting (Hollander, Berlin, & Stein, 2009). Brain-imaging research supports these observations, with one study finding damage in areas of the brain associated with poor decision making (inferior frontal regions) (Grant, Correia, & Brennan-Krohn, 2006).

There appears to be high comorbidity between kleptomania and mood disorders and a lesser comorbidity with substance misuse and dependence (Zerbo & Deringer, 2015). Some refer to kleptomania as an "antidepressant" behavior or a reaction on the part of some to relieve unpleasant feelings through stealing (Fishbain, 1987). To date, few reports of treatment exist, and these involve either behavioral interventions or use of antidepressant medication. In one exception, naltrexone—the opioid antagonist used in the treatment of excessive alcohol use—was somewhat effective in reducing the urge to steal in persons diagnosed with kleptomania (Grant, Kim, & Odlaug, 2009).

Pyromania

Just as we know that someone who steals does not necessarily have kleptomania, it is also true that not everyone who sets fires is considered to have **pyromania**—an impulse-control disorder that

Pool/Getty Images

In 2002, actress Winona Ryder was found guilty of shoplifting items worth several thousand dollars from a Beverly Hills department store.

involves having an irresistible urge to set fires. Again, the pattern parallels that of kleptomania, where the person feels a tension or arousal before setting a fire and a sense of gratification or relief while the fire burns. These individuals will also be preoccupied with fires and the associated equipment involved in setting and putting out these fires (Nanayakkara, Ogloff, McEwan, & Ducat, in press). Also rare, pyromania is diagnosed in only about 3% of arsonists (Lindberg, Holi, Tani, & Virkkunen, 2005) because arsonists can include people who set fires for monetary gain or revenge rather than to satisfy a physical or psychological urge. Because so few people are diagnosed with this disorder, research on etiology and treatment is limited (Nanayakkara et al., in press). Research that has been conducted follows the general group of arsonists (of which only a small percentage have pyromania) and examines the role of a family history of fire setting along with comorbid impulse disorders (antisocial personality disorder and alcohol misuse). Treatment is generally cognitive-behavioral and involves helping the person identify the signals that initiate the urges and teaching coping strategies to resist the temptation to start fires (Bumpass, Fagelman, & Brix, 1983; McGrath, Marshall, & Prior, 1979).

Concept Check 11.5

Match the following disorders with their corresponding symptoms: (a) gambling disorder, (b) intermittent explosive disorder, (c) kleptomania, and (d) pyromania.

1. This rarely diagnosed disorder is characterized by episodes of aggressive impulses and can sometimes be treated with cognitive-behavioral interventions, drug treatments, or both. ____________
2. This disorder begins with the person feeling a sense of tension that is released and followed with pleasure after they have committed a robbery. ____________
3. This disorder affects somewhere between 3% and 5% of the adult American population and is characterized by the need to gamble. ____________
4. Individuals with this disorder are preoccupied with fires and the equipment involved in setting and putting out fires. ____________

DSM Controversies: *Are Substance Dependency and Substance Misuse the Same?*

One of the changes to DSM-5 that caused concern among some in the field of substance-related disorders was dropping the distinction between dependence on a substance and misuse of that substance (G. Edwards, 2012; Hasin, 2012; Schuckit, 2012). Although there is general agreement that abusing a substance (such as binge drinking) and being dependent on that substance (such as increasing tolerance to alcohol and going through withdrawal symptoms if drinking is stopped) are different processes, research shows that, practically speaking, they tend to go together. In other words, if someone is routinely abusing a drug, that person will likely become dependent on it (O'Brien, 2011). From a scientific point of view, therefore, there is an obvious difference between misuse and dependence, but from a clinical perspective (which is the main function of the DSM), the argument was made that having these as separate diagnoses was more complicated than was necessary.

In addition, a second major change was the addition of "Addictive Disorder"—specifically, gambling disorder—to the substance-related disorders section. Here again the science suggests that the phenomena are quite similar with both substance-related disorders and gambling disorder showing patterns of dependence, cravings, and working on similar brain pathways (Ashley & Boehlke, 2012). However, this potentially opens up the category for the inclusion of many different kinds of addictive disorders. Other problems that cause real dysfunction among some people include the new DSM-5 disorder under further study—internet gaming disorder (Block, 2008; Van Rooij, Schoenmakers, Vermulst, Van Den Eijnden, & Van De Mheen, 2011) and even tanning addiction (Poorsattar & Hornung, 2010), and they are being taken seriously as similar types of problems. It is likely that many activities have the potential for causing dependence because they activate the reward systems in our brains in much the same way as the substances described. The difference in whether or not they constitute a "disorder" may come back to whether or not they cause the harmful distress that is part of most psychological diagnoses.

Summary

Perspectives on Substance-Related Disorders

- In DSM-5, substance-related and addictive disorders include problems with the use of depressants (alcohol, barbiturates, and benzodiazepines), stimulants (amphetamines, cocaine, nicotine, and caffeine), opiates (heroin, codeine, and morphine), and hallucinogens (cannabis and LSD) as well as gambling.
- Specific diagnoses are further categorized as substance intoxication and substance withdrawal.
- Nonmedical drug use in the United States has declined in recent times, although it continues to cost billions of dollars and seriously impairs the lives of millions of people each year.

Depressants, Stimulants, Opioids, and Hallucinogens

- Depressants are a group of drugs that decrease central nervous system activity. The primary effect is to reduce our levels of physiological arousal and help us relax. Included in this group are alcohol and sedative, hypnotic, and anxiolytic drugs, such as those prescribed for insomnia.
- Stimulants, the most commonly consumed psychoactive drugs, include caffeine (in coffee, chocolate, and many soft drinks), nicotine (in tobacco products such as cigarettes), amphetamines, and cocaine. In contrast to the depressant drugs, stimulants make us more alert and energetic.
- Opiates include opium, morphine, codeine, and heroin; they have a narcotic effect—relieving pain and inducing sleep. The broader term *opioids* is used to refer to the family of substances that includes these opiates and synthetic variations created by chemists (such as methadone) and the similarly acting substances that occur naturally in our brains (enkephalins, beta-endorphins, and dynorphins).
- Hallucinogens essentially change the way the user perceives the world. Sight, sound, feelings, and even smell are distorted, sometimes in dramatic ways, in a person under the influence of drugs such as cannabis and LSD.

Causes and Treatment of Substance-Related Disorders

- Most psychotropic drugs seem to produce positive effects by acting directly or indirectly on the dopaminergic mesolimbic system (the pleasure pathway). In addition, psychosocial factors such as expectations, stress, and cultural practices interact with the biological factors to influence drug use.
- Substance dependence is treated successfully only in a minority of those affected, and the best results reflect the motivation of the drug user and a combination of biological and psychosocial treatments.
- Programs aimed at preventing drug use may have the greatest chance of significantly affecting the drug problem.

Gambling Disorder

- Problem gamblers display the same types of cravings and dependence as persons who have substance-related disorders.
- Similar brain systems appear to be involved with those addicted to gambling as seen in persons with substance-related disorders.

Impulse-Control Disorders

- In DSM-5, impulse-control disorders include three separate disorders: intermittent explosive disorder, kleptomania, and pyromania.

Key Terms

substance-related and addictive disorders, 401
impulse-control disorders, 401
alcohol use disorder, 401
psychoactive substance, 402
substance use, 402
substance intoxication, 402
substance use disorders, 402
physiological dependence, 403
tolerance, 403
withdrawal, 403
substance dependence, 403
depressants, 405
stimulants, 405
opiates, 405
hallucinogens, 405
other commonly misused drugs, 405
gambling disorder, 405
alcohol, 405
alcohol-related disorders, 405
withdrawal delirium (delirium tremens/DTs), 407
Wernicke-Korsakoff syndrome, 407
fetal alcohol syndrome (FAS), 407
alcohol dehydrogenase (ADH), 407
barbiturates, 410
benzodiazepines, 410
amphetamines, 411
amphetamine use disorders, 412
cocaine use disorders, 414
tobacco-related disorders, 416
caffeine use disorders, 418
opioid-related disorders, 418
cannabis (*Cannabis sativa*) (marijuana), 419
cannabis use disorders, 419
LSD (*d*-lysergic acid diethylamide), 421
hallucinogen use disorders, 421
agonist substitution, 432
nicotine, 432
nicotine patch, 432
antagonist drugs, 433
controlled drinking, 434
relapse prevention, 435
gambling disorder, 437
intermittent explosive disorder, 439
kleptomania, 439
pyromania, 439

Answers to Concept Checks

11.1

Part A

1. c; 2. b; 3. d; 4. a

Part B

5. c; 6. d; 7. b; 8. a

11.2

1. False (the use of crack by pregnant mothers adversely affects only some babies); 2. True; 3. True; 4. False (cannabis produces the most variable reactions in people); 5. False (amphetamines are produced in labs); 6. True; 7. False (stimulants occur naturally)

11.3

Part A

1. f; 2. c; 3. d; 4. a; 5. e; 6. b

Part B

7. T; 8. T; 9. F (all have an effect); 10. F (they would still act uninhibited); 11. T

11.4

1. f; 2. c; 3. d; 4. i; 5. j; 6. g; 7. b; 8. e; 9. h; 10. a

11.5

1. b; 2. c; 3. a; 4. d

Exploring Substance Use Disorders

- Many kinds of problems can develop when people use and abuse substances that alter the way they think, feel, and behave.
- Once seen as due to personal weakness, drug abuse and dependence are now thought influenced by both biological and psychosocial factors.

Trigger

Social influences

- Exposure to drugs—through media, peers, parents, or lack of parental monitoring—versus no exposure to drugs
- Social expectations and cultural norms for use
- Family/culture/society and peers (all or some) supportive versus unsupportive of drug use

Psychological influences

Not to use:

- Fear of effects of drug use
- Decision not to use drugs
- Feeling of confidence and self-esteem without drug use

To use:

- Drug use for pleasure; association with "feeling good" (positive reinforcement)
- Drug use to avoid pain and escape unpleasantness by "numbing out" (negative reinforcement)
- Feeling of being in control
- Positive expectations/urges about what drug use will be like
- Avoidance of withdrawal symptoms
- Presence of other psychological disorders: mood anxiety, etc.

Causes

Drug use and drug abuse

Biological influences

- Inherited genetic vulnerability affects:
  - Body's sensitivity to drug (ADH gene)
  - Body's ability to metabolize drug (presence of specific enzymes in liver)
- Drugs activate natural reward center ("pleasure pathway") in brain
- Neuroplasticity increases drug-seeking and relapse

TREATMENT: BEST TO USE MULTIPLE APPROACHES

Psychosocial treatments

- Aversion therapy—to create negative associations with drug use (shocks with drinking, imagining nausea with cocaine use)
- Contingency management to change behaviors by rewarding chosen behaviors
- Alcoholics Anonymous and its variations
- Inpatient hospital treatment (can be expensive)
- Controlled use
- Community reinforcement
- Relapse prevention

Biological treatments

- Agonist substitution
  - Replacing one drug with a similar one (methadone for heroin, nicotine gum and patches for cigarettes)
- Antagonist substitution
  - Blocking one drug's effect with another drug (naltrexone for opiates and alcohol)
- Aversive treatments
  - Making taking drug very unpleasant (using Antabuse, which causes nausea and vomiting when mixed with alcohol, to treat alcoholism)
- Drugs to help recovering person deal with withdrawal symptoms (clonidine for opiate withdrawal, sedatives for alcohol, etc.)

TYPES OF DRUGS

	Examples	Effects
Depressants	Alcohol, barbiturates (sedatives: Amytal, Seconal, Nembutal), benzodiazepines (antianxiety: Valium, Xanax, Halcion)	■ Decreased central nervous system activity ■ Reduced levels of body arousal ■ Relaxation
Stimulants	Amphetamines, cocaine, nicotine, caffeine	■ Increased physical arousal ■ User feels more alert and energetic
Opiates	Heroin, morphine, codeine	■ Narcotic—reduce pain and induce sleep and euphoria by mirroring opiates in the brain (endorphins, etc.)
Hallucinogens	Cannabis, LSD, Ecstasy	■ Altered mental and emotional perception ■ Distortion (sometimes dramatic) of sensory perceptions

Exploring Impulse-Control Disorders

Characterized by inability to resist acting on a drive or temptation. Sufferers often perceived by society as having a problem simply due to a lack of "will."

TYPES OF IMPULSE-CONTROL DISORDERS

Disorder		Characteristics	Treatment
Intermittent Explosive	 Ollyy/Shutterstock.com	■ Acting on aggressive impulses that result in assaults or destruction of property ■ Current research is focused on how neurotransmitters and testosterone levels interact with psychosocial influences (stress, parenting styles)	Cognitive-behavioral interventions (helping person identify and avoid triggers for aggressive outbursts) and approaches modeled after drug treatments appear most effective
Kleptomania	 Robert Kneschke/Shutterstock.com	■ Recurring failure to resist urges to steal unneeded items ■ Feeling tense just before stealing, followed by feelings of pleasure or relief when committing the theft ■ High comorbidity with mood disorders and, to a lesser degree, with substance abuse/dependence	Behavioral interventions or antidepressant medication
Pyromania	 Dale A Stork/Shutterstock.com	■ Irresistible urge to set fires ■ Feeling aroused prior to setting fire then a sense of gratification or relief while the fire burns ■ Rare; diagnosed in less than 4% of arsonists	Cognitive-behavioral interventions (helping person identify signals triggering urges, and teaching coping strategies to resist setting fires)

12 Personality Disorders

lunamarina/Shutterstock.com

Learning Objectives

LO12.1 Distinguish personality disorders from other forms of psychopathology according to their key features as described in DSM-5.

LO12.2 Discuss how individuals with schizoid personality disorder differ from those with schizotypal personality disorder.

LO12.3 Contrast antisocial personality disorder with the related concept of psychopathy.

LO12.4 Identify the key symptoms involved in the presentation of borderline personality disorder.

LO12.5 Differentiate obsessive-compulsive personality disorder from obsessive-compulsive disorder.

LO12.6 Explain how the difficulties of treating personality disorders impact treatment prognosis.

An Overview of Personality Disorders

We all think we know what a personality is. It is all the characteristic ways a person behaves and thinks: "Rafael tends to be shy"; "Kai likes to be dramatic"; "Juan is always suspicious of others"; "Luna is outgoing"; "Bruce seems to be sensitive and gets upset easily over minor things"; "Sean has the personality of an eggplant!" We tend to type people as behaving in one way in many situations. For example, like Rafael, many of us are shy with people we do not know, but we will not be shy around our friends. A truly shy person is shy even among people they have known for some time. The shyness is part of the way the person behaves in most situations. We also have all probably behaved in all the other ways noted here (dramatic, suspicious, outgoing, easily upset). However, when personality characteristics interfere with relationships with others, cause the person distress, or in general disrupt activities of daily living, we consider these to be "personality disorders" (Skodol, 2012). In this chapter, we look at characteristic ways of behaving in relation to a number of specific personality disorders. First, we examine how we conceptualize personality disorders and the issues related to them; then we describe the disorders themselves.

Aspects of Personality Disorders

What if a person's characteristic ways of thinking and behaving cause significant distress to the self or others? What if the person cannot change this way of relating to the world and is unhappy? We might consider this person to have a personality disorder. Unlike many of the disorders we have already discussed, personality disorders are chronic; they do not come and go but originate in childhood and continue throughout adulthood (Hopwood et al., 2018). Because these chronic problems affect personality, they pervade every aspect of a person's life. For example, if a woman is overly suspicious (a sign of a possible paranoid personality disorder), this trait will affect almost everything she does, including her employment (she may change jobs often if she believes coworkers conspire against her), her relationships (she may not be able to sustain a lasting relationship if she can't trust anyone), and even her living situation (she may move often if she suspects her landlords are out to get her).

A **personality disorder** is a persistent pattern of emotions, cognitions, and behavior that results in enduring emotional distress for the person affected and/or for others and may cause difficulties with work and relationships (American Psychiatric Association, 2013). DSM-5 notes that having a personality disorder may distress the affected person. Individuals with personality disorders may not feel any subjective distress, however, and others may be the ones who acutely feel distress because of the actions of the person with the disorder. This is particularly common with antisocial personality disorder because the individual may show a blatant disregard for the rights of others and yet exhibit no remorse (DeLisi, Drury, & Elbert, 2019). In certain cases, someone other than the person with the personality disorder must decide whether the disorder is causing significant functional impairment because the affected person often cannot make such a judgment.

DSM-5 lists 10 specific personality disorders. Although the prospects for treatment success for people who have personality disorders may be more optimistic than previously thought (Choi-Kain & Gunderson, 2019; DeLisi et al., 2019), unfortunately, as you will see later, many people who have personality disorders in addition to other psychological problems (for example, major depression) tend to do poorly in treatment. One factor important to the success (or lack of success) of treatment is how the therapist feels about the client. The emotions of therapists brought out by clients (called "countertransference" by Sigmund Freud) tend to be negative for those diagnosed with personality disorders, especially those (as you will see next) in Cluster A (the odd or eccentric cluster) and Cluster B (the dramatic, emotional, or erratic cluster) (Michaud et al., 2020). Therapists especially need to guard against letting their personal feelings interfere with treatment when working with people who have personality disorders.

Prior to DSM-5, most disorders we discuss in this book were in Axis I of the DSM-IV-TR, which included the traditional disorders. The personality disorders were included in a separate axis, Axis II, because as a group they were seen as distinct. It was thought that the characteristic traits were more ingrained and inflexible in people who have personality disorders, and the disorders themselves were less likely to be successfully modified. With the changes made with DSM-5, these separate axes were eliminated, and now the personality disorders are listed with the rest of the DSM-5 disorders (American Psychiatric Association, 2013).

You may be surprised to learn that the category of personality disorders is controversial because it involves a number of unresolved issues. Examining these issues can help you understand all the disorders described in this book.

Categorical and Dimensional Models

Most of us are sometimes suspicious of others and a little paranoid, overly dramatic, too self-involved, or reclusive. Fortunately, these characteristics do not last long or are not overly intense; they have not significantly impaired how we live and work. People with personality disorders, however, display problem characteristics over extended periods and in many situations, which can cause great emotional pain for themselves, others, or both (Widiger, 2012). Their difficulty, then, can be seen as one of *degree* rather than *kind.* In other words, the problems of people with personality disorders may just be extreme versions of the problems many of us experience temporarily, such as being shy or suspicious (Hopwood et al., 2018).

The distinction between problems of degree and problems of kind is usually described in terms of *dimensions* instead of *categories.* The issue that continues to be debated in the field is whether personality disorders are extreme versions of otherwise typical personality variations (dimensions) or ways of relating that are different from psychologically healthy behavior (categories) (Skodol, 2012). You can see the difference between dimensions and categories in everyday life. For example, society tends to look at gender categorically. Society views people as being "male" or "female," despite other gender categories existing. Yet many believe it is more accurate to look at gender in terms of dimensions. For example, we know that gender identity can include a range of choices in "masculine" or "feminine" expressions (for example, clothing, body modifications, and personal grooming). We could just as easily place people along a continuum of masculine and feminine rather than in the absolute categories of male or female. A continuum includes those who do not view their gender expression or identity in terms of categories of "male" or "female." We also often label people's size categorically, as tall, average, or short. But height, too, can be viewed dimensionally, in inches or centimeters.

Many researchers and clinicians in this field see personality disorders as extremes on one or more personality dimensions. Yet because of the way people are diagnosed with the DSM, the personality disorders—like most other disorders—end up being viewed in categories. You have two choices—either you do ("yes") or you do not ("no") have a disorder. For example, either you have antisocial personality disorder or you do not. DSM diagnoses do not rate how dependent you are; if you meet the criteria, you are labeled as having dependent personality disorder. There is no "somewhat" when it comes to personality disorders.

To begin to address the personality dimensions, the DSM-5 Alternative Model of Personality Disorders (AMPD) was created in a different section of DSM (Section III, Emerging Measures and Models). A similar decision was made for the international version of the DSM—the World Health Organization's *International Statistical Classification of Diseases and Related Health Problems*, 11th version (ICD-11) (Bach, Christensen, Kongerslev, Sellbom, & Simonsen, 2020). The DSM-5 and the ICD-11 classification of personality disorders (PD) are largely commensurate, and, when combined, they delineate six trait domains: negative affectivity, detachment, antagonism/dissociality, disinhibition, anankastia, and psychoticism (Bach et al., 2020). More work on the usefulness of these alternatives is necessary to evaluate these alternatives.

There are advantages to using categorical models of behavior, the most important being their convenience. With simplification, however, come problems. One is that the mere act of using categories leads clinicians to reify them; that is, to view disorders as real "things," comparable to the realness of an infection or a broken arm. Some argue that personality disorders are not things that exist but points at which society decides a particular way of relating to the world has become a problem. There is the important unresolved issue again: Are personality disorders just an extreme variant of normal personality, or are they distinctly different disorders?

Some have proposed that the DSM-5 personality disorders section be replaced or at least supplemented by a dimensional model (Hopwood et al., 2018) in which individuals would not only be given categorical diagnoses but also would be rated on a series of personality dimensions. Widiger and colleagues (Widiger & Simonsen, 2005; Widiger & Trull, 2007; Widiger, 2011) have argued for decades that such a system would have at least three advantages over a purely categorical system: (1) It would retain more information about each individual, (2) it would be more flexible because it would permit both categorical and dimensional differentiations among individuals, and (3) it would avoid the often arbitrary decisions involved in assigning a person to a diagnostic category. Currently, there is an alternative model of personality disorders included in the section on "emerging measures and models" in DSM-5 that is included for further study (American Psychiatric Association, 2013). This model focuses on a continuum of disturbances of "self" (that is, how you view yourself and your ability to be self-directed) and interpersonal (that is, your ability to empathize and be intimate with others) functioning. It remains to be seen how this alternative model will be used in the future.

Although no general consensus exists about what the basic personality dimensions might be, there are several contenders (South et al., 2011). One of the more widely accepted is called the *five-factor model,* or the "Big Five," and is taken from work on normal personality (Hopwood & Thomas, 2012; McCrae & Costa Jr., 2008). In this model, people can be rated on a series of personality dimensions, and the combination of five components describes why people are so different. The five factors or dimensions are *extroversion* (talkative, assertive, and active versus silent, passive, and reserved); *agreeableness* (kind, trusting, and warm versus hostile, selfish, and mistrustful); *conscientiousness* (organized, thorough, and reliable versus careless, negligent, and unreliable); *neuroticism* (even-tempered versus nervous, moody, and temperamental); and *openness to experience* (imaginative, curious, and creative versus shallow and imperceptive) (Oltmanns & Widiger, 2020). On each dimension, people are rated high, low, or somewhere between.

Cross-cultural research establishes the relatively universal nature of the five dimensions—although there are individual differences across cultures (Valchev et al., 2013; Carlo, Knight, Roesch, Opal, & Davis, 2014). One study examined Big Five traits in high school students across six different cultures and found, for example, that young adults in Turkey reported higher levels of conscientiousness and extraversion than those in China, whereas students in Taiwan reported about as much openness as those in Slovenia (Vazsonyi, Ksinan, Mikuška, & Jiskrova, 2015). A number of researchers are trying to determine whether people with personality disorders can also be rated in a meaningful way along the Big Five dimensions and whether the system will help us better understand these disorders (Oltmanns & Widiger, 2020).

Personality Disorder Clusters

DSM-5 divides the personality disorders into three groups, or clusters; this will probably continue until a strong scientific basis is established for viewing them differently (American Psychiatric Association, 2013) (see Table 12.1). The cluster division is based on resemblance (Arbanas, 2021). Cluster A is called the odd or eccentric cluster; it includes paranoid, schizoid, and schizotypal personality disorders. Cluster B is the dramatic, emotional, or erratic cluster; it consists of antisocial, borderline, histrionic, and narcissistic personality disorders. Cluster C is the anxious or fearful cluster; it includes avoidant, dependent, and obsessive-compulsive personality disorders. We follow this order in our review.

Statistics and Development

Because many people with these problems do not seek help on their own as do those with many of the other DSM-5 disorders, gathering information about the prevalence of personality disorders is difficult and therefore varies a great deal. An important population survey suggests that as many as 1 in 10 adults in the United States may have a diagnosable personality disorder (Lenzenweger, Lane, Loranger, & Kessler, 2007), which makes them relatively common (see Table 12.2). In a Danish study, 11.3% of a community sample met the screening criteria for a personality disorder, which was slightly higher for woman and younger people (Bach, Kongerslev, & Simonsen, 2020). Numbers vary somewhat across countries, but worldwide about 6% of adults may have at least one personality disorder (Huang et al., 2009). Differences in prevalence estimates may be the result of different survey methods: surveying people in clinical settings versus surveying the general population—even those not seeking assistance (Torgersen, 2012). Similarly, gender differences in the disorders—for example, more women were diagnosed with borderline personality disorder, and more men identified with antisocial personality disorder—are highly variable when surveying the general population. There may be several reasons for these differences in diagnoses, including bias in diagnoses and differences in help-seeking behavior and tolerance of behavior in a culture. We discuss several of these concerns later in the chapter.

Table 12.1 Personality Disorders

Personality Disorder	Description
Cluster A: Odd or Eccentric Disorders	
Paranoid personality disorder	A pervasive distrust and suspiciousness of others such that their motives are interpreted as malevolent
Schizoid personality disorder	A pervasive pattern of detachment from social relationships and a restricted range of expression of emotions in interpersonal settings
Schizotypal personality disorder	A pervasive pattern of social and interpersonal deficits marked by acute discomfort with reduced capacity for close relationships, as well as by cognitive or perceptual distortions and eccentricities of behavior
Cluster B: Dramatic, Emotional, or Erratic Disorders	
Antisocial personality disorder	A pervasive pattern of disregard for and violation of the rights of others
Borderline personality disorder	A pervasive pattern of instability of interpersonal relationships, self-image, affects, and control over impulses
Histrionic personality disorder	A pervasive pattern of excessive emotion and attention seeking
Narcissistic personality disorder	A pervasive pattern of grandiosity (in fantasy or behavior), need for admiration, and lack of empathy
Cluster C: Anxious or Fearful Disorders	
Avoidant personality disorder	A pervasive pattern of social inhibition, feelings of inadequacy, and hypersensitivity to negative evaluation
Dependent personality disorder	A pervasive and excessive need to be taken care of, which leads to submissive and clinging behavior and fears of separation
Obsessive-compulsive personality disorder	A pervasive pattern of preoccupation with orderliness, perfectionism, and mental and interpersonal control, at the expense of flexibility, openness, and efficiency

Source: Reprinted, with permission, from American Psychiatric Association, 2013, *Diagnostic and statistical manual of mental disorders* (5th ed.). © 2013 American Psychiatric Association.

Table 12.2 Statistics and Development of Personality Disorders

Disorder	Prevalence*	Gender Differences*	Course
Paranoid personality disorder	In the clinical population: 6.3%–9.6% In the general population: 1.5%–1.8%	Approximately equal among men and women	Insufficient information
Schizoid personality disorder	In the clinical population: 1.4%–1.9% In the general population: 0.9%–1.2%	Slightly more common among men	Insufficient information
Schizotypal personality disorder	In the clinical population: 6.4%–5.7% In the general population: 0.7%–1.1%	Slightly more common among men	Chronic; some go on to develop schizophrenia
Antisocial personality disorder	In the clinical population: 3.9%–5.9% In the general population: 1.0%–1.8%	Much more common among men	Dissipates after age 40 (Hare, McPherson, & Forth, 1988)
Borderline personality disorder	In the clinical population: 28.5% In the general population: 1.4%–1.6%	Approximately equal among men and women	Symptoms gradually improve if individuals survive into their 30s (Zanarini et al., 2006); approximately 6% die by suicide (Perry, 1993)
Histrionic personality disorder	In the clinical population: 8.0%–9.7% In the general population: 1.2%–1.3%	Slightly more common among women	Chronic
Narcissistic personality disorder	In the clinical population: 5.1%–10.1% In the general population: 0.1%–0.8%	Slightly more common among men	May improve over time (Cooper & Ronningstam, 1992; Gunderson, Ronningstam, & Smith, 1991)
Avoidant personality disorder	In the clinical population: 21.5%–24.6% In the general population: 1.4%–2.5%	Slightly more common among women	Insufficient information
Dependent personality disorder	In the clinical population: 13.0%–15.0% In the general population: 0.9%–1.0%	Much more common among women	Insufficient information
Obsessive-compulsive personality disorder	In the clinical population: 6.1%–10.5% In the general population: 1.9%–2.1%	Slightly more common among men	Insufficient information

*Population data and gender data reported in S. Torgersen, 2012, Epidemiology, in T. A. Widiger (Ed.), *The Oxford handbook of personality disorders* (pp. 186–205), Oxford University Press.

Personality disorders were thought to originate in childhood and continue into the adult years (Cloninger & Svakic, 2009). More sophisticated analyses suggest that personality disorders can remit over time (Zanarini, Frankenburg, Hennen & Silk, 2006, 2014); however, they may be replaced by other symptoms (Martino et al., 2020). In other words, a person could receive a diagnosis of one personality disorder at one point in time and then years later no longer meet the criteria for their original problem but now have characteristics of a second (or third) personality disorder. Our relative lack of information about such important features of personality disorders as their developmental course is a repeating theme. The gaps in our knowledge of the course of about half these disorders are visible in Table 12.2. One reason for this dearth of research is that many individuals seek treatment not in the early developmental phases of their disorder but only after years of distress. This makes it difficult to study people with personality disorders from the beginning, although a few research studies have helped us understand the development of several disorders (Hecht, Cicchetti, Rogosch, & Crick, 2014).

People with borderline personality disorder are characterized by their volatile and unstable relationships; they tend to have persistent problems in early adulthood, with frequent hospitalizations, unstable personal relationships, severe depression, and suicidal gestures. Individuals with borderline personality disorder die by suicide at a rate about 50 times higher than the general population, with most research suggesting that 8% to 10% of patients with this illness have taken their own lives (Gunderson, 2011;

Björkenstam, Björkenstam, Holm, Gerdin, & Ekselius, 2015). On the bright side, their symptoms gradually improve if they survive into their 30s (Zanarini et al., 2006, 2014), although elderly individuals may still experience higher than average interpersonal difficulties (Powers, Gleason, & Oltmanns, 2013). People with antisocial personality disorder display a characteristic disregard for the rights and feelings of others; they tend to continue their destructive behaviors of lying and manipulation through adulthood. Fortunately, some tend to "burn out" in middle adulthood, reflected in a decline in the prevalence of antisocial personality disorder across the lifespan (Vachon et al., 2013). As a group, however, the problems of people with personality disorders continue, as shown when researchers follow their progress over the years (Torgersen, 2012).

Gender Differences

Men diagnosed with a personality disorder tend to display traits characterized as more aggressive, structured, self-assertive, and detached, and women tend to present with characteristics that are more submissive, emotional, and insecure (Torgersen, 2012). It is not surprising, then, that antisocial personality disorder is present more often in males and dependent personality disorder more often in females. Historically, histrionic and borderline personality disorders were identified by clinicians more often in women (Dulit, Marin, & Frances, 1993; Stone, 1993), but according to more recent studies of their prevalence in the general population, equal numbers of males and females may have histrionic and borderline personality disorders (see Table 12.2). If this observation holds up in future studies, why have these disorders been predominantly diagnosed among females in general clinical practice and in other studies?

Do the disparities indicate differences between men and women in certain basic experiences that are genetic, sociocultural, or both, or do they represent biases on the part of the clinicians who make the diagnoses? Take, for example, a classic study by Maureen Ford and Thomas Widiger (1989), who sent fictitious case histories to clinical psychologists for diagnosis. One case described a person with *antisocial personality disorder,* which is characterized by irresponsible and reckless behavior and usually diagnosed in males; the other case described a person with *histrionic personality disorder,* which is characterized by excessive emotionality and attention seeking and more often diagnosed in females. The subject was identified as male in some versions of each case and as female in others, although everything else was identical. As the graph in ■ Figure 12.1 shows, when the antisocial personality disorder case was labeled male, most psychologists gave the correct diagnosis. When the same case of antisocial personality disorder was labeled female, however, most psychologists diagnosed it as histrionic personality disorder rather than antisocial personality disorder. In the case of histrionic personality disorder, being labeled a woman increased the likelihood of that diagnosis.

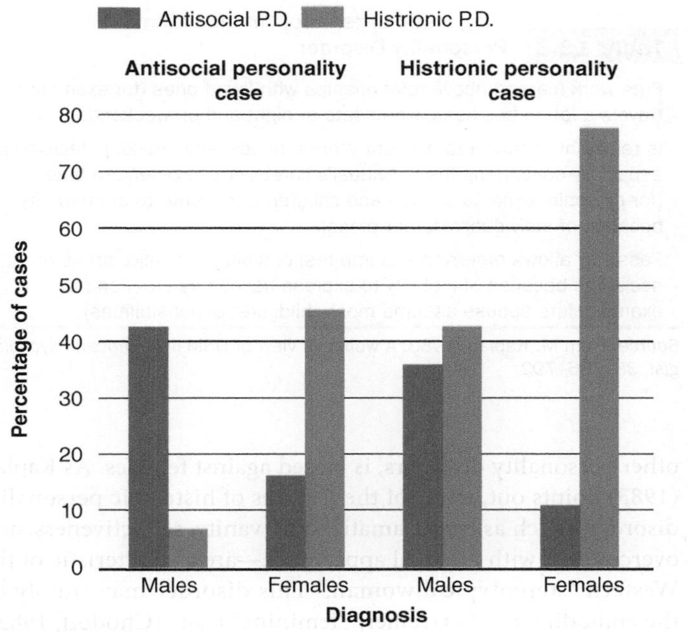

Figure 12.1

Gender bias in diagnosing personality disorders (P.D.). Data are shown for the percentage of cases clinicians rated as antisocial personality disorder or histrionic personality disorder, depending on whether the case was described as a male or a female. From M. R. Ford & T. A. Widiger, 1989, Sex bias in the diagnosis of histrionic and antisocial personality disorders, *Journal of Consulting and Clinical Psychology, 57,* 301–305.

Ford and Widiger (1989) concluded that the psychologists incorrectly diagnosed more women as having histrionic personality disorder.

This gender difference in diagnosis has also been criticized by other authors (see, for example, Kaplan, 1983) on the grounds that histrionic personality disorder, like several of the

SolStock/E+/Getty Images

Personality disorders tend to begin in childhood.

Table 12.3 Diagnostic Criteria for "Independent" Personality Disorder

Puts work (career) above relationships with loved ones (for example, travels a lot on business, works late at night and on weekends)
Is reluctant to take into account others' needs when making decisions, especially concerning the individual's career or use of leisure time (for example, expects spouse and children to relocate to another city because of individual's career plans)
Passively allows others to assume responsibility for major areas of social life because of inability to express necessary emotion (for example, lets spouse assume most childcare responsibilities)

Source: From M. Kaplan, 1983, A woman's view of DSM-III, *American Psychologist, 38,* 786–792.

other personality disorders, is biased against females. As Kaplan (1983) points out, many of the features of histrionic personality disorder—such as overdramatization, vanity, seductiveness, and overconcern with physical appearance—are characteristic of the Western "stereotypical woman." This disorder may simply be the embodiment of extremely "feminine" traits (Chodoff, 1982); branding such an individual mentally ill, according to Kaplan, reflects society's inherent bias against females. (See Table 12.3 for a humorous take on a male version of a personality disorder.) Interestingly, the "macho" personality (Mosher & Sirkin, 1984), in which the individual possesses stereotypically masculine traits, is nowhere to be found in the DSM.

The issue of gender bias in diagnosing personality disorder remains highly controversial (Masuda, Qina'au, Juberg, & Martin, 2020). Remember, however, that just because certain disorders are observed more in men or women does not necessarily indicate bias (Lilienfeld, VanValkenburg, Larntz, & Akiskal, 1986). When it is present, bias can occur at different stages of the diagnostic process. Widiger and Spitzer (1991) point out that the criteria for the disorder may themselves be biased *(criterion gender bias),* or the assessment measures and the way they are used may be biased *(assessment gender bias).* In general, the criteria themselves do not appear to have strong gender bias, although there may be some tendency for clinicians to use their own bias when using the criteria and therefore diagnose males and females differently (Oltmanns & Powers, 2012). As studies continue, researchers will try to make the diagnosis of personality disorders more accurate with respect to gender and more useful to clinicians.

Comorbidity

Looking at Table 12.2 and adding up the prevalence rates across the personality disorders, you might conclude that up to 25% of all people are affected. In fact, the percentage of people in the population with a personality disorder is likely closer to 10% (Huang et al., 2009; Lenzenweger et al., 2007). What accounts for this discrepancy? A major concern with the personality disorders is that people tend to be diagnosed with more than one. The term *comorbidity* historically describes the condition in which a person has multiple diseases (Caron & Rutter, 1991). A fair amount of disagreement is ongoing about whether the term should be used with psychological disorders because of the frequent overlap

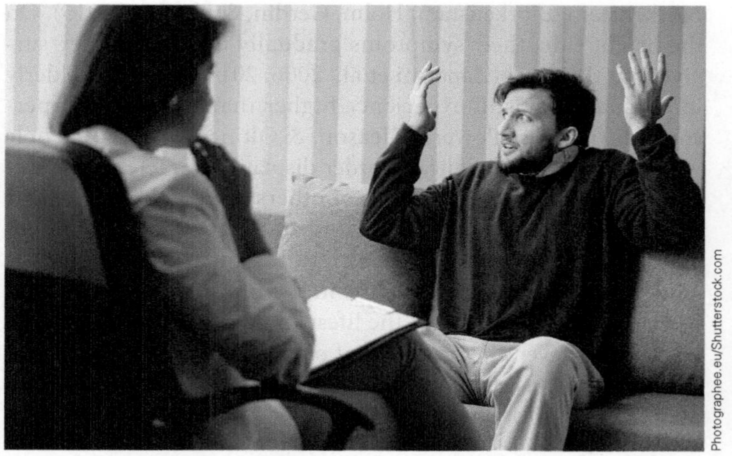

Gender bias may affect the diagnosis of clinicians who associate certain behavioral characteristics with certain sexes.

of different disorders (Skodol, 2005). In just one example, Zimmerman, Rothschild, and Chelminski (2005) conducted a study of 859 psychiatric outpatients and assessed how many had one or more personality disorders. Table 12.4 shows the odds that a person with a particular personality disorder would also meet the criteria for other disorders. For example, a person identified with borderline personality disorder is also likely to receive diagnoses of paranoid, schizotypal, antisocial, narcissistic, avoidant, or dependent personality disorders.

Do people really tend to have more than one personality disorder? Are the ways we define these disorders inaccurate, and do we need to improve our definitions so that they do not overlap? Or did we divide the disorders in the wrong way, and do we need to rethink the categories? Complicating this issue is the phenomenon that people will change diagnoses over time (Bangash, 2020). Such questions about comorbidity are just a few of the important issues faced by researchers who study personality disorders.

Personality Disorders under Study

We started this chapter by noting difficulties in categorizing personality disorders. For example, there is much overlap of the categories, which suggests there may be other ways to arrange these pervasive difficulties of character. It shouldn't surprise you to learn that other personality disorders have been studied for inclusion in the DSM—for example, sadistic personality disorder, which includes people who receive pleasure by inflicting pain on others (Gunay-Oge, Pehlivan, & Isikli, 2020), and passive-aggressive personality disorder, which includes people who are defiant and refuse to cooperate with requests—attempting to undermine authority figures (Lewis, Ridenour, Pitman, & Roche, 2020). The existence of these disorders as distinct personality disorders remains controversial, however, so they were not included in DSM-5 (Wetzler & Jose, 2012).

We now review the personality disorders currently in DSM-5, 10 in all. Table 12.5 provides a simplified look at how people with different personality disorders view the world.

Table 12.4 Diagnostic Overlap of Personality Disorders

Odds Ratio† of People Qualifying for Other Personality Disorder Diagnoses										
Diagnosis	**Paranoid**	**Schizoid**	**Schizotypal**	**Antisocial**	**Borderline**	**Histrionic**	**Narcissistic**	**Avoidant**	**Dependent**	**Obsessive-Compulsive**
Paranoid		2.1	37.3*	2.6	12.3*	0.9	8.7*	4.0*	0.9	5.2*
Schizoid	2.1		19.2	1.1	2.0	3.9	1.7	12.3*	2.9	5.5*
Schizotypal	37.3*	19.2		2.7	15.2*	9.4	11.0	3.9*	7.0	7.1
Antisocial	2.6	1.1	2.7		9.5*	8.1*	14.0*	0.9	5.6	0.2
Borderline	12.3*	2.0	15.2*	9.5*		2.8	7.1*	2.5*	7.3*	2.0
Histrionic	0.9	3.9	9.4	8.1*	2.8		13.2*	0.3	9.5	1.3
Narcissistic	8.7*	1.7	11.0	14.0*	7.1*	13.2*		0.3	4.0	3.7*
Avoidant	4.0*	12.3*	3.9*	0.9	2.5*	0.3	0.3		2.0	2.7
Dependent	0.9	2.9	7.0	5.6	7.3*	9.5	4.0	2.0		0.9
Obsessive-compulsive	5.2*	5.5*	7.1	0.2	2.0	1.3	2.0	2.7	0.9	

†The "odds ratio" indicates how likely it is that a person would have both disorders. The odds ratios with an asterisk (*) indicate that, statistically, people are likely to be diagnosed with both disorders—with a higher number meaning people are more likely to have both. Some higher odds ratios are not statistically significant because the number of people with the disorder in this study was relatively small.

Source: Reprinted, with permission, from M. Zimmerman, L. Rothschild, & I. Chelminski, 2005, The prevalence of DSM-IV personality disorders in psychiatric outpatients, *American Journal of Psychiatry, 162,* 1911–1918. © 2005 American Psychiatric Association.

Concept Check 12.1

Fill in the blanks to complete the following statements about personality disorders.

1. ____________ refers to meeting diagnostic criteria for multiple disorders, which is particularly common among individuals with personality disorders.
2. The personality disorders are divided into three clusters or groups: ____________ contains the odd or eccentric disorders; ____________ contains the dramatic, emotional, and erratic disorders; and ____________ contains the anxious and fearful disorders.
3. It's debated whether personality disorders are extreme versions of otherwise normal personality variations (therefore classified as dimensions) or ways of relating that are different from psychologically healthy behavior (classified as ____________).
4. Personality disorders are described as ____________ because unlike many disorders, they originate in childhood and continue throughout adulthood.
5. Although gender differences are evident in the research of personality disorders, some differences in the findings may be the result of ____________.

Table 12.5 Main Beliefs Associated with Specific Personality Disorders

Personality Disorder	Main Belief
Paranoid	I cannot trust people.
Schizotypal	It's better to be isolated from others.
Schizoid	Relationships are messy, undesirable.
Histrionic	People are there to serve or admire me.
Narcissistic	Since I am special, I deserve special rules.
Borderline	I deserve to be punished.
Antisocial	I am entitled to break rules.
Avoidant	If people knew the "real" me, they would reject me.
Dependent	I need people to survive, be happy.
Obsessive-compulsive	People should do better, try harder.

Source: Reprinted with permission from J. Lobbestael & A. Arntz, 2012, Cognitive contributions to personality disorders, in T. A. Widiger (Ed.), *The Oxford handbook of personality disorders* (p. 326), Oxford University Press.

Cluster A Personality Disorders

Three personality disorders—paranoid, schizoid, and schizotypal—share common features that resemble some of the psychotic symptoms seen in schizophrenia. These odd or eccentric personality disorders are described next.

Paranoid Personality Disorder

Although it is probably adaptive to be a little wary of other people and their motives, being too distrustful can interfere with making friends, working with others, and, in general, getting through daily interactions in a functional way. People with **paranoid personality disorder** are excessively mistrustful and suspicious of others, without any justification. They assume other people are out to harm or trick them; therefore, they tend not to confide in others. Consider the case of Jake.

Clinical Description

The defining characteristic of people with paranoid personality disorder is a pervasive unjustified distrust (Wong, 2020). Certainly, there may be times when someone is deceitful and "out to get you"; however, people with paranoid personality disorder are suspicious in situations in which most other people would agree their suspicions are unfounded. Even events that have nothing to do with them are interpreted as personal attacks (Lewis & Ridenour, 2020). These people would view a neighbor's barking dog or a delayed airline flight as a deliberate attempt to annoy them. Unfortunately, such mistrust often extends to people close to them and makes meaningful relationships difficult. Imagine what a lonely existence this must be. Suspiciousness and mistrust can show themselves in a number of ways. People with paranoid personality disorder may be argumentative, may complain, or may be quiet. This style of interaction is communicated, sometimes nonverbally, to others, often resulting in discomfort among those who come in contact with them because of this volatility. These individuals are sensitive to criticism and have an excessive need for autonomy (American Psychiatric Association, 2013). Having this disorder increases the risk of attempts to take their life and violent behavior, and these people tend to have a poor overall quality of life (Wong, 2020).

Causes

Evidence for biological contributions to paranoid personality disorder is limited. Some research suggests the disorder may be slightly more common among the relatives of people who have

Jake... Research Victim

Jake grew up in a middle-class neighborhood, and although he never got in serious trouble, he had a reputation in high school for arguing with teachers and classmates. After high school, he enrolled in the local community college, but he flunked out after the first year. Jake's lack of success in school was partly attributable to his failure to take responsibility for his poor grades. He began to develop conspiracy theories about fellow students and professors, believing they worked together to see him fail. Jake bounced from job to job, each time complaining that his employer was spying on him at work and at home.

At age 25—and against his parents' wishes—he moved out of his parents' home to a small town out of state. Unfortunately, the letters Jake wrote home daily confirmed his parents' worst fears. He was becoming increasingly preoccupied with theories about people who were out to harm him. Jake spent enormous amounts of time on his computer, exploring websites, and he developed an elaborate theory about how research had been performed on him in childhood. His letters home described his belief that researchers working with the CIA drugged him as a child and implanted something in his ear that emitted microwaves. These microwaves, he believed, were being used to cause him to develop cancer.

Over 2 years, he became increasingly preoccupied with this theory, writing letters to various authorities trying to convince them he was being slowly killed. After he threatened harm to some local college administrators, his parents were contacted, and they brought him to a psychologist who diagnosed him with paranoid personality disorder and major depression.

DSM 5 Table 12.1

Diagnostic Criteria for Paranoid Personality Disorder

A. A pervasive distrust and suspiciousness of others such that their motives are interpreted as malevolent, beginning by early adulthood and present in a variety of contexts, as indicated by four (or more) of the following:

1. Suspects, without sufficient basis, that others are exploiting, harming, or deceiving him or her.
2. Is preoccupied with unjustified doubts about the loyalty or trustworthiness of friends or associates.
3. Is reluctant to confide in others because of unwarranted fear that the information will be used maliciously against him or her.
4. Reads hidden demeaning or threatening meanings into benign remarks or events.
5. Persistently bears grudges (i.e., is unforgiving of insults, injuries, or slights).
6. Perceives attacks on his or her character or reputation that are not apparent to others and is quick to react angrily or to counterattack.
7. Has recurrent suspicions, without justification, regarding fidelity of spouse or sexual partner.

B. Does not occur exclusively during the course of schizophrenia, a bipolar disorder or depressive disorder with psychotic features, or another psychotic disorder and is not attributable to the physiological effects of another medical condition.

Note: If criteria are met prior to the onset of schizophrenia, add "premorbid," i.e., "paranoid personality disorder (premorbid)."

American Psychiatric Association. (2022). *Diagnostic and statistical manual of mental disorders* (5th ed., Text Revision).

schizophrenia (Lewis & Ridenour, 2020), although the association does not seem to be strong (Tienari et al., 2003). In other words, relatives of individuals with schizophrenia may be more likely to have paranoid personality disorder than people who do not have a relative with schizophrenia. In general, there appears to be a strong role for genetics in paranoid personality disorder (Kendler et al., 2015). As you will see later with the other odd or eccentric personality disorders in Cluster A, there seems to be some relationship with schizophrenia (Bolinskey et al., 2015), causing some to suggest eliminating it as a separate disorder from the DSM (Triebwasser, Chemerinski, Roussos, & Siever, 2013).

Psychological contributions to this disorder are even less certain, although some interesting speculations have been made. Retrospective research—asking people with this disorder to recall events from their childhood—suggests that early mistreatment or traumatic childhood experiences may play a role in the development of paranoid personality disorder (Iacovino, Jackson, & Oltmanns, 2014). Caution is warranted when interpreting these results because there may be strong bias in the recall of these individuals who are already prone to viewing the world as a threat.

Some psychologists point directly to the thoughts (also referred to as *schemas*) of people with paranoid personality disorder as a way of explaining their behavior (Lewis & Ridenour, 2020). One view is that people with this disorder have the following basic mistaken assumptions about others: "People are malevolent and deceptive," "They'll attack you if they get the chance," and "You can be okay only if you stay on your toes" (Lobbestael & Arntz, 2012). This is a maladaptive way to view the world, yet it seems to pervade every aspect of the lives of these individuals. Although we do not know why they develop these perceptions, some speculation is that the roots are in their early upbringing. Their parents may teach them to be careful about making mistakes and may impress on them that they are different from other people. This vigilance causes them to see signs that other people are deceptive and malicious (Triebwasser, Chemerinski, Roussos, & Siever, 2013). It is certainly true that people are not always benevolent and sincere, and our interactions are sometimes ambiguous enough to make other people's intentions unclear. Looking too closely at what other people say and do can sometimes lead you to misinterpret them.

Andrej Andric/Shutterstock.com

People with paranoid personality disorder often believe that impersonal situations exist specifically to annoy or otherwise disturb them.

Cultural factors have also been implicated in paranoid personality disorder. Certain groups of people—such as prisoners, refugees, people with hearing impairments, and older adults—are thought to be particularly susceptible because of their unique experiences (Iacovino et al., 2014; Raza, DeMarce, Lash, & Parker, 2014; Ryder, Sunohara, & Kirmayer, 2015). Additionally, signs of paranoia are often one of the initial symptoms noticed in individuals who later develop severe cognitive disorders, such as Alzheimer's dementia (Lewis & Ridenour, 2020). Imagine how someone might view other people if they were an immigrant who had difficulty with the language and the customs of a new culture. Such innocuous things as other people laughing or talking quietly might be interpreted as somehow directed at them. The late musician Jim Morrison of the Doors described this phenomenon in his song "People Are Strange" (1967): "People are strange, / When you're a stranger, / Faces look ugly, / When you're alone."

You have seen how someone could misinterpret ambiguous situations as malevolent. Therefore, cognitive and cultural factors may interact to produce the suspiciousness observed in some people with paranoid personality disorder.

Treatment

Because people with paranoid personality disorder are mistrustful of everyone, they are unlikely to seek professional help when they need it, and they have difficulty developing the trusting relationships necessary for successful therapy (Lewis & Ridenour, 2020; Wong, 2020). Establishing a meaningful therapeutic alliance between the client and the therapist therefore becomes an important first step (Lewis & Ridenour, 2020). When these individuals finally do seek therapy, the trigger is usually a crisis in their lives—such as Jake's threats to harm strangers—or other problems such as anxiety or depression, not necessarily their personality disorder (Kelly, Casey, Dunn, Ayuso-Mateos, & Dowrick, 2007).

Therapists try to provide an atmosphere conducive to developing a sense of trust (Lewis & Ridenour, 2020). They often use cognitive therapy to counter the person's mistaken assumptions about others, focusing on changing the person's beliefs that all people are malevolent and most people cannot be trusted (Beck, Davis, & Freeman, 2015). Be forewarned, however, that to date there are no confirmed demonstrations that any form of treatment can significantly improve the lives of people with paranoid personality disorder. A survey of mental health professionals indicated that only 11% of therapists who treat paranoid personality disorder thought these individuals would continue in therapy long enough to be helped (Quality Assurance Project, 1990).

Schizoid Personality Disorder

Do you know someone who is a "loner"? Someone who would choose a solitary walk over an invitation to a party? A person who comes to class alone, sits alone, and leaves alone? Now, magnify this preference for isolation many times over and you can begin to grasp the impact of **schizoid personality disorder** (Hopwood & Thomas, 2012). People with this personality disorder show a

Mr. Z... All on His Own

A 39-year-old scientist was referred after his return from a tour of duty in Antarctica where he stopped cooperating with others, withdrew to his room, and began drinking on his own. Mr. Z. was orphaned at age 4, raised by an aunt until age 9, and subsequently looked after by an aloof housekeeper. At university, he excelled at physics, but chess was his only contact with others. Throughout his subsequent life, he made no close friends and engaged primarily in solitary activities. Until the tour of duty in Antarctica, he had been quite successful in his research work in physics. He was now, some months after his return, drinking at least a bottle of schnapps each day, and his work continued to deteriorate. He presented as self-contained and unobtrusive and was difficult to engage effectively. He was at a loss to explain his colleagues' anger at his aloofness in Antarctica and appeared indifferent to their opinion of him. He did not appear to require any interpersonal relations, although he did complain of some tedium in his life and at one point during the interview became sad, expressing longing to see his uncle in Germany, his only living relation.

Source: Cases and excerpts reprinted, with permission of the Royal Australian and New Zealand College of Psychiatrists, from Quality Assurance Project, 1990, Treatment outlines for paranoid, schizotypal and schizoid personality disorders, *Australian and New Zealand Journal of Psychiatry, 24*, 339–350.

pattern of detachment from social relationships and a limited range of emotions in interpersonal situations. They seem aloof, cold, and indifferent to other people. The term *schizoid* is relatively old, having been used by Bleuler (1924) to describe people who have a tendency to turn inward and away from the outside world. These people were said to lack emotional expressiveness and pursued vague interests. Consider the case of Mr. Z.

Clinical Description

Individuals with schizoid personality disorder seem neither to desire nor to enjoy closeness with others, including romantic or sexual relationships. As a result, they appear cold and detached and do not seem affected by praise or criticism. One of the changes in DSM-IV-TR from previous versions was the recognition that at least some people with schizoid personality disorder are sensitive to the opinions of others but are unwilling or unable to express this emotion. For them, social isolation may be extremely painful. Unfortunately, living on the street appears to be prevalent among people with this personality disorder, perhaps as a result of their lack of close friendships and lack of dissatisfaction about not having a sexual relationship with another person (Rouff, 2000; Angstman & Rasmussen, 2011).

The social deficiencies of people with schizoid personality disorder are similar to those of people with paranoid personality disorder, although they are more extreme. As Beck and Freeman (1990, p. 125) put it, they "consider themselves to be observers rather than participants in the world around them." They do not seem to have the unusual thought processes that characterize the other disorders in Cluster A (Cloninger & Svakic, 2009) (see Table 12.6). For example, people with paranoid and schizotypal personality disorders often have *ideas of reference,* mistaken beliefs that meaningless events relate just to them. In contrast, those with schizoid personality disorder share the social isolation, poor rapport, and constricted affect (showing neither positive nor negative emotion) seen in people with paranoid personality disorder. You will see in Chapter 13 that this distinction among psychotic-like symptoms is important to understanding people with schizophrenia, some of whom show the "positive" symptoms (actively unusual behaviors such as ideas of reference) and others only the "negative" symptoms (the more passive manifestations of social isolation or poor rapport with others).

Table 12.6 Grouping Schema for Cluster a Disorders

	Psychotic-Like Symptoms	
Cluster A Personality Disorder	Positive (for example, ideas of reference, magical thinking, and perceptual distortions)	Negative (for example, social isolation, poor rapport, and constricted affect)
Paranoid	Yes	Yes
Schizoid	No	Yes
Schizotypal	Yes	No

Source: Adapted from L. J. Siever, 1992, Schizophrenia spectrum personality disorders, in A. Tasman & M. B. Riba (Eds.), *Review of psychiatry* (Vol. 11, pp. 25–42), American Psychiatric Press.

Causes and Treatment

Extensive research on the genetic, neurobiological, and psychosocial contributions to schizoid personality disorder remains to be conducted. In fact, very little empirical research has been published on the nature and causes of this disorder (Triebwasser et al., 2012). Early findings suggest that the brainstem inhibitory dysfunction was more pronounced under fear and sadness in schizoid personality disorder (C. Wang et al., 2020). Childhood shyness is reported as a precursor to later adult schizoid personality disorder. It may be that this personality trait is inherited and serves as an important determinant in the development of this disorder. Abuse and neglect in childhood are also reported among individuals with this disorder (Carr, Keenleyside, & Fitzhenry, 2015; Lobbestael, Arntz, & Bernstein, 2010). Research over the past several decades points to biological causes of autism spectrum disorder (ASD) (a disorder we discuss in more detail in Chapter 14), and research demonstrates significant overlap in the occurrence of ASD and schizoid personality disorder (Cook, Zhang, & Constantino, 2020). It is possible that a biological dysfunction found in both ASD and schizoid personality disorder combines with early learning or early problems with interpersonal relationships to produce the social deficits that define schizoid personality disorder (Hopwood & Thomas, 2012).

It is rare for a person with this disorder to request treatment except in response to a crisis such as extreme depression or losing a job (Kelly et al., 2007). Therapists often begin treatment by pointing out the value in social relationships. The person with the disorder may even need to be taught the emotions felt by others to learn empathy (Skodol & Gunderson, 2008). Because their social skills were never established or have atrophied through lack of use (Caballo, Salazar, Irurtia, Olivares, & Olivares, 2014), people with schizoid personality disorder often receive social skills training. The therapist takes the part of a friend or significant other in a technique known as *role-playing* and helps the patient practice establishing and maintaining social relationships (Skodol & Gunderson, 2008). This type of social skills training is helped by identifying a social network—a person or people who will be supportive (Bender, 2005). Outcome research on this type of approach is unfortunately quite limited, so we must be cautious in evaluating the effectiveness of treatment for people with schizoid personality disorder.

Schizotypal Personality Disorder

People with **schizotypal personality disorder** are typically socially isolated, like those with schizoid personality disorder. In addition, they also behave in ways that would seem unusual to many of us, and they tend to be suspicious and to have odd beliefs (Dong, Liu, Hodgson, & Medoff-Cooper, in press). Schizotypal personality disorder is considered by some to be on a continuum (that is, on the same spectrum) with schizophrenia—the severe disorder we discuss in the next chapter—but without some of the more debilitating symptoms, such as hallucinations and delusions. In fact, because of this close connection, DSM-5 includes this disorder under both the heading of a personality disorder and the heading of a schizophrenia spectrum disorder (American Psychiatric Association, 2013). Consider the case of Mr. S.

DSM 5

Table 12.2

Diagnostic Criteria for Schizoid Personality Disorder

A. A pervasive pattern of detachment from social relationships and a restricted range of expression of emotions in interpersonal settings, beginning by early adulthood and present in a variety of contexts, as indicated by four (or more) of the following:

1. Neither desires nor enjoys close relationships, including being part of a family.
2. Almost always chooses solitary activities.
3. Has little, if any, interest in having sexual experiences with another person.
4. Takes pleasure in few, if any, activities.
5. Lacks close friends or confidants other than first-degree relatives.
6. Appears indifferent to the praise or criticism of others.
7. Shows emotional coldness, detachment, or flattened affectivity.

B. Does not occur exclusively during the course of schizophrenia, a bipolar disorder or depressive disorder with psychotic features, another psychotic disorder, or autism spectrum disorder and is not attributable to the physiological effects of another medical condition.

Note: If criteria are met prior to the onset of schizophrenia, add "premorbid," e.g., "schizoid personality disorder (premorbid)."

American Psychiatric Association. (2022). *Diagnostic and statistical manual of mental disorders* (5th ed., Text Revision).

Mr. S... All on His Own

Mr. S. was a 35-year-old chronically unemployed man who had been referred by a physician because of a vitamin deficiency. This was thought to have eventuated because Mr. S. avoided any foods that "could have been contaminated by machine." He had begun to develop alternative ideas about diet in his 20s and soon left his family and began to study an Eastern religion. "It opened my third eye; corruption is all about," he said.

He now lived by himself on a small farm, attempting to grow his own food, bartering for items he could not grow himself. He spent his days and evenings researching the origins and mechanisms of food contamination and, because of this knowledge, had developed a small band who followed his ideas. He had never married and maintained little contact with his family: "I've never been close to my father. I'm a vegetarian."

He said he intended to do an herbalism course to improve his diet before returning to his life on the farm. He had refused medication from the physician and became uneasy when the facts of his deficiency were discussed with him.

Source: Cases and excerpts reprinted, with permission of the Royal Australian and New Zealand College of Psychiatrists, from Quality Assurance Project, 1990, Treatment outlines for paranoid, schizotypal and schizoid personality disorders, *Australian and New Zealand Journal of Psychiatry, 24,* 339–350.

Clinical Description

People given a diagnosis of schizotypal personality disorder have psychotic-like (but not psychotic) symptoms (such as believing everything relates to them personally), social deficits, and sometimes cognitive impairments or paranoia (Dong et al., in press). These individuals are often considered odd or bizarre because of how they relate to other people, how they think and behave, and even how they dress. They have *ideas of reference*; for example, they may believe that somehow everyone on a passing city bus is talking about them, yet they may be able to acknowledge this is unlikely (Salaminios et al., in press). Again, as you will see in Chapter 13, some people with schizophrenia also have ideas of reference, but they are usually not able to "test reality" or see the illogic of their ideas.

Individuals with schizotypal personality disorder also have odd beliefs or engage in "magical thinking," believing, for example, that they are clairvoyant or telepathic (Furnham & Crump, 2014). In addition, they report unusual perceptual experiences, including such illusions as feeling the presence of another person when they are alone. Notice the subtle but important difference between *feeling* as if someone else is in the room and the more extreme perceptual distortion in people with schizophrenia who might report there *is* someone else in the room when there isn't. Unlike people who simply have unusual interests or beliefs, those with schizotypal personality disorder tend to be suspicious and have paranoid thoughts, express little emotion, and may dress or behave in unusual ways (for example, wear many layers of clothing in the summertime or mumble to themselves) (Salaminios et al., in press). Prospective research on children who later develop schizotypal personality disorder found that they tend to exhibit extreme social anxiety, hypersensitivity, being teased for oddness, and peculiar thoughts and language (Rimsky & Cain, 2017).

Because persons with schizotypal personality disorder often have beliefs around religious or spiritual themes (Bennett, Shepherd, & Janca, 2013), clinicians must be aware that different cultural beliefs or practices may lead to a mistaken diagnosis of this disorder. For example, some people who practice certain religious rituals—such as speaking in tongues, practicing voodoo, or mind reading—may do so with such obsessiveness as to make them seem extremely unusual, thus leading to a misdiagnosis (American Psychiatric Association, 2013). Mental health workers have to be particularly sensitive to cultural practices that may differ from their own and can distort their view of certain seemingly unusual behaviors.

DSM 5 **Table 12.3**

Diagnostic Criteria for Schizotypal Personality Disorder

A. A pervasive pattern of social and interpersonal deficits marked by acute discomfort with, and reduced capacity for, close relationships, as well as by cognitive or perceptual distortions and eccentricities of behavior, beginning by early adulthood and present in a variety of contexts, as indicated by five (or more) of the following:

1. Ideas of reference (excluding delusions of reference).
2. Odd beliefs or magical thinking that influences behavior and is inconsistent with subcultural norms (e.g., superstitiousness, belief in clairvoyance, telepathy, or "sixth sense"; in children and adolescents, bizarre fantasies or preoccupations).
3. Unusual perceptual experiences, including bodily illusions.
4. Odd thinking and speech (e.g., vague, circumstantial, metaphorical, overelaborate, or stereotyped).
5. Suspiciousness or paranoid ideation.
6. Inappropriate or constricted affect.
7. Behavior or appearance that is odd, eccentric, or peculiar.
8. Lack of close friends or confidants other than first-degree relatives.
9. Excessive social anxiety that does not diminish with familiarity and tends to be associated with paranoid fears rather than negative judgments about self.

B. Does not occur exclusively during the course of schizophrenia, a bipolar disorder or depressive disorder with psychotic features, another psychotic disorder, or autism spectrum disorder.

Note: If criteria are met prior to the onset of schizophrenia, add "premorbid," e.g., ""schizotypal personality disorder (premorbid)."

American Psychiatric Association. (2022). *Diagnostic and statistical manual of mental disorders* (5th ed., Text Revision).

Causes

Historically, the word *schizotype* was used to describe people who were predisposed to develop schizophrenia (Meehl, 1962; Rado, 1962). Schizotypal personality disorder is viewed by some to be one phenotype of a schizophrenia genotype (Rimsky & Cain, 2017). Recall that a *phenotype* is one way a person's genetics is expressed. A *genotype* is the gene or genes that make up a particular disorder. Depending on a variety of other influences, however, the way you turn out—your phenotype—may vary from other persons with a similar genetic makeup. Some people are thought to have "schizophrenia genes" (the genotype) yet, because of the relative lack of biological influences (for example, prenatal and early postnatal factors include season of birth, influenza, birth complications, parental age), some will have the less severe schizotypal personality disorder (the phenotype) (Dong et al., in press; Rimsky & Cain, 2017).

The idea of a relationship between schizotypal personality disorder and schizophrenia arises partly from the way people with the disorders behave. Many characteristics of schizotypal personality disorder—including ideas of reference, illusions, and paranoid thinking—are similar but milder forms of behaviors observed among people with schizophrenia. Genetic research also seems to support a relationship. Family, twin, and adoption studies have shown an increased prevalence of schizotypal personality disorder among relatives of people with schizophrenia who do not also have schizophrenia themselves (Rimsky & Cain, 2017). These studies also tell us, however, that the environment can strongly influence schizotypal personality disorder. Some research suggests that schizotypal symptoms are strongly associated with childhood maltreatment among men, and this childhood maltreatment seems to result in posttraumatic stress disorder (PTSD) symptoms (see Chapter 5) among women (Berenbaum, Thompson, Milanak, Boden, & Bredemeier, 2008).

Cognitive assessment of people with this disorder points to mild to moderate decrements in their ability to perform on tests involving memory and learning, suggesting some damage in the left hemisphere (Siever & Davis, 2004). Other research, using magnetic resonance imaging, points to generalized brain abnormalities in those with schizotypal personality disorder (Attademo, Bernardini, & Verdolini, in press; Y. Wang et al., 2020).

Treatment

People with schizotypal personality disorder who request clinical help often seek assistance due to anxiety or depression. Relatedly, the presence of schizotypal personality disorder significantly

Concept Check 12.2

Which personality disorders are described here?

1. Heidi trusts no one and wrongly believes other people want to harm her or cheat her out of her life earnings. She is sure her husband is secretly planning to leave her and take their three boys, although she has no proof. She no longer confides in friends or divulges any information to coworkers for fear that it will be used in a plot against her. She is usually tense and ready to argue about harmless comments made by family members.

   ____

2. Amara lives alone in the country with her birds and has little contact with relatives or any other individuals in a nearby town. She is extremely concerned with pollution, fearing that harmful chemicals are in the air and water around her. She has developed her own water purification system and makes her own clothes. If it is necessary for her to go outside, she covers her body with excessive clothing and wears a face mask to avoid the contaminated air.

   ____

3. Santiago is a college student who has no close friends. He comes to class every day and sits in a corner and is sometimes seen having lunch alone on the park bench. Most students find him difficult to engage and complain about his lack of involvement in class activities, but he appears indifferent to what others say. He has no desire for close or intimate relationships and expresses no desire to have sex. He is meeting with a therapist only because his family tricked him into going.

   ____

increases the risk for developing major depressive disorder even years later (Skodol et al., 2011). Treatment includes some of the medical and psychological treatments for depression (Rimsky & Cain, 2017).

Controlled studies of attempts to treat groups of people with schizotypal personality disorder are few. There is now growing interest in treating this disorder, however, because it is being viewed as a precursor to schizophrenia (McClure et al., 2010). One study used a combination of approaches—including antipsychotic medication, community treatment (a team of support professionals providing therapeutic services), and social skills training—to treat the symptoms experienced by individuals with this disorder. Researchers found that this combination of approaches either reduced their symptoms or postponed the onset of later schizophrenia (Nordentoft et al., 2006). The idea of treating younger persons who have symptoms of schizotypal personality disorder with some combination of antipsychotic medication, cognitive behavior therapy, and social skills training in order to avoid the onset of schizophrenia is proving to be a promising prevention strategy (Correll, Hauser, Auther, & Cornblatt, 2010; Graff, McClure & Siever, 2014; Nordentoft et l., 2015; Weiser, 2011).

Cluster B Personality Disorders

People diagnosed with the Cluster B personality disorders—antisocial, borderline, histrionic, and narcissistic—all have behaviors that have been described as dramatic, emotional, or erratic. These personality disorders are described next.

Antisocial Personality Disorder

People with **antisocial personality disorder** are among the most puzzling of the individuals a clinician will see in a practice and are characterized as having a history of failing to comply with social norms. They perform actions most of us would find unacceptable, such as stealing from friends and family. They also tend to be irresponsible, impulsive, and deceitful (Choy, 2020). Robert Hare, a pioneer in the study of people with psychopathy (a subgroup of persons with antisocial personality disorder that we outline later in the chapter), describes them as "social predators who charm, manipulate, and ruthlessly plow their way through life, leaving a broad trail of broken hearts, shattered expectations, and empty wallets. Completely lacking in conscience and empathy, they selfishly take what they want and do as they please, violating social norms and expectations without the slightest sense of guilt or regret" (Hare, 1993, p. xi). Although first identified as a "medical" problem by Philippe Pinel at the start of the nineteenth century (1801/1962), descriptions of individuals with these antisocial tendencies can be found in ancient stone texts found in Mesopotamia dating as far back as 670 B.C. (Abdul-Hamid & Stein, 2012). Just who are these people with antisocial personality disorder? Consider the case of Caleb.

Caleb... The Thrill Seeker

I first met Caleb on his 17th birthday. Unfortunately, he was celebrating the event in a psychiatric hospital. He had been truant from school for several months and had gotten into some trouble. The local judge who heard his case had recommended psychiatric evaluation one more time, even though Caleb had been hospitalized six previous times, all for problems related to drug use and truancy. He was a veteran of the system and already knew most of the staff. I interviewed him to assess why he was admitted this time and to recommend treatment.

My first impression was that Caleb was cooperative and pleasant. He pointed out a tattoo on his arm that he had made himself, saying that it was a "stupid" thing to have done and that he now regretted it. He regretted many things and was looking forward to moving on with his life. I later found out that he was never truly remorseful for anything.

Our second interview was quite different. In the 48 hours since our first interview, Caleb had done a number of things that showed why he needed a great deal of help. The most serious incident involved a 15-year-old girl named Ann who attended class with Caleb in the hospital school. Caleb had told her that he was going to get himself discharged, get in trouble, and be sent to the same prison Ann's father was in, where he would rape her father. Caleb's threat so upset Ann that she hit her teacher and several of the staff. When I spoke to Caleb about this, he smiled slightly and said he was bored and that it was fun to upset Ann. When I asked whether it bothered him that his behavior might extend her stay in the hospital, he looked puzzled and said, "Why should it bother me? She's the one who'll have to stay in this hell hole!"

Just before Caleb's admittance, a teenager in his town was murdered. A group of teens went to the local cemetery at night to perform satanic rituals, and a young man was stabbed to death, apparently over a drug purchase. Caleb was in the group, although he did not stab the boy. He told me that they occasionally dug up graves to get skulls for their parties—not because they really believed in the devil but because it was fun and it scared the younger kids. I asked, "What if this was the grave of someone you knew, a relative or a friend? Would it bother you that strangers were digging up the remains?" He shook his head. "They're dead, man; they don't care. Why should I?"

Caleb told me he loved PCP, or "angel dust," and that he would rather be dusted than anything else. He routinely made the 2-hour trip to New York City to buy drugs in a particularly dangerous neighborhood. He denied that he was ever nervous. This wasn't machismo; he really seemed unconcerned.

Caleb made little progress. I discussed his future in family therapy sessions, and we talked about his pattern of showing supposed regret and remorse and then stealing money from his parents and going back onto the street. Most of our discussions centered on trying to give his parents the courage to say no to him and not to believe his lies.

One evening, after many sessions, Caleb said he had seen the "error of his ways" and that he felt bad he had hurt his parents. If they would only take him home this one last time, he would be the son he should have been all these years. His speech moved his parents to tears, and they looked at me gratefully as if to thank me for curing their son. When Caleb finished talking, I smiled, applauded, told him it was the best performance I had ever seen. His parents turned on me in anger. Caleb paused for a second, then he, too, smiled and said, "It was worth a shot!" Caleb's parents were astounded that he had again tricked them into believing him; he hadn't meant a word of what he had just said. Caleb was eventually discharged to a drug rehabilitation program. Within 4 weeks, he had convinced his parents to take him home, and within 2 days, he had stolen all their cash and disappeared; he apparently went back to his friends and to drugs.

When he was in his 20s, after one of his many arrests for theft, he was diagnosed as having antisocial personality disorder. His parents never summoned the courage to turn him out or refuse him money, and he continues to con them into providing him with a means of buying more drugs.

Clinical Description

Individuals with antisocial personality disorder tend to have long histories of violating the rights of others (Choy, 2020). They are often described as being aggressive because they take what they want, indifferent to the concerns of other people. Lying and cheating seem to be second nature to them, and often they appear unable to tell the difference between the truth and the lies they make up to further their own goals. They show no remorse or concern over the sometimes devastating effects of their actions. Substance use disorder is common in people with antisocial personality disorder and appears to be a lifelong pattern among these individuals (Wojciechowski, 2020). The long-term outcome for people with antisocial personality disorder is usually poor, regardless of gender (Black, 2013; Colman et al., 2009). One classic study, for example, followed 1,000 delinquent and nondelinquent boys over a 50-year period (Laub & Vaillant, 2000). Many of the delinquent boys would today receive a diagnosis of conduct disorder, which you will see later may be a precursor to antisocial personality disorder in adults. The delinquent boys were more than twice as likely to die an unnatural death (for example, accident, suicide, or homicide) as their nondelinquent peers, which may be attributed to factors such as excessive alcohol use and poor self-care (for example, infections and reckless behavior).

Antisocial personality disorder has had a number of names over the years. Philippe Pinel (1801/1962) identified what he called *manie sans délire* (mania without delirium) to describe people with unusual emotional responses and impulsive rages but no deficits in reasoning ability (Charland, 2010). Other labels have included moral insanity, egopathy, sociopathy, and psychopathy. A great deal has been written about these labels; we focus on the two that have figured most prominently in psychological research: **psychopathy** and DSM-5's antisocial personality disorder. There continues to be debate in the field if these really are two distinct disorders (Anderson, Sellbom, Wygant, Salekin, & Krueger, 2014; Douglas et al., 2015; Venables, Hall, & Patrick 2014; Wall, Wygant, & Sellbom, 2015; Werner, Few, & Buckholtz, 2015).

Defining Criteria

Hervey Cleckley (1941/1982), a psychiatrist who spent much of his career working with the "psychopathic personality," identified a constellation of 16 major characteristics, most of which are personality traits and are sometimes referred to as the "Cleckley criteria." Hare and his colleagues, building on the descriptive work of Cleckley, researched the nature of psychopathy (see, for example, Hare, 1970; Harpur, Hare, & Hakstian, 1989) and developed a 20-item checklist that serves as an assessment tool. Six of the criteria that Hare includes in his Revised Psychopathy Checklist (PCL-R) are as follows (Hare et al., 2012, p. 480):

1. Glibness/superficial charm
2. Grandiose sense of self-worth
3. Pathological lying
4. Conning/manipulative
5. Lack of remorse or guilt
6. Callous/lack of empathy

With some training, clinicians are able to gather information from interviews with a person, along with material from significant others or institutional files (for example, prison records), and assign the person scores on the checklist, with high scores indicating psychopathy (Hare & Neumann, 2006).

The Cleckley/Hare criteria focus primarily on underlying *personality traits* (for example, being self-centered or manipulative). Earlier versions of the DSM criteria for antisocial personality focused almost entirely on observable *behaviors* (for example, "impulsively and repeatedly changes employment, residence, or sexual partners"). The framers of the previous DSM criteria felt that trying to assess a personality trait—for example, whether someone was manipulative—would be more difficult than determining whether the person engaged in certain behaviors, such as repeated fighting. The DSM-5, however, moved closer to the trait-based criteria and includes some of the same language included in Hare's PCL-R (such as callousness, manipulativeness, and deceitfulness) (Colins, Fanti, & Andershed, in press). Unfortunately, research on identifying persons with antisocial personality disorder suggests that this new definition reduces the reliability of the diagnosis (Regier et al., 2013). Additional work will be needed to improve the reliability of this diagnosis while maintaining the core traits that characterize these individuals.

Antisocial Personality Disorder and Criminality

Although Cleckley did not deny that many psychopaths are at greatly elevated risk for criminal and antisocial behaviors, he did emphasize that some have few or no legal or interpersonal difficulties. In other words, some psychopaths are not criminals, and some do not display outward aggressiveness that was included in the DSM-IV-TR criteria for antisocial personality disorder. What separates many in this group from those who get into trouble with the law may be their intelligence quotient (IQ). In a classic prospective, longitudinal study, White, Moffitt, and Silva (1989) followed almost 1,000 children, beginning at age 5, to see what predicted antisocial behavior at age 15. They found that, of the 5-year-olds determined to be at high risk for later delinquent behavior, 16% did indeed have run-ins with the law by the age of 15, and 84% did not. What distinguished these two groups? In general, the at-risk children with lower IQs were the ones who got in trouble. This suggests that having a higher IQ may help protect some people from developing more serious problems, or it may at least prevent them from getting caught.

Some psychopaths function quite successfully in certain segments of society (for example, politics, business, and entertainment). Because of the difficulty in identifying these people, such "successful" or "subclinical" psychopaths (who meet some of the criteria for psychopathy) have not been the focus of much research. In a clever exception, Widom (1977, p. 677) recruited a sample of subclinical psychopaths through advertisements in underground newspapers that appealed to those with many of the major personality characteristics of psychopathy. For example, one of the advertisements read as follows:

> Wanted: charming, aggressive, carefree people who are impulsively irresponsible but are good at handling people and at looking after number one.

Widom found that her sample appeared to possess many of the same characteristics as imprisoned psychopaths. For example, a large percentage of them received low scores on questionnaire measures of empathy and socialization, and their parents tended to have higher rates of psychopathology, including alcoholism. But many of these individuals had stable occupations and had managed to stay out of prison. Widom's study, although lacking a control group, shows that at least some individuals with psychopathic personality traits avoid repeated contact with the legal system and may even function successfully in society (Forster & Lund, 2018).

Identifying psychopaths among the criminal population seems to have important implications for predicting their future criminal behavior (Vitacco, Neumann, & Pardini, 2014). As you can imagine, having personality characteristics such as a lack of remorse and impulsivity can lead to difficulty staying out of trouble with the legal system. In general, most research has found that people who score high on measures of psychopathy commit crimes at a higher rate than those with lower scores and are at greater risk for more violent crimes and recidivism (repeating offenses) (for example, Widiger, 2006), although some research has found psychopathy to be a less reliable predictor of criminality (Virtanen et al., 2020).

As we review the literature on antisocial personality disorder, note that the people included in the research may be members of only one of the three groups (those with antisocial personality disorder, psychopathy, and criminals) we have described. For example, genetic research is usually conducted with criminals because they and their families are easier to identify than members of the other groups. As you now know, the criminal group may include people other than those with antisocial personality disorder or psychopathy. Keep this in mind as you read on.

Conduct Disorder

It is important to note the developmental nature of antisocial behavior. DSM-5 provides a separate diagnosis for children who engage in behaviors that violate society's norms: *conduct disorder.* It provides for the designation of two subtypes—*childhood-onset type* (the onset of at least one criterion characteristic of CD prior to age 10 years) or *adolescent-onset type* (the absence of any criteria characteristic of CD prior to age 10 years). An additional subtype, new to the DSM-5, is called "with a callous-unemotional presentation" (Koutsogiorgi, Lordos, Fanti, & Michaelides, 2020). This designation is an indication that the young person presents

Courtesy of Robert Hare

Robert Hare has made extensive studies of people with psychopathic personalities.

in a way that suggests personality characteristics similar to an adult with psychopathy.

Many children with conduct disorder—most often diagnosed in boys—become juvenile offenders and tend to become involved with drugs. Caleb fits into this category. More important, the lifelong pattern of antisocial behavior is evident because young children who display antisocial behavior are likely to continue these behaviors as they grow older (Yazgan et al., 2021). Data from long-term follow-up research indicate that many adults with antisocial personality disorder or psychopathy had conduct disorder as children (Davidson, 2014; Kasen, Cohen, Skodol, Johnson, & Brook, 2014; Robins, 1978; Salekin, 2006); the likelihood of an adult having antisocial personality disorder increases if, as a child, they had both conduct disorder and attention deficit/hyperactivity disorder (Biederman, Mick, Faraone, & Burback, 2001; Moffitt, Caspi, Rutter, & Silva, 2001). In many cases, the types of norm violations that an adult would engage in—irresponsibility regarding work or family—appear as younger versions in conduct disorder, such as truancy from school or running away from home. Some children with conduct disorder do feel remorseful about their behavior, which is why DSM-5 included the qualifier "with a callous-unemotional presentation" in order to better differentiate these two groups.

There is a tremendous amount of interest in studying a group that includes individuals who cause a great deal of harm to society. Research has been conducted for a number of years, and so we know a great deal more about antisocial personality disorder than about most of the other personality disorders.

Genetic Influences

Family, twin, and adoption studies all suggest a genetic influence on both antisocial personality disorder and criminality (Goldman, Ducci, & Gitik, 2020). For example, in a classic study, Crowe (1974) examined children whose mothers were felons and who were later adopted by other families and compared them with adopted children of mothers who were not felons. All were separated from their mothers as newborns, minimizing the possibility that environmental factors from their biological families were responsible for the results. Crowe found that the adopted offspring of felons had significantly higher rates of arrests, conviction, and antisocial personality than did the adopted offspring of mothers who were not felons, which suggests at least some genetic influence on criminality and antisocial behavior.

Crowe found something else quite interesting, however: The adopted children of felons who themselves later became criminals had spent more time in interim orphanages than either the adopted children of felons who did not become criminals or the adopted children of mothers who were not felons. As Crowe points out, this suggests a gene–environment interaction. In other words, genetic factors may be important only in the presence of certain environmental influences (alternatively, certain environmental influences are important only in the presence of certain genetic predispositions). Epigenetics (as described in Chapter 2) is the study of factors other than inherited DNA sequence (such as new learning or stress) that alter the phenotypic expression of genes; it can have an influence on the DNA by changing the gene expression. Therefore, genetic factors may present a vulnerability, but actual development of criminality may require environmental factors (epigenetics), such as a deficit in early, high-quality contact with parents or parent surrogates (Goldman et al., 2020).

This gene–environment interaction was demonstrated most clearly by Cadoret, Yates, Troughton, Woodworth, and Stewart (1995), who studied adopted children and their likelihood of developing conduct problems. If the children's biological parents had a history of antisocial personality disorder and their adoptive families exposed them to chronic stress through marital, legal, or psychiatric problems, the children were at greater risk for conduct problems. Again, research shows that genetic influence does not necessarily mean certain disorders are inevitable. Genetic research on conduct disorder points to an interaction between genetic and environmental influences, such as academic difficulty, peer problems, low family income, neglect, and harsh

DSM 5 **Table 12.4**
Diagnostic Criteria for Antisocial Personality Disorder

A. A pervasive pattern of disregard for and violation of the rights of others, occurring since age 15 years, as indicated by three (or more) of the following:

1. Failure to conform to social norms with respect to lawful behaviors, as indicated by repeatedly performing acts that are grounds for arrest.
2. Deceitfulness, as indicated by repeated lying, use of aliases, or conning others for personal profit or pleasure.
3. Impulsivity or failure to plan ahead.
4. Irritability and aggressiveness, as indicated by repeated physical fights or assaults.
5. Reckless disregard for safety of self or others.
6. Consistent irresponsibility, as indicated by repeated failure to sustain consistent work behavior or honor financial obligations.
7. Lack of remorse, as indicated by being indifferent to or rationalizing having hurt, mistreated, or stolen from another.

B. The individual is at least age 18 years.

C. There is evidence of conduct disorder with onset before age 15 years.

D. The occurrence of antisocial behavior is not exclusively during the course of schizophrenia or bipolar disorder.

American Psychiatric Association. (2022). *Diagnostic and statistical manual of mental disorders* (5th ed., Text Revision).

discipline from parents (Beaver, Barnes, May, & Schwartz, 2011; Kendler, Aggen, & Patrick, 2013; Knopik et al., 2014; Silberg, Maes, & Eaves, 2012).

If you remember back to Chapter 4, we introduced the concept of an *endophenotype*—underlying aspects of a disorder that might be more directly influenced by genes. In the case of antisocial personality disorder, gene researchers are looking for genetic differences that may influence factors such as serotonin and dopamine levels or the relative lack of anxiety or fear seen in these individuals (which we discuss next) (Hare et al., 2012). Although this research is at its early stages, it is refining the search for genes—not for ones that "cause" antisocial personality disorder but for genes that create the unusual aspects of an antisocial personality, such as fearlessness, aggressiveness, impulsivity, and lack of remorse.

Neurobiological Influences

A great deal of research has focused on neurobiological influences that may be specific to antisocial personality disorder. One thing seems clear: General brain damage does not explain why some people become psychopaths or criminals; these individuals appear to score as well on neuropsychological tests as the rest of us (Hart, Forth, & Hare, 1990). Such tests are designed to detect only significant damage in the brain, however, and will not pick up subtle changes in chemistry or structure that could affect behavior.

Arousal Theories

The fearlessness, seeming insensitivity to punishment, and thrill-seeking behaviors characteristic of those with antisocial personality disorder (especially those with psychopathy) sparked interest in what neurobiological processes might contribute to these unusual reactions. Early theoretical work on people with antisocial personality disorder emphasized two hypotheses: the underarousal hypothesis and the fearlessness hypothesis. According to the *underarousal hypothesis*, psychopaths have abnormally low levels of cortical arousal (Junewicz & Billick, 2020). There appears to be an inverted U-shaped relation between arousal and performance, the Yerkes-Dodson curve, which suggests people with either high or low levels of arousal tend to experience negative affect and perform poorly in many situations, whereas individuals with intermediate levels of arousal tend to be relatively content and perform satisfactorily in most situations.

According to the underarousal hypothesis, the abnormally low levels of cortical arousal characteristic of psychopaths are the primary cause of their antisocial and risk-taking behaviors; they

DSM 5 Table 12.5
Diagnostic Criteria for Conduct Disorder

A. A repetitive and persistent pattern of behavior in which the basic rights of others or major age-appropriate societal norms or rules are violated, as manifested by the presence of at least three of the following 15 criteria in the past 12 months from any of the categories below, with at least one criterion present in the past 6 months:

Aggression to People and Animals

1. Often bullies, threatens, or intimidates others.
2. Often initiates physical fights.
3. Has used a weapon that can cause serious physical harm to others (e.g., a bat, brick, broken bottle, knife, gun).
4. Has been physically cruel to people.
5. Has been physically cruel to animals.
6. Has stolen while confronting a victim (e.g., mugging, purse snatching, extortion, armed robbery).
7. Has forced someone into sexual activity.

Destruction of Property

8. Has deliberately engaged in fire setting with the intention of causing serious damage.
9. Has deliberately destroyed others' property (other than by fire setting).

Deceitfulness or Theft

10. Has broken into someone else's house, building, or car.
11. Often lies to obtain goods or favors or to avoid obligations (i.e., "cons" others).
12. Has stolen items of nontrivial value without confronting a victim (e.g., shoplifting, but without breaking and entering; forgery).

Serious Violations of Rules

13. Often stays out at night despite parental prohibitions, beginning before age 13 years.
14. Has run away from home overnight at least twice while living in the parental or parental surrogate home, or once without returning for a lengthy period.
15. Is often truant from school, beginning before age 13 years.

B. The disturbance in behavior causes clinically significant impairment in social, academic, or occupational functioning.

C. If the individual is age 18 years or older, criteria are not met for antisocial personality disorder.

Specify whether:

Childhood-onset type: Individuals show at least one symptom characteristic of conduct disorder prior to age 10 years.

Adolescent-onset type: Individuals show no symptom characteristic of conduct disorder prior to age 10 years.

Unspecified onset: Criteria for a diagnosis of conduct disorder are met, but there is not enough information available to determine whether the onset of the first symptom was before age 10 years.

Specify current severity:

Mild: Few if any conduct problems in excess of those required to make the diagnosis are present, and conduct problems cause relatively minor harm to others (e.g., lying, truancy, staying out after dark without permission, other rule breaking).

Moderate: The number of conduct problems and the effect on others are intermediate between those specified "mild" and those in "severe" (e.g., stealing without confronting a victim, vandalism).

Severe: Many conduct problems in excess of those required to make the diagnosis are present, or conduct problems cause considerable harm to others (e.g., forced sex, physical cruelty, use of a weapon, stealing while confronting a victim, breaking and entering)

American Psychiatric Association. (2022). *Diagnostic and statistical manual of mental disorders* (5th ed., Text Revision).

seek stimulation to boost their chronically low levels of arousal. This means that Caleb lied, took drugs, and dug up graves to achieve the same level of arousal we might get from talking on the phone with a good friend or watching television. Several researchers have examined childhood and adolescent psychophysiological predictors of adult antisocial behavior and criminality. Raine, Venables, and Williams (1990), for example, assessed a sample of 15-year-olds on a variety of autonomic and central nervous system variables. They found that future criminals had lower skin conductance activity, lower heart rate during rest periods, and more slow-frequency brain wave activity, all indicative of low arousal.

According to the fearlessness hypothesis, psychopaths possess a higher threshold for experiencing fear than most other individuals (Lykken, 1957, 1982). In other words, things that greatly frighten the rest of us have little effect on the psychopath (Syngelaki, Fairchild, Moore, Savage, & Goozen, 2013). Remember that Caleb was unafraid of going alone to dangerous neighborhoods to buy drugs. According to proponents of this hypothesis, the fearlessness of the psychopath gives rise to all the other major features of the syndrome.

Theorists have tried to connect what we know about the workings of the brain with clinical observations of people with antisocial personality disorder, especially those with psychopathy. Several theorists have applied Jeffrey Gray's (1987) model of brain functioning to this population (Fowles, 1988; Quay, 1993). According to Gray, three major brain systems influence learning and emotional behavior: the behavioral inhibition system (BIS), the reward system, and the fight/flight system. Two of these systems, the BIS and the reward system, have been used to explain the behavior of people with psychopathy. The BIS is responsible for our ability to stop or slow down when we are faced with impending punishment, nonreward, or novel situations; activation of this system leads to anxiety and frustration. The BIS is thought to be located in the septohippocampal system and involves the noradrenergic and serotonergic neurotransmitter systems. The reward system is responsible for how we behave—in particular, our approach to positive rewards—and is associated with hope and relief. This system probably involves the dopaminergic system in the mesolimbic area of the brain, which we previously noted as the "pleasure pathway" for its role in substance use and abuse (Chen, 2020) (see Chapter 11).

If you think about the behavior of psychopaths, the possible malfunctioning of these systems is clear. An imbalance between the BIS and the reward system may make the fear and anxiety produced by the BIS less apparent and the positive feelings associated with the reward system more prominent (Byrd, Loeber, & Pardini, 2014; Hoppenbrouwers, Neumann, Lewis, & Johansson, 2015; Levenston, Patrick, Bradley, & Lang, 2000; Quay, 1993). Theorists have proposed that this type of neurobiological dysfunction may explain why psychopaths are not anxious about committing the antisocial acts that characterize their disorder (Chen, 2020).

Researchers continue to explore how differences in neurotransmitter function (for example, serotonin) and neurohormone function (for example, androgens such as testosterone and the stress neurohormone cortisol) in the brains of these individuals can explain the callousness, superficial charm, lack of remorse, and impulsivity that characterize people with psychopathy. Integrative theories that link these differences to both genetic and environmental influences are just now beginning to be outlined (DeLisi & Vaughn, 2015; Hyde, Shaw, & Hariri, 2013; Poppa &

ELIJAH NOUVELAGE/REUTERS/Alamy Stock Photo

Many prisons allow visits between inmates and their children, partly to help reduce later psychological problems in those children.

Bechara, 2015; Waller, Dotterer, & Hyde, 2015; Hare et al., 2012) and may lead to better understanding and treatments for this debilitating disorder.

Psychological and Social Dimensions

What goes on in the mind of a psychopath? In one of several studies of how psychopaths process reward and punishment, Newman, Patterson, and Kosson (1987) set up a card-playing task on a computer; they provided five-cent rewards and fines for correct and incorrect answers to psychopathic and nonpsychopathic criminal offenders. The game was constructed so that at first players were rewarded about 90% of the time and fined only about 10% of the time. Gradually, the odds changed until the probability of getting a reward was 0%. Despite feedback that reward was no longer forthcoming, the psychopaths continued to play and lose, while those without psychopathy stopped playing. As a result of this and other studies, the researchers hypothesized that once psychopaths set their sights on a reward goal, they are less likely than nonpsychopaths to be deterred despite signs the goal is no longer achievable (Dvorak-Bertscha, Curtin, Rubinstein, & Newman, 2009). Again, considering the reckless and daring behavior of some psychopaths (robbing banks without a mask and getting caught immediately), failure to abandon an unattainable goal fits the overall picture, although this relationship may be more complicated (Gao & Zhang, in press).

Gerald Patterson's influential work suggests that aggression in children with antisocial personality disorder may escalate, partly as a result of their interactions with their parents (Granic & Patterson, 2006; Patterson, 1982). He found that the parents often give in to the problem behaviors displayed by their children. For example, a boy's parents ask him to make his bed and he refuses. One parent yells at the boy. The boy yells back and becomes abusive. At some point, his interchange becomes so aversive that the parent stops fighting and walks away, thereby ending the fight but also letting the son not make his bed. Giving in to these problems results in short-term gains for both the parent (calm is restored in the house) and the child (he gets what he wants), but it results in continuing problems. The child has learned to continue fighting and not give up, and the parent learns that the only way to "win" is to withdraw all demands. This "coercive family process" combines with other factors—such as genetic influences, parental depression, poor monitoring of their child's activities, and less parental involvement—to help maintain the aggressive behaviors (Chronis et al., 2007; Patterson, DeBaryshe, & Ramsey, 1989). Coercive parenting—along with genetics—appears to be at least modestly involved with the callous-unemotional traits that seem related to later psychopathy (LoBraico, Bray, Feinberg, & Fosco, in press).

Although little is known about which environmental factors play a direct role in causing antisocial personality disorder and psychopathy (as opposed to childhood conduct disorders), evidence from adoption studies strongly suggests that shared environmental factors—that tend to make family members similar—are important to the etiology of criminality and perhaps antisocial personality disorder. For example, in the adoption study by Sigvardsson, Cloninger, Bohman, and von Knorring (1982), low social status of the adoptive parents increased the risk of nonviolent criminality among females. Like children with conduct disorders, individuals with antisocial personality disorder come from homes with inconsistent parental discipline (see, for example, Robins, 1966).

Developmental Influences

As children move into adulthood, the forms of antisocial behaviors change—from truancy and stealing from friends to extortion, assaults, armed robbery, or other crimes. Fortunately, clinical lore, as well as scattered empirical reports (Robins, 1966), suggest that rates of antisocial behavior begin to decline rather markedly around the age of 40. In their classic study, Hare, McPherson, and Forth (1988) provided empirical support for this phenomenon. They examined the conviction rates of male psychopaths and male nonpsychopaths who had been incarcerated for a variety of crimes. The researchers found that between the ages of 16 and 45 the conviction rates of nonpsychopaths remained relatively constant. In contrast, the conviction rates of psychopaths remained relatively constant up until about 40, at which time they decreased markedly (see ■ Figure 12.2). Why antisocial behavior often declines around middle age remains unanswered (Hare et al., 2012).

An Integrative Model

How can we put all this information together to get a better understanding of people with antisocial personality disorder? Remember that the research just discussed sometimes involved

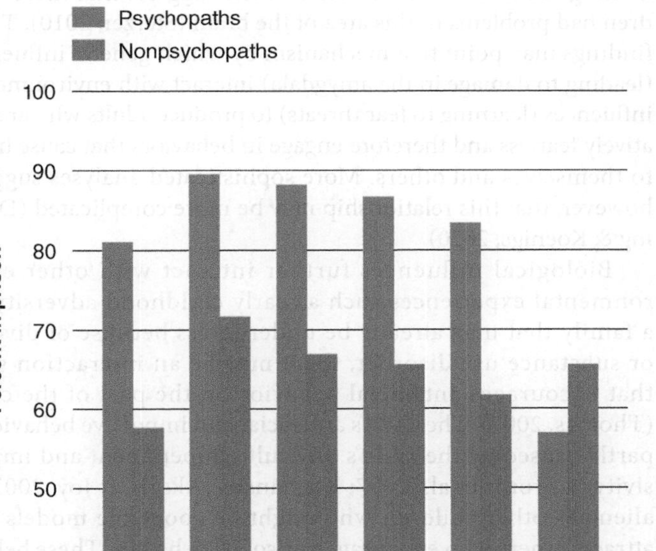

Figure 12.2

Lifetime course of criminal behavior in psychopaths and nonpsychopaths. Based on R. D. Hare, L. M. McPherson, & A. E. Forth, 1988, Male psychopaths and their criminal careers, *Journal of Consulting and Clinical Psychology, 56,* 710–714.

people labeled as having antisocial personality disorder but at other times included people labeled as psychopathic or even criminals. Whatever the label, it appears these people have a genetic vulnerability to antisocial behaviors and personality traits. As you have seen, genetics may lead to differences in neurotransmitter and neurohormone (dopamine and serotonin) function that influences aggressiveness, as well as differences in neurohormone (cortisol) function that affects the way people deal with stress. These brain differences may lead to personality traits such as callousness, impulsivity, and aggressiveness that characterize people with psychopathy (Hare et al., 2012).

One potential gene–environment interaction may be seen in the role of fear conditioning in children. If you remember back to Chapter 1 and Chapter 5, we discussed how we learn to fear things that can harm us (for example, a hot stove) through the pairing of an unconditioned stimulus (such as heat from burner) and a conditioned stimulus (such as a parent's warning to stay away), resulting in avoidance of the conditioned stimulus. But what if this conditioning is somehow impaired, and you do not learn to avoid things that can harm you? An important study looked at whether abnormal responses to fear conditioning as a young child could be responsible for later antisocial behavior in adults (Gao, Raine, Venables, Dawson, & Mednick, 2010). This large 20-year study assessed fear conditioning in a group of 1,795 children at age 3, and then looked to see who had a criminal record at age 23. They found that offenders showed significantly reduced fear conditioning at age 3 compared with matched comparison participants, with many of these children showing no fear conditioning at all. Deficits in amygdala functioning are thought to make individuals unable to recognize cues that signal threat, making them relatively fearless, which suggests that these children had problems in this area of the brain (Sterzer, 2010). These findings may point to a mechanism by which genetic influences (leading to damage in the amygdala) interact with environmental influences (learning to fear threats) to produce adults who are relatively fearless and therefore engage in behaviors that cause harm to themselves and others. More sophisticated analyses suggest, however, that this relationship may be more complicated (Deming & Koenigs, 2020).

Biological influences further interact with other environmental experiences such as early childhood adversity. In a family that may already be under stress because of divorce or substance use disorder, there may be an interaction style that encourages antisocial behavior on the part of the child (Thomas, 2009). The child's antisocial and impulsive behavior—partly caused by the child's difficult temperament and impulsivity (Chronis et al., 2007; Kochanska, Aksan, & Joy, 2007)—alienates other children who might be good role models and attracts others who encourage antisocial behavior. These behaviors may also result in the child's dropping out of school and a poor occupational history in adulthood, which help create increasingly frustrating life circumstances that further incite acts against society (Thomas, 2009).

This is, admittedly, an abbreviated version of a complex scenario. The important element is that in this integrative model of antisocial behavior, biological, psychological, and cultural factors combine in intricate ways to create someone like Caleb.

Treatment

One of the major problems with treating people in this group is typical of numerous personality disorders: They rarely identify themselves as needing treatment. Because of this and because they can be manipulative even with their therapists, most clinicians are pessimistic about the outcome of treatment for adults who have antisocial personality disorder, and there are few documented success stories (National Collaborating Centre for Mental Health, 2010). In general, therapists agree with incarcerating these people to deter future antisocial acts. Clinicians encourage identification of high-risk children so that treatment can be attempted before they become adults (National Collaborating Centre for Mental Health, 2010; Thomas, 2009). One large study with violent offenders found that cognitive behavior therapy could reduce the likelihood of violence 5 years after treatment (Olver, Lewis, & Wong, 2013), but treatment success was negatively correlated with ratings on the PCL-R for traits of "selfish, callous, and remorseless use of others." In other words, the higher the score on this trait (which we have seen is related to psychopathy), the less successful this group was in refraining from violence after their treatment. More contemporary approaches try to directly address the cognitive deficits that those with antisocial personality disorder present. These approaches are geared to enabling individuals to examine their own states of mind and understand others' minds and to behave more prosocially (Fonagy et al., 2020). These treatments are in early stages.

The most common treatment strategy for children involves parent training (Patterson, 1986; Presnall, Webster-Stratton, & Constantino, 2014; Scott, Briskman, & O'Connor, 2014). Many of these programs are being tested using an online format to give wider access to parent training (Diaz-Stransky, Rowley, Zecher, Grodberg, & Sukhodolsky, 2020; Ortiz, Vidair, Acri, Chacko, & Kobak, 2020). Parents are taught to recognize behavior problems early and to use praise and privileges to reduce problem behavior and encourage prosocial behaviors. Treatment studies typically show that these types of programs can significantly improve the behaviors of many children who display antisocial behaviors (Conduct Problems Prevention Research Group, 2010). A number of factors, however, put families at risk either for not succeeding in treatment or for dropping out early. These include cases with a high degree of family dysfunction, socioeconomic disadvantage, high family stress, a parent's history of antisocial behavior, and severe conduct disorder on the part of the child (Kaminski, Valle, Filene, & Boyle, 2008).

Prevention

We have seen a dramatic increase in the amount of research on prevention strategies focused on children at risk for later antisocial personality disorder. The aggressive behaviors of young children are remarkably stable, meaning that children who hit, insult, and threaten others are likely to continue these behaviors as they grow older. Unfortunately, these behaviors become more serious over time, and, though some individuals become less aggressive after adolescence (Jennings & Reingle, 2012), they are oftentimes early signs of the homicides and assaults seen among some adults (Eron & Huesmann, 1990; Singer & Flannery, 2000; Wright, Tibbetts, & Daigle, 2015).

Amani A/Alamy Stock Photo

Children with conduct disorder may become adults with antisocial personality disorder.

Approaches to change this aggressive course are being implemented mainly in school and preschool settings and emphasize behavioral supports for good behavior and skills training to improve social competence (Reddy, Newman, De Thomas, & Chun, 2009). A number of types of these programs are under evaluation, and the results look promising. For example, research using parent training for young children (toddlers from 1½ to 2½ years old) suggests that early intervention may be particularly helpful (Shaw, Dishion, Supplee, Gardner, & Arnds, 2006). Aggression can be reduced and social competence (for example, making friends and sharing) can be improved among young children, and these results generally are maintained over a few years (Conduct Problems Prevention Research, 2010; Reddy et al., 2009). One study found that the association between childhood conduct disorder and adult antisocial behavior was weaker among those adolescents who participated in high school sports, pointing to the possible utility of activities that disrupt delinquent habits (Samek, Elkins, Keyes, Iacono, & McGue, 2015). It is too soon to assess the impact of targeted prevention programs on adult antisocial behaviors typically observed among people with this personality disorder (Ingoldsby, Shelleby, Lane, & Shaw, 2012). Given the ineffectiveness of treatment for adults, however, prevention may be the best approach to this problem.

Claire... A Stranger Among Us

I have known Claire for more than 50 years and have watched her through the good but mostly bad times of her often shaky and erratic life as a person with borderline personality disorder. Claire and I went to school together from the eighth grade through high school, and we've kept in touch periodically. My earliest memory of her is of her hair, which was cut short and rather unevenly. She told me that when things were not going well, she cut her own hair severely, which helped to "fill the void." I later found out that the long sleeves she usually wore hid scars and cuts that she had made herself.

Claire was the first of our friends to smoke. What was unusual about this and her later drug use was not that they occurred (this was in the 1960s when "If it feels good, do it" hadn't been replaced by "Just say no") or that they began early. It was that she didn't seem to use them to get attention, like everyone else. Claire was also one of the first whose parents divorced, and both of them seemed to abandon her emotionally. She later told me that her father was an alcoholic who had regularly beaten her and her mother. She did poorly in school and had a low opinion of herself. She often said she was stupid and ugly, yet she was neither.

Throughout our school years, Claire left town periodically, without any explanation. I learned many years later that she was in psychiatric facilities to get help with her suicidal depression. She often threatened to kill herself, although we didn't guess that she was serious.

In our later teens, we all drifted away from Claire. She had become increasingly unpredictable, sometimes berating us for a perceived slight ("You're walking too fast. You don't want to be seen with me!") and at other times desperate to be around us. We were confused by her behavior. With some people, emotional outbursts can bring you closer together. Unfortunately for Claire, these incidents and her overall demeanor made us feel that we didn't know her. As we all grew older, the "void" she described in herself became overwhelming and eventually shut us all out.

Claire married twice, and both times had passionate but stormy relationships interrupted by hospitalizations. She tried to stab her first husband during a particularly violent rage. She tried a number of drugs but mainly used alcohol to "deaden the pain."

Now, in her mid-60s, things have calmed down some, although she says she is rarely happy. Claire does feel a little better about herself and is doing well as a travel agent. Although she is seeing someone, she is reluctant to become involved because of her personal history. Claire was ultimately diagnosed with depression and borderline personality disorder.

Borderline Personality Disorder

People with **borderline personality disorder** lead tumultuous lives. Their moods and relationships are unstable, and usually they have a poor self-image. These people often feel empty and are at great risk of dying by their own hands. Consider the case of Claire.

Clinical Description

Borderline personality disorder is one of the most common personality disorders observed in clinical settings. It is observed in every culture, is seen in about 1% to 2% of the general population (Choi-Kain & Gunderson, 2019), and constitutes 20% to 25% of all psychiatric admissions (Gunderson & Palmer, 2019). Claire's life illustrates the instability characteristic of people with borderline personality disorder. They tend to have turbulent relationships, fearing abandonment but lacking control over their emotions (Hooley, Cole, & Gironde, 2012). They often engage in behaviors that are suicidal, self-mutilative, or both, cutting, burning, or punching themselves. Claire sometimes used her cigarette to burn her palm or forearm, and she carved her initials in her arm. As mentioned previously, a significant proportion—nearly 10%—die by taking their own lives (Björkenstam, Björkenstam, Holm, Gerdin, & Ekselius, 2015; Gunderson, 2011). Fortunately, the long-term outcome for people with borderline personality disorder is encouraging (Winsper, in press). Approximately nine out of ten patients with borderline personality disorder achieve remission in the decade after seeking treatment (Gunderson et al., 2011; Keuroghlian et al., 2015).

People with this personality disorder are often intense, going from anger to deep depression in a short time. Dysfunction in the area of emotion is sometimes considered one of the core features of borderline personality disorder (Choi-Kain & Gunderson, 2019) and is one of the best predictors of suicide in this group (McGirr et al., 2009). The characteristic of instability (in emotion, interpersonal relationships, self-concept, and behavior) is seen as a core feature with some describing this group as being "stably unstable" (Hooley et al., 2012).

This instability extends to impulsivity, which can be seen in their drug misuse and self-mutilation. Although not so obvious as to why, the self-injurious behaviors, such as cutting, sometimes are described as tension-reducing by people who engage in these behaviors (McKenzie & Gross, 2014; Nock, 2010). Claire's empty feeling is also common; these people are sometimes described as chronically bored and have difficulties with their own identities (Linehan & Dexter-Mazza, 2008). The mood disorders discussed in Chapter 7 are common among people with borderline personality disorder. One study of inpatients with this disorder found that more than 80% also had major depression and approximately 10% had bipolar II disorder (Zanarini et al., 1998). Eating disorders are also common, with approximately 65% having some form of eating and feeding disorder (for example, Khosravi, 2020). Approximately 25% of people with borderline personality disorder also have bulimia (see Chapter 8); while 20% meet criteria for anorexia (Zanarini et al., 1998). Up to 64% of the people with borderline personality disorder are also diagnosed with at least one substance use disorder (Zanarini et al., 1998). Substance use in this population appears to be a way of coping with their unstable emotions (Vest & Tragesser, 2020). As with antisocial personality disorder, people with borderline personality disorder tend to improve during their 30s and 40s, although they may continue to have difficulties into old age (Zanarini et al., 2012).

Causes

The results from numerous family studies suggest that borderline personality disorder is more prevalent in families with the disorder and somehow linked with mood disorders (Amad, Ramoz, Thomas, Jardri, & Gorwood, 2014). Studies of monozygotic (identical) and dizygotic (fraternal) twins indicated a higher concordance rate among monozygotic twins, further supporting the role of genetics in the expression of borderline personality disorder (Streit, Colodro-Conde, Hall, & Witt, 2020).

The emotional reactivity that is a central aspect of borderline personality disorder has led researchers to look at this personality trait for clues about inherited influences (endophenotypes). Important genetic studies are investigating genes associated with the neurochemical serotonin because dysfunction in this system has been linked to the emotional instability, suicidal behaviors, and impulsivity seen in people with this disorder (Joyce, Stephenson, Kennedy, Mulder, & McHugh, 2013; Soloff, Chiappetta, Mason, Becker, & Price, 2014). This research is in its early stages, and there are, as yet, no solid answers for how genetic differences lead to the symptoms of borderline personality disorder (Streit et al., 2020).

Neuroimaging studies, designed to locate areas in the brain contributing to borderline personality disorder, point to the limbic network (Vandekerckhove, Berens, Wang, Quirin, & De Mey, 2020). Significantly, this area in the brain is involved in emotion regulation and dysfunctional serotonin neurotransmission, linking these findings with genetic research. Low serotonergic activity is involved with the regulation of mood and impulsivity, making it a target for extensive study in this group (Hooley et al., 2012).

To further understand the nature of this disorder, it is necessary to refine the concept of emotional reactivity in borderline personality disorder. When asked about their experiences, people with this disorder will report greater emotional fluctuations and greater emotional intensity, primarily in negative emotions such as anger and anxiety (Khosravani, Berk, Sharifi Bastan, Samimi Ardestani, & Wrobel, in press). Some research is looking at how sensitive these individuals are to the emotions of others. Using morphing technology, one study tested how people with and without borderline personality disorder could correctly identify the emotion of a face that was morphing on screen (changing slowly from a neutral expression to an emotional expression such as anger) and found those with borderline personality disorder were more accurate than controls (Fertuck et al., 2009).

In one study, the emotion "shame" was explored in people with this disorder (Rusch et al., 2007). For example, people were given the following scenario: "You attend your coworker's housewarming party, and you spill red wine on a new cream-colored carpet, but you think no one notices." Participants were then

DSM 5 **Table 12.6**
Diagnostic Criteria for Borderline Personality Disorder

A pervasive pattern of instability of interpersonal relationships, self-image, and affects, and marked impulsivity, beginning by early adulthood and present in a variety of contexts, as indicated by five (or more) of the following:

1. Frantic efforts to avoid real or imagined abandonment. (*Note:* Do not include suicidal or self-mutilating behavior covered in Criterion 5.)
2. A pattern of unstable and intense interpersonal relationships characterized by alternating between extremes of idealization and devaluation.
3. Identity disturbance: markedly and persistently unstable self-image or sense of self.
4. Impulsivity in at least two areas that are potentially self-damaging (e.g., spending, sex, substance abuse, reckless driving, binge eating). (*Note:* Do not include suicidal or self-mutilating behavior covered in criterion 5.)
5. Recurrent suicidal behavior, gestures, or threats, or self-mutilating behavior.
6. Affective instability due to a marked reactivity of mood (e.g., intense episodic dysphoria, irritability, or anxiety usually lasting a few hours and only rarely more than a few days).
7. Chronic feelings of emptiness.
8. Inappropriate, intense anger or difficulty controlling anger (e.g., frequent displays of temper, constant anger, recurrent physical fights).
9. Transient, stress-related paranoid ideation or severe dissociative symptoms.

American Psychiatric Association. (2022). *Diagnostic and statistical manual of mental disorders* (5th ed., Text Revision).

asked to say which of the following four reactions they would have (Rusch et al., 2007, p. 317):

- "You would wish you were anywhere but at the party." (indicating shame proneness)
- "You would stay late to help clean up the stain after the party." (guilt proneness)
- "You think your coworker should have expected some accidents at such a big party." (detachment)
- "You would wonder why your coworker chose to serve red wine with the new light carpet." (externalization)

This study found that women with borderline personality disorder (no men were included in this study) were more likely to report shame than healthy women and women with social phobia. The researchers also found that this elevated tendency to experience shame was associated with low self-esteem, low quality of life, and high levels of anger and hostility (Buchman-Wildbaum et al., 2021). Shame has also been found to be related to self-inflicted injury (for example, cutting) in this population (Wiklander et al., 2012). This incorporation of shame in interpreting certain situations has also been observed in children and youth with characteristics of borderline personality disorder (Hawes, Helyer, Herlianto, & Willing, 2013).

Cognitive factors in borderline personality disorder are just beginning to be explored. Here, the questions are, how do people with this disorder process information, and does this contribute to their difficulties? One study that looked at the thought processes of these individuals asked people with and without borderline personality disorder to look at words projected on a computer screen and to try to remember some of the words and forget others (Korfine & Hooley, 2000). When the words were not related to the symptoms of borderline personality disorder—for example, "celebrate," "charming," and "collect"—both groups performed equally well. However, when they were presented with words that might be relevant to the disorder—for example, "abandon," "suicidal," and "emptiness"—individuals with borderline personality disorder remembered more of these words despite being instructed to forget them. This preliminary evidence for a memory bias may hold clues to the nature of this disorder and may someday be helpful in designing more effective treatment (Baer, Peters, Eisenlohr-Moul, Geiger, & Sauer, 2012; Winter, Elzinga, & Schmahl, 2013).

An important environmental risk factor in a gene–environment interaction explanation for borderline personality disorder is the possible contribution of early trauma, especially sexual and physical abuse. Numerous studies show that people with this disorder are more likely to report abuse than are healthy individuals or those with other psychiatric conditions (see, for example, Bandelow et al., 2005; Kuo, Khoury, Metcalf, Fitzpatrick, & Goodwill, 2015; Zanarini et al., 2014). Unfortunately, these types of studies (based on recollection and a correlation between the two phenomena) do not tell us directly whether abuse and neglect cause later borderline personality disorder. In an important study, researchers followed 500 children who had documented cases of childhood physical and sexual abuse and neglect and compared them in adulthood with a control group (no history of reported abuse or neglect) (Widom, Czaja, & Paris, 2009). Significantly, more abused and neglected children went on to develop borderline personality disorder compared with controls. This finding is particularly significant for girls and women because girls are two or three times more likely to be sexually abused than boys (Bebbington et al., 2009).

It is clear that a majority of people who receive the diagnosis of borderline personality disorder have suffered terrible abuse or neglect from parents, sexual abuse, physical abuse by others, or a combination of these (Kleindienst, Löffler, Herzig, Bertsch, & Bekrater-Bodmann, 2020; Mainali, Rai, & Rutkofsky, 2020; Temes et al., 2020). For those who have not reported such histories, some research is examining just how they could develop borderline personality disorder. For example, factors such as temperament (emotional nature, such as being impulsive, irritable, or hypersensitive) or neurological impairments (being exposed prenatally to alcohol or drugs) and the ways they interact with parental styles may account for some cases of borderline personality disorder (Graybar & Boutilier, 2002).

Symptoms of borderline personality disorder have been observed among people who have gone through rapid cultural changes. The problems of identity, emptiness, fears of abandonment, and low anxiety threshold have been found in child and adult immigrants (Laxenaire, Ganne-Vevonec, & Streiff, 1982; Skhiri, Annabi, Bi, & Allani, 1982). These observations further support the possibility that prior trauma may, in some individuals, lead to borderline personality disorder.

Remember, however, that a history of childhood trauma, including sexual and physical abuse, occurs in people with other disorders, such as schizoid personality disorder, somatic symptom disorder (see Chapter 6), panic disorder (see Chapter 5), and dissociative identity disorder (see Chapter 6). In addition, a portion of individuals with borderline personality disorder have no apparent history of such abuse (Cloninger & Svakic, 2009). Although childhood sexual abuse and physical abuse and neglect seem to play an important role in the etiology of borderline personality disorder (Kleindienst et al., 2020; Mainali et al., 2020; Temes et al., 2020), neither appears to be necessary or sufficient to produce the syndrome.

An Integrative Model

Although there is no currently accepted integrative model for this disorder, it is tempting to borrow from the work on anxiety disorders to outline a possible view. In Chapter 5, we describe the *triple vulnerability theory* (Barlow, 2002; Suárez, Bennett, Goldstein, & Barlow, 2008). The first vulnerability (or diathesis) is a generalized biological vulnerability. We can see the genetic vulnerability to emotional reactivity in people with borderline personality disorder and the ways this affects specific brain function. The second vulnerability is a generalized psychological vulnerability. People with this personality disorder tend to view the world as threatening and to react strongly to real and perceived threats. The third vulnerability is a specific psychological vulnerability learned from early environmental experiences; this is where early trauma, abuse, or both may advance this sensitivity to threats. When a person is stressed, their biological tendency to be overly reactive interacts with the psychological tendency to feel threatened. This may result in the outbursts and suicidal behaviors commonly observed in this group. This preliminary model awaits validation and further research.

Treatment

In stark contrast to individuals with antisocial personality disorder, who rarely acknowledge requiring help, those with borderline personality disorder appear quite distressed and are more likely to seek treatment even than people with anxiety and mood disorders (Ansell, Sanislow, McGlashan, & Grilo, 2007; Bender et al., 2014). Reviews of research on the use of medical treatment for people with this disorder suggest that symptomatic treatment may not be helpful (Stoffers-Winterling, Storebø, & Lieb, in press). Efforts to provide successful treatment are complicated by problems with drug misuse, noncompliance with treatment, and attempts to take their own lives. As a result, many clinicians are reluctant to work with people who have borderline personality disorder.

One of the most thoroughly researched cognitive-behavioral treatments was developed by Marsha Linehan (Linehan et al., 2006; Linehan et al., 1999; Linehan & Dexter-Mazza, 2008). This approach—called **dialectical behavior therapy (DBT)**—involves helping people cope with the stressors that seem to trigger suicidal behaviors and other maladaptive responses. Priority in treatment is first given to those behaviors that may result in harm (suicidal behaviors), then those behaviors that interfere with therapy, and, finally, those that interfere with the patient's quality of life. Weekly individual sessions provide support, and patients are taught how to identify and regulate their emotions. Problem solving is emphasized so that patients can handle difficulties more effectively. In addition, they receive treatment similar to that used for people with PTSD, in which prior traumatic events are reexperienced to help extinguish the fear associated with them (see Chapter 5). In the final stage of therapy, clients learn to trust their own responses rather than depend on the validation of others, sometimes by visualizing themselves not reacting to criticism (Lynch & Cuper, 2012).

Results from a number of studies suggest that DBT may help reduce suicide attempts, dropouts from treatment, and hospitalizations (Linehan et al., 2015; Linehan & Dexter-Mazza, 2008; McMain, Guimond, Streiner, Cardish, & Links, 2013). A follow up of 39 women who received either dialectical behavior therapy or general therapeutic support (called "treatment as usual") for 1 year showed that, during the first 6 months of follow up, the women in the DBT group were less suicidal, less angry, and better adjusted socially (Linehan & Kehrer, 1993). Another study examined how treating these individuals with DBT in an inpatient setting (a psychiatric hospital) for approximately 5 days would improve their outcomes (Yen, Johnson, Costello, & Simpson, 2009). The participants improved in a number of areas, such as with a reduction in depression, hopelessness, anger expression, and dissociation. A growing body of evidence is now available to document the effectiveness of this approach to aid many individuals with this debilitating disorder (Linehan, 2014). Unfortunately, longitudinal studies provide substantial evidence for a high rate of symptomatic remission in borderline personality disorder (BPD) (Zeitler et al., 2020).

Probably some of the most intriguing research we describe in this book involves using the techniques in brain imaging to see how psychological treatments influence brain function. One pilot study examined emotional reactions to upsetting photos (for example, pictures of women being attacked) in controls and in women with borderline personality disorder (Schnell & Herpertz, 2007). This study found that among the women who benefited from treatment, arousal (in the amygdala and hippocampus) to the upsetting photos improved over time as a function of treatment. No changes occurred in controls or in women who did not have positive treatment experiences. This type of integrative research holds enormous promise for our understanding of borderline personality disorder and the mechanisms underlying successful treatment.

Histrionic Personality Disorder

Individuals with **histrionic personality disorder** tend to be overly dramatic and often seem almost to be acting, which is why the term *histrionic,* which means theatrical in manner, is used. Consider the case of Dariya.

Dariya... Always Onstage

When we first met, Dariya seemed to radiate enjoyment of life. She was single in her mid-30s and was going to night school for her master's degree. She often dressed flamboyantly. During the day, she taught children with disabilities, and when she didn't have class, she was often out late on a date. When I first spoke with her, she enthusiastically told me how impressed she was with my work in the field of developmental disabilities and that she had been extremely successful in using some of my techniques with her students. She was clearly overdoing the praise, but who wouldn't appreciate such flattering comments?

Because some of our research included children in her classroom, I saw Dariya often. Over a period of weeks, however, our interactions grew strained. She often complained of various illnesses and injuries (falling in the parking lot, twisting her neck looking out a window) that interfered with her work. She was disorganized, often leaving to the last minute tasks that required considerable planning. Dariya made promises to other people that were impossible to keep but seemed to be aimed at winning their approval. When she broke the promise, she usually made up a story designed to elicit sympathy and compassion. For example, she promised the mother of one of her students that she would put on a "massive and unique" birthday party for her daughter but forgot about it until the mother showed up with cake and juice. Upon seeing her, Dariya flew into a rage and blamed the principal for keeping her late after school, although there was no truth to this accusation.

Dariya often interrupted meetings about research to talk about her latest boyfriend. The boyfriends changed almost weekly, but her enthusiasm ("Like no other man I have ever met!") and optimism about the future ("He's the guy I want to spend the rest of my life with!") remained high for each of them. Wedding plans were seriously discussed with almost every one, despite their brief acquaintance. Dariya was ingratiating, especially to the male teachers, who often helped her out of trouble she got into because of her disorganization.

When it became clear that she would probably lose her teaching job because of her poor performance, Dariya managed to manipulate several of the male teachers and the assistant principal into recommending her for a new job in a nearby school district. A year later, she was still at the new school but had been moved twice to different classrooms. According to teachers she worked with, Dariya still lacked close interpersonal relationships, although she described her current romantic relationship as "deeply involved." After a rather long period of depression, Dariya sought help from a psychologist, who diagnosed her as also having histrionic personality disorder.

Clinical Description

People with histrionic personality disorder are inclined to express their emotions in an exaggerated fashion—for example, hugging someone they have just met or crying uncontrollably during a sad movie (Lengel, 2020). They also tend to be vain, self-centered, and uncomfortable when they are not in the limelight. They are often seductive in appearance and behavior, and they are typically concerned about their looks. (Dariya, for example, spent a great deal of money on unusual jewelry and was sure to point it out to anyone who would listen.) In addition, they seek reassurance and approval constantly and may become upset or angry when others do not attend to them or praise them. People with histrionic personality disorder also tend to be impulsive and have great difficulty delaying gratification.

The cognitive style associated with histrionic personality disorder is impressionistic (Beck, Freeman, & Davis, 2007), characterized by a tendency to view situations in global, black-and-white terms. Speech is often vague, lacking in detail, and characterized by exaggeration (American Psychiatric Association, 2013; Nestadt et al., 2009). For example, when Dariya was asked about a date she had had the night before, she might say it was "amazing" but fail to provide more detailed information.

The high rate of this diagnosis among women versus men raises questions about the nature of the disorder and its diagnostic criteria (Boysen, Ebersole, Casner, & Coston, 2014). As we discuss in the beginning of this chapter, there is some thought that the features of histrionic personality disorder—such as

Jose Luis Pelaez Inc/DigitalVision/Getty Images

People with histrionic personality disorder tend to be vain, extravagant, and seductive.

overdramatization, vanity, seductiveness, and overconcern with physical appearance—are characteristic of the Western "stereotypical female" and may lead to an overdiagnosis among women. Sprock (2000) examined this important question and found some evidence for a bias among psychologists and psychiatrists to associate the diagnosis with women rather than men.

Causes

Despite its long history, little research has been done on the causes or treatment of histrionic personality disorder (Lengel, 2020). The ancient Greek philosophers believed that many unexplainable problems of women were caused by the uterus (hysteria) migrating within the body (Abse, 1987; Ussher, 2013). As has been shown, however, histrionic personality disorder also occurs among men.

One hypothesis involves a possible relationship with antisocial personality disorder. Evidence suggests that histrionic personality and antisocial personality co-occur more often than chance would account for. Lilienfeld and colleagues (1986), for example, found that roughly two-thirds of people with a histrionic personality also met criteria for antisocial personality disorder. The evidence for this association has led to the suggestion (see, for example, Cloninger, 1978; Lilienfeld, 1992) that histrionic personality and antisocial personality may be sex-typed alternative expressions of the same unidentified underlying condition. Women with the underlying condition may be predisposed to exhibit a predominantly histrionic pattern, whereas males with the underlying condition may be predisposed to exhibit a predominantly antisocial pattern. Whether this association exists remains a controversial issue, however, and further research on this potential relationship is needed (Dolan & Völlm, 2009; Salekin, Rogers, & Sewell, 1997), particularly given that borderline personality disorder has also been conceptualized as a female variant of psychopathy (Sprague, Javdani, Sadeh, Newman, & Verona, 2012).

Treatment

Although a great deal has been written about ways of helping people with histrionic personality disorder, little of the research demonstrates success (Lengel, 2020). Some therapists have tried to modify the attention-getting behavior. Kass, Silvers, and

DSM 5 **Table 12.7**
Diagnostic Criteria for Histrionic Personality Disorder

A pervasive pattern of excessive emotionality and attention seeking, beginning by early adulthood and present in a variety of contexts, as indicated by five (or more) of the following:

1. Is uncomfortable in situations in which he or she is not the center of attention.
2. Interaction with others is often characterized by inappropriate sexually seductive or provocative behavior.
3. Displays rapidly shifting and shallow expression of emotions.
4. Consistently uses physical appearance to draw attention to self.
5. Has a style of speech that is excessively impressionistic and lacking in detail.
6. Shows self-dramatization, theatricality, and exaggerated expression of emotion.
7. Is suggestible (i.e., easily influenced by others or circumstances).
8. Considers relationships to be more intimate than they actually are.

American Psychiatric Association. (2022). *Diagnostic and statistical manual of mental disorders* (5th ed., Text Revision).

Abrams (1972) worked with five women, four of whom had been hospitalized for attempts to take their own lives and all of whom were later diagnosed with histrionic personality disorder. The women were rewarded for appropriate interactions and fined for attention-getting behavior. The therapists noted improvement after an 18-month follow-up, but they did not collect scientific data to confirm their observation.

A large part of therapy for these individuals usually focuses on the problematic interpersonal relationships. They often manipulate others through emotional crises, using charm, sex, seductiveness, or complaining (Beck et al., 2007). People with histrionic personality disorder often need to be shown how the short-term gains derived from this interactional style result in long-term costs, and they need to be taught more appropriate ways of negotiating their wants and needs.

Narcissistic Personality Disorder

We all know people who think highly of themselves—perhaps exaggerating their real abilities. They consider themselves somehow different from others and deserving of special treatment. In **narcissistic personality disorder**, this tendency is taken to its extreme (Pincus, 2020). In Greek mythology, Narcissus was a youth who spurned the love of Echo, so enamored was he of his own beauty. He spent his days admiring his own image reflected in a pool of water. Psychoanalysts, including Freud, used the term *narcissistic* to describe people who show an exaggerated sense of self-importance and are preoccupied with receiving attention (Ronningstam, 2012). Consider the case of Jae.

Jae... It's All About Me

Jae was an office assistant in a small law firm. Now in his early 30s, Jae had an extremely poor job history. He never stayed employed at the same place for more than 2 years, and he spent considerable time working through temporary employment agencies. Your first encounter, however, would make you believe that he was extremely competent and that he ran the office. If you entered the waiting room, you were greeted by Jae, even though he wasn't the receptionist. He would be extremely solicitous, asking how he could be of assistance, offer you coffee, and ask you to make yourself comfortable in "his" reception area. Jae liked to talk, and any conversation was quickly redirected in a way that kept him the center of attention.

This type of ingratiating manner was welcomed at first but soon annoyed other staff. This was especially true when he referred to the other workers in the office as his staff, even though he was not responsible for supervising any of them. The conversations with visitors and staff often consumed a great deal of his time and the time of other staff, and this was becoming a problem.

He quickly became controlling in his job—a pattern revealed in his other positions as well—eagerly taking charge of duties assigned to others. Unfortunately, he did not complete these tasks well, and this created a great deal of friction.

When confronted with any of these difficulties, Jae would first blame others. Ultimately, however, it would become clear that Jae's self-centeredness and controlling nature were at the root of many of the office inefficiencies. During a disciplinary meeting with all of the law firm's partners, an unusual step, Jae became explosively abusive and blamed them for being out to get him. He insisted that his performance was exceptional at all of his previous positions—something contradicted by his previous employers—and that they were at fault. After calming down, he revealed a previous drinking problem, a history of depression, and multiple family problems, all of which he believed contributed to any difficulties he experienced.

The firm recommended he be seen at a university clinic as a condition of his continued employment, where he was diagnosed with major depression, as well as narcissistic personality disorder. Ultimately, his behavior—including lateness and incomplete work—resulted in his termination. In a revealing turn of events, Jae reapplied for another position at the same firm 2 years later. A mix-up in records failed to reveal his previous termination, but he lasted only 3 days—showing up late to work on his second and third days. He was convinced he could be successful, yet he could not change his behavior to conform to even the minimal standards needed to be successful at work.

Clinical Description

People with narcissistic personality disorder have an unreasonable sense of self-importance and are so preoccupied with themselves that they lack sensitivity and compassion for other people (Pincus, 2020). They are not comfortable unless someone is admiring them. Their exaggerated feelings and their fantasies of greatness, called *grandiosity,* create a number of negative attributes. They require and expect a great deal of special attention—the best table in the restaurant, the illegal parking space in front of the movie theater. They also tend to use or exploit others for their own interests and show little empathy. When confronted with other successful people, they can be extremely envious and arrogant. And because they often fail to live up to their own expectations, they are often depressed.

Causes and Treatment

We start out as infants being self-centered and demanding, which is part of our struggle for survival. Part of the socialization process, however, involves teaching children empathy and altruism. Some writers, including Kohut (1971, 1977), believe that narcissistic personality disorder arises largely from a profound failure by the parents of modeling empathy early in a child's development. As a consequence, the child remains fixated at a self-centered, grandiose stage of development. In addition, the child (and later the adult) becomes involved in an essentially endless and fruitless search for the ideal person who will meet their unfulfilled empathic needs.

In a sociological view, Christopher Lasch (1978) wrote in his popular book *The Culture of Narcissism* that this personality disorder is increasing in prevalence in most Western societies, primarily as a consequence of large-scale social changes, including greater emphasis on short-term hedonism, individualism, competitiveness, and success. According to Lasch, the "me generation" ("baby boomers" born between 1946 and 1954) produced more than its share of individuals with narcissistic personality disorder. Indeed, reports confirm that narcissistic personality disorder is increasing in prevalence (Huang et al., 2009). However, this apparent rise may be a consequence of increased interest in and research on the disorder.

Research on treatment options is extremely limited in both number of studies and reports of success (Cloninger & Svakic, 2009; Dhawan, Kunik, Oldham, & Coverdale, 2010; Ronningstam, 2014). When therapy is attempted with these individuals, it often focuses on their grandiosity, their hypersensitivity to evaluation, and their lack of empathy toward others (Beck et al., 2007; Campbell & Miller, 2011). Cognitive therapy strives to replace their fantasies with a focus on the day-to-day pleasurable experiences that are truly attainable. Coping strategies such as relaxation training are used to help them face and accept criticism. Helping them focus on the feelings of others is also a goal. Because individuals with this disorder are vulnerable to severe depressive episodes, particularly in middle age, treatment is often initiated for the depression. It is impossible to draw any conclusions, however, about the impact of such treatment on the actual narcissistic personality disorder.

DSM 5 **Table 12.8**

Diagnostic Criteria for Narcissistic Personality Disorder

A pervasive pattern of grandiosity (in fantasy or behavior), need for admiration, and lack of empathy, beginning by early adulthood and present in a variety of contexts, as indicated by five (or more) of the following:

1. Has a grandiose sense of self-importance (e.g., exaggerates achievements and talents, expects to be recognized as superior without commensurate achievements).
2. Is preoccupied with fantasies of unlimited success, power, brilliance, beauty, or ideal love.
3. Believes that he or she is "special" and unique and can only be understood by, or should associate with, other special or high-status people (or institutions).
4. Requests excessive admiration.
5. Has a sense of entitlement (i.e., unreasonable expectations of especially favorable treatment or automatic compliance with his or her expectations).
6. Is interpersonally exploitative (i.e., takes advantage of others to achieve his or her own ends).
7. Lacks empathy: is unwilling to recognize or identify with the feelings and needs of others.
8. Is often envious of others or believes that others are envious of him or her.
9. Shows arrogant, haughty behaviors or attitudes.

American Psychiatric Association. (2022). *Diagnostic and statistical manual of mental disorders* (5th ed., Text Revision).

Concept Check 12.3

Correctly identify the type of personality disorder described here.

1. Kayla has low self-esteem and usually feels empty unless she does dangerous and exciting things. She is involved in drugs and has casual unprotected sexual encounters, even with strangers. She threatens to take her own life if her partner suggests getting help or if they talk about leaving her. She alternates between passionately loving and hating them, sometimes going from one extreme to the next in a short time. ________
2. Lance is 19 and has been in trouble with the law for the past 2 years. He lies to his parents, vandalizes buildings in the community, and often fights with others. He shows no remorse for the people he injures or the grief that he causes his ailing parents. ________
3. Madison thinks she is the best at everything. She thinks her performance is always excellent and is extremely critical of anyone else's success. She constantly looks for admiration and reassurance from others. ________
4. Tyesha is known for being overly dramatic. She cries uncontrollably during sad movies, and her friends sometimes think that she is acting. She is vain and self-centered, interrupting many of class conversations to discuss her personal life.

Cluster C Personality Disorders

People diagnosed with the next three personality disorders we highlight—avoidant, dependent, and obsessive-compulsive—share common features with people who have anxiety disorders. These anxious or fearful personality disorders are described next.

Avoidant Personality Disorder

As the name suggests, people with **avoidant personality disorder** are extremely sensitive to the opinions of others, and although they desire social relationships, their anxiety leads them to avoid such associations. Their extremely low self-esteem—coupled with a fear of rejection—causes them to be limited in their friendships and dependent on those they feel comfortable with (Lerner, Teitelbaum, & Meehan, 2020). Consider the case of Jane.

Jane... Not Worth Noticing

Jane was raised by a mother with alcohol use disorder who had borderline personality disorder and who abused her verbally and physically. As a child, she made sense of her mother's abusive treatment by believing that she (Jane) must be an intrinsically unworthy person to be treated so badly. As an adult in her late 20s, Jane still expected to be rejected when others found out that she was inherently unworthy and bad.

Jane was highly self-critical and predicted that she would not be accepted. She thought that people would not like her, that they would see she was a loser, and that she would not have anything to say. She became upset if she perceived that someone in even the most fleeting encounter was reacting negatively or neutrally. If a newspaper vendor failed to smile at her, or a sales clerk was slightly curt, Jane automatically thought it must be because she (Jane) was somehow unworthy or unlikable. She then felt quite sad. Even when she was receiving positive feedback from a friend, she discounted it. As a result, Jane had few friends and certainly no close ones.

Source: Case and excerpt reprinted, with permission, from A.T. Beck & A. Freeman, 1990, *Cognitive therapy of personality disorders,* Guilford Press. ©1990 Guilford Press.

Clinical Description

Theodore Millon (1981), who initially proposed this diagnosis, notes that it is important to distinguish between individuals who are asocial because they are apathetic, affectively flat, and relatively uninterested in interpersonal relationships (comparable to what DSM-5 terms schizoid personality disorder) and individuals who are asocial because they are interpersonally anxious and fearful of rejection. The latter fit the criteria of avoidant personality disorder (Millon & Martinez, 1995). These individuals feel chronically rejected by others and are pessimistic about their future.

Causes

Some evidence has found that avoidant personality disorder is related to other subschizophrenia-related disorders, occurring more often in relatives of people who have schizophrenia (Lerner et al., 2020). A number of theories have been proposed that integrate biological and psychosocial influences as the cause of avoidant personality disorder. Millon (1981), for example, suggests that these individuals may be born with a difficult temperament or personality characteristics. As a result, their parents may reject them or at least not provide them with enough early, uncritical love. This rejection, in turn, may result in low self-esteem and social alienation, conditions that persist into adulthood. Limited support does exist for psychosocial influences in the cause of avoidant personality disorder. For example, Stravynski, Elie, and Franche (1989) questioned a group of people with avoidant personality disorder and a group of control participants about their early treatment by their parents. Those with the disorder remembered their parents as more rejecting, more guilt engendering, and less affectionate than the control group, suggesting parenting may contribute to the development of this disorder. Similarly, research has consistently found that these individuals are more likely to report childhood experiences of neglect, isolation, rejection, and conflict with others (Eikenaes, Egeland, Hummelen, & Wilberg, 2015; Meyer & Carver, 2000).

Treatment

In contrast to the scarcity of research into most other personality disorders, there are a number of well-controlled studies on approaches to therapy for people with avoidant personality disorder (Leahy & McGinn, 2012). Behavioral intervention techniques for anxiety and social skills problems have had some success (Lerner et al., 2020). Because of the similarity between avoidant personality disorder and social phobia (see Chapter 5), research has looked at medical interventions for anxiety (several benzodiazepines, selective serotonin reuptake inhibitors, and monoamine oxidase inhibitors) and found that they were effective in treating avoidant personality disorder (Lerner et al., 2020). Therapeutic alliance—the collaborative connection between therapist and client—appears to be an important predictor for treatment success in this group (Strauss et al., 2006).

Dependent Personality Disorder

We all know what it means to be dependent on another person. People with **dependent personality disorder**, however, rely on others to make ordinary decisions as well as important ones, which results in an unreasonable fear of abandonment. Consider the case of Karen.

DSM 5 Table 12.9
Diagnostic Criteria for Avoidant Personality Disorder

A pervasive pattern of social inhibition, feelings of inadequacy, and hypersensitivity to negative evaluation, beginning by early adulthood and present in a variety of contexts, as indicated by four (or more) of the following:

1. Avoids occupational activities that involve significant interpersonal contact because of fears of criticism, disapproval, or rejection.
2. Is unwilling to get involved with people unless certain of being liked.
3. Shows restraint within intimate relationships because of the fear of being shamed or ridiculed.
4. Is preoccupied with being criticized or rejected in social situations.
5. Is inhibited in new interpersonal situations because of feelings of inadequacy.
6. Views self as socially inept, personally unappealing, or inferior to others.
7. Is unusually reluctant to take personal risks or to engage in any new activities because they may prove embarrassing.

American Psychiatric Association. (2022). *Diagnostic and statistical manual of mental disorders* (5th ed., Text Revision).

Karen... Whatever You Say

Karen was a 45-year-old married woman who was referred for treatment by her physician for problems with panic attacks. During the evaluation, she appeared to be worried, sensitive, and naive. She was easily overcome with emotion and cried on and off throughout the session. She was self-critical at every opportunity throughout the evaluation. For example, when asked how she got along with other people, she reported that "others think I'm dumb and inadequate," although she could give no evidence as to what made her think that. She reported that she didn't like school because "I was dumb" and that she always felt that she was not good enough.

Karen described staying in her first marriage for 10 years, even though "it was hell." Her husband had affairs with many other women and was verbally abusive. She tried to leave him many times but gave in to his repeated requests to return. She was finally able to divorce him, and shortly afterward she met and married her current husband, whom she described as kind, sensitive, and supportive. Karen stated that she preferred to have others make important decisions and agreed with other people to avoid conflict. She worried about being left alone without anyone to take care of her and reported feeling lost without other people's reassurance. She also reported that her feelings were easily hurt, so she worked hard not to do anything that might lead to criticism.

Source: Case and excerpt reprinted, with permission, from A. T. Beck & A. Freeman, 1990, *Cognitive therapy of personality disorders*, Guilford Press. © 1990 by Guilford Press.

Clinical Description

Individuals with dependent personality disorder sometimes agree with other people when their own opinion differs so as not to be rejected (Bornstein, 2012). Their desire to obtain and maintain supportive and nurturing relationships may lead to their other behavioral characteristics, including submissiveness, timidity, and passivity. People with this disorder are similar to those with avoidant personality disorder in their feelings of inadequacy, sensitivity to criticism, and need for reassurance. However, people with avoidant personality disorder respond to these feelings by avoiding relationships, whereas those with dependent personality disorder respond by clinging to relationships (Bornstein, 2012; Disney, 2013). It is important to note that in certain cultures (such as East Asian Confucianism) dependence and submission may be viewed as a desired interpersonal state (Chen, Nettles, & Chen, 2009).

Causes and Treatment

We are all born dependent on other people for food, physical protection, and nurturance. Part of the socialization process in most cultures involves helping us live independently (Bornstein, 1992). It was thought that such disruptions as the early death of a parent or neglect or rejection by caregivers could cause people to grow up fearing abandonment (Stone, 1993). It also is clear, however, that genetic influences are important in the development of this disorder (for example, Gjerde et al., 2012). What is not yet understood are the physiological factors underlying this genetic influence and the ways they interact with environmental influences (Sanislow et al., 2012).

The treatment literature for this disorder is mostly descriptive; little research exists to show whether a particular treatment is effective (Borge et al., 2010; Paris, 2008). On the surface, because of their attentiveness and eagerness to give responsibility for their problems to the therapist, people with dependent personality disorder can appear to be ideal patients. That very submissiveness, however, negates one of the major goals of therapy, which is to make the person more independent and personally responsible (Leahy & McGinn, 2012). Therapy therefore progresses gradually as the patient develops confidence in his ability to make decisions independently (Maccaferri et al., 2020). There is a particular need for care that the patient does not become overly dependent on the therapist.

DSM 5 **Table 12.10**
Diagnostic Criteria for Dependent Personality Disorder

A pervasive and excessive need to be taken care of that leads to submissive and clinging behavior and fears of separation, beginning by early adulthood and present in a variety of contexts, as indicated by five (or more) of the following:

1. Has difficulty making everyday decisions without an excessive amount of advice and reassurance from others.
2. Needs others to assume responsibility for most major areas of his or her life.
3. Has difficulty expressing disagreement with others because of fear of loss of support or approval. (***Note:*** Do not include realistic fears of retribution.)
4. Has difficulty initiating projects or doing things on his or her own (because of a lack of self-confidence in judgment or abilities rather than a lack of motivation or energy).
5. Goes to excessive lengths to obtain nurturance and support from others, to the point of volunteering to do things that are unpleasant.
6. Feels uncomfortable or helpless when alone because of exaggerated fears of being unable to care of himself or herself.
7. Urgently seeks another relationship as a source of care and support when a close relationship ends.
8. Is unrealistically preoccupied with fears of being left to take care of himself or herself.

American Psychiatric Association. (2022). *Diagnostic and statistical manual of mental disorders* (5th ed., Text Revision).

Obsessive-Compulsive Personality Disorder

People who have **obsessive-compulsive personality disorder** are characterized by a fixation on things being done "the right way" (Grant, Pinto, & Chamberlain, 2020). Although many might envy their persistence and dedication, this preoccupation with details prevents them from completing much of anything. Consider the case of Rami.

Rami... Getting It Exactly Right

Each day at exactly 8 a.m., Rami arrived at his office at the university where he was a graduate student in psychology. On his way, he always stopped at the 7-Eleven for coffee and the *New York Times*. From 8 a.m. to 9:15 a.m., he drank his coffee and read the paper. At 9:15 a.m., he reorganized the files that held the hundreds of papers related to his doctoral dissertation, now several years overdue. From 10 a.m. until noon, he read one of these papers, highlighting relevant passages. Then he took the paper bag that held his lunch (always a peanut butter and jelly sandwich and an apple) and went to the cafeteria to purchase a soda and eat by himself. From 1 p.m. until 5 p.m., he held meetings, organized his desk, made lists of things to do, and entered his references into a new database program on his computer. At home, Rami had dinner with his wife and then worked on his dissertation until after 11 p.m., although much of the time was spent trying out new features of his home computer.

Rami was no closer to completing his dissertation than he had been 4.5 years ago. His wife was threatening to leave him because he was equally rigid about everything at home and she didn't want to remain in this limbo of graduate school forever. When Rami eventually sought help from a therapist for his anxiety over his deteriorating marriage, he was diagnosed as having obsessive-compulsive personality disorder.

DSM 5 **Table 12.11**
Diagnostic Criteria for Obsessive-Compulsive Personality Disorder

A pervasive pattern of preoccupation with orderliness, perfectionism, and mental and interpersonal control, at the expense of flexibility, openness, and efficiency, beginning by early adulthood and present in a variety of contexts, as indicated by four (or more) of the following:

1. Is preoccupied with details, rules, lists, order, organization, or schedules to the extent that the major point of the activity is lost.
2. Shows perfectionism that interferes with task completion (e.g., is unable to complete a project because his or her own overly strict standards are not met).
3. Is excessively devoted to work and productivity to the exclusion of leisure activities and friendships (not accounted for by obvious economic necessity).
4. Is overconscientious, scrupulous, and inflexible about matters of morality, ethics, or values (not accounted for by cultural or religious identification).
5. Is unable to discard worn-out or worthless objects even when they have no sentimental value.
6. Is reluctant to delegate tasks or to work with others unless they submit to exactly his or her way of doing things.
7. Adopts a miserly spending style toward both self and others; money is viewed as something to be hoarded for future catastrophes.
8. Shows rigidity and stubbornness.

American Psychiatric Association. (2022). *Diagnostic and statistical manual of mental disorders* (5th ed., Text Revision).

Clinical Description

Like many with this personality disorder, Rami is work oriented, spending little time going to movies or parties or doing anything that isn't related to his graduate studies. Because of their general rigidity, these people tend to have poor interpersonal relationships (Samuels & Costa, 2012).

This personality disorder seems to be only distantly related to obsessive-compulsive disorder, one of the anxiety disorders we described in Chapter 5 (Samuels & Costa, 2012). People like Rami tend not to have the obsessive thoughts and the compulsive behaviors seen in the like-named obsessive-compulsive disorder. Although people with the anxiety disorder sometimes show characteristics of the personality disorder, they show the characteristics of other personality disorders as well (for example, avoidant, histrionic, or dependent) (Melca, Yücel, Mendlowicz, de Oliviera-Souza, & Fontenelle, 2015; Trull, Scheiderer, & Tomko, 2012).

Obsessive-compulsive personality disorder is one of the most common personality disorders in the general population (Burkauskas & Fineberg, 2020). DSM-5 estimates the prevalence of this disorder to be between 2.1% and 7.9% (American Psychiatric Association, 2013, p. 681). Despite the prevalence of this disorder, more research has been conducted on borderline and antisocial personality disorders (Grant et al., 2020), perhaps because these disorders can be more disruptive.

An intriguing theory suggests that the psychological profiles of many serial killers point to the role of obsessive-compulsive personality disorder (Williams, 2020). Ferreira (2000) notes that these individuals do not often fit the definition of someone with a severe mental illness—such as schizophrenia—but are "masters of control" in manipulating their victims. Their need to control all aspects of the crime fits the pattern of people with obsessive-compulsive personality disorder, and some combination of this disorder and unfortunate childhood experiences may lead to this disturbing behavior pattern (Williams, 2020). Obsessive-compulsive personality disorder may also play a role among some sex offenders—in particular, pedophiles. Brain-imaging research on pedophiles suggests that brain functioning in these individuals is similar to those with obsessive-compulsive personality disorder (Schiffer et al., 2007). At the other end of the behavioral spectrum, it is also common to find obsessive-compulsive personality disorder among gifted children, whose quest for perfectionism can be quite debilitating (Nugent, 2000).

Causes and Treatment

There seems to be a moderate genetic contribution to obsessive-compulsive personality disorder (Stein & Lochner, 2020). Some people may be predisposed to favor structure in their lives, but to reach the level it did with Rami may require parental reinforcement of conformity and neatness.

Therapy often attacks the fears that seem to underlie the need for orderliness (Pinto, 2015). These individuals are often afraid that what they do will be inadequate, so they procrastinate and excessively ruminate about important issues and minor details alike. Therapists help the individual relax or use cognitive

People with obsessive-compulsive personality disorder are preoccupied with doing things "the right way."

reappraisal techniques to reframe compulsive thoughts. This form of cognitive-behavioral therapy—following along the lines of treatment for obsessive-compulsive disorder (see Chapter 5)—appears to be effective for people with this personality disorder (Pinto, 2020).

Concept Check 12.4

Match the following scenarios with the correct personality disorder.

1. During a therapy session, Jorge gets up for a glass of water. Ten minutes later, Jorge still is not back. He first had to clean the fountain area and neatly arrange the glasses before pouring his glass of water. ____________
2. Whitney is self-critical and claims she is unintelligent and has no skills. She is also afraid to be alone and seeks constant reassurance from her family and friends. She says and does nothing about her cheating husband because she thinks that if she shows any resolve or initiative, she will be abandoned and will have to take care of herself. ____________
3. Jamar has no social life because of his great fear of rejection. He disregards compliments and reacts excessively to criticism, which feeds his pervasive feelings of inadequacy. Jamar takes everything personally. ____________

DSM Controversies: *The Battle for the Personality Disorders*

Discussion about the personality disorders in DSM-5 included proposals for a number of major changes to this category. As we have seen, the elimination of the distinction between Axis I and Axis II disorders elevated the personality disorders into the mainstream of problems experienced by individuals. However, other major changes that appeared to be ready for inclusion in DSM-5 never occurred. The goal of creating dimensions of different personality traits along the lines of the "Big 5" rather than the specific disorders outlined in this chapter (such as borderline personality disorder and antisocial personality disorder) never materialized. In part, this proposal was not included in DSM-5 due to the difficulty in making a diagnosis (too many permutations) and potential problems in using that information to design treatments (Skodol, 2012).

However, one of the biggest changes proposed was to completely eliminate four of the personality disorders (paranoid, schizoid, histrionic, avoidant, and dependent personality disorders). Instead, people previously diagnosed with these disorders would be identified as having a general personality disorder with the traits specified (such as suspiciousness, emotional liability, and hostility). The rationale for their removal included a relative lack of research on these disorders and significant overlap among the disorders (comorbidity) (Skodol, 2012). In anticipation of this significant change, one set of researchers authored a paper with the title "The Death of Histrionic Personality Disorder" (Blashfield et al., 2012), and the personality disorders community of researchers in general was divided over this change (Pull, 2013). Ultimately, the final draft retained these disorders and left for a later time any proposals for dealing with the problems of lack of research and specificity. This back and forth on how to carve up diagnoses exemplifies the difficulties that continue to exist for any diagnostic system, even after decades of arduous and dedicated research.

Summary

An Overview of Personality Disorders

- The personality disorders represent long-standing and ingrained ways of thinking, feeling, and behaving that can cause significant distress. Because people may display two or more of these maladaptive ways of interacting with the world, considerable disagreement remains over how to categorize the personality disorders.
- DSM-5 includes 10 personality disorders that are divided into three clusters: Cluster A (odd or eccentric) includes paranoid, schizoid, and schizotypal personality disorders; Cluster B (dramatic, emotional, or erratic) includes antisocial, borderline, histrionic, and narcissistic personality disorders; and Cluster C (anxious or fearful) includes avoidant, dependent, and obsessive-compulsive personality disorders.

Cluster A Personality Disorders

- People with paranoid personality disorder are excessively mistrustful and suspicious of other people, without any justification. They tend not to confide in others and expect other people to do them harm.
- People with schizoid personality disorder show a pattern of detachment from social relationships and a limited range of emotions in interpersonal situations. They seem aloof, cold, and indifferent to other people.
- People with schizotypal personality disorder are typically socially isolated and behave in ways that would seem unusual to most of us. In addition, they tend to be suspicious and have odd beliefs about the world.

Cluster B Personality Disorders

- People with antisocial personality disorder have a history of failing to comply with social norms. They perform actions most of us would find unacceptable, such as stealing from friends and family. They also tend to be irresponsible, impulsive, and deceitful.
- In contrast to the DSM-5 criteria for antisocial personality, which focus almost entirely on observable behaviors (for example, impulsively and repeatedly changing employment, residence, or sexual partners), the related concept of psychopathy primarily reflects underlying personality traits (for example, self-centeredness or manipulativeness).
- People with borderline personality disorder lack stability in their moods and in their relationships with other people, and they usually have poor self-esteem. These individuals often feel empty and are at great risk of suicide.
- Individuals with histrionic personality disorder tend to be overly dramatic and often appear almost to be acting.
- People with narcissistic personality disorder think highly of themselves—beyond their real abilities. They consider themselves somehow different from others and deserving of special treatment.

Cluster C Personality Disorders

- People with avoidant personality disorder are extremely sensitive to the opinions of others and therefore avoid social relationships. Their extremely low self-esteem, coupled with a fear of rejection, causes them to reject the attention of others.
- Individuals with dependent personality disorder rely on others to the extent of letting them make everyday decisions, as well as major ones; this results in an unreasonable fear of being abandoned.
- People who have obsessive-compulsive personality disorder are characterized by a fixation on things being done "the right way." This preoccupation with details prevents them from completing much of anything.
- Treating people with personality disorders is often difficult because they usually do not see that their difficulties are a result of the way they relate to others.
- Personality disorders are important for the clinician to consider because they may interfere with efforts to treat more specific problems such as anxiety, depression, or substance abuse. Unfortunately, the presence of one or more personality disorders is associated with a poor treatment outcome and a generally negative prognosis.

Key Terms

personality disorder, 445
paranoid personality disorder, 452
schizoid personality disorder, 453
schizotypal personality disorder, 455
antisocial personality disorder, 457
psychopathy, 458
borderline personality disorder, 465
dialectical behavior therapy (DBT), 468
histrionic personality disorder, 469
narcissistic personality disorder, 470
avoidant personality disorder, 472
dependent personality disorder, 473
obsessive-compulsive personality disorder, 474

Answers to Concept Checks

12.1

1. comorbidity; 2. Cluster A, Cluster B, Cluster C; 3. categories; 4. chronic; 5. bias

12.2

1. paranoid; 2. schizotypal; 3. schizoid

12.3

1. borderline; 2. antisocial; 3. narcissistic; 4. histrionic

12.4

1. obsessive-compulsive; 2. dependent; 3. Avoidant

Exploring Personality Disorders

- People with personality disorders think and behave in ways that cause distress to themselves and/or the people who care about them.
- There are three main groups, or clusters, of personality disorders, which usually begin in childhood.

CLUSTER A
Odd or Eccentric

Gazelle Technologies

Paranoid
extreme suspicion

Psychological Influences
- Thoughts that people are malicious, deceptive, and threatening
- Behavior based on mistaken assumptions about others

Biological Influences
- Possible but unclear link with schizophrenia

Causes

Social/Cultural Influences
- "Outsiders" may be susceptible because of unique experiences (e.g., prisoners, refugees, people with hearing impairments, and the elderly)
- Parents' early teaching may influence

Treatment
- Difficult because of client's mistrust and suspicion
- Cognitive work to change thoughts
- Low success rate

Schizoid
social isolation

Psychological Influences
- Very limited range of emotions
- Apparently cold and unconnected
- Unaffected by praise or criticism

Biological Influences
- May be associated with lower density of dopamine receptors

Causes

Treatment
- Learning value of social relationships
- Social skills training with role playing

Social/Cultural Influences
- Preference for social isolation
- Lack of social skills
- Lack of interest in close relationships, including romantic or sexual

Schizotypal
suspicion and odd behavior

Psychological Influences
- Unusual beliefs, behavior, or dress
- Suspiciousness
- Believing insignificant events are personally relevant ("ideas of reference")
- Expressing little emotion
- Symptoms of major depressive disorder

Biological Influences
- Genetic vulnerability for schizophrenia but without the biological or environmental stresses present in that disorder

Causes

Treatment
- Teaching social skills to reduce isolation and suspicion
- Medication (haloperidol) to reduce ideas of reference, odd communication, and isolation
- Low success rate

Social/Cultural Influences
- Preference for social isolation
- Excessive social anxiety
- Lack of social skills

CLUSTER C
Anxious or Fearful

Photodisc/Getty Images

Dependent
pervasive need to be taken care of

Psychological Influences
- Early "loss" of caretaker (death, rejection, or neglect) leads to fear of abandonment
- Timidity and passivity

Biological Influences
- Each of us born dependent for protection, food, and nurturance

Causes

Social/Cultural Influences
- Agreement for the sake of avoiding conflict
- Similar to Avoidant in
  – inadequacy
  – sensitivity to criticism
  – need for reassurance

BUT

for those same shared reasons
- Avoidants withdraw
- Dependents cling

Treatment
- Very little research Appear as ideal clients
- Submissiveness negates independence

CLUSTER B Dramatic, Emotional, or Erratic

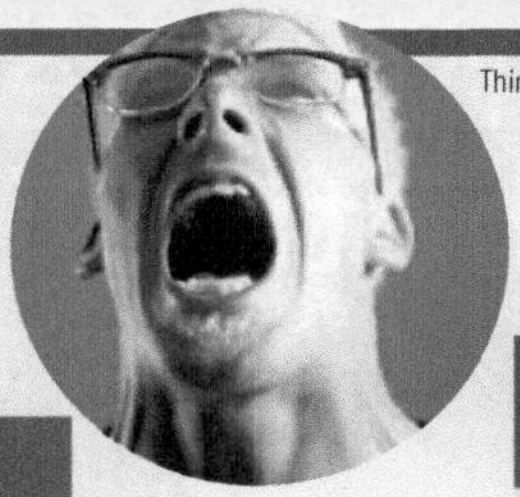

Thinkstock/Getty Images

Narcissistic
excessive interest in oneself

Psychological Influences

- May be influenced by lack of parental modeling of empathy
- Later this influences the child's ability to empathize with others

Biological Influences

- Unclear how biology plays a role in this disorder

Causes

Social/Cultural Influences

- Changes in societal norms that emphasize short-term hedonism, individualism, competitiveness, and success

Treatment

- Cognitive therapy to focus on the day-to-day pleasurable experiences that are attainable
- Teaching coaching strategies to use and accept criticism

Antisocial
violation of others' rights

Psychological Influence

- Difficulty learning to avoid punishment
- Indifferent to concerns of others

Biological Influences

- Genetic vulnerability combined with environmental influences
- Abnormally low cortical arousal
- High fear threshold

Causes

Social/Cultural Influences

- Criminality
- Stress/exposure to trauma
- Inconsistent parental discipline
- Socioeconomic disadvantage

Treatment

- Seldom successful (incarceration instead)
- Parent training if problems are caught early
- Prevention through preschool programs

Borderline
tumultuous instability

Psychological Influences

- Suicidal
- Erratic moods
- Impulsivity

Biological Influences

- Familial link to mood disorders
- Possibly inherited tendencies (impulsivity or volatility)

Causes

Social/Cultural Influences

- Early trauma, especially sexual/physical abuse
- Rapid cultural changes (immigration) may trigger symptoms

Treatment

- Dialectical behavior therapy (DBT)
  Medication:
  – tricyclic antidepressants
  – minor tranquilizers
  – lithium

Histrionic
excessively emotional

Psychological Influences

- Vain and self-centered
- Easily upset if ignored
- Vague and hyperbolic
- Impulsive; difficulty delaying gratification

Biological Influences

- Possible link to antisocial disorder
  – women histrionic/men antisocial

Causes

Treatment

- Little evidence of success
- Rewards and fines
- Focus on interpersonal relations

Social/Cultural Influences

- Overly dramatic behavior attracts attention
- Seductive
- Approval-seeking

Avoidant
inhibition

Psychological Influences

- Low self-esteem
- Fear of rejection, criticism leads to fear of attention
- Extreme sensitivity
- Resembles social phobia

Biological Influences

- Innate characteristics may cause rejection

Causes

Social/Cultural Influences

- Insufficient parental affection

Treatment

- Behavioral intervention techniques sometimes successful
  – systematic desensitization
  – behavioral rehearsal
- Improvements usually modest

Obsessive-Compulsive
fixation on details

Biological Influences

- Distant relation to OCD
- Probable weak genetic role
  – predisposition to structure combined with parental reinforcement

Psychological Influences

- Generally rigid
- Dependent on routines
- Procrastinating

Causes

Social/Cultural Influences

- Very work-oriented
- Poor interpersonal relationships

Treatment

- Little information
- Therapy
  – attack fears behind need
  – relaxation or distraction techniques redirect compulsion to order

13 Schizophrenia Spectrum and Other Psychotic Disorders

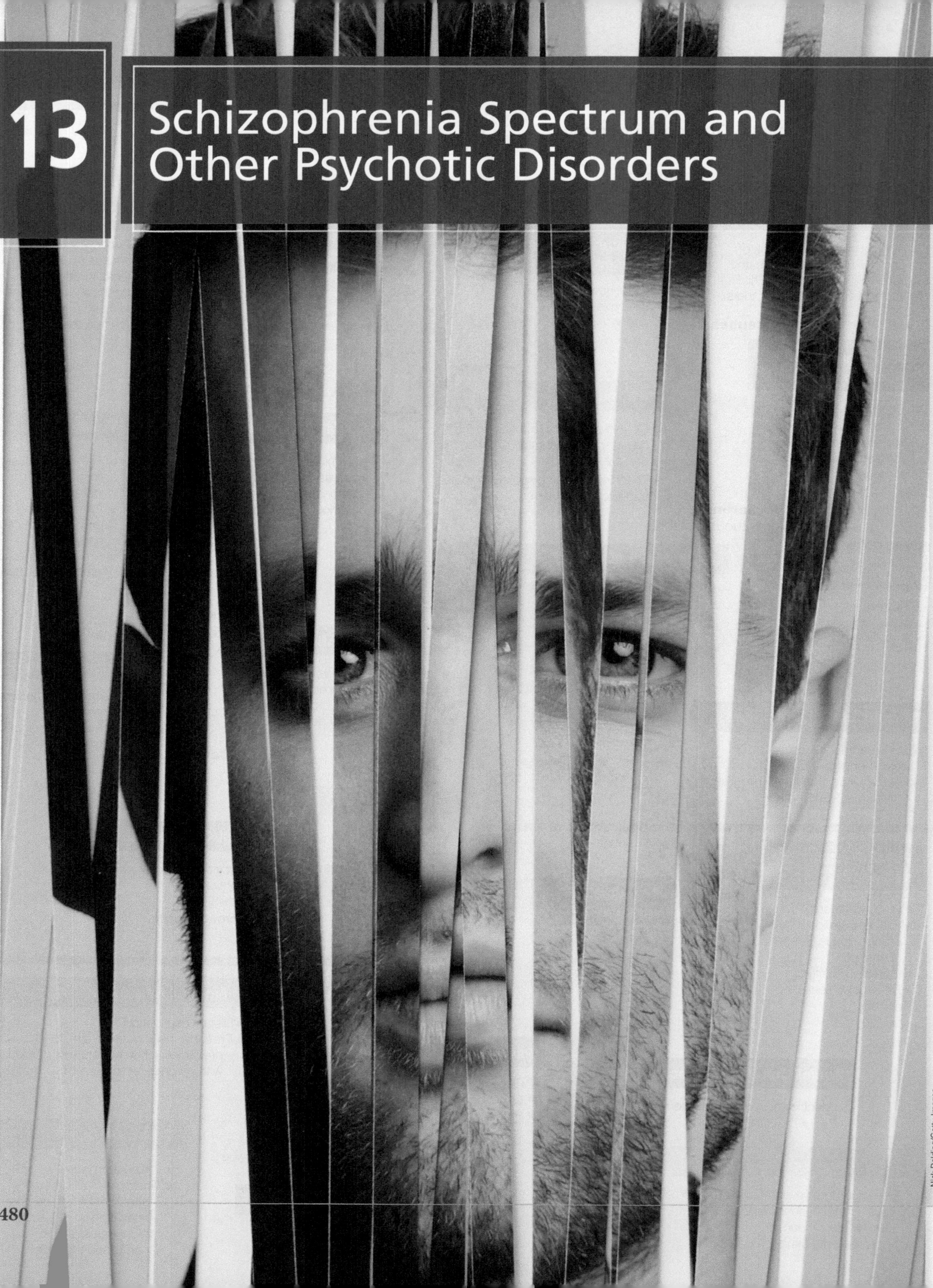

Nick Dolding/Getty Images

Learning Objectives

LO13.1 Describe the historical perspectives on schizophrenia reflected in 19th- and 20th-century definitions of the disorder.

LO13.2 Define schizophrenia according to its clinical symptoms and criteria as presented in the DSM-5.

LO13.3 Differentiate among positive, negative, and disorganized symptoms of schizophrenia.

LO13.4 Explain how factors such as genes, neurotransmitter imbalances, and expressed emotion contribute to the development of schizophrenia.

LO13.5 Explain how antipsychotic medications, employment support, community-based and family interventions, and psychosocial approaches can work together to treat schizophrenia.

Perspectives on Schizophrenia

A middle-aged man walks the streets of New York City with aluminum foil on the inside of his hat so Martians cannot read his mind. A young woman sits in her college classroom and hears the voice of God telling her she is a vile and disgusting person. You try to strike up a conversation with the supermarket bagger, but he stares at you vacantly and says only one or two words in a flat, toneless voice. Each of these people may have **schizophrenia**, the startling disorder characterized by a broad spectrum of cognitive and emotional dysfunctions including delusions and hallucinations, disorganized speech and behavior, and inappropriate emotions.

Schizophrenia is a complex syndrome that inevitably has a devastating effect on the lives of the person affected and on family members. This disorder can disrupt a person's perception, thought, speech, and movement: almost every aspect of daily functioning. Society often devalues these individuals. People with these severe mental health problems are more likely to be stigmatized and discriminated against than those without schizophrenia (Valery & Prouteau, 2020). Moreover, despite important advances in treatment, full recovery from schizophrenia has a low base rate of 1 in 7 patients (Jääskeläinen et al., 2013). This catastrophic disorder takes a tremendous emotional toll on everyone involved. In addition to the emotional costs, the financial drain is considerable. The annual cost of schizophrenia in the United States is estimated to exceed $150 billion when factors such as family caregiving, lost wages, and treatment are considered (Keepers et al., 2020). Because schizophrenia is so widespread, affecting approximately 1 of every 100 people at some point in their lives, and because its consequences are so severe, research on its causes and treatment has expanded rapidly. Given the attention it has received, you would think the question "What is schizophrenia?" would by now be answered easily. It is not.

In this chapter, we explore this intriguing disorder and review efforts to determine whether schizophrenia is distinct or a combination of disorders. The search is complicated by the presence of subtypes: different presentations and combinations of symptoms such as hallucinations, delusions, and disorders of speech, emotion, and socialization (Lawrence & First, 2020). After discussing the characteristics of people with schizophrenia, we describe research into its causes and treatment.

Early Figures in Diagnosing Schizophrenia

The history of schizophrenia as it has evolved over the years is unparalleled by any other disorder covered in this book. Knowing something about this history will help you understand that the nature of the disorder is multifaceted and treatment is correspondingly complex.

In *Observations on Madness and Melancholy*, published in 1809, John Haslam eloquently portrayed what he called "a form of insanity." In the following passage, Haslam mentions some symptoms that inform our current conception of schizophrenia:

> The attack is almost imperceptible; some months usually elapse before it becomes the subject of particular notice; and fond relatives are frequently deceived by the hope that it is only an abatement of excessive vivacity, conducting to a prudent reserve, and steadiness of character. A degree of apparent thoughtfulness and inactivity precede, together with a diminution of the ordinary curiosity, concerning that which is passing before them; and they therefore neglect those objects and pursuits which formerly proved courses of delight and instruction. The sensibility appears to be considerably blunted: they do not bear the same affection towards their parents and relations: they become unfeeling to kindness, and careless of reproof. … I have painfully witnessed this hopeless and degrading change, which in a short time has transformed the most promising and vigorous intellect into a slavering and bloated idiot. (Haslam, 1809/1976, pp. 64–67)

About the same time Haslam was writing his description in England, the French physician Philippe Pinel was writing about people we would describe as having schizophrenia (Pinel, 1801/1962, 1809). Some 50 years later, another physician, Benedict Morel, used the French term *démence* (loss of mind) *précoce* (early, premature) because the onset of the disorder is often during adolescence.

Toward the end of the 19th century, the German psychiatrist Emil Kraepelin (1899) built on the writings of Haslam, Pinel, and Morel (among others) to give us what stands today as the most enduring description and categorization of schizophrenia. Two of Kraepelin's accomplishments are especially important. First, he combined several symptoms of "insanity" that had usually been viewed as reflecting separate and distinct disorders: **catatonia** (alternating immobility and excited agitation), **hebephrenia** (silly and immature emotionality), and **paranoia** (delusions of grandeur or persecution). Kraepelin thought these symptoms shared similar underlying features and included them under the Latin term **dementia praecox**. Although the clinical manifestation might differ from person to person, Kraepelin believed an early onset at the heart of each disorder develops into "mental weakness."

Eugen Bleuler (1857–1939), a Swiss psychiatrist, introduced the term *schizophrenia* and was a pioneer in the field.

In a second important contribution, Kraepelin (1898) distinguished dementia praecox from manic-depressive illness (now called bipolar disorder). For people with dementia praecox, an early age of onset and a poor outcome were characteristic; in contrast, these patterns were not essential to manic depression (Lewis, Escalona, & Keith, 2009). Kraepelin also noted the numerous symptoms in people with dementia praecox, including hallucinations, delusions, negativism, and stereotyped behavior.

A second major figure in the history of schizophrenia was Kraepelin's contemporary, Eugen Bleuler (1908), a Swiss psychiatrist who introduced the term *schizophrenia* (Berrios, 2011; Fusar-Poli & Politi, 2008). The label was significant because it signaled Bleuler's departure from Kraepelin on what he thought was the core problem. *Schizophrenia*, which comes from the combination of the Greek words for "split" (*skhizein*) and "mind" (*phren*), reflected Bleuler's belief that underlying all the unusual behaviors shown by people with this disorder was an **associative splitting** of the basic functions of personality. This concept emphasized the "breaking of associative threads," or the destruction of the forces that connect one function to the next. Furthermore, Bleuler believed that a difficulty keeping a consistent train of thought characteristic of all people with this disorder led to the many and diverse symptoms they displayed. Whereas Kraepelin focused on early onset and poor outcomes, Bleuler highlighted what he believed to be the universal underlying problem. Unfortunately, the concept of "split mind" inspired the common but incorrect use of the term *schizophrenia* to mean split or multiple personality. (For a summary of the early contributors to the concept of schizophrenia, see Table 13.1.)

Identifying Symptoms

It is not easy to point to one thing that characterizes a person with schizophrenia. As you read about different disorders in this book, you have learned that a particular behavior, way of thinking, or emotion usually defines or is characteristic of each disorder. For example, depression always includes feelings of sadness, and panic disorder is always accompanied by intense feelings of anxiety. Surprisingly, this is not the case for schizophrenia. Schizophrenia is a number of behaviors or symptoms that are not necessarily shared by all people who are given this diagnosis. Kraepelin described the situation when he outlined his view of dementia praecox in the late 1800s:

> The complexity of the conditions which we observe in the domain of dementia praecox is very great, so that their inner connection is at first recognizable only by their occurring one after the other in the course of the same disease. In any case certain fundamental disturbances, even though they cannot for the most part be regarded as characteristic, yet return frequently in the same form, but in the most diverse combinations. (Kraepelin, 1919, p. 5)

This mix of symptoms was also highlighted by Bleuler in the title of his 1911 book, *Dementia Praecox, or the Group of Schizophrenias*, which emphasizes the complexity of the disorder. The varied nature of schizophrenia is something we come back to throughout this chapter. Individuals who have schizophrenia have varying symptoms, and we find that the causes vary as well.

Despite these complexities, researchers have identified clusters of symptoms that make up the disorder of schizophrenia. Later we describe these dramatic symptoms, such as seeing or hearing things that others do not (*hallucinations*) or having beliefs that are unrealistic, bizarre, and not shared by others in the same culture (*delusions*). But first, consider the following case of an individual who had an intense but relatively rare short-term episode of psychotic behavior.

What caused Amrit to act so strangely? Was it being laid off from his job? Was it the death of his father? Was it a genetic

Table 13.1 Early Figures in the History of Schizophrenia

Date	Historical Figure	Contribution
1809	John Haslam (1764–1844)	A superintendent of a British hospital. In *Observations on Madness and Melancholy*, he outlined a description of the symptoms of schizophrenia.
1801/1809	Philippe Pinel (1745–1826)	A French physician who described cases of schizophrenia
1852	Benedict Morel (1809–1873)	A physician at a French institution who used the term *démence précoce* (in Latin, *dementia praecox*), meaning early or premature (*précoce*) loss of mind (*démence*) to describe schizophrenia
1898/1899	Emil Kraepelin (1856–1926)	A German psychiatrist who unified the distinct categories of schizophrenia (hebephrenic, catatonic, and paranoid) under the name *dementia praecox*
1908	Eugen Bleuler (1857–1939)	A Swiss psychiatrist who introduced the term *schizophrenia*, meaning "splitting of the mind"

Amrit... Saving the Children

We first met 22-year-old Amrit at an outpatient clinic in a psychiatric hospital. Amrit's family was extremely concerned and upset by his unusual behavior and was desperately seeking help for him. They said that he was "sick" and "talking like a crazy man," and they were afraid he might harm himself.

Amrit had a normal childhood in a middle-class suburban neighborhood. His parents had been happily married until his father's death several years earlier. Amrit was an average student throughout school and had completed an associate's degree in junior college. His family seemed to think he regretted not continuing on to receive a bachelor's degree. Amrit had worked in a series of temporary jobs, and his mother reported that he seemed satisfied with what he was doing. He lived and worked in a major city, some 15 minutes from his mother and his married brother and sister.

Amrit's family said that about 3 weeks before he came to the clinic, he had started speaking strangely. He had been laid off from his job a few days before because of cutbacks and hadn't communicated with any of his family members for several days. When they next spoke with him, his behavior startled them. Although he had always been idealistic and anxious to help other people, he now talked about saving all the starving children in the world with his "secret plan." At first, his family assumed this was just an example of Amrit's sarcastic wit, but his demeanor changed to one of extreme concern and he spoke nonstop about his plans. He began carrying several spiral notebooks that he claimed contained his scheme for helping starving children; he said he would reveal it only at the right time to the right person. Suspecting that Amrit might be taking drugs, which could explain the sudden and dramatic change in his behavior, his family searched his apartment. Although they didn't find any evidence of drug use, they did find his checkbook and noticed a number of strange entries. Over the past several weeks, Amrit's handwriting had deteriorated, and he had written notes instead of the usual check information ("Start to begin now"; "This is important!"; "They must be saved"). He had also made unusual notes in several of his most prized books, a particularly alarming development given his reverence for these books.

As the days went on, Amrit showed dramatic changes in emotion, often crying and acting apprehensive. He stopped wearing socks and underwear and, despite the extremely cold weather, wouldn't wear a jacket when he went outdoors. At the family's insistence, he moved into his mother's apartment. He slept little and kept the family up until the early morning. His mother said it was like being in a living nightmare. Each morning she would wake up with a knot in her stomach, not wanting to get out of bed because she felt so helpless to do anything to rescue Amrit from his obvious distress.

The family's sense of alarm grew as Amrit revealed more details of his plan. He said that he was going to the German embassy because that was the only place people would listen to him. He would climb the fence at night when everyone was asleep and present his plan to the German ambassador. Fearing that Amrit would be hurt trying to enter the embassy grounds, his family contacted a local psychiatric hospital, described Amrit's condition, and asked that he be admitted. Much to their surprise and disappointment, they were told that Amrit could commit himself but that they couldn't bring him in involuntarily unless he was in danger of doing harm to himself or others. The fear that Amrit might be harmed wasn't sufficient reason to admit him involuntarily.

His family finally talked Amrit into meeting the staff at the outpatient clinic. In our interview, it was clear he was delusional, firmly believing in his ability to help all starving children. After some cajoling, I finally convinced him to let me see his books. He had written random thoughts (for example, "The poor, starving souls"; "The moon is the only place") and made drawings of rocket ships. Parts of his plan involved building a rocket ship that would go to the moon, where he would create a community for all malnourished children, a place where they could live and be helped. After a few brief comments on his plan, I began to ask him about his health.

"You look tired; are you getting enough sleep?"

"Sleep isn't really needed," he noted. "My plans will take me through, and then they can all rest."

"Your family is worried about you," I said. "Do you understand their concern?"

"It's important for all concerned to get together, to join together," he replied.

With that, he got up and walked out of the room and out of the building, after telling his family that he would be right back. After 5 minutes, they went to look for him, but he had disappeared. He was missing for 2 days, which caused his family a great deal of concern about his health and safety. In an almost miraculous sequence of events, they found him walking the streets of the city. He acted as if nothing had happened. Gone were his notebooks and the talk of his secret plan.

predisposition to have schizophrenia or another disorder that kicked in during a period of stress? Unfortunately, we will never know exactly what happened to Amrit to make him behave so bizarrely and then recover so quickly and completely. Research that we discuss next may shed some light on schizophrenia and potentially help other Amrits and their families.

Clinical Description, Symptoms, and Subtypes

The case of Amrit shows the range of problems experienced by people with schizophrenia or other psychotic disorders. The term **psychotic behavior** has been used to characterize many unusual behaviors, although in its strictest sense, it usually involves delusions (irrational beliefs) and/or hallucinations (sensory experiences in the absence of external events). Schizophrenia is one of the disorders that involve psychotic behavior; we describe others in more detail later.

Schizophrenia can affect all the functions we rely on each day. Before we describe the symptoms, it is important to look carefully at the specific characteristics of people who exhibit these behaviors, partly because we constantly see distorted images of people with schizophrenia. Headlines such as "Ex-Mental Patient Kills Family" falsely imply that everyone with schizophrenia is dangerous and violent. Popular accounts also contribute to this misinformation. Evidence for violence among people with schizophrenia suggests that although they may be more likely to commit violent acts than the general population, traits such as anger and antisocial personality are better predictors of violence than psychosis (Lawrence & First, 2020). Despite this information, the majority of characters with schizophrenia in English language movies between 1990 and 2010 were portrayed as violent, with more than one third depicted as murderers and one fourth as wanting to take their own life (Owen, 2012). As in mistakenly assuming that *schizophrenia* means "split personality," the popular press misrepresents psychopathology to the detriment of people who experience these debilitating disorders.

Schizophrenia spectrum disorder constitutes the group of diagnoses we cover in this chapter, as recognized by those in the field of schizophrenia. In fact, Eugen Bleuler, who coined the term *schizophrenia*, identified the different variants that were all included within this spectrum (Ritsner & Gottesman, 2011). Previous editions of the DSM struggled with this concept in its varied presentations over the years, and, as we describe in this chapter, DSM-5 currently includes schizophrenia as well as other related psychotic disorders that fall under this heading (including schizophreniform, schizoaffective, delusional, and brief psychotic disorders). In addition, a personality disorder (schizotypal personality disorder, discussed in Chapter 12) is also considered to be included under this umbrella category of schizophrenia spectrum disorders. All of these difficulties seem to share features of extreme reality distortion (for example, hallucinations, delusions). Later we discuss the symptoms the person experiences during the disorder (active phase symptoms), the course of the disorder, and spectrum of disorders included in this category (Lawrence & First, 2020).

Mental health workers typically distinguish between positive and negative symptoms of schizophrenia. A third dimension, disorganized symptoms, also appears to be an important aspect of the disorder (Lawrence & First, 2020). **Positive symptoms** generally refer to symptoms around distorted reality. **Negative symptoms** involve deficits in normal behavior in such areas as speech, blunted affect (or lack of emotional reactivity), and motivation (Foussias et al., 2014). **Disorganized symptoms** include rambling speech, erratic behavior, and inappropriate affect (for example, smiling when you are upset). A diagnosis of schizophrenia requires that two or more positive, negative, and/or disorganized symptoms be present for at least 1 month, with at least one of these symptoms including delusions, hallucinations, or disorganized speech. DSM-5 also includes a dimensional assessment that rates the severity of the individual's symptoms on a 0 to 4 scale with 0 indicating a symptom is not present, 1 indicating equivocal evidence (that is, not sure), 2 indicating it is present but mild, 3 that it is present and moderate, and 4 that it is present and severe (American Psychiatric Association, 2013). A great deal of research has focused on the different symptoms of schizophrenia, each of which is described here in some detail.

Positive Symptoms

We next describe the positive symptoms of schizophrenia, which are the more obvious signs of psychosis. These include the disturbing experiences of delusions and hallucinations. Between 60% and 80% of people with schizophrenia experience hallucinations, and approximately 70% experience delusions (Lawrence & First, 2020).

Delusions

A belief that would be seen by most members of a society as a misrepresentation of reality is called a *disorder of thought content*, or a **delusion**. Because of its importance in schizophrenia, delusion has been called "the basic characteristic of madness" (Jaspers, 1963, p. 93). If, for example, you believe that squirrels are aliens sent to earth on a reconnaissance mission, you would be considered as having a delusion. The media often portray people with schizophrenia as believing they are famous or important people (such as Napoleon or Jesus Christ), although this is only one type of delusion. Amrit's belief that he could end starvation for all the world's children is also a *delusion of grandeur* (a mistaken belief that the person is famous or powerful) (Knowles, McCarthy-Jones, & Rowse, 2011).

A common delusion in people with schizophrenia is that others are "out to get them." Called *delusions of persecution*, these beliefs can be most disturbing. One of us worked with a world-class cyclist who was on her way to making the Olympic team. Tragically, however, she developed a belief that other competitors were determined to sabotage her efforts, which forced her to stop riding for years. She believed opponents would spray her bicycle with chemicals that would take her strength away, and they would slow her down by putting small pebbles in the road that only she would ride over. These thoughts created a great deal of anxiety, and she refused even to go near her bicycle for some time.

Other more unusual delusions include Capgras syndrome, in which the person believes someone they know has been replaced by a double (Ventriglio et al., 2020), and Cotard's syndrome, in which the person believes they are dead (Tomasetti et al., 2020).

One man struggling to understand and come to grips with his strange thoughts frankly describes his delusional experiences (Timlett, 2013):

> I once considered that I was a kind of human-robot (perhaps severely autistic), and had been stuck in the same routine for years which meant that everyone knew me and recognized me and always knew exactly what I was thinking. I thought that I was in fact the subject of some kind of experiment designed to cure me from being so predictable and obvious in my behavior and thoughts. On my way

DSM 5 **Table 13.1**
Diagnostic Criteria for Schizophrenia

A. Two (or more) of the following, each present for a significant portion of time during a 1-month period (or less if successfully treated). At least one of these must be (1), (2), or (3):
  1. Delusions
  2. Hallucinations
  3. Disorganized speech (e.g., frequent derailment or incoherence)
  4. Grossly disorganized or catatonic behavior
  5. Negative symptoms (i.e., diminished emotional expression or avolition)

B. For a significant portion of the time since the onset of the disturbance, level of functioning in one or more major areas, such as work, interpersonal relations, or self-care, is markedly below the level achieved prior to the onset (or when the onset is in childhood or adolescence, there is failure to achieve expected level of interpersonal, academic, or occupational functioning).

C. Continuous signs of the disturbance persist for at least 6 months. This 6-month period must include at least 1 month of symptoms (or less if successfully treated) that meet Criterion A (i.e., active-phase symptoms) and may include periods of prodromal or residual symptoms. During these prodromal or residual periods, the signs of the disturbance may be manifested by only negative symptoms or by two or more symptoms listed in Criterion A present in an attenuated form (e.g., odd beliefs, unusual perceptual experiences).

D. Schizoaffective disorder and depressive or bipolar disorder with psychotic features have been ruled out because either (1) no major depressive or manic episodes have occurred concurrently with the active-phase symptoms or (2) if mood episodes have occurred during active-phase symptoms, they have been present for a minority of the total duration of the active and residual periods of the illness.

E. The disturbance is not attributable to the physiological effects of a substance (e.g., a drug of abuse, a medication) or another medical condition.

F. If there is a history of autistic spectrum disorder or a communication disorder of childhood onset, the additional diagnosis of schizophrenia is made only if prominent delusions or hallucinations, in addition to the other required symptoms of schizophrenia, are also present for at least 1 month (or less if successfully treated).

Specify if: With catatonia

American Psychiatric Association. (2022). *Diagnostic and statistical manual of mental disorders* (5th ed., Text Revision).

home and at work this explained why it is I thought that people I didn't know actually recognized me, and why I also believed they were secretly all wishing me well and why they now thought I might have been cured because I was now behaving differently and less predictably (p. 245).

Why would someone come to believe such obviously improbable things (for example, that you were a human robot repeating the same things endlessly)? A number of theories exist and can be summarized into two themes—motivational or deficit theories (McKay, Langdon, & Coltheart, 2007). A *motivational view of delusions* would look at these beliefs as attempts to deal with and relieve anxiety and stress. A person develops "stories" around some issue—for example, a famous person is in love with her (erotomania)—that in a way helps the person make sense out of uncontrollable anxieties in a tumultuous world. Preoccupation with the delusion distracts the individual from the upsetting aspects of the world, such as hallucinations. In contrast, a *deficit view of delusion* sees these beliefs as resulting from brain dysfunction that creates these disordered cognitions or perceptions. Much work remains to develop an integrative account for these intriguing but debilitating symptoms of schizophrenia (Lawrence & First, 2020).

Hallucinations

Have you ever thought you heard someone call your name, only to discover that no one was there? Did you ever think you saw something move by you, yet nothing did? We all have fleeting moments when we think we see or hear something that is not there. For many people with schizophrenia, however, these perceptions are real and occur regularly. The experience of sensory events without any input from the surrounding environment is called a **hallucination**. The case of Luis illustrates the phenomena of hallucinations, as well as other disorders of thought that are common among people with schizophrenia.

Luis... Missing Uncle Benjamin

Luis was 25 years old when I met him. He had been living in a psychiatric hospital for about 3 years. He was a little overweight and of average height; he typically dressed in a T-shirt and jeans and tended to be active. I first encountered him while I was talking to another man who lived on the same floor. Luis interrupted us by pulling on my shoulder. "My Uncle Benjamin is a good man. He treats me well." Not wanting to be impolite, I said, "I'm sure he is. Maybe after I've finished talking to Michael here, we can talk about your uncle." Luis persisted, "He can kill fish with a knife. Things can get awfully sharp in your mind, when you go down the river. I could kill you with my bare hands—taking things into my own hands. ... I know you know!" He was now speaking quickly and had gained emotionality, along with speed, as he spoke. I talked to him quietly until he calmed down for the moment; later, I looked into Luis's file for some information about his background.

Luis was brought up on a farm by his Aunt Katie and Uncle Benjamin. His father's identity is unknown, and his mother, who had an intellectual disability, couldn't care for him. Luis, too, was diagnosed as having an intellectual disability, although his functioning was only mildly impaired, and he attended school. The year Luis's Uncle Benjamin died, his high school teachers first reported unusual behavior. Luis occasionally talked to his deceased Uncle Benjamin in class. Later, he became increasingly agitated and verbally aggressive toward others and was diagnosed as having schizophrenia. He managed to graduate from high school but never obtained a job after that; he lived at home with his aunt for several years. Although his aunt sincerely wanted him to stay with her, his threatening behavior escalated to the point that she requested he be seen at the local psychiatric hospital.

I spoke with Luis again and had a chance to ask him a few questions. "Why are you here in the hospital, Luis?" "I really don't want to be here," he told me. "I've got other things to do. The time is right, and you know, when opportunity knocks." He continued for a few minutes until I interrupted him. "I was sorry to hear that your Uncle Benjamin died a few years ago. How are you feeling about him these days?" "Yes, he died. He was sick and now he's gone. He likes to fish with me, down at the river. He's going to take me hunting. I have guns. I can shoot you, and you'd be dead in a minute."

Luis's conversational speech resembled a ball rolling down a rocky hill. Like an accelerating object, his speech gained momentum the longer he went on, and, as if bouncing off obstacles, the topics almost always went in unpredictable directions. If he continued for too long, he often became agitated and spoke of harming others. Luis also told me that his uncle's voice spoke to him repeatedly. He heard other voices also, but he couldn't identify them or tell me what they said. We return to Luis's case later in this chapter when we discuss causes and treatments.

Hallucinations can involve any of the senses, although hearing things that aren't there, or *auditory hallucination*, is the most common form experienced by people with schizophrenia, with 70% to 80% of those with the diagnosis endorsing this type (Langlois et al., 2020). Luis had frequent auditory hallucinations, usually of his uncle's voice. When Luis heard a voice that belonged to his Uncle Bill, he often could not understand what his uncle was saying; on other occasions, the voice was clearer. "He told me to turn off the TV. He said, 'It's too damn loud, turn it down, turn it down." This is consistent with recent views of hallucinations as being related to metacognition or "thinking about thinking." In other words, metacognition is a phrase to describe examining your own thoughts. Most of us have had an occasional intrusive thought that we try not to focus on (for example, thinking, "I wish she were dead!" when you know that is not appropriate). People who experience hallucinations appear to have intrusive thoughts, but they believe they are coming from somewhere or someone else (Luis thinking he is hearing his uncle's voice when it is probably his own thoughts he is "hearing"). They then worry about having these thoughts and engage in *meta-worry*—or worrying about worrying (Lawrence & First, 2020). Unfortunately, meta-worry has been linked to increased anxiety and depression symptoms for those experiencing hallucinations (Zhuo et al., 2020).

Exciting research on hallucinations uses sophisticated brain-imaging techniques to try to localize these phenomena in the brain. In one of the first studies of its kind, researchers in London used single-photon emission computed tomography (SPECT) to study the cerebral blood flow of men with schizophrenia who also had auditory verbal hallucinations and made a surprising discovery (McGuire, Shah, & Murray, 1993). The researchers used the brain-imaging technique while the men were experiencing hallucinations and while they were not, and they found that the part of the brain most active during hallucinations was Broca's area (see ■ Figure 13.1). This is surprising because Broca's area is known to be involved in speech *production*, rather than language *comprehension*. Because auditory verbal hallucinations usually involve understanding the "speech" of others, you might expect more activity in Wernicke's area, which involves language comprehension. These observations support the metacognition theory that people who are hallucinating are *not* hearing the voices of others but are listening to their own thoughts or their own voices and cannot recognize the difference

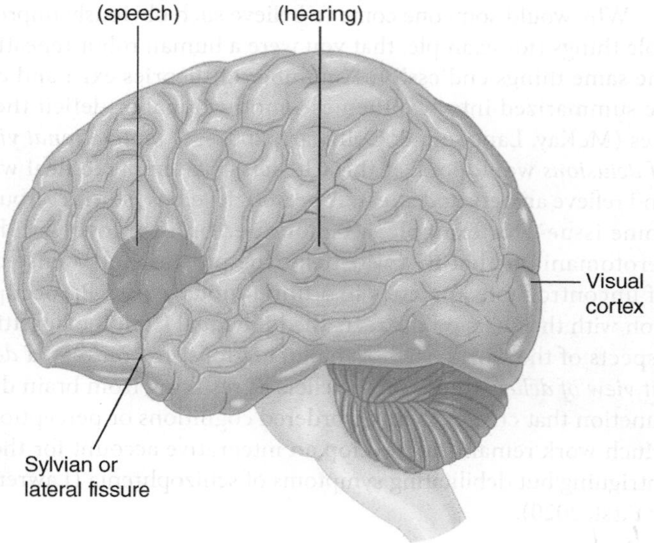

Figure 13.1

Major areas of functioning of the cerebral cortex. In most people, only the left hemisphere is specialized for language.

(Lawrence & First, 2020). One possible explanation for this problem is referred to as poor "emotional prosody comprehension" (Lucarini et al., 2020). Prosody is that aspect of our spoken language that communicates meaning and emotion through our pitch, amplitude, pauses, and so on. We can often tell when a person is asking a question, for example, not just by the words themselves but also by the way it is said (for example, "Hungry?"). Research suggests that emotional prosody is deficient in persons with auditory verbal hallucinations, contributing to the confusion both with others as well as when interpreting "inner voices" (Alba-Ferrara, Fernyhough, Weis, Mitchell, & Hausmann, 2012).

Negative Symptoms

In contrast to the active presentations that characterize the positive symptoms of schizophrenia, the negative symptoms usually indicate the absence or insufficiency of typical behavior. They include apathy, poverty of (that is, limited) thought or speech, and emotional and social withdrawal, and approximately 60% of people with schizophrenia display these symptoms (Correll & Schooler, 2020).

Avolition

Combining the prefix *a* (meaning "without") and *volition* (which means "an act of willing, choosing, or deciding"), **avolition** is the inability to initiate and persist in activities (Lawrence & First, 2020). People with this symptom (also referred to as *apathy*) show little interest in performing even the most basic day-to-day functions, including those associated with personal hygiene.

Alogia

Derived from the combination of *a* ("without") and *logos* ("words"), **alogia** refers to the relative absence of speech. A person with alogia may respond to questions with brief replies that have little content and may appear uninterested in the conversation. For example, to the question, "Do you have any children?" most parents might reply, "Oh yes, I have two beautiful children, a boy and a girl. My son is 6 and my daughter is 12." In the following exchange, someone with alogia responds to the same question:

INTERVIEWER: Do you have any children?
CLIENT: Yes.
I: How many children do you have?
C: Two
I: How old are they?
C: Six and twelve.

Such deficiency in communication is believed to reflect a negative thought disorder rather than inadequate communication skills. Some researchers, for example, suggest that people with alogia may have trouble finding the right words to formulate their thoughts (Andreasen, 2012). Sometimes alogia takes the form of delayed comments or slow responses to questions. Talking with individuals who manifest this symptom can be extremely frustrating, making you feel as if you are "pulling teeth" to get them to respond.

Anhedonia

A related symptom is called **anhedonia**, which derives from the combination of *a* ("without") and the word *hedonic* ("pertaining to pleasure"). Anhedonia is the presumed lack of pleasure experienced by some people with schizophrenia. Like some mood disorders, anhedonia signals an indifference to activities that would typically be considered pleasurable, including eating, social interactions, and sexual relations.

Asociality

This symptom may seem very similar to avolition or related to anhedonia. However, asociality (*a* meaning "without" and *social* meaning "relating to society or its organization") has been recognized as a separate symptom of schizophrenia spectrum disorders. This symptom captures a lack of interest in social interactions (American Psychiatric Association, 2013). Unfortunately, this symptom can also result from or be worsened by limited opportunities to interact with others, particularly for severely ill patients (Reddy, Horan, & Green, 2016).

Justin Paget/DigitalVision/Getty Images

Negative symptoms of schizophrenia include social withdrawal and apathy.

Affective Flattening

Imagine that people wore masks at all times: You could communicate with them verbally, but you wouldn't be able to see their emotional reactions. Approximately one quarter of the people with schizophrenia exhibit what is called **flat affect** (Lewis et al., 2009; Simonsen et al., 2012). They are similar to people wearing masks because they do not show emotions when you would normally expect them to. They may stare at you vacantly, speak in a flat and toneless manner, and seem unaffected by things going on around them. However, although they do not react openly to emotional situations, they may be responding on the inside.

Howard Berenbaum and Thomas Oltmanns (1992) compared people with schizophrenia who had flat (or "blunted") affect with those who did not. The two groups were shown clips from comedies and dramas selected to create emotional reactions in the viewer. Berenbaum and Oltmanns found that the people with flat affect showed little change in facial expression, although they reported experiencing the appropriate emotions. The authors concluded that the flat affect in schizophrenia may represent difficulty expressing emotion, not a lack of feeling. Researchers can now use computer analyses of facial expressions to more objectively assess the emotional expressiveness of people with disorders such as schizophrenia (Kring & Elis, 2013). One such study confirmed the difficulty of people with this disorder to express themselves properly with facial expressions (Hamm, Pinkham, Gur, Verma, & Kohler, 2014). The expression of affect—or the lack of this expression—may be an important symptom of the development of schizophrenia. In a particularly innovative study, researchers videotaped high-risk children (those with one or more parents who had schizophrenia) eating lunch in 1972 and followed them up almost 20 years later (Schiffman et al., 2004). The researchers were able to show that children who later went on to develop schizophrenia typically displayed less positive and more negative affect than those children who did not develop the disorder. This suggests that emotional expression may be one way to identify potential schizophrenia in children.

Disorganized Symptoms

Perhaps the least studied and therefore the least understood symptoms of schizophrenia are referred to as the "disorganized symptoms" (Lawrence & First, 2020). These include a variety of erratic behaviors that affect speech, motor behavior, and emotional reactions. The prevalence of these behaviors among those with schizophrenia is unclear.

Disorganized Speech

A conversation with someone who has schizophrenia can be particularly frustrating. If you want to understand what is bothering or upsetting this person, eliciting relevant information is especially difficult. For one thing, people with schizophrenia often lack *insight*, an awareness that they have a problem. In addition, they experience what Bleuler called "associative splitting" and what researcher Paul Meehl called "cognitive slippage" (Bleuler, 1908; Meehl, 1962). These phrases help describe the speech problems of people with schizophrenia: Sometimes they jump from topic to topic, and at other times they talk illogically. DSM-5 uses the term **disorganized speech** to describe such communication problems. Let's go back to our conversation with Luis to demonstrate the symptom:

> THERAPIST: Why are you here in the hospital, Luis?
>
> LUIS: I really don't want to be here. I've got other things to do. The time is right, and you know, when opportunity knocks. …

Luis didn't really answer the question he was asked. This type of response is called *tangentiality*—that is, going off on a tangent instead of answering a specific question. Luis also abruptly changed the topic of conversation to unrelated areas, a behavior that has variously been called *loose association* or *derailment* (Liddle, 2012):

> THERAPIST: I was sorry to hear that your Uncle Benjamin died a few years ago. How are you feeling about him these days?
>
> LUIS: Yes, he died. He was sick, and now he's gone. He likes to fish with me, down at the river. He's going to take me hunting. I have guns. I can shoot you, and you'd be dead in a minute.

Again, Luis did not answer the question. It was unclear whether he did not understand the question, could not focus his attention, or found it too difficult to talk about his uncle. You can see why people spend a great deal of time trying to interpret all the hidden meanings behind this type of conversation. Unfortunately, however, such analyses have yet to provide us with useful information about the nature of schizophrenia or its treatment.

Inappropriate Affect and Disorganized Behavior

Occasionally, people with schizophrenia display **inappropriate affect**, laughing or crying at improper times (Lawrence & First, 2020). Sometimes they exhibit bizarre behaviors such as hoarding objects or acting in unusual ways in public. People with schizophrenia engage in a number of other "active" behaviors that are usually viewed as unusual. For example, catatonia is one of the most curious symptoms in some individuals with schizophrenia; it involves motor dysfunctions that range from wild agitation to immobility (Dean et al., 2020). DSM-5 now includes catatonia as a separate schizophrenia spectrum disorder. On the active side of the continuum, some people pace excitedly or move their fingers or arms in stereotyped ways. At the other end of the extreme, people hold unusual postures, as if they were fearful of something terrible happening if they moved (**catatonic immobility**) (Dean et al., 2020). This manifestation can also involve *waxy flexibility*, or the tendency to keep their bodies and limbs in the position they are put in by someone else.

Again, to receive a diagnosis of schizophrenia, a person must display two or more of the major symptoms (that is, delusions, hallucinations, disorganized speech, grossly abnormal psychomotor behavior—including catatonia—or negative symptoms such as diminished emotional expression or avolition) for a significant portion of time for 1 month. At least one of the symptoms

DSM 5 **Table 13.2**

Diagnostic Criteria for Catatonia Associated with Another Mental Disorder (Catatonia Specifier)

A. The clinical picture is dominated by three or more of the following symptoms:

1. Stupor (i.e., no psychomotor activity; not actively relating to environment)
2. Cataplexy (i.e., passive induction of a posture held against gravity)
3. Waxy flexibility (i.e., slight, even resistance to positioning by examiner)
4. Mutism (i.e., no, or very little, verbal response [exclude if known aphasia])
5. Negativism (i.e., opposition or no response to instructions or external stimuli)
6. Posturing (i.e., spontaneous and active maintenance of a posture against gravity)
7. Mannerism (i.e., odd, circumstantial caricature of normal actions
8. Stereotypy (i.e., repetitive, abnormally frequent, non-goal-directed movements)
9. Agitation, not influenced by external stimuli
10. Grimacing
11. Echolalia (i.e., mimicking another's speech)
12. Echopraxia (i.e., mimicking another's movements)

American Psychiatric Association. (2022). *Diagnostic and statistical manual of mental disorders* (5th ed., Text Revision).

San Francisco Chronicle/Hearst Newspapers via Getty Images

People who live on the streets and who suffer from schizophrenia often bear the additional burden of persecutory delusions, which interfere with outside efforts to help.

must include delusions, hallucinations, or disorganized speech (American Psychiatric Association, 2013). Depending on the combination of symptoms displayed, two people could receive the same diagnosis but behave differently—for example, one having marked hallucinations and delusions and the other displaying disorganized speech and some negative symptoms. Proper treatment depends on differentiating individuals in terms of their varying symptoms.

Historic Schizophrenia Subtypes

As we noted earlier, the search for subtypes of schizophrenia began before Kraepelin described his concept of schizophrenia. Three divisions have historically been identified: paranoid (delusions of grandeur or persecution), disorganized (or hebephrenic; silly and immature emotionality), and catatonic (alternate immobility and excited agitation). Although these categories continued to be used in DSM-IV-TR, they were dropped from the diagnostic criteria for DSM-5 (American Psychiatric Association, 2013). Part of the rationale for omitting these subtypes was that they were not used frequently in clinical work, and the nature of an individual's symptoms can change over the course of their illness so people could move from one category to another (Tandon et al., 2013). The dimensional assessment of severity is now used instead of the three schizophrenia subtypes (Pagsberg, 2013).

In the next section, we describe the disorders that are included under the broader heading of "Schizophrenia Spectrum and Other Psychotic Disorders."

Other Psychotic Disorders

The psychotic behaviors of some individuals do not fit neatly under the heading of schizophrenia as we have just described. Several other categories of disorders depict these significant variations.

Schizophreniform Disorder

Some people experience the symptoms of schizophrenia for a few months only; they can usually resume normal lives. The symptoms sometimes disappear as the result of successful treatment, but they often do so for reasons unknown. The label **schizophreniform disorder** classifies these symptoms, but because relatively few studies are available on this disorder, data on important aspects of it are sparse. It appears, however, that the lifetime prevalence is approximately 0.2% (Erlich, Smith, Horwath, & Cournos, 2014). The DSM-5 diagnostic criteria for schizophreniform disorder include onset of psychotic symptoms within 4 weeks of the first noticeable change in usual behavior, confusion at the height of the psychotic episode, good *premorbid* (before the psychotic episode) social and occupational functioning, and the absence of blunted or flat affect (Garrabe & Cousin, 2012).

Schizoaffective Disorder

Historically, people who had symptoms of schizophrenia and who exhibited the characteristics of mood disorders (for example, depression or bipolar disorder) were lumped in the category of schizophrenia. Now, however, this mixed bag of problems is diagnosed as **schizoaffective disorder** (Lawrence & First, 2020). The prognosis is similar to the prognosis for people with schizophrenia—that is, individuals tend not to get better on their own and are likely to continue experiencing major life difficulties for many years. DSM-5 criteria for schizoaffective disorder require, in addition to the presence of a mood disorder, delusions or hallucinations for at least 2 weeks in the absence of prominent mood symptoms (American Psychiatric Association, 2013).

Delusional Disorder

Delusions are beliefs that are not generally held by other members of a society. The major feature of **delusional disorder** is a persistent belief that is contrary to reality, in the absence of other characteristics of schizophrenia (González-Rodríguez & Seeman, 2020). For example, a woman who believes without any evidence that coworkers are tormenting her by putting poison in her food and spraying her apartment with harmful gases may have a delusional disorder. This disorder is characterized by a persistent delusion that is not the result of an organic factor (such as brain seizures) or of any severe psychosis. Individuals with delusional disorder tend not to have flat affect, anhedonia, or other negative symptoms of schizophrenia, but they may become socially isolated because they are suspicious of others. The delusions are often long-standing, sometimes persisting over several years (Munro, 2012).

DSM-5 recognizes the following delusional subtypes: erotomanic, grandiose, jealous, persecutory, and somatic. An *erotomanic type* of delusion is the irrational belief that one is loved by another person, usually of higher status. Some individuals who stalk celebrities appear to have erotomanic delusional disorder. The *grandiose type* of delusion involves believing in one's inflated worth, power, knowledge, identity, or special relationship to a deity or famous person (Knowles et al., 2011). A person with the *jealous type* of delusion believes the sexual partner is unfaithful. The *persecutory type* of delusion involves believing oneself (or someone close) is being malevolently treated in some way. Finally, with the *somatic delusions* the person feels afflicted by a physical defect or general medical condition. Typically, these delusions differ from the more bizarre types often found in people with schizophrenia because in delusional disorder *the imagined events could be happening but aren't* (for example, mistakenly believing you are being followed). In schizophrenia, however, delusions tend to fall in the bizarre category (for example, believing your brain waves broadcast your thoughts to other people around the world). DSM-5 allows for one bizarre delusion, which separates it from a diagnosis of schizophrenia, which requires more than one delusion to be present (Heckers et al., 2013).

Previous versions of DSM included a separate delusional disorder—**shared psychotic disorder (folie à deux)**, the condition in which an individual develops delusions simply as a result of a close relationship with a delusional individual (Jerrom et al., 2020). The content and nature of the delusion originate with the

DSM 5

Table 13.3 Diagnostic Criteria for Schizophreniform Disorder

A. Two (or more) of the following, each present for a significant portion of time during a 1-month period (or less if successfully treated). At least one of these must be (1), (2), or (3):

1. Delusions
2. Hallucinations
3. Disorganized speech (e.g., frequent derailment or incoherence)
4. Grossly disorganized or catatonic behavior
5. Negative symptoms (i.e., diminished emotional expression or avolition)

B. An episode of the disorder lasts at least 1 month but less than 6 months. When the diagnosis must be made without waiting for recovery, it should be qualified as "provisional."

C. Schizoaffective disorder and depressive or bipolar disorder with psychotic features have been ruled out because either (1) no major depressive or manic episodes have occurred concurrently with the active-phase symptoms or (2) if mood episodes have occurred during active-phase symptoms, they have been present for a minority of the total duration of the active and residual periods of the illness.

D. The disturbance is not attributable to the physiological effects of a substance (e.g., a drug of abuse, a medication) or another medical condition.

Specify if:

With good prognostic features: This specifier requires the presence of at least two of the following features: onset of prominent psychotic symptoms within 4 weeks of the first noticeable change in usual behavior or functioning; confusion or perplexity; good premorbid social and occupational functioning; and absence of blunted or flat affect.

Without good prognostic features: This specifier is applied if two or more of the above features have not been present.

Specify if: With catatonia

American Psychiatric Association. (2022). *Diagnostic and statistical manual of mental disorders* (5th ed., Text Revision).

DSM 5 **Table 13.4**

Diagnostic Criteria for Schizoaffective Disorder

A. An uninterrupted period of illness during which there is a major mood episode (major depressive or manic) concurrent with Criterion A of schizophrenia. *Note:* The major depressive episode must include Criterion A1.

B. Delusions or hallucinations for 2 or more weeks in the absence of a major mood episode (depressive or manic) during the lifetime duration of the illness.

C. Symptoms that meet criteria for a major mood episode are present for the majority of the total durance of the active and residual portions of the illness.

D. The disturbance is not attributable to the effects of a substance (e.g., a drug of abuse, a medication) or another medical condition.

Specify whether:

Bipolar type: This subtype applies if a manic episode is part of the presentation. Major depressive episodes may also occur.

Depressive type: This subtype applies only if only major depressive episodes are part of the presentation.

Specify if: With catatonia

American Psychiatric Association. (2022). *Diagnostic and statistical manual of mental disorders* (5th ed., Text Revision).

partner and can range from the relatively bizarre (such as believing enemies are sending harmful gamma rays through your house) to the fairly ordinary (such as believing you are about to receive a major promotion despite evidence to the contrary). DSM-5 now includes this type of delusion under delusional disorder with a specifier to indicate if the delusion is shared (American Psychiatric Association, 2013).

Delusional disorder seems to be relatively rare, affecting 24 to 60 people out of every 100,000 in the general population (de Portugal, González, Haro, Autonell, & Cervilla, 2008; Ibanez-Casas & Cervilla, 2012). Among those people with psychotic disorders in general, between 2% and 8% are thought to have delusional disorder (Blaney, 2015; Vahia & Cohen, 2009). Researchers cannot be confident about the percentages because they know that many of these individuals have no contact with the mental health system.

The onset of delusional disorder is relatively late: The average age of first admission to a psychiatric facility is between 35 and 55 (Ibanez-Casas & Cervilla, 2012). Because many people with this disorder can lead relatively typical lives, they may not seek treatment until their symptoms become most disruptive. Delusional disorder seems to afflict more women than men (55% and 45%, respectively, of the affected population).

In an important longitudinal study, Opjordsmoen (1989) followed 53 people with delusional disorder for an average of 30 years and found they tended to fare better in life than people with schizophrenia but not as well as those with some other psychotic

DSM 5 **Table 13.5**

Diagnostic Criteria for Delusional Disorder

A. The presence of one (or more) delusions with a duration of 1 month or longer.

B. Criterion A for schizophrenia has never been met.

Note: Hallucinations, if present, are not prominent and are related to the delusional theme (e.g., the sensation of being infested with insects associated with delusions of infestation).

C. Apart from the impact of the delusion(s) or its ramifications, functioning is not markedly impaired, and behavior is not obviously bizarre or odd.

D. If manic or major depressive episodes have occurred, these have been brief relative to the duration of the delusional periods.

E. The disturbance is not attributable to the physiological effects of a substance or another medical condition and is not better explained by another mental disorder, such as body dysmorphic disorder or obsessive-compulsive disorder.

Specify whether:

Erotomanic type: This subtype applies when the central theme of the delusion is that another person is in love with the individual.

Grandiose type: This subtype applies when the central theme of the delusion is the conviction of having some great (but unrecognized) talent or insight or having made some important discovery.

Jealous type: This subtype applies when the central theme of the individual's delusion is that his or her spouse or lover is unfaithful.

Persecutory type: This subtype applies when the central theme of the delusion involves the individual's belief that he or she is being conspired against, cheated, spied on, followed, poisoned or drugged, maliciously maligned, harassed, or obstructed in the pursuit of long-term goals.

Somatic type: This subtype applies when the central theme of the delusion involves bodily functions or sensations.

Mixed type: This subtype applies when no delusional theme predominated.

Unspecified type: This subtype applies when the dominant delusional belief cannot be clearly determined or is not described in the specific types (e.g., referential delusions without a prominent persecutory or grandiose component).

American Psychiatric Association. (2022). *Diagnostic and statistical manual of mental disorders* (5th ed., Text Revision).

disorders, such as schizoaffective disorder. About 80% of the 53 individuals had been married at some time, and half were employed, which demonstrates an ability to function relatively well despite delusions.

There is much conflicting evidence about either the biological or the psychosocial influences on delusional disorder (Ibanez-Casas & Cervilla, 2012). Research on families suggests that the characteristics of suspiciousness, jealousy, and secretiveness may occur more often among the relatives of people with delusional disorder than among the population at

DSM 5 **Table 13.6**
Diagnostic Criteria for Substance/Medication-Induced Psychotic Disorder

A. Presence of one or both of the following symptoms:
  1. Delusions
  2. Hallucinations

B. There is evidence from the history, physical examination, or laboratory findings of both (1) and (2):
  1. The symptoms in Criterion A developed during, or soon after, substance intoxication or withdrawal or after exposure to a medication.
  2. The involved substance/medication is capable of producing the symptoms in Criterion A.

C. The disturbance is not better explained by a psychotic disorder that is not substance/medication-induced. Such evidence of an independent psychotic disorder could include the following: The symptoms preceded the onset of substance/medication use; the symptoms persist for a substantial period of time (e.g., about 1 month) after the cessation of acute withdrawal or severe intoxication; or there is other evidence of an independent nonsubstance/medication-induced psychotic disorder (e.g., a history of recurrent nonsubstance/medication-related episodes).

D. The disturbance does not occur exclusively during the course of a delirium.

E. The disturbance causes clinically significant distress or impairment in social, occupational, or other important areas of functioning.

Note: This diagnosis should be made instead of a diagnosis of substance intoxication or substance withdrawal only when the symptoms in Criterion A predominate in the clinical picture and when they are sufficiently severe to warrant clinical attention.

American Psychiatric Association. (2022). *Diagnostic and statistical manual of mental disorders* (5th ed., Text Revision).

DSM 5 **Table 13.7**
Diagnostic Criteria for Psychotic Disorder Associated with Another Medical Condition

A. Prominent hallucinations or delusions.

B. There is evidence from the history, physical examination, or laboratory findings that the disturbance is the direct pathophysiological consequence of another medical condition.

C. The disturbance is not better explained by another mental disorder.

D. The disturbance does not occur exclusively during the course of a delirium.

American Psychiatric Association. (2022). *Diagnostic and statistical manual of mental disorders* (5th ed., Text Revision).

large, suggesting some aspect of this disorder may be inherited (Kendler & Walsh, 2007).

A number of other disorders can cause delusions, and their presence should be ruled out before diagnosing delusional disorder. For example, abuse of amphetamines, alcohol, and cocaine can cause delusions, as can brain tumors, Huntington's disease, and Alzheimer's disease (Blaney, 2015). DSM-5 includes two categories of these disorders: **substance-induced psychotic disorder** and **psychotic disorder associated with another medical condition**—so that clinicians can qualify the nature of these difficulties.

Brief Psychotic Disorder

Recall the puzzling case of Amrit, who suddenly experienced the delusion that he could save the world and whose intense emotional swings lasted for only a few days. He would receive the DSM-5 diagnosis of **brief psychotic disorder**, which is characterized by the presence of one or more positive symptoms such as delusions, hallucinations, or disorganized speech or behavior lasting 1 month or less. Individuals like Amrit regain their previous ability to function well in day-to-day activities. Brief psychotic disorder is often precipitated by extremely stressful situations. One case study in Italy found an increase in hospitalizations for brief psychotic disorders during the COVID-19 pandemic. Of the six individuals admitted (none of whom had a previous psychiatric disorder), three presented the somatic delusion of being infected with COVID, and all six cases had religious/spiritual delusions and hallucinatory content (D'Agostino et al., 2021).

Attenuated Psychosis Syndrome

Some individuals who start to develop psychotic symptoms such as hallucinations or delusions are often sufficiently distressed to seek help from mental health professionals. They can be at high risk for developing schizophrenia and may be at an early stage of the disorder (called *prodromal*). Although they may not meet the full criteria for schizophrenia, they may be good candidates for early intervention in an effort to prevent symptoms from worsening. To focus attention on these individuals, DSM-5 is proposing a potentially new psychotic disorder for further study—**attenuated psychosis syndrome** (de Pablo, Catalan, & Fusar-Poli, 2020). Again, these people may have some of the symptoms of schizophrenia but are aware of the troubling and bizarre nature of these symptoms.

Schizotypal personality disorder, discussed in Chapter 12, is a related psychotic disorder. As you may recall, the characteristics are similar to those experienced by people with schizophrenia but are less severe. Some evidence also suggests that schizophrenia and schizotypal personality disorder may be genetically related as part of a "schizophrenia spectrum."

Remember that although people with related psychotic disorders display many of the characteristics of schizophrenia, these disorders differ significantly.

Concept Check 13.1

Part A

Determine which symptoms or types of schizophrenia spectrum disorders are described in each scenario.

1. Jayla has spent the past half hour staring in the mirror. As you approach her, she turns away and giggles. When you ask what she's laughing at, she answers, but you're having difficulty understanding what she says. ___________
2. Noah has experienced hallucinations and bizarre delusions for the past four months. ___________
3. Roberto's cognitive skills and affect are relatively intact. He, however, often has delusions and hallucinations that convince him enemies are out to persecute him. ___________
4. Hailey usually holds an unusual posture and is sometimes seen grimacing. ___________
5. Parker has started to hear voices, and this is very disturbing to him. He told his parents and recognizes that he needs to see a mental health professional for help. ___________

Part B

Diagnose the type of psychotic disorders described in each of the following. Choose from (a) schizophreniform disorder, (b) schizoaffective disorder, (c) delusional disorder, and (d) shared psychotic disorder.

6. Lately, Guillermo has become more isolated because he believes his coworkers are conspiring to get him fired. He becomes agitated whenever he sees a group of employees talking and laughing because he believes that they are plotting against him. ___________
7. Laylah reveals to her therapist that she hears numerous voices talking to her and giving her orders. Her doctor has just sent her to this therapist for what he believes to be a major depressive episode. She had begun to sleep all the time and contemplated suicide often. ___________
8. If Jelani's schizophrenic symptoms disappeared after about 4 months and he returned to his normal life, what diagnosis might he have received?

 ____

9. Amari believes the government is out to get him. He thinks agents follow him daily, monitor his calls, and read his mail. His roommate Dontrell tries to convince him otherwise. After a year of this, however, Dontrell begins to believe Amari is correct and the government is out to get him, too.

 ____

DSM 5 Table 13.8

Diagnostic Criteria for Brief Psychotic Disorder

A. Presence of one (or more) of the following symptoms. At least one of these must be (1), (2), or (3):

1. Delusions
2. Hallucinations
3. Disorganized speech (e.g., frequent derailment or incoherence)
4. Grossly disorganized or catatonic behavior

Note: Do not include a symptom if it is a culturally sanctioned response.

B. Duration of an episode of the disturbance is at least 1 day but less than 1 month, with eventual full return to premorbid level of functioning.

C. The disturbance is not better explained by major depressive or bipolar disorder with psychotic features or by another psychotic disorder such as schizophrenia or catatonia, and is not attributable to the physiological effects of a substance (e.g., a drug of abuse, a medication) or another medical condition.

Specify if:

With marked stressor(s) (brief reactive psychosis): If symptoms occur in response to events that, singly or together, would be markedly stressful to almost anyone in similar circumstances in the individual's culture.

Without marked stressor(s): If symptoms do not occur in response to events that, singly or together, would be markedly stressful to almost anyone in similar circumstances in the individual's culture.

With postpartum onset: If onset is during pregnancy or within 4 weeks postpartum.

Specify if: With catatonia

American Psychiatric Association. (2022). *Diagnostic and statistical manual of mental disorders* (5th ed., Text Revision).

Prevalence and Causes of Schizophrenia

Studying schizophrenia reveals the many levels on which we must decipher what makes us behave the way we do. To uncover the causes of this disorder, researchers look in several areas: (1) the possible genes involved in schizophrenia, (2) the chemical action of the drugs that help many people with this disorder, (3) abnormalities in the working of the brains of people with schizophrenia, and (4) environmental risk factors that may precipitate the onset of the symptoms (Harrison, 2012; Murray & Castle, 2012). As we survey the work of many specialists, we examine many state-of-the-art techniques for studying both biological and psychosocial influences, a process that may be slow going at times but will bring new insight to your understanding of psychopathology. We now examine the nature of schizophrenia and learn how researchers have attempted to understand and treat people who have it.

Statistics

Schizophrenia sometimes defies our desire for simplicity. We have seen how different symptoms can be displayed by individuals who would all be considered to have the disorder; in some people, the symptoms develop slowly, and in others they occur suddenly. Schizophrenia is generally chronic, and most people with the disorder have a difficult time functioning in society (Lieberman, Stroup, Perkins, & Dixon, 2020). This is especially true of their ability to relate to others; they tend not to establish or maintain significant relationships, so many people with schizophrenia never marry or have children. Unlike the delusions of people with other psychotic disorders, the delusions of people with schizophrenia are likely to be outside the realm of possibility. Finally, even when individuals with schizophrenia improve with treatment, they are likely to experience difficulties throughout their lives (Bornheimer, Li, Im, Taylor, & Himle, 2020). In fact, loneliness is a major problem among these individuals and is being studied extensively (Badcock, Adery, & Park, 2020).

Worldwide, the lifetime prevalence rate of schizophrenia is roughly equivalent for men and women, and it is estimated to be 0.2% to 1.5% in the general population, which means the disorder will affect about 1% of the population at some point (Erlich et al., 2014). People with schizophrenia tend to live 10 to 15 years less than average (Ng, Martinez, Koh, Tohen, & Gangwisch, 2020), partly because of the higher rate of suicide and accidents among people with schizophrenia. Although there is some disagreement about the distribution of schizophrenia between men and women, the difference between the sexes in age of onset is clear. For men, the likelihood of onset diminishes with age, but it can still first occur after the age of 75. The frequency of onset for women is lower than for men until age 36, when the relative risk for onset switches, with more women than men being affected later in life (Jablensky, 2012). Women appear to have more favorable outcomes than do men.

Development

The more severe symptoms of schizophrenia first occur in late adolescence or early adulthood, although we saw that there may be signs of the development of the disorder in early childhood (Murray & Castle, 2012). Children who go on to develop schizophrenia show early clinical features such as mild physical abnormalities, poor motor coordination, and mild cognitive and social problems (Golembo-Smith et al., 2012; Matheson et al., 2013; Welham et al., 2008). Unfortunately, these types of early problems are not specific enough to schizophrenia—meaning they could also be signs of other problems, such as the neurodevelopmental disorders we review in Chapter 14—to be able to say for sure that a particular child will later develop schizophrenia.

Up to 85% of people who later develop schizophrenia go through a **prodromal stage**—a 1- to 2-year period before the serious symptoms occur but when less severe yet unusual behaviors start to show themselves (Lawrence & First, 2020). These behaviors (which you may recognize from Chapter 12 as symptoms seen in schizotypal personality disorders) include ideas of reference (thinking insignificant events relate directly to them), magical thinking (believing they have special abilities such as being clairvoyant or telepathic), and illusions (such as feeling the presence of another person when they are alone). In addition, other symptoms are common, such as isolation, marked impairment in functioning, and a lack of initiative, interests, or energy (Addington et al., 2015).

Once symptoms begin to appear, it can take anywhere from 2 years to around 10 years before a person at high risk (such as mild positive symptoms) meets full criteria for a psychotic disorder (Lawrence & First, 2020). The highest period of risk for patients to develop a full-fledged psychotic disorder is during the first two years following their first displays of mild symptoms. Risk factors for going from high risk to developing the disorder include the length of duration of symptoms before seeking help, baseline functioning, as well as the presence of negative symptoms and disorganized symptoms (Addington et al., 2015, Nelson et al., 2013). Part of the delay in seeking help may be the result of hiding symptoms from others (sometimes because of increasing paranoia). Personality factors and the amount and quality of social support may also play a role in the amount of time it takes a person to first seek treatment for psychotic symptoms (Ruiz-Veguilla et al., 2012). Once treated, patients with this disorder will often improve. Unfortunately, most will also go through a pattern of relapse and recovery (Medalia, Saperstein, & Grant, 2020). This relapse rate is important when discussing the course of schizophrenia. For example, the data from one classic study show the course of schizophrenia among four prototypical groups (Zubin, Steinhauer, & Condray, 1992). About 22% of the group had one episode of schizophrenia and improved without lasting impairment. The remaining 78% experienced several episodes with differing degrees of impairment between them. People with schizophrenia have a poorer prognosis than those with most of the other disorders we describe in this book—including a high risk of suicide—although a significant number of individuals can experience long periods of recovery (Jablensky, 2012). Relapses are an important subject in the field of schizophrenia; we return to this phenomenon when we discuss causes and treatment. To illustrate this complex developmental picture, ■ Figure 13.2 graphically depicts the developmental course of schizophrenia. Life stages (from before birth to the end of life) are listed across the top of the graph, with the colored regions showing periods of decline and recovery.

Cultural Factors

Because schizophrenia is so complex, the diagnosis itself can be controversial. Some have argued that "schizophrenia" does not really exist but is a derogatory label for people who behave in ways outside the cultural norm (see, for example, Laing, 1967; Sarbin & Mancuso, 1980; Szasz, 1961). This concern takes us back to our discussions in the first chapter about the difficulty defining what is psychopathology. Although the idea that schizophrenia exists only in the minds of mental health professionals is certainly provocative, this extreme view is contradicted by

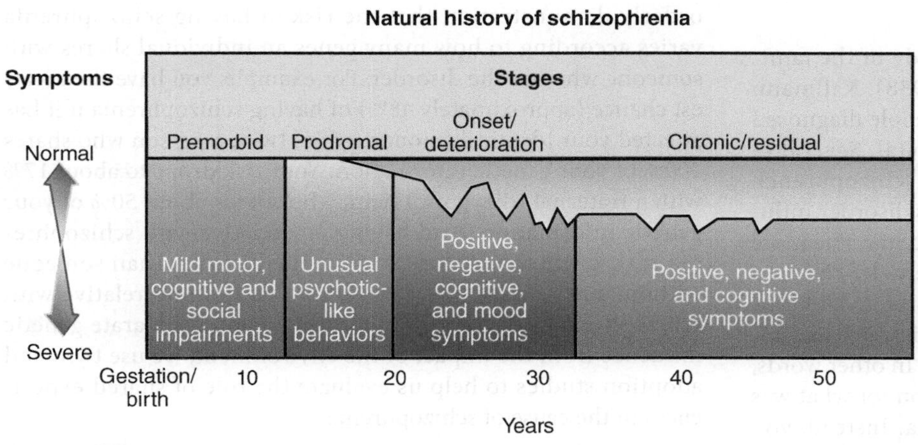

Figure 13.2

The longitudinal course of schizophrenia is depicted starting at birth through old age. The severity of the symptoms is showing on the left axis, and the changes in symptoms across each phase (premorbid, prodromal, onset, and chronic) are labeled. Adapted from J. A. Lieberman, D. Perkins, A. Belger, M. Chakos, F. Jarskog, K. Boteva, & J. Gilmore, 2001, The early stages of schizophrenia: Speculations on pathogenesis, pathophysiology, and therapeutic approaches, *Biological Psychiatry*, *50*, 885.

experience. We have had a great deal of contact with people who have this disorder and with their families and friends, and the tremendous amount of emotional pain resulting from schizophrenia gives definite credence to its existence. In an interesting historical note, Kraepelin, who we described as developing the modern-day view of schizophrenia, traveled to Asia at the turn of the past century to confirm that this unusual set of behaviors was experienced by cultures other than those of Western Europe (Lauriello, Bustillo, & Keith, 2005). We now know that people in widely diverging cultures have the symptoms of schizophrenia, which supports the notion that it is a reality for many people worldwide. Schizophrenia is thus universal, affecting all racial and cultural groups studied so far. There are even shared neuroanatomical similarities that provide evidence of schizophrenia's presence across individuals from different cultures (Gong et al., 2015).

DSM-5 introduced the Cultural Formulation Interview (CFI) (Aggarwal & Lewis-Fenandez, 2020). The CFI is a guide that helps clinicians examine any biases they may have when interviewing people from other cultures. For example, one type of question asks, "Why do you think this is happening to you? What are the causes of your [problem]?" The clinician is then prompted to follow up on the answer: "Some people may explain their problem as a result of bad things that happen in their life, problems with others, a physical illness, a spiritual reason, or many other causes" (American Psychiatric Association, 2013). This type of guidance can assist clinicians to follow up on ideas clients might have that would not typically be assessed (Aggarwal & Lewis-Fenandez, 2020).

The course and outcome of schizophrenia vary from culture to culture. For example, the stressors associated with significant political, social, and economic problems that are prevalent in many areas of Africa, Latin America, and Asia may contribute to poorer outcomes for people with schizophrenia in these countries (Aggarwal & Lewis-Fenandez, 2020). The lack of an adequate mental health infrastructure in low- and middle-income countries is also a problem for providing appropriate and consistent care to those suffering from schizophrenia. Efforts to increase several countries' capacity to care for those with schizophrenia have had some preliminary success in upper middle–income countries like China and Brazil (Patel, 2015). More initiatives focused on schizophrenia and other mental health disorders worldwide are starting to gain momentum.

In the United States, proportionately more African Americans receive the diagnosis of schizophrenia than European Americans (Aggarwal & Lewis-Fenandez, 2020). Research from both England and the United States suggests that people from devalued ethnic minority groups (Afro-Caribbean in England and African Americans and Puerto Ricans in the United States) may be victims of bias and stereotyping (Jones & Gray, 1986; Lewis, Croft-Jeffreys, & Anthony, 1990). In other words, they may be more likely to receive a diagnosis of schizophrenia than members of a dominant group. One prospective study of schizophrenia among different ethnic groups in London found that although the outcomes of schizophrenia appear similar across these groups, Blacks were more likely to be detained against their will, brought to the hospital by police, and given emergency injections (Goater et al., 1999). The differing rates of schizophrenia, therefore, may be partially the result of *misdiagnosis* rather than the result of any real cultural distinctions. An additional factor contributing to this imbalance may be the levels of stress associated with factors such as stigma, isolation, and discrimination (Anglin, Lighty, Greenspoon, & Ellman, 2014; Pinto, Ashworth, & Jones, 2008).

Genetic Influences

We could argue that few areas of psychopathology so clearly illustrate the enormous complexity and intriguing mystery of genetic influences on behavior as does the phenomenon of schizophrenia (Goff, 2020; Keshavan, Lizano, Perry, Prasad, & Licinio, 2020). Despite the possibility that schizophrenia may be several different disorders, we can safely make one generalization: *Genes are responsible for making some individuals vulnerable to schizophrenia*. We look at a range of research findings from family, twin, adoptee, offspring of twins, and linkage and association studies. We conclude by discussing the compelling reasons that no one gene is responsible for schizophrenia; rather, multiple gene variances combine to produce vulnerability (Murray & Castle, 2012).

Family Studies

In 1938, Franz Kallmann published a major study of the families of people with schizophrenia (Kallmann, 1938). Kallmann examined family members of more than 1,000 people diagnosed with schizophrenia in a Berlin psychiatric hospital. Several of his observations continue to guide research on schizophrenia. Kallmann showed that the severity of the parent's disorder influenced the likelihood of the child having schizophrenia: The more severe the parent's schizophrenia, the more likely the children were to develop it. Another observation was important: All forms of schizophrenia (for example, the historic categories such as catatonic and paranoid) were seen within the families. In other words, it does not appear that you inherit a predisposition for what was previously diagnosed as paranoid schizophrenia. Instead, you may inherit a general predisposition for schizophrenia that manifests in the same form or differently from that of your parent. More recent research confirms this observation and suggests that families that have a member with schizophrenia are at risk not just for schizophrenia alone or for all psychological disorders; instead, there appears to be some familial risk for a spectrum of psychotic disorders related to schizophrenia.

In a classic analysis, Gottesman (1991) summarized the data from about 40 studies of schizophrenia, as shown in ■ Figure 13.3. The most striking feature of this graph is its orderly demonstration that the risk of having schizophrenia varies according to how many genes an individual shares with someone who has the disorder. For example, you have the greatest chance (approximately 48%) of having schizophrenia if it has affected your identical (monozygotic) twin, a person who shares 100% of your genetic information. Your risk drops to about 17% with a fraternal (dizygotic) twin, who shares about 50% of your genetic information. And having any relative with schizophrenia makes you more likely to have the disorder than someone without such a relative (about 1% if you have no relative with schizophrenia). Because family studies cannot separate genetic influence from the impact of the environment, we use twin and adoption studies to help us evaluate the role of shared experiences in the cause of schizophrenia.

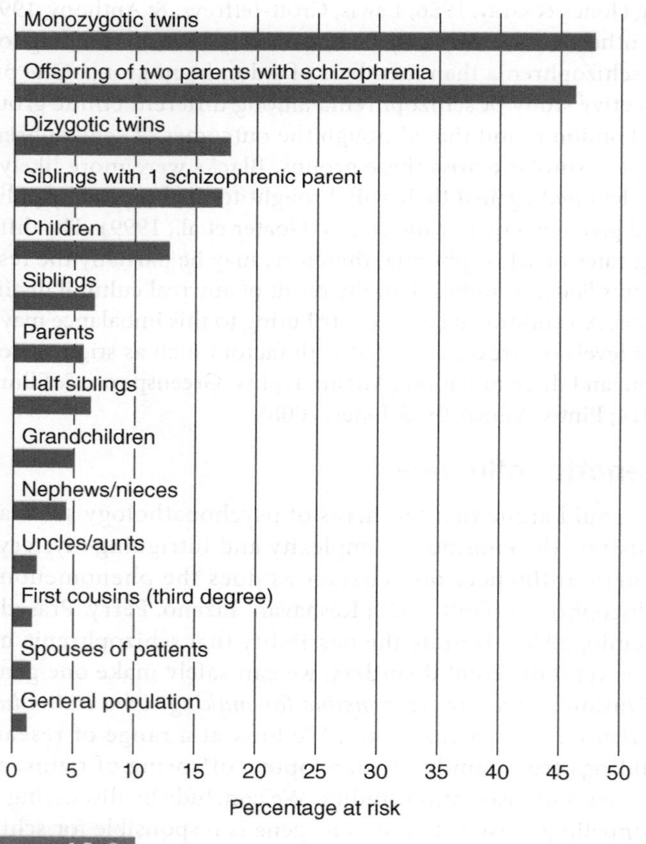

Figure 13.3

Risk of developing schizophrenia. Based on I. I. Gottesman, 1991, *Schizophrenia genesis: The origins of madness*, W. H. Freeman.

Twin Studies

If twins are raised together, identical twins share 100% of their genes and 100% of their environment, whereas fraternal twins share only about 50% of their genes and 100% of their environment. If the environment is solely responsible for schizophrenia, we would expect little difference between identical and fraternal twins with regard to this disorder. If only genetic factors are relevant, both identical twins would always have schizophrenia (be concordant), and the fraternal twins would both have it about 50% of the time. Research from twin studies indicates that the truth is somewhere in the middle (Goff, 2020; Keshavan et al., 2020).

In one of the most fascinating of "nature's experiments," identical quadruplets, all of whom have schizophrenia, have been studied extensively. Nicknamed the "Genain" quadruplets (from the Greek, meaning "dreadful gene"), these women were followed by David Rosenthal and his colleagues at the National Institute of Mental Health (NIMH) for a number of years (Rosenthal, 1963). The fictitious names of the women reported in studies of their lives—Nora, Iris, Myra, and Hester—represent the letters NIMH for the National Institute of Mental Health. In a sense, the women represent the complex interaction between genetics and environment. All four shared the same genetic predisposition, and all were brought up in the same particularly dysfunctional household; yet the time of onset for schizophrenia, the symptoms and diagnoses, the course of the disorder, and, ultimately, their outcomes, differed significantly from sister to sister.

Another family studied by the NIMH is the Galvin family, whose fascinating story was chronicled by Robert Kolker (Kolker, 2020). Don and Mimi Galvin had 12 children between 1945 and 1965—two girls and 10 boys. Six of the 10 Galvin boys were eventually diagnosed with schizophrenia. These six boys all expressed their diagnoses in different ways. One brother went from a diagnosis of schizophrenia to bipolar disorder. Another one was also diagnosed with mania (periods of great excitement or euphoria, delusions, and overactivity) (Kolker, 2020).

One genetic explanation for these differences may be the presence of *de novo* mutations in the family members. These are genetic mutations that can occur as a result of a mutation in a germ cell (egg or sperm) of one of the parents or, perhaps in the case of these family members, in the fertilized egg after conception. The case of the Genain quadruplets also reveals an important consideration in studying genetic influences on behavior—*unshared environments* (Plomin, 1990). We tend to think that siblings, and especially identical multiples, are brought up exactly the same way. The impression is that "good" parents expose their children to favorable environments and "bad" parents give them unstable experiences. Even identical siblings can have different prenatal and family experiences and can therefore be exposed to varying degrees of biological and environmental stress. For example, Hester, one of the Genain sisters, was described by her disturbed parents as a habitual masturbator, and she had more social problems than her sisters as she grew up. Hester was the first to experience severe symptoms of schizophrenia, at age 18, but her sister Myra was not hospitalized until 6 years later. This unusual case demonstrates that even siblings who are close in every aspect of their lives can still have considerably different experiences physically and socially as they grow up, which may result in vastly different outcomes. A follow-up on the lives of these women showed the progression of their disorder stabilized and in some cases improved when they were assessed at age 66 (Mirsky et al., 2000).

Adoption Studies

Several adoption studies have distinguished the roles of the environment and genetics as they affect schizophrenia. These studies often span many years. Because people often do not show the first signs of schizophrenia until middle age, researchers need to be sure all the offspring reach that point before drawing conclusions. Many schizophrenia studies are conducted in Europe, primarily because of the extensive and comprehensive records kept in countries where socialized medicine is practiced.

The largest adoption study was conducted in Finland (Tienari, 1991). From a sample of almost 20,000 women with schizophrenia, the researchers found 190 children who had been given up for adoption. The data from this study support the idea that schizophrenia represents a spectrum of related disorders, all of which overlap genetically. If an adopted child had a biological mother with schizophrenia, that child had about a 5% chance of having the disorder (compared to about only 1% in the general population). However, if the biological mother had schizophrenia or one of the related psychotic disorders (for example, delusional disorder or schizophreniform disorder), the risk that the adopted child would have one of these disorders rose to about 22% (Tienari et al., 2003; Tienari, Wahlberg, & Wynne, 2006). Even when raised away from their biological parents, children of parents with schizophrenia have a much higher chance of having the disorder themselves. At the same time, there appears to be a protective factor if these children are brought up in healthy supportive homes. In other words, a gene–environment interaction was observed in this study, with a good home environment reducing the risk of schizophrenia (Gilmore, 2010; Wynne et al., 2006).

The Offspring of Twins

Twin and adoption studies strongly suggest a genetic component for schizophrenia, but what about children who develop schizophrenia even though their parents do not? For example, the study by Tienari and colleagues (2003, 2006) we just discussed found that 1.7% of the children with parents without schizophrenia developed schizophrenia. Does this mean you can develop schizophrenia without "schizophrenic genes"? Or are some people carriers, having the genes for schizophrenia but for some reason not showing the disorder themselves? An important clue to this question comes from research on the children of twins with schizophrenia.

In a study begun in 1971 by Margit Fischer and later continued by Irving Gottesman and Aksel Bertelsen, 21 identical twin pairs and 41 fraternal twin pairs with a history of schizophrenia were identified, along with their children (Fischer, 1971; Gottesman & Bertelsen, 1989). The researchers wanted to determine the relative likelihood that a child would have schizophrenia if their parent did and if the parent's twin had schizophrenia but the parent did not. ■ Figure 13.4 illustrates the findings

Dr. Allan F. Mirsky/National Institute of Mental Health

The Genain quadruplets all had schizophrenia but exhibited different symptoms over the years.

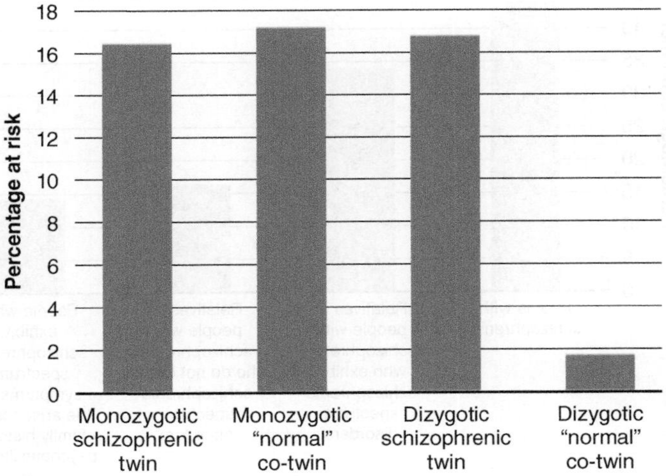

Figure 13.4

Risk for schizophrenia among children of twins.

from this study. For example, if your parent is an identical (monozygotic) twin with schizophrenia, you have about a 17% chance of having the disorder yourself, a figure that holds if you are the child of an unaffected identical twin whose co-twin has the disorder.

On the other hand, look at the risks for the child of a fraternal (dizygotic) twin. If your parent is the twin with schizophrenia, you have about a 17% chance of having schizophrenia yourself. If your parent does not have schizophrenia but your parent's fraternal twin does, your risk is only about 2%. The only way to explain this finding is through genetics. The data clearly indicate that you can have genes that predispose you to schizophrenia, not show the disorder yourself, but still pass on the genes to your children. In other words, you can be a "carrier" for schizophrenia. This is some of the strongest evidence yet that people are genetically vulnerable to schizophrenia. Remember, however, there is only a 17% chance of inheritance if your parent has schizophrenia, meaning that other factors help determine who will have this disorder.

Linkage and Association Studies

Recall from Chapter 4 that genetic linkage and association studies rely on traits such as blood types (whose exact location on the chromosome is already known) inherited in families with the disorder you are looking for—in this case, schizophrenia. Because researchers have determined the location of the genes for these traits (called *marker genes*), they can make a rough guess about the location of the disorder genes inherited with them. To date, researchers have looked at several sites for genes that may be responsible for schizophrenia. For example, regions of chromosomes 1, 2, 3, 5, 6, 8, 10, 11, 13, 20, and 22 are implicated in this disorder (Keshavan et al., 2020). Three of the most reliable genetic influences that make one susceptible to schizophrenia include sections on chromosome 8 (called Neuregulin 1 or NRG1), chromosome 6 (called dystrobrevin-binding protein 1 or DTNBP1), and chromosome 22 (called catecholamine O-methyl transferase or COMT) (Murray & Castle, 2012). The COMT gene is of particular interest to scientists because it plays a role in dopamine metabolism, which we will see appears to be disrupted in persons with this disorder. A study that combined one of the largest samples (36,989 cases of individuals with schizophrenia and 113,075 controls) identified 128 independent associations and 108 loci that meet genome-wide significance, 83 of which were new. This further strengthens that genetic risk arises from a large number of common genes each with a small effect that might be detected by genome-wide association studies (Ripke et al., 2014).

Endophenotypes

Genetic research on schizophrenia is evolving, and the information on the findings from these sophisticated studies is now being combined with advances in our understanding of specific deficits found in people with this disorder. Remember, in complex disorders such as this, researchers are not looking for a "schizophrenia gene" or genes. Instead, researchers try to find basic processes that contribute to the behaviors or symptoms of the disorder and then find the gene or genes that cause these difficulties—a strategy called *endophenotyping* (Keshavan et al., 2020).

Several potential candidates for endophenotypes for schizophrenia have been studied over the years. One of the more highly researched is called *smooth-pursuit eye movement*, or eye-tracking. Keeping their head still, typical people are able to track a moving pendulum, back and forth, with their eyes. The ability to track objects smoothly across the visual field is deficient in many people who have schizophrenia (Morita, Miura, Kasai, & Hashimoto, 2020); it does not appear to be the result of drug treatment or institutionalization (Lieberman et al., 1993). It also seems to be a problem for relatives of those with schizophrenia (Ivleva et al., 2014). ■ Figure 13.5 shows the decreasing likelihood of observing this abnormal eye-tracking ability the further a person is genetically from someone with schizophrenia. When all these observations are combined, they suggest an eye-tracking deficit may be an endophenotype for schizophrenia that could be used in further study.

Other such research focuses on the social, cognitive, and emotional deficits characteristic of schizophrenia. One study, for example, looked at multiple generations of families who had someone with schizophrenia (Gur et al., 2007). They tested them on a variety of skills for identified cognitive deficits in areas we described previously—such as emotion identification—and showed that specific problems were inherited in the same manner as schizophrenia (suggesting that these cognitive deficits might be endophenotypes for schizophrenia). A number of endophenotypes are being explored by a large group of scientists (the Consortium on the Genetics of Schizophrenia) that is studying

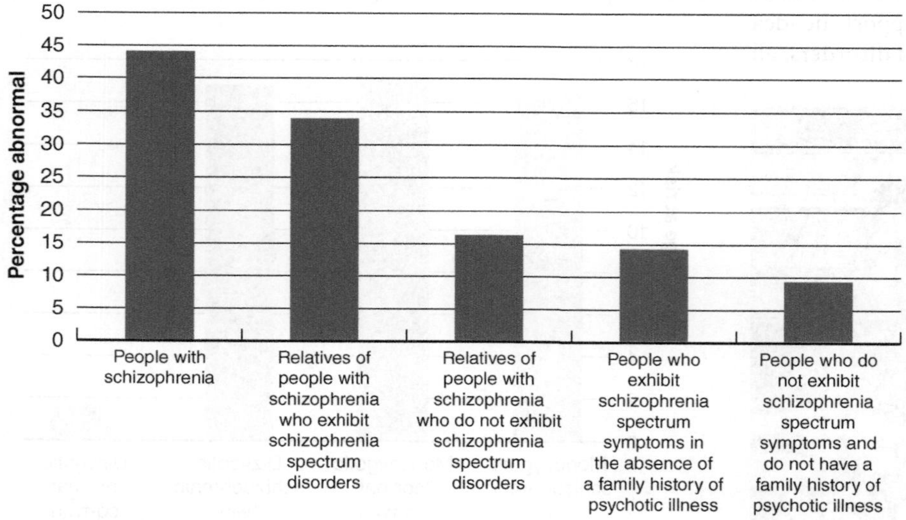

Figure 13.5

Abnormal smooth-pursuit eye movements and schizophrenia. Adapted, with permission, from G. K. Thaker & M. Avila, 2003, Schizophrenia, V: Risk markers, *American Journal of Psychiatry*, *160*, 1578. © 2003 American Psychiatric Association.

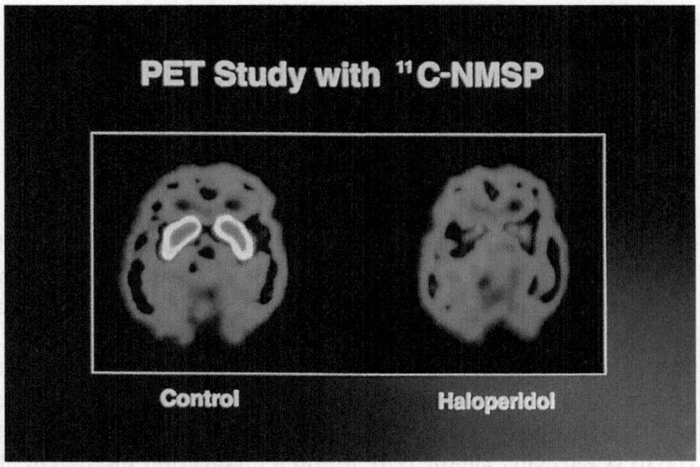

These PET images show the brain of a man with schizophrenia who had never been medicated (left) and after he received haloperidol (right). The red and yellow areas indicate activity in the D_2 receptors; haloperidol evidently reduced dopamine activity.

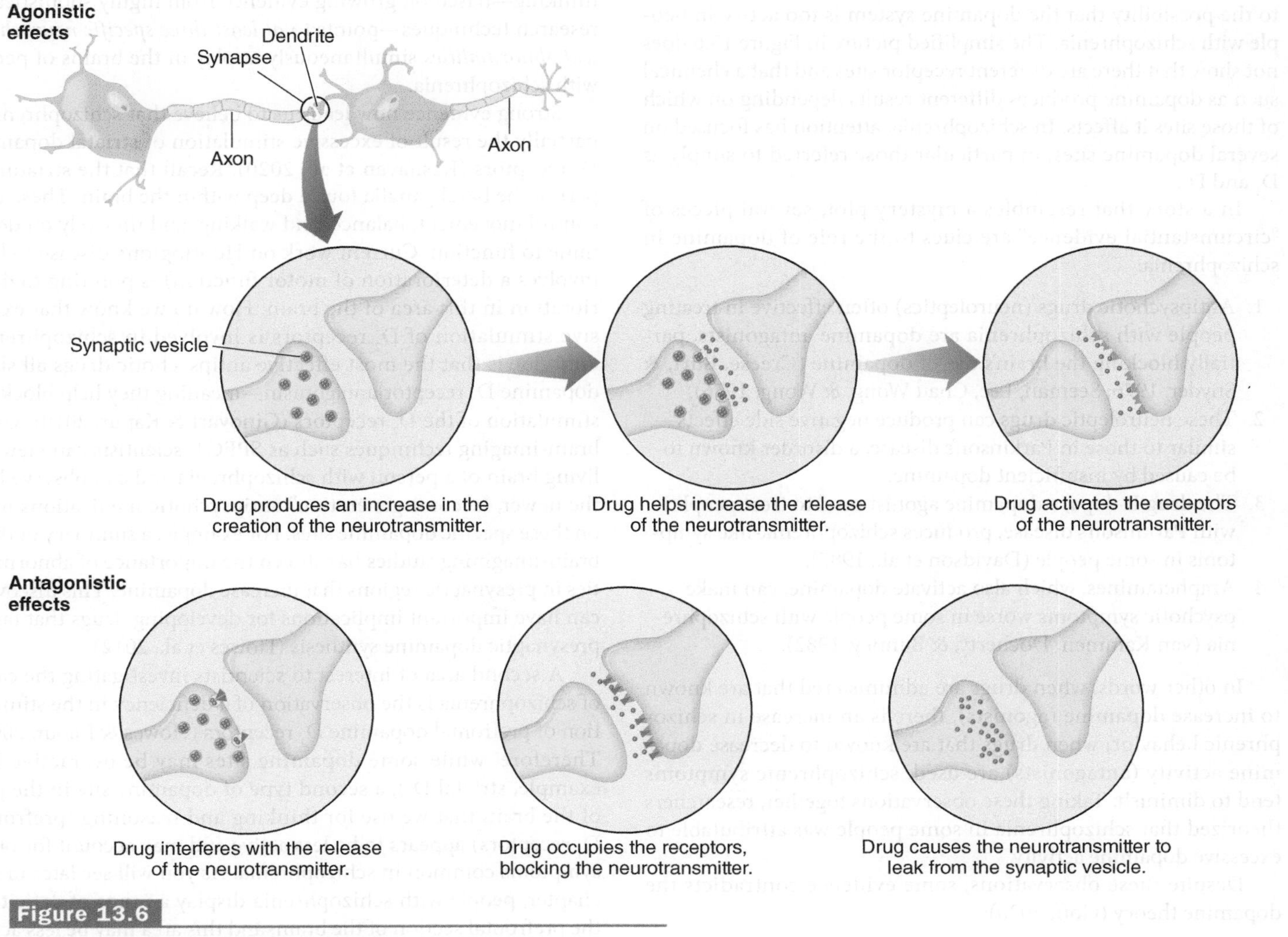

Figure 13.6
Some ways drugs affect neurotransmission.

more than 1,200 individuals with schizophrenia and their families (Lee et al., 2020).

Neurobiological Influences

The belief that schizophrenia involves a malfunctioning brain goes back as far as the writings of Kraepelin (1856–1926). It is therefore not surprising that a great deal of research has focused on the brain.

Dopamine

One of the most enduring yet controversial theories of the cause of schizophrenia involves the neurotransmitter *dopamine* (Goff, 2020). Before we consider the research, however, let's review briefly how neurotransmitters operate in the brain and how they are affected by neuroleptic medications, which reduce hallucinations and delusions. In Chapter 2, we discuss the sensitivity of specific neurons to specific neurotransmitters and describe how they cluster throughout the brain. The top of ■ Figure 13.6 shows two neurons and the important synaptic gap that separates them. Neurotransmitters are released from the storage vessels (synaptic vesicles) at the end of the axon, cross the gap, and are taken up by receptors in the dendrite of the next axon. Chemical "messages" are transported in this way from neuron to neuron throughout the brain.

This process can be influenced in a number of ways, and the rest of Figure 13.6 illustrates some of them. The chemical messages can be increased by agonistic agents or decreased by antagonistic agents. (Remember the word *antagonistic* means hostile or unfriendly; in some way, this is the effect of antagonistic agents on the chemical messenger service.) Antagonistic effects slow or stop messages from being transmitted by preventing the release of the neurotransmitter, blocking uptake at the level of the dendrite, or causing leaks that reduce the amount of neurotransmitter released. On the other hand, agonistic effects assist with the transference of chemical messages and, if extreme, can produce too much neurotransmitter activity by increasing production or release of the neurotransmitter and by affecting more receptors at the dendrites.

What we have learned about antipsychotic medications points to the possibility that the dopamine system is too active in people with schizophrenia. The simplified picture in Figure 13.6 does not show that there are different receptor sites and that a chemical such as dopamine produces different results depending on which of those sites it affects. In schizophrenia, attention has focused on several dopamine sites, in particular those referred to simply as D_1 and D_2.

In a story that resembles a mystery plot, several pieces of "circumstantial evidence" are clues to the role of dopamine in schizophrenia:

1. Antipsychotic drugs (neuroleptics) often effective in treating people with schizophrenia are dopamine antagonists, partially blocking the brain's use of dopamine (Creese, Burt, & Snyder, 1976; Seeman, Lee, Chau Wong, & Wong, 1976).
2. These neuroleptic drugs can produce negative side effects similar to those in Parkinson's disease, a disorder known to be caused by insufficient dopamine.
3. The drug L-dopa, a dopamine agonist used to treat people with Parkinson's disease, produces schizophrenia-like symptoms in some people (Davidson et al., 1987).
4. Amphetamines, which also activate dopamine, can make psychotic symptoms worse in some people with schizophrenia (van Kammen, Docherty, & Bunney, 1982).

In other words, when drugs are administered that are known to increase dopamine (agonists), there is an increase in schizophrenic behavior; when drugs that are known to decrease dopamine activity (antagonists) are used, schizophrenic symptoms tend to diminish. Taking these observations together, researchers theorized that schizophrenia in some people was attributable to excessive dopamine activity.

Despite these observations, some evidence contradicts the dopamine theory (Goff, 2020):

1. A significant number of people with schizophrenia are not helped by the use of dopamine antagonists.
2. Although the neuroleptics block the reception of dopamine quite quickly, the relevant symptoms subside only after several days or weeks, more slowly than we would expect.
3. These drugs are only partly helpful in reducing the negative symptoms (for example, flat affect or anhedonia) of schizophrenia.

In addition to these concerns, there is evidence of a "double-edged sword" with respect to schizophrenia. A medication called *olanzapine*—along with a family of similar drugs—is effective with many people who were not helped with traditional neuroleptic medications (Meftah, Deckler, Citrome, & Kantrowitz, 2020). That's the good news. The bad news for the dopamine theory is that olanzapine and these other new medications are weak dopamine antagonists, much less able to block the sites than other drugs (Javitt & Laruelle, 2006). Why would a medication inefficient at blocking dopamine be effective as a treatment for schizophrenia if schizophrenia is caused by excessive dopamine activity?

The answer may be that although dopamine is involved in the symptoms of schizophrenia, the relationship is more complicated than once thought (Keshavan et al., 2020). Current thinking—based on growing evidence from highly sophisticated research techniques—points to *at least three specific neurochemical abnormalities* simultaneously at play in the brains of people with schizophrenia.

Strong evidence now leads us to believe that schizophrenia is partially the result of excessive stimulation of striatal dopamine D_2 receptors (Keshavan et al., 2020). Recall that the striatum is part of the basal ganglia found deep within the brain. These cells control movement, balance, and walking, and they rely on dopamine to function. Current work on Huntington's disease (which involves a deterioration of motor function) is pointing to deterioration in this area of the brain. How do we know that excessive stimulation of D_2 receptors is involved in schizophrenia? One clue is that the most effective antipsychotic drugs all share dopamine D_2 receptor antagonism—meaning they help block the stimulation of the D_2 receptors (Ginovart & Kapur, 2010). Using brain-imaging techniques such as SPECT, scientists can view the living brain of a person with schizophrenia and can observe how the newer, "second-generation" antipsychotic medications work on these specific dopamine sites. For example, a summary of these brain-imagining studies has shown the importance of abnormalities in presynaptic regions that increase dopamine. This discovery can have important implications for developing drugs that target presynaptic dopamine synthesis (Howes et al., 2012).

A second area of interest to scientists investigating the cause of schizophrenia is the observation of a deficiency in the stimulation of prefrontal dopamine D_1 receptors (Howes & Kapur, 2009). Therefore, while some dopamine sites may be overactive (for example, striatal D_2), a second type of dopamine site in the part of the brain that we use for thinking and reasoning (prefrontal D_1 receptors) appears to be less active and may account for other symptoms common in schizophrenia. As you will see later in this chapter, people with schizophrenia display a range of deficits in the prefrontal section of the brain, and this area may be less active in people with schizophrenia (a condition known as *hypofrontality*, discussed later).

Finally, a third area of neurochemical interest involves research on alterations in prefrontal activity involving glutamate transmission (Keshavan et al., 2020). Glutamate is an excitatory neurotransmitter that is found in all areas of the brain and is only now being studied in earnest. Just as we saw with dopamine (for example, D_1 and D_2 receptors), glutamate has different types of receptors, and the ones being studied for their role in schizophrenia are the *N*-methyl-d-aspartate (NMDA) receptors. And, just as researchers were led to the study of dopamine by observations from the effects of dopamine-specific drugs on behavior, the effects of certain drugs that affect NMDA receptors point to clues to schizophrenia. Two recreational drugs described in Chapter 11—phencyclidine (PCP) and ketamine—can result in psychotic-like behavior in people without schizophrenia and can exacerbate psychotic symptoms in those with schizophrenia. Both PCP and ketamine are also NMDA antagonists, suggesting that a deficit in glutamate or blocking of NMDA sites may be involved in some symptoms of schizophrenia (Bianciardi & Uhlhaas, in press).

You can see that research on these two neurotransmitters and their relationship to each other is complex and awaits further clarification. However, advances in technology are leading us closer to the clues behind this enigmatic disorder and closer still to better treatments.

Brain Structure

Evidence for neurological damage in people with schizophrenia comes from a number of observations. Many children with a parent who has the disorder, and who are therefore at risk, tend to show subtle but observable neurological problems, such as abnormal reflexes and inattentiveness (Buka, Seidman, Tsuang, & Goldstein, 2013). These difficulties are persistent: Adults who have schizophrenia show deficits in their ability to perform certain tasks and to attend during reaction time exercises (Cleghorn & Albert, 1990). Such findings suggest that brain damage or dysfunction may cause or accompany schizophrenia, although no one site is probably responsible for the whole range of symptoms (Goff, 2020).

One of the most reliable observations about the brain in people with schizophrenia involves the size of the ventricles (see ■ Figure 13.7). As early as 1927, these liquid-filled cavities showed enlargement in some brains examined in people with schizophrenia (Jacobi & Winkler, 1927). Since then, more sophisticated techniques have been developed for observing the brain, and in the dozens of studies conducted on ventricle size, the great majority show abnormally large lateral and third ventricles in people with schizophrenia (Costas-Carrera, Garcia-Rizo, Bitanihirwe, & Penadés, in press). Ventricle size may not be a problem, but the dilation (enlargement) of the ventricles indicates that adjacent parts of the brain either have not developed fully or have atrophied, thus allowing the ventricles to become larger.

Ventricle enlargement is not seen in everyone who has schizophrenia. Several factors seem to be associated with this finding. For example, enlarged ventricles are observed more often in men than in women (Abel, Drake, & Goldstein, 2010). Also, ventricles seem to enlarge in proportion to age and to the duration of the schizophrenia. One study found that individuals with schizophrenia who were exposed to influenza prenatally may be more likely to have enlarged ventricles (Takei, Lewis, Jones, Harvey, & Murray, 1996). (The possible role of prenatal exposure to influenza in the development of schizophrenia is described in the next section.)

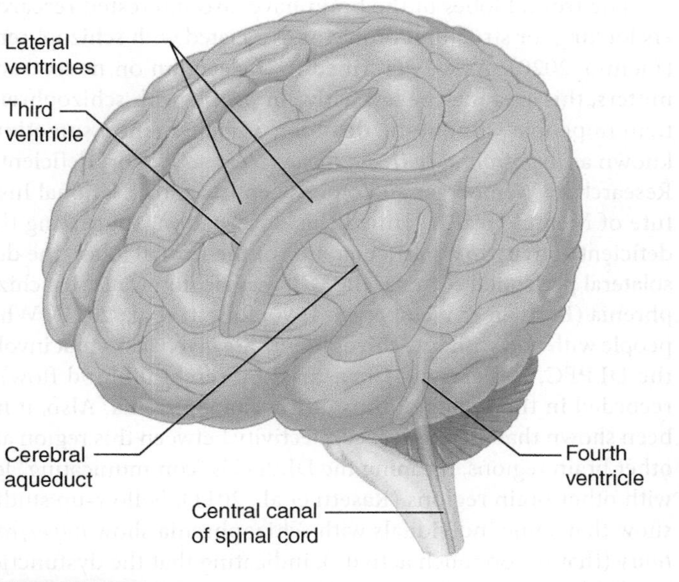

Figure 13.7
Location of the cerebrospinal fluid in the human brain. This extracellular fluid surrounds and cushions the brain and spinal cord. It also fills the four interconnected cavities (cerebral ventricles) within the brain and the central canal of the spinal cord.

In a study of ventricle size, researchers investigated the possible role of genetics (van Haren et al., 2012). Using a brain-imaging technique, magnetic resonance imaging (MRI), investigators pooled data to compare brain structure among twin pairs (both identical and fraternal) from several European countries for a total of 684 people. They compared twin pairs in which both twins had schizophrenia, twin pairs in which only one twin had schizophrenia, as well as healthy twin pairs. The results showed that lower white matter volume and larger third ventricular volume were associated with the risk for schizophrenia, and these differences appeared to be influenced by genetic factors.

We touched on the concept of unshared environments in the section on genetics (Jang, 2005; Plomin, 1990). Although twins are identical genetically, they can experience a number of environmental differences, even before they are born. For instance, in the intrauterine environment, twins must compete for nutrients, and they may not be equally successful. In addition, birth complications, such as the loss of oxygen (anoxia), could affect only one of the twins (Murray & Castle, 2012). Obstetrical complications appear often in one of a pair of twins who develops schizophrenia and among the more severely affected if both twins have schizophrenia (McNeil, 1987). Different experiences among twins already predisposed to the disorder could damage the brain and cause the types of symptoms we associate with schizophrenia.

The frontal lobes of the brain have also interested researchers looking for structural problems associated with schizophrenia (Licinio, 2020). As we described in the section on neurotransmitters, this area may be less active in people with schizophrenia than in people without the disorder, a phenomenon sometimes known as *hypofrontality* (*hypo* means "less active" or "deficient"). Research by Weinberger and other scientists at the National Institute of Mental Health refined this observation, suggesting that deficient activity in a particular area of the frontal lobes, the dorsolateral prefrontal cortex (DLPFC), may be implicated in schizophrenia (Berman & Weinberger, 1990; Rasetti et al., 2011). When people with and without schizophrenia are given tasks that involve the DLPFC, less activity (measured by cerebral blood flow) is recorded in the brains of those with schizophrenia. Also, it has been shown that there is less connectivity between this region and other brain regions, meaning the DLPFC is "communicating" less with other brain regions (Rasetti et al., 2011). Follow-up studies show that some individuals with schizophrenia show *hyperfrontality* (that is, too much activity), indicating that the dysfunction is reliable, but hyperfrontality displays itself differently in different people (Callicott et al., 2003; Garrity et al., 2007).

It appears that several brain sites are implicated in the cognitive dysfunction observed among people with schizophrenia, especially the prefrontal cortex, various related cortical regions, and subcortical circuits, including the thalamus and the striatum (Licinio, 2020). Remember that this dysfunction seems to occur *before the onset* of schizophrenia. In other words, brain variations may develop progressively, beginning before the symptoms of the disorder are apparent, perhaps prenatally (Harrison, 2012).

Prenatal and Perinatal Influences

There is evidence that the prenatal (before birth) and perinatal (around the time of birth) environment are correlated with the development of schizophrenia (Keshavan et al., 2020). Fetal exposure to viral infection, pregnancy complications, and delivery complications are among the environmental influences that seem to affect whether or not someone develops schizophrenia.

Several studies have shown that schizophrenia may be associated with prenatal exposure to influenza, viruses, or infections. For example, Sarnoff Mednick and colleagues followed a large number of people after a severe Type A2 influenza epidemic in Helsinki, Finland, and found that those whose mothers were exposed to influenza during the second trimester of pregnancy were more likely to have schizophrenia than others (Cannon, Barr, & Mednick, 1991). This observation has been confirmed by some researchers (see, for example, O'Callaghan, Sham, Takei, Glover, & Murray, 1991; Venables, 1996) but not by others (Buchanan & Carpenter, 2005; Selten, Frissen, Lensvelt-Mulders, & Morgan, 2009). The indications that viruslike diseases may cause injury to the fetal brain, which later may cause the symptoms of schizophrenia, are suggestive and may help explain why some people with schizophrenia behave the way they do (Murray & Castle, 2012).

The evidence of pregnancy complications (for example, bleeding) and delivery complications (for example, asphyxia or lack of oxygen) and their relationship to later schizophrenia suggest, on the surface, that this type of environmental stress combined with genetic and other variables may trigger the expression of the disorder (Keshavan et al., 2020). It is possible, however, that the genes carried by the fetus that make it vulnerable to schizophrenia may themselves contribute to the birth complications (van Os & Allardyce, 2009).

The chronic and early use of marijuana (cannabis) is also being studied as a potential influence on the onset of schizophrenia (Keshavan et al., 2020). Some research suggests that people who use cannabis in high doses have an increased likelihood of developing schizophrenia for those with COMT and AKT1 genotypes (Keshavan et al., 2020) and that people with schizophrenia are more likely to have a cannabis use disorder than individuals without schizophrenia (Corcoran et al., 2008; Martins & Gorelick, 2011). The link between these two problems is not yet clearly understood, and there are conflicting findings about whether or not other factors may be responsible for this correlation (Murray & Castle, 2012).

Psychological and Social Influences

That one identical twin may develop schizophrenia and the other may not suggests that schizophrenia involves something in addition to genes. We know that early brain trauma, perhaps resulting from a second-trimester viruslike attack or obstetrical complications, may generate physical stress that contributes to schizophrenia. All these observations show clearly that schizophrenia does not fall neatly into a few simple causal packages. For instance, not all people with schizophrenia have enlarged ventricles, nor do they all have a hypofrontality or disrupted activity in their dopamine systems. The causal picture may be further complicated by psychological and social factors. We next look at research into psychosocial factors. Do emotional stressors or family interaction patterns *initiate* the symptoms of schizophrenia? If so, how might those factors cause people to relapse after a period of improvement?

Stress

It is important to learn how much and what kind of stress makes a person with a predisposition for schizophrenia develop the disorder. Think back to the two cases we present at the beginning of this chapter. Did you notice any precipitating events? Amrit's father had died several years earlier, and Amrit was laid off from his job around the time his symptoms first appeared. Luis's uncle had died the same year he began acting strangely. Were these stressful events just coincidences, or did they contribute to the men's later problems?

Researchers have studied the effects of a variety of stressors on schizophrenia. Living in a large city, for example, is associated with an increased risk of developing schizophrenia—suggesting the stress of urban living may precipitate its onset (Boydell & Allardyce, 2012). Dohrenwend and Egri (1981) observed that otherwise healthy people who engage in combat during a war often display temporary symptoms that resemble those of schizophrenia. In a classic study, Brown and Birley (1968; Birley & Brown, 1970) examined people whose onset of schizophrenia could be dated within a week. These individuals had experienced a high number of stressful life events in the 3 weeks before they started showing signs of the disorder. In a large-scale study sponsored by the World Health Organization, researchers also looked at the role of life events in the onset of schizophrenia (Day et al., 1987). This cross-national study confirmed the findings of Brown and Birley across eight research centers.

Seasonality of birth is one of the most replicated influences on schizophrenia (Keshavan et al., 2020). More specifically, being born during the winter increases a person's chance for later developing schizophrenia by 5% to 8% (Torrey, Miller, Rawlings, & Yolken, 1997). Unfortunately, the neurobiological mechanisms underlying this influence is currently unknown (Keshavan et al., 2020).

The *retrospective* nature of such research creates problems. Each study relies on after-the-fact reports, collected after the person showed signs of schizophrenia. One always wonders whether such reports are biased in some way and therefore misleading. At the same time, there are strong individual differences in how people experience the same life events, and people with schizophrenia may experience events differently than those without the disorder (Keshavan et al., 2020).

Do the symptoms of schizophrenia become worse as a result of stressful life experiences? This vulnerability–stress model of schizophrenia suggests that this is the case, and it may be helpful in predicting problems. One research study used a natural disaster—the 1994 Northridge, California, earthquake—to assess how people with schizophrenia would react to this stress when compared with those with bipolar disorder and healthy controls (Horan et al., 2007). Both patient groups reported more stress-related symptoms compared with the controls; however, the people with schizophrenia reported lower levels of self-esteem after the disaster and were more likely to engage in avoidance coping (not thinking about the problem or becoming resigned to difficulties) than the other two groups. Research on sociocultural stress, such as poverty, homelessness, early life adversity, growing up in an urban environment, minority group position, and the stress of being in a new country (Lataster, Myin-Germeys, Lieb, Wittchen, & van Os, 2012; van Os, Kenis, & Rutten, 2010), suggests that these psychosocial stressors influence onset and possibly development of schizophrenia. Onset of symptoms usually happens as a result of environmental stressors, showing that these stressors may have their impact during sensitive periods in development. For example, stressors in early life may influence development of psychosis, possibly by increasing stressors later in life, making individuals more sensitive to later stressors, or both (Lataster et al., 2012).

A simple vulnerability can develop into a severe disorder from the interchange between gene–environment. Important research will isolate the gene–environment interactions in this area. For example, some studies now show that particular gene variances may predict which individuals with schizophrenia will be more likely to react negatively (such as relapse) with increased stress (Ascher-Svanum et al., 2010). These types of studies point to how stress can impact people with schizophrenia and may suggest useful treatments (such as cognitive-behavioral therapy to help them cope more appropriately) (Ascher-Svanum et al., 2010).

Families and Relapse

Jill Hooley of Harvard University is a noted researcher of expressed emotion in families with schizophrenia.

A great deal of research has studied how interactions within the family affect people who have schizophrenia. For example, the term **schizophrenogenic mother** was used for a time to describe a mother whose cold, dominant, and rejecting nature was thought to cause schizophrenia in her children (Fromm-Reichmann, 1948). In addition, the term **double bind communication** was used to portray a communication style that produced conflicting messages, which, in turn, caused schizophrenia to develop (Bateson, 1959). Here, the parent presumably communicates messages that have two conflicting meanings; for example, a mother responds coolly to her child's embrace but says, "Don't you love me anymore?" when the child withdraws. Although these theories are no longer supported, they have been—and in some cases continue to be—destructive, producing guilt in parents who are persuaded that their early mistakes caused devastating consequences.

Recent work has focused more on how family interactions contribute not to the onset of schizophrenia but to relapse after initial symptoms are observed. You will see that this research is similar to the work on vulnerability to stress in general that was just discussed. Research has focused on a particular emotional communication style known as **expressed emotion (EE)**. This concept was formulated by George W. Brown and his colleagues in London. Following a sample of people who had been discharged from the hospital after an episode of schizophrenic symptoms, the researchers found that former patients who had limited contact with their relatives did better than the patients who spent longer periods with their families (Brown, 1959). Additional research results indicated that if the levels of criticism (disapproval), hostility (animosity), and emotional overinvolvement (intrusiveness) expressed by the families were high, patients tended to relapse (Brown, Monck, Carstairs, & Wing, 1962).

Other researchers have since found that ratings of high expressed emotion in a family are a good predictor of relapse among people with chronic schizophrenia (Hinojosa-Marqués, Domínguez-Martínez, Kwapil, & Barrantes-Vidal, 2020). If an individual has schizophrenia and lives in a family with high expressed emotion, they are 3.7 times more likely to relapse than if they lived in a family with low expressed emotion (Kavanagh, 1992; Parker & Hadzi-Pavlovic, 1990). Here are examples of interviews that show how families of people with schizophrenia might communicate expressed emotion:

High Expressed Emotion

- I always say, "Why don't you pick up a book, do a crossword or something like that to keep your mind off it?" That's even too much trouble.

- I've tried to jolly him out of it and pestered him into doing things. Maybe I've overdone it, I don't know.

Low Expressed Emotion

- I know it's better for her to be on her own, to get away from me and try to do things on her own.
- Whatever she does suits me.
- I just tend to let it go because I know that when she wants to speak she will speak. (Hooley, 1985, p. 134)

This style suggests that families with high expressed emotion view the symptoms of schizophrenia as controllable and that the hostility arises when family members think that patients just do not want to help themselves (Hooley & Campbell, 2002; McNab, Haslam, & Burnett, 2007). The literature on expressed emotion is valuable to our understanding of why symptoms of schizophrenia recur and may show us how to treat people with this disorder and their families so that they do not experience further psychotic episodes (Hinojosa-Marqués et al., 2020).

An interesting issue that arises when studying family influences is whether what we see is unique to our culture or universal. Looking at expressed emotion across different cultures may help us learn whether expressed emotion is a *cause* of schizophrenia (Breitborde, López, & Kopelowicz, 2010; Kymalainen & Weisman de Mamani, 2008). Remember that the rate of schizophrenia is observed to be about the same worldwide, with a prevalence of about 1% in the global population. If a factor like high expressed emotion in families is a causal agent, we should see the same rates in families across cultures; however, they differ, as you can see in ■ Figure 13.8. These data come from an analysis of the concept of expressed emotion in several studies from India, Mexico, United Kingdom, and the United States (Jenkins & Karno, 1992). The differences suggest that there are cultural variations in how families react to someone with schizophrenia and their reactions do not cause the disorder (Singh, Harley, & Suhail, 2013). In addition, what may appear to be over-involvement in one culture may be viewed as supportive in other cultures.

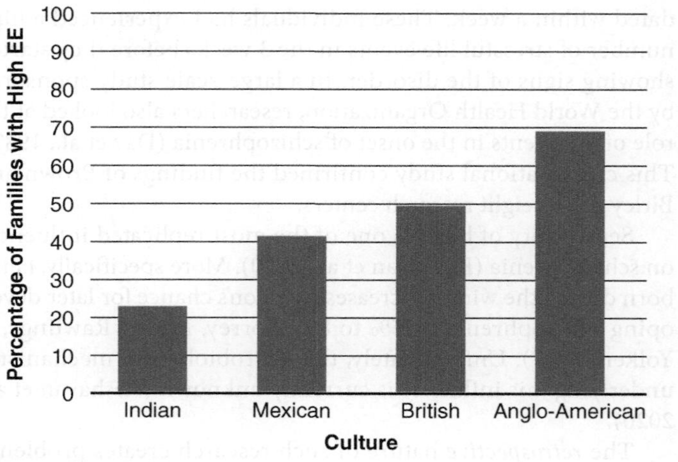

Figure 13.8

Cultural differences in expressed emotion.

Concept Check 13.2

Check your understanding of genetic vulnerability by filling in the blanks of the statements associated with family, twin, and adoption studies. Choose from (a) higher, (b) lower, (c) equal, (d) severity, (e) type, (f) identical twin, (g) specific, (h) fraternal twin, and (i) general.

1. The greatest risk of having schizophrenia is in those who have a(n) __________ or __________ with schizophrenia. Any relative with schizophrenia will make your chances of developing the disorder __________ than those of the general population.
2. Raised in a home other than that of their biological parents, adopted children of parents with schizophrenia have a(n) __________ chance of having the disorder themselves. Children of people with schizophrenia adopted into families without schizophrenia have a __________-than-average chance of having schizophrenia.
3. The likelihood of a child's having schizophrenia is influenced by the __________ of the parent's disorder. One may inherit a predisposition for __________ schizophrenia that is the same or different from that of the parent.

Treatment of Schizophrenia

If you remember our descriptions of Amrit and Luis, you will recall their families' concern for them. Amrit's mother spoke of the "living nightmare," and Luis's aunt expressed concern for both her safety and Luis's. In each case, the family was desperate to help, but what do you do for someone who has delusions, hears his dead uncle's voice, or cannot communicate complete thoughts? The search for help has taken many paths, sometimes down some disturbing roads. For example, in the 1500s, primitive surgery was conducted to remove the "stone of madness," which was thought to cause disturbed behavior. As barbaric as this practice may seem today, it is not different from the prefrontal lobotomies performed on people with schizophrenia as late as the 1950s (Almeida, Aquino, & Silva, 2020). This procedure severed the frontal lobes from the lower portion of the brain, which sometimes calmed the patient but also caused cognitive and emotional deficits. Even today, some societies use crude surgical procedures to eliminate the symptoms of schizophrenia. In Kenya, for instance, Kisii tribal doctors listen to their patients to find the location of the noises in their heads (hallucinations), then get them drunk, cut out a piece of scalp, and scrape the skull in the area of the voices (Marangu, 2020).

In the Western world today, treatment usually begins with one of the neuroleptic drugs invaluable in reducing the symptoms of schizophrenia for many people. They are typically used with a variety of psychosocial treatments to reduce relapse, compensate for skills deficits, and improve cooperation for taking the medications (Keepers et al., 2020).

An early 16th-century painting of psychosurgery, in which part of the brain is removed to treat mental disorders.

Table 13.2 Commonly Used Antipsychotic Medications

Class	Example*	Degree of Extrapyramidal Side Effects
Conventional antipsychotics:		
Phenothiazines	Chlorpromazine/*Thorazine*	Moderate
	Fluphenazine/*Prolixin*	High
	Mesoridazine/*Serentil*	Low
	Perphenazine/*Trilafon*	High
	Thioridazine/*Mellaril*	Low
	Trifluoperazine/*Stelazine*	High
Butyrophenone	Haloperidol/*Haldol*	High
Others	Loxapine/*Loxitane*	High
	Molindone/*Moban*	Low
	Thiothixene/*Navane*	High
Second-generation agents:		
	Aripiprazole/*Abilify*	Low
	Clozapine/*Clozaril*	Low
	Olanzapine/*Zyprexa*	Low
	Quetiapine/*Seroquel*	Low
	Risperidone/*Risperdal*	Low
	Ziprasidone/*Geodon*	Low

*The trade name is in italics.

Source: Adapted from American Psychiatric Association, 2004, *Practice guideline for the treatment of patients with schizophrenia*, (2nd ed.), *American Journal of Psychiatry*, *161*(Suppl.), 1–56.

Biological Interventions

Researchers have assumed for more than 100 years that schizophrenia requires some form of biological intervention. Kraepelin, who so eloquently described dementia praecox in the late 19th century, saw the disorder as a brain disease. Lacking a biological treatment, he routinely recommended that the physician use "good patience, kindly disposition, and self-control" to calm excited patients (Nagel, 1991). This approach was seen as only a temporary way of helping the person through disturbing times and was not thought to be an actual treatment.

During the 1930s, several novel biological treatments were tried. One approach was to inject massive doses of insulin—the drug that given in smaller doses is used to treat diabetes—to induce comas in people suffering from schizophrenia. Insulin coma therapy was thought for a time to be helpful, but closer examination showed it carried great risk of serious illness and death. During this time, *psychosurgery*, including prefrontal lobotomies (also known as a leucotomy), was introduced, and in the late 1930s, electroconvulsive therapy (ECT) was advanced as a treatment for schizophrenia. As with earlier drastic treatments, initial enthusiasm for ECT faded because it was found not to be beneficial for most people with schizophrenia—although it is still used with a limited number of people today, sometimes in combination with antipsychotic medications (Sanghani, Petrides, & Kellner, 2018). As we explain in Chapter 7, ECT is sometimes recommended for people who experience severe episodes of depression.

Antipsychotic Medications

A breakthrough in the treatment of schizophrenia came during the 1950s with the introduction of several drugs that relieved symptoms in many people (Cunningham Owens & Johnstone, 2012). Called *neuroleptics* (meaning "taking hold of the nerves"), these medications provided the first real hope that help was available for people with schizophrenia. When they are effective, neuroleptics help people think more clearly and reduce hallucinations and delusions. They work by affecting the positive symptoms (delusions, hallucinations, and agitation) and to a lesser extent the negative and disorganized ones, such as social deficits. Table 13.2 shows the classes of these drugs (based on their chemical structure) and their trade names.

Recall from our discussion of the dopamine theory of schizophrenia that the neuroleptics are dopamine antagonists. One of their major actions in the brain is to interfere with the dopamine neurotransmitter system. They can also affect other systems, however, such as the serotonergic and glutamate system. We are just beginning to understand the mechanisms by which these drugs work.

In general, each drug is effective with some people and not with others. Clinicians and patients often must go through a trial-and-error process to find the medication that works best, and some individuals do not benefit significantly from any of them. The earliest neuroleptic drugs, called conventional or first-generation antipsychotics (such as Haldol and Thorazine), are effective for approximately 60% to 70% of people who try them (Cunningham, Owens, & Johnstone, 2012). Many people are not helped by antipsychotics, however, or they experience unpleasant side effects. Fortunately, some people respond well to newer medications—sometimes called atypical or second-generation antipsychotics; the most common are risperidone and olanzapine. These newer drugs were in part developed to help patients who were previously unresponsive to medications. A comparison of multiple clinical trials shows better efficacy, though small, in preventing symptoms reemergence for these newer drugs over the previous ones (Kishimoto et al., 2013). Initially, it was thought that the newer drugs had fewer serious side effects than the conventional antipsychotics. However, two large-scale studies—one conducted in the United States (called the "Clinical Antipsychotic Trials of Intervention Effectiveness" or CATIE) (Stroup & Lieberman, 2010) and one in the United Kingdom (called the "Cost Utility of the Latest Antipsychotic Drugs in Schizophrenia Study" or CUtLASS) (Jones et al., 2006)—found that the second-generation drugs were no more effective or better tolerated than the older drugs (Lieberman & Stroup, 2011).

Another large and long-term study looked at the efficacy of antipsychotic medications on people with schizophrenia and other psychotic disorders (Harrow, Jobe, & Tong, in press). They followed 139 participants for 20 years to assess the effects of their medication use on recovery, remission, employment, symptom presentation, social outcomes, and antipsychotic medication effects. One of the important findings was that participants with schizophrenia who were not on antipsychotics after the first 2 years had better outcomes than participants prescribed antipsychotics (Harrow et al., in press). These results point out how important it is to carefully study the outcomes of all new treatments.

Noncompliance with Medication: Why?

Despite the optimism generated by the effectiveness of antipsychotics, they work only when they are taken properly, and many people with schizophrenia do not routinely take their medication (Patel, Sreeram, Vadukapuram, & Baweja, 2020). Luis frequently "cheeked" the Haldol pills that were helpful in reducing his hallucinations, holding them in his mouth until he was alone and then spitting them out. In one large-scale study, 74% of those studied had stopped taking their medications 18 months after initial use (Lieberman & Stroup, 2011).

A number of factors seem to be related to patients' noncompliance with a medication regimen, including negative doctor–patient relationships, cost of the medication, stigma, and poor social support (Haddad, Brain, & Scott, 2014). Not surprisingly, negative side effects are a major factor in patient refusal. Antipsychotics can produce a number of unwanted physical symptoms, such as grogginess, blurred vision, and dryness of the mouth. Because the drugs affect neurotransmitter systems, more serious side effects, called *extrapyramidal symptoms*, can also result (Stroup, Perkins, & Javitt, 2020). These symptoms include the motor difficulties similar to those experienced by people with Parkinson's disease, sometimes called Parkinsonian symptoms. *Akinesia* is one of the most common; it includes an expressionless face, slow motor activity, and monotonous speech. Another extrapyramidal symptom is *tardive dyskinesia*, which involves involuntary movements of the tongue, face, mouth, or jaw and can include protrusions of the tongue, puffing of the cheeks, puckering of the mouth, and chewing movements. Tardive dyskinesia seems to result from long-term use of high doses of antipsychotic medication and is often irreversible. Studies have shown that up to 20% to 50% of all patients treated with antipsychotics develop tardive dyskinesia with lower risk for younger people (only 3% to 5% of younger people taking this medication display tardive dyskinesia, with the risk increasing over time) (Waln & Jankovic, 2013). These serious negative side effects have justifiably concerned people who otherwise benefit from the drugs.

To learn what patients themselves say, Windgassen (1992) questioned 61 people who had had recent onsets of schizophrenia. About half reported the feeling of sedation or grogginess as an unpleasant side effect: "I always have to fight to keep my eyes open," "I felt as though I was on drugs … drowsy, and yet really wound up" (p. 407). Other complaints included deterioration in the ability to think or concentrate (18%), problems with salivation (16%), and blurred vision (16%). Although a third of the patients felt the medications were beneficial, about 25% had a negative attitude toward them. A significant number of people who could benefit from antipsychotic medications find them unacceptable as a treatment, which may explain the relatively high rates of refusal and noncompliance (Sendt, Tracy, & Bhattacharyya, 2015; Yamada et al., 2006).

Researchers have made this a major treatment issue in schizophrenia, realizing that medications cannot be successful if they are not taken regularly. Researchers hoped compliance rates would improve with the introduction of injectable medications. Instead of taking an oral antipsychotic every day, patients can have their medications injected every few weeks. Long-acting injectable antipsychotics (LAIs), which are administered once every 2 or 4 weeks (depending on the specific drug) rather than daily, are one option to help address nonadherence. LAIs have been associated with both reduced hospitalization rates and care costs (Potkin, Bera, Zubek, & Lau, 2013). Psychosocial interventions are now used

Radius Images/Jupiter Images

One of the major obstacles to drug treatment for schizophrenia is compliance. Patients discontinue their medication for a variety of reasons, including the negative side effects.

not only to treat schizophrenia but also to increase medication-taking compliance by helping patients communicate better with professionals about their concerns.

Additional Biological Treatments

An interesting treatment for the hallucinations experienced by many people with schizophrenia involves exposing the individual to magnetic fields. Called *transcranial magnetic stimulation*, this technique uses wire coils to repeatedly generate magnetic fields—up to 50 times per second—that pass through the skull to the brain. This input seems to interrupt temporarily the normal communication to that part of the brain (Marzouk, Winkelbeiner, Azizi, Malhotra, & Homan, 2020). Hoffman and colleagues (2000, 2003) used this technique to stimulate the area of the brain involved in hallucinations for individuals with schizophrenia who experienced auditory hallucinations. They found that many of the individuals experienced improvement following transcranial magnetic stimulation. Subsequent studies have also shown promising results (Dougall, Maayan, Soares-Weiser, McDermott, & McIntosh, 2015), but more stringent clinical trials are needed to demonstrate that this treatment works (Marzouk et al., 2020). Additionally, follow-up data is needed to test whether the improvements last. Preliminary research has shown that though this intervention may modestly improve auditory hallucinations, its effects last less than a month (Slotema, Aleman, Daskalakis, & Sommer, 2012).

Psychosocial Interventions

Historically, a number of psychosocial treatments have been tried for schizophrenia, reflecting the belief that the disorder results from problems in adapting to the world because of early experiences (Keepers et al., 2020). Many therapists have thought that individuals who could achieve insight into the presumed role of their personal histories could be safely led to deal with their current situations. Although clinicians who take a traditional psychodynamic or psychoanalytic approach to therapy continue to use this type of treatment, research suggests that their efforts at best may not be beneficial and at worst may be harmful (Mueser & Berenbaum, 1990; Scott & Dixon, 1995).

Today, few believe that psychological factors cause people to have schizophrenia or that traditional psychotherapeutic approaches will cure them. Nevertheless, you will see that psychological methods have an important role. Despite the great promise of drug treatment, the problems with ineffectiveness, inconsistent use, and relapse suggest that by themselves drugs may not be effective with many people. As with a number of the disorders discussed in this text, recent work in the area of psychosocial intervention has suggested the value of an approach that uses both kinds of treatment (Mueser & Marcello, 2011).

Until relatively recently, most people with severe and chronic cases of schizophrenia were treated in hospital settings. During the 19th century, inpatient care involved "moral treatment," which emphasized improving patients' socialization, helping them establish routines for self-control, and showing them the value of work and religion (Tenhula et al., 2009). Various types of such "milieu" treatments (changing the physical and social environment—usually to make institutional settings more homelike) have been popular, but, with one important exception: None seems to have helped people with schizophrenia.

Gordon Paul and Robert Lentz conducted pioneering work in the 1970s at a mental health center in Illinois (Paul & Lentz, 1977). Borrowing from the behavioral approaches used by Ted Ayllon and Nate Azrin (1968), Paul and Lentz designed an environment for inpatients that encouraged appropriate socialization, participation in group sessions, and self-care such as bed making while discouraging violent outbursts. They set up an elaborate **token economy**, in which residents could earn access to meals and small luxuries by behaving appropriately. A patient could, for example, buy cigarettes with the tokens he earned for keeping his room neat. On the other hand, a patient would be fined (lose tokens) for being disruptive or otherwise acting inappropriately. This incentive system was combined with a full schedule of daily activities. Paul and Lentz compared the effectiveness of applied behavioral (or social learning) principles with traditional inpatient environments. In general, they found that patients who went through their program did better than others on social, self-care, and vocational skills, and more of them could be discharged from the hospital. This study was one of the first to show that people experiencing the debilitating effects of schizophrenia can learn to perform some skills they need to live more independently.

During the years since 1955, many efforts have combined to halt the routine institutionalization of people with schizophrenia in the United States (Fakhoury & Priebe, 2007). This trend has occurred partly because of court rulings that limit involuntary hospitalization (as we saw in Amrit's case) and partly because of the relative success of antipsychotic medication. The bad news is that policies of deinstitutionalization have often been ill conceived, with the result that many people who have schizophrenia or other serious psychological disorders are homeless—the number is estimated at between 150,000 and 200,000 people in the United States alone (Foster, Gable, & Buckley, 2012; Pearson, Montgomery, & Locke, 2009). The good news is that more attention is being focused on supporting these people in their communities, among their friends and families. The trend is away from creating better hospital environments and toward the perhaps more difficult task of addressing complex problems in the less predictable and insecure world outside. So far, only a small fraction of the growing number of homeless individuals with mental disorders is being helped.

One of the more insidious effects of schizophrenia is its negative impact on a person's ability to relate to other people. Although not as dramatic as hallucinations and delusions, problems with social skills can be the most visible impairment displayed by people with schizophrenia and can prevent them from getting and keeping jobs and making friends. Clinicians attempt to reteach social skills such as basic conversation, assertiveness, and relationship building to people with schizophrenia (Keepers et al., 2020).

Therapists divide complex social skills into their component parts, which they model. Then the clients do role-playing and ultimately practice their new skills in the "real world," all the while receiving feedback and encouragement at signs of progress. This isn't as easy as it may sound. For example, how would you teach

A mother is glad to have her daughter home from a psychiatric hospital but acknowledges that "Now the real struggle begins."

someone to make a friend? Many skills are involved, such as maintaining eye contact when you talk to someone and providing the prospective friend with some (but not too much) positive feedback on their own behavior ("I really enjoy talking to you"). Such individual skills are practiced and then combined until they can be used naturally (Kayo et al., 2020). The challenge of teaching social skills, as with all therapies, is to maintain the effects over a long period.

In addition to social skills, programs often teach a range of ways people can adapt to their disorder yet live in the community. At the Independent Living Skills Program at the University of California, Los Angeles, for example, the focus is on helping people take charge of their own care by such methods as identifying signs that warn of a relapse and learning how to manage their medication (see Table 13.3) (Liberman, 2007). Preliminary evidence indicates that this type of training may help prevent relapses by people with schizophrenia, although longer-term outcome research is needed to see how long the effects last (Cunningham Owens & Johnstone, 2012). To address some obstacles to this much-desired maintenance, such programs combine skills training with the support of a multidisciplinary team that provides services directly in the community, which seems to reduce hospitalization (Cunningham Owens & Johnstone, 2012). The more time and effort given to these services, the more likely the improvement.

Is there a role for newer technologies in the diagnosis and treatment of schizophrenia? Creative researchers are answering this question in a number of exciting developments for the field. One study looked to improve the understanding of schizophrenia by using virtual reality technology to simulate multiple cognitive tasks (Fernández-Sotos, Fernández-Caballero, & Rodriguez-Jimenez, 2020). Researchers created game-like tasks to test aspects of working memory and perseveration (focusing on the same things repeatedly) and found not only that this approach could create real-life simulations that revealed deficits but also that the tasks could be fun. A study carried out at King's

Table 13.3 Independent Living Skills Program at UCLA

Module	Skill Areas	Learning Objectives
Symptom management	Identifying warning signs of relapse	To identify personal warning signs To monitor personal warning signs with assistance from others
	Managing warning signs	To obtain assistance from health-care providers in differentiating personal warning signs from persistent symptoms, medication side effects, and variations in mood To develop an emergency plan for responding to warning signs
	Coping with persistent symptoms	To recognize and monitor persistent personal symptoms To obtain assistance from health-care providers in differentiating persistent symptoms from warning signs, medication side effects, and variations in mood To use specific techniques for coping with persistent symptoms To monitor persistent symptoms daily
	Avoiding alcohol and street drugs	To identify adverse effects of alcohol and illicit drugs and benefits of avoiding them To refuse offers of alcohol and street drugs To know how to resist using these substances in coping with anxiety, low self-esteem, or depression To discuss openly use of alcohol and drugs with health-care providers
Medication management	Obtaining information on antipsychotic medication	To understand how these drugs work, why maintenance drug therapy is used, and what the benefits of taking medication are
	Knowing correct self-administration and evaluation	To follow the appropriate procedures for taking medication To evaluate responses to medication daily
	Identifying side effects of medication	To know which specific side effects sometimes result from taking medication and what to do when these problems occur
	Negotiating medication issues with health-care providers	To practice ways of obtaining assistance when problems occur with medication

Source: Reprinted, with permission, from T. A. Eckman, W. C. Wirshing, S. R. Marder, R. P. Liberman, K. Johnston-Cronk, K. Zimmermann, & J. Mintz, 1992, Techniques for training schizophrenic patients in illness self-management: A controlled trial, *American Journal of Psychiatry*, *149*, 1549–1555. © 1992 American Psychiatric Association.

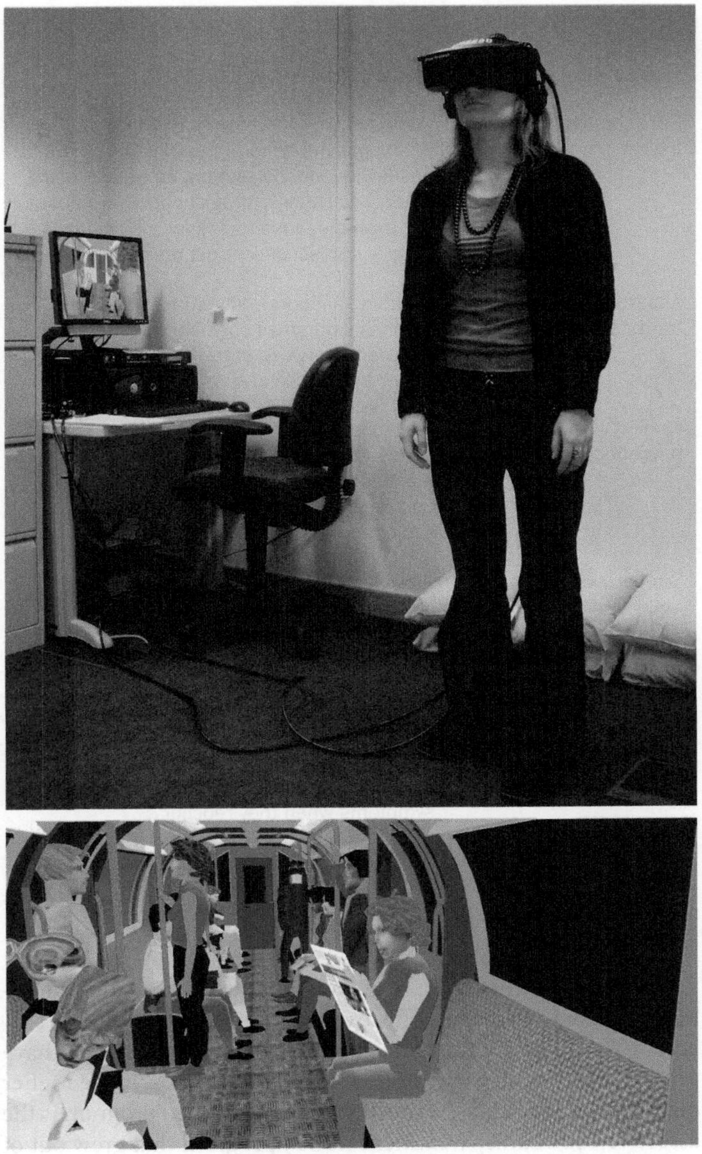

Courtesy of Daniel Freeman

Courtesy Daniel Freeman

Researchers are using virtual reality technology to better understand the complexity of schizophrenia. The photo at the top illustrates a participant in a study of paranoia. The bottom photo shows what the participants see. This technology allows researchers to closely control positions and facial expressions of the virtual people on the subway.

College in London tested the nature of paranoia in a virtual reality environment among groups with low paranoia, with nonclinical paranoia, and with persecutory delusions (Freeman, Pugh, Vorontsova, Antley, & Slater, 2010). Researchers constructed a virtual scene that depicts a London subway and created avatars as passengers that at times would look at the study participant (see accompanying photos).

Across the groups, there were meaningful differences in levels of anxiety, worry, interpersonal sensitivity, and depression according to their previous levels of paranoia. This type of assessment provided a safe environment in which to assess and study persecutory paranoia in the groups. Other research is using this technology to assist older persons with schizophrenia improve their cognitive and general motor skills (for example, by having them push away colorful balls that are floating toward them in a virtual world) (Chan, Ngai, Leung, & Wong, 2010). Again, these virtual assessments and treatments provide clinicians with controllable and safer environments in which to study and treat persons with schizophrenia.

Another psychosocial intervention for schizophrenia is cognitive remediation aimed at improving cognitive processes, such as attention, executive functioning, and memory, all of which are associated with impairments over the course of schizophrenia. Impairment in these cognitive areas predicts patients' overall functioning and poor response to other treatments (such as psychological rehabilitation or social skills training) (Mueser, Deavers, Penn, & Cassisi, 2013). Thus, a primary goal of cognitive remediation is to improve cognitive processes for those with schizophrenia in order to increase these individuals' functioning in the community. The intervention consists of cognitive practice exercises and learning cognitive strategies. This intervention seems to improve cognitive abilities and overall functioning, especially when combined with other treatments, such as psychological rehabilitation (Mueser et al., 2013). Also, studies suggest that patients' functioning improves more when a strategy-based approach is taken (Wykes, Huddy, Cellard, McGurk, & Czobor, 2011).

In our discussion of the psychosocial influences on schizophrenia, we review some work linking the person's social and emotional environments to the recurrence of schizophrenic episodes (Medalia et al., 2020). It is logical to ask whether families could be helped by learning to reduce their level of expressed emotion and whether this would result in fewer relapses and better overall functioning for people with schizophrenia (Hinojosa-Marqués et al., 2020). Several studies have addressed these issues in a variety of ways (Falloon et al., 1985; Hogarty et al., 1986, 1991), and behavioral family therapy has been used to teach the families of people with schizophrenia to be more supportive (Dixon & Lehman, 1995; Mueser, Liberman, & Glynn, 1990). Research on professionals who provide care for people who have schizophrenia, and who may display high levels of expressed emotion, is also an active area of study (Cunningham Owens & Johnstone, 2012).

In contrast to traditional therapy, behavioral family therapy resembles classroom education (Medalia et al., 2020). Family members are informed about schizophrenia and its treatment, relieved of the myth that they caused the disorder, and taught practical facts about antipsychotic medications and their side effects. They are also helped with communication skills so that they can become more empathic listeners, and they learn constructive ways of expressing negative feelings to replace the harsh criticism that characterizes some family interactions. In addition, they learn problem-solving skills to help them resolve conflicts that arise. Like the research on social skills training, outcome research suggests that the effects of behavioral family therapy are significant during the first year but less robust 2 years after intervention (Cunningham Owens & Johnstone, 2012). This type of

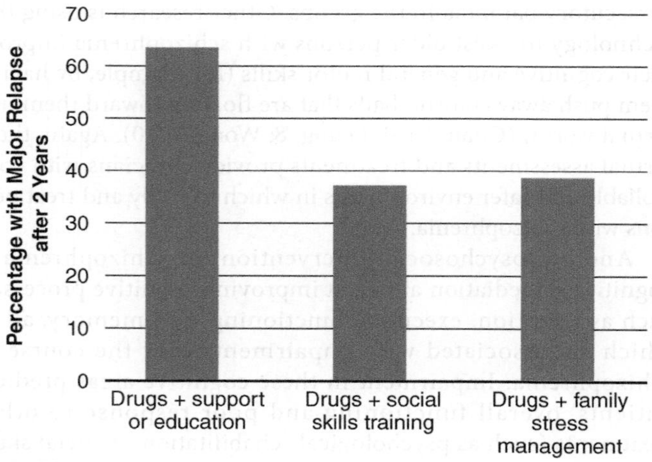

Figure 13.9

Studies on treatment of schizophrenia from 1980 to 1992. Adapted from I. R. H. Falloon, C. Brooker, & V. Graham-Hole, 1992, Psychosocial interventions for schizophrenia, *Behaviour Change*, *9*, 238–245.

therapy, therefore, must be ongoing if patients and their families are to benefit from it.

Adults with schizophrenia face great obstacles to maintaining gainful employment. Their social skills deficits make reliable job performance and adequate employee relationships a struggle. To address these difficulties, some programs focus on vocational rehabilitation, such as supportive employment. Supportive employment involves providing coaches who give on-the-job training, and these efforts can help some people with schizophrenia maintain meaningful jobs (Medalia et al., 2020).

Research suggests that individual social skills training, family intervention, and vocational rehabilitation may be helpful additions to biological (drug) treatment for schizophrenia. Significant relapses may be avoided or delayed by such psychosocial interventions. ■ Figure 13.9 illustrates the studies reviewed by one group (Falloon, Brooker, & Graham-Hole, 1992), which show that multilevel treatments reduce the number of relapses among people receiving drug therapy in comparison with simple social support or educational efforts.

Where treatment occurs, it has expanded over the years from locked wards in large psychiatric hospitals, to family homes, to local communities. In addition, the services have expanded to include self-advocacy and self-help groups. Former patients have organized programs such as Fountain House in New York City to provide mutual support. Psychosocial clubs have differing models, but all are "person centered" and focus on obtaining positive experiences through employment opportunities, friendship, and empowerment. Many see this consumer-run self-help model as an added component to more specific interventions such as social skills training, family intervention, and medical management of symptoms. Some research indicates that participation may help reduce relapses, but as it is also possible that those who participate may be a distinct group of individuals, it is difficult to interpret improvements (Davidson, Chinman, Sells, & Rowe, 2006; Goering et al., 2006).

Table 13.4 An Integrative Treatment Approach

Treatment	Description
Collaborative psychopharmacology	Using antipsychotic medications to treat the main symptoms of the disorder (hallucinations, delusions), as well as using other medications for secondary symptoms (for example, antidepressant medication for people with secondary depression)
Assertive community treatment	Providing support in the community, with emphasis on small caseloads for care providers, services in the community setting rather than a clinic, and 24-hour coverage
Family psychoeducation	Assisting family members, including educating them about the disorder and its management, helping them reduce stress and tension in the home, and providing social support
Supportive employment	Providing sufficient support before and during employment so that the person can find and keep a meaningful job
Illness management and recovery	Helping the individual become an active participant in treatment, including providing education about the disorder, teaching effective use of medication strategies for collaborating with clinicians, and coping with symptoms when they reoccur
Integrated dual-disorders treatment	Treating coexisting substance use

Because schizophrenia is a complex disorder that affects multiple areas of functioning, effective treatment is carried out at several levels. Table 13.4 lists six approaches to treatment that have proved effective in assisting these individuals to achieve higher quality lives. Probably the most extensively studied program is the assertive community treatment (ACT) program that grew out of work by researchers in Madison, Wisconsin (Swartz et al., 2006). ACT involves using a multidisciplinary team of professionals to provide broad-ranging treatment across all domains, including medication management, psychosocial treatment, and vocational training and support. As you can see, one approach alone is not sufficient to address the many needs of people with schizophrenia and their families (Cunningham Owens & Johnstone, 2012; Mueser & Marcello, 2011).

Treatment across Cultures

Treatment of schizophrenia and its delivery differ from one country to another and across cultures within countries (Marangu, 2020). For example, the vast majority of the Xhosa people of South Africa who have schizophrenia report using traditional healers who sometimes recommend the use of oral treatments to induce vomiting, enemas, and the slaughter of cattle to appease the spirits (Koen, Niehaus, Muller, & Laurent, 2008). Latino/as may be less likely than other groups to seek help in institutional

Treatment for the symptoms of schizophrenia vary widely by culture—from humane approaches using empirically validated interventions to simply removing the person from society.

settings, relying instead on family support (Hernandez, Barrio, & Yamada, 2013; Liberman & Kopelowicz, 2009). Adapting treatments to make them culturally relevant—in this case, adding important relatives to the social skills training of Latino/as with schizophrenia—is essential for effectiveness (Kopelowicz et al., 2012). In one interesting study, beliefs about symptoms and treatments were compared between British and Chinese populations (Furnham & Wong, 2007). Native Chinese hold more religious beliefs about both the causes and the treatments of schizophrenia than those living in England—for example, endorsing statements such as "Schizophrenia is due to evil done in a previous life" and "Ancestor worship (burning candles and joss sticks) will help treat schizophrenia." These different beliefs translate into practice—with the British using more biological, psychological, and community treatments, and the Chinese relying more on alternative medicine (Furnham & Wong, 2007). Supernatural beliefs about the cause of schizophrenia among family members in Bali lead to limited use of antipsychotic medication in treatment (Kurihara, Kato, Reverger, & Gusti Rai Tirta, 2006). In many countries in Africa, people with schizophrenia are kept in prisons, primarily because of the lack of adequate alternatives (Mustafa, 1990). In general, the movement from housing people in large institutional settings to community care is ongoing in most Western countries.

Prevention

One strategy for preventing a disorder such as schizophrenia—which typically first shows itself in early adulthood—is to identify and treat children who may be at risk for getting the disorder later in life. In our discussion of genetics, we noted that approximately 17% of the children born to parents who have schizophrenia are likely themselves to develop the disorder. These high-risk children have been the focus of several studies.

A classic at-risk study was initiated in the 1960s by Sarnoff A. Mednick and Fini Schulsinger (1965, 1968). They identified 207 Danish children of mothers who had severe cases of schizophrenia and 104 control children born to mothers who had no history of the disorder. The average age of these children was about 15 when they were first identified, and the researchers followed them for 10 more years to determine whether any factors had predicted who would and would not develop schizophrenia. We have already discussed pregnancy- and delivery-related complications. Mednick and Schulsinger also identified *instability of early family rearing environment*, which suggests that environmental influences may trigger the onset of schizophrenia (Cannon et al., 1991). Poor parenting may place additional strain on a vulnerable person who is already at risk.

One approach to prevention of schizophrenia receiving increased attention is the treatment of persons in the prodromal stages of the disorder. Here the individual is beginning to show early mild signs of schizophrenia (such as hallucinations or delusions) but is aware of these changes. Efforts to intervene with these individuals are being investigated as a means of either stopping to progression of the disorder or preventing relapses (Cunningham Owens & Johnstone, 2012).

Concept Check 13.3

Read the descriptions, and then match them to the following words: (a) olanzapine, (b) extrapyramidal symptoms, (c) serotonin, (d) dopamine, (e) metabolites, (f) token economy, (g) vocational rehabilitation, (h) social skills training, (i) family intervention.

1. Setting up an elaborate ______________ in which patients are fined for disruptive or inappropriate behavior and rewarded for appropriate behavior is beneficial in hospitals.
2. In ______________, clinicians attempt to reteach such behaviors as basic conversation, assertiveness, and relationship building to people with schizophrenia.
3. Aside from social skills training, two psychosocial treatments for schizophrenia—______________ (teaching family members to be supportive) and ______________ (teaching meaningful jobs)—may be helpful.
4. Recent studies sometimes indicate that the relationship of the neurotransmitters ______________ and ______________ may explain some positive symptoms of schizophrenia.
5. Because antipsychotic medications may cause serious side effects, some patients stop taking them. One serious side effect is called ______________, which may include Parkinsonian symptoms.
6. Difficult cases of schizophrenia seem to improve with a serotonin and dopamine antagonist called ______________.

DSM Controversies: *Attenuated Psychosis Syndrome*

One of the most discussed changes in DSM-5 related to schizophrenia spectrum and other psychotic disorders was the possible inclusion of a new diagnosis, attenuated psychosis syndrome. Recall that this diagnosis would be given to a person who is beginning to experience one or more of the symptoms of schizophrenia such as hallucinations or delusions but is aware that these are unusual experiences and are not typical for a healthy person (that is, relatively intact reality testing). They are at high risk for having more severe symptoms as displayed in schizophrenia spectrum disorder. The argument for including this set of symptoms as a new disorder is that catching the person in these early stages might prove helpful for early intervention efforts (Pagsberg, 2013). It is possible that getting the symptoms under control before they become severe might save the person from years of suffering (Woods, Walsh, Saksa, & McGlashan, 2010).

On the other hand, some argue against focusing attention on this select group of individuals. From a public health perspective, some suggest that rather than limit prevention efforts to this group, that broader attention should be paid to the mental health status of the general population to screen for and provide services for any person showing signs of these disturbances (van Os, 2011). DSM-5 "cut the baby in half" by including the disorder in its section "condition for further study." It remains to be seen if this set of criteria will eventually make its way into the DSM and what impact that will have on treatment and outcomes for those affected.

Summary

Perspectives on Schizophrenia

- Schizophrenia is a complex syndrome that has been recognized for many years. Perhaps the earliest and best description of this disorder was published in 1809 by John Haslam in his book *Observations on Madness and Melancholy*.
- A number of historic figures during the 19th and early 20th century contributed to the evolving definitions and possible causes of this spectrum of disorders.

Clinical Description, Symptoms, and Subtypes

- Schizophrenia is characterized by a broad spectrum of cognitive and emotional dysfunctions that include delusions and hallucinations, disorganized speech and behavior, and inappropriate emotions.
- The symptoms of schizophrenia can be divided into positive, negative, and disorganized. Positive symptoms are active manifestations of psychopathology, or an excess or distortion of normal behavior, and include delusions and hallucinations. Negative symptoms involve deficits in normal behavior on such dimensions as affect, speech, and motivation. Disorganized symptoms include rambling speech, erratic behavior, and inappropriate affect.
- Psychotic behaviors, such as hallucinations and delusions, characterize several other disorders; these include schizophreniform disorder (which includes people who experience the symptoms of schizophrenia for less than 6 months); schizoaffective disorder (which includes people who have symptoms of schizophrenia and who exhibit the characteristics of mood disorders, such as depression and bipolar affective disorder); delusional disorder (which includes people with a persistent belief that is contrary to reality, in the absence of the other characteristics of schizophrenia); and brief psychotic disorder (which includes people with one or more positive symptoms, such as delusions, hallucinations, or disorganized speech or behavior over the course of less than a month).
- A proposed new disorder—attenuated psychosis syndrome—includes one or more of the symptoms of schizophrenia (such as hallucinations or delusions), but the individual is aware that these are unusual experiences and are not typical for a healthy person. This is included in the Appendix of DSM-5 as a disorder in need of further study.

Prevalence and Causes of Schizophrenia

- A number of causative factors have been implicated for schizophrenia, including genetic influences, neurotransmitter imbalances, structural damage to the brain caused by a prenatal viral infection or birth injury, and psychological stressors.
- Relapse appears to be triggered by hostile and critical family environments characterized by high expressed emotion.

Treatment of Schizophrenia

- Successful treatment for people with schizophrenia rarely includes complete recovery. The quality of life for these individuals can be meaningfully affected, however, by combining antipsychotic medications with psychosocial approaches, employment support, and community-based and family interventions.
- Treatment typically involves antipsychotic drugs that are usually administered with a variety of psychosocial treatments, with the goal of reducing relapse and improving skills in deficits and compliance in taking the medications. The effectiveness of treatment is limited because schizophrenia is typically a chronic disorder.

Key Terms

schizophrenia, 481
catatonia, 481
hebephrenia, 481
paranoia, 481
dementia praecox, 481
associative splitting, 482
psychotic behavior, 483
positive symptoms, 484
negative symptoms, 484
disorganized symptoms, 484
delusion, 484
hallucination, 485
avolition, 487
alogia, 487
anhedonia, 487
flat affect, 488
disorganized speech, 488
inappropriate affect, 488
catatonic immobility, 488
schizophreniform disorder, 489
schizoaffective disorder, 490
delusional disorder, 490
shared psychotic disorder (folie à deux), 490
substance-induced psychotic disorder, 492
psychotic disorder associated with another medical condition, 492
brief psychotic disorder, 492
attenuated psychosis syndrome, 492
schizotypal personality disorder, 492
prodromal stage, 494
schizophrenogenic mother, 503
double bind communication, 503
expressed emotion (EE), 503
token economy, 507

Answers to Concept Checks

13.1

Part A

1. disorganized; 2. Schizophreniform disorder; 3. Delusional disorder; 4. catatonic; 5. Attenuated psychosis syndrome

Part B

6. c; 7. b; 8. a; 9. d

13.2

1. f, h, a; 2. a, a; 3. d, i

13.3

1. f; 2. h; 3. i, g; 4. d, c; 5. b; 6. a

Exploring Schizophrenia

- Schizophrenia disrupts perception of the world, thought, speech, movement, and almost every other aspect of daily functioning.
- Usually chronic with a high relapse rate; complete recovery from schizophrenia is rare.

- Stressful, traumatic life event
- High expressed emotion (family criticism, hostility, and/or intrusion)
- Sometimes no obvious trigger

Trigger

Biological Influences

- Inherited tendency (multiple genes) to develop disease
- Prenatal/birth complications—viral infection during pregnancy/birth injury affect child's brain cells
- Brain chemistry (abnormalities in the dopamine and glutamate systems)
- Brain structure (enlarged ventricles)

Causes

Dynamic Graphics/Jupiter Images

Behavioral Influences

- **Positive symptoms:**
  - —Active manifestations of abnormal behavior (delusions, hallucinations, disorganized speech, odd body movements, or catatonia)
- **Negative symptoms:**
  - —Flat affect (lack of emotional expression)
  - —Avolition (lack of initiative, apathy)
  - —Alogia (relative absence in amount or content of speech)

Emotional and Cognitive Influences

- Interaction styles that are high in criticism, hostility, and emotional overinvolvement can trigger a relapse

Social Influences

- Environment (early family experiences) can trigger onset
- Culture influences interpretation of disease/symptoms (hallucinations, delusions)

Photodisc/Getty Images

TREATMENT OF SCHIZOPHRENIA

Treatment		
Individual, Group, and Family Therapy		■ Can help patient and family understand the disease and symptom triggers. ■ Teaches families communication skills. ■ Provides resources for dealing with emotional and practical challenges.
Social Skills Training		■ Can occur in hospital or community settings. ■ Teaches the person with schizophrenia social, self-care, and vocational skills.
Medications	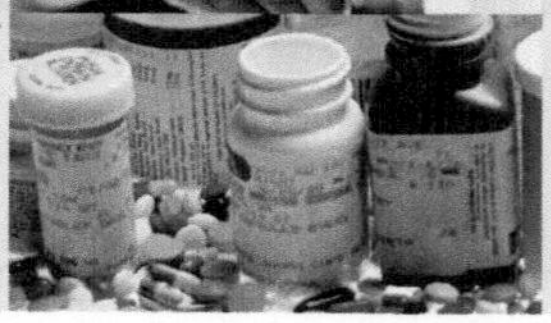	■ Taking neuroleptic medications may help people with schizophrenia to: —Clarify thinking and perceptions of reality —Reduce hallucinations and delusions ■ Drug treatment must be consistent to be effective. Inconsistent dosage may aggravate existing symptoms or create new ones.

Photos: ©Photodisc/Getty Images

SYMPTOMS OF SCHIZOPHRENIA

People with schizophrenia do not all show the same kinds of symptoms.
Symptoms vary from person to person and may be cyclical. Common symptoms include:

Symptoms

Delusions

Photodisc/Getty Images

- Unrealistic and bizarre beliefs not shared by others in the culture
- May be delusions of grandeur (that you are really Mother Teresa or Napoleon) or delusions of persecution (the cyclist who believed her competitors were sabotaging her by putting pebbles in the road)

Hallucinations

Photodisc/Getty Images

- Sensory events that aren't based on any external event (hearing voices, seeing people who have died)
- Many have auditory hallucinations (David hears his dead uncle talking to him)

Disorganized Speech

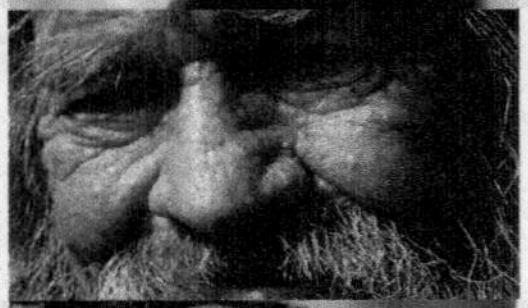

Royalty Free/Corbis

- Jumping from topic to topic
- Talking illogically (not answering direct questions, going off on tangents)
- Speaking in unintelligible words and sentences

Behavioral Problems

Dynamic Graphics/Jupiter Images

- Pacing excitably, wild agitation
- Catatonic immobility
- Waxy flexibility (keeping body parts in the same position when they are moved by someone else)
- Inappropriate dress (coats in the summer, shorts in the winter)
- Inappropriate affect
- Ignoring personal hygiene

Withdrawal

Photodisc/Getty Images

- Lack of emotional response (flat speech, little change in facial expressions)
- Apathy (little interest in day-to-day activities)
- Delayed and brief responses in conversation
- Loss of enjoyment in pleasurable activities (eating, socializing, sex)

14 Neurodevelopmental Disorders

Denis Kuvaev/Shutterstock.com

Learning Objectives

LO14.1 Define developmental psychopathology as a subfield of clinical psychology in terms of its key features and areas of study.

LO14.2 Discuss the primary characteristics of attention-deficit/hyperactivity disorder according to its criteria as listed in the DSM-5.

LO14.3 Distinguish between specific learning disorders and communication and motor disorders in terms of their symptoms and primary features.

LO14.4 Explain how biological conditions and psychosocial factors influence the development of autism spectrum disorder.

LO14.5 Contrast the three intellectual disabilities described in the text according to their causes, ages of onset, and impacts on functioning.

LO14.6 Discuss efforts to prevent neurodevelopmental disorders.

Overview of Neurodevelopmental Disorders

Almost all disorders described in this book are developmental disorders in the sense that they change over time. Most disorders originate in childhood, although the full presentation of the problem may not manifest itself until much later. Disorders that show themselves early in life often persist as the person grows older, so the term *childhood disorder* may be misleading. Because the developmental disorders in this group are all believed to be neurologically based, DSM-5 categorizes them as **neurodevelopmental disorders** (American Psychiatric Association, 2013). In this chapter, we cover those disorders that are revealed in a clinically significant way during a child's developing years and are of concern to families and educators. Remember, however, that these difficulties often persist through adulthood and are typically life-long problems, not problems unique to children.

Again, a number of difficulties and, indeed, distinct disorders begin in childhood. In certain disorders, some children are fine except for difficulties with talking. Others have problems relating to their peers. Still other children have a combination of conditions that significantly hinder their development, as illustrated by the case of Ryan.

As clinicians have grown to appreciate the far-reaching effects of childhood problems and the importance of early intervention in treating most disorders, they have become more interested in understanding the diversity of severe problems experienced in early life. Ryan was diagnosed with "autism" (now referred to as *autism spectrum disorder*) in the early 1970s. More than five decades later, we know more—although still not enough—about how to help children who have autism spectrum disorder. Who can say what the prognosis for Ryan might be today, especially if he were diagnosed and treated at age 2 instead of at age 7?

Ryan... The Boy Who Looked Right through You

Ryan, a beautiful blond baby, was born with the umbilical cord wrapped around his neck, so he had been without oxygen for an unknown period. Nonetheless, he appeared to be a healthy little boy. His mother later related that he was a good baby who rarely cried, although she was concerned he didn't like to be picked up and cuddled. His family became worried about his development when he was 2 years old and didn't talk (his older sister had at that age). They also noticed that he didn't play with other children; he spent most of his time alone, spinning plates on the floor, waving his hands in front of his face, and lining up blocks in a certain order.

The family's pediatrician assured them that Ryan was just developing at a different rate and would grow out of it. When, at age 3, Ryan's behavior persisted, his parents consulted a second pediatrician. Neurological examinations revealed nothing unusual but suggested, on the basis of Ryan's delay in learning such basic skills as talking and feeding himself, that he had severe intellectual disability.

Ryan's mother did not accept this diagnosis, and over the next few years she consulted numerous other professionals and received numerous diagnoses (including childhood schizophrenia, childhood psychosis, and developmental delay). By age 7, Ryan still didn't speak or play with other children, and he was developing aggressive and self-injurious behaviors. His parents brought him to a clinic for children with severe disabilities. Here, Ryan was diagnosed as having autism.

The clinic specialists recommended a comprehensive educational program of intensive behavioral intervention to help Ryan with language and socialization and to counter his increasing tendency to engage in tantrums. The work continued daily for approximately 10 years, both at the clinic and at home. During this time, Ryan learned to say only three words: "soda," "cookie," and "Mama." Socially, he appeared to like other people (especially adults), but his interest seemed to center on their ability to get him something he wanted, such as a favorite food or drink. If his surroundings were changed in even a minor way, Ryan became disruptive and violent to the point of hurting himself. To minimize his self-injurious behavior, the family took care to ensure that his surroundings stayed the same as much as possible. No real progress was made toward eliminating his violent behavior, however, and as he grew bigger and stronger, he became increasingly difficult to work with; he hurt his mother physically on several occasions. With great reluctance, she institutionalized Ryan when he was 17.

What Is Typical? What Is Not Typical?

Before we discuss specific disorders, we need to address the broad topic of development in relation to disorders usually first diagnosed in infancy, childhood, or adolescence. What can we learn from children like Ryan, and what effect do the early disruptions in their skills have on their later lives? Does it matter when in the developmental period certain problems arise? Are disruptions in development permanent, thus making any hope for treatment doubtful?

Recall that in Chapter 2 we described developmental psychopathology as the study of how disorders arise and how they change with time (Nigg, 2015). Childhood is considered particularly important because the brain changes significantly for several years after birth; this is also when critical developments occur in social, emotional, cognitive, and other important competency areas. These changes mostly follow a pattern: The child develops one skill before acquiring the next, and subsequent skills often build on one another. Although this pattern of change is only one aspect of development, it is an important concept at this point because it implies that any disruption in the development of early skills will, by the very nature of this sequential process, disrupt the development of later skills. For example, some researchers believe that people with autism spectrum disorder suffer from a disruption in early social development, which prevents them from developing important social relationships, even with their parents (Durand, 2014). From a developmental perspective, the absence of early and meaningful social relationships has serious consequences. Children whose motivation to interact with others is disrupted may have a more difficult time learning to communicate; that is, they may not want to learn to speak if other people are not important to them. Researchers don't know whether a disruption in communication skills is a direct outcome of the disorder or a by-product of disrupted early social development.

Understanding this type of developmental relationship is important for several reasons. Knowing what processes are disrupted will help us understand the disorder better and may lead to more appropriate intervention strategies. It may be important to identify children with attention-deficit/hyperactivity disorder, for example, because their problems with impulsivity may interfere with their ability to create and maintain friendships, an important developmental consideration. Similarly, identifying a disorder such as autism spectrum disorder at an early age is important for these children so that their social deficits can be addressed before they affect other skill domains, such as social communication. Too often, people see early and pervasive disruptions in developmental skills (such as you learned with Ryan) and expect a negative prognosis, with the problems predetermined and permanent. Remember, however, that biological and psychosocial influences continuously interact with each other. Therefore, even for disorders such as attention-deficit/hyperactivity disorder and autism spectrum disorder that have clear biological bases, the presentation of the disorder is different for each individual. Changes at the biological or the psychosocial level may reduce the impact of the disorder.

One note of caution is appropriate here. There is real concern in the profession, especially among developmental psychologists, that some workers in the field may view aspects of typical development as symptoms of psychopathology. For example, *echolalia*, which involves repeating the speech of others, was once thought to be a sign of autism spectrum disorder. When we study the development of speech in children without disorders, however, we find that repeating what someone else says is an intermediate step in language development. In children with autism spectrum disorder, therefore, echolalia is just a sign of relatively delayed language skills and not a symptom of their disorder (Roberts, 2014). Knowledge of development is important for understanding the nature of psychological disorders.

With that caveat in mind, we now examine several disorders usually diagnosed first in infancy, childhood, or adolescence, including *attention-deficit/hyperactivity disorder*, which involves characteristics of inattention or hyperactivity and impulsivity, and *specific learning disorder*, which is characterized by one or more difficulties in areas such as reading and writing. We then focus on *autism spectrum disorder*, a more severe disability, in which the child shows significant impairment in social communication and has restricted patterns of behavior, interest, and activities. Finally, we examine *intellectual disability*, which involves considerable deficits in cognitive abilities. Communication and motor disabilities, which are also considered neurodevelopmental disorders, are described in Table 14.1.

Attention-Deficit/Hyperactivity Disorder

Do you know people who flit from activity to activity, who start many tasks but seldom finish one, who have trouble concentrating, and who do not seem to pay attention when others speak? These people may have **attention-deficit/hyperactivity disorder (ADHD)**, one of the most common reasons children are referred for mental health services in the United States. The primary characteristics of such people include a pattern of inattention (such as being disorganized or forgetful about school or work-related tasks) or of hyperactivity and impulsivity. These characteristics can significantly disrupt academic efforts, as well as social relationships. Consider the case of Corey.

Clinical Description

Corey has many characteristics of ADHD. Like Corey, people with this disorder have a great deal of difficulty sustaining their attention on a task or activity (Barkley, 2015c). As a result, their tasks are often unfinished, and they often seem not to be listening when someone else is speaking. In addition to this serious disruption in attention, some people with ADHD display motor hyperactivity. Children with this disorder are often described as fidgety in school, unable to sit still for more than a few minutes. Corey's restlessness in his classroom was a considerable source of concern for his teacher and peers, who were frustrated by his impatience and excessive activity. In addition to hyperactivity and problems sustaining attention, impulsivity—acting apparently

Table 14.1 Common Communication and Motor Disorders.

Clinical Description	Statistics	Etiology	Treatment
Childhood-Onset Fluency Disorder			
A disturbance in speech fluency that includes a number of problems with speech, such as repeating syllables or words, prolonging certain sounds, making obvious pauses, or substituting words to replace ones that are difficult to articulate (Black & Andreasen, 2021).	Occurs twice as often among boys as among girls. Begins most often in children by the age of 6, and 98% of cases occur before the age of 10 (Maguire, Yeh, & Ito, 2012). Approximately 80% of children who stutter before they enter school will no longer stutter after they have been in school a year or so (Kroll & Beitchman, 2005).	Rather than anxiety causing childhood-onset fluency disorder, this problem makes people socially anxious (Ezrati-Vinacour & Levin, 2004). Multiple brain pathways appear to be involved, and genetic influences may be a factor (Maguire et al., 2012).	Parents are counseled about how to talk to their children. *Regulated-breathing method* is a promising behavioral treatment in which the person is instructed to stop speaking when a stuttering episode occurs and then to take a deep breath (exhale, then inhale) before proceeding (Onslow, Jones, O'Brian, Packman, & Menzies, 2012). Altered auditory feedback (electronically changing speech feedback to people who stutter) can improve speech, as can using forms of self-monitoring, in which people modify their own speech for the words they stutter (Onslow et al., 2012).
Language Disorder			
Clinical Description	**Statistics**	**Etiology**	**Treatment**
Limited speech in *all* situations. *Expressive language* (what is said) is significantly below *receptive language* (what is understood); the latter is usually average (Black & Andreasen, 2021).	Occurs in 10% to 15% of children younger than 3 years of age (Johnson & Beitchman, 2005) and is almost five times as likely to affect boys as girls (Whitehurst et al., 1988).	An unfounded psychological explanation is that the children's parents may not speak to them enough. A biological theory is that middle ear infection is a contributory cause.	May be self-correcting and may not require special intervention (Whitehurst et al., 1988).
Social (Pragmatic) Communication Disorder			
Clinical Description	**Statistics**	**Etiology**	**Treatment**
Difficulties with the social aspects of verbal and nonverbal communication, including verbosity, prosody, excessive switching of topics, and dominating conversations (Adams et al., 2012). Does not have the restricted and repetitive behaviors found in ASD (Black & Andreasen, 2021).	Exact estimates not yet available, but the number of cases identified appears to be rising with increasing awareness (Baird et al., 2006; Bishop, 2000).	Limited information.	Individualized social skills training (for example, modeling, role playing) with an emphasis on teaching important rules necessary for carrying on conversations with others (for example, what is too much and too little information) (Adams et al., 2012).
Tourette's Disorder			
Clinical Description	**Statistics**	**Etiology**	**Treatment**
Involuntary motor movements *(tics)*, such as head twitching, or vocalizations, such as grunts, that often occur in rapid succession, come on suddenly, and happen in idiosyncratic or stereotyped ways. Vocal tics often include the involuntary repetition of obscenities (Girgis & Pringsheim, in press).	Of all children, up to 20% show some tics during their growing years, and 1 to 10 children out of every 1,000 have Tourette's disorder (Jummani & Coffey, 2009). Usually develops before the age of 14. High comorbidity between tics and ADHD, as well as obsessive-compulsive disorder (Jummani & Coffey, 2009).	There are likely multiple vulnerability genes that influence the form and severity of tics (Jummani & Coffey, 2009).	*Psychological:* Self-monitoring, relaxation training, and habit reversal (Mingbunjerdsuk & Zinner, in press).

Adapted from (Durand, 2011).

Corey... The Boy Who Couldn't Sit Still

Corey, a handsome 9-year-old boy, was referred to us because of his difficulties at school and at home. Corey had a great deal of energy and loved playing most sports, especially baseball. Academically, his work was adequate, although his teacher reported that his performance was diminishing and she believed he would do better if he paid more attention in class. Corey rarely spent more than a few minutes on a task without some interruption: He would get up out of his seat, rifle through his desk, or constantly ask questions. His peers were frustrated with him because he was equally impulsive during their interactions. He never finished a game, and in sports he tried to play all positions simultaneously.

At home, Corey was considered a handful. His room was in a constant mess because he became engaged in a game or activity only to drop it and initiate something else. Corey's parents reported that they often scolded him for not carrying out some task, although the reason seemed to be that he forgot what he was doing rather than that he deliberately tried to defy them. They also said that, out of their own frustration, they sometimes grabbed him by the shoulders and yelled, "Slow down!" because his hyperactivity drove them crazy.

without thinking—is a common complaint made about people with ADHD. For instance, during meetings at baseball practice, Corey often shouted responses to the coach's questions even before the coach had a chance to finish his sentence.

For ADHD, DSM-5 differentiates two categories of symptoms. The first includes problems of *inattention*. People may appear not to listen to others; they may lose necessary school assignments, books, or tools; and they may not pay enough attention to details, making careless mistakes. The second category of symptoms includes *hyperactivity and impulsivity*. Hyperactivity includes fidgeting, having trouble sitting for any length of time, and always being on the go. Impulsivity includes blurting out answers before questions have been completed and having trouble waiting turns. Either the first (inattention) or the second and third (hyperactivity and impulsivity) set of symptoms must be present for someone to be diagnosed with ADHD (American Psychiatric Association, 2013). These different presentations are called *subtypes*, and they include the inattentive subtype (what some may call ADD, noting the absence of hyperactivity, although this is not an official diagnostic label) and the hyperactive/impulsive subtype. Other individuals meet criteria for both inattention and hyperactivity/impulsivity, and these individuals are labeled with the *combined* subtype.

Inattention, hyperactivity, and impulsivity often cause other problems that appear secondary to ADHD. Academic performance often suffers, especially as the child progresses in school. The cause of this poor performance is not known. It could be a result of inattention and impulsivity, and in some children, this can be made worse by factors such as concurrent learning disabilities. Genetic research on both ADHD and learning disabilities suggests that they may share a common biological cause (DuPaul, Gormley, & Laracy, 2013). Children with ADHD are likely to be unpopular and rejected by their peers (McQuade & Hoza, 2015). This, too, may be the result of genetic factors as well as environmental influences such as a hostile home environment and gene–environment interactions. For example, some research shows that having a specific genotype (that is, a dopamine transporter —DAT1; and a serotonin transporter) and psychosocial distress can predict ADHD in children (Lambacher et al., 2020).

Statistics

An important analysis of prevalence of ADHD suggests that the disorder is found in about 4% of the U.S. population of children (Mohammadi et al., 2021) and in 5.2% of the child populations across all regions of the world (Polanczyk, de Lima, Horta, Biederman, & Rohde, 2007). This finding of comparable rates of ADHD worldwide is important because debates continue to rage about the validity of ADHD as a real disorder. Some people believe that children who are just "active" are being misdiagnosed with ADHD. Previously, geographic differences were noted in the number of people diagnosed with this disorder. Children were more likely to receive the label of ADHD in the United States than anywhere else. For example, an analysis of data from surveying parents over the phone suggests that 11% of children in the United States aged 4 to 17 were labeled with ADHD between 2011 and 2012 (Centers for Disease Control and Prevention, 2013). But more sophisticated analyses show the levels more comparable to other countries (Mohammadi et al., 2021).

Based on these different rates of diagnosis, some have argued that ADHD in children is simply a cultural construct—meaning that the behavior of these children is typical from a developmental perspective and that Western society's intolerance (due to the loss of extended family support, pressure to succeed academically, and busy family life) causes labeling ADHD as a disorder (Timimi & Taylor, 2004). The best data suggest, however, that from 5% to 7% of the worldwide population of children currently meet the criteria for ADHD and 3% to 5% have symptoms that significantly interfere with their quality of life (Roberts, Milich, & Barkley, 2015).

Boys are 2 to 3 times more likely to be diagnosed with ADHD than girls, and this discrepancy increases for children being seen in clinics (Mohammadi et al., 2021). The reason for this gender difference is largely unknown. It may be that adults are more tolerant of hyperactivity among girls, who tend to be less active than boys with ADHD. Boys tend to be more aggressive, which will more likely result in attention by mental health professionals (Rucklidge, 2010). Girls with ADHD, on the other hand, tend to display more behaviors referred to as "internalizing"—specifically, anxiety and depression (Owens et al., 2015).

The higher prevalence of boys identified as having ADHD has led some to question whether the DSM-5 diagnostic criteria for this disorder are applicable to girls. Here is the quandary: Most research over the past several decades has used young boys as participants. This focus on boys may have been the result of their active and disruptive behaviors, which caused concern among families and school personnel and therefore prompted research into the nature, causes, and treatment of these problems. More boys displayed these behaviors, which made it easier to find participants to study. But did this almost singular focus on boys result in ignoring how young girls experience this disorder?

This concern is being raised by some psychologists, including Kathleen Nadeau (a clinical psychologist who specializes in girls with ADHD), who argues that more research is needed on ADHD in girls: "Girls experience significant struggles that are often overlooked because their ADHD symptoms bear little resemblance to those of boys" (Crawford, 2003, p. 28). She says that girls with ADHD were neglected because their symptoms differ so dramatically from boys' symptoms, and there is some evidence for these differences (Mayes, Castagna, & Waschbusch, 2020). Just as researchers are now exploring ADHD among adults, in addition to children, more research is now addressing the relative lack of research on girls and women. This expansion of research across age and gender bodes well for a fuller understanding of the disorder.

Children with ADHD are first identified as different from their peers around age 3 or 4; their parents describe them as active, mischievous, slow to toilet train, and oppositional (Taylor, 2012). However, in one study, much younger children at risk for ADHD were identified as having early signs of ADHD. Infants with an older sibling or parent diagnosed with ADHD were distinguishable from infants with no family history of ADHD as early as 12 months of age based on directly observed and examiner reports of behavior, particularly with respect to hyperactive-impulsive behavior (Miller et al., 2020). Parents of infants at familial risk for ADHD also reported significantly more behavior/temperament concerns as early as 12 months of age compared to parents of infants at low risk for ADHD.

The symptoms of inattention, impulsivity, and hyperactivity become increasingly obvious during the school years. Despite the perception that children grow out of ADHD, their problems usually continue: A significant portion children with ADHD have ongoing difficulties through adulthood (such as anxiety and/or depression) (Stern et al., 2020). Over time, children with ADHD seem to be less impulsive, although inattention persists. During adolescence, the impulsivity manifests itself in different areas; for example, teens with ADHD are at greater risk for pregnancy and contracting sexually transmitted infections. They are also more likely to have driving difficulties, such as crashes; to be cited for speeding; and to have their licenses suspended (Barkley, 2015b; Fabiano & Schatz, 2015).

What happens to children and adolescents with ADHD as they become adults? Rachel Klein and her colleagues followed up on more than 200 boys with this disorder and reported on their status 33 years later (Klein et al., 2012). When compared with a group without ADHD, the majority of these men (84%) were employed but in jobs with significantly lower positions than the comparison group. They also had 2.5 fewer years of education and were much less likely to hold higher degrees. These men were also more likely to be divorced and to have substance use problems and antisocial personality disorder (Klein et al., 2012). In addition, the effects of their tendency to be impulsive may account for their increased risk of displaying risky driving, having a sexually transmitted disease, increased chance of having a head injury, and more emergency department admissions (Ramos Olazagasti et al., 2013). In short, although the manifestations of ADHD change as people grow older, many of their problems persist.

Diagnosing children with ADHD is complicated. Several other DSM-5 disorders, also found in children, appear to overlap significantly with this disorder. Specifically, oppositional defiant disorder (ODD), conduct disorder, and bipolar disorder all have characteristics seen in children with ADHD. ODD is a DSM-5 disorder that includes behaviors such as "often loses temper," "argues with adults," "often deliberately annoys people," "touchy and easily annoyed by others," and "often spiteful and vindictive" (Toth, de Lacy, & King, 2016). The impulsivity and hyperactivity observed in children with ADHD can manifest themselves in some of these symptoms. Similarly, conduct disorder—which, as you saw in Chapter 12, can be a precursor to antisocial personality disorder—is also observed in many children with ADHD (Toth et al., 2016). Bipolar disorder (which, you may recall from Chapter 7, is one of the mood disorders) also overlaps significantly with ADHD (Pliszka, 2015). This overlap can complicate diagnosis in these children.

Causes

Important information about the genetics of ADHD is beginning to be uncovered (Barkley, 2015a). Researchers have known for some time that ADHD is more common in families in which one person has the disorder. For example, the relatives of children with ADHD have been found to be more likely to have ADHD themselves than would be expected in the general population (Fliers et al., 2009). It is important to note that these families display an increase in psychopathology in general, including conduct disorder, mood disorders, anxiety disorders, and substance use disorder (Barkley, 2015a). This research and the comorbidity in the children themselves suggest that some shared genetic deficits may contribute to the problems experienced by individuals with these disorders (Brown, 2009).

ADHD is considered to be highly influenced by genetics (Grimm, Kranz, & Reif, 2020). Environmental influences play a relatively small role in the cause of the disorder when compared with many other disorders we discuss in this book. As with other disorders, researchers are finding that multiple genes are responsible for ADHD (Nikolas & Burt, 2010). In its simplest form, we tend to think of genetic "problems" in terms of having genes turned off (not making proteins) when they should be turned on and vice versa. Research on ADHD (and on other disorders) is finding that in many cases, however, mutations occur that either create extra copies of a gene on one chromosome or result in the deletion of genes (called **copy number variants**—CNVs) (Harich et al., 2020). Because our DNA is structured to function with corresponding or matching pairs of genes on each chromosome, the additions or deletions of one or more genes result in disrupted development.

DSM 5 **Table 14.1**

Diagnostic Criteria for Attention Deficit/Hyperactivity Disorder

A. A persistent pattern of inattention and/or hyperactivity-impulsivity that interferes with functioning or development, as characterized by (1) and/or (2):

1. *Inattention:* Six (or more) of the following symptoms have persisted for at least 6 months to a degree that is inconsistent with developmental level and that negatively impacts directly on social and academic/occupational activities:

Note: The symptoms are not solely a manifestation of oppositional behavior, defiance, hostility, or failure to understand tasks or instructions. For older adolescents and adults (aged 17 and older), at least five symptoms are required.

a. Often fails to give close attention to details or makes careless mistakes in schoolwork, at work, or during other activities (e.g., overlooks or misses details, work is inaccurate).

b. Often has difficulty sustaining attention in tasks or play activities (e.g., has difficulty remaining focused during lectures, conversations, or lengthy reading).

c. Often does not seem to listen when spoken to directly (e.g., mind seems elsewhere, even in the absence of any obvious distraction).

d. Often does not follow through on instructions and fails to finish schoolwork, chores, or duties in the workplace (e.g., starts tasks but quickly loses focus and is easily sidetracked).

e. Often has difficulty organizing tasks and activities (e.g., difficulty managing sequential tasks; difficulty keeping materials and belongings in order; messy, disorganized work; has poor time management; fails to meet deadlines).

f. Often avoids, dislikes, or is reluctant to engage in tasks that require sustained mental effort (e.g., schoolwork or homework; for older adolescents and adults, preparing reports, completing forms, reviewing lengthy papers).

g. Often loses things necessary for tasks or activities (e.g., school materials, pencils, books, tools, wallets, keys, paperwork, eyeglasses, or mobile telephones).

h. Is often easily distracted by extraneous stimuli (for older adolescents and adults, may include unrelated thoughts).

i. Is often forgetful in daily activities (e.g., chores, running errands; for older adolescents and adults, returning calls, paying bills, keeping appointments).

2. *Hyperactivity and impulsivity:* Six (or more) of the following symptoms have persisted for at least 6 months to a degree that is inconsistent with developmental level and that negatively impacts directly on social and academic/occupational activities:

Note: The symptoms are not solely a manifestation of oppositional behavior, defiance, hostility, or failure to understand tasks or instructions. For older adolescents and adults (age 17 and older), at least five symptoms are required.

a. Often fidgets with or taps hands or feet or squirms in seat.

b. Often leaves seat in situations when remaining seated is expected (e.g., leaves his or her place in the classroom, in the office or other workplace, or in other situations that require remaining in place).

c. Often runs about or climbs in situations where it is inappropriate. *Note:* In adolescents or adults, may be limited to feeling restless.

d. Often unable to play or engage in leisure activities quietly.

e. Is often "on the go," acting as if "driven by a motor" (e.g., is unable to be or uncomfortable being still for an extended time, as in restaurants, meetings; may be experienced by others as being restless or difficult to keep up with).

f. Often talks excessively.

g. Often blurts out an answer before a question has been completed (e.g., completes people's sentences; cannot wait for turn in conversation).

h. Often has difficulty waiting his or her turn (e.g., while waiting in line).

i. Often interrupts or intrudes on others (e.g., butts into conversations, games, or activities; may start using other people's things without asking or receiving permission; for adolescents or adults, may intrude into or take over what others are doing).

B. Several inattentive or hyperactive-impulsive symptoms were present prior to age 12 years.

C. Several inattentive or hyperactive-impulsive symptoms are present in two or more settings (e.g., at home, school, or work; with friends or relatives; in other activities).

D. There is clear evidence that the symptoms interfere with, or reduce the quality of, social, academic, or occupational functioning.

E. The symptoms do not occur exclusively during the course of schizophrenia or another psychotic disorder and are not better explained by another mental disorder (e.g., mood disorder, anxiety disorder, dissociative disorder, personality disorder, substance intoxication or withdrawal).

Specify whether:

Combined presentation: If both Criterion A1 (inattention) and Criterion A2 (hyperactivity-impulsivity) are met for the past 6 months.

Predominantly inattentive presentation: If Criterion A1 (inattention) is met but Criterion A2 (hyperactivity-impulsivity) is not met for the past 6 months.

Predominantly hyperactive/impulsive presentation: If Criterion A2 (hyperactivity-impulsivity) is met and Criterion A1 (inattention) is not met for the past 6 months.

American Psychiatric Association. (2022). *Diagnostic and statistical manual of mental disorders* (5th ed., Text Revision).

Most attention to date focuses on genes associated with the neurochemical dopamine, although norepinephrine, serotonin, and gamma-aminobutyric acid (GABA) are also implicated in the cause of ADHD. More specifically, there is strong evidence that ADHD is associated with the dopamine D_4 receptor gene, the dopamine transporter gene (DAT1), and the dopamine D_5 receptor gene. DAT1 is of particular interest because methylphenidate (Ritalin)—one of the most common medical treatments for ADHD—inhibits this gene and increases the amount of dopamine available (Davis et al., 2007; de Azeredo et al., 2014). Such research helps us understand at a microlevel what might be going wrong and how to design new interventions.

As with several other disorders we have discussed, researchers are looking for endophenotypes, those basic deficits—such as specific attentional problems—characteristic of ADHD. The goal is to link these deficits to specific brain dysfunctions. Not surprisingly, specific areas of current interest for ADHD are the brain's attention system, working memory functions, inattentiveness, and impulsivity. Researchers are now trying to tie specific genetic defects to these cognitive processes to make the link between genes and behavior. Some research indicates that poor "inhibitory control" (the ability to stop responding to a task when signaled) may be common among both children with ADHD and their unaffected family members (siblings and parents) and may be one genetic marker (an endophenotype) for this disorder (Gui et al., 2020).

The strong genetic influence in ADHD does not rule out any role for the environment (Black & Andreasen, 2021). In one of a growing number of gene–environment interaction studies of ADHD, for example, researchers found that children with a specific mutation involving the dopamine system (called the DAT1 genotype) were more likely to exhibit the symptoms of ADHD if their mothers smoked during pregnancy (Russell, Ford, Williams, & Russell, 2016). Prenatal smoking seemed to interact with this genetic predisposition to increase the risk for hyperactive and impulsive behavior. Other research is now pointing to additional environmental factors, such as maternal stress and alcohol use, and parental marital instability and discord, as involved in these gene–environment interactions (Black & Andreasen, 2021).

The association between ADHD and maternal smoking is one of the more consistent findings in this area. In addition, a variety of other pregnancy complications (for example, maternal alcohol consumption and low birth weight) may play a role in increasing the chance that a child with a genetic predisposition for ADHD will display the symptoms characteristic of this disorder (Barkley, 2006c). Unfortunately, many of the studies in this area confound socioeconomic and genetic factors (for example, there is an increased likelihood of smoking among women who also have low socioeconomic status or are under other stressors) (He, Chen, Zhu, Hua, & Ke, 2020).

For several decades, ADHD has been thought to involve brain damage, and this notion is reflected in the previous use of labels such as "minimal brain damage" or "minimal brain dysfunction" (Ross & Pelham, 1981). The rapid advances in scanning technology now permit us to see just how the brain may be involved in this disorder. A great deal of research on the structure and the function of the brain for children with this disorder has been conducted over the past few years. In general, researchers now know that the overall volume of the brain in those with this disorder is slightly smaller (3% to 4%) than in children without this disorder (He et al., 2020). A number of areas in the brains of those with ADHD appear affected, especially those involved in self-organizational abilities (Valera, Faraone, Murray, & Seidman, 2007). These changes seem less pronounced in persons who received medication (Taylor, 2012). In fact, a number of studies now point to a "growth-enhancing effect" of stimulant medication, suggesting that brain development progresses in a more typical fashion in children receiving medication for ADHD versus those who do not (Frodl & Skokauskas, 2012; Rubia et al., 2014).

A variety of toxins such as allergens and food additives have been considered as possible causes of ADHD over the years, although little evidence supports the association. The theory that food additives such as artificial colors, flavorings, and preservatives are responsible for the symptoms of ADHD has been highly controversial. Feingold (1975) presented this view, along with recommendations for eliminating these substances as a treatment for ADHD. As a result, hundreds of thousands of families put their children on the Feingold diet, despite arguments by some that the diet has little or no effect on the symptoms of ADHD (Barkley, 1990; Kavale & Forness, 1983). Some large-scale research now suggests that there may be a small but measurable impact of artificial food colors and additives on the behavior of young children (Hurt & Arnold, 2015). One study found that 3-year-old and 8- to 9-year-old children who consumed typical amounts of preservatives (sodium benzoate) and food colorings had increased levels of hyperactive behaviors (inattention, impulsivity, and overactivity) (McCann et al., 2007). Other research now points to the possible role of toxins such as the pesticides found in foods as contributing to an increased risk of ADHD (Barkley, 2015a; Bouchard, Bellinger, Wright, & Weisskopf, 2010).

Psychological and social dimensions of ADHD may further influence the disorder itself—especially how the child fares over time. Negative responses by parents, teachers, and peers to the affected child's impulsivity and hyperactivity may contribute to feelings of low self-esteem, especially in children who are also depressed (Black & Andreasen, 2021). Years of constant reminders by teachers and parents to behave, sit quietly, and pay attention may create a negative self-image in these children, which, in turn, can negatively affect their ability to make friends, and these effects can last into adulthood (Murphy, 2015). Thus, the possible biological influences on impulsivity, hyperactivity, and attention, combined with attempts to control these children, may lead to rejection and consequent poor self-image. An integration of the biological and psychological influences on ADHD suggests that both need to be addressed when designing effective treatments (Black & Andreasen, 2021).

Treatment of ADHD

Treatment for ADHD has proceeded on two fronts: psychosocial and biological interventions (Smith & Shapiro, 2015). Psychosocial treatments generally focus on broader issues such as improving academic performance, decreasing disruptive behavior, and improving social skills. Typically, the goal of biological treatments

BSIP SA / Alamy Stock Photo

A child with ADHD is likely to behave inappropriately regardless of the setting.

is to reduce the children's impulsivity and hyperactivity and to improve their attention skills. Current thinking in this area points to using parent- and/or teacher-delivered behavioral interventions for young children before attempting medication (Black & Andreasen, 2021).

Psychosocial Interventions

Multiple psychosocial interventions are effective for children and adolescents with attention-deficit/hyperactivity disorder (ADHD), including behavioral parent training, behavioral classroom management, behavioral peer interventions, and organization training programs (DuPaul, Evans, Mautone, Owens, & Power, 2020). In general, the programs set such goals as increasing the amount of time the child remains seated, the number of math papers completed, or appropriate play with peers. Reinforcement programs reward the child for improvements and, at times, punish misbehavior with loss of rewards. Other parent education programs teach families how to respond constructively to their child's behaviors and how to structure the child's day to help prevent difficulties (DuPaul et al., 2020). Social skills training for these children, which includes teaching them how to interact appropriately with their peers, also seems to be an important treatment component, although the effect sizes in these studies are relatively small (Powell, Parker, Weighall, & Harpin, 2021). For adults with ADHD, cognitive-behavioral intervention to reduce distractibility and improve organizational skills appears quite helpful (Fullen, Jones, Emerson, & Adamou, 2020). Most clinicians typically recommend a combination of approaches designed to individualize treatments for those with ADHD, targeting both short-term management issues (decreasing hyperactivity and impulsivity) and long-term concerns (preventing and reversing academic decline and improving social skills).

Biological Interventions

The first types of medication used for children with ADHD were stimulants. Since the use of stimulant medication for children with ADHD was first described (Bradley, 1937), hundreds of studies have documented the effectiveness of this kind of medication in reducing the core symptoms (hyperactivity, impulsiveness) of the disorder. It is estimated that 3.5% of the children living in the United States are being treated with medication for symptoms of ADHD (Zuvekas & Vitiello, 2012). Drugs such as methylphenidate (Ritalin, Adderall) and several nonstimulant medications such as atomoxetine (Strattera), guanfacine (Tenex), and clonidine have proved helpful in reducing the core symptoms of hyperactivity and impulsivity and in improving concentration on tasks (Black & Andreasen, 2021).

Originally, it seemed paradoxical or contrary to expect that children would calm down after taking a stimulant. However, on the same low doses, children and adults with and without ADHD react in the same way. It appears that stimulant medications reinforce the brain's ability to focus attention during problem-solving tasks (Black & Andreasen, 2021). Although the use of stimulant medications remains controversial, especially for children, most clinicians recommend them temporarily, in combination with psychosocial interventions, to help improve children's social and academic skills.

The concerns over the use of stimulant medications now include their potential for misuse. In Chapter 11, we discussed that drugs such as Ritalin and Adderall are sometimes misused for their ability to create elation and reduce fatigue (Thornton, Dodd, & Weed, 2020). Also of great concern are the widespread misperceptions that these prescription medications are harmless and that they improve academic performance (they are frequently used for this purpose on college campuses) (Watson, Arcona, & Antonuccio, 2015). This is particularly worrisome for children with ADHD because they are at increased risk for later substance misuse (Elkins et al., 2020). As mentioned previously, other nonstimulant drugs such as atomoxetine (Strattera) also appear effective for some children with ADHD. This drug is a selective norepinephrine-reuptake inhibitor and therefore does not produce the same "highs" when used in larger doses. Research suggests that other drugs, such as some antidepressants (imipramine) and a drug used for treating high blood pressure (clonidine) may have similar effects as atomoxetine on people with ADHD (Connor, 2015). Not all children with ADHD have depression or high blood pressure (although depression can be a problem in some of these children), but these drugs work on the same neurotransmitter systems (norepinephrine and dopamine) involved in ADHD (Subcommittee on Attention-Deficit/Hyperactivity Disorder & Management, 2011). All these drugs seem to improve compliance and decrease negative behaviors in many children, and their effects do not usually last when the drugs are discontinued.

Psychopharmacogenetics is the study of how your genetic makeup influences your response to certain drugs. The hope for this field is that medications can be matched or even "designed" for individuals to better complement their specific needs (Jain, 2015). For example, one study looked at the use of methylphenidate (Ritalin) for children and adolescents with ADHD (Polanczyk, Zeni, et al., 2007). For those who had a specific gene defect—the adrenergic alpha-2A receptor gene (ADRA2A)—methylphenidate had a strong positive effect, especially on their problems with inattention. This was not the case for those with ADHD who did not have the ADRA2A gene defect. Currently, the use of drug treatments tends to be by trial and error: A medication is attempted at a particular dose; if it is not effective, the dose is changed. If that does not work, a different medication is tried. This new study holds the promise of potentially eliminating this guesswork by tailoring the treatment to the individual.

This exciting new approach to medical treatment for mental illness brings with it some weighty concerns. Central to these concerns are issues of privacy and confidentiality. Genetic screening to identify defects is likely to identify any number of potential genetic problems in each of us. How will schools, employment sites, and insurance companies view this information if they have access? The concern is that people will be discriminated against based on this information (for example, having the genes that may or may not lead to having ADHD or another disorder). Will the desire to better target drug treatments outweigh these types of ethical and privacy concerns? Most new technical advances, like those promised with psychopharmacogenetics, also uncover new problems, and it is essential that ethical issues be part of the discussion as researchers move forward in this area.

Some portion of children with ADHD do not respond to medications, and most children who do respond show improvement in ability to focus their attention but do not show gains in the important areas of academics and social skills. In addition, the medications often result in unpleasant side effects, such as insomnia, drowsiness, or irritability (Black & Andreasen, 2021).

Combined Approach to Treatment

To determine whether or not a combined approach to treatment is the most effective, a large-scale study initiated by the National Institute of Mental Health was conducted by six teams of researchers (Jensen et al., 2001). Labeled the Multimodal Treatment of Attention-Deficit/Hyperactivity Disorder (MTA) study, this 14-month study included 579 children who were randomly assigned to one of four groups. One group of the children received routine care without medication or specific behavioral interventions (community care). The three treatment groups consisted of medication management (usually methylphenidate), intensive behavioral treatment, and a combination of the two treatments. Initial reports from the study suggested that the combination of behavioral treatments and medication and medication alone were superior to behavioral treatment alone and community intervention for ADHD symptoms. For problems that went beyond the specific symptoms of ADHD, such as social skills, academics, parent–child relations, oppositional behavior, and anxiety or depression, results suggested slight advantages of combination over single treatments (medication management, behavioral treatment) and community care.

Some controversy surrounds the interpretation of these findings—specifically, whether the combination of behavioral and medical treatments is superior to medication alone (Biederman, Spencer, Wilens, & Greene, 2001; Pelham, 1999). One of the concerns surrounding the study was that although medication continued to be dispensed, the behavioral treatment was faded over time, which may account for the observed differences.

Practically, if there is no difference between these two treatments, most parents and therapists would opt for simply providing medication for these children because of its ease of use and lower time commitment (Connor, 2015). Behavioral interventions have the added benefit, however, of improving aspects of the child and family that are not directly affected by medication (Pelham Jr. & Altszuler, 2020). Reinterpretations of the data from this large-scale study continue, and more research likely will be needed to clarify the combined and separate effects of these two approaches to treatment (Connor, 2015; Ollendick & Shirk, 2010). Despite these advances, however, children with ADHD continue to pose a considerable challenge to their families and to the educational system.

Specific Learning Disorder

Academic achievement is highly valued in our society. We often compare the performance of our schoolchildren with that of children in other cultures to estimate whether we are succeeding or failing as a world leader and economic force. On a personal level, because parents often invest a great deal of time, resources, and emotional energy to ensure their children's academic success, it can be extremely upsetting when a child with no obvious intellectual deficits does not achieve as expected. In this section, we describe **specific learning disorder**—which is characterized by performance that is substantially below what would be expected given the person's age, intelligence quotient (IQ) score, and education (Black & Andreasen, 2021). We also look briefly at disorders that involve how we communicate. Consider the case of Chloe.

Clinical Description

According to DSM-5 criteria, Chloe would be diagnosed as having a specific learning disorder (in her case especially in the area of reading), which is defined as a significant discrepancy between a person's academic achievement and what would be expected for someone of the same age—referred to by some as

Chloe... Taking a Learning Disorder to College

Chloe, a 20-year-old college student, sought help because of her difficulty in several of her classes. She reported that she had enjoyed school and had been a good student until about the sixth grade, when her grades suffered significantly. Her teacher informed her parents that she wasn't working up to her potential and she needed to be better motivated. Chloe had always worked hard in school but promised to try harder. However, with each report card, her mediocre grades made her feel worse about herself. She managed to graduate from high school, but by that time she felt she was not as bright as her friends.

Chloe enrolled in the local community college and again found herself struggling with the work. Over the years, she had learned several tricks that seemed to help her study and at least get passing grades. She read the material in her textbooks aloud to herself; she had earlier discovered that she could recall the material much better this way than if she just read silently to herself. In fact, reading silently, she could barely remember any of the details just minutes later.

After her sophomore year, Chloe transferred to the university, which she found even more demanding and where she failed most of her classes. After our first meeting, I suggested that she be formally assessed to identify the source of her difficulty. As suspected, Chloe had a specific learning disorder.

Scores from an IQ test placed her slightly above average, but she was assessed to have significant difficulties with reading. Her comprehension was poor, and she could not remember most of the content of what she read. We recommended that she continue with her trick of reading aloud because her comprehension for what she heard was adequate. In addition, Chloe was taught how to analyze her reading—that is, how to outline and take notes. She was even encouraged to audiotape her lectures and play them back to herself as she drove around in her car. Although Chloe did not become an A student, she was able to graduate from the university, and she now works with young children who themselves have learning disabilities.

"unexpected underachievement" (Black & Andreasen, 2021). More specifically, the criteria require that the person perform academically at a level significantly below that of a typical person of the same age, cognitive ability (as measured on an IQ test), and educational background. In addition, a diagnosis of specific learning disorder requires that the person's disability not be caused by a sensory difficulty, such as trouble with sight or hearing, and should not be the result of poor or absent instruction. DSM-IV-TR listed specific disorders in reading, mathematics, and written expression as separate disorders, but because of the significant overlap in these disabilities, they are now combined to assist clinicians in taking a broader view of the individual's learning styles (Black & Andreasen, 2021). Clinicians can use the specifiers for *disorders of reading, written expression*, or *mathematics* to highlight specific problems for remediation. As with other disorders, clinicians rate the disorder on levels of severity.

Historically, a specific learning disorder would be defined as a discrepancy of more than 2 standard deviations between achievement and IQ. There was considerable controversy, however, over using the discrepancy between IQ and achievement as part of the process of identifying children with learning disorders (Cavendish, 2013). Part of the criticism involves the delay between when learning problems occur and when they finally result in a large enough difference between IQ scores and achievement scores —which may not be measurable until later in a child's academic life. An alternative approach—called *response to intervention*— is now being used by many clinicians (Grigorenko et al., 2020; Vaughn et al., 2020). It involves identifying a child as having a specific learning disorder when the response to a known effective intervention (for example, an early reading program) is significantly inferior to the performance by peers (Grigorenko et al., 2020). This provides an early warning system and focuses on providing effective instruction.

Statistics

The prevalence of specific learning disorders has been estimated between 5% and 15% across youth of various ages and cultures (American Psychological Association, 2013). A study of more than 1,600 German elementary schoolers found that approximately 7% showed significant deficits in reading, 9% in spelling (that is, written expression), and 5% in arithmetic (Moll, Kunze, Neuhoff, Bruder, & Schulte-Körne, 2014). Another study of Brazilian children in second through sixth grades estimated the prevalence of specific learning disorders to be between 5% and 8% across categories of written expression, reading, arithmetic and global impairment (Fortes et al., 2015). In the United States, approximately 6.5 million students between the ages of 3 and 21 were receiving services for specific learning disorder between 2009 and 2010 (U.S. Department of Education, 2012). The frequency of this diagnosis appears to increase in wealthier regions of the country, suggesting that with better access to diagnostic services, more children are identified (see ■ Figure 14.1). Difficulties with reading are the most common of the learning disorders and occur in some form in 7% of the general population (Pennington & Bishop, 2009; Peterson & Pennington, 2012). Mathematics disorder appears in approximately 5% to 6% of the population (Pierce, 2016), but there is limited information about the prevalence of disorder of written expression among children and adults. Early studies suggested that boys were more likely to have a reading disorder than girls, although other research indicates that boys and girls may be equally affected by this disorder (Feinstein & Phillips, 2006). Students with learning disorders are more likely

DSM 5 **Table 14.2**
Diagnostic Criteria for Specific Learning Disorder

A. Difficulty learning and using academic skills, as indicated by the presence of at least one of the following symptoms that have persisted for at least 6 months, despite the provision of interventions that target those difficulties:

1. Inaccurate or slow and effortful word reading (e.g., reads single words aloud incorrectly or slowly and hesitantly, frequently guesses words, has difficulty sounding out words).
2. Difficulty understanding the meaning of what is read (e.g., may read text accurately but not understand the sequence, relationships, inferences, or deeper meanings of what is read).
3. Difficulties with spelling (e.g., may add, omit, or substitute vowels or consonants).
4. Difficulties with written expression (e.g., makes multiple grammatical or punctuation errors within sentences; employs poor paragraph organization, written expression of ideas lacks clarity).
5. Difficulties mastering number sense, number facts, or calculation (e.g., has poor understanding of numbers, their magnitude, and relationships; counts on fingers to add single-digit numbers instead of recalling the math fact as peers do; gets lost in the midst of arithmetic computation and may switch procedures.
6. Difficulties with mathematical reasoning (e.g., has severe difficulty applying mathematical concepts, facts, or procedures to solve quantitative problems).

B. The affected academic skills are substantially and quantifiably below those expected for the individual's chronological age and cause significant interference with academic or occupational performance, or with activities of daily living, as confirmed by individually administered standardized achievement measures and comprehensive clinical assessment. For individuals aged 17 years and older, a documented history of impairing learning difficulties may be substituted for the standardized assessment.

C. The learning difficulties begin during school-age years but may not become fully manifest until the demands for those affected academic skills exceed the individual's limited capacities (e.g., as in timed tests, reading or writing lengthy, complex reports for a tight deadline, excessively heavy academic loads).

D. The learning difficulties are not better accounted for by intellectual disabilities, uncorrected visual or auditory acuity, other mental or neurological disorders, psychosocial adversity, lack of proficiency in the language of academic instruction, or inadequate educational instruction.

Note: The four diagnostic criteria are to be met based on clinical synthesis of the individual's history (developmental, medical, family, educational), school reports, and psychoeducational assessment.

Specify if:

With impairment in reading:
Word reading accuracy
Reading rate or fluency
Reading comprehension

With impairment in expression:
Spelling accuracy
Grammar and punctuation accuracy
Clarity or organization of written expression

With impairment in mathematics:
Number sense
Memorization of arithmetic facts
Accurate or fluent calculation
Accurate math reasoning

American Psychiatric Association. (2022). *Diagnostic and statistical manual of mental disorders* (5th ed., Text Revision).

to drop out of school (Lerma & Chen, 2020), more likely to be unemployed (Gerber, 2012), and more likely to have suicidal thoughts and attempt suicide (Daniel et al., 2006). Reading and mathematics performance at age 15 predict literacy and numeracy skills and education, workforce, and life outcomes at age 19 (Mamedova, Stephens, Liao, & Sirma, 2021). However, the negative outcomes for adults may be mitigated by providing the proper supports, such as having a positive relationship with caring adults and providing accommodations in postsecondary educational and employment settings (Lerma & Chen, 2020).

Interviews with adults who have specific learning disorder reveal that their school experiences were generally negative, and

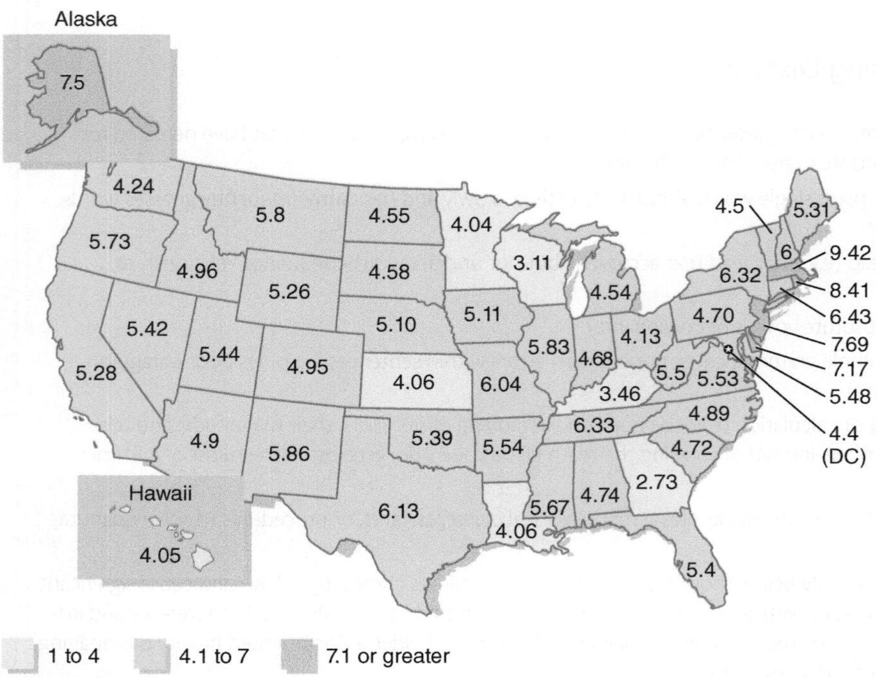

Figure 14.1

Uneven distribution. The highest percentages of schoolchildren diagnosed with learning disabilities are in the wealthiest states.

the effects often lasted beyond graduation. One man who did not have special assistance during school reports the following:

> I faked my way through school because I was very bright. I resent most that no one picked up my weaknesses. Essentially I judge myself on my failures. ... [I] have always had low self-esteem. In hindsight, I feel that I had low self-esteem in college. ... I was afraid to know myself. A blow to my self-esteem when I was in school was that I could not write a poem or a story. ... I could not write with a pen or pencil. The computer has changed my life. I do everything on my computer. It acts as my memory. I use it to structure my life and for all of my writing since my handwriting and written expression has always been so poor. (Polloway, Schewel, & Patton, 1992, p. 521)

A group of disorders loosely identified as *communication disorders* seems closely related to specific learning disorder (American Psychiatric Association, 2013). These disorders can appear deceptively benign, yet their presence early in life can cause wide-ranging problems later. For a brief overview of these disorders, which include **childhood-onset fluency disorder** (previously called **stuttering**) and **language disorder** (which combines DSM-IV-TR expressive and mixed receptive–expressive language disorders), see Table 14.1.

Causes

Theories about the causes of specific learning disorder include genetic, neurobiological, and environmental factors (Grigorenko et al., 2020). The genetic research in this area is particularly complex. It is clear that learning disorders run in families, and sophisticated family and twin studies bear this out (for example, Christopher et al., 2013). Yet analyses of the genes involved suggest that many effects are not specific—meaning that there are not different genes responsible for reading disorders and mathematics disorders. Instead, there are genes that affect learning, and they may contribute to problems across domains (reading, mathematics, writing) (Petrill, 2013; Plomin & Kovas, 2005).

The different problems associated with learning themselves have different origins. For example, children (and adults) often have very different problems associated with reading. Reading disorders are sometimes broken into problems with word recognition (difficulty decoding single words—sometimes called *dyslexia*), fluency (problems being able to read words and sentences smoothly and automatically), and comprehension (difficulty getting meaning from what is read) (Siegel & Mazabell, 2013; Tannock, 2009b). Most research to date focuses on problems with word recognition, and there is evidence that some develop these problems primarily through their genes, whereas others develop problems as a result of environmental factors (Siegel & Mazabell, 2013). Genes located on chromosomes 1, 2, 3, 6, 11, 12, 15, and 18 have all been repeatedly linked to these difficulties (Cope et al., 2012; Zou et al., 2012). At the same time, environmental influences such as the home reading habits of families can significantly affect outcomes—especially with skills such as word recognition—suggesting that reading to children at risk for reading disorders can lessen the impact of the genetic influence (Grigorenko et al., 2020).

Various forms of subtle brain impairment have also been thought responsible for learning disabilities; some of the earliest theories involve a neurological explanation (Hinshelwood, 1896). Research suggests structural, as well as functional, differences in the brains of people with learning disabilities. Specifically, three areas of the left hemisphere appear to be involved in problems with dyslexia (word recognition)—Broca's area (which affects articulation and word analysis), an area in the left parietotemporal area (which affects word analysis), and an area in the left occipitotemporal area (which affects recognizing word form) (Peterson & Pennington, 2012). A different area in the left hemisphere—the intraparietal sulcus—seems to be critical for the development of a sense of numbers and is implicated in mathematics disorder (Ashkenazi, Black, Abrams, Hoeft, & Menon, 2013). In contrast, there is no current evidence for specific deficits responsible for disorders of written expression.

Disorders of reading have been diagnosed more often in English-speaking countries. Although some have thought that this may simply be a difference in diagnostic practices, biological research now suggests it may involve the relative complexity of the written word in English. Researchers tested individuals who displayed reading disorders and who spoke English, French, or

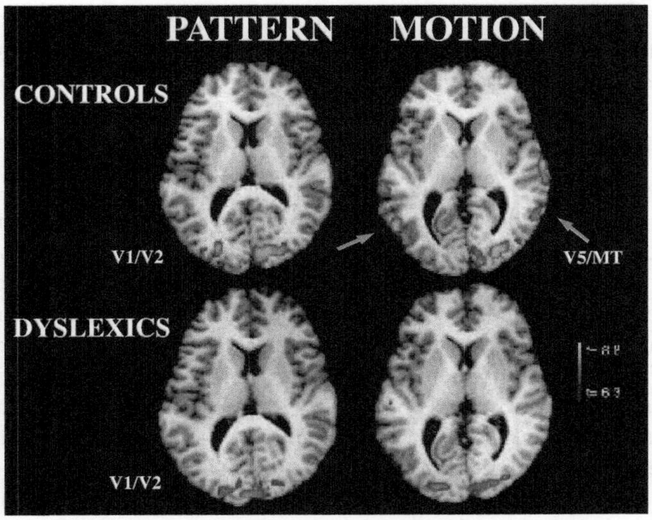

Courtesy National Institutes of Mental Health

These functional MRI scans of composite data from six adults with dyslexia and eight controls show a horizontal slice through the brain, with the face at the top. Imaging shows atypical brain activity associated with dyslexia. The scans were performed while participants tracked a pattern of moving dots on a computer screen. A brain area (V5/MT) typically active during such motion tasks did not switch on in those with dyslexia (right). Their brain activity was more similar to that of controls during a pattern recognition task (left).

Italian (Paulesu et al., 2001). Although those who spoke Italian did better on tests of reading, brain imaging (positron emission tomography) while participants were reading indicated that all of these people with reading disorders experienced the same reduced activity in the left temporal lobe. It was hypothesized that characteristics of the English and French languages may make them more difficult languages to read, thus accounting for these cultural differences in rates of diagnosis for reading disorders.

You saw that Chloe persisted despite the obstacles caused by her specific learning disorder, as well as by the reactions of teachers and others. What helped her continue toward her goal when others choose, instead, to drop out of school? Psychological and motivational factors that have been reinforced by others seem to play an important role in the eventual outcome of people with learning disorders. Factors such as socioeconomic status, cultural expectations, parental interactions and expectations, and child management practices, together with existing neurological deficits and the types of support provided in the school, seem to determine outcome (Grigorenko et al., 2020).

Treatment of Learning Disorders

As you will see in the case of intellectual disability, learning disorders primarily require educational intervention. Biological (drug) treatment is typically restricted to those individuals who may also have comorbid ADHD, which, as we discussed, involves impulsivity and an inability to sustain attention and can be helped with certain stimulant medications, such as methylphenidate (Ritalin or Adderall). Educational efforts can be broadly categorized into (1) specific skills instruction, including instruction on vocabulary, finding the main idea, and finding facts in readings, and (2) strategy instruction, which includes efforts to improve cognitive skills through decision making and critical thinking (Grigorenko et al., 2020).

Many programs are used to assist children with their problems related to learning. One approach that has received considerable research support is called Direct Instruction (Kame'enui, Fien, & Korgesaar, 2013). This program includes several components; among them are systematic instruction (using highly scripted lesson plans that place students together in small groups based on their progress) and teaching for mastery (teaching students until they understand all concepts). In addition, children are constantly assessed, and plans are modified based on progress or lack of progress. Direct Instruction and several related training programs appear to significantly improve academic skills in children with specific learning disorder (Kame'enui et al., 2013).

How do these behavioral and educational approaches help children with reading difficulties? Are they just tricks or adaptations to learning, or do these treatments have a more profound effect on the way these children process information? Exciting research using brain-imaging technology is allowing us to answer these important questions. One study used functional magnetic resonance imaging scanning (fMRI) to compare how children with and without reading disorders processed simple tasks (Temple et al., 2003). The children with reading difficulties were then exposed to 8 weeks of intensive training on a computer program that helped them work on their auditory and language-processing skills. Not only did the children improve their reading skills, but also their brains started functioning in a way similar to the brains of their peers who were good readers. This and similar studies (Peterson & Pennington, 2012) mirror results seen with other disorders—namely, that behavioral interventions can change the way the brain works and that we can use such interventions to help individuals with significant problems.

Used with permission of Laureate Learning Systems, Inc.

Specially designed computer games may help children with learning disorders improve their language skills.

Concept Check 14.1

Assign a label to each of the following cases: (a) ADHD, (b) social (pragmatic) communication disorder, (c) Tourette's disorder, or (d) specific learning disorder.

1. Trent's developmental disorder is characterized by uncontrollable yelps, sniffs, and grunting noises. __________
2. Ten-year-old Cole can be frustrating to his parents, teachers, and friends. He has trouble waiting his turn during games and does things seemingly without thinking. He often calls out answers in school, sometimes before the complete question is asked. __________
3. In school, 6-year-old Miley appears extremely awkward. She does not understand when other children are being sarcastic and misses many social communication cues. __________
4. Kelly was a good student until the sixth grade. Her grades slowly began to drop, despite her increased studying. Now, as a high school senior concerned about graduation and with hopes of going to college, Kelly has sought help. She places above average on an IQ test but shows significant problems with reading and comprehension. __________
5. Eight-year-old Chandra is described by everyone as a "handful." She fidgets constantly in class, drumming her fingers on the desk, squirming in her chair, and getting up and down. She has trouble waiting her turn at work or at play, and she sometimes has violent outbursts. __________

Autism Spectrum Disorder

Autism spectrum disorder (ASD) is a neurodevelopmental disorder that, at its core, affects how one perceives and socializes with others (Durand, 2014). DSM-5 combined most of the disorders previously included under the umbrella term "pervasive developmental disorders" (for example, autistic disorder, Asperger's disorder, and **childhood disintegrative disorder**) and included them into this one category (American Psychiatric Association, 2013). Moreover, **Rett disorder**, a genetic condition that affects mostly females and is characterized by hand wringing and poor coordination, is diagnosed as ASD with the qualifier "associated with Rett syndrome" or "associated with MeCP2 mutation" (the gene involved in Rett syndrome). And the designation "not otherwise specified," which was applied to other disorders prior to DSM-5, was deleted. A disorder new to DSM-5—social (pragmatic) communication disorder—includes the difficulties in social communication seen in ASD but without restricted, repetitive patterns of behavior (Adams & Gaile, 2020). These individuals do not easily learn the social rules when communicating with others (such as interrupting, talking too loud, not listening to others). Certain individuals previously diagnosed with pervasive developmental disorder—not otherwise specified may fall into this category.

Clinical Description

Two major characteristics of ASD are expressed in DSM-5: (1) impairments in social communication and social interaction and (2) restricted, repetitive patterns of behavior, interests, or activities (American Psychiatric Association, 2013). In addition, DSM-5 recognizes that the impairments are present in early childhood and that they limit daily functioning. It is the degree of impairment in each of these characteristics that presumably distinguish individuals previously diagnosed with the separate disorders of autistic disorder, Asperger's disorder, and **pervasive developmental disorder—not otherwise specified.**

To accommodate the range of difficulties in the two symptom clusters (social/communication interaction and restricted, repetitive patterns of behavior, interests, or activities), DSM-5 introduced three levels of severity: Level 1, "Requiring support"; Level 2, "Requiring substantial support"; and Level 3, "Requiring very substantial support." Separate ratings are provided for social/communication interaction and for restricted interests and repetitive behaviors. Each level of support is described qualitatively and, as yet, has no quantitative equivalent. This subjectivity makes assigning the appropriate level of support needed somewhat problematic if the person with ASD does not perform at the extreme ends of these categories (Durand, 2014). Consider the case of Amy.

Amy... In Her Own World

Amy, 3 years old, spends much of her day picking up pieces of lint. She drops the lint in the air and then watches intently as it falls to the floor. She also licks the back of her hands and stares at the saliva. She hasn't spoken yet and can't feed or dress herself. Several times a day, she screams so loudly that the neighbors at first thought she was being abused. She doesn't seem to be interested in her mother's love and affection but will take her mother's hand to lead her to the refrigerator. Amy likes to eat butter—whole pats of it, several at a time. Her mother uses the pats of butter that you get at some restaurants to help Amy learn and to keep her well-behaved. If Amy helps with dressing herself or if she sits quietly for several minutes, her mother gives her some butter. Amy's mother knows that the butter isn't good for her, but it is the only thing that seems to get through to the child. The family's pediatrician has been concerned about Amy's developmental delays for some time and has recently suggested that she be evaluated by specialists. The pediatrician thinks Amy may have autism spectrum disorder, and the child and her family will probably need extensive support.

Impairment in Social Communication and Social Interaction

One of the defining characteristics of people with ASD is that they do not develop age-appropriate social relationships (Davis & Carter, 2014). Amy never made friends among her peers and often limited her contact with adults to using them as tools—for example, taking the adult's hand to reach for something she wanted. Research on the symptoms of ASD including communication difficulties and social difficulties (which were listed independently as part of DSM-IV-TR) revealed the considerable overlap of these symptoms (Frazier et al., 2012; Skuse, 2012). DSM-5 combines these two areas into one general symptom cluster (social communication and social interaction). Difficulties with social communication and interaction are further defined by the inclusion of three aspects—problems with social reciprocity (a failure to engage in back-and-forth social interactions), nonverbal communication, and initiating and maintaining social relationships—all three of which must be present to be diagnosed with ASD.

Social reciprocity for individuals with more severe symptoms of ASD (previously diagnosed with autistic disorder) involves the inability to engage in **joint attention** (Ambrose, MacKenzie, & Ghanouni, 2020). If a toddler without ASD sees a toy she likes, she might look at her mother, smile, look at the toy, and look at her mother again. This social act communicates not only interest in the toy but also the desire to share this interest with another person. This action is limited in persons with ASD (Ambrose et al., 2020). Among persons with milder symptoms of ASD (previously diagnosed with Asperger's disorder), this lack of social reciprocity might present itself as appearing self-focused and not showing interest in things other people care about.

Research using sophisticated eye-tracking technology shows how social deficits evolve as the person develops. In one classic study, scientists showed an adult man with ASD some scenes from movies and compared how he looked at social scenes with how a man without ASD did so (Klin, Jones, Schultz, Volkmar, & Cohen, 2002). You can see from the illustration that the man with ASD (indicated by the purple lines) scanned nonsocial aspects of the scene (the actors' mouth and jacket), while the man without ASD looked at the socially meaningful sections (looking from eye to eye of the people conversing). This research suggests that people with ASD—for reasons not yet fully understood—may not be interested in social situations.

DSM 5 Table 14.3

Diagnostic Criteria for Autism Spectrum Disorder

A. Persistent deficits in social communication and social interaction across multiple contexts, as manifested by all of the following, currently or by history (examples are illustrative, not exhaustive; see text):

1. Deficits in social-emotional reciprocity; ranging, for example, from abnormal social approach and failure of normal back-and-forth conversation; to reduced sharing of interests, emotions, and affect; to failure to initiate or respond to social interactions.
2. Deficits in nonverbal communicative behaviors used for social interaction, ranging, for example, from poorly integrated verbal and nonverbal communication; to abnormalities in eye contact and body language or deficits in understanding and use of gestures; to a total lack of facial expressions and nonverbal communication.
3. Deficits in developing, maintaining, and understanding relationships, ranging, for example, from difficulties adjusting behavior to suit various social contexts; to difficulties in sharing imaginative play and in making friends; to absence of interest in peers.

B. Restricted, repetitive patterns of behavior, interests, or activities, as manifested by at least two of the following, currently or by history (examples are illustrative, not exhaustive; see text):

1. Stereotyped or repetitive motor movements, use of objects, or speech (e.g., simple motor stereotypies, lining up toys or flipping objects, echolalia, idiosyncratic phrases).
2. Insistence on sameness, inflexible adherence to routines, or ritualized patterns of verbal or nonverbal behavior (e.g., extreme distress at small changes, difficulties with transitions, rigid thinking patterns, greeting rituals, need to take same route or eat same food every day).
3. Highly restricted, fixated interests that are abnormal in intensity or focus (e.g., strong attachment to or preoccupation with unusual objects, excessively circumscribed or perseverative interests).
4. Hyper- or hyporeactivity to sensory input or unusual interest in sensory aspects of the environment (e.g., apparent indifference to pain/temperature, adverse response to specific sounds or textures, excessive smelling or touching of objects, visual fascination with lights or movement).

C. Symptoms must be present in the early developmental period (but may not become fully manifest until social demands exceed limited capacities, or may be masked by learned strategies in later life).

D. Symptoms cause clinically significant impairment in social, occupational, or other important areas of current functioning.

E. The disturbances are not better explained by intellectual developmental disorder (intellectual disability) or global developmental delay. Intellectual disability and autism spectrum disorder frequently co-occur; to make comorbid diagnoses of autism spectrum disorder and intellectual disability, social communication should be below that expected for general developmental level.

American Psychiatric Association. (2022). *Diagnostic and statistical manual of mental disorders* (5th ed., Text Revision).

A person with Autism Spectrum Disorder: ▬ A person without Autism Spectrum Disorder: ▬

Researchers are exploring how people with ASD view social interactions among other people. Adapted from A. Klin, W. Jones, R. Schultz, F. Volkmar, & D. Cohen, 2002, Defining and quantifying the social phenotype in autism, *American Journal of Psychiatry, 159,* 895–908. © A. Klin, W. Jones, R. Schultz, F. Volkmar, & D. Cohen, 2002.

Deficits in nonverbal communication can involve problems with a range of actions in persons with severe forms of ASD (such as not pointing to things you want) and among those with milder forms of ASD (such as standing too close to someone). Individuals with the less severe form of ASD may also lack appropriate facial expressions or tone of voice (also known as "**prosody**") (Durand, 2014) when speaking or just give the appearance of general nonverbal awkwardness. Finally, the deficits in social reciprocity and nonverbal communication can combine to influence the third symptom—problems maintaining social relationships.

Approximately 10% to 33% of individuals with ASD do not develop speech proficiency sufficient to communicate their needs effectively (Lord, Elsabbagh, Baird, & Veenstra-Vanderweele, 2018). In those with some speech, sometimes their communication is unusual. Some repeat the speech of others, a pattern called *echolalia,* which we referred to earlier as a sign of delayed speech development. If you say, "My name is Eileen. What's yours?" they will repeat all or part of what you said: "Eileen, what's yours?" And often, not only are your words repeated, but so is your intonation. On the other end of the autism spectrum, these individuals can be very verbal, but because of the social deficits and their tendency to have restricted interests, they often have one-sided conversations about the topics they want to discuss (Durand, 2014).

Restricted, Repetitive Patterns of Behavior, Interests, or Activities

The more striking characteristics of ASD include *restricted, repetitive patterns of behavior, interests, or activities.* Amy appeared to like things to stay the same: She became extremely upset if even a small change was introduced (such as moving her toys in her room). This intense preference for the status quo has been called *maintenance of sameness.* Often, people with ASD spend countless hours in *stereotyped* and *ritualistic behaviors,* making such stereotyped movements as spinning around in circles, waving their hands in front of their eyes with their heads cocked to one side, or biting their hands (Durand, 2014). For individuals with less severe ASD, these behaviors can take the form of an almost obsessive interest in certain, very specific subjects (such as following airline schedules or memorizing ZIP codes). This tendency to be much more interested in esoteric facts than in people further helps to interfere with social relationships.

Statistics

Current estimates of the rates of ASD are based on the previous DSM-IV-TR and ICD-10 criteria (Lord & Bishop, 2010). ASD was once thought to be a rare disorder (such as 1 in 10,000 births), although more recent estimates of its occurrence show an increase in its prevalence. For example, estimates as reported by the Centers for Disease Control and Prevention suggest that an average of 1 in 68 8-year-old children in the United States had a diagnosis under the category of ASD (Centers for Disease Control and Prevention, 2014). In the United States, approximately 1.5 million children ages 3 to 17 years have been diagnosed with ASD (Dietz, Rose, McArthur, & Maenner, 2020). The majority of the rise in the rates may be the result of changes between versions of the DSM (Miller et al., 2013) as well as increased awareness on the part of professionals and the general public. The reasons behind these changes are complex, however, and other environmental factors (such as prenatal exposure to toxins) cannot yet be ruled out as partially contributing to the rise in rates (Lord et al., 2018).

Gender differences are apparent in ASD, with the average reported male to female estimate being 4.5 to 1 (Centers for Disease Control and Prevention, 2014). ASD appears to be a universal phenomenon, identified in every part of the world, including Sweden (Gillberg, 1984), Japan (Sugiyama & Abe, 1989), Russia (Lebedinskaya & Nikolskaya, 1993), and Hong Kong (Chung, Luk, & Lee, 1990).

People with ASD have a range of IQ scores. It is estimated that approximately 31% of individuals with ASD have intellectual disabilities (defined as an IQ score less than 70, comparable deficits in adaptive functioning, and present before the age of 18) (Centers for Disease Control and Prevention, 2014). IQ measures are used to determine prognosis: The higher children score on IQ tests, the less likely they are to need extensive support by family members or people in the helping professions. Conversely, young children with ASD who score lower on IQ tests are more likely to be severely delayed in acquiring communication skills and to need a great deal of educational and social support as they grow older. Usually, language abilities and IQ scores are reliable predictors of how children with ASD will fare later in life: The better the language skills and IQ test performance, the better the prognosis (Lord et al., 2018).

Causes: Psychological and Social Dimensions

ASD is a complex condition that does not appear to have a single cause (Lord et al., 2018). Instead, a number of biological contributions may combine with psychosocial influences. Because historical context is important to research, it is helpful to examine past, as well as more recent, theories of ASD. (In doing this, we are departing from this book's usual format of providing biological dimensions first.)

Historically, ASD was wrongly seen as the result of failed parenting (Bettelheim, 1967; Ferster, 1961; Tinbergen & Tinbergen, 1972). Parents of children with the more severe form of ASD were characterized as perfectionistic, cold, and aloof (Kanner, 1949), with relatively high socioeconomic status (Allen, DeMyer, Norton, Pontius, & Yang, 1971; Cox, Rutter, Newman, & Bartak, 1975) and higher IQs than the general population (Kanner, 1943). Descriptions such as these inspired theories that held parents responsible for their children's unusual behaviors. These views were devastating to a generation of parents, who felt guilty and responsible for their children's problems. Imagine being accused of such coldness toward your own child as to cause serious and permanent disabilities! More sophisticated research using larger samples of children and families suggests that the parents of individuals with autism may not differ substantially from parents of children without disabilities (Bhasin & Schendel, 2007).

Other theories about the origins of ASD were based on the unusual speech patterns of some individuals—namely, their tendency to avoid first-person pronouns such as *I* and *me* and to use *he* and *she* instead. For example, if you ask a child with ASD, "Do you want something to drink?" he might say, "He wants something to drink" (meaning "I want something to drink"). This observation led some theorists to wonder whether ASD involves a lack of self-awareness (Goldfarb, 1963; Mahler, 1952). Imagine, if you can, not understanding that your existence is distinct. There is no "you," only "them." Such a debilitating view of the world was used to explain the unusual ways people with ASD behaved. Theorists suggested that the withdrawal seen among people with ASD reflected a lack of awareness of their own existence.

Later research has shown, however, that some people with ASD do seem to have self-awareness (Lind & Bowler, 2009) and that it follows a developmental progression. Just like children without a disability, those with cognitive abilities below the level expected for a child of 18 to 24 months show little or no self-recognition, but people with more advanced abilities do demonstrate self-awareness. Self-concept may be lacking when people with ASD also have cognitive disabilities or delays, not because of the disorder itself.

Myths about people with ASD are perpetuated when the idiosyncrasies of the disorder are highlighted. These perceptions are furthered by portrayals such as Dustin Hoffman's in the movie *Rain Man*. His character could, for instance, instantaneously and accurately count hundreds of toothpicks falling to the floor. This type of exceptional cognitive ability—referred to as "savant skills"—does not occur in all individuals with ASD. It is estimated that approximately one third of individuals with ASD have these unusual skills, although no persons with the more severe form of ASD appear to have savant abilities (Howlin, Goode, Hutton, & Rutter, 2010; Rutter & Pickles, 2015). These special skills typically occur in five areas—music, art, calendar calculating, mathematics, or mechanical/visual-spatial skills—and are usually associated with outstanding memory that is restricted to the area of expertise (Daniel & Menashe, 2020). These exceptional skills appear to be the result of possessing superior working memory and highly focused attention (Bennett & Heaton, 2012). It is important always to separate myth from reality and to be aware that such portrayals do not accurately represent the full range of manifestations of this complex disorder.

The phenomenon of echolalia, repeating a word or phrase spoken by another person, was once believed to be an unusual characteristic of this disorder. Subsequent work in developmental psychopathology, however, has demonstrated that repeating the speech of others is part of the typically developing language skills observed in most young children (Dawson, Mottron, & Gernsbacher, 2008). Even a behavior as disturbing as the self-injurious behavior (such as head banging) sometimes seen in people with ASD is observed in milder forms among typically developing infants (de Lissovoy, 1961). This type of research has helped clinicians isolate the facts from the myths about ASD and clarify the role of development in the disorder. One generally accepted conclusion is that social deficiencies are the primary distinguishing characteristic of people with ASD.

Causes: Biological Dimensions

Deficits in such skills as social communication and the characteristic restricted and repetitive behaviors and interests appear to be biological in origin (Lord et al., 2018). The role of biological influences on the origins of ASD, examined next, has received much empirical support.

Genetic Influences

It is now clear that ASD has a significant genetic component. What is also evident is that the genetics of ASD are highly complex (Wang et al., 2015) with a moderate genetic heritability (Hallmayer et al., 2011; Rutter, 2011a). Numerous genes on a number of our chromosomes have already been implicated in some way in the presentation of ASD (Li, Zou, & Brown, 2012). And as with other psychological disorders such as schizophrenia, many genes are involved, but each one has only a relatively small effect.

Families that have one child with ASD have about a 20% chance of having another child with the disorder (Ozonoff et al., 2011). This rate is more than 100 times the risk in the general population, providing strong evidence of a genetic component in the disorder. The exact genes involved in the development of ASD remain elusive. One area that is receiving attention involves the genes responsible for the brain chemical oxytocin. Because oxytocin is shown to have a role in how we bond with others and in our social memory, researchers are looking at whether genes responsible for this neurochemical are involved with the disorder. Preliminary work identifies an association between ASD and an oxytocin receptor gene (Andari et al., 2020).

There appears to be an increased risk of having a child with ASD among older parents. One group of researchers in Israel, for example, found that fathers 40 years old and up were more than five times more likely to have a child with ASD than fathers under the age of 30 (Reichenberg et al., 2006). The same correlation does seem to hold up for maternal age (Croen, Najjar, Fireman, & Grether, 2007; Durkin et al., 2008; Parner et al., 2012). These findings suggest that mutations may occur in the sperm of fathers or the eggs of mothers (called *de novo* mutations) that influence the development of ASD.

Neurobiological Influences

As in the area of genetics, many neurobiological influences are being studied to help explain the social communication and behavior problems observed in ASD (Fein, 2011). One intriguing theory involves research on the amygdala—the area of the brain that (as you saw in Chapter 5) is involved in emotions such as anxiety and fear. Researchers studying the brains of people with ASD after they died note that adults with and without the disorder have an amygdala of about the same size but that those with ASD have fewer neurons in this structure (Schumann & Amaral, 2006). Earlier research showed that young children with ASD actually have a larger amygdala. The theory being proposed is that the amygdala in children with ASD is enlarged early in life—causing excessive anxiety and fear (perhaps contributing to their social withdrawal). With continued stress, the release of the stress hormone cortisol damages the amygdala, causing the relative absence of these neurons in adulthood. The damaged amygdala may account for the different way people with ASD respond to social situations (Lombardo, Chakrabarti, & Baron-Cohen, 2009).

An additional neurobiological influence we mentioned in the section on genetics involves the neuropeptide oxytocin. Remember that this is an important social neurochemical that influences bonding and is found to increase trust and reduce fear. Some research on children with ASD found lower levels of oxytocin in their blood (Modahl et al., 1998), and giving oxytocin to people with ASD improved their ability to remember and process information with emotion content (such as remembering happy faces), a problem that is symptomatic of ASD (Huang, Huang, Ebstein, & Yu, 2021). This is one of a number of theories being explored as possible contributors to this puzzling disorder.

One highly controversial theory is that mercury—specifically, the mercury previously used as a preservative in childhood vaccines (thimerosal)—is responsible for the increases seen in ASD. Large epidemiological studies conducted in Denmark show that there is no increased risk of ASD in children who are vaccinated (Madsen et al., 2002; Parker, Schwartz, Todd, & Pickering, 2004). Additional research shows that the number of vaccinations—also a cause of concern by some families—also does not contribute to an increased risk of ASD (DeStefano, Price, & Weintraub, 2013). Despite this and other convincing evidence, the correlation between when a child is vaccinated for measles, mumps, and rubella (12 to 15 months) and when the symptoms of ASD first become evident (before 3 years), continues to fuel the belief by many families that there must be some connection. The negative consequence of this concern is that some parents are not vaccinating their children, and this is thought to contribute to a significant increase in cases of measles and mumps in the United States and other countries (Centers for Disease Control and Prevention, 2011).

The study of ASD is a relatively young field and still awaits an integrative theory of how biological, psychological, and social factors work together to put an individual at risk for developing autism. It is likely, however, that further research will identify the biological mechanisms that may explain the social aversion experienced by many people with the disorder. Also to be outlined are the psychological and social factors that interact early with the biological influences, producing deficits in socialization and communication, as well as the characteristic unusual behaviors.

Treatment of Autism Spectrum Disorder

Most treatment research has focused on children with the more severe form of ASD, so we primarily discuss treatment research for these individuals. There are a growing number of studies aimed at persons displaying less severe forms of ASD—typically focused on teaching social skills—and we describe this research as well. One generalization that can be made about ASD is that no completely effective treatment exists. Attempts to eliminate the social communication problems experienced by these individuals have not been successful to date (Durand, 2014). Rather, most efforts at treating people with ASD focus on enhancing their communication and daily living skills and on reducing problem behaviors, such as tantrums and self-injury (Durand, 2014). We describe some of these approaches next, including important work on early intervention for young children with ASD.

Psychosocial Treatments

Early psychodynamic treatments were based on the belief that ASD is the result of improper parenting, and they encouraged ego development (the creation of a self-image) (Bettelheim, 1967). Given our current understanding about the nature of the disorder, we should not be surprised to learn that treatments based solely on ego development have not had a positive impact on the lives of people with ASD (Kanner & Eisenberg, 1955). Greater success has been achieved with behavioral approaches that focus on skill building and behavioral treatment of

Matt Nager/Redux Pictures

Temple Grandin has a Ph.D. in animal science and a successful career designing humane equipment for handling livestock. She also was diagnosed with ASD.

problem behaviors. This approach is based on the early work of Charles Ferster (1961) and Ivar Lovaas. Although the work of Ferster and Lovaas has been greatly refined over the past few decades, the basic premise—that people with ASD can learn and that they can be taught some skills they lack—remains central. There is a great deal of overlap between the treatment of ASD and the treatment of intellectual disability. With that in mind, we highlight several treatment areas that are particularly important for people with ASD, including communication and socialization.

Problems with communication and language are among the defining characteristics of this disorder. A significant portion of people with ASD often do not acquire meaningful speech; they tend either to have limited speech or to use unusual speech, such as echolalia. Teaching people to speak in a useful way is difficult. Think about how we teach languages: It mostly involves imitation. Imagine how you would teach a young girl to say the word *spaghetti*. You could wait for several days until she said a word that sounded something like *spaghetti* (maybe *confetti*) and then reinforce her. You could then spend several days or weeks trying to shape *confetti* into something closer to *spaghetti*. Or you could just prompt, "Say 'spaghetti.'" Fortunately, most children can imitate and learn to communicate efficiently. But a child who has ASD can't or won't imitate.

In the mid-1960s, the late Ivar Lovaas and his colleagues took a monumental first step toward addressing the difficulty of getting children with the more severe forms of ASD to respond. They used the basic behavioral procedures of shaping and discrimination training to teach these nonspeaking children to imitate others verbally (Lovaas, Berberich, Perloff, & Schaeffer, 1966). The first skill the researchers taught the children was to imitate other people's speech. They began by reinforcing a child with food and praise for making any sound while watching the teacher. After the child mastered that step, they reinforced the child only if she made a sound after the teacher made a request—such as the phrase, "Say 'ball'" (a procedure known as *discrimination training*). Once the child reliably made some sound after the teacher's request, the teacher used *shaping* to reinforce only approximations of the requested sound, such as the sound of the letter "b." Sometimes the teacher helped the child with physical prompting—in this case, by gently holding the lips together to help the child make the sound of "b." Once the child responded successfully, a second word was introduced—such as "mama"—and the procedure was repeated. This continued until the child could correctly respond to multiple requests, demonstrating imitation by copying the words or phrases made by the teacher. Once the children could imitate, speech was easier, and progress was made in teaching some of them to use labels, plurals, sentences, and other more complex forms of language (Lovaas, 1977).

More recently, several different approaches have brought this type of teaching in typical settings, bringing the instruction away from a desk with one child and one teacher to regular settings at home, in school, and in the community and attempting to use more child-directed versus adult-directed techniques (**naturalistic teaching strategies**) (Akemoglu & Tomeny, 2020; Dunn Davison, Qi, & Kaiser, 2020). These teaching strategies include arranging the environment so that the child initiates an interest (such as placing a favorite toy just out of reach), and this is used as a teaching opportunity (for example, "Say, 'I want truck.'"). Various evidence-based treatment packages use aspects of this approach, including incidental teaching (McGee, Morrier, & Daly, 1999), pivotal response training (Koegel & Koegel, 2012), and milieu teaching (Hancock & Kaiser, 2012). These techniques seem to increase a variety of social communication skills (such as making requests, interactions with peers, joint-attention skills, play skills) among some children with more severe forms of ASD (Goldstein, 2002). Despite the success of some children in learning speech, other children do not respond to this training, and workers sometimes use alternatives to vocal speech, such as pointing to pictures or using devices that have vocal output and can literally "speak" for the child (such as iPads) (Aspiranti, Larwin, & Schade, 2020; Wainwright, Allen, & Cain, 2020).

One of the most striking features of people with ASD is their unusual reactions to other people. Although social deficits are among the more obvious problems experienced by people with autism, they can also be the most difficult to teach. A number of approaches are now used to teach social skills (for example, how to carry on a conversation and ask questions of other people), including the use of peers who do not have ASD as trainers, and there is evidence that those with ASD can improve their socialization skills (Durand, 2014).

Lovaas and his colleagues at the University of California, Los Angeles, reported on their early intervention efforts with young children (Lovaas, 1987). They used intensive behavioral treatment for communication and social skills problems for 40 hours or more per week, which seemed to improve intellectual and educational functioning. Follow-up suggests that these improvements are long lasting (Smith & Iadarola, 2015). Subsequent research on early intervention for toddlers with ASD include programs specifically targeting joint attention and play skills—the absence of which are some of the earliest signs of problematic social development. Focusing on these skills in the early years is important for helping the child develop more sophisticated social repertoires (Moody & Laugeson, 2020; Soares et al., 2021). A growing research base suggests that these skills can be facilitated among very young children with ASD (Lawton & Kasari, 2012; Wong & Kasari, 2012) and preliminary follow-up data suggest this approach may facilitate later development of language (Kasari, Gulsrud, Freeman, Paparella, & Hellemann, 2012). Some exciting research suggests that intensive early behavioral intervention may make the functioning of the developing brain in these children more similar to typically developing children compared with children with ASD who do not receive this treatment (Dawson et al., 2012; Voos et al., 2013).

Because some children and adolescents with ASD seem to enjoy the use of technology—perhaps due to the nonsocial nature of these activities (such as video modeling, computer-assisted instruction, computer games, and virtual worlds)—some have begun to use these techniques to encourage social skills. For example, one study explored the use of a virtual reality (VR)–based social skills learning environment for children with ASD (Ke, Moon, & Sokolikj, 2020). Data were gathered by way screen recording and observation of play- and design-oriented social skills enactment and pre- and postintervention questionnaires. Participants demonstrated an increased level of successful social skills performance from the baseline to the intervention phase. The findings provided preliminary evidence for the usage of a VR-based social skills learning environment for children with ASD (Ke et al., 2020).

Individuals with less severe forms of ASD do not have the cognitive delays often found in persons with more severe forms, and can—with support—do well academically in school. However, their social difficulties and common comorbid problems (such as ADHD or anxiety) complicate their interactions with peers and teachers and can lead to disruptive behavior problems. A number of different programs exist to help school-aged children improve skills such as appropriate social interaction, problem-solving, self-control, recognizing emotions in others, expanding their often narrow range of interests, and improving their understanding of nonliteral idioms (for example, understanding that the phrase "get off my back" means something very different from its literal meaning) (for example, Karkhaneh et al., 2010; Koning, Magill-Evans, Volden, & Dick, 2011). This work is in its infancy, and future research should tell us how best to improve these abilities in persons with ASD.

Biological Treatments

Medical intervention has had little positive impact on the core symptoms of social and language difficulties (Durand, 2014). A variety of pharmacological treatments are used to decrease agitation, with the major tranquilizers and serotonin-specific reuptake inhibitors being most helpful (Greydanus, Kaplan, & Patel, 2015). Because ASD may result from a variety of deficits, it is unlikely that one drug will work for everyone with this disorder. Much current work is focused on finding pharmacological treatments for specific behaviors or symptoms.

Integrating Treatments

Early intervention for very young children with ASD holds the most hope for significant changes in the core symptoms of this disorder. The treatment of choice for older children and those not responsive to early intervention combines various approaches to the many facets of this disorder. For children, most therapy consists of school education with special psychological supports for problems with communication and socialization. Behavioral approaches have been most clearly documented as benefiting children in this area. Pharmacological treatments can help some of them temporarily. Parents also need support because of the great demands and stressors involved in living with and caring for such children. As children with ASD grow older, intervention focuses on efforts to integrate them into the community, often with supported living arrangements and work settings. Because the range of abilities of people with ASD is so great, however, these efforts differ dramatically. Some people are able to live in their own apartments with only minimal support from family members. Others, with more severe forms of cognitive impairment, require more extensive efforts to support them in their communities.

Concept Check 14.2

Determine how well you are able to diagnose the disorder in each of the following situations by labeling them (a) ASD requiring very substantial support, (b) ASD requiring support, (c) Rett disorder, (d) social (pragmatic) communication disorder.

1. At an early age, Dwight became preoccupied with geography and could name all of the state capitals. His speech development was not delayed, but he does not like to play with other children or to be touched or held. ________
2. Six-year-old Tangelique has a low IQ and enjoys sitting in the corner by herself, where she arranges her toys or spins around in circles. She is unable to communicate verbally. She throws temper tantrums when her routine is changed even in the slightest way or when her parents try to get her to do something she doesn't want to do. ________
3. Six-year-old Megan experiences many problems in communicating and does not seem to understand the "rules" when speaking with other children. ________
4. Five-year-old Alicia has increasingly severe intellectual disability and is beginning to have trouble walking on her own. One of the characteristics of her disorder is constant hand wringing. ________

Intellectual Disability (Intellectual Developmental Disorder)

Intellectual disability (ID) is a disorder evident in childhood as significantly below-average intellectual and adaptive functioning (Black & Andreasen, 2021). People with ID experience difficulties with day-to-day activities to an extent that reflects both the severity of their cognitive deficits and the type and amount of assistance they receive. DSM-5 identifies difficulties in three domains: conceptual (skill deficits in areas such as language, reasoning, knowledge, and memory), social (problems with social judgment and the ability to make and retain friendships), and practical (difficulties managing personal care or job responsibilities) (American Psychiatric Association, 2013). Perhaps more than any other group you have studied in this text, people with ID have throughout history received treatment that can best be described as shameful (Scheerenberger, 1983). With notable exceptions, societies throughout the ages have devalued individuals whose intellectual abilities are deemed less than adequate. DSM-IV-TR previously used the term *mental retardation*, but this was changed in DSM-5 to *intellectual disability* (or *intellectual developmental disorder*) to be consistent with changes in terminology in this field (American Psychiatric Association, 2013).

The field of ID has undergone dramatic and fundamental changes during the past few decades. What it means to have an

ID, how to define it, how to label it, and how people with this disorder are treated have been scrutinized, debated, and fought over by a variety of concerned groups (Black & Andreasen, 2021). We describe the disorder in the context of these important changes, explaining both the status of people who have ID and our current understanding of its causes and treatment.

Kathy Hutchins/Shutterstock.com

Lauren Potter (an actress with Down syndrome) played Becky Jackson in the popular television show *Glee*.

The manifestations of ID are varied. Some individuals function quite well, even independently, in our complex society. For example, Lauren Potter (an actor with Down syndrome) played a cheerleader in the television show *Glee*. Others with ID have significant cognitive and physical impairments and require considerable assistance to carry on day-to-day activities. Consider the case of Ethan.

Ethan... Up to the Challenge

Ethan's mother contacted us because he was disruptive at school and at work. Ethan was 17 and attended the local high school. He had Down syndrome and was described as likable and, at times, mischievous. He enjoyed skiing, bike riding, and many other activities common among teenage boys. His desire to participate was a source of some conflict between him and his mother: He wanted to take the driver's education course at school, which his mother felt would set him up for failure, and he had a girlfriend he wanted to date, a prospect that also caused his mother concern.

School administrators complained because Ethan didn't participate in activities such as physical education, and at the work site that was part of his school program, he was often sullen, sometimes lashing out at the supervisors. They were considering moving him to a program with more supervision and less independence.

Ethan's family had moved often during his youth, and they experienced striking differences in the way each community responded to Ethan and his intellectual disability. In some school districts, he was immediately placed in classes with other children his age, and his teachers were provided with additional assistance and consultation. In others, it was just as quickly recommended that he be taught separately. Sometimes the school district had a special classroom in the local school for children with intellectual disabilities. Other districts had programs in other towns, and Ethan would have to travel an hour to and from school each day.

Every time he was assessed in a new school, the evaluation was similar to earlier ones. He received scores on his IQ tests in the range of 40 to 50, which placed him in the moderate range of intellectual disability. Each school gave him the same diagnosis: Down syndrome with moderate intellectual disability. At each school, the teachers and other professionals were competent and caring individuals who wanted the best for Ethan and his mother. Yet some believed that to learn skills Ethan needed a separate program with specialized staff. Others felt they could not provide a program with specialized staff. Still others felt they could provide a comparable education in a regular classroom and that to have peers without disabilities would be an added benefit.

In high school, Ethan had several academic classes in a separate classroom for children with learning problems, but he participated in some classes, such as gym, with students who did not have intellectual disability. His current difficulties in gym (not participating) and at work (being oppositional) were jeopardizing his placement in both programs. When I spoke with Ethan's mother, she expressed frustration that the work program was beneath him because he was asked to do boring, repetitious work such as folding paper. Ethan expressed a similar frustration, saying that he was treated like a baby. He could communicate fairly well when he wanted to, although he sometimes would become confused about what he wanted to say and it was difficult to understand everything he tried to articulate.

On observing him at school and at work, and after speaking with his teachers, we realized that a common paradox had developed. Ethan resisted work he thought was too easy. His teachers interpreted his resistance to mean that the work was too hard for him, and they gave him even simpler tasks. He resisted or protested more vigorously, and they responded with even more supervision and structure.

Clinical Description

People with ID display a broad range of abilities and personalities. Individuals like Ethan, who have mild or moderate impairments, can, with proper preparation, carry out most of the day-to-day activities expected of any of us. Many can learn to use mass transportation, purchase groceries, and hold a variety of jobs. Those with more severe impairments may need help to eat, bathe, and dress themselves, although with proper training and support, they can achieve a degree of independence (Black & Andreasen, 2021). These individuals experience impairments that affect most areas of functioning. Language and communication skills are often the most obvious. Ethan was only mildly impaired in this area, needing help with articulation. In contrast, people with more severe forms of ID may never learn to use speech as a form of communication, requiring alternatives such as sign language or special communication devices to express even their most basic needs. Because many cognitive processes are adversely affected, individuals with intellectual disability have difficulty learning, the level of challenge depending on how extensive the cognitive disability is.

Before examining the specific criteria for ID, note that, like the personality disorders we describe in Chapter 12, ID was previously included on Axis II of DSM-IV-TR. The rationale for placing these disorders on a separate axis was that they tend to be more chronic and less amenable to treatment and that clinicians should consider whether these disorders, if present, were affecting an Axis I disorder. People could be diagnosed on both Axis I (for example, generalized anxiety disorder) and Axis II (for example, mild intellectual disability). DSM-5 no longer has a separate axis for these disorders (American Psychiatric Association, 2013).

The DSM-5 criteria for ID no longer include numeric cutoffs for IQ scores, which were present in previous versions. They are still included in the narrative of the broader description, but the goal was to deemphasize these numbers in favor of a comprehensive assessment of functioning. To be diagnosed with ID, a person must have significant atypical intellectual functioning, a determination made with one of several IQ tests with a cutoff score set by DSM-5 of approximately 70. The American Association on Intellectual and Developmental Disabilities (AAIDD), which has its own, similar definition of intellectual disability, has a cutoff score of approximately 70 to 75 (Toth et al., 2016).

The second criterion calls for concurrent deficits or impairments in adaptive functioning. In other words, scoring "approximately 70 or below" on an IQ test is not sufficient for a diagnosis of ID. A person must also have significant difficulty in areas such

DSM 5 **Table 14.4**

Diagnostic Criteria for Intellectual Developmental Disorder (Intellectual Disability)

Intellectual developmental disorder (intellectual disability) is a disorder with onset during the developmental period that includes both intellectual and adaptive functioning deficits in conceptual, social, and practical domains. The following three criteria must be met:

A. Deficits in intellectual functions, such as reasoning, problem solving, planning, abstract thinking, judgment, academic learning, and learning from experience, confirmed by both clinical assessment and individualized, standardized intelligence testing.

B. Deficits in adaptive functioning that result in failure to meet developmental and sociocultural standards for personal independence and social responsibility. Without ongoing support, the adaptive deficits limit functioning in one or more activities of daily life, such as communication, social participation, and independent living, across multiple environments such as home, school, work, and community.

C. Onset of intellectual and adaptive deficits during the developmental period.

American Psychiatric Association. (2022). *Diagnostic and statistical manual of mental disorders* (5th ed., Text Revision).

as communication, self-care, home living, social and interpersonal skills, use of community resources, self-direction, functional academic skills, work, leisure, health, and safety. To illustrate, although Ethan had many strengths, such as his ability to communicate and his social and interpersonal skills (he had several good friends), he was not as proficient as other teenagers at caring for himself in areas such as home living, health, and safety or in academic areas. This aspect of the definition is important because it excludes people who can function quite well in society but for various reasons do poorly on IQ tests. For instance, someone whose primary language is not English may do poorly on an IQ test but may still function at a level comparable with those of peers. This person would not be considered to have ID even with a score of below 70 on the English-based IQ test.

The final criterion for ID is the age of onset. The characteristic below-average intellectual and adaptive abilities must be evident before the person is 18. This cutoff is designed to identify affected individuals when the brain is developing and therefore when any problems should become evident. The age criterion rules out the diagnosis of ID for adults who suffer from brain trauma or forms of dementia that impair their abilities. The age of 18 is somewhat arbitrary, but it is the age at which most children leave school, when our society considers a person an adult.

The imprecise definition of ID brings up an important issue: Intellectual disability, perhaps more than any of the other disorders, is defined by society. The cutoff score of 70 or 75 is based on a statistical concept (two or more standard deviations from the mean), not on qualities inherent in people who supposedly have ID. There is little disagreement about the diagnosis for people with the most severe disabilities; however, the majority of people diagnosed with ID are in the mild range of cognitive impairment (Black & Andreasen, 2021). They need some support and assistance, but remember that the criteria for using the label of ID are based partly on a somewhat arbitrary cutoff score for IQ that can (and does) change with changing social expectations.

People with ID differ significantly in their degree of disability. Almost all classification systems have differentiated these individuals in terms of their ability or on the cause of the ID (Holland, 2012). Traditionally, classification systems have identified four levels of ID: *mild*, which is identified by an IQ score between 50–55 and 70; *moderate*, with a range of 35–40 to 50–55; *severe*, ranging from 20–25 to 35–40; and *profound*, which includes people with IQ scores below 20–25. It is difficult to categorize each level of ID according to "average" individual achievements by people at each level. A person with severe or profound ID tends to have extremely limited formal communication skills (no spoken speech or only one or two words) and may require great or even total assistance in dressing, bathing, and eating. Yet people with these diagnoses have a range of skills that depend on training and the availability of other supports. Similarly, people like Ethan, who have mild or moderate ID, should be able to live independently or with minimal supervision; again, however, their achievement depends partly on their education and the community support available to them.

Perhaps the most controversial change introduced in the AAIDD definition of ID is its description of different levels of this disorder, which are based on the level of support or

Although this man cannot speak, he is learning to communicate with an eye-gaze board, pointing to or simply looking at the image that conveys his message.

assistance people need: *intermittent*, *limited*, *extensive*, or *pervasive* (Papazoglou, Jacobson, McCabe, Kaufmann, & Zabel, 2014; Thompson et al., 2009). The important difference is that the AAIDD system identifies the role of "needed supports" in determining level of functioning, whereas DSM-5 implies that the ability of the person is the sole determining factor. The AAIDD system focuses on specific areas of assistance a person needs that can then be translated into training goals. Whereas Ethan's DSM-5 diagnosis might be "moderate intellectual disability," he might receive the following AAIDD diagnosis: "a person with intellectual disability who needs limited supports in home living, health and safety, and in academic skills." The AAIDD definition emphasizes the types of support that Ethan and others require, and it highlights the need to identify what assistance is available when considering a person's abilities and potential.

Statistics

Approximately 90% of people with ID fall under the label of mild intellectual disability (IQ of 50 to 70). When you add individuals with moderate, severe, and profound ID (IQ below 50), the total population of people with this disorder represents approximately 1% to 3% of the general population (Black & Andreasen, 2021).

The course of ID is chronic, meaning that people do not go through periods of remission, such as with substance use disorders or anxiety disorders. The prognosis for people with this disorder varies considerably, however. Given appropriate training and support, individuals with less severe forms of ID can live relatively independent and productive lives. People with more severe impairments require more assistance to participate in work and community life.

Over the past century, a curious thing has occurred: IQ scores have risen. This phenomenon is known as the Flynn effect (Flynn, 1984). As these scores rise, those who make up IQ tests adjust the assessments every decade or two to keep the average score around 100. For most people, these changes have no practical effect. However, for people hovering at the cutoff point for ID, this may mean the difference between receiving the diagnosis or not (Billeiter, Froiland, Allen, & Hajovsky, 2021). In one study, the number of people scoring just below 70 (the cutoff for mild ID) tripled when they were administered one of the revised IQ tests (Kanaya, Scullin, & Ceci, 2003). These results emphasize the caution we need to take when interpreting who does or does not have ID.

Causes

There are literally hundreds of known causes of intellectual disability, including the following:

Environmental: For example, deprivation, physical or emotional abuse, and neglect

Prenatal: For instance, exposure to disease or drugs while still in the womb

Perinatal: Such as difficulties during labor and delivery

Postnatal: For example, infections and head injury

As we mention in Chapter 11, heavy use of alcohol among expecting mothers can produce a disorder in their children called *fetal alcohol syndrome*, a condition that can lead to severe learning disabilities (Wozniak et al., 2020). Other prenatal factors that can produce ID include the pregnant woman's exposure to disease and chemicals and poor nutrition. In addition, lack of oxygen (anoxia) during birth and malnutrition and head injuries during the developmental period can lead to severe cognitive impairments (Black & Andreasen, 2021).

Biological Dimensions

Most research on the causes of ID focuses on biological influences. We next look at biological dimensions that appear to be responsible for the more common forms of ID.

Genetic Influences

Multiple genetic influences appear to contribute to ID, including chromosomal disorders (such as having an extra 21st chromosome, as in Down syndrome), single-gene disorders, mitochondrial disorders (defects in mitochondria, which are compartments found in most human cells that generate the majority of energy needed by the cells to function) and multiple genetic mutations (Black & Andreasen, 2021). A portion of the people with more severe ID have identifiable single-gene disorders, involving a *dominant gene* (which expresses itself when paired with a typical gene), a *recessive gene* (which expresses itself only when paired with another copy of itself), or an *X-linked gene* (present on the X or sex chromosome).

Before we discuss known genetic causes of ID, it is important to recognize that as many as 30% of cases of ID have no identified etiology (Black & Andreasen, 2021). Important research using sophisticated genetic analysis techniques is pointing to genetic causes that went previously undetected. One study of children from Germany and Switzerland found that a variety of genetic mutations including *de novo* disorders (genetic mutations occurring in the sperm or egg or after fertilization) were present in those children with ID of unknown origin (Rauch et al.,

Monkey Business Images/Shutterstock.com

Intellectual disability can be defined in terms of the level of support people need.

2012). This work is important not only because it helps identify new causes of ID but also because it helps explain why a child could have a genetically based disorder without that mutation being present in either parent. Mutations in genetic material can occur at various points in development, and this helps explain the causes of previously puzzling cases of ID.

Only a few dominant genes result in ID, probably because of natural selection: Someone who carries a dominant gene that results in ID is less likely to have children and thus less likely to pass the gene to offspring. Therefore, this gene becomes less likely to continue in the population. Some people, however, especially those with mild ID, do marry and have children, thus passing on their genes. One example of a dominant gene disorder, *tuberous sclerosis complex (TSC)*, is relatively rare, occurring in 1 of approximately every 30,000 births. About 60% of the people with this disorder have ID, and most have seizures (uncontrolled electrical discharges in the brain) and characteristic bumps on the skin that during their adolescence resemble acne (Tye et al., 2020).

The next time you drink a diet soda, notice the warning, "Phenylketonurics: Contains Phenylalanine." This is a caution for people with the recessive disorder called **phenylketonuria (PKU)**, which affects 1 of every 10,000 newborns and is characterized by an inability to break down a chemical in our diets called phenylalanine (Black & Andreasen, 2021; Christ et al., 2020). Until the mid-1960s, the majority of people with this disorder had ID, seizures, and behavior problems, resulting from high levels of this chemical. Researchers developed a screening technique, however, that identifies the existence of PKU; infants are now routinely tested at birth, and any individuals identified with PKU can be successfully treated with a special diet that avoids the chemical phenylalanine. This is a rare example of the successful prevention of one form of ID.

Because untreated maternal PKU can harm the developing fetus, there is concern now that individuals with PKU who are of childbearing age may not stick to their diets and inadvertently cause PKU-related ID in their children before birth. Many physicians recommend dietary restriction through the person's lifetime, especially during the childbearing period—thus the warnings on products with phenylalanine (Widaman, 2009).

Lesch-Nyhan syndrome, an X-linked disorder, is characterized by ID, signs of cerebral palsy (spasticity or tightening of the muscles), and self-injurious behavior, including finger and lip biting (Nyhan, 1978). Only men are affected because a recessive gene is responsible; when it is on the X chromosome in men, it does not have a typical gene to balance it because men do not have a second X chromosome. Women with this gene are carriers and do not show any of the symptoms.

As our ability to detect genetic defects improves, more disorders will be identified genetically. The hope is that our increased knowledge will be accompanied by improvements in our ability to treat or, as in the case of PKU, prevent intellectual disability and other negative outcomes.

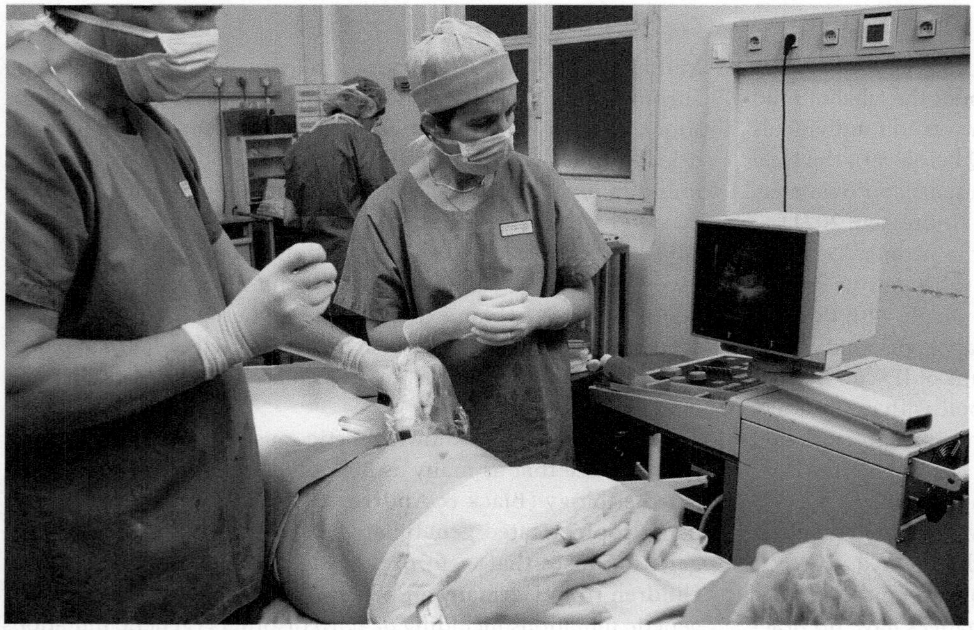

ASTIER/BSIP/Maxx Images

Amniocentesis can detect the presence of Down syndrome in a fetus. Guided by an ultrasound image, the doctor withdraws amniotic fluid for analysis.

Chromosomal Influences

Approximately 65 years ago the number of chromosomes—46—was correctly identified in human cells (Tjio & Levan, 1956). Three years later, researchers found that people with Down syndrome (the disorder Ethan displayed) had an additional small chromosome (Lejeune, Gauthier, & Turpin, 1959). Since that time, a number of other chromosomal aberrations that result in intellectual disability have been identified. We describe Down syndrome and fragile X syndrome in some detail, but there are hundreds of other ways in which changes among the chromosomes can lead to ID (Toth et al., 2016).

Down syndrome, the most common chromosomal form of ID, was first identified by the British physician Langdon Down in 1866. Down had tried to develop a classification system for people with ID based on their resemblance to people of other races; he described individuals with this particular disorder as "mongoloid" because they resembled people from Mongolia (Scheerenberger, 1983). The term *mongoloidism* was used for some time but has been replaced with the term *Down syndrome*. The disorder is caused by the presence of an extra 21st chromosome and is therefore sometimes referred to as *trisomy 21*. For reasons not completely understood, during cell division, two of the 21st chromosomes stick together (a condition called *nondisjunction*), creating one cell with one copy that dies and one cell with three copies that divide to create a person with Down syndrome.

People with Down syndrome have characteristic facial features, including folds in the corners of their upwardly slanting eyes, a flat nose, and a small mouth with a flat roof that makes the tongue protrude somewhat. Like Ethan, they tend to have congenital heart malformations. Adults with Down syndrome also have a greatly increased risk of dementia of the Alzheimer's type, a degenerative brain disorder that causes impairments in memory and other cognitive disorders (McGlinchey, McCallion, & McCarron, 2020). This disorder among people with Down syndrome occurs earlier than usual (sometimes in their early 20s) and has led to the finding that at least one form of Alzheimer's disease is attributable to a gene on the 21st chromosome.

The incidence of children born with Down syndrome has been tied to maternal age: As the age of the mother increases, so does her chance of having a child with this disorder (see ■ Figure 14.2). A woman at age 20 has a 1 in 2,000 chance of having a child with Down syndrome; at the age of 35, this risk increases to 1 in 500; and at the age of 45, it increases again to 1 in 18 births (Girirajan, 2009). Despite these numbers, many more children

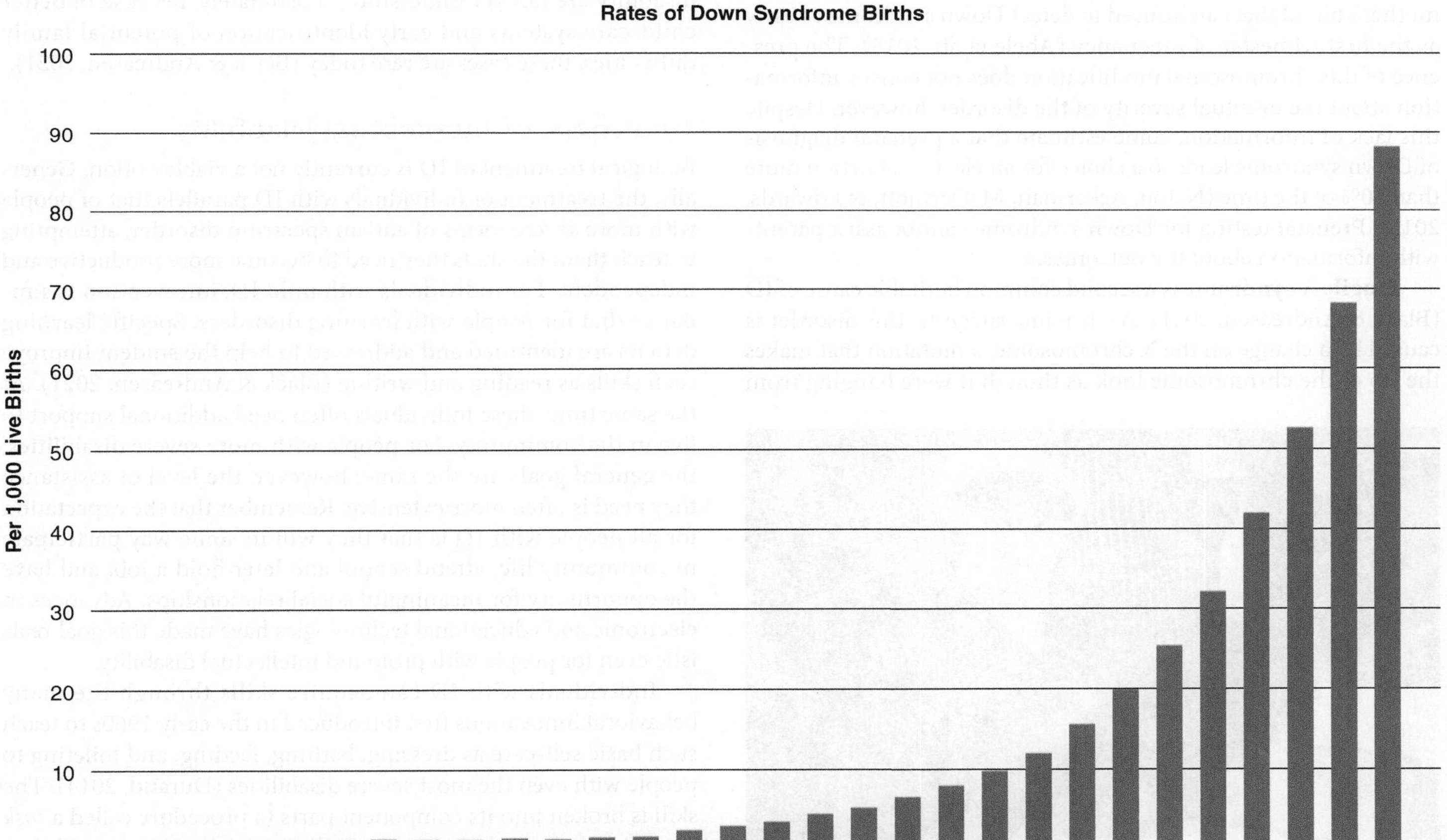

Figure 14.2

The increasing likelihood of Down syndrome with maternal age. Based on data from E. B. Hook, 1982, Epidemiology of Down syndrome, in S. M. Pueschel & J. E. Rynders (Eds.), *Down syndrome: Advances in biomedicine and the behavioral sciences* (pp. 11–88), Ware Press. © 1982 Ware University Press.

with Down syndrome are born to younger mothers simply because younger mothers have more children. The reason for the rise in incidence with maternal age is not clear. Some suggest that because a woman's ova (eggs) are all produced in youth, the older ones have been exposed to toxins, radiation, and other harmful substances over longer periods. One study found that certain occupations (such as food preparation and serving-related occupations) were associated with chemical solvent exposure and increased the likelihood of having a child with Down syndrome (Keen et al., 2020). This exposure may interfere with the typical meiosis (division) of the chromosomes, creating an extra 21st chromosome (Pueschel & Goldstein, 1991). It may also be that the hormonal changes that occur as future mothers age contribute to this error in cell division (Pandya, Mevada, Patel, & Suthar, 2013).

For some time, it has been possible to detect the presence of Down syndrome—but not the degree of ID—through **amniocentesis**, a procedure that involves removing and testing a sample of the fluid that surrounds the fetus in the amniotic sac, and through **chorionic villus sampling (CVS)** in which a small piece of placenta tissue is removed and tested. These types of test are not always desirable because they involve an invasive procedure (inserting a needle that could cause unwanted damage to the developing fetus). There are now more sophisticated tests of a mother's blood that can be used to detect Down syndrome as early as the first trimester of pregnancy (Abele et al., 2015). The presence of this chromosomal modification does not convey information about the eventual severity of the disorder, however. Despite this lack of information, some estimate that a prenatal diagnosis of Down syndrome leads to a choice for an elective abortion more than 50% of the time (Natoli, Ackerman, McDermott, & Edwards, 2012). Prenatal testing for Down syndrome cannot assist parents with information about the outcomes.

Fragile X syndrome is a second common heritable cause of ID (Black & Andreasen, 2021). As its name suggests, this disorder is caused by a change on the X chromosome, a mutation that makes the tip of the chromosome look as though it were hanging from a thread, giving it the appearance of fragility (Lubs, Stevenson, & Schwartz, 2012). As with Lesch-Nyhan syndrome, which also involves the X chromosome, fragile X primarily affects men because they do not have a second X chromosome with a typical gene to balance out the mutation. Unlike Lesch-Nyhan carriers, however, women who carry fragile X syndrome commonly display mild-to-severe learning disabilities (Santoro, Bray, & Warren, 2012). Men with the disorder display moderate-to-severe levels of ID and have higher rates of hyperactivity, short attention spans, gaze avoidance, and perseverative speech (repeating the same words again and again). In addition, such physical characteristics as large ears, testicles, and head circumference are common. Estimates are that 1 of every 4,000 men and 1 of every 8,000 women are born with fragile X syndrome (Black & Andreasen, 2021).

David Tothill/Photofusion Picture Library / Alamy Stock Photo

By participating in a training program for people with specific learning disabilities, this young man with Down syndrome is acquiring skills to earn a living.

Psychological and Social Dimensions

Cultural influences that may contribute to ID can include abuse, neglect, and social deprivation. Sometimes referred to as **cultural–familial intellectual disability**, people with these characteristics are thought to have cognitive impairments that result from a combination of psychosocial and biological influences, although the specific mechanisms that lead to this type of intellectual disability are not yet understood. Fortunately, because of better child-care systems and early identification of potential family difficulties, these cases are rare today (Black & Andreasen, 2021).

Treatment of Intellectual Disability

Biological treatment of ID is currently not a viable option. Generally, the treatment of individuals with ID parallels that of people with more severe forms of autism spectrum disorder, attempting to teach them the skills they need to become more productive and independent. For individuals with mild ID, intervention is similar to that for people with learning disorders. Specific learning deficits are identified and addressed to help the student improve such skills as reading and writing (Black & Andreasen, 2021). At the same time, these individuals often need additional support to live in the community. For people with more severe disabilities, the general goals are the same; however, the level of assistance they need is often more extensive. Remember that the expectation for all people with ID is that they will in some way participate in community life, attend school and later hold a job, and have the opportunity for meaningful social relationships. Advances in electronic and educational technologies have made this goal realistic even for people with profound intellectual disability.

Individuals with ID can acquire skills through the many behavioral innovations first introduced in the early 1960s to teach such basic self-care as dressing, bathing, feeding, and toileting to people with even the most severe disabilities (Durand, 2014). The skill is broken into its component parts (a procedure called a *task analysis*), and people are taught each part in succession until they can perform the whole skill. Performance on each step is encouraged by praise and by access to objects or activities the people desire (reinforcers). Success in teaching these skills is usually measured by the level of independence people can attain by using them. Typically, most individuals, regardless of their disability, can be taught to perform some skills.

Communication training is important for people with ID. Making their needs and wants known is essential for personal satisfaction and for participation in most social activities. The goals of communication training differ, depending on the existing skills. For people with mild levels of ID, the goals may be relatively minor (for example, improving articulation) or more extensive (for example, organizing a conversation) (Berney, 2012; Heath, Ganz, Parker, Burke, & Ninci, 2015). Some, like Ethan, have communication skills that are already adequate for day-to-day needs.

For individuals with the most severe disabilities, communication skills training can be particularly challenging, because they may have multiple physical or cognitive deficits that make spoken communication difficult or impossible. Creative researchers, however, use alternative systems that may be easier for these individuals, including sign language, used primarily by people with hearing disabilities, and *augmentative communication strategies*. Augmentative strategies may use picture books, teaching the person to make a request by pointing to a picture—for instance, pointing to a picture of a cup to request a drink (Heath et al., 2015). A variety of computer-assisted devices including tablet computers can be programmed so that the individual presses a button to produce complete spoken sentences (for example, "Would you come here? I need your help."). People with limited communication skills can be taught to use these devices, which helps them reduce the frustration of not being able to relate their feelings and experiences to other people (Durand, 2011).

Concern is often expressed by parents, teachers, and employers that some people with ID can be physically or verbally aggressive or may hurt themselves. Considerable debate has ensued over the proper way to reduce these behavior problems; the most heated discussions involve whether to use painful punishers (Repp & Singh, 1990). Alternatives to punishment that may be equally effective in reducing behavior problems such as aggression and self-injury include teaching people how to communicate their need or desire for such things as attention that they seem to be getting with their problem behaviors (Durand & Moskowitz, 2015). Important advances are being made in significantly reducing even severe behavior problems for some people.

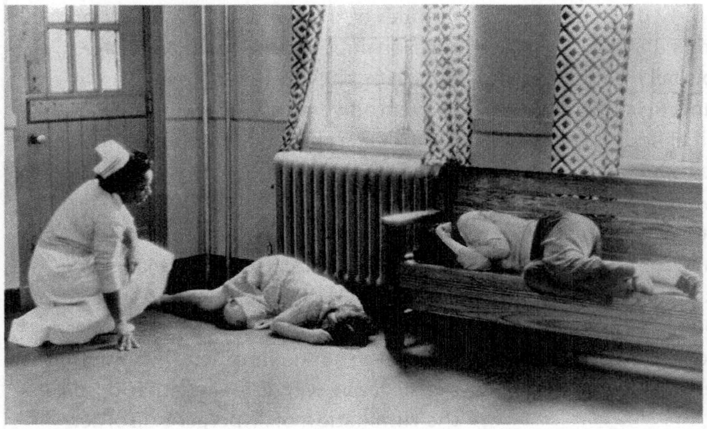
Research Collections/University Archive/Lovejoy Library

Although institutionalization was previously commonplace, efforts have been made to keep people with intellectual disability and other mental disorders within the comfort and support networks of their homes and communities.

In addition to ensuring that people with ID are taught specific skills, caretakers focus on the important task of supporting them in their communities. "Supported employment" involves helping an individual find and participate satisfactorily in a competitive job (Drake, Bond, & Becker, 2012). Research has shown not only that people with ID can be placed in meaningful jobs but also that, despite the costs associated with supported employment, it can be cost-effective (Cimera, 2012). The benefits to people who achieve the satisfaction of being a productive part of society are incalculable.

There is general agreement about *what* should be taught to people with ID. The controversy in recent years has been over *where* this teaching should take place. Should people with ID, especially the severe forms, be taught in specially designed separate classrooms or workshops, or should they attend their neighborhood public schools and work at local businesses? Increasingly, teaching strategies to help these students learn are being used in regular classrooms and in preparing them to work at jobs in the community (Foley, Dyke, Girdler, Bourke, & Leonard, 2012). The current prevention and treatment efforts suggest that meaningful changes can be achieved in the lives of those with ID.

Prevention of Neurodevelopmental Disorders

Prevention efforts for the neurodevelopmental disorders outlined in this chapter are in their early stages. One such effort—early intervention—has been described for ASD and appears to hold considerable promise for some children. In addition, early intervention can target and assist children who, because of inadequate environments, are at risk for developing cultural–familial ID (Eldevik, Jahr, Eikeseth, Hastings, & Hughes, 2010). The national Head Start program is one such effort at early intervention; it combines educational, medical, and social supports for these children and their families. One project identified a group of children shortly after birth and provided them with an intensive preschool program, along with medical and nutritional supports. This intervention continued until the children began formal education in kindergarten (Martin, Ramey, & Ramey, 1990). The researchers of this study found that for all but one of the children in a control group who received medical and nutritional support but not the intensive educational experiences, each had IQ scores below 85 at age 3, but that 3-year-olds in the experimental group all tested above 85. Such findings are important because they show the potential for creating a lasting impact on the lives of children with developmental disorders and their families.

Although it appears that many children can make significant progress if interventions are initiated early in life (Eldevik et al., 2010), a number of important questions remain regarding early intervention efforts. Not all children, for example, benefit significantly from such efforts, and future research will need to resolve a number of lingering concerns. For example, researchers need to determine how best to identify children and families who will benefit from such programs, how early in the child's development programs should begin, and how long to continue these early intervention programs to produce desirable outcomes.

Given recent advances in genetic screening and technology, it may someday be possible to detect and correct genetic and chromosomal modifications; related ongoing research could fundamentally change our approach to children with developmental disorders. For example, one study used mice that were genetically engineered to model fragile X syndrome found in many individuals with intellectual disability (Suvrathan, Hoeffer, Wong, Klann, & Chattarji, 2010). Researchers found that they could improve the functioning of certain glutamate receptors in the amygdala of the mice with a drug that blocks these receptors. The results were more typical functioning between these neurons, a potential early medical intervention for children with fragile X disorder (Krueger & Bear, 2011; Suvrathan, Hoeffer, Wong, Klann, & Chattarji, 2010). Someday, it may be possible for similar research to be performed prenatally on children identified as having syndromes associated with ID. For example, it may soon be possible to conduct prenatal gene therapy, where a developing fetus that has been screened for a genetic disorder may be the target of intervention before birth. This prospect is not without its difficulties, however.

Advances in biomedical technology will need support from psychological researchers to make sure that any needed treatments are carried out properly. For example, biological risk factors for several developmental disorders include malnutrition and exposure to toxins such as lead and alcohol. Although medical researchers can identify the role of these biological events in cognitive development, psychologists will need to support these efforts. Behavioral intervention for safety training (for example, involving lead-based paints in older homes), substance-use treatment and prevention, and behavioral medicine (for example, "wellness" efforts) are examples of crucial roles played by psychologists in helping to prevent certain forms of developmental disorders.

Concept Check 14.3

In the following situations, label each level of intellectual disability as mild, moderate, severe, or profound. Also label the corresponding levels of necessary support: intermittent, limited, extensive, or pervasive.

1. Kevin received an IQ score of 20. He needs help with all his basic needs, including dressing, bathing, and eating. ________, ________
2. Adam received an IQ score of 45. He lives in a fully staffed group home and needs a great deal of help with many tasks. He is beginning to receive training for a job in the community. ________, ________
3. Jessica received an IQ score of 30. She lives in a fully staffed group home where she is trained in basic adaptive skills and communication. She is improving over time and can communicate by pointing or using her eye-gaze board. ________, ________
4. Ledel received an IQ score of 65. He lives at home, goes to school, and is preparing to work when he is through with school. ________, ________

DSM Controversies: *Losing a Valued Label*

One of the most talked about and debated changes in the DSM-5 was the elimination of separate categories for "autistic disorder" and "Asperger's disorder"—which were present in DSM-IV. The rationale behind this reorganization of the separate autism related disorders under one rubric was that ASDs could be reliably distinguished from other disorders, but within this category there were considerable inconsistencies (Frazier et al., 2012; Rutter, 2011b). In other words, it was not always clear if someone had a milder form of autistic disorder (for example, with more speech) or had Asperger's disorder. They all share the pervasive deficits in social communication skills as well as the restricted patterns of behaviors. It was argued that the main differences among the disorders are ones involving the severity of the symptoms, language level, and levels of intellectual deficit and therefore could be grouped together as autism spectrum disorder—with varying degrees of severity.

One of the first concerns was that these new criteria might exclude some individuals who previously met DSM-IV criteria and result in the denial of treatment services for those left out. This concern was precipitated by researchers who evaluated cases that received a DSM-IV diagnosis of autism or a related disorder and tried to see how many would now fall into the new ASD category (McPartland, Reichow, & Volkmar, 2012). Their initial findings caused considerable alarm since they concluded that almost 40% of individuals would not meet the DSM-5 criteria. Although subsequent analyses found this number to be lower (e.g., approximately 9% in one study; Huerta, Bishop, Duncan, Hus, & Lord, 2012), there remains a concern that some individuals will no longer be eligible for needed services.

In addition to the concern about combining this disorder into the generic autism spectrum disorder, many of those individuals who have been previously diagnosed with Asperger's disorder feel that this decision takes away part of their identity (Pellicano & Stears, 2011). Rather than feeling shame or embarrassment about receiving this diagnosis, a good number of these individuals embrace their distinctiveness. Some advocate for seeing these differences in terms of "neurodiversity," or viewing their "disorder" as just a different and not "abnormal" way to view the world (Armstrong, 2010; Singer, 1999). In fact, the word "Aspies" is sometimes used with pride by individuals with this label (e.g., Beardon & Worton, 2011), and those who do not have this disorder are often referred to as "neurotypical"—sometimes in a negative way. It is likely that despite the elimination of Asperger's disorder from DSM-5, some in this community will continue to hold on to the label with pride.

Summary

Overview of Neurodevelopmental Disorders

- Developmental psychopathology is the study of how disorders arise and change with time. These changes usually follow a pattern, with the child mastering one skill before acquiring the next. This aspect of development is important because it implies that any disruption in the acquisition of early skills will, by the very nature of the developmental process, also disrupt the development of later skills.

Attention-Deficit/Hyperactivity Disorder

- The primary characteristics of people with attention-deficit/hyperactivity disorder are a pattern of inattention (such as not paying attention to school- or work-related tasks), impulsivity, and/or hyperactivity. These deficits can significantly disrupt academic efforts and social relationships.

Specific Learning Disorder

- DSM-5 describes specific learning disorder as academic performance that is substantially below what would be expected given the person's age, intelligence quotient (IQ) score, and education. These problems can be seen as difficulties with reading, mathematics, and/or written expression. All are defined by performance that falls far short of expectations based on intelligence and school preparation.
- Communication and motor disorders seem closely related to specific learning disorder. They include childhood speech fluency disorder (stuttering), a disturbance in speech fluency; language disorder, limited speech in all situations but without the types of cognitive deficits that lead to language problems in people with intellectual disability or one of the pervasive developmental disorders; and **Tourette's disorder**, which includes involuntary motor movements such as head twitching and vocalizations such as grunts that occur suddenly, in rapid succession, and in idiosyncratic or stereotyped ways.

Autism Spectrum Disorder

- People with ASD all experience trouble progressing in language, socialization, and cognition. This is not a relatively minor problem (like specific learning disorder) but is a condition that significantly affects how individuals live and interact with others.
- Autistic spectrum disorder is a childhood disorder characterized by significant impairment in social communication skills and restricted, repetitive patterns of behavior, interests, or activities. This disorder does not have a single cause; instead, a number of biological conditions may contribute, and these, in combination with psychosocial influences, result in the unusual behaviors displayed by people with ASD.
- Impressive advances have been made in improving outcomes for many young children with ASD using early intervention programs. Treatment for older children involves behavioral interventions focused on their social communication deficits and the restricted, repetitive patterns of behavior, interests, or activities.

Intellectual Disability

- The definition of intellectual disability has three parts: significantly subaverage intellectual functioning, concurrent deficits or impairments in present adaptive functioning, and an onset before the age of 18.
- Down syndrome is a type of intellectual disability caused by the presence of an extra 21st chromosome. It is possible to detect the presence of Down syndrome in a fetus through a process known as amniocentesis.
- Two other types of intellectual disability are common: fragile X syndrome, which is caused by a chromosomal modification of the tip of the X chromosome, and cultural–familial intellectual disability, a rare problem resulting from adverse environmental conditions.

Key Terms

neurodevelopmental disorders, 517
attention-deficit/hyperactivity disorder (ADHD), 518
copy number variants, 521
specific learning disorder, 525
childhood-onset fluency disorder (stuttering), 528
language disorder, 528
autism spectrum disorder (ASD), 530
childhood disintegrative disorder, 530
Rett disorder, 530
pervasive developmental disorder—not otherwise specified, 530
joint attention, 531
prosody, 532
naturalistic teaching strategies, 535
intellectual disability (ID), 536
phenylketonuria (PKU), 540
Lesch-Nyhan syndrome, 540
Down syndrome, 541
amniocentesis, 542
chorionic villus sampling (CVS), 542
fragile X syndrome, 542
cultural–familial intellectual disability, 542
Tourette's disorder, 545

Answers to Concept Checks

14.1

1. c; 2. a; 3. b; 4. d; 5. a

14.2

1. b; 2. a; 3. d; 4. c

14.3

1. profound, pervasive support; 2. moderate, limited support; 3. severe, extensive support; 4. mild, intermittent support

Exploring Neurodevelopmental Disorders

Disorders that appear early in life disrupt the normal course of development.

- Interrupting or preventing the development of one skill impedes mastery of the skill that is normally acquired next.
- Knowing what skills are disrupted by a particular disorder is essential to developing appropriate intervention strategies.

COGNITION

LANGUAGE

SOCIALIZATION

Photos: ©Photodisc/Getty Images

TYPES OF NEURODEVELOPMENTAL DISORDERS

	Description	Causes	Treatment
Attention-Deficit Hyperactivity Disorder (ADHD)  Suzanne Tucker/Shutterstock.com	■ Inattentive, overactive, and impulsive behavior ■ Disrupted schooling and relationships ■ Symptoms may change with maturity, but problems persist. ■ More prevalent in boys than girls	■ Research suggests hereditary factor. ■ Abnormal neurology ■ Possible link with maternal smoking ■ Negative responses by others create low self-esteem.	■ Biological (medication) – improves compliance – decreases negative behaviors – effects not long term ■ Psychological (behavioral) – goal setting and reinforcement
Specific Learning Disorder  Courtesy of Laureate Learning Systems Inc.	■ Reading, math, and written expression fall behind IQ, age, and education. ■ May also be accompanied by ADHD	■ Theories assume genetic, neurobiological, and environmental factors.	■ Education intervention – basic processing – cognitive and behavioral skills

	Types	Description	Treatment
Communication and Motor Disorders Closely related to learning disorders, but comparatively benign. Early appearance, wide range of problems later in life	Childhood Onset Fluency Disorder (Stuttering)	Disturbance in speech fluency (repeating words, prolonging sounds, extended pauses)	■ Psychological ■ Pharmacological
	Language Disorder	Limited speech in all situations	■ Psychological ■ Some cases may be self-correcting
	Social (Pragmatic) Communication Disorder	Problems with the social aspects of verbal and nonverbal communication	■ Psychological
 Photodisc/Getty Images	Tourette's Disorder	Involuntary motor movements (tics), such as physical twitches or vocalizations	■ Psychological ■ Pharmacological

PERVASIVE DEVELOPMENTAL DISORDERS

	Description	Causes	Treatment
Autism Spectrum Disorder  Photodisc/Getty Images	■ Severely impaired social communication ■ Restricted, repetitive patterns of behavior, interests, or activities ■ Symptoms often develop before 36 months of age. ■ Manifests across a wide range of functioning, from individuals who have limited communication skills to those who can converse with others but lack the social pragmatic skills to be able to make and maintain meaningful social relationships.	■ Little conclusive data ■ Numerous biological factors – clear genetic component – evidence of brain damage (cognitive deficits) combined with psychosocial influences	■ Behavioral focus – communication – socialization – living skills ■ Inclusive schooling ■ Temporary benefits from medication

INTELLECTUAL DISABILITY

	Description	Causes	Treatment
 Moodboard Stock Photography Ltd./Getty Images	■ Adaptive and intellectual functioning significantly below average ■ Language and communication impairments ■ Wide range of impairment—from mild to profound—in daily activities (90% of affected individuals have mild impairments).	■ Hundreds of identified factors – genetic – prenatal – perinatal – postnatal – environmental ■ Nearly 75% of cases cannot be attributed to any known cause.	■ No biological intervention ■ Behavioral focus similar to that for autism ■ Prevention – genetic counseling – biological screening – maternal care

15 Neurocognitive Disorders

Syldavia/Getty Images

Learning Objectives

LO15.1 Define *delirium* according to its clinical symptoms and causes.

LO15.2 Identify the deficits in cognitive abilities that reflect a diagnosis of neurocognitive disorder.

LO15.3 Describe the biological and genetic factors involved in the development of Alzheimer's disease.

LO15.4 Discuss approaches to treatment for neurocognitive disorders.

Research on the brain and its role in psychopathology has increased at a rapid pace, and we have described many of the latest advances throughout this book. All the disorders we have reviewed are in some way influenced by the brain. You have seen, for example, that relatively subtle changes in neurotransmitter systems can significantly affect mood, cognition, and behavior. Unfortunately, the brain is sometimes affected profoundly, and when this happens, drastic changes occur. In earlier editions of this book, the tone of this chapter was quite dark given the lack of information on these cognitive disorders that impair all aspects of mental functioning. The typically poor prognosis of the people afflicted led to pessimistic conclusions. However, a great deal of more contemporary research is leading us to be more optimistic about the future. For example, we used to think that once neurons died, there was no hope of any replacement, yet we now know brain cells can regenerate even in the aging brain (Kandasamy et al., 2020; Levin, Carnegie, & Celermajer, 2020). In this chapter, we examine this exciting work related to the brain disorders that affect cognitive processes such as learning, memory, and consciousness.

Perspectives on Neurocognitive Disorders

Most neurocognitive disorders develop much later in life, whereas intellectual disability and specific learning disorder are believed to be present from birth (see Chapter 14). In this chapter, we review two classes of cognitive disorders: *delirium*, an often temporary condition displayed as confusion and disorientation; and *mild or major neurocognitive disorder*, a progressive condition marked by gradual deterioration of a range of cognitive abilities (Black & Andreasen, 2021).

The label *neurocognitive disorders* in DSM-5 reflects a shift in the way these disorders are viewed (American Psychiatric Association, 2013). In early editions of the DSM, they were labeled *organic mental disorders*, along with mood, anxiety, personality, hallucinosis (an abnormal mental state involving hallucinations), and delusional disorders. The word *organic* indicated that brain injury or dysfunction was believed to be involved. The *organic mental disorders* category, however, covered so many disorders that the distinction was meaningless. Consequently, the traditional organic disorders (delirium, dementia, and amnestic disorders) were kept together, and the others (organic mood, anxiety, personality, hallucinosis, and delusional disorders) were categorized with disorders that shared their symptoms (such as anxiety and mood disorders).

Once the term *organic* was dropped, attention moved to developing a better label for delirium, dementia, and the amnestic disorders. The label *cognitive disorders* was used in DSM-IV to signify that their predominant feature is the impairment of such cognitive abilities as memory, attention, perception, and thinking. Although disorders such as schizophrenia, autism spectrum disorder, and depression also involve cognitive problems, cognitive issues are not believed to be primary characteristics (Ganguli et al., 2011; Sachdev et al., 2014). Problems still existed with the *cognitive disorder* label, however, because although the cognitive disorders usually first appear in older adults, intellectual disability and specific learning disorder (which are apparent early) also have cognitive impairment as a predominant characteristic. Finally, in DSM-5, *neurocognitive disorders* is now the category name for the various forms of dementia and amnestic disorders, with "major" or "mild" subtypes; DSM-5 retains the *delirium* label (American Psychiatric Association, 2013). This categorization was created because of the overlap of the different types of dementia (such as Alzheimer's disease) and amnestic disorder found in people, such that one person may actually experience multiple types of neurocognitive impairments or disorders (Ganguli et al., 2011; Sachdev et al., 2014).

As with certain other disorders, it may be useful to clarify why neurocognitive disorders are discussed in a textbook on psychopathology. Because they clearly have organic causes, you could argue that they are purely medical concerns. You will see, however, that the consequences of a neurocognitive disorder often include profound changes in a person's behavior and personality. Intense anxiety, depression, or both are common, especially among people with major neurocognitive disorders. In addition, paranoia is often reported, as are extreme agitation and aggression. Families and friends are also profoundly affected by such changes (Walaszek, 2020). Families and friends may experience emotional distress as a loved one is transformed into a different person, often one who no longer remembers who their families and friends are or what their history together is. The deterioration of cognitive ability, behavior, and personality and the effects on others are major concerns for mental health professionals.

Delirium

The disorder known as **delirium** is characterized by impaired consciousness and cognition during the course of several hours or days. Delirium is one of the earliest recognized mental disorders: Descriptions of people with these symptoms were written more than 2,400 years ago (Solai, 2009). Consider the case of Mr. J., whose scenario is played out daily in most major metropolitan hospital emergency rooms.

Clinical Description and Statistics

People with delirium appear confused, disoriented, and out of touch with their surroundings. They cannot focus and sustain their attention on even the simplest tasks. There are marked impairments in memory and language (Black & Andreasen, 2021). Mr. J. had trouble speaking; he was not only confused but also

Mr. J... Sudden Distress

Mr. J., an older gentleman, was brought to the hospital emergency room. He didn't know his own name, and at times he didn't seem to recognize his daughter, who was with him. Mr. J. appeared confused, disoriented, and a little agitated. He had difficulty speaking clearly and could not focus his attention to answer even the most basic questions. Mr. J.'s daughter reported that he had begun acting this way the night before, had been awake most of the time since then, was frightened, and seemed even more confused today. She told the nurse that this behavior was not normal for him, and she was worried that he was becoming "senile." She mentioned that his doctor had just changed his hypertension medication and wondered whether the new medication could be causing her father's distress. Mr. J. was ultimately diagnosed as having substance-induced delirium (a reaction to his new medication). Once the medication was stopped, he improved significantly over the course of the next 2 days.

could not remember basic facts, such as his own name. As you saw, the symptoms of delirium do not come on gradually but develop over hours or a few days, and they can vary over the course of a day.

Delirium is estimated to be present in approximately 10% to 15% of patients who are admitted into acute care facilities such as emergency rooms (Black & Andreasen, 2021). It is most prevalent among older adults, people undergoing medical procedures, cancer patients, and people with acquired immune deficiency syndrome (AIDS). Delirium subsides relatively quickly. Once thought to be only a temporary problem, more recent work indicates that the effects of delirium may be more lasting (Cole, Ciampi, Belzile, & Zhong, 2009; Meagher, Adamis, Trzepacz, & Leonard, 2012). Some individuals continue to have problems on and off; some even lapse into a coma and may die. Approximately 40% to 50% of persons with delirium die within one year (Black & Andreasen, 2021). Concern by medical professionals is increasing—perhaps because of the increased number of adults living longer—leading some to recommend that delirium be included as one of the "vital signs" (along with heartbeat, breathing rate, temperature, and blood pressure) that physicians routinely check when seeing older adults (Black & Andreasen, 2021).

Many medical conditions that impair brain function have been linked to delirium, including intoxication by drugs and poisons; withdrawal from drugs such as alcohol and sedative, hypnotic, and anxiolytic drugs; infections; head injury; and various other types of brain trauma (Williams, Dhesi, & Partridge, 2020). DSM-5 recognizes several causes of delirium among its subtypes. The diagnosis of delirium—that received by Mr. J., which was substance-induced delirium, as well as delirium not otherwise specified—includes disruptions in the person's ability to direct, focus, sustain, and shift attention. The rise in the use of designer drugs such as Ecstasy or "Molly" (methylenedioxymethamphetamine) and more recently "bath salts" (methylenedioxypyrovalerone) is of particular concern because of such drugs' potential to produce delirium (Penders, Gestring, & Vilensky 2012; Solai, 2009). Substance-induced delirium indicates the often complex nature of this condition.

That delirium can be brought on by the improper use of medication is a particular problem for older adults because they tend to use prescription medications more than any other age group. The risk of problems among older adults is increased further because they tend to eliminate drugs from their systems less efficiently than younger individuals. It is not surprising, then, that adverse drug reactions resulting in hospitalization are almost six times higher among older adults than in other age groups (Budnitz, Lovegrove, Shehab, & Richards, 2011; Olivier et al., 2009). And it is believed that delirium is responsible for many of the falls that cause debilitating hip fractures in older individuals (Seitz, Adunuri, Gill, & Rochon, 2011; Stenvall et al., 2006). Although there has been some improvement in the use of medication among older adults with physicians using more care with drug dosages and the use of multiple drugs, improper use continues to produce serious side effects, including symptoms of delirium (Budnitz et al., 2011; Olivier et al., 2009). Because possible combinations of illnesses and medications are so numerous, determining the cause of delirium is extremely difficult (Solai, 2009).

Delirium may be experienced by children who have high fevers or who are taking certain medications and is often mistaken as noncompliance (Kelly & Frosch, 2012). It often occurs during the course of dementia; as many as 50% of people with dementia suffer at least one episode of delirium (Fong, Davis, Growdon, Albuquerque, & Inouye, 2015; Kwok, Lee, Lam, & Woo, 2008). Because many of the primary medical conditions can be treated, delirium is often reversed within a relatively short time. Yet those who develop delirium while in the hospital have a one-and-a-half times increased risk for death in the following year, and this risk of mortality increases to two to four times for those in critical care with delirium (Inouye, Westendorp, & Saczynski, 2014). However, factors other than medical conditions can trigger delirium. Age itself is an important factor; older adults are more susceptible to developing delirium as a result of mild infections or medication changes (Inouye et al., 2014). Sleep deprivation, immobility, and excessive stress can also cause delirium (Black & Andreasen, 2021).

Researchers studying the brain functioning of persons with and without delirium are beginning to understand the mechanisms underlying this disorder of attention. In one study, scientists assessed brain activity using fMRI scanning during and after active episodes of delirium and found both lasting disruptions of connectivity (between the dorsolateral prefrontal cortex with the posterior cingulate cortex) as well as reversible disruptions (such as between the thalamus with the reticular activating system) (Choi et al., 2012; Slooter & de Groot, 2014). Although such research is potentially important for efforts to both prevent and treat delirium, there are potential ethical concerns. For example, a person experiencing delirium is not capable of providing informed consent for participating in such research and therefore someone else (such as a spouse or relative) must agree. In addition, fMRI testing can be anxiety-provoking for many people and was possibly very frightening for someone already so disoriented (Gaudreau, 2012). We discuss these issues in more detail in Chapter 16.

DSM 5 **Table 15.1**
Diagnostic Criteria for Delirium

A. A disturbance in attention (i.e., reduced ability to direct, focus, sustain, and shift attention) accompanied by reduced awareness of the environment.

B. The disturbance develops over a short period of time (usually hours to a few days), represents a change from baseline attention and awareness, and tends to fluctuate in severity during the course of a day.

C. An additional disturbance in cognition (e.g., memory deficit, disorientation, language, visuospatial ability, or perception).

D. The disturbances in Criteria A and C are not better explained by another preexisting, established, or evolving neurocognitive disorder and do not occur in the context of a severely reduced level of arousal, such as coma.

E. There is evidence from the history, physical examination, or laboratory findings that the disturbance is a direct physiological consequence of another medical condition, substance intoxication or withdrawal (i.e., due to a drug of abuse or to a medication), or exposure to a toxin, or is due to multiple etiologies.

American Psychiatric Association. (2022). *Diagnostic and statistical manual of mental disorders* (5th ed., Text Revision).

Treatment

The first step for the treatment of delirium is addressing underlying causes. For example, delirium brought on by withdrawal from alcohol or other drugs is usually treated with haloperidol or other antipsychotic medications, which help calm the individual (Black & Andreasen, 2021). Infections, brain injury, and tumors are given the necessary and appropriate medical intervention, which often then resolves the accompanying delirium. The antipsychotic drugs haloperidol and olanzapine are also prescribed for individuals in acute delirium when the cause is unknown (Meagher & Trzapacz, 2012).

The recommended first line of treatment for a person experiencing delirium is psychosocial intervention. The goal of nonmedical treatment is to reassure the individual to help them deal with the agitation, anxiety, and hallucinations of delirium. The inclusion of a family member in the care for patients with delirium, such as overnight stays with the patient, may be a great comfort to the patient. Similarly, familiar personal belongings such as family photographs may also be an easy and comforting intervention (Burne, Birkett, Bennet, & Shetty, 2021; Wilson et al., 2020). Also, a patient who is included in all treatment decisions retains a sense of control that can aid in the patient's ability to cope with anxiety and agitation due to the delirium. This type of psychosocial treatment can help the person manage during this disruptive period until the medical causes are identified and addressed (Breitbart & Alici, 2012). Some evidence suggests that this type of support can also delay institutionalization for older patients (Rahkonen et al., 2001).

Prevention

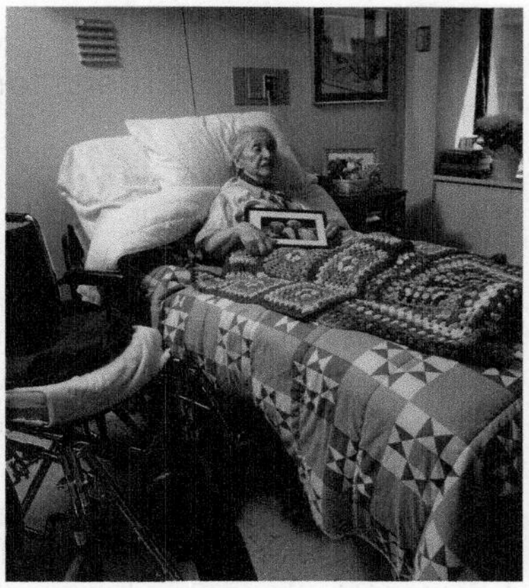
Richard Hutchings/Science Source

Older Adults patients with delirium in care facilities are often comforted by having their personal belongings nearby.

Preventive efforts may be most successful in assisting people who are susceptible to delirium. Proper medical care for illnesses and therapeutic drug monitoring can play significant roles in preventing delirium (Wilson et al., 2020). For example, the increased number of older adults involved in managed care and patient counseling on drug use appear to have led to more appropriate use of prescription drugs among older individuals (U.S. General Accounting Office, 1995). In addition, structured multidisciplinary interventions that target the prevention of delirium during hospital stays in older patients are very effective (for more information, see Hospital Elder Life Program; Inouye et al., 2014). These types of programs are implemented by an interdisciplinary team of doctors, nurses, and volunteers and consist of all of the following: reorientating the patient, providing vision and hearing aids as needed, increasing sleep and physical activity, maintaining proper hydration and nutrition, involving the patient in therapeutic activities, and reducing dosages of psychoactive drugs. One downside is that these programs require a great deal of resources from hospitals to put it into place consistently with all those who are at risk for delirium.

Concept Check 15.1

Match the terms with the following descriptions of delirium: (a) memory, (b) cause, (c) counseling, (d) confused, (e) elderly, and (f) trauma.

1. Managed care and patient ____________ have been successful in preventing delirium in older adults.
2. Treatment of delirium depends on the ____________ of the episode and can include medications, psychosocial intervention, or both.
3. Delirium severely affects people's ____________, making tasks such as recalling one's own name difficult.
4. The ____________ population is at the greatest risk of experiencing delirium resulting from improper use of medications.
5. Various types of brain ____________, such as head injury or infection, have been linked to delirium.
6. People who suffer from delirium appear to be ____________ or out of touch with their surroundings.

DSM-5 Table 15.2
Diagnostic Criteria for Major Neurocognitive Disorder

A. Evidence of significant cognitive decline from a previous level of performance in one or more cognitive domains (complex attention, executive function, learning and memory, language, perceptual-motor, or social cognition) based on:
  1. Concern of the individual, a knowledgeable informant, or the clinician that there has been a significant decline in cognitive function; and
  2. A substantial impairment in cognitive performance, preferably documented by standardized neuropsychological testing or, in its absence, another quantified clinical assessment.

B. The cognitive deficits interfere with independence in everyday activities (i.e., at a minimum, requiring assistance with complex instrumental activities of daily living such as paying bills or managing medications).

C. The cognitive deficits do not occur exclusively in the context of a delirium.

D. The cognitive deficits are not better explained by another mental disorder (e.g., major depressive disorder, schizophrenia).

Specify whether due to:
Alzheimer's disease
Frontotemporal lobar degeneration
Lewy body disease
Vascular disease
Traumatic brain injury
Substance/medication use
HIV infection
Prion disease
Parkinson's disease
Huntington's disease
Another medical condition
Multiple etiologies
Unspecified

American Psychiatric Association. (2022). *Diagnostic and statistical manual of mental disorders* (5th ed., Text Revision).

DSM-5 Table 15.3
Diagnostic Criteria for Mild Neurocognitive Disorder

A. Evidence of modest cognitive decline from a previous level of performance in one or more cognitive domains (complex attention, executive function, learning and memory, language, perceptual motor, or social cognition) based on:
  1. Concern of the individual, a knowledgeable informant, or the clinician that there has been a mild decline in cognitive function; and
  2. A modest impairment in cognitive performance, preferably documented by standardized neuropsychological testing or, in its absence, another quantified clinical assessment.

B. The cognitive deficits do not interfere with capacity for independence in everyday activities (i.e., complex instrumental activities of daily living such as paying bills or managing medications are preserved, but greater effort, compensatory strategies, or accommodation may be required).

C. The cognitive deficits do not occur exclusively in the context of a delirium.

D. The cognitive deficits are not better explained by another mental disorder (e.g., major depressive disorder, schizophrenia).

Specify whether due to:
Alzheimer's disease
Frontotemporal lobar degeneration
Lewy body disease
Vascular disease
Traumatic brain injury
Substance/medication use
HIV infection
Prion disease
Parkinson's disease
Huntington's disease
Another medical condition
Multiple etiologies
Unspecified

American Psychiatric Association. (2022). *Diagnostic and statistical manual of mental disorders* (5th ed., Text Revision).

Major and Mild Neurocognitive Disorders

Few things are more frightening than the possibility of one day not recognizing those you love, not being able to perform the most basic of tasks and, worse yet, being acutely aware of this failure of your mind. When family members show these signs, initially adult children often deny any difficulty, coming up with excuses ("I forget things, too") for their parents' failing abilities. **Major neurocognitive disorder** (previously labeled **dementia**) is a gradual deterioration of brain functioning that affects memory, judgment, language, and other advanced cognitive processes. **Mild neurocognitive disorder** is a new DSM-5 disorder that was created to focus attention on the early stages of cognitive decline (Walaszek, 2020). Here the person has modest impairments in cognitive abilities but can, with some accommodations (for example, making extensive lists of things to do or creating elaborate schedules), continue to function independently.

Causes of neurocognitive disorders include several medical conditions and the use or misuse of drugs or alcohol that produce negative changes in cognitive functioning. Some of these conditions—for instance, infection or depression—can cause neurocognitive impairment, although it is often reversible through treatment of the primary condition. Some forms of the disorder, such as Alzheimer's disease, are at present irreversible (Walaszek, 2020). Although delirium and neurocognitive disorder can occur together, neurocognitive disorder has a gradual

Pat Summitt ...
Grit and Determination

At the age of 57, Pat Summitt was a highly successful basketball coach and mother, but she was beginning to experience lapses in her memory:

> Friends starte asking, "Are you having trouble with your memory?" Finally I admitted, "Sometimes I draw blanks." I grew uncertain, and then a little frightened. I began staying in bed until late in the morning, which was unlike me. I'd always been a bolter, the first person up and the most energetic one, too, and I'd always gone to work earlier than anyone on my staff. But I began to dread going into the office. (p. 11)

Despite having cognitive difficulties, not all of her memories were lost to her in this initial stage of the disease. She began her memoir with the things she remembered:

> I remember a tiny saloon in the Tennessee hills where the bartender squirted bourbon shots from a squeeze bottle, straight into the customers' mouths. I remember teaching a clinic to other coaches and opening the floor for questions, and a guy raised his hand and asked if I had any advice when it came to "coaching women." I remember leveling him with a death ray stare and then relaxing and curling up the corner of my mouth and saying, "Don't worry about coaching 'women.' Just go home and coach 'basketball.'" (p. 6)
>
> I remember the night my son was born. The doctor placed him on my chest and I said, "Hey, Tyler, I've been waitin' on you." (pp. 6–7)

Her memory for important experiences that occurred years ago remained intact. However, recent experiences and facts were more elusive. She then goes on to describe some of the things she no longer remembered:

> Sometimes, when I first wake up, I don't remember where I am. For a moment I'm disoriented and uneasy, and I have to lie there until it comes to me.
>
> Occasionally when I'm asked a question, I begin to answer it but then I forget the subject—it slips away like a thread through my fingers.
>
> I struggle to remember directions. There are moments when I'm driving to someplace I should know, and I have to ask, "Do I go left or right here?"
>
> I tend not to remember what hotel room I'm in. I don't remember what times my appointments are. (p. 7)

Many people who begin to have these cognitive difficulties retell these initial experiences as incredibly frightening. However, Pat Summitt was known for her tough determination both on the basketball court and now battling Alzheimer's disease. Her reaction to her diagnosis and her doctor's recommendations show an incredible level of courage and strength:

Simon Bruty/Sports Illustrated/Getty Images

> In my case, symptoms began to appear when I was only 57. In fact, the doctors believe early-onset Alzheimer's has a strong genetic predictor, and that it may have been progressing hidden in me for some years before I was diagnosed. I'd been walking around with a slow-ticking, slow-exploding bomb in my brain cells, and it only became apparent when it began to seriously interfere with my work. (p. 9)
>
> The doctor told me that given my diagnosis, frankly, he felt I could no longer work at all. I should step down immediately, because in his opinion the dementia would progress rapidly. I needed to quit, and get myself out of the public eye as quickly as possible, or I would "embarrass" myself and ruin my legacy. As he spoke, I felt my fist clench. It was all I could do not to lunge across the desk and drop him with one punch. Who did he think he was? Even if I had an irreversible brain disease—even if I did—what right did he have to tell me how to cope with it? Quit? Quit? (pp. 17–18)

She goes on to write about her unusually practical and optimistic perspective on having Alzheimer's disease—a view of this degenerative disease that should serve as a role model for the millions of people impacted by this disorder:

> Above all, I know that Alzheimer's has brought me to a point that I was going to arrive at someday anyway. With or without this diagnosis, I was going to experience diminishment. We all do. It's our fate. No, I can't size up a court of ten players anymore, see the clock out of one eye and the shifting schemes of opposing players with the other, and order up a countermove by hollering "Five!" or "Motion!" But I can suggest that people with mild to moderate stages of dementia have far more abilities than incapacities. I can suggest that just because certain circuits of memory or swiftness of synapses may fail, thought and awareness and consciousness do not. (p. 375)

Source: P. H. Summitt, 2013, *Sum it up: A thousand and ninety-eight victories, a couple of irrelevant losses, and a life in perspective, Crown Archetype.*

progression as opposed to delirium's acute onset; people with neurocognitive disorders are not disoriented or confused in the early stages, unlike people with delirium. Like delirium, however, neurocognitive disorder has many causes, including a variety of traumas to the brain such as stroke (which destroys blood vessels), the infectious diseases of syphilis and HIV, severe head injury, the introduction of certain toxic or poisonous substances, and diseases such as Parkinson's, Huntington's, and, the most common cause of dementia, Alzheimer's. Consider the personal account by Pat Summitt, the most successful NCAA basketball coach of all time. She coached the Tennessee Lady Vols basketball team from 1974 to 2012—winning a record-setting 1,098 games—until her symptoms of neurocognitive disorder due to Alzheimer's disease prevented her from working with the team full-time. Unfortunately, Pat Summitt passed away in 2016 at the age of 64 as the result of complications due to Alzheimer's. Before she died, she courageously wrote of her experiences with this disorder (Summitt, 2013).

After several evaluations—which included neurological evaluations, magnetic resonance imaging (MRI) showing some damage in several parts of her brain, and a spinal tap that showed the presence of beta amyloid protein—Pat Summitt's neurologist concluded that she had early onset neurocognitive disorder due to Alzheimer's disease. People at the same stage of decline as she will continue to deteriorate and eventually may die (as she did in 2016) from complications of their disorder.

Clinical Description and Statistics

Depending on the individual and the cause, the gradual progression of neurocognitive disorder may have somewhat different symptoms, although all aspects of cognitive functioning are eventually affected. In the initial stages, memory impairment is typically seen as an inability to register ongoing events. In other words, a person can remember how to talk and may remember events from many years ago but will have trouble remembering what happened in the past hour. For example, Pat Summitt had vivid recollections about her childhood but could not remember which direction to drive in familiar places.

Pat Summitt could not find her way home because visuospatial skills are impaired among people with neurocognitive disorder. **Agnosia**, the inability to recognize and name objects, is one of the most familiar symptoms. **Facial agnosia**, the inability to recognize even familiar faces, can be extremely distressing to family members. A general deterioration of intellectual function results from impairment in memory, planning, and abstract reasoning (Walaszek, 2020).

Perhaps partly because people with neurocognitive disorder are aware that they are deteriorating mentally, emotional changes often occur as well. Common side effects are delusions (irrational beliefs), depression, agitation, aggression, and apathy (Lovestone, 2012). One study found that confinement during the COVID-19 increased the side effects among some patients (Boutoleau-Bretonnière et al., in press). It is difficult, however, to establish the cause-and-effect relationship. It is not known how much behavioral change is caused by progressive brain deterioration directly and how much is a result of the frustration and discouragement that inevitably accompany the loss of function and the isolation of "losing" loved ones. Cognitive functioning continues to deteriorate until the person requires almost total support to carry out day-to-day activities. Ultimately, death occurs as the result of inactivity, combined with the onset of other illnesses, such as pneumonia.

Globally, it is estimated that one new case of major neurocognitive disorder is identified every 7 seconds (Ferri et al., 2005). Major neurocognitive disorder can develop at almost any age, although this disorder is more frequent in older adults. The methodology for estimating the number of those with major neurocognitive disorder has resulted in sometimes diverging numbers (Launer, 2011). Current estimates in the United States suggest a prevalence of around 5 million people with major neurocognitive disorder (Alzheimer's Association, 2011), with rates of a little more than 5% in people older than 65 and 50% in those older than 90 (Black & Andreasen, 2021). The increasing number of people with just one form of neurocognitive disorder—due to Alzheimer's disease—is alarming. A dramatic rise in Alzheimer's disease is predicted through the year 2050 as larger numbers of people are expected to live beyond 85 years of age. ■ Figure 15.1 illustrates how the prevalence of neurocognitive disorder due to Alzheimer's disease is projected to greatly increase in older adults, partly as a result of the increase of baby boomers who will become senior citizens (Hebert, Weuve, Scherr, & Evans, 2013). Among the eldest of adults, research on centenarians (people 100 years and older) indicates that up to 100% showed signs of neurocognitive

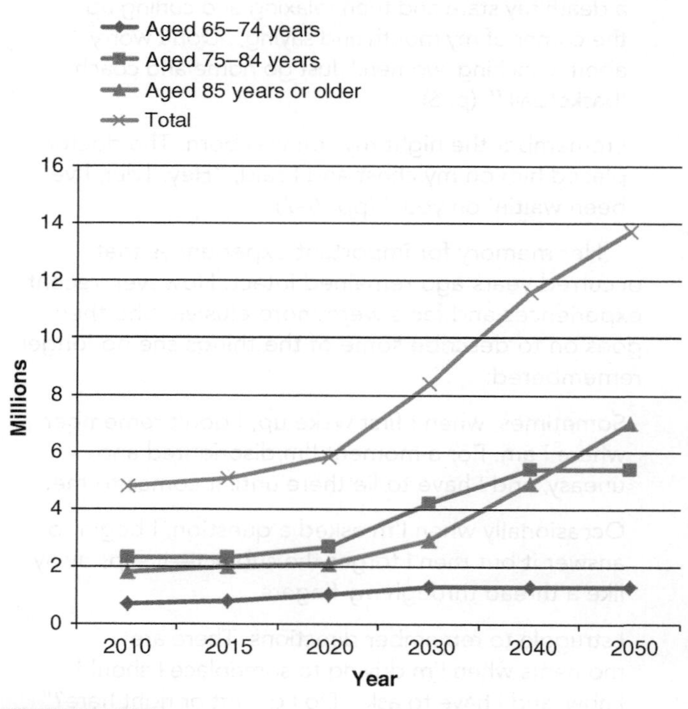

Figure 15.1

With the increasing numbers of persons living longer, the rate of Alzheimer's disease is predicted to escalate dramatically through the year 2050. From L. E. Hebert, J. Weuve, P. A. Scherr, & D. A. Evans, 2013, Alzheimer disease in the United States (2010–2050) estimated using the 2010 census, *Neurology, 80*(19), 1778–1783.

disorder (Davey et al., 2013; Imhof et al., 2007). Neurocognitive disorder due to Alzheimer's disease rarely occurs in people under 45 years of age.

Estimates of the prevalence of the new DSM-5 diagnosis—mild neurocognitive disorder—have been studied by the Einstein Aging Study at Yeshiva University (Katz et al., 2012). Researchers recruited 1,944 adults aged 70 or older and assessed them for mild neurocognitive disorder as well as mild amnestic neurocognitive disorder in this group. This latter disorder—in its more severe state—was previously a separate DSM disorder (*amnestic disorder*) but has been folded into the general neurocognitive disorder group. Almost 10% of those over 70 had mild neurocognitive disorder, and 11.6% met the criteria for mild amnestic neurocognitive disorder. Race also seemed to be a factor, with Black men and women at higher risk for mild neurocognitive disorder than White men and women (Katz et al., 2012).

A problem with confirming prevalence figures for neurocognitive disorder is that survival rates alter the outcomes. Because adults are generally living longer and are therefore more at risk of developing neurocognitive disorder, it is not surprising that the disorder is more prevalent. Incidence studies, which count the number of new cases in a year, may thus be the most reliable method for assessing the frequency of neurocognitive disorder, especially among the elderly. Research shows that the rate for new cases doubles with every 5 years of age after age 75. Many studies find greater increases of neurocognitive disorder among women (Carter, Resnick, Mallampalli, & Kalbarczyk, 2012). Neurocognitive disorder due to Alzheimer's disease may, as we discuss later, be more prevalent among women. Together, results suggest that neurocognitive disorder is relatively common among older adults, and the chances of developing it increase rapidly after the age of 75.

In addition to the human costs of neurocognitive disorder, the financial costs are staggering. Estimates of the costs of caring for people with neurocognitive disorder due to Alzheimer's disease are often quoted to be about $100 billion per year in the United States. One estimate indicates that the total worldwide societal cost of major neurocognitive disorder is more than $818 billion (Maresova, Hruska, Klimova, Barakovic, & Krejcar, 2020), including informal care and direct medical costs. Also, many times, family members care for an afflicted person around the clock, which is an inestimable personal and financial commitment (Lovestone, 2012).

4x5 Coll-Francisco Cruz / SuperStock

People with facial agnosia, a common symptom of neurocognitive disorder, are unable to recognize faces, even the faces of their closest friends and relatives.

DSM-5 identifies classes of neurocognitive disorder based on etiology: (1) Alzheimer's disease, (2) vascular injury, (3) frontotemporal degeneration, (4) traumatic brain injury, (5) Lewy body disease, (6) Parkinson's disease, (7) HIV infection, (8) substance use, (9) Huntington's disease, (10) prion disease, and (11) another medical condition. We emphasize neurocognitive disorder due to Alzheimer's disease because of its prevalence (almost half of those with neurocognitive disorder exhibit this type) and the relatively large amount of research conducted on its etiology and treatment.

Neurocognitive Disorder Due to Alzheimer's Disease

In 1907, the German psychiatrist Alois Alzheimer first described the disorder that bears his name. He wrote of a 51-year-old woman who had a "strange disease of the cerebral cortex" that manifested as progressive memory impairment and other behavioral and cognitive impairments, including suspiciousness (Richards & Sweet, 2009). He called the disorder an "atypical form of senile dementia"; thereafter, it was referred to as **Alzheimer's disease**.

Description and Statistics

The DSM-5 diagnostic criteria for **neurocognitive disorder due to Alzheimer's disease** include multiple cognitive deficits that develop gradually and steadily. Predominant are impairment of memory, orientation, judgment, and reasoning. The inability to integrate new information results in failure to learn new associations. Individuals with Alzheimer's disease forget important events and lose objects. Their interest in nonroutine activities narrows. They tend to lose interest in others and, as a result, become more socially isolated. As the disorder progresses, they can become agitated, confused, depressed, anxious, or even combative. Many of these difficulties become more pronounced late in the day—in a phenomenon referred to as "sundowner syndrome"—perhaps as a result of fatigue or a disturbance in the brain's biological clock (Shih, Pai, Lin, Sung, & Wang, 2020; Todd, 2020).

People with neurocognitive disorder due to Alzheimer's disease also display one or more other cognitive disturbances, including aphasia (difficulty with language), apraxia (impaired motor functioning), agnosia (failure to recognize objects), or difficulty with activities such as planning, organizing, sequencing, or abstracting information. These cognitive impairments have a serious negative impact on social and occupational functioning, and they represent a significant decline from previous abilities.

Research using brain scans is being conducted on people with mild neurocognitive disorder to see whether changes in brain structure early in the development of Alzheimer's disease can be detected, which could lead to early diagnosis (Dolui, Li, Nasrallah, Detre, & Wolk, 2020; Vogt et al., 2020). In the past, a definitive diagnosis of Alzheimer's disease could be made only after an autopsy determined that certain characteristic types of injury were present in the brain. There is now growing evidence, however, that the use of sophisticated brain scans along with new chemical tracers may soon be able to help clinicians identify the presence of Alzheimer's disease before the significant declines in cognitive abilities (through a project called the Alzheimer's Disease Neuroimaging Initiative [ADNI]) or death (Canevelli et al., 2021; Karikari et al., 2020). In addition, research on the presence of certain markers for Alzheimer's (such as beta amyloid—the substance in the amyloid plaques found in the brains of persons with this disease) in spinal fluid also appears to increase the accuracy of a diagnosis (Vanderstichele et al., 2012). Currently, to make a diagnosis without direct examination of the brain, the course and presence of the following symptoms should be observed—slow, progressive decline, typically in this order: memory, language, visuospatial function (that is, skills needed for movement, depth and distance perception, and spatial navigation), and executive function (that is, a set of mental skills that include working memory, flexible thinking, and self-control) (Walaszek, 2020).

In an interesting, somewhat controversial study—referred to as the "Nun Study"—the writings of a group of Catholic nuns collected over several decades appeared to indicate early in life which women were most likely to develop Alzheimer's disease later (Snowdon et al., 1996). Researchers observed that samples from the nuns' journals over the years differed in the number of ideas each contained, which the scientists called "idea density." In other words, some sisters described events in their lives simply: "I was born in Eau Claire, Wis, on May 24, 1913 and was baptized in St. James Church." Others were more elaborate in their prose: "The happiest day of my life so far was my First Communion Day which was in June nineteen hundred and twenty when I was but eight years of age, and four years later in the same month I was confirmed by Bishop D. D. McGavich" (Snowdon et al., 1996, p. 530). When findings of autopsies on 14 of the nuns were correlated with idea density, the simple writing (low idea density) occurred among all 5 nuns with Alzheimer's disease (Snowdon et al., 1996). This is an elegant research study because the daily lives of the nuns were similar, which ruled out many other possible causes. There is some concern, however, about overgeneralizing from this one study, and we must be cautious about depending too much on these observations because only a small number of people were examined.

Promising preliminary research on the early signs of neurocognitive disorder due to Alzheimer's disease has identified some small changes in neurocognitive functioning that research continues to attempt to pin down and measure reliably. For example, by continuously measuring the cognitive functioning of a person, it may be possible to start detecting when some of this person's cognitive functioning may start to decline (de la Fuente Garcia, Ritchie, & Luz, in press). Early detection before individuals meet clinical criteria is especially important because early intervention has been shown to have the biggest impact (Rentz et al., 2013).

Cognitive deterioration with Alzheimer's disease is slow during the early and later stages but more rapid during the middle stages (Ito et al., 2011; Richards & Sweet, 2009). The average survival time is estimated to be about 4 to 8 years, although many individuals live dependently for more than 20 years. In some forms, the disease can occur relatively early, during the 40s or 50s (sometimes referred to as *early onset*), but it usually appears during the 60s or 70s. Approximately 60% to 70% of the cases of neurocognitive disorder are found to be the result of Alzheimer's disease, which is believed to affect more than 50 million people worldwide and 5.5 million in the United States (World Health Organization, 2020).

Some early research on prevalence suggested that Alzheimer's disease may occur more often in people who have a limited education (Amieva et al., 2014; Fratiglioni et al., 1991). Greater impairment among these individuals might indicate a much earlier onset, suggesting that Alzheimer's disease causes intellectual dysfunction that, in turn, hampers educational efforts. Or there could be something about educational achievement that prevents or delays the onset of symptoms of the disorder. Later research seems to confirm the latter explanation. It appears that educational level may predict a delay in the observation of symptoms (Sheladia & Hemachandra Reddy, 2021). Unfortunately, people who attain a higher level of education also decline more rapidly once the symptoms become more severe (Scarmeas, Albert, Manly, & Stern, 2006), suggesting that education does not prevent Alzheimer's disease but just provides a buffer period of better functioning. Educational attainment may somehow create a mental "reserve," a learned set of skills that help someone cope longer with the cognitive deterioration that marks the beginning of neurocognitive deficits. Some people may adapt more successfully than others and thus escape detection longer. Brain deterioration may thus be comparable for both groups, but better-educated individuals may be able to function successfully on a day-to-day basis for a longer period. This tentative hypothesis may prove useful in designing treatment strategies, especially during the early stages of the disorder.

A biological version of this theory—the *cognitive reserve hypothesis*—suggests that the more synapses a person develops throughout life, the more neuronal death must take place before the signs of dementia are obvious (Nelson, Jester, Petkus, & Andel, 2021). Mental activity that occurs with education presumably builds up this reserve of synapses and serves as an initial protective factor in the development of the disorder. It is likely that both skill development and the changes in the brain with education may contribute to how quickly the disorder progresses.

Research suggests that Alzheimer's disease may be more prevalent among women (Walaszek, 2020), even when women's higher survival rate is factored into the statistics. In other words, because women live longer than men on average, they are more likely to experience Alzheimer's and other diseases, but longevity alone does not account for the higher prevalence of the disorder among women. A tentative explanation involves the hormone estrogen (Uddin et al., 2020). Women lose estrogen as they grow older, so perhaps estrogen is protective against the disease. A large and important study—the Women's Health Initiative Memory Study—looked at hormone use among women and its effect on Alzheimer's disease (Lobo, 2013; Shumaker et al., 2004). In its initial findings, the study followed women over age 65 using a type of combined estrogen plus progestin known as Prempro, and, contrary to the belief that giving women estrogen would decrease their chance of developing neurocognitive disorder, they observed an *increased* risk for Alzheimer's disease (Coker et al., 2010; Maki & Henderson, 2012). More research is ongoing into the individual effects of these two types of hormones on dementia (Song et al., 2020).

Finally, there appear to be questions about the prevalence of Alzheimer's disease according to cultural and/or racial identity. Early research seemed to suggest that certain populations (such as those with Japanese, Nigerian, certain Native American, and Amish backgrounds) were less likely to be affected (for example, see Pericak-Vance et al., 1996; Rosenberg et al., 1996). Similarly, prevalence rates of Alzheimer's disease in low- and middle-income countries have also been reportedly lower than higher-income countries (Sosa-Ortiz, Acosta-Castillo, & Prince, 2012). More recent work indicates, however, that some of these differences may be due to lower numbers in those who seek assistance (possibly due to stigma as well high levels of social care from family members), as well as differences in education and the ways the disorders were measured (Sosa-Ortiz et al., 2012; Wilson et al., 2010). For example, individuals in low- and middle-income countries did not meet DSM criteria for the disorder given that they did not have much social or occupational interference because their families were taking care of them (Sosa-Ortiz et al., 2012). Black and Hispanic Americans are more likely to develop this disorder compared to non-Hispanic White Americans, and some early research suggests higher rates among Native Americans (Walaszek, 2020). As you will see, findings like these help bring us closer to understanding the causes of this devastating disease.

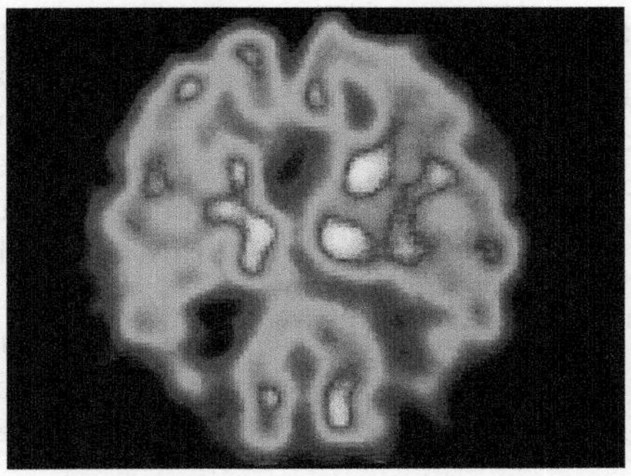
Tim Beddow/Science Source

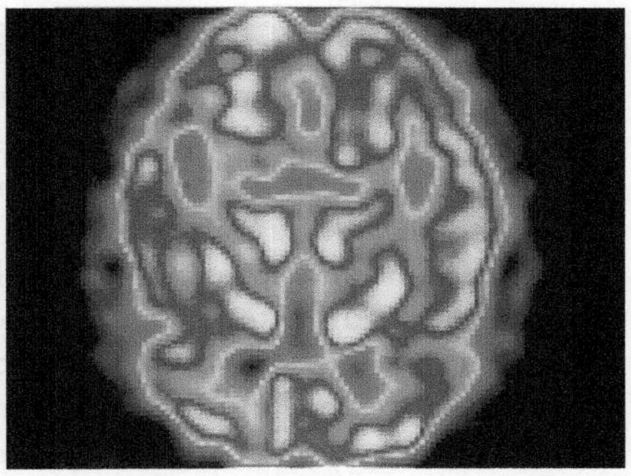
Tim Beddow/Science Source

The PET scan of a brain afflicted with Alzheimer's disease (left) shows significant tissue deterioration in comparison with a normal brain (right).

DSM 5 **Table 15.4**

Diagnostic Criteria for Major or Mild Neurocognitive Disorder due to Alzheimer's Disease

A. The criteria are met for major or mild neurocognitive disorder.

B. There is insidious onset and gradual progression of impairment in one or more cognitive domains (for major neurocognitive disorder, two domains must be impaired).

C. Criteria are met for either probable or possible Alzheimer's disease as follows:

For major neurocognitive disorder:

Probable Alzheimer's disease is diagnosed if either of the following is present; otherwise, possible Alzheimer's disease should be diagnosed.

1. Evidence of a causative Alzheimer's disease genetic mutation from family history or genetic testing
2. All three of the following are present:
   a. Clear evidence of decline in memory and learning and at least one other cognitive domain (based on detailed history or serial neuropsychological testing).
   b. Steadily progressive, gradual decline in cognition, without extended plateaus.
   c. No evidence of mixed etiology (i.e., absence of other neurodegenerative or cerebrovascular disease, or another neurological, mental, or systemic disease or condition likely contributing to cognitive decline).

For mild neurocognitive disorder:

Probable Alzheimer's disease is diagnosed if there is evidence of a causative Alzheimer's disease genetic mutation from either genetic testing or family history.

Possible Alzheimer's disease is diagnosed if there is no evidence of a causative Alzheimer's disease genetic mutation from either genetic testing or family history, and all three of the following are present:

1. Clear evidence of decline in memory and learning.
2. Steadily progressive, gradual decline in cognition, without extended plateaus.
3. No evidence of mixed etiology (i.e., absence of other neurodegenerative or cerebrovascular disease, or another neurological or systemic disease or condition likely contributing to cognitive decline).

D. The disturbance is not better explained by cerebrovascular disease, another neurodegenerative disease, the effects of a substance, or another mental, neurological, or systemic disorder.

American Psychiatric Association. (2022). *Diagnostic and statistical manual of mental disorders* (5th ed., Text Revision).

Vascular Neurocognitive Disorder

Each year, 500,000 people die from strokes (any diseases or traumas to the brain that result in restriction or cessation of blood flow). Although stroke is the third leading cause of death in the United States, many people survive, but one potential long-term consequence can be severely debilitating. **Vascular neurocognitive disorder** is a progressive brain disorder that is a common cause of neurocognitive deficits. It is one of the more common causes of neurocognitive disorder, second only to Alzheimer's disease (Black & Andreasen, 2021).

Description and Statistics

The word *vascular* refers to blood vessels. When the blood vessels in the brain are blocked or damaged and no longer carry oxygen and other nutrients to certain areas of brain tissue, damage results. Because multiple sites in the brain can be damaged, the profile of degeneration—the particular skills that are impaired—differs from person to person. DSM-5 lists as criteria for vascular neurocognitive disorder cognitive disturbances such as declines in speed of information processing and executive functioning (such as complex decision making) (Black & Andreasen, 2021). In contrast, those with Alzheimer's disease have memory problems as their initial cognitive disturbance.

Compared with research on neurocognitive disorder due to Alzheimer's type, there are fewer studies on vascular neurocognitive disorder, perhaps because of its lower incidence rates. The prevalence of vascular neurocognitive disorder is approximately 1.5% in people 70 to 75 years of age and increases to 15% for those over the age of 80 (Neugroschi, Kolevzon, Samuels, & Marin, 2005). The risk for men is slightly higher than among women, in contrast with the higher risk among women for Alzheimer's type dementia, and this has been reported in many developed and developing countries (Kalaria et al., 2008). The relatively high rate of cardiovascular disease among men in general may account for their increased risk of vascular neurocognitive disorder. The onset of vascular dementia is typically more sudden than the onset for the Alzheimer's type, probably because the disorder is the result of stroke, which inflicts brain injury immediately. The outcome, however, is similar for people with both types: Ultimately, they will require formal nursing care until they succumb to an infectious disease such as pneumonia, to which they are susceptible because of weakening of the immune system (Black & Andreasen, 2021).

Other Medical Conditions That Cause Neurocognitive Disorder

In addition to Alzheimer's disease and vascular damage, a number of other neurological and biochemical processes can lead to neurocognitive disorder. DSM-5 identifies eight specific causes in addition to Alzheimer's disease and vascular damage: frontotemporal degeneration, traumatic brain injury, Lewy body disease, Parkinson's disease, HIV infection, substance use, Huntington's disease, and prion disease (Black & Andreasen, 2021). Each of these is discussed here. In addition, a final category—neurocognitive disorder due to another medical condition—is provided for other causes. Other medical conditions that can lead to neurocognitive disorder include normal pressure hydrocephalus (excessive water in the cranium, resulting from brain shrinkage), hypothyroidism (an underactive thyroid gland), brain tumor, and vitamin B_{12} deficiency. There is increasing recognition of neurocognitive disorder among athletes who receive repeated blows to the head. In the past, this type of neurocognitive disorder was referred to as *dementia pugilistica* (which suggested that it was restricted to boxers or pugilists), but it is currently referred to as *chronic traumatic encephalopathy (CTE)*. CTE is caused by repetitive **head trauma** that can provoke distinctive neurodegeneration

DSM 5 **Table 15.5**

Diagnostic Criteria for Major or Mild Vascular Neurocognitive Disorder

A. The criteria are met for major or mild neurocognitive disorder.

B. The clinical features are consistent with a vascular etiology as suggested by either of the following:

1. Onset of the cognitive deficits is temporally related to one or more cerebrovascular events.
2. Evidence for decline is prominent in complex attention (including processing speed) and frontal-executive function.

C. There is evidence of the presence of cerebrovascular disease from history, physical examination, and/or neuroimaging considered sufficient to account for the neurocognitive deficits.

D. The symptoms are not better explained by another brain disease or systemic disorder. Probable vascular neurocognitive disorder is diagnosed if one of the following is present, otherwise, possible vascular neurocognitive disorder should be diagnosed:

1. Clinical criteria are supported by neuroimaging evidence of significant parenchymal injury attributed to cerebrovascular disease (neuroimaging-supported).
2. The neurocognitive syndrome is temporally related to one or more documented cerebrovascular events.
3. Both clinical and genetic (e.g., cerebral autosomal dominant arteriopathy with subcortical infarcts and leukoencephalopathy) evidence of cerebrovascular disease is present.

Possible vascular neurocognitive disorder is diagnosed if the clinical criteria are met but neuroimaging is not available and the temporal relationship of the neurocognitive syndrome with one or more cerebrovascular events is not established.

American Psychiatric Association. (2022). *Diagnostic and statistical manual of mental disorders* (5th ed., Text Revision).

(Bieniek et al., 2020). In their effect on cognitive ability, all of these disorders are comparable to the other forms of neurocognitive disorder we have discussed so far.

Descriptions and Statistics

Frontotemporal neurocognitive disorder is an overarching term used to categorize a variety of brain disorders that damage the frontal or temporal regions of the brain—areas that affect personality, language, and behavior (Black & Andreasen, 2021). DSM-5 identifies two variants of frontotemporal neurocognitive disorder—through declines in appropriate behavior (such as socially inappropriate actions, apathy, making poor judgments) or language (such as problems with speech, finding the right word, naming objects). One of the disorders in this category of neurocognitive disorders is **Pick's disease**, a rare neurological condition—occurring in about 5% of those people with neurocognitive impairment—that produces symptoms similar to that of Alzheimer's disease. The course of this disease is believed to last from 5 to 10 years and appears to have a genetic component (Gustafson & Brun, 2012). Pick's disease usually occurs relatively early in life—during a person's 40s or 50s—and is therefore considered an example of early onset neurocognitive disorder.

Jim McIsaac/Staff/Getty Images Sport/Getty Images

Junior Seau was an NFL star football player who committed suicide in 2012. The National Institutes of Health—at the request of his family—found he had brain abnormalities consistent with repetitive blows to the head, resulting in chronic traumatic encephalopathy (CTE).

Severe trauma to the head causes the brain to sustain lasting injuries (called **traumatic brain injury** or **TBI**) that can lead to neurocognitive disorder (Black & Andreasen, 2021). **Neurocognitive disorder due to traumatic brain injury** includes symptoms that persist for at least a week following the trauma, including executive dysfunction (such as difficulty planning complex activities) and impairments in learning and memory. Those who are at greatest risk for TBI are teens and young adults, especially accompanied by excessive alcohol use or lower socio-economic class (Fleminger, 2012). Traffic accidents, assaults, falls, and suicide attempts are common causes, as is being exposed to bomb blasts in combat.

Another common type of neurocognitive disorder is **neurocognitive disorder due to Lewy body disease** (Walaszek, 2020). Lewy bodies are microscopic deposits of a protein that damage brain cells over time. The signs of this disorder come on gradually and include impairment in

DSM 5 **Table 15.6**

Diagnostic Criteria for Major or Mild Frontotemporal Neurocognitive Disorder

A. The criteria are met for major or mild neurocognitive disorder.
B. The disturbance has insidious onset and gradual progression.
C. Either (1) or (2):
  1. Behavioral variant:
    a. Three or more of the following behavioral symptoms:
      i. Behavioral disinhibition
      ii. Apathy or inertia
      iii. Loss of sympathy or empathy
      iv. Perseverative, stereotyped, or compulsive/ritualistic behavior
      v. Hyperorality and dietary changes
    b. Prominent decline in social cognition and/or executive abilities.
  2. Language variant:
    a. Prominent decline in language ability, in the form of speech production, word finding, object naming, grammar, or word comprehension
D. Relative sparing of learning and memory and perceptual-motor function.
E. The disturbance is not better explained by cerebrovascular disease, another neurodegenerative disease, the effects of a substance, or another mental, neurological, or systemic disorder.

Probable frontotemporal neurocognitive disorder is diagnosed if either of the following is present; otherwise, possible frontotemporal neurocognitive disorder should be diagnosed:

1. Evidence of a causative frontotemporal neurocognitive disorder genetic mutation, from either family history or genetic testing
2. Evidence of disproportionate frontal and/or temporal lobe involvement from neuroimaging

Possible frontotemporal neurocognitive disorder is diagnosed if there is no evidence of a genetic mutation, and neuroimaging has not been performed.

American Psychiatric Association. (2022). *Diagnostic and statistical manual of mental disorders* (5th ed., Text Revision).

alertness and attention, vivid visual hallucinations, and motor impairment as seen in Parkinson's disease. In fact, there is some overlap between this disorder and **neurocognitive disorder due to Parkinson's disease** (Walaszek, 2020).

Parkinson's disease is a degenerative brain disorder that affects about 930,000 people in the United States (Marras et al., 2018), though estimates vary widely due to challenges in diagnosing the disorder (Wirdefeldt, Adami, Cole, Trichopoulos, & Mandel, 2011). Movie and television star Michael J. Fox and former U.S. Attorney General Janet Reno (who died from the disease in 2016) both were diagnosed with this progressive disorder. Motor problems are characteristic among people with Parkinson's disease, who tend to have stooped posture, slow body movements (called *bradykinesia*), tremors, and jerkiness in walking. The voice is also affected; afflicted individuals speak in a soft monotone. The changes in motor movements are the result of damage to dopamine pathways. Because dopamine is involved in complex movement, a reduction in this neurotransmitter makes affected individuals increasingly unable to control their muscle movements, which leads to tremors and muscle weakness (Walaszek, 2020). In addition to degeneration of these pathways, Lewy bodies are also present in the brains of affected persons. The course of the disease varies widely, with some individuals functioning well with treatment. It is estimated that about 75% of people who survive more than 10 years with Parkinson's disease develop neurocognitive disorder; conservative estimates place the rate at 4 to 6 times that found in the general population (Aarsland & Kurz, 2010; Svenningsson, Westman, Ballard, & Aarsland, 2012).

The **human immunodeficiency virus type 1 (HIV-1)**, which causes AIDS, can also cause neurocognitive disorder (called **neurocognitive disorder due to HIV infection**) (Wang et al., 2020).

DSM 5

Table 15.8

Diagnostic Criteria for Major or Mild Neurocognitive Disorder with Lewy Bodies

A. The criteria are met for major or mild neurocognitive disorder.

B. The disorder has an insidious onset and gradual progression.

C. The disorder meets a combination of core diagnostic features and suggestive diagnostic features for either probable or possible neurocognitive disorder with Lewy bodies.

For probable major or mild neurocognitive disorder with Lewy bodies, the individual has two core features, or one suggestive feature with one or more core features.

For possible major or mild neurocognitive disorder with Lewy bodies, the individual has only one core feature, or one or more suggestive features.

1. Core diagnostic features:
   - **a.** Fluctuating cognition with pronounced variations in attention and alertness
   - **b.** Recurrent visual hallucinations that are well formed and detailed
   - **c.** Spontaneous features of parkinsonism, with onset subsequent to the development of cognitive decline
2. Suggestive diagnostic features:
   - **a.** Meets criteria for rapid eye movement sleep behavior disorder
   - **b.** Severe neuroleptic sensitivity

D. The disturbance is not better explained by cerebrovascular disease, another neurodegenerative disease, the effects of a substance, or another mental, neurological, or systemic disorder.

American Psychiatric Association. (2022). *Diagnostic and statistical manual of mental disorders* (5th ed., Text Revision).

DSM 5

Table 15.7

Diagnostic Criteria for Major or Mild Neurocognitive Disorder due to Traumatic Brain Injury

A. The criteria are met for major or mild neurocognitive disorder.

B. There is evidence of a traumatic brain injury—that is, an impact to the head or other mechanisms of rapid movement or displacement of the brain within the skull, with one or more of the following:

1. Loss of consciousness
2. Posttraumatic amnesia
3. Disorientation and confusion
4. Neurological signs (e.g., neuroimaging demonstrating injury; a new onset of seizures; a marked worsening of a preexisting seizure disorder; visual field cuts; anosmia; hemiparesis)

C. The neurocognitive disorder presents immediately after the occurrence of the traumatic brain injury or immediately after recovery of consciousness and persists past the acute post-injury period.

American Psychiatric Association. (2022). *Diagnostic and statistical manual of mental disorders* (5th ed., Text Revision).

This impairment seems to be independent of the other infections that accompany HIV; in other words, the HIV infection itself seems to be responsible for the neurological impairment. The early symptoms of neurocognitive disorder resulting from HIV are cognitive slowness, impaired attention, and forgetfulness. Affected individuals also tend to be clumsy, to show repetitive movements such as tremors and leg weakness, and to become apathetic and socially withdrawn.

People with HIV seem particularly susceptible to impaired thinking in the later stages of HIV infection, although significant declines in cognitive abilities may occur earlier. Cognitive impairments were highly common among those infected with HIV, but with the introduction of new medications (highly active antiretroviral therapies, or HAARTs), less than 10% of patients now experience neurocognitive disorder (Wang et al., 2020). HIV-1 accounts for a relatively small percentage of people with neurocognitive disorder compared to Alzheimer's disease and vascular causes, but its presence can complicate an already devastating set of medical conditions.

Like neurocognitive disorder from Parkinson's disease and several other causes, neurocognitive disorder resulting from HIV is sometimes referred to as *subcortical dementia* because it affects primarily the inner areas of the brain, below the outer layer called the cortex (de Lacerda & Caixeta, 2020). The distinction between cortical (including neurocognitive disorder due to Alzheimer's disease) and subcortical dementia is important because of the different expressions of neurocognitive disorder in these two categories (see Table 15.1). **Aphasia**, which involves impaired language skills, occurs among people with neurocognitive disorder due to Alzheimer's disease but not among people with subcortical dementia. In contrast, people with subcortical dementia are more likely to experience severe depression and anxiety than those with neurocognitive disorder due to Alzheimer's disease. In general, motor skills including speed and coordination are impaired early on among those with subcortical dementia. The differing patterns of impairment can be attributed to the different areas of the brain affected by the disorders causing the neurocognitive disorder.

DSM 5 Table 15.9
Diagnostic Criteria for Neurocognitive Disorder due to Parkinson's Disease

A. The criteria are met for major or mild neurocognitive disorder.
B. The disturbance occurs in the setting of established Parkinson's disease.
C. There is insidious onset and gradual progression of impairment.
D. The neurocognitive disorder is not attributable to another medical condition and is not better explained by another mental disorder.

Major or mild neurocognitive disorder probably due to Parkinson's disease should be diagnosed if 1 and 2 are both met. Major or mild neurocognitive disorder possibly due to Parkinson's disease should be diagnosed if 1 or 2 is met:

1. There is no evidence of mixed etiology (i.e., absence of other neurodegenerative or cerebrovascular disease or another neurological, mental, or systemic disease or condition likely contributing to cognitive decline).
2. The Parkinson's disease clearly precedes the onset of neurocognitive disorder.

American Psychiatric Association. (2022). *Diagnostic and statistical manual of mental disorders* (5th ed., Text Revision).

Huntington's disease is a genetic disorder that initially affects motor movements, typically in the form of *chorea*, involuntary limb movements (Wijeratne et al., 2020). People with Huntington's disease can live for 20 years after the first signs of the disease appear, although skilled nursing care is often required during the final stages. Just as with Parkinson's disease, only a portion of people with Huntington's disease go on to display cognitive deficits; 42.5% of new Huntington's disorder cases also present with *mild* cognitive impairment (Robbins & Cools, 2014). Estimates of how many individuals go on to develop neurocognitive disorders vary widely from 20% to 80%—although some researchers believe that all patients with Huntington's disease would eventually display neurocognitive impairments if they lived long enough (Marsh & Margolis, 2009). **Neurocognitive disorder due to Huntington's disease** also follows the subcortical pattern.

The search for the gene responsible for Huntington's disease reads like a detective story. For some time, researchers have known that the disease is inherited as an autosomal dominant disorder, meaning that approximately 50% of the offspring of an

DSM 5 Table 15.10
Diagnostic Criteria for Major or Mild Neurocognitive Disorder due to HIV Infection

A. The criteria are met for major or mild neurocognitive disorder.
B. There is documented infection with human immunodeficiency virus (HIV).
C. The neurocognitive disorder is not better explained by non-HIV conditions, including secondary brain diseases such as progressive multifocal leukoencephalopathy or cryptococcal meningitis.
D. The neurocognitive disorder is not attributable to another medical condition and is not better explained by a mental disorder.

American Psychiatric Association. (2022). *Diagnostic and statistical manual of mental disorders* (5th ed., Text Revision).

Table 15.1 Characteristics of Neurocognitive Disorders

Characteristic	Dementia of the Alzheimer's Type	Subcortical Dementias
Language	Aphasia (difficulties with articulating speech)	No aphasia
Memory	Impaired recall and recognition	Impaired recall; normal or less impaired recognition
Visuospatial skills	Impaired	Impaired
Mood	Less severe depression and anxiety	More severe depression and anxiety
Motor speed	Normal	Slowed
Coordination	Normal until late in the progression	Impaired

Source: Adapted, with permission of Oxford University Press, from J. L. Cummings (Ed.), 1990, *Subcortical dementia*, Oxford University Press. © 1990 Jeffrey L. Cummings.

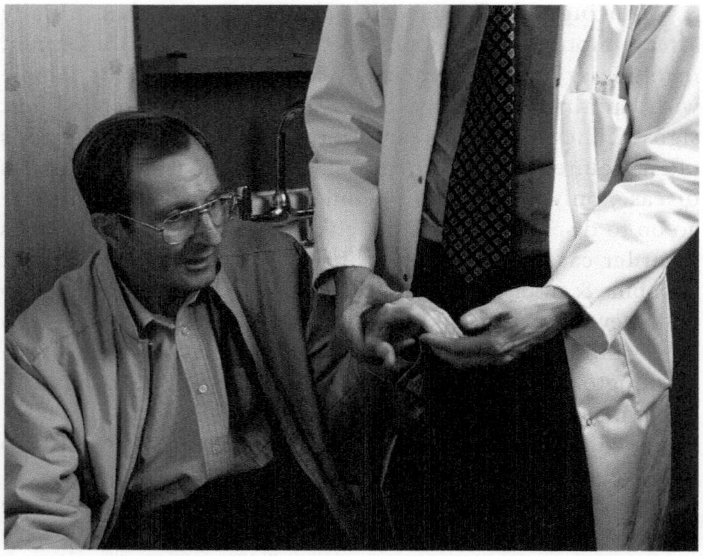

Simon Fraser/Royal Victoria Infirmary, Newcastle upon Tyne/Science Source

The AIDS virus may cause neurocognitive disorder in the later stages.

adult with Huntington's disease will develop the disease. Since 1979, behavioral scientist Nancy Wexler and a team of researchers have been studying the largest known extended family in the world afflicted by Huntington's disease in small villages in Venezuela. The villagers have cooperated with the research, partly because Wexler herself lost her mother, three uncles, and her maternal grandfather to Huntington's disease, and she announced in 2020 that she too had the disorder (Grady, 2020). Using genetic linkage analysis techniques (see Chapter 4), these researchers first mapped the deficit to an area on chromosome 4 (Gusella et al., 1983) and then identified the elusive gene (Huntington's Disease Collaborative Research Group, 1993). Finding that one gene that causes a disease is unusual; research on other inherited mental disorders typically points to multiple gene (polygenic) influences.

Neurocognitive disorder due to prion disease is a rare progressive neurodegenerative disorder caused by *prions*—proteins that can reproduce themselves and cause damage to brain cells, leading to neurocognitive decline (Vallabh et al., 2020). Unlike other infectious agents such as bacteria or viruses, prions are thought by some to have no DNA or RNA that can be destroyed by chemicals or radiation. As a result, there is no known treatment for prion disease, and the course of this disorder is always fatal. On the positive side, prions are not contagious in humans and have only been contracted through cannibalism (causing kuru) or accidental inoculations (such as through blood transfusions from an infected person) (Vallabh et al., 2020). One type of prion disease, **Creutzfeldt-Jakob disease**, is believed to affect only one in every million individuals (Vallabh et al., 2020). An alarming development in the study of Creutzfeldt-Jakob disease is the finding of 10 cases of a new variant that may be linked to bovine spongiform encephalopathy, more commonly referred to as "mad cow disease" (Ebringer, 2015; Neugroschi et al., 2005). This discovery led to a ban on exporting beef from the United Kingdom for a number of years because the disease might be transmitted from infected cattle to humans. We do not yet have definitive information about the link between mad cow disease and the new form of Creutzfeldt-Jakob disease (Vallabh et al., 2020).

Harry Hamburg / New York Daily News Archive / Getty Images

Michael J. Fox provides his time and celebrity status to efforts to cure Parkinson's disease, a degenerative disease that is severely affecting his life.

DSM 5 Table 15.11

Diagnostic Criteria for Major or Mild Neurocognitive Disorder due to Huntington's Disease

A. The criteria are met for major or mild neurocognitive disorder.
B. There is insidious onset and gradual progression.
C. There is clinically established Huntington's disease or risk for Huntington's disease based on family history or genetic testing.
D. The neurocognitive disorder is not attributable to another medical condition and is not better explained by another mental disorder.

American Psychiatric Association. (2022). *Diagnostic and statistical manual of mental disorders* (5th ed., Text Revision).

DSM 5 Table 15.12

Diagnostic Criteria for Neurocognitive Disorder due to Prion Disease

A. The criteria are met for major or mild neurocognitive disorder.
B. There is insidious onset, and rapid progression of impairment is common.
C. There are motor features of prion disease, such as myoclonus or ataxia, or biomarker evidence.
D. The neurocognitive disorder is not attributable to another medical condition and is not better explained by another mental disorder.

American Psychiatric Association. (2022). *Diagnostic and statistical manual of mental disorders* (5th ed., Text Revision).

Substance/Medication-Induced Neurocognitive Disorder

Prolonged drug use, especially combined with poor diet, can damage the brain and, in some circumstances, can lead to neurocognitive disorder. This impairment unfortunately lasts beyond the period involved in intoxication or withdrawal from these substances.

Description and Statistics

As many as 50% to 70% of chronic heavy alcohol users show cognitive impairment (Sico et al., 2014), and 7% of those with an alcohol use disorder also meet criteria for a neurocognitive disorder (Neugroschi et al., 2005). The long-term misuse of a number of drugs can lead to symptoms of neurocognitive disorder, including alcohol, inhalants such as glue or gasoline (which some people inhale for the euphoric feeling they produce), and sedative, hypnotic, and anxiolytic drugs (Toledo-Fernández et al., 2020) (see Chapter 11). These drugs pose a threat because they create physiological dependence, making it difficult for a user to stop ingesting them. The resulting brain damage can be permanent and can cause the same symptoms as seen in neurocognitive disorder due to Alzheimer's type. The DSM-5 criteria for **substance/medication-induced neurocognitive disorder** are essentially the same as many of the other forms of neurocognitive disorder. They include memory impairment and at least one of the following cognitive disturbances: aphasia (language disturbance), apraxia (inability to carry out motor activities despite intact motor function), agnosia (failure to recognize or identify objects despite intact sensory function), or a disturbance in executive functioning (such as planning, organizing, sequencing, and abstracting).

Causes of Neurocognitive Disorder

As our technology for studying the brain advances, so does our understanding of the many and varied causes of neurocognitive disorder. A complete description of what is known about the origins of this type of brain impairment is beyond the scope of this book, but we highlight some insights available for more common forms of this disorder.

Biological Influences

Cognitive abilities can be adversely compromised in many ways. As you have seen, neurocognitive disorder can be caused by a number of processes: Alzheimer's disease, Huntington's disease, Parkinson's disease, head trauma, substance misuse, and others (Walaszek, 2020). The most common cause of neurocognitive disorder, Alzheimer's disease, is also the most mysterious. Because of its prevalence and our relative ignorance about the factors responsible for it, Alzheimer's disease has held the attention of many researchers who are trying to find the cause and ultimately a treatment or cure for this devastating condition.

Findings from Alzheimer's research seem to appear almost daily. We should be cautious when interpreting the output of this fast-paced and competitive field; too often, as you have seen in other areas, findings are heralded prematurely as conclusive and important. Remember that "discoveries" of a single gene for bipolar disorder, schizophrenia, and alcoholism were later shown to be based on overly simplistic accounts. Similarly, findings from Alzheimer's research are sometimes too quickly sanctioned as accepted truths before they have been replicated, an essential validation process.

One lesson in scientific caution comes from research that demonstrates a negative correlation between cigarette smoking and Alzheimer's disease (Brenner et al., 1993). In other words, the study found that smokers are less likely than nonsmokers to develop Alzheimer's disease. Does this mean smoking has a protective effect, shielding a person against the development of this disease? On close examination, the finding may instead be the result of the differential survival rates of those who smoke and those who do not. In general, nonsmokers tend to live longer and are thereby more likely to develop Alzheimer's disease, which appears later in life. Some even believe the relative inability of cells to repair themselves, a factor that may be more pronounced among people with Alzheimer's disease, may interact with cigarette smoking to shorten the lives of smokers who are at risk for Alzheimer's disease (Riggs, 1993). Put another way, smoking may exacerbate the degenerative process of Alzheimer's disease, causing people with the disease who also smoke to die earlier than nonsmokers who have Alzheimer's disease (Ashare, Karlawish, Wileyto, Pinto, & Lerman, 2012). These types of studies and the conclusions drawn from them should make us sensitive to the complicated nature of the disorders.

What do we know about Alzheimer's disease, the most common cause of neurocognitive disorder? After the death of the patient he described as having a "strange disease of the cerebral cortex," Alois Alzheimer performed an autopsy. He found that the brain contained large numbers of tangled, strandlike filaments within the brain cells (referred to as *neurofibrillary tangles*). This type of damage occurs in everyone with Alzheimer's disease.

DSM 5 Table 15.13

Diagnostic Criteria for Substance/Medication-Induced Major or Mild Neurocognitive Disorder

A. The criteria are met for major or mild neurocognitive disorder.

B. The neurocognitive impairments do not occur exclusively during the course of a delirium and persist beyond the usual duration of intoxication and acute withdrawal.

C. The involved substance or medication and duration and extent of use are capable of producing the neurocognitive impairment.

D. The temporal course of the neurocognitive deficits is consistent with the timing of substance or medication use and abstinence (e.g., the deficits remain stable or improve after a period of abstinence).

E. The neurocognitive disorder is not attributable to another medical condition and is not better explained by another mental disorder.

American Psychiatric Association. (2022). *Diagnostic and statistical manual of mental disorders* (5th ed., Text Revision).

A second type of degeneration results from gummy protein deposits—called *amyloid plaques* (also referred to as *neuritic* or *senile plaques*)—that accumulate between the neurons in the brains of people with this disorder. Amyloid plaques are also found in older adults who do not have symptoms of neurocognitive disorder, but they have far fewer of them than do individuals with Alzheimer's disease (Richards & Sweet, 2009). Both forms of damage—neurofibrillary tangles and amyloid plaques—accumulate over the years and are believed to produce the characteristic cognitive disorders we have been describing (Weiner et al., 2012).

These two types of degeneration affect extremely small areas and can be detected only by a microscopic examination of the brain. As mentioned earlier, however, scientists are close to developing the neuroimaging technology and measures to assess amyloid proteins in spinal fluid that may soon detect the early development of these types of brain cell damage without having to rely on an autopsy (Weiner et al., 2012). In addition to having neurofibrillary tangles and amyloid plaques, over time the brains of many people with Alzheimer's disease atrophy (shrink) to a greater extent than would be expected through typical/usual aging (Lovestone, 2012). Because brain shrinkage has many causes, however, only by observing the tangles and plaques can a diagnosis of Alzheimer's disease be properly made.

Rapid advances are being made toward uncovering the genetic bases of Alzheimer's disease (Sims, Hill, & Williams, 2020). Genes play a strong role in Alzheimer's disease, with late-onset Alzheimer's disease showing heritability of 58% to 79% and early-onset Alzheimer's disease showing over 90%. As with most other behavioral disorders we have examined, multiple genes seem to be involved in the development of Alzheimer's disease. Table 15.3 illustrates what we know so far. Genes on chromosomes 1, 12, 14, 19, and 21 have all been linked to certain forms of Alzheimer's disease (Neugroschi et al., 2005). The link to chromosome 21 was discovered first, and it resulted from the unfortunate observation that individuals with Down syndrome, who have three copies of chromosome 21 instead of the usual two, developed the disease at an unusually high rate (Report of the Advisory Panel on Alzheimer's Disease, 1995). Additional research has located relevant genes on other chromosomes. These discoveries indicate that there is more than one genetic cause of Alzheimer's disease. Some forms, including the one associated with chromosome 14, have an early onset. Pat Summitt was diagnosed with an early-onset form. In contrast, Alzheimer's disease associated with chromosome 19 seems to be a late-onset form of the disease that has an effect only after the age of about 60.

Table 15.2 Genetic Factors in Alzheimer's Disease

Gene	Chromosome	Age of Onset (years)
Amyloid precursor protein (APP)	21	43 to 59
Presenilin 1	14	33 to 60
Presenilin 2	1	50 to 90
Apolipoprotein E4 (apo E4)	19	60

Source: S. Lovestone, 2012, Dementia: Alzheimer's disease, in M. G. Gelder, N. C. Andreasen, J. J. Lopez Jr., & J. R. Geddes (Eds.), *New Oxford textbook of psychiatry* (2nd. ed., Vol. 1, pp. 333–343), Oxford University Press.

Some genes that are now identified are **deterministic**, meaning that if you have one of these genes, you have a nearly 100% chance of developing Alzheimer's disease (Bettens, Sleegers, & Van Broeckhoven, 2010). Deterministic genes—such as the precursor gene for small proteins called *amyloid beta peptides* (also referred to as *beta amyloid* or *Ab*) and the *Presenilin 1* and *Presenilin 2* genes—will inevitably lead to Alzheimer's disease, but these genes are also rare in the general population. For treatment purposes, this means that even if researchers can find a way to prevent these genes from leading to Alzheimer's disease, it will help only a relatively small number of people. On the other hand, some genes—including the *apolipoprotein E4 (apo E4)* gene—are known as **susceptibility** genes. These genes only slightly increase the risk of developing Alzheimer's disease, but in contrast to the deterministic genes, these are more common in the general population (Walaszek, 2020). If future research can find ways to interfere with the *apo E4* gene, many people will be helped.

Although closing in on the genetic origins of Alzheimer's disease has not brought immediate treatment implications, researchers are nearer to understanding how the disease develops, which may result in medical interventions. Genetic research has advanced our knowledge of how the amyloid plaques develop in the brains of people with Alzheimer's disease and may hold a clue to its origins. In the core of the plaques is a solid waxy substance made up of a peptide called *amyloid beta (Ab)*. Just as cholesterol buildup on the walls of blood vessels chokes the blood supply, deposits of Ab are believed by some researchers to cause the cell death associated with Alzheimer's disease (Walaszek, 2020). An important question, then, is "Why does this protein accumulate in the brain cells of some people but not of others?"

Two mechanisms that may account for amyloid protein buildup are being studied. The first involves *amyloid precursor protein (APP)*, a large protein that is eventually broken down into the *amyloid protein* found in the amyloid plaques. Important work resulted in identifying the gene responsible for producing APP on chromosome 21 (Lovestone, 2012). This finding may help integrate two observations about Alzheimer's disease: (1) APP produces the amyloid protein found in the amyloid plaques, and (2) Down syndrome, associated with an extra 21st chromosome, results in a higher incidence of the disease (see Chapter 14). The gene responsible for producing APP and, ultimately, amyloid protein may be responsible for the relatively infrequent early-onset form of the disease, and its location could explain why people with Down syndrome—who have an extra 21st chromosome and therefore an extra APP gene—are more likely than the general population to develop Alzheimer's disease.

A second, more indirect way that amyloid protein may build up in brain cells is through *apolipoprotein E (apo E)*, which normally helps transport cholesterols, including amyloid protein, through the bloodstream. There are at least three forms of this transporter protein: *apo E2*, *apo E3*, and *apo E4*. Individuals who have late-onset Alzheimer's disease, the most common form, are likely to carry the gene associated with *apo E4*, located on chromosome 19. Researchers have found that the majority of people with Alzheimer's disease who also have a family history of the disease will have at least one gene for *apo E4* (Lovestone, 2012). In contrast, approximately 64% of individuals with Alzheimer's disease who have no family history of the disease have at least one gene for *apo E4*, and only 31% of nonaffected individuals have the gene. Having two genes for *apo E4* (one on each member of the chromosome 19 pair) increases the risk for Alzheimer's disease: As many as 90% of people with two genes developed Alzheimer's disease (Reiman et al., 2007). In addition, having two *apo E4* genes seemed to decrease the mean age of onset from 84 years to 68 years. These results suggest that *apo E4* may be responsible for late-onset Alzheimer's disease and that a gene on chromosome 19 is responsible.

What is still not completely understood is how *apo E4* causes amyloid proteins to build up in the neurons of people who ultimately exhibit Alzheimer's disease and whether this process is responsible for the disease. One study examined the role of high blood pressure in creating amyloid proteins when interacting with *apo E4* genotype in healthy adults. The study found that hypertension alone or *apo E4* alone did not increase amyloid deposits. However, healthy individuals with at least one *apo E4* gene and untreated high blood pressure had the greatest risk for amyloid proteins deposits. Also, the higher the blood pressure, the more amyloid proteins deposits were found. On the other hand, those with high blood pressure under medical control had only slightly higher levels of amyloid deposits than people without it (Rodrigue et al., 2013).

The *transactive response DNA binding protein (TDP-43)* has long been characterized as a main hallmark of *amyotrophic lateral sclerosis (ALS)* and *frontotemporal lobar degeneration* (Chang, Tan, Tan, & Yu, 2016). Several studies have indicated TDP-43 deposits in Alzheimer's disease brains and have robust connection with AD clinical phenotype. TDP-43 may contribute to Alzheimer's disease through both beta-amyloid (Ab)-dependent and Ab-independent pathways. TDP-43 modulation is being examined as a potential therapeutic strategy for Alzheimer's disease. However, to date, little of pieces of the research on TDP-43 have been performed to investigate the role in Alzheimer's disease; more investigations need to be confirmed in the future (Chang et al., 2016).

Researchers are also examining potential gene–environment interactions in development of Alzheimer's disease. Several studies suggest a few areas of promise. One study found that having the *apo E4* genotype was more likely to produce cognitive decline in those persons living in stressful environments—suggesting a gene (*apo E4*) and environment (stress) interaction (Boardman, Barnes, Wilson, Evans, & de Leon, 2012). Another study found that among African Americans, having low levels of cholesterol seemed to reduce risk of Alzheimer's disease—but only among those who did not carry the *apo E4* gene (Evans et al., 2000). Finally, researchers found that physical exercise reduced the likelihood of developing the disease but, like the previous study, only among those without the *apo E4* gene (Podewils et al., 2005). This type of research holds the potential for better understanding the complex nature of Alzheimer's disease and may lead to important prevention strategies (such as lowering cholesterol levels and exercising regularly) (Pedersen, 2010).

For all disorders described in this book, we have identified the role of biological, psychological, or both types of stressors as partially responsible for the onset of the disorder. Does neurocognitive disorder due to Alzheimer's disease—which appears to be a strictly biological event—follow the same pattern? One of the leading candidates for an external contributor to this disorder is head trauma. As we have seen, it appears that repeated blows to the head can bring on neurocognitive disorder (*chronic traumatic encephalopathy* or *CTE*). Fighters who carry the *apo E4* gene may be at greater risk for developing neurocognitive disorder attributed to head trauma (Jordan et al., 1997). In addition to boxers, new research suggests links to the trauma experienced by NFL players and the development of CTE in these former athletes (Stamm et al., 2015). Head trauma may be one of the stressors that initiate the onset of neurocognitive disorder of varying types. Other such stressors include having diabetes, high blood pressure, or herpes simplex virus-1 (Richards & Sweet, 2009). As with each of the disorders discussed, psychological and biological stressors may interact with physiological processes to produce Alzheimer's disease.

We opened the section with a word of caution, which it is appropriate at this point to repeat. Some of the findings just

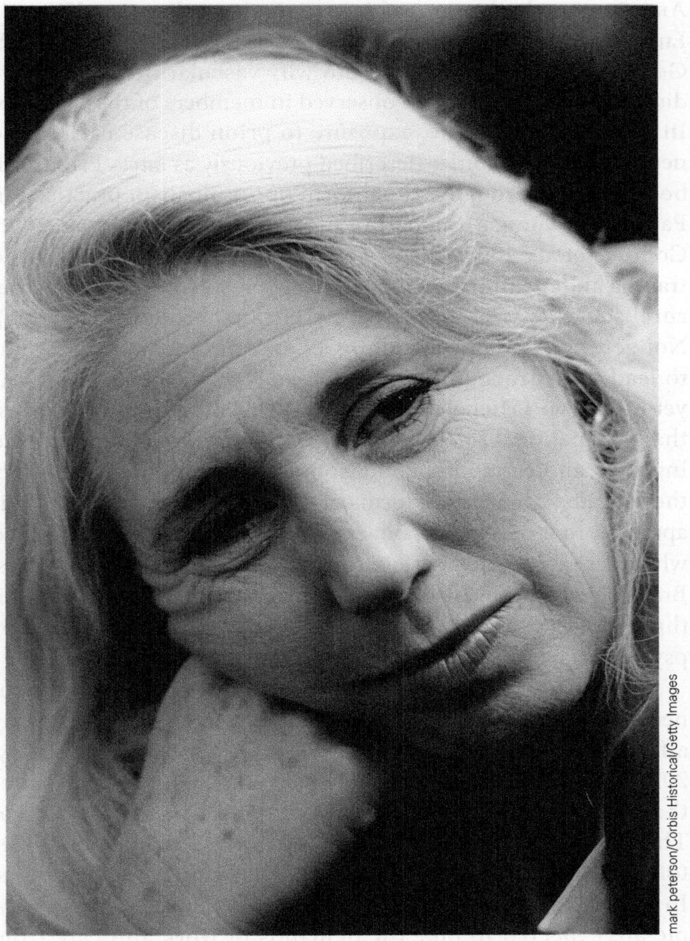

Nancy Wexler headed the team of scientists who found the gene for Huntington's disease.

reviewed are considered controversial, and many questions remain to be answered about neurocognitive disorder and one of its most common causes, Alzheimer's disease.

Psychological and Social Influences

Research has focused mostly on the biological conditions that produce neurocognitive disorder. Although few would claim that psychosocial influences directly cause the type of brain deterioration seen in people with neurocognitive disorder, they may help determine onset and course. For example, a person's lifestyle may involve contact with factors that can cause neurocognitive disorder. You saw, for instance, that substance abuse can lead to neurocognitive disorder and that (as discussed in Chapter 11) whether a person abuses drugs is determined by a combination of biological and psychosocial factors. In the case of vascular neurocognitive disorder, a person's biological vulnerability to vascular disease will influence the chances of strokes that can lead to this form of disorder. Lifestyle issues such as diet, exercise, and stress influence cardiovascular disease and therefore help determine who experiences vascular neurocognitive disorder (see Chapter 9).

Cultural factors may also affect this process. For example, hypertension and strokes are more prevalent among African Americans and subgroups of Asian Americans than non-Hispanic European Americans (Howard et al., 2013; King, Mainous III, & Geesey, 2007). This may explain why vascular neurocognitive disorder is also more often observed in members of these groups. In an extreme example, exposure to prion disease can lead to neurocognitive disorder described previously as *kuru*. Prions can be passed on through a ritual form of cannibalism practiced in Papua New Guinea as a part of mourning (Collinge et al., 2006; Collinge et al., 2008). Neurocognitive disorder caused by head trauma and malnutrition are relatively prevalent in preindustrial rural societies (Del Parigi, Panza, Capurso, & Solfrizzi, 2006). Not getting enough of vitamins B_9 and B_{12} in particular seems to lead to neurocognitive disorder, although the process is as yet unknown (Michelakos et al., 2013). These findings suggest that occupational safety (such as protecting workers from head injuries) and economic conditions influencing diet also affect the prevalence of certain forms of neurocognitive disorders. It is apparent that psychosocial factors help influence who does and who does not develop certain forms of neurocognitive disorders. Brain deterioration is a biological process, but, as you have seen throughout this text, even biological processes are influenced by psychosocial factors.

Psychosocial factors themselves influence the course of neurocognitive disorder. Recall that educational attainment may affect the onset of dementia (Sheladia & Hemachandra Reddy, 2021). Having certain skills may help some people cope better than others with the early stages of neurocognitive disorder. The early stages of confusion and memory loss may be better tolerated in cultures with lowered expectations of older adults. In certain cultures, including in China and India, younger people are expected to take the demands of work and care from older adults after a certain age, and symptoms of dementia are viewed as a sign of typical/usual aging (Motta-Ochoa et al., 2021). Neurocognitive disorder may go undetected for years in these societies (Sosa-Ortiz et al., 2012).

Much remains to be learned about the cause and course of most types of neurocognitive disorder. As you saw with Alzheimer's disease and Huntington's disease, certain genetic factors make some individuals vulnerable to progressive cognitive deterioration. In addition, brain trauma, some diseases, and exposure to certain drugs (such as alcohol, inhalants, and sedative, hypnotic, and anxiolytic drugs) can cause the characteristic decline in cognitive abilities. We also noted that psychosocial factors can help determine who is subject to these causes and how they cope with the condition. Looking at neurocognitive disorder from this integrative perspective should help you view treatment approaches in a more optimistic light. It may be possible to protect people from conditions that lead to neurocognitive disorder and to support them in dealing with the devastating consequences of having it. We next review attempts to help from both biological and psychosocial perspectives.

Treatment

For many of the disorders discussed in other chapters, treatment prospects are fairly good. Clinicians can combine various strategies to reduce subjective distress significantly. Even when treatment does not bring expected improvements, mental health professionals have usually been able to stop problems from progressing. This is not the case in the treatment of neurocognitive disorder.

One factor preventing major advances in the treatment of neurocognitive disorder is the nature of the damage caused by this disorder. The brain contains billions of neurons, many more than are used. Damage to some can be compensated for by others because of plasticity. There is a limit to where and how many neurons can be destroyed, however, before vital functioning is disrupted. Researchers are closing in on how to use the brain's natural process of regeneration to potentially reverse the damage caused in neurocognitive disorder (for example, Wright, Kawas, & Harding, 2015). Currently, however, with extensive brain damage, no known treatment can restore lost abilities. The goals of treatment therefore become (1) trying to prevent certain conditions (such as substance abuse or strokes) that may bring on neurocognitive disorder; (2) trying to delay the onset of symptoms to provide better quality of life; and (3) attempting to help these individuals and their caregivers cope with the advancing deterioration. Most efforts in treating neurocognitive disorder have focused on the second and third goals, with biological treatments aimed at stopping the cerebral deterioration and psychosocial treatments directed at helping patients and caregivers cope.

A troubling statistic further clouds the tragic circumstances of neurocognitive disorder. In one study, more than 60% of caregivers of people with neurocognitive disorder—usually relatives—have the symptoms characteristic of one or more anxiety disorders (55% of these caregivers had anxiety) and/or clinical depression (37% of the caregivers had depression) (Joling et al., 2015). Compared with the public, these caregivers use more psychotropic medications (designed to reduce symptoms of various psychological disorders) and report stress symptoms at three times the typical/usual rate. Caring for people with neurocognitive disorder, especially in its later stages, is clearly a trying experience (Pierse, Keogh, Challis, & O'Shea, in press). In fact, there is some evidence to suggest that the stress associated with caring for a person with neurocognitive disorder may place the caregiver at greatly increased risk for developing neurocognitive disorder themselves (Norton et al., 2010). As a result, clinicians are becoming increasingly sensitive to the needs of these caregivers, and research is now exploring interventions that are easy to disseminate (such as over the Internet) to assist them in caring for people with neurocognitive disorders. Preliminary results from such interventions are promising and have important implications for the caregivers of the "baby-boomer" generation (Blom, Bosmans, Cuijpers, Zarit, & Pot, 2013).

Biological Treatments

Neurocognitive disorder resulting from known infectious diseases, nutritional deficiencies, and depression can be treated if it is caught early. Unfortunately, however, no known treatment exists for the types of neurocognitive disorder that account for the vast majority of cases. Neurocognitive disorder caused by stroke, Parkinson's disease, or Huntington's disease is not currently treatable because there is no effective treatment for the primary disorder. However, exciting research in several related areas has brought us closer to helping individuals with these forms of neurocognitive disorder. A substance that may help preserve and perhaps restore neurons—glial cell–derived neurotrophic factor—may someday be used to help reduce or reverse the progression of degenerative brain diseases (Lu, Nagappan, Guan, Nathan, & Wren, 2013). Researchers are also looking into the possible benefits of transplanting stem cells (fetal brain tissue) into the brains of people with such diseases. Initial results from these studies are still preliminary but appear promising (Pen & Jensen, 2016). Neurocognitive disorder brought on by strokes may now be more preventable by new drugs that help prevent much of the damage inflicted by the blood clots characteristic of stroke (Walaszek, 2020). Most current attention is on a treatment for dementia of the Alzheimer's type because it affects so many people. Here, too, however, success has been modest at best.

Much work has been directed at developing drugs that will enhance the cognitive abilities of people with neurocognitive disorder due to Alzheimer's type. Many seem to be effective initially, but long-term improvements have not been observed in placebo-controlled studies (Black & Andreasen, 2021). Several drugs (called *cholinesterase inhibitors*) have had a modest impact on cognitive abilities in some patients and include donepezil (Aricept), rivastigmine (Exelon), and galantamine (Reminyl) (Trinh, Hoblyn, Mohanty, & Yaffe, 2003). *Tacrine hydrochloride* (Cognex), another in this family of drugs, is rarely used today because of the potential for liver damage (Rabins, 2006). These drugs prevent the breakdown of the neurotransmitter acetylcholine (which is deficient in people with Alzheimer's disease), thus making more acetylcholine available to the brain. Research suggests that, when using these drugs, people's cognitive abilities improve to the point where they were 6 months earlier (Kimchi & Lyketos, 2015). But the gain is not permanent. Even people who respond positively do not stabilize but continue to experience the cognitive decline associated with Alzheimer's disease. In addition, if they stop taking the drug—as almost three quarters of the patients do because of negative side effects such as liver damage and nausea—they lose even that 6-month gain (Kimchi & Lyketos, 2015). Newer drugs are now being investigated for the treatment of Alzheimer's disease. These include drugs that target the beta amyloid (plaques) in the brain, and it is hoped that these advances will finally provide a positive prognosis for this devastating disease (Lukiw, 2012; McClam, Marano, Rosenberg, & Lyketsos, 2015).

There is considerable controversy surrounding one new drug that was designed to reduce the beta amyloid (plaques) in the brain. Aduhelm (aducanumab), a new drug that received clearance from the U.S. Food and Drug Administration (FDA) in 2021, was supposed to offer that kind of change. It is the first federally approved drug that seeks to slow the underlying biological process of Alzheimer's rather than simply mitigate symptoms. However, several issues emerged after this approval. First, scientists familiar with the research behind this drug's effects questioned its effectiveness, suggesting there were limited data that it slowed the progression of the cognitive decline among people with this disorder (Servick, 2021). An additional concern was the cost of this drug. Aduhelm has a list price of $56,000 per year (Servick, 2021), a great deal of money, especially for a drug with limited data on its effectiveness. Future research may help settle these controversies.

Several other medical approaches are being explored to slow the course of Alzheimer's disease, but initial excitement generated by these approaches has waned with the findings from researchers. For example, many people have heard of using *Ginkgo biloba* (maidenhair) to improve memory. Initial research suggested that this herbal remedy may produce modest improvements in the memory of people with Alzheimer's disease, but other studies have not replicated this benefit (Vellas et al., 2012). Similarly, the effects of vitamin E have been evaluated. A few large studies have found that among individuals with moderately severe impairment, high doses of the vitamin (2,000 international units per day) delayed progression compared with a placebo (Dysken et al., 2014; Sano et al., 1997), but it did not prevent the development of the disease. Further research, in fact, indicates that taking high doses of vitamin E may actually increase mortality and therefore this intervention is no longer recommended (Richards & Sweet, 2009). Modest slowing of the progression of the disease also may be obtained by introducing exercise to patients (Paillard, Rolland, & de Souto Barreto, 2015). To date, however, no medical interventions are available that directly treat and therefore stop the progression of the conditions that cause the cerebral damage in Alzheimer's disease.

Medical interventions for neurocognitive disorder also include the use of drugs to help with some associated symptoms. A variety of antidepressants—such as serotonin-specific reuptake inhibitors—are commonly recommended to alleviate the depression and anxiety that too often accompany the cognitive decline. Antipsychotic medication is sometimes used for those who become unusually agitated (Walaszek, 2020).

Other researchers are targeting vaccines that would potentially treat and prevent—rather than just delay—the symptoms of Alzheimer's disease. Much of the research is attempting to get the immune system to attack the process that overproduces the small proteins (Ab) that lead to cell death. Prior efforts had to be abandoned because of the severe negative side effects of the vaccine, which included serious brain inflammation. More recent research with humans and animals indicates that there may be several vaccines that could be effective in preventing the damage caused by Ab formation and therefore represent the first glimmer of hope for patients and their families (Kabir et al., 2020; Mantile & Prisco, 2020).

This type of research currently begins with transgenic mice—mice in which the DNA has been altered. In the case of testing an Alzheimer's vaccine, the mice DNA is engineered to produce the same small proteins thought to be responsible for the neurocognitive disorder. Mice are good subjects because they age rapidly, with a 22-month-old mouse equivalent to a 65-year-old human (Davtyan et al., 2013; Morgan, 2007). This allows researchers to study how the brain reacts to the potential vaccine if it has already started the progression of Alzheimer's. If the results are promising in these transgenic mice, only then do researchers try small studies with humans. Researchers are optimistic that there may finally be intervention approaches that would reverse the current trend of increasing numbers of people with neurocognitive disorder. Next, we describe psychosocial approaches that are used with medication to address the variety of problems that accompany memory difficulties.

Psychosocial Treatments

Psychosocial treatments are now receiving a great deal of attention for their ability to delay the onset of severe cognitive decline. These efforts focus on enhancing the lives of people with neurocognitive disorder, as well as those of their families.

People with neurocognitive disorder can be taught skills to compensate for their lost abilities. Some researchers have evaluated formal adaptations to help people in the early stages of neurocognitive disorder. Michelle Bourgeois (2007) created "memory wallets" to help people with Alzheimer's disease carry on conversations. On white index cards inserted into a plastic wallet are printed declarative statements such as, "My husband John and I have three children," or "I was born on January 6, 1921, in Pittsburgh." In one of her studies, Bourgeois (1992) found that adults with neurocognitive disorder due to Alzheimer's disease could, with minimal training, use this memory aid to improve their conversations with others. With advances in technology such as tablet computers that can be programmed to "speak" for the person, adaptations such as these can help people communicate with others, help them remain aware of their surroundings, and reduce the frustration that comes with the awareness of their own decline (Fried-Oken et al., 2012).

Cognitive stimulation—encouraging people with neurocognitive disorder to practice learning and memory skills—seems to be an effective method for delaying the onset of the more severe cognitive effects of this disorder (Aguirre, Woods, Spector, & Orrell, 2013; Woods, Aguirre, Spector, & Orrell, 2012). These activities include word games, tests of memory of famous and familiar faces, and practice with numbers (for example, how much change you would receive back from a purchase). These types of skill-building exercises can maintain cognitive activity and improve the quality of life in those patients when compared with controls (Choi & Twamley, 2013).

What impact do the medical and nonmedical treatments have on those with Alzheimer's disease? Figure 15.2 illustrates how these interventions may delay the worst of the symptoms—essentially compressing the time when the person is most impaired (Becker, Mestre, Ziolko, & Lopez, 2007). The red line illustrates the typical course of the disease, which results in 3 to 5 years of severe impairment before death. However, with the interventions we highlighted (illustrated by the purple line), people are able to live more fully for a longer period, despite the still-inevitable impairment and death. Families find this extra time with their loved ones to be invaluable, and more advancements may lead to progress on improving mortality rates of this progressive disease.

Individuals with advanced neurocognitive disorder are not able to feed, bathe, or dress themselves. They cannot communicate with or recognize even familiar family members. They may wander away from home and become lost. Because they are no longer aware of social stigma, they may engage in public displays of sexual behavior, such as masturbation. They may be frequently agitated or even physically violent. To help both the person with dementia and the caregiver, researchers have explored interventions for dealing with these consequences of the disorder (Lovestone, 2012). For example, some research indicates that a combination of exercise for patients and instruction for caregivers on how to handle behavior problems can improve the overall health and the depression in people with Alzheimer's disease (Potter, Ellard, Rees, & Thorogood, 2011; Teri et al., 2003).

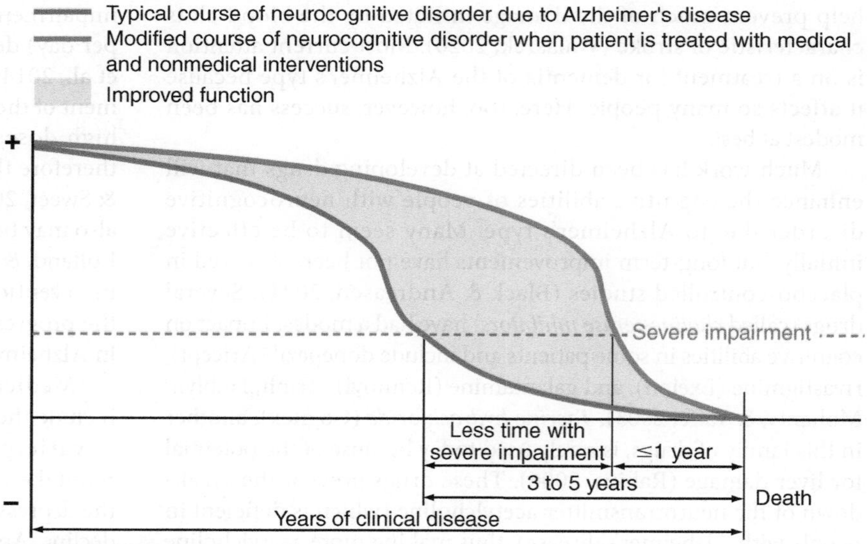

FIGURE 15.2

Improving the course of Alzheimer's disease with medical and nonmedical interventions. From J. T. Becker, L. T. Mestre, S. Ziolko, & O. L. Lopez, 2007, Gene–environment interactions with cognition in late life and compression of morbidity, *American Journal of Psychiatry, 164*, 849–852.

Of great concern is the tendency of people with neurocognitive disorder to wander. Sometimes they wind up in places or situations that may be dangerous (for example, stairwells or the street). Sometimes the person may be sedated or tied to a chair or bed to prevent roaming. Unfortunately, physical and medical restraint has its own risks, including additional medical complications; it also adds greatly to the loss of control and independence that already plague the person with neurocognitive disorder. Psychological treatment as an alternative to restraint sometimes involves providing cues for people to help them safely navigate around their home or other areas. New innovations in surveillance technology—creating a "smart home" that can monitor the location of the patient and warn caregivers—may provide more piece of mind for those who care for these patients. At the same time, ethical concerns are being raised about the use of this technology because of its ability to invade privacy (Bharucha et al., 2009; Chung, Demiris, & Thompson, 2016).

Someone with neurocognitive disorder can become agitated and sometimes verbally and physically aggressive. This behavior is understandably stressful for people trying to provide care. In these situations, medical intervention is often used, although many times with only modest results (Testad, Ballard, Brønnick, & Aarsland, 2010). Some research suggests that teaching communication skills in a manner similar to programs for persons with autism spectrum disorder (Durand & Moskowitz, 2019) may help reduce aggressive behavior in persons with neurocognitive disorder (Livingston et al., 2014). In addition, caregivers are often given assertiveness training to help them deal with hostile behaviors (see Table 15.3). Some caregivers may either passively accept all criticism inflicted by the person with neurocognitive disorder, which increases stress, or become angry and aggressive in return. This last response is of particular concern because of the potential for elder abuse. Withholding food or medication or inflicting physical abuse is most common among caregivers of elderly people who have cognitive deficits. Research has also shown that elder abuse occurs in nursing homes and assisted living facilities, with neglect and emotional abuse being the most common in these settings (Myhre, Saga, Malmedal, Ostaszkiewicz, & Nakrem, 2020). It is important

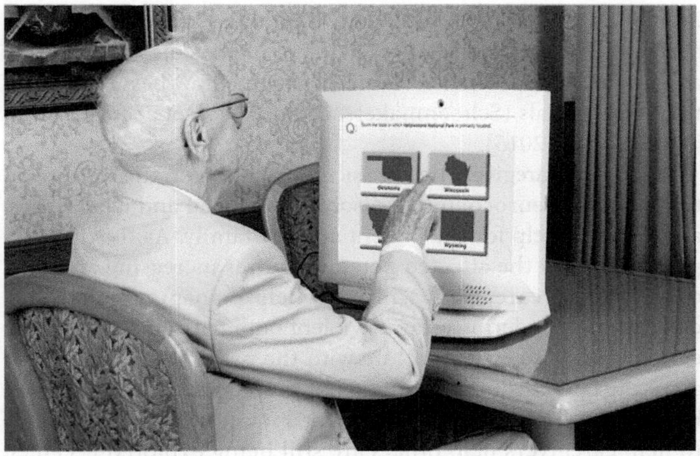

Dakim BrainFitness System: Kara Kenna photographer, www.dakim.com

A resident of an assistive living facility practices cognitive stimulation using one of several computer-based systems (the Dakim [m]Power Brain Fitness System).

to teach caregivers how to handle stressful circumstances so that they do not escalate into abusive situations. Not a great deal of objective evidence supports the usefulness of assertiveness training for reducing caregiver stress, and more research is needed to guide future efforts.

In general, families of people with mild to moderate neurocognitive disorder can benefit from supportive counseling to help them cope with the frustration, depression, guilt, and loss that take a heavy emotional toll. Clinicians must first recognize, however, that the ability to adapt to stressors differs among people. One study, for example, found cultural differences in the coping styles of caregivers. In one area of rural Alabama, White caregivers used acceptance and humor as coping strategies, and Black caregivers used religion and denial (Kosberg, Kaufman, Burgio, Leeper, & Sun, 2007). Another large-scale study of 555 principal caregivers over a 3-year period identified a number of steps that can be taken to support caregivers through this difficult time (Aneshensel, Pearlin,

Table 15.3 Sample Assertive Responses

Patient Behavior	Assertive Response
	Calmly but firmly say:
The patient refuses to eat, bathe, or change clothes.	"We agreed to do this at this time so that we will be able to (give specific activity or reward)."
The patient wants to go home.	"I know you miss some of the places we used to be. This is our home now, and together we are safe and happy here."
The patient demands immediate gratification.	"It's not possible to have everything we want. As soon as I've finished (describe specific task or action), we can discuss other things we want to do."
The patient accuses the caregiver of taking the patient's possessions.	"We both enjoy our own things. I'll help you look for (specific item missing) so that you can enjoy it just as soon as I have finished (describe specific task or action)."
The patient is angry, rebellious, or both.	"I like to be treated fairly just as you do. Let's discuss what's bothering you so that we can go back to our usual good relationship."

Source: Adapted, with permission, from A. J. Edwards, 1994, *When memory fails: Helping the Alzheimer's and dementia patient,* Plenum Press, p. 174. © 1994 Plenum Press.

Mullan, Zarit, & Whitlatch, 1995). Despite numerous studies aimed at supporting caregivers, however, the results to date remain weak, and additional work is needed to determine how best to support these individuals (Schoenmakers, Buntinx, & DeLepeleire, 2010; Tremont et al., 2015).

Early on, caregivers need basic information on the causes and treatment of neurocognitive disorder, financial and legal issues, and locating help for the patient and the family. As the disorder progresses and the affected person requires increasing amounts of assistance, caregivers will need help managing behavioral difficulties (wandering away or violent outbursts) and developing effective ways to communicate with the patient. Clinicians also assist the family with decisions about hospitalizations and, finally, help them adjust during bereavement. However, the best methods to help caregivers help others are still being explored (Peeters, Van Beek, Meerveld, Spreeuwenberg, & Francke, 2010; Zabalegui et al., 2014).

Overall, the outlook for slowing (but not stopping) the cognitive decline characteristic of neurocognitive disorder is optimistic. The best available medications provide some recovery of function, but they do not stop the progressive deterioration. Psychological interventions may help people cope more effectively with the loss of cognitive abilities, especially in the earlier stages of this disorder. In addition, emphasis is placed on helping caregivers—the other individuals affected by neurocognitive disorder—as the person they care for continues to decline.

Prevention

Without treatment, there is a need to rely even more heavily on prevention strategies for neurocognitive disorder. You can imagine that it is difficult to study prevention efforts for neurocognitive disorder because of the need to follow individuals for long periods to see whether the efforts are effective. One major study conducted in Sweden—where socialized medicine provides complete medical histories of all residents—looked at many of the risk factors (those factors that increase the chance of having neurocognitive disorder) and protective factors (those that decrease the risk) under study today (Fratiglioni & Qiu, 2009; Fratiglioni, Winblad, & von Strauss, 2007). They looked at the medical records of 1,810 participants who were older than 75 at the time and followed them for about 13 years. Through interviews and medical histories, they came to three major conclusions: Control your blood pressure, do not smoke, and lead an active physical and social life! These recommendations came out as the major factors that individuals can change—because you cannot change your genetics, for example—that will decrease the chances of developing neurocognitive disorder (Rizzuto, Orsini, Qiu, Wang, & Fratiglioni, 2012). Additional prevention research is ongoing, and there may be other potentially fruitful research areas that can lead to the successful prevention of this devastating disorder.

Concept Check 15.2

Identify the following symptoms of dementia from the descriptions: (a) facial agnosia, (b) agnosia, and (c) aphasia.

1. Timmy's elderly grandmother does not recognize her own home any more. ________
2. She can no longer form complete, coherent sentences. ________
3. She no longer recognizes Timmy when he visits, even though he is her only grandchild. ________

Identify the cognitive disorders described.

4. Julian is recovering from alcohol use disorder. When asked about his wild adventures as a young man, his stories usually end quickly because he can't remember the whole tale. He even has to write down things he has to do in a notebook; otherwise, he's likely to forget. ________
5. Mr. Brown has suffered from a number of strokes but can still care for himself. His ability to remember important things, however, has been declining steadily for the past few years. ________
6. A decline in cognitive functioning that is gradual and continuous and has been associated with neurofibrillary tangles and amyloid plaques. ________

DSM Controversies: *Is Normal Aging a Mental Disorder?*

Researchers and clinicians have, for some time, recognized that many older adults begin to show cognitive decline in areas such as memory that is more pronounced than expected for their age and begins to affect their daily functioning (Petersen et al., 1999). This interest in the distinction between the normal forgetting that occurs as we age and the onset of neurocognitive disorder is motivated by a desire to both understand the progression of the cognitive changes that accompany neurocognitive disorder and to attempt early intervention. In response to this concern, DSM-5 introduced a new psychiatric disorder—*mild neurocognitive disorder*—to categorize the condition and bring it to the attention of clinicians (Ganguli et al., 2011).

This proposed distinction is consistent with some of the breakthroughs in diagnoses involving improved brain scanning and identification of biomarkers that we covered earlier in this chapter (Weiner et al., 2012). Researchers are becoming more sophisticated in their ability to identify beginning signs of neurocognitive disorder, which not only allows for early diagnosis but also can highlight for clinicians the need to track cognitive abilities over time. However, this new disorder raised concerns among some in the field (Rabins & Lyketsos, 2011).

First, the distinction between "major" and "mild" neurocognitive disorder is a difficult one to make. DSM-5 attempts to quantify the declines by tying the diagnosis to cognitive test performance in the range of 122 standard deviations below what would be expected for a person of that age (American Psychiatric Association, 2013). Below-average performance does not necessarily mean, however, that the person has declining cognitive function. That can be assessed only if performance was measured through cognitive assessment *before* the decline occurred. But it has been argued that routine cognitive testing is not typically done on adults until after some concern is raised, making conclusions about changes in functioning problematic (Frances, 2010).

A second concern is one that is relevant for a number of other disorders as well. The addition of new disorders (such as mild neurocognitive disorder as well as others, such as premenstrual mood dysphoric disorder) and the broadening of the definitions of others have some concerned that eventually most people will meet the criteria for one or more psychiatric disorders. In the case of mild neurocognitive disorder, will we be labeling people—and perhaps prescribing drugs—to those who exhibit normal forgetting related to age? As a whole, the consequences of these changes across DSM-5 are not trivial (Frances, 2010). Pharmaceutical companies are incentivized to find more customers for psychiatric drugs, and therefore expanding the number of people with a diagnosis could increase business. The legal system could be impacted with a greater number of people using "mental illness" as a mitigating factor in their defense. These issues are far from being resolved, and it is important to note that DSM-5 is a work in progress that will hopefully evolve with our expanding scientific understanding of the nature and causes of all of the maladies impacting us.

Summary

Delirium

- Delirium is a temporary state of confusion and disorientation that can be caused by brain trauma, intoxication by drugs or poisons, surgery, and a variety of other stressful conditions, especially among older adults.

Major and Mild Neurocognitive Disorders

- Neurocognitive disorder is a progressive and degenerative condition marked by gradual deterioration of a range of cognitive abilities, including memory, language, and planning, organizing, sequencing, and abstracting information.
- Mild neurocognitive disorder is a condition in which there are early signs of cognitive decline such that it begins to interfere with activities of daily living.
- Alzheimer's disease is the leading cause of neurocognitive disorder, affecting approximately 5.5 million people in the United States; there is currently no known cause or cure.
- To date, there is no effective treatment for the irreversible neurocognitive disorder caused by Alzheimer's disease, Lewy bodies, vascular disease, Parkinson's disease, Huntington's disease, and various less common conditions that produce progressive cognitive impairment. Treatment often focuses on helping patients cope with the continuing loss of cognitive skills and helping caregivers deal with the stress of caring for affected individuals.

Key Terms

delirium, 549
major neurocognitive disorder (dementia), 552
mild neurocognitive disorder, 552
agnosia, 554
facial agnosia, 554
Alzheimer's disease, 555
neurocognitive disorder due to Alzheimer's disease, 555
vascular neurocognitive disorder, 558
head trauma, 558
frontotemporal neurocognitive disorder, 559
Pick's disease, 559
traumatic brain injury (TBI), 559
neurocognitive disorder due to traumatic brain injury, 559
neurocognitive disorder due to Lewy body disease, 559
neurocognitive disorder due to Parkinson's disease, 560
Parkinson's disease, 560
human immunodeficiency virus type 1 (HIV-1), 560
neurocognitive disorder due to HIV infection, 560
aphasia, 561
Huntington's disease, 561
neurocognitive disorder due to Huntington's disease, 561
neurological disorder due to prion disease, 562
Creutzfeldt-Jakob disease, 562
substance/medication-induced neurocognitive disorder, 563
deterministic, 564
susceptibility, 564

Answers to Concept Checks

15.1

1. c; **2.** b; **3.** a; **4.** e; **5.** f; **6.** d

15.2

1. b; **2.** c; **3.** a
4. substance-induced neurocognitive disorder; **5.** vascular neurocognitive disorder; **6.** neurocognitive disorder due to Alzheimer's disease

Exploring Neurocognitive Disorders

- When the brain is damaged, the effects are irreversible, accumulating until learning, memory, or consciousness are obviously impaired.
- Neurocognitive disorders develop much later than intellectual disability and other learning disorders, which are believed to be present at birth.

TYPES OF NEUROCOGNITIVE DISORDERS

	Description	Causes (subtypes)	Treatment
Delirium	■ Impaired consciousness and cognition for several hours or days – confusion, disorientation, inability to focus ■ Most prevalent among older adults, people with AIDS, and patients on medication	■ Delirium due to a general medical condition ■ Substance-induced delirium ■ Delirium due to multiple etiologies ■ Delirium not otherwise specified	■ Pharmacological – benzodiazepines – antipsychotics ■ Psychosocial – reassurance – presence of personal objects – inclusion in treatment decisions

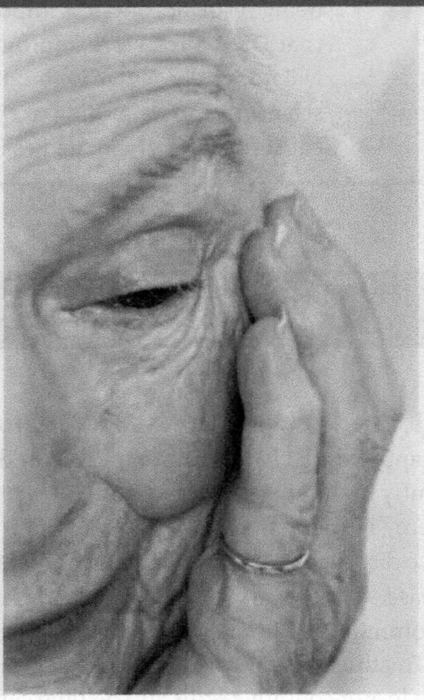

Photodisc/Getty Images

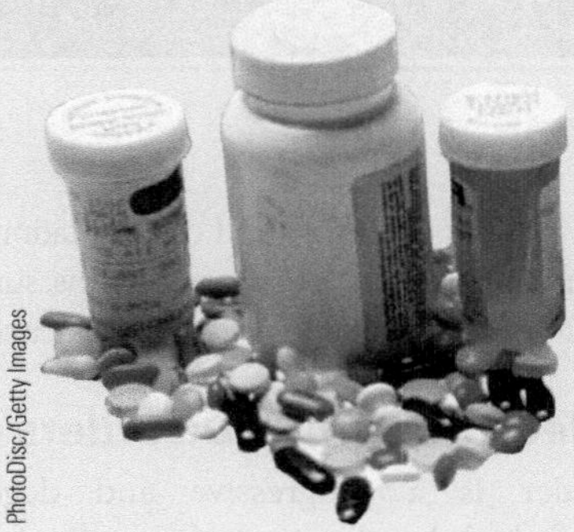

PhotoDisc/Getty Images

Major and Mild Neurocognitive Disorders

- Gradual deterioration of brain functioning that affects judgment, memory, language, and other advanced cognitive processes
- Caused by medical condition or drug abuse
- Some forms are irreversible; some are resolved by treatment of primary condition.

TYPES OF NEUROCOGNITIVE DISORDERS

	Description	Causes	Treatment
Neurocognitive Disorder Due to Alzheimer's Disease  Christian Martinez Kempin/E+/Getty Images	■ Increasing memory impairment and other multiple behavioral and cognitive deficits, affecting language, motor functioning, ability to recognize people or things, and/or planning ■ Most prevalent neurocognitive disorder ■ Subject of most research	■ Progressive brain damage, evident in neurofibrillary tangles and neuritic plaque, confirmed by autopsy but assessed by simplified mental status exam ■ Involves multiple genes	■ No cure so far, but hope lies in genetic research and amyloid protein. ■ Management may include lists, maps, and notes to help maintain orientation. ■ New medications that prevent acetylcholine breakdown and vitamin therapy delay but do not stop progression of decline.
Substance-Induced Neurocognitive Disorder 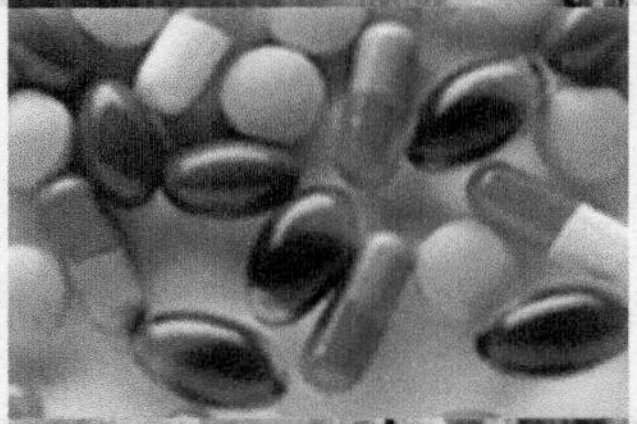 Photodisc/Getty Images	■ Caused by brain damage due to prolonged drug use, especially in combination with poor diet, as in alcohol dependency; other substances may include inhalants, and the sedative, hypnotic, and anxiolytic drugs ■ Treatment focuses on prevention.		
Vascular Neurocognitive Disorder 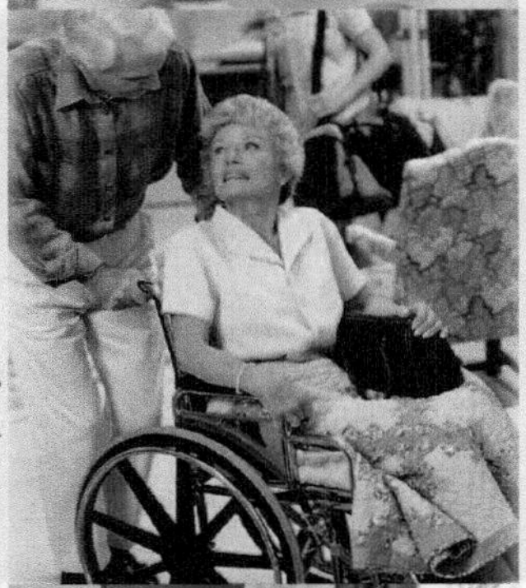 Photodisc/Getty Images	■ Permanent deterioration due to blocked or damaged blood vessels in the brain (stroke) ■ Symptoms include declines in speed of information processing and executive functioning (for example, complex decision making) and may also include problems with walking and weakness of limbs. ■ Treatment focuses on coping.		
Neurocognitive Disorders Due to Other Medical Conditions 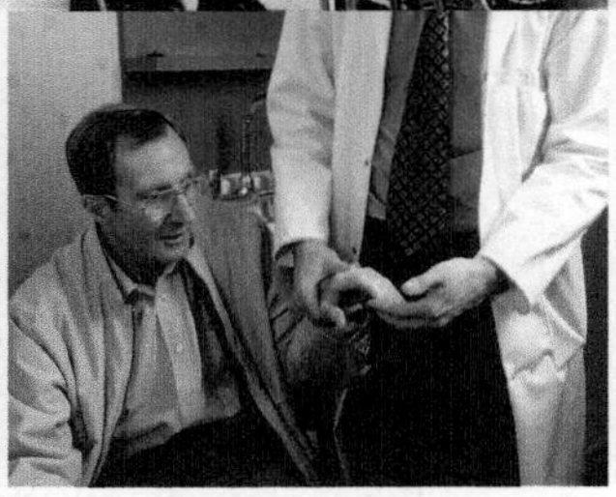 Simon Fraser / Royal Victoria Infirmary, Newcastle upon Tyne / Science Source	■ Similar in effect to other cognitive disorders, but caused by: – head trauma – Lewy bodies, HIV, Parkinson's, Huntington's, Pick's, or Creutzfeldt-Jakob disease – hydrocephalus, hypothyroidism, brain tumor, and vitamin B_{12} deficiency ■ Treatment of primary condition is sometimes possible.		

16 Mental Health Services: Legal and Ethical Issues

iStockphoto.com/Wolfgang Lienbacher

Learning Objectives

LO16.1 Compare the liberal and conservative eras as they pertain to mental health law.

LO16.2 Explain the purpose of civil commitment laws.

LO16.3 Identify the historical conditions under which a person may be involuntary committed.

LO16.4 Explain the role of transinstitutionalization as it pertains to the movement calling for a return to broader civil commitment procedures.

LO16.5 Contrast the foundations of criminal commitment as described in the M'Naghten rule with the more recent criteria established by the American Law Institute.

LO16.6 Discuss how the legal "duty to warn" standard applies to therapists, clients, and potential victims.

LO16.7 Explain the right to treatment, informed consent, and the impact of patients' mental status on the observation of these rights in mental health facilities.

Perspectives on Mental Health Law

We begin this chapter with a return to Amrit, whom we describe in Chapter 13 as having psychotic symptoms. Revisiting the case from his family's perspective reveals the complexities of mental health law and the ethical aspects of working with people who have psychological disorders.

Amrit suffered from what is known as brief psychotic disorder (see Chapter 13). Fortunately for him, this is one of the few psychotic disorders that is not chronic. What is important here is to see how the mental health system responded. Because Amrit had not hurt himself or someone else, he had to seek help on his own before the hospital would assist him, even though everyone involved realized that such action on his part was unlikely. This response by the mental health system added one more layer of helplessness to the family's already desperate emotional state. Why wouldn't the mental health facility admit Amrit, who was clearly out of touch with reality and in need of help? Why couldn't his own family authorize the mental health facility to act? What would have happened if Amrit had entered the German embassy and hurt or, worse, killed someone? Would he have gone to jail, or would he have finally received help from the mental health community? Would Amrit have been held responsible if he hurt other people while he was delusional? These are just a few of the many issues that surface when we try to balance the rights of people who have psychological disorders with the responsibilities of society to provide care.

Mental health professionals face such questions daily. They must both diagnose and treat people and consider individual and societal rights and responsibilities. As we describe how systems of ethics and legal concepts have developed, remember they change with time and with shifting societal and political perspectives on mental illness. How we treat people with psychological disorders is partly a function of how society views these people. For example, do people with mental illness need help and protection, or does society need protection from them? As public opinion about people with mental illness changes, so do the relevant laws and legal and ethical issues affect both research and practice. As you will see, the issues affecting research and practice are often complementary. For example, confidentiality is required to protect the identity of a participant in a research study and of a patient seeking help for a psychological disorder. Because people who receive mental health services often simultaneously participate in research studies, we must consider the concerns of both constituencies.

Amrit... A Family's Dilemma

As you remember, Amrit was brought to our clinic by family members because he was speaking and acting strangely. He talked incessantly about his "secret plan" to save all the starving children in the world. His family's concern intensified when Amrit said he was planning to break into the German embassy and present his plan to the German ambassador. Alarmed by his increasingly inappropriate behavior and fearing he would be hurt, the family was astounded to learn they could not force him into a psychiatric hospital. Amrit could admit himself—which was not likely, given his belief that his behaviors and beliefs were not unusual—but they had no power to admit him involuntarily unless he was in danger of doing harm to himself or others. Even if they sincerely believed some harm might be forthcoming, this wasn't sufficient reason to admit him involuntarily. The family coped with this emergency as best they could for several weeks until the most concerning of Amrit's behaviors began to diminish.

Civil Commitment

The legal system exercises significant influence over the mental health system, for better or for worse. Laws have been designed to protect people who display pathological behavior and to protect society. Often, achieving this protection is a delicate balancing act, with the scales sometimes thought to be tipped in favor of the rights of individuals and at other times in favor of society. For example, each state has **civil commitment laws** that detail when a person can be legally declared to have a mental illness and be placed in a hospital for treatment (Morris, 2020). When Amrit's family tried to have him involuntarily committed to a mental health facility, hospital officials decided that because he was not in imminent danger of hurting himself or others he could not be committed against his will. In this case, the laws protected Amrit from involuntary commitment, but they also put him and others at potential risk by not compelling him to get help.

In a now-classic book, La Fond and Durham (1992) argue that two clear trends in mental health law are evident in the recent history of the United States. According to these authors, a "liberal era" from 1960 to 1980 was characterized by a commitment to

AP Images / Sergey Ponomarev
Moch Bustomi/Anadolu Agency/Getty Images
AP Images/Leslie Brody

People with mental illness are treated differently in different cultures.

individual rights and fairness. In contrast, 1980 to the present has been a "neoconservative era" (partly in reaction to the liberal reforms of the 1960s and 1970s) that focused on majority concerns, including law and order. In the liberal era, the rights of people with mental illness dominated; in the neoconservative era, the rights of people with mental illness have been limited to provide greater protection to society.

Civil commitment laws in the United States date back to the late 19th century. Before this time, almost all people with severe mental illness were cared for by family members or the community or were left to care for themselves. An alarming trend accompanied the development of a large public hospital system devoted to treating such individuals: involuntary commitment of people for reasons unrelated to mental illness (Simon & Shuman, 2009). There were even instances in which women were committed to psychiatric hospitals by their husbands simply for holding differing personal or political views. In the 1800s, Mrs. E. P. W. Packard crusaded for better civil commitment laws after being involuntarily confined to a psychiatric hospital for 3 years because her husband felt her religious views were "dangerous to the spiritual interests of his children and the community" (Packard & Olsen, 1871; p. 11).

Criteria for Civil Commitment

Historically, states have permitted commitment when several conditions have been met: (1) The person has a "mental illness" and is in need of treatment, (2) the person is dangerous to themself or others, or (3) the person is unable to care for themself, a situation considered a "grave disability." How these conditions are interpreted has varied over the years and has always been controversial. Two types of authority permit the government to take actions that are against a citizen's will: police power and *parens patriae* ("state or country as the parent") power. Under police power, the government takes responsibility for protecting the public health, safety, and welfare and can create laws and regulations to ensure this protection. Criminal offenders are held in custody if they are a threat to society. The state applies *parens patriae* power when citizens are not likely to act in their own best interest—for example, to assume custody of children who have no living parents (Higdon, 2020). Similarly, it is used to commit individuals with severe mental illness to mental health facilities when it is believed that they might be harmed because they are unable to secure the basic necessities of life, such as food and shelter (grave disability), or because they do not recognize their need for treatment (Nunley et al., 2013). Under *parens patriae* power, the state acts as a surrogate parent, presumably in the best interests of a person who needs help.

A person in need of help can always voluntarily request admission to a mental health facility; after an evaluation by a mental health professional, a patient may be accepted for treatment. When an individual does not voluntarily seek help but others feel that treatment or protection is necessary, however, the formal process of civil commitment can be initiated. The specifics of this process differ from state to state, but it usually begins with a petition by a relative or mental health professional to a judge. The court may then request an examination to assess psychological status, ability for self-care, need for treatment, and potential for harm. The judge considers this information and decides whether commitment is appropriate. This process is similar to other legal proceedings, and the person under question has all the rights and protections provided by the law. In most states, the person can even request that a jury hear the evidence and make a determination. In all cases, the person must be notified that the civil commitment proceedings are taking place, must be present during the trial, must have representation by an attorney, and can examine the witnesses and request an independent evaluation. These safeguards are built into the civil commitment process to guarantee the rights of the person being examined and to ensure that no one is involuntarily committed to a psychiatric facility for other than legitimate reasons (Black & Andreasen, 2021).

Another route to civil commitment is being adopted by some states: court-ordered *assisted outpatient treatment (AOT)* (Yanos, O'Connor, DeLuca, Fregenti, & Reji, 2020). In this option, the person with severe mental illness agrees to receive treatment as a condition for continuing to live in the community. These AOT laws provide a balance between the individual's right to live independently and the community's concerns about safety (Yanos et al., 2020).

In emergency situations, when there is clearly immediate danger, a short-term commitment can be made without the formal proceedings required of a civil commitment. Family members or sometimes police officers certify that the person presents a "clear and present danger" to themself or to others (Black & Andreasen, 2021). Amrit's family was unsuccessful in having him admitted on an emergency basis because it was not clear that anyone was in immediate danger, only that someone might be hurt. Again, deciding what is a "clear and present danger" sometimes requires a great deal of subjective judgment from the court and from mental health professionals.

Defining Mental Illness

The concept of mental illness figures prominently in civil commitment, and it is important to understand how it is defined. **Mental illness** is a legal concept, typically meaning severe emotional or thought disturbances that negatively affect an individual's health and safety (Black & Andreasen, 2021). Each state has its own definition. For example, in New York, "'Mental illness means an affliction with a mental disease or mental condition which is manifested by a disorder or disturbance in behavior, feeling, thinking, or judgment to such an extent that the person afflicted requires care, treatment and rehabilitation" (New York Mental Hygiene Law, 1992). In contrast, in Connecticut, "'Mentally ill person' means a person who has a mental or emotional condition that has substantial adverse effects on his or her ability to function and who requires care and treatment, and specifically excludes a person who is an alcohol-dependent person or a drug-dependent person" (Connecticut General Statutes Annotated, 1992). Many states exclude cognitive disability or substance-related disorders from the definition of mental illness.

Mental illness is *not* synonymous with psychological disorder; in other words, receiving a diagnosis according to the *Diagnostic and Statistical Manual* (DSM-5) does not necessarily mean that a person's condition fits the legal definition of mental illness. Although the DSM is quite specific about criteria that must be met for diagnosis, there is considerable ambiguity about what constitutes a "mental condition" or what are "adverse effects on his or her ability to function." This allows flexibility in making decisions individually, but it also maintains the possibility of subjective impression and bias as influences on these decisions.

Dangerousness

Assessing whether someone is a danger to self or others is a critical determinant of the civil commitment process. **Dangerousness** is a particularly controversial concept to describe people with mental illness: According to popular opinion, people with a mental illness are more dangerous than those who are not (Kobau, DiIorio, Chapman, & Delvecchio, 2010; Schomerus et al., 2012). Although this conclusion is questionable, it is still widespread, partly because of sensational media reports. Such views are important to the process of civil commitment if they bias a determination of dangerousness and unfairly link it with severe mental illness.

The results of research on dangerousness and mental illness are often mixed, but evidence points to a moderately increased rate of violence among people with mental illness (Whiting & Fazel, 2020). Closer examination of this kind of research reveals that although having a mental illness generally does increase the likelihood of future violence, specific factors such as a high anger predisposition, recent stressors (such as victimization), and substance use are likely responsible for the increased risk of violence (Whiting & Fazel, 2020). It is also the presence of these risk factors that may predict the reoccurrence of perpetrated violent crimes by individual with mental illness.

Unfortunately, the widely held misperception that people with mental illness are more dangerous may differentially affect ethnic minorities (Vinkers, de Vries, van Baars, & Mulder, 2010). Black males are often perceived as dangerous, even when they don't exhibit any violent behavior, which may partly explain why Black individuals are overrepresented among those who are involuntarily committed to state psychiatric institutions (Misra et al., in press).

How do you determine whether a person is dangerous to others? How accurate are mental health professionals at predicting who will and who will not later be violent? The answers bear directly on the process of civil commitment, as well as on protection for society. If we can't accurately predict dangerousness, how can we justify involuntary commitment?

Research using functional imaging technologies reveals that our ability to "feel the pain" of other people—feeling empathetic to others in distress—involves activation of the prefrontal cortex (Escobar et al., 2014; Hillis, 2014;

KieferPix/Shutterstock.com

The government can exert *parens patriae* to protect people from hurting themselves.

Robertson et al., 2007), and injury to this area prevents people from using empathy to make moral decisions (Damasio, 2007; Decety & Skelly, 2013). This important research is now being used in court proceedings to help decide guilt or innocence (Mobbs, Lau, Jones, & Frith, 2009). Will it be argued that defendants who have psychopathy (see Chapter 12), for example, should be judged not responsible for their behavior because their inability to empathize with others has its origin in the brain? This "brain blame" will become more prominent in coming years because our definitions of insanity have not kept up with our understanding of the combined contributions of the environment and biology to mental illness and criminal behavior (Greely & Simpson, 2012).

Numerous risk assessment tools are routinely used to determine if someone is likely to be dangerous to society—including the Psychopathy Checklist-Revised (PCL-R) (Hare & Vertommen, 2003; Neumann, Johansson, & Hare, 2013), described in Chapter 12, that is used to identify persons with psychopathy. Evidence from numerous studies suggest that these tools are best at identifying persons at low risk of being violent but only marginally successful at accurately detecting who will be violent at a later point (Fazel, Singh, Doll, & Grann, 2012). Mental health professionals can identify groups of people who are at greater risk than the general population for being violent—such as having a previous history of both violence and drug or alcohol dependence—and can so advise the court. What clinicians cannot yet do is predict with certainty whether a particular person will or will not become violent.

Procedural Changes Affecting Civil Commitment

Clearly, there are significant problems with the process of civil commitment. In particular, deciding whether a person has a mental illness or is dangerous requires considerable subjective judgment, and, because of varying legal language, this determination can differ from state to state. These problems have resulted in a number of significant legal developments. We look next at how changes in civil commitment procedures have resulted in significant economic and social consequences, including an impact on one of our more important social problems: homelessness.

The Supreme Court and Civil Commitment

In 1957, the parents of Kenneth Donaldson had him committed to the Florida State Hospital for treatment of paranoid schizophrenia. Donaldson was not considered dangerous, yet, despite repeated offers of placement in a halfway house or with a friend, Dr. O'Connor, the superintendent of the hospital, refused to release him for almost 15 years, during which Donaldson received virtually no treatment (Donaldson, 1976). Donaldson successfully sued Dr. O'Connor for damages, winning $48,500. In deciding the case, the U.S. Supreme Court found that "a State cannot constitutionally confine … a non-dangerous individual who is capable of surviving safely in freedom by himself or with the help of willing and responsible family and friends" (*O'Connor v. Donaldson*, 1975).

Here, and in a subsequent decision known as *Addington v. Texas* (1979), the U.S. Supreme Court said that more than just a promise of improving quality of life is required to commit someone involuntarily. If nondangerous people with mental illness can survive in the community with the help of others, they should not be detained against their will. Needing treatment or having a grave disability was not sufficient to commit someone involuntarily with a mental illness. The effect of this decision substantially limited the government's ability to commit individuals unless they were dangerous (Black & Andreasen, 2021).

Criminalization

Because of the tightened restrictions on involuntary commitment that prevailed in the 1960s and 1970s, many people who would historically have been committed to mental health facilities for treatment were instead being handled by the criminal justice system. In other words, people with severe mental illness were now living in the community, but many were not receiving the mental health services they needed and would eventually run afoul of the legal system because of their behavior. This "criminalization" of people with mental illness was of great concern because the criminal justice system was not prepared to care for these individuals (Chaimowitz, 2012; Lamb, 2009; Lamb & Weinberger, 2009). Family members were increasingly frustrated that they could not obtain treatment for their loved ones, who were instead languishing in jail without help.

Deinstitutionalization and Homelessness

In addition to criminalization, two other trends emerged at this time, starting in the 1980s: an increase in the number of people who were homeless and **deinstitutionalization**, the movement of people with severe mental illness out of institutions (Scull, 2021). Remember that homelessness is not exclusively a problem of those with mental illness. Approximately 2 million to 3 million people will experience a night of homelessness in the United States each year, and estimates place the numbers of homeless

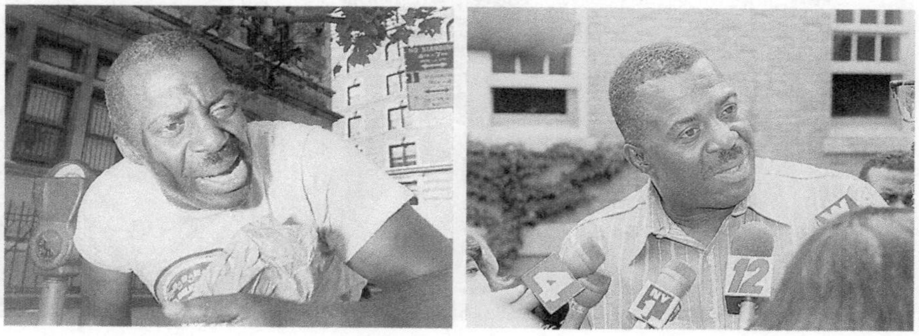

AP Images / Andrew Savulich

AP Images / Ed Bailey

Larry Hogue was involuntarily committed to a psychiatric hospital because, homeless and under the influence of drugs (left), he terrorized residents of a New York City neighborhood for years. Once off drugs (right), Hogue was able to control himself.

people at more than 400,000 on any given night (Substance Abuse and Mental Health Services Administration, 2011). The estimates of psychological disorders among those who are homeless vary, in part because of the difficulty in tracking these individuals. Best estimates suggest that diagnoses of severe mental illness (for example, schizophrenia and bipolar disorder) among homeless persons is about 30% (Substance Abuse and Mental Health Services Administration, 2011). For reasons not yet fully understood, ethnicity may also play a part in who among people with mental illness becomes homeless. In a large study in San Diego County, for example, Latino/as and Asian Americans with mental illness were less likely to become homeless, but African Americans were more likely to be homeless (Folsom et al., 2005).

Information on the characteristics of people who are homeless is important because it provides us with clues about why people become homeless, and it dispels the notion that all homeless people have mental health problems. For a time, homelessness was blamed on strict civil commitment criteria and deinstitutionalization (Scull, 2021); that is, policies to severely limit who can be involuntarily committed, the limits placed on the hospital stays of people with severe mental illness, and the concurrent closing of large psychiatric hospitals were held responsible for the substantial increase in homelessness during the 1980s. Although a sizable percentage of homeless people have mental illness, the rise in homelessness is also the result of such economic factors as increased unemployment and a shortage of low-income housing (Nooe & Patterson, 2010). Yet the perception that civil commitment restrictions and deinstitutionalization caused homelessness resulted in movements to change commitment procedures.

Reforms in civil commitment that made it more difficult to commit someone involuntarily occurred at the same time the policy of deinstitutionalization was closing large psychiatric hospitals (Black & Andreasen, 2021). Deinstitutionalization had two goals: (1) to close the large state mental hospitals and (2) to create a network of community mental health centers where the released individuals could be treated. Although the first goal appears to have been substantially accomplished, with about a 75% decrease in the number of hospitalized patients (Kiesler & Sibulkin, 1987), the essential goal of providing alternative community care appears not to have been attained. Instead, there was **transinstitutionalization**, or the movement of people with severe mental illness from large psychiatric hospitals to nursing homes or other group residences, including jails and prisons, many of which provide only marginal services (Mullan, 2021). Because of the deterioration in care for many people who had previously been served by the mental hospital system, deinstitutionalization is largely considered a failure. Although many praise the ideal of providing community care for people with severe mental illness, the support needed to provide this type of care has been severely deficient.

Reactions to Strict Commitment Procedures

Amrit's psychotic reaction and his family's travails in trying to get help occurred during the mid-1970s, a time characterized by greater concern for individual freedom than for society's rights and by the belief that people with mental illness were not properly served by being forced into treatment. Others, however, especially relatives of afflicted people, felt that by not coercing some individuals into treatment, the system was sanctioning their mental decline and placing them at grave risk of harm. The culmination of a number of factors—such as the lack of success with deinstitutionalization, the rise in homelessness, and the criminalization of people with severe mental illness—gave rise to a backlash against their perceived causes, including the strict civil commitment laws. The case of Joyce Brown captures this clash of concerns between individual freedoms for people with mental illness and society's responsibility to treat them.

This case is important because it illustrates the conflicting interests over civil commitment. Brown's family had for some time been concerned about her well-being and had tried unsuccessfully to have her involuntarily committed. Although she had never hurt anyone or tried to commit suicide, they felt that living on the streets of New York City was too hazardous, and they feared for her welfare. City officials expressed concern for Brown and others like her, especially during the dangerously cold winter, although some suspected that this was an excuse to remove people with disturbing behavior from the streets of affluent sections (Kasindorf, 1988). Brown chose not to seek treatment and resisted efforts to place her in alternative settings. At times, she could be quite articulate in making a case for her freedom of choice. Only weeks after she was released from the hospital, she was again living on the streets. Brown was involuntarily committed to a mental health facility again in early 1994 and was released at her insistence a short time later. This continued a pattern that lasted for years (Failer, 2002).

Rulings such as *O'Connor v. Donaldson* and *Addington v. Texas* argued that mental illness and dangerousness should be criteria for involuntary commitment. Because of cases like Brown's and concerns about homelessness and criminalization, however, a movement emerged calling for a return to broader civil procedures that would

Joyce Brown... Homeless but Not Helpless

During a 1988 winter emergency in New York City, Mayor Ed Koch ordered that all people who were homeless and who appeared to have a mental illness should be involuntarily committed to a mental health facility for their protection. He used the legal principle of *parens patriae* to justify this action, citing the need to protect these individuals from the cold and from themselves. One of the people who was taken off the streets, 40-year-old Joyce Brown, was picked up against her will and admitted to Bellevue Hospital, where she received a diagnosis of paranoid schizophrenia. She had been homeless for some time, swearing at people as they walked by; at one point, she adopted the name Billie Boggs after a New York television personality with whom she fantasized a relationship. Supported by the New York Civil Liberties Union, Brown contested her commitment and was released after 3 months (Tushnet, 2008).

Michal Besser / Alamy Stock Photo

People experience homelessness because of many factors, including economic conditions, mental health status, and drug use.

permit commitment not only of those who showed dangerousness to self or others but also of individuals in need of treatment and those with grave disability—and not dangerous—an opinion that continues to be shared by many today (Gordon, 2015). Groups including the National Alliance on Mental Illness, a coalition of family members of people with mental illness, argued for legal reform to make involuntary commitment easier—an emotional response to the failure to protect and treat people with mental illness. Several states in the late 1970s and early 1980s changed their civil commitment laws in an attempt to address these concerns. For example, the state of Washington revised its laws in 1979 to allow commitment of people who were judged to be in need of treatment, which produced a 91% increase in the number of involuntary commitments in the first year it was in effect (Durham & La Fond, 1985). There was essentially no change in the size of the hospital population at this time, only in the status under which patients were committed (La Fond & Durham, 1992). Whereas people were previously detained because of violence, they were now admitted under *parens patriae* powers; also, whereas most admissions had been voluntary, they were now involuntary. Hospitals began to fill up because of longer stays and repeated admissions, and they accepted only involuntary admissions; therefore, the result of easing the procedure for involuntarily committing people with mental illness was only to change the authority under which they were admitted.

The special case of sex offenders has attracted public attention in recent years, and the issue of how to treat repeat offenders is at the heart of the concerns over civil commitment. In the years between 1930 and 1960, some states passed "sexual psychopath laws" that provided hospitalization instead of incarceration, but for an indefinite period (Lussier, McCuish, & Cale, 2021). Sex offenders (rapists and pedophiles) could be civilly committed until they demonstrated that treatment was effective. However, because treatment is often unsuccessful when attempted with uncooperative clients (see Chapter 10) and because public opinion moved from a priority to treat to a priority to punish, these laws were repealed or went unused. Recent efforts have focused on incarcerating sex offenders for their crimes and, if they are judged still dangerous at the end of their sentences, civilly committing them. Such "sexual predator" laws were first enacted in 1990, and the Kansas version was upheld as constitutional by the U.S. Supreme Court (*Kansas v. Hendricks*, 1997). Confinement of this type was viewed by the court as acceptable because it was seen as treatment, even though the justices conceded that such treatment is often ineffective (Zonana & Buchanan, 2009). Some are greatly concerned that these types of laws give the government too much latitude in using civil commitment (as opposed to incarceration) just to keep certain individuals away from others in society (La Fond, 2005). However, those who are incarcerated and released from prison face many legal restrictions (such as housing) that may have negative effects by limiting rehabilitation and reintegration into society (Bonnar-Kidd, 2010).

An Overview of Civil Commitment

What should the criteria be for involuntarily committing someone with severe mental illness to a mental health facility? Should imminent danger to self or others be the only justification, or should society act as a parent and coerce people who appear to be in distress and in need of asylum or safety? How do we address the concerns of families like Amrit's who see their loved ones overcome by psychological problems? And what of our need not to be verbally harassed by people like Joyce Brown? When do these rights take precedence over the rights of an individual to be free from unwanted incarceration? It is tempting to conclude that the legal system has failed to address these issues and reacts only to the political whims of the times.

Allan Tannenbaum / Getty Images

A significant number of the homeless are individuals with mental disorders, many of whom live with their children in shelters or on the streets.

From another point of view, however, the periodic change in laws is a sign of a healthy system that responds to the limitations of previous decisions. The reactions by the Supreme Court in the 1970s to the coercive and arbitrary nature of civil commitment were as understandable as more recent attempts to make it easier to commit people in obvious need of help. As the consequences of these changes become apparent, the system responds to correct injustices. Although improvements may seem excruciatingly slow and may not always correctly address the issues in need of reform, the fact that laws can be changed should make us optimistic that the needs of individuals and of society can ultimately be addressed through the courts.

Concept Check 16.1

Check your understanding of civil commitment by filling in the blanks.

Several conditions must be met before the state is permitted to commit a person involuntarily: The person has a(n) (1) ___________ and is in need of treatment, the person is considered (2) ___________ to themselves or others, and the person is unable to care for themselves, also known as (3) ___________.

Mental illness is a(n) (4) ___________ concept, typically meaning severe emotional or thought disturbances that negatively affect an individual's health and safety, although this definition differs from state to state. When the laws about civil commitment emerged, (5) ___________ (movement of disabled individuals out of mental institutions) and (6) ___________ (movement of disabled individuals to a less restrictive facility) also occurred.

Criminal Commitment

What would have happened if Amrit had been arrested for trespassing on embassy grounds or, worse yet, if he had hurt or killed someone in his effort to present his plan for saving starving children? Would he have been held responsible for his actions, given his obvious disturbed mental state? How would a jury have responded to him when he seemed fine just several days later? If he was not responsible for his behavior then, why does he seem so normal now?

These questions are of enormous importance as we debate whether people should be held responsible for their criminal behavior despite the possible presence of mental illness. Cases such as that of Andrea Yates, who was first convicted and sentenced to life in prison for drowning her five children in a bathtub in 2001 but later found *not guilty by reason of insanity (NGRI)*, causes some to wonder whether the laws have gone too far. **Criminal commitment** is the process by which people are held because (1) they have been accused of committing a crime and are detained in a mental health facility until they can be assessed as fit or unfit to participate in legal proceedings against them or (2) they have been found not guilty of a crime by reason of insanity (Black & Andreasen, 2021).

The Insanity Defense

The purpose of our criminal justice system is to protect our lives, our liberty, and our pursuit of happiness, but not all people are punished for criminal behavior. The law recognizes that, under certain circumstances, people are not responsible for their behavior and it would be unfair and perhaps ineffective to punish them. Current views originate from a case recorded more than 150 years ago in England. Daniel M'Naghten today might receive the diagnosis of paranoid schizophrenia. He held the delusion that the English Tory party was persecuting him, and he set out to kill the British prime minister. He mistook the man's secretary for the prime minister and killed the secretary instead. In what has become known as the M'Naghten rule, the English court decreed that people are not responsible for their criminal behavior if they do not know what they are doing or if they don't know that what they are doing is wrong. This ruling was, in essence, the beginning of the *insanity defense* (see summary in Table 16.1). For more than 100 years, this rule was used to determine culpability when a person's mental state was in question.

In the intervening years, other standards have been introduced to modify the M'Naghten rule because many critics felt that simply relying on an accused person's knowledge of right or wrong was too limiting and a broader definition was needed (Devlin, 2020). Mental illness alters a person's cognitive abilities and also the person's emotional functioning, and mental health professionals believed the entire range of functioning should be taken into account when a person's responsibility was determined. One influential decision, known as the Durham rule, was initiated in 1954 by Judge David Bazelon of the Federal Circuit Court of Appeals for the District of Columbia and based on the case *Durham v. United States* (1954). The Durham rule broadened the criteria for responsibility from knowledge of right or wrong to state that the "accused is not criminally responsible if his unlawful act was the product of mental disease or mental defect" (see Table 16.1). This decision was initially hailed by mental health professionals because it allowed them to present to a judge or jury a complete picture of the person with mental illness. Unfortunately, it was soon apparent that mental health professionals did not have the expertise to assess reliably whether a person's mental illness caused the criminal behavior in question and therefore that decisions were being based on unscientific opinions (Gunn & Wheat, 2012). Although the Durham rule is no longer used, it caused a reexamination of the criteria used in the insanity defense.

An influential study of the question surrounding the definition of culpability was conducted around the same time as the Durham decision by a group of attorneys, judges, and law scholars who belonged to the American Law Institute (ALI). Their challenge was to develop criteria for determining whether a person's mental competence makes him answerable for criminal behavior. The ALI first reaffirmed the importance of distinguishing the behavior of people with mental illness from that of people without mental disorders. Its members pointed

Table 16.1 Important Factors in the Evolution of the Insanity Defense

Factor	Date	Quotation
M'Naghten rule	1843	[I]t must be clearly proved that at the time of committing the act, the party accused was labouring under such a defect of reason, from disease of the mind, as not to know the nature and quality of the act he was doing; or if he did know it, that he did not know he was doing what was wrong. (101 Cl. & F. 200, 8 Eng. Rep. 718, H.L. 1843)
Durham rule	1954	An accused is not criminally responsible if his unlawful act was the product of mental disease or mental defect. (*Durham v. United States*, 1954)
American Law Institute (ALI) rule	1962	1. A person is not responsible for criminal conduct if at the time of such conduct as a result of mental disease or defect he lacks substantial capacity either to appreciate the criminality (wrongfulness) of his conduct or to conform his conduct to the requirements of law. 2. As used in the Article, the terms "mental disease or defect" do not include an abnormality manifested only by repeated criminal or otherwise antisocial conduct. (American Law Institute, 1962)
Diminished capacity	1978	Evidence of abnormal mental condition would be admissible to affect the degree of crime for which an accused could be convicted. Specifically, those offenses requiring intent or knowledge could be reduced to lesser included offenses requiring only reckless or criminal neglect. (New York State Department of Mental Hygiene, 1978)
Insanity Defense Reform Act	1984	A person charged with a criminal offense should be found not guilty by reason of insanity if it is shown that, as a result of mental disease or mental retardation, he was unable to appreciate the wrongfulness of his conduct at the time of his offense. (American Psychiatric Association, 1983, p. 685)

Source: Reprinted, with permission, from E. Silver, C. Cirincione, & H. J. Steadman, 1994, Demythologizing inaccurate perceptions of the insanity defense, *Law and Human Behavior, 18*, 63–70. © 1994 Plenum Press.

out that the threat of punishment was unlikely to deter someone who had severe mental illness; the group's position was that these individuals should instead be treated until they improve and should then be released. (This recommendation is discussed further when we examine recent developments and criticisms of the insanity defense.) The ALI concluded that people are not responsible for their criminal behavior if, because of their mental illness, they cannot recognize the inappropriateness of their behavior or control it (American Law Institute, 1962). The criteria shown in Table 16.1, known as the ALI test, stipulate that a person must either be unable to distinguish right from wrong (as set forth in the M'Naghten rule) or be incapable of self-control to be shielded from legal consequences.

The ALI also included provisions for the concept of **diminished capacity** (see Table 16.1), which holds that people's ability to understand the nature of their behavior and therefore their criminal intent can be diminished by their mental illness. The theory of criminal intent—otherwise called *mens rea*, or having a "guilty mind"—is important legally because to convict someone of a crime, there must be proof of the physical act (*actus rea*) and the mental state (*mens rea*) of the person committing the act (Gunn & Wheat, 2012). For example, if a woman accidentally hits someone who steps in front of her car and the person subsequently dies, the woman would not be held criminally responsible. Although a person was killed, there was no criminal intent: the driver didn't deliberately hit the person and attempt murder. The diminished capacity concept proposes that a person with mental illness who commits a criminal offense may not, because of the illness, have criminal intent and therefore cannot be held responsible.

Reactions to the Insanity Defense

Judicial rulings through the 1960s and 1970s regarding criminal responsibility parallel the course of civil commitment. An effort was made to focus on the needs of people with mental illness who also broke the law, providing mental health treatment instead of punishment. The successful use of concepts such as *insanity* or *diminished capacity* in criminal cases alarmed large segments of the population, however. For instance, in 1979 a man successfully pleaded NGRI after being arrested for writing bad checks. His case was based on the testimony of an expert witness who said he suffered from pathological gambling disorder and he therefore could not distinguish right from wrong (*State v. Campanaro*, 1980). Other successful defenses were based on disorders in the DSM, such as posttraumatic stress disorder and kleptomania (Novak, 2010), and on disorders not covered in the DSM, including battered wife syndrome (Cookson, 2009).

Alex Wong / Staff / Getty Images News / Getty Images

James Brady, President Ronald Reagan's press secretary, was wounded in 1981 by a gunman attempting to assassinate the president. In 1994, Brady and his wife, Sarah, celebrated the passage of the Brady Act, which imposed stricter controls on the possession of handguns.

Without question, the case that prompted the strongest outrage against the insanity defense and the most calls for its abolition is that of John W. Hinckley Jr. (Zapf, Zottoli, & Pirelli, 2009). On March 31, 1981, as then President Ronald Reagan walked out of the Washington Hilton Hotel, Hinckley fired several shots, hitting and seriously wounding the president, a Secret Service agent, a police officer, and James Brady, the president's press secretary. In an instant, Secret Service agents tackled and disarmed Hinckley. Hinckley was obsessed with actress Jodie Foster and claimed he tried to kill the president to impress her. Hinckley was judged by a jury to be NGRI, using the ALI standard. The verdict sent shock waves throughout the country and legal community (Zapf et al., 2009). One of the many consequences of this event was that the late James Brady and his now deceased wife, Sarah, became advocates for stricter gun control laws and saw the ultimate passage of the Brady Act in 1994.

Although the insanity defense had already been criticized in the United States, about 75% of the states substantially changed their insanity defense rules after Hinckley's verdict, making it more difficult to use this defense (Simon & Shuman, 2014). As you have seen before, such impulses often are based more on emotion than on fact. Highly publicized cases—such as those of Hinckley, Charles Manson, Jeffrey Dahmer, and Ted Kaczynski—have led many people to associate mental illness with violence, thereby creating an unfavorable public perception of the insanity defense. One telephone survey study found that 91% of people who responded agreed with the statement, "judges and juries have a hard time telling whether the defendants are really sane or insane" (Hans, 1986). Almost 90% agreed the "insanity plea is a loophole that allows too many guilty people to go free." In a similar study, 90% of people agreed "the insanity plea is used too much. Too many people escape responsibilities for crimes by pleading insanity" (Pasewark & Seidenzahl, 1979). Is there hard evidence that the insanity defense is used too often?

A study of the public's impression of the insanity defense compared it with the actual use of the defense and its outcomes (Silver, Cirincione, & Steadman, 1994). As Table 16.2 shows, the public's perception that this defense is used in 37% of all felony cases is a gross overestimate; the actual figure is less than 1%. The public also overestimates how often the defense is successful, as well as how often people judged NGRI are set free. People tend to underestimate the length of hospitalization of those who are acquitted. This last issue is important: In contrast to public perceptions, the length of time a person is confined to a hospital after being judged NGRI may exceed the time the person would have spent in jail had that person been convicted of the crime (Simon & Shuman, 2014). Hinckley, for example, was a patient in St. Elizabeth's Hospital for more than 30 years until he was released in 2016. Other research shows that individuals with mental illness who are found guilty of *nonviolent* crimes can be committed more than eight times as long as those people without mental illness placed in prison (Perlin, 2000). In contrast to public perception, people with mental illness apparently do not often avoid justice as a result of being judged NGRI.

Despite sound evidence that it is not used excessively and does not result in widespread early release of dangerous individuals, major changes were made in the criteria for the insanity defense after the Hinckley verdict. Both the American Psychiatric Association (1983) and the American Bar Association (1984) recommended modifications, moving back toward M'Naghten-like definitions. Shortly afterward, Congress passed the Insanity Defense Reform Act of 1984, which incorporated these suggestions and made successful use of the insanity defense more difficult.

Table 16.2 Comparison of Public Perceptions with the Actual Occurrence of the Insanity Defense

	Public Perception (%)	Actual Occurrence (%)
Use of Insanity Defense		
Felony indictments resulting in an insanity plea	37.0	0.9
Insanity pleas resulting in acquittal	44.0	26.0
Disposition of Insanity Acquittees		
Insanity acquittees sent to a mental hospital	50.6	84.7
Insanity acquittees set free	25.6	15.3
Conditional release		11.6
Outpatient		2.6
Release		1.1
Length of Confinement of Insanity Acquittees (in months)		
All crimes	21.8	32.5
Murder		76.4

Source: Reprinted, with permission, from E. Silver, C. Cirincione, & H. J. Steadman, 1994, Demythologizing inaccurate perceptions of the insanity defense, *Law and Human Behavior, 18,* 63–70. © 1994 Plenum Press.

Another attempt at reforming the insanity plea has been to replace the NGRI verdict with a verdict of *guilty but mentally ill (GBMI)* (Bloom & Kirkorsky, in press). Although there are several versions of the GBMI verdict, the shared premise is that the consequences for a person ruled GBMI are different from those for a person who is NGRI. People found to be NGRI are not sent to prison but are evaluated at a psychiatric facility until such time as they are judged ready for release. A person determined to be no longer have a mental illness must be released. If Amrit had committed a crime and was found NGRI, because his brief psychotic disorder was quickly resolved, he would probably have been released immediately. In contrast, one version of the GBMI verdict in theory allows the system both to treat and to punish the individual. The person found guilty is given a prison term just as if there were no question of mental illness. Whether the person is incarcerated in prison or in a mental health facility is decided by legal authorities. If the person recovers from mental illness before the sentence has passed, that person can be confined in prison for the maximum length of the term. If Amrit were found GBMI under this system, he could serve a full prison sentence, even though his mental illness was resolved. This version of GBMI has been adopted by a number of states (Simon & Shuman, 2014).

Pima County Sheriff's Forensic Unit/Getty Images News/Getty Images

Jared Loughner, who shot Congresswoman Gabrielle Giffords and killed six other people, was forcibly medicated to make him fit to stand trial for his crimes. He ultimately pleaded guilty and received a sentence of life in prison without parole.

The second version of GBMI is even harsher for the mentally ill offender. Convicted individuals are imprisoned, and prison authorities may provide mental health services if they are available. The verdict itself is simply a declaration by the jury that the person was mentally ill at the time the crime was committed and does not result in differential treatment for the perpetrator. Idaho, Montana, and Utah have abandoned the insanity defense altogether and have adopted this version of GBMI ("The Evolving Insanity Defense," 2006).

As noted, the GBMI verdict was a reaction to the perceived loophole provided by the insanity defense. It has been used in several states for a number of years, and its effects have been investigated by researchers. Two studies have shown that people who receive the GBMI verdict are more likely to be imprisoned and to receive longer sentences than people pleading NGRI (Callahan, McGreevy, Cirincione, & Steadman, 1992; Keilitz, 1987). Research also indicates that individuals receiving GBMI verdicts are no more likely to receive treatment than other prisoners who have mental illness (Keilitz, 1987; Smith & Hall, 1982). Currently, the type of verdicts available (NGRI versus GBMI) depends on the laws of the particular state where the crimes were committed. Overall, some estimate that there are more than three times the number of people with severe mental illness in jails than in hospitals, pointing to the consequences of these changes in mental health laws (Torrey, Eslinger, Lamb, & Pavle, 2010). ■ Figure 16.1 illustrates how people with severe mental illness are increasingly being placed in prisons rather than in special mental health facilities. The percentage of placements in prisons is approaching rates comparable to that of those more than 150 years ago, before adequate services were available.

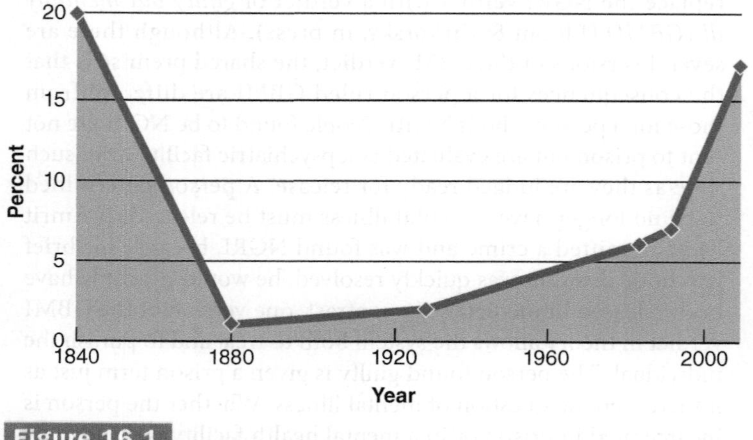

Figure 16.1

The percentage of jail and prison inmates with serious mental illness. The graph shows the increasing trend over the past few decades to incarcerate people with severe mental illness rather than to provide treatment. From E. Torrey, S. Eslinger, R. Lamb, & J. Pavle, 2010, *More mentally ill persons are in jails and prisons than hospitals: A survey of the states*, Treatment Advocacy Center, p. 13.

Therapeutic Jurisprudence

There is a built-in tension between the judicial system and the mental health system. The legal system is, by design, adversarial. In other words, it was created with prosecutors and defendants, winners and losers. In contrast, the mental health system is set up to find solutions to important psychological problems without placing blame on any parties. The goal is for both sides to "win." Fortunately, there is an increasing recognition in the legal system that a strict adversarial approach to dealing with people with mental health problems may be harmful to everyone. As a result of this change in thinking, when individuals with psychological disorders break the law, they may now find themselves in one of a variety of "problem-solving courts" (Barsky, Cucolo, & Sisti, 2020; Frailing, Alfonso, & Taylor, 2020). These courts are designed to address the unique needs of people with specific problems. For example, today in many states you can find drug treatment courts, domestic violence courts, and mental health courts, among others. Interestingly, models of problem-solving courts have their roots in the legal systems of Indigenous peoples in the United States, Canada, Australia, and New Zealand (King & Wexler, 2010).

These problem-solving courts are based on the concept of therapeutic jurisprudence—in essence, using what we know about behavior change to help people in trouble with the law. In drug treatment court, for example, a judge might be assigned to all criminal cases involving defendants who have substance use disorder. The judge would have the leeway to delay sentencing under the condition that the accused obtained and held a job for 6 months, received drug treatment during that time, and remained drug free. Similarly, a defendant in a mental health court might be helped by referrals to existing programs in the community and involvement of family members. Rather than simply trying to decide between prison and freedom, the court can serve as an instrument of social change. This evolving concept may provide effective alternatives in the criminal justice system for people with severe mental illness (Barsky et al., 2020; Frailing et al., 2020).

Society has long recognized the need to identify criminals who may not be in control of their behavior and who may not benefit from simple incarceration. The challenge is in trying to do what may be impossible: determining whether the person knew what she was doing, knew right from wrong, and could control her behavior. Mental health professionals cannot assess mental health retrospectively. An additional dilemma is the desire, on the one hand, to provide care to people with mental illness and, on the other, to treat them as responsible individuals. Finally, we must resolve the simultaneous and conflicting interests of wanting to assist people with mental illness and wanting to be protected from them. The recent trend of using problem-solving courts may be one way to address these concerns. We must reach a national consensus about the basic value of people with mental illness to decide how they should be dealt with legally. We hope the recent trend of favoring law and order over the rights of people with mental illness can be moderated to provide attention to both concerns.

Competence to Stand Trial

Before people can be tried for a criminal offense, they must be able to understand the charges against them and to assist with their own defense, criteria outlined by the U.S. Supreme Court in *Dusky v. United States* (1960). Thus, in addition to interpreting a person's state of mind during the criminal act, experts must also anticipate the person's state of mind during the subsequent legal proceedings. A person could be ruled NGRI because of his mental illness at the time of the criminal act yet still be competent to stand trial, a situation that would have occurred in Amrit's case had he committed a crime.

A person determined to be incompetent to stand trial typically loses the authority to make decisions and faces commitment. Because a trial requires a determination of **competence**, most people with obvious and severe impairments who commit crimes are never tried. Some observers estimate that for every person who receives a verdict of NGRI, 45 others are committed to a mental health facility with a diagnosis of severe mental illness (Butler, 2006). The length of stay is the time it takes the committed person to regain competence. Because this period can be drawn out, the courts have ruled that it cannot be indefinite and that, after a reasonable amount of time, the person must be found competent, set free, or committed under civil law (*Jackson v. Indiana*, 1972). Laws are often not precise in their language, and the phrase "reasonable amount of time" is open to a great deal of interpretation.

A final issue relates to the legal concept of burden of proof, the weight of evidence needed to win a case. In decisions of competence to stand trial, an important ruling placed responsibility on the defendant to provide the burden of proof—in this case, that she is incompetent to stand trial (*Medina v. California*, 1992). Again, public concern that dangerous individuals with mental illness are routinely acquitted and let loose on society after committing multiple violent offenses flies in the face of the facts. More realistically, a person with mental illness commits a nonviolent crime and receives treatment through legal actions, such as the competence proceedings.

Duty to Warn

Do mental health professionals have any responsibility for the actions of the people they serve? This is especially important when we consider the dangerous behavior exhibited by a minority of people with severe mental illness. What are the responsibilities of professionals who suspect that someone with whom they are working may hurt or even kill another person? Must they contact the appropriate authority or the person who may be harmed, or are they forbidden to discuss information disclosed during therapy sessions?

These issues were the subject of a tragic case known as *Tarasoff v. Regents of the University of California* (1974, 1976). In 1969, Prosenjit Poddar, a graduate student at the University of California, Berkeley, killed a fellow student, Tatiana Tarasoff, who had previously rejected his romantic advances. At the time of the murder, he was being seen by two therapists at the University Health Center and had received a diagnosis of paranoid schizophrenia. At his last session, Poddar hinted that he was going to kill Tarasoff. His therapist believed this threat was serious and contacted the campus police, who investigated the allegation and received assurances from Poddar that he would leave Tarasoff alone. Weeks later, after repeated attempts to contact her, Poddar shot and stabbed Tarasoff until she died.

After learning of the therapists' role in the case, Tarasoff's family sued the university, the therapists, and the university police, saying they should have warned Tarasoff that she was in danger. The court agreed, and the Tarasoff case has been used ever since as a standard for therapists concerning their **duty to warn** a client's potential victims. Related cases have further defined the role of the therapist in warning others (Felthous et al., 2020; Hall & Tardif, 2020). Courts have generally ruled that the threats must be specific. In *Thompson v. County of Alameda* (1980), the California Supreme Court ruled that a therapist does not have a duty to warn when a person makes nonspecific threats against nonspecific people. It is difficult for therapists to know their exact responsibilities for protecting third parties from their clients. Good clinical practice dictates that any time they are in doubt, they should consult with colleagues. A second opinion can be just as helpful to a therapist as to a client.

Mental Health Professionals as Expert Witnesses

Judges and juries often have to rely on **expert witnesses**, individuals who have specialized knowledge, to assist them in making decisions (Black & Andreasen, 2021). We have alluded to several instances in which mental health professionals serve in such a capacity, providing information about a person's dangerousness or ability to understand and participate in the defense. The public perceives expert witnesses ambivalently. On one hand, they see the value of persuasive expert testimony in educating a jury; on the other, they see expert witnesses who are biased and whose opinions suit the side that pays their bills (Simon & Shuman, 2009). How reliable are the judgments of mental health professionals who act as expert witnesses?

To take one example, in deciding whether someone should be civilly committed, the assessor must determine the person's potential for future violence. Research suggests that mental health professionals can make reliable predictions of dangerousness over the short term, for 2 to 20 days after the evaluation (Scott et al., 2008). They have not, however, been able to make reliable predictions of violence after longer periods (Fazel et al., 2012). It seems that the assessment tools that professionals use to assess danger may impact accuracy. Assessment tools that were designed to assess danger of violence in specific groups of patients (such as juvenile offenders) were more accurate than general assessment tools (Singh, Grann, & Fazel, 2011). A second area in which mental health professionals are often asked to provide consultation is in assigning a diagnosis. In Chapter 3, we discussed the development of systems to ensure the reliability of diagnoses.

AP Images / Don Shrubshell, Pool

Elizabeth Loftus, a psychologist at the University of California, Irvine and an expert in human memory, testifies during the pretrial hearing of former White House official Lewis "Scooter" Libby.

Recent revisions of diagnostic criteria, most notably DSM-IV-TR and DSM-5, have addressed this issue directly, thus helping clinicians make diagnoses that are generally reliable. Remember, however, that the legal definition of mental illness is not matched by a comparable disorder in DSM-5. Therefore, statements about whether someone has a "mental illness" reflect determinations made by the court, not by mental health professionals.

Mental health professionals appear to have expertise in identifying *malingering* and in assessing competence. Remember that to malinger is to fake or grossly exaggerate symptoms, usually to be absolved from blame. For example, a person might claim to have been actively hallucinating at the time of the crime and therefore not responsible. Research indicates that the Minnesota Multiphasic Personality Inventory test is mostly accurate in revealing malingering in people claiming to have serious mental illness. The examiners look for true symptoms but those that people with mental illness rarely report. Malingerers, in their rush to fake their illness, will often overreport these problems, perhaps to convince others they are mentally ill (Sellbom, Toomey, Wygant, Kucharski, & Duncan, 2010; Tarescavage, Wygant, Gervais, & Ben-Porath, 2013). Mental health professionals also appear capable of providing reliable information about a person's competence, or ability to understand and assist with a defense (Shulman, Cohen, Kirsh, Hull, & Champine, 2007). Overall, mental health professionals can provide judges and juries with reliable and useful information in certain areas (Black & Andreasen, 2021).

The research described here does not indicate how accurate expert testimony is under everyday conditions. In other words, under the right circumstances experts can make accurate determinations of the short-term risks that a person will commit an act of violence, is faking certain symptoms, or is competent to stand trial and of what diagnosis should be made. Still, other factors conspire to influence expert testimony. Personal and professional opinions that exceed the competence of the expert witness can influence what information is or is not presented, as well as how it is relayed to the court (Drogin, Commons, Gutheil, Meyer, & Norris, 2012). For instance, if the expert witness believes generally that people should not be involuntarily committed to mental health facilities, this opinion will likely influence how the witness presents clinical information in civil commitment court proceedings.

Concept Check 16.2

Check your understanding of criminal commitment by identifying the following concepts: (a) competence to stand trial, (b) diminished capacity, (c) American Law Institute rule, (d) Durham rule, (e) M'Naghten rule, (f) malingering, (g) expert witness, and (h) duty to warn.

1. The defendant does not go to trial because she is unable to understand the proceedings and assist in the defense. ________
2. The person could not distinguish between right and wrong at the time of the crime. ________
3. The person is not responsible for the crime if he is not able to appreciate the wrongfulness of behavior caused by mental disease or defect. ________
4. One of my clients threatened his mother's life during his session today. Now I must decide whether I have a(n) ________.
5. A mental disorder could lessen a person's ability to understand criminal behavior and to form criminal intent. ________
6. Dr. Z testified in court that the defendant was faking and exaggerating symptoms to evade responsibility. Dr. Z is acting as a(n) ________, and the defendant is ________.
7. The person is not criminally responsible if the crime was the result of "mental disease or mental defect." ________

Patients' Rights and Clinical Practice Guidelines

Until about 40 years ago, people in mental health facilities were accorded few rights. What treatment they received and whether they could make phone calls, send and receive mail, or have visitors were typically decided by hospital personnel who rarely consulted with the patient. Abuses of this authority, however, led to legal action and subsequent rulings by the courts concerning the rights of people in these facilities.

The Right to Treatment

One of the most fundamental rights of people in mental health facilities is the right to treatment (Dvoskin, Knoll, & Silva, 2020).

For too many and for too long, conditions were poor and treatment was lacking in numerous large mental health facilities. Starting in the early 1970s, a series of class-action lawsuits (filed on behalf of many individuals) helped establish the rights of people with mental illness and intellectual disabilities. A landmark case, *Wyatt v. Stickney* (1972), grew out of a lawsuit filed by the employees of large institutions in Alabama who were fired because of funding difficulties. The case also established, for the first time, the minimum standards that facilities had to meet in relation to the people who were hospitalized. Among the standards set by *Wyatt v. Stickney* were minimum staff–patient ratios and physical requirements, such as a certain number of showers and toilets for a given number of residents. The case also mandated that facilities make positive efforts to attain treatment goals for their patients.

Wyatt v. Stickney went further and expanded on a concept called the "least restrictive alternative," indicating that, wherever possible, people should be provided with care and treatment in the least confining and limiting environment possible. For example, the court noted the following for those with intellectual disabilities:

> Residents shall have a right to the least restrictive conditions necessary to achieve the purpose of habilitation. To this end the institution shall make every attempt to move residents from (1) more to less structured living; (2) large to smaller facilities; (3) large to smaller living units; (4) group to individual residences; (5) segregated from the community to integrated into the community; (6) dependent living to independent living. (*Wyatt v. Stickney*, 1972)

Despite this movement to secure treatment for people in mental health facilities, a gap was left as to what constituted proper treatment. The case of *Youngberg v. Romeo* (1982) reaffirmed the need to treat people in nonrestrictive settings but essentially left to professionals the decision about the type of treatment to be provided (Kelly, McBride, & Hearn, 2019). This concerned patient advocates because, historically, leaving treatment to professional judgment has not always resulted in the intended end for the people in need of help. In 1986, Congress provided a number of safeguards by passage of the Protection and Advocacy for Mentally Ill Individuals Act (Woodside & Legg, 1990), which established a series of protection and advocacy agencies in each state to investigate allegations of abuse and neglect and to act as legal advocates. This layer of protection has resulted in a balance between professional concerns and needs and rights of patients in mental health facilities.

The Right to Refuse Treatment

One of the most controversial issues in mental health today is the right of people, especially those with severe mental illness, to refuse treatment (Kelly et al., 2019). In recent times, the argument has centered on the use of antipsychotic medications. On one side of the issue are the mental health professionals who believe that, under certain circumstances, people with severe mental illness are not capable of making a decision in their own best interest and that the clinician is therefore responsible for providing treatment, despite the protestations of the affected people. On the other side, patients and their advocates argue that all people have a fundamental right to make decisions about their own treatment, even if doing so is not in their own best medical interests.

Although this controversy is not yet resolved, one court case has responded to a related question: Can people be "forced" to become competent to stand trial? This is an interesting dilemma: If people facing criminal charges are delusional or have such frequent severe hallucinations that they cannot fully participate in the legal proceedings, can they be forced against their will to take medication to reduce these symptoms, thereby making them competent to stand trial? A Supreme Court ruling, *Riggins v. Nevada* (1992), stated that, because of the potential for negative side effects (such as the involuntary motor movements associated with tardive dyskinesia), people cannot be forced to take antipsychotic medication. Other rulings, however, make allowances for involuntary medication following a *Harper* hearing (*Washington v. Harper*, 1990)—a due process hearing that allows mental health professionals to argue for the merits of medication use and the patient to provide a counterargument. This process was used to involuntarily medicate Jared Loughner—the man who eventually pleaded guilty to 19 charges of murder and attempted murder for a 2011 attack in Tucson, Arizona, in which U.S. Representative Gabrielle Giffords was severely injured and six other people were killed.

The Rights of Research Participants

Throughout this text we describe research conducted worldwide with people who have psychological disorders. We also touch briefly in Chapter 4 on the issue of the rights of these individuals. In general, people who participate in psychological research have the following rights (American Psychological Association, 2010a, 2010b):

1. The right to be informed about the purpose of the research study
2. The right to privacy
3. The right to be treated with respect and dignity
4. The right to be protected from physical and mental harm
5. The right to choose to participate or to refuse to participate without prejudice or reprisals
6. The right to anonymity in the reporting of results
7. The right to the safeguarding of their records

These rights are particularly important for people with psychological disorders who may not be able to understand them fully (Bloch & Green, 2012). One of the most important concepts in research is that those who participate must be fully informed about the risks and benefits of the study. Simple consent is not sufficient; it must be *informed consent*, or formal agreement by the subject to participate after being fully apprised of all important aspects of the study, including any possibility of harm. An important case underlines the significance of informed consent and the sometimes-gray areas that exist in applied research.

Greg Aller... Concerned about Rights

In 1988, 23-year-old Greg Aller signed a consent form agreeing to participate in a treatment study at the University of California at Los Angeles (UCLA) Neuropsychiatric Institute (Willwerth, 1993). Since the previous year, Greg had experienced vivid and frightening hallucinations and delusions about space aliens. His parents had contacted UCLA for assistance. They learned that the university was initiating a new study to evaluate people in the early stages of schizophrenia and to assess the effects of the withdrawal of medication. If Greg participated, he could receive extremely expensive drug therapy and counseling free. After taking the drug Prolixin for 3 months as part of the study, he improved dramatically; the hallucinations and delusions were gone. He was now able to enroll in college, and he made the dean's list.

Although overjoyed with the results, Greg's parents were concerned about the second phase of the study, which involved taking him off the medication. They were reassured by the researchers that this was an important and normal part of treatment for people with schizophrenia and that the potential for negative side effects of taking the drug for too long was great. They were also told the researchers would put Greg back on the medication if he grew considerably worse without it.

Toward the end of 1989, Greg was slowly taken off the drug, and he soon started having delusions about former President Ronald Reagan and space aliens. Although his deterioration was obvious to his parents, Greg did not indicate to the researchers that he needed the medication or tell them of his now-continuous hallucinations and delusions. Greg continued to deteriorate, at one point threatening to kill his parents. After several more months, Greg's parents persuaded him to ask for more medication. Although better than he was earlier, Greg has still not returned to the much-improved state he achieved following his first round of medication. •

This case highlights the conflicts that can arise when researchers attempt to study important questions in psychopathology. Administrators at the National Institutes of Health reported that the UCLA researchers did not give Greg and his family all the information about the risks of treatment and the possibility of other approaches (Aller & Aller, 1997). Critics claim that informed consent in this and similar situations are too often not fully met and that information is often altered to ensure participation. The UCLA researchers note, however, that what they did was no different from what would have happened outside the research study: They attempted to remove Greg from potentially dangerous antipsychotic medication. The controversy emerging from this case should be an added warning to researchers about their responsibilities to people who participate in their studies and their obligation to design added safeguards to protect the welfare of their study subjects. Some are now exploring methods to assess formally whether participants with mental illness fully understand the risks and benefits associated with these studies (for example, Harmell, Palmer, & Jeste, 2012; Palmer, Savla, Roesch, & Jeste, 2013).

© Mojgan B. Azimi

Greg Aller (right, with his parents) participated in a drug study at UCLA and suffered a severe relapse of psychotic symptoms when medication was withdrawn. He and his family subsequently raised the issue of informed consent for such research.

Evidence-Based Practice and Clinical Practice Guidelines

Health-care delivery systems around the world have become extremely interested in determining whether treatments commonly used for both physical and psychological disorders are effective. This concern stems partly from the greatly increased expense of health care and from the fact that much of the cost is picked up by governments around the world. As a result, governments and health-care policy makers are increasingly promoting *evidence-based practice (EBP)*: health-care practices supported by research findings demonstrating that they are effective. EBP is one of those ideas that comes along occasionally and takes the world by storm. Although some tenets of EBP have been around for decades, only in the past 20 years has EBP been formally identified as a systematic method of delivering clinical care (Institute of Medicine, 2001; Sackett, Strauss, Richardson, Rosenberg, & Haynes, 2000). In the United States, the President's New Freedom Commission on Mental Health (2003, p. 21) made the principal recommendation of its final report to advance EBPs and "expand the workforce providing evidence-based mental health services and supports." The American Psychological Association Presidential Task Force in 2006 adopted as policy a report describing EBP in psychology and encouraging wide adoption of the notion of basing principles of psychological practice on evidence (American Psychological Association, 2006).

As described throughout this book, evidence has accumulated on the effectiveness of psychological treatments for specific disorders both in research clinics and in clinics that serve the public directly (Barlow, Bullis, Comer, & Ametaj, 2013; IOM, 2015). When this evidence is put in the form of recommendations on how to treat a particular problem, these recommendations are called *clinical practice guidelines* (Hollon et al., 2014; IOM, 2011). In 1989, legislation established a new branch of the federal government called the Agency for Health Care Policy and Research. In 1999, this agency was reauthorized by Congress and renamed the Agency for Healthcare Research and Quality. The purpose of this agency is to establish uniformity in the delivery of effective health and mental health care and to communicate to practitioners, policy makers, and patients alike throughout the country the latest developments in treating certain disorders effectively. The agency is also responsible for research into improving systems for the delivery of health and mental health services. Since the passage in 2010 of legislation to provide a form of national health insurance in the United States—the Patient Protection and Affordable Care Act (ACA) or "Obamacare"—making health care more efficient and effective is more important than ever.

The government hopes to reduce costs by eliminating unnecessary or ineffective treatments and also to facilitate the utilization of effective interventions based on research evidence (IOM, 2015). In recent years, governments have allocated billions of dollars to facilitate dissemination and implementation of evidence-based psychological treatments in various health-care systems such as the Veterans Health Administration in the United States and the National Health Service in the United Kingdom (McHugh & Barlow, 2010, 2012). Treating people effectively—alleviating their pain and distress—is the most important way to reduce health-care costs because these individuals will no longer request one treatment after another in an unending search for relief. To this end, as part of the ACA, Congress enabled the Patient-Centered Outcomes Research Institute to facilitate research on which treatments for what conditions are most effective and to disseminate this information widely (Dickersin, 2010).

Anticipating the importance of this trend and the necessity that clinical practice guidelines be sound and valid, a task force of the American Psychological Association composed a template, or set, of principles for constructing and evaluating guidelines for clinical interventions for both psychological disorders and psychosocial aspects of physical disorders. These principles were published in 1995 and most recently revised in 2021 with relatively few changes (American Psychological Association, 2021).

The task force decided that clinical practice guidelines for specific disorders should be constructed on the basis of two simultaneous considerations, or axes: the clinical efficacy axis and the clinical utility axis. The **clinical efficacy axis** is a thorough consideration of the scientific evidence to determine whether the intervention in question is effective. This evidence would answer the question: Is the treatment effective when compared with an alternative treatment or with no treatment in a controlled clinical research context? In Chapter 4, we review the various research strategies used to determine whether an intervention is effective.

As you will remember, for many reasons, a treatment might seem effective when it is not. For instance, if patients improve on their own while being treated simply because of the passage of time or the natural healing process, the treatment had little to do with the improvement. It is possible that nonspecific effects of the treatment—perhaps just meeting with a caring health professional—are enough to make someone feel better without any contribution from the particular treatment technique. To determine clinical efficacy, experiments called *clinical trials* must establish whether the intervention in question is better than no therapy, better than a nonspecific therapy, or better than an alternative therapy. (The latter finding provides the highest level of evidence for a treatment's effectiveness.) Clinicians might also rely on information collected from various clinics where a large number of practitioners are treating the disorder in question. If these clinicians collect systematic data on the outcomes of their patients, they can ascertain how many are "cured," how many improve somewhat without recovering, and how many fail to respond to the intervention. Such data are referred to as *quantified clinical observations* or *clinical replication series*. Finally, a *clinical consensus* of leading experts is also a valuable source of information, although not as valuable as data from quantified clinical observations or randomized controlled trials (in which individuals are assigned randomly to a treatment or a control condition to evaluate the efficacy of the treatment).

The **clinical utility axis** is concerned with the effectiveness of the intervention in the practice setting in which it is to be applied, regardless of research evidence on its efficacy. In other words, will an intervention with proven efficacy in a research setting also be effective in the various clinical settings where the interventions are most often applied? Also, is application of the intervention in the settings where it is needed feasible and cost-effective? This axis is concerned with *external validity*—the extent to which an internally valid intervention is effective in different settings or under different circumstances from those where it was tested—and how easily it can be disseminated and implemented in those settings.

The first major issue to consider on the clinical utility axis is *feasibility*. Will patients accept the intervention and comply with its requirements, and is it relatively easy to administer? As noted in Chapter 7, electroconvulsive therapy is an effective treatment for severe depression in many cases, but it is extremely frightening to patients, many of whom refuse it. The treatment also requires sophisticated procedures and close supervision by medical personnel, usually in a hospital setting. Therefore, it is not particularly feasible and is used only as a last resort.

A second issue on the clinical utility axis is *generalizability*, which refers to the extent to which an intervention is effective with patients of differing backgrounds (ethnicity, age, or sex), as well as in different settings (inpatient, outpatient, or community) or with different therapists. Again, an intervention could be effective in a research setting with one group of patients but generalize poorly across different ethnic groups. In summary, a treatment can be highly effective as determined by the clinical efficacy axis, but unless the treatment is widely generalizable, feasible, and cost-effective, it is unlikely to be disseminated or implemented. For a summary of these two axes, see Table 16.3.

In reading the disorder chapters (Chapters 5–15 of this book), you will have noted a number of effective treatments, both psychosocial and medical. In the future, we will see a great deal of additional research to establish both the clinical efficacy and the clinical utility of various interventions for psychological disorders, and the development of ever more sophisticated clinical practice guidelines (Barlow et al., 2013; IOM, 2015). In 2010, the American Psychological Association decided to develop its own set of clinical practice guidelines on providing the best evidence-based psychological care for people with psychological disorders (Hollon et al., 2014), which continues to evolve (American Psychological Association, 2021).

In Chapter 1, we reviewed various activities that make up the role of scientist-practitioners in the mental health professions, who take a scientific approach to their clinical work to provide the most effective assessment procedures and interventions.

Table 16.3 Overview of Template for Constructing Psychological Intervention Guidelines

Clinical Efficacy (Internal Validity)	Clinical Utility (External Validity)
A. Better than alternative therapy (randomized controlled trials, or RCTs)	**A.** Feasibility
B. Better than nonspecific therapy (RCTs)	**1.** Patient acceptability (cost, pain, duration, side effects, and so on)
C. Better than no therapy (RCTs)	**2.** Patient choice in face of relatively equal efficacy
D. Quantified clinical observations	**3.** Probability of compliance
E. Clinical consensus	**4.** Ease of dissemination (number of practitioners with competence, requirements for training, opportunities for training, need for costly technologies or additional support personnel, and so on)
1. Strongly positive	**B.** Generalizability
2. Mixed	**1.** Patient characteristics
3. Strongly negative	**a.** Cultural background issues
4. Contradictory evidence	**b.** Gender issues
	c. Developmental level issues
	2. Other relevant patient characteristics
	a. Therapist characteristics
	b. Issues of robustness when applied in practice settings with different time frames, and so on
	3. Contextual factors regarding setting in which treatment is delivered
	C. Costs and benefits
	1. Costs of delivering intervention to individual and society
	2. Costs to individual and society of withholding intervention

Note: Confidence in treatment efficacy is based on both (a) absolute and relative efficacy of treatment and (b) quality and replicability of studies in which this judgment is made.

Note: Confidence in clinical utility as reflected on these three dimensions should be based on systematic and objective methods and strategies for assessing these characteristics of treatment as they are applied in actual practice. In some cases, randomized controlled trials will exist. More often, data will be in the form of quantified clinical observations (clinical replication series) or other strategies, such as health economic calculations.

Source: American Psychological Association Board of Professional Affairs Task Force on Psychological Intervention Guidelines, 1995, *Template for developing guidelines: Interventions for mental disorders and psychosocial aspects of physical disorders*, Approved by APA Council of Representatives, February 1995, American Psychological Association.

Changes in the delivery of mental health services are likely to be accompanied by considerable disruption because this is a major system that affects millions of people. But the change will also bring opportunities. Scientist-practitioners will contribute to the process of guidelines development in several ways. For example, as attempts are made to assess the clinical utility or external validity of interventions, the collected experience of thousands of mental health professionals will be immensely valuable. Most information relevant to clinical utility or external validity will be collected by these clinicians in the course of their practice. Thus, they will truly fulfill the scientist-practitioner role to the benefit of patients being treated for mental health issues.

Conclusions

Therapy and scientific progress do not occur in a vacuum. People who study and treat psychopathology are responsible not only for mastering the wealth of information we have only touched on in this book but also for understanding and appreciating their role in society and in the world. Every facet of life—from the biological to the social, political, and legal—interacts with every other facet; if we are to help people, we must appreciate this complexity.

We hope we have given you a good sense of the challenges faced by workers in the field of mental health and have spurred some of you to join us in this rewarding work.

Concept Check 16.3

Identify the following situation using one of these terms: (a) informed consent, (b) refuse treatment, (c) clinical utility, (d) clinical efficacy, and (e) reduce costs.

1. Recently, clinical practice guidelines were established on two axes. The __________ axis is a consideration of the scientific evidence to determine whether the intervention in question is effective.
2. The __________ axis is concerned with an intervention's effectiveness in the clinical setting where it will be applied, not in the research setting.
3. The clinical researcher knows the potential for harm of the participants is slight but is nevertheless careful to tell them about it and asks them whether they agree to give their __________.
4. Clinical practice guidelines are designed to safeguard clients and __________.
5. The Supreme Court ruling in *Riggins v. Nevada* helped support a patient's right to __________.

Summary

Perspectives on Mental Health Law

- Societal views of people with mental illness change with time, often as responses to perceived problems with and as intended improvements of relevant laws. According to researchers, a "liberal era" between 1960 and 1980 in the United States was characterized by a commitment to individual rights and fairness; the "neoconservative era" that followed focuses on majority concerns and on law and order.

Civil Commitment

- Civil commitment laws determine the conditions under which a person may be certified legally to have a mental illness and therefore to be placed in a hospital, sometimes in conflict with the person's own wishes.
- Historically, states have permitted commitment when several conditions have been met: (1) the person has a mental illness and is in need of treatment, (2) the person is dangerous to himself or to others, or (3) the person is unable to care for himself.
- *Mental illness* as used in legal system language is not synonymous with *psychological disorder*; each state has its own definition of mental illness, usually meant to include people with severe disturbances that negatively affect their health and safety.
- Having a mental illness does not seem to increase the likelihood of dangerousness—that is, that a person will commit violent acts in the future—although having symptoms of hallucinations and delusions does seem to indicate more risk for behaving violently.
- The combination of the lack of success with deinstitutionalization, which has resulted instead in transinstitutionalization; the rise in homelessness; and the criminalization of people with severe mental illness led to a backlash against the perceived causes of these factors, including the strict civil commitment laws.

Criminal Commitment

- Criminal commitment is the process by which people are held for one of two reasons: (1) They have been accused of committing a crime and are detained in a mental health facility until they can be determined fit or unfit to participate in legal proceedings against them, or (2) they have been found not guilty of a crime by reason of insanity.
- The insanity defense is defined by a number of legal rulings: The M'Naghten rule states that people are not responsible for criminal behavior if they do not know what they are doing or if they do know and they don't know it is wrong. The Durham rule broadened the criteria for responsibility from knowledge of right or wrong to the presence of a "mental disease or defect." The American Law Institute criteria concluded that people were not responsible for their criminal behavior if, because of their mental illness, they lacked either the cognitive ability to recognize the inappropriateness of their behavior or the ability to control their behavior.
- The concept of diminished capacity holds that people's ability to understand the nature of their behavior and therefore their criminal intent could be lessened by their mental illness.
- A determination of competence must be made before an individual can be tried for a criminal offense: To stand trial, people must be competent—able to understand the charges against them and to assist with their own defense.
- Duty to warn is a standard that sets forth the responsibility of the therapist to warn potential victims that a client may attempt to hurt or kill them.
- Individuals who have specialized knowledge and who assist judges and juries in making decisions, especially about such issues as competence and malingering, are called expert witnesses.

Patients' Rights and Clinical Practice Guidelines

- One of the more fundamental rights of patients in mental health facilities is their right to treatment; that is, they have a legal right to some sort of ongoing effort to both define and strive toward treatment goals. By contrast, a great deal of controversy exists over whether all patients are capable of making a decision to refuse treatment. This is an especially difficult dilemma in the case of antipsychotic medications that may improve patients' symptoms but bring with them severe negative side effects.
- Participants who are enrolled in any research study must be fully informed of the risks and benefits and formally give their informed consent to indicate they have been fully informed.
- Clinical practice guidelines can play a major role in providing information about types of interventions that are likely to be effective for a specific disorder, thereby setting the stage for evidence-based practice. Critical to such a determination are measures of clinical efficacy (internal validity) and clinical utility (external validity); in other words, the former is a measure of whether a treatment works, and the latter is a measure of whether the treatment is effective in a variety of settings and can be implemented in those settings.

Key Terms

civil commitment laws, 575
mental illness, 577
dangerousness, 577
deinstitutionalization, 578
transinstitutionalization, 579
criminal commitment, 581
diminished capacity, 582
competence, 585
duty to warn, 585
expert witnesses, 585
clinical efficacy axis, 589
clinical utility axis, 589

Answers to Concept Checks

16.1

1. mental disorder; **2.** dangerous; **3.** grave disability; **4.** legal; **5.** deinstitutionalization; **6.** transinstitutionalization

16.2

1. a; **2.** e; **3.** c; **4.** h; **5.** b; **6.** g, f; **7.** d

16.3

1. d; **2.** c; **3.** a; **4.** e; **5.** b

Appendix

A DSM-5 Classifications

Neurodevelopmental Disorders

Intellectual Disabilities

Intellectual Disability (Intellectual Developmental Disorder)/ Global Developmental Delay/Unspecified Intellectual Disability (Intellectual Developmental Disorder)

Communication Disorders

Language Disorder/Speech Sound Disorder/Childhood-Onset Fluency Disorder (Stuttering)/Social (Pragmatic) Communication Disorder/Unspecified Communication Disorder

Autism Spectrum Disorder

Autism Spectrum Disorder

Attention-Deficit/Hyperactivity Disorder

Attention-Deficit/Hyperactivity Disorder/Other Specified Attention-Deficit/Hyperactivity Disorder/Unspecified Attention-Deficit/Hyperactivity Disorder

Specific Learning Disorder

Motor Disorders

Developmental Coordination Disorder/Stereotypic Movement Disorder

Tic Disorders

Tourette's Disorder/Persistent (Chronic) Motor or Vocal Tic Disorder/Provisional Tic Disorder/Other Specified Tic Disorder/Unspecific Tic Disorder

Other Neurodevelopmental Disorders

Other Specified Neurodevelopmental Disorder/Unspecified Neurodevelopmental Disorder

Schizophrenia Spectrum and Other Psychotic Disorders

Schizotypal (Personality) Disorder
Delusional Disorder
Brief Psychotic Disorder
Schizophreniform Disorder
Schizophrenia
Schizoaffective Disorder
Substance/Medication-Induced Psychotic Disorder
Psychotic Disorder Due to Another Medical Condition
Catatonia Associated with Another Mental Disorder
Catatonic Disorder Due to Another Medical Condition
Unspecified Catatonia
Other Specified Schizophrenia Spectrum and Other Psychotic Disorder
Unspecified Schizophrenia Spectrum and Other Psychotic Disorder

Bipolar and Related Disorders

Bipolar I Disorder/Bipolar II Disorder/Cyclothymic Disorder/ Substance/Medication-Induced Bipolar and Related Disorder/ Bipolar and Related Disorder Due to Another Medical Condition/Other Specified Bipolar and Related Disorder/ Unspecified Bipolar and Related Disorder

Depressive Disorders

Disruptive Mood Dysregulation Disorder/Major Depressive Disorder/Persistent Depressive Disorder (Dysthymia)/ Premenstrual Dysphoric Disorder/Substance/Medication-Induced Depressive Disorder/Depressive Disorder Due to Another Medical Condition/Other Specified Depressive Disorder/Unspecified Depressive Disorder

Anxiety Disorders

Separation Anxiety Disorder/Selective Mutism/Specific Phobia/ Social Anxiety Disorder (Social Phobia)/Panic Disorder/Panic Attack Specifier/Agoraphobia/Generalized Anxiety Disorder/ Substance/Medication-Induced Anxiety Disorder/Anxiety Disorder Due to Another Medical Condition/Other Specified Anxiety Disorder/Unspecified Anxiety Disorder

Obsessive-Compulsive and Related Disorders

Obsessive-Compulsive Disorder/Body Dysmorphic Disorder/ Hoarding Disorder/Trichotillomania (Hair-Pulling Disorder)/ Excoriation (Skin-Picking) Disorder/Substance/Medication-Induced Obsessive-Compulsive and Related Disorder/ Obsessive-Compulsive and Related Disorder Due to Another Medical Condition/Other Specified Obsessive-Compulsive and Related Disorder/Unspecified Obsessive-Compulsive and Related Disorder

Trauma- and Stressor-Related Disorders

Reactive Attachment Disorder/Disinhibited Social Engagement Disorder/Posttraumatic Stress Disorder (includes Posttraumatic Stress Disorder for Children 6 Years and

Younger)/Acute Stress Disorder/Adjustment Disorders/Prolonged Grief Disorder/Other Specified Trauma- and Stressor-Related Disorder/Unspecified Trauma- and Stressor-Related Disorder

Dissociative Disorders

Dissociative Identity Disorder/Dissociative Amnesia/Depersonalization/Derealization Disorder/Other Specified Dissociative Disorder/Unspecified Dissociative Disorder

Somatic Symptom and Related Disorders

Somatic Symptom Disorder/Illness Anxiety Disorder/Conversion Disorder (Functional Neurological Symptom Disorder)/Psychological Factors Affecting Other Medical Conditions/Factitious Disorder (includes Factitious Disorder Imposed on Self, Factitious Disorder Imposed on Another)/Other Specified Somatic Symptom and Related Disorder/Unspecified Somatic Symptoms and Related Disorder

Feeding and Eating Disorders

Pica/Rumination Disorder/Avoidant/Restrictive Food Intake Disorder/Anorexia Nervosa (Restricting type, Binge-eating/Purging type)/Bulimia Nervosa/Binge-Eating Disorder/Other Specified Feeding or Eating Disorder/Unspecified Feeding or Eating Disorder

Elimination Disorders

Enuresis/Encopresis/Other Specified Elimination Disorder/Unspecified Elimination Disorder

Sleep–Wake Disorders

Insomnia Disorder

Hypersomnolence Disorder/Narcolepsy

Breathing-Related Sleep Disorders

Obstructive Sleep Apnea Hypopnea/Central Sleep Apnea/Sleep-Related Hypoventilation/Circadian Rhythm Sleep–Wake Disorders

Parasomnias

Nonrapid Eye Movement Sleep Arousal Disorders/Nightmare Disorder/Rapid Eye Movement Sleep Behavior Disorder/Restless Legs Syndrome/Substance/Medication-Induced Sleep Disorder/Other Specified Insomnia Disorder/Unspecified Insomnia Disorder/Other Specified Hypersomnolence Disorder/Unspecified Hypersomnolence Disorder/Other Specified Sleep–Wake Disorder/Unspecified Sleep–Wake Disorder

Sexual Dysfunctions

Delayed Ejaculation/Erectile Disorder/Female Orgasmic Disorder/Female Sexual Interest/Arousal Disorder/Genito-Pelvic Pain/Penetration Disorder/Male Hypoactive Sexual Desire Disorder/Premature (Early) Ejaculation/Substance/Medication-Induced Sexual Dysfunction/Other Specified Sexual Dysfunction/Unspecified Sexual Dysfunction

Gender Dysphoria

Gender Dysphoria/Other Specified Gender Dysphoria/Unspecified Gender Dysphoria

Disruptive, Impulse-Control, and Conduct Disorders

Oppositional Defiant Disorder/Intermittent Explosive Disorder/Conduct Disorder/Antisocial Personality Disorder/Pyromania/Kleptomania/Other Specified Disruptive, Impulse-Control, and Conduct Disorder/Unspecified Disruptive, Impulse-Control, and Conduct Disorder

Substance-Related and Addictive Disorders

Substance-Related Disorders

Alcohol-Related Disorders: Alcohol Use Disorder/Alcohol Intoxication/Alcohol Withdrawal/Other Alcohol-Induced Disorders/Unspecified Alcohol-Related Disorder

Caffeine-Related Disorders: Caffeine Intoxication/Caffeine Withdrawal/Other Caffeine-Induced Disorders/Unspecified Caffeine-Related Disorder

Cannabis-Related Disorders: Cannabis Use Disorder/Cannabis Intoxication/Cannabis Withdrawal/Other Cannabis-Induced Disorders/Unspecified Cannabis-Related Disorder

Hallucinogen-Related Disorders: Phencyclidine Use Disorders/Other Hallucinogen Use Disorder/Phencyclidine Intoxication/Other Hallucinogen Intoxication/Hallucinogen Persisting Perception Disorder/Other Phencyclidine-Induced Disorders/Other Hallucinogen-Induced Disorders/Unspecified Phencyclidine-Related Disorders/Unspecified Hallucinogen-Related Disorders

Inhalant-Related Disorders: Inhalant Use Disorder/Inhalant Intoxication/Other Inhalant-Induced Disorders/Unspecified Inhalant-Related Disorders

Opioid-Related Disorders: Opioid Use Disorder/Opioid Intoxication/Opioid Withdrawal/Other Opioid-Induced Disorders/Unspecified Opioid-Related Disorder

Sedative-, Hypnotic-, or Anxiolytic-Related Disorders: Sedative, Hypnotic, or Anxiolytic Use Disorder/Sedative, Hypnotic, or Anxiolytic Intoxication/Sedative, Hypnotic, or Anxiolytic Withdrawal/Other Sedative-, Hypnotic-, or Anxiolytic-Induced Disorders/Unspecified Sedative-, Hypnotic-, or Anxiolytic-Related Disorder

Stimulant-Related Disorders: Stimulant Use Disorder/Stimulant Intoxication/Stimulant Withdrawal/Other Stimulant-Induced Disorders/Unspecified Stimulant-Related Disorder

Tobacco-Related Disorders: Tobacco Use Disorder/Tobacco Withdrawal/Other Tobacco-Induced Disorders/Unspecified Tobacco-Related Disorder

Other (or Unknown) Substance-Related Disorders: Other (or Unknown) Substance Use Disorder/Other (or Unknown) Substance Intoxication/Other (or Unknown) Substance Withdrawal/Other (or Unknown) Substance-Induced Disorders/Unspecified Other (or Unknown) Substance-Related Disorder

Non-Substance-Related Disorders

Gambling Disorder

Neurocognitive Disorders

Delirium

Major and Mild Neurocognitive Disorders

Major or Mild Neurocognitive Disorder Due to Alzheimer's Disease
Major or Mild Frontotemporal Neurocognitive Disorder
Major or Mild Neurocognitive Disorder with Lewy Bodies
Major or Mild Vascular Neurocognitive Disorder
Major or Mild Neurocognitive Disorder Due to Traumatic Brain Injury
Substance/Medication-Induced Major or Mild Neurocognitive Disorder
Major or Mild Neurocognitive Disorder Due to HIV Infection
Major or Mild Neurocognitive Disorder Due to Prion Disease
Major or Mild Neurocognitive Disorder Due to Parkinson's Disease
Major or Mild Neurocognitive Disorder Due to Huntington's Disease
Major or Mild Neurocognitive Disorder Due to Another Medical Condition
Major and Mild Neurocognitive Disorders Due to Multiple Etiologies
Unspecified Neurocognitive Disorder

Personality Disorders

Cluster A Personality Disorders

Paranoid Personality Disorder/Schizoid Personality Disorder/Schizotypal Personality Disorder

Cluster B Personality Disorders

Antisocial Personality Disorder/Borderline Personality Disorder/Histrionic Personality Disorder/Narcissistic Personality Disorder

Cluster C Personality Disorders

Avoidant Personality Disorder/Dependent Personality Disorder/Obsessive-Compulsive Personality Disorder

Other Personality Disorders

Personality Change Due to Another Medical Condition/Other Specified Personality Disorder/Unspecified Personality Disorder

Paraphilic Disorders

Voyeuristic Disorder/Exhibitionist Disorder/Frotteuristic Disorder/Sexual Masochism Disorder/Sexual Sadism Disorder/Pedophilic Disorder/Fetishistic Disorder/Transvestic Disorder/Other Specified Paraphilic Disorder/Unspecified Paraphilic Disorder

Other Mental Disorders

Other Specified Mental Disorder Due to Another Medical Condition/Unspecified Mental Disorder Due to Another Medical Condition/Other Specified Mental Disorder/Unspecified Mental Disorder

Medication-Induced Movement Disorders and Other Adverse Effects of Medication

Neuroleptic-Induced Parkinsonism/Other Medication-Induced Parkinsonism/Neuroleptic Malignant Syndrome/Medication-Induced Acute Dystonia/Medication-Induced Acute Akathisia/Tardive Dyskinesia/Tardive Dystonia/Tardive Akathisia/Medication-Induced Postural Tremor/Other Medication-Induced Movement Disorder/Antidepressant Discontinuation Syndrome/Other Adverse Effect of Medication

Other Conditions That May Be a Focus of Clinical Attention

Relational Problems

Problems Related to Family Upbringing
Other Problems Related to Primary Support Group

Abuse and Neglect

Child Maltreatment and Neglect Problems
Adult Maltreatment and Neglect Problems

Educational and Occupational Problems

Educational Problems
Occupational Problems

Housing and Economic Problems

Housing Problems
Economic Problems

Other Problems Related to the Social Environment

Problems Related to Crime or Interaction with the Legal System

Other Health Service Encounters for Counseling and Medical Advice

Problems Related to Other Psychosocial, Personal, and Environment Circumstances

Other Circumstances of Personal History

Problems Related to Access to Medical and Other Health Care
Nonadherence to Medical Treatment

Appendix B

DSM-5 Disorders for Further Study

The DSM-5 Task Force judged that these disorders do not currently have sufficient supporting data for inclusion in DSM-5 and therefore require further study. In fact, only a few of these proposed disorders will ultimately meet criteria, and others will be excluded from further consideration. Many of the more interesting disorders are discussed in one or more appropriate chapters.

Attenuated Psychosis Syndrome

Key features include delusions, hallucinations, or disorganized speech that distresses and disables the individual; the symptoms are like psychosis but not extreme enough to be considered a full psychotic disorder.

Depressive Episodes with Short-Duration Hypomania

Key features of this disorder are depressive episodes and episodes resembling hypomanic episodes but having a shorter duration (at least 2 days but below the 4-day minimum for hypomanic episodes).

Caffeine Use Disorder

Key features of this disorder are constant caffeine use and an inability to control use.

Internet Gaming Disorder

Key features of this disorder are the fixation on internet games and continually playing them, at the expense of school, work, and/or social interactions.

Neurobehavioral Disorder Associated with Prenatal Alcohol Exposure

The key feature is diminished behavioral, cognitive, or adaptive functioning due to prenatal alcohol exposure.

Suicidal Behavior Disorder

Key feature is a suicide attempt within the past 2 years that is not related to confusion or delirium.

Nonsuicidal Self-Injury

Key feature is repeated, yet nonserious, self-inflicted bodily damage. The individual engages in these acts due to interpersonal problems, negative feelings, or uncontrollable and/or intense thoughts about the act of injuring themselves.

Source: American Psychiatric Association. (2013). *Diagnostic and statistical manual of mental disorders* (5th ed.). Arlington, VA: American Psychiatric Association.

Glossary

Note: Many familiar words have specialized meanings and usage in psychology. A number of these, used in the text, are defined here.

abnormal behavior Psychological dysfunction within an individual that is associated with distress or impairment in functioning and a response that is not typical or culturally expected.

actigraph Small electronic device that is worn on the wrist like a watch and records body movements. This device can be used to record sleep–wake cycles.

action potentials Short periods of electrical activity at the membrane of a neuron, responsible for the transmission of signals within the neuron.

acute grief Grief occurring in the initial period after loss. Includes feelings of longing, yearning and sadness as well as anxiety, anger or guilt. Characterized by intense preoccupation with thoughts about the person who died and difficulty concentrating on other matters.

acute pain Pain that typically follows an injury and disappears once the injury heals or is effectively treated.

acute stress disorder Severe reaction immediately following a terrifying event, often including amnesia about the event, emotional numbing, and **derealization.** If symptoms persist beyond one month, victims are diagnosed with **posttraumatic stress disorder.**

adjustment disorders Clinically significant emotional and behavioral symptoms in response to one or more specific stressors.

adoption studies In genetics research, the study of first-degree relatives reared in different families and environments. If they share common characteristics, such as a disorder, this finding suggests that those characteristics have a genetic component.

affect Conscious, subjective aspect of an **emotion** that accompanies an action at a given time.

agnosia Inability to recognize and name objects; may be a symptom of **major neurocognitive disorder** or other brain disorders.

agonist Chemical substance that effectively increases the activity of a **neurotransmitter** by imitating its effects.

agonist substitution Replacement of a drug on which a person is dependent with one that has a similar chemical makeup, an **agonist.** Used as a treatment for **substance dependence.**

agoraphobia Anxiety disorder characterized by anxiety about being in places or situations from which escape might be difficult in the event of panic symptoms or other unpleasant physical symptoms (e.g., incontinence).

AIDS-related complex (ARC) Group of minor health problems such as weight loss, fever, and night sweats that appears after HIV infection but before development of full-blown AIDS.

alcohol By-product of the fermentation of yeasts, sugar, and water; the most commonly used and abused **depressant** substance.

alcohol dehydrogenase (ADH) Enzyme that helps humans metabolize **alcohol.** Different levels of its subtypes may account for different susceptibilities to disorders such as **fetal alcohol syndrome.**

alcohol-related disorders Cognitive, biological, behavioral, and social problems associated with **alcohol** use and abuse.

alcohol use disorder The misuse of **alcohol** to alter the way users think, feel, and behave.

alogia Deficiency in the amount or content of speech, a disturbance often seen in people with **schizophrenia.**

alters Shorthand term for alter egos, the different personalities or identities in **dissociative identity disorder.**

Alzheimer's disease "Strange disease of the cerebral cortex" that causes an "atypical form of senile dementia," discovered in 1906 by German psychiatrist Alois Alzheimer.

amniocentesis Prenatal medical procedure that allows the detection of abnormalities (for example, **Down syndrome**) in the developing fetus. It involves removal and analysis of amniotic fluid from the mother.

amphetamine A **stimulant** medication used to treat hypersomnia by keeping the person awake during the day, and to treat **narcolepsy,** including sudden onset episodes, by suppressing **rapid eye movement sleep.**

amphetamine use disorders Severe intoxication or overdose through the use of amphetamines, including significant behavioral impairments and physiological symptoms.

analog model Approach to research that employs subjects who are similar to clinical clients, allowing replication of a clinical problem under controlled conditions.

anhedonia Inability to experience pleasure, associated with some **mood** and schizophrenic disorders.

animal phobia Unreasonable, enduring **fear** of animals or insects that usually develops early in life.

anorexia nervosa Eating disorder characterized by recurrent food refusal, leading to dangerously low body weight.

antagonist In **neuroscience,** a chemical substance that decreases or blocks the effects of a **neurotransmitter.**

antagonist drugs Medications that block or counteract the effects of psychoactive drugs.

antigens Foreign materials that enter the body, including bacteria and parasites.

antisocial personality disorder Cluster B (dramatic, emotional, or erratic) **personality disorder** involving a pervasive pattern of disregard for and violation of the rights of others.

anxiety A **mood** state characterized by marked negative affect and bodily symptoms of tension in which a person apprehensively anticipates future danger or misfortune. Anxiety may involve feelings, behaviors, and physiological responses.

aphasia Impairment or loss of language skills resulting from brain damage caused by **stroke, Alzheimer's disease,** or other illness or trauma.

apnea See **sleep apnea.**

association studies Research strategies for comparing **genetic markers** in groups of people with and without a particular disorder.

associative splitting Separation among basic functions of human personality (for example, cognition, **emotion,** and perception) seen by some as the defining characteristic of **schizophrenia.**

attachment disorders Developmentally inappropriate behaviors in which a child is unable or unwilling to form normal attachment relationships with caregiving adults.

attention deficit/hyperactivity disorder (ADHD) Developmental disorder featuring maladaptive levels of inattention, excessive activity, and impulsiveness.

attenuated psychosis syndrome Disorder involving the onset of psychotic symptoms such as hallucinations and delusions, which puts a person at high risk for schizophrenia; designated for further study by *DSM-5*.

autism spectrum disorder (autism) A **neurodevelopmental disorder** characterized by significant impairment in social interactions and communication and restricted patterns of behavior, interest, and activity.

autoimmune disease Condition in which the body's **immune system** attacks healthy tissue rather than **antigens.**

avoidant personality disorder Cluster C (anxious or fearful) **personality disorder** featuring a pervasive pattern of social inhibition, feelings of inadequacy, and hypersensitivity to criticism.

avoidant/restrictive food intake disorder (ARFID) Type of eating disorder where people limit their food intake not because they are concerned about weight or body shape but because they are not interested in eating or food or because they avoid certain sensory characteristics or consequences of food or eating.

avolition *Apathy,* or the inability to initiate or persist in important activities.

barbiturates Sedative (and addictive) drugs including Amytal, Seconal, and Nembutal that are used as sleep aids.

bariatric surgery Surgical approach to extreme **obesity,** usually accomplished by stapling the stomach to create a small stomach pouch or bypassing the stomach through gastric bypass surgery.

baseline Measured rate of a behavior before introduction of an intervention that allows comparison and assessment of the effects of the intervention.

behavior therapy Array of therapy methods based on the principles of behavioral and **cognitive science,** as well as principles of learning as applied to clinical problems. It considers specific behaviors rather than inferred conflicts as legitimate targets for change.

behavioral assessment Measuring, observing, and systematically evaluating (rather than inferring) the client's thoughts, feelings, and behavior in the actual problem situation or context.

behavioral inhibition system (BIS) Brain circuit in the limbic system that responds to threat signals by inhibiting activity and causing **anxiety.**

behavioral medicine Interdisciplinary approach applying behavioral science to the prevention, **diagnosis,** and treatment of medical problems.

behavioral model Explanation of human behavior, including dysfunction, based on principles of learning and adaptation derived from experimental psychology.

behaviorism Explanation of human behavior, including dysfunction, based on principles of learning and adaptation derived from experimental psychology.

benzodiazepines Antianxiety drugs including Valium, Xanax, Dalmane, and Halcion also used to treat insomnia. Effective against **anxiety** (and, at high potency, panic disorder), they show some side effects, such as some cognitive and motor impairment, and may result in **substance dependence.** Relapse rates are extremely high when the drug is discontinued.

binge Relatively brief episode of uncontrolled, excessive consumption, usually of food or **alcohol.**

binge-eating disorder (BED) Pattern of eating involving distress-inducing **binges** not followed by purging behaviors; being considered as a new *DSM* diagnostic category.

biofeedback Use of physiological monitoring equipment to make individuals aware of their own bodily functions, such as blood pressure or brain waves, that they cannot normally access, with the purpose of controlling these functions.

bipolar I disorder Alternation of **major depressive episodes** with full manic episodes.

bipolar II disorder Alternation of **major depressive episodes** with **hypomanic episodes** (not full manic episodes).

blood–injection–injury phobia Unreasonable **fear** and avoidance of exposure to blood, injury, or the possibility of an injection. Victims experience fainting and a drop in blood pressure.

body dysmorphic disorder (BDD) Disorder featuring a disruptive preoccupation with some imagined defect in appearance ("imagined ugliness"). Now classified among obsessive-compulsive and related disorders; previously grouped with DSM-IV somatoform disorders.

borderline personality disorder Cluster B (dramatic, emotional, or erratic) **personality disorder** involving a pervasive pattern of instability of interpersonal relationships, self-image, affects, and control over impulses.

brain circuits The **neurotransmitter** currents or neural pathways in the brain.

brain-gut connection The influence of the gut bacteria on physical and mental health.

breathing-related sleep disorders Sleep disruption leading to excessive sleepiness or insomnia, caused by a breathing problem such as interrupted **(sleep apnea)** or labored (hypoventilation) breathing.

brief psychotic disorder Psychotic disturbance involving **delusions, hallucinations,** or **disorganized speech** or behavior but lasting less than 1 month; often occurs in reaction to a stressor.

bulimia nervosa Eating disorder involving recurrent episodes of uncontrolled excessive **(binge)** eating followed by compensatory actions to remove the food (for example, deliberate vomiting, laxative abuse, and excessive exercise).

caffeine use disorders Cognitive, biological, behavioral, and social problems associated with the use and abuse of caffeine.

cancer Category of often-fatal medical conditions involving abnormal cell growth and malignancy.

cannabis See **marijuana.**

cannabis (*Cannabis sativa*) (marijuana) The dried parts of the cannabis or hemp plant.

cannabis use disorders Problematic pattern of cannabis use leading to clinically significant impairment or distress.

cardiovascular disease Afflictions in the mechanisms, including the heart, blood vessels, and their controllers, responsible for transporting blood to the body's tissues and organs. Psychological factors may play important roles in such diseases and their treatments.

case study method Research procedure in which a single person or small group is studied in detail. The method does not allow conclusions about cause-and-effect relationships, and findings can be generalized only with great caution (contrast with **single-case experimental design**).

castration anxiety In **psychoanalysis,** the **fear** in young boys that they will be mutilated genitally because of their lust for their mothers.

catalepsy Motor movement disturbance seen in people with some psychoses and **mood disorders** in which body postures are waxy and can be "sculpted" to remain fixed for long periods.

catatonia Disorder of movement involving immobility or excited agitation. Sometimes accompanies psychotic disorders or mood disorders.

catatonic immobility Disturbance of motor behavior in which the person remains motionless, sometimes in an awkward posture, for extended periods.

catharsis Rapid or sudden release of emotional tension thought to be an important factor in psychoanalytic therapy.

childhood disintegrative disorder A **pervasive developmental disorder** involving severe regression in language, adaptive behavior, and motor skills after a 2- to 4-year period of normal development.

childhood-onset speech fluency disorder (stuttering) Repetitions of words or parts of words, as well as prolongations of speech sounds.

chorionic villus sampling (CVS) A genetic test conducted during early pregnancy that samples cells found in the placenta (chorionic villi) and assesses possible genetic or chromosomal problems in the fetus.

chronic fatigue syndrome (CFS) Incapacitating exhaustion following only minimal exertion, accompanied by fever, headaches, muscle and joint pain, depression, and **anxiety.**

chronic pain Enduring pain that does not decrease over time; may occur in muscles, joints, and the lower back, and may be caused by enlarged blood vessels or degenerating or cancerous tissue. Other significant factors are social and psychological.

chronotype The tendency of the body to prefer the morning or evening, which is regulated by the body's circadian clock, genetic variations in the clock genes, and the environment.

circadian rhythm sleep disorders Sleep disturbances resulting in sleepiness or insomnia, caused by the body's inability to synchronize its sleep patterns with the current pattern of day and night.

circumplex model of emotions A model describing different emotions as points in a two-dimensional space of valence and arousal.

civil commitment laws Legal proceedings that determine a person is mentally disordered and may be hospitalized, even involuntarily.

classical categorical approach A **classification** method founded on the assumption of clear-cut differences among disorders, each with a different known cause.

classical conditioning Fundamental learning process first described by Ivan Pavlov. An event that automatically elicits a response is paired with another stimulus event that does not (a neutral stimulus). After repeated pairings, the neutral stimulus becomes a conditioned stimulus that by itself can elicit the desired response.

classification Assignment of objects or people to categories on the basis of shared characteristics.

clinical assessment Systematic evaluation and measurement of psychological, biological, and social factors in a person presenting with a possible **psychological disorder.**

clinical description Details of the combination of behaviors, thoughts, and feelings of an individual that make up a particular disorder.

clinical efficacy axis One of a proposed set of guidelines for evaluating clinical interventions on the evidence of their effectiveness (compare with **clinical utility axis**).

clinical significance Degree to which research findings have useful and meaningful applications to real problems.

clinical utility axis One of a proposed set of guidelines for evaluating clinical interventions by whether they can be applied effectively and cost effectively in real clinical settings (compare with **clinical efficacy axis**).

cocaine Derivative of coca leaves used medically as a local anesthetic and narcotic; often a substance of abuse.

cocaine use disorders Severe intoxication or overdose through the use of cocaine, including significant behavioral impairments and physiological symptoms.

cognitive-behavioral model Model that combines insights from the behavioral, cognitive, and social learning models, which brought the systematic development of a more scientific approach to the psychological aspects of psychopathology.

cognitive science Field of study that examines how humans and other animals acquire, process, store, and retrieve information.

cognitive therapy Treatment approach that involves identifying and altering negative thinking styles related to **psychological disorders** such as depression and **anxiety** and replacing them with more positive beliefs and attitudes and, ultimately, more adaptive behavior and coping styles.

cohort Participants in each age group of a study with a **cross-sectional design.**

cohort effect Observation that people of different age groups differ in their values and experiences.

collective unconscious Accumulated wisdom of a culture collected and remembered across generations, a psychodynamic concept introduced by Carl Jung.

comorbidity Presence of two or more disorders in an individual at the same time.

comparative treatment research Outcome research that contrasts two or more treatment methods to determine which is most effective.

competence Ability of legal defendants to participate in their own defense and understand the charges and the roles of the trial participants.

compulsions Repetitive, ritualistic, time- consuming behaviors or mental acts a person feels driven to perform to suppress obsessions.

confound Any factor occurring in a study that makes the results uninterpretable because its effects cannot be separated from those of the variables being studied.

confounding variable Variable in a research study that was not part of the intended design and that may contribute to changes in the **dependent variable.**

control group Group of individuals in a study who are similar to the experimental subjects in every way but are not exposed to the treatment received by the experimental group. Their presence allows for a comparison of the differential effects of the treatment.

controlled drinking An extremely controversial treatment approach to **alcohol** dependence, in which severe abusers are taught to drink in moderation.

conversion disorder (functional neurological symptom disorder) Physical malfunctioning, such as blindness or paralysis, suggesting neurological impairment but with no organic pathology to account for it.

copy number variants Genes that are deleted as a result of mutations; these deletions may play a role in the development of ADHD and other disorders.

coronary heart disease (CHD) Blockage of the arteries supplying blood to the heart muscle; a major cause of death in Western culture, with social and psychological factors involved.

correlation Degree to which two variables are associated. In a **positive correlation,** the two variables increase or decrease together. In a **negative correlation,** one variable decreases as the other increases.

correlation coefficient Computed statistic reflecting the strength and direction of any association between two variables. It can range from −1.00 through 0.00 (indicating no association) to +1.00, with the absolute value indicating the strength and the sign reflecting the direction.

course Pattern of development and change of a disorder over time.

covert sensitization Cognitive-behavioral intervention to reduce unwanted behaviors by having clients imagine the extremely aversive consequences of the behaviors and establish negative rather than positive associations with them.

Creutzfeldt–Jakob disease Extremely rare type of **prion disease** that may result from a number of sources, including the consumption of beef from cattle with "mad cow disease."

criminal commitment Legal procedure by which a person found not guilty of a crime by reason of **insanity** must be confined in a psychiatric hospital.

cross-generational effect Limit on the **generalizability** of longitudinal research because the group under study may differ from others in culture and experience.

cross-sectional design Methodology to examine a characteristic by comparing individuals of different ages (contrast with **longitudinal design**).

cultural–familial intellectual disability Mild **intellectual disability** that may be caused largely by environmental influences.

cyclothymic disorder Chronic (at least 2 years) **mood disorder** characterized by alternating **mood** elevation and depression levels that are not as severe as manic or **major depressive episodes**.

dangerousness Tendency to violence that, contrary to popular opinion, is not more likely among mental patients.

defense mechanisms Common patterns of behavior, often adaptive coping styles when they occur in moderation, observed in response to particular situations. In **psychoanalysis,** these are thought to be **unconscious** processes originating in the **ego.**

deinstitutionalization Systematic removal of people with severe mental illness or **intellectual disability** from institutions like psychiatric hospitals.

delayed ejaculation Disorder in which a man achieves orgasm only with great difficulty.

delirium Rapid-onset reduced clarity of consciousness and cognition, with confusion, disorientation, and deficits in memory and language.

delusion A **psychotic symptom** involving disorder of thought content and presence of strong beliefs that are misrepresentations of reality.

delusional disorder Psychotic disorder featuring a persistent belief contrary to reality **(delusion)** but no other symptoms of **schizophrenia.**

dementia Obsolete term for **major neurocognitive disorder.**

dementia praecox Latin term meaning "premature loss of mind," an early label for what is now called **schizophrenia,** emphasizing the disorder's frequent appearance during adolescence. Called *démence précoce* in France.

dependent personality disorder Cluster C (anxious or fearful) **personality disorder** characterized by a person's pervasive and excessive need to be taken care of, a condition that leads to submissive and clinging behavior and fears of separation.

dependent variable In an experimental study, the phenomenon that is measured and expected to be influenced (compare with **independent variable**).

depersonalization/derealization disorder A **dissociative disorder** in which feelings of depersonalization are so severe they dominate the client's life and prevent normal functioning.

depressants The **psychoactive substances** that result in behavioral sedation, including **alcohol** and the sedative, hypnotic, and anxiolytic drugs.

depressive cognitive triad Thinking errors in depressed people negatively focused in three areas: themselves, their immediate world, and their future.

derealization Situation in which the individual loses a sense of the reality of the external world.

deterministic In genetics, **genes** that lead to nearly a 100% chance of developing the associated disorder. These are rare in the population.

diagnosis Process of determining whether a **presenting problem** meets the established criteria for a specific **psychological disorder.**

dialectical behavioral therapy (DBT) Promising treatment for **borderline personality disorder** that involves exposing the client to stressors in a controlled situation, as well as helping the client regulate **emotions** and cope with stressors that might trigger suicidal behavior.

diathesis–stress model A **hypothesis** that both an inherited tendency (a **vulnerability**) and specific stressful conditions are required to produce a disorder.

dimensional approach Method of categorizing characteristics on a continuum rather than on a binary, either-or, or all-or-none basis.

diminished capacity Evidence of an abnormal mental condition in people that causes criminal charges against them requiring intent or knowledge to be reduced to lesser offenses requiring only reckless or criminal neglect.

directionality Possibility that when two variables, A and B, are correlated variable A causes variable B or variable B causes variable A.

disinhibited social engagement disorder Condition in which a child shows no inhibitions whatsoever in approaching adults.

disorder of arousal Category of sleep disorder during NREM sleep that includes **sleepwalking** and **sleep terrors.**

disorganized speech Style of talking often seen in people with **schizophrenia,** involving incoherence and a lack of typical logic patterns.

disorganized symptoms (of schizophrenia) Symptoms of **schizophrenia** that include rambling speech, erratic behavior, and inappropriate affect (for example, smiling when you are upset).

disruptive mood dysregulation disorder Condition in which a child has chronic negative moods such as anger and irritability without any accompanying mania.

dissociative amnesia A **dissociative disorder** featuring the inability to recall personal information, usually of a stressful or traumatic nature.

dissociative disorder Disorder in which individuals feel detached from themselves or their surroundings and reality, experience, and identity may disintegrate.

dissociative fugue Type of dissociative amnesia featuring sudden, unexpected travel away from home, along with an inability to recall the past, sometimes with assumption of a new identity.

dissociative identity disorder (DID) Formerly known as multiple personality disorder; a disorder in which as many as 100 personalities or fragments of personalities coexist within one body and mind.

dissociative trance disorder Altered state of consciousness in which people firmly believe they are possessed by spirits; considered a disorder only where there is distress and dysfunction.

dopamine **Neurotransmitter** whose generalized function is to activate other **neurotransmitters** and to aid in exploratory and pleasure-seeking behaviors (thus balancing **serotonin**). A relative excess of **dopamine** is implicated in **schizophrenia** (although contradictory evidence suggests the connection is not simple), and its deficit is involved in **Parkinson's disease.**

double bind communication According to an obsolete, unsupported theory, the practice of transmitting conflicting messages that was thought to cause **schizophrenia.**

double depression Severe mood disorder typified by major depressive episodes superimposed over a background of **persistent dysthymic mood**. Also called "Persistent depressive disorder with intermittent major depressive episodes."

double-blind control Procedure in outcome studies that prevents bias by ensuring that neither the subjects nor the providers of the experimental treatment know who is receiving treatment and who is receiving placebo.

Down syndrome Type of **intellectual disability** caused by a chromosomal aberration (chromosome 21) and involving characteristic physical appearance. Sometimes known as trisomy 21.

dream analysis Psychoanalytic therapy method in which dream contents are examined as symbolic of **id** impulses and **intrapsychic conflicts.**

duty to warn Mental health professional's responsibility to break confidentiality and notify the potential victim whom a client has specifically threatened.

dyssomnias Problems in getting to sleep or in obtaining sufficient quality sleep.

dysthymia See **Persistent depressive disorder.**

effect size Statistical measure that shows the amount of difference among the members of a group in a clinical study.

ego In **psychoanalysis**, the psychical entity responsible for finding realistic and practical ways to satisfy **id** drives.

ego psychology Derived from **psychoanalysis,** this theory emphasizes the role of the **ego** in development and attributes **psychological disorders** to failure of the ego to manage impulses and internal conflicts. Also known as *self-psychology.*

electroconvulsive therapy (ECT) Biological treatment for severe, chronic depression involving the application of electrical impulses through the brain to produce seizures. The reasons for its effectiveness are unknown.

electroencephalogram (EEG) Measure of electrical activity patterns in the brain, taken through electrodes placed on the scalp.

emotion Pattern of action elicited by an external event and a feeling state, accompanied by a characteristic physiological response.

endogenous opioids Substances occurring naturally throughout the body that function like **neurotransmitters** to shut down pain sensation even in the presence of marked tissue damage. These may contribute to psychological problems such as eating disorders. Also known as *endorphins* or *enkephalins.*

endophenotypes Genetic mechanisms that contribute to the underlying problems causing the symptoms and difficulties experienced by people with **psychological disorders.**

epidemiology A **psychopathology** research method examining the prevalence, distribution, and consequences of disorders in populations.

epigenetics The study of factors other than inherited DNA sequence, such as new learning or stress, that alter the phenotypic expression of genes.

equifinality Developmental psychopathology principle that a behavior or disorder may have several causes.

erectile disorder Recurring inability in some men to attain or maintain adequate penile erection until completion of sexual activity.

essential hypertension High blood pressure with no verifiable physical cause, which makes up the overwhelming majority of high blood pressure cases.

etiology Cause or source of a disorder.

excitatory Causing excitation; activating.

excoriation (skin picking disorder) Recurrent, difficult-to-control picking of one's skin leading to significant impairment or distress.

exhibitionistic disorder Sexual gratification attained by exposing genitals to unsuspecting strangers.

exorcism Religious ritual that attributes disordered behavior to possession by demons and seeks to treat the individual by driving the demons from the body.

experiment Research method that can establish causation by manipulating the variables in question and controlling for alternative explanations of any observed effects.

expert witness Person who because of special training and experience is allowed to offer opinion testimony in legal trials.

expressed emotion (EE) Hostility, criticism, and overinvolvement demonstrated by some families toward a family member with a **psychological disorder.** This can often contribute to the person's **relapse.**

external validity Extent to which research findings generalize, or apply, to people and settings not involved in the study.

extinction Learning process in which a response maintained by **reinforcement** in operant conditioning or pairing in **classical conditioning** decreases when that reinforcement or pairing is removed; also the procedure of removing that reinforcement or pairing.

facial agnosia Type of **agnosia** characterized by a person's inability to recognize even familiar faces.

factitious disorder Nonexistent physical or **psychological disorder** deliberately faked for no apparent gain except possibly sympathy and attention.

false negative Assessment error in which no pathology is noted (that is, test results are negative) when one is actually present.

false positive Assessment error in which pathology is reported (that is, test results are positive) when none is actually present.

familial aggregation The extent to which a disorder is found among a patient's relatives.

family studies Genetic studies that examine patterns of traits and behaviors among relatives.

fear The **emotion** of an immediate alarm reaction to present danger or life-threatening emergencies.

female orgasmic disorder Recurring delay or absence of orgasm in some women following a normal sexual excitement phase, relative to their prior experience and current stimulation. Also known as *inhibited orgasm* (female).

female sexual interest/arousal disorder Recurrent inability in some women to attain or maintain adequate lubrication and sexual excitement swelling responses until completion of sexual activity.

fetal alcohol syndrome (FAS) Pattern of problems including learning difficulties, behavior deficits, and characteristic physical flaws, resulting from heavy drinking by the victim's mother when she was pregnant with the victim.

fetishistic disorder Long-term, recurring, intense sexually arousing urges, fantasies, or behavior that involve the use of nonliving, unusual objects and that cause distress or impairment in life functioning.

fight/flight system (FFS) Brain circuit in animals that when stimulated causes an immediate alarm and escape response resembling human **panic.**

flat affect Apparently emotionless demeanor (including toneless speech and vacant gaze) when a reaction would be expected.

flight or fight response Biological reaction to alarming stressors that musters the body's resources (for example, blood flow and respiration) to resist or flee a threat.

fragile X syndrome Pattern of abnormality caused by a defect in the X chromosome resulting in **intellectual disability,** learning problems, and unusual physical characteristics.

free association Psychoanalytic therapy technique intended to explore threatening material repressed into the **unconscious.** The patient is instructed to say whatever comes to mind without censoring.

frontotemporal neurocognitive disorder Condition that damages the frontal or temporal regions of the brain; behavior or language is negatively affected.

frotteuristic disorder A **paraphilic disorder** in which the person gains sexual gratification by rubbing against unwilling victims in crowds from which they cannot escape.

gambling disorder Persistent and recurrent problematic gambling behavior leading to clinically significant impairment or distress

gamma-aminobutyric acid (GABA) A **neurotransmitter** that reduces activity across the synapse and thus inhibits a range of behaviors and **emotions,** especially generalized **anxiety.**

gender-affirming surgery Nonreversible altering of anatomy physically to be consistent with gender identity.

gender dysphoria Psychological dissatisfaction with biological gender, a disturbance in the sense of identity as a male or female. The primary goal is not sexual arousal but rather to live the life of the opposite gender.

gender nonconformity A phenomenon in which pre-pubescent children do not identify with their biological sex, but instead identify strongly with the gender of the opposite sex and display varying degrees of behavior more characteristic of the opposite sex.

gene–environment correlation model A **hypothesis** that people with a genetic predisposition for a disorder may also have a genetic tendency to create environmental risk factors that promote the disorder.

general adaptation syndrome (GAS) Sequence of reactions to sustained **stress** described by Hans Selye. These stages are alarm, resistance, and exhaustion, which may lead to death.

generalizability Extent to which research results apply to a range of individuals not included in the study.

generalized amnesia Loss of memory of all personal information, including identity.

generalized anxiety disorder (GAD) Anxiety disorder characterized by intense, uncontrollable, unfocused, chronic, and continuous worry that is distressing and unproductive, accompanied by physical symptoms of tenseness, irritability, and restlessness.

genes Long deoxyribonucleic acid (DNA) molecules, the basic physical units of heredity that appear as locations on chromosomes. A single gene is a subunit of DNA that determines inherited traits in living things.

genetic linkage analysis Study that seeks to match the inheritance pattern of a disorder to that of a **genetic marker.** This helps researchers establish the location of the **gene** responsible for the disorder.

genetic marker Inherited characteristic for which the chromosomal location of the responsible **gene** is known.

genito-pelvic pain/penetration disorder Sexual dysfunction in which a woman experiences pain or difficulty with penetration during intercourse; may include **vaginismus.**

genotype Specific genetic makeup of an individual.

glutamate Amino acid **neurotransmitter** that excites many different **neurons,** leading to action.

hallucinations The **psychotic symptoms** of perceptual disturbance in which things are seen, heard, or otherwise sensed although they are not actually present.

hallucinogen Any **psychoactive substance** such as **LSD** or **marijuana** that can produce **delusions, hallucinations, paranoia,** and altered sensory perception.

hallucinogen use disorders Cognitive, biological, behavioral, and social problems associated with the use and abuse of hallucinogenic substances.

head trauma Injury to the head and, therefore, to the brain, typically caused by accidents; can lead to cognitive impairments, including memory loss.

health psychology Subfield of **behavioral medicine** that studies psychological factors important in health promotion and maintenance.

hebephrenia Silly and immature emotionality, a characteristic of some types of **schizophrenia.**

heterosexual behavior Sexual activity with members of the opposite gender.

histrionic personality disorder Cluster B (dramatic, emotional, or erratic) **personality disorder** involving a pervasive pattern of excessive emotionality and attention seeking.

hormone Chemical messenger produced by the endocrine glands.

human genome project Ongoing scientific attempt to develop a comprehensive map of all human **genes.**

human immunodeficiency virus type 1 (HIV-1) Disease that causes AIDS.

Huntington's disease Genetic disorder marked by involuntary limb movements and progressing to **major neurocognitive disorder.**

hypersomnolence disorder Sleep dysfunction involving an excessive amount of sleep that disrupts normal routines.

hypertension Major risk factor for **stroke** and heart and kidney disease that is intimately related to psychological factors. Also known as *high blood pressure.*

hypomanic episode Less severe and less disruptive version of a **manic episode** that is one of the criteria for several **mood disorders.**

hypothesis Educated guess or statement to be tested by research.

id In **psychoanalysis,** the **unconscious** psychical entity present at birth representing basic sexual and aggressive drives.

idiographic strategy Close and detailed investigation of an individual emphasizing what makes that person unique (compare with **nomothetic strategy**).

illness anxiety disorder A **somatic symptom disorder** (previously known as *somatoform disorder*) involving severe **anxiety** over belief in having a disease process without any evident physical cause.

immune system Body's means of identifying and eliminating any foreign materials (for example, bacteria, parasites, and even transplanted organs) that enter.

implicit memory Condition of memory in which a person cannot recall past events despite acting in response to them (contrast with explicit memory).

impulse-control disorders Disorders in which a person acts on an irresistible, but potentially harmful, impulse.

inappropriate affect Emotional displays that are improper for the situation.

incest Deviant sexual attraction **(pedophilia)** directed toward a family member; often the attraction of a father toward a daughter who is maturing physically.

incidence Number of new cases of a disorder appearing during a specific period (compare with **prevalence**).

independent variable Phenomenon manipulated by the experimenter in a study and expected to influence the **dependent variable.**

informed consent Ethical requirement whereby research subjects agree to participate in a study only after they receive full disclosure about the nature of the study and their own role in it.

inhibitory Causing inhibition; suppressing.

insomnia disorder Condition in which insufficient sleep interferes with normal functioning.

integrated grief Grief that evolves from acute grief into a condition in which the individual accepts the finality of a death and adjusts to the loss.

intellectual disability (ID) A diagnosis received when one achieves a significantly below-average score on a test of intelligence and by limitations in the ability to function in areas of daily life.

intelligence quotient (IQ) Score on an intelligence test estimating a person's deviation from average test performance.

intermittent explosive disorder Episodes during which a person acts on aggressive impulses that result in serious assaults or destruction of property.

internal validity Extent to which the results of a study can be attributed to the **independent variable** after confounding alternative explanations have been ruled out.

interpersonal psychotherapy (IPT) Brief treatment approach that emphasizes resolution of interpersonal problems and stressors, such as role disputes, in marital conflict or forming relationships in marriage or a new job. It has demonstrated effectiveness for such problems as depression.

intrapsychic conflicts In **psychoanalysis**, the struggles among the **id, ego,** and **superego.**

introspection Early, nonscientific approach to the study of psychology involving systematic attempts to report thoughts and feelings that specific stimuli evoked.

inverse agonist Chemical substance that produces effects opposite those of a particular **neurotransmitter.**

joint attention Attention shared by two persons toward an object after one person has indicated interest in the object to the other person; this social interaction is limited or absent in people with **autism spectrum disorder.**

kleptomania Recurrent failure to resist urges to steal things not needed for personal use or their monetary value.

labeling Applying a name to a phenomenon or a pattern of behavior. The label may acquire negative connotations or be applied erroneously to the person rather than that person's behaviors.

language disorder Getting one's meaning or message across to others (expressive language disorder), or understanding the message coming from others (receptive language disorder).

learned helplessness Martin Seligman's theory that people become anxious and depressed when they make an attribution that they have no control over the **stress** in their lives (whether or not they do in reality).

learned helplessness theory of depression The theory according to which depression is the result of perceived or real absence of control over the outcome of an undesirable situation.

Lesch-Nyhan syndrome X-linked disorder characterized by **intellectual disability,** signs of cerebral palsy, and self-injurious behavior.

level Degree of behavior change with different interventions (for example, high or low).

localized or selective amnesia Memory loss limited to specific times and events, particularly traumatic events.

longitudinal design Systematic study of changes in the same individual or group examined over time (contrast with **cross-sectional design**).

LSD (*d*-lysergic acid diethylamide) Most common hallucinogenic drug; a synthetic version of the grain fungus ergot.

maintenance treatment Combination of continued **psychosocial treatment,** medication, or both designed to prevent **relapse** following therapy.

major depressive disorder, single or recurrent episode A **mood disorder** involving one *(single episode)* or more (separated by at least 2 months without depression, *recurrent)* **major depressive episodes.**

major depressive episode Most common and severe experience of depression, including feelings of worthlessness, disturbances in bodily activities such as sleep, loss of interest, and inability to experience pleasure, persisting at least 2 weeks.

major neurocognitive disorder (dementia) Gradual deterioration of brain functioning that affects memory, judgment, language, and other advanced cognitive processes.

male erectile disorder See **erectile disorder.**

male hypoactive sexual desire disorder Dysfunction in which a man feels distress from having little or no sexual interest.

malingering Deliberate faking of a physical or **psychological disorder** motivated by gain.

mania Period of abnormally excessive elation or euphoria, associated with some **mood disorders.**

marijuana *(Cannabis sativa)* Dried flowers and leaves of the hemp plant; a **hallucinogen** that is the most widely used illegal substance.

mental disorder See **psychological disorder.**

mental hygiene movement Mid-19th-century effort to improve care of the mentally disordered by informing the public of their mistreatment.

mental illness Term formerly used to mean **psychological disorder** but less preferred because it implies that the causes of the disorder can be found in a medical disease process.

mental status exam Relatively brief preliminary test of a client's judgment, orientation to time and place, and emotional and mental state; typically conducted during an initial interview.

microbiota Entirety of the microorganisms (such as fungi, viruses, and bacteria) that populate the intestines. The combined genome of these organisms is called the *microbiome*. The influence of the microbiome of the gut on psychological well-being is called the *psychobiome*.

microsleeps Short, seconds-long periods of sleep that occur in people who have been deprived of sleep.

mild neurocognitive disorder Modest impairment in cognitive abilities that can be overcome with accommodations such as extensive lists or elaborate schedules.

mixed features Condition in which the individual experiences both elation and depression or **anxiety** at the same time. Also known as *dysphoric manic episode* or *mixed manic episode.*

modeling (also known as *observational learning*) Learning through observation and imitation of the behavior of other individuals and consequences of that behavior.

mood Enduring period of emotionality.

mood disorders Group of disorders involving severe and enduring disturbances in emotionality ranging from elation to severe depression.

mood-stabilizing drug A medication used in the treatment of **mood disorders**, particularly bipolar disorder, that is effective in preventing and treating pathological shifts in mood.

moral therapy Psychosocial approach in the 19th century that involved treating patients as normally as possible in normal environments.

multidimensional integrative approach Approach to the study of **psychopathology** that holds **psychological disorders** as always being the products of multiple interacting causal factors.

multiple baseline A **single-case experimental design** in which measures are taken on two or more behaviors or on a single behavior in two or more situations. A particular intervention is introduced for each at different times. If behavior change is coincident with each introduction, this is strong evidence the intervention caused the change.

Munchausen syndrome A **factitious disorder** suggesting that the person is faking an illness, just as the original Baron von Münchhausen lied about his adventures. The symptoms are under voluntary control, and there is no obvious reason for producing the symptoms except, possibly, to assume the sick role and receive increased attention.

narcissistic personality disorder Cluster B (dramatic, emotional, or erratic) **personality disorder** involving a pervasive pattern of grandiosity in fantasy or behavior, need for admiration, and lack of empathy.

narcolepsy Sleep disorder involving sudden and irresistible sleep attacks.

natural environment phobia Fear of situations or events in nature, especially heights, storms, and water.

naturalistic teaching strategies Instructional techniques that are used with children having neurodevelopmental disorders and that move away from traditional desk instruction toward more natural social interactions.

negative correlation Association between two variables in which one increases as the other decreases.

negative symptoms Less outgoing symptoms, such as **flat affect** and poverty of speech, displayed by some people with **schizophrenia.**

negative symptoms (of schizophrenia) Symptoms of **schizophrenia** that involve deficits in normal behavior in such areas as speech, blunted affect (or lack of emotional reactivity), and motivation.

neurocognitive disorder due to Alzheimer's type Condition resulting from a disease that develops most often in people 50 and older, characterized by multiple cognitive defects that develop gradually and steadily.

neurocognitive disorder due to HIV infection Less common type of neurocognitive disorder that affects people who have HIV; may lead to impaired thinking in advanced stages.

neurocognitive disorder due to Huntington's disease Neurological disorder that follows a subcortical pattern and is notable for causing involuntary limb movements.

neurocognitive disorder due to Lewy body disease Neurological impairment that affects people with Lewy body disease, in which protein deposits damage brain cells and gradually cause motor impairments and loss of alertness.

neurocognitive disorder due to Parkinson's disease Disorder characterized by progressive decline in motor movements; results from damage to dopamine pathways.

neurocognitive disorder due to prion disease Rare progressive neurodegenerative disorder caused by prions, proteins that can reproduce themselves and cause damage to brain cells.

neurocognitive disorder due to traumatic brain injury Condition resulting from jarring of the brain caused by a blow to the head or other impact; symptoms persist for at least a week after the initial trauma.

neurodevelopmental disorders Neurologically based disorders that are revealed in a clinically significant way during a child's developing years.

neurohormones The **hormones** that affect the brain and are increasingly the focus of study in **psychopathology.**

neuroimaging Sophisticated computer-aided procedures that allow nonintrusive examination of nervous system structure and function.

neuron Individual nerve cell; responsible for transmitting information.

neuropsychological testing Assessment of brain and nervous system functioning by testing an individual's performance on behavioral tasks.

neuroscience Study of the nervous system and its role in behavior, thoughts, and **emotions.**

neurosis Obsolete psychodynamic term for **psychological disorder** thought to result from **unconscious** conflicts and the **anxiety** they cause. Plural is *neuroses.*

neurotransmitters Chemicals that cross the **synaptic cleft** between nerve cells to transmit impulses from one **neuron** to the next. Their relative excess or deficiency is involved in several **psychological disorders.**

nicotine Toxic and addictive substance found in tobacco leaves.

nicotine patch Patch placed on the skin that delivers **nicotine** to smokers without the carcinogens in cigarette smoke. Somewhat more successful than nicotine gum because it requires less effort by the wearer and delivers the drug more consistently; should be coupled with counseling to stop smoking and avoid **relapse.**

nicotine use disorders See **tobacco-related disorders.**

night eating syndrome Consuming a third or more of daily food intake after the evening meal and getting out of bed at least once during the night to have a high-calorie snack. In the morning, however, individuals with night eating syndrome are not hungry and do not usually eat breakfast. These individuals do not **binge** during their night eating and seldom purge.

nightmares Frightening and anxiety-provoking dreams occurring during **rapid eye movement sleep**. The individual recalls the bad dreams and recovers alertness and orientation quickly.

nomenclature In a naming system or **nosology,** the actual labels or names that are applied. In **psychopathology,** these include **mood disorders** and eating disorders.

nomothetic strategy Identification and examination of large groups of people with the same disorder to note similarities and develop general laws (compare with **idiographic strategy**).

nonbinary Referring to a spectrum of gender identities that are neither female nor male.

norepinephrine (also **noradrenaline)** The **neurotransmitter** active in the **central** and **peripheral nervous systems**, controlling heart rate, blood pressure, and respiration, among other functions. Because of its role in the body's alarm reaction, it may also contribute generally and indirectly to **panic attacks** and other disorders.

nosology The **classification** and naming system for medical and psychological phenomena.

obesity Excess of body fat resulting in a body mass index (BMI, a ratio of weight to height) of 30 or more.

object relations Modern development in psychodynamic theory involving the study of how children incorporate the memories and values of people who are close and important to them.

obsessions Recurrent intrusive thoughts or impulses the client seeks to suppress or neutralize while recognizing they are not imposed by outside forces.

obsessive-compulsive disorder (OCD) A **disorder** involving unwanted, persistent, intrusive thoughts and impulses, as well as repetitive actions intended to suppress them.

obsessive-compulsive personality disorder Cluster C (anxious or fearful) **personality disorder** featuring a pervasive pattern of preoccupation with orderliness, perfectionism, and mental and interpersonal control at the expense of flexibility, openness, and efficiency.

opiates Addictive **psychoactive substances** such as heroin, **opium,** and **morphine** that cause temporary euphoria and analgesia (pain reduction).

opioid-related disorders Severe intoxication or overdose through the use of **opiates,** which have a narcotic effect.

orgasmic reconditioning Learning procedure to help clients strengthen appropriate patterns of sexual arousal by pairing appropriate stimuli with the pleasurable sensations of masturbation.

other commonly misused substances Other substances (such as inhalants, anabolic steroids, and other over-the-counter and prescription medications) that produce psychoactive effects and that are misused but do not fit neatly into other categories.

panic Sudden, overwhelming fright or terror.

panic attack Abrupt experience of intense **fear** or discomfort accompanied by a number of physical symptoms, such as dizziness or heart palpitations.

panic control treatment (PCT) Cognitive-behavioral treatment for **panic attacks,** involving gradual exposure to feared somatic sensations and modification of perceptions and attitudes about them.

panic disorder Recurrent unexpected panic attacks accompanied by concern about future attacks and/or a lifestyle change to avoid future attacks.

paranoia People's irrational beliefs that they are especially important **(delusions of grandeur)** or that other people are seeking to do them harm.

paranoid personality disorder Cluster A (odd or eccentric) **personality disorder** involving pervasive distrust and suspiciousness of others such that their motives are interpreted as malevolent.

paraphilic disorders Sexual disorders and deviations in which sexual arousal occurs almost exclusively in the context of inappropriate objects or individuals.

parasomnias Various **abnormal behaviors** such as **nightmares** or **sleepwalking** that occur during sleep.

Parkinson's disease Degenerative brain disorder principally affecting motor performance (for example, tremors and stooped posture) associated with reduction in **dopamine. Major neurocognitive disorder** may be a result as well.

patient uniformity myth Tendency to consider all members of a category as more similar than they are, ignoring their individual differences.

pedophilia Paraphilia involving strong sexual attraction toward children.

persistent depressive disorder (dysthymia) A **mood disorder** involving persistently depressed **mood,** with low self-esteem, **withdrawal,** pessimism, or despair, present for at least 2 years, with no absence of symptoms for more than 2 months.

personality disorders Enduring maladaptive patterns for relating to the environment and self, exhibited in a range of contexts that cause significant functional impairment or subjective distress.

personality inventories Self-report questionnaires that assess personal traits by asking respondents to identify descriptions that apply to them.

person-centered therapy Therapy method in which the client, rather than the counselor, primarily directs the course of discussion, seeking self-discovery and self-responsibility.

pervasive developmental disorder not otherwise specified Wide-ranging, significant, and long-lasting dysfunctions that appear before the age of 18.

phenotype Observable characteristics or behaviors of an individual.

phenylketonuria (PKU) Recessive disorder involving the inability to break down a food chemical whose buildup causes intellectual disability, seizures, and behavior problems. PKU can be detected by infant screening and prevented by a specialized diet.

phobia A **psychological disorder** characterized by marked and persistent **fear** of an object or situation.

physiological dependence The use of increasingly greater amounts of a drug to experience the same effect (**tolerance**) and a negative physical response when the substance is no longer ingested (**withdrawal**).

Pick's disease Rare condition that results in early onset neurocognitive disorder.

placebo control group In an outcome **experiment,** a **control group** that does not receive the experimental manipulation but is given a similar procedure with an identical expectation of change, allowing the researcher to assess any **placebo effect.**

placebo effect Behavior change resulting from the person's expectation of change rather than from the experimental manipulation itself.

polysomnographic (PSG) evaluation Assessment of sleep disorders in which a client sleeping in the lab is monitored for heart, muscle, respiration, brain wave, and other functions.

polysubstance use Use of multiple mind- and behavior-altering substances, such as drugs.
positive correlation Association between two variables in which one increases as the other increases.
positive symptoms (of schizophrenia) Symptoms of **schizophrenia** that generally refer to symptoms around distorted reality such as hallucinations and delusions.
posttraumatic stress disorder (PTSD) Enduring, distressing emotional disorder that follows exposure to severe helplessness or a fear-inducing threat. The victim reexperiences the trauma, avoids stimuli associated with it, and develops a numbing of responsiveness and an increased vigilance and arousal.
premature ejaculation Recurring ejaculation before the person wishes it, with minimal sexual stimulation.
premenstrual dysphoric disorder Clinically significant emotional problems that can occur during the premenstrual phase of the reproductive cycle of a woman.
prepared learning An ability that has been adaptive for evolution, allowing certain associations to be learned more readily than others.
presenting problem Original complaint reported by the client to the therapist. The actual treated problem may sometimes be a modification derived from the presenting problem.
prevalence Number of people displaying a disorder in the total population at any given time (compare with **incidence**).
primary insomnia Difficulty in initiating, maintaining, or gaining from sleep; not related to other medical or psychological problems.
proband In genetics research, the individual displaying the trait or characteristic being studied.
prodromal stage Second of E. Morton Jellinek's four stages identified in the progression of alcoholism, featuring heavy drinking but with few outward signs of a problem.
prognosis Predicted future development of a disorder over time.
projective tests Psychoanalytically based measures that present ambiguous stimuli to clients on the assumption that their responses will reveal their **unconscious** conflicts. Such tests are inferential and lack high **reliability** and **validity.**
prolonged grief disorder (PGD) Prolonged adaptation to loss associated with intense longing for and preoccupation with the deceased, leading to difficulty moving on with life even after a year or more has passed.
prosody Vocal characteristics such as tone and stress; people with **autism spectrum disorder** often have trouble recognizing and interpreting these vocal cues.
prototypical approach System for categorizing disorders using both essential, defining characteristics and a range of variation on other characteristics.
psychoactive substances Substances, such as drugs, that alter **mood** or behavior.
psychoanalysis Psychoanalytic assessment and therapy, which emphasizes exploration of, and insight into, **unconscious** processes and conflicts, pioneered by Sigmund Freud.
psychoanalyst Therapist who practices **psychoanalysis** after earning either an M.D. or a Ph.D. degree and receiving additional specialized postdoctoral training.
psychoanalytic model Complex and comprehensive theory originally advanced by Sigmund Freud that seeks to account for the development and structure of personality, as well as the origin of **abnormal behavior,** based primarily on inferred inner entities and forces.
psychodynamic psychotherapy Contemporary version of **psychoanalysis** that still emphasizes **unconscious** processes and conflicts but is briefer and more focused on specific problems.
psychological autopsy Postmortem psychological profile of a suicide victim constructed from interviews with people who knew the person before death.
psychological disorder Psychological dysfunction associated with distress or impairment in functioning that is not a typical or culturally expected response.
psychological factors affecting medical condition A **somatic symptom disorder** with the presence of a diagnosed medical condition (such as asthma, diabetes, or severe pain) clearly caused by a known medical condition (such as cancer) that is adversely affected by one or more psychological or behavioral factors.
psychoncology Study of psychological factors involved in the **course** and treatment of **cancer**.
psychoneuroimmunology (PNI) Study of psychological influences on the neurological responding involved in the body's immune response.
psychopathology Scientific study of **psychological disorders.**
psychopathy Non-*DSM-5* category similar to **antisocial personality disorder** but with less emphasis on overt behavior. Indicators include superficial charm, lack of remorse, and other personality characteristics.
psychophysiological assessment Measurement of changes in the nervous system reflecting psychological or emotional events such as **anxiety, stress,** and sexual arousal.
psychosexual stages of development In **psychoanalysis,** the sequence of phases a person passes through during development. Each stage is named for the location on the body where **id** gratification is maximal at that time.
psychosocial treatment Treatment practices that focus on social and cultural factors (such as family experience), as well as psychological influences. These approaches include cognitive, behavioral, and interpersonal methods.
psychotic behavior Severe **psychological disorder** category characterized by **hallucinations** and loss of contact with reality.
psychotic disorder associated with another medical condition Condition that is characterized by hallucinations or delusions and that is the direct result of another physiological disorder, such as stroke or brain tumor.
psychotic symptoms The **delusions** and **hallucinations** that may appear during depressive or **manic episodes.**
purging disorder An eating disorder where people influence their weight by self-induced vomiting, using laxatives, diuretics, or other medications but do not show **binge-eating disorder** or other eating disorders.
purging techniques In the eating disorder **bulimia nervosa,** the self-induced vomiting or laxative abuse used to compensate for excessive food ingestion.
pyromania An **impulse-control disorder** that involves having an irresistible urge to set fires.
randomization Method for placing individuals into research groups that assures each an equal chance of being assigned to any group, thus eliminating any systematic differences across groups.
rapid eye movement (REM) sleep Periodic intervals of sleep during which the eyes move rapidly from side to side, and dreams occur, but the body is inactive.
reactive attachment disorder Attachment disorder in which a child with disturbed behavior neither seeks out a caregiver

nor responds to offers of help from one; fearfulness and sadness are often evident.

rebound insomnia In a person with insomnia, the worsened sleep problems that can occur when medications are used to treat insomnia and then withdrawn.

recurrent Repeatedly occurring.

reinforcement In **operant conditioning,** consequences for behavior that strengthen it or increase its frequency. Positive reinforcement involves the contingent delivery of a desired consequence. Negative reinforcement is the contingent escape from an aversive consequence. Unwanted behaviors may result from their reinforcement or the failure to reinforce desired behaviors.

relapse prevention Extending therapeutic progress by teaching the client how to cope with future troubling situations.

relaxation response Active components of meditation methods, including repetitive thoughts of a sound to reduce distracting thoughts and closing the mind to other intruding thoughts, that decrease the flow of stress hormones and **neurotransmitters** and cause a feeling of calm.

reliability Degree to which a measurement is consistent, for example, over time or among different raters.

repeated measurement When responses are measured on more than two occasions (not just before and after intervention) to assess trends.

research design Plan of experimentation used to test a **hypothesis.**

retrospective information Literally "the view back"; data collected by examining records or recollections of the past. It is limited by the accuracy, **validity,** and thoroughness of the sources.

Rett disorder Progressive neurodevelopmental disorder featuring constant hand- wringing, **intellectual disability,** and impaired motor skills.

reuptake Action by which a **neurotransmitter** is quickly drawn back into the discharging **neuron** after being released into a **synaptic cleft.**

rheumatoid arthritis Painful, degenerative disease in which the **immune system** essentially attacks itself, resulting in stiffness, swelling, and even destruction of the joints. **Cognitive-behavioral treatments** can help relieve pain and stiffness.

same-sex sexual behavior Sexual activity with members of the same **gender.**

schizoaffective disorder Psychotic disorder featuring symptoms of both **schizophrenia** and major **mood disorder.**

schizoid personality disorder Cluster A (odd or eccentric) **personality disorder** featuring a pervasive pattern of detachment from social relationships and a restricted range of expression of **emotions.**

schizophrenia Devastating psychotic disorder that may involve characteristic disturbances in thinking **(delusions)**, perception **(hallucinations)**, speech, **emotions,** and behavior.

schizophreniform disorder Psychotic disorder involving the symptoms of **schizophrenia** but lasting less than 6 months.

schizophrenogenic mother According to an obsolete, unsupported theory, a cold, dominating, and rejecting parent who was thought to cause **schizophrenia** in her offspring.

schizotypal personality disorder Cluster A (odd or eccentric) **personality disorder** involving a pervasive pattern of interpersonal deficits featuring acute discomfort with, and reduced capacity for, close relationships, as well as cognitive or perceptual distortions and eccentricities of behavior.

scientist-practitioners Mental health professionals who are expected to apply scientific methods to their work. They must keep current in the latest research on **diagnosis** and treatment, they must evaluate their own methods for effectiveness, and they may generate their own research to discover new knowledge of disorders and their treatment.

seasonal affective disorder (SAD) A **mood disorder** involving a cycling of episodes corresponding to the seasons of the year, typically with depression occurring during the winter.

self-actualizing Process emphasized in humanistic psychology in which people strive to achieve their highest potential against difficult life experiences.

self-efficacy Perception of having the ability to cope with **stress** or challenges.

self-monitoring Action by which clients observe and record their own behaviors as either an assessment of a problem and its change or a treatment procedure that makes them more aware of their responses. Also called self-observation.

self-psychology See **ego psychology.**

separation anxiety disorder Excessive, enduring fear in some individuals that harm will come to them or their loved ones when they are apart.

sequential design Combination of the **cross-sectional** and **longitudinal designs** involving repeated study of different **cohorts** over time.

serotonin A **neurotransmitter** involved in processing of information and coordination of movement, as well as inhibition and restraint. It also assists in the regulation of eating, sexual, and aggressive behaviors, all of which may be involved in different **psychological disorders.** Its interaction with **dopamine** is implicated in **schizophrenia.**

sexual dysfunction Sexual disorder in which the client finds it difficult to function adequately while having sex.

sexual masochism A **paraphilia** in which sexual arousal is associated with experiencing pain or humiliation.

sexual sadism A **paraphilia** in which sexual arousal is associated with inflicting pain or humiliation.

shaping In **operant conditioning**, the development of a new response by reinforcing successively more similar versions of that response. Both desirable and undesirable behaviors may be learned in this manner.

shared psychotic disorder (folie à deux) Psychotic disturbance in which individuals develop a **delusion** similar to that of a person with whom they share a close relationship.

single-case experimental design Research tactic in which an **independent variable** is manipulated for a single individual, allowing cause-and-effect conclusions but with limited **generalizability** (contrast with **case study method**).

situational phobia An **anxiety** involving enclosed places (for example, claustrophobia) or public transportation (for example, **fear** of flying).

sleep apnea Disorder involving brief periods when breathing ceases during sleep.

sleep efficiency (SE) Percentage of time actually spent sleeping of the total time spent in bed.

sleep terrors Episodes of apparent awakening from sleep, accompanied by signs of **panic,** followed by disorientation and amnesia for the incident. These occur during **nonrapid eye movement sleep** and so do not involve frightening dreams.

sleepwalking A **parasomnia** that involves leaving the bed during **nonrapid eye**

movement sleep. See also **somnambulism.**

social anxiety disorder (also called social phobia) Extreme, enduring, irrational **fear** and avoidance of social or performance situations.

social jet lag The repeated switching of a daily schedule because of social factors, similar to changing time zones when traveling. It is associated with sleep problems and other health issues, such as **obesity**.

somatic symptom disorder Disorder involving extreme and long-lasting focus on multiple physical symptoms for which no medical cause is evident. Previously known as *somatization disorder*.

somnambulism Repeated **sleepwalking** that occurs during **nonrapid eye movement sleep** and so is not the acting out of a dream. The person is difficult to waken and does not recall the experience.

specific learning disorder Neurodevelopmental disorder characterized by academic performance that is substantially below what would be expected given the person's age, intelligence quotient (IQ) score, and education.

specific phobia Unreasonable **fear** of a specific object or situation that markedly interferes with daily life functioning.

standardization Process of establishing specific norms and requirements for a measurement technique to ensure it is used consistently across measurement occasions. This includes instructions for administering the measure, evaluating its findings, and comparing these to data for large numbers of people.

statistical significance Probability that obtaining the observed research findings merely by chance is small.

stimulants Any **psychoactive substances** that elevate **mood,** activity, and alertness, including **amphetamines,** caffeine, **cocaine,** and **nicotine.**

stress Body's physiological response to a stressor, which is any event or change that requires adaptation.

stroke/cerebral vascular accident (CVA) Temporary blockage of blood vessels supplying the brain, or a rupture of vessels in the brain, resulting in temporary or permanent loss of brain functioning.

substance abuse Pattern of **psychoactive substance** use leading to significant distress or impairment in social and occupational roles and in hazardous situations.

substance dependence Maladaptive pattern of substance use characterized by the need for increased amounts to achieve the desired effect, negative physical effects when the substance is withdrawn, unsuccessful efforts to control its use, and substantial effort expended to seek it or recover from its effects. Also known as *addiction*.

substance intoxication The psychological reaction to ingested substances, such as drunkenness or getting high. Variables that interact include type of drug taken, amount ingested, and individual biological reaction. It can be experienced as impaired judgment, mood changes, and lowered motor ability (including problems walking or talking).

substance use The ingestion of psychoactive substances in moderate amounts that does not significantly interfere with social, educational, or occupational functioning.

substance/medication-induced neurocognitive disorder Brain damage caused by prolonged use of drugs, often in combination with a poor diet.

substance-induced psychotic disorder Psychosis caused by the ingestion of medications, psychoactive drugs, or toxins.

substance-related and addictive disorders Range of problems associated with the use and abuse of drugs such as **alcohol, cocaine,** heroin, and other substances people use to alter the way they think, feel, and behave. These are extremely costly in human and financial terms.

substance use disorders Drug use that significantly interferes with the user's education, job, or relationships with others or puts the user in physically dangerous situations.

suicidal attempts Efforts made to kill oneself.

suicidal ideation Serious thoughts about committing suicide.

suicidal plans The formulation of a specific method of killing oneself.

superego In **psychoanalysis,** the psychical entity representing the internalized moral principles of parents and society.

susceptibility In genetics, **genes** that only slightly increase the risk of developing the disorder, but in contrast to the **deterministic** genes, these are more common in the general population.

synaptic cleft Space between nerve cells where chemical transmitters act to move impulses from one **neuron** to the next.

systematic desensitization Behavioral therapy technique to diminish excessive **fears,** involving gradual exposure to the feared stimulus paired with a positive coping experience, usually relaxation.

taxonomy System of naming and **classification** (for example, of specimens) in science.

terminal button The end of an axon (of a neuron) where neurotransmitters are stored before release.

testability Ability of a **hypothesis**, for example, to be subjected to scientific scrutiny and to be accepted or rejected, a necessary condition for the **hypothesis** to be useful.

tobacco-related disorders Cognitive, biological, behavioral, and social problems associated with the use and abuse of **nicotine.**

token economy Social learning behavior modification system in which individuals earn items they can exchange for desired rewards by displaying appropriate behaviors.

tolerance Need for increased amounts of a substance to achieve the desired effect, and a diminished effect with continued use of the same amount.

Tourette's disorder Developmental disorder featuring multiple dysfunctional motor and vocal tics.

transference Psychoanalytic concept suggesting that clients may seek to relate to the therapist as they do to important authority figures, particularly their parents.

transinstitutionalization Movement of people with severe mental illness from large psychiatric hospitals to smaller group residences.

transvestic disorder A **paraphilia** in which individuals, usually males, are sexually aroused or receive gratification by wearing clothing of the opposite sex.

traumatic brain injury (TBI) Brain damage caused by a blow to the head or other trauma that injures the brain and results in diminished neurocognitive capacity.

trend Direction of change of a behavior or behaviors (for example, increasing or decreasing).

trichotillomania (hair pulling disorder) People's urge to pull out their own hair from anywhere on the body, including the scalp, eyebrows, and arm.

twin studies In genetics research, the comparison of twins with unrelated or less closely related individuals. If twins, particularly monozygotic twins who share identical **genotypes,** share common characteristics such as a disorder, even if they were reared in different environments, this is strong evidence of genetic involvement in those characteristics.

type A behavior pattern Cluster of behaviors including excessive competitiveness, time-pressured impatience, accelerated speech, and anger, originally thought to promote high risk for heart disease.

type B behavior pattern Cluster of behaviors including a relaxed attitude, indifference to time pressure, and less forceful ambition; originally thought to promote low risk for heart disease.

unconditional positive regard Acceptance by the counselor of the client's feelings and actions without judgment or condemnation.

unconscious Part of the psychic makeup that is outside the awareness of the person.

vaginismus Recurring involuntary muscle spasms in the outer third of the vagina that interfere with sexual intercourse.

validity Degree to which a technique measures what it purports to measure.

variability Degree of change in a phenomenon over time.

vascular neurocognitive disorder Progressive brain disorder involving loss of cognitive functioning, caused by blockage of blood flow to the brain, that appears concurrently with other neurological signs and symptoms.

voyeuristic disorder A **paraphilic disorder** in which sexual arousal is derived from observing unsuspecting individuals undressing or naked.

vulnerability A **susceptibility** or tendency to develop a disorder.

vulvodynia Chronic pain in the area on the outside of a woman's genitals (the vulva).

Wernicke–Korsakoff syndrome Organic brain syndrome resulting from prolonged heavy **alcohol** use, involving confusion, unintelligible speech, and loss of motor coordination. It may be caused by a deficiency of thiamine, a vitamin metabolized poorly by heavy drinkers.

withdrawal Severely negative physiological reaction to removal of a **psychoactive substance,** which can be alleviated by the same or a similar substance.

withdrawal delirium (delirium tremens/DTs) Frightening hallucinations and body tremors that result when a heavy drinker withdraws from **alcohol.**

withdrawal design Removing a treatment to note whether it has been effective. In **single-case experimental designs,** a behavior is measured **(baseline)**, an **independent variable** is introduced (intervention), and then the intervention is withdrawn. Because the behavior continues to be measured throughout (repeated measurement), any effects of the intervention can be noted. Also called *reversal design.*

References

Aaronson, C. J., Shear, M. K., Goetz, R. R., Allen, L. B., Barlow, D. H., White, K. S., & Gorman, J. M. (2008). Predictors and time course of response among panic disorder patients treated with cognitive-behavioral therapy. *Journal of Clinical Psychiatry, 69*(3), 418–424.

Aarsland, D., & Kurz, M. W. (2010). The epidemiology of dementia associated with Parkinson disease. *Journal of the Neurological Sciences, 289*(1–2), 18–22.

Abbey, S. E., & Garfinkel, P. E. (1991). Neurasthenia and chronic fatigue syndrome: The role of culture in the making of a diagnosis. *American Journal of Psychiatry, 148,* 1638–1646.

Abbott, D. W., de Zwaan, M., Mussell, M. P., Raymond, N. C., Seim, H. C., Crow, S. J., & Mitchell J. E. (1998). Onset of binge eating and dieting in overweight women: Implications for etiology, associated features and treatment. *Journal of Psychosomatic Research, 44,* 367–374.

Abbott, S. M., Soca, R., & Zee, P. C. (2014). Circadian Rhythm Sleep Disorders. In *Primary Care Sleep Medicine* (pp. 297–309). Springer New York.

Abdul-Hamid, W. K., & Stein, G. (2012). The Surpu: Exorcism of antisocial personality disorder in ancient Mesopotamia. *Mental Health, Religion & Culture.* doi: 10.1080/13674676.2012.713337

Abdul-Hamid, W. K., & Stein, G. (2012). The Surpu: Exorcism of antisocial personality disorder in ancient Mesopotamia. *Mental Health, Religion & Culture. 16*(7), 671–685. doi: 10.1080/13674676.2012.713337

Abel, G. G. (1989). Behavioral treatment of child molesters. In A. J. Stunkard & A. Baum (Eds.), *Perspectives in behavioral medicine: Eating, sleeping and sex* (pp. 223–242). Hillsdale, NJ: Erlbaum.

Abel, G. G., Barlow, D. H., Blanchard, E. B., & Guild, D. (1977). The components of rapists' sexual arousal. *Archives of General Psychiatry, 34,* 895–903.

Abel, G. G., Becker, J. V., Cunningham-Rathner, J., Mittelman, M., & Rouleau, J. L. (1988). Multiple paraphilic diagnoses among sex offenders. *Bulletin of the American Academy of Psychiatry and Law, 16,* 153–168.

Abel, K. M., Drake, R., & Goldstein, J. M. (2010). Sex differences in schizophrenia. *International Review of Psychiatry, 22*(5), 417–428.

Abela, J. R., & Hankin, B. L. (2011). Rumination as a vulnerability factor to depression during the transition from early to middle adolescence: A multiwave longitudinal study. *Journal of Abnormal Psychology, 120*(2), 259–271.

Abela, J. R., & Skitch, S. A. (2007). Dysfunctional attitudes, self-esteem, and hassles: Cognitive vulnerability to depression in children of affectively ill parents. *Behaviour Research and Therapy, 45*(6), 1127–1140.

Abela, J. R., Stolow, D., Mineka, S., Yao, S., Zhu, X. Z., & Hankin, B. L. (2011). Cognitive vulnerability to depressive symptoms in adolescents in urban and rural Hunan, China: A multiwave longitudinal study. *Journal of Abnormal Psychology, 120*(4), 765–778.

Abele, H., Wagner, P., Sonek, J., Hoopmann, M., Brucker, S., Artunc-Ulkumen, B., & Kagan, K. O. (2015). First trimester ultrasound screening for Down syndrome based on maternal age, fetal nuchal translucency and different combinations of the additional markers nasal bone, tricuspid and ductus venosus flow. *Prenatal Diagnosis, 35*(12), 1182–1186.

Abrahamson, D. J., Barlow, D. H., Sakheim, D. K., Beck, J. G., & Athanasiou, R. (1985). Effects of distraction on sexual responding in functional and dysfunctional men. *Behavior Therapy, 16,* 503–515.

Abramowitz, J. S., & Jacoby, R. J. (2015). Obsessive-compulsive and related disorders: A critical review of the new diagnostic class. *Annual Review of Clinical Psychology, 11,* 165–186.

Abramowitz, J. S., Taylor, S., & McKay, D. (2012). Exposure-based treatment for obsessive compulsive disorder. In G. Steketee (Ed.), *The Oxford handbook of obsessive compulsive and spectrum disorders* (pp. 322–364). New York, NY: Oxford University Press.

Abramson, L. Y., Metalsky, G. I., & Alloy, L. B. (1989). Hopelessness depression: A theory-based subtype of depression. *Psychological Review, 96*(2), 358–372.

Abramson, L. Y., Seligman, M. E. P., & Teasdale, J. D. (1978). Learned helplessness in humans: Critique and reformulation. *Journal of Abnormal Psychology, 87,* 49–74.

Abse, D. W. (1987). *Hysteria and related mental disorders: An approach to psychological medicine*. Bristol, UK: Wright.

Adachi, Y., Sato, C., Nishino, N., Ohryoji, F., Hayama, J., & Yamagami, T. (2009). A brief parental education for shaping sleep habits in 4-month-old infants. *Clinical Medicine & Research, 7*(3), 85–92. doi: 10.3121/cmr.2009.814

Adams, C., & Gaile, J. (2020). Evaluation of a parent preference–based outcome measure after intensive communication intervention for children with social (pragmatic) communication disorder and high-functioning autism spectrum disorder. *Research in Developmental Disabilities, 105,* 103752.

Adams, C., Lockton, E., Freed, J., Gaile, J., Earl, G., McBean, K., & Law, J. (2012). The Social Communication Intervention Project: A randomized controlled trial of the effectiveness of speech and language therapy for school-age children who have pragmatic and social communication problems with or without autism spectrum disorder. *International Journal of Language & Communication Disorders, 47*(3), 233–244. doi: 10.1111/j.1460-6984.2011.00146.x

Adams, T. D., Davidson, L. E., Litwin, S. E., Kolotkin, R. L., LaMonte, M. J., Pendleton, R. C., & Hunt, S. C. (2012). Health benefits of gastric bypass surgery after 6 years. *JAMA: Journal of the American Medical Association, 308*(11), 1122–1131. doi: 10.1001/2012.jama.11164

Adams, T. D., Gress, R. E., Smith, S. C., Halverson, R. C., Simper, S. C., Rosamond, W. D., & Hunt, S. C. (2007). Long-term mortality after gastric bypass surgery. *New England Journal of Medicine, 357*(8), 753–761.

Addington v. Texas, 99 S. Ct. 1804 (1979).

Addington, J., Liu, L., Buchy, L., Cadenhead, K. S., Cannon, T. D., Cornblatt, B. A., . . . Woods, S. W. (2015). North American prodrome longitudinal study (NAPLS 2): the prodromal symptoms. *The Journal of Nervous and Mental Disease, 203*(5), 328–335.

Addis, M. E. (2008). Gender and depression in men. *Clinical Psychology: Science and Practice, 15*(3), 153–168.

Ader, R., & Cohen, N. (1975). Behaviorally conditioned immunosuppression. *Psychosomatic Medicine, 37,* 333–340.

Ader, R., & Cohen, N. (1993). Psychoneuroimmunology: Conditioning and stress. *Annual Review of Psychology, 44,* 53–85.

Adler, N. E. (2013). Health Disparities Taking on the Challenge. *Perspectives on Psychological Science, 8*(6), 679–681.

Afari, N., & Buchwald, D. (2003). Chronic fatigue syndrome: A review. *American Journal of Psychiatry, 160*, 221–236.

Agatisa, P., Matthews, K., Bromberger, J., Edmundowicz, D., Chang, Y., & Sutton-Tyrell, K. (2005). Coronary and aortic calcification in women with major depression history. *Archives of Internal Medicine, 165*, 1229–1236.

Aggarwal, N. K., Nicasio, A. V., DeSilva, R., Boiler, M., & Lewis-Fernández, R. (2013). Barriers to implementing the *DSM-5* cultural formulation interview: A qualitative study. *Culture, Medicine, and Psychiatry, 37*(3), 505–533.

Agras W. S., Hammer L. D., Huffman L. C., Mascola, A., Bryson, S. W. , & Danaher, C. (2012). Improving healthy eating in families with a toddler at risk for overweight: A cluster randomized controlled trial. *Journal of Developmental and Behavioral Pediatrics, 33*(7), 529–534.

Agras, W. S. (1987). *Eating disorders: Management of obesity, bulimia, and anorexia nervosa.* Elmsford, NY: Pergamon.

Agras, W. S. (2001). The consequences and costs of eating disorders. *Psychiatric Clinics of North America, 24*, 371–379.

Agras, W. S., Lock, J., Brandt, H., Bryson, S. W., Dodge, E., Halmi, K. A., . . . Woodside, B. (2014). Comparison of 2 family therapies for adolescent anorexia nervosa: a randomized parallel trial. *JAMA Psychiatry, 71*(11), 1279–1286.

Agras, W. S., Sylvester, D., & Oliveau, D. (1969). The epidemiology of common fears and phobia. *Comprehensive Psychiatry, 10*, 151–156.

Agras, W. S., Telch, C. F., Arnow, B., Eldredge, K., & Marnell, M. (1997). One year follow-up of cognitive-behavioral therapy of obese individuals with binge eating disorder. *Journal of Consulting and Clinical Psychology, 65*, 343–347.

Agras, W. S., Walsh, B. T., Fairburn, C. G., Wilson, G. T., & Kraemer, H. C. (2000). A multicenter comparison of cognitive-behavioral therapy and interpersonal psychotherapy for bulimia nervosa. *Archives of General Psychiatry, 57*, 459–466.

Aguirre, E., Woods, R. T., Spector, A., & Orrell, M. (2013). Cognitive stimulation for dementia: a systematic review of the evidence of effectiveness from randomised controlled trials. *Ageing Research Reviews, 12*(1), 253–262.

Ahima, R. S., & Lazar, M. A. (2013). The health risk of obesity—better metrics imperative. *Science, 341*(6148), 856–858.

Ahlers, C. J., Schaefer, G. A., Mundt, I. A., Roll, S., Englert, H., Willich, S. N., & Beier, K. M. (2011). How unusual are the contents of paraphilias? Paraphilia-associated sexual arousal patterns in a community based sample of men. *Journal of Sexual Medicine, 8*(5), 1362–1370.

Ahmad, F. B., Cisewski, J. A., Miniño, A., & Anderson, R. N. (2021). Provisional mortality data: United States, 2020. *Morbidity and Mortality Weekly Report (MMWR), 70*, 519–522. doi: http://dx.doi.org/10.15585/mmwr.mm7014e1external icon

Ahmadiankalati, M., Steins-Loeber, S., & Paslakis, G. (2020). Review of randomized controlled trials using e-health interventions for patients with eating disorders. *Frontiers in Psychiatry, 11*. doi: 10.3389/fpsyt.2020.00568

Ahmed, A. O., Green, B. A., Goodrum, N. M., Doane, N. J., Birgenheir, D., & Buckley, P. F. (2013). Does a latent class underlie schizotypal personality disorder? Implications for schizophrenia. *Journal of Abnormal Psychology, 122*, 475–491. doi:10.1037/a0032713

Ahmed, I., & Thorpy, M. (2012). Narcolepsy and idiopathic hypersomnia. In M. S. Badr (Ed.), *Essentials of sleep medicine: An approach for clinical pulmonology* (pp. 297–314). New York, NY: Humana Press.

Aikins, D. E., & Craske, M. G. (2001). Cognitive theories of generalized anxiety disorder. *Psychiatric Clinics of North America, 24*, 57–74.

Ajina, S., & Bridge, H. (2017). Blindsight and unconscious vision: What they teach us about the human visual system. *Neuroscientist, 23*(5), 529–541. doi: 10.1177/1073858416673817

Akemoglu, Y., & Tomeny, K. R. (2020). A parent-implemented shared-reading intervention to promote communication skills of preschoolers with autism spectrum disorder. *Journal of Autism and Developmental Disorders*, 1–14.

Akiskal, H. (2006). Special issue on circular insanity and beyond: Historic contributions of French psychiatry to contemporary concepts and research on bipolar disorder. *Journal of Affective Disorders, 96*, 141–143.

Akiskal, H. S. (2009). Dysthymia, cyclothymia, and hyperthymia. In M. G. Gelder, N. C. Andreasen, J. J. López-Ibor Jr., & J. R. Geddes (Eds.), *New Oxford textbook of psychiatry* (2nd ed., Vol. 1, pp. 680–692). Oxford, UK: Oxford University Press.

Akiskal, H. S., & Cassano, G. B. (Eds.) (1997). *Dysthymia and the spectrum of chronic depressions.* New York, NY: Guilford.

al'Absi, M., & Wittmers, L. E., Jr. (2003). Enhanced adrenocortical responses to stress in hypertension-prone men and women. *Annals of Behavioral Medicine, 25*, 25–33.

Alba-Ferrara, L., Fernyhough, C., Weis, S., Mitchell, R. L. C., & Hausmann, M. (2012). Contributions of emotional prosody comprehension deficits to the formation of auditory verbal hallucinations in schizophrenia. *Clinical Psychology Review, 32*(4), 244–250. doi: 10.1016/j.cpr.2012.02.003

Albano, A. M., & Barlow, D. H. (1996). Breaking the vicious cycle: Cognitive-behavioral group treatment for socially anxious youth. In E. D. Hibbs & P. S. Jensen (Eds.), *Psychosocial treatments for child and adolescent disorders* (pp. 43–62). Washington, DC: American Psychological Association.

Albano, A. M., & Hack, S. (2004). Children and adolescents. In R. G. Heimberg, C. L. Turk, & D. S. Mennin (Eds.), *Generalized anxiety disorder: Advances in research and practice* (pp. 383–408). New York, NY: Guilford.

Albano, A. M., Chorpita, B. F., & Barlow, D. H. (1996). Childhood anxiety disorders. In E. J. Mash & R. A. Barkley (Eds.), *Child psychopathology* (pp. 196–241). New York, NY: Guilford.

Albano, A. M., Miller, P. P., Zarate, R., Côté, G., & Barlow, D. H. (1997). Behavioral assessment and treatment of PTSD in prepubertal children: Attention to development factors and innovative strategies in the case study of a family. *Cognitive and Behavioral Practice, 4*, 245–262.

Albert, C., Chae, C., Rexrode, K., Manson, J., & Kawachi, I. (2005). Phobic anxiety and risk of coronary heart disease and sudden cardiac among women. *Circulation, 111*, 480–487.

Albertini, R. S., & Phillips, K. A. (1999). Thirty-three cases of body dysmorphic disorder in children and adolescents. *Journal of the American Academy of Child and Adolescent Psychiatry, 38*(4), 453–459.

Albon, T., & Schneider, S. (2007). Psychotherapy of childhood anxiety disorders: A meta-analysis. *Psychother Psychosom, 76*, 15–24.

Albright, J. A., Stevens, S. A., & Beussman, D. J. (2012). Detecting ketamine in beverage residues: Application in date rape detection. *Drug Testing and Analysis, 4*(5), 337–341. doi: 10.1002/dta.335

Alda, M. (2015). Lithium in the treatment of bipolar disorder: Pharmacology and pharmacogenetics. *Molecular Psychiatry, 20*, 661–670.

Alessi, S. M., Roll, J. M., Reilly, M. P., & Johanson, C. E. (2002). Establishment of a diazepam preference in human volunteers following a differential-conditioning history of placebo versus diazepam choice. *Experimental and Clinical Psychopharmacology, 10,* 77–83.

Alexander, F. G. (1939). Emotional factors in essential hypertension: Presentation of a tentative hypothesis. *Psychosomatic Medicine, 1,* 175–179.

Alexander, F. G. (1950). *Psychosomatic medicine.* New York, NY: Norton.

Alexander, F. G., & Selesnick, S. T. (1966). *The history of psychiatry: An evaluation of psychiatric thought and practice from prehistoric times to the present.* New York, NY: Harper & Row.

Alexopoulos, G. S. (2005). Depression in the elderly. *Lancet, 365,* 1961–1970.

Alexopoulos, G., Katz, I., Bruce, M., Heo, M., Have, T., Raue, P., & Reynolds, C. F., III., (2005). Remission in depressed geriatric primary care patients: A report from the PROSPECT study. *American Journal of Psychiatry, 162,* 718–724.

Alharbi, Y. N. (2020). Current legal status of medical marijuana and cannabidiol in the United States. *Epilepsy & Behavior, 112,* 107452.

Ali, S. R., Liu, W. M., & Humedian, M. (2004). Islam 101: Understanding the religion and therapy implications. *Professional Psychology: Research and Practice, 35*(6), 635.

Alim, T. N., Feder, A., Graves, R. E., Wang, Y., Weaver, J., Westphal, M., & Charney, D. S. (2008). Trauma, resilience, and recovery in a high-risk African-American population. *The American Journal of Psychiatry, 165*(12), 1566–1575.

Allan, R., & Ungar, M. (2014). Resilience-building interventions with children, adolescents, and their families. In S. Prince-Embury & D. H., Saklofske (Eds.). *Resilience Interventions for Youth in Diverse Populations* (pp. 447–462). Springer: New York.

Allen, J. J., & Movius, H. L. (2000). The objective assessment of amnesia in dissociative identity disorder using event-related potentials. *International Journal of Psychophysiology, 38,* 21–41.

Allen, J. L., Lavallee K. L., Herren C., Ruhe, K., & Schneider, S. (2010). DSM-IV criteria for childhood separation anxiety disorder: Informant, age, and sex differences. *Journal of Anxiety Disorders, 24*(8), 946–952. doi: 10.1016/j.janxdis.2010.06.022

Allen, J., DeMyer, M. K., Norton, J. A., Pontius, W., & Yang, G. (1971). Intellectuality in parents of psychotic, subnormal, and normal children. *Journal of Autism and Childhood Schizophrenia, 1*(3), 311–326.

Allen, K. L., Byrne, S. M., Oddy, W. H., & Crosby, R. D. (2013). *DSM-IV–TR* and *DSM-5* eating disorders in adolescents: Prevalence, stability, and psychosocial correlates in a population-based sample of male and female adolescents. *Journal of Abnormal Psychology, 122*(3), 720–732.

Allen, K., Bloscovitch, J., & Mendes, W. B. (2002). Cardiovascular reactivity in the presence of pets, friends, and spouses: The truth about cats and dogs. *Psychosomatic Medicine, 64,* 727–739.

Allen, L. A., Woolfolk, R. L., Escobar, J. I., Gara, M. A., & Hamer, R. M. (2006). Cognitive-behavioral therapy for somatization disorder: A randomized controlled trial. *Archives of Internal Medicine, 166*(14), 1512–1518.

Allen, L. B., White, K. S., Barlow, D. H., Shear, M. K., Gorman, J. M., & Woods, S. W. (2010). Cognitive-behavior therapy (CBT) for panic disorder: Relationship of anxiety and depression comorbidity with treatment outcome. *Journal of Psychopathology & Behavioral Assessment, 32*(2), 185–192.

Allen, L. S., & Gorski, R. A. (1992). Sexual orientation and the size of the anterior commissure in the human brain. *Proceedings of the National Academy of Science, 89,* 7199–7202.

Allen, N. J., & Barres, B. A. (2009). Neuroscience: Glia—more than just brain glue. *Nature, 457*(7230), 675–677.

Allen, P., & Modinos, G. (2012). Structural neuroimaging in psychotic patients with auditory verbal hallucinations. In J. D. Blom & I. E. C. Sommer (Eds.), *Hallucinations* (pp. 251–265). New York, NY: Springer.

Allender, S., Peto, V., Scarborough, P., Boxer, A., & Rayner, M. (2007). *Coronary heart disease statistics.* Oxford, England: British Heart Foundation & Stroke Association.

Aller, R., & Aller, G. (1997). An institutional response to patient/family complaints. In A. E. Shamoo (Ed.), *Ethics in neurobiological research with human subjects: The Baltimore Conference on Ethics* (pp. 155–172). Amsterdam, The Netherlands: Gordon and Breach.

Alley, Z. M., Kerr, D. C., & Bae, H. (2020). Trends in college students' alcohol, nicotine, prescription opioid and other drug use after recreational marijuana legalization: 2008–2018. *Addictive Behaviors, 102,* 106212.

Alloy, L. B., & Abramson, L. Y. (2010). The role of the behavioral approach system (BAS) in bipolar spectrum disorders. *Current Directions in Psychological Science, 19*(3), 189–194.

Alloy, L. B., Abramson, L. Y., Urosevic, S., Bender, R. E., & Wagner, C. A. (2009). Longitudinal predictors of bipolar spectrum disorders: A behavioral approach system (BAS) perspective. *Clinical Psychology* (New York), *16*(2), 206–226.

Alloy, L. B., Bender, R. E., Whitehouse, W. G., Wagner, C. A., Liu, R. T., Grant, D. A., & Abramson, L. Y. (2012). High Behavioral Approach System (BAS) sensitivity, reward responsiveness, and goal-striving predict first onset of bipolar spectrum disorders: A prospective behavioral high-risk design. *Journal of Abnormal Psychology, 121*(2), 339–351.

Alloy, L. B., Ng, T. H., Titone, M. K., & Boland, E. M. (2017). Circadian rhythm dysregulation in bipolar spectrum disorders. *Current Psychiatry Reports, 19*(4). doi: 10.1007/s11920-017-0772-z

Alloy, L. B., Nusslock, R., & Boland, E. M. (2015). The development and course of bipolar spectrum disorders: An integrated reward and circadian rhythm dysregulation model. *Annual Review of Clinical Psychology, 11,* 213.

Alloy, L., & Abramson, L. (2006). Prospective incidence of first onsets and recurrences of depression in individuals at high and low cognitive risk for depression. *Journal of Abnormal Psychology, 115,* 145–156.

Alloy, L., Abramson, L. Y., Hogan, M. E., Whitehouse, W. G., Rose, D. T., Robinson, M. S., & Lapkin, J. B. (2000). The Temple-Wisconsin cognitive vulnerability to depression project: Lifetime history of axis I psychopathology in individuals at high and low cognitive risk for depression. *Journal of Abnormal Psychology, 109,* 403–418.

Alloy, L., Abramson, L., Safford, S., & Gibb, B. (2006). The cognitive vulnerability to depression (CVD) project: Current findings and future directions. In L. B. Alloy & J. H. Riskind (Eds.), *Cognitive vulnerability to emotional disorders* (pp. 33–61). Hillsdale, NJ: Erlbaum.

Almklov, E. L., Drummond, S. P., Orff, H., & Alhassoon, O. M. (2015). The effects of sleep deprivation on brain functioning in older adults. *Behavioral Sleep Medicine, 13*(4), 324–345.

Alpers, G. W. (2009). Ambulatory assessment of panic disorder and specific phobia. *Psychological Assessment, 21,* 476–485.

Alter, H. J., Mikovits, J. A., Switzer, W. M., Ruscetti, F. W., Lo, S. C., Klimas, N., Komaroff, A. L., Montoya, J. G., Bateman, L., Levine, S., Peerson, D., Levin, B., Hanson, M. R., Genfi, A., Bhat, M., Zheng, H., Wang, R., Li, B., Hung, G.-C., Lee, L. L., Sameroff, S., Heneine, W., Coffin, J., Horning, M., & Lipkin, W. I. (2012). A multicenter blinded analysis indicates no association between chronic fatigue syndrome/myalgic encephalomyelitis and either xenotropic murine leukemia virus-related virus or polytropic murine leukemia virus. *MBio, 3*(5), e00266-12.

Althof, S. (2006). The psychology of premature ejaculation: Therapies and consequences. *Journal of Sexual Medicine, 3,* 324–331.

Althof, S. E. (2007). Treatment of rapid ejaculation: Psychotherapy, pharmacotherapy, and combined therapy. In S. R. Leiblum (Ed.), *Principles and practice of sex therapy* (4th ed., pp. 212–240). New York, NY: Guilford.

Altman, M., & Wilfley, D. E. (2015). Evidence update on the treatment of overweight and obesity in children and adolescents. *Journal of Clinical Child & Adolescent Psychology, 44*(4), 521–537.

Altshuler, L. L., Kupka, R. W., Hellemann, G., Frye, M. A., Sugar, C. A., McElroy, S. L., & Suppes, T. (2010). Gender and depressive symptoms in 711 patients with bipolar disorder evaluated prospectively in the Stanley Foundation bipolar treatment outcome network. *American Journal of Psychiatry, 167*(6), 708–715.

Alzheimer's Association. (2011). Alzheimer's disease facts and figures. *Alzheimer's & Dementia: The Journal of the Alzheimer's Association, 7,* 208–244.

Amad, A., Ramoz, N., Thomas, P., Jardri, R., & Gorwood, P. (2014). Genetics of borderline personality disorder: systematic review and proposal of an integrative model. *Neuroscience & Biobehavioral Reviews, 40,* 6–19.

Amat, J., Baratta, B. V., Paul, E., Bland, S. T., Watkins, L. R., & Maier, S. F. (2005). Medial prefrontal cortex determines how stressor controllability affects behavior and dorsal raphe nucleus. *Nature Neuroscience, 8,* 365–371.

Ambrose, D., MacKenzie, D. E., & Ghanouni, P. (2020). The impact of person–environment–occupation transactions on joint attention in children with autism spectrum disorder: A scoping review. *British Journal of Occupational Therapy, 83*(6), 350–362.

American Bar Association Standing Committee on Association Standards for Criminal Justice. (1984). *Criminal justice and mental health standards.* Chicago, IL: Author.

American College of Obstetricians and Gynecologists. (2002). Clinical management guidelines for obstetricians–gynecologists: Premenstrual syndrome. *ACOG Practice Bulletin.* No. 15. Washington, DC: American College of Obstetricians and Gynecologists.

American Law Institute. (1962). *Model penal code: Proposed official draft.* Philadelphia, PA: Author.

American Psychiatric Association Practice Guideline. (2010). *Practice guideline for the treatment of patients with major depressive disorder* (3rd ed.). Washington, DC: American Psychiatric Association. Retrieved from http://www.psychiatryonline.com/pracGuide/pracGuideTopic_7.aspx

American Psychiatric Association. (1980). *Diagnostic and statistical manual of mental disorders* (3rd ed.). Washington, DC: Author.

American Psychiatric Association. (1983). American Psychiatric Association statement on the insanity defense. *American Journal of Psychiatry, 140,* 681–688.

American Psychiatric Association. (2000a). *Diagnostic and statistical manual of mental disorders* (4th ed., text revision). Washington, DC: Author.

American Psychiatric Association. (2000b). Substance use disorders: Alcohol, cocaine, opioids. In *Practice guidelines for the treatment of psychiatric disorders: Compendium 2000* (pp. 139–238). Washington, DC: Author.

American Psychiatric Association. (2004). Practice guideline for the treatment of patients with schizophrenia (2nd ed.). *American Journal of Psychiatry, 161*(Suppl.), 1–56.

American Psychiatric Association. (2006). Practice guideline for the psychiatric evaluation of adults (2nd ed.). *American Journal of Psychiatry, 163*(Suppl.), 1–36.

American Psychiatric Association. (2007). Practice guidelines for the treatment of patients with substance use disorders (2nd ed.). *American Journal of Psychiatry, 164*(Suppl.), 1–14.

American Psychiatric Association. (2010). Clinical practice guidelines. *American Journal of Psychiatry, 167*(10).

American Psychiatric Association. (2010a). *APA practice guidelines for treatment of patients with eating disorders* (3rd ed.). Retrieved from http://www .psychiatryonline.com/content.aspx?aID5138866

American Psychiatric Association. (2010b). DSM-5 Development: Sleep–Wake Disorders. Retrieved November 6, 2012, from http://www.dsm5.org/ProposedRevision/Pages/Sleep-WakeDisorders.aspx

American Psychiatric Association. (2013). *Diagnostic and statistical manual of mental disorders: DSM-5.* Washington, D.C.: American PsychiatricAassociation.

American Psychiatric Association. (2013). *Diagnostic and statistical manual of mental disorders: DSM-5.* Washington, DC: American PsychiatricAassociation.

American Psychological Association Presidential Task Force. (2006). Evidence-based practice in psychology. *American Psychologist, 61,* 271–285.

American Psychological Association Task Force on Gender Identity and Gender Variance. (2008). *Report of the Task Force on Gender Identity and Gender Variance.* Washington, DC: Author.

American Psychological Association. (2002a). Ethical principles of psychologists and code of conduct. *American Psychologist, 57,* 1060–1073.

American Psychological Association. (2010a). 2010 Amendments to the 2002 "Ethical principles of psychologists and code of conduct." *American Psychologist, 65*(5), 493–493.

American Psychological Association. (2010b). Report of the ethics committee, 2009. *American Psychologist, 65*(5), 483–492.

American Psychological Association. (2012). *The APA guidelines for the undergraduate psychology major version 2.0.* Washington, D.C.: American Psychological Association.

American Psychological Association. (2013). *APA guidelines for the undergraduate psychology major.* Washington, DC: Author.

American Psychological Association. (2016). Revision of Ethical Standard 3.04 of the Ethical Principles of Psychologists and Code of Conduct (2002, as amended 2010). *The American Psychologist, 71*(9), 900.

American Psychological Association. (2021). Professional practice guidelines for evidence-based psychological practice in health care. Retrieved from https://www.apa.org/about/policy/evidence-based-psychological-practice-health-care.pdf

American Society of Plastic Surgeons. (2012). National cosmetic procedures. Retrieved from http://www.plasticsurgery.org/news-and-resources/2012-plastic-surgery-statistics.html

Ames, G. E., Patel, R. H., McMullen, J. S., Thomas, C. S., Crook, J. E., Lynch, S. A., & Lutes, L. D. (2014). Improving maintenance of lost weight following a commercial liquid meal replacement program: a preliminary study. *Eating Behaviors, 15*(1), 95–98.

Amieva, H., Mokri, H., Le Goff, M., Meillon, C., Jacqmin-Gadda, H., Foubert-Samier, A., . . . Dartigues, J. F. (2014). Compensatory mechanisms in higher-educated subjects with Alzheimer's disease: a study of 20 years of cognitive decline. *Brain, 137*(4), 1167–1175.

Anandam, A., Akinnusi, M., Kufel, T., Porhomayon, J., & El-Solh, A. A. (2013). Effects of dietary weight loss on obstructive sleep apnea: a meta-analysis.Sleep and Breathing, 17(1), 227–234.

Andari, E., Nishitani, S., Kaundinya, G., Caceres, G. A., Morrier, M. J., Ousley, O., … Young, L. J. (2020). Epigenetic modification of the oxytocin receptor gene: Implications for autism symptom severity and brain functional connectivity. *Neuropsychopharmacology, 45*(7), 1150–1158.

Andersen, B. L., & Cyranowski, J. M. (1994). Women's sexual self-schema. *Journal of Personality and Social Psychology, 67*(6), 1079–1100.

Andersen, B. L., Cyranowski, J. M., & Espindle, D. (1999). Men's sexual self-schema. *Journal of Personality and Social Psychology, 76*(4), 645–661.

Andersen, B. L., Farrar, W. B., Golden-Kreutz, D., Emery, C. F., Glaser, R., Crespin, T., & Carson, W. E., III. (2007). Distress reduction from a psychological intervention contributes to improved health for cancer patients. *Brain, Behavior, and Immunity, 21,* 953–961.

Andersen, B. L., Yang, H., Farrar, W. B., Golden-Kreutz, D. M., Emery, C. F., Thornton, L. M., & Carson, W. E., III. (2008). Psychologic intervention improves survival for breast cancer patients: A randomized clinical trial. *Cancer, 113,* 3450–3458.

Anderson, J. L., Sellbom, M., Wygant, D. B., Salekin, R. T., & Krueger, R. F. (2014). Examining the associations between DSM-5 Section III antisocial personality disorder traits and psychopathy in community and university samples. *Journal of Personality Disorders, 28*(5), 675–697.

Anderson-Fye, E. P., & Lin, J. (2009). Belief and behavior aspects of the EAT-26: The case of schoolgirls in belize. Culture, Medicine and Psychiatry, 33(4), 623–638. doi:10.1007/s11013-009-9154-

Andersson, E., Hedman, E., Enander, J., Djurfeldt, D. R., Ljótsson, B., Cervenka, S., Isung, J., Svanborg, C., Mataix-Cols, D., Kaldo, V., Andersson, G., Lindefors, N., & Rück, C. (2015). D-Cycloserine vs placebo as adjunct to cognitive behavioral therapy for obsessive-compulsive disorder and interaction with antidepressants: A randomized clinical trial. *JAMA Psychiatry, 72*(7):659–667.

Andrasik, F. (2000). Biofeedback. In D. I. Mostofsky & D. H. Barlow (Eds.), *The management of stress and anxiety in medical disorders* (pp. 66–83). Needham Heights, MA: Allyn & Bacon.

Andreasen, N. C. (1987). Creativity and mental illness: Prevalence rates in writers and their first-degree relatives. *American Journal of Psychiatry, 144*(10), 1288–1292.

Andreasen, N. C. (2012). Schizophrenia: A conceptual history. In M. G. Gelder, N. C. Andreasen, J. J. Lopez-Ibor, Jr., & J. R. Geddes (Eds.), *New Oxford textbook of psychiatry* (2nd ed., Vol. 1, pp. 521-526). New York, NY: Oxford University Press.

Andrews, G., Hobbs, M. J., Borkovec, T. D., Beesdo, K., Craske, M. G., Heimberg, R. G., & Stanley, M. A. (2010). Generalized worry disorder: A review of DSM-IV generalized anxiety disorder and options for DSM-V. *Depression and Anxiety, 27*(2), 134–147. doi: 10.1002/da.20658

Aneshensel, C. S., Pearlin, L. I., Mullan, J. T., Zarit, S. H., & Whitlatch, C. J. (1995). *Profiles in caregiving: The unexpected career*. San Diego, CA: Academic.

Anglin, D. M., Lighty, Q., Greenspoon, M., & Ellman, L. M. (2014). Racial discrimination is associated with distressing subthreshold positive psychotic symptoms among US urban ethnic minority young adults. *Social Psychiatry and Psychiatric Epidemiology, 49*(10), 1545–1555.

Angst, J. (2009). Course and prognosis of mood disorders. In M. G. Gelder, N. C. Andreasen, J. J. López-Ibor, Jr., & J. R. Geddes (Eds.), *New Oxford textbook of psychiatry* (2nd ed., Vol. 1, pp. 665–669). Oxford, UK: Oxford University Press.

Angst, J., & Grobler, C. (2015) Unipolar mania: A necessary diagnostic concept. *European Archives of Psychiatry and Clinical Neuroscience, 265,* 273–280.

Angst, J., & Sellaro, R. (2000). Historical perspectives and natural history of bipolar disorder. *Biological Psychiatry, 48*(6), 445–457.

Angst, J., Cui, L. H., Swendsen, J., Rothen, S., Cravchik, A., & Merikangas, K. R. (2010). Major depressive disorder with subthreshold bipolarity in the National Comorbidity Survey Replication. *American Journal of Psychiatry, 167*(10), 1194–1201.

Angstman, K. B., & Rasmussen, N. H. (2011). Personality disorders: review and clinical application in daily practice. *American Family Physician, 84*(11), 1253.

Anisman, H., Zaharia, M. D., Meaney, M. J., & Merali, Z. (1998). Do early life events permanently alter behavioral and hormonal responses to stressors? *International Journal of Developmental Neuroscience, 16*(3–4), 149–164.

Anker, J. J., & Kushner, M. G. (2019). Co-occurring alcohol use disorder and anxiety: Bridging psychiatric, psychological, and neurobiological perspectives. *Alcohol Research, 40*(1). doi: 10.35946/arcr.v40.1.03

Ansell, E., Sanislow, C., McGlashan, T., & Grilo, C. (2007). Psychosocial impairment and treatment utilization by patients with borderline personality disorder, other personality disorders, mood and anxiety disorders, and a healthy comparison group. *Comprehensive Psychiatry, 48*(4), 329–336.

Anson, M., Veale, D., & de Silva, P. (2012). Social-evaluative versus self-evaluative appearance concerns in body dysmorphic disorder. *Behavior Research and Therapy, 50*(12), 753–760. doi: 10.1016/j.brat.2012.09.003

Anstey, K. J., Peters, R., Zheng, L., Barnes, D. E., Brayne, C., Brodaty, H., … Yaffe, K. (2020). Future directions for dementia risk reduction and prevention research: An International Research Network on Dementia Prevention consensus. *Journal of Alzheimer's Disease, 78,* 3–12. doi: 10.3233/JAD-200674

Anton, B., & Leff, L. P. (2006). A novel bivalent morphine/heroin vaccine that prevents relapse to heroin addiction in rodents. *Vaccine, 24*(16), 3232–3240.

Anton, R. F., Voronin, K. E., Book, S. W., Latham, P. K., Randall, P. K., Glen, W. B., … Schacht, J. P. (2020). Opioid and dopamine genes interact to predict naltrexone response in a randomized alcohol use disorder clinical trial. *Alcoholism: Clinical and Experimental Research, 44*(10), 2084–2096.

Antoni, M. H. (2012). *Stress, coping, and health in HIV/AIDS.* The Oxford Handbook of Stress, Heath, and Coping. Oxford, UK: Oxford University Press.

Antoni, M. H., & Dhabhar, F. S. (2019). The impact of psychosocial stress and stress management on immune responses in patients with cancer. *Cancer, 125*(9), 1417–1431. doi: 10.1002/cncr.31943

Antoni, M. H., & Lutgendorf, S. (2007). Psychosocial factors and disease progression in cancer. *Current Directions in Psychological Science, 16,* 42–46.

Antoni, M. H., Cruess, D. G., Cruess, S., Lutgendorf, S., Kumar, M., Ironson, G., & Schneiderman, N. (2000). Cognitive-behavioral stress management intervention effects on anxiety, 24-hr urinary norepinephrine output, and T-cytotoxic/suppressor cells over time among symptomatic HIV-infected gay men. *Journal of Consulting and Clinical Psychology, 68,* 31–45.

Antoni, M. H., Lechner, S., Diaz, A., Vargas, S., Holley, H., Phillips, K., & Blombery, B. (2009). Cognitive behavioral stress management effects on psychosocial and psychological adaptation in women undergoing treatment for breast cancer. *Brain, Behavior, and Immunity, 23,* 580–591.

Antoni, M. H., Lechner, S., Kazi, A., Wimberly, S., Sifre, T., Urcuyo, K., & Carver, C. S. (2006). How stress management improves quality of life after treatment for breast cancer. *Journal of Consulting and Clinical Psychology, 74,* 1143–1152.

Antony, M. M., & Barlow, D. H. (2002). Specific phobias. In D. H. Barlow, *Anxiety and its disorders: The nature and treatment of anxiety and panic* (2nd ed.). New York, NY: Guilford.

Antony, M. M., & Barlow, D. H. (Eds.). (2010). *Handbook of assessment and treatment planning for psychological disorders* (2nd ed.). New York, NY: Guilford.

Antony, M. M., Brown, T. A., & Barlow, D. H. (1997a). Heterogeneity among specific phobia types in DSM-IV. *Behavior Research and Therapy, 35,* 1089–1100.

Antony, M. M., Brown, T. A., & Barlow, D. H. (1997b). Response to hyperventilation and 5.5% CO_2 inhalation of subjects with types of specific phobia, panic disorder, or no mental disorder. *American Journal of Psychiatry, 154,* 1089–1095.

Antony, M. M., Craske, M. G., & Barlow, D. H. (2006). *Mastering your fears and phobias: Workbook.* New York, NY: Oxford University Press.

Anttila, V., Bulik-Sullivan, B., Finucane, H. K., Walters, R. K., Bras, J., Duncan, L., … The Brainstorm Consortium. (2018). Analysis of shared heritability in common disorders of the brain. *Science, 360*(6395) doi: 10.1126/science.aap8757

Aouizerate, B., Rotge, J., Martin-Guehl, C., Cuny, E., Rougier, A., Guehl, D., & Tignol, J. (2006). A systematic review of psychsurgical treatments for obsessive-compulsive disorder: Does deep brain stimulation represent the future trend in psychosurgery? *Clinical Neuropsychiatry, 3*(6), 391–403.

Apfelbaum, B. (2000). Retarded ejaculation: A much misunderstood syndrome. In S. R. Leiblum & R. C. Rosen (Eds.), *Principles and practice of sex therapy* (3rd ed., pp. 205–241). New York, NY: Guilford.

Apple, R. F., Lock, J., & Peebles, R. (2006). Is weight loss surgery right for yo? New York, NY: Oxford University Press. ISBN: 978-0-19-531315-4

Arai, J. A., Li, S., Hartley, D. M., & Feig, L. A. (2009). Transgenerational rescue of a genetic defect in long-term potentiation and memory formation by juvenile enrichment. *The Journal of Neuroscience, 29*(5), 1496–1502.

Arbanas, G. (2021). Personality disorders. In M. Lew-Starowicz, A. Giraldi, & T. H. C. Krüger (Eds.), *Psychiatry and sexual medicine: A comprehensive guide for clinical practitioners* (pp. 309–320). Cham, Switzerland: Springer.

Arcelus J., Mitchell, A. J., Wales, J., & Nielsen, S. (2011). Mortality rates in patients with anorexia nervosa and other eating disorders: A meta-analysis of 36 studies. *Archives of General Psychiatry, 68*(7), 724–731. doi: 10.1001/archgenpsychiatry.2011.74

Archer, M., Harwood, H., Stevelink, S., Rafferty, L., & Greenberg, N. (2020). Community reinforcement and family training and rates of treatment entry: A systematic review. *Addiction, 115*(6), 1024–1037.

Arenkiel, B. R., & Ehlers, M. D. (2009). Molecular genetics and imaging technologies for circuit-based neuroanatomy. *Nature, 461*(7266), 900–907.

Arias, A. J., Welch, W., & Kaminer, Y. (2020). Bioassays and detection of substances of abuse in youth. In Y. Kaminer & K. C. Winters (Eds.), *Clinical manual of youth addictive disorders* (pp. 97–122). Washington, D.C.: American Psychiatric Association Publishing.

Armbruster, D., Mueller, A., Moser, D. A., Lesch, K. P., Brocke, B., & Kirschbaum, C. (2009). Interaction effect of D4 dopamine receptor gene and serotonin transporter promoter polymorphism on the cortisol stress response. *Behavioral Neuroscience, 123*(6), 1288–1295.

Armstrong, T. (2010). *Neurodiversity: Discovering the extraordinary gifts of autism, ADHD, dyslexia, and other brain differences.* Boston: Da Capo Press.

Aronow, E., Weiss, K. A., & Reznikoff, M. (2013). *A practical guide to the Thematic Apperception Test: The TAT in clinical practice.* London: Routledge.

Arria, A. M., Garnier-Dykstra, L. M., Cook, E. T., Caldeira, K. M., Vincent, K. B., Baron, R. A., & O'Grady, K. E. (2013). Drug use patterns in young adulthood and post-college employment. *Drug and Alcohol Dependence, 127*(1–3), 23–30. doi: http://dx.doi.org/10.1016/j.drugalcdep.2012.06.001

Arrindell, W. A., Eisemann, M., Richter, J., Oei, T. P. S., Caballo, V. E., van der Ende, J., & Hudson, B. L. (2003a). Phobic anxiety in 11 nations Part I: Dimensional constancy of the five-factor model. *Behaviour Research and Therapy, 41,* 461–479.

Arrindell, W. A., Eisemann, M., Richter, J., Oei, T. P. S., Caballo, V. E., van der Ende, J., & Zaldívar, F. (2003b). Masculinity–feminity as a national characteristic and its relationship with national agoraphobic fear levels: Fodor's sex role hypothesis revitalized. *Behaviour Research and Therapy, 41,* 795–807.

Arterburn, D. E., & Fisher, D. P. (2014). The current state of the evidence for bariatric surgery. *Journal of the American Medical Association, 312*(9), 898–899.

Arterburn, D. E., Olsen, M. K., Smith, V. A., Livingston, E. H., Van Scoyoc, L., Yancy, W. S., . . . Maciejewski, M. L. (2015). Association between bariatric surgery and long-term survival. *JAMA, 313*(1), 62–70.

Asberg, M., Nordstrom, P., & Traskman-Bendz, L. (1986). Cerebrospinal fluid studies in suicide: An overview. *Annals of the American Academy of Science, 487,* 243–255.

Ascher-Svanum, H., Zhu, B., Faries, D. E., Salkever, D., Slade, E. P., Peng, X., & Conley, R. R. (2010). The cost of relapse and the predictors of relapse in the treatment of schizophrenia. *BMC Psychiatry, 10*(1), 2.

Aschoff, J., & Wever, R. (1962). Spontanperiodik des Menschen die Ausschulus aller Zeitgeber. *Die Naturwissenschaften, 49,* 337–342.

Ashare, R. L., Karlawish, J. H., Wileyto, E. P., Pinto, A., & Lerman, C. (2012). APOE _4, an Alzheimer's disease susceptibility allele, and smoking cessation. *The Pharmacogenomics Journal.* doi: 10.1038/tpj.2012.49

Ashkenazi, S., Black, J. M., Abrams, D. A., Hoeft, F., & Menon, V. (2013). Neurobiological underpinnings of math and reading learning disabilities. *Journal of Learning Disabilities.* doi: 10.1177/0022219413483174

Ashley, L. L., & Boehlke, K. K. (2012). Pathological gambling: A general overview. *Journal of Psychoactive Drugs, 44*(1), 27–37. doi: 10.1080/02791072.2012.662078

Ask, H., Cheesman, R., Jami, E. S., Levey, D. F., Purves, K. L., & Weber, H. (2021). Genetic contributions to anxiety disorders: Where we are and where we are heading. *Psychological Medicine.* doi: 10.1017/S0033291720005486

Askew, C., Hagel, A., & Morgan, J. (2015). Vicarious learning of children's social-anxiety-related fear beliefs and emotion Stroop bias. *Emotion, 15,* 501–510.

Asmundson, G. J., & Carleton, R. N. (2009). Fear of pain. In M. M. Antony & M. B. Stein (Eds.), *Oxford handbook of anxiety and related disorders* (pp. 551–561). Oxford, UK: Oxford University Press.

Asnaani, A., Gutner, C., Hinton, D., & Hofmann, S. G. (2009). Panic disorder, panic attacks, and panic attack symptoms across race-ethnic groups: Results of the Collaborative Psychiatric Epidemiology Survey. *CNS Neuroscience and Therapeutics, 15,* 249–254.

Asnaani, A., Richey, J. A., Dimaite, R., Hinton, D. E., & Hofmann, S. G. (2010). A cross-ethnic comparison of lifetime prevalence rates of anxiety disorders. *Journal of Nervous and Mental Disease, 198*(8), 551–555. doi: 10.1097/NMD.0b013e3181ea169f

Aspiranti, K. B., Larwin, K. H., & Schade, B. P. (2020). iPads/tablets and students with autism: A meta-analysis of academic effects. *Assistive Technology, 32*(1), 23–30.

Assumpção, A. A., Garcia, F. D., Garcia, H. D., Bradford, J. M., & Thibaut, F. (2014). Pharmacologic treatment of paraphilias. *Psychiatric Clinics of North America, 37*(2), 173–181.

Atchley, R., & Bedford, C. (2021). Dissociative symptoms in posttraumatic stress

disorder: A systematic review. *Journal of Trauma and Dissociation, 22*(1), 69–88. doi: 10.1080/15299732.2020.1760410
Atkinson, B. E., & Vernon, P. A. (2020). Twin studies and personality. In B. J. Carducci & C. S. Nave (Eds.), *The Wiley encyclopedia of personality and individual differences: Measurement and assessment* (Vol. 3, pp. 461–464). Hoboken, NJ: Wiley & Sons.
Attademo, L., Bernardini, F., & Verdolini, N. (in press). Neural correlates of schizotypal personality disorder: A systematic review of neuroimaging and EEG studies. *Current Medical Imaging.*
Attia, E., & Roberto, C. A. (2009). Should amenorrhea be a diagnostic criterion for anorexia nervosa? *International Journal of Eating Disorders, 42*(7), 581–589.
Attie, I., & Brooks-Gunn, J. (1995). The development of eating regulation across the life span. In D. Cicchetti & D. J. Cohen (Eds.), *Developmental psychopathology* (Vol. 2) (pp. 332–368). New York, NY: Wiley.
Atwood, M. E., & Friedman, A. (2020). A systematic review of enhanced cognitive behavioral therapy (CBT-E) for eating disorders. *International Journal of Eating Disorders, 53*(3), 311–330. doi: 10.1002/eat.23206
Augedal, A. W., Hansen, K. S., Kronhaug, C. R., Harvey, A. G., & Pallesen, S. (2013). Randomized controlled trials of psychological and pharmacological treatments for nightmares: A meta-analysis. *Sleep Medicine Reviews 17*(2), 143–152. doi: 10.1016/j.smrv.2012.06.001
Aurora, R. N., Zak, R. S., Auerbach, S. H., Casey, K. R., Chowdhuri, S., Karippot, A., & Bista, S. R. (2010). Best practice guide for the treatment of nightmare disorder in adults. *Journal of Clinical Sleep Medicine: JCSM: Official Publication of the American Academy of Sleep Medicine, 6*(4), 389.
Auyeng, B., Baron-Cohen, S., Ashwin, E., Knickmeyer, R., Taylor, K., Hackett, G., & Hines, M. (2009). Fetal testosterone predicts sexually differentiated childhood behavior in girls and boys. *Psychological Science, 20,* 144–148.
Avinun, R. (2020). The E is in the G: Gene–environment–trait correlations and findings from genome-wide association studies. *Perspectives on Psychological Science, 15*(1), 81–89.
Avis, N. E., Zhao, X., Johannes, C. B., Ory, M., Brockwell, S., & Greendal, G. A. (2018). Correlates of sexual function among multi-ethnic middle-aged women: Results from the study of women's health across the nation (SWAN). *Menopause, 25*(11), 1244–1255. doi: 10.1097/GME.0000000000001226
Axelsson, E., & Hedman-Lagerlöf, E. (2019). Cognitive behavior therapy for health anxiety: Systematic review and meta-analysis of clinical efficacy and health economic outcomes. *Expert Review of Pharmacoeconomics and Outcomes Research, 19*(6), 663–676. doi: 10.1080/14737167.2019.1703182
Ayala, E. S., Meuret, A. E., & Ritz, T. (2009). Treatments for blood-injury-injection phobia: A critical review of current evidence. *Journal of Psychiatric Research, 43*(15), 1235–1242.
Ayearst, L. E., & Bagby, R. M. (2010). Evaluating the psychometric properties of psychological measures. In M. M. Antony & D. H. Barlow (Eds.), *Handbook of assessment and treatment planning for psychological disorders* (2nd ed.). New York, NY: Guilford.
Ayers, C. R., Saxena, S., Golshan, S., & Wetherell, J. L. (2010). Age at onset and clinical features of late life compulsive hoarding. *International Journal of Geriatric Psychiatry, 25*(2), 142–149. doi: 10.1002/gps.2310
Ayers, C. R., Thorp, S. R., & Wetherell, J. L. (2009). Anxiety disorders and hoarding in older adults. In M. M. Antony & M. B. Stein (Eds.), *Oxford handbook of anxiety and related disorders.* (pp. 625–635). New York, NY: Oxford University Press.
Ayllon, T., & Azrin, N. H. (1968). *The token economy: A motivational system for therapy and rehabilitation.* New York, NY: Appleton-Century-Crofts.
Azmitia, E. C. (1978). The serotonin-producing neurons of the midbrain median and dorsal raphe nuclei. In L. Iverson, S. Iverson, & S. Snyder (Eds.), *Handbook of psychopharmacology: Vol. 9. Chemical pathways in the brain* (pp. 233–314). New York, NY: Plenum.
Babyak, M., Blumenthal, J. A., Herman, S., Khatri, P., Doraiswamy, M., Moore, K., & Krishnan, K. R. (2000). Exercise treatment for major depression: Maintenance of therapeutic benefit at 10 months. *Psychosomatic Medicine, 62,* 633–638.
Bach, A. K., Barlow, D., & Wincze, J. (2004). The enhancing effects of manualized treatment for erectile dysfunction among men using slidenafil: A preliminary investigation. *Behaviour Therapy, 35,* 55–73.
Bach, A. K., Brown, T. A., & Barlow, D. H. (1999). The effects of false negative feedback on efficacy expectancies and sexual arousal in sexually functional males. *Behavior Therapy, 30,* 79–95.
Bach, A. K., Wincze, J. P., & Barlow, D. H. (2001). Sexual dysfunction. In D. H. Barlow (Ed.), *Clinical handbook of psychological disorders: A step-by-step treatment manual* (3rd ed., pp. 562–608). New York, NY: Guilford.
Bach, B., Christensen, S., Kongerslev, M. T., Sellbom, M., & Simonsen, E. (2020). Structure of clinician-reported ICD-11 personality disorder trait qualifiers. *Psychological Assessment, 32*(1), 50.
Bach, B., Kongerslev, M. T., & Simonsen, E. (2020). Prevalence and structure of self-other problems in SAPAS screening for personality disorder in a national sample. *Personality and Mental Health, 14*(2), 175–185.
Bade, R., White, J. M., Chen, J., Baz-Lomba, J. A., Been, F., Bijlsma, L., … Celma, A. (2021). International snapshot of new psychoactive substance use: Case study of eight countries over the 2019/2020 new year period. *Water Research,* 116891.
Badr, M. S. (2012). Central sleep apnea. In M. S. Badr (Ed.), *Essentials of sleep medicine* (pp. 219–232). New York, NY: Humana Press.
Baek, J. H., Eisner, L. R., & Nierenberg, A. A. (2014). Epidemiology and course of unipolar mania: Results from the National Epidemiologic Survey on Alcohol and Related Conditions (NESARC). *Depression and Anxiety, 31,* 746–755.
Baer, R. A., Peters, J. R., Eisenlohr-Moul, T. A., Geiger, P. J., & Sauer, S. E. (2012). Emotion-related cognitive processes in borderline personality disorder: a review of the empirical literature. *Clinical Psychology Review,32*(5), 359-369.
Bahji, A., Stephenson, C., Tyo, R., Hawken, E. R., & Seitz, D. P. (2020). Prevalence of cannabis withdrawal symptoms among people with regular or dependent use of cannabinoids: A systematic review and meta-analysis. *JAMA Network Open, 3*(4), e202370–e202370.
Bailey, J. A. (2009). Addressing common risk and protective factors can prevent a wide range of adolescent risk behaviors. *Journal of Adolescent Health, 45*(2), 107–108.
Bailey, J. M. (2003). *The man who would be queen: The science of gender-bending and transsexualism.* Washington, DC: National Academy.
Bailey, J. M., & Benishay, D. S. (1993). Familial aggregation of female sexual orientation. *American Journal of Psychiatry, 150*(2), 272–277.
Bailey, J. M., & Pillard, R. C. (1991). A genetic study of male sexual orientation. *Archives of General Psychiatry, 48,* 1089–1096.

Bailey, J. M., Pillard, R. C., Dawood, K., Miller, M. B., Farrer, L. A., Trivedi, S., & Murphy, R. L. (1999). A family history study of male sexual orientation using three independent samples. *Behavior Genetics, 29,* 79–86.

Bailey, J. M., Pillard, R. C., Neale, M. C., & Agyei, Y. (1993). Heritable factors influence sexual orientation in women. *Archives of General Psychiatry, 50,* 217–223.

Bailey, R. C., & Baillie, A. J. (2012). The relationship between placebo alcohol and affect: Motives for drinking. *Drug and Alcohol Review, 32*(2), 162–169. doi: 10.1111/j.1465-3362.2012.00500.x

Baird, G., Simonoff, E., Pickles, A., Chandler, S., Loucas, T., Meldrum, D., & Charman, T. (2006). Prevalence of disorders of the autism spectrum in a population cohort of children in South Thames: The Special Needs and Autism Project (SNAP). *The Lancet, 368*(9531), 210–215.

Baker, C. D., & DeSilva, P. (1988). The relationship between male sexual dysfunction and belief in Zilbergeld's myths: An empirical investigation. *Sexual and Marital Therapy, 3*(2), 229–238.

Baldelli, L., Calandra-Buonaura, G., Provini, F., & Cortelli, P. (in press). Fatal familial insomnia. *Autonomic Nervous System and Sleep*, 199.

Baldessarini, R. J., Tondo, L., Pinna, M., Nuñez, N., & Vázquez, G. H. (2019). Suicidal risk factors in major affective disorders. *British Journal of Psychiatry, 215*(4), 621–626. doi: 10.1192/bjp.2019.167

Baldessarini, R. J., Vázquez, G. H., & Tondo, L. (2020). Bipolar depression: A major unsolved challenge. *International Journal of Bipolar Disorders, 8*(1). doi: 10.1186/s40345-019-0160-1

Baldessarini, R., Pompili, M., & Tondo, L. (2006). Suicidal risk in antidepressant drug trials. *Archives of General Psychiatry, 63,* 246–248.

Baldwin, J. D., & Baldwin, J. I. (1989). The socialization of homosexuality and heterosexuality in a non-Western society. *Archives of Sexual Behavior, 18,* 13–29.

Baldwin, J. R., Reuben, A., Newbury, J. B., & Danese, A. (2019). Agreement between prospective and retrospective measures of childhood maltreatment: A systematic review and meta-analysis. *JAMA Psychiatry, 76*(6), 584–593. doi: 10.1001/jamapsychiatry.2019.0097

Baldwin, R. (2009). Mood disorders in the elderly. In M. G. Gelder, N. C. Andreasen, J. J. López-Ibor, Jr., & J. R. Geddes (Eds.), *New Oxford textbook of psychiatry* (2nd ed., Vol. 2, pp. 1550–1558). Oxford, UK: Oxford University Press.

Ball, J., & Links, P. (2009). Borderline personality disorder and childhood trauma: Evidence for a causal relationship. *Current Psychiatry Reports, 11*(1), 63–68. doi: 10.1007/s11920-009-0010-4

Ballantyne, J. C. (2012). Opioids and other analgesics. In J. C. Verster, K. Brady, M. Galanter, & P. Conrod (Eds.), *Drug abuse and addiction in medical illness* (pp. 241–250). New York, NY: Springer.

Balon, R. (2006). SSRI-associated sexual dysfunction. *American Journal of Psychiatry, 163,* 1504–1512.

Balon, R., Segraves, R., & Clayton, A. (2007). Issues for DSM-V: Sexual dysfunction, disorder, or variation along normal distribution—Toward rethinking DSM criteria of sexual dysfunctions. *American Journal of Psychiatry, 164,* 198–200.

Balter, M. (2015). Can epigenetics explain the homosexuality puzzle? *Science, 350(*6257), 148.

Balthazart, J. (2020). Sexual partner preference in animals and humans. *Neuroscience and Biobehavioral Reviews, 115,* 34–47. doi: 10.1016/j.neubiorev.2020.03.02

Bancroft, J. (1989). *Human sexuality and its problems* (2nd ed.). New York, NY: Churchill Livingstone.

Bancroft, J. (1994). Homosexual orientation: The search for a biological basis. *British Journal of Psychiatry, 164,* 437–440.

Bancroft, J. (1997). Sexual problems. In D. M. Clark & C. G. Fairburn (Eds.), *Science and practice of cognitive behavior therapy* (pp. 243–257). New York, NY: Oxford University Press.

Bancroft, J., Loftus, J., & Long, J. S. (2003). Distress about sex: A national survey of women in heterosexual relationships. *Archives of Sexual Behavior, 32,* 193–208.

Bandelow, B., Krause, J., Wedekind, D., Broocks, A., Hajak, G., & Ruther, E. (2005). Early traumatic life events, parental attitudes, family history, and birth risk factors in patients with borderline personality disorder and healthy controls. *Psychiatry Research, 134,* 169–179.

Bandura, A. (1973). *Aggression: A social learning analysis.* Englewood Cliffs, NJ: Prentice Hall.

Bandura, A. (1986). *Social foundations of thought and action: A social cognitive theory.* Englewood Cliffs, NJ: Prentice Hall.

Bandura, A., O'Leary, A., Taylor, C. B., Gauthier, J., & Gossard, D. (1987). Perceived self- efficacy and pain control: Opioid and nonopioid mechanisms. *Journal of Personality and Social Psychology, 53,* 563–571.

Bangash, A. (2020). Personality disorders in later life: Epidemiology, presentation and management. *BJPsych Advances, 26*(4), 208–218.

Barbosa-Leiker, C., Campbell, A. N., Pavlicova, M., Scodes, J., Burlew, A. K., Hatch-Maillette, M., … Nunes, E. V. (2020). Substance use and mental health in emerging adult vs older adult men and women with opioid use disorder. *American Journal on Addictions, 29*(6), 536–542.

Barclay, N. L., & Gregory, A. M. (2013). Quantitative genetic research on sleep: a review of normal sleep, sleep disturbances and associated emotional, behavioural, and health-related difficulties. Sleep Medicine Reviews, 17(1), 29–40.

Bardone-Cone, A. M., Schaefer, L. M., Maldonado, C. R., Fitzsimmons, E. E., Harney, M. B., Lawson, M. A., . . . Smith, R. (2010). Aspects of self-concept and eating disorder recovery: What does the sense of self look like when an individual recovers from an eating disorder? *Journal of Social and Clinical Psychology, 29*(7), 821–846.

Bardone-Cone, A. M., Thompson, K. A., & Miller, A. J. (2020). The self and eating disorders. *Journal of Personality, 88*(1), 59–75. doi: 10.1111/jopy.12448

Barger, L. K., Flynn-Evans, E. E., Kubey, A., Walsh, L., Ronda, J. M., Wang, W., Wright Jr, K. P., & Czeisler, C. A. (2014). Prevalence of sleep deficiency and use of hypnotic drugs in astronauts before, during, and after spaceflight: an observational study. *The Lancet Neurology, 13*(9), 904–912.

Bargh, J. A., & Chartrand, T. L. (1999). The unbearable automaticity of being. *American Psychologist, 54,* 462–479.

Bar-Haim, Y., Larry, D., Pergamin, L., Bakermans-Kranenburg, M. J., & Van Ijzendoorn, M. H. (2007). Threat-related attentional bias in anxious and nonanxious individuals: A meta-analytic study. *Psychological Bulletin, 133,* 1–24.

Barik, J., Marti, F., Morel, C., Fernandez, S. P., Lanteri, C., Godeheu, G., & Tronche, F. (2013). Chronic stress triggers social aversion via glucocorticoid receptor in dopaminoceptive neurons. *Science, 339*(6117), 332–335. doi: 10.1126/science.1226767

Barker, C., Pistrang, N., & Elliot, R. (2015). *Research methods in clinical psychology.* West Sussex, UK: John Wiley and Sons Inc.

Barkley, R. A. (2006). Attention-deficit hyperactivity disorder: A handbook for diagnosis and treatment (3rd ed.). Guilford Press.

Barkley, R. A. (1990). *Attention-deficit hyperactivity disorder: A handbook for diagnosis and treatment.* New York, NY: Guilford.

Barkley, R. A. (2006a). ADHD in adults: Developmental course and outcome of children with ADHD, and ADHD in clinic-referred adults. In R. A. Barkley (Ed.), *Attention-deficit hyperactivity disorder: A handbook for diagnosis and treatment* (3rd ed., pp. 248–296). New York, NY: Guilford.

Barkley, R. A. (2006b). Etiologies. In R. A. Barkley (Ed.), *Attention-deficit hyperactivity disorder: A handbook for diagnosis and treatment* (3rd ed., pp. 219–247). New York, NY: Guilford.

Barkley, R. A. (2015a). Etiologies of ADHD. In R. A. Barkley (Ed.), *Attention-deficit hyperactivity disorder: A handbook for diagnosis & treatment* (4th ed., pp. 356–390). New York, NY: The Guilford Press.

Barkley, R. A. (2015b). Health problems and related impairments in children and adults with ADHD. In R. A. Barkley (Ed.), *Attention-deficit hyperactivity disorder: A handbook for diagnosis & treatment* (4th ed., pp. 267–313). New York, NY: The Guilford Press.

Barkley, R. A. (Ed.). (2015c). *Attention-deficit hyperactivity disorder: A handbook for diagnosis & treatment* (4th ed.). New York, NY: The Guilford Press.

Barlow, D. H., Curreri, A. J., & Woodard, L. S. (2021). Neuroticism and disorders of emotion: A new synthesis. *Current Directions in Psychological Science, 30*(5), 410–417.

Barlow, D. H., Harris, B. A., Eustis, E. H., & Farchione, T. J. (2020, June). The unified protocol for transdiagnostic treatment of emotional disorders. World Psychiatry. 19(2):245–246. doi: 10.1002/wps.20748.

Barlow, D. H. (1986). Causes of sexual dysfunction: The role of anxiety and cognitive interference. *Journal of Consulting and Clinical Psychology, 54,* 140–148.

Barlow, D. H. (1988). *Anxiety and its disorders: The nature and treatment of anxiety and panic.* New York, NY: Guilford.

Barlow, D. H. (1991). Disorders of emotion. *Psychological Inquiry, 2*(1), 58–71.

Barlow, D. H. (2000). Unraveling the mysteries of anxiety and its disorders from the perspective of emotion theory. *American Psychologist, 55,* 1245–1263.

Barlow, D. H. (2002). *Anxiety and its disorders: The nature and treatment of anxiety and panic* (2nd ed.). New York, NY: Guilford.

Barlow, D. H. (2004). Covert sensitization for paraphilia. In D. Wedding & R. J. Corsini (Eds.), *Case studies in psychotherapy* (4th ed., pp. 105–113). Belmont, CA: Thomson. Reprinted from *Covert conditioning casebook* (1st ed., pp. 187–207) by J. R. Cautela & A. J. Kearney, Eds., 1993, Belmont, CA: Brooks /Cole.

Barlow, D. H., & Craske, M. G. (2007). *Mastery of your anxiety and panic* (4th ed.). New York, NY: Oxford University Press.

Barlow, D. H., & Lehman, C. L. (1996). Advances in the psychosocial treatment of anxiety disorders: Implications for national health care. *Archives of General Psychiatry, 53,* 727–735.

Barlow, D. H., & Liebowitz, M. R. (1995). Specific and social phobias. In H. I. Kaplan & B. J. Sadock (Eds.), *Comprehensive textbook of psychiatry: VI* (pp. 1204–1217). Baltimore, MD: Williams & Wilkins.

Barlow, D. H., & Nock, M. K. (2009). Why can't we be more idiographic in our research? *Perspectives on Psychological Science, 4,* 19–21.

Barlow, D. H., & Wincze, J. P. (1980). Treatment of sexual deviations. In S. R. Leiblum & L. A. Pervin (Eds.), *Principles and practice of sex therapy* (pp. 347–375). New York, NY: Guilford.

Barlow, D. H., Allen, L. B., & Basden, S. (2007). Psychological treatments for panic disorders, phobias, and generalized anxiety disorder. In P. E. Nathan & J. M. Gorman (Eds.), *A guide to treatments that work* (3rd ed.). New York, NY: Oxford University Press.

Barlow, D. H., Allen, L. B., & Choate, M. L. (2004). Toward a unified treatment for emotional disorders. *Behavior Therapy, 35,* 205–230.

Barlow, D. H., Becker, R., Leitenberg, H., & Agras, W. S. (1970). A mechanical strain gauge for recording penile circumference change. *Journal of Applied Behavior Analysis, 3,* 73–76.

Barlow, D. H., Brown, T. A., & Craske, M. G. (1994). Definitions of panic attacks and panic disorder in DSM-IV: Implications for research. *Journal of Abnormal Psychology, 103,* 553–554.

Barlow, D. H., Bullis, J. R., Comer, J. S., & Ametaj, A. A. (2013). Evidence-based psychological treatments: An update and a way forward. In S. Nolen-Hoeksema, T.D. Cannon, & T. Widiger (Eds.), *Annual Review of Clinical Psychology* (Vol. 9, pp. 1–27). Palo Alto, CA: Annual Reviews.

Barlow, D. H., Chorpita, B. F., & Turovsky, J. (1996). Fear, panic, anxiety, and disorders of emotion. In D. A. Hope (Ed.), *Perspectives on anxiety, panic and fear* (The 43rd Annual Nebraska Symposium on Motivation) (pp. 251–328). Lincoln, NE: Nebraska University Press.

Barlow, D. H., Ellard, K. K., Sauer-Zavala, S., Bullis, J. R., & Carl, J. R. (2014). The origins of neuroticism. *Perspectives on Psychological Science, 9,* 481–496.

Barlow, D. H., Farchione, T. J., Bullis, J. R., Gallagher, M. W., Murray-Latin, H., Sauer-Zavala, S., Bentley, K. H., Thompson-Hollands, J., Conklin, L. R., Boswell, J. F., Ametaj, A., Carl, J. R., Boettcher, H. T., & Cassiello-Robbins, C. (2017). The unified protocol for transdiagnostic treatment of emotional disorders compared with diagnosis-specific protocols for anxiety disorders: A randomized clinical trial. *JAMA Psychiatry, 74*(9), 875–884. doi: 10.1001/jamapsychiatry.2017.2164

Barlow, D. H., Farchione, T. J., Fairholme, C. P., Ellard, K. K., Boisseau, C. L., Allen, L. B., & Ehrenreich-May, J. (2012b). *Unified protocol for the transdiagnostic treatment of emotional disorders* (Therapist Guide). New York, NY: Oxford University Press.

Barlow, D. H., Gorman, J. M., Shear, K. M., & Woods, S. W. (2000). Cognitive-behavioral therapy, imipramine, or their combination for panic disorder: A randomized controlled trial. *JAMA: Journal of the American Medical Association, 283*(19), 2529–2536.

Barlow, D. H., Hayes, S. C., & Nelson, R. O. (1984). *The scientist practitioner: Research and accountability in clinical and educational settings.* Boston, MA: Allyn & Bacon.

Barlow, D. H., Levitt, J. T., & Bufka, L. F. (1999). The dissemination of empirically supported treatments: A view to the future. *Behaviour Research and Therapy, 37*(Suppl. 1), S147–162.

Barlow, D. H., Moscovitch, D. A., & Micco, J. A. (2004). Psychotherapeutic interventions for phobias: A review. In M. Maj, H. S. Akiskal, J. L. Lopez-Ibor, & A. Okasha (Eds.), *Phobias.* (pp.179–210). Hoboken, NJ: Wiley.

Barlow, D. H., Nock, M. K., & Hersen, M. (2009). *Single case experimental designs: Strategies for studying behavior change* (3rd ed.). New York, NY: Allyn & Bacon.

Barlow, D. H., Pincus, D. B., Heinrichs, N., & Choate, M. L. (2003). Anxiety disorders. In I. B. Weiner (Series Ed.), G. S. Stricker, & T. A. Widiger (Vol. Eds.), *Handbook of psychology.* Hoboken, NJ: Wiley.

Barlow, D. H., Rapee, R. M., & Parini, S. (2014). *10 steps to mastering Stress: A lifestyle approach.* New York, NY: Oxford University Press.

Barlow, D. H., Sakheim, D. K., & Beck, J. G. (1983). Anxiety increases sexual arousal. *Journal of Abnormal Psychology, 92,* 49–54.

Barlow, D. H., Sauer-Zavala, S., Carl, J. R., Bullis, J. R., & Ellard, K. K. (2014). The nature, diagnosis, and treatment of neuroticism: Back to the future. *Clinical Psychological Science, 2,* 344–365.

Barmish, A. J., & Kendall, P. C. (2005). Should parents be co-clients in cognitive behavioral therapy for anxious youth? *Journal of Clinical Child and Adolescent Psychology, 34*(3), 69–581. doi: 10.1207/s15374424jccp3403

Barnard, A. (2000, September 12). When plastic surgeons should just say "no." *Boston Globe,* pp. E1, E3.

Barnhofer, T., Crane, C., Brennan, K., Duggan, D. S., Crane, R. S., Eames, C., Radford, S., Silverton, S., Fennell, M. J., & Williams, J. M. (2015). Mindfulness-based cognitive therapy (MBCT) reduces the association between depressive symptoms and suicidal cognitions in patients with a history of suicidal depression. *Journal of Consulting and Clinical Psychology, 83*(6):1013–1020.

Baron, M., Risch, N., Hamburger, R., Mandel, B., Kushner, S., Newman, M., . . . Belmaker, R. H. (1987). Genetic linkage between X-chromosome markers and bipolar affective illness. *Nature, 326*(6110), 289–292.

Barrett, L. F. (2009). Variety is the spice of life: A psychological construction approach to understanding variability in emotion. *Cognition and Emotion, 23*(7), 1284–1306.

Barrett, L. F. (2012). Emotions are real. *Emotion, 12*(3), 413-429. doi: 10.1037/a0027555

Barry, C. T., Golmaryami, F. N., Rivera-Hudson, N., & Frick, P. J. (2012). Evidence-based assessment of conduct disorder: Current considerations and preparation for DSM-5. *Professional Psychology: Research and Practice, 44*(1), 56–63.

Barry, K., & Finke, J. (2020). Nicotine replacement therapy for smoking cessation. *American Family Physician, 102*(1), 17–18.

Barsaglini, A., Sartori, G., Benetti, S., Pettersson-Yeo, W., Mechelli, A. (2014, March). The effects of psychotherapy on brain function: a systematic and critical review. Prog Neurobiol. 114:1-14. doi: 10.1016/j.pneurobio.2013.10.006.

Barsky, A. J., & Ahern, D. K. (2005). Cognitive behavior therapy for hypochondriasis: A randomized controlled trial. *JAMA: Journal of the American Medical Association, 291,* 1464–1470.

Barsky, A. J., Orav, E., & Bates, D. (2005). Somatization increases medical utilization and costs independent of psychiatric and medical comorbidity. *Archives of General Psychiatry, 62,* 903–910.

Barsky, B. A., Cucolo, H. E., & Sisti, D. A. (2020). Expanding therapeutic jurisprudence across the federal judiciary. *Journal of the American Academy of Psychiatry and the Law.*

Barsky, B. A., Cucolo, H. E., & Sisti, D. A. (2020). Expanding therapeutic jurisprudence across the federal judiciary. *Journal of the American Academy of Psychiatry and the Law.*

Barthelemy, O. J., Richardson, M. A., Rose-Jacobs, R., Forman, L. S., Cabral, H. J., & Frank, D. A. (2016). Effects of intrauterine substance and postnatal violence exposure on aggression in children. *Aggressive Behavior, 42,* 209–221.

Bartholomew, R. E., Wessely, S., & Rubin, G. J. (2012). Mass psychogenic illness and the social network: Is it changing the pattern of outbreaks? *Journal of the Royal Society of Medicine, 105*(12), 509–512.

Bartlett, N., & Vasey, P. (2006). A retrospective study of childhood gender-atypical behavior in Samoan Fa'afafine. *Archives of Sexual Behavior, 35,* 695–666.

Bartlik, B., & Goldberg, J. (2000). Female sexual arousal disorder. In S. R. Leiblum & R. C. Rosen (Eds.), *Principles and practice of sex therapy* (3rd ed., pp. 85–117). New York, NY: Guilford.

Barwick, F. (2021). Nonpharmacological treatment of insomnia. In E. H. During & C. A. Kushida (Eds.), *Clinical sleep medicine: A comprehensive guide for mental health and other medical professionals* (pp. 79–97). Washington, D.C.: American Psychiatric Association Publishing.

Basson, R. (2007). Sexual desire/arousal disorders in women. In S. R. Leiblum (Ed.), *Principles and practice of sex therapy* (4th ed., pp. 25–53). New York, NY: Guilford.

Basson, R., Wierman, M., van Lankveld, J., & Brotto, L. (2010). Summary of the recommendations on sexual dysfunctions in women. *Journal of Sexual Medicine,* 7(1, pt. 2), 314–326.

Bateson, G. (1959). Cultural problems posed by a study of schizophrenic process. In A. Auerback (Ed.), *Schizophrenia: An integrated approach* (pp. 125–148). New York, NY: Ronald.

Baumann, M. H. (2014). Awash in a sea of 'bath salts': Implications for biomedical research and public health. Addiction, 109(10), 1577-1579.

Baumann, M. H., Partilla, J. S., Lehner, K. R., Thorndike, E. B., Hoffman, A. F., Holy, M., . . . Brandt, S. D. (2013). Powerful cocaine-like actions of 3, 4-methylenedioxypyrovalerone (MDPV), a principal constituent of psychoactive 'bath salts' products. *Neuropsychopharmacology, 38*(4), 552–562.

Baxter, L. R. (1992). Neuroimaging studies of obsessive compulsive disorder. *Psychiatric Clinics of North America, 15*(4):871–884.

Beach, S. R. H., Jones, D. J., & Franklin, K. J. (2009). Marital, family, and interpersonal therapies for depression in adults. In I. H. Gotlib & C. L. Hammen (Eds.), *Handbook of depression* (2nd ed., pp. 624–641). New York, NY: Guilford.

Beach, S. R. H., Sandeen, E. E., & O'Leary, K. D. (1990). Depression in marriage: A model for etiology and treatment. In D. H. Barlow (Ed.), *Treatment manuals for practitioners* (pp. 53–86). New York, NY: Guilford.

Beach, S. R., & O'Leary, K. D. (1992). Treating depression in the context of marital discord: Outcome and predictors of response of marital therapy versus cognitive therapy. *Behavior Therapy, 23*(4), 507–528.

Beals, J., Manson, S., Whitesell, N., Mitchell, C., Novins, D., Simpson, S., & Spicer, P. (2005). Prevalence of major depressive episode in two American Indian reservation populations: Unexpected findings with a structured interview. *American Journal of Psychiatry, 162,* 1713–1722.

Bear, R. E., Fitzgerald, P., Rosenfeld, J. V., & Bittar, R. G. (2010). Neurosurgery for obsessive-compulsive disorder: Contemporary approaches. *Journal of Clinical Neuroscience, 17*(1), 1–5. doi: 10.1016/j.jocn.2009.02.043

Beard, G. M. (1869). Neurasthenia or nervous exhaustion. *Boston Medical Surgical Journal, 3,* 217–221.

Beardon, L., & Worton, D. (2011). *Aspies on mental health: Speaking for ourselves.* London, U.K.: Jessica Kingsley.

Beardslee, W. R., Brent, D. A., Weersing, V. R., Clarke, G. N., Porta, G., Hollon, S. D., Gladstone, T. R., Gallop, R., Lynch, F. L., Iyengar, S., DeBar, L., & Garber, J. (2013). Prevention of depression in at-risk adolescents: Longer-term effects. *JAMA Psychiatry, 70,* 1161–1170.

Beaulieu, J. M., & Gainetdinov, R. R. (2011, March). The physiology, signaling, and pharmacology of dopamine receptors. Pharmacol Rev. 63(1):182-217. doi: 10.1124/pr.110.002642.

Beaver, K. M., Barnes, J. C., May, J. S., & Schwartz, J. A. (2011). Psychopathic personality traits, genetic risk, and gene-environment correlations. *Criminal Justice and Behavior, 38*(9), 896–912.

Bebbington, P., Cooper, C., Minot, S., Brugha, T., Jenkins, R., Meltzer, H., & Dennis, M. (2009). Suicide attempts, gender, and sexual abuse: Data from the 2000 British Psychiatric Morbidity Survey. *American Journal of Psychiatry, 166*(10), 1135.

Bech, P. (2009). Clinical features of mood disorders and mania. In M. G. Gelder, N. C. Andreasen, J. J. López-Ibor, Jr., & J. R. Geddes (Eds.), *New Oxford textbook of psychiatry* (2nd ed., Vol. 1, pp. 632–637). Oxford, UK: Oxford University Press.
Beck, A. T. (1967). *Depression: Clinical, experimental and theoretical aspects.* New York, NY: Harper & Row.
Beck, A. T. (1976). *Cognitive therapy and the emotional disorders.* New York, NY: International Universities Press.
Beck, A. T. (1986). Hopelessness as a predictor of eventual suicide. *Annals of the New York Academy of Science, 487,* 90–96.
Beck, A. T., & Freeman, A. (1990). *Cognitive therapy of personality disorders.* New York, NY: Guilford.
Beck, A. T., Epstein, N., & Harrison, R. (1983). Cognitions, attitudes and personality dimensions in depression. *British Journal of Cognitive Psychotherapy, 1*(1), 1–16.
Beck, A. T., Freeman, A., & Davis, D. D. (2007). *Cognitive therapy of personality disorders* (2nd ed.). New York, NY: Guilford.
Beck, A. T., Davis, D. D., & Freeman, A., Eds. (2015). *Cognitive therapy of personality disorders* (3rd ed.) New York, NY: Guilford.
Beck, J. G. (1993). Vaginismus. In W. O'Donohue & J. H. Geer (Eds.), *Handbook of sexual dysfunctions: Assessment and treatment* (pp. 381–397). Boston, MA: Allyn & Bacon.
Beck, J. G., & Averill, P. M. (2004). Older adults. In R. G. Heimberg, C. L. Turk, & D. S. Mennin (Eds.), *Generalized anxiety disorder: Advances in research and practice* (pp. 409–433). New York, NY: Guilford.
Beck, J. G., & Sloan, D. M. (Eds.). (2012). *The Oxford handbook of traumatic stress disorders.* New York, NY: Oxford University Press.
Beck, J. G., & Stanley, M. A. (1997). Anxiety disorders in the elderly: The emerging role of behavior therapy. *Behavior Therapy, 28,* 83–100.
Becker, C. B., Smith, L. M., & Ciao, A. C. (2005). Reducing eating disorder risk factors in sorority members: A randomized trial. *Behavior Therapy, 36,* 245–253.
Becker, J. T., Mestre, L. T., Ziolko, S., & Lopez, O. L. (2007). Gene-environment interactions with cognition in late life and compression of morbidity. *American Journal of Psychiatry, 164*(6), 849–852.
Becker, J. V. (1990). Treating adolescent sexual offenders. *Professional Psychology: Research and Practice, 21,* 362–365.
Becvar, D. S. (2013). *Handbook of family resilience.* New York, NY: Springer.
Beekman, A. T., Geerlings, S. W., Deeg, D. J., Smit, J. H., Schoevers, R. S., de Beurs, E., & van Tilberg, W. (2002). The natural history of late-life depression: A 6-year prospective study in the community. *Archives of General Psychiatry, 59,* 605–611.
Beesdo, K., Pine, D. S., Lieb, R., & Wittchen, H.-U. (2010). Incidence and risk patterns of anxiety and depressive disorders and categorization of generalized anxiety disorder. *Archives of General Psychiatry, 67*(1), 47–57.
Beesdo-Baum, K., Klotsche, J., Knappe, S., Craske, M. G., LeBeau, R. T., Hoyer, J., & Wittchen, H.-U. (2012). Psychometric properties of the dimensional anxiety scales for DSM-5 in an unselected sample of German treatment seeking patients. *Depression and Anxiety, 29*(12), 1014–1024.
Béjot, Y., Juenet, N., Garrouty, R., Maltaverne, D., Nicolleau, L., Giroud, M., & Didi-Roy, R. (2010). Sexsomnia: An uncommon variety of parasomnia. *Clinical Neurology and Neurosurgery, 112*(1), 72–75.
Belik, S. L., Sareen, J., & Stein, M. B. (2009). Anxiety disorders and physical comorbidity. In M. M. Antony & M. B. Stein (Eds.), *Oxford handbook of anxiety and related disorders.* (pp. 596–610). New York, NY: Oxford University Press.
Bell, C. C., Dixie-Bell, D. D., & Thompson, B. (1986). Further studies on the prevalence of isolated sleep paralysis in black subjects. *Journal of the National Medical Association, 78*(7), 649–659.
Bell, I. R. (1994). Somatization disorder: Health care costs in the decade of the brain. *Biological Psychiatry, 35,* 81–83.
Bellak, L. (1975). *The thematic apperception test, the children's apperception test, and the senior apperception technique in clinical use* (3rd ed.). New York, NY: Grune & Stratton.
Benbadis, R. R., & Allen-Hauser, W. (2000). An estimate of the prevalence of psychogenic non-epileptic seizures. *Seizure, 9*(4), 280–281.
Bender, D. S. (2005). Therapeutic alliance. In J. M. Oldham, A. E. Skodol, & D. S. Bender (Eds.), *Textbook of personality disorders* (pp. 405–420). Washington, DC: American Psychiatric Publishing.
Bender, D. S., Dolan, R. T., Skodol, A. E., Sanislow, C. A., Dyck, I. R., McGlashan, T. H., . . . Gunderson, J. G. (2014). Treatment utilization by patients with personality disorders. *American Journal of Psychiatry.*
Bender, E. (2004). Data show wide variation in addiction treatment costs. *Psychiatric News, 39,* 11.
Benjamin, C. L., Harrison, J. P., Settipani, C. A., Brodman, D. M., & Kendall, P. C. (2013). Anxiety and related outcomes in young adults 7 to 19 years after receiving treatment for child anxiety. *Journal of Consulting and Clinical Psychology, 81,* 865.
Bennett, E., & Heaton, P. (2012). Is talent in autism spectrum disorders associated with a specific cognitive and behavioural phenotype? *Journal of Autism and Developmental Disorders, 42*(12), 2739–2753.
Bennett, K., Shepherd, J., & Janca, A. (2013). Personality disorders and spirituality. *Current Opinion in Psychiatry, 26*(1), 79–83.
Benowitz, N. (2008). Neurobiology of nicotine addiction: Implications for smoking cessation treatment. *The American Journal of Medicine, 121* (4A), S3–S10.
Ben-Porath, Y. S., & Tellegen, A. (2008). *MMPI-2-RF: Manual for administration, scoring and interpretation.* Minnesota: University of Minnesota Press.
Benson, H. (1975). *The relaxation response.* New York, NY: William Morrow.
Benson, H. (1984). *Beyond the relaxation response.* New York, NY: Times Books.
Berenbaum, H., & Oltmanns, T. F. (1992). Emotional experience and expression in schizophrenia and depression. *Journal of Abnormal Psychology, 101,* 37–44.
Berenbaum, H., Thompson, R. J., Milanak, M. E., Boden, M. T., & Bredemeier, K. (2008). Psychological trauma and schizotypal personality disorder. *Journal of Abnormal Psychology, 117*(3), 502–519.
Bergeron, S., Reed, B. D., Wesselmann, U., & Bohm-Starke, N. (2020). Vulvodynia. *Nature Reviews Disease Primers, 6*(1). doi: 10.1038/s41572-020-0164-
Berghöfer, A., Pischon, T., Reinhold, T., Apovian, C. M., Sharma, A. M., & Willich, S. N. (2008). Obesity prevalence from a European perspective: A systematic review. *BMC Public Health, 8,* 200.
Berkley, A. S., Carter, P. A., Yoder, L. H., Acton, G., & Holahan, C. K. (2020). The effects of insomnia on older adults' quality of life and daily functioning: A mixed-methods study. *Geriatric Nursing, 41*(6), 832–838.
Berkman, L. F., & Syme, S. L. (1979). Social networks, host resistance, and mortality: A nine-year follow-up study of Alameda county residents. *American Journal of Epidemiology, 109,* 186.
Berman, A. L. (2009). Depression and suicide. In I. H. Gotlib & C. L. Hammen (Eds.), *Handbook of depression* (2nd ed., pp. 510–530). New York, NY: Guilford.
Berman, A. L., & Jobes, D. A. (1991). *Adolescent suicide: Assessment and intervention.* Washington, DC: American Psychological Association.

Berman, J. R., Berman, L. A., Toler, S. M., Gill, J., & Haughie, S., for the Sildenafil Study Group. (2003). Safety and efficacy of sildenafil citrate for the treatment of female sexual arousal disorder: A double-blind, placebo controlled study. *The Journal of Urology, 170*, 2333–2338.

Berman, K. F., & Weinberger, D. R. (1990). Lateralization of cortical function during cognitive tasks: Regional cerebral blood flow studies of normal individuals and patients with schizophrenia. *Journal of Neurology, Neurosurgery and Psychiatry, 53*, 150–160.

Berman, M. E., McCloskey, M. S., Fanning, J. R., Schumacher, J. A., & Coccaro, E. F. (2009). Serotonin augmentation reduces response to attack in aggressive individuals. *Psychological Science, 20*(6), 714–720. doi: 10.1111/j.1467-9280.2009.02355.x

Bernat, J. A., Calhoun, K. S., & Adams, H. E. (1999). Sexually aggressive and nonaggressive men: Sexual arousal and judgments in response to acquaintance rape and consensual analogues. *Journal of Abnormal Psychology, 108*, 662–673.

Berner, L. A., Shaw, J. A., Witt, A. A., & Lowe, M. R. (2013). The relation of weight suppression and body mass index to symptomatology and treatment response in anorexia nervosa. *Journal of Abnormal Psychology, 122*(3), 694–708.

Berney, T. P. (2012). Methods of treatment. In M. G. Gelder, N. C. Andreasen, J. J. Lopez -Ibor, Jr., & J. R. Geddes (Eds.), *New Oxford textbook of psychiatry* (2nd ed., Vol. 2, pp. 1871–1877). New York, NY: Oxford University Press.

Bernstein, D. M., & Loftus, E. F. (2009). How to tell if a particular memory is true or false. *Perspectives on Psychological Science, 4*(4), 370–374.

Bernstein, D. P., & Useda, J. (2007). Paranoid personality disorder. In W. O'Donohue, K. Fowler, & S. Lilienfeld (Eds.), *Personality disorders: Toward the DSM-V* (pp. 41–62). Thousand Oaks, CA: Sage.

Berntsen, D., Johannessen, K. B., Thornsen, Y. D., Bertelsen, M., Hoyle, R. H., & Rubin, D. C. (2012). Peace and war: Trajectories of posttraumatic stress disorder symptoms before, during, and after military deployment in Afghanistan. *Psychological Science, 23*, 1557–1565.

Berridge, K. C., & Kringelbach, M. L. (2015). Pleasure systems in the brain. *Neuron, 86*(3), 646–664.

Berrios, G. E. (2011). Eugen Bleuler's place in the history of psychiatry. *Schizophrenia Bulletin, 37*(6), 1095–1098.

Berton, O., McClung, C. A., DiLeone, R. J., Krishnan, V., Renthal, W., Russo, S. J., & Nestler, E. J. (2006). Essential role of BDNF in the mesolimbic dopamine pathway in social defeat stress. *Science, 311*, 864–868.

Bes-Rastrollo, M., Sayon-Orea, C., Ruiz-Canela, M., & Martinez-Gonzalez, M. A. (2016). Impact of sugars and sugar taxation on body weight control: A comprehensive literature review. *Obesity, 24*(7), 1410–1426. doi: 10.1002/oby.21535

Bettelheim, B. (1967). *The empty fortress*. New York, NY: Free Press.

Bettens, K., Sleegers, K., & Van Broeckhoven, C. (2010). Current status on Alzheimer disease molecular genetics: From past, to present, to future. *Human Molecular Genetics, 19*(R1), R4–11.

Bhagwanjee, A., Parekh, A., Paruk, Z., Petersen, I., & Subedar, H. (1998). Prevalence of minor psychiatric disorders in an adult African rural community in South Africa. *Psychological Medicine, 28*, 1137–1147.

Bharucha, A., Anand, V., Forlizzi, J., Dew, M., Reynolds, C., III, Stevens, S., & Wactlar, H. (2009). Intelligent assistive technology applications to dementia care: Current capabilities, limitations, and future challenges. *The American Journal of Geriatric Psychiatry: Official Journal of the American Association for Geriatric Psychiatry, 17*(2), 88.

Bhasin, T., & Schendel, D. (2007). Sociodemographic risk factors for autism in a U.S. metropolitan area. *Journal of Autism and Developmental Disorders, 37*, 667–677.

Biederman, J., Faraone, S. V., Wozniak, J., Mick, E., Kwon, A., Cayton, G. A., & Clark, S. V. (2005). Clinical correlates of bipolar disorder in a large, referred sample of children and adolescents. *Journal of Psychiatric Research, 39*(6), 611–622.

Biederman, J., Mick, E., Faraone, S. V., Spencer, T., Wilens, T. E., & Wozniak, J. (2000). Pediatric mania: A developmental subtype of bipolar disorder? *Biological Psychiatry, 48*(6), 458–466.

Biederman, J., Spencer, T., Wilens, T., & Greene, R. (2001). Attention-deficit /hyperactivity disorder. In G. O. Gabbard (Ed.), *Treatment of psychiatric disorders* (3rd ed., Vol. 1, pp. 145–176). Washington, DC: American Psychiatric Publishing.

Bieniek, K. F., Blessing, M. M., Heckman, M. G., Diehl, N. N., Serie, A. M., Paolini, M. A., … Dickson, D. W. (2020). Association between contact sports participation and chronic traumatic encephalopathy: a retrospective cohort study. *Brain Pathology, 30*(1), 63–74.

Bierut, L. J., Heath, A. C., Bucholz, K. K., Dinwiddie, S. H., Madden, P. A., Statham, D. J., & Martin, N. G. (1999). Major depressive disorder in a community-based twin sample: Are there different genetic and environmental contributions for men and women? *Archives of General Psychiatry, 56*(6), 557–563.

Billeiter, K. B., Froiland, J. M., Allen, J. P., & Hajovsky, D. B. (2021). Neurodiversity and intelligence: Evaluating the Flynn effect in children with autism spectrum disorder. *Child Psychiatry & Human Development*, 1–9.

Billy, J. O. G., Tanfer, K., Grady, W. R., & Klepinger, D. H. (1993). The sexual behavior of men in the United States. *Family Planning Perspectives, 25*, 52–60.

Binder, E. B., Bradley, R. G., Liu, W., Epstein, M. P., Deveau, T. C., Mercer, K. B., & Ressler, K. J. (2008). Association of FKBP5 polymorphisms and childhood abuse with risk of posttraumatic stress disorder symptoms in adults. *JAMA: Journal of the American Medical Association, 299*(11), 1291–1305.

Binik, Y. M. (2010). The DSM diagnostic criteria for dyspareunia. *Archives of Sexual Behavior, 39*, 292–303.

Binik, Y. M., Bergeron, S., & Kalifé, S. (2007). Dyspareunia and vaginismus: So-called sexual pain. In S. R. Leiblum (Ed.), *Principles and practice of sex therapy* (4th ed., pp. 124–156). New York, NY: Guilford.

Binzer, M., Andersen, P. M., & Kullgren, G. (1997). Clinical characteristics of patients with motor disability due to conversion disorder: A prospective control group study. Journal of Neurology, Neurosurgery, and Psychiatry, 63(1), 83–88.

Birkmeyer, J. D., Finks, J. F., O'Reilly, A., Oerline, M., Carlin, A. M., Nunn, A. R., . . . Birkmeyer, N. J. (2013). Surgical skill and complication rates after bariatric surgery. *New England Journal of Medicine, 369*(15), 1434–1442.

Birley, J., & Brown, G. W. (1970). Crisis and life changes preceding the onset or relapse of acute schizophrenia: Clinical aspects. *British Journal of Psychiatry, 16*, 327–333.

Birmaher, B., Axelson, D., Goldstein, B., Strober, M., Gill, M. K., Hunt, J., & Keller, M. (2009). Four-year longitudinal course of children and adolescents with bipolar spectrum disorders: The Course and Outcome of Bipolar Youth (COBY) study. *American Journal of Psychiatry, 166*(7), 795–804.

Bishop, D. V. M. (2000). Pragmatic language impairment: A correlate of SLI, a distinct subgroup, or part of the autistic continuum. In D. V. M. Bishop & L. B. Leonard (Eds.), *Speech and language impairments in children: Causes, characteristics, intervention and outcome* (pp. 99–113). East Sussex, UK: Psychology Press.

Björkenstam, E., Björkenstam, C., Holm, H., Gerdin, B., & Ekselius, L. (2015). Excess cause-specific mortality in

in-patient-treated individuals with personality disorder: 25-year nationwide population-based study. *The British Journal of Psychiatry, 207*(4):339–345.
Bjorntorp, P. (1997). Obesity. *Lancet, 350*, 423–426.
Black, D. W. (2013). *Bad Boys, Bad Men: Confronting Antisocial Personality Disorder (Sociopathy).* New York, NY: Oxford University Press.
Black, D. W., & Andreasen, N. C. (2021). Legal issues. In D. W. Black & N. C. Andreasen (Eds.), *Introductory textbook of psychiatry* (7th ed., pp. 439–448). Washington, D.C.: American Psychiatric Association Publishing.
Black, D. W., & Andreasen, N. C. (2021). Neurocognitive disorders. In D. W. Black & N. C. Andreasen (Eds.), *Introductory textbook of psychiatry* (7th ed., pp. 375–399). Washington, D.C.: American Psychiatric Association Publishing.
Black, D. W., & Andreasen, N. C. (2021). Neurodevelopmental (child) disorders. In D. W. Black & N. C. Andreasen (Eds.), *Introductory textbook of psychiatry* (7th ed., pp. 79–114). Washington, D.C.: American Psychiatric Association Publishing.
Black, D. W., & Andreasen, N. C. (2021). Substance-related and addictive disorders. In D. W. Black & N. C. Andreasen (Eds.), *Introductory textbook of psychiatry* (7th ed., pp. 341–373). Washington, D.C.: American Psychiatric Association Publishing.
Black, D. W., & Andreasen, N. C. (2021a). Interviewing and assessment. In D. W. Black & N. C. Andreasen (Eds.), *Introductory textbook of psychiatry* (7th ed., pp. 15–53). Washington, DC: American Psychiatric Association Publishing.
Black, D. W., & Andreasen, N. C. (2021b). Neurobiology and genetics of mental illness. In D. W. Black & N. C. Andreasen (Eds.), *Introductory textbook of psychiatry* (7th ed., pp. 55–75). Washington, DC: American Psychiatric Association Publishing.
Black, J. A., White, B., Viner, R. M., & Simmons, R. K. (2013). Bariatric surgery for obese children and adolescents: a systematic review and meta-analysis. *Obesity Reviews, 14*(8), 634–644.
Blacker, D. (2005). Psychiatric rating scales. In B. J. Sadock & V. A. Sadock (Eds.), *Kaplan & Sadock's comprehensive textbook of psychiatry* (pp. 929–955). Philadelphia, PA: Lippincott Williams & Wilkins.
Blagys, M. D., & Hilsenroth, M. J. (2000). Distinctive features of short-term psychodynamic–interpersonal psychotherapy: A review of the comparative psychotherapy process literature. *Clinical Psychology: Science and Practice, 7*, 167–188.
Blair, K., Shaywitz, J., Smith, B. W., Rhodes, R., Geraci, M., Jones, M., & Pine, D. S. (2008). Response to emotional expressions in generalized social phobia and generalized anxiety disorder: Evidence for separate disorders. *American Journal of Psychiatry, 165*(9), 1193–1202. doi: 10.1176/appi.ajp.2008.07071060
Blanchard, E. B. (1992). Psychological treatment of benign headache disorders. Special issue: Behavioral medicine: An update for the 1990s. *Journal of Consulting and Clinical Psychology, 60*(4), 537–551.
Blanchard, E. B., & Andrasik, F. (1982). Psychological assessment and treatment of headache: Recent developments and emerging issues. *Journal of Consulting and Clinical Psychology, 50*(6), 859–879.
Blanchard, E. B., & Epstein, L. H. (1977). *A biofeedback primer.* Reading, MA: Addison-Wesley.
Blanchard, R. (2008). Sex ration of older siblings in heterosexual and homosexual, right-handed and non-right-handed men. *Archives of Sexual Behavior, 37*, 977–981.
Blanchard, R. (2010). The DSM diagnostic criteria for pedophilia. *Archives of Sexual Behavior, 39*, 304–314.
Blanchard, R. (2018). Fraternal birth order, family size, and male homosexuality: Meta-analysis of studies spanning 25 years. *Archives of Sexual Behavior, 47*(1). doi: 10.1007/s10508-017-1007-4
Blanchard, R., & Bogaert, A. (1996). Homosexuality in men and number of older brothers. *American Journal of Psychiatry, 153*, 27–31.
Blanchard, R., & Bogaert, A. (1998). Birth order in homosexual versus heterosexual sex offenders against children, pubescents, and adults. *Archives of Sexual Behavior, 27*(6), 595–603.
Blanchard, R., & Steiner, B. W. (1992). *Clinical management of gender identity disorders in children and adults.* Washington, DC: American Psychiatric Press.
Blanco, C., Goodwin, R., Liebowitz, M. R., Schmidt, A. B., Lewis-Fernandez, R., & Olfson, M. (2004). Use of psychotropic medications for patients with office visits who receive a diagnosis of panic disorder. *Medical Care, 42*(12), 1242–1246.
Blanco, C., Rubio, J., Wall, M., Wang, S., Jiu, C. J., & Kendler, K. S. (2014). Risk factors for anxiety disorders: Common and specific effects in a national sample, *Depression and Anxiety, 31*, 756–774.
Blanco, C., Vesga-Lopez, O., Stewart, J. W., Liu, S.-M., Grant, B. F., & Hasin, D. S. (2012). Prevalence, correlates, comorbidity and treatment-seeking among individuals with a lifetime major depressive episode with and without atypical features: Results from the National Epidemiologic Survey on Alcohol and Related Conditions. *Journal of Clinical Psychiatry, 73*(2), 224–232.
Blaney, P. H. (2015). Paranoid and delusional disorders. In P. H. Blaney, R. F. Krueger, Robert F., & T. Millon (Eds), *Oxford textbook of psychopathology* (3rd ed., pp. 383–417). New York, NY: Oxford University Press.
Blasco-Fontecilla, H. (2013). On suicide clusters: More than contagion. *The Australian and New Zealand Journal of Psychiatry, 47*(5), 490–491.
Blascovich, J., & Tomaka, J. (1996). The biopsychosocial model of arousal regulation. *Advances in Experimental Social Psychology, 28*, 1–51.
Blascovich, J., Spencer, S. J., Quinn, D., & Steele, C. (2001). African Americans and high blood pressure: The role of stereotype threat. *Psychological Science, 12*(3), 225–229.
Blashfield, R. K., Keeley, J. W., Flanagan, E. H., & Miles, S. R. (2014). The cycle of classification: *DSM-I* through *DSM-5*. *Annual review of clinical psychology, 10*, 25–51. doi: 10.1146/annurev-clinpsy-032813-153639
Blashfield, R. K., Reynolds, S. M., & Stennett, B. (2012). The death of histrionic personality disorder. In T. A. Widiger (Ed.), *The Oxford handbook of personality disorders* (pp. 603–627). New York, NY: Oxford University Press.
Blazer, D. (2020). Social isolation and loneliness in older adults: A mental health/public health challenge. *JAMA Psychiatry, 77*(10), 990–991. doi: 10.1001/jamapsychiatry.2020.1054
Blazer, D. G. (2003). Depression in late life: Review and commentary. *Journal of Gerontology—Series A Biological Sciences and Medical Science, 58*, 249–265.
Blazer, D. G., & Hybels, C. F. (2009). Depression in later life: Epidemiology, assessment, impact, and treatment. In I. H. Gotlib & C. L. Hammen (Eds.), *Handbook of depression* (2nd ed., pp. 492–509). New York, NY: Guilford.
Blazer, D. G., George, L., & Hughes, D. (1991). The epidemiology of anxiety disorders: An age comparison. In C. Salzman & B. Liebowitz (Eds.), *Anxiety disorders in the elderly* (pp. 17–30). New York, NY: Springer.
Blehar, M. C., & Rosenthal, N. E. (1989). Seasonal affective disorder and phototherapy. *Archives of General Psychiatry, 46*, 469–474.
Bleiberg, K. L., & Markowitz, J. C. (in press). Interpersonal psychotherapy for depression. In D. H. Barlow (Ed.), *Clinical*

handbook of psychological disorders: A step-by-step treatment manual (5th ed.). New York, NY: Guilford.

Bleuler, E. (1908). Die prognose der dementia praecox (schizophreniegruppe). *Allgemeine Zeitschrift für Psychiatrie, 65,* 436–464.

Bleuler, E. (1911). *Dementia praecox or the group of schizophrenias* (J. Zinkin, Trans.). New York, NY: International Universities Press.

Bleuler, E. (1924). *Textbook of psychiatry* (A. A. Brill, Trans.). New York, NY: Macmillan.

Bliss, E. L. (1984). A symptom profile of patients with multiple personalities including MMPI results. *Journal of Nervous and Mental Diseases, 172,* 197–211.

Bloch, M. H., Landeros-Weisenberger, A., Rosario, M. C., Pittenger, C., & Leckman, J. F. (2008). Meta-analysis of the symptom structure of obsessive-compulsive disorder. *American Journal of Psychiatry, 165*(12), 1532–1542. doi: 10.1176/appi.ajp.2008.08020320

Bloch, M., Schmidt, P. J., & Rubinow, D. R. (2014). Premenstrual syndrome: Evidence for symptom stability across cycles. *American Journal of Psychiatry, 154*(12), 1741–1746.

Bloch, S., & Green, S. (2012). Psychiatric ethics. In M. G. Gelder, N. C. Andreasen, J. J. Lopez-Ibor, Jr., & J. R. Geddes (Eds.), *New Oxford textbook of psychiatry* (2nd ed., Vol. 1, pp. 28-32). New York, NY: Oxford University Press.

Block, J. J. (2008). Issues for DSM-V: Internet addiction. *American Journal of Psychiatry, 165*(3), 306–307. doi: 10.1176/appi.ajp.2007.07101556

Blom, M. M., Bosmans, J. E., Cuijpers, P., Zarit, S. H., & Pot, A. M. (2013). Effectiveness and cost-effectiveness of an internet intervention for family caregivers of people with dementia: design of a randomized controlled trial. *BMC Psychiatry, 13*(1), 1.

Bloom, F. E., & Kupfer, D. J. (1995). *Psychopharmacology: The fourth generation of progress.* New York, NY: Raven.

Bloom, F. E., Nelson, C. A., & Lazerson, A. (2001). *Brain, mind, & behavior* (3rd ed.). New York, NY: Worth.

Bloom, J. D., & Kirkorsky, S. E. (in press). Mens rea, competency to stand trial, and guilty but mentally ill. *Journal of the American Academy of Psychiatry and the Law.*

Blum, D. J., & Zeitzer, J. M. (2021). Irregular sleep-wake, non-24-hour sleep wake, jet lag, and shift work sleep disorders. In E. H. During & C. A. Kushida (Eds.), *Clinical sleep medicine: A comprehensive guide for mental health and other medical professionals* (pp. 245–271.). Washington, D.C.: American Psychiatric Association Publishing.

Blum, K., Baron, D., McLaughlin, T., & Gold, M. S. (2020). Molecular neurological correlates of endorphinergic/dopaminergic mechanisms in reward circuitry linked to endorphinergic deficiency syndrome (EDS). *Journal of the Neurological Sciences, 411,* 116733.

Blumenthal, J. A., Sherwood, A., Babyak, M., Watkins, L., Waugh, R., Georgiades, A., & Hinderliter, A. (2005). Effects of exercise and stress management training on markers of cardiovascular risk in patients with ischemic heart disease. *JAMA: Journal of the American Medical Association, 293,* 1626–1634.

Blumenthal, S. J. (1990). An overview and synopsis of risk factors, assessment, and treatment of suicidal patients over the life cycle. In S. J. Blumenthal & D. J. Kupfer (Eds.), *Suicide over the life cycle: Risk factors, assessment and treatment of suicidal patients* (pp. 685–734). Washington, DC: American Psychiatric Press.

Blumenthal, S. J., & Kupfer, D. J. (1988). Clinical assessment and treatment of youth suicide. *Journal of Youth and Adolescence, 17,* 1–24.

Blundell, J. E. (2002). The psychobiological approach to appetite and weight control. In K. D. Brownell & C. G. Fairburn (Eds.), *Eating disorders and obesity: A comprehensive handbook* (2nd ed., pp. 13–20). New York, NY: Guilford.

Blythin, S. P. M., Nicholson, H. L., Macintyre, V. G., Dickson, J. M., Fox, J. R. E., & Taylor, P. J. (2020). Experiences of shame and guilt in anorexia and bulimia nervosa: A systematic review. *Psychology and Psychotherapy: Theory, Research and Practice, 93*(1), 134–159. doi: 10.1111/papt.12198

Boardman, J. D., Barnes, L. L., Wilson, R. S., Evans, D. A., & de Leon, C. F. M. (2012). Social disorder, APOE-E4 genotype, and change in cognitive function among older adults living in Chicago. *Social Science & Medicine, 74*(10), 1584–1590. doi: http://dx.doi.org/10.1016/j.socscimed.2012.02.012

Bob, P. (2003). Dissociation and neuroscience: History and new perspectives. *International Journal of Neuroscience, 113,* 903–914.

Bockoven, J. S. (1963). *Moral treatment in American psychiatry.* New York, NY: Springer.

Bockting, C. L., Hollon, S. D., Jarrett, R. B., Kuyken, W., & Dobson, K. (2015). A lifetime approach to major depressive disorder: The contributions of psychological interventions in preventing relapse and recurrence. *Clinical Psychology Review, 41,* 16–25.

Bodell, L. P., & Keel, P. K. (2015). Weight suppression in bulimia nervosa: Associations with biology and behavior. *Journal of Abnormal Psychology, 124*(4), 994–1002.

Boden, J. M., Fergusson, D. M., & Horwood, L. J. (2012). Alcohol misuse and violent behavior: Findings from a 30-year longitudinal study. *Drug and Alcohol Dependence, 122*(1), 135–141.

Bodlund, O., & Kullgren, G. (1996). Transsexualism—General outcome and prognostic factors: A five-year follow-up study of nineteen transsexuals in the process of changing sex. *Archives of Sexual Behavior, 25,* 303–316.

Bodnar, R. J. (2012). Endogenous opiates and behavior. *Peptides, 38*(2), 463–522.

Boehm, J. K., & Kubzansky, L. D. (2012). The heart's content: The association between positive psychological well-being and cardiovascular health. *Psychological bulletin, 138*(4), 655–691.

Bøen, H., Dalgard, O. S., & Bjertness, E. (2012). The importance of social support in the associations between psychological distress and somatic health problems and socio-economic factors among older adults living at home: a Cross sectional study. *BMC Geriatrics, 12*(1), 27.

Bogaert, A. F., & Skorska, M. (2011). Sexual orientation, fraternal birth order, and the maternal immune hypothesis: A review. *Frontiers in Neuroendocrinology, 32*(2), 247–254.

Bogan, R. K., Roth, T., Schwartz, J., & Miloslavsky, M. (2014). Time to response with sodi-um oxybate for the treatment of excessive daytime sleepiness and cataplexy in patients with narcolepsy. Journal of clinical sleep medicine: JCSM: official publication of the American Academy of Sleep Medicine, 11(4), 427–432.

Bogart, A. F. (2010). Physical development and sexual orientation in men and women: An analysis of NATSL-2000. *Archives of Sexual Behavior, 39,* 110–116.

Bögels, S. M., Alden, L., Beidel, D. C., Clark, L. A., Pine, D. S., Stein, M. B., & Voncken, M. (2010). Social anxiety disorder: Questions and answers for the DSM-V. *Depression and Anxiety, 27*(2), 168–189. doi: 10.1002/da.20670

Boland, R. J., & Keller, M. B. (2009). Course and outcome of depression. In I. H. Gotlib & C. L. Hammen (Eds.), *Handbook of depression* (2nd ed., pp. 23–43). New York, NY: Guilford.

Bolinskey, P. K., James, A. V., Cooper-Bolinskey, D., Novi, J. H., Hunter, H. K., Hudak, D. V., . . . Lenzenweger, M. F. (2015). Revisiting the blurry boundaries of schizophrenia:

Spectrum disorders in psychometrically identified schizotypes. *Psychiatry Research, 225*(3), 335–340.

Bonanno, G. (2006). Is complicated grief a valid construct? *Clinical Psychology Science Practice, 13,* 129–134.

Bonanno, G. A., & Kaltman, S. (2001). The varieties of grief experience. *Clinical Psychology Review, 21,* 705–734.

Bonanno, G. A., (2004). Loss, trauma, and human resilience: Have we underestimated the human capacity to thrive after extremely aversive events? *American Psychologist, 59,* 20–28.

Bonanno, G. A., Westphal, M., & Mancini, A. D. (2011). Resilience to loss and potential trauma. *Annual Review of Clinical Psychology, 7*(1), 511–535. doi: 10.1146/annurev-clinpsy-032210-104526

Bonanno, G., & Kaltman, S. (1999). Toward an integrative perspective on bereavement. *Psychological Bulletin, 125*(6), 1004–1008.

Bond, A., & Lader, M. (2012). Anxiolytics and sedatives. In J. C. Verster, K. Brady, M. Galanter, & P. Conrod (Eds.), *Drug abuse and addiction in medical illness: Causes, consequences and treatment* (pp. 231–239). New York, NY: Springer.

Bonnar-Kidd, K. K. (2010). Sexual offender laws and prevention of sexual violence or recidivism. *American Journal of Public Health, 100*(3), 412–419.

Booij, L., & Van der Does, A. J. (2007). Cognitive and serotonergic vulnerability to depression: Convergent findings. *Journal of Abnormal Psychology, 116*(1), 86–94.

Boon, S., & Draijer, N. (1993). Multiple personality disorder in the Netherlands: A clinical investigation of 71 cases. *American Journal of Psychiatry, 150,* 489–494.

Boone, L., Soenens, B., Vansteenkiste, M., & Braet, C. (2012). Is there a perfectionist in each of us? An experimental study on perfectionism and eating disorder symptoms. *Appetite, 59*(2), 531–540.

Boot, W. R., Simons, D. J., Stothart, C., & Stutts, C. (2013). The pervasive problem with placebos in psychology why active control groups are not sufficient to rule out placebo effects. *Perspectives on Psychological Science, 8*(4), 445–454. doi: 10.1177/1745691613491271

Borg, L., Buonora, M., Butelman, E. R., Ducat, E., Ray, B. M., & Kreek, M. J. (2015). The pharmacology of opioids. In R. K. Ries, D. A. Fiellin, S. C. Miller, & R. Saitz (Eds.), *The ASAM principles of addiction medicine* (5th ed., pp. 135–150). New York, NY: Wolters Kluwer.

Borge, F.-M., Hoffart, A., Sexton, H., Martinsen, E., Gude, T., Hedley, L. M., & Abrahamsen, G. (2010). Pre-treatment predictors and in-treatment factors associated with change in avoidant and dependent personality disorder traits among patients with social phobia. *Clinical Psychology & Psychotherapy, 17*(2), 87–99.

Borgelt, L. M., Franson, K. L., Nussbaum, A. M., & Wang, G. S. (2013). The pharmacologic and clinical effects of medical cannabis. *Pharmacotherapy: The Journal of Human Pharmacology and Drug Therapy, 33*(2), 195–209.

Borges, G., Nock, M. K., Abad, J. M. H., Hwang, I., Sampson, N. A., Alonso, J., & Kessler, R. C. (2010). Twelve month prevalence of and risk factors for suicide attempts in the WHO World Mental Health Surveys. *The Journal of Clinical Psychiatry, 71*(12), 1617–1628.

Borkovec, T. D., & Costello, E. (1993). Efficacy of applied relaxation and cognitive-behavioral therapy in the treatment of generalized anxiety disorder. *Journal of Consulting and Clinical Psychology, 61*(4), 611–619.

Borkovec, T. D., & Hu, S. (1990). The effect of worry on cardiovascular response to phobic imagery. *Behaviour Research and Therapy, 28,* 69–73.

Borkovec, T. D., & Ruscio, A. (2001). Psychotherapy for generalized anxiety disorder. *Journal of Clinical Psychiatry, 62,* 37–45.

Borkovec, T. D., Shadick, R., & Hopkins, M. (1991). The nature of normal and pathological worry. In R. M. Rapee & D. H. Barlow (Eds.), *Chronic anxiety, generalized anxiety disorder, and mixed anxiety depression.* New York, NY: Guilford.

Bornstein, R. F. (1992). The dependent personality: Developmental, social, and clinical perspectives. *Psychological Bulletin, 112,* 3–23.

Bornstein, R. F. (2012). Dependent personality disorder. In T. A. Widiger (Ed.), *The Oxford handbook of personality disorders* (pp. 505-526). New York, NY: Oxford University Press.

Borodinsky, L. N., Root, C. M., Cronin, J. A., Sann, S. B., Gu, X., & Spitzer, N. C. (2004). Activity-dependent homeostatic specification of transmitter expression in embryonic neurons. *Nature, 429,* 523–530.

Boskind-Lodahl, M. (1976). Cinderella's stepsisters: A feminist perspective on anorexia nervosa and bulimia. *Signs, 2,* 342–356.

Bosson, J. K., Parrott, D. J., Swan, S. C., Kuchynka, S. L., & Schramm, A. T. (2015). A dangerous boomerang: Injunctive norms, hostile sexist attitudes, and male-to-female sexual aggression. *Aggressive Behavior, 41*(6), 580–593.

Bouchard, C. (2002). Genetic influences on body weight and shape. In K. D. Brownell & C. G. Fairburn (Eds.), *Eating disorders and obesity: A comprehensive handbook* (2nd ed., pp. 21–26). New York, NY: Guilford.

Bouchard, M. F., Bellinger, D. C., Wright, R. O., & Weisskopf, M. G. (2010). Attention-deficit/hyperactivity disorder and urinary metabolites of organophosphate pesticides. *Pediatrics, 125*(6), e1270–1277.

Bouchard, T. J., Jr., Lykken, D. T., McGue, M., Segal, N. L., & Tellegen, A. (1990). Sources of human psychological differences: The Minnesota study of twins reared apart. *Science, 250,* 223–228.

Bouman, T. K. (2014). Psychological treatments for hypochondriasis: A narrative review. *Current Psychiatry Reviews, 10,* 58–69.

Bourgeois, M. S. (1992). Evaluating memory wallets in conversations with persons with dementia. *Journal of Speech and Hearing Research, 35,* 1344–1357.

Bourgeois, M. S. (2007). *Memory books and other graphic cuing systems: Practical communication and memory aids for adults with dementia.* Baltimore, MD: Health Professions.

Boutoleau-Bretonnière, C., Pouclet-Courtemanche, H., Gillet, A., Bernard, A., Laure Deruet, A., Gouraud, I., … Kapogiannis, D. (in press). The effects of confinement on neuropsychiatric symptoms in Alzheimer's disease during the COVID-19 crisis. *Journal of Alzheimer's Disease.*

Bouton, M. E. (2005). Behavior systems and the contextual control of anxiety, fear, and panic. In L. Feldman Barrett, P. Niedenthal, & P. Winkielman (Eds.), *Emotion: Conscious and unconscious* (pp. 205–227). New York, NY: Guilford.

Bouton, M. E., Mineka, S., & Barlow, D. H. (2001). A modern learning-theory perspective on the etiology of panic disorder. *Psychological Review, 108,* 4–32.

Bower, B. (1999). Personality conflicts: A clinical upstart elbows its way into the personality-assessment fray. *Science News, 156,* 88–90.

Bower, J. E., Moskowitz, J. T., & Epel, E. (2009). Is benefit finding good for your health? Pathways linking positive life changes after stress and physical health outcomes. *Current Directions in Psychological Science, 18,* 337–341.

Bowers, J. S., & Marsolek, C. J. (2003). *Rethinking implicit memory.* New York, NY: Oxford University Press.

Bowlby, J. (1980). *Attachment and loss.* New York, NY: Basic Books.

Bowman, E. S., & Coons, P. M. (2000). The differential diagnosis of epilepsy, pseudoseizures, dissociative identity disorder, and dissociative disorder not otherwise specified. *Bulletin of the Menninger Clinic, 64,* 164–180.

Boyce, N. (2011). Suicide clusters: The undiscovered country. *The Lancet, 378*(9801), 1452.

Boydell, J., & Allardyce, J. (2011). Does urban density matter? In A. S. David, S. Kapur, P. McGuffin, & R. M. Murray (Eds.), *Schizophrenia: The final frontier—A festschrift for Robin M. Murray* (pp. 273–280). New York, NY: Routledge.

Boyer, P., & Liénard, P. (2008). Ritual behavior in obsessive and normal individuals: Moderating anxiety and reorganizing the flow of action. *Current Directions in Psychological Science, 17*(4), 291–294.

Boysen, G., Ebersole, A., Casner, R., & Coston, N. (2014). Gendered mental disorders: Masculine and feminine stereotypes about mental disorders and their relation to stigma. *The Journal of Social Psychology, 154*(6), 546–565.

Bradford, A., & Meston, C. M. (2006). The impact of anxiety on sexual arousal in women. *Behaviour Research and Therapy, 44,* 1067–1077.

Bradford, A., & Meston, C. M. (2011). Sex and gender disorders. In D. H. Barlow (Ed.), *Oxford handbook of clinical psychology.* New York, NY: Oxford University Press.

Bradford, J. (1997). Medical interventions in sexual deviance. In D. R. Laws & W. O'Donohue (Eds.), *Sexual deviance: Theory, assessment and treatment* (pp. 449–464). New York, NY: Guilford.

Bradley, B. P., Mogg, K., White, J., Groom, C., & de Bono, J. (1999). Attentional bias for emotional faces in generalized anxiety disorder. *British Journal of Clinical Psychology, 38,* 267–278.

Bradley, R. G., Binder, E. B., Epstein, M. P., Tang, Y., Nair, H. P., Liu, W., & Ressler, K. J. (2008). Influence of child abuse on adult depression: Moderation by the corticotropin-releasing hormone receptor gene. *Archives of General Psychiatry, 65*(2), 190–200.

Bradley, W. (1937). The behavior of children receiving Benzedrine. *American Journal of Psychiatry, 94,* 577–585.

Braff, D., Schork, N. J., & Gottesman, I. I. (2007). Endophenotyping schizophrenia. *American Journal of Psychiatry, 164,* 705–707.

Brakefield, T. A., Mednick, S. C., Wilson, H. W., De Neve, J. E., Christakis, N. A., & Fowler, J. H. (2014). Same-sex sexual attraction does not spread in adolescent social networks. *Archives of Sexual Behavior, 43*(2), 335–344.

Brand, B. L., Webermann, A. R., Snyder, B. L., & Kaliush, P. R. (2019). Detecting clinical and simulated dissociative identity disorder with the test of memory malingering. *Psychological Trauma: Theory, Research, Practice, and Policy, 11*(5), 513–520. doi: 10.1037/tra0000405

Brand, B., Classen, C., Lanins, R., Loewenstein, R., McNary, S., Pain, C., & Putnam, F. (2009). A naturalistic study of dissociative identity disorder and dissociative disorder not otherwise specified patients treated by community clinicians. *Psychological Trauma: Theory, Research, Practice, and Policy, 1*(2), 153–171.

Brandão, D. J., Fontenelle, L. F., da Silva, S. A., Menezes, P. R., & Pastor-Valero, M. (2019). Depression and excess mortality in the elderly living in low- and middle-income countries: Systematic review and meta-analysis. *International Journal of Geriatric Psychiatry, 34*(1), 22–30. doi: 10.1002/gps.5008

Brannigan, G. G., & Decker, S. L. (2006). The Bender-Gestalt II. *American Journal of Orthopsychiatry, 76*(1), 10–12.

Brauchi, J. T., & West, L. J. (1959). Sleep deprivation. *Journal of the American Medical Association, 171*(1), 11–14.

Brawman-Mintzer, O. (2001). Pharmacologic treatment of generalized anxiety disorder. *Psychiatric Clinics of North America, 24,* 119–137.

Bray, G. A. (2012). Diet and exercise for weight loss. *Journal of American Medical Association, 307*(24), 2641–2642.

Breckenridge, J., Salter, M., & Shaw, E. (2012). *Use and abuse: Understanding the intersections of childhood abuse, alcohol and drug use and mental health.* Sydney, Australia: University of New South Wales.

Breeksema, J. J., Niemeijer, A. R., Krediet, E., Vermetten, E., & Schoevers, R. A. (2020). Psychedelic treatments for psychiatric disorders: A systematic review and thematic synthesis of patient experiences in qualitative studies. *CNS Drugs, 34*(9), 925–946. doi: 10.1007/s40263-020-00748-y

Breitbart, W., & Alici, Y. (2012). Evidence-based treatment of delirium in patients with cancer. *Journal of Clinical Oncology, 30*(11), 1206-1214. doi: 10.1200/jco.2011.39.8784

Breitborde, N. J., López, S. R., & Kopelowicz, A. (2010). Expressed emotion and health outcomes among Mexican-Americans with schizophrenia and their caregiving relatives. *The Journal of Nervous and Mental Disease, 198*(2), 105–109.

Bremner, J. D. (1999). Does stress damage the brain? *Biological Psychiatry, 45,* 797–805.

Bremner, J. D., Randall, P. R., Scott, T. M., Bronen, R. A., Seibyl, J. P., Southwick, S. M., & Innis, R. R. (1995). MRI-based measurement of hippocampal volume in patients with combat-related posttraumatic stress disorder. *American Journal of Psychiatry, 152,* 973–981.

Brenes, G. A., Miller, M. E., Stanley, M. A., Williamson, J. D., Knudson, M., & McCall, W. V. (2009). Insomnia in older adults with generalized anxiety disorder. *American Journal of Geriatric Psychiatry, 17,* 465–472.

Brenner, D. E., Kukull, W. A., van Belle, G., Bowen, J. D., McCormick, W. C., Teri, L., & Larson, E. B. (1993). Relationship between cigarette smoking and Alzheimer's disease in a population-based case-control study. *Neurology, 43,* 293–300.

Brent, D. A., & Kolko, D. J. (1990). The assessment and treatment of children and adolescents at risk for suicide. In S. J. Blumenthal & D. J. Kupfer (Eds.), *Suicide over the life cycle: Risk factors, assessment and treatment of suicidal patients.* Washington, DC: American Psychiatric Press.

Brent, D. A., & Mann, J. J. (2005). Family genetic studies, suicide, and suicidal behavior. *American Journal of Medical Genetics, 133*(1), 13–24.

Brent, D. A., Brunwasser, S. M., Hollon, S. D., Weersing, V. R., Clarke, G. N., Beardless, W. R., Gladstone, T. R. G., Porta, G., Lynch, F. L., Iyengar, S., & Garber, J. (2015). Effect of a cognitive-behavioral prevention program on depression 6 years after implementation among at-risk adolescents: A randomized clinical trial. *JAMA Psychiatry, 72,* 1110–1118.

Brent, D. A., Melhem, N. M., Oquendo, M., Burke, A., Birmaher, B., Stanley, B., Biernesser, C., Keilp, J., Kalka, D., Ellis, S., Porta, G., Zelazny, J., Iyengar, S., & Mann, J. J. (2015). Familial pathways to early-onset suicide attempt: A 5.6-year prospective study. *JAMA Psychiatry, 72,* 160–168.

Brent, D. A., Oquendo, M., Birmaher, B., Greenhill, L., Kolko, D., Stanley, B., & Mann, J. J. (2002). Familial pathways to early-onset suicide attempt risk for suicidal behavior in offspring of mood-disordered suicide attempters. *Archives of General Psychiatry, 59,* 801–807.

Brent, D. A., Oquendo, M., Birmaher, B., Greenhill, L., Kolko, D., Stanley, B., & Mann, J. J. (2003). Peripubertal suicide attempts in offspring of suicide attempters with siblings concordant for suicidal behavior. *American Journal of Psychiatry, 160,* 1486–1493.

Brent, D. A., Perper, J. A., Goldstein, C. E., Kolko, D. J., Allan, M. J., Allman, C. J., & Zellenak, J. P. (1988). Risk factors for adolescent suicide: A comparison of adolescent suicide victims with suicidal inpatients. *Archives of General Psychiatry, 45,* 581–588.

Brent, D., & Birmaher, B. (2009). Paediatric mood disorders. In M. G. Gelder, N. C. Andreasen, J. J. López-Ibor, Jr., & J. R. Geddes (Eds.), *New Oxford textbook of psychiatry* (2nd ed., Vol. 2, pp. 1669–1680). Oxford, UK: Oxford University Press.

Brent, D., Emslie, G., Clarke, G., Wagner, K. D., Asarnow, J. R., Keller, M., & Zelazny, J. (2008). Switching to another SSRI or to venlafaxine with or without cognitive behavioral therapy for adolescents with SSRI-resistant depression: The TORDIA randomized controlled trial. *JAMA: Journal of the American Medical Association, 299*(8), 901–913.

Brent, D., Melhem, N., Donohoe, M. B., & Walker, M. (2009). The incidence and course of depression in bereaved youth 21 months after the loss of a parent to suicide, accident, or sudden natural death. *American Journal of Psychiatry, 166*(7), 786–794.

Brentjens, M. H., Yeung-Yue, K. A., Lee, P. C., & Tyring, S. K. (2003). Recurrent genital herpes treatments and their impact on quality of life. *Pharmacoeconomics, 21,* 853–863.

Breslau, N. (2012). Epidemiology of posttraumatic stress disorder in adults. In J. G. Beck & D. M. Sloan (Eds.), *The Oxford handbook of traumatic stress disorders* (pp. 84–97). New York, NY: Oxford University Press.

Breslau, N., Davis, G. C., & Andreski, M. A. (1995). Risk factors for PTSD-related traumatic events: A prospective analysis. *American Journal of Psychiatry, 152,* 529–535.

Breslau, N., Lucia, V. C., & Alvarado, G. F. (2006). Intelligence and other predisposing factors in exposure to trauma and posttraumatic stress disorder. *Archives of General Psychiatry, 63,* 1238–1245.

Breuer, J., & Freud, S. (1957). *Studies on hysteria.* New York, NY: Basic Books. (Original work published in 1895.)

Brewer, S., Gleditsch, S. L., Syblik, D., Tietjens, M. E., & Vacik, H. W. (2006). Pediatric anxiety: Child life intervention in day surgery. *Journal of Pediatric Nursing,* 21, 13–22.

Brewerton, T. D., Rance, S. J., Dansky, B. S., O'Neil, P. M., & Kilpatrick, D. G. (2014). A comparison of women with child-adolescent versus adult onset binge eating: Results from the National Women's Study. *International Journal of Eating Disorders, 47*(7), 836–843.

Briganti, A., Salonia, A., Gallina, A., Saccà, A., Montorsi, P., Rigatti, P., & Montorsi, F. (2005). Drug insight: Oral phosphodiesterase type 5 inhibitors for erectile dysfunction. *Nature Clinical Practice Urology, 2*(5), 239–247. doi: 10.1038/ncpuro0186

Britton, J. C., Grillon, C., Lissek, S., Norcross, M. A., Szuhany, K., Chen, G., Ernst, M., Nelson, E. E., Leibenluft, E., Shechner, T., & Pine, D. S. (2013). Response to learned threat: An fMRI study in adolescent and adult anxiety. *American Journal of Psychiatry, 170,* 1195–1204.

Brody, A. L., Saxena, S., Stoessel, P., Gillies, L. A., Fairbanks, L. A., Alborzian, S., & Baxter, L. R., Jr. (2001). Regional brain metabolic changes in patients with major depression treated with either paroxetine or interpersonal therapy. *Archives of General Psychiatry, 48,* 631–640.

Brody, H., & Miller, F. G. (2011). Lessons from recent research about the placebo effect —from art to science. *JAMA: Journal of the American Medical Association, 306*(23), 2612–2613. doi: 10.1001/jama.2011.1850

Brody, M. J., Walsh, B. T., & Devlin, M. J. (1994). Binge eating disorder: Reliability and validity of a new diagnostic category. *Journal of Consulting and Clinical Psychology, 62,* 381–386.

Broft, A., Berner, L. A., & Walsh, B. T. (2010). Pharmacotherapy for bulimia nervosa. In C. M. Grilo & J. E. Mitchell (Eds.), *The treatment of eating disorders: A clinical handbook.* (pp. 388–401). New York, NY: Guilford.

Bromet, E., Andrade, L. H., Hwang, I., Sampson, N. A., Alonso, J., de Girolamo, G., & Kessler, R. C. (2011). Cross-national epidemiology of DSM-IV major depressive episode. *BMC Medicine, 9*(1), 90.

Brondolo, E., Grantham, K. I., Karlin, W., Taravella, J., Mencia-Ripley, A., Schwartz, J. E., & Contrada, R. J. (2009). Trait hostility and ambulatory blood pressure among traffic enforcement agents: The effects of stressful social interactions. *Journal of Occupational Health Psychology, 14*(2), 110–121.

Brotman, M. A., Schmajuk, M., Rich, B. A., Dickstein, D. P., Guyer, A. E., Costello, E. J., & Leibenluft, E. (2006). Prevalence, clinical correlates, and longitudinal course of severe mood dysregulation in children. *Biological Psychiatry, 60*(9), 991–997.

Brotto, L. (2015). Filbanserin. *Archives of Sexual Behavior, 44*(8), 2103–2105. doi 10.1007/s10508-015-0643-9

Brotto, L. A. (2006). Psychologic-based desire and arousal disorders: Treatment strategies and outcome results. In I. Goldstein, C. M. Meston, S. R. Davis, & A. M. Traish (Eds.), *Women's sexual function and dysfunction: Study, diagnosis, and treatment* (pp. 441–448). New York, NY: Taylor and Francis.

Brotto, L. A. (2010). The DSM diagnostic criteria for hypoactive sexual desire disorder in women. *Archives of Sexual Behavior, 39,* 222–239.

Brotto, L., & Luria, M. (2014). *Sexual interest /arousal disorder in women.* In Y. M. Binik & K. S. K. Hall (Eds.). Principles and Practice of Sex Therapy 5th edition (pp. 17–42). The Guildford Press: New York.

Broude, G. J., & Greene, S. J. (1980). Cross-cultural codes on 20 sexual attitudes and practices. In H. Barry, III, & A. Schlegel (Eds.), *Cross-cultural samples and codes* (pp. 313–333). Pittsburgh, PA: University of Pittsburgh Press.

Broughton, R. J. (2000). NREM arousal parasomnias. In M. H. Kryger, T. Roth, & W. C. Dement (Eds.), *Principles and practice of sleep medicine* (3rd ed., pp. 693–706). Philadelphia, PA: W. B. Saunders.

Broughton, R., Billings, R., & Cartwright, R. (1994). Homicidal somnambulism: A case report. *Sleep, 17,* 253–264.

Broussard, L. (2020). Inhalants. In B. S. Levine & S. Kerrigan (Eds.), *Principles of forensic toxicology* (pp. 561–568). Cham: Springer International.

Brown, A., Scales, U., Beever, W., Rickards, B., Rowley, K., & O'Dea, K. (2012). Exploring the expression of depression and distress in aboriginal men in central Australia: A qualitative study. *BMC Psychiatry, 12*(1), 97.

Brown, D. R., Ahmed, F., Gary, L. E., & Milburn, N. G. (1995). Major depression in a community sample of African Americans. *American Journal of Psychiatry, 152,* 373–378.

Brown, G. W. (1959). Experiences of discharged chronic schizophrenic mental hospital patients in various types of living group. *Millbank Memorial Fund Quarterly, 37,* 105–131.

Brown, G. W., & Birley, J. L. T. (1968). Crisis and life change and the onset of schizophrenia. *Journal of Health and Social Behavior, 9,* 203–214.

Brown, G. W., Monck, E. M., Carstairs, G. M., & Wing, J. K. (1962). Influence of family life on the course of schizophrenic illness. *British Journal of Preventive and Social Medicine, 16,* 55–68.

Brown, J., & Finn, P. (1982). Drinking to get drunk: Findings of a survey of junior and senior high school students. *Journal of Alcohol and Drug Education, 27,* 13–25.

Brown, M. M., Bell, D. S., Jason, L. A., Christos, C., & Bell, D. E. (2012). Understanding long term outcomes of chronic fatigue syndrome. *Journal of Clinical Psychology, 68*(9), 1028–1035.

Brown, P. L. (2006, December 2). Supporting boys or girls when the line isn't clear. *New York Times.* Retrieved from http://www.nytimes.com/2006/12/02/us/02child.html

Brown, R. J., & Lewis-Fernandez, R. (2011). Culture and conversion disorder: Implications for DSM-5. *Psychiatry, 74*(3), 187–206. doi: 10.1521/psyc.2011.74.3.187

Brown, R., & LeDoux, J. (2020). Higher-order memory schema and consciousness experience. *Cognitive Neuropsychology, 37*(3–4), 213–215. doi: 10.1080/02643294.2020.1729713

Brown, T. A., & Barlow, D. H. (2005). Dimensional versus categorical classification of mental disorders in the fifth edition of the diagnostic and statistical manual of mental disorders and beyond: Comment on the special section. Special issue: Toward a dimensionally based taxonomy of psychopathology. *Journal of Abnormal Psychology, 114*(4), 551–556.

Brown, T. A., & Barlow, D. H. (2009). A proposal for a dimensional classification system based on the shared features of the DSM-IV anxiety and mood disorders: Implications for assessment and treatment. *Psychological Assessment, 21*(3), 256–271.

Brown, T. A., & Barlow, D. H. (2014). *Anxiety and related disorders interview schedule for DSM-5 (ADIS-5L): Client interview schedule.* New York, NY: Oxford University Press.

Brown, T. A., & Barlow, D. H. (in press). *Anxiety Disorders Interview Schedule for DSM-5* (AVIS.5). New York, NY: Oxford University Press.

Brown, T. A., & Naragon-Gainey, K. (2013). Evaluation of the unique and specific contributions of dimensions of the triple vulnerability model to the prediction of DSM-IV anxiety and mood disorder constructs. *Behavior Therapy, 44*(2), 277–292.

Brown, T. A., Barlow, D. H., & Liebowitz, M. R. (1994). The empirical basis of generalized anxiety disorder. *American Journal of Psychiatry, 15*(9), 1272–1280.

Brown, T. A., Campbell, L. A., Lehman, C. L., Grisham, J. R., & Mancill, R. B. (2001). Current and lifetime comorbidity of the DSM-IV anxiety and mood disorders in a large clinical sample. *Journal of Abnormal Psychology.*

Brown, T. A., Chorpita, B. F., & Barlow, D. H. (1998). Structural relationships among dimensions of the DSM-IV anxiety and mood disorders and dimensions of negative affect, positive affect, and autonomic arousal. *Journal of Abnormal Psychology, 107*(2), 179–192.

Brown, T. A., Marten, P. A., & Barlow, D. H. (1995). Discriminant validity of the symptoms comprising the DSM-III-R and DSM-IV associated symptom criterion of generalized anxiety disorder. *Journal of Anxiety Disorders, 9,* 317–328.

Brown, T. A., White, K. S., & Barlow, D. H. (2005). A psychometric reanalysis of the Albany panic and phobia questionnaire. *Behaviour Research and Therapy, 43,* 337–355.

Brown, T. E. (Ed.). (2009). *ADHD comorbidities: Handbook for ADHD complications in children and adults.* Arlington, VA: American Psychiatric Publishing.

Brown, W. M., Finn, C. J., Cooke, B. M., & Breedlove, S. M. (2002). Differences in finger length ratios between self-identified "butch" and "femme" lesbians. *Archives of Sexual Behavior, 31,* 123–127.

Browne, H. A., Hansen, S. N., Buxbaum, J. D., Gair, S. L., Nissen, J. B., Nikolajsen, K. H., Schendel, D. E., Reichenberg, A., Parner, E. T., & Grice, D. E. (2015). Familial clustering of tic disorders and obsessive-compulsive disorder. *JAMA psychiatry,72,* 359–366.

Brownell, K. D., & Ludwig, D. S. (2011). The supplemental nutrition assistance program, soda, and USDA policy: Who benefits? *Journal of American Medical Association, 306,* 1370–1371.

Brownell, K. D. (1991). Dieting and the search for the perfect body: Where physiology and culture collide. *Behavior Therapy, 22,* 1–12.

Brownell, K. D., (2002). Eating disorders in athletes. In K. D. Brownell & C. G. Fairburn (Eds.), *Eating disorders and obesity: A comprehensive handbook* (2nd ed., pp. 191–196). New York, NY: Guilford.

Brownell, K. D. (2003). *Food fight: The inside story of the food industry, America's obesity crisis and what we can do about it.* New York, NY: McGraw-Hill.

Brownell, K. D., & Fairburn, C. G. (Eds.) (1995). *Eating disorders and obesity: A comprehensive handbook.* New York, NY: Guilford.

Brownell, K. D., & Frieden, T. R. (2009). Ounces of prevention—the public policy case for taxes on sugared beverages. *New England Journal of Medicine, 360*(18), 1805–1808.

Brownell, K. D., & Rodin, J. (1994). The dieting maelstrom: Is it possible and advisable to lose weight? *American Psychologist, 49*(9), 781–791.

Brownell, K. D., & Yach, D. (2005). The battle of the bulge. *Foreign Policy,* 26–27.

Brownell, K. D., Farley, T., Willett, W. C., Popkin, B. M., Chaloupka, F. J., Thompson, J. W., & Ludwig, D. S. (2009). The public health and economic benefits of taxing sugar-sweetened beverages. *New England Journal of Medicine, 361*(16), 1599–1605.

Brownell, K. D., Hayes, S. C., & Barlow, D. H. (1977). Patterns of appropriate and deviant sexual arousal: The behavioral treatment of multiple sexual deviations. *Journal of Consulting and Clinical Psychology, 45*(6), 1144–1155.

Brownell, K. D., Kersh, R., Ludwig, D. S., Post, R. C., Puhl, R. M., Schwartz, M. B., & Willett, W. C. (2010). Personal responsibility and obesity: A constructive approach to a controversial issue. *Health Affairs, 29*(3), 379–387.

Bruce, B. B., & Newman, N. J. (2010). Functional visual loss. *Neurologic Clinic, 28,* 789-802.

Bruce, M. L. (2002). Psychosocial risk factors for depressive disorders in late life. *Biological Psychiatry, 52,* 175–184.

Bruce, S. E., Yonkers, K. A., Otto, M. W., Eisen, J. L., Weisberg, R. B., Pagano, M., & Keller, M. B. (2005). Influence of psychiatric comorbidity on recovery and recurrence in generalized anxiety disorder, social phobia, and panic disorder: A 12-year prospective study. *American Journal of Psychiatry, 162,* 1179–1187.

Bruch, H. (1973). *Eating disorders: Obesity, anorexia nervosa, and the person within.* New York, NY: Basic Books.

Bruch, H. (1985). Four decades of eating disorders. In D. M. Garner & P. E. Garfinkel (Eds.), *Handbook of psychotherapy for anorexia nervosa and bulimia* (pp. 7–18). New York, NY: Guilford.

Bruch, M. A., & Heimberg, R. G. (1994). Differences in perceptions of parental and personal characteristics between generalized and non-generalized social phobics. *Journal of Anxiety Disorders, 8,* 155–168.

Bruck, M., Ceci, S., Francouer, E., & Renick, A. (1995). Anatomically detailed dolls do not facilitate preschoolers' reports of a pediatric examination involving genital touching. *Journal of Experimental Psychology: Applied, 1,* 95–109.

Bruni, O., Melegari, M. G., Esposito, A., Sette, S., Angriman, M., Apicella, M., … Ferri, R. (2020). Executive functions in preschool children with chronic insomnia. *Journal of Clinical Sleep Medicine, 16*(2), 231–241.

Brunoni, A. R., Valiengo, L., Baccaro, A., Zanao, T., de Oliveira, J. F., Goulart, A., & Fregni, F. (2013). The sertraline versus electrical current therapy for treating depression clinical study: Results from a factorial, randomized, controlled trial. *JAMA Psychiatry, 70*(4), 383–391.

Bryant, R. A. (2010). The complexity of complex PTSD. *American Journal of Psychiatry, 167,* 879–881.

Bryant, R. A., & Das, P. (2012). The neural circuitry of conversion disorder and its recovery. *Journal of Abnormal Psychology, 121*(1), 289–296. doi: 10.1037/a0025076

Bryant, R. A., Friedman, M. J., Spiegel, D., Ursano, R., & Strain, J. (2011). A review of acute stress disorder in DSM-5. *Depression and Anxiety, 28*(9), 802–817. doi: 10.1002/da.20737

Bryant, R. A., Kenny, L., Joscelyne, A., Rawson, N., Maccallum, F., Cahill, C., Hopwood, S., Aderka, I., & Nickerson, A. (2014). Treating prolonged grief disorder: A randomized clinical trial. *JAMA Psychiatry, 71,* 1332–1339.

Bryant, R. A., Moulds, M. L., & Nixon, R. V. D. (2003). Cognitive behavior therapy of acute stress disorder: A four-year follow-up. *Behaviour Research and Therapy, 41,* 489–494.

Bryant, R. A., O'Donnell, M. L., Creamer, M., McFarlane, A., & Silove, D. (2013). A multisite analysis of the fluctuating course of posttraumatic stress disorder. *JAMA Psychiatry, 70,* 839–846.

Buchanan, R. W., & Carpenter, W. T. (2005). Schizophrenia and other psychotic disorders. In B. J. Sadock & V. A. Sadock (Eds.), *Kaplan & Sadock's comprehensive textbook of psychiatry* (pp. 1329–1345). Philadelphia, PA: Lippincott, Williams & Wilkins.

Buchfuhrer, D. O., & Buchfuhrer, M. (2021). Restless legs syndrome and periodic limb moverments. In E. H. During & C. A. Kushida (Eds.), *Clinical sleep medicine: A comprehensive guide for mental health and other medical professionals* (pp. 333–355). Washington, D.C.: American Psychiatric Association Publishing.

Buchman-Wildbaum, T., Unoka, Z., Dudas, R., Vizin, G., Demetrovics, Z., & Richman, M. J. (2021). Shame in borderline personality disorder: Meta-analysis. *Journal of Personality Disorders, 35* (Suppl. A), 149–161.

Buchwald, H., Avidor, Y., Braunwald, E., Jensen, M. D., Pories, W., Fahrbach, K., & Schoelles, K. (2004). Bariatric surgery: A systematic review and meta-analysis. *JAMA: Journal of the American Medical Association, 292,* 1724–1737.

Buckingham-Howes, S., Berger, S. S., Scaletti, L. A., & Black, M. M. (2013). Systematic review of prenatal cocaine exposure and adolescent development. *Pediatrics, 131* (6), e1917–e1936.

Budnitz, D. S., Lovegrove, M. C., Shehab, N., & Richards, C. L. (2011). Emergency hospitalizations for adverse drug events in older Americans. *New England Journal of Medicine, 365*(21), 2002–2012.

Bufferd, S. J., Dougherty, L. R., Carlson, G. A., Rose, S., & Klein, D. N. (2012). Psychiatric disorders in preschoolers: Continuity from ages 3 to 6. *American Journal of Psychiatry, 169,* 1157–1164.

Buffum, J. (1982). Pharmacosexology: The effects of drugs on sexual function—A review. *Journal of Psychoactive Drugs, 14,* 5–44.

Buhle, J. T., Stevens, B. L., Friedman, J. J., & Wager, T. D. (2012). Distraction and placebo: two separate routes to pain control. *Psychological Science, 23*(3), 246–253.

Buhlmann, U., Reese, H. E., Renaud, S., & Wilhelm, S. (2008). Clinical considerations for the treatment of body dysmorphic disorder with cognitive-behavioral therapy. *Body Image, 5*(1), 39–49.

Buka, S. L., Seidman, L. J., Tsuang, M. T., & Goldstein, J. M. (2013). The New England family study high-risk project: Neurological impairments among offspring of parents with schizophrenia and other psychoses. *American Journal of Medical Genetics Part B: Neuropsychiatric Genetics, 162*(7), 653–660.

Bulik, C. M., Sullivan, P. F., & Kendler, K. S. (2000). An empirical study of the classification of eating disorders. *American Journal of Psychiatry, 157*(6), 886–895.

Bulik, C. M., Sullivan, P. F., Tozzi, F., Furberg, H., Lichtenstin, P., & Pedersen, N. L. (2006). Prevalence, heritability, and prospective risk factors, for anorexia nervosa. *Archives of General Psychiatry, 63*(3), 305–312.

Bulik, C. M., Thornton, L., Pinheiro, A. P., Plotnicov, K., Klump, K. L., Brandt, H., . . . Kaye, W. H. (2008). Suicide attempts in anorexia nervosa. *Psychosomatic Medicine, 70*(3), 378-383.

Bumpass, E. R., Fagelman, F. D., & Brix, R. J. (1983). Intervention with children who set fires. *American Journal of Psychotherapy, 37*(3), 328–345.

Burgess, C. R., & Scammell, T. E. (2012). Narcolepsy: neural mechanisms of sleepiness and cataplexy. *The Journal of Neuroscience, 32*(36), 12305–12311.

Burkauskas, J., & Fineberg, N. A. (2020). History and epidemiology of OCPD. In J. E. Grant, A. Pinto, & S. R. Chamberlain (Eds.), *Obsessive-compulsive personality disorder* (pp. 1–26). Washington, D.C.: American Psychiatric Association Publishing.

Burkhalter, H., Wirz-Justice, A., Denhaerynck, K., Fehr, T., Steiger, J., Venzin, R. M., . . . De Geest, S. (2015). The effect of bright light therapy on sleep and circadian rhythms in renal transplant recipients: A pilot randomized, multicentre wait-list controlled trial. *Transplant International, 28*(1), 59–70.

Burne, R., Birkett, R., Bennet, W., & Shetty, A. (2021). An unusual presentation of prolonged delirium. *bmj, 373.*

Burnett, A. L., Nehra, A., Breau, R. H., Culkin, D. J., Faraday, M. M., Hakim, L. S., … Shindel, A. W. (2018). Erectile dysfunction: AUA guideline. *Journal of Urology, 200*(3), 633–641. doi: 10.1016/j.juro.2018.05.004

Burnette, M. M., Koehn, K. A., Kenyon-Jump, R., Hutton, K., & Stark, C. (1991). Control of genital herpes recurrences using progressive muscle relaxation. *Behavior Therapy, 22,* 237–247.

Burnham, M. M., & Gaylor, E. E. (2011). Sleep environments of young children in post-industrial societies. In M. El-Sheikh (Ed.), *Sleep and development: Familial and socio-cultural considerations* (pp. 195–218). New York, NY: Oxford University Press.

Burns, J. W., Glenn, B., Bruehl, S., Harden, R. N., & Lofland, K. (2003). Cognitive factors influence outcome following multidisciplinary chronic pain treatment: A replication and extension of a cross-lagged panel analysis. *Behaviour Research and Therapy, 41,* 1163–1182.

Burns, J. W., Nielson, W. R., Jensen, M. P., Heapy, A., Czlapinski, R., & Kerns, R. D. (2015). Specific and general therapeutic mechanisms in cognitive behavioral treatment of chronic pain. *Journal of Consulting and Clinical Psychology, 83*(1), 1–11.

Burri, A., Spector, T., & Rahman, Q. (2013). A discordant monozygotic twin approach to testing environmental influences on sexual dysfunction in women. *Archives of Sexual Behavior, 42*(6), 961–972.

Burton, R. (1977). *Anatomy of melancholy.* (Reprint edition). New York, NY: Random House. (Original work published in 1621.)

Busatto, G. F. (2013). Structural and functional neuroimaging studies in major depressive disorder with psychotic features: A critical review. *Schizophrenia Bulletin, 39*(4), 776–786. doi: 10.1093/schbul/sbt054

Buscher, A. L., & Giordano, T. P. (2010). Gaps in knowledge in caring for HIV survivors long-term. *JAMA: Journal of the American Medical Association, 304,* 340–341.

Bushman, B. J. (1993). Human aggression while under the influence of alcohol and other drugs: An integrative research review. *Psychological Science, 2,* 148–152.

Butcher, J. N. (2009). Clinical personality assessment: History, evolution, contemporary models, and practical applications. In J. N. Butcher (Ed.), *Oxford handbook of personality assessment* (pp. 5–21). New York, NY: Oxford University Press.

Butcher, J. N., Graham, J. R., Williams, C. L., & Ben-Porath, Y. S. (1990). *Development and use of the MMPI-2 content scales.* Minneapolis: University of Minnesota Press.

Butler, B. (2006). NGRI revisited: Venirepersons' attitudes toward the insanity defense. *Journal of Applied Social Psychology, 36,* 1833–1847.

Butler, L. D., Duran, R. E. F., Jasiukaitis, P., Koopman, C., & Spiegel, D. (1996). Hypnotizability and traumatic experience: A diathesis stress model of dissociative symptomatology. *American Journal of Psychiatry, 153,* 42–63.

Buysse, D. J., Strollo, P. J., Black, J. E., Zee, P. G., & Winkelman, J. W. (2008). Sleep disorders. In R. E. Hales, S. C. Yudofsky, & G. O. Gabbard (Eds.), *The American Psychiatric Publishing textbook of psychiatry* (5th ed., pp. 921–969). Arlington, VA: American Psychiatric Publishing.

Buzzella, B. A., Ehrenreich-May, J. T., & Pincus, D. B. (2011). Comorbidity and family factors associated with selective mutism. *Child Development Research,* 2011, 1–9.

Bye, E. K. (2007). Alcohol and violence: Use of possible confounders in a time-series analysis. *Addiction, 102,* 369–376.

Byers, A. L., Yaffe, K., Covinsky, K. E., Friedman, M. B., & Bruce, M. L. (2010). High occurrence of mood and anxiety disorders among older adults: The National Comorbidity Survey Replication. *Archives of General Psychiatry, 67*(5), 489–496. doi: 10.1001/archgenpsychiatry.2010.35

Byne, W., & Parsons, B. (1993). Human sexual orientation: The biologic theories reappraised. *Archives of General Psychiatry, 50,* 228–239.

Byne, W., Bradley, S. J., Coleman, E., Eyler, A. E., Green, R., Menvielle, E. J., & Tompkins, D. A. (2012). Report of the American Psychiatric Association Task Force on treatment of gender identity disorder. *Archives of Sexual Behavior, 41*(4), 759–796.

Byne, W., Lasco, M. S., Kemether, E., Edgar, M. A., Morgello, S., Jones, L. B., & Tobet, S. (2000). The interstitial nuclei of the human anterior hypothalamus: An investigation of sexual variation in volume and cell size, number and density. *Brain Research, 856,* 254–258.

Byrd, A. L., Loeber, R., & Pardini, D. A. (2014). Antisocial behavior, psychopathic features and abnormalities in reward and punishment processing in youth. *Clinical Child and Family Psychology review, 17*(2), 125-156.

Byrne, D., & Schulte, L. (1990). Personality dispositions as mediators of sexual responses. *Annual Review of Sex Research, 1,* 93–117.

Byrne, E. M., Johnson, J., McRae, A. F., Nyholt, D. R., Medland, S. E., Gehrman, P. R., & Chenevix-Trench, G. (2012). A genome-wide association study of caffeine-related sleep disturbance: Confirmation of a role for a common variant in the adenosine receptor. *Sleep, 35*(7), 967–975.

Caballero, B. (2007). The global epidemic of obesity: An overview. *Epidemiologic Reviews, 29,* 1–5.

Caballo, V. E., Salazar, I. C., Irurtia, M. J., Olivares, P., & Olivares, J. (2014). The relationship between social skills and social anxiety and personality styles/disorders. *Behavioral Psychology, 22,* 401–422.

Cacioppo, J. T., Cacioppo, S., Dulawa, S., & Palmer, A. A. (2014). Social neuroscience and its potential contribution to psychiatry. World Psychiatry, 13(2), 131–139. doi:10.1002/wps.20118

Cacioppo, S., Grippo, A. J., London, S., Goossens, L., & Cacioppo, J. T. (2015). Loneliness: Clinical import and interventions. Perspectives on Psychological Science, 10(2), 238–249. doi:10.1177/1745691615570616

Cacioppo, J. T., & Patrick, W. (2008). *Loneliness: Human nature and the need for social connection.* New York, NY: Norton.

Cacioppo, J. T., Amaral, D. G., Blanchard, J. J., Cameron, J. L., Carter, C. S., Crews, D., & Quinn, K. J. (2007). Social neuroscience: Progress and implications for mental health. *Perspectives on Psychological Science, 2*(2), 99–123.

Cadoret, R. J. (1978). Psychopathology in the adopted-away offspring of biologic parents with antisocial behavior. *Archives of General Psychiatry, 35,* 176–184.

Cadoret, R. J., Yates, W. R., Troughton, E., Woodworth, G., & Stewart, M. A. (1995). Genetic-environment interaction in the genesis of aggressivity and conduct disorders. *Archives of General Psychiatry, 52,* 916–924.

Cafri, G., Yamamiya, Y., Brannick, M., & Thompson, J. K. (2005). The influence of sociocultural factors on body image: A meta-analysis. *Clinical Psychology: Science and Practice, 12,* 421–433.

Caglayan, A. O. (2010). Genetic causes of syndromic and non-syndromic autism. *Developmental Medicine & Child Neurology, 52*(2), 130–138. doi: 10.1111/j.1469-8749.2009.03523.x

Cai, N., Choi, K. W., & Fried, E. I. (2020). Reviewing the genetics of heterogeneity in depression: Operationalizations, manifestations and etiologies. *Human molecular genetics, 29*(R1), R10–R18.

Cain, A. S., Epler, A. J., Steinley, D., & Sher, K. J. (2010). Stability and change in patterns of concerns related to eating, weight, and shape in young adult women: A latent transition analysis. *Journal of Abnormal Psychology, 119*(2), 255–267.

Cain, V. S., Johannes, C. B., Avis, N. E., Mohr, B., Schocken, M., Skurnick, J., & Ory, M. (2003). Sexual functioning and practices in a multi-ethnic study of midlife women: Baseline results from SWAN. *Journal of Sex Research, 40*(3), 266–276.

Calabrese, J., Shelton, M., Rapport, D., Youngstrom, E., Jackson, K., Bilali, S., & Findling, R. L. (2005). A 20-month, double-blind, maintenance trial of lithium versus divalproex, in rapid-cycling bipolar disorder. *American Journal of Psychiatry, 162,* 2152–2161.

Calamari, J. E., Chik, H. M., Pontarelli, N. K., & DeJong, B. L. (2012). Phenomenology and epidemiology of obsessive compulsive disorder. In G. Steketee (Ed.), *The Oxford handbook of obsessive compulsive and spectrum disorders* (pp. 11–47). New York, NY: Oxford University Press.

Calamari, J. E., Wiegartz, P. S., Riemann, B. C., Cohen, R. J., Greer, A., Jacobi, D. M., & Carmin, C. (2004). Obsessive-compulsive disorder subtypes: An attempted replication and extension of symptom-based taxonomy. *Behavior Research and Therapy, 42,* 647–670.

Calati, R., Gressier, F., Balestri, M., & Serretti, A. (2013). Genetic modulation of borderline personality disorder: systematic review and meta-analysis. *Journal of Psychiatric Research, 47*(10), 1275–1287.

Caldirola, D., Alciati, A., Riva, A., & Perna, G. (2018). Are there advances in pharmacotherapy for panic disorder? A systematic review of the past five years. *Expert Opinion on Pharmacotherapy, 19*(12), 1357–1368. doi: 10.1080/14656566.2018.1504921

Caligor, E., Levy, K. N., & Yeomans, F. E. (2015). Narcissistic personality disorder: diagnostic and clinical challenges. *American Journal of Psychiatry, 172*(5).

Callahan, L. A., McGreevy, M. A., Cirincione, C., & Steadman, H. (1992). Measuring the effects of the guilty but mentally ill (GBMI) verdict: Georgia's 1982 GBMI reform. *Law and Human Behavior, 16,* 447–462.

Callanan, V. J., & Davis, M. S. (2012). Gender differences in suicide methods. *Social Psychiatry and Psychiatric Epidemiology, 47*(6), 857–869.

Callicott, J. H., Mattay, V. S., Verchinski, B. A., Marenco, S., Egan, M. F., & Weinberger, D. R. (2003). Complexity of prefrontal cortical dysfunction in schizophrenia:

More than up or down. *American Journal of Psychiatry, 160,* 2209–2215.
Cameron, N. M., Champagne, F. A., Parent, C., Fish, E. W., Ozaki-Kuroda, K., & Meaney, M. J. (2005). The programming of individual differences in defensive responses and reproductive strategies in the rat through variations in maternal care. *Neuroscience and Biobehavioral Reviews, 29,* 843–865.
Campbell, A. N., Miele, G. M., Nunes, E. V., McCrimmon, S., & Ghitza, U. E. (2012). Web-based, psychosocial treatment for substance use disorders in community treatment settings. *Psychological Services, 9*(2), 212.
Campbell, D. E., Snyder, J. L., & Austin, T. (2020). Neurocognitive testing. In D. S. Patel (Ed.), *Concussion management for primary care* (pp. 63–75). Cham, Switzerland: Springer Nature Switzerland AG.
Campbell, J. M., & Oei, T. P. (2010). A cognitive model for the intergenerational transference of alcohol use behavior. *Addictive Behaviors, 35*(2), 73–83. doi: 10.1016/j.addbeh.2009.09.013
Campbell, J., & Oei, T. P. (2013). The intergenerational transference of addiction. In P. M. Miller, A. W. Blume, D. J. Kavanagh, K. M. Kampman, M. E. Bates, M. E. Larimer, N. M. Petry, P. De Witte, & S. A. Ball (Eds), *Principles of addiction: Comprehensive addictive behaviors and disorders,* (Vol.1, 313–322). Waltham, MA: Elsevier Academic Press.
Campbell, W. K., & Miller, J. D. (2011). *The handbook of narcissism and narcissistic personality disorder: Theoretical approaches, empirical findings, and treatments.* John Wiley & Sons.
Campbell-Sills, L., & Brown, T. A. (2010). Generalized anxiety disorder. In M. M. Antony & D. H. Barlow (Eds.), *Handbook of assessment and treatment planning for psychological disorders* (2nd ed., pp. 224–266). New York, NY: Guilford.
Campbell-Sills, L., Ellard, K. K., & Barlow, D. H. (2015). Emotion regulation in anxiety disorders. In J. J. Gross (Ed.), *Handbook of Emotion Regulation* (2nd ed.). New York, NY: Guilford.
Camplain, R., Camplain, C., Trotter, R. T., Pro, G., Sabo, S., Eaves, E., … Baldwin, J. A. (2020). Racial/ethnic differences in drug-and alcohol-related arrest outcomes in a southwest county from 2009 to 2018. *American Journal of Public Health, 110*(S1), S85–S92.
Campo, J. A., Nijman, H., Merckelbach, H., & Evers, C. (2003). Psychiatric comorbidity of gender identity disorders: A survey among Dutch psychiatrists. *American Journal of Psychiatry, 160,* 1332–1336.
Campo, J. V., & Negrini, B. J. (2000). Case study: Negative reinforcement and behavioral management of conversion disorder. *Journal of the American Academy of Child and Adolescent Psychiatry, 39*(6), 787–790.
Canan, F., & North, C. S. (2019). A study of dissociation in survivors of 5 disasters. *Psychiatry Research, 279,* 77–82. doi: 10.1016/j.psychres.2019.07.00
Canevelli, M., Arisi, I., Bacigalupo, I., Arighi, A., Galimberti, D., Vanacore, N., … Bruno, G. (2021). Biomarkers and phenotypic expression in Alzheimer's disease: exploring the contribution of frailty in the Alzheimer's Disease Neuroimaging Initiative. *GeroScience, 43*(2), 1039–1051.
Canli, T., & Lesch, K.-P. (2007). Long story short: The serotonin transporter in emotion regulation and social cognition. *Nature Neuroscience, 10,* 1103–1109.
Cannon, T. D., Barr, C. E., & Mednick, S. A. (1991). Genetic and perinatal factors in the etiology of schizophrenia. In E. F. Walker (Ed.), *Schizophrenia: A life-course developmental perspective* (pp. 9–31). New York, NY: Academic.
Cannon, W. B. (1929). *Bodily changes in pain, hunger, fear and rage* (2nd ed.). New York, NY: Appleton-Century-Crofts.
Cannon, W. B. (1942). Voodoo death. *American Anthropologist, 44,* 169–181.
Cano, M., Oh, S., Salas-Wright, C. P., & Vaughn, M. G. (2020). Cocaine use and overdose mortality in the United States: Evidence from two national data sources, 2002–2018. *Drug and Alcohol Dependence, 214,* 108148. doi: https://doi.org/10.1016/j.drugalcdep.2020.108148
Cantor, J. M., Blanchard, R., Paterson, A. D., & Bogaert, A. F. (2002). How many gay men owe their sexual orientation to fraternal birth order? *Archives of Sexual Behavior, 31,* 63–71.
Capobianco, D. J., Swanson, J. W., & Dodick, D. W. (2001). Medication-induced (analgesic rebound) headache: Historical aspects and initial descriptions of the North American experience. *Headache, 41,* 500–502.
Cardeña, E. A., & Gleaves, D. H. (2003). Dissociative disorders: Phantoms of the self. In M. Hersen & S. M. Turner (Eds.), *Adult psychopathology and diagnosis* (4th ed., pp. 476–404). Hoboken, NJ: Wiley.
Cardeña, E., & Carlson, E. (2011). Acute stress disorder revisited. *Annual Review of Clinical Psychology, 7,* 245–267. doi: 10.1146/annurev-clinpsy-032210-104502
Cardeña, E., Lewis-Fernandez, R., Bear, D., Pakianathan, I., & Spiegel, D. (1996). Dissociative disorders. In T. A. Widiger, A. J. Frances, H. A. Pincus, R. Ross, M. B. First, & W. W. Davis (Eds.), *DSM-IV sourcebook* (Vol. 2, pp. 973–1005). Washington, DC: American Psychiatric Press.
Cardi, V., Esposito, M., Clarke, A., Schifano, S., & Treasure, J. (2015). The impact of induced positive mood on symptomatic behaviour in eating disorders. An experimental, AB/BA crossover design testing a multimodal presentation during a test-meal. *Appetite, 87,* 192–198.
Carlo, G., Knight, G. P., Roesch, S. C., Opal, D., & Davis, A. (2014). Personality across cultures: A critical analysis of Big Five research and current directions. In F. T. L. Leong, L. Comas-Díaz, G. C. Nagayama Hall, V. C. McLoyd, & J. E. (Eds.), *APA handbook of multicultural psychology, Vol. 1: Theory and research,* (pp. 285–298). Washington, DC: American Psychological Association.
Carlson, G. A. (1990). Annotation: Child and adolescent mania—Diagnostic considerations. *Journal of Child Psychology and Psychiatry, 31*(3), 331–341.
Carlson, G. A., & Klein, D. N. (2014). How to understand divergent views on bipolar disorder in youth. *Annual Review of Clinical Psychology, 10,* 529–551.
Carlson, G. A., & Meyer S. E. (2006). Phenomenology and diagnosis of bipolar disorder in children, adolescents, and adults: Complexities and developmental issues. *Development and Psychopathology, 18,* 939–969.
Caron, C., & Rutter, M. (1991). Comorbidity in childhood psychopathology: Concepts, issues, and research strategies. *Journal of Child Psychology and Psychiatry, 32,* 1063–1080.
Carpenter, A. L., Pulfiafico, A. C., Kurtz, S. M., Pincus, D. B., & Comer, J. S. (2014). Extending parent-child interaction therapy for early childhood internalizing problems: New advances for ana overlooked population. *Clinical Child and Family Psychology Review, 17,* 340–356.
Carpenter, J. K., Andrews, L. A., Witcraft, S. M., Powers, M. B., Smits, J. A. J., & Hofmann, S. G. (2018). Cognitive behavioral therapy for anxiety and related disorders: A meta-analysis of randomized placebo-controlled trials. *Depression and Anxiety, 35*(6), 502–514. doi: 10.1002/da.22728
Carpenter, J. S., Crouse, J. J., Scott, E. M., Naismith, S. L., Wilson, C., Scott, J., … Hickie, I. B. (2021). Circadian depression: A mood disorder phenotype. *Neuroscience and Biobehavioral Reviews, 126,* 79–101. doi: 10.1016/j.neubiorev.2021.02.04
Carpenter, M. J., Jardin, B. F., Burris, J. L., Mathew, A. R., Schnoll, R. A., Rigotti, N.

A., & Cummings, K. M. (2013). Clinical strategies to enhance the efficacy of nicotine replacement therapy for smoking cessation: a review of the literature. *Drugs, 73*(5), 407–426.

Carpenter, W. T., & van Os, J. (2011). Should attenuated psychosis syndrome be a DSM-5 diagnosis? *American Journal of Psychiatry, 168*(5), 460-463.

Carpentier, M., Silovsky, J., & Chaffin, M. (2006). Randomized trial of treatment for children with sexual behavior problems: Ten-year follow-up. *Journal of Consulting and Clinical Psychology, 74,* 482–488.

Carr, A., Keenleyside, M., & Fitzhenry, M. (2015). *The Waterford Mental Health Survey.* University College Dublin School of Psychology, Health Services Executive.

Carr, E. G., & Durand, V. M. (1985). Reducing behavior problems through functional communication training. *Journal of Applied Behavior Analysis, 18,* 111–126.

Carrico, A. W., & Antoni, M. H. (2008). Effects of psychological interventions on neuroendocrine hormone regulation and immune states in HIV-positive persons: A review of randomized controlled trials. *Psychosomatic Medicine, 70,* 575–584.

Carrier, S., Brock, G. B., Pommerville, P. J., Shin, J., Anglin, G., Whittaker, S., & Beasley, C. M., Jr. (2005). Efficacy and safety of oral tadalafil in the treatment of men in Canada with erectile dysfunction: A randomized, double-blind, parallel, placebo-controlled clinical trial. *Journal of Sexual Medicine, 2,* 685–698.

Carroll, B. J., Feinberg, M., Greden, J. F., Haskett, R. F., James, N. M., Steiner, M., & Tarika, J. (1980). Diagnosis of endogenous depression: Comparison of clinical, research, and neuroendocrine criteria. *Journal of Affective Disorders, 2,* 177–194.

Carroll, B. J., Martin, F. I., & Davies, B. (1968). Resistance to suppression by dexamethasone of plasma 11-O.H.C.S. levels in severe depressive illness. *British Medical Journal, 3,* 285–287.

Carroll, R. A. (2007). Gender dysphoria and transgender experiences. In S. R. Leiblum (Ed.), *Principles and practice of sex therapy* (4th ed., pp. 477–508). New York, NY: Guilford.

Carson, C. C., Burnett, A. L., Levine, L. A., & Nehra, A. (2002). The efficacy of sildenafil citrate (Viagra) in clinical populations: an update. *Urology, 60*(2 Suppl. 2), 12–27. doi: 10.1016/s0090-4295(02)01687-4

Carson, R. C. (1991). Discussion: Dilemmas in the pathway of DSM-IV. *Journal of Abnormal Psychology, 100,* 302–307.

Carson, R. C. (1996). Aristotle, Galileo, and the *DSM* taxonomy: The case of schizophrenia. *Journal of Consulting and Clinical Psychology, 64*(6), 1133–1139.

Carstensen, L. L., Charles, S. T., Isaacowitz, D., & Kennedy, Q. (2003). Life-span personality development and emotion. In R. J. Davidson, K. Scherer, & H. H. Goldsmith (Eds.), *Handbook of affective sciences* (pp. 931–951). Oxford, UK: Oxford University Press.

Carstensen, L. L., Turan, B. Scheibe, S., Ram, N., Ersner-Hershfield, H., Samanez-Larkin, G. R., Brooks, K. P., & Nesselroad, J. R. (2011), Emotional experience improves with age: Evidence based on over 10 years of experience sampling. *Psychology and Aging, 26,* 21–33.

Carter, C. L., Resnick, E. M., Mallampalli, M., & Kalbarczyk, A. (2012). Sex and gender differences in Alzheimer's disease: Recommendations for future research. *Journal of Women's Health, 21*(10), 1018–1023.

Carter, J. C., & Fairburn, C. G. (1998). Cognitive-behavioral self-help for binge eating disorder: A controlled effectiveness study. *Journal of Consulting and Clinical Psychology, 66,* 616–623.

Carter, J. C., McFarlane, T. L., Bewell, C., Olmsted, M. P., Woodside, D. B., Kaplan, A. S., & Crosby, R. D. (2009). Maintenance treatment for anorexia nervosa: A comparison of cognitive behavior therapy and treatment as usual. *International Journal of Eating Disorders, 42*(3), 202–207.

Carter, J. S., & Garber, J. (2011). Predictors of the first onset of a major depressive episode and changes in depressive symptoms across adolescence: Stress and negative cognitions. *Journal of Abnormal Psychology, 120*(4), 779–796.

Carter, J. S., Garber, J., Cielsa, J., & Cole, D. (2006). Modeling relations between hassles and internalizing and externalizing symptoms in adolescents: A four-year prospective study. *Journal of Abnormal Psychology, 115,* 428–442.

Carter, R. M., Wittchen, H.-U., Pfister, H., & Kessler, R. C. (2001). One-year prevalence of subthreshold and threshold DSM-IV generalized anxiety disorder in a nationally representative sample. *Depression & Anxiety, 13,* 78–88.

Cartwright, R. D. (2006). Sleepwalking. In T. Lee-Chiong (Ed.), *Sleep: A comprehensive handbook* (pp. 429–433). Hoboken, NJ: Wiley.

Carvalho, A. F., Firth, J., & Vieta, E. (2020). Bipolar disorder. *New England Journal of Medicine, 383*(1), 58–66. doi: 10.1056/NEJMra1906193

Carvalho, M., Carmo, H., Costa, V., Capela, J., Pontes, H., Remião, F., & Bastos, M. D. (2012). Toxicity of amphetamines: An update. *Archives of Toxicology, 86*(8), 1167–1231. doi: 10.1007/s00204-012-0815-5

Carver, C. S., Johnson, S. L., & Joormann, J. (2009). Two-mode models of self-regulation as a tool for conceptualizing effects of the serotonin system in normal behavior and diverse disorders. *Current Directions in Psychological Science, 18*(4), 195–199.

Caspi, A., McClay, J., Moffitt, T. E., Mill, J., Martin, J., Craig, I. W., & Poulton, R. (2002). Role of genotype in the cycle of violence in maltreated children. *Science, 297,* 851–853.

Caspi, A., Sugden, K., Moffitt, T. E., Taylor, A., Craig, I. W., Harrington, H., & Poulton, R. (2003). Influence of life stress on depression: Moderation by a polymorphism in the 5-HTT gene. *Science, 301,* 386–389.

Cassano, G., Rucci, P., Frank, E., Fagiolini, A., Dell'Osso, L., Shear, K., & Kupfer, D. J. (2004). The mood spectrum in unipolar and bipolar disorder: Arguments for a unitary approach. *American Journal of Psychiatry, 161,* 1264–1269.

Cassidy, F., Yatham, L. N., Berk, M., & Grof, P. (2008). Pure and mixed manic subtypes: A review of diagnostic classification and validation. *Bipolar Disorders, 10,* 131–143.

Castell, B. D., Kazantzis, N., & Moss-Morris, R. E. (2011). Cognitive behavioral therapy and graded exercise for chronic fatigue syndrome: A meta-analysis. *Clinical Psychology: Science and Practice, 18*(4), 311–324.

Castonguay, L. G., Eldredge, K. L., & Agras, W. S. (1995). Binge eating disorder: Current state and directions. *Clinical Psychology Review, 15,* 815–890.

Castro, F. G., & Nieri, T. (2010). Cultural factors in drug use etiology: Concepts, methods, and recent findings. In L. M. Scheier (Ed.), *Handbook of drug use etiology: Theory, methods, and empirical findings* (pp. 305–324). Washington, DC: American Psychological Association.

Castro, F. G., & Nieri, T. (2010). Cultural factors in drug use etiology: Concepts, methods, and recent findings. In L. M. Scheier (Ed.), *Handbook of drug use etiology: Theory, methods, and empirical findings* (pp. 305–324). Washington, D.C.: American Psychological Association.

Cautela, J. R. (1966). Treatment of compulsive behavior by covert sensitization. *Psychological Record, 16,* 33–41.

Cautela, J. R. (1967). Covert sensitization. *Psychological Reports, 20,* 459–468.

Cavendish, W. (2013). Identification of learning disabilities: Implications of proposed DSM-5 criteria for school-based Assessment. *Journal of Learning Disabilities, 46*(1), 52–57. doi: 10.1177/0022219412464352

Cechnicki, A., Bielańska, A., Hanuszkiewicz, I., & Daren, A. (2013). The predictive validity of Expressed Emotions (EE) in schizophrenia. A 20-year prospective study. *Journal of Psychiatric Research, 47*(2), 208–214. doi: http://dx.doi.org/10.1016/j.jpsychires.2012.10.004

Ceci, S. J. (1995). False beliefs: Some developmental and clinical considerations. In D. L. Schacter (Ed.), *Memory distortion: How minds, brains, and societies reconstruct the past* (pp. 91–125). Cambridge, MA: Harvard University Press.

Ceci, S. J. (2003). Cast in six ponds and you'll reel in something: Looking back on 25 years of research. *American Psychologist, 58*, 855–867.

Cederlöf, M., Thornton, L. M., Baker, J., Lichtenstein, P., Larsson, H., Rück, C., . . . Mataix-Cols, D. (2015). Etiological overlap between obsessive-compulsive disorder and anorexia nervosa: a longitudinal cohort, multigenerational family and twin study. *World Psychiatry, 14*(3), 333–338.

Celeghin, A., Bagnis, A., Diano, M., Méndez, C. A., Costa, T., & Tamietto, M. (2019). Functional neuroanatomy of blindsight revealed by activation likelihood estimation meta-analysis. *Neuropsychologia, 128*, 109–118. doi: 10.1016/j.neuropsychologia.2018.06.007

Celio, A. A., Winzelberg, A. J., Dev, P., & Taylor, C. B. (2002). Improving compliance in on-line, structured self-help programs: Evaluation of an eating disorder prevention program. *Journal of Psychiatric Practice, 8*, 14–20.

Celio, A. A., Zabinski, M. F., & Wilfley, D. E. (2002). African American body images. In T. F. Cash & T. Pruzinsky (Eds.), *Body image: A handbook of theory, research and clinical practice* (pp. 234–242). New York, NY: Guilford.

Centers for Disease Control and Prevention. (2015). *Incidence, prevalence, and cost of sexually transmitted infections in the United States.* http://www.cdc.gov/std/herpes/std-fact-herpes-detailed.htm.

Centers for Disease Control and Prevention. (2007). Cigarette smoking among adults—United States, 2006. *Morbidity and Mortality Weekly Report* [serial online]; *56*(44): 1157–1161. Retrieved from http://www.cdc.gov/mmwr/preview/mmwrhtml/mm5644a2.htm

Centers for Disease Control and Prevention. (2008). Annual smoking-attributable mortality, year, and potential life lost, and productivity losses—United States, 2000–2004. *Morbidity and Mortality Weekly Report* [serial online]; *57*(45): 1226–1228. Retrieved from http://www.cdc.gov/mmwr/preview/mmwrhtml/mm5745a3.htm

Centers for Disease Control and Prevention. (2010a). *Diagnosis of HIV infection and AIDS in the United States and dependent areas, 2008* (HIV Surveillance Report, Volume 20). Retrieved from http://www.cdc.gov/hiv/surveillance/resources/reports/2008report/index.htm

Centers for Disease Control and Prevention. (2010b). Fatal injury data. Retrieved from http://www.cdc.gov/injury/wisqars/fatal.html

Centers for Disease Control and Prevention. (2010c). Web-based Injury Statistics Query and Reporting System (WISQARS). Retrieved from http://www.cdc.gov/ncipc/wisqars

Centers for Disease Control and Prevention. (2011a). Prevalence of hypertension and controlled hypertension—United States, 2005–2008. *Morbidity and Mortality Weekly Report, 60*(1), 94–97.

Centers for Disease Control and Prevention. (2011b). Measles—United States, January-May 20, 2011. *Morbidity and Mortality Weekly Report, 60*(20), 666–668.

Centers for Disease Control and Prevention. (2012). Prevalence of autism spectrum disorders—Autism and Developmental Disabilities Monitoring Network, 14 sites, United States, 2008. *Morbity and Mortality Weekly Report, 61*(SS-03), 1–19. Retrieved from http://www.cdc.gov/mmwr/preview/mmwrhtml/ss6103a1.htm?s_cid=ss6103a1_e

Centers for Disease Control and Prevention. (2013a). *National Center for Health Statistics, State and Local Area Integrated Telephone Survey. 2011–2012 National Survey of Children's Health*. Rockville, M.D.: U.S. Department of Health and Human Services.

Centers for Disease Control and Prevention. (2013b). Human immunodeficiency virus (HIV) disease death rates among men aged 25–54 years, by race and age group—national vital statistics. *Morbidity and Mortality Weekly Report, 62*(9), 175.

Centers for Disease Control and Prevention. (2013c). Suicide among adults aged 35–64 Years—United States, 1999–2010. *Morbidity and Mortality Weekly Report, 62*(17), 321–325.

Centers for Disease Control and Prevention. (2014). *Prevalence of Autism Spectrum Disorders Among Children 8 Years — Autism and Developmental Disabilities Monitoring Network, 11 Sites, United States, 2010.* MMWR 2014;63, (No. SS-02):1–19. Retrieved from: http://www.cdc.gov/mmwr/preview/mmwrhtml/ss6103a1.htm?s_cid=ss6103a1_e

Centers for Disease Control and Prevention. (2020). Estimated HIV incidence and prevalence in the United States, 2014–2018. *HIV Surveillance Supplemental Report, 25*(1). http://www.cdc.gov/ hiv/library/reports/hiv-surveillance.html.

Centers for Disease Control and Prevention. (2021). *Sexually transmitted infections: Prevalence, incidence and cost in the United States.* https://www.cdc.gov/std/herpes/stats.htm

Centers for Disease Control, National Center for Health Statistics. (2014). *Multiple cause-of-death data, 1999–2013.* Retrieved from http://wonder.cdc.gov.ezproxy.bu.edu/mcd.html.

Černis, E., Evans, R., Ehlers, A., & Freeman, D. (2020). Dissociation in relation to other mental health conditions: An exploration using network analysis: Dissociation across mental health. *Journal of Psychiatric Research.* doi: 10.1016/j.jpsychires.2020.08.023

Cespedes Feliciano, E. M., Rifas-Shiman, S. L., Quante, M., Redline, S., Oken, E., & Taveras, E. M. (2019). Chronotype, social jet lag, and cardiometabolic risk factors in early adolescence. *JAMA Pediatrics, 173*(11), 1049–1057. doi: 10.1001/jamapediatrics.2019.3089

Cha, C. B., Najmi, S., Park, J. M., Finn, C. T., & Nock, M. J. (2010). Attentional bias toward suicide-related stimuli predicts suicidal behavior. *Journal of Abnormal Psychology, 119*, 616–622.

Chaimowitz, G. (2012). The criminalization of people with mental illness. *Canadian Journal of Psychiatry, 57*(2), 129.

Chakravarti, D., LaBella, K. A., & DePinho, R. A. (2021). Telomeres: History, health, and hallmarks of aging. *Cell, 184*(2), 306–322. doi: 10.1016/j.cell.2020.12.028

Chalder, T., Cleare, A., & Wessely, S. (2000). The management of stress and anxiety in chronic fatigue syndrome. In D. I. Mostofsky & D. H. Barlow (Eds.), *The management of stress and anxiety in medical disorders* (pp. 160–179). Needham Heights, MA: Allyn & Bacon.

Chalder, T., Deary, V., Husain, K., & Walwyn, R. (2010). Family-focused cognitive behavior therapy versus psycho-education for chronic fatigue syndrome in 11- to 18-year-olds: A randomized controlled treatment trial. *Psychological Medicine, 40*(8), 1269–1279.

Chamberlain, S. R., Menzies, L., Hampshire, A., Suckling, J., Fineberg, N. A., Campo, N., & Sahakien, B. J. (2008). Orbitofrontal dysfunction in patients with obsessive-compulsive disorder and their unaffected relatives. *Science, 321*, 421–422.

Chamberlain, S. R., Menzies, L., Sahakian, B. J., & Fineberg, N. A. (2007). Lifting the veil on trichotillomania. *American Journal of Psychiatry, 164*, 568–574.

Champagne, F. A. (2018). Social and behavioral epigenetics: Evolving perspectives on nature-nurture interplay, plasticity, and inheritance. In M. Meloni, J. Cromby, D. Fitzgerald, & S. Lloyd (Eds.), *The Palgrave handbook of biology and society.* London: Palgrave Macmillan.

Chan, C., Ngai, E., Leung, P., & Wong, S. (2010). Effect of the adapted virtual reality cognitive training program among Chinese older adults with chronic schizophrenia: A pilot study. *International Journal of Geriatric Psychiatry, 25*(6), 643–649.

Chandra, A., Mosher, W. D., & Casey, C. (2011). *Sexual behavior, sexual attraction, and sexual identity in the United States: data from the 2006–2008 National Survey of Family Growth.* Atlanta, GA: US Department of Health and Human Services, Centers for Disease Control and Prevention, National Center for Health Statistics.

Chang, X.-L., Tan, M.-S., Tan, L., & Yu, J.-T. (2016). The role of TDP-43 in Alzheimer's disease. *Molecular Neurobiology, 53*(5), 3349–3359.

Chao, Y. M., Pisetsky, E. M., Dierker, L. C., Dohm, F.-A., Rosselli, F., May, A., & Striegel-Moore, R. H. (2008). Ethnic differences in weight control practices among U.S. adolescents from 1995 to 2005. *International Journal of Eating Disorders, 41*(2), 97–193. doi: https://doi.org/10.1002/eat.20479

Chaouloff, F., & Groc, L. (2010). Temporal modulation of hippocampal excitatory transmission by corticosteroids and stress. *Frontiers in Neuroendocrinology.* Advance online publication. *32*(1), 25–42 doi: 10.1016/j.yfrne.2010.07.004

Chapman, A. L., Dixon-Gordon, K. L., Butler, S. M., & Walters, K. N. (2015). Emotional reactivity to social rejection versus a frustration induction among persons with borderline personality features. *Personality Disorders: Theory, Research, and Treatment, 6*(1), 88.

Charland, L. C. (2008). A moral line in the sand: Alexander Crichton and Philippe Pinel on the psychopathology of the passions. In L. C. Charland & P. Zachar (Eds.), *Fact and value in emotion* (pp. 15–34). Amsterdam, The Netherlands: John Benjamins.

Charland, L. C. (2010). Science and morals in the affective psychopathology of Philippe Pinel. *History of Psychiatry, 21*(1), 38–53.

Charles, S. T., & Carstensen, L. L. (2010). Social and emotional aging. *Annual Review of Psychology, 61*, 383–409.

Charney, D. S. (2004). Psychobiological mechanisms of resilience and vulnerability: Implications for successful adaptation to extreme stress. *The American Journal of Psychiatry, 161*(2), 195–216.

Charney, D. S., & Drevets, W. C. (2002). Neuro-biological basis of anxiety disorders. In K. L. Davis, D. Charney, J. T. Coyle, & C. Nemeroff (Eds.), *Neuropsychopharmacology: The fifth generation of progress* (pp. 901–951). Philadelphia, PA: Lippincott Williams & Wilkins.

Charney, D. S., Barlow, D. H., Botteron, K., Cohen, J. D., Goldman, D., Raquel, E. G., & Zalcman, S. J. (2002). Neuroscience research agenda to guide development of a pathophysiologically based classification system. In D. J. Kupfer, M. B. First, & D. A. Regier (Eds.), *A research agenda for DSM-V* (pp. 31–83). Washington, DC: American Psychiatric Association.

Charney, D. S., Woods, S. W., Price, L. H., Goodman, W. K., Glazer, W. M., & Heninger, G. R. (1990). Noradrenergic dysregulation in panic disorder. In J. C. Ballenger (Ed.), *Neurobiology of panic disorder* (pp. 91–105). New York, NY: Wiley-Liss.

Chartrand, H., Sareen, J., Toews, M., & Bolton, J. M. (2012). Suicide attempts versus nonsuicidal self-injury among individuals with anxiety disorders in a nationally representative sample. *Depression and Anxiety, 29*, 172–179.

Chassin, L., Pillow, D. R., Curran, P. J., Molina, B. S. G., & Barrera, M. (1993). Relation of parental alcoholism to early adolescent substance use: A test of three mediating mechanisms. *Journal of Abnormal Psychology, 102*, 3–19.

Chassin, L., Presson, C. C., Rose, J. S., & Sherman, S. J. (2001). From adolescence to adulthood: Age-related changes in beliefs about cigarette smoking in a Midwestern community sample. *Health Psychology, 20*(5), 377–386.

Chasson, G. S., Buhlmann, U., Tolin, D. F., Rao, S. R., Reese, H. E., Welsh, K. S., & Wilhelm, S. (2010). Need for speed: Evaluating slopes of OCD recovery in behavior therapy enhanced with d-cycloserine. *Behavior Research and Therapy, 48*, 675–679.

Chavez, M., & Insel, T. R. (2007). Eating disorders: National Institute of Mental Health perspective. *American Psychologist, 62*, 159–166.

Check, J. R. (1998). Munchausen syndrome by proxy: An atypical form of child abuse. *Journal of Practical Behavioral Health, 4*, 340–345.

Checknita, D., Maussion, G., Labonté, B., Comai, S., Tremblay, R. E., Vitaro, F., . . . Turecki, G. (2015). Monoamine oxidase A gene promoter methylation and transcriptional downregulation in an offender population with antisocial personality disorder. *The British Journal of Psychiatry, 206*(3), 216-222.

Chemerinski, E., Triebwasser, J., Roussos, P., & Siever, L. J. (2013). Schizotypal personality disorder. *Journal of Personality Disorders, 27*(5), 652–679.

Chen, F. R. (2020). Behavioral inhibition system function as the mediator in the pathway from electrodermal fear conditioning to antisocial behavior: Integrating the reinforcement sensitivity theory. *Personality and Individual Differences, 166*, 110179.

Chen, M. C., Hamilton, J. P., & Gotlib, I. H. (2010). Decreased hippocampal volume in healthy girls at risk of depression. *Archives of General Psychiatry, 67*(3), 270–276.

Chen, Y., Nettles, M. E., & Chen, S.-W. (2009). Rethinking dependent personality disorder: Comparing different human relatedness in cultural contexts. *Journal of Nervous and Mental Disease, 197*(11), 793–800.

Chen, Y., Yu, S., Hu, Y., Li, C., Artaud, F., Carcaillon-Bentata, L., … Lee, P. (2021). Risk of suicide among patients with Parkinson disease. *JAMA Psychiatry, 78*(3), 293–301. doi: 10.1001/jamapsychiatry.2020.4001

Chesney, M. A. (1986, November). *Type A behavior: The biobehavioral interface.* Keynote address presented at the annual meeting of the Association for Advancement of Behavior Therapy, Chicago.

Cheung, F. M. (1995). Facts and myths about somatization among the Chinese. In T. Y. Lin, W. S. Tseng, & E. K. Yeh (Eds.), *Chinese societies and mental health* (pp. 156–166). Hong Kong: Oxford University Press.

Cheung, F. M. (2012). Mainstreaming culture in psychology. *American Psychologist, 67*(8), 721–730. doi: 10.1037/a0029876

Cheung, F. M., van de Vijver, F. J., & Leong, F. T. (2011). Toward a new approach to the study of personality in culture. *American Psychologist, 66*(7), 593–603. doi: 10.1037/a0022389

Cheung, Y., Law, C., Chan, B., Liu, K., & Yip, P. (2006). Suicidal ideation and suicidal attempts in a population based study of Chinese people: Risk attributable to hopelessness, depression, and social factors. *Journal of Affective Disorders, 90*, 193–199.

Chevalier, J. M., & Buckles, D. J. (2013). *Participatory action research: Theory and methods for engaged inquiry.* New York, NY: Routledge.

Chiappini, S., Guirguis, A., John, A., Corkery, J. M., & Schifano, F. (2020). COVID-19: The hidden impact on mental health and drug addiction. *Frontiers in Psychiatry, 11*, 767.

Chida, Y., & Mao, X. (2009). Does psychosocial stress predict symptomatic herpes simplex virus recurrence? A meta-analytic

investigation on prospective studies. *Brain, Behavior, and Immunity, 23,* 917–925.
Chida, Y., & Steptoe, A. (2009). The association of anger and hostility with future coronary heart disease: A meta-analytic review of prospective evidence. *Journal of the American College of Cardiology, 53*(11), 936–946.
Chida, Y., & Steptoe, A. (2010). Greater cardiovascular responses to laboratory mental stress are associated with poor subsequent cardiovascular risk status: A meta-analysis of prospective evidence. *Hypertension, 55*(4), 1026–1032.
Chioqueta, A., & Stiles, T. (2004). Suicide risk in patients with somatization disorder. *Crisis: The Journal of Crisis Intervention and Suicide Prevention, 25*(1), 3–7.
Chisuwa, N., & O'Dea, J. A. (2010). Body image and eating disorders amongst Japanese adolescents: A review of the literature. *Appetite, 54,* 5–15.
Chivers, M. L., & Bailey, J. M. (2000). Sexual orientation of female-to-male transsexuals: A comparison of homosexual and nonhomosexual types. *Archives of Sexual Behavior, 29*(3), 259–279.
Chivers, M. L., Rieger, G., Latty, E., & Bailey, M. (2004). A sex difference in the specificity of sexual arousal. *Psychological Science, 15,* 736–744.
Chmielewski, M., Clark, L. A., Bagby, R. M., & Watson, D. (2015). Method matters: Understanding diagnostic reliability in *DSM-IV* and *DSM-5. Journal of Abnormal Psychology, 124*(3), 764–769. http://dx.doi.org/10.1037/abn0000069
Cho, H. J., Lavretsky, H., Olmstead, R., Levin, M. J., Oxman, M. N., & Irwin, M. R. (2008). Sleep disturbance and depression recurrence in community-dwelling older adults: A prospective study. *American Journal of Psychiatry, 165*(12), 1543–1550.
Choate, M. L., Pincus, D. B., Eyberg, S. M., & Barlow, D. B. (2005). Parent–child interaction therapy for treatment of separation anxiety disorder: A pilot study. *Cognitive and Behavioral Practice, 12*(1), 126–135.
Chobanian, A. V., Bakris, G. L., Black, H. R., Cushman, W. C., Green, L. A., Izzo, J. L., & National High Blood Pressure Education Program Coordinating Committee. (2003). Seventh report of the Joint National Committee on prevention, detection, evaluation, and treatment of high blood pressure. *Hypertension, 42,* 1206–1252.
Chodoff, P. (1982). Hysteria in women. *American Journal of Psychiatry, 139,* 545–551.
Choi, J., & Twamley, E. W. (2013). Cognitive rehabilitation therapies for Alzheimer's disease: A review of methods to improve treatment engagement and self-efficacy. *Neuropsychology Review, 23*(1), 48–62. doi: 10.1007/s11065-013-9227-4
Choi, S.-H., Lee, H., Chung, T.-S., Park, K.-M., Jung, Y.-C., Kim, S. I., & Kim, J.-J. (2012). Neural network functional connectivity during and after an episode of delirium. *American Journal of Psychiatry, 169*(5), 498–507. doi: 10.1176/appi.ajp.2012.11060976
Choi-Kain, L. W., & Gunderson, J. G. (2019). *Applications of good psychiatric management for borderline personality disorder: A practical guide.* Washington, D.C.: American Psychiatric Publishing.
Chorpita, B. F., & Barlow, D. H. (1998). The development of anxiety: The role of control in the early environment. *Psychological Bulletin, 124*(1), 3–21.
Chosak, A., Marques, L., Greenberg, J. L., Jenike, E., Dougherty, D. D., & Wilhelm, S. (2008). Body dysmorphic disorder and obsessive-compulsive disorder: Similarities, differences and the classification debate. *Expert Review of Neurotherapeutics, 8*(8), 1209–1218.
Chou, T., Asnaani, A., & Hofmann, S. G. (2012). Perception of racial discrimination and psychopathology across three U.S. ethnic minority groups. *Cultural Diversity and Ethnic Minority Psychology, 18,* 74–81. doi: 10.1037/a0025432
Choy, O. (2020). Antisocial personality disorder. In B. J. Carducci, C. S. Nave, A. D. Fabio, D. H. Saklofske, & C. Stough (Eds.), *The Wiley encyclopedia of personality and individual differences: Clinical, applied, and cross-cultural research* (Vol. 3, pp. 97–101). Hoboken, N.J.: Wiley.
Christ, S. E., Clocksin, H. E., Burton, B. K., Grant, M. L., Waisbren, S., Paulin, M.-C., … Saville, C. (2020). Executive function in phenylketonuria (PKU): Insights from the Behavior Rating Inventory of Executive Function (BRIEF) and a large sample of individuals with PKU. *Neuropsychology, 34*(4), 456.
Christakis, N. A., & Fowler, J. H. (2007). The spread of obesity in a large social network over 32 years. *New England Journal of Medicine, 357*(4), 370–379.
Christensen, Z. P., Freedman, E. G., & Foxe, J. J. (2021). Caffeine exposure in utero is associated with structural brain alterations and deleterious neurocognitive outcomes in 9–10 year old children. *Neuropharmacology, 186,* 108479.
Christopher, J. C., Wendt, D. C., Marecek, J., & Goodman, D. M. (2014). Critical cultural awareness: Contributions to a globalizing psychology. *American Psychologist, 69*(7), 645–655.
Christopher, M. E., Hulslander, J., Byrne, B., Samuelsson, S., Keenan, J. M., Pennington, B., & Olson, R. K. (2013). Modeling the etiology of individual differences in early reading development: Evidence for strong genetic influences. *Scientific Studies of Reading, 17*(5), 350–368.
Chronis, A. M., Lahey, B. B., Pelham, W. E., Jr., Williams, S. H., Baumann, B. L., Kipp, H., & Rathouz, P. J. (2007). Maternal depression and early positive parenting predict future conduct problems in young children with attention-deficit/hyperactivity disorder. *Developmental Psychology, 43,* 70–82.
Chung, K.-F., Yeung, W.-F., Ho, F. Y.-Y., Yung, K.-P., Yu, Y.-M., & Kwok, C.-W. (2015). Cross-cultural and comparative epidemiology of insomnia: the Diagnostic and statistical manual (DSM), International classification of diseases (ICD) and International classification of sleep disorders (ICSD). *Sleep Medicine, 16*(4), 477–482.
Chung, J., Demiris, G., & Thompson, H. J. (2016). Ethical Considerations Regarding the Use of Smart Home Technologies for Older Adults: An Integrative Review. *Annual Review of Nursing Research, 34*(1), 155–181.
Chung, S. Y., Luk, S. L., & Lee, P. W. H. (1990). A follow-up study of infantile autism in Hong Kong. *Journal of Autism and Developmental Disorders, 20,* 221–232.
Chung, T., & Martin, C. S. (2009). Subjective stimulant and sedative effects of alcohol during early drinking experiences predict alcohol involvement in treated adolescents. *Journal of Studies on Alcohol and Drugs, 70*(5), 660–667.
Cicchetti, D. (1991). A historical perspective on the discipline of developmental psychopathology. In J. Rolf, A. S. Masten, D. Cicchetti, K. H. Nuechterlein, & S. Weintraub (Eds.), *Risk and protective factors in the development of psychopathology* (pp. 2–28). New York, NY: Cambridge University Press.
Cimera, R. E. (2012). The economics of supported employment: What new data tell us. *Journal of Vocational Rehabilitation, 37*(2), 109.
Ciraulo, D. A., Barlow, D. H., Gulliver, S. B., Farchione, T., Morissette, S. B., Kamholz, B. W., Eisenmenger, K., Brown, B., Devine, E., Brown, T. A., & Knapp, C. M. (2013). The effects of venlafaxine and cognitive behavioral therapy alone and combined in the treatment of co-morbid alcohol use-anxiety disorders. *Behaviour Research and Therapy, 51,* 729–735.
Clance, P. R., & Imes, S. A. (1978). The imposter phenomenon in high achieving women: Dynamics and therapeutic intervention. *Psychotherapy: Theory, Research & Practice, 15*(3), 241–247.

Clancy, S. A., McNally, R. J., Schacter, D. L., Lenzenweger, M. F., & Pitman, R. K. (2002). Memory distortion in people reporting abduction by aliens. *Journal of Abnormal Psychology, 111*, 455–461.

Clark, C. J., Henderson, K. M., de Leon, C. F., Guo, H., Lunos, S., Evans, D. A., & Everso Rose, S. A. (2012). Latent constructs in psychosocial factors associated with cardiovascular disease: An examination by race and sex. *Frontiers in Psychiatry, 3*, 5.

Clark, D. A., & O'Connor, K. (2005). Thinking is believing: Ego-dystonic intrusive thoughts in obsessive-compulsive disorder. In D. A. Clark (Ed.), *Intrusive thoughts in clinical disorders* (pp. 145–174). New York, NY: Guilford.

Clark, D. A., & Rhyno, S. (2005). Unwanted intrusive thoughts in nonclinical individuals: Implications for clinical disorders. In D. A. Clark (Ed.), *Intrusive thoughts in clinical disorders* (pp. 1–29). New York, NY: Guilford.

Clark, D. M. (1986). A cognitive approach to panic. *Behaviour Research and Therapy, 24*, 461–470.

Clark, D. M. (1996). Panic disorder: From theory to therapy. In P. Salkovskis (Ed.), *Frontiers of cognitive therapy* (pp. 318–344). New York, NY: Guilford.

Clark, D. M., Ehlers, A., Hackman, A., McManus, F., Fennell, M., Grey, N., & Wild, J. (2006). Cognitive therapy versus exposure and applied relaxation in social phobia: A randomized controlled trial. *Journal of Consulting and Clinical Psychology, 74*, 568–578.

Clark, D. M., Ehlers, A., McManus, F., Hackman, A., Fennell, M. J. V., Campbell, H., & Louis, B. (2003). Cognitive therapy versus fluoxetine in generalized social phobia: A randomized placebo-controlled trial. *Journal of Consulting and Clinical Psychology, 71*, 1058–1067.

Clark, D. M., Salkovskis, P. M., Hackmann, A., Middleton, H., Anastasiades, P., & Gelder, M. (1994). A comparison of cognitive therapy, applied relaxation and imipramine in the treatment of panic disorder. *British Journal of Psychiatry, 164*(6), 759–769.

Clark, L. A. (2005). Temperament as a unifying basis for personality and psychopathology [Special issue]. *Journal of Abnormal Psychology, 114*, 505–521.

Clark, R. (2003). Parental history of hypertension and coping responses predict blood pressure changes in black college volunteers undergoing a speaking task about perceptions of racism. *Psychosomatic Medicine, 65*, 1012–1019.

Clarkin, J. F., Howieson, D. B., & McClough, J. (2008). The role of psychiatric measures in assessment and treatment. In R. E. Hales, S. C. Yudofsky, & G. O. Gabbard (Eds.), *The American Psychiatric Publishing textbook of psychiatry* (5th ed., pp. 73–110). Arlington, VA: American Psychiatric Publishing.

Clayton, A. H., Croft, H. A., & Handiwala, L. (2014). Antidepressants and sexual dysfunction: Mechanisms and clinical implications. *Postgraduate Medicine, 126*(2), 91–99.

Clayton, E. W. (2015). Beyond myalgic encephalomyelitis/chronic fatigue syndrome: An IOM report on redefining an illness. *JAMA, 313*(11), 1101–1102.

Cleckley, H. M. (1982). *The mask of sanity* (6th ed.). St. Louis, MO: Mosby. (Original work published in 1941.)

Cleghorn, J. M., & Albert, M. L. (1990). Modular disjunction in schizophrenia: A framework for a pathological psychophysiology. In A. Kales, C. N. Stefanis, & J. A. Talbot (Eds.), *Recent advances in schizophrenia* (pp. 59–80). New York, NY: Springer-Verlag.

Clemenson, G. D., Deng, W., & Gage, F. H. (2015). Environmental enrichment and neurogenesis: from mice to humans, Current Opinion in Behavioral Sciences, 4, 56–62. https://doi.org/10.1016/j.cobeha.2015.02.005.

Clement, U. (1990). Surveys of heterosexual behavior. *Annual Review of Sex Research, 1*, 45–74.

Clementz, B. A., & Sweeney, J. A. (1990). Is eye movement dysfunction a biological marker for schizophrenia? A methodological review. *Psychological Bulletin, 108*, 77–92.

Cloninger, C. R. (1978). The link between hysteria and sociopathy: An integrative model of pathogenesis based on clinical, genetic, and neurophysiological observations. In H. S. Akiskal & W. L. Webb (Eds.), *Psychiatric diagnosis: Exploration of biological predictors* (pp. 189–218). New York, NY: Spectrum.

Cloninger, C. R., & Svakic, D. M. (2009). Personality disorders. In B. J. Sadock, V. A. Sadock, & P. Ruiz (Eds.), *Kaplan & Sadock's comprehensive textbook of psychiatry* (9th ed., Vol. II, pp. 2197–2240). Philadelphia, PA: Lippincott Williams & Wilkins.

Closser, M. H. (1992). Cocaine epidemiology. In T. R. Kosten & H. D. Kleber (Eds.), *Clinician's guide to cocaine addiction: Theory, research, and treatment* (pp. 225-240). New York, NY: Guilford.

Coates, T. J. (1990). Strategies for modifying sexual behavior for primary and secondary prevention of HIV disease. *Journal of Consulting and Clinical Psychology, 58*(1), 57–69.

Cobb, S. (1976). Social support as a moderator of life stress. *Psychosomatic Medicine, 38*, 300.

Cobham, V. E., Dadds, M. R., Spence, S. H., & McDermott, B. (2010). Parental anxiety in the treatment of childhood anxiety: A different story three years later. *Journal of Clinical Child and Adolescent Psychology, 39*(3), 410–420. PMID 20419581

Coccaro, E. F. (2012). Intermittent explosive disorder as a disorder of impulsive aggression for DSM-5. *American Journal of Psychiatry, 169*(6), 577–588.

Coccaro, E. F. (2020). The Overt Aggression Scale Modified (OAS-M) for clinical trials targeting impulsive aggression and intermittent explosive disorder: Validity, reliability, and correlates. *Journal of Psychiatric Research, 124*, 50–57.

Coccaro, E. F., & McCloskey, M. (2010). Intermittent explosive disorder: Clinical aspects. In E. Aboujaoude & L. M. Koran (Eds.), *Impulse control disorders* (pp. 221–232). New York, NY: Cambridge University Press.

Cocores, J. A., Miller, N. S., Pottash, A. C., & Gold, M. S. (1988). Sexual dysfunction in abusers of cocaine and alcohol. *American Journal of Drug and Alcohol Abuse, 14*, 169–173.

Coderre, T. J., Katz, J., Vaccarino, A. L., & Melzack, R. (1993). Contribution of central neuroplasticity to pathological pain: Review of clinical and experimental evidence. *Pain, 52*, 259–285.

Coe, C. L. (2010). Immunity in primates within a psychobiological perspective. In G. E. Demas & R. J. Nelson (Eds.) *Ecoimmunology.* New York, NY: Oxford University Press.

Cohen, A. S., Barlow, D. H., & Blanchard, E. B. (1985). Psychophysiology of relaxation-associated panic attacks. *Journal of Abnormal Psychology, 94*, 98.

Cohen, C. I., Natarajan, N., Araujo, M., & Solanki, D. (2013). Prevalence of negative symptoms and associated factors in older adults with schizophrenia spectrum disorder. *American Journal of Geriatric Psychiatry, 21*(2), 100–107. doi: 10.1097/JGP.1090b1013e3182447b3182443

Cohen, D., & Pressman, S. D. (2006). Positive affect and health. *Current Directions in Psychological Science, 15*, 122–125.

Cohen, J. (2002). Confronting the limits of success. *Science, 296*, 2320–2324.

Cohen, J. (2011). AIDS research: Complexity surrounds HIV prevention advances. *Science, 333*(6041), 393.

Cohen, J. B., & Reed, D. (1985). Type A behavior and coronary heart disease among Japanese men in Hawaii. *Journal of Behavioral Medicine, 8*, 343–352.

Cohen, J. S., Edmunds, J. M., Brodman, D. M., Benjamin, C. L., & Kendall, P. C. (2012). Using self-monitoring: Implementation of collaborative empiricism in cognitive-behavioral therapy. *Cognitive and Behavioral Practice. 20*(4), 419–428. doi: 10.1016/j.cbpra.2012.06.002

Cohen, J., & Avidan, A. Y. (2021). Other parasomnias: Nightmare disorder, recurrent isolated sleep paralysis, sleep-related hallucinations, exploding head sndrme, sleep enuresis. In E. H. During & C. A. Kushida (Eds.), *Clinical sleep medicine: A comprehensive guide for mental health and other medical professionals* (pp. 311–331). Washington, D.C.: American Psychiatric Association Publishing.

Cohen, L., Soares, C., Vitonis, A., Otto, M., & Harlow, B. (2006). Risk for new onset of depression during the menopausal transition. *Archive General Psychiatry, 63,* 385–390.

Cohen, S. (1996). Psychological stress, immunity, and upper respiratory infections. *Current Directions in Psychological Science, 5,* 86–90.

Cohen, S., & Herbert, T. B. (1996). Health psychology: Psychological factors and physical disease from the perspective of human psychoneuroimmunology. *Annual Review of Psychology, 47,* 113–142.

Cohen, S., & Janicki-Deverts, D. (2009). Can we improve our physical health by altering our social networks? *Perspectives on Psychological Science, 4,* 375–378.

Cohen, S., Doyle, W. J., & Skoner, D. P. (1999). Psychological stress, cytokine production, and severity of upper respiratory illness. *Psychosomatic Medicine, 61,* 175–180.

Cohen, S., Doyle, W. J., Skoner, D. P., Fireman, P., Gwaltney, J. M., Jr., & Newsome, J. T. (1995). State and trait negative affect as predictors of objective and subjective symptoms of respiratory viral infections. *Journal of Personality and Social Psychology, 68,* 159–169.

Cohen, S., Doyle, W. J., Turner, R., Alper, C. M., & Skoner, D. P. (2003). Sociability and susceptibility to the common cold. *Psychological Science, 14*(5), 389–395.

Cohen, S., Doyle, W., Skoner, D. P., Rabin, B. S., & Gwaltney, J. M. (1997). Social ties and susceptibility to the common cold. *JAMA: Journal of the American Medical Association, 277,* 1940–1944.

Cohen-Kettenis, P. T., & Pfäfflin, F. (2010). The DSM diagnostic criteria for gender identity disorder in adolescents and adults. *Archives of Sexual Behavior, 39,* 499–513.

Coker, L. H., Espeland, M. A., Rapp, S. R., Legault, C., Resnick, S. M., Hogan, P., . . . Shumaker, S. A. (2010). Postmenopausal hormone therapy and cognitive outcomes: The Women's Health Initiative Memory Study (WHIMS). *The Journal of Steroid Biochemistry and Molecular Biology, 118*(4–5), 304–310.

Cole, M. G., Ciampi, A., Belzile, E., & Zhong, L. (2009). Persistent delirium in older hospital patients: A systematic review of frequency and prognosis. *Age and Ageing, 38*(1), 19–26.

Cole, S. W. (2008). Psychosocial influences on HIV-1 disease progression: Neural, endocrine, and virologic mechanisms. *Psychosomatic Medicine, 70,* 562–568.

Cole, S. W. (2011). Socioenvironmental effects on gene expression. In K. S. Kendler, S. Jaffee, & D. Romer (Eds.), *The dynamic genome and mental health: The role of genes and environments in youth development* (pp. 195–228). New York, NY: Oxford University Press.

Coleman, E., Bockting, W. O., & Gooren, L. (1993). Homosexual and bisexual identity in sex-reassigned female-to-male transsexuals. *Archives of Sexual Behavior, 22,* 37–50.

Coleman, E., Colgan, P., & Gooren, L. (1992). Male cross-gender behavior in Myanmar (Burma): A description of the acault. *Archives of Sexual Behavior, 21*(3), 313–321.

Colibazzi, T., Posner, J., Wang, Z., Gorman, D., Gerber, A., Yu, S., Zhu, H., Kangarlu, A., Duan, Y., Russell, J. A., & Peterson, B. S. (2010). Neural systems subserving valence and arousal during the experience of induced emotions. *Emotion, 10*(3), 377–389. https://doi.org/10.1037/a0018484

Colins, O. F., Andershed, H., & Pardini, D. A. (2015). Psychopathic traits as predictors of future criminality, intimate partner aggression, and substance use in young adult men. *Law & Human Behavior, 39*(6), 547–558.

Colins, O. F., Fanti, K. A., & Andershed, H. (in press). The *DSM-5* limited prosocial emotions specifier for conduct disorder: Comorbid problems, prognosis, and antecedents. *Journal of the American Academy of Child & Adolescent Psychiatry.*

Colles, S. L., & Dixon, J. B. (2012). The relationship of night eating syndrome with obesity, bariatric surgery, and physical health. In J. D. Lundgren, K. C. Allison, & A. J. Stunkard (Eds.), *Night eating syndrome: Research, assessment and treatment* (pp. 85–107). New York, NY: Guilford.

Colles, S. L., Dixon, J. B., & O'Brien, P. E. (2007). Night eating syndrome and nocturnal snacking: Association with obesity, binge eating, and psychological distress. *International Journal of Obesity, 31,* 1722–1730.

Collinge, J., Whitfield, J., McKintosh, E., Beck, J., Mead, S., Thomas, D. J., & Alpers, M. P. (2006). Kuru in the 21st century: An acquired human prion disease with very long incubation periods. *Lancet, 367*(9528), 2068–2074.

Collinge, J., Whitfield, J., McKintosh, E., Frosh, A., Mead, S., Hill, A. F., . . . Alpers, M. P. (2008). A clinical study of kuru patients with long incubation periods at the end of the epidemic in Papua New Guinea. Philosophical Transactions of the Royal Society of London B: *Biological Sciences, 363*(1510), 3725–3739.

Colloca, L., Lopiano, L., Lanotte, M., & Benedetti, F. (2004). Overt versus covert treatment for pain, anxiety, and Parkinson's disease. *Lancet Neurology, 3*(11), 679–684. doi: 10.1016/S1474-4422(04)00908-1

Colman, I., Murray, J., Abbott, R., Maughan, B., Kuh, D., Croudace, T., & Jones, P. B. (2009). Outcomes of conduct problems in adolescence: 40 year follow-up of national cohort. *British Medical Journal, 338,* a2981.

Comas-Diaz, L. (1981). Puerto Rican *espiritismo* and psychotherapy. *American Journal of Orthopsychiatry, 51*(4), 636–645.

Comer, J. S., Blanco, C., Hasin, D. S., Liu, S.-M., Grant, B. F., Turner, J. B., & Olfson, M. (2011). Health-related quality of life across the anxiety disorders: results from the national epidemiologic survey on alcohol and related conditions (NESARC). *Journal of Clinical Psychiatry, 72,* 43–50.

Comer, J. S., Mojtabai, R., & Olfson, M. (2011). National trends in the antipsychotic treatment of psychiatric outpatients with anxiety disorders. *American Journal of Psychiatry, 168,* 1057–1065.

Compare, A., Bigi, R., Orrego, P. S., Proietti, R., Grossi, E., & Steptoe, A. (2013). Type d personality is associated with the development of stress cardiomyopathy following emotional triggers. *Annals of Behavioral Medicine, 45*(3), 299–307.

Compas, B. E., Boyer, M., Stanger, C., Colletti, R., & Thomsen, A. (2006). Latent variable analysis of coping, anxiety/depression, and somatic symptoms in adolescents with chronic pain. *Journal of Consulting and Clinical Psychology, 74,* 1132–1142.

Compas, B. E., Forehand, R., Keller, G., Champion, J. E., Rakow, A., Reeslund, K. L., & Cole, D. A. (2009). Randomized controlled trial of a family cognitive-behavioral preventive intervention for children of depressed parents. *Journal of Consulting and Clinical Psychology, 77*(6), 1007–1020.

Compas, B. E., Oppedisano, G., Connor, J. K., Gerhardt, C. A., Hinden, B. R., Achenbach, T. M., & Hammen, C. (1997). Gender differences in depressive symptoms in adolescence: Comparison of national samples of clinically referred and nonreferred youths. *Journal of Consulting and Clinical Psychology, 65,* 617–626.

Compton, S. N., Peris, T. S., Almirall, D., Birmaher, B., Sherrill, J., Kendall, P. C., March, J. S., Gosch, E. A., Ginsburg, G. S., Rynn, M. A., Piacentini, J. C., McCracken, J. T., Keeton, C. P., Suveg, C. M., Aschenbrand, S.

G., Sakolsky, D., Iyengar, S., Walkup, J. T., & Albano, A. M. (2014). Predictors and moderators of treatment response in childhood anxiety disorders: results from the CAMS trial. *Journal of Consulting and Clinical Psychology, 82*(2), 212–224.

Compton, W. M., Boyle, M., & Wargo, E. (2015). Prescription opioid abuse: problems and responses. *Preventive Medicine, 80,* 5–9.

Condon, W., Ogston, W., & Pacoe, L. (1969). Three faces of Eve revisited: A study of transient microstrabismus. *Journal of Abnormal Psychology, 74,* 618–620.

Conduct Problems Prevention Research Group. (2010). The effects of a multi-year universal social-emotional learning program: The role of student and school characteristics. *Journal of Consulting and Clinical Psychology, 78*(2), 156–168.

Connecticut General Statutes Annotated, 319: Part II, 17a-495 (1992).

Connor, D. F. (2015). Stimulant and nonstimulant medications for childhood ADHD. In R. A. Barkley (Ed.), *Attention-deficit hyperactivity disorder: A handbook for diagnosis & treatment* (4th ed., pp. 666–685). New York, NY: The Guilford Press.

Conti, C. R., Pepine, C. J., & Sweeney, M. (1999). Efficacy and safety of sildenafil citrate in the treatment of erectile dysfunction in patients with ischemic heart disease. *American Journal of Cardiology, 83,* 29C–34C.

Convit, A. (2012). Obesity is associated with structural and functional brain abnormalities: Where do we go from here? *Psychosomatic Medicine, 74,* 673–674.

Conwell, Y., Duberstein, P. R., & Caine, E. D. (2002). Risk factors for suicide in later life. *Biological Psychiatry, 52,* 193–204.

Conwell, Y., Duberstein, P. R., Cox, C., Hermmann, J. H., Forbes, N. T., & Caine, E. D. (1996). Relationships of age and axis I diagnoses in victims of completed suicide: A psychological autopsy study. *American Journal of Psychiatry, 153,* 1001–1008.

Cook, B. J., Wonderlich, S. A., Mitchell, J. E., Thompson, R., Sherman, R., & McCallum, K. (2016). Exercise in eating disorders treatment: Systematic review and proposal of guidelines. *Medicine and Science in Sports and Exercise, 48*(7), 1408–1414. doi: 10.1249/MSS.0000000000000912

Cook, E. W., Hodes, R. L., & Lang, P. J. (1986). Preparedness and phobia: Effects of stimulus content on human visceral conditioning. *Journal of Abnormal Psychology, 95*(3), 195–207. https://doi.org/10.1037/0021-843X.95.3.195

Cook, M. L., Zhang, Y., & Constantino, J. N. (2020). On the continuity between autistic and schizoid personality disorder trait burden: A prospective study in adolescence. *Journal of Nervous and Mental Disease, 208*(2), 94–100.

Cook, P. J. (1993). The matter of tobacco use. *Science, 262,* 1750–1751.

Cookson, C. (2009). Confronting our fear: Legislating beyond battered woman syndrome and the law of self-defense in Vermont. *Vermont Law Review, 34,* 415.

Coolidge, F. L., Marle, P. D., Rhoades, C. S., Monaghan, P., & Segal, D. L. (2013). Psychometric properties of a new measure to assess autism spectrum disorder in DSM-5. *American Journal of Orthopsychiatry, 83*(1), 126.

Coolidge, F., Thede, L., & Young, S. (2002). The heritability of gender identity disorder in a child and adolescent twin sample. *Behavior Genetics, 32,* 251–257.

Coons, P. M. (1994). Confirmation of childhood abuse in child and adolescent cases of multiple personality disorder not otherwise specified. *Journal of Nervous & Mental Disease, 182,* 461–464.

Coons, P. M., Bowman, E. S., Kluft, R. P., & Milstein, V. (1991). The cross cultural occurrence of NPD: Additional cases from a recent survey. *Dissociation, 4,* 124–128.

Cooper, A. J. (1988). Sexual dysfunction and cardiovascular disease. *Stress Medicine, 4,* 273–281.

Cooper, A. M., & Ronningstam, E. (1992). Narcissistic personality disorder. In A. Tasman & M. B. Riba (Eds.), *Review of psychiatry* (Vol. 11, pp. 80–97). Washington, DC: American Psychiatric Press.

Cooper, J. A., Arulpragasam, A. R., & Treadway, M. T. (2018). Anhedonia in depression: Biological mechanisms and computational models. *Current Opinion in Behavioral Sciences, 22,* 128–135. doi: 10.1016/j.cobeha.2018.01.024

Cooper, J., Kapur, N., Webb, R., Lawlor, M., Guthrie, E., Mackway-Jones, K., & Appleby, L. (2005). Suicide after deliberate self-harm: A 4-year cohort study. *American Journal of Psychiatry, 162,* 297–303.

Cooper, L. .L, Rong, J., Pahlevan, N. M., Rinderknecht, D. G., Benjamin, E. J., Hamburg, N. M., Vasan, R. S., Larson, M. G., Gharib, M., & Mitchell, G. F. (2021). Intrinsic frequencies of carotid pressure waveforms predict heart failure events: The Framingham Heart Study. *Hypertension, 77*(2), 338–346. doi: 10.1161/HYPERTENSI-ONAHA.120.15632

Cooper, N. S., Feder, A., Southwick, S. M., & Charney, D. S. (2007). Resilience and vulnerability to trauma: Psychobiological mechanisms. In D. Romer & E. F. Walker (Eds.), *Adolescent psychopathology and the developing brain: Integrating brain and prevention science* (pp. 347–372). New York, NY: Oxford University Press.

Cooper, S.-A., & Smiley, E. (2012). Prevalence of intellectual disabilities and epidemiology of mental ill-health in adults with intellectual disabilities. In M. G. Gelder, N. C. Andreasen, J. J. Lopez-Ibor, Jr., & J. R. Geddes (Eds.), *New Oxford textbook of psychiatry* (2nd ed., Vol. 2, pp. 1825–1829). New York, NY: Oxford University Press.

Cooperberg, J., & Faith, M. S. (2004). Treatment of obesity II: Childhood and adolescent obesity. In J. K. Thompson (Ed.), *Handbook of eating disorders and obesity* (pp. 443–450). New York, NY: Wiley.

Cope, M. B., Fernandez, J. R., & Allison, D. (2004). Genetic and biological risk factors. In J. K. Thompson (Ed.), *Handbook of eating disorders and obesity* (pp. 323–338). New York, NY: Wiley.

Cope, N., Eicher, J. D., Meng, H., Gibson, C. J., Hager, K., Lacadie, C., & Gruen, J. R. (2012). Variants in the DYX2 locus are associated with altered brain activation in reading-related brain regions in subjects with reading disability. *NeuroImage, 63*(1), 148–156. doi: http://dx.doi.org/10.1016/j.neuroimage.2012.06.037

Copeland, W. E., Shanahan, L., Egger, H., Angold, A., & Costello, E. J. (2014). Adult diagnostic and functional outcomes of DSM-5 disruptive mood dysregulation disorder. *American Journal of Psychiatry, 171,* 668–674.

Copen, C. E., Chandra, A., & Febo-Vazquez, I. (2016). Sexual behavior, sexual attraction, and sexual orientation among adults aged 18–44 in the United States: Data from the 2011–2013 National Survey of Family Growth. *National Health Statistics Reports, 7*(88), 1–14.

Coplan, J. D., Trost, R. C., Owens, M. J., Cooper, T. B., Gorman, J. M., Nemeroff, C. B., & Rosenblum, L. A. (1998). Cerebrospinal fluid concentrations of somatostatin and biogenic amines in grown primates reared by mothers exposed to manipulated foraging conditions. *Archives of General Psychiatry, 55,* 473–477.

Corcoran, C. M., Kimhy, D., Stanford, A., Khan, S., Walsh, J., Thompson, J., & Malaspina, D. (2008). Temporal association of cannabis use with symptoms in individuals at clinical high risk for psychosis. *Schizophrenia Research, 106,* 286–293.

Corker, E. A., Beldie, A., Brain, C., Jakovljevic, M., Jarema, M., Karamustafalioglu, O., . . . Waern, M. (2015). Experience of stigma and discrimination reported by people experiencing the first episode of schizophrenia and those with a first episode of depression: The FEDORA project. *International Journal of Social Psychiatry, 61*(5), 438–445.

Correll, C. U., Hauser, M., Auther, A. M., & Cornblatt, B. A. (2010). Research in people with psychosis risk syndrome: A review of the current evidence and future directions. *Journal of Child Psychology and Psychiatry, 51*(4), 390–431.

Corrigan, P. W., Druss, B. G., & Perlick, D. A. (2014). The impact of mental illness stigma on seeking and participating in mental health care. *Psychological Science in the Public Interest, 15*(2), 37–70. doi: 10.1177/1529100614531398

Corson, P. W., & Andersen, A. E. (2002). Body image issues among boys and men. In T. F. Cash & T. Pruzinsky (Eds.), *Body image: A handbook of theory, research and clinical practice* (pp. 192–199). New York, NY: Guilford.

Cortiella, C., & Horowitz, S. H. (2014). *The State of Learning Disabilities: Facts, Trends and Emerging Issues* (3rd ed.). New York, NY: National Center for Learning Disabilities.

Cortoni, F., & Gannon, T. A. (2011). Female sexual offenders. In D. P. Boer, R. Eher, L. A. Craig, M. H. Miner, & F. Pfafflin (eds.). *International perspectives on the assessment and treatment of sex offenders: Theory, practice and research,* (pp. 35–54). John Wiley & Sons: New York.

Cortoni, F., & Gannon, T. A. (2016). Female Sexual Offenders: An Overview. In A. Phenix & H. M. Hoberman (Eds.). *Sexual Offending* (pp. 213–224). Springer: New York.

Coryell, W., Endicott, J., & Keller, M. (1992). Rapid cycling affective disorder: Demo-graphics, diagnosis, family history, and course. *Archives of General Psychiatry, 49,* 126–131.

Coryell, W., Endicott, J., Maser, J. D., Keller, M. B., Leon, A. C., & Akiskal, H. S. (1995). Long-term stability of polarity distinctions in the affective disorders. *American Journal of Psychiatry, 152,* 385–390.

Coryell, W., Solomon, D., Turvey, C., Keller, M., Leon, A. C., Endicott, J., & Mueller, T. (2003). The long-term course of rapid-cycling bipolar disorder. *Archives of General Psychiatry, 60,* 914–920.

Costa e Silva, J. A., & De Girolamo, G. (1990). Neurasthenia: History of a concept. In N. Sartorius, D. Goldberg, G. De Girolamo, J. A. Costa e Silva, Y. Lecrubier, & U. Wittchen (Eds.), *Psychological disorders in general medical settings* (pp. 699–81). Toronto, Canada: Hogrefe and Huber.

Costa Jr, P. T., & McCrae, R. R. (2013). The five-factor model of personality and its relevance to personality disorders. *Personality and Personality Disorders: The Science of Mental Health, 7,* 17.

Costa, E. (1985). Benzodiazepine-GABA interactions: A model to investigate the neurobiology of anxiety. In A. H. Tuma & J. D. Maser (Eds.), *Anxiety and the anxiety disorders.* Hillsdale, NJ: Erlbaum.

Costantino, A., Cerpolini, S., Alvisi, S., Morselli, P. G., Venturoli, S., & Meriggiola, M. C. (2013). A prospective study on sexual function and mood in female-to-male transsexuals during testosterone administration and after sex reassignment surgery. *Journal of Sex & Marital Therapy, 39*(4), 321–335.

Costin, V., & Vignoles, V. L. (2020). Meaning is about mattering: Evaluating coherence, purpose, and existential mattering as precursors of meaning in life judgments. *Journal of Personality and Social Psychology, 118*(4), 864.

Cottone, P., Sabino, V., Roberto, M., Bajo, M., Pockros, L., Frihauf, J. B., & Zorrilla, E. P. (2009). CRF system recruitment mediates dark side of compulsive eating. *PNAS: Proceedings of the National Academy of Sciences of the United States of America, 106,* 20016–20020.

Courcoulas, A. P. (2012). Progress in filling the gaps in bariatric surgery. *JAMA: Journal of the American Medical Association, 308,* 1160–1161. doi: 10.1001/jama.2012.12337

Courcoulas, A. P., Christian, N. J., Belle, S. H., Berk, P. D., Flum, D. R., Garcia, L., . . . Wolfe, B. M. (2013). Weight change and health outcomes at 3 years after bariatric surgery among individuals with severe obesity. *JAMA, 310*(22), 2416–2425.

Cowley, G., & Spingen, K. (1990, March). The promise of Prozac. *Newsweek, 115*(13), 38.

Cox, A. C., Weed, N. C., & Butcher, J. N. (2009). The MMPI-2: History, interpretation, and clinical issues. In J. N. Butcher (Ed.), *Oxford handbook of personality assessment* (pp. 250–276). New York, NY: Oxford University Press.

Cox, A., Rutter, M., Newman, S., & Bartak, L. (1975). A comparative study of infantile autism and specific developmental receptive language disorder: II. Parental characteristics. *British Journal of Psychiatry, 126,* 146–159.

Cox, B. C., Swinson, R. P., Schulman, I. D., Kuch, K., & Reikman, J. T. (1993). Gender effects in alcohol use in panic disorder with agoraphobia. *BRAT, 31*(4), 413–416.

Cozanitis, D. A. (2004). One hundred years of barbiturates and their saint. *Journal of the Royal Society of Medicine, 97,* 594–598.

Crabbe, J. C., Wahlsten, D., & Dudek, B. C. (1999). Genetics of mouse behavior: Interactions with laboratory environment. *Science, 284,* 1670–1672.

Craddock, N., & Jones, I. (2001). Molecular genetics of bipolar disorder. *British Journal of Psychiatry, 41,* 128–133.

Crago, M., Shisslak, C. M., & Estes, L. S. (1997). Eating disturbances among American minority groups: A review. *The International Journal of Eating Disorders, 19,* 239–248.

Craighead, W. E., Hart, A. B., Craighead, L. W., & Ilardi, S. S. (2002). Psychosocial treatments for major depressive disorder. In P. E. Nathan & J. M. Gorman (Eds.), *A guide to treatments that work* (2nd ed., pp. 245–261). New York, NY: Oxford University Press.

Craske, M. G., & Barlow, D. H. (1988). A review of the relationship between panic and avoidance. *Clinical Psychology Review, 8,* 667–685.

Craske, M. G., & Barlow, D. H. (2006). *Mastery of your anxiety and worry.* New York, NY: Oxford University Press.

Craske, M. G., & Barlow, D. H. (2014). Panic disorder and agoraphobia. In D. H. Barlow, *Clinical handbook of psychological disorders* (pp. 1–61). New York, NY: Guilford Press.

Craske, M. G., & Barlow, D. H. (2014). Panic disorder. In D. H. Barlow (Ed.), *Clinical handbook of psychological disorders* (pp. 1–61). New York, NY: Guilford.

Craske, M. G., & Rowe, M. K. (1997). Nocturnal panic. *Clinical Psychology: Science & Practice, 4,* 153–174.

Craske, M. G., Antony, M. M., & Barlow, D. H. (2006). *Mastering your fears and phobias: Therapist guide.* New York, NY: Oxford University Press.

Craske, M. G., Barlow, D. H., Clark, D. M., Curtis, G. C., Hill, E. M., Himle, J. A., & Warwick, H. M. C. (1996). Specific (simple) phobia. In T. A. Widiger, A. J. Frances, H. A. Pincus, R. Ross, M. B. First, & W. W. Davis (Eds.), *DSM-IV sourcebook* (Vol. 2, pp. 473–506). Washington, DC: American Psychiatric Association.

Craske, M. G., Brown, T. A., & Barlow, D. H. (1991). Behavioral treatment of panic disorder: A two-year follow-up. *Behavior Therapy, 22,* 289–304.

Craske, M. G., Golinelli, D., Stein, M. B., Roy-Byrne, P., Bystritsky, A., & Sherbourne, C. (2005). Does the addition of cognitive behavioral therapy improve panic disorder treatment outcome relative to medication alone in the primary-care setting? *Psychological Medicine, 35*(11), 1645–1654. doi: 10.1017/S003329170500557X

Craske, M. G., Hermans, D., & Vansteenwegen, D. (2006). *Fear and learning.* Washington, DC: American Psychological Association.

Craske, M. G., Kircanski, K., Epstein, A., Wittchen, H.-U., Pine, D. S.,

Lewis-Fernández, R., & Hinton, D. (2010). Panic disorder: A review of DSM-IV panic disorder and proposals for DSM-V. *Depression and Anxiety, 27*(2), 93–112.

Craske, M. G., Lang, A. J., Mystkowski, J. L., Zucker, B. G., & Bystritsky, A. (2002). Does nocturnal panic represent a more severe form of panic disorder? *Journal of Nervous and Mental Disease, 190,* 611–618.

Craske, M. G., Stein, M. B., Sullivan, G., Sherbourne, C., Bystritsky, A., Rose, R. D., & Roy-Byrne, P. (2011). Disorder-specific impact of coordinated anxiety learning and management treatment for anxiety disorders in primary care. *Archives of General Psychiatry, 68,* 378–388. doi: 10.1001/archgenpsychiatry.2011.25

Crawford, N. (2003). ADHD: A women's issue. *Monitor on Psychology, 35,* 28–30.

Creed, F., & Barsky, A. (2004). A systematic review of the epidemiology of somatisation disorder and hypochondriasis. *Journal of Psychosomatic Research, 56,* 391–408.

Creese, I., Burt, D. R., & Snyder, S. H. (1976). Dopamine receptor binding predicts clinical and pharmacological potencies of antischizophrenic drugs. *Science, 192,* 481–483.

Cremniter, D., Jamin, S., Kollenbach, K., Alvarez, J. C., Lecrubier, Y., Gilton, A., & Spreux-Varoquaux, O. (1999). CSF 5-HIAA levels are lower in impulsive as compared to nonimpulsive violent suicide attempts and control subjects. *Biological Psychiatry, 45*(12), 1572–1579.

Crerand, C., Sarwer, D., Magee, L., Gibbons, L., Lowe, M., Bartlett, S., & Whitaker, L. A. (2004). Rate of body dysmorphic disorder among patients seeking facial plastic surgery. *Psychiatric Annals, 34, 958–965.*

Crichton, P., & Morey, S. (2003). Treating pain in cancer patients. In D. C. Turk & R. J. Gatchel (Eds.), *Psychological approaches to pain management: A practitioner's handbook* (2nd ed., pp. 501–514). New York, NY: Guilford.

Crisp, A. H., Callender, J. S., Halek, C., & Hsu, L. K. G. (1992). Long-term mortality in anorexia nervosa: A 20-year follow-up of the St. George's and Aberdeen cohorts. *British Journal of Psychiatry, 161,* 104–107.

Cristancho, M. A., Kocsis, J. H., & Thase, M. E. (2012). Dysthymic disorder and other chronic depressions. *FOCUS, 10,* 422–427.

Critelli, J. W., & Bivona, J. M. (2008). Women's erotic rape fantasies: An evaluation of theory and research. *Journal of Sex Research, 45,* 57–70.

Critser, G. (2003). *Fat land: How Americans became the fattest people in the world.* Boston, MA: Houghton Mifflin.

Croen, L. A., Najjar, D. V., Fireman, B., & Grether, J. K. (2007). Maternal and paternal age and risk of autism spectrum disorders. *Archives of Pediatrics & Adolescent Medicine, 161*(4), 334.

Crouse, K. (2013, January 3). A fun-loving, carefree, spirit becomes the face of anxiety. *New York Times.* Retrieved from http://www.nytimes.com/2013/01/04/sports/golf/charlie-beljan-lives-a-life-of-high-anxiety-and-low-golf-scores.html?pagewanted=all

Crow, S. J., Mitchell, J. E., Roerig, J. D., & Steffen, K. (2009). What potential role is there for medication treatment in anorexia nervosa? *International Journal of Eating Disorders, 42*(1), 1–8.

Crow, S. J., Thuras, P., Keel, P. K., & Mitchell, J. E. (2002). Long-term menstrual and reproductive function in patients with bulimia nervosa. *American Journal of Psychiatry, 159,* 1048–1050.

Crowe, R. R. (1974). An adoption study of antisocial personality. *Archives of General Psychiatry, 31,* 785–791.

Crowley, T., Richardson, D., & Goldmeir, D. (2006). Recommendation for the management of vaginismus: BASHH special interest group for sexual dysfunction. *International Journal of STD and AIDS, 17,* 14–18.

Crump, C., Sundquist, K., Winkleby, M. A., & Sundquist, J. (2013). Comorbidities and mortality in bipolar disorder: a Swedish national cohort study. *JAMA Psychiatry, 70*(9):931–939.

Cryan, J. F., & Dinan, T. G. (2012). Mind-altering microorganisms: The impact of the gut microbiota on brain and behaviour. *Nature Reviews Neuroscience, 13*(10), 701–712.

Csordas, T. J. (2015). Cultural phenomenology and psychiatric illness. In L. J. Kirmayer, R. Lemelson, & C. A. Cummings (Eds.). *Re-visioning psychiatry: Cultural phenomenology, critical neuroscience, and global mental health* (117–140). New York, NY: Cambridge University Press.

Cuffee, Y., Ogedegbe, C., Williams, N. J., Ogedegbe, G., & Schoenthaler, A. (2014). Psychosocial risk factors for hypertension: An update of the literature. *Current hypertension reports, 16*(10), 1–11.

Cuijpers, P. (2015). Psychotherapies for adult depression: Recent developments. *Current Opinion in Psychiatry, 28,* 24–29.

Cuijpers, P., Beekman, A. T., & Reynolds III, C. F. (2012). Preventing depression: A global priority. *JAMA: The Journal of the American Medical Association, 307*(10), 1033–1034.

Cuijpers, P., Geraedts, A. S., van Oppen, P., Andersson, G., Markowitz, J. C., & van Straten, A. (2011). Interpersonal psychotherapy for depression: a meta-analysis. *American Journal of Psychiatry, 168*(6), 581–592.

Cuijpers, P., Sijbrandji, M., Koole, S., Huibers, M., Berking, M., & Andersson, G. (2014). Psychological treatment of generalized anxiety disorder: A meta-analysis. *Clinical Psychology Review, 34,* 130–140.

Cummings, J. L. (Ed.). (1990). *Subcortical dementia.* New York, NY: Oxford University Press.

Cunningham Owens, D. G., & Johnstone, E. C. (2012). Treatment and management of schizophrenia. In M. G. Gelder, N. C. Andreasen, J. J. López-Ibor, Jr., & J. R. Geddes (Eds.), *New Oxford textbook of psychiatry* (2nd ed., Vol. 1, pp. 578-595). New York, NY: Oxford University Press.

Cunningham, J., Yonkers, K. A., O'Brien, S., & Eriksson, E. (2009). Update on research and treatment of premenstrual dysphoric disorder. *Harvard Review of Psychiatry, 17*(2), 120–137.

Curatolo, P., Bombardieri, R., & Jozwiak, S. (2008). Tuberous sclerosis. *The Lancet, 372*(9639), 657–668.

Currier, J. M., Neimeyer, R. A., & Berman, J. S. (2008). The effectiveness of psychotherapeutic interventions for bereaved persons: A comprehensive quantitative review. *Psychological Bulletin, 134*(5), 648–661.

Curry, S. J., Krist, A. H., Owens, D. K., Barry, M. J., Caughey, A. B., Davidson, K. W., … Wong, J. B. (2019). Interventions to prevent perinatal depression: U.S. preventive services task force recommendation statement. *JAMA: Journal of the American Medical Association, 321*(6), 580–587. doi: 10.1001/jama.2019.0007

Curtis, G. C., Hill, E. M., & Lewis, J. A. (1990). *Heterogeneity of DSM-III-R simple phobia and the simple phobia/agoraphobia boundary: Evidence from the ECA study.* Preliminary report to the Simple Phobia subcommittee of the DSM-IV Anxiety Disorders Work Group.

Curtis, G. C., Himle, J. A., Lewis, J. A., & Lee, Y-J. (1989). *Specific situational phobias: Variant of agoraphobia?* Paper requested by the Simple Phobia subcommittee of the DSM-IV Anxiety Disorders Work Group.

Cyranowski, J. M., Aarestad, S. L., & Andersen, B. L. (1999). The role of sexual self-schema in a diathesis-stress model of sexual dysfunction. *Applied & Preventative Psychology, 8,* 217–228.

Cyranowski, J. M., Frank, E., Young, E., & Shear, M. K. (2000). Adolescent onset of the gender difference in lifetime rates of major depression. *Archives of General Psychiatry, 57,* 21–27.

D'Hulst, C., Atack, J. R., & Kooy, R. F. (2009). The complexity of the GABAA receptor shapes unique pharmacological profiles. *Drug Discovery Today, 14*(17–18), 866–875. doi: 10.1016/j.drudis.2009.06.009

D'Onofrio, B. M., Rickert, M. E., Langström, N., Donahue, K. L., Coyne, C. A., Larsson, H., & Rathouz, P. J. (2012). Familial confounding of the association between maternal smoking during pregnancy and offspring substance use and problems. *JAMA Psychiatry, 69*(11), 1140–1150.

D'Onofrio, B. M., Turkheimer, E., Emery, R. E., Slutske, W. S., Heath, A. C., Madden, P. A., & Martin, N. G. (2006). A genetically informed study of the processes underlying the association between parental marital instability and offspring adjustment. *Developmental Psychology, 42*, 486–499.

Daamen, A. P., Penning, R., Brunt, T., & Verster, J. C. (2012). Cocaine. In J. C. Verster, K. Brady, M. Galanter, & P. Conrod (Eds.), *Drug abuse and addiction in medical illness* (pp. 163–173). New York, NY: Springer.

Dahlem, C. H., Scalera, M., Anderson, G., Tasker, M., Ploutz-Snyder, R., McCabe, S. E., & Boyd, C. J. (2020). Recovery opioid overdose team (ROOT) pilot program evaluation: A community-wide post-overdose response strategy. *Substance Abuse*, 1–5.

Dalack, G. W., Glassman, A. H., & Covey, L. S. (1993). Nicotine use. In D. L. Dunner (Ed.), *Current psychiatric therapy* (pp. 114–118). Philadelphia, PA: W. B. Saunders.

Dalenberg, C. J., Brand, B. L., Gleaves, D. H., Dorahy, M. J., Loewenstein, R. J., Cardeña, E., Frewen, P. A., Carlson, E. B., & Spiegel, D. (2012). Evaluation of the evidence for the trauma and fantasy models of dissociation. *Psychological Bulletin, 138*(3), 550–588.

Dalle Grave, R., Calugi, S., Doll, H. A., & Fairburn, C. G. (2013). Enhanced cognitive behaviour therapy for adolescents with anorexia nervosa: An alternative to family therapy? *Behaviour Research and Therapy, 51*, R9–R12.

Daly, R. J. (1983). Samuel Pepys and post traumatic stress disorder. *British Journal of Psychiatry, 143*, 64–68.

Damasio, A. (2007). Neuroscience and ethics: Intersections. *American Journal of Bioethics, 7*(1), 3–7.

Dan, O., Sagi-Schwartz, A., Bar-haim, Y., & Eshel, Y. (2011). Effects of early relationships on children's perceived control: A longitudinal study. *International Journal of Behavioral Development, 35*(5), 449–456.

Dana, R. H. (1996). The Thematic Apperception Test (TAT). In C. S. Newmark (Ed.), *Major psychological assessment instruments* (pp. 166–205). Boston, MA: Allyn & Bacon.

Daniel, E., & Menashe, I. (2020). Exploring the familial role of social responsiveness differences between savant and nonsavant children with autism. *Scientific Reports, 10*(1), 1–8.

Daniel, S. S., Walsh, A. K., Goldston, D. B., Arnold, E. M., Reboussin, B. A., & Wood, F. B. (2006). Suicidality, school dropout, and reading problems among adolescents. *Journal of Learning Disabilities, 39*, 507–514.

Daniels, A., Adams, N., Carroll, C., & Beinecke, R. (2009). A conceptual model for behavioral health and primary care integration: Emerging challenges and strategies for improving international mental health services. *International Journal of Mental Health, 38*(1), 100–112.

Dansinger, M. L., Gleason, J. A., Griffith, J. L., Selker, H. P., & Schaefer, E. J. (2005). Comparison of the Atkins, Ornish, Weight Watchers, and Zone diets for weight loss and heart disease risk reduction: A randomized trial. *JAMA: Journal of the American Medical Association, 293*, 43–53.

Darcangelo, S. (2008). Fetishism: Psychopathology and theory. In D. R. Laws & W. T. O'Donohue (Eds.), *Sexual deviance: Theory, assessment, and treatment* (2nd ed., pp. 108–118). New York, NY: Guilford.

Darwin, C. R. (1872). *The expression of emotions in man and animals.* London, UK: John Murray.

Davey, A., Dai, T., Woodard, J. L., Miller, L. S., Gondo, Y., Johnson, M. A., . . . Stabler, S. P. (2013). Profiles of cognitive functioning in a population-based sample of centenarians using factor mixture analysis. *Experimental Aging Research, 39(2)*, 125–144.

Davey, G. (2006). Cognitive mechanisms in fear acquisition and maintenance. In M. G. Craske, D. Hermans, & D. Vansteenwegen (Eds.), *Fear and learning from basic processes to clinical implications.* (pp. 99–116). Washington, DC: American Psychological Association.

David Klonsky, E., Kotov, R., Bakst, S., Rabinowitz, J., & Bromet, E. J. (2012). Hopelessness as a predictor of attempted suicide among first admission patients with psychosis: A 10-year cohort study. *Suicide and Life-Threatening Behavior, 42*(1), 1–10.

Davidson, A. J., Sellix, M. T., Daniel, J., Yamazaki, S., Menaker, M., & Block, G. D. (2006). Chronic jet-lag increases mortality in aged mice. *Current Biology, 16*, R914–R916.

Davidson, J. R. T., Foa, E. B., & Huppert, J. D. (2004). Fluoxetine, comprehensive Cognitive behavioral therapy, and placebo in generalized social phobia. *Archives of General Psychiatry, 61*, 1005–1013.

Davidson, K. W., Mostofsky, E., & Whang, W. (2010). Don't worry, be happy: Positive affect and reduced 10-year incident coronary heart disease: The Canadian Nova Scotia Health Survey. *European Heart Journal, 31*(9), 1065–1070.

Davidson, K., MacGregor, M. W., Stuhr, J., Dixon, K., & MacLean, D. (2000). Constructive anger verbal behavior predicts blood pressure in a population-based sample. *Health Psychology, 19*, 55–64.

Davidson, L., Chinman, M., Sells, D., & Rowe, M. (2006). Peer support among adults with serious mental illness: a report from the field. *Schizophrenia Bulletin, 32*(3), 443–450.

Davidson, M., Keefe, R. S. E., Mohs, R. C., Siever, L. J., Losonczy, M. F., Horvath, T. B., & Davis, K. L. (1987). L-Dopa challenge and relapse in schizophrenia. *American Journal of Psychiatry, 144*, 934–938.

Davidson, R. J. (1993). Cerebral asymmetry and emotion: Methodological conundrums. *Cognition and Emotion, 7*, 115–138.

Davidson, R. J., Pizzagalli, D. A., & Nitschke, J. B. (2009). Representation and regulation of emotion in depression: Perspectives from affective neuroscience. In I. H. Gotlib & C. L. Hammen (Eds.), *Handbook of depression* (2nd ed., pp. 218–248). New York, NY: Guilford.

Davidson, R., Pizzagalli, D., Nitschke, J., & Putnam, K. (2002). Depression: Perspectives from affective neuroscience. *Annual Review of Psychology, 53*, 545–574.

Davidson, S. L. (2014). Relationship between Childhood Conduct Disorder and Antisocial Personality Disorder in Adulthood: An Argument in Favor of Mandatory Life Sentences without Parole for Juvenile Homicide Offenders. *Law and Psychology Review, 39*, 239.

Davies, M. N., Verdi, S., Burri, A.,Trzaskowski, M., Lee, M., Hettema, J. M., Jansen, R., Boomsma, D. I., & Spector, T. D. (2015). Generalized anxiety disorder: A twin study of genetic architecture, genome-wide association and differential gene expression. *PlosOne, 10*(8), e0134865

Davis, C., Levitan, R. D., Kaplan, A. S., Carter, J., Reid, C., Curtis, C., & Kennedy, J. L. (2007). Dopamine transporter gene (DAT1) associated with appetite suppression to methylphenidate in a case–control study of binge eating disorder. *Neuropsychopharmacology, 32*(10), 2199–2206.

Davis, L. (2014). Paraphilic Disorders in Women: Mental Illness or a Reaction to Untreated Trauma?. In N. L., Ishibashi (Eds.). *Arguing with the DSM-5: Reflections for the perspective of social work*, (pp. 29–39). Lulu.com: Chicago, Il.

Davis, M. (2002). Neural circuitry of anxiety and stress disorders. In K. L. Davis, D. Charney, J. T. Coyle, & C. Nemeroff (Eds.), *Neuropsychopharmacology: The fifth generation of progress* (pp. 901–930). Philadelphia, PA: Lippincott Williams & Wilkins.

Davis, N. O., & Carter, A. S. (2014). Social development in autism. In F. Volkmar, S. Rogers, R. Paul, & K. A. Pelphrey (Eds.), *Handbook of autism and pervasive developmental disorders* (4th ed., pp. 212–229). New York, NY: Wiley.

Davison, G. C. (1968). Elimination of a sadistic fantasy by a client-controlled counter- conditioning technique: A case study. *Journal of Abnormal Psychology, 73,* 91–99.

Davison, S., & Janca, A. (2012). Personality disorder and criminal behaviour: what is the nature of the relationship? *Current Opinion in Psychiatry, 25*(1), 39–45.

Davtyan, H., Ghochikyan, A., Petrushina, I., Hovakimyan, A., Davtyan, A., Poghosyan, A., . . . Larsen, A. K. (2013). Immunogenicity, efficacy, safety, and mechanism of action of epitope vaccine (Lu AF20513) for Alzheimer's disease: prelude to a clinical trial. *The Journal of Neuroscience, 33*(11), 4923–4934.

Dawson, D. A., Goldstein, R. B., & Grant, B. F. (2012). Differences in the profiles of DSM-IV and DSM-5 alcohol use disorders: Implications for clinicians. *Alcoholism: Clinical and Experimental Research,* Volume 37, Issue Supplement S1, pages E305–E313 doi: 10.1111/j.1530-0277.2012.01930.x

Dawson, D. A., Grant, B. F., Stinson, F. S., Chou, P. S., Huang, B., & Ruan, W. J. (2005). Recovery from DSM-IV alcohol dependence: United States, 2001–2002. *Addiction, 100,* 281–292.

Dawson, G., Jones, E. J. H., Merkle, K., Venema, K., Lowy, R., Faja, S., & Webb, S. J. (2012). Early behavioral intervention is associated with normalized brain activity in young children with autism. *Journal of the American Academy of Child and Adolescent Psychiatry, 51*(11), 1150–1159.

Dawson, M., Mottron, L., & Gernsbacher, M. (2008). Learning in autism. In J. H. Byrne & H. L. Roediger (Eds.), *Learning and memory: A comprehensive reference: Cognitive psychology* (pp. 759–772). New York, NY: Elsevier.

Day, R., Nielsen, J. A., Korten, A., Ernberg, G., Dube, K. C., Gebhart, J., & Olatawura, M. (1987). Stressful life events preceding the acute onset of schizophrenia: A cross-national study from the World Health Organization. *Cultural Medicine and Psychiatry, 11,* 123–205.

de Azeredo, L. A., Rovaris, D. L., Mota, N. R., Polina, E. R., Marques, F. Z., Contini, V., . . . Grevet, E. H. (2014). Further evidence for the association between a polymorphism in the promoter region of SLC6A3/DAT1 and ADHD: findings from a sample of adults. *European archives of psychiatry and clinical neuroscience, 264*(5), 401–408.

De Backer, G., Kittel, F., Kornitzer, M., & Dramaix, M. (1983). Behavior, stress, and psychosocial traits as risk factors. *Preventative Medicine, 12,* 32–36.

De Brito, S. A., & Hodgins, S. (2009). Antisocial personality disorder. In M. McMurran & R. C. Howard (Eds.), *Personality, personality disorder and violence: An evidence based approach* (pp. 133–154). New York, NY: Wiley.

De Dios, J. A. A., & Brass, S. D. (2012). New and unconventional treatments for obstructive sleep apnea. *Neurotherapeutics, 9*(4), 702–709.

De Gregorio, D., Aguilar-Valles, A., Preller, K. H., Heifets, B. D., Hibicke, M., Mitchell, J., & Gobbi, G. (2021). Hallucinogens in mental health: Preclinical and clinical studies on LSD, psilocybin, MDMA, and ketamine. *Journal of Neuroscience, 41*(5), 891–900.

de Jong, J. C., Maroda, A. J., Camacho, M., & Chen, P. G. (2020). The impact of playing a musical instrument on obstructive sleep apnea: A systematic review. *Annals of Otology, Rhinology & Laryngology, 129*(9), 924–929.

de Kleine, R. A., Hendriks, G. J., Kusters, W. J., Broekman, T. G., & van Minnen, A. (2012): A randomized placebo-controlled trial of d-cycloserine to enhance exposure therapy for posttraumatic stress disorder. *Biological Psychiatry, 71,* 962–968.

de la Fuente Garcia, S., Ritchie, C., & Luz, S. (in press). Artificial intelligence, speech, and language processing approaches to monitoring Alzheimer's disease: A systematic review. *Journal of Alzheimer's Disease.*

de Lacerda, M. C. C., & Caixeta, L. F. (2020). Neuropsychological profile of language alterations in subcortical dementia of the white and gray matter: Neuropsychology/neuropsychological profiles of dementia: Valid biomarkers? *Alzheimer's & Dementia, 16,* e044030.

de Lissovoy, V. (1961). Head banging in early childhood. *Child Development, 33,* 43–56.

de Portugal, E., González, N., Haro, J. M., Autonell, J., & Cervilla, J. A. (2008). A descriptive case-register study of delusional disorder. *European Psychiatry, 23*(2), 125–133.

De Raedt, R., Vanderhasselt, M.-A., & Baeken, C. (2015). Neurostimulation as an intervention for treatment resistant depression: From research on mechanisms towards targeted neurocognitive strategies. *Clinical Psychology Review, 41,* 61–69.

de Wit, H., & Phillips, T. J. (2012). Do initial responses to drugs predict future use or abuse? *Neuroscience & Biobehavioral Reviews, 36*(6), 1565–1576. doi: http://dx.doi.org/10.1016/j.neubiorev.2012.04.005

de Zambotti, M., Claudatos, S., Inkelis, S., Colrain, I. M., & Baker, F. C. (2015). Evaluation of a consumer fitness-tracking device to assess sleep in adults. *Chronobiology international, 32*(7), 1024–1028.

Deakin, J. F. W., & Graeff, F. G. (1991). Critique: 5-HT and mechanisms of defence. *Journal of Psychopharmacology, 5*(4), 305–315.

Deale, A., Chalder, T., Marks, I., & Wessely, S. (1997). Cognitive behavior therapy for chronic fatigue syndrome: A randomized controlled trial. *American Journal of Psychiatry, 154,* 408–414.

Deale, A., Husain, K., Chalder, T., & Wessely, S. (2001). Long-term outcome of cognitive behavioral therapy versus relaxation therapy for chronic fatigue syndrome: A 5-year follow-up study. *American Journal of Psychiatry, 158,* 2038–2042.

Debruyne, H., & Audenaert, K. (2012). Towards understanding Cotard's syndrome: An overview. *Neuropsychiatry, 2*(6), 481–486.

Decety, J., & Skelly, L. R. (2013). The neural underpinnings of the experience of empathy: Lessons for psychopathy. In K. N. Ochsner & S. M. Kosslyn (Eds), *The Oxford handbook of cognitive neuroscience, volume 2: The cutting edges* (pp. 228–243). New York, NY: Oxford University Press.

Deckersbach, T., Moshier, S. J., Tuschen-Caffier, B., & Otto, M. W. (2011). Memory dysfunction in panic disorder: An investigation of the role of chronic benzodiazepine use. *Depression and Anxiety, 28,* 999–1007. doi: 10.1002/da.20891

Deckersbach, T., Peters, A. T., Sylvia, L., Urdahl, A., Magalhães, P. V., Otto, M. W., . . . Nierenberg, A. (2014). Do comorbid anxiety disorders moderate the effects of psychotherapy for bipolar disorder? Results from STEP-BD. *American Journal of Psychiatry, 171*(2), 178–186.

Del Parigi, A., Panza, F., Capurso, C., & Solfrizzi, V. (2006). Nutritional factors, cognitive decline, and dementia. *Brain Research Bulletin, 69*(1), 1–19.

DeLamater, J., & Sill, M. (2005). Sexual desire in latter life. *Journal of Sex Research, 42,* 138–149.

Delano-Wood, L., & Abeles, N. (2005). Late-life depression: Detection, risk, reduction, and somatic intervention. *Clinical Psychology Science Practice, 12,* 207–217.

DeLisi, L. E., Maurizio, A., Yost, M., Papparozzi, C. F., Fulchino, C., Katz, C. L., Altesman, J., Biel, M., Lee, J., & Stevens, P. (2003). A survey of New Yorkers after the Sept. 11, 2001, terrorist attacks. *American Journal of Psychiatry, 160*(4), 780–783.

DeLisi, M., & Vaughn, M. G. (2015). Ingredients for criminality require genes, temperament, and psychopathic personality. *Journal of Criminal Justice, 43*(4), 290–294.

DeLisi, M., Drury, A. J., & Elbert, M. J. (2019). The etiology of antisocial personality disorder: The differential roles of adverse childhood experiences and childhood psychopathology. *Comprehensive Psychiatry, 92*, 1–6.

Delizonna, L. L., Wincze, J. P., Litz, B. T., Brown, T. A., & Barlow, D. H. (2001). A comparison of subjective and physiological measures of mechanically produced and erotically produced erections. (Or, is an erection an erection?) *Journal of Sex and Marital Therapy, 27*, 21–31.

Dell, P. F. (1998). Axis II pathology in outpatients with dissociative identity disorder. *Journal of Nervous and Mental Disease, 186*(6), 352–356.

Dell, P. F., & O'Neil, J. A. (Eds.). (2009). *Dissociation and the dissociative disorders.* New York, NY: Routledge.

Demartini, B., Nisticò, V., Edwards, M. J., Gambini, O., & Priori, A. (2021). The pathophysiology of functional movement disorders. *Neuroscience and Biobehavioral Reviews, 120*, 387–400. doi: 10.1016/j.neubiorev.2020.10.019

Dembroski, T. M., & Costa, P. T., Jr. (1987). Coronary prone behavior: Components of the Type A pattern and hostility. *Journal of Personality, 55*(2), 211–235.

Demers, C. H., Bogdan, R., & Agrawal, A. (2014). The genetics, neurogenetics and pharmacogenetics of addiction. *Current Behavioral Neuroscience Reports, 1*(1), 33–44.

Deming, P., & Koenigs, M. (2020). Functional neural correlates of psychopathy: A meta-analysis of MRI data. *Translational Psychiatry, 10*(1), 1–8.

Denis, C., Fatséas, M., & Auriacombe, M. (2012). Analyses related to the development of DSM-5 criteria for substance use related disorders: 3. An assessment of pathological gambling criteria. *Drug and Alcohol Dependence, 122*(1–2), 22–27. doi: http://dx.doi.org/10.1016/j.drugalcdep.2011.09.006

Denomme, W. J., & Shane, M. S. (2020). History of withdrawal modulates drug-and food-cue reactivity in cocaine dependent participants. *Drug and Alcohol Dependence, 208*, 107815.

Dent, M. F., & Bremner, J. D. (2009). Pharmacotherapy for posttraumatic stress disorder and other trauma-related disorders. In M. M. Antony & M. B. Stein (Eds.), *Oxford handbook of anxiety and related disorders.* (pp. 405–416). New York, NY: Oxford University Press.

Denys, D., Mantione, M., Figee, M., van den Munckhof, P., Koerselman, F., Westenberg, H., & Schuurman, R. (2010). Deep brain stimulation of the nucleus accumbens for treatment-refractory obsessive-compulsive disorder. *Archives of General Psychiatry, 67*(10), 1061–1068. doi: 10.1001/archgenpsychiatry.2010.122

Denzin, N. K. (1987). *The recovering alcoholic.* Newbury Park, CA: Sage.

Depue, R. A., Luciana, M., Arbisi, P., Collins, P., & Leon, A. (1994). Dopamine and the structure of personality: Relation of agonist-induced dopamine activity to positive emotionality. *Journal of Personality and Social Psychology, 67*, 485–498.

DeRogatis, L. R., Komer, L., Katz, M., Moreau, M., Kimura, T., Garcia, M. J., & . . . Pyke, R. (2012). Treatment of Hypoactive Sexual Desire Disorder in premenopausal women: Efficacy of flibanserin in the VIOLET Study. *Journal Of Sexual Medicine, 9*, 1074–1085. doi:10.1111/j.1743-6109.2011.02626.x

Dersh, J., Polatin, P. B., & Gatchel, R. J. (2002). Chronic pain and psychopathology: Research findings and theoretical considerations. *Psychosomatic Medicine, 64*, 773–786.

DeRubeis, R., Gelfand, L. A., Tang, T. Z., & Simons, A. D. (1999). Medications versus cognitive behavior therapy for severely depressed outpatients: Mega-analysis of four randomized comparisons. *American Journal of Psychiatry, 156*, 1007–1013.

DeRubeis, R., Hollon, S., Amsterdam, J., Shelton, R., Young, P., & Gallop, R. (2005). Cognitive therapy vs. medications in the treatment of moderate to severe depression. *Archives of General Psychiatry, 62*, 409–416.

Desantis, A., & Hane, A. (2010). "Adderall is definitely not a drug": Justifications for the illegal use of ADHD stimulants. *Substance Use & Misuse, 45*(1–2), 31–46.

DeStefano, F., Price, C. S., & Weintraub, E. S. (2013). Increasing exposure to antibody-stimulating proteins and polysaccharides in vaccines is not associated with risk of autism. *Journal of Pediatrics, 163*(2), 561–567. doi: http://dx.doi.org/10.1016/j.jpeds.2013.02.001

Devanand, D. P. (2002). Comorbid psychiatric disorders in late life depression. *Biological Psychiatry, 52*, 236–242.

Deveci, A., Taskin, O., Dinc, G., Yilmaz, H., Demet, M. M., Erbay-Dundar, P., & Ozman, E. (2007). Prevalence of pseudoneurologic conversion disorder in an urban community in Manisa, Turkey. *Social Psychiatry and Psychiatric Epidemiology, 42*(11), 857–864.

developments. Oxford: Oxford University Press.

Devlin, L. (2020). Mental abnormality and the criminal law. *Changing legal objectives* (pp. 71–86). Toronto: University of Toronto Press.

DeWall, C. N., MacDonald, G., Webster, G. D., Masten, C. L., Baumeister, R. F., Powell, C., & Eisenberger, N. I. (2010). Acetaminophen reduces social pain: Behavioral and neural evidence. *Psychological Science, 21*, 931–937.

Dhawan, N., Kunik, M. E., Oldham, J., & Coverdale, J. (2010). Prevalence and treatment of narcissistic personality disorder in the community: A systematic review. *Comprehensive Psychiatry, 51*(4), 333–339. doi: 10.1016/j.comppsych.2009.09.003

Dhejne, C., Öberg, K., Arver, S., & Landén, M. (2014). An analysis of all applications for sex reassignment surgery in Sweden, 1960–2010: Prevalence, incidence, and regrets. *Archives of Sexual Behavior, 43*(8), 1535–1545.

Di Cesare, M., Bentham, J., Stevens, G. A., Zhou, B., Danaei, G., Lu, Y., … NCD Risk Factor Collaboration (NCD-RisC). (2016). Trends in adult body-mass index in 200 countries from 1975 to 2014: A pooled analysis of 1698 population-based measurement studies with 19.2 million participants. *The Lancet, 387*(10026), 1377–1396. doi: 10.1016/S0140-6736(16)30054-X

Di Lodovico, L., Hatteea, H., Couton, C., Duriez, P., Treasure, J., & Gorwood, P. (2021). Physical exercise-related endophenotypes in anorexia nervosa. *International Journal of Eating Disorders*, doi: 10.1002/eat.23503

Diamond, L. M. (2007). A dynamical systems approach to the development and expression of female same-sex sexuality. *Perspectives on Psychological Science, 2*, 142–161.

Diamond, L. M. (2012). The desire disorder in research on sexual orientation in women: Contributions of dynamical systems theory. *Archives of Sexual Behavior, 41*(1), 73–83.

Diamond, L. M., Alley, J., Dickenson, J., & Blair, K. L. (2020). Who counts as sexually fluid? Comparing four different types of sexual fluidity in women. *Archives of Sexual Behavior, 49*(7), 2389–2403. doi: 10.1007/s10508-019-01565-

Diamond, L. M., Butterworth, M. R., & Savin-Williams, R. C. (2011). Working with sexual-minority individuals. In D. H. Barlow (Ed.), *Oxford handbook of clinical psychology.* New York, NY: Oxford University Press.

Diamond, M. (1995). Biological aspects of sexual orientation and identity. In L. Diamant & R. D. McAnulty (Eds.), *The psychology of sexual orientation, behavior, and identity.* Westport, CT: Greenwood Press.

Diamond, M., & Sigmundson, K. (1997). Sex reassignment at birth: Long-term review and clinical implications. *Archives of Pediatric and Adolescent Medicine, 151*, 298–304.

Diaz-Stransky, A., Rowley, S., Zecher, E., Grodberg, D., & Sukhodolsky, D. G. (2020). Tantrum tool: Development and open pilot study of online parent training for irritability and disruptive behavior. *Journal of Child and Adolescent Psychopharmacology, 30*(9), 558–566.

Dick, D. M. (2011). Gene-environment interaction in psychological traits and disorders. *Annual Review of Clinical Psychology, 7*, 383–409. doi: 10.1146/annurev-clinpsy-032210-104518

Dickens, G., & Sugarman, P. (2012). Adult firesetters: Prevalence, characteristics and psychopathology. In G. L. Dickens, P. A. Sugarman, & T. A. Gannon (Eds.), *Firesetting and mental health: Theory, research and practice* (pp. 3–27). London: RCPsych Publications.

Dickens, W. T., Turkheimer, E., & Beam, C. (2011). The social dynamics of the expression of genes for cognitive ability. In K. S. Kendler, S. Jaffee, & D. Romer (Eds.), *The dynamic genome and mental health: The role of genes and environments in youth development* (pp. 103–127). New York, NY: Oxford University Press.

Dickersin, K. (2010). To reform U.S. health care, start with systematic reviews. *Science, 329*, 516.

DiClemente, R. J., Crittenden, C. P., Rose, E., Sales, J. M., Wingood, G. M., Crosby, R. A., & Salazar, L. F. (2008). Psychosocial predictors of HIV-associated sexual behaviors and the efficacy of prevention interventions in adolescents at-risk for HIV infection: What works and what doesn't work? *Psychosomatic Medicine, 70*, 598–605.

DiClemente, R. J., Wingwood, G. M., Harrington, K. F., Lang, D. L., Davies, S. L., Hook, E. W., & Robillard, A. (2004). Efficacy of an HIV prevention intervention for African American adolescent girls: A randomized controlled trial. *JAMA: Journal of the American Medical Association, 292*, 171–179.

Diedrich, A., & Voderholzer, U. (2015). Obsessive–compulsive personality disorder: A current review. *Current Psychiatry Reports, 17*(2), 1-10.

Diener, E. (2000). Subjective well-being: The science of happiness, and a proposal for a national index. *American Psychologist, 55*, 34–43.

Diener, E., Oishi, S., & Lucas, R. E. (2003). Personality, culture, and subjective well-being: Emotional and cognitive evaluations of life. *Annual Review of Psychology, 54*, 403–425.

Dietz, P. M., Rose, C. E., McArthur, D., & Maenner, M. (2020). National and state estimates of adults with autism spectrum disorder. *Journal of Autism and Developmental Disorders, 50*(12), 4258–4266.

Dimberg, U., & Öhman, A. (1983). The effects of directional facial cues on electrodermal conditioning to facial stimuli. *Psychophysiology, 20*, 160–167.

Dimidjian, S., Barrera Jr., M., Martell, C., Muñoz, R. F., & Lewinsohn, P. M. (2011). The origins and current status of behavioral activation treatments for depression. *Annual Review of Clinical Psychology, 7*, 1–38.

Dimidjian, S., Martell, C., Herman-Dunn, R., & Hubley, S. (in press). Behavior activation for depression. In D. H. Barlow (Ed.), *Clinical handbook of psychological disorders: A step-by-step treatment manual* (5th ed.). New York, NY: Guilford.

Dimon, L. (2013). What witchcraft is Facebook? *The Atlantic*. Retrieved October 19, 2015 from http://www.theatlantic.com/health/archive/2013/09/what-witchcraft-is-facebook/279499/

DiNardo, P. A., Guzy, L. T., Jenkins, J. A., Bak, R. M., Tomasi, S. F., & Copeland, M. (1988). Etiology and maintenance of dog fears. *Behaviour Research and Therapy, 26*, 241–244.

Dinnel, D. L., Kleinknecht, R. A., & Tanaka-Matsumi, J. (2002). A cross-cultural comparison of social phobia symptoms. *Journal of Psychopathology and Behavioral Assessment, 24*, 75–82.

Dishion, T. J., Patterson, G. R., & Reid, J. R. (1988). Parent and peer factors associated with drug sampling in early adolescence: Implications for treatment. In E. R. Rahdert & J. Gabowski (Eds.), *Adolescent drug abuse: Analyses of treatment research* (NIDA Research Monograph No. 77, DHHS Publication No. ADM88-1523, pp. 69–93). Rockville, MD: National Institute on Drug Abuse.

Disney, K. L. (2013). Dependent personality disorder: A critical review. *Clinical Psychology Review, 33*(8), 1184-1196.

Dixon, L. B., & Lehman, A. F. (1995). Family interventions for schizophrenia. *Schizophrenia Bulletin, 21*, 631–643.

Dixon-Gordon, K. L., Weiss, N. H., Tull, M. T., DiLillo, D., Messman-Moore, T., & Gratz, K. L. (2015). Characterizing emotional dysfunction in borderline personality, major depression, and their co-occurrence. *Comprehensive Psychiatry, 62*, 187–203.

Djernes, J. K. (2006). Prevalence and predictors of depression in populations of elderly: A review. *Acta Psychiatrica Scandinavica, 113*(5), 372–387.

Docter, R. F., & Prince, V. (1997). Transvestism: A survey of 1032 cross-dressers. *Archives of Sexual Behavior, 26*, 589–605.

Doehrmann, O., Ghosh, S. S., Polli, F. E., Reynolds, G. O., Whitfield-Gabrieli, S., Hofmann, S. G., Pollack, M., & Gabrieli, J. D. (2013). Predicting treatment response in social anxiety disorder from functional magnetic resonance imaging. *JAMA Psychiatry, 70*, 87–97.

Dogan, S. (2009). Vaginismus and accompanying sexual dysfunctions in a Turkish clinical sample. *Journal of Sexual Medicine, 6*, 184–192.

Dohrenwend, B. P. Yager, T. J., Wall, M. M., & Adams, B. G. (2012). The roles of combat exposure, personal vulnerability, and involvement in harm to civilians or prisoners in Vietnam-war-related posttraumatic stress disorder. *Clinical Psychological Science, 1*, 223–238.

Dohrenwend, B. P., & Dohrenwend, B. S. (1981). Socioenvironmental factors, stress and psychopathology. *American Journal of Community Psychology, 9*(2), 128–164.

Dohrenwend, B. P., & Egri, G. (1981). Recent stressful life events and episodes of schizophrenia. *Schizophrenia Bulletin, 7*, 12–23.

Dohrenwend, B. P., Turner, J. B., & Turse, N. A. (2006). The psychological risks of Vietnam for U.S. veterans: A revisit with new data and methods. *Science, 313*, 979–982.

Dolan, M., & Völlm, B. (2009). Antisocial personality disorder and psychopathy in women: A literature review on the reliability and validity of assessment instruments. *International Journal of Law and Psychiatry, 32*(1), 2–9.

Dolui, S., Li, Z., Nasrallah, I. M., Detre, J. A., & Wolk, D. A. (2020). Arterial spin labeling versus 18F-FDG-PET to identify mild cognitive impairment. *NeuroImage: Clinical, 25*, 102146.

Dominé, F., Berchtold, A., Akré, C., Michaud, P.-A., & Suris, J.-C. (2009). Disordered eating behaviors: What about boys? *Journal of Adolescent Health, 44*(2), 111–117.

Domínguez-Salas, S., Gómez-Salgado, J., Andrés-Villas, M., Díaz-Milanés, D., Romero-Martín, M., & Ruiz-Frutos, C. (2020). Psycho-emotional approach to the psychological distress related to the COVID-19 pandemic in Spain: A cross-sectional observational study. *Healthcare (Basel), 8*(3), 190.

Domino, E. F., & Miller, S. C. (2015). The pharmacology of dissociatives. In R. K. Ries, D. A. Fiellin, S. C. Miller, & R. Saitz (Eds.), *The ASAM principles of addiction medicine* (5th ed., pp. 256–266). New York, NY: Wolters Kluwer.

Domschke, K., & Dannlowski, U. (2010). Imaging genetics of anxiety disorders. *NeuroImage, 53*, 822–831.

Donaldson, K. (1976). *Insanity inside out*. New York, NY: Crown.

Donath, C., Gräßel, E., Baier, D., Pfeiffer, C., Bleich, S., & Hillemacher, T. (2012). Predictors of binge drinking in adolescents: ultimate and distal factors—a representative study. *BMC Public Health, 12*(1), 263–278.

Dong, F., Liu, J., Hodgson, N. A., & Medoff-Cooper, B. (in press). Early life factors of schizotypal personality disorder in adolescents: A systematic review. Journal of Psychiatric and Mental Health Nursing. doi: https://doi.org/10.1111/jpm.12733

Dougall, N., Maayan, N., Soares-Weiser, K., McDermott, L. M., & McIntosh, A. (2015). Transcranial magnetic stimulation for schizophrenia. *Schizophrenia Bulletin, 41*(6), 1220–1222.

Dougherty, D. D., Rauch, S. L., & Jenike, M. A. (2012). Pharmacological treatments for obsessive compulsive disorder. In G. Steketee (Ed.), *The Oxford handbook of obsessive compulsive and spectrum disorders* (pp. 291–306). New York, NY: Oxford University Press.

Douglas, K. S., Guy, L. S., & Hart, S. D. (2009). Psychosis as a risk factor for violence to others: A meta-analysis. *Psychological Bulletin, 135*(5), 679–706. doi: 10.1037/a0016311

Douglas, K. S., Nikolova, N. L., Kelley, S. E., Edens, J. F., Cutler, B. L. (Ed.), & Zapf, P. A. (Ed.). (2015). *APA handbook of forensic psychology, Vol. 1: Individual and situational influences in criminal and civil contexts.* Washington, DC: American Psychological Association.

Douzgou, S., Breen, C., Crow, Y. J., Chandler, K., Metcalfe, K., Jones, E., & Clayton-Smith, J. (2012). Diagnosing fetal alcohol syndrome: new insights from newer genetic technologies. *Archives of Disease in Childhood, 97*(9), 812–817. doi: 10.1136/archdischild-2012-302125

Dowling, N., Smith, D., & Thomas, T. (2007). A comparison of individual and group cognitive-behavioural treatment for female pathological gambling. *Behaviour Research and Therapy 45*(9), 2192–2202.

Dragioti, E., Dimoliatis, I., Fountoulakis, K. N., & Evangelou, E. (2015). A systematic appraisal of allegiance effect in randomized controlled trials of psychotherapy. *Annals of General Psychiatry, 14*(1), 25–33. doi:10.1186/s12991-015-0063-1

Dragioti, E., Dimoliatis, I., Fountoulakis, K. N., & Evangelou, E. (2015). A systematic appraisal of allegiance effect in randomized controlled trials of psychotherapy. *Annals of General Psychiatry, 14*(1), 1–9.

Drake, R., Bond, G., & Becker, D. (2012). *Individual placement and support: An evidence-based approach to supported employment.* New York, NY: Oxford.

Drogin, E. Y., Commons, M. L., Gutheil, T. G., Meyer, D. J., & Norris, D. M. (2012). "Certainty" and expert mental health opinions in legal proceedings. *International Journal of Law and Psychiatry, 35*(5–6), 348-353. doi: http://dx.doi.org/10.1016/j.ijlp.2012.09.002

Drummond, K. D., Bradley, S. J., Peterson-Badali, M., & Zucker, K. J. (2008). A follow-up study of girls with gender identity disorder. *Developmental Psychology, 44*, 34–45.

Du, J., Fan, N., Zhao, M., Hao, W., Liu, T., Lu, L., … Lan, X. (2020). Expert consensus on the prevention and treatment of substance use and addictive behaviour-related disorders during the COVID-19 pandemic. *General Psychiatry, 33*(4).

Dubovsky, S. L. (1983). Psychiatry in Saudi Arabia. *American Journal of Psychiatry, 140*(11), 1455–1459.

Duclos, J., Vibert, S., Mattar, L., & Godart, N. (2012). Expressed emotion in families of patients with eating disorders: a review of the literature. *Current Psychiatry Reviews, 8*(3), 183–202.

Dugas, M. J., Schwartz, A., & Francis, K. (2012). Intolerance of uncertainty, fear of anxiety, and adolescent worry. *Journal of Abnormal Child Psychology, 40*, 863–870.

Dulit, R. A., Marin, D. B., & Frances, A. J. (1993). Cluster B personality disorders. In D. L. Dunner (Ed.), *Current psychiatric therapy* (pp. 405–411). Philadelphia, PA: W. B. Saunders.

Duman, R. (2004). Depression: A case of neuronal life and death? *Biological Psychiatry, 56*, 140–145.

Dummit, E. S., Klein, R. G., Tancer, N. K., Asche, B., Martin, J., & Fairbanks, J. A. (1997). Systematic assessment of 50 children with selective mutism. *Journal of the American Academy of Child and Adolescent Psychiatry, 36*(5), 653–660. doi: 10.1097/00004583-199705000-00016

Dunlop, B. W., & Nemeroff, C. B. (2007). The role of dopamine in the pathophysiology of depression. *Archives of General Psychiatry, 64*(3), 327–337.

Dunn Davison, M., Qi, C. H., & Kaiser, A. P. (2020). Enhanced milieu teaching strategies for preschool children with autism spectrum disorder. *Young Exceptional Children*, 1096250620928335.

DuPaul, G. J., Evans, S. W., Mautone, J. A., Owens, J. S., & Power, T. J. (2020). Future directions for psychosocial interventions for children and adolescents with ADHD. *Journal of Clinical Child & Adolescent Psychology, 49*(1), 134–145.

DuPaul, G. J., Gormley, M. J., & Laracy, S. D. (2013). Comorbidity of LD and ADHD: Implications of DSM-5 for assessment and treatment. *Journal of Learning Disabilities, 46*(1), 43–51. doi: 10.1177/0022219412464351

Durand, V. M. (1990). *Severe behavior problems: A functional communication training approach*. New York, NY: Guilford.

Durand, V. M. (1998). *Sleep better: A guide to improving the sleep of children with special needs.* Baltimore, MD: Paul H. Brookes.

Durand, V. M. (1999). Functional communication training using assistive devices: Recruiting natural communities of reinforcement. *Journal of Applied Behavior Analysis, 32*(3), 247–267.

Durand, V. M. (2001). Future directions for children and adolescents with mental retardation. *Behavior Therapy, 32*, 633–650.

Durand, V. M. (2006). Sleep terrors. In J. E. Fisher & W. T. O'Donohue (Eds.), *Evidence-based psychotherapy* (pp. 654–659). Reno, NV: Springer.

Durand, V. M. (2008). *When children don't sleep well: Interventions for pediatric sleep disorders, Therapist guide*. New York, NY: Oxford University Press.

Durand, V. M. (2011). Disorders of development. In D. H. Barlow, (Ed.), *Oxford handbook of clinical psychology* (pp., 551–573). New York, NY: Oxford University Press.

Durand, V. M. (2014). *Autism spectrum disorder: A clinical guide for general practitioners*. Washington, D.C.: American Psychological Association.

Durand, V. M. (2014b). *Disorders of development.* In D. H. Barlow (Ed.), Oxford handbook of clinical psychology: Revised edition (pp. 558–581). New York, NY: Oxford University.

Durand, V. M. (2014c). *Sleep better!: A guide to improving sleep for children with special needs (revised edition).* Baltimore, MD: Paul H. Brookes.

Durand, V. M. (in press). Supporting families with children who display severe challenging behavior. *Research and Practice for Persons with Severe Disabilities.*

Durand, V. M., & Carr, E. G. (1992). An analysis of maintenance following functional communication training. *Journal of Applied Behavior Analysis, 25*(4), 777–794.

Durand, V. M., & Hieneman, M. (2008). *Helping parents with challenging children: Positive family intervention, Facilitator's guide*. New York, NY: Oxford University Press.

Durand, V. M., & Mindell, J. A. (1999). Behavioral intervention for childhood sleep terrors. *Behavior Therapy, 30*, 705–715.

Durand, V. M., & Moskowitz, L. (2015). Functional communication training: Thirty years of treating challenging behavior. *Topics in Early Childhood Special Education, 35*(2), 116–126. doi: 10.1177/0271121415569509

Durand, V. M., & Moskowitz, L. (2019). Functional communication training: Thirty years of treating challenging behavior. *Topics in Early Childhood Special Education, 6*(3), 138–144. doi: 10.1177/0271121415569509

Durand, V. M., & Wang, M. (2011). Clinical trials. In J. C. Thomas & M. Hersen (Eds.), *Understanding research in clinical and counseling psychology,* (pp. 201–228). New York, NY: Routledge.

Durand, V. M., Hieneman, M., Clarke, S., Wang, M., & Rinaldi, M. (2013). Positive family intervention for severe challenging behavior I: A multi-site randomized clinical trial. *Journal of Positive Behavior Interventions, 15*(3), 133–143.

Durand, V. M. (2014a). *Autism spectrum disorder: A clinical guide for general practitioners*. Washington, D.C.: American Psychological Association.

Durant, C., Christmas, D., & Nutt, D. (2010). The pharmacology of anxiety. *Current Topics in Behavioral Neurosciences, 2,* 303–330.

Durham v. United States, 214 F.2d, 862, 874-875 (D.C. Cir., 1954).

Durham, M. L., & La Fond, J. Q. (1985). The empirical consequences and policy implications of broadening the statutory criteria for civil commitment. *Yale Law and Policy Review, 3,* 395–446.

During, E. H. (2021a). Introduction. In E. H. During & C. A. Kushida (Eds.), *Clinical sleep medicine: A comprehensive guide for mental health and other medical professionals* (pp. 1–15). Washington, D.C.: American Psychiatric Association Publishing.

During, E. H. (2021b). Pharmacological treatment of insomnia. In E. H. During & C. A. Kushida (Eds.), *Clinical sleep medicine: A comprehensive guide for mental health and other medical professionals* (pp. 61–77). Washington, D.C.: American Psychiatric Association Publishing.

Durkheim, E. (1951). *Suicide: A study in sociology.* (J. A. Spaulding & G. Simpson, Trans.). New York, NY: Free Press.

Durkin, M. S., Maenner, M. J., Newschaffer, C. J., Lee, L. C., Cunniff, C. M., Daniels, J. L., & Zahorodny, W. (2008). Advanced parental age and the risk of autism spectrum disorder. *American Journal of Epidemiology, 168*(11), 1268–1276.

Dürsteler, K. M., Berger, E. M., Strasser, J., Caflisch, C., Mutschler, J., Herdener, M., & Vogel, M. (2015). Clinical potential of methylphenidate in the treatment of cocaine addiction: a review of the current evidence. *Substance abuse and rehabilitation, 6,* 61–74.

Dusky v. United States, 362 U.S. 402 (1960).

Dusseldorp, E., van Elderen, T., Maes, S., Meulman, J., & Kraaij, V. (1999). A meta-analysis of psychoeducational programs for coronary heart disease patients. *Health Psychology, 18,* 506–519.

Dustin, M. L., & Long, E. O. (2010). Cytotoxic immunological synapses. *Immunological Review, 235,* 24–34.

Dvorak-Bertscha, J., Curtin, J., Rubinstein, T., & Newman, J. (2009). Psychopathic traits moderate the interaction between cognitive and affective processing. *Psychophysiology, 46*(5), 913.

Dvoskin, J. A., Knoll, J. L., & Silva, M. (2020). A brief history of the criminalization of mental illness. *CNS Spectrums, 25*(5), 638–650.

Dwyer, J. B., Aftab, A., Widge, A., Rodriguez, C. I., Carpenter, L. L., Nemeroff, C. B., … Kalin, N. H. (2020). Hormonal treatments for major depressive disorder: State of the art. *American Journal of Psychiatry, 177*(8), 686–705. doi: 10.1176/appi.ajp.2020.19080848

Dysken, M. W., Sano, M., Asthana, S., Vertrees, J. E., Pallaki, M., Llorente, M., . . . Prieto, S. (2014). Effect of vitamin E and memantine on functional decline in Alzheimer disease: the TEAM-AD VA cooperative randomized trial. *JAMA, 311*(1), 33–44.

Dzau, V. J., & Pizzo, P. A. (2014). Relieving Pain in America: Insights from an Institute of Medicine committee. *JAMA, 312*(15), 1507–1508.

Eastman, C. I., Young, M. A., Fogg, L. F., Liu, L., & Meaden, P. M. (1998). Bright light treatment of winter depression: A placebo-controlled trial. *Archives of General Psychiatry, 55*(10), 883–889.

Eaton, W. W., Kessler, R. C., Wittchen, H.-U., & McGee, W. J. (1994). Panic and panic disorder in the United States. *American Journal of Psychiatry, 151,* 413–420.

Eaton, W. W., Shao, H., Nestadt, G., Lee, H. B., Bienvenu, O. J., & Zandi, P. (2008). Population-based study of first onset and chronicity in major depressive disorder. *Archives of General Psychiatry, 65*(5), 513–520.

Ebigno, P. (1982). Development of a culture- specific screening scale of somatic complaints indicating psychiatric disturbance. *Culture, Medicine, and Psychiatry, 6*(1), 29–43.

Ebigno, P. O. (1986). A cross sectional study of somatic complaints of Nigerian females using the Enugu Somatization Scale. *Culture, Medicine, and Psychiatry, 10,* 167–186.

Ebringer, A. (2015). *Creutzfeldt-Jakob Disease and its variants.* In Multiple sclerosis, mad cow disease and acinetobacter (pp. 141–152). London, UK: Springer International Publishing.

Eckman, T. A., Wirshing, W. C., Marder, S. R., Liberman, R. P., Johnston-Cronk, K., Zimmermann, K., & Mintz, J. (1992). Techniques for training schizophrenic patients in illness self-management: A controlled trial. *American Journal of Psychiatry, 149,* 1549–1555.

Eddy, K. T., Dorer, D. J., Franko, D. L., Tahilani, K., Thompson-Brenner, H., & Herzog, D. B. (2008). Diagnostic crossover in anorexia nervosa and bulimia nervosa: Implications for DSM-V. *American Journal of Psychiatry, 165*(2), 245–250.

Eddy, K. T., Keel, P. K., Dorer, D. J., Delinsky, S. S., Franko, D. L., & Herzog, D. B. (2002). A longitudinal comparison of anorexia nervosa subtypes. *International Journal of Eating Disorders, 31,* 191–201.

Edwards, A. C., & Kendler, K. S. (2012). A twin study of depression and nicotine dependence: Shared liability or causal relationship? *Journal of Affective Disorders, 142*(1–3), 90–97. doi: http://dx.doi.org/10.1016/j.jad.2012.03.048

Edwards, A. J. (1994). *When memory fails: Helping the Alzheimer's and dementia patient.* New York, NY: Plenum Press.

Edwards, G. (2012). "The Evil Genius of the Habit": DSM-5 seen in historical context. *Journal of Studies on Alcohol and Drugs, 73*(4), 699.

Edwards, R. R., Campbell, C., Jamison, R. N., & Wiech, K. (2009). The neurobiological underpinnings of coping with pain. *Current Directions in Psychological Science, 18,* 237–241.

Eelen, P., & Vervliet, B. (2006). Fear conditioning and clinical implications: What can we learn from the past? In M. G. Craske, D. Hermans, & D. Vansteenwegen, *Fear and learning: From basic processes to clinical implications* (pp. 17–35). Washington, DC: American Psychological Association.

Eftekhari, A., Ruzek, J. L., Crowley, J. J., Rosen, C. S., Greenbaum, M. A., & Karlin, B. E. (2013). Effectiveness of national implementation of prolonged exposure therapy in veterans affairs care. *JAMA Psychiatry, 70,* 949–955.

Egan, B. M., Zhao, Y., & Axon, R. N. (2010). US trends in prevalence, awareness, treatment, and control of hypertension. *JAMA: Journal of the American Medical Association, 303,* 2043–2050.

Egeland, J. A., Gerhard, D. S., Pauls, D. L., Sussex, J. N., Kidd, K. K., Alien, C. R., . . . Housman, D. E. (1987). Bipolar affective

disorders linked to DNA markers on chromosome 11. *Nature, 325*(6107), 783–787.
Ehlers, A., & Clark, D. M. (2003). Early psychological interventions for adult survivors of trauma: A review. *Biological Psychiatry, 53,* 817–826.
Ehlers, A., Clark, D. M., Hackmann, A., McManus, F., Fennell, M., Herbert, C., & Mayou, R. (2003). A randomized controlled trial of cognitive therapy, a self-help booklet, and repeated assessments as early interventions for posttraumatic stress disorder. *Archives of General Psychiatry, 60,* 1024–1032.
Ehlers, A., Hackmann, A., Grey, N., Wild, J., Liness, S., Albert, I., Deale, A., Stott, R., & Clark, D. M. (2014). A randomized controlled trial of 7-day intensive and standard weekly cognitive therapy for PTSD and emotion-focused supportive therapy. *American Journal of Psychiatry, 171,* 294–304.
Ehlers, A., Hofmann, S. G., Herda, C. A., & Roth, W. T. (1994). Clinical characteristics of driving phobia. *Journal of Anxiety Disorders, 8,* 323–339.
Ehrenreich, J. T., Goldstein, C. R., Wright, L. R., & Barlow, D. H. (2009). Development of a unified protocol for the treatment of emotional disorders in youth. *Child & Family Behavior Therapy, 31*(1), 20–37.
Ehrhardt, A. A., & Meyer-Bahlburg, H. F. L. (1981). Effects of prenatal sex hormones on gender-related behavior. *Science, 211,* 1312–1318.
Ehrhardt, A. A., Meyer-Bahlburg, H. F. L., Rosen, L. R., Feldman, J. F., Veridiano, N. P., Zimmerman, I., & McEwen, B. (1985). Sexual orientation after prenatal exposure to exogenous estrogen. *Archives of Sexual Behavior, 14*(1), 57–77.
Eikenaes, I., Egeland, J., Hummelen, B., & Wilberg, T. (2015). Avoidant Personality Disorder versus Social Phobia: The Significance of Childhood Neglect. *PloS one, 10*(3), e0122846.
Eikenæs, I., Pedersen, G., & Wilberg, T. (2016). Attachment styles in patients with avoidant personality disorder compared with social phobia. *Psychology and Psychotherapy: Theory, Research and Practice. 89*(3), 245–260.
Eilert, N., Enrique, A., Wogan, R., Mooney, O., Timulak, L., & Richards, D. (2021). The effectiveness of internet-delivered treatment for generalized anxiety disorder: An updated systematic review and meta-analysis. *Depression and Anxiety, 38*(2), 196–219. doi:10.1002/da.23115
Eisenberger, N. I. (2012). The neural bases of social pain: Evidence for shared representations with physical pain. *Psychosomatic Medicine, 74*(2), 126–135.
Eisler, I., Dare, C., Hodes, M., Russell, G. F. M., Dodge, E., & Le Grange, D. (2000). Family therapy for adolescent anorexia nervosa: The results of a controlled comparison of two family interventions. *Journal of Child Psychology and Psychiatry, 41,* 727–736.
Ekstrand, M. L., & Coates, T. J. (1990). Maintenance of safer sexual behaviors and predictors of risky sex: The San Francisco men's health study. *American Journal of Public Health, 80,* 973–977.
Elbedour, S., Shulman, S., & Kedem, P. (1997). Children's fears: Cultural and developmental perspectives. *Behavior Research and Therapy, 35,* 491–496.
Eldevik, S., Jahr, E., Eikeseth, S., Hastings, R. P., & Hughes, C. J. (2010). Cognitive and adaptive behavior outcomes of behavioral intervention for young children with intellectual disability. *Behavior Modification, 34*(1), 16–34.
Eley, T. C. (2011). The interplay between genes and environment in the development of anxiety and depression. In K. S. Kendler, S. Jaffee, & D. Romer (Eds.), *The dynamic genome and mental health: The role of genes and environments in youth development* (pp. 229–254). New York, NY: Oxford University Press.
El-Gabalawy, R., Mackenzie, C. S., Thibodeau, M. A., Asmundson, G. J. G., & Sareen, J. (2013). Health anxiety disorders in older adults: Conceptualizing complex conditions in late life. *Clinical Psychology Review, 33,* 1096–1105.
Elkins, I. J., Saunders, G. R., Malone, S. M., Wilson, S., McGue, M., & Iacono, W. G. (2020). Differential implications of persistent, remitted, and late-onset ADHD symptoms for substance abuse in women and men: A twin study from ages 11 to 24. *Drug and Alcohol Dependence, 212,* 107947.
Ellason, J. W., & Ross, C. A. (1997). Two-year follow up of inpatients with dissociative identity disorder. *American Journal of Psychiatry, 154,* 832–839.
Ellis, P. M., & Dronsfield, A. T. (2013). Antabuse's diamond anniversary: Still sparkling on? *Drug and Alcohol Review, 32*(4), 342–344.
Elovainio, M., Kivimäki, M., Viikari, J., Ekelund, J., & Keltikangas-Järvinen, L. (2005). The mediating role of novelty seeking in the association between the type 4 dopamine receptor gene polymorphism and cigarette-smoking behavior. *Personality and Individual Differences, 38*(3), 639–645.
Emery, C. F., Anderson, D. R., & Andersen, B. L. (2011). Psychological interventions in health care settings. In D. H. Barlow (Ed.), *Oxford handbook of clinical psychology.* (pp. 701–716). New York, NY: Oxford University Press.
Emmelkamp, P. M. G., Benner, A., Kuipers, A., Feiertag, G. A., Koster, H. C., & van Apeldoorn, F. J. (2006). Comparison of brief dynamic and cognitive-behavioural therapies in avoidant personality disorder. *The British Journal of Psychiatry, 189*(1), 60–64.
Emsley, R., Chiliza, B., Asmal, L., & Harvey, B. H. (2013). The nature of relapse in schizophrenia. *BMC Psychiatry, 13*(1), 50.
England, P., & Bearak, J. (2014). The sexual double standard and gender differences in attitudes toward casual sex among US university students. *Demographic Research, 30,* 1327–1338.
Epperson, C. N., Steiner, M., Hartlage, S. A., Eriksson, E., Schmidt, P. J., Jones, I., & Yonkers, K. A. (2012). Premenstrual dysphoric disorder: Evidence for a new category for DSM-5. *American Journal of Psychiatry, 169*(5), 465–475.
Epstein, D. R., Sidani, S., Bootzin, R. R., & Belyea, M. J. (2012). Dismantling multicomponent behavioral treatment for insomnia in older adults: A randomized controlled trial. *Sleep, 35*(6), 797–805.
Epstein, L. H., Myers, M. D., Raynor, H., & Saelens, B. E. (1998). Treatment of pediatric obesity. *Pediatrics, 101,* 554–570.
Eranti, S., Mogg, A., Pluck, G., Landau, S., Purvis, R., Brown, R. G., & McLoughlin, D. M. (2007). A randomized, controlled trial with 6-month follow-up of repetitive transcranial magnetic stimulation and electroconvulsive therapy for severe depression. *American Journal of Psychiatry, 164*(1), 73–81.
Erath, S. A., Bierman, K. L., & Conduct Problems Prevention Research Group. (2006). Aggressive marital conflict, maternal harsh punishment, and child aggressive-disruptive behavior: Evidence for direct and mediated relations. *Journal of Family Psychology, 20,* 217–226.
Erikson, E. (1982). *The life cycle completed.* New York, NY: Norton.
Erlangsen, A., Stenager, E., Conwell, Y., Andersen, P. K., Hawton, K., Benros, M. E., … Stenager, E. (2020). Association between neurological disorders and death by suicide in Denmark. *JAMA, 23*(5), 444–454. doi: 10.1001/jama.2019.21834
Erlich, M. D., Smith, T. E., Horwath, E., & Cournos, F. (2014). Schizophrenia and other psychotic disorders. In J. L. Cutler (Ed), *Psychiatry* (pp. 97–128). New York, NY: Oxford University Press.
Eroglu, C., & Barres, B. A. (2010). Regulation of synaptic connectivity by glia. *Nature, 468*(7321), 223–231. doi: 10.1038/nature 09612

Eron, L., & Huesmann, R. (1990). The stability of aggressive behavior: Even unto the third generation. In M. Lewis & S. Miller (Eds.), *Handbook of developmental psychopathology* (pp. 147–156). New York, NY: Plenum.

Ersche, K. D., Jones, P. S., Williams, G. B., Robbins, T. W., & Bullmore, E. T. (2012). Cocaine dependence: A fast-track for brain ageing? *Molecular Psychiatry. 18*, 134–135. doi: http://www.nature.com/mp/journal/vaop/ncurrent/suppinfo/mp201231s1.html

Escobar, J. I., Gara, M. A., Diaz-Martinez, A. M., Interian, A., Warman, M., Allen, L. A., & Rodgers, D. (2007). Effectiveness of a time-
limited cognitive behavior therapy type intervention among primary care patients with medically unexplained symptoms. *Annals of Family Medicine, 5*(4), 328–335.

Escobar, M. J., Huepe, D., Decety, J., Sedeño, L., Messow, M. K., Baez, S., . . . Schröeder, J. (2014). Brain signatures of moral sensitivity in adolescents with early social deprivation. *Scientific Reports, 4*.

Eser, D., Schule, C., Baghai, T. C., Romeo, E., & Rupprecht, R. (2006). Neuroactive steroids in depression and anxiety disorders: Clinical studies. *Neuroendocrinology, 84*(4), 244–254.

Eslinger, P. J., & Damasio, A. R. (1985). Severe disturbance of higher cognition after bilateral frontal lobe ablation: Patient EVR. *Neurology, 35*, 1731–1741.

Esparza-Romero, J., Valencia, M. E., Urquidez-Romero, R., Chaudhari, L. S., Hanson, R. L., Knowler, W. C., . . . Schulz, L. O. (2015). Environmentally driven increases in type 2 diabetes and obesity in Pima Indians and non-Pimas in Mexico over a 15-year period: the Maycoba Project. *Diabetes Care, 38*(11), 2075–2082.

Essex, M. J., Klein, M. H., Slattery, M. J., Goldsmith, H. H., & Kalin, N. H. (2010). Early risk factors and developmental pathways to chronic high inhibition and social anxiety disorder in adolescence. *American Journal of Psychiatry, 167*(1), 40–46. doi: 10.1176/appi.ajp.2009.07010051

Eth, S. (1990). Posttraumatic stress disorder in childhood. In M. Hersen & C. G. Last (Ed.), *Handbook of child and adult psychopathology: A longitudinal perspective*. Elmsford, NY: Pergamon Press.

Etkin, A., & Schatzberg, A. F. (2011). Common abnormalities and disorder-specific compensation during implicit regulation of emotional processing in generalized anxiety and major depressive disorders. *American Journal of Psychiatry, 168*(9), 968–978.

Etter, J. (2009). Dependence on the nicotine gum in former smokers. *Addictive Behaviors, 34*(3), 246–251.

Ettinger, A. B., Devinsky, O., Weisbrot, D. M., Ramakrishna, R. K., & Goyal, A. (1999). A comprehensive profile of clinical, psychiatric, and psychosocial characteristics of patients with psychogenic nonepileptic seizures. *Epilepsia, 40*(9), 1292–1298.

Eva, A., Imane, B., Jean-Baptiste, H., Aminata, S., Françoise, A.-L., Déborah, S., & Jean-Luc, R. (2021). International study of the prevalence and factors associated with insomnia in the general population. *Sleep Medicine*.

Evans, R. M., Emsley, C. L., Gao, S., Sahota, A., Hall, K. S., Farlow, M. R., & Hendrie, H. (2000). Serum cholesterol, APOE genotype, and the risk of Alzheimer's disease: A population-based study of African Americans. *Neurology, 54*, 240–242.

Evans, R., Widman, L., Stokes, M. N., Javidi, H., Hope, E. C., & Brasileiro, J. (2020). Association of sexual health interventions with sexual health outcomes in black adolescents: A systematic review and meta-analysis. *JAMA Pediatrics, 174*(7), 676–689. doi: 10.1001/jamapediatrics.2020.0382

Evans, S. M., & Reed, S. C. (in press). Impulsivity and the effects of alcohol in women with a history of childhood sexual abuse: A pilot study. *Experimental and Clinical Psychopharmacology*.

Evrensel, A., & Tarhan, K. N. (2021). Emerging role of gut-microbiota-brain axis in depression and therapeutic implication. *Progress in Neuro-Psychopharmacology and Biological Psychiatry, 106*. doi: 10.1016/j.pnpbp.2020.110138

Exner, J. E. (2003). *The Rorschach: A comprehensive system. Basic foundations and principles of interpretation* (4th ed.). New York, NY: Wiley.

Eysenck, M. W. (1992). Anxiety: The cognitive perspective. Lawrence Erlbaum Associates, Inc. Eysenck, H. J. (Ed.) (1967). *The biological basis of personality*. Springfield, IL: Charles C. Thomas.

Ezrati-Vinacour, R., & Levin, I. (2004). The relationship between anxiety and stuttering: A multidimensional approach. *Journal of Fluency Disorders, 29*(2), 135–148.

Ezzati, M., & Riboli, E. (2012). Can noncommunicable diseases be prevented? Lessons from studies of populations and individuals. *Science, 337*(6101), 1482–1487.

Ezzel, C. (1993). On borrowed time: Long-term survivors of HIV-l infection. *Journal of NIH Research, 5*, 77–82.

Fabiano, G. A., & Schatz, N. K. (2015). Driving risk interventions for teens with ADHD. In R. A. Barkley (Ed.), *Attention-deficit hyperactivity disorder: A handbook for diagnosis & treatment* (4th ed., pp. 705–727). New York, NY: The Guilford Press.

Fagan, P. J., Wise, T. N., Schmidt, C. W., & Berlin, M. D. (2002). Pedophilia. *JAMA: Journal of the American Medical Association, 288*, 2458–2465.

Fagundes, C. P., & Way, B. (2014). Early-life stress and adult inflammation. *Current Directions in Psychological Science, 23*(4), 277–283.

Fagundes, C. P., Glaser, R., Johnson, S. L., Andridge, R. R., Yang, E. V., Di Gregorio, M. P., & Kiecolt-Glaser, J. K. (2012). Basal cell carcinoma: Stressful life events and the tumor environment. *Archives of General Psychiatry, 69*(6), 618–626.

Fahrner, E. M. (1987). Sexual dysfunction in male alcohol addicts: Prevalence and treatment. *Archives of Sexual Behavior, 16*(3), 247–257.

Failer, J. L. (2002). *Who qualifies for rights? Homelessness, mental illness, and civil commitment*. Ithaca, NY: Cornell University Press.

Fairburn, C. G., Cooper, Z., & Shafran, R. (2003, May). Cognitive behaviour therapy for eating disorders: a "transdiagnostic" theory and treatment. Behav Res Ther. 41(5):509–28. doi: 10.1016/s0005-7967(02)00088-8.

Fairburn, C. G. (1985). Cognitive
-behavioral treatment for bulimia. In D. M. Garner & P. E. Garfinkel (Eds.), *Handbook of psychotherapy for anorexia nervosa and bulimia* (pp. 160–192). New York, NY: Guilford.

Fairburn, C. G. (2008). *Cognitive behavior therapy and eating disorders*. New York, NY: Guilford.

Fairburn, C. G. (2013). *Overcoming binge eating* (2nd ed.). New York, NY: Guilford.

Fairburn, C. G., & Bohn, K. (2005). Eating disorder NOS (EDNOS): An example of the troublesome 'not otherwise specified' (NOS) category in DSM-IV. *Behaviour Research and Therapy, 43*(6), 691–701.

Fairburn, C. G., & Brownell, K. D. (2002). *Eating disorders and obesity: A comprehensive handbook* (2nd ed.). New York, NY: Guilford.

Fairburn, C. G., & Cooper, Z. (1993). The eating disorder examination. In C. G. Fairburn & G. T. Wilson (Eds.), *Binge eating: Nature, assessment, and treatment*. (pp. 317–360). New York, NY: Guilford.

Fairburn, C. G., & Cooper, Z. (in press). Eating disorders: A transdiagnostic protocol. In D. H. Barlow (Ed.), *Clinical handbook of psychological disorders: A step-by-step treatment manual* (5th ed.). New York, NY: Guilford.

Fairburn, C. G., Agras, W. S., & Wilson, G. T. (1992). The research on the treatment of bulimia nervosa: Practical and theoretical implications. In G. H. Anderson & S. H. Kennedy (Eds.), *The biology of feast and famine: Relevance to eating disorders* (pp. 317–340). New York, NY: Academic Press.

Fairburn, C. G., Cooper, Z., & Cooper, P. J. (1986). The clinical features and maintenance of bulimia nervosa. In K. D. Brownell & J. P. Foreyt (Eds.), *Handbook of eating disorders: Physiology, psychology, and treatment of obesity, anorexia, and bulimia* (pp. 389–404). New York, NY: Basic Books.

Fairburn, C. G., Cooper, Z., & Shafran, R. (2003). Cognitive behavior therapy for eating disorders: A "transdiagnostic" theory and treatment. *Behaviour Research and Therapy, 41*, 509–528.

Fairburn, C. G., Cooper, Z., Bohn, K., O'Connor, M. E., Doll, H. A., & Palmer, R. L. (2007). The severity and status of eating disorder NOS: Implications for DSM-V. *Behavior Research and Therapy, 45*, 1705–1715.

Fairburn, C. G., Cooper, Z., Doll, H. A., & Davies, B. A. (2005). Identifying dieters who will develop an eating disorder: A prospective, population-based study. *American Journal of Psychiatry, 162*, 2249–2255.

Fairburn, C. G., Cooper, Z., Doll, H. A., & Welch, S. L. (1999). Risk factors for anorexia nervosa: Three integrated case-control comparisons. *Archives of General Psychiatry, 56*, 468–476.

Fairburn, C. G., Cooper, Z., Doll, H. A., Norman, P., & O'Connor, M. (2000). The natural course of bulimia nervosa and binge eating disorder in young women. *Archives of General Psychiatry, 57*, 659–665.

Fairburn, C. G., Cooper, Z., Doll, H. A., O'Connor, M. E., Bohn, K., Hawker, D. M., & Palmer, R. L. (2009). Transdiagnostic cognitive-behavioral therapy for patients with eating disorders: A two-site trial with 60-week follow-up. *American Journal of Psychiatry, 166*, 311–319.

Fairburn, C. G., Cooper, Z., Doll, H. A., Palmer, R. L., & Dalle Grave, R. (2013). Enhanced cognitive behaviour therapy for adults with anorexia nervosa: A UK-Italy study. *Behaviour Research and Therapy, 51*(1), R2–R8.

Fairburn, C. G., Cowen, P. J., & Harrison, P. J. (1999). Twin studies and the etiology of eating disorders. *International Journal of Eating Disorders, 26*(4), 349–358.

Fairburn, C. G., Doll, H. A., Welch, S. L., Hay, P. J., Davies, B. A., & O'Connor, M. E. (1998). Risk factors for binge eating disorder. *Archives of General Psychiatry, 55*, 425–432.

Fairburn, C. G., Jones, R., Peveler, R. C., Hope, R. A., & O'Connor, M. (1993). Psychotherapy and bulimia nervosa: The longer-term effects of interpersonal psychotherapy, behaviour therapy and cognitive behaviour therapy. *Archives of General Psychiatry, 50*, 419–428.

Fairburn, C. G., Shafran, R., & Cooper, Z. (1999). A cognitive behavioural theory of anorexia nervosa. *Behaviour Research and Therapy, 37*, 1–13.

Fairburn, C. G., Stice, E., Cooper, Z., Doll, H. A., Norman, P. A., & O'Connor, M. E. (2003). Understanding persistence in bulimia nervosa: A 5-year naturalistic study. *Journal of Consulting and Clinical Psychology, 71*, 103–109.

Fairburn, C. G., Welch, S. L., Doll, S. A., Davies, B. A., & O'Connor, M. E. (1997). Risk factors for bulimia nervosa: A community-based case-control study. *Archives of General Psychiatry, 54*, 509–517.

Fairholme, C. P., Boisseau, C. L., Ellard, K. K., Ehrenreich, J. T., & Barlow, D. H. (2010). Emotions, emotion regulation, and psychological treatment: A unified perspective. In A. M. Kring & D. M. Sloan (Eds.), *Emotion regulation and psychopathology: A transdiagnostic approach to etiology and treatment* (pp. 283–309). New York, NY: Guilford.

Fakhoury, W., & Priebe, S. (2007). Deinstitutionalization and reinstitutionalization: Major changes in the provision of mental healthcare. *Psychiatry, 6*(8), 313–316. doi: 10.1016/j.mppsy.2007.05.008

Fallon, A. E., & Rozin, P. (1985). Sex differences in perceptions of desirable body shape. *Journal of Abnormal Psychology, 94*, 102–105.

Fallon, B. A., Altamash, I., Qureshi, A. I., Schneier, F. R., Sanchez-Lacay, A., Vermes, D., & Liebowitz, M. R. (2003). An open trial of fluvoxamine for hypochondriasis. *Psychosomatics, 44*, 298–303.

Falloon, I. R. (Ed.). (2015). *Handbook of behavioural family therapy*. London, UK: Routledge.

Falloon, I. R. H., Boyd, J. L., McGill, C. W., Williamson, M., Razani, J., Moss, H. B., & Simpson, G. M. (1985). Family management in the prevention of morbidity of schizophrenia. *Archives of General Psychiatry, 42*, 887–896.

Falloon, I. R. H., Brooker, C., & Graham-Hole, V. (1992). Psychosocial interventions for schizophrenia. *Behaviour Change, 9*, 238–245.

Fang, A., & Hofmann, S. G. (2010). Relationship between social anxiety disorder and body dysmorphic disorder. *Clinical Psychology Review, 30*, 1040–1048.

Fang, A., & Wilhelm, S. (2015). Clinical features, cognitive biases, and treatment of body dysmorphic disorder. *Annual Review of Clinical Psychology, 11*, 187–212.

Fang, H., Tu, S., Sheng, J., & Shao, A. (2019). Depression in sleep disturbance: A review on a bidirectional relationship, mechanisms and treatment. *Journal of Cellular and Molecular Medicine, 23*(4), 2324–2332. doi: 10.1111/jcmm.14170

Farnam, F., Janghorbani, M., Merghati-Khoei, E., & Raisi, F. (2014). Vaginismus and its correlates in an Iranian clinical sample. *International Journal of Impotence Research, 26*(6), 230–234.

Farrelly, S., Clement, S., Gabbidon, J., Jeffery, D., Dockery, L., Lassman, F., . . . Thornicroft, G. (2014). Anticipated and experienced discrimination amongst people with schizophrenia, bipolar disorder and major depressive disorder: A cross sectional study. *BMC Psychiatry, 14*(1), 157.

Farrokh, S., Roels, C., Owusu, K. A., Nelson, S. E., & Cook, A. M. (in press). Alcohol withdrawal syndrome in neurocritical care unit: Assessment and treatment challenges. *Neurocritical Care*, 1–15.

Fatemi, S. H., Aldinger, K. A., Ashwood, P., Bauman, M. L., Blaha, C. D., Blatt, G. J., & Welsh, J. P. (2012). Consensus paper: Pathological role of the cerebellum in autism. *Cerebellum, 11*(3), 777–807. doi: 10.1007/s12311-012-0355-9

Fauci, A. S. (2017). An HIV vaccine is essential for ending the HIV/AIDS pandemic. *JAMA, 318*(16), 1535–1536. doi: 10.1001/jama.2017.1350

Fauci, A. S., & Folkers, G. K. (2012). Toward an AIDS-free generation. *JAMA: Journal of the American Medical Association, 308*(4), 343-344.

Fauci, A. S., Redfield, R. R., Sigounas, G., Weahkee, M. D., & Giroir, B. P. (2019). Ending the HIV epidemic: A plan for the United States. *JAMA, 321*(9), 844–845. doi: 10.1001/jama.2019.1343

Faurholt-Jepsen, M., Frost, M., Ritz, C., Christensen, E. M., Jacoby, A. S., Mikkelsen, R. L., . . . Kessing, L. V. (2015). Daily electronic self-monitoring in bipolar disorder using smartphones–the MONARCA I trial: a randomized, placebo-controlled, single-blind, parallel group trial. *Psychological Medicine, 45*(13):2691–2704.

Fausto-Sterling, A. (2000a). The five sexes, revisited. *The Sciences, 40*(4), 19–23.

Fausto-Sterling, A. (2000b). *Sexing the body.* New York, NY: Basic.

Fausto-Sterling, A. (2015). Intersex: Concept of multiple sexes is not new. *Nature, 519*(7543), 291–291.

Fava, G. A., Cosci, F., & Sonino, N. (2017). Current psychosomatic practice. *Psychotherapy and Psychosomatics, 86*(1), 13–30. doi: 10.1159/000448856

Fava, G. A., Grandi, S., Rafanelli, C., Fabbri, S., & Cazzaro, M. (2000). Explanatory therapy in hypochondriasis. *Journal of Clinical Psychiatry, 61*(4), 317–322.

Fava, G. A., Ruini, C., Rafanelli, C., Finos, L., Conti, S., & Grandi, S. (2004). Six-year outcome of cognitive behavior therapy for prevention of recurrent depression. *American Journal of Psychiatry, 161,* 1872–1876.

Favrod-Coune, T., & Broers, B. (2021). Addiction to caffeine and other xanthines. In N. el-Guebaly, G. Carrà, M. Galanter, & A. M. Baldacchino (Eds.), *Textbook of addiction treatment* (pp. 215–228). Cambridge, MA: Springer.

Fazel, S., & Runeson, B. (2020). Suicide. *New England Journal of Medicine, 382*(3), 266–274. doi: 10.1056/NEJMra1902944

Fazel, S., Singh, J. P., Doll, H., & Grann, M. (2012). Use of risk assessment instruments to predict violence and antisocial behaviour in 73 samples involving 24,827 people: Systematic review and meta-analysis. *BMJ: British Medical Journal, 345,* e4692. doi: http://dx.doi.org/10.1136/bmj.e4692

Federoff, J. P., Fishell, A., & Federoff, B. (1999). A case series of women evaluated for paraphilic sexual disorders. *Canadian Journal of Human Sexuality, 8*(2), 127–140.

Fein, D. A. (2011). *The neuropsychology of autism*. New York, NY: Oxford University Press.

Feinberg, M., & Carroll, B. J. (1984). Biological "markers" for endogenous depression: Effect of age, severity of illness, weight loss and polarity. *Archives of General Psychiatry, 41,* 1080–1085.

Feingold, B. F. (1975). *Why your child is hyperactive*. New York, NY: Random House.

Feinstein, C., & Phillips, J. M. (2006). Developmental disorders of communication, motor skills, and learning. In M. K. Dulcan & J. M. Wiener (Eds.), *Essentials of child and adolescent psychiatry* (pp. 203–231). Washington, DC: American Psychiatric Publishing.

Feldman, H. A., Goldstein, I., Hatzichristou, D. G., Krane, R. J., & McKunlay, J. B. (1994). Impotence and its medical and psychosocial correlates: Results of the Massachusetts Male Aging Study. *Journal of Urology, 151,* 54–61.

Feldman, M. B., & Meyer, I. H. (2007). Childhood abuse and eating disorders in gay and bisexual men. *International Journal of Eating Disorders, 40*(5), 418–423.

Feldman, M. D., & Christensen, J. F. (Eds.). (2014). *Behavioral medicine: A guide for clinical practice,* 4th edition. McGraw-Hill Medical.

Felmingham, K. L., & Bryant, R. A. (2012). Gender differences in the maintenance of response to cognitive behavior therapy for posttraumatic stress disorder. Journal of Consulting and Clinical Psychology, 80(2), 196–200. doi:10.1037/a0027156

Felthous, A. R., O'Shaughnessy, R., Kuten, J., François-Purssell, I., Medrano, J., & Carabellese, F. (2020). The clinician's duty to warn or protect: In the United States, England, Canada, New Zealand, France, Spain, and Italy. *The Wiley international handbook on psychopathic disorders and the law* (pp. 121–153). Hoboken, N.J.: John Wiley.

Fergus, T. A., & Valentiner, D. P. (2010). Disease phobia and disease conviction are separate dimensions underlying hypochondriasis. *Journal of Behavior Therapy and Experimental Psychiatry, 41,* 438–444.

Ferguson, C. J., & Negy, C. (2014). Development of a brief screening questionnaire for histrionic personality symptoms. *Personality and Individual Differences, 66,* 124–127.

Fergusson, D., & Woodward, L. J. (2002). Mental health, educational, and social role outcomes of adolescents with depression. *Archives of General Psychiatry, 59,* 225–231.

Fergusson, D., Horwood, J., Ridder, E., & Beautrais, A. (2005). Subthreshold depression in adolescence and mental health outcomes in adulthood. *Archives of General Psychiatry, 62,* 66–72.

Ferreira, C. (2000). Serial killers: Victims of compulsion or masters of control? In D. H. Fishbein (Ed.), *The science, treatment, and prevention of antisocial behaviors: Application to the criminal justice system* (pp. 15-1–15-18). Kingston, NJ: Civic Research Institute.

Ferri, C. P., Prince, M., Brayne, C., Brodaty, H., Fratiglioni, L., Ganguli, M., & Scazufca, M. (2005). Global prevalence of dementia: A Delphi consensus study. *The Lancet, 366*(9503), 2112–2117. doi: http://dx.doi.org/10.1016/S0140-6736(05)67889-0

Ferster, C. B. (1961). Positive reinforcement and behavioral deficits of autistic children. *Child Development, 32,* 437–456.

Ferster, C. B., & Skinner, B. F. (1957). *Schedules of reinforcement.* New York, NY: Appleton-Century-Crofts.

Fertuck, E. A., Jekal, A., Song, I., Wyman, B., Morris, M. C., Wilson, S. T., & Stanley, B. (2009). Enhanced "Reading the Mind in the Eyes" in borderline personality disorder compared to healthy controls. *Psychological Medicine, 39*(12), 1979–1988.

Feusner, J. D., Phillips, K. A., & Stein, D. J. (2010). Olfactory reference syndrome: Issues for DSM-V. *Depression and Anxiety, 27*(6), 592–599. doi: 10.1002/da.20688

Ficks, C. A., & Waldman, I. D. (2014). Candidate genes for aggression and antisocial behavior: a meta-analysis of association studies of the 5HTTLPR and MAOA-uVNTR. *Behavior Genetics, 44*(5), 427–444.

Field, A. E., Cheung, L., Wolf, A. M., Herzog, D. B., Gortmaker, S. L., & Colditz, G. A. (1999). Exposure to the mass media and weight concerns among girls. *Pediatrics, 103,* e36.

Field, A. E., Sonneville, K. R., Crosby, R. D., Swanson, S. A., Eddy, K. T., Camargo, C. A., . . . Micali, N. (2014). Prospective associations of concerns about physique and the development of obesity, binge drinking, and drug use among adolescent boys and young adult men. *JAMA Pediatrics, 168*(1), 34–39.

Fielder, R. L., Carey, K. B., & Carey, M. P. (2013). Are hookups replacing romantic relationships? A longitudinal study of first-year female college students. *Journal of Adolescent Health, 52*(3), 657–659.

Fields, B. W., & Fristad, M. A. (2009). Assessment of childhood bipolar disorder. *Clinical Psychology: Science and Practice, 16*(2), 166–181.

Fileborn, B., Thorpe, R., Hawkes, G., Minichiello, V., Pitts, M., & Dune, T. (2015). Sex, desire and pleasure: Considering the experiences of older Australian women. *Sexual and Relationship Therapy,* 30(1), 117–130.

Filippi, M. (Ed.). (2015). *Oxford textbook of neuroimaging.* Oxford, UK: Oxford University Press.

Fincham, F. D., Beach, S. R. H., Harold, G. T., & Osborne, L. N. (1997). Marital satisfaction and depression: Different causal relationships for men and women? *Psychological Science, 8*(5), 351–357.

Fineberg, N. A., Potenza, M. N., Chamberlain, S. R., Berlin, H. A., Menzies, L., Bechara, A., & Hollander, E. (2010). Probing compulsive and impulsive behaviors, from animal models to endophenotypes: A narrative review. *Neuropsychopharmacology, 35*(3), 591–604.

Finger, S., & Zaromb, F. (2006). Benjamin Franklin and shock-induced amnesia. *American Psychologist, 61,* 240–248.

Finkenbine, R., & Miele, V. J. (2004). Globus hystericus: A brief review. *General Hospital Psychiatry, 26, 78–82.*

First, M. B., & Pincus, H. A. (2002). The DSM-IV text revision: Rationale and potential impact on clinical practice. *Psychiatric Services, 53,* 288–292.

Fischer, M. (1971). Psychoses in the offspring of schizophrenic monozygotic twins and their normal co-twins. *British Journal of Psychiatry, 118,* 43–52.

Fishbain, D. A. (1987). Kleptomania as risk-taking behavior in response to depression. *American Journal of Psychotherapy, 41,* 598–603.

Fisher, C. B., & Vacanti-Shova, K. (2012). The responsible conduct of psychological research: An overview of ethical principles, APA Ethics Code standards, and federal regulations. In S. J. Knapp, M. C., Gottlieb, M. M. Handelsman, & L. D. VandeCreek (Eds.), *APA handbook of ethics in psychology, Vol 2: Practice, teaching, and research* (pp. 335–369). Washington, DC: American Psychological Association.

Fisher, P. L., & Wells, A. (2009). Psychological models of worry and generalized anxiety disorder. In M. M. Antony & M. B. Stein (Eds.), *Oxford handbook of anxiety and related disorders* (pp. 225–237). New York, NY: Oxford University Press.

Fiske, A., Wetherell, J. L., & Gatz, M. (2009). Depression in older adults. *Annual Review of Clinical Psychology, 5,* 363–389.

Fitts, S. N., Gibson, P., Redding, C. A., & Deiter, P. J. (1989). Body dysmorphic disorder: Implications for its validity as a DSM-III-R clinical syndrome. *Psychological Reports, 64,* 655–658.

Flanagan, J. (2015). Epigenome-wide association studies (EWAS): Past, present, and future. In M. Verma (Ed.), *Cancer Epigenetics* (Vol. 1238, pp. 51–63). New York, NY: Springer.

Flegal, K. M., Carroll, M. D., Kit, B. K., & Ogden, C. L. (2012). Prevalence of obesity and trends in the distribution of body mass index among US adults, 1999–2010. *JAMA: Journal of the American Medical Association, 307*(5), 491–497.

Flegal, K. M., Carroll, M. D., Ogden, C. L., & Curtin, L. R. (2010). Prevalence and trends in obesity among US adults, 1999–2008. *JAMA: Journal of the American Medical Association, 303*(3), 235–241.

Flegal, K. M., Graubard, B. I., Williamson, D. F., & Gail, M. H. (2005). Excess deaths associated with underweight, overweight, and obesity. *JAMA: Journal of the American Medical Association, 293,* 1861–1867.

Flegal, K. M., Kit, B. K., Orpana, H., & Graubard, B. I. (2013). Association of all-cause mortality with overweight and obesity using standard body mass index categories: A systematic review and meta-analysis. *JAMA: Journal of the American Medical Association, 309*(1), 71–82. doi: 10.1001/jama.2012.113905

Flegal, K. M., Kruszon-Moran, D., Carroll, M. D., Fryar, C. D., & Ogden, C. L. (2016). Trends in obesity among adults in the United States, 2005 to 2014. *JAMA, 315*(21), 2284–2291.

Fleischer, M., Schäfer, M., Coogan, A., Häßler, F., & Thome, J. (2012). Sleep disturbances and circadian CLOCK genes in borderline personality disorder. *Journal of Neural Transmission, 119*(10), 1105–1110. doi: 10.1007/s00702-012-0860-5

Fleminger, S. (2012). The neuropsychiatry of head injury. In M. G. Gelder, N. C. Andreasen, J. J. Lopez-Ibor, Jr., & J. R. Geddes (Eds.), *New Oxford Textbook of Psychiatry* (2nd ed., Vol. 1, pp. 387–399). New York, NY: Oxford University Press.

Flemming, K. (2010). The use of morphine to treat cancer-related pain: A synthesis of quanti-tative and qualitative research. *Journal of Pain and Symptom Management, 39*(1), 139–154.

Fletcher, J. M., Lyon, G. R., Fuchs, L. S., & Barnes, M. A. (2007). *Learning disabilities: From identification to intervention.* New York, NY: Guilford.

Fletcher, R. B., & Hattie, J. (2011). *Intelligence and intelligence testing.* New York, NY: Routledge.

Fliers, E., Vermeulen, S., Rijsdijk, F., Altink, M., Buschgens, C., Rommelse, N., & Franke, B. (2009). ADHD and poor motor performance from a family genetic perspective. *Journal of the American Academy of Child & Adolescent Psychiatry, 48*(1), 25–34.

Flint, A., Schaffer, A., Meyers, B., Rothschild, A., & Mulsant, B. (2006). Research assessment of patients with psychotic depression: The STOP-PD approach. *Psychiatric Annals, 36,* 48–56.

Flint, J. (2009). Molecular genetics. In M. G. Gelder, N. C. Andreasen, J. J. Lopez-Ibor, Jr., & J. R. Geddes (Eds.), *New Oxford textbook of psychiatry* (2nd ed., Vol. 1, pp. 222–233). Oxford, UK: Oxford University Press.

Flor, H., & Turk, D. C. (2011). *Chronic Pain: An Integrated Biobehavioral Approach.* Seattle: International Association for the Study of Pain Press.

Flor, H., Elbert, T., Kenecht, S., Weinbruch, C., Pantev, C., Birbaumer, N., & Taub, E. (1995). Phantom limb pain as a perceptual correlate of cortical reorganization following arm amputation. *Nature, 375,* 482–484.

Flores, B., & Schatzberg, A. (2006). Psychotic depression. In D. J. Stein, D. J. Kupfer, & A. F. Schatzberg (Eds.). *The American Psychiatric Publishing textbook of mood disorders* (pp. 561–571). Arlington, VA: American Psychiatric Publishing.

Flynn, J. R. (1984). The mean IQ of Americans: Massive gains 1932 to 1978. *Psychological Bulletin, 95,* 29–51.

Foa, E. B., Gillihan, S. J., & Bryant, R. A. (2013). Challenge and successes in dissemination of evidence-based treatment for posttraumatic stress: Lessons learned from prolonged exposure therapy for PTSD. *Psychological Science in the Public Interest (Supplement), 14,* 65–11.

Foa, E. B., Jenike, M., Kozak, M. J., Joffe, R., Baer, L., Pauls, D., & Turner, S. M. (1996). Obsessive-compulsive disorder. In T. A. Widiger, A. J. Frances, H. A. Pincus, M. R. Ross, M. B. First, & W. W. Davis (Eds.), *DSM-IV sourcebook* (Vol. 2, pp. 549–576). Washington, DC: American Psychiatric Association.

Foa, E. B., Liebowitz, M. R., Kozak, M. J., Davies, S., Campeas, R., Franklin, M. E., & Tu, X. (2005). Randomized, placebo- controlled trial of exposure and ritual prevention, clomipramine, and their combination in the treatment of obsessive-compulsive disorder. *American Journal of Psychiatry, 162,* 151–161.

Foa, E. B., McLean, C. P., Capaldi, S., & Rosenfield, D. (2013). Prolonged exposure vs. supportive counseling for sexual abuse-related PTSD in adolescent girls: A ranomized controlled trial. *JAMA,* 310, 2650–2657.

Fogelson, D. L., Asarnow, R. A., Sugar, C. A., Subotnik, K. L., Jacobson, K. C., Neale, M. C., . . . Nuechterlein, K. H. (2010). Avoidant personality disorder symptoms in first-degree relatives of schizophrenia patients predict performance on neurocognitive measures: the UCLA family study. *Schizophrenia Research, 120*(1), 113–120.

Fogelson, D. L., Nuechterlein, K. H., Asarnow, R. A., Payne, D. L., Subotnik, K. L., Jacobson, K. C., & Kendler, K. S. (2007). Avoidant personality disorder is a separable schizophrenia-spectrum personality disorder even when controlling for the presence of paranoid and schizotypal personality disorders: The UCLA family study. *Schizophrenia Research, 91,* 192–199.

Foldes-Busque, G., Dionne, C. E., Turcotte, S., Tully, P. J., Tremblay, M., Poirier, P., & Denis, I. (2021). Epidemiology and prognostic implications of panic disorder and generalized anxiety disorder in patients with coronary artery disease: Rationale and design for a longitudinal cohort study. *BMC Cardiovascular Disorders, 21*(1). doi: 10.1186/s12872-021-01848

Foley, E., Baillie, A., Huxter, M., Price, M., & Sinclair, E. (2010). Mindfulness-based cognitive therapy for individuals whose lives have been affected by cancer: A randomized controlled-trial. *Journal of Consulting and Clinical Psychology, 78,* 72–79.

Foley, K. R., Dyke, P., Girdler, S., Bourke, J., & Leonard, H. (2012). Young adults with intellectual disability transitioning from school to post-school: A literature review framed within the ICF. *Disability and Rehabilitation, 34*(20), 1747–1764.

Folsom, D. P., Hawthorne, W., Lindamer, L., Gilmer, T., Bailey, A., Golshan, S., & Jeste, D. V. (2005). Prevalence and risk factors for homelessness and utilization of mental health services among 10,340 patients with serious mental illness in a large public mental health system. *American Journal of Psychiatry, 162,* 370–376.

Folstein, M. F., Folstein, S. E., & McHugh, P. R. (1975). "Mini-mental state": a practical method for grading the cognitive state of patients for the clinician. *Journal of Psychiatric Research, 12*(3), 189–198.

Fonagy, P., Yakeley, J., Gardner, T., Simes, E., McMurran, M., Moran, P., … Cameron, A. (2020). Mentalization for offending adult males (MOAM): Study protocol for a randomized controlled trial to evaluate mentalization-based treatment for antisocial personality disorder in male offenders on community probation. *Trials, 21*(1), 1–17.

Fong, T. G., Davis, D., Growdon, M. E., Albuquerque, A., & Inouye, S. K. (2015). The interface between delirium and dementia in elderly adults. *The Lancet Neurology, 14*(8), 823–832.

Fonseca, A., Ganho-Ávila, A., Lambregtse-van den Berg, M., Lupatelli, A., Rodriguez-Muñoz, M. D. L. F., Ferreira, P., … Bina, R. (2020). Emerging issues and questions on peripartum depression prevention, diagnosis and treatment: A consensus report from the cost action riseup-PPD. *Journal of Affective Disorders, 274,* 167–173. doi: 10.1016/j.jad.2020.05.112

Forand, N. R., & Derubeis, R. J. (2013). Pretreatment anxiety predicts patterns of change in cognitive behavioral therapy and medications for depression. *Journal of Consulting and Clinical Psychology. 81*(5), *774–782.* doi: 10.1037/a0032985

Ford, C., & Beach, F. (1951). *Patterns of sexual behavior.* New York, NY: Harper & Row.

Ford, E. S, Croft, J. B., Posner, S. F., Goodman, R. A., & Giles, W. H. (2013). Co-Occurrence of Leading Lifestyle-Related Chronic Conditions Among Adults in the United States, 2002-2009. *Preving Chronic Disease.* 2013 Apr 25;10:E6. http://www.cdc.gov/pcd/issues/2013/12_0316.htm

Ford, H., & Cortoni, F. (2008). Sexual deviance in females: Assessment and treatment. In D. R. Laws & W. T. O'Donohue (Eds.), *Sexual deviance: Theory, assessment, and treatment* (2nd ed., pp. 508–526). New York, NY: Guilford.

Ford, J. B., Sutter, M. E., Owen, K. P., & Albertson, T. E. (2014). Volatile substance misuse: an updated review of toxicity and treatment. *Clinical Reviews in Allergy & Immunology, 46*(1), 19–33.

Ford, M. R., & Widiger, T. A. (1989). Sex bias in the diagnosis of histrionic and antisocial personality disorders. *Journal of Consulting and Clinical Psychology, 57,* 301–305.

Fordyce, W. E. (1988). Pain and suffering: A reappraisal. *American Psychologist, 43*(4), 276–283.

Forster, N., & Lund, D. W. (2018). Identifying and dealing with functional psychopathic behavior in higher education. *Global Business and Organizational Excellence, 38*(1), 22–31.

Fortes, I. S., Paula, C. S., Oliveira, M. C., Bordin, I. A., de Jesus Mari, J., & Rohde, L. A. (2015). A cross-sectional study to assess the prevalence of DSM-5 specific learning disorders in representative school samples from the second to sixth grade in Brazil. *European Child & Adolescent Psychiatry,* 1–13.

Forti, G., Corona, G., Vignozzi, L., & Maggi, M. (2011) Testosterone and Other Hormonal Therapies (Antiestrogen, DHEA, Thyroid Hormones) for Erectile Dysfunction. In M. Maggi (Eds). *Hormonal Therapy for Male Sexual Dysfunction* (pp. 42–54). Wiley-Blackwell: Oxford, UK.

Foster, A., Gable, J., & Buckley, J. (2012). Homelessness in schizophrenia. *The Psychiatric Clinics of North America, 35*(3), 717.

Fournier, J. C., DeRubeis, R. J., Hollon, S. D., Dimidjian, S., Amsterdam, J. D., Shelton, R. C., & Fawcett, J. (2010). Antidepressant drug effects and depression severity: A patient-level meta-analysis. *JAMA: Journal of the American Medical Association, 303*(1), 47–53.

Foussias, G., Agid, O., Fervaha, G., & Remington, G. (2014). Negative symptoms of schizophrenia: clinical features, relevance to real world functioning and specificity versus other CNS disorders. *European Neuropsychopharmacology, 24*(5), 693–709.

Fowler, J. C. (2012). Suicide risk assessment in clinical practice: Pragmatic guidelines for imperfect assessments. *Psychotherapy, 49*(1), 81–90.

Fowles, D. C. (1988). Psychophysiology and psychopathy: A motivational approach. *Psychophysiology, 25,* 373–391.

Fox, E., & Damjanovic, L. (2006) The eyes are sufficient to produce a threat superiority effect. *Emotion, 6,* 534–539.

Foy, D. W., Resnick, H. S., Sipprelle, R. C., & Carroll, E. M. (1987). Premilitary, military and postmilitary factors in the development of combat related posttraumatic stress disorder. *The Behavior Therapist, 10,* 3–9.

Frailing, K., Alfonso, B., & Taylor, R. (2020). Therapeutic jurisprudence in swift and certain probation. *American Behavioral Scientist, 64*(12), 1768–1785.

Frances, A. (2009). Whither DSM-V? *British Journal of Psychiatry, 195,* 391–392.

Frances, A. (2010, February 11). Opening pandora's box: The 19 worst suggestions for DSM-5. *Psychiatric Times.*

Frances, A. J. (2012). DSM 5 is guide not bible—Ignore its ten worst changes. *Psychology Today.* Retrieved from http://www.psychologytoday.com/blog/dsm5-in-distress/201212/dsm-5-is-guide-not-bible-ignore-its-ten- worst-changes/comments

Frances, A. J., & Widiger, T. (2012). Psychiatric diagnosis: Lessons from the *DSM-IV* past and cautions for the *DSM-5* future. In S. Nolen-Hoeksema, T. D. Cannon, & T. Widiger (Eds.), *Annual review of clinical psychology* (Vol. 8, pp. 109–130). Palo Alto, CA: Annual Reviews.

Frances, A., & Widiger, T. A. (1986). Methodo-logical issues in personality disorder diagnosis. In T. Millon & G. L. Klerman (Eds.), *Contemporary directions in psychopathology: Toward the DSM-IV* (pp. 381–400). New York, NY: Guilford.

Francis, D. D., Diorio, J., Plotsky, P. M., & Meaney, M. J. (2002). Environmental enrichment reverses the effects of maternal separation on stress reactivity. *Journal of Neuroscience, 22,* 7840–7843.

Francis, D., Diorio, J., Liu, D., & Meaney, M. J. (1999). Nongenomic transmission across generations of maternal behavior and stress responses in the rat. *Science, 286,* 1155–1158.

Frank, E., Anderson, C., & Rubinstein, D. (1978). Frequency of sexual dysfunction in "normal" couples. *New England Journal of Medicine, 299,* 111–115.

Frank, E., Nimgaonkar, V. L., Philips, M. L., & Kupfer, D. J. (2015). All the world's a (clinical) stage: Rethinking bipolar disorder from a longitudinal perspective. *Molecular Psychiatry, 20,* 23–31.

Frank, E., Swartz, H. A., Mallinger, A. G., Thase, M. E., Weaver, E. V., & Kupfer, D. J. (1999). Adjunctive psychotherapy for bipolar disorder: Effects of changing treatment modality. *Journal of Abnormal Psychology, 108*(4), 579–587.

Franklin, J. E., & Frances, R. J. (1999). Alcohol and other psychoactive substance use disorders. In R. E. Hales, S. C. Yudofsky, & J. A. Talbott (Eds.), *Textbook of psychiatry* (3rd ed., pp. 363–423). Washington, DC: American Psychiatric Press.

Franklin, K. A., & Lindberg, E. (2015). Obstructive sleep apnea is a common disorder in the population—a review on the epidemiology of sleep apnea. *Journal of Thoracic Disease, 7*(8), 1311.

Franklin, M. E., & Foa, E. B. (2014). Obsessive-compulsive disorder. In D. H. Barlow (Ed.), *Clinical handbook of psychological disorders: A step-by-step treatment manual* (5th ed.). New York, NY: Guilford.

Franko, D. L., Keshaviah, A., Eddy, K. T., Krishna, M., Davis, M. C., Keel, P. K., & Herzog, D. B. (2013). A longitudinal investigation of mortality in anorexia nervosa and bulimia nervosa. *American Journal of Psychiatry, 170*(8), 917–925.

Franko, D. L., Thompson-Brenner, H., Thompson, D. R., Boisseau, C. L., Davis, A., Forbush, K. T., & Wilson, G. T. (2012). Racial/ethnic differences in adult participants in randomized clinical trials of binge eating disorder. *Journal of Consulting and Clinical Psychology, 80,* 186–195.

Franko, D. L., Wonderlich, S. A., Little, D., & Herzog, D. B. (2004). Diagnosis and classification of eating disorders. In J. K. Thompson (Ed.), *Handbook of eating disorders and obesity* (pp. 58–80). New York, NY: Wiley.

Frasure-Smith, N., & Lesperance, F. (2005). Depression and coronary heart disease: Complex synergism of mind, body, and environment. *Current Directions in Psychological Science, 14,* 39–43.

Frasure-Smith, N., Lesperance, F., Juneau, M., Talajic, M., & Bourassa, M. G. (1999). Gender, depression, and one-year prognosis after myocardial infarction. *Psychosomatic Medicine, 61,* 26–37.

Fratiglioni, L., & Qiu, C. (2009). Prevention of common neurodegenerative disorders in the elderly. *Experimental Gerontology, 44*(1), 46–50.

Fratiglioni, L., Grut, M., Forsell, Y., Viitanen, M., Grafstrom, M., Holmen, K., & Winblad, B. (1991). Prevalence of Alzheimer's disease and other dementias in an elderly urban population: Relationship with age, sex and education. *Neurology, 41,* 1886–1892.

Fratiglioni, L., Winblad, B., & von Strauss, E. (2007). Prevention of Alzheimer's disease and dementia: Major findings from the Kungsholmen Project. *Physiology & Behavior, 92*(1–2), 98–104.

Frazier, T. W., Youngstrom, E. A., Speer, L., Embacher, R., Law, P., Constantino, J. N., & Eng, C. (2012). Validation of proposed DSM-5 criteria for autism spectrum disorder. *Journal of the American Academy of Child & Adolescent Psychiatry, 51*(1), 28–40.e23. doi: 10.1016/j.jaac.2011.09.021

Fredrikson, M., & Matthews, K. A. (1990). Cardiovascular responses to behavioral stress and hypertension: A meta-analytic review. *Annals of Behavioral Medicine, 12*(1), 30–39.

Fredrikson, M., Annas, P., & Wik, G. (1997). Parental history, aversive exposure and the development of snake and spider phobia in women. *Behavior Research and Therapy, 35,* 23–28.

Freedman, M., King, J., & Kennedy, E. (2001). Popular diets: A scientific review. *Obesity Research, 9*(Suppl.), S1–S38.

Freeman, D., Pugh, K., Vorontsova, N., Antley, A., & Slater, M. (2010). Testing the continuum of delusional beliefs: An experimental study using virtual reality. *Journal of Abnormal Psychology, 119*(1), 83–92.

Freeman, E. W., Rickels, K., Sammel, M. D., Lin, H., & Sondheimer, S. J. (2009). Time to relapse after short- or long-term treatment of severe premenstrual syndrome with sertraline. *Archives of General Psychiatry, 66*(5), 537–544.

Freeman, E., Sammel, M., Lin, H., & Nelson, D. (2006). Associations of hormones and menopausal status with depressed mood in women with no history of depression. *Archive General Psychiatry, 63,* 375–382.

French-Belgian Collaborative Group. (1982). Ischemic heart disease and psychological patterns: Prevalence and incidence studies in Belgium and France. *Advances in Cardiology, 29,* 25–31.

Frenda, S. J., Nichols, R. M., & Loftus, E. F. (2011). Current issues and advances in misinformation research. *Current Directions in Psychological Science, 20*(1), 20–23. doi: 10.1177/0963721410396620

Freud, A. (1946). *Ego and the mechanisms of defense.* New York, NY: International Universities Press.

Freud, S. (1974). On coca. In R. Byck (Ed.), *Cocaine papers by Sigmund Freud* (pp. 49–73). New York, NY: Stonehill. (Original work published in 1885.)

Freund, K., Seto, M. C., & Kuban, M. (1996). Two types of fetishism. *Behaviour Research and Therapy, 34,* 687–694.

Frick, P. J. (2012). Developmental pathways to conduct disorder: Implications for future directions in research, assessment, and treatment. *Journal of Clinical Child & Adolescent Psychology, 41*(3), 378–389. doi: 10.1080/15374416.2012.664815

Fridlund, A. J., Beck, H. P., Goldie, W. D., & Irons, G. (2012). Little Albert: A neurologically impaired child. *History of Psychology, 15*(4), 302–327.

Friedberg, F., & Sohl, S. (2009). Cognitive-behavior therapy in chronic fatigue syndrome: Is improvement related to physical activity? *Journal of Clinical Psychology, 65,* 423–442.

Frieden, T. R., Foti, K. E., & Mermin, J. (2015). Applying public health principles to the HIV epidemic: How are we doing? *New England Journal of Medicine, 373*(23), 2281–2287. doi: 10.1056/NEJMms1513641

Friedl, M. C., & Draijer, N. (2000). Dissociative disorders in Dutch psychiatric inpatients. *American Journal of Psychiatry, 157*(6), 1012–1013.

Friedman, A. F., Bolinskey, P. K., Levak, R. W., & Nichols, D. S. (2014). *Psychological Assessment with the MMPI-2/MMPI-2-RF.* London: Routledge.

Friedman, J. M. (2009). Obesity: Causes and control of excess body fat. *Nature, 459*(7245), 340–342.

Friedman, M. J. (2009). Phenomenology of posttraumatic stress disorder and acute stress disorder. In M. M. Antony & M. B. Stein (Eds.), *Oxford handbook of anxiety and related disorders* (pp. 65–72). New York, NY: Oxford University Press.

Friedman, M. J., Resick, P. A., Bryant, R. A., Strain, J., Horowitz, M., & Spiegel, D. (2011). Classification of trauma and stressor-related disorders in DSM-5. *Depression and Anxiety, 28*(9), 737–749. doi: 10.1002/da.20845

Friedman, M., & Rosenman, R. H. (1959). Association of specific overt behavior pattern with blood and cardiovascular findings. *JAMA: Journal of the American Medical Association, 169,* 1286.

Friedman, M., & Rosenman, R. H. (1974). *Type A behavior and your heart.* New York, NY: Knopf.

Fried-Oken, M., Rowland, C., Daniels, D., Dixon, M., Fuller, B., Mills, C., & Oken, B. (2012). AAC to support conversation in persons with moderate Alzheimer's disease. *Augmentative and Alternative Communication, 28*(4), 219–231.

Fritz, C. O., Morris, P. E., & Richler, J. J. (2012). Effect size estimates: Current use, calculations, and interpretation. *Journal of Experimental Psychology: General, 141*(1), 2–18.

Frodl, T., & Skokauskas, N. (2012). Meta-analysis of structural MRI studies in children and adults with attention deficit hyperactivity disorder indicates treatment effects. *Acta Psychiatrica Scandinavica, 125*(2), 114–126.

Fromm-Reichmann, F. (1948). Notes on the development of treatment of schizophrenics by psychoanalytic psychotherapy. *Psychiatry, 11,* 263–273.

Frost, R. O., & Rasmussen, J. L. (2012). Phenomenology and characteristics of compulsive hoarding. In G. Steketee (Ed.), *The Oxford handbook of obsessive compulsive and spectrum disorders* (pp. 70–88). New York, NY: Oxford University Press.

Frost, R. O., Patronek, G., & Rosenfield, E. (2011). Comparison of object and animal hoarding. *Depression and Anxiety, 28*(10), 885–891. doi: 10.1002/da.20826

Frost, R. O., Steketee, G., & Tolin, D. F. (2012). Diagnosis and assessment of hoarding disorder. *Annual Review of Clinical Psychology, 8*, 219–242. doi: 10.1146/annurev-clinpsy-032511-143116

Frühauf, S., Gerger, H., Schmidt, H. M., Munder, T., & Barth, J. (2013). Efficacy of psychological interventions for sexual dysfunction: a systematic review and meta-analysis. *Archives of Sexual Behavior, 42*(6), 915–933.

Fugl-Meyer, A. R., & Sjogren Fugl-Meyer, K. (1999). Sexual disabilities, problems, and satisfaction in 18–74 year old Swedes. *Scandinavian Journal of Sexology, 3*, 79–105.

Fuji, D. E., Tsushima, V., Murakami-Brundage, J., & Kamath, V. (2014). *Assessing for schizophrenia in Asian Americans. In guide to psychological assessment with Asians* (pp. 305–326). Springer New York.

Fukuda, K., Straus, S. E., Hickie, I., Sharpe, M. B., Dobbins, J. G., & Komaroff, A. L. (1994). Chronic fatigue syndrome: A comprehensive approach to its diagnosis and management. *Annals of Internal Medicine, 121*, 953–959.

Fullana, M. A., Mataix-Cols, D., Caspi, A., Harrington, H., Grisham, J. R., Moffitt, T. E., & Poulton, R. (2009). Obsessions and compulsions in the community: Prevalence, interference, help-seeking, developmental stability, and co-occurring psychiatric conditions. *American Journal of Psychiatry, 166*(3), 329–336. doi: 10.1176/appi.ajp.2008.08071006

Fullen, T., Jones, S. L., Emerson, L. M., & Adamou, M. (2020). Psychological treatments in adult ADHD: A systematic review. *Journal of Psychopathology and Behavioral Assessment*, 1–19.

Fulton, H. G., Krank, M. D., & Stewart, S. H. (2012). Outcome expectancy liking: A self-generated, self-coded measure predicts adolescent substance use trajectories. *Psychology of Addictive Behaviors, 26*(4), 870.

Fulton, J. J., Kiel, E. J., Tull, M. T., & Gratz, K. L. (2014). Associations between perceived parental overprotection, experiential avoidance, and anxiety. *Journal of Experimental Psychopathology, 5*, 200–211. doi: 10.5127/jep.034813

Functional visual loss. *Neurologic Clinics, 28*(3), 789–802.

Furberg, H., Olarte, M., Afari, N., Goldberg, J., Buchwald, D., & Sullivan, P. (2005). The prevalence of self-reported chronic fatigue in a U.S. twin registry. *Journal of Psychosomatic Research, 59*, 283–290.

Furman, D., Campisi, J., Verdin, E., Carrera-Bastos, P., Targ, S., Franceschi, C., Ferrucci, L., Gilroy, D. W., Fasano, A., Miller, G. W., Miller, A. H., Mantovani, A., Weyand, C. M., Barzilai, N., Goronzy, J. J., Rando, T. A., Effros, R. B., Lucia, A., Kleinstreuer, N., & Slavich, G. M. (2019). Chronic inflammation in the etiology of disease across the life span. *Nature Medicine, 25*, 1822–1832. doi: 10.1038/s41591-019-0675-0

Furman, W., & Collibee, C. (2014). Sexual activity with romantic and nonromantic partners and psychosocial adjustment in young adults. *Archives of Sexual Behavior, 43*(7), 1327–1341.

Furnham, A., & Crump, J. (2014). A bright side, facet analysis of Schizotypal Personality Disorder: The relationship between the HDS Imaginative Factor, the NEO-PI-R personality trait facets in a large adult sample. *Thinking Skills and Creativity, 11*, 42–47.

Furnham, A., & Wong, L. (2007). A cross-cultural comparison of British and Chinese beliefs about the causes, behaviour manifestations and treatment of schizophrenia. *Psychiatry Research, 151*, 123–138.

Furr, J. M., Comer, J. S., Sacks, H., Chan, P. T., Kerns, C. E., Feinberg, L., & Kurtz, S. M. S. (2012, November). *The Boston University Brave Buddies Program: A replication of the Brave Buddies intensive, outpatient treatment program for children with selective mutism.* Paper presented at the 46th annual meeting of the Association for Behavioral and Cognitive Therapies, National Harbor, MD.

Furr, J. M., Tiwari, S., Suveg, C., & Kendall, P. C. (2009). Anxiety disorders in children and adolescents. In M. M. Antony & M. B. Stein (Eds.), *Oxford handbook of anxiety and related disorders* (pp. 636–656). New York, NY: Oxford University Press.

Fusar-Poli, P., & Politi, P. (2008). Paul Eugen Bleuler and the birth of schizophrenia (1908). *American Journal of Psychiatry, 165*(11), 1407. doi: 10.1176/appi.ajp.2008.08050714

Fusar-Poli, P., Carpenter, W. T., Woods, S. W., & McGlashan, T. H. (2014). Attenuated psychosis syndrome: ready for DSM-5.1? *Annual review of clinical psychology, 10*, 155–192.

Fushimi, N., Wang, L., Ebisui, S., Cai, S., & Mikage, M. (2008). Studies of ephedra plants in Asia. Part 4.1. Morphological differences between Ephedra sinica Stapf and E. intermedia Schrenk et C.A. Meyer, and the botanical origin of Ma-huang produced in Qinghai Province. *Journal of Traditional Medicines, 25*(3), 61–66.

Fyer, A. J., Mannuzza, S., Chapman, T. F., Liebowitz, M. R., & Klein, D. F. (1993). A direct interview family study of social phobia. *Archives of General Psychiatry, 50*, 286–293.

Fyer, A. J., Mannuzza, S., Gallops, M. S., Martin, L. Y., Aaronson, C., Gorman, J. M., et al. (1990). Familial transmission of simple phobias and fears: A preliminary report. *Archives of General Psychiatry, 47*, 252–256.

Fyer, A., Liebowitz, M., Gorman, J., Compeas, R., Levin, A., Davies, S., et al. (1987). Discontinuation of alprazolam treatment in panic patients. *American Journal of Psychiatry, 144*, 303–308.

Gagnon, J. H. (1990). The explicit and implicit use of the scripting perspective in sex research. *Annual Review of Sex Research, 1*, 1–43.

Galatzer-Levy, I. R., & Bonanno, G. A. (2014). Optimism and death predicting the course and consequences of depression trajectories in response to heart attack. *Psychological Science, 25*, 2177–2178.

Galea, S., Ahern, J., Resnick, H., Kilpatrick, D., Bucuvalas, M., Gold, J., & Vlahov, D. (2002). Psychological sequelae of the September 11 terrorist attacks in New York City. *New England Journal of Medicine, 346*, 982–987.

Gallagher, M. W., Bentley, K. H., & Barlow, D. H. (2014). Perceived control and vulnerability to anxiety disorders: A meta-analytic review. *Cognitive Therapy and Research, 38*, 571–584.

Gallant, A. R., Lundgren, J., & Drapeau, V. (2012). The night-eating syndrome and obesity. *Obesity Reviews, 13*(6), 528–536.

Galletta, A. (2013). *Mastering the semi-structured interview and beyond: From research design to analysis and publication.* New York : NYU Press.

Gallo, L., & Matthews, K. (2003). Understanding the association between socioeconomic status and physical health: Do negative emotions play a role? *Psychological Bulletin, 129*, 10–51.

Galmiche, M., Déchelotte, P., Lambert, G., & Tavolacci, M. P. (2019). Prevalence of eating disorders over the 2000–2018 period: A systematic literature review. *American Journal of Clinical Nutrition, 109*(5), 1402–1413. doi: 10.1093/ajcn/nqy342

Gandaglia, G., Briganti, A., Jackson, G., Kloner, R. A., Montorsi, F., Montorsi, P., & Vlachopoulos, C. (2014). A systematic review of the association between erectile dysfunction and cardiovascular disease. *European Urology, 65*(5), 968–978.

Ganguli, M., Blacker, D., Blazer, D. G., Grant, I., Jeste, D. V., Paulsen, J. S., & Sachdev, P. S. (2011). Classification of neurocognitive disorders in DSM-5: A work in progress. *American Journal of Geriatric Psychiatry, 19*(3), 205–210.

Ganna, A., Verweij, K. J. H., Nivard, M. G., Maier, R., Wedow, R., Busch, A. S., …

Zietsch, B. P. (2019). Large-scale GWAS reveals insights into the genetic architecture of same-sex sexual behavior. *Science, 365*(6456). doi: 10.1126/science.aat7693

Gansler, D. A., McLaughlin, N. C., Iguchi, L., Jerram, M., Moore, D. W., Bhadelia, R., et al. (2009). A multivariate approach to aggression and the orbital frontal cortex in psychiatric patients. *Psychiatry Research: Neuroimaging, 171*(3), 145–154.

Gao, Y., & Zhang, W. (in press). Reward processing and psychopathic traits in children. *Personality Disorders: Theory, Research, and Treatment.*

Gao, Y., Raine, A., Venables, P. H., Dawson, M. E., & Mednick, S. A. (2010). Association of poor childhood fear conditioning and adult crime. *American Journal of Psychiatry, 167*(1), 56–60. doi: 10.1176/appi.ajp.2009.09040499

Garber, J., & Carter, J. S. (2006). Major depression. In R. T. Ammerman (Ed.), *Comprehensive handbook of personality and psychopathology. Volume III: Child psychopathology* (pp. 165–216). Hoboken, NJ: Wiley.

Garber, J., Clarke, G. N., Weersing, V. R., Beardslee, W. R., Brent, D. A., Gladstone, T. R., & Iyengar, S. (2009). Prevention of depression in at-risk adolescents: A randomized controlled trial. *JAMA: Journal of the American Medical Association, 301*(21), 2215–2224.

Garber, J., Gallerani, C. M., & Frankel, S. A. (2009). Depression in children. In I. H. Gotlib & C. L. Hammen (Eds.), *Handbook of depression* (2nd ed., pp. 405–443). New York, NY: Guilford.

Garcia, G., Kincannon, H. T., Poston Jr, D. L., & Walther, C. S. (2014). *Patterns of Sexual Activity in China and the United States.* In D. L. Poston, Jr., W. S. Yang, & D. N. Farris (Eds.), The Family and Social Change in Chinese Societies (pp. 99–116). Springer: Netherlands.

Garcia, J., McGowan, B. K., & Green, K. F. (1972). Biological constraints on conditioning. In A. H. Black & W. F. Prokasy (Eds.), *Classical conditioning II: Current research and theory.* New York, NY: Appleton-Century-Crofts.

Garcia-Campayo, J., Claraco, L. M., Sanz-Carrillo, C., Arevalo, E., & Monton, C. (2002). Assessment of a pilot course on the management of somatization disorder for family doctors. *General Hospital Psychiatry, 24,* 101–105.

Garcia-Lopez, L. J., Olivares, J., Beidel, D., Albano, A., Turner, S., & Rosa, A. (2006). Efficacy of three treatment protocols for adolescents with social anxiety disorder: A 5-year follow-up assessment. *Journal of Anxiety Disorders*, 20(2), 175–191. doi: 10.1016/j.janxdis.2005.01.003

Gardiner, C., Kiazand, A., Alhassan, S., Soowon, K., Stafford, R., Balise, R., & King, A. C. (2007). Comparison of the Atkins, Zone, Ornish, and LEARN diets for change in weight and related risk factors among overweight premenopausal women. *JAMA: Journal of the American Medical Association, 297,* 969–977.

Garfield, A. F., & Zigler, E. (1993). Adolescent suicide prevention: Current research and social policy implications. *American Psychologist, 48*(2), 169–182.

Garfinkel, P. E. (1992). Evidence in support of attitudes to shape and weight as a diagnostic criterion of bulimia nervosa. *International Journal of Eating Disorders, 11*(4), 321–325.

Garland, E. L., Howard, M. O., Vaughn, M. G., & Perron, B. E. (2011). Volatile substance misuse in the United States. *Substance Use & Misuse, 46*(Supplement 1), 8–20.

Garlow, S., & Nemeroff, C. B. (2003). Neurobiology of depressive disorders. In R. J. Davidson, K. R. Scherer, & H. H. Goldsmith (Eds.)., *Handbook of affective sciences* (pp. 1021–1043). New York, NY: Oxford University Press.

Garlow, S., Boone, E., Li, W., Owens, M., & Nemeroff, C. (2005). Genetic analysis of the hypothalamic corticotrophin releasing factor system. *Endocrinology, 146,* 2362–2368.

Garmezy, N., & Rutter, M. (Eds.) (1983). *Stress, coping and development in children.* New York, NY: McGraw-Hill.

Garner, D. M., & Fairburn, C. G. (1988). Relationship between anorexia nervosa and bulimia nervosa: Diagnostic implications. In D. M. Garner & P. E. Garfinkel (Eds.), *Diagnostic issues in anorexia nervosa and bulimia nervosa.* New York, NY: Brunner/Mazel.

Garner, D. M., Garfinkel, P. E., Rockert, W., & Olmsted, M. P. (1987). A prospective study of eating disturbances in the ballet. Ninth World Congress of the International College of Psychosomatic Medicine, Sydney, Australia. *Psychotherapy and Psychosomatics, 48*(1–4), 170–175.

Garnier-Dykstra, L. M., Caldeira, K. M., Vincent, K. B., O'Grady, K. E., & Arria, A. M. (2012). Nonmedical use of prescription stimulants during college: Four-year trends in exposure opportunity, use, motives, and sources. *Journal of American College Health, 60*(3), 226–234. doi: 10.1080/07448481.2011.589876

Garrabe, J., & Cousin, F. R. (2012). Acute and transient psychotic disorders. In M. G. Gelder, N. C. Andreasen, J. J. Lopez-Ibor, Jr., & J. R. Geddes (Eds.), *New Oxford textbook of psychiatry* (2nd ed., Vol. 1, pp. 602–608). New York, NY: Oxford University Press.

Garrity, A. G., Pearlson, G. D., McKiernan, K., Lloyd, D., Kiehl, K. A., & Calhoun, V. D. (2007). Aberrant "default mode" functional connectivity in schizophrenia. *American Journal of Psychiatry, 164*(3), 450–457.

Gatchel, R. (2005). *Clinical essentials of pain management.* Washington, DC: American Psychological Association.

Gatchel, R. J., & Dersh, J. (2002). Psychological disorders and chronic pain: Are there cause-and-effect relationships? In D. C. Turk & R. J. Gatchel (Eds.), *Psychological approaches to pain management: A practitioner's handbook* (2nd ed., pp. 30–51). New York, NY: Guilford.

Gatchel, R. J., & Turk, D. C. (Eds.) (1999). *Psychosocial factors in pain: Critical perspectives.* New York, NY: Guilford.

Gatchel, R. J., Peng, Y. B., Peters, M. L., Fuchs, P. N., & Turk, D. C. (2007). The biopsychosocial approach to chronic pain: Scientific advances and future directions. *Psychological Bulletin, 133,* 581–624.

Gaudreau, J.-D. (2012). Insights into the neural mechanisms underlying delirium. *American Journal of Psychiatry, 169*(5), 450–451. doi: 10.1176/appi.ajp.2012.12020256

Gavin, A. M. (2003). The asylum at Quaise: Nantucket's antebellum poor farm. *Historic Nantucket, 52*(4), 17–20.

Gavin, N. I., Gaynes, B. N., Lohr, K. N., Meltzer-Brody, S., Gartlehner, G., & Swinson, T. (2005). Perinatal depression—A systematic review of prevalence and incidence. *Obstetrics and Gynecology, 106*(5), 1071–1083.

Gaw, A. C. (2008). Cultural issues. In R. E. Hales, S. C. Yudofsky, & G. O. Gabbard (Eds.), *The American Psychiatric Publishing textbook of psychiatry* (5th ed., pp. 1529–1547). Arlington, VA: American Psychiatric Publishing.

Ge, X., Conger, R., & Elder, G. (1996). Coming of age too early: Pubertal influences on girls' vulnerability to psychological distress. *Child Development, 67,* 3386–3400.

Gearhardt, A. N., Bragg, M. A., Pearl, R. L., Schvey, N. A., Roberto, C. A., & Brownell, K. D. (2012). Obesity and public policy. In S. Nolen-Hoeksema, T. D. Cannon, & T. Widiger (Eds.), *Annual review of clinical psychology* (Vol. 8, pp. 404–430). Palo Alto, CA: Annual Reviews.

Gearhardt, A. N., Yokum, S., Orr, P. T., Stice, E., Corbin, W. R., & Brownell, K. D. (2011). Neural correlates of food addiction. *Archives of General Psychiatry, 68*(8), 808–815.

Gearhart, J. P. (1989). Total ablation of the penis after circumcision electrocautery: A method of management and long term follow-up. *Journal of Urology, 42,* 789–801.

Geddes, J., Andreasen, N., Goodwin, G., & Halmi, K. (2020–2003). Epidemiology and primary prevention of feeding and eating disorders. In *New Oxford Textbook of Psychiatry*. Oxford: Oxford University Press. Retrieved 10 Mar. 2021, from https://oxfordmedicine.com/view/10.1093/med/9780198713005.001.0001/med-9780198713005-chapter-103

Geer, J. H., Morokoff, P., & Greenwood, P. (1974). Sexual arousal in women: The development of a measurement device for vaginal blood volume. *Archives of Sexual Behavior, 3,* 559–564.

Geers, A. L., & Caplandies, F. C. (2021). Placebo and nocebo effects. In R. H. Paul, L. E. Salminen, J. Heaps, & L. M. Cohen (Eds.), *The Wiley encyclopedia of health psychology* (Vol. 1, pp. 475–483). Hoboken, NJ: Wiley.

Geller, B., Cooper, T. B., Graham, D. L., Fetaer, H. M., Marsteller, F. A., & Wells, J. M. (1992). Pharmacokinetically designed double blind placebo controlled study of nortriptyline in 6–12 year olds with major depressive disorder: Outcome: Nortriptyline and hydroxy-nortriptyline plasma levels; EKG, BP and side effect measurements. *Journal of the American Academy of Child and Adolescent Psychiatry, 31,* 33–44.

Gendron, M., & Feldman Barrett, L. (2009). Reconstructing the past: A century of ideas about emotion in psychology. *Emotion Review, 1*(4), 316–339.

Generations United. (2006). *Meth and child welfare: Promising solutions for children, their parents and grandparents*. Washington, DC: Author.

Gentile, J. P., Dillon, K. S., & Gillig, P. M. (2013). Psychotherapy and pharmacotherapy for patients with dissociative identity disorder. *Innovations in Clinical Neuroscience, 10*(2), 22–29

George, M. S., Taylor, J. J., & Short, E. B. (2013). The expanding evidence base for rTMS of depression. *Current Opinions in Psychiatry, 26,* 13–18.

Geraerts, E., Lindsay, D. S., Merckelbach, H., Jelicic, M., Raymaekers, L., Arnold, M. M., & Schooler, J. S. (2009). Cognitive mechanisms underlying recovered memory experiences of childhood sexual abuse. *Psychological Science, 20,* 92–98.

Gerard, D. L. (1997). Chiarugi and Pinel considered: Soul's brain/person's mind. *Journal of the History of the Behavioral Sciences,* 33(4), 381–403.

Gerber PJ (2012). The impact of learning disabilities on adulthood: a review of the evidenced-based literature for research and practice in adult education. *Journal of Learning Disabilities, 45*(1), 31–46, 201210.1177/00222194114266858

Gerritsen, L., Hägg, S., Reynolds, C. A., & Pedersen, N. L. (2020). The association of individual changes in stressful life events and telomere length over time in twins 50 years and older. *Psychosomatic Medicine, 82*(6), 614–622. doi: 10.1097/PSY.0000000000000826

Gershon, E. S., Kelsoe, J. R., Kendler, K. S., & Watson, J. D. (2001). It's time to search for susceptibility genes for major mental illnesses. *Science, 294,* 5.

Gerstein, D. R., Volberg, R. A., Toce, M. T., Harwood, H., Johnson, R. A., & Bule, T., & Tucker, A. (1999). *Gambling impact and behavior study: Report to the national gambling impact study commission*. Chicago, IL: National Opinion Research Center at the University of Chicago.

Geschwind, D. H., & Flint, J. (2015). Genetics and genomics of psychiatric disease. *Science, 349,* 1489–1494.

Gesquiere, L. R., Learn, N. H., Simao, M. C. M., Onyango, P. O., Alberts, S. C., & Altmann, J. (2011). Life at the top: Rank and stress in wild male baboons. *Science, 333*(6040), 357–360.

Giannotti, F., & Cortesi, F. (2009). Family and cultural influences on sleep development. *Child and Adolescent Psychiatric Clinics of North America, 18*(4), 849–861. doi: 10.1016/j.chc.2009.04.003

Gibbons, R., Hur, K., Bhaumik, D., & Mann, J. (2006). The relationship between antidepressant prescription rates and rate of early adolescent suicide. *American Journal of Psychiatry, 163,* 1898–1904.

Giedke, H., & Schwarzler, F. (2002). Therapeutic use of sleep deprivation in depression. *Sleep Medicine Reviews, 6,* 361–377.

Gielen, A. C., McDonald, E. M., & Shields, W. (20154). Unintentional home injuries across the life span: Problems and solutions. *Annual Review of Public Health, 36,* 231–253.

Gielen, A. C., Sleet, D., & DiClemente, R. (Eds). 2006. *Injury and Violence Prevention: Behavioral Science Theories, Methods, and Applications.* San Francisco, CA: Jossey-Bass.

Giesbrecht, T., Lynn, S. J., Lilienfeld, S. O., & Merckelbach, H. (2008). Cognitive processes in dissociation: An analysis of core theoretical assumptions. *Psychological Bulletin, 134*(5), 617–647.

Giesbrecht, T., Smeets, T., Leppink, J., Jelicic, M., & Merckelbach, H. (2007). Acute dissociation after 1 night of sleep loss. *Journal of Abnormal Psychology, 116*(3), 599–606.

Giese-Davis, J., Collie, K., Rancourt, K. M., Neri, E., Kraemer, H. C., & Spiegel, D. (2011). Decrease in depression symptoms is associated with longer survival in patients with metastatic breast cancer: A secondary analysis. *Journal of Clinical Oncology, 29*(4), 413–420.

Gillberg, C. (1984). Infantile autism and other childhood psychoses in a Swedish urban region: Epidemiological aspects. *Journal of Child Psychology and Psychiatry, 25,* 35–43.

Gillespie, C. F., & Nemeroff, C. B. (2007). Corticotropin-releasing factor and the psychobiology of early-life stress. *Current Directions in Psychological Science, 16*(2), 85–89.

Gillespie-Lynch, K., Sepeta, L., Wang, Y., Marshall, S., Gomez, L., Sigman, M., & Hutman, T. (2012). Early childhood predictors of the social competence of adults with autism. *Journal of Autism and Developmental Disorders, 42*(2), 161–174. doi: 10.1007/s10803-011-1222-0

Gilmore, J. H. (2010). Understanding what causes schizophrenia: A developmental perspective. *American Journal of Psychiatry, 167*(1), 8–10. doi: 10.1176/appi.ajp.2009.09111588

Gilmour, G. S., Nielsen, G., Teodoro, T., Yogarajah, M., Coebergh, J. A., Dilley, M. D., … Edwards, M. J. (2020). Management of functional neurological disorder. *Journal of Neurology, 267*(7), 2164–2172. doi: 10.1007/s00415-020-09772-w

Giltay, E., Geleijnse, J., Zitman, F., Hoekstra, T., & Schouten, E. (2004). Dispositional optimism and all-cause and cardiovascular mortality in a prospective cohort of elderly Dutch men and women. *Archives of the General Psychiatry, 61,* 1126–1135.

Ginovart, N., & Kapur, S. (2010). Dopamine receptors and the treatment of schizophrenia. In K. A. Neve (Ed.), *The dopamine receptors* (2nd ed., pp. 431–477). New York, NY: Humana Press.

Ginsburg, G. S., & Silverman, W. K. (2000). Gender role orientation and fearfulness in children with anxiety disorders. *Journal of Anxiety Disorders, 14*(1), 57–67.

Ginsburg, G. S., Becker, E. M., Keeton, C. P., Sakolsky, D., Piacentini, J., Albano, A. M., Compton, S. N., Iyengar, S., Sullivan, K., Caporino, N., Peris, T., Birmaher, B., Rynn, M., March, J., & Kendall, P. C. (2014). Naturalistic follow-up of youths treated for pediatric anxiety disorders. *JAMA Psychiatry, 71,* 310.

Ginsburg, G. S., Drake, K. L., Tein, J-Y, Teetsel, R., & Riddle, M. A. (2015). Preventing onset of anxiety disorders in offspring of anxious parents: A randomized controlled trial of a family-based intervention. *American Journal of Psychiatry, 172,* 1207–1214.

Girault, J. A., & Greengard, P. (2004). The neurobiology of dopamine signaling. *Archives of Neurology, 61*(5), 641–644.

Girgis, J., & Pringsheim, T. (in press). Prenatal risk factors for Tourette syndrome:

A systematic review update. *Current Developmental Disorders Reports.*

Girirajan, S. (2009). Parental-age effects in Down syndrome. *Journal of Genetics, 88*(1), 1–7. doi: 10.1007/s12041-009-0001-6

Gislason, I. L. (1988). Eating disorders in childhood (ages 4 through 11 years). In B. J. Blinder, B. F. Chaitin, & R. S. Goldstein (Eds.), *The eating disorders: Medical and psychological bases of diagnosis and treatment* (pp. 285–293). New York, NY: PMA.

Gitlin, M. J. (2009). Pharmacotherapy and other somatic treatments for depression. In I. H. Gotlib & C. L. Hammen (Eds.), *Handbook of depression* (2nd ed., pp. 554–585). New York, NY: Guilford.

Gjerde, L. C., Czajkowski, N., Røysamb, E., Ørstavik, R. E., Knudsen, G. P., Østby, K., & Reichborn-Kjennerud, T. (2012). The heritability of avoidant and dependent personality disorder assessed by personal interview and questionnaire. *Acta Psychiatrica Scandinavica, 126*(6), 448–457. doi: 10.1111/j.1600-0447.2012.01862.x

Gjerde, L. C., Czajkowski, N., Røysamb, E., Ystrom, E., Tambs, K., Aggen, S. H., . . . Knudsen, G. P. (2015). A longitudinal, population-based twin study of avoidant and obsessive-compulsive personality disorder traits from early to middle adulthood. *Psychological Medicine, 45*(16), 3539–3548.

Glaser, D. (2020). Fabricated or induced illness: From "Munchausen by proxy" to child and family-oriented action. *Child Abuse and Neglect, 108.* doi: 10.1016/j.chiabu.2020.104649

Glaser, R., & Kiecolt-Glaser, J. K. (2005). Stress-induced immune dysfunction: Implications for health. *Nature Reviews Immunology, 5*(3), 243–251.

Glaser, R., Kennedy, S., Lafuse, W. P., Bonneau, R. H., Speicher, C. E., Hillhouse, J., & Kiecolt-Glaser, J. K. (1990). Psychological stress-induced modulation of IL-2 receptor gene expression and IL-2 production in peripheral blood leukocytes. *Archives of General Psychiatry, 47,* 707–712.

Glaser, R., Rice, J., Sheridan, J., Fertel, R., Stout, J., Speicher, C., et al. (1987). Stress-related immune suppression: Health implications. *Brain, Behavior, and Immunity, 1,* 7–20.

Glasper, E. R., Schoenfeld, T. J., & Gould, E. (2012). Adult neurogenesis: Optimizing hippocampal function to suit the environment. *Behavioural Brain Research, 227*(2), 380–383.

Glaus, J., Vandeleur, C., Gholam-Rezaee, M., Castelao, E., Perrin, M., Rothen, S., & Preisig, M. (2012). Atypical depression and alcohol misuse are related to the cardiovascular risk in the general population. *Acta Psychiatrica Scandinavica,* 1–12.

Gleason, M. M., Fox, N. A., Drury, S., Smyke, A., Egger, H. L., Nelson, C. A., & Zeanah, C. H. (2011). Validity of evidence-derived criteria for reactive attachment disorder: Indiscriminately social/disinhibited and emotionally withdrawn/inhibited types. *Journal of the American Academy of Child and Adolescent Psychiatry, 50*(3), 216–231.e3. doi: 10.1016/j.jaac.2010.12.012

Gleaves, D. H. (1996). The sociocognitive model of dissociative identity disorder: A reexamination of the evidence. *Psychological Bulletin, 120,* 42–59.

Gleaves, D. H., Smith, S. M., Butler, L. D., & Spiegel, D. (2004). False and recovered memories in the laboratory and clinic: A review of experimental and clinical evidence. *Clinical Psychology: Science and Practice. 11*(1), 3–28.

Goater, N., King, M., Cole, E., Leavey, G., Johnson-Sabine, E., Blizard, R., & Hoar, A. (1999). Ethnicity and outcomes of psychosis. *British Journal of Psychiatry, 175,* 34–42.

Godart, N. T., Perdereau, F., Rein, Z., Berthoz, S., Wallier, J., Jeammet, P., & Falment, M. F. (2007). Comorbidity studies of eating disorders and mood disorders. Critical review of the literature. *Journal of Affective Disorders, 97*(1–3), 37–49.

Goel, A. K., Talwar, D., & Jain, S. K. (2015). Evaluation of short-term use of nocturnal nasal continuous positive airway pressure for a clinical profile and exercise capacity in adult patients with obstructive sleep apnea-hypopnea syndrome. *Lung India, 32*(3), 225.

Goel, M. S., McCarthy, E. P., Phillips, R. S., & Wee, C. C. (2004). Obesity among U.S. immigrant subgroups by duration of residence. *JAMA: Journal of the American Medical Association, 292,* 2860–2867.

Goering, P., Durbin, J., Sheldon, C. T., Ochocka, J., Nelson, G., & Krupa, T. (2006). Who uses consumer-run self-help organizations? *American Journal of Orthopsychiatry, 76,* 367–373.

Goff, D. C., & Coyle, J. T. (2001). The emerging role of glutamate in the pathophysiology and treatment of schizophrenia. *American Journal of Psychiatry, 158,* 1367–1377.

Gold, J. H. (1997). Premenstrual dysphoric disorder: What's that? *JAMA: Journal of the American Medical Association, 278,* 1024–1025.

Gold, J. H. (1999). Premenstrual dysphoric disorder: An update. *Journal of Practical Psychiatry and Behavioral Health, 5,* 209–215.

Gold, J. H., Endicott, J., Parry, B. L., Severino, S. K., Stotland, N., & Frank, E. (1996). Late luteal phase dysphoric disorder. In T. A. Widiger, A. J. Frances, H. A. Pincus, Ross, R., First, M. B., & Davis, W. W. (Eds.), *DSM-IV sourcebook* (Vol. 2, pp. 317–394). Washington, DC: American Psychiatric Association.

Gold, S. N., & Seibel, S. L. (2009). Treating dissociation: A contextual approach. In P. F. Dell & J. A. O'Neil (Eds.), *Dissociation and the dissociative disorders: DSM-V and beyond.* (pp. 625–636). New York, NY: Routledge/Taylor & Francis Group.

Goldberg, D., & Fawcett, J. (2012). The importance of anxiety in both major depression and bipolar disorder. *Depression and Anxiety, 29*(6), 471–478.

Goldberg, J. F., Perlis, R. H., Bowden, C. L., Thase, M. E., Miklowitz, D. J., Marangell, L. B., & Sachs, G. S. (2009). Manic symptoms during depressive episodes in 1,380 patients with bipolar disorder: Findings from the STEP-BD. *American Journal of Psychiatry, 166*(2), 173–181.

Goldberg, S. B., Pace, B. T., Nicholas, C. R., Raison, C. L., & Hutson, P. R. (2020). The experimental effects of psilocybin on symptoms of anxiety and depression: A meta-analysis. *Psychiatry Research, 284,* 112749.

Golden, C. J., Hammeke, T. A., & Purisch, A. D. (1980). *The Luria-Nebraska Battery manual.* Palo Alto, CA: Western Psychological Services.

Golden, R., Gaynes, B., Ekstrom, R., Hmaer, R., Jacobsen, F., & Nemeroff, C. B. (2005). The efficacy of light therapy in the treatment of mood disorders: A review and meta-analysis of the evidence. *American Journal of Psychiatry, 162,* 656–662.

Goldfarb, M. R., & Trudel, G. (2019). Marital quality and depression: A review. *Marriage and Family Review, 55*(8), 737–763. doi: 10.1080/01494929.2019.1610136

Goldfarb, W. (1963). Self-awareness in schizophrenic children. *Archives of General Psychiatry, 8,* 63–76.

Goldin, A. P., Sigman, M., Braier, G., Golombek, D. A., & Leone, M. J. (2020). Interplay of chronotype and school timing predicts school performance. *Nature Human Behaviour, 4*(4), 387–396. doi: 10.1038/s41562-020-0820-2

Goldin, P. R., Manber, T., Hakimi, S., Canli, T., & Gross, J. J. (2009). Neural bases of social anxiety disorder: Emotional reactivity and cognitive regulation during social and physical threat. *Archives of General Psychiatry, 66*(2), 170–180.

Goldin, P. R., Ziv, M., Jazaieri, H., Hahn, K., Heimberg, R., & Gross, J. J. (2013). Impact of cognitive behavioral therapy for social anxiety disorder on the neural dynamics of cognitive reappraisal of negative self-beliefs: randomized clinical trial. *JAMA Psychiatry, 70*(10), 1048–1056.

Goldman, D., Ducci, F., & Gitik, M. (2020). Familial genetics of psychopathic disorders. In A. R. Felthous & H. Saß (Eds.), *The Wiley international handbook on psychopathic disorders and the law* (pp. 159–187). Hoboken, N.J.: Wiley.

Goldman, N., Glei, D. A., Lin, Y., & Weinstein, M. (2010). The serotonin transporter polymorphism (5-HTTLPR): Allelic variation and links with depressive symptoms. *Depression and Anxiety, 27*(3), 260-269.

Goldmeier, D., Garvey, L., & Barton, S. (2008). Does chronic stress lead to increased rates of recurrences of genital herpes?—A review of the psychoneuroimmunilogical evidence. *International Journal of STD and AIDS, 19,* 359–362.

Goldschmidt, A. B., Hilbert, A., Manwaring, J. L., Wilfley, D. E., Pike, K. M., Fairburn, C. G., & Striegel-Moore, R. (2010). The significance of overvaluation of shape and weight in binge eating disorder. *Behaviour Research and Therapy, 48*(3), 187–193.

Goldstein, G., & Shelly, C. (1984). Discriminative validity of various intelligence and neuropsychological tests. *Journal of Consulting and Clinical Psychology, 52,* 383–389.

Goldstein, H. (2002). Communication intervention for children with autism: A review of treatment efficacy. *Journal of Autism and Developmental Disorders, 32*(5), 373–396. doi: 10.1023/a:1020589821992

Goldstein, I., Lue, T. F., Padma-Nathan, H., Rosen, R. C., Steers, W. D., & Wicker, P. A., for the Sildenafil Study Group. (1998). Oral sildenafil in the treatment of erectile dysfunction. *New England Journal of Medicine, 338,* 1397–1404.

Goldstein, J. M., & Lewine, R. R. J. (2000). Overview of sex differences in schizophrenia: Where have we been and where do we go from here? In D. J. Castle, J. McGrath, & J. Kulkarni (Eds.), *Women and schizophrenia* (pp. 111–143). Cambridge, UK: Cambridge University Press.

Goldstein, S., & Brooks, R. B. (Eds.). (2013). *Handbook of resilience in children* (2nd ed.). New York, NY: Springer.

Goldstein, Z., Rosen, B., Howlett, A., Anderson, M., & Herman, D. (2020). Interventions for paternal perinatal depression: A systematic review. *Journal of Affective Disorders, 265,* 505–510. doi: 10.1016/j.jad.2019.12.029

Goldston, D. B., Molock, S. D., Whitbeck, L. B., Murakami, J. L., Zayas, L. H., & Hall, G. C. N. (2008). Cultural considerations in adolescent suicide prevention and psychosocial treatment. *American Psychologist, 63*(1), 14–31.

Goldston, D., Reboussin, B., & Daniel, S. (2006). Predictors of suicide attempts: State and trait components. *Journal of Abnormal Psychology, 115,* 842–849.

Golembo-Smith, S., Schiffman, J., Kline, E., Sørensen, H. J., Mortensen, E. L., Stapleton, L., . . . Mednick, S. (2012). Premorbid multivariate markers of neurodevelopmental instability in the prediction of adult schizophrenia-spectrum disorder: a high-risk prospective investigation. *Schizophrenia Research, 139*(1), 129–135.

Goleva, S. B., Lake, A. M., Torstenson, E. S., Haas, K. F., & Davis, L. K. (2020). Epidemiology of functional seizures among adults treated at a university hospital. *JAMA Network Open, 3*(12), e2027920. doi: 10.1001/jamanetworkopen.2020.27920

Golier, J., Yehuda, R., Lupien, S., Harvey, P., Grossman, R., & Elkin, A. (2002). Memory performance in Holocaust survivors with posttraumatic stress disorder. *American Journal of Psychiatry, 159,* 1682–1688.

Gomez-Caminero, A., Blumentals, W. A., Russo, L., Brown, R. R., & Castilla-Puentes, R. (2005). Does panic disorder increase the risk of coronary heart disease? A cohort study of a national managed care database. *Psychosomatic Medicine, 67,* 688–691.

Gomez-Gil, E., Steva, I., Almaraz, M. C., Pasara, E., Segovia, S., & Guillamon, A. (2010). Familiality of gender identity disorder in non-twin siblings. *Archives of Sexual Behavior, 39,* 546–552.

Gong, Q., Dazzan, P., Scarpazza, C., Kasai, K., Hu, X., Marques, T. R., . . . David, A. S. (2015). A neuroanatomical signature for schizophrenia across different ethnic groups. *Schizophrenia Bulletin,* sbv109.

Gonzalez, J. S., Batchelder, A. W., Psaros, C. P., & Safren, S. A. (2011). Depression and HIV/AIDS treatment nonadherence: A review and meta-analysis. *Journal of Acquired Immune Deficiency Syndromes, 58*(2), 181–187.

Gonzalez, J. S., Hendriksen, E. S., Collins, E. M., Duran, R. E., & Safren, S. A. (2009). Latinos and HIV/AIDS: Examining factors related to disparity and identifying opportunities for psychosocial intervention research. *AIDS and Behavior, 13*(3), 582–602.

Good, B. J., & Kleinman, A. M. (1985). Culture and anxiety: Cross-cultural evidence for the patterning of anxiety disorders. In A. H. Tuma & J. D. Maser (Eds.), *Anxiety and the anxiety disorders* (pp. 297–313). Hillsdale, NJ: Erlbaum.

Goodkin, K., Baldewicz, T. T., Asthana, D., Khamis, I., Blaney, N. T., Kumar, M., & Shapshak, P. (2001). A bereavement support group intervention affects plasma burden of human immunodeficiency virus type 1. Report of a randomized controlled trial. *Journal of Human Virology, 4,* 44–54.

Goodman, G. S., Ghetti, S., Quas, J. A., Edelstein, R. S., Alexander, K. W., Redlich, A. D., Cordon, I. M., & Jones, D. P. H. (2003). A prospective study of memory for child sexual abuse: New findings relevant to the repressed/lost memory controversy. *Psychological Science, 14*(2), 113–118.

Goodman, G. S., Quas, J. A., & Ogle, C. M. (2010). Child maltreatment and memory. *Annual Reviews of Psychology, 61,* 325–351. doi: 10.1146/annurev.psych.093008.100403

Goodman, R., & Scott, S. (2012). Sleep disorders. In R. Goodman & S. Scott (Eds.), *Child and adolescent psychiatry* (3rd ed., pp. 163–170).

Goodnough, A. (2002). Post-9/11 pain found to linger in young minds. Available at http://www.nytimes.com/2002/05/02/health/02SCHO.html?todaysheadlines

Goodpaster, B. H., DeLany, J. P.,
Otto, A. D., et al. (2010). Effects of Diet and Physical Activity Interventions on Weight Loss and Cardiometabolic Risk Factors in Severely Obese Adults: A Randomized Trial. *JAMA.* 304(16): 1795–1802. doi:10.1001/jama.2010.1505

Goodrick, S. (2014). Defining narcolepsy. *The Lancet Neurology, 13*(6), 542.

Goodwin, D. W., & Gabrielli, W. F. (1997). Alcohol: Clinical aspects. In J. H. Lowinson, P. Ruiz, R. B. Millman, & J. G. Langrod (Eds.), *Substance abuse: A comprehensive textbook* (pp. 142–148). Baltimore, MD: Williams & Wilkins.

Goodwin, D. W., & Guze, S. B. (1984). *Psychiatric diagnosis* (3rd ed.). New York, NY: Oxford University Press.

Goodwin, F. K., & Ghaemi, S. N. (1998). Understanding manic-depressive illness. *Archives of General Psychiatry, 55*(1), 23–25.

Goodwin, F. K., & Jamison, K. R. (Eds.) (2007). *Manic depressive illness: Bipolar disorders and recurrent depression* (2nd ed.). New York, NY: Oxford University Press.

Goodwin, F. K., Fireman, B., Simon, G. E., Hunkeler, E. M., Lee, J., & Revicki, D. (2003). Suicide risk in bipolar disorder during treatment with lithium and divalproex. *JAMA: Journal of the American Medical Association, 290,* 1467–1473.

Goodwin, G. M. (2009). Neurobiological aetiology of mood disorders. In M. G. Gelder, N. C. Andreasen, J. J. Lopez-Ibor, Jr., & J. R. Geddes (Eds.), *New Oxford textbook of psychiatry* (2nd ed., Vol. 1, pp. 658–664). Oxford, UK: Oxford University Press.

Goos, L. M., Crosbie, J., Payne, S., & Schachar, R. (2009). Validation and extension of the endophenotype model in ADHD patterns of inheritance in a family study of inhibitory control. *American Journal of Psychiatry, 166*(6), 711–717.

Gordis, E. (2000). Alcohol, the brain, and behavior: Mechanisms of addiction. *Alcohol Research & Health, 24*(1), 12–15.

Gordon, J. A. (2002). Anxiolytic drug targets: Beyond the usual suspects. *Journal of Clinical Investigation, 110*(7), 915–917.

Gordon, L., Joo, J. E., Powell, J. E., Ollikainen, M., Novakovic, B., Li, X., & Saffery, R. (2012). Neonatal DNA methylation profile in human twins is specified by a complex interplay between intrauterine environmental and genetic factors, subject to tissue-specific influence. *Genome Research, 22*(8), 1395–1406. doi: 10.1101/gr.136598.111

Gordon, S. (2015). The danger zone: How the dangerousness standard in civil commitment proceedings harms people with serious mental illness. *Utah Law Review*, paper 911.

Gore-Felton, C., & Koopman, C. (2008). Behavioral mediation of the relationship between psychosocial factors and HIV disease progression. *Psychosomatic Medicine, 70,* 569–574.

Gorenstein, E. E., & Newman, J. P. (1980). Disinhibitory psychopathology: A new perspective and a model for research. *Psychological Review, 87,* 301–315.

Gotlib, I. H., & Abramson, L. Y. (1999). Attributional theories of emotion. In T. Dagleish & M. J. Power (Eds.), *Handbook of cognition and emotion* (pp. 613–636). Chichester, U.K: Wiley.

Gotlib, I. H., & Hammen, C. L. (2009). *Handbook of depression* (2nd ed.). New York, NY: Guilford.

Gotlib, I. H., & Joormann, J. (2010). Cognition and depression: Current status and future directions. *Annual Review of Clinical Psychology, 6,* 285–312.

Gotlib, I. H., & Krasnoperova, E. (1998). Biased information processing as a vulnerability factor for depression. *Behavior Therapy, 29,* 603–617.

Gotlib, I. H., & Nolan, S. A. (2001). Depression. In A. S. Bellack & M. Hersen (Eds.), *Psychopathology in adulthood* (2nd ed., pp. 252–277). Boston, MA: Allyn & Bacon.

Gotlib, I. H., Joormann, J., & Foland-Ross, L. C. (2014). Understanding familial risk for depression: A 25-year perspective. *Perspectives on Psychological Science, 9,* 94–108.

Gotlib, I. H., Ranganath, C., & Rosenfeld, J. P. (1998). Frontal EEG alpha asymmetry, depression, and cognitive functioning. *Cognition and Emotion, 12,* 449–478.

Gotlib, I. H., Roberts, J. E., & Gilboa, E. (1996). Cognitive interference in depression. In I. G. Sarason, G. R. Pierce, & B. R. Sarason (Eds.), *Cognitive interference: Theories, methods, and findings* (pp. 347–377). Mahwah, NJ: Erlbaum.

Gottesman, I. I., & Bertelsen, A. (1989). Dual mating studies in psychiatry: Offspring of inpatients with examples from reactive (psychogenic) psychoses. *International Review of Psychiatry, 1,* 287–296.

Gottesman, I. I., & Erlenmeyer-Kimling, L. (2001). Family and twin strategies as a head start in defining prodromes and endophenotypes for hypothetical early-interventions in schizophrenia. *Schizophrenia Research, 51*(1), 93–102.

Gottfredson, L., & Saklofske, D. H. (2009). Intelligence: Foundations and issues in assessment. *Canadian Psychology/Psychologie canadienne, 50*(3), 183–195.

Gottlieb, G. (1998). Normally occurring environmental and behavioral influences on gene activity: From central dogma to probabilistic epigenesis. *Psychological Review, 105,* 492–802.

Gould, M. (1990). Suicide clusters and media exposure. In S. J. Blumenthal & D. J. Kupfer (Eds.), *Suicide over the life cycle: Risk factors, assessment and treatment of suicidal patients* (pp. 517–532). Washington, DC: American Psychiatric Press.

Gould, M. S. (2001). Suicide and the media. *Annals of the New York Academy of Sciences, 932,* 200–221; discussion 221–224.

Gould, M., Marrocco, F., Kleinman, M., Thomas, J., Mostkoff, K., Cote, J., & Davies, M. (2005). Evaluating iatrogenic risk of youth suicide screening programs. *JAMA: Journal of the American Medical Association, 293,* 1635–1643.

Gould, S. J. (1991). The chain of reason versus the chain of thumbs. In *Bully for brontosaurus: Reflections in natural history* (pp. 182–197). New York, NY: Norton.

Goyal, M., Singh, S., Sibinga, E. M., Gould, N. F., Rowland-Seymour, A., Sharma, R., Berger, Z., Sleicher, D., Maron, D. D., Shihab, H. M., Ranasinghe, P. D., Linn, S., Saha, S., Bass, E. B., & Haythornwaite, J. A. (2014). Meditation programs for psychological stress and well-being: A systematic review and meta-analysis. *JAMA Internal Medicine, 174*(3), 357–368.

Grabbe, K. L., & Bunnell, R. (2010). Reframing HIV prevention in sub-saharan Africa using couple-centered approaches. *JAMA: Journal of the American Medical Association, 304,* 346–347.

Grabe, S., & Hyde, J. S. (2006). Ethnicity and body dissatisfaction among women in the United States: A meta-analysis. *Psychological Bulletin, 132,* 622–640.

Grabe, S., Ward, L. M., & Hyde, J. S. (2008). The role of the media in body image concerns among women: A meta-analysis of experimental and correlational studies. *Psychological Bulletin, 134*(3), 460–476.

Grados, M. A., Riddle, M. A., Samuels, J. F., Liang, K-Y., Hoehn-Saric, R., Bienvenu, O. J., & Nestadt, J. (2001). The familial phenotype of obsessive-compulsive disorder in relation to tic disorders: The Hopkins OCD family study. *Biological Psychiatry, 50,* 559–565.

Grady, D. (2020, March, 10). Haunted by a gene. *New York Times.*

Grady-Weliky, T. (2003). Premenstrual dysphoric disorder. *New England Journal of Medicine, 345,* 433–438.

Graeff, F. G. (1993). Role of 5-ht in defensive behavior and anxiety. *Review in the Neurosciences, 4,* 181–211.

Graeff, F. G. (2004). Serotonin, the periaqueductal gray and panic. *Neuroscience and Biobehavioral Reviews, 28,* 239–259.

Graff, F. S., McClure, M. M., & Siever, L. J. (2014). Remediation and Cognitive Enhancers in Schizotypal Personality Disorder. *Current Treatment Options in Psychiatry, 1*(4), 369–375.

Graham, C. A. (2010). The DSM criteria for female orgasmic disorder. *Archives of Sexual Behavior, 39,* 256–270.

Grandjean, J., Buehlmann, D., Buerge, M., Sigrist, H., Seifritz, E., Vollenweider, F. X., … Rudin, M. (2021). Psilocybin exerts distinct effects on resting state networks associated with serotonin and dopamine in mice. *NeuroImage, 225,* 117456.

Granic, I., & Patterson, G. R. (2006). Toward a comprehensive model of antisocial development: A dynamic systems approach. *Psychological Review, 113,* 101–131.

Granillo, M. T., Perron, B. E., Jarman, C., & Gutowski, S. M. (2013). Cognitive behavioral therapy with substance use disorders: Theory, evidence, and practice. In M. G. Vaughn & B. E. Perron (Eds.), *Social work practice in the addictions* (pp. 101–118). New York, NY: Springer.

Grant, B. F., Hasin, D. S., Stinson, F. S., Dawson, D. A., Ruan, J., Goldstein, R. B., Smith, S. M., Saha, T. D., & Huang, B. (2005). Prevalence, correlates, comorbidity, and comparative disability of *DSM-IV* generalized anxiety disorder in the USA: Results from the National Epidemiological Survey of Alcohol and Related Conditions. *Psychological Medicine, 35,* 747–759.

Grant, B. F., Stinson, F. S., Dawson, D. A., Chou, S. P., DuFour, M. C., Compton,

W., Pickering, R. P., & Kaplan, K. (2004). Prevalence and co-occurrence of substance use disorders and independent mood and anxiety disorders: Results from the national survey on alcohol and related conditions. *Archives of General Psychiatry, 61,* 807–816.

Grant, B., Chou, S., Goldstein, R., Huang, B., Stinson, F., Saha, T., & Pickering, R, P. (2008). Prevalence, correlates, disability, and comorbidity of DSM-IV borderline personality disorder: Results from the Wave 2 National Epidemiologic Survey on Alcohol and Related Conditions. *The Journal of Clinical Psychiatry, 69*(4), 533.

Grant, I., Patterson, T. L., & Yager, J. (1988). Social supports in relation to physical health and symptoms of depression in the elderly. *American Journal of Psychiatry, 145*(10), 1254–1258.

Grant, J. E. (2003). Family history and psychiatric comorbidity in persons with kleptomania. *Comprehensive Psychiatry, 44*(6), 437–441.

Grant, J. E., & Kim, S. W. (2002). Temperament and early environmental influences in kleptomania. *Comprehensive Psychiatry, 43,* 223–229.

Grant, J. E., Correia, S., & Brennan-Krohn, T. (2006). White matter integrity in kleptomania: A pilot study. *Psychiatry Research: Neuroimaging, 147,* 233–237.

Grant, J. E., Kim, S. W., & Odlaug, B. L. (2009). A double-blind, placebo-controlled study of the opiate antagonist, naltrexone, in the treatment of kleptomania. *Biological Psychiatry, 65*(7), 600–606.

Grant, J. E., Odlaug, B. L., & Kim, S. W. (2010). Kleptomania: Clinical characteristics and relationship to substance use disorders. *The American Journal of Drug and Alcohol Abuse, 36*(5), 291–295.

Grant, J. E., Pinto, A., & Chamberlain, S. R. (2020). *Obsessive-compulsive personality disorder*. Washington, D.C.: American Psychiatric Association Publishing.

Grant, J. E., Stein, D. J., Woods, D. W., & Keuthen, N. J. (Eds.). (2012). *Trichotillomania, skin picking, and other body-focused repetitive behaviors.* Arlington, VA: American Psychiatric Publishing.

Grant, J. E., Odlaug, B. L., & Schreiber, L. R. N. (2015). Pathologic gambling: Clinical characteristics and treatment. In R. K. Ries, D. A. Fiellin, S. C. Miller, & R. Saitz (Eds.), *The ASAM principles of addiction medicine* (5th ed., pp. 575–587). New York, NY: Wolters Kluwer.

Grant, K. E., Compas, B. E., Thurm, A. E., McMahon, S. D., & Gipson, P. Y. (2004). Stressors and child and adolescent psychopathology: Measurement issues and prospective effects. *Journal of Clinical Child and Adolescent Psychology, 33*(2), 412–425.

Gray, J. A. (1982). *The neuropsychology of anxiety.* New York, NY: Oxford University Press.

Gray, J. A. (1985). Issues in the neuropsychology of anxiety. In A. H. Tuma & J. D. Maser (Eds.), *Anxiety and the anxiety disorders* (pp. 5–25). Hillside, NJ: Erlbaum.

Gray, J. A. (1987). *The psychology of fear and stress* (2nd ed.). New York, NY: Cambridge University Press.

Gray, J. A., & Buffery, A. W. H. (1971). Sex differences in emotional and cognitive behavior in mammals including man: Adaptive and neural bases. *Acta Psychologica, 35,* 89–111.

Gray, J. A., & McNaughton, N. (1996). The neuropsychology of anxiety: Reprise. In D. A. Hope (Ed.), *Perspectives on anxiety, panic and fear* (The 43rd Annual Nebraska Symposium on Motivation) (pp. 61–134). Lincoln: Nebraska University Press.

Gray, J. A., & McNaughton, N. (2003). *The neuropsychology of anxiety: An enquiry into the function of the septo-hippocampal system.* Oxford, UK: Oxford University Press.

Gray, K. M., & Milin, R. (2021). Adolescent substance misuse/use disorders: Management. *Textbook of addiction treatment* (pp. 1495–1500). New York, NY: Springer.

Graybar, S. R., & Boutilier, L. R. (2002). Nontraumatic pathways to borderline personality disorder. *Psychotherapy: Theory/Research /Practice/Training, 39,* 152–162.

Grazzi, L., Andrasik, F., D'Amico, D., Leone, M., Usai, S., Kass, S. J., & Bussone, G. (2002). Behavioral and pharmacologic treatment of transformed migraine with analgesic overuse: Outcome at 3 years. *Headache, 42,* 483–490.

Grebb, J. A., & Carlsson, A. (2009). Introduction and considerations for a brain-based diagnostic system in psychiatry. In B. J. Sadock, V. A. Sadock, & P. Ruiz (Eds.), *Kaplan & Sadock's comprehensive textbook of psychiatry* (9th ed., Vol. I, pp. 1–5). Philadelphia, PA: Lippincott Williams & Wilkins.

Greely, H., & Simpson, J. R. (2012). *Neuroimaging in forensic psychiatry: From the clinic to the courtroom.* New York, NY: Wiley.

Green McDonald, P., O'Connell, M., & Suls, J. (2015). Cancer control falls squarely within the province of the psychological sciences. *American Psychologist, 70*(2), 61.

Green, B. L., Grace, M. C., Lindy, J. D., Titchener, J. L., & Lindy, J. G. (1983). Levels of functional impairment following a civilian disaster: The Beverly Hills Supper Club fire. *Journal of Consulting and Clinical Psychology, 51,* 573–580.

Green, C. R., Ndao-Brumblay, S. K., & Hart-Johnson, T. (2009). Sleep problems in a racially diverse chronic pain population. *The Clinical Journal of Pain, 25*(5), 423–430.

Green, R. (1987). *The "sissy boy syndrome" and the development of homosexuality.* New Haven, CT: Yale University Press.

Green, R., & Money, J. (1969). *Transsexualism and sex reassignment.* Baltimore, MD: Johns Hopkins Press.

Greenberg, B. D., Rauch, S. L., & Haber, S. N. (2010). Invasive circuitry-based neurotherapeutics: Stereotactic ablation and deep brain stimulation for OCD. *Neuropsychopharmacology, 35*(1), 317–336. doi: 10.1038/npp.2009.128

Greenberg, D. R., & LaPorte, D. L. (1996). Racial differences in body type preferences of men for women. *International Journal of Eating Disorders, 19,* 275–278.

Greenberg, H. R. (2005). Impulse-control disorders not elsewhere classified. In B. J. Sadock & V. A. Sadock (Eds.), *Kaplan & Sadock's comprehensive textbook of psychiatry* (8th ed., pp. 2035–2054). Philadelphia, PA: Lippincott, Williams & Wilkins.

Greenough, W. T., Withers, G. S., & Wallace, C. S. (1990). Morphological changes in the nervous system arising from behavioral experience: What is the evidence that they are involved in learning and memory? In L. R. Squire & E. Lindenlaub (Eds.), *The biology of memory, Symposia Medica Hoescht 23* (pp. 159–183). Stuttgart/New York, NY: Schattauer Verlag.

Greenwood, T. A., Lazzeroni, L. C., Calkins, M. E., Freedman, R., Green, M. F., Gur, R. E., . . . Radant, A. D. (2016). Genetic assessment of additional endophenotypes from the Consortium on the Genetics of Schizophrenia Family Study. *Schizophrenia Research, 170*(1), 30–40.

Greenwood, T. A., Lazzeroni, L. C., Murray, S. S., Cadenhead, K. S., Calkins, M. E., Dobie, D. J., . . . Braff, D. L. (2014). Analysis of 94 candidate genes and 12 endophenotypes for schizophrenia from the Consortium on the Genetics of Schizophrenia. *American Journal of Psychiatry, 168*(9), 930–946. http://dx.doi.org/10.1176/appi.ajp.2011.10050723

Greenwood, T. A., Swerdlow, N. R., Gur, R. E., Cadenhead, K. S., Calkins, M. E., Dobie, D. J., & Braff, D. L. (2013). Genome-wide linkage analyses of 12 endophenotypes for schizophrenia from the Consortium on the Genetics of Schizophrenia. *American Journal of Psychiatry, 170*(5), 521–532.

Greeven, A., Van Balkom, A., Visser, S., Merkelbach, J., Van Rood, Y., Van Dyck, R., & Spinhoven, P. (2007). Cognitive behavior therapy and paroxetine in the treatment of hypochondriasis: A

randomized controlled trial. *American Journal of Psychiatry, 164*, 91–99.
Gregg, N. (2013). Adults with learning disabilities: Factors contributing to persistence. In H. L. Swanson, K. R. Harris, & S. Graham (Eds.), *Handbook of learning disabilities* (2nd ed., pp. 85–103). New York, NY: Guilford.
Gregoire, A. (1992). New treatments for erectile impotence. *British Journal of Psychiatry, 160*, 315–326.
Grenier, S., Payette, M., Gunther, B., Askari, S., Desjardins, F. F., Raymond, B., & Berbiche, D. (2019). Association of age and gender with anxiety disorders in older adults: A systematic review and meta-analysis. *International Journal of Geriatric Psychiatry,34*(3), 397–407. doi: 10.1002/gps.5035
Greydanus, D. E., Kaplan, G., & Patel, D. R. (2015). Pharmacology of autism spectrum disorder. In S. H. Fatemi (Ed.), *Molecular basis of autism* (pp. 173–194). New York, NY: Springer.
Griebel, G., & Holmes, A. (2013). 50 years of hurdles and hope in anxiolytic drug discovery. *Nat Rev Drug Discov* 12, 667–687 (2013). https://doi.org/10.1038/nrd4075
Griffith, E. E. H., English, T., & Mayfield, U. (1980). Possession, prayer and testimony: Therapeutic aspects of the Wednesday night meeting in a black church. *Psychiatry, 43*(5), 120–128.
Griffiths, R. R., Richards, W. A., McCann, U., & Jesse, R. (2006). Psilocybin can occasion mystic-type experiences having substantial and sustained personal meaning and spiritual significance. *Psychopharmacology, 187*, 268–283.
Griffiths, R., Richards, W., Johnson, M., McCann, U., & Jesse, R. (2008). Mystical-type experiences occasioned by psilocybin mediate the attribution of personal meaning and spiritual significance 14 months later. *Journal of Psychopharmacology, 22*(6), 621.
Grigorenko, E. L., Compton, D. L., Fuchs, L. S., Wagner, R. K., Willcutt, E. G., & Fletcher, J. M. (2020). Understanding, educating, and supporting children with specific learning disabilities: 50 years of science and practice. *American Psychologist, 75*(1), 37.
Grilo, C. M., Crosby, R. D., Wilson, G. T., & Masheb, R. M. (2012). 12-Month follow-up of fluoxetine and cognitive behavioral therapy for binge eating disorder. *Journal of Consulting and Clinical Psychology, 80*(6), 1108–1113.
Grilo, C. M., Masheb, R. M., & White, M. A. (2010). Significance of overvaluation of shape/weight in binge-eating disorder: Comparative study with overweight and bulimia nervosa. *Obesity, 18*, 499–504.
Grilo, C. M., Masheb, R. M., & Wilson, G. T. (2001). Subtyping binge eating disorder. *Journal of Consulting and Clinical Psychology, 69*, 1066–1072.
Grilo, C. M., Masheb, R. M., & Wilson, G. T. (2005). Efficacy of cognitive behavioral therapy and fluoxetine for the treatment of binge eating disorder: A randomized double-blind placebo-controlled comparison. *Biological Psychiatry, 57*(3), 301–309.
Grilo, C. M., Masheb, R. M., & Wilson, G. T. (2006). Rapid response to treatment for binge eating disorder. *Journal of Consulting and Clinical Psychology, 74*, 602–613.
Grilo, C. M., Masheb, R. M., Wilson, G. T., Gueorguieva, R., & White, M. A. (2011). Cognitive-behavioral therapy, behavioral weight loss, and sequential treatment for obese patients with binge-eating disorder: A randomized controlled trial. *Journal of Consulting and Clinical Psychology, 79*(5), 675–685.
Grimm, O., Kranz, T. M., & Reif, A. (2020). Genetics of ADHD: What should the clinician know? *Current Psychiatry Reports, 22*(4), 18. doi: 10.1007/s11920-020-1141-x
Grinspoon, L., & Bakalar, J. B. (1980). Drug dependence: Non-narcotic agents. In H. I. Kaplan, A. M. Freedman, & B. J. Sadock (Eds.), *Comprehensive textbook of psychiatry* (3rd ed., pp. 1614–1629). Baltimore, MD: Williams & Wilkins.
Grisham, J. R., & Barlow, D. H. (2005). Compulsive hoarding: Current research and theory. *Journal of Psychopathology and Behavioral Assessment, 27*, 45–52.
Grisham, J. R., Norberg, M. M., & Certoma, S. P. (2012). Treatment of compulsive hoarding. In G. Steketee (Ed.), *The Oxford handbook of obsessive compulsive and spectrum disorders* (pp. 422–435). New York, NY: Oxford University Press.
Grisham, J., Frost, R. O., Steketee, G., Kim, H. J., & Hood, S. (2006). Age of onset of compulsive hoarding. *Journal of Anxiety Disorders, 20*, 675–686.
Grizenko, N., Fortier, M.-E., Zadorozny, C., Thakur, G., Schmitz, N., Duval, R., & Joober, R. (2012). Maternal stress during pregnancy, ADHD symptomatology in children and genotype: Gene-environment interaction. *Journal of the Canadian Academy of Child and Adolescent Psychiatry, 21*(1), 9.
Grogan, S. (2016). Body image: Understanding body dissatisfaction in men, women and children (3rd ed.). Abingdon, UK: Routledge. doi: org/10.4324/9781315681528
Gross, J. J. (2015). *Handbook of emotion regulation* (2nd ed.). New York, NY: Guilford.
Grossardt, B. R., Bower, J. H., Geda, Y. E., Colligan, R. C., & Rocca, W. A. (2009). Pessimistic, anxious, and depressive personality traits predict all-cause mortality: The Mayo Clinic Cohort Study of Personality and Aging. *Psychosomatic Medicine, 71*, 491–500.
Grossbard, J. R., Neighbors, C., & Larimer, M. E. (2011). Perceived norms for thinness and muscularity among college students: What do men and women really want? *Eating Behaviors, 12*,192–199.
Grossman, C. I., Purcell, D. W., Rotheram-Borus, M. J., & Veniegas, R. (2013). Opportunities for HIV combination prevention to reduce racial and ethnic health disparities. *American Psychologist, 68*(4), 237–246.
Grosz, H. J., & Zimmerman, J. (1970). A second detailed case study of functional blindness: Further demonstration of the contribution of objective psychological laboratory data. *Behavior Therapy, 1*, 115–123.
Gruber, J., Johnson, S. L., Oveis, C., & Keltner, D. (2008). Risk for mania and positive emotional responding: Too much of a good thing? *Emotion, 8*(1), 23–33.
Gu, D., Kelly, T. N., Wu. X., Chen, J., Samet, J. M., Huang, J. F., & He, J. (2009). Mortality attributable to smoking in China. *New England Journal of Medicine, 360*, 150–159.
Gu, P. K., & Sullivan, S. S. (2021). Pediatric obstructive sleep apnea. In E. H. During & C. A. Kushida (Eds.), *Clinical sleep medicine: A comprehensive guide for mental health and other medical professionals* (pp. 171–185). Washington, D.C.: American Psychiatric Association Publishing.
Guedeney, N. (2007). Withdrawal behavior and depression in infancy. *Infant Mental Health Journal, 28*, 393–408.
Guerdjikova, A. I., Mori, N., Casuto, L. S., & McElroy, S. L. (2019). Update on binge eating disorder. *Medical Clinics of North America, 103*(4), 669–680. doi: 10.1016/j.mcna.2019.02.003
Gui, A., Mason, L., Gliga, T., Hendry, A., Ali, J. B., Pasco, G., … Johnson, M. H. (2020). Look duration at the face as a developmental endophenotype: Elucidating pathways to autism and ADHD. *Development and Psychopathology, 32*(4), 1303–1322.
Guilleminault, C. (1989). Clinical features and evaluation of obstructive sleep apnea. In M. H. Kryger, T. Roth, & W. C. Dement (Eds.), *Principles and practice of sleep medicine* (pp. 552–558). Philadelphia, PA: W. B. Saunders.
Gulliksson, M., Burell, G., Vessby, B., Lundin, L., Toss, H., & Svärdsudd, K. (2011). Randomized controlled trial of cognitive behavioral therapy vs standard treatment to prevent recurrent cardiovascular events in patients with coronary heart disease: Secondary Prevention in Uppsala Primary Health Care project (SUPRIM). *Archives of Internal Medicine, 171*(2), 134–140.

Gunay-Oge, R., Pehlivan, F. Z., & Isikli, S. (2020). The effect of positive childhood experiences on adult personality psychopathology. *Personality and Individual Differences, 158*, 109862.

Gündel, H., O'Connor, M. F., Littrell, L., Fort, C., & Lane, R. D. (2003). Functional neuroanatomy of grief: An FMRI study. *American Journal of Psychiatry, 160*, 1946–1953.

Gunderson, J. G. (2011). Borderline personality disorder. *New England Journal of Medicine, 364*, 2037–2042.

Gunderson, J. G., & Palmer, B. A. (2019). Inpatient psychiatric units. In L. W. Choi-Kain & J. G. Gunderson (Eds.), *Applications of good psychiatric management for borderline personality disorder: A practical guide* (pp. 11–35). Washington, D.C.: American Psychiatric Association Publishing.

Gunderson, J. G., Ronningstam, E., & Smith, L. E. (1991). Narcissistic personality disorder: A review of data on DSM-III-R descriptions. *Journal of Personality Disorders, 5*, 167–177.

Gunderson, J. G., Stout, R. L., McGlashan, T. H., Shea, M. T., Morey, L. C., . . . Zanarini, M. C. (2011). Ten-year course of borderline personality disorder: psychopathology and function from the Collaborative Longitudinal Personality Disorders study. *Archives of General Psychiatry, 68*(8), 827–837.

Gunn, M., & Wheat, K. (2012). General principles of law relating to people with mental disorder. In M. G. Gelder, N. C. Andreasen, J. J. Lopez-Ibor, Jr., & J. R. Geddes (Eds.), *New Oxford Textbook of Psychiatry* (2nd ed., Vol. 2, pp. 1895–1907). New York, NY: Oxford University Press.

Gunnar, M. R., & Fisher, P. A. (2006). Bringing basic research on early experience and stress neurobiology to bear on preventive interventions for neglected and maltreated children. *Development and Psychopathology, 18*(3), 651–677.

Gupta, S., & Bonanno, G. A. (2011). Complicated grief and deficits in emotional expressive flexibility. *Journal of Abnormal Psychology, 120*(3), 635–643.

Gur, R. E., Nimgaonkar, V. L., Almasy, L., Calkins, M. E., Ragland, J. D., Pogue-Geile, M. F., & Gur, R. C. (2007). Neurocognitive endophenotypes in a multiplex multigenerational family study of schizophrenia. *American Journal of Psychiatry, 164*, 813–819.

Guralnik, O., Giesbrecht, T., Knutelska, M., Sirroff, B., & Simeon, D. (2007). Cognitive functioning in depersonalization disorder. *Journal of Nervous and Mental Disease, 195*(12), 983–988.

Guralnik, O., Schmeidler, J., & Simeon, D. (2000). Feeling unreal: Cognitive processes in depersonalization. *American Journal of Psychiatry, 157*(1), 103–109.

Gureje, O. (2004). What can we learn from a cross-national study of somatic distress? *Journal of Psychosomatic Research, 56*, 409–412.

Gureje, O., Simon, G. E., Ustun, T. B., & Goldberg, D. P. (1997). Somatization in cross-cultural perspective: A World Health Organization study in primary care. *American Journal of Psychiatry, 154*, 989–995.

Gurvits, T. V., Shenton, M. E., Hokama, H., Ohta, H., Lasko, N. B., Gilbertson, M. W., & Pitman, R. K. (1996). Magnetic resonance imaging study of hippocampal volume in chronic, combat-related posttraumatic stress disorder. *Biological Psychiatry, 40*, 1091–1099.

Gusella, J. F., Wexler, N. S., Conneally, P. M., Naylor, S. L., Anderson, M. A., Tanzi, R. E., & Martin, J. B. (1983). A polymorphic DNA marker genetically linked to Huntington's disease. *Nature, 306*, 234–239.

Gustad, J., & Phillips, K. A. (2003). Axis I comorbidity in body dysmorphic disorder. *Comprehensive Psychiatry, 44*, 270–276.

Gustafson, L., & Brun, A. (2012). Frontotemporal dementias. In M. G. Gelder, N. C. Andreasen, J. J. Lopez-Ibor, Jr., & J. R. Geddes (Eds.), *New Oxford Textbook of Psychiatry* (2nd ed., Vol. 1, pp. 344–350). New York, NY: Oxford University Press.

Gutierrez, D., Crowe, A., Mullen, P. R., Pignato, L., & Fan, S. (2020). Stigma, help seeking, and substance use. *Professional Counselor, 10*(2), 220–234.

Guttmannova, K., Bailey, J. A., Hill, K. G., Lee, J. O., Hawkins, J. D., Woods, M. L., & Catalano, R. F. (2011). Sensitive periods for adolescent alcohol use initiation: Predicting the lifetime occurrence and chronicity of alcohol problems in adulthood. *Journal of Studies on Alcohol and Drugs, 72*(2), 221–231.

Guze, S. B., Cloninger, C. R., Martin, R. L., & Clayton, P. J. (1986). A follow-up and family study of Briquet's syndrome. *British Journal of Psychiatry, 149*, 17–23.

Haber, S. N., & Barchas, P. R. (1983). The regulatory effect of social rank on behavior after amphetamine administration. In P. R. Burchas (Ed.), Social hierarchies: Essays toward a sociophysiological perspective (pp. 119–132). Westport, CT: Greenwood Press.

Hackett, T. P., & Cassem, N. H. (1973). Psychological adaptation to convalescence in myocardial infarction patients. In J. P. Naughton, H. K. Hellerstein, & I. C. Mohler (Eds.), *Exercise testing and exercise training in coronary heart disease.* New York, NY: Academic Press.

Haddad, P. M., Brain, C., & Scott, J. (2014). Nonadherence with antipsychotic medication in schizophrenia: challenges and management strategies. *Patient Related Outcome Measures, 5*, 43–62.

Hadland, S. E., Austin, S. B., Goodenow, C. S., & Calzo, J. P. (2014). Weight misperception and unhealthy weight control behaviors among sexual minorities in the general adolescent population. *Journal of Adolescent Health, 54*(3), 296–303.

Hadley, S., Kim, S., Priday, L., & Hollander, E. (2006). Pharmacologic treatment of body dysmorphic disorder. *Primary Psychiatry*, 13, 61–69.

Haeffel, G. J., & Hames, J. L. (2014). Cognitive vulnerability to depression can be contagious. *Clinical Psychological Science, 2*, 75–85.

Haenen, M. A., de Jong, P. J., Schmidt, A. J. M., Stevens, S., & Visser, L. (2000). Hypochondriacs' estimation of negative outcomes: Domain-specificity and responsiveness to reassuring and alarming information. *Behaviour Research and Therapy, 38*, 819–833.

Hahn, T., Kircher, T., Straube, B., Wittchen, H-U., Konrad, C., Ströhle, A., Wittmann, A., Pfleiderer, B., Reif, A., Arolt, V., & Lueken, U. (2015). Predicting treatment response to cognitive behavioral therapy in panic disorder with agoraphobia by integrating local neural information. *JAMA Psychiatry, 72*, 68–74.

Halahakoon, D. C., Kieslich, K., O'Driscoll, C., Nair, A., Lewis, G., & Roiser, J. P. (2020). Reward-processing behavior in depressed participants relative to healthy volunteers: A systematic review and meta-analysis. *JAMA Psychiatry, 77*(12), 1286–1295. doi:10.1001/jamapsychiatry.2020.2139

Hall, K. (2007). Sexual dysfunction and childhood sexual abuse: Gender differences and treatment implications. In S. R. Leiblum (Ed.), *Principles and practice of sex therapy* (4th ed., pp. 350–378). New York, NY: Guilford.

Hall, L. S., & Love, C. T. (2003). Finger-length ratios in female monozygotic twins discordant for sexual orientation. *Archives of Sexual Behavior, 32*, 23–28.

Hall, R. C., & Tardif, I. (2020). Florida law enforcement policies for and experience with Tarasoff-like reporting. *Journal of the American Academy of Psychiatry and the Law.*

Halliburton, A. E., & Bray, B. C. (2016). Long-Term Prevalence and Demographic Trends in US Adolescent Inhalant Use: Implications for Clinicians and Prevention Scientists. *Substance Use & Misuse*, 1–14.

Hallmayer, J., Cleveland, S., Torres, A., Phillips, J., Cohen, B., Torigoe, T., & Smith, K. (2011). Genetic heritability and shared environmental factors among twin pairs with autism. *Archives of General Psychiatry*, archgenpsychiatry. 2011.2076 v2011.

Halmi, K. A., Bellace, D., Berthod, S., Ghosh, S., Berrettini, W., Brandt, H. A., . . . Strober, M. (2012). An examination of early childhood perfectionism across anorexia nervosa subtypes. *International Journal of Eating Disorders, 45*(6), 800–807.

Hamer, D. H., Hu, S., Magnuson, V. L., Hu, N., & Pattatucci, A. M. (1993). A linkage between DNA markers on the X chromosome and male sexual orientation. *Science, 261,* 321–327.

Hamilton, J. L., Stange, J. P., Abramson, L. Y., & Alloy, L. B. (in press). Stress and the development of cognitive vulnerabilities to depression explain sex differences in depressive symptoms during adolescence. *Clinical Psychological Science,* 2167702614545479.

Hamilton, J. L., Stange, J. P., Abramson, L. Y., & Alloy, L. B. (2015). Stress and the development of cognitive vulnerabilities to depression explain sex differences in depressive symptoms during adolescence. *Clinical Psychological Science, 3*(5), 702–714. doi: 10.1177/2167702614545479

Hamm, J., Pinkham, A., Gur, R. C., Verma, R., & Kohler, C. G. (2014). Dimensional information-theoretic measurement of facial emotion expressions in schizophrenia. *Schizophrenia Research and Treatment, 2014,* ID 243907.

Hammen, C. (2005). Stress and depression. *Annual Review of Clinical Psychology, 1,* 293–319.

Hammen, C. (2009). Children of depressed parents. In I. H. Gotlib & C. Hammen (Eds.), *Handbook of depression* (2nd ed., pp. 275–297). New York, NY: Guilford.

Hammen, C., & Keenan-Miller, D. (2013). In G. Stricker, T. A. Widiger, & I. B. Weiner (Eds.), *Handbook of psychology, Volume 8: Clinical psychology* (pp. 121–146). Hoboken, NJ: Wiley.

Hammer, S., Saag, M., Scheechter, M., Montaner, J., Schooley, R., Jacobsen, D., & the International AIDS Society-USA Panel. (2006). Treatment for adult HIV infection: 2006 recommendations of the International AIDS Society-USA panel. *JAMA: Journal of the American Medical Association, 296,* 827–843.

Hammond, C. J., Hendrickson, B., & Fishman, M. (2020). Youth opioid use. In Y. Kaminer & K. C. Winters (Eds.), *Clinical manual of youth addictive disorders* (pp. 203–227). Washington, D.C.: American Psychiatric Association Publishing.

Hampton, T. (2010). Depression care effort brings dramatic drop in large HMO population's suicide rate. *JAMA: Journal of the American Medical Association, 303*(19), 1903–1905.

Hancock, T. B., & Kaiser, A. P. (2012). Implementing enhanced milieu teaching with children who have autism spectrum disorders. In P. A. Prelock & R. J. McCauley (Eds.), *Treatment of autism spectrum disorders: Evidence based-intervention strategies for communication and social interactions* (pp. 163–187). Baltimore, MD: Paul H. Brookes.

Hankin, B. L., & Abramson, L. Y. (2001). Development of gender differences in depression: An elaborated cognitive vulnerability–transactional stress theory. *Psychological Bulletin, 127,* 773–796.

Hankin, B. L., Wetter, E., & Cheely, C. (2007). Sex differences in adolescent depression: A developmental psychopathological approach. In J. R. Z. Abela & B. L. Hankin (Eds.), *Handbook of depression in children and adolescents* (pp. 377–414). New York, NY: Guilford.

Hanlon, E. C., & Knutson, K. L. (2014). Sleep deprivation and metabolism. In *Sleep Deprivation and Disease* (pp. 111–129). Springer.

Hanlon, E. C., & Van Cauter, E. (2011). Quantification of sleep behavior and of its impact on the cross-talk between the brain and peripheral metabolism. *Proceedings of the National Academy of Sciences, 108*(Supplement 3), 15609–15616. doi: 10.1073/pnas.1101338108

Hanna, G. L. (1995). Demographic and clinical features of obsessive-compulsive disorder in children and adolescents. *Journal of the American Academy of Child and Adolescent Psychiatry, 34,* 19–27.

Hannema, S., Schagen, S., Hoekzema, E., Kreukels, B., Veltman, D., Cohen-Kettenis, P., & Bakker, J. (2014). *Brain Structure and Function in Gender Dysphoric Adolescents.* Poster presented at 53rd Annual ESPE Meeting, Dublin, Ireland.

Hans, V. P. (1986). An analysis of public attitudes toward the insanity defense. *Criminology, 4,* 393–415.

Hanson, R. K., Gordon, A., Harris, A. J. R., Marques, J. K., Murphy, W., Quinsey, V. L., & Seto, M. C. (2002). First report on the collaborative outcome data project on the effectiveness of psychological treatment for sex offenders. *Sexual Abuse: A Journal of Research and Treatment, 14,* 169–194.

Hanson, R. K., Steffy, R. A., & Gauthier, R. (1993). Long-term recidivism of child molesters. *Journal of Consulting and Clinical Psychology, 61,* 646–652.

Hantouche, E., Akiskal, H., Azorin, J., Chatenet-Duchene, L., & Lancrenon, S. (2006). Clinical and psychometric characterization of depression in mixed mania: A report from the French National Cohort of 1090 manic patients. *Journal of Affective Disorders, 96,* 225–232.

Hara, K., Adachi, N., Akanuma, N., Ito, M., Okazaki, M., Matsubara, R., Adachi, T., Ishii, R., Kanemoto, K., Matsuura, M., Hara, J., Kato, M., & Onuma, T. (2015). Dissociative experiences in epilepsy: Effects of epilepsy-related factors on pathological dissociation. *Epilepsy and Behavior, 44,* 185–191.

Harbert, T. L., Barlow, D. H., Hersen, M., & Austin, J. B. (1974). Measurement and modification of incestuous behavior: A case study. *Psychological Reports, 34,* 79–86.

Harburg, E., Kaciroti, N., Gleiberman, L., Julius, M., & Schork, M. A. (2008). Marital pair anger-coping types may act as an entity to affect mortality: Preliminary findings from a prospective study (Tecumseh, Michigan, 1971–1988). *Journal of Family Communication, 8*(1), 44–61.

Hardie, T. L., Moss, H. B., & Lynch, K. G. (2006). Genetic correlations between smoking initiation and smoking behaviors in a twin sample. *Addictive Behaviors, 31*(11), 2030–2037.

Hare, R. D. (1970). *Psychopathy: Theory and research.* New York, NY: Wiley.

Hare, R. D. (1993). *Without conscience: The disturbing world of the psychopaths among us.* New York, NY: Pocket Books.

Hare, R. D., & Neumann, C. S. (2006). The PCL-R assessment of psychopathology: Development, structural properties, and new directions. In C. J. Patrick (Ed.), *Handbook of psychopathy* (pp. 58–88). New York, NY: Guilford.

Hare, R. D., & Vertommen, H. (2003). *The Hare psychopathy checklist—revised.* Toronto, Canada: Multi-Health Systems.

Hare, R. D., McPherson, L. M., & Forth, A. E. (1988). Male psychopaths and their criminal careers. *Journal of Consulting and Clinical Psychology, 56,* 710–714.

Hare, R. D., Neumann, C. S., & Widiger, T. A. (2012). Psychopathy. In T. A. Widiger (Ed.), *The Oxford handbook of personality disorders* (pp. 478–504). New York, NY: Oxford University Press.

Harich, B., van der Voet, M., Klein, M., Čížek, P., Fenckova, M., Schenck, A., & Franke, B. (2020). From rare copy number variants to biological processes in ADHD. *American Journal of Psychiatry, 177*(9), 855–866.

Hariri, A. R., Mattay, V. S., Tessitore, A., Kolachana, B., Fera, F., Goldman, D., & Weinberger, D. R. (2002). Serotonin transporter genetic variation and the response of the human amygdala. *Science, 297,* 400–402.

Harmell, A. L., Palmer, B. W., & Jeste, D. V. (2012). Preliminary study of a web-based tool for enhancing the informed consent process in schizophrenia research. *Schizophrenia Research, 141*(2–3), 247–250. doi: http://dx.doi.org/10.1016/j.schres.2012.08.001

Harmer, C. J. (2008). Serotonin and emotional processing: Does it help explain antidepressant drug action? *Neuropharmacology, 55*(6), 1023–1028.

Harmer, C. J., O'Sullivan, U., Favaron, E., Massey-Chase, R., Ayres, R., Reinecke, A., & Cowen, P. J. (2009). Effect of acute antidepressant administration on negative affective bias in depressed patients. *The American Journal of Psychiatry, 166*(10), 1178–1184.

Harp, K. L., & Bunting, A. M. (2020). The racialized nature of child welfare policies and the social control of Black bodies. *Social Politics: International Studies in Gender, State & Society, 27*(2), 258–281.

Harper, L. V. (2005). Epigenetic inheritance and the intergenerational transfer of experience. *Psychological Bulletin, 131,* 340–360.

Harpur, T. J., Hare, R. D., & Hakstian, A. R. (1989). Two-factor conceptualization of psychopathy: Construct validity and assessment implications. *Psychological Assessment: A Journal of Consulting and Clinical Psychology, 1,* 6–17.

Harrer, M., Adam, S. H., Messner, E., Baumeister, H., Cuijpers, P., Bruffaerts, R., ... Ebert, D. D. (2020). Prevention of eating disorders at universities: A systematic review and meta-analysis. *International Journal of Eating Disorders, 53*(6), 813–833. doi: 10.1002/eat.23224

Harrison, B. J., Pujol, J., Cardoner, N., Deus, J., Alonso, P., Lopez-Sola, M., & Soriano-Mas, C. (2013). Brain corticostriatal systems and the major clinical symptom dimensions of obsessive-compulsive disorder. *Biological Psychiatry, 73*(4), 321–328. doi: 10.1016/j.biopsych.2012.10.006

Harrison, M. A., & Frederick, E. J. (in press). Interested in serial killers? Morbid curiosity in college students. *Current Psychology.*

Harrison, P. J. (2012). The neurobiology of schizophrenia. In M. G. Gelder, N. C. Andreasen, J. J. Lopez-Ibor, Jr., & J. R. Geddes (Eds.), *New Oxford Textbook of Psychiatry* (2nd ed., Vol. 1, pp. 561–568). New York, NY: Oxford University Press.

Hart, S. D., Forth, A. E., & Hare, R. D. (1990). Performance of criminal psychopaths on selected neuropsychological tests. *Journal of Abnormal Psychology, 99,* 374–379.

Harte, C. B., & Meston, C. M. (2008a). Acute effects of nicotine on physiological and subjective sexual arousal in nonsmoking men: A randomized, double-blind, placebo-controlled trial. *The Journal of Sexual Medicine, 5*(1), 110–121.

Harte, C. B., & Meston, C. M. (2008b). The inhibitory effects of nicotine on physiological sexual arousal in nonsmoking women: Results from a randomized, double-blind, placebo-controlled, cross-over trial. *The Journal of Sexual Medicine, 5*(5), 1184–1197.

Hartlage, S. A., Freels, S., Gotman, N., & Yonkers, K. (2012). Criteria for premenstrual dysphoric disorder: Secondary analyses of relevant data sets. *Archives of General Psychiatry, 69*(3), 300–305.

Hartvigsen, J., Hancock, M. J., Kongsted, A., Louw, Q., Ferreira, M. L., Genevay, S., ... Lancet Low Back Pain Series Working Group. (2018). What low back pain is and why we need to pay attention. *The Lancet, 391*(10137), 2356–2367. doi: 10.1016/S0140-6736(18)30480-X

Hartwell, E. E., Feinn, R., Morris, P. E., Gelernter, J., Krystal, J., Arias, A. J., ... Schacht, J. P. (2020). Systematic review and meta-analysis of the moderating effect of rs1799971 in OPRM1, the mu-opioid receptor gene, on response to naltrexone treatment of alcohol use disorder. *Addiction, 115*(8), 1426–1437.

Harvey, A. G. (2008). Sleep and circadian rhythms in bipolar disorder: Seeking synchrony, harmony, and regulation. *The American Journal of Psychiatry, 165*(7), 820–829.

Harvey, A. G., Soehner, A. M., Kaplan, K. A., Hein, K., Lee, J., Kanady, J., Li, D., Rabe-Hesketh, S., Ketter, T. A., Nylan, T. C., & Buysse, D. J. (2015). Treating insomnia improves mood state, sleep, and functioning in bipolar disorder: A pilot randomized controlled trial. *Journal of Consulting and Clinical Psychology, 83,* 564–577.

Harvey, A. G., Talbot, L. S., & Gershon, A. (2009). Sleep disturbance in bipolar disorder across the lifespan. *Clinical Psychology: Science and Practice, 16*(2), 256–277.

Harvey, P. D., & Bowie, C. R. (2013). Schizophrenia spectrum conditions. In I. B. Weiner (Series Ed.), G. Stricker, & T. A. Widiger (Vol. Eds.), *Handbook of psychology: Vol. 8, Clinical psychology* (pp. 240–261). Hoboken, NJ: John Wiley & Sons.

Harvey, S. B., & Wessely, S. (2009). Chronic fatigue syndrome: Identifying zebras among the horses. *BMC Medicine, 7,* 58. doi: 10.1186/1741-7015-7-58

Harvey, S. B., Wadsworth, M., Wessely, S., & Hotopf, M. (2008). Etiology of chronic fatigue syndrome: Testing popular hypotheses using a national birth cohort study. *Psychosomatic Medicine, 70,* 488–495.

Hasin, D. S. (2012). Combining abuse and dependence in DSM-5. *Journal of studies on alcohol and drugs, 73*(4), 702–704.

Hasin, D. S., Sarvet, A. L., Meyers, J. L., Saha, T. D., Ruan, W. J., Stohl, M., & Grant, B. F. (2018). Epidemiology of adult *DSM-5* major depressive disorder and its specifiers in the United States. *JAMA Psychiatry, 75*(4), 336–346. doi: 10.1001/jamapsychiatry.2017.4602

Hasin, D., Fenton, M. C., Skodol, A., Krueger, R., Keyes, K., ... Grant, B. Personality disorders and the 3-year course of alcohol, drug, and nicotine use disorders. *Archives of General Psychiatry, 68*(11), 68, 1158–1167.

Hasin, D., Goodwin, R., Stinson, F., & Grant, B. (2005). Epidemiology of major depressive disorder. *Archives of General Psychiatry, 62,* 1097–1106.

Haslam, J. (1976). *Observations on madness and melancholy.* New York, NY: Arno Press. (Original work published in 1809.)

Hatfield, E., Cacioppo, J. T., & Rapson, R. L. (1994). *Emotional contagion.* Cambridge: Cambridge University Press.

Hathaway, S. R., & McKinley, J. C. (1943). *Manual for the Minnesota Multiphasic Personality Inventory.* New York, NY: Psychological Corporation.

Haukkala, A., Konttinen, H., Laatikainen, T., Kawachi, I., & Uutela, A. (2010). Hostility, anger control, and anger expression as predictors of cardiovascular disease. *Psychosomatic Medicine, 72*(6), 556–562.

Hauner, K. K., Mineka, S., Voss, J. L., & Paller, K. A. (2012). Exposure therapy triggers lasting reorganization of neural fear processing. *Proceedings of the National Academy of Sciences of the United States, 109*(23), 9203–9208. doi: 10.1073/pnas.1205242109

Hausteiner, C., Klupsch, D., Emeny, R., Baumert, J., Ladwig, K. H., & Investigators. (2010). Clustering of negative affectivity and social inhibition in the community: Prevalence of type D personality as a cardiovascular risk marker. *Psychosomatic Medicine, 72*(2), 163–171.

Hawes, D. J., Helyer, R., Herlianto, E. C., & Willing, J. (2013). Borderline personality features and implicit shame-prone self-concept in middle childhood and early adolescence. *Journal of Clinical Child*

& Adolescent Psychology, 42(3), 302–308. doi: 10.1080/15374416.2012.723264

Hawker, C., Merkouris, S., Youssef, G., & Dowling, N. (2021). Exploring the associations between gambling cravings, self-efficacy, and gambling episodes: An ecological momentary assessment study. *Addictive Behaviors, 112*, 106574.

Hawkley, L. C., & Cacioppo, J. T. (2007). Aging and loneliness: Downhill quickly? *Current Directions in Psychological Science, 16*, 187–191.

Hawkley, L. C., Thisted, R. A., Masi, C. M., & Cacioppo, J. T. (2010). Loneliness predicts increased blood pressure: 5-year cross-lagged analyses in middle-aged and older adults. *Psychology and Aging, 25*(1), 132–141.

Hawton, K. (1995). Treatment of sexual dysfunctions of sex therapy and other approaches. *British Journal of Psychiatry, 167*, 307–314.

Hawton, K., Houston, K., Haw, C., Townsend, E., & Harriss, L. (2003). Comorbidity of axis I and axis II disorders in patients who attempted suicide. *American Journal of Psychiatry, 160*, 1494–1500.

Hay, P. J., & Fairburn, C. (1998). The validity of the DSM-IV scheme for classifying bulimic eating disorders. *International Journal of Eating Disorders, 23*, 7–15.

Hay, P. J., & Hall, A. (1991). The prevalence of eating disorders in recently admitted psychiatric in-patients. *British Journal of Psychiatry, 159*, 562–565.

Hayes, S. C., & Hofmann, S. G. (Eds.) (2020). *Beyond the DSM: Toward a process-based alternative for diagnosis and mental health treatment.*

Hayes, S. C., Barlow, D. H., & Nelson-Gray, R. O. (1999). *The scientist-practitioner: Research and accountability in the age of managed care* (2nd ed.). Boston, MA: Allyn & Bacon.

Hayes-Skelton, S. A., Roemer, L., & Orsillo, S. M. (2013), A randomized clinical trial comparing an acceptance-based behavior therapy to applied relaxation for generalized anxiety disorder. *Journal of Consulting and Clinical Psychology, 81*, 761–773.

Hayley, A. C., Williams, L. J., Venugopal, K., Kennedy, G. A., Berk, M., & Pasco, J. A. (2015). The relationships between insomnia, sleep apnoea and depression: findings from the American National Health and Nutrition Examination Survey, 2005–2008. *Australian & New Zealand Journal of Psychiatry, 49*(2), 156–170.

Haynes, S. G., & Matthews, K. A. (1988). Area review: Coronary-prone behavior: Continuing evolution of the concept: Review and methodologic critique of recent studies on type A behavior and cardiovascular disease. *Annals of Behavioral Medicine, 10*(2), 47–59.

Haynes, S. N., O'Brien, W., & Kaholokula, J. (2011). *Behavioral assessment and case formulation.* New York, NY: Wiley.

Haynes, S. N., Yoshioka, D. T., Kloezeman, K., & Bello, I. (2009). Clinical applications of behavioral assessment. In J. N. Butcher (Ed.), *Oxford handbook of personality assessment* (pp. 226–249). New York, NY: Oxford University Press.

Haynos, A. F., & Fruzzetti, A. E. (2011). Anorexia nervosa as a disorder of emotion dysregulation: Evidence and treatment implications. *Clinical Psychology: Science and Practice, 18*(3), 183–202.

Hazell, P., O'Connell, D., Heathcote, D., Robertson, J., & Henry, D. (1995). Efficacy of tricyclic drugs in treating child and adolescent depression: A meta-analysis. *British Medical Journal, 8*, 897–901.

Hazlett-Stevens, H., & Bernstein, D. A. (2012). Relaxation. In W. T. O'Donohue & J. E. Fisher (Eds.), *Cognitive Behavior Therapy: Core Principles for Practice* (pp. 105–132). Hoboken, NJ: Wiley

He, Y., Cai, B., Shin, H.-C., Beresovsky, V., Parsons, V., Irimata, K., Scanlon, P., & Parker, J. (2020). The National Center for Health Statistics' 2015 and 2016 research and development surveys. *Vital Health Statistics, 59*, 1–60.

He, Y., Chen, J., Zhu, L.-H., Hua, L.-L., & Ke, F.-F. (2020). Maternal smoking during pregnancy and ADHD: Results from a systematic review and meta-analysis of prospective cohort studies. *Journal of Attention Disorders, 24*(12), 1637–1647.

Heath, A. K., Ganz, J. B., Parker, R., Burke, M., & Ninci, J. (2015). A Meta-analytic Review of Functional Communication Training Across Mode of Communication, Age, and Disability. *Review Journal of Autism and Developmental Disorders, 2*(2), 155–166.

Hebert, L. E., Weuve, J., Scherr, P. A., & Evans, D. A. (2013). Alzheimer disease in the United States (2010–2050) estimated using the 2010 census. *Neurology, 80*(19), 1778–1783.

Hecht, K. F., Cicchetti, D., Rogosch, F. A., & Crick, N. R. (2014). Borderline personality features in childhood: The role of subtype, developmental timing, and chronicity of child maltreatment. *Development and Psychopathology, 26*(03), 805–815.

Heckers, S., Barch, D. M., Bustillo, J., Gaebel, W., Gur, R., Malaspina, D., . . . Van Os, J. (2013). Structure of the psychotic disorders classification in DSM-5. *Schizophrenia Research, 150*(1), 11–14.

Heilig, M., & Spanagel, R. (2021). Neurobiology of alcohol. In K. T. Brady, F. R. Levin, M. D. Galanter, & H. D. Kleber (Eds.), *The American Psychiatric Association Publishing textbook of substance use disorder treatment* (pp. 117–140). Washington, D.C.: American Psychiatric Association Publishing.

Heim, C., Plotsky, P., & Nemeroff, C. (2004). Importance of studying the contributions of early adverse experience to neurobiological findings in depression. *Neuropsychopharmacology, 29*, 641–648.

Heim, C., Wagner, D., Maloney, E., Papanicolaou, D., Dimitris, A., Solomon, L., & Reeves, W. C. (2006). Early adverse experience and risk for chronic fatigue syndrome. *Archives of General Psychiatry, 63*, 1258–1266.

Heiman, J. R. (2000). Orgasmic disorders in women. In S. R. Leiblum & R. C. Rosen (Eds.), *Principles and practice of sex therapy* (3rd ed., pp. 118–153). New York, NY: Guilford.

Heiman, J. R. (2007). Orgasmic disorders in women. In S. R. Leiblum (Ed.), *Principles and practice of sex therapy* (4th ed., pp. 84–123). New York, NY: Guilford.

Heiman, J. R., & LoPiccolo, J. (1983). Clinical outcome of sex therapy: Effects of daily versus weekly treatment. *Archives of General Psychiatry, 40*, 443–449.

Heiman, J. R., & LoPiccolo, J. (1988). *Becoming orgasmic: A sexual and personal growth program for women* (rev. ed.). New York, NY: Prentice Hall.

Heiman, J. R., & Meston, C. M. (1997). Empirically validated treatment for sexual dysfunction. *Annual Review of Sex Research, 8*, 148–195.

Heimberg, R. G., & Magee, L. (2014). Social anxiety disorder. In D. H. Barlow (Ed.), *Clinical handbook of psychological disorders: A step-by-step treatment manual* (5th ed.). New York, NY: Guilford

Helgeson, V. (2005). Recent advances in psychosocial oncology. *Journal of Consulting and Clinical Psychology, 73*, 268–271.

Heller, W., & Nitschke, J. B. (1997). Regional brain activity in emotion: A framework for understanding cognition in depression. *Cognition and Emotion, 11*(5–6), 737–661.

Helzer, J. E., Kraemer, H. C., Krueger, R. F., Wittchen, H.-U., Sirovatka, P. J., & Regier, D. A. (Eds.) (2008). *Dimensional approaches in diagnostic classification: Refining the research agenda for DSM-V.* Washington, DC: American Psychiatric Association.

Helzer, J. E., Wittchen, H.-U., Krueger, R. F., & Kraemer, H. C. (2008). Dimensional options for DSM-V: The way forward. In J. E. Helzer, H. C. Kraemer, R. F. Krueger,

H.-U. Wittchen, P. J. Sirovatka, & D. A. Regier (Eds.), *Dimensional approaches in diagnostic classification: Refining the research agenda for DSM-V* (pp. 115–127). Washington, D.C.: American Psychiatric Association.

Henderson, K. E., & Brownell, K. D. (2004). The toxic environment and obesity: Contribution and cure. In J. K. Thompson (Ed.), *Handbook of eating disorders and obesity* (pp. 339–348). New York, NY: Wiley.

Hendriks, G. J., Kampman, M., Keijsers, G. P., Hoogduin, C. A., & Voshaar, R. C. O. (2014). Cognitive-behavioral therapy for panic disorder with agoraphobia in older people: A comparison with younger patients. *Depression and Anxiety, 31,* 669–677.

Henningsen, P., Gündel, H., Kop, W. J., Löwe, B., Martin, A., Rief, W., … Van Den Bergh, O. (2018). Persistent physical symptoms as perceptual dysregulation: A neuropsychobehavioral model and its clinical implications. *Psychosomatic Medicine, 80*(5), 422–431. doi: 10.1097/psy.0000000000000588

Henquet, C., Krabbendam, L., Spauwen, J., Kaplan, C., Lieb, R., Wittchen, H.-U., & van Os, J. (2005). Prospective cohort study of cannabis use, predisposition for psychosis, and psychotic symptoms in young people. *British Medical Journal, 330,* 11.

Herbert, T. B., & Cohen, S. (1993). Depression and immunity: A meta-analytic review. *Psychological Bulletin, 113*(3), 472–486.

Herdt, G. H. (1987). *The Sambia: Ritual and gender in New Guinea.* New York, NY: Holt, Rinehart and Winston.

Herdt, G. H., & Stoller, R. J. (1989). Commentary to "The socialization of homosexuality and heterosexuality in a non-Western society." *Archives of Sexual Behavior, 18,* 31–34.

Herlitz, C. A., & Forsberg, M. (2010). Sexual behavior and risk assessment in different age cohorts in the general population of Sweden (1989-2007). *Scandinavian Journal of Public Health, 38,* 32–39.

Hermans, E. J., Henckens, M. J. A. G., Joels, M., & Fernandez, G. (2014). Dynamic adaptation of large-scale brain networks in response to acute stressors. *Trends in Neurosciences, 37,* 304–314.

Hermans, E. J., van Marle, H. J., Ossewaarde, L., Henckens, M. J., Qin, S., van Kesteren, M. T., & Fernández, G. (2011). Stress-related noradrenergic activity prompts large-scale neural network reconfiguration. *Science, 334*(6059), 1151–1153. doi: 10.1126/science.1209603

Hernandez, M., Barrio, C., & Yamada, A. M. (2013). Hope and burden among Latino families of adults with schizophrenia. *Family Process, 52*(4), 697–708.

Heron, J., Barker, E. D., Joinson, C., Lewis, G., Hickman, M., Munafò, M., & Macleod, J. (2013). Childhood conduct disorder trajectories, prior risk factors and cannabis use at age 16: birth cohort study. *Addiction, 108*(12), 2129–2138.

Hershberger, S., & Segal, N. (2004). The cognitive, behavioral, and personality profiles of a male monozygotic triplet set discordant for sexual orientation. *Archives of Sexual Behavior, 33,* 497–514.

Herzog, D. B., Dorer, D. J., Keel, P. K., Selwyn, S. E., Ekeblad, E. R., Flores, A. T., & Keller, M. B. (1999). Recovery and relapse in anorexia and bulimia nervosa: A 7.5-year follow-up study. *Journal of the American Academy of Child and Adolescent Psychiatry, 38*(7), 829–837.

Heshka, S., Anderson, J. W., Atkinson, R. L., Greenway, F. L., Hill, J. O., Phinney, S. D., & Pi-Sunyer, F. X. (2003). Weight loss with self-help compared with a structured commercial program: A randomized trial. *JAMA: Journal of the American Medical Association, 289,* 1792–1798.

Hetherington, M. M., & Cecil, J. E. (2010). Gene-environment interactions in obesity. *Forum of Nutrition, 63,* 195–203.

Hettema, J. M., Neale, M. C., & Kendler, K. S. (2001). A review and meta-analysis of the genetic epidemiology of anxiety disorders. *American Journal of Psychiatry, 158,* 1568–1578.

Hettema, J. M., Prescott, C. A., Myers, J. M., Neale, M. C., & Kendler, K. S. (2005). The structure of genetic and environmental risk factors for anxiety disorders in men and women. *Archives of General Psychiatry, 62,* 182–189.

Heylens, G., De Cuypere, G., Zucker, K. J., Schelfaut, C., Elaut, E., Vanden Bossche, H., . . . T'Sjoen, G. (2012). Gender identity disorder in twins: A review of the case report literature. *The Journal of Sexual Medicine, 9*(3), 751–757.

Higdon, M. J. (2020). Parens patriae and the disinherited child. *Washington Law Review, 95,* 619.

Higgins, A. (2021, August 9). Albania's fading fraternity of women who declare themselves men. *New York Times.* https://www.nytimes.com/2021/08/08/world/europe/sworn-virgins-albania.html?referringSource=articleShare

Higgins, S. T., Heil, S. H., Dantona, R., Donham, R., Matthews, M., & Badger, G. J. (2006). Effects of varying the monetary value of voucher-based incentives on abstinence achieved during and following treatment among cocaine-dependent outpatients. *Addiction, 102,* 271–281.

Higgins, S. T., Sigmon, S. C., & Heil, S. H. (2014). Drug use disorders. In D. H. Barlow (Ed.), *Clinical handbook of psychological disorders: A step-by-step treatment manual.* New York, NY: Guilford.

Higuchi, S., Matsushita, S., Imazeki, H., Kinoshita, T., Takagi, S., & Kono, H. (1994). Aldehyde dehydrogenase genotypes in Japanese alcoholics. *Lancet, 343,* 741–742.

Hilbert, A., Hildebrandt, T., Agras, W. S., Wilfley, D. E., & Wilson, G. T. (2015). Rapid response in psychological treatments for binge eating disorder. *Journal of consulting and clinical psychology, 83*(3), 649–654.

Hilbert, A., Petroff, D., Herpertz, S., Pietrowsky, R., Tuschen-Caffier, B., Vocks, S., & Schmidt, R. (2019). Meta-analysis of the efficacy of psychological and medical treatments for binge-eating disorder. *Journal of Consulting and Clinical Psychology, 87*(1), 91–105. doi: 10.1037/ccp0000358

Hilbert, A., Petroff, D., Herpertz, S., Pietrowsky, R., Tuschen-Caffier, B., Vocks, S., & Schmidt, R. (2020). Meta-analysis on the long-term effectiveness of psychological and medical treatments for binge-eating disorder. *International Journal of Eating Disorders, 53*(9), 1353–1376. doi: 10.1002/eat.23297

Hilgard, E. R. (1992). Divided consciousness and dissociation. *Consciousness & Cognition, 1,* 16–31.

Hill, C. (2011). Practitioner Review: Effective treatment of behavioural insomnia in children. *Journal of Child Psychology and Psychiatry, 52*(7), 731–740.

Hill, K. G., Bailey, J. A., Hawkins, J. D., Catalano, R. F., Kosterman, R., Oesterle, S., & Abbott, R. D. (2014). The onset of STI diagnosis through age 30: Results from the Seattle Social Development Project intervention. *Prevention Science, 15*(1), 19–32.

Hiller, W., Leibbrand, R., Rief, W., & Fichter, M. (2005). Differentiating hypochondriasis from panic disorder. *Journal of Anxiety Disorders, 19,* 29–49.

Hillis, A. E. (2014). Inability to empathize: brain lesions that disrupt sharing and understanding another's emotions. *Brain, 137*(4), 981–997.

Hindmarch, I. (1990). Cognitive impairment with anti-anxiety agents: A solvable problem? In D. Wheatley (Ed.), *The anxiolytic jungle: Where, next?* (pp. 49–61). Chichester, UK: Wiley.

Hinshaw, S. P., & Stier, A. (2008). Stigma as related to mental disorders. *Annual Review of Clinical Psychology, 4,* 367–393.

Hinshelwood, J. A. (1896). A case of dyslexia: A peculiar form of word-blindness. *Lancet, 2,* 1451–1454.

Hinton, D. E., & Good, B. J. (Eds.). (2009). *Culture and panic disorder*. Stanford: Stanford University Press.

Hinton, D. E., Chong, R., Pollack, M. H., Barlow, D. H., & McNally, R. J. (2008). Ataque de nervios: Relationship to anxiety sensitivity and dissociation predisposition. *Depression and Anxiety, 25,* 489–495.

Hinton, D. E., Hofmann, S. G., Pitman, R. K., Pollack, M. H., & Barlow, D. H. (2008). The panic attack-posttraumatic stress disorder model: Applicability to orthostatic panic among Cambodian refugees. *Cognitive Behavioral Therapy, 37*(2), 101–16.

Hinton, D. E., Lewis-Fernandez, R., & Pollack, M. H. (2009). A model of the generation of ataque de nervios: The role of fear of negative affect and fear of arousal symptoms. *CNS Neuroscience Therapeutics, 15*(3), 264–275.

Hinton, D. E., Park, L., Hsia, C., Hofmann, S., & Pollack, M. H. (2009). Anxiety disorder presentations in Asian populations: A review. *CNS Neuroscience & Therapeutics, 15*(3), 295–303.

Hinton, D. E., Seponski, D. M., Khann, S., Armes, S. E., Lahar, C. J., Kao, S., & Schunert, T. (2019). Culturally sensitive assessment of anxious-depressive distress in the Cambodian population: Avoiding category truncation. *Transcultural Psychiatry, 56*(4), 643–666. doi: 10.1177/1363461519851609

Hinton, D., Pich, V., Chhean, D., Pollack, M. H., & Barlow, D. H. (2004). Olfactory-triggered panic attacks among Cambodian refugees attending a psychiatric clinic. *General Hospital Psychiatry, 26*(5), 390–397.

Hinton, D., Pollack, M. H., Pich, V., Fama, J. M., & Barlow, D. H. (2005). Orthostatically induced panic attacks among Cambodian refugees: Flashbacks, catastrophic cognitions, and associated psychopathology. *Cognitive Behavioral Practice, 12,* 301–311.

Hirschfeld, D. R., Rosenbaum, J. F., Biederman, J., Bolduc, E. A., Farone, S. V., Snidman, N., & Kagan, J. (1992). Stable behavioral inhibition and its association with anxiety disorder. *Journal of the American Academy of Child and Adolescent Psychiatry, 31,* 103–111.

Hirschfeld, R. M. A., Keller, M. M., Panico, S., Arons, B. S., Barlow, D., Davidoff, F., & Wyatt, R. J. (1997). The National Depressive and Manic-Depressive Association consensus statement on the undertreatment of depression. *JAMA: Journal of the American Medical Association, 277*(4), 333–340.

Hirschtritt, M. E., Olfson, M., & Kroenke, K. (2021). Balancing the risks and benefits of benzodiazepines. *JAMA, 325*(4), 347–348. doi: 10.1001/jama.2020.22106

Hirshkowitz, M., Seplowitz, R. G., & Sharafkhaneh, A. (2009). Sleep disorders. In B. J. Sadock, V. A. Sadock, & P. Ruiz (Eds.), *Kaplan & Sadock's comprehensive textbook of psychiatry* (9th ed., Vol. I, pp. 2150–2177). Philadelphia, PA: Lippincott Williams & Wilkins.

Hitchcock, P. B., & Mathews, A. (1992). Interpretation of bodily symptoms in hypochondriasis. *Behaviour Research and Therapy, 30*(3), 223–234.

Hlastala, S. A., Kotler, J. S., McClellan, J. M., & McCauley, E. A. (2010). Interpersonal and social rhythm therapy for adolescents with bipolar disorder: Treatment development and results from an open trial. *Depression and Anxiety, 27*(5), 457–464.

Ho, B. C., Wassink, T. H., Ziebell, S., & Andreasen, N. C. (2011). Cannabinoid receptor 1 gene polymorphisms and marijuana misuse interactions on white matter and cognitive deficits in schizophrenia. *Schizophrenia Research, 128*(1), 66–75.

Ho, J. F. V., Yaakup, H., Low, G. S. H., Wong, S. L., Tho, L. M., & Tan, S. B. (2020). Morphine use for cancer pain: A strong analgesic used only at the end of life? A qualitative study on attitudes and perceptions of morphine in patients with advanced cancer and their caregivers. *Palliative Medicine, 34*(5), 619–629.

Hodder, R. K., Freund, M., Wolfenden, L., Bowman, J., Nepal, S., Dray, J., … Wiggers, J. (2017). Systematic review of universal school-based "resilience" interventions targeting adolescent tobacco, alcohol or illicit substance use: a meta-analysis. *Preventive Medicine, 100,* 248–268.

Hodgson, K., & McGuffin, P. (2013). The genetic basis of depression. *Current Topics in Behavioral Neurosciences, 14,* 81–99.

Hoek, H. W. (2002). The distribution of eating disorders. In K. D. Brownell & C. G. Fairburn (Eds.), *Eating disorders and obesity: A comprehensive handbook* (2nd ed., pp. 207–211). New York, NY: Guilford.

Hoek, H. W., van Harten, P. N., Hermans, K. M. E., Katzman, M. A., Matroos, G. E., & Susser, E. S. (2005). The incidence of anorexia nervosa on Curacao. *American Journal of Psychiatry, 162,* 748–752.

Hoffman, B., Papas, R., Chatkoff, D., & Kerns, R. (2007). Meta-analysis of psychological interventions for chronic low back pain. *Health Psychology, 26,* 1–9.

Hoffman, R. E., Boutros, N. N., Hu, S., Berman, R. M., Krystal, J. H., & Charney, D. S. (2000). Transcranial magnetic stimulation and auditory hallucinations in schizophrenia. *Lancet, 355,* 1073–1075.

Hoffman, R. E., Hawkins, K. A., Gueorguieva, R., Boutros, N. N., Rachid, F., Carroll, K., & Krystal, J. H. (2003). Transcranial magnetic stimulation of left temporoparietal cortex and medication-resistant auditory hallucinations. *Archives of General Psychiatry, 60,* 49–56.

Hofmann S. G., & Otto, M. W. (2008). *Cognitive-behavior therapy of social anxiety disorder: Evidence-based and disorder specific treatment techniques.* New York, NY: Routledge.

Hofmann, S. G. (2007a). Enhancing exposure-based therapy from a translational research perspective. *Behaviour Research and Therapy, 45*(9), 1987–2001.

Hofmann, S. G. (2007b). Cognitive factors that maintain social anxiety disorder: A comprehensive model and its treatment implications. *Cognitive Behaviour Therapy, 36*(4), 195–209.

Hofmann, S. G. (2014). D-cycloserine for treating anxiety disorders: Making good exposures better and bad exposures worse. *Depression and Anxiety, 31,* 175.

Hofmann, S. G. (2016). *Emotion in therapy: From science to practice.* New York, N.Y.: Guilford Press.

Hofmann, S. G. (2020) The age of depression and its treatment. *JAMA Psychiatry, 77,* 667–668. doi: 10.1001/jamapsychiatry.2020.0158

Hofmann, S. G. (2020). *The anxiety skills workbook: Simple CBT and mindfulness strategies for overcoming anxiety, fear, and worry.* Oakland, CA: New Harbinger Press.

Hofmann, S. G., & Barlow, D. H. (1996). Ambulatory psychophysiological monitoring: A potentially useful tool when treating panic relapse. *Cognitive and Behavioral Practice, 3,* 53–61.

Hofmann, S. G., & Barlow, D. H. (2002). Social phobia (social anxiety disorder). In D. H. Barlow, *Anxiety and its disorders: The nature and treatment of anxiety and panic* (2nd ed.). New York, NY: Guilford.

Hofmann, S. G., & Doan, S. N. (2018). *The social foundations of emotion: Developmental, cultural, and clinical dimensions.* Washington, D.C.: American Psychological Association

Hofmann, S. G., & Hay, A. C. (2018). Rethinking avoidance: Toward a balanced approach to avoidance in treating anxiety disorders. *Journal of Anxiety Disorders, 55,* 14–21. doi: 10.1016/j.janxdis.2018.03.004

Hofmann, S. G., & Hayes, S. C. (2019). The future of intervention science: Process-based therapy. *Clinical Psychological Science, 7,* 37–50. doi: 10.1177/2167702618772296

Hofmann, S. G., & Hinton, D. E. (2014). Cross-cultural aspects of anxiety disorders. *Current Psychiatry Reports, 16,* 450.

Hofmann, S. G., & Smits, J. A. (2008). Cognitive-behavioral therapy for adult anxiety disorders: A meta-analysis of randomized placebo-controlled trials. *Journal of Clinical Psychiatry, 69*(4), 621–632.

Hofmann, S. G., Alpers, G. W., & Pauli, P. (2009). Phenomenology of panic and phobic disorders. In M. M. Antony & M. B. Stein (Eds.), *Oxford handbook of anxiety and related disorders* (pp. 34–46). New York, NY: Oxford University Press.

Hofmann, S. G., Asnaani, A., & Hinton, D. E. (2010). Cultural aspects in social anxiety and social anxiety disorder. *Depression and Anxiety, 27*(12), 1117–1127.

Hofmann, S. G., Asnaani, A., Vonk, J. J., Sawyer, A. T., & Fang, A. (2012). The efficacy of cognitive behavioral therapy: A review of meta-analyses. *Cognitive Therapy and Research, 36,* 427–440.

Hofmann, S. G., Lehman, C. L., & Barlow, D. H. (1997). How specific are specific phobias? *Journal of Behavior Therapy and Experimental Psychiatry, 28,* 233–240.

Hofmann, S. G., Meuret, A. E., Smitts, J. A. J., Simon, N. M., Pollack, M. H., Eisenmenger, K., & Otto, M. W. (2006). Augmentation of exposure therapy with D-cycloserine for social anxiety disorder. *Archives of General Psychiatry, 63*(3), 298–304.

Hofmann, S. G., Moscovitch, D. A., Litz, B. T., Kim, H.-J., Davis, L., & Pizzagalli, D. A. (2005). The worried mind: Autonomic and prefrontal activation during worrying. *Emotion, 5,* 464–475.

Hofmann, S. G., Sawyer, A. T., & Asnaani, A. (2012). D-cycloserine as an augmentation strategy for cognitive behavioral therapy of anxiety disorders: An update. *Current Pharmaceutical Design, 18*(35), 5659–5662.

Hofmann, S. G., Sawyer, A. T., Witt, A., & Oh, D. (2010). The effect of mindfulness-based therapy on anxiety and depression: A meta-analytic review. *Journal of Consulting and Clinical Psychology, 78,* 169–183.

Hofmann, S. G., Smits, J. A., Rosenfield, D., Simon, N., Otto, M. W., Meuret, A. E., & Pollack, M. H. (2013). D-cycloserine as an augmentation strategy with cognitive-behavioral therapy for social anxiety disorder. *American Journal of Psychiatry, 170*(7), 751–758. doi: 10.1176/appi.ajp.2013

Hogarty, G. E., Anderson, C. M., Reiss, D. J., Kornblith, S. J., Greenwald, D. P., Javna, C. D., & Madonia, M. J. (1986). Family psychoeducation, social skills training, and maintenance chemotherapy in the aftercare treatment of schizophrenia: I. One year effects of a controlled study on relapse and expressed emotion. *Archives of General Psychiatry, 43,* 633–642.

Hogarty, G. E., Anderson, C. M., Reiss, D. J., Kornblith, S. J., Greenwald, D. P., Ulrich, R. F., Carter, M., & The Environmental–Personal Indicators in the Course of Schizophrenia (EPICS) Research Group. (1991). Family psychoeducation, social skills training, and maintenance chemotherapy in the aftercare treatment of schizophrenia. *Archives of General Psychiatry, 48,* 340–347.

Holden, C. (2005). Obesity in the east. *Science, 307,* 38.

Holder, H. D., Gruenewald, P. J., Ponicki, W. R., Treno, A. J., Grube, J. W., Saltz, R. F., & Roeper, P. (2000). Effect of community-based interventions on high-risk drinking and alcohol-related injuries. *JAMA: Journal of the American Medical Association, 284,* 2341–2347.

Holland, A. J. (2012). Classification, diagnosis, psychiatric assessment, and needs assessment. In M. G. Gelder, N. C. Andreasen, J. J. Lopez-Ibor, Jr., & J. R. Geddes (Eds.), *New Oxford textbook of psychiatry* (2nd ed., Vol. 2, pp. 1819–1824). New York, NY: Oxford University Press.

Holland, J. M., & Gallagher-Thompson, D. (2011). Interventions for mental health problems in later life. In D. H. Barlow (Ed.), *Oxford handbook of clinical psychology* (pp. 810–836). New York, NY: Oxford University Press.

Hollander, E., Allen, A., Kwon, J., Aronwoitz, B., Schmeidler, J., Wong, C., & Simeon, D. (1999). Clomipramine vs. desipramine crossover trial in body dysmorphic disorder: Selective efficacy of a serotonin reuptake inhibitor in imagined ugliness. *Archives of General Psychiatry, 56*(11), 1033–1039.

Hollander, E., Berlin, H. A., & Stein, D. J. (2009). Impulse-control disorders not elsewhere classified. In J. A. Bourgeois, R. E. Hales, J. S. Young, & S. C. Yudofsky (Eds.), *The American Psychiatric Publishing Board review guide for psychiatry* (pp. 469–482). Arlington, VA: American Psychiatric Publishing.

Hollander, J. A., & Kenny, P. J. (2012). Compulsive drug use and brain reward systems. In J. C. Verster, K. Brady, M. Galanter, & P. Conrod (Eds.), *Drug Abuse and Addiction in Medical Illness* (pp. 63–72). New York, NY: Springer.

Hollis, J. F., Connett, J. E., Stevens, V. J., & Greenlick, M. R. (1990). Stressful life events, Type A behavior, and the prediction of cardiovascular and total mortality over six years. *Journal of Behavioral Medicine, 13*(3), 263–280.

Hollon, S. D, DeRubeis, R. J., Fawcett, J., Amsterdam, J. D., Shelton, R. C., Zajecka, J., Young, P. R., & Gallop, R. (2014). Effect of cognitive therapy with antidepressant medications vs antidepressants alone on the rate of recovery in major depressive disorder: A randomized clinical trial. *JAMA Psychiatry, 71,* 1157–1164.

Hollon, S. D. (2011). Cognitive and behavior therapy in the treatment and prevention of depression. *Depression and Anxiety, 28*(4), 263–266.

Hollon, S. D., & Dimidjian, S. (2009). Cognitive and behavioral treatment of depression. In I. H. Gotlib & C. L. Hammen (Eds.), *Handbook of depression* (2nd ed., pp. 586–603). New York, NY: Guilford.

Hollon, S. D., Areán, P. A., Craske, M. G., Crawford, K. A., Kivlahan, D. R., Magnavita, J. J., . . . Kurtzman, H. (2014). Development of Clinical Practice Guidelines. *Annual Review of Clinical Psychology, 10*(1), 213–241. doi: 10.1146/annurev-clinpsy-050212-185529

Hollon, S. D., DeRubeis, R. J., Shelton, R. C., Amsterdam, J. D., Salomon, R. M., O'Reardon, J. P., & Gallop, R. (2005). Prevention of relapse following cognitive therapy vs. medications in moderate to severe depression. *Archives of General Psychiatry, 62,* 417–422.

Hollon, S. D., Stewart, M. O., & Strunk, D. (2006). Cognitive behavior therapy has enduring effects in the treatment of depression and anxiety. *Annual Review of Psychology, 57,* 285–315.

Holroyd, K. A., & Penzien, D. B. (1986). Client variables in the behavioral treatment of current tension headache: A meta-analytic review. *Journal of Behavioral Medicine, 9,* 515–536.

Holroyd, K. A., Andrasik, F., & Noble, J. (1980). A comparison of EMG biofeedback and a credible pseudotherapy in treating tension headache. *Journal of Behavioral Medicine, 3,* 29–39.

Holroyd, K. A., Penzien, D. B., Hursey, K. G., Tobin, D. L., Rogers, L., Holm, J. E., & Chila, A. G. (1984). Change mechanisms in EMG biofeedback training. Cognitive changes underlying improvements in tension headache. *Journal of Consulting and Clinical Psychology, 52,* 1039–1053.

Holt-Lunstad, J., Birmingham, W. A., & Light, K. C. (2008). Influence of a "warm touch" support enhancement intervention among married couples on ambulatory blood pressure, oxytocin, alpha amylase, & cortisol. *Psychosomatic Medicine, 70,* 976–985.

Holt-Lunstad, J., Smith, T. B., & Layton, J. B. (2010). Social relationships and mortality risk: A meta-analytic review. *PLoS Med, 7*(7), e1000316. doi: 10.1371/journal.pmed.1000316

Holzman, P. S., & Levy, D. L. (1977). Smooth pursuit eye movements and functional psychoses: A review. *Schizophrenia Bulletin, 3,* 15–27.

Hong, Y., & Kim, S. (2020). Influence of presumed media influence for health prevention: How mass media indirectly promote health prevention behaviors through descriptive norms. *Health Communication, 35*(14), 1800–1810.
Hook, E. B. (1982). Epidemiology of Down syndrome. In S. M. P. J. E. Rynders (Ed.), *Down syndrome: Advances in biomedicine and the behavioral sciences* (pp. 11–88). Cambridge, MA: Ware Press.
Hooley, J. M. (1985). Expressed emotion: A review of the critical literature. *Clinical Psychology Review, 5,* 119–139.
Hooley, J. M., & Campbell, C. (2002). Control and controllability: Beliefs and behaviour in high and low expressed emotion relatives. *Psychological Medicine, 32,* 1091–1099.
Hooley, J. M., Cole, S. H., & Gironde, S. (2012). Borderline personality disorder. In T. A. Widiger (Ed.), *The Oxford handbook of personality disorders* (pp. 409–436). New York, NY: Oxford University Press.
Hoon, P. W., Wincze, J. P., & Hoon, E. F. (1977). A test of reciprocal inhibition: Are anxiety and sexual arousal in women mutually inhibitory? *Journal of Abnormal Psychology, 86,* 65–74.
Hoppenbrouwers, S., Neumann, C. S., Lewis, J., & Johansson, P. (2015). A latent variable analysis of the Psychopathy Checklist–Revised and behavioral inhibition system/behavioral activation system factors in North American and Swedish offenders. *Personality Disorders: Theory, Research, and Treatment, 6*(3), 251–260.
Hopwood, C. J., & Thomas, K. M. (2012). Paranoid and schizoid personality disorders. In T. A. Widiger (Ed.), *The Oxford handbook of personality disorders* (pp. 582–602). New York, NY: Oxford University Press.
Hopwood, C. J., Kotov, R., Krueger, R. F., Watson, D., Widiger, T. A., Althoff, R. R., … Blais, M. A. (2018). The time has come for dimensional personality disorder diagnosis. *Personality and mental health, 12*(1), 82.
Horan, W. P., Ventura, J., Mintz, J., Kopelowicz, A., Wirshing, D., Christian-Herman, J., Foy, D., & Liberman, R. P. (2007). Stress and coping responses to a natural disaster in people with schizophrenia. *Psychiatry Research, 151,* 77–86.
Horowitz, J., & Garber, J. (2006). The prevention of depressive symptoms in children and adolescents: A meta-analytic review. *Journal of Consulting and Clinical Psychology, 74,* 401–415.
Horwath, E., & Weissman, M. (1997). Epidemiology of anxiety disorders across cultural groups. In S. Friedman (Ed.), *Cultural issues in the treatment of anxiety* (pp. 21–39). New York, NY: Guilford.
Horwath, E., & Weissman, M. M. (2000). The epidemiology and cross-national presentation of obsessive-compulsive disorder. *Psychiatric Clinics of North America, 23*(3), 493–507.
Hostinar, C. E., Sullivan, R. M., & Gunnar, M. R. (2013, April 22). Psychobiological mechanisms: Review of animal models and human studies across development. *Psychological Bulletin.* Advance online publication.
House, J. S., Landis, K. R., & Umberson, D. (1988). Social relationships and health. *Science, 241,* 540–545.
House, J. S., Robbins, C., & Metzner, H. M. (1982). The association of social relationships and activities with mortality: Prospective evidence from the Tecumseh community health study. *American Journal of Epidemiology, 116,* 123.
Houston, B. K., Chesney, M. A., Black, G. W., Cates, D. S., & Hecker, M. H. L. (1992). Behavioral clusters and coronary heart disease risk. *Psychosomatic Medicine, 54*(4), 447–461.
Hovenkamp-Hermelink, J. H. M., Jeronimus, B. F., Myroniuk, S., Riese, H., & Schoevers, R. A. (2021). Predictors of persistence of anxiety disorders across the lifespan: A systematic review. *The Lancet Psychiatry*. doi: 10.1016/S2215-0366(20)30433-8
Howard, G., Lackland, D. T., Kleindorfer, D. O., Kissela, B. M., Moy, C. S., Judd, S. E., . . . Howard, V. J. (2013). Racial differences in the impact of elevated systolic blood pressure on stroke risk. *JAMA Internal Medicine,173*(1), 46–51.
Howe, M. L. (2007). Children's emotional false memories. *Psychological Science, 18*(10), 856–860.
Howe, M. L., & Knott, L. M. (2015). The fallibility of memory in judicial processes: Lessons from the past and their modern consequences. *Memory, 23*(5), 633–656. doi: 10.1080/09658211.2015.1010709
Howell, M. (2012). Parasomnias: An updated review. *Neurotherapeutics, 9*(4), 753–775. doi: 10.1007/s13311-012-0143-8
Howes, O. D., & Kapur, S. (2009). The dopamine hypothesis of schizophrenia: Version III—The final common pathway. *Schizophrenia Bulletin, 35*(3), 549–562. doi: 10.1093/schbul/sbp006
Howes, O. D., & Murray, R. M. (2014). Schizophrenia: an integrated sociodevelopmental-cognitive model. *The Lancet, 383*(9929), 1677–1687.
Howes, O. D., Kambeitz, J., Kim, E., Stahl, D., Slifstein, M., Abi-Dargham, A., & Kapur, S. (2012). The nature of dopamine dysfunction in schizophrenia and what this means for treatment: meta-analysis of imaging studies. *Archives of General Psychiatry, 69*(8), 776–786.
Howland, R. H., Rush, A. J., Wisniewski, S. R., Trivedi, M. H., Warden, D., Fava, M., & Gallop, R. (2009). Concurrent anxiety and substance use disorders among outpatients with major depression: Clinical features and effect on treatment outcome. *Drug and Alcohol Dependence, 99*(1-3), 248–260.
Howlin, P., Goode, S., Hutton, J., & Rutter, M. (2010). Savant skills in autism: Psychometric approaches and parental reports. In F. Happé & U. Frith (Eds.), *Autism and talent* (pp. 13–24). New York, NY: Oxford University Press.
Hser, Y. I., Evans, E., Grella, C., Ling, W., & Anglin, D. (2015). Long-term course of opioid addiction. *Harvard Review of Psychiatry, 23*(2), 76–89.
Hsu, L. K. G. (1988). The outcome of anorexia nervosa: A reappraisal. *Psychological Medicine, 18,* 807–812.
Hsu, L. K. G. (1990). *Eating disorders.* New York, NY: Guilford.
Hsu, L. K. G., & Zimmer, B. (1988). Eating disorders in old age. *International Journal of Eating Disorders, 7,* 133–138.
https://doi.org/10.1016/j.ncl.2010.03.012
Huang, Y. C., Lin, C. C., Hung, Y. Y., & Huang, T. L. (2013). Rapid relief of catatonia in mood disorder by lorazepam and diazepam. *Biomedical Journal, 36*(1), 35–39.
Huang, Y., Huang, X., Ebstein, R. P., & Yu, R. (2021). Intranasal oxytocin in the treatment of autism spectrum disorders: A multilevel meta-analysis. *Neuroscience & Biobehavioral Reviews.*
Huang, Y., Kotov, R., de Girolamo, G., Preti, A., Angermeyer, M., Benjet, C., & Kessler, R. C. (2009). DSM-IV personality disorders in the WHO World Mental Health Surveys. *The British Journal of Psychiatry, 195*(1), 46–53. doi: 10.1192/bjp.bp.108.058552
Hubbard, N. A., Siless, V., Frosch, I. R., Goncalves, M., Lo, N., Wang, J., Bauer, C. C. C., Conroy, K., Cosby, E., Hay, A., Jones, R., Pinaire, M., Vaz De Souza, F., Vergara, G., Ghosh, S., Henin, A., Hirshfeld-Becker, D. R., Hofmann, S. G., Rosso, I. M., … Whitfield-Gabrieli, S. (2020). Brain function and clinical characterization in the Boston adolescent neuroimaging of depression and anxiety study. *Neuroimage: Clinical, 27,* 102240.
Hubert, N. C., Jay, S. M., Saltoun, M., & Hayes, M. (1988). Approach-avoidance and distress in children undergoing preparation for painful medical procedures. *Journal of Clinical Child Psychology, 17*(3), 194–202.
Hucker, S. J. (1997). Sexual sadism: Psychopathology and theory. In D. R. Laws & W. T.

O'Donohue (Eds.), *Sexual deviance: Theory, assessment, and treatment* (pp. 194–209). New York, NY: Guilford.
Hucker, S. J. (2008). Sexual masochism: Psychopathology and theory. In D. R. Laws & W. T. O'Donohue (Eds.), *Sexual deviance: Theory, assessment, and treatment* (2nd ed., pp. 250–263). New York, NY: Guilford.
Hudson, A. N., Van Dongen, H. P., & Honn, K. A. (2020). Sleep deprivation, vigilant attention, and brain function: a review. *Neuropsychopharmacology, 45*(1), 21–30.
Hudson, J. I., Hiripi, E., Pope, H. G., Jr., & Kessler, R. C. (2007). The prevalence and correlates of eating disorders in the national comorbidity survey replication. *Biological Psychiatry, 61,* 348–358.
Hudson, J. I., Lalonde, J. K., Berry, J. M., Pindych, L. J., Bulik, C. M., Crow, S. J., & Pope, H. G. (2006). Binge-eating disorder as a distinct familial phenotype in obese individuals. *Archives of General Psychiatry, 63,* 313–319.
Hudson, J. I., Mangweth, B., Pope, H. G., Jr., De Col, C., Hausmann, A., Gutweniger, S., & Tsaung, M. T. (2003). Family study of affective spectrum disorder. *Archives of General Psychiatry, 60,* 170–177.
Huerta, M., Bishop, S. L., Duncan, A., Hus, V., & Lord, C. (2012). Application of DSM-5 criteria for autism spectrum disorder to three samples of children with DSM-IV diagnoses of pervasive developmental disorders. *American Journal of Psychiatry, 169*(10), 1056–1064.
Hughes, J. R. (2009). Nicotine-related disorders. In B. J. Sadock, V. A. Sadock, & P. Ruiz (Eds.), *Kaplan & Sadock's comprehensive textbook of psychiatry* (9th ed., Vol. I, pp. 1353–1360). Philadelphia, PA: Lippincott Williams & Wilkins.
Hummelen, B., Pedersen, G., Wilberg, T., & Karterud, S. (2014). Poor Validity of the DSM-IV Schizoid Personality Disorder Construct as a Diagnostic Category. *Journal of Personality Disorders,* 1–13.
Humphrey, L. L. (1989). Observed family interactions among subtypes of eating disorders using structural analysis of social behavior. *Journal of Consulting and Clinical Psychology, 57,* 206–214.
Hunsley, J., & Mash, E. J. (2011). Evidence based assessment. In D. H. Barlow (Ed.), *Oxford handbook of clinical psychology.* (pp. 76–97). New York, NY: Oxford University Press.
Hunt, W. A. (1980). History and classification. In A. E. Kazdin, A. S. Bellack, & M. Hersen (Eds.), *New perspectives in abnormal psychology.* New York, NY: Oxford University Press.
Hunter, E., Sierra, M., & David, A. (2004). The epidemiology of depersonalisation and derealisation: A systematic review. *Social Psychiatry and Psychiatric Epidemiology, 39,* 9–18.
Hunter, J. A., Jr., & Mathews, R. (1997). Sexual deviance in females. In D. R. Laws & W. T. O'Donohue (Eds.), *Sexual deviance: Theory, assessment, and treatment* (pp. 465–490). New York, NY: Guilford.
Huntington's Disease Collaborative Research Group. (1993). A novel gene containing a trinucleotide repeat that is expanded and unstable on Huntington's disease chromosomes. *Cell, 72,* 971–983.
Huntjens, R. J., Peters, M., Woertman, L., Bovenschen, L., Loes, M., Martin, R., & Postma, A. (2006). Inter-identity amnesia in dissociative identity disorder: A simulated memory impairment? *Psychological Medicine, 36,* 857–863.
Huntjens, R. J., Postma, A., Hamaker, E. L., Woertman, L., van der Hart, O., & Peters, M. (2002). Perceptual and conceptual priming in patients with dissociative identity disorder. *Memory & Cognition, 30,* 1033–1043.
Huntjens, R. J., Postma, A., Peters, M., Woertman, L., & van der Hart, O. (2003). Interidentity amnesia for neutral, episodic information in dissociative identity disorder. *Abnormal Psychology,* 112, 290–297.
Huppert, J. D. (2009). Anxiety disorders and depression comorbidity. In M. M. Antony & M. B. Stein (Eds.), *Oxford handbook of anxiety and related disorders* (pp. 576–586). New York, NY: Oxford University Press.
Hurt, E., & Arnold, L. E. (2015). Dietary management of ADHD. In R. A. Barkley (Ed.), *Attention-deficit hyperactivity disorder: A handbook for diagnosis & treatment* (4th ed., pp. 630–640). New York, NY: The Guilford Press.
Hurt, S. W., Schnurr, P. P., Severino, S. K., Freeman, E. W., Gise, L. H., Rivera-Tovar, A., & Steege, J. F. (1992). Late luteal phase dysphoric disorder in 670 women evaluated for premenstrual complaints. *American Journal of Psychiatry, 149*(4), 525–530.
Husain, M., & Chalder, T. (2021). Medically unexplained symptoms: Assessment and management. *Clinical Medicine, Journal of the Royal College of Physicians of London, 21*(1), 13–18. doi: 10.7861/CLINMED.2020-0947
Hutchinson, D. M., & Rapee, R. M. (2007). Do friends share similar body image and eating problems? The role of social networks and peer influences in early adolescence. *Behaviour Research and Therapy, 45*(7), 1557–1577.
Hyde, L. W., Shaw, D. S., & Hariri, A. R. (2013). Understanding youth antisocial behavior using neuroscience through a developmental psychopathology lens: review, integration, and directions for research. *Developmental Review, 33*(3), 168–223.
Hyman, S. E. (2009). How adversity gets under the skin. *Nature Neuroscience, 12*(3), 241–243.
Hypericum Depression Trial Study Group. (2002). Effect of *Hypericum perforatum* (St John's wort) in major depressive disorder: A randomized controlled trial. *JAMA: Journal of the American Medical Association, 287,* 1853–1854.
Iacono, W. G., Bassett, A. S., & Jones, B. D. (1988). Eye tracking dysfunction is associated with partial trisomy of chromosome 5 and schizophrenia. *Archives of General Psychiatry, 45*(12), 1140–1141.
Iacovino, J. M., Jackson, J. J., & Oltmanns, T. F. (2014). The relative impact of socioeconomic status and childhood trauma on Black-White differences in paranoid personality disorder symptoms. *Journal of Abnormal Psychology,123*(1), 225.
Ibanez-Casas, I., & Cervilla, J. A. (2012). Neuropsychological research in delusional disorder: A comprehensive review. *Psychopathology, 45*(2), 78–95.
Ikramuddin, S., & Livingston, E. H. (2013). New insights on bariatric surgery outcomes. *JAMA, 310*(22), 2401–2402.
Imhof, A., Kovari, E., von Gunten, A., Gold, G., Rivara, C.-B., Herrmann, F. R., & Giannakopoulos, P. (2007). Morphological substrates of cognitive decline in nonagenarians and centenarians: A new paradigm? *Journal of the Neurological Sciences, 257*(1–2), 72–79.
Immonen, S., Launes, J., Järvinen, I., Virta, M., Vanninen, R., Schiavone, N., … Michelsson, K. (2020). Moderate alcohol use is associated with decreased brain volume in early middle age in both sexes. *Scientific Reports, 10*(1), 1–8.
Ingoldsby, E. M., Shelleby, E., Lane, T., & Shaw, D. S. (2012). Extrafamilial contexts and children's conduct problems. In V. Maholmes & R. B. King (Eds.), *The Oxford handbook of poverty and child development* (pp. 404–422). New York, NY: Oxford University Press.
Ingram, R., Miranda, J., & Segal, Z. (2006). Cognitive vulnerability to depression. In L. B. Alloy and J. H. Riskind (Eds.)., *Cognitive vulnerability to emotional disorders* (pp. 63–91). Mahwah, NJ: Erlbaum.
Inouye, S. K., Westendorp, R. G., & Saczynski, J. S. (2014). Delirium in elderly people. *The Lancet, 383*(9920), 911–922.
Insel, T. R. (1992). Toward a neuroanatomy of obsessive-compulsive disorder. *Archives of General Psychiatry, 49,* 739–744.

Insel, T. R. (2006). Beyond efficacy: The STAR*D trial. *American Journal of Psychiatry, 163,* 5–7.
Insel, T. R., Scanlan, J., Champoux, M., & Suomi, S. J. (1988). Rearing paradigm in a nonhuman primate affects response to B-CCE challenge. *Psychopharmacology, 96,* 81–86.
Institute of Medicine. (1999). *Reducing the burden of injury: Advancing prevention and treatment.* Washington, DC: National Academies Press.
Institute of Medicine. (2001). *Crossing the quality chasm: A new health system for the 21st century.* Washington, DC: National Academies Press.
Institute of Medicine. (2002). *Reducing suicide: A national imperative.* Washington, DC: National Academies Press.
IOM. (2011). *Clinical Practice Guidelines We Can Trust.* Washington, DC: The National Academies Press.
IOM. (2015). *Psychosocial interventions for mental and substance use disorders: A framework for establishing evidence-based standards.* Washington, DC: The National Academies Press.
Iqbal, A., Khera, R. A., Hanif, M. A., Ayub, M. A., & Zafar, M. N. (2020). Ma-huang. In M. A. Hanif, H. Nawaz, M. M. Khan, & H. J. Byrne (Eds.), *Medicinal plants of South Asia* (pp. 479–494). Cambridge, MA: Elsevier.
Irfan, M., Schenck, C. H., & Howell, M. J. (2021). Non-REM parasomnias. In E. H. During & C. A. Kushida (Eds.), *Clinical sleep medicine: A comprehensive guide for mental health and other medical professionals* (pp. 273–291). Washington, D.C.: American Psychiatric Association Publishing.
Iribarren, C., Sidney, S., Bild, D. E., Liu, K., Markovitz, J. H., Roseman, J. M., & Matthews, K. (2000). Association of hostility with coronary artery calcification in young adults. *JAMA: Journal of the American Medical Association, 283*(19), 2546–2551.
Ironson, G., Taylor, C. B., Boltwood, M., Bartzokis, T., Dennis, C., Chesney, M., & Segal, G. M. (1992). Effects of anger on left ventricular ejection fraction in coronary artery disease. *American Journal of Cardiology, 70,* 281–285.
Isaacowitz, D., Smith, T. T., & Carstensen, L. L. (2003). Socioemotional selectivity, positive bias, and mental health among trauma survivors in old age. *Ageing International, 28,* 181–199.
Isenberg-Grzeda, E., Kutner, H. E., & Nicolson, S. E. (2012). Wernicke-Korsakoff-syndrome: Under-recognized and under-treated. *Psychosomatics, 53*(6), 507–516. doi: http://dx.doi.org/10.1016/j.psym.2012.04.008
Ishak, A., Ramsay, M., Hart, N., & Steier, J. (2020). BPAP is an effective second-line therapy for obese patients with OSA failing regular CPAP: A prospective observational cohort study. *Respirology, 25*(4), 443–448.
Ito, K., Corrigan, B., Zhao, Q., French, J., Miller, R., Soares, H., . . . Fullerton, T. (2011). Disease progression model for cognitive deterioration from Alzheimer's Disease Neuroimaging Initiative database. *Alzheimer's & Dementia, 7*(2), 151-160.
Ivanov, I. (2009). Disulfiram and acamprosate. In B. J. Sadock, V. A. Sadock, & P. Ruiz (Eds.), *Kaplan & Sadock's comprehensive textbook of psychiatry* (9th ed., Vol. II, pp. 3099–3105). Philadelphia, PA: Lippincott Williams & Wilkins.
Iverson, S. D., & Iverson, L. L. (2007). Dopamine: 50 years in perspective. Trends in neurosciences, *30*(5), 188–193.
Iverson, L. (2006). Neurotransmitter transporters and their impact on the development of psychopharmacology. *British Journal of Pharmacology, 147*(Suppl. 1), S82–S88.
Ivleva, E. I., Moates, A. F., Hamm, J. P., Bernstein, I. H., O'Neill, H. B., Cole, D., . . . Tamminga, C. A. (2014). Smooth pursuit eye movement, prepulse inhibition, and auditory paired stimuli processing endophenotypes across the schizophrenia-bipolar disorder psychosis dimension. *Schizophrenia Bulletin,* 40(3), 642-652.
Izard, C. E. (1992). Basic emotions, relations among emotions, and emotion–cognition relations. *Psychological Review, 99*(3), 561–565.
Jääskeläinen, E., Juola, P., Hirvonen, N., McGrath, J. J., Saha, S., Isohanni, M., . . . Miettunen, J. (2013). A systematic review and meta-analysis of recovery in schizophrenia. *Schizophrenia Bulletin, 39*(6), 1296–1306.
Jablensky, A. (2012). Epidemiology of schizophrenia. In M. G. Gelder, N. C. Andreasen, J. J. Lopez-Ibor, Jr., & J. R. Geddes (Eds.), *New Oxford Textbook of Psychiatry* (2nd ed., Vol. 1, pp. 540–553). New York, NY: Oxford University Press.
Jackson v. Indiana, 406 U.S. 715 (1972).
Jackson, C., Brown, J. D., & L'Engle, K. L. (2007). R-rated movies, bedroom televisions, and initiation of smoking by white and black adolescents. *Archives of Pediatrics & Adolescent Medicine, 161,* 260–268.
Jackson, G., Rosen, R., Kloner, R., & Kostis, J. (2006). The second Princeton consensus on sexual dysfunction and cardiac risk: New guidelines for sexual medicine. *Journal of Sexual Medicine, 3*(1), 28–36.
Jackson, J. S., Knight, K. M., & Rafferty, J. A. (2010). Race and unhealthy behaviors: Chronic stress, the HPA axis, and physical and mental health disparities over the life course. *American Journal of Public Health, 100*(5), 933–939. doi: 10.2105/AJPH.2008.143446
Jackson, T., & Chen, H. (2011). Risk factors for disordered eating during early and middle adolescence: Prospective evidence from mainland Chinese boys and girls. *Journal of Abnormal Psychology, 120*(2), 454–464.
Jacobi, W., & Winkler, H. (1927). Encephalographische studien an chronischen schizophrenen. *Archives fur Psychiarrie und Nervenkrunkheiten, 81*(1), 299–332.
Jacobsen, P. B., & Andrykowski, M. A. (2015). Tertiary prevention in cancer care: Understanding and addressing the psychological dimensions of cancer during the active treatment period. *American Psychologist, 70*(2), 134–145.
Jacobson, K. A., Gao, Z. G., Matricon, P., Eddy, M. T., & Carlsson, J. (2020). Adenosine A2A receptor antagonists: From caffeine to selective non-xanthines. *British Journal of Pharmacology.*
Jacobson, N. S., Dobson, K. S., Truax, P. A., Addis, M. E., Koerner, K., Gollan, J. K., & Prince, S. E. (1996). A component analysis of cognitive-behavioral treatment for depression. *Journal of Consulting and Clinical Psychology, 64,* 295–304.
Jacobson, N. S., Fruzzetti, A. E., Dobson, K., Whisman, M., & Hops, H. (1993). Couple therapy as a treatment for depression: II. The effects of relationship quality and therapy on depressive relapse. *Journal of Consulting and Clinical Psychology, 61*(3), 516–519.
Jacobson, N. S., Martell, C. R., & Dimidjian, S. (2001). Behavioral activation treatment for depression: Returning to contextual roots. *Clinical Psychology: Science and Practice, 8*(3), 255–270.
Jaffe, J. H., Rawson, R. A., & Ling, W. (2005). Cocaine-related disorders. In B. J. Sadock & V. A. Sadock (Eds.), *Kaplan & Sadock's comprehensive textbook of psychiatry* (8th ed., pp. 1220–1238). Philadelphia, PA: Lippincott, Williams & Wilkins.
Jaffee, S. (2011). Genotype-environment correlations: Definitions, methods of measurement, and implications for research on adolescent psychopathology. In K. S. Kendler, S. Jaffee, & D. Romer (Eds.), *The dynamic genome and mental health: The role of genes and environments in youth development* (pp. 79–102). New York, NY: Oxford University Press.

Jager, G. (2012). Cannabis. In J. C. Verster, K. Brady, M. Galanter, & P. Conrod (Eds.), *Drug abuse and addiction in medical illness* (pp. 151–162). New York, NY: Springer.
Jain, K. K. (2015). Personalized management of psychiatric disorders. In K. K. Jain (Ed.), *Textbook of Personalized Medicine* (2nd ed., pp. 461–478): Springer New York.
Jakicic, J. M., Tate, D. F., Lang, W., Davis, K. K., Polzien, K., Rickman, A. D., & Finkelstein, E. A. (2012). Effect of a stepped-care intervention approach on weight loss in adults: A randomized clinical trial. *JAMA: Journal of the American Medical Association, 307*(24), 2617–2626.
James, B. O., Jenkins, R., & Lawani, A. O. (2012). Depression in primary care: the knowledge, attitudes and practice of general practitioners in Benin City, Nigeria. *South African Family Practice, 54*(1), 55–60.
James, E., Robertshaw, T. L., Hoskins, M., & Sessa, B. (2020). Psilocybin occasioned mystical-type experiences. *Human Psychopharmacology: Clinical and Experimental, 35*(5), e2742.
James, P. A., Oparil, S., Carter, B. L., Cushman, W. C., Dennison-Himmelfarb, C., Handler, J., Lackland, D. T., LeFevre, M. L., MacKenzie, T. D., Ogedegbe, O., Smith Jr., S. C., Svetkey, LP., Taler, S. J., Townsend, R. R., Wright Jr., J. T., Narva, A. S., & Ortiz, E. (2014). 2014 evidence-based guideline for the management of high blood pressure in adults: report from the panel members appointed to the Eighth Joint National Committee (JNC 8). *JAMA, 311*(5), 507–520.
Jamison, K. R. (1989). Mood disorders and patterns of creativity in British writers and artists. *Psychiatry, 52*(2), 125–134.
Jamison, K. R. (1993). *Touched with fire: Manic depressive illness and the artistic temperament.* New York, NY: Macmillan.
Jamison, R. N., & Virts, K. L. (1990). The influence of family support on chronic pain. *Behaviour Research and Therapy, 28*(4), 283–287.
Jang, K. L. (2005). *The behavioral genetics of psychopathology: A clinical guide.* Mahwah, NJ: Lawrence Erlbaum Associates.
Jang, S. H., Kim, D. I., & Choi, M. S. (2014). Effects and treatment methods of acupuncture and herbal medicine for premenstrual syndrome/premenstrual dysphoric disorder: systematic review. *BMC Complementary and Alternative Medicine, 14*(1), 11. doi:10.1186/1472-6882-14-11
Jannini, E. A., Burri, A., Jern, P., & Novelli, G. (2015). Genetics of human sexual behavior: Where we are, where we are going. *Sexual Medicine Reviews, 3*(2), 65–77.
Jansen, A. G., Mous, S. E., White, T., Posthuma, D., & Polderman, T. J. (2015). What twin studies tell us about the heritability of brain development, morphology, and function: A review. *Neuropsychology Review, 25*(1), 27–46.
Janszky, I., Ahnve, S., Lundberg, I., & Hemmingsson, T. (2010). Early-onset depression, anxiety, and risk of subsequent coronary heart disease: 37-year follow-up of 49,321 young Swedish men. *Journal of the American College of Cardiology, 56*(1), 31–37.
Jarrett, R. B., Minhajuddin, A., Gershenfeld, H., Friedman, E. S., & Thase, M. E. (2013). Preventing depressive relapse and recurrence in higher-risk cognitive therapy responders: a randomized trial of continuation phase cognitive therapy, fluoxetine, or matched pill placebo. *JAMA Psychiatry, 70,* 1152–1160.
Jason, L. A., Fennell, P. A., & Taylor, R. R. (2003). *Handbook of chronic fatigue syndrome.* Hoboken, NJ: Wiley.
Jason, L. A., Richman, J. A., Rademaker, A. W., Jordan, K. M., Plioplys, A. V., Taylor, R. R., & Plioplys, S. (1999). A community-based study of chronic fatigue syndrome. *Archives of Internal Medicine, 159,* 2129–2137.
Jason, L. A., Roesner, N., Porter, N., Parenti, B., Mortensen, J., & Till, L. (2010). Provision of social support to individuals with chronic fatigue syndrome. *Journal of Clinical Psychology, 66,* 249–258.
Jaspers, K. (1963). *General psychopathology* (J. Hoenig & M. W. Hamilton, Trans.). Manchester, UK: Manchester University Press.
Jaussent, I., Dauvilliers, Y., Ancelin, M. L., Dartigues, J. F., Tavernier, B., Touchon, J., & Besset, A. (2011). Insomnia symptoms in older adults: Associated factors and gender differences. *The American Journal of Geriatric Psychiatry, 19*(1), 88.
Javitt, D. C., & Laruelle, M. (2006). Neurochemical theories. In J. A. Lieberman, T. S. Stroup, & D. O. Perkins (Eds.), *The American Psychiatric Publishing textbook of schizophrenia* (pp. 85–116). Washington, DC: American Psychiatric Publishing.
Javitt, D. C., & Zukin, S. R. (2009). Phencyclidine (or phencyclidine-like)-related disorders. In B. J. Sadock, V. A. Sadock, & P. Ruiz (Eds.), *Kaplan & Sadock's comprehensive textbook of psychiatry* (9th ed., Vol. I, pp. 1337–1397). Philadelphia, PA: Lippincott Williams & Wilkins.
Jellinek, E. M. (1946). Phases in the drinking histories of alcoholics. *Quarterly Journal of Studies on Alcohol, 7,* 1–88.
Jellinek, E. M. (1952). Phases of alcohol addiction. *Quarterly Journal of Studies on Alcohol, 13,* 673–684.
Jellinek, E. M. (1960). *The disease concept of alcohol.* New Brunswick, NJ: Hillhouse Press.
Jenike, M. A., Baer, L., Ballantine, H. T., Martuza, R. L., Tynes, S., Giriunas, I., & Cassem, N. H. (1991). Cingulotomy for refractory obsessive-compulsive disorder: A long-term follow-up of 33 patients. *Archives of General Psychiatry, 48,* 548–555.
Jenkins, J. H., & Karno, M. (1992). The meaning of expressed emotion: Theoretical issues raised by cross-cultural research. *American Journal of Psychiatry, 149,* 9–21.
Jenni, O. G., & O'Connor, B. B. (2005). Children's sleep: An interplay between culture and biology. *Pediatrics, 115*(1), 204–216. doi: 10.1542/peds.2004-0815B
Jennings, W. G., & Reingle, J. M. (2012). On the number and shape of developmental/life-course violence, aggression, and delinquency trajectories: A state-of-the-art review. *Journal of Criminal Justice, 40*(6), 472–489.
Jensen, E., Schmidt, E., Pedersen, B., & Dahl, R. (1991). Effect on smoking cessation of silver acetate, nicotine and ordinary chewing gum. *Psychopharmacology, 104*(4), 470–474.
Jensen, H. M., Gron, R., Lidegaard, O., Pedersen, L. H., Andersen, P. K., & Kessing, L. V. (2013). Maternal depression, antidepressant use in pregnancy and Apgar scores in infants. *British Journal of Psychiatry, 202*(5), 347–351.
Jensen, P. S., Hinshaw, S. P., Swanson, J. M., Greenhill, L. L., Conners, C. K., Arnold, L. E., & Wigal, T. (2001). Findings from the NIMH Multimodal Treatment Study of ADHD (MTA): Implications and applications for primary care providers. *Journal of Developmental and Behavioral Pediatrics, 22*(1), 60–73.
Jeuring, H. W., Comijs, H. C., Deeg, D. J. H., Hoogendijk, E. O., Beekman, A. T. F., Stek, M. L., & Huisman, M. (2018). Secular trends in excess mortality of late-life depression. *Journal of Affective Disorders, 234,* 28–33. doi: 10.1016/j.jad.2018.02.068
Jiang, W., Samad, Z., Boyle, S., Becker, R. C., Williams, R., Kuhn, C., & Velazquez, E. J. (2013). Prevalence and clinical characteristics of mental stress-induced myocardial ischemia in patients with coronary heart disease. *Journal of the American College of Cardiology, 61*(7), 714–722.
Jiann, B. P., Su, C. C., Yu, C. C., Wu, T. T., & Huang, J. K. (2009). Risk factors for individual domains of female sexual function. *The Journal of Sexual Medicine, 6*(12), 3364–3375.
Jilek, W. G. (1982). Altered states of consciousness in North American Indian ceremonials. *Ethos, 10*(4), 326–343.

Jin, X., Zhang, Y., Celniker, S. E., Xia, Y., Mao, J.-H., Snijders, A. M., & Chang, H. (2021). Gut microbiome partially mediates and coordinates the effects of genetics on anxiety-like behavior in collaborative cross mice. *Scientific Reports, 11,* 270.

Jindal, R. D., Thase, M. E., Fasiczka, A. L., Friedman, E. S., Buysse, D. J., Frank, E., & Kupfer, D. J. (2002). Electroencephalographic sleep profiles in single-episode and recurrent unipolar forms of major depression: II. Comparison during remission. *Biological Psychiatry, 1,* 230–236.

Jockin, V., McGue, M., & Lykken, D. T. (1996). Personality and divorce: A genetic analysis. *Journal of Personality and Social Psychology, 71,* 288–299.

Joe, S., Baser, R., Breeden, G., Neighbors, H., & Jackson, J. (2006). Prevalence of and risk factors for lifetime suicide attempts among blacks in the United States. *JAMA: Journal of the American Medical Association, 296,* 2112–2123.

Johannes, C. B., Araujo, A. B., Feldman, H. A., Derby, C. A., Kleinman, K. P., & McKinlay, J. B. (2000). Incidence of erectile dysfunction in men 40 to 69 years old: Longitudinal results from the Massachusetts male aging study. *Journal of Urology, 163,* 460–463.

Johansson, A., Sundbom, E., Höjerback, T., & Bodlund, O. (2010). A five-year follow-up study of Swedish adults with gender identity disorder. *Archives of Sexual Behavior, 39*(6), 1429–1437.

John, J. (2010). Economic perspectives on pediatric obesity: impact on health care expenditures and cost-effectiveness of preventive interventions. Nestle Nutr Workshop Ser Pediatr Program. 66:111–24. doi: 10.1159/000318952.

Johnson, A. M., Mercer, C. H., Erens, B., Copas, A. J., McManus, S., Wellings, K., & Field, J. (2001). Sexual behaviour in Britain: Partnerships, practices, and HIV risk behaviours. *The Lancet, 358,* 1835–1842.

Johnson, A. M., Wadsworth, J., Wellings, K., Bradshaw, S., & Field, J. (1992). Sexual lifestyles and HIV risk. *Nature, 360,* 410–412.

Johnson, C. J., & Beitchman, J. H. (2005). Expressive language disorder. In B. J. Sadock & V. A. Sadock (Eds.), *Kaplan & Sadock's comprehensive textbook of psychiatry* (pp. 3136–3142). Philadelphia: Lippincott, Williams & Wilkins.

Johnson, J. G., Cohen, P., Kasen, S., & Brook, J. S. (2002). Eating disorders during adolescence and the risk for physical and mental disorders during early adulthood. *Archives of General Psychiatry, 59,* 545–552.

Johnson, J. G., Cohen, P., Kasen, S., & Brook, J. S. (2006). Dissociative disorders among adults in the community, impaired functioning, and Axis I and Axis II comorbidity. *Journal of Psychiatric Research, 40,* 131–140.

Johnson, J. G., Cohen, P., Pine, D. S., Klein, D. F., Kasen, S., & Brook, J. S. (2000). Association between cigarette smoking and anxiety disorders during adolescence and early adulthood. *JAMA: Journal of the American Medical Association, 284,* 2348–2351.

Johnson, J. G., Weissman, M. M., & Klerman, G. L. (1990). Panic disorder, comorbidity and suicide attempts. *Archives of General Psychiatry, 47,* 805–808.

Johnson, S. L., & Miller, I. (1997). Negative life events and time to recovery from episodes of bipolar disorder. *Journal of Abnormal Psychology, 106*(3), 449–457.

Johnson, S. L., Cuellar, A. K., & Miller, C. (2009). Bipolar and unipolar depression: A comparison of clinical phenomenology, biological vulnerability, and psychosocial predictors. In I. H. Gotlib & C. L. Hammen (Eds.), *Handbook of depression* (2nd ed., pp. 142–162). New York, NY: Guilford.

Johnson, S. L., Cuellar, A. K., Ruggero, C., Winett-Perlman, C., Goodnick, P., White, R., & Miller, I. (2008). Life events as predictors of mania and depression in bipolar I disorder. *Journal of Abnormal Psychology, 117*(2), 268–277.

Johnson, S. L., Gruber, J. L., & Eisner, L. R. (2007). Emotion and bipolar disorder. In J. Rottenberg & S. L. Johnson (Eds.), *Emotion and psychopathology* (pp. 123–150). Washington, DC: American Psychological Association.

Johnson, S. L., Winett, C. A., Meyer, B., Greenhouse, W. J., & Miller, I. (1999). Social support and the course of bipolar disorder. *American Psychological Association, 180*(4), 558–566.

Johnson, W., Turkheimer, E., Gottesman, I. I., & Bouchard, T. J., Jr. (2009). Beyond heritability: Twin studies in behavioral research. *Current Directions in Psychological Science, 18*(4), 217–220.

Johnston, B. C., Kanters, S., Bandayrel, K., Wu, P., Naji, F., Siemieniuk, R. A., . . . Mills, E. J. (2014). Comparison of weight loss among named diet programs in overweight and obese adults: a meta-analysis. *JAMA, 312*(9), 923–933.

Johnston, C. A., Rost, S., Miller-Kovach, K., Moreno, J. P., & Foreyt, J. P. (2013). Multi-component access to a commercially available weight loss program: A randomized controlled trial. *The FASEB Journal, 27*(1_MeetingAbstracts), 851–852.

Johnston, L. D., Miech, R. A., O'Malley, P. M., Bachman, J. G., Schulenberg, J. E., & Patrick, M. E. (2019). *Monitoring the Future national survey results on drug use 1975–2018: Overview, key findings on adolescent drug use.* Ann Arbor: Institute for Social Research, University of Michigan.

Johnston, L. D., O'Malley, P. M., Bachman, J. G., & Schulenberg, J. E. (2012). *Monitoring the future: National survey results on drug use, 1975–2011. Volume II: College Students & Adults Ages 19–50.* Ann Arbor MI: Institute for Social Research, University of Michigan.

Joiner, T. E. (2014). *The perversion of virtue: Understanding murder-suicide.* New York, NY: Oxford University Press.

Joiner, T. E., Jr. (1997). Shyness and low social support as interactive diatheses, with loneliness as mediator: Testing an interpersonal–personality view of vulnerability to depressive symptoms. *Journal of Abnormal Psychology, 106*(3), 386–394.

Joiner, T. E., Jr. (1999). A test of interpersonal theory of depression in youth psychiatric inpatients. *Journal of Abnormal Child Psychology, 27*(1), 77–85.

Joiner, T. E., Jr., & Rudd, M. D. (1996). Toward a categorization of depression-related psychological constructs. *Cognitive Therapy and Research, 20,* 51–68.

Joiner, T. E., Jr., & Rudd, M. D. (2000). Intensity and duration of suicidal crises vary as a function of previous suicide attempts and negative life events. *Journal of Consulting and Clinical Psychology, 68*(5), 909–916.

Joiner, T. E., Jr., & Timmons, K. A. (2009). Depression in its interpersonal context. In I. H. Gotlib & C. L. Hammen (Eds.), *Handbook of depression* (2nd ed., pp. 322–339). New York, NY: Guilford.

Joiner, T. E., Jr., Heatherton, T. F., & Keel, P. K. (1997). Ten year stability and predictive validity of five bulimia-related indicators. *American Journal of Psychiatry, 154,* 1133–1138.

Joiner, T., Kalafat, J., Draper, J., Stokes, H., Knudson, M., Berman, A. L., & McKeon, R. (2007). Establishing standards for the assessment of suicide risk among callers to the national suicide prevention lifeline. *Suicide and Life-Threatening Behavior, 37*(3), 353–365.

Joling, K. J., van Marwijk, H. W., Veldhuijzen, A. E., van der Horst, H. E., Scheltens, P., Smit, F., & van Hout, H. P. (2015). The two-year incidence of depression and anxiety disorders in spousal caregivers of persons with dementia: who is at the greatest risk? *The American Journal of Geriatric Psychiatry, 23*(3), 293–303.

Jones, M. C. (1924a). A laboratory study of fear: The case of Peter. *The Pedagogical Seminary. 31* (4): 308–315. doi:10.1080/08856559.1924.9944851

Jones, M. C. (1924b).The elimination of children's fears. Journal of Experimental Psychology, 7, 382–390.
Jones, B. E., & Gray, B. A. (1986). Problems in diagnosing schizophrenia and affective disorders in blacks. *Hospital and Community Psychiatry, 37,* 61–65.
Jones, J. C., & Barlow, D. H. (1990). The etiology of posttraumatic stress disorder. *Clinical Psychology Review, 10,* 299–328.
Jones, P., Barnes, T., Davies, L., Dunn, G., Lloyd, H., Hayhurst, K., & Lewis, S. W. (2006). Randomized controlled trial of the effect on quality of life of second- vs first-generation antipsychotic drugs in schizophrenia: Cost Utility of the Latest Antipsychotic Drugs in Schizophrenia Study (CUtLASS 1). *Archives of General Psychiatry, 63*(10), 1079.
Jones, R. T. (2009). Hallucinogen-related disorders. In B. J. Sadock, V. A. Sadock, & P. Ruiz (Eds.), *Kaplan & Sadock's comprehensive textbook of psychiatry* (9th ed., Vol. I, pp. 1331–1340). Philadelphia, PA: Lippincott Williams & Wilkins.
Joo, E. Y., Yoon, C. W., Koo, D. L., Kim, D., & Hong, S. B. (2012). Adverse effects of 24 hours of sleep deprivation on cognition and stress hormones. *Journal of Clinical Neurology, 8*(2), 146–150.
Joormann, J. (2009). Cognitive aspects of depression. In I. H. Gotlib & C. L. Hammen (Eds.), *Handbook of depression* (2nd ed., pp. 298–321). New York, NY: Guilford.
Jordan, B. D., Relkin, N. R., Ravdin, L. D., Jacobs, A. R., Bennett, A., & Gandy, S. (1997). Apolipoprotein E Epsilon 4 associated with chronic traumatic brain injury in boxing. *JAMA: Journal of the American Medical Association, 278,* 136–140.
Joslyn, G., Ravindranathan, A., Brush, G., Schuckit, M., & White, R. L. (2010). Human variation in alcohol response is influenced by variation in neuronal signaling genes. *Alcoholism: Clinical and Experimental Research, 34*(5), 800–812.
Joudrey, P. J., Chadi, N., Roy, P., Morford, K. L., Bach, P., Kimmel, S., … Calcaterra, S. L. (2020). Pharmacy-based methadone dispensing and drive time to methadone treatment in five states within the United States: A cross-sectional study. *Drug and Alcohol Dependence, 211*, 107968.
Joyce, P. R., Stephenson, J., Kennedy, M., Mulder, R. T., & McHugh, P. C. (2013). The presence of both serotonin 1A receptor (HTR1A) and dopamine transporter (DAT1) gene variants increase the risk of borderline personality disorder. *Frontiers in Genetics, 4,* 313.
Joyner, M. J., Charkoudian, N., & Wallin, B. G. (2010). Sympathetic nervous system and blood pressure in humans: Individualized patterns of regulation and their implications. *Hypertension, 56*(1), 10–16.
Judd, L. L. (2000). Course and chronicity of unipolar major depressive disorder: Commentary on Joiner. *Child Psychology Science and Practice, 7*(2), 219–223.
Judd, L. L. (2012). Dimensional paradigm of the long-term course of unipolar major depressive disorder. *Depression and Anxiety, 29*(3), 167–171.
Judd, L. L., Akiskal, H., Schettler, P., Coryell, W., Endicott, J., Maser, J., & Keller, M. B. (2003). A prospective investigation of the natural history of the long-term weekly symptomatic status of bipolar II disorder. *Archives of General Psychiatry, 60,* 261–269.
Judge, B., & Rusyniak, D. (2009). Illicit drugs I: Amphetamines. In M. R. Dobbs (Ed.), *Clinical neurotoxicology: Syndromes, substances, environments, expert consult* (pp. 303–313). Philadelphia, PA: WB Saunders.
Judge, C., O'Donovan, C., Callaghan, G., Gaoatswe, G., & O'Shea, D. (2014). Gender dysphoria–prevalence and co-morbidities in an Irish adult population. *Frontiers in Endocrinology, 5*(87), 1–5.
Jufer-Phipps, R. A., & Levine, B. S. (2020). Benzodiazepines. In B. S. Levine & S. Karrigan (Eds.), *Principles of forensic toxicology* (pp. 317–331). Cham: Springer.
Juliano, L. M., Ferré, S., & Griffiths, R. R. (2015). Tha pharmacology of caffeine. In R. K. Ries, D. A. Fiellin, S. C. Miller, & R. Saitz (Eds.), *The ASAM principles of addiction medicine* (5th ed., pp. 180–200). New York, NY: Wolters Kluwer.
Jummani, R., & Coffey, B. J. (2009). Tic disorders. In B. J. Sadock, V. A. Sadock, & P. Ruiz (Eds.), *Kaplan & Sadock's comprehensive textbook of psychiatry* (9th ed., Vol. II, pp. 3609–3623). Philadelphia, PA: Lippincott Williams & Wilkins.
Junewicz, A., & Billick, S. B. (2020). Conduct disorder: Biology and developmental trajectories. *Psychiatric Quarterly, 91*(1), 77–90.
Junginger, J. (1997). Fetishism: Assessment and treatment. In D. R. Laws & W. O'Donohue (Eds.), *Sexual deviance: Theory, assessment and treatment* (pp. 92–110). New York, NY: Guilford.
Kabir, M. T., Uddin, M., Mathew, B., Das, P. K., Perveen, A., & Ashraf, G. M. (2020). Emerging promise of immunotherapy for Alzheimer's disease: A new hope for the development of Alzheimer's vaccine. *Current Topics in Medicinal Chemistry, 20*(13), 1214–1234.
Kafka, M. P. (2010). The DSM diagnostic criteria for fetishism. *Archives of sexual behavior, 39*(2), 357–362.
Kafka, M. P., & Hennen, J. (2003). Hypersexual desire in males: Are males with paraphilias difference from males with paraphilia-related disorders? *Sexual Abuse: A Journal of Research & Treatment, 4,* 307–321.
Kagan, J. (2014a). Temperamental contributions to the development of psychological profiles: I. Basic issues. In S. G. Hofmann and P. D. DiBartolo (Eds.), *Social anxiety: Clinical, developmental, and social perspectives (third edition)* (pp. 377–418). Amsterdam, The Netherlands: Elsevier/Academic Press.
Kagan, J. (2014b). Temperamental contributions to the development of psychological profiles: II. Two candidates. In S. G. Hofmann and P. D. DiBartolo (Eds.), *Social anxiety: Clinical, developmental, and social perspectives (third edition)* (pp. 419–450). Amsterdam, The Netherlands: Elsevier/Academic Press.
Kahler, C. W., Litvin Bloom, E., Leventhal, A. M., & Brown, R. A. (2015). Behavioral interventions in smoking cessation. In R. K. Ries, D. A. Fiellin, S. C. Miller, & R. Saitz (Eds.), *The ASAM principles of addiction medicine* (5th ed., pp. 894–911). New York, NY: Wolters Kluwer.
Kahn, R. S., Khoury, J., Nichols, W. C., & Lanphear, B. P. (2003). Role of dopamine transporter genotype and maternal prenatal smoking in childhood hyperactive-impulsive, inattentive, and oppositional behaviors. *The Journal of Pediatrics, 143*(1), 104–110.
Kahn, X., King, X., Abelson, X., & Liberzon, X. (2009). Au to provide reference.
Kaiser, J. (2006). Differences in immune cell "brakes" may explain chimp–human split on AIDS. *Science Magazine, 312,* 672–673.
Kaiser, T., Herzog, P., Voderholzer, U., & Brakemeier, E. (2021). Unraveling the comorbidity of depression and anxiety in a large inpatient sample: Network analysis to examine bridge symptoms. *Depression and Anxiety, 38*(3), 307–317. doi: 10.1002/da.23136
Kalaria, R., Maestre, G., Arizaga, R., Friedland, R., Galasko, D., Hall, K., & Potocnik, F. (2008). Alzheimer's disease and vascular dementia in developing countries: Prevalence, management, and risk factors. *Lancet Neurology, 7*(9), 812.
Kalat, J. W. (2013). *Biological psychology* (11th ed.). Belmont, CA: Wadsworth, Cengage Learning.
Kalivas, P. W. (2005). New directions pharmacotherapy for addiction or can we forget to be addicted? *Clinical Neuroscience Research, 5,* 147–150.
Kallmann, F. J. (1938). *The genetics of schizophrenia.* New York, NY: Augustin.

Kalra, G., Christodoulou, G., Jenkins, R., Tsipas, V., Christodoulou, N., Lecic-Tosevski, D., . . . Bhugra, D. (2012). Mental health promotion: guidance and strategies. *European Psychiatry, 27*(2), 81–86. doi:10.1016/j.eurpsy.2011.10.001

Kame'enui, E. J., Fien, H., & Korgesaar, J. (2013). Direct instruction as *eo nomine* and contronym: Why the right words and the details matter. In H. L. Swanson, K. R. Harris, & S. Graham (Eds.), *Handbook of learning disabilities* (2nd ed.). New York, NY: Guilford.

Kamen, C., Tejani, M. A., Chandwani, K., Janelsins, M., Peoples, A. R., Roscoe, J. A., & Morrow, G. R. (2014). Anticipatory nausea and vomiting due to chemotherapy. *European journal of pharmacology, 722,* 172–179.

Kaminen-Ahola, N. (2020). Fetal alcohol spectrum disorders: Genetic and epigenetic mechanisms. *Prenatal Diagnosis, 40*(9), 1185–1192.

Kaminski, J. W., Valle, L., Filene, J., & Boyle, C. (2008). A meta-analytic review of components associated with parent training program effectiveness. *Journal of Abnormal Child Psychology, 36*(4), 567–589.

Kanai, R., Bahrami, B., Roylance, R., & Rees, G. (2012). Online social network size is reflected in human brain structure. *Proceedings of the Royal Society: Biological Sciences, 279*(1732), 1327–1334. doi: 10.1098/rspb.2011.1959

Kanaya, T., Scullin, M. H., & Ceci, S. J. (2003). The Flynn effect and U.S. policies: The impact of rising IQ scores on American society via mental retardation diagnoses. *American Psychologist, 58,* 778–790.

Kanayama, G., Barry, S., & Pope, H. G. (2006). Body image and attitudes toward male roles in anabolic-androgenic steroid users. *American Journal of Psychiatry, 163,* 697–703.

Kandasamy, M., Anusuyadevi, M., Aigner, K. M., Unger, M. S., Kniewallner, K. M., de Sousa, D. M. B., … Aigner, L. (2020). TGF-β signaling: A therapeutic target to reinstate regenerative plasticity in vascular dementia? *Aging and Disease, 11*(4), 828.

Kandel, E. R., Dudai, Y., & Mayford, M. R. (2014, March).The molecular and systems biology of memory. Cell. 157(1):163–86. doi: 10.1016/j.cell.2014.03.001.

Kandel, E. R., Schwartz, J., & Jessell, T. M. (2000). *Principles of neural science* (4th ed.). New York, NY: McGraw-Hill.

Kane, J. M., Stroup, S., & Marder, S. R. (2009). Schizophrenia: Pharmacological treatment. In B. J. Sadock, V. A. Sadock, & P. Ruiz (Eds.), *Kaplan & Sadock's comprehensive textbook of psychiatry* (9th ed., Vol. I, pp. 1547–1556). Philadelphia, PA: Lippincott Williams & Wilkins.

Kanigel, R. (1988, October/November). Nicotine becomes addictive. *Science Illustrated, 2,* 19–21.

Kanner, L. (1943). Autistic disturbances of affective contact. *Nervous Child, 2,* 217–250.

Kanner, L. (1949). Problems of nosology and psychodynamics of early infantile autism. *American Journal of Orthopsychiatry, 19,* 416–426.

Kanner, L., & Eisenberg, L. (1955). Notes on the follow-up studies of autistic children. In P. H. J. Zubin (Ed.), *Psychopathology of childhood* (pp. 227–239). New York, NY: Grune & Stratton.

Kansas v. Hendricks, 117 S. Ct. 2072 (1997).

Kaplan, H. S. (1979). *Disorders of sexual desire.* New York, NY: Brunner/Mazel.

Kaplan, M. (1983). A woman's view of DSM-III. *American Psychologist, 38,* 786–792.

Kaplan, S. A., Reis, R. B., Kohn, I. J., Ikeguchi, E. F., Laor, E., Te, A. E., & Martins, A. C. (1999). Safety and efficacy of sildenafil in postmenopausal women with sexual dysfunction. *Urology, 53,* 481–486.

Kaptchuk, T. J., Kelley, J. M., Conboy, L. A., Davis, R. B., Kerr, C. E., & Lembo, A. J. (2008). Components of placebo effect: Randomised controlled trial in patients with irritable bowel syndrome. *BMJ, 336*(7651), 999–1003. doi: 10.1136/bmj.39524.439618.25

Karg, K., Burmeister, M., Shedden, K., & Sen, S. (2011). The serotonin transporter promoter variant (5-HTTLPR), stress, and depression meta-analysis revisited: Evidence of genetic moderation. *Archives of General Psychiatry, 68*(5), 444–454. doi: 10.1001/archgenpsychiatry.2010.189

Karikari, T. K., Benedet, A. L., Ashton, N. J., Rodriguez, J. L., Snellman, A., Suárez-Calvet, M., … Rial, A. M. (2020). Diagnostic performance and prediction of clinical progression of plasma phospho-tau181 in the Alzheimer's Disease Neuroimaging Initiative. *Molecular Psychiatry*, 1–14.

Karin, O., Raz, M., & Alon, U. (2021). An opponent process for alcohol addiction based on changes in endocrine gland mass. *Iscience, 24*(3), 102127.

Kariuki-Nyuthe, C., & Stein, D. J. (2015). Anxiety and related disorders and physical illness. *Key Issues in Mental Health, 179,* 81–97.

Karkhaneh, M., Clark, B., Ospina, M. B., Seida, J. C., Smith, V., & Hartling, L. (2010). Social Stories™ to improve social skills in children with autism spectrum disorder. *Autism, 14*(6), 641–662. doi: 10.1177/1362361310373057

Karlin, B. E., Trockel, M., Spira, A. P., Taylor, C. B., & Manber, R. (2015). National evaluation of the effectiveness of cognitive behavioral therapy for insomnia among older versus younger veterans. *International Journal of Geriatric Psychiatry, 30*(3), 308–315.

Karsinti, E., Labaeye, M., Piani, K., Fortias, M., Brousse, G., Bloch, V., … Vorspan, F. (2020). Network analysis of psychotic manifestations among cocaine users. *Journal of Psychiatric Research, 130,* 300–305.

Kasari, C., Gulsrud, A., Freeman, S., Paparella, T., & Hellemann, G. (2012). Longitudinal follow-up of children with autism receiving targeted interventions on joint attention and play. *Journal of the American Academy of Child & Adolescent Psychiatry, 51*(5), 487–495. doi: http://dx.doi.org/10.1016/j.jaac.2012.02.019

Kasen, S., Cohen, P., Skodol, A. E., Johnson, J. G., & Brook, J. S. (1999). Influence of child and adolescent psychiatric disorders on young adult personality disorder. *American Journal of Psychiatry, 156*(10), 1529-1535.

Kasindorf, J. (1988, May 2). The real story of Billie Boggs: Was Koch right—Or the civil libertarians? *New York,* pp. 36–44.

Kaslow, N. J., Davis, S. P., & Smith, C. O. (2009). Biological and psychosocial interventions for depression in children and adolescents. In I. H. Gotlib & C. L. Hammen (Eds.), *Handbook of depression* (2nd ed., pp. 642–672). New York, NY: Guilford.

Kass, A. E., Trockel, M., Safer, D. L., Sinton, M. M., Cunning, D., Rizk, M. T., . . . Taylor, C. B. (2014). Internet-based preventive intervention for reducing eating disorder risk: A randomized controlled trial comparing guided with unguided self-help. *Behaviour Research and Therapy, 63,* 90–98.

Kass, D. J., Silvers, F. M., & Abrams, G. M. (1972). Behavioral group treatment of hysteria. *Archives of General Psychiatry, 26,* 42–50.

Kate, M., Hopwood, T., & Jamieson, G. (2020). The prevalence of dissociative disorders and dissociative experiences in college populations: A meta-analysis of 98 studies. *Journal of Trauma and Dissociation, 21*(1), 16–61. doi: 10.1080/15299732.2019.1647915

Kato, K., Sullivan, P., Evengard, B., & Pederson, N. (2006). Premorbid predictors of chronic fatigue. *Archives of General Psychiatry, 63,* 1267–1272.

Katon, W. (1993). Somatization disorder, hypochondriasis, and conversion disorder. In D. L. Dunner (Ed.), *Current psychiatric therapy* (pp. 314–320). Philadelphia, PA: W. B. Saunders.

Katon, W. J. (2003). Clinical and health services relationships between major depression, depressive symptoms, and general medical illness. *Biological Psychiatry, 54,* 216–226.

Katz, J., & Gagliese, L. (1999). Phantom limb pain: A continuing puzzle. In R. J. Gatchel & D. C. Turk (Eds.), *Psychosocial factors in pain: Critical perspectives* (pp. 284–300). New York, NY: Guilford.

Katz, M. J., Lipton, R. B., Hall, C. B., Zimmerman, M. E., Sanders, A. E., Verghese, J., & Derby, C. A. (2012). Age-specific and sex-specific prevalence and incidence of mild cognitive impairment, dementia, and Alzheimer dementia in blacks and whites: A report from the Einstein Aging Study. *Alzheimer Disease & Associated Disorders, 26*(4), 335–343. doi: 310.1097/WAD.1090b1013e31823dbcfc

Katz, M., DeRogatis, L. R., Ackerman, R., Hedges, P., Lesko, L., Garcia, M. J., & Sand, M. (2013). Efficacy of flibanserin in women with hypoactive sexual desire disorder: Results from the BEGONIA trial. *Journal Of Sexual Medicine, 10,* 1807–1815. doi:10.1111/jsm.12189

Kaufman, C. E., Beals, J., Croy, C., Jiang, L., Novins, D. K., & The AI-SUPERPFP Team. (2013). Multilevel context of depression in two American Indian tribes. *Journal of Consulting and Clinical Psychology, 81,* 1040–1051.

Kaufman, J. C. (2001). The Sylvia Plath effect: Mental illness in eminent creative writers. *The Journal of Creative Behavior, 35,* 37–50.

Kaufman, J. C. (2002). Creativity and confidence: Price of achievement. *American Psychologist, 57,* 375–376.

Kaufman, J. C., & Baer, J. (2002). I bask in dreams of suicide: Mental illness, poetry, and women. *Review of General Psychology, 6,* 271–286.

Kavale, K. A., & Forness, S. R. (1983). Hyperactivity and diet treatment: A meta-analysis of the Feingold hypothesis. *Journal of Learning Disabilities, 16,* 324–330.

Kavanagh, D. J. (1992). Recent developments in expressed emotion and schizophrenia. *British Journal of Psychiatry, 160,* 601–620.

Kay, C., & Green, J. (2013). Reactive attachment disorder following early maltreatment: Systematic evidence beyond the institution. *Journal of Abnormal Child Psychology, 41*(4), 571–586. doi: 10.1007/s10802-012-9705-9

Kaye, W. (2008). Neurobiology of anorexia and bulimia nervosa. *Physiology and Behavior, 94*(1), 121–135.

Kaye, W. H., Bulik, C. M., Thornton, L., Barbarich, N., Masters, K., & Price Foundation Collaborative Group. (2014). Comorbidity of anxiety disorders with anorexia and bulimia nervosa. *American Journal of Psychiatry, 161*(12), 2215–2221.

Kaye, W. H., Weltzin, T. E., Hsu, L. K. G., McConaha, C. W., & Bolton, B. (1993). Amount of calories retained after binge eating and vomiting. *American Journal of Psychiatry, 150*(6), 969–971.

Kazak, A. E., & Noll, R. B. (2015). The integration of psychology in pediatric oncology research and practice: Collaboration to improve care and outcomes for children and families. *American Psychologist, 70*(2), 146–158.

Kazak, A. E., Boeving, C. A., Alderfer, M. A., Hwang, W., & Reilly, A. (2005). Posttraumatic stress symptoms during treatment in parents of children with cancer. *Journal of Clinical Oncology, 23,* 7405–7410.

Kazdin, A. E. (2011). *Single-case research designs: Methods for clinical and applied settings.* New York, NY: Oxford University Press.

Ke, F., Moon, J., & Sokolikj, Z. (2020). Virtual reality–based social skills training for children with autism spectrum disorder. *Journal of Special Education Technology,* 0162643420945603.

Keane, T. M., & Barlow, D. H. (2002). Posttraumatic stress disorder. In D. H. Barlow, *Anxiety and its disorders: The nature and treatment of anxiety and panic.* (2nd ed., pp. 418–453). New York, NY: Guilford.

Keane, T. M., & Miller, M. W. (2012). Future of classification in posttraumatic stress disorder. In J. G. Beck & D. M. Sloan (Eds.), *The Oxford handbook of traumatic stress disorders* (pp. 54–66). New York, NY: Oxford University Press.

Keane, T. M., Marx, B. P., Sloan, D. M., & DePrince, A. (2011). Trauma, dissociation, and post-traumatic stress disorder. In D. H. Barlow (Ed.), *The Oxford handbook of clinical psychology* (pp. 359–386). New York, NY: Oxford University Press.

Kearney, A. J. (2006). A primer of covert sensitization. *Cognitive and Behavioral Practice, 13*(2), 167–175. doi: 10.1016/j.cbpra.2006.02.002

Kearns, M. C., Ressler, K. J., Zatzick, D., & Rothbaum, B. O. (2012). Early interventions for PTSD: A review. *Depression and Anxiety, 29,* 833–842. doi: 10.1002/da.21997

Keck, P. E., & McElroy, S. L. (2002). Pharmacological treatments for bipolar disorder. In P. E. Nathan & J. M. Gorman (Eds.), *A guide to treatments that work* (2nd ed., pp. 277–299). New York, NY: Oxford University Press.

Keefe, D. L. (2002). Sex hormones and neural mechanisms. *Archives of Sexual Behavior, 31*(5), 401–403.

Keefe, F. J., & France, C. R. (1999). Pain: Biopsychosocial mechanisms and management. *Current Directions in Psychological Science, 8,* 137–141.

Keefe, F. J., Dunsmore, J., & Burnett, R. (1992). Behavioral and cognitive-behavioral approaches to chronic pain: Recent advances and future directions. Special issue: Behavioral medicine: An update for the 1990s. *Journal of Consulting and Clinical Psychology, 60*(4), 528–536.

Keel, P. K. (2019). Purging disorder: Recent advances and future challenges. *Current Opinion in Psychiatry, 32*(6), 518–524. doi: 10.1097/YCO.0000000000000541

Keel, P. K., & Forney, K. J. (2013). Psychosocial risk factors for eating disorders. *International Journal of Eating Disorders, 46*(5), 433–439.

Keel, P. K., Brown, T. A., Holland, L. A., & Bodell, L. P. (2012). Empirical classification of eating disorders. *Annual Review of Clinical Psychology, 8,* 381–404.

Keel, P. K., Dorer, D. J., Eddy, K. T., Franko, D., Charatan, D. L., & Herzog, D. B. (2003). Predictors of mortality in eating disorders. *Archives of General Psychiatry, 60,* 179–183.

Keel, P. K., Fichter, M., Quadflieg, N., Bulik, C. M., Baxter, M. G., Thornton, L., & Kaye, W. H. (2004). Application of a latent class analysis to empirically define eating disorder phenotypes. *Archives of General Psychiatry, 61,* 192–200.

Keel, P. K., Heatherton, T. F., Dorer, D. J., Joiner, T, E., & Zalta, A. K. (2006). Point prevalence of bulimia nervosa in 1982, 1992, and 2002. *Psychological Medicine, 36,* 119–127.

Keel, P. K., Mitchell, J. E., Miller, K. B., Davis, T. L., & Crow, S. J. (2000). Predictive validity of bulimia nervosa as a diagnostic strategy. *American Journal of Psychiatry 157*(1), 136–138.

Keen, C., Hunter, J. E., Allen, E. G., Rocheleau, C., Waters, M., & Sherman, S. L. (2020). The association between maternal occupation and Down syndrome: A report from the national Down syndrome project. *International Journal of Hygiene and Environmental Health, 223*(1), 207–213.

Keilitz, I. (1987). Researching and reforming the insanity defense. *Rutgers Law Review, 39,* 289–322.

Keitner, G. I., Ryan, C. E., Miller, I. W., Kohn, R., Bishop, D. S., & Epstein, N. B. (1995). Role of the family in recovery and major depression. *American Journal of Psychiatry, 152,* 1002–1008.

Keller, M. B., & Wunder, J. (1990). Bipolar disorder in childhood. In M. Hersen & C. G. Last (Eds.), *Handbook of child and adult psychopathology: A longitudinal perspective.* Elmsford, NY: Pergamon Press.

Keller, M. B., Lavori, P. W., Endicott, J., Coryell, W., & Klerman, G. L. (1983). "Double depression": Two year follow-up. *American Journal of Psychiatry, 140*(6), 689–694.

Keller, M. B., McCollough, J. P., Klein, D. N., Arnow, B., Dunner, D. L., Gelenberg, A. J., & Zajecka, J. (2000). A comparison of nefazodone, the cognitive behavioral-analysis system of psychotherapy, and their combination for the treatment of chronic depression. *New England Journal of Medicine, 342*(20), 1462–1470.

Kellner, C. H., Greenberg, R. M., Murrough, J. W., Bryson, E. O., Briggs, M. C., & Pasculli, R. M. (2012). ECT in treatment-resistant depression. *American Journal of Psychiatry, 169*(12), 1238–1244.

Kellner, D. (2008). Media spectacle and the "massacre at Virginia Tech." In B. Agger & T. W. Luke (Eds.), *There is a gunman on campus: Tragedy and terror at Virginia Tech* (pp. 29–54). Lanham, MD: Rowman & Littlefield.

Kelly, B. D., Casey, P., Dunn, G., Ayuso-Mateos, J. L., & Dowrick, C. (2007). The role of personality disorder in "difficult to reach" patients with depression: Findings from the ODIN study. *European Psychiatry, 22,* 153–159.

Kelly, J. F. (2013). Alcoholics Anonymous science update: Introduction to the special issue. *Substance Abuse, 34*(1), 1–3. doi: 10.1080/08897077.2012.691447

Kelly, J. F., Abry, A., Ferri, M., & Humphreys, K. (2020). Alcoholics anonymous and 12-step facilitation treatments for alcohol use disorder: A distillation of a 2020 Cochrane review for clinicians and policy makers. *Alcohol and Alcoholism, 55*(6), 641–651.

Kelly, J. F., Stout, R. L., Magill, M., Tonigan, J. S., & Pagano, M. E. (2010). Mechanisms of behavior change in alcoholics anonymous: Does Alcoholics Anonymous lead to better alcohol use outcomes by reducing depression symptoms? *Addiction, 105*(4), 626–636.

Kelly, M. P., Strassberg, D. S., & Kircher, J. R. (1990). Attitudinal and experiential correlates of anorgasmia. *Archives of Sexual Behavior, 19*(2), 165–177.

Kelly, M., McBride, A., & Hearn, J. (2019). Legal considerations in psychiatry. *Textbook of Psychiatry* (pp. 201–224). Washington, D.C.: American Psychiatric Association Publishing.

Kelly, P., & Frosch, E. (2012). Recognition of delirium on pediatric hospital services. *Psychosomatics, 53*(5), 446–451.

Kemeny, M. E. (2003). The psychobiology of stress. *Current Directions in Psychological Science, 12*(4), 124–129.

Kemp, S. (1990). *Medieval psychology.* New York, NY: Greenwood Press.

Kendall, P. C., & Peterman, J. S. (2015). CBT for adolescents with anxiety: Mature yet still developing. *American Journal of Psychiatry, 172,* 519–530.

Kendall, P. C., Hudson, J. L., Gosch, E., Flannery-Schroeder, E., & Suveg, C. (2008). Cognitive behavioral therapy for anxiety disordered youth: A randomized clinical trial evaluating child and family modalities. *Journal of Consulting and Clinical Psychology*, 76(2), 282–297. doi: 10.1037/0022-006X.76.2.282

Kendler, K. S. (2001). Twin studies of psychiatric illness. *Archives of General Psychiatry, 58,* 1005–1013.

Kendler, K. S. (2005). Psychiatric genetics: A methodological critique. In N. C. Andreasen (Ed.), *Research advances in genetics and genomics: Implications for psychiatry* (pp. 5–25). Washington, DC: American Psychiatric Publishing.

Kendler, K. S. (2006). Reflections on the relationship between psychiatric genetics and psychiatric nosology. *American Journal of Psychiatry, 163,* 1138–1146.

Kendler, K. S. (2011). A conceptual overview of gene-environment interaction and correlation in a developmental context. In K. S. Kendler, S. Jaffee, & D. Romer (Eds.), *The dynamic genome and mental health: The role of genes and environments in youth development* (pp. 5–28). New York, NY: Oxford University Press.

Kendler, K. S. (2013). What psychiatric genetics has taught us about the nature of psychiatric illness and what is left to learn. *Molecular Psychiatry, 18*(10), 1058–1066. doi: 10.1038 /mp.1013.50

Kendler, K. S. (2021). Kraepelin's final views on manic-depressive illness. *Journal of Affective Disorders, 282,* 979–990. doi: 10.1016/j.jad.2020.12.200

Kendler, K. S., & Gardner, C. O. (2010). Dependent stressful life events and prior depressive episodes in the prediction of major depression: the problem of causal inference in psychiatric epidemiology. *Archives of General Psychiatry, 67*(11), 1120–1127.

Kendler, K. S., & Gardner, C. O. (2014). Sex differences in the pathways to major depression: A study of opposite-sex twin Pairs. *American Journal of Psychiatry, 171,* 426–435.

Kendler, K. S., & Gardner, C. O. (2014). Sex differences in the pathways to major depression: A study of opposite-sex twin pairs. *American Journal of Psychiatry, 171*(4), 426–435. doi: 10.1176/appi.ajp.2013.13101375

Kendler, K. S., & Prescott, C. A. (2006). *Genes, environment, and psychopathology: Understanding the causes of psychiatric and substance use disorders.* New York, NY: Guilford.

Kendler, K. S., Aggen, S. H., & Neale, M. C. (2013). Evidence for multiple genetic factors underlying DSM-IV criteria for major depression. *JAMA Psychiatry, 70*(6), 599–607. doi: 10.1001/jamapsychiatry.2013.751

Kendler, K. S., Aggen, S. H., & Patrick, C. J. (2013). Familial influences on conduct disorder reflect 2 genetic factors and 1 shared environmental factor. *JAMA Psychiatry, 70*(1), 78–86.

Kendler, K. S., Aggen, S. H., Neale, M. C., Knudsen, G. P., Krueger, R. F., Tambs, K., . . . Reichborn-Kjennerud, T. (2015). A longitudinal twin study of cluster A personality disorders. *Psychological Medicine, 45*(07), 1531-1538.

Kendler, K. S., Chen, X., Dick, D., Maes, H., Gillespie, N., Neale, M. C., & Riley, B. (2012). Recent advances in the genetic epidemiology and molecular genetics of substance use disorders. *Nature Neuroscience, 15*(2), 181–189. doi: 10.1038/nn.3018.

Kendler, K. S., Czajkowski, N., Tambs, K., Torgersen, S., Aggen, S. H., Neale, M. C., & Reichborn-Kjennerud, T. (2006). Dimensional representations of DSM-IV cluster A personality disorders in a population-based sample of Norwegian twins: A multivariate study. *Psychological Medicine, 36,* 1583–1591.

Kendler, K. S., Gatz, M., Gardner, C. O., & Pedersen, N. L. (2007). Clinical indices of familial depression in the Swedish Twin Registry. *Acta Psychiatrica Scandinavica, 115*(3), 214–220.

Kendler, K. S., Hettema, J. M., Butera, F., Gardner, C. O., & Prescott, C. A. (2003). Life event dimensions of loss, humiliation, entrapment, and danger in the prediction of onsets of major depression and generalized anxiety. *Archives of General Psychiatry, 60,* 789–796.

Kendler, K. S., Jacobson, K. C., Prescott, C. A., & Neale, M. C. (2003). Specificity of genetic and environmental risk factors for use and abuse/dependence of cannabis, cocaine, hallucinogens, sedatives, stimulants, and opiates in male twins. *American Journal of Psychiatry, 160,* 687–695.

Kendler, K. S., Jaffee, S., & Romer, D. (2011). *The dynamic genome and mental health: The role of genes and environments in youth development.* New York, NY: Oxford University Press.

Kendler, K. S., Karkowski, L. M., & Prescott, C. A. (1999a). The assessment of dependence in the study of stressful life events: Validation using a twin design. *Psychological Medicine, 29*(6), 1455–1460.

Kendler, K. S., Karkowski, L. M., & Prescott, C. A. (1999b). Causal relationship between stressful life events and the onset of major depression. *American Journal of Psychiatry, 156*(6), 837–841.

Kendler, K. S., Kuhn, J., Vittum, J., Prescott, C. A., & Riley, B. (2005). The interaction of stressful life events and a serotonin transporter polymorphism in the prediction of episodes of major depression. *Archives of General Psychiatry, 62,* 529–535.

Kendler, K. S., Larsson Lönn, S., Morris, N. A., Sundquist, J., Långström, N., & Sundquist, K. (2014). A Swedish national adoption study of criminality. *Psychological Medicine, 44*(09), 1913–1925.

Kendler, K. S., MacLean, C., Neale, M., Kessler, R., Heath, A., & Eaves, L. (1991). The genetic epidemiology of bulimia nervosa. *American Journal of Psychiatry, 148*(12), 1627–1637.

Kendler, K. S., Myers, J., & Prescott, C. A. (2005). Sex differences in the relationship between social support and risk for major depression: A longitudinal study of opposite-sex twin pairs. *American Journal of Psychiatry, 162,* 250–256.

Kendler, K. S., Myers, J., & Zisook, S. (2008). Does bereavement-related major depression differ from major depression associated with other stressful life events? *American Journal of Psychiatry, 165*(11), 1449–1455.

Kendler, K. S., Neale, M. C., Kessler, R. C., Heath, A. C., & Eaves, L. J. (1992a). Generalized anxiety disorder in women: A population-based twin study. *Archives of General Psychiatry, 49,* 267–272.

Kendler, K. S., Neale, M. C., Kessler, R. C., Heath, A. C., & Eaves, L. J. (1993). A longitudinal twin study of 1-year prevalence of major depression in women. *Archives of General Psychiatry, 50,* 843–852.

Kendler, K. S., Neale, M. C., MacLean, C. J., Heath, A. C., Eaves, L. J., & Kessler, R. C. (1993). Smoking and major depression: A causal analysis. *Archives of General Psychiatry, 50,* 36–43.

Kendler, K., & Walsh, D. (2007). Schizophreniform disorder, delusional disorder and psychotic disorder not otherwise specified: Clinical features, outcome and familial psychopathology. *Acta Psychiatrica Scandinavica, 91*(6), 370–378.

Kendrick, D., Young, B., Mason-Jones, A. J., Ilyas, N., Achana, F. A., et al. (2012). Home safety education and provision of safety equipment for injury prevention. Cochrane Database Syst. Rev. 9:CD005014.

Kennard, B. D., Clarke, G. N., Weersing, V. R., Asarnow, J. R., Shamseddeen, W., Porta, G., & Brent, D. A. (2009). Effective components of TORDIA cognitive–behavioral therapy for adolescent depression: Preliminary findings. *Journal of Consulting and Clinical Psychology, 77*(6), 1033–1041.

Kennedy, J. L., Altar, C. A., Taylor, D. L., Degtiar, I., & Hornberger, J. C. (2014). The social and economic burden of treatment-resistant schizophrenia: A systematic literature review. *International Clinical Psychopharmacology, 29*(2), 63–76.

Kennedy, S. (2000). Psychological factors and immunity in HIV infection: Stress, coping, social support, and intervention outcomes. In D. I. Mostofsky & D. H. Barlow (Eds.), *The management of stress and anxiety in medical disorders* (pp. 194–205). Needham Heights, MA: Allyn & Bacon.

Kennedy, S. H., Giacobbe, P., Rizvi, S. J., Placenza, F. M., Nishikawa, Y., Mayberg, H. S., & Lozano, A. M. (2011). Deep brain stimulation for treatment-resistant depression: Follow-up after 3 to 6 years. *American Journal of Psychiatry, 168*(5), 502–510.

Kennedy, S. H., Konarski, J. Z., Segal, Z. V., Lau, M. A., Bieling, P. J., McIntyre, R. S., & Mayberg, H. S. (2007). Differences in brain glucose metabolism between responders to CBT and venlafaxine in a 16-week randomized controlled trial. *The American Journal of Psychiatry, 164*(5), 778–788.

Kennedy, W. K., Leloux, M., Kutscher, E. C., Price, P. L., Morstad, A. E., & Carnahan, R. M. (2010). Acamprosate. *Expert Opinion on Drug Metabolism & Toxicology, 6*(3), 363–380.

Kerns, R. D., Rosenberg, R., & Otis, J. D. (2002). Self-appraised problem solving and pain-relevant social support as predictors of the experience of chronic pain. *Annals of Behavioral Medicine, 24,* 100–105.

Kerns, R. D., Sellinger, J., & Goodin, B. R. (2011). Psychological treatment of chronic pain. *Annual Review of Clinical Psychology, 7,* 411–434.

Kerr, M., Stattin, H., & Burk, W. J. (2010). A reinterpretation of parental monitoring in longitudinal perspective. *Journal of Research on Adolescence, 20*(1), 39–64. doi: 10.1111/j.1532-7795.2009.00623.x

Kersting, A., Brahler, E., Glaesmer, H., & Wagner, B. (2011). Prevalence of complicated grief in a representative population-based sample. *Journal of Affective Disorders, 131*(1–3), 339–343.

Keshaviah, A., Edkins, K., Hastings, E. R., Krishna, M., Franko, D. L., Herzog, D. B., . . . Eddy, K. T. (2014). Re-examining premature mortality in anorexia nervosa: A meta-analysis redux. *Comprehensive Psychiatry, 55*(8), 1773–1784. doi: 10.1016/j.comppsych.2014.07.017

Keski-Rahkonen, A., Hoek, H. W., Susser, E. S., Linna, M. S., Sihvola, E., Raevuori, A., & Rissanen, A. (2007). Epidemiology and course of anorexia nervosa in the community. *American Journal of Psychiatry, 164*(8), 1259–1265.

Kessler, R. C. (2006). The epidemiology of depression among women. In C. Keyes &, S. Goodman (Eds.), *A handbook for the social, behavioral, and biomedical sciences: Women and depression* (pp. 22–37). New York, NY: Cambridge University Press.

Kessler, R. C., & Bromet, E. J. (2013). The epidemiology of depression across cultures. *Annual Review of Public Health, 34,* 119–138.

Kessler, R. C., & Wang, P. S. (2009). Epidemiology of depression. In I. H. Gotlib & C. L. Hammen (Eds.), *Handbook of depression* (2nd ed., pp. 5–22). New York, NY: Guilford.

Kessler, R. C., Avenevoli, S., & Ries Merikangas, K. (2001). Mood disorders in children and adolescents: An epidemiologic perspective. *Biological Psychiatry, 49*(12), 1002–1014.

Kessler, R. C., Avenevoli, S., Costello, E. J., Georgiades, K., Green, J. G., Gruber, M. J., … Merikangas, K. R. (2012). Prevalence, persistence, and sociodemographic correlates of *DSM-IV* disorders in the national comorbidity survey replication adolescent supplement. *Archives of General Psychiatry, 69*(4), 372–380. doi:10.1001/archgenpsychiatry.2011.160

Kessler, R. C., Berglund, P., Borges, G., Nock, M., & Wang, P. (2005). Trends in suicide ideation, plans, gestures, and attempts in the United States, 1990–1992 to 2001–2003. *JAMA: Journal of the American Medical Association, 293,* 2487–2495.

Kessler, R. C., Berglund, P., Demler, O., Jin, R., Koretz, D., Merikangas, K. R., & National Comorbidity Survey Replication. (2003). The epidemiology of major depressive disorder: Results from the National Comorbidity Survey Replication (NCS-R). *JAMA: Journal of the American Medical Association, 289,* 3095–3105.

Kessler, R. C., Berglund, P., Demler, O., Jin, R., Merikangas, K. R., & Walters, E. E. (2005). Lifetime prevalence and age-of-onset distributions of DSM-IV disorders in the National Comorbidity Survey Replication. *Archives of General Psychiatry, 62,* 593–602.

Kessler, R. C., Chiu, W. T., Demler, O., & Walters, E. E. (2005). Prevalence, severity, and comorbidity of 12-month DSM-IV disorders in the National Comorbidity Survey replication. *Archives of General Psychiatry, 62,* 617–627.

Kessler, R. C., Chiu, W. T., Jin, R., Ruscio, A. M., Shear, K., & Walters, E. E. (2006). The epidemiology of panic attacks, panic disorder, and agoraphobia in the National Comorbidity Survey Replication. *Archives of General Psychiatry, 63*(4), 415–424. doi: 10.1001/archpsyc.63.4.415

Kessler, R. C., Coccaro, E. F., Fava, M., Jaeger, S., Jin, R., & Walters, E. (2006). The prevalence and correlates of DSM-IV intermittent explosive disorder in the National Comorbidity Survey Replication. *Archives of General Psychiatry, 63*(6), 669–679.

Kessler, R. C., Galea, S., Jones, R. T., & Parker, H. A. (2006). *Mental illness and suicidality after Hurricane Katrina.* Bulletin of the World Health Organization (WHO Publication No. 06-033019).

Kessler, R. C., McGonagle, K. A., Zhao, S., Nelson, C. B., Hughes, M., Eshleman, S., & Kendler, K. S. (1994). Lifetime and 12-month prevalence of DSM-III-R psychiatric disorders among persons aged 15–54 in the United States: Results from the National Comorbidity Survey. *Archives of General Psychiatry, 5*, 8–19.

Kessler, R. C., Petukhova, M., Sampson, N. A., Zaslavsky, A. M., & Wittchen, H. U. (2012). Twelve-month and lifetime prevalence and lifetime morbid risk of anxiety and mood disorders in the United States. *International Journal of Methods in Psychiatric Research, 21*, 169.

Keuroghlian, A. S., Gunderson, J. G., Pagano, M. E., Markowitz, J. C., Ansell, E. B., Shea, M. T., . . . Stout, R. L. (2015). Interactions of Borderline Personality Disorder and Anxiety Disorders Over 10 Years. *The Journal of Clinical Psychiatry, 76*(11), 1–478.

Keys, A., Brozek, J., Henschel, A., Michelson, O., & Taylor, H. L. (1950). *The biology of human starvation* (Vol. 1). Minneapolis: University of Minnesota Press.

Khachaturian, Z. S. (2007). Alzheimer's 101. *Alzheimer's and Dementia, 3*, 1–2.

Khan, S., King, A. P., Abelson, J. L, & Liberzon, I. (2009). Neuroendocrinology of anxiety disorders. In M. M. Antony & M. B. Stein (Eds.), *Oxford handbook of anxiety and related disorders*. Oxford, UK: Oxford University Press.

Khokhar, J., Ferguson, C., Zhu, A., & Tyndale, R. (2010). Pharmacogenetics of drug dependence: Role of gene variations in susceptibility and treatment. *Annual Review of Pharmacology and Toxicology, 50*(1), 39–61.

Khosravani, V., Berk, M., Sharifi Bastan, F., Samimi Ardestani, S. M., & Wrobel, A. (in press). The effects of childhood emotional maltreatment and alexithymia on depressive and manic symptoms and suicidal ideation in females with bipolar disorder: Emotion dysregulation as a mediator. *International Journal of Psychiatry in Clinical Practice*, 1–13.

Khosravi, M. (2020). Eating disorders among patients with borderline personality disorder: Understanding the prevalence and psychopathology. *Journal of Eating Disorders, 8*(1), 1–9.

Khoury, B., Lecomte, T., Fortin, G., Masse, M., Therien, P., Bouchard, V., Chapleau, M.-A., Paquin, K., & Hofmann, S. G. (2013). Mindfulness-based therapy: A comprehensive meta-analysis. *Clinical Psychology Review, 33*, 763–771.

Kiecolt-Glaser, J. K., & Newton, T. L. (2001). Marriage and health: His and hers. *Psychological Bulletin, 127*, 475–503.

Kiecolt-Glaser, J. K., Loving, T., Stowell, J., Malarkey, W., Lemeshow, S., & Dickinson, S., & Glaser, R. (2005). Hostile marital interactions, proinflammatory cytokine production, and wound healing. *Archives of General Psychiatry, 62*, 1377–1384.

Kiesler, C. A., & Sibulkin, A. E. (1987). *Mental hospitalization: Myths and facts about a national crisis*. Beverly Hills, CA: Sage.

Kiesler, D. J. (1966). Some myths of psychotherapy research and the search for a paradigm. *Psychological Bulletin, 65*, 110–136.

Kihlstrom, J. F. (1992). Dissociation and dissociations: A commentary on consciousness and cognition. *Consciousness & Cognition, 1*, 47–53.

Kihlstrom, J. F. (1997). Memory, abuse, and science. *American Psychologist, 52*, 994–995.

Kihlstrom, J. F. (2005a). Dissociative disorders. In S. Nolen-Hoeksema, T. D. Cannon, & T. Widiger (Eds.), *Annual review of clinical psychology* (Vol. 1). Palo Alto, CA: Annual Reviews.

Kihlstrom, J. F. (2005b). Dissociative disorders. *Annual Review of Clinical Psychology, 1*, 227–253.

Kihlstrom, J. F., Glisky, M. L., & Anguilo, M. J. (1994). Dissociative tendencies and dissociative disorders. *Journal of Abnormal Psychology, 103*, 117–124.

Killerman, S. (2015). Retrieved from: http://itspronounced-metrosexual.com/2013/01/a-comprehensive-list-of-lgbtq-term-definitions/

Killgore, W. D. S., Cotting, D. I., Thomas, J. L., Cox, A. L., McGurk, D., Vo, A. H., & Hoge, C. W. (2008). Post-combat invincibility: Violent combat experiences are associated with increased risk-taking propensity following deployment. *Journal of Psychiatric Research, 42*(13), 1112–1121. doi: 10.1016/j.jpsychires.2008.01.001

Kilpatrick, D. G., Koenen, K. C., Ruggiero, K. J., Acierno, R., Galea, S., Resnick, H. S., & Gelernter, J. (2007). The serotonin transporter genotype and social support and moderation of posttraumatic stress disorder and depression in hurricane-exposed adults. *The American Journal of Psychiatry, 164*(11), 1693–1699.

Kilpatrick, D. G., Resnick, H. S., & Friedman, M. J. (2010). National Stressful Events Survey PTSD Short Scale (NSESSS-PTSD).

Kilzieh, N., & Akiskal, H. S. (1999). Rapid-cycling bipolar disorder: An overview of research and clinical experience. *Psychiatric Clinics of North America, 22*(3), 585–607.

Kim, E. D., & Lipshultz, L. I. (1997, April 15). Advances in the treatment of organic erectile dysfunction. *Hospital Practice*, 101–120.

Kim, H. F., Schulz, P. E., Wilde, E. A., & Yudofsky, S. C. (2008). Laboratory testing and imaging studies in psychiatry. In R. E. Hales, S. C. Yudofsky, & G. O. Gabbard (Eds.), *The American Psychiatric Publishing textbook of psychiatry* (5th ed., pp. 19–72). Arlington, VA: American Psychiatric Publishing.

Kim, J. M., & López, S. R. (2014). The expression of depression in Asian Americans and European Americans. *Journal of Abnormal Psychology, 123*, 745–763.

Kimchi, E. Z., & Lyketos, C. G. (2015). Dementia and milder cognitive symptoms. In D. C. Steffens, D. G. Blazer, & M. E. Thakur (Eds.), *The American Psychiatric Publishing textbook of geriatric psychiatry* (5th ed., pp.177–242). Washington, D.C.: American Psychiatric Publishing.

King, D. E., Mainous III, A. G., & Geesey, M. E. (2007). Turning back the clock: Adopting a healthy lifestyle in middle age. *The American Journal of Medicine, 120*(7), 598–603.

King, D. W., King, L. A., Foy, D. W., & Gudanowski, D. M. (1996). Prewar factors in combat related posttraumatic stress disorder: Structural equation modeling with a national sample of female and male Vietnam veterans. *Journal of Consulting and Clinical Psychology, 64*, 520–531.

King, L. A., Pless, A. P., Schuster, J. L., Potter, C. M., Park, C. L., Spiro, A., & King, D. W. (2012). Risk and protective factors for traumatic stress disorder. In J. G. Beck & D. M. Sloan (Eds.), *The Oxford handbook of traumatic stress disorders* (pp. 333–346). New York, NY: Oxford University Press.

King, M., & Wexler, D. (2010). Therapeutic jurisprudence. In J. M. Brown & E. A. Campbell (Eds.), *The Cambridge handbook of forensic psychology* (pp. 126–132). Cambridge, UK: Cambridge University Press.

Kinzie, J. D., Leung, P. K., Boehnlein, J., & Matsunaga, D. (1992). Psychiatric epidemiology of an Indian village: A 19-year replication study. *Journal of Nervous and Mental Disease, 180*(1), 33–39.

Kirmayer, L. J., & Sartorius, N. (2007). Cultural models and somatic syndromes. *Psychosomatic Medicine, 69*(9), 832–840.

Kirmayer, L. J., & Weiss, M. (1993). *On cultural considerations for somatoform disorders in the DSM-IV.* In cultural proposals and supporting papers for DSM-IV. Submitted to the DSM-IV Task Force by the Steering Committee, NIMH-Sponsored Group on Culture and Diagnosis.

Kirmayer, L. J., Looper, K. J., & Taillefer, S. (2003). Somatoform disorders. In M. Hersen & S. M. Turner (Eds.), *Adult psychopathology and diagnosis* (4th ed., pp. 420–475). New York, NY: Wiley.

Kirov, G., & Owen, M. J. (2009). Genetics of schizophrenia. In B. J. Sadock, V. A. Sadock, & P. Ruiz (Eds.), *Kaplan & Sadock's comprehensive textbook of psychiatry* (9th ed., Vol. I, pp. 1462–1475). Philadelphia, PA: Lippincott Williams & Wilkins.

Kishimoto, T., Agarwal, V., Kishi, T., Leucht, S., Kane, J. M., & Correll, C. U. (2013). Relapse prevention in schizophrenia: a systematic review and meta-analysis of second-generation antipsychotics versus first-generation antipsychotics. *Molecular Psychiatry, 18*(1), 53–66.

Kishimoto, T., Robenzadeh, A., Leucht, C., Leucht, S., Watanabe, K., Mimura, M., . . . Correll, C. U. (2012). Long-acting injectable vs oral antipsychotics for relapse prevention in schizophrenia: A meta-analysis of randomized trials. *Schizophrenia Bulletin,* sbs150.

Kistner, J. A. (2009). Sex differences in child and adolescent psychopathology: An introduction to the special section. *Journal of Clinical Child and Adolescent Psychology, 38*(4), 453–459.

Kivimaki, M., Nyberg, S. T., Batty, G. D., Fransson, E. I., Heikkila, K., Alfredsson, L., & Consortium, I. P.-W. (2012). Job strain as a risk factor for coronary heart disease: a collaborative meta-analysis of individual participant data. *Lancet, 380*(9852), 1491–1497.

Kjernisted, K. D., Enns, M. W., & Lander, M. (2002). An open-label clinical trial of nefazodone in hypochondriasis. *Psychosomatics, 43,* 290–294.

Klaus, K., Rief, W., Brähler, E., Martin, A., Glaesmer, H., & Mewes, R. (2015). Validating psychological classification criteria in the context of somatoform disorders: A one-and four-year follow-up. *Journal of Abnormal Psychology, 124*(4):1092–1101.

Klein, D. F. (1989). The pharmacological validation of psychiatric diagnosis. In L. Robins & J. Barrett (Eds.), *Validity of psychiatric diagnosis.* New York, NY: Raven Press.

Klein, D. N. (2008). Classification of depressive disorders in the DSM-V: Proposal for a two-dimension system. *Journal of Abnormal Psychology, 117*(3), 552–560.

Klein, D. N. (2010). Chronic depression: Diagnosis and classification. *Current Directions in Psychological Science, 19*(2), 96–100.

Klein, D. N., Glenn, C. R., Kosty, D. B., Seeley, J. R., Rohde, P., & Lewinsohn, P. M. (2013). Predictors of first lifetime onset of major depressive disorder in young adulthood. *Journal of Abnormal Psychology, 122,* 1–6.

Klein, D. N., Lewinsohn, P. M., Rohde, P., Seeley, J. R., & Durbin, C. E. (2002). Clinical features of major depressive disorder in adolescents and their relatives: Impact on familial aggregation, implications for phenotype definition, and specificity of transmission. *Journal of Abnormal Psychology, 111,* 98–106.

Klein, D. N., Schwartz, J. E., Rose, S., & Leader, J. B. (2000). Five-year course and outcome of dysthymic disorder: A prospective, naturalistic follow-up study. *American Journal of Psychiatry, 157*(6), 931–939.

Klein, D. N., Shankman, S., & Rose, S. (2006). Ten-year prospective follow-up study of the naturalistic course of dysthymic disorder and double depression. *American Journal of Psychiatry, 163,* 872–880.

Klein, D. N., Taylor, E. B., Dickstein, S., & Harding, K. (1988). The early–late onset distinction in DSM-III-R dysthymia. *Journal of Affective Disorders, 14*(1), 25–33.

Klein, R. G., Mannuzza, S., Ramos Olazagasti, M. A., Roizen, E., Jesse A. Hutchison, J. A., Lashua, E. C., & Castellanos, F. X. (2012). Clinical and functional outcome of childhood attention-deficit/hyperactivity disorder 33 years later. *Archives of General Psychiatry, 69*(12), 1295–1303. doi: 10.1001/archgenpsychiatry.2012.271

Kleindienst, N., Löffler, A., Herzig, M., Bertsch, K., & Bekrater-Bodmann, R. (2020). Evaluation of the own body in women with current and remitted borderline personality disorder: Evidence for long-lasting effects of childhood sexual abuse. *European Journal of Psychotraumatology, 11*(1), 1764707.

Kleinknecht, R. A., Dinnel, D. L., Kleinknecht, E. E., Hiruma, N., & Harada, N. (1997). Cultural factors in social anxiety: A comparison of social phobia symptoms and *taijin kyofusho. Journal of Anxiety Disorders, 11,* 157–177.

Kleinman, A. (1986). *Social origins of distress and disease: Depression, neurasthenia, and pain in modern China.* New Haven, CT: Yale University Press.

Kleinman, A. (2004). Culture and depression. *New England Journal of Medicine, 351,* 951–953.

Kleinplatz, F. J., Moser, C., & Lev, A. I. (2012). Sex and gender identity disorders. In I. B. Weiner, G. Stricker, & T. A. Widiger (Eds.), *Handbook of psychology, Clinical psychology* (2nd ed., Vol. 8, pp. 171–192). Hoboken, NJ: Wiley.

Kleinplatz, P. J. (2018). *History of the treatment of female sexual dysfunction(s).* doi: 10.1146/annurev-clinpsy-050817-084802

Kleinstäuber, M., Allwang C, Bailer, J., Berking, M., Brünahl, C., Erkic, M., Gitzen, H., Gollwitzer, M., Gottschalk, J. M., Heider, J., Hermann, A., Lahmann, C., Löwe, B., Martin, A., Rau, J., Schröder, A., Schwabe, J., Schwarz, J., Stark, R., Weiss, F. D., & Rief, W. (2019). Cognitive behaviour therapy complemented with emotion regulation training for patients with persistent physical symptoms: A randomised clinical trial. *Psychotherapy and Psychosomatic,s 88*(5), 287–299. doi: 10.1159/000501621.

Kleinstäuber, M., Witthöft, M., & Hiller, W. (2011). Efficacy of short-term psychotherapy for multiple medically unexplained physical symptoms: A meta-analysis. *Clinical Psychology Review, 31,* 146–160.

Klerman, G. L., & Weissman, M. M. (1989). Increasing rates of depression. *JAMA: Journal of the American Medical Association, 261,* 2229–2235.

Klerman, G. L., Weissman, M. M., Rounsaville, B. J., & Chevron, E. S. (1984). *Interpersonal psychotherapy of depression.* New York, NY: Basic Books.

Klimas, N., Koneru, A. O., & Fletcher, M. A. (2008). Overview of HIV. *Psychosomatic Medicine, 70,* 523–530.

Klin, A., Jones, W., Schultz, R., Volkmar, F., & Cohen, D. (2002). Defining and quantifying the social phenotype in autism. *American Journal of Psychiatry, 159,* 895–908.

Kluft, R. P. (1984). Treatment of multiple personality disorder. *Psychiatric Clinics of North America, 7,* 9–29.

Kluft, R. P. (1991). Multiple personality disorder. In A. Tasman & S. W. Goldinger (Eds.), *Review of psychiatry* (Vol. 10). Washington, DC: American Psychiatric Press.

Kluft, R. P. (1996). Treating the traumatic memories of patients with dissociative identity disorder. *American Journal of Psychiatry, 153,* 103–110.

Kluft, R. P. (1999). Current issues in dissociative identity disorder. *Journal of Practical Psychology and Behavioral Health, 5,* 3–19.

Kluft, R. P. (2009). A clinician's understanding of dissociation: Fragments of an acquaintance.

In P. F. Dell & J. A. O'Neil (Eds.), *Dissociation and the dissociative disorders.* New York, NY: Routledge.

Klump, K. L., Kaye, W. H., & Strober, M. (2001). The evolving genetic foundations of eating disorders. *The Psychiatric Clinics of North America, 24,* 215–225.

Klump, K. L., Racine, S. E., Hildebrandt, B., Burt, S. A., Neale, M., Sisk, C. L., . . . Keel, P. K. (2014). Influences of Ovarian Hormones on Dysregulated Eating A Comparison of Associations in Women With Versus Women Without Binge Episodes. *Clinical Psychological Science, 2*(5), 545–559.

Klumpp, H., Fitzgerald, D. A., & Phan, K. L. (2013). Neural predictors and mechanisms of cognitive behavioral therapy on threat processing in social anxiety disorder. *Progress in Neuro-Psychopharmacology & Biological Psychiatry, 45,* 83–91.

Knapp, S. J., Gottlieb, M. C., Handelsman, M. M., & VandeCreek, L. D. (2012a). *APA handbook of ethics in psychology, Vol 1: Moral foundations and common themes.* Washington, DC: American Psychological Association.

Knapp, S. J., Gottlieb, M. C., Handelsman, M. M., & VandeCreek, L. D. (2012b). *APA handbook of ethics in psychology, Vol 2: Practice, teaching, and research.* Washington, DC: American Psychological Association.

Knappe, S., Beesdo-Baum, K., Nocon, A., & Wittchen, H.-U. (2012). Re-examining the differential familial liability of agoraphobia and panic disorder. *Depression and Anxiety, 29*(11), 931–938.

Knoop, H., Prins, J. B., Moss-Morris, R., & Bleijenberg, G. (2010). The central role of cognitive processes in the perpetuation of chronic fatigue syndrome. *Journal of Psychosomatic Research, 68,* 489–494.

Knopf, A. (2020). Genomics and addiction treatment: The wave of the future. *Alcoholism & Drug Abuse Weekly, 32*(42), 1–5.

Knopik, V. S., Bidwell, L. C., Flessner, C., Nugent, N., Swenson, L., Bucholz, K. K., . . . Heath, A. C. (2014). DSM-IV defined conduct disorder and oppositional defiant disorder: an investigation of shared liability in female twins. *Psychological Medicine, 44*(05), 1053-1064.

Knowles, R., McCarthy-Jones, S., & Rowse, G. (2011). Grandiose delusions: A review and theoretical integration of cognitive and affective perspectives. *Clinical Psychology Review, 31*(4), 684–696. doi: 10.1016/j.cpr.2011.02.009

Ko, H-C., Lee, L-R., Chang, R-B., & Huang, K-E. (1996). Comorbidity of premenstrual depression and postpartum blues among Chinese women. *Biological Psychiatry, 39,* 648.

Kobau, R., DiIorio, C., Chapman, D., & Delvecchio, P. (2010). Attitudes about mental illness and its treatment: Validation of a generic scale for public health surveillance of mental illness associated stigma. *Community Mental Health Journal, 46*(2), 164–176.

Koch, P., Mansfield, P., Thurau, D., & Carey, M. (2005). "Feeling frumpy": The relationship between body image and sexual response changes in midlife women. *Journal of Sex Research, 42,* 215–223.

Kochanek, K. D., Xu, J. Q., & Arias, E. (2020). Mortality in the United States, 2019. NCHS Data Brief, no 395. Hyattsville, MD: National Center for Health Statistics

Kochanska, G., Aksan, N., & Joy, M. E. (2007). Children's fearfulness as a moderator of parenting in early socialization: Two longitudinal studies. *Developmental Psychology, 43,* 222–237.

Kochman, F. J., Hantouche, E. G., Ferrari, P., Lancrenon, S., Bayart, D., & Akiskal, H. S. (2005). Cyclothymic temperament as a prospective predictor of bipolarity and suicidality in children and adolescents with major depressive disorder. *Journal of Affective Disorders, 85,* 181–189.

Koegel, R. L., & Koegel, L. K. (2012). *The PRT pocket guide: Pivotal response treatment for autism spectrum disorders.* Baltimore, MD: Paul H. Brookes.

Koen, L., Niehaus, D., Muller, J., & Laurent, C. (2008). Use of traditional treatment methods in a Xhosa schizophrenia population. *South African Medical Journal, 93*(6), 443.

Kogon, M. M., Biswas, A., Pearl, D., Carlson, R. W. L., & Spiegel, D. (1997). Effects of medical and psychotherapeutic treatment on the survival of women with metastatic breast carcinoma. *Cancer, 80,* 225–230.

Kohn, R., Wintrob, R. M., & Alarcón, R. D. (2009). Transcultural psychiatry. In B. J. Sadock, V. A. Sadock, & P. Ruiz (Eds.), *Kaplan & Sadock's comprehensive textbook of psychiatry* (9th ed., Vol. I, pp. 734–753). Philadelphia, PA: Lippincott Williams & Wilkins.

Kohut, H. (1971). *The analysis of self.* New York, NY: International Universities Press.

Kohut, H. (1977). *The restoration of the self.* Chicago, IL: University of Chicago Press.

Kolb, B., & Whishaw, I. Q. (1998). Possible regeneration of rat medial front cortex following neonatal frontal lesions. *Behavioral Brain Research, 91,* 127–141.

Kolb, B., Gibb, R., & Gorny, G. (2003). Experience-dependent changes in dendritic arbor and spine density in neocortex vary qualitatively with age and sex. *Neurobiology of Learning & Memory, 79,* 1–10.

Kolb, B., Gibb, R., & Robinson, T. E. (2003). Brain plasticity and behavior. *Current Directions in Psychological Science, 12*(1), 1–5.

Kolla, B. P., Auger, R., & Morgenthaler, T. (2012). Circadian rhythm sleep disorders. *ChronoPhysiology and Therapy, 2,* 19–34.

Kollei, I., Schieber, K., de Zwaan, M., Svitak, M., & Martin, A. (2013). Body dysmorphic disorder and nonweight-related body image concerns in individuals with eating disorders. *International Journal of Eating Disorders, 46*(1), 52–59. doi: 10.1002/eat.22067

Kollins, S. (2008). ADHD, substance use disorders, and psychostimulant treatment: Current literature and treatment guidelines. *Journal of Attention Disorders, 12*(2), 115.

Kong, G., & Krishnan-Sarin, S. (2020). Youth tobacco use. In Y. Kaminer & K. C. Winters (Eds.), *Clinical manual of youth addictive disorders* (pp. 157–173). Washington, D.C.: American Psychiatric Association Publishing.

Kong, L. L., Allen, J. J., & Glisky, E. L. (2008). Interidentity memory transfer in dissociative identity disorder. *Journal of Abnormal Psychology, 117*(3), 686–692.

Koning, C., Magill-Evans, J., Volden, J., & Dick, B. (2011, September 15). Efficacy of cognitive behavior therapy-based social skills intervention for school-aged boys with autism spectrum disorders. *Research in Autism Spectrum Disorders.* doi: 10.1016/j.rasd.2011.07.011

Koob, A. (2009). *The root of thought.* Upper Saddle River, NJ: FT Press.

Kopelowicz, A., Zarate, R., Wallace, C. J., Liberman, R. P., Lopez, S. R., & Mintz, J. (2012). The ability of multifamily groups to improve treatment adherence in Mexican Americans with schizophrenia. *Archives of General Psychiatry, 69*(3), 265.

Koran, L. M., Abujaoude, E., Large, M. D., & Serpe, R. T. (2008). The prevalence of body dysmorphic disorder in the United States adult population. *CNS Spectrums, 13*(4), 316–322.

Korfine, L., & Hooley, J. M. (2000). Directed forgetting of emotional stimuli in borderline personality disorder. *Journal of Abnormal Psychology, 109,* 214–221.

Kosberg, J. I., Kaufman, A. V., Burgio, L. D., Leeper, J. D., & Sun, F. (2007). Family caregiving to those with dementia in rural Alabama: Racial similarities and differences. *Journal of Aging and Health, 19,* 3–21.

Kotlicka-Antczak, M., Pawełczyk, A., Rabe-Jabłońska, J., Śmigielski, J., & Pawełczyk, T. (2014). Obstetrical complications and Apgar score in subjects at risk of psychosis. *Journal of Psychiatric Research, 48*(1), 79–85.

Koutsogiorgi, C. C., Lordos, A., Fanti, K. A., & Michaelides, M. P. (2020). Factorial structure and nomological network of the inventory of callous-unemotional traits accounting for item keying variance. *Journal of Personality Assessment*, 1–12.

Kovacs, M., Akiskal, H. S., Gatsonis, C., & Parrone, P. L. (1994). Childhood-onset dysthymic disorder. *Archives of General Psychiatry, 51,* 365–374.

Kovacs, M., Goldston, D., & Gatsonis, C. (1993). Suicidal behaviors and childhood-onset depressive disorders: A longitudinal investigation. *Journal of the American Academy of Child and Adolescent Psychiatry, 32,* 8–20.

Kraemer, H. C. (2014). The reliability of clinical diagnoses: State of the art. *Annual Review of Clinical Psychology, 10,* 111–130. doi: 10.1146/annurev-clinpsy-032813-153739

Kraepelin, E. (1898). *The diagnosis and prognosis of dementia praecox.* Paper presented at the 29th Congress of Southwestern German Psychiatry, Heidelberg.

Kraepelin, E. (1899). *Kompendium der psychiatrie* (6th ed.). Leipzig, Germany: Abel.

Kraepelin, E. (1913). *Psychiatry: A textbook for students and physicians.* Leipzig, Germany: Barth.

Kraepelin, E. (1919). *Dementia praecox and paraphrenia* (R. M. Barclay & G. M. Robertson, Trans.). New York, NY: R. E. Krieger.

Kral, J. G. (2002). Surgical interventions for obesity. In K. D. Brownell & C. G. Fairburn (Eds.), *Eating disorders and obesity: A comprehensive handbook* (2nd ed., pp. 510–515). New York, NY: Guilford.

Krenek, M., & Maisto, S. A. (2013). Life events and treatment outcomes among individuals with substance use disorders: A narrative review. *Clinical Psychology Review, 33*(3), 470–483. doi: http://dx.doi.org/10.1016/j.cpr.2013.01.012

Kreutzmann, J., Havekes, R., Abel, T., & Meerlo, P. (2015). Sleep deprivation and hippocampal vulnerability: changes in neuronal plasticity, neurogenesis and cognitive function. *Neuroscience, 309,* 173–190. Kring, A. M. (2012). Emotion deficits in people with schizophrenia. *Annual Review of Clinical Psychology, 9,* 409–433.

Kring, A. M., & Elis, O. (2013). Emotion deficits in people with schizophrenia. Annual review of clinical psychology, 9, 409–433.

Kring, A. M., & Sloan, D. M. (2010). *Emotion regulation and psychopathology: A transdiagnostic approach to etiology and treatment.* New York, NY: Guilford.

Kroenke, K. (2007). Efficacy of treatment for somatoform disorders: A review of randomized controlled trials. *Psychosomatic Medicine, 69*(9), 881–888.

Kroll, R., & Beitchman, J. H. (2009). Stuttering. In B. J. Sadock, V. A. Sadock, & P. Ruiz (Eds.), *Kaplan & Sadock's comprehensive textbook of psychiatry* (9th ed., Vol. II, pp. 3528–3533). Philadelphia, PA: Lippincott Williams & Wilkins.

Krueger, D. D., & Bear, M. F. (2011). Toward fulfilling the promise of molecular medicine in fragile X syndrome. *Annual Review of Medicine, 62,* 411.

Krueger, R. B. (2010a). The DSM diagnostic criteria for sexual sadism. *Archives of Sexual Behavior, 39*(2), 325–345.

Krueger, R. B. (2010b). The DSM diagnostic criteria for sexual masochism. *Archives of sexual behavior, 39*(2), 346–356.

Krueger, R. B., & Kaplan, M. S. (2015). Paraphilic Disorders. In A. Tasman, J. Kay, J. A. Lieberman, M. B. First, & M. B. Riba (Eds.). *Psychiatry, Fourth Edition* (pp.1749–1758). John Wiley & Sons, Ltd: Chichester, UK.

Krueger, R. F., & Markon, K. E. (2014). The role of the *DSM-5* personality trait model in moving toward a quantitative and empirically based approach to classifying personality and psychopathology. *Annual Review of Clinical Psychology, 10,* 477–501. doi: 10.1146/annurev-clinpsy-032813-153732

Krueger, R. F., Hopwood, C. J., Wright, A. G., & Markon, K. E. (2014). *DSM-5* and the path toward empirically based and clinically useful conceptualization of personality and psychopathology. *Clinical Psychology: Science and Practice, 21*(3), 245–261. doi: 10.1111/cpsp.12073

Krueger, R. F., Markon, K. E., Patrick, C. J., & Iacono, W. G. (2005). Externalizing psychopathology in adulthood: A dimensional-spectrum conceptualization and its implications for DSM-V. *Journal of Abnormal Psychology, 114*(4), 537–550. doi:10.1037/0021-843x.114.4.537

Krueger, R. F., Watson, D., & Barlow, D. H. (2005). Introduction to the special section: Toward a dimensionally based taxonomy of psychopathology [Special issue]. *Journal of Abnormal Psychology, 114,* 491–493.

Krug, E. G., Kresnow, M.-J., Peddicord, J. P., Dahlberg, L. L., Powell, K. E., Crosby, A. E., & Annest, J. L. (1998). Suicide after natural disasters. *New England Journal of Medicine, 338*(6), 373–378.

Krupitsky, E., & Blokhina, E. (2010). Long-acting depot formulations of naltrexone for heroin dependence: A review. *Current Opinion in Psychiatry, 23*(3), 210.

Kube, T., Rozenkrantz, L., Rief, W., & Barsky, A. (2020). Understanding persistent physical symptoms: Conceptual integration of psychological expectation models and predictive processing accounts. *Clinical Psychology Review, 76,* 101829. doi: 10.1016/j.cpr.2020.101829

Kucharska-Newton, A. M., Williams, J. E., Chang, P. P., Stearns, S. C., Sueta, C. A., Blecker, S. B., & Mosley, T. H. (2014, December). Anger proneness, gender, and the risk of heart failure. J Card Fail. 20(12):1020-6. doi: 10.1016/j.cardfail.2014.09.010.

Kuehn, B. M. (2010). Sibutramine warning. *JAMA: Journal of the American Medical Association, 303,* 322.

Kumar, A., Sharma, A., Bansal, P., Bahetra, M., Gill, H. K., & Kumar, R. (2020). A comparative study on the safety and efficacy of naltrexone versus baclofen versus acamprosate in the management of alcohol dependence. *Indian Journal of Psychiatry, 62*(6), 650.

Kumpulainen, K. (2002). Phenomenology and treatment of selective mutism. *CNS Drugs, 16*(3), 175–180.

Kuo, J. R., Khoury, J. E., Metcalfe, R., Fitzpatrick, S., & Goodwill, A. (2015). An examination of the relationship between childhood emotional abuse and borderline personality disorder features: The role of difficulties with emotion regulation. *Child Abuse and Neglect, 39,* 147–155.

Kuo, W. H., Gallo, J. J., & Tien, A. Y. (2001). Incidence of suicide ideation and attempts in adults: The 13-year follow-up of a community sample in Baltimore, Maryland. *Psychological Medicine, 31,* 1181–91.

Kuperman, S., Chan, G., Kramer, J. R., Wetherill, L., Bucholz, K. K., Dick, D., & Schuckit, M. A. (2013). A model to determine the likely age of an adolescent's first drink of alcohol. *Pediatrics, 131*(2), 242–248. doi: 10.1542/peds.2012-0880

Kupfer, D. J. (1995). Sleep research in depressive illness: Clinical implications—A tasting menu. *Biological Psychiatry, 38,* 391–403.

Kupfer, D. J., First, M. B., & Regier, D. A. (2002). *A research agenda for DSM-V.* Washington, DC: American Psychiatric Association.

Kupfer, D. J., Frank, E., & Ritchey, F. C. (2015). Staging bipolar disorder: What data and what models are needed? *Lancet Psychiatry, 6,* 564–570.

Kupka, R., Luckenbaugh, D., Post, R., Suppes, T., Altshuler, L., Keck, P., & Nolen, W. A. (2005). Comparison of rapid-cycling and non-rapid-cycling bipolar disorder based on prospective mood ratings in 539 outpatients. *American Journal of Psychiatry, 162,* 1273–1280.

Kurihara, T., Kato, M., Reverger, R., & Gusti Rai Tirta, I. (2006). Beliefs about causes of schizophrenia among family members: A community-based survey in Bali. *Psychiatric Services, 57,* 1795–1799.

Kurtz, M. M., & Richardson, C. L. (2012). Social cognitive training for schizophrenia: A meta-analytic investigation of controlled research. *Schizophrenia Bulletin, 38*(5), 1092–1104.

Kurtz, T. W. (2010). Genome-wide association studies will unlock the genetic basis of hypertension: Con side of the argument. *Hypertension, 56*(6), 1021–1025.

Kuyken, W., Hayes, R., Barrett, B., Byng, R., Dalgleish, T., Kessler, D., Lewis, G., Watkins, E., Brejcha, C., Cardy, J., Causley, A., Cowderoy, S., Evans, A., Gradinger, F., Kaur, S., Lanham, P., Morant, N., Richards, J., Shah, P., Sutton H., Vicary, R., Weaver, A., Wilks, J., Williams, M., Taylor, R. S., & Byford, S. (2015). Effectiveness and cost-effectiveness of mindfulness-based cognitive therapy compared with maintenance antidepressant treatment in the prevention of depressive relapse or recurrence (PREVENT): a randomised controlled trial. *Lancet, 386*, 63–73.

Kuypers, K., Verkes, R., Van den Brink, W., Van Amsterdam, J., & Ramaekers, J. (2020). Intoxicated aggression: Do alcohol and stimulants cause dose-related aggression? A review. *European Neuropsychopharmacology, 30*, 114–147.

Kwapil, T. R., & Barrantes-Vidal, N. (2012). Schizotypal personality disorder: An integrative review. In T. A. Widiger (Ed.), *The Oxford handbook of personality disorders* (pp. 437–477). New York, NY: Oxford University Press.

Kwok, T., Lee, J., Lam, L., & Woo, J. (2008). Vitamin B12 supplementation did not improve cognition but reduced delirium in demented patients with vitamin B12 deficiency. *Archives of Gerontology and Geriatrics, 46*(3), 273–282.

Kymalainen, J., & Weisman de Mamani, A. G. (2008). Expressed emotion, communication deviance, and culture in families of patients with schizophrenia: A review of the literature. *Cultural Diversity and Ethnic Minority Psychology, 14*(2), 85–91.

La Fond, J. Q. (2005). *Preventing sexual violence: How society should cope with sex offenders*. Washington, DC: American Psychological Association.

La Fond, J. Q., & Durham, M. L. (1992). *Back to the asylum: The future of mental health law and policy in the United States*. New York, NY: Oxford University Press.

La Greca, A. M., & Prinstein, M. J. (2002). Hurricanes and earthquakes. In A. N. La Greca, W. K. Silverman, & M. C. Roberts (Eds.), *Helping Children Cope with Disasters and Terrorism* (Vol. 1, pp. 107–138). Washington, DC: American Psychological Association.

La Greca, A. M., Silverman, W. K., Lai, B., & Jaccard, J. (2010). Hurricane-related exposure experiences and stressors, other life events, and social support: Concurrent and prospective impact on children's persistent posttraumatic stress symptoms. *Journal of Consulting and Clinical Psychology, 78*, 794–805. doi: 10.1037/a0020775

Laan, E., & Tiefer, L. (2014). *The sham drug idea of the year: Pink Viagra*. L. A. Times. Retrieved from http://www.latimes.com/opinion/op-ed/la-oe-laan-tiefer-pink-viagra-20141114-story.html

Lacey, J. H. (1992). The treatment demand for bulimia: A catchment area report of referral rates and demography. *Psychiatric Bulletin, 16*, 203–205.

Lack, L. C., Gradisar, M., Van Someren, E. J. W., Wright, H. R., & Lushington, K. (2008). The relationship between insomnia and body temperatures. *Sleep Medicine Reviews, 12*(4), 307–317.

Lader, M. H. (1975). *The psychophysiology of mental illness*. London, U.K.: Routledge & Kegan Paul.

Laing, R. D. (1967). *The politics of experience*. New York, NY: Pantheon.

Lakes, K., Vaughan, E., Jones, M., Burke, W., Baker, D., & Swanson, J. (2012). Diverse perceptions of the informed consent process: Implications for the recruitment and participation of diverse communities in the National Children's Study. *American Journal of Community Psychology, 49*(1), 215–232. doi: 10.1007/s10464-011-9450-1

Lakin, M. M., Montague, D. K., Vanderbrug Medendorp, S., Tesar, L., & Schover, L. R. (1990). Intracavernous injection therapy: Analysis of results and complications. *Journal of Urology, 143*, 1138–1141.

Lalumière, M. L., Blanchard, R., & Zucker, K. J. (2000). Sexual orientation and handedness in men and women: A meta-analysis. *Psychological Bulletin, 126*, 575–592.

Lam, R. W., & Lavitan, R. D. (2000). Pathophysiology of seasonal affective disorder: A review. *Journal of Psychiatry and Neuroscience, 25*, 469–480.

Lam, R., Levitt, A., Levitan, R., Enns, M., Morehouse, R., Michalak, E., & Tam, S. E. (2006). The Can-Sad study: A randomized controlled trial of the effectiveness of light therapy and fluoxetine in patients with winter seasonal affective disorder. *American Journal of Psychiatry, 163*, 805–812.

Lam, T. H., Ho, S. Y., Hedley, A. J., Mak, K. H., & Peto, R. (2001). Mortality and smoking in Hong Kong: Case-control study of all adult deaths in 1998. *British Medical Journal, 323*, 361–362.

Lamb, H. R. (2009). Reversing criminalization. *American Journal of Psychiatry, 166*(1), 8–10. doi: 10.1176/appi.ajp.2008.08101515

Lamb, H. R., & Weinberger, L. E. (2009). Criminalization of persons with severe mental illness. In B. J. Sadock, V. A. Sadock, & P. Ruiz (Eds.), *Kaplan & Sadock's comprehensive textbook of psychiatry* (9th ed., Vol. II, pp. 4380–4395). Philadelphia, PA: Lippincott Williams & Wilkins.

Lambacher, G., Pascale, E., Pucci, M., Mangiapelo, S., D'Addario, C., & Adriani, W. (2020). Search for an epigenetic biomarker in ADHD diagnosis, based on the DAT1 gene 5'-UTR methylation: A new possible approach. *Psychiatry Research, 291*, 113154.

Lamberg, L. (2003). All night diners: Researchers take a new look at night eating syndrome. *JAMA: Journal of the American Medical Association, 290*, 1442.

Lamis, D. A., Malone, P. S., Langhinrichsen-Rohling, J., & Ellis, T. E. (2010). Body investment, depression, and alcohol use as risk factors for suicide proneness in college students. *Crisis: The Journal of Crisis Intervention and Suicide Prevention, 31*(3), 118–127.

Lander, E. S., Linton, L. M., Birren, B., Nusbaum, C., Zody, M. C., Baldwin, J., … Morgan, M. J. (2001). Initial sequencing and analysis of the human genome. *Nature, 409*(6822), 860–921. doi: 10.1038/35057062

Landis, S., & Insel, T. R. (2008, November 7). The "neuro" in neurogenetics. *Science, 322*, 821.

Lang, P. J. (1985). The cognitive psychophysiology of emotion: Fear and anxiety. In A. H. Tuma & J. D. Maser (Eds.), *Anxiety and the anxiety disorders*. Hillsdale, NJ: Erlbaum.

Lang, P. J. (1995). The emotion probe: Studies of motivation and attention. *American Psychologist, 50*, 372–385.

Lang, P. J., Bradley, M. M., & Cuthbert, B. N. (1998). Emotion, motivation, and anxiety: Brain mechanisms and psychophysiology. *Biological Psychiatry, 44*, 1248–1263.

Långström, N., & Seto, M. (2006). Exhibitionistic and voyeuristic in a Swedish national population survey. *Archives of Sexual Behavior, 35*, 427–435.

Långström, N., & Zucker, K. (2005). Transvestic fetishism in the general population: Prevalence and correlates. *Journal of Sex & Marital Therapy, 31*, 87–95.

Långström, N., Rahman, Q., Carlström, E., & Lichtenstein, P. (2010). Genetic and environmental effects on same-sex sexual behavior: A population study of twins in Sweden. *Archives of Sexual Behavior, 39*, 75–80.

Lanius, R. A., Brand, B., Vermetten, E., Frewen, P. A., & Spiegel, D. (2012). The dissociative subtype of posttraumatic stress disorder: Rationale, clinical and neurobiological evidence, and implications. *Depression and Anxiety, 29,* 701–708. doi: 10.1002/da.21889

Lantz Lesser, E., Smith, K. E., Strauman, T. J., Crosby, R. D., Engel, S. G., Crow, S. J., Peterson, C. B., & Wonderlich, S. A. (2021). Relationships between nonappearance self-discrepancy, weight discrepancy, and binge eating disorder symptoms. *Eating and Weight Disorders, 26*(5), 1571–1580. doi: 10.1007/s40519-020-00975-8

Lapierre, S., Erlangsen, A., Waern, M., De Leo, D., Oyama, H., Scocco, P., & Quinnett, P. (2011). A systematic review of elderly suicide prevention programs. *Crisis: The Journal of Crisis Intervention and Suicide Prevention, 32*(2), 88–98.

Larsen, B. A., Darby, R. S., Harris, C. R., Nelkin, D. K., Milam, P. E., & Christenfeld, N. J. (2012). The immediate and delayed cardiovascular benefits of forgiving. *Psychosomatic Medicine, 74*(7), 745–750. doi: 10.1097/PSY .0b013e31825fe96c

Larson, N. C., Barger, S. D., & Sydeman, S. J. (2013). Type D personality is not associated with coronary heart disease risk in a North American sample of retirement-aged adults. *International Journal of Behavioral Medicine, 20*(2), 277–285.

Lasch, C. (1978). *The culture of narcissism: American life in an age of diminishing expectations.* New York, NY: W. W. Norton.

Lataster, J., Myin-Germeys, I., Lieb, R., Wittchen, H. U., & Van Os, J. (2012). Adversity and psychosis: A 10-year prospective study investigating synergism between early and recent adversity in psychosis. *Acta Psychiatrica Scandinavica, 125*(5), 388–399.

Latfi, R., Kellum, J. M., DeMaria, E. J., & Sugarman, H. J. (2002). Surgical treatment of obesity. In T. A. Wadden & A. J. Stunkard (Eds.), *Handbook of obesity treatment* (pp. 339–356). New York, NY: Guilford.

Lau, J. Y. F., & Eley, T. C. (2010). The genetics of mood disorders. *Annual Review of Clinical Psychology, 6,* 313–337.

Laub, J. H., & Vaillant, G. E. (2000). Delinquency and mortality: A 50-year follow-up study of 1,000 delinquent and nondelinquent boys. *American Journal of Psychiatry, 157,* 96–102.

Laumann, E. O., Nicolosi, A., Glasser, D. B., Paik, A., Gingell, C., Moreira, E., & Wang, T. (2005). Sexual problems among women and men aged 40–80 years: Prevalence and correlates identified by the Global Study of Sexual Attitudes and Behaviors. *International Journal of Impotence Research, 17,* 39–57.

Laumann, E., Gagnon, J., Michael, R., & Michaels, S. (1994). *The social organization of sexuality: Sexual practices in the United States.* Chicago, IL: University of Chicago Press.

Laumann, E., Paik, A., & Rosen, R. C. (1999). Sexual dysfunction in the United States. Prevalence and predictors. *JAMA: Journal of the American Medical Association, 281,* 537–544.

Laumann, E., Paik, A., Glasser, D., Kang, J., Wang, T., Levinson, B., & Gingell, C. (2006). A cross-national study of subjective sexual well-being among older women and men: Findings from the global study of sexual attitudes and behaviors. *Archives of Sexual Behavior, 35,* 145–161.

Launer, L. J. (2011). Counting dementia: there is no one "best" way. *Alzheimer's & Dementia, 7*(1), 10–14.

Lauriello, J., Bustillo, J. R., & Keith, S. J. (2005). Schizophrenia: Scope of the problem. In B. J. Sadock & V. A. Sadock (Eds.), *Kaplan & Sadock's comprehensive textbook of psychiatry* (pp. 1345–1354). Philadelphia, PA: Lippincott, Williams & Wilkins.

Lavender, E., Hirasawa-Fujita, M., & Domino, E. F. (2020). Ketamine's dose related multiple mechanisms of actions: Dissociative anesthetic to rapid antidepressant. *Behavioural Brain Research,* 112631.

Lawrence, A. (2005). Sexuality before and after male-to-female sex reassignment surgery. *Archives of Sexual Behavior, 34,* 147–166.

Lawrence, A. A. (2013). Debating the Meaning of Autogynephilia. In A. A. Lawrence (Eds.). *Men Trapped in Men's Bodies* (pp. 95–110; 161–178). Springer: New York.

Laws, D. R., & O'Donohue, W. (Eds.) (1997). *Sexual deviance: Theory, assessment and treatment.* New York, NY: Guilford.

Laws, D. R., & O'Donohue, W. T. (2008). Introduction. In D. R. Laws & W. T. O'Donohue (Eds.), *Sexual deviance: Theory, assessment, and treatment* (2nd ed., pp. 1–20). New York, NY: Guilford.

Lawton, K., & Kasari, C. (2012). Teacher-implemented joint attention intervention: Pilot randomized controlled study for preschoolers with autism. *Journal of Consulting and Clinical Psychology, 80*(4), 687.

Laxenaire, M., Ganne-Vevonec, M. O., & Streiff, O. (1982). Les problèmes d'identité chez les enfants des migrants. *Annales Medico-Psychologiques, 140,* 602–605.

Lazare, D. (1989, October 14). Drugs 'R' Us. *In These Times,* 12–13.

Lazarus, R. S. (1968). Emotions and adaptation: Conceptual and empirical relations. In W. J. Arnold (Ed.), *Nebraska Symposium on Motivation* (Vol. 16). Lincoln: University of Nebraska Press.

Lazarus, R. S. (1991). Progress on a cognitive-motivational relational theory of emotion. *American Psychologist, 46*(8), 819–834.

Lazarus, R. S. (1995). Psychological stress in the workplace. In R. Crandall & P. L. Perrewe (Eds.), *Occupational stress: A handbook* (pp. 3–14). Philadelphia, PA: Taylor & Francis.

Le Foll, B., Gallo, A., Le Strat, Y., Lu, L., & Gorwood, P. (2009). Genetics of dopamine receptors and drug addiction: A comprehensive review. *Behavioural Pharmacology, 20*(1), 1–17.

le Grange, D., Crosby, R. D., Rathouz, P. J., & Leventhal, B. L. (2007). A randomized controlled comparison of family-based treatment and supportive psychotherapy for adolescent bulimia nervosa. *Archives of General Psychiatry, 64*(9), 1049–1056.

Le Grange, D., Lock, J., Agras, W. S., Bryson, S. W., & Jo, B. (2015). Randomized Clinical Trial of Family-Based Treatment and Cognitive-Behavioral Therapy for Adolescent Bulimia Nervosa. *Journal of the American Academy of Child & Adolescent Psychiatry, 54*(11), 886–894.

le Grange, D., Lock, J., Loeb, K., & Nicholls, D. (2010). Academy for eating disorders position paper: The role of the family in eating disorders. *International Journal of Eating Disorders, 43,* 1–5.

Le, T. M., Zhornitsky, S., Zhang, S., & Li, C.-S. R. (2020). Pain and reward circuits antagonistically modulate alcohol expectancy to regulate drinking. *Translational Psychiatry, 10*(1), 1–10.

Leahy, R. L., & McGinn, L. K. (2012). Cognitive therapy for personality disorders. In T. A. Widiger (Ed.), *The Oxford handbook of personality disorders* (pp. 727–750). New York, NY: Oxford University Press.

LeBeau, R. T., Glenn, D. E., Hanover, L. N., Beesdo-Baum, K., Wittchen, H.-U., & Craske, M. G. (2012). A dimensional approach to measuring anxiety for DSM-5. *International Journal of Methods in Psychiatric Research, 21*(4), 258–272.

LeBeau, R. T., Glenn, D., Liao, B., Wittchen, H.-U., Beesdo-Baum, K., Ollendick, T., & Craske, M. G. (2010). Specific phobia: A review of DSM-IV specific phobia and preliminary recommendations for DSM-V. *Depression and Anxiety, 27*(2), 148–167.

LeBeau, R. T., Mischel, E. R., Simpson, H. B., Mataix-Cols, D., Phillips, K. A., Stein, D. J., & Craske, M. G. (2013). Preliminary assessment of obsessive–compulsive spectrum disorder scales for *DSM-5. Journal of Obsessive-Compulsive and Related Disorders, 2*(2), 114–118.

LeBeau, R., Bogels, S., Moller, E., & Craske, M. (2015). Integrating dimensional assessment and categorical diagnosis in *DSM-5*: The benefits and challenges of the

paradigm shift for the anxiety disorders. *Psychopathology Review, 2*(1), 83-99.
LeBeau, R., Mischel, E., Resnick, H., Kilpatrick, D., Friedman, M., & Craske, M. (2014). Dimensional assessment of posttraumatic stress disorder in *DSM-5. Psychiatry Research, 218*(1), 143–147. doi:10.1016/j.psychres.2014.03.032
Lebedinskaya, K. S., & Nikolskaya, O. S. (1993). Brief report: Analysis of autism and its treatment in modern Russian defectology. *Journal of Autism and Developmental Disorders, 23,* 675–697.
Lebel, S., Mutsaers, B., Tomei, C., Leclair, C. S., Jones, G., Petricone-Westwood, D., … Dinkel, A. (2020). Health anxiety and illness-related fears across diverse chronic illnesses: A systematic review on conceptualization, measurement, prevalence, course, and correlates. *PLoS ONE, 15*(7 July). doi: 10.1371/journal.pone.0234124
Lechner, S., & Antoni, M. (2004). Posttraumatic growth and group based intervention for persons dealing with cancer: What have we learned so far? *Psychological Inquiry, 15,* 35–41.
Leckman, J. F., Denys, D., Simpson, H. B., Mataix-Cols, D., Hollander, E., Saxena, S., & Stein, D. (2010). Obsessive-compulsive disorder: A review of the diagnostic criteria and possible subtypes and dimensional specifiers for DSM-V. *Depression and Anxiety, 27*(6), 507–527. doi: 10.1002/da.20669
Leckman, J. F., Grice, D. E., Boardman, J., Zhang, H., Vitali, A., Bondi, C., & Pauls, D. (1997). Symptoms of obsessive-compulsive disorder. *American Journal of Psychiatry, 154,* 911–917.
Lecrubier, Y., Bakker, A., Dunbar, G., & the Collaborative Paroxetine Panic Study Investigators. (1997). A comparison of paroxetine, clomipramine and placebo in the treatment of panic disorder. *Acta Psychiatrica Scandinavica, 95,* 145–152.
Lecrubier, Y., Judge, R., & the Collaborative Paroxetine Panic Study Investigators. (1997). Long term evaluation of paroxetine, clomipramine and placebo in panic disorder. *Acta Psychiatrica Scandinavica, 95,* 153–160.
Ledford, H. (2015). First cancer-fighting virus approved. *Nature, 526,* 622–623.
LeDoux, J. (2015). *Anxious: Using the brain to understand and treat fear and anxiety.* New York, NY: Viking.
LeDoux, J. E. (1996). *The emotional brain: The mysterious underpinnings of emotional life.* New York, NY: Simon & Schuster.
LeDoux, J. E. (2002). *Synaptic self: How our brains become who we are.* New York, NY: Penguin Books.
Ledoux, J. E., & Brown, R. (2017). A higher-order theory of emotional consciousness. *Proceedings of the National Academy of Sciences of the United States of America, 114*(10), E2016–E2025. doi: 10.1073/pnas.1619316114
LeDoux. J. E, & Hofmann, S. G. (2018). The subjective experience of emotion: A fearful view. *Current Opinion in Behavioral Sciences, 19,* 67–72. doi: 10.1016/j.cobeha.2017.09.011.
Lee, C. C., Czaja, S. J., & Schulz, R. (2010). The moderating influence of demographic characteristics, social support, and religious coping on the effectiveness of a multicomponent psychosocial caregiver intervention in three racial ethnic groups. *The Journals of Gerontology Series B: Psychological Sciences and Social Sciences, 65B*(2), 185–194.
Lee, C. K. (1992). Alcoholism in Korea. In J. Helzer & G. Canino (Eds.), *Alcoholism—North America, Europe and Asia: A coordinated analysis of population data from ten regions* (pp. 247–262). London, U.K.: Oxford University Press.
Lee, M. A., & Shlain, B. (1992). *Acid dreams: The complete social history of LSD: The CIA, the sixties, and beyond.* New York, NY: Grove Press.
Lee, P.-F., Ho, C.-C., Yeh, D.-P., Hung, C.-T., Chang, Y.-C., Liu, C.-C., … Hsieh, X.-Y. (2020). Cross-sectional associations of physical fitness performance level and sleep duration among older adults: Results from the national physical fitness survey in Taiwan. *International Journal of Environmental Research and Public Health, 17*(2), 388.
Lee, S. H., Han, D. H., Oh, S., Lyoo, I. K., Lee, Y. S., Renshaw, P. F., & Lukas, S. (2009). Quantitative electroencephalographic (qEEG) correlates of craving during virtual reality therapy in alcohol-dependent patients. *Pharmacology Biochemistry and Behavior, 91*(3), 393–397. doi: 10.1016/j.pbb.2008.08.014
Lee, S. Y., & Chung, J. (2020). Risk factors of binge drinking in adults across gender and age groups: Sixth Korea National Health and Nutrition Examination Survey 2014. *Journal of Addictions Nursing, 31*(4), E27–E37.
Lee, T. M., Chen, E. Y., Chan, C. C., Paterson, J. G., Janzen, H. L., & Blashko, C. A. (1998). Seasonal affective disorder. *Clinical Psychology: Science and Practice, 5,* 275–290.
Lees, B., Meredith, L. R., Kirkland, A. E., Bryant, B. E., & Squeglia, L. M. (2020). Effect of alcohol use on the adolescent brain and behavior. *Pharmacology Biochemistry and Behavior, 192,* 172906.
Lefley, H. (2009). *Family psychoeducation in serious mental illness: Models, outcomes, applications.* New York, NY: Oxford University Press.
Lefrancois, G. R. (1990). *The lifespan* (3rd ed.). Belmont, CA: Wadsworth.
Lehman, B. J., Taylor, S. E., Kiefe, C. I., & Seeman, T. E. (2009). Relationship of early life stress and psychological functioning to blood pressure in the CARDIA study. *Health Psychology, 28*(3), 338–346.
Leibbrand, R., Hiller, W., & Fichter, M. M. (2000). Hypochondriasis and somatization: Two distinct aspects of somatoform disorders? *Journal of Clinical Psychology, 56,* 63–72.
Leibenluft, E. (2011). Severe mood dysregulation, irritability, and the diagnostic boundaries of bipolar disorder in youths. *American Journal of Psychiatry, 168*(2), 129–142.
Leibenluft, E., & Rich, B. A. (2008). Pediatric bipolar disorder. *Annual Review of Clinical Psychology, 4,* 163–187.
Leiblum, S. R. (2010). *Treating sexual desire disorders: A clinical casebook.* New York, NY: Guilford.
Leiblum, S. R., & Rosen, R. C. (Eds.) (2000). *Principles and practice of sex therapy* (3rd ed.). New York, NY: Guilford.
Leitenberg, H., Detzer, M. J., & Srebnik, D. (1993). Gender differences in masturbation and the relation of masturbation experience in preadolescence and/or early adolescence to sexual behavior and sexual adjustment in young adulthood. *Archives of Sexual Behavior, 22*(2), 87–98.
Lejeune, J., Gauthier, M., & Turpin, R. (1959). Étude des chromosomes somatiques de neuf enfants mongoliens. *Comptes Rendus Hebdomadaires des Séances de l' Académie des Sciences. D: Sciences Naturelles (Paris), 248,* 1721–1722.
Lener, M. S., Wong, E., Tang, C. Y., Byne, W., Goldstein, K. E., Blair, N. J., . . . Hazlett, E. A. (2014). White matter abnormalities in schizophrenia and schizotypal personality disorder. *Schizophrenia Bulletin, 41*(1), 300–310.
Lengel, G. J. (2020). Histrionic personality disorder. In B. J. Carducci, C. S. Nave, A. D. Fabio, D. H. Saklofske, & C. Stough (Eds.), *The Wiley encyclopedia of personality and individual differences: Clinical, applied, and cross-cultural research* (Vol. 1, pp. 97–101). Hoboken, N.J.: Wiley.
Lenze, E. J., Mulsant, B. H., Shear, M. K., Schulberg, H. C., Dew, M. A., Begley, A. E., Pollock, B. G., & Reynolds, C. F. (2000). Comorbid anxiety disorders in depressed elderly patients. *Am J Psychiatry, 157*(5):722–728.

Lenze, E. J., Miller, A. R., Munir, Z. B., Pornoppadol, C., & North, C. S. (1999). Psychiatric symptoms endorsed by somatization disorder patients in a psychiatric clinic. *Annals of Clinical Psychiatry, 11*(2), 73–79.

Lenzenweger, M. F., & Dworkin, R. H. (1996). The dimensions of schizophrenia phenomenology. Note one or two, at least three, perhaps four. *British Journal of Psychiatry, 168,* 432–440.

Lenzenweger, M. F., McLachlan, G., & Rubin, D. B. (2007). Resolving the latent structure of schizophrenia endophenotypes using expectation-maximization-based finite mixture modeling. *Journal of Abnormal Psychology, 116,* 16–29.

Lenzenweger, M., Lane, M., Loranger, A., & Kessler, R. (2007). DSM-IV personality disorders in the National Comorbidity Survey Replication. *Biological Psychiatry, 62*(6), 553–564.

Lerma, P., & Chen, R. K. (2020). Adults with learning disabilities in postsecondary education and the workforce. *Journal of Disability Studies, 6*(2), 70–78.

Lerner, E., Teitelbaum, J., & Meehan, K. B. (2020). Avoidant personality disorder. In V. Zeigler-Hill & T. K. Shackelford (Eds.), *Encyclopedia of personality and individual differences* (pp. 351–358). Hoboken, N.J.: Springer.

Lerner, R., Kibler, J. L., & Zeichner, S. B. (2013). Relationship between mindfulness-based stress reduction and immune function in cancer and HIV/AIDS. *Cancer and Clinical Oncology, 2*(1), 62–72.

Leserman, J. (2008). Role of depression, stress, and trauma in HIV disease progression. *Psychosomatic Medicine, 70,* 539–545.

Leserman, J., Petitto, J. M., Golden, R. N., Gaynes, B. N., Gu, H., Perkins, D. O., & Evans, D. L. (2000). Impact of stressful life events, depression, social support, coping, and cortisol on progression to AIDS. *American Journal of Psychiatry, 157,* 1221–1228.

Leslie, M., Lambert, E., & Treasure, J. (2019). Towards a translational approach to food addiction: Implications for bulimia nervosa. *Current Addiction Reports, 6*(3), 258–265. doi: 10.1007/s40429-019-00264-0

Leuchter, A. F., Cook, I. A., Witte, E. A., Morgan, M., & Abrams, M. (2002). Changes in brain function of depressed subjects during treatment with placebo. *American Journal of Psychiatry, 159*(1)122–129.tf vtcr c

LeVay, S. (1991). A difference in hypothalamic structure between heterosexual and homosexual men. *Science, 253,* 1034–1037.

Levenston, G. K., Patrick, C. J., Bradley, M. M., & Lang, P. J. (2000). The psychopath as observer: emotion and attention in picture processing. *Journal of Abnormal Psychology, 109*(3), 373.

Leventhal, A. M., & Zvolensky, M. J. (2015). Anxiety, deperssion, and cigarette smoking: A transdiagnostc vulnerability framework to understand emotion-smoking comorbidity. *Psychological Bulletin, 141,* 176–212.

Levesque, R. J. (2012). Sadistic personality disorder. In *Encyclopedia of Adolescence* (pp. 2445–2446). Springer US.

Levin, F. R., Evans, S. M., Brooks, D. J., & Garawi, F. (2007). Treatment of cocaine dependent treatment seekers with adult ADHD: Double-blind comparison of methylphenidate and placebo. *Drug and Alcohol Dependence, 87,* 20–29.

Levin, R. A., Carnegie, M. H., & Celermajer, D. S. (2020). Pulse pressure: An emerging therapeutic target for dementia. *Frontiers in Neuroscience, 14,* 669.

Levine, J. A., Lanningham-Foster, L. M., McCrady, S. K., Krizan, A. C., Olson, L. R., Kane, P. H., Jensen, M. D., & Clark, M. M. (2005). Interindividual variation in posture allocation: Possible role in human obesity. *Science,* 307, 584–586.

Levine, M. P., & Smolak, L. (1996). Media as a context for the development of disordered eating. In L. Smolak, M. P. Levine, & R. Striegel-Moore (Eds.), *The developmental psychopathology of eating disorders: Implications for research, prevention, and treatment* (pp. 235–257). Mahwah, NJ: Erlbaum.

Levine, S. B., (2015). Filbanserin. *Archives of Sexual Behavior, 44*(8), 2107–2109. doi: 10.1007/s10508-015-0617-y

Levinson, D. F. (2009). Genetics of major depression. In I. H. Gotlib & C. L. Hammen (Eds.), *Handbook of depression* (2nd ed., pp. 165–186). New York, NY: Guilford.

Levitt, A. J., Joffe, R. T., Moul, D. F., Lam, R. W., Teicher, M. H., Lebegue, B., & Buchanan, A. (1993). Side effects of light therapy in seasonal affective disorder. *American Journal of Psychiatry, 150,* 650–652.

Levitt, A., & Boyle, M. (2002). The impact of latitude on the prevalence of seasonal depression. *Canadian Journal of Psychiatry, 46,* 650–654.

Levy, B. R., Slade, M. D., Kunkel, S. R., & Kasl, S. V. (2002). Longevity increased by positive self-perceptions of aging. *Journal of Personality and Social Psychology, 83,* 261–270.

Levy, D. T., Warner, K. E., Cummings, K. M., Hammond, D., Kuo, C., Fong, G. T., … Borland, R. (2019). Examining the relationship of vaping to smoking initiation among U.S. youth and young adults: A reality check. *Tobacco Control, 28(6),* 629–635.

Levy, K. B., O'Grady, K. E., Wish, E. D., & Arria, A. M. (2005). An in-depth qualitative examination of the ecstasy experience: Results of a focus group with Ecstasy-using college students. *Substance Use and Misuse, 40*(9–10), 1427–1441. doi: 10.1081/ja-200066886

Lewinsohn, P. M., Allen, N. B., Seeley, J. R., & Gotlib, I. H. (1999). First onset versus recurrence of depression: Differential processes of psychosocial risk. *Journal of Abnormal Psychology, 108*(3), 483–489.

Lewis, B. A., Statt, E., & Marcus, B. H. (2011). Behavioral interventions in public health settings: Physical activity, weight loss, and smoking. In D. H. Barlow (Ed.), *Oxford handbook of clinical psychology* (pp. 717–738). New York, NY: Oxford University Press.

Lewis, D. O., Yeager, C. A., Swica, Y., Pincus, J. H., & Lewis, M. (1997). Objective documentation of child abuse and dissociation in 12 murderers with dissociative identity disorder. *American Journal of Psychiatry, 154,* 1703–1710.

Lewis, F. M., Brandt, P. A., Cochrane, B. B., Griffith, K. A., Grant, M., Haase, J. E., Houldin, A. D., Post-White, J., Zahlis, E. H., & Shands, M. E. (2015). The Enhancing Connections Program: A six-state randomized clinical trial of a cancer parenting program. *Journal of Consulting and Clinical Psychology, 83*(1), 1–12.

Lewis, G., Croft-Jeffreys, C., & Anthony, D. (1990). Are British psychiatrists racist? *British Journal of Psychiatry, 157,* 410–415.

Lewis, G., David, A., Andreasson, S., & Allsbeck, P. (1992). Schizophrenia and city life. *Lancet, 340,* 137–140.

Lewis, K. C., & Ridenour, J. M. (2020). Paranoid personality disorder. In V. Zeigler-Hill & T. K. Shackelford (Eds.), *Encyclopedia of personality and individual differences* (pp. 3413–3421). Cham, Switzerland: Springer.

Lewis, K. C., Ridenour, J. M., Pitman, S., & Roche, M. (2020). Evaluating stable and situational expressions of passive-aggressive personality disorder: A multimethod experience sampling case study. *Journal of Personality Assessment,* 1–13.

Lewis, S., Escalona, R., & Keith, S. J. (2009). Phenomenology of schizophrenia. In B. J. Sadock, V. A. Sadock, & P. Ruiz (Eds.), *Kaplan & Sadock's comprehensive textbook of psychiatry* (9th ed., Vol. I, pp. 1433–1451). Philadelphia, PA: Lippincott Williams & Wilkins.

Lewis, T. T., Everson-Rose, S. A., Powell, L. H., Matthews, K. A., Brown, C., & Wesley, D. (2006). Chronic exposure to everyday discrimination and coronary artery calcification in African-American women: The SWAN heart study. *Psychosomatic Medicine, 68,* 362–368.

Lewis, T., DiLillo, D., & Peterson, L. (2004). Parental beliefs regarding developmental benefits of childhood injuries. *American Journal of Health Behavior, 28*(Suppl. 1) S61–S68.

Lewis-Fernandez, R., Hinton, D. E., Laria, A. J., Patterson, E. H., Hofmann, S. G., Craske, M. G., Stein, D. J., Asnaani, A., & Liao, B. (2010, February). Culture and the anxiety disorders: recommendations for DSM-V. Depress Anxiety. 27(2):212–29. doi: 10.1002/da.20647.

Lewis-Fernández, R., Hinton, D. E., Laria, A. J., Patterson, E. H., Hofmann, S. G., Craske, M. G., & Liao, B. (2010). Culture and the anxiety disorders: Recommendations for DSM-V. *Depression and Anxiety, 27*(2), 212–229.

Lewy, A. J., & Sack, R. L. (1987). Light therapy of chronobiological disorders. In A. Halaris (Ed.), *Chronobiology and psychiatric disorders* (pp. 181–206). New York, NY: Elsevier.

Lewy, A. J., Bauer, V. K., Cutler, N. L., Ahmed, S., Thomas, K. H., Blood, M. L., & Letham Jackson, J. M. (1998). Morning vs. evening light treatment of patients with winter depression. *Archives of General Psychiatry, 55,* 890–896.

Lewy, A. J., Kern, H. E., Rosenthal, N. E., & Wehr, T. A. (1982). Bright artificial light treatment of a manic-depressive patient with a seasonal mood cycle. *American Journal of Psychiatry, 139,* 1496–1498.

Lewy, A. J., Tutek, J., Havel, L. L., & Nikia, M. N. (2014). The role of circadian rhythms, light and melatonin in SAD and nonseasonal affective and anxiety disorders. *Current Psychiatry Reviews, 10,* 214–222.

Leyfer, O., & Brown, T. A. (2011). The anxiety-depression spectrum. In D. H. Barlow (Ed.), *Oxford handbook of clinical psychology* (pp. 279–293). New York, NY: Oxford University Press.

Lezak, M. D., Howieson, D. B., Bigler, E. D., & Tranel, D. (2012). *Neuropsychological assessment* (5th ed.). New York, NY: Oxford University Press.

Li, X., Zou, H., & Brown, W. T. (2012). Genes associated with autism spectrum disorder. *Brain Research Bulletin, 88*(6), 543–552. doi: 10.1016/j.brainresbull.2012.05.017

Li, Z., Wei, J., Zhang, G., Huang, J. J., Zingg, B., Wang, X., … Zhang, L. I. (2021). Corticostriatal control of defense behavior in mice induced by auditory looming cues. *Nature Communications, 12*(1). doi: 10.1038/s41467-021-21248-7

Liberman, R. P. (2007). Dissemination and adoption of social skills training: Social validation of an evidence-based treatment for the mentally disabled. *Journal of Mental Health, 16,* 595–623.

Liberman, R., & Kopelowicz, A. (2009). Training skills for illness self-management in the rehabilitation of schizophrenia: A family-assisted program for Latinos in California. *Salud Mental, 31,* 93–105.

Liddell, H. S. (1949). The role of vigilance in the development of animal neurosis. In P. Hoch & J. Zubin (Eds.), *Anxiety.* New York, NY: Grune & Stratton.

Liddle, P. F. (2012). Descriptive clinical features of schizophrenia. In M. G. Gelder, N. C. Andreasen, J. J. Lopez-Ibor, Jr., & J. R. Geddes (Eds.), *New Oxford textbook of psychiatry* (2nd ed., Vol. 1, pp. 526–531). New York, NY: Oxford University Press.

Lieb, R. (2015). Epidemiological perspectives on comorbidity between substance use disorders and other mental disorders. In G. Dom & F. Moggy (Eds),*Co-occurring addictive and psychiatric disorders* (pp. 3–12). Berlin, Germany: Springer Heidelberg.

Lieb, R., Wittchen, H-U., Hofler, M., Fuetsch, M., Stein, M. B., & Merikangas, K. R. (2000). Parental psychopathology, parenting styles, and the risk of social phobia in offspring. *Archives of General Psychiatry, 57,* 859–866.

Lieb, R., Zimmermann, P., Friis, R. H., Hofler, M., Tholen, S., & Wittchen, H.-U. (2002). The natural course of DSM-IV somatoform disorders and syndromes among adolescents and young adults: A prospective-longitudinal community study. *European Psychiatry, 17,* 321–331.

Lieberman, J. A., & Stroup, T. S. (2011). The NIMH-CATIE schizophrenia study: What did we learn? *American Journal of Psychiatry, 168*(8), 770–775. doi: 10.1176/appi.ajp.2011.11010039

Lieberman, J. A., Jody, D., Alvir, J. M. J., Ashtari, M., Levy, D. L., Bogerts, B., & Cooper, T. (1993). Brain morphology, dopamine, and eye-tracking abnormalities in first-episode schizophrenia. *Archives of General Psychiatry, 50,* 357–368.

Lieberman, J. A., Perkins, D., Belger, A., Chakos, M., Jarskog, F., Boteva, K., & Gilmore, J. (2001). The early stages of schizophrenia: Speculations on pathogenesis, pathophysiology, and therapeutic approaches. *Biological Psychiatry, 50,* 885.

Liebeskind, J. (1991). Pain can kill. *Pain, 44,* 3–4.

Liebman, R. E., & Burnette, M. (2013). It's not you, it's me: An examination of clinician- and client-level influences on countertransference toward borderline personality disorder. *American Journal of Orthopsychiatry, 83*(1), 115–125. doi: 10.1111/ajop.12002

Liebowitz, M. R., Schneier, F., Campeas, R., Hollander, E., Hatterer, J., Fyer, A., Gully, R. (1992). Phenelzine vs. atenolol in social phobia: A placebo controlled comparison. *Archives of General Psychiatry, 49,* 290–300.

Lilenfeld, L. R. R., Wonderlich, S., Riso, L. P., Crosby, R., & Mitchell, J. (2006). Eating disorders and personality: A methodological and empirical review. *Clinical Psychology Review, 26,* 299–320.

Lilienfeld, S. O. (1992). The association between antisocial personality and somatization disorders: A review and integration of theoretical models. *Clinical Psychology Review, 12,* 641–662.

Lilienfeld, S. O. (2014). *DSM-5:* Centripetal scientific and centrifugal antiscientific forces. *Clinical Psychology: Science and Practice, 21*(3), 269–279. doi: 10.1111/cpsp.12075

Lilienfeld, S. O., & Hess, T. H. (2001). Psychopathic personality traits and somatization: Sex differences and the mediating role of negative emotionality. *Journal of Psychopathology and Behavioral Assessment, 23,* 11–24.

Lilienfeld, S. O., & Marino, L. (1995). Mental disorder as a Roschian concept: A critique of Wakefield's 'harmful dysfunction' analysis. *Journal of Abnormal Psychology, 104*(3), 411–420.

Lilienfeld, S. O., & Marino, L. (1999). Essentialism revisited: Evolutionary theory and the concept of mental disorder. *Journal of Abnormal Psychology, 108,* 400–411.

Lilienfeld, S. O., Kirsch, I., Sarbin, T. R., Lynn, S. J., Chaves, J. F., & Ganaway, G. K. (1999). Dissociative identity disorder and the sociocognitive model: Recalling the lessons of the past. *Psychological Bulletin, 125*(5), 507–523.

Lilienfeld, S. O., VanValkenburg, C., Larntz, K., & Akiskal, H. S. (1986). The relationship of histrionic personality to antisocial personality and somatization disorders. *American Journal of Psychiatry, 143,* 718–722.

Lima, E. N., Stanley, S., Kaboski, B., Reitzel, L. R., Richey, A., Castro, Y., & Jakobsons, L. J. (2005). The incremental validity of the MMPI-2: When does therapist access not enhance treatment outcome? *Psychological Assessment, 17*(4), 462–468.

Lin, K. M., Hwu, H. G., & Tsuang, M. T. (2012). Schizophrenia and other psychosis in Asians and Asian Americans. In E. C. Chang (Ed.), *Handbook of Adult Psychopathology in Asians: Theory, Diagnosis, and Treatment* (p. 83). New York, NY: Oxford University Press.

Linardon, J., Cuijpers, P., Carlbring, P., Messer, M., & Fuller-Tyszkiewicz, M. (2019). The efficacy of app-supported smartphone interventions for mental health problems: A meta-analysis of randomized controlled trials. *World Psychiatry,18*(3), 325–336. doi: 10.1002/wps.20673

Lind, M. J., Aggen, S. H., Kirkpatrick, R. M., Kendler, K. S., & Amstadter, A. B. (2015). A longitudinal twin study of insomnia symptoms in adults. *Sleep, 38*(9), 1423–1430.

Lind, S., & Bowler, D. (2009). Delayed self-recognition in children with autism spectrum disorder. *Journal of Autism and Developmental Disorders, 39*(4), 643–650. doi: 10.1007/s10803-008-0670-7

Lindau, S. T., Schumm, L. P., Laumann, E. O., Levinson, W., O'Muircheartaigh, C. A., & Waite, L. J. (2007). A study of sexuality and health among older adults in the United States. *New England Journal of Medicine, 357*(8), 762–774.

Lindberg, N., Holi, M. M., Tani, P., & Virkkunen, M. (2005). Looking for pyromania: Characteristics of a consecutive sample of Finnish male criminals with histories of recidivist fire-setting between 1973 and 1993. *BMC Psychiatry, 5*(1), 47–52.

Lindblad, F., & Hjern, A. (2010). ADHD after fetal exposure to maternal smoking. *Nicotine & Tobacco Research, 12*(4), 408–415.

Lindenmayer, J., & Khan, A. (2006). Psychopathology. In J. A. Lieberman, T. S. Stroup, & D. O. Perkins (Eds.), *Textbook of schizophrenia* (pp. 187–221). Washington, DC: American Psychiatric Publishing.

Linehan, M. (2014). *DBT? Skills training manual.* Guilford Publications.

Linehan, M. M. (2015). *DBT® Skills Training Manual.* New York, NY: Guilford.

Linehan, M. M., & Dexter-Mazza, E. T. (2008). Dialectical behavior therapy for borderline personality disorder. In D. H. Barlow (Ed.), *Clinical handbook of psychological disorders* (4th ed., pp. 365–420). New York, NY: Guilford.

Linehan, M. M., & Kehrer, C. A. (1993). Borderline personality disorder. In D. H. Barlow (Ed.), *Clinical handbook of psychological disorders: A step by step treatment manual* (pp. 396–441). New York, NY: Guilford.

Linehan, M., Comtois, K., Murray, A., Brown, M., Gallop, R., Heard, H., & Lindenboim, N. (2006). Two-year randomized controlled trial and follow-up of dialectical behavior therapy vs therapy by experts for suicidal behaviors and borderline personality disorder. *Archives of General Psychiatry, 63*(7), 757.

Linehan, M., Schmidt, H., Dimeff, L., Craft, J., Kanter, J., & Comtois, K. (1999). Dialectical behavior therapy for patients with borderline personality disorder and drug-dependence. *American Journal on Addictions, 8*(4), 279–292.

Linton, S. J., Kecklund, G., Franklin, K. A., Leissner, L. C., Sivertsen, B., Lindberg, E., . . . Björkelund, C. (2015). The effect of the work environment on future sleep disturbances: a systematic review. *Sleep Medicine Reviews, 23,* 10–19.

Liotti, M., Mayberg, H. S., McGinnis, S., Brannan, S. L., & Jerabek, P. (2002). Unmasking disease-specific cerebral blood flow abnormalities: Mood challenge in patients with remitted unipolar depression. *American Journal of Psychiatry, 159,* 1807–1808.

Lipchik, G. L., Holroyd, K. A., & Nash, J. M. (2002). Cognitive-behavioral management of recurrent headache disorders: A minimal-therapist-contact approach. In D. C. Turk & R. J. Gatchel (Eds.), *Psychological approaches to pain management: A practitioner's handbook* (2nd ed.) (pp. 365–389). New York, NY: Guilford.

Lipsitch, M., Swerdlow, D. L., & Finelli, L. (2020). Defining the epidemiology of covid-19: Studies needed. *New England Journal of Medicine, 382*(13), 1194–1196.

Lissek, S., & Grillon, C. (2012). Learning models of PTSD. In J. G. Beck & D. M. Sloan (Eds.), *The Oxford handbook of traumatic stress disorders* (pp. 175–190). New York, NY: Oxford University Press.

Lissek, S., Kaczkurkin, A. N., Rabin, S., Geraci, M., Pine, D. S., & Grillon, C. (2014). Generalized anxiety disorder is associated with overgeneralization of classically conditioned fear. *Biological psychiatry, 75*(11), 909–915.

Litvin, E. B., Ditre, J. W., Heckman, B. W., & Brandon, T. H. (2012). Nicotine. In J. C. Verster, K. Brady, M. Galanter, & P. Conrod (Eds.), *Drug abuse and addiction in medical illness* (pp. 137–150). New York, NY: Springer.

Litz, B. T., Salters-Pedneault, K., Steenkamp, M., Hermos, J. A., Bryant, R. A., Otto, M. W., & Hofmann, S. G. (2012). A randomized placebo-controlled trial of d-cycloserine and exposure therapy for post-traumatic stress disorder. *Journal of Psychiatric Research, 46,* 1184–1190.

Liu, N. H., Wu, C., Pérez-Stable, E. J., & Muñoz, R. F. (2021). Longitudinal association between smoking abstinence and depression severity in those with baseline current, past, and no history of major depressive episode in an international online tobacco cessation study. *Nicotine and Tobacco Research, 23*(2), 267–275.

Liu, X., Zhou, H., Jiang, C., Xue, Y., Zhou, Z., & Wang, J. (2020). Cognitive control deficits in alcohol dependence are a trait- and state-dependent biomarker: An ERP study. *Frontiers in Psychiatry, 11,* 1389.

Livesley, W. J., & Jang, K. L. (2008). The behavioral genetics of personality disorder. *Annual Review of Clinical Psychology, 4,* 247–274.

Livesley, W. J., Jang, K. L., & Vernon, P. A. (1998). Phenotypic and genotypic structure of traits delineating personality disorder. *Archives of General Psychiatry, 55,* 941–948.

Livhits, M., Mercado, C., Yermilov, I., Parikh, J. A., Dutson, E., Mehran, A., . . . Gibbons, M. M. (2012). Preoperative predictors of weight loss following bariatric surgery: systematic review. *Obesity Surgery, 22*(1), 70–89.

Livingston, E. H. (2007). Obesity, mortality, and bariatric surgery death rates. *JAMA: Journal of the American Medical Association, 298*(20), 2406–2408.

Livingston, E. H. (2010). Surgical treatment of obesity in adolescence. *JAMA: Journal of the American Medical Association, 303*(6), 559–560.

Livingston, E. H. (2012). Inadequacy of BMI as an indicator for bariatric surgery. *Journal of American Medical Association, 307,* 88–89.

Llewellyn, C. H., Trzaskowski, M., van Jaarsveld, C. H., Plomin, R., & Wardle, J. (2014). Satiety mechanisms in genetic risk of obesity. *JAMA Pediatrics, 168*(4), 338–344.

Lloyd, E. A. (2005). *The case of the female orgasm: Bias in the science of evolution.* Cambridge, MA: Harvard University Press.

Lo, C. C., & Cheng, T. C. (2018). Social status, discrimination, and minority individuals' mental health: A secondary analysis of US national surveys. *Journal of Racial and Ethnic Health Disparities, 5*(3), 485–494. doi: 10.1007/s40615-017-0390-9

Lo, S. C., Pripuzova, N., Li, B., Komaroff, A. L., Hung, G. C., Wang, R., & Alter, H. J. (2010). Detection of MLV-related virus gene sequences in blood of patients with chronic fatigue syndrome and healthy blood donors. *Proceedings of the National Academy of Sciences, 107*(36), 15874–15879.

Lo, S. C., Pripuzova, N., Li, B., Komaroff, A. L., Hung, G. C., Wang, R., & Alter, H. J. (2012). Retraction for Lo et al., Detection of MLV-related virus gene sequences in blood of patients with chronic fatigue syndrome and healthy blood donors. *Proceedings of the National Academy of Sciences of the United States of America, 109*(1), 346–346.

Lobbestael, J., & Arntz, A., (2012). Cognitive contributions to personality disorders. In T. A. Widiger (Ed.), *The Oxford handbook of personality disorders* (pp. 325–344). New York, NY: Oxford University Press.

Lobbestael, J., Arntz, A., & Bernstein, D. P. (2010). Disentangling the relationship between different types of childhood maltreatment and personality disorders. *Journal of Personality Disorders, 24,* 285–295.

Lobo, R. A. (2013). Where are we 10 years after the Women's Health Initiative? *The Journal of Clinical Endocrinology & Metabolism, 98*(5), 1771–1780.

LoBraico, E. J., Bray, B. C., Feinberg, M. E., & Fosco, G. M. (in press). Constellations of family risk for long-term adolescent antisocial behavior. *Journal of Family Psychology*.

Lochner, C., Grant, J. E., Odlaug, B. L., Woods, D. W., Keuthen, N. J., & Stein, D. J. (2012). DSM-5 field survey: Hair-pulling disorder (trichotillomania). *Depression and Anxiety, 29,* 1025–1031. doi: 10.1002/da.22011

Lock, J., Le Grange, D., Agras, S., Moye, A., Byrson, S. W., & Jo, B. (2010). Randomized clinical trial comparing family-based treatment with adolescent-focused individual therapy for adolescents with anorexia nervosa. *Archives of General Psychiatry, 67*(10), 1025–1032.

Lock, J., Le Grange, D., Agras, W. S., & Dare, C. (2001). *Treatment manual for anorexia nervosa: A family-based approach.* New York, NY: Guilford.

Lock, J., Le Grange, D., Agras, W. S., Fitzpatrick, K. K., Jo, B., Accurso, E., . . . Stainer, M. (2015). Can adaptive treatment improve outcomes in family-based therapy for adolescents with anorexia nervosa? Feasibility and treatment effects of a multi-site treatment study. *Behaviour Research and Therapy, 73,* 90–95.

Loehlin, J. C. (1992). *Genes and environment in personality development.* Newbury Park, CA: Sage.

Loehlin, J., McFadden, D., Medland, S., & Martin, N. (2006). Population differences in finger-length ratios: Ethnicity or latitude? *Archives of Sexual Behavior, 35,* 739–742.

Loewenstein, R. J. (2018). Dissociation debates: Everything you know is wrong. *Dialogues in Clinical Neuroscience, 20*(3), 229–242.

Loftus, E. F. (2003). Make-believe memories. *American Psychologist, 58,* 867–873.

Loftus, E. F., Coan, J. A., & Pickrell, J. E. (1996). Manufacturing false memories using bits of reality. In L. Reder (Ed.), *Implicit memory and metacognition* (pp. 195–220). Mahwah, NJ: Erlbaum.

Loftus, E., & Davis, D. (2006). Recovered memories. *Annual Review of Clinical Psychology, 2,* 469–498.

Logan, C. (2009). Sexual deviance in females: Psychopathology and theory. In D. R. Laws & W. T. O'Donohue (Eds.), *Sexual deviance: Theory, assessment, and treatment* (2nd ed., pp. 486–507). New York, NY: Guilford.

Lombardi, V. C., Ruscetti, F. W., Gupta, J. D., Pfost, M. A., Hagen, K. S., Peterson, D. L., Ruscetti, S. K., Bagni, R. K., Petrow-Sadowski, C., Gold, B., Dean, M. Silverman, R. H., & Mikovits, J. A. (2009). Detection of an infectious retrovirus, XMRV, in blood cells of patients with chronic fatigue syndrome. *Science, 326*(5952), 585–589.

Lombardo, M. V., Chakrabarti, B., & Baron-Cohen, S. (2009). The amygdala in autism: not adapting to faces? *American Journal of Psychiatry, 166*(4), 395–397.

Lonczak, H. S. P., Abbott, R. D. P., Hawkins, J. D. P., Kosterman, R. P., & Catalano, R. F. P. (2002). Effects of the Seattle Social Development Project on sexual behavior, pregnancy, birth, and sexually transmitted disease outcomes by age 21 years. *Archives of Pediatrics & Adolescent Medicine, 156*(5), 438–447.

Loomans, E. M., Hofland, L., van der Stelt, O., van der Wal, M. F., Koot, H. M., Van den Bergh, B. R. H., & Vrijkotte, T. G. M. (2012). Caffeine intake during pregnancy and risk of problem behavior in 5- to 6-year-old children. *Pediatrics, 130*(2), e305–e313. doi: 10.1542/peds.2011-3361

López, S. R., & Guarnaccia, P. J. (2012). Cultural dimensions of psychopathology: The social world's impact on mental disorders. In J. E. Maddux & B. A. Winstead (Eds.), *Psychopathology: Foundations for a contemporary understanding* (pp. 45–68). New York, NY: Routledge.

LoPiccolo, J., Heiman, J. R., Hogan, D. R., & Roberts, C. W. (1985). Effectiveness of single therapists versus cotherapy teams in sex therapy. *Journal of Consulting and Clinical Psychology, 53*(3), 287–294.

Lord, C., & Bishop, S. L. (2010). Autism spectrum disorders. *Social Policy Report, 24*(2), 3–21.

Lord, C., Elsabbagh, M., Baird, G., & Veenstra-Vanderweele, J. (2018). Autism spectrum disorder. *The Lancet, 392*(10146), 508–520.

Lösel, F., & Schmucker, M. (2005). The effectiveness of treatment for sexual offenders: A comprehensive meta-analysis. *Journal of Experimental Criminology, 1,* 117–146.

Lotti, F., & Maggi, M. (2018). Sexual dysfunction and male infertility. *Nature Reviews Urology, 15*(5), 287–307. doi: 10.1038/nrurol.2018.20

Lovaas, O. I. (1977). *The autistic child: Language development through behavior modification.* New York, NY: Irvington.

Lovaas, O. I. (1987). Behavioral treatment and normal educational and intellectual functioning in young autistic children. *Journal of Consulting and Clinical Psychology, 55,* 3–9.

Lovaas, O. I., Berberich, J. P., Perloff, B. F., & Schaeffer, B. (1966). Acquisition of imitative speech by schizophrenic children. *Science, 151,* 705–707.

Lovallo, W. R. (2010). Cardiovascular responses to stress and disease outcomes: a test of the reactivity hypothesis. *Hypertension, 55*(4), 842–843.

Lovestone, S. (2012). Dementia: Alzheimer's disease. In M. G. Gelder, N. C. Andreasen, J. J. Lopez-Ibor, Jr., & J. R. Geddes (Eds.), *New Oxford textbook of psychiatry* (2nd ed., Vol. 1, pp. 333–343). New York, NY: Oxford University Press.

Lovibond, P. (2006). Fear and avoidance: An integrated expectancy model. In M. G. Craske, D. Hermans, & D. Vansteenwegen, *Fear and learning: From basic processes to clinical implications* (pp. 117–132). Washington, DC: American Psychological Association.

Löwe, B., & Gerloff, C. (2018). Functional somatic symptoms across cultures: Perceptual and health care issues. *Psychosomatic Medicine, 80*(5), 412–415. doi: 10.1097/PSY.0000000000000594

Lowe, M. R., Miller-Kovach, K., Frie, N., & Phelan, S. P. (1999). An initial evaluation of a commercial weight loss program: Short-term effects on weight, eating behavior, and mood. *Obesity Research, 7,* 51–59.

Lozano, A. M., Giacobbe, P., Hamani, C., Rizvi, S. J., Kennedy, S. H., Kolivakis, T. T., Debonnel, G., Sadikot, A. F., Lam, R. W., Howard, A. K., Ilcewicz-Klimek, M., Honey, C. R., & Mayberg, H. S. (2012). A multicenter pilot study of subcallosal cingulate area deep brain stimulation for treatment-resistant depression. *Journal of Neurosurgery, 116,* 15–22.

Lu, B., Nagappan, G., Guan, X., Nathan, P. J., & Wren, P. (2013). BDNF-based synaptic repair as a disease-modifying strategy for neurodegenerative diseases. *Nature Reviews Neuroscience, 14*(6), 401–416.

Lubinski, D. (2004). Introduction to the special section of cognitive abilities: 100 years after Spearman's (1904) "'General intelligence,' objectively determined and measured." *Journal of Personality and Social Psychology, 86,* 96–111.

Lubs, H. A., Stevenson, R. E., & Schwartz, C. E. (2012). Fragile X and X-linked intellectual disability: Four decades of discovery.

The American Journal of Human Genetics, 90(4), 579–590. doi: http://dx.doi.org/10.1016/j.ajhg.2012.02.018

Luby, J. L. (2012). Dispelling the "They'll Grow Out of It" myth: Implications for intervention. *American Journal of Psychiatry, 169,* 1128–1129.

Luby, J. L., Gaffrey, M. S., Tillman, R., April, L. M., & Belden, A. C. (2014). Trajectories of preschool disorders to full DSM depression at school age and early adolescence: Continuity of preschool depression. *American Journal of Psychiatry, 171,* 768–776.

Luby, J. L., Mrakotsky, C., Heffelfinger, A., Brown, K., Hessler, M., & Spitznagel, E. (2003). Modification of DSM-IV criteria for depressed preschool children. *American Journal of Psychiatry, 160,* 1169–1172.

Ludescher, B., Leitlein, G., Schaefer, J. E., Vanhoeffen, S., Baar, S., Machann, J., & Eschweiler, G. (2009). Changes of body composition in bulimia nervosa: Increased visceral fat and adrenal gland size. *Psychosomatic Medicine, 71*(1), 93–97.

Ludwig, A. M. (1995). *The price of greatness: Resolving the creativity and madness controversy.* New York, NY: Guilford Publications.

Ludwig, A., Brandsma, J., Wilbur, C., Bendfeldt, F., & Jameson, D. (1972). The objective study of a multiple personality. *Archives of General Psychiatry, 26,* 298–310.

Ludwig, D. S. (2012). Weight loss strategies for adolescents: A 14-year-old struggling to lose weight. *JAMA: Journal of the American Medical Association, 307,* 498–508.

Lugnegård, T., Hallerbäck, M. U., & Gillberg, C. (2012). Personality disorders and autism spectrum disorders: what are the connections? *Comprehensive Psychiatry, 53*(4), 333–340.

Lukiw, W. J. (2012). Amyloid beta (Ab) peptide modulators and other current treatment strategies for Alzheimer's disease (AD). *Expert Opinion on Emerging Drugs, 17*(1), 43–60.

Lundgren, J. D., Allison, K. C., & Stunkard, A. J. (Eds.)(2012). *Night eating syndrome: Research, assessment and treatment.* New York, NY: Guilford.

Lundh, L.-G., & Öst, L.-G. (1996). Recognition bias for critical faces in social phobics. *BRAT, 34,* 787–794.

Lundorff, M., Holmgren, H., Zachariae, R., Farver-Vestergaard, I., & O'Connor, M. (2017). Prevalence of prolonged grief disorder in adult bereavement: A systematic review and meta-analysis. *Journal of Affective Disorders, 212,* 138–149.

Lundstrom, B., Pauly, I., & Walinder, J. (1984). Outcome of sex reassignment surgery. *Acta Psychiatrica Scandinavica, 70,* 289–294.

Lurigio, A., & Harris, A. (2009). Mental illness, violence, and risk assessment: An evidence-based review. *Victims & Offenders, 4*(4), 341–347.

Lussier, P., & Piché, L. (2008). Frotteurism: Psychopathology and theory. In D. R. Laws & W. T. O'Donohue (Eds.), *Sexual deviance: Theory, assessment, and treatment* (2nd ed., pp. 131–149). New York, NY: Guilford.

Lussier, P., McCuish, E. C., & Cale, J. (2021). The construction of sexual offending as a social problem: A historical perspective. *Understanding Sexual Offending* (pp. 29–63). New York, NY: Springer.

Lutgendorf, S. K., & Andersen, B. L. (2015). Biobehavioral approaches to cancer progression and survival: Mechanisms and interventions. *American Psychologist, 70*(2), 186–197

Lutgendorf, S. K., Antoni, M. H., Ironson, G., Klimas, N., Kumar, M., Starr, K., & Schneiderman, N. (1997). Cognitive-behavioral stress management decreases dysphoric mood and herpes simplex virus-type 2 antibody titers in symptomatic HIV-seropositive gay men. *Journal of Consulting and Clinical Psychology, 65,* 31–43.

Lutgendorf, S., Costanzo, E., & Siegel, S. (2007). Psychosocial influences in oncology: An expanded model of biobehavioral mechanisms. In R. Ader, R. Glaser, N. Cohen, & M. Irwin (Eds.), *Psychoneuroimmunology* (4th ed., pp. 869–895). New York, NY: Academic Press.

Lydiard, R. B., Brawman-Mintzer, O., & Ballenger, J. C. (1996). Recent developments in the psychopharmacology of anxiety disorders. *Journal of Consulting & Clinical Psychology, 64,* 660–668.

Lyketsos, C. G., & Olin, J. (2002). Depression in Alzheimer's disease: Overview and treatment. *Biological Psychiatry, 52,* 243–252.

Lykken, D. T. (1957). A study of anxiety in the sociopathic personality. *Journal of Abnormal and Social Psychology, 55,* 6–10.

Lykken, D. T. (1982). Fearfulness: Its carefree charms and deadly risks. *Psychology Today, 16,* 20–28.

Lynam, D. R., & Vachon, D. D. (2012). Antisocial personality disorder in DSM-5: Missteps and missed opportunities. *Personality Disorders: Theory, Research, and Treatment, 3*(4), 483–495. doi: 10.1037/per0000006

Lynch, F. L., Dickerson, J. F., Clarke, G., Vitiello, B., Porta, G., Wagner, K. D., & Brent, D. (2011). Incremental cost-effectiveness of combined therapy vs medication only for youth with selective serotonin reuptake inhibitor-resistant depression: Treatment of SSRI-resistant depression in adolescents trial findings. *Archives of General Psychiatry, 68*(3), 253.

Lynch, H. F., & Rosenfeld, S. (2020). Institutional Review Board quality, private equity, and promoting ethical human subjects research. *Annals of Internal Medicine, 173*(7), 558–562.

Lynch, S. K., Turkheimer, E., D'Onofrio, B. M., Mendle, J., Emery, R. E., Slutske, W. S., & Martin, N. G. (2006). A genetically informed study of the association between harsh punishment and offspring behavioral problems. *Journal of Family Psychology, 20,* 190–198.

Lynch, T. R., & Cuper, P. F. (2012). Dialectical behavior therapy of borderline and other personality disorders. In T. A. Widiger (Ed.), *The Oxford handbook of personality disorders* (pp. 785–793). New York, NY: Oxford University Press.

Lynn, S. J., Lilienfeld, S. O., Merckelbach, H., Giesbach T., McNally, R. J., Loftus, E. F., Bruck, M., Garry, M., & Malaktaris, A. (2014). The trauma model of dissociation: Inconvenient truths and stubborn fictions. Comment on Dahlberg et al. (2012). *Psychological Bulletin, 140,* 896–910.

Lynn, S. J., Maxwell, R., Merckelbach, H., Lilienfeld, S. O., Kloet, D. V. H., & Miskovic, V. (2019). Dissociation and its disorders: Competing models, future directions, and a way forward. *Clinical Psychology Review, 73.* doi: 10.1016/j.cpr.2019.101755

Lyons, M. J., Eisen, S. A., Goldberg, J., True, W., Lin, N., Meyer, J. M., & Tsuang, M. T. (1998). A registry-based twin study of depression in men. *Archives of General Psychiatry, 55,* 468–472.

Lyons, M. J., True, W. R., Eisen, S. A., Goldberg, J., Meyer, J. M., Faraone, S. V., & Tsuang, M. (1995). Differential heritability of adult and juvenile antisocial traits. *Archives of General Psychiatry, 52,* 906–915.

Lyons, M. J., York, T. P., Franz, C. E., Grant, M. D., Eaves, L. J., Jacobson, K. C., & Kremen, W. S. (2009). Genes determine stability and the environment determines change in cognitive ability during 35 years of adulthood. *Psychological Science, 20*(9), 1146–1152.

Lyubomirsky, S. (2001). Why are some people happier than others? The role of cognitive and motivational processes in well-being. *American Psychologist, 56,* 239–249.

Ma, S., Hoang, M. A., Samet, J. M., Wang, J., Mei, C., Xu, X., & Stillman, F. A. (2008). Myths and attitudes that sustain smoking in China. *Journal of Health Communication, 13,* 654–666.

Maccaferri, G. E., Dunker-Scheuner, D., De Roten, Y., Despland, J.-N., Sachse, R., & Kramer, U. (2020). Psychotherapy of dependent personality disorder: The relationship of patient–therapist interactions to outcome. *Psychiatry, 83*(2), 179–194. doi: 10.1080/00332747.2019.1675376

Maccallum, F., & Bryant, R. A. (2011). Imagining the future in complicated grief. *Depression and Anxiety, 28*(8), 658–665.

Macdonald, P. T., Waldorf, D., Reinarman, C., & Murphy, S. (1988). Heavy cocaine use and sexual behavior. *Journal of Drug Issues, 18,* 437–455.

MacDougall, J. M., Dembroski, T. M., Dimsdale, J. E., & Hackett, T. P. (1985). Components of Type A, hostility, and anger-in: Further relationships to angiographic findings. *Health Psychology, 4*(2), 137–152.

Mace, C. J. (1992). Hysterical conversion II: A critique. *British Journal of Psychiatry, 161,* 378–389.

Macedo, M., Marques, A., & Queirós, C. (2015). Virtual reality in assessment and treatment of schizophrenia: a systematic review. *Jornal Brasileiro de Psiquiatria, 64*(1), 70–81.

Maciejewski, P., Zhang, B., Block, S., & Prigerson, H. (2007). An empirical examination of the stage theory of grief. *JAMA: Journal of the American Medical Association, 297*(7), 716–723.

MacKinnon, D. F., Zandi, P. P., Gershon, E. S., Nurnberger, J. I., & DePaulo, J. R. (2003). Association of rapid mood switching with panic disorder and familial panic risk in familial bipolar disorder. *American Journal of Psychiatry, 160,* 1696–1698.

MacLeod, C., & Mathews, A. M. (1991). Cognitive-experimental approaches to the emotional disorders. In P. R. Martin (Ed.), *Handbook of behavior therapy and psychological science: An integrative approach* (pp. 116–150). Elmsford, NY: Pergamon Press.

Macleod, J., Oakes, R., Copello, A., Crome, I., Egger, M., Hickman, M., & Davey Smith, G. (2004). Psychological and social sequelae of cannabis and other illicit drug use by young people: A systematic review of longitudinal, general population studies. *Lancet, 363,* 1579–1588.

Macy, J. T., Chassin, L., & Presson, C. C. (2012). The association between implicit and explicit attitudes toward smoking and support for tobacco control measures. *Nicotine & Tobacco Research.* doi: 10.1093/ntr/nts117

Madsen, K. M., Hviid, A., Vestergaard, M., Schendel, D., Wohlfahrt, J., Thorsen, P., & Melbye, M. (2002). A population-based study of measles, mumps, and rubella vaccination and autism. *New England Journal of Medicine, 347,* 1477–1482.

Maeng, L. Y., & Milad, M. R. (2015). Sex differences in anxiety disorders: Interactions between fear, stress, and gonadal hormones. *Hormones and Behavior, 76,* 106–117.

Magee, W. J., Eaton, W. W., Wittchen, H.-U., McGonagle, K. A., & Kessler, R. C. (1996). Agoraphobia, simple phobia, and social phobia in the National Comorbidity Survey. *Archives of General Psychiatry, 53,* 159–168.

Magne-Ingvar, U., Ojehagen, A., & Traskman-Bendz, L. (1992). The social network of people who attempt suicide. *Acta Psychiatrica Scandinavica, 86,* 153–158.

Magruder, K., Serpi, T., Kimerling, R., Kilbourne, A. M., Collins, J. F., Cypel, Y., Frayne, S. M., Furey, J., Huang, G. D., Gleason, T., Reinhard, M. J., Spiro, A., & Kang, H. (2015). Prevalence of posttraumatic stress disorder in Vietnam-era women veterans: The health of Vietnam-era Women's Study (HealthVIEWS). *JAMA Psychiatry, 72,* 1127–1134.

Maguire, G. A., Yeh, C. Y., & Ito, B. S. (2012). Overview of the diagnosis and treatment of stuttering. *Journal of Experimental & Clinical Medicine, 4*(2), 92–97.

Maher, B. A., & Maher, W. B. (1985a). Psychopathology: I. From ancient times to the eighteenth century. In G. A. Kimble & K. Schlesinger (Eds.), *Topics in the history of psychology* (pp. 251–294). Hillsdale, NJ: Erlbaum.

Maher, B. A., & Maher, W. B. (1985b). Psychopathology: II. From the eighteenth century to modern times. In G. A. Kimble & K. Schlesinger (Eds.), *Topics in the history of psychology* (pp. 295–329). Hillsdale, NJ: Erlbaum.

Maher, J. J. (1997). Exploring alcohol's effects on liver function. *Alcohol Health & Research World, 21,* 5–12.

Mahler, M. (1952). On childhood psychosis and schizophrenia: Autistic and symbiotic infantile psychosis. *Psychoanalytic Study of the Child, 7,* 286–305.

Mahmood, S. S., Levy, D., Vasan, R. S., & Wang, T. J. (2014). The Framingham Heart Study and the epidemiology of cardiovascular disease: A historical perspective. *The Lancet, 383*(9921), 999–1008. doi: 10.1016/S0140-6736(13)61752-3

Mahoney, D. F., Purtilo, R. B., Webbe, F. M., Alwan, M., Bharucha, A. J., Adlam, T. D., & Becker S. A. (2007). In-home monitoring of persons with dementia: Ethical guidelines for technology research and development. *Alzheimer's & Dementia, 3*(3), 217–226.

Mai, F. (2004). Somatization disorder: A practical review. *Canadian Journal of Psychiatry, 49,* 652–662.

Maier, S. F., & Seligman, M. E. (1976). Learned helplessness: Theory and evidence. *Journal of Experimental Psychology: General, 105*(1), 3–46.

Mainali, P., Rai, T., & Rutkofsky, I. H. (2020). From child abuse to developing borderline personality disorder into adulthood: Exploring the neuromorphological and epigenetic pathway. *Cureus, 12*(7).

Mainz, V., Schulte-Rüther, M., Fink, G. R., Herpertz-Dahlmann, B., & Konrad, K. (2012). Structural brain abnormalities in adolescent anorexia nervosa before and after weight recovery and associated hormonal changes. *Psychosomatic Medicine, 74,* 574–582.

Maj, M. (2008). Depression, bereavement and "understandable" intense sadness: Should the DSM-IV approach be revised? *American Journal of Psychiatry, 165*(11), 1373–1375.

Maj, M., Pirozzi, R., Magliano, L., & Bartoli, L. (2002). The prognostic significance of "switching" in patients with bipolar disorder: A 10-year prospective follow-up study. *American Journal of Psychiatry, 159,* 1711–1717.

Maj, M., Stein, D. J., Parker, G., Zimmerman, M., Fava, G. A., De Hert, M., … Wittchen, H. (2020). The clinical characterization of the adult patient with depression aimed at personalization of management. *World Psychiatry, 19*(3), 269–293. doi: 10.1002/wps.20771

Maki, P. M., & Henderson, V. W. (2012). Hormone therapy, dementia, and cognition: the Women's Health Initiative 10 years on. *Climacteric, 15*(3), 256–262.

Malatesta, V. J., & Adams, H. E. (2001). Sexual dysfunctions. In H. E. Adams & P. B. Sutker (Eds.), *Comprehensive handbook of psychopathology* (3rd ed., pp. 713–748). New York, NY: Kluwer Academic/Plenum.

Malavige, L. S., & Jayawickrema, S. (2015). Premature ejaculation and its management. *Sri Lanka Journal of Diabetes Endocrinology and Metabolism, 5*(1), 13–19.

Maldonado, J. R., Butler, L. D., & Spiegel, D. (1998). Treatments for dissociative disorders. In P. E. Nathan & J. M. Gorman (Eds.), *A guide to treatments that work.* New York, NY: Oxford University Press.

Maletzky, B. (2002). The paraphilias: Research and treatment. In P. E. Nathan & J. M. Gorman (Eds.), *A guide to treatments that work* (2nd ed., pp. 525–557). New York, NY: Oxford University Press.

Maletzky, B. M. (1991). *Treating the sexual offender.* Newbury Park, CA: Sage.

Mallan, K. M., Lipp, O. V., & Cochrane B. (2013). Slithering snakes, angry men and out-group members: what and whom are we evolved to fear? Cogn Emot. 27(7):1168–80. doi: 10.1080/02699931.2013.778195.

Malm, H., Sourander, A., Gissler, M., Gyllenberg, D., Hinkka-Yli-Salomäki, S., McKeague, I. W., Artama, M., & Brown, A. S. (2015). Pregnancy complications following prenatal exposure to SSRIs or maternal psychiatric disorders: Results from population-based national register data. *American Journal of Psychiatry.* doi: 10.1176/appi.ajp.2015.14121575

Malow, B. A., Adkins, K. W., Reynolds, A., Weiss, S. K., Loh, A., Fawkes, D., Katz, T., Goldman, S. E., Madduri, N., & Hundley, R. (2014). Parent-based sleep education for children with autism spectrum disorders. *Journal of autism and developmental disorders, 44*(1), 216–228.

Mamedova, S., Stephens, M., Liao, Y. S., J., & Sirma, P. (2021). *2012–2016 Program for International Student Assessment Young Adult Follow-up Study (PISA YAFS): How reading and mathematics performance at age 15 relate to literacy and numeracy skills and education, workforce, and life outcomes at age 19 (NCES 2021-029).* Washington, D.C.: National Center for Educaiton Statistics. Retrieved from https://nces.ed.gov /pubsearch/pubsinfo.asp?pubid=2021029

Manber, R., Edinger, J. D., Gress, J. L., San Pedro-Salcedo, M. G., Kuo, T. F., & Kalista, T. (2008). Cognitive behavioral therapy for insomnia enhances depression outcome in patients with comorbid major depressive disorder and insomnia. *Sleep, 31*(4), 489–495.

Mancuso, S., Knoesen, N., & Castle, D. J. (2010). Delusional vs. nondelusional body dysmorphic disorder. *Comprehensive Psychiatry, 51*(2), 177–182.

Mandalos, G. E., & Szarek, B. L. (1990). Dose-related paranoid reaction associated with fluoxetine. *Journal of Nervous and Mental Disease, 178*(1), 57–58.

Mandell, D. S., Thompson, W. W., Weintraub, E. S., DeStefano, F., & Blank, M. B. (2005). Trends in Diagnosis Rates for Autism and ADHD at Hospital Discharge in the Context of Other Psychiatric Diagnoses. *Psychiatric Services, 56*(1), 56–62. doi: 10.1176/appi.ps.56.1.56

Maness, C., & Trotti, L. M. (2021). Idiopathec hypersomnia. In E. H. During & C. A. Kushida (Eds.), *Clinical sleep medicine: A comprehensive guide for mental health and other medical professionals* (pp. 129–146). Washington, D.C.: American Psychiatric Association Publishing.

Manicavasagar, V., Marnane, C., Pini, S., Abelli, M., Rees, S., Eapen, V., & Silove, D. (2010). Adult separation anxiety disorder: A disorder comes of age. *Current Psychiatry Reports, 12*(4), 290–297. doi: 10.1007 /s11920-010-0131-9

Mann, J. J., Brent, D. A., & Arango, V. (2001). The neurobiology and genetics of suicide and attempted suicide: a focus on the serotonergic system. *Neuropsychopharmacology, 24*(5), 467–477.

Mann, J. J., Malone, K. M., Diehl, D. J., Perel, J., Cooper, T. B., & Mintun, M. A. (1996). Demonstration in vivo of reduced serotonin responsivity in the brain of untreated depressed patients. *American Journal of Psychiatry, 153,* 174–182.

Mann, J. J., Waternaux, C., Haas, G. L., & Malone, K. M. (1999). Toward a clinical model of suicidal behavior in psychiatric patients. *American Journal of Psychiatry, 156*(2), 181–189.

Mann, J., Apter, A., Bertolote, J., Beautrais, A., Currier, D., Haas, A., & Hendin, H. (2005). Suicide prevention strategies: A systematic review. *JAMA: Journal of the American Medical Association, 294,* 2064–2074.

Mann, K., Klingler, T., Noe, S., Röschke, J., Müller, S., & Benkert, O. (1996). Effects of yohimbine on sexual experiences and nocturnal penile tumescence and rigidity in erectile dysfunction. *Archives of Sexual Behavior, 25,* 1–16.

Mann, T., Tomiyama, A. J., & Ward, A. (2015). Promoting Public Health in the Context of the "Obesity Epidemic" False Starts and Promising New Directions. *Perspectives on Psychological Science, 10*(6), 706–710.

Manne, S. L., & Ostroff, J. S. (2008). *Coping with breast cancer: A couples-focused group intervention: Therapist guide.* New York, NY: Oxford University Press.

Manni, R., Ratti, M. T., & Tartara, A. (1997). Nocturnal eating: Prevalence and features in 120 insomniac referrals. *Sleep, 20,* 734–738.

Mannino, D. M., Klevens, R. M., & Flanders, W. D. (1994). Cigarette smoking: An independent risk factor for impotence? *American Journal of Epidemiology, 140,* 1003–1008.

Manson, J. E., Willett, W. C., Stampfer, M. J., Colditz, G. A., Hunter, D. J., Hankinson, S. E., & Speizer, F. E. (1995). Body weight and mortality among women. *New England Journal of Medicine, 333,* 677–685.

Manson, S. M., & Good, B. J. (1993, January). *Cultural considerations in the diagnosis of DSM-IV mood disorders.* Cultural proposals and supporting papers for DSM-IV. Submitted to the DSM-IV Task Force by the Steering Committee, NIMH-Sponsored Group on Culture and Diagnosis.

Månsson, K. N. T., Carlbring, P., Frick, A., Engman, J., Olsson, C. J., Bodlund, O., Furmark, T., & Andersson, G. (2013). Altered neural correlates of affective processing after internet-delivered cognitive behavior therapy for social anxiety disorder. *Psychiatry Research, 214*(3), 229–237.

Mantile, F., & Prisco, A. (2020). Vaccination against β-amyloid as a strategy for the prevention of Alzheimer's disease. *Biology, 9*(12), 425.

Mantovani, A., Pavlicova, M., Avery, D., Nahas, Z., McDonald, W. M., Wajdik, C. D., & Lisanby, S. H. (2012). Long-term efficacy of repeated daily prefrontal transcranial magnetic stimulation (TMS) in treatment- resistant depression. *Depression and Anxiety, 29*(10), 883–890.

Manuel, J. K., Houck, J. M., & Moyers, T. B. (2012). The impact of significant others in motivational enhancement therapy: Findings from Project MATCH. *Behavioural and cognitive psychotherapy, 40*(3), 297.

Marangell, L., Rush, A., George, M., Sackheim, H., Johnson, C, Husain, M., & Lisanby, S. H. (2002). Vagus nerve stimulation (VNS) for major depressive episodes: One year outcomes. *Biological Psychiatry, 51,* 280–287.

March, J. S., & Vitiello, B. (2009). Clinical messages from the Treatment for Adolescents with Depression Study (TADS). *American Journal of Psychiatry, 166*(10), 1118–1123.

Marcolini, E., & Tolchin, B. (2021). Functional seizures. *Emergency Medicine Clinics of North America, 39*(1), 123–132. doi: 10.1016/j.emc.2020.09.007

Marcus, E. (2010). *Why suicide? Questions and answers about suicide, suicide prevention and coping with the suicide of someone you Know.* New York, NY: Harper Collins.

Marcus, S. C., & Olfson, M. (2010). National trends in the treatment for depression from 1998 to 2007. *Archives of General Psychiatry, 67*(12), 1265–1273.

Maremmani, I., Pacini, M., Pani, P. P., Popovic, D., Romano, A., Maremmani, A. G. I., & Perugi, G. (2009). Use of street methadone in Italian heroin addicts presenting for opioid agonist treatment. *Journal of Addictive Diseases, 28*(4), 382–388.

Maresova, P., Hruska, J., Klimova, B., Barakovic, S., & Krejcar, O. (2020). Activities of daily living and associated costs in the most widespread neurodegenerative diseases: A systematic review. *Clinical Interventions in Aging, 15,* 1841.

Marinelli, M., & McCutcheon, J. E. (2014). Heterogeneity of dopamine neuron activity across traits and states. Neuroscience, 282, 176–197. doi:10.1016/j.neuroscience.2014.07.034

Markova, V., Sandal, G. M., & Guribye, E. (2020). What do immigrants from various cultures think is the best way to cope with depression? Introducing the cross-cultural coping inventory. *Frontiers in Psychology, 11*, 1599.

Marks, I. M. (1969). *Fears and phobias.* New York, NY: Academic.

Marks, I. M. (1985). Behavioural treatment of social phobia. *Psychopharmacology Bulletin, 21*, 615–618.

Marlatt, G. A., & Donovan, D. M. (2005). *Relapse prevention: Maintenance strategies in the treatment of addictive behaviors.* New York, NY: Guilford.

Marlatt, G. A., & Gordon, J. R. (1985). *Relapse prevention: Maintenance strategies in the treatment of addictive behaviors.* New York, NY: Guilford.

Marlatt, G. A., Larimer, M. E., Baer, J. S., & Quigley, L. A. (1993). Harm reduction for alcohol problems: Moving beyond the controlled drinking controversy. *Behavior Therapy, 24*, 461–504.

Marmar, C. R., Schlenger, W., Henn-Haase, C., Qian, M., Purchia, E., Li, M., Corry, N., Williams, C. S., Ho, C.-L., Horesh, D., Karstoft, K.-I., Shalev, A., & Kulka,R. A. (2015). Course of posttraumatic stress disorder 40 years after the Vietnam war. Findings from the National Vietnam Veterans Longitudinal Study. *JAMA Psychiatry, 72*, 875–881.

Marmot, M. G., & Syme, S. L. (1976). Acculturation and coronary heart disease in Japanese Americans. *American Journal of Epidemiology, 104*, 225–247.

Marques, A., Roquet, D., Matar, E., Taylor, N. L., Pereira, B., O'Callaghan, C., & Lewis, S. J. (in press). Limbic hypoconnectivity in idiopathic REM sleep behaviour disorder with impulse control disorders. *Journal of Neurology*, 1–10.

Marques, J. K., Wiederanders, M., Day, D. M., Nelson, C., & van Ommeren, A. (2005). Effects of a relapse prevention program on sexual recidivism: Final results from California's Sex Offender Treatment and Evaluation Project (SOTEP). *Sexual Abuse: A Journal of Research and Treatment, 17*(1), 79–107.

Marques, L., Alegria, M., Becker, A. E., Chen, C.-N., Fang, A., Chosak, A., & Diniz, J. B. (2011). Comparative prevalence, correlates of impairment, and service utilization for eating disorders across US ethnic groups: Implications for reducing ethnic disparities in health care access for eating disorders. *International Journal of Eating Disorders, 44*(5), 412–420.

Marques, M. M., De Gucht, V. Gouveia, M. J., Leal, I., & Maes, S. (2015). Differential effects of behavioral interventions with a graded physical activity componenet in patients suffering from chronic fatigue (syndrome): An updated systematic review and meta-analysis. *Clinical Psychology Review, 40*, 123–137.

Marras, C., Beck, J. C., Bower, J. H., Roberts, E., Ritz, B., Ross, G. W., … C. M. Tanner on behalf of the Parkinson's Foundation P4 Group. (2018). Prevalence of Parkinson's disease across North America. *npj Parkinson's Disease, 4*(1), 21. doi: 10.1038/s41531-018-0058-0

Marsac, M. L., Kassam-Adams, N., Hildenbrand, A. K., Kohser, K. L., & Winston, F. K. (2011). After the injury: Initial evaluation of a web-based intervention for parents of injured children. *Health Education Research, 26*(1), 1–12.

Marsh, L., & Margolis, R. L. (2009). Neuropsychiatric aspects of movement disorders. In B. J. Sadock, V. A. Sadock, & P. Ruiz (Eds.), *Kaplan & Sadock's comprehensive textbook of psychiatry* (9th ed., Vol. I, pp. 481–503). Philadelphia, PA: Lippincott Williams & Wilkins.

Marsh, R., Horga, G., Wang, Z., Wang, P., Klahr, K. W., Berner, L. A., & Peterson, B. S. (2011). An fMRI study of self-regulatory control and conflict resolution in adolescents with bulimia nervosa. *American Journal of Psychiatry, 168*, 1210–1220.

Marshall, W. L. (1997). Pedophilia: Psychopathology and theory. In D. R. Laws & W. O'Donohue (Eds.), *Sexual deviance: Theory, assessment and treatment* (pp. 152–174). New York, NY: Guilford.

Marshall, W. L., & Barbaree, H. E. (1990). An integrated theory of the etiology of sexual offending. In W. L. Marshall, D. R. Laws, & H. E. Barbaree (Eds.), *Handbook of sexual assault: Issues, theories, and treatment of the offender* (pp. 257–725). New York, NY: Plenum.

Marshall, W. L., Barbaree, H. E., & Christophe, D. (1986). Sexual offenders against female children: Sexual preferences for age of victims and type of behavior. *Canadian Journal of Behavioral Science, 18*, 424–439.

Marteau, T. M., Hollands, G. J., & Fletcher, P. C. (2012). Changing human behavior to prevent disease: The importance of targeting automatic processes. *Science, 337*(6101), 1492–1495.

Marten, P. A., Brown, T. A., Barlow, D. H., Borkovec, T. D., Shear, M. K., & Lydiard, R. B. (1993). Evaluation of the ratings comprising the associated symptom criterion of DSM-III-R generalized anxiety disorder. *Journal of Nervous and Mental Disease, 181*(11), 676–682.

Martens, E. J., de Jonge, P., Na, B., Cohen, B. E., Lett, H., & Whooley, M. A. (2010). Scared to death? Generalized anxiety disorder and cardiovascular events in patients with stable coronary heart disease. *Archives of General Psychiatry, 67*, 750–758.

Martensson, B., Petterson, A., Berglund,L., & Ekselius, L. (2015). Bright white light therapy in depression: A critical review of the evidence. *Journal of Affective Disorders, 182*, 1–7.

Martin, I. (1983). Human classical conditioning. In A. Gale & J. A. Edward (Eds.), *Physiological correlates of human behavior: Vol. 2. Attention and performance.* London, UK: Academic Press.

Martin, J., O'Donovan, M. C., Thapar, A., Langley, K., & Williams, N. (2015). The relative contribution of common and rare genetic variants to ADHD. *Transl Psychiatry, 5*, e506. doi: 10.1038/tp.2015.5

Martin, P. R., & MacLeod, C. (2009). Behavioral management of headache triggers: avoidance of triggers is an inadequate strategy. *Clinical Psychology Review, 29*, 483–495.

Martin, P. R., Reece, J., Callan, M., MacLeod, C., Kaur, A., Gregg, K., & Goadsby, P. J. (2014). Behaviorl management of the triggers of recurrent headache: A randomized controlled trial. *Behavioural Research and Therapy, 61*, 1–11.

Martin, S. D., Martin, E., Rai, S. S., Richardson, M. A., & Royall, R. (2001). Brain blood flow changes in depressed patients treated with interpersonal psychotherapy or venlafaxine hydrochloride. *Archives of General Psychiatry, 58*, 641–648.

Martin, S. L., Ramey, C. T., & Ramey, S. L. (1990). The prevention of intellectual impairment in children of impoverished families: Findings of a randomized trial of educational daycare. *American Journal of Public Health, 80*, 844–847.

Martinez, A. G., Piff, P. K., Mendoza-Denton, R., & Hinshaw, S. P. (2011). The power of a label: Mental illness diagnoses, ascribed humanity, and social rejection. *Journal of Social and Clinical Psychology, 30*(1), 1–23. doi: 10.1521/jscp.2011.30.1.1

Martinez, A. P., Dorahy, M. J., Nesbit, A., Palmer, R., & Middleton, W. (2020). Delusional beliefs and their characteristics: A comparative study between dissociative identity disorder and schizophrenia spectrum disorders. *Journal of Psychiatric Research, 131*, 263–268. doi: 10.1016/j.jpsychires.2020.09.015

Martinez, M. A., & Craighead, L. W. (2015). Toward Person (ality)-Centered Treatment: How Consideration of Personality and Individual Differences in Anorexia Nervosa May Improve Treatment Outcome. *Clinical Psychology: Science and Practice, 22*(3), 296–314.

Martínez-Fernández, E., Aragón-Poce, F., Márquez-Espinós, C., Pérez-Pérez, A., Pérez-Bustamante, F., & Torres-Morera, L. (2002). The history of opiates. In J. C. Diz, A. Franco, D. R. Bacon, J. Rupreht, & J. Alvarez (Eds.), *The history of anesthesia: Proceedings of the fifth International Symposium on the History of Anesthesia, Santiago, Spain, September 19–23, 2001* (pp. 75–77). Amsterdam, The Netherlands: Elsevier Science.

Martino, F., Gammino, L., Sanza, M., Berardi, D., Pacetti, M., Sanniti, A., … Menchetti, M. (2020). Impulsiveness and emotional dysregulation as stable features in borderline personality disorder outpatients over time. *Journal of Nervous and Mental Disease, 208*(9), 715–720.

Martin-Pichora, A. L., & Antony, M. M. (2011). Successful treatment of olfactory reference syndrome with cognitive behavioral therapy: A case study. *Cognitive and Behavioral Practice, 18,* 545–554.

Martins, S. S., & Gorelick, D. A. (2011). Conditional substance abuse and dependence by diagnosis of mood or anxiety disorder or schizophrenia in the US population. *Drug and Alcohol Dependence, 119*(1), 28–36.

Marx, W., Lane, M., Hockey, M., Aslam, H., Berk, M., Walder, K., … Jacka, F. N. (2021). Diet and depression: Exploring the biological mechanisms of action. *Molecular Psychiatry, 26*(1), 134–150. doi: 10.1038/s41380-020-00925-x

Maser, J. D. (1985). List of phobias. In A. H. Tuma & J. D. Maser (Eds.), *Anxiety and the anxiety disorders.* Hillsdale, NJ: Erlbaum.

Masia-Warner, C., Klein, R. G., Dent, H. C., Fisher, P. H., Alvir, J., Albano, A., & Guardino, M. (2005). School-based intervention for adolescents with social anxiety disorder: Results of a controlled study. *Journal of Abnormal Child Psychology,* 33(6), 707–722. doi: 10.1007/s10802-005-7649-z

Mason, F. L. (1997). Fetishism: Psychopathology and theory. In D. R. Laws & W. O'Donohue (Eds.), *Sexual deviance: Theory, assessment and treatment* (pp. 75–91). New York, NY: Guilford.

Mason, T. B., Lavender, J. M., Wonderlich, S. A., Crosby, R. D., Engel, S. G., Strauman, T. J., … Peterson, C. B. (2016). Self-discrepancy and eating disorder symptoms across eating disorder diagnostic groups. *European Eating Disorders Review, 24*(6), 541–545. doi: 10.1002/erv.2483

Master, S. L., Eisenberger, N. I., Taylor, S. E., Naliboff, B. D., Shirinyan, D., & Lieberman, M. D. (2009). A picture's worth: Partner photographs reduce experimentally induced pain. *Psychological Science, 20,* 1316–1318.

Masters, W. H., & Johnson, V. E. (1966). *Human sexual response.* Boston, MA: Little, Brown.

Masters, W. H., & Johnson, V. E. (1970). *Human sexual inadequacy.* Boston, MA: Little, Brown.

Masuda, A., Qina'au, J., Juberg, M., & Martin, T. (2020). Bias in the *Diagnostic and Statistical Manual 5* and psychopathology. In L. T. Benuto, M. P. Duckworth, A. Masuda, & W. O'Donohue (Eds.), *Prejudice, stigma, privilege, and oppression: A behavioral health handbook* (pp. 215–234). Cham, Switzerland: Springer.

Mataix-Cols, D., Boman, M., Monzani, B., Rück, C., Serlachius, E., Långström, N., & Lichtenstein, P. (2013). Population-based, multigenerational family clustering study of obsessive-compulsive disorder. *JAMA psychiatry, 70,* 709–717.

Mataix-Cols, D., Frost, R. O., Pertusa, A., Clark, L. A., Saxena, S., Leckman, J. F., & Wilhelm, S. (2010). Hoarding disorder: A new diagnosis for DSM-V? *Depression and Anxiety, 27*(6), 556–572. doi: 10.1002/da.20693

Mathes, B. M., Timpano, K. R., Raines, A. M., & Schmidt, N. B. (2020). Attachment theory and hoarding disorder: A review and theoretical integration. *Behaviour Research and Therapy, 125.* doi: 10.1016/j.brat.2019.103549

Matheson, S. L., Vijayan, H., Dickson, H., Shepherd, A. M., Carr, V. J., & Laurens, K. R. (2013). Systematic meta-analysis of childhood social withdrawal in schizophrenia, and comparison with data from at-risk children aged 9–14 years. *Journal of Psychiatric Research, 47*(8), 1061–1068.

Mathew, S. J., & Hoffman, E. J. (2009). Pharmacotherapy for generalized anxiety disorder. In M. M. Antony & M. B. Stein (Eds.), *Oxford handbook of anxiety and related disorders* (pp. 350–363). New York, NY: Oxford University Press.

Mathews, C. A. (2009). Phenomenology of obsessive-compulsive disorder. In M. M. Antony & M. B. Stein (Eds.), *Oxford handbook of anxiety and related disorders.* Oxford, UK: Oxford University Press.

Matsubayashi, T., Sawada, Y., & Ueda, M. (2012). Natural disasters and suicide: Evidence from Japan. *Social Science & Medicine, 82,* 126–133.

Matsumoto, D. (1996). *Culture and psychology.* Pacific Grove, CA: Brooks/Cole.

Matthews, K. (2005). Psychological perspectives on the development of coronary heart disease. *American Psychologist, 60,* 780–796.

Matthews, K. A. (1988). Coronary heart disease and Type A behaviors: Update on and alternative to the Booth-Kewley and Friedman (1987) quantitative review. *Psychological Bulletin, 104*(3), 373–380.

Matthews, K. A. (2013). Matters of the heart: Advancing psychological perspectives on cardiovascular diseases. *Perspectives on Psychological Science, 8,* 676–678.

Matthews, K. A., Schott, L. L., Bromberger, J., Cyranowski, J., Everson-Rose, S. A., & Sowers, M. F. (2007). Associations between depressive symptoms and inflammatory/hemostatic markers in women during the menopausal transition. *Psychosomatic Medicine, 69,* 124–130.

Matthews-Ewald, M. R., Zullig, K. J., & Ward, R. M. (2014). Sexual orientation and disordered eating behaviors among self-identified male and female college students. *Eating Behaviors, 15*(3), 441–444.

Mattis, S. G., & Ollendick, T. H. (2002). Nonclinical panic attacks in late adolescence prevalence and associated psychopathology. *Journal of Anxiety Disorders, 16,* 351–367.

Matza, L. S., Revicki, D. A., Davidson, J. R., & Stewart, J. W. (2003). Depression with atypical features in the National Comorbidity Survey: Classification, description, and consequences. *Archives of General Psychiatry, 60,* 817–826.

Mauler, B. I., Hamm, A. O., Weike, A. I., & Tuschen-Caffier, B. (2006). Affect regulation and food intake in bulimia nervosa: Emotional responding to food cues after deprivation and subsequent eating. *Journal of Abnormal Psychology, 115,* 567–579.

Maust, D., Cristancho, M., Gray, L., Rushing, S., Tjoa, C., & Thase, M. E. (2012). *Psychiatric rating scales.* In T. E. Schlaepfer & C. B. Nemeroff (eds.). Handbook of Clinical Neurology (pp. 227–237) Amsterdam: Elsevier

Maxwell, J. C., & Brecht, M.-L. (2011). Methamphetamine: Here we go again? *Addictive Behaviors, 36*(12), 1168–1173. doi: 10.1016/j.addbeh.2011.07.017

May, D. G., Shaffer, V. N., & Yoon, K. L. (2020). Treatment of double depression: A meta-analysis. *Psychiatry Research, 291.* doi: 10.1016/j.psychres.2020.113262

Mayberg, H., Lozano, A., Voon, V., McNeely, H., Seminowicz, D., Hanani, C., & Kennedy, S. H. (2005). Deep brain stimulation for treatment resistant depression. *Neuron, 45,* 651–660.

Mayer, K. H., Nelson, L., Hightow-Weidman, L., Mimiaga, M. J., Mena, L., Reisner, S., … Sullivan, P. S. (2021). The persistent and evolving HIV epidemic in American men who have sex with men. *The Lancet, 397*(10279), 1116–1126. doi: 10.1016/S0140-6736(21)00321-4

Mayes, S. D., Castagna, P. J., & Waschbusch, D. A. (2020). Sex differences in externalizing and internalizing symptoms in ADHD, autism, and general population samples. *Journal of Psychopathology and Behavioral Assessment*, 1–8.

Mayou, R., Phil, M., Kirmayer, L., Simon, G., Kroenke, G., & Sharpe, M. (2005). Somato- form disorders: Time for a new approach in DSM-V. *American Journal of Psychiatry, 162,* 847–855.

Mayville, S., Katz, R. C., Gipson, M. T., & Cabral, K. (1999). Assessing the prevalence of body dysmorphic disorder in an ethnically diverse group of adolescents. *Journal of Child and Family Studies, 8*(3), 357–362.

Mazure, C. M. (1998). Life stressors as risk factors in depression. *Clinical Psychology: Science and Practice, 5*(3), 291–313.

Mazure, C. M., Bruce, M. L., Maciejewski, P. K., & Jacobs, S. C. (2000). Adverse life events and cognitive-personality characteristics in the prediction of major depression and antidepressant response. *American Journal of Psychiatry, 157*(6), 896–903.

Mbata, G., & Chukwuka, J. (2012). Obstructive sleep apnea hypopnea syndrome. *Annals of Medical and Health Sciences Research, 2*(1), 74–77.

McCabe, M., & Wauchope, M. (2005). Behavioral characteristics of men accused of rape: Evidence for different types of rapists. *Archives of Sexual Behavior, 34,* 241–253.

McCabe, R., Antony, M. M., Summerfeldt, L. J., Liss, A., & Swinson, R. P. (2003). Preliminary examination of the relationship between anxiety disorders in adults and self-reported history of teasing or bullying experiences. *Cognitive Behaviour Therapy, 32,* 187–193.

McCabe, S. E., Arterberry, B. J., Dickinson, K., Evans-Polce, R. J., Ford, J. A., Ryan, J. E., & Schepis, T. S. (2021). Assessment of changes in alcohol and marijuana abstinence, co-use, and use disorders among U.S. young adults from 2002 to 2018. *JAMA Pediatrics, 175*(1), 64–72.

McCabe, S. E., West, B. T., Teter, C. J., & Boyd, C. J. (2012). Co-ingestion of prescription opioids and other drugs among high school seniors: Results from a national study. *Drug and Alcohol Dependence, 126*(1–2), 65–70. doi: http://dx.doi.org/10.1016/j.drugalcdep.2012.04.017

McCaffery, J. M., Papandonatos, G. D., Stanton, C., Lloyd-Richardson, E. E., & Niaura, R. (2008). Depressive symptoms and cigarette smoking in twins from the national longitudinal study of adolescent health. *Health Psychology, 27* (3, Supplement 1), S207–S215.

McCaffrey, R. J., Lynch, J. K., & Westervelt, H. J. (2011). Clinical neuropsychology. In D. H. Barlow (Ed.), *Oxford handbook of clinical psychology* (pp. 680–700). New York, NY: Oxford University.

McCann, D., Barrett, A., Cooper, A., Crumpler, D., Dalen, L., Grimshaw, K., & Prince, E. (2007). Food additives and hyperactive behaviour in 3-year-old and 8/9-year-old children in the community: A randomised, double-blinded, placebo-controlled trial. *The Lancet, 370*(9598), 1560–1567.

McCann, U. D., & Ricaurte, G. A. (2009). Amphetamine (or amphetamine-like)-related disorders. In B. J. Sadock, V. A. Sadock, & P. Ruiz (Eds.), *Kaplan & Sadock's comprehensive textbook of psychiatry* (9th ed., Vol. I, pp. 1288–1296). Philadelphia, PA: Lippincott Williams & Wilkins.

McCann, U. D., Sgambati, F. P., Schwartz, A. R., & Ricaurte, G. A. (2009). Sleep apnea in young abstinent recreational MDMA ("ecstasy") consumers. *Neurology, 73*(23), 2011–2017.

McClam, T. D., Marano, C. M., Rosenberg, P. B., & Lyketsos, C. G. (2015). Interventions for neuropsychiatric symptoms in neurocognitive impairment due to Alzheimer's disease: A Review of the Literature. *Harvard Review of Psychiatry, 23*(5), 377–393.

McClearn, G. E., Johansson, B., Berg, S., Pedersen, N. L., Ahern, F., Petrill, S. A., & Plomin, R. (1997). Substantial genetic influence on cognitive abilities in twins 80 or more years old. *Science, 276,* 1560–1563.

McClellan, J., & King, M. C. (2010). Genomic analysis of mental illness: A changing landscape. *JAMA: Journal of the American Medical Association, 303*(24), 2523–2524.

McClellan, J., Kowatch, R., & Findling, R. L. (2007). Practice parameter for the assessment and treatment of children and adolescents with bipolar disorder. *Journal of the American Academy of Child and Adolescent Psychiatry, 46*(1), 107–125.

McCloskey, M. S., Noblett, K. L., Deffenbacher, J. L., Gollan, J. K., & Coccaro, E. F. (2008). Cognitive-behavioral therapy for intermittent explosive disorder: A pilot randomized clinical trial. *Journal of Consulting and Clinical Psychology, 76*(5), 876–886.

McClure, M., Harvey, P., Goodman, M., Triebwasser, J., New, A., Koenigsberg, H., & Siever, L. J. (2010). Pergolide treatment of cognitive deficits associated with schizotypal personality disorder: Continued evidence of the importance of the dopamine system in the schizophrenia spectrum. *Neuropsychopharmacology, 35,* 1356–1362.

McCrady, B. S., & Tonigan, J. S. (2015). Recent research into the Twelve-Step programs. In R. K. Ries, D. A. Fiellin, S. C. Miller, & R. Saitz (Eds.), *The ASAM principles of addiction medicine* (5th ed., pp. 1043–1059). New York, NY: Wolters Kluwer.

McCrady, B. S. (2014). Alcohol use disorders. In D. H. Barlow (Ed.), *Clinical handbook of psychological disorders: A step-by-step treatment manual.* New York, NY: Guilford.

McCrae, R. R. (2002). NEO PI-R data from 36 cultures: Further intercultural comparisons. In R. McCrae & J. Allik (Eds.), *The five-factor model of personality across cultures* (pp. 105–126). New York, NY: Kluwer Academic/Plenum.

McCrae, R., & Costa P., Jr., (2008). The five-factor theory of personality. In O. P. John, R. W. Robins, & L. A. Pervin (Eds.), *Handbook of personality: Theory and research* (3rd ed., pp. 159–181). New York, NY: Guilford.

McCullough, J. P., Jr. (2000). *Treatment for chronic depression: Cognitive Behavioral Analysis System of Psychotherapy (CBASP).* New York, NY: Guilford.

McCullough, J. P., Jr. (in press). Introduction and state-of-the-art issues for CBASP. In M. Belz, F. Caspar, & E. Schramm (Eds.), *CBASP in Practice: Basic concepts and new developments.* Munich, Germany: Elsevier.

McCullough, J. P., Jr., Klein, D. N., Keller, M. B., Holzer, C. E., III, Davis, S. M., Kornstein, S. G., & Harrison, W. M. (2000). Comparison of DSM-III-R chronic major depression and major depression superimposed on dysthymia (double depression): Validity of the distinction. *Journal of Abnormal Psychology, 109,* 419–427.

McEwen, B. S., & Karatsoreos, I. N. (2015). Sleep deprivation and circadian disruption: stress, allostasis, and allostatic load. *Sleep medicine clinics, 10*(1), 1–10. McEwen BS. The Brain on Stress: Toward an Integrative Approach to Brain, Body, and Behavior. *Perspectives on Psychological Science.* 2013;8(6):673–675. doi:10.1177/1745691613506907

McEwen, B. S. (2020). Hormones and behavior and the integration of brain-body science. *Hormones and Behavior, 119.* doi: 10.1016/j.yhbeh.2019.104619

McEwen, B. S., & Magarinos, A. M. (2004). Does stress damage the brain? In J. M. Gorman,

Fear and anxiety: The benefits of translational research (pp. 23–45). Washington, DC: American Psychiatric Publishing.

McFadden, D., Loehlin, J., Breedlove, S., Lippa, R., Manning, J., & Rahman, Q. (2005). A reanalysis of five studies on sexual orientation and the relative length of the 2nd and 4th fingers (the 2D: 4D ratio). *Archives of Sexual Behavior, 34,* 341–356.

McGee, G. G., Morrier, M. J., & Daly, T. (1999). An incidental teaching approach to early intervention for toddlers with autism. *Research and Practice for Persons with Severe Disabilities, 24*(3), 133–146.

McGirr, A., Paris, J., Lesage, A., Renaud, J., & Turecki, G. (2009). An examination of DSM-IV borderline personality disorder symptoms and risk for death by suicide: A psychological autopsy study. *Canadian Journal of Psychiatry, 54*(2), 87.

McGlinchey, E., McCallion, P., & McCarron, M. (2020). Down syndrome and dementia: Advances in the field. *Current Opinion in Psychiatry, 33*(3), 278–283.

McGoldrick, M., Loonan, R., & Wohlsifer, D. (2007). Sexuality and culture. In S. R. Leiblum (Ed.), *Principles and practice of sex therapy* (4th ed., pp. 416–441). New York, NY: Guilford.

McGough, J. J. (2005). Adult manifestations of attention-deficit/hyperactivity disorder. In B. J. Sadock & V. A. Sadock (Eds.), *Kaplan & Sadock's comprehensive textbook of psychiatry* (pp. 3198–3204). Philadelphia, PA: Lippincott, Williams & Wilkins.

McGovern, M. P., Xie, H., Segal, S. R., Siembab, L., & Drake, R. E. (2006). Addiction treatment services and co-occurring disorders: Prevalence estimates, treatment practices, and barriers. *Journal of Substance Abuse Treatment, 31*(3), 267–275.

McGovern, P. E. (2007). *Ancient wine: The search for the origins of viniculture.* Princeton, NJ: Princeton University Press.

McGrath, P., Marshall, P. G., & Prior, K. (1979). A comprehensive treatment program for a fire setting child. *Journal of Behavior Therapy and Experimental Psychiatry, 10*(1), 69–72.

McGrath, R. E., & Carroll, E. J. (2012). The current status of "projective" "tests." In H. Cooper, P. M. Camic, D. L. Long, A. T. Panter, D. Rindskopf, & K. Sher (Eds.), *APA handbook of research methods in psychology, Vol 1: Foundations, planning, measures, and psychometrics* (pp. 329–348). Washington, D.C.: American Psychological Association.

McGuffin, P., Rijsdijk, F., Andrew, M., Sham, P., Katz, R., & Cardno, A. (2003). The heritability of bipolar affective disorder and the genetic relationship to unipolar depression. *Archives of General Psychiatry, 60,* 497–502.

McGuire, J. F., Piacentini, J., Scahill, L., Woods, D. W., Villarreal, R., Wilhelm, S., Walkup, J. T., & Peterson, A. L. (2015). Bothersome tics in patients with chronic tic disorders: Characteristics and individualized treatment response to behavior therapy. *Behaviour Reearch and Therapy, 70,* 56–62.

McGuire, P. K., Shah, G. M. S., & Murray, R. M. (1993). Increased blood flow in Broca's area during auditory hallucinations in schizophrenia. *Lancet, 342,* 703–706.

McHugh, R. K. (2015). Treatment of co-occurring anxiety disorders and substance use disorders. *Harvard Review of Psychiatry, 23,* 99–111.

McHugh, R. K., & Barlow, D. H. (2010). The dissemination and implementation of evidence-based psychological treatments: A review of current efforts. *American Psychologist, 65,* 73–84.

McHugh, R. K., & Barlow, D. H., Eds. (2012). *Dissemination and implementation of evidence-based psychological interventions.* New York, NY: Oxford University Press.

McIntyre, R. S., Berk, M., Brietzke, E., Goldstein, B. I., López-Jaramillo, C., Kessing, L. V., … Mansur, R. B. (2020). Bipolar disorders. *The Lancet, 396*(10265), 1841–1856. doi: 10.1016/S0140-6736(20)31544-0

McKay, D., Todaro, J., Neziroglu, F., Campisi, T., Moritz, E. K., & Yaryura-Tobias, J. A. (1997). Body dysmorphic disorder: A preliminary evaluation of treatment and maintenance using exposure with response prevention. *Behaviour Research and Therapy, 35,* 67–70.

McKay, R., & Dennett, D. (2010). The evolution of misbelief. *Behavioral and Brain Sciences, 32*(6), 493–510.

McKay, R., Langdon, R., & Coltheart, M. (2007). Models of misbelief: Integrating motivational and deficit theories of delusions. *Consciousness and Cognition, 16*(4), 932–941.

McKenna, B. S., & Eyler, L. T. (2012). Overlapping prefrontal systems involved in cognitive and emotional processing in euthymic bipolar disorder and following sleep deprivation: A review of functional neuroimaging studies. *Clinical Psychology Review, 32*(7), 650–663. doi: 10.1016/j.cpr.2012.07.003

McKenzie, K. C., & Gross, J. J. (2014). Nonsuicidal self-injury: an emotion regulation perspective. *Psychopathology, 47*(4), 207-219.

McKenzie, S. J., Williamson, D. A., & Cubic, B. A. (1993). Stable and reactive body image disturbances in bulimia nervosa. *Behavior Therapy, 24,* 195–207.

McKetin, R., Coen, A., & Kaye, S. (2015). A comprehensive review of the effects of mixing caffeinated energy drinks with alcohol. *Drug and Alcohol Dependence, 151,* 15–30.

McLaughlin, N. C. R., & Greenberg, B. D. (2012). In G. Steketee (Ed.), *The Oxford handbook of obsessive compulsive and spectrum disorders* (pp. 307–321). New York, NY: Oxford University Press.

McLean, C. P., Asnaani, A., Litz, B. T., & Hofmann, S. G. (2011). Gender differences in anxiety disorders: Prevalence, course of illness, comorbidity, and burden of illness. *Journal of Psychiatric Research, 45,* 1027–1035. doi: 10.1016/j.jpsychires.2011.03.006

McLean, P., & Taylor, S. (1992). Severity of unipolar depression and choice of treatment. *Behaviour Research and Therapy, 30*(5), 443–451.

McMain, S. F., Guimond, T., Streiner, D. L., Cardish, R. J., & Links, P. S. (2014). Dialectical behavior therapy compared with general psychiatric management for borderline personality disorder: clinical outcomes and functioning over a 2-year follow-up. *American Journal of Psychiatry, 169,* 650–671.

McMain, S., Links, P. S., Guimond, T., Wnuk, S., Eynan, R., Bergmans, Y., & Warwar, S. (2013). An exploratory study of the relationship between changes in emotion and cognitive processes and treatment outcome in borderline personality disorder. *Psychotherapy Research, 23*(6), 658-673.

McNab, C., Haslam, N., & Burnett, P. (2007). Expressed emotion, attributions, utility beliefs, and distress in parents of young people with first episode psychosis. *Psychiatry Research, 151,* 97–106.

McNally, R. (2003). *Remembering trauma.* Cambridge, MA: Belknap Press.

McNally, R. J. (1996). Cognitive bias in the anxiety disorders. In D. A. Hope (Ed.), *Perspectives on anxiety, panic and fear* (The 43rd Annual Nebraska Symposium on Motivation) (pp. 211–250). Lincoln, NE: Nebraska University Press.

McNally, R. J. (1999). EMDR and mesmerism: A comparative historical analysis. *Journal of Anxiety Disorders, 13,* 225–236.

McNally, R. J. (2001). On Wakefield's harmful dysfunction analysis of mental disorder. *Behaviour Research and Therapy, 39*(3), 309–314. doi: 10.1016/s0005-7967(00)00068-1

McNally, R. J. (2011). *What is mental illness?* Cambridge, MA: Harvard University Press.

McNally, R. J. (2012a). Explaining "memories" of space alien abduction and past lives: An experimental psychopathology approach. *Journal of Experimental Psychopathology, 3*(1), 2–16.

McNally, R. J. (2012b). Are we winning the war against posttraumatic stress disorder? *Science, 336*(6083), 872–874. doi: 10.1126/science.1222069

McNally, R. J., & Geraerts, E. (2009). A new solution to the recovered memory debate. *Perspectives on Psychological Science, 4*(2), 126–134.

McNeil, T. F. (1987). Perinatal influences in the development of schizophrenia. In H. Helmchen & F. A. Henn (Eds.), *Biological perspectives of schizophrenia* (pp. 125–138). New York, NY: Wiley.

McPartland, J. C., Reichow, B., & Volkmar, F. R. (2012). Sensitivity and specificity of proposed DSM-5 diagnostic criteria for autism spectrum disorder. *Journal of the American Academy of Child & Adolescent Psychiatry, 51*(4), 368–383. doi: 10.1016/j.jaac.2012.01.007

McQuade, J. D., & Hoza, B. (2015). Peer relationships of children with ADHD. In R. A. Barkley (Ed.), *Attention-deficit hyperactivity disorder: A handbook for diagnosis & treatment* (4th ed., pp. 210–222). New York, NY: The Guilford Press.

McQuillan, G., Kruszon-Moran, D., Flagg, E. W., & Paulose-Ram, R. (2018). Prevalence of herpes simplex virus type 1 and type 2 in persons aged 14–49: United States, 2015–2016. NCHS Data Brief, no 304. Hyattsville, MD: National Center for Health Statistics.

McWilliams, J. M., Meara, E., Zaslavsky, A. M., & Ayanian, J. Z. (2009). Differences in control of cardiovascular disease and diabetes by race, ethnicity, and education: U.S. trends from 1999 to 2006 and effects of Medicare coverage. *Annals of Internal Medicine, 150*(8), 505–515.

Mead, G. E., Morley, W., Campbell, P., Greig, C. A., McMurdo, M., & Lawlor, D. A. (2009). Exercise for depression. *Cochrane Database of Systematic Reviews, 3*, CD004366. doi: 10.1002/14651858.CD004366.pub4

Meagher, D., & Trzapacz, P. (2012). Delirium. In M. G. Gelder, N. C. Andreasen, J. J. Lopez-Ibor, Jr., & J. R. Geddes (Eds.), *New Oxford textbook of psychiatry* (2nd ed., Vol. 1, pp. 325–333). New York, NY: Oxford University Press.

Meagher, D., Adamis, D., Trzepacz, P., & Leonard, M. (2012). Features of subsyndromal and persistent delirium. *The British Journal of Psychiatry, 200*(1), 37–44.

Meaney, M. J. (2010). Epigenetics and the biological definition of gene X environment interactions. *Child Development, 81*(1), 41–79. doi: 10.1111/j.1467 8624.2009.01381.x

Meaney, M. J., & Szyf, M. (2005). Maternal care as a model for experience-dependent chromatin plasticity? *Trends in Neurosciences, 28*(9), 456–463.

Means, M. K., & Edinger, J. D. (2006). Nonpharmacologic therapy of insomnia. In T. Lee-Chiong (Ed.), *Sleep: A comprehensive handbook* (pp. 133–136). Hoboken, NJ: Wiley.

Mechoulam, R., & Parker, L. A. (2013). The endocannabinoid system and the brain. *Annual Review of Psychology, 64*, 21–47.

Medina v. California, 112 S. Ct. 2575 (1992).

Mednick, S. A., & Schulsinger, F. (1965). A longitudinal study of children with a high risk for schizophrenia: A preliminary report. In S. Vandenberg (Ed.), *Methods and goals in human behavior genetics* (pp. 255–296). New York, NY: Academic Press.

Mednick, S. A., & Schulsinger, F. (1968). Some premorbid characteristics related to breakdown in children with schizophrenic mothers. *Journal of Psychiatric Research, 6*, 267–291.

Meehl, P. E. (1945). The dynamics of "structured" personality tests. *Journal of Clinical Psychology, 1*, 296–303.

Meehl, P. E. (1962). Schizotaxia, schizotypy, schizophrenia. *American Psychologist, 17*, 827–838.

Meehl, P. E. (1989). Schizotaxia revisited. *Archives of General Psychiatry, 46*, 935–944.

Mehler, P. S. (2017). Medical complications of anorexia nervosa and bulimia nervosa. In S. Agras and A. Robinson, *The Oxford handbook of eating disorders*, 2nd ed (pp. 222–228). Oxford: Oxford University Press. doi: 10.1093/oxfordhb/9780190620998.013.29

Mehler, P. S., Birmingham, L. C., Crow, S. J., & Jahraus, J. P. (2010). Medical complications of eating disorders. In C. M. Grilo & J. E. Mitchell (Eds.), *The treatment of eating disorders: A clinical handbook* (pp. 66–80). New York, NY: Guilford.

Melca, I. A., Yücel, M., Mendlowicz, M. V., de Oliveira-Souza, R., & Fontenelle, L. F. (2015). The correlates of obsessive–compulsive, schizotypal, and borderline personality disorders in obsessive–compulsive disorder. *Journal of Anxiety Disorders, 33*, 15–24.

Melhem, N. M., Porta, G., Shamseddeen, W., Payne, M. W., & Brent, D. A. (2011). Grief in adolescents bereaved by sudden parental death. *Archives of General Psychiatry, 68*(9), 911–919.

Meltzer-Brody, S., Stuebe, A., Dole, N., Savitz, D., Rubinow, D., & Thorp, J. (2011). Elevated corticotropin releasing hormone (CRH) during pregnancy and risk of postpartum depression (PPD). *Journal of Clinical Endocrinology & Metabolism, 96*(1), E40–E47.

Melzack, R. (1999). From the gate to the neuromatrix. *Pain* (Suppl. 6), S121–S126.

Melzack, R. (2005). Evolution of the neuromatrix theory of pain. *Pain Practice, 5*, 85–94.

Melzack, R., & Wall, P. D. (1965). Pain mechanisms: A new theory. *Science, 150*, 971–979.

Melzack, R., & Wall, P. D. (1982). *The challenge of pain*. New York, NY: Basic Books.

Mendis, S. (2010). The contribution of the Framingham Heart Study to the prevention of cardiovascular disease: A global perspective. *Progress in Cardiovascular Diseases, 53*(1), 10–14. doi: 10.1016/j.pcad.2010.01.001

Mendoza-Azpur, G., Cruz, M., Bahamonde, A., Ponce, C., Mauricio, J. M., & Shibli, J. A. (2021). Clinical and histological manifestations of chronic coca leaf chewing in a Peruvian population: A cross-sectional study. *Journal of the International Academy of Periodontology, 23*(1), 11–16.

Mennes, C. E., Ben Abdallah, A., & Cottler, L. B. (2009). The reliability of self-reported cannabis abuse, dependence and withdrawal symptoms: Multisite study of differences between general population and treatment groups. *Addictive Behaviors, 34*(2), 223–226. doi: 10.1016/j.addbeh.2008.10.003

Menza, M. (2006). STAR*D: The results begin to roll in. *American Journal of Psychiatry, 163*, 1123–1125.

Mercer, K. B., Orcutt, H. K., Quinn, J. F., Fitzgerald, C. A., Conneely, K. N., Barfield, R. T., & Ressler, K. J. (2012). Acute and posttraumatic stress symptoms in a prospective gene x environment study of a university campus shooting. *Archives of General Psychiatry, 69*(1), 89–97. doi: 10.1001/archgenpsychiatry.2011.109

Meredith, S. E., Juliano, L. M., Hughes, J. R., & Griffiths, R. R. (2013). Caffeine use disorder: a comprehensive review and research agenda. *Journal of Caffeine Research, 3*(3), 114–130.

Merens, W., Willem Van der Does, A. J., & Spinhoven, P. (2007). The effects of serotonin manipulations on emotional information processing and mood. *Journal of Affective Disorders, 103*(1–3), 43–62.

Merikangas, K. R., & Pato, M. (2009). Recent developments in the epidemiology of bipolar disorder in adults and children: Magnitude, correlates, and future directions. *Clinical Psychology: Science and Practice, 16*(2), 121–133.

Merikangas, K. R., & Risch, N. (2014). Will the genomics revolution revolutionize psychiatry?. *American Journal of Psychiatry 160*(4), 625–635. http://dx.doi.org/10.1176/appi.ajp.160.4.625

Merikangas, K. R., Akiskal, H. S., Angst, J., Greenberg, P. E., Hirschfeld, R. M., Petukhova, M., & Kessler, R. C. (2007). Lifetime and 12-month prevalence of bipolar spectrum disorder in the National Comorbidity Survey Replication. *Archives of General Psychiatry, 64*(5), 543–552.

Merikangas, K. R., Cui, L., Kattan, G., Carlson, G. A., Youngstrom, E. A., & Angst, J. (2012). Mania with and without depression in a community sample of US adolescents. *Archives of General Psychiatry, 69*(9), 943–951.

Merikangas, K. R., Jin, R., He, J. P., Kessler, R. C., Lee, S., Sampson, N. A., & Zarkov, Z. (2011). Prevalence and correlates of bipolar spectrum disorder in the World Mental Health Survey Initiative. *Archives of General Psychiatry, 68*(3), 241–251.

Merikanto, I., Kantojärvi, K., Partonen, T., Pesonen, A., & Paunio, T. (2021). Genetic variants for morningness in relation to habitual sleep-wake behavior and diurnal preference in a population-based sample of 17,243 adults. *Sleep Medicine, 80*, 322–332. doi: 10.1016/j.sleep.2021.01.054

Mermin, J., & Fenton, K. A. (2012). The future of HIV prevention in the United States. *JAMA: Journal of the American Medical Association, 308*(4), 347–348.

Mesri, B., Xiong, Y., Marjorie Barnes-Horowitz, N., & Craske, M. G. (2020). Avoidance moderates cognitive behavioral therapy for panic disorder and agoraphobia. *Journal of Nervous and Mental Disease, 208*(10), 785–793. doi: 10.1097/NMD.0000000000001195

Meston, C. M., & Lorenz, T. A. (2013). Physiological stress responses predict sexual functioning and satisfaction differently in women who have and have not been sexually abused in childhood. *Psychological Trauma: Theory, Research, Practice, and Policy, 5*(4), 350–358.

Meston, C. M., & Gorzalka, B. B. (1995). The effects of sympathetic activation on physiological and subjective sexual arousal in women. *Behaviour Research and Therapy, 33*, 651–664.

Meuret, A. E., Rosenfield, D., Wilhelm, F. H., Zhou, E., Conrad, A., Ritz, T., & Roth, W. T. (2011). Do unexpected panic attacks occur spontaneously? *Biological Psychiatry, 70*, 985–991. doi: 10.1016/j.biopsych.2011.05.027

Mewton, L., Hodge, A., Gates, N., Visontay, R., Lees, B., & Teesson, M. (2020). A randomised double-blind trial of cognitive training for the prevention of psychopathology in at-risk youth. *Behaviour Research and Therapy, 132*, 103672.

Meyer, A. J., Nash, J. D., McAlister, A. L., Maccoby, M., & Farquhar, J. W. (1980). Skills training in a cardiovascular health education campaign. *Journal of Consulting and Clinical Psychology, 2*, 129–142.

Meyer, B., & Carver, C. S. (2000). Negative childhood accounts, sensitivity and pessimism: A study of avoidant personality disorder features in college students. *Journal of Personality Disorders, 14*, 233–248.

Meyer-Bahlburg, H. F. (2010). From mental disorder to iatrogenic hypogonadism: Dilemmas in conceptualizing gender identity variants as psychiatric conditions. *Archives of Sexual Behavior, 39*(2), 461–476.

Meyer-Bahlburg, H., Dolezal, C., Baker, S., Carlson, A., Obeid, J., & New, M. (2004). Prenatal androgenization affects gender-related behavior but not gender identity in 5–12 year old girls with congenital adrenal hyperplasia. *Archives of Sexual Behavior, 33*, 97–104.

Meyerowitz, B. E. (1983). Postmastectomy coping strategies and quality of life. *Health Psychology, 2*, 117–132.

Myers, K. M., & Davis, M. (2002). Systems-level reconsolidation: Reengagement of the hippocampus with memory reactivation. Neuron, 36(3), 340–343. doi:10.1016/S0896-6273(02)01017-6

Mezick, E. J., Matthews, K. A., Hall, M., Kamarck, T. W., Strollo, P. J., Buysse, D. J., & Reis, S. E. (2010). Low life purpose and high hostility are related to an attenuated decline in nocturnal blood pressure. *Health Psychology, 29*(2), 196–204.

Mezzich, J. E., Kleinman, A., Fabrega, H., Jr., Good, B., Johnson-Powell, G., Lin, K. M., & Parron, D. (1992). *Cultural proposals for DSM-IV.* Submitted to the DSM-IV Task Force by the Steering Committee, NIMH-Sponsored Group on Culture and Diagnosis.

Michalak, J., Schultze, M., Heidenreich, T., & Schramm, E. (2015). A randomized controlled trial on the efficacy of mindfulness-based cognitive therapy and a group version of cognitive behavioral analysis system for chronically depressed patients. *Journal of Consulting and Clinical Psychology, 83*, 951–963.

Michaud, L., Ligier, F., Bourquin, C., Corbeil, S., Saraga, M., Stiefel, F., … Richard-Devantoy, S. (2020). Differences and similarities in instant countertransference towards patients with suicidal ideation and personality disorders. *Journal of Affective Disorders, 265*, 669–678.

Michelakos, T., Kousoulis, A. A., Katsiardanis, K., Dessypris, N., Anastasiou, A., Katsiardani, K.-P., & Petridou, E. T. (2013). Serum folate and B12 levels in association with cognitive impairment among seniors: Results from the VELESTINO study in Greece and meta-analysis. *Journal of Aging and Health, 25*(4), 589-616. doi: 10.1177/0898264313482488

Michultka, D. M., Blanchard, E. B., Appelbaum, K. A., Jaccard, J., & Dentinger, M. P. (1989). The refractory headache patient: II. High medication consumption (analgesic rebound) headache. *Behaviour Research and Therapy, 27*, 411–420.

Mihura, J. L., Meyer, G. J., Dumitrascu, N., & Bombel, G. (2012). The validity of individual Rorschach variables: Systematic reviews and meta-analyses of the Comprehensive System. *Psychological Bulletin 139*(3), 548–605. doi: 10.1037/10029406

Miklowitz, D. J., Otto, M. W., Frank, E., Reilly-Harrington, N. A., Wisniewski, S. R., Kogan, J. N., Nierenberg, A. A., Calabrese, J. R., Marangell, L. B., Gyulai, L., Araga, M., Gonzalez, J. M., Shirley, E. R., Thase, M. E., & Sachs, G. S. (2007). Psychosocial treatments for bipolar depression: a 1-year randomized trial from the Systematic Treatment Enhancement Program. *Arch Gen Psychiatry, 64*(4):419–426.

Miklowitz, D. J. (2014). Bipolar disorder. In D. H. Barlow (Ed.), *Clinical handbook of psychological disorders: A step-by-step treatment manual* (5th ed.). New York, NY: Guilford.

Miklowitz, D. J., Efthimiou, O., Furukawa, T. A., Scott, J., McLaren, R., Geddes, J. R., & Cipriani, A. (2021). Adjunctive psychotherapy for bipolar disorder: A systematic review and component network meta-analysis. *JAMA Psychiatry, 78*(2), 141–150. doi: 10.1001/jamapsychiatry.2020.2993

Miklowitz, D. J., George, E. L., Richards, J. A., Simoneau, T. L., & Suddath, R. L. (2003). A randomized study of family-focused psychoeducation and pharmacotherapy in the outpatient management of bipolar disorder. *Archives of General Psychiatry, 60*, 904–912.

Miklowitz, D. J., Schneck, C. D., Singh, M. K., Taylor, D. O., George, E. L., Cosgrove, M. E., Howe, M. E., Dickinson, L. M., Garber, J., & Chang, K. D. (2013). Early intervention for symptomatic youth for bipolar disorder: A randomized trial of family-focused therapy. *Journal of the American Academy of Child and Adolescent Psychiatry, 52*, 121–131.

Mill, J. (2011). Epigenetic effects on gene function and their role in mediating gene-enviroment interactions. In K. S. Kendler, S. Jaffee, & D. Romer (Eds.), *The dynamic genome and mental health: The role of genes and environments in youth development* (pp. 145–171). New York, NY: Oxford University Press.

Millan, M. J., Fone, K., Steckler, T., & Horan, W. P. (2014). Negative symptoms of schizophrenia: Clinical characteristics, pathophysiological substrates, experimental models and prospects for improved treatment. *European Neuropsychopharmacology, 24*(5), 645–692.

Millar, H. R., Qrdell, F., Vyvyan, J. P., Naji, S. A., Prescott, G. J., & Eagles, J. M. (2005). Anorexia nervosa mortality in northeast Scotland 1965–1999. *American Journal of Psychiatry, 162,* 753–757.

Miller, G. (2011). Social neuroscience. Why loneliness is hazardous to your health. *Science, 331*(6014), 138–140. doi: 10.1126/science.331.6014.138

Miller, G., & Blackwell, E. (2006). Turning up the heat: Inflammation as a mechanism linking chronic stress, depression, and heart disease. *Current Directions in Psychological Science, 15,* 269–277.

Miller, I. W., & Norman, W. H. (1979). Learned helplessness in humans: A review and attribution- theory model. *Psychological Bulletin, 86*(1), 93–118.

Miller, I. W., Norman, W. H., & Keitner, G. I. (1989). Cognitive-behavioral treatment of depressed inpatients: Six- and twelve-month follow-up. *American Journal of Psychiatry, 146,* 1274–1279.

Miller, J. N., & Black, D. W. (2020). Bipolar disorder and suicide: A review. *Current Psychiatry Reports, 22*(2). doi: 10.1007/s11920-020-1130-0

Miller, J., Bilder, D., Farley, M., Coon, H., Pinborough-Zimmerman, J., Jenson, W., & McMahon, W. (2013). Autism spectrum disorder reclassified: A second look at the 1980s Utah/UCLA Autism Epidemiologic Study. *Journal of Autism and Developmental Disorders 43*(1), 200–210. doi: 10.1007/s10803-012-1566-0

Miller, M. W., Wolf, E. J., & Keane, T. M. (2014). Posttraumatic stress disorder in DSM-5: New criteria and controversies. *Clinical Psychology: Science and Practice, 21,* 208–220.

Miller, M., Iosif, A.-M., Bell, L. J., Farquhar-Leicester, A., Hatch, B., Hill, A., … Ozonoff, S. (2020). Can familial risk for ADHD be detected in the first two years of life? *Journal of Clinical Child & Adolescent Psychology*, 1–13.

Miller, N. E. (1969). Learning of visceral and glandular responses. *Science, 163,* 434–445.

Miller, S. D. (1989). Optical differences in cases of multiple personality disorder. *Journal of Nervous and Mental Disease, 177*(8), 480–486.

Miller, T. Q., Smith, T. W., Turner, C. W., Guijarro, M. L., & Hallet, A. J. (1996). A meta-analytic review of research on hostility and physical health. *Psychological Bulletin, 119*(2), 322–348.

Miller, W. R., & Hester, R. K. (1986). Inpatient alcoholism treatment: Who benefits? *American Psychologist, 41,* 794–805.

Miller, W. R., & Rollnick, S. (2002). *Motivational interviewing: Lessons preparing people for change*. New York, NY: Guildford.

Miller, W. R., & Rollnick, S. (2012). *Motivational interviewing: Helping people change.* New York, NY: Guilford Press.

Millon, T. (1981). *Disorders of personality: DSM-III, Axis II.* New York, NY: Wiley.

Millon, T. (1991). Classification in psychopathology: Rationale, alternatives, and standards. *Journal of Abnormal Psychology, 100*(3), 245–261.

Millon, T. (2004). *Masters of the mind.* Hoboken, NJ: Wiley.

Millon, T., & Martinez, A. (1995). Avoidant personality disorder. In W. J. Livesley (Ed.), *The DSM-IV personality disorders* (pp. 218–233). New York, NY: Guilford.

Mills, P. J., Adler, K. A., Dimsdale, J. E., Perez, C. J., Ziegler, M. G., Ancoli-Israel, S., & Grant, I. (2004). Vulnerable caregivers of Alzheimer disease patients have a deficit in beta 2-adrenergic receptor sensitivity and density. *American Journal of Geriatric Psychiatry, 12,* 281–286.

Mindell, J. A., & Owens, J. A. (2015). *A clinical guide to pediatric sleep: diagnosis and management of sleep problems* (3rd ed.). Philadelphia, PA: Lippincott Williams & Wilkins.

Mineka, S. (1985). The frightful complexity of the origins of fears. In F. R. Bruch & J. B. Overmier (Eds.), *Affect, conditioning, and cognition: Essays on the determinants of behavior.* Hillsdale, NJ: Erlbaum.

Mineka, S., & Sutton, J. (2006). In M. G. Craske, D. Hermans, & D. Vansteenwegen, *Fear and learning: From basic processes to clinical implications* (pp. 75–97), Washington, DC: American Psychological Association.

Mineka, S., & Zinbarg, R. (1996). Conditioning and ethological models of anxiety disorders: Stress-in-dynamic-context anxiety models. In D. A. Hope (Ed.), *Perspectives on anxiety, panic and fear* (The 43rd Annual Nebraska Symposium on Motivation) (pp. 135–210). Lincoln, NE: Nebraska University Press.

Mineka, S., & Zinbarg, R. (1998). Experimental approaches to understanding the mood and anxiety disorders. In J. Adair (Ed.), *Advances in psychological research, Vol. 2: Social, personal, and cultural aspects* (pp. 429–454). Hove, UK: Psychology Press/Erlbaum.

Mineka, S., & Zinbarg, R. (2006). A contemporary learning theory perspective on the etiology of anxiety disorders. *American Psychologist, 61,* 10–26.

Mineka, S., Watson, D., & Clark, L. A. (1998). Comorbidity of anxiety and unipolar mood disorders. *Annual Review of Psychology, 49,* 377–412.

Mingbunjerdsuk, D., & Zinner, S. H. (in press). Coping with tics in school and with peers. *Current Developmental Disorders Reports.*

Minino, A. M., Arias, E., Kochanek, K. D., Murphy, S. L., & Smith, B. L. (2002). Deaths: Final data for 2000. *National Vital Statistics Reports, 50,* 1–119.

Minuchin, S., Rosman, B. L., & Baker, L. (1978). *Psychosomatic families.* Cambridge, MA: Harvard University Press.

Mirosevic, S., Jo, B., Kraemer, H. C., Ershadi, M., Neri, E., & Spiegel, D. (2019). "Not just another meta-analysis": Sources of heterogeneity in psychosocial treatment effect on cancer survival. *Cancer Medicine, 8*(1), 363–373. doi: 10.1002/cam4.1895

Mirsky, A. F., Bieliauskas, L. A., French, L. M., van Kammen, D. P., Jonsson, E., & Sedvall, G. (2000). A 39-year follow-up of the Genain quadruplets. *Schizophrenia Bulletin, 26,* 699–708.

Misra, S., Jackson, V. W., Chong, J., Choe, K., Tay, C., Wong, J., & Yang, L. H. (in press). Systematic review of cultural aspects of stigma and mental illness among racial and ethnic minority groups in the United States: Implications for interventions. *American Journal of Community Psychology.*

Mistry, H., Bhugra, D., Chaleby, K., Khan, F., & Sauer, J. (2009). Veiled communication: is uncovering necessary for psychiatric assessment? *Transcultural Psychiatry, 46*(4), 642–650. doi: 10.1177/1363461509351366

Mitchell, D. C., Knight, C. A., Hockenberry, J., Teplansky, R., & Hartman, T. J. (2014). Beverage caffeine intakes in the US. *Food and Chemical Toxicology, 63,* 136–142.

Mitchell, D. C., Knight, C. A., Hockenberry, J., Teplansky, R., & Hartman, T. J. (2014). Beverage caffeine intakes in the U.S. *Food and Chemical Toxicology, 63,* 136–142.

Mitchell, W. B., DiBartolo, P. M., Brown, T. A., & Barlow, D. H. (1998). Effects of positive and negative mood on sexual arousal in sexually functional males. *Archives of Sexual Behavior, 27*(2), 197–207.

Mobbs, D., Lau, H., Jones, O., & Frith, C. (2009). Law, responsibility, and the brain. In N. Murphy, G. Ellis, & T. O'Connor (Eds.), *Downward causation and the neurobiology of free will* (pp. 243–260). New York, NY: Springer.

Mock, S. E., & Eibach, R. P. (2012). Stability and change in sexual orientation identity over a 10-year period in adulthood. *Archives of sexual behavior, 41*(3), 641–648.

Modahl, C., Green, L., Fein, D., Morris, M., Waterhouse, L., Feinstein, C., & Levin, H. (1998). Plasma oxytocin levels in autistic children. *Biological Psychiatry, 43,* 270–277.

Modinos, G., Mechelli, A., Ormel, J., Groenewold, N., Aleman, A., & McGuire, P. (2009). Schizotypy and brain structure: A voxel-based morphometry study. *Psychological Medicine, 40,* 1423–1431.

Modrego, P. J. (2010). Depression in Alzheimer's disease. Pathophysiology, diagnosis, and treatment. *Journal of Alzheimer's Disease, 21,* 1077–1087.

Moene, F. C., Landberg, E. H., Hoogduin, K. A., Spinhoven, P., Hertzberger, L. I., Kleyweg, R. P., & Weeda, J. (2000). Organic syndromes diagnosed as conversion disorder: Identification and frequency in a study of 85 patients. *Journal of Psychosomatic Research, 49,* 7–12.

Moene, F. C., Spinhoven, P., Hoogduin, K. A., & van Dyck, R. (2002). A randomised controlled clinical trial on the additional effect of hypnosis in a comprehensive treatment programme for in-patients with conversion disorder of the motor type. *Psychotherapy and psychosomatics, 71,* 66–76.

Moene, F. C., Spinhoven, P., Hoogduin, K. A., & van Dyck, R. (2003). A randomized controlled clinical trial of a hypnosis-based treatment for patients with conversion disorder, motor type. *International Journal of Clinical and Experimental Hypnosis, 51*(1), 29–50.

Moffitt, T. E., Caspi, A., Rutter, M., & Silva, P. A. (2001). *Sex differences in antisocial behaviour: Conduct disorder, delinquency, and violence in the Dunedin longitudinal study*. Cambridge, UK: Cambridge University Press.

Mogg, K., Bradley, B. P., Millar, N., & White, J. (1995). A follow-up study of cognitive bias in generalized anxiety disorder. *BRAT, 33,* 927–935.

Mogg, K., Philippot, P., & Bradley, B. P. (2004). Selective attention to angry faces in clinical social phobia. *Journal of Abnormal Psychology, 113,* 160–165.

Mogil, J. S., Sternberg, W. F., Kest, B., Marek, P., & Liebeskind, J. C. (1993). Sex differences in the antagonism of swim stress-induced analgesia: Effects of gonadectomy and estrogen replacement. *Pain, 53,* 17–25.

Mohammadi, M.-R., Zarafshan, H., Khaleghi, A., Ahmadi, N., Hooshyari, Z., Mostafavi, S.-A., … Salmanian, M. (2021). Prevalence of ADHD and its comorbidities in a population-based sample. *Journal of Attention Disorders, 25*(8), 1058–1067.

Mohlman, J., Bryant, C., Lenze, E. J., Stanley, M. A., Gum, A., Flit, A., & Craske, M. G. (2012). Improving recognition of late life anxiety disorders in Diagnostic and Statistical Manual of Mental Disorders, Fifth Edition: Observations and recommendations of the Advisory Committee to the Lifespan Disorders Work Group. *International Journal of Geriatric Psychiatry, 27,* 549–556. doi: 10.1002/gps.2752

Moll, K., Kunze, S., Neuhoff, N., Bruder, J., & Schulte-Korne, G. (2014) Specific Learning Disorder: Prevalence and Gender Differences. *PLoS ONE 9*(7): e103537.

Molosh, A. I., Dustrude, E. T., Lukkes, J. L., Fitz, S. D., Caliman, I. F., Abreu, A. R. R., … Shekhar, A. (2020). Panic results in unique molecular and network changes in the amygdala that facilitate fear responses. *Molecular Psychiatry, 25*(2), 442–460. doi: 10.1038/s41380-018-0119-0

Momen, N. C., Plana-Ripoll, O., Agerbo, E., Benros, M. E., Børglum, A. D., Christensen, M. K., … McGrath, J. J. (2020). Association between mental disorders and subsequent medical conditions. *New England Journal of Medicine, 382*(18), 1721–1731. doi: 10.1056/NEJMoa1915784

Money, J., & Ehrhardt, A. (1972). *Man and woman, boy and girl.* Baltimore, MD: Johns Hopkins University Press.

Monroe, S. M., & Reid, M. W. (2009). Life stress and major depression. *Current Directions in Psychological Science, 18*(2), 68–72.

Monroe, S. M., Anderson, S. F., & Harkness, K. L. (2019). Life stress and major depression: The mysteries of recurrences. *Psychology Review, 126*(6), 791–816. doi: 10.1037/rev0000157.

Monroe, S. M., Kupfer, D. J., & Frank, E. (1992). Life stress and treatment course of recurrent depression: I. Response during index episode. *Journal of Consulting and Clinical Psychology, 60*(5), 718–724.

Monroe, S. M., Roberts, J. E., Kupfer, D. J., & Frank, E. (1996). Life stress and treatment course of recurrent depression: II. Postrecovery associations with attrition, symptom course, and recurrence over 3 years. *Journal of Abnormal Psychology, 105*(3), 313–328.

Monroe, S. M., Rohde, P., Seeley, J. R., & Lewinsohn, P. M. (1999). Life events and depression in adolescence: For first onset of major depressive disorder. *Journal of Abnormal Psychology, 108*(4), 606–614.

Monroe, S. M., Slavich, G. M., & Georgiades, K. (2009). The social environment and life stress in depression. In I. H. Gotlib & C. L. Hammen (Eds.), *Handbook of depression* (2nd ed., pp. 340–360). New York, NY: Guilford.

Monson, C. M., Fredman, S. J., Macdonald, A., Pukay-Martin, N. D., Resick, P. A., & Schnurr, P. P. (2012). Effect of cognitive-behavioral couple therapy for PTSD: A randomized controlled trial. *Journal of American Medical Association, 308,* 700–709. doi: 10.1001/jama.2012.9307

Monson, C. M., Resick, P. A., & Rizvi, S. L. (2014). Posttraumatic stress disorder. In D. H. Barlow (Ed.), *Clinical handbook of psychological disorders: A step-by-step treatment manual* (5th ed.). New York, NY: Guilford.

Montejo-Gonzalez, A. L., Liorca, G., Izquierdo, J. A., Ledesma, A., Bousono, M., Calcedo, A., & Vincens, E. (1997). SSRI-induced sexual dysfunction: Fluoxetine, paroxetine, sertraline, and fluvoxamine in a prospective, multicenter, and descriptive clinical study of 344 patients. *Journal of Sex and Marital Therapy, 23,* 176–194.

Monti, J. M., Pandi-Perumal, S. R., & Möhler, H. (2010). *Gaba and sleep: Molecular, functional and clinical aspects.* Springer Science & Business Media.

Moody, C. T., & Laugeson, E. A. (2020). Social skills training in autism spectrum disorder across the lifespan. *Child & Adolescent Psychiatric Clinics, 29*(2), 359–371.

Moore, D. S. (2001). *The dependent gene: The fallacy of "nature vs. nurture."* New York, NY: Henry Holt.

Moore, M. (2012). Behavioral sleep problems in children and adolescents. *Journal of Clinical Psychology in Medical Settings, 19*(1), 77–83.

Moreno, A., Azar, M., Warren, N., Dickerson, T., Koob, G., & Janda, K. (2010). A critical evaluation of a nicotine vaccine within a self-administration behavioral model. *Molecular pharmaceutics, 7*(2), 431–441.

Moreno, C., Laje, G., Blanco, C., Jiang, H., Schmidt, A. B., & Olfson, M. (2007). National trends in the outpatient diagnosis and treatment of bipolar disorder in youth. *Archives of General Psychiatry, 64*(9), 1032–1039.

Morenz, B., & Becker, J. (1995). The treatment of youthful sexual offenders. *Applied & Preventive Psychology, 4,* 247–256.

Morey, J. N., Boggero, I. A., Scott, A. B., & Segerstrom, S. C. (2015). Current directions in stress and human immune function. *Current Opinion in Psychology, 5,* 13–17.

Morgan, D. (2007). The rationale for an immunological approach to Alzheimer's therapeutics. In A. C. Cuello (Ed.), *Pharmacological mechanisms in Alzheimer's therapeutics* (pp. 141–148). New York, NY: Springer.

Morgan, H. W. (1981). *Drugs in America: A social history, 1800–1980.* Syracuse, NY: Syracuse University Press.

Morin, C. M., & Benca, R. (2012). Chronic insomnia. *The Lancet, 379*(9821), 1129–1141. doi: 10.1016/s0140-6736(11)60750-2

Morin, C. M., Savard, J., & Ouellet, M. C. (2012). Nature and treatment of insomnia. In I. B. Weiner, A. M. Nezu, C. M. Nezu, & P. A. Geller (Eds.), *Handbook of psychology, Health psychology* (Vol. 9, pp. 318–339).

Morneau-Vaillancourt, G., Coleman, J. R. I., Purves, K. L., Cheesman, R., Rayner, C., Breen, G., & Eley, T. C. (2020). The genetic and environmental hierarchical structure of anxiety and depression in the UK biobank. *Depression and Anxiety, 37*(6), 512–520. doi: 10.1002/da.22991

Morokoff, P. J., & Heiman, J. R. (1980). Effects of erotic stimuli on sexually functional and dysfunctional women: Multiple measures before and after sex therapy. *Behaviour Research and Therapy, 18,* 127–137.

Morrato, E. H., & Allison, D. B. (2012). FDA approval of obesity drugs: A difference in risk-benefit perceptions. *JAMA: Journal of the American Medical Association, 308,* 1097–1098. doi: 10.1001/jama.2012.10007

Morris, J. K., Cook, D. G., & Shaper, A. G. (1994). Loss of employment and mortality. *British Medical Journal, 308,* 1135–1139.

Morris, J. S., Öhman, A., & Dolan, R. J. (1998). Conscious and unconscious emotion learning in the human amygdala. *Nature, 393,* 467–470.

Morris, N. P. (2020). Detention without data: Public tracking of civil commitment. *Psychiatric Services, 71*(7), 741–744.

Morrison, A. S., & Heimberg, R. G. (2013). Social anxiety and social anxiety disorder. *Annual Review of Clinical Psychology, 9,* 249–274.

Morrow, G. R., & Dobkin, P. L. (1988). Anticipatory nausea and vomiting in cancer patients undergoing chemotherapy treatment: Prevalence, etiology, and behavioral interventions. *Clinical Psychology Review, 8,* 517–556.

Mortberg, E., Clark, D. M., & Bejerot, S. (2011). Intensive group cognitive therapy and individual cognitive therapy for social phobia: Sustained improvement at 5-year follow-up. *Journal of Anxiety Disorders, 25,* 994–1000. doi: 10.1016/j.janxdis.2011.06.007

Mosher, D. L., & Sirkin, M. (1984). Measuring a macho personality constellation. *Journal of Research in Personality, 18,* 150–163.

Mosher, W. D., Chandra, A., & Jones, J. (2005). Sexual behavior and selected health measures: Men and women 15–44 years of age, United States, 2002. *Advance Data from Vital and Health Statistics, 362,* 1–55. Hyattsville, MD: National Center for Health Statistics.

Moskowitz, A. (2004). "Scared stiff": Catatonia as an evolutionary based fear response. *Psychological Review, 111,* 984–1002.

Mostofsky, D. I., & Barlow, D. H. (Eds.) (2000). *The management of stress and anxiety in medical disorders.* Needham Heights, MA: Allyn & Bacon.

Motta-Ochoa, R., Bresba, P., Da Silva Castanheira, J., Lai Kwan, C., Shaffer, S., Julien, O., … Blain-Moraes, S. (2021). "When I hear my language, I travel back in time and I feel at home": Intersections of culture with social inclusion and exclusion of persons with dementia and their caregivers. *Transcultural Psychiatry,* 13634615211001707.

Mucha, T. F., & Reinhardt, R. F. (1970). Conversion reactions in student aviators. *American Journal of Psychiatry, 127,* 493–497.

Mueller, T., Keller, M. B., Leon, A. C., Solomon, D. A., Shea, M. T., Coryell, W., & Endicott, J. (1996). Recovery after 5 years of unremitting major depressive disorder. *Archives of General Psychiatry, 53,* 794–799.

Mueser, K. T., & Berenbaum, H. (1990). Psychodynamic treatment of schizophrenia: Is there a future? *Psychological Medicine, 20,* 253–262.

Mueser, K. T., & Marcello, S. (2011). Schizophrenia. In D. H. Barlow (Ed.), *Oxford handbook of clinical psychology* (pp. 469–503). New York, NY: Oxford University.

Mueser, K. T., Deavers, F., Penn, D. L., & Cassisi, J. E. (2013). Psychosocial treatments for schizophrenia. *Annual Review of Clinical Psychology, 9,* 465–497.

Mueser, K. T., Liberman, R. P., & Glynn, S. M. (1990). Psychosocial interventions in schizophrenia. In A. Kales, C. N. Stefanis, & J. A. Talbott (Eds.), *Recent advances in schizophrenia* (pp. 213–235). New York, NY: Springer-Verlag.

Mufson, L., Pollack-Dorta, K., Wickramaratne, P., Nomura, Y., Olfson, M., & Weismann, M. (2004). A randomized effectiveness trial of interpersonal psychotherapy for depressed adolescents. *Archives of General Psychiatry, 61,* 577–584.

Muhuri, P. K., Gfroerer, J. C., & Davies, M. C. (2013). *Associations of nonmedical pain reliever use and initiation of heroin use in the United States Center for Behavioral Health Statistics and Quality.* Retrieved from http://www.samhsa.gov/data/2k13/DataReview/DR006/nonmedical-pain-reliever-use-2013.htm.

Mulder, R., Frampton, C., Luty, S., & Joyce, P. (2009). Eighteen months of drug treatment for depression: Predicting relapse and recovery. *Journal of Affective Disorders, 114*(1–3), 263–270.

Mullan, M. (2021). How U.S. society has treated those with mental illnesses. *Richmond Public Interest Law Review, 24*(2), 79–114.

Mullany, B., Barlow, A., Goklish, N., Larzelere-Hinton, F., Cwik, M., Craig, M., & Walkup, J. T. (2009). Toward understanding suicide among youths: Results from the White Mountain Apache tribally mandated suicide surveillance system, 2001–2006. *American Journal of Public Health, 99*(10), 1840–1848.

Müller, C. P., Schumann, G., Kornhuber, J., & Kalinichenko, L. S. (2020). The role of serotonin in alcohol use and abuse. *Handbook of behavioral neuroscience* (Vol. 31, pp. 803–827). London: Elsevier.

Mumford, D. B., Whitehouse, A. M., & Platts, M. (1991). Sociocultural correlates of eating disorders among Asian schoolgirls in Bradford. *British Journal of Psychiatry, 158,* 222–228.

Munder, T., Flückiger, C., Gerger, H., Wampold, B. E., & Barth, J. (2012). Is the allegiance effect an epiphenomenon of true efficacy differences between treatments? A meta-analysis. *Journal of Counseling Psychology, 59*(4), 631–637.

Munjack, D. J. (1984). The onset of driving phobias. *Journal of Behavior Therapy and Experimental Psychiatry, 15,* 305–308.

Muñoz, R. F., Beardslee, W. R., & Leykin, Y. (2012). Major depression can be prevented. *American Psychologist, 67*(4), 285–295.

Muñoz, R. F., Cuijpers, P., Smit, F., Barrera, A. Z., & Leykin, Y. (2010). Prevention of major depression. *Annual Review of Clinical Psychology, 6,* 181–212.

Muñoz, R. F., Le, H.-N., Clarke, G. N., Barrera, A. Z., & Torres, L. D. (2009). Preventing first onset and recurrence of major depressive episodes. In I. H. Gotlib & C. L. Hammen (Eds.), *Handbook of depression* (2nd ed., pp. 533–553). New York, NY: Guilford.

Munro, A. (2012). Persistent delusional symptoms and disorders. In M. G. Gelder, N. C. Andreasen, J. J. Lopez-Ibor, Jr., & J. R. Geddes (Eds.), *New Oxford textbook of psychiatry* (2nd ed., Vol. 1, pp. 609–628). New York, NY: Oxford University Press.

Muresanu, D. F., Stan, A., & Buzoianu, A. (2012). Neuroplasticity and impulse control disorders. *Journal of the Neurological Sciences, 316*(1–2), 15–20. doi: http://dx.doi.org/10.1016/j.jns.2012.01.016

Muris, P., & Field, A. P. (2010). The role of verbal threat information in the development of childhood fear. "Beware the Jabberwock." *Clinical Child and Family Psychology Review, 13,* 129–150.

Muronov, A. Y. (2020). Delirium tremens: Early diagnosis and intensive care guidelines. Review. *Alexander Saltanov Intensive Care Herald, 1,* 53–65.

Murphy, M., & Peterson, M. J. (2015). Sleep disturbances in depression. *Sleep medicine clinics, 10*(1), 17.

Murphy, J. A., & Byrne, G. J. (2012). Prevalence and correlates of the proposed DSM-5 diagnosis of chronic depressive disorder. *Journal of Affective Disorders, 139,* 172–180.

Murphy, K. R. (2015). Psychological counseling of adults with ADHD. In R. A. Barkley (Ed.), *Attention-deficit hyperactivity disorder: A handbook for diagnosis & treatment* (4th ed., pp. 741–756). New York, NY: The Guilford Press.

Murphy, S. L., Xu, J., & Kochanek, K. D. (2013). *Deaths: Final data for 2010.* National Vital Statisctics Reports, *61*,(4).

Murphy, T. K., Storch, E. A., Lewin, A. B., Edge, P. J., & Goodman, W. K. (2012). Clinical factors associated with pediatric autoimmune neuropsychiatric disorders associated with streptococcal infections. *Journal of Pediatrics, 160,* 314–319. doi: 10.1016/j.jpeds.2011.07.012

Murphy, W. D., & Page, I. J. (2008). Exhibitionism: Psychopathology and theory. In D. R. Laws & W. T. O'Donohue (Eds.), *Sexual deviance: Theory, assessment, and treatment* (2nd ed., pp. 61–75). New York, NY: Guilford.

Murray, R. M., & Castle, D. J. (2012). Genetic and environmental risk factors for schizophrenia. In M. G. Gelder, N. C. Andreasen, J. J. Lopez-Ibor, Jr., & J. R. Geddes (Eds.), *New Oxford textbook of psychiatry* (2nd ed., Vol. 1, pp. 553–561). New York, NY: Oxford University Press.

Mustafa, G. (1990). Delivery systems for the care of schizophrenic patients in Africa-Sub-Sahara. In A. Kales, C. N. Stefanis, & J. A. Talbot (Eds.), *Recent advances in schizophrenia* (pp. 353–371). New York, NY: Springer-Verlag.

Mustanski, B. S., Bailey, J. M., & Kaspar, S. (2002). Dermatoglyphics, handedness, sex, and sexual orientation. *Archives of Sexual Behavior, 31,* 113–122.

Mustian, K. M., Devine, K., Ryan, J. L., Janelsins, M. C., Sprod, L. K., Peppone, L. J., Candelario, G. D., Mohile, S. G., & Morrow, G. R. (2011). Treatment of nausea and vomiting during chemotherapy. *U.S. Oncology & Hematology, 7*(2), 91–97.

Myers, J. K., Weissman, M. M., Tischler, C. E., Holzer, C. E., III, Orvaschel, H., Anthony, J. C., & Stoltzman, R. (1984). Six-month prevalence of psychiatric disorders in three communities. *Archives of General Psychiatry, 41,* 959–967.

Myhre, J., Saga, S., Malmedal, W., Ostaszkiewicz, J., & Nakrem, S. (2020). Elder abuse and neglect: An overlooked patient safety issue. A focus group study of nursing home leaders' perceptions of elder abuse and neglect. *BMC Health Services Research, 20*(1), 1–14.

My-pro-ana. (2013). Home page. Retrieved July 19, 2013, from http://www.myproana.com/

Na, K., Kang, J. M., & Cho, S. (2021). Prevalence of *DSM-5* mixed features: A meta-analysis and systematic review. *Journal of Affective Disorders, 282,* 203–210. doi: 10.1016/j.jad.2020.12.14

Nadeem, I. M., Shanmugaraj, A., Sakha, S., Horner, N. S., Ayeni, O. R., & Khan, M. (2020). Energy drinks and their adverse health effects: A systematic review and meta-analysis. *Sports Health,* 1941738120949181.

Nagata, J. M., Ganson, K. T., & Austin, S. B. (2020). Emerging trends in eating disorders among sexual and gender minorities. *Current Opinion in Psychiatry, 33*(6), 562–567. doi: 10.1097/YCO.0000000000000645

Nagata, J. M., Ganson, K. T., & Murray, S. B. (2020). Eating disorders in adolescent boys and young men: An update. *Current Opinion in Pediatrics, 32*(4), 476–481. doi: 10.1097/MOP.0000000000000091

Nagayama Hall, G. C. (1995). The preliminary development of theory-based community treatment for sexual offenders. *Professional Psychology: Research and Practice, 26*(5), 478–483.

Nagel, D. B. (1991). Psychotherapy of schizophrenia: 1900–1920. In J. G. Howells (Ed.), *The concept of schizophrenia: Historical perspectives* (pp. 191–201). Washington, DC: American Psychiatric Press.

Najavits, L. M. (2007). Psychosocial treatments for posttraumatic stress disorder. In P. E. Nathan & J. M. Gorman (Eds.), *A guide to treatments that work* (3rd ed.). New York, NY: Oxford University Press.

Nakajima, M., & al'Absi, M. (2012). Predictors of risk for smoking relapse in men and women: A prospective examination. *Psychology of Addictive Behaviors, 26*(3), 633–637.

Nakajima, S. (2018). Complicated grief: Recent developments in diagnostic criteria and treatment. *Philosophical Transactions of the Royal Society B: Biological Sciences, 373*(1754). doi: 10.1098/rstb.2017.0273

Nakajima, S. (2018). Complicated grief: Recent developments in diagnostic criteria and treatment. *Philosophical Transactions of the Royal Society B: Biological Sciences, 373*(1754). doi: 10.1098/rstb.2017.0273

Nanayakkara, V., Ogloff, J. R., McEwan, T. E., & Ducat, L. (in press). Firesetting among people with mental disorders: Differences in diagnosis, motives and behaviour. *International Journal of Forensic Mental Health,* 1–15.

Narrow, W. E., Clarke, D. E., Kuramoto, S. J., Kraemer, H. C., Kupfer, D. J., Greiner, L., & Regier, D. A. (2013). *DSM-5* field trials in the United States and Canada, Part III: Development and reliability testing of a cross-cutting symptom assessment for *DSM-5. American Journal of Psychiatry, 170*(1), 71–82.

Nash, W. P., Boasso, A. M., Steenkamp, M. M., Larson, J. L., Lubin, R. E., & Litz, B. T. (2014). Posttraumatic stress in deployed marines: Prospective trajectories of early adaptation. *Journal of Abnormal Psychology, 124,* 155–171.

Nasser, M. (1988). Eating disorders: The cultural dimension. *Social Psychiatry and Psychiatric Epidemiology, 23,* 184–187.

National Collaborating Centre for Mental Health. (2010)London, UK: British Psychological Society & Royal College of Psychiatrists. https://www.rcpsych.ac.uk/improving-care/nccmh

National Collaborating Centre for Mental Health. (2009). *Borderline personality disorder: The NICE GUIDELINE on treatment and management, Clinical practice guideline no. 78.* London, UK: British Psychological Society & Royal College of Psychiatrists.

National Institute of Drug Abuse. (2013) ([field_revisiondate_1]). MDMA (Ecstasy or Molly) Retrieved from http://www.drugabuse.gov/publications/drugfacts/mdma-ecstasy-or-molly on September 14, 2014

National Institute of Mental Health. (2003). *Breaking ground, breaking through: The strategic plan for mood disorders research* (NIH Publication No. 03-5121). Washington, DC: U.S. Government Printing Office.

National Institute of Mental Health. (2020). *NIMH Strategic Plan for Research* (NIH Publication No. 20-MH-8096). Washington, DC: U.S. Government Printing Office.

National Institute on Alcohol Abuse and Alcoholism. (1997). *Alcohol alert: Alcohol-metabolism* (No. 35, PH 371). Bethesda, MD: Author.

National Institute on Drug Abuse (NIDA). (2009). *Principles of addiction treatment: A research-based guide, 2nd edition* (NIH Publication No. 09-4180). Rockville, MD: National Institute on Drug Abuse.

National Institutes of Health. (n.d.). Human Connectome. Accessed 2021.

National Safety Council. (2013). Estimating the cost of unintentional injuries. Retrieved from http://www.nsc.org/news_resources/injury_and_death_statistics/Pages/EstimatingtheCostsofUnintentional Injuries.aspx

National Sleep Foundation. (2005). *2005 sleep in America poll.* Washington, DC: Author.

National Sleep Foundation. (2009). *2009 sleep in America poll.* Washington, DC: Author.

Natoli, J. L., Ackerman, D. L., McDermott, S., & Edwards, J. G. (2012). Prenatal diagnosis of Down syndrome: A systematic review of termination rates (1995–2011). *Prenatal diagnosis, 32*(2), 142–153.

Navarrete, C. D., Olsson, A., Ho, A. K., Mendes, W. B., Thomsen, L., & Sidanius, J. (2009). Fear extinction to an out-group face: The role of target gender. *Psychological Science, 20*(2), 155–158. doi: 10.1111/j.1467-9280.2009.02273.x

Neal-Barnett, A. M., & Smith, J., Sr. (1997). African Americans. In S. Friedman (Ed.), *Cultural issues in the treatment of anxiety* (pp. 154–174). New York, NY: Guilford.

Neimeyer, R. A., & Currier, J. M. (2009). Grief therapy: Evidence of efficacy and emerging directions. *Current Directions in Psychological Science, 18*(6), 352–356.

Nelles, W. B. N., & Barlow, D. H. (1988). Do children panic? *Clinical Psychology Review, 8*(4), 359–372.

Nelson, B., Yuen, H. P., Wood, S. J., Lin, A., Spiliotacopoulos, D., Bruxner, A., . . . & Francey, S. M. (2013). Long-term follow-up of a group at ultra high risk ("prodromal") for psychosis: The PACE 400 study. *JAMA Psychiatry, 70*(8), 793–802.

Nelson, D. L., Beutler, L. E., & Castonguay, L. G. (2012). Psychotherapy integration in the treatment of personality disorders: A commentary. *Journal of Personality Disorders, 26*(1), 7–16.

Nelson, M. E., Jester, D. J., Petkus, A. J., & Andel, R. (2021). Cognitive reserve, Alzheimer's neuropathology, and risk of dementia: A systematic review and meta-analysis. *Neuropsychology Review*, 1–18.

Nelson, R. O., & Barlow, D. H. (1981). Behavioral assessment: Basic strategies and initial procedures. In D. H. Barlow (Ed.), *Behavioral assessment of adult disorders.* New York, NY: Guilford.

Nemeroff, C. (2004). Early-life adversity, CRF dysregulation, and vulnerability to mood and anxiety disorders. *Psychopharmacology Bulletin, 38*, 14–20.

Nemeroff, C. B. (2013). Psychoneuroimmunoendocrinology: The biological basis of mind-body physiology and pathophysiology. *Depression and Anxiety, 30*(4), 285–287.

Nepon, J., Belik, S. L., Bolton, J., & Sareen, J. (2010). The relationship between anxiety disorders and suicide attempts: Findings from the national epidemiologic survey on alcohol and related conditions. *Depression and Anxiety, 27*, 791–798.

Nestadt, G., Romanoski, A., Chahal, R., Merchant, A., Folstein, M., Gruenberg, E., & McHugh, P. R. (2009). An epidemiological study of histrionic personality disorder. *Psychological Medicine, 20*(2), 413–422.

Nestler, E. J., Hyman, S. E., & Malenka, R. C. (2008). *Molecular neuropharmacology* (2nd ed.). New York, NY: McGraw-Hill.

Neubauer, D. (2009). New directions in the pharmacologic treatment of sleep disorders. *Primary Psychiatry, 16*(2), 52–58.

Neubauer, D. N. (2021). Diagnosis of insomnia. In E. H. During & C. A. Kushida (Eds.), *Clinical sleep medicine: A comprehensive guide for mental health and other medical professionals* (pp. 39–59). Washington, D.C.: American Psychiatric Association Publishing.

Neugroschi, J. A., Kolevzon, A., Samuels, S. C., & Marin, D. B. (2005). Dementia. In B. J. Sadock & V. A. Sadock (Eds.), *Kaplan & Sadock's comprehensive textbook of psychiatry* (pp. 1068–1093). Philadelphia, PA: Lippincott, Williams & Wilkins.

Neumann, C. S., Johansson, P. T., & Hare, R. D. (2013). The Psychopathy Checklist-Revised (PCL-R), low anxiety, and fearlessness: A structural equation modeling analysis. *Personality Disorders: Theory, Research, and Treatment, 4*(2), 129–137.

Neumark-Sztainer, D., & Eisenberg, M. E. (2014). Body Image Concerns, Muscle-Enhancing Behaviors, and Eating Disorders in Males. *JAMA, 312*(20), 2156–2157.

Neumark-Sztainer, D., & Haines, J. (2004). Psychosocial and behavioral consequences of obesity. In J. K. Thompson (Ed.), *Handbook of eating disorders and obesity* (pp. 349–371). New York, NY: Wiley.

Neumark-Sztainer, D., Wall, M. M., Larson, N., Story, M., Fulkerson, J. A., Eisenberg, M. E., & Hannan, P. J. (2012). Secular trends in weight status and weight-related attitudes and behaviors in adolescents from 1999 to 2010. *Preventive Medicine, 54*(1), 77–81. doi: 10.1016/j.ypmed.2011.10.003

Neumark-Sztainer, D., Wall, M., Larson, N. I., Eisenberg, M. E., & Loth, K. (2011). Dieting and disordered eating behaviors from adolescence to young adulthood: findings from a 10-year longitudinal study. *Journal of the American Dietetic Association, 111*(7), 1004–1011.

Nevsimalova, S. (2009). Narcolepsy in childhood. *Sleep Medicine Reviews, 13*(2), 169–180. doi: 10.1016/j.smrv.2008.04.007

New York Mental Hygiene Law § 1.03 (20) (1992).

Newman, J. P., Patterson, C. M., & Kosson, D. S. (1987). Response perseveration in psychopaths. *Journal of Abnormal Psychology, 96*, 145–148.

Newman, J. P., Widom, C. S., & Nathan, S. (1985). Passive-avoidance in syndromes of disinhibition: Psychopathy and extraversion. *Journal of Personality and Social Psychology, 50*, 624–630.

Newman, M. G., Castonguay, L. G., Borkovec, T. D., Fisher, A. J., Boswell, J. F., Szkodny, L. E., & Nordberg, S. S. (2011). A randomized controlled trial of cognitive-behavioral therapy for generalized anxiety disorder with integrated techniques from emotion-focused and interpersonal therapies. *Journal of Consulting and Clinical Psychology, 79*(2), 171–181. doi: 10.1037/a0022489

Newman, M. G., Llera, S. J., Erickson, T. M., Przeworski, A., & Castonguay, L. G. (2013). Worry and generalized anxiety disorder: A review and theoretical synthesis of evidence on nature, etiology, mechanisms, and treatment. *Annual Review of Clinical Psychology*, 275–297. doi: 10.1146/annurev-clinpsy-050212-185544

Newton, N. C., Conrod, P., Teesson, M., & Faggiano, F. (2012). School-based alcohol and other drug prevention. In J. C. Verster, K. Brady, M. Galanter, & P. Conrod (Eds.), *Drug abuse and addiction in medical illness* (pp. 545–560). New York, NY: Springer.

Neylan, T. C., Reynolds, C. F., III, & Kupfer, D. J. (2003). Sleep disorders. In R. E. Hales & S. C. Yudofsky (Eds.), *Textbook of clinical psychiatry* (4th ed., pp. 975–1000). Washington, DC: American Psychiatric Publishing.

Nezu, C. M., Nezu, A. M., Friedman, S. H., Houts, P. S., DelliCarpini, L., Bildner, C., & Faddis, S. (1999). Cancer and psychological distress: Two investigations regarding the role of social problem-solving. *Journal of Psychosocial Oncology, 16*(3–4), 27–40.

Ng, A. C. T., Delgado, V., Borlaug, B. A., & Bax, J. J. (2021). Diabesity: The combined burden of obesity and diabetes on heart

disease and the role of imaging. *Nature Reviews Cardiology, 18*(4), 291–304. doi: 10.1038/s41569-020-00465-5
Ng, B. Y., Yap, A. K., Su, A., Lim, D., & Ong, S. H. (2002). Personality profiles of patients with dissociative trance disorder in Singapore. *Comprehensive psychiatry, 43,* 121–126.
Ng, M., Fleming, T., Robinson, M., Thomson, B., Graetz, N., Margono, C., . . . Gupta, R. (2014). Global, regional and national prevalence of overweight and obesity in children and adults 1980-2013: A systematic analysis. *Lancet (London, England), 384*(9945), 766–781.
Nicassio, P. M., Greenberg, M. A., & Motivala, S. J. (2010). Clinical psychology and health psychology: Toward an integrated perspective on health. In J. M. Suls, Davidson, K. W., & Kaplan, R. M. (Eds.), *Handbook of health psychology and behavioral medicine.* New York, NY: Guilford.
Nichols, D. S. (2011). *Essentials of MMPI-2 assessment* (2nd ed.). Hoboken, NJ: Wiley.
Niederkrotenthaler, T., Voracek, M., Herberth, A., Till, B., Strauss, M., Etzersdorfer, E., … Sonneck, G. (2010). Role of media reports in completed and prevented suicide: Werther v. Papageno effects. *British Journal of Psychiatry, 197*(3), 234–243. doi: 10.1192/bjp.bp.109.074633
Nielsen, D., Ji, F., Yuferov, V., Ho, A., Chen, A., Levran, O., Ott, J., & Kreek, M. (2008). Genotype patterns that contribute to increased risk for or protection from developing heroin addiction. *Molecular Psychiatry, 13*(4), 417–428.
Nierenberg, A. A., Akiskal, H. S., Angst, J., Hirschfeld, R. M., Merikangas, K. R., Petukhova, M., & Kessler, R. C. (2010). Bipolar disorder with frequent mood episodes in the National Comorbidity Survey Replication (NCS-R). *Molecular Psychiatry, 15*(11), 1075–1087.
Nierenberg, A. A., Friedman, E. S., Bowden, C. L., Sylvia, L. G., Thase, M. E., Ketter, T., & Calabrese, J. R. (2013). Lithium treatment moderate-dose use study (LiTMUS) for bipolar disorder: A randomized comparative effectiveness trial of optimized personalized treatment with and without lithium. *American Journal of Psychiatry, 170*(1), 102–110.
Nigg, J. T. (2015). Editorial: The shape of the nosology to come in developmental psychopathology. *Journal of Child Psychology and Psychiatry, 56*(4), 397–399. doi: 10.1111/jcpp.12408
Nigg, J. T., Nikolas, M., & Burt, S. A. (2010). Measured gene-by-environment interaction in relation to Attention-Deficit/Hyperactivity Disorder. *Journal of the American Academy of Child & Adolescent Psychiatry, 49*(9), 863–873. doi: 10.1016/j.jaac.2010.01.025
Nijmeijer, J. S., Minderaa, R. B., Buitelaar, J. K., Mulligan, A., Hartman, C. A., & Hoekstra, P. J. (2008). Attention-deficit/hyperactivity disorder and social dysfunctioning. *Clinical Psychology Review, 28*(4), 692–708.
Nijs, J., Paul, L., & Wallman, K. (2008). Chronic fatigue syndrome: An approach combining self-management with graded exercise to avoid exacerbations. *Journal of Rehabilitation Medicine, 40,* 241–247.
Nikolas, M. A., & Nigg, J. T. (2015). Moderators of neuropsychological mechanism in Attention-Deficit Hyperactivity Disorder. *Journal of Abnormal Child Psychology, 43*(2), 271–281. doi: 10.1007/s10802-014-9904-7
Nikolas, M., & Burt, S. (2010). Genetic and environmental influences on ADHD symptom dimensions of inattention and hyperactivity: A meta-analysis. *Journal of Abnormal Psychology, 119*(1), 1.
Nisbett, R. E., & Ross, L. (1980). *Human inference: Strategies and shortcomings in social judgment.* New York, NY: Century.
Nithianantharajah, J., & Hannan, A. J. (2006, September). Enriched environments, experience-dependent plasticity and disorders of the nervous system. *Nature Reviews Neuroscience.* 7(9):697-709. doi: 10.1038/nrn1970.
Nivard, M. G., Dolan, C. V., Kendler, K. S., Kan, K.-J., Willemsen, G., Van Beijsterveldt, C. E. M.. Lindauer, R. J. L., Van Beek, J. H. D. A., Geels, L. M., Bartels, M., Middeldorp, C. M., & Boomsma, D. I. (2015). Stability in symptoms of anxiety and depression as a function of genotype and environment: A longitudinal twin study from ages 3 to 63 years. *Psychological Medicine, 45,* 1039–1049.
Nivoli, A. M., Murru, A., & Vieta, E. (2010). Lithium: Still a cornerstone in the long-term treatment in bipolar disorder? *Neuropsychobiology, 62*(1), 27–35.
Nock, M. K. (2010). Self-injury. *Annual Review of Clinical Psychology, 6,* 339–363.
Nock, M. K., Borges, G., Bromet, E. J., Alonso, J., Angermeyer, M., Beautrais, A., & Williams, D. (2008). Cross-national prevalence and risk factors for suicidal ideation, plans and attempts. *British Journal of Psychiatry, 192*(2), 98–105.
Nock, M. K., Borges, G., Bromet, E. J., Cha, C. B., Kessler, R. C., & Lee, S. (2008). Suicide and suicidal behavior. *Epidemiologic Reviews, 30,* 133–154.
Nock, M. K., Cha, C. B., & Dour, H. J. (2011). Disorders of impulse-control and self-harm. In D. H. Barlow (Ed.), *Oxford handbook of clinical psychology* (pp. 504–529). New York, NY: Oxford University.
Nock, M. K., Cha, C. B., & Dour, H. J. (2011). Disorders of impulse-control and self-harm. In D. H. Barlow (Ed.), *Handbook of clinical psychology.* (pp. 504–529). New York, NY: Oxford University Press.
Nock, M. K., Hwang, I., Sampson, N. A., & Kessler, R. C. (2010). Mental disorders, comorbidity and suicidal behavior: Results from the National Comorbidity Survey Replication. *Molecular Psychiatry, 15,* 868–876.
Nock, M. K., Kazdin, A. E., Hiripi, E., & Kessler, R. C. (2006). Prevalence, subtypes, and correlates of DSM-IV conduct disorder in the National Comorbidity Survey Replication. *Psychological Medicine, 36*(05), 699–710.
Nock, M. K., Park, J. M., Finn, C. T., Deliberto, T. L., Dour, H. J., & Banaji, M. R. (2010). Measuring the suicidal mind: Implicit cognition predicts suicidal behavior. *Psychological Science, 21*(4), 511–517.
Nock, M., & Kessler, R. (2006). Prevalence of and risk factors for suicide attempts versus suicide gestures: Analysis of the National Comorbidity Survey. *Journal of Abnormal Psychology, 115,* 616–623.
Nofzinger, E. A., Schwartz, C. F., Reynolds, C. F., Thase, M. E., Jennings, J. R., Frank, E., & Kupfer, D. J. (1994). Affect intensity and phasic REM sleep in depressed men before and after treatment with cognitive-behavior therapy. *Journal of Consulting and Clinical Psychology, 62,* 83–91.
Nolen-Hoeksema, S. (1990). *Sex differences in depression.* Stanford, CA: Stanford University Press.
Nolen-Hoeksema, S. (2000). Further evidence for the role of psychosocial factors in depression chronicity. *Clinical Psychology: Science and Practice, 7*(2), 224–227.
Nolen-Hoeksema, S., & Aldao, A. (2011). Gender and age differences in emotion regulation strategies and their relationship to depressive symptoms. *Personality and Individual Differences, 51*(6), 704–708. doi: 10.1016/j.paid.2011.06.012
Nolen-Hoeksema, S., & Hilt, L. M. (2009). Gender differences in depression. In I. H. Gotlib & C. L. Hammen (Eds.), *Handbook of depression* (2nd ed., pp. 386–404). New York, NY: Guilford.
Nolen-Hoeksema, S., Girgus, J. S., & Seligman, M. E. P. (1992). Predictors and consequences of childhood depressive symptoms: A 5-year longitudinal study. *Journal of Abnormal Psychology, 101*(3), 405–422.
Nolen-Hoeksema, S., Wisco, B. E., & Lyubomirsky, S. (2008). Rethinking rumination. *Perspectives on Psychological Science, 3*(5), 400–424.

Nooe, R. M., & Patterson, D. A. (2010). The ecology of homelessness. *Journal of Human Behavior in the Social Environment, 20*(2), 105–152.

Nordentoft, M., Melau, M., Iversen, T., Petersen, L., Jeppesen, P., Thorup, A., . . . Jørgensen, P. (2015). From research to practice: how OPUS treatment was accepted and implemented throughout Denmark. *Early Intervention in Psychiatry, 9*(2), 156–162.

Nordentoft, M., Thorup, A., Petersen, L., Ohlenschlaeger, J., Melau, M., Christensen, T. O., & Jeppesen, P. (2006). Transition rates from schizotypal disorder to psychotic disorder for first-contact patients included in the opus trial: A randomized clinical trial of integrated treatment and standard treatment. *Schizophrenia Research, 83,* 29–40.

Normile, D. (2009). Asia grapples with unexpected wave of HIV infections. *Science, 27,* 1174.

Norrholm, S. D., & Ressler, K. J. (2009). Genetics of anxiety and trauma-related disorders. *Neuroscience, 164*(1), 272–287.

Norris, A. L., Marcus, D. K., & Green, B. A. (2015). Homosexuality as a discrete class. *Psychological Science, 26*(12), 1843–1853.

Norton, G. R., Harrison, B., Hauch, J., & Rhodes, L. (1985). Characteristics of people with infrequent panic attacks. *Journal of Abnormal Psychology, 94,* 216–221.

Norton, M. C., Smith, K. R., Østbye, T., Tschanz, J. T., Corcoran, C., Schwartz, S., & Welsh-Bohmer, K. A. (2010). Greater risk of dementia when spouse has dementia? The Cache County Study. *Journal of the American Geriatrics Society, 58*(5), 895–900.

Novak, B. (2010). Kleptomania and the law. In E. Aboujaoude (Ed.), *Impulse control disorders* (pp. 45–50). New York, NY: Cambridge University Press.

Novella, J., Gosselin, J. T., & Danowski, D. (2015). One size doesn't fit all: New continua of figure drawings and their relation to ideal body image. *Journal of American College Health, 63*(6), 353–360. doi: 10.1080/07448481.2015.1040410

Noyes, R., & Kletti, R. (1977). Depersonalization in response to life-threatening danger. *Comprehensive Psychiatry, 18,* 375–384.

Noyes, R., Garvey, M. J., Cook, B., & Suelzer, M. (1991). Controlled discontinuation of benzodiazepine treatment for patients with panic disorder. *American Journal of Psychiatry, 148,* 517–523.

Noyes, R., Jr., Stuart, S. P., & Watson, D. B. (2008). A reconceptualization of the somatoform disorders. *Psychosomatics, 49*(1), 14–22.

Noyes, R., Stuart, S. P., Langbehn, D. R., Happel, R. L., Longley, S. L., Muller, B. A., & Yagla, S. J. (2003). Test of an interpersonal model of hypochondriasis. *Psychomatic Medicine, 65,* 292–300.

Noyes, R., Watson, D., Carney, C., Letuchy, E., Peloso, P., Black, D., & Doebbeling, B. N. (2004). Risk factors for hypochondriacal concerns in a sample of military veterans. *Journal of Psychosomatic Research, 57,* 529–539.

Ntika, M., Sakellariou, I., Kefalas, P., & Stamatopoulou, I. (2014, June). Experiments with emotion contagion in emergency evacuation simulation. In *Proceedings of the 4th International Conference on Web Intelligence, Mining and Semantics (WIMS14)* (p. 49). ACM.

Nugent, S. A. (2000). Perfectionism: Its manifestations and classroom-based interventions. *Journal of Secondary Gifted Education, 11,* 215–221.

Nunes, K. L., Hermann, C. A., Malcom, J. R., & Lavoie, K. (2013). Childhood sexual victimization, pedophilic interest, and sexual recidivism. *Child Abuse & Neglect, 37*(9), 703–711.

Nunes, P., Wenzel, A., Borges, K., Porto, C., Caminha, R., & de Oliveira, I. (2009). Volumes of the hippocampus and amygdala in patients with borderline personality disorder: A meta-analysis. *Journal of Personality Disorders, 23*(4), 333–345.

Nunley, W., Nunley, B., Cutleh, D. L., Dentingeh, J., & McFahland, B. (2013). Involuntary civil commitment. In K. Yeager, D. Cutler, D. Svendsen, & G. M. Sills (Eds.), *Modern community mental health: An interdisciplinary approach* (pp. 49–61). New York, NY: Oxford University Press.

Nurnberger, J. I. (2012). Genetics of bipolar disorder: Where we are and where we are going. *Depression and Anxiety, 29,* 991–993.

Nurnberger, J. I., & Gershon, E. S. (1992). Genetics. In E. S. Paykel (Ed.), *Handbook of affective disorders* (pp. 126–145). New York, NY: Guilford.

Nusslock, R., Harmon-Jones, E., Alloy, L. B., Urosevic, S., Goldstein, K., & Abramson, L. Y. (2012). Elevated left mid-frontal cortical activity prospectively predicts conversion to bipolar I disorder. *Journal of Abnormal Psychology, 121*(3), 592–601.

Nutakor, J. A., Dai, B., Gavu, A. K., & Antwi, O.-A. (2020). Relationship between chronic diseases and sleep duration among older adults in Ghana. *Quality of Life Research, 29*(8), 2101–2110.

Nutt, D., & Carhart-Harris, R. (2021). The current status of psychedelics in psychiatry. *JAMA Psychiatry, 78*(2),121–122. doi: 10.1001/jamapsychiatry.2020.2171

Nyhan, W. L. (1978). The Lesch-Nyhan syndrome. *Developmental Medicine and Child Neurology, 20,* 376–387.

Nzwalo, H., Ferreira, L., Peralta, R., & Bentes, C. (2013). Sleep-related eating disorder secondary to zolpidem. *BMJ Case Reports,* bcr2012008003.

O'Brien, C. (2011). Addiction and dependence in DSM-V. *Addiction, 106*(5), 866–867.

O'Brien, M. E., Clark, R. A., Besch, C. L., Myers, L., & Kissinger, P. (2003). Patterns and correlates of discontinuation of the initial HAART regimen in an urban outpatient cohort. *Journal of Acquired Immune Deficiency Syndrome, 34*(4), 407–414.

O'Brien, P. E., Sawyer, S. M., Laurie, C., Brown, W. A., Skinner, S., Veit, F., & Dixon, J. B. (2010). Laparoscopic adjustable gastric banding in severely obese adolescents: A randomized trial. *JAMA: Journal of the American Medical Association, 303*(6), 519–526.

O'Brien, P. M., Backstrom, T., Brown, C., Dennerstein, L., Endicott, J., Epperson, C. N., & Yonkers, K. (2011). Towards a consensus on diagnostic criteria, measurement and trial design of the premenstrual disorders: The ISPMD Montreal consensus. *Archives of Women's Mental Health, 14*(1), 13-21. doi: 10.1007/s00737-010-0201-3

O'Callaghan, E., Sham, P., Takei, N., Glover, G., & Murray, R. M. (1991). Schizophrenia after prenatal exposure to 1957 A2 influenza epidemic. *Lancet, 337,* 1248–1250.

O'Carroll, P. W. (1990). Community strategies for suicide prevention and intervention. In S. J. Blumenthal & D. J. Kupfer (Eds.), *Suicide over the life cycle: Risk factors, assessment and treatment of suicidal patients.* Washington, DC: American Psychiatric Press.

O'Connor v. Donaldson, 95 S. Ct. 2486 (1975).

O'Connor, M. F., Wellisch, D. K., Stanton, A. L., Eisenberger, N. I., Irwin, M. R., & Lieberman, M. D. (2008). Craving love? Enduring grief activates brain's reward center. *Neuroimage, 42*(2), 969–972.

O'Donnell, M. L., Varker, T., Creamer, M., Fletcher, S., McFarlane, A. C., Silove, D., & Forbes, D. (2013). Exploration of delayed-onset posttraumatic stress disorder after severe injury. *Psychosomatic Medicine, 75,* 68–75. doi: 10.1097/PSY.0b013e3182761e8b

O'Donovan, A., Slavich, G. M., Epel, E. S., & Neylan, T. C. (2013). Exaggerated neurobiological sensitivity to threat as a mechanism linking anxiety with increased risk for diseases of aging. *Neuroscience and Biobehavioral Reviews, 37,* 96–108. doi: 10.1016/j.neubiorev.2012.10.013

O'Donovan, A., Tomiyama, A. J., Lin, J., Puterman, E., Adler, N. E., Kemeny, M., & Epel, E. S. (2012). Stress appraisals and cellular aging: A key role for anticipatory threat in the relationship between psychological stress and telomere length. *Brain, Behavior and Immunity, 26*(4), 573–579.

O'Hara, M. W., & McCabe, J. E. (2013). Postpartum depression: Current status and future directions. *Annual Review of Clinical Psychology, 9,* 379–407.

O'Hara, M. W., Stuart, S., Gorman, L. L., & Wenzel, A. (2000). Efficacy of interpersonal psychotherapy for postpartum depression. *Archives of General Psychiatry, 57,* 1039–1045.

O'Kearney, R., & Pech, M. (2014). General and sleep-specific worry in insomnia. *Sleep and Biological Rhythms, 12*(3), 212–215.Oades, R. D. (1985). The role of noradrenaline in tuning and dopamine in switching between signals in the CNS. *Neuroscience and Biobehavioral Reviews, 9,* 261–282.

Oakley, D. A., & Halligan, P. W. (2009). Hypnotic suggestion and cognitive neuroscience. *Trends in Cognitive Sciences, 13*(6), 264–270.

Oar, E. L., Farrell, L. J., Waters, A. M., Conlon, E. G., & Ollendick, T. H. (2015). One session treatment for pediatric blood-injection-injury phobia: A controlled multiple baseline trial. *Behaviour Research and Therapy, 73,* 131–142.

O'Connell, N., Nicholson, T. R., Wessely, S., & David, A. S. (2020). Characteristics of patients with motor functional neurological disorder in a large UK mental health service: A case-control study. *Psychological Medicine, 50*(3), 446–455. doi: 10.1017/S0033291719000266

Odlaug, B. L., & Grant, J. E. (2012). Pathological skin picking. In J. E. Grant, D. J. Stein, D. W. Woods, N. J. Keuthen (Eds.), *Trichotillomania, skin picking, and other body-focused repetitive behaviors* (pp. 21–41). Arlington, VA: American Psychiatric Publishing.

Ogden, C. L., Carroll, M. D., Curtin, L. R., Lamb, M. M., & Flegal, K. M. (2010). Prevalence of high body mass index in US children and adolescents, 2007–2008. *JAMA: Journal of the American Medical Association, 303*(3), 242–249.

Ogden, C. L., Carroll, M. D., Curtin, L. R., McDowell, M. A., Tabak, C. J., & Flegal, K. M. (2006). Prevalence of overweight and obesity in the United States, 1999–2004. *JAMA: Journal of the American Medical Association, 295,* 1549–1555.

Ogden, C. L., Carroll, M. D., Kit, B. K., & Flegal, K. M. (2012). Prevalence of obesity and trends in body mass index among US children and adolescents, 1999–2010. *JAMA: Journal of American Medical Association, 307,* 483–490.

Ogden, C. L., Carroll, M. D., Kit, B. K., & Flegal, K. M. (2014). Prevalence of childhood and adult obesity in the United States, 2011–2012. *JAMA, 311*(8), 806–814.

Ogden, C. L., Carroll, M. D., Lawman, H. G., Fryar, C. D., Kruszon-Moran, D., Kit, B. K., & Flegal, K. M. (2016). Trends in obesity prevalence among children and adolescents in the United States, 1988–1994 through 2013–2014. *JAMA, 315*(21), 2292–2299.

Ohayon, M. M., & Schatzberg, A. F. (2002). Prevalence of depressive episodes with psychotic features in the general population. *American Journal of Psychiatry, 159,* 1855–1861.

Ohayon, M. M., & Schatzberg, A. F. (2003). Using chronic pain to predict depressive morbidity in the general population. *Archives of General Psychiatry, 60,* 39–47.

Ohayon, M. M., Dauvilliers, Y., & Reynolds, C. F. (2012). Operational definitions and algorithms for excessive sleepiness in the general population: Implications for DSM-5 nosology. *Archives of General Psychiatry, 69*(1), 71–79. doi: 10.1001/archgenpsychiatry.2011.1240

Öhman, A. (1996). Preferential pre-attentive processing of threat in anxiety: Preparedness and attentional biases. In R. Rapee (Ed.), *Current controversies in the anxiety disorders* (pp. 253–290). New York, NY: Guilford.

Öhman, A., & Dimberg, U. (1978). Facial expressions as conditioned stimuli for electrodermal responses: A case of preparedness? *Journal of Personality and Social Psychology, 36*(11), 1251–1258.

Öhman, A., & Mineka, S. (2001). Fears, phobias, and preparedness: Toward an evolved model of fear and fear learning. *Psychological Review, 108*(3), 483–522.

Öhman, A., Flykt, A., & Lundqvist, D. (2000). Unconscious emotion: Evolutionary perspective, psychophysiological data, and neuropsychological mechanisms. In R. Lane & L. Nadel (Eds.), *The cognitive neuroscience of emotion* (pp. 296–327). New York, NY: Oxford University Press.

Okazaki, S., Okazaki, M., & Sue, S. (2009). Clinical personality assessment with Asian Americans. In J. N. Butcher (Ed.), *Oxford handbook of personality assessment* (pp. 377–395). New York, NY: Oxford University Press.

Oldenburg, B., de Courten, M., & Frean, E. (2010). The contribution of health psychology to the advancement of global health. In J. M. Suls, K. W. Davidson, & R. M. Kaplan, (Eds.), *Handbook of health psychology and behavioral medicine.* New York, NY: Guilford.

Olds, J. (1956). Pleasure centers in the brain. *Scientific American, 195,* 105–116.

Olds, J., & Milner, P. M. (1954). Positive reinforcement produced by electrical stimulation of septal area and other regions of rat brain. *Journal of Comparative and Physiological Psychology, 47,* 419–427.

Olfson, M., King, M., & Schoenbaum, M. (2015). Benzodiazepine use in the United States. *JAMA Psychiatry, 72,* 136–142.

Olfson, M., Marcus, S., & Schaffer, D. (2006). Antidepressant drug therapy and suicide in severely depressed children and adolescents. *Archives of General Psychiatry, 63,* 865–872.

Olfson, M., Shaffer, D., Marcus, S. C., & Greenberg, T. (2003). Relationship between antidepressant medication treatment and suicide in adolescents. *Archives of General Psychiatry, 60,* 978–82.

Olin, S. S., Raine, A., Cannon, T. D., Parnas, J., Schulsinger, F., & Mednick, S. A. (1997). Childhood behavior precursors of schizotypal personality disorder. *Schizophrenia Bulletin, 23,* 93–103.

Olivardia, R., Pope, H. G., & Hudson, J. I. (2000). Muscle dysmorphia in male weightlifters: A case-control study. *American Journal of Psychiatry, 157,* 1291–1296.

Oliver, M. B., & Hyde, J. S. (1993). Gender differences in sexuality: A meta-analysis. *Psychological Bulletin, 114*(1), 29–51.

Olives, C., Myerson, R., Mokdad, A. H., Murray, C. J., & Lim, S. S. (2013). Prevalence, awareness, treatment, and control of hypertension in United States counties, 2001–2009. *PLoS One, 8*(4), e60308.

Olivier B. Serotonin: a never-ending story. Eur J Pharmacol. 2015 Apr 15;753:2-18. doi: 10.1016/j.ejphar.2014.10.031.

Olivier, P., Bertrand, L., Tubery, M., Lauque, D., Montastruc, J.-L., & Lapeyre-Mestre, M. (2009). Hospitalizations because of adverse drug reactions in elderly patients admitted through the emergency department: A prospective survey. *Drugs & Aging, 26*(6), 475–482.

Ollendick, T. H., & Shirk, S. R. (2010). Clinical interventions with children and adolescents: Current status, future directions. In D. H. Barlow (Ed.), *Oxford handbook of clinical psychology* (pp. 762–788). New York, NY: Oxford University Press.

Olmstead, S. B., Pasley, K., & Fincham, F. D. (2013). Hooking up and penetrative hookups: Correlates that differentiate college men. *Archives of Sexual Behavior, 42*(4), 573–583.

Olsen, S., Smith, S. S., Oei, T. P. S., & Douglas, J. (2012). Motivational interviewing (MINT) improves continuous positive airway pressure (CPAP) acceptance and adherence: A randomized controlled trial. *Journal of Consulting and Clinical Psychology, 80*(1), 151.

Olson, K. R., Key, A. C., & Eaton, N. R. (2015). Gender cognition in transgender children. *Psychological Science, 26,* 476–474.

Oltmanns, J. R., & Widiger, T. A. (2020). The Five-Factor Personality Inventory for ICD-11: A facet-level assessment of the ICD-11 trait model. *Psychological Assessment, 32*(1), 60–71.

Oltmanns, T. F., & Powers, A. D. (2012). Gender and personality disorders. In T. A. Widiger (Ed.), *The Oxford handbook of personality disorders* (pp. 206–218). New York, NY: Oxford University Press.

Oluwoye, O., Kriegel, L., Alcover, K. C., McPherson, S., McDonell, M. G., & Roll, J. M. (2020). The dissemination and implementation of contingency management for substance use disorders: A systematic review. *Psychology of Addictive Behaviors, 34*(1), 99.

Olver, M. E., Lewis, K., & Wong, S. C. P. (2013). Risk reduction treatment of high-risk psychopathic offenders: The relationship of psychopathy and treatment change to violent recidivism. *Personality Disorders: Theory, Research, and Treatment, 4*(2), 160–167.

Omalu, B. I., Ives, D. G., Buhari, A. M., Lindner, J. L., Schauer, P. R., Wecht, C. H., & Kuller, L. H. (2007). Death rates and causes of death after bariatric surgery for Pennsylvania residents, 1995 to 2004. *Archives of Surgery, 142*(10), 923–928; discussion 929.

Ono, T., Matsumura, M., & Nishino, S. (2021). Narcolepsy. In E. H. During & C. A. Kushida (Eds.), *Clinical sleep medicine: A comprehensive guide for mental health and other medical professionals* (pp. 99–127). Washington, D.C.: American Psychiatric Association Publishing.

Onslow, M., Jones, M., O'Brian, S., Packman, A., & Menzies, R. (2012). Stuttering. In P. Sturmey & M. Hersen (Eds.), *Handbook of evidence-based practice in clinical psychology* (Vol. 1, pp. 185–208). New York, NY: John Wiley & Sons, Inc.

Opara, F., Hawkins, K., Sundaram, A., Merchant, M., Rasmussen, S., & Holmes, L., Jr. (2013). Impact of comorbidities onracial/ethnic disparities in hypertension in the United States. *ISRN Public Health, 2013,* e967518. doi: 10.1155/2013/967518.

Opjordsmoen, S. (1989). Delusional disorders: I. Comparative long-term outcome. *Acta Psychiatrica Scandinavica, 80,* 603–612.

Oquendo, M., Galfalvy, H., Russo, S., Ellis, S., Grunebaum, M., Burke, A., & Mann, J. J. (2004). Prospective study of clinical predictors of suicidal acts after a major depressive episode in patients with major depressive disorder or bipolar disorder. *American Journal of Psychiatry, 161,* 1433–1441.

Orford, J., & Keddie, A. (2006). Abstinence or controlled drinking in clinical practice: A test of the dependence and persuasion hypotheses. *Addiction, 81*(4), 495–504.

Organization for Economic Co-operation and Development. (2012). *Obesity Update 2012.* Retrieved from http://www.oecd.org/health/49716427.pdf

Orne, M. T., Dinges, D. F., & Orne, E. C. (1984). On the differential diagnosis of multiple personality in the forensic context. *International Journal of Clinical and Experimental Hypnosis, 32,* 118–169.

Orsillo, S. M., & Roemer, L. (2011). *The mindful way through anxiety: Break free from chronic worry and reclaim your life.* New York, NY: Guilford.

Orth-Gomer, K., Schneiderman, N., Wang, H. X., Walldin, C., Blom, M., & Jernberg, T. (2009). Stress reduction prolongs life in women with coronary disease: The Stockholm Women's Intervention Trial for Coronary Heart Disease (SWITCHD). *Circulation Cardiovascular Quality and Outcomes, 2*(1), 25–32.

Ortin, A., Lake, A. M., Kleinman, M., & Gould, M. S. (2012). Sensation seeking as risk factor for suicidal ideation and suicide attempts in adolescence. *Journal of Affective Disorders, 143,* 214–222.

Ortiz, C., Vidair, H. B., Acri, M., Chacko, A., & Kobak, K. (2020). Pilot study of an online parent-training course for disruptive behavior with live remote coaching for practitioners. *Professional Psychology: Research and Practice.*

Oslin, D. W., & Klaus, J. R. (2009). Drug and alcohol abuse. In B. J. Sadock & V. A. Sadock (Eds.), *Kaplan & Sadock's comprehensive textbook of psychiatry* (9th ed., Vol. 2, pp. 4088–4095). Philadelphia, PA: Lippincott Williams & Wilkins.

Öst, L. G. (1985). Mode of acquisition of phobias. *Acta Universitatis Uppsaliensis* (Abstracts of Uppsala Dissertations from the Faculty of Medicine), *529,* 1–45.

Öst, L. G. (1989). *Blood phobia: A specific phobia subtype in DSM-IV.* Paper requested by the Simple Phobia subcommittee of the DSM-IV Anxiety Disorders Work Group.

Öst, L. G. (1992). Blood and injection phobia: Background and cognitive, physiological, and behavioral variables. *Journal of Abnormal Psychology, 101*(1), 68–74.

Öst, L. G., & Sterner, U. (1987). Applied tension: A specific behavioural method for treatment of blood phobia. *Behaviour Research and Therapy, 25,* 25–30.

Öst, L. G., Svensson, L., Hellström, K., & Lindwall, R. (2001). One-session treatment of specific phobia in youths: A randomized clinical trial. *Journal of Consulting and Clinical Psychology, 69,* 814–824.

Osterberg, E. (1986). Alcohol-related problems in cross-national perspectives: Results of the ISACE study. Special issue: Alcohol and culture: Comparative perspectives from Europe and America. (T. Babot, Ed.). *Annals of the New York Academy of Sciences, 472,* 10–20.

Oswalt, S. B., & Wyatt, T. J. (2013). Sexual health behaviors and sexual orientation in a US national sample of college students. *Archives of Sexual Behavior, 42*(8), 1561–1572.

Otis, J. D., & Pincus, D. B. (2008). Chronic pain. In B. A. Boyer & I. Paharia (Eds.), *Comprehensive handbook of clinical health psychology* (pp. 349–370). Hoboken, NJ: Wiley.

Otis, J. D., Pincus, D. B., & Murawksi, M. E. (2011). Cognitive behavioral therapy in pain management. In M. E. Ebert & R. D. Kerns (Eds.), *Behavioral and psychopharmacological therapeutics in pain management* (pp. 184–200). New York, NY: Cambridge University Press.

Otis, J., Macdonald, A., & Dobscha, A. (2006). Integration and coordination of pain management in primary care. *Journal of Clinical Psychology, 62,* 1333–1343.

Otto, M. W., & Applebaum, A. J. (2011). The nature and treatment of bipolar disorder and the bipolar spectrum. In D. H. Barlow (Ed.), *Handbook of clinical psychology.* New York, NY: Oxford University Press.

Otto, M. W., Behar, E., Smits, J. A. J., & Hofmann, S. G. (2009). Combining pharmacological and cognitive behavioral therapy in the treatment of anxiety disorders. In M. M. Antony & M. B. Stein (Eds.), *Oxford handbook of anxiety and related disorders* (pp. 429–440). New York, NY: Oxford University Press.

Otto, M. W., Reilly-Harrington, N. A., Knauz, R. O., Henin, A., Kogan, J. N., & Sachs, G. S. (2008a). *Managing bipolar disorder: A cognitive-behavioral approach. (Therapist Guide).* New York, NY: Oxford University Press.

Otto, M. W., Reilly-Harrington, N. A., Knauz, R. O., Henin, A., Kogan, J. N., & Sachs, G. S. (2008b). *Managing bipolar disorder: A cognitive-behavioral approach. (Workbook).* New York, NY: Oxford University Press.

Otto, M. W., Tolin, D. F., Simon, N. M., Pearlson, G. D., Basden, S., Meunier, S. A., & Pollack, M. H. (2010). Efficacy of D-cycloserine for enhancing response to cognitive-behavior therapy for panic disorder. *Biological Psychiatry, 67*(4), 365–370.

Oude Luttikhuis, H., Baur, L., Jansen, H., Shrewsbury, V. A., O'Malley, C., Stolk, R. P., & Summerbell, C. D. (2009).

Interventions for treating obesity in children: Review. *Cochrane Database System Review, 1*: CD001871.

Ouellet-Morin, I., Boivin, M., Dionne, G., Lupien, S. J., Arseneault, L., Barr, R. G., & Tremblay, R. E. (2008). Variations in heritability of cortisol reactivity to stress as a function of early familial adversity among 19-month-old twins. *Archives of General Psychiatry, 65*(2), 211–218.

Overeem, S., & Reading, P. (Eds.). (2010). *Sleep disorders in neurology: A practical approach*. New York, NY: Wiley-Blackwell.

Ovsiew, F. (2005). Neuropsychiatry and behavioral neurology. In B. J. Sadock & V. A. Sadock (Eds.), *Kaplan & Sadock's comprehensive textbook of psychiatry* (pp. 323–349). Philadelphia: Lippincott Williams & Wilkins.

Owen, J. J., Rhoades, G. K., Stanley, S. M., & Fincham, F. D. (2010). "Hooking up" among college students: Demographic and psychosocial correlates. *Archives of Sexual Behavior, 39,* 653–663.

Owen, J., & Fincham, F. D. (2011). Effects of gender and psychosocial factors on "friends with benefits" relationships among young adults. *Archives of Sexual Behavior, 40*(2), 311–320.

Owen, P. R. (2012). Portrayals of schizophrenia by entertainment media: a content analysis of contemporary movies. *Psychiatric Services, 63* (7), 655–659.

Owens, E. B., Cardoos, S. L., & Hinshaw, S. P. (2015). Developmental progression and gender differences among individuals with ADHD. In R. A. Barkley (Ed.), *Attention-deficit hyperactivity disorder: A handbook for diagnosis & treatment* (4th ed., pp. 223–255). New York, NY: The Guilford Press.

Owens, M., Goodyer, I. M., Wilkinson, P., Bhardwaj, A., Abbott, R., Croudace, T., & Sahakian, B. J. (2012). 5-HTTLPR and early childhood adversities moderate cognitive and emotional processing in adolescence. *PLoS One, 7(11),* e48482. doi: 10.1371/journal.pone.0048482

Owens, Mulchahey, Taylor, Maloney, Dearborn, & Weiss 2009 ref from Chapter 9, MSP 8

Ozbay, F., Johnson, D. C., Dimoulas, E., Morgan, C. A., III, Charney, D., & Southwick, S. (2007). Social support and resilience to stress: From neurobiology to clinical practice. *Psychiatry, 4*(5), 35–40.

Ozonoff, S., Young, G. S., Carter, A., Messinger, D., Yirmiya, N., Zwaigenbaum, L., & Stone, W. L. (2011). Recurrence risk for autism spectrum disorders: A baby siblings research consortium study. *Pediatrics, 128*(3), e488–e495. doi: 10.1542/peds.2010-2825

Pace-Schott, E. F., Germain, A. Milad, M. R. (2015). Effects of sleep on memory for conditioned fear and fear extinction. *Psychological Bulletin, 141,* 835.

Packard, E. P. W., & Olsen, S. N. B. (1871). *The prisoners' hidden life, or insane asylums unveiled: As demonstrated by the report of the investigating committee of the legislature of Illinois, together with Mrs. Packard's coadjutors' testimony*. Chicago, IL: J. N. Clarke.

Padmanabhan, S., Caulfield, M., & Dominiczak, A. F. (2015). Genetic and molecular aspects of hypertension. *Circulation Research, 116*(6), 937–959.

Pagaling, G. T., Espiritu, A. I., Leochico, C. F. D., Andal, V. M. D., Blasco, K. A. R., Bagnas, M. A. C., & Pasco, P. M. D. (2020). Wernicke-Korsakoff syndrome in hyperemesis gravidarum: A case report and literature review. *The Neurohospitalist,* 1941874420953027.

Page, A. C., & Martin, N. G. (1998). Testing a genetic structure of blood–injury–injection fears. *American Journal of Medical Genetics (Neuropsychiatric Genetics), 81,* 377–384.

Page, G. G., Ben-Eliyahu, S., Yirmiya, R., & Liebeskind, J. C. (1993). Morphine attenuates surgery-induced enhancement of metastatic colonization in rats. *Pain, 54*(1), 21–28.

Pagsberg, A. K. (2013). Schizophrenia spectrum and other psychotic disorders. *European Child & Adolescent Psychiatry, 22*(1), 3–9. doi: 10.1007/s00787-012-0354-x

Pahlajani, G., Raina, R., Jones, S., Ali, M., & Zippe, C. (2012). Vacuum erection devices revisited: Its emerging role in the treatment of erectile dysfunction and early penile rehabilitation following prostate cancer therapy. *The Journal of Sexual Medicine, 9*(4), 1182–1189.

Paillard, T., Rolland, Y., & de Souto Barreto, P. (2015). Protective effects of physical exercise in Alzheimer's disease and Parkinson's disease: A narrative review. *Journal of Clinical Neurology, 11*(3), 212–219.

Palace, E. M. (1995). Modification of dysfunctional patterns of sexual response through autonomic arousal and false physiological feedback. *Journal of Consulting and Clinical Psychology, 63,* 604–615.

Palace, E. M., & Gorzalka, B. B. (1990). The enhancing effects of anxiety on arousal in sexually dysfunctional and functional women. *Journal of Abnormal Psychology, 99*(4), 403–411.

Palamar, J. J., & Barratt, M. J. (2016). Synthetic cannabinoids: undesirable alternatives to natural marijuana. *The American Journal of Drug and Alcohol Abuse,* Advance online publication. doi:# 10.3109/00952990.2016.1139584.

Palermo, D., & Sharkey, K. M. (2021). Delayed and advanced sleep-wake phase disorders. In E. H. During & C. A. Kushida (Eds.), *Clinical sleep medicine: A comprehensive guide for mental health and other medical professionals* (pp. 223–244). Washington, D.C.: American Psychiatric Association Publishing.

Palmer, B. W., Savla, G. N., Roesch, S. C., & Jeste, D. V. (2013). Changes in capacity to consent over time in patients involved in psychiatric research. *The British Journal of Psychiatry, 202*(6), 454–458.

Pan, A., Sun, Q., Okereke, O. I., Rexrode, K. M., & Hu, F. B. (2011). Depression and risk of stroke morbidity and mortality: A meta-analysis and systematic review. *JAMA: Journal of the American Medical Association, 306*(11), 1241–1249.

Pan, L., Blanck, H. M., Sherry, B., Dalenius, K., & Grummer-Strawn, L. M. (2012). Trends in the prevalence of extreme obesity among US preschool-aged children living in low-income families, 1998–2010. *JAMA: Journal of American Medical Association, 308,* 2563–2565.

Pandya, N. H., Mevada, A., Patel, V., & Suthar, M. (2013). Study of effects of advanced maternal age related risks for Down syndrome & other trisomies. *International Journal of Biomedical and Advance Research, 4*(2), 123–127.

Paniagua, F. A., & Yamada, A. M. (Eds.). (2013). *Handbook of multicultural mental health: Assessment and treatment of diverse populations.* Academic Press.

Pantaleo, G., Graziosi, C., & Fauci, A. S. (1993). The immunopathogenesis of human immunodeficiency virus infection. *New England Journal of Medicine, 328,* 327–335.

Panza, F., Frisardi, V., Seripa, D., Logroscino, G., Santamato, A., Imbimbo, B. P., & Solfrizzi, V. (2012). Alcohol consumption in mild cognitive impairment and dementia: Harmful or neuroprotective? *International Journal of Geriatric Psychiatry, 27*(12), 1218–1238. doi: 10.1002/gps.3772

Papadopoulos, F. C., Ekbom, A., Brandt, L., & Ekselius, L. (2009). Excess mortality, causes of death and prognostic factors in anorexia nervosa. *British Journal of Psychiatry, 194*(1), 10–17.

Papazoglou, A., Jacobson, L. A., McCabe, M., Kaufmann, W., & Zabel, T. A. (2014). To ID or not to ID? Changes in classification rates of intellectual disability using DSM-5. *Mental Retardation, 52*(3), 165–174.

Papillo, J. F., & Shapiro, D. (1990). The cardiovascular system. In J. T. Cacioppo & L. G. Tassinaryo (Eds.), *Principles of psychophysiology: Physical, social, and inferential elements.* New York, NY: Cambridge University Press.

Paquette, V., Lévesque, J., Mensour, B., Leroux, J-M., Beudoin, G., Bourgouin, P., & Beauregard, M. (2003). "Change the mind and you change the brain": Effects of cognitive-behavioral therapy on the neural correlates of spider phobia. *Neuroimage, 18,* 401–409.

Parcesepe, A. M., & Cabassa, L. J. (2013). Public stigma of mental illness in the United States: A systematic literature review. *Administration and Policy in Mental Health and Mental Health Services Research, 40*(5), 384–399.

Parchi, P., Capellari, S., & Gambetti, P. (2012). Fatal familial and sporadic insomnia. In W. Dickson & R. O. Weller (Eds.), *Neurodegeneration: The molecular pathology of dementia and movement disorders* (2nd ed., pp. 346–349). Oxford, UK: Wiley-Blackwell.

Pardini, D. A., Frick, P. J., & Moffitt, T. E. (2010). Building an evidence base for DSM-5 conceptualizations of oppositional defiant disorder and conduct disorder: Introduction to the special section. *Journal of Abnormal Psychology, 119*(4), 683–688.

Pardini, D., Lochman, J., & Wells, K. (2004). Negative emotions and alcohol use initiation in high-risk boys: The moderating effect of good inhibitory control. *Journal of Abnormal Child Psychology, 32,* 505–518.

Paris, J. (2008). Clinical trials of treatment for personality disorders. *Psychiatric Clinics of North America, 31*(3), 517–526. doi: 10.1016/j.psc.2008.03.013

Paris, J. (2019). Dissociative identity disorder: Validity and use in the criminal justice system. *BJPsych Advances, 25*(5), 287–293. doi: 10.1192/bja.2019.12

Park, C. L., Edmondson, D., Fenster, J. R., & Blank, T. O. (2008). Meaning making and psychological adjustment following cancer: The mediating roles of growth, life meaning, and restored just-world beliefs. *Journal of Consulting and Clinical Psychology, 76,* 863–875.

Park, D. C. (2007). Eating disorders: A call to arms. *American Psychologist,* 62, 158.

Parker, G., & Hadzi-Pavlovic, D. (1990). Expressed emotion as a predictor of schizophrenic relapse: An analysis of aggregated data. *Psychological Medicine, 20,* 961–965.

Parker, G., McCraw, S., & Fletcher, K. (2012). Cyclothymia. *Depression and Anxiety, 29*(6), 487–494.

Parker, G., McCraw, S., Blanch, B., Hadzi-Pavlovic, D., Synnot, H., & Rees, A. (2013). Discriminating melancholic and non- melancholic depression by prototypic clinical features. *Journal of Affective Disorders, 144,* 199–207.

Parker, R. N., McCaffree, K. J., & Alaniz, M. L. (2013). Alcohol availability and violence among Mexican American youth. In R. N. Parker & K. J. McCaffree (Eds.), *Alcohol and violence: The nature of the relationship and the promise of prevention* (pp. 31–38). Plymouth, U.K.: Lexington.

Parker, S., Schwartz, B., Todd, J., & Pickering, L. (2004). Thimerosal-containing vaccines and autistic spectrum disorder: A critical review of published original data. *Pediatrics, 114*(3), 793.

Parkinson, L., & Rachman, S. (1981a). Intrusive thoughts: The effects of an uncontrived stress. *Advances in Behaviour Research and Therapy, 3,* 111–118.

Parkinson, L., & Rachman, S. (1981b). Speed of recovery from an uncontrived stress. *Advances in Behaviour Research and Therapy, 3,* 119–123.

Parner, E. T., Baron-Cohen, S., Lauritsen, M. B., Jørgensen, M., Schieve, L. A., Yeargin-Allsopp, M., & Obel, C. (2012). Parental age and autism spectrum disorders. *Annals of Epidemiology, 22*(3), 143–150.

Parrott, A. C. (2012). MDMA and LSD. In J. C. Verster, K. Brady, M. Galanter, & P. Conrod (Eds.), *Drug abuse and addiction in medical illness* (pp. 175–188). New York, NY: Springer.

Parrott, D. J., Tharp, A. T., Swartout, K. M., Miller, C. A., Hall, G. C. N., & George, W. H. (2012). Validity for an integrated laboratory analogue of sexual aggression and bystander intervention. *Aggressive Behavior, 38*(4), 309–321. doi: 10.1002/ab.21429

Parry-Jones, B., & Parry-Jones, W. L. (2002). History of bulimia and bulimia nervosa. In K. D. Brownell & C. G. Fairburn (Eds.), *Eating disorders and obesity: A comprehensive handbook* (2nd ed., pp. 145–150). New York, NY: Guilford.

Parry-Jones, W. L., & Parry-Jones, B. (1994). Implications of historical evidence for the classification of eating disorders. *British Journal of Psychiatry, 165,* 287–292.

Pascale, A., Marchesi, N., Govoni, S., & Barbieri, A. (2020). Targeting the microbiota in pharmacology of psychiatric disorders. *Pharmacological Research, 157.*

Pasewark, R. A., & Seidenzahl, D. (1979). Opinions concerning the insanity plea and criminality among mental patients. *Bulletin of the American Academy of Psychiatry and Law, 7,* 199–202.

Passie, T., & Halpern, J. H. (2015). The pharmacology of hallucinogens. In R. K. Ries, D. A. Fiellin, S. C. Miller, & R. Saitz (Eds.), *The ASAM principles of addiction medicine* (5th ed., pp. 235–255). New York, NY: Wolters Kluwer.

Patel, S. R., White, D. P., Malhotra, A., Stanchina, M. L., & Ayas, N. T. (2003). Continuous positive airway pressure therapy for treating gess in a diverse population with obstructive sleep apnea: Results of a meta-analysis. *Archives of Internal Medicine, 163*(5), 565–571. doi: 10.1001/archinte.163.5.565

Patrick, D., Althof, S., Pryor, J., Rosen, R., Rowland, D., Ho, K., & Jamieson, C. (2005). Premature ejaculation: An observational study of men and their partners. *Journal of Sexual Medicine, 2,* 358–367.

Patterson, G. R. (1982). *Coercive family process.* Eugene, OR: Castalia.

Patterson, G. R. (1986). Performance models for antisocial boys. *American Psychologist, 41,* 432–444.

Patterson, G. R., DeBaryshe, B. D., & Ramsey, E. (1989). A developmental perspective on antisocial behavior. *American Psychologist, 44,* 329–335.

Patton, G. C., Johnson-Sabine, E., Wood, K., Mann, A. H., & Wakeling, A. (1990). Abnormal eating attitudes in London school girls—A prospective epidemiological study: Outcome at twelve month follow-up. *Psychological Medicine, 20,* 383–394.

Paul, G. L., & Lentz, R. J. (1977). *Psychosocial treatment of chronic mental patients: Milieu versus social learning programs.* Cambridge, MA: Harvard University Press.

Paul, T., Schroeter, K., Dahme, B., & Nutzinger, D. O. (2002). Self-injurious behavior in women with eating disorders. *American Journal of Psychiatry, 159,* 408–411.

Paulesu, E., Démonet, J. F., Fazio, F., McCrory, E., Chanoine, V., Brunswick, N., & Frith, U. (2001). Dyslexia: Cultural diversity and biological unity. *Science, 291*(5511), 2165–2167. doi: 10.1126/science.1057179

Pauli, P., & Alpers, G. W. (2002). Memory bias in patients with hypochondriasis and somatoform pain disorder. *Journal of Psychosomatic Research, 52,* 45–53.

Paulson, J. F., & Bazemore, S. D. (2010). Prenatal and postpartum depression in fathers and its association with maternal depression: A meta- analysis. *JAMA: Journal of the American Medical Association, 303*(19), 1961–1969.

Paxton, S. J., Schutz, H. K., Wertheim, E. H., & Muir, S. L. (1999). Friendship clique and peer influences on body image concerns, dietary restraint, extreme weight-loss behaviors, and binge eating in adolescent girls. *Journal of Abnormal Psychology, 108*(2), 255–266.

Paykel, E. S., & Scott, J. (2009). Treatment of mood disorders. In M. G. Gelder, N. C. Andreasen, J. J. López-Ibor, Jr., & J. R. Geddes (Eds.), *New Oxford textbook of psychiatry* (2nd ed., Vol. 1, pp. 669–680). Oxford, UK: Oxford University Press.

Payne, K., Reissing, E., Lahaie, M., Binik, Y., Amsel, R., & Khalife, S. (2005). What is sexual pain? A critique of DSM's classification of dyspareunia and vaginismus. In D. Karasic & J. Drescher (Eds.), *Sexual and gender diagnoses of the Diagnostic and Statistical Manual (DSM): A reevaluation* (pp. 141–154). New York, NY: Haworth.

Payne, L. A., White, K. S., Gallagher, M. W., Woods, S. W., Shear, K. M., Gorman, J. M., Farchione, T. J., & Barlow, D. H. (in press). Second-stage treatments for relative non-responders to cognitive-behavioral therapy (CBT) for panic disorder with or without agoraphobia—Continued CBT versus paroxetine: A randomized controlled trial. *Depression and Anxiety.*

Payne, L. A., White, K. S., Gallagher, M. W., Woods, S. W., Shear, M. K., Gorman, J. M., Farchione, T. J., & Barlow, D. H. (2016). Second-stage treatments for relative non-responders to cognitive behavioral therapy (CBT) for panic disorder with or without agoraphobia—Continued CBT versus SSRI: A randomized controlled trial. *Depression & Anxiety, 33*(5), 392–399. doi: 10.1002/da.22457.

Payne, L. A., White., K. S., Gallagher, M. W., Woods, S. W., Shear, M. K., Gorman, J. M., Farchione, T. J., & Barlow, D. H. (2016). Second-stage treatments for relative non-responders to cognitive-behavioral therapy (CBT) for panic disorder with or without agoraphobia: Continued CBT versus SSRI: A randomized controlled trial. *Depression and Anxiety, 33,* 392–399.

Peall, K. J., & Robertson, N. P. (2014). Narcolepsy: environment, genes and treatment. *Journal of Neurology, 261*(8), 1644–1646.

Pearlstein, T. (2010). Premenstrual dysphoric disorder: Out of the appendix. *Archives of Women's Mental Health, 13*(1), 21–23.

Pearlstein, T., & Steiner, M. (2008). Premenstrual dysphoric disorder: Burden of illness and treatment update. *Journal of Psychiatry & Neuroscience, 33*(4), 291–301.

Pearlstein, T., Yonkers, K. A., Fayyad, R., & Gillespie, J. A. (2005). Pretreatment pattern of symptom expression in premenstrual dysphoric disorder. *Journal of Affective Disorder, 85,* 275–282.

Pearson, C. M., Wonderlich, S. A., & Smith, G. T. (2015). A Risk and Maintenance Model for Bulimia Nervosa: From Impulsive Action to Compulsive Behavior, *Psychological Review, 122*(3), 516–533.

Pearson, C., Montgomery, A., & Locke, G. (2009). Housing stability among homeless individuals with serious mental illness participating in Housing First programs. *Journal of Community Psychology, 37*(3), 404–417.

Pearson, F. S., Prendergast, M. L., Podus, D., Vazan, P., Greenwell, L., & Hamilton, Z. (2012). Meta-analyses of seven of the National Institute on Drug Abuse's principles of drug addiction treatment. *Journal of Substance Abuse Treatment, 43*(1), 1–11.

Peat, C. M., Peyerl, N. L., & Muehlenkamp, J. J. (2008). Body image and eating disorders in older adults: A review. *The Journal of General Psychology, 135*(4), 343–358.

Peat, C., Mitchell, J. E., Hoek, H. W., & Wonderlich, S. A. (2009). Validity and utility of subtyping anorexia nervosa. *International Journal of Eating Disorders, 42*(7), 590–594.

Pedersen, C. B., & Mortensen, P. B. (2006). Are the cause(s) responsible for urban-rural differences in schizophrenia risk rooted in families or in individuals? *American Journal of Epidemiology, 163*(11), 971–978.

Pedersen, N. L. (2010). Reaching the limits of genome-wide significance in Alzheimer disease: Back to the environment. *JAMA: Journal of the American Medical Association, 303*(18), 1864–1865.

Peeters, J., Van Beek, A., Meerveld, J., Spreeuwenberg, P., & Francke, A. (2010). Informal caregivers of persons with dementia, their use of and needs for specific professional support: A survey of the National Dementia Programme. *BMC Nursing, 9*(1), 9. doi: 10.1186/1472-6955-9-9

Pehlivanturk, B., & Unal, F. (2002). Conversion disorder in children and adolescents: A 4-year follow-up study. *Journal of Psychosomatic Research, 52,* 187–191.

Pelham Jr., W. E., & Altszuler, A. R. (2020). Combined treatment for children with attention-deficit/hyperactivity disorder: Brief history, the multimodal treatment for attention-deficit/hyperactivity disorder study, and the past 20 years of research. *Journal of Developmental & Behavioral Pediatrics, 41,* S88–S98.

Pelham, W. E., Jr. (1999). The NIMH Multimodal Treatment Study for attention-deficit hyperactivity disorder: Just say yes to drugs alone? *Canadian Journal of Psychiatry, 44,* 981–990.

Pellicano, E., & Stears, M. (2011). Bridging autism, science and society: Moving toward an ethically informed approach to autism research. *Autism Research, 4*(4), 271–282. doi: 10.1002/aur.201

Pellowski, J. A., Kalichman, S. C., Matthews, K. A., & Adler, N. (2013). A pandemic of the poor: Social disadvantage and the U.S. HIV epidemic. *American Psychologist, 68*(4), 197–209.

Pen, A. E., & Jensen, U. B. (2016). Current status of treating neurodegenerative disease with induced pluripotent stem cells. *Acta Neurologica Scandinavica.* doi: 10.1111/ane.12545. [Epub ahead of print]

Penders, T. M., Gestring, R. E., & Vilensky, D. A. (2012). Intoxication delirium following use of synthetic cathinone derivatives. *The American Journal of Drug and Alcohol Abuse, 38*(6), 616–617.

Pendery, M. L., Maltzman, I. M., & West, L. J. (1982). Controlled drinking by alcoholics? New findings and a reevaluation of a major affirmative study. *Science, 217,* 169–175.

Penedo, F. J., Antoni, M. H., & Schneiderman, N. (2008). *Cognitive-behavioral stress management for prostate cancer recovery: Facilitator guide.* New York, NY: Oxford University Press.

Peng, T. (2008, November 23). Out of the Shadows. *Newsweek.*

Pennington, B., & Bishop, D. (2009). Relations among speech, language, and reading disorders. *Annual Review of Psychology, 60,* 283–306.

Penninx, B. W., Pine, D. S., Holmes, E. A., & Reif, A. (2021). Anxiety disorders. *The Lancet, 397*(10277), 914–927. doi: 10.1016/S0140-6736(21)00359-7

Peplau, L. A. (2003). Human sexuality: How do men and women differ? *Current Directions in Psychological Science, 12,* 37–40.

Perea, G., & Araque, A. (2007). Astrocytes potentiate transmitter release at single hippocampal synapses. *Science, 317,* 1083–1087.

Pereira, D. B., Antoni, M. H., Danielson, A., Simon, T., Efantis-Potter, J., Carver, C. S., & O'Sullivan, M. J. (2003). Stress as a predictor of symptomatic genital herpes virus recurrence in women with human immunodeficiency virus. *Journal of Psychosomatic Research, 54*(3), 237–244.

Pérez-Fuentes, G., Olfson, M., Villegas, L., Morcillo, C., Wang, S., & Blanco, C. (2013). Prevalence and correlates of child sexual abuse: A national study. *Comprehensive Psychiatry, 54*(1), 16–27.

Perez-Sales, P. (1990). Camptocormia. *British Journal of Psychiatry, 157,* 765–767.

Pericak-Vance, M. A., Johnson, C. C., Rimmler, J. B., Saunders, A. M., Robinson, L. C., D'Hondt, E. G., & Haines, J. L. (1996). Alzheimer's disease and apolipoprotein E-4 allele in an Amish population. *Annals of Neurology, 39,* 700–704.

Peris, T. S., Compton, S. N., Kendall, P. C., Birmaher, B., Sherrill, J., March, J., . . . Piacentini, J. (2015). Trajectories of change in youth anxiety during cognitive —behavior therapy. *Journal of Consulting and Clinical Psychology, 83*(2), 239.

Perkonigg, A., Pfister, H., Stein, M. B., Hofler, M., Lieb, R., Maercker, A., & Wittchen, H.-U. (2005). Longitudinal course of posttraumatic stress disorder and posttraumatic stress disorder symptoms in a community sample of adolescents and young adults. *American Journal of Psychiatry, 162,* 1320–1327.

Perlin, M. L. (2000). *The hidden prejudice: Mental disability on trial.* Washington, DC: American Psychological Association.

Perlis, M. L., Smith, L. J., Lyness, J. M., Matteson, S. R., Pigeon, W. R., Jungquist, C. R., & Tu, X. (2006). Insomnia as a risk factor for onset of depression in the elderly. *Behavioral Sleep Medicine, 4*(2), 104–113.

Perneczky, R., Wagenpfeil, S., Lunetta, K. L., Cupples, L. A., Green, R. C., DeCarli, C., & Kurz, A. (2009). Education attenuates the effect of medial temporal lobe atrophy on cognitive function in Alzheimer's disease: The MIRAGE Study. *Journal of Alzheimer's Disease, 17*(4), 855–862.

Perrault, R., Carrier, J., Desautels, A., Montplaisir, J., & Zadra, A. (2014). Electroencephalographic slow waves prior to sleepwalking episodes. *Sleep Medicine, 15*(12), 1468–1472.

Perrin, S., Bevan, D., Payne, S., & Bolton, D. (2019). GAD-specific cognitive behavioral treatment for children and adolescents: A pilot randomized controlled trial. *Cognitive Therapy and Research, 43*(6), 1051–1064. doi:10.1007/s10608-019-10020-3

Perron, B., & Howard, M. (2009). Adolescent inhalant use, abuse, and dependence. *Addiction, 104*(7), 1185–1192.

Perry, J. C. (1993). Longitudinal studies of personality disorders. *Journal of Personality Disorders, 7,* 63–85.

Perry, J. C., & Bond, M. (2012). Change in defense mechanisms during long-term dynamic psychotherapy and five-year outcome. *American Journal of Psychiatry, 169*(9), 916–925.

Perry, J. C., & Bond, M. (2014). Change in defense mechanisms during long-term dynamic psychotherapy and five-year outcome. *American Journal of Psychiatry, 169*(9), 916–925.

Person, D. C., & Borkovec, T. D. (1995, August). *Anxiety disorders among the elderly: Patterns and issues.* Paper presented at the 103rd annual meeting of the American Psychological Association. New York.

Perugi, G., Angst, J., Azorin, J. M., Bowden, C., Vieta, E., & Young, A. H. (2013). Is comorbid borderline personality disorder in patients with major depressive episode and bipolarity a developmental subtype? Findings from the international BRIDGE study. *Journal of Affective Disorders, 144,* 72–78.

Petersen, J. L., & Hyde, J. S. (2010). A meta-analytic review of research on gender differences in sexuality, 1993-2007. *Psychological Bulletin, 136,* 21–38.

Petersen, R. C., Smith, G. E., Waring, S. C., Ivnik, R. J., Tangalos, E. G., & Kokmen, E. (1999). Mild cognitive impairment: Clinical characterization and outcome. *Archives of Neurology, 56*(3), 303–308. doi: 10.1001/archneur.56.3.303

Peterson, L., & Roberts, M. C. (1992). Complacency, misdirection, and effective prevention of children's injuries. *American Psychologist, 47*(8), 1040–1044.

Peterson, L., & Thiele, C. (1988). Home safety at school. *Child and Family Behavior Therapy, 10*(1), 1–8.

Peterson, R. L., & Pennington, B. F. (2012). Developmental dyslexia. *The Lancet, 379*(9830), 1997–2007. doi: http://dx.doi.org/10.1016/S0140-6736(12)60198-6

Petit, D., Pennestri, M. H., Paquet, J., Desautels, A., Zadra, A., Vitaro, F., . . . Montplaisir, J. (2015). Childhood sleepwalking and sleep terrors: a longitudinal study of prevalence and familial aggregation. *JAMA Pediatrics, 169*(7), 653–658.

Petrill, S. A. (2013). Behavioral genetics, learning abilities, and disabilities. In H. L. Swanson, K. R. Harris, & S. Graham (Eds.), *Handbook of learning disabilities* (2nd ed., pp. 293–306). New York, NY: Guilford.

Petrovic, P., Kalso, E., Petersson, K. M., & Ingvar, M. (2002). Placebo and opioid analgesia—imaging a shared neuronal network. *Science, 295*(5560), 1737–1740.

Pettorruso, M., Zoratto, F., Miuli, A., De Risio, L., Santorelli, M., Pierotti, A., … di Giannantonio, M. (in press). Exploring dopaminergic transmission in gambling addiction: a systematic translational review. *Neuroscience & Biobehavioral Reviews.*

Phé, V., & Rouprêt, M. (2012). Erectile dysfunction and diabetes: a review of the current evidence-based medicine and a synthesis of the main available therapies. *Diabetes & metabolism, 38*(1), 1–13.

Phelan, S., & Wadden, T. A. (2004). Behavioral assessment of obesity. In J. K. Thompson (Ed.), *Handbook of eating disorders and obesity* (pp. 393–420). New York, NY: Wiley.

Phelps, E. A., & Hofmann, S. G. (2019). Memory editing: From science fiction to clinical practice. *Nature, 572,* 43–50. doi: 10.1038/s41586-019-1433-7

Phelps, E. A., & Hofmann, S. G. (2019). Memory editing from science fiction to clinical practice. *Nature, 572*(7767), 43–50. doi: 10.1038/s41586-019-1433-7

Philips, H. C., & Grant, L. (1991). Acute back pain: A psychological analysis. *Behaviour Research and Therapy, 29,* 429–434.

Phillips, K. A. (1991). Body dysmorphic disorder: The distress of imagined ugliness. *American Journal of Psychiatry, 148,* 1138–1149.

Phillips, K. A. (2005). *The broken mirror: Understanding and treating body dysmorphic disorder* (Rev. & expanded ed.). New York, NY: Oxford University Press.

Phillips, K. A., & Stout, R. (2006). Association in the longitudinal course of body dysmorphic disorder with major depression, obsessive compulsive disorder, and social phobia. *Journal of Psychiatric Research, 40,* 360–369.

Phillips, K. A., Albertini, R. S., & Rasmussen, S. A. (2002). A randomized placebo-controlled trial of fluoxetine in body dysmorphic disorder. *Evidence-Based Mental Health, 5,* 119.

Phillips, K. A., Dufresne, R. G., Wilkel, C. S., & Vittorio, C. C. (2000). Rate of body dysmorphic disorder in dermatology patients. *Journal of the American Academy of Dermatology, 42,* 436–441.

Phillips, K. A., Grant, J., Siniscalchi, J., & Albertini, R. S. (2001). Surgical and nonpsychiatric medical treatment of patients with body dysmorphic disorder. *Psychosomatics, 42,* 504–510.

Phillips, K. A., McElroy, S. L., Keck, P. E., Jr., Pope, H. G., Jr., & Hudson, J. I. (1993). Body dysmorphic disorder: 30 cases of imagined ugliness. *American Journal of Psychiatry, 150,* 302–308.

Phillips, K. A., Menard, W., & Fay, C. (2006). Gender similarities and differences in 200 individuals with body dysmorphic disorder. *Comprehensive Psychiatry, 47,* 77–87.

Phillips, K. A., Menard, W., Fay, C., & Pagano, M. E. (2005). Psychosocial functioning and quality of life in body dysmorphic disorder. *Comprehensive Psychiatry, 46*(4), 254–260.

Phillips, K. A., Menard, W., Fay, C., & Weisberg, R. (2005). Demographic characteristics, phenomenology, comorbidity, and family history in 200 individuals with body dysmorphic disorder. *Psychosomatics, 46,* 317–325.

Phillips, K. A., Menard, W., Pagano, M., Fay, C., & Stout, R. (2006). Delusional versus nondelusional body dysmorphic disorder: Clinical features and course of illness. *Journal of Psychiatric Research, 40,* 95–104.

Phillips, K. A., Pagano, M., Menard, W., & Stout, R. (2006). A 12-month follow-up study of the course of body dysmorphic disorder. *American Journal of Psychiatry, 163,* 907–912.

Phillips, K. A., Pinto, A., Hart, A. S., Coles, M. E., Eisen, J. L., Menard, W., & Rasmussen, S. A. (2012). A comparison of insight in body dysmorphic disorder and obsessive-compulsive disorder. *Journal of Psychiatric Research, 46,* 1293–1299. doi: 10.1016/j.jpsychires.2012.05.016

Phillips, K. A., Wilhelm, S., Koran, L. M., Didie, E., Fallon, B., Feusner, J., & Stein, D. J. (2010). Body dysmorphic disorder: Some key issues for DSM-V. *Depression and Anxiety, 27,* 573–591. doi: 10.1002/da.20709.

Phillips, K. A., Yen, S., & Gunderson, J. G. (2003). Personality disorders. In R. E. Hales & S. C. Yudofsky (Eds.), *Textbook of clinical psychiatry* (4th ed., pp. 804–832). Washington, DC: American Psychiatric Publishing.

Phillips, L. J., Francey, S. M., Edwards, J., & McMurray, N. (2007). Stress and psychosis: Towards the development of new models of investigation. *Clinical Psychology Review, 27,* 307–317.

Phillips, M. R., Li, X., & Zhang, Y. (2002). Suicide rates in China, 1995–99. *Lancet, 359,* 835–840.

Phillips, M. R., Shen, Q., Liu, X., Pritker, S., Streiner, D., Conner, K., & Yang, G. (2007). Assessing depressive symptoms in persons who die of suicide in mainland China. *Journal of Affective Disorders, 98,* 73–82.

Pick, S., Goldstein, L. H., Perez, D. L., & Nicholson, T. R. (2019). Emotional processing in functional neurological disorder: A review, biopsychosocial model and research agenda. *Journal of Neurology, Neurosurgery and Psychiatry, 90*(6), 704–711. doi: 10.1136/jnnp-2018-319201

Pierce, K. (2016). Neurodevelopmental disorders: Specific learning disorder, communication disorders, and motor disorders. In M. K. Dulcan (Ed.), *Dulcan's Textbook of Child and Adolescent Psychiatry* (2nd ed., pp. 157–171). Arlington, VA: American Psychiatric Publishing.

Pierce, K. A., & Kirkpatrick, D. R. (1992). Do men lie on fear surveys? *Behaviour Research and Therapy, 30,* 415–418.

Pierse, T., Keogh, F., Challis, D., & O'Shea, E. (in press). Resource allocation in dementia care: Comparing the views of people with dementia, carers and health and social care professionals under constrained and unconstrained budget scenarios. *Aging & Mental Health.*

Pike, K. M., & Rodin, J. (1991). Mothers, daughters, and disordered eating. *Journal of Abnormal Psychology, 100*(2), 198–204.

Pike, K. M., Hoek, H. W., & Dunne, P. E. (2014). Cultural trends and eating disorders. *Current Opinion in Psychiatry, 27*(6), 436–442.

Pike, K. M., Walsh, B. T., Vitousek, K., Wilson, G. T., & Bauer, J. (2003). Cognitive behavior therapy in the posthospitalization treatment of anorexia nervosa. *American Journal of Psychiatry, 160,* 2046–2048.

Pike, K., Hoek, H., & Dunne, P. (2014). Cultural trends and eating disorders. *Current Opinion in Psychiatry, 27,* 436–442.

Pincus, A. L. (2020). Commentary on the special issue: Complexity, pleomorphism, and dynamic processes in narcissistic personality disorder. *Journal of Personality Disorders, 34*(Suppl.), 204–206.

Pincus, D. B., Santucci, L. C., Ehrenreich, J. T., & Eyberg, S. M. (2008). The implementation of modified parent-child interaction therapy for youth with separation anxiety disorder. *Cognitive and Behavioral Practice, 15*(2), 118–125.

Pinel, P. (1962). *A treatise on insanity.* New York, NY: Hafner. (Original work published in 1801.)

Pinel, P. H. (1809). *Traité medico-philosophique sur l'aliénation mentale.* Paris, France: J. A. Brosson.

Pinto, A. (2015). Treatment of obsessive-compulsive personality disorder. In *Clinical Handbook of Obsessive-Compulsive and Related Disorders* (pp. 415–429). Springer International Publishing.

Pinto, A. (2020). Psychotherapy for OCPD. In J. E. Grant, A. Pinto, & S. R. Chamberlain (Eds.), *Obsessive-compulsive personality disorder* (pp. 143–177). Washington, D.C.: American Psychiatric Association Publishing.

Pinto, R., Ashworth, M., & Jones, R. (2008). Schizophrenia in black Caribbeans living in the UK: An exploration of underlying causes of the high incidence rate. *The British Journal of General Practice, 58*(551), 429.

Piomelli, D. (2003). The molecular logic of endocannabinoid signalling. *Nature Reviews Neuroscience, 4*(11), 873–884.

Piomelli, D. (2014). More surprises lying ahead. The endocannabinoids keep us guessing. *Neuropharmacology, 76,* 228–234.

Pires, G. N., Tufik, S., & Andersen, M. L. (2015). Sleep deprivation and anxiety in humans and rodents—Translational considerations and hypotheses. *Behavioral neuroscience, 129*(5), 621.

Pisetsky, E. M., Thornton, L. M., Lichtenstein, P., Pedersen, N. L., & Bulik, C. M. (2013). Suicide attempts in women with eating disorders. *Journal of Abnormal Psychology, 122*(4), 1042–1056.

Pizzagalli, D. A. (2014). Depression, stress, and anhedonia: Toward a synthesis and integrated model. *Annual Review of Clinical Psychology, 10,* 393–432.

Pjrek, E., Friedrich, M., Cambioli, L., Dold, M., Jäger, F., Komorowski, A., … Winkler, D. (2020). The efficacy of light therapy in the treatment of seasonal affective disorder: A meta-analysis of randomized controlled trials. *Psychotherapy and Psychosomatics, 89*(1), 17–24. doi: 10.1159/000502891

Plans, L., Barrot, C., Nieto, E., Rios, J., Schulze, T. J., Papiol, S., Mitjans, M., Vieta, E., & Bennabarre, A. (2019). Association between completed suicide and bipolar disorder: A systematic review of the literature. *Journal of Affective Disorders 242,* 111–122.

Pletcher, M. J., Vittinghoff, E., Kalhan, R., Richman, J., Safford, M., Sidney, S., & Kertesz, S. (2012). Association between marijuana exposure and pulmonary function over 20 years. *JAMA: Journal of the American Medical Association, 307*(2), 173–181. doi: 10.1001/jama.2011.1961

Pliszka, S. R. (2015). Comorbid psychiatric disorders in children with ADHD. In R. A. Barkley (Ed.), *Attention-deficit hyperactivity disorder: A handbook for diagnosis & treatment* (4th ed., pp. 140–168). New York, NY: The Guilford Press.

Plomin, R. (1990). The role of inheritance in behavior. *Science, 248,* 183–188.

Plomin, R., & Davis, O. S. P. (2009). The future of genetics in psychology and psychiatry: Microarrays, genome-wide association, and non-coding RNA. *Journal of Child Psychology and Psychiatry, 50*(1–2), 63–71.

Plomin, R., & Kovas, Y. (2005). Generalist genes and learning disabilities. *Psychological Bulletin, 131*(4), 592–617.

Plomin, R., DeFries, J. C., McClearn, G. E., & Rutter, M. (1997). *Behavioral genetics: A primer* (3rd ed.). New York, NY: Freeman.

Plomin, R., McClearn, G. E., Smith, D. L., Skuder, P., Vignetti, S., Chorney, M. J., & McGuffin, P. (1995). Allelic association between 100 DNA markers and high versus low IQ. *Intelligence, 21,* 31–48.

Pocock, S. J. (2013). *Clinical trials: a practical approach.* Hoboken, NJ: John Wiley & Sons.

Podewils, L. J., Guallar, E., Kuller, L. H., Fried, L. P., Lopez, O. L., Carlson, M., & Lyketsos, C. G. (2005). Physical activity, APOE genotype, and dementia risk: Findings from the Cardiovascular Health Cognition Study. *American Journal of Epidemiology, 161,* 639–651.

Polanczyk, G., de Lima, M. S., Horta, B. L., Biederman, J., & Rohde, L. A. (2007). The worldwide prevalence of ADHD: A systematic review and metaregression analysis. *American Journal of Psychiatry, 164,* 942–948.

Polanczyk, G., Zeni, C., Genro, J. P., Guimaraes, A. P., Roman, T., Hutz, M. H., & Rohde, L. A. (2007). Association of the adrenergic a2A receptor gene with methylphenidate improvement of inattentive symptoms in children and adolescents with attention-deficit/hyperactivity disorder. *Archives of General Psychiatry, 64,* 218–224.

Polivy, J. M., & Herman, C. P. (1993). Etiology of binge eating: Psychological mechanisms. In C. G. Fairburn & G. T. Wilson (Eds.), *Binge eating: Nature, assessment, and treatment.* New York, NY: Guilford.

Polivy, J., & Herman, C. P. (2002). Dieting and its relation to eating disorder. In K. D. Brownell & C. G. Fairburn (Eds.), *Eating disorders and obesity: A comprehensive handbook* (2nd ed., pp. 83–86). New York, NY: Guilford.

Pollack, M. H. (2005). The pharmacotherapy of panic disorder. *Journal of Clinical Psychiatry, 66,* 23–27.

Pollack, M. H., & Simon, N. M. (2009). Pharmacotherapy for panic disorder and agoraphobia. In M. M. Antony & M. B. Stein (Eds.), *Oxford handbook of anxiety and related disorders* (pp. 295–307). New York, NY: Oxford University Press.

Polloway, E. A., Schewel, R., & Patton, J. R. (1992). Learning disabilities in adulthood: Personal perspectives. *Journal of Learning Disabilities, 25,* 520–522.

Polonsky, D. C. (2000). Premature ejaculation. In S. R. Leiblum & R. C. Rosen (Eds.), *Principles and practice of sex therapy* (3rd ed., pp. 305–332). New York, NY: Guilford.

Pompili, M., Serafini, G., Innamorati, M., Biondi, M., Siracusano, A., Di Giannantonio, M., & Möller-Leimkühler, A. M. (2012). Substance abuse and suicide risk among adolescents. *European Archives of Psychiatry and Clinical Neuroscience, 262*(6), 469–485.

Pompili, M., Serafini, G., Innamorati, M., Möller-Leimkühler, A. M., Giupponi, G., Girardi, P., & Lester, D. (2010). The hypothalamic-pituitary-adrenal axis and serotonin abnormalities: A selective overview for the implications of suicide prevention. *European Archives of Psychiatry and Clinical Neuroscience, 260*(8), 583–600.

Ponseti, J., Granert, O., Jansen, O., Wolff, S., Beier, K., Neutze, J., & Bosinski, H. (2012). Assessment of pedophilia using hemodynamic brain response to sexual stimuli. *Archives of General Psychiatry, 69*(2), 187.

Poole, K. L., Van Lieshout, R. J., & Schmidt, L. A. (2017). Exploring relations between shyness and social anxiety disorder: The role of sociability. *Personality and Individual Differences, 110,* 55–59. doi: 10.1016/j.paid.2017.01.020

Poon, K., Watson, L., Baranek, G., & Poe, M. D. (2012). To what extent do joint attention, imitation, and object play behaviors in infancy predict later communication and intellectual functioning in ASD? *Journal of Autism and Developmental Disorders, 42*(6), 1064–1074. doi: 10.1007/s10803-011-1349-z

Poorsattar, S., & Hornung, R. (2010). Tanning addiction: Current trends and future treatment. *Expert Review of Dermatology, 5*(2), 123–125.

Pope Jr, H. G., Gruber, A. J., Mangweth, B., Bureau, B., Jouvent, R., & Hudson, J. I. (2014). Body image perception among men in three countries. *American Journal of Psychiatry, 157*(8), 1297–1301.

Pope, C., Pope, H., Menard, W., Fay, C., Olivardia, R., & Phillips, K. (2005). Clinical features of muscle dysmorphia among males with body dysmorphic disorder. *Body Image, 4,* 395–400.

Pope, H. G., Jr., & Kanayama, G. (2012). Anabolic–androgenic steroids. In J. C. Verster, K. Brady, M. Galanter, & P. Conrod (Eds.), *Drug Abuse and Addiction in Medical Illness* (pp. 251–264). New York, NY: Springer.

Pope, H. G., Jr., Gruber, A. J., Mangweth, B., Bureau, B., deCol, C., Jouvent, R., & Hudson, J. I. (2000). Body image perception among men in three countries. *American Journal of Psychiatry, 157,* 1297–1301.

Pope, H. G., Jr., Oliva, P. S., Hudson, J. I., Bodkin, J. A., & Gruber, A. J. (1999). Attitudes toward DSM-IV dissociative disorders diagnoses among board-certified American psychiatrists. *American Journal of Psychiatry, 156*(2), 321–323.

Pope, K. S. (1996). Memory, abuse and science: Questioning claims about the false memory syndrome epidemic. *American Psychologist, 51,* 957–974.

Pope, K. S. (1997). Science as careful questioning: Are claims of a false memory syndrome epidemic based on empirical evidence? *American Psychologist, 52,* 997–1006.

Poppa, T., & Bechara, A. (2015). A neural perspective of immoral behavior and psychopathy. *AJOB Neuroscience, 6*(3), 15–24.

Portenoy, R., & Mathur, G. (2009). Cancer pain. In S.-C. J. Yeung, C. P. Escalante, & R. F. Gagel (Eds.), *Medical care of the cancer patient* (pp. 60–71). Shelton, CT: PMPH USA Ltd.

Post, L., Page, C., Conner, T., & Prokhorov, A. (2010). Elder abuse in long-term care: Types, patterns, and risk factors. *Research on Aging, 32*(3), 323.

Post, R. M. (1992). Transduction of psychosocial stress into the neurobiology of recurrent affective disorder. *American Journal of Psychiatry, 149*(8), 999–1010.

Post, R. M., Rubinow, D. R., Uhde, T. W., Roy-Byrne, P. P., Linnoila, M., Rosoff, A., & Cowdry, R. (1989). Dysphoric mania: Clinical and biological correlates. *Archives of General Psychiatry, 46,* 353–358.

Potenza, M. N., Steinberg, M. A., Skudlarski, P., Fulbright, R. K., Lacadie, C. M., Wilber, M. K., & Wexler, B. E. (2003). Gambling urges in pathological gambling: A functional magnetic resonance imaging study. *Archives of General Psychiatry, 60,* 828–836.

Potter, R., Ellard, D., Rees, K., & Thorogood, M. (2011). A systematic review of the effects of physical activity on physical functioning, quality of life and depression in older people with dementia. *International Journal of Geriatric Psychiatry, 26*(10), 1000–1011.

Poulsen, S., Lunn, S., Daniel, S. I. F., Folke, S., Mathiesen, B. B., Katznelson, H., & Fairburn, C. G. (2014). A randomized controlled trial of psychoanalytic psychotherapy versus cognitive behavior therapy for bulimia nervosa. *American Journal of Psychiatry, 171,* 109–116.

Powell, L. A., Parker, J., Weighall, A., & Harpin, V. (2021). Psychoeducation intervention effectiveness to improve social skills in young people with ADHD: A meta-analysis. *Journal of Attention Disorders,* 1087054721997553.

Powell, R. A., & Howell, A. J. (1998). Effectiveness of treatment for dissociative identity disorder. *Psychological Reports, 83,* 483–490.

Powers, A. D., Gleason, M. E., & Oltmanns, T. F. (2013). Symptoms of borderline personality disorder predict interpersonal (but not independent) stressful life events in a community sample of older adults. *Journal of Abnormal Psychology, 122*(2), 469.

Prause, N., & Janssen, E. (2006). Blood flow: Vaginal photoplethysmography. In I. Goldstein, C. M. Meston, S. R. Davis, & A. M. Traish (Eds.), *Women's sexual function and dysfunction: Study, diagnostic and treatment* (pp. 359–367). New York, NY: Taylor and Francis.

Prelior, E. F., Yutzy, S. H., Dean, J. T., & Wetzel, R. D. (1993). Briquet's syndrome, dissociation and abuse. *American Journal of Psychiatry, 150,* 1507–1511.

Prenoveau, J. M., Craske, M. G., Liao, B., & Ornitz, E. M. (2013). Human fear conditioning and extinction: Timing is everything . . . or is it? *Biological psychology, 92*(1), 59–68.

President's New Freedom Commission on Mental Health. (2003). *Achieving the promise: Transforming mental health care in America—Final report* (DHHS Pub. No. SMA-03-3832). Rockville, MD: Substance Abuse and Mental Health Services Administration.

Presley, C. A., & Meilman, P. W. (1992). *Alcohol and drugs on American college campuses: A report to college presidents.* Carbondale: Southern Illinois University Press.

Presnall, N., Webster-Stratton, C. H., & Constantino, J. N. (2014). Parent training: Equivalent improvement in externalizing behavior for children with and without familial risk. *Journal of the American Academy of Child & Adolescent Psychiatry, 53*(8), 879–887.

Price, A. M. H., Wake, M., Ukoumunne, O. C., & Hiscock, H. (2012). Outcomes at six years of age for children with infant sleep problems: Longitudinal community-based study. *Sleep Medicine, 13*(8), 991–998. doi: 10.1016/j.sleep.2012.04.014

Price, J. R., Mitchell, E., Tidy, E., & Hunot, V. (2008). Cognitive behaviour therapy for chronic fatigue syndrome in adults. *Cochrane Database of Systematic Reviews, 3,* CD001027. doi: 10.1002/14651858.CD001027.pub2

Price, S. R., Hilchey, C. A., Darredeau, C., Fulton, H. G., & Barrett, S. P. (2010). Energy drink co-administration is associated with increased reported alcohol ingestion. *Drug and Alcohol Review, 29*(3), 331–333.

Pridal, C. G., & LoPiccolo, J. (2000). Multielement treatment of desire disorders: Integration of cognitive, behavioral and systemic therapy. In S. R. Leiblum & R. C. Rosen (Eds.), *Principles and practice of sex therapy* (3rd ed., pp. 57–81). New York, NY: Guilford.

Prince, M. (1906–1907). Hysteria from the point of view of dissociated personality. *Journal of Abnormal Psychology, 1,* 170–187.

Prins, J., van der Meer, J., & Bleijenberg, G. (2006). Chronic fatigue syndrome. *Lancet, 367,* 346–355.

pro-ana-nation. (2010). Home page. Retrieved April 28, 2010, from http://www.pro-ana-nation.com/v1/index.php

Proulx, T., & Heine, S. J. (2009). Connections from Kafka: Exposure to meaning threats improves implicit learning of an artificial grammar. *Psychological Science, 20*(9), 1125–1131.

Pruzinsky, T. (1988). Collaboration of plastic surgeon and medical psychotherapist: Elective cosmetic surgery. *Medical Psychotherapy, 1,* 1–13.

Pueschel, S. M., & Goldstein, A. (1991). Genetic counseling. In J. L. Matson & J. A. Mulick (Eds.), *Handbook of mental retardation* (2nd ed., pp. 279–291). Elmsford, NY: Pergamon Press.

Pugliese, M. T., Weyman-Daun, M., Moses, N., & Lifshitz, F. (1987). Parental health beliefs as a cause of nonorganic failure to thrive. *Pediatrics, 80,* 175–182.

Puhan, M. A., Suarez, A., Cascio, C. L., Zahn, A., Heitz, M., & Braendli, O. (2006). Didgeridoo playing as alternative treatment for obstructive sleep apnoea syndrome: randomised controlled trial. *BMJ 332*(7536), 266–270.

Puliafico, A. C., Comer, J. S., & Pincus, D. B. (2012). Adapting parent-child interaction therapy to treat anxiety disorders in young children. *Child and Adolescent Psychiatry Clinics of North America, 21,* 607–619.

Pulkki-Raback, L., Kivimäki, M., Ahola, K., Joutsenniemi, K., Elovainio, M., & Virtanen, M. (2012). Living alone and antidepressant medication use: A prospective study in a working-age population. *BMC Public Health, 12*(1), 236. doi: 10.1186/1471-2458-12-236

Pull, C. B. (2013). Too few or too many? Reactions to removing versus retaining specific personality disorders in DSM-5. *Current Opinion in Psychiatry, 26*(1), 73–78.

Purdon, C. (2009). Psychological approaches to understanding obsessive-compulsive disorder. In M. Anthony and M. B. Stein (Eds)., *Oxford handbook of anxiety and related disorders,* 238–249. New York, NY: Oxford University Press.

Purdy, D., & Frank, E. (1993). Should postpartum mood disorders be given a more prominent or distinct place in DSM-IV? *Depression, 1,* 59–70.

Purves, K. L., Coleman, J. R. I., Meier, S. M., Rayner, C., Davis, K. A. S., Cheesman, R., … Eley, T. C. (2020). A major role for common genetic variation in anxiety disorders. *Molecular Psychiatry, 25*(12), 3292–3303. doi: 10.1038/s41380-019-0559-1

Pury, C. L. S., & Mineka, S. (1997). Covariation bias for blood–injury stimuli and aversion outcomes. *Behavior Research and Therapy, 35,* 35–47.

Putnam, F. W. (1991). Dissociative phenomena. In A. Tasman & S. M. Goldinger (Eds.), *American Psychiatric Press review of psychiatry* (Vol. 10). Washington, DC: American Psychiatric Press.

Putnam, F. W. (1992). Altered states: Peeling away the layers of a multiple personality. *Sciences, 32*(6), 30–36.

Putnam, F. W. (1997). *Dissociation in children and adolescents: A developmental perspective.* New York, NY: Guilford.

Putnam, F. W., & Loewenstein, R. J. (1993). Treatment of multiple personality disorder: A survey of current practices. *American Journal of Psychiatry, 150,* 1048–1052.

Putnam, F. W., Guroff, J. J., Silberman, E. K., Barban, L., & Post, R. M. (1986). The clinical phenomenology of multiple personality disorder: Review of 100 recent cases. *Journal of Clinical Psychiatry, 47,* 285–293.

Puzziferri, N., Roshek, T. B., Mayo, H. G., Gallagher, R., Belle, S. H., & Livingston, E. H. (2014). Long-term follow-up after bariatric surgery: a systematic review. *JAMA, 312*(9), 934–942.

Qian, M., Wu, Q., Wu, P., Hou, Z., Liang, Y., Cowling, B. J., & Yu, H. (2020). Psychological responses, behavioral changes and public perceptions during the early phase of the COVID-19 outbreak in China: A population based cross-sectional survey. *MedRxiv.*

Quality Assurance Project. (1990). Treatment outlines for paranoid, schizotypal and schizoid personality disorders. *Australian and New Zealand Journal of Psychiatry, 24,* 339–350.

Quay, H. C. (1993). The psychobiology of undersocialized aggressive conduct disorder: A theoretical perspective. *Development and Psychopathology, 5,* 165–180.

Quinsey, V. L. (2010). Coercive paraphilic disorder. *Archives of Sexual Behavior, 39,* 405–410.

Quoidbach, J., Gilbert, D. T., & Wilson, T. D. (2013). The end of history illusion. *Science, 339*(6115), 96–98. doi: 10.1126/science.1229294

Rabe, S., Zoellner, T., Beauducel, A., Maercker, A., & Karl, A. (2008). Changes in brain electrical activity after cognitive behavioral therapy for posttraumatic stress disorder in patients injured in motor vehicle accidents. *Psychosomatic Medicine, 70*(1), 13–19.

Raber, J., Arzy, S., Bertolus, J. B., Depue, B., Haas, H. E., Hofmann, S. G. Kangas, M., Kensinger, E., Lowry, C. A., Marusak, H. A., Minnier, J., Mouly, A. M., Muehlberger, A., Norrholm, S. D., Peltonen, K., Pinna, G., Rabinak, C., Shiban. Y., Soreq, H., … Boutros, S. W. (2019). Current understanding of fear learning and memory in humans and animal models and the value of a linguistic approach for analyzing fear learning and memory in humans. *Neuroscience and Biobehavioral Reviews, 105,* 136–177. doi: 10.1016/j.neubiorev.2019.03.015

Rabins, P. V. (2006). *Guideline watch: Practice guidelines for the treatment of patients with Alzheimer's disease and other dementias of late life.* Washington, DC: American Psychiatric Association.

Rabins, P. V., & Lyketsos, C. G. (2011). A commentary on the proposed DSM revision regarding the classification of cognitive disorders. *American Journal of Geriatric Psychiatry, 19*(3), 201–204.

Rachman, S. (1978). *Fear and courage.* San Francisco: W. H. Freeman.

Rachman, S. (1991). Neo-conditioning and the classical theory of fear acquisition. *Clinical Psychology Review, 11,* 155–173.

Rachman, S. (2006). *Fear of contamination.* New York, NY: Oxford University Press.

Rachman, S., & de Silva, P. (1978). Abnormal and normal obsessions. *Behaviour Research and Therapy, 16,* 233–248.

Rachman, S., & Hodgson, R. (1968). Experimentally induced "sexual fetishism": Replication and development. *Psychological Record, 18*(1), 25–27.

Racine, M., Tousignant-Laflamme, Y., Kloda, L. A., Dion, D., Dupuis, G., & Choinire, M. (2012b). A systematic literature review of 10 years of research on sex/gender and pain perception: Part 2, Do biopsychosocial factors alter pain sensitivity differently in women and men? *Pain, 153*(3), 619–635. doi: 10.1016/j.pain.2011.11.02

Racine, M., Tousignant-Laflamme, Y., Kloda, L. A., Dion, D., Dupuis, G., & Choinire, M. (2012a). A systematic literature review of 10 years of research on sex/gender and experimental pain perception: Part 1, Are there really differences between women and men? *Pain, 153*(3), 602–618. doi: 10.1016/j.pain.2011.11.02

Racine, N., Devereaux, C., Cooke, J. E., Eirich, R., Zhu, J., & Madigan, S. (2021). Adverse childhood experiences and maternal anxiety and depression: A meta-analysis. *BMC Psychiatry, 21*(1). doi: 10.1186 /s12888-020-03017-w

Racine, S. E., & Wildes, J. E. (2015). Dynamic longitudinal relations between emotion regulation difficulties and anorexia nervosa symptoms over the year following intensive treatment. *Journal of Clinical and Consulting Psychology, 83*(4), 785–795.

Rado, S. (1962). Theory and therapy: The theory of schizotypal organization and its application to the treatment of decompensated schizotypal behavior. In S. Rado (Ed.), *Psychoanalysis of behavior* (Vol. 2, pp. 127–140). New York, NY: Grune & Stratton.

Radomsky, A. S., & Taylor, S. (2005). Subtyping OCD: Prospects and problems. *Behavior Therapy, 36,* 371–379.

Rahkonen, T., Eloniemi-Sulkava, U., Paanila, S., Halonen, P., Sivenius, J., & Sulkava, R. (2001). Systematic intervention for supporting community care of elderly people after a delirium episode. *International Psychogeriatrics, 13*(1), 37–49.

Raine, A., Venables, P. H., & Williams, M. (1990). Relationships between central and autonomic measures of arousal at age 15 years and criminality at age 24 years. *Archives of General Psychiatry, 47,* 1003–1007.

Raison, C. L., Klein, H. M., & Steckler, M. (1999). The moon and madness reconsidered. *Journal of Affective Disorders, 53*(1), 99–106.

Rakison, D. H. (2009). Does women's greater fear of snakes and spiders originate in infancy? *Evolution and Human Behavior, 30*(6), 438–444.

Ramachandran, V. S. (1993). Filling in the gaps in perception II: Scotomas and phantom limbs. *Current Directions in Psychological Science, 2,* 56–65.

Ramaekers, J. G., Mason, N. L., & Theunissen, E. L. (2020). Blunted highs: Pharmacodynamic and behavioral models of cannabis tolerance. *European Neuropsychopharmacology, 36,* 191–205. doi: https://doi.org/10.1016/j.euroneuro.2020.01.006

Ramchandani, P., Stein, A., Evans, J., O'Connor, T., & the ALSPAC Study Team. (2005). Paternal depression in the postnatal period and child development: A prospective population study. *Lancet, 365,* 2201–2205.

Ramos Olazagasti, M. A., Klein, R. G., Mannuzza, S., Belsky, E. R., Hutchison, J. A., Lashua-Shriftman, E. C., & Xavier Castellanos, F. (2013). Does childhood attention-deficit/hyperactivity disorder predict risk-taking and medical illnesses in adulthood? *Journal of the American Academy of Child & Adolescent Psychiatry, 52*(2), 153–162.e154. doi: http://dx.doi.org/10.1016/j.jaac.2012.11.012

Ramrakha, S., Paul, C., Bell, M. L., Dickson, N., Moffitt, T. E., & Caspi, A. (2013). The relationship between multiple sex partners and anxiety, depression, and substance dependence disorders: A cohort study. *Archives of Sexual Behavior, 42*(5), 863–872.

Ramsawh, H. J., Morgentaler, A., Covino, N., Barlow, D. H., & DeWolf, W. C. (2005). Quality of life following simultaneous placement of penile prosthesis with radical prostatectomy. *Journal of Urology, 174*(4, Part 1 of 2), 1395–1398.

Ramsawh, H., Raffa, S. D., White, K. S., & Barlow, D. H. (2008). Risk factors for isolated sleep paralysis in an African American sample: A preliminary study. *Behavior Therapy 39*(4), 386–397. doi: 10.1016/j.beth.2007.11.002.

Ranjith, G., & Mohan, R. (2004). Dhat syndrome: A functional somatic syndrome? (Letter to the editor). *British Journal of Psychiatry,* pp. 200–209.

Ranson, M. B., Nichols, D. S., Rouse, S. V., & Harrington, J. L. (2009). Changing or replacing an established psychological assessment standard: Issues, goals, and problems with special reference to recent developments in the MMPI-2. In J. N. Butcher (Ed.), *Oxford handbook of personality assessment* (pp. 112–139). New York, NY: Oxford University Press.

Rapee, R. M., & Melville, L. F. (1997). Recall of family factors in social phobia and panic disorder: Comparison of mother and offspring reports. *Depression and Anxiety, 5,* 7–11.

Rapee, R. M., Schniering, C. A., & Hudson, J. L. (2009). Anxiety disorders during childhood and adolescence: Origins and treatment. *Annual Review of Clinical Psychology, 5,* 311–341.

Rapkin, A. J., Chang, L. C., & Reading, A. E. (1989). Mood and cognitive style in premenstrual syndrome. *Obstetrics and Gynecology, 74,* 644–649.

Rasetti, R., Sambataro, F., Chen, Q., Callicott, J. H., Mattay, V. S., & Weinberger, D. R. (2011). Altered cortical network dynamics: a potential intermediate phenotype for schizophrenia and association with ZNF804A. *Archives of General Psychiatry, 68*(12), 1207–1217.

Rash, C. J., & Petry, N. M. (2015). Gambling disorder. In M. S. Ascher & P. Levounis (Eds.), *The behavioral addictions* (pp. 53–65). Arlington, VA: American Psychiatric Publishing.

Rasmussen, S. A., & Eisen, J. L. (1990). Epidemiology of obsessive-compulsive disorder. *Journal of Clinical Psychiatry, 51,* 10–14.

Rasmusson, A. M., Anderson, G. M., Krishnan-Sarin, S., Wu, R., & Paliwal, P. (2006). A decrease in plasma DHEA to cortisol ratio during smoking abstinence may predict relapse: A preliminary study. *Psychopharmacology, 186,* 473–480.

Rassin, E., & Koster, E. (2003). The correlation between thought–action fusion and religiosity in a normal sample. *Behaviour Research and Therapy, 41,* 361–368.

Rathod, N. H., Addenbrooke, W. M., & Rosenbach, A. F. (2005). Heroin dependence in an English town: 33-year follow-up. *British Journal of Psychiatry, 187,* 421–425.

Rauch, A., Wieczorek, D., Graf, E. R., Wieland, T., Endele, S., Schwarzmayr, T., & Strom, T. M. (2012). Range of genetic mutations associated with severe non-syndromic sporadic intellectual disability: An exome sequencing study. *The Lancet, 380*(9854), 1674–1682.

Rauch, S. A. M., King, A. P., Abelson, J., Tuerk, P. W., Smith, E., Rothbaum, B. O., Clifton, E., Defever, A, & Liberzon, I.

(2014). Biological and symptom changes in posttraumatic disorder treatment: A randomized clinical trial. *Depression and Anxiety, 32,* 204–212.

Rauch, S. L., Phillips, K. A., Segal, E., Markis, N., Shin, L. M., Whalen, P. J., & Kennedy, D. N. (2003). A preliminary morphometric magnetic resonance imaging study of regional brain volumes in body dysmorphic disorder. *Psychiatry Research, 122,* 13–19.

Ravussin, E., Valencia, M. E., Esparza, J., Bennett, P. H., & Schulz, L. O. (1994). Effects of a traditional lifestyle on obesity in Pima Indians. *Diabetes Care, 17,* 1067–1074.

Ray, L. A. (2012). Clinical neuroscience of addiction: Applications to psychological science and practice. *Clinical Psychology: Science and Practice, 19*(2), 154–166. doi: 10.1111/j.1468-2850.2012.01280.x

Ray, W. A., Gurwitz, J., Decker, M. D., & Kennedy, D. L. (1992). Medications and the safety of the older driver: Is there a basis for concern? Special issue: Safety and mobility of elderly drivers: II. *Human Factors, 34*(1), 33–47.

Raymond, N. C., Coleman, E., Ohlerking, F., Christenson, G. A., & Miner, M. (1999). Psychiatric comorbidity in pedophilic sex offenders. *American Journal of Psychiatry, 156,* 786–788.

Rayner, K. E., Schniering, C. A., Rapee, R. M., Taylor, A., & Hutchinson, D. M. (2012). Adolescent girls' friendship networks, body dissatisfaction, and disordered eating: Examining selection and socialization processes. *Journal of Abnormal Psychology, 122*(1), 93–104. doi: 10.1037/a0029304

Raza, G. T., DeMarce, J. M., Lash, S. J., & Parker, J. D. (2014). Paranoid Personality Disorder in the United States: The Role of Race, Illicit Drug Use, and Income. *Journal of Ethnicity in Substance Abuse, 13*(3), 247–257.

Razran, G. (1961). The observable unconscious and the inferable conscious in current Soviet psychophysiology: Interoceptive conditioning, semantic conditioning, and the orienting reflex. *Psychological Review, 68,* 81–150.

Rea, M., Tompson, M. C., & Miklowitz, D. J. (2003). Family-focused treatment versus individual treatment for bipolar disorder: Results of a randomized clinical trial. *Journal of Consulting and Clinical Psychology, 71,* 482–492.

Reames, B. N., Finks, J. F., Bacal, D., Carlin, A. M., & Dimick, J. B. (2014). Changes in bariatric surgery procedure use in Michigan, 2006-2013. *JAMA, 312*(9), 959–961.

Reas, D. L., & Grilo, C. M. (2014). Current and emerging drug treatments for binge eating disorder. *Expert Opinion on Emerging Drugs, 19*(1), 99–142.

Rebocho, M. F., & Silva, P. (2014). Target selection in rapists: The role of environmental and contextual factors. *Aggression and Violent Behavior, 19*(1), 42–49.

Record, N. B., Onion, D. K., Prior, R. E., Dixon, D. C., Record, S. S., Fowler, F. L., Cayer, G. R., Amos, C. I., & Pearson, T. A. (2015). Community-wide cardiovascular disease prevention programs and health outcomes in a rural county, 1970–2010. *JAMA, 313*(2), 147–155.

Redd, W. H., & Andrykowski, M. A. (1982). Behavioral intervention in cancer treatment: Controlling aversion reactions to chemotherapy. *Journal of Consulting and Clinical Psychology, 50,* 1018–1029.

Reddy, L. A., Newman, E., De Thomas, C. A., & Chun, V. (2009). Effectiveness of school-based prevention and intervention programs for children and adolescents with emotional disturbance: A meta-analysis. *Journal of School Psychology, 47*(2), 77–99.

Reddy, L. F., Horan, W. P., & Green, M. F. (2016). Motivational deficits and negative symptoms in schizophrenia: Concepts and assessments. *Current Topics in Behavioral Neuroscience, 27,* 357-373.

Reeves, G. M., Nijjar, G. V., Langenberg, P., Johnson, M. A., Khabazghazvini, B., Sleemi, A., & Postolache, T. T. (2012). Improvement in depression scores after 1 hour of light therapy treatment in patients with seasonal affective disorder. *The Journal of Nervous and Mental Disease, 200*(1), 51–54.

Regier, D. A., Narrow, W. E., Clarke, D. E., Kraemer, H. C., Kuramoto, S. J., Kuhl, E. A., & Kupfer, D. J. (2013). DSM-5 field trials in the United States and Canada, part II: Test-retest reliability of selected categorical diagnoses. *American Journal of Psychiatry, 170*(1), 59–70.

Regier, D. A., Narrow, W. E., Clarke, D. E., Kraemer, H. C., Kuramoto, S. J., Kuhl, E. A., & Kupfer, D. J. (2013). *DSM-5* field trials in the United States and Canada, Part II: Test-retest reliability of selected categorical diagnoses. *American Journal of Psychiatry, 170*(1), 59–70. doi: 10.1176/appi.ajp.2012.12070999

Regier, D. A., Narrow, W. E., Kuhl, E. A., & Kupfer, D. J. (2009). The conceptual development of DSM-V. *American Journal of Psychiatry, 166*(6), 645–650.

Rehm, J., Marmet, S., Anderson, P., Gual, A., Kraus, L., Nutt, D. J., . . . Wiers, R. W. (2013). Defining substance use disorders: Do we really need more than heavy use? *Alcohol and Alcoholism, 48*(6), 633–640.

Rehse, B., & Pukrop, R. (2003). Effects of psychosocial interventions on quality of life in adult cancer patients: Meta analysis of 37 published controlled outcome studies. *Patient Education and Counseling, 50*(2), 179–186. doi: 10.1016/S0738-3991(02)00149-0

Reichborn-Kjennerud, T., Czajkowski, N., Ystrøm, E., Ørstavik, R., Aggen, S. H., Tambs, K., . . . Kendler, K. S. (2015). A longitudinal twin study of borderline and antisocial personality disorder traits in early to middle adulthood. *Psychological Medicine, 45*(14), 3121–3131.

Reichenberg, A., Gross, R., Weiser, M., Bresnahan, M., Silverman, J., Harlap, S., & Lubin, G. (2006). Advancing paternal age and autism. *Archives of General Psychiatry, 63*(9), 1026.

Reilly-Harrington, N. A., Alloy, L. B., Fresco, D. M., & Whitehouse, W. G. (1999). Cognitive styles and life events interact to predict bipolar and unipolar symptomatology. *Journal of Abnormal Psychology, 108*(4), 567–578.

Reilly-Harrington, N. A., Deckersbach, T., Knauz, R., Wu, Y., Tran, T., Eidelman, P., & Nierenberg, A. A. (2007). Cognitive behavioral therapy for rapid-cycling bipolar disorder: A pilot study. *Journal of Psychiatric Practice, 13*(5), 291–297.

Reiman, E. M., Webster, J. A., Myers, A. J., Hardy, J., Dunckley, T., Zismann, V. L., & Stephan, D. (2007). GAB2 alleles modify Alzheimer's risk in APOE ′4 carriers. *Neuron, 54*(5), 713–720.

Reinders, A. A. T. S., Marquand, A. F., Schlumpf, Y. R., Chalavi, S., Vissia, E. M., Nijenhuis, E. R. S., . . . Veltman, D. J. (2019). Aiding the diagnosis of dissociative identity disorder: Pattern recognition study of brain biomarkers. *British Journal of Psychiatry, 215*(3), 536–544. doi: 10.1192/bjp.2018.255

Reiss, S. (1991). Expectancy model of fear, anxiety and panic. *Clinical Psychology Review, 11,* 141–153.

Reitan, R. M., & Davison, I. A. (1974). *Clinical neuropsychology: Current status and applications.* Washington, DC: V. H. Winston.

Rekers, G. A., Kilgus, M., & Rosen, A. C. (1990). Long-term effects of treatment for gender identity disorder of childhood. *Journal of Psychology & Human Sexuality, 3*(2), 121–153.

Rentz, D. M., Parra Rodriguez, M. A., Amariglio, R., Stern, Y., Sperling, R., & Ferris, S. (2013). Promising developments in neuropsychological approaches for the detection of preclinical Alzheimer's disease: a selective review. *Alzheimers Research & Therapy, 5*(6), 58.

Report of the Advisory Panel on Alzheimer's Disease. (1995). *Alzheimer's disease and related dementias: Biomedical update.* U.S.

Department of Health and Human Services. Washington, DC: U.S. Government Printing Office.

Repp, A. C., & Singh, N. N. (1990). *Perspectives on the use of nonaversive and aversive interventions for persons with developmental disabilities*. Sycamore, IL: Sycamore.

Rescorla, R. A. (1988). Pavlovian conditioning: It's not what you think it is. *American Psychologist, 43*(3), 151–160.

Resick, P. A., Williams, L. F., Suvak, M. K., Monson, C. M., & Gradus, J. L. (2012). Long-term outcomes of cognitive-behavioral treatments for posttraumatic stress disorder among female rape survivors. *Journal of Consulting and Clinical Psychology, 80*, 201–210. doi: 10.1037/a0026602

Ressler, K. J., & Rothbaum, B. O. (2013). Augmenting obsessive-compulsive disorder treatment from brain to mind. *JAMA Psychiatry, 70*, 1129–1131.

Reynolds, C. F. (2011). Troubled sleep, troubled minds, and DSM-5. *Archives of General Psychiatry, 68*(10), 990–991. doi: 10.1001/archgenpsychiatry.2011.104

Reynolds, C. F., III. (2009). Prevention of depressive disorders: A brave new world. *Depression and Anxiety, 26*(12), 1062–1065.

Rhebergen, D., & Graham, R. (2014). The re-labelling of dysthymic disorder to persistent depressive disorder in DSM-5: Old wine in new bottles? *Current Opinions in Psychiatry, 27*, 27–31.

Ricciardelli, L. A., & McCabe, M. P. (2004). A biopsychosocial model of disordered eating and the pursuit of muscularity in adolescent boys. *Psychological Bulletin, 130*, 170–205.

Rice, F., Riglin, L., Thapar, A. K., Heron, J., Anney, R., O'Donovan, M. C., & Thapar, A. (2019). Characterizing developmental trajectories and the role of neuropsychiatric genetic risk variants in early-onset depression. *JAMA Psychiatry, 76*(3), 306–313. doi: 10.1001/jamapsychiatry.2018.3338

Rice, G., Anderson, C., Risch, N., & Ebers, G. (1999). Male homosexuality: Absence of linkage to microsatellite markers at Xq28. *Science, 284*, 665–667.

Rice, M. E., & Harris, G. T. (2002). Men who molest their sexually immature daughters: Is a special explanation required? *Journal of Abnormal Psychology, 111*, 329–339.

Richards, R., Kinney, D. K., Lunde, I., Benet, M., & Merzel, A. P. C. (1988). Creativity in manic depressives, cyclothymes, their normal relatives, and control subjects. *Journal of Abnormal Psychology, 97*(3), 281–288.

Richards, S. S., & Sweet, R. A. (2009). Dementia. In B. J. Sadock, V. A. Sadock, & P. Ruiz (Eds.), *Kaplan & Sadock's comprehensive textbook of psychiatry* (9th ed., Vol. I, pp. 1167–1198). Philadelphia, PA: Lippincott Williams & Wilkins.

Richardson, G. S. (2006). Shift work sleep disorder. In T. Lee-Chiong (Ed.), *Sleep: A comprehensive handbook* (pp. 395–399). Hoboken, NJ: Wiley.

Richardson, G., Goldschmidt, L., & Willford, J. (2009). Continued effects of prenatal cocaine use: Preschool development. *Neurotoxicology and Teratology, 31*(6), 325–333.

Richmond-Rakerd, L. S., D'Souza, S., Milne, B. J., Caspi, A., & Moffitt, T. E. (2021). Longitudinal associations of mental disorders with physical diseases and mortality among 2.3 million New Zealand citizens. *JAMA Network Open, 4*(1) doi: 10.1001/jamanetworkopen.2020.33448

Richters, J., de Visser, R. O., Badcock, P. B., Smith, A. M., Rissel, C., Simpson, J. M., & Grulich, A. E. (2014). Masturbation, paying for sex, and other sexual activities: the Second Australian Study of Health and Relationships. *Sexual Health, 11*(5), 461–471.

Rickels, K., Rynn, M., Ivengar, M., & Duff, D. (2006). Remission of generalized anxiety disorder: A review of the paroxetine clinical trials database. *Journal of Clinical Psychiatry, 67*, 41–47.

Rickels, K., Schweizer, E., Case, W. G., & Greenblatt, D. J. (1990). Long-term therapeutic use of benzodiazepines: I. Effects of abrupt discontinuation. *Archives of General Psychiatry, 47*, 899–907.

Ridenour, T. A., & Howard, M. O. (2012). Inhalants abuse: Status of etiology and intervention. In J. C. Verster, K. Brady, M. Galanter, & P. Conrod (Eds.), *Drug abuse and addiction in medical illness* (pp. 189–199). New York, NY: Springer.

Riding, A. (1992, November 17). New catechism for Catholics defines sins of modern world. *New York Times*, pp. A1, A16.

Ridley, N. J., Draper, B., & Withall, A. (2013). Alcohol-related dementia: An update of the evidence. *Alzheimers Research & Therapy, 5*(3), 1–8.

Rief, W., & Martin, A. (2014). How to use the new *DSM-5* somatic symptom disorder diagnosis in research and practice: A critical evaluation and a proposal for modifications. *Annual Review of Clinical Psychology, 10*, 339–367.

Rief, W., Hiller, W., & Margraf, J. (1998). Cognitive aspects of hypochondriasis and the somatization syndrome. *Journal of Abnormal Psychology, 107*, 587–595.

Rieger, G., & Savin-Williams, R. C. (2012). Gender nonconformity, sexual orientation, and psychological well-being. *Archives of Sexual Behavior, 41*(3), 611–621.

Riemann, D., Berger, M., & Voderholzer, U. (2001). Sleep and depression—Results from psychobiological studies: An overview. *Biological Psychology, 57*, 67–103.

Riggins v. Nevada, 112 S. Ct. 1810 (1992).

Riggs, J. E. (1993). Smoking and Alzheimer's disease: Protective effect or differential survival bias? *Lancet, 342*, 793–794.

Riihimäki, K., Vuorilehto, M., Melartin, T., Haukka, J., & Isometsä, E. (2013). Incidence and predictors of suicide attempts among primary-care patients with depressive disorders: A 5-year prospective study. *Psychological Medicine*, 1–12.

Rimsky, L., & Cain, N. M. (2017). Schizotypal personality disorder. In V. Zeigler-Hill & T. K. Shackelford (Eds.), *Encyclopedia of personality and individual differences* (pp. 627–628). Cham, Switzerland: Springer.

Ripke, S., Neale, B. M., Corvin, A., Walters, J. T., Farh, K. H., Holmans, P. A., . . . Pers, T. H. (2014). Biological insights from 108 schizophrenia-associated genetic loci. *Nature, 511*(7510), 421.

Risch, N., Herrell, R., Lehner, T., Liang, K. Y., Eaves, L., Hoh, J., & Merikangas, K. R. (2009). Interaction between the serotonin transporter gene (5-HTTLPR), stressful life events, and risk of depression: A meta-analysis. *Journal of American Medical Association, 301*(23), 2462–2471. doi: 10.1001/jama.2009.878

Ritsner, M. S., & Gottesman, I. I. (2011). The schizophrenia construct after 100 years of challenges. In M. S. Ritsner (Ed), *Handbook of schizophrenia spectrum disorders* (Vol 1, pp. 1–44). Heidelberg, Germany: Springer.

Ritterband, L. M., Thorndike, F. P., Gonder-Frederick, L. A., Magee, J. C., Bailey, E. T., Saylor, D. K., & Morin, C. M. (2009). Efficacy of an internet-based behavioral intervention for adults with insomnia. *Arch Gen Psychiatry, 66*(7), 692–698. doi: 10.1001/archgenpsychiatry.2009.66

Ritz, T., Meuret, A. E., & Ayala, E. S. (2010). The psychophysiology of blood-injection-injury phobia: Looking beyond the diphasic response. *International Journal of Psychophysiology, 78*, 50–67.

Riva, P., Romero Lauro, L. J., Dewall, C. N., & Bushman, B. J. (2012). Buffer the pain away: Stimulating the right ventrolateral prefrontal cortex reduces pain following social exclusion. *Psychological Science, 23*(12), 1473–1475.

Rivera-Tovar, A. D., & Frank, E. (1990). Late luteal phase dysphoric disorder in young women. *American Journal of Psychiatry, 147*, 1634–1636.

Rivera-Tovar, A. D., Pilkonis, P., & Frank, E. (1992). Symptom patterns in late luteal-phase dysphoric disorder. *Journal of Psychopathology and Behavioral Assessment, 14,* 189–199.

Rizzuto, D., Orsini, N., Qiu, C., Wang, H.-X., & Fratiglioni, L. (2012). Lifestyle, social factors, and survival after age 75: Population based study. *BMJ: British Medical Journal, 345,* e5568.

Ro, A., Geronimus, A., Bound, J., Griffith, D., & Gee, G. (2015). Cohort and Duration Patterns Among Asian Immigrants: Comparing Trends in Obesity and Self-Rated Health. *Biodemography and Social Biology, 61*(1), 65–80.

Robbins, T. W., & Cools, R. (2014). Cognitive deficits in Parkinson's disease: a cognitive neuroscience perspective. *Movement Disorders, 29*(5), 597–607.

Roberts, A., Cash, T., Feingold, A., & Johnson, B. (2006). Are black–white differences in females' body dissatisfaction decreasing? A meta-analytic review. *Journal of Consulting and Clinical Psychology, 74,* 1121–1131.

Roberts, J. M. (2014). Echolalia and language development in children with autism. In J. Arciuli & J. Brock (Eds.), *Communication in Autism* (Vol. 11, pp. 55–74). Philadelphia: John Benjamins Publishing Company.

Roberts, R. E., Kaplan, G. A., Shema, S. J., & Strawbridge, W. J. (1997). Does growing old increase the risk for depression? *American Journal of Psychiatry, 154,* 1384–1390.

Roberts, R. E., Roberts, C. R., & Chen, I. G. (2000). Ethnocultural differences in sleep complaints among adolescents. *The Journal of Nervous and Mental Disease, 188,* 222–229.

Roberts, W., Milich, R., & Barkley, R. A. (2015). Primary symptoms, diagnostic criteria, subtyping, and prevalence of ADHD. In R. A. Barkley (Ed.), *Attention-deficit hyperactivity disorder: A handbook for diagnosis & treatment* (4th ed., pp. 51–80). New York, NY: The Guilford Press.

Robertson, D., Snarey, J., Ousley, O., Harenski, K., Bowman, F. D., Gilkey, R., & Kilts, C. (2007). The neural processing of moral sensitivity to issues of justice and care. *Neuropsychologia, 45*(4), 755–766.

Robertson, N. (1988). *Getting better: Inside Alcoholics Anonymous.* New York, NY: William Morrow.

Robinaugh, D. J., & McNally, R. J. (2013). Remembering the past and envisioning the future in bereaved adults with and without complicated grief. *Clinical Psychological Science, 1*(3), 290–300. doi: 10.1177/2167702613476027.

Robins, L. N. (1966). *Deviant children grown up: A sociological and psychiatric study of sociopathic personality*. Baltimore, MD: Williams & Wilkins.

Robins, L. N. (1978). Sturdy childhood predictors of adult antisocial behavior: Replications from longitudinal studies. *Psychological Medicine, 8,* 611–622.

Robinson, G. E., Fernald, R. D., & Clayton, D. F. (2008, November 7). Genes and social behavior. *Science, 322,* 896–899.

Robinson, R. G., Jorge, R. E., Moser, D. J., Acion, L., Solodkin, A., Small, S. L., & Arndt, S. (2008). Escitalopram and problem-solving therapy for prevention of poststroke depression: A randomized controlled trial: Correction. *JAMA: Journal of the American Medical Association, 301*(10).

Robles, T., Glaser, R., & Kiecolt-Glaser, J. (2005). Out of balance: A new look at chronic stress, depression, and immunity. *Current Directions in Psychological Science, 14,* 111–115.

Rock, C. L., Flatt, S. W., Sherwood, N. E., Karanja, N., Pakiz, B., & Thomson, C. A. (2010). Effect of a free prepared meal and incentivized weight loss program on weight loss and weight loss maintenance in obese and overweight women: A randomized controlled trial. *JAMA: Journal of American Medical Association, 304,* 1803–1810.

Rockney, R. M., & Lemke, T. (1992). Casualties from a junior–senior high school during the Persian Gulf war: Toxic poisoning or mass hysteria? *Developmental and Behavioral Pediatrics, 13*(5), 339–342.

Rodin, J., & Langer, E. J. (1977). Long-term effects of a controlled relevant intervention with the institutionalized aged. *Journal of Personality and Social Psychology, 35*(12), 897–902.

Rodin, J., & Salovey, P. (1989). Health psychology. *Annual Review of Psychology, 40,* 533–579.

Rodrigue, K. M., Rieck, J. R., Kennedy, K. M., Devous, M. D., Diaz-Arrastia, R., & Park, D. C. (2013). Risk factors for b-amyloid deposition in healthy aging: vascular and genetic effects. *JAMA Neurology, 70*(5), 600–606.

Roelofs, K., Keijsers, G. P., Hoogduin, K. A., Naring, G. W., & Moene, F. C. (2002). Childhood abuse in patients with conversion disorder. *American Journal of Psychiatry, 159,* 1908–1913.

Roemer, L., & Orsillo, S. M. (2013). An acceptance-based behavioral therapy for generalized anxiety disorder. In D. H. Barlow (Ed.), *Clinical handbook of psychological disorders: A step-by-step treatment manual* (5th ed.). New York, NY: Guilford.

Roemer, L., Orsillo, S. M., & Barlow, D. H. (2002). Generalized anxiety disorder. In D. H. Barlow, *Anxiety and its disorders: The nature and treatment of anxiety and panic* (2nd ed.). New York, NY: Guilford.

Roenneberg, T., Pilz, L. K., Zerbini, G., & Winnebeck, E. C. (2019). Chronotype and social jetlag: a (self-) critical review. *Biology, 8*(3), 54. Roenneberg, T., Pilz, L., Zerbini, G., & Winnebeck, E. (2019). Chronotype and social jetlag: A (self-) critical review. *Biology, 8,* 54. doi: 10.3390/biology8030054

Rohan, K. J. (2009). *Coping with the seasons: A cognitive-behavioral approach to seasonal affective disorder: Therapist guide.* New York, NY: Oxford University Press.

Rohan, K. J., Roecklein, K. A., Lacy, T. J., & Vacek, P. M. (2009). Winter depression recurrence one year after cognitive-behavioral therapy, light therapy, or combination treatment. *Behavioral Therapy, 40*(3), 225–238.

Rohan, K. J., Roecklein, K. A., Tierney Lindsey, K., Johnson, L. G., Lippy, R. D., Lacy, T. M., & Barton, F. B. (2007). A randomized controlled trial of cognitive-behavioral therapy, light therapy, and their combination for seasonal affective disorder. *Journal of Consulting and Clinical Psychology, 75,* 489–500.

Rohan, K. J., Sigmon, S. T., & Dorhofer, D. M. (2003). Cognitive-behavioral factors in seasonal affective disorder. *Journal of Consulting and Clinical Psychology, 71,* 22–30.

Rohan, M. J., Meyerhoff, J., Ho, S. Y., Evans, M., Postolache, T. T., & Vacek, P. M. (2015). Outcomes one and two winters following cognitive-behavioral therapy or light therapy for seasonal affective disorder. *American Journal of Psychiatry.* doi: appiajp201515060773

Rohde, P., Lewinsohn, P. M., Klein, D. N., Seeley, J. R., & Gau, J. M. (2013). Key characteristics of major depressive disorder occurring in childhood, adolescence, emerging adulthood, and adulthood. *Clinical Psychological Science, 1*(1), 41–53.

Roid, G. H. (2003). *Stanford-binet intelligence scales (SB5).* Rolling Meadows, IL: Riverside.

Roid, G. H., & Pomplun, M. (2005). Interpreting the Stanford-Binet intelligence scales (5th ed.). In D. P. Flanagan & P. L. Harrison (Eds.), *Contemporary intellectual assessment: Theories, tests, and issues* (2nd ed., pp. 325–343). New York, NY: Guilford.

Rojo, L., Conesa, L., Bermudez, O., & Livianos, L. (2006). Influence of stress in the onset of eating disorders: Data from a two stage epidemiologic controlled study. (2006). *Psychosomatic Medicine, 68,* 628–635.

Rollman, B. L., Belnap, B. H., Mazumdar, S., Houck, P. R., Zhu, F., Gardner, W., & Shear, M. K. (2005). A randomized trial to improve the quality of treatment for panic and generalized anxiety disorders in primary care. *Archives of General Psychiatry, 62,* 1332–1341. doi: 10.1001/archpsyc.62.12.1332

Romanelli, R. J., Wu, F. M., Gamba, R., Mojtabai, R., & Segal, J. B. (2014). Behavioral therapy and serotonin reuptake inhibitor pharmacotherapy in the treatment of obsessive-compulsive disorder: A systematic review and meta-analysis of head-to-head randomized controlled trials, *Depression and Anxiety, 31,* 641–652.

Ronningstam, E. (2012). Narcissistic personality disorder: The diagnostic process. In T. A. Widiger (Ed.), *The Oxford handbook of personality disorders* (pp. 527–548). New York, NY: Oxford University Press.

Ronningstam, E. (2014). Introduction to the special series on "Narcissistic personality disorder—New perspectives on diagnosis and treatment." *Personality Disorders: Theory, Research, and Treatment, 5*(4), 419.

Room, R., & Greenfield, T. (2006). Alcoholics Anonymous, other 12-step movements and psychotherapy in the US population, 1990. *Addiction, 88*(4), 555–562.

Root, T. L., Pinheiro, A. P., Thornton, L., Strober, M., Fernandez-Aranda, F., Brandt, H., & Bulk, C. M. (2010). Substance use disorders in women with anorexia nervosa. *International Journal of Eating Disorders, 43*(1), 14–21.

Rorabaugh, W. J. (1991). Alcohol in America. *OAH Magazine of History, 6*(2), 17–19.

Rorschach, H. (1951). *Psychodiagnostics.* New York, NY: Grune & Stratton. (Original work published in 1921.)

Roscoe, J. A., Morrow, G. R., Aapro, M. S., Molassiotis, A., & Olver, I. (2011). Anticipatory nausea and vomiting. *Support Care Cancer, 19*(10), 1533–1538.

Rosell, D. R., Futterman, S. E., McMaster, A., & Siever, L. J. (2014). Schizotypal personality disorder: a current review. *Current Psychiatry Reports, 16*(7), 1–12.

Rosellini, A. J., Boettcher, H., Brown, T. A., & Barlow, D. H. (2015). A transdiagnostic temperament-phenotype profile approach to emotional disorder classification: An update. *Psychopathology Review, 2*(1), 110–128.

Rosen, J. C., Reiter, J., & Orosan, P. (1995). Cognitive-behavioral body image therapy for body dysmorphic disorder. *Journal of Consulting Clinical Psychology, 63,* 263–269.

Rosen, R. C. (2000). Medical and psychological interventions for erectile dysfunction: Toward a combined treatment approach. In S. R. Leiblum & R. C. Rosen (Eds.), *Principles and practice of sex therapy* (3rd ed., pp. 276–304). New York, NY: Guilford.

Rosen, R. C. (2007). Erectile dysfunction: Integration of medical and psychological approaches. In S. R. Leiblum (Ed.), *Principles and practice of sex therapy* (4th ed., pp. 277–312). New York, NY: Guilford.

Rosen, R. C., & Beck, J. G. (1988). *Patterns of sexual arousal: Psychophysiological processes and clinical applications.* New York, NY: Guilford.

Rosen, R. C., Connor, M. K., Miyasato, G., Link, C., Shifren, J. L., Fisher, W. A., . . . Schobelock, M. J. (2012). Sexual desire problems in women seeking healthcare: a novel study design for ascertaining prevalence of hypoactive sexual desire disorder in clinic-based samples of US women. *Journal of Women's Health, 21*(5), 505–515.

Rosen, R., Janssen, E., Wiegel, M., Bancroft, J., Althof, S., Wincze, J., & Barlow, D. H. (2006). Psychological and interpersonal correlates in men with erectile dysfunction and their partners: A pilot study of treatment outcome with sildenafil. *Journal of Sex & Marital Therapy, 32,* 215–234.

Rosen, R., Wing, R., Schneider, S., & Gendrano, N. (2005). Epidemiology of erectile dysfunction: The role of medical comorbidities and lifestyle factors. *Urological Clinics of North America, 32,* 403–417.

Rosenberg, R. N., Richter, R. W., Risser, R. C., Taubman, K., Prado-Farmer, I., Ebalo, E., & Schellenberg, G. D. (1996). Genetic factors for the development of Alzheimer's disease in the Cherokee Indian. *Archives of Neurology, 53,* 997–1000.

Rosengren, A., Tibblin, G., & Wilhelmsen, L. (1991). Self-perceived psychological stress and incidence of coronary artery disease in middle-aged men. *American Journal of Cardiology, 68,* 1171–1175.

Rosenman, R. H., Brand, R. J., Jenkins, C. D., Friedman, M., Straus, R., & Wurm, M. (1975). Coronary heart disease in the Western Collaborative Group Study: Final follow-up experience of 8 years. *JAMA: Journal of the American Medical Association, 233,* 872–877.

Rosenthal, D. (Ed.). (1963). *The Genain quadruplets: A case study and theoretical analysis of heredity and environment in schizophrenia.* New York, NY: Basic Books.

Rosenthal, M., Gratz, K., Kosson, D., Cheavens, J., Lejuez, C., & Lynch, T. (2008). Borderline personality disorder and emotional responding: A review of the research literature. *Clinical Psychology Review, 28*(1), 75–91.

Rosenthal, P. A., & Rosenthal, S. (1984). Suicidal behavior by preschool children. *American Journal of Psychiatry, 141,* 520–525.

Rösler, A., & Witztum, M. D. (1998). Treatment of men with paraphilia with a long-acting analogue of gonadotropin-releasing hormone. *New England Journal of Medicine, 338,* 416–422.

Ross, A. O., & Pelham, W. E. (1981). Child psychopathology. *Annual Review of Psychology, 32,* 243–278.

Ross, C. A. (1997). *Dissociative identity disorder.* New York, NY: Wiley.

Ross, C. A. (2009). Dissociative amnesia and dissociative fugue. In P. F. Dell & J. A. O'Neil (Eds.), *Dissociation and the dissociative disorders* (pp. 429–434). New York, NY: Routledge.

Ross, C. A. (2020). Voices: Are they dissociative or psychotic? *Journal of Nervous and Mental Disease, 208*(9), 658–662. doi: 10.1097/NMD.0000000000001206

Ross, C. A., Anderson, G., Fleisher, W. P., & Norton, G. R. (1991). The frequency of multiple personality disorder among psychiatric inpatients. *American Journal of Psychiatry, 148,* 1717–1720.

Ross, C. A., Miller, S. D., Reagor, P., Bjornson, L., Fraser, G. A., & Anderson, G. (1990). Structured interview data on 102 cases of multiple personality disorder from four centers. *American Journal of Psychiatry, 147,* 596–601.

Rossow, I., & Bye, E. K. (2012). The problem of alcohol-related violence: An epidemiological and public health perspective. In M. McMurran (Ed.), *Alcohol-related violence* (pp. 1–18). Chichester, U.K.: Wiley.

Rost, M., Nast, R., Elger, B. S., & Shaw, D. (2020). Trust trumps comprehension, visceral factors trump all: A psychological cascade constraining informed consent to clinical trials. A qualitative study with stable patients. *Research Ethics,* 1747016120914335.

Rothbaum, B. O., Price, M., Jovanovic, T., Norrholm, S. D., Gerardi, M., Dunlop, B., Davis, M., Bradley, B., Duncan, E. J., Rizzo, A., & Ressler, K. J. (2014): A randomized, double-blind evaluation of D-cycloserine or alprazolam combined with virtual reality exposure therapy for posttraumatic stress disorder in Iraq and Afghanistan War veterans. *American Journal of Psychiatry, 171,* 640–648.

Rothblum, E. D. (2002). Gay and lesbian body images. In T. F. Cash & T. Pruzinsky (Eds.), *Body image: A handbook of theory, research and clinical practice* (pp. 257–265). New York, NY: Guilford.

Rothschild, A. J. (2013). Challenges in the treatment of major depressive disorder with psychotic features. *Schizophrenia Bulletin, 39*(4), 787–796. doi: 10.1093/schbul/sbt046

Rottenberg, J., & Johnson, S. L. (2007). *Emotion and psychopathology: Bridging affective and clinical science*. Washington, DC: American Psychological Association.

Rotton, J., & Kelly, I. W. (1985). Much ado about the full moon: A meta-analysis of lunar-lunacy research. *Psychological Bulletin, 97*(2), 286–306.

Rouff, L. (2000). Schizoid personality traits among the homeless mentally ill: A quantitative and qualitative report. *Journal of Social Distress and the Homeless, 9,* 127–141.

Roush, W. (1997). Herbert Benson: Mind–body maverick pushes the envelope. *Science, 276,* 357–359.

Rowe, J. B. (2010). Conversion disorder: Understanding the pathogenic links between emotion and motor systems in the brain. *Brain, 133*(Pt 5), 1295–1297.

Rowell, E. A., & Rowell, R. (1939). *On the trail of marihuana: The weed of madness*. Mountain View, CA: Pacific Press.

Roy, A. K., Lopes, V., & Klein, R. G. (2014). Disruptive mood dysregulation disorder: A new diagnostic approach to chronic irritability in youth. *American Journal of Psychiatry, 171,* 918–924.

Roy-Byrne, P. P., & Katon, W. (2000). Anxiety management in the medical setting: Rationale, barriers to diagnosis and treatment, and proposed solutions. In D. I. Mostofsky & D. H. Barlow (Eds.), *The management of stress and anxiety in medical disorders* (pp. 1–14). Needham Heights, MA: Allyn & Bacon.

Roydeva, M. I., & Reinders, A. A. T. S. (2021). Biomarkers of pathological dissociation: A systematic review. *Neuroscience and Biobehavioral Reviews, 123,* 120–202. doi: 10.1016/j.neubiorev.2020.11.019

Rubia, K., Alegria, A. A., Cubillo, A. I., Smith, A. B., Brammer, M. J., & Radua, J. (2014). Effects of stimulants on brain function in Attention-Deficit/Hyperactivity Disorder: A systematic review and meta-analysis. *Biological Psychiatry, 76*(8), 616–628. doi: 10.1016/j.biopsych.2013.10.016

Rubio, J. M., Markowitz, J. C., Alegria, A., Perez-Fuentes, G., Liu, S.-M., Lin, K.-H., & Blanco, C. (2011). Epidemiology of chronic and nonchronic major depressive disorder: Results from the national epidemiology survey on alcohol and related conditions. *Depression and Anxiety, 28,* 622–631.

Ruchkin, V., Schwab-Stone, M., Jones, S., Cicchetti, D. V., Koposov, R., & Vermeiren, R. (2005). Is posttraumatic stress in youth a culture-bound phenomenon? A comparison of symptom trends in selected U.S. and Russian communities. *American Journal of Psychiatry, 162,* 538–544.

Rück, C., Karlsson, A., Steele, J. D., Edman, G., Meyerson, B. A., Ericson, K., & Svanborg, P. (2008). Capsulotomy for obsessive-compulsive disorder: Long-term follow-up of 25 patients. *Archives of General Psychiatry, 65*(8), 914–921. doi: 10.1001/archpsyc.65.8.914.

Rucklidge, J. J. (2010). Gender differences in attention-deficit/hyperactivity disorder. *The Psychiatric Clinics of North America, 33*(2), 357–373.

Rudaz, M., Craske, M. G., Becker, E. S., Ledermann, T., & Margraf, J. (2010). Health anxiety and fear of fear in panic disorder and agoraphobia vs. social phobia: A prospective longitudinal study. *Depression and Anxiety, 27,* 404–411.

Rudd, M. D., Joiner, Y., & Rajab, M. H. (2001). *Treating suicidal behavior*. New York, NY: Guilford.

Rudd, M. D., Rajab, M. H., Orman, D. T., Stulman, D. A., Joiner, T., & Dixon, W. (1996). Effectiveness of an outpatient intervention targeting suicidal young adults: Preliminary results. *Journal of Consulting and Clinical Psychology, 64,* 179–190.

Rudolph, K. D. (2009). Adolescent depression. In I. H. Gotlib & C. L. Hammen (Eds.), *Handbook of depression* (2nd ed., pp. 444–466). New York, NY: Guilford.

Ruffin, R., Ironson, G., Fletcher, M. A., Balbin, E., & Schneiderman, N. (2012). Health locus of control beliefs and healthy survival with AIDS. *International Journal of Behavioral Medicine, 19*(4), 512–517.

Ruiz, F. S., Andersen, M. L., Martins, R. C. S., Zager, A., Lopes, J. D., & Tufik, S. (2012). Immune alterations after selective rapid eye movement or total sleep deprivation in healthy male volunteers. *Innate Immunity, 18*(1), 44–54.

Ruiz-Veguilla, M., Luisa Barrigón, M., Diaz, F. J., Ferrin, M., Moreno-Granados, J., Dolores Salcedo, M., & Gurpegui, M. (2012). The duration of untreated psychosis is associated with social support and temperament. *Psychiatry Research, 200*(2–3), 687–692. doi: http://dx.doi.org/10.1016/j.psychres.2012.03.024

Rupprecht, R., Rammes, G., Eser, D., Baghai, T. C., Schule, C., Nothdurfter, C., & Kucher, K. (2009). Translocator protein (18 kD) as target for anxiolytics without benzodiazepine-like side effects. *Science, 325*(5939), 490–493.

Rusch, N., Lieb, K., Gottler, I., Hermann, C., Schramm, E., Richter, H., & Bohus, M. (2007). Shame and implicit self-concept in women with borderline personality disorder. *American Journal of Psychiatry, 164*(3), 500–508.

Ruscio, J. (2004). Diagnoses and the behaviors they denote: A critical evaluation of the labeling theory of mental illness. *Scientific Review of Mental Health Practice, 3,* 5–22.

Rush, A. (2007). STAR *D: What have we learned? *American Journal of Psychiatry, 164,* 201–204.

Rush, A. J., Erman, M. K., Giles, D. E., Schlesser, M. A., Carpenter, G., Vasavada, N., & Roffwarg, H. P. (1986). Polysomnographic findings in recently drug-free and clinically remitted depressed patients. *Archives of General Psychiatry, 43,* 878–884.

Rush, A. J., Giles, D. E., Schlesser, M. A., Orsulak, P. J., Weissenburger, J. E., Fulton, C. L., & Roffwarg, P. (1997). Dexamethasone response, thyrotropin-releasing hormone stimulation, rapid eye movement latency, and subtypes of depression. *Biological Psychiatry, 41,* 915–928.

Rush, B. (1812). *Medical inquiries and observations upon the diseases of the mind*. Philadelphia, PA: Kimber and Richardson.

Russell, A. E., Ford, T., Williams, R., & Russell, G. (2016). The association between socioeconomic disadvantage and attention deficit/hyperactivity disorder (ADHD): A systematic review. *Child Psychiatry & Human Development, 47*(3), 440–458.

Russell, A. E., Ford, T., Williams, R., & Russell, G. (in press). The association between socioeconomic disadvantage and Attention Deficit/Hyperactivity Disorder (ADHD): A systematic review. *Child Psychiatry & Human Development*, 1–19. doi: 10.1007/s10578-015-0578-3

Russell, G. (2009). Disorders of eating: Anorexia nervosa. In M. G. Gelder, N. C. Andreasen, J. J. López-Ibor, Jr., & J. R. Geddes (Eds.), *New Oxford textbook of psychiatry* (2nd ed., pp. 777–800). New York, NY: Oxford University Press.

Russell, G. F. M. (1979). Bulimia nervosa: An ominous variant of anorexia nervosa. *Psychological Medicine, 9,* 429–448.

Russell, G. F. M. (2009). Disorders of Eating: Anorexia Nervosa. In M. G. Gelder, N. C. Andreasen, J. J. López-Ibor, Jr., & J. R. Geddes (Eds.), *New Oxford textbook of psychiatry* (2nd ed., pp. 777–800). New York, NY: Oford University Press.

Russell, G. F. M., Szmukler, G. I., Dare, C., & Eisler, I. (1987). An evaluation of family therapy in anorexia nervosa and bulimia nervosa. *Archives of General Psychiatry, 44,* 1047–1056.

Russo, S. J., Dietz, D. M., Dumitriu, D., Morrison, J. H., Malenka, R. C., & Nestler, E. J. (2010). The addicted synapse: mechanisms of synaptic and structural plasticity in nucleus accumbens. *Trends in neurosciences, 33*(6), 267–276.

Rutledge, T., Groesz, L., Linke, S., Woods, G., & Herbst, K. (2011). Behavioural weight management for the primary careprovider. *Obesity Reviews, 12*(5), e290–e297.

Rutter, M. (2002). The interplay of nature, nurture, and developmental influences: The challenge ahead for mental health. *Archives of General Psychiatry, 59,* 996–1000.

Rutter, M. (2006). *Genes and behavior: Nature–nurture interplay.* Oxford, UK: Blackwell.

Rutter, M. (2010). Gene-environment interplay. *Depression and Anxiety, 27*(1), 1–4.

Rutter, M. (2011a). Progress in understanding autism: 2007–2010. *Journal of Autism and Developmental Disorders, 41*(4), 395–404. doi: 10.1007/s10803-011-1184-2

Rutter, M. (2011b). Research review: Child psychiatric diagnosis and classification: Concepts, findings, challenges and potential. *Journal of Child Psychology and Psychiatry, 52*(6), 647–660. doi: 10.1111/j.1469-7610.2011.02367.x

Rutter, M., & Giller, H. (1984). *Juvenile delinquency: Trends and perspectives.* New York, NY: Guilford.

Rutter, M., & Pickles, A. (2016). Annual Research Review: Threats to the validity of child psychiatry and psychology. *Journal of Child Psychology and Psychiatry 57*(3), 398–416.

Rutter, M., Moffitt, T. E., & Caspi, A. (2006). Gene–environment interplay and psychopathology: Multiple varieties but real effects. *Journal of Child Psychology and Psychiatry, 47,* 226–261.

Ruzek, J. I. (2012). Community-based early intervention with trauma survivors. In J. G. Beck & D. M. Sloan (Eds.), *The Oxford handbook of traumatic stress disorders* (pp. 347–362). New York, NY: Oxford University Press.

Ruzek, J. I., Karlin, B. E., & Zeiss, A. (2012). Implementation of evidence-based psychological treatments in the Veterans Health Administration. In R. K. McHugh & D. H. Barlow (Eds.), *Dissemination and implementation of evidence-based psychological interventions* (pp. 78–96). New York, NY: Oxford University Press.

Ryan, D. H., & Kushner, R. (2010). The state of obesity and obesity research. *JAMA: Journal of American Medical Association, 304,* 1835–1836.

Ryan, W. D. (1992). The pharmacologic treatment of child and adolescent depression. *Psychiatric Clinics of North America, 15,* 29–40.

Ryder, A. G., Sunohara, M., & Kirmayer, L. J. (2015). Culture and personality disorder: from a fragmented literature to a contextually grounded alternative. *Current opinion in psychiatry, 28*(1), 40–45.

Ryder, A. G., Yang, J., Zhu, X., Yao, S., Yi, J., Heine, S. J., & Bagby, R. M. (2008). The cultural shaping of depression: Somatic symptoms in China, psychological symptoms in North America? *Journal of Abnormal Psychology, 117*(2), 300–313.

Saab, P. G., Llabre, M. M., Hurwitz, B. E., Frame, C. A., Reineke, I., Fins, A. I., & Schneiderman, N. (1992). Myocardial and peripheral vascular responses to behavioral challenges and their stability in black and white Americans. *Psychophysiology, 29*(4), 384–397.

Sachdev, P. S., Blacker, D., Blazer, D. G., Ganguli, M., Jeste, D. V., Paulsen, J. S., & Petersen, R. C. (2014). Classifying neurocognitive disorders: The DSM-5 approach. *Nature Reviews Neurology, 10*(11), 634–642.

Sachs, G. S., & Rush, A. J. (2003). Response, remission, and recovery in bipolar disorders: What are the realistic treatment goals? *Journal of Clinical Psychiatry, 64,* 18–22.

Sachs, G. S., Nierenberg, A. A., Calabrese, J. R., Marangell, L. B., Wisniewski, S. R., Gyulai, L., & Thase, M. E. (2007). Effectiveness of adjunctive antidepressant treatment for bipolar depression. *New England Journal of Medicine, 356*(17), 1711–1722.

Sack, R. L., Auckley, D., Auger, R. R., Carskadon, M. A., Wright, K. P., Jr., Vitiello, M. V., & American Academy of Sleep Medicine. (2007). Circadian rhythm sleep disorders: Part II, Advanced sleep phase disorder, delayed sleep phase disorder, free-running disorder, and irregular sleep-wake rhythm. *Sleep, 30*(11), 1484–1501.

Sackeim, H. A., & Devanand, D. P. (1991). Dissociative disorders. In M. Hersen & S. M. Turner (Eds.), *Adult psychopathology & diagnosis* (2nd ed., pp. 279–322). New York, NY: Wiley.

Sackett, D. L., Strauss, S. E., Richardson, W. S., Rosenberg, W., & Haynes, R. B. (2000). *Evidence-based medicine: How to practice and teach EBM* (2nd ed.). London, UK: Churchill Livingstone.

Sacks, H., Comer, J. S., Pincus, D. B., Comacho, M., & Hunter, L. (2013). Effective interventions for students with separation anxiety disorder. In C. Franklin, M. B. Harris, & P. Allen-Meares (Eds.), *The school services sourcebook* (2nd ed.). New York, NY: Oxford University Press.

Sacks, J. A., Comer, J. S., Furr, J. M., Pincus, D. B., & Kurtz, S. M. S. (2011, November). *Daily speech changes across an intensive group behavioral treatment program for early childhood selective mutism.* Poster presented at the 45th annual meeting of the Association of Behavioral and Cognitive Therapies, Child and Adolescent Anxiety Special Interest Group Exposition. Toronto, Canada.

Safford, M. M., Brown, T. M., Muntner, P. M., Durant, R. W., Glasser, S., Halanych, J. H., Shikany, J. M., Prineas, R. J., Samdarshi, T., Bittner, V. A., Lewis, C. E., Gamboa, C., Cushman, M., Howard, V., & Howard, G. (2012). Association of race and sex with risk of incident acute coronary heart disease events. *JAMA, 308*(17), 1768–1774.

Sahler, O., Fairclough, D., Phipps, S., Mukhern, R., Dolgin, M., & Noll, R. (2005). Using problem solving skills training to reduce negative affectivity in mothers of children with newly diagnosed cancer: Report of a multisite randomized trial. *Journal of Consulting and Clinical Psychology, 73,* 272–283.

Saigh, P. A. (1984). Pre- and postinvasion anxiety in Lebanon. *Behavior Therapy, 15,* 185–190.

Sakel, M. (1958). *Schizophrenia.* Philosophical Library

Sakheim, D. K., Barlow, D. H., Abrahamson, D. J., & Beck, J. G. (1987). Distinguishing between organogenic and psychogenic erectile dysfunction. *Behaviour Research and Therapy, 25,* 379–390.

Salaminios, G., Morosan, L., Toffel, E., Tanzer, M., Eliez, S., Badoud, D., … Debbané, M. (in press). Associations between schizotypal personality features, mentalizing difficulties and thought problems in a sample of community adolescents. *Early Intervention in Psychiatry.*

Salekin, R. T. (2006). Psychopathy in children and adolescents: Key issues in conceptualization and assessment. In C. J. Patrick (Ed.), *Handbook of psychopathy* (pp. 389–414). New York, NY: Guilford.

Salekin, R. T., Rogers, R., & Sewell, K. W. (1997). Construct validity of psychopathy in a female offender sample: A multitrait–multimethod evaluation. *Journal of Abnormal Psychology, 106*(4), 576–585. doi: 10.1037/0021-843x.106.4.576

Salkovskis, P. M., & Campbell, P. (1994). Thought suppression induces intrusion in naturally occurring negative intrusive thoughts. *Behaviour Research and Therapy, 32*(1), 1–8.

Salkovskis, P., Warwick, H., & Deale, A. (2003). Cognitive-behavioral treatment for severe and persistent health anxiety. *Brief Treatment and Crisis Intervention, 3,* 353–367.

Sallet, J., Mars, R. B., Noonan, M. P., Andersson, J. L., O'Reilly, J. X., & Rushworth, M. F. (2011). Social network size affects neural circuits in macaques. *Science, 334*(6056), 697–700. doi: 10.1126/science.1210027

Salvatore, J. E., Larsson Lönn, S., Sundquist, J., Sundquist, K., & Kendler, K. S. (2018). Genetics, the rearing environment, and the intergenerational transmission of divorce: A Swedish national adoption study. *Psychological Science, 29*(3), 370–378. doi: 10.1177/0956797617734864

Salvatore, P., Bhuvaneswar, C., Tohen, M., Khalsa, H. M., Maggini, C., & Baldessarini, R. J. (2014). Capgras' syndrome in first-episode psychotic disorders. *Psychopathology, 47*(4), 261–269.

Samek, D. R., Elkins, I. J., Keyes, M. A., Iacono, W. G., & McGue, M. (2015). High school sports involvement diminishes the association between childhood conduct disorder and adult antisocial behavior. *Journal of Adolescent Health, 57*(1), 107–112.

Samson, L., & Janssen, E. (2014). Sexual and affective responses to same-and opposite-sex stimuli in heterosexual and homosexual men: Assessment and manipulation of visual attention. *Archives of Sexual Behavior, 43*(5), 917–930.

Samuels, J., & Costa, P. T. (2012). Obsessive-compulsive personality disorder. In T. A. Widiger (Ed.), *The Oxford handbook of personality disorders* (pp. 566–581). New York, NY: Oxford University Press.

Sanchez-Roige, S., & Palmer, A. A. (2020). Emerging phenotyping strategies will advance our understanding of psychiatric genetics. *Nature Neuroscience, 23*(4), 475–480.

Sandal, C. (2020). Drug-facilitated sexual assault. *Workplace Health & Safety, 68*(3), 155–155.

Sanderson, W. C., & Barlow, D. H. (1990). A description of patients diagnosed with DSM-III-R generalized anxiety disorder. *Journal of Nervous and Mental Disease, 178,* 588–591.

Sandi C, Haller J. Stress and the social brain: behavioural effects and neurobiological mechanisms. Nat Rev Neurosci. 2015 May;16(5):290-304. doi: 10.1038/nrn3918.

Sandin, B., Chorot, P., Santed, M., & Valiente, R. (2004). Differences in negative life events between patients with anxiety disorders, depression and hypochondriasis. *Anxiety, Stress & Coping: An International Journal, 17,* 37–47.

Sanislow, C. A., da Cruz, K. L., Gianoli, M. O., & Reagan, E. M. (2012). Avoidant personality disorder, traits, and type. In T. A. Widiger (Ed.), *The Oxford handbook of personality disorders* (pp. 549–565). New York, NY: Oxford University Press.

Sankey, A., Hill, C., Brown, J., Quinn, L., & Fletcher, A. (2006). A follow-up study of chronic fatigue syndrome in children and adolescents: Symptoms persistence and school absenteeism. *Clinical Child Psychology and Psychiatry, 11,* 126–138.

Sano, M., Ernesto, C., Thomas, R. G., Klauber, M. R., Schafer, K., Grundman, M., & Thal, L. J. (1997). A controlled trial of selegiline, alpha-tocopherol, or both as treatment for Alzheimer's disease. *New England Journal of Medicine, 336,* 1216–1222.

Santarelli, L., Saxe, M., Gross, C., Surget, A., Battaglia, F., Dulawa, S., & Hen, R. (2003). Requirement of hippocampal neurogenesis for the behavioral effects of antidepressants. *Science, 301,* 805–809.

Santoro, M. R., Bray, S. M., & Warren, S. T. (2012). Molecular mechanisms of fragile X syndrome: A twenty-year perspective. *Annual Review of Pathology: Mechanisms of Disease, 7,* 219–245.

Santosa, C. M., Strong, C. M., Nowakowska, C., Wang, P. W., Rennicke, C. M., & Ketter, T. A. (2007). Enhanced creativity in bipolar disorder patients: A controlled study. *Journal of Affective Disorders, 100*(1–3), 31–39.

Santosh, P. J. (2009). Medication for children and adolescents: Current issues. In M. G. Gelder, N. C. Andreasen, J. J. Lopez-Ibor, Jr., & J. R. Geddes (Eds.), *New Oxford textbook of psychiatry* (2nd ed., Vol. 2, pp. 1793–1798). Oxford, UK: Oxford University Press.

Santry, H. P., Gillen, D. L., & Lauderdale, D. S. (2005). Trends in bariatric surgical procedures. *JAMA: Journal of the American Medical Association,* 294, 1909–1917.

Santucci, L. C., Ehrenreich, J. T., Trosper, S. E., Bennett, S. M., & Pincus, D. B. (2009). Development and preliminary evaluation of a one-week summer treatment program for separation anxiety disorder. *Cognitive and Behavioral Practice, 16,* 317–331. doi: 10.1016/j.cbpra.2008.12.005

Sapolsky, R. (2004). Is impaired neurogenesis relevant to the affective symptoms of depression? *Biological Psychiatry, 56,* 137–139.

Sapolsky, R. M. (1990). Stress in the wild. *Scientific American, 262,* 116–123.

Sapolsky, R. M. (2007). Stress, stress-related disease, and emotional regulation. In J. J. Gross (Ed.), *Handbook of emotion regulation* (pp. 606–615). New York, NY: Guilford.

Sapolsky, R. M., & Meaney, M. J. (1986). Maturation of the adrenal stress response: Neuroendocrine control mechanisms and the stress hyporesponsive period. *Brain Research Review, 11,* 65–76.

Sapolsky, R. M., & Ray, J. C. (1989). Styles of dominance and their endocrine correlates among wild, live baboons. *American Journal of Primatology, 18*(1), 1–13.

Sarbin, T., & Mancuso, J. (1980). *Schizophrenia: Medical diagnosis or moral verdict?* Elmsford, NY: Pergamon Press.

Sareen, J., Afifi, T. O., McMillan, K. A., & Asmundson, G. J. G. (2011). Relationship between household income and mental disorders: Findings from a population-based longitudinal study. *Archives of General Psychiatry 68*(4), 419–427. doi: 10.1001/archgenpsychiatry.2011.15

Sareen, J., Jacobi, F., Cox, B. J., Belik, S., Clara, I., & Stein, B. M. (2006). Disability and poor quality of life associated with comorbid anxiety disorders and physical conditions. *Archives of Internal Medicine, 166,* 2109–2116.

Sari, Y., Johnson, V. R., & Weedman, J. M. (2011). Role of the serotonergic system in alcohol dependence: from animal models to clinics. *Progress in Molecular Biology and Translational Science, 98,* 401–443.

Sarkar, A., & Adshead, G. (Eds.) (2012). *Clinical Topics in Personality Disorder.* London: RJPsych Publications.

Sarrel, P. M., & Masters, W. H. (1982). Sexual molestation of men by women. *Archives of Sexual Behavior, 11,* 117–131.

Sarwer, D. B., Foster, G. D., & Wadden, T. A. (2004). Treatment of obesity I: Adult obesity. In J. K. Thompson (ed.), *Handbook of eating disorders and obesity* (pp. 421–442). New York, NY: Wiley.

Saudino, J. J., Pedersen, N. L., Lichenstein, P., McClearn, G. E., & Plomin, R. (1997). Can personality explain genetic influence on life events? *Journal of Personality & Social Psychology, 72*(1), 196–206.

Saudino, K. J., Wang, M., Flom, M., & Asherson, P. (2018). Genetic and environmental links between motor activity level and attention problems in early childhood. *Developmental Science, 21*(5). doi: 10.1111/desc.12630

Savard, J., Savard, M.-H., & Morin, C. M. (2011). Insomnia. In M. M. Antony & D. H. Barlow (Eds.), *Handbook of assessment and treatment planning for psychological disorders* (2nd ed. (pp. 633–670). New York, NY: Guilford.

Savin-Williams, R. (2006). Who's gay? Does it matter? *Current Directions in Psychological Science, 15,* 40–44.

Saxe, G. N., Stoddard, F., Hall, E., Chawla, N., Lopez, C., Sheridan, R., & Yehuda, R. (2005). Pathways to PTSD: Part I. Children with burns. *American Journal of Psychiatry, 162,* 1299–1304.

Saxe, G. N., van der Kolk, B. A., Berkowitz, R., Chinman, G., Hall, K., Leiberg, G., & Schwartz, J. (1993). Dissociative disorders in psychiatric inpatients. *American Journal of Psychiatry, 150,* 1037–1042.

Saxena, S., & Prasad, K. (1989). DSM-III subclassifications of dissociative disorders applied to psychiatric outpatients in India. *American Journal of Psychiatry, 146,* 261–262.

Saxena, S., Winograd, A., Dunkin, J. J., Maidment, K., Rosen, R., Vapnik, T., & Bystritsky, A. (2001). A retrospective review of clinical characteristics and treatment response in body dysmorphic disorder versus obsessive-compulsive disorder. *Journal of Clinical Psychiatry, 62,* 67–72.

Scanlon, D. (2013). Specific learning disability and its newest definition: Which is comprehensive? and which is insufficient? *Journal of Learning Disabilities, 46*(1), 26–33. doi: 10.1177/0022219412464342

Scarella, T. M., Boland, R. J., & Barsky, A. J. (2019). Illness anxiety disorder: Psychopathology, epidemiology, clinical characteristics, and treatment. *Psychosomatic Medicine, 81*(5), 398–407. doi: 10.1097/PSY.0000000000000691

Scarlett, S., Nolan, H., Kenny, R. A., & O'Connell, M. D. (2020). Objective sleep duration in older adults: Results from the Irish longitudinal study on ageing. *Journal of the American Geriatrics Society, 68*(1), 120–128.

Scarmeas, N., Albert, S. M., Manly, J. J., & Stern, Y. (2006). Education and rates of cognitive decline in incident Alzheimer's disease. *Journal of Neurology, Neurosurgery, and Psychiatry, 77*(3), 308–316.

Schacter, D. L., Chiu, P., & Ochsner, K. N. (1993). Implicit memory: A selective review. *Annual Review of Neuroscience, 16,* 159–182.

Schaffer, A., Isometsä, E. T., Tondo, L. H., Moreno, D., Turecki, G., Reis, C., Cassidy, F., Sinyor, M., Azorin, J. M., Kessing, L. V., Ha, K., Goldstein, T., Weizman, A., Beautrais, A., Chou, Y. H., Diazgranados, N., Levitt, A. J., Zarate Jr., C. A., Rihmer, Z., & Yatham, L. N. (2015). International Society for Bipolar Disorders Task Force on Suicide: Meta-analyses and meta-regression of correlates of suicide attempts and suicide deaths in bipolar disorder. *Bipolar Disorders, 17,* 1–16.

Scharfstein, L. A., Beidel, D., Finnell, L. R., Distler, A., & Carter, N. T. (2011). Do pharmacological and behavioral interventions differentially affect treatment outcome for children with social phobia? *Behavior Modification*, 35(5), 451–467. doi: 10.1177/0145445511408590

Schatzberg, A. (2000). New indications for antidepressants. *Journal of Clinical Psychiatry, 61*(Suppl. 11), 9–17.

Schatzberg, A., Rush, J., Arnow, B., Banks, P., Blalock, J., Borian, F., Howland, R., & Keller, M. B. (2005). Chronic depression: Medication (Nefazodone) or psychotherapy (CBASP) is effective when the other is not. *Archives of General Psychiatry, 62,* 513–520.

Scheerenberger, R. C. (1983). *A history of mental retardation*. Baltimore, MD: Paul H. Brookes.

Scheidt, P. C., Harel, Y., Trumble, A. C., Jones, D. H., Overpeck, M. D., & Bijur, P. E. (1995). The epidemiology of nonfatal injuries among U.S. children and youth. *American Journal of Public Health, 85,* 932–938.

Scheidt, P. C., Overpeck, M. D., Trifiletti, L. B., & Cheng, T. (2000). Child and adolescent injury research in 1998: A summary of abstracts submitted to the Ambulatory Pediatrics Association and the American Public Health Association. *Archives of Pediatrics and Adolescent Medicine, 154,* 442–445.

Scheier, M. F., Matthews, K. A., Owens, J. F., Magovern, G. J., Sr., Lefebvre, R. C., Abbott, R. A., & Carver, C. S. (1989). Dispositional optimism and recovery from coronary artery bypass surgery: The beneficial effects on physical and psychological well-being. *Journal of Personality and Social Psychology, 57*(6), 1024–1040.

Schenck, C. H., Arnulf, I., & Mahowald, M. W. (2007). Sleep and sex: What can go wrong? A review of the literature on sleep related disorders and abnormal sexual behaviors and experiences. *Sleep, 30*(6), 683.

Schiavi, R. C. (1990). Chronic alcoholism and male sexual dysfunction. *Journal of Sex and Marital Therapy, 16,* 23–33.

Schiavi, R. C., White, D., Mandeli, J., & Levine, A. C. (1997). Effect of testosterone administration on sexual behavior and mood in men with erectile dysfunction. *Archives of Sexual Behavior, 26,* 231–241.

Schiele, M. A., Gottschalk, M. G., & Domschke, K. (2020). The applied implications of epigenetics in anxiety, affective and stress-related disorders: A review and synthesis on psychosocial stress, psychotherapy and prevention. *Clinical Psychology Review, 77,* 101830.

Schiele, M. A., Gottschalk, M. G., & Domschke, K. (2020). The applied implications of epigenetics in anxiety, affective and stress-related disorders: A review and synthesis on psychosocial stress, psychotherapy and prevention. *Clinical Psychology Review, 77*. doi: 10.1016/j.cpr.2020.101830

Schietecatte, I., Roeyers, H., & Warreyn, P. (2012). Exploring the nature of joint attention impairments in young children with autism spectrum disorder: Associated social and cognitive skills. *Journal of Autism and Developmental Disorders, 42*(1), 1–12. doi: 10.1007/s10803-011-1209-x

Schifano, F., Napoletano, F., Arillotta, D., Zangani, C., Gilgar, L., Guirguis, A., … Vento, A. (2020). The clinical challenges of synthetic cathinones. *British Journal of Clinical Pharmacology, 86*(3), 410–419.

Schiffer, B., Peschel, T., Paul, T., Gizewski, E., Forsting, M., Leygraf, N., & Krueger, T. H. C. (2007). Structural brain abnormalities in the frontostriatal system and cerebellum in pedophilia. *Journal of Psychiatric Research, 41,* 753–762.

Schiffman, J., Walker, E., Ekstrom, M., Schulsinger, F., Sorensen, H., & Mednick, S. (2004). Childhood videotaped social and neuromotor precursors of schizophrenia: A prospective investigation. *American Journal of Psychiatry, 161*(11), 2021–2027.

Schildkraut, J. J. (1965). The catecholamine hypothesis of affective disorders: A review of supporting evidence. *American Journal of Psychiatry, 122,* 509–522.

Schiller, C., & Allen, P. J. (2005). Follow-up of infants prenatally exposed to cocaine. *Pediatric Nursing, 31,* 427–436.

Schmaling, K. B., Fiedelak, J. I., Katon, W. J., Bader, J. O., & Buchwald, D. S. (2003). Prospective study of the prognosis of unexplained chronic fatigue in a clinic-based cohort. *Psychosomatic Medicine, 65,* 1047–1054.

Schmidt, U., Lee, S., Beecham, J., Perkins, S., Treasure, J., Yi, I., & Eisler, I. (2007). A randomized controlled trial of family therapy and cognitive behavior therapy guided self-care for adolescents with bulimia nervosa and related disorders. *American Journal of Psychiatry, 164*(4), 591–598.

Schneck, C. D., Miklowitz, D. J., Miyahara, S., Araga, M., Wisniewski, S., Gyulai, L., & Sachs, G. S. (2008). The prospective course of rapid-cycling bipolar disorder: Findings from the STEP-BD. *American Journal of Psychiatry, 165*(3), 370–377; quiz 410.

Schneck, C., Miklowitz, D., Calabrese, J., Allen, M., Thomas, M., Wisniewski, S., & Sachs, G. S. (2004). Phenomenology of rapid-cycling bipolar disorder: Data from the first 500 participants in the systematic treatment enhancement program. *American Journal of Psychiatry, 161,* 1902–1908.

Schneider, S., Blatter-Meunier, J., Herren, C., In-Albon, T., Adornetto, C., Meyer, A., & Lavallee, K. L. (2013). The efficacy of a family-based cognitive-behavioral treatment for separation anxiety disorder in children aged 8-13: A randomized comparison with a general anxiety program. *Journal of Consulting and Clinical Psychology, 81,* 932.

Schneiderman, N. (2004). Psychosocial, behavioral, and biological aspects of chronic diseases. *Current Directions in Psychological Science, 13,* 247–251.

Schneier, F. R., Neria, Y., Pavlicova, M., Hembree, E., Suh, E. J., Amsel, L., & Marshall, R. D. (2012). Combined prolonged exposure therapy and paroxetine for PTSD related to the World Trade Center attack: A randomized controlled trial. *American Journal of Psychiatry, 169,* 80–88. doi: 10.1176/appi.ajp.2011.11020321

Schnell, K., & Herpertz, S. C. (2007). Effects of dialectic-behavioral-therapy on the neural correlates of affective hyperarousal in borderline personality disorder. *Journal of Psychiatric Research, 41,* 837–847.

Schoenbach, V. J., Kaplan, B. H., Fredman, L., & Kleinbaum, D. G. (1986). Social ties and mortality in Evans County, Georgia. *American Journal of Epidemiology, 123,* 577.

Schoenberg, M. R., Marsh, P. J., & Benbadis, S. R. (2012). Where are somatoform disorders going? An update on the DSM-V. *Expert Review of Neurotherapeutics, 12,* 1371–1374. doi: 10.1586/ern.12.136

Schoeneman, T. J. (1977). The role of mental illness in the European witchhunts of the sixteenth and seventeenth centuries: An assessment. *Journal of the History of the Behavioral Sciences, 13,* 337–351.

Schoenmakers, B., Buntinx, F., & DeLepeleire, J. (2010). Supporting the dementia family caregiver: The effect of home care intervention on general well-being. *Aging & Mental Health, 14*(1), 44–56.

Schomerus, G., Schwahn, C., Holzinger, A., Corrigan, P. W., Grabe, H. J., Carta, M. G., & Angermeyer, M. C. (2012). Evolution of public attitudes about mental illness: A systematic review and meta-analysis. *Acta Psychiatrica Scandinavica, 125*(6), 440–452.

Schramm, E., Klein, D. N., Elsaesser, M., Furukawa, T. A., & Domschke, K. (2020). Review of dysthymia and persistent depressive disorder: History, correlates, and clinical implications. *The Lancet Psychiatry, 7*(9), 801–812. doi: 10.1016/s2215-0366(20)30099-7

Schredl, M. (2010). Nightmare frequency and nightmare topics in a representative German sample. *European Archives of Psychiatry and Clinical Neuroscience, 260*(8), 565–570.

Schreiner-Engel, P., & Schiavi, R. C. (1986). Lifetime psychopathology in individuals with low sexual desire. *Journal of Nervous and Mental Disease, 174,* 646–651.

Schuck, P. F., Malgarin, F., Cararo, J. H., Cardoso, F., Streck, E. L., & Ferreira, G. C. (2015). Phenylketonuria pathophysiology: On the role of metabolic alterations. *Aging and disease, 6*(5), 390–399.

Schuckit, M. A. (1994). Low level of response to alcohol as a predictor of future alcoholism. *American Journal of Psychiatry, 151,* 184–189.

Schuckit, M. A. (1998). Biological, psychological and environmental predictors of alcoholism risk: A longitudinal study. *Journal of Studies on Alcohol, 59,* 485–494.

Schuckit, M. A. (2009b). Alcohol-use disorders. *The Lancet, 373(9662),* 492–501.

Schuckit, M. A. (2012). Editor's corner: Editorial in reply to the comments of Griffith Edwards. *Journal of Studies on Alcohol and Drugs, 73*(4), 521.

Schuckit, M. A. (2014a). A brief history of research on the genetics of alcohol and other drug use disorders. *Journal of Studies on Alcohol and Drugs: Supplement, 75(*Suppl 17), 59–67.

Schuckit, M. A. (2014b). Recognition and management of withdrawal delirium (delirium tremens). *New England Journal of Medicine, 371*(22), 2109–2113.

Schuckit, M. A., Smith, T. L., Anthenelli, R., & Irwin, M. (1993). Clinical course of alcoholism in 636 male inpatients. *American Journal of Psychiatry, 150,* 786–792.

Schulberg, H. C., Block, M. R., Madonia, M. J., Scott, C. P., Rodriguez, E., Imber, S. D., & Coulehan, J. L. (1996). Treating major depression in primary care practice: Eight-month clinical outcomes. *Archives of General Psychiatry, 53,* 913–919.

Schulz, R., Drayer, R. A., & Rollman, B. L. (2002). Depression as a risk factor for non-suicide mortality in the elderly. *Biological Psychiatry, 52,* 205–225.

Schulze, L., Schmahl, C., & Niedtfeld, I. (2016). Neural correlates of disturbed emotion processing in borderline personality disorder: a multimodal meta-analysis. *Biological psychiatry, 79*(2), 97–106.

Schumann, C. M., & Amaral, D. G. (2006). Stereological analysis of amygdala neuron number in autism. *Journal of Neuroscience, 26,* 7674–7679.

Schurger, A., Pereira, F., Treisman, A., & Cohen, J. D. (2010). Reproducibility distinguishes conscious from nonconscious neural representations. *Science, 327,* 97–99.

Schutter, D. J. (2009). Antidepressant efficacy of high-frequency transcranial magnetic stimulation over the left dorsolateral prefrontal cortex in double-blind sham-controlled designs: A meta-analysis. *Psychological Medicine, 39*(1), 65–75.

Schwalberg, M. D., Barlow, D. H., Alger, S. A., & Howard, L. J. (1992). Comparison of bulimics, obese binge eaters, social phobics, and individuals with panic disorder or comorbidity across DSM-III-R anxiety. *Journal of Abnormal Psychology, 101,* 675–681.

Schwartz, A. J. (2011). Rate, relative risk, and method of suicide by students at 4-year colleges and universities in the United States, 2004–2005 through 2008–2009. *Suicide and Life-Threatening Behavior, 41*(4), 353–371.

Schwartz, B. I., Mansbach, J. M., Marion, J. G., Katzman, D. K., & Forman, S. (2008). Variations in admission practices for adolescents with anorexia nervosa: North American sample. *Journal of Adolescent Health, 43*(5), 425-431.

Schwartz, I. M. (1993). Affective reactions of American and Swedish women to the first premarital coitus: A cross-cultural comparison. *Journal of Sex Research, 30*(1), 18–26.

Schwartz, M. B., & Brownell, K. D. (2007). Actions necessary to prevent childhood obesity: Creating the climate for change. *Journal of Law, Medicine, & Ethics, 35,* 78–89.

Schwartz, M. S., & Andrasik, F. (Eds.) (2003). *Biofeedback: A practitioner's guide* (3rd ed.). New York, NY: Guilford.

Schwartz, R. P., Brooner, R. K., Montoya, I. D., Currens, M., & Hayes, M. (2010). A 12-year follow-up of a methadone medical maintenance program. *The American Journal on Addictions, 8*(4), 293–299.

Schwartz, R. P., Jaffe, J. H., O'Grady, K. E., Das, B., Highfield, D. A., & Wilson, M. E. (2009). Scaling-up interim methadone maintenance: Treatment for 1,000 heroin-addicted individuals. *Journal of Substance Abuse Treatment, 37*(4), 362–367. doi: 10.1016/j.jsat.2009.04.002

Schwartz, R., & Feisthamel, K. (2009). Disproportionate diagnosis of mental disorders among African American versus European American clients: Implications for counseling theory, research, and practice. *Journal of Counseling & Development, 87*(3), 295–301.

Schwartz, J. M., Stoessel, P. W., Baxter, L. R., Martin, K. M., & Phelps, M. E. (1996). Systematic changes in cerebral glucose metabolic rate after successful behavior modification treatment of obsessive-compulsive disorder. *Archives of General Psychiatry, 53*(2), 109–113. https://doi.org/10.1001/archpsyc.1996.01830020023004

Schwarzkopf, D. S., & Rees, G. (2010). Brain activity to rely on? *Science, 327,* 43–44.

Scoriels, L., Jones, P. B., & Sahakian, B. J. (2013). Modafinil effects on cognition and emotion in schizophrenia and its neurochemical modulation in the brain. *Neuropharmacology, 64,* 168–184.

Scott, C. L., Hilty, D. M., & Brook, M. (2003). Impulse-control disorders not elsewhere classified. In R. E. Hales & S. C. Yudofsky (Eds.), *Textbook of clinical psychiatry* (4th ed., pp. 781–802). Washington, DC: American Psychiatric Publishing.

Scott, C. L., Quanbeck, C. D., & Resnick, P. J. (2008). Assessment of dangerousness. In R. E. Hales, S. C. Yudofsky, & G. O. Gabbard (Eds.), *The American Psychiatric Publishing textbook of psychiatry* (5th ed., pp. 1655–1672). Arlington, VA: American Psychiatric Publishing.

Scott, J. E., & Dixon, L. B. (1995). Psychological interventions for schizophrenia. *Schizophrenia Bulletin, 21,* 621–630.

Scott, K. M., Lim, C., Al-Hamzawi, A., Alonso, J., Bruffaerts, R., Caldas-De-Almeida, J. M., … Kessler, R. C. (2016). Association of mental disorders with subsequent chronic physical conditions: World mental health surveys from 17 countries. *JAMA Psychiatry, 73*(2), 150–158. doi: 10.1001/jamapsychiatry.2015.2688

Scott, K. M., Lim, C., Al-Hamzawi, A., Alonso, J., Bruffaerts, R., Caldas-De-Almeida, J. M., . . . Kessler, R. C. (2016). Association of mental disorders with subsequent chronic physical conditions: World mental health surveys from 17 countries. JAMA Psychiatry, 73(2), 150–158. doi:10.1001/jamapsychiatry.2015.2688

Scott, K. M., Lim, C., Al-Hamzawi, A., Alonso, J., Bruffaerts, R., Caldas-de-Almeida, J. M., Florescu, S., de Girolamo, G., Hu, C., de Jonge, P., Kawakami, N., Medina-Mora, M. E., Moskalewicz, J., Navarro-Mateu, F., O'Neill, S., Piazza, M., Posada-Villa, J., Torres, Y., & Kessler R. C. (in press). Association of mental disorders with subsequent chronic physical conditions: World mental health surveys from 17 countries. *JAMA Psychiatry.* doi: 10.1001/jamapsychiatry.2015.2688

Scott, S., Briskman, J., & O'Connor, T. G. (2014). Early prevention of antisocial personality: long-term follow-up of two randomized controlled trials comparing indicated and selective approaches. *American Journal of Psychiatry, 171*(6), 649–657.

Scull, A. (2021). "Community care": Historical perspective on deinstitutionalization. *Perspectives in Biology and Medicine, 64*(1), 70–81.

Sedlak, T. W., & Kaplin, A. I. (2009). Novel neurotransmitters. In B. J. Sadock, V. A. Sadock, & P. Ruiz (Eds.), *Kaplan & Sadock's comprehensive textbook of psychiatry* (9th ed., Vol. I, pp. 102–118). Philadelphia, PA: Lippincott Williams & Wilkins.

Seedat, S., Scott, K. M., Angermeyer, M. C., Berglund, P., Bromet, E. J., Brugha, T. S., & Kessler, R. C. (2009). Cross-national associations between gender and mental disorders in the WHO World Mental Health Surveys. *Archives of General Psychiatry, 66*(7), 785.

Seeman, P., Lee, T., Chau Wong, M., & Wong, K. (1976). Antipsychotic drug doses and neuroleptic/dopamine receptors. *Nature, 261,* 717–719.

Segal, N. (2006). Two monozygotic twin pairs discordant for female to male transsexualism. *Archives of Sexual Behavior, 35,* 347–358.

Segal, Z. V., Bieling, P., Young, T., MacQueen, G., Cooke, R., Martin, L., & Levitan, R. D. (2010). Antidepressant monotherapy vs sequential pharmacotherapy and mindfulness-based cognitive therapy, or placebo, for relapse prophylaxis in recurrent depression. *Archives of General Psychiatry, 67*(12), 1256.

Segal, Z. V., Williams, J. M. G., & Teasdale, J. D. (2002). *Mindfulness-based cognitive therapy for depression: A new approach to preventing relapse.* New York, NY: Guilford.

Segerstrom, S. C., & Sephton, S. E. (2010). Optimistic expectancies and cell-mediated immunity: The role of positive affect. *Psychological Science, 21,* 448–455.

Seglem, K. B., Waaktaar, T., Ask, H., & Torgersen, S. (2015). Genetic and environmental influences on adolescents' smoking involvement: a multi-informant twin study. *Behavior Genetics, 45*(2), 171–180.

Segraves, R., & Althof, S. (1998). Psychotherapy and pharmacotherapy of sexual dysfunctions. In P. E. Nathan & J. M. Gorman (Eds.), *A guide to treatments that work* (pp. 447–471). New York, NY: Oxford University Press.

Segraves, R., & Woodard, T. (2006). Female hypoactive sexual desire disorder: History and current status. *Journal of Sexual Medicine, 3,* 408–418.

Seitz, D. P., Adunuri, N., Gill, S. S., & Rochon, P. A. (2011). Prevalence of dementia and cognitive impairment among older adults with hip fractures. *Journal of the American Medical Directors Association, 12(*8), 556–564.

Seligman, M. E. P. (1971). Phobias and preparedness. *Behavior Therapy, 2,* 307–320.

Seligman, M. E. P. (1975). *Helplessness: On depression, development and death.* San Francisco, CA: W. H. Freeman.

Seligman, M. E. P. (1998). *Learned optimism* (2nd ed.). New York, NY: Simon & Schuster.

Seligman, M. E. P. (2002). *Authentic happiness: Using the new positive psychology to realize your potential for lasting fulfillment.* New York, NY: Free Press/Simon & Schuster.

Seligman, M. E. P., Schulman, P., DeRubeis, R. J., & Hollon, S. D. (1999). The prevention of depression and anxiety. *Prevention and Treatment, 2,* 8.

Sellbom, M., Toomey, J. A., Wygant, D. B., Kucharski, L. T., & Duncan, S. (2010). Utility of the MMPI–2-RF (restructured form) validity scales in detecting malingering in a criminal forensic setting: A known-groups design. *Psychological Assessment, 22*(1), 22–31.

Selten, J. P., Frissen, A., Lensvelt-Mulders, G., & Morgan, V. A. (2009). Schizophrenia and 1957 pandemic of influenza: meta-analysis. *Schizophrenia Bulletin,* sbp147.

Selye, H. (1936). A syndrome produced by diverse noxious agents. *Nature, 138,* 32.

Selye, H. (1950). *The physiology and pathology of exposure to stress.* Montreal, Canada: Acta.

Semans, J. H. (1956). Premature ejaculation: A new approach. *Southern Medical Journal, 49,* 353–358.

Semple, R. J., & Burke, C. A. (2012). Mindfulness based treatment for children and adolescents. In P. C. Kendall (Ed.), *Child and adolescent therapy: Cognitive-behavioral procedures* (4th ed., pp. 411–426). New York, NY: Guilford.

Sendt, K. V., Tracy, D. K., & Bhattacharyya, S. (2015). A systematic review of factors influencing adherence to antipsychotic medication in schizophrenia-spectrum disorders. *Psychiatry Research, 225*(1), 14–30.

Senn, S., Odenwald, M., Sehrig, S., Haffke, P., Rockstroh, B., Pereyra Kröll, D., … Rösner, S. (2020). Therapeutic success in relapse prevention in alcohol use disorder: The role of treatment motivation and drinking-related treatment goals. *Journal of Addictive Diseases,* 1–8.

Sentissi, O., Popovic, D., Moeglin, C., Stukalin, Y. B., Mosheva, M., Vieta, E., … Souery, D. (2019). Predominant polarity in bipolar disorder patients: The COPE bipolar sample. *Journal of Affective Disorders, 250,* 43–50. doi: 10.1016/j.jad.2019.02.053

Serefoglu, E. C., & Saitz, T. R. (2012). New insights on premature ejaculation: a review of definition, classification, prevalence and treatment. *Asian J Androl, 14*(6), 822–829.

Servick, K. (2021). Alzheimer's drug approved despite murky results. *Science, 372*(6547), 1141.

Seto, M. C. (2009). Pedophilia. In S. Nolen-Hoeksema, T. D. Cannon, & T. Widiger, (Eds.), *Annual review of clinical psychology* (Vol. 5, pp. 391–408). Palo Alto, CA: Annual Reviews.

Seto, M. C. (2012). Is pedophilia a sexual orientation? *Archives of Sexual Behavior, 41*(1), 231–236.

Seto, M. C., Kingston, D. A., & Bourget, D. (2014). Assessment of the Paraphilias. *Psychiatric Clinics of North America, 37*(2), 149–161.

Seto, M. C., Lalumière, M. L., Harris, G. T., & Chivers, M. L. (2012). The sexual responses of sexual sadists. *Journal of abnormal psychology, 121,* 739–753.

Seto, M., Cantor, J., & Blanchard, R. (2006). Child pornography offenses are a valid diagnostic indicator of pedophilia. *Journal of Abnormal Psychology, 115,* 610–615.

Severino, S. K., & Moline, M. L. (1989). *Premenstrual syndrome: A clinician's guide.* New York, NY: Guilford.

Shaffer, D. R. (1993). *Developmental psychology: Childhood and adolescence* (3rd ed.). Pacific Grove, CA: Brooks/Cole.

Shafran, R., Cooper, Z., & Fairburn, C. G. (2002). Clinical perfectionism: A cognitive-behavioural analysis. *Behaviour Research Therapy,* 40, 773–791.

Shafran, R., Lee, M., Payne, E., & Fairburn, C. G. (2006). The impact of manipulating personal standards on eating attitudes and behaviour. *Behaviour Research and Therapy, 44,* 897–906.

Shalev, A. Y., Ankri, Y., Israeli-Shalev, Y., Peleg, T., Adessky, R., & Freedman, S. (2012). Prevention of posttraumatic stress disorder by early treatment: Results from the Jerusalem Trauma Outreach and Prevention study. *Archives of General Psychiatry, 69,* 166–176. doi: 10.1001/archgenpsychiatry.2011.127

Shamloul, R., & Ghanem, H. (2013). Erectile dysfunction. *The Lancet,* 381(9861), 153–165.

Shamloul, R., & Ghanem, H. (2013). Erectile dysfunction. *Lancet, 381*(9861), 153–165. doi: 10.1016/S0140-6736(12)60520-0

Shapiro, D. (1974). Operant-feedback control of human blood pressure: Some clinical issues. In P. A. Obrist, A. H. Black, J. Brener, & L. V. DiCara (Eds.), *Cardiovascular psychophysiology: Current issues in response mechanisms, biofeedback, and methodology.* Chicago, IL: Aldine.

Shapiro, J. R., Berkman, N. D., Brownley, K. A., Sedway, J. A., Lohr, K. N., & Bulik, C. M. (2007). Bulimia nervosa treatment: A systematic review of randomized controlled trials. *International Journal of Eating Disorders, 40*(4), 321–336.

Sharma, M. P., & Manjula, M. (2013). Behavioral and psychological management of somatic symptom disorder: An overview. *International Review of Psychiatry, 25,* 116–124.

Sharpe, M. (1992). Fatigue and chronic fatigue syndrome. *Current Opinion in Psychiatry, 5,* 207–212.

Sharpe, M. (1993). *Chronic fatigue syndrome* (pp. 298–317). Chichester, UK: Wiley.

Sharpe, M. (1997). Chronic fatigue. In D. M. Clark & C. G. Fairburn (Eds.), *Science and practice of cognitive behavior therapy* (pp. 381–414). Oxford, UK: Oxford University Press.

Sharpe, M., Clements, A., Hawton, K., Young, A., Sargent, P., & Cowen, P. (1996). Increased prolactin response to buspirone in chronic fatigue syndrome. *Journal of Affective Disorders, 41,* 71–76.

Sharpless, B. A., & Barber, J. P. (2011). Lifetime prevalence rates of sleep paralysis: A systematic review. *Sleep Medicine Reviews, 15,* 311–315.

Sharpless, B. A., & Kliková, M. (2019). Clinical features of isolated sleep paralysis. *Sleep Medicine, 58,* 102–106. doi: 10.1016/j.sleep.2019.03.007

Sharpless, B., & Doghramji, K. (2015). *Sleep Paralysis: Historical, Psychological, and Medical Perspectives.* Oxford University Press.

Shatkin, J. P., & Ivanenko, A. (2009). Pediatric sleep disorders. In B. J. Sadock, V. A. Sadock, & P. Ruiz (Eds.), *Kaplan & Sadock's comprehensive textbook of psychiatry* (9th ed., Vol. I, pp. 3903–3908). Philadelphia, PA: Lippincott Williams & Wilkins.

Shaw, D. S., Dishion, T. J., Supplee, L., Gardner, F., & Arnds, K. (2006). Randomized trial of a family-centered approach to the prevention of early conduct problems: 2-year effects of the family check-up in early childhood. *Journal of Consulting and Clinical Psychology, 74,* 1–9.

Shaw, J., & Porter, S. (2015). Constructing rich false memories of committing crime. *Psychological Science, 26,* 291–301.

Shear, K., Frank, E., Houck, P. R., & Reynolds, C. F. (2005). Treatment of complicated grief: A randomized controlled trial. *JAMA, 293*(21), 2601–2608.

Shear, K., Jin, R., Ruscio, A. M., Walters, E. E., & Kessler, R. C. (2006). Prevalence and correlates of estimated DSM-IV child and adult separation anxiety disorder in the National Comorbidity Survey Replication. *American Journal of Psychiatry, 163*(6), 1074–1083. doi: 10.1176/appi.ajp.163.6.107

Shear, M. K. (2012). Getting straight about grief. *Depression and Anxiety, 29,* 461–464.

Shear, M. K., Brown, T. A., Barlow, D. H., Money, R., Sholomskas, D. E., Woods, S. W., & Papp, L. A. (1997). Multicenter collaborative panic disorder severity scale. *American Journal of Psychiatry, 154,* 1571–1575.

Shear, M. K., Reynolds, C. F., Simon, N. M., Zisook, S., Wang, Y., Mauro, C., Duan, N., Lebowitz, B., & Skritskaya, N. (2016). Optimizing treatment of complicated grief: A randomized clinical trial. *JAMA Psychiatry, 73*(7), 685–694.

Shear, M. K., Simon, N., Wall, M., Zisook, S., Neimeyer, R., Duan, N., & Keshaviah, A. (2011). Complicated grief and related bereavement issues for DSM-5. *Depression and Anxiety, 28,* 103–117.

Shear, M. K., Simon, N., Wall, M., Zisook, S., Neimeyer, R., Duan, N., … Keshaviah, A. (2011). Complicated grief and related bereavement issues for *DSM-5. Depression and Anxiety, 28*(2), 103–117. doi: 10.1002/da.20780

Shear, M. K., Wang, Y., Skritskaya, N., Duan, N., Mauro, C., & Ghesquiere, A. (2014). Treatment of complicated grief in elderly persons: A randomized clinical trial. *JAMA Psychiatry, 71,* 1287–1295.

Sheets, E. S., & Craighead, W. E. (2014). Comparing chronic interpersonal and noninterpersonal stress domains as predictors of depression recurrence in emerging adults, *Behaviour Research and Therapy, 63,* 36–42.

Sheikh, J. I. (1992). Anxiety and its disorders in old age. In J. E. Birren, K. Sloan, & G. D. Cohen (Eds.), *Handbook of mental health and aging* (pp. 410–432). New York, NY: Academic Press.

Sheladia, S., & Hemachandra Reddy, P. (2021). Age-related chronic diseases and Alzheimer's disease in Texas: A Hispanic-focused study. *Journal of Alzheimer's Disease Reports* (Preprint), 1–13.

Shen, B., Avivi, Y. E., Todaro, J. F., Spiro, A., III., Laurenceau, J., Ward, K. D., & Niaura, R. (2008). Anxiety characteristics independently and prospectively predict myocardial infarction in men: The unique contribution of anxiety among psychologic factors. *Journal of the American College of Cardiology, 51,* 113–119.

Shenton, M. E., & Kubicki, M. (2009). Structural brain imaging in schizophrenia. In B. J. Sadock, V. A. Sadock, & P. Ruiz (Eds.), *Kaplan & Sadock's comprehensive textbook of psychiatry* (9th ed., Vol. I, pp. 1494–1507). Philadelphia, PA: Lippincott Williams & Wilkins.

Sheperis, C. J., Lionetti, T. M., & Snook, J. (2015). Substance-related disorders. In B. Flamez & C. J. Sheperis (Eds), *Diagnosing and treating children and adolescents: A guide for mental health professionals* (pp. 413–440). Hoboken, NJ: Wiley & Sons.

Sheppes, G., Luria, R., Fukuda, K., & Gross, J. J. (2013). There's more to anxiety than meets the eye: Isolating threat-related attentional engagement and disengagement biases. *Emotion, 13,* 520–528.

Sher, K. J., Martinez, J. A., & Littlefield, A. K. (2011). Alcohol use and alcohol use disorders. In D. H. Barlow (Ed.), *Oxford handbook of clinical psychology*. New York, NY: Oxford University.

Sherbourne, C. D., Hays, R. D., & Wells, K. B. (1995). Personal and psychosocial risk factors for physical and mental health outcomes and course of depression among depressed patients. *Journal of Consulting and Clinical Psychology, 63,* 345–355.

Shih, Y. H., Pai, M. C., Lin, H. S., Sung, P. S., & Wang, J. J. (2020). Effects of walking on sundown syndrome in community-dwelling people with Alzheimer's disease. *International Journal of Older People Nursing, 15*(2), e12292.

Shin, L. M., & Liberzon, I. (2010). The neurocircuitry of fear, stress, and anxiety disorders. *Neuropsychopharmacology, 35*(1), 169–191.

Shin, L. M., Lasko, N. B., Macklin, M. L., Karpf, R. D., Milad, M. R., Orr, S. P., & Pitman, R. K. (2009). Resting metabolic activity in the cingulate cortex and vulnerability to posttraumatic stress disorder. *Archives of General Psychiatry, 66*(10), 1099–1107. doi: 10.1001/archgenpsychiatry.2009.138

Shin, L. M., Shin, P. S., Heckers, S., Krangel, T. S., Macklin, M. L., Orr, S. P., & Rauch, S. L. (2004). Hippocampal function in posttraumatic stress disorder. *Hippocampus, 14,* 292–300.

Shingleton, R. M., Thompson-Brenner, H., Thompson, D. R., Pratt, E. M., & Franko, D. L. (2015). Gender differences in clinical trials of binge eating disorder: An analysis of aggregated data. *Journal of Consulting and Clinical Psychology, 83*(2), 382–386.

Shneidman, E. S. (1989). Approaches and commonalities of suicide. In R. F. W. Diekstra, R. Mariss, S. Platt, A. Schmidtke, & G. Sonneck (Eds.), *Suicide and its prevention: The role of attitude and imitation. Advances in Suicidology* (Vol. 1). Leiden, Netherlands: E. J. Brill.

Shneidman, E. S., Farberow, N. L., & Litman, R. E. (Eds.) (1970). *The psychology of suicide.* New York, NY: Science House.

Shohat, S., Amelan, A., & Shifman, S. (2020). Convergence and divergence in the genetics of psychiatric disorders from pathways to developmental stages. *Biological Psychiatry, 89*(1), 32–40. doi: 10.1016/j.biopsych.2020.05.019

Shriane, A. E., Ferguson, S. A., Jay, S. M., & Vincent, G. E. (2020). Sleep hygiene in shift workers: A systematic literature review. *Sleep Medicine Reviews, 53,* 101336. doi: 10.1016/j.smrv.2020.101336

Shulman, K. I., Cohen, C. A., Kirsh, F. C., Hull, I. M., & Champine, P. R. (2007). Assessment of testamentary capacity and vulnerability to undue influence. *American Journal of Psychiatry, 164*(5), 722–727.

Shumaker, S. A., Legault, C., Kuller, L., Rapp, S. R., Thal, L., Lane, D. S., Coker, L. H., & Women's Health Initiative Memory Study. (2004). Conjugated equine estrogens and incidence of probable dementia and mild cognitive impairment in postmenopausal women: Women's Health Initiative Memory Study. *JAMA: Journal of the American Medical Association, 291,* 3005–3007.

Sibrava, N. J., Beard, C., Bjornsson, A. S., Moitra, E., Weisberg, R. B., & Keller, M. B. (2013). Two-year course of generalized anxiety disorder, social anxiety disorder, and panic disorder in a longitudinal sample of African American adults. *Journal of Consulting and Clinical Psychology, 81,* 1052.

Sico, J. J., Amin, H., Sorokin, A., Volpe, D. C., Hamid, H., Machado, D., … Brust, J. C. M. (2014). Neurologic disorders related to alcohol and other drug use. In R. K. Ries, D. A. Fiellin, S. C. Miller, & R. Saitz (Eds.), *The ASAM principles of addiction medicine,* (5th ed., pp. 1178–1194). New York, NY: Wolters Kluwer.

Siddiqui, F., & D'Ambrosio, C. (2012). Sleep disorders in older patients. In M. Pisani (Ed.), *Aging and lung disease* (pp. 173–188). New York, NY: Humana Press.

Siegel, L. S., & Mazabell, S. (2013). Basic cognitive processes and reading disabilities. In H. L. Swanson, K. R. Harris, & S. Graham (Eds.), *Handbook of learning disabilities* (2nd ed., pp. 186–213). New York, NY: Guilford.

Sierra, M., & Berrios, G. E. (1998). Depersonalization: Neurobiological perspectives. *Society of Biological Psychiatry, 44,* 898–908.

Sierra, M., Senior, C., Dalton, J., McDonough, M., Bond, A., Phillips, M. L., & David, A. S. (2002). Autonomic response in depersonalization disorder. *Archives of General Psychiatry, 59,* 833–838.

Siever, L. J., & Davis, K. L. (2004). The pathophysiology of schizophrenia disorders: Perspectives from the spectrum. *American Journal of Psychiatry, 161,* 398–413.

Siever, L. J., Davis, K. L., & Gorman, L. K. (1991). Pathogenesis of mood disorders. In K. Davis, H. Klar, & J. T. Coyle (Eds.), *Foundations of psychiatry.* Philadelphia, PA: W. B. Saunders.

Siffre, M. (1964). *Beyond time* (H. Briffaul, Trans.). New York, NY: McGraw-Hill.

Sigafoos, J., Green, V. A., Schlosser, R., O'Reilly, M. F., Lancioni, G. E., Rispoli, M., Lang, R. (2009). Communication intervention in Rett syndrome: A systematic review. *Research in Autism Spectrum Disorders, 3*(2), 304–318. doi: 10.1016/j.rasd.2008.09.006

Silberg, J. L., Maes, H., & Eaves, L. J. (2012). Unraveling the effect of genes and environment in the transmission of parental antisocial behavior to children's conduct disturbance, depression and hyperactivity. *Journal of Child Psychology and Psychiatry, 53*(6), 668–677.

Silove, D. M., Marnane, C. L., Wagner, R., Manicavasagar, V. L., & Rees, S. (2010). The prevalence and correlates of adult separation anxiety disorder in an anxiety clinic. *BMC Psychiatry, 10,* 21.

Silva, F. R. d., Guerreiro, R. d. C., Andrade, H. d. A., Stieler, E., Silva, A., & de Mello, M. T. (2020). Does the compromised sleep and circadian disruption of night and shiftworkers make them highly vulnerable to 2019 coronavirus disease (COVID-19)? *Chronobiology International, 37*(5), 607–617.

Silver, E., Cirincione, C., & Steadman, H. J. (1994). Demythologizing inaccurate perceptions of the insanity defense. *Law and Human Behavior, 18,* 63–70.

Silverman, W. K., & La Greca, A. M. (2002). Children experiencing disasters: Definitions, reactions and predictors of outcomes. In A. N. La Greca, W. K. Silverman, & M. C. Roberts (Eds.), *Helping children cope with disasters and terrorism* (Vol. 1, pp. 11–33). Washington, DC: American Psychological Association.

Silverman, W. K., & Rabian, B. (1993). Simple phobias. *Child and Adolescent Psychiatric Clinics of North America, 2,* 603–622.

Silverstone, T. (1985). Dopamine in manic depressive illness: A pharmacological synthesis. *Journal of Affective Disorders, 8*(3), 225–231.

Simeon, D. (2009). Neurobiology of depersonalization disorder. In P. F. Dell & J. A. O'Neil (Eds.), *Dissociation and the dissociative disorders* (pp. 367–372). New York, NY: Routledge.

Simeon, D., & Abugal, J. (2006). *Feeling unreal: Depersonalization disorder and the loss of the self.* Oxford, UK: Oxford University Press.

Simeon, D., Guralnik, O., Hazlett, E. A., Spiegel-Cohen, J., Hollander, E., & Buchsbaum, M. S. (2000). Feeling unreal: A PET study of depersonalization disorder. *American Journal of Psychiatry, 157,* 1782–1788.

Simeon, D., Guralnik, O., Knutelska, M., Hollander, E., & Schmeidler, J. (2001). Hypothalamic–pituitary–adrenal axis dysregulation in depersonalization disorder. *Neuropsychopharmacology, 25,* 793–795.

Simeon, D., Guralnik, O., Schmeidler, J., & Knutelska, M. (2004). Fluoxetine therapy in depersonalization disorder: Randomised controlled trial. *British Journal of Psychiatry, 185,* 31–36.

Simmons, R., & Blyth, D. (1987). *Moving into adolescence: The impact of pubertal change and school context.* New York, NY: Aldine de Gruyter.

Simms, L. J., Prisciandaro, J. J., Krueger, R. F., & Goldberg, D. P. (2012). The structure of depression, anxiety, and somatic symptoms in primary care. *Psychological Medicine, 42,* 15–28.

Simon, G. (2006). How can we know whether antidepressants increase suicide risk? *American Journal of Psychiatry, 163,* 1861–1863.

Simon, G. E., Gureje, O., & Fullerton, C. (2001). Course of hypochondriasis in an international primary care study. *General Hospital Psychiatry, 23,* 51–55.

Simon, G. E., von Koff, M., Saunders, K., Miglioretti, D. L., Crane, P. K., van Belle, G., & Kessler, R. C. (2006). Association between obesity and psychiatric disorders in the U.S. adult population. *Archives of General Psychiatry, 63,* 824–830.

Simon, N. M. (2012). Is complicated grief a post-loss stress disorder? *Depression and Anxiety, 29,* 541–544.

Simon, N. M. (2013). Treating complicated grief. *JAMA, 310,* 416–423.

Simon, N. M., Hofmann, S. G., Rosenfield, D., Hoeppner, S. S., Hoge, E. A., Bui, E., & Khalsa, S. B. S. (2021). Yoga, cognitive-behavioral therapy or stress education control for generalized anxiety disorder: A randomized clinical trial. *JAMA Psychiatry, 78,* 13–20. doi: 10.1001/jamapsychiatry.2020.2496

Simon, R. I., & Shuman, D. W. (2014). Clinical issues in psychiatry and the law. In R. E. Hales, S. C. Yudofsky, & L. Weiss Roberts (Eds), *The American Psychiatric Publishing textbook of psychiatry* (6th ed., pp.175–204). Washington, DC: American Psychiatric Publishing, Inc.

Simon, R. I., & Shuman, D. W. (2008). Psychiatry and the law. In R. E. Hales, S. C. Yudofsky, & G. O. Gabbard (Eds.), *The American Psychiatric Publishing textbook of psychiatry* (5th ed., pp. 1555–1599). Arlington, VA: American Psychiatric Publishing.

Simon, R. I., & Shuman, D. W. (2009). Clinical-legal issues in psychiatry. In B. J. Sadock, V. A. Sadock, & P. Ruiz (Eds.), *Kaplan & Sadock's comprehensive textbook of psychiatry* (9th ed., Vol. II, pp. 4427–4439). Philadelphia, PA: Lippincott Williams & Wilkins.

Simon, W., & Gagnon, J. H. (1986). Sexual scripts: Permanence and change. *Archives of Sexual Behavior, 15*(2), 97–120.

Simoneau, T. L., Miklowitz, D. J., Richards, J. A., Saleem R., & George, E. L. (1999). Bipolar disorder and family communication: Effects of a psychoeducational treatment program. *Journal of Abnormal Psychology, 108,* 588–597.

Simonetti, J. A., Mackelprang, J. L., Rowhani-Rahbar, A., Zatzick, D., & Rivara, F. P. (2015). Psychiatric comorbidity, suicidality, and in-home firearm access among a nationally representative sample of adolescents. *JAMA Psychiatry, 72,* 152–159.

Simons, J. S., Dvorak, R. D., & Lau-Barraco, C. (2009). Behavioral inhibition and activation systems: Differences in substance use expectancy organization and activation in memory. *Psychology of Addictive Behaviors, 23*(2), 315–328. doi:10.1037/a0015834

Simpson, C. A., Diaz-Arteche, C., Eliby, D., Schwartz, O. S., Simmons, J. G., & Cowan, C. S. M. (2021). The gut microbiota in anxiety and depression: A systematic review. *Clinical Psychology Review, 83.* doi: 10.1016/j.cpr.2020.101943

Simpson, G. K., Tate, R. L., Whiting, D. L., & Cotter, R. E. (2011). Suicide prevention after traumatic brain injury: A randomized controlled trial of a program for the psychological treatment of hopelessness. *The Journal of Head Trauma Rehabilitation, 26*(4), 290–300.

Simpson, H. B., Foa, E. B., Liebowitz, M. R., Huppert, J. D., Cahill, S., Maher, M. J., McLean, C. P., Bender, J., Marcus, S. M., Williams, M. T., Weaver, J., Vermes, D., Van Meter, P., Rodriguez, C. I., Powers, M., Pinto, A., Imms, P., Hahn, C.-G., & Campeas, R. (2013). Cognitive-behavioral therapy vs. resperidone for augmenting serotonin reuptake inhibitors in obsessive-compulsive disorder: A randomized clinical trial. *JAMA Psychiatry, 70,* 1190–1199.

Sims, R., Hill, M., & Williams, J. (2020). The multiplex model of the genetics of Alzheimer's disease. *Nature Neuroscience, 23*(3), 311–322.

Singer, J. (1999). "Why can't you be normal for once in your life?" From a "problem with no name" to the emergence of a new category of difference. In M. Corker & S. French (Eds.), *Disability discourse* (pp. 59–67). Buckingham, U.K.: Open University Press.

Singer, M., & Flannery, D. J. (2000). The relationship between children's threats of violence and violent behaviors. *Archives of Pediatrics and Adolescent Medicine, 154,* 785–790.

Singh, G. (2021). Central sleep apneas. In E. H. During & C. A. Kushida (Eds.), *Clinical sleep medicine: A comprehensive guide for mental health and other medical professionals* (pp. 199–222). Washington, D.C.: American Psychiatric Association Publishing.

Singh, J. P., Grann, M., & Fazel, S. (2011). A comparative study of violence risk assessment tools: A systematic review and metaregression analysis of 68 studies involving 25,980 participants. *Clinical Psychology Review, 31*(3), 499–513.

Singh, S. P., Harley, K., & Suhail, K. (2013). Cultural specificity of emotional overinvolvement: A systematic review. *Schizophrenia Bulletin, 39*(2), 449–463. doi: 10.1093/schbul/sbr170

Singh, S., Basu, D., Kohli, A., & Prabhakar, S. (2009). Auditory P300 event-related potentials and neurocognitive functions in opioid dependent men and their brothers. *American Journal on Addictions, 18*(3), 198–205.

Sisask, M., & Värnik, A. (2012). Media roles in suicide prevention: A systematic review. *International Journal of Environmental Research and Public Health, 9*(1), 123–138.

Sit, D., Rothschild, A. J., & Wisner, K. L. (2006). A review of postpartum psychosis. *Journal of Womens Health, 15*(4), 352–368.

Sivalokanathan, S., Małek, Ł. A., & Malhotra, A. (2021). The cardiac effects of performance-enhancing medications: Caffeine vs. anabolic androgenic steroids. *Diagnostics, 11*(2), 324.

Sjöström, L., Peltonen, M., Jacobson, P., Sjöström, C. D., Karason, K., Wedel, H., . . . Carlsson, L. M. S. (2012). Bariatric surgery and long-term cardiovascular events. *JAMA: Journal of American Medical Association, 307,* 56–65.

Skeem, J., Kennealy, P., Monahan, J., Peterson, J., & Appelbaum, P. (2016). Psychosis uncommonly and inconsistently precedes violence among high-risk individuals. *Clinical Psychological Science, 4*(1), 40–49.

Skeldon, A. C., Derks, G., & Dijk, D.-J. (2016). Modelling changes in sleep timing and duration across the lifespan: Changes in circadian rhythmicity or sleep homeostasis? *Sleep Medicine Reviews, 28,* 96–107. https://doi.org/10.1016/j.smrv.2015.05.011

Skhiri, D., Annabi, S., Bi, S., & Allani, D. (1982). Enfants d'immigrés: Facteurs de liens ou de rupture? *Annales Medico-Psychologiques, 140,* 597–602.

Skidmore, W., Linsenmeier, J., & Bailey, J. (2006). Gender nonconformity and psychological distress in lesbians and gay men. *Archives of Sexual Behavior, 35,* 685–697.

Skinner, B. F. (1938). *The behavior of organisms: An experimental analysis.* Appleton-Century. Oxford: England.

Skinner, B. F. (1948). *Walden two.* New York, NY: Macmillan.

Skinner, B. F. (1971). *Beyond freedom and dignity.* New York, NY: Knopf.

Skodol, A. E. (2005). Manifestations, clinical diagnosis, and comorbidity. In J. M. Oldham, A. E. Skodol, & D. S. Bender

(Eds.), *Textbook of personality disorders* (pp. 57–87). Washington, DC: American Psychiatric Publishing.

Skodol, A. E. (2012). Personality disorders in DSM-5. *Annual Review of Clinical Psychology, 8*, 317–344.

Skodol, A. E., & Gunderson, J. G. (2008). Personality disorders. In R. E. Hales, S. C. Yudofsky, & G. O. Gabbard (Eds.), *The American Psychiatric Publishing textbook of psychiatry* (5th ed., pp. 821–860). Arlington, VA: American Psychiatric Publishing.

Skodol, A. E., Bender, D. S., Morey, L. C., Clark, L. A., Oldham, J. M., Alarcon, R. D., & Siever, L. J. (2011). Personality disorder types proposed for DSM-5. *Journal of Personality Disorders, 25*(2), 136–169.

Skodol, A. E., Grilo, C. M., Keyes, K. M., Geier, T., Grant, B. F., & Hasin, D. S. (2011). Relationship of personality disorders to the course of major depressive disorder in a nationally representative sample. *American Journal of Psychiatry, 168*(3), 257–264.

Skóra, M. N., Pattij, T., Beroun, A., Kogias, G., Mielenz, D., de Vries, T., … Müller, C. P. (2020). Personality driven alcohol and drug abuse: New mechanisms revealed. *Neuroscience & Biobehavioral Reviews, 116*, 64–73.

Skorucak, J., Hertig-Godeschalk, A., Schreier, D. R., Malafeev, A., Mathis, J., & Achermann, P. (2020). Automatic detection of microsleep episodes with feature-based machine learning. *Sleep, 43*(1), zsz225.

Skuse, D. H. (2012). DSM-5's conceptualization of autistic disorders. *Journal of the American Academy of Child and Adolescent Psychiatry, 51*(4), 344–346. doi: 10.1016/j.jaac.2012.02.009

Slade, E., Keeney, E., Mavranezouli, I., Dias, S., Fou, L., Stockton, S., … Kendall, T. (2018). Treatments for bulimia nervosa: A network meta-analysis. *Psychological Medicine, 48*(16), 2629–2636. doi: 10.1017/S00332917 18001071

Slater, M. E., & Alpert, H. R. (2020). Apparent per capita alcohol consumption: National, state, and regional trends, 1977–2018. Surveillance Report #115. Washington, D.C.: U.S. Department of Health and Human Services, Public Health Service, National Institutes of Health.

Slavich, G. M. (2020). Social safety theory: A biologically based evolutionary perspective on life stress, health, and behavior. *Annual Review of Clinical Psychology, 16*, 265–295. doi: 10.1146/annurev-clinpsy-032816-045159

Slavich, G. M., & Irwin, M. R. (2014). From stress to inflammation and major depressive disorder: A social signal transduction theory of depression. *Psychological Bulletin, 140*, 774–815.

Slavova, S., Rock, P., Bush, H. M., Quesinberry, D., & Walsh, S. L. (2020). Signal of increased opioid overdose during COVID-19 from emergency medical services data. *Drug and Alcohol Dependence, 214*, 108176.

Slaymaker, E., Scott, R. H., Palmer, M. J., Palla, L., Marston, M., Gonsalves, L., Say, L., & Wellings, K. (2020). Trends in sexual activity and demand for and use of modern contraceptive methods in 74 countries: A retrospective analysis of nationally representative surveys. *Lancet Global Health, 8*(4), e567–e579. doi: 10.1016/S2214-109X(20)30060-7

Sleet, D. A., Hammond, R., Jones, R., Thomas, N., & Whitt, B. (2003). Using psychology for injury and violence prevention in the community. In R. H. Rozensky, N. G. Johnson, C. D. Goodheart, & R. Hammond (Eds.), *Psychology builds a healthy world* (pp. 185–216). Washington, DC: American Psychological Association.

Slooter, A. J. C., & de Groot, J.-C. (2014). Neuroimaging of delirium. In R. A. J. O. Dierckx, A. Otte, E. F. J. de Vries, A. van Waarde (Eds), *PET and SPECT in psychiatry* (pp. 463–470). Berlin, Germany: Springer Berlin Heidelberg.

Slotema, C. W., Aleman, A., Daskalakis, Z. J., & Sommer, I. E. (2012). Meta-analysis of repetitive transcranial magnetic stimulation in the treatment of auditory verbal hallucinations: Update and effects after one month. *Schizophrenia Research, 142*(1–3), 40-45. doi: http://dx.doi.org/10.1016/j.schres.2012.08.025

Smeets, G., de Jong, P. J., & Mayer, B. (2000). If you suffer from a headache, then you have a brain tumour: Domain-specific reasoning "bias" and hypochondriasis. *Behaviour Research and Therapy, 38*, 763–776.

Smith, B. H., & Shapiro, C. J. (2015). Combined treatments for ADHD. In R. A. Barkley (Ed.), *Attention-deficit hyperactivity disorder: A handbook for diagnosis & treatment* (4th ed., pp. 686–704). New York, NY: The Guilford Press.

Smith, D. E., Marcus, M. D., & Kaye, W. (1992). Cognitive-behavioral treatment of obese binge eaters. *International Journal of Eating Disorders, 12*, 257–262.

Smith, Frederick H. (2008). *The archaeology of alcohol and drinking.* Gainesville, FL: University of Florida Press.

Smith, G. A., & Hall, J. A. (1982). Evaluating Michigan's guilty but mentally ill verdict: An empirical study. *Journal of Law Reform, 16*, 75–112.

Smith, G. P., & Gibbs, J. (2002). Peripheral physiological determinants for eating and body weight. In K. D. Brownell & C. G. Fairburn (Eds.), *Eating disorders and obesity: A comprehensive handbook* (2nd ed., pp. 8–12). New York, NY: Guilford.

Smith, G. T., & Oltmanns, T. F. (2009). Scientific advances in the diagnosis of psychopathology: Introduction to the special section. *Psychological Assessment, 21*(3), 241–242.

Smith, G. T., Simmons, J. R., Flory, K., Annus, A. M., & Hill, K. K. (2007). Thinness and eating expectancies predict subsequent binge-eating and purging behavior among adolescent girls. *Journal of Abnormal Psychology, 116*, 188–197.

Smith, N. S., & Capron, D. W. (2020). Expanding fear of loss of vigilance: Intolerance of uncertainty, responsibility for harm, and fear of sleep for predicting nocturnal panic. *Behavioral Sleep Medicine*, 1–15. doi: 10.1080/15402002.2020.1860988

Smith, T. C., Ryan, M. A., Wingard, D. L., Slymen, D. J., Sallis, J. F., Kritz-Silverstein, D., & Millennium Cohort Study Team. (2008). New onset and persistent symptoms of post-traumatic stress disorder self reported after deployment and combat exposures: Prospective population based US military cohort study. *BMJ: British Medical Journal, 336*(7640), 366–371. doi: 10.1136/bmj.39430.638241.AE

Smith, T. W. (1992). Hostility and health: Current status of a psychosomatic hypothesis. *Health Psychology, 11*(3), 139–150.

Smith, T., & Iadarola, S. (2015). Evidence base update for autism spectrum disorder. *Journal of Clinical Child & Adolescent Psychology, 44*(6), 897–922. doi: 10.1080/15374416.2015.1077448

Smith, T., Horwath, E., & Cournos, F. (2010). Scizophrenia and other psychotic disorders. In J. L. Cutler & E. R. Marcus (Eds.), *Psychiatry* (2nd ed., pp. 101–131). New York, NY: Oxford University Press.

Smith, W., Noonan, C., & Buchwald, D. (2006). Mortality in a cohort of chronically fatigued patients. *Psychological Medicine, 36*, 1301–1306.

Smitherman, T. A., Burch, R., Sheikh, H., & Loder, E. (2013). The prevalence, impact, and treatment of migraine and severe headaches in the United States: A review of statistics from national surveillance studies. *Headache*, 53(3), 427–436.

Smits, J. A. J., Pollack, M. H., Rosenfield, D., Otto, M. W., Dowd, S., Carpenter, J., Dutcher, C. D., Lewis, E. M., Witcraft, S. M., Papini, S., Curtiss, J., Andrews, L., Kind, S., Conroy, K., & Hofmann, S. G. (2020). Dose timing of D-cycloserine to augment exposure therapy for social anxiety disorder: A randomized clinical trial. *JAMA Network Open, 3*(6), e206777. doi: 10.1001/jamanetworkopen.2020.6777

Smolak, L., & Levine, M. P. (1996). Adolescent transitions and the development of eating problems. In L. Smolak, M. P. Levine, & R. Striegel-Moore (Eds.), *The developmental psychopathology of eating disorders: Implications for research, prevention, and treatment* (pp. 207–233). Mahwah, NJ: Erlbaum.

Smoller, J. W., Block, S. R., & Young, M. M. (2009). Genetics of anxiety disorders: The complex road from DSM to DNA. *Depression and Anxiety, 26*(11), 965–975. doi: 10.1002/da.20623

Smoller, J. W., Yamaki, L. H., & Fagerness, J. A. (2005). The corticotropin-releasing hormone gene and behavioral inhibition in children at risk for panic disorder. *Biological Psychiatry, 57,* 1485–1492.

Snelling, J., Sahai, A., & Ellis, H. (2003). Attitudes of medical and dental students to dissection. *Clinical Anatomy, 16,* 165–172.

Sneyers, B., Duceppe, M.-A., Frenette, A. J., Burry, L. D., Rico, P., Lavoie, A., … Williamson, D. R. (2020). Strategies for the prevention and treatment of iatrogenic withdrawal from opioids and benzodiazepines in critically ill neonates, children and adults: A systematic review of clinical studies. *Drugs*, 1–23.

Snowdon, D. A., Kemper, S. J. , Mortimer, J. A., Greiner, L. H., Wekstein, D. R., & Markesbery, W. R. (1996). Linguistic ability in early life and cognitive function and Alzheimer's disease in late life: Findings from the nun study. *JAMA: Journal of the American Medical Association, 275*(7), 528–532.

Snyder, J. S., Soumier, A., Brewer, M., Pickel, J., & Cameron, H. A. (2011). Adult hippocampal neurogenesis buffers stress responses and depressive behaviour. *Nature, 476*(7361), 458–U112.

Snyder, L. (2012). American College of Physicians ethics manual. *Annals of Internal Medicine, 156*(1_Part_2), 73-104. doi:10.7326/0003-4819-156-1-201201031-00001

Snyder, S. H. (1976). The dopamine hypothesis of schizophrenia: Focus on the dopamine receptor. *American Journal of Psychiatry, 133,* 197–202.

Snyder, S. H. (1981). Opiate and benzodiazepine receptors. *Psychosomatics, 22*(11), 986–989.

Snyder, S. H., Burt, D. R., & Creese, I. (1976). Dopamine receptor of mammalian brain: Direct demonstration of binding to agonist and antagonist states. *Neuroscience Symposia, 1,* 28–49.

Soares, E. E., Bausback, K., Beard, C. L., Higinbotham, M., Bunge, E. L., & Gengoux, G. W. (2021). Social skills training for autism spectrum disorder: A meta-analysis of in-person and technological interventions. *Journal of Technology in Behavioral Science, 6*(1), 166–180. doi: 10.1007/s41347-020-00177-0

Sobell, M. B., & Sobell, L. C. (1978). *Behavioral treatment of alcohol problems*. New York, NY: Plenum Press.

Sobell, M. B., & Sobell, L. C. (1993). *Problem drinkers: Guided self-change treatment.* New York, NY: Guilford.

Society for Research in Child Development. (2007). *Ethical standards for research with children.* Available from www.srcd.org/ethicalstandards.html.

Soeiro-de-Souza, M. G., Dias, V. V., Bio, D. S., Post, R. M., & Moreno, R. A. (2011). Creativity and executive function across manic, mixed and depressive episodes in bipolar I disorder. *Journal of Affective Disorders, 135*(1–3), 292–297.

Sohn, C., & Lam, R. (2005). Update on the biology of seasonal affective disorder. *CNS Spectrums, 10,* 635–646.

Sohn, M., & Bosinski, H. A. G. (2007). Gender identity disorders: Diagnostic and surgical aspects. *Journal of Sexual Medicine, 4,* 1193–1208.

Solai, L. K. K. (2009). Delirium. In B. J. Sadock, V. A. Sadock, & P. Ruiz (Eds.), *Kaplan & Sadock's comprehensive textbook of psychiatry* (9th ed., Vol. I, pp. 1153–1167). Philadelphia, PA: Lippincott Williams & Wilkins.

Solmi, M., Wade, T. D., Byrne, S., Del Giovane, C., Fairburn, C. G., Ostinelli, E. G., … Cipriani, A. (2021). Comparative efficacy and acceptability of psychological interventions for the treatment of adult outpatients with anorexia nervosa: A systematic review and network meta-analysis. *The Lancet Psychiatry, 8*(3), 215–224. doi: 10.1016/S2215-0366(20)30566-6

Soloff, P. H., Chiappetta, L., Mason, N. S., Becker, C., & Price, J. C. (2014). Effects of serotonin-2A receptor binding and gender on personality traits and suicidal behavior in borderline personality disorder. *Psychiatry Research: Neuroimaging, 222*(3), 140–148.

Soloff, P. H., Lynch, K. G., Kelley, T. M., Malone, K. M., & Mann, J. J. (2000). Characteristics of suicide attempts of patients with major depressive episode and borderline personality disorder: A comparative study. *American Journal of Psychiatry, 157*(4), 601–608.

Solomon, D. A., Leon, A. C., Coryell, W. H., Endicott, J., Li, C., Fiedorowicz, J. G., & Keller, M. B. (2010). Longitudinal course of bipolar I disorder: Duration of mood episodes. *Archives of General Psychiatry, 67*(4), 339–347.

Solomon, D. A., Leon, A. C., Endicott, J., Coryell, W. H., Mueller, T. I., Posternak, M. A., & Keller, M. B. (2003). Unipolar mania over the course of a 20-year follow-up study. *American Journal of Psychiatry, 160,* 2049–2051.

Solomon, R. L. (1980). The opponent-process theory of acquired motivation: The costs of pleasure and the benefits of pain. *American Psychologist, 35,* 691–712.

Solomon, R. L., & Corbit, J. D. (1974). An opponent process theory of motivation: I. Temporal dynamics of affect. *Psychological Review, 81*, 119–145.

Song, Y.-j., Li, S.-r., Li, X.-w., Chen, X., Wei, Z.-x., Liu, Q.-s., & Cheng, Y. (2020). The effect of estrogen replacement therapy on Alzheimer's disease and Parkinson's disease in postmenopausal women: A meta-analysis. *Frontiers in Neuroscience, 14,* 157.

Soreca, I., Frank, E., & Kupfer, D. J. (2009). The phenomenology of bipolar disorder: What drives the high rate of medical burden and determines long-term prognosis? *Depression and Anxiety, 26*(1), 73–82.

Sorkin, A., Weinshall, D., Modai, I., & Peled, A. (2006). Improving the accuracy of the diagnosis of schizophrenia by means of virtual reality. *American Journal of Psychiatry, 163,* 512–520.

Sosa-Ortiz, A. L., Acosta-Castillo, I., & Prince, M. J. (2012). Epidemiology of dementias and Alzheimer's disease. *Archives of Medical Research, 43*(8), 600–608.

Souery, D., Zaninotto, L., Calati, R., Linotte, S., Mendlewicz, J., Sentissi, O., & Serretti, A. (2012). Depression across mood disorders: Review and analysis in a clinical sample. *Comprehensive Psychiatry, 53,* 24–38.

South, S. C., Oltmanns, T. F., & Krueger, R. F. (2011). The spectrum of personality disorders. In D. H. Barlow (Ed.), *Oxford handbook of clinical psychology* (pp. 530–550). New York, NY: Oxford University.

Spangler, D. L., Simons, A. D., Monroe, S. M., & Thase, M. E. (1996). Gender differences in cognitive diathesis-stress domain match: Implications for differential pathways to depression. *Journal of Abnormal Psychology, 105,* 653–657.

Spangler, D. L., Simons, A. D., Monroe, S. M., & Thase, M. E. (1997). Comparison of cognitive models of depression: Relationships between cognitive constructs and cognitive diathesis-stress match. *Journal of Abnormal Psychology, 106,* 395–403.

Spanos, N. P. (1996). *Multiple identities and false memories: A sociocognitive prospective.* Washington, DC: American Psychological Association.

Spanos, N. P., Cross, P. A., Dickson, K., & DuBreuil, S. C. (1993). Close encounters: An examination of UFO experiences. *Journal of Abnormal Psychology, 102,* 624–632.

Speisman, R. B., Kumar, A., Rani, A., Foster, T. C., & Ormerod, B. K. (2013). Daily exercise improves memory, stimulates hippocampal neurogenesis and modulates immune and neuroimmune cytokines in aging rats. *Brain, Behavior and Immunity, 28,* 25–43. doi: 10.1016/j.bbi.2012.09.013.

Spencer, T. J., Biederman, J., & Mick, E. (2007). Attention-deficit/hyperactivity disorder: Diagnosis, lifespan, comorbidities, and neurobiology. *Ambulatory Pediatrics, 7*(1, Suppl. 1), 73–81.

Spichak, S., Bastiaanssen, T. F. S., Berding, K., Vlckova, K., Clarke, G., Dinan, T. G., & Cryan, J. F. (2021). Mining microbes for mental health: Determining the role of microbial metabolic pathways in human brain health and disease. *Neuroscience and Biobehavioral Reviews, 125,* 698–761. doi: 10.1016/j.neubiorev.2021.02.044

Spiegel, D. (2010). Dissociation in DSM-5. *Journal of Trauma and Dissociation, 11(3), 261–265.*

Spiegel, D. (2013). Tranceformations: Hypnosis in brain and body. *Depression and Anxiety, 30,* 342–352.

Spiegel, D., Bloom, J. R., Kramer, H. C., & Gotheil, E. (1989). Effect of psychosocial treatment on survival of patients with metastatic breast cancer. *Lancet, 14,* 888–891.

Spiegel, D., Lewis-Fernandez, R., Lanius, R., Vermetten, E., Simeon, D., & Friedman, M. (2013). Dissociative disorders in DSM-5. *Annual Review of Clinical Psychology, 9,* 299–326.

Spiegel, D., Loewenstein, R. J., Lewis-Fernandez, R., Sar, V., Simeon, D., Vermetten, E., & Dell, P. F. (2011). Dissociative disorders in DSM-5. *Depression and Anxiety, 28,* 824–852. doi: 10.1002/da.20874

Spielberger, C. D., & Frank, R. G. (1992). Injury control: A promising field for psychologists. *American Psychologist, 47*(8), 1029–1030.

Spielman, A. J., & Glovinsky, P. (1991). The varied nature of insomnia. In P. J. Hauri (Ed.), *Case studies in insomnia* (pp. 1–15). New York, NY: Plenum Press.

Spinella, M. (2005). Mood in relation to subclinical symptoms. *International Journal of Neuroscience, 115,* 433–443.

Spinelli, M. G., & Endicott, J. (2003). Controlled clinical trial of interpersonal psychotherapy versus parenting education program for depressed pregnant women. *American Journal of Psychiatry, 160,* 555–562.

Spinelli, S., Chefer, S., Suomi, S. J., Higley, J. D., Barr, C. S., & Stein, E. (2009). Early-life stress induces long-term morphologic changes in primate brain. *Archives of General Psychiatry, 66*(6), 658–665.

Spira, A., Bajos, N., Bejin, A., Beltzer, N., Bozon, M., Ducot, M., & Touzard, H. (1992). AIDS and sexual behavior in France. *Nature, 360,* 407–409.

Spitzer, C., Spelsberg, B., Grabe, H. J., Mundt, B., & Freyberger, H. J. (1999). Dissociative experiences and psychopathology in conversion disorders. *Journal of Psychosomatic Research, 46*(3), 291–294.

Spitzer, R. L. (1999). Harmful dysfunction and the DSM definition of mental disorder. *Journal of Abnormal Psychology, 108,* 430–432.

Spitzer, R. L., Yanovski, S. Z., Wadden, T., Wing, R., Marcus, M., Stunkard, A., & Horne, R. L. (1993). Binge eating disorder: Its further validation in a multi-site study. *International Journal of Eating Disorders, 13,* 137–153.

Spoont, M. R. (1992). Modulatory role of serotonin in neural information processing: Implications for human psychopathology. *Psychological Bulletin, 112*(2), 330–350.

Sprague, J., Javdani, S., Sadeh, N., Newman, J. P., & Verona, E. (2012). Borderline personality disorder as a female phenotypic expression of psychopathy? *Personality Disorders: Theory, Research, and Treatment, 3*(2), 127.

Sprock, J. (2000). Gender-typed behavioral examples of histrionic personality disorder. *Journal of Psychopathology and Behavioral Assessment, 22,* 107–122.

Spurrell, E. B., Wilfley, D. E., Tanofsky, M. B., & Brownell, K. D. (1997). Age of onset for binge eating: Are there different pathways to binge eating? *International Journal of Eating Disorders, 21,* 55–65.

Srivastava, S., Childers, M. E., Baek, J. H., Strong, C. M., Hill, S. J., Warsett, K. S., & Ketter, T. A. (2010). Toward interaction of affective and cognitive contributors to creativity in bipolar disorders: A controlled study. *Journal of Affective Disorders, 125,* 27–34.

Staal, W. G., Pol, H. E. H., Schnack, H. G., Hoogendoorn, M. L. C., Jellema, K., & Kahn, R. S. (2000). Structural brain abnormalities in patients with schizophrenia and their healthy siblings. *American Journal of Psychiatry, 157,* 416–421.

Stahl, S. M. (2008). *Stahl's essential psychopharmacology* (3rd ed.). New York, NY: Cambridge University Press.

Stall, R., McKusick, L., Wiley, J., Coates, T. J., & Ostrow, D. G. (1986). Alcohol and drug use during sexual activity and compliance with safe sex guidelines for AIDS. *Health Education Quarterly, 13,* 359–371.

Stamm, J. M., Bourlas, A. P., Baugh, C. M., Fritts, N. G., Daneshvar, D. H., Martin, B. M., . . . Stern, R. A. (2015). Age of first exposure to football and later-life cognitive impairment in former NFL players. *Neurology, 84*(11), 1114–1120.

Stangier, U., Hilling, C., Heidenreich, T., Risch, A. K., Barocka, A., Schlösser, R., Kronfeld, K., Ruckes, C., Berger, H., Röschke, J., Weck, F., Volk, S., Hambrecht, M., Serfling, R., Erkwoh, R., Stirn, A., Sobanski, T., & Hautzinger, M. (2013). Maintenance Cognitive-Behavioral Therapy and Manualized Psychoeducation in the Treatment of Recurrent Depression: A Multicenter Prospective Randomized Controlled Trial. *American Journal of Psychiatry, 170,* 624–632.

Stangier, U., Schramm, E., Heidenreich, T., Berger, M., & Clark, D. M. (2011). Cognitive therapy vs. interpersonal therapy in social anxiety disorder: A randomized controlled trial. *Archives of General Psychiatry, 68,* 692–700. doi: 10.1001/archgenpsychiatry.2011.67

Stanley, M. A., Beck, J. G., Novy, D. M., Averill, P. M., Swann, A. C., Diefenbach, G. J., & Hopko, D. R. (2003). Cognitive-behavioral treatment of late-life generalized anxiety disorder. *Journal of Consulting and Clinical Psychology, 71*(2), 309–319.

Stanley, M. A., Wilson, N. L., Novy, D. M., Rhoades, H. M., Wagener, P. D., Greisinger, A. J., & Kunik, M. E. (2009). Cognitive behavior therapy for generalized anxiety disorder among older adults in primary care: A randomized clinical trial. *JAMA: Journal of the American Medical Association, 301*(14), 1460–1467. doi: 10.1001/jama.2009.458

Stappenbeck, C. A., Hellmuth, J. C., Simpson, T., & Jakupcak, M. (2014). The effects of alcohol problems, PTSD, and combat exposure on nonphysical and physical aggression among Iraq and Afghanistan war veterans. *Psychological Trauma: Theory, Research, Practice, and Policy, 6*(1), 65–72.

Starkman, M. N., Giordani, B., Gebarski, S. S., Berent, S., Schork, M. A., & Schteingart, D. E. (1999). Decrease in cortisol reverses human hippocampal atrophy following treatment of Cushing's disease. *Biological Psychiatry, 46,* 1595–1602.

State v. Campanaro, Nos. 632-79, 1309-79, 1317-79, 514-80, & 707-80 (S. Ct. N.J. Criminal Division, Union County 1980).

Stathopoulou, G., Powers, M. B., Berry, A. C., Smits, J. A. J., & Otto, M. W. (2006). Exercise interventions for mental health: A quantitative and qualitative review. *Clinical Psychology: Science and Practice, 13*(2), 179–193.

Stech, E. P., Lim, J., Upton, E. L., & Newby, J. M. (2020). Internet-delivered cognitive behavioral therapy for panic disorder with or without agoraphobia: A systematic review and meta-analysis. *Cognitive Behaviour Therapy, 49*(4), 270–293. doi: 10.1080/16506073.2019.1628808

Steenkamp, M. M., Litz, B. T., & Marmar, C. R. (2020). First-line psychotherapies for military-related PTSD. *JAMA, 323*(7), 656–657. doi: 10.1001/jama.2019.20825

Steiger, A. (2008). Hormones and sleep. In S. R. Pandi-Perumal & J. Verster (Eds.), *Sleep disorders: Diagnosis and therapeutics* (pp. 457–466). Boca Raton, FL: Taylor & Francis.

Steiger, H., Bruce, K. R., & Groleau, P. (2011). Neural circuits, neurotransmitters, and behavior: Seratonin and temperament in bulimic syndromes. *Current Topics in Behavioral Neurosciences, 6,* 125–138.

Steiger, H., Bruce, K. R., Israël, M. (2013). Eating disorders: Anorexia nervosa, bulimia nervosa, and binge eating disorder. In I. B. Weiner (Series Ed.), G. Stricker, & T. A. Widiger (Vol. Eds.), *Handbook of psychology: Vol. 8 Clinical psychology* (pp. 147–170). Hoboken, NJ: Wiley.

Stein, D. J., & Lochner, C. (2020). Psychobiology of OCPD. In J. E. Grant, A. Pinto, & S. R. Chamberlain (Eds.), *Obsessive-compulsive personality disorder* (pp. 127–142). Washington, D.C.: American Psychiatric Association Publishing.

Stein, D. J., Bass, J. K., & Hofmann, S. G. (2019). *Global mental health and psychotherapy: Adapting psychotherapy for low- and middle-income countries.* doi: 10.1016/C2017-0-01830-X

Stein, D. J., Phillips, K. A., Bolton, D., Fulford, K. W. M., Sadler, J. Z., & Kendler, K. S. (2010). What is a mental/psychiatric disorder? From DSM-IV to DSM-V. *Psychological Medicine, 40*(11), 1759–1765.

Stein, M. B., Goldin, P. R., Sareen, J., Zorrilla, L. T., & Brown, G. G. (2002). Increased amygdala activation to angry and contemptuous faces in generalized social phobia. *Archives of General Psychiatry, 59,* 1027–1034.

Stein, M. B., Liebowitz, M. R., Lydiard, R. B., Pitts, C. D., Bushnell, W., & Gergel, I. (1998). Paroxetine treatment of generalized social phobia (social anxiety disorder). A randomized clinical trial. *JAMA: Journal of the American Medical Association, 280,* 708–713.

Stein, M. B., Schork, N. J., & Gelernter, J. (2007). Gene-by-environment (serotonin transporter and childhood maltreatment) interaction for anxiety sensitivity, an intermediate phenotype for anxiety disorders. *Neuropsychopharmacology, 33*(2), 312–319.

Stein, M. I. (1978). Thematic apperception test and related methods. In B. B. Wolman (Ed.), *Clinical diagnosis of mental disorders: A handbook* (pp. 179–235). New York, NY: Plenum Press.

Stein, M., Hilsenroth, M., Slavin-Mulford, J., & Pinsker, J. (2011). *Social Cognition and Object Relations Scale: Global Rating Method (SCORS-G).*Unpublished manuscript, Massachusetts General Hospital and Harvard Medical School, Boston, MA, 1(2).

Steinberg, A. B., & Phares, V. (2001). Family functioning, body image, and eating disturbances. In J. K. Thompson & L. Smolak (Eds.), *Body image, eating disorders, and obesity in youth: Assessment, prevention and treatment* (127–147). Washington, DC: American Psychological Association.

Steinglass, P., Weisstub, E., & Kaplan De-Nour, A. K. (1988). Perceived personal networks as mediators of stress reactions. *American Journal of Psychiatry, 145,* 1259–1264.

Steketee, G., & Barlow, D. H. (2002). Obsessive-compulsive disorder. In D. H. Barlow, *Anxiety and its disorders: The nature and treatment of anxiety and panic* (2nd ed.). New York, NY: Guilford.

Steketee, G., & Frost, R. O. (2007a). *Compulsive hoarding and acquiring: Client workbook.* New York, NY: Oxford University Press.

Steketee, G., & Frost, R. O. (2007b). *Compulsive hoarding and acquiring: Therapist guide.* New York, NY: Oxford University Press.

Steketee, G., Gibson, A., Frost, R. O., Alabiso, J., Arluke, A., & Patronek, G. (2011). Characteristics and antecedents of people who hoard animals: An exploratory comparative interview study. *Review of General Psychology, 15(2),* 114–124.

Steketee, G., Quay, S., & White, K. (1991). Religion and guilt in OCD patients. *Journal of Anxiety Disorders, 5,* 359–367.

Stenvall, M., Olofsson, B., Lundstrom, M., Svensson, O., Nyberg, L., & Gustafson, Y. (2006). Inpatient falls and injuries in older patients treated for femoral neck fracture. *Archives of Gerontology and Geriatrics, 43*(3), 389–399.

Steptoe, A., & Wardle, J. (2012). Enjoying life and living longer. *Archives of Internal Medicine, 172*(3), 273–275. doi: 10.1001/archinternmed.2011.1028

Stern, A., Agnew-Blais, J. C., Danese, A., Fisher, H. L., Matthews, T., Polanczyk, G. V., … Arseneault, L. (2020). Associations between ADHD and emotional problems from childhood to young adulthood: A longitudinal genetically sensitive study. *Journal of Child Psychology and Psychiatry, 61*(11), 1234–1242.

Sterzer, P. (2010). Born to be criminal? What to make of early biological risk factors for criminal behavior. *American Journal of Psychiatry, 167*(1), 1–3. doi:10.1176/appi.ajp.2009.09111601

Stevens, R. G., & Zhu, Y. (2015). Electric light, particularly at night, disrupts human circadian rhythmicity: is that a problem? *Philosophical Transactions of the Royal Society of London B: Biological Sciences, 370*(1667), 20140120.

Stewart, S. E., Jenike, E., & Jenike, M. A. (2009). Biological treatment for obsessive-compulsive disorder. In M. M. Antony & M. B. Stein (Eds.), *Oxford handbook of anxiety and related disorders* (pp. 375–390). New York, NY: Oxford University Press.

Stice, E., & Shaw, H. (2004). Eating disorder prevention programs: A meta-analytic review. *Psychological Bulletin, 130,* 206–227.

Stice, E., Akutagawa, D., Gaggar, A., & Agras, W. S. (2000). Negative affect moderates the relation between dieting and binge eating. *International Journal of Eating Disorders, 27,* 218–229.

Stice, E., Cameron, R. P., Killen, J. D., Hayward, C., & Taylor, C. B. (1999). Naturalistic weight-reduction efforts prospectively predict growth in relative weight and onset of obesity among female adolescents. *Journal of Consulting and Clinical Psychology, 67,* 967–974.

Stice, E., Gau, J. M., Rohde, P., & Shaw, H. (2017). Risk factors that predict future onset of each *DSM-5* eating disorder: Predictive specificity in high-risk adolescent females. *Journal of Abnormal Psychology, 126*(1), 38–51. doi: 10.1037/abn0000219

Stice, E., Marti, C. N., & Rohde, P. (2013). Prevalence, incidence, impairment, and course of the proposed DSM-5 eating disorder diagnoses in an 8-year prospective community study of young women. *Journal of Abnormal Psychology, 122*(2), 445–457.

Stice, E., Marti, C. N., Shaw, H., & Jaconis, M. (2009). An 8-year longitudinal study of the natural history of threshold, subthreshold, and partial eating disorders from a community sample of adolescents. *Journal of Abnormal Psychology, 118*(3), 587–597.

Stice, E., Ng, J., & Shaw, H. (2010). Risk factors and prodromal eating pathology. *Journal of Child Psychology and Psychiatry and Allied Disciplines, 51*(4), 518–525.

Stice, E., Presnell, K., Shaw, H., & Rohde, P. (2005). Psychological and behavioral risk factors for obesity onset in adolescent girls: A prospective study. *Journal of Consulting and Clinical Psychology, 73,* 195–202.

Stice, E., Rohde, P., Butryn, M. L., Shaw, H., & Marti, C. N. (2015). Effectiveness Trial of a Selective Dissonance-based Eating

Disorder Prevention Program with Female College Students: Effects at 2-and 3-Year Follow-up. *Behaviour Research and Therapy, 71,* 21–26.

Stice, E., Rohde, P., Durant, S., & Shaw, H. (2012). A preliminary trial of a prototype internet dissonance-based eating disorder prevention program for young women with body image concerns. *Journal of Consulting and Clinical Psychology, 80,* 907–916.

Stice, E., Rohde, P., Shaw, H., & Marti, C. N. (2012). Efficacy trial of a selective prevention program targeting both eating disorder symptoms and unhealthy weight gain among female college students. *Journal of Consulting and Clinical Psychology, 80,* 164–170.

Stice, E., Shaw, H., & Marti, C. N. (2006). A meta-analytic review of obesity prevention programs for children and adolescents: The skinny on interventions that work. *Psychological Bulletin, 132*(5), 667–691.

Stice, E., Shaw, H., & Marti, C. N. (2007). A meta-analytic review of eating disorder prevention programs: Encouraging findings. *Annual Review of Clinical Psychology, 3,* 207–231.

Stinson, F. S., Dawson, D. A., Goldstein, R. B., Chou, S. P., Huang, B., Smith, S. M., & Pickering, R. P. (2008). Prevalence, correlates, disability, and comorbidity of DSM-IV narcissistic personality disorder: Results from the Wave 2 National Epidemiologic Survey on Alcohol and Related Conditions. *Journal of Clinical Psychiatry, 69*(7), 1033.

Stoffers-Winterling, J., Storebø, O. J., & Lieb, K. (in press). Pharmacotherapy for borderline personality disorder: An update of published, unpublished and ongoing studies. *Current Psychiatry Reports, 22,* 1–10.

Stokes, A., & Preston, S. H. (2016). Revealing the burden of obesity using weight histories. *Proceedings of the National Academy of Sciences, 113*(3), 572–577.

Stoller, R. J. (1976). Two feminized male American Indians. *Archives of Sexual Behavior, 5,* 529–538.

Stone, A. B., Pearlstein, T. B., & Brown, W. A. (1991). Fluoxetine in the treatment of late luteal phase dysphoric disorder. *Journal of Clinical Psychiatry, 52*(7), 290–293.

Stone, J., Carson, A., Aditya, H., Prescott, R., Zaubi, M., Warlow, C., Sharpe, M. (2009). The role of physical injury in motor and sensory conversion symptoms: A systematic and narrative review. *Journal of Psychosomatic Research, 66*(5), 383–390.

Stone, J., Carson, A., Duncan, R., Coleman, R., Roberts, R., Warlow, C., Hibberd, C., Murray, G., Cull, R., Pelosi, A., Cavanagh, J., Matthews, K., Goldbeck, R., Smyth, R., Walker, J., MacMahon, A. D., & Sharpe, M.(2009). Symptoms 'unexplained by organic disease' in 1144 new neurology out-patients: How often does the diagnosis change at follow-up? *Brain,* 132(Pt 10), 2878–2888.

Stone, J., Kotoula, V., Dietrich, C., De Simoni, S., Krystal, J. H., & Mehta, M. A. (2015). Perceptual distortions and delusional thinking following ketamine administration are related to increased pharmacological MRI signal changes in the parietal lobe. *Journal of Psychopharmacology, 29*(9), 1025–1028.

Stone, J., LaFrance, W. C., Levenson, J. L., & Sharpe, M. (2010). Issues for DSM-5: Conversion disorder. *American Journal of Psychiatry, 167,* 626–627.

Stone, J., Smyth, R., Carson, A., Lewis, S., Prescott, R., Warlow, C., & Sharpe, M. (2005). Systematic review of misdiagnosis of conversion symptoms and hysteria. *British Medical Journal, 331, no pagination specified.*

Stone, J., Smyth, R., Carson, A., Warlow, C., & Sharpe, M. (2006). La belle indifference in conversion symptoms and hysteria: Systematic review. *British Journal of Psychiatry, 188,* 204–209.

Stone, M. H. (1993). Cluster C personality disorders. In D. L. Dunner (Ed.), *Current psychiatric therapy* (pp. 411–417). Philadelphia, PA: W. B. Saunders.

Stone, M. H. (2013). A new look at borderline personality disorder and related disorders: hyper-reactivity in the limbic system and lower centers. *Psychodynamic Psychiatry, 41*(3), 437–466.

Strain, E. C. (2009). Substance-related disorders. In B. J. Sadock, V. A. Sadock, & P. Ruiz (Eds.), *Kaplan & Sadock's comprehensive textbook of psychiatry* (9th ed., Vol. I, pp. 1237–1268). Philadelphia, PA: Lippincott Williams & Wilkins.

Strain, E. C., Lofwall, M. R., & Jaffe, J. H. (2009). Opioid-related disorders. In B. J. Sadock, V. A. Sadock, & P. Ruiz (Eds.), *Kaplan & Sadock's comprehensive textbook of psychiatry* (9th ed., Vol. I, pp. 1360–1387). Philadelphia, PA: Lippincott Williams & Wilkins.

Strain, J. J., & Friedman, M. J. (2011). Considering adjustment disorders as stress response syndromes for DSM-5. *Depression and Anxiety, 28,* 818–823. doi: 10.1002/da.20782

Strandwitz, P. (2018). Neurotransmitter modulation by the gut microbiota. *Brain Research, 1693,* 128–133.

Strandwitz, P., Kim, K. H., Terekhova, D., Liu, J. K., Sharma, A., Levering, J., … Lewis, K. (2019). GABA-modulating bacteria of the human gut microbiota. *Nature Microbiology, 4*(3), 396–403.

Stratta, P., Capanna, C., Riccardi, I., Carmassi, C., Piccinni, A., Dell'Osso, L., & Rossi, A. (2012). Suicidal intention and negative spiritual coping one year after the earthquake of L'Aquila (Italy). *Journal of Affective Disorders, 136*(3), 1227–1231.

Straus, S. E., Tosato, G., Armstrong, G., Lawley, T., Preble, O. T., Henle, W., & Blaese, R. M. (1985). Persisting illness and fatigue in adults with evidence of Epstein Barr virus infection. *Annals of Internal Medicine, 102,* 7–16.

Strauss, J. L., Hayes, A. M., Johnson, S. L., Newman, C. F., Brown, G. K., Barber, J. P., & Beck, A. T. (2006). Early alliance, alliance ruptures, and symptom change in a nonrandomized trial of cognitive therapy for avoidant and obsessive-compulsive personality disorders. *Journal of Consulting and Clinical Psychology, 74,* 337–345.

Stravynski, A., Elie, R., & Franche, R. L. (1989). Perception of early parenting by patients diagnosed with avoidant personality disorder: A test of the overprotection hypothesis. *Acta Psychiatrica Scandinavica, 80,* 415–420.

Streit, F., Colodro-Conde, L., Hall, A. S., & Witt, S. H. (2020). Genomics of borderline personality disorder. In B. T. Baune (Ed.), *Personalized psychiatry* (pp. 227–237). Amsterdam, Netherlands: Elsevier.

Striegel-Moore, R. H., & Franko, D. L. (2002). Body image issues among girls and women. In T. F. Cash & T. Pruzinsky (Eds.), *Body image: A handbook of theory, research and clinical practice* (pp. 183–191). New York, NY: Guilford.

Striegel-Moore, R. H., & Franko, D. L. (2008). Should binge eating disorder be included in the DSM-V? A critical review of the state of the evidence. *Annual Review of Clinical Psychology, 4,* 305–324.

Striegel-Moore, R. H., Cachelin, F. M., Dohm, F. A., Pike, M., Wilfley, D. E., & Fairburn, C. G. (2001). Comparison of binge eating disorder and bulimia nervosa in a community sample. *International Journal of Eating Disorders, 29,* 157–165.

Striegel-Moore, R. H., Dohm, F. A., Kraemer, H. C., Taylor, C. B., Daniels, S., Crawford, P. B., & Schreiber, G. B. (2003). Eating disorders in white and black women. *American Journal of Psychiatry, 160,* 1326–1331.

Striegel-Moore, R. H., Franko, D. L., & Garcia, J. (2009). The validity and clinical utility of night eating syndrome. *International Journal of Eating Disorders, 42*(8), 720–738.

Striegel-Moore, R. H., Silberstein, L. R., & Rodin, J. (1986). Toward an understanding of risk factors for bulimia. *American Psychologist, 3,* 246–263.

Striegel-Moore, R. H., Silberstein, L. R., & Rodin, J. (1993). The social self in bulimia nervosa: Public self-consciousness, social anxiety, and perceived fraudulence. *Journal of Abnormal Psychology, 102*(2), 297–303.

Striegel-Moore, R. H., Wilson, G. T., DeBar, L., Perrin, N., Lynch, F., Rosselli, F., & Kraemer, H. C. (2010). Cognitive behavioral guided self-help for the treatment of recurrent binge eating. *Journal of Consulting and Clinical Psychology, 78*(3), 312–321.

Striegel-Moore, R., Rosselli, F., Wilson, G., Perrin, N., Harvey, K., & DeBar, L. (2010). Nocturnal eating: Association with binge eating, obesity, and psychological distress. *Clinical Psychology & Psychotherapy, 11*, 13.

Strike, P. C., & Steptoe, A. (2005). Behavioral and emotional triggers of acute coronary syndromes: A systematic review and critique. *Psychosomatic Medicine, 67*, 179–186.

Strober, M. (2002). Family–genetic perspectives on anorexia nervosa and bulimia nervosa. In K. D. Brownell & C. G. Fairburn (Eds.), *Eating disorders and obesity: A comprehensive handbook* (2nd ed., pp. 212–218). New York, NY: Guilford.

Strober, M., Freeman, R., Lampert, C., Diamond, J., & Kaye, W. (2000). Controlled family study of anorexia nervosa and bulimia nervosa: Evidence of shared liability and transmission of partial syndromes. *American Journal of Psychiatry, 157*, 393–401.

Stroebe, M., Stroebe, W., & Abakoumkin, G. (2005). The broken heart: Suicidal ideation in bereavement. *American Journal of Psychiatry, 162*, 2178–2180.

Strokoff, J., Owen, J., & Fincham, F. D. (2014). Diverse reactions to hooking up among US university students. *Archives of Sexual Behavior, 44*(4), 935–943.

Strong, C. M., Nowakowska, C., Santosa, C. M., Wang, P. W., Kraemer, H. C., & Ketter, T. A. (2007). Temperament-creativity relationships in mood disorder patients, healthy controls and highly creative individuals. *Journal of Affective Disorders, 100*(1–3), 41–48.

Strong, S. M., Williamson, D. A., Netemeyer, R. G., & Geer, J. H. (2000). Eating disorder symptoms and concerns about body differ as a function of gender and sexual orientation. *Journal of Social and Clinical Psychology, 19*, 240–255.

Stroup, T. S., & Lieberman, J. A. (Eds.). (2010). *Antipsychotic trials in schizophrenia: The CATIE project*. Cambridge, UK: Cambridge University Press.

Stunkard, A., Allison, K., & Lundgren, J. (2008). Issues for DSM-V: Night eating syndrome. *American Journal of Psychiatry, 165*(4), 424.

Suarez, E. C., Lewis, J. G., & Kuhn, C. (2002). The relation of aggression, hostility, and anger to lipopolysaccharide-stimulated tumor necrosis factor (TNF) by blood monocytes from normal men. *Behavior and Immunity, 16*, 675–684.

Suárez, L., Bennett, S., Goldstein, C., & Barlow, D. H. (2009). Understanding anxiety disorders from a "triple vulnerabilities" framework. In M. M. Antony & M. B. Stein (Eds.), *Oxford handbook of anxiety and related disorders* (pp. 153–172). New York, NY: Oxford University Press.

Subcommittee on Attention-Deficit/Hyperactivity Disorder, Steering Committee on Quality Improvement, & Management. (2011). ADHD: Clinical practice guidelines for the diagnosis, evaluation, and treatment of attention- deficit/hyperactivity disorder in children and adolescents. *Pediatrics, 128*(5), 1007–1022. doi: 10.1542/peds.2011-2654

Subramanian, S., Bandopadhyay, D., Mishra, P. K., Mathew, M., & John, M. (2010). Design and development of non-fibrillar amyloid b as a potential Alzheimer vaccine. *Biochemical and Biophysical Research Communications, 394*(2), 393–397.

Substance Abuse and Mental Health Services Administration (SAMHSA). (2020). *Key substance use and mental health indicators in the United States: Results from the 2018 National Survey on Drug Use and Health.* HHS Publication No. PEP19-5068, NSDUH Series H-54. Rockville, MD: Center for Behavioral Statistics and Quality, Substance Ause and Mental Health Services Administration.

Substance Abuse and Mental Health Services Administration (SAMHSA). (2011). *The DAWN Report: Trends in Emergency Department Visits Involving Underage Alcohol Use: 2005 to 2009.* Rockville, MD: Substance Abuse and Mental Health Services Administration; 2011.

Substance Abuse and Mental Health Services Administration, Office of Applied Studies. (2002). *Emergency department trends from the Drug Abuse Warning Network, final estimates 1994–2001.* (DAWN Series D-21, DHHS Publication No. (SMA) 02-3635). Rockville, MD: Author.

Substance Abuse and Mental Health Services Administration, Office of Applied Studies. (2009). *Results from the 2008 National Survey on Drug Use and Health: National findings* (NSDUH Series H-36, DHHS Publication No. (SMA) 09-4434). Rockville, MD: Author.

Substance Abuse and Mental Health Services Administration. (2011, July). Current statistics on the prevalence and characteristics of people experiencing homelessness in the United States. Retrieved May 12, 2013, from http://homeless.samhsa.gov/ResourceFiles/hrc_factsheet.pdf

Substance Abuse and Mental Health Services Administration. (2012). *Results from the 2011 National Survey on Drug Use and Health: Summary of national findings* (NSDUH Series H-44, DHHS Publication No. (SMA) 12-4713). Rockville, MD: Author.

Substance Abuse and Mental Health Services Administration. (2014). *Results from the 2013 National Survey on Drug Use and Health: Summary of National Findings,* NSDUH Series H-48, HHS Publication No. (SMA) 14-4863. Rockville, MD: Substance Abuse and Mental Health Services Administration.

Substance Abuse and Mental Health Services Administration. (2014). *National Survey on Drug Use and Health.* Retrieved from: http://www.samhsa.gov/data/sites/default/files/NSDUH-FRR1-2014/NSDUH-FRR1-2014.pdf

Sue, S., Yan Cheng, J. K., Saad, C. S., & Chu, J. P. (2012). Asian American mental health: A call to action. *American Psychologist, 67*(7), 532.

Sugiyama, T., & Abe, T. (1989). The prevalence of autism in Nagoya, Japan: A total population study. *Journal of Autism and Developmental Disorders, 19*, 87–96.

Sullivan, G. M., & LeDoux, J. E. (2004). Synaptic self: Conditioned fear, developed adversity, and the anxious individual. In J. M. Gorman (Ed.), *Fear and anxiety: The benefits of translational research* (pp. 1–22). Washington, DC: American Psychiatric Publishing.

Sullivan, G. M., Kent, J. M., & Coplan, J. D. (2000). The neurobiology of stress and anxiety. In D. I. Mostofsky & D. H. Barlow (Eds.), *The management of stress and anxiety in medical disorders* (pp. 15–35). Needham Heights, MA: Allyn & Bacon.

Sullivan, P. F., Neale, M. C., & Kendler, K. S. (2000). Genetic epidemiology of major depression: Review and meta-analysis, *American Journal of Psychiatry, 157*, 1552–1562.

Sullivan, P. S., Satcher Johnson, A., Pembleton, E. S., Stephenson, R., Justice, A. C., Althoff, K. N., … Beyrer, C. (2021). Epidemiology of HIV in the USA: Epidemic burden, inequities, contexts, and responses. *The Lancet, 397*(10279), 1095–1106. doi: 10.1016/S0140-6736(21)00395-0

Sullivan, S. (2012). Update on emerging drugs for insomnia. *Expert Opinion on Emerging Drugs, 17*(3), 295–298. doi: 10.1517/14728214.2012.693158

Sullivan, S., & Guilleminault, C. (2009). Emerging drugs for insomnia: New frontiers for old and novel targets. *Expert Opinion on Emerging Drugs, 14*(3), 411–422.

Sulloway, F. (1979). *Freud, biologist of the mind.* London, UK: Burnett.

Suls, J., & Bunde, J. (2005). Anger, anxiety, and depression as risk factors for cardiovascular disease: The problems and implications of overlapping affective dispositions. *Psychological Bulletin, 131,* 260–300.

Summerfeldt, L. J., Kloosterman, P. H., & Antony, M. M. (2010). Structured and semi-structured interviews. In M. M. Antony & D. H. Barlow (Eds.), *Handbook of assessment and treatment planning for psychological disorders* (2nd ed.). New York, NY: Guilford.

Summitt, P. H. (2013). *Sum it up: A thousand and ninety-eight victories, a couple of irrelevant losses, and a life in perspective.* New York, NY: Crown Archetype.

Sun, J. (2011). Seasonality of suicide in Shandong, China, 991–2009: Associations with gender, age, area and methods of suicide. *Journal of Affective Disorders, 135*(1–3), 258–266.

Sun, N., Li, Y., Cai, Y., Chen, J., Shen, Y., Sun, J., & Zhang, K. (2012). A comparison of melancholic and nonmelacholic recurrent major depression in Han Chinese women. *Depression and Anxiety, 29,* 4–9.

Suneel, I., & Siddique, S. (2020). Impact of covert sensitization on recovery of alcoholics in Pakistan. *Rawal Medical Journal, 45*(3), 573–576.

Suomi, S. J. (1999). Attachment in rhesus monkeys. In J. Cassidy & P. Shaver (Eds.), *Handbook of attachment: Theory, research, and clinical applications* (pp. 181–197). New York, NY: Guilford.

Suomi, S. J. (2000). A biobehavioral perspective on developmental psychopathology. In A. J. Sameroff, J. Lewis, & S. M. Miller (Eds.), *Handbook of developmental psychopathology* (pp. 237–256). New York, NY: Kluwer Academic/Plenum.

Sutherland, K., & Cistulli, P. A. (2015). Recent advances in obstructive sleep apnea pathophysiology and treatment. *Sleep and Biological Rhythms, 13*(1), 26–40.

Sutin, A. R., Stephan, Y., & Terracciano, A. (2015). Weight Discrimination and Risk of Mortality. *Psychological Science, 26*(11), 1803–1811.

Sutin, A. R., Terracciano, A., Milaneschi, Y., An, Y., Ferrucci, L., & Zonderman, A. B. (2013). The trajectory of depressive symptoms across the adult life span. *JAMA Psychiatry, 70,* 803–811.

Suvisaari, J. M., Taxell-Lassas, V., Pankakoski, M., Haukka, J. K., Lönnqvist, J. K., & Häkkinen, L. T. (2013). Obstetric complications as risk factors for schizophrenia spectrum psychoses in offspring of mothers with psychotic disorder. *Schizophrenia Bulletin, 39*(5), 1056–1066.

Suvrathan, A., Hoeffer, C. A., Wong, H., Klann, E., & Chattarji, S. (2010). Characterization and reversal of synaptic defects in the amygdala in a mouse model of fragile X syndrome. *Proceedings of the National Academy of Sciences, 107*(25), 11591–11596.

Svaldi, J., Schmitz, F., Baur, J., Hartmann, A. S., Legenbauer, T., Thaler, C., … Tuschen-Caffier, B. (2019). Efficacy of psychotherapies and pharmacotherapies for bulimia nervosa. *Psychological Medicine, 49*(6), 898–910. doi: 10.1017/S0033291718003525

Svartberg, M., Stiles, T. C., & Seltzer, M. H. (2004). Randomized, controlled trial of the effectiveness of short-term dynamic psychotherapy and cognitive therapy for cluster C personality disorders. *American Journal of Psychiatry, 161,* 810–817.

Svenningsson, P., Westman, E., Ballard, C., & Aarsland, D. (2012). Cognitive impairment in patients with Parkinson's disease: diagnosis, biomarkers, and treatment. *The Lancet Neurology, 11*(8), 697–707.

Svetkey, L. P., Stevens, V. J., Brantley, P. J., Appel, L. J., Hollis, J. F., Loria, C. M., & Aicher, K. (2008). Comparison of strategies for sustaining weight loss: The weight loss maintenance randomized controlled trial. *JAMA: Journal of the American Medical Association, 299*(10), 1139–1148.

Swami, V., Frederick, D. A., Aavik, T., Alcalay, L., Allik, J., Anderson, D., … Zivcic-Becirevic, I. (2010). The attractive female body weight and female body dissatisfaction in 26 countries across 10 world regions: Results of the international body project I. *Personality and Social Psychology Bulletin, 36*(3), 309–325. doi: 10.1177/014616720935970

Swann, A. C., Lafer, B., Perugi, G., Frye, M., Bauer, M., Bahk, W.-M., & Suppes, T. (2013). Bipolar mixed states: An international society for bipolar disorders task force report on symptom structure, course of illness, and diagnosis. *American Journal of Psychiatry, 170*(1), 31–42.

Swanson, S. A., Crow, S. J., Le Grange, D., Swendsen, J., & Merikangas, K. R. (2011). Prevalence and correlates of eating disorders in adolescents. *Archives of General Psychiatry, 68,* 714–723.

Swartz, M. S., Lauriello, J., & Drake, R. E. (2006). Psychosocial therapies. In J. A. Lieberman, T. S. Stroup, & D. O. Perkins (Eds.), *The American Psychiatric Publishing textbook of schizophrenia* (pp. 327–340). Washington, DC: American Psychiatric Publishing.

Swartz, M., Blazer, D., George, L., & Landerman, R. (1986). Somatization disorder in a community population. *American Journal of Psychiatry, 143,* 1403–1408.

Swedo S. E., Leckman J. F., & Rose, N. R. (2012). From research subgroup to clinical syndrome: Modifying the PANDAS criteria to describe PANS (pediatric acute-onset neuropsychiatric syndrome). *Pediatrics & Therapeutics, 2*(2), 1–8. doi: 10.4172/2161-0665.1000113

Swendeman, D., Ramanathan, N., Baetscher, L., Medich, M., Scheffler, A., Comulada, W. S., & Estrin, D. (2015). Smartphone self-monitoring to support self-management among people living with HIV: perceived benefits and theory of change from a mixed-methods randomized pilot study. *JAIDS Journal of Acquired Immune Deficiency Syndromes, 69,* S80–S91.

Sylvers, P., Ryan, S., Alden, S., & Brennan, P. (2009). Biological factors and the development of persistent criminality. In J. Savage (Ed.), *The development of persistent criminality* (pp. 141–162). New York, NY: Oxford University Press.

Syngelaki, E. M., Fairchild, G., Moore, S. C., Savage, J. C., & Goozen, S. H. M. (2013). Fearlessness in juvenile offenders is associated with offending rate. *Developmental Science, 16*(1), 84–90.

Sysko, R., & Wilson, G. T. (2011). Eating disorders. In D. H. Barlow (Ed.), *Handbook of clinical psychology*. (pp. 387–404). New York, NY: Oxford University Press.

Szasz, T. (1961). *The myth of mental illness: Foundations of a theory of personal conduct.* New York, NY: Hoeber-Harper.

Takahasi, T. (1989). Social phobia syndrome in Japan. *Comprehensive Psychiatry, 30,* 45–52.

Takei, N., Lewis, S., Jones, P., Harvey, I., & Murray, R. M. (1996). Prenatal exposure to influenza and increased cerebrospinal fluid spaces in schizophrenia. *Schizophrenia Bulletin, 22,* 521–534.

Talbot, L. S., Stone, S., Gruber, J., Hairston, I. S., Eidelman, P., & Harvey, A. G. (2012). A test of the bidirectional association between sleep and mood in bipolar disorder and insomnia. *Journal of Abnormal Psychology, 121*(1), 39–50.

Tan, E. S. (1980). Transcultural aspects of anxiety. In G. D. Burrows & B. Davies (Eds.), *Handbook of studies on anxiety.* Amsterdam, The Netherlands: Elsevier/North-Holland.

Tandon, R., & Carpenter, W. T. (2012). DSM-5 status of psychotic disorders: 1 year prepublication. *Schizophrenia Bulletin, 38*(3), 369–370. doi: 10.1093/schbul/sbs048

Tandon, R., Gaebel, W., Barch, D. M., Bustillo, J., Gur, R. E., Heckers, S., . . . Van Os, J. (2013). Definition and description of schizophrenia in the DSM-5. *Schizophrenia research, 150*(1), 3–10.

Taneli, T., Guo, Y.-H., & Mushtaq, S. (2015). Internet gaming disorder: Virtual or real? In M. S. Ascher & P. Levounis (Eds.), *The behavioral addictions* (pp. 67–80). Arlington, VA: American Psychiatric Publishing.

Tang, A. L., & Thomas, S. J. (2020). Relationships between depressive symptoms, other psychological symptoms, and quality of life. *Psychiatry Research, 289*. doi: 10.1016/j.psychres.2020.113049.

Tannock, R. (2009a). Mathematics disorder. In B. J. Sadock, V. A. Sadock, & P. Ruiz (Eds.), *Kaplan & Sadock's comprehensive textbook of psychiatry* (9th ed., Vol. II, pp. 3485–3493). Philadelphia, PA: Lippincott Williams & Wilkins.

Tannock, R. (2009b). Reading disorder. In B. J. Sadock, V. A. Sadock, & P. Ruiz (Eds.), *Kaplan & Sadock's comprehensive textbook of psychiatry* (9th ed., Vol. II, pp. 3475–3485). Philadelphia, PA: Lippincott Williams & Wilkins.

Tapert, S. F., & Jacobus, J. (2012). Neurotoxic effects of alcohol in adolescence. *Annual review of clinical psychology, 9*(1).

Tarasoff v. Regents of University of California ("Tarasoff I"), 529 P.2d 553 (Cal. S. Ct. 1974).

Tarasoff v. Regents of University of California ("Tarasoff II"), 551 P.2d 334 (Cal. S. Ct. 1976).

Tarescavage, A. M., Wygant, D. B., Gervais, R. O., & Ben-Porath, Y. S. (2013). Association between the MMPI-2 Restructured Form (MMPI-2-RF) and malingered neurocognitive dysfunction among non-head injury disability claimants. *The Clinical Neuropsychologist, 27*(2), 313–335.

Tarullo, A. R., & Gunnar, M. R. (2006). Child maltreatment and the developing HPA axis. *Hormones and Behavior, 50,* 632–639.

Tau, G. Z., & Peterson, B. S. (2010). Normal development of brain circuits. *Neuropsychopharmacology, 35*(1), 147–168.

Taugher, R. J., Dlouhy, B. J., Kreple, C. J., Ghobbeh, A., Conlon, M. M., Wang, Y., & Wemmie, J. A. (2020). The amygdala differentially regulates defensive behaviors evoked by CO2. *Behavioural Brain Research,377*. doi: 10.1016/j.bbr.2019 .112236

Taylor, D., Gehrman, P., Dautovich, N. D., Lichstein, K. L., & McCrae, C. S. (2014). Causes of Insomnia. In D. Taylor, P. Gehrman, N. D. Dautovich, K. L. Lichstein, & C. S. McCrae (Eds.), *Handbook of Insomnia* (pp. 11–27). New York, NY: Springer.

Taylor, E. (2012). Attention deficit and hyperkinetic disorders in childhood and adolescence. In M. G. Gelder, N. C. Andreasen, J. J. Lopez-Ibor, Jr., & J. R. Geddes (Eds.), *New Oxford textbook of psychiatry* (2nd ed., Vol. 2, pp. 1643–1654). New York, NY: Oxford University Press.

Taylor, G. T., Maloney, S., Dearborn, J., & Weiss, J. (2009). Hormones in the mentally disturbed brain: Steroids and peptides in the development and treatment of psychopathology. *Central Nervous System Agents in Medicinal Chemistry, 9,* 331–360.

Taylor, J., & Lang, A. R. (2006). Psychopathy and substance use disorders. In C. J. Patrick (Ed.), *Handbook of psychopathy* (pp. 495–511). New York, NY: Guilford.

Taylor, R. R., Jason, L. A., Richman, J. A., Torres-Harding, S. R., King, C., & Song, S. (2003). Epidemiology. In L. A. Jason, P. A. Fennell, & R. R. Taylor (Eds.), *Handbook of chronic fatigue syndrome* (pp. 3–25). Hoboken, NJ: Wiley.

Taylor, S. E. (2002). *The tending instinct: How nurturing is essential to who we are and how we live.* New York, NY: Henry Holt.

Taylor, S. E. (2006). Tend and befriend: Biobehavioral bases of affiliation under stress. *Current Directions in Psychological Science, 15*(6), 273–277.

Taylor, S. E. (2009). *Health psychology* (7th ed.). New York, NY: McGraw-Hill.

Taylor, S. E., Klein, L. C., Lewis, B. P., Gruenewald, T. L., Gurung, R. A. R., & Updegraff, J. A. (2000). Biobehavioral responses to stress in females: Tend-and-befriend, not fight- or-flight. *Psychological Review, 107,* 411–429.

Taylor, S. E., Repetti, R. L., & Seeman, T. (1997). Health psychology: What is an unhealthy environment and how does it get under the skin? *Annual Review of Psychology, 48,* 411–447.

Taylor, S., & Asmundson, G. J. G. (2004). *Treating health anxiety: A cognitive behavioral approach.* New York, NY: Guilford.

Taylor, S., & Asmundson, G. J. G. (2009). Hypochondriasis and health anxiety. In M. M. Antony & M. B. Stein (Eds.), *Oxford handbook of anxiety and related disorders* (pp. 525–540). Oxford, UK: Oxford University Press.

Taylor, S., Abramowitz, J. S., McKay, D., & Cuttler, C. (2012). Cognitive approaches to understanding obsessive compulsive and related disorders. In G. Steketee (Ed.), *The Oxford handbook of obsessive compulsive and spectrum disorders* (pp. 233–252). New York, NY: Oxford University Press.

Taylor, S., Asmundson, G., & Coons, M. (2005). Current directions in the treatment of hypochondriasis. *Journal of Cognitive Psychotherapy: An International Quarterly, 19,* 285–304.

Taylor, S., Thordarson, D. S., Jang, K. L., & Asmundson, G. J. (2006). Genetic and environmental origins of health anxiety: A twin study. *World Psychiatry, 5*(1), 47–50.

Tazici, O. (2014). Unipolar mania: A distinct entity. *Journal of Affective Disorders, 152–154,* 52–56.

Teachman, B. A., Joormann, J., Steinman, S. A., & Gotlib, I. H. (2012). Automaticity in anxiety disorders and depressive disorder. *Clinical Psychology Review, 32,* 575–603.

Teasdale, J. D. (1993). Emotion and two kinds of meaning: Cognitive therapy and applied cognitive science. *Behaviour Research and Therapy, 31*(4), 339–354.

Teasdale, J. D., Scott, J., Moore, R. G., Hayhurst, H., Pope, M., & Paykel, E. S. (2001). How does cognitive therapy prevent relapse in residual depression? Evidence from a controlled trial. *Journal of Consulting and Clinical Psychology, 69,* 347–357.

Teasdale, J. D., Segal, Z. V., Williams, J. M., Ridgeway, V. A., Soulsby, J. M., & Lau, M. A. (2000). Prevention of relapse/recurrence in major depression by mindfulness-based cognitive therapy. *Journal of Consulting and Clinical Psychology, 4,* 615–623.

Teh, C. F., Zaslavsky, A. M., Reynolds, C. F., & Cleary, P. D. (2009). Effect of depression treatment on chronic pain outcomes. *Psychosomatic Medicine, 72,* 61–67.

Teicher, M. H., Glod, C., & Cole, J. O. (1990). Emergence of intense suicidal preoccupation during fluoxetine treatment. *American Journal of Psychiatry, 147*(1), 207–210.

Telch, C. F., & Agras, W. S. (1993). The effects of a very low calorie diet on binge eating. *Behavior Therapy, 24,* 177–193.

Telch, M. J., Lucas, J. A., & Nelson, P. (1989). Nonclinical panic in college students: An investigation of prevalence and symptomatology. *Journal of Abnormal Psychology, 98,* 300–306.

Telch, M. J., Rosenfield, D., Lee, H.-J., & Pai, A. (2012). Emotional reactivity to a single inhalation of 35% carbon dioxide and its association with later symptoms of posttraumtic stress disorders and anxiety n soldiers deployed to Iraq. *Archives of General Psychiatry, 69,* 1161–1168.

Temes, C. M., Magni, L. R., Aguirre, B. A., Goodman, M., Ridolfi, M. E., & Zanarini, M. C. (2020). Parameters of reported childhood sexual abuse and assault in adolescents and adults with borderline personality disorder. *Personality and Mental Health, 14*(3), 254–262.

Temoshok, L. R., Wald, R. L., Synowski, S., & Garzino-Demo, A. (2008). Coping as a multisystem construct associated with pathways mediating HIV-relevant immune function and disease progression. *Psychosomatic Medicine, 70,* 555–561.

Temple, E., Deutsch, G. K., Poldrack, R. A., Miller, S. L., Tallal, P., Merzenich, M. M., & Gabrieli, J. D. (2003). Neural deficits in children with dyslexia ameliorated by behavioral remediation: Evidence from functional MRI. *Proceedings of the National Academy of Sciences, 100*(5), 2860-2865.

Temple, E., Deutisch, G. K., Poldrack, R. A., Miller, S. L., Tallal, P., Merzenich, M. M., & Gabrieli, J. (2003). Neural deficits in children with dyslexia ameliorated by behavioral remediation: Evidence from functional MRI. *Proceedings of the National Academy of Sciences, 100,* 2860–2865.

Tenhula, W. N., Bellack, A. S., & Drake, R. E. (2009). Schizophrenia: Psychosocial approaches. In B. J. Sadock, V. A. Sadock, & P. Ruiz (Eds.), *Kaplan & Sadock's comprehensive textbook of psychiatry* (9th ed., Vol. I, pp. 1557–1572). Philadelphia, PA: Lippincott Williams & Wilkins.

Teodoro, T., & Afonso, P. (2020). Culture-bound syndromes and cultural concepts of distress in psychiatry. *Revista Portuguesa de Psiquiatria e Saúde Mental, 6*(3), 118–126.

ter Kuile, M. M., Melles, R., de Groot, H. E., Tuijnman-Raasveld, C. C., & van Lankveld, J. J. (2013). Therapist-aided exposure for women with lifelong vaginismus: A randomized waiting-list control trial of efficacy. *Journal of Consulting and Clinical Psychology, 81*(6), 1127–1136.

ter Kuile, M., van Lankveld, J., Jacques, J., de Groot, E., Melles, R., Neffs, J., & Zanbergen, M. (2007). Cognitive-behavioral therapy for women with lifelong vaginismus: Process and prognostic factors. *Behaviour Research and Therapy, 45,* 359–373.

Teri, L., Gibbons, L. E., McCurry, S. M., Logsdon, R. G., Buchner, D. M., Barlow, W. E., & Larson, E. B. (2003). Exercise plus behavioral management in patients with Alzheimer disease: A randomized controlled trial. *JAMA: Journal of the American Medical Association, 290*(15), 2015–2022.

Terman, J. S., Terman, M., Lo, E., & Cooper, T. B. (2001). Circadian time of morning light administration and therapeutic response in winter depression. *Archives of General Psychiatry, 58,* 69–75.

Terman, M., Terman, J. S., & Ross, D. C. (1998). A controlled trial of timed bright light and negative air ionization of treatment of winter depression. *Archives of General Psychiatry, 55,* 875–882.

Testad, I., Ballard, C., Brønnick, K., & Aarsland, D. (2010). The effect of staff training on agitation and use of restraint in nursing home residents with dementia: A single-blind, randomized controlled trial. *The Journal of Clinical Psychiatry, 71*(1), 80.

Teti, D. M., & Crosby, B. (2012). Maternal depressive symptoms, dysfunctional cognitions, and infant night waking: The role of maternal nighttime behavior. *Child Development, 83*(3), 939–953. doi: 10.1111/j.1467-8624.2012.01760.x

Tetrault, J. M., Holt, S. R., Cavallo, D. A., O'Connor, P. G., Gordon, M. A., Corvino, J. K., … Carroll, K. M. (2020). Computerized cognitive behavioral therapy for substance use disorders in a specialized primary care practice: A randomized feasibility trial to address the RT component of SBIRT. *Journal of Addiction Medicine, 14*(6), e303–e309.

Thaker, G. K., & Avila, M. (2003). Schizophrenia, V: Risk markers. *American Journal of Psychiatry, 160,* 1578.

Thapar, A., & McGuffin, P. (2009). Quantitative genetics. In M. G. Gelder, N. C. Andreasen, J. J. Lopez-Ibor, Jr., & J. R. Geddes (Eds.), *New Oxford textbook of psychiatry* (2nd ed., Vol. 1, pp. 212–221). Oxford, UK: Oxford University Press.

Thase, M. E. (1990). Relapse and recurrence in unipolar major depression: Short-term and long-term approaches. *Journal of Clinical Psychiatry, 51*(Suppl. 6), 51–57.

Thase, M. E. (2005). Major depressive disorder. In F. Andrasik (Ed.), *Comprehensive handbook of personality and psychopathology. Volume 2: Adult psychopathology* (pp. 207–230). New York, NY: Wiley.

Thase, M. E. (2009). Neurobiological aspects of depression. In I. H. Gotlib & C. L. Hammen (Eds.), *Handbook of depression* (2nd ed., pp. 187–217). New York, NY: Guilford.

Thase, M. E., & Denko, T. (2008). Pharmacotherapy of mood disorders. *Annual Review of Clinical Psychology, 4,* 53–91.

Thase, M. E., & Kupfer, D. J. (1996). Recent developments in the pharmacotherapy of mood disorders. *Journal of Consulting and Clinical Psychology, 64,* 646–659.

Thase, M. E., Simons, A. D., & Reynolds, C. F., III. (1996). Abnormal electroencephalographic sleep profiles in major depression. *Archives of General Psychiatry, 53,* 99–108.

Thayer, J. F., Friedman, B. H., & Borkovec, T. D. (1996). Autonomic characteristics of generalized anxiety disorder and worry. *Biological Psychiatry, 39,* 255–266.

The Evolving Insanity Defense. (2006). *ABA Journal, 92,* 37.

The Oregon Research Institute. (2013). *eBody Project.* Retrieved from https://www.ebodyproject.org/

Thibodeau, M. A., Welch, P. G., Sareen, J., & Asmundson, G. L. G. (2013). Anxiety disorders are independently associated with suicide ideation and attempts: Propensity score matching in two epidemiological samples. *Depression and Anxiety, 30,* 947–954.

Thirthalli, J., & Rajkumar, R. P. (2009). Statistical versus clinical significance in psychiatric research—An overview for beginners. *Asian Journal of Psychiatry, 2*(2), 74–79.

Thomas, C. R. (2009). Oppositional defiant disorder and conduct disorder. In M. K. Dulcan (Ed.), *Dulcan's textbook of child and adolescent psychiatry* (pp. 223–239). Arlington, VA: American Psychiatric Publishing.

Thompson v. County of Alameda, 614 P.2d 728 (Cal. S. Ct. 1980).

Thompson, J. K., & Kinder, B. (2003). Eating disorders. In M. Hersen & S. Turner (Eds.), *Handbook of adult psychopathology* (4th ed., pp. 555–582). New York, NY: Plenum.

Thompson, J. K., & Stice, E. (2001). Thin-idea internalization: Mounting evidence for a new risk factor for body-image disturbance and eating pathology. *Current Directions in Psychological Science, 11,* 181–183.

Thompson, J. R., Bradley, V. J., Buntinx, W. H. E., Schalock, R. L., Shogren, K. A., Snell, M. E., & Yeager, M. (2009). Conceptualizing supports and the support needs of people with intellectual disability. *Intellectual and Developmental Disabilities, 47*(2), 135–146.

Thompson, M. A., Aberg, J. A., Cahn, P., Montaner, J. S. G., Rizzardini, G., Telenti, A., & Schooley, R. T. (2010). Antiretroviral treatment of adult HIV infection. *JAMA: Journal of the American Medical Association, 304,* 321–333.

Thompson, M. A., Mugavero, M. J., Amico, K. R., Cargill, V. A., Chang, L. W., Gross, R., & Nachega, J. B. (2012). Guidelines for improving entry into and retention in care and antiretroviral adherence for persons with HIV: Evidence-based recommendations from an International Association of Physicians in AIDS Care panel. *Annals of Internal Medicine, 156*(11), 817–833, W-284–W-294.

Thompson, P. M., Jahanshad, N., Ching, C. R. K., Salminen, L. E., Thomopoulos, S. I., Bright, J., Baune, B. T., Bertolín, S., Bralten, J., Bruin, W. B., Bülow, R., Chen, J., Chye, Y., Dannlowski, U., de Kovel. C. G. F., Donohoe, G., Eyler, L. T., Faraone, S. V., Favre, P., … ENIGMA Consortium. (2020). ENIGMA and global neuroscience: A decade of large-scale studies of the brain in health and disease across more than 40 countries. *Translational Psychiatry,10*(1),100

Thompson-Brenner, H., Boisseau, C. L., & St. Paul, M. S. (2011). Representations of ideal figure-size in *Ebony* magazine: A content analysis. *Body Image, 8*(4), 373–378.

Thompson-Brenner, H., Glass, S., & Westen, D. (2003). A multidimensional meta-analysis of psychotherapy for bulimia nervosa. *Clinical Psychology: Science and Practice, 10*, 269–287.

Thoresen, C. E., & Powell, L. H. (1992). Type A behavior pattern: New perspectives on theory, assessment and intervention. Special issue: Behavioral medicine: An update for the 1990s. *Journal of Consulting and Clinical Psychology, 60*(4), 595–604.

Thorlton, J., Colby, D. A., & Devine, P. (2014). Proposed actions for the US Food and Drug Administration to implement to minimize adverse effects associated with energy drink consumption. *American Journal of Public Health, 104*(7), 1175–1180.

Thorndike, A. N., Riis, J., Sonnenberg, L. M., & Levy, D. E. (2014). Traffic-light labels and choice architecture: promoting healthy food choices. *American journal of Preventive Medicine, 46*(2), 143–149.

Thorndike, A. N., Sonnenberg, L., Riis, J., Barraclough, S., & Levy, D. E. (2012). A 2-phase labeling and choice architecture intervention to improve healthy food and beverage choices. *American Journal of Public Health, 102*(3), 527–533.

Thornton, L. M., Mazzeo, S. E., & Bulik, C. M. (2010). The heritability of eating disorders: Methods and current findings. *Current Topics in Behavioral Neurosciences, 6*, 141–156. doi. org/10.1007/7854_2010_91

Thornton, V. A., Dodd, C. G., & Weed, N. C. (2020). Assessment of prescription stimulant misuse among college students using the MMPI-2-RF. *Addictive Behaviors, 110*, 106511.

Thorpe, G. L., & Burns, L. E. (1983). *The agoraphobic syndrome.* New York, NY: Wiley.

Thorson, J., & Öberg, P. (2003). Was there a suicide epidemic after Goethe's *Werther*? *Archives of Suicide Research, 7*(1), 69–72. doi: 10.1080/13811110301568

Thurston, R. C., & Kubzansky, L. D. (2009). Women, loneliness, and incident coronary heart disease. *Psychosomatic Medicine, 71*(8), 836–842.

Thurstone, C., & Kaminer, Y. (2020). Youth cannabis use. In Y. Kaminer & K. C. Winters (Eds.), *Clinical manual of youth addictive disorders* (pp. 175–201). Washington, D.C.: American Psychiatric Association Publishing.

Thyer, B. A. (1993). Childhood separation anxiety disorder and adult-onset agoraphobia: Review of evidence. In C. Last (Ed.), *Anxiety across the lifespan: A developmental perspective* (pp. 128–145). New York, NY: Springer.

Tienari, P. (1991). Interaction between genetic vulnerability and family environment: The Finnish adoptive family study of schizophrenia. *Acta Psychiatrica Scandinavica, 84*, 460–465.

Tienari, P., Wahlberg, K.-E., & Wynne, L. C. (2006). Finnish adoption study of schizophrenia: Implications for family interventions. *Families, Systems & Health, 24*, 442–451.

Tienari, P., Wynne, L. C., Laksy, K., Moring, J., Nieminen, P., Sorri, A., & Wahlberg, K. E. (2003). Genetic boundaries of the schizophrenia spectrum: Evidence from the Finnish adoptive family study of schizophrenia. *American Journal of Psychiatry, 160*, 1567–1594.

Tienari, P., Wynne, L. C., Moring, J., Lahti, I., Naarala, M., Sorri, A., & Moring, J. (1994). The Finnish adoptive family study of schizophrenia: Implications for family research. *British Journal of Psychiatry, 23*(Suppl. 164), 20–26.

Tiggemann, M. (2002). Media influences on body image development. In T. F. Cash & T. Pruzinsky (Eds.), *Body image: A handbook of theory, research and clinical practice* (pp. 91–98). New York, NY: Guilford.

Tiggemann, M., & Lynch, J. E. (2001). Body image across the life span in adult women: The role of self-objectification. *Developmental Psychology*, *37*, 243–253.

Timimi, S., & Taylor, E. (2004). ADHD is best understood as a cultural construct. *British Journal of Psychiatry, 184*, 8–9.

Timlett, A. (2013). Controlling bizarre delusions. *Schizophrenia Bulletin, 39*(2), 244–246. doi: 10.1093/schbul/sbs137

Tinbergen, E. A., & Tinbergen, N. (1972). *Early childhood autism: An ethological approach.* Berlin, Germany: Parey.

Tingelstad, J. B. (1991). The cardiotoxicity of the tricyclics. *Journal of the American Academy of Child and Adolescent Psychiatry, 30*, 845–846.

Tishelman, A. C., Kaufman, R., Edwards-Leeper, L., Mandel, F. H., Shumer, D. E., & Spack, N. P. (2015). Serving transgender youth: Challenges, dilemmas, and clinical examples. *Professional Psychology: Research and Practice, 46*(1), 37–45.

Tishler, C. L., Reiss, N. S., & Rhodes, A. R. (2007). Suicidal behavior in children younger than twelve: A diagnostic challenge for emergency department personnel. *Academic Emergency Medicine, 14*(9), 810–818.

Tjio, J. H., & Levan, A. (1956). The chromosome number of man. *Hereditas, 42*, 1–6.

Tober, D. M., & Budiani, D. (2014). Introduction: Why Islam health and body? *Body and Society, 13*(3), 1–13.

Todaro, J. F., Shen, B., Raffa, S. D., Tilkemeier, P. L., & Niaura, R. (2007). Prevalence of anxiety disorders in men and women with established coronary heart disease. *Journal of Cardiopulmonary Rehabilitation and Prevention, 27*, 86–91.

Todd, W. D. (2020). Potential pathways for circadian dysfunction and sundowning-related behavioral aggression in Alzheimer's disease and related dementias. *Frontiers in Neuroscience, 14*, 910.

Toledo-Fernández, A., Marín-Navarrete, R., Villalobos-Gallegos, L., Salvador-Cruz, J., Benjet, C., & Roncero, C. (2020). Exploring the prevalence of substance-induced neurocognitive disorder among polysubstance users, adding subjective and objective evidence of cognitive impairment. *Psychiatry Research, 288*, 112944.

Tolin, D. F. (2011). Challenges and advances in treating hoarding. *Journal of Clinical Psychology, 67*, 451–455. doi: 10.1002/jclp.20796

Tolin, D. F., Frost, R. O., Steketee, G., & Muroff, J. (2015). Cognitive behavioral therapy for hoarding disorder: A meta-analysis. *Depression and Anxiety, 32*, 158–166.

Tolin, D. F., Stevens, M. C., Villavicencio, A. L., Norberg, M. M., Calhoun, V. D., Frost, R. O., & Pearlson, G. D. (2012). Neural mechanisms of decision making in hoarding disorder. *Archives of General Psychiatry, 69*, 832–841. doi: 10.1001 /archgenpsychiatry.2011.1980

Tomarken, A., & Keener, A. (1998). Frontal brain asymmetry and depression: A self-regulatory perspective. *Cognition and Emotion, 12*, 387–420.

Tomarken, A., Dichter, G., Garber, J., & Simien, C. (2004). Relative left frontal hypo- activation in adolescents at risk for depression. *Biological Psychology, 67*, 77–102.

Tomenson, B., McBeth, J., Chew-Graham, C. A., MacFarlane, G., Davies, I., Jackson, J., & Creed, F. H. (2012). Somatization and health anxiety as predictors of health care use. *Psychosomatic Medicine, 74*(6), 656–664. doi: 10.1097/PSY.0b013e31825cb140

Tondo, L., Jamison, K. R., & Baldessarini, R. J. (1997). Effect of lithium maintenance on suicidal behavior in major mood disorders. In D. M. Stoff & J. J. Mann (Eds.), *The neurobiology of suicide: From the bench to the clinic* (Vol. 836, pp. 339–351). New York, NY: Academy of Sciences.

Toomey, R., Faraone, S. V., Simpson, J. C., & Tsuang, M. T. (1998). Negative, positive, and disorganized symptom dimensions in schizophrenia, major depression, and bipolar disorder. *Journal of Nervous and Mental Disorders, 186,* 470–476.

Topiwala, A., Allan, C. L., Valkanova, V., Zsoldos, E., Filippini, N., Sexton, C., ... Mackay, C. E. (2017). Moderate alcohol consumption as risk factor for adverse brain outcomes and cognitive decline: Longitudinal cohort study. *British Medical Journal, 357,* 2353.

Torales, J., González, I., Castaldelli-Maia, J. M., & Ventriglio, A. (2020). Kleptomania as a neglected disorder in psychiatry. *International Review of Psychiatry, 32*(5–6), 451–454.

Torgersen, S. (1986). Genetics of somatoform disorder. *Archives of General Psychiatry, 43,* 502–505.

Torgersen, S. (2012). Epidemiology. In T. A. Widiger (Ed.), *The Oxford handbook of personality disorders* (pp. 186–205). New York, NY: Oxford University Press.

Torrey, E., Eslinger, S., Lamb, R., & Pavle, J. (2010). *More mentally ill persons are in jails and prisons than hospitals: A survey of the states.* Arlington, VA: Treatment Advocacy Center.

Tortorella, A., Fabrazzo, M., Monteleone, A. M., Steardo, L., & Monteleone, P. (2014). The role of drug therapies in the treatment of anorexia and bulimia nervosa: a review of the literature. *Journal of Psychopathology, 20,* 50–65.

Toth, K., de Lacy, N., & King, B. H. (2016). Intelectual disability. In M. K. Dulcan (Ed.), *Dulcan's Textbook of Child and Adolescent Psychiatry* (2nd ed., pp. 105–133). Arlington, VA: American Psychiatric Publishing.

Toth, S. L., Harris, L. S., Goodman, G. S., & Cicchetti, D. (2011). Influence of violence and aggression on children's psychological development: Trauma, attachment, and memory. In P. R. Shaver & M. Mikulincer (Eds.), *Human aggression and violence: Causes, manifestations, and consequences* (pp. 351–365). Washington, DC: American Psychological Association. doi: 10.1037/12346-019

Townsend, J. M., & Wasserman, T. H. (2011). Sexual hookups among college students: Sex differences in emotional reactions. *Archives of Sexual Behavior, 40*(6), 1173–1181.

Trace, S. E., Baker, J. H., Penas-Lledo, E., & Bulik, C. M. (2013). The genetics of eating disorders. Annu Rev Clin Psychol. 9:589–620. doi: 10.1146/annurev-clinpsy-050212-185546.

Tracey, S. A., Chorpita, B. F., Douban, J., & Barlow, D. H. (1997). Empirical evaluation of DSM-IV generalized anxiety disorder criteria in children and adolescents. *Journal of Clinical Child Psychology, 26,* 404–414.

Trauer, J. M., Qian, M. Y., Doyle, J. S., Rajaratnam, S. M., & Cunnington, D. (2015). Cognitive Behavioral Therapy for Chronic Insomnia: A Systematic Review and Meta-analysis. *Annals of Internal Medicine, 163*(3), 191–204.

Treasure, J., Duarte, T. A., & Schmidt, U. (2020). Eating disorders. *The Lancet, 395*(10227), 899–911. doi: 10.1016/S0140-6736(20)30059-

Treasure, J., Duarte, T. A., & Schmidt, U. (2020). Eating disorders. *The Lancet, 395*(10227), 899–911. doi: 10.1016/S0140-6736(20)30059-3

Treatment for Adolescents with Depression Study Team (TADS). (2004). Fluoxetine, cognitive-behavioral therapy, and their combination for adolescents with depression. *JAMA: Journal of the American Medical Association, 292,* 807–820.

Treatment for Adolescents with Depression Study Team. (2009). The Treatment for Adolescents with Depression Study (TADS): Outcomes over 1 year of naturalistic follow-up. *American Journal of Psychiatry, 166,* 1141–1149.

Tremblay, M., Baydala, L., Khan, M., Currie, C., Morley, K., Burkholder, C., ... Stillar, A. (2020). Primary substance use prevention programs for children and youth: A systematic review. *Pediatrics, 146*(3).

Tremont, G., Davis, J. D., Papandonatos, G. D., Ott, B. R., Fortinsky, R. H., Gozalo, P., ... Bishop, D. S. (2015). Psychosocial telephone intervention for dementia caregivers: A randomized, controlled trial. *Alzheimer's & Dementia, 11*(5), 541–548.

Triebwasser, J., Chemerinski, E., Roussos, P., & Siever, L. J. (2012). Schizoid personality disorder. *Journal of Personality Disorders, 26*(6), 919–926.

Triebwasser, J., Chemerinski, E., Roussos, P., & Siever, L. J. (2013). Paranoid personality disorder. *Journal of Personality Disorders, 27*(6), 795–805.

Trinh, N., Hoblyn, J., Mohanty, S., & Yaffe, K. (2003). Efficacy of cholinesterase inhibitors in the treatment of neuropsychiatric symptoms and functional impairment in Alzheimer disease: A meta-analysis. *JAMA, 289*(2), 210–216. doi: 10.1001/jama.289.2.210

Trivedi, M., Rush, A., Wisniewski, S., Nierenberg, A., Warden, D., Ritz, L., & STAR*D Study Team. (2006). Evaluation of outcomes with citalopram for depression using measurement-based care in STAR *D: Implications for clinical practice. *American Journal of Psychiatry, 163,* 28–40.

True, W. R., Rice, J., Eisen, S. A., Heath, A. C., Goldberg, J., Lyons, M. J., & Nowak, J. (1993). A twin study of genetic and environmental contributions to liability for posttraumatic stress symptoms. *Archives of General Psychiatry, 50,* 257–264.

Trull, T. J., Scheiderer, E. M., & Tomko, R. L. (2012). Axis II comorbidity. In T. A. Widiger (Ed.), *The Oxford handbook of personality disorders* (pp. 566–581). New York, NY: Oxford University Press.

Trull, T. J., Carpenter, R. W., & Widiger, T. A. (2013). Personality disorders. In I. B. Weiner (Series Ed.), G. Stricker, & T. A. Widiger (Vol. Eds.), *Handbook of psychology: Vol. 8 Clinical psychology* (pp. 94–120). Hoboken, NJ: John Wiley & Sons.

Truong, T., Liquet, B., Menegaux, F., Plancoulaine, S., Laurent-Puig, P., Mulot, C., ... Guénel, P. (2014). Breast cancer risk, nightwork, and circadian clock gene polymorphisms. *Endocrine-related cancer, 21*(4), 629–638.

Tsai, A. C., Lucas, M., & Kawachi, I. (2015). Association between social integration and suicide among women in the United States. *JAMA Psychiatry, 72,* 987.

Tsai, G. E., Condie, D., Wu, M. T., & Chang, I. W. (1999). Functional magnetic resonance imaging of personality switches in a woman with dissociative identity disorder. *Harvard Review of Psychiatry, 7*(2), 119–122.

Tsao, J. C. I., Mystkowski, J. L., Zucker, B. G., & Craske, M. G. (2002). Effects of cognitive-behavioral therapy for panic disorder on comorbid conditions: Replication and extension. *Behavior Therapy, 33,* 493–509.

Tsuang, M. T., Stone, W. S., & Faraone, S. V. (2012). Schizoaffective and schizotypal disorders. In M. G. Gelder, N. C. Andreasen, J. J. Lopez-Ibor, Jr., & J. R. Geddes (Eds.), *New Oxford textbook of psychiatry* (2nd ed., Vol. 1, pp. 595–602). New York, NY: Oxford University Press.

Tuchman, B. (1978). *A distant mirror.* New York, NY: Ballantine Books.

Tucker, J. A., Murphy, J. G., & Kertesz, S. G. (2011). Substance use disorders. In M. Antony & D. H. Barlow (Eds.), *Handbook of assessment and treatment planning for psychological disorders* (2nd ed.). New York, NY: Guilford.

Tunnell, N. C., Ritz, T., Wilhelm, F. H., Roth, W. T., & Meuret, A. E. (2021). Habituation or normalization? Experiential and respiratory recovery from voluntary hyperventilation in treated versus untreated patients with panic disorder. *Behavior Therapy, 52*(1), 124–135. doi: 10.1016/j.beth.2020.03.003

Turk, D. C., & Monarch, E. S. (2002). Biopsychosocial perspective on chronic pain. In D. C. Turk & R. J. Gatchel (Eds.),

Psychological approaches to pain management: A practitioner's handbook (2nd ed., pp. 3–29). New York, NY: Guilford.

Turkheimer, E. (1998). Heritability and biological explanation. *Psychological Review, 105,* 782–791.

Turkheimer, E., Haley, A., Waldron, M., D'Onofrio, B., & Gottesman, I. I. (2003). Socioeconomic status modifies heritability of IQ in young children. *Psychological Science, 14,* 623–628.

Turner, C., Spinks, A., McClure, R., & Nixon, J. (2004). Community-based interventions for the prevention of burns and scalds in children. *Cochrane Database Syst. Rev.* 3:CD004335

Turner, J., Mancl, L., & Aaron, L. (2006). Short- and long-term efficacy of brief cognitive behavioral therapy for patients with chronic temporomandibular disorder pain: A randomized, controlled trial. *Pain, 121,* 181–194.

Turner, S. M., Beidel, D. C., & Jacob, R. G. (1994). Social phobia: A comparison of behavior therapy and atenolol. *Journal of Consulting Psychology, 62,* 350–358.

Tushnet, M. (2008). Who qualifies for rights? [Review of the book *Homelessness, mental illness and civil commitment]. The Journal of Politics, 66*(02), 626–628.

Twenge, J. M., Sherman, R. A., & Wells, B. E. (2015). Changes in American adults' sexual behavior and attitudes, 1972–2012. *Archives of Sexual Behavior, 44(8), 2273–2285.* doi: 10.1007/s10508-015-0540-2

Tye, C., Mcewen, F. S., Liang, H., Underwood, L., Woodhouse, E., Barker, E. D., … Group, T. S. S. (2020). Long-term cognitive outcomes in tuberous sclerosis complex. *Developmental Medicine & Child Neurology, 62*(3), 322–329.

Tyler, D. B. (1955). Psychological changes during experimental sleep deprivation. *Diseases of the Nervous System, 16,* 293–299.

Tylš, F., Páleníček, T., & Horáček, J. (2014). Psilocybin–summary of knowledge and new perspectives. *European Neuropsychopharmacology, 24*(3), 342–356.

Tynes, L. L., White, K., & Steketee, G. S. (1990). Toward a new nosology of obsessive-compulsive disorder. *Comprehensive Psychiatry, 31,* 465–480.

U.S. Department of Education, National Center for Education Statistics. (2012). *Digest of education statistics, 2011*(NCES 2012-001).

U.S. Department of Energy Office of Science. (2009). *Human genome project information.* Retrieved from http://www.ornl.gov/sci/techresources/Human_Genome/home.shtml

U.S. Department of Health and Human Services. (1991). *Health and behavior research.* National Institutes of Health: Report to Congress.

U.S. Department of Health and Human Services. (2014). *The health consequences of smoking: 50 years of progress. A report of the Surgeon General.* Atlanta, GA: U.S. Department of Health and Human Services, Centers for Disease Control and Prevention, National Center for Chronic Disease Prevention and Health Promotion, Office on Smoking and Health.

U.S. Department of Health and Human Services. The Health Consequences of Smoking—50 Years of Progress: A Report of the Surgeon General. Atlanta, GA: U.S. Department of Health and Human Services, Centers for Disease Control and Prevention, National Center for Chronic Disease Prevention and Health Promotion, Office on Smoking and Health, 2014. http://www.surgeongeneral.gov/library/reports/50-years-of-progress/exec-summary.pdf

U.S. General Accounting Office. (1995). *Prescription drugs and the elderly: Many still receive potentially harmful drugs despite recent improvements.* (GOA/HEHS-95-152). United States General Accounting Office: Report to Congress.

Uchino, B. N. (2009). Understanding the link between social support and physical health: A life-span perspective with emphasis on the separability of perceived and received support. *Perspectives on Psychological Science, 4,* 236–255.

Uddin, M. S., Rahman, M. M., Jakaria, M., Rahman, M. S., Hossain, M. S., Islam, A., … Barreto, G. E. (2020). Estrogen signaling in Alzheimer's disease: Molecular insights and therapeutic targets for Alzheimer's dementia. *Molecular Neurobiology, 57*(6), 2654–2670.

Uddin, M., Amstadter, A. B., Nugent, N. R., & Koenen, K. C. (2012). Genetics and genomics of posttraumatic stress disorder. In J. G. Beck & D. M. Sloan (Eds.), *The Oxford handbook of traumatic stress disorders* (pp. 143–158). New York, NY: Oxford University Press.

Uebelacker, L., & Whisman, M. (2006). Moderators of the association between relationship discord and major depression in a national population-based sample. *Journal of Family Psychology, 20,* 40–46.

Uehara, T., Yamasaki, T., Okamoto, T., Koike, T., Kan, S., Miyauchi, S., & Tobimatsu, S. (2013). Efficiency of a "small-world" brain network depends on consciousness level: A resting-state fMRI study. *Cerebral Cortex*. doi: 10.1093/cercor/bht004

Uhde, T. (1994). The anxiety disorder: Phenomenology and treatment of core symptoms and associated sleep disturbance. In M. Kryger, T. Roth, & W. Dement (Eds.), *Principles and practice of sleep medicine* (pp. 871–898). Philadelphia, PA: Saunders.

Uher, R. (2011). Gene-enviroment interactions. In K. S. Kendler, S. Jaffee, & D. Romer (Eds.), *The dynamic genome and mental health: The role of genes and environments in youth development* (pp. 29–58). New York, NY: Oxford University Press.

Uleman, J. S., Saribay, S. A., & Gonzalez, C. M. (2008). Spontaneous inferences, implicit impressions, and implicit theories. *Annual Review of Psychology, 59,* 329–360.

Umberger, W., & Gaddis, L. (2020). The science of addiction through the lens of opioid treatment for chronic noncancer pain. *Pain Management Nursing, 21*(1), 57–64.

UNAIDS. (2009). *AIDS epidemic update 2009.* Geneva: Joint United Nations Programme on HIV/AIDS (UNAIDS). Retrieved from http://www.who.int/hiv/pub/epidemiology/epidemic/en/index.html

Unger, J. B., Yan, L., Chen, X., Jiang, X., Azen, S., Qian, G., & Johnson, C. (2001). Adolescent smoking in Wuhan, China: Baseline data from the Wuhan Smoking Prevention Trial. *American Journal of Preventive Medicine, 21*(3), 162–169.

Unutzer, J., Katon, W., Callahan, C. M., Williams, J. W., Hunkeler, E., Harpole, L., & Langston, C. (2002). Collaborative care management of late-life depression in the primary care setting: A randomized controlled trial. *JAMA: Journal of the American Medical Association, 288,* 2836–2845.

Urbina, S. (2014). *Essentials of psychological testing.* Hoboken, NJ: John Wiley & Sons.

Ursano, R. J., Sonnenberg, S. M., & Lazar, S. G. (2008). Psychodynamic psychotherapy. In R. E. Hales, S. C. Yudofsky, & G. O. Gabbard (Eds.), *The American Psychiatric Publishing textbook of psychiatry* (5th ed., pp. 1171–1190). Arlington, VA: American Psychiatric Publishing.

Ussher, J. M. (2013). Diagnosing difficult women and pathologising femininity: Gender bias in psychiatric nosology. *Feminism & Psychology, 23*(1), 63–69.

Vachon, D. D., Lynam, D. R., Widiger, T. A., Miller, J. D., McCrae, R. R., & Costa, P. T. (2013). Basic Traits Predict the Prevalence of Personality Disorder Across the Life Span The Example of Psychopathy. *Psychological Science, 24*(5), 698–705.

Vahia, I. V., & Cohen, C. I. (2009). Schizophrenia and delusional disorders. In B. J. Sadock, V. A. Sadock, & P. Ruiz (Eds.), *Kaplan &*

Sadock's comprehensive textbook of psychiatry (9th ed., Vol. II, pp. 4073–4081). Philadelphia, PA: Lippincott Williams & Wilkins.
Vaillant, G. E. (1979). Natural history of male psychological health. *New England Journal of Medicine, 301,* 1249–1254.
Vaillant, G. E. (1992). *Ego mechanisms of defense: A guide for clinicians and researchers.* Washington, D.C.: American Psychiatric Press.
Vaillant, G. E. (2012). Lifting the field's "repression" of defenses. *American Journal of Psychiatry, 169*(9), 885–887.
Valchev, V. H., Nel, J. A., Van de Vijver, F. J., Meiring, D., De Bruin, G. P., & Rothmann, S. (2013). Similarities and differences in implicit personality concepts across Ethnocultural groups in South Africa. *Journal of Cross-Cultural Psychology, 44*(3), 365–388.
Valera, E. M., Faraone, S. V., Murray, K. E., & Seidman, L. J. (2007). Meta-analysis of structural imaging findings in attention-deficit/hyperactivity disorder. *Biological Psychiatry, 61,* 1361–1369.
Vallabh, S. M., Minikel, E. V., Williams, V. J., Carlyle, B. C., McManus, A. J., Wennick, C. D., … Nobuhara, C. K. (2020). Cerebrospinal fluid and plasma biomarkers in individuals at risk for genetic prion disease. *BMC Medicine, 18*(1), 1–12.
Valles-Colomer, M., Falony, G., Darzi, Y., Tigchelaar, E. F., Wang, J., Tito, R. Y., … Raes, J. (2019). The neuroactive potential of the human gut microbiota in quality of life and depression. *Nature Microbiology, 4*(4), 623–632.
Valtonen, H. M., Suominen, K., Mantere, O., Leppämäki, S., Arvilommi, P., & Isometsä, E. (2007). Suicidal behaviour during different phases of bipolar disorder. *Journal of Affective Disorders, 97,* 101–107.
Van Ameringen, M., Mancini, C., Patterson, B., & Simpson, W. (2009). Pharmacotherapy for social anxiety disorder: An update. *The Israel Journal of Psychiatry and Related Sciences, 46*(1), 53–61.
van Amsterdam, J., & van den Brink, W. (2013). Reduced-risk drinking as a viable treatment goal in problematic alcohol use and alcohol dependence. *Journal of Psychopharmacology, 27*(11), 987–997.
van Beijsterveldt, C., Hudziak, J., & Boomsma, D. (2006). Genetic and environmental influences on cross-gender behavior and relation to behavior problems: A study of Dutch twins at ages 7 and 10 years. *Archives of Sexual Behavior, 35,* 647–658.
Van den Bergh, O., Witthöft, M., Petersen, S., & Brown, R. (2017). Symptoms and the body: Taking the inferential leap. *Neuroscience & Biobehavioral Reviews.* https://doi.org/10.1016/j.neubiorev.2017.01.015
van der Hart, O., & Nijenhuis, E. R. S. (2009). Dissociative disorders. In P. H. Blaney & T. Millon (Eds.), *Oxford textbook of psychopathology* (2nd ed., pp. 452–481). New York, NY: Oxford University Press.
van der Kloet, D., Giesbrecht, T., Lynn, S. J., Merckelbach, H., & de Zutter, A. (2012). Sleep normalization and decrease in dissociative experiences: Evaluation in an inpatient sample. *Journal of Abnormal Psychology, 121,* 140–150. doi: 10.1037/a0024781
van der Wal, S. J., Vermetten, E., & Elbert, G. (2020). Long-term development of post-traumatic stress symptoms and associated risk factors in military service members deployed to Afghanistan: Results from the PRISMO 10-year follow-up. *European Psychiatry: The Journal of the Association of European Psychiatrists, 64*(1), e10. doi: 10.1192/j.eurpsy.2020.11
van Dongen, J., Ehli, E. A., Slieker, R. C., Bartels, M., Weber, Z. M., Davies, G. E., … Boomsma, D. I. (2014). Epigenetic variation in monozygotic twins: a genome-wide analysis of DNA methylation in buccal cells. *Genes, 5*(2), 347–365. doi:10.3390/genes5020347
van Duijil, M., Cardena, E., & de Jong, J. (2005). The validity of DSM-IV dissociative disorders in southwest Uganda. *Transcultural Psychiatry, 42,* 219–241.
Van Dycke, K. C., Rodenburg, W., van Oostrom, C. T., van Kerkhof, L. W., Pennings, J. L., Roenneberg, T., … van der Horst, G. T. (2015). Chronically Alternating Light Cycles Increase Breast Cancer Risk in Mice. *Current Biology, 25*(14), 1932–1937.
van Haren, N. E., Rijsdijk, F., Schnack, H. G., Picchioni, M. M., Toulopoulou, T., Weisbrod, M., … Boomsma, D. I. (2012). The genetic and environmental determinants of the association between brain abnormalities and schizophrenia: the schizophrenia twins and relatives consortium. *Biological Psychiatry, 71*(10), 915–921.
van Hoeken, D., Veling, W., Sinke, S., Mitchell, J. E., & Hoek, H. W. (2009). The validity and utility of subtyping bulimia nervosa. *International Journal of Eating Disorders, 42*(7), 595–602.
van Kammen, D. P., Docherty, J. P., & Bunney, W. E. (1982). Prediction of early relapse after pimozide discontinuation by response to d-amphetamine during pimozide treatment. *Biological Psychiatry, 17,* 223–242.
van Laar, M., Volkerts, E., & Verbaten, M. (2001). Subchronic effects of the GABA-agonist lorazepam and the 5-HT2A/2C antagonist ritanserin on driving performance, slow wave sleep and daytime sleepiness in healthy volunteers. *Psychopharmacology (Berlin), 154,* 189–197.
van Maanen, A., Meijer, A. M., van der Heijden, K. B., & Oort, F. J. (2016). The effects of light therapy on sleep problems: A systematic review and meta-analysis. *Sleep Medicine Reviews, 29,* 52–62. doi: 10.1016/j.smrv.2015.08.009
Van Orden, K. A., Witte, T. K., Cukrowicz, K. C., Braithwaite, S. R., Selby, E. A., & Joiner, T. E., Jr. (2010). The interpersonal theory of suicide. *Psychological Review, 117*(2), 575–600.
van Os, J. (2011). Should attenuated psychosis syndrome be a DSM-5 diagnosis? *American Journal of Psychiatry, 168*(5), 460–463.
van Os, J., & Allardyce, J. (2009). The clinical epidemiology of schizophrenia. In B. J. Sadock, V. A. Sadock, & P. Ruiz (Eds.), *Kaplan & Sadock's comprehensive textbook of psychiatry* (9th ed., Vol. I, pp. 1475–1487). Philadelphia, PA: Lippincott Williams & Wilkins.
van Os, J., Kenis, G., & Rutten, B. P. (2010). The environment and schizophrenia. *Nature, 468*(7321), 203–212.
van Overveld, M., de Jong, P. J., & Peters, M. L. (2011). The Multi-Dimensional Blood/Injury Phobia Inventory: Its psychometric properties and relationship with disgust propensity and disgust sensitivity. *Journal of Anxiety Disorders, 25*(3), 319–325. doi: http://dx.doi.org/10.1016/j.janxdis.2010.10.004
Van Praag, H. M., & Korf, J. (1975). Central monamine deficiency in depressions: Causative of secondary phenomenon? *Pharmakopsychiatr Neuropsychopharmakol, 8,* 322–326.
Van Rooij, A. J., Schoenmakers, T. M., Vermulst, A. A., Van Den Eijnden, R. J. J. M., & Van De Mheen, D. (2011). Online video game addiction: Identification of addicted adolescent gamers. *Addiction, 106*(1), 205–212. doi: 10.1111/j.1360-0443.2010.03104.x
Van Ryzin, M. J., Fosco, G. M., & Dishion, T. J. (2012). Family and peer predictors of substance use from early adolescence to early adulthood: An 11-year prospective analysis. *Addictive Behaviors, 37*(12), 1314–1324. doi: 10.1016/j.addbeh.2012.06.020
van't Veer-Tazelaar, P. J., van Marwijk, H. W. J., van Oppen, P., van Hout, H. P. J., van der Horst, H. E., Cuijpers, P., & Beekman, A. T. (2009). Stepped-care prevention of anxiety and depression in late life: A randomized controlled trial. *Archives of General Psychiatry, 66*(3), 297–304.
Vandekerckhove, M., Berens, A., Wang, Y., Quirin, M., & De Mey, J. (2020). Alterations in the fronto-limbic network and corpus callosum in borderline-personality disorder. *Brain and Cognition, 138,* 103596.

Vander Wal, J. S. (2012). Night eating syndrome: a critical review of the literature. *Clinical Psychology Review, 32*(1), 49–59.

Vanderstichele, H., Bibl, M., Engelborghs, S., Le Bastard, N., Lewczuk, P., Molinuevo, J. L., & Blennow, K. (2012). Standardization of preanalytical aspects of cerebrospinal fluid biomarker testing for Alzheimer's disease diagnosis: A consensus paper from the Alzheimer's Biomarkers Standardization Initiative. *Alzheimer's & Dementia, 8*(1), 65–73. doi: http://dx.doi.org/10.1016/j.jalz.2011.07.004

Vanek, J., Prasko, J., Ociskova, M., Hodny, F., Holubova, M., Minarikova, K., … Nesnidal, V. (2021). Insomnia in patients with borderline personality disorder. *Nature and science of sleep, 13*, 239–250. doi: 10.2147/NSS.S295030

Vanitallie, T. B., & Lew, E. A. (1992). Assessment of morbidity and mortality risk in the overweight patient. In T. A. Wadden and T. B. Vanitallie (Eds.), *Treatment of the seriously obese patient.* New York, NY: Guilford.

Vannucchi, G., Masi, G., Toni, C., Dell'Osso, L., Marazziti, D., & Perugi, G. (2014). Clinical features, developmental course, and psychiatric comorbidity of adult autism spectrum disorders. *CNS Spectrums, 19*(02), 157–164.

Vargas, I., Nguyen, A. M., Muench, A., Bastien, C. H., Ellis, J. G., & Perlis, M. L. (2020). Acute and chronic insomnia: What has time and/or hyperarousal got to do with it? *Brain sciences, 10*(2), 71.

Vassos, E., Pedersen, C. B., Murray, R. M., Collier, D. A., & Lewis, C. M. (2012). Meta-analysis of the association of urbanicity with schizophrenia. *Schizophrenia bulletin, 38*(6), 1118–1123.

Vasterling, J. J., Brailey, K., Constans, J. I., & Sotker, P. B. (1998). Attention and memory dysfunction in posttraumatic stress disorders. *Neuropsychology, 12*(1), 125–133.

Vaughn, S., Capin, P., Scammacca, N., Roberts, G., Cirino, P., & Fletcher, J. M. (2020). The critical role of word reading as a predictor of response to intervention. *Journal of Learning Disabilities, 53*(6), 415–427.

Vazques, G. H., Holtzman, J. N., Tondo, L., & Baldessarini, R. J. (2015). Efficacy and tolerability of treatment for bipolar depression. *Journal of Affective Disorders, 183,* 258–262.

Vazsonyi, A. T., Ksinan, A., Mikuška, J., & Jiskrova, G. (2015). The Big Five and adolescent adjustment: An empirical test across six cultures. *Personality and Individual Differences, 83,* 234–244.

Veale, D. (2000). Outcome of cosmetic surgery and "DIY" surgery inpatients with body dysmorphic disorder. *Psychiatric Bulletin, 24*(6), 218–221.

Veale, D., & Riley, S. (2001). Mirror, mirror on the wall, who is the ugliest of them all? The psychopathology of mirror gazing in body dysmorphic disorder. *Behaviour Research and Therapy, 39,* 1381–1393.

Veale, D., Boocock, A., Gournay, K., Dryden, W., Shah, F., & Walburn, J. (1996). Body dysmorphic disorder: A survey of 50 cases. *British Journal of Psychiatry, 169,* 196–201.

Veale, D., Ennis, M., & Lambrou, C. (2002). Possible association of body dysmorphic disorder with an occupation or education in art and design. *American Journal of Psychiatry, 159,* 1788–1790.

Veale, D., Gournay, K., Dryden, W., Boocock, A., Shah, F., Willson, R., & Walburn, J. (1996). Body dysmorphic disorder: A cognitive behavioral model and pilot randomized control trial. *Behaviour Research and Therapy, 34,* 717–729.

Veith, I. (1965). Hysteria: *The history of a disease.* Chicago: University of Chicago Press.

Vellas, B., Coley, N., Ousset, P. J., Berrut, G., Dartigues, J. F., Dubois, B., . . . Touchon, J. (2012). Long-term use of standardised Ginkgo biloba extract for the prevention of Alzheimer's disease (GuidAge): a randomised placebo-controlled trial. *The Lancet Neurology, 11*(10), 851–859.

Venables, N. C., Hall, J. R., & Patrick, C. J. (2014). Differentiating psychopathy from antisocial personality disorder: A triarchic model perspective. *Psychological Medicine, 44*(05), 1005–1013.

Venables, P. H. (1996). Schizotypy and maternal exposure to influenza and to cold temperature: The Mauritius study. *Journal of Abnormal Psychology, 105,* 53–60.

Verma, K. K., Khaitan, B. K., & Singh, O. P. (1998). The frequency of sexual dysfunction in patients attending a sex therapy clinic in North India. *Archives of Sexual Behavior, 27,* 309–314.

Vermetten, E., Schmahl, C., Lindner, S., Loewenstein, R., & Bremner, J. (2006). Hippocampal and amygdalar volumes in dissociative identity disorder. *American Journal of Psychiatry, 163,* 630–636.

Vermund, S. H., Sheldon, E. K., & Sidat, M. (2015). Southern Africa: The highest priority region for HIV prevention and care interventions. *Current HIV/AIDS Report, 12,* 191–195.

Vernberg, E. M., LaGreca, A. M., Silverman, W. K., & Prinstein, M. J. (1996). Prediction of posttraumatic stress symptoms in children after Hurricane Andrew. *Journal of Abnormal Psychology, 105,* 237–248.

Vest, N. A., & Tragesser, S. (2020). Coping motives mediate the relationship between borderline personality features and alcohol, cannabis, and prescription opioid use disorder symptomatology in a substance use disorder treatment sample. *Personality Disorders: Theory, Research, and Treatment, 11*(3), 230–236. doi: 10.1037/per0000385

Vesuna, S., Kauvar, I. V., Richman, E., Gore, F., Oskotsky, T., Sava-Segal, C., … Deisseroth, K. (2020). Deep posteromedial cortical rhythm in dissociation. *Nature, 586*(7827), 87–94. doi: 10.1038/s41586-020-2731-9

Viana, A. G., Beidel, D. C., & Rabian, B. (2009). Selective mutism: A review and integration of the last 15 years. *Clinical Psychology Review, 29*(1), 57–67. doi: 10.1016/j.cpr.2008.09.009

Vicario, S., Pérez-Rivas, A., de Guevara-Miranda, D. L., Santín, L., & Sampedro-Piquero, P. (2020). Cognitive reserve mediates the severity of certain neuropsychological deficits related to cocaine use disorder. *Addictive Behaviors, 107*, 106399.

Viguera, A. C., Tondo, L., Koukopoulos, A. E., Reginaldi, D., Lepri, B., & Baldessarini, R. (2011). Episodes of mood disorders in 2,252 pregnancies and postpartum periods. *American Journal of Psychiatry, 168*(11), 1179–1185.

Vingerhoets, A. J. J. M., Rottenberg, J., Cevaal, A., & Nelson, J. K. (2007). Is there a relationship between depression and crying? A review. *Acta Psychiatrica Scandinavica, 115,* 340–351.

Vinkers, D., de Vries, S., van Baars, A., & Mulder, C. (2010). Ethnicity and dangerousness criteria for court ordered admission to a psychiatric hospital. *Social Psychiatry and Psychiatric Epidemiology, 45*(2), 221–224.

Virag, R. (1999). Indications and early results of sildenafil (Viagra) in erectile dysfunction. *Urology, 54,* 1073–1077.

Virtanen, S., Latvala, A., Andershed, H., Lichtenstein, P., Tuvblad, C., Colins, O. F., … Lundström, S. (2020). Do psychopathic personality traits in childhood predict subsequent criminality and psychiatric outcomes over and above childhood behavioral problems? *Journal of Criminal Justice*, 101761.

Vitacco, M. J., Neumann, C. S., & Caldwell, M. F. (2010). Predicting antisocial behavior in high-risk male adolescents: Contributions of psychopathy and instrumental violence. *Criminal Justice and Behavior, 37*(8), 833–846.

Vitacco, M. J., Neumann, C. S., & Pardini, D. A. (2014). Predicting future criminal offending in a community-based sample of males using self-reported psychopathy. *Criminal Justice and Behavior, 41*(3), 345–363.

Vitiello, B., & Lederhendler, I. (2000). Research on eating disorders: Current status and future prospects. *Biological Psychiatry, 47*, 777–786.

Vlaeyen, J. W. S., Maher, C. G., Wiech, K., Van Zundert, J., Meloto, C. B., Diatchenko, L., … Linton, S. J. (2018). Low back pain. *Nature Reviews Disease Primers, 4*(1) doi: 10.1038/s41572-018-0052-1

Voderholzer, U., Schwartz, C., Thiel, N., Kuelz, A. K , Hartmann, A., Scheidt, C. E., Schlegl, S., & Zeeck, A. (2014). A comparison of schemas, schema modes and childhood traumas in obsessive-compulsive disorder, chronic pain disorder and eating disorders. Psychopathology. 47(1):24–31. doi: 10.1159/000348484.

Vogel, S. A., & Reder, S. (1998). Educational attainment of adults with learning disabilities. In S. A. Vogel & S. Reder (Eds.), *Learning disabilities, literacy, and adult education* (pp. 5–28). Baltimore, MD: Paul H. Brookes.

Vogt, N. M., Hunt, J. F., Adluru, N., Dean III, D. C., Johnson, S. C., Asthana, S., … Bendlin, B. B. (2020). Cortical microstructural alterations in mild cognitive impairment and Alzheimer's disease dementia. *Cerebral Cortex, 30*(5), 2948–2960.

Vohs, K. D., Bardone, A. M., Joiner, T. E., Jr., Abramson, L. Y., & Heatherton, T. F. (1999). Perfectionism, perceived weight status, and self-esteem interact to predict bulimic symptoms: A model of bulimic symptom development. *Journal of Abnormal Psychology, 108*, 695–700.

Voigt, K., Nagel, A., Meyer, B., Langs, G., Braukhaus, C., & Lowe, B. (2010). Towards positive diagnostic criteria: A systematic review of somatoform disorder diagnoses and suggestions for future classification. *Journal of Psychosomatic Research, 68*(5), 403–414.

Voigt, K., Wollburg, E., Weinmann, N., Herzog, A., Meyer, B., Langs, G., & Lowe, B. (2012). Predictive validity and clinical utility of DSM-5 somatic symptom disorder—Comparison with DSM-IV somatoform disorders and additional criteria for consideration. *Journal of Psychosomatic Research, 73*(5), 345–350. doi: 10.1016/j.jpsychores.2012.08.020

Volkow, N. D., & Morales, M. (2015). The Brain on Drugs: From Reward to Addiction. *Cell, 162*(4), 712–725. https://doi.org/10.1016/j.cell.2015.07.046

Volkow, N. D., Baler, R. D., Compton, W. M., & Weiss, S. R. (2014). Adverse health effects of marijuana use. *New England Journal of Medicine, 370*(23), 2219–2227.

Volkow, N. D., Wang, G. J., Kollins, S. H., Wigal, T. L., Newcorn, J. H., Telang, F., & Swanson, J. M. (2009). Evaluating dopamine reward pathway in ADHD: Clinical implications. *JAMA: Journal of the American Medical Association, 302*(10), 1084–1091.

Voon, V., Gallea, C., Hattori, N., Bruno, M., Ekanayake, V., & Hallett, M. (2010). The involuntary nature of conversion disorder. *Neurology, 74*(3), 223–228.

Voos, A., Pelphrey, K., Tirrell, J., Bolling, D., Wyk, B., Kaiser, M., & Ventola, P. (2013). Neural mechanisms of improvements in social motivation after pivotal response treatment: Two case studies. *Journal of Autism and Developmental Disorders, 43*(1), 1–10. doi: 10.1007/s10803-012-1683-9

Vriends, N., Pfaltz, M. C., Novianti, P., & Hadiyono, J. (2013). Taijin kyofusho and social anxiety and their clinical relevance in Indonesia and Switzerland. *Frontiers in Psychology, 4*, 3. doi: 10.3389/fpsyg.2013.00003

Vrshek-Schallhorn, S., Stroud, C. B., Mineka, S., Hammen, C., Zinbarg, R. E., Wolitzky-Taylor, K.,& Craske, M. G. (2015). Chronic and episodic interpersonal stress as statistically unique predictors of depression in two samples of emerging adults. *Journal of Abnormal Psychology, 124*(4), 918.

Vyas, C. M., Donneyong, M., Mischoulon, D., Chang, G., Gibson, H., Cook, N. R., Manson, J. E., Reynolds III, C. F., & Okereke, O. I. (2020). Association of race and ethnicity with late-life depression severity, symptom burden, and care. *JAMA Network Open, 3*(3), e201606. doi: 10.1001/jamanetworkopen.2020.1606

Wadden, T. A., & Osei, S. (2002). The treatment of obesity: An overview. In T. A. Wadden & A. J. Stunkard (Eds.), *Handbook of obesity treatment* (pp. 229–248). New York, NY: Guilford.

Wadden, T. A., Brownell, K. D., & Foster, G. D. (2002). Obesity: Responding to the global epidemic. *Journal of Consulting and Clinical Psychology, 70*, 510–525.

Wadden, T. A., Butryn, M. L., Hong, P. S., & Tsai, A. G. (2014). Behavioral treatment of obesity in patients encountered in primary care settings: a systematic review. *JAMA, 312*(17), 1779–1791.

Wade, T. D., Bulik, C. M., Prescott, C. A., & Kendler, K. S. (2004). Sex influences on shared risk factors for bulimia nervosa and other psychiatric disorders. *Archives of General Psychiatry, 61*, 251–256.

Wade, T. D., Tiggemann, M., Bulik, C. M., Fairburn, C. G., Wray, N. R., & Martin, N. G. (2008). Shared temperament risk factors for anorexia nervosa: A twin study. *Psychosomatic Medicine, 70*(2), 239–244.

Wager, T. D., & Atlas, L. Y. (2015). The neuroscience of placebo effects: connecting context, learning and health. *Nature Reviews Neuroscience, 16*(7), 403–418. Wager, T. (2005). The neural bases of placebo effects in pain. *Current Directions in Psychological Science, 14*, 175–179.

Wagner, B. M. (1997). Family risk factors for child and adolescent suicidal behavior. *Psychological Bulletin, 121*, 246–298.

Wagner, G., Penelo, E., Wanner, C., Gwinner, P., Trofaier, M. L., Imgart, H., . . . Karwautz, A. F. (2013). Internet-delivered cognitive–behavioural therapy v. conventional guided self-help for bulimia nervosa: long-term evaluation of a randomised controlled trial. *The British Journal of Psychiatry, 202*(2), 135–141.

Wainwright, B. R., Allen, M. L., & Cain, K. (2020). Symbolic understanding and word–picture–referent mapping from iPads in autism spectrum condition: The roles of iconicity and engagement. *Journal of Autism and Developmental Disorders*, 1–16.

Wakefield, J. C. (1999). Evolutionary versus prototype analyses of the concept of disorder. *Journal of Abnormal Psychology, 108*, 3, 374–399.

Wakefield, J. C. (2003). Dysfunction as a factual component of disorder. *Behavior Research and Therapy, 41*, 969–990.

Wakefield, J. C. (2009). Mental disorder and moral responsibility: Disorders of personhood as harmful dysfunctions, with special reference to alcoholism. *Philosophy, Psychiatry, & Psychology, 16*(1), 91–99.

Wakefield, J. C., Schmitz, M. F., First, M. B., & Horwitz, A. V. (2007). Extending the bereavement exclusion for major depression to other losses: Evidence from the national comorbidity survey. *Archives of General Psychiatry, 64*, 433–440

Walaszek, A. (2020). *Behavioral and psychological symptoms of dementia*. Washington, D.C.: American Psychiatric Association Publishing.

Walker, D. L., Ressler, K. J., Lu, K.-T., & Davis, M. (2002). Facilitation of conditioned fear extinction by systemic administration or intra-amygdala infusions of D-cycloserine assessed with fear-potentiated startle. *Journal of Neuroscience, 22*, 2343–2351.

Walkup, J. T., Albano, A. M., Piacentini, J., Birmaher, B., Compton, S. N., Sherrill, J. T., & Kendall, P. C. (2008). Cognitive behavioral therapy, sertraline, or a combination in childhood anxiety. *New England Journal of Medicine, 359*(26), 2753–2766. doi: 10.1056/NEJMoa0804633

Wall, T. D., Wygant, D. B., & Sellbom, M. (2015). Boldness explains a key difference between psychopathy and antisocial personality disorder. *Psychiatry, Psychology and Law, 22*(1), 94–105.

Wallace, C. S., Kilman, V. L., Withers, G. S., & Greenough, W. T. (1992). Increases in dendritic length in occipital cortex after 4 days of differential housing in weanling rats. *Behavioral and Neural Biology, 58,* 64–68.

Wallace, J., & O'Hara, M. W. (1992). Increases in depressive symptomatology in the rural elderly: Results from a cross-sectional and longitudinal study. *Journal of Abnormal Psychology, 101*(3), 398–404.

Waller, N. G., & Ross, C. A. (1997). The prevalence and biometric structure of pathological dissociation in the general population: Taxometric and behavior genetic findings. *Journal of Abnormal Psychology, 106,* 499–510.

Waller, N. G., Putnam, F. W., & Carlson, E. B. (1996). Types of dissociation and dissociative types: A taxometric analysis of dissociative experiences. *Psychological Methods, 1,* 300–321.

Waller, R., Dotterer, H. L., & Hyde, L. W. (2015). A Gene-Environment Approach to Understanding Youth Antisocial Behavior. *Emerging Trends in the Social and Behavioral Sciences: An Interdisciplinary, Searchable, and Linkable Resource.* 1–33.

Waller, R., Gardner, F., Hyde, L. W., Shaw, D. S., Dishion, T. J., & Wilson, M. N. (2012). Do harsh and positive parenting predict parent reports of deceitful-callous behavior in early childhood? *Journal of Child Psychology and Psychiatry, 53*(9), 946–953.

Waller, R., Gardner, F., Shaw, D. S., Dishion, T. J., Wilson, M. N., & Hyde, L. W. (2015). Callous-unemotional behavior and early-childhood onset of behavior problems: the role of parental harshness and warmth. *Journal of Clinical Child & Adolescent Psychology, 44*(4), 655–667.

Waln, O., & Jankovic, J. (2013). An update on tardive dyskinesia: From phenomenology to treatment. *Tremor and Other Hyperkinetic Movements, 3,* pii: tre-03-161-4138-1.

Walsh, B. T. (1991). Fluoxetine treatment of bulimia nervosa. *Journal of Psychosomatic Research, 35,* 471–475.

Walsh, B. T. (1995). Pharmacotherapy of eating disorders. In K. D. Brownell & C. G. Fairburn (Eds.), *Eating disorders and obesity: A comprehensive handbook* (pp. 313–317). New York, NY: Guilford.

Walsh, B. T. (2010). Eating disorders in DSM-V: Review of existing literature (Part 3). *International Journal of Eating Disorders, 43*(2), 97.

Walsh, B. T., Agras, W. S., Devlin, M. J., Fairburn, C. G., Wilson, G. T., Kahn, C., & Chally, M. K. (2000). Fluoxetine for bulimia nervosa following poor response to psychotherapy. *American Journal of Psychiatry, 157,* 1332–1334.

Walsh, B. T., Hadigan, C. M., Devlin, M. J., Gladis, M., & Roose, S. P. (1991). Long-term outcome of antidepressant treatment of bulimia nervosa. *Archives of General Psychiatry, 148,* 1206–1212.

Walsh, B. T., Kaplan, A. S., Attia, E., Olmsted, M., Parides, M., Carter, J. C., & Rockert, W. (2006). Fluoxetine after weight restoration in anorexia nervosa. *JAMA: Journal of the American Medical Association, 295,* 2605–2612.

Walsh, B. T., Wilson, G. T., Loeb, K. L., Devlin, M. J., Pike, K. M., Roose, S. P., Fleiss, J., & Waternaux, C. (1997). Medication and psychotherapy in the treatment of bulimia nervosa. *American Journal of Psychiatry, 154,* 523–531.

Walsh, J. K., Mayleben, D., Guico-Pabia, C., Vandormael, K., Martinez, R., & Deacon, S. (2008). Efficacy of the selective extrasynaptic GABA A agonist, gaboxadol, in a model of transient insomnia: A randomized, controlled clinical trial. *Sleep Medicine, 9*(4), 393–402.

Walsh, K., Danielson, C. K., McCauley, J. L., Saunders, B. E., Kilpatrick, D. G., & Resnick, H. S. (2012). National prevalence of posttraumatic stress disorder among sexually revictimized adolescent, college, and adult household-residing women. *Archives of General Psychiatry, 69*(9), 935–942. doi: 10.1001/archgenpsychiatry.2012.132

Walters, E. E., & Kendler, K. S. (1995). Anorexia nervosa and anorexia-like syndromes in a population based female twin sample. *American Journal of Psychiatry, 152,* 64–71.

Wan, M., Abel, K., & Green, J. (2008). The transmission of risk to children from mothers with schizophrenia: A developmental psychopathology model. *Clinical Psychology Review, 28*(4), 613–637.

Wan, Y. Y. (2010). Multitasking of helper T cells. *Immunology, 130,* 166–171.

Wang, C., Nieri, T., Do, K. A., & Llanes, E. (2020). Parenting factors predicting substance use and aggression among Latino/a adolescents: The moderating role of cultural values. *Journal of Child and Family Studies, 29*(10), 2710–2721.

Wang, C., Shao, X., Jia, Y., Zhang, B., Shen, C., & Wang, W. (2020). Inhibitory brainstem reflexes under external emotional-stimuli in schizoid and histrionic personality disorders. *Personality and Individual Differences, 158,* 109843.

Wang, H., Troy, L. M., Rogers, G. T., Fox, C. S., McKeown, N. M., Meigs, J. B., & Jacques, P. F. (2014). Longitudinal association between dairy consumption and changes of body weight and waist circumference: *The Framingham Heart Study. International Journal of Obesity, 38*(2), 299–305. doi:10.1038/ijo.2013.78

Wang, P. S., Berglund, P., Olfson, M., Pincus, H. A., Wells, K. B., & Kessler, R. C. (2005). Failure and delay in initial treatment contact after first onset of mental disorders in the national comorbidity survey replication. *Archives of General Psychiatry, 62,* 603–613.

Wang, P. S., Bohn, R. L., Glynn, R. J., Mogun, H., & Avorn, J. (2001). Hazardous benzodiazepine regimens in the elderly: Effects of half-life, dosage, and duration on risk of hip fracture. *American Journal of Psychiatry, 158,* 892–898.

Wang, S. (2006). Contagious behavior. *Psychological Science, 19,* 22–26.

Wang, S., & Blazer, D. G. (2015). Depression and cognition in the elderly. *Annual Review of Clinical Psychology, 11,* 331.

Wang, T., Collet, J.-P., Shapiro, S., & Ware, M. A. (2008). Adverse effects of medical cannabinoids: A systematic review. *CMAJ, 178*(13), 1669–1678. doi: 10.1503/cmaj.071178

Wang, X., Wang, D., & Shen, J. (2006). The effects of social support on depression in the aged. *Chinese Journal of Clinical Psychology, 14,* 73.

Wang, Y., Harding, I. H., Testa, R., Tonge, B., Jones, H., Seal, M., … Abu-Akel, A. (2020). Structural and functional brain abnormalities in children with schizotypal disorder: A pilot study. *npj Schizophrenia, 6*(1), 1–4.

Wang, Y., Liu, M., Lu, Q., Farrell, M., Lappin, J. M., Shi, J., … Bao, Y. (2020). Global prevalence and burden of HIV-associated neurocognitive disorder: A meta-analysis. *Neurology, 95*(19), e2610–e2621.

Wang, Y., Wang, P., Xu, X., Goldstein, J., McConkie, A., Cheung, S. W., & Jiang, Y.-H. (2015). Genetics of autism spectrum disorders: The opportunity and challenge in the genetics clinic. In S. H. Fatemi (Ed.), *Molecular basis of autism* (pp. 33–66). New York, NY: Springer.

Wang, Z., Baker, D. G., Harrer, J., Hamner, M., Price, M., & Amstadter, A. (2011). The relationship between combat-related posttraumatic stress disorder and the 5-HTTLPR/rs25531 polymorphism. *Depression and Anxiety, 28,* 1067–1073. doi: 10.1002/da.20872

Wang, Z., Neylan, T. C., Mueller, S. G., Lenoci, M., Truran, D., Marmar, C. R., & Schuff, N. (2010). Magnetic resonance imaging of hippocampal subfields in posttraumatic stress disorder. *Archives of General Psychiatry, 67*(3), 296–303. doi: 10.1001/archgenpsychiatry.2009.205

Ward, M. M., Swan, G. E., & Chesney, M. A. (1987). Arousal-reduction treatments for mild hypertension: A meta-analysis of recent studies. *Handbook of Hypertension, 9,* 285–302.

Ward, T., & Beech, A. R. (2008). An integrated theory of sexual offending. In D. R. Laws & W. T. O'Donohue (Eds.), *Sexual deviance: Theory, assessment, and treatment* (2nd ed., pp. 21–36). New York, NY: Guilford.

Ward, Z. J., Bleich, S. N., Cradock, A. L., Barrett, J. L., Giles, C. M., Flax, C., … Gortmaker, S. L. (2019). Projected U.S. state-level prevalence of adult obesity and severe obesity. *New England Journal of Medicine, 381*(25), 2440–2450. doi: 10.1056/NEJMsa1909301

Warren, E. C., & Kolodny, A. (2021). Trends in heroin treatment admissions in the United States by race, sex, and age. *JAMA Network Open, 4*(2), e2036640–e2036640.

Warshaw, M. G., Dolan, R. T., & Keller, M. B. (2000). Suicidal behavior in patients with current or past panic disorder: Five years of prospective data from the Harvard/Brown Anxiety Research Program. *American Journal of Psychiatry, 157,* 1876–1878.

Warwick, H. M., & Salkovskis, P. M. (1990). Hypochondriasis. *Behavior Research Therapy, 28,* 105–117.

Washington v. Harper, 494 U.S. 210 C.F.R. (1990).

Waters, E., de Silva-Sanigorski, A., Hall, B. J., Brown, T. Campbell, K. J., Gao, Y., & Summerbell, C. D. (2011). Interventions for preventing obesity in children. *Cochrane Database System Review, 12:* CD001871.

Waters, F., Allen, P., Aleman, A., Fernyhough, C., Woodward, T. S., Badcock, J. C., … Vercammen, A. (2012). Auditory hallucinations in schizophrenia and nonschizophrenia populations: a review and integrated model of cognitive mechanisms. *Schizophrenia Bulletin, 38*(4), 683–693.

Watson, G. L., Arcona, A. P., & Antonuccio, D. O. (2015). The ADHD drug abuse crisis on American college campuses. *Ethical Human Psychology and Psychiatry, 17*(1), 5–21.

Watson, J. B. (1913). Psychology as a behaviorist views it. *Psychology Review, 20,* 158–177.

Weaver, J. C. G., Cervoni, N., Champagne, F. A., D'Alessio, A. C., Charma, S., Seckl, J., & Meaney, M. J. (2004). Epigenetic programming by maternal behavior. *Nature Neuroscience, 7,* 847–854.

Weber, H., Richter, J., Straube, B., Lueken, U., Domschke, K., Schartner, C., Klauke, B., Baumann, C., Pané-Farré, C., Jacob. C. P., Scholz, C. J., Zwanzger, P., Lang, T., Fehm, L., Jansen, A., Konrad, C., Fydrich, T., Wittmann, A., Pfleiderer, B., … Reif, A. (2016). Allelic variation in CRHR1 predisposes to panic disorder: evidence for biased fear processing. *Molecular Psychiatry, 21*(6), 813–822. doi: 10.1038/mp.2015.125

Wechsler, H., Lee, J. E., Kuo, M., Seibring, M., Nelson, T. F., & Lee, H. (2002). Trends in college binge drinking during a period of increased prevention efforts: Findings from 4 Harvard School of Public Health College Alcohol Study surveys: 1993–2001. *Journal of American College Health, 50*(5):203–217.

Weck, F., Neng, J. M. B., Richtberg, S., Jakob, M., & Stangier, U. (2015). Cognitive therapy versus exposure therapy for hypochondriasis (health anxiety): A randomized controlled trial. *Journal of Consulting and Clinical Psychology, 83,* 665–676.

Weems, C. F., Silverman, W. K., & La Greca, A. M. (2000). What do youths referred for anxiety problems worry about?: Worry and its relation to anxiety and anxiety disorders in children and adolescents. *Journal of Abnormal Child Psychology, 28,* 63–72.

Wegner, D. (1989). *White bears and other unwanted thoughts.* New York, NY: Viking.

Wehr, T. A., Duncan, W. C., Jr., Sher, L., Aeschbach, D., Schwartz, P. J., Turner, E. H., & Rosenthal, N. E. (2001). A circadian signal of change of season in patients with seasonal affective disorder. *Archives of General Psychiatry, 58,* 1108–1114.

Weight Watchers International. (2010). Company overview. Retrieved from http://www.weightwatchersinternational.com/phoenix.zhtml?c5130178&p5irol-irhome

Weinberg, M. S., Lottes, I. L., & Shaver, F. M. (1995). Swedish or American youth: Who is more permissive? *Archives of Sexual Behavior, 24,* 409–437.

Weinberger, A. H., Gbedemah, M., Martinez, A. M., Nash, D., Galea, S., & Goodwin, R. D. (2018). Trends in depression prevalence in the USA from 2005 to 2015: Widening disparities in vulnerable groups. *Psychological Medicine, 48*(8), 1308–1315. doi: 10.1017/S0033291717002781

Weinberger, D. R., Berman, K. F., & Chase, T. N. (1988). Mesocortical dopaminergic function and human cognition. *Annals of the New York Academy of Sciences, 537,* 330–338.

Weiner, D. B. (1979). The apprenticeship of Philippe Pinel: A new document, 'Observations of Citizen Pussin on the insane.' *The American Journal of Psychiatry, 136*(9), 1128–1134.

Weiner, D. N. (1996). *Premature ejaculation: An evaluation of sensitivity to erotica.* Unpublished doctoral dissertation, State University of New York, Albany.

Weiner, L., & Avery-Clark, C. (2014). Sensate Focus: clarifying the Masters and Johnson's model. *Sexual and Relationship Therapy, 29*(3), 307–319.

Weiner, M. W., Aisen, P. S., Jack, Jr., C. R., Jagust, W. J., Trojanowski, J. Q., Shaw, L., & Schmidt, M. (2010). The Alzheimer's Disease Neuroimaging Initiative: Progress report and future plans. *Alzheimer's and Dementia, 6*(3), 202–211, e207.

Weiner, M. W., Veitch, D. P., Aisen, P. S., Beckett, L. A., Cairns, N. J., Green, R. C., & Trojanowski, J. Q. (2012). The Alzheimer's Disease Neuroimaging Initiative: A review of papers published since its inception. *Alzheimer's & Dementia, 8*(1, Supplement), S1–S68. doi: http://dx.doi.org/10.1016/j.jalz.2011.09.172

Weinstock, H., Berman, S., & Cates, W. (2004). Sexually transmitted diseases in American youth: Incidence and prevalence estimates. *Perspectives on Sexual and Reproductive Health, 36,* 6–10.

Weisberg, R. B., Maki, K. M., Culpepper, L., & Keller, M. B. (2005). Is anyone really M.A.D.?: The occurrence and course of mixed anxiety-depressive disorder in a sample of primary care patients. *Journal of Nervous and Mental Disease, 193*(4), 223–230.

Weisburg, R. B., Brown, T. A., Wincze, J. P., & Barlow, D. H. (2001). Causal attributions and male sexual arousal: The impact of attributions for a bogus erectile difficulty on sexual arousal, cognitions, and affect. *Journal of Abnormal Psychology, 110*(2), 324–334.

Weiser, M. (2011). Early intervention for schizophrenia: The risk-benefit ratio of antipsychotic treatment in the prodromal phase. *American Journal of Psychiatry, 168*(8), 761–763. doi: 10.1176/appi.ajp.2011.11050765

Weiskrantz, L. (1980). Varieties of residual experience. *Quarterly Journal of Experimental Psychology, 32,* 365–386.

Weiskrantz, L. (1992, September/October). Unconscious vision: The strange phenomenon of blindsight. *The Sciences,* pp. 23–28.

Weiskrantz, L. (2009). *Blindsight: A case study spanning 35 years and new*

Weiss, B., & Garber, J. (2003). Developmental differences in the phenomenology of depression. *Development and Psychopathology, 15,* 403–430.

Weiss, L. G., Locke, V., Pan, T., Harris, J. G., Saklofske, D. H., & Prifitera, A. (2015). WISC-V Use in Societal Context. In L. G.

Weiss, D. H. Saklofske, J. A. Holdnack, & A. Prifitera (Eds.), *WISC-V Assessment and Interpretation: Scientist-Practitioner Perspectives*, 123–176. San Diego, CA: Elsevier.

Weiss, R. D., & Iannucci, R. A. (2009). Cocaine-related disorders. In B. J. Sadock, V. A. Sadock, & P. Ruiz (Eds.), *Kaplan & Sadock's comprehensive textbook of psychiatry* (9th ed., Vol. I, pp. 1318–1331). Philadelphia, PA: Lippincott Williams & Wilkins.

Weisse, C. S., Pato, C. W., McAllister, C. G., Littman, R., & Breier, A. (1990). Differential effects of controllable and uncontrollable acute stress on lymphocyte proliferation and leukocyte percentages in humans. *Brain, Behavior, and Immunity, 4,* 339–351.

Weissman, M. (1995). *Mastering depression: A patient's guide to interpersonal psychotherapy.* New York, NY: Oxford University Press.

Weissman, M. M., & Olfson, M. (1995). Depression in women: Implications for health care research. *Science, 269,* 799–801.

Weissman, M. M., Bland, R. C., Canino, G. J., Greenwald, S., Hwu, H. G., Lee, C. K., et al. (1994). The cross national epidemiology of obsessive compulsive disorder. The Cross National Collaborative Group. *Journal of Clinical Psychiatry, 55*(Supplement), 5–10.

Weissman, M. M., Bruce, M. L., Leaf, P. J., Florio, L. P., & Holzer, C. (1991). Affective disorders. In L. N. Robins & D. A. Regier (Eds.), *Psychiatric disorders of America: The epidemiologic catchment area study* (pp. 53–80). New York, NY: Free Press.

Weissman, M. M., Klerman, G. L., Markowitz, J. S., & Ouellette, R. (1989). Suicidal ideation and suicide attempts in panic disorder and attacks. *New England Journal of Medicine, 321,* 1209–1214.

Weissman, M. M., Wolk, S., Wickramaratne, P., Goldstein, R. B., Adams, P., Greenwald, S., & Steinberg, D. (1999). Children with prepubertal-onset major depressive disorder and anxiety grow up. *Archives of General Psychiatry, 56,* 794–801.

Weissman, M., Bland, R., Canino, G., Greenwald, S., Hwo, H., Lee, C., & Eng-Kung, Y. (1994). The cross national epidemiology of obsessive compulsive disorder. *Journal of Clinical Psychiatry, 55,* 5–10.

Weissman, M., Wickramaratne, P., Nomura, Y., Verdeli, H., Pilowsky, D., Grillon, C., & Bruder, G. (2005). Families at high and low risk for depression: A 3-generation study. *Archives of General Psychiatry, 62,* 29–36.

Weitz, E. S., Hollon, S. D., Twisk, J., van Straten, A., Huibers, M. J., David, D., DeRubeis, R. J., Dimidjian, S., Dunlop, B. W., Cristea, I. A., Faramarzi, M., Hegerl, U., Jarrett, R. B., Kheirkhah, F., Kennedy, S. H., Mergl, R., Miranda, J., Mohr, D. C., Rush, A. J., Segal, Z. V., Siddique, J., Simons, A. D., Vittengl, J. R., & Cuijpers, P. (in press). Baseline depression severity as moderator of depression outcomes between cognitive behavioral therapy vs pharmacotherapy: An individual patient data meta-analysis. *JAMA Psychiatry.* doi:10.1001/jamapsychiatry.2015.1516

Weitz, E. S., Hollon, S. D., Twisk, J., Van Straten, A., Huibers, M. J. H., David, D., ... Cuijpers, P. (2015). Baseline depression severity as moderator of depression outcomes between cognitive behavioral therapy vs pharmacotherapy: An individual patient data meta-analysis. *JAMA Psychiatry, 72*(11), 1102–1109. doi: 10.1001/jamapsychiatry.2015.1516

Weitze, C., & Osburg, S. (1996). Transsexualism in Germany: Empirical data on epidemiology and application of the German transsexuals' act during its first ten years. *Archives of Sexual Behavior, 25,* 409–465.

Welch, P. G., Carleton, R. N., & Asmundson, G. J. (2009). Measuring health anxiety: Moving past the dichotomous response option of the original Whiteley Index. *Journal of Anxiety Disorders, 23,* 1002–1007. doi: 10.1016/j.janxdis.2009.05.006

Welham, J., Scott, J., Williams, G., Najman, J., Bor, W., O'Callaghan, M., & McGrath, J. (2008). Emotional and behavioural antecedents of young adults who screen positive for non-affective psychosis: A 21-year birth cohort study. *Psychological Medicine, 39*(4), 625–634.

Wellings, K., Collumbien, M., Slaymaker, E., Singh, S., Hodges, Z., Patel, D., & Bajos, N. (2006). Sexual behaviour in context: A global perspective. *Lancet, 368*(9548), 1706–1728. doi: 10.1016/S0140-6736(06)69479-8

Wells, A.,Welford, M., King, P., Papageorgiou, C., Wisely, J., & Mendel, E. (2010). A pilot randomized trial of metacognitive therapy vs applied relaxation in the treatment of adults with generalized anxiety disorder. *Behaviour Research and Therapy, 48,* 429–434.

Wells, B., & Twenge, J. (2005). Changes in young people's sexual behavior and attitudes, 1943–1999: A cross-temporal meta-analysis. *Review of General Psychology, 9,* 249–261.

Wells, D. L., & Ott, C. A. (2011). The "new" marijuana. *The Annals of Pharmacotherapy, 45*(3), 414–417. doi: 10.1345/aph.1P580

Wells, K. B., Stewart, A., Hays, R. D., Burnam, M. A., Rogers, W., Daniels, M., & Ware J. (1989). The functioning and well-being of depressed patients: Results from the medical outcomes study. *JAMA: Journal of the American Medical Association, 262*(7), 914–919.

Wendt, O., & Rindskopf, D. (2020). Exploring new directions in statistical analysis of single-case experimental designs. *Evidence-Based Communication Assessment and Intervention, 14*(1–2), 1–5. doi: 10.1080/17489539.2020.1741842

Wermter, A.-K., Kamp-Becker, I., Hesse, P., Schulte-Körne, G., Strauch, K., & Remschmidt, H. (2010). Evidence for the involvement of genetic variation in the *oxytocin receptor gene* (*OXTR*) in the etiology of autistic disorders on high-functioning level. *American Journal of Medical Genetics Part B: Neuropsychiatric Genetics, 153B*(2), 629–639.

Werner, K. B., Few, L. R., & Bucholz, K. K. (2015). Epidemiology, Comorbidity, and Behavioral Genetics of Antisocial Personality Disorder and Psychopathy. *Psychiatric Annals, 45*(4), 195.

Wertz, J., Caspi, A., Ambler, A., Broadbent, J., Hancox, R. J., Harrington, H., ... Moffitt, T. E. (2021). Association of history of psychopathology with accelerated aging at midlife. *JAMA Psychiatry.* doi: 10.1001/jamapsychiatry.2020.4626

Westen, D. (1991). Social cognition and object relations. *Psychological Bulletin, 109,* 429–455.

Wetherell, J. L., Ayers, C. R., Nuevo, R., Stein, M. B., Ramsdell, J., & Patterson, T. L. (2010). Medical conditions and depressive, anxiety, and somatic symptoms in older adults with and without generalized anxiety disorder. *Aging and Mental Health, 14,* 764–768.

Wetherell, J. L., Gatz, M., & Craske, M. G. (2003). Treatment of generalized anxiety disorder in older adults. *Journal of Consulting and Clinical Psychology, 71,* 31–40.

Wetherell, J. L., Lenze, E. J., & Stanley, M. (2005). Evidence-based treatment of geriatric anxiety disorders. *Psychiatric Clinics of North America, 28,* 871–896.

Wetherell, J. L., Thorp, S. R., Patterson, T. L., Golshan, S., Jeste, D. V., & Gatz, M. (2004). Quality of life in geriatric generalized anxiety disorder: A preliminary investigation. *Journal of Psychiatric Research, 38,* 305–312.

Wetzler, S., & Jose, A. (2012). Passive-aggressive personality disorder: The demise of a syndrome. In T. A. Widiger (Ed.), *The Oxford handbook of personality disorders* (pp. 674–693). New York, NY: Oxford University Press.

Wheeler, J., Newring, K. A. B., & Draper, C. (2008). Transvestic fetishism: Psychopathology and theory. In D. R. Laws & W. T. O'Donohue (Eds.), *Sexual deviance: Theory, assessment, and treatment* (2nd ed., pp. 286–304). New York, NY: Guilford.

Whisman, M. A., Johnson, D. P., & Smolen, A. (2011). Dysfunctional attitudes and the serotonin transporter promoter polymorphism (5-HTTLPR). *Behavior Therapy, 42*(2), 300–305.

Whisman, M., Weinstock, L., & Tolejko, N. (2006). Marriage and depression. In L. M. Corey & S. Goodman (Eds.), *A handbook for the social, behavioral, and biomedical sciences* (pp. 219–240). Boulder, CO: Cambridge University Press.

Whitbourne, S. K., & Skultety, K. M. (2002). Body image development: Adulthood and aging. In T. M. Cash & T. Pruzinsky (Eds.), *Body image: A handbook of theory, research, and clinical practice* (pp. 83–90). New York, NY: Guilford.

White, A., & Hingson, R. (2014). The burden of alcohol use: Excessive alcohol consumption and related consequences among college students. *Alcohol Research: Current Reviews, 35*(2), 201–218.

White, J. L., Moffitt, T. E., & Silva, P. A. (1989). A prospective replication of the protective effects of IQ in subjects at high risk for juvenile delinquency. *Journal of Consulting and Clinical Psychology, 57,* 719–724.

White, K. S., & Barlow, D. H. (2002). In D. H. Barlow (Ed.), *Anxiety and its disorders: The nature and treatment of anxiety and panic* (2nd ed.). New York, NY: Guilford.

White, K. S., Brown, T. A., Somers, T. J., & Barlow, D. H. (2006). Avoidance behavior in panic disorder: The moderating influence of perceived control. *Behaviour Research and Therapy, 44,* 147–157.

White, K. S., Payne, L. A., Gorman, J. M., Shear, M. K., Woods, S. W., Saksa, J. R., & Barlow, D. H. (2013). Does maintenance CBT contribute to long-term treatment response of panic disorder with or without agoraphobia? A randomized controlled clinical trial. *Journal of Consulting and Clinical Psychology, 81,* 47–57.

White, P. D., Goldsmith, K. A., Johnson, A. L., Potts, L., Walwyn, R., DeCesare, J. C., & Group, P. T. M. (2011). Comparison of adaptive pacing therapy, cognitive behavior therapy, graded exercise therapy, and specialist medical care for chronic fatigue syndrome (PACE): A randomised trial. *Lancet, 377*(9768), 823–836.

White, W., & Kurtz, E. (2008). Twelve defining moments in the history of Alcoholics Anonymous. In M. Galanter & L. A. Kaskutas (Eds.), *Research on Alcoholics Anonymous and spirituality in addiction recovery: The twelve-step program model, spiritually oriented recovery, twelve-step membership, effectiveness and outcome research* (pp. 37–57). New York, NY: Springer Verlag.

Whitehurst, G. J., Fischel, J. E., Lonigan, C. J., Valdez-Menchaca, M. C., DeBaryshe, B. D., & Caulfield, M. B. (1988). Verbal interaction in families of normal and expressive-language-delayed children. *Developmental Psychology, 24,* 690–699.

Whiteside, U., Bittinger, J. N., Kilmer, J. R., Lostutter, T. W., & Larimer, M. E. (2015). College student drinking. In R. K. Ries, D. A. Fiellin, S. C. Miller, & R. Saitz (Eds.), *The ASAM principles of addiction medicine* (5th ed., pp. 562–574). New York, NY: Wolters Kluwer.

Whitfield-Gabrieli, S., Ghosh, S. S., Nieto-Castanon, A., Saygin, Z., Doehrmann, O., Chai, X. J., Reynold, G. O., Hofmann, S. G., Pollack, M. H., & Gabrieli, J. D. E. (2016). Brain connectomics predict response to treatment in social anxiety disorder. *Molecular Psychiatry, 21*(5), 680–685.

Whitfield-Gabrieli, S., Ghosh, S. S., Nieto-Castanon, A., Saygin, Z., Doehrmann, O., Chai, X. J., Reynold, G. O., Hofmann, S. G., Pollack, M. H., & Gabrieli, J. D. E. (2016). Brain connectomics predict response to treatment in social anxiety disorder. *Molecular Psychiatry, 21,* 680–685. doi: 10.1038/mp.2015.109

Whiting, D., & Fazel, S. (2020). Epidemiology and risk factors for violence in people with mental disorders *Violence and Mental Disorders* (pp. 49–62). New York, NY: Springer.

Whitnam, F. L., Diamond, M., & Martin, J. (1993). Homosexual orientation in twins: A report on 61 pairs and three triplet sets. *Archives of Sexual Behavior, 22*(3), 187–206.

Whittal, M. L., & Robichaud, M. (2012). Cognitive treatment for OCD. In G. Steketee (Ed.), *The Oxford handbook of obsessive compulsive and spectrum disorders* (pp. 345–364). New York, NY: Oxford University Press.

Whittal, M. L., Agras, W. S., & Gould, R. A. (1999). *Behavior Therapy, 30,* 117–135.

World Health Organization. (2015). World health statistics 2015. World Health Organization. https://apps.who.int/iris/handle/10665/170250

Whooley, M. A., & Wong, J. M. (2013). Depression and cardiovascular disorders. *Annual Review of Clinical Psychology, 9,* 327–354.

Whooley, M. A., de Jonge, P., Vittinghoff, E., Otte, C., Moos, R., Carney, R. M., & Browner, W. S. (2008). Depressive symptoms, health behaviors, and risk of cardiovascular events in patients with coronary heart disease. *JAMA: Journal of the American Medical Association, 300,* 2379–2388.

Widaman, K. F. (2009). Phenylketonuria in children and mothers: Genes, environments, behavior. *Current Directions in Psychological Science, 18*(1), 48c52.

Widiger, T. A. (1991). Personality disorder dimensional models proposed for the DSM-IV. *Journal of Personality Disorders, 5,* 386–398.

Widiger, T. A. (2006). Psychopathy and DSM-IV psychopathology. In C. J. Patrick (Ed.), *Handbook of psychopathy* (pp. 156–171). New York, NY: Guilford.

Widiger, T. A. (2011). The DSM-5 dimensional model of personality disorder: Rationale and empirical support. *Journal of Personality Disorders, 25*(2), 222–234.

Widiger, T. A. (2012). Historical developments and current issues. In T. A. Widiger (Ed.), *The Oxford handbook of personality disorders* (pp. 13–34). New York, NY: Oxford University Press.

Widiger, T. A., & Coker, L. A. (2003). Mental disorders as discrete clinical conditions: Dimensional versus categorical classification. In M. Hersen & S. M. Turner (Eds.), *Adult psychopathology and diagnosis* (4th ed., pp. 3–35). New York, NY: Wiley.

Widiger, T. A., & Crego, C. (2013). Diagnosis and classification. In I. B. Weiner (Series Ed.), G. Stricker, & T. A. Widiger (Vol. Eds.), *Handbook of psychology: Vol. 8 Clinical psychology* (pp. 3-18). Hoboken, NJ: John Wiley & Sons.

Widiger, T. A., & Edmundson, M. (2011). Diagnoses, dimensions, and DSM V. In D. H. Barlow (Ed.), *Handbook of clinical psychology.* New York, NY: Oxford University Press.

Widiger, T. A., & Samuel, D. B. (2005). Diagnostic categories or dimensions? A question for the diagnostic and statistical manual of mental disorders (5th ed.). *Journal of Abnormal Psychology, 114,* 494–504.

Widiger, T. A., & Sankis, L. M. (2000). Adult psychopathology: Issues and controversies. *Annual Review of Psychology, 51,* 377–404.

Widiger, T. A., & Simonsen, E. (2005). Alternative dimensional models of personality disorder: Finding a common ground. *Journal of Personality Disorders, 19*(2), 110–130.

Widiger, T. A., & Spitzer, R. L. (1991). Sex bias in the diagnosis of personality disorders: Conceptual and methodological issues. *Clinical Psychology Review, 11,* 1–22.

Widiger, T. A., Cadoret, R., Hare, R., Robins, L., Rutherford, M., Zanarini, M., . . . Hart, S. (1996). DSM—IV antisocial personality disorder field trial. *Journal of Abnormal Psychology, 105*(1), 3.

Widiger, T. A., Frances, A. J., Pincus, H. A., Ross, R., First, M. B., Davis, W., & Kline, M. (Eds.) (1998). *DSM-IV sourcebook* (Vol. 4). Washington, DC: American Psychiatric Association.

Widiger, T. A., Livesley, W. J., & Clark, L. A. (2009). An integrative dimensional classification of personality disorder. *Psychological Assessment, 21*(3), 243–255.

Widiger, T., & Trull, T. (2007). Plate tectonics in the classification of personality disorder: Shifting to a dimensional model. *American Psychologist, 62*(2), 71.

Widiger, T. A. (2013). Classification and diagnosis: Historical development and contemporary issues. In J. Maddux & B. Winstead (Eds.), *Psychopathology: Foundations for a contemporary understanding* (3rd ed.). New York, NY: Erlbaum.

Widom, C. S. (1977). A methodology for studying noninstitutionalized psychopaths. *Journal of Consulting and Clinical Psychology, 45,* 674–683.

Widom, C. S. (1984). Sex roles, criminality, and psychopathology. In C. S. Widom (Ed.), *Sex roles and psychopathology* (pp. 183–217). New York, NY: Plenum Press.

Widom, C. S., Czaja, S. J., & Paris, J. (2009). A prospective investigation of borderline personality disorder in abused and neglected children followed up into adulthood. *Journal of Personality Disorders, 23*(5), 433–446.

Wiebe, S. T., Cassoff, J., & Gruber, R. (2012). Sleep patterns and the risk for unipolar depression: A review. *Nature and Science of Sleep, 4,* 63–71.

Wiech, K., Ploner, M., & Tracey, I. (2008). Neurocognitive Aspects of Pain Perception. *Trends in Cognitive Sciences, 12,* 306–313.

Wiegel, M. (2008). *Women who sexually abuse minors: Description and instrument validation.* (Unpublished doctoral dissertation). Boston University, Boston, MA.

Wiegel, M., Scepkowski, L., & Barlow, D. (2006). Cognitive and affective processes in female sexual dysfunctions. In I. Goldstein, C. Meston, S. Davis, & A. Traish (Eds.), *Women's sexual function and dysfunction: Study, diagnosis and treatment* (pp. 85–92). London, UK: Taylor & Francis.

Wiegel, M., Wincze, J. P., & Barlow, D. H. (2002). Sexual dysfunction. In M. M. Antony & D. H. Barlow (Eds.), *Handbook of assessment and treatment planning for psychological disorders* (pp. 481–522). New York, NY: Guilford.

Wiger, D. E., & Mooney, N. B. (2015). Mental Status Exam. In R. L. Cautin (Eds.), *The Encyclopedia of Clinical Psychology* (1-5). Hoboken, NJ : John Wiley & Sons. doi 10.1002/9781118625392.wbecp104

Wijeratne, P. A., Johnson, E. B., Eshaghi, A., Aksman, L., Gregory, S., Johnson, H. J., … Georgiou-Karistianis, N. (2020). Robust markers and sample sizes for multicenter trials of Huntington disease. *Annals of Neurology, 87*(5), 751–762.

Wiklander, M., Samuelsson, M., Jokinen, J., Nilsonne, Å., Wilczek, A., Rylander, G., & Åsberg, M. (2012). Shame-proneness in attempted suicide patients. *BMC Psychiatry, 12*(1), 50.

Wilcox, H. C., Arria, A. M., Caldeira, K. M., Vincent, K. B., Pinchevsky, G. M., & O'Grady, K. E. (2010). Prevalence and predictors of persistent suicide ideation, plans, and attempts during college. *Journal of Affective Disorders, 127*(1), 287–294.

Wilcox, H. C., Storr, C. L., & Breslau, N. (2009). Posttraumatic stress disorder and suicide attempts in a community sample of urban American young adults. *Archives of General Psychiatry, 66*(3), 305–311. doi: 10.1001/archgenpsychiatry.2008.557

Wildes, J. E., Emery, R. E., & Simons, A. D. (2001). The roles of ethnicity and culture in the development of eating disturbance and body dissatisfaction: A meta-analytic review. *Clinical Psychology Review, 21*(4), 521–551. doi: 10.1016/S0272-7358(99) 00071-9

Wilfley, D. E., & Rodin, J. (1995). Cultural influences on eating disorders. In K. D. Brownell & C. G. Fairburn (Eds.), *Eating disorders and obesity: A comprehensive handbook.* New York, NY: Guilford, pp. 78–82.

Wilfley, D. E., Welch, R., Stein, R. I., Spurrell, E. B., Cohen, L. R., Saelens, B. E., & Matt, G. E. (2002). A randomized comparison of group cognitive-behavioral and group interpersonal psychotherapy for treatment of overweight individuals with binge-eating disorder. *Archives of General Psychiatry, 59,* 713–721.

Wilhelm, S., Buhlmann, U., Tolin, D. F., Meunier, S. A., Pearlson, G. D., Reese, H. E., Cannistraro, P., Jenike, M. A., & Rauch, S. L. (2008). Augmentation of behavior therapy with D-cycloserine for obsessive-compulsive disorder. *American Journal of Psychiatry. 165,* 335–341.

Wilhelm, S., Otto, M. W., Lohr, B., & Deckersbach, T. (1999). Cognitive behavior group therapy for body dysmorphic disorder: A case series. *Behaviour Research and Therapy, 37,* 71–75.

Wilk, K., & Hegerl, U. (2010). Time of mood switches in ultra-rapid cycling disorder: A brief review. *Psychiatry Research, 180,* 1–4.

Williams, C. J., & Weinberg, M. S. (2003). Zoophilia in men: A study of sexual interest in animals. *Archives of Sexual Behavior, 32,* 523–535.

Williams, D. (2020). Is serial sexual homicide a compulsion, deviant leisure, or both? Revisiting the case of Ted Bundy. *Leisure Sciences, 42*(2), 205–223.

Williams, D. R., Lawrence, J. A., & Davis, B. A. (2019). *Racism and health: Evidence and needed research. Annual Review of Public Health, 40,* 105–125. doi: 10.1146/annurev-publhealth-040218-043750

Williams, R. B, Haney, T. L., Lee, K. L., Kong, Y.-H., Blumenthal, J. A., & Whalen, R. E. (1980). Type a behavior, hostility, and coronary atherosclerosis. *Psychosomatic Medicine, 42*(6), 539–549. https://doi.org/10.1097/00006842-198011000-00002

Williams, J. M. G., Teasdale, J. D., Segal, Z. V., & Kabat-Zinn, J. (2007). *The mindful way through depression: Freeing yourself from chronic unhappiness.* New York, NY: Guilford.

Williams, J., Hadjistavropoulos, T., & Sharpe, D. (2006). A meta-analysis of psychological and pharmacological treatments for body dysmorphic disorder. *Behaviour Research and Therapy, 44,* 99–111.

Williams, L. (1994). Recall of childhood trauma: A prospective study of women's memories of child sexual abuse. *Journal of Consulting and Clinical Psychology, 62,* 1167–1176.

Williams, M. R., Chaudhry, R., Perera, S., Pearce, R. K. B., Hirsch, S. R., Ansorge, O., . . . Maier, M. (2013). Changes in cortical thickness in the frontal lobes in schizophrenia are a result of thinning of pyramidal cell layers. *European Archives of Psychiatry and Clinical Neuroscience, 263*(1), 25–39.

Williams, R. B., & Schneiderman, N. (2002). Resolved: Psychosocial interventions can improve clinical outcomes in organic disease (Pro). *Psychosomatic Medicine, 64,* 552–557.

Williams, R. B., Barefoot, J. C., & Schneiderman, N. (2003). Psychosocial risk factors for cardiovascular disease; More than one culprit at work. *JAMA: Journal of the American Medical Association, 290,* 2190–2192.

Williams, R. B., Marchuk, D. A., Gadde, K. M., Barefoot, J. C., Grichnik, K., Helms, M. J., & Siegler, I. C. (2001). Central nervous system serotonin function and cardiovascular responses to stress. *Psychosomatic Medicine, 63,* 300–305.

Williams, S. T., Dhesi, J. K., & Partridge, J. S. (2020). Distress in delirium: Causes, assessment and management. *European Geriatric Medicine, 11*(1), 63–70.

Williamson, K., Nimegeer, A., & Lean, M. (2020). Rising prevalence of BMI ≥40 kg/m2: A high-demand epidemic needing better documentation. *Obesity Reviews, 21*(4). doi: 10.1111/obr.1298

Willwerth, J. (1993, August 30). Tinkering with madness. *Time,* pp. 40–42.

Wilson, B. M., Mickes, L., Stolarz-Fantino, S., Evrard, M., & Fantino, E. (2015).

Increased false-memory susceptibility after mindfulness meditation. *Psychological Science, 26,* 1567–1573.

Wilson, G. T., & Fairburn, C. G. (2007). Treatments for eating disorders. In P. E. Nathan & J. M. Gorman (Eds.), *A guide to treatments that work* (3rd ed., pp. 579–610). New York, NY: Oxford University Press.

Wilson, G. T., & Zandberg, L. (2012). Cognitive-behavioral guided self-help for eating disorders: Effectiveness and scalability. *Clinical Psychology Review, 32,* 343–357.

Wilson, G. T., Loeb, K. L., Walsh, B. T., Labouvie, E., Petkova, E., Liu, S., & Waternaux, C. (1999). Psychological versus pharmacological treatments of bulimia nervosa: Predictors and processes of change. *Journal of Consulting and Clinical Psychology, 67,* 451–459.

Wilson, G. T., Wilfley, D. E., Agras, W. S., & Bryson, S. W. (2010). Psychological treatments of binge eating disorder. *Archives of General Psychiatry, 67*(1), 94–101.

Wilson, J. E., Mart, M. F., Cunningham, C., Shehabi, Y., Girard, T. D., MacLullich, A. M., … Ely, E. W. (2020). Delirium. *Nature Reviews Disease Primers, 6*(1), 1–26.

Wilson, R. S., Aggarwal, N. T., Barnes, L. L., Mendes de Leon, C. F., Hebert, L. E., & Evans, D. A. (2010). Cognitive decline in incident Alzheimer disease in a community population. *Neurology, 74*(12), 951–955.

Wimmer, G. E., & Shohamy, D. (2012, October). Preference by association: how memory mechanisms in the hippocampus bias decisions. Science. 338(6104): 270–3. doi: 10.1126/science.1223252.

Winchel, R. M., Stanley, B., & Stanley, M. (1990). Biochemical aspects of suicide. In S. J. Blumenthal & D. J. Kupfer (Eds.), *Suicide over the life cycle: Risk factors, assessment and treatment of suicidal patterns* (pp. 97–126). Washington, DC: American Psychiatric Press.

Wincze, J. P. (2009). *Enhancing sexuality: A problem-solving approach to treating dysfunction: Therapist guide* (2nd ed). New York, NY: Oxford University Press.

Wincze, J. P., & Carey, M. P. (2001). *Sexual dysfunction: A guide for assessment and treatment.* New York, NY: Guilford.

Wincze, J. P., & Weisberg, R. B. (2015). *Sexual dysfunction: A guide for assessment and treatment.* Guilford Publications: New York.

Wincze, J. P., Bach, A., & Barlow, D. H. (2008). Sexual dysfunction. In D. H. Barlow (Ed.), *Clinical handbook of psychological disorders: A step-by-step treatment manual* (4th ed., pp. 615–661). New York, NY: Guilford.

Windgassen, K. (1992). Treatment with neuroleptics: The patient's perspective. *Acta Psychiatrica Scandinavica, 86,* 405–410.

Wing, J. K., Cooper, J. E., & Sartorius, N. (1974). *The measurement and classification of psychiatric symptoms.* Cambridge, UK: Cambridge University Press.

Wing, R. R. (2010). Treatment options for obesity: Do commercial weight loss programs have a role? *Journal of American Medical Association, 304,* 1837–1838.

Winkelman, J. W. (2006). Efficacy and tolerability of open-label topiramate in the treatment of sleep-related eating disorder: A retrospective case series. *Journal of Clinical Psychiatry, 67,* 1729–1734.

Winsper, C. (in press). Borderline personality disorder: Course and outcomes across the lifespan. *Current Opinion in Psychology.*

Winter, A. (1998). *Mesmerized powers of mind in Victorian Britain.* University of Chicago Press: Chicago.

Winter, D., Elzinga, B., & Schmahl, C. (2013). Emotions and memory in borderline personality disorder. *Psychopathology, 47*(2), 71–85.

Winters, R. W., & Schneiderman, N. (2000). Anxiety and coronary heart disease. In D. I. Mostofsky & D. H. Barlow (Eds.), *The management of stress and anxiety in medical disorders* (pp. 206–219). Needham Heights, MA: Allyn & Bacon.

Winzelberg, A. J., Eppstein, D., Eldredge, K. L., Wilfley, D., Dasmahapatra, R., Dev, P., & Taylor, C. B. (2000). Effectiveness of an Internet-based program for reducing risk factors for eating disorders. *Journal of Consulting and Clinical Psychology, 68,* 346–350.

Winzelberg, A. J., Taylor, C. B., Sharpe, T., Eldredge, K. L., Dev, P., & Constantinou, P. S. (1998). Evaluation of a computer-mediated eating disorder intervention program. *International Journal of Eating Disorders, 24,* 339–349.

Wirdefeldt, K., Adami, H. O., Cole, P., Trichopoulos, D., & Mandel, J. (2011). Epidemiology and etiology of Parkinson's disease: A review of the evidence. *European Journal of Epidemiology, 26*(1), 1–58.

Wirz-Justice, A. (1998). Beginning to see the light. *Archives of General Psychiatry, 55,* 861–862.

Wise, M. G., Hilty, D. M., & Cerda, G. M. (2001). Delirium due to a general medical condition, delirium due to multiple etiologies, and delirium not otherwise specified. In G. O. Gabbard (Ed.), *Treatment of psychiatric disorders* (3rd ed., Vol. 1, pp. 387–412). Washington, DC: American Psychiatric Publishing.

Wiseman, F. K., Alford, K. A., Tybulewicz, V. L. J., & Fisher, E. M. C. (2009). Down syndrome—recent progress and future prospects. *Human Molecular Genetics, 18*(R1), R75–83.

Wisner, K. L, Bogen, D. L., Sit, D., McShea, M., Hughes, C., Rizzo, D., Confer, A., Luther, J., Eng, H., & Wisniewski, S. W. (2013). Does fetal exposure to SSRIs or maternal depression impact infant growth? *American Journal of Psychiatry, 170*(5), 485–493.

Wisner, K. L., Moses-Kolko, E. L., & Sit, D. K. (2010). Postpartum depression: A disorder in search of a definition. *Archives of Women's Mental Health, 13*(1), 37–40.

Wisner, K. L., Parry, B. L., & Piontek, C. M. (2002). Postpartum depression. *New England Journal of Medicine, 347,* 194–199.

Wisner, K. L., Sit, D. K. Y., McShea, M. C., Rizzo, D., Zoretich, R. A., Hughes, C. L. . . . Hanusa, B. H. (2013). Onset timing, thoughts of self-harm, and diagnoses in postpartum women with screen-positive depression findings. *JAMA Psychiatry, 70*(5), 490–498.

Witherington, R. (1988). Suction device therapy in the management of erectile impotence. *Urologic Clinics of North America, 15,* 123–128.

Witkiewitz, K., & Marlatt, G. A. (2004). Relapse prevention for alcohol and drug problems: That was Zen, this is Tao. *American Psychologist, 59,* 224–235.

Wittchen, H.-U. (2002). Generalized anxiety disorder: Prevalence, burden, and cost to society. *Depression and Anxiety, 16,* 162–171.

Wittchen, H.-U. (2012). The burden of mood disorders. *Science, 338,* 15.

Wittchen, H.-U., Gloster, A. T., Beesdo-Baum, K., Fava, G. A., & Craske, M. G. (2010). Agoraphobia: A review of the diagnostic classificatory position and criteria. *Depression and Anxiety, 27,* 113–133.

Wittchen, H.-U., Knäuper, B., & Kessler, R. C. (1994). Lifetime risk of depression. *British Journal of Psychiatry, 165* (Suppl. 26), 116–122.

Wittchen, H.-U., Zhao, S., Kessler, R. C., & Eaton, W. W. (1994). DSM-III-R generalized anxiety disorder in the national comorbidity survey. *Archives of General Psychiatry, 51,* 355–364.

Witthöft, M., & Hiller, W. (2010). Psychological approaches to origins and treatments of somatoform disorders. *Annual Review of Clinical Psychology, 6,* 257–283.

Wittmann, M., Dinich, J., Merrow, M., & Roenneberg, T. (2006). Social jetlag: Misalignment of biological and social time. *Chronobiology*

International, 23(1–2), 497–509. doi: 10.1080/07420520500545979

Wittstein, I., Thiemann, D., Lima, J., Baughman, K., Sculman, S., Gerstenblith, G., & Champion, H. C. (2005). Neurohumoral features of myocardial stunning due to sudden emotional stress. *New England Journal of Medicine, 352,* 539–548.

Wojciechowski, T. W. (2020). The salience of antisocial personality disorder for predicting substance use and violent behavior: The moderating role of deviant peers. *Journal of Drug Issues, 50*(1), 35–50.

Wolf, E. J., Lunney, C. A., Miller, M. W., Resick, P. A., Friedman, M. J., & Schnurr, P. P. (2012). The dissociative subtype of PTSD: A replication and extension. *Depression and Anxiety, 29,* 679–688. doi: 10.1002/da.21946

Wolf, E. J., Miller, M. W., Reardon, A. F., Ryabchenko, K. A., Castillo, D., & Freund, R. (2012). A latent class analysis of dissociation and posttraumatic stress disorder: Evidence for a dissociative subtype. *Archives of General Psychiatry, 69,* 698–705. doi: 10.1001/archgenpsychiatry.2011.1574

Wolf, M. M. (1978). Social validity: The case for subjective measurement or how applied behavior analysis is finding its heart. *Journal of Applied Behavior Analysis, 11,* 203–214.

Wolfe, B. M., & Belle, S. H. (2014). Long-term risks and benefits of bariatric surgery: A research challenge. *JAMA, 312*(17), 1792–1793.

Wolff, K. (2012). Ketamine. In J. C. Verster, K. Brady, M. Galanter, & P. Conrod (Eds.), *Drug Abuse and Addiction in Medical Illness* (pp. 201–211). New York, NY: Springer.

Wolf-Maier, K., Cooper, R. S., Banegas, J. R., Giampaoli, S., Hense, H., Joffres, M., & Vescio, F. (2003). Hypertension prevalence and blood pressure levels in 6 European countries, Canada, and the United States. *JAMA: Journal of the American Medical Association, 289,* 2362–2369.

Wolitzky-Taylor, K. B., Castriotta, N., Lenze, E. J., Stanley, M. A., & Craske, M. G. (2010). Anxiety disorders in older adults: A comprehensive review. *Depression and Anxiety, 27*(2), 190–211. doi: 10.1002/da.20653

Wollburg, E., Voigt, K., Braukhaus, C., Herzog, A., & Lowe, B. (2013). Construct validity and descriptive validity of somatoform disorders in light of proposed changes for the DSM-5. *Journal of Psychosomatic Research, 74*(1), 18–24. doi: 10.1016/j.jpsychores.2012.09.015

Wolpe, J. (1958). *Psychotherapy by reciprocal inhibition.* Stanford, CA: Stanford University Press.

Wonderlich, S. A., Gordon, K. H., Mitchell, J. E., Crosby, R. D., & Engel, S. G. (2009). The validity and clinical utility of binge eating disorder. *International Journal of Eating Disorders, 42*(8), 687–705.

Wong, C., & Kasari, C. (2012). Play and joint attention of children with autism in the preschool special education classroom. *Journal of Autism and Developmental Disorders, 42*(10), 2152–2161. doi: 10.1007/s10803-012-1467-2

Wong, K. K. Y. (2020). Paranoid Personality Disorder. In B. J. Carducci, C. S. Nave, A. D. Fabio, D. H. Saklofske, & C. Stough (Eds.), *The Wiley encyclopedia of personality and individual differences: Clinical, applied, and cross-cultural research* (Vol. 3, pp. 175–179). Hoboken, N.J.: Wiley.

Wood, J. J., Kendall, P. C., Wood, K. S., Kerns, C. M., Seltzer, M., Small, B. J., … Storch, E. A. (2020). Cognitive behavioral treatments for anxiety in children with autism spectrum disorder: A randomized clinical trial. *JAMA Psychiatry, 77*(5), 474–483.

Wood, J. M., Garb, H. N., Nezworski, M. T., Lilienfeld, S. O., & Duke, M. C. (2015). A second look at the validity of widely used Rorschach indices: Comment on Mihura, Meyer, Dumitrascu, and Bombel (2013). *Psychology Bulletin, 141*(1):236–249.

Woodman, C. L., Noyes, R., Black, D. W., Schlosser, S., & Yagla, S. J. (1999). A 5-year follow-up study of generalized anxiety disorder and panic disorder. *Journal of Nervous and Mental Disease, 187,* 3–9.

Woods, B., Aguirre, E., Spector, A. E., & Orrell, M. (2012). Cognitive stimulation to improve cognitive functioning in people with dementia. *Cochrane Database Systematic Review, 2,* CD005562.

Woods, E. R., Lin, Y. G., Middleman, A., Beckford, P., Chase, L., & DuRant, R. H. (1997). The associations of suicide attempts in adolescents. *Pediatrics, 99,* 791–796.

Woods, S. W., Miller, T. J., Davidson, L., Hawkins, K. A., Sernyak, M. J., & McGlashan, T. H. (2001). Estimated yield of early detection of prodromal or first episode patients by screening first-degree relatives of schizophrenic patients. *Schizophrenia Research, 52,* 21–27.

Woods, S. W., Walsh, B. C., Saksa, J. R., & McGlashan, T. H. (2010). The case for including attenuated psychotic symptoms syndrome in DSM-5 as a psychosis risk syndrome. *Schizophrenia Research, 123*(2–3), 199.

Woodside, M. R., & Legg, B. H. (1990). Patient advocacy: A mental health perspective. *Journal of Mental Health Counseling, 12,* 38–50.

Woolfolk, R. L., & Allen, L. A. (2011). Somatoform and physical disorders. In D. H. Barlow (Ed.), Oxford handbook of clinical psychology (pp. 334–358). New York, NY: Oxford University Press.

Worell, J., & Remer, P. (1992). *Feminist perspectives in therapy: An empowerment model for women.* New York, NY: Wiley.

Workman, J. L., Barha, C. K., & Galea, L. A. M. (2012). Endocrine substrates of cognitive and affective changes during pregnancy and postpartum. *Behavioral Neuroscience, 126*(1), 54–72.

World Health Organization. (1992). *The ICD-10 classification of mental and behavioural disorders: Clinical descriptions and diagnostic guidelines.* Geneva, Switzerland: World Health Organization.

World Health Organization. (2000). *Women and HIV/AIDS: Fact sheet no. 242.* Retrieved from http://www.who.int/inf-fs/en/fact242.html

World Health Organization. (2001). *Mental Health: New Understanding, New Hope.* Geneva, Switzerland: World Health Organization.

World Health Organization. (2003). Global summary of the HIV/AIDS epidemic, December 2003. Retrieved from http://www.who.int/hiv/pub/epidemiology/epi2003/en

World Health Organization. (2004). *Global status report on alcohol 2004* (2nd ed.). Geneva, Switzerland: World Health Organization.

World Health Organization. (2011). Mental health atlas: 2011. Italy: World Health Organization. doi:10.1093/schbul/sbp137

World Health Organization. (2020). Dementia. Retrieved from https://www.who.int/news-room/fact-sheets/detail/dementia

Wozniak, J. R., Fink, B. A., Fuglestad, A. J., Eckerle, J. K., Boys, C. J., Sandness, K. E., … Brearley, A. M. (2020). Four-year follow-up of a randomized controlled trial of choline for neurodevelopment in fetal alcohol spectrum disorder. *Journal of Neurodevelopmental Disorders, 12*(1), 1–13.

Wright, J. (2009). *Address unknown: The homeless in America.* New Brunswick, NJ: Transaction.

Wright, J. P., Tibbetts, S. G., & Daigle, L. E. (2015). *Criminals in the making: Criminality across the life course.* Sage Publications.

Wright, J. W., Kawas, L. H., & Harding, J. W. (2015). The development of small molecule angiotensin IV analogs to treat Alzheimer's and Parkinson's diseases. *Progress in Neurobiology, 125,* 26–46.

Wu, C., & Guilleminault, C. (2021). Adult obstructive sleep apnea. In E. H. During & C. A. Kushida (Eds.), *Clinical sleep medicine:*

A comprehensive guide for mental health and other medical professionals (pp. 147–169). Washington, D.C.: American Psychiatric Association Publishing.
Wu, E., Birnbaum, H., Shi, L., Ball, D., Kessler, R., Moulis, M., Aggarwal, J. (2005). The economic burden of schizophrenia in the United States in 2002. *Journal of Clinical Psychiatry, 66*(9), 1122–1129.
Wu, F. (2009). *Suicide and Justice: A Chinese Perspective.* New York, NY: Routledge.
Wu, L.-T., Blazer, D. G., Li, T.-K., & Woody, G. E. (2011). Treatment use and barriers among adolescents with prescription opioid use disorders. *Addictive Behaviors, 36*(12), 1233–1239. doi: 10.1016/j.addbeh.2011.07.033
Wu, L.-T., Parrott, A., Ringwalt, C., Patkar, A., Mannelli, P., & Blazer, D. (2009). The high prevalence of substance use disorders among recent MDMA users compared with other drug users: Implications for intervention. *Addictive Behaviors, 34*(8), 654–661.
Wulfert, E., Franco, C., Williams, K., Roland, B., & Maxson, J. H. (2008). The role of money in the excitement of gambling. *Psychology of Addictive Behaviors, 22*(3), 380–390.
Wulfert, E., Maxson, J., & Jardin, B. (2009). Cue-specific reactivity in experienced gamblers. *Psychology of Addictive Behaviors, 23*(4), 731–735. doi: 10.1037/a0017134
Wyatt v. Stickney, 344 F. Supp. 373 (Ala. 1972).
Wykes, T., Huddy, V., Cellard, C., McGurk, S. R., & Czobor, P. (2011). A meta-analysis of cognitive remediation for schizophrenia: methodology and effect sizes. *American Journal of Psychiatry, 168,* 472–485.
Wynne, L. C., Tienari, P., Nieminen, P., Sorri, A., Lahti, I. O., Moring, J., & Miettunen, J. (2006). I. Genotype-environment interaction in the schizophrenia spectrum: Genetic liability and global family ratings in the Finnish Adoption Study. *Family Process, 45*(4), 419–434.
Xiao, D., Chen, Z., Wu, S., Huang, K., Xu, J., Yang, L., … Chen, S. (2020). Prevalence and risk factors of small airway dysfunction, and association with smoking, in china: Findings from a national cross-sectional study. *The Lancet Respiratory Medicine, 8*(11), 1081–1093. doi: 10.1016/S2213-2600(20)30155-7
Xing, G., Zhang, L., Russell, S., & Post, R. (2006). *Schizophrenia Research, 84,* 36–56.
Yach, D., Struckler, D., & Brownell, K. D. (2006). Epidemiologic and economic consequences of the global epidemics of obesity and diabetes. *Nature Medicine, 12(1),* 62–66.
Yaden, D. B., Yaden, M. E., & Griffiths, R. R. (2020). Psychedelics in psychiatry: Keeping the renaissance from going off the rails. *JAMA Psychiatry,* December 2. doi: 10.1001/jamapsychiatry.2020.3672
Yamada, K. (2015). Unremembered nocturnal eating syndrome: 8 case reports. *Reactions, 1541,* 148–147.
Yamada, K., Watanabe, K., Nemoto, N., Fujita, H., Chikaraishi, C., Yamauchi, K., & Kanba, S. (2006). Prediction of medication noncompliance in outpatients with schizophrenia: 2-year follow-up study. *Psychiatry Research, 141,* 61–69.
Yamamoto, J., Silva, A., Sasao, T., Wang, C., & Nguyen, L. (1993). Alcoholism in Peru. *American Journal of Psychiatry, 150,* 1059–1062.
Yan, L. L., Liu, K., Matthews, K. A., Daviglus, M. L., Ferguson, T. F., & Kiefe, C. I. (2003). Psychosocial risk factors and risk of hypertension: The coronary artery risk development in young adults (CARDIA) study. *JAMA: Journal of the American Medical Association, 290,* 2138–2148.
Yanez, B., Edmondson, D., Stanton, A. L., Park, C. L., Kwan, L., Ganz, P. A., & Blank, T. O. (2009). Facets of spirituality as predictors of adjustment to cancer: Relative contributions of having faith and finding meaning. *Journal of Consulting and Clinical Psychology, 77,* 730–741.
Yanos, P. T., O'Connor, L. K., DeLuca, J. S., Fregenti, S., & Reji, P. M. (2020). Assisted outpatient treatment orders and the therapeutic relationship in assertive community treatment: A mixed-methods study. *Psychosis, 12*(1), 23–33.
Yanovski, S. Z., & Yanovski, J. A. (2014). Long-term drug treatment for obesity: A systematic and clinical review. *JAMA, 311*(1), 74–86.
Yates, G., & Bass, C. (2017). The perpetrators of medical child abuse (Munchausen syndrome by proxy): A systematic review of 796 cases. *Child Abuse and Neglect, 72,* 45–53. doi: 10.1016/j.chiabu.2017.07.008
Yates, P. M., Hucker, S. J., & Kingston, D. A. (2008). Sexual sadism: Psychopathology and theory. In D. R. Laws & W. T. O'Donohue (Eds.), *Sexual deviance: Theory, assessment, and treatment* (2nd ed., pp. 213–230). New York, NY: Guilford.
Yatham, L. N., Kennedy, S., O'Donovan, C., Parikh, Sagar, V., MacQueen, G., & Beaulieu, S. (2006). Canadian Network for Mood and Anxiety Treatments (CANMAT) guidelines for the management of patients with bipolar disorder: Update 2007. *Bipolar Disorders, 8,* 721–739.
Yatham, L. N., Liddle, P. F., Sossi, V., Erez, J., Vafai, N., Lam, R. W., & Blinder, S. (2012). Positron emission tomography study of the effects of tryptophan depletion on brain serotonin2 receptors in subjects recently remitted from major depression. *Archives of General Psychiatry, 69*(6), 601–609.
Yau, Y. H. C., Yip, S. W. & Potenza, M. N. (2015). Understanding "behavioral addictions": insights from research. In R. K. Ries, D. A. Fiellin, S. C. Miller, & R. Saitz (Eds.), *The ASAM principles of addiction medicine* (5th ed., pp. 55–81). New York, NY: Wolters Kluwer.
Yazgan, I., Hanson, J. L., Bates, J. E., Lansford, J. E., Pettit, G. S., & Dodge, K. A. (2021). Cumulative early childhood adversity and later antisocial behavior: The mediating role of passive avoidance. *Development and Psychopathology, 33*(1), 340–350.
Yeaton, W. H., & Bailey, J. S. (1978). Teaching pedestrian safety skills to young children: An analysis and one-year follow-up. *Journal of Applied Behavior Analysis, 11,* 315–329.
Yeh, S.-R., Fricke, R. A., & Edwards, D. H. (1996, January 19). The effect of social experience on serotonergic modulation of escape circuit of crayfish. *Science, 271,* 355–369.
Yehuda, R., Pratchett, L., & Pelcovitz, M. (2012). Biological contributions to PTSD: Differentiating normative from pathological response. In J. G. Beck & D. M. Sloan (Eds.), *The Oxford handbook of traumatic stress disorders* (pp. 159–174). New York, NY: Oxford University Press.
Yen, S., Johnson, J., Costello, E., & Simpson, E. (2009). A 5-day dialectical behavior therapy partial hospital program for women with borderline personality disorder: Predictors of outcome from a 3-month follow-up study. *Journal of Psychiatric Practice, 15*(3), 173.
Yeo, G. S., & Heisler, L. K. (2012). Unraveling the brain regulation of appetite: lessons from genetics. *Nature Neuroscience, 15*(10), 1343–1349.
Yerkes, R. M., & Dodson, J. D. (1908). The relation of strength of stimulus to rapidity of habit-formation. *Journal of Comparative Neurology and Psychology, 18,* 459–482.
Yilmaz, Z., Halvorsen, M., Bryois, J., Yu, D., Thornton, L. M., Zerwas, S., … Eating Disorders Working Group of the Psychiatric Genomics Consortium, Tourette Syndrome/Obsessive-Compulsive Disorder Working Group of the Psychiatric Genomics Consortium. (2020). Examination of the shared genetic basis of anorexia nervosa and obsessive–compulsive disorder. *Molecular Psychiatry, 25*(9), 2036–2046. doi: 10.1038/s41380-018-0115-4
Yim, I. S., Glynn, L. M., Dunkel-Schetter, C., Hobel, C. J., Chicz-DeMet, A., & Sandman, C. A. (2009). Risk of postpartum depressive symptoms with elevated

corticotropin-releasing hormone in human pregnancy. *Archives of General Psychiatry, 66*(2), 162–169.
Yin, R. K. (2012). *Applications of case study research* (3rd ed.). Thousand Oaks, CA: Sage.
Yonkers, K. A., Kornstein, S. G., Gueorguieva, R., Merry, B., Van Steenburgh, K., & Altemus, M. (2015). Symptom-onset dosing of sertraline for the treatment of premenstrual dysphoric disorder: A randomized clinical trial. *JAMA Psychiatry, 72*(10):1037–1044.
Yonkers, K. A., Warshaw, M., Massion, A. O., & Keller, M. B. (1996). Phenomenology and course of generalized anxiety disorder. *British Journal of Psychiatry, 168,* 308–313.
Young, A. M., & Herling, S. (1986). Drugs as reinforcers: Studies in laboratory animals. In S. R. Goldberg & I. P. Stolerman (Eds.), *Behavioral analysis of drug dependence* (pp. 9–67). Orlando, FL: Academic Press.
Young, J. E., Rygh, J. L., Weinberger, A. D., & Beck, A. T. (in press). Cognitive therapy for depression. In D. H. Barlow (Ed.), *Clinical handbook of psychological disorders: A step-by-step treatment manual* (5th ed.). New York, NY: Guilford.
Young, R. M. (2013). Cravings and expectancies. In P. M. Miller, A. W. Blume, D. J. Kavanagh, K. M. Kampman, M. E. Bates, M. E. Larimer, N. M. Petry, P. De Witte, & S. A. Ball (Eds), *Principles of addiction: Comprehensive addictive behaviors and disorders,* (Vol.1, 425–434). Waltham, MA: Elsevier Academic Press.
Youngberg v. Romeo, 457 U.S. 307 (1982).
Youngstrom, E. A. (2009). Definitional issues in bipolar disorder across the life cycle. *Clinical Psychology: Science and Practice, 16*(2), 140–160.
Young-Wolff, K. C., Enoch, M.-A., & Prescott, C. A. (2011). The influence of gene-environment interactions on alcohol consumption and alcohol use disorders: A comprehensive review. *Clinical Psychology Review, 31*(5), 800–816. doi: 10.1016/j.cpr.2011.03.005
Yu, B., Chen, X., Chen, X., & Yan, H. (2020). Marijuana legalization and historical trends in marijuana use among U.S. residents aged 12–25: results from the 1979–2016 National Survey on drug use and health. *BMC Public Health, 20*(1), 156.
Yu, X., Tam, W. W., Wong, P. T., Lam, T. H., & Stewart, S. M. (2012). The Patient Health Questionnaire-9 for measuring depressive symptoms among the general population in Hong Kong. *Comprehensive Psychiatry, 53*(1), 95–102. doi:10.1016/j.comppsych.2010.11.002
Yuen, W. S., Chan, G., Bruno, R., Clare, P., Mattick, R., Aiken, A., … Peacock, A. (2020). Adolescent alcohol use trajectories: Risk factors and adult outcomes. *Pediatrics, 146*(4), e20200440. doi: 10.1542/peds.2020-0440
Zabalegui, A., Hamers, J. P., Karlsson, S., Leino-Kilpi, H., Renom-Guiteras, A., Saks, K., . . . Cabrera, E. (2014). Best practices interventions to improve quality of care of people with dementia living at home. *Patient Education and Counseling, 95*(2), 175–184.
Zachar, P., & Kendler, K. S. (2014). A diagnostic and statistical manual of mental disorders history of premenstrual dysphoric disorder. *The Journal of Nervous and Mental Disease,* 202(4), 346–352. doi: 10.1097/NMD.0000000000000128
Zadra, A., & Donderi, D. C. (2000). Nightmares and bad dreams: Their prevalence and relationship to well-being. *Journal of Abnormal Psychology, 109,* 273–281.
Zajonc, R. B. (1984). On the primacy of affect. *American Psychologist, 39*(2), 117–123.
Zajonc, R. B. (1998). Emotions. In D. Gilbert, S. T. Fiske, & G. Lindzey (Eds.), *Handbook of social psychology* (Vol. 1, 4th ed., pp. 591–632). New York, NY: McGraw-Hill.
Zakowski, S. G., McAllister, C. G., Deal, M., & Baum, A. (1992). Stress, reactivity, and immune function in healthy men. *Health Psychology, 11,* 223–232.
Zanarini, M. C., Frankenburg, F. R., Dubo, E. D., Sickel, A. E., Trikha, A., Levin, A., & Reynolds, V. (1998). Axis I comorbidity of borderline personality disorder. *American Journal of Psychiatry, 155*(12), 1733–1739.
Zanarini, M. C., & Wedig, M. M. (2014). Childhood adversity and the development of borderline personality disorder. In *Handbook of Borderline Personality Disorder in Children and Adolescents* (pp. 265–276). Springer New York.
Zanarini, M. C., Frankenburg, F. R., & Fitzmaurice, G. M. (2014). Severity of anxiety symptoms reported by borderline patients and Axis II comparison subjects: description and prediction over 16 years of prospective follow-up. *Journal of Personality Disorders, 28*(6), 767-777.
Zanarini, M. C., Frankenburg, F. R., Dubo, E. D., Sickel, A. E., Trikha, A., Levin, A., Reynolds, V. Weiss, L. G., Locke, V., Pan, T., Harris, J. G., Saklofske, D. H., & Prifitera, A. (2015). WISC-V Use in Societal Context. In L. G. Weiss, D. H. Saklofske, J. A. Holdnack, & A. Prifitera (Eds.), *WISC-V Assessment and Interpretation: Scientist-Practitioner Perspectives,* 123–176. San Diego, CA: Elsevier.
Zanarini, M. C., Frankenburg, F. R., Hennen, J., Reich, D. B., & Silk, K. R. (2006). Prediction of the 10-year course of borderline personality disorder. *American Journal of Psychiatry, 163,* 827–832.
Zanarini, M. C., Frankenburg, F. R., Reich, D. B., & Fitzmaurice, G. (2012). Attainment and stability of sustained symptomatic remission and recovery among patients with borderline personality disorder and axis II comparison subjects: a 16-year prospective follow-up study. *American Journal of Psychiatry, 169*(5), 476–483.
Zanarini, M. C., Reichman, C. A., Frankenburg, F. R., Reich, D. B., & Fitzmaurice, G. (2010). The course of eating disorders in patients with borderline personality disorder: A 10-year follow-up study. *International Journal of Eating Disorders, 43*(3), 226–232.
Zanos, P., Moaddel, R., Morris, P. J., Riggs, L. M., Highland, J. N., Georgiou, P., … Gould, T. D. (2018). Ketamine and ketamine metabolite pharmacology: Insights into therapeutic mechanisms. *Pharmacological Reviews, 70*(3), 621–660. doi: 10.1124/pr.117.015198
Zapf, P., Zottoli, T., & Pirelli, G. (2009). Insanity in the courtroom: Issues of criminal responsibility and competency to stand trial. In D. A. Krauss & J. D. Lieberman (Eds.), *Psychological expertise in court: Psychology in the courtroom* (pp. 79–101). Surrey, England: Ashgate.
Zarate, C. A., Jr., Singh, J. B., Carlson, P. J., Brutsche, N. E., Ameli, R., Luckenbaugh, D. A., Charney, D. S., & Manji, H. K. (2006). A randomized trial of an N-methyl-D-aspartate antagonist in treatment-resistant major depression. *Archives of General Psychiatry, 63*(8), 856–864. doi: 10.1001/archpsyc.63.8.856
Zautra, A., Johnson, L., & Davis, M. (2005). Positive affect as a source of resilience for women in chronic pain. *Journal of Consulting and Clinical Psychology, 73,* 212–220.
Zeanah, C. H., & Gleason, M. M. (2010). *Reactive attachment disorders: A review for DSM-V.* Retrieved December 29, 2010 from http://stage .dsm5.org/Proposed%20Revision%20Attachments/APA%20DSM-5%20 Reactive%20Attachment%20Disorder%20Review.pdf
Zeitler, M.-L., Bohus, M., Kleindienst, N., Knies, R., Ostermann, M., Schmahl, C., & Lyssenko, L. (2020). How to assess recovery in borderline personality disorder: Psychosocial functioning and satisfaction with life in a sample of former DBT study patients. *Journal of Personality Disorders, 34*(3), 289–307.
Zemore, S. E., Subbaraman, M., & Tonigan, J. S. (2013). Involvement in 12-step activities

and treatment outcomes. *Substance Abuse, 34*(1), 60–69. doi: 10.1080/08897077.2012.691452

Zerbo, E., & Deringer, E. (2015). Kleptomania: To steal or not to steal. That is the question. In M. S. Ascher & P. Levounis (Eds.), *The behavioral addictions* (pp. 113–135). Arlington, VA: American Psychiatric Publishing.

Zervas, I. M., Theleritis, C., & Soldatos, C. R. (2012). Using ECT in schizophrenia: A review from a clinical perspective. *World Journal of Biological Psychiatry, 13*(2), 96–105.

Zhai, L., Zhang, H., & Zhang, D. (2015). Sleep duration and depression among adults: A meta-analysis of prospective studies. *Depression and Anxiety, 32,* 644–670.

Zhang, H., & Cai, B. (2003). The impact of tobacco on lung health in China. *Respirology, 8,* 17–21.

Zhang, J., Palmer, A., Zhang, N., & Gewirtz, A. H. (in press). Coercive parenting mediates the relationship between military fathers' emotion regulation and children's adjustment. *Journal of Abnormal Child Psychology*.

Zhang, T., Wang, K., Qu, M., Jiang, H., Chen, X., & Luo, J. (2020). The effect of physical activity on drug cravings of drug addicts with AIDS: The dual mediating effect of internal inhibition. *Frontiers in Psychology, 11*.

Zheng, G., Yang, Y., Zhu, X., & Elston, R. C. (2012). *Analysis of genetic association studies*. New York, NY: Springer.

Zhou, J. N., Hofman, M. A., Gooren, L. J., & Swaab, D. F. (1995). A sex difference in the human brain and its relation to transsexuality. *Nature, 378,* 68–70.

Zhou, X., Teng, T., Zhang, Y., Del Giovane, C., Furukawa, T. A., Weisz, J. R., … Xie, P. (2020). Comparative efficacy and acceptability of antidepressants, psychotherapies, and their combination for acute treatment of children and adolescents with depressive disorder: A systematic review and network meta-analysis. *The Lancet Psychiatry, 7*(7), 581–601. doi: 10.1016/S2215-0366(20)30137-1

Zigler, E., & Hodapp, R. M. (1986). *Understanding mental retardation*. Cambridge, UK: Cambridge University Press.

Zilbergeld, B. (1999). *The new male sexuality*. New York, NY: Bantam Books.

Zilboorg, G., & Henry, G. (1941). *A history of medical psychology*. New York, NY: W. W. Norton.

Zillmann, D. (1983). Arousal and aggression. In R. G. Geen & E. Donnerstein (Eds.), *Aggression: Theoretical and empirical reviews* (Vol. 1, pp. 75–102). New York, NY: Academic Press.

Zimmerman, M., & Mattia, J. I. (1998). Body dysmorphic disorder in psychiatric outpatients: Recognition, prevalence, comorbidity, demographic, and clinical correlates. *Comprehensive Psychiatry, 39*(5), 265–270.

Zimmerman, M., Rothschild, L., & Chelminski, I. (2005). The prevalence of DSM-IV personality disorders in psychiatric outpatients. *American Journal of Psychiatry, 162,* 1911–1918.

Zinbarg, R. E., & Barlow, D. H. (1996). Structure of anxiety and the anxiety disorders: A hierarchical model. *Journal of Abnormal Psychology, 105,* 181–193.

Zinbarg, R. E., Barlow, D. H., Liebowitz, M. R., Street, L., Broadhead, E., Katon, W., & Kraemer, H. (1998). The DSM-IV field trial for mixed anxiety-depression. In T. A. Widiger, A. J. Frances, H. A. Pincus, R. Ross, M. B. First, W. Davis, & M. Kline (Eds.), *DSM-IV sourcebook* (Vol. 4, pp. 735–799). Washington, DC: American Psychiatric Association.

Zinbarg, R. E., Barlow, D. H., Liebowitz, M., Street, L., Broadhead, E., Katon, W., & Kraemer, H. (1994). The DSM-IV field trial for mixed anxiety depression. *American Journal of Psychiatry, 151,* 1153–1162.

Zinbarg, R. E., Craske, M. G., & Barlow, D. H. (2006). *Mastery of your anxiety and worry: Therapist guide*. New York, NY: Oxford University Press.

Zingmond, D. S., McGory, M. L., & Ko, C. Y. (2005). Hospitalization before and after gastric bypass surgery. *JAMA: Journal of the American Medical Association,* 294, 1918–1924.

Zisook, S., Corruble, E., Duan, N., Inglewicz, A., Karam, E., Lanouette, N., & Young, I. T. (2012). The bereavement exclusion and DSM-5. *Depression and Anxiety, 29,* 425–443.

Zonana, H., & Buchanan, A. (2009). Ethical issues in the treatment of sex offenders. In F. M. Saleh, A. J. Grudzinskas, J. M. Bradford, & B. D. M. (Eds.), *Sex offenders: Identification, risk assessment, treatment, and legal issues* (pp. 425–440). New York, NY: Oxford University Press.

Zou, L., Chen, W., Shao, S., Sun, Z., Zhong, R., Shi, J., & Song, R. (2012). Genetic variant in KIAA0319, but not in DYX1C1, is associated with risk of dyslexia: An integrated meta-analysis. *American Journal of Medical Genetics Part B: Neuropsychiatric Genetics, 159B*(8), 970–976. doi: 10.1002/ajmg.b.32102

Zubieta, J., Bueller, J., Jackson, L., Scott, D., Xu, Y., & Koeppe, R., & Stohler, C. S. (2005). Placebo effects mediated by endogenous opioid activity on u-opioid receptors. *Journal of Neuroscience, 25,* 7754–7762.

Zubin, J., Steinhauer, S. R., & Condray, R. (1992). Vulnerability to relapse in schizophrenia. *British Journal of Psychiatry, 161,* 13–18.

Zuccato, C., & Cattaneo, E. (2009). Brain-derived neurotrophic factor in neurodegenerative diseases. *Nature Reviews Neurology, 5*(6), 311–322.

Zuchner, S., Cuccaro, M. L., Tran-Viet, K. N., Cope, H., Krishnan, R. R., Pericak-Vance, M. A., & Ashley-Koch, A. (2006). SLITRK1 mutations in trichotillomania. *Molecular Psychiatry, 11,* 887–889.

Zucker, K. J. (2005). Measurement of psychosexual differentiation. *Archives of Sexual Behavior, 34,* 375–388.

Zucker, K. J. (2010). The DSM diagnostic criteria for gender identity disorder in children. *Archives of Sexual Behavior, 39,* 477–498.

Zuvekas, S. H., & Vitiello, B. (2012). Stimulant medication use in children: A 12-year perspective. *American Journal of Psychiatry, 169*(2), 160–166. doi: doi:10.1176/appi.ajp.2011.11030387

Zvolensky, M. J., Bakhshaie, J., Shepherd, J. M., Peraza, N., Viana, A. G., Walker, R. L., Garza, M., Ochoa-Perez, M., & Lemaire, C. (2020). Anxiety sensitivity and acculturative stress: Concurrent relations to mental health among Spanish-speaking Latinx in primary care. *Transcultural Psychiatry,* September 15, 1363461520946557. doi: 10.1177/1363461520946557

Zwahlen, M., & Egger, M. (2006). *Progression and mortality of untreated HIV-positive individuals living in resource-limited settings: Update of literature review and evidence synthesis* (UNAIDS Obligation HQ/05/42204). Retrieved from http://data.unaids.org/pub/periodical/2006/zwahlen_unaids_hq_05_422204_2007_en.pdf

Zwaigenbaum, L., Bryson, S., & Garon, N. (2013). Early identification of autism spectrum disorders. *Behavioural Brain Research, 251,* 133–146.

Zych, A. D., & Gogolla, N. (2021). Expressions of emotions across species. *Current Opinion in Neurobiology, 68,* 57–66. doi: 10.1016/j.conb.2021.01.003

Name Index

B

Bermudez, O., 283
Bernardini, F., 456
Bernat, J. A., 382
Berner, L. A., 272, 284
Berney, T. P., 543
Bernstein, D. A., 89
Bernstein, D. M., 203, 204
Berntsen, D., 159
Berridge, K. C., 425
Berrios, G. E., 195, 482
Berry, A. C., 250
Bertelsen, A., 497
Berton, O., 55
Bertsch, K., 468
Besch, C. L., 328
Bettelheim, B., 533
Bettens, K., 564
Bevan, D., 136
Bhagwanjee, A., 134
Bharucha, A., 569
Bhattacharyya, S., 506
Bhugra, D., 120
Bi, S., 468
Biederman, J., 223, 460, 520, 525
Bieniek, K. F., 559
Bierut, L. J., 233
Bigler, E. D., 86
Billeiter, K. B., 539
Billick, S. B., 461
Binder, E. B., 38
Binik, Y. M., 368, 377
Bio, D. S., 232
Birkett, R., 551
Birley, J., 502
Birmaher, B., 227, 228, 229
Birmingham, W. A., 334
Birren, B., 35
Bishop, D., 526
Bishop, D. V. M., 519
Bishop, S. L., 532, 544
Biswas, A., 330
Bittar, R. G., 52–53
Bittinger, J. N., 408
Bivona, J. M., 357
Bjertness, E., 255
Björkenstam, C., 449
Björkenstam, E., 466
Black, D. W., 80, 87, 227, 402–404, 410, 412–414, 417, 432, 458, 519, 523–526, 528, 539, 540, 542, 549–551, 554, 558, 559, 567–579, 581, 585, 586
Black, G. W., 336
Blackwell, E., 320, 325
Blagys, M. D., 22
Blair, K., 153
Blanchard, E., 345
Blanchard, E. B., 345, 382, 383
Blanchard, R., 361, 380, 382, 383, 393
Blanco, C., 131, 143, 215, 222–223
Blaney, P. H., 491, 492
Blank, T. O., 331
Blasco-Fontecilla, H., 259
Blascovich, J., 324, 332
Blashfield, R. K., 5, 90–93, 99
Blazer, D. G., 148, 229, 231
Bleiberg, K. L., 250, 251
Bleijenberg, G., 342, 343
Bleuler, E., 488
Bliss, E. L., 199
Bloch, M., 98
Bloch, M. H., 166, 587
Block, S., 221
Blokhina, E., 433
Blom, M. M., 567
Bloom, F. E., 47
Bloom, J. D., 583
Bloom, J. R., 330
Bloscovitch, J., 65
Blum, K., 419
Blumentals, W. A., 131
Blumenthal, J. A., 62, 335
Blumenthal, S. J., 255, 258
Blythin, S. P. M., 271
Boardman, J. D., 565
Boasso, A. M., 159
Bob, P., 203
Bockoven, J. S., 13, 15, 16
Bockting, C. L., 252
Bockting, W. O., 391
Bodell, L. P., 285
Boden, J. M.,410
Boden, M. T., 456
Bodkin, J. A., 200
Bodlund, O., 393
Bodnar, R. J., 340
Boehlke, K. K., 438
Boehm, J. K., 334
Boehnlein, J., 231
Boen, H., 255
Boettcher, H., 96
Boeving, C. A., 331
Bogaert, A., 361
Bogaert, A. F., 361, 362
Bogart, A. F., 361
Bogels, S., 5, 91
Bogels, S. M., 152, 156
Bohn, K., 285
Bohn, R. L., 135
Boiler, M., 96
Boisseau, C. L., 61, 63, 278
Boland, E. M., 238
Boland, R. J., 182, 215, 220
Bolinskey, P. K., 85, 453
Bolton, B., 270
Bolton, D., 4, 136
Bolton, J., 132
Bombel, G., 82–83
Bonanno, G. A., 221, 222, 231
Bond, A., 48, 543
Bond, M., 20
Bonnar-Kidd, K. K., 580
Bono, C., 391
Boocock, A., 171
Booij, L., 243
Boomsma, D., 391
Boon, S., 201
Boone, E., 233
Boone, L., 282
Boot, W. R., 121
Borg, L., 425
Borge, F.-M., 474
Borges, G., 255, 256, 257
Borkovec, T. D., 133, 135, 136
Borlaug, B.A., 268
Bornstein, R. F., 474
Borodinsky, L. N., 47
Bosinski, H. A. G., 391
Boskind-Lodahl, M., 274
Bosmans, J. E., 567
Bosson, J. K., 81
Bouchard, M. F., 523
Bouchard, T. J. Jr., 35, 116
Bouman, T. K., 187
Bourassa, M. G., 337
Bourget, D., 379
Bourke, J., 543
Boutilier, L. R., 468
Bouton, M. E., 23, 57, 129, 130, 141
Bower, J. E., 331
Bower, J. H., 337
Bowers, J. S., 59
Bowie, C. R., 99
Bowlby, J., 129
Bowler, D., 533
Bowman, E. S., 201, 203
Boxer, A., 335
Boyce, N., 259
Boyd, C. J., 418
Boydell, J., 66
Boyer, P., 167
Boyle, C., 464
Boyle, M., 219, 418
Boysen, G., 469
Bradford, A., 363, 368, 370, 372, 373–374, 376, 379, 382, 385
Bradford, J., 388
Bradford, J. M., 388
Bradley, B. P., 135, 153
Bradley, M. M., 60–61, 462
Bradley, R. G., 233, 235
Bradley, S. J., 393, 395
Bradley, W., 524
Bradshaw, S., 358
Braet, C., 282
Brahler, E., 221
Brailey, K., 162
Brain, C., 506
Brakefield, T. A., 361
Brakemeier, E., 125
Brand, B., 157
Brand, B. L., 200, 205
Brandao, D. J., 229
Brandsma, J., 198
Brannan, S. L., 243
Brannigan, G. G., 87
Braukhaus, C., 183
Brawman-Mintzer, O., 136, 168
Bray, B. C., 422, 463
Bray, G. A., 291
Bray, S. M., 542
Brecht, M.-L., 413
Bredemeier, K., 456
Breeden, G., 258
Breedlove, S. M., 361
Breeksema, J. J., 49
Breier, A., 324
Breitbart, W., 551
Breitborde, N. J., 504
Bremner, J., 203
Bremner, J. D., 162, 163
Brenes, G. A., 133
Brennan-Krohn, T., 439
Brenner, D. E., 563
Brent, D., 221–222, 228, 229
Brent, D. A., 254, 257, 258
Breslau, N., 158, 159, 161
Breuer, J., 18
Brewer, M., 235
Brewer, S., 331
Brewerton, T. D., 274
Bridge, H., 191
Briganti, A., 377
Briskman, J., 464
Britton, J. C., 129
Brix, R. J., 440
Brodman, D. M., 155
Brody, H., 53
Broekman, T. G., 163
Broers, B., 418
Broft, A., 284
Bromet, E. J., 231, 255, 256, 257
Brondolo, E., 334
Brønnick, K., 569
Brook, J. S., 195
Brook, M., 174
Brooker, C., 510
Brooks, D. J., 427
Brooks, R. B., 69
Brotman, M. A., 223
Brotto, L., 363
Brotto, L. A., 377
Broude, G. J., 360

Chamberlain, S. R., 51–52, 175, 474
Champagne, F. A., 40
Champine, P. R., 586
Champoux, M., 54
Chan, B., 258
Chan, C., 509
Chandra, A., 357
Chandwani, K., 23
Chang, I. W., 200
Chang, L. C., 98
Chang, R-B., 98
Chang, X.-L., 565
Chaouloff, F., 321
Chapman, D., 577
Chapman, T. F., 155
Charkoudian, N., 334
Charland, L. C., 458
Charles, S. T., 67, 68
Charney, D. S., 48, 50, 69, 99, 234
Chartrand, H., 132
Chartrand, T. L., 59
Chassin, L., 119, 427
Chasson, G. S., 156
Chatkoff, D., 347
Chattarji, S., 544
Chau Wong, M., 500
Check, J. R., 190
Cheely, C., 68
Chemerinski, E., 453
Chen, S., 419, 462, 523, 527
Chen, S.-W., 474
Chen, Y., 255
Cheng, T., 348
Cheng, T. C., 139
Chesney, M. A., 62, 336, 347
Cheung, F. M., 67, 185
Cheung, Y., 258
Chevalier, J. M., 122
Chevron, E. S., 250
Chhean, D., 148
Chiappetta, L., 466
Chiappini, S., 404
Chida, Y., 320, 331, 335, 336
Chik, H. M., 167
Chinman, M., 510
Chioqueta, A., 185
Chiu, P., 59
Chiu, W. T., 133, 138, 141, 152, 167
Chivers, M. L., 359, 382, 391
Chmielewski, M., 92
Cho, S., 214
Choate, M. L., 63, 150, 151, 250
Chobanian, A. V., 332
Chodoff, P., 450
Choi, J., 568
Choi, K. W., 114–115
Choi, M. S., 98
Choi, S.-H., 550
Choi-Kain, L. W., 445, 466
Chong, R., 139
Chorney, M. J., 35
Chorot, P., 187
Chorpita, B. F., 99, 129, 133, 135
Chosak, A., 170
Chou, T., 139
Choy, O., 457, 458
Christ, S. E., 540
Christensen, J. F., 320
Christensen, Z. P., 418
Christenson, G. A., 379
Christmas, D., 127
Christophe, D., 383
Christopher, M. E., 528
Christos, C., 341
Chronis, A. M., 463, 464
Chun, V., 465
Chung, J., 569
Chung, S. Y., 532
Chung, T., 410
Ciampi, A., 550
Cicchetti, D., 68, 203, 448
Cielsa, J., 237
Cimera, R. E., 543
Ciraulo, D. A., 131, 143
Cirincione, C., 583, 584
Clance, P. R., 283
Clancy, S. A., 204
Claraco, L. M., 188
Clark, C. J., 335
Clark, D., 142
Clark, D. A., 165, 167, 168
Clark, D. M., 143, 155, 163
Clark, L. A., 92, 99, 173
Clark, R., 334
Clark, R. A., 328
Clarke, A., 105
Clarke, G. N., 228
Clarke, S., 80, 121
Clarkin, J. F., 81
Clayton, A. H., 371
Clayton, A., 363
Clayton, D. F., 36
Clayton, E. W., 342
Clayton, P. J., 187
Cleary, P. D., 339
Cleghorn, J. M., 501
Clemenson, G. D., 55
Clement, U., 359
Cloninger, C. R., 187, 448, 454, 468, 470, 471
Closser, M. H., 414
Coan, J. A., 204
Coates, T. J., 350
Cobb, S., 65
Cobham, V. E., 155
Coccaro, E. F., 49, 439
Cochrane, B., 59
Cocores, J. A., 371
Coderre, T. J., 344
Coe, C. L., 320, 324, 326
Coffey, B. J., 519
Cohen, C. A., 586
Cohen, C. I., 491
Cohen, D., 324, 531
Cohen, J., 328
Cohen, J. B., 336
Cohen, J. D., 59
Cohen, L., 230
Cohen, N., 326
Cohen, P., 195
Cohen, S., 65, 320, 324–326
Cohen-Kettenis, P. T., 389
Coker, L. H., 557
Colby, D. A., 417
Cole, D., 237
Cole, J. O., 245
Cole, M. G., 550
Cole, P., 560
Cole, S. H., 466
Cole, S. W., 35, 328
Coleman, E., 379, 391, 395
Colgan, P., 391
Colibazzi, T., 61
Collibee, C., 359
Collier, D. A., 66
Colligan, R. C., 337
Collinge, J., 566
Collins, E. M., 329
Collins, P., 51
Colloca, L., 53
Colman, I., 458
Colodro-Conde, L., 466
Coltheart, M., 485
Comacho, M., 151
Comas-Diaz, L., 198
Comer, J. S., 131, 143, 151, 156, 157, 588
Comijs, H. C., 229
Commons, M. L., 586
Compare, A., 335, 337
Compas, B. E., 68, 237, 252, 348
Compton, S. N., 136, 418, 420
Condie, D., 200
Condray, R., 494
Conesa, L., 283
Conlon, E. G., 150–151
Connett, J. E., 336
Connor, D. F., 525
Conrod, P., 437
Constans, J. I., 162
Constantino, J. N., 454, 464
Convit, A., 268
Conwell, Y., 231, 255, 258
Cook, A. M., 433
Cook, B., 136
Cook, B. J., 270
Cook, E. W., 59
Cook, I. A., 53
Cook, M. L., 454
Cook, P. J., 437
Cooke, B. M., 361
Cookson, C., 582
Coolidge, F., 391
Cools, R., 561
Coons, M., 187
Coons, P. M., 201, 203, 204, 205
Cooper, Z., 270
Cooper, A. J., 370
Cooper, J., 258
Cooper, J. A., 213
Cooper, J. E., 76
Cooper, L. L., 336
Cooper, N. S., 69
Cooper, T. B., 219
Cooper, Z., 271, 272, 281, 282
Cope, N., 528
Copeland, W. E., 224
Copen, C. E., 357
Coplan, J. D., 55, 128
Corbit, J. D., 427
Corcoran, C. M., 502
Corkery, J. M., 404
Cornblatt, B. A., 457
Corona, G., 377
Correia, S., 439
Correll, C. U., 457
Corson, P. W., 280
Cortoni, F., 384, 386
Coryell, W., 226, 227
Cosci, F., 329
Costa e Silva, J. A., 341
Costa, E., 43
Costa, P. Jr., 446
Costa, P. T., 336, 475
Costantino, A., 393
Costanzo, E., 329
Costello, E., 136, 468
Costello, E. J., 224
Costin, V., 103
Coston, N., 469
Cotter, R. E., 258
Cournos, F., 490
Cousin, F. R., 490
Couton, C., 270
Coverdale, J., 471
Covey, L. S., 416
Covino, N., 378
Covinsky, K. E., 134, 229
Cowen, P. J., 281
Cowling, B. J., 118
Cox, A., 533
Cox, A. C., 85
Cox, L., 391
Cozanitis, D. A., 410

Crabbe, J. C., 40
Crago, M., 277
Craig, I. W., 37
Craighead, L. W., 251, 282
Craighead, W. E., 240, 251
Craske, M., 91
Craske, M. G., 5, 23, 126, 127, 131, 135–141, 143–145, 147, 148, 150, 183, 184
Crawford, N., 521
Creamer, M., 159
Creed, F., 183, 185
Creese, I., 51, 500
Crego, C., 4, 5, 90, 99
Cremniter, D., 258
Crerand, C., 173
Crichton, P., 347
Crick, N. R., 448
Cristancho, M. A., 215
Critelli, J. W., 357
Croft, H. A., 371
Croft-Jeffreys, C., 495
Crosby, R., 282
Crosby, R. D., 273, 274, 286
Crouse, K., 142
Crow, S. J., 270, 273
Crowe, A., 431
Crowley, J. J., 163
Crowley, T., 368
Crump, C., 227
Crump, J., 456
Cryan, J. F., 56
Csordas, T. J., 119
Cucolo, H. E., 584
Cuellar, A. K., 217
Curreri, A. J., 164
Cuffee, Y., 334, 335
Cuijpers, P., 136, 214, 250–252, 567
Cunningham Owens, D. G., 505, 508, 510, 511
Cunningham, J., 98
Cunningham-Rathner, J., 379
Cuper, P. F., 468
Curran, P. J., 427
Currier, J. M., 221, 222
Curry, S. J., 218
Curtin, J., 463
Curtis, G. C., 147
Cuthbert, B. N., 60–61
Cuttler, C., 168
Cyranowski, J. M., 241, 359–360, 374
Czaja, S. J., 467
Czobor, P., 509

D

D'Hulst, C., 48
D'Onofrio, B., 35
D'Onofrio, B. M., 107, 416
da Silva, S. A., 229
Daamen, A. P., 413
Dadds, M. R., 155
Dahl, R., 433
Dahlem, C. H., 431, 439
Dahme, B., 283
Dahmer, J., 382
Dai, B., 110
Daigle, L. E., 464
Dalack, G. W., 416
Dalgard, O. S., 255
Daly, R. J., 158
Damasio, A., 578
Damasio, A. R., 52
Damjanovic, L., 153
Dan, O., 129
Dana, R. H., 83
Daniel, E., 533
Daniel, S., 258
Daniel, S. S., 527
Dannlowski, U., 127
Danowski, D., 278
Dansky, B. S., 274
Darcangelo, S., 379
Darredeau, C., 417
Das, P., 193
Daskalakis, Z. J., 507
Davey, A., 555
Davey, G., 58
David Klonsky, E., 258
David, A., 66, 193
Davidson, A. J., 510
Davidson, J. R., 218
Davidson, J. R. T., 155
Davidson, K. W., 337
Davidson, M., 500
Davidson, R., 236
Davidson, R. J., 236
Davidson, S. L., 460
Davies, B, 235
Davies, M. C., 418
Davies, M. N., 134
Davis, D., 203, 204, 205
Davis, D. D., 469, 523
Davis, G. C., 161
Davis, J. D., 453, 550
Davis, K. L., 43, 456
Davis, L., 384
Davis, M., 57, 156, 338, 446, 531
Davis, M. S., 256
Davis, O. S. P., 35
Davison, G., 387
Davison, I. A., 87
Davison, S., 382
Davtyan, A., 568
Davtyan, H., 568
Dawson, D. A., 403, 404
Dawson, M., 533
Dawson, M. E., 464
Day, D. M., 388
Day, R., 503
de Azeredo, L. A., 523
De Backer, G., 336
de Bono, J., 135
de Courten, M., 321
De Girolamo, G., 341
De Gregorio, D., 422
de Groot, H. E., 377
de Groot, J.-C., 550
De Gucht, V., 343
de Guevara-Miranda, D. L., 414
de Jong, J., 198
de Jong, P. J., 31, 184, 187
de Kleine, R. A., 163
de Lacerda, M. C. C., 561
de Lacy, N., 521
de Leon, C. F. M., 565
de Lima, M. S., 520
de Lissovoy, V., 533
De Mey, J., 466
de Portugal, E., 491
De Raedt, R., 248, 249
de Silva, P., 173
de Souto Barreto, P., 567
De Thomas, C. A., 465
de Vries, S., 577
de Wit, H., 429
de Zutter, A., 203
de Zwaan, M., 172
Deal, M., 324
Deale, A., 185, 343, 347
Dean, III, D. C., 488
Deary, V., 343
Deavers, F., 509
DeBaryshe, B., 463
Decety, J., 578
Déchelotte, P., 267
Decker, S. L., 87
Decker, M. D., 135
Deckersbach, T., 94, 144, 172
Deeg, D. J. H., 229
Deffenbacher, J. L., 439
DeFries, J. C., 234
Deiter, P. J., 171
DeJong, B. L., 167
Del Parigi, A., 566
DeLamater, J., 364, 365
Delano-Wood, L., 229, 230, 245
DeLepeleire, J., 570
Delgado, V., 268
DeLisi, L. E., 108–109
DeLisi, M., 445, 462
Delizonna, L. L., 377, 378
Dell, P. F., 194–195
DeLuca, J. S., 576
Delvecchio, P., 577
Demartini, B., 189
Dembroski, T. M., 62, 336
Deming, P., 464
Demiris, G., 569
Demler, O., 133, 134, 138–139, 147, 152, 167, 229
DeMyer, M. K., 533
Deng, W., 55
Denko, T., 245
Denomme, W. J., 415
Dent, M. F., 163
Denys, D., 52–53
Denzin, N. K., 434
DePaulo, J. R., 226
DePinho, R. A., 39
DePrince, A., 157, 193
Depue, R. A., 51
Deringer, E., 439
DeRogatis, L. R., 377
Dersh, J., 182, 338, 339
DeRubeis, R., 251, 253
DeSilva, P., 374
DeSilva, R., 96
de Silva-Sanigorski, A., 291
Detre, J. A., 555
Devanand, D. P., 196, 201, 202, 230
Deveci, A., 191
Devine, K., 23
Devine, P., 417
Devinsky, O., 191–192
Devlin, L., 581
Devlin, M. J., 284
DeWall, C. N., 341
DeWolf, W. C., 378
Dexter-Mazza, E. T., 466, 468
Dhabhar, F. S., 330
Dhawan, N., 471
Dhejne, C., 393
Dhesi, J. K., 550
Di Cesare, M., 268
Di Lodovico, L., 270
Diamond, L. M., 360, 362
Diamond, M., 361, 362, 392
Dias, V. V., 232
Diaz-Milanes, D., 118
Diaz-Stransky, A., 464
DiBartolo, P. M., 372
Dichter, G., 236
Dick, D. M., 36
Dickens, W. T., 35, 40
Dickersin, K., 589
DiClemente, R., 348
DiClemente, R. J., 350
Diener, E., 58, 63
Dietz, P. M., 532
DiIorio, C., 577
DiLillo, D., 348
Dillon, K. S., 205
Dimaite, R., 153
Dimberg, U., 153

Dimidjian, S., 212, 250, 251
Dimoliatis, I., 110
Dimon, L., 11
Dimsdale, J. E., 62
Dinan, T. G., 56
DiNardo, P. A., 149
Dinges, D. F., 199
Dinnel, D. L., 153
Diorio, J., 39, 129
Dishion, T. J., 428, 465
Disney, K. L., 474
Distler, A., 155
Dixie-Bell, D. D., 141
Dixon, K., 494
Dixon, L. B., 507, 509
Djernes, J. K., 230
Do, K. A., 429
Doan, S. N., 61, 62
Dobkin, P. L., 23
Dobson, K., 251, 252
Docherty, J. P., 500
Docter, R. F., 381
Dodd, C. G., 524
Dodick, D. W., 347
Dodson, J. D., 125
Doehrmann, O., 54, 155
Dogan, S., 374, 393
Dohrenwend, B. P., 159, 159–161, 237
Dohrenwend, B. S., 237
Dolan, M., 470
Dolan, R. J., 58
Doll, H., 578
Dolui, S., 555
Dominé, F., 274
Dominguez-Salas, S., 118
Domino, E. F., 424
Domschke, K., 40, 116, 127, 215
Donaldson, K., 578
Donath, C., 408
Dong, F., 455, 456
Donohoe, M. B., 221
Dorhofer, D. M., 219
Dotterer, H. L., 463
Douban, J., 133
Dougall, N., 507
Dougherty, D. D., 168
Douglas, K. S., 458
Dour, H. J., 175
Dowling, N., 438
Dowrick, C., 453
Doyle, W., 65
Doyle, W. J., 324
Dragioti, E., 110
Draijer, N., 201
Drake, K. L., 155
Drake, R., 501, 543
Dramaix, M., 336
Draper, C., 380
Drayer, R. A., 230
Drevets, W. C., 48, 50, 234
Drogin, E. Y., 586
Dronsfield, A. T., 433
Drummond, K. D., 393
Drury, A. J., 445
Du, J., 431
Duan, N., 164
Duarte, T. A., 269, 270
Duberstein, P. R., 231, 255
Dubovsky, S. L., 120
Ducat, L., 440
Ducci, F., 460
Duclos, J., 281
Dudai, Y., 55
Dudek, B. C., 40
Duff, D., 136
Dufresne, R. G., 171–172
Dugas, M. J., 137
Dulit, R. A., 449
Dumitrascu, N., 82–83
Dummit, E. S., 156
Dunbar, G., 143
Duncan, A., 544
Duncan, R., 191
Duncan, S., 586
Dunlop, B. W., 51, 234
Dunn, G., 453
Dunne, P. E., 267, 277
DuPaul, G. J., 520, 524
Duran, R. E. F., 202
Duran, R. E., 329
Durand, V. M., 80, 106, 109, 113, 120, 121, 141, 518, 530, 532, 542, 543, 569
Durant, C., 127
Durbin, C. E., 233
Durham, M. L., 580
Duriez, P., 270
Durkheim, E., 257
Dursteler, K. M., 427
Dusseldorp, E., 335
Dustin, M. L., 326
Dvorak, R. D., 427
Dvorak-Bertscha, J., 463
Dvoskin, J. A., 586
Dwyer, J. B., 47
Dyke, P., 543
Dysken, M. W., 567

E

Eastman, C. I., 219
Eaton, N. R., 394
Eaton, W. W., 134, 138–139, 148, 214, 215
Eaves, L. J., 35, 233, 461
Ebersole, A., 469
Ebigno, P., 119
Ebigno, P. O., 185
Ebringer, A., 562
Eddy, K. T., 272, 275, 283
Eddy, M. T., 418
Edge, P. J., 167
Edmondson, D., 331
Edmundson, M., 91, 92, 99
Edwards, A. C., 542
Edwards, D. H., 55
Edwards, J. G., 417
Edwards, R. R., 339, 340
Eelen, P., 57
Eftekhari, A., 163
Egan, B. M., 332
Egeland, J., 473
Egeland, J. A., 117
Egger, H., 224
Egger, M., 327
Ehlers, A., 148, 163, 181
Ehlers, M. D., 47
Ehrenreich, J. T., 61, 63, 150, 151, 224
Ehrenreich-May, J. T., 156
Ehrhardt, A. A., 361, 392
Eibach, R. P., 360, 362
Eikenaes, I., 473
Eikeseth, S., 543
Eilert, N., 136
Eisen, J. L., 167
Eisenberg, M. E., 278–280
Eisenberger, N. I., 341
Eisenlohr-Moul, T. A., 467
Eisner, L. R., 213
Ekelund, J., 51
Ekselius, L., 219, 449, 466
Ekstrand, M. L., 350
Elbedour, S., 64
Elbert, G., 158
Elbert, M. J., 445
Eldevik, S., 543
Eldredge, K. L., 273
Eley, T. C., 38, 233, 234
El-Gabalawy, R., 185
Elger, B. S., 121
Elis, O., 488
Elkins, I. J., 465, 524
Ellard, D., 568
Ellard, K. K., 56, 61, 63, 129, 130, 174, 250, 323
Ellason, J. W., 201, 205
Ellis, H., 433
Ellis, T. E., 258
Ellman, L. M., 495
Elovainio, M., 51
Elsabbagh, M., 532
Elsaesser, M., 215
Elzinga, B., 467
Emeny, R., 337
Emerson, L. M., 524
Emery, C. F., 329, 330, 335, 337
Emery, R. E., 275
Endicott, J., 251
Engel, S. G., 273
England, P., 359
English, T., 192
Ennis, M., 171
Enns, M. W., 188
Enoch, M.-A., 430
Epel, E., 331
Epel, E. S., 321
Epler, A. J., 275
Epperson, C. N., 98, 222
Epstein, L. H., 344
Eranti, S., 249
Erikson, E., 68
Eriksson, E., 98
Erlangsen, A., 255
Erlenmeyer- Kimling, L., 35, 36
Erlich, M. D., 490, 494
Eroglu, C., 43
Eron, L., 464
Escalona, R., 482
Escobar, J. I., 185, 188
Escobar, M. J., 577
Eser, D., 48
Eshel, Y., 129
Eslinger, P. J., 52
Eslinger, S., 584
Espindle, D., 359–360
Esposito, M., 105
Essex, M. J., 128, 153
Estes, L. S., 277
Etter, J., 432
Ettinger, A. B., 191–192
Evangelou, E., 110
Evans, D. A., 554, 565
Evans, E., 418
Evans, J., 218
Evans, R., 181, 524
Evans, R. M., 328, 565
Evans, S. M., 427
Evengard, B., 342
Evers, C., 394
Evrard, M., 203–204
Exner, J. E., 82–83
Eyberg, S. M., 150, 151
Eysenck, M. W., 63
Ezrati-Vinacour, R., 519
Ezzati, M. 320, 348
Ezzel, C., 328

F

Fabbri, S., 187
Fabiano, G. A., 521
Fabrazzo, M., 284
Fagan, P. J., 383, 385, 387, 388
Fagelman, F. D., 440
Fagerness, J. A., 128
Faggiano, F., 437

Fagundes, C. P., 325, 329, 330
Fahrner, E. M., 371
Failer, J. L, 579
Fairburn, C., 270, 271
Fairburn, C. G., 269–273, 275, 278, 280–282, 284, 285
Fairchild, G., 462
Fairholme, C. P., 61, 63
Fakhoury, W., 507
Fallon, B. A., 188
Falloon, I. R., 510
Falloon, I. R. H., 509
Fama, J. M., 139
Fan, S., 431
Fang, A., 129, 169–170, 172–173
Fanning, J. R., 49
Fanti, K. A., 459
Fantino, E., 203–204
Faraone, S. V., 523
Farberow, N. L., 257
Farnam, F., 374
Farquhar, J. W., 351
Farrell, L. J., 150–151
Farrokh, S., 433
Farver-Vestergaard, I., 164
Fatemi, S. H., 44
Fauci, A. S., 321, 327–329
Faurholt-Jepsen, M., 81
Fausto-Sterling, A., 394–395
Fava, G. A., 137, 187, 214, 329
Favrod-Coune, T., 418
Fawcett, J., 217
Fay, C., 170, 171, 173
Fayyad, R., 98
Fazel, S., 255, 577, 578, 585
Febo-Vazquez, I., 357
Feder, A., 69
Federoff, B. 384
Federoff, J. P., 384, 386
Feig, L. A., 40
Feinberg, M., 235
Feinberg, M. E., 463
Feingold, A., 171
Feinstein, C., 526
Feldman, H. A., 365, 370
Feldman, M. B., 280
Feldman, M. D., 320
Felmingham, K. L., 64
Felthous, A. R., 585
Fennell, P. A., 342
Fenster, J. R., 331
Fenton, K. A., 321, 328, 329, 349
Fergus, T. A., 184
Fergusson, D., 230
Fergusson, D. M., 410
Fernald, R. D., 36
Fernandez, G., 127
Fernyhough, C., 487
Ferre, S., 418
Ferri, C. P., 554
Ferri, M., 434
Ferster, C. B., 25, 533
Fertuck, E. A., 466
Feusner, J. D., 153
Few, L. R., 458
Fichter, M., 184
Fichter, M. M., 183
Fiedelak, J. I., 342
Field, A. E., 274, 277, 279
Field, A. P., 149
Field, J., 358
Fielder, R. L., 359
Fields, B. W., 230
Fien, H., 529
Fileborn, B., 364
Filene, J., 464
Filippi, M., 87, 88
Fincham, F. D., 241, 359
Fineberg, N. A., 47, 175, 475
Finelli, L., 108
Finger, S., 14
Finke, J., 432
Finkenbine, R., 189
Finn, C. J., 361
Finn, C. T., 260
Finn, P., 118
Finnell, L. R., 155
First, M. B., 93, 94, 99, 481, 484, 486, 487, 488, 490, 494
Firth, J., 227
Fischer, M., 497
Fishbain, D. A., 439
Fishell, A., 384
Fisher, P. A., 162
Fisher, P. L., 135
Fishman, M., 418
Fiske, A., 229, 230, 231, 255
Fitts, S. N., 171
Fitzgerald, D. A., 155
Fitzgerald, P., 52–53
Fitzhenry, M., 454
Fitzpatrick, S., 467
Flanagan, E. H., 5, 90
Flanagan, J., 117
Flanders, W. D., 371
Flannery, D. J., 464
Flannery-Schroeder, E., 155
Flegal, K.M., 268
Fleisher, W. P., 201
Fleminger, S., 559
Fletcher, K., 225
Fletcher, M. A., 327, 328
Fletcher, P. C., 319
Fletcher, R. B., 86
Flint, A., 217
Flint, J., 35, 36
Flom, M., 35
Flor, H., 338, 339, 344
Flores, B., 217
Flory, K., 277
Flykt, A., 58, 61
Flynn, J. R., 539
Foa, E. B., 155, 163, 166, 168, 169
Fogg, L. F., 219
Foldes-Busque, G., 131
Foley, E., 330
Foley, K. R., 543
Folkers, G. K., 321, 327
Folsom, D. P., 579
Fonagy, P., 464
Fong, T. G., 550
Fonseca, A., 218
Fontenelle, L. F., 229, 475
Ford, E. S., 321
Ford, H., 386
Ford, T., 523
Fordyce, W. E., 338
Forness, S. R., 523
Forsberg, M., 360
Forster, N., 459
Fort, C., 222
Fortes, I. S., 526
Forth, A. E., 461
Forti, G., 377
Fosco, G. M., 428, 463
Foster, A., 507
Foster, G. D., 291
Fountoulakis, K. N., 110
Fournier, J. C., 245, 251
Fowler, J. C., 260
Fowles, D. C., 462
Fox, E., 153
Foxe, J. J., 418
Foy, D. W., 161
Frailing, K., 584
France, C. R., 338, 344
Frances, A., 92, 96, 99, 570, 571
Frances, A. J., 312, 449
Frances, R. J., 410
Francis, D., 39
Francis, D. D., 129
Francis, K., 137
Francouer, E., 204
Frank, E., 98, 164, 236, 237, 241, 254
Frankel, S. A., 220
Frankenburg, F. R., 448
Franklin, J. E., 410
Franklin, M. E., 168, 169
Franko, D. L., 269, 270, 273, 277
Franz, C. E., 35
Frasure-Smith, N., 337
Fratiglioni, L., 556, 570
Frazier, T. W., 531, 544
Frean, E., 321
Frederick, E. J., 107
Fredman, L., 65
Fredrikson, M., 58, 334
Freedman, E. G., 418
Freels, S., 98, 222
Freeman, A., 453, 469
Freeman, D., 181, 509
Freeman, E. W., 98
Fregenti, S., 576
Frenda, S. J., 203, 205
Freud, S., 18, 257
Freund, K., 381
Frewen, P. A., 157
Freyberger, H. J., 192
Fricke, R. A., 55
Fridlund, A. J., 24
Fried, E. I., 114–115
Friedberg, F., 343
Frieden, T. R., 327
Friedl, M. C., 201
Friedman, A. F., 85
Friedman, B. H., 135
Friedman, E. S., 253
Friedman, J. J., 341
Friedman, J. M., 159, 161
Friedman, M., 335
Friedman, M. B., 134, 229
Friedman, M. J., 94, 157, 158, 164
Fried-Oken, M., 568
Frissen, A., 502
Fristad, M. A., 230
Frith, C., 578
Fritz, C. O., 106
Frodl, T., 523
Froiland, J. M., 539
Fromm-Reichmann, F., 503
Frosch, E., 550
Frost, R. O., 173, 174
Frühauf, S., 376
Fruzzetti, A. E., 251, 283
Fugl-Meyer, A. R., 363
Fuji, D. E., 120
Fukuda,K., 135
Fulford, K. W. M., 4, 5
Fullana, M. A., 167
Fullen, T., 524
Fullerton, C., 183
Fulton, H. G., 417, 427
Fulton, J. J., 129
Furberg, H., 342
Furman, D., 321
Furman, W., 359
Furnham, A., 511
Furr, J. M., 133, 136, 157
Furukawa, T. A., 215
Fusar-Poli, P., 482
Fyer, A. J., 143, 149, 155

G

Gable, J., 507
Gaddis, L., 430

Gorman, J. M., 144
Gorman, L. K., 43
Gorman, L. L., 251
Gormley, M. J., 520
Gorny, G., 56, 68
Gorski, R. A., 361
Gorwood, P., 51, 270, 466
Gorzalka, B. B., 371, 372
Gosch, E., 155
Gosselin, J. T., 278
Gotheil, E., 330
Gotlib, I. H., 135, 229, 236, 239
Gotman, N., 98, 222
Gottesman, I. I., 35, 36, 116, 484, 497
Gottschalk, M. G., 40, 116, 127
Gould, E., 235
Gould, M., 258, 259, 260
Gould, R. A., 284
Gould, S. J., 17
Gournay, K., 172
Gouveia, M. J., 343
Goyal, A., 191–192
Goyal, M., 345
Grabbe, K. L., 350
Grabe, H. J., 192
Grabe, S., 277
Grace, M. C., 158
Grados, M. A., 167
Gradus, J. L., 163
Grady, D., 562
Graeff, F. G., 128
Graff, F. S., 457
Graham, C. A., 363, 366, 367
Graham, J. R., 85
Graham, R., 215
Graham-Hole, V., 510
Grandi, S., 187
Grandjean, J., 422
Granic, I., 463
Grann, M., 578, 585
Grant, B., 213, 229
Grant, B. F., 134, 139, 403
Grant, I., 67
Grant, J., 173
Grant, J. E., 174, 175, 408, 439, 474, 475, 494
Grant, K. E., 237
Grant, M. D., 35
Gratz, K. L., 129
Graubard, B. I., 268
Gray, B. A., 495
Gray, J. A., 48, 50, 127, 128
Gray, K. M., 403
Graybar, S. R., 468
Graziosi, C., 327
Greely, H., 578
Green McDonald, P., 330
Green, B. A., 358
Green, B. L., 158
Green, J., 165
Green, J. G., 587
Green, K. F., 59
Green, M. F., 487
Green, R., 392, 395
Greenbaum, M. A., 163
Greenberg, B. D., 52–53, 169
Greenberg, H. R.., 437
Greenberg, M. A., 320
Greenberg, N., 435
Greenblatt, D. J, 136
Greene, R., 525
Greene, S. J., 360
Greenfield, T., 434
Greenlick, M. R., 336
Greenough, W. T., 55
Greenspoon, M., 495
Greenwood, P., 369
Greeven, A., 188
Gregoire, A., 377
Grella, C., 418
Grenier, S., 139
Griebel, G., 48
Griffith, E. E. H., 192, 198
Griffiths, R. R., 417, 418, 421
Griffiths, R., 421
Grigorenko, E. L., 526, 528, 529
Grillon, C., 23, 162
Grilo, C., 468
Grilo, C. M., 274, 284
Grimm, O., 521
Grinspoon, L., 414
Grippo, A. J., 65
Grisham, J., 174
Grisham, J. R., 131, 173
Grobler, C., 213
Groc, L., 321
Grodberg, D., 464
Grof, P., 214
Grogan, S., 279
Groleau, P., 282
Groom, C., 135
Gross, J. J., 60–63, 135, 153, 466
Grossardt, B. R., 337
Grossbard, J. R., 279
Grossman, C. I., 329, 349
Growdon, M. E., 550
Gruber, A. J., 200
Gruber, J., 243
Gu, D., 350
Guan, X., 567
Guedeney, N., 229
Guerdjikova, A. I., 285
Gui, A., 523
Guijarro, M., 334
Guild, D., 382
Guilleminault, C., 48
Guimond, T., 468
Guirguis, A., 404
Gulliksson, M., 335
Gunay-Oge, R., 450
Gundel, H., 222
Gunderson, J. G., 445, 448, 455, 466
Gunn, M., 581, 582
Gunnar, M. R., 162, 330
Guo, Y.-H., 438
Gupta, S., 221
Gur, R. C., 488, 498
Gur, R. E., 498
Guralnik, O., 195
Gureje, O., 183, 185
Guribye, E., 119
Guroff, J. J., 199
Gurvits, T. V., 162
Gurwitz, J.,135
Gusella, J. F., 562
Gustad, J., 170, 171–172
Gustafson, L., 559
Gusti Rai Tirta, I., 511
Gutheil, T. G., 586
Gutierrez, D., 431
Gutner, C., 139
Guttmannova, K., 409
Guze, S. B., 187
Gwaltney, J. M., 65

H

Haber, S. N., 52–53, 65–66, 169
Hack, S., 133, 136
Hackett, T., 62
Haddad, P. M., 506
Hadigan, C. M., 284
Hadiyono, J., 153
Hadjistavropoulos, T., 172
Hadland, S. E., 280
Hadley, S., 172
Hadzi-Pavlovic, D., 503
Haeffel, G. J., 238, 240
Haenen, M. A., 184, 187
Hagel, A., 148
Hahn, T., 129
Hajovsky, D. B., 539
Hakimi, S., 153
Hakstian, A. R., 458
Halahakoon, D. C., 213
Haley, A., 35
Hall, A. S., 466, 585
Hall, B. J., 291
Hall, J. A., 584
Hall, J. R., 458
Hall, K., 374
Haller, J., 55
Hallet, A. J., 334
Halliburton, A. E., 422
Hallmayer, J., 533
Halpern, J. H., 421
Hamaker, E. L., 200
Hamer, R. M., 185
Hames, J. L., 238, 240
Hamilton, J. L., 228
Hamm, J., 488
Hammeke, T. A., 87
Hammen, C., 235, 237, 252
Hammen, C. L., 229
Hammer, S., 327, 328
Hammond, C. J., 418
Hammond, R., 348
Handiwala, L., 371
Haney, T. L., 62
Hanif, M. A., 411
Hankin, B. L., 68, 241
Hanna, G. L., 167
Hannan, A. J., 68
Hannema, S., 392
Hanover, L. N., 5
Hans, V. P., 583
Hanson, R. K., 388
Hantouche, E., 214, 257
Hara, K., 203
Harada, N., 153
Harburg, E., 62
Harden, R. N., 339
Hardie, T. L., 424
Harding, J. W., 566
Hare, R. D., 457–459, 461, 463, 464, 578
Harich, B., 521
Hariri, A. R., 462
Harley, K., 504
Harlow, B., 230
Harmell, A. L., 588
Harmer, C. J., 47, 49
Haro, J. M., 491
Harold, G. T., 241
Harp, K. L., 414
Harpin, V., 524
Harpur, T. J., 458
Harrington, H., 37
Harrington, J. L., 85
Harris, G. T., 382, 383, 387
Harris, L. S., 203
Harrison, B. J., 51–52
Harrison, B., 141
Harrison, J. P., 155
Harrison, M. A., 107
Harrison, P. J., 281,493, 502
Harriss, L., 258
Hart, A. B., 251
Hart, S. D., 461
Harte, C. B., 371
Hartlage, S. A., 98, 222
Hartley, D. M., 40
Hartman, T. J., 417
Hartvigsen, J., 338
Hartwell, E. E., 425

Harvey, A. G., 236
Harvey, I., 501
Harvey, P. D., 99
Harvey, S. B., 342
Harwood, H., 435
Hasin, D., 213, 227, 228–229, 231
Haslam, N., 504
Hastings, R. P., 543
Hatfield, E., 11, 61
Hathaway, S. R., 83, 85
Hatteea, H., 270
Hattie, J., 86
Hatzichristou, D. G., 365
Hauch, J., 141
Haukka, J., 257
Haukkala, A., 334
Hauner, K. K., 53, 150, 151
Hauser, M., 457
Hausmann, M., 487
Hausteiner, C., 337
Havel, L. L., 219
Haw, C., 258
Hawes, D. J., 467
Hawken, E. R., 419
Hawker, C., 438
Hawkins, J. D. P., 118
Hawkley, L. C., 320, 324, 334
Hawton, K., 258, 364, 365, 367
Hay, A. C., 129
Hay, P. J., 270
Hayes, M., 331
Hayes, S. C., 6, 96, 99, 131, 379
Hayes-Skelton, S. A., 136
Haynes, R. B., 588
Haynes, S. N., 81
Haynos, A. F., 283
Hazell, P., 68
Hazlett-Stevens, H., 89
He, Y., 410, 523
Hearn, J., 587
Heath, A. C., 233
Heath, A. K., 543
Heathcote, D., 68
Heatherton, T. F., 282
Heaton, P., 533
Hebert, L. E., 554
Hecht, K. F., 448
Hecker, M. H. L., 336
Heckers, S., 490
Hedley, A. J., 350
Hedman- Lagerlof, E., 187
Hegerl, U., 226
Heidenreich, T., 155, 250
Heil, S. H., 403
Heilig, M., 426, 427
Heim, C., 235
Heiman, J. R., 366, 372, 376
Heimberg, R. G., 152, 155
Heinrichs, N., 151
Helgeson, V., 329
Heller, W., 236
Hellmuth, J. C., 427
Hellstrom, K., 150–151
Helyer, R., 467
Helzer, J. E., 5, 91, 92
Hemachandra Reddy, P., 556
Hemmingsson, T., 337
Henckens, M. J. A. J., 127
Henderson , K. E., 268
Henderson, K. M., 557
Hendrickson, B., 418
Hendriks, G. J., 144, 163
Hendriksen, E. S., 329
Hennen, J., 379
Hennen, J., 2014, 448
Henningsen, P., 181
Henry, D., 68
Henry, G., 10, 15
Henschel, A., 280
Herbert, T. B., 325, 326
Herda, C. A., 148
Herdt, G. H., 360
Herlianto, E. C., 467
Herling, S., 426
Herlitz, C. A., 360
Herman, C. P., 281
Herman, D., 218
Hermann, C. A., 385
Hermans, D., 23
Hermans, E. J., 127
Hernandez, M., 511
Heron, J., 230
Herpertz, S. C., 469
Herren, C., 151
Hershberger, S., 361
Herzig, M., 468
Herzog, A., 183
Herzog, D. B., 269
Herzog, P., 125
Hester, R. K., 433
Hettema, J. M., 36, 134, 149, 237
Heylens, G., 391
Hieneman, M., 80, 121
Higdon, M. J., 576
Higgins, A., 393
Higgins, S. T., 403, 431, 435
Higuchi, S., 429
Hilchey, C. A., 417
Hildenbrand, A. K., 349
Hilgard, E. R., 59
Hill, E. M., 147
Hill, K. G., 118
Hill, K. K., 277
Hill, M., 564
Hiller, W., 183–185, 187, 188
Hillis, A. E., 577
Hilsenroth, M., 83
Hilsenroth, M. J., 22
Hilt, L. M., 228
Hilty, D. M., 174
Himle, J. A., 147
Hindmarch, I., 135
Hingson, S. T., 408
Hinshaw, S. P., 67, 96, 97
Hinshelwood, J. A., 528
Hinton, D. E., 139, 148, 153
Hirasawa-Fujita, M., 424
Hirschfeld, D. R., 153
Hirschfeld, R. M. A., 245
Hirschtritt, M. E., 134
Hiruma, N., 153
Hitchcock, P. B., 187
Hlastala, S. A., 254
Ho, S. Y., 350, 404
Hoblyn, J., 567
Hockenberry, J., 417
Hodder, R. K., 436
Hodes, R. L., 59
Hodge, A., 105
Hodgson, K., 233
Hodgson, N. A., 455
Hodgson, R., 385
Hoeffer, C. A., 544
Hoeft, F., 528
Hoek, H. W., 267, 270, 272, 276, 277
Hoekstra, T., 337
Hoffman, B., 347
Hoffman, E. J., 135, 136
Hofman, M. A., 392
Hofmann, S., 148
Hofmann, S. G., 61–63, 96, 99, 125, 126, 129–131, 135, 136, 139, 143, 146, 147, 152, 153, 155, 156, 163, 172–173, 203, 230, 240, 250, 345
Hogan, D. R., 376
Hogarty, G. E., 509
Höjerback, T., 393
Holder, H. D., 437
Holi, M. M., 440
Holland, J. M., 67, 325
Holland, L. A., 285
Hollander, E., 172, 195
Hollander, J. A., 428
Hollands, G. J., 319
Hollis, J. F., 336
Hollon, S. D., 143, 214, 250, 251, 252, 253, 588, 589
Holm, H., 449, 466
Holmes, A., 48
Holmes, E. A., 125
Holmgren, H., 164
Holroyd, K. A., 341, 345
Holt-Lunstad, J., 65, 334
Holtzman, J. N., 248
Hong, Y., 428
Hood, S., 174
Hoogduin, C. A., 144
Hoogduin, K. A., 192, 193
Hoogendijk, E. O., 229
Hooley, J. M., 466, 467, 504
Hoon, E. F., 371
Hoon, P. W., 371
Hopkins, M., 135
Hoppenbrouwers, S., 462
Hops, H., 251
Hopwood, C. J., 92, 445, 446, 453, 454
Hopwood, T., 195
Horan, W. P., 487, 503
Horowitz, J., 251
Horowitz, M., 164
Horta, B. L., 520
Horwath, E., 167, 490
Horwood, J., 230
Horwood, L. J., 410
Hoskins, M., 421
Hostinar, C. E., 330
Hotopf, M., 342
Hou, Z., 118
Houck, P. R., 164
House, J. S., 65, 66
Houston, B. K., 336
Houston, K., 258
Hovenkamp-Hermelink, J. H. M., 126
Howard, G. 566
Howard, A. K., 422
Howard, L. J., 270
Howard, M. O., 422
Howe, M. L., 204
Howell, A. J., 205
Howes, O. D., 500
Howieson, D. B., 81, 86
Howland, R. H., 94
Howlett, A., 218
Howlin, P., 533
Hoyer, J., 5
Hoza, B., 520
Hruska, J., 555
Hser, Y. I., 418
Hsia, C., 148
Hsu, L. K. G., 271, 272, 281
Hu, S., 135
Hua, L.-L., 523
Huang, J. K., 374
Huang, K-E., 98
Huang, T. L., 217
Huang, Y. C., 217
Huang, Y., 447, 450, 471
Hubbard, N. A., 88
Hubert, N. C., 331
Hucker, S. J., 382
Huddy, V., 509

Hudson, J. I., 171, 200, 234, 270, 275
Hudson, J. L., 151, 155
Hudziak, J., 391
Huerta, M., 544
Huesmann, R., 464
Hughes, C. J., 543, 417
Hughes, D., 148
Hughes, J. R., 417, 432
Huisman, M., 229
Hull, I. M., 586
Humedian, M., 120
Hummelen, B., 473
Humphreys, K., 434
Hung, Y. Y., 217
Hunot, V., 343
Hunsley, J., 74
Hunt, W. A., 14
Hunter, E., 193
Hunter, J. A., Jr., 386
Hunter, L., 151
Huntjens, R. J., 200
Huppert, J. D., 131, 155
Hurt, E., 523
Hurt, S. W., 98
Hus, V., 544
Husain, K., 343
Husain, M., 185, 187
Hutchinson, D. M., 279
Hutson, P. R., 422
Hutton, J., 533
Huxter, M., 330
Hwang, I., 258
Hwang, W., 331
Hybels, C. F., 229, 231
Hyde, J. S., 277, 359
Hyde, L. W., 462, 463
Hyman, S. E., 47

I

Iacono, W. G., 465
Iacovino, J. M., 453
Iannucci, R. A., 414
Ibanez-Casas, I., 491
Ilardi, S. S., 251
Imes, S. A., 283
Imhof, A., 555
Immonen, S., 407
Ingoldsby, E. M., 465
Ingram, R., 240
Ingvar, M., 53
Inouye, S. K., 550
Insel, T. R., 36, 52, 54, 55
Iqbal, A., 411
Irons, G., 24
Ironson, G., 62, 328
Irurtia, M. J., 455
Irwin, M., 409
Irwin, M. R., 234
Isaacowitz, D., 68
Isenberg-Grzeda, E., 407
Isikli, S., 450
Isometsa, E., 257
Ito, B. S., 519
Ito, K., 556
Ivanov, I., 433
Ivengar, M., 136
Iverson, L. L., 47
Iverson, S. D., 47
Ivleva, E. I., 498
Izard, C. E., 61

J

Jääskeläinen, E., 481
Jablensky, A., 494
Jaccard, J., 162
Jackson, G., 370, 453
Jackson, J., 258
Jacob, R. G., 155
Jacobi, W., 501
Jacobsen, P. B., 330
Jacobson, K. A., 418
Jacobson, K. C., 35, 425
Jacobson, N., 251
Jacobson, N. S., 250, 251
Jacobson, P., 292–293
Jacoby, R. J., 164
Jaconis, M., 274
Jaffe, J. H., 413, 418
Jaffee, S., 35, 36, 38, 234, 237
Jager, G., 419
Jahr, E., 543
Jain, S. K., 525
Jakob, M., 188
Jakupcak, M., 427
James, B. O., 119
James, E., 421
Jameson, D., 198
Jamieson, G., 195
Jamison, K. R., 219, 226, 227, 232, 235, 254
Janca, A., 382, 456
Janelsins, M., 23
Janelsins, M. C., 23
Jang, K. L., 99, 187, 501
Jang, S. H., 98
Janghorbani, M., 374
Janicki-Devarts, D., 320, 324
Jankovic, J., 506
Janssen, E., 359, 369
Janszky, I., 337
Jardri, R., 466
Jarrett, R. B., 252, 253
Jasiukaitis, P., 202
Jason, L. A., 341, 342
Javdani, S., 470
Javitt, D. C., 500
Jay, S. M., 331
Jayawickrema, S., 373–374, 376
Jelicic, M., 193
Jellinek, E. M., 409
Jenike, E., 168
Jenike, M. A., 168
Jenkins, J. H., 504
Jenkins, R., 119
Jenner, C., 391
Jennings, W. G., 464
Jensen, E., 433
Jensen, P. S., 525
Jensen, U. B., 567
Jerabek, P., 243
Jesse, R., 421
Jessell, T. M., 47
Jeste, D. V., 588
Jester, D. J., 556
Jeuring, H. W., 229
Jiang, H., 222–223
Jiang, W., 335
Jiann, B. P., 374
Jilek, W. G., 198
Jin, R., 133, 134, 138, 139, 151, 229
Jin, X., 56
Jiskrova, G., 446
Jiu, C. J., 131
Jobes, D. A., 256
Jockin, V., 38
Joe, S., 258
Joels, M., 127
Johannes, C. B., 365
Johanson, C. E., 427
Johansson, A., 393, 394
Johansson, B., 35
Johansson, P., 462
Johansson, P. T., 578
John, A., 404
Johnson, A. M., 358
Johnson, B., 171
Johnson, J., 468
Johnson, J. G., 129, 131, 195, 201
Johnson, L., 338, 519
Johnson, S. L., 60, 63, 217, 227, 243
Johnson, V., 375, 376
Johnson, V. E., 107, 371, 375
Johnson, W., 116
Johnston, E. C., 408
Johnston, L. D., 134
Johnstone, E. C., 505, 508–511
Joiner, T., 260
Joiner, T. E., Jr., 250, 258, 259, 282
Joiner, Y., 261
Joling, K. J., 566
Jones, A. J., 519
Jones, B. E., 495
Jones, G., 524
Jones, J. C., 162
Jones, M. C., 24
Jones, P., 501, 506
Jones, R., 348, 495
Jones, R. T., 159, 421, 578
Jones, S., 378
Jones, W., 531
Joormann, J., 135
Jordan, B. D., 565
Jose, A., 450
Joslyn, G., 405
Joudrey, P. J., 431
Joy, M. E., 464
Joyce, P. R., 466
Joyner, M. J., 334
Juberg, M., 450
Judd, L. L., 214, 215, 220, 227
Judge, B., 411
Judge, C., 391
Judge, R., 143
Jufer-Phipps, R. A., 410
Juliano, L. M., 417, 418
Julius, M., 62
Jummani, R., 519
Juneau, M., 337
Junewicz, A., 461
Junginger, J., 379

K

Kabat-Zinn, J., 250
Kabir, M. T., 568
Kaciroti, N., 62
Kaczkurkin, A. N., 23
Kafka, M. P., 379
Kagan, J., 153
Kahler, C. W., 416
Kaiser, J., 328, 342
Kaiser, T., 125
Kalaria, R., 558
Kalat, J. W., 47
Kalbarczyk, A., 555
Kalichman, S. C., 327
Kalin, N. H., 128
Kalinichenko, L. S., 407
Kallmann, F. J., 496
Kalra, G., 117
Kalso, E., 53
Kaltman, S., 221
Kamath, V., 120
Kaméenui, E. J., 529
Kamen, C., 23
Kaminen-Ahola, N., 407
Kaminer, Y., 418, 419
Kaminski, J. W., 464
Kampman, M., 144
Kanai, R., 55
Kanaya, T., 539
Kanayama, G., 279, 280, 423
Kandasamy, M., 549
Kandel, E. R., 47, 55, 59
Kang, J. M., 214
Kanigel, R., 416

L

Leventhal, B. L., 286
Levin, F. R., 427
Levin, I., 519
Levin, R. A., 549
Levine, A. C., 377
Levine, B. S., 410
Levine, M. P., 283
Levine, S. B., 377
Levinson, D. F., 233
Levitt, A., 219
Levitt, J. T., 144
Levy, B. R., 58
Levy, D. T., 417
Levy, K. B., 412
Lewin, A. B., 167
Lewinsohn, P. M., 212, 220, 233
Lewis, B. A., 321, 348
Lewis, C. M., 66
Lewis, D. O., 202
Lewis, F. M., 330, 462
Lewis, G., 66, 495
Lewis, J. A., 147
Lewis, K., 464
Lewis, K. C., 450, 452, 453
Lewis, M., 202
Lewis, S., 189, 482, 488, 501
Lewis, T., 348
Lewis, T. T., 332
Lewis-Fernandez, R., 96, 139, 191, 192, 193–195, 203
Lewy, A. J., 219
Leyfer, O., 234
Leykin, Y., 251
Lezak, M. D., 86
Li, B., 533
Li, S., 40
Li, W., 233
Li, X., 256
Li, Z., 126, 427, 494, 555
Liang, Y., 118
Liao, B., 23
Liao, Y. S. J., 527
Liberman, R., 511
Liberman, R. P., 508, 509
Liberzon, I., 128, 129
Lichenstein, P., 38
Lichtenstein, P., 361
Liddell, H. S., 125
Liddle, P. F., 488
Lieb, K., 468
Lieb, R., 134, 155, 185, 404, 503
Lieberman, J. A., 498, 506
Liebeskind, J., 338
Liebeskind, J. C., 341, 344
Liebowitz, M. R., 133, 146, 155
Lienard, P., 167
Lifshitz, F., 279
Light, K. C., 334
Lighty, Q., 495
Lilenfeld, L. R. R., 282
Lilienfeld, S. O., 5, 91, 93, 96, 99, 193–194, 200, 203, 205, 450, 470
Lim, D., 198
Lim, S. S., 332
Lin, C. C., 217
Lin, H., 98, 230
Lin, H. S., 555
Lin, K.-H., 215
Lin, Y., 38
Linardon, J., 144
Lind, S., 533
Lindau, S. T., 358
Lindberg, N., 440
Lindner, S., 203
Lindwall, R., 150–151
Lindy, J. D., 158
Lindy, J. G., 158
Linehan, M., 468
Linehan, M. M., 466, 468
Ling, W., 413, 418
Links, P. S., 468
Linsenmeier, J., 392
Linton, L. M., 35
Lionetti, T. M., 404
Liotti, M., 243
Lipchik, G. L., 341, 347
Lipp, O. V., 59
Lipshultz, L. I., 365, 377–378
Lipsitch, M., 108
Liss, A., 154
Lissek, S., 23, 162
Litman, R. E., 257
Little, D., 269
Littman, R., 324
Littrell, L., 222
Litvin Bloom, E., 416
Litz, B. T., 152, 159, 163, 377
Liu, D., 39
Liu, K., 258
Liu, L., 219
Liu, N. H., 416
Liu, S.-M., 215
Liu, W. M., 120
Liu, X., 426
Livesley, W. J., 99
Livianos, L., 283
Livingston, E. H., 569
Llanes, E., 429
Lloyd, E. A., 367
Lo, C. C., 139
Lo, E., 219
Lo, S. C., 342
Lobbestael, J., 453
Lobo, R. A., 556
LoBraico, E. J., 463
Lochman, J., 427
Lochner, C., 174, 475
Lock, J., 281
Locke, G., 507
Loder, E., 341
Loeb, K., 281
Loeber, R., 462
Loehlin, J., 361
Loehlin, J. C., 35
Loewenstein, R., 203
Loewenstein, R. J., 193–195, 205
Löffler, A., 468
Lofland, K., 339
Loftus, E. F., 203, 204, 205
Loftus, J., 363
Lofwall, M. R., 418
Logan, C., 384, 386
Lohr, B., 172
Lombardi, V. C., 342
Lonczak, H. S. P., 118
London, S., 65
Long, E. O., 326
Long, J. S., 363
Loomans, E. M., 418
Loonan, R., 360
Looper, K. J., 187
Lopes, V., 223
Lopez, O. L., 568
Lopez, S. R., 231, 504
Lopiano, L., 53
LoPiccolo, J., 364, 376, 377
Loranger, A., 447
Lord, C., 532, 533, 544
Lordos, A., 459
Lorenz, T. A., 374
Lösel, F., 388
Lostutter, T. W., 408
Loth, K., 278
Lottes, I. L., 360
Lotti, F., 363
Lovallo, W. R., 322
Lovegrove, M. C., 550
Lovestone, S., 554, 555, 564, 565, 568
Lovibond, P., 58
Lowe, B., 183, 193
Lowe, M. R., 272
Lozano, A. M., 249
Lu, B., 567
Lu, K.-T., 156
Lu, L., 51
Lubin, R. E., 159
Lubs, H. A., 542
Luby, J. L., 229
Lucas, J. A., 141
Lucas, M., 243
Lucas, R. E., 63
Lucia, V. C., 161
Luciana, M., 51
Ludescher, B., 270
Ludwig, A. M., 231, 232
Ludwig, A., 198, 200
Ludwig, D. S., 291
Luk, S. L., 532
Lukiw, W. J., 567
Lund, D. W., 459
Lundberg, I., 337
Lunde, I., 232
Lundh, L.-G., 153
Lundorff, M., 164
Lundqvist, D., 58, 61
Lundstrom, B., 393
Lunney, C. A., 157
Luria, M., 363
Luria, R., 135
Lussier, P., 379, 580
Lutgendorf, S., 329, 330
Lutgendorf, S. K., 328, 330
Lydiard, R. B., 168
Lyketos, C. G., 567
Lyketsos, C. G., 230, 567, 570
Lykken, D. T., 35, 38, 462
Lynch, F. L., 252
Lynch, H. F., 122
Lynch, J. E., 278
Lynch, J. K., 87
Lynch, K. G., 258
Lynch, S. K., 107, 424
Lynch, T. R., 468
Lynn, S. J., 181, 193, 194, 203–205
Lyons, M. J., 35, 116, 233
Lyubomirsky, S., 58

M

Maayan, N., 507
Maccaferri, G. E., 474
Maccallum, F., 221
Maccoby, M., 351
Macdonald, P. T., 371
MacDougall, J. M., 62
Mace, C. J., 189
Maciejewski, P., 221
Mackenzie, C. S., 185
MacKenzie, D. E., 531
MacKinnon, D. F., 226
MacLeod, C., 135, 347
Macy, J. T., 119
Maeng, L. Y., 64
Maenner, M., 532
Maes, H., 461
Maes, S., 335, 343
Magarinos, A. M., 162
Magee, L., 155
Magee, W. J., 148, 152
Maggi, M., 363, 377, 428
Magliano, L., 226
Magne-Ingvar, U., 257
Magruder, K., 158
Maguire, G. A., 519
Maher, B. A., 9, 12, 15

Maher, J. J., 405
Maher, W. B., 9, 12, 15
Mahler, M., 533
Mahmood, S. S., 336
Mai, F., 188
Maier, S., 58
Mainali, P., 468
Mainous III, A. G., 566
Maisto, S. A., 409
Maj, M., 226, 251, 253, 262
Mak, K. H., 350
Maki, P. M., 557
Malatesta, V. J., 371
Malavige, L. S., 373–374, 376
Malcom, J. R., 385
Maldonado, J. R., 201, 205
Malenka, R. C., 47
Maletzky, B., 387, 388
Malhotra, A., 423
Mallampalli, M., 555
Mallan, K. M., 59
Malmedal, W., 569
Malone, K. M., 258
Malone, P. S., 258
Maltzman, I. M., 434
Mamedova, S., 527
Manber, R., 109
Manber, T., 153
Mancill, R. B., 131
Mancini, A. D., 221
Mancini, C., 155
Mancl, L., 347
Mancuso, J., 494
Mancuso, S., 171
Mandalos, G. E., 245
Mandel, J., 560
Mandeli, J., 377
Manicavasagar, V., 151
Manjula, M., 187
Manly, J. J., 556
Mann, J., 257, 258
Mann, J. J., 258, 377
Manne, S. L., 330
Mannino, D. M., 371
Mannuzza, S., 155
Mansfield, P., 374
Manson, J., 337
Manson, S. M., 231
Mansson, K. N. T., 155
Mantile, F., 568
Mantovani, A., 249
Mao, X., 320
Marangell, L., 249
Marano, C. M., 567
Marcello, S., 507, 510
Marcolini, E., 191
Marcus, B. H., 321
Marcus, D. C., 358
Marcus, E., 255
Marcus, M. D., 286
Marcus, S. C., 245
Marek, P., 341
Maremmani, I., 432
Maresova, P., 555
Margolis, R. L., 561
Margraf, J., 141, 183
Marin, D. B., 449, 558
Marinelli, M., 55
Marino, L., 5
Markon, K. E., 92
Markova, V., 119
Markowitz, J. C., 215, 250, 251
Markowitz, J.S., 131
Marks, I., 343
Marks, I. M., 93
Marlatt, G. A., 435
Marmar, C. R., 159, 163
Marmot, M. G., 336
Marnane, C. L., 151
Marques, J. K., 388
Marques, L., 277
Marques, M. M., 343
Marras, C., 560
Marsac, M. L., 349
Marsh, L., 561
Marsh, P. J., 191
Marshall, P. G., 440
Marshall, W. L., 383, 385, 388
Marsolek, C. J., 59
Marteau, T. M., 319
Martell, C., 212
Martell, C. R., 250
Marten, P. A., 135
Martens, E. J., 337
Martensson, B., 219
Marti, C. N., 274
Martin, A., 172, 182
Martin, F. I., 235
Martin, J., 361
Martin, K. M., 53
Martin, L. Y., 543
Martin, N., 361
Martin, N. G., 149
Martin, P. R., 347, 410
Martin, R. L., 187
Martin, T., 450
Martinez, A., 473
Martinez, A. G., 96
Martinez, A. M., 228
Martinez, A. P., 201, 494
Martinez, M. A., 282
Martinez-Fernandez, E., 432
Martino, F., 448
Martin-Pichora, A. L., 153
Martins, S. S., 502
Marx, B. P., 157, 193
Maser, J. D., 145
Mash, E. J., 74
Masheb, R. M., 274
Masi, C. M., 334
Masia-Warner, C., 155
Mason, F. L., 379
Mason, N. L., 419
Mason, N. S., 466
Mason, T. B., 270
Master, S. L., 339
Masters, W., 375, 376
Masters, W. H., 107, 371, 375
Masuda, A., 450
Mataix-Cols, D., 167, 174
Mathes, B. M., 173
Matheson, S. L., 494
Mathew, S. J., 135, 136
Mathews, A., 187
Mathews, A.M., 135
Mathews, C. A., 166
Mathews, R., 386
Matricon, P., 418
Matsubayashi, T., 258
Matsumoto, D., 336
Matsunaga, D., 231
Mattar, L., 281
Matthews, K., 335–337
Matthews, K. A., 327, 334, 336, 337
Matthews-Ewald, M. R., 274
Mattia, J. I., 170, 171
Mattis, S. G., 141
Matza, L. S., 218
Maust, D., 81
Mauro, C., 164
Mautone, J. A., 524
Maxwell, R., 193–194
Maxwell, J. C., 413
May, D. G., 215
May, J. S., 461
Mayberg, H., 249
Mayberg, H. S., 243
Mayer, B., 187
Mayer, K. H., 328
Mayes, S. D., 521
Mayfield, U., 192
Mayford, M. R., 55
Mayou, R., 206
Mayville, S., 171
Mazabell, S., 528
Mazure, C. M., 237
Mazzeo, S. E., 273
McAlister, L., 351
McAllister, C. G., 324
McArthur, D., 532
McBride, A., 587
McCabe, J. E., 218
McCabe, M., 382
McCabe, M. P., 274
McCabe, R., 154
McCabe, S. E., 408, 418
McCaffree, K. J., 429
McCaffrey, R. J., 87
McCall, W. V., 133
McCallion, P., 541
McCann, D., 523
McCann, U., 421
McCann, U. D., 412
McCarron, M., 541
McCarthy, E. P., 276
McCarthy-Jones, S., 484
McCauley, E. A., 254
McClam, T. D., 567
McClearn, G. E., 35, 38, 234
McClellan, J., 234
McClellan, J. M., 254
McCloskey, M. S., 49, 439
McClough, J., 81
McClure, M., 457
McClure, M. M., 457
McConaha, C. W., 270
McCrady, B. S., 409, 434, 435
McCrae, R., 446
McCraw, S., 217, 225
McCuish, E. C., 580
McCullough, J. P., Jr., 220, 250, 252
McCutcheon, J. E., 55
McDermott, B., 155
McDermott, L. M., 507
McDermott, S., 542
McDonald, E. M., 348
McElroy, S. L., 171, 285
McEwan, T. E., 440
McEwen, B. S., 46, 162, 321
McFadden, D., 361
McFarlane, A., 159
McGee, W. J., 138–139
McGinn, L. K., 473, 474
McGinnis, S., 243
McGirr, A., 466
McGlashan, T., 468
McGlashan, T. H., 512
McGlinchey, E., 541
McGoldrick, M., 360, 374
McGonagle, K. A., 148
McGovern, P. E., 405
McGowan, B. K., 59
McGrath, P., 440
McGreevy, M. A., 584
McGue, M., 35, 38, 465
McGuffin, P., 35, 38, 233
McGuire, J. F., 167
McGuire, P. K., 486
McGurk, S. R., 509
McHugh, P. C., 466
McHugh, R. K., 139, 144, 589
McIntosh, A., 507
McIntyre, R. S., 224
McKay, D., 168, 169, 172

McKay, R., 485
McKenzie, K. C., 466
McKinley, J. C., 83, 85
McKunlay, J. B., 365
McLaughlin, N. C. R., 169
McLaughlin, T., 419
McLean, C. P., 152, 163
McLean, P., 251
McMahon, S. D., 237
McMain, S., 468
McNab, C., 504
McNally, R., 203–205
McNally, R. J., 4, 17, 59, 139, 158, 221
McNaughton, N., 50, 127–128
McNeil, T. F., 501
McPartland, J. C., 544
McQuade, J. D., 520
McQuillan, G., 320
McWilliams, J. M., 332
Mead, G. E., 250
Meaden, P. M., 219
Meagher, D., 550, 551
Meaney, M. J., 35, 39, 40, 129
Meaney, M., 322
Meara, E., 332
Mechelli, A., 53
Mechoulam, R., 420
Medland, S., 361
Mednick, S. A., 464, 502
Medoff-Cooper, B., 455
Meehan, K. B., 472
Meehl, P. E., 83, 96, 456, 488
Meerveld, J., 570
Mehler, P. S., 270, 273
Meijer, A. M., 219
Meilman, P. W., 408
Melartin, T., 257
Melca, I. A., 475
Melhem, N., 221–222
Melles, R., 377
Meltzer-Brody, S., 218
Melville, L. F., 155
Melzack, R., 339, 344
Menard, W., 170–173
Menashe, I., 533
Mendel, E., 137
Mendes, W. B., 65
Mendis, S., 336
Mendlowicz, M. V., 475
Mendoza- Denton, R., 96
Mendoza-Azpur, G., 413
Menezes, P. R., 229
Menon, V., 528
Menzies, L., 175
Menzies, R., 519
Merali, Z., 39
Mercer, K. B., 38, 161
Merckelbach, H., 193, 194, 203, 394
Meredith, L. R., 405
Meredith, S. E., 417
Merens, W., 49
Merghati-Khoei, E., 374
Merikangas, K. R., 133, 134, 138–139, 213, 227–229, 270
Merkouris, S., 438
Mermin, J., 321, 328, 329, 349
Merzel, A. P. C., 232
Mesri, B., 138
Meston, C. M., 363, 368, 370–374, 376, 377, 379, 382, 385
Mestre, L. T., 568
Metalsky, G. I., 239
Metzner, H. M., 65
Meulman, J., 335
Meuret, A. E., 31, 126, 129–130, 149, 150
Mevada, A., 542
Mewton, L., 105
Meyer S. E., 230
Meyer, A. J., 351
Meyer, B., 473, 586
Meyer, G. J., 82–83
Meyer, I. H., 280
Meyer-Bahlburg, H. F. L., 392, 393
Meyers, B., 217
Mezick, E. J., 334
Mezzich, J. E., 198
Micco, J. A., 150
Michael, R., 374
Michaelides, M. P., 459
Michaels, S., 374
Michalak, J., 250
Michaud, L., 445
Michaud, P.-A., 274
Michelakos, T., 566
Michelson, O., 280
Mickes, L., 203–204
Miele, V. J., 189
Mihura, J. L., 82–83
Miklowitz, D. J., 254
Mikuška, J., 446
Milad, M. R., 64, 163
Milanak, M. E., 456
Milburn, N. G., 228
Miles, S. R., 5, 90
Milich, R., 520
Milin, R., 403
Mill, J., 40
Miller, A. J., 270, 521
Miller, A. R., 185
Miller, C., 217
Miller, F. G., 53
Miller, G., 55, 65, 320, 325
Miller, I., 503
Miller, I. W., 58, 238, 251
Miller, J. D., 471, 532
Miller, J. N., 227
Miller, M. E., 133
Miller, M. W., 157, 158
Miller, N. E., 344
Miller, N. S., 371
Miller, S. C., 424
Miller, S. D., 200
Miller, T. Q., 334, 336
Miller, W. R., 433
Millon, T., 15, 90, 92, 96, 473
Mills, P. J., 325
Milner, P. M., 425
Milstein, V., 201
Mineka, S., 53, 57, 58, 129, 150, 153
Miner, M., 379
Mingbunjerdsuk, D., 519
Minhajuddin, A., 253
Minino, A. M., 256
Miranda, J., 240
Mirosevic, S., 331
Mirsky, A. F., 497
Miskovic, V., 193–194
Mistry, H., 120
Mitchell, D. C., 417
Mitchell, E., 343
Mitchell, J., 282
Mitchell, J. E., 270, 272, 273
Mitchell, R. L. C., 487
Mitchell, W. B., 372
Mittelman, M., 379
Mobbs, D., 578
Mock, S. E., 360, 362
Modrego, P. J., 230
Moene, F. C., 190, 191, 193
Moffitt, T. E., 35, 37, 64, 99, 460
Mogg, K., 135, 153
Mogil, J. S., 341
Mogun, H., 135
Mohammadi, M.-R., 520
Mohan, R., 185
Mohanty, S., 567
Mohile, S. G., 23
Mohler, H., 48
Mohlman, J., 139
Mojtabai, R., 143, 169
Mokdad, A. H., 332
Molassiotis, A., 23
Molina, B. S. G., 427
Moline, M. L., 98
Moll, K., 526
Moller, E., 5, 91
Molosh, A. I., 126
Momen, N. C., 323
Monarch, E. S., 347
Monck, E. M., 503
Money, J., 392
Monroe, S. M., 237
Monson, C. M., 162, 163
Montague, D. K., 377
Montejo-Gonzalez, A. L., 371
Monteleone, A. M., 284
Monteleone, P., 284
Montgomery, A., 507
Monti, J. M., 48
Monton, C., 188
Mooney, N. B., 76
Moore, D. S., 40
Moore, S. C., 462
Moreno, C., 222–223
Moreno, R. A., 232
Morenz, B., 388
Morey, J. N., 325
Morey, S., 347
Morgan, D., 568
Morgan, H. W., 433
Morgan, J., 148
Morgan, M., 53
Morgan, M. J., 35
Morgan, V. A., 502
Morgentaler, A., 378
Mori, N., 285
Morneau-Vaillancourt, G., 234
Morokoff, P., 369, 372
Morris, J. S., 58
Morris, P. E., 106
Morrison, A. S., 152
Morrow, G. R., 23
Mortberg, E., 155
Mortensen, P. B., 66
Moscovitch, D. A., 150
Moser, C., 364
Moses, N., 279
Moses-Kolko, E. L., 218
Mosher, D. L., 450
Mosher, W. D., 358
Moshier, S. J., 144
Moskowitz, A., 218
Moskowitz, J. T., 331
Moskowitz, L., 543, 569
Moss, H. B., 424
Moss-Morris, R., 343
Moss-Morris, R. E., 343
Mostofsky, D. I., 321
Mostofsky, E., 337
Motivala, S. J., 320
Motta-Ochoa, R., 566
Mottron, L., 533
Moulds, M. L., 163
Movius, H. L., 200
Mucha, T. F., 191
Muehlenkamp, J. J., 278
Mueller, T., 220
Mueser, K. T., 418, 507, 509, 510
Mufson, L., 251
Mulder, C., 577

Mulder, R. T., 466
Mullan, J. T., 570
Mullan, M., 579
Mullany, B., 255
Mullen, P. R., 431
Muller, C. P., 407
Muller, J., 510
Mulsant, B., 217
Munder, T., 376
Mundt, B., 192
Munir, Z. B., 185
Munoz, R. F., 212, 251, 416
Munro, A., 490
Murakami- Brundage, J., 120
Murawski, M. E., 338
Muresanu, D. F., 438
Muris, P., 149
Muroff, J., 174
Muronov, A. Y., 407
Murphy, J. A., 215, 217
Murphy, M., 523
Murphy, S., 371
Murphy, T. K., 167
Murphy, W. D., 380
Murray, C. J., 332
Murray, K. E., 523
Murray, R. M., 66, 486, 493–495, 498, 501, 502
Murray, S. B., 274
Murru, A., 248
Mushtaq, S., 438
Mustafa, G., 511
Mustanski, B. S., 361
Mustian, K. M., 23
Myers, J. K., 36, 134, 139, 145
Myers, K. M., 57
Myers, L., 328
Myerson, R., 332
Myhre, J., 569
Myin-Germeys, I., 503
Mystkowski, J. L., 131, 140

N

Na, K., 214
Nadeem, I. M., 410
Nagappan, G., 567
Nagata, J. M., 274
Nagayama Hall, G. C., 388
Nagel, D. B., 505
Najavits, L. M., 162, 163
Najmi, S., 260
Nakajima, M., 416
Nakajima, S., 221, 222, 262
Nakrem, S., 569
Nanayakkara, V., 440
Naragon-Gainey, K., 130
Naring, G. W., 192
Narrow, W. E., 5, 91, 94
Nash, D., 228
Nash, J., 351
Nash, J. M., 341
Nash, W. P., 159
Nasrallah, I. M., 555
Nasser, M., 276
Nast, R., 121
Nathan, P. J., 567
Natoli, J. L., 542
Navarrete, C. D., 153
Neal-Barnett, A. M., 141
Neale, M. C., 36, 134, 233, 361, 425
Negrini, B. J., 193
Neighbors, C., 279
Neighbors, H., 258
Neimeyer, R. A., 221
Nelles, W. B. N., 139
Nelson, B., 494
Nelson, C., 388
Nelson, C. A., 47
Nelson, D., 230
Nelson, J. K., 213
Nelson, L., 556
Nelson, P., 141
Nelson, R. O., 6, 73–74, 76
Nelson, S. E., 433
Nelson-Gray, R. O., 6
Nemeroff, C., 233
Nemeroff, C. B., 51, 55, 234, 235, 330
Neng, J. M. B., 188
Nepon, J., 132
Nestadt, G., 469
Nestler, E. J., 47
Nettles, M. E., 474
Neugroschi, J. A., 558, 562–564
Neumann, C. S., 459, 462, 578
Neumark-Sztainer, D., 278–280
Newman, E., 463, 465
Newman, J. P., 470
Newman, M. G., 135, 136
Newman, N. J., 189
Newman, S., 533
Newring, K. A. B., 380
Newton, N. C., 437
Newton, T. L., 324
Neylan, T. C., 321
Nezu, A. M., 330
Nezu, C. M., 330
Ng, A. C. T., 268
Ng, B. Y., 198
Ng, J., 281
Ngai, E., 509
Niaura, R., 337
Nicasio, A. V., 96
Nicassio, P. M., 320
Nicholas, C. R., 422
Nicholls, D., 281
Nichols, D. S., 83–86
Nichols, R. M., 203
Nicolson, S. E., 407
Niederkrotenthaler, T., 259
Niehaus, D., 510
Nielsen, D., 425
Nierenberg, A. A., 213, 226
Nieri, T., 429
Nigg, J. T., 518
Nijenhuis, E. R. S., 194
Nijman, H., 394
Nijs, J., 342
Nikia, M. N., 219
Nikolas, M., 521
Nikolskaya, O. S., 532
Nimegeer, A., 268
Nimgaonkar, V. L., 214
Ninci, J., 543
Nisbett, R. E., 107
Nithianantharajah, J., 68
Nitschke, J. B., 236
Nivard, M. G., 238
Nivoli, A. M., 248
Nixon, R. V. D., 163
Noble, J., 345
Noblett, K. L., 439
Nock, M. J., 260
Nock, M. K., 90, 175, 255–258, 260, 466
Nolan, H., 110
Nolen-Hoeksema, S., 228, 238–239
Noll, R. B., 331
Nooe, R. M., 579
Noonan, C., 342
Norberg, M. M., 174
Nordentoft, M., 457
Nordstrom, P., 258
Norman, W. H., 58, 238, 251
Normile, D., 327
Norrholm, S. D., 161
Norris, A. L., 358
Norris, D. M., 586
North, C. S., 157, 185
Norton, G. R., 141, 201
Norton, J. A., 533
Norton, M. C., 567
Novak, B., 582
Novella, J., 278
Novianti, P., 153
Noyes, R., 136, 187, 202
Noyes, R., Jr., 206
Ntika, M., 11
Nugent, N. R., 161
Nugent, S. A., 475
Nunes, K. L., 385
Nunez, N., 227
Nunley, B., 576
Nunley, W., 576
Nurnberger, J. I., 226, 233
Nusbaum, C., 35
Nusslock, R., 236, 238
Nutakor, J. A., 110
Nutt, D., 49, 127
Nutzinger, D. O., 283
Nyhan, W. L., 540

O

O'Brian, S., 519
O'Brien, C., 98, 403
O'Brien, M. E., 328
O'Brien, S., 98
O'Callaghan, E., 502
O'Carroll, P. W., 259
O'Connell, D., 68
O'Connell, M., 330
O'Connor, K., 165, 168
O'Connor, M., 164
O'Connor, M. F., 222
O'Connor, P. G., 576
O'Connor, T., 218
O'Connor, T. G., 464
O'Donnell, M. L., 158, 159
O'Donohue, W., 379, 388
O'Donovan, A., 321, 331
O'Donovan, C., 391
O'Donovan, M. C., 230
O'Grady, K. E., 412
O'Hara, M. W., 218, 230, 251
O'Leary, K. D., 251
O'Malley, P. M., 408
O'Neil, J. A., 194
O'Neil, P. M., 274
O'Shea, D., 391
O'Shea, E., 567
Oar, E. L., 150–151
Öberg, K., 393
Oberg, P., 259
Ochsner, K. N., 59
Oddy, W. H., 274
Odlaug, B. L., 175, 439
Ogle, C. M., 205
Ogloff, J. R., 440
Oh, D., 136, 250
Oh, S., 414
Ohayon, M. M., 217, 338
Ohlerking, F., 379
Ohman, A., 58, 61, 153
Oishi, S., 63
Ojehagen, A., 257
Okazaki, M., 83
Okazaki, S., 83
Oldenburg, B., 321
Oldham, J., 471
Olds, J., 425
Olfson, M., 134, 143, 222–223
Olin, J., 230
Oliva, P. S., 200
Olivares, J., 455

Q

R

Reichow, B., 544
Reid, J. R., 428
Reid, M. W., 237
Reif, A., 125, 521
Reilly, A., 331
Reilly, M. P., 427
Reilly-Harrington, N. A., 254
Reiman, E. M., 565
Reimer, D., 393
Reinarman, C., 371
Reinders, A. A. T. S., 203
Reingle, J. M., 464
Reinhardt, R. F., 191
Reiss, N. S., 256
Reiss, S., 129
Reitan, R. M., 87
Reiter, J., 172
Reji, P. M., 576
Rekers, G. A., 394
Remer, P., 85
Renaud, S., 172
Renick, A., 204
Rentz, D. M., 556
Repp, A. C., 543
Rescorla, R., 57
Rescorla, R. A., 23
Resick, P. A., 162, 164
Resnick, H. S., 94, 161, 555
Ressler, K. J., 156, 161, 163, 169
Reverger, R., 511
Revicki, D. A., 218
Rexrode, K., 337
Reynolds, C. F., 164
Reznikoff, M., 83
Rhebergen, D., 215
Rhoades, G. K., 359
Rhodes, A. R., 256
Rhodes, L., 141
Rhyno, S., 167
Riboli, E., 320, 348
Ricaurte, G. A., 412
Ricciardelli, L. A., 274
Rice, F., 230
Rice, M. E., 383, 387
Rich, B. A., 222–223, 230
Richards, C. L., 550
Richards, J. A., 254
Richards, R., 232
Richards, S. S., 555–567
Richards, W., 421
Richards, W. A., 421
Richardson, D., 368
Richardson, G., 414
Richardson, W. S., 588
Richey, J. A., 153
Richler, J. J., 106
Richmond-Raker, L. S., 323
Richtberg, S., 188
Rickels, K., 98, 136
Ridder, E., 230
Riddle, M. A., 155
Ridenour, J. M., 450, 452, 453
Ridenour, T. A., 422
Riding, A., 401
Rief, W., 181–185, 187
Rieger, G., 359, 394
Ries Merikangas, K., 228
Riggs, J. E., 563
Riglin, L., 230
Riihimaki, K., 257
Riley, B., 238
Riley, S., 170
Rimsky, L., 456, 457
Rinaldi, M., 80, 121
Rindskopf, D., 111, 113
Ripke, S., 498
Risch, N., 38
Riso, L. P., 282
Ritchey, F. C., 214
Ritsner, M. S., 484
Ritz, T., 31, 149, 150
Riva, P., 341
Rivera-Tovar, A. D., 98
Rizvi, S. L., 162
Rizzuto, D., 570
Robbins, C., 65
Robbins, T. W., 561
Roberto, C. A., 273
Roberts, A., 171
Roberts, C. W., 376
Roberts, J. E., 237
Roberts, J. M., 518
Roberts, M. C., 348
Roberts, W., 520
Robertshaw, T. L., 421
Robertson, D., 578
Robertson, J., 68
Robertson, N., 434
Robichaud, M., 169
Robinaugh, D. J., 221
Robins, L. N., 460, 463
Robinson, G. E., 36
Robinson, R. G., 252
Robinson, T. E., 55, 68
Robles, T., 323, 325
Rocca, W. A., 337
Roche, M., 450
Rochon, P. A., 550
Rock, P., 418
Rockney, R. M., 11
Rodin, J., 277, 278, 282, 336
Rodrigue, K. M., 565
Roelofs, K., 192
Roels, C., 433
Roemer, L. 135, 136
Roesch, S. C., 446, 588
Rogers, R., 470
Rogosch, F. A., 448
Rohan, K. J., 219, 220
Rohde, L. A., 520
Rohde, P., 220, 228, 233, 274
Roid, G. H., 86
Rojo, L., 283
Roll, J. M., 427
Rolland, Y., 567
Rollman, B. L., 136, 230
Romanelli, R. J., 169
Romeo, E., 48
Romer, D., 35, 36, 234, 237
Romero Lauro, L. J., 341
Romero-Martin, M., 118
Ronningstam, E., 470, 471
Room, R., 434
Roose, S. P., 284
Root, T. L., 273
Rorschach, H., 82
Rosario, M. C., 166
Roscoe, J. A., 23
Rose, C. E., 532
Rose, J. S., 119
Rose, N. R., 167
Rose, S., 215, 220
Rosellini, A. J., 96, 99
Rosen, A. C., 394
Rosen, B., 218
Rosen, C. S., 163
Rosen, J. C., 172
Rosen, R., 365, 366, 369, 370
Rosen, R. C., 364–368, 369, 370, 375–377
Rosenbach, A. F., 418
Rosenberg, P. B., 567
Rosenberg, R., 339
Rosenberg, R. N., 557
Rosenberg, W., 588
Rosenfeld, J. P, 236
Rosenfeld, J. V., 52–53
Rosenfeld, S., 122
Rosenfield, D., 161, 163
Rosenfield, E., 174
Rosengren, A., 335
Rosenman, R. H., 335, 336
Rosenthal, D., 496
Rosenthal, P. A., 256
Rosenthal, S., 256
Rösler, A., 388
Ross, A. O., 523
Ross, C. A., 196, 201–203, 205
Ross, D. C., 219
Ross, L., 107
Rossow, I., 410
Rost, M., 121
Roth, W. T., 148
Rothbaum, B. O., 163, 169
Rothblum, E. D., 64, 274
Rotheram-Borus, M. J., 329, 349
Rothschild, A., 217
Rothschild, A. J., 218
Rottenberg, J., 60, 63, 213
Rotton, J., 11
Rouff, L., 454
Rouleau, J. L., 379
Rounsaville, B. J., 250
Rouprêt, M., 370
Rouse, S. V., 85
Roush, W., 345
Roussos, P., 453
Rowe, J. B., 191, 193
Rowe, M., 510
Rowe, M. K., 140
Rowell, E. A., 419
Rowell, R., 419
Rowley, S., 464
Rowse, G., 484
Roy, A. K., 223
Roy-Byrne, P. P., 134
Roydeva, M. I., 203
Roylance, R., 55
Rozenkrantz, L., 181
Rubia, K., 523
Rubin, G. J., 11
Rubinow, D. R., 98
Rubinstein, T., 463
Rubio, J., 131
Rubio, J. M., 215
Ruchkin, V., 161
Ruck, C., 169
Rucklidge, J. J., 520
Rudaz, M., 141
Rudd, M. D., 258, 261
Rudolph, K. D., 228
Ruffin, R., 328
Ruhe, K., 151
Ruiz-Frutos, C., 118
Ruiz-Veguilla, M., 494
Runeson, B., 255
Rupprecht, R., 48
Rusch, N., 466, 467
Ruscio, A. M., 151
Russell, A. E., 523
Russell, G., 272, 273, 279, 281, 282, 523
Russell, G. F. M., 274
Russell, S., 47
Russo, L., 131
Russo, S. J., 430
Rusyniak, D., 411
Rutkofsky, I. H., 468

Rutten, B. P., 503
Rutter, M., 35, 36, 38, 40, 64, 69, 99, 107, 234, 429, 450, 453, 460, 533, 544
Ruzek, J. I., 161, 163
Ryan, J. L., 23
Ryder, A. G., 231, 453
Rynn, M., 136

S

Sachdev, P. S., 549
Sackeim, H. A., 196, 201, 202, 248
Sackett, D. L., 588
Sacks, H., 151
Sacks, J. A., 157
Saczynski, J. S., 550
Sadeh, N., 470
Sadler, J. Z., 4, 5
Safford, M. M., 332
Safford, S., 240
Safren, S. A., 328, 329
Saga, S., 569
Sagi-Schwartz, A., 129
Sahakian, B. J., 175
Saigh, P. A., 158
Saitz, T. R., 367
Sakel, M., 14
Sakellariou, I., 11
Sakheim, D. K., 370, 371, 372
Saksa, J. R., 512
Salaminios, G., 456
Salas-Wright, C. P., 414
Salazar, I. C., 455
Saleem, R., 254
Salekin, R. T., 458, 460, 470
Salkovskis, P. M., 168
Salkovskis, P., 185
Sallet, J., 55
Salovey, P., 336
Saltoun, M., 331
Salvatore, J. E., 38
Samek, D. R., 465
Samimi Ardestani, S. M., 466
Sammel, M., 230
Sammel, M. D., 98
Sampedro-Piquero, P., 414
Sampson, N. A., 258
Samson, L., 359
Samuel, D. B., 92, 99
Samuels, J., 475
Samuels, S. C., 558
Sanchez-Roige, S., 115
Sandal, C., 410
Sandal, G. M., 119
Sanderson, W. C., 134
Sandi, C., 55
Sandin, B., 187
Sanislow, C. A., 474
Sanislow, C., 468
Sankis, L. M., 5
Sano, M., 567
Santed, M., 187
Santín, L., 414
Santoro, M. R., 542
Santosa, C. M., 232
Santosh, P. J., 68
Santucci, L. C., 150, 151
Sanz-Carrillo, C., 188
Sapolsky, R. M., 321–323
Sar, V., 194–195
Sarbin, T., 494
Sareen, J., 131, 132, 153, 185
Saribay, S. A., 59
Sarrel, P. M., 371
Sartori, G., 53
Sartorius, N., 76, 185
Sarwer, D. B., 291
Saudino, K. J., 35, 38
Sauer, J., 120
Sauer, S. E., 467
Sauer-Zavala, S., 56, 63, 323
Savage, J. C., 462
Savin-Williams, R., 391
Savin-Williams, R. C., 394
Savla, G. N., 588
Sawada, Y., 258
Sawyer, A. T., 63, 129, 136, 156, 250
Saxe, G. N., 161, 201
Saxena, S., 172, 174, 198
Scanlan, J., 54
Scarborough, P., 335
Scarella, T. M., 182
Scarlett, S., 110
Scarmeas, N., 556
Scepkowski, L., 371
Schacter, D. L., 59, 204
Schaffer, A., 217, 227
Scharfstein, L. A., 155
Schatz, N. K., 521
Schatzberg, A. F., 217, 338
Schatzberg, A., 136, 252
Scheerenberger, R. C., 541
Scheiderer, E. M., 475
Scheidt, P. C., 348
Scheier, M. F., 348
Scherr, P. A., 554
Schewel, R., 528
Schiavi, R. C., 364, 371, 377
Schieber, K., 172
Schiele, M. A., 40, 116, 127
Schifano, F., 404, 424
Schifano, S., 105
Schiffer, B., 475
Schiffman, J., 488
Schildkraut, J. J., 43
Schmahl, C., 203, 467
Schmaling, K. B., 342
Schmeidler, J., 195
Schmidt, A. B., 222–223
Schmidt, A. J. M., 184
Schmidt, C. W., 383
Schmidt, E., 433
Schmidt, H. M., 376
Schmidt, L. A., 152
Schmidt, P. J., 98
Schmidt, U., 269, 270
Schmucker, M., 388
Schneck, C. D., 226
Schneider, S., 144, 151, 155, 365
Schneiderman, N., 320, 320, 325, 328–337
Schneier, F. R., 163
Schnell, K., 469
Schniering, C. A., 151, 279
Schoenbach, V. J., 65
Schoenbaum, M., 134
Schoenberg, M. R., 191
Schoeneman, T. J., 9
Schoenfeld, T. J., 235
Schoenmakers, B., 570
Schomerus, G., 577
Schork, M. A., 62
Schork, N. J., 129
Schouten, E., 337
Schover, L. R., 377
Schramm, E., 155, 215, 250
Schreiner-Engel, P., 364
Schroeter, K., 283
Schuckit M. A., 405, 407, 409, 410, 426, 433
Schulberg, H. C., 251
Schule, C., 48
Schulenberg, J. E., 408
Schulman, P., 251
Schulte, L., 374
Schulte-Körne, G., 526
Schultz, R., 531
Schultze, M., 250
Schulz, P. E., 89
Schulz, R., 230
Schumacher, J. A., 49
Schumann, J. E., 407
Schurger, A., 59
Schutter, D. J., 249
Schwalberg, M. D., 270
Schwartz, A., 137
Schwartz, A. J., 257, 461
Schwartz, C. E., 542
Schwartz, J., 47
Schwartz, J. E., 220
Schwartz, J. M., 53
Schwartz, M. S., 344
Schwarzkopf, D. S., 59
Schwarzler, F., 236
Schweizer, E., 136
Scott, C. L., 174, 585
Scott, J., 251
Scott, J. E., 507
Scott, K. M., 323, 325
Scott, S., 464, 506
Scull, A., 578, 579
Scullin, M. H., 539
Sedlak, T. W., 420
Seeley, J. R., 220, 233
Seeman, P., 500
Seeman, T. E., 334
Segal, J. B., 169
Segal, N., 361, 391
Segal, N. L., 35
Segal, Z., 240
Segal, Z. V., 250
Segerstrom, S. C., 325, 327
Seglem, K. B., 424
Segraves, R., 363, 376, 378
Seibel, S. L., 205
Seidenzahl, D., 583
Seidman, L. J., 501, 523
Seitz, D. P., 419, 550
Selesnick, S. T., 9, 12, 14
Seligman, M. E., 58
Seligman, M. E. P., 238–239, 251
Sellaro, R., 227
Sellbom, M., 458, 586
Sellinger, J., 344
Sells, D., 510
Selten, J. P., 502
Selye, H., 321
Semans, J. H., 376
Semple, R. J., 136
Sen, S., 38
Sendt, K. V., 506
Senn, S., 435
Sentissi, O., 214
Sephton, S. E., 325, 327
Serefoglu, E. C., 367
Serpe, R. T., 171
Servick, K., 567
Sessa, B., 421
Seto, M. C., 379–384
Settipani, C. A., 155
Severino, S. K., 98
Sewell, K. W., 470
Shadick, R., 135
Shaffer, D. R., 68
Shaffer, V. N., 215
Shafran, R., 281, 282
Shah, G. M. S., 486

T

U

V

W

X

Y

Z

Subject Index

Antisocial personality disorder
arousal theories for, 461–463
case studies, 457–458
clinical description of, 458
conduct disorder and, 459–460
criminality in, 459
defining criteria, 458–459
developmental influences, 463
diagnosis, reliability of, 459
diagnostic criteria for, 461–462
gender differences in, 449
genetic influences, 460–461
integrative model for, 463–464
neurobiological influences, 461
prevention of, 464–465
psychopathy in, 459
psychosocial factors, 463
substance misuse and, 404
treatments for, 464
Anxiety
case study, 238
castration, 20
conversion disorder and, 191–192
defined, 125
effects of, 125–126
fear and, 126
neurobiology of, 129
panic and, 63, 138
sexual arousal and, 372
sexual dysfunction and, 372
stress and, 323–324
Anxiety and Related Disorder Interview Schedule for DSM-5 (ADIS-5), 78
Anxiety disorders, 125. *See also* Panic disorders
biological contributions, 127–129
brain structure and, 128
causes of, 126–130
characterization of, 61
children with, 7
comorbidity of, 130–131
depression and, 230
generalized, 132–137
genetic factors, 234
illness anxiety disorder and, 187
insomnia disorder and, 298
integrated model for, 130
panic and, 63
physical disorders and, 131
psychological factors, 129–130
social factors, 130
social phobias, 151–157
specific phobia, 145–151
suicide and, 131–132
summary, 175–176
terms, definitions of, 125–126
Anxiety sensitivity, 129, 134
Anxiolytic drugs, 410
Anxious distress specifier, 217
Aphasia, 563
Apolipoprotein E4 (apo E4), 564
Appearance, mental status exam and, 76
Arbitrary inference, 239
ARC. *See* AIDS-related complex (ARC)
Arousal
antisocial personality disorder, 461–463
anxiety and, 372
pedophilic disorder and, 383
Asclepiad Temples, 15
Asociality, 487
Asperger's disorder, 544. *See also* Autism spectrum disorder
Assertiveness training, 347
Assessment. *See* Clinical assessment
Assessment gender bias, 450
Association studies, 115, 498
Associative splitting, 482
Asylum reform, 16–17
Asylums, 16
Ataques de nervios, 139
Atherosclerosis, 335
Atomoxetine, 524–525
Attachment disorders, 165
Attention deficit/hyperactivity disorder (ADHD)
adults with, 524
biological interventions, 524–525
case study, 520
causes of, 521, 523
clinical description, 518, 520
defined, 518
diagnosis of, 520–521
diagnostic criteria for, 522
learning disorders and, 529
mood disorders and, 230
psychosocial interventions, 524
statistics, 520–521
treatments for, 523–524
Attenuated psychosis syndrome, 492, 512
Attribution, 58
Atypical behavior, 4–5
Atypical features specifier, 217
Auditory hallucinations, 217, 486
Augmentative communication strategies, 543
Autism spectrum disorder
Asperger's disorder *vs.*, 544
biological factors, 533
case study, 530
characteristics of, 532
clinical description, 530
defined, 530
diagnostic criteria for, 531
genetic influences, 533–53
history of, 533
neurobiological factors, 534
psychosocial factors, 532–533
social communication impairment in, 531–53
social interaction impairment in, 531–532
statistics, 532
treatments for, 534–536
Autogynephilia, 381, 391
Autohypnotic model, 202
Autonomic inflexibility, 135
Autonomic nervous system, 45
Autonomic restrictors, 135
Aversive treatment, 433
Avoidant personality disorder
case study, 472
causes of, 473
clinical description, 473
diagnostic criteria for, 473
treatments for, 473
Avolition, 487
Axons, 42

B

Baby blues, 218
Barbiturates. *See also specific drugs*
clinical description of, 410
defined, 410
statistics, 410–411
Bariatric surgery, 293
Basal ganglia, 44, 45
Baseline, 113
Basic genetic epidemiology, 115
B cells, 325–326
BDD. *See* Body dysmorphic disorder (BDD)
BED. *See* Binge-eating disorder (BED)
Behavior. *See also* Health-related behavior
abstinence, 403
across cultures, 114–115
assessment of, 80–82
disorganized, 488–489
drug-seeking, 403
genes, developments, 35–36
heterosexual, 357
homosexual, 357
mental status exam and, 76
modification of, 348–349
nongenomic inheritance of, 39–40
personality disorder and, 447
rating scales, 81
researching over time, 117
types, 335
Behavioral assessment, 80–82
Behavioral medicine, 320
Behaviorism, 17, 24
The Behavior of Organisms (Skinner), 24
Behavior rating scales, 81
Behavior therapy, 24
Bender Visual–Motor Gestalt Test, 87
Benzodiazepines, 14, 134
clinical description of, 410
defined, 410
GAD, 135–136
panic disorders, 143
statistics, 410–411
Beta-adrenergic receptors, 49
Beta amyloid, 564
Beta-blockers, 49, 155, 375
Beyond Freedom and Dignity (Skinner), 25
Bianchi, Kenneth, 199
Binge-eating disorder (BED)
characterization, 273–274
controversial *DSM-5* inclusion of, 312
cultural factors, 275–276
defined, 267
diagnostic criteria for, 274
drug treatment for, 283–284
treatments for, 286–287
Binge-eating/purging type of anorexia nervosa, 272
Bini, Lucio, 14
Biofeedback, 89, 344–345
Biological markers, 34
Biological model
American, 13
anxiety disorders, 127–129
autism, 533
Chinese, 12
consequences of, 15
defined, 8
DID and, 202–203
eating disorders, 281–282
Greek, 12–13
intellectual disability, 539
mood disorders, 233–236
neurocognitive disorder, 563–566
nineteenth century, 13
panic disorders and, 141
PTSD, 162
Roman, 12–13
substance-related disorders, 424–426
treatment development, 14

C

D

E

Extrapyramidal symptoms, 506
Eysenck, Hans, 24

F

Face validity, 83
Facial agnosia, 554
Factitious disorders, 191
Failure to thrive syndrome, 279
False memory syndrome, 204–205
False negatives, 87
False positives, 87
Familial aggregation, 93
Familial factors
borderline personality disorder and, 466
characterization of, 116
eating disorders, 281
psychopathy, 464
schizophrenia and, 496, 503–504
substance misuse, 424–425
suicide, 257–258
Family-based treatment (FBT), 288
FAS. *See* Fetal alcohol syndrome (FAS)
Fatalistic suicides, 257
Fearlessness hypothesis, 461–462
Fear memory reconsolidation, 163
Fears. *See also* Cluster C personality disorders
cultural aspects of, 63–64
defined, 126
emotions of, 60–61
physiology of, 60
prevalence of, 148
reaction to, 126
Female orgasmic disorder, 366
Female sexual interest/arousal disorder, 363
diagnostic criteria for, 366
Fetishistic disorder, 379
FFS. *See* Fight/flight system (FFS)
Fight/flight system (FFS), 128
Fight response, 60
Five-factor model, 446
Fixation, 20
Flat affect, 490
Flibanserin, 377
Flight of ideas, 213
Fluency disorder in children, 528
Fluoxetine, 245, 253, 283
fMRI. *See* Functional magnetic
Folie à deux, 490
Food taxes, 293
Forebrain, 43
Formal observation, 81
Foster, Jodie, 583
Fragile X syndrome, 541, 542
Franklin, Benjamin, 14, 17
Fraternal birth order hypothesis, 361
Free association, 21
Frenzy witchcraft, 198
Freud, Anna, 20, 21
Freud, Sigmund, 17, 413
basic observations of, 18
defense mechanism theory of, 19–20
mind structure theory of, 18–19
psychosexual theory of, 20
Fright disorders, 63
Frigo phobia, 148
Fromm, Erich, 21
Frontal lobes, 45, 502
Frontotemporal neurocognitive disorders, 559
diagnostic criteria for, 559
Frotteuristic disorder, 379, 380
Fugue, dissociative, 195–198
Functional communication training
defined, 113
intellectual disabled children, 543
Functional genomics, 425
Functional magnetic resonance imaging (fMRI), 59, 88
Functional neurological symptom disorder, 189–193
Functional seizures, 192

G

GABA. *See* Gamma-aminobutyric acid (GABA)
GABA-benzodiazepine system, 48, 128
GAD. *See* Generalized anxiety disorder (GAD)
Galen, 12–13
Galvanic skin response (GSR), 89
Gambling disorder, 405, 437–438
Gamma-aminobutyric acid (GABA), 43, 48
ADHD and, 523
alcohol use and, 405
anxiety disorders and, 127
anxiolytic substance, 410
benzodiazepines and, 48
characterization of, 48
function of, 48
hypnotic substances, 410
sedatives, 410
stress response and, 326
substance misuse and, 425
Gamma-hydroxybutyrate (GHB), 424
Gate control theory of pain, 339
GBMI. *See* Guilty but mentally ill (GBMI)
Gender affirming surgery, 393–394
Gender differences
ADHD, 520
Alzheimer's disease, 556
antisocial personality disorder, 449
BDD, 171
body sizes, 278
bulimia nervosa, 64–65, 274–275
in casual sex, 359–360
chronic pain, 340–341
conversion disorder, 191
depression, 64
histrionic personality disorder, 469
homosexuality attitudes of, 351
insomnia disorder, 299
learning disorders, 526
mood disorders, 64–65, 240–241
OCD, 64
panic attack, 139
paraphilic disorders, 384
personality disorders, 449–450
psychopathology and, 64–65
response to, 64
schizophrenia, 494
sex reassignment surgery, 393–394
sexual dysfunction, 363
sexuality, 359–360
somatic symptom disorder, 187
Gender dysphoria, 97, 357, 390
case studies, 37, 392
causes of, 391–393
defined, 357
defining criteria for, 390–391
diagnostic criteria for, 390
exploration of, 398
treatments for, 393
Gender nonconformity, 394
Gender roles, 64
Gene–environment correlation model, 36, 237
Gene–environment interaction
adoption studies, 116
Alzheimer's disease, 565
basic approaches, 115
borderline personality disorder and, 467
conduct disorder, 464
diathesis–stress model for, 36–38
twin studies, 116
Gene finding, 115
Generalizability, 105
Generalized amnesia, 195
Generalized anxiety disorder (GAD)
cardiac vagal tone and, 135
case study, 132–133
causes, 134–135
clinical description of, 133
diagnostic criteria for, 133
integrative model of, 136
onset, 134
statistics, 133–134
symptoms of, 133
treatment for, 135–137
Generalized biological vulnerability, 130, 134, 135, 141
Generalized psychological vulnerability
anxiety, 130
panic disorders, 142
PTSD, 161
General paresis, 13
Genes. *See also* Chromosomes
Alzheimer's disease-associated, 564
behavior, developments, 35–36
depression/anxiety link, 234
effects of, 35
expression of, 35
independent influences, 39
nature of, 34–35
substance misuse, 424–425, 429
Gene therapy, 544
Genetic linkage analysis, 116
Genetic markers, 117
Genetics. *See also* Genes
ADHD, 523
Alzheimer's disease, 564
analyses, 116
antisocial personality disorder, 461
autism spectrum disorder, 533–534
borderline personality disorder, 466
family studies, 116
hypersomnolence disorder, 301–302
intellectual disability, 539–540
mood disorders, 233–234
schizophrenia, 495–499
schizotypal personality disorder, 456

H

I

Insanity defense. *See* Not guilty by reason of insanity (NGRI)
Insanity Defense Reform Act, 583
Insidious onset, 7
Insight, 17
Insomnia
medications for, 307–308
rebound, 300
Insomnia disorder
case study, 298
causes of, 299
clinical description, 298
integrative model of, 299–301
statistics, 298–299
Institutionalization policies, 507
Institutional review board (IRB), 122
Insulin shock therapy, 14
Integrated grief, 222
Integrative model
antisocial personality disorder, 463–464
anxiety disorders, 130
borderline personality disorder, 468–469
brain function studies, 55–56
case study, 31–33
characterization of, 25–26
eating disorders, 283, 284
generalized anxiety disorder, 134
hypochondriasis, 187
insomnia disorder, 299–301
mood disorders, 244
multidimensional, 31–33
panic disorders, 144
schizophrenia treatment, 510–511
substance misuse, 429–430
suicidal behavior, 260
Intellectual disability
biological influences, 539
case study, 537
causes of, 539–543
chromosomal influences, 541–542
clinical description, 537–539
communication skills and, 543
defined, 536
degrees of, 538–539
de novo disorders and, 539
diagnostic criteria for, 538
Down syndrome, 539–540
fragile X syndrome, 541, 542
genetic influences, 539–540
Lesch-Nyhan syndrome, 540
psychosocial factors, 542
statistics, 539
treatments for, 542–543
Intellectual functioning, 76
Intelligence quotient (IQ)
antisocial personality disorder and, 459
calculation of, 86
intellectual disability, 538
specific learning disorders and, 525
Intelligence testing, 86
Intermittent explosive disorder, 439
Internal validity, 103, 104–105
International Classification of Diseases (ICD-10), 93
International Classification of Diseases and Related Health Problems (ICD), 93
Interoceptive avoidance, 138
Interpersonal and social rhythm therapy (IPSRT), 254
Interpersonal psychotherapy (IPT), 250
bulimia nervosa, 285
depression, 251, 253
elderly and, 67
mood disorders, 250–251
Interpersonal theory of suicide, 258
Interrater reliability, 75, 82
Intersexuality, 390, 394–395
Intervention guidelines, 590
Interviews
clinical assessment, 75–79
function of, 75–79
mental status exam, 76–78
motivational, 307
OCD sample questions, 78–79
semistructured clinical, 78
sexual behavior, 369
Intoxication
alcohol, 405
amphetamine, 411–413
anxiolytic drugs, 410
cannabis, 419–420
characterization of, 402
diagnostic criteria for, 406
hypnotic drugs, 410
opioid, 418
sedative, 410
Intrapsychic conflicts, 19
Introspection, 24
Inverse agonists, 48
IPSRT. *See* Interpersonal and social rhythm therapy (IPSRT)
IPT. *See* Interpersonal psychotherapy (IPT)
IQ. *See* Intelligence quotient (IQ)
IRB. *See* Institutional review board (IRB)
Irregular sleep–wake type, 305
Ischemia, 335
Isolated sleep paralysis, 141, 303

J

Jackson v. Indiana, 585
Jet lag sleep disorder, 305
Johnson, Lennox, 416
Jones, Mary Cover, 24
Jung, Carl, 21, 22

K

Kaczynski, Ted, 583
Kansas v. Hendricks, 580
Ketamine, 501
Killer T cells, 326
Kleptomania, 439
Kohut, Heinz, 21
Koro, 185
Kraepelin, Emil, 15, 91, 93, 481
Kyol goeu, 139

L

Labeling, 96, 520
La belle indifférence, 189, 193
Lady Gaga, 5
Language disorder, 528
Late luteal phase dysphoric disorder (LLPDD), 98
Lavitra, 377
Law of effect, 25
Learned alarms, 141
Learned helplessness, 58, 238–240
Learned optimism, 58
Learning disorders
causes of, 528–529
clinical description of, 525–526
diagnostic criteria for, 527
statistics, 526–528
treatments for, 529
Leary, Timothy, 421
Lesch-Nyhan syndrome, 540
Leukocytes, 325
Lewy body disease, neurocognitive disorder due to, 559
Libido, 18
Life-span development, 7
focus of, 67
mood disorder and, 229–230
principles of, 67–68
Life-span developmental psychopathology, 7
Light therapy, 220
Limbic system, 44, 45
Linkage studies, 498
Lithium, 247–248
Lithium carbonate, 247
LL. *See* Long allele (LL)
LLPDD. *See* Late luteal phase dysphoric disorder (LLPDD)
Localized amnesia, 195
Long allele (LL), 37
Longitudinal designs, 118–119
Loose association, 76
LSD (*d*-lysergic acid diethylamide), 421
Lunacy, 11
Luria-Nebraska Neuropsychological Battery, 87
Lymphocytes, 325
Lysergic acid amide, 421

M

Macrophages, 325
Madden, John, 126
Magical thinking, 455
Magnetic resonance imaging (MRI), 87
Ma-huang *(Ephedra sinica)*, 411
Maintenance treatment, 253
Major depressive disorders, recurrent, 214
genetic factors, 234
Major depressive episodes
defined, 214
diagnostic criteria for, 92, 214
duration of, 215
length of, 220
prevalence, 228
Major neurocognitive disorder. *See also* Neurocognitive disorder
alcohol abuse and, 407
biological treatments, 567–568
causes of, 563–566
characteristics of, 561
classes of, 555
clinical description of, 554–555
defined, 549
diagnostic criteria for, 549
exploration of, 572
prevention of, 570
psychosocial factors, 566
psychosocial treatments, 568–570
statistics, 554–555
subcortical, 560
substance induced, 563–564
treatments for, 566–570

N

National Institute of Mental Health (NIMH), 26
Natural environment phobia, 147
Naturalistic teaching strategies, 535
Natural opioids, 340
Negative cognitive styles, 239
Negative correlation, 107
Negative reinforcement, 427
Nervous system, divisions of, 41
Neurasthenia, 341
Neurobiological factors. *See also* Brain functioning; Brain structure
  antisocial personality disorder, 461
  anxiety, 129
  autism spectrum disorder, 534
  hypertension, 334
  panic, 129
  schizophrenia, 499–502
  substance misuse, 425–426
Neurocognitive disorders. *See also specific disorder*
  Alzheimer's disease, 555–563
  classes of, 549, 555
  delirium, 550
  diagnostic criteria for, 552, 557, 561
  exploration of, 572
  HIV/AIDS-related, 560–561
  Huntington's disease-related, 561
  major, 552–554
  medical condition-associated, 558–562
  mild, 552–554, 573
  overview of, 549
  prevalence of, 566
  prion disease-related, 562
  substance/medication-induced, 563
  summary, 571
  vascular, 558
Neurodevelopmental disorders, 517
  Neurofibrillary tangles, 563
  Neurohormones, 235
Neuroimaging
  brain functioning, 88
  brain structure, 87–88
  defined, 87
Neuroleptics, 14, 500, 505
Neurons, 43
  transmission of information, 42
Neuroplasticity, 430
Neuropsychological testing, 86–87
Neuroscience, 41
Neuroses, 20
Neurosis, 21, 22, 181
Neurosurgery, 52, 165, 169
Neurotransmitters. *See also specific biochemicals*
  abnormal activity of, 47
  defined, 42
  discovery of, 47
  excitatory, 43
  inhibitory, 43
  mood disorders and, 234
  paths of, 47
  release of, 48
  types of, 48–51
NGRI. *See* Not guilty by reason of insanity (NGRI)
Nicotine
  characterization of, 416
  negative effects of, 416
  withdrawal, 416
Nicotine patch, 432
Nicotine use disorder. *See also* Cigarette smoking
Night eating syndrome, 290, 291
Nightmare disorders, 309–310
NIMH. *See* National Institute of Mental Health (NIMH)
NMDA. *See N*-methyl-d-aspartate (NMDA)
N-methyl-d-aspartate (NMDA), 501
Nocebo effect, 110
Nocturnal eating syndrome, 311
Nocturnal panic, 140–141
Nomenclature, 90
Nomothetic strategy, 90
Nondemand pleasuring, 375
Non-24-hour sleep–wake type, 305
Nonrapid eye movement (NREM), 302
Noradrenaline. *See* Norepinephrine
Norepinephrine, 43, 49–50
Norepinephrine pathways, 50
Normal behavior
  in childhood, 518
  sexuality, 357–362
  social standard of, 4
Nosology, 90
Not culturally expected behavior, 4–5
Not guilty by reason of insanity (NGRI)
  factors in, 581
  history of, 581–582
  public reactions to, 583
  reform efforts, 583
NREM. *See* Nonrapid eye movement (NREM)
Nun Study, 556

O

Obesity
  causes of, 291
  eating disorders and, 267
  eating patterns and, 290
  onset of, 279
  prevention of, 294
  statistics, 289–290
  treatments for, 291–295
Object relations, 21
Observational assessment, 81
Observational learning, 58
Observations on Madness and Melancholy (Haslam), 481
Obsessions, 166, 167
Obsessive-compulsive disorder (OCD), 78
  anorexia nervosa-associated, 273
  assessment questionnaire, 78–79
  BDD and, 170, 172
  brain functioning, 52–54
  case study, 165–166
  causes, 168
  clinical description, 165
  defined, 165
  diagnostic criteria for, 166
  hoarding and, 173–174
  statistics, 167
  tic disorder and, 167
  treatment for, 168–169
  types of, 166–167
Obsessive-compulsive personality disorder
  case study, 474–475
  causes of, 475–476
  clinical description of, 475
  diagnostic criteria for, 475
  pedophiles and, 475
  serial killers and, 475
  treatment for, 475–476
Obstructive sleep apnea hypopnea syndrome, 304
Occipital lobe, 45
OCD. *See* Obsessive-compulsive disorder (OCD)
O'Connor v. Donaldson, 578, 579
Odd behavior. *See* Cluster A personality disorders
Oedipus complex, 20
Oedipus Rex, 20
Olanzapine, 500
Olfactory reference syndrome, 153
Oncology, 329
One-trail learning, 59
Operant conditioning, 24–25
Operant control of pain, 339
Operational definition, 81
Opiates, 405
Opioids
  characterization of, 418–419
  endogenous, 340
  marijuana, 419–420
  withdrawal from, 418
Opioid use disorder, 418–419
Opponent-process theory, 427
Oppositional defiant disorder (ODD), 521
Orbital surface, 52
Oresme, Nicholas, 10
Orgasm disorders, 366–368
Orgasmic reconditioning, 387
Overgeneralization, 239

P

Pain. *See also* Chronic pain
  physical and psychological experience of, 337–339
  sexual, 368
Pain behaviors, 338
Pa-leng, 148
P300 amplitude, 426
Panic
  anxiety disorders and, 63, 137
  defined, 126
  neurobiology of, 129
  nocturnal, 140–141
  psychological aspects, 129–130
  stress and, 130
Panic attacks
  causes of, 144
  defined, 126
  diagnostic criteria for, 127
  gender differences, 139
  prevalence of, 139
  types, 126
Panic control treatment (PCT), 143
Panic disorders. *See also* Anxiety disorders
  case study, 137
  causes of, 141–142
  in childhood, 7
  clinical description of, 137–138
  cultural factors, 139
  diagnostic criteria for, 140
  evolution of, 142
  psychological intervention for, 143–144

Q

R

S